R. Gupta's®

**Popular Master Guide**

NATIONAL TESTING AGENCY (NTA)

# CUET-UG

Common University Entrance Test for Under Graduate Courses/Programmes

# B.Com (Hons.)

## Entrance Exam

*by*

**RPH Editorial Board**

**2026-27**
EDITION

RAMESH PUBLISHING HOUSE, NEW DELHI

## CUET Guidance Note For B.COM (HONS.) Aspirants

Dear students choosing the Right CUET paper combination is paramount for your chosen career. The distinction between a correct combination and a hasty choice can influence your chances of admission. This book specifically contains the precise CUET paper combinations vital for your admission. Also note here that different Universities might have slightly different combinations but this book encompasses all the major paper combinations required for your admission but you are still advised to refer the latest admission notification of your chosen University.

***Published by***

O.P. Gupta *for* Ramesh Publishing House

***Admin. Office***

12-H, New Daryaganj Road, Opp. Officers' Mess,
New Delhi-110002 ✆ 23275224, 23245124

**E-mail:** info@rameshpublishinghouse.com
**For Online Shopping:** www.rameshpublishinghouse.com

***Showroom***

- Balaji Market, Nai Sarak, Delhi-6 ✆ 23282525 📱 9354373464
- 4457, Nai Sarak, Delhi-110006



**Book Code: R-2588**

**ISBN: 978-93-5477-445-4**

**Price: ₹ 1065**

**Printed at: Deepak Offset, Delhi**

# CONTENTS

## PREVIOUS YEARS' PAPERS (With explanatory answers)



## ENGLISH



## BUSINESS STUDIES



## MATHEMATICS

## ACCOUNTANCY/BOOK KEEPING



## GENERAL TEST



★ ★ ★ ★ ★

Previous Years' Paper

# Common University Entrance Test for UG Programmes

# CUET-UG—ENGLISH LANGUAGE

## Entrance Exam, 2025

(Exam held on 27-05-2025)

## Subject Code: 101

**Directions (Qs. No. 1-4):** *Read the given passage and answer the questions that follow:*

Virtues are the result of repeated actions, as habits lay the foundation of moral excellence. Right from the beginning of their lives, children are taught good habits by their parents and teachers. Magnanimity, helpfulness and sacrifice are great virtues which need to be well cultivated in human beings. Trees give shade for the benefit of others, while they themselves stand enduring the scorching heat of the sun. They selflessly bear the fruit which is consumed by birds, animals and human beings. Rivers travel hundreds of kilometers, irrigating the land and providing water for all living beings. Flowers spread their scent to make the environment pleasant. Nature teaches us to tolerate pain for the sake of service to others. Henna yields its reddish hue when ground into a paste. Sugarcane yields sweet juice when it is pressed. Flowers get pierced through with a needle to embellish us with garlands.

The character of virtuous men and women is also like the above things and elements of Nature. What is the use of this perishable and mortal frame if it is not used for the benefit of others? To live our life only for ourselves is to live like cats and dogs. People who are noble at heart do not abandon human virtues even if they have to lose their lives. A Sanskrit couplet says—"Whether men praise them or no, whether they get riches or no, whether they live long or soon die, the virtuous will never waver from the path of righteousness."

**1.** Which of the following is NOT mentioned in the passage?
1. Being truthful is the most important sign of virtuosity.
2. Nature teaches us to endure pain and serve others.
3. A self-centred existence is a bestial existence.
4. Not abandoning the right path even in the face of death.

**2.** In the passage, what is meant by "mortal frame"?
1. Nature
2. Animals
3. Land
4. Human body

**3.** According to the passage, which of the following is NOT true?
1. Parents and teachers inculcate good habits in children from the early stages.
2. There are parallels between the character of virtuous human beings and Nature.
3. Ethical behaviour is not dependent upon praise or reward.
4. The virtuous deviate from their path, if they aren't duly acknowledged.

**4.** Which of the following does not exemplify 'endurance', according to the passage?
1. Trees enduring the scorching heat of the Sun.
2. Sugarcane getting pressed to yield juice.
3. Trees bearing fruit and flowers spreading fragrance.
4. Henna being ground and turned into a paste.

**Directions (Qs. No. 5-8):** *Read the given passage and answer the questions that follow:*

Uma could not sing; but since learning to write, she had developed the habit of writing down any song she heard, to lessen the pain of not being able to sing it. Today the beggar woman was singing...

Resentful anguish welled up in Uma's heart. She called the singer secretly to her room, shut the door and began to write down the song in her eccentric spelling.

Tilakmanjari, Kanakmanjari and Anangamanjari observed everything through the crack in the door, and burst out, clapping their hands, "Boudidi, we've seen what you're doing!"

Uma quickly unfastened the door and began to plead with them, "Darling sisters, please don't tell anybody. I beg you, please don't. I'll never do it again. I'll never write again..."

**1.** 1 **2.** 4 **3.** 4 **4.** 3

At length, Uma noticed that Tilakmanjari was eyeing her exercise-book. She ran and clutched the book to her chest. Her sisters-in-law tried to take it away from her by force, but when they did not succeed, Anangamanjari went to summon her brother.

Pyarimohan arrived and sat down grimly on the bed. He said in a voice like thunder, "Give me the exercise-book."

The little girl clasped the exercise-book to her chest and directed a glance of utter supplication at her husband's face. But when she saw Pyarimohan was getting up to snatch the book from her, she flung it down, covered her face with her hands and collapsed on the floor.

**5.** Pyarimohan is bound to Uma by ............ .
1. paternal-ties
2. the bond of friendship
3. marital-ties
4. fraternal-ties

**6.** What is meant by "eccentric" in the passage?
1. neat and beautiful
2. strange and incorrect
3. written in the upper case
4. written in European languages

**7.** Why did Uma develop the habit of writing down any song she heard?
1. To alleviate her anguish at her lack of skill at singing.
2. To work upon and enhance her recently acquired skill at writing.
3. To compile all the songs in her exercise book.
4. To be able to learn to sing the song later.

**8.** What does the phrase 'a glance of utter supplication' mean in the passage?
1. an extremely angry and irritated look
2. a look of total excitement
3. a look showing celebration
4. a look of request and prayer

**Directions (Qs. No. 9-12):** *Read the given passage and answer the questions that follow:*

Solace. He turned the roll of paper between his fingers and wondered if that had not been his error—to search always for solace when there was other game to hunt in the forest. Had he had more spirit, more nerve, more desire and ambition, then perhaps he would have instead hunted for success, distinction, magic. Perhaps he would have followed in pursuit of an art, published a book of poetry, earned a name for himself, a little fame, even gold bangles for Sarla...

But the thought was puerile that it was made him spit out a bitter shred of tobacco. Every effort he had made had ended in defeat: most of the poems he had written and sent to Murad had been rejected, his monograph never published; his wife and son eyed him with blatant disappointment; nor had he won the regard of his colleagues or students. The inherent weakness in his father that had made him an ineffectual, if harmless, teacher and householder, had been passed on to him. He felt it inside him like an empty hole, one he had been staring at all his years, intimidated by its blackness and blankness. Even his attempt to fill it with a genuine and heartfelt homage to a true poet, a man who had distinguished himself as he would have liked to do, had been defeated by all the obstacles that sprang up in his life like shards and pebbles sent up at every step. It was one more blow, and perhaps the bitterest of all.

**9.** Choose a word similar in meaning to the word-Puerile
1. childish  2. melancholy
3. cosmopolitan  4. precocious

**10.** What does the word 'game' in the given phrase symbolise, 'other games to hunt in the forest'
1. Wild animals in the forest
2. Desires or goals being pursued
3. Playful activities
4. Rules of a competition.

**11.** On the basis of your reading identify the tone of the passage.
1. Contemptuous  2. Mournful
3. Satarical  4. Disillusioned

**12.** Who does Deven blame for his failure in life?
1. His wife and son
2. His lack of creativity
3. His father's submissive and timid nature
4. His inherited activism and assertiveness

**13.** Arrange the parts in the correct sequence to form a meaningful sentence:
(A) peeps into the dark abyss of human consciousness,
(B) Neruda conceives poetry not as something which has
(C) its deliberate relation with things of beauty, but rather as an art which
(D) something which has the ability to perceive suffering

Choose the **correct** answer from the options given below:
1. (B), (C), (A), (D)  2. (A), (D), (C), (B)
3. (C), (A), (B), (D)  4. (D), (B), (C), (A)

| **5.** 3 | **6.** 2 | **7.** 1 | **8.** 4 | **9.** 1 | **10.** 2 | **11.** 2, 4 | **12.** 3 | **13.** 1 |
|---|---|---|---|---|---|---|---|---|

**14.** Select the correct antonym for the word: HEGEMONY

1. Supremacy 2. Leadership
3. Prosperity 4. Independence

**15.** Arrange the following parts in the correct sequence to form a meaningful sentence:
(A) the three best hypotheses
(B) ask them to get together
(C) the group has come up with
(D) in fours and decide on
Choose the **correct** answer from the options given below:
1. (A), (D), (C), (B) 2. (C), (B), (D), (A)
3. (B), (D), (A), (C) 4. (D), (B), (C), (A)

**16.** Complete the idioms given in List-I with their second part given in List-II:

| List-I (Idiom's first part) | List-II (Idiom's second part) |
|---|---|
| (A) To hit the nail | (I) to injury |
| (B) To add insult | (II) before the horse |
| (C) To put the cart | (III) in the air |
| (D) To build castles | (IV) on the head |

Choose the **correct** answer from the options given below:
1. (A) - (I), (B) - (III), (C) - (II), (D) - (IV)
2. (A) - (II), (B) - (IV), (C) - (III), (D) - (I)
3. (A) - (IV), (B) - (I), (C) - (II), (D) - (III)
4. (A) - (III), (B) - (IV), (C) - (I), (D) - (II)

**17.** Select the correct synonym for the word: DISCONCERTING
1. Embarrasing 2. Comfortable
3. Suave 4. Adroit

**18.** Select the correct antonym for the word: Valiant
1. Nervous 2. Kind
3. Coward 4. Brave

**19.** Arrange the following parts in the correct sequence to form a meaningful sentence:
(A) tell a lie to the teacher
(B) he is between the devil
(C) neither betray his friend nor
(D) and the deep sea as he can
Choose the **correct** answer from the options given below:
1. (A), (C), (B). (D) 2. (B), (D), (C), (A)
3. (C), (B), (D), (A) 4. (D), (A), (B), (C)

**20.** Rearrange the following parts in the correct sequence to form a meaningful sentence
(A) better known as the shifting cultivation
(B) garia is a folk dance performed in
(C) Tripura revolves around the Jhum culture,
(D) Tripura where the life and culture of the people of
Choose the **correct** answer from the options given below:
1. (C), (A), (B), (D) 2. (D), (C), (B), (A)
3. (A), (B), (D), (C) 4. (B), (D), (C), (A)

**21.** Fill in the blank in the given sentence with the correct option:
The person who studies the structure and composition of the earth to know about its history and antiquity is called a .............. .
1. Botanist 2. Geologist
3. Cartographer 4. Geographer

**22.** The little priest was not an interesting man to look at, having stubby brown hair and a round and stolid face which did not give away anything.
The word STOLID in the above sentence means:
1. Frowning 2. Darkish
3. Emotionless 4. Hateful

**23.** Fill in the blanks in the sentences given in List-I with the appropriate words given in List-II.

| List-I (Sentences) | List-II (Words) |
|---|---|
| (A) The ........ silence in the courtroom was broken only by the sound of a pen tapping. | (I) eccentric |
| (B) Her ......... behaviour raised eyebrows at the otherwise formal event. | (II) penetrating |
| (C) The ........... weather made the trek arduous for the beginners. | (III) oppressive |
| (D) The professor gave a ........ analysis of the painting, revealing hidden layers of meaning. | (IV) inclement |

Choose the **correct** answer from the options given below:
1. (A) - (I), (B) - (III), (C) - (II), (D) - (IV)
2. (A) - (III), (B) - (I), (C) - (IV), (D) - (II)
3. (A) - (II), (B) - (IV), (C) - (I), (D) - (III)
4. (A) - (IV), (B) - (II), (C) - (III), (D) - (I)

**24.** Which of the following words does not refer to one of the movements of a horse?
1. Trotting 2. Cantering
3. Galloping 4. Spinning

**14.** 4 **15.** 3 **16.** 3 **17.** 1 **18.** 3 **19.** 2 **20.** 4 **21.** 2 **22.** 3 **23.** 2 **24.** 4

**25.** Match the words given in List-I with the appropriate definitions in List-II.

| List-I (Words) | List-II (Definitions) |
|---|---|
| (A) Neurologist | (I) one who treats heart diseases |
| (B) Orthodontist | (II) one who studies causes and diagnosis of diseases |
| (C) Cardiologist | (III) one who corrects and straightens irregular teeth |
| (D) Pathologist | (IV) one who cures nerve-related diseases |

Choose the **correct** answer from the options given below:

1. (A) - (I), (B) - (III), (C) - (IV), (D) - (II)
2. (A) - (IV), (B) - (III), (C) - (I), (D) - (II)
3. (A) - (II), (B) - (IV), (C) - (I), (D) - (III)
4. (A) - (III), (B) - (I), (C) - (II), (D) - (IV)

**26.** Rearrange the following parts in the correct sequence to form a meaningful sentence

(A) the lives of labourers
(B) *Pahala Pandhav* is
(C) Shrilal Shukla's
(D) a realistic portrayal of

Choose the **correct** answer from the options given below:-

1. (A), (B), (C), (D) 2. (A), (B), (D), (C)
3. (B), (A), (D), (C) 4. (C), (B), (D), (A)

**27.** Arrange the following parts in the correct sequence to form a meaningful sentence:

(A) who is a doctor, (B) for his higher studies
(C) has gone to America (D) my brother Jagan,

Choose the **correct** answer from the options given below:

1. (A), (D), (B), (C) 2. (B), (C), (D), (A)
3. (D), (A), (C), (B) 4. (C), (A), (D), (B)

**28.** Select the word closest in meaning to the word 'ARDUOUS' from the options given below:

1. Mysterious 2. Continuous
3. Supportive 4. Difficult

**29.** Match the words given in List-I with their corresponding definitions in List-II.

| List-I (Words) | List-II (Definitions) |
|---|---|
| (A) Meteorologist | (I) One who studies election and trends in voting |
| (B) Cosmologist | (II) One who studies fossils and the history of life forms on the earth |
| (C) Psephology | (III) One who studies and predicts atmospheric phenomena |
| (D) Paleontologist | (IV) One who studies the universe, its origin, expanse etc. |

Choose the **correct** answer from the options given below:

1. (A) - (II), (B) - (I), (C) - (IV), (D) - (III)
2. (A) - (IV), (B) - (II), (C) - (III), (D) - (I)
3. (A) - (I), (B) - (III), (C) - (II), (D) - (IV)
4. (A) - (III), (B) - (IV), (C) - (I), (D) - (II)

**30.** Rearrange the following parts in the correct sequence to form a meaningful sentence:

(A) technology, political opinions, military capacities, education, lifestyle, inter alia
(B) there has been growing awareness and rise in urge to be at par with
(C) with increasing purchasing power and larger disposable incomes
(D) current trends in different countries across the world in terms of science,

Choose the **correct** answer from the options given below:-

1. (D), (B), (C), (A) 2. (A), (B), (C), (D)
3. (C), (B), (D), (A) 4. (C), (A), (B), (D)

**31.** Select the correct antonym for the word: PLACATE

1. Provoke 2. Appease
3. Hate 4. Nullify

**32.** Select the correct antonym for the word: PURGE

1. Contaminate 2. Truncate
3. Conceal 4. Complicate

**33.** Choose the correct synonym for the word: DISDAIN

1. Astonish 2. Contempt
3. Destruction 4. Exhaustion

**34.** Select the correct expression to complete the sentence: It ........... since morning.

1. has been raining 2. has raining
3. will raining 4. rain

**35.** Rearrange the following parts in the correct sequence to form a meaningful sentence:

(A) culture is a characteristic
(B) the vision
(C) way of life inspired by
(D) and values of life.

Choose the **correct** answer from the options given below:

1. (A), (C), (B), (D) 2. (A), (B), (C), (D)
3. (B), (A), (D), (C) 4. (C), (B), (D), (A)

**25.** 2 **26.** 4 **27.** 3 **28.** 4 **29.** 4 **30.** 3 **31.** 1 **32.** 1 **33.** 2 **34.** 1 **35.** 1

**36.** Select the correct antonym for the word: BELLIGERENT

1. Brave
2. Friendly
3. Hostile
4. Bemused

**37.** Match the words given in List-I with the appropriate definitions in List-II.

| List-I (Words) | List-II (Definitions) |
|---|---|
| (A) Aviator | (I) controls and operates the flight of an aircraft |
| (B) Jurist | (II) knows several languages, mainly foreign |
| (C) Lexicographer | (III) an expert in the legal field |
| (D) Linguist | (IV) writer of a dictionary |

Choose the **correct** answer from the options given below:

1. (A) - (I), (B) - (II), (C) - (IV), (D) - (III)
2. (A) - (II), (B) - (IV), (C) - (III), (D) - (I)
3. (A) - (I), (B) - (III), (C) - (IV), (D) - (II)
4. (A) - (III), (B) - (I), (C) - (II), (D) - (IV)

**38.** Select the correct antonym for the word: Zenith

1. Horizon
2. Nadir
3. Savage
4. Sober

**39.** Select the correct expression to complete the sentence What is the time ............ ?

1. for your watch
2. at your watch
3. by your watch
4. from your watch

**40.** Choose the appropriate word to fill in the blank in the given sentence:
............ they had been waiting in line all night, I was sure they'd get the tickets for the show.

1. As though
2. Because of
3. Since
4. Until

**41.** Select the correct antonym for the word: INIQUITOUS

1. Unfair
2. Wicked
3. Virtuous
4. Hilarious

**42.** Choose the correct word from the given options to fill the blank in the sentence given below:
"Pakhom ............ with him and the deal was closed at one thousand Rupees."

1. played
2. negotiated
3. disagreed
4. fought

**43.** Match the words given in List-I with their definitions in List-II.

| List-I (Words) | List-II (Definitions) |
|---|---|
| (A) Theology | (I) A branch of philosophy that deals with the nature of existence |
| (B) Epistemology | (II) The study of the origin of the human race, its customs, beliefs and development |
| (C) Ontology | (III) A part of philosophy that deals with knowledge |
| (D) Anthropology | (IV) The study of religion and beliefs |

Choose the **correct** answer from the options given below:

1. (A) - (I), (B) - (II), (C) - (III), (D) - (IV)
2. (A) - (I), (B) - (III), (C) - (II), (D) - (IV)
3. (A) - (IV), (B) - (III), (C) - (I), (D) - (II)
4. (A) - (III), (B) - (IV), (C) - (I), (D) - (II)

**44.** Match the idioms given in List-I with the underlined part of the sentences given in List-II.

| List-I (Idioms) | List-II (Sentences) |
|---|---|
| (A) turned over a new leaf | (I) This unexpected new difficulty <u>roused me to do my best.</u> |
| (B) set his face against | (II) It is a matter of gratification that he <u>changed for the better.</u> |
| (C) put me on my mettle | (III) It is pointless to <u>worry about</u> the result before it's declared. |
| (D) to meet trouble half-way | (IV) As a social reformer, he <u>sternly opposed</u> child labour. |

Choose the **correct** answer from the options given below:-

1. (A) - (I), (B) - (II), (C) - (III), (D) - (IV)
2. (A) - (II), (B) - (IV), (C) - (I), (D) - (III)
3. (A) - (II), (B) - (I), (C) - (IV), (D) - (III)
4. (A) - (III), (B) - (IV), (C) - (I), (D) - (II)

**45.** Select the correct synonym for the word: BENEDICTION

1. benefit
2. forgiveness
3. blessing
4. calmness

**46.** Select the correct synonym for the word: EPHEMERAL

1. Putrid
2. Invisible
3. Temporary
4. Permanent

**36.** 2 **37.** 3 **38.** 2 **39.** 3 **40.** 3 **41.** 3 **42.** 2 **43.** 3 **44.** 2 **45.** 3 **46.** 3

**47.** Rearrange the following parts in the correct sequence to form a meaningful sentence
(A) producing harmones, proteins lend satiety, prevent
(B) hunger pangs at bay, managing both weight and calories
(C) apart from building muscle, repair tissues and
(D) quick breakdown of sugar in the blood and keep
Choose the **correct** answer from the options given below:
1. (C), (A), (D), (B)
2. (A), (B), (C), (D)
3. (D), (C), (A), (B)
4. (D), (B), (C), (A)

**48.** Select the correct meaning of the underlined word in the sentence given below:
His desultory efforts at studying made it clear that he was not serious about passing the exam.
1. cautious
2. impetuous
3. guileful
4. unenthusiastic

**49.** Match the sentences given in List-I with the correct figures of speech given in List-II:

| List-I (Sentences) | List-II (Figures of speech) |
|---|---|
| (A) The wind whispered through the trees. | (I) Alliteration |
| (B) A plumber's house always has a leaking tap. | (II) Oxymoron |
| (C) She opened her eyes to the deafening silence | (III) Irony |
| (D) The buzzing bees drew attention. | (IV) Personification |

Choose the **correct** answer from the options given below:
1. (A) - (IV), (B) - (III), (C) - (II), (D) - (I)
2. (A) - (III), (B) - (I), (C) - (II), (D) - (IV)
3. (A) - (I), (B) - (IV), (C) - (III), (D) - (II)
4. (A) - (II), (B) - (III), (C) - (IV), (D) - (I)

**50.** Rearrange the following parts in the correct sequence to form a meaningful sentence:
(A) had left before Namita
(B) the large group
(C) reached the venue for her performance
(D) of Sattriya dancers
Choose the **correct** answer from the options given below:
1. (B), (C), (A), (D)
2. (B), (A), (D), (C)
3. (B), (D), (A), (C)
4. (C), (B), (D), (A)

# EXPLANATORY ANSWERS

**1. (1):** Being truthful is the most important sign of virtuosity: This point is not found in the passage. The author emphasizes virtues like magnanimity, helpfulness, sacrifice, and righteousness, but never mentions truthfulness as a key virtue. Therefore, this option is correctly identified as not mentioned.

**2. (4):** The term "mortal frame" refers to the human body, which is described as perishable. The passage suggests that if the body is not used for the benefit of others, it serves no noble purpose. Thus, using one's life selflessly is seen as true virtue.

**3. (4):** The virtuous deviate from their path, if they aren't duly acknowledged: This is not true as per the passage. It clearly states that virtuous people stay committed to righteousness, regardless of praise, wealth, or life span. The Sanskrit couplet confirms this idea strongly.

**4. (3):** Trees bearing fruit and flowers spreading fragrance: These acts are beneficial but do not show "endurance" or suffering. The passage defines endurance through actions like facing the sun's heat or being pressed or pierced. Hence, this option does not truly reflect endurance.

**5. (3):** The passage identifies Pyarimohan as Uma's husband, especially when it says "a glance of utter supplication at her husband's face." This clearly establishes that the bond between them is marital, not paternal or fraternal. His commanding tone and her pleading reaction further indicate a traditional husband-wife relationship.

**6. (2):** The word "eccentric" in "eccentric spelling" means that Uma wrote words in a peculiar and incorrect manner. Since she was newly literate, her spellings were likely unconventional. The passage implies she spelled words phonetically or in her own unique way, not neatly or correctly.

**7. (1):** Uma couldn't sing and felt deep pain because of it. She started writing songs she heard as a way to reduce this sorrow. The passage clearly states she developed this habit "to lessen the pain of not being able to sing," which makes option 1 the accurate reason.

**8. (4):** "Utter supplication" means a deep and humble plea. Uma looks at her husband with such a pleading expression, silently begging him not to take away her book. The tone is one of desperation and emotional appeal, fitting the meaning of request and prayer.

**9. (1):** The word "puerile" means childish or immature. In the passage, the thought that achieving fame and success could still be possible is called "puerile," indicating that Deven himself sees it as naive or juvenile, not grounded in reality.

**10. (2):** The phrase "other game to hunt in the forest" is metaphorical. Here, "game" symbolizes ambitions or goals like success, art, poetry, and fame that Deven feels he failed to pursue due to his constant search for solace or comfort.

**47.** 1 **48.** 4 **49.** 1 **50.** 3

**11. (2, 4):** Both "mournful" and "disillusioned" tones are present in the passage. The narrator expresses mournful regret over missed opportunities and failed ambitions. At the same time, there is a clear sense of disillusionment—he once hoped for recognition, poetry, success, and meaning, but now sees all those dreams shattered. He even calls his hope "puerile," showing that he no longer believes in it. Therefore, the combined tone is rightly described as mournful and disillusioned, and 2 & 4 is the correct answer.

**12. (3):** Deven blames his father's weakness, which he believes was passed on to him. He feels this inherited trait made both of them ineffectual in life. He sees it as a black hole inside him that prevented him from achieving anything meaningful.

**13. (1):** The correct sequence is: Neruda conceives poetry not as something which has (B), its deliberate relation with things of beauty, but rather as an art which (C), peeps into the dark abyss of human consciousness, (A), something which has the ability to perceive suffering (D). This order forms a logical and grammatically correct sentence describing Neruda's view of poetry.

**14. (4):** Hegemony means dominance or leadership, especially by one state or group over others. The opposite of dominance is independence, where no control or influence is exerted by another power. Hence, Independence is the correct antonym.

**15. (3):** The meaningful sentence is: Ask them to get together (B), in fours and decide on (D), the three best hypotheses (A), the group has come up with (C). This sequence maintains proper structure and meaning in a collaborative task context.

**16. (3):** (A) - (IV), (B) - (I), (C) - (II), (D) - (III)

(A) To hit the nail on the head (IV) – means to describe exactly what is causing a situation.

(B) To add insult to injury (I) – means to make a bad situation worse.

(C) To put the cart before the horse (II) – means to do things in the wrong order.

(D) To build castles in the air (III) – means to make unrealistic plans or dreams.

**17. (1):** The word "disconcerting" refers to something that causes discomfort, confusion, or embarrassment. It unsettles a person and makes them feel uneasy or awkward. Among the given options, "embarrassing" is the closest synonym in both tone and meaning.

**18. (3):** "Valiant" means showing courage, bravery, or heroism. Its direct opposite would be someone who lacks courage, i.e., a "coward." A coward avoids danger or challenge due to fear, which is the antonym of being valiant.

**19. (2):** The correct sentence is: He is between the devil (B), and the deep sea as he can (D), neither betray his friend nor (C), tell a lie to the teacher (A). This describes a dilemma with no good outcome.

**20. (4):** The meaningful sentence is: Garia is a folk dance performed in (B), Tripura where the life and culture of the people of (D), Tripura revolves around the Jhum culture, (C), better known as the shifting cultivation (A). This forms a coherent and informative statement.

**21. (2):** A geologist studies the Earth's structure, materials, and processes to understand its history and formation. The question mentions learning about the Earth's structure and antiquity, which directly relates to the work of a geologist, not a geographer or cartographer.

**22. (3):** The term "stolid" means showing little or no emotion. In the sentence, the priest's face "did not give away anything," which supports the meaning of being unexpressive or emotionless.

**23. (2):** (A) - (III), (B) - (I), (C) - (IV), (D) - (II)

(A) **Oppressive silence:** Refers to a tense, heavy quietness, often making people feel uncomfortable or pressured—common in intense places like courtrooms.

(B) **Eccentric behaviour:** Means odd or unusual conduct; at a formal event, such behaviour would naturally draw attention.

(C) **Inclement weather:** Describes harsh or severe weather—like rain, storms, or cold—making physical activity like trekking difficult.

(D) **Penetrating analysis:** Means a deep and insightful examination that uncovers hidden details or meanings, often used in intellectual or academic contexts.

**24. (4):** Trotting, cantering, and galloping are standard horse gaits, each indicating a specific speed or movement pattern. Spinning, however, is not a recognized horse gait and does not describe movement used in equestrian contexts.

**25. (2):** (A) - (IV), (B) - (III), (C) - (I), (D) - (II)

(A) **Neurologist:** treats nervous system disorders (IV)

(B) **Orthodontist:** specializes in correcting teeth alignment (III)

(C) **Cardiologist:** deals with heart-related issues (I)

(D) **Pathologist:** studies disease causes and diagnosis (II)

**26. (4):** The correct sequence is: Shrilal Shukla's (C), *Pahala Pandhav* is (B), a realistic portrayal of (D), the lives of labourers (A). This forms a clear and meaningful sentence introducing the author and theme of the work.

**27. (3):** The sentence becomes: My brother Jagan, (D) who is a doctor, (A) has gone to America (C) for his higher studies (B). This flows smoothly and logically describes the subject and his action.

**28. (4):** The word "arduous" means something that is difficult, strenuous, or requiring great effort. It does not relate to mystery, supportiveness, or continuity, making "difficult" the correct synonym.

**29. (4):** (A) - (III), (B) - (IV), (C) - (I), (D) - (II)

**(A) Meteorologist – (III):** A meteorologist studies and predicts weather and atmospheric conditions such as rainfall, storms, and temperature changes.

**(B) Cosmologist – (IV):** A cosmologist is concerned with the study of the universe, including its origin, structure, and overall dynamics like the Big Bang theory.

**(C) Psephology – (I):** Psephology is the branch of political science that deals with the study of elections and voting trends.

**(D) Paleontologist – (II):** A paleontologist examines fossils and ancient life forms to understand Earth's biological history.

Each word is matched with its correct scientific field, making Option 4 the correct answer.

**30.** **(3):** The sentence reads: With increasing purchasing power and larger disposable incomes (C), there has been growing awareness and rise in urge to be at par with (B), current trends in different countries across the world in terms of science, (D), technology, political opinions, military capacities, education, lifestyle, inter alia (A).
This sequence builds logically from cause to effect and covers all aspects clearly.

**31.** **(1):** Placate means to calm, pacify, or soothe someone who is angry. The opposite of calming is to provoke, which means to stir up anger or annoyance. Therefore, provoke is the correct antonym.

**32.** **(1):** Purge means to cleanse or remove impurities. The opposite would be to make something impure or dirty, which is contaminate. So, contaminate is the correct antonym.

**33.** **(2):** Disdain means a strong feeling of dislike or contempt for someone or something considered unworthy. It does not relate to astonishment or exhaustion. Hence, contempt is the correct synonym.

**34.** **(1):** The sentence refers to a continuous action starting in the past and still ongoing, which calls for the present perfect continuous tense. So, "It has been raining since morning" is grammatically correct.

**35.** **(1):** The sentence reads: Culture is a characteristic (A), way of life inspired by (C), the vision (B), and values of life (D). This sequence is grammatically logical and meaningful.

**36.** **(2):** Belligerent means hostile or aggressive, especially in a confrontational way. The opposite of being aggressive is friendly, which indicates a peaceful and kind attitude. Hence, friendly is the correct antonym.

**37.** **(3):** (A) - (I), (B) - (III), (C) - (IV), (D) - (II)
(A) **Aviator – (I):** One who operates or flies aircraft.
(B) **Jurist – (III):** A legal expert or authority in law.
(C) **Lexicographer – (IV):** A person who writes or compiles dictionaries.
(D) **Linguist – (II):** Someone who knows or studies multiple languages, especially foreign ones.

**38.** **(2):** Zenith means the highest point or peak. Its antonym is nadir, which means the lowest point. The two are direct opposites in figurative and literal usage, making nadir the correct answer.

**39.** **(3):** The correct phrase is "What is the time by your watch?", which is the standard and idiomatic way of asking someone the time based on their watch. Other options are grammatically or idiomatically incorrect.

**40.** **(3):** The sentence is giving a reason for the speaker's certainty that the people would get the tickets. "Since" means because, which fits perfectly: "Since they had been waiting in line all night..." conveys both cause and context.

**41.** **(3):** Iniquitous means extremely wicked, immoral, or unjust. The correct antonym is virtuous, which refers to someone who is morally good, righteous, or ethical. Hence, virtuous is the correct opposite.

**42.** **(2):** The sentence "Pakhom ............ with him and the deal was closed at one thousand Rupees" refers to reaching a deal. The word negotiated best fits here, as it means discussing terms to arrive at an agreement. Other options do not suit the context of closing a deal.

**43.** **(3):** (A) - (IV), (B) - (III), (C) - (I), (D) - (II)
(A) **Theology – (IV):** Theology is the study of religion and beliefs, focusing on divine concepts, scriptures, and spiritual matters.
(B) **Epistemology – (III):** Epistemology is a branch of philosophy that deals with knowledge—its nature, sources, and limits.
(C) **Ontology – (I):** Ontology studies the nature of existence and being, examining what entities exist and how they relate.
(D) **Anthropology – (II):** Anthropology is the study of human beings, including their origins, development, cultural customs, and evolution.

**44.** **(2):** (A) - (II), (B) - (IV), (C) - (I), (D) - (III)
(A) **Turned over a new leaf – (II):** This idiom means to reform or start afresh, which matches the sentence where someone changed for the better.
(B) **Set his face against – (IV):** This means to firmly oppose something, matching the context of sternly opposing child labour.
(C) **Put me on my mettle – (I):** Means to test someone's strength or ability, as in the sentence about a difficulty that made someone do their best.
(D) **To meet trouble half-way – (III):** Refers to anticipating or worrying about trouble before it happens, matching the idea of worrying before results are declared.

**45.** **(3):** Benediction means a blessing or expression of good wishes, especially at the end of a religious service. Among the options, blessing is the most accurate synonym.

**46.** **(3):** Ephemeral means lasting for a very short time. The best synonym among the options is temporary, which also refers to something not permanent or enduring.

**47.** **(1):** The sentence becomes:
(C) Apart from building muscle, repair tissues and
(A) producing hormones, proteins lend satiety, prevent
(D) quick breakdown of sugar in the blood and keep
(B) hunger pangs at bay, managing both weight and calories.
This arrangement logically explains the multiple roles of proteins in the body.

**48.** **(4):** Desultory means lacking a plan, purpose, or enthusiasm. In the sentence, it reflects that his studying was aimless and showed no real effort, making unenthusiastic the correct meaning.

**49.** **(1):** (A) - (IV), (B) - (III), (C) - (II), (D) - (I)
(A) The wind whispered... – Personification (IV): giving human traits to wind
(B) A plumber's house always has a leaking tap – Irony (III): unexpected contradiction
(C) Deafening silence – Oxymoron (II): two opposite terms used together
(D) Buzzing bees... – Alliteration (I): repetition of initial consonant sounds

**50.** **(3):** The correct sequence is:
(B) The large group
(D) of Sattriya dancers
(A) had left before Namita
(C) reached the venue for her performance.
This order forms a clear, grammatically correct sentence.

Previous Years' Paper

# Common University Entrance Test for UG Programmes

# CUET–UG—BUSINESS STUDIES

## Entrance Exam, 2025

(Exam held on 24-05-2025)

## Subject Code: 305

**1.** Which of the following shows the relationship between planning and controlling?
1. Both reinforce each other
2. Both are unrelated to each other
3. Both are substitutes of each other
4. Both are seperable twins of management

**2.** Arrange the following steps involved in selection process in the proper sequence.
(A) Preliminary screening
(B) Employment interview
(C) Reference and background checks
(D) Selection test
Choose the **correct** answer from the options given below:
1. (A), (C), (B), (D)    2. (A), (B), (C), (D)
3. (A), (D), (B), (C)    4. (C), (B), (D), (A)

**3.** Which of the following is NOT a limitation of formal organisation?
1. No clear-cut structure
2. Social interaction
3. Personal satisfaction
4. Rigidly laid down policies

**4.** "Not being afraid of the risks associated with business and relying on one's capabilities to successfully manage these". Identify the entrepreneurial competency highlighted in the aforesaid statement.
1. Assertiveness    2. Persistence
3. Self-confidence    4. Systematic Planning

**5.** Which principle of management is violated if a worker takes orders from two or more superiors?
1. Unity of direction
2. Unity of command
3. Order
4. Discipline

**6.** Which of the following statements is NOT true?
1. Price is an important element of the marketing mix.
2. Marketing is a social process.
3. Use of agressive selling techniques to make customers buy their products is marketing .
4. Placement is described as the set of marketing tools that firms use in a target market.

**7.** Match List-I with List-II.

| List-I | List-II |
|---|---|
| (A) Standards | (I) Setting of Reduction of defects from 10 pc to 5 pc per lot |
| (B) Management by exception | (II) Assigning additional workers and equipment to the project. |
| (C) Critical Control Point | (III) An attempt to control everything results in controlling nothing. |
| (D) Corrective Action | (IV) Focusing on KRAs |

Choose the **correct** answer from the options given below:
1. (A) - (II), (B) - (I), (C) - (III), (D) - (IV)
2. (A) - (I), (B) - (III), (C) - (IV), (D) - (II)
3. (A) - (I), (B) - (II), (C) - (IV), (D) - (III)
4. (A) - (III), (B) - (I), (C) - (IV), (D) - (II)

**8.** Which among the options given below is NOT a feature of management as a profession?
1. Restricted Entry
2. Professional Association
3. Service Motive
4. Personalised Application

**9.** Which of the following is a career oriented process?
1. Training    2. Development
3. Selection    4. Reference check

| **1.** 1 | **2.** 3 | **3.** 4 | **4.** 3 | **5.** 2 | **6.** 3, 4 | **7.** 2 | **8.** 4 | **9.** 2 |
|---|---|---|---|---|---|---|---|---|

**10.** Arrange the following steps involved in the process of organising in logical sequence:

(A) The activities which are similar in nature are grouped together.

(B) Jobs are allocated to the members of each department in accordance to their skills and competencies.

(C) Authority and reporting relationships are established to create a hierarchal structure.

(D) The work is divided into manageable activities so that duplication can be avoided.

Choose the **correct** answer from the options given below:

1. (A), (C), (B), (D)
2. (A), (B), (C), (D)
3. (D), (A), (B), (C)
4. (C), (B), (D), (A)

**11.** The importance of the business environment includes:

(A) Identifying first mover advantage

(B) Improving business performance

(C) Performance appraisal

(D) Coping with rapid changes

Choose the **correct** answer from the options given below:

1. (A), (B) and (D) only
2. (A), (B) and (C) only
3. (A), (B), (C) and (D)
4. (B), (C) and (D) only

**12.** Match List-I with List-II.

| List-I | List-II |
|---|---|
| (A) Responsibility | (I) Right to command subordinates and to give orders and exact obedience. |
| (B) Authority | (II) Downward transfer of authority from a superior to a subordinate. |
| (C) Accountability | (III) Obligation of a subordinate to perform the duty or tasks assigned to him. |
| (D) Delegation | (IV) Answerability for the accomplishment of the task assigned by the superior to his subordinate. |

Choose the **correct** answer from the options given below:

1. (A) - (II), (B) - (I), (C) - (III), (D) - (IV)
2. (A) - (I), (B) - (II), (C) - (III), (D) - (IV)
3. (A) - (III), (B) - (I), (C) - (IV), (D) - (II)
4. (A) - (III), (B) - (IV), (C) - (I), (D) - (II)

**13.** Span of management refers to:

1. Number of subordinates at lower level
2. Total number of managers
3. Number of subordinates under a superior
4. Number of levels in the organisation

**14.** Match List-I with List-II.

| List-I (Dimensions of business environment) | List-II (Elements) |
|---|---|
| (A) Social | (I) Literacy rates |
| (B) Economic | (II) Public Debt (internal and external) |
| (C) Technological | (III) Monopolistic Restrictive Trade Practices Act |
| (D) Legal | (IV) Scientific improvements |

Choose the **correct** answer from the options given below:

1. (A) - (I), (B) - (II), (C) - (IV), (D) - (III)
2. (A) - (II), (B) - (I), (C) - (III), (D) - (IV)
3. (A) - (IV), (B) - (II), (C) - (I), (D) - (III)
4. (A) - (III), (B) - (IV), (C) - (I), (D) - (II)

**15.** Match List-I with List-II.

| List-I. | List-II |
|---|---|
| (A) Physiological needs | (I) Friendship |
| (B) Safety and Security needs | (II) Status |
| (C) Esteem needs | (III) Confirmed job |
| (D) Social needs | (IV) Food |

Choose the **correct** answer from the options given below:

1. (A) - (IV), (B) - (III), (C) - (II), (D) - (I)
2. (A) - (I), (B) - (II), (C) - (III), (D) - (IV)
3. (A) - (II), (B) - (III), (C) - (IV), (D) - (I)
4. (A) - (III), (B) - (IV), (C) - (I), (D) - (II)

**16.** Identify the correct statements in the context of the planning.

(A) Planning will be a futile exercise if it is not acted upon or implemented.

(B) Planning implies a process which coordinates human efforts and assembles resources.

(C) Planning is closely connected with creativity and innovation.

(D) Planning is what managers at all levels do.

Choose the **correct** answer from the options given below:

1. (A) and (B) only
2. (A), (B) and (D) only
3. (A), (C) and (D) only
4. (B) and (D) only

**17.** Which of the following concepts is not related to F.W. Taylor?

1. Scalar Chain
2. Harmony, not discord
3. Standardisation and simplification of work
4. Cooperation, not individualism

**10.** 3 **11.** 1 **12.** 3 **13.** 3 **14.** 1 **15.** 1 **16.** 3 **17.** 1

**18.** In India, the advertisements for alcoholic beverages are banned, the dimension of business environment referred to here is:

1. Economic  2. Social
3. Political  4. Legal

**19.** Who is popularly known as the 'Father of Scientific Management'?

1. Frederick Taylor  2. A.H. Maslow
3. Douglas McGregor  4. Henry Fayol

**20.** Fayol says that discipline requires:

(A) Good supervisors at all levels
(B) Agreements should be clear and fair
(C) Removal of the employee
(D) Penalties should be fairly imposed

Choose the **correct** answer from the options given below:

1. (A), (B) and (D) only
2. (A), (C) and (D) only
3. (A), (B), (C) and (D)
4. (B), (C) and (D) only

**21.** Arrange the following steps of the planning process in a logical sequence.

(A) Establishing Objectives
(B) Developing Premises
(C) Evaluation of Alternatives
(D) Selecting a Course of Action

Choose the **correct** answer from the options given below:

1. (A), (B), (D), (C)
2. (A), (B), (C), (D)
3. (B), (A), (D), (C)
4. (C), (B), (D), (A)

**22.** Management is considered as art because of which of the following features?

(A) Systematized body of knowledge
(B) Existence of theoretical knowledge
(C) Personalized application
(D) Being based on practice and creativity

Choose the **correct** answer from the options given below:

1. (A), (B) and (D) only
2. (A), (B) and (C) only
3. (A), (B), (C) and (D)
4. (B), (C) and (D) only

**23.** When the demand of a product is inelastic, the firm is in a better position to fix?

1. Higher Prices  2. Lower Prices
3. Similar Prices  4. Competitive Prices

**24.** Money required for carrying out business activity is called:

1. Debt capital  2. Equity capital
3. Personal fund  4. Business Finance

**25.** To oversee the efforts of the workforce is the function of:

1. Supervisory level  2. Middle level
3. Top level  4. Top & middle level

**26.** Arrange the following steps involved in the process of financial planning in logical sequence.

(A) Sales forecast is made.
(B) Requirement of fixed capital and working capital is estimated.
(C) Expected profits are estimated.
(D) Sources of finance are identified.

Choose the **correct** answer from the options given below:

1. (A), (B), (C), (D)
2. (B), (D), (C), (A)
3. (C), (A), (D), (B)
4. (C), (B), (D), (A)

**27.** The criteria against which actual performance is measured in the process of controlling are called:

1. Grades  2. Classes
3. Standards  4. Appraisals

**28.** Arrange the following steps of controlling the process in a logical sequence.

(A) Reporting of deviation and their causes after comparison.
(B) Projecting the future and determining the goals and standards.
(C) Taking corrective action at an appropriate level.
(D) Measuring the work in terms of control standards.

Choose the **correct** answer from the options given below:

1. (B), (D), (A), (C)
2. (A), (B), (C), (D)
3. (B), (A), (D), (C)
4. (C), (B), (D), (A)

**29.** The nature of relationship of our country with foreign countries is an example of which dimension of the business environment?

1. Economic environment  2. Social environment
3. Legal environment  4. Political environment

**30.** Financial leverage is believed to be favorable if:

1. ROI is lower than cost of debt
2. ROI is higher than cost of debt
3. Debt is not easily available
4. If the interest rate is high

**18.** 4 **19.** 1 **20.** 1 **21.** 2 **22.** 4 **23.** 1 **24.** 4 **25.** 1 **26.** 1 **27.** 3 **28.** 1 **29.** 4 **30.** 2

**31.** Match List-I with List-II.

| List-I | List-II |
|---|---|
| (A) Net Working Capital | (I) Investments in long term assets. |
| (B) Fixed Capital Decision | (II) Proportion of debt in the overall capital. |
| (C) Financial Leverage | (III) Excess of current assets over current liabilities. |
| (D) Trading on Equity | (IV) Increase in profit earned by the equity shareholders due to the presence of fixed financial charges. |

Choose the **correct** answer from the options given below:

1. (A) - (IV), (B) - (II), (C) - (III), (D) - (I)
2. (A) - (I), (B) - (II), (C) - (III), (D) - (IV)
3. (A) (II), (B) (I), (C) - (IV), (D) - (III)
4. (A) - (III), (B) - (I), (C) - (II), (D) - (IV)

**32.** The process of earning profits and increasing wealth while posing characteristics such as risk taking, management, leadership and innovation is called:

1. Business development
2. Entrepreneurship
3. Planning
4. Business Process

**33.** "Planning requires logical and systematic thinking rather than guess work or wishful thinking". Identify the feature of planning highlighted in the aforesaid statement.

1. Planning is futuristic
2. Planning involves decision making
3. Planning is a mental exercise
4. Planning is pervasive

**34.** ............ is an impersonal form of communication by a marketer to promote a product.

1. Personal Selling
2. Advertising
3. Labelling
4. Packaging

**35.** Identify the type of plan which provides the prescribed ways or manner in which a task has to be performed considering the objective?

1. Rules
2. Strategies
3. Method
4. Procedures

**36.** Which of the following is the importance of delegation?

(A) High morale of subordinates
(B) Develops initiatives among employees
(C) Promotes centralisation
(D) Dilutes span of management

Choose the **correct** answer from the options given below:

1. (A), (B) and (D) only
2. (A) and (B) only
3. (B) and (D) only
4. (B), (C) and (D) only

**37.** Under which method of the training, a trainee is put under the guidance of a master worker?

1. Apprenticeship programme
2. Internship training
3. Vestibule training
4. Job rotation

**38.** The process whereby an executive develops an orderly pattern of group effort among his subordinates and secures unity of action is known as:

1. Control
2. Coordination
3. Reporting
4. Organising

**39.** Classifying products into different groups on the basis of their important features is called:

1. Grading
2. Branding
3. Labelling
4. Packaging

**40.** "Marketing methods used" is an important factor affecting which 'P' of marketing mix?

1. Product
2. Place
3. Price
4. Promotion

**Directions (Qs. No. 41-45):** *Read the given passage and answer the questions that follow:*

Manoj purchased a car from DD Motors invoiced at 10 lacs. The company offered many attractive gifts, like free insurance for the first two years, free pick-up and drop facilities for free servicing of upto 20,000 km etc. But after a few days, he noticed that the pick-up of the car was not good and there was some problem with the engine of the car. The company serviced the car for free, but even then, Manoj was not satisfied with the performance of the car. Manoj again called the customer care services of DD Motors, but DD Motors did not give him the due response. So he filed a complaint with the District Commission after but was not satisfied with the decision. He was very disturbed and, after a month, decided to appeal against it.

**41.** Manoj filed a complaint with the District Commission but was not satisfied with the decision. To which authority can he file an appeal against the decision?

1. National Commission
2. National Law Commission
3. State Commission
4. Supreme Court

**42.** Which rights of Manoj are violated by DD Motors?

1. Right to be informed and Right to safety
2. Right to be heard and Right to seek redressal
3. Right to choose/be assured and Right to safety
4. Right to consumer education and Right to be heard

**31.** 4 **32.** 2 **33.** 3 **34.** 2 **35.** 3 **36.** 2 **37.** 1 **38.** 2 **39.** 1 **40.** 3 **41.** 3 **42.** 2

**43.** Which of the following relief is NOT available to Manoj?
1. To remove the defect in car
2. To replace the defective car with a new one
3. To return the car and get refund of the price paid for the car
4. To retain the car and get a refund of the price paid for the car

**44.** Which of the following ways/means of consumer protection has been indicated in the above case?
1. Self regulation by the business
2. Business associations
3. Consumer organisations
4. Consumer awareness

**45.** Identify the responsibility which Manoj kept in mind in the above case?
1. Read labels carefully
2. Obtaining Bill/Invoice
3. Focusing on gifts only
4. Having a driving license

**Directions (Qs. No. 46-50):** *Read the given passage and answer the questions that follow:*

Sarah is the manager of a customer service team at a growing e-commerce company. The company has recently faced an influx of customer queries due to an increase in online orders. As the manager, Sarah's role is crucial in ensuring her team is aligned with the company's goals and capable of meeting the growing demand.

To begin, Sarah holds a team meeting where she clearly communicates the new expectations for handling customer inquiries, including targets for response times and quality standards. She provides clear guidelines on how to manage the increased workload and sets specific deadlines for individual tasks. Sarah integrates employees' efforts and ensures that the team understands the importance of customer satisfaction and how it contributes to the company's reputation and success.

Additionally, Sarah motivates her team by recognizing their achievements, offering constructive feedback, and providing training sessions to improve their skills. She fosters open communication, encouraging her team to express any challenges they encounter. Her leadership style includes delegation of responsibilities, which helps employees feel trusted and empowered.

Under Sarah's direction, the team becomes more efficient, delivering timely and high-quality customer service, which ultimately boosts customer satisfaction and supports the company's growth.

**46.** Which of the following is a key responsibility of Sarah when directing a team?
1. Establishing budget
2. Planning company strategy
3. Preparing a setting for initiating action
4. Hiring new employees

**47.** Which element of directing, does Sarah follow in encouraging employees to meet performance standards?
1. Delegation
2. Decentralisation
3. Control
4. Motivation

**48.** The above case clearly depicts that directing is the heart of management because Sarah:
1. Ensures managers plan all the work
2. Empowers employees and improves their engagement
3. Reduces employee responsibility
4. Limits feedback opportunities

**49.** What is the primary purpose of directing in management?
1. Setting company goals
2. Communicating with employees and guiding their actions
3. Developing new products
4. Analyzing market trends

**50.** Effective communication of Sarah in directing helps to:
1. Align employee efforts with organizational goals
2. Create confusion
3. Increase turnover
4. Avoid delegating tasks

# EXPLANATORY ANSWERS

**1. (1):** Planning and controlling are interrelated and mutually reinforcing functions of management. Planning sets objectives and outlines what needs to be done, while controlling ensures that actual performance aligns with the planned objectives. If deviations are found during controlling, it leads to revision in plans, and thus, the cycle continues.

**2. (3):** The correct order of the selection process is:
(A) Preliminary Screening – initial shortlisting of applications,
(D) Selection Test – to evaluate candidate's aptitude or skills,
(B) Employment Interview – face-to-face assessment,
(C) Reference and Background Checks – verification of candidate's credibility and past records.

**3. (4):** A major limitation of formal organisation is its dependence on fixed rules, procedures, and rigidly laid down policies. This restricts flexibility and adaptability in decision-making. Employees must follow strict hierarchies and cannot easily take initiative or respond quickly to dynamic situations. While formal structure ensures order and clarity, its rigidity often reduces creativity and slows response to change.

| **43.** 4 | **44.** 4 | **45.** 2 | **46.** 3 | **47.** 4 | **48.** 2 | **49.** 2 | **50.** 1 |
|---|---|---|---|---|---|---|---|

**4. (3):** The statement highlights the entrepreneur's belief in their own ability to face business risks and manage successfully. This reflects self-confidence, which is a core entrepreneurial competency involving assurance in one's own decisions and actions.

**5. (2):** According to Fayol's principles of management, unity of command states that each employee should receive orders from only one superior. Violation leads to confusion, conflict, and inefficiency in operations.

**6. (4): Use of aggressive selling techniques to make customers buy their products is marketing:** This statement is not true because marketing is a broader concept that focuses on identifying customer needs and satisfying them through value creation, not just pushing products through aggressive selling. Modern marketing emphasizes customer satisfaction, building relationships, and delivering value, whereas aggressive selling is a narrow and outdated view.

**(4) Placement is described as the set of marketing tools that firms use in a target market:** This is also not true. The set of marketing tools used by firms in a target market is known as the marketing mix, which includes Product, Price, Place (Placement), and Promotion — commonly referred to as the 4Ps. "Placement" alone refers only to distribution or the way the product reaches the consumer, not the entire set of tools. Hence, both options 3 and 4 are NOT true.

**7. (2):** (A) - (I), (B) - (III), (C) - (IV), (D) - (II):

(A) Standards – (I): Standards define the expected level of performance, such as reducing defects from 10 pc to 5 pc per lot.

(B) Management by Exception – (III): This principle says that trying to control everything is ineffective; focus should be on deviations or exceptions only.

(C) Critical Control Point – (IV): It involves identifying Key Result Areas (KRAs) where control is most effective.

(D) Corrective Action – (II): This refers to measures like assigning extra workers/equipment to fix deviations from plans.

**8. (4):** Management as a profession is expected to follow a standardized and impersonal approach based on principles, codes of conduct, and professional ethics. While restricted entry, professional association, and service motive are accepted features of any profession, personalised application is not. Personal discretion or subjective decision-making based on personal bias goes against the professional nature of management. A profession is supposed to apply knowledge objectively and uniformly, not personally.

**9. (2):** Development is a career-oriented and long-term process focused on overall growth of the individual. It helps employees grow their capabilities for future responsibilities and roles. Unlike training, which is job-specific and short-term, development enhances conceptual, interpersonal, and decision-making skills that shape career progression. Selection and reference checks are hiring processes, not focused on career building.

**10. (3):** The correct logical sequence in the process of organising is:

(D) The work is divided into manageable activities so that duplication can be avoided: The first step is to identify and divide the total work into smaller tasks or activities. This is called division of work, and it helps avoid overlap and confusion.

(A) The activities which are similar in nature are grouped together: This step is known as departmentalisation, where related tasks are grouped into departments like finance, marketing, HR, etc.

(B) Jobs are allocated to the members of each department in accordance to their skills and competencies: This step involves assignment of duties. Each person is given a specific task that suits their skills.

(C) Authority and reporting relationships are established to create a hierarchal structure: This step creates the organizational structure by defining lines of authority, who reports to whom, and levels of responsibility.

Thus, the sequence D $\rightarrow$ A $\rightarrow$ B $\rightarrow$ C reflects the natural progression from planning the work to creating a structured hierarchy.

**11. (1):** The business environment is important for several reasons:

(A) **Identifying first mover advantage:** By analysing environmental trends, businesses can launch innovative products or services before competitors.

(B) **Improving business performance:** Understanding external factors helps in adapting better and making informed decisions, improving overall performance.

(D) **Coping with rapid changes:** A dynamic business environment requires quick adaptation. Awareness helps businesses survive and grow.

(C) **Performance appraisal,** however, is an internal HR activity, not directly linked to external business environment analysis.

**12. (3):** (A) - (III), (B) - (I), (C) - (IV), (D) - (II):

(A) Responsibility – (III): It is the obligation to perform assigned tasks.

(B) Authority – (I): It is the right to command and issue orders.

(C) Accountability – (IV): It is the answerability for fulfilling responsibilities.

(D) Delegation – (II): It is the downward transfer of authority from superior to subordinate.

These four are fundamental concepts in organizing and ensure clarity in task distribution and command relationships.

**13. (3):** Span of management, also called span of control, refers to how many subordinates report directly to one manager. A wider span means more subordinates per manager; a narrower span means fewer. It affects the structure of the organisation—wider spans create flatter structures, while narrow spans lead to more hierarchical levels.

**14. (1):** (A) - (I), (B) - (II), (C) - (IV), (D) - (III):

(A) Social – (I) Literacy rates: Social environment includes elements like education levels, lifestyles, and cultural values. Literacy rate is a key social factor.

(B) Economic – (II) Public Debt: Economic environment covers factors like national income, inflation, interest rates, and public debt.

(C) Technological – (IV) Scientific improvements: Technological environment includes research, innovation, and technological advancements.

(D) Legal – (III) Monopolistic Restrictive Trade Practices Act: Legal environment includes laws and regulations like MRTP Act, Consumer Protection Act, etc., which affect business operations.

**15. (1):** This is based on Maslow's hierarchy of needs:

(A) Physiological needs – (IV) Food: Basic needs for survival like food, water, shelter.

(B) Safety and Security needs – (III) Confirmed job: Includes job security, financial security, health, and safety.

(C) Esteem needs – (II) Status: Desire for respect, recognition, and status.

(D) Social needs – (I) Friendship: The need for belonging, love, and interpersonal relationships.

**16. (3):** (A), (C) and (D) only:

(A) Planning becomes meaningless without execution. Action is essential to give effect to any plan.

(C) Planning involves foresight, setting goals, and devising new ideas, which directly connects it to creativity and innovation.

(D) Planning is a universal function performed by managers at all levels, from top to operational.

(B) is incorrect because coordination and assembling resources relate more to organising, not planning.

**17. (1):** Scalar Chain is a principle given by Henry Fayol, not F.W. Taylor. Taylor's scientific management includes concepts like:

- Harmony, not discord
- Standardisation and simplification of work
- Cooperation, not individualism

These were part of Taylor's efforts to improve efficiency and reduce conflict in industrial settings.

**18. (4):** A ban on advertisements of alcoholic beverages refers to government regulations and legal restrictions imposed on business practices. This reflects the legal environment, which includes laws, rules, and legal policies affecting businesses.

**19. (1):** Frederick Winslow Taylor is known as the Father of Scientific Management. He introduced techniques like time study, motion study, standardisation, and functional foremanship to improve industrial productivity.

**20. (1):** Henri Fayol emphasized discipline as one of his 14 principles of management. According to him:

(A) Good supervisors at all levels ensure proper guidance and rule enforcement.

(B) Agreements should be clear and fair so employees understand expectations.

(D) Penalties should be fairly imposed to maintain consistency and justice.

(C) Removal of an employee is an extreme measure, not a direct requirement of discipline as per Fayol's principle.

**21. (2):** The correct sequence of the planning process is:

(A) **Establishing Objectives:** First step—defining what the organisation wants to achieve.

(B) **Developing Premises:** Assumptions about future conditions are made to base planning decisions.

(C) **Evaluation of Alternatives:** Various options to achieve objectives are analysed.

(D) **Selecting a Course of Action:** The most suitable alternative is chosen for implementation.

**22. (4):** Management is considered an art because:

(B) It involves theoretical knowledge, but not in a rigid scientific format.

(C) It requires personalized application, meaning each manager applies principles differently.

(D) It is based on practice and creativity, as managers develop skills through experience.

(A) It refers more to the science aspect of management, not the artistic side.

**23. (1):** When the demand is inelastic, it means that consumers will continue buying the product even if the price increases. In such cases, the firm has greater flexibility to fix higher prices without significantly affecting demand. This typically occurs for essential goods or products with no close substitutes.

**24. (4):** The money needed to carry out various business operations such as purchasing assets, paying salaries, or producing goods is collectively called business finance. It includes both short-term and long-term capital requirements from various sources like equity, debt, or retained earnings.

**25. (1):** The supervisory level of management is directly responsible for overseeing and guiding the efforts of workers. They ensure day-to-day operations run smoothly, maintain discipline, monitor work, and provide feedback to the workforce. This level acts as a link between workers and middle management.

**26. (1):** The correct logical sequence in the financial planning process is:

(A) **Sales forecast is made:** Estimating future sales is the first step as it influences other financial aspects.

(B) **Requirement of fixed and working capital is estimated:** Based on sales expectations, the capital needed for assets and operations is calculated.

(C) **Expected profits are estimated:** Profit projections depend on cost and revenue analysis.

(D) **Sources of finance are identified:** Once capital needs and profit potential are clear, suitable funding sources are chosen.

**27. (3):** In the process of controlling, performance is evaluated by comparing it to predefined standards. Standards act as benchmarks or criteria that define the expected level of performance. If actual performance deviates from these standards, corrective action is taken.

**28. (1):** The correct sequence of steps in the controlling process is:

(B) **Projecting the future and determining the goals and standards:** This is the first step where performance standards are set.

(D) **Measuring the work in terms of control standards:** Actual performance is measured.

(A) **Reporting of deviation and their causes after comparison:** Deviations are identified and analyzed.

(C) **Taking corrective action at an appropriate level:** Necessary actions are taken to fix the issues and align future performance.

**29. (4):** The relationship of our country with foreign nations reflects the political environment. This includes diplomatic relations, trade policies, stability of government, taxation policies on foreign investments, etc., all of which directly impact businesses operating internationally.

**30. (2):** Financial leverage is said to be favorable when the Return on Investment (ROI) exceeds the cost of debt. In such cases, the use of borrowed funds adds to the returns of shareholders, increasing the profitability of the firm. If ROI is lower than the interest on debt, leverage becomes unfavorable.

**31. (4):** (A) - (III), (B) - (I), (C) - (II), (D) - (IV):

(A) Net Working Capital – (III): It is calculated as Current Assets minus Current Liabilities, reflecting short-term liquidity.

(B) Fixed Capital – (I): Refers to investments in long-term assets like buildings, machinery, etc., essential for production.

(C) Financial Leverage – (II): Indicates the proportion of debt used in total capital structure.

(D) Trading on Equity – (IV): Occurs when fixed financial charges like interest on debt lead to increased earnings for equity shareholders due to higher return on capital employed than cost of debt.

**32. (2):** Entrepreneurship is the process of creating and running a business venture while taking risks and showing qualities like innovation, leadership, planning, and risk-taking. Its main aim is wealth creation and profit generation through new ideas or market opportunities.

**33. (3):** This feature highlights that planning is based on rational thinking, analysis, and forecasting, not guesswork or emotional decisions. It requires a logical and systematic approach, involving intellect and foresight to choose the best course of action.

**34. (2):** Advertising is an impersonal form of communication where a marketer communicates with a large audience to promote a product or service through mass media (TV, print, digital, etc.). Unlike personal selling, there is no direct interaction with individuals; the message is one-way and aimed at creating awareness or persuading buyers.

**35. (3):** A method is a specific and prescribed way of performing a task or activity. It is a type of plan that defines the step-by-step manner in which a job is to be done, considering the objectives. Methods are part of procedures and help in standardizing how activities are performed efficiently.

**36. (2):** The importance of delegation lies in empowering subordinates and building a capable workforce.

(A) High morale of subordinates: When responsibility and authority are delegated, it shows trust, which boosts confidence and motivation.

(B) Develops initiatives among employees: Delegation gives employees autonomy to take decisions, enhancing their decision-making and leadership skills.

(C) Promotes centralisation is incorrect because delegation actually supports decentralisation.

(D) Dilutes span of management is also not a key importance of delegation; rather, it helps manage workload but doesn't directly relate to altering span of control.

**37. (1):** In the apprenticeship training method, a trainee learns by working under the direct supervision of an experienced master worker. This method is commonly used in technical trades like carpentry, plumbing, and engineering, where practical, hands-on skills are essential and developed over a long period.

**38. (2):** Coordination refers to the process by which a manager ensures harmony of efforts among different individuals and departments to achieve common objectives. It involves aligning group efforts and maintaining unity of action, which is essential for organizational efficiency.

**39. (1):** Grading is the process of classifying products into different categories or classes based on their features, quality, size, or other characteristics. It helps in standardization and enables customers to easily compare and choose products of desired quality.

**40. (3):** The phrase "marketing methods used" influences the Price component of the marketing mix when it refers to how a company positions its product and uses different pricing techniques based on marketing strategies. For example, heavy promotional costs, premium branding, or niche targeting through marketing can lead to higher pricing decisions. Thus, the pricing strategy is often shaped by the marketing methods employed, such as cost-based pricing, value-based pricing, or competition-based pricing.

**41. (3):** Since Manoj first approached the District Commission and was not satisfied with its decision, he can appeal to the State Commission. As per the Consumer Protection Act, an appeal against the decision of the District Commission must be filed before the State Commission within the prescribed time.

**42. (2):** DD Motors ignored Manoj's complaints and did not respond adequately to his dissatisfaction. This violates his Right to be heard, which ensures that consumers can voice complaints and concerns. It also violates the Right to seek redressal, which ensures that consumers are entitled to fair settlement of genuine grievances.

**43. (4):** A consumer cannot retain the product and simultaneously claim a full refund, as it amounts to unjust enrichment. The legal relief includes repair, replacement, or return for refund—but not retention with full refund. Hence, this option is not a valid relief.

**44. (4):** The case shows that Manoj was aware of his consumer rights and proceeded to file a complaint and appeal—this reflects consumer awareness, a key way of consumer protection through individual vigilance and informed action.

**45. (2):** Manoj filed a formal complaint, which implies he had proper documentation like a bill/invoice. This reflects a responsible consumer behavior, as such proof is necessary to seek legal redressal in consumer forums.

**46. (3):** Sarah's role in holding meetings, setting expectations, assigning tasks, and guiding employees shows she is creating an environment where action can begin, which is a key part of the directing function in management. This prepares the team to act efficiently toward goals.

**47. (4):** By recognizing achievements, giving constructive feedback, and offering training, Sarah is encouraging employees to perform better. These are actions rooted in motivation, a vital element of directing that energizes individuals to achieve desired results.

**48. (2):** The passage emphasizes how Sarah delegates responsibilities, fosters open communication, and offers support, all of which empower the team and increase their involvement and commitment. This shows how directing is central to successful management.

**49. (2):** The main objective of directing is to guide, supervise, communicate, and lead employees so their actions align with the organization's goals. Sarah performs all these functions, highlighting the true purpose of directing in management.

**50. (1):** Sarah's clear communication regarding expectations, targets, and the importance of customer satisfaction ensures that employee actions are in sync with company goals, which is the core benefit of effective communication in directing.

## Previous Years' Paper

# Common University Entrance Test for UG Programmes

# CUET–UG—MATHEMATICS

# Entrance Exam, 2025

(Exam held on 14-05-2025)

## Section-A : (Mandatory)

**1.** Let $A = [a_{ij}]_{n \times n}$ be a matrix. Then Match List-I with List-II.

| List-I | List-II |
|---|---|
| A. $A^T = A$ | I. A is a singular matrix |
| B. $A^T = -A$ | II. A is a non-singular matrix |
| C. $\|A\| = 0$ | III. A is a skew symmetric matrix |
| D. $\|A\| \neq 0$ | IV. A is symmetric matrix |

Choose the ***correct*** answer from the options given below:

1. A-IV, B-III, C-II, D-I
2. A-IV, B-III, C-I, D-II
3. A-I, B-II, C-III, D-IV
4. A-I, B-II, C-IV, D-III

**2.** If $A = \begin{bmatrix} 1 & 0 \\ 0 & -1 \end{bmatrix}$ and $B = \begin{bmatrix} 0 & 1 \\ 1 & 0 \end{bmatrix}$ then the matrix AB is equal to:

1. $\begin{bmatrix} 0 & 0 \\ 0 & 0 \end{bmatrix}$
2. $\begin{bmatrix} 0 & -1 \\ 1 & 0 \end{bmatrix}$
3. $\begin{bmatrix} 0 & 1 \\ -1 & 0 \end{bmatrix}$
4. $\begin{bmatrix} 1 & 1 \\ 1 & -1 \end{bmatrix}$

**3.** If A is a square matrix and I is the identity matrix of same order such that $A^2 = I$, then $(A - I)^3 + (A + I)^3 - 3A$ is equal to:

1. A
2. 2A
3. 3A
4. 5A

**4.** If $A = \begin{bmatrix} 0 & 0 & \sqrt{3} \\ 0 & \sqrt{3} & 0 \\ \sqrt{3} & 0 & 0 \end{bmatrix}$, then $|adj\ A|$ is equal to:

1. 3
2. 9
3. 27
4. 81

**5.** If $y = 3e^{2x} + 2e^{3x}$, then $\frac{d^2y}{dx^2} + 6y$ is equal to:

1. $\frac{dy}{dx}$
2. $5\frac{dy}{dx}$
3. $6\frac{dy}{dx}$
4. $30\frac{dy}{dx}$

**6.** The interval, on which the function $f(x) = x^2e^{-x}$ is increasing, is equal to:

1. $(-\infty, \infty)$
2. $(-\infty, 2) \cup (2, \infty)$
3. $(-2, 0)$
4. $(0, 2)$

**7.** If the maximum value of the function $f(x) = \frac{\log_e x}{x}$, $x > 0$ occurs at $x = a$, then $a^2f''(a)$ is equal to:

1. $\frac{5}{e}$
2. $-\frac{1}{e}$
3. $-\frac{1}{e^3}$
4. $-5e^3$

**8.** $\int_1^4 |x - 2|\, dx$ is equal to:

1. 5
2. $\frac{7}{2}$
3. $\frac{3}{2}$
4. $\frac{5}{2}$

| 1. 2 | 2. 3 | 3. 4 | 4. 3 | 5. 2 | 6. 4 | 7. 2 | 8. 4 |
|---|---|---|---|---|---|---|---|

**9.** The integral $I = \int \frac{e^{5\log_e x} - e^{4\log_e x}}{e^{3\log_e x} - e^{2\log_e x}} dx$ is equal to:

1. $\frac{x}{2} + C$, where C is the constant of integration
2. $\frac{x^2}{2} + C$, where C is the constant of integration
3. $\frac{x^3}{3} + C$, where C is the constant of integration
4. $\frac{x^4}{4} + C$, where C is the constant of integration

**10.** The area (in sq. units) of the region bounded by the parabola $y^2 = 4x$ and the line $x = 1$ is:

1. $\frac{1}{3}$ 2. $\frac{4}{3}$
3. $\frac{5}{3}$ 4. $\frac{8}{3}$

**11.** Which of the following are linear first order differential equations?

A. $\frac{dy}{dx} + P(x)y = Q(x)$ B. $\frac{dx}{dy} + P(y)x = Q(y)$

C. $(x - y)\frac{dy}{dx} = x + 2y$ D. $(1 + x^2)\frac{dy}{dx} + 2xy = 2$

Choose the ***correct*** answer from the options given below:

1. A, B and D only 2. A and B only
3. A, B and C only 4. A, B, C and D

**12.** The solution of the differential equation

$\log_e \left(\frac{dy}{dx}\right) = 3x + 4y$ is given by:

1. $4e^{3x} + 3e^{-4y} + C = 0$, where C is constant of integration
2. $3e^{3x} + 4e^{-4y} + C = 0$, where C is constant of integration
3. $4e^{-3x} + 3e^{4y} + C = 0$, where C is constant of integration
4. $3e^{-3x} + 4e^{4y} + C = 0$, where C is constant of integration

**13.** The probability distribution of a random variable X is given by

| X | 0 | 1 | 2 |
|---|---|---|---|
| P(X) | $1 - 7a^2$ | $\frac{1}{2}a + \frac{1}{4}$ | $a^2$ |

If $a > 0$, then $P(0 < x \le 2)$ is equal to:

1. $\frac{1}{16}$ 2. $\frac{3}{18}$
3. $\frac{7}{16}$ 4. $\frac{9}{16}$

**14.** The corner points of the feasible region associated with the LLP: Maximise $Z = px + qy$, $p, q > 0$ subject to $2x + y \le 10$, $x + 3y \le 15$, $x, y \ge 0$ are (0, 0), (5, 0), (3, 4) and (0, 5). If optimum value occurs at both (3, 4) and (0, 5), then:

1. $p = q$ 2. $p = 2q$
3. $p = 3q$ 4. $q = 3p$

**15.** Consider the LPP: Minimize $Z = x + 2y$ subject to $2x + y \ge 3$, $x + 2y \ge 6$, $x, y \ge 0$. The optimal feasible solution occurs at:

1. (6, 0) only
2. (0, 3) only
3. Neither (6, 0) nor (0, 3)
4. Both (6, 0) and (0, 3)

## Section-B : Core (Optional)*

**16.** Let $f : R \to R$ be defined as $f(x) = 10x$. Then (Where R is the set of real numbers)

1. $f$ is both one-one and onto
2. $f$ is onto but not one-one
3. $f$ is one-one but not onto
4. $f$ is neither one-one nor onto

**17.** Let A = {1, 2, 3}. Then, the number of relations containing (1, 2) and (1, 3), which are reflexive and symmetric but not transitive, is:

1. 1 2. 2
3. 3 4. 4

**18.** For $|x| < 1$, $\sin(\tan^{-1} x)$ equal to:

1. $\frac{1}{\sqrt{1+x^2}}$ 2. $\frac{1}{\sqrt{1-x^2}}$
3. $\frac{x}{\sqrt{1-x^2}}$ 4. $\frac{x}{\sqrt{1+x^2}}$

**19.** Let $A = \begin{bmatrix} 1 & 2 & 1 \\ -1 & 3 & 2 \\ 2 & 4 & 1 \end{bmatrix}$ and $M_{ij}$, $A_{ij}$ respectively denote the minor, co-factor of an element $a_{ij}$ of matrix A, then which of the following are true?

A. $M_{22} = -1$ B. $A_{23} = 0$
C. $A_{32} = 3$ D. $M_{23} = 1$
E. $M_{32} = -3$

Choose the ***correct*** answer from the options given below:

1. A and B only 2. A, B, C and E only
3. A, D and E only 4. A, C and E only

| 9. 3 | 10. 4 | 11. 1 | 12. 1 | 13. 3 | 14. 4 | 15. 4 | 16. 1 | 17. 1 | 18. 4 | 19. 1 |
|---|---|---|---|---|---|---|---|---|---|---|

* In this book we have included Mathematics (core) only, Mathematics (applied) have not been included.

**20.** Let $A = \begin{bmatrix} \cos\theta & -\sin\theta \\ \sin\theta & \cos\theta \end{bmatrix}$ and $I = \begin{bmatrix} 1 & 0 \\ 0 & 1 \end{bmatrix}$.

If $A^T + A = I$, then:

1. $\theta = 2n\pi + \frac{\pi}{3}, n \in \mathbb{Z}$
2. $\theta = n\pi, n \in \mathbb{Z}$
3. $\theta = (2n+1)\frac{\pi}{2}, n \in \mathbb{Z}$
4. $\theta = 2n\pi + \frac{\pi}{6}, n \in \mathbb{Z}$

**21.** If A and B are skew-symmetric matrices, then which one of the following is NOT true?

1. $A^3 + B^5$ is skew-symmetric
2. $A^{19}$ is skew-symmetric
3. $B^{14}$ is symmetric
4. $A^4 + B^5$ is symmetric

**22.** If A and B are invertible matrices then which of the following statement is NOT correct?

1. $\text{adj}A = |A|A^{-1}$
2. $(A + B)^{-1} = A^{-1} + B^{-1}$
3. $|A^{-1}| = |A|^{-1}$
4. $(AB)^{-1} = B^{-1}A^{-1}$

**23.** Let $A = [a_{ij}]_{2\times3}$ and $B = [b_{ij}]_{3\times2}$, then $|5AB|$ is equal to:

1. $5^2 \cdot |A| \cdot |B|$
2. $5^3 \cdot |A| \cdot |B|$
3. $5^2 |AB|$
4. $5^3 |AB|$

**24.** Let AX = B be a system of three linear equations in three variables. Then the system has:

A. a unique solutions if $|A| = 0$
B. a unique solutions if $|A| \neq 0$
C. no solutions if $|A| = 0$ and $(\text{adj } A)\, B \neq 0$
D. infinitely many solutions if $|A| = 0$ and $(\text{adj } A)B = 0$

Choose the ***correct*** answer from the options given below:

1. A, C and D only
2. B, C and D only
3. B only
4. B and C only

**25.** If the function $f(x) = \begin{cases} \dfrac{k\cos x}{\pi - 2x} & : x \neq \dfrac{\pi}{2} \\ 3 & : x = \dfrac{\pi}{2} \end{cases}$ is continuous at $x = \frac{\pi}{2}$, then $k$ is equal to:

1. 6
2. 5
3. –6
4. 4

**26.** Match List-I with List-II.

| List-I | List-II |
|---|---|
| A. $f(x) = \lvert x\rvert$ | I. Not differentiable at $x = -2$ only |
| B. $f(x) = \lvert x + 2\rvert$ | II. Not differentiable at $x = 0$ only |
| C. $f(x) = \lvert x^2 - 4\rvert$ | III. Not differentiable at $x = 2$ only |
| D. $f(x) = \lvert x - 2\rvert$ | IV. Not differentiable at $x = 2, -2$ only |

Choose the ***correct*** answer from the options given below:

1. A-I, B-II, C-III, D-IV
2. A-II, B-I, C-IV, D-III
3. A-II, B-I, C-III, D-IV
4. A-IV, B-III, C-II, D-I

**27.** Let $y = \sin(\cos x^2)$, then the value of $\frac{dy}{dx}$ at $x = \frac{\sqrt{\pi}}{2}$ is equal to:

1. $\frac{-\sqrt{\pi}}{2}\cos\left(\frac{1}{\sqrt{2}}\right)$
2. $-\sqrt{\frac{\pi}{2}}\cos\left(\frac{1}{\sqrt{2}}\right)$
3. $-\sqrt{\frac{\pi}{2}}\sin\left(\frac{1}{\sqrt{2}}\right)$
4. $\sqrt{\frac{\pi}{2}}\sin\left(\frac{1}{\sqrt{2}}\right)$

**28.** Match List-I with List-II.

| List-I | List-II |
|---|---|
| A. The minimum value of $f(x) = (2x - 1)^2 + 3$ | I. 4 |
| B. The maximum value of $f(x) = -\lvert x + 1\rvert + 4$ | II. 10 |
| C. The minimum value of $f(x) = \sin(2x) + 6$ | III. 3 |
| D. The maximum value of $f(x) = -(x - 1)^2 + 10$ | IV. 5 |

Choose the ***correct*** answer from the options given below:

1. A-I, B-II, C-III, D-IV
2. A-III, B-II, C-I, D-IV
3. A-III, B-I, C-IV, D-II
4. A-III, B-IV, C-I, D-II

| **20.** 1 | **21.** 4 | **22.** 2 | **23.** 3 | **24.** 2 | **25.** 1 | **26.** 2 | **27.** 2 | **28.** 3 |
|---|---|---|---|---|---|---|---|---|

**29.** The function $f(x) = \tan x - x$.

1. is a decreasing function on $\left[0, \frac{\pi}{2}\right)$
2. is an increasing function on $\left[0, \frac{\pi}{2}\right)$
3. is a constant function
4. is neither increasing nor decreasing function on $\left[0, \frac{\pi}{2}\right)$

**30.** The rate of change of area of a circle with respect to its circumference when radius is 4 cm, is:

1. 2 $cm^2/cm$
2. 4 $cm^2/cm$
3. 8 $cm^2/cm$
4. 16 $cm^2/cm$

**31.** $\int_{\pi/6}^{\pi/3} \frac{\tan x}{\tan x + \cot x} dx$ is equal to:

1. $\frac{\pi}{4}$
2. 0
3. $\frac{\pi}{6}$
4. $\frac{\pi}{12}$

**32.** Match List-I with List-II.

| List-I (Definite integral) | List-II (Value) |
|---|---|
| A. $\int_0^1 \frac{2x}{1+x^2} dx$ | I. 2 |
| B. $\int_{-1}^1 \sin^3 x \cos^4 x\, dx$ | II. $\log_e\left(\frac{3}{2}\right)$ |
| C. $\int_0^\pi \sin x\, dx$ | III. $\log_e 2$ |
| D. $\int_2^3 \frac{2}{x^2-1} dx$ | IV. 0 |

Choose the ***correct*** answer from the options given below:

1. A-I, B-II, C-III, D-IV
2. A-III, B-II, C-I, D-IV
3. A-III, B-I, C-IV, D-II
4. A-III, B-IV, C-I, D-II

**33.** The integral $I = \int e^x \left(\frac{x-1}{3x^2}\right) dx$ is equal to:

1. $\frac{1}{3}\left(\frac{x^2}{2} - x\right) + C$, where C is constant of integration
2. $\left(\frac{x^2}{2} - x\right)e^x + C$, where C is constant of integration
3. $\frac{1}{3x^2} e^x + C$, where C is constant of integration
4. $\frac{1}{3x} e^x + C$, where C is constant of integration

**34.** The area (in sq. units) of the region bounded by the curve $y = x^5$, the $x$-axis and the ordinates $x = -1$ and $x = 1$ is equal to:

1. $\frac{1}{6}$
2. $\frac{1}{3}$
3. $\frac{1}{2}$
4. $\frac{2}{3}$

**35.** The area (in sq. units) of the region bounded by $y = 2\sqrt{1-x^2}$, $x \in [0, 1]$ and $x$-axis is equal to:

1. 1
2. 2
3. $\frac{\pi}{2}$
4. $\frac{\pi}{4}$

**36.** The integrating factor of the differential equation $(x \log_e x)\frac{dy}{dx} + y = 2\log_e x$ is:

1. $\log_e x$
2. $x$
3. $\frac{1}{x}$
4. $\frac{1}{\log_e x}$

**37.** Consider the differential equation,

$$x\frac{dy}{dx} = y(\log_e y - \log_e x + 1),$$

then which of the following are true?

A. It is a linear differential equation

B. It is a homogenous differential equation

C. Its general solution is $\log_e\left(\frac{y}{x}\right) = Cx$, where C is constant of integration

D. Its general solution is $\log_e\left(\frac{x}{y}\right) = Cy$, where C is constant of integration

E. If $y(1) = 1$, then its particular solution is $y = x$

Choose the ***correct*** answer from the options given below:

1. A, D and E only
2. A and D only
3. B and C only
4. B, C and E only

| **29.** 2 | **30.** 2 | **31.** 4 | **32.** 4 | **33.** 4 | **34.** 2 | **35.** 3 | **36.** 1 | **37.** 4 |
|---|---|---|---|---|---|---|---|---|

**38.** If $\hat{i}$, $\hat{j}$ and $\hat{k}$, are unit vector along co-ordinates axes OX, OY and OZ respectively, then which of the following is/are true?

A. $\hat{i} \times \hat{i} = \vec{0}$ B. $\hat{i} \times \hat{k} = \hat{j}$

C. $\hat{i} \cdot \hat{i} = 1$ D. $\hat{i} \cdot \hat{j} = 0$

Choose the ***correct*** answer from the options given below:

1. A and B only 2. A, C and D only
3. A only 4. A, B, C and D

**39.** If the points A, B, C with position vectors $20\hat{i} + \lambda\hat{j}$, $5\hat{i} - \hat{j}$ and $10\hat{i} - 13\hat{j}$ respectively are collinear, then the value of $\lambda$ is:

1. 12 2. −37
3. 37 4. −12

**40.** If $\vec{a} + \vec{b} + \vec{c} = \vec{0}$ and $|\vec{a}| = 3$, $|\vec{b}| = 5$, $|\vec{c}| = 7$, then the angle between $\vec{a}$ and $\vec{b}$ is:

1. $\frac{\pi}{2}$ 2. $\frac{\pi}{3}$

3. $\frac{\pi}{4}$ 4. $\frac{\pi}{6}$

**41.** Let $\vec{a} = \hat{i} + 4\hat{j}$, $\vec{b} = 4\hat{j} + \hat{k}$ and $\vec{c} = \hat{i} - 2\hat{k}$. If $\vec{d}$ is a vector perpendicular to both $\vec{a}$ and $\vec{b}$ such that $\vec{c} \cdot \vec{d} = 16$, then $|\vec{d}|$ is equal to:

1. $\sqrt{33}$ 2. $2\sqrt{33}$
3. $3\sqrt{33}$ 4. $4\sqrt{33}$

**42.** If a line makes angles $\alpha$, $\beta$, $\gamma$ with the positive directions of $x$-axis, $y$-axis and $z$-axis respectively, then $\sin^2 \alpha + \sin^2\beta + \sin^2\gamma$ is equal to:

1. 1 2. 2
3. 3 4. −2

**43.** Consider the line $\vec{r} = \hat{i} - 2\hat{j} + 4\hat{k} + \lambda(-\hat{i} + 2\hat{j} - 4\hat{k})$

Match List-I with List-II.

| List-I | List-II |
|---|---|
| A. A point on the given line | I. $\left(\frac{-1}{\sqrt{21}}, \frac{2}{\sqrt{21}}, \frac{-4}{\sqrt{21}}\right)$ |
| B. direction ratios of the line | II. (4, −2, −2) |
| C. direction cosines of the line | III. (1, −2, 4) |
| D. direction ratios of a line perpendicular to given line | IV. (−1, 2, −4) |

Choose the ***correct*** answer from the options given below:

1. A-IV, B-III, C-II, D-I
2. A-III, B-IV, C-II, D-I
3. A-III, B-IV, C-I, D-II
4. A-IV, B-III, C-I, D-II

**44.** The shortest distance between the lines $\frac{x-1}{2} = \frac{y-2}{3} = \frac{z-3}{4}$ and $\frac{x-2}{4} = \frac{y-4}{6} = \frac{z-5}{8}$ is equal to:

1. 0 2. $\sqrt{\frac{29}{5}}$

3. $\sqrt{\frac{5}{29}}$ 4. $\sqrt{5}$

**45.** Which one of the following set of constraints does the given shaded region represent?

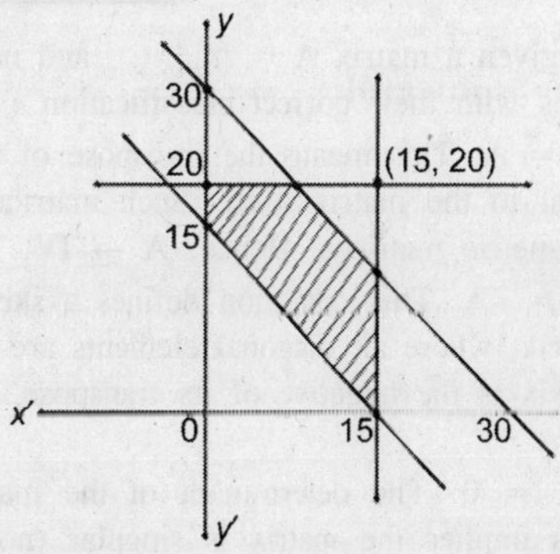


1. $x + y \le 30$, $x + y \ge 15$, $x \le 15$, $y \le 20$, $x, y \ge 0$
2. $x + y \le 30$, $x + y \ge 15$, $y \le 15$, $x \le 20$, $x, y \ge 0$
3. $x + y \ge 30$, $x + y \le 15$, $x \le 15$, $y \le 20$, $x, y \ge 0$
4. $x + y \ge 30$, $x + y \le 15$, $y \le 15$, $x \le 20$, $x, y \ge 0$

**46.** The corner points of the feasible region of the LPP: Minimize Z = $-50x + 20y$ subject to $2x - y \ge -5$, $3x + y \ge 3$, $2x - 3y \le 12$ and $x, y \ge 0$ are:

1. (0, 5), (0, 6), (1, 0), (6, 0)
2. (0, 3), (0, 5), (3, 0), (6, 0)
3. (0, 3), (0, 5), (1, 0), (6, 0)
4. (0, 5), (0, 6), (1, 0), (3, 0)

| **38.** 2 | **39.** 2 | **40.** 2 | **41.** 4 | **42.** 2 | **43.** 3 | **44.** 3 | **45.** 1 | **46.** 3 |
|---|---|---|---|---|---|---|---|---|

**47.** If A and B are any two events such that P(B) = P(A and B), then which of the following is correct?

1. $P(B|A) = 1$
2. $P(A|B) = 1$
3. $P(B|A) = 0$
4. $P(A|B) = 0$

**48.** If A is any event associated with sample space and If $E_1$, $E_2$, $E_3$ are mutually exclusive and exhaustive events. Then which of the following are true?

A. $P(A) = P(E_1)P(E_1|A) + P(E_2)P(E_2|A) + P(E_3)P(E_3|A)$

B. $P(A) = P(A|E_1)P(E_1) + P(A|E_2)P(E_2) + P(A|E_3)P(E_3)$

C. $P(E_i|A) = \dfrac{P(A|E_i)P(E_i)}{\sum_{i=1}^{3} P(A|E_i)P(E_i)}, i = 1, 2, 3$

D. $P(A|E_i) = \dfrac{P(E_i|A)P(E_i)}{\sum_{i=1}^{3} P(E_i|A)P(E_i)}, i = 1, 2, 3$

Choose the ***correct*** answer from the options given below:

1. A and C only
2. A and D only
3. B and D only
4. B and C only

**49.** Match List-I with List-II.

Let A and B are two events such that P(A) = 0.8, P(B) = 0.5, P(B|A) = 0.4

| List-I | List-II |
|---|---|
| A. $P(A \cap B)$ | I. 0.2 |
| B. $P(A|B)$ | II. 0.32 |
| C. $P(A \cup B)$ | III. 0.64 |
| D. $P(A')$ | IV. 0.98 |

Choose the ***correct*** answer from the options given below:

1. A-II, B-IV, C-III, D-I
2. A-II, B-III, C-IV, D-I
3. A-III, B-IV, C-II, D-I
4. A-III, B-II, C-I, D-IV

**50.** A black and a red die are rolled simultaneously. The probability of obtaining a sum greater than 9, given that the black resulted in a 5 is:

1. 1/2
2. 1
3. 2/3
4. 1/3

# EXPLANATORY ANSWERS

**1.** We are given a matrix $A = [a_{ij}]_{n \times n}$ and need to match properties with their correct classification.

A. $A^T = A$: This means the transpose of the matrix is equal to the matrix itself. Such matrices are called symmetric matrices. Hence, A → IV.

B. $A^T = -A$: This condition defines a skew-symmetric matrix, where all diagonal elements are zero and the matrix is the negative of its transpose. Hence B → III.

C. $|A| = 0$: The determinant of the matrix is zero. This implies the matrix is singular (not invertible). Hence, C → I.

D. $|A| \neq 0$: If the determinant is non-zero, the matrix is non-singular (invertible). Hence D → II.

So the correct matching is: A-IV, B-III, C-I, D-II.

**2.** We are given:

$$A = \begin{bmatrix} 1 & 0 \\ 0 & -1 \end{bmatrix}, B = \begin{bmatrix} 0 & 1 \\ 1 & 0 \end{bmatrix}$$

We need to calculate AB.

$$AB = \begin{bmatrix} 1 & 0 \\ 0 & -1 \end{bmatrix}\begin{bmatrix} 0 & 1 \\ 1 & 0 \end{bmatrix}$$

Step-by-step multiplication:

- First row, first column:

  $(1 \times 0) + (0 \times 1) = 0$

- First row, second column:

  $(1 \times 1) + (0 \times 0) = 1$

- Second row, first column:

  $(0 \times 0) + (-1 \times 1) = -1$

- Second row, second column:

  $(0 \times 1) + (-1 \times 0) = 0$

So, $$AB = \begin{bmatrix} 0 & 1 \\ -1 & 0 \end{bmatrix}$$

Now, comparing with the given options:

1. $\begin{bmatrix} 0 & 0 \\ 0 & 0 \end{bmatrix}$ → Not matching
2. $\begin{bmatrix} 0 & -1 \\ 1 & 0 \end{bmatrix}$ → Signs do not match
3. $\begin{bmatrix} 0 & 1 \\ -1 & 0 \end{bmatrix}$ → Correct
4. $\begin{bmatrix} 1 & 1 \\ 1 & -1 \end{bmatrix}$ → Not matching

**3.** We are given:

$$A^2 = I$$

where I is the identity matrix. We need to evaluate:

$$(A - I)^3 + (A + I)^3 - 3A$$

**Step 1:** $(A - I)^3$

$$(A - I)^3 = A^3 - 3A^2I + 3AI^2 - I^3$$

| 47. 2 | 48. 4 | 49. 2 | 50. 4 |
|---|---|---|---|

Since $A^2 = I$ and $AI = A$:

$$(A - I)^3 = A^3 - 3I + 3A - I$$

$$(A - I)^3 = A^3 + 3A - 4I$$

**Step 2: Expand** $(A + I)^3$

$$(A + I)^3 = A^3 + 3A^2I + 3AI^2 + I^3$$

Substitute $A^2 = I$, $AI = A$:

$$(A + I)^3 = A^3 + 3I + 3A + I$$

$$(A + I)^3 = A^3 + 3A + 4I$$

**Step 3: Add them together**

$$(A - I)^3 + (A + I)^3 = (A^3 + 3A - 4I) + (A^3 + 3A + 4I)$$

$$= 2A^3 + 6A$$

**Step 4: Subtract 3A**

$$(A - I)^3 + (A + I)^3 - 3A = 2A^3 + 6A - 3A$$

$$= 2A^3 + 3A$$

**Step 5: Simplify using** $A^3 = A \cdot A^2$

$$= A \cdot I = A$$

$$2A^3 + 3A = 2A + 3A = 5A.$$

**4.** We are given:

$$A = \begin{bmatrix} 0 & 0 & \sqrt{3} \\ 0 & \sqrt{3} & 0 \\ \sqrt{3} & 0 & 0 \end{bmatrix}$$

We need to find $|\text{adj}(A)|$

**Step 1: Recall property of adjoint determinant**

For an $n \times n$ matrix A,

$$|\text{adj}(A)| = |A|^{n-1}$$

Here $n = 3$.

So, $|\text{adj}(A)| = |A|^2$

**Step 2: Find determinant of A**

$$|A| = \begin{vmatrix} 0 & 0 & \sqrt{3} \\ 0 & \sqrt{3} & 0 \\ \sqrt{3} & 0 & 0 \end{vmatrix}$$

Expanding along the first row:

$$|A| = 0 \cdot M_{11} - 0 \cdot M_{12} + \sqrt{3} \cdot M_{13}$$

So,

$$|A| = \sqrt{3} \cdot \begin{vmatrix} 0 & \sqrt{3} \\ \sqrt{3} & 0 \end{vmatrix}$$

$$= \sqrt{3} \cdot \left(0 \cdot 0 - \sqrt{3} \cdot \sqrt{3}\right)$$

$$= \sqrt{3} \cdot \left(\sqrt{3}\right) = -3\sqrt{3}$$

**Step 3: Compute** $|\text{adj}(A)|$

$$|\text{adj}(A)| = |A^2| = \left(-3\sqrt{3}\right)^2 = 27.$$

**5.** Given: $y = 3e^{2x} + 2e^{3x}$.

$$\frac{dy}{dx} = 6e^{2x} + 6e^{3x} = (6^{2x} + e^{3x})$$

$$\frac{d^2y}{dx^2} = 12e^{2x} + 18e^{3x}$$

Now,

$$\frac{d^2y}{dx^2} + 6y = (12e^{2x} + 18e^{3x}) + 6(3e^{2x} + 2e^{3x})$$

$$= (12 + 18)e^{2x} + (18 + 12)e^{3x}$$

$$= 30(e^{2x} + e^{3x})$$

Since $6(e^{2x} + e^{3x}) = \dfrac{dy}{dx}$, we get

$$\frac{d^2y}{dx^2} + 6y = 5\frac{dy}{dx}.$$

**6.** We are given:

$$f(x) = x^2e^{-x}$$

**Step 1: Differentiate** $f(x)$

$$f'(x) = \frac{d}{dx}\left(x^2e^{-x}\right)$$

Using product rule:

$$f'(x) = (x^2)' \cdot e^{-x} + x^2 \cdot (e^{-x})'$$

$$f'(x) = (2x)e^{-x} + x^2(-e^{-x})$$

$$f'(x) = e^{-x}(2x - x^2)$$

**Step 2: Simplify derivative**

$$f'(x) = e^{-x} \cdot x(2 - x)$$

Since $e^{-x} > 0$ for all $x$, the sign of $f'(x)$ depends on $x(2 - x)$.

**Step 3: Find where $f'(x) > 0$**

$$x(2 - x) > 0$$

This inequality holds when $0 < x < 2$

**Step 4: Conclusion**

The function is increasing in interval (0, 2).

**7.** We are given the function:

$$f(x) = \frac{\ln x}{x}, \; x > 0$$

We need $a^2f''(a)$, where maximum occurs at $x = a$.

**Step 1: Differentiate** $f(x)$

$$f(x) = \frac{\ln x}{x}$$

Using quotient rule:

$$f'(x) = \frac{(1/x) \cdot x - (\ln x) \cdot 1}{x^2}$$

$$f'(x) = \frac{1 - \ln x}{x^2}$$

**Step 2: Find critical point**

For maximum, set $f'(x) = 0$:

$$1 - \ln x = 0 \Rightarrow \ln x = 1 \Rightarrow x = e$$

So, maximum occurs at $a = e$.

**Step 3: Compute second derivative** $f''(x)$

$$f'(x) = \frac{1 - \ln x}{x^2}$$

Differentiate again:

$$f''(x) = \frac{d}{dx}\left(\frac{1 - \ln x}{x^2}\right)$$

Let numerator $u = 1 - \ln x$, denominator $v = x^2$.

$$f''(x) = \frac{u'v - uv'}{v^2}$$

$$u = -1/x$$
$$v = x^2, \text{ so } v' = 2x$$

$$f''(x) = \frac{\left(-\frac{1}{x}\right)(x^2) - (1 - \ln x)(2x)}{x^4}$$

$$f''(x) = \frac{-x - 2x(1 - \ln x)}{x^4}$$

$$f''(x) = \frac{-x - 2x + 2x \ln x}{x^4}$$

$$f''(x) = \frac{-3x + 2x \ln x}{x^4}$$

$$f''(x) = \frac{2 \ln x - 3}{x^3}$$

**Step 4: Evaluate at $x = a = e$**

$$f''(e) = \frac{2 \ln e - 3}{e^3} = \frac{2(1) - 3}{e^3} = \frac{-1}{e^3}$$

**Step 5: Compute $a^2 f''(a)$**

$$a^2 f''(a) = e^2 \cdot \frac{-1}{e^3} = -\frac{1}{e}.$$

**8.** Break at the kink $x = 2$:

$$\int_1^4 |x - 2|\, dx = \int_1^2 (2 - x)dx + \int_2^4 (x - 2)dx$$

Compute:

$$\int_1^2 (2 - x)dx = \left[2x - \frac{x^2}{2}\right]_1^2 = \frac{1}{2},$$

$$\int_2^4 (x - 2)dx = \left[\frac{x^2}{2} - 2x\right]_2^4 = 2.$$

$$\text{Sum} = \frac{1}{2} + 2 = \frac{5}{2}.$$

**9.** We are given:

$$I = \int \frac{e^{5 \ln x} - e^{4 \ln x}}{e^3 \ln x - e^{2 \ln x}} dx$$

**Step 1: Simplify exponentials**

$$e^{k \ln x} = x^k$$

So numerator:

$$e^{5 \ln x} - e^{4 \ln x} = x^5 - x^4$$

Denominator:

$$e^{3 \ln x} - e^{2 \ln x} = x^3 - x^2$$

Thus, $$I = \int \frac{x^5 - x^4}{x^3 - x^2} dx$$

**Step 2: Factorize**

$$\frac{x^5 - x^4}{x^3 - x^2} = \frac{x^4(x - 1)}{x^2(x - 1)} = x^2 \ (x \neq 1)$$

So, $$I = \int x^2 dx$$

**Step 3: Integrate**

$$I = \frac{x^3}{3} + C.$$

**10.** Parabola: $y^2 = 4x \Rightarrow x = \frac{y^2}{4}$ (open right).

Line: $x = 1$. Their intersection satisfy $y^2 = 4 \Rightarrow y = \pm 2$. Area betweeen the vertical line and the parabola from $y = -2$ to $y = 2$:

$$\text{Area} = \int_{-2}^{2} \left[1 - \frac{y^2}{4}\right] dy = \left[y - \frac{y^3}{12}\right]_{-2}^{2}$$

$$= \left(2 - \frac{8}{12}\right) - \left(-2 + \frac{8}{12}\right)$$

$$= \frac{4}{3} - \left(-\frac{4}{3}\right) = \frac{8}{3}.$$

**11.** A linear first-order differential equation has the form:

$$\frac{dy}{dx} + P(x)y = Q(x)$$

or equivalently if roles are reversed,

$$\frac{dx}{dy} + P(y)x = Q(y).$$

The key condition is: the dependent variable and its derivative must appear only in the first power and not multiplied together.

A. $\frac{dy}{dx} + P(x)y = Q(x)$

This is exactly the standard linear form.

B. $\frac{dx}{dy} + P(y)x = Q(y)$

This is linear in $x$ (with $y$ as the independent variable).

C. $(x - y)\frac{dy}{dx} = x + 2y$

Rearrange:

$$\frac{dy}{dx} = \frac{x + 2y}{x - y}$$

Here, $y$ appears in denominator with $x$-$y$. This makes it non-linear.

D. $(1 + x^2)\frac{dy}{dx} + 2xy = 2$

Divide through by $(1 + x^2)$:

$$\frac{dy}{dx} + \frac{2x}{1 + x^2} y = \frac{2}{1 + x^2}$$

This is linear first order.

**12.** We are given:

$$\ln\left(\frac{dy}{dx}\right) = 3x + 4y$$

**Step 1: Exponentiate both side**

$$\frac{dy}{dx} = e^{3x + 4y}$$

**Step 2: Rearrange for variable separable form**

$$e^{-4y}\,dy = e^{3x}\,dx$$

**Step 3: Integrate both side**

$$\int e^{-4y}dy = \int e^{3x}dx$$

Left side:

$$\int e^{-4y}dy = \frac{e^{-4y}}{-4} = -\frac{1}{4}e^{-4y}$$

Right side:

$$\int e^{3x}dx = \frac{1}{3}e^{3x}$$

So, $-\frac{1}{4}e^{-4y} = \frac{1}{3}e^{3x} + C$

**Step 4: Simplify**

Multiply through by 12:

$$-3e^{-4y} = 4e^{3x} + 12C$$

Rearranging,

$4e^{3x} + 3e^{-4y} + C = 0$

**Step 5: Compare with options**

This matches Option 1.

**13.** Given the pmf:

$$P(X = 0) = 1 - 7a^2,$$

$$P(X = 1) = \frac{1}{2}a + \frac{1}{4},$$

$$P(X = 2) = a^2 \text{ with } a > 0.$$

Use $\Sigma P = 1$:

$$(1 - 7a^2) + \left(\frac{1}{2}a + \frac{1}{4}\right) + a^2 = 1$$

$$\Rightarrow -6a^2 + \frac{1}{2}a + \frac{1}{4} = 0$$

$$\Rightarrow 24a^2 - 2a - 1 = 0$$

$$a = \frac{2 \pm \sqrt{100}}{48} = \left\{\frac{1}{4}, -\frac{1}{6}\right\}$$

$$\Rightarrow \quad a = \frac{1}{4}(a > 0).$$

Then

$$P(0 < x \le 2) = P(X = 1) + P(X = 2)$$

$$= \left(\frac{1}{2}a + \frac{1}{4}\right) + a^2$$

$$= \frac{1}{8} + \frac{1}{4} + \frac{1}{16} = \frac{7}{16}.$$

**14.** At both optimal points the object must have equal value:

$$Z(3, 4) = 3p + 4q,$$

$$Z(0, 5) = 0 \cdot p + 5q$$

Equate for common optimum:

$$3p + 4q = 5q \Rightarrow 3p = q \Rightarrow q = 3p.$$

**15.** Feasible set:

$$2x + y \ge 3,\ x + 2y \ge 6,\ x, y \ge 0.$$

Intersection of the two boundary lines:

$$2x + y = 3,\ x + 2y = 6$$

$$\Rightarrow \quad x = 0,\ y = 3.$$

Check the corner (6, 0): it also satisfies both constraints and

$$Z = x + 2y : Z(0, 3) = 6,$$

$$Z(6, 0) = 6.$$

Thus both yield the minimum (indeed the whole segment between them gives Z = 6).

**16.** $f : \mathbb{R} \to \mathbb{R}$, $f(x) = 10x$.

For any $y \in \mathbb{R}$ there exists $x = \frac{y}{10}$ with

$$f(x) = y \Rightarrow \text{onto.}$$

If $f(x_1) = f(x_2) \Rightarrow 10x_1 = 10x_2$

$\Rightarrow x_1 = x_2$

$\Rightarrow$ one-one. Hence bijective.

**17.** On A = {1, 2, 3}, reflexive $\Rightarrow$ (1, 1), (2, 2), (3, 3) must be in R. Given (1, 2), (1, 3) and symmetry $\Rightarrow$ also (2, 1), (3, 1). The only remaining symmetric choice is whether to include (2, 3) and (3, 2).

- Without (2, 3), (3, 2): relation $R_0$ is reflexive and symmetric, but not transitive since (2, 1) and (1, 3) hold while (2, 3) does not.
- With (2, 3), (3, 2): relation becomes the complete relation (all 9 pairs), which is transitive.

Hence exactly one relation meets "reflexive & symmetric but not transitive."

**18.** We need $\sin(\tan^{-1} x)$ for $|x| < 1$.

**Step 1: Let $\theta = \tan^{-1} x$.**

So, $\tan\theta = x$

**Step 2: Construct right triangle.**

Take opposite side = $x$, adjacent side = 1.

Then hypotenuse = $\sqrt{1 + x^2}$

**Step 3: Find $\sin\theta$.**

$$\sin\theta = \frac{\text{opposite}}{\text{hypotenuse}} = \frac{x}{\sqrt{1 + x^2}}.$$

Thus, $\sin(\tan^{-1} x) = \dfrac{x}{\sqrt{1 + x^2}}.$

**19.** Matrix $A = \begin{bmatrix} 1 & 2 & 1 \\ -1 & 3 & 2 \\ 2 & 4 & 1 \end{bmatrix}$.

$M_{ij}$ = minor, $A_{ij}$ = cofactor = $(-1)^{i+j} M_{ij}$.

- $M_{22}$: delete row 2, col 2 $\Rightarrow \begin{vmatrix} 1 & 1 \\ 2 & 1 \end{vmatrix} = 1 - 2 = -1.$

  So A is true.

- $M_{23}$: delete row 2, col 3 $\Rightarrow \begin{vmatrix} 1 & 2 \\ 2 & 4 \end{vmatrix} = 4 - 4 = 0.$

  Then $A_{23} = (-1)^{2+3} M_{23} = -0 = 0$. So B is true; D is false.

- $M_{32}$: delete row 3, col 2 $\Rightarrow \begin{vmatrix} 1 & 1 \\ -1 & 2 \end{vmatrix} = 2 - (-1) = 3.$

  Hence $A_{32} = (-1)^{3/2} M_{32} = -3$. So C is false; E is false.

Thus only A and B are correct.

**20.** We have

$$A = \begin{bmatrix} \cos\theta & -\sin\theta \\ \sin\theta & \cos\theta \end{bmatrix}, I = \begin{bmatrix} 1 & 0 \\ 0 & 1 \end{bmatrix}$$

Condition: $A^T + A = I$.

**Step 1: Compute $A^T$**

$$A^T = \begin{bmatrix} \cos\theta & \sin\theta \\ -\sin\theta & \cos\theta \end{bmatrix}$$

So, $$A^T + A = \begin{bmatrix} 2\cos\theta & 0 \\ 0 & 2\cos\theta \end{bmatrix}$$

**Step 2: Equate with I**

$$\begin{bmatrix} 2\cos\theta & 0 \\ 0 & 2\cos\theta \end{bmatrix} = \begin{bmatrix} 1 & 0 \\ 0 & 1 \end{bmatrix}$$

Thus $$2\cos\theta = 1 \Rightarrow \cos\theta = \frac{1}{2}$$

**Step 3: Solve for θ**

$$\cos\theta = \frac{1}{2} \Rightarrow \theta = 2n\pi \pm \frac{\pi}{3}, n \in \mathbb{Z}$$

So correct option is $\theta = 2n\pi + \frac{\pi}{3}$.

**21.** For a skew-symmetric matrix A, $A^T = -A$.
Hence $(A^n)^T = (A^T)^n = (-A)^n = (-1)^n$
$A^n$: odd powers are skew-symmetric; even powers are symmetric.

- $A^3$ and $B^5$ are skew-symmetric $\Rightarrow A^3 + B^5$ is skew-symmetric (sum of skew-symmetric matrices).
- $A^{19}$ is skew-symmetric (odd power).
- $B^{14}$ is symmetric (even power).
- $A^4$ is symmetric (even) and $B^5$ is skew-symmetric (odd); their sum is not symmetric in general.

**22.** Known identities for invertible matrices:

- adj $A = |A|\, A^{-1}$ (true).
- $|A^{-1}| = |A|^{-1}$ (true).
- $(AB)^{-1} = B^{-1}A^{-1}$ (true).
- $(A + B)^{-1} = A^{-1} + B^{-1}$ is not generally valid.

**23.** A is $2 \times 3$ and B is $3 \times 2 \Rightarrow$ AB is $2 \times 2$ (square).
For any $2 \times 2$ matrix M, $|kM| = k^2|M|$.
Thus $$|5AB| = 5^2\, |AB|.$$

**24.** For the system AX = B with A $3 \times 3$:

- Unique solution iff $|A| \neq 0$ (invertible).
- If $|A| = 0$ and (adj A)B $\neq 0 \Rightarrow$ inconsistent $\Rightarrow$ no solution.
- If $|A| = 0$ and (adj A)B $= 0 \Rightarrow$ consistent with rank $< 3 \Rightarrow$ infinitely many solutions.

Hence B, C, and D are correct; A is not.

**25.** We are given

$$f(x) = 2n\pi + \frac{\pi}{3} \cdot \begin{cases} \dfrac{k\cos x}{\pi - 2x}, & x \neq \dfrac{\pi}{2} \\ 3, & x = \dfrac{\pi}{2} \end{cases}$$

For continuity at $x = \frac{\pi}{2}$,

$$\lim_{x\to\pi/2} \frac{k\cos x}{\pi - 2x} = 3.$$

**Step 1: Check limit form**

At $x = \frac{\pi}{2}$, numerator $k\cos(\pi/2) = 0$,

denominator $\pi - 2(\pi/2) = 0$.
So, limit is in 0/0 form $\Rightarrow$ apply L'Hôpital's rule.

**Step 2; Apply L'Hôpital**

$$\lim_{x\to\pi/2} \frac{k\cos x}{\pi - 2x} = \lim_{x\to\pi/2} \frac{-k\sin x}{-2} = \frac{k}{2} \lim_{x\to\pi/2} \sin x.$$

Since $\sin(\pi/2) = 1$:

$$\lim_{x\to\pi/2} \frac{k\cos x}{\pi - 2x} = \frac{k}{2}$$

**Step 3: Continuity condition**

$$\frac{k}{2} = 3 \Rightarrow k = 6.$$

**26.** We need to check where each absolute value function is not differentiable (the "kink" points).

A. $f(x) = |x|$
Not differentiable at $x = 0$. → II

B. $f(x) = |x + 2|$
Not differentiable at $x = -2$. → I

C. $f(x) = |x^2 - 4|$
Inside: $x^2 - 4 = 0 \Rightarrow x = \pm 2$.
Not differentiable at $x = 2, -2$. → IV

D. $f(x) = |x - 2|$
Not differentiable at $x = 2$. → III

Correct matching: A-II, B-I, C-IV, D-III.

**27.** We are given:

$$y = \sin(\cos(x^2))$$

We need $\frac{dy}{dx}$ at $x = \frac{\sqrt{\pi}}{2}$.

**Step 1: Differentiate using chain rule**

$$\frac{dy}{dx} = \cos(\cos(x^2)) \cdot \frac{d}{dx}[\cos(x^2)]$$

$$\frac{d}{dx}[\cos(x^2)] = -\sin(x^2) \cdot 2x$$

So, $$\frac{dy}{dx} = -2x\sin(x^2)\cos(\cos(x^2))$$

**Step 2: Substitute $x = \frac{\sqrt{\pi}}{2}$**

$$x^2 = \left(\frac{\sqrt{\pi}}{2}\right)^2 = \frac{\pi}{4}$$

So, $$\frac{dy}{dx} = -2\left(\frac{\pi}{2}\right)\sin\left(\frac{\pi}{4}\right)\cos\left(\cos\left(\frac{\pi}{4}\right)\right)$$

$$= -\sqrt{\pi} \cdot \frac{1}{\sqrt{2}} \cdot \cos\left(\frac{1}{\sqrt{2}}\right)$$

**Step 3: Simplify**

$$\frac{dy}{dx} = -\sqrt{\frac{\pi}{2}}\cos\left(\frac{1}{\sqrt{2}}\right).$$

**28.** A. $(2x - 1)^2 + 3$: square term $\geq 0$, minimum at $2x - 1 = 0 \Rightarrow$ value $3 \rightarrow$ III.

B. $-|x + 1| + 4$: maximum when $|x + 1| = 0 \Rightarrow$ value $4 \rightarrow$ I.

C. $\sin(2x) + 6$: minimum when $\sin(2x) = -1 \Rightarrow$ value $5 \rightarrow$ IV.

D. $-(x - 1)^2 + 10$: maximum when $(x - 1)^2 = 0 \Rightarrow$ value $10 \rightarrow$ II.

So, A–III, B–I, C–IV, D–II.

**29.** We are given:

$$f(x) = \tan x - x$$

**Step 1: Differentiate**

$$f'(x) = \sec^2 x - 1 = \tan^2 x$$

**Step 2: Analyze sign of derivative**

On $\left(0, \frac{\pi}{2}\right)$, $\tan^2 x > 0$

At $x = 0$, $\tan^2 0 = 0$

So $f'(x) \geq 0$ on $\left[0, \frac{\pi}{2}\right)$

That means $f(x)$ is an increasing function.

**30.** Area of circle $A = \pi r^2$

Circumference $C = 2\pi r$

We need $\frac{dA}{dC}$ at $r = 4$

**Step 1: Differentiate both**

$$\frac{dA}{dr} = 2\pi r, \quad \frac{dC}{dr} = 2\pi$$

**Step 2: Use chain rule**

$$\frac{dA}{dC} = \frac{\frac{dA}{dr}}{\frac{dC}{dr}} = \frac{2\pi r}{2\pi} = r$$

**Step 3: Substitute $r = 4$**

$$\frac{dA}{dC} = 4 \text{ cm}^2/\text{cm}.$$

**31.** We are given:

$$I = \int_{\pi/6}^{\pi/3} \frac{\tan x}{\tan x + \cot x}dx$$

**Step 1: Simplify denominator**

$$\tan x + \cot x = \frac{\sin x}{\cos x} + \frac{\cos x}{\sin x}$$

$$= \frac{\sin^2 x + \cos^2 x}{\sin x \cos x} = \frac{1}{\sin x \cos x}$$

**Step 2: Simplify integrand**

$$\frac{\tan x}{\tan x + \cot x} = \tan x\,(\sin x \cdot \cos x)$$

$$= \frac{\sin x}{\cos x} \cdot \sin x \cos x = \sin^2 x$$

So, $$I = \int_{\pi/6}^{\pi/3} \sin^2 x\, dx$$

**Step 3: Use identity**

$$\sin^2 x = \frac{1 - \cos 2x}{2}$$

$$I = \int_{\pi/6}^{\pi/3} \frac{1 - \cos 2x}{2}dx$$

$$= \frac{1}{2}\int_{\pi/6}^{\pi/3} 1 dx - \frac{1}{2}\int_{\pi/6}^{\pi/3} \cos 2x\, dx$$

**Step 4: Evaluate**

First part:

$$\frac{1}{2}[x]_{\pi/6}^{\pi/3} = \frac{1}{2}\left(\frac{\pi}{3} - \frac{\pi}{6}\right) = \frac{1}{2} \cdot \frac{\pi}{6} = \frac{\pi}{12}$$

Second part:

$$\frac{1}{2}\int_{\pi/6}^{\pi/3} \cos 2x\, dx = -\frac{1}{2} \cdot \frac{1}{2} \sin 2x \Big|_{\pi/6}^{\pi/3}$$

$$= -\frac{1}{4}\left(\sin\frac{2\pi}{3} - \sin\frac{\pi}{3}\right)$$

$$= -\frac{1}{4}\left(\frac{\sqrt{3}}{2} - \frac{\sqrt{3}}{2}\right) = 0$$

**Step 5: Final result**

$$I = \frac{\pi}{12}.$$

**32.** Compute each integral:

A. $\int_0^1 \frac{2x}{1 + x^2}dx$

Put $u = 1 + x^2 \Rightarrow du = 2x\, dx$. Limit $1 \rightarrow 2$.

$= \int_1^2 \frac{du}{u} = \ln 2. \rightarrow$ III

B. $\int_{-1}^{1} \sin^3 x \cos^4 x\, dx$

$\sin(-x) = -\sin x$, $\cos(-x) = \cos x \Rightarrow$ integrand is odd $\Rightarrow$ integral $= 0. \rightarrow$ IV

C. $\int_0^\pi \sin x\, dx = [-\cos x]_0^\pi = 2. \rightarrow$ I

D. $\int_2^3 \frac{2}{x^2 - 1}dx = \int_2^3 \left(\frac{1}{x-1} - \frac{1}{x+1}\right)dx$

$= [\ln(x - 1) - \ln(x + 1)]_2^3 = \ln\frac{3}{2}. \rightarrow$ II

Correct matching: A-III, B-IV, C-I, D-II.

**33.** We are given:

$$I = \int e^x\left(\frac{x-1}{3x^2}\right)dx$$

**Step 1: Observe form**

This looks like a derivative of something like $\frac{e^x}{3x^2}$. Let's check:

$$\frac{d}{dx}\left(\frac{e^x}{3x^2}\right) = \frac{(e^x)(3x^2)-(e^x)(6x)}{9x^4}$$

Simplify numerator:

$$= \frac{e^x(3x^2-6x)}{9x^4} = \frac{e^x(x^2-2x)}{3x^3}$$

But this does not exactly match. Let's recheck carefully.

**Step 2: Simplify integrand**

$$\frac{x-1}{3x^2} = \frac{1}{3}\left(\frac{x}{x^2}-\frac{1}{x^2}\right) = \frac{1}{3}\left(\frac{1}{x}-\frac{1}{x^2}\right)$$

So integrand:

$$I = \frac{1}{3}\int e^x\left(\frac{1}{x}-\frac{1}{x^2}\right)dx$$

**Step 3: Look for derivative structure**

Consider $\frac{d}{dx}\left(\frac{e^x}{3x}\right)$:

$$\frac{d}{dx}\left(\frac{e^x}{3x}\right) = \frac{e^x\cdot 3x-e^x\cdot 3}{9x^2} = \frac{e^x(x-1)}{3x^2}$$

That, eactcly matches the integrand!

**Step 4: Integrate**

$$I = \int\frac{d}{dx}\left(\frac{e^x}{3x}\right)dx = \frac{e^x}{3x}+C.$$

**34.** Curve $y = x^5$ is odd and symmetric about the origin. The required area between the curve and the $x$-axis for $-1$ to $1$ is

$$2\int_0^1 x^5 dx = 2\left[\frac{x^6}{6}\right]_0^1 = 2\cdot\frac{1}{6} = \frac{1}{3}$$

**35.** We are given the curve

$$y = 2\sqrt{1-x^2},\quad x \in [0, 1]$$

We need the area under this curve above the $x$-axis.

**Step 1: Write area integral**

$$A = \int_0^1 2\sqrt{1-x^2}\,dx$$

**Step 2: Recognize geometry**

$\sqrt{1-x^2}$ is the upper semicircle of radius 1.

So $2\sqrt{1-x^2}$ is twice that height.

Thus the curve represents a semicircle of radius 1, but scaled by factor 2 vertically.

Better to evaluate directly.

**Step 3: Substitution**

Put $x = \sin\theta \Rightarrow dx = \cos\theta\, d\theta,\ \theta \in [0, \pi/2]$

Then

$$A = \int_0^{\pi/2} 2\sqrt{1-\sin^2\theta}\cdot\cos\theta\, d\theta$$

$$= \int_0^{\pi/2} 2\cos\theta\cdot\cos\theta\, d\theta$$

$$= 2\int_0^{\pi/2}\cos^2\theta\, d\theta$$

**Step 4: Evaluate**

$$\cos^2\theta = \frac{1+\cos 2\theta}{2}$$

$$\text{So, } 2\int_0^{\pi/2}\cos^2\theta\, d\theta = 2\int_0^{\pi/2}\frac{1+\cos 2\theta}{2}\, d\theta$$

$$= 2\int_0^{\pi/2}(1+\cos 2\theta)\, d\theta$$

$$= \left[\theta+\frac{1}{2}\sin 2\theta\right]_0^{\pi/2} = \frac{\pi}{2}+0 = \frac{\pi}{2}.$$

**36.** Given $(x \ln x)\frac{dy}{dx}+y = 2\ln x$. Divide by $x \ln x$ to get linear form:

$$\frac{dy}{dx}+\frac{1}{x\ln x}y = \frac{2}{x}$$

Here $P(x) = \frac{1}{x\ln x}$. The integrating factor is

$$IF = e^{\int P(x)dx} = e^{\int\frac{dx}{x\ln x}} = e^{\ln(\ln x)} = \ln x.$$

**37.** Given $x\frac{dy}{dx} = y(\ln y - \ln x + 1) = y\left[\ln\left(\frac{y}{x}\right)+1\right]$

Set $v = \frac{y}{x} \Rightarrow y = vx,\ \frac{dy}{dx} = v+x\frac{dv}{dx}$. Then

$$v+x\frac{dv}{dx} = v\ln v + v \Rightarrow x\frac{dv}{dx} = v\ln v$$

which is separable:

$$\frac{dv}{v\ln v} = \frac{dx}{x} \Rightarrow \ln(\ln v) = \ln x + C$$

$$\ln v = Cx \Rightarrow \ln\left(\frac{y}{x}\right) = Cx$$

Hence the equation is homogeneous (depends on $y/x$), not linear.

With $y(1) = 1$: $\ln(1) = C \Rightarrow C = 0$, giving $y = x$.

So true statements: B (homogeneous), C (general solution $\ln(y/x) = Cx$) E (particular solution $y = x$).

**38.** We know that standard unit vectors along coordinate axes:

$$i = (1, 0, 0),\ j = (0, 1, 0),$$
$$k = (0, 0, 1)$$

A. $i \times i = 0$. True

B. $i \times k = -j$, not j. False

C. $i \cdot i = 1$. True

D. $i \cdot j = 0$. true

So correct: A, C, D only.

**39.** Let A(20, λ), B(5, –1), C(10, –13).

For collinearity, $\overline{AB}$ and $\overline{AC}$ must be proportionl.

$$\overline{AB} = (-15, -1 - \lambda),$$
$$\overline{AC} = (-10, -13 - \lambda)$$

Thus,
$$\frac{-15}{-10} = \frac{-1-\lambda}{-13-\lambda} \Rightarrow \frac{3}{2} = \frac{-1-\lambda}{-13-\lambda}$$

Cross-multiply:
$$3(-13 - \lambda) = 2(-1 - \lambda)$$
$$\Rightarrow \quad -39 - 3\lambda = -2 - 2\lambda \Rightarrow \lambda = -37.$$

**40.** We are given:
$$\vec{a}+\vec{b}+\vec{c} = 0 \Rightarrow \vec{a}+\vec{b} = -\vec{c}$$

Take magnitudes:
$$|\vec{a}+\vec{b}| = |\vec{c}| = 7$$

Now,
$$|\vec{a}+\vec{b}|^2 = |\vec{a}|^2 + |\vec{b}|^2 + 2\vec{a}\cdot\vec{b}$$
$$7^2 = 3^2 + 5^2 + 2|\vec{a}||\vec{b}|\cos\theta$$
$$49 = 9 + 25 + 2(3)(5)\cos\theta$$
$$49 = 34 + 30\cos\theta$$
$$15 = 30\cos\theta \Rightarrow \cos\theta = \frac{1}{2}$$
$$\theta = \frac{\pi}{3}.$$

**41.** Since $\vec{d}$ is perpendicular to both $\vec{a}$ and $\vec{b}$,

let
$$\vec{d} = t(\vec{a}\times\vec{b}).$$
$$\vec{a} = (1, 4, 0), \quad \vec{b} = (0, 4, 1)$$
$$\Rightarrow \quad \vec{a}\times\vec{b} = \begin{vmatrix} i & j & k \\ 1 & 4 & 0 \\ 0 & 4 & 1 \end{vmatrix} = (4, -1, 4)$$

Given $\vec{c}\cdot\vec{d} = 16$ with $\vec{c} = (1, 0, -2)$:
$$\vec{c}\cdot\vec{d} = t\,\vec{c}\cdot(\vec{a}\times\vec{b})$$
$$= t(4 - 8) = -4t = 16 \Rightarrow t = -4$$

Hence $\vec{d} = -4(4, -1, 4)$ and
$$|\vec{d}| = 4|(4, -1, 4)|$$
$$= 4\sqrt{4^2 + (-1)^2 + 4^2} = 4\sqrt{33}.$$

**42.** If a line make angle α, β, γ with positive *x*, *y*, *z* axes, then the diretion cosines satisfy:
$$\cos^2\alpha + \cos^2\beta + \cos^2\gamma = 1$$

We want $\sin^2\alpha + \sin^2\beta + \sin^2\gamma$

Now,
$$\sin^2\alpha = 1 - \cos^2\alpha,$$
$$\sin^2\beta = 1 - \cos^2\beta, \ \sin^2\gamma = 1 - \cos^2\gamma$$

So, $\sin^2\alpha + \sin^2\beta + \sin^2\gamma$
$$= 3 - (\cos^2\alpha + \cos^2\beta + \cos^2\gamma)$$
$$= 3 - 1 = 2.$$

**43.** For the line $\vec{r} = (1, -2, 4) + \lambda(-1, 2, -4)$:

- A point on the line is given by the position vector (1, –2, 4) → III.
- Direction ratios are the components of the direction vector (–1, 2, 4) → IV.
- Direction cosines are the unit vector along (–1, 2, –4): magnitude $= \sqrt{1+4+16} = \sqrt{21}$;

  hence $\left(-\frac{1}{\sqrt{21}}, \frac{2}{\sqrt{21}}, -\frac{4}{\sqrt{21}}\right) \to$ I.
- A line perpendicular must have direction ratios orthogonal to (–1, 2, –4). Check (4, –2, –2): (–1) · 4 + 2 · (–2) + (–4) · (–2) = –4 – 4 + 8 = 0 → perpendicular → II.

Answer. 3: A–III, B–IV, C–I, D–II

**44.** We are given two lines:
$$\frac{x-1}{2} = \frac{y-2}{3} = \frac{z-3}{4}, \quad \frac{x-2}{4} = \frac{y-4}{6} = \frac{z-5}{8}$$

**Step 1: Write parametric form**

First line: let parameter λ.
$$x = 1 + 2\lambda, \ y = 2 + 3\lambda,$$
$$z = 3 + 4\lambda$$

So point A(1, 2, 3), direction $\vec{d_1} = (2, 3, 4)$

Second line: let parameter μ.
$$x = 2 + 4\mu, \ y = 4 + 6\mu,$$
$$z = 5 + 8\mu$$

So point B(2, 4, 5) direction $\vec{d_2} = (4, 6, 8)$
$$= 2(2, 3, 4).$$

**Step 2: Check direction vectors**
$$\vec{d_2} = 2\vec{d_1}$$

Thus lines are parallel.

**Step 3: Shortest distance formula (parallel lines)**

If lines are parallel, distance between them is
$$D = \frac{|(\vec{B}-\vec{A})\times\vec{d_1}|}{|\vec{d_1}|}$$
$$\vec{B}-\vec{A} = (1, 2, 2)$$
$$\vec{d_1} = (2, 3, 4)$$

**Step 4: Compute cross product**
$$(1, 2, 2)\times(2, 3, 4) = \begin{vmatrix} i & j & k \\ 1 & 2 & 2 \\ 2 & 3 & 4 \end{vmatrix}$$
$$= (2\cdot4 - 2\cdot3)i - (1\cdot4 - 2\cdot2)j + (1\cdot3 - 2\cdot2)k$$
$$= (8 - 6)i - (4 - 4)j + (3 - 4)k$$
$$= 2i + 0j - 1k$$

So, Vector = (2, 0, –1)

$$\text{Magnitude} = \sqrt{2^2 + 0^2 + (-1)^2} = \sqrt{5}$$

**Step 5: Denominator**

$$|\vec{d}_1| = \sqrt{2^2+3^2+4^2} = \sqrt{29}$$

**Step 6: Distance**

$$D = \frac{\sqrt{5}}{\sqrt{29}} = \sqrt{\frac{5}{29}}.$$

**45.** The shaded strip lies between the two diagonals $x + y = 15$ and $x + y = 30$.

It is further bounded on the right by the vertical line $x = 15$ and above by the horizontal line $y = 20$.

The region is in the first quadrant, so $x \geq 0$, $y \geq 0$.

Hence the constraints are:

$x + y \leq 30$, $x + y \geq 15$, $x \leq 15$, $y \leq 20$, $x \geq 0$, $y \geq 0$.

**46.** Feasible region constraints:

$2x - y \geq -5 \Rightarrow y \leq 2x + 5$; $3x + y \geq 3$

$\Rightarrow y \geq 3 - 3x$; $2x - 3y \leq 12$

$\Rightarrow y \geq \frac{2x-12}{3}$; and $x, y \geq 0$.

On $x = 0$: $3 \leq y \leq 5 \Rightarrow (0, 3), (0, 5)$

On $y = 0$: $1 \leq x \leq 6 \Rightarrow (1, 0), (6, 0)$

Other pairwise intersections either lies outside $x \geq 0$, $y \geq 0$. Hence, corner points are

(0, 3), (0, 5), (1, 0), (6, 0).

**47.** Given $P(B) = P(A \cap B)$. This means all of B occurs within A (*i.e.*, $B \subseteq A$). Then

$$P(A|B) = \frac{P(A \cap B)}{P(B)} = \frac{P(B)}{P(B)} = 1.$$

**48.** We use Law of Total Probability and Bayes' theorem.

A. $P(A) = P(E_1)P(E_1|A) + P(E_2)P(E_2|A) + P(E_3)P(E_3|A)$.

Wrong: this is not the law of total probability (reversed conditional).

B. $P(A) = P(A|E_1)P(E_1) + P(A|E_2)P(E_2) + P(A|E_3)P(E_3)$.

Correct: this is Law of Total Probability.

C. $P(E_i|A) = \frac{P(A|E_i)P(E_i)}{\sum_{j=1}^{3} P(A|E_j)P(E_j)}$.

Correct: this is Bayes' theorem.

D. $P(A|E_i) = \frac{P(E_i|A)P(A)}{\sum_{j=1}^{3} P(E_j|A)P(A)}$.

Wrong: denominator is not correct, should simply be $P(E_i)$.

So true statements are B and C only.

**49.** Given: $P(A) = 0.8$, $P(B) = 0.5$, $P(B|A) = 0.4$

A. $P(A \cap B) = P(A)P(B|A) = 0.8 \times 0.4 = 0.32. \rightarrow$ II

B. $P(A|B) = \frac{P(A \cap B)}{P(B)} = \frac{0.32}{0.5} = 0.64. \rightarrow$ III

C. $P(A \cup B) = P(A) + P(B) - P(A \cap B) = 0.8 + 0.5 - 0.32 = 0.98. \rightarrow$ IV

D. $P(A') = 1 - P(A) = 0.2. \rightarrow$ I

Correct match: A-II, B-III, C-IV, D-I.

**50.** Two dice: black (given fixed at 5) and red.

So sum = 5 + R.

Condition: sum $> 9 \Rightarrow 5 + R > 9 \Rightarrow R > 4$.

So red must be 5 or 6. Probability $= 2/6 = \frac{1}{3}$.

YOUR SPACE

**YOUR SPACE**

Previous Years' Paper

# Common University Entrance Test for UG Programmes

# CUET–UG—ACCOUNTANCY/BOOK KEEPING

## Entrance Exam, 2025

(Exam held on 15-05-2025)

**Subject Code: 301**

**1.** To calculate interest coverage ratio; steps followed will be:

Net Profit after tax ₹ 60,000; 12% Long-term debt 20,00,000; and Tax rate 40%.

(A) Calculate Net Profit before tax
(B) Divide Net Profit before Interest and Tax by Interest on long-term debt
(C) Calculate Net profit before interest and tax
(D) Calculate Interest on Long-term Debt

Choose the **correct** answer from the options given below:

1. (A), (D), (C), (B)
2. (A), (B), (C), (D)
3. (B), (A), (D), (C)
4. (C), (B), (D), (A)

**2.** Which of the following is **not** one of the method of valuation of goodwill?

1. Average profit method
2. Super profit method
3. Average Capitalisation weighted method
4. Capitalisation method

**3.** The amount on any call should not exceed ............ of the face value of shares.

1. 20% 2. 25%
3. 30% 4. 15%

**4.** If the premium amount has not been received, in respect of the shares forfeited, the Securities Premium Reserve Account:

1. will not be mentioned at the time of forfeiture
2. will be debited at the time of forfeiture
3. will be credited at the time of forfeiture
4. will be considered at the time of reissue of shares

**5.** A and B are partners, they admit C into partnership. C was asked to pay ₹ 2,50,000 though his share of capital was estimated ₹ 2,00,000 only. For what ₹ 50,000 extra was asked from C?

1. Capital 2. Reserve
3. Liabilities 4. Goodwill

**6.** Which of the following will lead to dissolution of partnership firm?

1. Admission of a partner
2. With the consent of all the partners.
3. Death of a partner
4. Retirement of a partner

**7.** Match List-I with List-II.

| List-I | List-II |
|---|---|
| (A) Calls in Advance A/c Dr. To Particular Call A/c | (I) For Interest due on Calls in Advance |
| (B) Interest on Calls in Advance A/c Dr. To Sundry Shareholder's A/c | (II) For Interest Paid on Calls in Advance |
| (C) Sundry Shareholder's A/c Dr. To Bank A/c | (III) Calls in advance adjusted with the call money due |
| (D) Bank A/c Dr. To Calls in Arrears A/c To Interest on Calls in Arrears A/c | (IV) Calls in arrears received with interest |

Choose the **correct** answer from the options given below:

1. (A) - (I), (B) - (II), (C) - (III), (D) - (IV)
2. (A) - (I), (B) - (III), (C) - (II), (D) - (IV)
3. (A) - (III), (B) - (I), (C) - (II), (D) - (IV)
4. (A) - (III), (B) - (IV), (C) - (I), (D) - (II)

**1.** 1 **2.** 3 **3.** 2 **4.** 2 **5.** 4 **6.** 2 **7.** 3

**8.** How many blank worksheets are shown when a new workbook is created?

1. One 2. Two
3. Three 4. Four

**9.** In which of the following case court can order dissolution of a partnership firm?

1. On the death of a partner
2. On the expiry of term of partnership
3. When business cannot be carried on except at a loss.
4. When a partner become insolvent.

**10.** The order in which following items appear in the cash flow statement:

(A) Cash and cash equivalents at the end
(B) Cash and cash equivalents at the beginning
(C) Purchase of property
(D) Proceeds from Issuance of Bonds

Choose the **correct** answer from the options given below:

1. (C), (D), (A), (B)
2. (C), (B), (A), (D)
3. (C), (D), (B), (A)
4. (C), (B), (D), (A)

**11.** The following ratios primarily measure risk:

(A) Liquidity
(B) Activity
(C) Debts
(D) Profitability

Choose the **correct** answer from the options given below:

1. (A), (B) and (D) only
2. (A), (C) and (D) only
3. (A), (B), (C) and (D)
4. (B), (C) and (D) only

**12.** A and B are partners, sharing profits equally. Their fixed capitals were ₹ 2,00,000 and ₹ 3,00,000 respectively. Interest on capital as provided under partnership deed @10% p.a was omitted. Select the correct option from the following:

1. A capital account will be debited by 25,000
2. A capital account will be debited by 5,000
3. B capital account will be debited by 5,000
4. B capital account will be debited by 25,000

**13.** Net loss of the firm as per profit and loss account for the year ending March 31, 2024 amounted to ₹ 75,000. Yaduvanshi, Madhulika and Vidushi are partners, sharing profits and losses in the ratio of 2 : 2 : 1. Their fixed capitals on April 01, 2019 were: Yaduvanshi ₹ 5,00,000, Madhulika ₹ 4,00,000 and Vidushi ₹ 3,50,000. On the basis of the above information, pass the necessary journal entry

1. Yaduvanshi capital A/c Dr. 30,000
   Madhulika capital A/c Dr. 30,000
   Vidushi capital A/c Dr. 15,000
   To profit & loss appropriation A/c 75,000
2. Yaduvanshi current A/c Dr. 30,000
   Madhulika current A/c Dr. 30,000
   Vidushi current A/c Dr. 15,000
   To profit & loss appropriation A/c 75,000
3. Profit & loss appropriation A/c Dr. 75,000
   To Yaduvanshi capital A/c 30,000
   To Madhulika capital A/c 30,000
   To Vidushi capital A/c 15,000
4. Profit & loss appropriation A/c Dr. 75,000
   To Yaduvanshi current A/c 30,000
   To Madhulika current A/c 30,000
   To Vidushi current A/c 15,000

**14.** Neil, Kapil, Sunil started a furniture business in partnership. After one year of their operation, they started exporting Opium by keeping them in blank spaces between the furniture. As authorities came to know about the illegal business of the firm, they will compel them for:

1. Changing partner's
2. Dissolution by Agreement
3. To continue business by imposing fine
4. Compulsory Dissolution

**15.** Which of the following will be included in case debenture's are issued to vendor at a discount for purchase consideration other than cash?

(A) % Debenture A/c is credited.
(B) Vendor A/c is debited.
(C) Discount on issue of Debenture A/c is debited.
(D) Securities Premium Reserve A/c is credited.

Choose the **correct** answer from the options given below:

1. (A), (B), (C) and (D)
2. (A), (C) and (D) only
3. (A), (B) and (C) only
4. (B), (C) and (D) only

| **8.** 3 | **9.** 3 | **10.** 3 | **11.** 2 | **12.** 2 | **13.** 2 | **14.** 4 | **15.** 3 |
|---|---|---|---|---|---|---|---|

**16.** Arrange following in correct sequence related to issue of shares:

(A) Letters of allotment, and letters of regret are sent

(B) Prospective investors would make an application along with the application money

(C) The company issues the prospectus to the public

(D) Subsequent installment are called

Choose the **correct** answer from the options given below:

1. (C), (D), (A), (B)
2. (C), (B), (A), (D)
3. (C), (A), (D), (B)
4. (C), (B), (D), (A)

**17.** Convertible debentures cannot be issued at a discount if:

1. They are not to be immediately converted
2. They are to be immediately converted
3. Shareholder opts for redemption in cash
4. Not recited approval from SEBI

**18.** In case of dissolution of a partnership firm, losses, including deficiencies of capital, shall be paid first out of:

1. Capital of partners
2. Profits
3. Partners individual contribution in their profit sharing ratio
4. Borrowings

**19.** Match List-I with List-II.

| List-I | List-II |
|---|---|
| (A) Accounting standard rules | (I) 2013 |
| (B) Companies Act | (II) 1932 |
| (C) Financial statement of company | (III) 2006 |
| (D) Partnership Act | (IV) Schedule III |

Choose the **correct** answer from the options given below:

1. (A) - (III), (B) - (I), (C) - (IV), (D) - (II)
2. (A) - (IV), (B) - (I), (C) - (III), (D) - (II)
3. (A) - (III), (B) - (I), (C) - (II), (D) - (IV)
4. (A) - (III), (B) - (IV), (C) - (I), (D) - (II)

**20.** It is available only for the creditors on winding up of the company.

1. Registered capital
2. Subscribed capital
3. Capital reserve
4. Reserve capital

**21.** The manner prescribed in the revised schedule III to the companies act, 2013, the particulars of balance sheet will appear in the order:

(A) Deferred tax assets

(B) Deferred tax liabilities

(C) Reserves and Surplus

(D) Short-term provisions

Choose the **correct** answer from the options given below:

1. (A), (B), (C), (D) 2. (A), (D), (C), (B)
3. (C), (A), (D), (B) 4. (C), (B), (D), (A)

**22.** Which of the following items are included under Reserve and Surplus?

(A) Security Premium reserve

(B) Revaluation reserve

(C) Share option outstanding account

(D) Reserve Capital

Choose the **correct** answer from the options given below:

1. (A), (B) and (C) only
2. (A), (C) and (D) only
3. (A), (B) and (D) only
4. (B), (C) and (D) only

**23.** L, N and T are partners sharing profits in the ratio of 5 : 3 : 2. If N retires, the gaining ratio of L & T would be:

1. 3 : 2 2. 5 : 2
3. 5 : 3 4. 2 : 3

**24.** High Land India Ltd. invited applications for 50,000 Shares of ₹ 100 each per share. Applications were received for 70,000 shares and pro-rata allotment was made on the application for 50,000 shares. Rohan to whom 600 shares were allotted failed to pay the allotment money and his shares were forfeited immediately after allotment. Of the shares forfeited, 500 share were reissued as fully paid-up for ₹ 80 per share.

Order to be followed for recording entries will be:

(A) Forfeiture of shares

(B) Calculation of amount received on allotment

(C) Adjustment of excess money received on application towards allotment

(D) Reissue of shares

Choose the **correct** answer from the options given below:

1. (A), (B), (C), (D) 2. (A), (B), (D), (C)
3. (C), (B), (A), (D) 4. (C), (B), (D), (A)

**16.** 2 **17.** 2 **18.** 2 **19.** 1 **20.** 4 **21.** 4 **22.** 1 **23.** 2 **24.** 3

**25.** If a new partner does not bring his share of goodwill in cash, the following treatment shall be made:
1. crediting old partners capital A/c in new ratio and debiting new partner capital A/c
2. crediting old partners capital A/c in sacrificing ratio and debiting new partner current A/c
3. crediting all partners in the new ratio and debiting premium account
4. no entry is made when new partner does not bring his share of goodwill in cash

**26.** Match List-I with List-II.

Match the accounts with their purpose:

| List-I | List-II |
|---|---|
| (A) Profit and Loss adjustment A/c | (I) Changes in amount of capital |
| (B) Profit and Loss appropriation A/c | (II) Generally no change in amount of capital |
| (C) Fixed capital A/c | (III) Errors and omissions found after preparation of final A/c |
| (D) Fluctuating capital method | (IV) Extention of Profit & Loss A/c |

Choose the **correct** answer from the options given below:
1. (A) - (I), (B) - (II), (C) - (III), (D) - (IV)
2. (A) - (I), (B) - (III), (C) - (II), (D) - (IV)
3. (A) - (III), (B) - (IV), (C) - (I), (D) - (II)
4. (A) - (III), (B) - (IV), (C) - (II), (D) - (I)

**27.** Method of Codification should be:
1. Easy to process data
2. An identification mark
3. Easy to understand, cryptic, and leads to grouping of accounts
4. Such that it leads to grouping of accounts

**28.** Accounting treatment for a partnership firm is similar to that of a sole proprietorship business except the following aspects:

(A) Distribution of Profit and Loss among the partners

(B) Dissolution of Partnership Firm

(C) Raising Capital through public offering

(D) Adjustments for Wrong Appropriation of Profits in the Past

Choose the **correct** answer from the options given below:
1. (A), (B) and (C) only
2. (A), (B), (C) and (D)
3. (A), (B) and (D) only
4. (B), (C) and (D) only

**29.** Zomato Ltd. decided to offer 10% of its issued capital to its employees at a price lower than its market value. The scheme adopted by Zomato Ltd. is:
1. Private placement of shares
2. Employees Stock Option Plan
3. Issue of bonus shares
4. Employers contribution to EPFO

**30.** Which of the following are shown under capital account in case capital of partner's are fixed?

(A) Fresh capital introduced

(B) Permanent capital withdrawn

(C) Interest on capital

(D) Amount of capital brought down from the previous year

Choose the **correct** answer from the options given below:
1. (A), (B) and (C) only
2. (A), (B) and (D) only
3. (A), (C) and (D) only
4. (B), (C) and (D) only

**31.** On the basis of information given below the closing Inventory will be:

| | |
|---|---|
| Opening inventory | 20,000 |
| Average inventory | 40,000 |

1. 20,000 2. 40,000
3. 60,000 4. 80,000

**32.** Where there is no articles of association of its own, which of the following provisions applies as per Table A?
1. A minimum of 15 days' notice is given to the shareholders to pay the amount
2. Calls must be made on a uniform basis on all shares of all class.
3. A period of one month must elapse between two calls
4. The amount of call should not exceed 20% of the face value of the share

**33.** In order to bring clarity regarding the identity of ultimate owners of the company, disclosure of shares in the company held by each shareholder is required, holding more than ........... shares, specifying the number of shares held.
1. 5% 2. 10%
3. 12% 4. 15%

| | | | | | | | | |
|---|---|---|---|---|---|---|---|---|
| **25.** 2 | **26.** 4 | **27.** 4 | **28.** 3 | **29.** 2 | **30.** 2 | **31.** 3 | **32.** 3 | **33.** 1 |

**34.** Match List-I with List-II.

Match the statements with their respective Provisions/ other name.

| List-I | List-II |
|---|---|
| (A) AS-3 | (I) Statement of Profit & Loss |
| (B) Schedule 3 of Companies Act | (II) Cash flow statement |
| (C) Financial status of the undertaking | (III) Final accounts of company |
| (D) Performance report | (IV) Balance sheet |

Choose the **correct** answer from the options given below:

1. (A) - (II), (B) - (III), (C) - (I), (D) - (IV)
2. (A) - (II), (B) - (III), (C) - (IV), (D) - (I)
3. (A) - (I), (B) - (II), (C) - (IV), (D) - (III)
4. (A) - (III), (B) - (IV), (C) - (I), (D) - (II)

**35.** Which of the following event take place in the case of dissolution of a partnership firm?

1. Court does not intervene
2. Business is not terminated
3. Economic relations between the partners comes to an end.
4. Assets and Liabilities are revalued

**36.** To write off Discount on issue of debentures following entry is made:

1. Shareholder A/c Dr.
   To Discount on issue of Debentures A/c
2. Capital reserve A/c Dr.
   To Discount on issue of Debentures A/c
3. Securities Premium Reserve A/c./Statement of Profit and Loss Dr.
   To Discount on Issue of Debentures A/c.
4. Share forfeiture A/c Dr.
   To Discount on issue of Debentures A/c

**37.** Which of the following entry shows withdrawal of excess capital by partner's?

1. Partner's capital A/c is debited and Cash/Bank A/c is credited.
2. Cash/Bank A/c is debited and partner's capital A/c is credited.
3. Drawings A/c is debited and profit and loss A/c is credited.
4. Profit and loss A/c is debited and Drawings A/c is credited.

**38.** In line with what is prescribed by the Accounting Standard, goodwill appearing in the balance sheet is written off at the time of:

1. Firm's dissolution
2. Revaluation of assets and liabilities
3. Firm's reconstitution
4. Preparation of Realisation A/c

**39.** Match List-I with List-II.

If the partnership deed is silent regarding the items provided in List-I.

| List-I | List-II |
|---|---|
| (A) Interest on Capital | (I) to be shared equally |
| (B) Interest on Loan | (II) not charged |
| (C) Interest on Drawings | (III) not payable |
| (D) Sharing of Profits | (IV) @6% p.a. |

Choose the **correct** answer from the options given below:

1. (A) - (I), (B) - (II), (C) - (III), (D) - (IV)
2. (A) - (I), (B) - (III), (C) - (II), (D) - (IV)
3. (A) - (III), (B) - (IV), (C) - (II), (D) - (I)
4. (A) - (III), (B) - (IV), (C) - (I), (D) - (II)

**40.** Money received against share warrants' is to be disclosed as a separate item under which head/sub-head:

1. Shareholder's fund
2. Reserves and Surplus
3. Non-current Liabilities
4. Notes to accounts

**Directions (Qs. No. 41-45):** *Answer the questions from based on following paragraph.*

Preeti, Kabir and Shershah are partners in a firm. Kabir retires from the firm. On his date of retirement, ₹ 1,00,000 became due to him. Preeti and Shershah promised to pay him in four yearly equal installments plus interest @ 12% p.a. on the unpaid balance every year at the end of the year, to which he agreed.

**41.** The amount of interest payable at the end of fourth year will be:

1. ₹ 9,000
2. ₹ 6,000
3. ₹ 3,000
4. ₹ 2,500

**42.** Gaining ratio among remaining partners Preeti and Shershah is:

1. 1 : 2
2. 1 : 1
3. 2 : 1
4. 3 : 2

**43.** In case at the time of retirement of Kabir, his share of goodwill is valued at ₹ 15,000, then what will be the total value of firm valued goodwill on his retirement?

1. 15,000
2. 30,000
3. 45,000
4. 60,000

**34.** 2 **35.** 3 **36.** 3 **37.** 1 **38.** 3 **39.** 3 **40.** 1 **41.** 3 **42.** 2 **43.** 3

**44.** Net Amount of installment payable at the end of 2nd year to Kabir is:

1. ₹ 25,000
2. ₹ 34,000
3. ₹ 31,000
4. ₹ 37,000

**45.** The dues of Kabir is to be paid in 4 yearly installment. The amount of each installment will be:

1. ₹ 20,000
2. ₹ 25,000
3. ₹ 37,000
4. ₹ 34,000

**Directions (Qs. No. 46-50):** *Based on the information provided below, compute and answer.*

**Comparative Balance Sheet of Amrit Limited as at March 31, 2023 and March 31, 2024**

(₹ in Lakhs)

| Particulars | March 31, 2023 | March 31, 2024 | Absolute Increase (+) or Decrease (–) | Percentage Increase (+) or Decrease (–) |
|---|---|---|---|---|
| **I. Equity and Liabilities** | | | | |
| Shareholders' funds | | | | |
| Share capital | 15 | 20 | 5 | .... |
| Reserves and surplus | 14 | .... | (1) | (7.14) |
| **Non-current liabilities** | | | | |
| Long-term borrowings | .... | 19 | 3 | 18.75 |
| **Current liabilities** | | | | |
| Trade payables | 2 | 3 | 1 | 50 |
| **Total** | **47** | **55** | **8** | **17.02** |
| **II. Assets** | | | | |
| **Non-current assets** | | | | |
| Fixed assets | | | | |
| Tangible assets | 15 | .... | 5 | 33.33 |
| Intangible assets | 16 | 19 | 3 | 18.75 |
| **Current assets** | | | | |
| Inventories | 14 | 13 | (1) | (7.14) |
| Cash and Cash Equivalents | 2 | 3 | 1 | .... |
| **Total** | **47** | **55** | **8** | **17.02** |

**46.** Percentage change in cash and cash equivalents:

1. 50%
2. 20%
3. 33.33%
4. 66.67%

**47.** Value of reserves and surplus on 31 March, 2024 stood at:

1. 15,00,000
2. 14,00,000
3. 13,00,000
4. 16,00,000

**48.** The value of long term borrowings as on 31 March, 2023:

1. 22,00,000
2. 16,00,000
3. 18,00,000
4. 7,00,000

**49.** What is the value of tangible assets as on 31 March 2024?

1. 15,00,000
2. 5,00,000
3. 20,00,000
4. 10,00,000

**50.** What is the percentage change in share capital?

1. 30%
2. 33.33%
3. 40%
4. 25%

**44.** 2 **45.** 2 **46.** 1 **47.** 3 **48.** 2 **49.** 3 **50.** 2

# EXPLANATORY ANSWERS

1. **(1):** To compute the Interest Coverage Ratio (ICR), which shows how easily a company can pay interest from its operating earnings, we follow a logicai sequence:

(A) Calculate Net Profit before Tax (NPBT):

Given: Net Profit after tax = ₹ 60,000,

and Tax rate = 40%

Net Profit before tax = ₹ 60,000 ÷ (1 – 0.40) = ₹ 60,000 ÷ 0.60 = ₹ 1,00,000

(D) Calculate Interest on Long-term Debt:

12% of ₹ 20,00,000 = ₹ 2,40,000

(C) Calculate Net Profit before Interest and Tax (EBIT):

EBIT = Net Profit before tax + Interest

= ₹ 1,00,000 + ₹ 2,40,000 = ₹ 3,40,000

(B) Divide EBIT by Interest to get ICR:

ICR = ₹ 3,40,000 ÷ ₹ 2,40,000 ≈ 1.42 times

Thus, the correct sequence is: (A), (D), (C), (B).

2. **(3):** This option is not a recognized method for goodwill valuation. The accepted methods include:

- **Average Profit Method:** Uses average past profits × number of years' purchase.
- **Super Profit Method:** Uses profits exceeding normal profits (super profit × years).
- **Capitalisation Method:** Converts average/super profit into capitalized value to calculate goodwill.

The term "Average Capitalisation weighted method" is not a valid or commonly used technique and does not appear in standard accounting frameworks.

3. **(2):** According to Section 49 of the Companies Act, the company cannot make a call exceeding 25% of the nominal (face) value of shares at any one time. This restriction ensures shareholders are not overburdened in a single call. For example, for a ₹ 10 share, the company may ask for a maximum of ₹ 2.50 per call.

4. **(2):** When shares are issued at a premium but the premium amount hasn't been received and the shares are later forfeited, the premium is treated as not earned. Therefore:

- The Securities Premium Reserve Account must be debited to cancel out the earlier credit entry.
- This restores the account to reflect only the premium actually received.

Hence, the correct treatment is a debit to the Securities Premium Reserve at the time of forfeiture.

5. **(4):** When a new partner is asked to bring more money than their capital share, the extra amount is usually attributed to Goodwill.

Here, C's capital share is ₹ 2,00,000, but he is asked to bring ₹ 2,50,000.

- The extra ₹ 50,000 is not for capital contribution or reserves, but for compensating existing partners for sharing future profits.
- This is treated as Goodwill brought in by the new partner.

6. **(2):** A partnership firm can be dissolved voluntarily when all partners give their consent, as per Section 40 of the Indian Partnership Act, 1932. This is a recognized and valid mode of dissolution.

While death of a partner may lead to dissolution, it does not necessarily cause dissolution if the partnership agreement specifies continuity. Therefore, option 2 is more universally correct since consent of all partners always leads to dissolution.

7. **(3):** Let's now recheck the entries carefully:

(A) Calls in Advance A/c Dr. To Particular Call A/c → This is passed when calls in advance are adjusted against the due call → (III)

(B) Interest on Calls in Advance A/c Dr. To Sundry Shareholder's A/c → This is for interest due on calls in advance → (I)

(C) Sundry Shareholder's A/c Dr. To Bank A/c → This is used when interest on calls in advance is paid, cash goes out → (II)

(D) Bank A/c Dr. To Calls in Arrears A/c To Interest on Calls in Arrears A/c → This entry is passed when arrears and interest on arrears are received → (IV)

Thus, the corrected matching is:

(A)-(III), (B)-(I), (C)-(II), (D)-(IV).

8. **(3):** By default, Microsoft Excel creates a new workbook with three blank worksheets named Sheet1, Sheet2, and Sheet3. This can be customized in settings, but the standard default is **three**.

**9. (3):** Under the Indian Partnership Act, a court can order dissolution when:

- The business can be carried on only at a loss
- Partner becomes insane or incapable
- Persistent breach of the agreement, etc.

Death or expiry of term automatically dissolves or leads to reconstitution but loss-based continuation is a specific legal ground for court-ordered dissolution.

**10. (3):** The standard format of a Cash Flow Statement is:

(C) Purchase of property – under investing activities

(D) Proceeds from bond issue – under financing activities

(B) Cash and equivalents at beginning – disclosed in reconciliation

(A) Cash and equivalents at end – closing reconciliation figure

Thus, logical order: C → D → B → A.

**11. (2):** We are to identify which ratios primarily measure risk. Let's examine:

(A) **Liquidity Ratios (like Current Ratio, Quick Ratio):** Measure short-term solvency risk – the firm's ability to meet short-term obligations.

✓ This is a risk-related ratio.

(C) **Debt Ratios (like Debt-to-Equity, Interest Coverage):** Directly measure financial risk arising from leverage.

✓ Definitely a risk measure.

(D) **Profitability Ratios (like Net Profit Margin, Return on Equity):** While primarily measuring performance, poor profitability increases sustainability risk.

✓ Considered under risk assessment as well.

(B) **Activity Ratios (like Inventory Turnover, Debtors Turnover):** These measure efficiency, not direct financial risk. They are operational indicators, not risk-focused.

✗ Hence, not primarily risk-measuring.

So, the correct answer is: (A), (C), and (D) only.

**12. (2):** Given:

- A & B share profits equally
- Fixed capitals:
  A = ₹ 2,00,000;
  B = ₹ 3,00,000
- Interest @10% omitted

Interest due:

- A = ₹ 20,000
- B = ₹ 30,000

Difference = ₹ 10,000

→ But they share profits equally, so each partner should effectively bear ₹ 25,000 in interest allocation.

Since A was under-credited by ₹ 5,000 and B was over-credited by ₹ 5,000, the adjusting journal entry would be:

- A's capital account will be debited by ₹ 5,000
- B's capital account will be credited by ₹ 5,000

This implies A gave ₹ 5,000 more than his fair share, and must be debited.

Correct answer: A capital account will be debited by ₹ 5,000.

**13. (2):** Yaduvanshi current A/c Dr. 30,000

Madhulika current A/c Dr. 30,000

Vidushi current A/c Dr. 15,000

To Profit & Loss Appropriation A/c 75,000

Given:

- Net Loss = ₹ 75,000
- Ratio = 2 : 2 : 1
- Fixed capitals (so adjustments go through current accounts)

Loss distribution:

- Yaduvanshi = ₹ 30,000
- Madhulika = ₹ 30,000
- Vidushi = ₹ 15,000

Journal entry (as loss is being debited from partners' accounts):

Yaduvanshi Current A/c Dr. ₹ 30,000

Madhulika Current A/c Dr. ₹ 30,000

Vidushi Current A/c Dr. ₹ 15,000

To Profit & Loss Appropriation A/c ₹ 75,000

Correct answer: Option 2.

**14. (4):** When a partnership is engaged in unlawful activities, such as exporting opium, the court mandates compulsory dissolution under Section 39 of the Indian Partnership Act, 1932.

- The business becomes illegal, and continuation is not allowed.
- Authorities can take legal action and forcibly dissolve the firm.

**15. (3):** When debentures are issued at a discount to a vendor (i.e., not for cash):

- Vendor A/c is debited – as vendor is to be paid
- % Debentures A/c is credited – to recognize liability
- Discount on Issue of Debentures A/c is debited – to record the discount loss
- Securities Premium Reserve A/c is not involved here, as debentures are at discount, not at a premium.

**16. (2):** Correct chronological process for issue of shares:

(C) The company first issues a prospectus inviting the public to subscribe.

(B) Interested investors submit applications along with application money.

(A) After scrutiny, letters of allotment or regret are sent to applicants.

(D) Then, subsequent installments like allotment or call money are collected.

Thus, the correct sequence is: Prospectus → Application → Allotment → Installments.

**17. (2):** As per SEBI guidelines and Companies Act, convertible debentures which are to be immediately converted into equity shares cannot be issued at a discount, because it would indirectly mean issuing shares at a discount, which is not allowed under law.

Thus, immediate conversion triggers the restriction.

**18. (2):** At the time of dissolution, the order of payment is:

1. Losses including capital deficiency are first set off against profits,
2. If insufficient, then against capital of partners,
3. Then partners may bring in money in their profit-sharing ratio,
4. Borrowings are liabilities and are repaid as part of outside debts.

Hence, the first source to meet losses is profits.

**19. (1):** (A) - (III), (B) - (I), (C) - (IV), (D) - (II)

(A) Accounting Standard Rules – Notified in 2006 under Companies (Accounting Standards) Rules. → (III)

(B) Companies Act – Latest applicable act is Companies Act, 2013 → (I)

(C) Financial Statements – Prepared as per Schedule III of Companies Act → (IV)

(D) Partnership Act – Established in 1932 → (II).

**20. (4):** Reserve capital is that portion of uncalled share capital which a company decides not to call up except on winding up.

- It is available only to creditors during liquidation.
- This ensures a fund cushion for settling external liabilities.

**21. (4):** As per Revised Schedule III to the Companies Act, 2013, the balance sheet items are arranged under major headings and subheadings in a particular order.

For liabilities side:

(C) Reserves and Surplus appear under "Shareholders' Funds" at the top.

(B) Deferred Tax Liabilities come under "Non-Current Liabilities".

(D) Short-term Provisions fall under "Current Liabilities".

(A) Deferred Tax Assets are shown on the asset side, typically under "Non-Current Assets".

So, among given options, the most logical sequence for liability items:

Reserves and Surplus → Deferred Tax Liabilities → Short-term Provisions → Deferred Tax Assets.

**22. (1):** Under Reserves and Surplus, the following are included:

(A) Securities Premium Reserve – Yes, it's part of reserves.

(B) Revaluation Reserve – Yes, it's a capital reserve.

(C) Share Option Outstanding Account – Shown under reserves in equity.

(D) Reserve Capital – Not included; it's a portion of uncalled capital, not a reserve.

Hence, correct grouping: A, B, and C only.

**23. (2):** Profit-sharing ratio of L : N : T = 5 : 3 : 2

When N retires, L and T will gain N's share in some agreed ratio.

If no specific agreement is given, assume gaining ratio = old ratio among continuing partners.

So, L and T will share N's 3/10 in the ratio of L : T = 5 : 2.

Thus, gaining ratio = 5 : 2.

**24. (3):** In the case of pro-rata allotment, the correct sequence of accounting entries is as follows:

(C) **Adjustment of excess money received on application towards allotment:** Since applications were received for 70,000 shares but only 50,000 were allotted, excess application money must be adjusted against the allotment dues. Rohan, being allotted 600 shares on pro-rata basis, would have paid extra at the time of application which is adjusted before checking for allotment payment default.

(B) **Calculation of amount received on allotment:** After adjusting the excess from the application, calculate the net unpaid amount on allotment for Rohan's shares. Only then can it be determined that he defaulted.

(A) **Forfeiture of shares:** Once it's confirmed that Rohan failed to pay the allotment money even after adjustments, his 600 shares are forfeited. This step comes after identifying the default.

(D) **Reissue of shares:** 500 out of the forfeited shares are reissued as fully paid-up at ₹ 80 each.

Hence, the proper sequence of entries is: (C), (B), (A), (D).

**25. (2):** If goodwill is not brought in cash by the new partner:

- The old partners must still be compensated for the sacrifice they made in the profit share.
- This is done by crediting old partners' capital accounts in sacrificing ratio and debiting the new partner's current account or capital account (depending on arrangement).
- No premium account is involved.

Correct treatment: Option 2.

**26. (4):** (A) - (III), (B) - (IV), (C) - (II), (D) - (I)

(A) Profit and Loss Adjustment A/c → (III): Used for rectifying errors or omissions discovered after the preparation of final accounts.

(B) Profit and Loss Appropriation A/c → (IV): This account is an extension of Profit & Loss A/c and is used to distribute profits among partners.

(C) Fixed Capital A/c → (II): Under this method, there is generally no change in the capital balance except for fresh capital or permanent withdrawal.

(D) Fluctuating Capital method → (I): Here, the capital changes frequently with interest on capital, drawings, salary, etc.

**27. (4):** The primary objective of codification in accounting is to enable the systematic grouping of accounts. It helps in organizing ledger accounts in a way that related accounts are placed together for easier classification, analysis, and reporting. While other options mention helpful features like ease of processing or identification, the fundamental reason for codifying accounts is to ensure logical grouping and structure within the accounting system.

Hence, the correct answer is: Option 4.

**28. (3):** Accounting treatment of partnership firms is broadly similar to sole proprietorship, except for aspects that involve multiple partners, such as:

(A) Profit and Loss distribution among partners

(B) Dissolution procedures are different

(D) Adjustment for wrong profit appropriations must account for multiple partners

(C) Raising capital through public offering is not allowed for either sole proprietorship or partnership. Only companies can do this.

So, correct differences are A, B, and D only.

**29. (2):** When a company offers its shares to employees at a price lower than market value, it is done through the Employee Stock Option Plan (ESOP). This is a benefit scheme allowing employees to purchase shares after a vesting period.

- It is not a private placement, bonus issue, or EPFO contribution.

**30. (2):** Under the fixed capital method, only permanent changes in capital (like new capital or withdrawal of capital) are shown in the capital account.

(A) Fresh capital introduced – Yes

(B) Permanent capital withdrawn – Yes

(D) Brought forward balance from last year – Yes

(C) Interest on capital – No, this is shown in the current account under fixed capital method.

So, the correct items: A, B, D only.

**31. (3):** We are given:

- Opening Inventory = ₹ 20,000
- Average Inventory = ₹ 40,000

Formula:

Average Inventory = (Opening Inventory + Closing Inventory) / 2

⇒ ₹ 40,000 = (₹ 20,000 + Closing Inventory) / 2

Multiply both sides by 2:

₹ 80,000 = ₹ 20,000 + Closing Inventory

⇒ Closing Inventory

= ₹ 80,000 − ₹ 20,000

= ₹ 60,000.

**32. (3):** As per Regulation 13 of Table A of the Companies Act (applicable when a company does not have its own Articles of Association), a minimum interval of one month must elapse between two calls on shares.

This provision ensures adequate time for shareholders to arrange funds and maintain fairness in the call process.

**33. (1):** Under the Companies Act, 2013, to improve transparency in ownership, a company must disclose details of all shareholders holding more than 5% of the shares.

This ensures that the identity of significant shareholders (those potentially influencing company decisions) is known.

**34. (2):** (A) - (II), (B) - (III), (C) - (IV), (D) - (I)

(A) AS-3 → (II): AS-3 relates to Cash Flow Statement

(B) Schedule III of Companies Act → (III): It provides the format of Final Accounts for companies

(C) Financial status → (IV): Represents the Balance Sheet

(D) Performance report → (I): Refers to Statement of Profit & Loss

**35. (3):** In the dissolution of a partnership firm, the economic relationship between partners ends.

- They no longer share profits/losses
- The firm is wound up
- Assets are realized, liabilities are paid

Thus, the partnership ceases to exist, and the mutual business relationship ends permanently.

**36. (3):** The discount on issue of debentures is a capital loss and must be amortized over the life of the debentures. It is written off by debited to Securities Premium Reserve (if available) or else to the Statement of Profit and Loss if no premium reserve exists. Hence, the correct accounting entry is:

Securities Premium Reserve A/c / Statement of Profit and Loss A/c Dr.

To Discount on Issue of Debentures A/c.

**37. (1):** When a partner withdraws excess capital from the firm, it reduces the firm's obligation toward that partner.

Therefore, the partner's capital account is debited and the Cash or Bank account is credited, indicating outflow of funds. This reflects withdrawal of capital, not drawings.

**38. (3):** As per the applicable accounting standards and partnership principles, goodwill appearing in the books is adjusted during reconstitution of the firm, which includes events like admission, retirement, or change in profit-sharing ratio. At this time, existing goodwill is either written off or adjusted among partners based on the new arrangement. It is not specifically written off only at the time of dissolution — that treatment is handled through the Realisation Account.

Hence, goodwill is written off or adjusted at the time of firm's reconstitution, making option 3 correct.

**39. (3):** (A) - (III), (B) - (IV), (C) - (II), (D) - (I)

When the partnership deed is silent, the default provisions under the Indian Partnership Act, 1932 are:

(A) Interest on Capital → (III): Not payable

(B) Interest on Loan → (IV): Payable @6% p.a.

(C) Interest on Drawings → (II): Not charged

(D) Sharing of Profits → (I): To be shared equally.

**40. (1):** Money received against share warrants is considered a part of Shareholder's Fund but is disclosed as a separate line item under that head until shares are actually allotted. It represents a right to subscribe to shares and is treated as equity in nature.

**41. (3):** The principal due to Kabir = ₹ 1,00,000

Payment is made in 4 equal annual installments,

so installment = ₹ 1,00,000 ÷ 4

= ₹ 25,000

At the start of 4th year,

Kabir has received 3 installments → ₹ 75,000 paid

→ balance = ₹ 25,000

Interest @12% on ₹ 25,000

= ₹ 3,000 (for the 4th year).

**42. (2):** Since no original profit-sharing ratio is given, it is assumed Kabir was sharing profits equally with Preeti and Shershah, i.e., 1 : 1 : 1.

Kabir retires, and his 1/3 share is divided among Preeti and Shershah.

If not specified, it is assumed to be divided equally. Hence, gaining ratio = 1 : 1.

**43. (3):** Kabir's share of goodwill = ₹ 15,000

His share = 1/3 (from equal partnership among 3)

So, total goodwill of the firm

= ₹ 15,000 ÷ (1/3)

= ₹ 45,000.

**44. (2):** Total amount due to Kabir = ₹ 1,00,000, to be paid in 4 equal annual installments

→ each principal installment = ₹ 25,000.

At the start of the second year, Kabir has received one installment,

so balance = ₹ 75,000.

Interest for the second year

= 12% of ₹ 75,000

= ₹ 9,000

Therefore, the installment payable at the end of the second year

= ₹ 25,000 (principal) + ₹ 9,000 (interest)

= ₹ 34,000.

**45. (2):** Total due to Kabir = ₹ 1,00,000

To be paid in 4 equal yearly installments

→ ₹ 1,00,000 ÷ 4 = ₹ 25,000 per installment (excluding interest)

So, each principal installment = ₹ 25,000

**46. (1):** Cash and Cash Equivalents increased from ₹ 2 lakhs in 2023 to ₹ 3 lakhs in 2024.

Percentage change = (3 − 2) ÷ 2 × 100

= 1 ÷ 2 × 100 = 50%.

**47. (3):** Reserves and Surplus show a decrease of ₹ 1 lakh, with the percentage change given as (−7.14%).

So, closing balance = ₹ 14 lakhs − ₹ 1 lakh

= ₹ 13,00,000.

**48. (2):** Long-term borrowings in 2024 = ₹ 19 lakhs, and increase = ₹ 3 lakhs.

So, value in 2023 = ₹ 19 lakhs − ₹ 3 lakhs

= ₹ 16,00,000.

**49. (3):** Tangible assets increased by ₹ 5 lakhs, and value in 2023 = ₹ 15 lakhs.

Therefore, value in 2024

= ₹ 15 lakhs + ₹ 5 lakhs.

= ₹ 20,00,000.

**50. (2):** Share capital increased from ₹ 15 lakhs to ₹ 20 lakhs.

Percentage change = (5 ÷ 15) × 100

= 33.33%.

Previous Years' Paper

# Common University Entrance Test for UG Programmes

# CUET–UG—GENERAL TEST

## Entrance Exam, 2025

(Exam held on 27-05-2025)

## Subject Code: 501

**1.** Jatin is ninth from the front in a column of boys. There were thrice as many behind him as there were in front. How many boys are there between Jatin and the fifth boy from the end of the column?

1. 33
2. 20
3. 21
4. 19

**2.** Earth Hour, the voluntary one hour blackout observed by 187 countries on 23rd day of March every year, to mark a battle against global warming, was first organized by which organization of the following:

1. Green Peace
2. World Health Organization
3. World Wildlife Fund for Nature
4. People for Ethical Treatment of Animals

**3.** Which one of the following is credited as the 'pioneer of rocket technology' in India?

1. Haider Ali
2. Sher Shah Suri
3. Tipu Sultan
4. Alauddin Khilji

**4.** C is to the East of B, which is to the North of D. If A is to the South of D, then in which general direction of C is A?

1. South
2. South-West
3. North
4. North-East

**5.** Earthquake refers to the vibration on the earth's surface caused by catastrophic endogenetic forces.

(A) The magnitude or intensity of energy released by an earthquake is not measured by the modified Mercalli Intensity Scale.

(B) The place on the ground surface which is perpendicular to the focus is called the epicenter.

(C) Seismology is the special branch of geology that deals with the study of earthquakes.

(D) Shadow zones are some specific areas where earthquake waves do not occur or occur rarely.

Choose the **correct** answer from the options given below:

1. (A), (B) and (D) only
2. (A), (C) and (D) only
3. (A), (B) and (C) only
4. (B), (C) and (D) only

**6.** A, B, C, D, E, F and G are sitting around a circular table facing the center. E is second to the right of F, who is sitting on the immediate right of C. A & D are the only persons sitting between G & E.

(A) B is third to the right of G.

(B) C is the immediate right of G.

(C) D is the immediate right of B.

(D) G is second to the left of F.

Choose the **correct** answer from the options given below:

1. (C) and (D) only
2. (A), (B) and (D) only
3. (A), (B) and (C) only
4. (A), (B), (C) and (D)

**7.** Arrange the sequence of national events in the order of their occurrence.

(A) Inauguration of Prerna Sthal.

(B) Droupadi Murmu takes oath as the 15th President of India.

(C) Karpoori Thakur, referred to as 'Jan Nayak', became the 49th recipient of the Bharat Ratna.

(D) India became the first country to prepare a full list of fauna, called 'Fauna of India'.

Choose the **correct** answer from the options given below:

1. (A), (B), (C), (D)
2. (B), (A), (D), (C)
3. (B), (C), (A), (D)
4. (C), (B), (D), (A)

| **1.** 4 | **2.** 3 | **3.** 3 | **4.** 2 | **5.** 4 | **6.** 2 | **7.** 3 |
|---|---|---|---|---|---|---|

**8.** A trader sells wheat at 10% profit and uses weight 10% less than the actual measure. What is his actual percentage gain?

1. 18.18% 2. 20%
3. 22.22% 4. 10%

**9.** Choose the number which is different from the others.

1. 295 2. 552
3. 729 4. 906

**10.** Which of the following is called the 'Tiger of the Ganges' along with the distinction of being the 'National Aquatic Animal'?

1. Ghariyal 2. Dolphin
3. Royal Bengal Tiger 4. Hippopotamus

**11.** How many degrees will the hour hand move, in the time within which the minute hand moves 240°?

1. 20° 2. 18°
3. 24° 4. 22°

**12.** 'Amar Sonar Bangla', the national anthem of present day Bangladesh was written by which of the following poets?

1. Bankim Das Chatterjee
2. Rabindra Nath Tagore
3. Ashfaq Ullah Khan
4. Sarojini Naidu

**13.** Who among the following emperors fought the 'First Battle of Panipat'?

1. Babur and Sikandar Lodhi
2. Akbar and Hemu
3. Humayun and Sher Shah Suri
4. Babur and Ibrahim Lodhi

**14.** When seen through a mirror, an analog clock shows quarter to four. The correct time shows by the clock:

1. 9:15 2. 9:45
3. 8:15 4. 8:45

**15.** If the slant height of a cone is decreased by 15 per cent and the radius of its base is increased by 20 per cent, then by what per cent will its curved surface area change?

1. 2 per cent decrease
2. 2.5 per cent decrease
3. 2.5 per cent increase
4. 2 per cent increase

**16.** Match the following missions to their respective purposes:

| List-I (Mission) | List-II (Purpose) |
|---|---|
| (A) Chandrayaan-3 | (I) Development and launch of a dual-frequency synthetic aperture radar satellite |
| (B) Gaganyaan-3 | (II) Attempt for soft landing on moon |
| (C) NISAR | (III) Solar Observatory Mission |
| (D) Aditya-L1 | (IV) India's first crewed (human) space mission |

Choose the **correct** answer from the options given below:

1. (A) - (II), (B) - (IV), (C) - (I), (D) - (III)
2. (A) - (I), (B) - (III), (C) - (II), (D) - (IV)
3. (A) - (IV), (B) - (I), (C) - (III), (D) - (II)
4. (A) - (III), (B) - (IV), (C) - (I), (D) - (II)

**17.** Manish is eighteenth from the right end and Rahul is fifth from the left end in a row of boys. If there are seven boys between Manish and Rahul, how many boys are there in the row?

1. 29 2. 30
3. 31 4. 41

**18.** The partition of Bengal in 1905 was realized during the Viceroyship of:

1. Lord Mountbatten
2. Lord Dalhousie
3. Lord Irwin
4. Lord Curzon

**19.** Trace out the figure, from among the following options, in which the figure (X) is embedded:

(X)

1. 

2. 

3. 

4. 

| | | | | | |
|---|---|---|---|---|---|
| **8.** 3 | **9.** 1 & 3 | **10.** 2 | **11.** 1 | **12.** 2 | **13.** 4 |
| **14.** 3 | **15.** 4 | **16.** 1 | **17.** 2 | **18.** 4 | **19.** 4 |

**20.** A bag contains 3 red, 2 blue, 5 green and 4 yellow balls. If two balls are picked at random, what is the probability that either both are red or both are blue?

1. 1/7　　2. 3/91
3. 4/91　　4. 5/91

**21.** The sum of $n$ terms of the series

$1+\frac{3}{2}+2+\frac{5}{2}+3+\frac{7}{2}+......$

1. $\frac{n(n+1)}{2}$　　2. $\frac{n(n+3)}{4}$
3. $\frac{(n+1)(n+2)}{4}$　　4. $\frac{n(n+3)}{2}$

**22.** The component of the blood which helps to fight infections is:

1. Erythrocytes　　2. Plasma
3. Platelets　　4. Leukocytes

**23.** A boy travels between point A and point B at a speed of 6 km/h and returns at a speed of 9 km/h. If the total time taken by him is 1 hour 15 min, the distance between A and B is:

1. 6.5 km　　2. 5.5 km
3. 4.5 km　　4. 9 km

**24.** In the given question, a statement is followed by two assumptions. You have to decide which of the assumptions is implicit in the statement and choose your answer accordingly.

**Statement:** Over The Top (OTT) platform has become indispensable for the entertainment of people.

**Assumptions:**

I. People enjoy watching content on OTT.
II. OTT is the only medium of entertainment.

1. Only assumption II is implicit.
2. Only assumption I is implicit.
3. Both I and II are implicit.
4. Neither I nor II is implicit.

**25.** In the letter series, some of the letters are missing, which are given in the alternatives (A), (B), (C) and (D).

m n o n o p q o p q r _ _ _ _ s t u

(A) r　　(B) s
(C) q　　(D) p

Choose the **correct** sequence from the options given below:

1. (C), (B), (D), (A)　　2. (A), (B), (C), (D)
3. (B), (A), (D), (C)　　4. (B), (D), (C), (A)

**26.** The value of gravity ($g$) on the Moon is .......... of that on the earth's surface.

1. 1/2　　2. 1/3
3. 1/6　　4. 1/9

**27.** In the given question, find out which of the following answer figures completes the figure matrix?

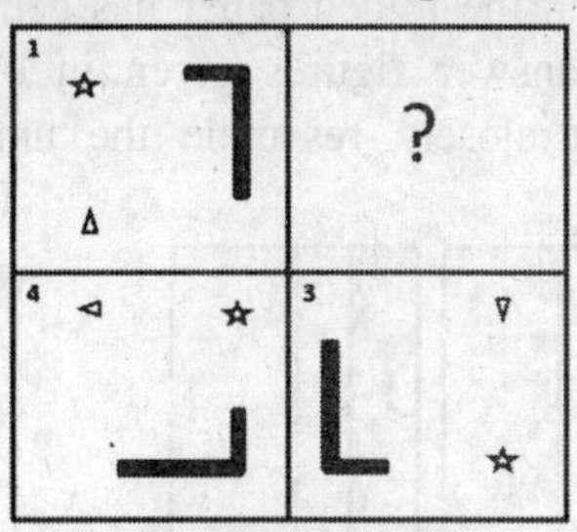

1. 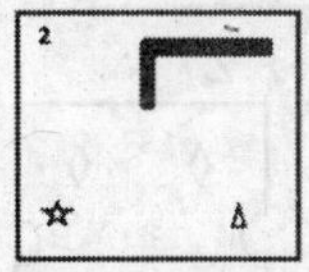　　2. 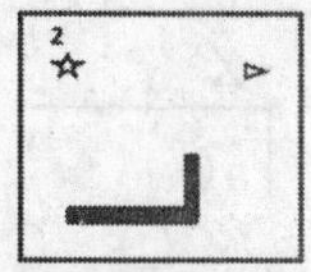

3. 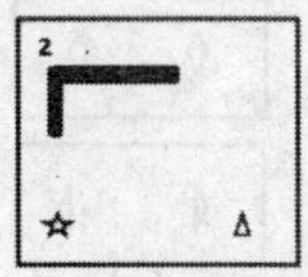　　4. 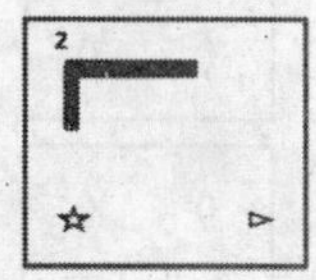

**28.** P and Q together can do a piece of work in 60 days. Q and R together can do it in 120 days. P and R together can do it in 90 days. In what time can Q alone do the same work?

1. 144 days　　2. 720 days
3. 360 days　　4. 720/7 days

**29.** Soap consists of:

1. Alkali salts of higher fatty acids
2. Calcium carbonate, aluminum silicate and gypsum
3. Sodium silicate and silicate of a base, like calcium or lead
4. Sodium silicate and ammonium nitrate

**30.** Match List-I with List-II.

| List-I | List-II |
|---|---|
| (A) Remainder when $17^{35234}$ is divided by 8 | (I) 0 |
| (B) Remainder when 4444 is divided by 9 | (II) 1 |
| (C) Unit's digit of $(34)^{15}+(34)^{16}$ | (III) 2 |
| (D) Unit digit of $7^4-9^3$ | (IV) 7 |

Choose the **correct** answer from the options given below:

1. (A) - (II), (B) - (IV), (C) - (I), (D) - (III)
2. (A) - (I), (B) - (II). (C) - (III), (D) - (IV)
3. (A) - (II), (B) - (IV), (C) - (III), (D) - (I)
4. (A) - (IV), (B) - (II), (C) - (I), (D) - (III)

| **20.** 3 | **21.** 4 | **22.** 4 | **23.** 3 | **24.** 2 | **25.** 4 | **26.** 3 | **27.** 4 | **28.** 1 | **29.** 1 | **30.** 1 |
|---|---|---|---|---|---|---|---|---|---|---|

31. The number of diagonals in a Hexagon is:

1. 6     2. 7
3. 8     4. 9

**32.** The figures X, Y and Z given below show a sequence of folding of paper. The fig. (Z) shows the manner in which the folded paper has been cut. Choose from the answer figures given in options which would most closely resemble the unfolded form of fig. (Z).

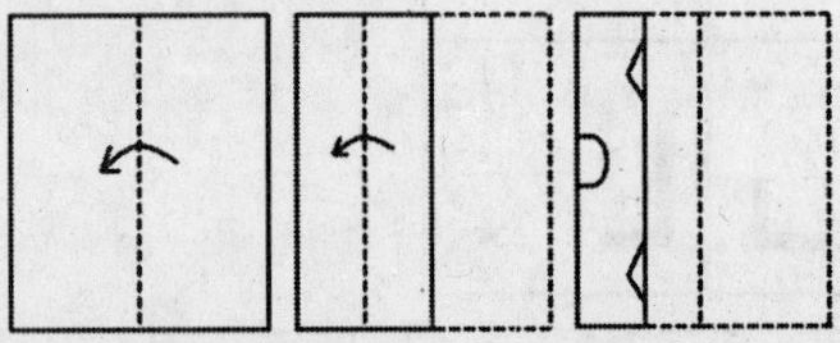

X     Y     Z

1. 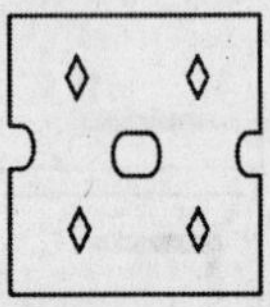    2. 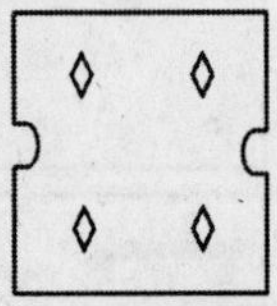

3. 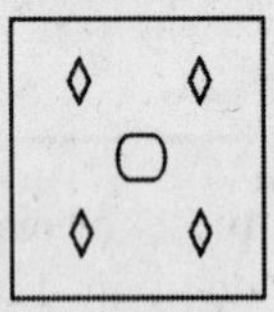    4. 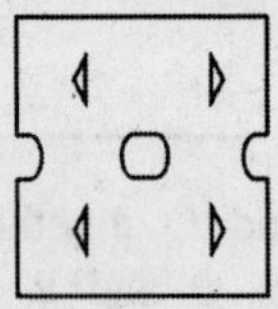

**33.** If the area of an equilateral triangle is $36\sqrt{3}$ $cm^2$, then the length of the side is:

1. 12 cm     2. 9 cm
3. 6 cm     4. 3 cm

**34.** Arrange the sequence of the stages of human progress in order of their occurrence.

(A) The Palaeolithic Age
(B) The Chalcolithic Age
(C) The Neolithic Age
(D) The Mesolithic Age

Choose the **correct** answer from the options given below:

1. (A), (B), (C), (D)
2. (B), (A), (D), (C)
3. (D), (A), (B), (C)
4. (A), (D), (C), (B)

**35.** Select a suitable figure from the answer figures which will substitute this question mark so that a series is formed in order.

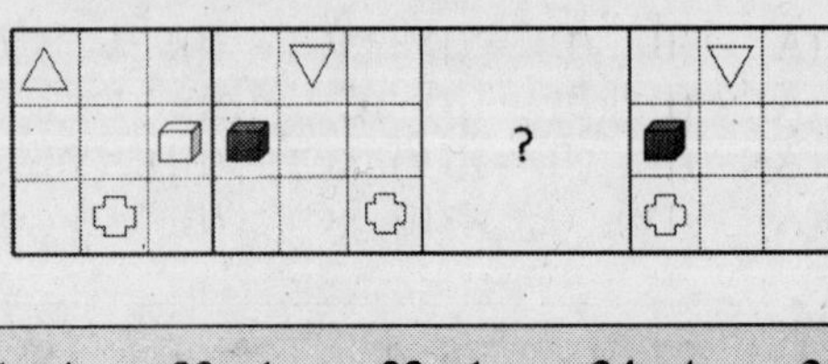

1. 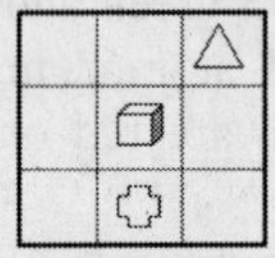    2. 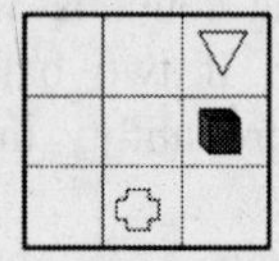

3. 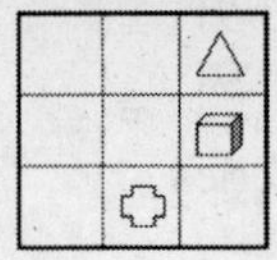    4. 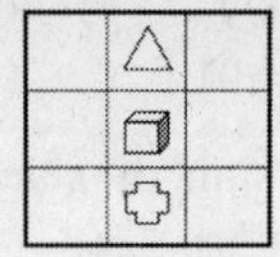

**36.** The sum of the digits of a 4-digit number is subtracted from the number. The resulting number is always:

1. divisible by 6     2. divisible by 9
3. divisible by 4     4. divisible by 8

**37.** Trace out the alternative figure from among the following options in which the figure (X) is embedded (rotation is not allowed):

(X)

1.     2. 

3.     4. 

**38.** 3 men or 15 boys can do a piece of work in 30 days. In how many days will 2 men and 5 boys do this work?

1. 15 days     2. 25 days
3. 30 days     4. 40 days

**39.** The nearest integer to 6650 which is exactly divisible by 429 is:

1. 6864     2. 6435
3. 6436     4. 6535

**40.** Which of the following nicknames would you most likely relate to Thailand?

1. Land of Thousand Elephants
2. Land of Morning Calm
3. Land of White Elephants
4. Land of Tigers

**41.** If 10% of X = 15% of Y = 1/5 of Z, then X : Y : Z is:

1. 6 : 3 : 4     2. 10 : 15 : 18
3. 15 : 10 : 18     4. 6 : 4 : 3

**31.** 4   **32.** 1   **33.** 1   **34.** 4   **35.** 3   **36.** 2   **37.** 2   **38.** 3   **39.** 1   **40.** 3   **41.** 4

**42.** In the given question, a statement is followed by two conclusions numbered I and II. You have to assume everything in the statement to be true, then consider the two conclusions together and decide which of them logically follows beyond a reasonable doubt from the information given in the statement.

**Statement:** Birds of same feather flock together.

**Conclusions:**

I. Similar people tend to associate with each other.
II. A group of birds have beautiful feathers.

1. Only conclusion I follows
2. Only conclusion II follows
3. Both I and II follow
4. Neither I nor II follows

**43.** Choose the correct water image of the given figure, amongst the following answer figures:

1. 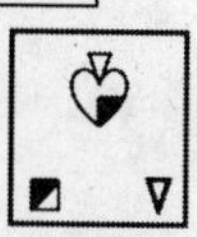
2. 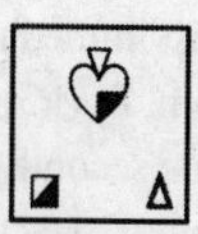
3. 
4. 

**44.** The relation between Mean, Median and Mode for symmetrical distribution is:

1. Mode = 2 Median – 5 Mean
2. Mode = 4 Median – Mean
3. Mean = Median = Mode
4. Mode = 2 Median = Mean

**45.** Which one of the following answer figures completes the figure matrix given below:

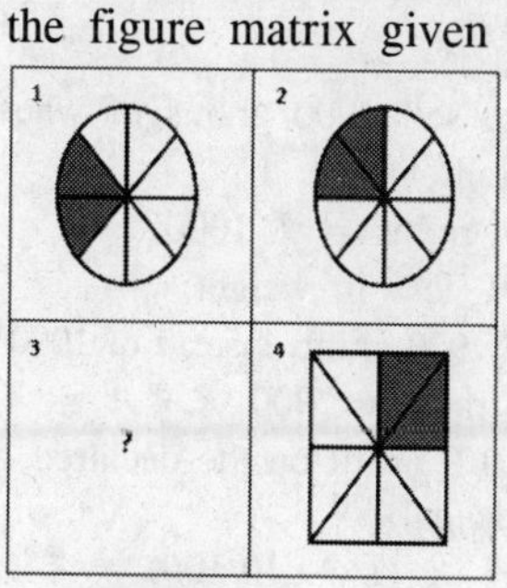


1. 
2. 
3. 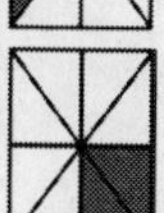
4. 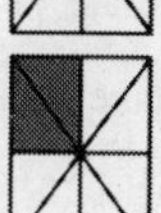

**46.** Mohiniyattam is a solo female dance form known for its rhythmic and unbroken flow of body movements.

(A) The love and devotion to god Vishnu is usually the theme of this dance form.
(B) This dance form belongs to the state of Andhra Pradesh.
(C) Mohiniyattam has the grace and elegance of Bharatanatyam and the vigor of Kathakali.
(D) The dancers attire in a beautiful white and gold bordered Kasavu sari with distinctive white jasmine flowers around a French bun at the side of her head.

Choose the **correct** answer from the options given below:

1. (A), (B) and (C) only
2. (A), (B) and (D) only
3. (A), (C) and (D) only
4. (B), (C) and (D) only

**47.** The question below consists of a question and two statements numbered I and II given below it. You have to decide whether the data provided in the statements is sufficient to answer the question.

The last Tuesday of February 2024 fell on which date?

I. The first Tuesday of that month fell on 6th.
II. The last day of that month was Thursday.

1. The data in the statement I alone is sufficient to answer the question.
2. The data in the statement II alone is sufficient to answer the question.
3. The data in both statements I and II together are necessary to answer the question.
4. The data either in statement I alone or in statement II alone are sufficient to answer the question.

**48.** By looking in a mirror, it appears that it is 6:05 on an analog clock. What is the actual time?

1. 11:30
2. 5:50
3. 5:55
4. 11:28

**49.** For what value of $k$, the system of equations $3x - ky - 3 = 0$ and $2x - 3y - 4 = 0$ has no solution?

1. 6
2. 9
3. 5
4. 9/2

**50.** Paris Olympics 2024 was held in the vicinity of which river?

1. Seine
2. Thames
3. Colorado
4. Nile

**42.** 1 **43.** 3 **44.** 3 **45.** 2 **46.** 3 **47.** 4 **48.** 3 **49.** 4 **50.** 1

# EXPLANATORY ANSWERS

**1.** Jatin is 9th from the front, so there are 8 boys ahead of him. According to the question, the number of boys behind him is three times the number in front:
$8 \times 3 = 24$ boys behind Jatin.
Therefore, total number of boys
= 8 (in front) + 1 (Jatin himself) + 24 (behind)
= 33 boys.
The fifth boy from the end will be at position number
$= 33 - 5 + 1 = 29$ from the front.
Jatin is 9th from the front.
The number of boys between Jatin (9th) and the fifth from end (29th) $= 29 - 9 - 1 = 19$ boys.

**2.** Earth Hour was first initiated by the World Wide Fund for Nature (WWF) in 2007 in Sydney, Australia. It is observed annually on the 23rd of March in over 180 countries, encouraging individuals, communities, and businesses to turn off non-essential lights for one hour to raise awareness about global warming and environmental conservation.

**3.** Tipu Sultan is regarded as the pioneer of rocket technology in India. He and his father Haider Ali developed iron-cased rockets which were used effectively during wars against the British, especially in the Anglo-Mysore wars. These Mysorean rockets influenced later European military rocket designs.

**4.** C is to the east of B, and B is to the north of D, so C is northeast of D. A is to the south of D.
Thus, from C's position (northeast of D), A would lie toward the southwest.
Hence, A is in the south-west direction from C.

**5.** (B), (C) and (D) only

**(A) is incorrect** because the Modified Mercalli Intensity Scale does measure the intensity of shaking, not magnitude, so the statement is factually wrong.

**(B) is correct:** the epicenter is the point on the earth's surface directly above the earthquake's focus.

**(C) is correct:** seismology is the branch of geology that studies earthquakes.

**(D) is correct:** shadow zones are regions where seismic waves are not recorded due to the wave refraction and absorption patterns inside Earth.

**6.** We are given:
- E is second to the right of F,
- F is sitting on the immediate right of C,
- A and D are the only persons sitting between G and E.

Let's fix positions clockwise using the given information.
Start by placing C at position P1, then:
- F is to the immediate right of C ⇒ F at P2
- E is second to the right of F ⇒ E at P4

So far:
P1 – C  P2 – F
P3 – (unknown)  P4 – E
Now use the clue: A and D are the only persons sitting between G and E.
So G _ A D _ E (clockwise), placing A and D between G and E.
Try placing:
- E at P4
- Then P5 = A, P6 = D, P7 = G

Now filled:
P1 – C  P2 – F
P3 – B (only person left)  P4 – E
P5 – A  P6 – D
P7 – G
Complete clockwise arrangement:
C – F – B – E – A – D – G
Now check each option:
(A) B is third to the right of G
From G (P7), count clockwise:
1st = C (P1), 2nd = F (P2), 3rd = B (P3) ⇒ True
(B) C is immediate right of G
From G (P7), immediate right is P1 = C ⇒ True
(C) D is immediate right of B
From B (P3), immediate right is P4 = E ⇒ False
(D) G is second to the left of F
From F (P2), moving left:
1st left = C (P1), 2nd left = G (P7) ⇒ True
So, only (A), (B), and (D) are correct.
Answer: 2: (A), (B) and (D) only.

**7.** Let's arrange the events with year:
(B) Droupadi Murmu became President in July 2022
(C) Karpoori Thakur awarded Bharat Ratna in January 2024
(A) Prerna Sthal inaugurated in February 2024
(D) 'Fauna of India' list launched in March 2024
Correct sequence of occurrence:
(B) → (C) → (A) → (D)
Answer: 3: (B), (C), (A), (D).

**8.** Let the trader claims to sell 1000 grams of wheat.
Cost Price (CP) per gram = Re. 1
So, actual CP of 1000 grams = ₹ 1000
However, he gives 10% less in weight.
That means he gives only 900 grams instead of 1000 grams.
So, actual cost to the trader = 900 × ₹ 1 = ₹ 900
He sells the wheat at 10% profit on the declared quantity (1000 grams), not on actual.
So, SP = 1000 × ₹ 1 × (1 + 10/100) = ₹ 1100
Thus, for 900 grams of wheat, the trader receives ₹ 1100.
His gain = ₹ 1100 – ₹ 900 = ₹ 200
Now calculate percentage gain:

$$\text{Percentage gain} = \frac{\text{Gain}}{\text{Actual CP}} \times 100 = \frac{200}{900} \times 100$$

$$= 22.22\%.$$

**9.** This question allows for two valid interpretations, each highlighting a different number as the odd one out based on distinct logical reasoning:

Logic 1 – Perfect Power Logic:

- 729 is a perfect cube ($9^3$) and also a perfect sixth power ($3^6$), making it unique among the given numbers.
- 295, 552, and 906 are not perfect squares, cubes, or higher powers.

So, 729 stands out due to its special mathematical structure.

Logic 2 – Divisibility by 5:

- 295 ends in 5 ⇒ divisible by 5.
- 552, 729, and 906 do not end in 0 or 5, so they are not divisible by 5.

Thus, 295 is the only number in the group divisible by 5. Since both logics are equally valid and highlight different numbers, both 295 and 729 are correct answers, depending on the reasoning applied.

Answer: 1 and 3: 295 and 729.

**10.** The Ganges River Dolphin is referred to as the 'Tiger of the Ganges' due to its importance in the river ecosystem. It is also officially declared as the National Aquatic Animal of India by the Government.

**11.** The minute hand of a clock moves 6° per minute (360° in 60 minutes).

To move 240°, time taken = 240 ÷ 6 = 40 minutes.

The hour hand moves 0.5° per minute (360° in 12 hours = 0.5° per minute).

So, in 40 minutes, hour hand moves = 0.5 × 40 = 20°.

**12.** 'Amar Sonar Bangla' is the national anthem of Bangladesh. It was written by Rabindra Nath Tagore in 1905 during the Swadeshi movement, as a protest against the partition of Bengal by the British. The first ten lines of this song were adopted as the national anthem by Bangladesh in 1971.

**13.** The First Battle of Panipat took place in 1526 between Babur, the founder of the Mughal Empire, and Ibrahim Lodhi, the last ruler of the Delhi Sultanate.

Babur's victory marked the beginning of Mughal rule in India and the end of the Lodhi dynasty.

**14.** When a clock shows 3:45 in the mirror, the actual time is calculated by subtracting from 12:00.

12:00 – 3:45 = 8:15

Therefore, the actual time shown by the clock is 8:15.

**15.** Curved Surface Area (CSA) of a cone

$$= \pi \times r \times l$$

Let original radius = 100, slant height = 100

$$\text{Original CSA} = \pi \times 100 \times 100 = 10000\pi$$

$$\text{New radius} = 100 + 20\% = 120$$

$$\text{New slant height} = 100 - 15\% = 85$$

$$\text{New CSA} = \pi \times 120 \times 85 = 10200\pi$$

$$\% \text{ change} = \frac{10200 - 10000}{10000} \times 100 = 2\%$$

So, the curved surface area increases by 2%.

**16.** Let's match the missions correctly:

**(A) Chandrayaan-3 → (II) Attempt for soft landing on the moon:** Chandrayaan-3 was ISRO's mission to achieve a successful soft landing on the Moon. It succeeded in August 2023.

**(B) Gaganyaan-3 → (IV) India's first crewed (human) space mission:** Gaganyaan aims to send Indian astronauts (Gagannauts) into space. Gaganyaan-3 is part of this human spaceflight programme.

**(C) NISAR → (I) Development and launch of a dual-frequency synthetic aperture radar satellite:** NISAR (NASA-ISRO Synthetic Aperture Radar) is a joint Earth observation mission with a dual-frequency radar for climate and disaster monitoring.

**(D) Aditya-L1 → (III) Solar Observatory Mission:** Aditya-L1 is India's first solar mission, launched to study the Sun's outer atmosphere (corona and solar wind).

Answer: 1: (A) – (II), (B) – (IV), (C) – (I), (D) – (III).

**17.** Given:

- Manish is 18th from the right end
- Rahul is 5th from the left end
- 7 boys are between them

So, total boys = (Position of Manish from right) + (Position of Rahul from left) + (Number of boys between them) = 18 + 5 + 7 = 30.

**18.** The Partition of Bengal was carried out in 1905 during the viceroyalty of Lord Curzon. The stated purpose was administrative efficiency, but it was widely seen as an attempt to divide and weaken nationalist sentiments in Bengal. The partition was strongly opposed and later annulled in 1911.

**19.** The given figure (X) is a "Y" shaped structure — it consists of a vertical line with two diverging arms at the top, forming a symmetric "Y".

Now let's carefully examine each option:

- **Option 1:** Contains a combination of hexagonal lines and verticals, but the structure does not form a Y shape. *(Incorrect)*
- **Option 2:** Has intersecting triangles forming an hourglass or "X" shape, which is not similar to figure (X). *(Incorrect)*
- **Option 3:** Shows a triangle with internal divisions but does not clearly form a Y-shaped structure. The lines do not match the alignment of figure (X). *(Incorrect)*
- **Option 4:** If you closely observe the center, you can clearly identify the "Y" shape embedded within. It consists of a vertical line with two lines diverging upwards, exactly as in figure (X). *(Correct)*

Therefore, figure (X) is correctly embedded in Option 4.

**20.** Total number of balls in the bag

= 3 red + 2 blue + 5 green + 4 yellow = 14 balls

We are required to find the probability that either both balls are red or both are blue when two balls are drawn at random.

Total number of ways to choose 2 balls out of 14

$$= {}^{14}C_2 = \frac{14 \times 13}{2} = 91$$

Now, Number of ways to choose 2 red balls = ${}^{3}C_2$ = 3

Number of ways to choose 2 blue balls = ${}^{2}C_2$ = 1

So, favourable outcomes = 3 + 1 = 4

Therefore, required probability = 4/91.

**21.** The given series is: $1+\frac{3}{2}+2+\frac{5}{2}+3+\frac{7}{2}+...$

Observe the pattern:

- Odd-positioned terms: 1, 2, 3, ... form an arithmetic sequence of natural numbers
- Even-positioned terms: $\frac{3}{2}, \frac{5}{2}, \frac{7}{2}, ...$ also form an arithmetic sequence

Let's calculate the sum of first few terms and test the formulas:

For $n = 1 : 1 \rightarrow$ Sum $= 1$

Check Option 2:

$$1\times\frac{1+3}{2} = \frac{4}{2} = 2 \rightarrow \textit{(Incorrect)}$$

$$n = 2: \quad 1+\frac{3}{2} = \frac{5}{2}$$

$$\text{Option 2:} \quad 2\times\frac{2+3}{2} = 2\times\frac{5}{2} = 5 \rightarrow \textit{(Incorrect)}$$

$$n = 4: \quad 1+\frac{3}{2}+2+\frac{5}{2} = \left(\frac{1}{2}\right)+\left(\frac{3}{2}+\frac{5}{2}\right)$$

$$= 3 + 4 = 7$$

$$\text{Option 2:} \quad 4\times\frac{4+3}{2} = 4\times\frac{7}{2} = 14 = 14 \rightarrow \textit{(Correct)}$$

$$n = 5: \quad 1+\frac{3}{2}+2+\frac{5}{2}+3 = (1+2+3)+\frac{3}{2}+\frac{5}{2}$$

$$= 6 + 4 = 10$$

$$\text{Option 2:} \quad 5\times\frac{5+3}{2} = 5\times\frac{8}{2} = 20 \rightarrow \textit{(Correct)}$$

Hence, the formula that correctly represents the sum of $n$ terms of the series is: $\frac{n(n+3)}{2}$.

**22.** The component of blood that helps in fighting infections is known as Leukocytes, or white blood cells (WBCs). They are part of the immune system and function to identify and destroy harmful pathogens like bacteria, viruses, and other foreign invaders.

Other options:

- **Erythrocytes (RBCs):** Carry oxygen
- **Plasma:** Transport medium for cells and nutrients
- **Platelets:** Help in blood clotting

Only leukocytes have the defensive role against infections.

**23.** Let the distance between A and B be $x$ km.

Time taken to go from A to B at 6 km/h $= \frac{x}{6}$ hours

Time taken to return from B to A at 9 km/h $= \frac{x}{9}$ hours

Total time = 1 hour 15 minutes
= 1.25 hours

$$\text{So,} \quad \frac{x}{6}+\frac{x}{9} = 1.25$$

Take LCM of 6 and 9 = 18

$$\frac{3x+2x}{18} = 1.25 \Rightarrow \frac{5x}{18} = 1.25$$

$$\Rightarrow \quad x = \frac{1.25\times 18}{5} = \frac{22.5}{5} = 4.5$$

Therefore, the distance between A and B is 4.5 km.

**24.** Statement: "Over The Top (OTT) platform has become indispensable for the entertainment of people."

- **Assumption I:** People enjoy watching content on OTT — Implicit, because unless people find OTT entertaining, it wouldn't be considered indispensable.
- **Assumption II:** OTT is the only medium of entertainment — Not implicit, as the statement says OTT is indispensable, not exclusive.

Only the first assumption logically follows from the statement. Answer: 2: Only assumption I is implicit.

**25.** Given sequence:

m n o | n o p | q o p | q r _ _ _ _ s t u

Break the series into overlapping trios:

- m n o
- n o p
- o p q
- p q r
- q r s
- r s t
- s t u

So, missing letters after "q r" must be:

s, t, p, q ⇒ But needs to fit full letter structure.

However, based on the pattern, after "q r", the correct 4-letter gap to reach "s t u" should be:

s, t, u, v, but that conflicts.

Let's look again:

From "m n o", next trio = shift one forward each time:

n o p
o p q
p q r
q r s
r s t
s t u

So the missing letters are: s, t, u, v — but since the sequence given already ends at "s t u", the missing 4 letters just before that are: r, s, t, u

Therefore: The missing letters are: (B) s, (D) p, (C) q, (A) r.

But reordered correctly, matching pattern: (B), (D), (C), (A).

**26.** The gravitational acceleration on the Moon is approximately 1/6th of that on Earth.

- Earth's gravity ≈ 9.8 m/s$^2$
- Moon's gravity ≈ 1.63 m/s$^2$

$$\frac{1.63}{9.8} \approx \frac{1}{6}.$$

**27.** To solve this figure matrix, let's analyze both shapes and symbols row-wise and column-wise.

**Step 1: Analyze arrow shapes (thick L-shapes):**

- In the first row, images (1) and (2) both have an L-shape rotated differently.
- In the second row, images (4) and (3) also have L-shapes in different orientations.

Now observe the positions of the thick L-shapes:

- From left to right in the top row: shape rotates 90° clockwise from 1 to 2.

- From left to right in the bottom row: shape rotates 90° clockwise from 4 to 3.

So, following the same logic, the L-shape in the missing figure (top right) must be a 90° clockwise rotation of the shape in cell (2).

Looking at cell (2), the shape is a vertical L. Its 90° clockwise rotation is the horizontal L found in option 4.

**Step 2: Analyze the small symbols (triangle, star, etc.):**

Each box contains a triangle and a star, and their positions also follow a consistent diagonal symmetry or shifting across rows/columns.

Following the same position trend of symbols (as seen in cells 1, 2, 3, and 4), the triangle and star in the missing cell match the placement seen in option 4.

Thus, both the thick L-shape and the symbol positions match in option 4.

**28.** Let the total work be 1 unit.

We are given:

- P and Q together can complete the work in 60 days $\Rightarrow$ (P + Q)'s 1-day work = 1/60
- Q and R together can complete the work in 120 days $\Rightarrow$ (Q + R)'s 1-day work = 1/120
- P and R together can complete the work in 90 days $\Rightarrow$ (P + R)'s 1-day work = 1/90

Now, add all three equations:

$$(P + Q) + (Q + R) + (P + R) = \frac{1}{60} + \frac{1}{120} + \frac{1}{90}$$

$$\Rightarrow \quad 2(P + Q + R) = \text{LCM of } 60, 120, 90 = 360$$

Convert each to a common denominator:

$$\frac{1}{60} = \frac{6}{360}; \ \frac{1}{120} = \frac{3}{360}; \ \frac{1}{90} = \frac{4}{360}$$

$$\Rightarrow \quad \text{Sum} = \frac{6+3+4}{360} = \frac{13}{360}$$

$$\text{So,} \quad 2(P + Q + R) = \frac{13}{360}$$

$$\Rightarrow \quad P + Q + R = \frac{13}{720}$$

Now subtract (P + R)'s work to get Q's work:

$$Q = (P + Q + R) - (P + R)$$

$$= \frac{13}{720} - \frac{1}{90}$$

Convert 1/90 to denominator 720:

$$\frac{1}{90} = \frac{8}{720} \Rightarrow Q = \frac{13-8}{720} = \frac{5}{720}$$

Therefore, Q alone can complete the work in:

$$= \frac{720}{5} = 144 \text{ days.}$$

**29.** Soap is formed by saponification, where alkali (such as NaOH or KOH) reacts with fatty acids or triglycerides. This forms alkali salts of higher fatty acids, which we commonly call soap.

Other options refer to ingredients used in glass, ceramics, or fertilizers.

**30.** Let's solve each part of List-I and match with the correct element from List-II:

**(A) Remainder when $17^{(35234)}$ is divided by 8:**

Use modulo patterns.

Since $17 \equiv 1 \pmod 8$, then $17^n \equiv 1^n \equiv 1 \pmod 8$ for any $n$.

$\Rightarrow$ Remainder = 1 $\rightarrow$ Matches with (II)

**(B) Remainder when $4^{4444}$ is divided by 9:**

Powers of 4 modulo 9 cycle as:

$$4^1 \equiv 4 \pmod 9$$
$$4^2 \equiv 7 \pmod 9$$
$$4^3 \equiv 1 \pmod 9$$

Cycle: 4, 7, 1 (length 3)

Now, 4444 ÷ 3 gives remainder 1

$\Rightarrow$ So, $4^{4444} \equiv 4^1 \equiv 4 \pmod 9$ $\rightarrow$ Matches with (IV)

**(C) Unit digit of $(34)^{15} + (34)^{16}$:**

Look at unit digit pattern of 4:

$$4^1 = 4$$
$$4^2 = 16 \rightarrow \text{unit digit } 6$$

Cycle: 4, 6 (length 2)

For $4^{15}$ $\rightarrow$ odd $\Rightarrow$ unit digit = 4

For $4^{16}$ $\rightarrow$ even $\Rightarrow$ unit digit = 6

Sum = 4 + 6 = 10 $\Rightarrow$ Unit digit = 0 $\rightarrow$ Matches with (I)

(D) Unit digit of $7^4 - 9^3$:

$7^4$: powers cycle $\rightarrow$ 7, 9, 3, 1 $\Rightarrow 7^4 \Rightarrow$ unit digit = 1

$9^3$: powers cycle $\rightarrow$ 9, 1 $\Rightarrow 9^3 \Rightarrow$ unit digit = 9

Now 1 − 9 = -8 $\Rightarrow$ take unit digit = 2

$\rightarrow$ Matches with (III)

Correct matching: (1): (A)-II), (B)-(IV), (C)-(I), (D)-(III).

**31.** Formula for number of diagonals in an $n$-sided polygon $= \dfrac{n(n-3)}{2}$

For a hexagon ($n = 6$): $= \dfrac{6(6-3)}{2} = 6 \times \dfrac{3}{2} = 9$.

**32.** Let's analyze the folding and cutting step by step:

- **Figure X:** The paper is first folded vertically in half, from left to right.
- **Figure Y:** Then the paper is again folded vertically from right to left, making a total of two vertical folds. So, the paper is folded into quarters (1/4th of its original width).
- **Figure Z:** Shows cuts made on the folded paper: One semicircular cut on the vertical edge (middle of the folded sheet)

  Two diamond-shaped cuts at the top and bottom

Now, when the paper is unfolded, the cuts will mirror along both fold lines.

- The semicircular cut, made at the center fold, will mirror to form two symmetrical semicircles on either side, resulting in two full circular notches on the middle of left and right edges.
- The diamond cuts on the folded sheet will replicate four times upon full unfolding (mirroring across both folds).

Among the options:

- Option 1 shows:
  4 diamond shapes — correctly placed due to mirroring
  2 semicircular edge notches — correct as per the central vertical cut

Thus, the unfolded paper must look like Option 1.

**33.** We are given that the area of an equilateral triangle is: $36\sqrt{3}$ $cm^2$

The formula for the area of an equilateral triangle with side length aaa is:

$$\text{Area} = \frac{\sqrt{3}}{4}a^2$$

Substitute the given area into the formula:

$$\frac{\sqrt{3}}{4}a^2 = 36\sqrt{3}$$

Divide both sides by $\sqrt{3}$ :

$$\frac{1}{4}a^2 = 36$$

Multiply both sides by 4: $a^2 = 144$

Take the square root of both sides: $a = \sqrt{144} = 12$

Therefore, the length of each side of the equilateral triangle is 12 cm.

**34.** The correct chronological order of the prehistoric ages of human progress is:

**(A) Palaeolithic Age – Old Stone Age:** beginning of human tools and hunting

**(D) Mesolithic Age – Middle Stone Age:** transition phase, microliths used

**(C) Neolithic Age – New Stone Age:** agriculture, domestication begins

**(B) Chalcolithic Age – Copper-Stone Age:** early use of metal tools

Therefore, the correct sequence is:

Palaeolithic → Mesolithic → Neolithic → Chalcolithic.

**35.** Let's analyze the movement and transformation of the three elements in the figure across the series from left to right:

Top row (Triangle) – 1st Item:

Pattern:

- It moves one step forward in each frame (left to right)
- It also alternates its orientation (inverted every time)

Sequence:

1. ▲ in column 1
2. ▼ in column 2
3. ▲ in column 3
4. ? → should be in column 4 and inverted ⇒ ▼
5. ▼ in column 5
6. ?

So, triangle in column 4, facing downward (▼)

**Middle row (Cube) – 2nd Item:**

Pattern:

- Moves 2 steps at a time, alternating forward and backward
- Also alternates color between white and black

Sequence (position and colour):

1. White cube in column 2
2. Black cube in column 3 (→ moved forward 1 step, and changed colour)
3. ? → Now should move 2 steps back, from column 3 → column 1, and colour switches to white
4. Then black cube reappears in column 2 in the next image

So, cube should be white, placed in column 1

Bottom row (Plus symbol) – 3rd Item:

Pattern:

- Remains in same shape and colour, and moves 1 step forward each time

Sequence:

1. **Column 3**
2. **Column 4**
3. **Column 5**

So, in the missing frame, it should be in column 6

But we are to find the missing figure before that — so before it reaches column 5, it was in column 4

→ It must be in column 4 in the missing image

Final Expected Configuration:

- Top row: ▼ in column 4
- Middle row: White cube in column 1
- Bottom row: White plus in column 4

Check which option matches:

Option 3 shows:

- ▼ (triangle) in column 4
- White cube in column 1
- White cross in column 4

Perfect match.

**36.** Let the 4-digit number be represented as N.

Let the sum of its digits be S.

We are given: The number N – S is always divisible by a certain number.

**General Rule:** For any number, if you subtract the sum of its digits from the number itself, the result is always divisible by 9.

Why? Let's prove it algebraically:

Let the number be:

$N = 1000a + 100b + 10c + d$ where $a, b, c, d$ are the digits of the number

Sum of digits $= a + b + c + d = S$

Then,

$N - S = (1000a + 100b + 10c + d) - (a + b + c + d)$
$= 999a + 99b + 9c$

Each term on the right-hand side is divisible by 9:

$999a = 9 \times 111a,\ 99b = 9 \times 11b,\ 9c = 9 \times c$

Hence, $N - S$ is divisible by 9

This is a known divisibility property for all whole numbers.

**37.** We are given a base figure (X), which consists of two intersecting thin lines forming an 'X' shape, where each line has a small outward bend at its ends. The figure is formed by two clean, curved strokes crossing each other. The task is to identify which of the given options contain this exact figure embedded without rotation.

Let's analyze each option carefully:

Option 1:

- Contains thick, straight overlapping bands.
- The structure is geometrically rigid and lacks the distinctive outward curves found in figure (X).
- No accurate embedding of (X) is observed.

Not a match.

Option 2:

- Among all the lines in the structure, the inner intersecting lines are thin and angled, matching the curved outward strokes of figure (X).
- These lines exactly replicate the direction, style, and bending of figure (X) without rotation.

Perfect match

Option 3:

- Composed of thick, diagonal strips with squared ends.
- The distinctive curving ends of figure (X) are not present.
- The lines do not replicate the gentle bend seen in (X).

Not a match

Option 4:

- Similar to Option 3, features wide angular bands.
- No visible trace of the specific curve-ended X shape from figure (X).

Not a match

Hence, only Option 2 correctly embeds figure (X) without rotation and preserves the exact style, shape, and orientation of the curved intersecting lines.

**38.** We are given:

3 men or 15 boys can complete the work in 30 days.

From this, we calculate total work:

Work = 3 men × 30 days = 90 men-days

This is the same as 15 boys × 30 days = 450 boys-days

We are asked: In how many days will 2 men and 5 boys complete the same work?

Let's convert all workers into a common unit, say man-days:

From the given, 3 men = 15 boys ⇒ 1 man = 5 boys

So, 1 boy = 1/5 man

Now, 2 men = 2 man

5 boys = 5 × (1/5) = 1 man

Total workforce = 2 + 1 = 3 men

Therefore, 2 men and 5 boys together are equivalent to 3 men, and since 3 men can do the work in 30 days, 2 men and 5 boys will also complete the work in 30 days.

**39.** We are asked to find the nearest integer to 6650 that is exactly divisible by 429.

Step 1: Divide 6650 by 429

$6650 \div 429 \approx 15.5$

So, the two closest multiples of 429 are:

- 429 × 15 = 6435
- 429 × 16 = 6864

Step 2: Compare both with 6650:

- $|6650 - 6435| = 215$
- $|6864 - 6650| = 214$

Since 6864 is only 214 away and 6435 is 215 away, 6864 is numerically closer to 6650.

Also, both 6435 and 6864 are divisible by 429, but the question specifically asks for the nearest such number. Among the options, Option 1 is 6864, which is the correct choice.

**40.** Thailand is commonly referred to as the "Land of White Elephants." This nickname comes from the cultural and historical reverence for white elephants in Thai royal traditions.

Other options:

- Land of Thousand Elephants = Laos
- Land of Morning Calm = South Korea
- Land of Tigers = India (also used loosely for Southeast Asia)

Answer: 3: Land of White Elephants.

**41.** Given: 10% of X = 15% of Y = 1/5 of Z

Let the common value be $k$

Then, $10X/100 = k \Rightarrow X = 10k$

$15Y/100 = k \Rightarrow Y = (20k)/3$

$(1/5)Z = k \Rightarrow Z = 5k$

Now find the ratio X : Y : Z

$X = 10k,\ Y = 20k/3,\ Z = 5k$

Now take LCM of denominators (1 and 3): Multiply all by 3:

$X : Y : Z = 30k : 20k : 15k$

Now divide all by 5: = 6 : 4 : 3.

**42. Statement:** "Birds of same feather flock together."

**Meaning:** People who are similar in nature or interests stick together.

- Conclusion I: Similar people tend to associate with each other → *True*
- Conclusion II: A group of birds have beautiful feathers → *This is not implied*

Only the first conclusion logically follows.

**43.** We are asked to find the water image of the given figure — this is a vertical reflection over a horizontal axis. In a water image:

- The top and bottom elements swap places.
- The left and right sides remain unchanged.
- All shapes are also inverted vertically.

Let's break down the original figure (from top to bottom):

- **Top-left:** Small black square
- **Top-right:** White triangle pointing upwards
- **Center:** Spade pointing upwards with a downward-pointing triangle inside it
- **Bottom-center:** (None visible in original, triangle is at the base of the spade)

Applying the water image transformation:

1. Black square (top-left) → moves to bottom-left, remains black square
2. White triangle (top-right, pointing up) → moves to bottom-right, becomes downward-pointing
3. Spade with triangle:
   Spade inverts → now points downward
   Internal triangle (was pointing down) → now becomes pointing up
4. No new elements appear at the top

Now check the options:

- Option 1: Spade triangle is still downward → *(Incorrect)*
- Option 2: White triangle on bottom-right is pointing up → *(Incorrect)*
- Option 3: Spade is correctly inverted
  Internal triangle is now upward — *(Correct)*
  Black square is at bottom-left — *(Correct)*
  White triangle is at bottom-right, pointing downward — *(Correct)*

Matches all water image rules

- Option 4: Black square is misplaced, triangle is on the wrong side — *(Incorrect)*.

**44.** In a symmetrical distribution, particularly a normal distribution (bell-shaped curve), the values of Mean, Median, and Mode are all equal and located at the center of the distribution. This is a fundamental property of symmetric distributions, where the data is evenly distributed around a central value.

So, Mean = Median = Mode

This condition does not hold for skewed distributions, but for symmetrical ones, it is always true.

**45.** We are given a 2 × 2 matrix of figures, where the top row contains circular figures and the bottom row contains square figures, all divided into 8 equal sectors.

Our task is to identify the logical relationship between the figures and determine which figure correctly completes the missing position (Box 3).

**Step 1: Analyze the top row (Figures 1 and 2)**

- **Figure 1 (Top-Left Circle):** Two adjacent sectors are shaded – they occupy the top-left and bottom-left positions (forming a vertical block on the left side).
- **Figure 2 (Top-Right Circle):** The shaded block has moved one sector clockwise. Now the shaded sectors are in the top-right and bottom-right.

So, the rule in the top row is: "Two adjacent sectors are shaded, and in the next figure, the pair shifts one position clockwise."

**Step 2: Analyze Figure 4 (Bottom-Right Square)**

- Figure 4 has two adjacent shaded sectors in the square – they are in the top-left and top-right.

To follow the same rule as the top row but in reverse, we should now move one sector backward (counter-clockwise) to determine the shading in Figure 3 (the missing figure).

So, if in Figure 4 the shaded sectors are:

- Top-left and top-right (adjacent on the top side), then in the previous step (Figure 3), the shaded sectors must have been:
- Left and top-left, which is one step back counter-clockwise.

**Step 3: Find the matching option**

Look for the option where the square has two adjacent shaded sectors in the left and top-left positions.

Option 2 matches this exactly.

**46.** Let's evaluate each statement:

(A) "The love and devotion to god Vishnu is usually the theme of this dance form."

*Correct.* Mohiniyattam is based on themes of love and devotion, often associated with Lord Vishnu, especially his female form Mohini, making this statement accurate.

(B) "This dance form belongs to the state of Andhra Pradesh."

*Incorrect.* Mohiniyattam is a classical dance form of Kerala, not Andhra Pradesh.

(C) "Mohiniyattam has the grace and elegance of Bharatanatyam and the vigor of Kathakali."

*Correct.* It blends the elegance and lasya (grace) of Bharatanatyam with the drama and energy of Kathakali, both of which are classical dance forms of South India.

(D) "The dancer's attire in a beautiful white and gold bordered Kasavu sari with jasmine flowers..."

*Correct.* This description accurately reflects the traditional costume worn in Mohiniyattam performances.

Hence, only statements (A), (C), and (D) are correct.

**47.** The data either in statement I alone or in statement II alone are sufficient to answer the question.

**Question:** What was the date of the last Tuesday in February 2024?

Statement I: The first Tuesday was on 6th February 2024.

If 6th is Tuesday, then subsequent Tuesdays are:

13th, 20th, and 27th ⇒ So, last Tuesday = 27th February

Statement I alone is sufficient.

Statement II: The last day of February 2024 was Thursday.

2024 is a leap year, so February has 29 days.

If 29th is Thursday, then 27th was Tuesday ⇒ Last Tuesday = 27th February

Statement II alone is also sufficient.

Thus, either statement alone is enough to answer the question.

**48.** To find the actual time from a mirror image of an analog clock, subtract the given time from 11:60.

Given mirror time = 6:05

Real time = 11:60 – 6:05 = 5:55

So, the actual time is 5:55.

**49.** We are given two equations:

1. $3x - ky = 3$  2. $2x - 3y = 4$

The condition for no solution in a system of linear equations is:

$$\frac{a_1}{a_2} = \frac{b_1}{b_2} \neq \frac{c_1}{c_2}$$

Let's apply: $\frac{3}{2} = \frac{k}{3} \Rightarrow k = \frac{3 \times 3}{2} = \frac{9}{2}$

Now check: $\frac{3}{2} = \frac{9/2}{3} = \frac{3}{2}$ But $\frac{-3}{-4} = \frac{3}{4} \neq \frac{3}{2}$

So, the condition is satisfied when $k = 9/2$.

**50.** The Paris Olympics 2024 are being held in venues located along and near the River Seine, which flows through the heart of Paris, France. Major events and even the opening ceremony are planned along this river.

Previous Years' Paper

# Common University Entrance Test for UG Programmes

# CUET (UG) B.Com (Hons.) Entrance Exam, 2024*

## ENGLISH

**1.** Re-arrange the following phrases in the right sequence to form a meaningful sentence.

(*a*) for seven hours but was hardly
(*b*) because of the absence of any motivation
(*c*) able to decide who the murderer was
(*d*) she worked on the case

Choose the **correct** answer from the options given below:

A. (*a*), (*c*), (*d*), (*b*) B. (*d*), (*a*), (*c*), (*b*)
C. (*d*), (*c*), (*b*), (*a*) D. (*a*), (*b*), (*c*), (*d*)

**2.** Fill in the blank with the **correct** option.

The candidate assured the interviewers that the dip in her grades during her second semester was an ____ since she had always been a top scorer in the first semester.

A. anomaly B. allay
C. adage D. abatement

**3.** Match the words in List-I with their definitions in List-II.

| List-I (Words) | List-II (Definitions) |
|---|---|
| (*a*) Theocracy | I. One who keeps drugs for sale and puts up prescriptions |
| (*b*) Megalomania | II. One who collects and studies objects or artistic works from the distant past |
| (*c*) Apothecary | III. A government by divine guidance or religious leaders |
| (*d*) Antiquarian | IV. A morbid delusion of one's power, importance or godliness |

Choose the **correct** answer from the options given below:

| | (*a*) | (*b*) | (*c*) | (*d*) |
|---|---|---|---|---|
| A. | III | IV | I | II |
| B. | IV | III | II | I |
| C. | I | III | IV | II |
| D. | III | IV | II | I |

**4.** Fill in the blank with the **correct** option.

A small ______ between two children ended up as a group fight.

A. altercation B. match
C. contest D. race

**5.** Replace the underlined word with the most appropriate SYNONYM.

For sometime now, we've been <u>toying</u> with the idea of transferring all our business from physical to online sales only.

A. launch
B. showing
C. considering
D. careful

**6.** Select the word opposite in meaning to the underlined word.

At first the workers were agreeable to the proposals of their Manager, but later they were <u>reconciled</u> to the new proposals.

A. resistant B. estranged
C. cooperate D. agreed

**1.** B **2.** A **3.** A **4.** A **5.** C **6.** A, B

*** This Previous Year Paper has been given here as a Combination of CUET (UG) 2024 different exams for the Subjects 'English, Business Studies, Mathematics, Accountancy/ Book Keeping and General Test', which have been mapped to this course.**

**7.** Complete the sentences given in List-I with the appropriate words given in List-II:

| List-I (Sentences) | List-II (Words) |
|---|---|
| (*a*) She was able to give a ______ explanation in the court for her presence near the crime scene. | I. collaborate/d |
| (*b*) The Rockland Hospital ______ with AIIMS to conduct a free cancer screening camp. | II. corroborate/ing |
| (*c*) Though she has shown only 4% improvement in achieving her target yet her efforts are ______. | III. credible |
| (*d*) The doctors give the prognosis by ______ their diagnosis with several tests. | IV. creditable |

Choose the **correct** answer from the options given below:

| | (*a*) | (*b*) | (*c*) | (*d*) |
|---|---|---|---|---|
| A. | I | II | III | IV |
| B. | I | III | II | IV |
| C. | III | I | IV | II |
| D. | II | IV | I | III |

**8.** Fill in the blank with the **correct** option.

Most of the guests arrived for the concert ______ bus.

A. by
B. with
C. from
D. through

**9.** Choose the word closest in meaning to the underlined word.

Why did you make that flippant remark about her choice of clothes?

A. sarcastic
B. disrespectful
C. casual
D. indifferent

**10.** Select the word OPPOSITE in meaning to the underlined word.

The thief showed his disbelief when informed that his partner had been arrested.

A. displayed
B. concealed
C. battled
D. marked

**11.** Fill in the blank with the **correct** option.

The President finally had to ______ the demands of the public for his resignation.

A. ignore
B. initiate
C. accede to
D. condone

**12.** Re-arrange the following parts of a sentence in their correct sequence to form a meaningful sentence.

(*a*) for organizations which provide
(*b*) services to customers on a face-to-face basis
(*c*) employees with whom they deal is very important
(*d*) the quality of the relationship between customers and

Choose the **correct** answer from the options given below:

A. (*a*), (*b*), (*d*), (*c*)
B. (*c*), (*a*), (*b*), (*d*)
C. (*b*), (*d*), (*a*), (*c*)
D. (*d*), (*a*), (*c*), (*b*)

**13.** Re-arrange the following parts of a sentence in their correct sequence to form a meaningful sentence.

(*a*) as a concept fundamental to
(*b*) especially with the injunction to treat equals equally
(*c*) justice is associated with the notion of equity and equality,
(*d*) ethical theory and political philosophy,

Choose the **correct** answer from the options given below:

A. (*d*), (*b*), (*c*), (*a*)
B. (*c*), (*a*), (*b*), (*d*)
C. (*b*), (*a*), (*d*), (*c*)
D. (*a*), (*d*), (*c*), (*b*)

**14.** Match the idioms in List-I with their meanings in List-II:

| List-I (Idioms) | List-II (Meanings) |
|---|---|
| (*a*) blow the gaff | I. feel unable to deal with something |
| (*b*) at the end of your tether | II. feel terribly ashamed and embarrassed |
| (*c*) be full of beans | III. divulge a secret |
| (*d*) want to curl up and die | IV. be full of energy |

Choose the **correct** answer from the options given below:

| | (*a*) | (*b*) | (*c*) | (*d*) |
|---|---|---|---|---|
| A. | III | I | IV | II |
| B. | II | IV | I | III |
| C. | IV | I | II | III |
| D. | III | IV | I | II |

**7.** C **8.** A **9.** B, C **10.** B **11.** C **12.** A **13.** D **14.** A

**15.** Match the blanks in List-I with the Preposition in List-II:

| List-I (Sentences) | List-II (Prepositions) |
|---|---|
| (*a*) The edited version of her article is indistinguishable _______ her first version. | I. with |
| (*b*) I just don't feel any affinity _____ his prose style. It's too caustic. | II. to |
| (*c*) Her ideas are not all that dissimilar _____ mine. | III. for |
| (*d*) It would be wrong to mistake his diffidence _____ his arrogance or coldness. | IV. from |

Choose the **correct** answer from the options given below:

| | (*a*) | (*b*) | (*c*) | (*d*) |
|---|---|---|---|---|
| A. | IV | I | II | III |
| B. | I | III | II | IV |
| C. | IV | II | I | III |
| D. | III | IV | I | II |

**16.** Re-arrange the parts in their correct sequence to form a meaningful sentence:

(*a*) students with tools for critical thinking
(*b*) cooperative learning is an
(*c*) that enhances creativity and provides
(*d*) eclectic and unique teaching method

Choose the **correct** answer from the options given below:

A. (*a*), (*c*), (*b*), (*d*) B. (*b*), (*d*), (*c*), (*a*)
C. (*b*), (*a*), (*d*), (*c*) D. (*c*), (*b*), (*d*), (*a*)

**Directions (Qs. No. 17-22):** *Read the given passage and answer the six questions that follow.*

When I was in my late teens and still undecided about which language I should write in, he told me that the language one is born into, one's mother tongue, can be the only possible medium of creative expression.

For most of his life, my father, Sripat Rai, had been a Hindi editor and critic. Off and on, he translated writings into English from Hindi. He was fond of saying that a failed writer becomes a critic. The weight of his literary expectation came, eventually, to rest on me. He seemed happy that I was showing an inclination for writing. "She will go far," he told my mother after reading the first story that I sent him from Melbourne.

My father's pronouncement on the mother tongue stayed with me when I later started writing fiction in Hindi. Another thing that I barely acknowledged even to myself was that I felt something like shame whenever I thought of writing in English. It seemed wrong for a granddaughter of Premchand even to be thinking so. Our family had a certain linguistic pride. I knew that Premchand was famous, but I had not at that time realised the extent of his popularity.

The fact that I was the granddaughter of Premchand, followed me everywhere. Everyone had a story to tell about their personal engagement with his fiction—the shopkeeper, the long time cook in my father's Delhi house, a tea vendor, etc. The list was long, for there was practically no one who had not read something by him that had moved them. However, it was this very ubiquity, the reverence and love that he inspired in people, that made of him something too large for me to comprehend in the early years of my life. It led also to the strange feeling that, without having read him and just by being related to him, I had somehow inhaled his writing. The reading happened much later.

**17.** The author grew up with the expectation that she would take up _______.

Fill in the blank with the **correct** option to complete the sentence.

A. editorship of a magazine.
B. translation of literary pieces.
C. creative writing.
D. the job of a critic.

**18.** When her father said, "She will go far", he meant that _______.

Fill in the blank with the **correct** option to complete the sentence.

A. she will travel widely.
B. she will achieve great heights in life.
C. she will go too far, one of these days.
D. she will settle in a far-off place.

**19.** Choose a Statement which is **not** true with respect to the passage:

A. The author felt pressurized to write in Hindi because of her father.
B. She felt obligated to carry on the legacy of Premchand.
C. Her family was chauvinistic about the English language.
D. She was in awe of the extensive reach of her grandfather's writings.

**15.** A **16.** B **17.** C **18.** B **19.** C

20. Premchand became too large for her to understand mainly because of _______.
   (*a*) his ability to connect with people from all walks of life.
   (*b*) the fact that she feared him.
   (*c*) the kind of love and reverence that he inspired in people.
   (*d*) her constant anxiety of failing him.

   Choose the **correct** answer from the options given below:
   A. (*a*) and (*d*) only
   B. (*a*) and (*c*) only
   C. (*b*) and (*c*) only
   D. (*c*) and (*d*) only

21. 'Inhaled his writing' refers to:

   Choose the **correct** option from the following:
   A. imbibing his style subconsciously.
   B. being compelled to write like him.
   C. being influenced by what people said about him.
   D. her father's expectation from her.

22. Choose the correct meaning of the word "Ubiquity" as it appears in the passage:
   A. Occasional
   B. Restricted
   C. Omnipresence
   D. Unwanted

**Directions (Qs. No. 23-28):** *Read the given passage and answer the six questions that follow.*

Free will is the ability to decide and act free from any influence of past events or environment. It implies complete freedom to make any choice absolutely. We clearly don't have free will. Our decisions and actions are never divorced from our past.

We have a conditioned mind. Our memories, past impressions and experiences bias and shape our thoughts and actions in the present. It is our karmic imprint. Not just what we are born with, but also what we accumulate while living. We can consider it as the result of our genetic code, upbringing and environment. It's our backstory.

The only way to experience free will is to get rid of all such conditioning; to neutralise our karmic imprint; to be independent of our psychological coding. That's possible only if we can purify our mind by letting go of all our ego, attachments and fixed beliefs. Then we can reside in the truth of our being.

The above is an exacting definition of free will. What we commonly mean by free will is that we have a choice in most situations like, who you choose to marry, what profession you pursue or how you react to someone's aggression. Sounds reasonable, But here's the catch. Our ability to make that choice too is significantly restricted, dictated by our predispositions.

This applies even to our ability to bring about change within ourselves. Despite a strong resolve to be calmer, kinder or less anxious, our ability to manifest that change depends, partly on our emotional and mental wiring. That's why some people succeed in such efforts more than the others.

If you wish to expand the scope of your agency, explore ways to engage in sustained inner work, deepen your self-awareness, examine and reform your conditioned beliefs. But then, I wonder if your inclination to embark on that journey too depends on your current karmic coding.

23. The author argues that humans don't have "free will" because _______.

   Fill in the blank with the **correct** option to complete the sentence.
   A. our decisions are shaped by past events and environmental influences.
   B. we are born with pre-determined choices that we are forced to make.
   C. we are always dictated by our mind to make irrational choices.
   D. human beings are born slaves of social constructs and expectations.

24. "Karmic imprint" referred to in the passage implies _______.

   Fill in the blank with the **correct** option to complete the sentence.
   A. the ability to bring about change in oneself.
   B. our genetic code, upbringing and environment.
   C. the truth of our being, our individuality.
   D. the wrong doings and vices of our past lives.

25. "Free will" can be experienced if _______.

   Fill in the blank with the **correct** option to complete the sentence.
   A. we embrace our past experiences and conditioning.
   B. we make choices without considering the consequences.
   C. we let go of our ego, attachments and fixed beliefs.
   D. we accumulate more and more karmic imprints.

| **20.** B | **21.** A | **22.** C | **23.** A | **24.** B | **25.** C |
|---|---|---|---|---|---|

**26.** The author proves that the idea of "free will" is a myth by suggesting that ________ .

Fill in the blank with the **correct** option to complete the sentence.

A. our ability to make a choice is restricted by our predispositions.
B. we are unable to bring a change in ourselves.
C. our choices are solely guided by the current environment.
D. our choices are completely independent of past events and our genetic code.

**27.** What does the author propose as a means to expand the scope of one's agency?

Choose the **correct** option.

A. Making choices frequently and impulsively.
B. Engaging in sustained inner work and self-awareness.
C. Holding on to fixed beliefs and stringent mindsets.
D. Ignoring one's past experiences and dispositions.

**28.** What do you think could be a suitable title for this passage?

Choose the **most appropriate** option.

A. Definition of "Free Will".
B. Our backstory—key to a successful life.
C. Do human beings really have "Free Will"?
D. Making Choices—Every Man's Prerogative!

**Directions (Qs. No. 29-34):** *Read the given passage and answer the six questions that follow.*

On a chilly winter evening, nothing warms you up better than a cup of hot cocoa. Chocolate was first consumed in liquid form by the Olmec people of northwestern Central America around 1500 BCE. It was even enjoyed by the Aztec Emperor Montezuma, and the Aztec word for it (*xocolatl*, pronounced *shoh-kwah-tl*) evolved into the English word Chocolate.

But the Aztecs didn't serve their cocoa hot. And since sugar had not yet arrived from Europe, back then, the drink was often flavoured with peppers and spices. It may not have been quite as indulgent as today's version, but it was more palatable if you believed, as the Aztecs did, that chocolate was a gift from the Gods and had healing properties.

After the Spanish arrived in the Americas in the 1500s, liquid chocolate made its way across the pond, where wealthy Europeans added sugar and drank it warm. In *Chocolate : History, Culture and Heritage,* author Bertram Gordon says hot chocolate became "the beverage of the aristocracy," as sugar was still a luxury.

Soon enough, though, hot chocolate caught on with the masses. Chocolate houses—a cross between cafes and casinos—started popping up around 17th-century Europe. In these lively places, hot chocolate was poured from gilded pots into elegant cups (for a posh experience, one can still find it today at the famed Parisian tearoom Angelina's, which is also in New York City). But by the end of the 18th century, chocolate houses had mostly died off, partly because the cost of chocolate was much higher than that of coffee or tea.

Taking a tour of international cups of cocoa, Italians serve it like a thick pudding. Colombians serve it with a dollop of soft cheese while Mexicans punch it up with vanilla, chilli powder and cinnamon. And Filipinos serve it with mango chunks.

**29.** Cocoa was first introduced by the:

A. American people
B. Olmec people
C. Aztec people
D. Spanish people

**30.** The Aztec people made their cocoa palatable by:

A. serving it cold
B. adding sugar to the drink
C. spiking it with spices
D. drinking it as a medicine

**31.** Why did hot chocolate become "the beverage of the aristocracy" in Europe?

A. The essential ingredient was out of reach of the commoners.
B. The Queen had a marked chocolate maker.
C. Only wealthy Europeans could buy it.
D. It was being consumed by the pharma companies.

**32.** The Chocolate Houses didn't survive past the 18th century as:

A. people preferred tea/coffee to hot chocolate.
B. it catered to the not so elite of the society.
C. chocolate was costlier than tea or coffee.
D. the supply of cocoa dwindled over the years.

**33.** Choose the correct statement from the following:

A. Italians serve hot chocolate flavoured with spices.
B. Mexicans serve hot chocolate topped with a dollop of cream.
C. Colombians serve hot chocolate topped with a dollop of cheese.
D. Filipinos served hot chocolate flavoured with peppers.

| **26.** A | **27.** B | **28.** A, C | **29.** B | **30.** C, D | **31.** A, C | **32.** C | **33.** C |
|---|---|---|---|---|---|---|---|

**34.** Choose the correct meaning of the underlined expression in the following sentence:

Soon enough, though, hot chocolate caught on with the masses.

A. was readily available in cafes.
B. became popular among the commoners.
C. hot chocolate did not appeal to people.
D. masses got attracted to the rich experience of drinking hot chocolate.

**Directions (Qs. No. 35-40):** *Read the given passage and answer the six questions that follow.*

Coffee's genetic make-up is no trivial concern; 10 million tonnes of the crop were grown and sold in 2022-23. The coffee that we drink comes from two species: Coffea Canephora, which is also known as Robusta and Coffea Arabica, known as Arabica. In many cases, beans from the two species are blended to make a brew. But the beans of single species are also roasted and sold. Overall, Arabica beans represent around 56% of all coffee sold.

Most genetic variation in living organisms comes from hybridization with other species. However, this is a relatively rare event for Coffea Arabica because it has more than two copies of each chromosome - a phenomenon called polyploidy. Coffea Canephora has two copies of each chromosome, but Coffea Arabica contains multiple copies. This makes it much more difficult for Arabica to interbreed with other species.

As a result, Coffea Arabica's main source of single nucleotide variation is mutation, which occurs at a steady rate over time. However, the species is also relatively young, having formed as a hybrid of Robusta and Coffea Eugenioides - another coffee species that is not widely cultivated - within the past 50,000 years. From that single plant, which has basically no variation, you create the whole species, and then the variation is only the novel mutations that have occurred since that event.

Despite this, there is substantial variation in the physical characteristics of the Arabica coffee plant, including different flavour profiles in the beans and variations in disease resistance, says emeritus geneticist Juan Medrano at the UC Davis Coffee Center at the University of California, Davis. "We're always talking about low variability fat the DNA level, but there is variability at the structural level, at the chromosomal level, at the level of deletions... and insertions," Medrano says.

**35.** Which of the following varieties of coffee is the most sold in the world?

A. Coffea Canephora
B. Coffea Arabica
C. Coffea Eugenioides
D. A blend of Coffea Canephora and Coffea Arabica

**36.** Which of the following species of coffee has more than two copies of each chromosome?

A. Arabica
B. Robusta
C. Coffea Eugenioides
D. A blend of Arabica and Robusta

**37.** Which of the following statements is true about coffea Arabica?

A. Hybridization is the main source of its genetic variation.
B. It has only two copies of each chromosome.
C. It displays the phenomenon of polyploidy.
D. It is easily interbred with other species.

**38.** Which of the following species of coffee developed only in the last 50,000 years?

A. Coffea Canephora  B. Coffea Eugenioides
C. Arabica  D. Robusta

**39.** Which of the following types of variability is not very high for Coffea Arabica?

A. Variability at the structural level.
B. Variability at the chromosomal level.
C. Variability at the level of deletions and insertions.
D. Variability at the DNA level.

**40.** Choose the statement that is factually **incorrect** from the options given below.

A. It is possible to roast the beans of a single species of coffee.
B. Two species of coffee can be blended to make a brew.
C. Due to its genetic make-up, novel mutations do not occur in the species Coffea Arabica.
D. Variations in disease resistance can be seen in the Arabica coffee plant.

**41.** Re-arrange the following phrases in correct sequence to form a meaningful sentence.

(*a*) created by human
(*b*) collective cultural heritage
(*c*) all languages
(*d*) communities are our

Choose the **correct** answer from the options given below:

A. (*a*), (*b*), (*d*), (*c*)  B. (*b*), (*a*), (*d*), (*c*)
C. (*c*), (*a*), (*d*), (*b*)  D. (*d*), (*b*), (*c*), (*a*)

**34.** B, D **35.** B **36.** A **37.** C **38.** * **39.** D **40.** C **41.** C

**42.** Fill in the blank with the **correct** option, to form a meaningful sentence.

The Principal addressed us in the assembly and ______ the rumours of an early summer break.

A. defended B. quashed
C. cleared D. rebuked

**43.** Complete the sentences given in List-I with the appropriate phrasal verbs given in List-II.

| List-I (Sentences) | List-II (Phrasal verbs) |
|---|---|
| (*a*) She was very ______ with him for his offensive remarks on women in politics. | I. give away |
| (*b*) I have plenty of interesting books to ______ to book lovers. | II. cut down |
| (*c*) Strange that people easily ______ to temptation and ruin their reputation! | III. cut up |
| (*d*) Rahul is trying to ______ on his smoking. | IV. give in |

Choose the **correct** answer from the options given below:

| | (*a*) | (*b*) | (*c*) | (*d*) |
|---|---|---|---|---|
| A. | I | II | III | IV |
| B. | II | IV | I | III |
| C. | I | II | IV | III |
| D. | III | I | IV | II |

**44.** Complete the sentences given in List-I with the appropriate adverbs given in List-II:

| List-I (Sentences) | List-II (Adverbs) |
|---|---|
| (*a*) I thought the restaurant would be expensive but it was ______ affordable. | I. badly |
| (*b*) It was a serious accident. But the car was ______ damaged. | II. reasonably |
| (*c*) The meeting was a disaster as it was very ______ organized. | III. quickly |
| (*d*) Mira is gifted, she has the ability to learn any language ______. | IV. hardly |

Choose the **correct** answer from the options given below:

| | (*a*) | (*b*) | (*c*) | (*d*) |
|---|---|---|---|---|
| A. | II | IV | I | III |
| B. | IV | II | III | I |
| C. | I | II | IV | III |
| D. | III | IV | I | II |

**45.** Choose the appropriate word pair to complete the sentence:

I didn't know Rahul was in the hospital. If I ______, I would ______ him.

A. knew, go
B. had known, have visited
C. have known, be going
D. know, had gone

**46.** Identify the option closest in meaning to the underlined word:

The movie star's biography is a glossy, <u>sycophantic</u> portrayal.

A. cowardly
B. domineering
C. flattering
D. insolent

**47.** Choose the correct ANTONYM of the underlined word:

The Minister unleashed a <u>compliment</u> against the newspaper for its biased editorial on illiteracy among women in his constituency.

A. denunciation
B. endorsement
C. regulation
D. speculation

**48.** Choose the correct SYNONYM for <u>redoubtable</u> from the options given below.

A. flimsy B. perplexing
C. formidable D. voluble

**49.** Choose the correct ANTONYM for <u>sullen</u> from the options given below.

A. morose B. reticent
C. timid D. genial

**50.** Rearrange the following parts in the correct sequence to make a meaningful sentence:

(*a*) are inborn but our
(*b*) constituents of flavour, are learned
(*c*) our responses to basic tastes
(*d*) perceptions of smells, the main

Choose the **correct** answer from the options given below:

A. (*b*), (*d*), (*a*), (*c*)
B. (*a*), (*c*), (*b*), (*d*)
C. (*c*), (*a*), (*d*), (*b*)
D. (*c*), (*b*), (*d*), (*a*)

**42.** B **43.** D **44.** A **45.** B **46.** C **47.** A **48.** C **49.** D **50.** C

# EXPLANATORY ANSWERS

1. **(B):**

   (*d*) She worked on the case – introduces the subject and the action.

   (*a*) for seven hours – specifies the duration of the action.

   (*c*) but was hardly able to decide who the murderer was – describes the result of her effort, indicating difficulty in solving the case.

   (*b*) because of the absence of any motivation – provides the reason behind the difficulty faced.

   The complete sentence would be: "She worked on the case for seven hours but was hardly able to decide who the murderer was because of the absence of any motivation."

2. **(A):** In the sentence, "anomaly" is the most suitable word because it refers to an irregularity or deviation from what is expected or usual. The candidate is explaining that the drop in her grades during the second semester was unusual compared to her consistent top performance in the first semester.

3. **(A):**

   (*a*) **Theocracy:** (*iii*) A theocracy is a system of government where religious leaders control the state, or where the state's policies are governed by divine principles or religious doctrines.

   The term reflects a political system where religious authority is central.

   (*b*) **Megalomania:** (*iv*) Megalomania is a psychological condition where an individual has an exaggerated sense of their own power, importance, or godliness.

   This delusion of grandeur is often marked by a belief in one's supreme abilities or dominance.

   (*c*) **Apothecary:** (*i*) An apothecary is a historical term for someone who prepares and sells medicines.

   This role is akin to that of a modern pharmacist, who manages prescriptions and medicinal products.

   (*d*) **Antiquarian:** (*ii*) An antiquarian is a person who studies, collects, or deals in antiques and historical artifacts.

   This term is used to describe someone who has a deep interest in historical objects or artistic works from the past.

4. **(A):** The sentence describes a situation that escalated from a small issue to a bigger conflict. "Altercation" means a noisy argument or disagreement, especially in public. Therefore, the sentence should read: "A small altercation between two children ended up as a group fight."

5. **(C):** The word "toying" in this context means considering or thinking about an idea in a casual or preliminary way. The most appropriate synonym for "toying" is "considering."

6. **(A, B):**

   (A) **Resistant:** This term means opposed to or unwilling to accept something. It is opposite to reconciled, which means to become resigned or accepting of a situation.

   (B) **Estranged:** This term refers to being alienated or disconnected, which is also opposite to reconciled, as it implies a lack of acceptance or harmony with the situation.

7. **(C):**

   (*a*) She was able to give a credible explanation in the court for her presence near the crime scene.

   (*iii*) "Credible" means believable or convincing, which fits the context of providing a reliable explanation.

   (*b*) The Rockland Hospital collaborated with AIIMS to conduct a free cancer screening camp.

   (*i*) "Collaborated" means worked together, which is appropriate for describing joint efforts between organizations.

   (*c*) Though she has shown only 4% improvement in achieving her target yet her efforts are creditable.

   (*iv*) "Creditable" means deserving praise or recognition, fitting for acknowledging her efforts despite modest improvement.

   (*d*) The doctors give the prognosis by corroborating their diagnosis with several tests.

   (*ii*) "Corroborating" means confirming or supporting with additional evidence, which is suitable for describing the process of validating a diagnosis.

8. **(A):** The preposition "by" is used to indicate the means or method of transport. Therefore, the sentence should read: "Most of the guests arrived for the concert by bus."

**9. (B & C):** The word "flippant" means not showing a serious or respectful attitude. "Disrespectful" is the closest in meaning as it directly indicates a lack of respect. "Casual" also fits because a flippant remark can be considered overly casual or not serious. Therefore, both "disrespectful" and "casual" are correct.

**10. (B):** The word "showed" means to display or exhibit something. The opposite of showing would be to conceal or hide. Therefore, the correct word is "concealed."

**11. (C):** The phrase needed must indicate yielding to demands. "Accede to" means to agree to a request or demand. Therefore, the correct sentence is: "The President finally had to accede to the demands of the public for his resignation."

**12. (A):**

(*a*) introduces the context: "For organizations which provide."

(*b*) specifies the type of service provided: "services to customers on a face-to-face basis."

(*d*) continues with the main point: "the quality of the relationship between customers and."

(*c*) concludes the thought: "employees with whom they deal is very important."

The sentence is "For organizations which provide services to customers on a face-to-face basis, the quality of the relationship between customers and employees with whom they deal is very important."

**13. (D):**

(*a*) introduces the topic: "as a concept fundamental to."

(*d*) specifies the field: "ethical theory and political philosophy."

(*c*) links the topic with the main point: "justice is associated with the notion of equity and equality."

(*b*) adds detail about the application: "especially with the injunction to treat equals equally."

The sentence is "Justice is associated with the notion of equity and equality, as a concept fundamental to ethical theory and political philosophy, especially with the injunction to treat equals equally."

**14. (A):**

(*a*) blow the gaff - III. divulge a secret: To reveal or disclose something that was supposed to be kept secret.

(*b*) at the end of your tether - I. feel unable to deal with something: To reach the limit of one's patience or endurance.

(*c*) be full of beans - IV. be full of energy: To be very lively, energetic, or enthusiastic.

(*d*) want to curl up and die - II. feel terribly ashamed and embarrassed: To feel extremely embarrassed or ashamed, often wanting to disappear or hide.

**15. (A):**

(*a*) The edited version of her article is indistinguishable from her first version. IV. from: Used to indicate that two things are not distinguishable from each other.

(*b*) I just don't feel any affinity with his prose style. I. with: Used to express a lack of connection or relationship with something.

(*c*) Her ideas are not all that dissimilar to mine. II. to: Used to show similarity or comparison between two things.

(*d*) It would be wrong to mistake his diffidence for his arrogance or coldness. III. for: Used to indicate a misunderstanding or misinterpretation of something.

**16. (B):**

(*b*) "Cooperative learning is an": This introduces the subject of the sentence, which is cooperative learning.

(*d*) "eclectic and unique teaching method": This describes what cooperative learning is—an eclectic and unique teaching method.

(*c*) "that enhances creativity and provides": This clause explains what the teaching method does, namely enhancing creativity and providing something.

(*a*) "students with tools for critical thinking": This completes the explanation by specifying what the teaching method provides—tools for critical thinking for students.

The Sentence is "Cooperative learning is an eclectic and unique teaching method that enhances creativity and provides students with tools for critical thinking."

**17. (C):** The passage indicates that the author grew up with the weight of her father's literary expectations, particularly in creative writing. Her father, a Hindi editor and critic, was happy that she showed an inclination for writing. Therefore, the author grew up with the expectation that she would take up creative writing.

**18. (B):** When her father said, "She will go far," he meant that she would achieve great heights in life. This interpretation aligns with the context of the father's pride in her writing abilities and his expectations for her future success.

**19. (C):** The statement "Her family was chauvinistic about the English language" is not true with respect to the passage. The passage mentions that her father had translated writings into English from Hindi and felt that the mother tongue should be the medium of creative expression, which indicates a preference for Hindi rather than chauvinism against English.

**20. (B):** Premchand became too large for her to understand mainly because of his ability to connect with people from all walks of life (*a*) and the kind of love and reverence that he inspired in people (*c*). The passage describes how everyone had a personal engagement with his fiction and how the reverence he inspired made him difficult for her to comprehend.

**21. (A):** 'Inhaled his writing' refers to imbibing his style subconsciously. The author felt that just by being related to Premchand, she had somehow absorbed his writing, even before she read his works.

**22. (C):** The word "ubiquity" in the passage means omnipresence. It refers to the widespread presence and influence of Premchand's writings, as practically everyone the author encountered had read something by him.

**23. (A):** The author argues that humans don't have "free will" because our decisions are shaped by past events and environmental influences. The passage explains that our memories, past impressions, and experiences bias and shape our thoughts and actions in the present.

**24. (B):** "Karmic imprint" referred to in the passage implies our genetic code, upbringing, and environment. The passage describes karmic imprint as the result of what we are born with and what we accumulate while living, influenced by our genetic code, upbringing, and environment.

**25. (C):** "Free will" can be experienced if we let go of our ego, attachments, and fixed beliefs. The passage states that to experience free will, one must get rid of all conditioning and be independent of psychological coding by letting go of ego, attachments, and fixed beliefs.

**26. (A):** The author proves that the idea of "free will" is a myth by suggesting that our ability to make a choice is restricted by our predispositions. The passage explains that even our ability to bring about change within ourselves is significantly restricted by our emotional and mental wiring.

**27. (B):** The author proposes engaging in sustained inner work and self-awareness as a means to expand the scope of one's agency. The passage suggests that to expand one's agency, one should engage in inner work, deepen self-awareness, and examine and reform conditioned beliefs.

**28. (A & C):** The most suitable title for this passage is "Do human beings really have 'Free Will'?" The passage questions the existence of free will and explores how our choices are influenced by past events, conditioning, and predispositions. The title "Definition of 'Free Will'" also fits as the passage provides a detailed explanation of what free will means and its constraints. Therefore, both options A and C are suitable titles.

**29. (B):** Cocoa was first introduced by the Olmec people. The passage mentions that chocolate was first consumed in liquid form by the Olmec people of northwestern Central America around 1500 BCE.

**30. (C & D):** The Aztec people made their cocoa palatable by spiking it with spices and believed that chocolate had healing properties. The passage notes that since sugar had not yet arrived from Europe, the Aztecs often flavored their drink with peppers and spices and believed that chocolate was a gift from the Gods with healing properties. Therefore, both options C and D are correct.

**31. (A & C):** Hot chocolate became "the beverage of the aristocracy" in Europe because the essential ingredient was out of reach of the commoners and only wealthy Europeans could buy it. The passage explains that after the Spanish arrived in the Americas, liquid chocolate made its way to Europe where wealthy Europeans added sugar and drank it warm, as sugar was still a luxury. Therefore, both options A and C are correct.

**32. (C):** The Chocolate Houses didn't survive past the 18th century as chocolate was costlier than tea or coffee. The passage states that by the end of the 18th century, chocolate houses had mostly died off partly because the cost of chocolate was much higher than that of coffee or tea.

**33. (C):** Colombians serve hot chocolate topped with a dollop of cheese. The passage describes that Colombians serve hot chocolate with a dollop of soft cheese.

**34. (B & D):** The underlined expression "caught on with the masses" means became popular among the commoners and masses got attracted to the rich experience of drinking hot chocolate. The passage mentions that soon enough, hot chocolate became popular and chocolate houses started popping up around 17th-century Europe, suggesting it appealed to a wider audience. Therefore, both options B and D are correct.

**35. (B):** The passage states that Arabica beans represent around 56% of all coffee sold, making Coffea Arabica the most sold variety of coffee in the world.

**36. (A):** The passage mentions that Coffea Arabica contains multiple copies of each chromosome, a phenomenon called polyploidy, indicating that Arabica has more than two copies of each chromosome.

**37. (C):** The passage states that Coffea Arabica displays the phenomenon of polyploidy, meaning it has more than two copies of each chromosome, making option C the true statement about Coffea Arabica.

**39. (D):** The passage highlights that Coffea Arabica has low variability at the DNA level compared to structural and chromosomal levels, as well as levels of deletions and insertions.

**40. (C):** The passage mentions that novel mutations do occur in the species Coffea Arabica since it has a steady rate of mutation over time.

Therefore, the statement that due to its genetic make-up, novel mutations do not occur in Coffea Arabica is factually incorrect.

**41. (C):**

(*c*) "All languages" introduces the subject of the sentence.

(*a*) "created by human" provides more detail about the subject, describing what all languages are.

(*d*) "communities are our" explains the relationship between the languages and human communities.

(*b*) "collective cultural heritage" concludes by defining what the languages represent.

The sentence is "All languages created by human communities are our collective cultural heritage."

**42. (B):** The Principal addressed us in the assembly and quashed the rumours of an early summer break. "Quashed" means to put an end to or suppress, which fits the context of addressing and ending rumours.

**43. (D):**

(*a*) - (*iii*) Correct phrasal verb: "cut up" (means to be very critical or upset).

So, the sentence should be: "She was very cut up with him for his offensive remarks on women in politics."

(*b*) - (*i*) Correct phrasal verb: "give away" (means to distribute something for free).

So, the sentence should be: "I have plenty of interesting books to give away to book lovers."

(*c*) - (*iv*) Correct phrasal verb: "give in" (means to surrender or yield).

So, the sentence should be: "Strange that people easily give in to temptation and ruin their reputation!"

(*d*) - (*ii*) Rahul is trying to ____________ on his smoking.

Correct phrasal verb: "cut down" (means to reduce or decrease).

So, the sentence should be: "Rahul is trying to cut down on his smoking."

**44. (A):**

(*a*) - (*ii*) Correct adverb: "reasonably" (means moderately or fairly).

So, the sentence should be: "I thought the restaurant would be expensive but it was reasonably affordable."

(*b*) - (*iv*) Correct adverb: "hardly" (means barely or not significantly).

So, the sentence should be: "It was a serious accident. But the car was hardly damaged."

(*c*) - (*i*) Correct adverb: "badly" (means poorly or ineffectively).

So, the sentence should be: "The meeting was a disaster as it was very badly organized."

(*d*) - (*iii*) Correct adverb: "quickly" (means at a fast pace).

So, the sentence should be: "Mira is gifted, she has the ability to learn any language quickly."

**45. (B):** "Had known" is the past perfect tense, which indicates that the knowledge of Rahul being in the hospital would have been relevant in the past.
"Have visited" is the past perfect conditional form of the verb, meaning that if the condition (knowing Rahul was in the hospital) had been met, the action of visiting him would have occurred.

So, the complete sentence would be: "I didn't know Rahul was in the hospital. If I had known, I would have visited him."

**46. (C):** Sycophantic means behaving or done in an obsequious way to gain advantage; essentially, it refers to excessively flattering or ingratiating oneself to someone in power. Flattering also means showing excessive praise or admiration, this aligns with the meaning of sycophantic.

**47. (A):** Compliment refers to an expression of praise or admiration. Denunciation is the action of publicly condemning or criticizing someone or something, which is the opposite of giving praise or admiration.

**48. (C):** Redoubtable means inspiring fear or awe; having a formidable presence. Formidable similarly means inspiring fear or respect through being impressively large, powerful, intense, or capable.

**49. (D):** Sullen describes a gloomy, sulky, or brooding mood or demeanor. Genial means friendly and cheerful, which is the opposite of being gloomy or sulky.

**50. (C):**

(*c*) "Our responses to basic tastes" introduces the subject of the sentence.

(*a*) "are inborn but our" follows logically, describing the nature of these responses.

(*d*) "perceptions of smells, the main" continues by shifting focus to another aspect related to the main constituents of flavour.

(*b*) "constituents of flavour, are learned" completes the thought by contrasting the inborn responses to learned perceptions.

So, the rearranged sentence is: "Our responses to basic tastes are inborn but our perceptions of smells, the main constituents of flavour, are learned."

# BUSINESS STUDIES

1. Match List-I with List-II.

| List-I | List-II |
|---|---|
| (*a*) Intelligence test | I. Indicator of a person's capacity to develop |
| (*b*) Aptitude test | II. Clues to a person's emotions, values, etc. |
| (*c*) Personality test | III. Measure existing skills of the individual |
| (*d*) Trade test | IV. Indicator of a person's learning ability and ability to make judgements |

Choose the **correct** answer from the options given below:

| | (*a*) | (*b*) | (*c*) | (*d*) |
|---|---|---|---|---|
| A. | I | II | III | IV |
| B. | IV | I | II | III |
| C. | II | III | I | IV |
| D. | I | III | IV | II |

2. Which of the following are advantages of functional structure of an organisation?
(*a*) Leads to occupational specialisation.
(*b*) Places less emphasis on organisational objectives.
(*c*) Promotes coordination and control within a department.
(*d*) Increases operational efficiency.

Choose the **correct** answer from the options given below:
A. (*a*), (*b*) and (*c*) only
B. (*a*) and (*b*) only
C. (*a*), (*c*) and (*d*) only
D. (*c*) and (*d*) only

3. "Management always works by keeping an end result or aim of the organisation. All activities of managers are directed towards the end result." From the above statement, Identify the feature of management.
A. Management is multidimensional
B. Management is continuous
C. Management is intangible
D. Management is a goal oriented process

4. The key position of top-level management is ________.
A. Managing Director
B. Production Manager
C. Marketing Manager
D. Plant Supervisor

**Directions (Qs. No. 5-9):** *On the basis of the information given in the case, answer the next five questions.*

"Just Foodie" is a food chain offering different snacks like chips, biscuits, chocochip cookies, cakes, etc through their own retail outlets. To make their products available to customers at right time, right place, they are also selling their products to grocery stores in addition to their own outlets. The taste, quality and packing are given utmost care. They are offering good quality, so they are able to charge higher price than their competitors. To increase their sales, they are using different offers like: Free gifts, Cash backs, etc. They are offering discounts to customers on various occasions. All these considerations have made "Just Foodie" a complete success and they are able to win over different competitors in thc market, and their market share is rising continuously.

5. In the above case "Just Foodie" is using various variables of Marketing Mix. Identify the variable used in the following statement:

"To make their products available to customers at right time, right place, they are also selling their products to grocery stores in addition to their own outlets."
A. Product
B. Price
C. Promotion
D. Physical distribution

6. "Identify the element of marketing mix in the following statement:

"The taste, quality and packing are given utmost care."
A. Product mix
B. Price mix
C. Promotion mix
D. Physical distribution mix

**1.** B **2.** C **3.** D **4.** A **5.** D **6.** A

**7.** "They are able to charge higher price than their competitors." Which element of marketing mix is discussed in the statement?

A. Product mix
B. Price mix
C. Promotion mix
D. Physical distribution mix

**8.** "To increase their sales, they are using different offers like: Free gifts, Cash backs etc. They are offering discounts to customers on various occasions. Identify the marketing mix element from the above statement.

A. Product mix
B. Price mix
C. Promotion mix
D. Physical distribution mix

**9.** "To increase their sales, they are using different offers like: Free gifts, Cash backs etc. They are offering discounts to customers on various occasions. Which tool of the promotion mix is used in the given statement.

A. Advertisement
B. Sales promotion
C. Personal selling
D. Publicity

**Directions (Qs. No. 10-14):** *On the basis of the information given in the case, answer the next five questions.*

**A Maharatna Company, Indian Oil**

Indian Oil is India's largest commercial organisation. It is the top ranked Indian company in the Fortune 'Global 500' listings (2017). Indian Oil's vision is driven by a group of dynamic leaders, who have made it a name to reckon with. With an over 34,000 strong workforce, a Maharatna Company, Indian Oil has been helping to meet India's energy demands and reaching petroleum products in every part of India for over five decades.

- It plans to increase its business operation all around the world.
- The company plans to invest ₹ 20,000 crore in 2017-18 acquisitions and plans to expand overseas. The company is always believed to be ahead of the demand. Last year too, IOC had invested close to ₹ 20,000 crore, including around ₹ 16,000 crore in various Indian projects and on acquisition for upstream in Russia.
- The company believed that if the goals are well defined, employees are aware of what the organisation has to do and what they must do to achieve those goals.
- Changes or events cannot be eliminated, but they can be anticipated and managerial responses to them can be developed. Policy formation serves as the basis of coordinating the activities and efforts of different divisions, departments and individuals.
- It helps in avoiding confusion and misunderstanding. Manager can look into the future and make a choice from amongst various alternative courses of action.

**10.** Identify the function of management highlighted in the above case.

A. Organising
B. Staffing
C. Directing
D. Planning

**11.** "If the goals are well defined, employees are aware of what the organisation has to do and what they must do to achieve those goals". Identify the significance of managerial function highlighted in this statement.

A. Facilitates decision making
B. Reduces overlapping and wasteful activities
C. Reduces risks of uncertainty
D. Provides direction

**12.** "Changes or events cannot be eliminated, but they can be anticipated and managerial responses to them can be developed." Identify the significance of managerial function highlighted in this statement.

A. Provides direction
B. Reduces risks of uncertainty
C. Reduces overlapping and wasteful activities
D. Facilitates decision making

**13.** "Policy formation serves as the basis of coordinating the activities and efforts of different divisions, departments and individuals. It helps in avoiding confusion and misunderstanding." Identify the significance of managerial function highlighted in this statement.

A. Facilitates decision making
B. Reduces risks of uncertainty
C. Provides direction
D. Reduces overlapping and wasteful activities

| **7.** B | **8.** C | **9.** B | **10.** D | **11.** D | **12.** B | **13.** D |
|---|---|---|---|---|---|---|

**14.** "Manager can look into the future and make a choice from amongst various alternative courses of action." Identify the significance of managerial function highlighted in this statement.

A. Provides direction
B. Reduces risks of uncertainty
C. Reduces overlapping and wasteful activities
D. Facilitates decision making

**15.** Identify the Principle of Management where Taylor pioneered the introduction of method of scientific inquiry into the domain of management practice.

A. Science, not rule of thumb
B. Harmony not discord
C. Cooperation, not individualism
D. Development of each and every person to the greatest efficiency and prosperity

**16.** Match List-I with List-II on the basis of Management Principles:

| List-I | List-II |
|---|---|
| (*a*) Obedience to organisational rules | I. Unity of direction |
| (*b*) One boss for every individual employee | II. Remuneration of employees |
| (*c*) One head and one plan | III. Discipline |
| (*d*) Remuneration should be just and equitable | IV. Unity of command |

Choose the **correct** answer from the options given below:

| | (*a*) | (*b*) | (*c*) | (*d*) |
|---|---|---|---|---|
| A. | I | II | III | IV |
| B. | I | III | II | IV |
| C. | I | II | IV | III |
| D. | III | IV | I | II |

**17.** The aim of which technique given by F.W. Taylor is to reduce a given line or a product to fixed types, sizes and characteristics?

A. Method study
B. Time study
C. Standardisation of work
D. Functional foremanship

**18.** Match List-I with List-II on the basis of Management Principles:

| List-I (Meaning) | List-II (Term) |
|---|---|
| (*a*) Employees turnover should be minimised | I. Stability of personnel |
| (*b*) Emphasises kindliness and justice | II. Equity |
| (*c*) Chain of authority and communication from top to bottom | III. Esprit de corps |
| (*d*) Promotes team spirit | IV. Scalar chain |

Choose the **correct** answer from the options given below:

| | (*a*) | (*b*) | (*c*) | (*d*) |
|---|---|---|---|---|
| A. | I | II | III | IV |
| B. | I | III | II | IV |
| C. | I | II | IV | III |
| D. | III | IV | I | II |

**19.** Under which dimension of business environment is "Online Booking of Air Tickets" included?

A. Legal dimension
B. Economic dimension
C. Technical dimension
D. Social dimension

**20.** Which of the following is an example of economic environment?

A. Money supply in economy
B. Constitution of the country
C. Life expectancy
D. Population shifts

**21.** Which of the following is an example of legal environment?

A. Death/Birth Ratio
B. Trade Union Act
C. Prevailing Political System
D. Public Debt

**22.** Which of the following does **not** characterise business environment?

A. Inter-related
B. External forces
C. Market orientation and product
D. Relativity

**23.** Identify the correct sequence of steps under the Planning function:

(*a*) Setting objectives
(*b*) Identifying alternative courses of action
(*c*) Developing premises
(*d*) Evaluating alternative courses of action

Choose the **correct** answer from the options given below:

A. (*a*), (*b*), (*c*), (*d*) B. (*a*), (*c*), (*b*), (*d*)
C. (*b*), (*a*), (*d*), (*c*) D. (*c*), (*b*), (*d*), (*a*)

**14.** D **15.** A **16.** D **17.** C **18.** C **19.** * **20.** A **21.** B **22.** C **23.** B

**24.** Identify the correct sequence of Selection process:

(*a*) Selection decision
(*b*) Employment interview
(*c*) Selection tests
(*d*) Reference checking

Choose the **correct** answer from the options given below:

A. (*a*), (*b*), (*c*), (*d*) B. (*a*), (*c*), (*b*), (*d*)
C. (*b*), (*a*), (*d*), (*c*) D. (*c*), (*b*), (*d*), (*a*)

**25.** "It is a joint programme of training in which educational institutions and business firms cooperate." Identify the method of training.

A. Vestibule training B. Apprenticeship training
C. Internship training D. Job rotation

**26.** Match List-I with List-II on the basis of meaning and name of the concept:

| List-I | List-II |
|---|---|
| (*a*) Choosing the most appropriate candidate | I. Selection |
| (*b*) Candidate is given an introduction to superiors | II. Orientation |
| (*c*) Learning the skills related to a job | III. Recruitment |
| (*d*) Searching for prospective employees | IV. Training |

Choose the **correct** answer from the options given below:

| | (*a*) | (*b*) | (*c*) | (*d*) |
|---|---|---|---|---|
| A. | I | II | III | IV |
| B. | I | III | II | IV |
| C. | I | II | IV | III |
| D. | III | IV | I | II |

**27.** Which of the following is a process of incitement or inducing subordinates to act in a desired manner to achieve organisational goals?

A. Motivation B. Supervision
C. Leadership D. Communication

**28.** Find the correct sequence of needs as given by Maslow in his Need Hierarchy Theory.

(*a*) Belongingness needs
(*b*) Safety and Security
(*c*) Self-actualisation needs
(*d*) Esteem needs

Choose the **correct** answer from the options given below:

A. (*a*), (*b*), (*c*), (*d*) B. (*a*), (*c*), (*b*), (*d*)
C. (*b*), (*a*), (*d*), (*c*) D. (*c*), (*b*), (*d*), (*a*)

**29.** "________ is a process of influencing the behaviour of people by making them strive voluntarily towards achievement of organisational goals."

A. Motivation B. Supervision
C. Leadership D. Communication

**30.** Which of the following is **not** a limitation of Controlling?

A. Costly affair
B. Resistance from employees
C. Ensure order and discipline
D. Little control on external factors

**31.** Identify the correct sequence of Controlling process:

(*a*) Analysing deviations
(*b*) Measurement of actual performance
(*c*) Setting up standards
(*d*) Comparison of actual performance with standards

Choose the **correct** answer from the options given below:

A. (*a*), (*b*), (*c*), (*d*) B. (*a*), (*c*), (*b*), (*d*)
C. (*b*), (*a*), (*d*), (*c*) D. (*c*), (*b*), (*d*), (*a*)

**32.** "Only a 5% increase in labour cost may be more troublesome than a 15% increase in postal charges." Identify the concept pointed out in the statement.

A. Deviation
B. Critical point control
C. Break-even analysis
D. Critical path method

**33.** Identify the function performed by Financial Market from the following statement:

"Holders of assets can readily sell their financial assets through the mechanism of the financial market."

A. Reduce the cost of transactions
B. Provide liquidity to financial assets
C. Facilitate price discovery
D. Mobilisation of savings and channelising them into the most productive uses

**34.** If any of the parties are not satisfied by the order of ________, they can appeal against such order to the State Commission on the grounds of facts or law within a period of forty-five days from the date of order.

A. District Commission
B. State Commission
C. National Commission
D. Local Court

**24.** D **25.** C **26.** C **27.** A **28.** C **29.** C **30.** C **31.** D **32.** B **33.** B **34.** A

**35.** Identify the importance of consumer protection discussed in the following lines—"Business organisation make money by selling goods and providing services to consumers. Thus, consumers form an important group among the many stakeholders of business and like other stakeholders, their interest has to be well taken care of".

A. Moral justification
B. Business uses society's resources
C. Social responsibility
D. Long-term interest of business

**36.** Identify the Consumer Right—"The consumer has the freedom to access variety of products at competitive prices. This implies that the marketers should offer a wide variety of products in terms of quality, brand, prices, size, etc."

A. Right to Safety
B. Right to Seek Redressal
C. Right to be Assured
D. Right to Consumer Education

**37.** Identity the method of floatation in Primary Market wherein a company sells securities enbloc at an agreed price to a broker.

A. Rights issue
B. Offer for sale
C. e-IPOs
D. Offer through Prospectus

**38.** Match List-I with List-II on the basis of meaning and the term:

| List-I (Meaning) | List-II (Term) |
|---|---|
| (*a*) Right to command | I. Answerability |
| (*b*) Obligation to perform task | II. Delegation |
| (*c*) Accountability | III. Authority |
| (*d*) Basis of management hierarchy | IV. Responsibility |

Choose the **correct** answer from the options given below:

| | (*a*) | (*b*) | (*c*) | (*d*) |
|---|---|---|---|---|
| A. | I | II | III | IV |
| B. | I | III | II | IV |
| C. | I | II | IV | III |
| D. | III | IV | I | II |

**39.** Identify the correct sequence of Organising function of management.

(*a*) Establishing authority and reporting relationships
(*b*) Departmentalisation
(*c*) Identification and division of work
(*d*) Assignment of duties

Choose the **correct** answer from the options given below:

A. (*a*), (*b*), (*c*), (*d*)
B. (*a*), (*c*), (*b*), (*d*)
C. (*b*), (*a*), (*d*), (*c*)
D. (*c*), (*b*), (*d*), (*a*)

**40.** The formal organisation can be better understood by a study of its features which are as follows:

(*a*) It specifies the relationships among various job positions and the nature of their inter-relationship. This clarifies who has to report to whom.
(*b*) It is a means to achieve the objectives specified in the plans, as it lays down rules and procedures essential for their achievement.
(*c*) Independent channels of communication without specified direction of flow of information are developed by group members.
(*d*) It is deliberately designed by the top management to facilitate the smooth functioning of the organisation.

Which of the following options are correct?

A. (*a*), (*b*) and (*d*) only
B. (*a*), (*b*) and (*c*) only
C. (*a*), (*b*), (*c*) and (*d*)
D. (*b*), (*c*) and (*d*) only

**41.** The informal organisation offers many benefits. Important among them are given below:

(*a*) Prescribed lines of communication are not followed. Thus, informal organisation leads to faster spread of information as well as quick feedback.
(*b*) It helps to fulfil the social needs of the members and allows them to find like minded people. This enhances their job satisfaction since it gives them a sense of belongingness in the organisation.
(*c*) It contributes towards fulfilment of organisational objectives by compensating for inadequacies in the formal organisation.
(*d*) Unity of command is maintained through an established chain of command.

Choose the **correct** answer from the options given below:

A. (*a*), (*b*) and (*d*) only
B. (*a*), (*b*) and (*c*) only
C. (*a*), (*b*), (*c*) and (*d*)
D. (*b*), (*c*) and (*d*) only

**35.** C **36.** C **37.** B **38.** D **39.** D **40.** A **41.** B

**42.** Identify the correct sequence of trading & settlement procedure:

(*a*) The investor has to sign a broker client agreement.

(*b*) The investor has to open a 'Demat' Account.

(*c*) An order confirmation slip is issued to the investor by the broker.

(*d*) The broker will then go online and connect to the main stock exchange.

Choose the **correct** answer from the options given below:

A. (*a*), (*b*), (*c*), (*d*) B. (*a*), (*c*), (*b*), (*d*)
C. (*b*), (*a*), (*d*), (*c*) D. (*c*), (*b*), (*d*), (*a*)

**43.** The market where existing securities are bought and sold is known as ______ .

A. Primary market B. Secondary market
C. Capital market D. Financial market

**44.** Qualities of sucessful entrepreneur do **not** include:

A. Initiative B. Self-confidence
C. Risk avoider D. Wealth creators

**45.** Identify the function performed by SEBI:

"It controls insider trading, takeover bids and imposes penalties for such practices."

A. Protective functions
B. Regulatory functions
C. Developmental functions
D. Preventive functions

**46.** Financial management aims at choosing the best investment and financing alternatives by focusing on their costs and benefits. Its objective is to:

A. Increase the shareholders' wealth
B. Decrease the shareholders' wealth
C. Increase the shareholders' capital
D. Decrease the shareholders' capital

**47.** A proper matching of funds requirements and their availability is sought to be achieved by ______ .

A. Financial planning
B. Financial control
C. Capital budgeting
D. Investment decisions

**48.** Debt is ______ but is more ______ for a business because the payment of interest and the return of principal is obligatory for the business.

A. Cheaper, risky B. Cheaper, safe
C. Expensive, risky D. Expensive, safe

**49.** "Coordination unifies unrelated interests into purposeful work activity." Identify the nature of coordination.

A. Coordination is an all pervasive function
B. Coordination is a continuous process
C. Coordination ensures unity of action
D. Coordination integrates group efforts

**50.** Akash Industries has installed a waste recycling plant in its premises and does not dump their waste material anymore. This plant is providing employment to many people. Identify the objective of management which the company is achieving by doing the aforesaid activity.

A. Social objective B. Economic objective
C. Personal objective D. Growth

# EXPLANATORY ANSWERS

**1. (B):** An intelligence test assesses an individual's overall mental capacity, which aligns with the description of "Indicator of a person's learning ability and ability to make judgements." Aptitude tests measure a person's capability to develop particular skills or perform specific tasks, matching the "Indicator of a person's capacity to develop." Personality tests are designed to reveal aspects of an individual's character or psychological makeup, correctly described as "Clues to a person's emotions, values, etc." Trade tests focus on assessing the skills already acquired by an individual in a particular field, fitting the description of "Measure existing skills of the individual."

**2. (C):** Functional structure of an organization offers several advantages, including "Leads to occupational specialization" where employees become experts in their specific functions, enhancing the operational efficiency. It also "Promotes coordination and control within a department" as the structure clearly defines roles and responsibilities within functional areas. Lastly, it "Increases operational efficiency" because specialized functions often streamline processes and improve performance across tasks.

**3. (D):** The statement highlights that management activities are inherently directed towards achieving the organizational goals. This feature of management

**42.** A **43.** B **44.** C **45.** A, B **46.** A **47.** A **48.** A **49.** D **50.** A

underscores its goal-oriented nature, where every action and decision is made with the aim of fulfilling specific objectives, marking management as a process that is fundamentally oriented towards achieving predetermined results.

4. **(A):** The key position in top-level management is typically held by the Managing Director. This role is pivotal as it involves overseeing the entire operation of the organization and making strategic decisions that affect the overall direction and success of the company.

   Other roles listed, such as Production Manager, Marketing Manager, and Plant Supervisor, while important, are generally considered mid-level or operational positions and do not encompass the broad strategic responsibilities of top-level management.

5. **(D):** The statement refers to "Just Foodie" expanding its distribution strategy by selling products through both its own retail outlets and grocery stores. This approach focuses on ensuring that products are available to customers at the right time and place, which is a key aspect of physical distribution. Physical distribution involves the logistics of getting products from production to consumers, and includes decisions about where and how products are sold, thus broadening their reach and accessibility.

6. **(A):** The statement emphasizes the attention given to the taste, quality, and packaging of the products, which are crucial elements of the product itself. This focus on enhancing the features and attributes of the product falls under the product mix of the marketing mix.

   The product mix involves decisions related to the design, quality, and packaging of the goods offered, aiming to meet customer expectations and differentiate from competitors.

7. **(B):** The statement addresses "Just Foodie's" ability to charge a higher price than competitors, which pertains to the pricing strategy of the marketing mix. This element involves setting and adjusting the price of products based on factors such as perceived value, costs, and competition.

   By charging a higher price, the company is leveraging its product's perceived quality and differentiation to achieve better profitability and market positioning.

8. **(C):** Utilizing offers such as free gifts, cash backs, and discounts are tactics within the "Promotion mix." These strategies are used to increase sales and enhance product appeal through various promotional activities aimed at stimulating demand. This element of the marketing mix focuses on communicating with customers to inform, persuade, and influence their purchase decisions.

9. **(B):** The promotional tools mentioned, including free gifts, cash backs, and discounts, are all part of "Sales promotion." This tool is designed to boost sales in the short term by creating additional value and incentives for purchase. Sales promotions are distinct from other promotional tools like advertising, personal selling, or publicity, as they directly incentivize the purchase decision with tangible benefits.

10. **(D):** The function of management highlighted here is "Planning." The description of Indian Oil's strategic investments and expansion both in India and overseas reflects a systematic process of thinking about future activities that the organization needs to undertake in order to meet its goals. Planning involves determining in advance what to do, how to do it, when to do it, and who should do it. This function guides the direction of organizational efforts and is crucial in setting the groundwork for other management functions.

11. **(D):** The significance of the managerial function highlighted is "Provides direction." When goals are well-defined, and employees are clear about the organizational objectives and their roles in achieving these goals, it essentially provides them with a direction.

    This clarity helps in aligning individual efforts with the organizational aims, ensuring everyone works toward the same end result, thereby enhancing the efficiency and effectiveness of the organizational operations.

12. **(B):** The statement emphasizes the importance of "Reduces risks of uncertainty." Anticipating changes and developing managerial responses is a critical aspect of managing risks and uncertainties that an organization faces.

    By being proactive and planning for possible changes, the management can significantly mitigate the impacts of unforeseen events, thus stabilizing the operational environment.

13. **(D):** The significance highlighted is "Reduces overlapping and wasteful activities." Policy formation plays a crucial role in coordinating the efforts

of different departments and individuals within the organization. By clearly defining policies, an organization can ensure that all parts work harmoniously towards common goals, which in turn minimizes redundancies and inefficiencies, making the process streamlined and focused.

**14. (D):** This statement highlights the significance of "Facilitates decision making." The ability of a manager to look into the future and choose from various alternatives is a fundamental part of the decision-making process.

Effective planning allows managers to evaluate different scenarios and make informed decisions that align with the strategic objectives of the organization, thus facilitating a more decisive and purposeful management approach.

**15. (A):** Frederick W. Taylor's principle of "Science, not rule of thumb" reflects his advocacy for the use of systematic study and analysis of work processes rather than relying on conventional wisdom or ad hoc decisions.

Taylor's introduction of scientific methods into management involved studying tasks with the aim of making them more efficient. This principle is foundational to the scientific management theory, which aims to improve economic efficiency and labor productivity through empirical studies and systematic methodology.

**16. (D):** Matching the given terms with the correct principles:

(*a*) **Obedience to organizational rules - Discipline:** Obedience to organizational rules is essential for maintaining discipline within the workplace. Discipline ensures that employees follow established guidelines and standards, contributing to an orderly and effective work environment.

(*b*) **One boss for every individual employee - Unity of command:** The principle of having one boss for each employee ensures clarity in reporting relationships and instructions. This avoids confusion and potential conflicts that might arise from receiving directives from multiple superiors.

(*c*) **One head and one plan - Unity of direction:** Unity of direction means that all activities within an organization should be aligned under one central leadership and a single plan. This ensures that all efforts are directed towards a common goal, promoting cohesion and coordination.

(*d*) **Remuneration should be just and equitable - Remuneration of employees:** The principle of fair and equitable remuneration ensures that employees are fairly compensated for their work. This motivates employees and supports their satisfaction, leading to better performance and retention.

**17. (C):** Standardization of work is a technique proposed by F.W. Taylor to achieve efficiency and consistency in production by setting fixed types, sizes, and characteristics for products or processes. By standardizing these elements, organizations can streamline operations, reduce variability, and enhance quality control, leading to more predictable and efficient production outcomes.

This approach aligns with Taylor's principles of scientific management, which aim to optimize work processes through uniformity and clear guidelines.

**18. (C):** Matching the meanings with the appropriate management terms:

(*a*) "Employees turnover should be minimized" aligns with "Stability of personnel," which emphasizes the importance of keeping turnover low to maintain operational efficiency, hence option I.

(*b*) "Emphasises kindliness and justice" matches "Equity," which involves treating employees fairly and justly, hence option II.

(*c*) "Chain of authority and communication from top to bottom" describes the "Scalar chain," which is the formal line of authority which moves from highest to lowest rank in a straight line, hence option IV.

(*d*) "Promotes team spirit" refers to "Esprit de corps," which focuses on building harmony and unity among the members of the organization, hence option III.

**20. (A):** The "Money supply in economy" is an example of the economic environment. The economic environment encompasses factors that influence business operations and decisions, including economic policies, economic conditions, and the economic system.

Money supply affects inflation, interest rates, and overall economic growth, all of which directly impact business operations and strategies.

**21. (B):** The "Trade Union Act" is part of the legal environment. The legal environment consists of laws and regulations that businesses must comply with.

The Trade Union Act, which regulates the operation of trade unions and their rights, directly influences how businesses manage their human resources and interact with unions.

**22. (C):** "Market orientation and product" does not characterize the business environment as it pertains more directly to strategic decisions made within the company rather than external factors influencing the company. The business environment typically refers to external forces like social, technological, economic, environmental, and political influences, not internal business strategies.

**23. (B):**

(*a*) **Setting Objectives:** This is the first step in the planning process. It involves defining clear, specific, and measurable goals that an organization aims to achieve. Objectives provide direction and a basis for making decisions throughout the planning process.

(*c*) **Developing Premises:** Once objectives are set, the next step is to establish the premises or assumptions about the future environment in which the plans will be executed. These premises might include economic conditions, market trends, resource availability, and other relevant factors that could impact the plan.

(*b*) **Identifying Alternative Courses of Action:** With objectives and premises in place, the next step is to identify various possible ways to achieve the objectives. This involves brainstorming and generating different strategies, approaches, and actions that could be taken.

(*d*) **Evaluating Alternative Courses of Action:** After identifying the alternatives, each option is evaluated to determine its feasibility, advantages, disadvantages, risks, and potential outcomes. This step helps in comparing the alternatives and selecting the most suitable one.

**24. (D):** The correct sequence of the selection process is:

- **Selection tests:** Assess candidates' abilities and fit for the role.
- **Employment interview:** Further evaluate the candidates' qualifications and suitability through direct interaction.
- **Reference checking:** Verify the information provided by candidates through their references.
- **Selection decision:** Make the final hiring decision based on the gathered information and assessments.

**25. (C):** "Internship training" is a method where educational institutions and business firms cooperate to provide practical experience to students. This type of training allows students to gain real-world skills and knowledge relevant to their field of study while still in an educational setting, making it a joint program between academia and industry.

**26. (C):** The correct matches between List-I and List-II based on the meanings and names of the concepts are as follows:

(*a*) Choosing the most appropriate candidate aligns with "Selection," indicating the process of selecting the best candidate from a pool of applicants, hence option I.

(*b*) A candidate is given an introduction to superiors, which pertains to "Orientation," where new hires are familiarized with the company, their roles, colleagues, and superiors, hence option II.

(*c*) Learning the skills related to a job is described by "Training," which involves improving the skills and competencies of employees to perform specific tasks, hence option IV.

(*d*) Searching for prospective employees is associated with "Recruitment," the process of finding and attracting capable applicants for employment, hence option III.

**27. (A):** "Motivation" is the process of incitement or inducing subordinates to act in a desired manner to achieve organizational goals. Motivation involves understanding the needs and desires of individuals and using that knowledge to influence their behaviors in ways that align with the organization's objectives.

**28. (C):**

(*b*) **Safety and Security Needs:** Once physiological needs are fulfilled, the need for safety and security becomes prominent. This includes personal and financial security, health and well-being, and protection from accidents and illness.

(*a*) **Belongingness and Love Needs:** After safety needs are addressed, social needs become important. These involve relationships, social connections, and a sense of belonging. This can be fulfilled through friendships, family, and intimate relationships.

(*d*) **Esteem Needs:** These needs pertain to the desire for respect, self-esteem, and recognition. There are two types of esteem needs: lower esteem (respect from others, status, fame, glory) and higher esteem (self-respect, confidence, competence, achievement).

(*c*) **Self-Actualisation Needs:** At the top of the hierarchy, self-actualisation refers to the realization of one's potential, self-fulfillment, seeking personal growth, and peak experiences. It is the desire to become the most that one can be.

**29. (C):** "Leadership" is defined as the process of influencing the behaviour of people by making them strive voluntarily towards the achievement of organizational goals. Leadership involves guiding, directing, and motivating others towards the successful completion of organizational objectives.

**30. (C):** "Ensure order and discipline" is not a limitation but rather a benefit of controlling. Controlling involves monitoring performance, comparing it with planned objectives, and taking corrective actions when necessary. This function helps to maintain order and ensures discipline within the organization by keeping activities on track. Limitations of controlling typically include being a costly affair, facing resistance from employees, and having limited control over external factors.

**31. (D):** The correct sequence of the controlling process is:

(*c*) **Setting up standards:** This step involves defining specific, measurable criteria or benchmarks that represent the desired level of performance. Standards can be based on past performance, industry norms, or organizational goals.

(*b*) **Measurement of actual performance:** Once standards are established, the next step is to gather and record data on the actual performance. This involves tracking how well the organization or its employees are performing in relation to the set standards.

(*d*) **Comparison of actual performance with standards:** This step involves analyzing the data collected to see how actual performance measures up against the established standards. This comparison helps in identifying whether performance meets, exceeds, or falls short of the set benchmarks.

(*a*) **Analysing deviations:** In this final step, the reasons for any discrepancies between actual performance and standards are investigated. This involves understanding why performance did not meet the expected levels and determining the underlying causes. This might include evaluating factors such as equipment malfunctions, employee training gaps, or process inefficiencies.

**32. (B):** The concept pointed out in the statement is "Critical point control." This concept involves identifying key areas or factors that have a significant impact on performance and are critical to the success of the operation. In the given statement, a smaller increase in labour costs is deemed more significant than a larger increase in postal charges, indicating that labour costs are a critical point that needs stringent control and monitoring.

**33. (B):** The function performed by financial markets in the given statement is "Provide liquidity to financial assets." Liquidity refers to the ease with which assets can be converted into cash without a significant loss of value. The financial market facilitates the buying and selling of financial assets like stocks and bonds, ensuring that holders can readily sell them, thus providing liquidity.

**34. (A):** If any of the parties are not satisfied with the order of the "District Commission," they can appeal against such order to the State Commission. This process is part of the hierarchical structure of consumer dispute redressal agencies established under the Consumer Protection Act, where appeals can be made from lower to higher levels within specified periods.

**35. (C):** The importance of consumer protection discussed in the statement is "Social responsibility." The statement highlights that businesses have a responsibility towards their consumers, who are a key stakeholder group. Protecting the interests of consumers is part of a business's social responsibility, ensuring that their rights are safeguarded and their welfare is promoted, which in turn supports the overall societal good.

**36. (C):** The "Right to be Assured" in consumer rights context refers to the consumer's freedom to access a variety of products at competitive prices, ensuring that marketers offer a wide assortment of products regarding quality, brand, prices, size, etc. This right implies that consumers should be able to choose from an array of products, enabling them to find goods that best meet their needs at fair prices.

**37. (B):** The method of flotation in the Primary Market where a company sells securities en bloc at an agreed price to a broker is known as "Offer for sale." In this method, the company does not directly issue securities to the public but instead sells them to an underwriting firm or broker who then sells the securities to the public, often at a predetermined price.

**38. (D):** Matching List-I (Meaning) with List-II (Term) based on their meanings:

(*a*) **Right to command:** "Authority" is the right given to a person to achieve the objectives of the organization, hence option III.

(*b*) **Obligation to perform task:** "Responsibility" refers to the obligation of an individual to perform assigned tasks, hence option IV.

(*c*) **Accountability:** "Answerability" denotes the obligation to report the performance and take responsibility for it, hence option I.

(*d*) **Basis of management hierarchy:** "Delegation" involves the transfer of authority from one individual to another while retaining accountability. It is fundamental in creating a management hierarchy, hence option II.

**39. (D):**

(*c*) **Identification and Division of Work:** The first step is to identify the total work to be done and divide it into manageable tasks. This ensures that work is not duplicated and resources are used efficiently.

(*b*) **Departmentalisation:** After dividing the work, similar tasks are grouped together to form departments or units. This helps in specialization and improves efficiency.

(*d*) **Assignment of Duties:** Once departments are created, specific tasks are assigned to individuals based on their skills and competencies. This ensures that each person knows what is expected of them.

(*a*) **Establishing Authority and Reporting Relationships:** Finally, a hierarchy is established by defining authority and reporting relationships. This step ensures that there is a clear chain of command and accountability within the organization.

**40. (A):** The correct options that describe the features of a formal organization are:

(*a*) It specifies the relationships among various job positions and the nature of their inter-relationship, clarifying who has to report to whom.

(*b*) It is a means to achieve the objectives specified in the plans, as it lays down rules and procedures essential for their achievement.

(*d*) It is deliberately designed by the top management to facilitate the smooth functioning of the organization.

Option (*c*) does not describe a feature of formal organization as formal organizations have specified channels of communication with a clear direction of information flow.

**41. (B):** The benefits of an informal organization include:

(*a*) Prescribed lines of communication are not followed, which leads to a faster spread of information and quicker feedback.

(*b*) It helps fulfill the social needs of the members and allows them to find like-minded people, enhancing job satisfaction and providing a sense of belonging.

(*c*) It compensates for inadequacies in the formal organization, contributing towards the fulfillment of organizational objectives.

Option (*d*), stating that "Unity of command is maintained through an established chain of command," is a characteristic of formal, not informal, organizations.

**42. (A):** The correct sequence of trading and settlement procedures is:

(*a*) The investor has to sign a broker-client agreement, which establishes the legal framework for the interaction between the broker and the client.

(*b*) The investor has to open a 'Demat' account, which is necessary for holding shares in electronic form.

(*c*) An order confirmation slip is issued to the investor by the broker, confirming the order placed by the investor.

(*d*) The broker will then go online and connect to the main stock exchange to execute the trade.

**43. (B):** The market where existing securities are bought and sold is known as the "Secondary market." This is distinct from the primary market, where securities are first issued. The secondary market allows investors to buy and sell securities they already own.

**44. (C):** Among the qualities of successful entrepreneurs, "Risk avoider" does not typically include. Entrepreneurs are generally known for their willingness to take calculated risks. The characteristic of avoiding risk is contrary to the entrepreneurial spirit, which often involves initiative, self-confidence, and the creation of wealth through new ventures.

**45. (A, B):** The function described—controlling insider trading, takeover bids, and imposing penalties for such practices—falls under both protective and regulatory functions of the Securities and Exchange Board of India (SEBI).

**(A) Protective Functions:** These functions aim to protect the interests of investors and ensure fair practices in the securities market.

Controlling insider trading and imposing penalties for such malpractices directly protect investors from unfair and illegal activities.

**(B) Regulatory Functions:** These functions involve establishing rules and regulations for the securities market and ensuring that these regulations are followed. By controlling insider trading and takeover bids, SEBI enforces its regulations to maintain the integrity of the market.

**46. (A):** Financial management aims primarily at increasing the shareholders' wealth. This objective is achieved by making investment and financing decisions that enhance the overall value of the firm. The focus is on selecting projects and financing options that offer the best balance of risk and return, thereby maximizing the market value of the shareholders' equity.

**47. (A):** "Financial planning" is the process of ensuring a proper matching of funds requirements with their availability. It involves forecasting financial needs and ensuring that sufficient funding options are available to meet these needs at the right time. This ensures the business can meet its obligations and invest in opportunities without facing liquidity crises.

**48. (A):** Debt is considered "cheaper" because the interest paid on debt is tax-deductible, which reduces the actual cost of debt to the business. However, it is also "risky" because the business is obligated to pay back the principal and interest regardless of its financial situation. This creates financial risk, especially if the business faces cash flow issues.

**49. (D):** "Coordination integrates group efforts" is a fundamental nature of coordination. It is about aligning the efforts of different parts of an organization towards a common purpose. By doing so, coordination ensures that different departments and individuals work together harmoniously and efficiently, avoiding conflicts and overlapping of efforts, thereby achieving the organization's objectives more effectively.

**50. (A):** By installing a waste recycling plant and providing employment to many people, Akash Industries is achieving its "Social objective." This activity demonstrates the company's commitment to environmental sustainability and community welfare. Such initiatives help the company to fulfill its social responsibilities by reducing environmental impact and improving societal well-being.

# MATHEMATICS

**1.** If A and B are symmetric matrices of the same order, then AB – BA is a:

A. symmetric matrix
B. zero matrix
C. skew symmetric matrix
D. identity matrix

**2.** If A is a square matrix of order 4 and $|A| = 4$, then $|2A|$ will be:

A. 8 B. 64
C. 16 D. 4

**3.** If $[A]_{3\times2}\ [B]_{x\times y} = [C]_{3\times1}$, then:

A. $x = 1,\ y = 3$ B. $x = 2,\ y = 1$
C. $x = 3,\ y = 3$ D. $x = 3,\ y = 1$

**4.** If a function $f(x) = x^2 + bx + 1$ is increasing in the interval [1, 2], then the least value of $b$ is:

A. 5 B. 0
C. –2 D. –4

**5.** Two dice are thrown simultaneously. If X denotes the number of fours, then the expectation of X will be:

A. $\frac{5}{9}$ B. $\frac{1}{3}$
C. $\frac{4}{7}$ D. $\frac{3}{8}$

**6.** For the function $f(x) = 2x^3 - 9x^2 + 12x - 5$, $x \in [0, 3]$, match List-I with List-II:

| **List-I** | **List-II** |
|---|---|
| (*a*) Absolute maximum value | I. 3 |
| (*b*) Absolute minimum value | II. 0 |
| (*c*) Point of maxima | III. –5 |
| (*d*) Point of minima | IV. 4 |

Choose the **correct** answer from the options given below:

| | (*a*) | (*b*) | (*c*) | (*d*) |
|---|---|---|---|---|
| A. | IV | II | I | III |
| B. | II | III | I | IV |
| C. | IV | III | II | I |
| D. | IV | III | I | II |

**7.** An objective function $Z = ax + by$ is maximum at points (8, 2) and (4, 6). If $a \geq 0$ and $b \geq 0$ and $ab = 25$, then the maximum value of the function is equal to:

A. 60
B. 50
C. 40
D. 80

**8.** The area of the region bounded by the lines $x + 2y = 12$, $x = 2$, $x = 6$ and $x$-axis is:

A. 34 sq. units
B. 20 sq. units
C. 24 sq. units
D. 16 sq. units

**9.** A dice is rolled thrice. What is the probability of getting a number greater than 4 in the first and the second throw of dice and a number less than 4 in the third throw?

A. $\frac{1}{3}$ B. $\frac{1}{6}$
C. $\frac{1}{9}$ D. $\frac{1}{18}$

**10.** The corner points of the feasible region determined by

$x + y \leq 8,\ 2x + y \geq 8,\ x \geq 0,\ y > 0$

are A(0, 8), B(4, 0) and C(8, 0). If the objective function $Z = ax + by$ has its maximum value on the line segment AB, then the relation between $a$ and $b$ is:

A. $8a + 4 = b$
B. $a = 2b$
C. $b = 2a$
D. $8b + 4 = a$

**11.** If $t = e^{2x}$ and $y = \log_e t^2$, then $\frac{d^2y}{dx^2}$ is:

A. 0 B. $4t$
C. $\frac{4e^{2t}}{t}$ D. $\frac{e^{2t}(4t-1)}{t^2}$

**1.** C **2.** B **3.** B **4.** C **5.** B **6.** D **7.** B **8.** D **9.** D **10.** B **11.** A

12. $\int \frac{\pi}{x^{n+1} - x} dx =$

A. $\frac{\pi}{n} \log_e \left| \frac{x^n - 1}{x^n} \right| + C$   B. $\log_e \left| \frac{x^n + 1}{x^n - 1} \right| + C$

C. $\frac{\pi}{n} \log_e \left| \frac{x^n + 1}{x^n} \right| + C$   D. $\pi \log_e \left| \frac{x^n}{x^n - 1} \right| + C$

13. The value of $\int_0^1 \frac{a - bx^2}{\left(a + bx^2\right)^2} dx$ is:

A. $\frac{a - b}{a + b}$   B. $\frac{1}{a - b}$

C. $\frac{a + b}{2}$   D. $\frac{1}{a + b}$

14. The second order derivative of which of the following functions is $5^x$?

A. $5^x \log_e 5$   B. $5^x (\log_e 5)^2$

C. $\frac{5^x}{\log_e 5}$   D. $\frac{5^x}{(\log_e 5)^2}$

15. The degree of the differential equation

$$\left(1 - \left(\frac{dy}{dx}\right)^2\right)^{3/2} = k\frac{d^2y}{dx^2} \text{ is:}$$

A. 1   B. 2

C. 3   D. $\frac{3}{2}$

16. Let R be the relation over the set A of all straight lines in a plane such that $l_1$ R $l_2 \Leftrightarrow l_1$ is parallel to $l_2$. Then R is:

A. Symmetric
B. An Equivalence relation
C. Transitive
D. Reflexive

17. The probability of not getting 53 Tuesdays in a leap year is:

A. 2/7
B. 1/7
C. 0
D. 5/7

18. The angle between two lines whose direction ratios are proportional to 1, 1, –2 and $\left(\sqrt{3} - 1\right), \left(-\sqrt{3} - 1\right), -4$ is:

A. $\pi/3$   B. $\pi$
C. $\pi/6$   D. $\pi/2$

19. If $\left(\vec{a} - \vec{b}\right).\left(\vec{a} + \vec{b}\right) = 27$ and $|\vec{a}| = 2|\vec{b}|$, then $|\vec{b}|$ is:

A. 3   B. 2
C. 5/6   D. 6

20. If $\tan^{-1}\left(\frac{2}{3^{-x} + 1}\right) = \cot^{-1}\left(\frac{3}{3^x + 1}\right)$, then which one of the following is true?

A. There is no real value of $x$ satisfying the above equation.
B. There is one positive and one negative real value of $x$ satisfying the above equation.
C. There are two real positive values of $x$ satisfying the above equation
D. There are two real negative values of $x$ satisfying the above equation

21. If A, B and C are three singular matrices given by

$$A = \begin{bmatrix} 1 & 4 \\ 3 & 2a \end{bmatrix}, B = \begin{bmatrix} 3b & 5 \\ a & 2 \end{bmatrix} \text{ and}$$

$$C = \begin{bmatrix} a + b + c & c + 1 \\ a + c & c \end{bmatrix},$$

then the value of $abc$ is:

A. 15   B. 30
C. 45   D. 90

22. The value of the integral $\int_{\log_e 2}^{\log_e 3} \frac{e^{2x} - 1}{e^{2x} + 1} dx$ is:

A. $\log_e 3$   B. $\log_e 4 - \log_e 3$
C. $\log_e 9 - \log_e 4$   D. $\log_e 3 - \log_e 2$

23. If $\vec{a}, \vec{b}$ and $\vec{c}$ are three vectors such that $\vec{a} + \vec{b} + \vec{c} = \vec{0}$, where $\vec{a}$ and $\vec{b}$ are unit vectors and $|\vec{c}| = 2$, then the angle between the vectors $\vec{b}$ and $\vec{c}$ is:

A. 60°   B. 90°
C. 120°   D. 180°

| | | | | | | | | | |
|---|---|---|---|---|---|---|---|---|---|
| **12.** A | **13.** D | **14.** B | **15.** B | **16.** B | **17.** D | **18.** A | **19.** A | **20.** B | **21.** C |
| **22.** B | **23.** D | | | | | | | | |

**24.** Let [x] denote the greatest integer function. Then match List-I with List-II:

| List-I | List-II |
|---|---|
| (*a*) $\lvert x-1\rvert + \lvert x-2\rvert$ | I. is differentiable everywhere except at $x = 0$ |
| (*b*) $x - \lvert x\rvert$ | II. is continuous everywhere |
| (*c*) $x - [x]$ | III. is not differentiable at $x = 1$ |
| (*d*) $x\,\lvert x\rvert$ | IV. is differentiable at $x = 1$ |

Choose the **correct** answer from the options given below:

| | (*a*) | (*b*) | (*c*) | (*d*) |
|---|---|---|---|---|
| A. | I | II | III | IV |
| B. | I | III | II | IV |
| C. | II | I | III | IV |
| D. | II | IV | III | I |

**25.** The rate of change (in $cm^2/s$) of the total surface area of a hemisphere with respect to radius $r$ at $r = \sqrt[3]{1.331}$ cm is:

A. $66\pi$ B. $6.6\pi$
C. $3.3\pi$ D. $4.4\pi$

**26.** The area of the region bounded by the lines $\frac{x}{7\sqrt{3}\,a} + \frac{y}{b} = 4$, $x = 0$ and $y = 0$ is:

A. $56\sqrt{3}\,ab$ B. $56a$
C. $ab/2$ D. $3ab$

**27.** If A is a square matrix and I is an identity matrix such that $A^2 = A$, then $A(I - 2A)^3 + 2A^3$ is equal to:

A. I + A B. I + 2A
C. I – A D. A

**28.** Match List-I with List-II:

| List-I | List-II |
|---|---|
| (*a*) Integrating factor of $xdy - (y + 2x^2)dx = 0$ | I. $1/x$ |
| (*b*) Integrating factor of $(2x^2 - 3y)dx = xdy$ | II. $x$ |
| (*c*) Integrating factor of $(2y + 3x^2)dx + xdy = 0$ | III. $x^2$ |
| (*d*) Integrating factor of $2xdy + (3x^3 + 2y)dx = 0$ | IV. $x^3$ |

Choose the **correct** answer from the options given below:

| | (*a*) | (*b*) | (*c*) | (*d*) |
|---|---|---|---|---|
| A. | I | III | IV | II |
| B. | I | IV | III | II |
| C. | II | I | III | IV |
| D. | III | IV | II | I |

**29.** If the function $f : \mathbb{N} \to \mathbb{N}$ is defined as

$$f(n) = \begin{cases} n-1, & \text{if } n \text{ is even} \\ n+1, & \text{if } n \text{ is odd} \end{cases}, \text{ then}$$

(*a*) $f$ is injective (*b*) $f$ is into
(*c*) $f$ is surjective (*d*) $f$ is invertible

Choose the **correct** answer from the options given below:

A. (*b*) only B. (*a*), (*b*) and (*d*) only
C. (*a*) and (*c*) only D. (*a*), (*c*) and (*d*) only

**30.** $\int_0^{\frac{\pi}{2}} \frac{1 - \cot x}{\operatorname{cosec} x + \cos x}\,dx =$

A. 0 B. $\frac{\pi}{4}$
C. $\infty$ D. $\frac{\pi}{12}$

**31.** If the random variable X has the following distribution:

| X | 0 | 1 | 2 | Otherwise |
|---|---|---|---|---|
| P(X) | $k$ | $2k$ | $3k$ | 0 |

Match List-I with List-II:

| List-I | List-II |
|---|---|
| (*a*) $k$ | I. $\frac{5}{6}$ |
| (*b*) $P(X < 2)$ | II. $\frac{4}{3}$ |
| (*c*) $E(X)$ | III. $\frac{1}{2}$ |
| (*d*) $P(1 \le X \le 2)$ | IV. $\frac{1}{6}$ |

Choose the **correct** answer from the options given below:

| | (*a*) | (*b*) | (*c*) | (*d*) |
|---|---|---|---|---|
| A. | I | II | III | IV |
| B. | IV | III | II | I |
| C. | I | II | IV | III |
| D. | III | IV | I | II |

**24.** C **25.** B **26.** A **27.** D **28.** B **29.** D **30.** A **31.** B

**32.** For a square matrix $A_{n \times n}$

(*a*) $|\text{adj } A| = |A|^{n-1}$

(*b*) $|A| = |\text{adj } A|^{n-1}$

(*c*) $A(\text{adj } A) = |A|$

(*d*) $|A^{-1}| = \dfrac{1}{|A|}$

Choose the **correct** answer from the options given below:

A. (*b*) and (*d*) only
B. (*a*) and (*d*) only
C. (*a*), (*c*) and (*d*) only
D. (*b*), (*c*) and (*d*) only

**33.** The matrix $\begin{bmatrix} 1 & 0 & 0 \\ 0 & 1 & 0 \\ 0 & 0 & 1 \end{bmatrix}$ is a:

(*a*) scalar matrix
(*b*) diagonal matrix
(*c*) skew-symmetric matrix
(*d*) symmetric matrix

Choose the **correct** answer from the options given below:

A. (*a*), (*b*) and (*d*) only
B. (*a*), (*b*) and (*c*) only
C. (*a*), (*b*), (*c*) and (*d*)
D. (*b*), (*c*) and (*d*) only

**34.** The feasible region represented by the constraints $4x + y \geq 80$, $x + 5y \geq 115$, $3x + 2y \leq 150$, $x, y \geq 0$ of an LPP is:

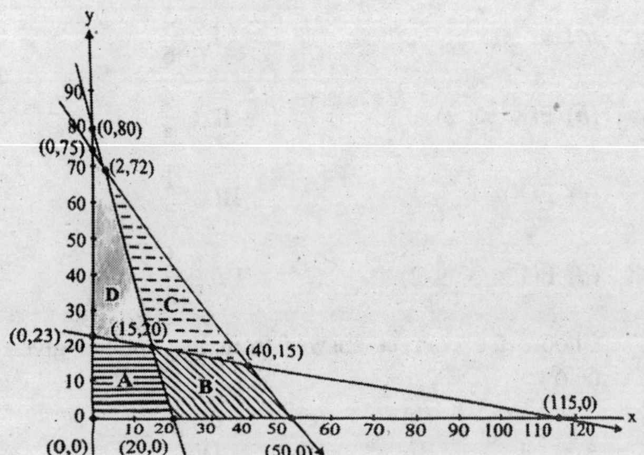


A. Region A
B. Region B
C. Region C
D. Region D

**35.** The area of the region enclosed between the curves $4x^2 = y$ and $y = 4$ is:

A. 16 sq. units
B. $\dfrac{32}{3}$ sq. units
C. $\dfrac{8}{3}$ sq. units
D. $\dfrac{16}{3}$ sq. units

**36.** $\int e^x \left(\dfrac{2x+1}{2\sqrt{x}}\right) dx =$

A. $\dfrac{1}{2\sqrt{x}} e^x + C$
B. $-e^x \sqrt{x} + C$
C. $-\dfrac{1}{2\sqrt{x}} e^x + C$
D. $e^x \sqrt{x} + C$

**37.** If $f(x)$, defined by $f(x) = \begin{cases} kx + 1 & \text{if } x \leq \pi \\ \cos x & \text{if } x > \pi \end{cases}$ is continuous at $x = \pi$, then the value of $k$ is:

A. 0
B. $\pi$
C. $\dfrac{2}{\pi}$
D. $-\dfrac{2}{\pi}$

**38.** If $P = \begin{bmatrix} -1 \\ 2 \\ 1 \end{bmatrix}$ and $Q = \begin{bmatrix} 2 & -4 & 1 \end{bmatrix}$ are two matrices, then $(PQ)'$ will be:

A. $\begin{bmatrix} 4 & 5 & 7 \\ -3 & -3 & 0 \\ 0 & -3 & -2 \end{bmatrix}$
B. $\begin{bmatrix} -2 & 4 & 2 \\ 4 & -8 & -4 \\ -1 & 2 & 1 \end{bmatrix}$
C. $\begin{bmatrix} 5 & 5 & 2 \\ 7 & 6 & 7 \\ -9 & -7 & 0 \end{bmatrix}$
D. $\begin{bmatrix} -2 & 4 & 8 \\ 7 & 5 & 7 \\ -8 & -2 & 6 \end{bmatrix}$

**39.** $\Delta = \begin{vmatrix} 1 & \cos x & 1 \\ -\cos x & 1 & \cos x \\ -1 & -\cos x & 1 \end{vmatrix}$

(*a*) $\Delta = 2(1 - \cos^2 x)$
(*b*) $\Delta = 2(2 - \sin^2 x)$
(*c*) Minimum value of $\Delta$ is 2
(*d*) Maximum value of $\Delta$ is 4

Choose the **correct** answer from the options given below:

A. (*a*), (*c*) and (*d*) only
B. (*a*), (*b*) and (*c*) only
C. (*a*), (*b*), (*c*) and (*d*)
D. (*b*), (*c*) and (*d*) only

| **32.** B | **33.** A | **34.** C | **35.** D | **36.** D | **37.** D | **38.** B | **39.** D |
|---|---|---|---|---|---|---|---|

**40.** $f(x) = \sin x + \frac{1}{2}\cos 2x$ in $\left[0, \frac{\pi}{2}\right]$

(*a*) $f'(x) = \cos x - \sin 2x$

(*b*) The critical points of the function are $x = \frac{\pi}{6}$ and $x = \frac{\pi}{2}$

(*c*) The minimum value of the function is 2

(*d*) The maximum value of the function is $\frac{3}{4}$

Choose the **correct** answer from the options given below:

A. (*a*), (*b*) and (*d*) only
B. (*a*), (*b*) and (*c*) only
C. (*a*), (*b*), (*c*) and (*d*)
D. (*b*), (*c*) and (*d*) only

**41.** The direction cosines of the line which is perpendicular to the lines with direction ratios 1, –2, –2 and 0, 2, 1 are:

A. $\frac{2}{3}, -\frac{1}{3}, \frac{2}{3}$ B. $-\frac{2}{3}, -\frac{1}{3}, \frac{2}{3}$

C. $\frac{2}{3}, -\frac{1}{3}, -\frac{2}{3}$ D. $\frac{2}{3}, \frac{1}{3}, \frac{2}{3}$

**42.** Let X denote the number of hours you play during a randomly selected day. The probability that X can take values $x$ has the following form, where $c$ is some constant.

$$P(X = x) = \begin{cases} 0.1 & , \text{ if } x = 0 \\ cx & , \text{ if } x = 1 \text{ or } x - 2 \\ c(5 - x) & , \text{ if } x = 3 \text{ or } x = 4 \\ 0 & , \text{ otherwise} \end{cases}$$

Match List-I with List-II:

| List-I | List-II |
|---|---|
| (*a*) $c$ | I. 0.75 |
| (*b*) $P(X \le 2)$ | II. 0.3 |
| (*c*) $P(X = 2)$ | III. 0.55 |
| (*d*) $P(X \ge 2)$ | IV. 0.15 |

Choose the **correct** answer from the options given below:

| | (*a*) | (*b*) | (*c*) | (*d*) |
|---|---|---|---|---|
| A. | I | II | III | IV |
| B. | IV | III | II | I |
| C. | I | II | IV | III |
| D. | III | IV | I | II |

**43.** If $\sin y = x \sin (a + y)$, then $\frac{dy}{dx}$ is:

A. $\frac{\sin^2 a}{\sin(a+y)}$ B. $\frac{\sin(a+y)}{\sin^2 a}$

C. $\frac{\sin(a+y)}{\sin a}$ D. $\frac{\sin^2(a+y)}{\sin a}$

**44.** The unit vector perpendicular to each of the vectors $\vec{a} + \vec{b}$ and $\vec{a} - \vec{b}$, where $\vec{a} = \hat{i} + \hat{j} + \hat{k}$ and $\vec{b} = \hat{i} + 2\hat{j} + 3\hat{k}$ is:

A. $\frac{1}{\sqrt{6}}\hat{i} + \frac{2}{\sqrt{6}}\hat{j} + \frac{1}{\sqrt{6}}\hat{k}$ B. $-\frac{1}{\sqrt{6}}\hat{i} + \frac{1}{\sqrt{6}}\hat{j} - \frac{1}{\sqrt{6}}\hat{k}$

C. $-\frac{1}{\sqrt{6}}\hat{i} + \frac{2}{\sqrt{6}}\hat{j} + \frac{2}{\sqrt{6}}\hat{k}$ D. $-\frac{1}{\sqrt{6}}\hat{i} + \frac{2}{\sqrt{6}}\hat{j} - \frac{1}{\sqrt{6}}\hat{k}$

**45.** The distance between the lines

$\vec{r} = \hat{i} - 2\hat{j} + 3\hat{k} + \lambda(2\hat{i} + 3\hat{j} + 6\hat{k})$ and

$\vec{r} = 3\hat{i} - 2\hat{j} + 1\hat{k} + \mu(4\hat{i} + 6\hat{j} + 12\hat{k})$ is:

A. $\frac{\sqrt{28}}{7}$ B. $\frac{\sqrt{199}}{7}$

C. $\frac{\sqrt{328}}{7}$ D. $\frac{\sqrt{421}}{7}$

**46.** If $f(x) = 2\left(\tan^{-1}(e^x) - \frac{\pi}{4}\right)$, then $f(x)$ is:

A. even and is strictly increasing in $(0, \infty)$
B. even and is strictly decreasing in $(0, \infty)$
C. odd and is strictly increasing in $(-\infty, \infty)$
D. odd and is strictly decreasing in $(-\infty, \infty)$

**47.** For the differential equation

$(x \log_e x)dy = (\log_e x - y)dx$

(*a*) Degree of the given differential equation is 1
(*b*) It is a homogeneous differential equation
(*c*) Solution is $2y \log_e x + A = (\log_e x)^2$, where A is an arbitrary constant
(*d*) Solution is $2y \log_e x + A = \log_e (\log_e x)$, where A is an arbitrary constant

Choose the **correct** answer from the options given below:

A. (*a*) and (*c*) only
B. (*a*), (*b*) and (*c*) only
C. (*a*), (*b*) and (*d*) only
D. (*a*) and (*d*) only

**40.** A **41.** A **42.** B **43.** D **44.** D **45.** C **46.** C **47.** A

**48.** There are two bags. Bag-1 contains 4 white and 6 black balls and Bag-2 contains 5 white and 5 black balls. A dice is rolled, if it shows a number divisible by 3, a ball is drawn from Bag-1, else a ball is drawn from Bag-2. If the ball drawn is not black in colour, the probability that it was not drawn from Bag-2 is:

A. $\frac{4}{9}$  B. $\frac{3}{8}$

C. $\frac{2}{7}$  D. $\frac{4}{19}$

**49.** Which of the following cannot be the direction ratios of the straight line $\frac{x-3}{2} = \frac{2-y}{3} = \frac{z+4}{-1}$?

A. 2, –3, –1
B. –2, 3, 1
C. 2, 3, –1
D. 6, –9, –3

**50.** Which one of the following represents the correct feasible region determined by the following constraints of an LPP?

$x + y \geq 10,\ 2x + 2y \leq 25,\ x \geq 0,\ y \geq 0$

A. 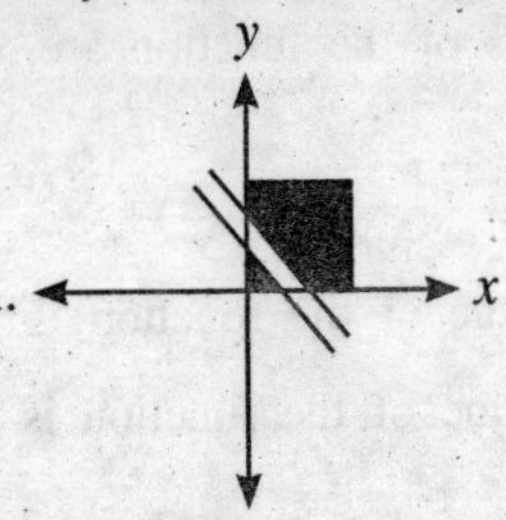


B. 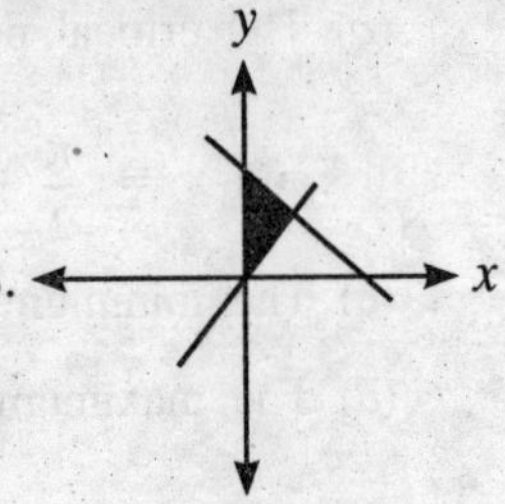


C. 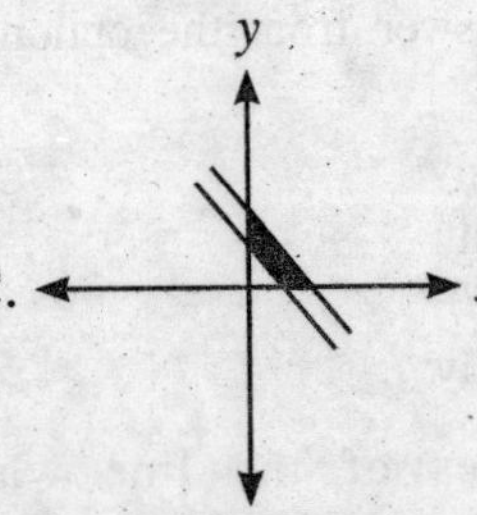


D. 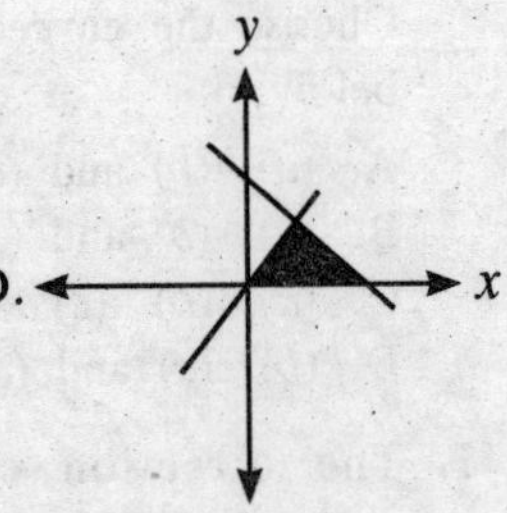


# EXPLANATORY ANSWERS

**1. (C):** Given, A and B are symmetric matrices of the same order

$\because$ $(AB - BA)^T = (AB)^T - (BA)^T$

$\Rightarrow$ $(AB - BA)^T = B^TA^T - A^TB^T$

$\Rightarrow$ $(AB - BA)^T = BA - AB$

$\Rightarrow$ $(AB - BA)^T = -(AB - BA)$

$\therefore$ AB – BA is a skew-symmetric matrix.

**2. (B):** Let A is a square matrix of order $n$

Then, $|KA| = K^n|A|$

because K is common from each row of KA

Given, A is a square matrix of order 4 and

$|A| = 4$

$\therefore$ $|2A| = 2^4|A| = 2^4 \times 4$

$= 16 \times 4 = 64$

$\Rightarrow$ $|2A| = 64.$

**3. (B):** Given, $[A]_{3 \times 2}\ [B]_{x \times y} = [C]_{3 \times 1}$

$\Rightarrow [A]_{3 \times 2}\ [B]_{2 \times 1} = [C]_{3 \times 1}$

$\therefore$ $x = 2$ and $y = 1.$

$[[a]_{m \times n}\ [b]_{n \times p} = [c]_{m \times p}]$

**4. (C):** Given, $f(x) = x^2 + bx + 1$

$\therefore$ $f'(x) = 2x + b$

and $f''(x) = 2$ for all $x$

Now, $f''(x) = 2$ for all $x \in (1, 2)$

$\Rightarrow$ $f''(x) > 0$ for all $x \in [1, 2]$

$\Rightarrow f'(x)$ is an increasing function on [1, 2]

$\Rightarrow f'(1)$ and $f'(2)$ are the least and the greatest values of $f'(x)$ on [1, 2]

This is possible when least value of $f'(x)$ i.e., $f'(1) > 0$

Now, $f'(1) > 0 \Rightarrow 2 + b > 0 \Rightarrow b > -2$

Thus, the least value of $b$ is –2.

**5. (B):** $\because$ Two dice thrown

$\therefore$ S = {(1, 1), (1, 2), (1, 3), ...(1, 6)
(2, 1), ... (2, 6)
(3, 1), ... (3, 6)
(4, 1), ... (4, 6)
(5, 1), ... (5, 6)
(6, 1), ... (6, 6)}

$\therefore$ $n(S) = 36$

Given X denotes 4

X can take value 0, 1, 2

(X = 0) = (4 not on any dice)

**48.** C **49.** C **50.** C

$$P(X = 0) = \frac{25}{36}$$

(X = 1) = 4 on any one dice

(X = 2) = 4 on both dice

$\therefore$ $$P(X = 1) = \frac{10}{36}$$

and $$P(X = 2) = \frac{1}{36}$$

$\therefore$ Expectation $E(X) = 0 \times \frac{25}{36} + 1 \times \frac{10}{36} + 2 \times \frac{1}{36}$

$= 0 + \frac{10}{36} + \frac{2}{36} = \frac{12}{36} = \frac{1}{3}.$

**6. (D):** Given, $f(x) = 2x^3 - 9x^2 + 12x - 5;$

$x \in [0. 3]$

Put $x = 0$

$\therefore$ $f(0) = -5$ (Minimum)

Put $x = 3$;

$\therefore$ $f(3) = 2 \times 27 - 9 \times 9 + 12 \times 3 - 5$

$= 54 - 81 + 36 - 5$

$= 90 - 86 = 4$ (Maximum)

$\therefore$ (*a*) Absolute maximum value = (*iv*) 4

(*b*) Absolute minimum value = (*iii*) –5

(*c*) Point of maxima = (*i*) 3

(*d*) Point of minima = (*ii*) 0.

**7. (B):** Given, $z = ax + by$

$\therefore$ Maximum value of points (8, 2) and (4, 6)

$\therefore$ $z = 8a + 2b = 4a + 6b$

$\Rightarrow$ $4a = 4b \Rightarrow a = b$ ...(*i*)

and given $ab = 25$ ...(*ii*)

From (*i*) and (*ii*),

$a = b = 5$

$\therefore$ Maximum value $= 8 \times 5 + 2 \times 5$

$= 40 + 10 = 50.$

**8. (D):** Given, straight line,

$$x + 2y = 12$$

$\Rightarrow$ $$y = \frac{12 - x}{2}$$

$\Rightarrow$ $$\frac{x}{12} + \frac{y}{6} = 1$$

This line cutting $x$ and $y$-axis of (12, 0) and (0, 6) and $x = 2$ and $x = 6$ are straight lines parallel to $y$-axis

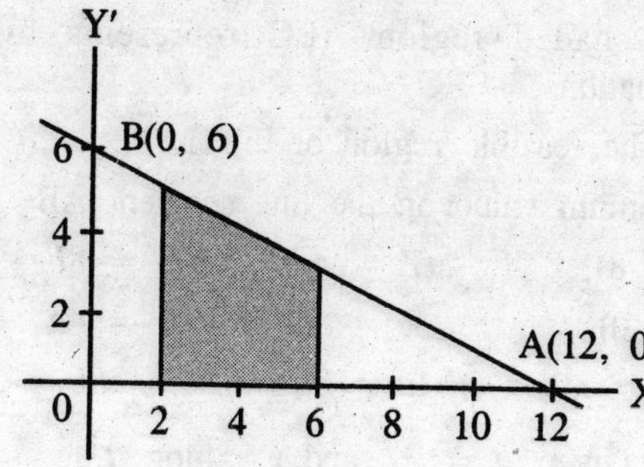


The area of the region bounded by given lines

= area of shaded region

$= \int_2^6 |y|\, dx = \int_2^6 y\, dx = \int_2^6 \left(\frac{12 - x}{2}\right) dx$

$= \int_2^6 \left(6 - \frac{x}{2}\right) dx = \left[6x - \frac{x^2}{4}\right]_2^6$

$= (36 - 9) - (12 - 1)$

$= 27 - 11 = 16$ sq. units.

**9. (D):** A dice is rolled thrice

$\therefore$ $n(S) = 6 \times 6 \times 6 = 6^3$

and getting a number greater than 4 in the first and the second throw of dice and less than 4 in the third throw

= (6 6 1), (6 6 2), (6 6 3), (6 5 1), (6 5 2), (6 5 3), (5 6 1), (5 6 2), (5 6 3), (5 5 1), (5 5 2), (5 5 3)

So, favourable number of elementary events

$$n(E) = 12$$

Hence, required probability $= \frac{n(E)}{n(S)} = \frac{12}{6^3}$

$= \frac{2 \times 6}{6^3} = \frac{2}{6^2} = \frac{2}{36} = \frac{1}{18}.$

**10. (B):** Given, $x + y \le 8$, $2x + y \ge 8$, $x \ge 0$, $y \ge 0$

Corner points are A(0, 8), B(4, 0) and C(8, 0) and $Z = ax + by$

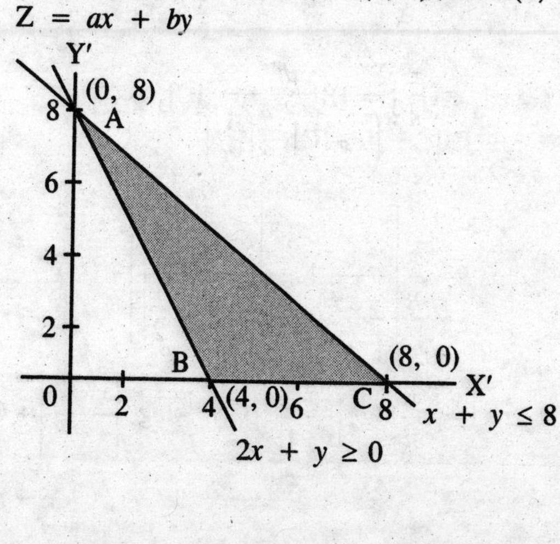

The shaded region ABC represents by given inequations

$\Rightarrow$ The feasible region of this LPP

Maximum value on the line segment AB

A(0, 8), $Z = a.0 + b.8 = 8b$

B(4, 0), $Z = a.4 + b.0 = 4a$

$\therefore$ $4a = 8b \Rightarrow a = 2b.$

**11. (A):** Given, $t = e^{2x}$ and $y = \log_e t^2$

$$\therefore \quad \frac{dt}{dx} = 2e^{2x}$$

$$\text{and} \quad \frac{dy}{dt} = 2t\frac{1}{t^2} = \frac{2}{t}$$

$$\therefore \quad \frac{dt}{dx} \times \frac{dy}{dt} = 2e^{2x} \times \frac{2}{t}$$

$$\Rightarrow \quad \frac{dy}{dx} = \frac{4e^{2x}}{e^{2x}}$$

$$\Rightarrow \quad \frac{dy}{dx} = 4$$

$$\therefore \quad \frac{d^2y}{dx^2} = 0.$$

**12. (A):** Let, $I = \int \frac{\pi}{x^{n+1} - x} dx =$

$$= \int \frac{\pi dx}{x(x^n - 1)} = \pi \int \frac{x^{n-1} dx}{x^n (x^n - 1)}$$

Let $x^n - 1 = t$ then $nx^{n-1}\ dx = dt$

$$\Rightarrow x^{n-1}\ dx = \frac{dt}{n}$$

$$\therefore \quad I = \pi \int \frac{dt}{n(t+1)t}$$

$$= \frac{\pi}{n}\int \frac{dt}{t^2 + t} = \frac{\pi}{n}\int \frac{dt}{t^2 + t + \frac{1}{4} - \frac{1}{4}}$$

$$= \frac{\pi}{n}\int \frac{dt}{\left(t + \frac{1}{2}\right)^2 - \left(\frac{1}{2}\right)^2}$$

$$= \frac{\pi}{n}\left[\frac{1}{2 \times \frac{1}{2}} \log_e \left|\frac{t + \frac{1}{2} - \frac{1}{2}}{t + \frac{1}{2} + \frac{1}{2}}\right|\right] + C$$

$$= \frac{\pi}{n}\log_e \left|\frac{t}{t+1}\right| + C = \frac{\pi}{n}\log_e \left|\frac{x^n - 1}{x^n}\right| + C.$$

**13. (D):** Let $I = \int_0^1 \frac{a - bx^2}{(a + bx^2)^2} dx$

Put $x = \sqrt{\frac{a}{b}} \tan x$

$$\Rightarrow \quad \tan\theta = x\sqrt{\frac{b}{a}}$$

$$\therefore \quad dx = \sqrt{\frac{a}{b}} \sec^2\theta\, d\theta$$

$$\theta = \tan^{-1}\left(x\sqrt{\frac{b}{a}}\right)$$

$\because$ $x = 0$

$\therefore$ $\theta = 0$

and $x = 1$

$$\therefore \quad \theta = \tan^{-1}\sqrt{\frac{b}{a}}$$

$$\text{Then, } I = \int_0^{\tan^{-1}\sqrt{\frac{b}{a}}} \frac{a - b \times \frac{a}{b}\tan^2\theta}{\left(a + b \times \frac{a}{b}\tan^2\theta\right)^2} \sqrt{\frac{a}{b}} \sec^2\theta d\theta$$

$$= \int_0^{\tan^{-1}\sqrt{\frac{b}{a}}} \frac{a(1 - \tan^2\theta)}{a^2(1 + \tan^2\theta)^2} \sqrt{\frac{a}{b}} \sec^2\theta d\theta$$

$$= \frac{1}{a}\sqrt{\frac{a}{b}} \int_0^{\tan^{-1}\sqrt{\frac{b}{a}}} \frac{(1 - \tan^2\theta)}{(1 + \tan^2\theta)(\sec^2\theta)} \sec^2\theta d\theta$$

$$= \frac{1}{a}\sqrt{\frac{a}{b}} \int_0^{\tan^{-1}\sqrt{\frac{b}{a}}} \frac{(1 - \tan^2\theta)}{(1 + \tan^2\theta)} d\theta = \frac{1}{a}\sqrt{\frac{a}{b}} \int_0^{\tan^{-1}\sqrt{\frac{b}{a}}} \cos 2\theta\, d\theta$$

$$= \frac{1}{a}\sqrt{\frac{a}{b}} \left[\frac{\sin 2\theta}{2}\right]_0^{\tan^{-1}\sqrt{\frac{b}{a}}}$$

$$= \frac{1}{2a}\sqrt{\frac{a}{b}} \left[\frac{2\tan\theta}{1 + \tan^2\theta}\right]_0^{\tan^{-1}\sqrt{\frac{b}{a}}}$$

$$= \frac{1}{2a}\sqrt{\frac{a}{b}} \left[\frac{2\sqrt{\frac{b}{a}}}{1 + \frac{b}{a}} - 0\right]$$

$$= \frac{1}{2a}\sqrt{\frac{a}{b}} \times 2\sqrt{\frac{b}{a}} \times \frac{a}{a+b} = \frac{1}{a+b}.$$

**14. (B):** Let $y = 5^x$

then, $\frac{dy}{dx} = 5^x \log_e 5$

$\therefore \quad \frac{d^2y}{dx^2} = \log_e 5 \ (5^x \log_e 5)$

$\Rightarrow \quad \frac{d^2y}{dx^2} = 5^x (\log_e 5)^2.$

**15. (B):** Given, differential equation,

$$\left(1-\left(\frac{dy}{dx}\right)^2\right)^{3/2} = k\frac{d^2y}{dx^2}$$

$$\Rightarrow \left(1-\left(\frac{dy}{dx}\right)^2\right)^3 = \left(k\frac{d^2y}{dx^2}\right)^2$$

$$\Rightarrow \left(1-\left(\frac{dy}{dx}\right)^2\right)^3 = k^2\left(\frac{d^2y}{dx^2}\right)^2$$

Here, order = 2

Degree = Power of the highest order derivative = 2.

**16. (B):** $l_1 \text{ R } l_2 \Leftrightarrow l_1$ is parallel to $l_2$ for reflexive

$(l_1, l_2) \in R$

$l_1$ is parallel to $l_2$

For symmetric:

$(l_1, l_2) \in R \Rightarrow (l_2, l_1) \in R$

It is also true.

For transitive:

$(l_1, l_2) \in R \ \& \ (l_2, l_3) \in R \Rightarrow (l_1, l_3) \in R$

It is also true.

$\therefore$ It is an equivalence relation.

**17. (D):** In a leap year there are 366 days

366 days = 52 weeks and 2 days

Thus a leap year has always 52 Tuesday

The remaining 2 days can be

Tuesday and Wednesday

Wednesday and Thursday

Thursday and Friday

Friday and Saturday

Saturday and Sunday

Sunday and Monday

Monday and Tuesday

$\therefore$ Total number of elementary events = 7

and favourable number of elementary events = 2

[Tuesday and Wednesday, Monday and Tuesday]

Hence, Probability (53 Tuesday) $= \frac{2}{7}$

Hence, probability (not getting 53 Tuesday in a leap year)

$= 1-\frac{2}{7} = \frac{5}{7}.$

**18. (A):** Let $\theta$ be the angle between the given lines

Given, $a_1 = 1, \ b_1 = 1, \ c_1 = -2$

and $a_2 = \left(\sqrt{3}-1\right)$

$b_2 = \left(-\sqrt{3}-1\right)$

$c_2 = -4$

$$\therefore \cos\theta = \frac{a_1a_2 + b_1b_2 + c_1c_2}{\sqrt{a_1^2+b_1^2+c_1^2}.\sqrt{a_2^2+b_2^2+c_2^2}}$$

$$= \frac{1\times\left(\sqrt{3}-1\right)+1\times\left(-\sqrt{3}-1\right)+-2\times-4}{\sqrt{1+1+4}\sqrt{\left(\sqrt{3}-1\right)^2+\left(\sqrt{3}+1\right)^2+16}}$$

$$= \frac{\sqrt{3}-1+-\sqrt{3}-1+8}{\sqrt{6}\sqrt{3+1-2\sqrt{3}+3+1+2\sqrt{3}+16}}$$

$$= \frac{6}{\sqrt{6}\sqrt{8+16}}$$

$$= \frac{6}{\sqrt{6\times 24}} = \frac{6}{\sqrt{144}} = \frac{6}{12} = \frac{1}{2}$$

$$\Rightarrow \cos\theta = \frac{1}{2} = \cos\frac{\pi}{3}$$

$$\Rightarrow \theta = \frac{\pi}{3}.$$

**19. (A):** Given, $\left(\vec{a}-\vec{b}\right).\left(\vec{a}+\vec{b}\right) = 27$

and $|\vec{a}| = 2|\vec{b}|$

$\because \left(\vec{a}-\vec{b}\right).\left(\vec{a}+\vec{b}\right) = 27$

$\therefore \quad |\vec{a}|^2 - |\vec{b}|^2 = 27$

$\Rightarrow \left(2|\vec{b}|\right)^2 - |\vec{b}|^2 = 27$

$\Rightarrow \quad 4|\vec{b}|^2 - |\vec{b}|^2 = 27$

$\Rightarrow \quad 3|\vec{b}|^2 = 27$

$\Rightarrow \quad |\vec{b}|^2 = 9$

$\Rightarrow \quad |\vec{b}| = 3.$

**20. (B):** Given, $\tan^{-1}\left(\frac{2}{3^{-x}+1}\right) = \cot^{-1}\left(\frac{3}{3^x+1}\right)$

$$\Rightarrow \cot^{-1}\left(\frac{3^{-x}+1}{2}\right) = \cot^{-1}\left(\frac{3}{3^x+1}\right)$$

$$\therefore \frac{3^{-x}+1}{2} = \frac{3}{3^x+1}$$

$$\Rightarrow \frac{\frac{1}{3^x}+1}{2} = \frac{3}{3^x+1}$$

$$\Rightarrow \frac{1+3^x}{2.3^x} = \frac{3}{3^x+1}$$

$$\Rightarrow (1+3^x)^2 = 3 \times 2 \times 3^x$$

$$\Rightarrow 1 + 3^{2x} + 2.3^x = 6.3^x$$

$$\Rightarrow 1 + 3^{2x} = 6.3^x - 2.3^x$$

$$\Rightarrow 1 + 3^{2x} = 4.3^x$$

Hence, there is no real value of $x$ satisfying the above equation.

**21. (C):** Given, A, B and C are three singular matrices

$$|A| = 0$$

$$\Rightarrow \begin{vmatrix} 1 & 4 \\ 3 & 2a \end{vmatrix} = 0$$

$$\Rightarrow 2a - 12 = 0 \Rightarrow a = 6$$

$$|B| = 0$$

$$\Rightarrow \begin{vmatrix} 3b & 5 \\ a & 2 \end{vmatrix} = 0$$

$$\Rightarrow 6b - 5a = 0$$

$$\Rightarrow 6b - 5 \times 6 = 0 \Rightarrow b = 5$$

and $|c| = 0$

$$\Rightarrow \begin{vmatrix} a+b+c & c+1 \\ a+c & c \end{vmatrix} = 0$$

$$\Rightarrow \begin{vmatrix} 6+5+c & c+1 \\ 6+c & c \end{vmatrix} = 0$$

$$\Rightarrow \begin{vmatrix} 11+c & c+1 \\ 6+c & c \end{vmatrix} = 0$$

$$\Rightarrow (11+c)c - (c+1)(6+c) = 0$$

$$\Rightarrow 11c + c^2 - 6c - c^2 - 6 - c = 0$$

$$\Rightarrow 4c - 6 = 0$$

$$\Rightarrow c = \frac{3}{2}$$

Thus, $abc = 6 \times 5 \times \frac{3}{2} = 45$.

**22. (B):** Let $I = \int_{\log_e 2}^{\log_e 3} \frac{e^{2x}-1}{e^{2x}+1}dx = \int_{\log_e 2}^{\log_e 3} \frac{\frac{e^{2x}-1}{e^x}}{\frac{e^{2x}+1}{e^x}}dx$

$$= \int_{\log_e 2}^{\log_e 3} \frac{e^x - e^{-x}}{e^x + e^{-x}}dx$$

Put $e^x + e^{-x} = t$; $(e^x - e^{-x})dx = dt$

$$\therefore I = \int_{\log_e 2}^{\log_e 3} \frac{dt}{t}$$

$$= [\log t]_{\log_e 2}^{\log_e 3} = \left[\log(e^x + e^{-x})\right]_{\log_e 2}^{\log_e 3}$$

$$= \log\left(e^{\log_e 3} + e^{-\log_e 3}\right) - \log\left(e^{\log_e 2} + e^{-\log_e 2}\right)$$

$$= \log\left(3+\frac{1}{3}\right) - \log\left(2+\frac{1}{2}\right)$$

$$= \log\frac{10}{3} - \log\frac{5}{2}$$

$$= \log_e \frac{10}{3} \times \frac{2}{5} = \log_e \frac{4}{3} = \log_e 4 - \log_e 3.$$

**23. (D):** $\because \vec{a}+\vec{b}+\vec{c} = 0$

$$\therefore \vec{b}+\vec{c} = -\vec{a}$$

Squaring both sides

$$|\vec{b}|^2 + |\vec{c}|^2 + 2\vec{b}.\vec{c} = |\vec{a}|^2$$

$$\Rightarrow 1+4+2|\vec{b}||\vec{c}|\cos\theta = 1$$

$$\Rightarrow 1 + 4 + 2 \times 2 \cos\theta = 1$$

$$\Rightarrow 5 + 4\cos\theta = 1$$

$$\Rightarrow 4\cos\theta = 1 - 5$$

$$\Rightarrow 4\cos\theta = -4$$

$$\Rightarrow \cos\theta = -1$$

$$\therefore \theta = 180^\circ.$$

**24. (C):** $|x - 1| + |x - 2|$ is continuous everywhere

$x - |x|$ is differentiable at everywhere except at $x = 0$

$x - [x]$ is not differentiable at $x = 1$

$x|x|$ is differentiable at $x = 1$.

**25. (B):** Given, $r = \sqrt[3]{1.331} = \left[(1.1)^3\right]^{1/3}$

$$= 1.1 \text{ cm}$$

$\because$ Total surface area of a hemisphere

$$= 2\pi r^2 + \pi r^2$$

$\Rightarrow \quad A = 3\pi r^2$

Differentiating w.r.t. to $r$ we obtain,

$$\frac{dA}{dr} = 3\pi \times 2r$$

$$= 6\pi r$$

$$= 6\pi \times 1.1$$

$$\Rightarrow \quad \frac{dA}{dr} = 6.6\pi.$$

**26.** **(A):** Given lines $\frac{x}{7\sqrt{3a}} + \frac{y}{b} = 4$

$x = 0$ and $y = 0$

$$\Rightarrow \quad \frac{x}{28\sqrt{3a}} + \frac{y}{4b} = 1$$

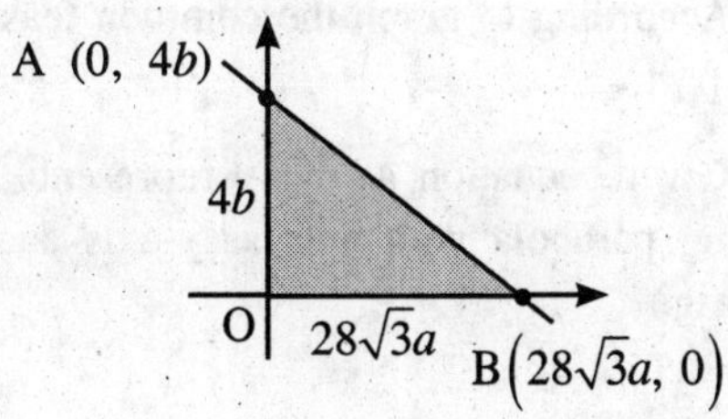


$$\therefore \quad \text{Area} = \frac{1}{2} \times \text{base} \times \text{height}$$

$$= \frac{1}{2} \times 28\sqrt{3a} \times 4b$$

$$= 14\sqrt{3a} \times 4b = 56\sqrt{3}ab$$

$\therefore$ The area of the region bounded by the given lines is $56\sqrt{3}ab$.

**27.** **(D):** Given, A is a square matrix and I is an identity matrix

$$A^2 = A$$

$\therefore A(I - 2A)^3 + 2A^3$

$= A[I^3 - 3I^2 . 2A + 3I . (2A)^2 - (2A)^3] + 2A^3$

$= A[I - 6AI + 12A^2I - 8A^3] + 2A^3$

$= A[I - 6A + 12A^2 - 8A^3] + 2A^3$ [$\because$ AI = A]

$= AI - 6AI + 12A^3 - 8A^4 + 2A^3$

$= A - 6A + 12A - 8A + 2A$

$= 15A - 14A = A.$

**28.** **(B):** (*a*) $xdy - (y + 2x^2)dx = 0$

$$\Rightarrow \quad \frac{dy}{dx} - \frac{y}{x} = 2x \qquad 2x\left[\text{form of } \frac{dy}{dx} + Py = Q\right]$$

$$\therefore \quad P = \frac{-1}{x}$$

$$\therefore \quad I.F. = e^{\int P dx} = e^{\int -\frac{1}{x} dx} = e^{-\log x}$$

$$= e^{\log_x -1} = x^{-1} = \frac{1}{x}$$

$$\Rightarrow \quad I.F. = \frac{1}{x}$$

(*b*) $(2x^2 - 3y)dx = xdy$

$$\Rightarrow \quad 2x - 3\frac{y}{x} = \frac{dy}{dx}$$

$$\Rightarrow \quad \frac{dy}{dx} + \frac{3}{x}y = 2x$$

$$\therefore \quad P = \frac{3}{x}$$

$$\therefore \quad I.F. = e^{\int P dx} = e^{\int \frac{3}{x} dx} = e^{3\log x}$$

$$= e^{\log x^3} = x^3$$

$$\Rightarrow \quad I.F. = x^3$$

(*c*) $(2y + 3x^2)dx + xdy = 0$

$$\Rightarrow \quad (2y + 3x^2) + x\frac{dy}{dx} = 0$$

$$\Rightarrow \quad \frac{dy}{dx} + 2\frac{y}{x} = -3x$$

$$\therefore \quad P = \frac{2}{x}$$

$$\therefore \quad I.F. = e^{\int P dx} = e^{\int \frac{2}{x} dx} = e^{2\log x}$$

$$= e^{\log x^2} = x^2$$

(*d*) $2xdy + (3x^3 + 2y)dx = 0$

$$\Rightarrow \quad 2x\frac{dy}{dx} + (3x^3 + 2y) = 0$$

$$\Rightarrow \quad \frac{dy}{dx} + \frac{y}{x} = \frac{-3}{2}x^2$$

$$\therefore \quad P = \frac{1}{x}$$

$$\therefore \quad I.F. = e^{\int P dx} = e^{\int \frac{1}{x} dx} = e^{\log x}$$

$$= x$$

Hence, option (B) is correct answer.

**29.** **(D):** $f : \mathbb{N} \to \mathbb{N}$

$$f(n) = \begin{cases} n-1, & \text{if } n \text{ is even} \\ n+1, & \text{if } n \text{ is odd} \end{cases},$$

This function is injective and subjective both and if function is bijective then it is also invertible.

**30. (A):**

Let $I = \int_0^{\pi/2} \frac{1-\cot x}{\operatorname{cosec} x + \cos x} dx = \int_0^{\pi/2} \frac{1 - \frac{\cos x}{\sin x}}{\frac{1}{\sin x} + \cos x} dx$

$\Rightarrow \quad I = \int_0^{\pi/2} \frac{\sin x - \cos x}{1 + \sin x \cos x} dx \quad \ldots(i)$

$\left[\text{Using} \int_0^a f(x)dx = \int_0^a f(a-x)dx\right]$

$\therefore \quad I = \int_0^{\pi/2} \frac{\sin\left(\frac{\pi}{2} - x\right) - \cos\left(\frac{\pi}{2} - x\right)}{1 + \sin\left(\frac{\pi}{2} - x\right)\cos\left(\frac{\pi}{2} - x\right)} dx$

$= \int_0^{\pi/2} \frac{\cos x - \sin x}{1 + \cos x \sin x} dx$

$I = \int_0^{\pi/2} \frac{\cos x - \sin x}{1 + \sin x \cos x} dx \quad \ldots(ii)$

From adding (*i*) and (*ii*), we obtain,

$2I = \int_0^{\pi/2} \frac{\sin x - \cos x + \cos x - \sin x}{1 + \sin x \cos x} dx$

$\Rightarrow \quad I = \frac{1}{2} \int_0^{\pi/2} \frac{0}{1 + \sin x \cos x} dx$

$\Rightarrow \quad I = 0.$

**31. (B):** Here, $k + 2k + 3k + 0 = 1$

$\Rightarrow \quad 6k = 1$

$\therefore \quad k = \frac{1}{6}$

$P(X < 2) = k + 2k$

$= \frac{1}{6} + \frac{2}{6}$

$= \frac{3}{6} = \frac{1}{2}$

$P(1 \le x \le 2) = 2k + 3k$

$= 5k$

$= \frac{5}{6}$

and $\quad E(X) = \frac{4}{3}$

Hence, option (B) is the correct answer.

**33. (A):** Let $A = \begin{bmatrix} 1 & 0 & 0 \\ 0 & 1 & 0 \\ 0 & 0 & 1 \end{bmatrix}$

Here A is a square matrix

$\because$ All the elements, except diagonal element are zero

$\therefore$ A is a diagonal matrix and diagonal elements are equal is called the scalar matrix.

$\therefore$ A is a scalar matrix

and $A^T = A$

$\therefore$ A is a symmetric matrix

Thus, A is scalar matrix, a diagonal matrix and a symmetric matrix.

**34. (C):** According to graph the common feasible region is C part.

**35. (D):** Given, equation $4x^2 = y$ represents an upward opening parabola with axis as *y*-axis and vertex at the origin

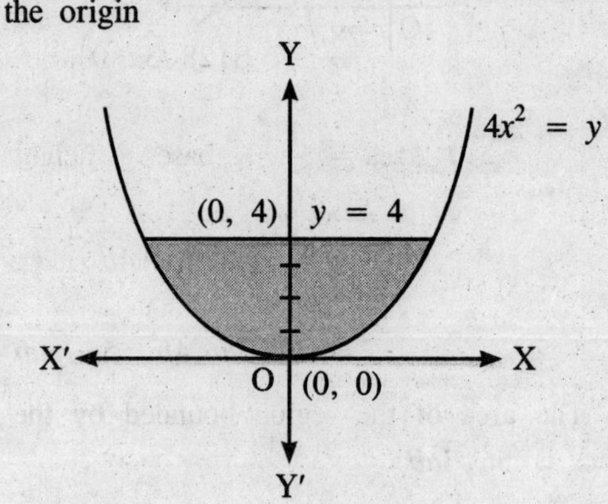


The shaded region is lying in the first quadrant and bounded by

$4x^2 = y$

and $y = 4$

$\therefore$ Area $= A = 2\int_0^4 |x| dy = 2\int_0^4 x\, dy = 2\int_0^4 \sqrt{\frac{y}{4}} dy$

$= 2\left[\frac{1}{2}\int_4^4 y^{1/2} dy\right] = \left[\frac{y^{3/2}}{3/2}\right]_0^4$

$= \frac{2}{3}\left[y^{3/2}\right]_0^4$

$= \frac{2}{3}\left[4^{3/2} - 0\right] = \frac{2}{3}[8] = \frac{16}{3}$

$\Rightarrow \quad A = \frac{16}{3}$ sq. units.

**36. (D):** Let, $I = \int e^x \left(\frac{2x+1}{2\sqrt{x}}\right) dx$

$= \int e^x \left(\sqrt{x} + \frac{1}{2\sqrt{x}}\right) dx$

$= \int e^x \sqrt{x} dx + \int e^x . \frac{1}{2\sqrt{x}} dx$ [Using ILATE]

$= \sqrt{x} \int e^x dx - \int \frac{d(\sqrt{x})}{dx} e^x dx + \int e^x . \frac{1}{2\sqrt{x}} dx$

$= \sqrt{x}e^x - \int \frac{1}{2\sqrt{x}} e^x dx + \int \frac{1}{2\sqrt{x}} e^x dx$

$= e^x \sqrt{x} + c.$

**37. (D):** When $x \le \pi$, we have $f(x) = kx + 1$

when, $x > \pi$, we have $f(x) = \cos x$

(LHL at $x = \pi$) $= \lim_{x \to \pi^-} f(x) = \lim_{x \to 2} (kx + 1) = k\pi + 1$

(RHL at $x = \pi$) $= \lim_{x \to \pi^+} f(x) = \lim_{x \to \pi} \cos x = \cos \pi = -1$

$\because f(x)$ is continuous at $x = \pi$

$\therefore \quad k\pi + 1 = -1$

$\Rightarrow \quad k = \frac{-2}{\pi}.$

**38. (B):** Given, $P = \begin{bmatrix} -1 \\ 2 \\ 1 \end{bmatrix}$

and $Q = [2 \quad -4 \quad 1]$

$(PQ) = \begin{bmatrix} -1 \\ 2 \\ 1 \end{bmatrix} [2 \quad -4 \quad 1]$

$= \begin{bmatrix} -2 & 4 & -1 \\ 4 & -8 & 2 \\ 2 & -4 & 1 \end{bmatrix}$

$(PQ)' = \begin{bmatrix} -2 & 4 & -1 \\ 4 & -8 & 2 \\ 2 & -4 & 1 \end{bmatrix}^1 = \begin{bmatrix} -2 & 4 & 2 \\ 4 & -8 & -4 \\ -1 & 2 & 1 \end{bmatrix}.$

**39. (D):** Given, $\Delta = \begin{vmatrix} 1 & \cos x & 1 \\ -\cos x & 1 & \cos x \\ -1 & -\cos x & 1 \end{vmatrix}$

Applying $C_1 = C_1 + C_3$

$\therefore \quad \Delta = \begin{vmatrix} 2 & \cos x & 1 \\ 0 & 1 & \cos x \\ 0 & -\cos x & 1 \end{vmatrix}$

$= 2\begin{vmatrix} 1 & \cos x \\ -\cos x & 1 \end{vmatrix} - 0 + 0$

$= 2(1 + \cos^2 x)$

$\Rightarrow \quad \Delta = 2(1 + 1 - \sin^2 x)$

$\Rightarrow \quad \Delta = 2(2 - \sin^2 x)$

$\because \quad -1 \le \sin x \le 1$

$\therefore \quad \Delta = 2[2 - (-1)^2]$

$= 2[2 - 1] = 2$

when $\sin x = -1$

and $\Delta = 2[2 - 1^2] = 2[2 - 1] = 2$

when $\sin x = 1$

$0 \le \sin x \le 1$

$\therefore \quad \Delta = 2[2 - 0] = 4$

when $\sin x = 0$

and $\Delta = 2[2 - 1^2] = 2$

when $\sin x = 1$

$\therefore$ Minimum value of $\Delta = 2$

and maximum value of $\Delta = 4$

Hence, option (D) is correct.

**40. (A):** Given, $f(x) = \sin x + \frac{1}{2}\cos 2x$ in $\left[0, \frac{\pi}{2}\right]$

$\therefore \quad f'(x) = \cos x - \sin 2x$

At critical point, we have

$f'(x) = 0 \Rightarrow \cos x = \sin 2x = 0$

$\Rightarrow \cos x - 2 \sin x \cos x = 0$

$\Rightarrow \quad \cos x (1 - 2 \sin x) = 0$

$\Rightarrow \quad \cos x = 0$ or $1 - 2 \sin x = 0$

or, $\quad \sin x = \frac{1}{2} = \sin\frac{\pi}{6}$

$\therefore \quad x = \frac{\pi}{2}$ and $\frac{\pi}{6}$ $\left[\because 0 \le x \le \frac{\pi}{2}\right]$

Now, Calculate the value of $f(x)$ at these points and at the end points of interval

$\therefore \quad f(0) = \sin 0° + \frac{1}{2}\cos 0° = 0 + \frac{1}{2} \times 1 = \frac{1}{2}$

and $\quad f\left(\frac{\pi}{6}\right) = \sin\frac{\pi}{6} + \frac{1}{2}\cos\frac{\pi}{3} = \frac{1}{2} + \frac{1}{2} \times \frac{1}{2}$

$= \frac{1}{2} + \frac{1}{4} = \frac{2+1}{4} = \frac{3}{4}$

$$f\left(\frac{\pi}{2}\right) = \sin\frac{\pi}{2} + \frac{1}{2}\cos\pi$$

$$= 1 - \frac{1}{2} = \frac{1}{2}$$

Hence, the critical points of the function are

$$x = \frac{\pi}{6} \text{ and } x = \frac{\pi}{2}$$

The minimum value of the function is $\frac{1}{2}$ and the maximum value of the function is $\frac{3}{4}$

Hence, option (A) is correct.

**41.** **(A):** Let $l$, $m$, $n$ be the direction cosines of the required line

Since it is perpendicular to the lines whose direction cosines are proportional to 1, –2, –2 and 0, 2, 1 respectively

$\therefore \quad l - 2m - 2n = 0 \qquad \ldots(i)$

and $0l + 2m + n = 0 \qquad \ldots(ii)$

On solving (*i*) and (*ii*), by cross-multiplication

$$\frac{l}{-2+4} = \frac{m}{0-1} = \frac{n}{2}$$

$$\Rightarrow \frac{l}{2} = \frac{m}{-1} = \frac{n}{2}$$

Thus, the direction ratios of the required line are proportional to 2, –1, 2

Hence, its direction cosines are

$$\frac{2}{\sqrt{2^2+(-1)^2+2^2}}, \frac{-1}{\sqrt{2^2+(-1)^2+2^2}}, \frac{2}{\sqrt{2^2+(-1)^2+2^2}}$$

or, $\frac{2}{3}, \frac{-1}{3}, \frac{2}{3}$.

**42.** **(B):** According to question

$$\sum_0^4 P(X) = 1$$

$\therefore$ P(X = 0) + P(X = 1) + P(X = 2) + P(X = 3) + P(X = 4) = 1

$\Rightarrow$ 0.1 + C + 2C + 2C + C = 1

$\Rightarrow$ 6C = 0.9 $\Rightarrow$ C = 0.15

$\therefore$ (*a*) C = 0.15

(*b*) P(X $\leq$ 2)

= P(X = 0) + P(X = 1) + P(X = 2)

= 0.1 + C + 2C

= 0.1 + 3C = 0.1 + 3 $\times$ 0.15

= 0.1 + 0.45 = 0.55

(*c*) P(X = 2) = 2C = 2 $\times$ 0.15 = 0.3

(*d*) P(X $\geq$ 2)

= P(X = 2) + P(X = 3) + P(X = 4)

= 2C + 2C + C = 5C

= 5 $\times$ 0.15 = 0.75

Hence, option (B) is the correct answer.

**43.** **(D):** Given, $\sin y = x \sin(a + y)$

Differentiating both sides w.r. to $x$, we obtain

$$\cos y\frac{dy}{dx} = \sin(a+y).1 + x\cos(a+y).\frac{dy}{dx}$$

$$\Rightarrow \cos y\frac{dy}{dx} = \sin(a+y) + x\cos(a+y)\frac{dy}{dx}$$

$$\Rightarrow \cos y\frac{dy}{dx} - x\cos(a+y)\frac{dy}{dx} = \sin(a+y)$$

$$\Rightarrow [\cos y - x\cos(a+y)]\frac{dy}{dx} = \sin(a+y)$$

$$\Rightarrow \left[\cos y - \frac{\sin y}{\sin(a+y)}\cos(a+y)\right]\frac{dy}{dx} = \sin(a+y)$$

$$\left[\because \sin y = x\sin(a+y) \quad \therefore x = \frac{\sin y}{\sin(a+y)}\right]$$

$$\Rightarrow \left[\frac{\sin(a+y)\cos y - \cos(a+y)\sin y}{\sin(a+y)}\right]\frac{dy}{dx} = \sin(a+y)$$

$$\Rightarrow \frac{\sin(a+y-y)}{\sin(a+y)}\frac{dy}{dx} = \sin(a+y)$$

$$\Rightarrow \frac{\sin a}{\sin(a+y)}\frac{dy}{dx} = \sin(a+y)$$

$$\Rightarrow \frac{dy}{dx} = \frac{\sin^2(a+y)}{\sin a}.$$

**44.** **(D):** Given, $\vec{a} = \hat{i} + \hat{j} + \hat{k}$

and $\vec{b} = \hat{i} + 2\hat{j} + 3\hat{k}$

$\therefore \quad \vec{a} + \vec{b} = 2\hat{i} + 3\hat{j} + 4\hat{k}$

and $\vec{a} - \vec{b} = 0\hat{i} - \hat{j} - 2\hat{k}$

Let $\vec{c} = x\hat{i} + y\hat{j} + z\hat{k}$ be a unit vector perpendicular to the vector $(\vec{a} + \vec{b})$ and $(\vec{a} - \vec{b})$

then, $\vec{c}.(\vec{a}+\vec{b}) = 0$

and $\vec{c}.(\vec{a}-\vec{b}) = 0$

$\Rightarrow (x\hat{i}+y\hat{j}+z\hat{k})(2\hat{i}+3\hat{j}+4\hat{k}) = 0$

and $(x\hat{i}+y\hat{j}+z\hat{k}).(0\hat{i}-\hat{j}-2\hat{k}) = 0$

$\Rightarrow 2x + 3y + 4z = 0$

and $0 - y - 2z = 0$

Using cross-multiplication

$$\frac{x}{-6+4} = \frac{y}{0+4} = \frac{z}{-2-0}$$

$$\Rightarrow \frac{x}{-2} = \frac{y}{4} = \frac{z}{-2} = \lambda$$

$$\Rightarrow x = -2\lambda,\ y = 4\lambda,\ z = -2\lambda$$

$\because \vec{c}$ is a unit vector

$\therefore |\vec{c}| = 1$

$\Rightarrow x^2 + y^2 + z^2 = 1$

$\Rightarrow 4\lambda^2 + 16\lambda^2 + 4\lambda^2 = 1$

$\Rightarrow 24\lambda^2 = 1$

$$\lambda = \pm\frac{1}{\sqrt{24}} = \pm\frac{1}{2\sqrt{6}}$$

$$\therefore x = \pm\frac{2}{2\sqrt{6}},\ \pm\frac{4}{2\sqrt{6}}$$

and $$z = \frac{-2}{2\sqrt{6}}$$

Hence, unit vector of $\vec{c}$ are $\frac{-1}{\sqrt{6}}\hat{i}+\frac{2}{\sqrt{6}}\hat{j}-\frac{1}{\sqrt{6}}\hat{k}$.

**45. (C):** Given lines,

$$l_1 : \vec{r} = (\hat{i}-2\hat{j}+3\hat{k})+\lambda(2\hat{i}+3\hat{j}+6\hat{k})$$

$$= \vec{a}_1+\lambda\vec{b}$$

$$l_2 : \vec{r} = 3\hat{i}-2\hat{j}+\hat{k}+\mu(4\hat{i}+6\hat{j}+12\hat{k})$$

$$= (3\hat{i}-2\hat{j}+\hat{k})+2\mu(2\hat{i}+3\hat{j}+6\hat{k})$$

$$= \vec{a}_2+2\mu\vec{b}$$

Both are parallel lines

$$\therefore \text{Distance} = \left|\frac{\vec{b}\times(\vec{a}_2-\vec{a}_1)}{|\vec{b}|}\right|$$

$$\Rightarrow \vec{a}_2-\vec{a}_1 = 2\hat{i}+0\hat{j}-2\hat{k}$$

and $\vec{b} = 2\hat{i}+3\hat{j}+6\hat{k}$

$$\therefore \vec{b}\times(\vec{a}_2-\vec{a}_1) = \begin{vmatrix}\hat{i} & \hat{j} & \hat{k}\\ 2 & 3 & 6\\ 2 & 0 & -2\end{vmatrix}$$

$$= \hat{i}(-6-0)-\hat{j}(-4-12)+\hat{k}(0-6)$$

$$= -6\hat{i}+16\hat{j}-6\hat{k}$$

$$\therefore |\vec{b}\times(\vec{a}_2-\vec{a}_1)| = \sqrt{36+256+36} = \sqrt{328}$$

and $|\vec{b}| = \sqrt{4+9+36} = \sqrt{49} = 7$

Hence, $$\text{Distance} = \left|\frac{\vec{b}\times(\vec{a}_2-\vec{a}_1)}{|\vec{b}|}\right| = \frac{\sqrt{328}}{7}.$$

**46. (C):** Given, $$f(x) = 2\left[\tan^{-1}(e^x)-\frac{\pi}{4}\right]$$

$$\therefore f'(x) = 2\left[\frac{1}{1+e^{2x}}.e^x-0\right]$$

$$\Rightarrow f'(x) = \frac{2e^x}{1+e^{2x}} > 0$$

$\therefore$ It is strictly increasing function and this is odd function.

**47. (A):** Given, $(x\log_e x)dy = (\log_e x - y)dx$

$$\Rightarrow \frac{dy}{dx} = \frac{1}{x}-\frac{1}{x\log_e x}.y$$

$$\Rightarrow \frac{dy}{dx}+\frac{1}{x\log_e x}y = \frac{1}{x}$$

Degree of the given differential equation is 1

It is a linear differential equation of the form

$$\frac{dy}{dx}+\text{P}y = \text{Q}$$

Where, $\text{P} = \frac{1}{x\log_e x}$ and $\text{Q} = \frac{1}{x}$

Now, $$\text{I.F.} = e^{\int \text{P}\,dx} = e^{\int\frac{1}{x\log_e x}dx} = \log_e x$$

$\Rightarrow \text{I.F.} = \log_e x$

Using $y(\text{I.F.}) = \int \text{Q(I.F.)}dx + c$

$$\therefore y(\log_e x) = \int\frac{1}{x}\log_e x\,dx + c \quad \ldots(i)$$

Let $$I = \int \frac{1}{x} \log_e x \, dx$$

$$= \log_e x \int \frac{1}{x} dx - \int \frac{1}{x} \log_e x \, dx$$

$\Rightarrow$ $$I = \log_e x \, . \, \log_e x - I$$

$\Rightarrow$ $$2I = (\log_e x)^2$$

$\Rightarrow$ $$I = \frac{1}{2}(\log_e x)^2 \quad \ldots(ii)$$

From (*i*) and (*ii*), we obtain,

$$y(\log_e x) = \frac{1}{2}(\log_e x)^2 + c$$

$\Rightarrow$ $$2y(\log_e x) = (\log_e x)^2 + 2c$$

$\Rightarrow$ $$2y(\log_e x) - 2c = (\log_e x)^2$$

$\Rightarrow$ $$2y \log_e x + A = (\log_e x)^2$$

Where A is constant.

**48. (B):** Let $E_1$ = Event that a ball is drawn from first bag

and $E_2$ = event that a ball is drawn from second bag

$\because$ Number divisible by 3 = 3, 6

$\therefore$ $$P(E_1) = \frac{2}{6} = \frac{1}{3}$$

$\therefore$ $$P(E_2) = 1 - \frac{1}{3} = \frac{2}{3}$$

Let A = Ball is drawn black ball

$\therefore$ $$P(A) = \frac{1}{3} \times \frac{6}{10} + \frac{2}{3} \times \frac{5}{10}$$

$$= \frac{1}{5} + \frac{1}{3} = \frac{8}{15}$$

$\therefore$ Probability of ball is drawn second bag

$$P\left(\frac{E_2}{A}\right) = \frac{\frac{2}{3} \times \frac{5}{10}}{\frac{8}{15}}$$

$$= \frac{2}{3} \times \frac{1}{2} \times \frac{15}{8} = \frac{5}{8}$$

$\therefore$ Ball is not drawn from Bag-2

$$= 1 - \frac{5}{8} = \frac{3}{8}.$$

**49. (C):** Given, Straight line,

$$\frac{x-3}{2} = \frac{2-y}{3} = \frac{z+4}{-1}$$

$\Rightarrow$ $$\frac{x-3}{2} = \frac{y-2}{3} = \frac{z+4}{-1}$$

$\therefore$ Direction ratio = 2, 3, –1

Hence, option (C) 2, 3, –1 can not be the direction ratio.

**50. (C):** $$x + y \geq 10$$

$$2x + 2y \leq 25$$

$$x \geq 0, \; y \geq 0$$

$\therefore$

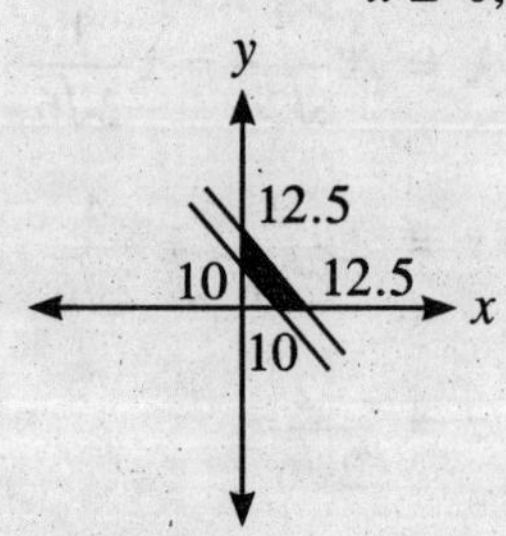


Hence, Option (C) is correct.

# ACCOUNTANCY/BOOK KEEPING

1. Identify the correct sequence of the following steps involved in calculating cash flows from operating activities of a company:

   (*a*) Operating profit before working capital changes
   (*b*) Cash generated from operations
   (*c*) Income tax paid
   (*d*) Net cash flow from operating activities
   (*e*) Goodwill amortised

   Choose the **correct** answer from the options given below:

   A. (*e*), (*c*), (*d*), (*a*), (*b*)
   B. (*e*), (*a*), (*d*), (*b*), (*c*)
   C. (*e*), (*a*), (*b*), (*c*), (*d*)
   D. (*a*), (*b*), (*c*), (*d*), (*e*)

2. Arrange the following in the correct order:

   (*a*) Subscribed Capital
   (*b*) Issued Capital
   (*c*) Authorised Capital
   (*d*) Paid-up Capital
   (*e*) Called-up Capital

   Choose the **correct** answer from the options given below:

   A. (*c*), (*b*), (*a*), (*d*), (*e*)
   B. (*b*), (*c*), (*a*), (*d*), (*e*)
   C. (*c*), (*b*), (*a*), (*e*), (*d*)
   D. (*b*), (*c*), (*a*), (*e*), (*d*)

3. The Deceased Partner's Capital Account includes the following amount/balances:

   (*a*) Opening balance of his capital
   (*b*) His share of profit/loss till the date of death
   (*c*) His share of General Reserve
   (*d*) His drawings till the date of death
   (*e*) Amount paid to his executors

   Choose the **correct** answer from the options given below:

   A. (*a*), (*b*), (*d*) and (*e*) only
   B. (*a*), (*b*), (*c*) and (*d*) only
   C. (*a*), (*b*) and (*c*) only
   D. (*a*), (*b*), (*c*) and (*e*) only

**Directions (Qs. No. 4-8):** *Read the following information carefully and answer the next five questions.*

| Particulars | ₹ |
|---|---|
| Revenue from Operations | 8,75,000 |
| Creditors | 90,000 |
| Bills Receivable | 48,000 |
| Bills Payable | 52,000 |
| Purchases | 4,20,000 |
| Trade Debtors | 59,000 |

4. Calculate Trade Receivables Turnover Ratio.

   A. 8.18 times  B. 8.23 : 1
   C. 8.18%  D. 8.81 : 1

5. Calculate Average Collection Period.

   A. 30 days  B. 60 days
   C. 45 days  D. 15 days

6. Calculate Trade Payables Turnover Ratio.

   A. 29.6 times  B. 2.96 times
   C. 29.6%  D. 2.69 : 1

7. Calculate Average Payment Period.

   A. 123 days
   B. 121 days
   C. 132 days
   D. 133 days

8. Trade Receivables Turnover Ratio and Trade Payables Turnover Ratio are categorised as:

   A. Liquidity Ratio
   B. Solvency Ratio
   C. Activity Ratio
   D. Profitability Ratio

**Directions (Qs. No. 9-13):** *Read the following information carefully and answer the next five questions.*

G, K and B were partners running a partnership for last 10 years, sharing profit and loss in the ratio of 5 : 3 : 2. Post Covid, their firm was affected badly and started incurring losses. On 31st March, 2023 they all decided to dissolve the firm due to continuous losses. Their capital balances were ₹ 4,00,000, ₹ 3,00,000 and

| 1. C | 2. C | 3. B | 4. A | 5. C | 6. B | 7. A | 8. C |
|---|---|---|---|---|---|---|---|

₹ 2,00,000 respectively. Firm had liabilities ₹ 80,000, Cash balance ₹ 40,000, other Sundry Assets ₹ 8,50,000 and P&L A/c constituted the rest. Assets realised at 80% and liabilities were paid in full. There was unrecorded liability of ₹ 50,000 which was settled at ₹ 40,000. Realisation expenses amounted to ₹ 30,000, being paid by G on behalf of the firm.

**9.** What is the mode of dissolution of the firm followed by G, K and B?

A. Dissolution of Agreement
B. On the happening of certain contingencies
C. Dissolution by Notice
D. Compulsory Dissolution

**10.** Determine the amount of Profit and Loss Account.

A. (Cr.) ₹ 90,000
B. (Dr.) ₹ 90,000
C. (Cr.) ₹ 1,30,000
D. (Dr.) ₹ 1,30,000

**11.** Determine Gain/Loss on Realisation.

A. Loss ₹ 2,40,000
B. Gain ₹ 24,000
C. Loss ₹ 1,70,000
D. Loss ₹ 2,10,000

**12.** The entry for realisation expenses in above case study will be:

A. Realisation A/c Dr.
    To Cash A/c
B. Realisation A/c Dr.
    To G's Capital A/c
C. G's Capital A/c Dr.
    To Realisation A/c
D. Cash A/c Dr.
    To Realisation A/c

**13.** Existing Profit and Loss Account in the books of the firm will be shared/borne by partners in the ratio:

A. 5 : 3 : 2
B. Equal Ratio
C. 4 : 3 : 2
D. Ratio of closing capital claims

**14.** Libraries run by charitable trusts are an example of:

A. Partnership
B. Not for profit organisation
C. Companies
D. Cooperatives

**15.** The main source of revenue for 'not for profit' organisation is:

A. Sale of goods
B. Sale of periodicals
C. Subscription from members
D. Sale of assets

**16.** Match List-I with List-II.

| List-I | List-II |
|---|---|
| (*a*) Share capital | I. Will be called at the time of winding up |
| (*b*) Reserves and surplus | II. Calls in advance |
| (*c*) Reserve capital | III. Subscribed but not fully paid |
| (*d*) Current liabilities | IV. Sinking fund |

Choose the **correct** answer from the options given below:

| | (*a*) | (*b*) | (*c*) | (*d*) |
|---|---|---|---|---|
| A. | I | II | III | IV |
| B. | I | III | II | IV |
| C. | I | II | IV | III |
| D. | III | IV | I | II |

**17.** Which of the following would affect the Revaluation Account at the time of reconstitution of a partnership firm?

A. Increase in assets
B. Drawings against capital
C. Interest on capital
D. Partner's salary

**18.** Identify the correct sequence to be followed while preparing of final account of a partnership firm:

(*a*) Profit and Loss Appropriation Account
(*b*) Profit and Loss Account
(*c*) Trading Account
(*d*) Balance Sheet

Choose the **correct** answer from the options given below:

A. (*c*), (*b*), (*a*), (*d*)
B. (*a*), (*c*), (*b*), (*d*)
C. (*b*), (*a*), (*d*), (*c*)
D. (*c*), (*b*), (*d*), (*a*)

**19.** Window dressing is a practice:

A. to manipulate the accounts to show a better picture of the financial position than the actual one.
B. to show excesive depreciation.
C. to avoid tax.
D. to reduce tax.

| 9. A | 10. B | 11. A | 12. B | 13. A | 14. B | 15. C | 16. D | 17. A | 18. A | 19. A |
|---|---|---|---|---|---|---|---|---|---|---|

**20.** Match List-I with List-II.

| List-I | List-II |
|---|---|
| (*a*) Salary to partner | I. Credit side of Partner's Capital Account |
| (*b*) Interest on partner's loan | II. Debit side of Partner's Current Account |
| (*c*) Interest on partner's drawings | III. Debit side of Profit and Loss Account |
| (*d*) Additional capital introduced | IV. Credit side of Partner's Current Account |

Choose the **correct** answer from the options given below:

| | (*a*) | (*b*) | (*c*) | (*d*) |
|---|---|---|---|---|
| A. | I | II | III | IV |
| B. | I | III | II | IV |
| C. | IV | III | II | I |
| D. | III | IV | I | II |

**21.** Which of the following would affect the Revaluation Account at the time of admission of a partner?

(*a*) Increase in assets
(*b*) Drawings against capital
(*c*) Recording of unrecorded assets
(*d*) Decrease in liabilities

Choose the **correct** answer from the options given below:

A. (*a*), (*b*) and (*c*) only
B. (*a*), (*b*) and (*d*) only
C. (*a*), (*c*) and (*d*) only
D. (*b*), (*c*) and (*d*) only

**22.** Match List-I with List-II.

| List-I (Items of cash flow) | List-II (Type of activity) |
|---|---|
| (*a*) Purchase of tangible assets | I. Operating activity |
| (*b*) Issue of shares | II. Cash and cash equivalents |
| (*c*) Increase in current assets | III. Investing activity |
| (*d*) Marketable securities | IV. Financing activity |

Choose the **correct** answer from the options given below:

| | (*a*) | (*b*) | (*c*) | (*d*) |
|---|---|---|---|---|
| A. | I | II | III | IV |
| B. | I | III | II | IV |
| C. | I | II | IV | III |
| D. | III | IV | I | II |

**23.** Which one of the following are correct in connection with the Common Size Statement?

(*a*) Expressed as a percentage on revenue from operation
(*b*) Horizontal analysis
(*c*) Vertical analysis
(*d*) Expressed as a percentage on total assets

Choose the **correct** answer from the options given below:

A. (*a*), (*b*) and (*d*) only
B. (*a*), (*b*) and (*c*) only
C. (*a*), (*c*) and (*d*) only
D. (*b*), (*c*) and (*d*) only

**24.** Calculate the resulting cash flow and state the nature of cash flow from the following information:

Acquired machinery for ₹ 3,50,000 by issuing cheque.

A. Investing activity and outflow ₹ 3,50,000
B. Investing activity and inflow ₹ 3,50,000
C. Investing activity and no flow
D. Operating activity and outflow ₹ 3,50,000

**25.** Arrange the following in proper sequence while preparing Cash Flow Statement:

(*a*) Net cash flow from operating activities
(*b*) Cash flow from financing activities
(*c*) Cash flow from investing activities
(*d*) Calculate net profit before tax and extraordinary items in working note

Choose the **correct** answer from the options given below:

A. (*a*), (*b*), (*c*), (*d*)  B. (*d*), (*a*), (*c*), (*b*)
C. (*b*), (*a*), (*d*), (*c*)  D. (*c*), (*b*), (*d*), (*a*)

**26.** The adjustment required for overvaluation of closing stock, while calculating adjusted profit for calculating goodwill is:

(*a*) reduction from concerned year's profit
(*b*) reduction from next year's profit
(*c*) addition to next year's profit
(*d*) addition to previous year's profit

Choose the **correct** answer from the options given below:

A. (*a*), (*b*) and (*d*) only  B. (*a*) and (*c*) only
C. (*a*) and (*d*) only  D. (*b*), (*c*) and (*d*) only

**27.** Oversubscription is a situation where the:

A. number of shares applied for is equal to the number of shares issued
B. number of shares applied for is more than the number of shares issued
C. number of shares applied for is less than the number of shares issued
D. face value of the share is less than the issue price of the share

| 20. C | 21. C | 22. D | 23. C | 24. A | 25. B | 26. B | 27. B |
|---|---|---|---|---|---|---|---|

**28.** 400 shares of ₹ 50 each issued at par were forfeited for non-payment of final call of ₹ 10 per share. These shares were reissued at ₹ 45 per share as fully paid-up. The amount transferred to capital reserve is:

A. ₹ 15,000 B. ₹ 14,000
C. ₹ 16,000 D. ₹ 13,000

**29.** When debentures are issued at a premium and redeemed at premium, the journal entry will have the following combination:

(*a*) Discount on issue of debentures account is credited
(*b*) Loss on issue of debentures account is debited
(*c*) Security premium account is credited
(*d*) Premium on redemption of debentures account is credited

Choose the **correct** answer from the options given below:

A. (*a*), (*b*) and (*d*) only
B. (*a*), (*b*) and (*c*) only
C. (*a*), (*b*), (*c*) and (*d*)
D. (*b*), (*c*) and (*d*) only

**30.** Match List-I with List-II.

| **List-I (Name of account to be debited or credited, when shares are forfeited)** | **List-II (Amount to be debited or credited)** |
|---|---|
| (*a*) Share Capital Account | I. Debited with amount not received |
| (*b*) Share Forfeited Account | II. Credited with amount not received |
| (*c*) Calls-in-arrears Account | III. Credited with amount received towards share capital |
| (*d*) Securities Premium Account | IV. Debited with amount called up |

Choose the **correct** answer from the options given below:

| | (*a*) | (*b*) | (*c*) | (*d*) |
|---|---|---|---|---|
| A. | I | II | III | IV |
| B. | IV | III | II | I |
| C. | I | II | IV | III |
| D. | III | IV | I | II |

**31.** Arrange the following in the correct sequence in the context of debenture.

(*a*) Payment to debenture-holders
(*b*) Creation of DRR
(*c*) Issue of debentures
(*d*) Redemption becomes due

Choose the **correct** answer from the options given below:

A. (*a*), (*b*), (*c*), (*d*) B. (*a*), (*c*), (*b*), (*d*)
C. (*b*), (*a*), (*d*), (*c*) D. (*c*), (*b*), (*d*), (*a*)

**32.** If a delay occurs beyond 8 days in refunding the subscription amount, failing to gather the minimum subscription, from the date of closure of the subscription list, the company shall be liable for interest at the rate of:

A. 15%
B. 12%
C. 6%
D. Prevailing in State Bank of India

**33.** A company can accept calls in advance, if authorised by:

A. Shareholders
B. Board of Directors
C. Articles of Association
D. Memorandum of Association

**34.** A, B and C are partners sharing profits in the ratio of 3 : 2 : 1. C died on 1st July, 2023. On this date, final accounts were prepared to ascertain profits for the period. It resulted in a profit of ₹ 1,75,000 to the firm. To give effect to the above:

A. Profit and Loss Account will be debited.
B. Profit and Loss Appropriation Account will be debited.
C. Profit and Loss Account will be credited.
D. Profit and Loss Appropriation Account will be credited.

**35.** On the date of admission of a partner there was a balance of ₹ 45,000 in the account of machinery. It was found undervalued by 10%. The value of machinery will appear in the new Balance Sheet at:

A. ₹ 49,500 B. ₹ 50,000
C. ₹ 40,000 D. ₹ 40,500

**36.** Dividend received is:

A. Operating activity
B. Financing activity
C. Investing activity
D. Cash and cash equivalents

**37.** A partnership can have maximum 50 partners. This limit has been set by the:

A. Indian Partnership Act, 1932
B. State Government
C. Indian Contract Act, 1872
D. Central Government

**28.** B **29.** D **30.** B **31.** D **32.** A **33.** C **34.** B **35.** B **36.** C **37.** D

**38.** Which of the following is an example of sequential code?

A. Using Code "CL001" for "Accounts of XYZ Ltd".
B. Using Code "100-199" for "Dealers of Small Pumps".
C. Using Code "SJ" for "Sales Journals".
D. Using Code "HQ" for "Headquarters".

**39.** If there is no claim against Workmen Compensation Reserve, it is __________ at the time of admission of a partner.

Fill in the blank with the **correct** answer from the options given below:

A. debited to old partners' capital account
B. credited to all partners' capital accounts
C. credited to old partners' capital accounts
D. debited to all partners' capital accounts

**40.** A, B and C are partners sharing profits in the ratio of 3 : 3 : 4. They decide to share the future profits equally. The sacrifice or gain of partners are:

A. A gains 1/30; B gains 1/30; C sacrifices 2/30
B. A gains 2/30; B gains 1/30; C sacrifices 3/30
C. A sacrifices 1/30; B gains 3/30; C sacrifices 2/30
D. A gains 2/30; B gains 3/30; C sacrifices 5/30

**41.** Match List-I with List-II.

| List-I (Equal amount of drawings made) | List-II (Number of month for which interest calculated) |
|---|---|
| (*a*) At the end of each half year | I. 4.5 months |
| (*b*) At the beginning of each quarter | II. 6.5 months |
| (*c*) At the beginning of each month | III. 7.5 months |
| (*d*) At the end of each quarter | IV. 3 months |

Choose the **correct** answer from the options given below:

| | (*a*) | (*b*) | (*c*) | (*d*) |
|---|---|---|---|---|
| A. | I | II | III | IV |
| B. | I | III | II | IV |
| C. | IV | II | I | III |
| D. | IV | III | II | I |

**42.** Kavita and Lalita are partners, sharing profits in the ratio of 2 : 1. They decide to admit Mohan for 1/4th share in future profits with a guaranteed amount of ₹ 25,000. Both Kavita and Lalita undertake to meet the liability arising due to the guaranteed amount to Mohan in their respective profit sharing ratio. The firm earned profits of ₹ 76,000 for the year 2022-23. The deficiency borne by Kavita is:

A. ₹ 4,000 B. ₹ 2,000
C. ₹ 6,000 D. ₹ 4,500

**43.** Anshu and Nitu are partners, sharing profits in the ratio of 3 : 2. They admitted Jyoti as a new partner for 3/10 share which she acquired 2/10 from Anshu and 1/10 from Nitu. Calculate the new profit sharing ratio of Anshu, Nitu and Jyoti.

A. 4 : 3 : 3 B. 3 : 4 : 3
C. 3 : 3 : 4 D. 3 : 2 : 1

**44.** The journal entry for treatment of goodwill, when a new partner brings his share of goodwill in cash and one of the old partners gains, involves the following:

(*a*) Gaining Partner's Capital Account is debited
(*b*) Premium for Goodwill Account is debited
(*c*) Sacrificing Partner's Capital Account is credited
(*d*) Gaining Partner's Capital Account is credited

Choose the **correct** answer from the options given below:

A. (*a*), (*b*) and (*d*) only
B. (*a*), (*b*) and (*c*) only
C. (*a*), (*b*), (*c*) and (*d*)
D. (*b*), (*c*) and (*d*) only

**45.** While preparing Cash Flow Statement, purchase of goodwill is treated as:

A. Operating activity B. Financing activity
C. Investing activity D. Extraordinary item

**46.** The components of Computerised Accounting System are:

A. Data, Report, Ledger, Hardware, Software
B. Data, People, Procedure, Hardware, Software
C. People, Procedure, Ledger, Data, Chart of Accounts
D. Data, Coding, Procedure, Rules, Output

**47.** The Sales and Accounts Receivable Subsystem deals with:

A. the recording of Sales, maintaining of Sales Ledger and Receivables
B. the preparation of Budget for the coming financial year
C. the preparation of Profit and Loss Account, Balance Sheet and Cash Flow Statement
D. the purchase and payment to creditors

**38.** A **39.** C **40.** A **41.** D **42.** A **43.** A **44.** B **45.** C **46.** B **47.** A

**48.** The common fields used in a relationship between tables are called:

A. Joint fields B. Main fields
C. Table fields D. Key fields

**49.** On dissolution of a firm, bank overdraft is transferred to:

A. Bank Account
B. Realisation Account
C. Partners' Capital Account
D. Partners' Loan Account

**50.** Arrange the following steps in the correct sequence of the life of a company:

(*a*) Commencement of Business
(*b*) Incorporation
(*c*) Promotion
(*d*) Floatation

Choose the **correct** answer from the options given below:

A. (*a*), (*b*), (*c*), (*d*) B. (*a*), (*c*), (*b*), (*d*)
C. (*b*), (*a*), (*d*), (*c*) D. (*c*), (*b*), (*d*), (*a*)

# EXPLANATORY ANSWERS

**1. (C):** The correct sequence for calculating cash flows from operating activities involves:

(*e*) First recognizing non-cash expenses and adjusting the operating profit accordingly. Goodwill amortised is such an expense that is added back to the operating profit as it does not involve cash outflow.

(*a*) Calculate the operating profit before working capital changes. This involves adjusting the initial operating profit with non-cash transactions and any gains or losses from investments and financing activities.

(*b*) Next, the adjustments for changes in working capital are made to arrive at the cash generated from operations. This step involves analyzing changes in inventory, receivables, and payables to determine the actual cash inflow or outflow from operations.

(*c*) Afterwards, the income tax paid is deducted as it represents a cash outflow that affects the net cash available from operating activities.

(*d*) Finally, the net cash flow from operating activities is calculated. This figure represents the total cash that the company has generated from its core business operations, after all adjustments and payments have been considered.

**2. (C):** The order of capital stages in a company is typically as follows:

(*c*) Authorised Capital is the maximum amount of share capital that a company is authorized to issue to shareholders. It sets the ceiling on how much can be raised via share issuance.

(*b*) Issued Capital is the portion of the authorised capital that is actually offered for sale to investors.

(*a*) Subscribed Capital is the portion of the issued capital that investors agree to purchase.

(*e*) Called-up Capital represents the amount of subscribed capital that the company has called upon the shareholders to deposit. It is not necessarily the full amount of subscribed capital.

(*d*) Paid-up Capital is the amount of called-up capital that has actually been paid by the shareholders. This is the actual capital that the company has received and can use.

**3. (B):** The Deceased Partner's Capital Account would include:

(*a*) The opening balance of his capital, representing his initial investment or the balance carried forward from the previous period.

(*b*) His share of profit or loss till the date of death, which adjusts his capital account for any earnings or losses incurred during the period he was active in the business up to his date of death.

(*c*) His share of General Reserve, which allocates a portion of the reserve profits to his account based on his ownership percentage at the time of death.

(*d*) His drawings till the date of death, which represents any amounts withdrawn from the business by the partner before his death, reducing his capital account.

(*e*) The amount paid to his executors is not included, as it refers to the actual disbursement from the partnership to settle the deceased partner's account, which is a transaction outside the capital account itself.

**4. (A): Net Credit Sales:** The Revenue from Operations is likely to represent the Net Credit Sales, assuming all are Credit Sales. Thus,

Net Credit Sales = 8,75,000

| **48.** D | **49.** A, B | **50.** D |
|---|---|---|

**Average Trade Receivables:** This should include both Trade Debtors and Bills Receivable, and if we had opening balances, it would be the average of the opening and closing balances. However, since we only have the ending balances:

1. Trade Debtors = 59,000
2. Bills Receivable = 48,000
3. Total Trade Receivables
   = 59,000 + 48,000 = 107,000

Given that we're using only the ending balance (in the absence of the opening balance), we will use this sum as our Average Trade Receivables for the calculation.

Thus, Average Trade Receivables = 107,000

Now, calculate the ratio:

Trade Receivables Turnover Ratio

$$= \frac{8,75,000}{107,000} \approx 8.18$$

This adjusted ratio of 8.18 means the receivables turnover happened approximately 8.18 times during the period, indicating how often the combined trade debtors and bills receivable are converted into cash or sales within the year. This is a more accurate reflection of the credit management efficiency.

**5. (C):** The Average Collection Period represents the average number of days taken by a company to collect its receivables from customers. It can be calculated using the formula:

Average Collection Period

$$= \frac{365}{\text{Trade Receivables Turnover Ratio}}$$

From the previous question, the Trade Receivables Turnover Ratio was found to be 8.18 times. Therefore, the calculation is:

$$\text{Average Collection Period} = \frac{365}{8.18} \approx 44.62 \text{ days}$$

This value rounds to approximately 45 days, which correlates with option C, indicating that on average, the company collects its receivables in about 45 days.

**6. (B):** The Trade Payables Turnover Ratio is a measure of how often a company pays off its suppliers in a year. It is calculated as follows:

Trade Payables Turnover Ratio

$$= \frac{\text{Purchases}}{\text{Average Trade Payables}}$$

Where:

- Purchases = 420,000.
- Average Trade Payables = 90000 + 52000 = 142,000

So, Trade Payables Turnover Ratio

$$= \frac{420,000}{142,000} \approx 2.96 \text{ times.}$$

**7. (A):** The Average Payment Period is calculated to determine the average number of days a company takes to pay its suppliers. The formula used is:

Average Payment Period

$$= \frac{365}{\text{Trade Payables Turnover Ratio}}$$

Assuming the Trade Payables Turnover Ratio is 2.96 times as determined is question 6, the calculation would be:

$$\text{Average Payment Period} = \frac{365}{2.96} \approx 123.31 \text{ days}$$

This rounds off to 123 days, which is option A, indicating the company pays its suppliers on average every 123 days.

**8. (C):** Trade Receivables Turnover Ratio and Trade Payables Turnover Ratio are classified under financial metrics that measure how efficiently a company manages its working capital and short-term operational efficiency. Both ratios are categorized as:

- Activity Ratios, which assess the effectiveness of a company's use of its assets.

This matches with option C, highlighting that these ratios are crucial for analyzing the company's operational performance in terms of asset management and operational efficiency.

**9. (A):** The mode of dissolution followed by G, K, and B is referred to as "Dissolution by Agreement." This method occurs when all partners mutually agree to terminate the partnership. The scenario describes that due to continuous losses, all partners decided to dissolve the firm on 31st March, 2023, which aligns with a dissolution based on a mutual agreement among the partners.

**10. (B):** To find the amount in the Profit and Loss Account, calculate the balance needed to equate the assets with the sum of liabilities and partners' capital. The sum of the capital accounts is 900,000 (400,000 + 300,000 + 200,000), and the total liabilities are 80,000, making a combined total of 980,000. The assets, including cash (40,000) and sundry assets (850,000), total 890,000. The P&L Account balance is derived by subtracting the total assets from the combined total of liabilities and capital:

P&L Account = 890,000 – 980,000 = –90,000.

This indicates a deficit or a debit balance of 90,000 in the P&L Account, which is in line with option B.

11. **(A):** To calculate the Gain or Loss on Realisation, compare the book values of assets against their realised values:

- Total book value of assets: 890,000 (cash of 40,000 + sundry assets of 850,000)
- Assets realised at 80% of book value: 680,000 (850,000 × 80%)
- Realisation expenses : 30,000

Loss on Realisation

= Book Value of Assets − Realised Value of Assets + Realisation expenses

= 890,000 − 680,000 + 30000 = 240,000.

12. **(B):** The entry to record realisation expenses paid by G on behalf of the firm is:

Realisation A/c Dr

To G's Capital A/c

This accounting entry is correct as it shows that the expense has been borne by G and thus increases his capital account while the Realisation Account reflects the cost associated with dissolving the firm. This matches option B.

13. **(A):** Existing balances in the Profit and Loss Account should be shared by the partners according to the agreed profit-sharing ratio, which is 5 : 3 : 2. This sharing ratio is typically applied to any accumulated profits or losses unless specified otherwise. Since the partners agreed to share profits and losses in this ratio, it applies to the P&L Account balances as well, confirming option A as correct.

14. **(B):** Libraries run by charitable trusts do not operate for profit but aim to serve the community, typically relying on donations, grants, and volunteer support rather than selling goods or services for profit. Such organizations are designed to provide public benefits and are usually registered as "Not for Profit Organizations," which fits the description given in the question. This differentiates them from partnerships, companies, and cooperatives, which are structured to generate profits or serve their members' specific interests.

15. **(C):** The main source of revenue for 'not for profit' organizations typically includes donations, grants, and subscriptions from members. Since the question specifies a regular, recurring source of revenue directly related to the organization's members, subscriptions are the most fitting answer. Subscriptions are payments made by members to support the organization's activities and services, aligning with option C.

16. **(D):** Matching List-I with List-II involves identifying the correct financial terminology:

(*a*) **Share capital:** This is the capital raised by a company through the issue of shares. The correct match would be "Subscribed but not fully paid" since share capital often includes amounts that have been subscribed by shareholders but not yet paid in full.

(*b*) **Reserves and surplus:** These are accumulated earnings, generally retained within the company to strengthen the financial structure or for specific purposes. A common use of reserves is a sinking fund (for debt repayment, asset replacement, etc.), matching with "Sinking fund."

(*c*) **Reserve capital:** This is a portion of the authorized capital which has not been called up and is available to be called up only in the event of liquidation, matching with "Will be called at the time of winding up."

(*d*) **Current liabilities:** These are short-term liabilities that are due within a year and not related to calls in advance. Therefore, the available options do not perfectly match typical financial definitions for current liabilities, suggesting a potential error or unconventional terminology usage.

17. **(A):** The Revaluation Account in a partnership is used during the reconstitution of a firm (like the admission of a new partner, retirement, or death of a partner) to adjust the book values of assets and liabilities to their fair market values. An "Increase in assets" would lead to a credit in the Revaluation Account, reflecting an increase in the firm's net assets. This revaluation does not affect other items like drawings against capital, interest on capital, or partner's salary, as these relate to the distribution or expenses of capital rather than asset valuation. Thus, an increase in assets directly impacts the Revaluation Account, matching with option A.

18. **(A):** The correct sequence for preparing the final accounts of a partnership firm starts with the Trading Account, where the firm calculates its gross profit or loss. Following this, the Profit and Loss Account is prepared to determine the net profit or loss by accounting for all other expenses and revenues. Next, the Profit and Loss Appropriation Account is prepared, where the net profit or loss is distributed according to the partnership agreement. Finally, the Balance Sheet is prepared to show the financial position of the firm. Thus, the sequence is:

(*c*) Trading Account

(*b*) Profit and Loss Account

(*a*) Profit and Loss Appropriation Account

(*d*) Balance Sheet

**19.** **(A):** Window dressing refers to the practice of presenting company accounts in a manner that makes the financial position of the company appear stronger than it actually is, typically by manipulating figures to enhance financial statements temporarily. This might involve shifting deadlines, unrealistically high valuations for inventory, or other such methods to embellish the financial results. Option A correctly describes this practice.

**20.** **(C):** Matching the financial terms with their respective account entries:

(*a*) Salary to partner is typically credited to the Partner's Capital Account to reflect an increase due to salary.

(*b*) Interest on partner's loan is debited from the Profit and Loss Account as it is an expense to the firm.

(*c*) Interest on partner's drawings is debited to the Partner's Current Account, representing a charge against the partner for drawing funds.

(*d*) Additional capital introduced by a partner increases the partner's stake in the firm and is credited to the Partner's Capital Account.

**21.** **(C):** When a new partner is admitted into a partnership, the Revaluation Account is impacted by changes that directly affect the valuation of the firm's assets and liabilities:

(*a*) Increase in assets increases the total value in the Revaluation Account.

(*c*) Recording of unrecorded assets also increases the value in the Revaluation Account as these assets were previously not accounted for.

(*d*) Decrease in liabilities effectively increases the firm's net assets, reflected as a credit in the Revaluation Account.

Option C is correct as it includes all changes that directly impact the firm's valuation through the Revaluation Account, without including (*b*) Drawings against capital, which does not affect the Revaluation Account.

**22.** **(D):** The correct classification of each item under cash flow activities can be identified as follows:

(*a*) Purchase of tangible assets is an Investing activity since it involves acquiring long-term assets.

(*b*) Issue of shares is a Financing activity because it relates to transactions involving equity or long-term liabilities.

(*c*) Increase in current assets does not directly correspond to any of the given types of activities. Typically, changes in current assets are considered under Operating activities if they relate to changes in working capital, but this is not listed in the options.

(*d*) Marketable securities can be classified as cash and cash equivalents or sold.

**23.** **(C):** Common Size Statements are financial tools used in analysis to see each line item as a percentage of a common figure:

(*a*) Expressed as a percentage on revenue from operation is a method used in common size income statements to show each income and expense as a proportion of total revenue.

(*c*) Vertical analysis is another term for the method described in (*a*), where each item on the financial statement is listed as a percentage of another item (typically sales for the income statement and total assets for the balance sheet).

(*d*) Expressed as a percentage on total assets is commonly used in the common size balance sheet, where each asset, liability, and equity item is shown relative to total assets.

Option C correctly includes (*a*), (*c*), and (*d*) as components of common size statements, emphasizing the use of percentages to standardize financial statements for comparison.

**24.** **(A):** Acquiring machinery by issuing a cheque for 3,50,000 is an Investing activity because it involves the purchase of a long-term asset. The cash flow associated with this transaction is an outflow because cash is paid out to acquire the machinery. The nature of this transaction does not involve any inflow or operational cash flow; hence, the correct answer is:

- Investing activity and outflow of 3,50,000.

**25.** **(B):** The proper sequence for preparing a Cash Flow Statement begins with:

(*d*) Calculate net profit before tax and extraordinary items in working notes to adjust for non-cash transactions and changes in working capital.

(*a*) Net cash flow from operating activities, derived from the net profit before tax adjusted for changes in working capital and other non-cash charges.

(*c*) Cash flow from investing activities, where cash flows from the purchase and sale of long-term assets are recorded.

(*b*) Cash flow from financing activities, which includes cash flows related to changes in equity and long-term debts.

This sequence allows for the systematic preparation of a cash flow statement, ensuring that all relevant cash flows are correctly recorded and classified. Option B is the correct sequence reflecting this process.

**26. (B):** When there is an overvaluation of closing stock, it artificially inflates the profit for that year. To adjust for the overvaluation while calculating adjusted profit for goodwill:

(*a*) Reduce from the concerned year's profit because the overvaluation affected that year's reported profit by making it higher than it should have been.

(*c*) Addition to next year's profit because the starting stock of the next year would be overvalued, needing a correction to reduce the profit impact it initially caused.

The correct answer, which accounts for the adjustments necessary in both the year of overvaluation and the following year, is therefore (*a*) and (*c*), corresponding to option B.

**27. (B):** Oversubscription in terms of share issuance occurs when the number of shares applied for exceeds the number of shares issued. This indicates a higher demand than the available supply of shares. Option B correctly describes this situation.

**29. (D):** When debentures are issued at a premium and redeemed at a premium, the accounting entries should reflect the premium transactions:

(*b*) Loss on issue of debentures account would be debited if the issuance expenses exceed the premium received.

(*c*) Securities premium account is credited when debentures are issued at a premium, representing the excess over their face value.

(*d*) Premium on redemption of debentures account is credited to recognize the additional amount payable over the face value at the time of redemption.

Option D, which includes (*b*), (*c*), and (*d*), correctly matches these entries.

**30. (B):** Matching the accounts with their correct treatment when shares are forfeited involves understanding the flow of funds and entries:

(*a*) Share Capital Account is debited with the amount called up on the forfeited shares.

(*b*) Share Forfeited Account is credited with the amount received towards share capital, representing the forfeiture of shares.

(*c*) Calls-in-arrears Account is credited with the amount not received, representing amounts due but unpaid at forfeiture.

(*d*) Securities Premium Account, if relevant to the share transaction, might be debited or credited based on the scenario, but it is typically related to amounts above the par value received during initial issuance.

The arrangement in option B aligns correctly with these typical account treatments.

**31. (D):** The correct sequence in the context of debentures involves:

(*c*) **Issue of debentures:** This is the first step where the company issues debentures to the public or private investors.

(*b*) **Creation of DRR (Debenture Redemption Reserve):** This is a reserve created out of profits for the purpose of redeeming debentures in the future, a requirement after issuing debentures.

(*d*) **Redemption becomes due:** This step marks the point when the redemption of debentures is scheduled according to the terms of issue.

(*a*) **Payment to debenture-holders:** This is the final step where actual payment is made to the debenture holders upon redemption.

Option D correctly orders these steps, showing the typical lifecycle of debentures from issuance to redemption.

**32. (A):** If a delay occurs beyond 8 days in refunding the subscription amount after failing to gather the minimum subscription, the company is legally bound to pay interest. As per the current regulatory framework, the company shall pay interest at 15% per annum. This is aimed at compensating investors for the delay in the refund of their subscription money.

**33. (C):** A company can accept calls in advance if authorized by its Articles of Association. The Articles of Association define the rules regarding the management of the company's internal affairs and its relationship with shareholders, including the handling of share capital such as calls in advance.

**34. (B):** When a partner dies, and the final accounts are prepared to ascertain profits for the period, adjustments related to profit allocation to deceased partner's account are made via the Profit and Loss Appropriation Account. This account deals with the distribution of profits among partners including any adjustments due to changes in the partnership such as the death of a partner. Therefore, the Profit and Loss Appropriation Account will be debited to allocate the share of profits up to the date of the partner's death, aligning with option B.

**35. (B):** On the date of admission of a new partner, if it was found that the machinery was undervalued by 10%, the correct revalued amount of the machinery would be calculated as follows:

- Original value = ₹ 45,000

- Undervaluation by 10% means it was 90% of the actual value, so:

$$\text{Actual Value} = \frac{45,000}{0.9} = ₹\ 50,000$$

Thus, in the new Balance Sheet post-revaluation, the value of the machinery will appear at ₹ 50,000, which corresponds to option B.

**36. (C):** Dividend received from investments in other companies is typically classified as an Investing activity. This is because it represents returns on investments made by the company in the equity of other companies. It is related to the income generated from investing capital, not from the primary operations or financing activities of the company. Therefore, the correct answer is option C.

**37. (D):** The limit of having a maximum of 50 partners in a partnership is set by the Companies Act, which is under the jurisdiction of the Central Government. The Indian Partnership Act, 1932, originally did not impose a strict upper limit on the number of partners, but amendments and provisions under the Companies Act have set this limit to manage the organizational structure and legal responsibilities more effectively. Therefore, the correct answer is option D.

**38. (A):** Sequential code typically involves a system where each item or category is labeled in a sequential format that follows a numerical or systematic series. Using Code "CL001" for "Accounts of XYZ Ltd" represents a sequential coding system where the code can continue as CL002, CL003, etc., for similar or related categories, thus making option A the correct example of a sequential code.

**39. (C):** If there is no claim against the Workmen Compensation Reserve at the time of the admission of a new partner, the reserve is usually distributed among the existing (old) partners since it was created during their tenure and not involving the new partner. This distribution would be credited to the old partners' capital accounts, effectively transferring the reserve into their capital and adjusting the equity according to the rights and contributions of the existing partners. Thus, the correct answer is option C.

**40. (A):** To calculate the gains and sacrifices of partners when changing their profit-sharing ratio, compare the old and new ratios:

- Old Ratio: A = 3/10, B = 3/10, C = 4/10
- New Ratio (equal sharing): A = 1/3, B = 1/3, C = 1/3

Calculate the difference in their shares to find gains and sacrifices:

- A's old share = 3/10, new share = 1/3 (or 3.33/10), gain = 0.33/10 = 1/30
- B's old share = 3/10, new share = 1/3, gain = 1/30
- C's old share = 4/10, new share = 1/3 (or 3.33/10), sacrifice = 0.67/10 = 2/30

Therefore, A and B each gain 1/30, while C sacrifices 2/30, making option A correct.

**41. (D):** To determine the number of months for which interest on drawings should be calculated based on the timing of the drawings:

(*a*) Drawings made at the end of each half year will have an average period for interest calculation of approximately 3 months, considering the mid-point of the period over which the interest accumulates.

(*b*) Drawings made at the beginning of each quarter will accumulate interest over approximately 7.5 months, considering three-quarters of a year (since interest starts accumulating from the beginning of the quarter).

(*c*) Drawings made at the beginning of each month would accrue interest for an average period of 6.5 months, taking into account the time from the start of the year to the midpoint of the 12 months.

(*d*) Drawings at the end of each quarter would have interest calculated for approximately 4.5 months, considering that the drawings would have three months till the next quarter plus additional time till the year-end.

**42. (A):** To determine the deficiency borne by Kavita due to the guaranteed amount:

- Total profit: ₹ 76,000
- Mohan's share (1/4th): ₹ 19,000
- Guaranteed amount: ₹ 25,000
- Deficiency: 25,000 – 19,000 = ₹ 6,000

Kavita and Lalita share the deficiency in their profit sharing ratio (2 : 1):

- Kavita's portion: 2/3 of 6,000 = 4,000

Kavita bears a deficiency of ₹ 4,000, aligning with option A.

**43. (A):** Anshu and Nitu shared profits in a 3:2 ratio and admitted Jyoti for a 3/10 share. Anshu and Nitu's remaining shares after Jyoti's acquisition:

- Anshu's old share: 3/5 – 2/10 (transferred to Jyoti) = 3/5 – 1/5 = 2/5
- Nitu's old share: 2/5 - 1/10 (transferred to Jyoti) = 2/5 – 1/10 = 3/10

Converting into a common denominator:

- Anshu: 4/10 • Nitu: 3/10 • Jyoti: 3/10

The new profit-sharing ratio of Anshu, Nitu, and Jyoti becomes 4:3:3, which is option A.

**44. (B):**

(*a*) **Gaining Partner's Capital Account is debited:** The new partner brings in cash as goodwill, which benefits the existing partners. To reflect this in the books, the capital account of the gaining partner (the one who benefits more from the new arrangement) is debited. This reduces their capital account to balance the benefit they receive from the goodwill.

(*b*) **Premium for Goodwill Account is debited:** When the new partner brings in goodwill in cash, this amount is first recorded as a premium for goodwill. This account is debited because it represents an asset coming into the business.

(*c*) **Sacrificing Partner's Capital Account is credited:** The existing partners who sacrifice a portion of their share to accommodate the new partner need to be compensated. Their capital accounts are credited to reflect this compensation.

**45. (C):** In the preparation of the Cash Flow Statement, the purchase of goodwill is classified as an Investing activity. This classification is because purchasing goodwill relates to acquiring long-term assets that are expected to generate future economic benefits. It is not related to the primary revenue-generating activities (Operating) nor to financing transactions. Thus, option C is correct.

**46. (B):** The components of a Computerised Accounting System include:

- **Data:** The raw financial information that needs to be processed.
- **People:** Users who interact with the system to input, process, and use the data.
- **Procedure:** The methods and processes used for handling and processing the data.
- **Hardware:** The physical devices like computers and servers on which the system runs.
- **Software:** The applications and programs that execute the accounting tasks.

This comprehensive approach ensures all aspects of a computerized accounting environment are covered, fitting with option B.

**47. (A):** The Sales and Accounts Receivable Subsystem primarily focuses on:

- **Recording of sales:** Capturing all sales transactions as they occur.
- **Maintaining the Sales Ledger:** Keeping track of all sales-related entries and their respective accounts.
- **Receivables:** Managing and tracking amounts owed by customers who have purchased goods on credit.

This subsystem ensures accurate recording and monitoring of sales and related receivables, aligning with option A.

**48. (D):** In database management, especially concerning relationships between tables, the common fields used to link tables are referred to as:

- **Key fields:** These are fields that serve as primary identifiers in one table and are used to establish connections or relationships with corresponding fields in another table, ensuring data consistency and integrity.

Key fields play a crucial role in maintaining relationships within a database, making option D correct.

**49. (A, B):**

(A) The Bank Account is used to handle all cash transactions during the normal operations of the business and also during the dissolution process. When assets are sold and liabilities are paid off during dissolution, these transactions are conducted through the Bank Account.

(B) On the dissolution of a firm, the bank overdraft is transferred to the Realisation Account. The Realisation Account is used to account for all the assets and liabilities of the firm during the dissolution process. It helps in determining the net gain or loss on realization, which is then distributed among the partners.

**50. (D):** The correct sequence in the life of a company involves:

(*c*) **Promotion:** Where the idea for the company is developed and initial capital gathering and planning occur.

(*b*) **Incorporation:** The legal process where the company is formally registered and recognized as a corporate entity.

(*d*) **Floatation:** Where shares are offered to the public, and the company begins to raise funds from investors.

(*a*) **Commencement of Business:** Once the necessary capital is raised, and legal formalities are completed, the company officially starts its business operations.

These stages follow the typical lifecycle from conceptualization to the actual start of business operations, correctly outlined in option D.

# GENERAL TEST

**1.** From the given options, which pass connects Jammu with Srinagar?

A. Banihal Pass
B. Nathu La Pass
C. Niti Pass
D. Rohtang Pass

**2.** Which of the following is not correctly matched regarding Padma Awards-2024?

A. Padma Vibhushan Award → Shri Konidela Chiranjeevi
B. Padma Shri Award → Mithun Chakraborty
C. Padma Bhushan Award → M. Fathima Beevi
D. Padma Bhushan Award → Sitaram Jindal

**3.** Match List-I with List-II.

| List-I (Person) | List-II (Area of Work) |
|---|---|
| (*a*) Vishakhadatta | I. Medicine |
| (*b*) Kartikeya Sarabhai | II. Poet |
| (*c*) Charaka | III. Environmentalist |
| (*d*) Satyendra Nath Bose | IV. Mathematics |

Choose the **correct** answer from the options given below:

| | (*a*) | (*b*) | (*c*) | (*d*) |
|---|---|---|---|---|
| A. | I | III | IV | II |
| B. | II | III | I | IV |
| C. | II | I | III | IV |
| D. | III | IV | I | II |

**4.** If $\sin A = \frac{4}{5}$, then $(3 - \tan A)(2 + \cos A) = ?$

A. $\frac{12}{5}$
B. $\frac{13}{3}$
C. $\frac{13}{5}$
D. 3

**5.** A man can row a boat at 8 km/h in still water. If the speed of the water current is 2 km/h and it takes him 2 hours to row to a place and come back, then how far off (in km) is the place?

A. 7.5
B. 6
C. 9.5
D. 10

**6.** The following states were formed after 1960. What was the correct sequence of their formation?

(*a*) Haryana
(*b*) Sikkim
(*c*) Nagaland
(*d*) Goa

Choose the **correct** answer from the options given below:

A. (*c*), (*b*), (*a*), (*d*)
B. (*c*), (*a*), (*b*), (*d*)
C. (*c*), (*d*), (*a*), (*b*)
D. (*d*), (*c*), (*a*), (*b*)

**7.** Out of the given options, which scheme's objective is to conduct an annual survey at the gram panchayat level to monitor the progress in the development process of the rural areas?

A. Mission Antyodaya (2022-23)
B. Mission Karmayogi (2022-23)
C. Mission Rashtriya Gokul (2022-23)
D. Mission Atmanirbhar Bharat (2022-23)

**8.** Which one of the following countries is **not** a member of the "Quadrilateral Security Dialogue", also known as "QUAD"?

A. China
B. Japan
C. India
D. Australia

**9.** Who has become the first woman chairperson of the Railway Board of India Railways in 2023?

A. Jaya Verma Sinha
B. Mita Vashishth
C. Ravneet Kaur
D. Vasudha Gupta

**10.** Match List-I with List-II.

| List-I (Country) | List-II (Currency) |
|---|---|
| (*a*) Myanmar | I. Ruble |
| (*b*) Russia | II. Ngultrum |
| (*c*) Malaysia | III. Kyat |
| (*d*) Bhutan | IV. Ringgit |

Choose the **correct** answer from the options given below:

| | (*a*) | (*b*) | (*c*) | (*d*) |
|---|---|---|---|---|
| A. | III | I | II | IV |
| B. | III | I | IV | II |
| C. | IV | I | III | II |
| D. | II | I | IV | III |

**1.** A **2.** B **3.** B **4.** B **5.** A **6.** B **7.** A **8.** A **9.** A **10.** B

**11.** "Jhulaghat Suspension Bridge" between India and which country has become fully operational now?

A. Bhutan B. Nepal
C. China D. Myanmar

**12.** Due to ocean acidification when the ocean becomes more acidic, what happens to the pH level of the ocean?

A. The pH level goes down.
B. The pH level stays the same.
C. The pH level goes up.
D. The pH level becomes zero.

**13.** Who is the first para-athlete to receive the Padma Bhushan award in India?

A. Bhavina Patel
B. Devendra Jhajharia
C. Avani Lekhara
D. Mariyappan Thangavelu

**14.** Zemu Glacier is located in which state of India?

A. Uttarakhand
B. Himachal Pradesh
C. Sikkim
D. Arunachal Pradesh

**15.** Who among the following is Chile's first woman President?

A. Mary Robinson
B. Michelle Bachelet
C. Kim Campbell
D. Jennifer Shipley

**16.** Which organisation developed and launched 'Ugram' Indigenous Assault Rifle for the armed forces?

A. ISRO B. BEL
C. HAL D. DRDO

**17.** Which of the following substances is a bad conductor of electricity?

A. Diamond
B. Gold
C. Silver
D. Graphite

**18.** Which of the following disease is caused due to the deficiency of proteins?

A. Arthritis
B. Kwashiorkor
C. Goitre
D. Night Blindness

**19.** Match List-I with List-II

| List-I (Navy–Institution) | List-II (Place) |
|---|---|
| (*a*) INS Chilka | I. Goa |
| (*b*) INS Hansa | II. Andhra Pradesh |
| (*c*) INS Satavahana | III. Kerala |
| (*d*) INS Garuda | IV. Odisha |

Choose the **correct** answer from the options given below:

| | (*a*) | (*b*) | (*c*) | (*d*) |
|---|---|---|---|---|
| A. | III | I | II | IV |
| B. | I | IV | II | III |
| C. | IV | I | III | II |
| D. | IV | I | II | III |

**20.** DRDO has conducted the first successful flight test of Agni-5 missile equipped with MIRV technology. What is the full form of MIRV?

A. Multiple Independently Targetable Re-Entry Vehicle
B. Mission India Target Re-Entry Vehicle
C. Multiple Independently Technology Re-Entry Vehicle
D. Multiple Indirect Targetable Re-Entry Vehicle

**21.** Which Indian has won the "Ramon Magsaysay Award-2023"?

A. Korvi Rakshand
B. Ashwini Kumar
C. Dipti Ranjan Sahoo
D. Dr. Ravi Kannan R.

**22.** Who has been appointed the Chairman of the 16th Finance Commission of India?

A. Ajay Narayan Jha
B. Smt. Annie George Mathew
C. Pradip Kumar Mohanty
D. Dr. Arvind Panagariya

**23.** Sri Ranganathswamy Temple which is situated in Tamil Nadu, is dedicated to which deity?

A. Lord Shiva B. Lord Vishnu
C. Goddess Durga D. Goddess Lakshmi

**24.** The Election Commission of India gets the power to conduct elections from which of the following articles?

A. Article 324 B. Article 280
C. Article 264 D. Article 26

| | | | | | | | |
|---|---|---|---|---|---|---|---|
| **11.** B | **12.** A | **13.** B | **14.** C | **15.** B | **16.** D | **17.** A | **18.** B |
| **19.** D | **20.** A | **21.** D | **22.** D | **23.** B | **24.** A | | |

**25.** Match List-I with List-II.

| List-I (Centre of Handicraft) | List-II (State) |
|---|---|
| (*a*) Mon | I. Arunachal Pradesh |
| (*b*) Nalbari | II. Assam |
| (*c*) Pasighat | III. Meghalaya |
| (*d*) Tura | IV. Nagaland |

Choose the **correct** answer from the options given below:

| | (*a*) | (*b*) | (*c*) | (*d*) |
|---|---|---|---|---|
| A. | IV | II | I | III |
| B. | I | III | IV | II |
| C. | IV | III | I | II |
| D. | I | II | IV | III |

**26.** In which state is "Amchang Wildlife Sanctuary" located?

A. Assam B. Rajasthan
C. Odisha D. Manipur

**27.** India's first 3-D printed Post Office has been inaugurated in:

A. Guwahati B. Kolkata
C. Mumbai D. Bengaluru

**28.** What should come in the place of the questions mark (?) in the following alphanumeric series?

A1X, B4P, E25J, J100F, ?

A. O289D B. O225E
C. Q289D D. Q225E

**29.** In the given analogy, choose the word which will replace the question mark :

NEGI : MVTR :: SING : ?

A. TRNS B. TRNT
C. FRMT D. HRMT

**30.** In a certain code language 'ki ru pi' means 'nobody like cruel', 'ki mi cha' means 'king was cruel' and 'ru pi cha' means 'nobody like king'. What is the code for 'was' in the given code language?

A. ki B. mi
C. cha D. ru

**31.** Read the following information carefully to choose the best option for the question:

'P % Q' means that 'P is the sister of Q'
'P + Q' means that 'P is the son of Q'
'P × Q' means that 'P is the husband of Q'
'P – Q' means that 'P is the brother of Q'

Which of the following means 'A is the son-in-law of G'?

A. A × U + S × G
B. A + S % U × G
C. A – S + U × G
D. A × U % S + G

**32.** If 26th January, 2020 was a Sunday, then what day of the week was it on 16th March of that year?

A. Sunday B. Monday
C. Tuesday D. Wednesday

**33.** What will be the measurement of the angle made by the hour and minute hands of a clock when the time is 'quarter past 3'?

A. $6\frac{1}{2}^\circ$ B. $10^\circ$
C. $7\frac{1}{2}^\circ$ D. $8\frac{1}{2}^\circ$

**34.** If in a certain code language, 'MERCURY' is coded as 'NGUGZXF', then how will 'ENTANGLE' be coded in the same code language?

A. FPXFSMSM B. FPWESMSM
C. FPWESNSN D. FPWFTNSM

**35.** The problem given below consists of a question and two statements numbered I and II. You have to decide whether the data provided in the statements are sufficient to answer the question.

How many sisters does Sunny have?

I. Sunny is the only son of his parents.
II. Sunny's parents have three children.

A. Only statement I alone is sufficient to answer the question.
B. Only statement II alone is sufficient to answer the question.
C. Statements I and II together are sufficient to answer the question.
D. Either statement I or II alone is sufficient to answer the questions.

**36.** A boy leaves his house. He travels 6 km towards South, then travels 8 km towards West and further travels 9 km towards South. How far and in which direction is he from his house now?

A. 13 km, South West
B. 17 km, South West
C. 17 km, North West
D. 13 km, West

**25.** A **26.** A **27.** D **28.** C **29.** D **30.** B **31.** D **32.** B **33.** C **34.** B **35.** C **36.** B

**37.** Find out which of the answer figures completes the figure matrix:

**Problem figure:**

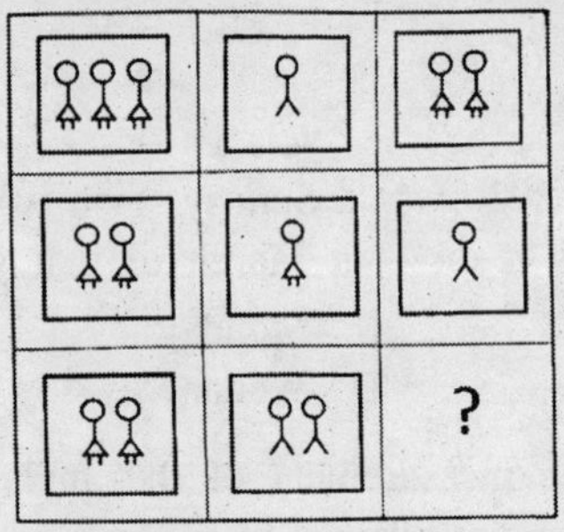

A.  B. 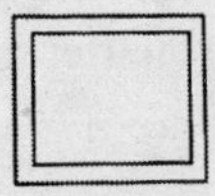

C.  D. 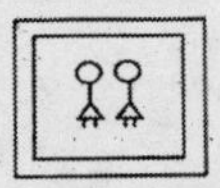

**38.** A clock seen through a mirror shows 'quarter to seven'. What is the correct time shown by the clock?

A. 6:15 B. 6:17

C. 5:17 D. 5:15

**39.** The sequence of folding a piece of paper and the manner in which the folded paper has been cut is shown in the following figures. How would this paper look when unfolded?

A. 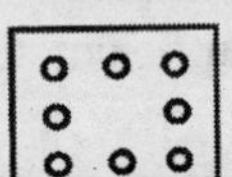 B. 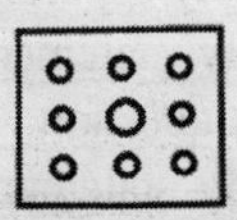

C. 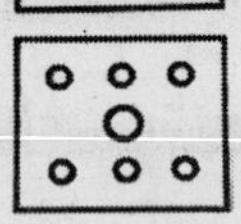 D. 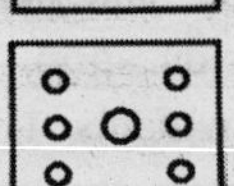

**40.** Find out the missing (?) number and letter.

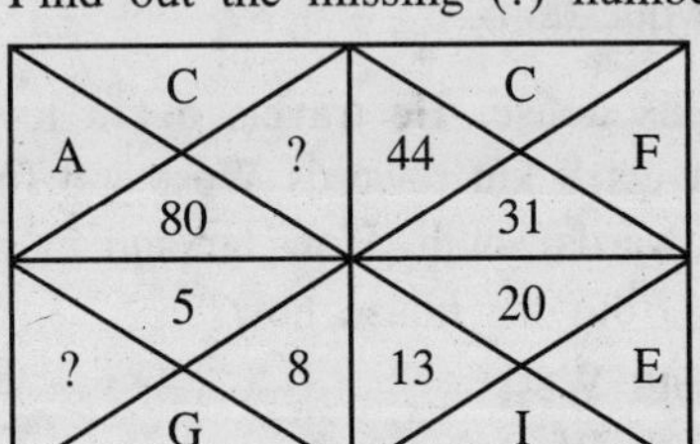


A. 59 and K B. 61 and L

C. 61 and K D. 59 and L

**41.** What will be the next number of the series

3, 6, 10.5, 17, 26, ?

A. 31 B. 38

C. 40 D. 41

**42.** In a class of 40 students, Anjali's rank is thrice that of Anita. There are 4 students who have ranks worse than that of Anjali. Anita's rank in the class is:

A. 9th B. 10th

C. 18th D. 12th

**43.** Six people E, H, K, M, S and U are seated in a circle facing the centre. U and H are immediate neighbours of M. E is the only person sitting between K and S. H is to the immediate right of S. Who is to the immediate right of U?

A. M B. E

C. K D. S

**44.** Find out which of the answer figures from the options can be formed using all the pieces given in the problem figure.

**Problem figure**

A.  B. 

C.  D. 

**45.** Read the given statements and conclusions carefully assuming that the information given in the statements is true, even if it appears to be at variance with commonly known facts. Decide which of the given conclusion(s) logically follows from the statements.

**Statements:**

No keyboard is a mouse

All mouses are computers.

All computers are laptops.

**Conclusions:**

I. All mouses are laptops.

II. All computers can never be keyboards.

A. Only conclusion I follows

B. Only conclusion II follows

C. Neither conclusion I nor II follows

D. Both conclusions I and II follow

| **37.** B | **38.** D | **39.** B | **40.** B | **41.** B | **42.** D | **43.** C | **44.** C | **45.** D |
|---|---|---|---|---|---|---|---|---|

**46.** Simplify: $24 \div 4 \times 2 + 8 - 4 = ?$

A. 1 B. 7
C. 16 D. 56

**47.** The difference of the greatest and the smallest of the fractions $\frac{1}{2}, \frac{8}{11}, \frac{7}{8}, \frac{7}{9}, \frac{5}{6}$ is:

A. $\frac{3}{8}$ B. $\frac{6}{7}$
C. $\frac{7}{9}$ D. $\frac{1}{3}$

**48.** The sum of LCM and HCF of two numbers is 854. If the LCM is 60 times the HCF and one of the numbers is 70, then the other number is:

A. 160 B. 164
C. 168 D. 172

**49.** The present age of Harish is 8 times the sum of the ages of his two sons at present. After 8 years, his age will be 2 times the sum of the ages of his two sons. The present age of Harish (in years) is:

A. 31 B. 32
C. 33 D. 34

**50.** In an examination, it is required to get 300 marks to pass. A student gets 225 marks and is declared fail by 10% marks. What are the maximum marks of the examinations?

A. 700 B. 750
C. 800 D. 850

**51.** In a class of 40 students, ratio of boys and girls is 3 : 2 and the average marks scored by boys is 42 and that by girls is 46. Then the average marks scored by the whole class is:

A. 43.4
B. 43.6
C. 43.8
D. 44

**52.** The sum of three numbers is 136. If the ratio between the first number and the second number is 2 : 3 and that between the second and third number is 5 : 3, then the first number is:

A. 42 B. 40
C. 36 D. 32

**53.** An item is sold for ₹ 504 after allowing 20% discount and still a profit of 5% has been earned. The marked price is how much more than the cost price?

A. ₹ 120 B. ₹ 135
C. ₹ 150 D. ₹ 160

**54.** A certain sum becomes ₹ 2,356 in 3 years and ₹ 2,660 in 5 years on simple interest. The value of sum is:

A. ₹ 1800 B. ₹ 1880
C. ₹ 1900 D. ₹ 1980

**55.** In a square, lengths of the diagonals are $(4k + 6)$ cm and $(7k - 3)$ cm. The area of the square (in $cm^2$) is:

A. 144 B. 162
C. 169 D. 172

**56.** The volume of a cylinder having base radius 3 cm is 396 $cm^3$. Find its curved surface area (in $cm^2$). (Use $\pi = 22/7$)

A. 280 B. 301.5
C. 264 D. 320.6

**57.** A tap can fill a tank in 6 hours. After half the tank is filled, three more similar taps are opened. What is the total time taken to fill the tank completely?

A. 4 hours
B. 5 hours
C. 3 hours 30 minutes
D. 3 hours 45 minutes

**58.** A train running at the speed of 80 km/h crosses a 350 m long tunnel in 36 seconds. The length of the train (in m) is:

A. 350 B. 380
C. 420 D. 450

**59.** If the mean of 3, 4, 9, $2k$, 10, 8, 6 and $(k + 6)$ is 8, and mode of 2, 2, 3, $2p$, $(2p + 1)$, 4, 4, 5 and 6 ($p$ is a natural number) is 4, then the value of $(k - 2p)$ is :

A. 0 B. 1
C. 2 D. 3

**60.** In a triangle ABC, points D and E are on AB and AC respectively such that DE is parallel to BC. If AD = 6 cm, DB = 4 cm, AE = 9 cm, then the length of EC (in cm) is:

A. 7 B. 6.4
C. 6 D. 5.5

| | | | | | | | |
|---|---|---|---|---|---|---|---|
| **46.** C | **47.** A | **48.** C | **49.** B | **50.** B | **51.** B | **52.** B | **53.** C |
| **54.** C | **55.** B | **56.** C | **57.** D | **58.** D | **59.** C | **60.** C | |

# EXPLANATORY ANSWERS

**1. (A):** The Banihal Pass connects Jammu with Srinagar, playing a crucial role in linking the Jammu region with the Kashmir Valley. Located in the Pir Panjal range at an elevation of about 2,832 meters (9,291 feet), it is traversed by the Banihal-Qazigund road tunnel, also known as the Jawahar Tunnel, which ensures all-weather connectivity between the two regions.

**2. (B):** Padma Shri Award — Mithun Chakraborty

The incorrect match regarding the Padma Awards-2024 is Mithun Chakraborty listed as a Padma Shri awardee. In reality, Mithun Chakraborty was honored with the Padma Bhushan for his significant contributions to Indian cinema.

**3. (B):**

(*a*) **Vishakhadatta - Poet (II):** Vishakhadatta was an ancient Indian poet and playwright, known for his work "Mudrarakshasa."

(*b*) **Kartikeya Sarabhai - Environmentalist (III):** Kartikeya Sarabhai is a renowned Indian environmentalist and founder of the Centre for Environment Education (CEE).

(*c*) **Charaka - Medicine (I):** Charaka was an ancient Indian physician, known as the author of the "Charaka Samhita," a seminal text on Ayurveda.

(*d*) **Satyendra Nath Bose - Mathematics (IV):** Satyendra Nath Bose was an Indian physicist and mathematician, best known for his work on quantum mechanics and the Bose-Einstein statistics.

**4. (B):** Given, $\sin A = \frac{4}{5}$

$$\therefore \quad \cos A = \sqrt{1-\sin^2 A} = \sqrt{1-\left(\frac{4}{5}\right)^2}$$

$$= \sqrt{1-\frac{16}{25}} = \sqrt{\frac{9}{25}} = \frac{3}{5}$$

$$\therefore \quad \tan A = \frac{\sin A}{\cos A} = \frac{\frac{4}{5}}{\frac{3}{5}} = \frac{4}{3}$$

$$\therefore (3 - \tan A)(2 + \cos A)$$

$$= \left(3-\frac{4}{3}\right)\left(2+\frac{3}{5}\right)$$

$$= \left(\frac{5}{3}\right)\left(\frac{13}{5}\right) = \frac{13}{3}.$$

**5. (A):** Given, speed of boat in still water = 8 km/h and speed of current = 2 km/h

$\therefore$ Speed upward = 8 – 2 = 6 km/h

and speed downward = 8 + 2 = 10 km/h

Let, distance = $d$

$$\text{Then,} \quad \frac{d}{6}+\frac{d}{10} = 2$$

$$\Rightarrow \quad d\left(\frac{1}{6}+\frac{1}{10}\right) = 2$$

$$\Rightarrow \quad d\left(\frac{5+3}{30}\right) = 2$$

$$\Rightarrow \quad d = \frac{2\times 30}{8}$$

$$\Rightarrow \quad d = \frac{15}{2} = 7.5 \text{ km}$$

Hence, required distance = $d$ = 7.5 km.

**6. (B):**

(*c*) **Nagaland:** Formed on December 1, 1963, becoming the 16th state of India. It was created to recognize the distinct identity and culture of the Naga people.

(*a*) **Haryana:** Formed on November 1, 1966, when it was separated from Punjab. This reorganization was based on linguistic lines to cater to the Hindi-speaking population.

(*b*) **Sikkim:** Became the 22nd state of India on May 16, 1975. Before this, Sikkim was a protectorate and then a kingdom under Indian suzerainty.

(*d*) **Goa:** Became the 25th state of India on May 30, 1987, through the 56th Amendment of the Constitution of India. The day is celebrated annually as Goa Statehood Day.

**7. (A):** Mission Antyodaya (2022-23) aims to enhance the living conditions of rural areas by conducting an annual survey at the gram panchayat level. This initiative monitors the progress in the development process, ensuring that various governmental schemes and programs are effectively implemented and yielding the desired outcomes.

**8. (A):** The "Quadrilateral Security Dialogue" (QUAD) is a strategic alliance comprising Japan, India, Australia, and the United States, aimed at enhancing cooperation on security and regional stability in the Indo-Pacific region. China is not a member of this dialogue.

9. **(A):** Jaya Verma Sinha made history in 2023 by becoming the first woman chairperson of the Railway Board of Indian Railways. Her appointment marks a significant milestone in the history of Indian Railways, reflecting progress towards gender equality in top administrative positions.

10. **(B):**

(*a*) **Myanmar - The Kyat (III)** is the official currency of Myanmar. It is used for all financial transactions within the country and is represented by the symbol "Ks." The Kyat is subdivided into 100 pyas, though smaller denominations are rarely used.

(*b*) **Russia - The Ruble (I)** is the currency of Russia, symbolized as "₽" or "RUB." It is one of the oldest currencies in the world and has been in use since the 13th century. The Ruble is subdivided into 100 kopecks and is crucial for everyday transactions within Russia.

(*c*) **Malaysia - The Ringgit (IV),** often abbreviated as MYR, is the currency of Malaysia. It is symbolized by "RM" and is subdivided into 100 sen. The Ringgit is used throughout Malaysia and is essential for domestic commerce and trade.

(*d*) **Bhutan - The Ngultrum (II)** is Bhutan's currency, represented by the symbol "Nu." It is pegged to the Indian Rupee and is used in all financial transactions within Bhutan. The Ngultrum is subdivided into 100 chetrum.

11. **(B):** The "Jhulaghat Suspension Bridge," connecting India and Nepal, has recently become fully operational, enhancing cross-border connectivity and facilitating easier movement of people and goods between the two countries. Located in the Uttarakhand region of India, this bridge is a significant infrastructure development aimed at strengthening bilateral ties and improving access to remote areas on both sides of the border.

12. **(A):** Ocean acidification occurs when excess carbon dioxide ($CO_2$) from the atmosphere dissolves in seawater, forming carbonic acid. This process decreases the pH level of the ocean, making it more acidic. As a result, the pH level goes down, which can negatively impact marine life, particularly organisms with calcium carbonate shells or skeletons, such as corals and shellfish, by affecting their ability to form and maintain these structures.

13. **(B):** Devendra Jhajharia is the first para-athlete to be honored with the Padma Bhushan, one of India's highest civilian awards. Known for his exceptional achievements in para-athletics, Jhajharia is a javelin thrower who has won multiple gold medals at the Paralympic Games, including in 2004 and 2016.

14. **(C):** The Zemu Glacier is located in Sikkim, India, within the Kanchenjunga range of the Himalayas. It is one of the largest glaciers in the eastern Himalayas and feeds several important rivers in the region. The glacier is renowned for its stunning natural beauty and is a crucial source of water for the surrounding ecosystems.

15. **(B):** Michelle Bachelet made history as Chile's first woman President, serving two non-consecutive terms from 2006 to 2010 and again from 2014 to 2018. Her presidency marked a significant milestone for gender equality in Chilean politics.

16. **(D):** The 'Ugram' Indigenous Assault Rifle was developed and launched by the Defence Research and Development Organisation (DRDO), which is India's premier defense research agency. This advanced assault rifle is designed to enhance the capabilities of the Indian armed forces with its modern features and improved performance.

17. **(A):** While diamond is a form of carbon and has a strong covalent bonding structure, it does not have free electrons or ions to conduct electricity, making it an insulator. In contrast, gold, silver, and graphite are good conductors of electricity.

18. **(B):** Kwashiorkor is a serious nutritional disorder caused by a deficiency in dietary protein, despite adequate caloric intake. It primarily affects young children and is characterized by symptoms such as swelling of the abdomen and legs (edema), irritability, liver damage, and skin changes. The condition arises when there is not enough protein in the diet to meet the body's needs for growth and repair, leading to severe physical and metabolic disturbances.

19. **(D):**

(*a*) **INS Chilka - Odisha (IV):** INS Chilka is the premier naval training establishment for the Indian Navy, located near Chilika Lake in Odisha.

(*b*) **INS Hansa - Goa (I):** INS Hansa is a significant naval air station located in Dabolim, Goa, serving as the base for the Indian Navy's aviation operations.

(*c*) **INS Satavahana - Andhra Pradesh (II):** INS Satavahana is a naval submarine training base located in Visakhapatnam, Andhra Pradesh, focusing on training submariners.

(*d*) **INS Garuda - Kerala (III):** INS Garuda is a naval air station situated in Kochi, Kerala, and plays a crucial role in naval aviation operations.

**20. (A):** MIRV, or Multiple Independently Targetable Re-Entry Vehicle, is a missile technology that enables a single missile to carry multiple warheads, each capable of being directed to a different target independently. This enhances the missile's effectiveness and strategic value, as it allows for a single launch to potentially strike several targets simultaneously, increasing the chances of mission success and complicating defense measures for adversaries.

**21. (D):** Dr. Ravi Kannan R. was awarded the Ramon Magsaysay Award in 2023 for his exemplary work in delivering quality healthcare to underserved communities in India. As a prominent oncologist, Dr. Kannan has dedicated his career to providing medical services to patients in remote and economically disadvantaged regions.

**22. (D):** Dr. Arvind Panagariya has been appointed the Chairman of the 16th Finance Commission of India. He is an esteemed economist and former Vice Chairman of NITI Aayog, known for his expertise in economic policy and development.

**23. (B):** The Sri Ranganathswamy Temple in Tamil Nadu is dedicated to Lord Vishnu, one of the principal deities in Hinduism. Located in Srirangam, it is one of the most significant Vaishnavite temples in India and is renowned for its grandeur and architectural excellence.

**24. (A):** Article 324 of the Indian Constitution provides for the establishment and powers of the Election Commission of India, empowering it to supervise, direct, and control the entire process of elections to the Parliament and State Legislatures, as well as the office of the President and Vice President of India.

**25. (A):**

(*a*) **Mon - Nagaland (IV):** Mon is a district in Nagaland known for its rich tradition of tribal crafts, including traditional weaving and basketry, reflecting the diverse cultural heritage of the Naga tribes.

(*b*) **Nalbari - Assam (II):** Nalbari in Assam is renowned for its traditional Assamese handicrafts, particularly handloom products like muga silk and traditional weaving techniques.

(*c*) **Pasighat - Arunachal Pradesh (I):** Pasighat in Arunachal Pradesh is noted for its indigenous crafts, including intricate woodwork and weaving, showcasing the craftsmanship of the local tribes.

(*d*) **Tura - Meghalaya (III):** Tura in Meghalaya is recognized for its traditional handicrafts, including weaving and bamboo crafts, which are integral to the cultural expressions of the Garo tribe.

**26. (A):** The Amchang Wildlife Sanctuary is located in Assam, near the city of Guwahati. This sanctuary is renowned for its rich biodiversity, including a variety of wildlife such as elephants, tigers, and several species of birds and reptiles. It serves as an important conservation area, protecting the natural habitat and promoting ecological balance in the region.

**27. (D):** India's first 3-D printed Post Office was inaugurated in Bengaluru, showcasing a groundbreaking approach in construction technology. The building, created using 3-D printing techniques, exemplifies innovation in architectural design and efficiency. This project reflects a move towards modernizing infrastructure and highlights India's commitment to adopting cutting-edge technology in various sectors.

**28. (C):**

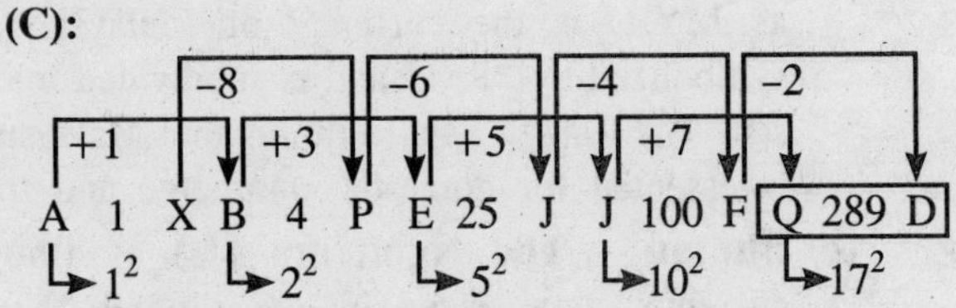


∴ Q289D should come in the place of the question mark in the series.

**29. (D):** Alphabets in natural series and reverse series

A = Z, B = Y, C = X, .... X = C, Y = B, Z = A

Given, NEGI : MVTR

⇒ N E G I
↓ ↓ ↓ ↓
M V T R

Similarly, S I N G
↓ ↓ ↓ ↓
H R M T

So, NEGI : MVTR :: SING : **HRMT**.

**30. (B):** Given, 'ki ru pi' = 'nobody like cruel' ...(*i*)

'ki mi cha' = 'king was cruel' ...(*ii*)

'ru pi cha' = 'nobody like king' ...(*iii*)

From (*i*) and (*ii*),

'cruel' = 'ki'

From (*ii*) and (*iii*),

king = cha

From (*ii*), mi = was

So, 'mi' is the code for 'was' in the given code language.

**31. (D):** (D) A × U % S + G

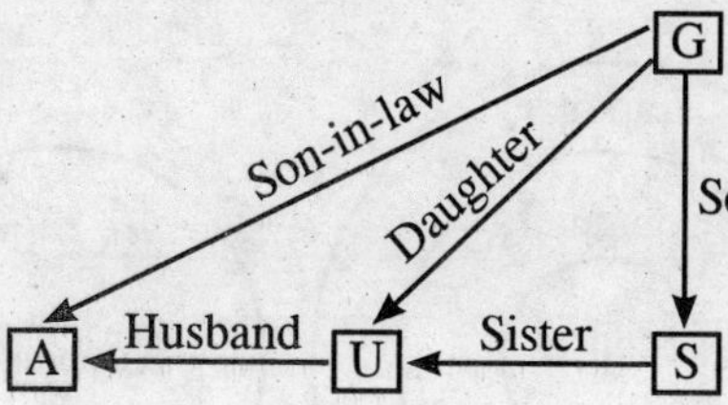


So, option (D) means 'A' is the son-in-law of 'G'.

**32. (B):** Given, 26 January, 2020 = Sunday

∴ 25 January, 2020 = Saturday

Number of day from 26 January, 2020 to 16 March, 2020

$$= 6 + 29 + 16 = 51 \text{ days}$$

$$= 7 \times 7 + 2 = 2 \text{ odd days}$$

∴ 16 March, 2020 = Saturday + 2 days

= Monday.

**33. (C):** Here, 'quarter past 3' = 3 hours 15 minutes

Angles traced by the hour hand in 12 hours = 360°

Angled traced by hour hand in 3 hours 15 minutes

$$i.e., = \frac{13}{4} \text{ hours}$$

$$= \frac{360°}{12} \times \frac{13}{4} = \frac{195}{2} = 97\frac{1}{2}^{\circ}$$

Angled traced by minute hand in 60 minutes = 360°

∴ Angle traced by it in 15 minutes

$$= \left(\frac{360°}{60} \times 15\right) = 90°$$

Hence, required angle $= \left(97\frac{1}{2}^{\circ} - 90°\right) = 7\frac{1}{7}^{\circ}$.

**34. (B):** Given,

M E R C U R Y
+1 +2 +3 +4 +5 +6 +7
N G U G Z X F

Similarly,

E N T A N G L E
+1 +2 +3 +4 +5 +6 +7 +8
F P W E S M S M

So, 'ENTANGLE' will be coded as 'FPWESMSM'.

**35. (C):** From given statements (I) and (II).

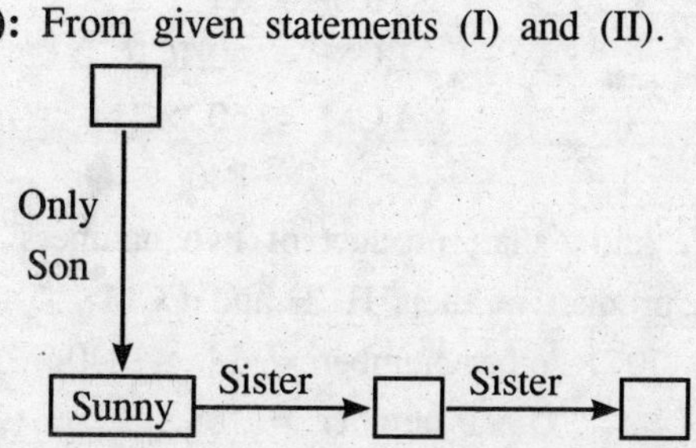


Sunny has 2 sisters.

So, Statements (I) and (II) together are sufficient to answer the question.

**36. (B):** Here, Starting point = A = house

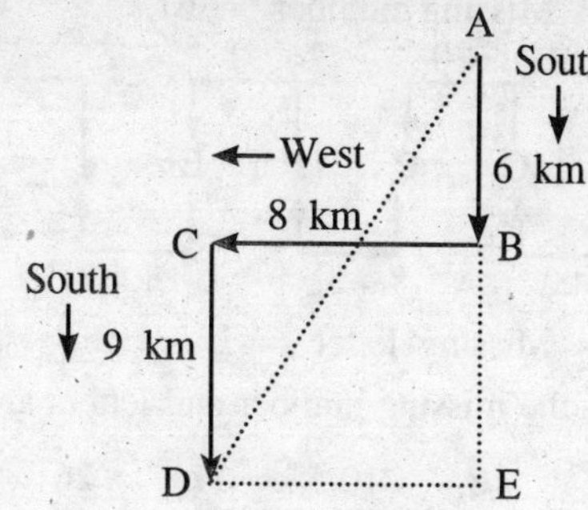


AB = 6 km

BC = 8 km

CD = 9 km

∵ AB + CD = 6 + 9

= 15 km = AE

and BC = ED

= 8 km

$$\therefore \quad AD = \sqrt{AE^2 + ED^2}$$

$$= \sqrt{(15)^2 + (8)^2}$$

$$= \sqrt{225 + 64} = \sqrt{289}$$

$$= 17 \text{ km}$$

He (D) is 17 km far and in South-West direction from his house now.

**38. (D):** A clock seen through a mirror show quarter to seven = 6:45

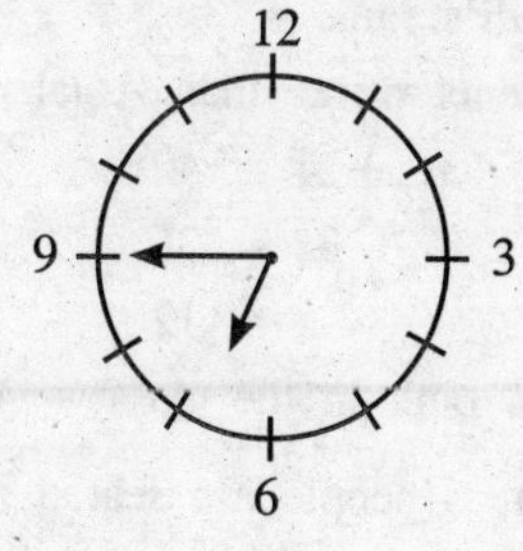


Now, correct time

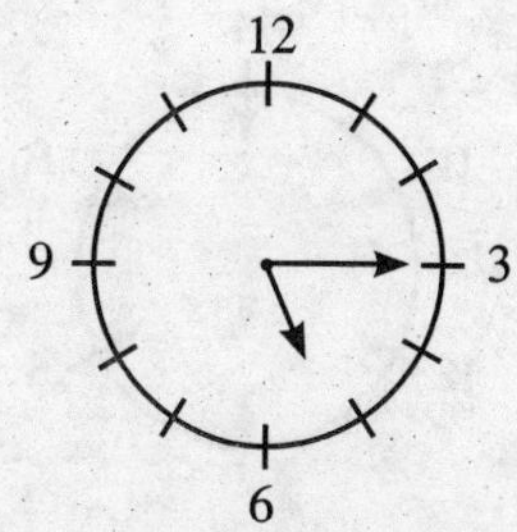


Hence, correct time show by the clock = 5:15.

**40. (B):** 5 8 13 20 31 44 [61] 80

+3 +5 +7 +11 +13 +17 +19

Here, 3, 5, 7, 11, 13, 17 and 19 are prime numbers.

$\therefore$ ? = Missing number = 61.

and

+0 −1 −2

A C C F E I G [L]

+2 +3 +4 +5

$\therefore$ ? = Missing letter = L

Hence, the missing number and letters are 61 and L.

**41. (B):** 3 6 10.5 17 26 [38]

+3 +4.5 +6.5 +9 +12

+1.5 +2 +2.5 +3

+1/2 +1/2 +1/2

? = the next number of the series = 38.

**42. (D):** Given, Number of students in a class = 40

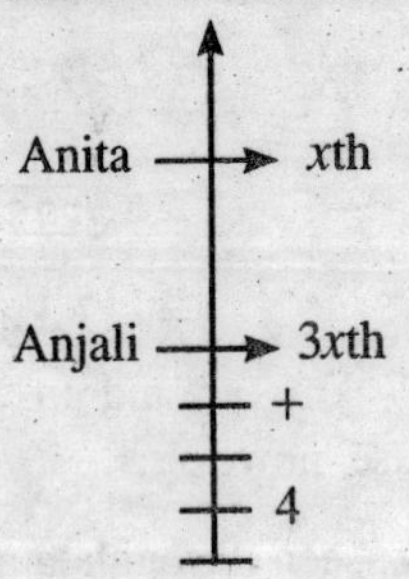


Let Anita's rank = $x$

Then, Anjali's rank = $3x$

and 4 students worse than Anjali

So, $3x + 4 = 40$

$\Rightarrow$ $3x = 36$

$\Rightarrow$ $x = 12$

So, Anita's rank in the class = 12th.

**43. (C):** Given, 6 people are seated in a circle facing the centre

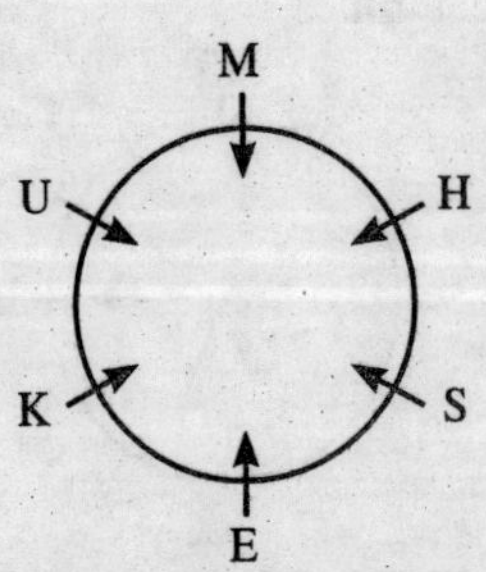


Here, K is the immediate right of U.

**45. (D):** From given statements:

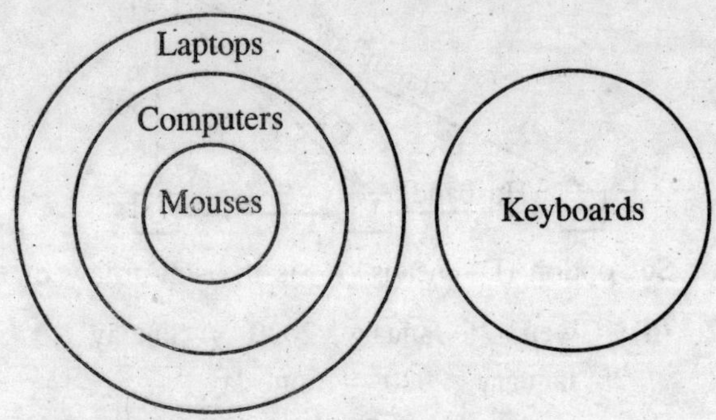


Conclusion:

I. All Mouses are laptops. (True)

II. All Computers can never be keyboards. (True)

Here, Both conclusions I and II follow.

**46. (C):** $24 \div 4 \times 2 + 8 - 4$

$= 6 \times 2 + 8 - 4$

$= 12 + 8 - 4$

$= 20 - 4 = 16.$

**47. (A):** $\because$ $\frac{1}{2} = 0.5$ $\frac{8}{11} = 0.72$

$\frac{7}{8} = 0.85$ $\frac{7}{9} = 0.77$

$\frac{5}{6} = 0.83$

$\therefore$ Greatest fraction = $\frac{7}{8}$

and smallest fraction = $\frac{1}{2}$

$\therefore$ Required difference = $\frac{7}{8} - \frac{1}{2} = \frac{7-4}{8} = \frac{3}{8}.$

**48. (C):** Given LCM + HCF = 854

and LCM = 60 HCF

$\therefore$ 60HCF + HCF = 854

$\Rightarrow$ 61HCF = 854

$\Rightarrow$ HCF = $\frac{854}{61} = 14$

$\Rightarrow$ HCF = 14

$\therefore$ LCM = 60HCF

$\Rightarrow$ LCM = $60 \times 14$

= 840

We know that, product of two numbers

= product of their HCF and LCM

$\Rightarrow$ $70 \times$ other number = $14 \times 840$

$\Rightarrow$ Other number = 168.

**49. (B):** Let present age of Harish be $z$ years and present ages of his two sons be $x$ years and $y$ years

Then, $z = 8(x + y)$ ...(*i*)

After 8 years,

$z + 8 = 2(x + y + 8 + 8)$

$\Rightarrow z + 8 = 2(x + y) + 32$ ...(*ii*)

From (*i*) and (*ii*),

$$z + 8 = 2 \times \frac{z}{8} + 32$$

$$\Rightarrow z + 8 = \frac{z}{4} + 32$$

$$\Rightarrow z - \frac{z}{4} = 32 - 8$$

$$\Rightarrow \frac{4z - z}{4} = 24$$

$$\Rightarrow \frac{3}{4}z = 24 \Rightarrow z = 32 \text{ years}$$

Hence, the present age of Harish is 32 years.

**50. (B):** Let the maximum marks of the examination $= x$

Then, $300 - 225 = x \times \frac{10}{100}$

$$\Rightarrow 75 = \frac{x}{10}$$

$$\Rightarrow x = 750.$$

**51. (B):** Given, number of students in a class = 40

Boys : Girls = 3 : 2

$\therefore$ Number of boys $= 40 \times \frac{3}{5} = 24$

and number of girls $= 40 \times \frac{2}{5} = 16$

Now, Total marks scored by boys

$= 24 \times 42 = 1008$

and total marks scored by girls

$= 16 \times 46 = 736$

Hence, the average marks scored by the whole class

$$= \frac{1008 + 736}{40} = \frac{1744}{40} = 43.6.$$

**52. (B):** Given, the sum of 3 numbers = 136

First : Second = 2 : 3 = 10 : 15

Second : Third = 5 : 3 = 15 : 9

$\therefore$ First : Second : Third = 10 : 15 : 9

Then, the first number $= 136 \times \frac{10}{10 + 15 + 9}$

$$= 136 \times \frac{10}{34} = 4 \times 10 = 40.$$

**53. (C):** Marked price $\times \frac{100 - 20}{100} = ₹\ 504$

$$\Rightarrow \text{M.P.} \times \frac{4}{5} = ₹\ 504$$

$$\Rightarrow \text{M.P.} = 504 \times \frac{5}{4}$$

$$\Rightarrow \text{M.P.} = 126 \times 5 = ₹\ 630$$

and cost price $\times \frac{105}{100} = ₹\ 504$

$$\Rightarrow \text{C.P.} = 504 \times \frac{105}{100} = 504 \times \frac{20}{21}$$

$$\Rightarrow \text{C.P.} = 24 \times 20 = 480$$

So, M.P. – C.P. = 630 – 480 = ₹ 150

Hence, the marked price is ₹ 150 more than the cost price.

**54. (C):** Given, sum become ₹ 2356 in 3 years and sum become ₹ 2660 in 5 years.

$\therefore$ Simple interest in 5 – 3 = 2 years

= 2660 – 2356 = ₹ 304

$\Rightarrow$ Simple interest in 3 years $= \frac{304}{2} \times 3$

= 152 × 3 = ₹ 456

$\therefore$ The value of sum = 2356 – 456 = ₹ 1900.

**55. (B):** In a square, length of diagonals are equal

$\therefore 4k + 6 = 7k - 3$

$\Rightarrow 7k - 6k = 6 + 3$

$\Rightarrow k = 9$

$\therefore$ Diagonal $= 4k + 6$

$= 12 + 6 = 18$ cm

and diagonal $= \text{Side}\sqrt{2}$

$\Rightarrow 18 = \text{Side}\sqrt{2} \Rightarrow \text{Side} = 9\sqrt{2}$

$\therefore$ Area of the square $= (\text{Side})^2 = (9\sqrt{2})^2$

$= 162 \text{ cm}^2.$

**56. (C):** The volume of a cylinder = 396

$\Rightarrow \pi r^2 h = 396$

$\Rightarrow \pi(3)^2 h = 396$

$$\Rightarrow \pi h = \frac{396}{9} = 44$$

$\Rightarrow \qquad \pi h = 44$

Its curved surface area $= 2\pi rh$

$= 2\pi h \times 3 \quad [\because \pi h = 44]$

$= 2 \times 44 \times 3$

$= 264 \text{ cm}^2.$

**57. (D):** A tap can fill a tank in 6 hours

$\Rightarrow$ A tap can fill $\frac{1}{2}$ tank in 3 hours

and remaining part of tank fill in $\frac{\frac{1}{2}}{\frac{4}{6}}$ hours

$= \frac{1}{2} \times \frac{6}{4} = \frac{3}{4}$ hours

$= \frac{3}{4} \times 60 = 45$ minutes

$\therefore$ The total time taken to fill the tank completely

$= 3$ hours $+ 45$ minutes

$= 3$ hours 45 minutes.

**58. (D):** Let the length of the train $= x$ m

Then, $\quad \dfrac{x + 350}{80 \times \frac{5}{18}} = 36$

$\Rightarrow \qquad x + 350 = 36 \times 80 \times \frac{5}{18}$

$= 2 \times 80 \times 5$

$\Rightarrow \qquad x + 350 = 160 \times 5 = 800$

$\Rightarrow \qquad x = 800 - 350$

$\Rightarrow \qquad x = 450$ m.

**59. (C):** Given, mean $= 8$

$\therefore \quad \dfrac{3 + 4 + 9 + 2k + 10 + 8 + 6 + (k + 6)}{8} = 8$

$\Rightarrow \qquad 46 + 3k = 8 \times 8$

$\Rightarrow \qquad 3k = 64 - 46 = 18$

$\Rightarrow \qquad k = 6$

and 2, 2, 3, $2p$, $(2p + 1)$, 4, 4, 5 ($p$ is a natural number)

$\Rightarrow$ 2, 2, 3, $2 \times 2$, $(2 \times 2 + 1)$, 4, 4, 5

$\Rightarrow$ 2, 2, 3, 4, 5, 4, 4, 5

Given, $\qquad$ Mode $= 4$

$\Rightarrow \qquad 2p = 4$

$\Rightarrow \qquad p = 2$

Henec, $\qquad (k - 2p) = 6 - 2$

$= 6$

**60. (C):** Given, in $\Delta$ABC

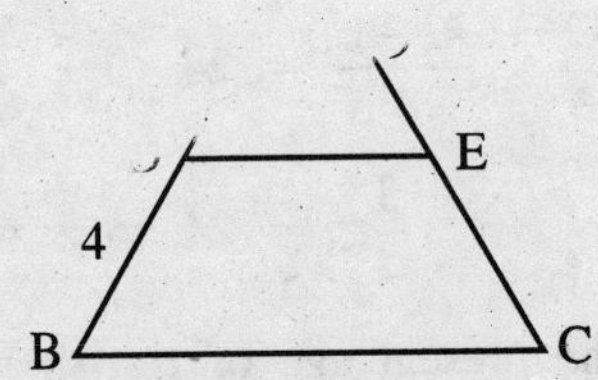


DE || BC

AD = 6 cm

DB = 4 cm

AE = 9 cm

From Thales theorem,

In $\Delta$ABC, $\qquad \dfrac{AD}{DB} = \dfrac{AE}{EC}$

$\Rightarrow \qquad \dfrac{6}{4} = \dfrac{9}{EC}$

$\Rightarrow \qquad 6EC = 9 \times 4$

$\Rightarrow \qquad EC = \dfrac{9 \times 4}{6} = \dfrac{36}{6} = 6$

$\Rightarrow \qquad EC = 6$ cm.

## Previous Years' Paper (Solved)

## (Common University Entrance Test for UG Programmes)

# CUET (UG)–B.Com (Hons.) Entrance Exam, 2023*

## ENGLISH

**Directions (Qs. No. 1-5):** *Read the following passage to answer question:*

The village school was located in a prominent place where apart from the school, there were a few shops, a small temple and a government dispensary. The headmaster of the school was a learned and scholarly man loved by all. The dispensary was looked after by a doctor and a male nurse. The doctor attended the dispensary very punctually and used to retire to his residence after the duty hours and never allowed anyone to visit his residence after the duty hours.

The school was housed in dilapidated building and very often the headmaster used to take the children out to the nearby garden where they could play and take part in various sports and games under the able supervision of the headmaster.

One day a stray dog entered the garden when the children were playing. One of them pelted a stone at the dog and it started barking and all of a sudden became boisterous and bit a child in the leg. The boy was very badly hurt and his leg started bleeding. The children who by this time became panicky rushed to the headmaster who together with a few students, took the child to the nearby dispensary and then to the doctors residence.

The headmaster knocked at the door of the doctor for help. But the doctor refused to open the door and made it clear that he would not attend to anyone howsoever serious he may be, during his leisure hours. However the headmaster continued to knock at the door and finally the doctor opened the door when he saw the headmaster trembling with fear and the student in agony and pain.

The doctor mellowed down now and took the child to the dispensary for bandaging and giving necessary injections and medicines. The doctor was impressed by the dedication and sincerity of the headmaster. He realized his folly and decided to attend to the needy and sick even during his leisure hours.

**1.** The village school was located near the:

A. Forest B. Market
C. Library D. Pond

**2.** After the duty hours the government dispensary doctor normally:

A. Slept and dreamt
B. Spent time with his family
C. went to his private clinic
D. Rested at home and never allowed visitors

**3.** All of a sudden a dog became boisterous and it bit a child in the leg. The dog got angry mainly because:

A. One boy did mischief
B. Dog was feeling hungry
C. Dog saw another dog
D. Boy did not give food to the dog

**4.** The head master was trembling with fear at the doctor's residence along with the injured boy. The doctor was:

A. afraid of higher officials
B. afraid of student's parents
C. not opening the door
D. impressed with the dedication of the headmaster

**5.** Find the synonym from a passage which means "To become less extreme in behaviour".

A. Stray B. boisterous
C. mellowed D. Folly

**Directions (Qs. No. 6-10):** *Read the following passage to answer question:*

The needs of a nations people are bigger and much more important than any other considerations. The mission of parliament is that it has to be alive and dynamic over issues vital to the existence of our very nationhood. Our freedom did not come as a gift. The whole country struggled for decades to achieve the first vision of independence, so

*** This Previous Year Paper has been given here as a Combination of CUET (UG) 2023 different exams for the Subjects 'English, Business Studies, Mathematics, Accountancy/ Book Keeping and General Test', which have been mapped to this course.**

we have to protect it. There were excellent leaders in all walks of life-science, education and industry. To preserve this freedom from intruders and others who would compromise it is our bounden duty and not a matter of choice and convenience. No ideology is above the security and prosperity of our country. No agenda is more important than harmony among the people. Students should get ready to transform India into a developed nation. Ignite your minds and think big.

A teacher once said, 'Give me a five-year-old child. After seven years, no God or Devil will be able to change the child.' Will all teachers be such gurus? The administrators have a great opportunity to link the people and political leaders. They should always take decisions that are good for the people I believe it is only executives like empowered district collectors who can assist transformation. The state-Central integrated fund has to be deployed in mission mode programmes.

**6.** We have to protect our nations Independence as we got it after:
A. excellent leader
B. War and Fight
C. Struggle for decades
D. Help from foreign country

**7.** To transform India into a Developed Nation Dr. A.P.J. Abdul Kalam expects his students to:
A. Ignite the minds B. Fire the mind
C. Use the mind D. Clean the mind

**8.** The one who can link the people and political leaders even to assist for transformation. They are known as:
A. Leader B. Administrators
C. Manager D. Major

**9.** The existence of Nation hood is maintained by:
A. Country B. Office
C. Collectorate D. Parliament

**10.** Find the synonym from the passage which means:
'Trespasser'
Choose the correct option:
A. Leader B. Teacher
C. Intruder D. Collector

**Directions (Qs. No. 11-15):** *Read the following passage to answer question:*

Village Resource Centres (VRCs) were established by the Indian Space Research Organisation (ISRO) as part of its societal mission of bringing space-based services emanating from Satellite Communication (SatCom) and Earth Observation (EO) to rural society. While SatCom provides the method for an effective delivery of information and services across vast regions, EO provides community-centric information regarding geo-referenced land records; natural resources; the environment; sites for exploiting ground water for potable use and recharging: wasteland and reclamation; watershed profile; and cropping patterns. It can also provide customized local area information. These systems are very useful for predicting disaster, giving early warning and vulnerability-related information.

ISRO has undertaken the mission of assisting the VRC programme with a portfolio of services which are being established in collaboration with forty partner agencies across twenty-two states. A total of 473 VRCs have been set up with plans for rapid expansion in the future. Each VRC essentially has digital connectivity; specialty health care providers enabled via the Indian National Satellite System (INSAT); Spatial information on natural resources facilities for primary health care and distance education.

**11.** Village resource centres were set up by the ______ to bring space based centres to rural society:
A. Sat com
B. Indian Space Research Organisation
C. Earth observation
D. Indian National Satellite system

**12.** ISRO has undertaken the mission of assisting the village Resource Centres Programme with forty partner agencies across ______ states.
A. Twenty One B. Twenty Two
C. Twenty Three D. Twenty Five

**13.** Match List-I with List-II:

| *List-I* | *List-II* |
|---|---|
| (*a*) SatCom | (*i*) Village Resource Centres |
| (*b*) VRCs | (*ii*) Indian National Satellite System |
| (*c*) ISRO | (*iii*) Satellite Communication |
| (*d*) INSAT | (*iv*) Indian Space Research Organisation |

Choose the correct answer from the options given below:

| | (*a*) | (*b*) | (*c*) | (*d*) |
|---|---|---|---|---|
| A. | (*iii*) | (*iv*) | (*i*) | (*ii*) |
| B. | (*iv*) | (*ii*) | (*iii*) | (*i*) |
| C. | (*ii*) | (*iv*) | (*i*) | (*iii*) |
| D. | (*iii*) | (*i*) | (*iv*) | (*ii*) |

**14.** Find a word from the passage that means the same as 'to assume things before it happens'.
A. Communications B. Observations
C. Information D. Prediction

**15.** Find a word from the passage that is an antonym of the word 'safe/secure'.
A. Exploitation B. Expansion
C. Vulnerable D. Collaboration

**16.** Fill in the blank with the correct determiner:
The teacher asked him ______ questions.
A. much B. a few
C. any D. every

**17.** Change the following into direct speech:

He requested me to shut the door.

A. He told, "The door should be shut."
B. He said, "Please shut the door."
C. He said, "Shut the door."
D. He ordered, "Close the door."

**18.** Fill in the blank with the correct adverb:

I ______ met him at the conference on Sunday but discussed a lot of things.

A. Always B. Never
C. Briefly D. Finally

**19.** Which of the following sentences does ***not*** use the correct modals.

(*a*) I swim across the river when I was young.
(*b*) It may rain next Friday
(*c*) I expected that I would get a first class
(*d*) One ought to respect the environmental laws
(*e*) This used to be a dense jungle.

Choose the ***correct answer*** from the options given below:

A. (*a*) and (*d*) only B. (*a*) only
C. (*e*) only D. (*c*) and (*d*) only

**20.** Complete the sentence by choosing the appropriate options:

He gave ______ European ______ one-rupee coin.

A. the, an B. a, a
C. an, an D. the, a

**21.** Complete the sentence by choosing the appropriate set of prepositions:

He is notoriously mean ______ his treatment ______ his servants.

A. in, of B. with, of
C. of, with D. for, of

**22.** Synonym of the word "alleviate".

(*a*) worsen (*b*) grow
(*c*) lessen (*d*) increase
(*e*) reduce

Choose the ***correct answer*** from the options given below:

A. (*a*) and (*e*) only B. (*c*) and (*e*) only
C. (*b*) and (*d*) only D. (*a*) only

**23.** Choose the correct Exclamatory sentence of the given sentence:

The Night is very beautiful.

A. How beautiful is the night!
B. Night is so beautiful!
C. What beautiful night!
D. Night is too beautiful!

**24.** Choose the option that has been correctly changed from Direct to Indirect speech.

Adesh said, "Please shut the door behind you."

(*a*) Adesh requested me to please shut the door behind me.
(*b*) Adesh said that I request you to shut the door behind you.
(*c*) Adesh said to shut the door behind you.
(*d*) Adesh said to me that I request to shut the door behind you.

Choose the ***correct answer*** from the options given below:

A. (*a*) only B. (*b*) only
C. (*c*) only D. (*d*) only

**25.** Match the underline phrases with their meanings:

| ***List-I (Phrases)*** | ***List-II (Meanings)*** |
|---|---|
| (*a*) I had so much work to do but the fever got the best of me | (*i*) Peaceful time |
| (*b*) They spent their halcyon days in a village | (*ii*) Vulnerable/Weak spot |
| (*c*) He earned really well but ended up penniless. Gambling was his achilles heel | (*iii*) Competent for a work |
| (*d*) A doctor worth his salt will advise people for healthy eating | (*iv*) Take advantage of something |

Choose the ***correct answer*** from the options given below:

| | (*a*) | (*b*) | (*c*) | (*d*) |
|---|---|---|---|---|
| A. | (*iv*) | (*i*) | (*ii*) | (*iii*) |
| B. | (*iv*) | (*ii*) | (*i*) | (*iii*) |
| C. | (*i*) | (*iii*) | (*ii*) | (*iv*) |
| D. | (*iv*) | (*iii*) | (*ii*) | (*i*) |

**26.** Choose the correct meaning of the underlined word from the following sentence:

The minister entered the hall with his entourage.

A. cars
B. belongings
C. following subordinates
D. police

**27.** Find out the adverbs from the given sentence and tick the correct option given below:

People often complain about foolish things and easily try to escape from the reality.

A. complain, reality
B. often, easily
C. easily, complain
D. often, escape

**28.** Choose the option with the same meaning:

Camouflage

(*a*) disguise (*b*) cover
(*c*) demonstrate (*d*) fabric

Choose the ***correct answer*** from the options given below:

A. (*a*) only B. (*b*) only
C. (*c*) only D. (*d*) only

**29.** Complete the sentence using the correct options:

When I reached the station, the train

A. been leaving
B. had been already leaving
C. had already left
D. has left

**30.** State the kind of clause for the underlined part of the given sentence:

The Children whom I teach in standard 8 are very disciplined.

A. Adverb clause B. Adjective clause
C. Noun clause D. Adverb clause of time

**31.** Match List-I with List-II to complete the idioms:

| *List-I* | *List-II* |
|---|---|
| (*a*) At one's | (*i*) tongue |
| (*b*) Hold one's | (*ii*) fingertips |
| (*c*) Lose one's | (*iii*) head |
| (*d*) Win | (*iv*) hands down |

Choose the ***correct answer*** from the options given below:

| | (*a*) | (*b*) | (*c*) | (*d*) |
|---|---|---|---|---|
| A. | (*ii*) | (*i*) | (*iii*) | (*iv*) |
| B. | (*i*) | (*ii*) | (*iii*) | (*iv*) |
| C. | (*iv*) | (*iii*) | (*ii*) | (*i*) |
| D. | (*ii*) | (*i*) | (*iv*) | (*iii*) |

**32.** Find the correct Antonym of the word 'Terrible':

A. scaring B. soothing
C. horrible D. frightening

**33.** Match List I with List II for suitable antonyms:

| *List-I* *(Word)* | *List-II* *(Antonym)* |
|---|---|
| (*a*) Charming | (*i*) Hide |
| (*b*) Occasional | (*ii*) Miser |
| (*c*) Generous | (*iii*) Hideous |
| (*d*) Exhibit | (*iv*) Regular |

Choose the correct answer from the options given below:

| | (*a*) | (*b*) | (*c*) | (*d*) |
|---|---|---|---|---|
| A. | (*iii*) | (*iv*) | (*ii*) | (*i*) |
| B. | (*iv*) | (*ii*) | (*iii*) | (*i*) |
| C. | (*iii*) | (*ii*) | (*i*) | (*iv*) |
| D. | (*ii*) | (*i*) | (*iv*) | (*iii*) |

**34.** Arrange the following in the correct sequence:

(*a*) With telling us about
(*b*) has been mainly occupied
(*c*) the finite world has been analysed
(*d*) the elements into which
(*e*) The language of man

Choose the correct answer from the options given below:

A. (*e*), (*b*), (*a*), (*d*), (*c*)
B. (*a*), (*e*), (*b*), (*d*), (*c*)
C. (*e*), (*a*), (*b*), (*d*), (*c*)
D. (*e*), (*d*), (*a*), (*b*), (*c*)

**35.** Match the phrases with their meaning:

| *List-I* | *List-II* |
|---|---|
| (*a*) Set in | (*i*) to treat with contempt |
| (*b*) Wind up | (*ii*) extinguished |
| (*c*) look down upon | (*iii*) begin |
| (*d*) put out | (*iv*) bring to an end |

Choose the correct answer from the options given below:

| | (*a*) | (*b*) | (*c*) | (*d*) |
|---|---|---|---|---|
| A. | (*ii*) | (*iii*) | (*iv*) | (*i*) |
| B. | (*iv*) | (*ii*) | (*iii*) | (*i*) |
| C. | (*iii*) | (*i*) | (*iv*) | (*ii*) |
| D. | (*iii*) | (*iv*) | (*i*) | (*ii*) |

**36.** Choose the option that gives the correct meaning of the foreign word:

'animus'

A. good intention B. bad intention
C. mean while D. self love

**37.** Identify the correct passive voice form of the following sentence:

One should keep one's promises.

A. Promises need to be kept.
B. Promises should be kept.
C. Nobody keeps promises.
D. One has kept one's promises.

**38.** Complete the sentence with suitable option:

You ______ stood by your friends in their bad times.

A. ought to have B. should
C. must D. can have

**39.** Choose the correct question tag for the given sentence:

She doesn't really know how to get out of the problem?

A. Isn't she? B. doesn't she
C. does she? D. Is it?

**40.** Choose the correct option to change the following sentence into passive voice.

Your behaviour astonished me.

A. I was astonished by you with your behaviour.
B. You are astonished by me with behaviour.
C. I was astonished by your behaviour.
D. With your behaviour you were astonished

**41.** Choose one word which can be substituted for the given sentence:

'One who acts against religion'.

A. Egoist B. Heretic
C. Optimist D. Stoic

**42.** Fill in the blank with the suitable homonym

Choose the correct one from the following.

Ravi <u>writes</u> in his note book today.

The marriage is performed as per Hindu ______.

A. Rites B. Wrights
C. Rights D. Raight

**43.** Parts of a sentence are given in a jumbled order. Arrange the parts in the correct sequence to form a meaningful sentence.

(*a*) the resistance (*b*) of
(*c*) depend on (*d*) what does
(*e*) a conductor

Choose the ***correct answer*** from the options given below:

A. (*d*), (*a*), (*e*), (*c*), (*b*) B. (*d*), (*a*), (*b*), (*e*), (*c*)
C. (*b*), (*a*), (*d*), (*e*), (*c*) D. (*d*), (*a*), (*c*), (*b*), (*e*)

**44.** Choose the correct idiomatic expression.

The staff agreed to <u>execute</u> the plans.

A. Carry away B. Lay out
C. Turn down D. Carry out

**45.** Complete the omitted/grammatically correct sentence:

"Asoka two lives, one as ruthless conqueror and the as a compassionate ruler"

(*a*) Asoka led two lives one as the most ruthless conqueror and the as a compassionate ruler.
(*b*) Asoka led two various lives, one ruthless conqueror and the as a compassionate ruler.
(*c*) Asoka led two live one as ruthless conqueror and the as a famous compassionate ruler.
(*d*) Asoka led two lives one as ruthless conqueror and the other as a compassionate ruler.
(*e*) Asoka led two lives one as ruthless conqueror so and the as a compassionate ruler.

Choose the correct answer from the options given below:

A. (*a*) only B. (*b*) only
C. (*e*) only D. (*d*) only

**46.** Choose the correct subject for a letter of enquiry for a course in Choreography:

A. Enquiry for choreography
B. Course in choreography
C. Enquiry regarding course in choreography
D. Enquiry in course of choreography

**47.** Choose the correct Assertive sentence of the given sentence:

Alas that youth should pass away!

A. It is sad that youth has passed away
B. It is sad to think that youth should pass away
C. It is sad that youth shall pass away
D. It is sad that youth passes away

**48.** Complete the sentence in List I with the correct preposition from List II:

| ***List-I*** | ***List-II*** |
|---|---|
| (*a*) ____ the street the piper slept | (*i*) in |
| (*b*) Little Jack Horner sat ____ a corner | (*ii*) into |
| (*c*) Old mother Hubbard went ____ the cupboard | (*iii*) over |
| (*d*) The cow jumped ____ the moon | (*iv*) to |

Choose the correct answer from the options given below:

| | (*a*) | (*b*) | (*c*) | (*d*) |
|---|---|---|---|---|
| A. | (*ii*) | (*i*) | (*iv*) | (*iii*) |
| B. | (*i*) | (*ii*) | (*iv*) | (*iii*) |
| C. | (*iii*) | (*ii*) | (*i*) | (*iv*) |
| D. | (*ii*) | (*iii*) | (*iv*) | (*i*) |

**49.** Find out which part of the sentence has an error.

The captain along with his team are practicing very hard for the forthcoming matches.

A. The Captain along with his team
B. are practicing very hard
C. for the
D. forthcoming matches

**50.** Spot the Error

(*a*) Copernicus proved (*b*) that Earth
(*c*) moves (*d*) round
(*e*) the sun

Choose the ***correct answer*** from the options given below:

A. (*b*) only B. (*c*) only
C. (*d*) only D. (*e*) only

# ANSWERS

1. **(B):** The village school's location is mentioned in the passage as being in a prominent place surrounded by some shops, a temple, and a government dispensary. There's no direct mention of the school being near a forest, library, or pond. However, the presence of shops suggests a market-like setting, which makes option B the most likely answer.

2. **(D):** The doctor's routine after his duty hours is clearly stated in the passage. It says that the doctor "used to retire to his residence after the duty hours and never allowed anyone to visit his residence after the duty hours." This directly indicates that he rested at his home and was strict about not entertaining visitors during that time.

3. **(A):** The primary reason the dog became aggressive and bit a child is directly linked to a particular action from one of the children. The passage mentions, "One of them pelted a stone at the dog." This act of mischief from the child triggered the dog's aggressive behavior. In this scenario, pelting a stone can be seen as a direct threat, leading to the dog's defensive reaction.

4. **(D):** The doctor's initial refusal to help was overridden when he saw the headmaster's state of extreme worry and the injured student's pain. The passage says, "the doctor opened the door when he saw the headmaster trembling with fear and the student in agony and pain." Following this, the doctor's subsequent actions and feelings were influenced by the headmaster's dedication. The doctor was "impressed by the dedication and sincerity of the headmaster." The headmaster's commitment to the well-being of his student is evident here, showcasing the strong bond and sense of responsibility educators often feel towards their students.

5. **(C):** The term "mellowed" in the passage refers to the doctor's change in behavior from strict and unyielding to more understanding and compassionate. The phrase "The doctor mellowed down now" indicates a reduction in his earlier stern behavior. In this context, "to mellow" means to become gentler or more lenient, which aligns with the definition of "to become less extreme in behavior."

6. **(C):** India's hard-won independence came after a prolonged "struggle for decades," as stated in the passage. This wasn't a result of wars or direct fights, nor was it a gift from excellent leaders or foreign aid. The mention of the prolonged struggle underscores the sacrifices, non-violent protests, negotiations, and relentless efforts made by the entire nation to free itself from colonial rule.

7. **(A):** Dr. A.P.J. Abdul Kalam, a visionary leader and former President of India, always emphasized on the power of the youth. In the passage, he inspires students to "ignite your minds" as a means to transform India into a developed nation. Igniting the mind symbolizes invoking curiosity, passion, and a thirst for knowledge and innovation.

8. **(B):** "Administrators" are pinpointed in the passage as having a significant role in bridging the gap between the people and political leaders, subsequently aiding in transformation. Administrators, in this context, likely refer to government officials and civil servants who are responsible for implementing policies and ensuring governance at the grassroots level.

9. **(D):** The "existence of our very nationhood" is closely tied to the mission of the "parliament," as highlighted in the passage. A nation's parliament is its supreme legislative body and represents the collective will of its people. It enacts laws, discusses national issues, and holds the government accountable.

10. **(C):** The term "intruder" is synonymous with 'trespasser'. An intruder is someone who enters a place without permission or authorization, often with malicious intent. In the context of the passage, the term is used to emphasize the importance of safeguarding India's hard-won freedom from those who might seek to harm or compromise it. The reference to intruders can be seen as a broader metaphor for any force or ideology that might threaten India's sovereignty, harmony, or security.

11. **(B):** The **Indian Space Research Organisation (ISRO)** is credited with setting up Village Resource Centres (VRCs) to extend space-based services to the rural populace. ISRO, established in 1969, has been instrumental in utilizing space technology for India's development, especially focusing on rural and remote areas.

12. **(B):** The passage clearly mentions that ISRO has collaborated with forty partner agencies spread out across **twenty-two states** for the VRC program. India, with its diverse geography and vast area, has always faced challenges in ensuring that the benefits of technology and development reach even the most remote corners. The initiative to span across twenty-two states shows the program's expansive reach, attempting to bring the advantages of space technology to a broader spectrum of the Indian population.

**13. (D):** Matching the terms with their respective meanings or representations, we get:

- SatCom (*a*) aligns with Satellite Communication (*iii*), which is a technology for relaying and broadcasting information using satellites.
- VRCs (*b*) stands for Village Resource Centres (*i*), which are centers established in rural regions to provide space-based services.
- ISRO (*c*) is the acronym for Indian Space Research Organisation (*iv*), the space agency of the Government of India.
- INSAT (*d*) matches with Indian National Satellite System (*ii*), a series of multipurpose geostationary satellites commissioned by ISRO to cater to telecommunications, broadcasting, meteorology, and search and rescue operations.

**14. (D):** The word **'Prediction'** means to foresee or anticipate an event before it takes place. In the realm of space technology and observation, prediction plays a pivotal role, especially in forecasting natural calamities, weather patterns, or any other potential events that could have significant societal implications.

**15. (C):** The term **'Vulnerable'** denotes a state of susceptibility or being prone to harm, danger, or risk. In contrast to being 'safe' or 'secure,' a vulnerable state means that there's potential exposure to harm. In the context of space-based observations, understanding vulnerabilities becomes vital. By identifying areas, populations, or resources that are vulnerable - be it to natural disasters, climate change, or any other threats - proactive measures can be adopted to mitigate adverse impacts. (B) The correct option is "a few." In this context, "questions" is a countable noun. The determiner "much" is used with uncountable nouns, "any" usually appears in negative or interrogative contexts, and "every" doesn't fit grammatically. "A few" is used to indicate a small number of countable nouns. Therefore, "The teacher asked him a few questions." is the appropriate construction.

**16. (B):** Direct speech is a direct quotation of what someone else said. The phrase "He requested me to shut the door." can be changed to direct speech as "He said, 'Please shut the door". The word "please" implies a request. The other options do not convey the sense of a request as directly and politely as option B does.

**17. (B)** **18. (C)** **19. (B)**

**20. (B):** The correct answer is "a European a one-rupee coin." In this case, "European" is used as a noun referring to a person from Europe. When we refer to a singular, unspecified entity, we use the indefinite article "a" before consonant sounds and "an" before vowel sounds. "European" starts with a "y" sound (a consonant sound) and "one-rupee coin" starts with a "w" sound (also a consonant sound). Therefore, "a" is the appropriate article for both nouns.

**21. (A):** The correct set of prepositions is "in" and "of." We use "in" to describe a manner or way in which something is done, and "of" to show possession or relation. Therefore, "He is notoriously mean in his treatment of his servants" implies that he treats his servants in a mean manner.

**22. (B):** The word "alleviate" means to make a situation or a pain less severe. Out of the given options, "lessen" and "reduce" are synonyms to "alleviate" as they both convey the idea of diminishing or decreasing something in intensity, degree, or amount.

**23. (A):** An exclamatory sentence is one that expresses strong emotion. In this context, "How beautiful is the night!" is the correct exclamatory form of "The night is very beautiful." This structure ("How [adjective] is [subject]!") is a common form of expressing admiration or surprise in English exclamatory sentences.

**24. (A):** When converting direct speech to indirect speech, the exact words of the speaker are paraphrased and certain changes are made to pronouns, tense, and words showing place and time. The correct conversion of "Adesh said, 'Please shut the door behind you.'" is "Adesh requested me to please shut the door behind me." This captures the essence of the request made by Adesh without directly quoting him.

**25. (A):** Matching the phrases with their meanings:

- (*a*) "I had so much work to do but the fever got the best of me" corresponds to (*iv*) "Take advantage of something." This phrase implies that the fever overcame or overwhelmed the person, preventing them from working.
- (*b*) "They spent their halcyon days in a village" matches with (*i*) "Peaceful time." "Halcyon days" is an idiom that means a calm, peaceful, or happy period in the past.
- (*c*) "He earned really well but ended up penniless. Gambling was his Achilles heel" aligns with (*ii*) "Vulnerable/Weak spot." An "Achilles heel" refers to a person's main weakness or vulnerability.
- (*d*) "A doctor worth his salt will advise people for healthy eating" pairs with (*iii*) "Competent for a work." The idiom "worth one's salt" means to be competent or deserving of one's salary or position.

**26. (C):** The word "entourage" refers to a group of people attending or surrounding an important person. In this context, it pertains to the minister's accompanying group, which can be his aides, assistants, or any other group of followers. Hence, the most accurate meaning among the given options is "following subordinates."

**27. (B):** An adverb is a word that modifies a verb, an adjective, or another adverb. In the given sentence, "often" modifies the verb "complain" and "easily" modifies the verb "try." Therefore, the correct adverbs from the sentence are "often" and "easily."

**28. (A):** The term "camouflage" means to disguise something, usually to make it blend in with its surroundings. Out of the given options, "disguise" directly captures the essence of "camouflage." Thus, the word "disguise" is synonymous with "camouflage."

**29. (C):** The sentence indicates a completed action in the past relative to another past action or event. The train had already departed by the time the speaker reached the station. The correct tense to denote this sequence of past events is the past perfect tense, which is formed using "had" + past participle. Therefore, "had already left" is the appropriate completion for the sentence.

**30. (B):** Clauses in English can function as different parts of speech and can be classified based on their function. In the sentence "The Children whom I teach in standard 8 are very disciplined," the underlined clause "whom I teach in standard 8" provides additional information about "The Children," making it an adjective clause. An adjective clause modifies a noun (in this case, "The Children") and often starts with relative pronouns like "who," "whom," "whose," "which," or "that."

**31. (A):** Idioms are fixed expressions with meanings not directly deducible from the individual words. For the given idioms: (*a*) "At one's fingertips" means having information or a skill readily available. (*b*) "Hold one's tongue" means to refrain from speaking. (*c*) "Lose one's head" suggests panicking or acting without thinking. (*d*) "Win hands down" means to win easily. Thus, the correct matches are (*ii*), (*i*), (*iii*), and (*iv*) respectively.

**32. (B):** Antonyms are words that have opposite meanings. The word 'Terrible' denotes something causing fear or dread. Among the given options, "soothing" suggests calmness and comfort, making it the opposite of "terrible."

**33. (A):** Matching words with their antonyms: (*a*) The opposite of "Charming," which means attractive, is "Hideous" implying ugly. (*b*) "Occasional" means happening from time to time, while "Regular" implies happening frequently. (*c*) "Generous" means giving more than is necessary or usual, while its opposite "Miser" denotes a person who hoards money and avoids spending. (*d*) "Exhibit" means to display or show, while "Hide" means to conceal. So, the correct antonyms are (*iii*), (*iv*), (*ii*), and (*i*).

**34. (A):** Arranging sentences in a logical order is essential for coherence. The correct sequence forms a comprehensible statement about human language: "The language of man (*e*) has been mainly occupied (*b*) with telling us about (*a*) the elements into which (*d*) the finite world has been analysed (*c*)."

**35. (D):** Understanding the meaning of phrases is essential for comprehension: (*a*) "Set in" means to begin or commence. (*b*) "Wind up" denotes bringing something to a conclusion or end. (*c*) "Look down upon" signifies treating someone with contempt or considering them inferior. (*d*) "Put out" means extinguished, usually in the context of a light or fire. The correct matches are (*iii*), (*iv*), (*i*), and (*ii*).

**36. (B):** The Latin word "animus" refers to a feeling of ill will, animosity, or hostility. Thus, the correct meaning of 'animus' in the given context is "bad intention."

**37. (B):** Changing a sentence to passive voice involves shifting the focus from the doer of the action to the receiver of the action. The sentence "One should keep one's promises" focuses on the act of keeping promises, so in passive form, it becomes "Promises should be kept," which emphasizes the promises themselves.

**38. (A):** The given sentence implies a sense of obligation or duty in the past that wasn't met. The phrase "ought to have" suggests a missed obligation or something that should have been done in the past but wasn't. Thus, "You ought to have stood by your friends in their bad times" indicates that it was expected or would have been right for the person to stand by their friends, but they didn't.

**39. (C):** Question tags are short questions at the end of statements. They're used mainly in speech. When the main part of the sentence is negative, the question tag is positive. "She doesn't really know" is negative, so the tag should be positive: "does she?"

**40. (C):** To form the passive, you use the appropriate form of verb "to be" + the past participle of the main verb. The given sentence, "Your behaviour astonished me," is in the active voice where "me" is the object. In its passive form, "me" becomes the subject and the focus shifts to the feeling, making it "I was astonished by your behaviour."

**41. (B):** A "heretic" is someone who holds beliefs that are contrary to the accepted beliefs of a particular religion. The definition provided "One who acts against religion" aligns closely with this term. An egoist is someone centered on their own needs, an optimist is someone who looks at the positive side of things, and a stoic is someone who endures pain without showing feelings.

**42. (A):** Homonyms are words that are pronounced the same but differ in meaning, derivation, or spelling. In this context, the word "Rites" (religious practices or ceremonies) is suitable. "Wrights" refers to makers or builders (like "wheelwright"), "Rights" are entitlements or freedoms, and "Raight" is not a standard English word.

**43. (B)**

**44. (D):** Idiomatic expressions are phrases that have a figurative meaning different from their literal meaning. The phrase "carry out" means to execute or perform an action, which aligns with the given statement about executing plans. "Carry away" means to become overly enthusiastic, "Lay out" is to present or explain something in detail, and "Turn down" means to reject or decline.

**45. (D):** Constructing the sentence, we need to establish a comparison between two types of lives led by Asoka. The sentence "Asoka led two lives one as ruthless conqueror and the other as a compassionate ruler" correctly juxtaposes the two contrasting phases of his life. It also uses correct parallel structure, using "one as" and "the other as" to introduce the two lives.

**46. (C):** "Enquiry regarding course in choreography" is the most comprehensive and clear subject for a letter of inquiry. It explicitly states that the inquiry is about a course specifically in choreography. While the other options also imply an inquiry about choreography, option C provides the most direct and clear phrasing for the context.

**47. (B):** An assertive sentence is a declarative statement. The original sentence, "Alas that youth should pass away!", is an exclamatory sentence that conveys a feeling of sadness about the passing of youth. The closest option that captures this sentiment in a declarative way is "It is sad to think that youth should pass away."

**48. (A)**

**49. (B):** The phrase "The captain along with his team" requires a singular verb because "along with" doesn't make the noun plural. So, the verb "are" should be changed to "is". The correct statement should be "The captain along with his team is practicing very hard for the forthcoming matches."

**50. (A):** Copernicus did not just prove "that Earth" but rather "that the Earth." Proper nouns like Earth, when referred to as the planet we live on, often take the definite article "the." The rest of the statement, "moves round the sun," is accurate, as it accurately captures the heliocentric theory that Copernicus is known for.

# BUSINESS STUDIES

**1.** Staffing is the part of which functional area of Management?
A. Marketing Management
B. Human Resource Management
C. Production Management
D. Financial Management

**2.** Social Environment includes:
A. Consumption habits and life expectancies
B. Money supply in the economy
C. Rate of savings
D. New ways of producing goods

**3.** Which element of Marketing Mix refers to activities that make firm's product available to the target customers?
A. Promotion B. Place
C. Price D. Product

**4.** Arrange the following functions of Management:
(*a*) Staffing (*b*) Planning
(*c*) Organizing (*d*) Controlling
(*e*) Directing

Choose the ***correct answer*** from the options given below:
A. (*a*), (*b*), (*c*), (*d*), (*e*) B. (*b*), (*c*), (*a*), (*e*), (*d*)
C. (*c*), (*b*), (*a*), (*d*), (*e*) D. (*b*), (*c*), (*a*), (*d*), (*e*)

**5.** Identify the trend in stock market when equity shares are more easily sold even at higher price:
A. Bearish B. Bullish
C. Horse trading D. Badla

**6.** Identify the market that is known as Stock Exchange:
A. Secondary Market B. Money Market
C. Capital Market D. Primary Market

**7.** Identify for the following under whose overall administrative control, SEBI functions:
A. Ministry of Corporate Affairs, GOI
B. Ministry of Home Affairs, GOI
C. Ministry of Finance, GOI
D. Ministry of External Affairs, GOI

**8.** Identify the specific forces of Business Environment from following:
(*a*) Investors
(*b*) Customers
(*c*) Social
(*d*) Political
(*e*) Competitors

Choose the ***correct answer*** from the options given below:
A. (*a*), (*b*), (*c*) and (*d*) only
B. (*a*), (*b*) and (*e*) only
C. (*c*) and (*d*) only
D. (*c*), (*d*) and (*e*) only

**9.** Match List I with List II:

| *List-I* | *List-II* |
|---|---|
| (*a*) District Commission | (*i*) One crore to Ten crore rupees |
| (*b*) State Commission | (*ii*) Appeal against National Commission in matter of its original jurisdiction |
| (*c*) National Commission | (*iii*) Upto one crore rupees |
| (*d*) Supreme Court | (*iv*) Exceeds Ten crore rupees |

Choose the ***correct answer*** from the options given below:

| | (*a*) | (*b*) | (*c*) | (*d*) |
|---|---|---|---|---|
| A. | (*i*) | (*ii*) | (*iii*) | (*iv*) |
| B. | (*iv*) | (*iii*) | (*ii*) | (*i*) |
| C. | (*iii*) | (*i*) | (*iv*) | (*ii*) |
| D. | (*iii*) | (*i*) | (*ii*) | (*iv*) |

**10.** Arrange the steps of Trading and Settlement procedure in Securities:
(*a*) Open a demat account
(*b*) Place an order with the broker
(*c*) Sign a broker-client agreement
(*d*) Broker match the share price available
(*e*) Broker issue a trade confirmation slip

Choose the ***correct answer*** from the options given below:
A. (*a*), (*b*), (*c*), (*d*), (*e*) B. (*e*), (*d*), (*c*), (*b*), (*a*)
C. (*c*), (*a*), (*b*), (*d*), (*e*) D. (*c*), (*a*), (*d*), (*b*), (*e*)

**11.** Salary is not a primary economic reward for an entrepreneur:
(*a*) A 'never say die' attitude of an entrepreneur is termed as self-confidence.
(*b*) Acting out of choice rather than compulsion is initiative
(*c*) Entrepreneur's concern for conservation of time and money is termed as 'assertiveness'
(*d*) Executive summary and operation strategies are included in Business Plan

Choose the ***correct answer*** from the options given below:
A. (*a*), (*c*), (*e*) only B. (*a*), (*b*), (*e*) only
C. (*a*), (*d*), (*e*) only D. (*a*), (*b*), (*c*) only

**12.** Process which provides for learning opportunities that helps employee growth is:

A. Education B. Development
C. Training D. Education and Training

**13.** Arrange the Channels of Distribution in order for a consumer product:

(*a*) Consumer (*b*) Retailer
(*c*) Wholesaler (*d*) Producer

Choose the ***correct answer*** from the option given below:

A. (*a*), (*b*), (*c*), (*d*) B. (*d*), (*c*), (*b*), (*a*)
C. (*c*), (*a*), (*b*), (*d*) D. (*a*), (*d*), (*c*), (*b*)

**14.** "Dependence on technological gadgets is comparatively higher in America than in India". Which feature of business environment is highlighted by the statement?

A. Relativity B. Uncertainity
C. Complexity D. Dynamic

**15.** Match List I with List II:

| *List-I* | *List-II* |
|---|---|
| (*a*) Job Enrichment | (*i*) Indicates the characteristics which describe an organisation |
| (*b*) Organisational Climate | (*ii*) Informal Communication |
| (*c*) Laissez-faire | (*iii*) Leadership Style |
| (*d*) Grapevine | (*iv*) Concerned with designing jobs that include greater variety of work content. |

Choose the ***correct answer*** from the options given below:

| | (*a*) | (*b*) | (*c*) | (*d*) |
|---|---|---|---|---|
| A. | (*iii*) | (*iv*) | (*ii*) | (*i*) |
| B. | (*iii*) | (*iv*) | (*i*) | (*ii*) |
| C. | (*iv*) | (*ii*) | (*iii*) | (*i*) |
| D. | (*iv*) | (*i*) | (*iii*) | (*ii*) |

**16.** Select from following who is considered Risk taker:

A. Manager
B. Customer
C. Entrepreneur
D. Government

**17.** Which of the following are the features of leadership:

(*a*) It tries to bring change in the behaviour of a person
(*b*) It is an internal feeling
(*c*) It indicates interpersonal relationship between leaders and followers
(*d*) It is a continuous process

Choose the ***correct answer*** from the options given below:

A. (*a*), (*c*) and (*d*) only
B. (*a*) and (*c*) only
C. (*a*), (*b*) and (*d*) only
D. (*c*) and (*d*) only

**18.** Match List I with List II:

| *List-I* | *List-II* |
|---|---|
| (*a*) Regulatory Function of SEBI | (*i*) Levying fee or other charges |
| (*b*) Development Function of SEBI | (*ii*) Training of intermediaries |
| (*c*) Protective Function of SEBI | (*iii*) Controlling insider training |
| (*d*) Objective of SEBI | (*iv*) Regulate stock exchanges |

Choose the ***correct answer*** from the options given below:

| | (*a*) | (*b*) | (*c*) | (*d*) |
|---|---|---|---|---|
| A. | (*i*) | (*ii*) | (*iv*) | (*iii*) |
| B. | (*i*) | (*ii*) | (*iii*) | (*iv*) |
| C. | (*iii*) | (*ii*) | (*iv*) | (*i*) |
| D. | (*iii*) | (*i*) | (*ii*) | (*iv*) |

**19.** Which technique of Scientific Management violates Unity of Command?

A. Time study
B. Standardisation of work
C. Functional Foremenship
D. Simplification of work

**20.** External Sources of recruitment does not include:

(*a*) Casual callers
(*b*) Employment exchange
(*c*) Transfer
(*d*) Advertising
(*e*) Promotions

Choose the ***correct answer*** from the options given below:

A. (*a*) and (*b*) only B. (*b*) and (*c*) only
C. (*c*) and (*e*) only D. (*d*) and (*e*) only

**21.** Match List I with List II:

| *List-I* | *List-II* |
|---|---|
| (*a*) Treasury Bill | (*i*) Mobilise large amount of money |
| (*b*) Commercial paper | (*ii*) Maturity period of one day to fifteen days |
| (*c*) Call money | (*iii*) Maturity period of 15 days to one year |
| (*d*) Certificate of Deposit | (*iv*) Issued by RBI |

Choose the ***correct answer*** from the options given below:

| | (*a*) | (*b*) | (*c*) | (*d*) |
|---|---|---|---|---|
| A. | (*iii*) | (*i*) | (*ii*) | (*iv*) |
| B. | (*ii*) | (*iii*) | (*iv*) | (*i*) |
| C. | (*iv*) | (*iii*) | (*ii*) | (*i*) |
| D. | (*iv*) | (*iii*) | (*i*) | (*ii*) |

**22.** Which quality of a leader requires that he should understand people and maintain good human relations with them:

A. Initiative
B. Communication skills
C. Integrity
D. Social Skills

**23.** Planning is pervasive because:
A. It is required in setting special goals
B. It is required at all levels of management
C. It is forward looking and backward looking
D. It lays down the base for other functions of management

**24.** Planning is an intellectual process that requires logic rather than wishful thinking. Which feature of planning is highlighted by the statement?
A. Futuristic B. Continuous
C. Mental exercise D. Pervasive

**25.** ______ refers to vertical shifting of employees in an organisation.
A. Promotion B. Transfer
C. Interview D. Placement

**26.** A company has replaced their obsolete machinery with a Hi-Tech machine as it could not achieve its target in the previous month due to slow production process. Which step in the process of controlling is executed by the company?
A. Measurement of actual performance
B. Comparing actual performance with standards
C. Analysing deviations
D. Taking Corrective action

**27.** Match List I with List II:

| ***List-I*** | ***List-II*** |
|---|---|
| (*a*) Convenience products | (*i*) Consumed in one or few uses |
| (*b*) Shopping products | (*ii*) Brand loyality of the highest order |
| (*c*) Speciality products | (*iii*) Purchased frequently |
| (*d*) Non durable products | (*iv*) Buyers devote considerable time |

Choose the ***correct answer*** from the options given below:

| | (*a*) | (*b*) | (*c*) | (*d*) |
|---|---|---|---|---|
| A. | (*iii*) | (*iv*) | (*ii*) | (*i*) |
| B. | (*iii*) | (*ii*) | (*iv*) | (*i*) |
| C. | (*iv*) | (*iii*) | (*ii*) | (*i*) |
| D. | (*i*) | (*ii*) | (*iii*) | (*iv*) |

**28.** According to which principle of management, "Organisation should have a chain of authority and communication that runs from top to bottom and should be followed by managers and the subordinates."
A. Centralisation and Decentralisation
B. Subordination of individual interest to general interest
C. Scalar chain
D. Espirit De Corps

**29.** Which technique of Scientific Management violates Fayol's principle of Equity?
A. Standardization of work
B. Motion Study
C. Differential Piece wage System
D. Mental Revolution

**30.** Which Marketing Management philosophy has main focus on existing product?
A. Selling concept B. Production concept
C. Product concept D. Marketing concept

**31.** Capital structure should emphasize on:
A. Increasing the turnover of firm
B. Increasing the assets and liabilities of firm
C. Increasing the shareholders wealth
D. Increasing voting right of shareholders

**32.** Identify the correct sequence of first five steps of staffing process:
(*a*) Estimating the manpower requirement
(*b*) Recruitment
(*c*) Training and development
(*d*) Placement and orientation
(*e*) Selection

Choose the ***correct answer*** from the options given below:
A. (*a*), (*b*), (*d*), (*c*), (*e*)
B. (*a*), (*b*), (*c*), (*d*), (*e*)
C. (*a*), (*b*), (*e*), (*d*), (*c*)
D. (*a*), (*c*), (*b*), (*d*), (*e*)

**33.** "The principles of management are not rigid prescriptions, these can be modified by the manager when the situation so demands."

What nature of principles of management has been indicated in above statement?
A. General guidelines
B. Flexible
C. Contingent
D. Mainly behavioural

**34.** Arrange following elements of communication process in a sequence:
(*a*) Sender
(*b*) Receiver
(*c*) Message
(*d*) Media
(*e*) Feedback

Choose the ***correct answer*** from the options given below:
A. (*a*), (*c*), (*b*), (*e*), (*d*) B. (*c*), (*a*), (*b*), (*d*), (*e*)
C. (*a*), (*c*), (*d*), (*b*), (*e*) D. (*a*), (*c*), (*b*), (*d*), (*e*)

**35.** Match List I with List II:

| *List-I* | *List-II* |
|---|---|
| (*a*) Advertising Expenditure | (*i*) Human Resource Management |
| (*b*) Quality | (*ii*) Finance and Accounting |
| (*c*) Labour Turnover | (*iii*) Marketing |
| (*d*) Liquidity | (*iv*) Production |

Choose the ***correct answer*** from the options given below:

| | (*a*) | (*b*) | (*c*) | (*d*) |
|---|---|---|---|---|
| A. | (*iii*) | (*iv*) | (*ii*) | (*i*) |
| B. | (*iii*) | (*iv*) | (*i*) | (*ii*) |
| C. | (*iv*) | (*iii*) | (*ii*) | (*i*) |
| D. | (*iv*) | (*iii*) | (*i*) | (*ii*) |

**36.** Identify the rights provided to consumers by the Consumer Protection Act 2019

(*a*) Right to Safety
(*b*) Right to be Informed
(*c*) Right to choose
(*d*) Right to be heard
(*e*) Right to be assured

Choose the ***correct answer*** from the options given below:

A. (*a*), (*b*), (*c*) and (*d*) only
B. (*a*), (*b*), (*c*) and (*e*) only
C. (*a*), (*b*), (*d*) and (*e*) only
D. (*a*), (*b*) and (*c*) only

**37.** Identify the Non Financial Incentive that give more autonomy and powers to subordinates:

A. Employee participation
B. Employee Empowerment
C. Organisational climate
D. Co-partnership

**38.** As per Consumer Protection Act, 2019, State commission has a jurisidiction to entertain complaints where value of goods and services paid as consideration:

A. Does not exceed one crore but more than 20 lakh rupees
B. Exceeds one crore but does not exceed ten crore rupees
C. Exceeds five crore but does not exceed ten crore rupees
D. Exceeds four crore but does not exceed five crores rupees

**39.** The primary aim of financial management is:

A. Maximise profit of firm
B. Maximise sales of firm
C. Maximise shareholders' wealth
D. Maximise number of customer of firm

**40.** Arrange the steps of Controlling process in a logical sequence.

(*a*) Measurement of Actual performance
(*b*) Setting performance standards
(*c*) Taking Corrective action
(*d*) Comparison of actual performance with standards
(*e*) Analysing deviations

Choose the ***correct answer*** from the options given below:

A. (*b*), (*a*), (*d*), (*e*), (*c*)
B. (*c*), (*d*), (*a*), (*b*), (*e*)
C. (*a*), (*b*), (*c*), (*d*), (*e*)
D. (*c*), (*e*), (*d*), (*b*), (*a*)

**Directions (Qs. No. 41-45):** *Read the case given below and attempt the following questions:*

Rohan is the Head Boy of Ethos Public School. The School is going to hold a covid vaccination camp for students of age group 12-14 yrs in the month of May. The entire Prefectorial Board is given the duties for the event under the leadership of Rohan. Rohan has shortlisted following activities:

1. Identification of students eligible for vaccination under 12-14 years.
2. Obtaining Aadhar card for registration of these students on the covid vaccination App
3. Consent letters of parents

He further divided the execution part activities. Later he grouped the similar natured activities into different units. Then he allocated these to different prefects under his prefectorial board. Thereafter he devised a computer software where each prefect was supposed to enter his data of vaccination for further submission to school headmistress.

**41.** ______ is the function of management discussed in the above passage:

A. Planning
B. Directing
C. Organising
D. Staffing

**42.** Rohan has shortlisted following activities

Identify the step highlighted in the above line in the process of organisation.

A. Setting objectives
B. Assignment of duties
C. Identifying the alternative courses of action
D. Identification and division of work

**43.** "Later he grouped the similar natured activities into different units"

Identify the step highlighted in the above line in the organisation process.

A. Implementing the plan
B. Measurement of actual performance
C. Departmentalisation
D. Selecting an alternative

**44.** "Then he allocated these to different prefects under his prefectorial board"

Which step of organisation process is discussed in these lines?

A. Assignment of duties
B. Implementing the plan

C. Division of activities
D. Follow up action

**45.** "Thereafter he devised a computer software where each prefect was supposed to enter his data of vaccination for further submission to school headmistress".

Identify the step of organisation process discussed in above statement.
A. Follow up action
B. Establishing reporting relationship
C. Corrective action
D. Assignment of duties

**Directions (Qs. No. 46-50):** *Read the case given below and attempt the following questions:*

Management is the process of planning, organising, staffing, directing and controlling the enterprise resources efficiently and effectively for achieving the goals of the organisation. Effectiveness in Management is concerned with doing the right task, completing activities and achieving goals. Efficiency means doing the task correctly with minimum cost.

**46.** Company's target production is 10,000 units in a year. To achieve this target the manager has to operate on double shifts due to power failure most of the time.

In the above case manager was:
A. Effective and efficient both
B. Only efficient
C. Efficient but not effective
D. Effective but not so efficient

**47.** Cutting down the cost but not achieving the target production is an example of:
A. Effective but not efficient
B. Effective and efficient both
C. Effecient but not effective
D. Neither efficient nor effective

**48.** ______ implies setting goals in advance and developing a way of achieving them efficiently and effectively.
A. Organising
B. Controlling
C. Planning
D. Coordination

**49.** ______ is the management function of monitoring organisational performance towards the attainment of organisational goals:
A. Planning B. Organising
C. Directing D. Controlling

**50.** ______ determines what activities and resources are required.
A. Planning B. Organising
C. Controlling D. Directing

## ANSWERS

**1. (B):** Staffing is a crucial part of Human Resource Management (HRM). It refers to the process of acquiring, developing, and retaining employees to ensure that an organization has the right people in the right positions to achieve its goals and objectives efficiently and effectively. Effective staffing within Human Resource Management is vital for building a capable and motivated workforce, which, in turn, contributes to the organization's growth and success.

**2. (A):** The social environment refers to the factors and conditions that influence the behaviour, beliefs, lifestyle, and values of individuals and groups within society. It encompasses various aspects of human life, including cultural norms, demographic trends, education levels, consumption patterns, and health-related factors like life expectancies.

**3. (B):** In the Marketing Mix, also known as the 4Ps of marketing, "Place" refers to the element that deals with the activities and strategies involved in making the firm's product available to the target customers. It focuses on the distribution channels, logistics, and locations where the product will be sold or delivered to the customers. Place decisions are crucial in ensuring that the product reaches the right customers at the right time and in the right quantities to satisfy their needs and preferences.

**4. (B):** (*b*) **Planning:** Planning is the first and most fundamental function of management. It involves setting organizational goals, determining the strategies and actions needed to achieve those goals, and developing comprehensive plans to guide the organiza-tion's activities. The planning process includes defining objectives, identifying tasks, allocating resources, and establishing timelines for accomplishing the desired outcomes.

(*c*) **Organizing:** Organizing is the function that involves arranging and structuring the resources of the organization to effectively carry out the plans. This includes defining roles, responsibilities, and relationships among employees, establishing reporting lines, and creating a framework that ensures the smooth flow of work. The goal of organizing is to maximize efficiency and facilitate coordination within the organization.

(*a*) **Staffing:** Staffing is the function responsible for acquiring, developing, and retaining a qualified and capable workforce to achieve organizational objectives. It involves recruit-ment, selection, training, and development of employees, as well as addressing their needs and ensuring their well-being in the workplace. Staffing aims to ensure that the right people with the right skills are in the right positions.

(*e*) **Directing:** Directing, also known as leading or guiding, is the function that focuses on influencing and motivating employees to achieve organizational goals. It involves communicating the vision and objectives, guiding and supervising employees' efforts, and providing support and encouragement to enhance their performance. Effective leadership is essential for maintaining a positive work environment and inspiring the team to perform at their best.

(*d*) **Controlling:** Controlling is the final function of management and involves monitoring, comparing, and correcting the actual performance against the planned objectives. This function ensures that the organization's activities are in line with the established plans and standards. If any deviations or issues arise, controlling involves taking corrective actions to bring the performance back on track and achieve the desired outcomes.

Each function is interconnected and contributes to the overall success of an organization. Effective management involves harmonizing these functions to work together seamlessly and guide the organization toward its goals in an efficient and coordinated manner.

**5. (B):** When equity shares are more easily sold, even at higher prices, it indicates a bullish trend in the stock market. In a bullish market,. investor confidence is high, and there is a general optimism about the future performance of the stock market. The ,demand for stocks is greater than the supply, leading to an increase in stock prices, and investors are willing to buy shares with the expectation of further price appreciation.

**6. (A):** The market that is known as the Stock Exchange is the Secondary Market. It is where securities that have been previously issued in the primary market (through initial public offerings or IPOs) are bought and sold among investors. In the secondary market, investors trade stocks, bonds, and other financial instruments with each other, and the prices are determined by the forces of supply and demand.

**7. (C):** SEBI (Securities and Exchange Board of India) functions under the overall administrative control of the Ministry of Finance, Government of India. SEBI is the regulatory body responsible for overseeing and regulating the securities market in India. Its main objective is to protect the interests of investors, ensure fair and transparent dealings in the securities market, and promote the development and regulation of the securities market in the country.

**8. (B):** (*a*) **Investors:** Investors are individuals, institutions, or entities that provide capital or financial resources to a business. They can be shareholders, venture capitalists, angel investors, or other funding sources. Investors play a crucial role in the growth and development of a business as they provide the necessary funds for expansion, research and development, and operational activities. In return for their investment, they may expect returns on their investment in the form of dividends, capital appreciation, or other financial benefits. Businesses need to attract and retain investors to ensure financial stability and support their long-term goals.

(*b*) **Customers:** Customers are the individuals or organizations that purchase goods and services from a business. They are the end-users of the products or services offered by the company. Customer preferences, demands, and feedback have a direct impact on a business's success. Understanding customer needs and providing high-quality products or services that meet those needs is essential for building customer loyalty and maintaining a competitive advantage in the market.

(*e*) **Competitors:** Competitors are other businesses or organizations operating in the same industry or offering similar products or services. Competition in the market affects a company's pricing strategy, marketing efforts, and overall performance. Businesses need to analyze their competitors' strengths and weaknesses to identify opportunities and threats in the market. Competing effectively against rivals is critical for gaining market share and sustaining growth.

**9. (C)**

**10. (C): (*c*) Sign a broker-client agreement:** Before trading in securities, an investor needs to sign a broker-client agreement with the brokerage firm. This agreement outlines the terms and conditions of the client's relationship with the broker.

(*a*) **Open a demat account:** A demat account is a digital account used to hold and trade securities in electronic form. Investors need to open a demat account with a depository participant (DP) to facilitate the electronic transfer of shares.

(*b*) **Place an order with the broker:** Once the demat account is set up, the investor can place an order with the broker to buy or sell specific securities. The order can be given through various means, such as phone, online trading platform, or mobile application.

(*d*) **Broker matches the share price available:** After receiving the order, the broker matches it with the available share prices in the market. If a suitable match is found, the trade is executed.

(*e*) **Broker issues a trade confirmation slip:** After the trade is executed, the broker issues a trade confirmation slip to the investor. This slip contains details of the transaction, including the quantity, price, and date of the trade.

**11. (*)**

**12. (B):** The process that provides learning opportunities to help employee growth is "Development." Employee development focuses on enhancing the skills, knowledge, and abilities of individuals within an organization to improve their performance, boost productivity, and prepare them for future roles and responsibilities. It includes activities such as workshops, seminars, coaching, mentoring, job rotations, and on-the-job learning experiences to develop employees' capabilities and potential. Unlike training, which tends to be more job-specific and focus on improving current job skills, employee development has a broader scope and aims to foster long-term career growth and personal development.

**13. (B):** (*d*) **Producer:** The producer is the entity that manufactures or produces the consumer product. They are the originators of the product and play a vital role in bringing it to the market.

(*c*) **Wholesaler:** Wholesalers are intermediaries who purchase goods in bulk from the producers and sell them in smaller quantities to retailers. They act as distributors and help in reaching the product to various retailers efficiently.

(*b*) **Retailer:** Retailers are the businesses that sell the product directly to the end consumers. They can be brick-and-mortar stores, online retailers, or any other form of businesses that provide the product to the final consumers.

(*a*) **Consumer:** The consumers are the ultimate end-users of the product who purchase and use it for personal consumption.

**14. (A):** The statement compares the dependence on technological gadgets between America and India, indicating that the level of dependence is relatively higher in America than in India. "Relativity" in the business environment context refers to the comparison or relative nature of various factors, such as economic conditions, technological advancements, consumer behaviour, and cultural practices, between different countries or regions. It acknowledges that the business environment can vary significantly from one place to another, and organizations need to adapt their strategies accordingly based on these relative differences.

**15. (D)**

**16. (C):** Entrepreneurs are considered risk-takers in the business context. An entrepreneur is an individual who starts and operates a new business venture, taking on financial and personal risks in the hope of achieving success and profitability. They invest their own resources, such as time, money, and effort, into their business ideas, and they are willing to face uncertainty and potential losses to pursue their vision and goals. Risk-taking is a significant characteristic of entrepreneurship, as entrepreneurs need to make critical decisions and navigate uncertainties to bring their ideas to fruition and create value in the market.

**17. (A):** The features of leadership from the given options are:

(*a*) **It tries to bring change in the behaviour of a person:** Leadership involves influencing and guiding others to achieve common goals. One of the key aspects of leadership is to inspire and motivate individuals to change their behaviour or actions in alignment with the shared vision.

(*c*) **It indicates interpersonal relationship between leaders and followers:** Successful leadership requires effective communication, collaboration, and a positive relationship between leaders and their followers. Interpersonal skills play a crucial role in fostering a strong team dynamic.

(*d*) **It is a continuous process:** Leadership is not a one-time event but an ongoing and continuous process. Effective leaders consistently work towards guiding and inspiring their team members, adapting to changing circumstances, and striving to achieve organizational goals over time.

**18. (B)**

**19. (C):** Functional Foremanship is a technique of Scientific Management that violates the principle of Unity of Command. In Functional Foremanship, a worker is placed under the supervision of multiple specialists or functional foremen, each responsible for a specific aspect of the worker's job. For example, one foreman may be responsible for planning and another for production, and the worker would have to report to both.

The Unity of Command principle states that a worker should have only one direct supervisor to avoid conflicting instructions and to maintain clear accountability and responsibility. With Functional Foremanship, the worker ends up reporting to multiple foremen, which can lead to confusion, inefficiency, and a lack of clarity in the chain of command.

**20. (C):** External sources of recruitment are those from which the organization brings in new employees from outside the company. Transfer and Promotions are not external sources of recruitment.

(*c*) **Transfer:** Transfer is an internal movement of employees from one position or department to another within the same organization. It is not an external source of recruitment.

(*e*) **Promotions:** Promotions refer to the advancement of current employees to higher-level positions within the organization. They are not external sources of recruitment.

**21. (C)**

**22. (D):** The quality of a leader that requires understanding people and maintaining good human relations with them is "Social Skills." Social skills refer to the ability to communicate effectively, empathize, and build rapport with others. Leaders with strong social skills can connect with their team members, understand their needs, and create a positive and supportive work environment. They can resolve conflicts, motivate their team, and foster collaboration among individuals. Social skills are essential for building strong relationships and promoting teamwork, which are crucial for successful leadership and achieving organizational goals.

**23. (B):** The reason planning is considered pervasive is that it is required at all levels of management within an organization. Planning is not limited to a specific level or department; instead, it is an essential function that takes place throughout the organization, from top-level strategic planning to middle-level tactical planning and lower-level operational planning.

All managers, regardless of their level in the organizational hierarchy, need to engage in planning to establish objectives, identify the actions required to achieve those objectives, allocate resources effectively, and set guidelines for decision-making and performance evaluation. This comprehensive approach to planning ensures that the organization's efforts are coordinated, aligned with its overall goals, and contribute to its success.

**24. (C):** The feature of planning highlighted by the statement is "Mental exercise." Planning is an intellectual and systematic process that involves using logic, analysis, and critical thinking to set objectives, identify alternative courses of action, and make decisions based on facts and data rather than wishful thinking or emotional impulses.

Through the process of planning, managers engage in mental exercises to evaluate various options, assess potential risks and benefits, and develop well-thought-out strategies to achieve organizational goals. This logical and analytical approach to planning helps in making informed decisions and increases the likelihood of successful outcomes.

**25. (A):** Promotion refers to the vertical shifting of employees in an organization. It involves the advancement of an employee to a higher-level position with increased responsibilities, authority, and often higher pay. Promotion is a form of recognition for an employee's performance and potential for growth within the organization. It is a way to reward employees for their hard work and dedication while providing them with new challenges and opportunities for career advancement.

**26. (D):** Taking corrective action is the step in the process of controlling where the organization implements measures to address the deviations or gaps between actual performance and the desired standards. When the company realizes that it could not achieve its target in the previous month due to slow production with the obsolete machinery, it decides to take corrective action by replacing the obsolete machinery with a Hi-Tech machine.

By taking corrective action, the company aims to resolve the identified issue of slow production and improve its performance. The Hi-Tech machine is expected to increase production efficiency, output, and overall performance, helping the company achieve its targets more effectively in the future.

**27. (A)**

**28. (C):** The principle of management that emphasizes that "organisation should have a chain of authority and communication that runs from top to bottom and should be followed by managers and the subordinates" is known as the "Scalar chain" principle.

The scalar chain principle states that there should be a clear and unbroken line of authority from the highest level of management to the lowest level of the organization. This chain of command ensures that there is a well-defined hierarchy, and communication flows through a specific path, promoting effective decision-making, coordination, and accountability within the organization.

Managers and subordinates are expected to follow this scalar chain of authority to ensure that orders, instructions, and information are passed down and up the hierarchy in an orderly manner. By adhering to the scalar chain principle, organizations can maintain a structured and efficient flow of communication and decision-making, which contributes to overall organizational effectiveness.

**29. (C):** The technique of Scientific Management that violates Fayol's principle of Equity is "Differential Piece wage System." Fayol's principle of Equity emphasizes treating employees with fairness and ensuring that they are compensated fairly for their work. It advocates for equitable remuneration and rewards for employees based on their contributions and efforts.

In contrast, the Differential Piece wage System, as a technique of Scientific Management, involves paying different wage rates to workers based on their individual performance or productivity. This can lead to inequality in pay among workers, as some employees may earn significantly more than others, even when their efforts and contributions are comparable.

The principle of Equity suggests that employees should be rewarded and remunerated fairly for their work, regardless of individual differences in performance. Implementing a wage system that leads to significant disparities in pay can create feelings of unfairness and demotivation among workers, thereby violating the principle of Equity.

**30. (A):** The marketing management philosophy that has the main focus on the existing product is the "Selling concept." The Selling concept philosophy is centered on the idea that consumers will not buy enough of a product unless the organization undertakes a significant selling and promotional effort. In this approach, the primary goal of the organization is to sell the existing products rather than focusing on understanding and fulfilling customer needs.

Organizations adopting the Selling concept often use aggressive advertising and sales techniques to convince customers to purchase their products. This philosophy assumes that customers need to be persuaded to buy the product, even if it may not precisely meet their needs or wants.

It is crucial to recognize that the Selling concept is just one of the various marketing management philosophies, and modern marketing practices tend to lean more towards customer-centric approaches such as the Marketing concept or the Societal Marketing concept, which prioritize customer needs and long-term customer relationships.

**31. (C):** Capital structure refers to the mix of different sources of funds, such as equity and debt, used by a company to finance its operations and investments. The primary objective of determining an optimal capital structure is to maximize the shareholders' wealth.

The capital structure decisions should aim to achieve a balance between debt and equity financing that minimizes the cost of capital and maximizes the overall value of the company. By optimizing the capital structure, the company can enhance its financial performance and increase the value of the shareholders' investments. This is typically achieved by choosing an appropriate mix of debt and equity that helps the company take advantage of financial leverage while also managing financial risks effectively. Ultimately, the goal is to create value for the shareholders, ensuring that their wealth and returns on investments are maximized.

**32. (C):** (*a*) **Estimating the manpower requirement:** This is the initial step in the staffing process where the organization assesses its current and future workforce needs based on the company's objectives, growth plans, and workload.

(*b*) **Recruitment:** After estimating the manpower requirement, the organization moves on to the recruitment phase. This step involves attracting potential candidates from both internal and external sources to apply for the available positions.

(*e*) **Selection:** The selection process involves evaluating and choosing the best-suited candidates from the pool of applicants who have applied for the positions.

(*d*) **Placement and orientation:** Once suitable candidates are selected through the recruitment process, they are placed in their respective job roles, and the company provides them with an orientation to familiarize them with the organization's policies, culture, and work environment.

(*c*) **Training and development:** After orientation, the new employees undergo training and development programs to acquire the necessary skills and knowledge to perform their jobs effectively.

**33. (B):** The statement highlights that the principles of management are not rigid prescriptions and can be modified by the manager when the situation demands. This flexibility in the application of management principles allows managers to adapt their approach to different situations, challenges, and organizational contexts. Rather than being fixed rules, the principles provide general guidelines that can be adjusted and tailored to fit specific circumstances, making them flexible in their application. This adaptability is essential in modern management practices, as it allows managers to be responsive and effective in diverse and ever-changing business environments.

**34. (C):** (*a*) **Sender:** The communication process begins with the sender, who initiates the communication by encoding the message and sending it to the receiver.

(*c*) **Message:** The message is the information, idea, or thoughts that the sender wants to convey to the receiver. It is encoded by the sender using words, symbols, or gestures.

(*d*) **Media:** The media refers to the channel or means through which the message is transmitted from the sender to the receiver. It can include various methods like face-to-face communication, written communication, phone calls, emails, etc.

(*b*) **Receiver:** The receiver is the person or group for whom the message is intended. They receive and decode the message to understand its meaning.

(*e*) **Feedback:** After receiving and understanding the message, the receiver provides feedback to the sender. Feedback is a crucial component of the communication process as it allows the sender to know whether the message was received and understood as intended.

**35. (B)**

**36. (C):** The Consumer Protection Act 2019 provides consumers with the following rights:

(*a*) **Right to Safety:** Consumers have the right to be protected against the marketing of goods and services that are hazardous to life and property. The Act ensures that products and services meet safety standards and do not pose any unreasonable risks to consumers.

(*b*) **Right to be Informed:** Consumers have the right to be informed about the quality, quantity, potency, purity, standard, and price of goods or services to make informed decisions. The Act mandates businesses to provide accurate and transparent information to consumers.

(*d*) **Right to be heard:** Consumers have the right to be heard and have their grievances addressed. The Act provides mechanisms for consumers to seek redressal in case of any unfair trade practices or deficiencies in goods and services.

(*e*) **Right to be assured:** Consumers have the right to be assured of access to various consumer goods and services at competitive prices. The Act emphasizes the availability of essential goods and services to consumers without any exploitation.

**37. (B):** Employee empowerment is a non-financial incentive that gives more autonomy and powers to subordinates. Empowerment involves delegating decision-making authority and responsibility to employees, allowing them to take ownership of their work, and giving them the freedom to make decisions related to their tasks and responsibilities.

When employees are empowered, they have the authority to make choices and take actions without constant supervision or approval from higher-level managers. This autonomy and power to make decisions can lead to increased job satisfaction, motivation, and a sense of ownership in their work, ultimately contributing to higher productivity and better organizational outcomes.

**38. (B):** As per the Consumer Protection Act, 2019, the State Commission has jurisdiction to entertain complaints where the value of goods or services paid as consideration exceeds one crore rupees but does not exceed ten crore rupees.

**39. (C):** The primary aim of financial management is to maximize shareholders' wealth. This means that the financial decisions and actions taken by the management of a company are geared towards increasing the value of the firm and, in turn, maximizing the wealth of the shareholders or owners of the company.

While increasing profits and sales are important aspects of running a business, the ultimate goal of financial management is to enhance the long-term value of the company's shares. By making sound financial decisions, such as investing in profitable projects, optimizing capital structure, and managing cash flows efficiently, the company can achieve sustainable growth and create value for its shareholders over time.

**40. (A):** (*b*) **Setting performance standards:** The first step in the controlling process is to establish performance standards or benchmarks that define the expected level of performance.

(*a*) **Measurement of Actual performance:** After setting the performance standards, the organization measures and gathers data on the actual performance of various processes, projects, or operations.

(*d*) **Comparison of actual performance with standards:** In this step, the organization compares the actual performance with the predetermined performance standards to identify any deviations or gaps between the two.

(*e*) **Analysing deviations:** After the comparison, the organization analyzes the reasons for the deviations between actual performance and the set standards. This analysis helps in understanding the root causes of the variations.

(*c*) **Taking Corrective action:** Once the actual performance is compared with the set standards and deviations are identified, the organization takes corrective action to address any discrepancies or issues that are hindering the achievement of desired performance.

**41. (C):** The function of management discussed in the above passage is "Organising."

Organising involves the process of dividing tasks and responsibilities, grouping similar activities together, and allocating them to specific individuals or teams within the organization. In the given passage, Rohan, as the Head Boy, is organizing the activities for the covid vaccination camp for students of age group 12-14 years.

He first shortlisted the activities, identified the eligible students, obtained Aadhar cards for registration, and collected consent letters from parents. Later, he divided the execution part activities and grouped similar activities into different units. He then allocated these activities to different prefects under his prefectorial board.

By doing so, Rohan is organizing the tasks and responsibilities and assigning them to specific individuals (the prefects) within the Prefectorial Board. This helps in creating a systematic and coordinated approach to the vaccination camp's preparation and execution.

**42. (D):** The step highlighted in the above line in the process of organization is "Identification and division of work." Rohan has shortlisted the activities and then divided them into different units based on their nature. This process involves identifying the specific tasks or work that needs to be done and then dividing them into manageable units or groups based on their similarities or relatedness. This step helps in creating a structured framework for assigning responsibilities and ensuring that the work is distributed effectively among the prefects under Rohan's leadership.

**43. (C):** The step highlighted in the above line in the organization process is "Departmentalisation." Rohan grouped the similar natured activities into different units, which means he created separate departments or units based on the similarity of the activities. This helps in organizing and coordinating the tasks more efficiently and ensures that related activities are grouped together under the responsibility of different prefects within the Prefectorial Board. Departmentalisation is an important aspect of organizing as it helps in achieving specialization and effective allocation of resources to achieve the objectives of the event smoothly.

**44. (A):** The step of the organization process discussed in the above lines is "Assignment of duties." Rohan allocated the different activities to different prefects under his prefectorial board. By assigning specific tasks and responsibilities to each prefect, he ensures that the event's various aspects are handled efficiently and coordinated effectively under his leadership. The assignment of duties is a crucial aspect of organizing as it clarifies who is responsible for what, allowing for better accountability and coordination within the team.

**45. (B):** The step of the organization process discussed in the above statement is "Establishing reporting relationship." Rohan devised a computer software where each prefect was supposed to enter his date of vaccination. This software allows the prefects to report their vaccination dates and details, creating a reporting relationship between the prefects and Rohan as the Head Boy. The software enables a smooth flow of information, updates, and data from the prefects to the school headmistress, ensuring effective communication and coordination in organizing the vaccination camp.

**46. (D):** In the given case, the manager is able to achieve the target production of 10,000 units in a year by operating on double shifts despite facing power failures most of the time. The manager is effective (achieving the goals of producing 10,000 units) but may not be very efficient due to the reliance on double shifts, which may lead to increased costs and other challenges.

**47. (C):** Cutting down the cost indicates efficiency (doing the task correctly with minimum cost). However, not achieving the target production indicates a lack of effectiveness (not achieving the goals).

**48. (C):** Planning is the management function that implies setting goals in advance and developing a way of achieving them efficiently and effectively. It involves determining the objectives or desired outcomes, identifying the actions and resources required to accomplish those objectives, and creating a roadmap to reach the goals. Planning provides a direction for the organization, and it serves as the foundation for other management functions like organizing, staffing, directing, and controlling. Without proper planning, an organization may lack direction and coherence in its activities, making it challenging to achieve its goals efficiently and effectively.

**49. (D):** Controlling is the management function of monitoring organizational performance towards the attainment of organizational goals. It involves comparing actual performance with planned performance, identifying deviations or variations, and taking corrective actions as needed to ensure that the organization's goals are achieved efficiently and effectively. Controlling is an essential function as it helps managers keep track of progress, identify areas that need improvement, and maintain alignment with the established objectives. By continuously evaluating and adjusting performance, controlling ensures that the organization stays on the right track and can make necessary adjustments to reach its goals successfully.

**50. (B)**

# MATHEMATICS

**1.** The value of the integral

$I = \int_{-1}^{1} (x + x^3 + x^5)dx$ is:

A. 2 B. −2
C. 0 D. 1

**2.** Which constraint correctly represents the situation "Mixture of $x$ and $y$ must be at least 8 units"?

A. $x + y > 8$
B. $x + y < 8$
C. $x + y \leq 8$
D. $x + y \geq 8$

**3.** A dice is thrown. If A is the event 'the number appearing is a multiple of 3 and B is the event 'the number appearing is even', then A and B are:

A. dependent events
B. independent events
C. $P(A \cap B) = \frac{1}{3}$
D. $P(B) = \frac{1}{3}$

**4.** The feasible region for the constrains $x \geq 0$, $x + y \leq 1$ and $x - y \leq 1$, is situated in:

(*a*) I and II Quadrant
(*b*) I Quadrant
(*c*) II and IV Quadrant
(*d*) IV Quadrant
(*e*) I, II, III and IV Quadrant

Choose the correct answer from the options given below:

A. (*a*) only B. (*b*) and (*d*) only
C. (*b*) and (*c*) only D. (*e*) only

**5.** Match List I with List II

| List-I (Differential Equations) | List-II (Degree) |
|---|---|
| (*a*) $\left(\frac{dy}{dx}\right)^3 + yx = 0$ | (*i*) 2 |
| (*b*) $e^{\frac{dy}{dx}} + y^2 + y'' = 0$ | (*ii*) 1 |
| (*c*) $xyy'' + x(y')^2 - yy' = 0$ | (*iii*) Not defined |
| (*d*) $(y'')^2 + y = 0$ | (*iv*) 3 |

Choose the correct answer from the options given below:

| | (*a*) | (*b*) | (*c*) | (*d*) |
|---|---|---|---|---|
| A. | (*iv*) | (*iii*) | (*ii*) | (*i*) |
| B. | (*i*) | (*ii*) | (*iii*) | (*iv*) |
| C. | (*ii*) | (*iii*) | (*iv*) | (*i*) |
| D. | (*iv*) | (*iii*) | (*i*) | (*ii*) |

**6.** Area of the region bounded by the curve $x^2 = 4y$, $x$-axis and $x = 3$ is:

A. $\frac{9}{2}$ sq. units B. $\frac{9}{4}$ sq. units
C. $\frac{9}{5}$ sq. units D. $\frac{9}{8}$ sq. units

**7.** If a matrix has 24 elements, which of the following cannot be the possible order of the matrix?

A. $6 \times 4$ B. $12 \times 12$
C. $8 \times 3$ D. $1 \times 24$

**8.** Any function $f(x)$ is an increasing function in $[a, b]$ if:

(*a*) $\forall\, x_1, x_2 \in [a, b], f(x_1) \geq f(x_2)$ if $x_1 < x_2$
(*b*) $\forall\, x_1, x_2 \in [a, b], f(x_1) \geq f(x_2)$ if $x_1 > x_2$
(*c*) $\forall\, x_1, x_2 \in [a, b], f(x_1) \leq f(x_2)$ if $x_1 < x_2$
(*d*) $\forall\, x_1, x_2 \in [a, b], f(x_1) < f(x_2)$ if $x_1 > x_2$

Choose the correct answer from the options given below:

A. (*a*), (*d*) only B. (*b*), (*d*) only
C. (*b*), (*c*) only D. (*a*), (*c*) only

**9.** The values of a for which, the function $f(x) = a^x$ is increasing on R are given by:

A. $0 < a < \infty$ B. $-\infty < a < \infty$
C. $1 < a < \infty$ D. $0 \leq a < \infty$

**10.** If $\begin{vmatrix} 2 & 4 \\ 5 & 1 \end{vmatrix} = \begin{vmatrix} 2x & 4 \\ 6 & x \end{vmatrix}$, then $x$ is equal to:

A. 1 B. $2\sqrt{3}$
C. $\pm\sqrt{3}$ D. $\pm 2\sqrt{3}$

**11.** If A and B are events such that $P(A|B) = P(B|A)$, then:

A. $A = B$ B. $A \cap B = \phi$
C. $A \subset B$ but $A \neq B$ D. $P(A) = P(B)$

**12.** The value of the integral $\int e^x \left(\frac{1}{x} - \frac{1}{x^2}\right)dx$ is:

A. $\frac{e^x}{x} + C$, where C is a constant

B. $\frac{e^{-x}}{x} + C$, where C is a constant

C. $e^x$ + C, where C is a constant

D. $e^{-x}$ + C, where C is a constant

**13.** Match List I with List II

| List-I (Equation of curves) | List-II (Slope of tangent at $x = 2$) |
|---|---|
| (*a*) $y = x^3 - x$ | (*i*) 8 |
| (*b*) $y = (x - 2)^2$ | (*ii*) 2/3 |
| (*c*) $y = 2x^2 + 3$ | (*iii*) 11 |
| (*d*) $y = \sqrt{4x+1} - 7$ | (*iv*) 0 |

Choose the correct answer from the options given below:

| | (*a*) | (*b*) | (*c*) | (*d*) |
|---|---|---|---|---|
| A. | (*ii*) | (*i*) | (*iv*) | (*iii*) |
| B. | (*i*) | (*ii*) | (*iv*) | (*iii*) |
| C. | (*iii*) | (*iv*) | (*i*) | (*ii*) |
| D. | (*iii*) | (*iv*) | (*ii*) | (*i*) |

**14.** The sum of the minor and the cofactor of the element 6 in the determinant

$$\Delta = \begin{vmatrix} 2 & 3 & 1 \\ 4 & 5 & 6 \\ 7 & 8 & 9 \end{vmatrix} \text{ is:}$$

A. –5 B. –10

C. 10 D. 0

**15.** If $(x + 1)e^y = 1$, then:

A. $\frac{d^2y}{dx^2} = y^2$ B. $\frac{d^2y}{dx^2} = \left(\frac{dy}{dx}\right)^2$

C. $\frac{d^2y}{dx^2} = -y^2$ D. $\frac{d^2y}{dx^2} = \frac{dy}{dx}$

**16.** Let $A = \begin{bmatrix} 1 & \cos\theta & 1 \\ -\cos\theta & 1 & \cos\theta \\ -1 & -\cos\theta & 1 \end{bmatrix}$ $0 \le \theta \le 2\pi$, then:

A. $|A| = 0$ B. $|A| \in [2, 4]$

C. $|A| \in (2, 4)$ D. $|A| \in (2, \infty)$

**17.** Which of the following statements is/are correct?

(*a*) $|x|$ is continuous every where in its domain.

(*b*) $|x|$ is differentiable every where in its domain.

(*c*) $|x|$ is continuous at every integral point.

(*d*) $|x|$ is discontinuous at every integral point.

Choose the correct answer from the options given below:

A. (*a*), (*c*) only B. (*b*), (*d*) only

C. (*b*), (*c*) only D. (*a*), (*d*) only

**18.** Vector in the direction of $\hat{i} + \hat{j} + \hat{k}$ with magnitude 5 units is:

A. $\frac{\hat{i} - \hat{j} + \hat{k}}{\sqrt{3}}$ B. $\frac{\hat{i} + \hat{j} + \hat{k}}{\sqrt{3}}$

C. $\frac{5(\hat{i} + \hat{j} + \hat{k})}{\sqrt{3}}$ D. $\frac{5}{3}(\hat{i} + \hat{j} + \hat{k})$

**19.** The general solution of the differential equation $ydx - (x + 2y^2)dy = 0$ is:

A. $x = 2y^2 + Cy$, C is a constant

B. $y = 2x^2 + Cy$, C is a constant

C. $y = 2x^2 + Cx$, C is a constant

D. $x = 2x^2 + Cy$, C is a constant

**20.** Which of the following is the correct equation to find the area of the shaded region, with reference to the figure given below?

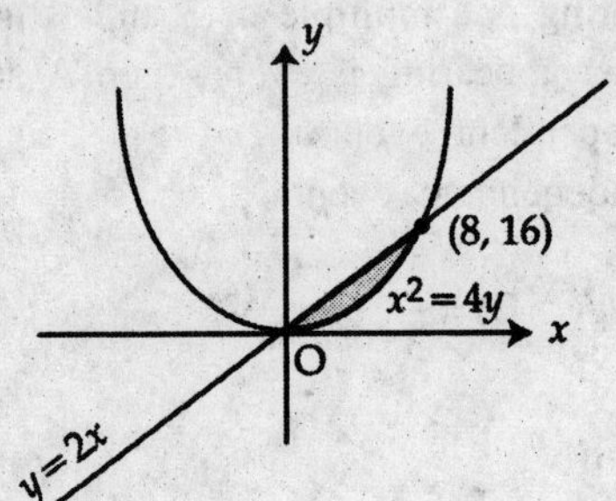


A. $A = 2\int_0^8 (2x - x^2)dx$

B. $A = 2\int_0^4 (2x - x^2)dx$

C. $A = 2\int_0^4 \left(2x - \frac{x^2}{4}\right)dx$

D. $A = \int_0^8 \left(2x - \frac{x^2}{4}\right)dx$

**21.** Corner points of the feasible region for a linear programming problem are (0, 2), (3, 0), (6, 0), (6, 8) and (0, 5). Let $F = 4x + 6y$ be the objective function. Then the minimum value of F occurs at:

A. (0, 2) only

B. (3, 0) only

C. The mid point of the line segment joining the points (0, 2) and (3, 0) only

D. Every point on the line segment joining the points (0, 2) and (3, 0)

**22.** The tangent to the curve $y = x^3 - 11x + 5$ at $x = 2$ is parallel to:

(*a*) $y = x + 1$ (*b*) $y = -x + 2$
(*c*) $2y = x + 3$ (*d*) $2y = 2x + 4$

Choose the correct answer from the options given below:

A. (*a*), (*b*) only B. (*b*), (*c*) only
C. (*a*), (*d*) only D. (*b*), (*d*) only

**23.** Consider a binary operation * on N defined as $a*b = a^3 + b^3$, choose the correct answer:

A. * is both associative and commutative
B. * is associative but not commutative
C. * is commutative but not associative
D. * is neither commutative nor associative

**24.** The value of $a + b + c + d$ if $\begin{bmatrix} 2a+b & a+2b \\ 2c+d & c+2d \end{bmatrix} = \begin{bmatrix} 8 & 4 \\ 3 & 3 \end{bmatrix}$ is:

A. 4 B. 2
C. 6 D. 8

**25.** The derivative of $\cos^{-1}\left(\frac{\sin x + \cos x}{\sqrt{2}}\right), -\frac{\pi}{4} < x < \frac{\pi}{4}$ with respect to $x$ is:

A. $\frac{1}{\sqrt{2}}$ B. 1
C. −1 D. $\frac{-1}{\sqrt{2}}$

**26.** If A is square matrix such that $A^2 = A$, then $(I + A)^3 - 8A$ is equal to:

A. I B. A
C. I − A D. 3A

**27.** Match List-I with List-II

| List-I (Function $y$) | List-II (Derivative $\frac{dy}{dx}$) |
|---|---|
| (*a*) $y = \cos\sqrt{x}$ | (*i*) $\frac{\sec(\tan\sqrt{x})\tan(\tan\sqrt{x})\sec^2\sqrt{x}}{2\sqrt{x}}$ |
| (*b*) $y = \sqrt{\sin x}$ | (*ii*) $-3x^2\cos(x^3)\sin(\sin(x^3))$ |
| (*c*) $y = \sec(\tan\sqrt{x})$ | (*iii*) $\frac{\cos x}{2\sqrt{\sin x}}$ |
| (*d*) $y = \cos(\sin(x^3))$ | (*iv*) $\frac{-1}{2\sqrt{x}}\sin\sqrt{x}$ |

Choose the correct answer from the options given below:

| | (*a*) | (*b*) | (*c*) | (*d*) |
|---|---|---|---|---|
| A. | (*i*) | (*iv*) | (*ii*) | (*iii*) |
| B. | (*iv*) | (*iii*) | (*i*) | (*ii*) |
| C. | (*iii*) | (*ii*) | (*iv*) | (*i*) |
| D. | (*ii*) | (*i*) | (*iii*) | (*iv*) |

**28.** The direction cosines of the normal to the plane $x - y + z = 4$ are:

A. $-\frac{1}{\sqrt{3}}, \frac{1}{\sqrt{3}}, \frac{1}{\sqrt{3}}$ B. $\frac{1}{\sqrt{3}}, \frac{1}{\sqrt{3}}, \frac{1}{\sqrt{3}}$
C. $\frac{1}{\sqrt{3}}, \frac{-1}{\sqrt{3}}, \frac{1}{\sqrt{3}}$ D. $\frac{-1}{\sqrt{3}}, \frac{-1}{\sqrt{3}}, \frac{1}{\sqrt{3}}$

**29.** The integral $I = \int e^x\left(\frac{1+\sin x}{1+\cos x}\right)dx$ is:

A. $e^x \tan x + C$, where C is a constant
B. $e^x \sec x + C$, where C is a constant
C. $e^x \tan\left(\frac{x}{2}\right) + C$, where C is a constant
D. $e^{-x} \tan\left(\frac{x}{2}\right) + C$, where C is a constant

**30.** The area lying between the curves $y^2 = 4x$ and $y = 2x$ is:

A. $\frac{2}{3}$ B. 1
C. $\frac{1}{3}$ D. $\frac{1}{4}$

**31.** The value(s) of $x$, for which the matrix

$A = \begin{bmatrix} x-1 & 1 & 1 \\ 1 & x-1 & 1 \\ 1 & 1 & x-1 \end{bmatrix}$ is singular, is/are:

A. 1 B. −1, 2
C. ± 1 D. 1, 2

**32.** If $A = [2\ -3\ 4]$ $B = \begin{bmatrix} 3 \\ 2 \\ 2 \end{bmatrix}$

$X = [1\ 2\ 3]$ $Y = \begin{bmatrix} 2 \\ 3 \\ 4 \end{bmatrix}$

then AB + XY =

A. [28] B. [24]
C. 28 D. 24

**33.** The maximum value of the $f(x) = \frac{1}{4x^2 + 2x + 1}$ is:

A. $\frac{4}{3}$ B. $\frac{3}{4}$
C. $\frac{-4}{3}$ D. $-\frac{3}{4}$

**34.** Match List-I with List-II:

| List-I (Functions) | List-II (Range) |
|---|---|
| (*a*) $\operatorname{cosec}^{-1}x$ | (*i*) $(0, \pi)$ |
| (*b*) $\sec^{-1}x$ | (*ii*) $\left[\frac{-\pi}{2}, \frac{\pi}{2}\right] - \{0\}$ |
| (*c*) $\tan^{-1}x$ | (*iii*) $\left(-\frac{\pi}{2}, \frac{\pi}{2}\right)$ |
| (*d*) $\cot^{-1}x$ | (*iv*) $[0, \pi] - \left\{\frac{\pi}{2}\right\}$ |

Choose the correct answer from the options given below:

| | (*a*) | (*b*) | (*c*) | (*d*) |
|---|---|---|---|---|
| A. | (*iv*) | (*i*) | (*ii*) | (*iii*) |
| B. | (*iii*) | (*i*) | (*iv*) | (*ii*) |
| C. | (*ii*) | (*iv*) | (*iii*) | (*i*) |
| D. | (*i*) | (*ii*) | (*iii*) | (*iv*) |

**35.** The value of $\frac{9}{4}\sin^{-1}\frac{2\sqrt{2}}{3}+\frac{9}{4}\sin^{-1}\frac{1}{3}$ is:

A. $\frac{9}{4}$ B. $\frac{9\pi}{4}$
C. $\frac{\pi}{8}$ D. $\frac{9\pi}{8}$

**36.** The two events E and F are independent. If P(E) = 0.3 and P(E∪F) = 0.5, then P(E/F) – P(F/E) is:

A. $\frac{2}{7}$ B. $\frac{3}{35}$
C. $\frac{1}{70}$ D. $\frac{1}{7}$

**37.** If $\vec{a}+\lambda\vec{b}$ is perpendicular to $\vec{c}$, where $\vec{a} = -\hat{i}+2\hat{j}+\hat{k}, \vec{b} = 3\hat{i}+2\hat{j}+k$ and $\vec{c}=\hat{i}-\hat{j}$ then:

A. $\lambda = -1$ B. $\lambda = -3$
C. $\lambda = 1$ D. $\lambda = 3$

**38.** The Greatest Integer Function $f$ : R → R given by $f(x) = [x]$, $x \in$ R and $[x]$, denotes the greatest integer less than or equal to $x$ is:

A. one-one
B. onto
C. both one-one and onto
D. neither one-one nor onto

**39.** For A = $\begin{bmatrix} a_{11} & a_{12} & a_{13} \\ a_{21} & a_{22} & a_{23} \\ a_{31} & a_{32} & a_{33} \end{bmatrix}$ if $M_{ij}$ and $A_{ij}$ are the minor and the cofactor of $a_{ij}$ respectively, then |A| equals to:

(*a*) $a_{11}A_{11} + a_{12}A_{12} + a_{13}A_{13}$
(*b*) $a_{21}A_{12} + a_{22}A_{22} + a_{23}A_{32}$
(*c*) $a_{11}M_{11} - a_{12}M_{12} + a_{13}M_{13}$
(*d*) $a_{11}M_{11} + a_{12}M_{12} + a_{13}M_{13}$

Choose the correct answer from the options given below:

A. (*a*), (*b*) only B. (*a*), (*c*) only
C. (*c*), (*d*) only D. (*a*), (*c*), (*d*) only

**40.** The value of the integral $\int_{-1}^{1}|x|\,dx$ is:

A. 2 B. $\frac{1}{2}$
C. 1 D. 0

**41.** The probability that A speaks the truth is $\frac{4}{5}$. He throws a dice and reports that it is a five. The probability that it is actually a five is:

A. $\frac{4}{9}$ B. $\frac{1}{2}$
C. $\frac{2}{9}$ D. $\frac{5}{9}$

**42.** The linear programming problem :
minimise $z = 3x + 2y$
subject to the constraints
$x + y \geq 8$,
$3x + 5y \leq 15, x \geq 0, y \geq 0$
has

A. one solution
B. two solutions
C. no feasible solution
D. infinitely many solutions

**43.** The general solution of the differential equation $\frac{dy}{dx} = \sin^{-1}x$ is:

A. $y = x\sin^{-1}x - \sqrt{1-x^2} + C$, where C is a constant
B. $y = x\sin^{-1}x + \sqrt{1+x^2} + C$, where C is a constant
C. $y = x\sin^{-1}x + \sqrt{1-x^2} + C$, where C is a constant
D. $y = -x\sin^{-1}x + \sqrt{1-x^2} + C$, where C is a constant

**44.** The distance of the point with position vector $(2\hat{i}+\hat{j}-\hat{k})$ from the plane $\vec{r}\cdot(-2\hat{i}+\hat{j}+3\hat{k}) = 8$ is:

A. $\frac{7}{\sqrt{14}}$ B. $2\sqrt{14}$

C. $\sqrt{14}$ D. $\frac{\sqrt{14}}{7}$

**45.** The rate of change of the area of a equilateral triangle with respect to its side when its side = 2 is:

A. $\frac{\sqrt{3}}{4}$ B. $\sqrt{3}$

C. $\frac{\sqrt{3}}{2}$ D. $2\sqrt{3}$

**46.** The relation R in the set A = {1, 2, 3} given by R = {(1, 2), (2, 1)} is:

A. Reflexive
B. Symmetric
C. Reflexive but not symmetric
D. Equivalence Relation

**47.** The function $f$ is given by

$$f(x)=\begin{cases} x^3+3 & , \text{if } x \neq 0 \\ 4 & , \text{if } x = 0 \end{cases}$$

Then number of points of discontinuity for this function is:

A. 0 B. 1
C. 2 D. 3

**48.** Which of the following functions satisfies Rolle's theorem?

A. $f(x) = x,\ x \in [1, 2]$
B. $f(x) = x^2,\ x \in [-1, 1]$
C. $f(x) = x^3,\ x \in [-1, 2]$
D. $f(x) = x^4,\ x \in [0, 2]$

**49.** Equation of a plane with intercept $\sqrt{3}$ on $z$-axis and parallel to XOY plane is:

A. $x=\sqrt{3}$ B. $z-\sqrt{3}=0$

C. $x+\sqrt{3}=0$ D. $z+\sqrt{3}=0$

**50.** Two ropes are tied along the two diagonals of a cubic room. Ropes are inclined to each other at:

A. 45° B. 30°

C. $\cos^{-1}\left(\frac{1}{\sqrt{3}}\right)$ D. $\cos^{-1}\left(\frac{1}{3}\right)$

# ANSWERS

**1. (C):** Given, I = $\int_{-1}^{1}(x+x^3+x^5)dx$

$$= \int_{-1}^{1} x\,dx + \int_{-1}^{1} x^3dx + \int_{-1}^{1} x^5dx$$

$$= \left[\frac{x^2}{2}\right]_{-1}^{1} + \left[\frac{x^4}{4}\right]_{-1}^{1} + \left[\frac{x^6}{6}\right]_{-1}^{1}$$

$$= \frac{1}{2}\left[x^2\right]_{-1}^{1} + \frac{1}{4}\left[x^4\right]_{-1}^{1} + \frac{1}{6}\left[x^6\right]_{-1}^{1}$$

$$= \frac{1}{2}\left[(1)^2-(-1)^2\right] + \frac{1}{4}\left[(1)^4-(-1)^4\right] + \frac{1}{6}\left[(1)^6-(-1)^6\right]$$

$$= \frac{1}{2}[1-1] + \frac{1}{4}[1-1] + \frac{1}{6}[1-1]$$

$$= \frac{1}{2}[0] + \frac{1}{4}[0] + \frac{1}{6}[0]$$

= 0 + 0 + 0 = 0

Hence, correct answer is (C).

**2. (D)**

**3. (B):** We have, S = {1, 2, 3, 4, 5, 6}

$\Rightarrow$ $n$ (S) = 6

A : Number appearing is a multiple of 3

A : {3, 6} $\Rightarrow$ $n(A) = 2$

B : Number of appearing is even

B : {2, 4, 6} $\Rightarrow$ $n(B) = 3$

$A \cap B = \{6\} \Rightarrow n(A \cap B) = 1$

$$P(A) = \frac{n(A)}{n(S)} = \frac{2}{6} = \frac{1}{3}$$

and $$P(B) = \frac{n(B)}{n(S)} = \frac{3}{6} = \frac{1}{2}$$

So, $$P(A \cap B) = \frac{1}{6} = P(A) \cdot P(B)$$

Thus, A and B are independent events.

Hence, correct answer is (B).

**4. (B):** Given, $x \geq 0,\ x + y \geq 1 \Rightarrow x + y = 1$ ...(1)

| $x$ | 0 | 1 |
|---|---|---|
| $y$ | 1 | 0 |

Now, $x - y \leq 1$

$\therefore$ $x - y = 1$ ...(2)

| $x$ | 0 | 1 |
|---|---|---|
| $y$ | −1 | 0 |

From equations (1) & (2), we get

$2x = 2 \Rightarrow x = 1$

$y = 0$ (1, 0)

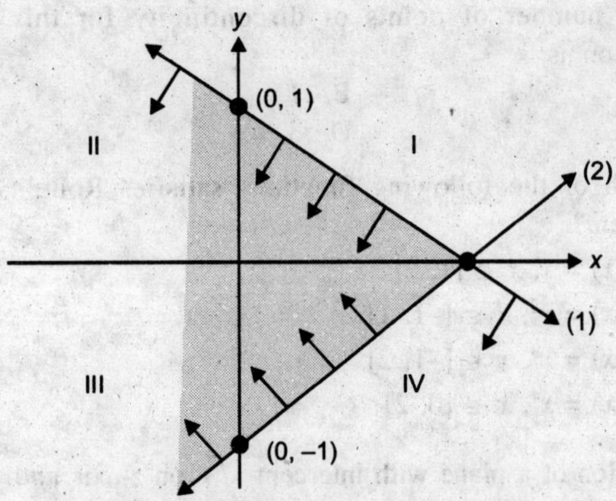


Hence, I & IV are correct answers.

**5. (A):** (*a*) $\left(\frac{dy}{dx}\right)^3 + yx = 0$

Differential Equation → Degree highest derivatives power $\left(\frac{dy}{dx}\right)^3 + yx = 0$

Highest derivative $\left(\frac{dy}{dx}\right)$, so degree is 3.

(*b*) $e^{\frac{dy}{dx}} + y^2 + y'' = 0$

When derivative is exponential power, so its degree is not defined.

(*c*) $xyy'' + x(y')^2 - yy' = 0$

Highest derivative is $y''$ , so its degree is 1.

(*d*) $(y'')^2 + y = 0$

Highest derivative is $y''$, so its degree is 2.

Hence, (*a*) – (*iv*), (*b*) – (*iii*), (*c*) – (*ii*), (*d*) – (*i*)

Thus, correct answer is (A).

**6. (B):** Given, $x^2 = 4y$ and $x = 3$

So, $x^2 = 4y$ at $y = 0$, $x = 0$

Then, bounds are $x = 0$ and $x = 3$

Area (A) enclosed

$$A = \int_{x=0}^{x=3} y\,dx = \int_0^3 \frac{x^2}{4}dx$$

$$= \frac{1}{4}\int_0^3 x^2 dx = \frac{1}{4}\left[\frac{x^3}{3}\right]_0^3$$

$$= \frac{1}{12}\left[x^3\right]_0^3$$

$$= \frac{1}{12}\times(3)^3 = \frac{27}{12} = \frac{9}{4} \text{ sq units}$$

Hence, correct answer is (B).

**7. (B):** Since matrix has 24 elements

$1 \times 24 = 24$
$2 \times 12 = 24$
$3 \times 8 = 24$
$4 \times 6 = 24$
$6 \times 4 = 24$
$8 \times 3 = 24$
$12 \times 2 = 24$
$24 \times 1 = 24$

∴ No. of rows × no. of columns = 24

Thus, the possible orders are

1 × 24, 2 × 12, 3 × 8, 4 × 6, 6 × 4, 8 × 3, 12 × 2 and 24 × 1.

Hence, 12 × 12 cannot be the possible order of matrix.

Hence, correct answer is (B).

**8. (C):** We have to prove that function is always increasing *i.e.*, $f(x) < f(x_2)$ for $x_1 < x_2$ where $x_1, x_2 \in [a, b]$ and $x_1 < x_2$.

In interval $[x_1, x_2]$

As $f$ is defined everywhere.

$f$ is continuous or differentiable in $[x_1, x_2]$

From mean value theorem

⇔ $c$ in $(x_1, x_2)$ *i.e.*, $c \in (x_1, x_2)$ s.t.

$$f'(c) = \frac{f(x_2) - f(x_1)}{x_2 - x_1}$$

Given that $f'(x) > 0\ \forall\ x \in (a, b)$

∴ $f'(c) > 0\ \ \forall\ c \in (x_1, x_2)$

$$\Rightarrow \frac{f(x_2) - f(x_1)}{x_2 - x_1} > 0 \Rightarrow f(x_2) - f(x_1) > 0$$

Then, for any two points $x_1, x_2$ in interval $[a, b]$ where $x_1 > x_2$.

∴ $f(x_2) > f(x_1)$. Thus $f$ increasing in the interval $[a, b]$.

Therefore, $\forall\ x_1, x_2 \in [a, b]$, $f(x_1) \geq f(x_2)$ if $x_1 > x_2$ and $\forall\ x_1, x_2 \in [a, b]$, $f(x_1) \leq f(x_2)$ if $x_1 < x_2$.

Thus, correct answer is (C).

**9. (C):** We have,

$f(x) = a^x$

∴ $f'(x) = a^x \log a$

Since, function $f(x)$ is increasing on R.

∴ $f'(x) > 0$

∴ $a^x \log a > 0$

Since, the logarithmic function is defined for positive values of $a$.

∴ $a > 0$

∴ $a^x > 0$

But $a^x \log a > 0$

It is possible, when $\log a^x > 0$ and $\log a > 0$ or $a^x < 0$ and $\log a < 0$

$\log a > 0$

$\therefore \quad a > 1$

Hence, $f(x)$ is increasing, when $a > 1$

Thus, $1 < a < \infty$.

So, correct answer is (C).

**10. (C):** Given, $\begin{vmatrix} 2 & 4 \\ 5 & 1 \end{vmatrix} = \begin{vmatrix} 2x & 4 \\ 6 & x \end{vmatrix}$

$\therefore (2 \times 1) - (4 \times 5) = 2x \times x - 4 \times 6$

$\Rightarrow \quad 2 - 20 = 2x^2 - 24$

$\Rightarrow \quad -18 = 2x^2 - 24$

$\Rightarrow \quad 2x^2 = 24 - 18$

$\Rightarrow \quad 2x^2 = 6$

$\Rightarrow \quad x^2 = \frac{6}{2} = 3$

$\therefore \quad x = \pm\sqrt{3}$

Hence, correct answer is (C).

**11. (*)**

**12. (A):** Given, $\int e^x\left(\frac{1}{x} - \frac{1}{x^2}\right)dx$

Property of integration

$\int e^x(f(x) + f'(x))dx = e^x f(x) + C$

Let $\quad f(x) = \frac{1}{x}$

Differential $\quad f'(x) = -\frac{1}{x^2}$

$\therefore \quad \int e^x\left(\frac{1}{x} - \frac{1}{x^2}\right)dx = \int e^x\left[\frac{1}{x} + \left(-\frac{1}{x^2}\right)\right]dx$

$= e^x \cdot \frac{1}{x} + C$

Where C is a constant

Thus, correct answer is (A).

**13. (C):** (*a*) $y^2 = x^3 - x$ slope of tangent at $x = 2$

Differential w.r.t. $x$, we get

$\frac{dy}{dx} = 3x^2 - 1 \quad ...(1)$

Putting $x = 2$ in equation (1), we get

$\left(\frac{dy}{dx}\right)_{x=2} = 3(2)^2 - 1$

$= 3 \times 4 - 1 = 12 - 1 = 11$

(*b*) $\quad y = (x - 2)^2$

$= x^2 - 4x + 4$

$\frac{dy}{dx} = 2x - 4 \quad ...(2)$

Putting $x = 2$ in equation (2), we get

$= 2 \times 2 - 4 = 4 - 4 = 0$

(*c*) $\quad y = 2x^2 + 3$

$\frac{dy}{dx} = 2 \times 2x = 2 \times 2 \times 2 = 8$

(*d*) $\quad y = \sqrt{4x+1} - 7$

$\frac{dy}{dx} = \frac{d}{dx}(4x + 1)^{1/2}$

$= 2(4x + 1)^{-1/2}$

$= 2(4 \times 2 + 1)^{-1/2}$

$= 2(8 + 1)^{-1/2} = 2 \times (9)^{-1/2}$

$= \frac{2}{9^{1/2}} = \frac{2}{3}$

Hence, (*a*) – (*iii*), (*b*) – (*iv*), (*c*) – (*i*), (*d*) – (*ii*)

Thus, correct answers is (C).

**14. (D):** Given, $\Delta = \begin{vmatrix} 2 & 3 & 1 \\ 4 & 5 & 6 \\ 7 & 8 & 9 \end{vmatrix}$

Since 6 lies in the second row and third column i.e., $a_{23} = 6$

Minor of $a_{23} = M_{23} = \begin{vmatrix} 2 & 3 & 1 \\ 4 & 5 & 6 \\ 7 & 8 & 9 \end{vmatrix}$

$= \begin{vmatrix} 2 & 3 \\ 7 & 8 \end{vmatrix}$

$= 16 - 21 = -5$

Thus, cofactor of element 6 in $\begin{vmatrix} 1 & 2 & 3 \\ 4 & 5 & 6 \\ 7 & 8 & 9 \end{vmatrix}$ is

$(-1)\begin{vmatrix} 2 & 3 \\ 7 & 8 \end{vmatrix} = (-1)(16 - 21) = (-1)(-5) = 5$

We got the matrix $\begin{vmatrix} 2 & 3 \\ 8 & 9 \end{vmatrix}$ after deleting column 1 and 2

$\therefore$ Sum of minor and cofactor $= -5 + 5 = 0$.

**15. (B):** Given, $(x + 1)e^y = 1$

Differential wrt $x$, we get

$\frac{d(e^y(x+1))}{dx} = \frac{d(1)}{dx}$

$\Rightarrow \quad \frac{d(e^y(x+1))}{dx} = 0$

Using product rule in $e^y(x + 1)$

As, $\quad (uv)' = u'v + v'u$

where $u = e^y$ and $v = x + 1$

$\frac{d(e^y)}{dx} \cdot (x+1) + \frac{d(x+1)}{dx} \cdot e^y = 0$

$\Rightarrow \quad \frac{d(e^y)}{dx} \times \frac{dy}{dx}(x+1) + \left(\frac{d(x)}{dx} + \frac{d(1)}{dx}\right) \cdot e^y = 0$

$\Rightarrow \quad \frac{d(d^y)}{dy} \times \frac{dy}{dx}(x+1) + (1+0) \cdot e^y = 0$

$\Rightarrow\quad e^y \times \frac{dy}{dx}(x+1) + e^y = 0$

$\Rightarrow\quad e^y\left(\frac{dy}{dx}\right)(x+1) = e^{-y}$

$\Rightarrow\quad \frac{dy}{dx} = \frac{e^{-y}}{e^y(x+1)}$

$\Rightarrow\quad \frac{dy}{dx} = \frac{-1}{(x+1)}$

Again differentiating wrt $x$, we get

$$\frac{d}{dx}\left(\frac{dy}{dx}\right) = \frac{d}{dx}\left(\frac{-1}{(x+1)}\right)$$

Using Quotient rule

As, $\left(\frac{u}{v}\right)' = \frac{u'v - v'u}{v^2}$

where $u = 1$ and $v = x + 1$.

$$\therefore\quad \frac{d^2y}{dx^2} = \left[\frac{\frac{d(1)}{dx}\cdot(x+1) - \frac{d(x+1)}{dx}\cdot 1}{(x+1)^2}\right]$$

$$= -\left[\frac{0\cdot(x+1) - \frac{d(x+1)}{dx}\cdot 1}{(x+1)^2}\right]$$

$$= -\left[\frac{0-(1+0)\cdot 1}{(x+1)^2}\right]$$

$$= -\left[\frac{-1}{(x+1)^2}\right] = \frac{1}{(x+1)^2}$$

Hence, $\frac{d^2y}{dx^2} = \frac{1}{(x+1)^2}$

$$= \left(\frac{-1}{x+1}\right)^2 = \left(\frac{dy}{dx}\right)^2$$

Thus, correct answer is (B).

**16. (B):** Given, $A = \begin{bmatrix} 1 & \cos\theta & 1 \\ -\cos\theta & 1 & \cos\theta \\ -1 & -\cos\theta & 1 \end{bmatrix}$ $0 \le \theta \le 2\pi$

$\therefore\quad |A| = \begin{bmatrix} 1 & \cos\theta & 1 \\ -\cos\theta & 1 & \cos\theta \\ -1 & -\cos\theta & 1 \end{bmatrix}$

$\Rightarrow\quad |A| = 1 - \cos^2\theta + \cos^2\theta - (-1 - \cos^2\theta - \cos^2\theta)$

$= 1 - 0 - (-1 - 2\cos^2\theta)$

$= 1 + 1 + 2\cos^2\theta = 2 + 2\cos^2\theta$

For $\theta$, $0 \le \theta \le 2\pi$

$|A|_{max}$ at $\theta = 0 \Rightarrow 2 + 2\cos^2(0) = 4$ [$\because \cos 0 = 1$]

and $|A|_{min}$ at $\theta = \frac{\pi}{2}$

$\Rightarrow\ 2 + 2\cos^2\left(\frac{\pi}{2}\right)$

$= 2 + 2\cos^2(90°)$ [$\because \cos 90° = 0$]

$= 2 + 0 = 2$

$\therefore\ |A| \in [2, 4]$

Thus, correct answer is (B).

**17. (D):** (*a*) Let $f(x) = x^{1/3} \rightarrow$ So $|x|$ is continuous every where in its domain. Hence, (*a*) is correct.

(*b*) $f(x) = \frac{1}{3x^{2/3}}$ $\rightarrow$ differentiable not possible at $n = 0$. $[x]$ not differentiable every where in its domain. Hence, (*b*) is false.

(*c*) If $f(x) = x - [x]$ is discontinuous at all integral points. Hence, $|x|$ denotes the greatest integer less than or equal to $x$. So, statement (*c*) is false.

(*d*) Let $n$ be an integer

Then, $g(n) = n - n = 0$

LHL at $x = n = \lim_{x\to n^-} g(x) = \lim_{x\to n^-}[x-(x)]$

$= n - (n - 1) = 1$

RHL at $x = n = \lim_{x\to n^+} g(x) = \lim_{x\to n^+}[x-(x)]$

$= n - n = 0$

Since LHL = RHL

Hence, $g$ is not continuous *i.e.*, discontinuous at $x = n$ *i.e.*, $g(x)$ is discontinuous at all integral point. So, $[x]$ is discontinous at every integral point. Hence statement (D) is true.

**18. (C):** Given, vector $\vec{a} = \hat{i} + \hat{j} + \hat{k}$

Let $\vec{a} = a_1\hat{i} + a_2\hat{j} + a_3\hat{k}$ is a vector, then the magnitude of the vector is given by

$$|\vec{a}| = \sqrt{a_1^2 + a_2^2 + a_3^2}$$

If $\vec{a} = a_1\hat{i} + a_2\hat{j} + a_3\hat{k}$ is a vector, then the unit vector is given by

$$\hat{a} = \frac{\vec{a}}{|a|}$$

We have, $\vec{a} = \hat{i} + \hat{j} + \hat{k}$

As, we know that if $\vec{a}$ is a vector, then the unit vector in the direction of $\vec{a}$ is given by

$$\hat{a} = \frac{\vec{a}}{|a|}$$

$$\Rightarrow\quad \hat{a} = \frac{\hat{i}+\hat{j}+\hat{k}}{\sqrt{1^2+1^2+1^2}} = \frac{\hat{i}+\hat{j}+\hat{k}}{\sqrt{3}}$$

$\therefore$ Vector of direction

$$d = 5\hat{a}$$

$$= \frac{5(\hat{i}+\hat{j}+\hat{k})}{\sqrt{3}}$$

Hence, correct answer is (C).

**19. (A):** Given, $ydx - (x + 2y^2)dy = 0$

$$\Rightarrow \quad \frac{ydx}{dy} = x + 2y^2$$

$$\Rightarrow \quad \frac{dx}{dy} = \frac{x}{y} + 2y$$

$$\Rightarrow \quad \frac{dx}{dy} - \frac{x}{y} = 2y$$

Differential equation in the form of $\frac{dx}{dy} + Px = Q$

Integrating factor (IF) $= e^{\int P dy}$

$$\text{IF} = e^{\int -\frac{1}{y} dy}$$

$$= e^{-\ln y} = \frac{1}{y}$$

Differential equation is given as

$$x \times \frac{1}{y} = \int \frac{1}{y} \times (2y) dy + C$$

$$\Rightarrow \quad \frac{x}{y} = 2y + C$$

$$\Rightarrow \quad x = 2y^2 + Cy$$

Where C is constant

Thus, correct answer is (A).

**20. (D):**

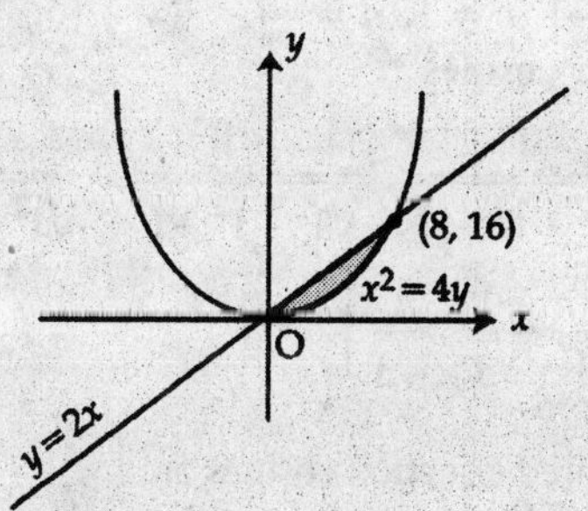


We have,

Area = Area underline – Area under curve

$$= \int_0^8 \left(2x - \frac{x^2}{4}\right) dx$$

Area = Area underline – Area under curve

$$= \int_0^8 2x\, dx - \int_0^8 \frac{x^2}{4} dx$$

Hence, area of the shaded region

$$= \int_0^8 \left(2x - \frac{x^2}{4}\right) dx$$

Hence, correct answer is (D).

**21. (D):** Given, $F = 4x + 6y$

For $z = 4x + 6y$

$z(0, 2) = 4(0) + 6(2)$

$z(0, 2) = 12$

$z(3, 0) = 4(3) + 6(0)$

$z(3, 0) = 12$

and $z(6, 0) = 4(6) + 6(0) = 24$

$\therefore$ $z(6, 0) = 24$

$z(6, 8) = 4(6) + 6(8)$

$= 24 + 48 = 72$

and $z(0, 5) = 4(0) + 6(5)$

$= 0 + 30 = 30$

| Points | Values of $z$ |
|---|---|
| (0, 2) | 12 |
| (3, 0) | 12 |
| (6, 0) | 24 |
| (6, 8) | 72 |
| (0, 5) | 30 |

$\therefore$ minimum $z$ occurs at (0, 2) and (3, 0).

$\therefore$ minimum value of $z$ occurs at any point on the line segment (0, 2) and (3, 0)

Thus, correct answer is (D).

**22. (C)** **23. (C)**

**24. (C):** Given, $\begin{bmatrix} 2a+b & a+2b \\ 2c+d & c+2d \end{bmatrix} = \begin{bmatrix} 8 & 4 \\ 3 & 3 \end{bmatrix}$

By equality of matrices, we have

$2a + b = 8$ ...(1)

$a + 2b = 4$ ...(2)

$2c + d = 3$ ...(3)

$c + 2d = 3$ ...(4)

From equations (1) & (2), we get

$$\begin{array}{r} 2a + b = 8 \\ a + 2b = 4 \\ \hline 2a + b = 8 \\ \underset{-}{2a} + \underset{-}{4b} = \underset{-}{8} \\ \hline -3b = 0 \end{array} \quad \Rightarrow b = 0$$

From equation (1), we get

$\therefore$ $2a + 0 = 8$

$\Rightarrow$ $2a = 8 \quad \Rightarrow a = 4$

Now, from equation (3) and (4), we get

$$\begin{array}{r} 2c + d = 3 \\ c + 2d = 3 \\ \hline 2c + d = 3 \\ \underset{-}{2c} + \underset{-}{4d} = \underset{-}{6} \\ \hline -3d = -3 \end{array} \quad \Rightarrow d = 1$$

Putting the value of $d$ in equation (3), we get

$2c + 1 = 3$

$\Rightarrow$ $2c = 2$

$\therefore$ $c = 1$

$\therefore$ $a + b + c + d = 4 + 0 + 1 + 1 = 6$

Hence, correct answer is (C).

**25. (C):** Let, $y = \cos^{-1}\left(\frac{\sin x + \cos x}{\sqrt{2}}\right)$

$$= \cos^{-1}\left(\frac{1}{\sqrt{2}}\sin x + \frac{1}{\sqrt{2}}\cos x\right)$$

$$= \cos^{-1}\left(\sin\frac{\pi}{4}\sin x + \cos\frac{\pi}{4}\cos x\right)$$

$$= \cos^{-1}\left(\cos\frac{\pi}{4}\cos x + \sin\frac{\pi}{4}\sin x\right)$$

$$= \cos^{-1}\left(\cos\frac{\pi}{4} - x\right)$$

$$\therefore \quad y \cos = \cos\left(\frac{\pi}{4} - x\right)$$

$$\Rightarrow \quad y = \frac{\pi}{4} - x$$

$$\Rightarrow \quad \frac{dy}{dx} = -1$$

Hence, correct answer is (C).

**26. (C):** Given, $A^2 = A$, $(I + A)^3 - 8A$

We have, $(I + A)^3 - 8A$

$= I^3 + A^3 + 3I^2A + 3IA^2 - 8A$

$= I + A^2 + 3A + 3A - 8A \quad [\because A^2 = A]$

$= I + 7A - 8A$

$= I - A$

Hence, correct answer is (C).

**27. (B):** (*a*) $y = \cos\sqrt{x}$

Differentiating wrt $x$, we get

$$\therefore \quad \frac{dy}{dx} = -\sin\sqrt{x} \times \frac{2}{2\sqrt{x}}$$

$$= \frac{-\sin\sqrt{x}}{2\sqrt{x}}$$

$$= \frac{-1}{2\sqrt{x}}\sin\sqrt{x}$$

(*b*) $y = \sqrt{\sin x}$

$\Rightarrow \quad y^2 = \sin x$

Differentiating wrt $x$, we get

$$\therefore \quad 2y\frac{dy}{dx} = \cos x$$

$$\Rightarrow \quad \frac{dy}{dx} = \frac{\cos x}{2y} = \cos x\frac{1}{2\sqrt{\sin x}}$$

(*c*) Given, $y = \sec\left(\tan\sqrt{x}\right)$

Differentiating wrt $x$, we get

$$y' = \frac{dy}{dx} = \left(\sec(\tan\sqrt{x})\right)'$$

$$= \sec(\tan\sqrt{x})\tan(\tan\sqrt{x})(\tan\sqrt{x})'$$

$$= \sec(\tan\sqrt{x})\tan(\tan\sqrt{x})\cdot\left(\sec^2\sqrt{x}\cdot(\sqrt{x})'\right)$$

$$= \sec(\tan\sqrt{x})\tan(\tan\sqrt{x})\cdot\sec^2\sqrt{x}\times\frac{1}{2\sqrt{x}}$$

$$= \frac{\sec(\tan\sqrt{x})\sec(\tan\sqrt{x})\sec^2\sqrt{x}}{2\sqrt{x}}$$

(*d*) Given, $y = \cos(\sin(x^3))$

$$\therefore \quad \frac{dy}{dx} = -\sin\left(\sin(x^3)\right)\frac{d}{dx}\left(\sin(x^3)\right)$$

$$= -\sin\left(\sin(x^3)\right)\cos x^3\frac{d}{dx}(x^3)$$

$$= -3x^2\sin\left(\sin(x^3)\right)\cos x^3$$

$$= -3x^2\cos(x^3)\sin\left(\sin(x^3)\right)$$

Hence, (*a*) – (*iv*), (*b*) – (*iii*), (*c*) – (*i*), (*d*) – (*ii*)

Thus, correct answer is (B).

**28. (C):** Given, $x - y + z = 4$

$\Rightarrow \quad x - y + z - 4 = 0$

Direction cosines of normal to a plane $ax + bx + cz + d = 0$ is

$$\pm\left(\frac{a}{\sqrt{a^2+b^2+c^2}}, \frac{b}{\sqrt{a^2+b^2+c^2}}, \frac{c}{\sqrt{a^2+b^2+c^2}}\right)$$

$\therefore$ Directional cosines of normal to the plane $x - y + z - 4 = 0$ are

$a = 1, b = -1, c = 1, d = -4$

$\therefore$ Direction cosines

$$= \pm\left(\frac{1}{\sqrt{1^2+1^2+1^2}}, \frac{-1}{\sqrt{1^2+1^2+1^2}}, \frac{1}{\sqrt{1^2+1^2+1^2}}\right)$$

$$= \pm\left(\frac{1}{\sqrt{3}}, \frac{-1}{\sqrt{3}}, \frac{1}{\sqrt{3}}\right)$$

Hence, required direction cosines are $\left(\frac{1}{\sqrt{3}}, \frac{-1}{\sqrt{3}}, \frac{1}{\sqrt{3}}\right)$.

**29. (C):** Given, $I = \int e^x\left(\frac{1+\sin x}{1+\cos x}\right)dx$

$\because \sin 2x = 2\sin x \operatorname{con} x$

Replacing $x$ by $\frac{x}{2}$, we get

$$\sin 2\left(\frac{x}{2}\right) = 2\sin\left(\frac{x}{2}\right)\cos\left(\frac{x}{2}\right)$$

$$\therefore \quad \sin x = 2\sin\frac{x}{2}\cos\frac{x}{2}$$

and $\quad \cos 2x = 2\cos^2 x - 1$

Replacing $x$ by $\frac{x}{2}$, we get

$$\cos 2\left(\frac{x}{2}\right) = 2\cos^2\left(\frac{x}{2}\right) - 1$$

$$\Rightarrow \quad 1 + \cos x = 2\cos^2 \frac{x}{2}$$

$$\therefore \quad e^x\left(\frac{1+\sin x}{1+\cos x}\right) = e^x\left(\frac{1+2\sin\left(\frac{x}{2}\right)\cos\left(\frac{x}{2}\right)}{2\cos^2\left(\frac{x}{2}\right)}\right)dx$$

Since $\sin^2 x + \cos^2 x = 1$

Replacing $x$ by $\frac{x}{2}$, we get $\sin^2\left(\frac{x}{2}\right)+\cos^2\left(\frac{x}{2}\right)=1$

$$\Rightarrow e^x\left(\frac{\sin^2\left(\frac{x}{2}\right)+\cos^2\left(\frac{x}{2}\right)+2\sin\frac{x}{2}\cos\frac{x}{2}}{2\cos^2\left(\frac{x}{2}\right)}\right)$$

$$= \frac{e^x}{2}\left(\frac{\sin\frac{x}{2}+\cos\frac{x}{2}}{\cos\frac{x}{2}}\right)^2$$

$$= \frac{e^x}{2}\left(\frac{\sin\frac{x}{2}}{\cos\frac{x}{2}}+\frac{\cos\frac{x}{2}}{\cos\frac{x}{2}}\right)^2$$

$$= \frac{e^x}{2}\left(\tan\frac{x}{2}+1\right)^2$$

$$= \frac{e^x}{2}\left(\tan^2\frac{x}{2}+1^2+2\left(\tan\frac{x}{2}\right)\cdot 1\right)$$

$$= \frac{e^x}{2}\left(\tan^2\frac{x}{2}+1+2\tan\frac{x}{2}\right) \qquad [\because 1 + \tan^2 x = \sec^2 x$$

Replacing $x$ by $\frac{x}{2}$, we get

$$1 + \tan^2\left(\frac{x}{2}\right) = \sec^2\left(\frac{x}{2}\right)$$

$$= \frac{e^x}{2}\left(\sec^2\left(\frac{x}{2}\right)+2\tan\left(\frac{x}{2}\right)\right)$$

$$= e^x\left(\frac{1}{2}\cdot\sec^2\left(\frac{x}{2}\right)+\frac{2}{2}\tan\left(\frac{x}{2}\right)\right)$$

$$= e^x\left(\tan\left(\frac{x}{2}\right)+\frac{1}{2}\sec^2\left(\frac{x}{2}\right)\right)$$

$\therefore$ Our integration becomes,

$$\int e^x\left(\frac{1+\sin x}{1+\cos x}\right)dx = \int e^x\left(\tan\left(\frac{x}{2}\right)+\frac{1}{2}\sec^2\left(\frac{x}{2}\right)\right)dx$$

It is of the form

$$\int e^x\,[f(x)+f'(x)]dx$$

$$= e^x f(x) + C, \text{ where } f(x) = \tan^{-1}x,\ f'(x) = \frac{1}{1+x^2}$$

$$\therefore \quad \int e^x\left(\frac{1+\sin x}{1+\cos x}\right)dx = e^x\tan\frac{x}{2}+C$$

Where C is constant.

Hence, correct answer is (C).

**30. (C):** Given, curves $y^2 = 4x$ and $y = 2x$

Equation of parabola, is $y^2 = 4x$

Also, $y = 2x$ passes through points (0, 0) and (1, 2)

Point (1, 2) lies in parabola $y^2 = 4x$

$\therefore$ Intersecting point at A = [1, 2]

So, Area required $y = 2x$

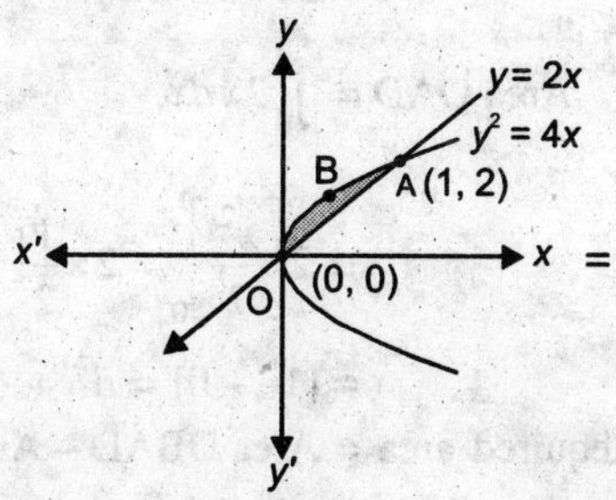


=

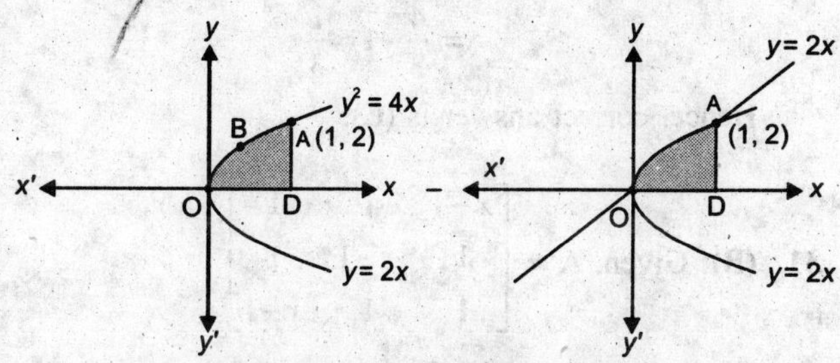


$\therefore$ Area required = Area OBAD – Area OAD

Area OBAD,

$$\text{Area OBAD} = \int_0^1 y\,dx$$

$y \rightarrow$ Equation of parabola

$$y^2 = 4x$$

$$\therefore \quad y = \sqrt{4x} = 2\sqrt{x}$$

$$\text{Hence, area OBAD} = \int_0^1 2\sqrt{x}dx$$

$$= 2\int_0^1 x^{1/2}dx$$

$$= 2\left[\frac{x^{\frac{1}{2}+1}}{\frac{1}{2}+1}\right]_0^1 = 2\left[\frac{x^{\frac{3}{2}}}{\frac{3}{2}}\right]_0^1$$

$$= 2\times\frac{2}{3}\left[x^{3/2}\right]_0^1$$

$$= \frac{4}{3}\left[1^{3/2}-(0)^{3/2}\right]$$

$$= \frac{4}{3}$$

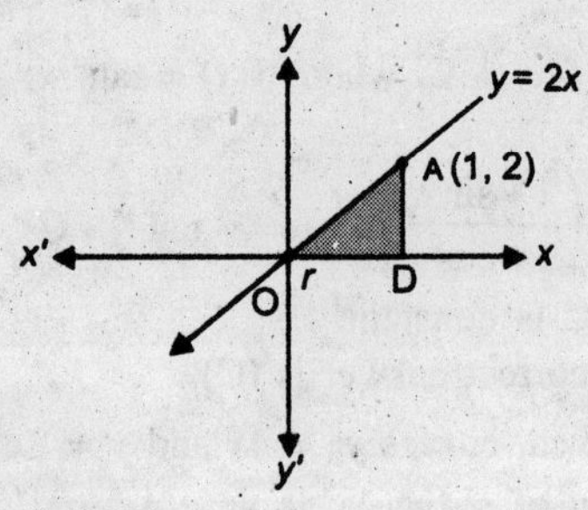


Now, Area OAD,

$$\text{area OAD} = \int_0^1 y\,dx$$

$y \rightarrow$ equation of line

$$y = 2x$$

$\therefore$ $$\text{Area OAD} = \int_0^1 2x\,dx$$

$$= 2\left[\frac{x^2}{2}\right]_0^1 = 2 \times \frac{1}{2}\left[x^2\right]_0^1$$

$$= [1^2 - 0] = 1$$

$\therefore$ Required area = Area OBAD – Area OAD

$$= \frac{4}{3} - 1 = \frac{1}{3}$$

Hence, correct answer is (C).

**31.** **(B)**: Given, $A = \begin{bmatrix} x-1 & 1 & 1 \\ 1 & x-1 & 1 \\ 1 & 1 & x-1 \end{bmatrix}$

Expanding along the first row, we get

$$|A| = (x-1)\begin{vmatrix} x-1 & 1 \\ 1 & x-1 \end{vmatrix} - 1\begin{vmatrix} 1 & 1 \\ 1 & x-1 \end{vmatrix} + \begin{vmatrix} 1 & x-1 \\ 1 & 1 \end{vmatrix}$$

$= (x-1)\{(x-1)(x-1) - 1 \times 1\} - 1\{(x-1) - 1 \times 1\}$
$\qquad + 1\{1 \times 1 - 1 \times (x-1)\}$

$= (x-1)(x^2 - 2x + 1 - 1) - 1(x - 1 - 1) + 1(1 - x + 1)$

$= (x-1)(x^2 - 2x) - 1(x-2) + (-x+2)$

$= x(x-1)(x-2) - 1(x-2) - (x-2)$

$= (x-2)\{x(x-1) - 1 - 1\}$

$= (x-2)(x^2 - x - 2)$

For singular $|A| = 0$

$\Rightarrow (x-2)(x^2 - x - 2) = 0$

$\Rightarrow (x-2)(x^2 - 2x + x - 2) = 0$

$\Rightarrow (x-2)(x(x-2) + 1)(x-2) = 0$

$\Rightarrow (x-2)(x-2)(x+1) = 0$

$\Rightarrow (x-2)^2 = 0,\ x + 1 = 0$

$\Rightarrow x - 2 = 0,\ x + 1 = 0$

$\Rightarrow x = 2,\ \ x = -1$

$\therefore$ The values of $x$ are –1, 2

Hence, correct answer is (B).

**32.** **(A)**: Given, $A = [2\ \ -3\ \ 4]$, $B = \begin{bmatrix} 3 \\ 2 \\ 2 \end{bmatrix}$

$$X = [1\ \ 2\ \ 3],\ y = \begin{bmatrix} 2 \\ 3 \\ 4 \end{bmatrix}$$

$$AB = [2\ \ -3\ \ 4]_{1 \times 3}\begin{bmatrix} 3 \\ 2 \\ 2 \end{bmatrix}_{3\times1}$$

$$= [6\ \ -6\ \ +8]$$
$$= [8]_{1 \times 1}$$

$$XY = [1\ \ 2\ \ 3]\begin{bmatrix} 2 \\ 3 \\ 4 \end{bmatrix}$$

$$= [2 + 6 + 12] = 20$$

$\therefore$ AB + XY = 8 + 20 = 28

Hence, correct answer is (A).

**33.** **(A): Apply quotient rule differentiation**

Given, $$f(x) = \frac{1}{4x^2 + 2x + 1}$$

$\because$ If $$f(x) = \frac{s(x)}{t(x)},$$

Then $$f'(x) = \frac{t(x) \times s'(x) - s(x) \times t(x)}{\{t(x)\}^2}$$

$$\therefore f'(x) = \frac{(4x^2 + 2x + 1) \times \frac{d}{dx}(1) - 1 \times \frac{d}{dx}(4x^2 + 2x + 1)}{(4x^2 + 2x + 1)^2}$$

$$\left[\because \frac{d}{dx}(\text{constant}) = 0 \text{ and } \frac{d}{dx}(x^n) = nx^{n-1}\right]$$

$$= \frac{-(8x + 2)}{(4x^2 + 2x + 1)^2}$$

For maxima or minima put $f'(x) = 0$

$$0 = 8x + 2$$

$\Rightarrow$ $$8x + 2 = 0$$

$$8x = -2$$

$\therefore$ $$x = -\frac{2}{8} = -\frac{1}{4}$$

Again differentiate, we get

$$f''(x) = \frac{-[(4x + 2x + 1)^2 8 - (8x + 2)2(4x^2 + 2x + 1)(8x + 2)]}{|4x^2 + 2x + 1|^4}$$

At $x = \frac{-1}{4}$, $f''(x)$ is negative.

The function $f(x)$ is maximum at $x = \frac{-1}{4}$.

Thus, the maximum value is

$$f\left(\frac{-1}{4}\right)_{max} = \frac{1}{4\times\frac{1}{16}-2\times\frac{1}{4}+1}$$

$$= \frac{1}{\frac{1}{4}-\frac{1}{2}+1}$$

$$= \frac{4}{1-2+4} = \frac{4}{3}$$

Thus, maximum value will be $\frac{4}{3}$.

**34. (C):** (*a*) Range of $\text{cosec}^{-1}x$ is nothing but domain of cosec $x$ which is $\left[\frac{-\pi}{2}, \frac{\pi}{2}\right] - \{0\}$

(*b*) sec $x$ is defined for all the values of $x$, except for $x = \frac{\pi}{2}$

We can see the range $\sec^{-1}x$ is $[0, \pi] - \left\{\frac{\pi}{2}\right\}$.

(*c*) $f(x) = \tan^{-1} x$

$$\frac{-\pi}{2} < f(x) < \frac{\pi}{2}$$

Interval Notation: $\left(\frac{-\pi}{2}, \frac{\pi}{2}\right)$

(*d*) $\cot^{-1}x \rightarrow$ for cot $x$ to be one-one, we restrict the domain R-$n\pi$ of cot $x$ to $(0, \pi)$. Therefore, the range of $\cot^{-1}x$ is $(0, \pi)$

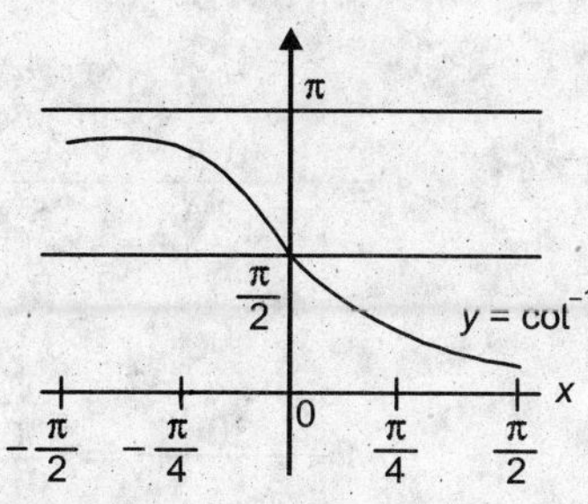


Hence, (*a*) – (*ii*), (*b*) – (*iv*), (*c*) – (*iii*), (*d*) – (*i*)

Thus, correct answer is (C).

**35. (D):** Given, $\frac{9}{4}\sin^{-1}\frac{2\sqrt{2}}{3}+\frac{9}{4}\sin^{-1}\frac{1}{3}$

Let $\frac{9}{4}\sin^{-1}\left(\frac{2\sqrt{2}}{3}\right)+\frac{9}{4}\sin^{-1}\left(\frac{1}{3}\right)=\frac{9\pi}{8}$

(From option (D))

$$\Rightarrow \frac{9\pi}{8}-\frac{9}{4}\sin^{-1}\frac{1}{3}=\frac{9}{4}\sin^{-1}\frac{2\sqrt{2}}{3}$$

$$\text{LHS} = \frac{9\pi}{8}-\frac{9}{4}\sin^{-1}\frac{1}{3}$$

$$= \frac{9}{4}\left(\frac{\pi}{2}-\sin^{-1}\frac{1}{3}\right)$$

$$= \frac{9}{4}\left(\cos^{-1}\frac{1}{3}\right)$$

Now, let $\cos^{-1}\left(\frac{1}{3}\right) = x$

Then, $\cos x = \frac{1}{3}$

$$\Rightarrow \quad \sin x = \sqrt{1-\left(\frac{1}{3}\right)^2} = \frac{2\sqrt{2}}{3}$$

$$\therefore \quad x = \sin^{-1}\left(\frac{2\sqrt{2}}{3}\right)$$

$$\Rightarrow \quad \cos^{-1}\frac{1}{3} = \sin^{-1}\left(\frac{2\sqrt{2}}{3}\right)$$

$$\therefore \quad \text{LHS} = \frac{9}{4}\sin^{-1}\frac{2\sqrt{2}}{3} = \text{RHS}$$

Thus, $\frac{9}{4}\sin^{-1}\frac{2\sqrt{2}}{3}-1\frac{9}{4}\sin^{-1}\frac{1}{3}=\frac{9\pi}{8}$

Hence, correct answer is (D).

**36. (C):** Given, $P(E) = 0.3$ and $P(E \cup F) = 0.5$

Since, E and F are independent

$$P(E \cup F) = P(E) + P(F) - P(E \cap F)$$

$$0.5 = 0.3 + P(F) - P(E) \cdot P(F)$$

$$\Rightarrow \quad 0.5 - 0.3 = P(F)\,[1 - P(E)]$$

$$\Rightarrow \quad 0.2 = P(F)[1 - P(E)]$$

$$= P(F)[1 - 0.3]$$

$$= P(F)(0.7)$$

$$\therefore \quad P(F) = \frac{0.2}{0.7} = \frac{2}{7}$$

Now, $P\left(\frac{E}{F}\right)-P\left(\frac{E}{F}\right)=\frac{P(E\cap F)}{P(F)}-\frac{P(E\cap F)}{P(E)}$

$$= \frac{P(E)\cdot P(F)}{P(F)}-\frac{P(E)\cdot P(F)}{P(E)}$$

$$= P(E) - P(F)$$

$$= 0.3 - \frac{2}{7}$$

$$= \frac{3}{10} - \frac{2}{7}$$

$$= \frac{21-20}{70} = \frac{1}{70}$$

Hence, correct answer is (C).

**37. (D):** Given, $\vec{a} = -\hat{i}+2\hat{j}+\hat{k}, \vec{b} = 3\hat{i}+2\hat{j}+k,$

$$\vec{c} = \hat{i} - \hat{j}$$

We need to find value of $a + \lambda b \perp c$

$\Rightarrow \quad (a+\lambda b)\cdot c = 0$

$\Rightarrow \quad a\cdot c + \lambda b \cdot c = 0$

$\Rightarrow \quad \lambda = -\dfrac{a\cdot c}{b\cdot c}$

$$= \frac{(-\hat{i}+2\hat{j}+\hat{k})\cdot(\hat{i}-\hat{j})}{(3\hat{i}+2\hat{j}+\hat{k})\cdot(\hat{i}-\hat{j})}$$

$$= \frac{-(-1-2+0)}{3-2+0} = -\frac{(-3)}{1} = +3$$

$\therefore \quad \lambda = 3$

Hence, correct answer is (D).

**38. (D):** Given, $f(x) = [x]$ = greatest integer less than equal to $x$

Example, [1] = 1, [1.01] = 1, [1.2] = 1, [1.9] = 1, [1.99] = 1, [2] = 2

A function $f : x \to y$ is one-one or injective, if for every.

$x_1, x_2 \in X, f(x_1) = f(x_2) \Rightarrow x_1 = x_2$

Assume, $x_1 = 2.1$ and $x_2 = 2.5$

$\therefore \quad f(2.1) = (2.1) = 2$

and $\quad f(2.5) = (2.5) = 2$

So, it is observed that $f(x_1) = f(x_2)$, but $x_1 \neq x_2$

Thus, $f$ is not one-one.

A function $f : x \to y$ is onto or surjective, if for every $y \in Y$

$\Leftrightarrow$ an element is X such that $f(x) = y$

For $2.5 \in R$, there does not exist any $x$ in R s.t.

$$f(x) = 2.5$$

$\therefore f$ is not onto.

Hence, the greatest integer function $f: R \to R$, defined by $f(x) = [x]$ is neither one-one nor onto.

**39. (B):** Given, $A = \begin{bmatrix} a_{11} & a_{12} & a_{13} \\ a_{21} & a_{22} & a_{23} \\ a_{31} & a_{32} & a_{33} \end{bmatrix}$

$M_{11} = (a_{22}\cdot a_{33}) - (a_{23}\cdot a_{32})$

$M_{12} = (a_{21}\cdot a_{33}) - (a_{23}\cdot a_{31})$

$M_{13} = (a_{21}\cdot a_{32}) - (a_{22}\cdot a_{31})$

$$A_{ij} = (-1)^{i+j} M_{ij}$$

$|A| = a_{11}[(a_{22}\cdot a_{33}) - (a_{23}\cdot a_{32})] - a_{12}[(a_{21}\cdot a_{33}) - (a_{23}\cdot a_{31})] + a_{13}[(a_{21}\cdot a_{32}) - (a_{22}\cdot a_{31})]$

$\Rightarrow |A| = a_{11}M_{11} - a_{12}M_{12} + a_{13}M_{13}$

From cofactor minor

$|A| = a_{11}A_{11} + a_{12}A_{12} + a_{13}A_{13}$

Hence, correct answers (*a*) and (*c*)

Then, correct option (B).

**40. (C):** Let $I = \int_{-1}^{1} |x|\,dx = -\int_{-1}^{0} x\,dx + \int_{0}^{1} x\,dx$

Since, $|x| = \begin{cases} x & \text{if } x \geq 0 \\ -x & \text{if } x \leq 0 \end{cases}$

$\therefore \; |x| = -x$, when $x$ lies between –1 and 0 and $|x| = x$, when $x$ lies between 0 and 1.

$$= -\left[\frac{x^2}{2}\right]_1^0 + \left[\frac{x^2}{2}\right]_0^1$$

$$= -\left[-\frac{1}{2}\right] + \left[\frac{1}{2}\right] = \frac{1}{2} + \frac{1}{2} = 1.$$

**41. (A):** Probability of speaking truth $P(A) = \dfrac{4}{5}$

Probability of getting five, $P(B) = \dfrac{1}{6}$

Probability of not getting five $P(\bar{A}) = 1 - \dfrac{1}{6} = \dfrac{5}{6}$

Probability of not getting five can be given by

$$P(\bar{B}) = 1 - \frac{4}{5} = \frac{1}{5}$$

Probability of actually getting five is calculated by Bayes's rule

$$P\left(\frac{A}{B}\right) = \frac{P\left(\frac{B}{A}\right)P(A)}{P(B)}$$

$$= \frac{\left(\frac{4}{5}\times\frac{1}{6}\right)}{\left(\frac{4}{5}\times\frac{1}{6}\right) + \left(\frac{1}{5}\times\frac{5}{6}\right)}$$

$$= \frac{\frac{4}{30}}{\left(\frac{4}{30}+\frac{5}{30}\right)} = \frac{\frac{4}{30}}{\frac{9}{30}} = \frac{4}{9}$$

Hence, the probability that it is actually five is $\dfrac{4}{9}$.

**42. (C):** Given, minimize $z = 3x + 2y$

Subject to, $\quad x + y \geq 8$

$3x + 5y \leq 15$

$x \geq 0, y \geq 0$

We have

$x + y \geq 8$ $\qquad$ $3x + 5y \leq 15$

| $x$ | 0 | 8 |
|---|---|---|
| $y$ | 8 | 0 |

| $x$ | 0 | 5 |
|---|---|---|
| $y$ | 3 | 0 |

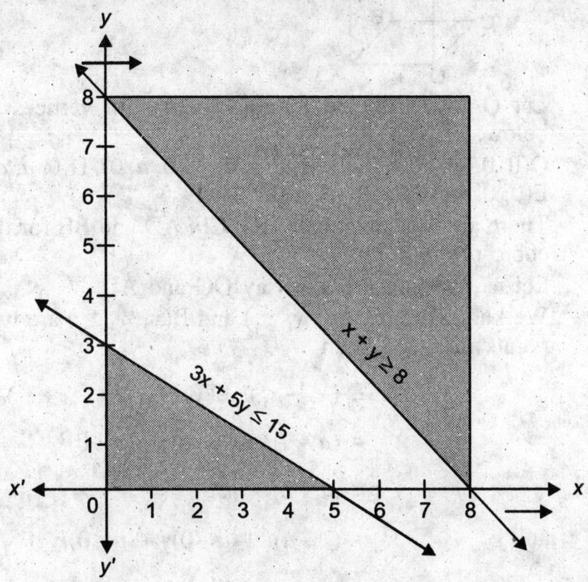


As, there is no common region, so there is no feasible region.

Hence, these is no minimum value of $z$.

Thus, correct answer is (C).

**43. (C):** Given, $\frac{dy}{dx} = \sin^{-1} x$

$\therefore \qquad dy = \sin^{-1}x \; dx$

Integrating on both sides, we get

$$\int dy = \int \sin^{-1} x \cdot 1 dx$$

Integrating by parts, we get

$$\int f(x)g(x)dx = f(x)\int g(x)dx - \int [f'(x)\int g(x)dx]dx$$

Take $f(x) = \sin^{-1}x$ and $g(x) = 1$

$$\therefore \qquad y = \sin^{-1} x\int 1dx - \int\left[\frac{1}{\sqrt{1-x^2}}\int 1\cdot dx\right]dx$$

$$\left[\because \frac{d(\sin^{-1} x)}{dx} = \frac{1}{\sqrt{1-x^2}}\right]$$

$$\Rightarrow \qquad y = \sin^{-1} x - \int \frac{x}{\sqrt{1-x^2}}dx$$

Let $\qquad t = 1 - x^2$

$\qquad dt = -2xdx$

$$\Rightarrow \qquad xdx = \frac{-dt}{2}$$

Hence, equation becomes

$$y = x\sin^{-1} x - \int \frac{-dt}{2\sqrt{t}}$$

$$= x\sin^{-1} x + \int \frac{dt}{2\sqrt{t}}$$

$$= x\sin^{-1} x + \frac{1}{2}\int t^{-\frac{1}{2}}dt$$

$$= x\sin^{-1} x + \frac{1}{2}\frac{t^{-\frac{1}{2}+1}}{\frac{-1}{2}+1} + C$$

$$= x\sin^{-1} x + \frac{1}{2}\frac{t^{\frac{1}{2}}}{\left(\frac{1}{2}\right)} + C$$

$$= x\sin^{-1} x + \sqrt{t} + C$$

$$= x\sin^{-1} x + \sqrt{1-x^2} + C$$

Hence, correct answer is (C).

**44. (C):** Given, position vector $= \left(2\hat{i} + \hat{j} - \hat{k}\right)$

$$\text{Plane} = \vec{r}\cdot\left(-2\hat{i} + \hat{j} + 3\hat{k}\right) = 8$$

*i.e.*, let $n = -2\hat{i} + \hat{j} + 3\hat{k}$ and $d = 8$

Let $\qquad \vec{a} = 2\hat{i} + \hat{j} - \hat{k}$

and $\qquad \vec{n} = -2\hat{i} + \hat{j} + 3\hat{k}$ and $d = 8$

$$\text{Distance} = \frac{|\vec{a}\cdot\vec{n} - d|}{\vec{n}}$$

$$= \frac{|(2\hat{i} + \hat{j} - \hat{k})\cdot(-2\hat{i} + \hat{j} + 3\hat{k}) - 8|}{-2\hat{i} + \hat{j} + 3\hat{k}}$$

$$= \frac{|-4+1-3-8|}{\sqrt{(-2)^2 + 1^2 + 3^2}}$$

$$= \frac{|-14|}{\sqrt{4+1+9}} = \frac{14}{\sqrt{14}}$$

$$= \frac{\sqrt{14}\times\sqrt{14}}{\sqrt{14}} = \sqrt{14}$$

Hence, required distance $= \sqrt{14}$.

**45. (B):** Side of equilateral triangle, $a = 2$

Area of equilateral triangle

$$A = \frac{\sqrt{3}}{4}a^2$$

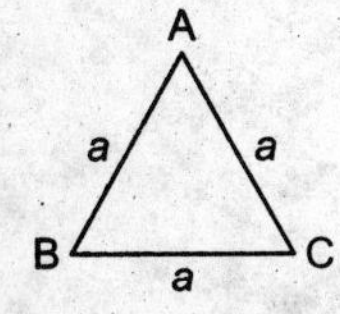


$$\therefore \qquad \frac{dA}{dt} = \frac{\sqrt{3}}{4}\cdot 2a$$

$$= \frac{\sqrt{3}}{4} \times 2 \times 2 = \sqrt{3}$$

Hence, rate of change of area of $\sqrt{3}$ sq units.

**46. (B):** Given, A = {1, 2, 3}, given, R = {(1, 2), (2, 1)}
Set = {1, 2, 3}
R = {(1, 2) (2, 1)}
If relation is reflexive, then $(a, a) \in R \ \forall \ a \in \{1, 2, 3\}$
as $(1, 1) \notin R$
So, R is not reflexive
If the relation is symmetric, then $(a, b)$ & $(b, a) \in R$
Here, (1, 2) & (2, 1) $\in$ R
So, R is symmetric
Hence, correct answer is (B).

**47. (B):** Given, $f(x) = \begin{cases} x^3 + 3 & , \text{ if } x \neq 0 \\ 4 & , \text{ if } x = 0 \end{cases}$

$$\lim_{x \to 0^-} (x^3 + 3) = 3$$

$$\lim_{x \to 0^+} (x^3 + 3) = 3$$

$$\text{By} \quad \lim_{x \to 3} x^3 + 3 = 4$$

Unit exists but not continuous as 0, then number of points of discontinuity for this function is 1.
Hence, correct answer is (B).

**48. (B):** We have, $f(x) = x^2$

(1) $f(x)$ is continuous on [–1, 1]

(2) $f(x)$ is differentiable on (–1, 1)

$f(-1) = 1 \qquad f(1) = 1$

$\exists$ point C, such that

$f'(C) = 0 \qquad -1 < C < 1$

$f(x) = x^2, \qquad f'(x) = 2x$

$f'(C) = 0 \qquad \Rightarrow 2C = 0$

Since, $\quad -1 < 0 < 1 \qquad C = 0$

Hence, $f(x) = x^2$, $x \in [-1, 1]$ satisfies the Rolle's theorem.

**49. (B):** The equation of the plane XOY is $z = 0$
Any plane parallel to the form $z = a$

Since, the $z$-intercept of the plane is $\sqrt{3}$.

$\therefore \qquad a = \sqrt{3}$

Thus, equation of the intercept the required plane is $z = \sqrt{3}$

$\therefore$ Equation is $z - \sqrt{3} = 0$
Hence, correct answer is (B).

**50. (D):**

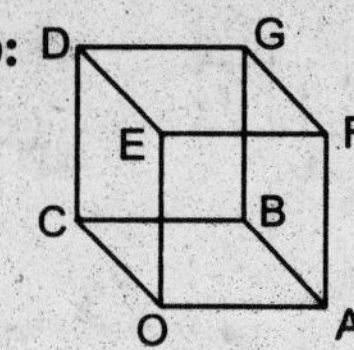


Let OABCDEFG be a cubic room with vertices as below:
O(0, 0, 0), A($a$, 0, 0), B($a$, $a$, 0), C(0, $a$, 0), D(0, $a$, $a$), E(0, 0, $a$), F ($a$, 0, $a$), G($a$, $a$, $a$)
There are four diagonals OG, CF, AD and BE for the cubic room.
Let us consider any two say OG and AD.
We know that if A($x_1$, $y_1$, $z_1$) and B($x_2$, $y_2$, $z_2$) are two points in space, then

$$\overrightarrow{AB} = (x_2 - x_1)\hat{i} + (y_2 - y_1)\hat{j} + (z_2 - z_1)\hat{k}$$

$$\Rightarrow \quad \overrightarrow{OG} = (a-0)\hat{i} + (a-0)\hat{j} + (a-0)\hat{k}$$

$$= a\hat{i} + a\hat{j} + a\hat{k}$$

$$\text{and} \quad \overrightarrow{AD} = (0-a)\hat{i} + (a-0)\hat{j} + (a-0)\hat{k}$$

$$= -a\hat{i} + a\hat{j} + a\hat{k}$$

$$\text{Thus,} \quad |\overrightarrow{OG}| = \sqrt{a^2 + a^2 + a^2}$$

$$= a\sqrt{3}$$

$$\text{and} \quad |\overrightarrow{AD}| = \sqrt{(-a)^2 + a^2 + a^2}$$

$$= a\sqrt{3}$$

$$\therefore \quad \overrightarrow{OG} \cdot \overrightarrow{AD} = -a^2 + a^2 + a^2 = a^2$$

We know that the angle between two vectors $\vec{a}$ and $\vec{b}$ is given by

$$\theta = \cos^{-1} \frac{\vec{a} \cdot \vec{b}}{|\vec{a}| \cdot |\vec{b}|}$$

Thus, angle between two diagonals $\overrightarrow{OG}$ and $\overrightarrow{AD}$ is

$$\theta = \cos^{-1} \frac{a^2}{a\sqrt{3} \times a\sqrt{3}}$$

$$= \frac{a^2}{a^2 \times 3} = \cos^{-1}\left(\frac{1}{3}\right)$$

Hence, correct answer is (D).

# ACCOUNTANCY/BOOK KEEPING

**1.** Which of the following will be shown on the credit side of Deceased Partner A/c?
(*a*) Revaluation Gain Share
(*b*) Goodwill written off
(*c*) Share of profit till date of death
(*d*) Drawings till date of death
(*e*) Interest on capital till date of death

Choose the ***correct answer*** from the options given below:
A. (*a*) and (*c*) only
B. (*b*), (*d*) and (*e*) only
C. (*a*), (*b*) and (*d*) only
D. (*a*), (*c*) and (*e*) only

**2.** Match List I with List II.

| ***List-I*** | ***List-II*** |
|---|---|
| (*a*) Interest on capital | (*i*) Admission of partner |
| (*b*) Gaining Ratio | (*ii*) Profit/Loss in the old profit sharing ratio |
| (*c*) Sacrificing ratio | (*iii*) Continuing partners |
| (*d*) Revaluation of Assets and Liabilities | (*iv*) When partnership deed specifically provide for it |

Choose the ***correct answer*** from the options given below:

| | (*a*) | (*b*) | (*c*) | (*d*) |
|---|---|---|---|---|
| A. | (*i*) | (*ii*) | (*iii*) | (*iv*) |
| B. | (*iii*) | (*iv*) | (*i*) | (*ii*) |
| C. | (*ii*) | (*iii*) | (*iv*) | (*i*) |
| D. | (*iv*) | (*iii*) | (*i*) | (*ii*) |

**3.** Capital gain tax paid on sale of fixed assets should be classified as ______.
A. Cash inflow from Operating Activities
B. Cash outflow from Operating Activities
C. Cash inflow from Investing Activities
D. Cash outflow from Investing Activities

**4.** On 1st July, 2022, Centaur Ltd. issued ₹ 25,00,000 8% debentures of ₹ 100 each as collateral security to first Level Bank against loan dues of ₹ 20,00,000. How much amount will be shown in the Balance sheet?
A. ₹ 25,00,000  B. ₹ 45,00,000
C. ₹ 20,00,000  D. ₹ 70,00,000

**5.** Identify the key that allows the access to the system.
A. Security  B. Encryption
C. Software  D. Password

**6.** On R's retirement, the amount payable to him after all adjustments, work out to be ₹ 60,000 but the remaining partners P and Q agreed to pay him ₹ 75,000 in full settlement of his claim. Identify the term which represent ₹ 15,000 extra, that is paid to R.
A. Share in Profits
B. Hidden Goodwill
C. Interest on his Capital
D. Compensation for Past work

**7.** Which command reverse the last action performed in the worksheet?
A. Ctrl + Z  B. Ctrl + P
C. Ctrl + Y  D. Ctrl + C

**8.** A, B and C are partners with equal profit sharing ratio. Their fixed capitals are ₹ 30,000, ₹ 25,000 and ₹ 30,000 respectively. C decided to take retirement A and B decided to continue the partnership firm and change their profit sharing ratio into Capital Ratio. What is the gaining Ratio of A and B?
A. 6 : 5  B. 1 : 1
C. 7 : 4  D. 3 : 2

**9.** A company can buy its own shares when:
A. The debt - Equity ratio is not more than 1 : 1 after the buy back.
B. The amount of buy back shares in any financial year not exceeding 20% of the paid-up capital and free reserves.
C. Partly paid up shares are considered buy back.
D. Article of Association must authorise and special resolution has been passed for the buy back of shares.

**10.** C Ltd. made a profit of ₹ 10,000 after charging depreciation of ₹ 2,000 on Assets, transfer to General Reserve ₹ 3,000. Written of Goodwill ₹ 700, Profit on sale of Asset ₹ 300, increase in Debtors ₹ 300, increase in creditors ₹ 600, increase in prepaid expenses ₹ 20 and decrease in outstanding expenses ₹ 200. What will be the cash from operating activities?
A. ₹ 15,500  B. ₹ 15,480
C. ₹ 15,000  D. ₹ 16,000

**11.** Identify the term that is used to show the amount received as per the will of a deceased person.
A. Specific Donations  B. Life membership fees
C. Subscription  D. Legacies

**12.** Trade payables to be settled beyond 12 months from the date of Balance sheet or beyond the operating cycle are classified under:
A. Long term provisions

B. Other long term liabilities
C. Deferred tax liabilities
D. Long term Borrowing

**13.** What is the correct sequence to prepare company's Balance Sheet as per the standard format given according to schedule III of Companies Act 2013?
(*a*) Non Current Liability
(*b*) Non Current Assets
(*c*) Shareholder's Fund
(*d*) Current Assets
(*e*) Current Liability

Choose the ***correct answer*** from the options given below:
A. (*c*), (*a*), (*b*), (*e*), (*d*) B. (*a*), (*b*), (*c*), (*d*), (*e*)
C. (*c*), (*a*), (*e*), (*b*), (*d*) D. (*a*), (*c*), (*e*), (*b*), (*d*)

**14.** In which of the following case, claim is valid if the partnership agreement is silent?
A. Sanjay is an active partner and wants a salary of ₹ 1,00,000 per year.
B. Monika had advanced a loan to the firm and claims interest @10% per annum.
C. Sanjay and Monika contributed ₹ 2,00,000 and ₹ 5,00,000 as capital respectively and Monika wants equal share.
D. Monika wants interest on capital to be credited @10% per annum.

**15.** Separate disclosure of cash flow arising from Financial Activities is important because:
A. It helps in identifying the investment activities.
B. It helps in gaining in investing activities.
C. It helps in making investing decision.
D. It is useful in predicting claims on future cash flow by providers of funds to the enterprise.

**16.** Find out cash from financing Activities from the following information.

| | |
|---|---|
| Issue of Equity Shares | ₹ 80,000 |
| Redemption of Preference Shares | ₹ 30,000 |
| Interim Dividend Paid | ₹ 25,000 |
| Interest on Debentures | ₹ 15,000 |
| Issue of Debentures | ₹ 30,000 |

A. Inflow ₹ 80,000 B. Outflow ₹ 80,000
C. Inflow ₹ 40,000 D. Outflow ₹ 40,000

**17.** When a company issues shares in open market and the amount is payable in instalments. What is the sequence of amount demanded by the company?
(*a*) Money received on calls
(*b*) Money due on calls
(*c*) Allotment money received
(*d*) Application money transferred to Share Capital A/c
(*e*) Allotment money due

Choose the ***correct answer*** from the options given below:
A. (*d*), (*c*), (*b*), (*a*), (*e*) B. (*d*), (*e*), (*c*), (*b*), (*a*)
C. (*d*), (*c*), (*a*), (*b*), (*e*) D. (*d*), (*e*), (*c*), (*a*), (*b*)

**18.** Select the sub-head under which loose tools will be shown in the Balance Sheet of a company:
A. Current Assets B. Trade Receivables
C. Inventories D. Other current Assets

**19.** Match List I with List II.

| ***List-I*** | ***List-II*** |
|---|---|
| (*a*) Loss on Revaluation | (*i*) Credited to old partners in old ratio |
| (*b*) Profit on Revaluation | (*ii*) Debited to profit and loss suspense A/c |
| (*c*) Premium brought by new partner | (*iii*) Credited to old partners in sacrificing ratio |
| (*d*) On the death of a partner, profit till the date of death is ₹ 2,000 | (*iv*) Debited to old partners in the old ratio |

Choose the ***correct answer*** from the options given below:

| | (*a*) | (*b*) | (*c*) | (*d*) |
|---|---|---|---|---|
| A. | (*i*) | (*iv*) | (*iii*) | (*ii*) |
| B. | (*iv*) | (*i*) | (*iii*) | (*ii*) |
| C. | (*ii*) | (*i*) | (*iv*) | (*iii*) |
| D. | (*iii*) | (*ii*) | (*iv*) | (*i*) |

**20.** Complete the sequence where interest on capital has to be provided as per partnership deed, but available profits are not sufficient to provide full amount of interest on capital.
(*a*) If it is appropriation, calculate interest on capital for all partners at given rate
(*b*) Divide the available amount in the capital for all partners at given rate
(*c*) Calculate ratio between capital of partners
(*d*) Consider the partnership deed and decide whether interest on capital is a charge or an appropriation
(*e*) Consider the available profit

Choose the ***correct answer*** from the options given below:
A. (*a*), (*b*), (*c*), (*d*), (*e*) B. (*b*), (*c*), (*d*), (*e*), (*a*)
C. (*d*), (*a*), (*e*), (*c*), (*b*) D. (*c*), (*d*), (*a*), (*b*), (*e*)

**21.** Arrange following in a sequence in which amount realised from Assets will be utilised to pay.
(*a*) Partner's Loan
(*b*) Partner's Capital
(*c*) Secured debts of the firm

(*d*) Unsecured debts of the firm
(*e*) Residue to partners

Choose the ***correct answer*** from the options given below:

A. (*c*), (*d*), (*e*), (*a*), (*b*)
B. (*c*), (*d*), (*e*), (*b*), (*a*)
C. (*c*), (*d*), (*a*), (*b*), (*e*)
D. (*c*), (*d*), (*a*), (*e*), (*b*)

**22.** In a partnership firm, partners share profit and loss in the ratio of 3 : 2. If firm incurred a loss of ₹ 10,000 during the year then calculate the amount of loss to be shared by partners.

A. Equally
B. According to profit sharing ratio
C. According to gaining ratio
D. According to sacrificing ratio

**23.** Out of the following when will the need for valuation of goodwill does not arise:

A. Admission of a partner
B. Retirement of a partner
C. Dissolution of partnership firm
D. Death of a partners

**24.** Read the following facts about admission of a partner:

(*a*) A new partner acquires his share from the old partners that reduces the old partners share in profits.
(*b*) The partner's capital must be adjusted so as to be proportionate to their new profit sharing ratio.
(*c*) Assets and Liabilities may be revalued and reassessed on admission of a partner.
(*d*) Adjustment for Reserves and Accumulated profits/loss is done.
(*e*) Profit sharing ratio of existing partners may change on admission of a new partner.

Choose the ***correct answer*** from the options given below:

A. (*a*), (*b*), (*c*) and (*d*) only
B. (*b*), (*c*), (*d*) and (*e*) only
C. (*c*), (*d*) and (*e*) only
D. (*a*), (*c*), (*d*) and (*e*) only

**25.** From the following identify the items which are payable to retiring partner, if mentioned in deed:

(*a*) Credit balance of his/her Capital/Current Account
(*b*) Share of goodwill
(*c*) Goodwill of the firm
(*d*) Share in revaluation gain/loss
(*e*) Share in accumulated profit (Reserves)

Choose the ***correct answer*** from the options given below:

A. (*a*), (*b*) only
B. (*a*), (*b*), (*d*), (*e*) only
C. (*b*), (*c*), (*d*), (*e*) only
D. (*a*), (*c*), (*d*), (*e*) only

**26.** A part of fixed Assets costing ₹ 2,00,000 (Book value ₹ 1,50,000) was sold at a gain of ₹ 10,000. How it will affect the cash flow statement?

A. Inflow ₹ 1,60,000 in Investing Activities and Add ₹ 10,000 in Operating Activities
B. Inflow ₹ 1,60,000 in Investing Activities and Less ₹ 10,000 in Operating Activities
C. Inflow ₹ 2,10,000 in Investing Activities Add ₹ 10,000 in Operating Activities
D. Inflow ₹ 2,10,000 in Investing Activities and Less ₹ 10,000 in Operating Activities

**27.** Identify those debentures on which no interest will be paid/provided.

A. Debentures issued to underwriters
B. Debentures issued for cash
C. Debentures issued to vendor
D. Debentures issued as Collateral Security

**28.** Identify the correct sequence where new partner is to bring proportionate capital.

(*a*) Calculation of Capital Balance of old partners
(*b*) Preparation of Revaluation A/c
(*c*) Determination of Revaluation gain/loss
(*d*) Presentation of Treatment of Goodwill
(*e*) Calculation of Capital to be brought in by the new partner

Choose the ***correct answer*** from the options given below:

A. (*c*), (*b*), (*d*), (*a*), (*e*)
B. (*d*), (*b*), (*c*), (*e*), (*a*)
C. (*d*), (*c*), (*b*), (*a*), (*e*)
D. (*b*), (*c*), (*d*), (*a*), (*e*)

**29.** Every company analyse its earning capacity of the business which is outcome of utilisation of resources employed in the business. To analyse profitability company can use:

(*a*) Dividend Payout Ratio
(*b*) Return on Net Worth
(*c*) Gross Profit Ratio
(*d*) Quick Ratio
(*e*) Inventory Turnover Ratio

Choose the ***correct answer*** from the option given below:

A. (*c*) and (*e*) only
B. (*c*), (*d*) and (*e*) only
C. (*a*), (*b*) and (*c*) only
D. (*a*), (*c*) and (*e*) only

**30.** Identify the ratio which is not computed for evaluating solvency of the business.

A. Debt-Equity Ratio
B. Proprietary Ratio
C. Operating Ratio
D. Interest Coverage Ratio

**31.** Match List I with List II.

| List-I | List-II |
|---|---|
| (*a*) Current Maturities of long term Debt | (*i*) Other Non-Current Liabilities |
| (*b*) Securities Premium | (*ii*) Short term Borrowing |
| (*c*) Outstanding salaries | (*iii*) Other Current Liability |
| (*d*) Premium on Redemption of Debentures | (*iv*) Reserves and Surplus |

Choose the ***correct answer*** from the options given below:

| | (*a*) | (*b*) | (*c*) | (*d*) |
|---|---|---|---|---|
| A. | (*iii*) | (*iv*) | (*ii*) | (*i*) |
| B. | (*ii*) | (*i*) | (*iii*) | (*iv*) |
| C. | (*ii*) | (*iv*) | (*iii*) | (*i*) |
| D. | (*iii*) | (*ii*) | (*i*) | (*iv*) |

**32.** Identify the term that indicate excess of Expenditure over Income, in case of a Non-for-profit Organisation.

A. Payment B. Expenditure
C. Deficit D. Loss

**33.** Identify the salient features of Income and Expenditure account from the following:

(*a*) It is prepared on accrual basis.
(*b*) It includes both revenue as well as capital items.
(*c*) It is prepared after taking into account the additional information regarding outstanding prepaid expenses and depreciation etc.
(*d*) Its result is surplus or deficit.
(*e*) It is prepared with the help of Receipts and Payments Account.

Choose the ***correct answer*** from the options given below:

A. (*a*), (*b*), (*c*) and (*d*) only
B. (*a*), (*b*), (*c*) and (*e*) only
C. (*b*), (*c*), (*d*) and (*e*) only
D. (*a*), (*c*), (*d*) and (*e*) only

**34.** W Ltd. has given you following information

| | |
|---|---|
| Machinery (opening Balance) | ₹ 50,000 |
| Machinery (closing Balance) | ₹ 60,000 |
| Accumulated Depreciation (opening balance) | ₹ 25,000 |
| Accumulated Depreciation (closing balance) | ₹ 15,000 |

During the year, a machine costing ₹ 25,000 with accumulated depreciation of ₹ 15,000 was sold for ₹ 13,000. Calculate Cash Flow from Investing Activity.

A. 22,000 B. (22,000)
C. (35,000) D. 13,000

**35.** Which of the following will be added to operating profit before working capital changes, while preparing Cash Flow statement from indirect method?

A. Increase in Trade Receivable by ₹ 80,000
B. Decrease in Inventory by ₹ 50,000
C. Increase in Prepaid Expenses by ₹ 30,000
D. Decrease in Trade Payable by ₹ 20,000

**36.** Match List I with List II.

| List-I | List-II |
|---|---|
| (*a*) Interest charges | (*i*) Employees Benefit Expenses |
| (*b*) Sale of services | (*ii*) Other incomes |
| (*c*) Salary | (*iii*) Revenue from Operations |
| (*d*) Dividend Income | (*iv*) Finance cost |

Choose the ***correct answer*** from the options given below:

| | (*a*) | (*b*) | (*c*) | (*d*) |
|---|---|---|---|---|
| A. | (*iv*) | (*iii*) | (*i*) | (*ii*) |
| B. | (*iv*) | (*ii*) | (*i*) | (*iii*) |
| C. | (*ii*) | (*i*) | (*iii*) | (*iv*) |
| D. | (*ii*) | (*iv*) | (*i*) | (*iii*) |

**37.** Match List I with List II.

| List-I | List-II |
|---|---|
| (*a*) Transfer of accumulated profits | (*i*) Realisation account |
| (*b*) Unrecorded asset sold on dissolution of firm | (*ii*) Profit and Loss Account |
| (*c*) Manager's commission | (*iii*) Profit and Loss Appropriation Account |
| (*d*) Partner's commission | (*iv*) Partner's Capital account |

Choose the ***correct answer*** from the options given below:

| | (*a*) | (*b*) | (*c*) | (*d*) |
|---|---|---|---|---|
| A. | (*iv*) | (*i*) | (*iii*) | (*ii*) |
| B. | (*iv*) | (*i*) | (*ii*) | (*iii*) |
| C. | (*iv*) | (*ii*) | (*iii*) | (*i*) |
| D. | (*iv*) | (*iii*) | (*ii*) | (*i*) |

**38.** Identify that account to which share of profit of a deceased partner is debited from the date of the last Balance Sheet to the date of his/her death.

A. His capital account
B. Profit and loss account
C. Profit and Loss Suspense account
D. Trading account

**39.** How many blank worksheet(s) are shown, by default when a new workbook is created?

A. One B. Two
C. Three D. Four

**40.** Select out of the following that leads to the need of codification.

A. The Encryption of data
B. To secure various accounts
C. To keep proper records
D. To allot codes

**Directions (Qs. No. 41-45):** *Read the following information carefully and answer these questions.*

A Ltd. with an Authorised Capital of ₹ 10,00,000 is divided into shares of ₹ 10 each, issued 50,000 shares at a premium of ₹ 2 per share payable as follows

| | |
|---|---|
| on Application | ₹ 3 per share |
| on Allotment | ₹ 5 per share (including premium) |
| on First and Final call | Balance amount |

Application were received for 60,000 shares and the directors allotted shares to all on proportionate basis. All money received except first and final call from Hari who had applied for 1200 shares. His shares were forfeited and later half of his forfeited shares were reissued at ₹ 8 per share as fully paid up.

**41.** Identify the number of shares with which A Ltd. is registered.

A. 1,00,000 Shares
B. 50,000 Shares
C. 60,000 Shares
D. 10,00,000 Shares

**42.** Select the amount received on Share Allotment Account:

A. ₹ 2,50,000
B. ₹ 1,50,000
C. ₹ 2,20,000
D. ₹ 3,00,000

**43.** Select the amount that is received from Hari's reissued shares:

A. ₹ 4,800 B. ₹ 4,000
C. ₹ 8,000 D. ₹ 9,600

**44.** Identify the account to which the discount allowed on reissue of forfeited shares should be debited.

A. Bank Account
B. Forfeited Share Account
C. Capital Reserve Account
D. Securities Premium Reserve Account

**45.** The balance, if any, left in the share forfeited account relating to reissued shares, should be transferred to ______.

A. Forfeited Share Account
B. Share Capital Account
C. Reserve Capital Account
D. Capital Reserve Account

**Directions (Qs. No. 46-50):** *Read the following information carefully and answer these questions.*

Meena and Tina are partners in a firm and sharing profit as 3 : 2. They decided to dissolve their firm on March 31, 2017 when their Balance Sheet was as follows:

**Balance Sheet Meena and Tina as on March 31, 2017**

| Liabilities | Amount (₹) | Assets | Amount (₹) |
|---|---|---|---|
| Capital | | Machinery | 70,000 |
| Meena 90,000 | | Investments | 50,000 |
| Tina 80,000 | 1,70,000 | Stock | 22,000 |
| Sundry creditors | 60,000 | Sundry Debtors | 1,03,000 |
| Bills payable | 20,000 | Cash at bank | 5,000 |
| | 2,50,000 | | 2,50,000 |

The assets and liabilities were disposed off as follows:

(*a*) Machinery were given to creditors in full settlement of their account and stock were given bills payable in full settlement.

(*b*) Investment were took over by Tina at book value, Sundry debitors of book value ₹ 50,000 took over by Meena at 10% less and remaining debtors realised ₹ 51,000.

(*c*) Realisation expenses amount to ₹ 2,000.

**46.** When a creditor accepts an asset whose value is more than the amount due to him, he will ______ the excess amount which will be credited to ______ Account.

A. Pay, Bank B. Not pay, Creditors
C. Pay, Realisation D. Not pay, Realisation

**47.** Which mode of dissolution is highlighted in the above case?

A. Compulsory Dissolution
B. Dissolution by agreement
C. Dissolution by court
D. Dissolution on happening of contingencies

**48.** Identify the amount realised in cash from Sundry Debtors.

A. ₹ 96,000 B. ₹ 1,03,000
C. ₹ 1,00,000 D. ₹ 51,000

**49.** State Journal entry for payment of realisation expenses.

| | | |
|---|---|---|
| A. Realisation Expenses A/c | Dr. ₹ 2,000 | |
| To Realisation A/c | | ₹ 2,000 |
| B. Realisation A/c | Dr. ₹ 2,000 | |
| To Realisation Expenses A/c | | ₹ 2,000 |
| C. Realisation A/c | Dr. ₹ 2,000 | |
| To Bank A/c | | ₹ 2,000 |
| D. Bank A/c | Dr. ₹ 2,000 | |
| To Realisation A/c | | ₹ 2,000 |

**50.** State Journal entry for realisation of investment.

| | | |
|---|---|---|
| A. Tina's capital A/c | Dr. ₹ 50,000 | |
| To Realisation A/c | | ₹ 50,000 |
| B. Tina's capital A/c | Dr. ₹ 30,000 | |
| Meena's capital A/c | Dr. ₹ 20,000 | |
| To Realisation A/c | | ₹ 50,000 |
| C. Realisation A/c | Dr. ₹ 50,000 | |
| To Tina's capital A/c | | ₹ 50,000 |
| D. Realisation A/c | Dr. ₹ 50,000 | |
| To Tina's capital A/c | | ₹ 30,000 |
| To Meena's capital A/c | | ₹ 20,00 |

# ANSWERS

1. **(D):** On the credit side of the Deceased Partner's Account, the following items will be shown:
   (*a*) **Revaluation Gain Share:** When a partner dies, the partnership often undergoes a revaluation of its assets and liabilities. If there is a gain resulting from this revaluation, it will be credited to the Deceased Partner's Account.
   (*c*) **Share of profit till the date of death:** The Deceased Partner is entitled to their share of the partnership's profits up until the date of their death. This amount will be credited to the Deceased Partner's Account.
   (*e*) **Interest on capital till the date of death:** The Deceased Partner is entitled to interest on their capital investment up until the date of their death. This interest amount will be credited to the Deceased Partner's Account.

2. **(D)**

3. **(D):** When capital gain tax is paid on the sale of fixed assets, it is considered a cash outflow from Investing Activities in the statement of cash flows. Investing Activities involve cash flows related to the acquisition and disposal of long-term assets, including the sale of fixed assets. The cash outflow associated with capital gain tax paid on the sale of fixed assets is considered part of the cash outflow from Investing Activities. Cash inflow from Investing Activities typically includes proceeds from the sale of fixed assets, while cash outflow includes expenses or taxes related to such transactions, such as capital gain tax.

4. **(C):** When Centaur Ltd. issued ₹ 25,00,000 8% debentures of ₹ 100 each as collateral security to the first Level Bank against loan dues of ₹ 20,00,000 the amount shown in the balance sheet will be the value of the loan dues, which is ₹ 20,00,000.
   The debentures issued serve as collateral security for the loan, and their value is equal to the loan amount. Therefore, the balance sheet will reflect the loan dues of ₹ 20,00,000 as the amount shown. The face value or total value of the debentures issued is not relevant in determining the amount shown in the balance sheet.

5. **(D):** A password is a secret and personal combination of characters that serves as a form of authentication and allows an individual to gain access to a system or account. It acts as a security measure to verify the identity of the user and grant them access to the system.

6. **(B):** Hidden Goodwill refers to the excess amount paid to a retiring partner or an outgoing party over and above their calculated share in the net assets of the partnership. It is an additional payment made as a gesture of goodwill or to maintain the partnership's reputation.
   In this case, ₹ 15,000 extra payment made to R represents Hidden Goodwill. It is an amount paid by the remaining partners P and Q to compensate R for the value of the goodwill they have built over the years. The partners agreed to pay ₹ 75,000, which includes the calculated settlement amount of ₹ 60,000 plus an additional ₹ 15,000 as Hidden Goodwill.

7. **(A):** Ctrl + Z is a keyboard shortcut that is commonly used to undo or reverse the most recent action in many software applications, including spreadsheets like Microsoft Excel or Google Sheets. By pressing Ctrl + Z, you can undo the last action performed in the worksheet, such as deleting a cell, formatting changes, or data entry.

8. **(C)**

9. **(D):** When a company decides to buy its own shares from the market, it is known as a share buy back or share repurchase. This process involves the company purchasing its own shares from existing shareholders. In order to carry out a share buy back, certain conditions must be met, including:
   Article of Association must authorize and a special resolution has been passed for the buy back of shares. The company's Articles of Association, which is a document containing rules and regulations governing the company, must specifically authorize the company to buy back its own shares. Additionally, a special resolution passed by the shareholders in a general meeting is required to authorize the buy back.

10. **(B)**

11. **(D):** Legacies refer to specific amounts of money or assets that are bequeathed to individuals or organizations through a will or testamentary document. When a deceased person leaves a specific amount of money or property to a recipient, it is considered a legacy.

12. **(B):** Trade payables that are to be settled beyond 12 months from the date of the balance sheet or beyond the operating cycle are classified as other long term liabilities.
    Trade payables are amounts owed by a company to its suppliers or vendors for goods or services received on credit. Normally, trade payables are classified as current liabilities, as they are expected to be settled within one year or the operating cycle of the business, whichever is longer. However, when trade payables

extend beyond 12 months or the operating cycle, they are considered other long term liabilities. This classification indicates that the company does not expect to settle the amount within the short-term, and it will be paid off over a longer time frame.

**13. (C):** (*c*) **Shareholder's Fund:** The balance sheet starts with the Shareholder's Fund, which includes the various components of the company's equity. This typically includes share capital, reserves, and any retained earnings.

(*a*) **Non-Current Liabilities:** After the Shareholder's Fund, the balance sheet presents the Non-Current Liabilities. These are long-term obligations that the company owes, such as long-term loans, debentures, or other borrowings that are not due within the next year.

(*e*) **Current Liabilities:** Following the Non-Current Liabilities, the balance sheet displays the Current Liabilities. These are short-term obligations that the company owes and are typically due within the next year. This includes accounts payable, accrued expenses, and any other current liabilities.

(*b*) **Non-Current Assets:** After the liabilities, the balance sheet presents the Non-Current Assets. These are long-term assets that the company owns, such as property, plant, and equipment, investments, intangible assets, and long-term investments.

(*d*) **Current Assets:** Lastly, the balance sheet shows the Current Assets. These are short-term assets that the company owns and are expected to be converted into cash within the next year. This includes cash and cash equivalents, accounts receivable, inventories, and other current assets.

**14. (C):** In the absence of any specific provision in the partnership agreement regarding the distribution of profits and losses, the default rule is that profits and losses are shared equally among the partners. This is known as the equal share rule.

In this case, since the partnership agreement is silent on the matter, Monika's claim for an equal share in the profits and losses would be valid. Even though Monika contributed 5,00,000 as capital, she can still be entitled to an equal share of the profits and losses along with Sanjay, who contributed 2,00,000 as capital.

Therefore, in this situation, if the partnership agreement is silent, Monika's claim for an equal share in the partnership's profits and losses would be valid.

**15. (D):** Separate disclosure of cash flow arising from Financial Activities is important because it provides valuable information about the cash flows related to the company's financing activities. This information is useful for assessing the company's ability to generate cash flow, meet its financial obligations, and predict future claims on cash flow by providers of funds to the enterprise.

Financial activities include activities related to the company's capital structure, such as issuing or repurchasing stocks, taking loans, paying dividends, and other financing transactions. By separately disclosing the cash flow arising from these activities, stakeholders, such as investors, creditors, and analysts, can gain insights into the company's financing decisions and understand the impact of these activities on its overall cash position.

This information is particularly relevant for providers of funds to the enterprise, as it allows them to assess the company's financial health, solvency, and its ability to generate sufficient cash flow to meet its obligations. It helps them make informed decisions regarding their investments or the provision of additional funds to the company.

**16. (C)**

**17. (B):** When a company issues shares in the open market and the amount is payable in installments, the sequence of amount demanded by the company is as follows:

(*d*) **Application money transferred to Share Capital A/c:** The first demand made by the company is for the application money received from the shareholders to be transferred to the Share Capital Account. This is done once the shares are allotted.

(*e*) **Allotment money due:** The next demand made by the company is for the allotment money that is due from the shareholders. Allotment money is the portion of the share price that is payable upon the allotment of shares.

(*c*) **Allotment money received:** Once the allotment money is paid by the shareholders, the company receives the payment and records it as allotment money received.

(*b*) **Money due on calls:** After the allotment is made and the allotment money is received, the next demand made by the company is for the money due on calls. Calls refer to the remaining amount payable on the shares, which is typically made in installments.

(*a*) **Money received on calls:** Finally, the company receives the payment from shareholders in response to the calls made, and this amount is recorded as money received on calls.

**18. (C):** Loose tools, which are tools or equipment used in the business operations, are typically categorized as part of the company's inventory. Inventories include various items that are held for sale, in the process of production, or in the form of raw materials, work in progress, or finished goods.

Loose tools are considered part of the company's assets and are recorded as inventory in the balance sheet. They are classified under the sub-head of Inventories, which falls under the Current Assets section of the balance sheet.

**19. (B)**

**20. (C):** When interest on capital has to be provided as per the partnership deed, but the available profits are not sufficient to provide the full amount of interest, the sequence of steps to be followed is as follows:

(*d*) **Consider the partnership deed and decide whether interest on capital is a charge or an appropriation:** The partnership deed will specify the terms and conditions regarding the payment of interest on capital. It is important to refer to the partnership deed to determine whether interest on capital is treated as a charge on profits or as an appropriation from profits.

(*a*) **If it is an appropriation, calculate interest on capital for all partners at the given rate:** If the partnership deed treats interest on capital as an appropriation from profits, the interest is calculated for each partner at the agreed-upon rate on their respective capital contributions.

(*e*) **Consider the available profit:** Assess the available profits of the partnership. If the available profits are sufficient to cover the calculated interest on capital for all partners, allocate the interest accordingly.

(*c*) **Calculate the ratio between capital of partners:** Determine the ratio of capital contributions between the partners. This ratio will be used to allocate the available profit or funds.

(*b*) **Divide the available amount in the capital for all partners at the given rate:** If the available profits are not sufficient to cover the full amount of interest on capital for all partners, the remaining amount can be divided among the partners in proportion to their capital contributions. This ensures that each partner receives a portion of the available funds based on their capital stake in the partnership.

**21. (C):** When the amount realized from assets it needs to be utilized to pay off various obligations, the sequence in which they are typically paid is as follows:

(*c*) **Secured debts of the firm:** Secured debts, which are obligations backed by specific assets of the firm, are usually given priority for payment. The amount realized from assets will be first used to pay off secured debts.

(*d*) **Unsecured debts of the firm:** After satisfying the secured debts, the amount realized from assets is then utilized to pay off unsecured debts. Unsecured debts are obligations that do not have specific assets assigned as collateral.

(*a*) **Partner's Loan:** Once the secured and unsecured debts of the firm are settled, any remaining amount can be used to repay the partner's loans. Partner's loans are loans provided to the firm by the partners.

(*b*) **Partner's Capital:** If there are still funds remaining after repaying the partner's loans, they can be used to repay the partner's capital contributions. Partner's capital represents the investments made by the partners into the firm.

(*e*) **Residue to partners:** Any remaining amount, known as the residue, after all the obligations mentioned above have been paid off, will be distributed among the partners in their profit sharing ratio or as specified in the partnership agreement.

**22. (B):** In a partnership firm, the partners' share of profit and loss is typically determined by their agreed-upon profit sharing ratio. The profit sharing ratio represents the proportion in which partners share the profits or losses of the firm.

In this scenario, the partners share profit and loss in the ratio of 3 : 2. If the firm incurred a loss of ₹ 10,000 during the year, the amount of loss to be shared by partners would be allocated according to their profit sharing ratio.

**23. (C):** Valuation of goodwill typically arises in certain situations involving changes in the partnership structure, such as admission or retirement of a partner, or death of a partner. The need for valuation arises to determine the value of the goodwill associated with the partnership and to make appropriate adjustments to the partners' capital accounts.

However, in the case of Dissolution of a partnership firm, the partnership is being completely terminated. In such a scenario, the goodwill is typically not valued as there is no ongoing business or partnership to which the goodwill is associated. The assets and liabilities are settled, and any remaining value is distributed among the partners according to their profit sharing or capital ratio.

**24.** **(D):** The given facts about the admission of a partner include:

(*a*) A new partner acquires their share from the old partners that reduces the old partners' share in profits. When a new partner is admitted, their share in the profits is typically taken from the existing partners' share, leading to a reduction in their profit share.

(*c*) Assets and liabilities may be revalued and reassessed on admission of a partner. Admission of a new partner often involves revaluation and reassessment of the partnership's assets and liabilities to adjust their values based on fair market values or the agreed terms.

(*d*) Adjustment for reserves and accumulated profits/loss is done. Upon the admission of a new partner, adjustments are made to allocate reserves and accumulated profits or losses among the partners, ensuring a fair distribution.

(*e*) Profit sharing ratio of existing partners may change on admission of a new partner. The admission of a new partner can lead to a change in the profit sharing ratio of the existing partners to accommodate the new partner's share of profits.

**25.** **(B):** From the given options, the items that are payable to a retiring partner, if mentioned in the partnership deed, include:

(*a*) **Credit balance of his/her Capital/Current Account:** If the partnership deed specifies that the retiring partner is entitled to the credit balance in their capital or current account, then this amount is payable to the retiring partner.

(*b*) **Share of goodwill:** If the partnership deed specifies that the retiring partner is entitled to a share of the goodwill, then this share of goodwill is payable to the retiring partner.

(*d*) **Share in revaluation gain/loss:** If the partnership deed specifies that the retiring partner is entitled to a share in the revaluation gain or loss of the firm, then this share is payable to the retiring partner.

(*e*) **Share in accumulated profit (Reserves):** If the partnership deed specifies that the retiring partner is entitled to a share in the accumulated profits or reserves of the firm, then this share is payable to the retiring partner.

**26.** **(B)**

**27.** **(D):** Debentures issued as collateral security are not intended to raise funds directly but are issued to secure a loan or other obligations of the issuer. In such cases, the debentures serve as a form of security or guarantee, and no interest is typically paid or provided on these debentures.

**28.** **(D):** When a new partner is joining a partnership and needs to bring in proportionate capital, the correct sequence of steps is as follows:

(*b*) **Preparation of Revaluation A/c:** Before determining the capital to be brought in by the new partner, a revaluation account is prepared. This account is used to record the adjustments in the values of assets and liabilities of the partnership due to the admission of the new partner.

(*c*) **Determination of Revaluation gain/loss:** After preparing the revaluation account, the revaluation gain or loss is determined. This is done by comparing the revalued values of assets and liabilities with their previous book values.

(*d*) **Presentation of Treatment of Goodwill:** After determining the revaluation gain or loss, the treatment of goodwill is presented. This involves making adjustments for the valuation of goodwill, if any, in the partnership's books.

(*a*) **Calculation of Capital Balance of old partners:** Once the revaluation gain or loss and the treatment of goodwill are determined, the capital balance of the old partners is calculated. This involves adjusting their existing capital accounts based on the revaluation and the treatment of goodwill.

(*e*) **Calculation of Capital to be brought in by the new partner:** Finally, after calculating the capital balance of the old partners, the new partner's capital contribution is determined. The new partner's capital is calculated based on the agreed-upon proportionate capital sharing arrangement.

**29.** **(C):** To analyze the profitability of a company, it can use various financial ratios. From the options provided, the ratios commonly used to assess profitability are:

(*a*) **Dividend Payout Ratio:** The Dividend Payout Ratio is calculated by dividing the dividends paid to shareholders by the net profit of the company. It indicates the portion of earnings that are distributed to shareholders as dividends. While it is more related to the distribution of profits, it can still provide insights into the company's profitability.

(*b*) **Return on Net Worth:** Return on Net Worth (also known as Return on Equity) is calculated by dividing the net profit after taxes by the shareholders' equity. It measures the profitability of a company in relation to the investment made by its shareholders. This ratio indicates the return earned by shareholders on their investment in the company.

(*c*) **Gross Profit Ratio:** The Gross Profit Ratio is calculated by dividing the gross profit by net sales. It measures the profitability of a company's core operations and indicates the proportion of sales revenue that is available to cover operating expenses and generate a profit. A higher gross profit ratio indicates better profitability.

**30. (C):** Operating Ratio is not computed for evaluating solvency of the business. Instead, it is a measure used to assess the operational efficiency of a company. It is calculated by dividing the operating expenses by the net sales and multiplying by 100. The operating ratio indicates the proportion of net sales that is consumed by operating expenses.

**31. (C)**

**32. (C):** In the context of a not-for-profit organization, a deficit refers to the excess of expenditure over income. It indicates that the organization's expenses have exceeded its revenues or funding sources during a specific period. A deficit is a financial shortfall that needs to be addressed, typically through additional fundraising efforts, cost-cutting measures, or adjustments in financial planning.

**33. (D):** The salient features of the Income and Expenditure account are as follows:

(*a*) **It is prepared on accrual basis:** The Income and Expenditure account is prepared on an accrual basis, which means that revenue and expenses are recognized when they are earned or incurred, regardless of the actual cash inflows or outflows.

(*c*) **It is prepared after taking into account additional information regarding outstanding prepaid expenses and depreciation etc.:** In the preparation of the Income and Expenditure account, adjustments are made for outstanding expenses, prepaid expenses, depreciation, and other items to reflect the true financial position of the organization.

(*d*) **Its result is surplus or deficit:** The result of the Income and Expenditure account is either a surplus or a deficit, which represents the excess of income over expenses or the excess of expenses over income, respectively.

(*e*) **It is prepared with the help of the Receipts and Payments Account:** The Income and Expenditure account is prepared with the help of the Receipts and Payments account, which records all the cash receipts and payments of the organization.

**34. (B)**

**35. (B):** A decrease in inventory suggests that inventory has been sold, and cash has been received or will be received soon. Therefore, this option would be added to operating profit before working capital changes.

**36. (A)** **37. (B)**

**38. (C):** The Profit and Loss Suspense account is a temporary account used to hold any unallocated profit or loss until it is appropriately allocated or resolved. In the case of a deceased partner, their share of profit from the date of the last Balance Sheet to the date of their death may need to be temporarily recorded in the Profit and Loss Suspense account until it is distributed or adjusted in accordance with the partnership agreement or legal requirements.

**39. (C):** When a new workbook is created in Microsoft Excel, by default, it includes three blank worksheets. These worksheets are labeled as "Sheet1", "Sheet2," and "Sheet3." Each worksheet provides a separate working space where you can enter and manipulate data.

The presence of multiple blank worksheets allows you to organize your data and calculations across different sheets within the same workbook. You can use these additional worksheets for different purposes, such as creating separate tabs for different categories of data or performing various calculations or analyses.

**40. (A):** Encryption is the process of converting data into a secure and unreadable format using encryption algorithms. It is commonly used to protect sensitive information and ensure data confidentiality. When data is encrypted, it is encoded with a specific key or algorithm that requires a decryption key to convert it back into its original readable form.

**41. (A):** The number of shares with which A Ltd. is registered can be calculated by dividing the Authorized Capital by the face value of each share.

Given:

Authorized Capital: 10,00,000

Face value of each share: 10

Number of shares = Authorized Capital/Face value of each share

Number of shares = 10,00,000/10

Number of shares = 1,00,000

Therefore, A Ltd. is registered with 1,00,000 shares.

**42. (C)** **43. (B)**

**44. (B):** The account to which the discount allowed on the reissue of forfeited shares should be debited is the Forfeited Share Account.

When shares are forfeited, they are typically recorded in a separate account called the Forfeited Share Account. This account is used to track the forfeited shares and any subsequent reissue or disposal of those shares.

In this scenario, half of Hari's forfeited shares were reissued at a price of ₹ 8 per share. The difference between the reissue price (8) and the nominal value of the shares (10) represents a discount. This discount allowed on the reissue of forfeited shares should be debited to the Forfeited Share Account.

**45. (D):** The balance left in the share forfeited account relating to the reissued shares should be transferred to the Capital Reserve Account.

When shares are forfeited and subsequently reissued, any balance remaining in the Forfeited Share Account, specifically relating to the reissued shares, is transferred to the Capital Reserve Account.

In this scenario, half of Hari's forfeited shares were reissued at a price of ₹ 8 per share. After accounting for the reissue, the remaining balance in the Forfeited Share Account, which pertains to these reissued shares, should be transferred to the Capital Reserve Account.

**46. (C):** When a creditor accepts an asset whose value is more than the amount due to him, he will pay the excess amount, which will be credited to the Realisation Account.

In the given scenario, the machinery was given to the creditors in full settlement of their account. Since the value of the machinery (₹ 70,000) is more than the amount due to the creditors (₹ 60,000), the excess amount of ₹ 10,000 will be paid by the creditor. This excess amount will be credited to the Realisation Account.

**47. (B):** In Dissolution by Agreement, the partners mutually agree to dissolve the firm and wind up its affairs. They reach a consensus to terminate the partnership and distribute the assets and liabilities among themselves or as agreed upon.

In the given scenario, Meena and Tina decided to dissolve their firm on March 31, 2017. They agreed on the disposal of assets and liabilities as mentioned in the question. The distribution and settlement of assets and liabilities were carried out based on their agreement.

**48. (D):** In the scenario, it is mentioned that Sundry Debtors had a book value of ₹ 1,03,000. However, Meena took over the Sundry Debtors at 10% less, which means she agreed to take over the debtors at a value of 90% of their book value.

10% less of 1,03,000 is 10,300 (10% of 1,03,000 = 10,300).

Therefore, Meena took over the Sundry Debtors at a value of ₹ 1,03,000 – 10,300 = ₹ 92,700.

Additionally, it is mentioned that the remaining debtors were realized for 51,000. This indicates that the actual amount realized in cash from Sundry Debtors is 51,000.

**49. (C)** **50. (A)**

# GENERAL TEST

1. Ministry of Health and Family Welfare has launched 'Nikshay Poshan Yojana' related to eradication of which of the following disease?
A. Dengue B. Malaria
C. Tuberculosis D. Kala-Azar

2. Match List-I with List-II.

| List-I (Important Days) | List-II (Date) |
|---|---|
| (*a*) National Youth Day | I. 28th February |
| (*b*) Army Day | II. 12th January |
| (*c*) National Science Day | III. 15th January |
| (*d*) National Safety Day | IV. 4th March |

Choose the ***correct*** answer from the options given below:

| | (*a*) | (*b*) | (*c*) | (*d*) |
|---|---|---|---|---|
| A. | II | III | IV | I |
| B. | II | III | I | IV |
| C. | III | II | I | IV |
| D. | IV | III | I | II |

3. If P(E) = 0.05, what is the probability of 'not E'?
A. 0.05 B. 0.45
C. 0.95 D. 0.55

4. Find the next term in the alpha-numeric series:
Z1A, W8C, T27E, Q64G, N125I, __?__
A. K216L B. K216K
C. L343K D. L343L

5. Which of the following statements are incorrect?
(*a*) Volume of a cone = $\frac{1}{3}\pi r^3 h$
(*b*) Volume of a cone = $\frac{1}{3}\pi r^2 h$
(*c*) Volume of a hemispere = $\frac{2}{3}\pi r^2$
(*d*) Volume of a hemispere = $\frac{2}{3}\pi r^3$
(*e*) Volume of a cylinder = $\frac{1}{3}\pi r^3 h$
Choose the ***correct*** answer from the options given below:
A. (*a*), (*b*) and (*d*) only
B. (*a*), (*b*) and (*c*) only
C. (*a*), (*c*) and (*e*) only
D. (*c*), (*d*) and (*e*) only

6. Five children Arun, Bhuvi, Charu, Deepak and Emmy are sitting along the corners of a pentagonal table facing the centre. Bhuvi is between Emmy and Charu. Deepak is to the right of Emmy. Who is to the left of Charu?
A. Bhuvi B. Arun
C. Charu D. Deepak

7. A man standing on the bank of a river observes that the angle subtended by a tree standing on the opposite bank is 60° on his side of Bank. When he moved away 24 m from the bank, he finds the angle to be 30°. Find the breadth of the river:
A. 12 B. 18
C. 26 D. 20

8. The first satellite in space was launched by:
A. U.S.A.
B. United Kingdom
C. U.S.S.R.
D. France

9. Given below are two statements: one is labelled as Assertion (A) and the other is labelled as Reason (R).
**Assertion (A):** Polar areas have high atmospheric pressure.
**Reason (R):** These areas receive minimum sunshine throughout the year.
In the light of the above statements, choose the ***most appropriate*** answer from the options given below:
A. Both (A) and (R) are correct and (R) is the correct explanation of (A)
B. Both (A) and (R) are true, but (R) is not the correct explanation of (A)
C. (A) is true, but (R) is false
D. (A) is false, but (R) is true

10. Which one of the following numbers is not a prime number?
A. 241 B. 337
C. 391 D. 571

11. If the mean of 5 observations $x$, $x + 2$, $x + 4$, $x + 6$ and $x + 8$ is 11, then value of $x$:
A. 7 B. 43
C. 51 D. 8

12. Amar is 16th from the left end in a row of boys and Vishal is 18th from the right end. Satish is 11th towards the right of Amar and 3rd towards the right of Vishal side end. How many boys are there is a row?

A. 45 B. 26
C. 39 D. 41

**13.** Following question is based on the information given below:

(*i*) 'R × S' means 'R is father of S'
(*ii*) 'R – S' means 'R is sister of S'
(*iii*) 'R + S' means 'R is mother of S'
(*iv*) 'R ÷ S' means 'R is brother of S'

In the expression A + B × C ÷ D how is C related to A?

A. Son
B. Grandson
C. Granddaughter
D. Grandmother

**14.** Given below are two statements:

**Statement (I):** Right to information has been granted to every citizen of India under Right to information Act, 2005 which came into force on 12th October, 2005.

**Statement (II):** Right to information is a fundamental Right.

In the light of the above statements, choose the ***most appropriate*** answer from the options given below:

A. Both Statement I and Statement II are true
B. Both Statement I and Statement II are false
C. Statement I is true, but Statement II is false
D. Statement I is false, but Statement II is true

**15.** Given below are two statements: one is labelled as Assertion (A) and the other is labelled as Reason (R).

**Assertion (A):** The 73rd Amendment granted constitutional states to the Gram Sabha.

**Reason (R):** The Balawant Rai Mehta committee mentioned the Gram Sabha.

In the light of the above statements, choose the ***most appropriate*** answer from the options given below:

A. Both (A) and (R) are correct and (R) is the correct explanation of (A)
B. Both (A) and (R) are correct, but (R) is not the correct explanation of (A)
C. (A) is true, but (R) is not false
D. (A) is false, but (R) is true

**16.** Select the figure from the options which will continue the series established by the problem figure:

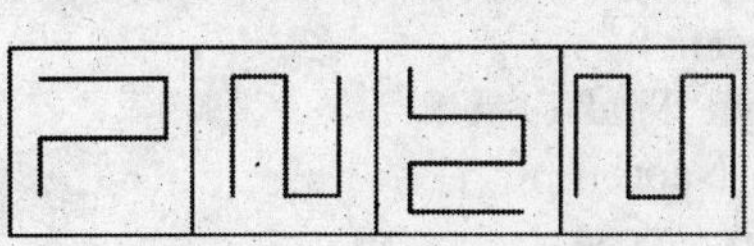

A. 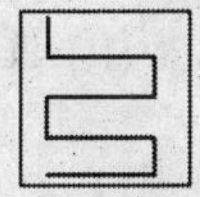
B. 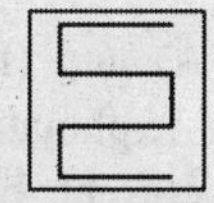
C. 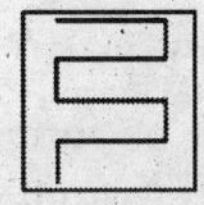
D. 

**17.** The sum of an Infinite geometric series is 4 and the sum of the cubes of the terms of the same GP is 192. The Common Ratio of the original geometric series is:

A. $\frac{1}{2}$ B. $-\frac{1}{2}$
C. $\frac{1}{4}$ D. $-\frac{1}{4}$

**18.** A clock is started at noon. By 20 minutes part 6, the hand had has turned through:

A. 175° B. 180°
C. 185° D. 190°

**19.** Match List-I with List-II.

| List-I (World Organization) | List-II (Headquarters) |
|---|---|
| (*a*) BRICS | I. Geneva (Switzerland) |
| (*b*) NATO | II. Shanghai (China) |
| (*c*) WTO | III. Kathmandu (Nepal) |
| (*d*) SAARC | IV. Brussels (Belgium) |

Choose the ***correct*** answer from the options given below:

| | (*a*) | (*b*) | (*c*) | (*d*) |
|---|---|---|---|---|
| A. | III | IV | I | II |
| B. | IV | II | I | III |
| C. | II | IV | I | III |
| D. | II | IV | III | I |

**20.** The Credit of inventing soap by using Mustard oil and some alkalies goes to which of the following scientist?

A. Chakrapani
B. Sushruta
C. Nagarjuna
D. Patayjali

**21.** Given below are two statements, one is labelled as Assertion (A) and the other is labelled as Reason (R).

**Assertion (A):** Clothes are not washed properly in hard water.

**Reason (R):** Hard water contains many minerals.

In the light of the above statements, choose the ***most appropriate*** answer from the options given below:

A. Both (A) and (R) are correct and (R) is the correct explanation of (A)

B. Both (A) and (R) are correct, but (R) is not the correct explanation of (A)
C. (A) is correct, but (R) is not correct
D. (A) is not correct, but (R) is correct

**22.** How many 3 digit even numbers can be formed from the digits (0-9) if repetition of digits are allowed?

A. 350 B. 400
C. 450 D. 1000

**23.** Which of the planet have no satellite?

(*a*) Mercury
(*b*) Neptune
(*c*) Satrun
(*d*) Venus

Choose the ***correct*** answer from the options given below:

A. (*b*) and (*d*) only
B. (*a*) and (*b*) only
C. (*b*), (*c*) and (*d*) only
D. (*a*) and (*d*) only

**24.** If CE || DB, what is the value of *x*:

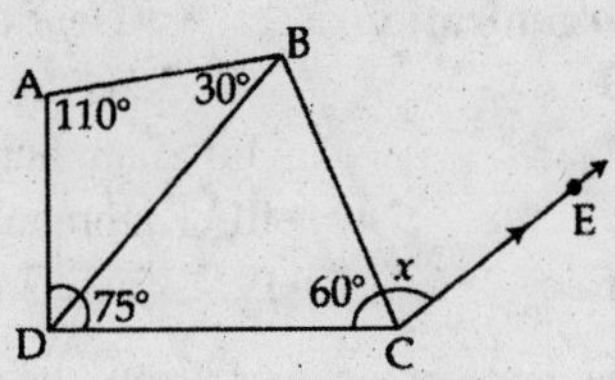


A. 45° B. 30°
C. 75° D. 85°

**25.** Who was the Chief Justice of India when public interest litigation (PIL) was introduced to the Indian Judicial system?

A. M. Hidayatullah
B. A.M. Ahmadi
C. P.N. Bhagwati
D. A.S. Anand

**26.** How many cubes are there in a group?

A. 10 B. 16
C. 18 D. 20

**27.** The only continent through which Tropic of Cancer, Equator and Tropic of Capricorn passes?

A. Asia B. Australia
C. Antarctica D. Africa

**28.** Facing towards North, Ravi walks 30 m. He then turns left and walks 50 m. He again turns left and walks 30 m. How far is he from his original position and towards which direction?

A. 30 m, North
B. 20 m, East
C. 20 m, South
D. 50 m, West

**29.** Find out the figure that can be formed from the piece given below:

A.  B. 

C.  D. 

**30.** Complete the picture series:

A.  B. 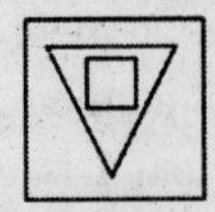

C.  D. 

**31.** Find from amongst the figure, the one which resembles the pattern formed when the transparent sheet is folded along the dotted line.

A.  B. 

C.  D. 

**32.** Who among the following gave the popular slogan "Home Rule is my birthright and I will have it"?

A. Annie Besant
B. Lokamanya Tilak
C. Dadabhai Naoroji
D. Aurobindo Ghose

**33.** ₹ 800 becomes ₹ 956 in 3 years at a certain rate of simple interest. If the rate of interest is increased by 4%, what will ₹ 800 amount to in 3 years:

A. ₹ 1,020.80 B. ₹ 1,025
C. ₹ 1,052 D. ₹ 1,050

**34.** Two statements in the following questions, followed by two conclusions I and II. Read the conclusion and decide most suitable answer.

**Statements** : All horses are goats.
No goat is a donkey.

**Conclusions** : I. No horse is a donkey.
II. Atleast some goats are horses.

A. If only conclusion I follows.
B. If only conclusion II follows.
C. If both conclusion I and II follows.
D. If none of the conclusion follows.

**35.** ISRO Launched "GSAT-6A" satellites on:

A. 31 August, 2017 B. 29 March, 2018
C. 05 June, 2017 D. 12 January, 2018

**36.** A trader sold half of his articles at 60% profit, half of the remaining at 20% loss and the rest was sold at the cost price. In total transaction his gain % or loss % will be:

A. Gain 20% B. Loss 5%
C. Gain 40% D. Gain 25%

**37.** Match List-I with List-II.

| **List-I (Name of City)** | **List-II (Famous for production of)** |
|---|---|
| (*a*) Ahmedabad | I. Machine tools |
| (*b*) Bangalore | II. Aluminium |
| (*c*) Bhilai | III. Textiles |
| (*d*) Renukoot | IV. Steel |

Choose the ***correct*** answer from the options given below:

| | (*a*) | (*b*) | (*c*) | (*d*) |
|---|---|---|---|---|
| A. | I | II | III | IV |
| B. | II | III | IV | I |
| C. | III | I | IV | II |
| D. | IV | III | II | I |

**38.** The 36th National Games 2022 was held in which of the following state?

A. Goa B. Gujarat
C. Haryana D. Karnataka

**39.** Find out the wrong number in the sequence:

40960, 10240, 2560, 640, 200, 40, 10

A. 40 B. 640
C. 200 D. 2560

**40.** The constitution authorises the president to make provisions for discharge of duties of Governor in extraordinary circumstances under the ______.

A. Article 160 B. Article 162
C. Article 165 D. Article 310

**41.** The fibre crop which is known as the Golden Fibre?

A. Cotton B. Hump
C. Natural Silk D. Jute

**42.** The first person to use crystal for radio wave detection was:

A. J.C. Bose B. H.C. Verma
C. S.N. Bose D. C.V. Raman

**43.** The surface area (in $m^2$) of a sphere of radius 7 cm is: (Use $\pi = 22/7$)

A. 0.0616 B. 6.16
C. 61.6 D. 0.616

**44.** By selling on book for ₹ 250, loss percentage is 10%. What is the cost price?

A. ₹ 277.7 B. ₹ 250
C. ₹ 285 D. ₹ 315

**45.** If $\frac{x}{(b-c)(b+c-2a)} = \frac{y}{(c-a)(c+a-2b)}$

$= \frac{z}{(a-b)(a+b-2c)}$ then value of $x + y + z$ is:

A. $a + b + c$ B. $a^2 + b^2 + c^2$
C. 0 D. 1

**46.** A completes $\frac{7}{20}$ of a work in 10 days. Then he completes the remaining work with the help of B in 5 days. The time required for A and B together to complete the entire work is:

A. $\frac{100}{29}$ days B. $\frac{100}{13}$ days
C. $\frac{100}{17}$ days D. $\frac{200}{13}$ days

**47.** Look at the statement and mark the correct answer on the conclusions that follows:

**Statements** : (*a*) Shubham is my cousin.
(*b*) A cousin may be a aunt's son, uncle's son or son of parent's step-siblings.

**Conclusions** : I. Shubham is my sisters son.
II. Shubham is my uncle's son.

A. Only conclusion I follows.
B. Only conclusion II follows.
C. Both conclusion I and II follows.
D. Neither conclusion I nor II follows.

**48.** If Today is Monday, After 62 it will be:

A. Wednesday B. Saturday
C. Sunday D. Thursday

**49.** The price of rice increases by 30%. A family reduced its consumption so that the expenditure of the rice is up only by 10%. If the total consumption of the rice before the price rise was 10 kg per month, then the consumption of rice per month at present (in kg) is:

A. $7\frac{6}{15}$ B. $8\frac{1}{15}$

C. $8\frac{6}{13}$ D. $8\frac{5}{13}$

**50.** The volume of a sphere of radius $r$ is obtained by multiplying its surface area with:

A. $\frac{4}{3}$ B. $\frac{r}{3}$

C. $\frac{4r}{3}$ D. $3r$

**51.** If EFFECTIVE is coded as FEGDDSJUF, then how RELATIVE can be written in that code?

A. TDNZVHXD B. TCNAVGXC

C. SDMZUHWD D. SCMAUGXD

**52.** A bag contains 6 red, 4 blue and 10 white balls. A ball is picked from the bag at random. What is the probability that it is neither white nor blue?

A. $\frac{20}{6}$ B. $\frac{3}{10}$

C. $\frac{2}{5}$ D. $\frac{1}{2}$

**53.** Find the area of an equilateral triangle each of whose sides measures 4 cm:

A. $4\sqrt{3}$ cm$^2$ B. $4\sqrt{3}$ m$^2$

C. $3\sqrt{3}$ cm$^2$ D. $3\sqrt{3}$ m$^2$

**54.** The difference between two numbers is 24. If one number is 2 times the second, then the two numbers will be:

A. 36, 12 B. 48, 24

C. 32, 8 D. 12, 6

**55.** Choose the correct mirror image:

A.  B. 

C.  D. 

**56.** Match List-I with List-II.

| List-I | List-II |
|---|---|
| (*a*) First speaker of Lok Sabha | I. Dr. Amartya Sen |
| (*b*) First Indian to get Bharat Ratna Award | II. G.V. Mavalankar |
| (*c*) First Indian recipient of Nobel Prize in Economics | III. Dr. S. Radhakrishnan |
| (*d*) First Indian Nobel Laureate | IV. Rabindra Nath Tagore |

Choose the ***correct*** answer from the options given below:

| | (*a*) | (*b*) | (*c*) | (*d*) |
|---|---|---|---|---|
| A. | II | III | I | IV |
| B. | II | III | IV | I |
| C. | III | II | I | IV |
| D. | IV | III | I | II |

**57.** Who has been honoured with the Golden ball award in the FIFA World Cup 2022?

A. Kylian Mbappe B. Luka Modric

C. Lionel Messi D. Enzo Fernandez

**58.** A boy is running at a speed of $p$ km/h to cover a distance of 1 km but due to slippery ground his speed is reduced by $q$ km/h ($p > q$). If he takes $r$ hours to cover the distance, which of the following condition is true:

A. $\frac{1}{r} = (p - q)$ B. $r = (p - q)$

C. $r = \frac{1}{p + q}$ D. $r = p + q$

**59.** What can be placed at '?' if both side of ': :' have same relationship between numbers:

85 : 42 :: 139 : ?

A. 68 B. 69

C. 70 D. 67

**60.** Commemoration of national days should always be encouraged in schools and colleges. Which of the following statement given below is a strong argument:

(*a*) This type of commemoration gives opportunity to children and youth to value to contribution of people who built our nation.

(*b*) There is nothing wrong in celebrating a day and enjoy once is a while.

(*c*) These events hamper the focus of students from regular study.

A. Argument (*a*) and (*b*) are strong

B. Only argument (*a*) is strong

C. Argument (*b*) and (*c*) are strong

D. Only argument (*c*) is strong

# ANSWERS

**1. (C)** **2. (B)**

**3. (C):** Required Probability of 'not E'.

$$= 1 - 0.05$$

$$= 1 - \frac{5}{100} = \frac{100 - 5}{100}$$

$$= \frac{95}{100} = 0.95.$$

**4. (B)** **5. (C)**

**6. (B):**

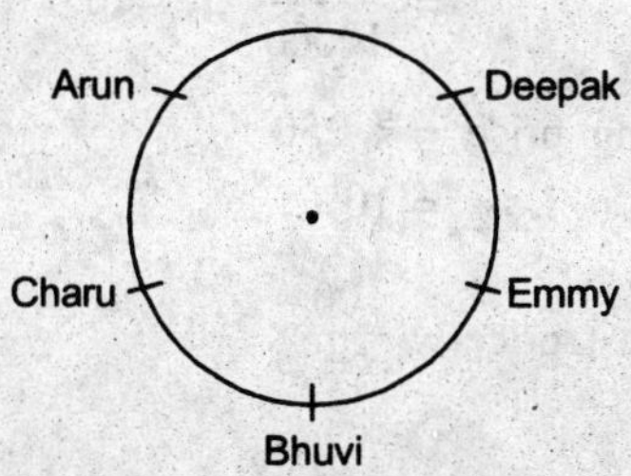


Clearly, Arun is left of Charu.

**7. (A):**

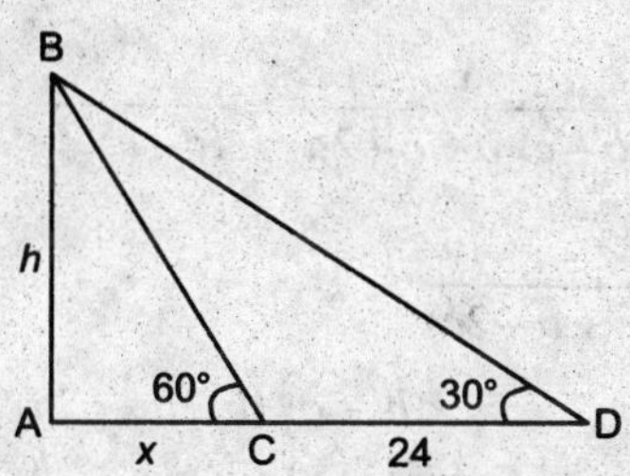


$$\tan 60° = \frac{h}{x}$$

$$\Rightarrow \sqrt{3} = \frac{h}{x}$$

$$\Rightarrow h = \sqrt{3}x$$

$$\tan 30° = \frac{h}{x + 24}$$

$$\Rightarrow \frac{1}{\sqrt{3}} = \frac{h}{x + 24}$$

$$\Rightarrow \sqrt{3}h = x + 24$$

$$\Rightarrow 3x = x + 24$$

$$\Rightarrow 2x = 24$$

$$\Rightarrow x = 12$$

Hence, breadth of the river = 12 m.

**8. (C)** **9. (B)**

**10. (C):** 391 is not a prime number because 391 is divided by 17 and 23.

**11. (A):** Total of 5 observations = 11 × 5 = 55

$$\therefore x + x + 2 + x + 4 + x + 6 + x + 8 = 55$$

$$\Rightarrow 5x + 20 = 55$$

$$\Rightarrow 5x = 35$$

$$\Rightarrow x = 7$$

Hence, the value of $x = 7$.

**12. (D)** **13. (B)** **14. (C)**

**15. (B)** **16. (C)**

**17. (B):**

$$S_{\infty} = \frac{a}{1 - r}$$

$$\Rightarrow 4 = \frac{a}{1 - r}$$

$$\Rightarrow \frac{a}{1 - r} = 4 \quad ...(i)$$

$$(a)^3 + a^3r^3 + a^3r^6 + ... = 192$$

$$\Rightarrow \frac{a^3}{1 - r^3} = 192 \quad ...(ii)$$

Divide the cube of (*i*) by (*ii*), we get,

$$\frac{a^3}{(1 - r)^3} \times \frac{(1 - r^3)}{a^3} = \frac{(4)^3}{192} = \frac{64}{192} = \frac{1}{3}$$

$$\Rightarrow \frac{1 - r^3}{(1 - r)^3} = \frac{1}{3}$$

$$\Rightarrow \frac{1^2 + r + r^2}{1 + r^2 - 2r} = \frac{1}{3}$$

$$\Rightarrow r^2 - 2r + 1 = 3(1 + r + r^2)$$

$$\Rightarrow r^2 - 2r + 1 - 3 - 3r - 3r^2 = 0$$

$$-2r^2 - 5r - 2 = 0$$

$$\Rightarrow 2r^2 + 5r + 2 = 0$$

$$\Rightarrow 2r^2 + 4r + r + 2 = 0$$

$$2r(r + 2) + 1(r + 2) = 0$$

$$(2r + 1)(r + 2) = 0$$

$$r = -\frac{1}{2}$$

or $r = -2$

Hence, common ratio = $-\frac{1}{2}$.

**18. (D)** **19. (C)** **20. (A)**

**21. (B)**

**22. (C):** For a number to be even, we must have 2, 4, 6, 8, 0 at the unit's place.

Since, digits can be repeated.

Hence, required number of numbers

$= 5 \times 10 \times 9 = 450.$

**23. (D)**

**24. (D):**

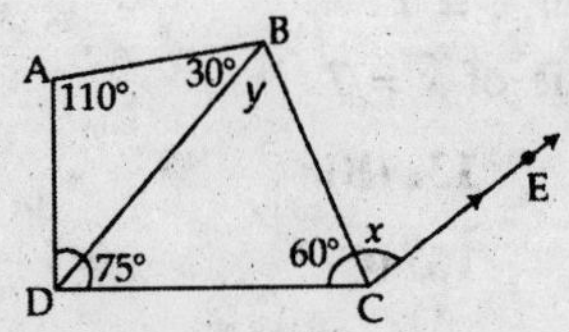


$\because$ CE || DB

$$\angle A + \angle B + \angle C + \angle D = 360°$$

$$\Rightarrow 110° + y + 30° + 60° + 75° = 360°$$

$$\Rightarrow y + 275° = 360°$$

$$\Rightarrow y = 360° - 275° = 85°$$

($\because$ CE || DB $\Rightarrow \angle x = \angle y$)

Hence, $x = y = 85°$.

**25. (C)** **26. (D)** **27. (D)**

**28. (D):**

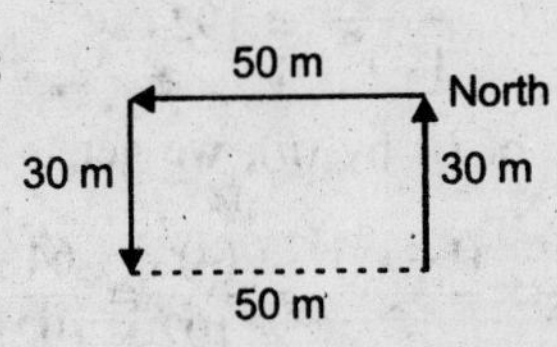


Ravi is 50 m away from his original position and towards west direction.

**29. (C)** **30. (D)** **31. (C)**

**32. (B)** **33. (C)** **34. (C)**

**35. (B)**

**36. (D):** Let total articles = 100

C.P. of each article = ₹ 100

Total C.P. = 100 × 100 = ₹ 10000

S.P. of half articles = $5000 \times \frac{160}{100}$ = ₹ 8000

S.P. of half of remaining articles

$= 2500 \times \frac{80}{100}$ = ₹ 2000

S.P. of rest articles = ₹ 2500

Total S.P. = ₹ 8000 + 2000 + 2500

= ₹ 12500

Profit = 12500 − 10000

= ₹ 2500

Profit % = $\frac{2500}{10000} \times 100 = 25\%$.

**37. (C)** **38. (B)**

**39. (C):**

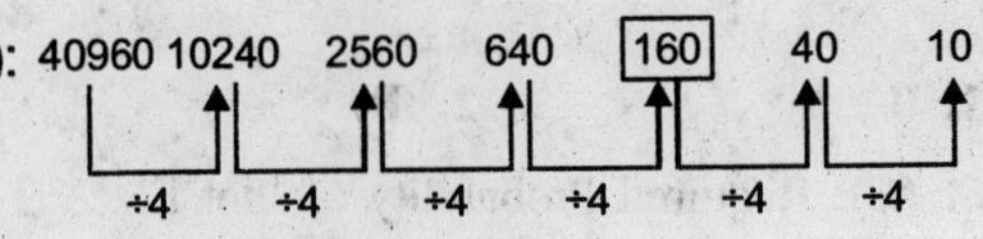


Hence, wrong number = 200.

**40. (A)** **41. (D)** **42. (A)**

**43. (A)** Surface area of sphere = $4\pi r^2$

$$= 4 \times \frac{22}{7} \times 7 \times 7 = 616 \text{ cm}^2$$

$$= \frac{616}{10000} \text{ m}^2 = 0.0616 \text{ m}^2.$$

**44. (A):** Selling price = ₹ 250

Loss = 10%

Then, Cost price = $\frac{100}{90} \times 250$

= ₹ $\frac{2500}{9}$ = ₹ 277.7

**45. (C):** Let $\frac{x}{(b-c)(b+c-2a)} = \frac{y}{(c-a)(c+a-2b)}$

$$= \frac{z}{(a-b)(a+b-2c)} = k$$

$\therefore$
$$x = k(b-c)(b+c-2a)$$
$$y = k(c-a)(c+a-2b)$$
$$z = k(a-b)(a+b-2c)$$

Now, $x + y + z = k[(b-c)(b+c-2a) + (c-a)(c+a-2b) + (a-b)(a+b-2c)]$

$= k[b^2 + bc - 2ab - bc - c^2 + 2ac + c^2 + ac - 2bc - ac - a^2 + 2ab + a^2 + ab - 2ac - ab - b^2 + 2bc]$

$= k[0] = 0.$

**46. (B):** $\because \frac{7}{20}$ part of a work A can do in 10 days

Remaining part $= 1 - \frac{7}{20} = \frac{13}{20}$ part of work

$\because$ (A + B)'s 5 days work = $\frac{13}{20}$ part

$\therefore$ (A + B)'s 1 day work = $\frac{13}{20 \times 5} = \frac{13}{100}$

Hence, (A + B) can do whole work in $\frac{100}{13}$ days.

**47. (D)**

**48. (C):** Today is Monday. After 63 days (7 × 9) it will be Monday.

Hence, after 62 days it will be Sunday.

**49. (C)**

**50. (B):** The Volume of sphere = $\frac{4}{3}\pi r^3$

Surface area of sphere = $4\pi r^2$

Hence, the volume of sphere of radius $r$ is obtained by multiplying its surface area with $\frac{r}{3}$.

**51. (C):** As,

| E | F | F | E | C | T | I | V | E |
|---|---|---|---|---|---|---|---|---|
| +1 ↓ | −1 ↓ | +1 ↓ | −1 ↓ | +1 ↓ | −1 ↓ | +1 ↓ | −1 ↓ | +1 ↓ |
| F | E | G | D | D | S | J | U | F |

Similarly,

| R | E | L | A | T | I | V | E |
|---|---|---|---|---|---|---|---|
| +1 ↓ | −1 ↓ | +1 ↓ | −1 ↓ | +1 ↓ | −1 ↓ | +1 ↓ | −1 ↓ |
| S | D | M | Z | U | H | W | D |

**52. (B):**

Red ball = 6

Blue ball = 4

White ball = 10

Required probability = $\frac{6}{20} = \frac{3}{10}$

**53. (A):** Area of an equilateral triangle

$$= \frac{\sqrt{3}}{4}(\text{Side})^2$$

$$= \frac{\sqrt{3}}{4} \times (4)^2 = \frac{\sqrt{3}}{4} \times 16$$

$$= 4\sqrt{3} \text{ cm}^2.$$

**54. (B):** Let second number = $x$

∴ One number = $2x$

According to the question,

$$2x - x = 24$$

$$\Rightarrow x = 24$$

$$\therefore 2x = 2 \times 24 = 48$$

Hence, number will be 48 and 24.

**55. (D)** **56. (A)** **57. (C)**

**58. (A):** Relative speed = $(p - q)$ km/hr

Distance = 1 km

Time = $r$ hours

$$\therefore \text{Speed} = \frac{\text{Distance}}{\text{Time}} = \frac{1}{r}$$

$$\Rightarrow (p - q) = \frac{1}{r}$$

Hence, $\frac{1}{r} = (p - q)$.

**59. (B):** 85 : 42 :: 139 : 69

$85 = \frac{85-1}{2} = \frac{84}{2} = 42$  $139 = \frac{139-1}{2} = \frac{138}{2} = 69$

Hence, 69 will come at the place of question mark.

**60. (B)**

# Previous Years' Paper (Solved)

## (Common University Entrance Test for UG Programmes)

# CUET (UG)–B.Com (Hons.) Entrance Exam, 2022*

## ENGLISH

**Directions (Qs. No. 1-6):** *Read the following passage to answer question:*

The first form did not really see very much of Erica because she did not have lessons with them. But even if they met her in a passage or in the art room or gym they looked the other way. In the common-room at night Erica had a miserable time. Not one of the second form girls also would have anything to do with her. Loud remarks about sneaks and cowards were made in her hearing. The only person who ever threw her a word at all was the bad-tempered Margery Fenworthy. Erica did not like Margery any more than the other girls did but she was so grateful to be spoken to even, by the surly first former that she almost began to like the girl.

'I'm surprised you speak to Erica, Margery,' said Pat, when she had heard Margery ask to borrow Erica's stationery said Margery, in her usual rude way. 'You're none of you friendly to me, and I know what it is to have people being beastly to you.' 'But Margery, it's your own fault,' said Pat in surprise. 'You're so rude and sullen. You never smile and joke.' Margery, 'you don't give me a chance.' 'Oh, Margery, what a fib'! Cried Pat. 'It's you who never give us a chance to be decent to you. You scowl and glower and frown all the time.' 'If you're going to pick me to pieces you can save yourself the trouble', said Margery, fiercely. 'I don't care tuppence for any of you. And if I want to speak to that wretched Erica, I shall. Who cares for a pack of silly girls, and a crowd of stuck-up teachers? I don't Pat was astonished. What a strange girl Margery was! Did she really want a chance of being friends with the others? Was she terribly shy? What was behind that funny manner of hers? Pat talked about it with her twin. 'Margery is always making enemies she said.' 'I spoke to her today about it and she accused us of never giving her a chance! Do you think we ought to do something about it?'

**1.** Match List-I with List-II.

| *List-I (Part A)* | *List-II (Part B)* |
|---|---|
| (*a*) Loud remarks about sneaks and cowards were made | (*i*) in the presence of Erica |
| (*b*) Margery Fenworthy | (*ii*) was very unpopular |
| (*c*) "Oh Margery ... it's you who never give us a chance to be decent" | (*iii*) said Pat |
| (*d*) The girl with a twin sister named | (*iv*) Pat |

Choose the correct answer from the options given below:

| | (*a*) | (*b*) | (*c*) | (*d*) |
|---|---|---|---|---|
| A. | (*i*) | (*ii*) | (*iv*) | (*iii*) |
| B. | (*i*) | (*ii*) | (*iii*) | (*iv*) |
| C. | (*ii*) | (*iv*) | (*iii*) | (*i*) |
| D. | (*iv*) | (*iii*) | (*i*) | (*ii*) |

**2.** From the given options, choose the one which is correct according to the passage.

The girls mentioned in the passage are:

(*a*) Erica, Margery and Pat
(*b*) Erica and Pat only
(*c*) Only Patricia
(*d*) Joan, Erica and Patricia

A. (*b*) B. (*a*)
C. (*c*) D. (*d*)

**3.** From the given options, select the one which is right and correct according to the passage:

A. "I am surprised you speak to Margery, Erica" said Pat
B. "I am surprised you speak to Erica, Pat" said Margery

*** This Previous Year Paper has been given here as a Combination of CUET (UG) 2022 different exams for the Subjects 'English, Business Studies, Mathematics, Accountancy/ Book Keeping and General Test', which have been mapped to this course.**

C. "I am surprised you speak to Margery, Pat" said Erica
D. "I am surprised you speak to Erica, Margery" said Pat

**4.** From the passage Margaret fenworthy comes across as ______. Select the option which is correct according to the passage.
A. A bad tempered, unpopular girl
B. Heroic and a strong mountaineer
C. Saintly and a recluse
D. A cynical middle aged woman

**5.** From the passage it may be concluded that Erica was very.

Select the option which is correct according to the passage.
A. Lonely, friendless and timid
B. Dominating and Arrogant
C. Cunning and stupid
D. Brilliant and very popular

**6.** From the passage it becomes clear that: (choose the correct option).

Not one of the First Form girls would have anything to do with Erica because:
A. She did not have any lessons with them
B. She used to mind her own business
C. She was unfriendly, rude and selfish
D. Erica was away on a holiday in Paris with her family

**Directions (Qs. No. 7-12):** *Read the following passage to answer question.*

She took me by the hand walked me into the lobby like a five-year old child. Didn't she know I was pushing 15? This was the third home Nancy was placing me in-in a span of eight months! I guess she felt a little sorry for me. The bright fluorescent lights threatened to burn my skin as I walked towards a bouncy-looking lady with curly hair and a sweetly-smiling man. They called themselves Allie and Alex. Cute, I thought.

After they exchanged the usual reams of paperwork, it was off in their Chevy Suburban to get situated into another new home. This time, there were no other foster children and nor another biological child. Anything could happen.

Over the next few weeks, Allie, Alex and I fell into quite a nice routine. She'd make pancakes for breakfast, or he'd fry up some sausage and eggs. They sang a lot, even danced as they cooked. They must have just bought the house because, most weekends, we were either painting a living room butter yellow or staining a coffee table mocha brown.

I kept waiting for the other shoe to drop. When would they start threatening a loss of pancakes if I didn't mow the lawn? When would the sausage and eggs be replaced with unidentifiable slosh because he didn't feel like cooking in the morning? But, it never happened. They kept cooking, singing and dancing like a couple of happy fools.

It was a Saturday afternoon when Allie decided it was time to paint the brick fireplace white. As we crawled closer to the dirty old firepit, we pulled out the petrified wood and noticed a teeny-tiny treasure box! We looked at each other in wonder and excitement. She actually said, "I wonder if the Leprechauns left it!"

**7.** Over the next few weeks who all fell into a nice comfortable routine?

Select the correct option.
A. Nancy
B. Allie and Nancy
C. The narrator, Allie and Alex
D. Only Alex

**8.** "She took me by the hand and walked me into the lobby...". The 'me' refers to the:
A. Narrator and the protagonist of the passage
B. Narrator and the footballer
C. A filmstar and a villain
D. The headmaster of an English school

**9.** On a Sunday afternoon, what did Allie decide to do?

Select the correct option.
(*a*) Crawl towards the dirty old garage
(*b*) Paint the brick firepit white
(*c*) Sing a song
(*d*) Write a letter to the President

Choose the correct answer from the options given below:

A. (*a*) B. (*b*)
C. (*c*) D. (*d*)

**10.** It appears from the passage that over the next few days the narrator and the other two characters were:

Select the correct option.
A. Relaxed and comfortable
B. Stressed and anxious
C. Depressed and gloomy
D. Plotting revenge

**11.** Match List-I with List-II:

| *List-I* | *List-II* |
|---|---|
| (*a*) Nancy | (*i*) Treated the narrator as if he was a 5 year old child |
| (*b*) Allie | (*ii*) Made pancakes for breakfast |
| (*c*) Alex | (*iii*) Fried sausages and eggs |
| (*d*) Narrator | (*iv*) Was placed in the 3rd home |

Choose the correct answer from the options given below:

| | (a) | (b) | (c) | (d) |
|---|---|---|---|---|
| A. | (i) | (ii) | (iii) | (iv) |
| B. | (iv) | (iii) | (ii) | (i) |
| C. | (iv) | (i) | (iii) | (ii) |
| D. | (ii) | (iv) | (i) | (iii) |

**12.** From the passage it may be assumed that the narrator was a 15 year old teenager without parents because the passage talks about.

Select the correct option.

A. Foster home for the narrator and other foster children
B. Cleaning firepits
C. Church and Chapels of Great Britain
D. Malls of a Metropolitan city

**Directions (Qs. No. 13-18):** *Read the following passage to answer question.*

### Workers and Slaves

The Pharaohs may have believed that it was their links with the Gods that kept Egypt going, but really it was the hard work of the ordinary people. It was they who dug the soil, worked in the mines and quarries, sailed the boats on the river Nile, marched with the army into Syria or Nubia, cooked food and raised children. Slavery was not very important in ancient Egypt, but it did exist. Most of the slaves were prisoners who had been captured during the many wars Egypt fought with their neighbours in the Near East. Slaves were usually treated well and were allowed to own property. Many Egyptian workers were serfs. This meant that their freedom was limited. They could be bought and sold along with the estates where they worked. Farmers had to be registered with the government. They had to sell crops at a fixed price and pay taxes in the form of produce. During the season of the Nile floods, when the fields lay under water, many workers were recruited into public building projects. Punishment for those who ran away was harsh.

**13.** From the passage we get to know that a distinct quality of ancient Egypt under the Pharaohs was the fact that.

Select the correct option.

A. Though slavery existed slaves were not treated harshly at all
B. The Pharaohs were very democratic and handsome
C. No Egyptian working in ancient Egypt worked as a serf
D. The river Nile would stop No flowing during the rains in Egypt

**14.** From the passage we get to know that in ancient Egypt many workers were known as serfs. These were people with:

Select the correct answer.

A. Workers with limited freedom in ancient Egypt
B. Students with limited Intelligence in modern Egypt
C. Nobility with limited power in medieval Egypt
D. Pharaohs with limited connection with the gods of Egyptian Gods

**15.** What according to the passage was the reason of ancient Egyptian progress and prosperity.

(*a*) The link the Pharaohs claimed they had with the Gods
(*b*) The labour and hard work of the ordinary men in ancient Egypt
(*c*) The mines and quarries full of germs armed with rockets and missiles and jewals in ancient Egypt
(*d*) The modern smart Egyptian army

Choose the correct answer from the options given below:

A. (*a*) B. (*b*)
C. (*c*) D. (*d*)

**16.** From the given passage options, select the one which is true according to the passage.

(*a*) Pharaohs believed that it was their link with the Gods that favoured Egypt
(*b*) The ordinary people worked overtime to destroy Egypt
(*c*) The Pharaohs did not believe they were connected to the Gods
(*d*) The Pharaohs were the hard working slaves of ancient Egypt

Choose the correct answer from the options given below:

A. (*c*) B. (*b*)
C. (*a*) D. (*d*)

**17.** Select the option that is **incorrect** according to the passage.

A. In the Egypt under the Pharaohs, slaves were allowed to own property
B. Most of the slaves were prisoners captured in the many wars Egypt fought with its neighbours in the NEAR EAST
C. Slaves were well treated in ancient Egypt
D. Slavery was extremely important in ancient Egypt

**18.** Match List-I with List-II.

| *List-I* | *List-II* |
|---|---|
| (*a*) Serfs could be | (*i*) Farmers |
| (*b*) Registered with the government | (*ii*) Recruited workers during the rainy season |
| (*c*) Public building projects | (*iii*) Bought and sold along with the estates were they worked |
| (*d*) Harsh punishment | (*iv*) For those who ran away |

Choose the correct answer from the options given below:

| | (a) | (b) | (c) | (d) |
|---|---|---|---|---|
| A. | (i) | (ii) | (iii) | (iv) |
| B. | (iv) | (iii) | (ii) | (i) |
| C. | (iii) | (i) | (ii) | (iv) |
| D. | (ii) | (iii) | (iv) | (i) |

**Directions (Qs. No. 19-22):** *From the given options select the one that is opposite in meaning to the given word:*

**19.** ACQUITTED
A. Promoted B. Burdened
C. Convicted D. Development

**20.** RELINQUISH
A. Garbage B. Harmonize
C. Beautify D. Possess

**21.** CAPACIOUS
A. Limited B. Charming
C. Foolish D. Colourful

**22.** FRAUDULENT
A. Candid B. Direct
C. Forthright D. Genuine

**Directions (Qs. No. 23-26):** *From the given options select the figure of speech of the poetic device used in expression.*

**23.** Both wry with the laboured ease of loss.
A. Simile B. Personification
C. Oxymoron D. Metaphor

**24.** Far Far from gusty waves.
A. Oxymoron B. Alliteration
C. Simile D. Personification

**25.** The smiling young trees provided a strange comfort.
A. Personification B. Metaphor
C. Simile D. Oxymoron

**26.** Like angels from heaven the paratrooper landed on earth.
A. Personification B. Oxymoron
C. Simile D. Pun

**Directions (Qs. No. 27-30):** *From the given options, select the one which correctly explains the expression.*

**27.** To be at sixes and sevens.
A. To be a primary school student
B. A state of total confusion and disorder
C. To be certain of batting well in a cricket match
D. To give away secrets

**28.** Once in a blue moon.
A. Most regularly B. Very often
C. Very rarely D. Once in a fortnight

**29.** A wild goose chase.
A. A Foolish and useless enterprises
B. To hunt wild life
C. A violent chase of criminals
D. To speak harshly

**30.** To burn a hole in the pocket.
A. To steal from someone's pocket
B. To destroy someone else's belongings
C. To burn address accidentally
D. To spend money very quickly

**Directions (Qs. No. 31-34):** *Choose the word from the given options that is closest in meaning to the given word.*

**31.** PUGNACIOUS
A. Rebellious B. Amusing
C. Quarrelsome D. Desirable

**32.** CLING
A. Attach B. Detach
C. Release D. Forward

**33.** ENCHANTING
A. Witty B. Pleasant
C. Comical D. Harmful

**34.** GIGANTIC
A. Miniature B. Monstrous
C. Diligent D. Awkward

**Directions (Qs. No. 35-38):** *From the given options, select the one that will rightly substitute the given expression.*

**35.** Period of 10 years.
A. Decade B. Fortnight
C. Annuity D. Millennium

**36.** One who loves and collects books.
A. Rockstar B. Bibliophile
C. Bellicose D. Bohemian

**37.** The killing of a new-born child.
A. Homicide B. Suicide
C. Massacre D. Infanticide

**38.** Detailed plan of a journey.
A. Passport B. Travelogue
C. Itinerary D. Timetable

**Directions (Qs. No. 39-42):** *From the given options, select the one that carries the same relation as.*

**39.** Attach : Detach
A. Barren : Fertile
B. Timid : Coward
C. Ridiculous : Funny
D. Jealous : Envious

**40.** Medley : Mixture
A. Iterate : Repeat
B. Coarse : Fine
C. Abundance : Scarcity
D. Triumph : Failure

**41.** Retreat : Advance
A. Garrulous : Talkative
B. Oblivion : Forgetfulness
C. Savage : Civilised
D. Obstinate : Stubborn

**42.** Meek : Modest
A. Blunt : Sharp
B. Finally : Eventually
C. Clever : Stupid
D. Condemn : Approve

**Directions (Qs. No. 43-46):** *From the given options, select the rightly spelt word:*

**43.** A. Katastrophic B. Catestrefic
C. Catastrophic D. Catostrofik

**44.** A. Kamunism B. Communism
C. Cummonism D. Cumunism

**45.** A. Cooperative B. Cauperative
C. Koperative D. Coperative

**46.** A. Pnemonia B. Pneumonia
C. Newmonia D. Nemonia

**Directions (Qs. No. 47-50):** *Rearrange the following jumbled group of words to make a meaningful sentence.*

**47.** (*a*) Penetrate the biological tissues
(*b*) Will produce unprecedented amount
(*c*) A large scale exchange of nuclear weapons
(*d*) Of radiation that can

Choose the correct answer from the options given below:
A. (*a*), (*b*), (*d*), (*c*)
B. (*c*), (*d*), (*a*), (*b*)
C. (*c*), (*b*), (*d*), (*a*)
D. (*a*), (*b*), (*c*), (*d*)

**48.** (*a*) During the last few years
(*b*) People in this area
(*c*) The mission has provided
(*d*) Able service to all the needy

Choose the correct answer from the options given below:
A. (*b*), (*d*), (*c*), (*a*)
B. (*c*), (*d*), (*b*), (*a*)
C. (*a*), (*b*), (*d*), (*c*)
D. (*c*), (*b*), (*a*), (*d*)

**49.** (*a*) Him to rush to his village immediately
(*b*) An urgent telegram asking
(*c*) He has received
(*d*) No other message other than

Choose the correct answer from the options given below:
A. (*c*), (*d*), (*b*), (*a*)
B. (*b*), (*c*), (*a*), (*d*)
C. (*c*), (*d*), (*a*), (*b*)
D. (*a*), (*b*), (*c*), (*d*)

**50.** (*a*) He managed to make sense
(*b*) It was the first time when
(*c*) Of the book even though
(*d*) He read anything on the subject

Choose the correct answer from the options given below:
A. (*d*), (*c*), (*a*), (*b*)
B. (*b*), (*a*), (*d*), (*c*)
C. (*a*), (*c*), (*b*), (*d*)
D. (*a*), (*b*), (*c*), (*d*)

## ANSWERS

**1. (B):** The question requires matching statements from List-I with appropriate statements from List-II. (*a*) "Loud remarks about sneaks and cowards were made" can be matched with (*i*) "in the presence of Erica" as the passage mentions that such remarks were made in Erica's hearing. (*b*) "Margery Fenworthy" matches with (*ii*) "was very unpopular" since the passage describes that nobody liked Margery except Erica, which indicates her unpopularity. (*c*) "Oh Margery ... it's you who never give us a chance to be decent" is a statement made by Pat as mentioned in the passage, so it matches with (*iii*) "said Pat". (*d*) The girl with a twin sister is named Pat, so this matches with (*iv*) "Pat".

**2. (B):** According to the passage, the girls mentioned are Erica, Margery, and Pat. Thus, option (*a*) is the correct answer.

**3. (D):** In the passage, the exact line reads, "'I'm surprised you speak to Erica, Margery,' said Pat," which directly matches with option (D).

**4. (A):** Margery Fenworthy is described in the passage as someone with a bad temper. It's mentioned that she is the only one who spoke to Erica and that she is not liked by the other girls. Hence, she comes across as "A bad tempered, unpopular girl".

**5. (A):** Erica is described as having a miserable time in the common room and no one from the second form girls wanted to have anything to do with her. This suggests that she was lonely and friendless. The fact that she was grateful to Margery, who was known to be bad-tempered, indicates her timidity. Hence, she comes across as "Lonely, friendless, and timid".

6. **(A):** The passage directly mentions "The first form did not really see very much of Erica because she did not have lessons with them". This indicates that the reason for the First Form girls not interacting with Erica was that she didn't have lessons with them. Therefore, the correct option is "She did not have any lessons with them".

7. **(C):** The passage mentions that "Over the next few weeks, Allie, Alex, and I fell into quite a nice routine." This clearly indicates that the narrator, along with Allie and Alex, settled into a comfortable daily pattern. This routine involved cooking breakfast together, singing, dancing, and doing house chores.

8. **(A):** The pronoun "me" in the line "She took me by the hand and walked me into the lobby..." refers to the individual narrating the events of the story. As the passage progresses, the experiences and emotions of this individual are described in the first person. The narrator is the protagonist, or the central character, of this passage.

9. **(B):** The passage states, "It was a Saturday afternoon when Allie decided it was time to paint the brick fireplace white." This clearly indicates that on that particular day, Allie's plan was to paint the fireplace. Thus, the correct answer is that she decided to "paint the brick firepit white."

10. **(A):** The characters' interactions, as depicted in the passage, showcase a harmonious environment. They engage in collaborative activities like cooking and house chores, enjoying music and dance. There's no indication of stress or discomfort, making the atmosphere appear "relaxed and comfortable."

11. **(A):** From the passage, we gather the following: (*a*) Nancy - "She took me by the hand walked me into the lobby like a five-year old child." Thus, Nancy treated the narrator as if he was very young, which matches with (*i*). (*b*) Allie - "She'd make pancakes for breakfast..." clearly aligns with Allie making pancakes or option (*ii*). (*c*) Alex - "or he'd fry up some sausage and eggs". This line directly refers to Alex's cooking activities, indicating (*iii*). (*d*) Narrator - "This was the third home Nancy was placing me in..." which means the narrator was being placed in multiple homes, corresponding with (*iv*).

12. **(A):** The passage's narrative revolves around the experiences of a teenager, presumably without parents, as indicated by mentions of foster care and multiple placements in different homes. The theme of the story underscores the trials and tribulations, as well as the moments of warmth, faced by children in foster care. The recurrent mention of "foster home" and the transition between them makes it evident that the narrator was in the care system, making the option about "foster home for the narrator and other foster children" the most logical inference from the story.

13. **(A):** Slavery existed in ancient Egypt but what set it apart from many other ancient civilizations was the treatment of slaves. The passage specifically states that "Slavery was not very important in ancient Egypt, but it did exist." It further clarifies that slaves were usually treated well and even had the right to own property. This contrasts with many ancient societies where slaves were often treated poorly and had very limited rights, if any at all.

14. **(A):** The term 'serfs' in the context of the passage refers to workers whose freedom was limited. They were tied to the land or estates where they worked, and they could be bought and sold along with these estates. This feudal-like system bound the serfs to the land, making their economic and personal freedoms restricted. In essence, while they weren't slaves, they lacked many of the rights associated with free citizens.

15. **(B):** While the Pharaohs believed that their connections with the Gods were responsible for Egypt's prosperity, it was, in reality, the hard work and labor of ordinary people that drove the nation forward. They worked in various sectors, from agriculture to mining, which contributed to the overall development and sustenance of the ancient Egyptian civilization. The strength of a civilization often rests on the shoulders of its everyday workers, and in ancient Egypt, this was no different.

16. **(C):** The passage clearly mentions that the Pharaohs had a strong belief that their connections with the Gods were what favored Egypt. This belief, however, contrasts with the reality, which was that the ordinary people's hard work and contributions were the actual foundation of Egypt's success.

17. **(D):** The passage explicitly states that "Slavery was not very important in ancient Egypt," which directly contradicts the statement "Slavery was extremely important in ancient Egypt." Thus, the latter statement is incorrect based on the information provided.

**18. (C):** By matching the provided lists: (*a*) "Serfs could be bought and sold along with the estates where they worked," which corresponds to (*iii*). (*b*) The passage says, "Farmers had to be registered with the government," aligning with (*i*). (*c*) During the season of the Nile floods, when fields lay underwater, "many workers were recruited into public building projects," matching with (*ii*). (*d*) The passage mentions a "harsh punishment for those who ran away," which correlates with (*iv*). Therefore, the correct match is (*a*)-(*iii*), (*b*)-(*i*), (*c*)-(*ii*) and (*d*)-(*iv*).

**19. (C):** Acquitted refers to the formal and legal declaration that someone is not guilty of a criminal charge. It is the conclusion of a judicial process that finds the accused innocent. On the other hand, "Convicted" means that a person has been found guilty of a criminal charge. Therefore, it stands as the direct opposite of "Acquitted".

**20. (D):** "Relinquish" means to voluntarily give up or let go of something, especially some rights, title, or possession. It signifies the act of releasing or parting with something one holds. Contrarily, "Possess" implies owning, holding, or having control over something. If you relinquish your right to something, you're giving up your claim or control over it. But if you possess something, it's in your ownership or control. This dynamic displays the contrasting nature of the two terms.

**21. (A):** "Capacious" is an adjective used to describe something that has the ability to contain a lot, often used in the context of a space or container being large in size or volume. Think of a capacious room or a capacious bag—they can hold much. The term "Limited" points towards something being confined, restricted, or not expansive. In the context of space or volume, "Limited" would mean that there's a lack of abundance or room. Thus, it serves as the antonym to "Capacious".

**22. (D):** The term "Fraudulent" relates to deceit, trickery, or wrongful deception with the intention to gain something (often monetary) or deceive someone. It's associated with acts that are not genuine or honest. "Genuine", conversely, denotes authenticity, realness, or being free from pretense, affectation, or deceit. A genuine item is real and not a counterfeit, and a genuine person is sincere and not trying to deceive. Given this contrast in their inherent meanings, "Genuine" stands opposite to "Fraudulent".

**23. (C):** The expression "laboured ease" stands out as a juxtaposition of contradictory terms. "Laboured" typically denotes something that requires effort or hard work, whereas "ease" signifies comfort or lack of difficulty. When combined, these words create an oxymoron, which is a figure of speech that merges contrasting ideas to portray complex emotions or situations. In this case, the oxymoron "laboured ease" conveys the paradoxical feeling of finding comfort or acceptance in loss, even though the process is painful.

**24. (B):** The phrase "Far Far from gusty waves" prominently displays the repetition of the initial sound "f" in both "Far" and "from". This deliberate use of the same initial consonant sound in closely positioned or consecutive words is called alliteration. Alliteration is employed in both prose and poetry to create rhythm, catch the reader's attention, and emphasize particular sections of the text.

**25. (A):** In the statement "The smiling young trees provided a strange comfort," trees are ascribed the human-like quality of "smiling." Trees, in reality, do not smile, but this attribution of a human trait to a non-human entity is called personification. Personification is a figurative device that endows animals, objects, or abstract ideas with human characteristics or behaviors, making them more relatable and allowing writers to create vivid imagery and emotional resonance.

**26. (C):** The phrase "Like angels from heaven the paratrooper landed on earth" draws a direct comparison between the paratrooper and angels using the word "like." This comparative statement that uses "like" or "as" to draw parallels between two dissimilar entities is known as a simile. Similes are a staple of poetic language, enabling poets to conjure imaginative visuals and evoke deeper emotions by juxtaposing familiar concepts with unfamiliar or unexpected ones. Here, the comparison magnifies the gracefulness and perhaps the surprise of the paratrooper's landing.

**27. (B):** The idiom "to be at sixes and sevens" signifies being in a state of confusion or disarray. It traces its origins to a dispute between two London guilds about their precedence in the 14th century. The guilds, the Merchant Taylors and the Skinners, were both founded in close succession, leading to the debate. In various processions, they rotated their positions annually between the sixth and seventh spots, hence the phrase. Over time, the term became more generalized, referring to any state of confusion or disorder, and not just about specific rankings.

**28. (C):** The expression "once in a blue moon" denotes an event that happens very infrequently. A blue moon refers to the rare occurrence when there are two full moons in one calendar month. Traditionally, each month has one full moon, but occasionally, the lunar cycle's timing aligns such that a second full moon, termed a "blue moon," appears. Although blue moons are not technically blue, the rarity of the phenomenon has led to the popularization of this phrase in English language, symbolizing something that doesn't happen often.

**29. (A):** To go on "a wild goose chase" means to pursue something that is unattainable or is a fruitless endeavor. Historically, a "wild goose chase" was a type of horse race in which the lead rider pursued a course of his choosing and others followed at set intervals, much like wild geese flying in formation. Over time, the phrase's meaning shifted, and it began to refer to a pointless or unattainable pursuit, mirroring the futility of chasing after a wild goose.

**30. (D):** The idiom "to burn a hole in the pocket" refers to the urge to spend money rapidly, especially when one has disposable income or newfound wealth. The visual imagery suggests money being so hot or uncomfortable that it "burns" its way out of one's pocket, emphasizing the impulsive nature of the spending. This expression underlines the human tendency to sometimes act irresponsibly with money, especially when one feels they have more than they're used to.

**31. (C):** The word "PUGNACIOUS" is derived from the Latin word "pugnare", which means "to fight". It refers to a person who is eager or quick to argue, quarrel, or fight. Thus, the word "Quarrelsome" best captures its essence. Pugnacious individuals are often confrontational and can be challenging to engage with in discussions because of their aggressive nature. Their readiness to dispute can make collaborations difficult, as they may often challenge perspectives aggressively, even if the situation doesn't warrant such a reaction.

**32. (A):** To "CLING" is to hold on tightly to something or someone. It can also refer to objects that stick closely to surfaces, like wet clothes that cling to the body. The word "Attach" closely resonates with this meaning. In a more abstract sense, people might cling to ideas, memories, or feelings, indicating a reluctance to let go or move on. Attachment can be both physical, like sticking or adhering to a surface, and emotional, like being closely bound or connected to a thought, feeling, or another person.

**33. (B):** The term "ENCHANTING" is used to describe something that is charming or captivating, often in a delightful or magical way. Something enchanting draws you in and holds your attention because of its beauty or charm. The word "Pleasant" is closely aligned with this sentiment. Enchanting experiences or sights can often evoke feelings of wonder and amazement. They often stand out in memory because of the strong positive emotions they generate. Such moments or things leave a lasting impact, making us want to relive or revisit them.

**34. (B):** "GIGANTIC" describes something that is very large or enormous in size. It emphasizes an extreme scale or magnitude that often surpasses ordinary standards or expectations. "Monstrous" in this context aligns closely with this meaning, emphasizing the vastness or enormity of something. When we refer to something as gigantic, we often compare it with regular-sized counterparts to underscore its impressive or overwhelming size. The term has its roots in the word "gigant", which historically referred to the Giants of Greek mythology, legendary beings renowned for their immense size and strength.

**35. (A):** A "Decade" specifically refers to a period of 10 years. Originating from the Greek word 'dekas', which means 'ten', it is commonly used to categorize historical, technological, cultural, or personal events and advancements. For instance, the 1960s is referred to as a decade, and it's often associated with cultural revolutions, civil rights movements, and significant shifts in music and fashion. It's a convenient way to encapsulate years that share common characteristics.

**36. (B):** A "Bibliophile" is an individual who has a great appreciation for or collects books. The term is derived from the Greek words 'biblion' (book) and 'philos' (loving). A bibliophile often possesses a deep reverence for books, not just for their content, but sometimes also for their physical form, binding, history, and even the art of bookmaking. While all bibliophiles love books, not all of them are collectors. Some might just enjoy reading and surrounding themselves with books without the intent of collecting rare or antique editions.

**37. (D):** "Infanticide" is the act of killing an infant, usually by a parent. The term comes from Latin 'infans', meaning unable to speak, and 'caedere', which means to kill. Historically and in some cultures, infanticide was practiced for various reasons, including economic distress, the undesirability of the child due to gender or deformities, or societal pressures. Modern societies largely condemn and criminalize infanticide, viewing it as a heinous act. However, it's essential to understand the underlying causes, such as postpartum depression or societal pressures, that might drive someone to commit such an act.

**38. (C):** An "Itinerary" is a detailed plan or route of a journey. It can be as basic as a list of places one intends to visit or as detailed as specifying dates, times, modes of transportation, and lodging details. People often use itineraries when planning trips to ensure they maximize their time and experiences. Travel agents, tour operators, or even individuals planning their vacations often draft itineraries. In a broader sense, an itinerary can also refer to a planned route or journey for business trips, political campaigns, or any event that requires traveling between multiple locations.

**39. (A):** "Attach" and "Detach" are antonyms. While "attach" means to fasten or join something to something else, "detach" refers to the act of separating or removing something. Similarly, "Barren" and "Fertile" are antonyms. A barren land is one that cannot produce or is too poor to produce vegetation, while fertile land is rich in nutrients and is conducive for the growth of plants. These terms often describe soil quality in agriculture. Fertile soils are sought after for farming because they can support a diverse range of crops and result in better yields.

**40. (A):** "Medley" and "Mixture" are synonymous. Both words refer to a combination of different things. For instance, in music, a medley is a blend of several tunes played one after another. Likewise, a mixture refers to a substance made by combining two or more different materials. Similarly, "Iterate" and "Repeat" convey the same idea. To iterate is to say or perform again, often used in the context of computer programming or design processes. Repeat, a more general term, simply implies doing something again.

**41. (C):** "Retreat" and "Advance" are antonyms. Retreat means to withdraw or move back, often used in military contexts when referring to troops moving away from enemy forces. On the other hand, advance means to move forward or make progress. Similarly, "Savage" and "Civilised" are opposites. A society described as savage is viewed as primitive or lacking the cultural and social refinements of a civilized society. It's essential to approach these terms with caution, as labeling a society "savage" can be ethnocentric and disrespectful. It's always crucial to respect cultural differences without imposing judgments based on one's own cultural standards.

**42. (B):** "Meek" and "Modest" are similar in their connotations. While meek implies a mild nature or submissive character, modest means having or showing a moderate estimation of one's abilities or achievements. It's about not being boastful or arrogant. Similarly, "Finally" and "Eventually" are synonymous. Both terms denote an outcome that follows a series of events or a period. For instance, "She finally/ eventually arrived at the party" means she arrived after some delay or events. Both words indicate the culmination of waiting or anticipation.

**43. (C):** The correct spelling is "Catastrophic." The term "catastrophic" refers to something that causes or involves a catastrophe, which is a sudden and widespread disaster. The root word "catastrophe" comes from the Greek "katastrophç," meaning an overturning or a sudden end. In contemporary usage, the word can describe natural disasters like earthquakes or human-made disasters like wars. It's also frequently used in casual speech to refer to significant failures or blunders.

**44. (B):** The rightly spelt word is "Communism." Communism is a sociopolitical and economic ideology and movement whose ultimate goal is the establishment of a communist society, which is a socioeconomic order structured upon the ideas of common ownership of the means of production and the absence of social classes, money, and the state.

**45. (A):** "Cooperative" is the correct spelling. A cooperative is a business organization owned and operated by a group of individuals for their mutual benefit. It can also describe a willingness to cooperate with others.

**46. (B):** "Pneumonia" is the correctly spelt term. Pneumonia is a type of infection that inflames the air sacs in one or both lungs. The air sacs may fill with fluid or pus, causing cough, fever, chills, and difficulty breathing. The "p" at the beginning of the word is silent, which can make the pronunciation and spelling tricky for some.

**47. (C):** The correct sequence is "(*c*) A large scale exchange of nuclear weapons (*b*) Will produce an unprecedented amount (*d*) Of radiation that can (*a*) Penetrate the biological tissues." From a grammatical perspective, this arrangement forms a subject-predicate-object construction, which is standard in English grammar. Here, "(*c*) A large scale exchange of nuclear weapons" acts as the subject, "(*b*) Will produce" is the verb phrase, and the remaining parts "(*d*) Of radiation" and "(*a*) Penetrate the biological tissues" work as the object and modifier, respectively, providing more details about the consequences of the action.

**48. (B):** The coherent arrangement is "(*c*) The mission has provided (*d*) Able service to all the needy (*b*) People in this area (*a*) During the last few years." This sequence begins with the main clause "(*c*) The mission has provided (*d*) Able service" which provides the core information. Following this, "(*b*) People in this area" acts as the qualifier, giving specifics about the recipients. Finally, "(*a*) During the last few years" serves as a temporal adverbial phrase, situating the action in time.

**49. (A):** The proper order is "(*c*) He has received (*d*) No other message other than (*b*) An urgent telegram asking (*a*) Him to rush to his village immediately." Starting with "(*c*) He has received" introduces the subject and the verb. The clause "(*d*) No other message other than" acts as a restrictive modifier, emphasizing the uniqueness of the message. The phrases "(*b*) An urgent telegram asking" and "(*a*) Him to rush to his village immediately" provide further details, functioning as object and purpose clause respectively.

**50. (C):** The correct sequence is "(*a*) He managed to make sense (*c*) Of the book even though (*b*) It was the first time when (*d*) He read anything on the subject." The main clause is "(*a*) He managed to make sense (*c*) Of the book," where "He" is the subject, "managed" is the verb, and "Of the book" is the prepositional phrase acting as an object. The clause "(*b*) It was the first time when (*d*) He read anything on the subject" is a subordinate clause providing a reason or condition for the main clause, with "It" referring to the act of understanding the book.

# BUSINESS STUDIES

**1.** Arrange the functions of Management in correct sequence:

(*a*) Staffing
(*b*) Organising
(*c*) Planning
(*d*) Controlling
(*e*) Directing

Choose the correct answer from the options given below:

A. (*a*), (*b*), (*c*), (*e*), (*d*)
B. (*b*), (*c*), (*d*), (*e*), (*a*)
C. (*b*), (*c*), (*a*), (*e*), (*d*)
D. (*c*), (*b*), (*a*), (*e*), (*d*)

**2.** A manager should not fall into the temptations of misusing her/his powers for individual family benefit at the cost of larger general interest of the workers/ company.

The relevant principle of management is:

A. Subordination of individual interest to general interest
B. Discipline
C. Unity of Direction
D. Initiative

**3.** The following statements explains the concept of standardization and simplification of work.

(*a*) They seek to determine the amount and frequency of rest intervals
(*b*) They aim at eliminating superfluous variety, sizes and dimension
(*c*) Unnecessary movements are eliminated so that less time is required to complete the jobs.
(*d*) They help to determine the number of workers to be employed
(*e*) They help the organisation in devising new varieties instead of existing one.

Choose the ***correct*** answer from the options given below:

A. (*a*) and (*b*) only  B. (*b*) and (*e*) only
C. (*c*) and (*a*) only  D. (*d*) and (*e*) only

**4.** According to Fayol lazy personnel should be dealt with sternly for sending the message that everyone is equal in the eyes of management. This will ensure loyalty and devotion. The relevant principle of management is ______.

A. Discipline  B. Equity
C. Espirit De Corps  D. Unity of command

**5.** Attitude towards product innovations, lifestyles and consumer preferences are influenced by:

A. Economic Environment
B. Social Environment
C. Cultural Environment
D. Ecological Environment

**6.** Match the List-I with List-II.

| ***List-I (Dimension of Business Environment)*** | ***List-II (Component)*** |
|---|---|
| (*a*) Economic | (*i*) Festivals |
| (*b*) Social | (*ii*) Court Judgments |
| (*c*) Political | (*iii*) Public Debt |
| (*d*) Legal | (*iv*) Ideology of ruling party |

Choose the ***correct*** answer from the options given below:

| | (*a*) | (*b*) | (*c*) | (*d*) |
|---|---|---|---|---|
| A. | (*ii*) | (*i*) | (*iv*) | (*iii*) |
| B. | (*iii*) | (*i*) | (*iv*) | (*ii*) |
| C. | (*iv*) | (*iii*) | (*ii*) | (*i*) |
| D. | (*iii*) | (*ii*) | (*iv*) | (*i*) |

**7.** Which of the following does NOT come under the dimensions of Business Environment?

A. Political  B. Legal
C. Social  D. Security

**8.** If there is a plan to increase production then more labour and more machinery will be required. This step would also involve organizing for labour and purchase of machinery. Identify this step in the process of planning.

A. Follow up action
B. Implementing the plan
C. Evaluating alternative courses
D. Developing premises

**9.** From the given options. Identify the statement that best describes planning is a continuous process:

A. It lays down the base for other functions of management
B. A plan is framed, it is implemented and is followed by another plan
C. It involves peeping into the future
D. It involve foresight, intelligent imagination and sound judgment

**10.** Amrit Lala, MD of Awasthi Ltd. retired after 33 years of service. The responsibility was given to Amit. Amit realized that there was lot of rivalry, confusion and misunderstanding among departmental heads. He detected inefficiencies, took corrective action and developed a master plan for the organisation to follow. This served as basis for coordinating the activities of all the departments, led to clarity of thought and action and the work got a smooth start.

Identify the importance of planning highlighted in the above paragraph.

A. Planning promote innovative ideas
B. Planning reduces overlapping and wasteful activities
C. Planning facilitates decision making
D. Planning provides direction

**11.** Interaction among people at work give rise to this type of organisation.

Identify the type of organisation highlighted in the above statement.

A. Formal Organisation
B. Informal Organisation
C. Administrative Organisation
D. Functional Organisation

**12.** Out of the following options, choose the correct combination that constitute parts of organizing process:

(*a*) Identification and division of work
(*b*) Setting up standards for performance
(*c*) Establishing authority and reporting relationships
(*d*) Developing Premises
(*e*) Assignment of duties

Choose the ***correct*** answer from the options given below:

A. (*b*), (*d*), (*e*) only
B. (*a*), (*b*), (*c*) only
C. (*a*), (*c*), (*e*) only
D. (*c*), (*d*), (*e*) only

**13.** Match the Set-A with Set-B.

| ***Set-A*** | ***Set-B*** |
|---|---|
| (*a*) Product specialization | (*i*) Span of management |
| (*b*) All decision making authority is kept with top level | (*ii*) Informal |
| (*c*) Arises out of personal qualities | (*iii*) Divisional Structure |
| (*d*) Number of subordinates that can be managed by a superior | (*iv*) Centralisation |

Choose the ***correct*** answer from the options given below:

| | (*a*) | (*b*) | (*c*) | (*d*) |
|---|---|---|---|---|
| A. | (*iii*) | (*iv*) | (*ii*) | (*i*) |
| B. | (*iii*) | (*ii*) | (*iv*) | (*i*) |
| C. | (*iii*) | (*i*) | (*ii*) | (*iv*) |
| D. | (*i*) | (*iii*) | (*iv*) | (*ii*) |

**14.** It is prerequisites to effective functioning of an organisation because it enables the manager to use his time on high priority activities.

A. Planning
B. Delegation
C. Decentralisation
D. Organisation Structure

**15.** Identify the function of marketing that is also undertaken to fulfil the 'right to be heard' right of a consumer under Consumer Protection Act.

A. Marketing Planning
B. Transportation
C. Physical Distribution
D. Customer Support Services

**16.** A brand or part of a brand that is given legal protection against its use by other firms. Identify the term of branding highlighted in the above statement.

A. Brand B. Brand Name
C. Brand Mark D. Trade Mark

**17.** The label on the package of a shaving cream mentions, '40% Extra free' or package of a toothpaste mentioning 'Free toothbrush inside' or save ₹ 15.' Identify the function of labelling.

A. Grading of product
B. Providing information required by law
C. Helps in promotion of products
D. Describe the product and specify its contents

**18.** Match the List-I with List-II.

| ***List-I (Source of Recruitment)*** | ***List-II (Condition)*** |
|---|---|
| (*a*) Casual Caller | (*i*) Thc application of Sohan, was forwarded by XYZ consultancies to the Company |
| (*b*) Advertisement | (*ii*) Raj sent his application to the company through the website Jobseekers.com |
| (*c*) Placement Agencies | (*iii*) Prateek has seen a job vacancy in the newspaper and decided to give his application |
| (*d*) Web publishing | (*iv*) Rohan went to XYZ Ltd. and gave his application for a job. |

Choose the ***correct*** answer from the options given below:

| | (*a*) | (*b*) | (*c*) | (*d*) |
|---|---|---|---|---|
| A. | (*iii*) | (*ii*) | (*i*) | (*iv*) |
| B. | (*iv*) | (*iii*) | (*i*) | (*ii*) |
| C. | (*iv*) | (*i*) | (*iii*) | (*ii*) |
| D. | (*iv*) | (*ii*) | (*iii*) | (*i*) |

**19.** Mr. Gaurav needs to add 20 people to their team of sales executives. He had given an advertisement in the newspaper and has received 200 applications. Help him to select the best 20 candidates by giving him the correct sequence.

(*a*) Selection Test
(*b*) Reference and Background checks
(*c*) Employment Interview
(*d*) Selection Decision
(*e*) Preliminary Screening

Choose the ***correct*** answer from the option given below:

A. (*e*), (*a*), (*c*), (*b*), (*d*)
B. (*a*), (*b*), (*c*), (*d*), (*e*)
C. (*e*), (*c*), (*b*), (*d*), (*a*)
D. (*e*), (*a*), (*b*), (*c*), (*d*)

**20.** Arrange the staffing process in sequence

(*a*) Recruitment
(*b*) Estimating the manpower requirement
(*c*) Placement and orientation
(*d*) Selection
(*e*) Training and Development

Choose the ***correct*** answer from the options given below:

A. (*b*), (*a*), (*d*), (*e*), (*c*)
B. (*b*), (*a*), (*d*), (*c*), (*e*)
C. (*b*), (*a*), (*c*), (*d*), (*e*)
D. (*a*), (*b*), (*d*), (*c*), (*e*)

**21.** One of the following is not an element of direction. Identify:

A. Communication
B. Delegation
C. Motivation
D. Supervision

**22.** Choose the correct statement/statements:

(*a*) Non-Financial Incentives mainly focus on satisfying psychological, social and emotional factors
(*b*) Money can satisfy all kinds of needs of individuals
(*c*) Career advancement opportunity, job security and employee empowerment are non-financial incentives
(*d*) Promotion, stock option and perquisites are non-financial incentives

Choose the ***correct*** answer from the options given below:

A. (*a*), (*b*) and (*c*) only
B. (*b*) and (*c*) only
C. (*c*) and (*d*) only
D. (*a*) and (*c*) only

**23.** Match the List-I with List-II.

| ***List-I*** | ***List-I*** |
|---|---|
| (*a*) Motivation | (*i*) Function to be performed at the operative level |
| (*b*) Supervision | (*ii*) Complex process as the individuals are generous in their expectations |
| (*c*) Communication | (*iii*) Process that tries to bring change in the behaviour of others |
| (*d*) Leadership | (*iv*) It implies common understanding |

Choose the ***correct*** answer from the options given below:

| | (*a*) | (*b*) | (*c*) | (*d*) |
|---|---|---|---|---|
| A. | (*i*) | (*ii*) | (*iii*) | (*iv*) |
| B. | (*iv*) | (*iii*) | (*ii*) | (*i*) |
| C. | (*ii*) | (*i*) | (*iv*) | (*iii*) |
| D. | (*i*) | (*ii*) | (*iv*) | (*iii*) |

**24.** Arrange the need hierarchy theory of motivation propounded by Abraham Maslow in hierarchical order from basic to highest level need.

(*a*) Basic Physiological Needs
(*b*) Esteem Needs
(*c*) Safety Needs
(*d*) Self actualisation needs
(*e*) Affiliation needs

Choose the ***correct*** answer from the options given below:

A. (*a*), (*b*), (*c*), (*d*) and (*e*)
B. (*a*), (*c*), (*e*), (*b*) and (*d*)
C. (*d*), (*b*), (*e*), (*c*) and (*a*)
D. (*d*), (*b*), (*e*), (*a*) and (*c*)

**25.** Identify one statement among the following that is NOT true about capital budgeting:

A. These decisions are very crucial for any business since they affect its long run earning capacity
B. The size of assets, profitability and competitiveness are all affected by these decisions
C. These are concerned with levels of cash, inventory and receivable
D. These decisions are irreversible except at a huge cost

**26.** A company will tend to pay lower rate of dividend if:

A. Lower amount of earnings, stable earning, potentials, no shortage of cash, easy access to capital market
B. Restrictive clauses imposed by lender, low access to capital market, falling short of cash, good growth opportunities available

C. Short of cash, good growth opportunities available, low access to capital market, enjoys stable earnings
D. Unstable earnings, falling short on cash, easy access to capital market, lower amount of earning

**27.** It is a process of estimating the fund requirement of a business and specifying the sources of funds:
A. Financial Management
B. Financing Decision
C. Financial Planning
D. Capital Budgeting

**28.** A firm's ability to borrow at a lower rate:
A. Decreases its capacity to employ higher debt
B. Increases its capacity to employ higher debt
C. Can or employ any amount of debt available from market
D. Unable to raise any amount of debt

**29.** Arrange the following current assets in order of their liquidity.
(*a*) Prepaid expenses
(*b*) Raw Material
(*c*) Debtors
(*d*) Finished goods inventory
(*e*) Bills receivable

Choose the ***correct*** answer from the options given below:
A. (*a*), (*b*), (*c*), (*d*) and (*e*)
B. (*e*), (*b*), (*d*), (*c*) and (*a*)
C. (*e*), (*c*), (*d*), (*b*) and (*a*)
D. (*e*), (*d*), (*c*), (*b*) and (*a*)

**30.** Treasury Bills are issued by:
A. Government of India
B. RBI (Reserve Bank of India)
C. Stock Exchange
D. NSE (National Stock Exchange)

**31.** Identify the objective of SEBI from the following:
(*a*) To protect the rights and interests of investors
(*b*) To regulate stock market and the securities industry to promote their orderly functions.
(*c*) Registration of brokers
(*d*) To prevent trading malpractices and achieve a balance between self regulation by securities industry and its statutory regulation
(*e*) Calling for information by undertaking inspection

Choose the ***correct*** answer from the options given below:
A. (*a*), (*b*) and (*c*) only B. (*b*), (*c*) and (*d*) only
C. (*d*), (*e*) and (*a*) only D. (*a*), (*b*) and (*d*) only

**32.** Name the market for financial securities which is also known as 'New Issue Market':
A. Primary Market B. Secondary Market
C. Money Market D. Capital Market

**33.** "Through this process of disinvestment and reinvestment, savings get channelized into their most productive investment avenues"— which function of stock exchange is highlighted by the given statement?
A. Providing liquidity and marketability of securities
B. Contributes to economic growth
C. Spreading of equity cult
D. Providing scope for speculation

**34.** "Holders of assets can readily sell their financial assets through the mechanism of the financial market"— This statement highlight one of the functions of financial market.

Identify
A. Facilitates price discovery
B. Provides liquidity to financial assets
C. Reducing the cost of transactions
D. Mobilisation of earnings and channeling them into the most productive uses

**35.** Match the List-I with List-II.

| ***List-I*** | ***List-I*** |
|---|---|
| (*a*) Right to consumer education | (*i*) Right to be protected against goods and services which are hazardous to life |
| (*b*) Right to be heard | (*ii*) Right to have complete information of the product |
| (*c*) Right to be informed | (*iii*) Right to file a complaint and be heard in case of dissatisfaction |
| (*d*) Right to safety | (*iv*) Right to acquire knowledge and to be well informed consumer |

Choose the ***correct*** answer from the options given below:

| | (*a*) | (*b*) | (*c*) | (*d*) |
|---|---|---|---|---|
| A. | (*iv*) | (*iii*) | (*ii*) | (*i*) |
| B. | (*i*) | (*ii*) | (*iii*) | (*iv*) |
| C. | (*iv*) | (*i*) | (*ii*) | (*iii*) |
| D. | (*iii*) | (*i*) | (*ii*) | (*iv*) |

**36.** Shikha wants to buy a Microwave. She goes to an outlet for the same. The sales person is convincing her to buy microwave of a particular brand only. Identify the consumer right which is being hindered here from the following:
A. Right to safety
B. Right to be informed
C. Right to choose
D. Right to be heard

**37.** Identify from the following phrase which means "Let the buyer beware"?

A. Caveat emptor B. Caveat venditor
C. Caveat vendor D. Consumer emptor

**38.** Who can file a complaint?

(*a*) Any Consumer
(*b*) Any Shopkeeper
(*c*) Any registered consumer association
(*d*) Any non-registered NGO
(*e*) A legal heir of a deceased consumer

Choose the ***correct*** answer from the options given below:

A. (*a*), (*b*) and (*c*) only B. (*a*), (*c*) and (*e*) only
C. (*a*), (*c*) and (*d*) only D. (*b*), (*d*) and (*e*) only

**39.** Identify from the following that cannot be termed as a 'Consumer' under Consumer Protection Act?

A. One who purchased a car on installments
B. One who got a car as a gift from parents
C. One who drives a car with the permission of owner
D. One who purchases cars for resale

**40.** Identify which one is not a step in the process of setting up a Business?

A. Assessment of feasibility of the idea
B. Reference and Background checks
C. Project commissioning and launch
D. Appraisal by funding agencies

**Directions (Qs. No. 41-50):** *Read the case given below and attempt the following questions:*

Anukriti, a III year B.Com student is very fond of home cooked food as her mother keeps experimenting with new tastes and varieties every now and then. Although the family is well off and reputed in society, her mother feels lack of recognition and self-respect for herself. The mother daughter duo decided to go ahead with their own start up and cater to various occasions like birthday parties, office events, festivities, food for elderly and patients and so on.

They assessed the number and type of human resources required and accordingly hired the calculated man-power for help from those introduced by their domestic help and some relatives. They ensured the quality standards for hygiene in kitchen, standardized the quality of vegetables, dry fruits and other raw materials to be purchased, made sure that the orders are delivered in time.

While Anukriti's mother took care of all cooking in Kitchen, she personally observed the helpers at work. Being a commerce student, Anukriti decided to take care of finances herself. She prepared budgets in terms of quality, time, cost of material, calculated a point with no profit, no loss to ensure earning of target profits.

As per the feedback received from customers, they improvised the dishes with lesser oil, spices, sugar.

As both of them were very understanding and positive towards feedback, their business grew well. Gradually, they trained their staff in cooking, packaging, inventory management. The employees are happy and satisfied as their basic remuneration and incentives are increased.

**41.** Mother feels lack of recognition and self-respect for herself. The category of need identified in the statement is:

A. Belonging Needs
B. Esteem Needs
C. Self-actualisation Needs
D. Safety security Needs

**42.** "Assessed the number and types of human resources required". The concept identified is:

A. Workload analysis
B. Workforce analysis
C. Staffing
D. Recruitment

**43.** Hired the calculated manpower for help from those introduced by their domestic help and some relatives.

Identify the source of recruitment:

A. Direct recruitment
B. Placement agencies
C. Labour contractors
D. Recommendations of Employees

**44.** 'They ensured quality standards for hygiene, standardized the quality of raw materials....'

This is a step in the process of one of the function of management. Identify the function.

A. Planning B. Organising
C. Marketing D. Controlling

**45.** Anukriti's mother took care of all cooking in kitchen and personally observed the helpers at work. Identify the technique of controlling:

A. Statistical reports
B. Responsibility accounting
C. Personal Observation
D. Management Information System

**46.** Identify the technique of control used by Anukriti when she prepares budgets of various types:

A. PERT and CPM
B. Ratio analysis
C. Return on Investment
D. Budgetary Control

**47.** She calculated a point with no profit, no loss to ensure earning of target profits. Identify the technique of control highlighted above:

A. Ratio analysis
B. Break even analysis
C. Return on investment
D. Budgetary control

48. As per the feedback received, they improvised the dishes with lesser oil, spices and sugar.

Identify the step in the process of control:

A. Setting Performance Standards
B. Measurement of performance
C. Taking collective actions
D. Comparison of actual performance with standards

49. In an organisation the employees are happy and satisfied ...

Identify the feature of management highlighted in the above statement".

A. Management is a group activity
B. Management is intangible
C. Management is all pervasive
D. Management is multi-dimensional

50. They trained their staff in cooking, packaging, inventory management. The employees are happy and satisfied as their basic remuneration and incentives also increased.

Identify the objective of management highlighted above here:

A. Personal Objectives
B. Social Objectives
C. Organisational Objectives
D. Economic Objectives

## ANSWERS

1. **(D):** Management is a universal term used for certain functions performed by individuals in an enterprise who are bound together in a hierarchy of relationships. Every individual in the hierarchy is responsible for successful completion of a particular task. To be able to fulfil that responsibility he is assigned a certain amount of authority or the right to take a decision. This authority-responsibility relationship binds individuals as superiors and subordinates and gives rise to different levels in an organisation.

   Management is described as the process of planning, organising, staffing, directing and controlling the efforts of organisational members and of using organisational resources to achieve specific goals.

2. **(A): Subordination of Individual Interest to General Interest:** The interests of an organisation should take priority over the interests of any one individual employee according to Fayol. Every worker has some individual interest for working in a company. The company has got its own objectives. For example, the company would want to get maximum output from its employees at a competitive cost (salary). On the other hand, an employee may want to get maximum salary while working the least. In another situation an individual employee may demand some concession, which is not admissible to any other employee like working for less time.

   In all the situations the interests of the group/company will supersede the interest of any one individual. This is so because larger interests of the workers and stakeholders are more important than the interest of any one person. For example, interests of various stakeholders, *i.e.*, owners, shareholders, creditors, debtors, financers, tax authorities, customers and the society at large cannot be sacrificed for one individual or a small group of individuals who want to exert pressure on the company. A manager can ensure this by her/his exemplary behaviour. For example, she/he should not fall into temptation of misusing her/his powers for individual/ family benefit at the cost of larger general interest of the workers/company. This will raise her/his stature in the eyes of the workers and at the same time ensure same behaviour by them.

3. **(B): Standardisation and Simplification of Work:** Simplification aims at eliminating superfluous varieties, sizes and dimensions while standardisation implies devising new varieties instead of the existing ones. Simplification aims at eliminating unnecessary diversity of products. It results in savings of cost of labour, machines and tools. It implies reduced inventories, fuller utilisation of equipment and increasing turnover.

   Most large companies like Nokia, Toyota and Microsoft etc. have successfully implemented standardisation and simplification. This is evident from their large share in their respective markets.

4. **(B): Equity:** Good sense and experience are needed to ensure fairness to all employees, who should be treated as fairly as possible, according to Fayol. This principle emphasises kindliness and justice in the behaviour of managers towards workers. This will ensure loyalty and devotion. Fayol does not rule out use of force sometimes. Rather he says that lazy personnel should be dealt with sternly to send the message that everyone is equal in the eyes of the management. There should be no discrimination against anyone on account of sex, religion, language, caste, belief or nationality etc. In practice we can observe that now-a-days in multinational corporations people of various nationalities work together in a discrimination free environment. Equal opportunities are available for everyone in such companies to rise.

**5. (B):** Major Elements of Social Environment:

- Attitudes towards product innovations, lifestyles, occupational distribution and consumer preferences
- Concern with quality of life
- Life expectancy
- Expectations from the workforce
- Shifts in the presence of women in the workforce
- Birth and death rates
- Population shifts
- Educational system and literacy rates
- Consumption habits
- Composition of family

**6. (B)**

**7. (D):** Dimensions of, or the factors constituting the business environment include economic, social, technological, political and legal conditions which are considered relevant for decision-making and improving the performance of an enterprise.

**8. (B): Implementing the plan:** This is the step where other managerial functions also come into the picture. The step is concerned with putting the plan into action, i.e., doing what is required. For example, if there is a plan to increase production then more labour, more machinery will be required. This step would also involve organising for labour and purchase of machinery.

**9. (B):** Plans are prepared for a specific period of time, may be for a month, a quarter, or a year. At the end of that period there is need for a new plan to be drawn on the basis of new requirements and future conditions. Hence, planning is a continuous process. Continuity of planning is related with the planning cycle. It means that a plan is framed; it is implemented, and is followed by another plan, and so on.

**10. (B): Planning reduces overlapping and wasteful activities:** Planning serves as the basis of coordinating the activities and efforts of different divisions, departments and individuals. It helps in avoiding confusion and misunderstanding. Since planning ensures clarity in thought and action, work is carried on smoothly without interruptions. Useless and redundant activities are minimised or eliminated. It is easier to detect inefficiencies and take corrective measures to deal with them.

**11. (B):** Interaction among people at work gives rise to a 'network of social relationships among employees' called the informal organisation. Informal organisation emerges from within the formal organisation when people interact beyond their officially defined roles. When people have frequent contacts they cannot be forced into a rigid formal structure. Rather, based on their interaction and friendship they tend to form groups which show conformity in terms of interest. Examples of such groups formed with common interest may be those who take part in cricket matches on Sundays, meet in the cafeteria for coffee, are interested in dramatics, etc. Informal organisation has no written rules, is fluid in form and scope and does not have fixed lines of communication.

**12. (C):** Organising involves a series of steps that need to be taken in order to achieve the desired goal. The following steps emerge in the process of organising:

- Identification and division of work
- Departmentalisation
- Assignment of duties
- Establishing authority and reporting relationships

**13. (A)**

**14. (B):** A manager, no matter how capable he is, cannot manage to do every task on his own. The volume of work makes it impractical for him to handle it all by himself. As a consequence, if he desires to meet the organisational goals, focus on objectives and ensure that all work is accomplished, he must delegate authority.

Delegation refers to the downward transfer of authority from a superior to a subordinate. It is a pre-requisite to the efficient functioning of an organisation because it enables a manager to use his time on high priority activities. It also satisfies the subordinate's need for recognition and provides them with opportunities to develop and exercise initiative.

Delegation helps a manager to extend his area of operations as without it, his activities would be restricted to only what he himself can do. However, delegation does not mean abdication. The manager shall still be accountable for the performance of the assigned tasks. Moreover, the authority granted to a subordinate can be taken back and redelegated to another person. Thus, irrespective of the extent of delegated authority, the manager shall still be accountable to the same extent as before delegation.

**15. (D): Right to be heard:** The consumer has a right to file a complaint and to be heard in case of dissatisfaction with a good or a service. It is because of this reason that many enlightened business firms have set up their own consumer service and grievance cells. Many consumer organisations are also working towards this direction and helping consumers in redressal of their grievances.

**16. (D):** A brand or part of a brand that is given legal protection is called trademark. The protection is given against its use by other firms. Thus the firm, which got its brand registered, gets the exclusive right for its use.

In that case, no other firm can use such name or mark in the country. Though branding adds to the cost e.g., to the cost of packaging, labelling, legal protection, and promotion, it provides several advantages to the sellers as well as the consumers.

17. **(C): Helps in Promotion of Products:** An important function of label is to aid in promotion of the products. A carefully designed label can attract attention and give reason to purchase. We see many product labels providing promotional messages for example, the pack of a popular Amla Hair Oil states, 'Baalon mein Dum, Life mein Fun'. The label on the package of a brand of Detergent Powder says, 'Keep cloth look good and your machine in top condition'. Labels play important role in sales promotional schemes launched by companies. For example the label on the package of a Shaving Cream mentions, '40% Extra Free' or package of a toothpaste mentioning, 'Free Toothbrush Inside', or 'Save ₹ 15'.

18. **(B)** 19. **(C)**

20. **(B): STAFFING PROCESS:**
- Estimating the Manpower Requirements
- Recruitment
- Selection
- Placement and Orientation
- Training and Development
- Performance Appraisal
- Promotion and career planning
- Compensation

21. **(B):** The process of directing involves guiding, coaching, instructing, motivating, leading the people in an organisation to achieve organisational objectives. Consider the following examples: (*i*) A supervisor explains a worker about operations to be carried by him on a lathe machine, (*ii*) A mining engineer explains about safety precautions to be followed while working in a coal mine, (*iii*) A Managing Director declares share in the profits to the managers for their contribution to inhance profits of the company, and (*iv*) A manager inspires his/her employees by playing a lead role in performing a work. All these examples and many other activities related to directing may broadly be grouped into four categories which are the elements of directing. These are:
- Supervision
- Motivation
- Leadership
- Communication

22. **(D):** Apart from the monetary and future security needs, an individual also has psychological, social and emotional needs. Satisfying these needs also plays an important role in their motivation. Non-financial incentives focus mainly on the fulfilment of these needs and thus cannot be measured in terms of money. However, there are chances that a particular non-financial incentive may also involve the financial incentive as well. For example, when a person is promoted his psychological needs are fulfilled as he gets more authority, his status increases but at the same time, he has benefitted monetarily also as he gets a rise in salary. The most common non-financial incentives are:

- **Status:** With reference to an organization, status refers to the position in the hierarchy of the organizational chart. The level of authority, responsibility, recognition, salary, perks, etc. determine the status of an employee in the organization.

  A person at the top level management has more authority, responsibility, recognition and salary and vice-versa. Status satisfies the self-esteem and psychological needs of an individual and in turn, motivates him to work hard.

- **Organizational Climate:** Organizational climate refers to the environmental characteristics of an organization that are perceived by its employees about the organization and have a major influence on their behaviour. Each organization has a different organizational climate that distinguishes it from other organizations.

  Some of the factors that influence the organizational climate of an enterprise are organizational structure, individual responsibility, rewards, risk and risk-taking, warmth and support and tolerance and conflict. When the organizational climate is positive employees tend to be more motivated.

- **Career Advancement Opportunity:** It is very important for an organization to have an appropriate skill development program and a sound promotion policy for its employees which works as a booster for them to perform well and get promoted.

  Every employee desires growth in an organization and when he gets promotion as an appreciation of his work he is motivated to work better.

- **Job Enrichment:** It refers to the designing of jobs in such a way that it involves a higher level of knowledge and skill, a variety of work content, more autonomy and responsibility of employees, meaningful work experience and more opportunities of growth. When the job is interesting, it itself serves as a source of motivation.

- **Job Security:** Job security provides future stability and a sense of security among the employees. The employees are not worried about the future and thus work with more enthusiasm. Owing to the unemployment problem in our country, job security works as a great incentive for the employees.

However, there is also a negative aspect of this incentive that employees tend to take their job for granted and not work efficiently.

- **Employee Recognition Programmes:** Recognition means acknowledgment and appreciation of work done by employees. Recognition in the organization boosts their self-esteem and they feel motivated. For example, declaring the best performer of the week or month, displaying their names on the notice board and giving them rewards, fall under the Employee recognition program.
- **Employee Participation:** Involving the employees in decision making regarding the issues related to them such as canteen committees, work committees, etc. also helps in motivating them and inducing a sense of belongingness in them.
- **Employee Empowerment:** Giving more autonomy and powers to subordinates also make them feel that they are important to the organization and in turn they serve the organization better.

**23. (C)**

**24. (B):** There are various views on human motivation; the most popular among these is given by Abraham H. Maslow. He attempted to portray a picture of human behaviour by arranging the various needs in a hierarchy. His viewpoint about motivation is very popular because of its theoretical and applied value which is popularly known as the "Theory of Self-actualisation".

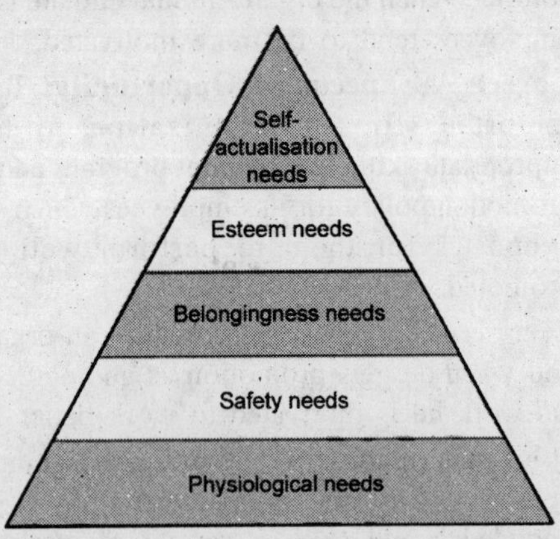


**25. (C):** Investment decision can be long-term or short-term. A long-term investment decision is also called a Capital Budgeting decision. It involves committing the finance on a long-term basis. For example, making investment in a new machine to replace an existing one or acquiring a new fixed asset or opening a new branch, etc. These decisions are very crucial for any business since they affect its earning capacity in the long run. The size of assets, profitability and competitiveness are all affected by capital budgeting decisions. Moreover, these decisions normally involve huge amounts of investment and are irreversible except at a huge cost. Therefore, once made, it is often almost impossible for a business to wriggle out of such decisions. Therefore, they need to be taken with utmost care. These decisions must be taken by those who understand them comprehensively.

**26. (D)**

**27. (C):** A proper matching of funds requirements and their availability is sought to be achieved by financial planning. This process of estimating the fund requirement of a business and specifying the sources of funds is called financial planning. Financial planning takes into consideration the growth, performance, investments and requirement of funds for a given period. Financial planning includes both short-term as well as long-term planning. Long-term planning relates to long term growth and investment. It focuses on capital expenditure programmes. Short-term planning covers short-term financial plan called budget. Typically, financial planning is done for three to five years. For longer periods it becomes more difficult and less useful. Plans made for periods of one year or less are termed as budgets. Budgets are example of financial planning exercise in greater details. They include detailed plan of action for a period of one year or less.

**28. (B):** When a firm is able to borrow at a lower rate, it increases the capacity to employ higher debt and can increase the debt component in the capital structure.

**29. (B):** Current Assets: Current assets are those which are either in the form of cash or can be converted into cash within a year. The examples of such assets are cash in hand/bank, bills receivable, stock of raw materials, semi-finished goods and finished goods, sundry debtors, short term investments, prepaid expenses, etc.

**30. (B):** A Treasury bill is basically an instrument of short-term borrowing by the Government of India maturing in less than one year. They are also known as Zero Coupon Bonds issued by the Reserve Bank of India on behalf of the Central Government to meet its short-term requirement of funds. Treasury bills are issued in the form of a promissory note. They are highly liquid and have assured yield and negligible risk of default. They are issued at a price which is lower than their face value and repaid at par. The difference between the price at which the treasury bills are issued and their redemption value is the interest receivable on them and is called discount. Treasury bills are available for a minimum amount of ₹ 25,000 and in multiples thereof.

**31. (D):** The overall objective of SEBI is to protect the interests of investors and to promote the development of, and regulate the securities market. This may be elaborated as follows:

- To regulate stock exchanges and the securities industry to promote their orderly functioning.
- To protect the rights and interests of investors, particularly individual investors and to guide and educate them.
- To prevent trading malpractices and achieve a balance between self regulation by the securities industry and its statutory regulation.
- To regulate and develop a code of conduct and fair practices by intermediaries like brokers, merchant bankers etc., with a view to making them competitive and professional.

**32. (A):** The primary market is also known as the New Issues Market. It deals with new securities being issued for the first time. The essential function of a primary market is to facilitate the transfer of investible funds from savers to entrepreneurs seeking to establish new enterprises or to expand existing ones through the issue of securities for the first time. The investors in this market are banks, financial institutions, insurance companies, mutual funds and individuals.

A company can raise capital through the primary market in the form of equity shares, preference shares, debentures, loans and deposits. Funds raised may be for setting up new projects, expansion, diversification, modernisation of existing projects, mergers and takeovers etc.

**33. (B): Contributes to Economic Growth:** A stock exchange is a market in which existing securities are resold or traded. Through this process of disinvestment and reinvestment savings get channelized into their most productive investment avenues. This leads to capital formation and economic growth.

**34. (B): Providing Liquidity to Financial Assets:** Financial markets facilitate easy purchase and sale of financial assets. In doing so they provide liquidity to financial assets, so that they can be easily converted into cash whenever required. Holders of assets can readily sell their financial assets through the mechanism of the financial market.

**35. (A):** The Consumer Protection Act provides for six rights of consumers. The consumer protection councils set up under the Act are intended to promote and protect the various rights of consumers. These rights include the following:

- **Right to Safety:** The consumer has a right to be protected against goods and services which are hazardous to life and health. For instance, electrical appliances which are manufactured with substandard products or do not conform to the safety norms might cause serious injury. Thus, consumers are educated that they should use electrical appliances which are ISI marked as this would be an assurance of such products meeting quality specifications.
- **Right to be Informed:** The consumer has a right to have complete information about the product he intends to buy including its ingredients, date of manufacture, price, quantity, directions for use, etc. It is because of this reason that the legal framework in India requires the manufactures to provide such information on the package and label of the product.
- **Right to Choose:** The consumer has the freedom to choose from a variety of products at competitive prices. This implies that the marketers should offer a wide variety of products in terms of quality, brand, prices, size, etc. and allow the consumer to make a choice from amongst these.
- **Right to be Heard:** The consumer has a right to file a complaint and to be heard in case of dissatisfaction with a good or a service. It is because of this reason that many enlightened business firms have set up their own consumer service and grievance cells. Many consumer organisations are also working towards this direction and helping consumers in redressal of their grievances.
- **Right to seek Redressal:** The consumer has a right to get relief in case the product or service falls short of his expectations. The Consumer Protection Act provides a number of reliefs to the consumers including replacement of the product, removal of defect in the product, compensation paid for any loss or injury suffered by the consumer, etc.
- **Right to Consumer Education:** The consumer has a right to acquire knowledge and to be a well informed consumer throughout life. He should be aware about his rights and the reliefs available to him in case of a product or service falling short of his expectations. Many consumer organisations and some enlightened businesses are taking an active part in educating consumers in this respect.

**36. (C)**

**37. (A):** Development of education and mass media and increasing competition in the market have made the consumer conscious of his right and power in determining market forces. The principle of caveat emptor (or let the buyer beware) has been substituted by the principle of 'customer is king'. Business enterprises have started following customer-oriented policies.

38. **(B):** A complaint before the appropriate consumer forum can be made by:
- Any consumer;
- Any registered consumers' association;
- The Central Government or any State Government;
- One or more consumers, on behalf of numerous consumers having the same interest; and
- A legal heir or representative of a deceased consumer.

39. **(D):** A 'consumer' is generally understood as a person who uses or consumes goods or avails of any service. Under the Consumer Protection Act, a consumer is defined as:
- Any person who buys any goods for a consideration, which has been paid or promised, or partly paid and partly promised, or under any scheme of deferred payment. It includes any user of such goods, when such use is made with the approval of the buyer, but does not include a person who obtains goods for re-sale or any commercial purpose.
- Any person who hires or avails of any service, for a consideration which has been paid or promised, or partly paid and partly promised, or under any system of deferred payment. It includes any beneficiary of services when such services are availed of with the approval of the person concerned, but does not include a person who avails of such services for any commercial purpose.

40. **(A):** The process of setting up a business is preceded by the decision to choose entrepreneurship as a career and identification of promising business ideas upon a careful examination of the entrepreneurial opportunities. Generation of ideas is not enough; the business ideas must stand the scrutiny from techno-economic, financial and legal perspectives. That is, after the initial screening of the ideas that do not seem promising prima facie, you should conduct an in-depth examination of the chosen three-four before settling for the one where you would like to exert your time, money and energies. You should prepare a business plan that will serve as the road map for effective venturing, whether you may require institutional funding (in which case it is necessary to do so) or not. Setting up of new business enterprises is a very challenging task; you are likely to encounter many problems en route. It's advisable to be aware of these problems as to forewarn means to fore arm!

**41. (C)** **42. (D)** **43. (A)**
**44. (D)** **45. (C)** **46. (D)**
**47. (A)** **48. (C)** **49. (A)**
**50. (C)**

# MATHEMATICS

**1.** In a sequence of Bernoulli trials with $p = 3/4$, the probability that first success occurs after four failures, is:

A. $\frac{3}{512}$ B. $\frac{3}{1024}$

C. $\frac{1}{2}$ D. $\frac{3}{4}$

**2.** If $\begin{bmatrix} x-4 & 2 & -1 \\ -2 & y-2 & 6 \\ 1 & -6 & z+3 \end{bmatrix}$ is skew-symmetric matrix, then the value of $\begin{vmatrix} x & y & z \\ y & z & x \\ z & x & y \end{vmatrix}$ is:

A. 144 B. 117

C. –117 D. 1

**3.** If A = $[2\ -1\ 6]_{1 \times 3}$ and B = $\begin{bmatrix} 1 \\ 4 \\ 6 \end{bmatrix}_{3\times1}$, then sum of elements of matrix BA is:

A. 11 B. 77

C. 88 D. 101

**4.** The function $f(x) = 2x^3 - 3x^2 - 36x + 10$ is strictly increasing in:

A. $(-\infty, -2) \cup (3, \infty)$ B. $(-\infty, -1) \cup (2, \infty)$

C. $(-\infty, 0)$ D. $(0, \infty)$

**5.** If $x = at^2$ and $y = 2at$, then the value of $\frac{d^2y}{dx^2}$ at $t = 2$ is:

A. $-\frac{1}{4a}$ B. $-\frac{1}{16}$

C. 0 D. $-\frac{1}{16a}$

**6.** The function $f(x) = x^3 + \frac{5}{2}x^2 - 2x - 3$, has:

A. two points of local maxima

B. two points of local minima

C. one point of local maxima and one point of local minima

D. no point of local maxima or minima

**7.** If $\int (x^2 + \sqrt{x})\,dx = ax^3 + bx^{\frac{3}{2}} + c$ where $a$, $b$ and $c$ are constants, then the value of $\frac{9}{5}(a^2 + b^2)$ is:

A. $\frac{5}{9}$ B. $\frac{1}{3}$

C. $\frac{2}{3}$ D. 1

**8.** $\int_{-4}^{4} \log_e\left(\frac{5+x}{5-x}\right)dx$ is equal to:

A. $2 \log_e 5$ B. $3 \log_e 5$

C. $-\frac{16}{9}$ D. 0

**9.** The area enclosed by two circles $x^2 + y^2 = a^2$ and $(x - a)^2 + y^2 = a^2$ is:

A. $\left(\frac{4\pi - \sqrt{3}}{6}\right)a^2$ B. $\left(\frac{4\pi - 3\sqrt{3}}{6}\right)a^2$

C. $\frac{\pi - \sqrt{3}}{6}a^2$ D. $\frac{2\sqrt{3} - \pi}{6}a^2$

**10.** The order and degree of the differential equation $\sqrt{x\frac{dy}{dx} + 1} = \frac{d^2y}{dx^2} + \frac{dy}{dx}$ are respectively:

A. 1 and 2 B. 2 and 1

C. 2 and 2 D. 1 and 1

**11.** The general solution of the differential equation $\frac{dx}{dy} = 2ye^{y^2 - x}$ is

A. $e^y = e^{x^2} + c$ B. $e^x = e^{y^2} + c$

C. $e^{-y} + e^{x^2} = c$ D. $e^{x^2} - y = c$

**12.** The differential equation representing the family of curves given by $y = e^{-x}(a + bx)$ is:

A. $\frac{d^2y}{dx^2} = e^x\left(\frac{dy}{dx}\right)$ B. $\frac{d^2y}{dx^2} + 2\frac{dy}{dx} + y = 0$

C. $\frac{d^2y}{dx^2} - \frac{dy}{dx} - y = 0$ D. $\frac{d^2y}{dx^2} + 2\frac{dy}{dx} + 7x = 0$

**13.** If the difference between mean and variance of a binomial distribution B($n$, $p$) is 1 and the difference of their squares is 15, then:

A. $n = 64, p = \frac{1}{8}$ B. $n = 64, p = \frac{7}{8}$

C. $n = 32, p = \frac{1}{8}$ D. $n = 32, p = \frac{7}{8}$

**14.** The variance of the first 16 natural number is:

A. $\frac{85}{4}$ B. $\frac{56}{3}$

C. 24 D. $\frac{133}{4}$

**15.** The corner points of the feasible region of an L.P.P. is shown in the Figure. The $s_1$ maximum and minimum values of the objective function $z = 2x + y$ is:

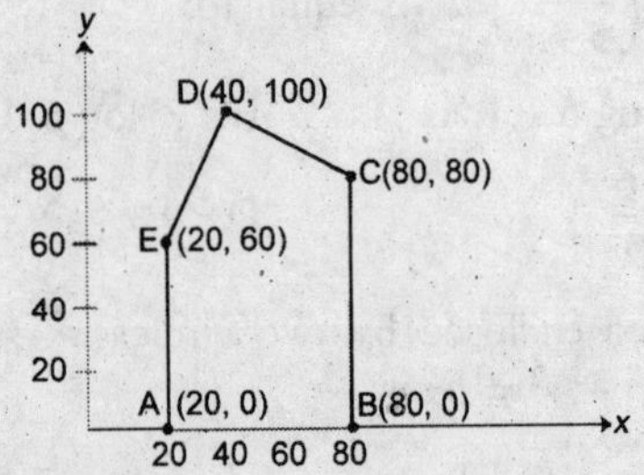


A. 180
B. 340
C. 260
D. 280

**16.** Let $f : R \to [0, \infty)$ be defined by $f(x) = x^2 + |x - 5|$. Then $f$ is:
A. one-one but not onto.
B. neither one-one nor onto.
C. one-one and onto.
D. onto but not one-one.

**17.** Let R be a relation on the set A = {1, 2, 3, 4, 5, 6} defined as R = $\{(x, y) : x + y$ is divisible by $y, x \le y\}$. Then R is:
A. reflexive but neither symmetric nor transitive.
B. reflexive and transitive but not symmetric.
C. an equivalences relation.
D. reflexive, symmetric but not transitive.

**18.** Let, $A = \begin{bmatrix} 2 & 3 \\ -1 & 1 \end{bmatrix}$ and $B = \frac{1}{5}\begin{bmatrix} a & b \\ c & d \end{bmatrix}$. If $B = A^{-1}$, then $(d - b)$ is equal to:

A. –1 B. 5
C. –5 D. 1

**19.** If the matrix

$$\begin{bmatrix} x^2 - 3x + 2 & 1 & 3 \\ -1 & 2x^2 - 3x + 1 & -7 \\ -3 & 7 & x^2 - 7x + 6 \end{bmatrix}$$

is skew symmetric, then $x$ is equal to:

A. 1 B. 2

C. 6 D. $\frac{1}{2}$

**20.** The value of $\int_{-\frac{\pi}{2}}^{\frac{\pi}{2}} \sin^7 x \, dx$ is:

A. 0 B. $\frac{5\pi}{16}$

C. $\pi$ D. $\frac{32}{5}$

**21.** $\int \frac{\cot^4 \sqrt{x} \, \text{cosec}^2 \sqrt{x}}{\sqrt{x}} dx$ is equal to:

A. $\frac{2}{5}\cot^5 \sqrt{x} + c$ B. $-\cot^5 \sqrt{x} + c$

C. $-\frac{2}{5}\cot^5 \sqrt{x} + c$ D. $-\frac{5}{2}\cot^5 \sqrt{x} + c$

**22.** $\int \frac{dx}{x\sqrt{ax - x^2}}$ is equal to:

A. $\frac{1}{a}\frac{\sqrt{x}}{\sqrt{a-x}} + C$ B. $-\frac{2}{a}\frac{\sqrt{x}}{\sqrt{a-x}} + C$

C. $\frac{\sqrt{a-x}}{\sqrt{x}} + C$ D. $-\frac{2}{a}\frac{\sqrt{a-x}}{\sqrt{x}} + C$

**23.** Match List-I with List-II.

| List-I | List-II |
|---|---|
| (a) $\int e^x\left(\frac{1}{x} - \frac{1}{x^2}\right)dx =$ | I. $e^x(x^2 - 2x + 2) + C$ |
| (b) $\int xe^x dx =$ | II. $-\frac{e^x}{x^2} + C$ |
| (c) $\int x^2 e^x dx =$ | III. $\frac{e^x}{x} + C$ |
| (d) $\int e^x\left(-\frac{1}{x^2} + \frac{2}{x^3}\right)dx =$ | IV. $e^x (x - 1) + C$ |

Choose the ***correct*** answer from the options given below:

| | (a) | (b) | (c) | (d) |
|---|---|---|---|---|
| A. | III | I | II | IV |
| B. | II | IV | I | III |
| C. | III | IV | II | I |
| D. | III | IV | I | II |

**24.** The value of $\int_0^1 \tan^{-1}\left(\frac{2x - 1}{1 + x - x^2}\right)dx$ is:

A. $\frac{\pi}{2}$ B. 0

C. 1 D. $\frac{\pi}{4}$

**25.** $\int_1^e \frac{\log_e x}{x} dx$ is equal to:

A. $\frac{1}{2}$ B. $e$

C. 1 D. $\frac{1}{4}$

**26.** The principal value of

$\cos^{-1}\left(\cos\frac{7\pi}{6}\right)+\sin^{-1}\left(\sin\frac{7\pi}{6}\right)$ is:

A. $\frac{4\pi}{3}$ B. $\frac{2\pi}{3}$

C. $\pi$ D. $\frac{\pi}{3}$

**27.** $f(x)=\begin{cases} ax+1, & x\le 3 \\ bx+3, & x>3 \end{cases}$ is continuous, then:

A. $2a + 2b = 3$ B. $3a + 3b = 2$

C. $3a - 3b = 2$ D. $2a - 2b = 3$

**28.** The sum of the ordinates of the points where the tangents to the curve $y = x^3 - 3x^2 - 9x + 7$ are parallel to the $x$-axis is:

A. –24 B. 16

C. –8 D. 56

**29.** The solution of the differential equation $\frac{dy}{dx}=\frac{x+y}{x-y}$ is:

A. $\tan^{-1}\left(\frac{y}{x}\right)=\log_e|x|+C$

B. $\tan^{-1}\left(\frac{y}{x}\right)=\frac{1}{2}\log_e(x^2+y^2)+C$

C. $\tan^{-1}\left(\frac{y}{x}\right)=\log_e\left(\frac{x^2+y^2}{x^2}\right)+C$

D. $x^2+y^2=C(x^2-y^2)$

**30.** If the lines $\frac{x+1}{3}=\frac{y+2}{2k}=\frac{z-3}{-2}$ and $\frac{x-1}{2k}=\frac{y-1}{-1}=\frac{z-1}{2}$ are perpendicular, then $k$ is equal to:

A. $-\frac{1}{2}$ B. –1

C. 1 D. 2

**31.** Out of the given statements, choose the correct statements:

(*a*) The line $\frac{x-1}{1}=\frac{y-2}{1}=\frac{z-3}{1}$ is parallel to the plane $2x - y - z = 3$.

(*b*) The direction ratios of the normal to the plane $x + y - z = 4$ is 1, 1, –1.

(*c*) The direction ratios of the line $\frac{x}{3}=\frac{y}{2}=\frac{z}{1}$ is 3, 2, 1.

(*d*) If $\vec{a}=\hat{i}+\hat{j}$, then the unit vector $\hat{a}=\frac{\hat{i}+\hat{j}}{\sqrt{3}}$

(*e*) If $\vec{a}=\hat{i}$ and $\vec{b}=\hat{k}$, then the angle between $\vec{a}$ and $\vec{b}$ is zero.

Choose the ***correct*** answer from the options given below:

A. (*a*), (*b*), (*d*) only B. (*a*), (*b*), (*e*) only

C. (*c*), (*d*), (*e*) only D. (*a*), (*b*), (*c*) only

**32.** The distance of the point (2, 5, –3) from the plane $\vec{r}.\left(6\hat{i}-3\hat{j}+2\hat{k}\right)=4$ is:

A. $\frac{17}{7}$ B. $\frac{29}{7}$

C. $\frac{1}{7}$ D. $\frac{13}{7}$

**33.** The acute angle between the two planes $2x + y - 2z = 5$ and $3x - 6y - 2z = 7$ is:

A. $\cos^{-1}\left(\frac{4}{21}\right)$ B. $\cos^{-1}\left(\frac{16}{21}\right)$

C. $\sin^{-1}\left(\frac{2}{21}\right)$ D. $\sin^{-1}\left(\frac{4}{21}\right)$

**34.** The differential equation representing family of curves $y = ae^x + be^{-2x}$, where $a$ and $b$ are arbitrary constants, is:

A. $\frac{d^2y}{dx^2}+\frac{dy}{dx}-y=0$

B. $2\frac{d^2y}{dx^2}+3\frac{dy}{dx}-4y=0$

C. $\frac{d^2y}{dx^2}+\frac{dy}{dx}-2y=0$

D. $\frac{d^2y}{dx^2}+4y=0$

**35.** The equation of the plane, containing line of intersection of planes $x + 3y - z = 5$ and $2x - y + z = 3$ and passes through (2, 1, –2) is:

A. $3x + 2y - 8 = 0$

B. $x + 3y + 2z - 8 = 0$

C. $3x + 2y + 2z - 4 = 0$

D. $x + y + z - 1 = 0$

**36.** If two sides of triangle are represented by the vectors $-\hat{i}+\hat{j}+2\hat{k}$ and $2\hat{i}-\hat{j}+4\hat{k}$, then area of triangle is:

A. $\frac{1}{2}\sqrt{101}$ B. $\frac{1}{2}\sqrt{51}$

C. $\sqrt{101}$ D. 5

**37.** The unit vectors perpendicular to planes $x + 2y + 3z - 1 = 0$ and $x + y - z + 8 = 0$ are:

A. $\pm\frac{1}{\sqrt{3}}(\hat{i}-\hat{j}+\hat{k})$ B. $\pm\frac{1}{7}(2\hat{i}-3\hat{j}+6\hat{k})$

C. $\pm\frac{1}{\sqrt{42}}(5\hat{i}-4\hat{j}+\hat{k})$ D. $\pm\frac{1}{\sqrt{11}}(3\hat{i}-\hat{j}-\hat{k})$

**38.** The optimal value of the linear programming problem
min($z$) = $3x + 9y$
subject to constraints
$x + 3y \le 60$,
$x + y \ge 10$,
$x \le y$,
$x \ge 0$ and $y \ge 0$ is:

A. 0 B. 30
C. 90 D. 60

**39.** Three identical boxes have 2 coins each as follows: box-1 has 2 gold coins, box-2 has 2 silver coins, box-3 has one gold and one silver coin. If a box is chosen at random and one gold coin is taken out from it, then the probability that the other coin in the box is also of gold is:

A. $\frac{2}{3}$ B. $\frac{2}{5}$

C. $\frac{1}{3}$ D. $\frac{1}{2}$

**40.** A person P fires 4 shots at a target. If the probability of each shot hitting the target is 0.7, then the probability that – P hits the target at least one is:

A. 0.2401 B. 0.0081
C. 0.9919 D. 0.7599

**Directions (Qs. No. 41-45):** *Read the data carefully and answer the following questions.*

Four two vectors $\vec{a}$ and $\vec{b}$, If $|\vec{a}| = 2$, $|\vec{b}| = 3$ and $|\vec{a}\times\vec{b}| = 2\sqrt{5}$.

**41.** $|\vec{a}-\vec{b}|$ is equal to:

A. 5 B. $\sqrt{5}$
C. 1 D. 3

**42.** $|\vec{a}+\vec{b}|$ is equal to:

A. $\sqrt{21}$ B. 21
C. $\sqrt{5}$ D. 5

**43.** The projection of $\vec{a}$ on $\vec{b}$ is:

A. 2 B. $\frac{8}{3}$

C. $\frac{4}{3}$ D. 6

**44.** If θ is the angle between the vectors $\vec{a}+\vec{b}$ and $\vec{a}-\vec{b}$ then $\sin^2\theta$ is equal to:

A. $\frac{5}{21}$ B. $\frac{20}{21}$

C. $\frac{5}{9}$ D. $\frac{16}{21}$

**45.** The area of the triangle formed by the vectors $\vec{a}$ and $\vec{b}$ is:

A. $\sqrt{5}$ B. $2\sqrt{5}$
C. 3 D. 6

**Directions (Qs. No. 46-50):** *Based on the given information answer the following questions:*

A man plans to jump and climb the stairs. If the path (as shown in the figure), he moves on for the first jump is given by the function $y = f(x) = 2x + \sqrt{4x - 12x^2}$, where $x$ (in meters) is the horizontal distance covered and $y$ (in meter) is the corresponding height attained. Assume that his initial position is origin.

**46.** The domain of the function is:

A. $\left[-\frac{1}{\sqrt{3}}, \frac{1}{\sqrt{3}}\right]$ B. $\left[0, \frac{1}{3}\right]$

C. $\left[0, \frac{2}{3}\right]$ D. $\left[\frac{1}{3}, 3\right]$

**47.** The function is strictly increasing in:

A. $\left(0, \frac{1}{3}\right)$ B. $\left(0, \frac{1}{4}\right)$

C. $\left(\frac{1}{4}, \frac{1}{3}\right)$ D. $\left(\frac{1}{12}, \frac{1}{3}\right)$

**48.** The value of $x$ for which $f'(x) = 0$ is:

A. $\frac{1}{2}$ B. $\frac{1}{4}$

C. $\frac{1}{6}$ D. $\frac{1}{12}$

**49.** The maximum height attained in the first jump is:

A. 1 B. $\frac{5}{4}$

C. $\frac{2}{3}$ D. $\frac{3}{4}$

**50.** The slope of the tangent to the curve $y = f(x)$ at the point when $x = \frac{1}{12}$ is:

A. 2 B. 4
C. $2+\sqrt{3}$ D. $2(1+\sqrt{3})$

# ANSWERS

**1. (B):** Probability for Success $(p) = \frac{3}{4}$

Probability for Failure $(q)$

$$= 1 - p = 1 - \frac{3}{4} = \frac{1}{4}$$

Now, Probability that first success occurs after 4 failures

$$= \text{(FFFFS)}$$

$$= \frac{1}{4} \times \frac{1}{4} \times \frac{1}{4} \times \frac{1}{4} \times \frac{3}{4} = \frac{3}{1024}.$$

**2. (C):** For a skew-symmetric matrix, all diagonal elements must be zero

$$\therefore \begin{bmatrix} x-4 & 2 & -1 \\ -2 & y-2 & 6 \\ 1 & -6 & z+3 \end{bmatrix} \text{ is skew-symmetric}$$

when, $x - 4 = 0 \Rightarrow x = 4$

$y - 2 = 0 \Rightarrow y = 2$

and $z + 3 = 0 \Rightarrow z = -3$

Now,

$$\begin{vmatrix} x & y & z \\ y & z & x \\ z & x & y \end{vmatrix} = x(yz - x^2) + y(xz - y^2) + z(xy - z^2)$$

$$= 3xyz - x^3 - y^3 - z^3$$

$$= 3(4)(2)(-3) - (4)^3 - (2)^3 - (-3)^3$$

$$= -72 - 64 - 8 + 27 = -117.$$

**3. (B):** $A = \begin{bmatrix} 2 & -1 & 6 \end{bmatrix}_{1\times3}$ and $B = \begin{bmatrix} 1 \\ 4 \\ 6 \end{bmatrix}_{3\times1}$

Now, $BA = \begin{bmatrix} 1 \\ 4 \\ 6 \end{bmatrix} \begin{bmatrix} 2 & -1 & 6 \end{bmatrix} = \begin{bmatrix} 2 & -1 & 6 \\ 8 & -4 & 24 \\ 12 & -6 & 36 \end{bmatrix}$

Sum of elements of BA

$$= 2 - 1 + 6 + 8 - 4 + 24 + 12 - 6 + 36$$

$$= 77.$$

**4. (A):** $f(x) = 2x^3 - 3x^2 - 36x + 10$

$f'(x) = 6x^2 - 6x - 36 + 0$

$= 6(x^2 - x - 6)$

$= 6(x + 2)(x - 3)$

Putting, $f'(x) = 0$

$6(x + 2)(x - 3) = 0$

$\therefore \quad x = -2$ and $3$

On number line,

For $x < -2$, $(x + 2) < 0$ and $(x - 3) < 0$

$\therefore \quad f'(x) > 0$ (Increasing)

For $-2 < x < 3$, $(x + 2) > 0$ and $(x - 3) < 0$

$\therefore \quad f'(x) < 0$ (Decreasing)

For $x > 3$, $(x + 2) > 0$ and $(x - 3) > 0$

$\therefore \quad f'(x) > 0$ (Increasing)

Hence, $f(x)$ is increasing in $(-\infty, -2) \cup (3, \infty)$.

**5. (D):** $x = at^2$, $y = 2at$

$$\frac{dx}{dt} = 2at \text{ and } \frac{dy}{dt} = 2a$$

Now, $$\frac{dy}{dx} = \frac{\frac{dy}{dt}}{\frac{dx}{dt}} = \frac{2a}{2at} = \frac{1}{t}$$

$$\frac{d^2y}{dx^2} = \frac{d}{dt}\left(\frac{dy}{dx}\right) \times \frac{dt}{dx} = \frac{d}{dt}\left(\frac{1}{t}\right) \times \frac{1}{2at}$$

$$= -\frac{1}{t^2} \times \frac{1}{2at} = -\frac{1}{2at^3}$$

At $t = 2$, $$\frac{d^2y}{dx^2} = -\frac{1}{2a(2)^3} = -\frac{1}{16a}.$$

**6. (C):** $f(x) = x^3 + \frac{5}{2}x^2 - 2x - 3$

For local maxima or local minima

$f'(x) = 0$

$f'(x) = 3x^2 + \frac{5}{2}(2x) - 2$

$= 3x^2 + 5x - 2$

$= 3x^2 + 6x - x - 2$

$= 3x(x + 2) - 1(x + 2)$

$= (x + 2)(3x - 1)$

When $f'(x) = 0$

$(x + 2)(3x - 1) = 0$

$\therefore \quad x = -2$ and $\frac{1}{3}$

Again, $f''(x) = 6x + 5$

when, $x = -2$, $f''(-2) = 6(-2) + 5 = -7 < 0$

$\therefore f(x)$ has local maxima at $x = -2$

and when $x = \frac{1}{3}$,

$$f''\left(\frac{1}{3}\right) = 6\left(\frac{1}{3}\right) + 5 = 7 > 0$$

$\therefore f(x)$ has local minima at $x = \frac{1}{3}$.

**7. (D):** $\int\left(x^2+\sqrt{x}\right).dx = ax^3+bx^{3/2}+c$

$$\frac{(x)^{(2+1)}}{(2+1)}+\frac{(x)^{\left(\frac{1}{2}+1\right)}}{\left(\frac{1}{2}+1\right)}+c = ax^3+bx^{3/2}+c$$

$$\frac{x^3}{3}+\frac{x^{3/2}}{\frac{3}{2}}+c = ax^3+bx^{3/2}+c$$

$$\therefore \qquad a = \frac{1}{3},\ b = \frac{2}{3}$$

$$\frac{9}{5}\left[\left(\frac{1}{3}\right)^2+\left(\frac{2}{3}\right)^2\right] = \frac{9}{5}\left[\frac{1}{9}+\frac{4}{9}\right]=\frac{9}{5}\times\frac{5}{9}=1.$$

**8. (D):** We know that by property

$$\int_{-a}^{a} f(x)dx = \int_{0}^{a}\{f(x)+f(-x)\}dx$$

$$\therefore \qquad I = \int_{-4}^{4}\log_e\left(\frac{5+x}{5-x}\right)dx$$

$$= \int_{0}^{4}\left\{\log_e\left(\frac{5+x}{5-x}\right)+\log_e\left(\frac{5-x}{5+x}\right)\right\}dx$$

$$= \int_{0}^{4}\left\{\log_e\frac{5+x}{5-x}.\frac{5-x}{5+x}\right\}dx$$

$$= \int_{0}^{4}\{\log_e 1\}dx = \int_{0}^{4}0\,dx = 0.$$

**9. (A):** Given equation:

$$x^2 + y^2 = a^2$$

and $\qquad (x - a)^2 + y^2 = a^2$

$\Rightarrow \qquad y^2 = a^2 - (x - a)^2$

Point of intersections:

$$x^2 + y^2 - a^2 = (x - a)^2 + y^2 - a^2$$

$$2ax = a^2$$

$$\Rightarrow x = \frac{a}{2}$$

$$y = \sqrt{a^2-\frac{a^2}{4}} = \frac{\sqrt{3}}{2}a$$

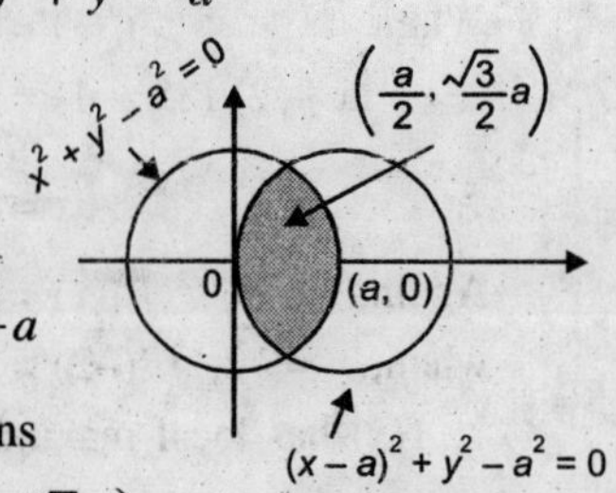


$\therefore$ Point of intersections

$$\left(\frac{a}{2},\frac{\sqrt{3}}{2}a\right) \text{ and } \left(\frac{a}{2},-\frac{\sqrt{3}}{2}a\right)$$

$$\text{Required Area} = 4\int_{x=0}^{\left(\frac{a}{2},\frac{\sqrt{3}}{2}a\right)}\int_{y=0}^{\sqrt{2xa-x^2}} dy.dx$$

$$= 4\int_{x=0}^{\left(\frac{a}{2},\frac{\sqrt{3}}{2}a\right)}\left(\sqrt{2xa-x^2}\right).dx$$

$$= 4\int_{0}^{\left(\frac{a}{2},\frac{\sqrt{3}}{4}a\right)}\left(\sqrt{a^2-(x-a)^2}\right).dx$$

$$= 4\left[\frac{x-a}{a}\sqrt{2xa-x^2}+\frac{a^2}{2}\sin^{-1}\left(\frac{x-a}{a}\right)\right]_0^{a/2}$$

$$= 4\left[\frac{-3a}{2}\sqrt{a^2-\frac{a^2}{4}}+\frac{a^2}{2}\sin^{-1}\left(-\frac{1}{2}\right)-\frac{a^2}{2}\sin^{-1}(-1)\right]$$

$$= \left(\frac{4\pi-\sqrt{3}}{6}\right).a^2.$$

**10. (C):** $\sqrt{x.\frac{dy}{dx}+1} = \frac{d^2y}{dx^2}+\frac{dy}{dx}$

$$\left(x.\frac{dy}{dx}+1\right) = \left(\frac{d^2y}{dx^2}+\frac{dy}{dx}\right)^2$$

This is equation of second degree and second order.

**11. (B):** $\frac{dx}{dy} = 2y.e^{y^2-x}$

$$\frac{dx}{dy} = 2y.\frac{e^{y^2}}{e^x}$$

$$e^x.\frac{dx}{dy} = 2y.e^{y^2}$$

$$e^x.dx = 2y.e^{y^2}.dy$$

Integrating both sides, we get,

$$\int e^x.dx = \int 2y.e^{y^2}.dy$$

$$e^x = \int 2y.e^{y^2}.dy$$

Let $y^2 = t \Rightarrow \quad 2y.dy = dt$

$$\therefore \qquad e^x = \int e^t.dt = e^t$$

$$e^x = e^{y^2}+c.$$

**12. (B):** $y = e^{-x}(a + bx) \qquad$ ...(*i*)

$$\frac{dy}{dx} = b.e^{-x} - e^{-x}(a + bx) \qquad \text{...(ii)}$$

$$\frac{d^2y}{dx^2} = -b.e^{-x} + e^{-x}(a + bx) - e^{-x}.b$$

$$\frac{d^2y}{dx^2} = e^{-x}(a + bx) - 2b.e^{-x} \qquad \text{...(iii)}$$

From $(i)$, $e^{-x}(a + bx) = y$

and from $(ii)$, $-be^{-x} = -e^{-x}(a+bx) - \frac{dy}{dx} = -y - \frac{dy}{dx}$

Putting in equation $(iii)$, we have,

$$\frac{d^2y}{dx^2} = y - 2y - \frac{2dy}{dx}$$

$$\frac{d^2y}{dx^2} + 2\frac{dy}{dx} + y = 0.$$

**13. (A):** Mean = $np$ and variance = $npq$

According to question,

$$\text{Mean} - \text{Variance} = 1$$

$$np - npq = 1$$

$$np(1 - q) = 1$$

And, $(np)^2 - (npq)^2 = 15$

$$(np)^2 [1 - q^2] = 15$$

$$\frac{\{np.(1-q)\}^2 (1+q)}{(1-q)} = 15$$

$$(1)^2 \frac{(1+q)}{(1-q)} = \frac{15}{1}$$

By componendo & dividendo,

$$\frac{(1+q)-(1-q)}{(1+q)+(1-q)} = \frac{15-1}{15+1}$$

$$q = \frac{7}{8}$$

then, $p = 1 - q = 1 - \frac{7}{8} = \frac{1}{8}$

and $np(1 - q) = 1$

$$n\left(\frac{1}{8}\right)\left(1-\frac{7}{8}\right) = 1$$

$$n = 8 \times 8 = 64.$$

**14. (A):** From formula, Variance of first $n$ natural number

$$\sigma^2 = \left\{\frac{\Sigma f_i d_i}{N} - \left(\frac{\Sigma f_i d_i}{N}\right)^2\right\}$$

Here, $n = 16$

$$= \frac{1^2+2^2+3^2+...+16^2}{16} - \left(\frac{1+2+3+...+16}{16}\right)^2$$

$$= \frac{16.(16+1).(2\times16+1)}{16\times6} - \left(\frac{16\times(16+1)}{16\times2}\right)^2$$

$$= \frac{17\times33}{6} - \left(\frac{17}{2}\right)^2 = \frac{17}{2}\left[11 - \frac{17}{2}\right] = \frac{85}{4}.$$

**15. (D):**

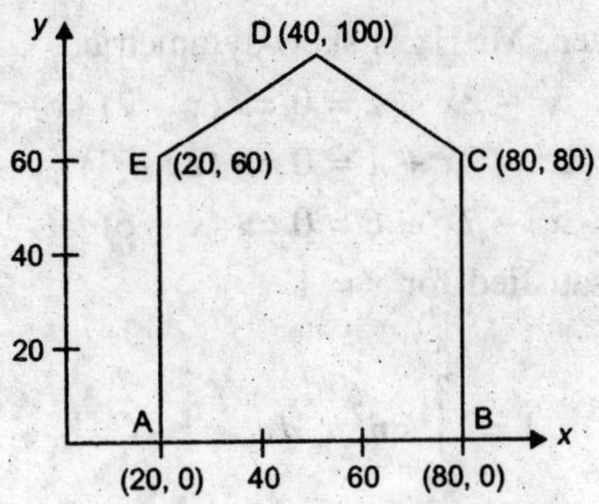


| Corner points | $z = (2x + y)$ |
|---|---|
| A – (20, 0) | – $z = 2 \times 20 + 0 = 40$ (Minimum) |
| B – (80, 0) | – $z = 2 \times 80 + 0 = 160$ |
| C – (80, 80) | – $z = 2 \times 80 + 80 = 240$ (Maximum) |
| D – (40, 100) | – $z = 2 \times 40 + 100 = 180$ |
| E – (20, 60) | – $z = 2 \times 20 + 60 = 100$ |

$\therefore$ Sum of Maximum & Minimum values

$$= 240 + 40 = 280.$$

**16. (B):** $y = f(x) = x^2 + |x - 5|$

For, $x = 0$, $y = 0 + |0 - 5| = 5$

$x = 1$, $y = 1 + |1 - 5| = 5$

As, $f(0) = f(1)$

$\therefore$ $f(x)$ is not ONE-ONE and also not onto function.

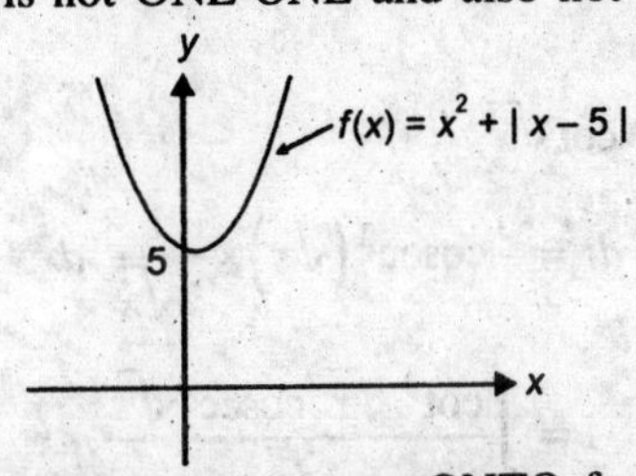


This is neither one-one nor ONTO function.

**17. (A):** Set A = {1, 2, 3, 4, 5, 6}

Relation (R) = $\{(x, y) : (x + y)$ is divisible by $y\}$

For $x = y$, $(y + y) \div y$, This is true.

Hence, Relation R is reflexive

Again, For, $z = (x + y) \div y, \neq y \div (x + y)$

Thus, this is not symmetric.

and for $(x + y) \div (y + z) \neq (z + x) \div (x + y)$

Thus, function is not transitive.

**18. (B):** $A = \begin{bmatrix} 2 & 3 \\ -1 & 1 \end{bmatrix}$

$$|A| = 2 \times 1 - 3 \times (-1) = 2 + 3 = 5$$

Now, $A^{-1} = \frac{\text{Adj}(A)}{|A|} = \frac{\begin{bmatrix} 1 & -3 \\ 1 & 2 \end{bmatrix}}{5} = \frac{1}{5}\begin{bmatrix} 1 & -3 \\ 1 & 2 \end{bmatrix}$

Now, $B = A^{-1} = \frac{1}{5}\begin{bmatrix} a & b \\ c & d \end{bmatrix} = \frac{1}{5}\begin{bmatrix} 1 & -3 \\ 1 & 2 \end{bmatrix}$

$$d = 2, b = -3$$

Then, $d - b = 2 - (-3) = 5$.

**19. (A):** Given, Matrix is skew-symmetric.

Then, $x^2 - 3x + 2 = 0 \Rightarrow (x-2)(x-1) = 0$

$2x^2 - 3x + 1 = 0 \Rightarrow (2x-1)(x-1) = 0$

$x^2 - 7x + 6 = 0 \Rightarrow (x-6)(x-1) = 0$

This is satisfied for $x = 1$.

**20. (A):** $$I = \int_{-\pi/2}^{\pi/2} \sin^7 x.dx$$

As, $\sin^7(-x) = -\sin^7(x)$

Therefore, sin $x$ is a odd function

$$\therefore \quad I = \int_{-\pi/2}^{\pi/2} \sin^7 x.dx = \int_{-\pi/2}^{0} \sin^7 x.dx + \int_{0}^{\pi/2} \sin^7 x.dx$$

$$= \int_{0}^{\pi/2} \sin^7(-x).dx + \int_{0}^{\pi/2} \sin^7(x).dx$$

$$= -\int_{0}^{\pi/2} \sin^7(x).dx + \int_{0}^{\pi/2} \sin^7(x).dx = 0.$$

**21. (C):** Let $\cot\sqrt{x} = t$

then, $$dt = -\text{cosec}^2\left(\sqrt{x}\right) \times \frac{1}{2\sqrt{x}}.dx$$

Now, $$I = \int \frac{\cot^4\sqrt{x}.\text{cosec}^2\sqrt{x}}{\sqrt{x}}.dx$$

$$= 2\int \cot^4\sqrt{x}\left\{\frac{\text{cosec}^2\sqrt{x}}{2\sqrt{x}}\right\}.dx$$

$$= 2\int t^4.(-dt) = -2.\frac{t^5}{5} = -\frac{2}{5}.\cot^5\sqrt{x} + c.$$

**22. (D):** $$I = \int \frac{dx}{x\sqrt{ax - x^2}}$$

Let $x = \frac{1}{t} \Rightarrow dx = -\frac{dt}{t^2}$

$$\therefore \quad I = \int \frac{dx}{x\sqrt{ax-x^2}} = \int \frac{-dt}{t^2 \times \frac{1}{t}.\sqrt{a \times \frac{1}{t} - \frac{1}{t^2}}}$$

$$= -\int \frac{dt}{\sqrt{at-1}} = \frac{-(at-1)^{1-\frac{1}{2}}}{\frac{1}{2}} \times \frac{1}{a} + c$$

$$= -2\frac{\sqrt{at-1}}{a} + c = \frac{-2}{a}\frac{\sqrt{a-x}}{\sqrt{x}} + c.$$

**23. (D):** (*a*) $$\int e^x.\left(\frac{1}{x} - \frac{1}{x^2}\right).dx = \int \frac{e^x}{x}.dx - \int \frac{e^x}{x^2}.dx$$

$$= \frac{1}{x}.\int e^x.dx - \int\left(\frac{d(1/x)}{dx}\int e^x.dx\right).dx - \int \frac{e^x}{x^2}.dx$$

$$= \frac{1}{x}.e^x + \int \frac{e^x}{x^2}.dx - \int \frac{e^x}{x^2}.dx + c = \frac{e^x}{x} + c \qquad ...(III)$$

(*b*) $$\int x.e^x.dx = x.\int e^x.dx - \int\left(\frac{dx}{dx}.\int e^x.dx\right).dx$$

$$= x.e^x - e^x + c = e^x(x-1) + c \qquad ...(IV)$$

(*c*) $$\int x^2.e^x.dx = x^2\int e^x.dx - \int\left(\frac{dx^2}{dx}.\int e^x.dx\right)dx$$

$$= x^2.e^x - 2\int x.e^x.dx$$

$$= x^2.e^x - 2e^x(x-1) + c$$

$$= e^x(x^2 - 2x + 2) + c \qquad ...(I)$$

(*d*) $$\int e^x\left(-\frac{1}{x^2} + \frac{2}{x^3}\right)dx$$

Here, $$\frac{d}{dx}\left(-\frac{1}{x^2}\right) = -2.(x)^{-(2+1)} = \frac{-2}{x^3}$$

$$\therefore \int e^x\left(-\frac{1}{x^2} + \frac{2}{x^3}\right)dx = \int e^x\left(f(x) + f'(x)\right).dx$$

$$= e^x.f(x) + c = -\frac{e^x}{x^2} + c \qquad ...(II)$$

Hence, correct code is

(*a*) → III, (*b*) → IV, (*c*) → I, (*d*) → II.

**24. (B):** Let, $$I = \int_0^1 \tan^{-1}\left(\frac{2x-1}{1+x-x^2}\right)dx$$

$$I = \int_0^1 \tan^{-1}\left[\frac{x+(x-1)}{1+x(1-x)}\right]dx$$

$$I = \int_0^1 \tan^{-1}\left[\frac{x+(x-1)}{1+x(x-1)}\right]dx$$

Using, $$\tan^{-1}x + \tan^{-1}(y) = \tan^{-1}\left[\frac{x+y}{1-xy}\right]$$

$$\therefore \quad I = \int_0^1\left[\tan^{-1}(x) + \tan^{-1}(x-1)\right]dx$$

$$I = \int_0^1 \tan^{-1}[-(x-1)]dx + \int_0^1 \tan^{-1}(-x)dx \qquad ...(i)$$

Using the Property, $P_4$

$$\therefore \int_0^a f(x)dx = \int_0^a f(a-x)dx$$

$\therefore \quad I = \int_0^1 \tan^{-1}(1-x)dx + \int_0^1 \tan^{-1}(1-x-1)\,dx$

$I = \int_0^1 \tan^{-1}[-(x-1)]\,dx + \int_0^1 \tan^{-1}(-x)\,dx$

$\tan^{-1}(-x) = -\tan^{-1}(x)$

$I = -\int_0^1 \tan^{-1}(x-1)\,dx - \int_0^1 \tan^{-1}(x)dx$ ...(*ii*)

Adding (*i*) and (*ii*)

$$I + I = \int_0^1 \tan^{-1}(x)\,dx + \int_0^1 \tan^{-1}(x-1)dx - \int_0^1 \tan^{-1}(x)\,dx - \int_0^1 \tan^{-1}(x-1)\,dx$$

$2I = 0$

$\therefore \quad I = 0.$

**25. (A):** $I = \int_1^e \frac{\log_e x}{x}.dx = \int_1^e \frac{\ln x}{x}.dx$

Let $\ln(x) = 2 \Rightarrow dz = \frac{1}{x}.dx$

$$I = \int_1^e z.dz = \left[\frac{z^2}{2}\right]_1^e = \left[\frac{\ln x}{2}\right]_1^e = \frac{\ln e}{2} - 0 = \frac{1}{2}.$$

**26. (B):** $\cos^{-1}\left(\cos\frac{7\pi}{6}\right) + \sin^{-1}\left(\sin\frac{7\pi}{6}\right)$

$= \cos^{-1}\left(\cos\left(\pi + \frac{\pi}{6}\right)\right) + \sin^{-1}\left(\sin\left(\pi + \frac{\pi}{6}\right)\right)$

$= \cos^{-1}\left(-\cos\frac{\pi}{6}\right) + \sin^{-1}\left(-\sin\frac{\pi}{6}\right)$

$= \cos^{-1}\left(-\frac{\sqrt{3}}{2}\right) + \sin^{-1}\left(-\frac{1}{2}\right) = \left(\pi - \frac{\pi}{6}\right) + \left(-\frac{\pi}{6}\right)$

Since, Principal value of $\cos^{-1}(\theta) \in [0, \pi]$

and $\sin^{-1}(\theta) \in \left[\frac{-\pi}{2}, \frac{\pi}{2}\right]$

$\therefore$ Principal values of the given expression

$$= \pi - \frac{2\pi}{6} = \frac{2\pi}{3}.$$

**27. (C):** $f(x)$ is continuous, then

$\lim_{x\to 3^-} f(x) = \lim_{x\to 3^+} f(x)$

$\lim_{x\to 3^-} (ax+1) = \lim_{x\to 3^+} bx+3$

$3a + 1 = 3b + 3$

$3a - 3b = 2.$

**28. (C):** Given curve $y = x^3 - 3x^2 - 9x + 7$

Slope of the tangent, $\frac{dy}{dx} = 3x^2 - 6x - 9$

As, Slope is parallel to the $x$-axis

then, $\frac{dy}{dx} = 0$

$\Rightarrow \quad 3x^2 - 6x - 9 = 0$

$3(x^2 - 2x - 3) = 0$

$3(x + 1)(x - 3) = 0$

$\therefore \quad x = -1, 3$

Ordinate of the point, when $x = -1$

$y = (-1)^3 - 3(-1)^2 - 9(-1) + 7$

$= 12$

when $x = 3$, $\quad y = (3)^3 - 3(3)^2 - 9(3) + 7 = -20$

Sum $= -20 + 12 = -8.$

**29. (B):** $\frac{dy}{dx} = \frac{x+y}{x-y}$

Let $y = V.x$, $\quad \frac{dy}{dx} = V.\frac{dx}{dx} + x.\frac{dV}{dx}$

$V + x.\frac{dV}{dx} = \frac{x+Vx}{x-Vx} = \frac{1+V}{1-V}$

$x.\frac{dV}{dx} = \frac{1+V}{1-V} - V = \frac{1+V^2}{1-V}$

$\left(\frac{1-V}{1+V^2}\right).dV = \frac{dx}{x}$

Integrating both sides, we have,

$\int\left(\frac{1-V}{1+V^2}\right).dV = \int\frac{dx}{x}$

$\int\frac{1}{1+V^2}.dV - \frac{1}{2}\int\frac{2V}{1+V^2}.dV = \int\frac{dx}{x}$

$\tan^{-1}(V) - \frac{1}{2}\log_e(1+V^2) = \log_e x + C$

Putting $V = \frac{y}{x}$

$\tan^{-1}\left(\frac{y}{x}\right) - \frac{1}{2}\log_e\left(\frac{x^2+y^2}{x^2}\right) = \log_e x + C$

$\tan^{-1}\left(\frac{y}{x}\right) - \log_e\left(\frac{x^2+y^2}{x^2}\right)^{1/2} = \log_e x + C$

$\tan^{-1}\left(\frac{y}{x}\right) = \log_e\left(\frac{\sqrt{x^2+y^2}}{x}\right) + \log_e x + C$

$\tan^{-1}\left(\frac{y}{x}\right) = \log_e\left(\frac{\sqrt{x^2+y^2}}{x} \times x\right) + C$

$\tan^{-1}\left(\frac{y}{x}\right) = \frac{1}{2}\log_e(x^2+y^2) + C.$

**30. (C):** Given equation:

$$\frac{x+1}{3}=\frac{y+2}{2k}=\frac{z-3}{-2}$$

and

$$\frac{x-1}{2k}=\frac{y-1}{-1}=\frac{z-1}{2}$$

$$\vec{a} = 3\hat{i}+2k\hat{j}-2\hat{k}$$

$$\vec{b} = 2k\hat{i}-\hat{j}+2\hat{k}$$

As, two lines are perpendicular, then

$$\vec{a}.\vec{b} = 0$$

$$\left(3\hat{i}+2k\hat{j}-2\hat{k}\right).\left(2k\hat{i}-\hat{j}+2\hat{k}\right) = 0$$

$$6k - 2k - 4 = 0$$

$$4k - 4 = 0$$

$$k = \frac{4}{4}=1.$$

**31. (D):** (*b*) Direction ratios to the normal to the plane $ax + by + cz = 4$ is $(a, b, -c)$

So, D.r. of the normal to the plane $x + y - z = 4$ is $(1, 1, -1)$

(*c*) D.r. of the line $\frac{x}{a}=\frac{y}{b}=\frac{z}{c}$ is $(a, b, c)$

So, D.r. of the line $\frac{x}{3}=\frac{y}{2}=\frac{z}{1}$ is (3, 2, 1)

(*a*) line $\frac{x-1}{1}=\frac{y-2}{1}=\frac{z-3}{1}$ is parallel to the plane $2x - y - z = 3$.

**32. (D):** The distance of a point with position vector $\vec{a}$ from the plane $\vec{r}$.

$\vec{n}=d$, where $\vec{n}$ is the normal to the plane is

$$\left|\frac{\vec{a}.\vec{n}-d}{|\vec{n}|}\right|$$

Given, the point is (2, 5, –3)

So, $\vec{a} = 2\hat{i}+5\hat{j}-3\hat{k}$

The equation of plane is $\vec{r}.\left(6\hat{i}-3\hat{j}+2\hat{k}\right) = 4$

Comparing with $\vec{r}.\vec{n}=d$,

$$\vec{n} = 6\hat{i}-3\hat{j}+2\hat{k} \text{ and } d = 4$$

Distance of point from plane $= \left|\frac{\vec{a}.\vec{n}-d}{|\vec{n}|}\right|$

$$= \left|\frac{(2\hat{i}+5\hat{j}-3\hat{k}).(6\hat{i}-3\hat{j}+2\hat{k})-4}{\sqrt{6^2+(-3)^2+2^2}}\right|$$

$$= \left|\frac{(2\times6)+(5\times-3)+(-3\times2)-4}{\sqrt{36+9+4}}\right|$$

$$= \left|\frac{12-15-6-4}{\sqrt{49}}\right| = \left|\frac{-13}{7}\right|=\frac{13}{7}.$$

**33. (A):** $2x + y - 2z = 5$

$\Rightarrow$ $2x + y - 2z - 5 = 0$

$3x - 6y - 2z = 7$

$\Rightarrow$ $3x - 6y - 2z - 7 = 0$

Comparing the given equation,

$$2x + y - 2z - 5 = 0$$

$$3x - 6y - 2z - 7 = 0$$

with $a_1x + b_1y + c_1z + d_1 = 0$

and $a_2x + b_2y + c_2z + d_2 = 0$

We get, $a_1 = 2, b_1 = 1, c_1 = -2$

and $a_2 = 3, b_2 = -6, c_2 = -2$

The angle between plane is,

$$\Rightarrow \cos\theta = \frac{a_1a_2+b_1b_2+c_1c_2}{\sqrt{a_1^2+b_1^2+c_1^2}\sqrt{a_2^2+b_2^2+c_2^2}}$$

$$= \frac{(2)(3)+(1)(-6)+(-2)(-2)}{\sqrt{(2)^2+(1)^2+(-2)^2}\sqrt{(3)^2+(-6)^2+(-2)^2}}$$

$$= \frac{6-6+4}{\sqrt{4+1+4}\sqrt{9+36+4}}=\frac{4}{\sqrt{9}\sqrt{49}}$$

$$= \frac{4}{3\times7}=\frac{4}{21} \Rightarrow \theta = \cos^{-1}\left(\frac{4}{21}\right).$$

**34. (C):** $y = ae^x + be^{-2x}$

$$\frac{dy}{dx} = a.e^x - 2b.e^{-2x}$$

$$\frac{d^2y}{dx^2} = a.e^x + 4b.e^{-2x}$$

Now, $\frac{d^2y}{dx^2}+\frac{dy}{dx} = ae^x + 4b.e^{-2x} + a.e^x - 2be^{-2x}$

$$= 2(a.e^x + be^{-2x}) = 2y$$

$$\therefore \frac{d^2y}{dx^2}+\frac{dy}{dx}-2y = 0.$$

**35. (A):** Given equation of plane

$$x + 3y - z = 5 \text{ and } 2x - y + z = 3$$

Equation of the plane, passing through point of intersection,

$$L_1 + \lambda L_2 = 0$$

$\Rightarrow$ $(x + 3y - z - 5) + \lambda(2x - y + z - 3) = 0$

$$(1 + 2\lambda)x + (3 - \lambda)y + (\lambda - 1)z - (5 + 3\lambda) = 0$$

As this passes through (2, 1, –2)

$$(1 + 2\lambda)(2) + (3 - \lambda)(1) + (\lambda - 1)(-2) - (5 + 3\lambda) = 0$$

$$4\lambda - \lambda - 2\lambda - 3\lambda + 2 + 3 + 2 - 5 = 0$$

$$2\lambda = 2$$

$$\therefore \lambda = 1$$

Hence, required equation:

$$(x + 3y - z - 5) + (2x - y + z - 3) = 0$$

$$3x + 2y - 8 = 0.$$

**36. (A):** Area of the triangle

$$A = \frac{1}{2}\left|\begin{vmatrix} \hat{i} & \hat{j} & \hat{k} \\ -1 & 1 & 2 \\ 2 & -1 & 4 \end{vmatrix}\right|$$

$$= \frac{1}{2}\left|(4+2)\hat{i}+(4+4)\hat{j}+(1-2)\hat{k}\right| = \frac{1}{2}\left|6\hat{i}+8\hat{j}-\hat{k}\right|$$

$$= \frac{1}{2}\left|\sqrt{(6)^2+(8)^2+(-1)^2}\right| = \frac{1}{2}\left|\sqrt{36+64+1}\right| = \frac{\sqrt{101}}{2}.$$

**37. (C):** We know that $\left(\vec{a}+\vec{b}\right)$ is perpendicular to both $\vec{a}$ and $\vec{b}$

So, perpendicular plane equation is cross product of two plane

$$= \begin{vmatrix} \hat{i} & \hat{j} & \hat{k} \\ 1 & 2 & 3 \\ 1 & 1 & -1 \end{vmatrix}$$

$$= (-2-3)\hat{i}+(3-(-1))\hat{j}+(1-2)\hat{k} = -5\hat{i}+4\hat{j}-\hat{k}$$

Unit vector

$$= \frac{\vec{a}}{|\vec{a}|} = \pm\frac{(-5\hat{i}+4\hat{j}-\hat{k})}{\sqrt{(-5)^2+(4)^2+(-1)^2}} = \pm\frac{(5\hat{i}-4\hat{j}+\hat{k})}{\sqrt{42}}.$$

**38. (D):** $x + 3y \le 60$ $\quad$ $x + y \ge 10$ $\quad$ $x \le y$

| $x$ | 0 | 60 |
|---|---|---|
| $y$ | 20 | 0 |

| $x$ | 0 | 10 |
|---|---|---|
| $y$ | 10 | 0 |

| $x$ | 0 | 20 |
|---|---|---|
| $y$ | 0 | 20 |

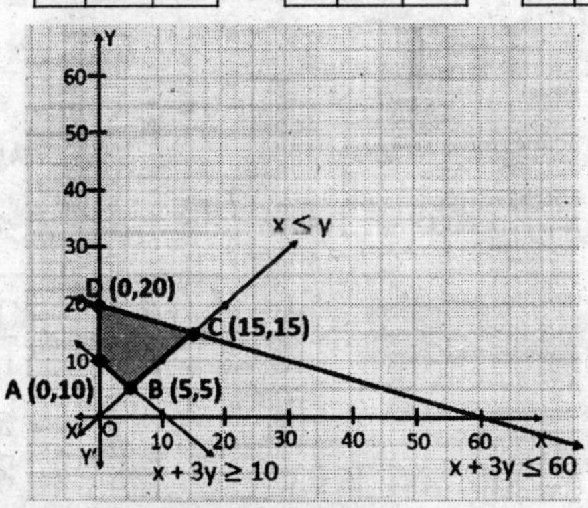


| Corner Points | Value of Z | |
|---|---|---|
| (0, 10) | 90 | |
| (5, 5) | 60 | → Minimum |
| (15, 15) | 180 | } Maximum |
| (0, 20) | 180 | |

$\therefore$ Z = 60 is minimum at (5, 5).

**39. (A):** Let B1 : Selecting Box 1 having two gold coins

B2 : Selecting Box 2 having two silver coins

B3 : Selecting Box 3 having one gold and one silver coin

G : The second coin is of gold

We need to find the Probability that the other coin in the box is also of gold, if the first coin is of gold i.e., $P(B_1 \mid G)$

$$= \frac{P(B_1).P(G \mid B_1)}{P(B_1).P(G \mid B_1)+P(B_2).P(G \mid B_2)+P(B_3).P(G \mid B_3)}$$

$P(B_1)$ = Probability of selecting Box 1 = $\frac{1}{3}$

$P(G \mid B_1)$ = Probability of second coin is of gold in box 1 = 1

$P(B_2)$ = Probability of selecting Box 2 = $\frac{1}{3}$

$P(G \mid B_2)$ = Probability that second coin is of gold in box 2 = 0

$P(B_3)$ = Probability of selecting Box 3 = $\frac{1}{3}$

$P(G \mid B_3)$ = Probability that second coin is of gold in box 3 = $\frac{1}{2}$

$$P(B_1 \mid G) = \frac{\frac{1}{3}\times 1}{\frac{1}{3}\times 1+\frac{1}{3}\times 0+\frac{1}{3}\times\frac{1}{2}} = \frac{\frac{1}{3}\times 1}{\frac{1}{3}\times\left[1+0+\frac{1}{2}\right]}$$

$$= \frac{1}{1+\frac{1}{2}} = \frac{1}{\frac{3}{2}} = \frac{2}{3}.$$

**40. (C):** Person hitting the target probability = 0.7

Person not htting the target probability = 1 – 0.7 = 0.3

Probability that person hit the target in atleast one attempt

= 1 – probability that he not hit target in 4 attempt

= 1 – $(0.3)^4$ = 1 – 0.0081 = 0.9919.

**41. (B):** $|\vec{a}| = 2,\ |\vec{b}| = 3,\ |\vec{a}\times\vec{b}| = 2\sqrt{5}$

$$|\vec{a}-\vec{b}|^2 = |\vec{a}|^2+|\vec{b}|^2-2|\vec{a}|.|\vec{b}|\cos\theta$$

Here $\theta$ is angle between $\vec{a}$ and $\vec{b}$

Now, $|\vec{a}\times\vec{b}| = |\vec{a}|.|\vec{b}|.\sin\theta$

$$2\sqrt{5} = 2\times 3\times\sin\theta$$

$$\therefore \quad \sin\theta = \frac{\sqrt{5}}{3}$$

and $\quad \cos\theta = \sqrt{1-\sin^2\theta} = \sqrt{1-\left(\frac{\sqrt{5}}{3}\right)^2} = \sqrt{\frac{4}{9}}$

$$\Rightarrow \quad \cos\theta = \frac{2}{3}$$

So, $\quad |\vec{a}-\vec{b}|^2 = (2)^2+(3)^2-2\times 2\times 3\times\frac{2}{3}$

$= 4 + 9 - 8 = 5$

$$\therefore \quad |\vec{a}-\vec{b}| = \sqrt{5}.$$

**42. (A):** $|\vec{a}+\vec{b}|^2 = |\vec{a}|^2 + |\vec{b}|^2 + 2|\vec{a}|.|\vec{b}|.\cos\theta$

$$= (2)^2 + (3)^2 + 2\times 2\times 3\times\frac{2}{3}$$

$$= 4 + 9 + 8 = 21$$

$\therefore$ $|\vec{a}+\vec{b}| = \sqrt{21}.$

**43. (C):**

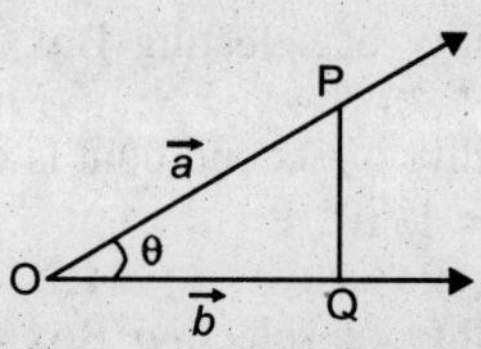


Projection of $\vec{a}$ and $\vec{b}$ is length OQ

From $\Delta$POQ, $|\overrightarrow{OQ}| = |\overrightarrow{OP}|.\cos\theta$

$$\overrightarrow{OQ} = \frac{\overrightarrow{OP}.\overrightarrow{OQ}}{|\overrightarrow{OQ}|} = \frac{\vec{a}.\vec{b}}{|\vec{b}|}$$

$$= |\vec{a}|.\cos\theta$$

$$= 2\times\frac{2}{3} = \frac{4}{3}.$$

**44. (D):** $(\vec{a}+\vec{b}).(\vec{a}-\vec{b}) = |\vec{a}+\vec{b}|.|\vec{a}-\vec{b}|.\cos\theta$

$$\vec{a}.\vec{a}-\vec{a}.\vec{b}+\vec{b}.\vec{a}-\vec{b}.\vec{b} = |\vec{a}+\vec{b}|.|\vec{a}-\vec{b}|.\cos\theta$$

$$|\vec{a}|^2 - |\vec{b}|^2 = |\vec{a}+\vec{b}|.|\vec{a}-\vec{b}|.\cos\theta$$

$$\{\because \vec{a}.\vec{b} = \vec{b}.\vec{a}\}$$

$$(2)^2 - (3)^2 = \sqrt{21}.\sqrt{5}.\cos\theta$$

$$-5 = \sqrt{105}.\cos\theta$$

$$\cos\theta = \frac{-5}{\sqrt{105}} = -\frac{\sqrt{5}}{\sqrt{21}}$$

$$\sin^2\theta = 1 - \cos^2\theta$$

$$= 1 - \left(-\frac{\sqrt{5}}{\sqrt{21}}\right)^2 = 1 - \frac{5}{21} = \frac{21-5}{21} = \frac{16}{21}.$$

**45. (A):** Area of the triangle formed by $\vec{a}$ and $\vec{b}$

$$|A| = \frac{1}{2}|\vec{a}\times\vec{b}| = \frac{1}{2}\times 2\sqrt{5} = \sqrt{5} \text{ unit square.}$$

**46. (B):** Given function, $y = 2x+\sqrt{4x-12x^2}$

Domain: $(4x - 12x^2) \geq 0$

$$4x(1 - 3x) \geq 0$$

$$1 - 3x \geq 0$$

$$x \leq \frac{1}{3}$$

$\therefore$ Domain $= \left[0, \frac{1}{3}\right]$.

**47. (B):** $y = f(x) = 2x+\sqrt{4x-12x^2}$

$$y' = f'(x) = 2+\frac{(4-24x)}{2\sqrt{4x-12x^2}}$$

$$= 2+\frac{2-12x}{\sqrt{4x-12x^2}} = 2+\frac{1-6x}{\sqrt{x-3x^2}}$$

As $y' > 0$ in $\left(0, \frac{1}{4}\right)$

$\therefore$ Function is strictly increasing in $\left(0, \frac{1}{4}\right)$ and strictly decreasing in $\left(\frac{1}{4}, \frac{1}{3}\right)$.

**48. (B):** $f'(x) = 2+\frac{4-24x}{2\sqrt{4x-12x^2}}$

when $f'(x) = 0$, $2+\frac{2-12x}{\sqrt{4x-12x^2}} = 0$

$$6x - 1 = \sqrt{4x-12x^2}$$

$$4x - 12x^2 = (6x - 1)^2$$

$$4x - 12x^2 = 36x^2 + 1 - 12x$$

$$48x^2 - 16x + 1 = 0$$

$$x = \frac{16\pm\sqrt{256-48\times 4}}{2\times 48}$$

$$= \frac{16\pm\sqrt{64}}{96} = \frac{16\pm 8}{96} = \frac{1}{4}, \frac{1}{12}$$

$\therefore$ $f'(x) = 0$ at $x = \frac{1}{4}$.

**49. (C):** $y' = 0$ at $x = \frac{1}{12}$ and $\frac{1}{4}$

$$y \text{ at } x = \frac{1}{12} = 2\times\frac{1}{12}+\sqrt{4\times\frac{1}{12}-12\times\left(\frac{1}{12}\right)^2}$$

$$= \frac{1}{6}+\sqrt{\frac{1}{3}-\frac{1}{12}} = \frac{1}{6}+\frac{1}{2} = \frac{4}{6} = \frac{2}{3}.$$

**50. (B):** Slope of the tangent

$$y' = 2+\frac{4-24x}{2\sqrt{4x-12x^2}} = 2+\frac{1-6x}{\sqrt{x-3x^2}}$$

$$y' \text{ at } x = \frac{1}{12} = 2+\frac{1-\frac{6}{12}}{\sqrt{\frac{1}{12}-\frac{3}{144}}} = 2+\frac{1-\frac{1}{2}}{\sqrt{\frac{1}{12}-\frac{1}{48}}}$$

$$= 2+\frac{\frac{1}{2}}{\sqrt{\frac{1}{16}}} = 2+\frac{\frac{1}{2}}{\frac{1}{4}} = 2+2 = 4.$$

# ACCOUNTANCEY/BOOK KEEPING

1. Match List-I with List-II.

| List-I | List-II |
|---|---|
| (*a*) Excess of purchase consideration over value of net assets | (*i*) Issue Debentures as collateral security |
| (*b*) Excess of net assets over purchase consideration | (*ii*) Goodwill |
| (*c*) Debenture Suspense Account | (*iii*) Issue of Debentures for consideration other than cash |
| (*d*) Assets received against Debentures | (*iv*) Capital Reserve |

Choose the ***correct*** answer from the options given below:

| | (*a*) | (*b*) | (*c*) | (*d*) |
|---|---|---|---|---|
| A. | (*iv*) | (*ii*) | (*i*) | (*iii*) |
| B. | (*ii*) | (*iv*) | (*i*) | (*iii*) |
| C. | (*ii*) | (*iv*) | (*iii*) | (*i*) |
| D. | (*iv*) | (*ii*) | (*iii*) | (*i*) |

2. Which among the following are the non-cash items?
(*a*) Deferred Tax
(*b*) Goodwill write-off
(*c*) Depreciation
(*d*) Increase in Stock

Choose the ***correct*** answer from the options given below:
A. (*b*) and (*c*) only
B. (*a*), (*b*) and (*d*) only
C. (*b*), (*c*) and (*d*) only
D. (*a*), (*b*) and (*c*) only

3. Operating Profit Ratio of XYZ Ltd. is 60%. The operating ratio of XYZ Ltd. is:
A. 30% B. 60%
C. 100% D. 40%

4. Which among the following are the modes of dissolution?
(*a*) Dissolution by Nature
(*b*) Compulsory Dissolution
(*c*) Dissolution by Agreement
(*d*) Dissolution by Notice

Choose the ***correct*** answer from the options given below:
A. (*b*), (*c*) and (*d*) only B. (*a*), (*c*) and (*d*) only
C. (*a*), (*b*) and (*c*) only D. (*a*), (*d*) and (*b*) only

5. In the absence of any information regarding the acquisition of share in the profit of retiring/deceased partner by the remaining partners, it is assumed that they will acquire his/her share in the:
A. Capital Ratio
B. Equal Ratio
C. New Profit Sharing Ratio
D. Old Profit Sharing Ratio

6. Extract of Receipt and Payment Account for the year ended on March 31, 2021 is given.
Calculate the amount of Stationery to be shown in Income and Expenditure A/c.
Payments for Stationery: ₹ 23,000
Additional Information:

| | 1 April, 2020 | 31 March, 2021 |
|---|---|---|
| Stock of Stationary | 4,000 | 3,000 |
| Creditors for Stationery | 9,000 | 2,500 |

A. ₹ 17,500 B. ₹ 20,500
C. ₹ 11,500 D. ₹ 23,000

7. ______ is the amount received as per the will of a deceased person.
A. Honorarium B. Entrance Fees
C. Donation D. Legacies

8. From the following information of I Ltd., calculate Net Increase/Decrease in cash and cash equivalents during the year 2021-22.
(*i*) Cash flow from Operating Activities: ₹ 2,35,000
(*ii*) Cash used in investing Activities: ₹ 4,35,000
(*iii*) Cash flow from financing activities: ₹ 2,35,000
A. ₹ 35,000 Decrease
B. ₹ 4,35,000 Decrease
C. ₹ 4,70,000 Increase
D. ₹ 35,000 Increase

9. Blue Prints Ltd. purchased a building worth ₹ 1,50,000, Machinery worth ₹ 1,40,000 and Furniture worth ₹ 10,000 from XYZ Co. and took over its liabilities of ₹ 20,000 for a purchase consideration of ₹ 3,15,000. Calculate the Goodwill/Capital Reserve to be recorded by Blue Print Ltd.
A. ₹ 35,000 Capital Reserve
B. ₹ 35,000 Goodwill
C. ₹ 3,15,000 Goodwill
D. ₹ 55,000 Goodwill

10. The Directors of Tivoli Plastics Ltd. resolved that 200 equity shares of ₹ 100 each be Forfeited of non-

payment of the second and final call of ₹ 30 per share. Out of these, 150 shares were reissued at ₹ 60 per share as fully paid-up. How much amount will be transferred to Capital Reserve Account?

A. ₹ 10,500 B. ₹ 4,500
C. ₹ 6,000 D. ₹ 8,000

**11.** On 1/4/22, X and Y decided to dissolve their firm. On that date of dissolution, Goodwill appeared at ₹ 5,00,000 in the Balance Sheet. Goodwill will be:

A. Transferred to the debit side of realisation A/c
B. Transferred to the credit side of partner's Capital A/c in their profit sharing ratio
C. Transferred to the credit side of realisation A/c
D. Transferred to cash account

**12.** From the following information, calculate interest on Capital of C, a partner for the year ended 31st March, 2022.

C's Capital on 31/3/2022: ₹ 12,00,000
Profit credited to C for the year ended 31/3/2022: ₹ 3,00,000
Drawings made during the year: ₹ 1,00,000
Additional Capital introduced on 1/10/21: ₹ 5,00,000
Rate of Interest = 12% p.a

A. ₹ 60,000 B. ₹ 1,44,000
C. ₹ 90,000 D. ₹ 1,20,000

**13.** If the total income earned by Saket Club, a Not-for-Profit organisation is ₹ 2,60,000 and surplus earned is ₹ 85,000, then total expenditure incurred will be:

A. ₹ 1,85,000 B. ₹ 1,75,000
C. ₹ 3,45,000 D. ₹ 85,000

**14.** If X share of profit was to be calculated on the basis of Average Profit of the last three years, which were ₹ 1,36,000 for 2018-19, ₹ 1,54,000 for 2019-20 and ₹ 1,00,000 for 2020-21. X share of profit for the period from April 01, 2020 to June 30, 2020 shall be calculated on the basis of Average Profit. The profit sharing ration is 4 : 5 : 1 between X, Y and Z.

His share of profit will be:

A. ₹ 26,000 B. ₹ 13,000
C. ₹ 10,000 D. ₹ 12,000

**15.** Correct sequence of issue of shares is:

(*a*) Receipt of Application
(*b*) Issue of Prospectus
(*c*) Letter of Allotment of Shares
(*d*) Letter of Regret

Choose the ***correct*** answer from the options:

A. (*a*), (*b*), (*c*), (*d*)
B. (*a*), (*b*), (*d*), (*c*)
C. (*b*), (*a*), (*c*), (*d*)
D. (*c*), (*b*), (*a*), (*d*)

**16.** For computing Goodwill by capitalisation of Average Profit method, the following sequence would be followed:

(*a*) Capitalise the average profit on the basis of Normal Rate of Return
(*b*) Ascertain the firm's Capital – Total Assets – Outside Liabilities
(*c*) Ascertain the average profits based on past years' performance
(*d*) Compute the volume of Goodwill

Choose the ***correct*** answer from the options:

A. (*b*), (*c*), (*a*), (*d*) B. (*c*), (*a*), (*b*), (*d*)
C. (*a*), (*b*), (*c*), (*d*) D. (*a*), (*c*), (*b*), (*d*)

**17.** Earning Capacity of a Company is measured by:

A. Working Capital Ratio
B. Profitability Ratio
C. Solvency Ratio
D. Liquidity Ratio

**18.** Separate disclosure of cash flows from _____ activities is important because they represent the extent to which expenditure have been made for resources intended to generate future income and cash flows:

A. Operating B. Investing
C. Financing D. Extraordinary

**19.** In common size statement, if revenue from operations are ₹ 23,00,000 and other incomes are ₹ 3,00,000, then the percentage of "Total Revenue from Operations" to "Revenue from operations" will be:

A. 110% B. 113.04%
C. 12.04% D. 110.04%

**20.** Which A/c is credited transfer of interest on Debenture Redemption Fund Investment?

A. Debenture Redemption Fund A/c
B. Debenture Redemption Fund Investment A/c
C. Bank A/c
D. Statement of P & L

**21.** The directors of a company forfeited 400 equity shares of ₹ 10 each fully called up on which ₹ 1,600 had been paid. All the forfeited shares were reissued upon payment of ₹ 3,000. Calculate the amount transferred to Capital Reserve.

A. ₹ 1,600 B. ₹ 600
C. ₹ 1,400 D. ₹ 2,400

**22.** Raman and Naman were in partnership sharing profit and losses as 3 : 2. Their partnership firm was dissolved on 31 March, 2022. On the date of dissolution, Naman's loan was ₹ 20,000. Naman agreed to take stock (already transferred to Realisation A/c) of ₹ 15,000 at ₹ 18,000 and balance in cash for the settlement of loan. Journal Entry for above transaction is:

A. Naman's Loan A/c Dr. 20,000
To Realisation A/c 18,000
To cash A/c 2,000

B. Naman's Loan A/c Dr. 20,000
To Realisation A/c 15,000
To cash A/c 5,000

C. Naman's Loan A/c Dr. 20,000
To Realisation A/c 20,000

D. Naman's Loan A/c Dr. 20,000
To Realisation A/c 12,000
To cash A/c 8,000

**23.** Calculate the amount of adjusted profit for the year ended 31 March, 2021 for the purpose of valuation of Goodwill from the following information:

Profit for the year ended 31 March, 2021: ₹ 80,000
On 1 July, 2020, a major plant repair was undertaken for ₹ 10,000 which was charged to Revenue. The said sum is to be capitalised for Goodwill valuation subject to adjustment of depreciation @ 10% p.a. on reducing balance method.

A. ₹ 90,000  B. ₹ 89,000
C. ₹ 89,750  D. ₹ 89,250

**24.** Match List-I with List-II.

| *List-I* | *List-II* |
|---|---|
| (*a*) Partner's Salary | (*i*) P & L A/c Dr. |
| (*b*) Manager's Salary | (*ii*) P & L Appropriation A/c Dr. |
| (*c*) Distribution of Loss | (*iii*) P & L A/c Cr. |
| (*d*) Commission Received | (*iv*) P & L Appropriation A/c Cr. |

Choose the ***correct*** answer from the options:

| | (*a*) | (*b*) | (*c*) | (*d*) |
|---|---|---|---|---|
| A. | (*i*) | (*ii*) | (*iii*) | (*iv*) |
| B. | (*ii*) | (*i*) | (*iv*) | (*iii*) |
| C. | (*iii*) | (*ii*) | (*iv*) | (*i*) |
| D. | (*iv*) | (*iii*) | (*ii*) | (*i*) |

**25.** How will you deal with the following items while preparing for the Bombay Women Cricket Club, its Income and Expenditure Account for the year ending 31st March, 2021 and its Balance Sheet, on the same date : Donation for the Pavilion construction ₹ 12,25,000, Expenditure incurred ₹ 10,80,000, Total estimate ₹ 25,00,000.

A. ₹ 1,45,000 to be shown in Liability side of Balance Sheet
B. ₹ 1,45,000 to be shown on the Asset side of the Balance sheet and ₹ 25,00,000 to be shown on Liability side
C. ₹ 12,75,000 to be shown on expenditure side of Income and Expenditure Account
D. ₹ 12,75,000 to be shown on Income side of Income and Expenditure Account

**26.** X Ltd. has a Current Ration of 3.5 : 1 and Quick Ratio of 2 : 1. If excess of current assets over quick assets represented by inventories is ₹ 24,000. Calculate current liabilities.

A. ₹ 16,000  B. ₹ 56,000
C. ₹ 36,000  D. ₹ 32,000

**27.** Comparative Statements are also known as:

A. Dynamic Analysis  B. Horizontal Analysis
C. Vertical Analysis  D. External Analysis

**28.** The company purchased plant with a book value of ₹ 1,90,000 from National Victory Company and agreed to pay via issuing 2000, 10% Debentures of ₹ 100 each at a discount of 5%.
Amount that will be credited to 10% Debenture A/c will be:

A. ₹ 1,90,000  B. ₹ 2,00,000
C. ₹ 2,40,000  D. ₹ 10,000

**29.** Valuation of Goodwill takes place on which of the following occasions:

(*a*) Incorporation of a new business
(*b*) Change in profit sharing ratio
(*c*) Amalgamation of partnership firm
(*d*) Admission of a partner
(*e*) Dissolution of firm or closure of business

Choose the ***correct*** answer from the options:

A. (*a*), (*b*) and (*d*) only
B. (*b*), (*c*) and (*d*) only
C. (*a*), (*c*), (*d*) only
D. (*a*), (*b*), (*e*) only

**30.** Following items are categorised under Operating Activities:

(*a*) Purchase of Goodwill
(*b*) Transfer to General Reserve
(*c*) Issue of fresh shares
(*d*) Gain on sale of machinery

Choose the ***correct*** answer from the options:

A. (*b*) and (*d*) only  B. (*a*) and (*b*) only
C. (*a*) and (*d*) only  D. (*b*) and (*c*) only

**31.** Match List-I with List-II.

| *List-I* | *List-II* |
|---|---|
| (*a*) Liquidity Ratio | (*i*) Proprietary Ratio |
| (*b*) Solvency Ratio | (*ii*) Current Ratio |
| (*c*) Activity Ratio | (*iii*) Earning per share |
| (*d*) Profitability Ratio | (*iv*) Current assets turnover ratio |

Choose the ***correct*** answer from the options:

| | (*a*) | (*b*) | (*c*) | (*d*) |
|---|---|---|---|---|
| A. | (*ii*) | (*i*) | (*iv*) | (*iii*) |
| B. | (*iii*) | (*iv*) | (*i*) | (*ii*) |
| C. | (*i*) | (*ii*) | (*iii*) | (*iv*) |
| D. | (*iii*) | (*ii*) | (*i*) | (*iv*) |

**32.** The money received from applicants to whom no debentures have been allotted will be ______.

A. Refunded
B. Adjusted
C. Used later on
D. Not refunded

**33.** What will be the share of deceased partner, whose ratio was 1/4, if the turnover in year of death till the date of death was ₹ 8,00,000 and in previous year was ₹ 20,00,000? Profit in previous year was ₹ 4,00,000.

A. ₹ 40,000 B. ₹ 13,333
C. ₹ 1,60,000 D. ₹ 1,00,000

**34.** If Amit, a partner, withdrew ₹ 10,000 per month in the end, what will be the amount of interest on drawing if it is calculated @ 8% p.a.?

A. ₹ 9,600 B. ₹ 4,800
C. ₹ 5,200 D. ₹ 4,400

**35.** Match List-I with List-II.

| *List-I* | *List-II* |
|---|---|
| (*a*) Share forfeiture | (*i*) Reserve Capital |
| (*b*) Uncalled Capital | (*ii*) Pro-rata allotment |
| (*c*) Over-subscription | (*iii*) Capital Reserve |
| (*d*) Discount on issue of shares | (*iv*) Reissue of shares |

Choose the ***correct*** answer from the options:

| | (*a*) | (*b*) | (*c*) | (*d*) |
|---|---|---|---|---|
| A. | (*iii*) | (*i*) | (*ii*) | (*iv*) |
| B. | (*iv*) | (*i*) | (*iii*) | (*ii*) |
| C. | (*ii*) | (*iii*) | (*iv*) | (*i*) |
| D. | (*i*) | (*ii*) | (*iv*) | (*iii*) |

**36.** X, Y, Z are partners who decided to dissolve their firm. Realisation expenses were to be borne by Y for which he was to be given remuneration of ₹ 10,000. Actual expenses were ₹ 12,000. How much amount will be transferred to Y's Capital A/c for it?

A. ₹ 22,000 B. ₹ 12,000
C. ₹ 2,000 D. ₹ 10,000

**37.** The default extension of MS Access (2007) file is:

A. .accbd B. .end
C. .doc D. .exe

**38.** Which of the following statement is not correct?

A. A spreadsheet is a configuration of rows and columns
B. A spreadsheet is different from worksheet
C. Spreadsheet application is a computer programme
D. Spread sheet can be used for making Graphs also

**39.** The data that is entered in a cell may be either:

(*a*) Numeric
(*b*) Alpha-Numeric
(*c*) Date
(*d*) Label

Choose the ***correct*** answer from the options:

A. (*c*) and (*d*) only
B. (*a*), (*b*) and (*d*) only
C. (*a*), (*c*) and (*d*) only
D. (*a*), (*b*) and (*c*) only

**40.** The computerised Accounting System refers to:

A. Processing of Balance Sheet only
B. Processing of Accounting related transactions and produce Records and Reports
C. Processing of accounting related data only
D. Printing of Balance Sheet and Profit and Loss Account

**Directions (Qs. No. 41-45):** *Read the following information to answer.*

On the basis of case study given below, answer the question which follows:

"Mikku on alumni of IIT Delhi, initiated his start-up "Gajanan Ltd.", in the year 2016. His profit in the year 2020-21 after all appropriation was ₹ 6,25,000. This profit was arrived after taking following items into consideration:

| | |
|---|---|
| Loss on Sale of Fixed Assets | ₹ 5,00,000 |
| Goodwill written off | ₹ 3,80,000 |
| Transfer to reserve | ₹ 3,55,000 |
| Provision for tax | ₹ 2,70,000 |
| Interest on Debentures paid | ₹ 1,65,000 |

Other Details are:

| Partculars | 2020 (in ₹) | 2021 (in ₹) |
|---|---|---|
| Prepaid Expenses | 25,000 | 10,000 |
| Accrued interest | 40,000 | 68,000 |
| Trade payables | 7,00,000 | 4,00,000 |
| Inventories | 6,50,000 | 5,50,000 |

**41.** Net profit before tax will be ₹ ______.

A. ₹ 9,80,000 B. ₹ 8,95,000
C. ₹ 12,50,000 D. ₹ 16,30,000

**42.** Operating Profit before working capital changes will be ₹ ______.

A. 22,95,000 B. 20,95,000
C. 23,95,000 D. 12,95,000

**43.** From among the following, choose the item which would be mentioned in financing activity also:

A. Provision for tax
B. Interest on Debenture
C. Goodwill written off
D. Loss on sale of fixed assets

**44.** Cash from operating activities before tax will be ₹ ___.

A. 27,38,000 B. 26,82,000
C. 23,78,000 D. 28,62,000

**45.** Cash flow from Operating Activities will be ₹ ______.
A. 30,72,000
B. 29,52,000
C. 26,82,000
D. 24,12,000

**Directions (Qs. No. 46-50):** *Read the following information to answer.*

Arun and Ram are partners in a restaurant business sharing profits and losses in capital ratio. Their fixed capital from the beginning of the firm was ₹ 2,00,000 and ₹ 1,50,000 respectively.

The profit for the year ended 31 March, 2022 before the appropriation of Salary and Interest on Capital was ₹ 2,20,000. Ram is allowed a salary of ₹ 2,000 per quarter and interest on capital @ 10 % p.a.

Due to the further expansion of the business, they decided to enter Sanjeev as a new partner for 1/5 share in profits. It was agreed that Sanjeev will bring ₹ 1,00,000 as capital and ₹ 50,000 as his share of Goodwill. It was decided that he will give ₹ 1,00,000 as loan to the firm for 3 years.

**46.** The amount of salary to be shown in the Dr. side of P & L Appropriation A/c will be:
A. ₹ 2,000
B. ₹ 8,000
C. ₹ 12,000
D. ₹ 24,000

**47.** Interest on capital will be shown on the Dr. side of Profit and Loss Appropriation A/c and ______ side of Partner's ______ A/c.
A. Cr, Capital
B. Dr, Current
C. Cr, Current
D. Dr, Capital

**48.** Rate of Interest on loan given by Sanjeev will be:
A. 8% P.A.
B. 10% P.A.
C. NIL
D. 6% P.A.

**49.** The amount of distributed profits of both the partner's will be:
A. ₹ 1,77,000
B. ₹ 2,20,000
C. ₹ 1,71,000
D. ₹ 2,00,000

**50.** The new profit sharing ratio of Arun, Ram and Sanjeev will be:
A. 1 : 1 : 1
B. 14 : 10 : 6
C. 16 : 12 : 7
D. 3 : 2 : 1

## ANSWERS

**1. (B):** Goodwill is an intangible asset that arises when one company purchases another for a premium value. Any excess of the amount of purchase consideration over the value of net assets of the transferor company acquired by the transferee company should be recognised as goodwill in the financial statements of Transferee Company.

Excess value of net assets over purchase consideration at the time of purchase of business is credited to capital reserve.

Debenture Suspense Account is a temporary account prepared by an entity to record the transaction of debenture when such an entity issues or agrees to issue a certain amount worth debentures as collateral security.

Generally, debentures are issued for cash. But, sometimes debentures can be issued for non-cash considerations. It may happen that a company has acquired any other company or purchased some assets from a vendor and then instead of paying by cash, the company has opted to settle the payment by issuing debentures to the vendors.

**2. (D):** Non-cash items are referred to as those entries on a cash flow statement or income statement that do not involve actual cash transactions. In other words, these are expenses that are listed in an income statement that do not involve cash payment. Examples of non-cash items include depreciation, amortization, deferred income tax, Goodwill write-off, stock based compensation that is provided to employees.

**3. (D):** Operating Ratio + Operating Profit Ratio = 100%

OR

Operating Profit Ratio = 100% – Operating Ratio
60% = 100% – Operating Ratio
Operating Ratio = 100% – 60% = 40%.

**4. (A):** Dissolution of partnership refers to a change in the existing relations among the various partners of a firm. It is noteworthy that such a change in the partners' relationship does not have any impact on the firm.

Modes of Dissolution of a Partnership Firm

**A. Voluntary Dissolution:** • By Agreement • Compulsory Dissolution • On the happening of certain contingencies • By notice of partnership at will

**B. Dissolution by Court Order:** •Insanity/Unsound Mind • Permanent Incapacity • Misconduct • Persistent Breach of the Agreement • Continuous/Perpetual Losses • Just and Equitable Grounds.

**5. (D):** As per Indian Partnership Act 1932, in the absence of any information regarding the acquisition of share in profit of the retiring/deceased partner by the remaining partners. It is assumed that they will acquires his/her shares in the old profit-sharing ratio.

**6. (A):** Statement of Medicine Consumed during the year 2020-21

| Expenditure | Amt |
|---|---|
| Stationery consumed: | |
| Purchases of Stationery during the year 2020-21 | 23000 |
| Add : Stock in the beginning | 4000 |
| Less : Stock at the end | (3000) |
| Add : Creditors at the end | 2500 |
| Less : Creditors in the beginning | (9000) |
| **Amount of Stationery be shown in Income and Expenditure Account** | 17,500 |

**7. (D):** Property received as a result of the will of the deceased person is called legacy.

**8. (D):** Cash Flow Statement

| Particulars | Amount (₹) |
|---|---|
| Cash flow from Operating Activities | 2,35,000 |
| Cash used in investing Activities | (4,35,000) |
| Cash flow from financing activities | 2,35,000 |
| Net (Increase) | 35,000 |

**9. (B):** Books of Blue Prints Limited

Journal

| Particulars | | L.F. | Dr. | Cr. |
|---|---|---|---|---|
| Building A/c | Dr. | | 1,50,000 | |
| Plant & Machinery A/c | Dr. | | 1,40,000 | |
| Furniture A/c | Dr. | | 10,000 | |
| Goodwill A/c* | Dr. | | 35,000 | |
| To Liabilities | | | | 20,000 |
| To XYZ Co | | | | 3,15,000 |
| (Purchase of assets and taking over of liabilities of XYZ Co.) | | | | |

** Since the purchase consideration is more than net assets taken over, the difference has been debited to goodwill account.*

**10. (B):**

Journal

| Particulars | | L.F. | Dr. | Cr. |
|---|---|---|---|---|
| Share Capital A/c | Dr. | | 20,000 | |
| To Forfeited Shares A/c | | | | 14,000 |
| To Share Second and Final Call A/c | | | | 6,000 |
| (200 shares forfeited for non-payment of final call at ₹ 30 per share) | | | | |
| Bank A/c | Dr. | | 9,000 | |
| Share Forfeiture A/c | Dr. | | 6,000 | |
| To Share Capital A/c | | | | 15,000 |
| (Reissue of 150 shares of ₹ 100 each, issued as fully paid for ₹ 60 each) | | | | |
| Share Forfeiture A/c | Dr. | | 4,500 | |
| To Capital Reserve A/c | | | | 4,500 |
| (Profit on reissue of 150 forfeited shares transferred to capital reserve) | | | | |

Working Notes: (₹)

- Total amount forfeited on 200 shares
  = 14,000 (200 shares ₹ 70)
- Amount forfeited on 150 shares
  = 10,500 (150 shares ₹ 70)
- Amount forfeited on 50 shares
  = 3,500 (50 shares ₹ 70)
- Amount of discount on reissue of 150 shares
  = 6,000 (150 shares ₹ 40)
- Amount of profit on reissued shares transferred to capital reserve = 4,500 (₹ 10,500 – ₹ 6,000)
- Balance left in share forfeited account
  = 4,500 (₹ 14,000 – ₹ 6,000)
  (equal to amount forfeited on 50 shares) – ₹ 3,500

**11. (A):** Treatment of goodwill is very easy in case of dissolution of a firm. In case, if goodwill is already appearing in the balance sheet, it is treated like any other asset, and is transferred to the realisation account at the value given in balance sheet. Following entry is passed for it.

Realisation A/c    Dr.
To Goodwill A/c

**12. (C):** Capital on 31/3/2022 = 12,00,000
Profit = 3,00,000
Drawings = 1,00,000
Add capital = 5,00,000
Rate of interest = 12% p.a
Interest amount?

Opening capital = Closing capital – Profit + Drawings – Add. capital
= 12,00,000 – 3,00,000 + 1,00,000 – 5,00,000
Opening cap. = 5,00,000

Int. on opening capital for 12 months

$$= \frac{12}{100} \times 5,00,000 = 60,000$$

Int. on add capital for 6 months

$$= \left[12\% \times \frac{6}{12} \text{ of } 5,00,000\right]$$

$$= \left[\frac{12}{100} \times \frac{6}{12} \times 5,00,000\right] = 30,000$$

Total interest = 60,000 + 30,000 = 90,000.

**13. (B):** Income – Expenditure = Surplus
2,60,000 – Expenditure = 85,000
2,60,000 – 85,000 = Expenditure
1,75,000 = Expenditure.

**14. (B):** Average Profit = Total profit of last 3 years/ number of years
= (1,36,000 + 1,54,000 + 1,00,000)/3 = 1,30,000
The profit sharing ration is 4 : 5 : 1 between X, Y and Z.

Z's annual share = (1,30,000 × 4)/10 = 52,000
Z's share for 3 months (April 01, 2020 to June 30, 2020) = (52000/12) × 3 = 13,000.

**15. (C):** Steps in issue of shares:
- appoint a manager for the purpose of issue of shares.
- issue of a prospectus
- application money is received
- minimum subscription is disclosed
- allotted securities are listed under a stock exchange.

**16. (B):** Steps in computing Goodwill by Capitalisation of Average Profits:
- Ascertain the average profits based on the past few years' performance.
- Capitalize the average profits on the basis of the normal rate of return to ascertain capitalised value of average profits
- Ascertain the actual capital employed (net assets) by deducting outside liabilities from the total assets
- Compute the value of goodwill by deducting net assets from the capitalised value of average profits.

**17. (B): Earning Capacity of a Company:**
- Working Capital Ratio is a measure of liquidity, meaning the business's ability to meet its payment obligations as they fall due.
- Profitability ratios assess a company's ability to earn profits from its sales or operations, balance sheet assets, or shareholders' equity. Profitability ratios indicate how efficiently a company generates profit and value for shareholders.
- Solvency ratio indicates whether a company's cash flow is sufficient to meet its long-term liabilities and thus is a measure of its financial health.
- A liquidity helps determine if a company can use its current, or liquid, assets to cover its current liabilities.

**18. (B):** Separate disclosure of cash flows from investing activities is important because they represent the extent to which expenditures have been made for resources intended to generate future income and cash flows.

**19. (B):** Total Revenue from Operations = Revenue from operations + Revenue from other incomes
= 23,00,000 + 3,00,00 = 26,00,000

Percentage of "Total Revenue from Operations" to "Revenue from operations" = Total Revenue from Operations/Revenue from operations × 100
= (26,00,000/23,00,00) × 100 = 113.04%.

**20. (D):** P & L A/c is credited transfer of interest on Debenture Redemption Fund Investment.

**21. (C):**

**Journal**

| Particulars | | L.F. | Dr. | Cr. |
|---|---|---|---|---|
| Share Capital A/c | Dr. | | 4,000 | |
| To Share Call A/c | | | | 1,600 |
| To Share forfeiture A/c | | | | 2,400 |
| (Forfeit of 400 equity shares.) | | | | |
| Bank A/c | Dr. | | 3,000 | |
| Share Forfeiture A/c | Dr. | | 1,000 | |
| To Share Capital A/c | | | | 4,000 |
| Share Forfeiture A/c | Dr. | | 1,400 | |
| To Capital Reserve A/c | | | | 1,400 |
| (Balance left in Share Forfeiture A/c, i.e., ₹ 2,400 – ₹ 1,000 = ₹ 1,400 transferred to Capital Reserve A/c) | | | | |

**22. (A):** Naman's Loan A/c Dr. 20,000
To Realisation A/c 18,000
To cash A/c 2,000.

**23. (B):** Profits = 80,000
Add: Repairs to Plant Capitalised = 10,000
Less: Depreciation @10% W.D.V = 1,000
Net Profit = ₹ 89,000.

**24. (B)**

**25. (A):** Books of Bombay Women Cricket Club
Balance Sheet as on March 31, 2021

| Liabilities | | Amount (₹) | Assets | Amount (₹) |
|---|---|---|---|---|
| Donation for Pavilion | 1225000 | | Construction of Pavilion in Progress | 1080000 |
| Less: Exp. on construction of Pavilion | (1080000) | 145000 | | |
| Add: Pavilion Construction | 1080000 | 1080000 | | |

**Reason**
- Donation for construction of Pavilion is a donation for specific purpose.
- Expenses on construction on Pavilion is a capital expenditure.

**26. (B):** Current Ratio = 3.5 : 1
Quick Ratio = 2 : 1
Let Current Liabilities = $x$
Current Assets = $3.5x$ and
Quick Assets = $2x$
Inventory = Current Assets – Quick Assets
24,000 = $3.5x - 2x = 1.5x$
$x$ = ₹ 16,000
Current Assets = $3.5x$ = 3.5 × ₹ 16,000
= ₹ 56,000.

**27. (B):** Comparative statements are the form of horizontal analysis. Common size statement shows the profitability and financial position of a firm for different periods of time in a comparative form to give an idea about position of two or more periods.

**28. (B):** Book value of plant 1,90,000

Issued 2000, 10% Debentures of ₹ 100 each at a discount of 5%

| Journal | | | | |
|---|---|---|---|---|
| Particulars | | L.F. | Dr. | Cr. |
| Vendor A/c | Dr. | | 1,90,000 | |
| Discount A/c | Dr. | | 10,000 | |
| To 10% debentures | | | | 2,00,000 |
| (Issue of 2,000 debentures of ₹ 100 each at 5% discount) calculated as follows: 2000 × 100 × 0.5 = 10,000 | | | | |

**29. (B):** Goodwill is one of the special aspects of partnership accounts which requires adjustment at the time of reconstitution of a firm, i.e., a change in the profit-sharing ratio, the admission of a partner or the retirement or death of a partner. The need for valuation of goodwill arises at the time of sale of a business. But goodwill may also arise in the following circumstances under partnership firm:

- Change in the profit-sharing ratio amongst the existing partners
- Admission of new partner
- Retirement of a partner
- Death of a partner
- Amalgamation of partnership firms

**30. (A):** Operating activities are the daily activities of a company involved in producing and selling its product, generating revenues, as well as general administrative and maintenance activities. Key operating activities for a company include manufacturing, sales, advertising, and marketing activities.

| | |
|---|---|
| Purchase of Goodwill | Investing Activity |
| Transfer to General Reserve | Operating Activity |
| Issue of Fresh shares | Financing Activities |
| Gain on sale of Machinery | Operating Activity |

**31. (A):** Types of Ratios

**Liquidity Ratios:** Current Ratio, Quick Ratio.

**Solvency Ratios:** Debt to Equity Ratio, Debt Ratio, Proprietary Ratio or Equity Ratio, Interest Coverage Ratio

**Activity Ratio:** Stock Turnover ratio or Inventory Turnover Ratio, Debtors Turnover ratio or Accounts Receivable Turnover Ratio, Creditors Turnover ratio or Accounts Payable Turnover Ratio, Working Capital turnover ratio, Investment Turnover Ratio

**Profitability Ratio:** Gross Profit Ratio, Operating Ratio, Operating Profit Ratio, Net Profit Ratio, Return on Investment (ROI), Return on Net Worth, Earnings per share, Book Value per share, Dividend Payout Ratio, Price Earnings Ratio

**32. (A):** The money received from applicants to whom no debentures have been allotted will be *Refunded.*

**33. (A):** In previous year, on a turnover of ₹ 20,00,000, profit was = 4,00,000

In the year of death, on a turnover of ₹ 8,00,000, profit would be = (4,00,000/20,00,000) × 8,00,000

= 1,60,000

Share of deceased partner = ¼ of 1,60,000 = 40,000.

**34. (A):** Total Drawings every month = 10,000

Total Drawings in the year = ₹ 1,20,000

Rate of Interest = 8% p.a.

Interest on Drawings = 1,20,000 × 8/100 = 9,600.

**35. (A):** When a company re-issues only a part of the forfeited shares, then it will transfer only the profit relating to this part to the capital reserve. When a company re-issues shares at a price more than their face value, it needs to transfer the excess amount to the Securities Premium A/c.

Reserve capital is a part of uncalled capital as uncalled capital represents the amount of share that is not called from the public.

A company may receive applications for shares more than the number of shares it has offered to the public. This is known as over-subscription of shares. At times of over-subscription of shares at a premium, sometimes a company adjusts the excess money by making pro-rata allotment.

When forfeited shares are originally issued at discount are reissued then discount allowed at the time of original issue is again applicable. On reissue of shares, the discount on issue of shares account is debited by the original discount amount.

**36. (D):** In this case, following journal entry would be made:

Realisation A/c Dr. 10,000

To Y's Capital A/c 10,000

Thus, 10,000 will be transferred to Y's Capital A/c.

**37. (A):**

| | **Default Extensions** |
|---|---|
| Access 2007 | .accbd |
| Arrow-Head Definition Table | .end |
| Word Documents | .doc |
| Excel files | .exe |

**38. (B):** A spreadsheet is a configuration of rows and columns. Rows are horizontal vectors while columns are vertical vectors. It is used to record, calculate and compare numerical or financial data. Each value can either be an independent (i.e. basic) value or it may be derived on the basis of values of other variables. The derived value is the outcome of an arithmetic expression and/or a function (i.e. a formula). Spreadsheet application (sometimes referred to simply as spreadsheet) is a computer program that allows us to add (i.e. enter) and process data. We shall understand spreadsheet with the help of MS-Excel (or simply, Excel), which is one of the Microsoft Office Suite of software. A spreadsheet is also known as a worksheet.

**39. (D):** The data that is entered in a cell may be either numeric or alpha-numeric or a date. As a data is typed in a cell, Excel is able to make out its type (i.e. numeric or alpha-numeric or date) depending on the nature of value typed in a cell.

**40. (B):** The Computerised Accounting System takes accounting transactions as inputs and processes them to generate journals, ledgers, trial balance and final accounts. Computerised Accounting System carries out all the function of manual accounting using a computer's hardware and software. It takes accounting transactions as input and processes it to produce reports and accounting information for the internal and external users.

**41. (C):** Net profit before Tax = Profit after all Appropriations + Provision for taxation + Transfer to General reserve

Net profit before Tax = 6,25,000 + 2,70,000 + 3,55,000

Net profit before Tax = 12,50,000.

**42. (A):**

**Cash Flow Statement**

| Particulars | Amount | Amount |
|---|---|---|
| Cash Flow from Operating Activities | | |
| Net Profit Before Taxation and Extraordinary Items | | 12,50,000 |
| Items to be Added: | | |
| Loss on Sale of fixed Assets | 5,00,000 | |
| Interest on Borrowings | 1,65,000 | |
| Goodwill Amortized | 3,80,000 | |
| Operating Profit before Working Capital Adjustments | | 22,95,000 |

**43. (B)**

**44. (B):** Cash from operating activities before tax = Operating Profit before Working Capital Adjustments + Decrease in Current Assets (Prepaid Expenses, Inventories) – Decrease in Current Liabilities (Trade Payables) – Increase in Current Assets (Prepaid Expenses, Inventories, Trade Receivables) + Increase in Current Liabilities

= 22,95,000 + 15,000 + 1,00,000 – 28,000 + 3,00,000

= 26,82,000.

**45. (D):** Cash flow from Operating Activities = Cash from operating activities before tax + Provision for tax

= 26,28,000 – 2,70,000 = 24,12,000.

**46. (B):** Ram is allowed a salary of 2,000 per quarter. Hence, the amount of salary to be shown in the Dr. side of P & L Appropriation A/c will be:

₹ 2,000 × 4 = ₹ 8,000.

**47. (A):** Interest on capital is an expense to the firm and is debited to the profit and loss appropriation account. Interest is payable to the partners and hence, the partner's capital account is credited with the amount of interest. In case of loss, no interest will be allowed on capital.

**48. (C):** Sanjeev was not entitled for interest on capital. Thus, Rate of Interest on loan given by Sanjeev will be nil.

**49. (A):** The profit for the year ended 31 March, 2022 before the appropriation of Salary and Interest on Capital = 2,20,000; Gross Profit = 2,20,000

Deductions, Interest on capital at 10% p.a.

= 10% of 3,50,000 = 35,000

Salary to Ram = 8,000

Thus, the amount of distributed profit of both the partner's = 2,20,000 – 35,000 – 8,000 = 1,77,000.

**50. (C):** Total Profit = 1, Sanjeev's share = 1/5

Remaining share = 1 – 1/5 = 4/5

Arun's Old Share = 4/7

Arun's New Share = 4/5 × 4/7 = 16/35

Ram's Old Share = 3/7

Ram's New Share = 4/5 × 3/7 = 12/35

Sanjeev's Share = 1/5 × 7/7 = 7/35

Thus, the new profit-sharing ratio of Arun, Ram and Sanjeev will be 16 : 12 : 7.

# GENERAL TEST

**1.** Who got the Major Dhyan Chand Khel Ratna Award 2021 for his excellent performance in cricket?

A. Mithali Raj  B. Shikhar Dhawan
C. Virat Kohli  D. M.S. Dhoni

**2.** UNESCO has added this festival to its 2021 list of Intangible Cultural Heritage:

A. Durga Puja  B. Diwali
C. Holi  D. Kali Puja

**3.** Which mission has been renamed as Pradhan Mantri Digital health Mission (PM-DHM)?

A. Ayushman Bharat
B. Awaz Health Insurance Scheme
C. Aam Aadmi Bima Yojna
D. National Digital Health Mission (NDHM)

**4.** The theme of 'Shikshak' Parv-2021 was:

A. Quality and Sustainable Schools: Learning from schools in India
B. Learning Outcomes
C. Quality Teachers for Quality Education
D. Holistic Development

**5.** Light Combat Helicopters (LCH) are developed by:

A. Bharat Electronics
B. Defence Research and Development Organisation
C. Hindustan Aeronautics Limited
D. Bharat Dynamics

**6.** Out of the alternatives choose the most appropriate description about the three given words.

Bangle : Anklet : Necklace

A. These are Games product
B. These are jewellery
C. These are metals
D. These are Stationery items

**7.** From the following pairs select the combination of right pair from the following options.

(*a*) Kuwait : Taka  (*b*) Greece : Dinnar
(*c*) Argentina : Peso  (*d*) Bangladesh : Taka
(*e*) Sweden : Krona

Choose the correct answer from the options given below.

A. (*c*), (*d*), (*e*)  B. (*a*), (*b*), (*c*)
C. (*b*), (*c*), (*d*)  D. (*a*), (*d*), (*e*)

**8.** Arrange the given words in the sequence in which they occur in the dictionary.

(*a*) Firmament  (*b*) Finish
(*c*) First  (*d*) Fissure
(*e*) Fiscal

Choose the correct answer from the options given below:

A. (*b*), (*c*), (*d*), (*a*), (*e*)  B. (*a*), (*b*), (*c*), (*d*), (*e*)
C. (*b*), (*a*), (*c*), (*e*), (*d*)  D. (*e*), (*a*), (*b*), (*c*), (*d*)

**9.** Match List-I with List-II:

| *List-I* | *List-II* |
|---|---|
| (*a*) Ellora caves | (*i*) Jaipur |
| (*b*) Amer Fort | (*ii*) Agra |
| (*c*) Golden Temple | (*iii*) Aurangabad |
| (*d*) Taj Mahal | (*iv*) Amritsar |

Choose the correct answer from the options given below:

| | (*a*) | (*b*) | (*c*) | (*d*) |
|---|---|---|---|---|
| A. | (*i*) | (*iii*) | (*iv*) | (*ii*) |
| B. | (*iii*) | (*i*) | (*iv*) | (*ii*) |
| C. | (*iv*) | (*iii*) | (*i*) | (*ii*) |
| D. | (*iii*) | (*iv*) | (*i*) | (*ii*) |

**10.** Match List-I with List-II.

| *List-I* (*River*) | *List-II* (*Continents*) |
|---|---|
| (*a*) Nile | (*i*) North America |
| (*b*) Mississippi | (*ii*) South America |
| (*c*) Ganga | (*iii*) Africa |
| (*d*) Amazon | (*iv*) India |

Choose the correct answer from the options given below:

| | (*a*) | (*b*) | (*c*) | (*d*) |
|---|---|---|---|---|
| A. | (*iii*) | (*i*) | (*iv*) | (*ii*) |
| B. | (*iii*) | (*ii*) | (*iv*) | (*i*) |
| C. | (*i*) | (*iii*) | (*iv*) | (*ii*) |
| D. | (*iii*) | (*iv*) | (*ii*) | (*i*) |

**11.** Among the four options given below three have similarities find the odd one out.

A. Scurvy  B. Influenza
C. Beri Beri  D. Rickets

**12.** Match List-I with List-II.

| *List-I* | *List-II* |
|---|---|
| (*a*) Saina Nehwal | (*i*) Boxing |
| (*b*) Mary Kom | (*ii*) Wrestling |
| (*c*) Mithali Raj | (*iii*) Badminton |
| (*d*) Geeta Phogat | (*iv*) Cricket |

Choose the correct answer from the options given below:

| | (*a*) | (*b*) | (*c*) | (*d*) |
|---|---|---|---|---|
| A. | (*iii*) | (*i*) | (*iv*) | (*ii*) |
| B. | (*iii*) | (*i*) | (*ii*) | (*iv*) |
| C. | (*iv*) | (*i*) | (*ii*) | (*iii*) |
| D. | (*iii*) | (*ii*) | (*iv*) | (*i*) |

**13.** Match List-I with List-II.

| *List-I* | *List-II* |
|---|---|
| (*a*) Hepatitis | (*i*) Blood |
| (*b*) Pneumonia | (*ii*) Joints |
| (*c*) Arthritis | (*iii*) Liver |
| (*d*) Thalassemia | (*iv*) Lungs |

Choose the correct answer from the options given below:

| | (*a*) | (*b*) | (*c*) | (*d*) |
|---|---|---|---|---|
| A. | (*iii*) | (*iv*) | (*ii*) | (*i*) |
| B. | (*iii*) | (*i*) | (*ii*) | (*iv*) |
| C. | (*iv*) | (*iii*) | (*i*) | (*ii*) |
| D. | (*ii*) | (*iii*) | (*iv*) | (*i*) |

**14.** In the following questions arrange the given words in the sequence that occur in the dictionary.

(*a*) Whiter (*b*) Wound
(*c*) Writer (*d*) Worked
(*e*) Worst

Choose the correct answer from the options given below:

A. (*a*), (*d*), (*b*), (*e*), (*c*) B. (*a*), (*d*), (*e*), (*b*), (*c*)
C. (*d*), (*a*), (*b*), (*e*), (*c*) D. (*d*), (*a*), (*e*), (*b*), (*c*)

**15.** Among the four options, three have the same property. Find the odd one out.

A. Mole Hills B. Nilgiri Hills
C. Aravali Hills D. Shivalik Hills

**16.** Which of the following is a leap year?

A. 1500 B. 700
C. 1300 D. 2000

**17.** Which one of the following diagram represents Automobile, Cars, Motorcycle?

A.  B. 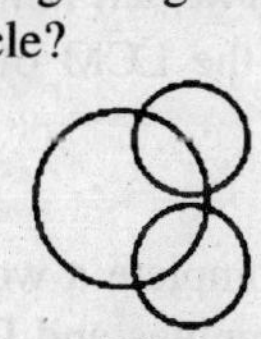

C. 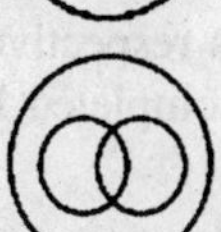 D. 

**18.** In the given questions select the related word from the alternatives.

Horse : Jockey : Car ______

A. Brake B. Chauffeur
C. Seatbelt D. Steering

**19.** Among the four options given below three have similar properties. Find the odd one out:

A. Ginger B. Beetroot
C. Carrot D. Cabbage

**20.** Monu rides his bicycle north wards, then turned left and rides one km and again turned left and rides 2 km. Monu found himself exactly one km west of his starting point. How far did he ride north wards initially?

A. 5 km B. 2 km
C. 3 km D. 4 km

**21.** Which among the following is the biggest planet of our solar system?

A. Saturn B. Jupiter
C. Mars D. Venus

**22.** From the given option which word can't be formed from the letters given in:

"PERMANENT"

A. MENTOR B. TRAMP
C. AMPERE D. REMANT

**23.** Arrange the following words as they occur in the english.

(*a*) Explosive (*b*) Explicit
(*c*) Exponent (*d*) Exposition
(*e*) Explore

Choose the correct answer from the options given below:

A. (*b*), (*e*), (*c*), (*a*), (*d*) B. (*e*), (*b*), (*c*), (*a*), (*d*)
C. (*e*), (*b*), (*a*), (*c*), (*d*) D. (*b*), (*e*), (*a*), (*c*), (*d*)

**24.** What is meaningful/logical order of the words given below?

(*a*) Type (*b*) Save
(*c*) Open (*d*) Print
(*e*) Close

Choose the correct answer from the options given below:

A. (*c*), (*a*), (*d*), (*b*), (*e*) B. (*a*), (*c*), (*b*), (*d*), (*e*)
C. (*c*), (*a*), (*b*), (*d*), (*e*) D. (*a*), (*c*), (*d*), (*b*), (*e*)

**25.** The pH value of human's urine in human is about:

A. 2.5 B. 4.0
C. 6.0 D. 9.0

**26.** HEAVY can be coded as 8, 5, 1, 22, 25, then LIGHT will be coded as.

A. 12, 7, 9, 8, 20 B. 12, 9, 7, 8, 20
C. 7, 8, 9, 12, 20 D. 9, 7, 8, 12, 20

**27.** Who is known as the 'Father of Green Revolution' in India?

A. Verghese Kurien B. M.S. Swaminathan
C. Dr. Lalji Singh D. Dr. Balram Jakhad

**28.** Justice is always related to ______.

A. Deceit B. Just
C. Generosity D. Nobility

**29.** In Rigveda, the river Jhelum is known as:

A. Sutridri B. Parushini
C. Vitasta D. Asikni

**30.** A person is going towards north in the night and he sees Dhruv tara and sees it on his left side. Which of the following statements justify the fact?

A. Always B. Sometimes
C. Generally D. Never

**31.** The first Indian women Fighter Pilot to fly a fighter jet is:
A. Avani Chaturvedi B. Gunjan Saxena
C. Shubhangi Swaroop D. Bhawana Kanth

**32.** Match List-I with List-II.

| ***List-I*** | ***List-II*** |
|---|---|
| (*a*) Pedology | (*i*) Study of muscles |
| (*b*) Pisciculture | (*ii*) Study of growing old |
| (*c*) Myology | (*iii*) Study of soils |
| (*d*) Gerontology | (*iv*) Study of fish |

Choose the correct answer from the options given below:

| | (*a*) | (*b*) | (*c*) | (*d*) |
|---|---|---|---|---|
| A. | (*ii*) | (*iv*) | (*iii*) | (*i*) |
| B. | (*ii*) | (*iii*) | (*i*) | (*iv*) |
| C. | (*iv*) | (*ii*) | (*i*) | (*iii*) |
| D. | (*iii*) | (*iv*) | (*i*) | (*ii*) |

**33.** The interest earned on ₹ 25000 in 5 years at simple interest is ₹ 1500. What is the rate of interest?
A. 1.1% B. 1.2%
C. 1.4% D. 1.6%

**34.** Given that $a : b = 5 : 3$ and $b : c = 2 : 5$

Which of the following is true?
A. $a < b < c$ B. $b < c < a$
C. $b < a < c$ D. $a < c < b$

**35.** Arrange the given ratios in descending order.
(*a*) 7 : 15 (*b*) 15 : 23
(*c*) 17 : 25 (*d*) 21 : 39

Choose the correct answer from the options given below:
A. (*c*) > (*a*) > (*b*) > (*d*) B. (*a*) > (*d*) > (*c*) > (*b*)
C. (*c*) > (*b*) > (*d*) > (*a*) D. (*d*) > (*a*) > (*b*) > (*c*)

**36.** A is younger than B by 7 years. If their ages are in the respective ratio of 7 : 9 then how old is A?
A. 31.5 years B. 16.5 years
C. 24.5 years D. 18.5 years

**37.** Match List-I with List-II.

| ***List-I*** | ***List-II*** |
|---|---|
| (*a*) First country to use Glass | (*i*) New Zealand |
| (*b*) First country to make Written Constitution | (*ii*) Russia |
| (*c*) First country to do Artificial Satellite Experiment | (*iii*) USA |
| (*d*) First Country to impose Carbon Tax | (*iv*) Egypt |

Choose the correct answer from the options given below:

| | (*a*) | (*b*) | (*c*) | (*d*) |
|---|---|---|---|---|
| A. | (*iv*) | (*iii*) | (*ii*) | (*i*) |
| B. | (*iii*) | (*iv*) | (*i*) | (*ii*) |
| C. | (*ii*) | (*i*) | (*iii*) | (*iv*) |
| D. | (*i*) | (*ii*) | (*iv*) | (*iii*) |

**38.** The average of 3 odd consecutive numbers is 15. What is the sum of first and last numbers?
A. 30 B. 20
C. 40 D. 35

**39.** In the formula "W = Fs cos θ", the angle between force and displacement (θ) is equal to 90°, the net work done will be:
A. Double B. Positive but not double
C. Negative D. Zero

**40.** What is the value of 70% of 420 + 30% of 280?
A. 284 B. 268
C. 368 D. 378

**41.** 2.56 expressed as a per cent of 1.6 is:
A. 16% B. 25%
C. 160% D. 90%

**42.** P can do a work in 12 days. Q can do the same work in 10 days. If P and Q come together, both of them can complete the same work in how many days?
A. $2\frac{2}{11}$ days B. $3\frac{3}{11}$ days
C. $5\frac{5}{11}$ days D. $4\frac{4}{11}$ days

**43.** $\frac{3}{4}$ part of tank is filled by a motor pump in 15 minutes, then the rest part of the tank will be filled in.
A. 3.5 minutes B. 5 minutes
C. 8 minutes D. 20 minutes

**44.** The ratio of two numbers is 5 : 6 and their HCF is 8. What is the LCM of these numbers?
A. 180 B. 240
C. 280 D. 140

**45.** A can complete a work in 4 minutes. B in 5 minutes, C in 6 minutes and D in 10 minutes respectively. The average number of units of work completed by them per minute will be:
A. 0.789 B. 0.179
C. 0.501 D. 0.800

**46.** The value of 2 ÷ 2 – 2.
A. 1 B. –1
C. 0 D. $\frac{1}{2}$

**47.** The network in the graphical area spread over countries, is known as:
A. LAN B. VAN
C. MAN D. WAN

**48.** A chair is sold for ₹ 96 at 20% loss. The cost price of the chair is:
A. ₹ 120 B. ₹ 80
C. ₹ 115.20 D. ₹ 76.80

**49.** The value of $\frac{(8.9)^2 - (2.1)^2}{8.9 - 2.1}$

A. 8.6 B. 6.8

C. 10.0 D. 11.0

**50.** The value of $\left(\frac{x}{y}\right)^{2a-3b} \times \left(\frac{x}{y}\right)^{3b-4c} \times \left(\frac{x}{y}\right)^{4c-2a}$.

A. $\frac{x}{y}$ B. 1

C. 0 D. $\left(\frac{x}{y}\right)^{2a+3b+4c}$

**51.** In parallelogram ABCD, angle A is greater than angle B by 10°, the measure of angle D is:

A. 95° B. 75°

C. 85° D. 65°

**52.** If the length of diagonals of a rhombus are 10 cm and 24 cm then the side of the rhombus is:

A. 26 cm B. 24 cm

C. 13 cm D. 12 cm

**53.** In the figure AOB is a straight line then the value of $x$ is:

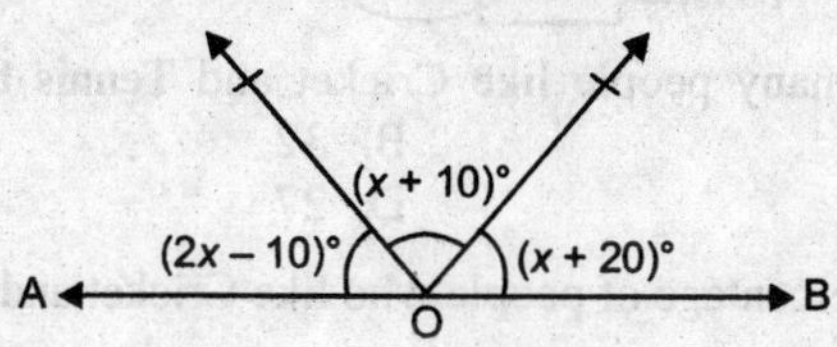


A. 60 B. 50

C. 40 D. 70

**54.** How much time, the Constituent Assembly took to complete the Constitution?

A. 02 years, 11 months and 18 days

B. 02 years, 18 months and 11 days

C. 03 years, 11 months and 18 days

D. 03 years, 18 months and 11 days

**Directions (Qs. No. 55-57):** *In the given figure ABCD is a square and radius of semi circle is 7 cm.*

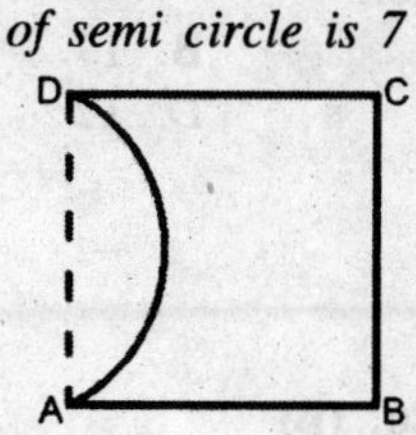


On the basis of the above information answer the questions.

**55.** The side of the square is:

A. $\frac{7}{2}$ cm B. 7 cm

C. 14 cm D. 12 cm

**56.** The perimeter of the figure is:

A. 42 cm B. 20 cm

C. 86 cm D. 64 cm

**57.** Area of the figure is:

A. 119 $cm^2$ B. 273 $cm^2$

C. 350 $cm^2$ D. 42 $cm^2$

**Directions (Qs. No. 58-60):** *The marks of 5 students in a unit test are given below:*

$x - 1, 2x + 1, 2x - 2, x - 1, 2x + 3$ where $x = 5$.

On the basis of above information answer the questions.

**58.** The mode of data in numerals is:

A. 11 B. 13

C. 4 D. 8

**59.** The median of data in numerals is:

A. 11 B. 4

C. 8 D. 13

**60.** The mean of the data in numerals is:

A. 4 B. 8

C. 13 D. 11

**61.** Some dens are rooms. All rooms are walls. Some walls are bricks. All bricks are plates.

(*a*) Some plates are walls

(*b*) Some walls are dens

(*c*) Some bricks are rooms

(*d*) Some plates are rooms

Choose the correct answer from the options given below:

A. (*a*) and (*c*) only B. (*b*) and (*c*) only

C. (*a*) and (*b*) only D. (*c*) and (*d*) only

**62.** If A means '–', B means '÷', C means '+' and D means '×', then 45B3C18A4D6 = ?

A. 179 B. 9

C. 18 D. 152

**63.** What will be next figure of the series?

A. 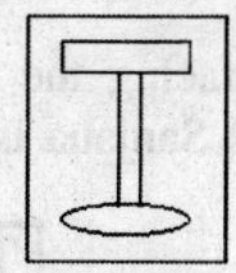 B. 

C.  D. 

**64.** Find the next figure of given series:

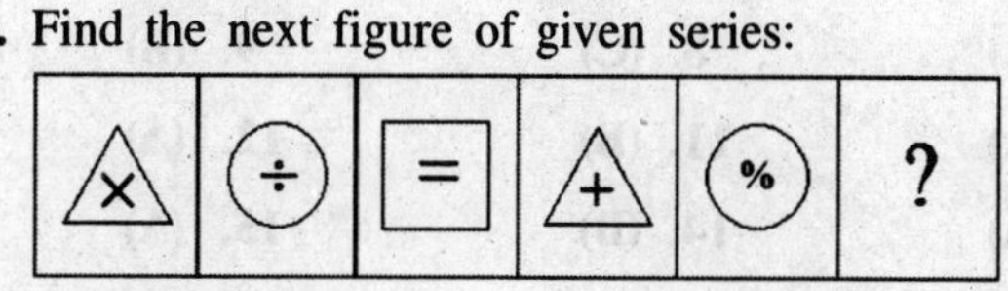

A.  B. 

C. 

D. 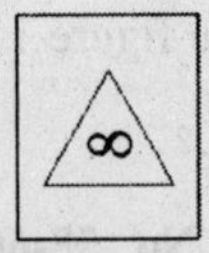

**65.** Find the next item of given series.

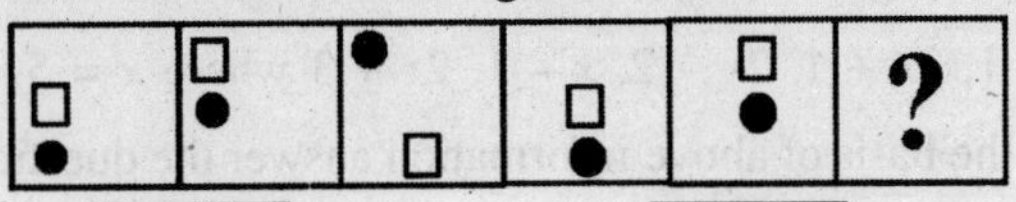

A. 

B. 

C. 

D. 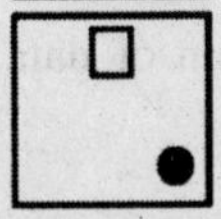

**66.** Out of the four alternatives choose the most appropriate description about the given words.

Sarnath : Kapilvastu : Sanchi

A. There are places having massive pillars
B. These are linked with lord Buddha
C. These are famous for stone caves
D. These have ancient Universities

**67.** A meaningful word starting with A is made from the first, the second, the fourth, the fifth and the sixth letters of the word 'CONTRACT'. Which of the following is the middle letter of the word?

A. T  B. O
C. C  D. R

**68.** Find the missing number from the following given option:

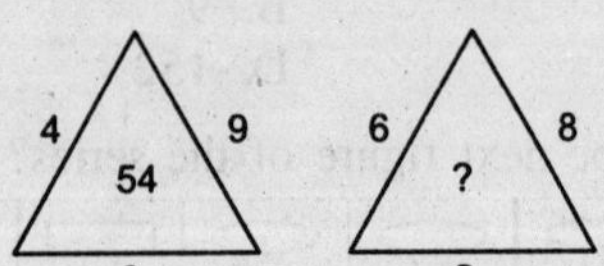


A. 72  B. 17
C. 10  D. 26

**69.** Forty girls are standing in a row facing the North. Amita is eleventh from left end and Sanjana is thirty first from the right end of the row. How for will Smita, who is third to the right to Amita in the row, be from Sanjana?

A. 3rd  B. 4th
C. 2nd  D. 5th

**70.** Find the missing number from the following given options.

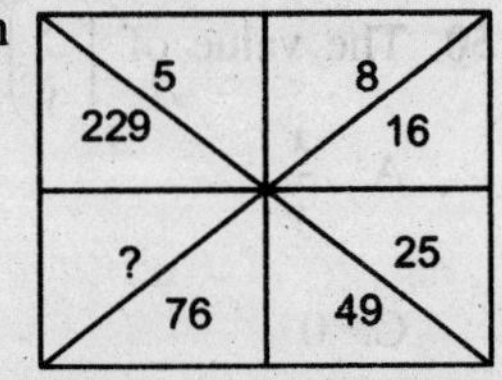


A. 150
B. 53
C. 125
D. 148

**71.** Among the options given below three have similarities. Find the odd one out.

A. Rice  B. Wheat
C. Chick peas  D. Corn

**Directions (Qs. No. 72-75):** *Read details carefully for questions.*

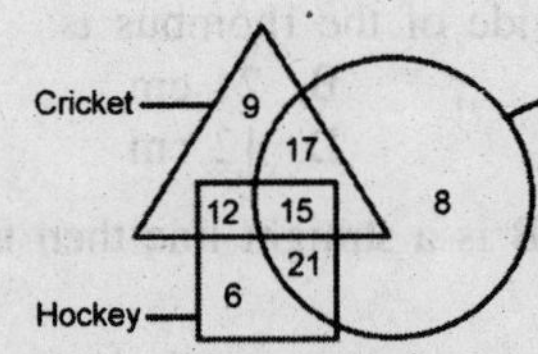


**72.** How many people like Cricket and Tennis both?

A. 17  B. 32
C. 15  D. 27

**73.** The percentage of people who like Cricket and Hockey both is ______.

A. 36.36%  B. 30.68%
C. 33.3%  D. 42.04%

**74.** Let C, H and T represents number of people who likes Cricket, Hockey and Tennis respectively. The ratio of C : H : T is:

A. 53 : 54 : 61  B. 61 : 54 : 53
C. 54 : 53 : 61  D. 54 : 61 : 53

**75.** How many people like Cricket, Tennis and Hockey games all together.

A. 21  B. 17
C. 15  D. 12

## ANSWERS

**1.** (A) **2.** (A) **3.** (D)
**4.** (A) **5.** (C) **6.** (*)
**7.** (A) **8.** (C) **9.** (B)
**10.** (A) **11.** (B) **12.** (A)
**13.** (A) **14.** (B) **15.** (A)
**16.** (D) **17.** (A) **18.** (D)
**19.** (D) **20.** (B) **21.** (B)
**22.** (A) **23.** (D) **24.** (C)
**25.** (C) **26.** (B) **27.** (B)
**28.** (*) **29.** (C) **30.** (*)
**31.** (A) **32.** (D)

**33.** **(B):** Rate of interest $= \frac{SI \times 100}{P \times t}$

$$= \frac{1500 \times 100}{25000 \times 5}$$

$$= \frac{6}{5} = 1.2\%.$$

**34. (C):** $a : b = 5 : 3$ and $b : c = 2 : 5$

$$a : b : c = 5 \times 2 : 3 \times 2 : 3 \times 5 = 10 : 6 : 15$$

$\therefore b < a < c$ is true.

**35. (C):** $\frac{7}{15} = 0.466$

$\frac{15}{23} = 0.652$

$\frac{17}{25} = 0.68$

$\frac{21}{39} = 0.538$

$\therefore \frac{17}{25}, \frac{15}{23}, \frac{21}{39}, \frac{7}{15}$ are is descending order.

Hence, (*c*) > (*b*) > (*d*) > (*a*).

**36. (C):** Let B's age $= x$ years

$\therefore$ A's age $= x - 7$ years

$$\frac{x-7}{x} = \frac{7}{9}$$

$\Rightarrow 9x - 63 = 7x$

$\Rightarrow 2x = 63$

$\Rightarrow x = \frac{63}{2} = 31.5$

$\therefore$ A's age $= 31.5 - 7 = 24.5$ years.

**37. (A)**

**38. (A):** Let three odd consecutive numbers are $x$, $x + 2$ and $x + 4$

$x + x + 2 + x + 4 = 15 \times 3$

$\Rightarrow 3x + 6 = 45$

$\Rightarrow 3x = 39 \Rightarrow x = 13$

$\therefore$ first no. = 13, last number = 13 + 4 = 17

$\therefore$ Sum of first no. and last no. = 13 + 17 = 30.

**39. (D):** W = Fs cos 90°

W = 0

$\therefore$ The net work done will be zero.

**40. (D):** 70% of 420 + 30% of 280

$$= \frac{70}{100} \times 420 + \frac{30}{100} \times 280 = 294 + 84 = 378.$$

**41. (C):** 2.56 = 1.6% of $x$

$\Rightarrow \frac{256}{100} = \frac{16x}{1000}$

$\Rightarrow x = \frac{256 \times 10}{16} = 160\%.$

**42. (C):** P's 1 day work $= \frac{1}{12}$

Q's 1 day work $= \frac{1}{10}$

(P + Q)'s 1 day work $= \frac{1}{12} + \frac{1}{10} = \frac{5+6}{60} = \frac{11}{60}$

$\therefore$ (P + Q) can do whole work $= \frac{60}{11} = 5\frac{5}{11}$ days.

**43. (B):** $\frac{3}{4}$ part of tank is filled in 15 minutes

$\therefore \frac{1}{4}$ part of tank is filled in $\frac{15 \times 4}{3} \times \frac{1}{4} = 5$ minutes.

**44. (B):** Let numbers are $5x$ and $6x$

HCF of $5x$ and $6x = x$

$\therefore x = 8$ [HCF = 8 given]

$\therefore$ Numbers are 40 and 48

$$\text{LCM} = \frac{40 \times 48}{8} = 40 \times 6 = 240.$$

**45. (B):** (A + B + C + D)'s 1 minute work

$$= \frac{1}{4} + \frac{1}{5} + \frac{1}{6} + \frac{1}{10} = \frac{15+12+10+6}{60} = \frac{43}{60}$$

$\therefore$ The average no. of units of work

$$= \frac{43}{60 \times 4} = \frac{43}{240} = 0.179.$$

**46. (B):** $2 \div 2 - 2 = 1 - 2 = -1.$

**47. (*)**

**48. (A):** Let C.P. = ₹ 100

Loss $= \frac{20}{100} \times 100 =$ ₹ 20

S.P. = 100 − 20 = ₹ 80

When S.P. ₹ 80 then C.P. = ₹ 100

When S.P. ₹ 96 then C.P. = ₹ $\frac{100}{80} \times 96$

$\therefore$ CP = ₹ 120.

**49. (D):** $\frac{(8.9)^2 - (2.1)^2}{8.9 - 2.1} = \frac{(8.9+2.1)(8.9-2.1)}{(8.9-2.1)} = 8.9 + 2.1 = 11.0.$

**50. (B):** $\left(\frac{x}{y}\right)^{2a-3b} \times \left(\frac{x}{y}\right)^{3b-4c} \times \left(\frac{x}{y}\right)^{4c-2a}$

$$= \left(\frac{x}{y}\right)^{2a-3b+3b-4c+4c-2a} = \left(\frac{x}{y}\right)^0 = 1.$$

**51. (C):**

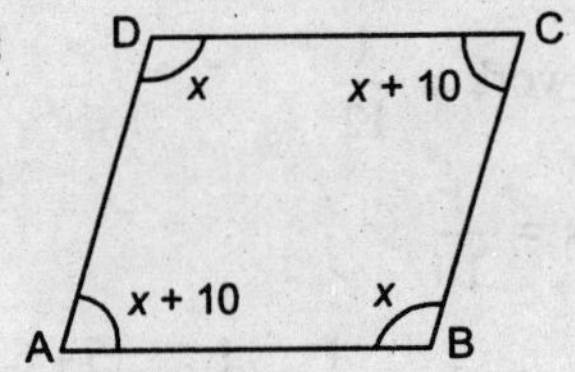


$\because$ ABCD is a ||gm

Let $\angle B = x°$

$\therefore$ $\angle A = (x + 10)°$

$\angle A + \angle B + \angle C + \angle D = 360°$

$\Rightarrow x + 10° + x + x + 10 + x = 360°$

$\Rightarrow$ $4x + 20° = 360°$

$\Rightarrow$ $4x = 340°$

$\Rightarrow$ $x = 85°$

$\therefore$ $\angle D = 85°$.

**52. (C):**

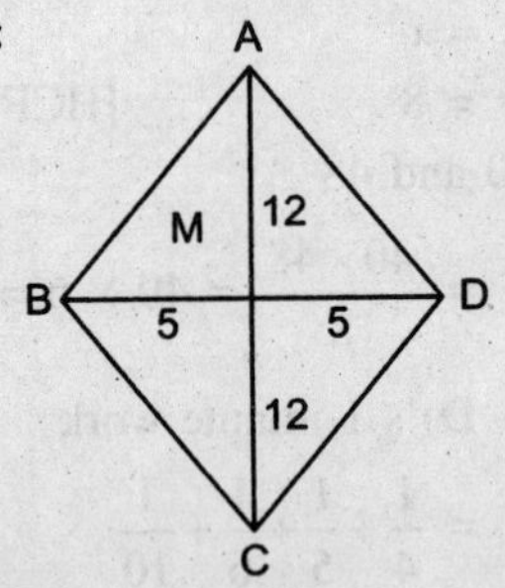


ABCD is a rhombus

In $\Delta ABM$,

$$(AB)^2 = (12)^2 + (5)^2 = 144 + 25 = 169$$

$\Rightarrow$ $AB = 13$ cm

Hence, the side of rhombus = 13 cm.

**53. (C):**

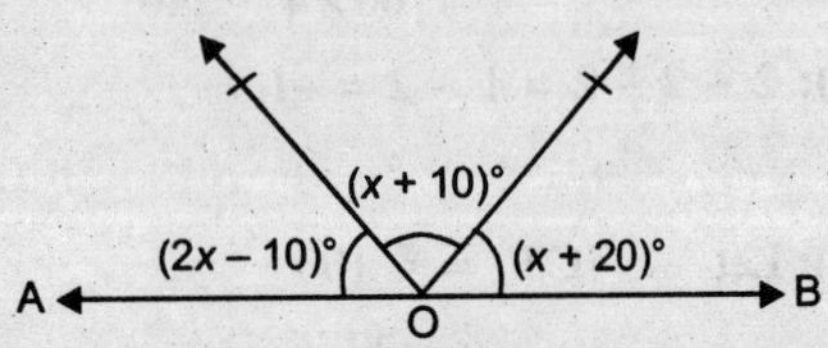


In the given figure, AOB is a straight line

$\therefore (2x - 10)° + (x + 10)° + (x + 20)° = 180°$

$\Rightarrow$ $4x + 20° = 180°$

$\Rightarrow$ $4x = 180° - 20° = 160°$

$\Rightarrow$ $x = 40°$.

**54. (A)**

**55. (C):** $\because$ Radius of semi circle = 7 cm

$\therefore$ Side of the square = 7 × 2 = 14 cm.

**56. (D)**

**57. (A):** Area of the figure = 119 cm$^2$.

**58. (C):** $x - 1,\ 2x - 1,\ 2x - 2,\ x - 1,\ 2x + 3$

$\because$ $x = 5$, then obtained marks are,

4, 9, 8, 4, 13

Mode of data = 4.

**59. (C):** First write the data in ascending order,

4, 4, 8, 9, 13

Here $n = 5$ which is odd

$\therefore$ median $= \dfrac{n+1}{2}$ th term

$= \dfrac{6}{2}$ th term

= 3rd term = 8

Hence, median = 8.

**60. (B):** Mean $= \dfrac{4+4+8+9+13}{5} = \dfrac{38}{5} = 7.6 = 8.$

**61. (C)**

**62. (B):** 'A' means –, 'B' means ÷, 'C' means +, 'D' means ×

$45 \div 3 + 18 - 4 \times 6$

$= 15 + 18 - 24 = 33 - 24 = 9.$

**63. (A)** **64. (C)** **65. (B)**

**66. (B)** **67. (A)**

**68. (A):**

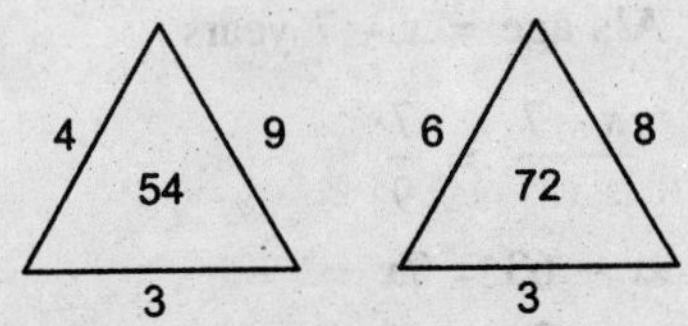


$4 \times 3 \times 9 \div 2 = 108 \div 2 = 54$

$6 \times 3 \times 8 \div 2 = 144 \div 2 = 72$

Hence, 72 will come at the place of question mark.

**69. (B)**

**70. (D):**

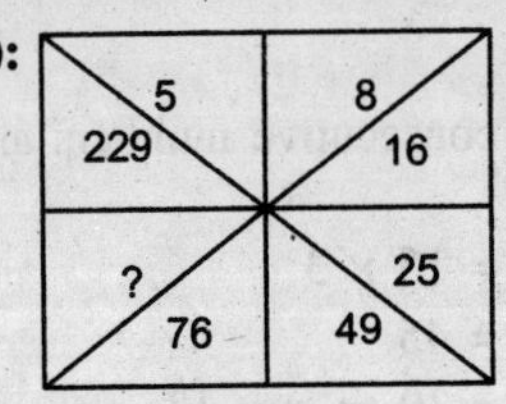


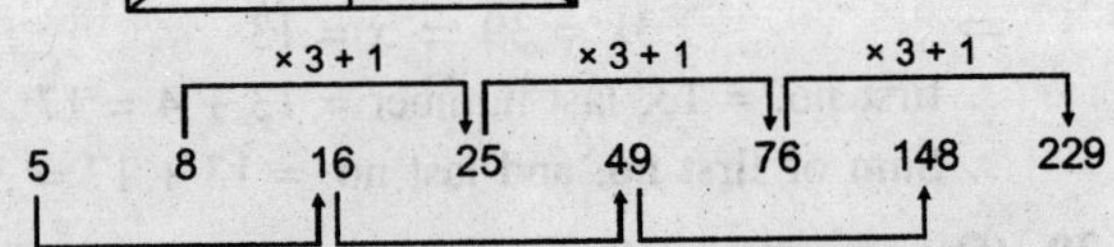


Hence, 148 will come at the place of question mark.

**71. (C)**

**72. (B):** 32 people like Cricket and Tennis both.

**73. (B):** Required % = 30.68%

**74. (A):** No. of people who likes Cricket

= 27 + 26 = 53

No. of people who likes Hockey = 27 + 27 = 54

No. of people who likes Tennis = 32 + 29 = 61

The ratio of C : H : T = 53 : 54 : 61.

**75. (C):** No. of people who likes Cricket, Tennis and Hockey all together = 15 which is common in all.

# CUET-UG

## SECTION-IA

# ENGLISH LANGUAGE

# Comprehension

Comprehension is a very important part of English paper. The questions on comprehension lay particular stress on understanding a given passage. You are required to read a passage or poem and answer a few questions based on it. Various comprehension questions are set solely with the objectives named below:

1. To test your ability to detect the central idea or the focal point in the given passage.
2. To test your ability to understand and interpret the given passage or poem.
3. To judge your capability to pick out the various arguments put forward by the writer for or against something.
4. To test your accuracy and richness of vocabulary.
5. To test your academic ability to understand the implied and the clearly and fully expressed ideas of the writer of the passage or poem.
6. To test, occasionally, your power of appreciating critically the views contained in the given passage or poem.

While answering comprehension questions, you must comply with the following important points:

1. First, read the whole passage or poem attentively, carefully and quickly.
2. Read it for the second time, slowly but steadily.
3. Work out the probable meaning of new words, from the context in which they have been used.
4. Underline and look for transitional words and phrases as an aid to comprehension.
5. The process of elimination should be used while selecting the correct answer.
6. Your answers should be brief and to the point, where-ever required.

## I. CLOZE TEST

A cloze test is a procedure in which a person is asked to supply words that have been removed from a passage as a test of his ability to comprehend text. Practise it regularly to score well.

**Directions:** *In each of the following passages some numbered blank spaces are given. For each numbered blank space answer choices are given. Pick out the one which is the most appropriate for that blank space. Keep the trend of the passage in mind.*

### PASSAGE-1

A drug which has been ....(1).... promoted here for fever and pain ....(2).... has invited medical ....(3).... over its ....(4).... side-effects following adverse reactions and its ....(5).... withdrawal in certain European countries. The scientific advisory committee has issued a ....(6).... advice on the ....(7).... of the drug ....(8).... some serious ....(9).... in the liver. While most doctors in India ....(10).... there is not need to ....(11).... yet, they also admit that they ....(12).... ....(13).... about it as most studies on the drug are industry ....(14).... .

### QUESTIONS

**1.** A. aggressively B. astonishingly C. surprisingly D. immensely

**2.** A. treatment B. relief C. cure D. removal

**3.** A. concern B. criticism C. discussion D. debate

**4.** A. probable B. probably C. possible D. possibly

**5.** A. unconditional B. immediate C. consequent D. subsequent

**6.** A. precautionary B. preliminary C. formal D. informal

7. A. sell B. purchase
C. recommendation D. marketing

8. A. reminding B. following
C. thinking D. caring

9. A. complications B. problem
C. complexity D. consequences

10. A. suggest B. insist
C. lay D. say

11. A. worry B. react
C. panic D. exorbitant

12. A. think B. know
C. knew D. known

13. A. a bit B. a little
C. a few D. little

14. A. based B. sponsored
C. surveyed D. experimented

## PASSAGE-2

I believe the biggest challenge ....(1).... the world is that of ....(2).... poverty across a large ....(3).... of the ....(4).... population and the continued ....(5).... between the rich and poor nations. The globalisation ....(6).... of the Nineties was ....(7).... to change all that and it has not made a significant impact as yet. Indeed, poverty today is the single biggest ....(8).... of place and democracy. It is high time that even the most ....(9).... rich citizen or indeed all of us ....(10).... people, realise that the only way to ....(11).... prosperity is to defeat poverty.

### QUESTIONS

1. A. confronting B. facing
C. spoiling D. destroying

2. A. acute B. continued
C. general D. common

3. A. proportion B. share
C. portion D. fraction

4. A. universal B. en bloc
C. entire D. global

5. A. disputation B. disparity
C. discrimination D. tensile

6. A. struggle B. efforts
C. wave D. air

7. A. considered B. perpetually
C. supposed D. perhaps

8. A. curse B. enemy
C. hurdle D. obstruction

9. A. complacent B. compliant
C. fatuous D. inconsiderate

10. A. well-to-do B. cultured
C. privileged D. developed

11. A. defend B. debilitate
C. protect D. save

## PASSAGE-3

What the daily newspapers nowadays ....(1).... carry are the reports of ...(2).... murders, killings, genocides and ....(3).... cleansing all over the world. India is not an exception ...(4).... For a moment one is sure ....(5).... the principle of religious tolerance, peace and ....(6)...., which were the ....(7).... of Indian society, that are now slowly but steadily ....(8).... hatred, anger, disgust and religious intolerance. Making things worse are the divisive practices being ....(9).... by some ....(10).... minds that have led to the rise of religious fundamentalism. And this is a ....(11)...., which is ....(12)..... in the form of hundreds of innocent lives being lost in all corners of the country.

### QUESTIONS

1. A. usually B. generally
C. regularly D. casually

2. A. huge B. massive
C. brutal D. mass

3. A. ethnic B. ethical
C. evasive D. eventual

4. A. to it B. in it
C. for it D. on it

5. A. of thinking
B. to think about
C. to think of
D. thinking about

6. A. conscientious B. compassion
C. rapacity D. sagacity

7. A. heart B. core
C. cornerstones D. milestones

8. A. are replaced with
B. replaced by
C. being replaced by
D. being replaced with

9. A. precluded B. precipitated
C. predisposed D. fabricated

10. A. perverted B. scrupulous
C. nefarious D. ruthless

11. A. calumny B. bane
C. crass D. denouncement

12. A. visible B. coming
C. taking its toll D. resulting its toll.

## PASSAGE-4

The outstanding ....(1).... of the development of science and technology can neither be realised nor enriched in an atmosphere with disturbed ....(2).... balance, ....(3).... to pollution hazards. The ....(4).... of pollution and conservation of the natural ecosystems in all the development efforts are ....(5).... not merely for the growth of our ....(6).... but for our very existence on this earth. It demands the ....(7)... that it deserves. Although ....(8).... is expressed in various circles for ....(9).... the environmental balance and ....(10).... of forests, but at the same time there is a large scale ....(11).... of forests, as ....(12).... evidenced in several river valley projects ....(13).... at the national level.

### QUESTIONS

**1.** A. capacity B. potential
C. possibility D. advancement

**2.** A. economical B. natural
C. ecological D. polluting

**3.** A. susceptible B. adversely
C. salubrious D. pernicious

**4.** A. removal B. eradication
C. discarding D. evolution

**5.** A. imperil B. imminent
C. impulsive D. imperative

**6.** A. status B. sociability
C. economy D. environment

**7.** A. importance B. attention
C. value D. care

**8.** A. interest B. enthusiasm
C. deep concern D. anxiety

**9.** A. maintaining B. evolving
C. developing D. rising

**10.** A. growing B. maintaining
C. maintenance D. regeneration

**11.** A. degeneration B. degradation
C. deprivation D. dereliction

**12.** A. blatantly B. vitally
C. vividly D. indiscreetly

**13.** A. executed B. planned
C. organised D. undertaken

## PASSAGE-5

India is a country where women ....(1).... worshipped and ....(2).... at the same time. If mantras have been chanted to ....(3)... the Goddesses, ....(4).... have also been hurled at a domestic wife questioning her devotion and ....(5)..... Their position has remained more or less the same ....(6).... . Though women have taken ....(7).... since the country achieved independence, they still are a ....(8).... of political, socio-economic and legal neglect. The current year has seen a number of government ....(9).... to empower women. Though these are ....(10)...., much will depend on the ....(11).... implementation of these schemes or else they ....(12).... achieve the targets, they have set for themselves.

### QUESTIONS

**1.** A. are B. were
C. has been D. have been

**2.** A. cursed B. blamed
C. crucified D. insulted

**3.** A. placate B. please
C. plead D. respect

**4.** A. curses B. expletives
C. obscenity D. objurgation

**5.** A. virginity B. purity
C. chastity D. fecundity

**6.** A. till date
B. over time
C. till now
D. until now.

**7.** A. remarkable progress
B. advancement
C. rapid strides
D. important steps

**8.** A. object B. subject
C. matter D. victim

**9.** A. machinery B. initiatives
C. project D. plannings

**10.** A. laudable B. languor
C. lascivious D. lassitude

**11.** A. efficient B. thorough
C. appropriate D. effective

**12.** A. would not B. should not
C. will not D. cannot

## PASSAGE-6

We are ....(1).... about our success and failure in every field. No doubt, we start our actions with ....(2).... but still in a corner of our mind ....(3).... about success and failure and ....(4).... makes us tense. And this tension sometimes ....(5).... that it effects our efficiency and performance. So, we ....(6).... remember that the mind is efficient ....(7).... it is cool, not hot or tense. The tease or excited mind ....(8).... produce rational concepts or ....(9).... thought processes. A calm person has his senses fully ....(10).... with the environment ....(11).... he places himself. A restless person ....(12).... notice anything, consequently he gets into trouble with himself and others and ....(13).... everything.

### QUESTIONS

1. A. always worried B. anxious always
   C. curious always D. in doubt-always
2. A. over-confidence B. full confidence
   C. full enthusiasm D. full effort
3. A. a doubt remains still
   B. remains a doubt
   C. still remians a doubt
   D. a doubt still remains
4. A. intentionally B. unnecessarily
   C. necessarily D. unconsciously
5. A. become so intense
   B. grow so much
   C. become so intensive
   D. become so serious
6. A. must B. have to
   C. will have to D. shall have to
7. A. when B. when only
   C. only then when D. only when
8. A. can never B. could not
   C. connot D. possibly
9. A. obnoxious B. obligatory
   C. objective D. orderly
10. A. engrossed B. paralleled
    C. identified D. sunk
11. A. on which B. in which
    C. at which D. where
12. A. do not B. does not
    C. did not D. cannot

## PASSAGE-7

Great books do not spring from something ....(1).... in the great men who wrote them. They are the ....(2).... of their very core, the ....(3).... of the life itself of the authors. And literature cannot be said to ....(4).... its true purpose. Until it ....(5).... translated into the actual life of him who reads. Literature is the ....(6).... of true ideas and high emotions and life is ....(7).... of ideas and emotions. In a world ....(8).... of literature, the intellectual and emotional activity of all ....(9)... exceptionally gifted men would quickly sink and ....(10).... to a narrow circle. The broad, the noble, the generous would tend to disappear ....(11).... accessible storage. And life would be ....(12).... degraded, because the ....(13).... idea and the pretty emotion would never feel the upward pull of the ideas and emotions of genius.

### QUESTIONS

1. A. accidental B. remarkable
   C. strange D. superficial
2. A. affluence B. effluence
   C. excellence D. magnificence
3. A. outcome B. offspring
   C. flow D. expression
4. A. have served B. done
   C. achieve D. accomplished
5. A. is B. has been
   C. gets D. has
6. A. store B. stock
   C. vast reservoir D. huge collection
7. A. expression B. expansion
   C. storage D. constituted
8. A. devout B. devolve
   C. deterrent D. deprived
9. A. but few B. except
   C. but a few D. people
10. A. die B. spoil
    C. dissolve D. retract
11. A. for want of B. desiring
    C. searching D. for
12. A. altogether B. correspondingly
    C. contrarily D. actually
13. A. beautiful B. ornamental
    C. stupid D. fallacious

## PASSAGE-8

Patriotism is one of the qualities that touches the heart of the ....(1).... countrymen. When a soldier fights and dies in saving his country from the enemy, his sacrifice in this way is termed as ....(2).... and attains the ....(3).... worthy of worship. Thus in a war the soldier gets ....(4).... without surrendering, by which he ....(5).... saved his life, ....(6).... the hearts of his fellow being. This situation is true not only in ....(7).... an enemy but anyone who struggles to acheive a ....(8).... aim without surrendering and ....(9).... his life. He ....(10).... succeeded but he leaves a ....(11).... for others to follow who will definitely win and attain the victory ....(12).... the adversaries..

### QUESTIONS

1. A. humble B. rustic
   C. fellow D. sophisticated
2. A. intelligent B. virtuous
   C. supreme D. courageous

3. A. death B. martyrdom
C. end D. goal

4. A. vanquished B. vanguard
C. reward D. award

5. A. would have had B. would be able to
C. would have D. could have

6. A. attracting B. winning
C. taking D. getting

7. A. struggling B. killing
C. winning D. fighting

8. A. esteemed B. high
C. patriotic D. laudable

9. A. offers B. sacrifices
C. lays D. present

10. A. could have B. could not have
C. may have D. may not have

11. A. trail B. trial
C. goal D. situation

12. A. upon B. over
C. on D. against

## PASSAGE-9

Our beautiful sunbright ....(1).... is being systematically damaged by industrial pollution ....(2).... into rivers like the Ganga and Jamuna, ....(3).... wastes from atomic plants ....(4).... into-the world's oceans, and poisonous gases ....(5).... with the ozonosphere. ....(6)...., tropical rain forests and green pastures are ....(7).... under the pressure of a ....(8).... population. Rivers like the Narmada are being dammed to change nature's ....(9).... surface ....(10).... between flora and fauna, and sloping mountain terrain is being ....(11).... into mini oceans to supply electricity to the ....(12).... industrial stomach of our age.

### QUESTIONS

1. A. ecology
B. ecosystem
C. environment
D. physical phenomena

2. A. directed B. channelled
C. scattered D. accumulated

3. A. atomic B. scientific
C. nuclear D. bumptious

4. A. diverted B. routed
C. outstretched D. overflown

5. A. channelled B. routed
C. scattered D. mixed

6. A. Besides B. Instead
C. Addition to D. Above all

7. A. diminishing B. reducing
C. minimising D. disappearing

8. A. proliferating B. profiting
C. projecting D. pronounceable

9. A. smooth B. well balanced
C. rough D. unequal

10. A. equilibrium B. equality
C. equation D. equity

11. A. contracted B. convulsed
C. conjured D. converted

12. A. hungry B. greedy
C. vacant D. ever starving

## PASSAGE-10

Only ....(1)...., people find a long journey by motor-car ....(2)... . Mostly a long journey by train is much more comfortable and ....(3).... . The tracks, the coaches and the smooth though swift motion ....(4).... the pleasantness of the train journey. ....(5).... at the beautiful countryside from a window seat in a fast moving train has a ....(6).... of its own. A night journey ....(7).... its pleasures too. One can experience a sense of adventure ....(8).... a restful sleep. Modern railway travel being ....(9)... comfortable than in the past, ....(10).... the childhood excitement of ....(11).... the train and its engine as ....(12).... of visual and imaginative delight.

### QUESTIONS

1. A. exceptionally B. ordinarily
C. unusually D. abnormally

2. A. disagreeable B. unenjoyable
C. strange D. agreeable

3. A. enjoyable B. suitable
C. appropriate D. enjoying

4. A. hike B. jolt
C. contribute D. all add to

5. A. Observing B. Enjoying
C. To look D. Looking

6. A. comfort B. complacence
C. delight D. satisfaction

7. A. had B. has
C. have D. has have

8. A. alongwith B. together with
C. addition to D. adding to

9. A. highly B. extensively
C. exceptionally D. so much more

10. A. revives B. vibrates
C. regenerates D. enliven

11. A. fancying B. enjoying
C. feeling D. dreaming

12. A. subjects B. objects
C. centre D. focus

## PASSAGE-11

Women were earlier considered as the kitchen keepers and house keepers – that was ....(1).... as their ....(2)... field of activity. ....(3)... women began to get educated and came out ....(4)... the social and potitical field and today they are there in all fields and are ....(5)... equal emloyment as the menfolk. Not only this they are ....(6)... themselves in those fields. Two important reasons behind the changed ....(7)... are : firstly, Womens are ....(8)... themselves duly qualified and want to use-their talents to seek an employment; and secondly, with the price-index ....(9).... everyday it is found necessary for the middle class families that the wife having ....(10).... academic qualifications working and ....(11).... the family income. This while giving them a social status, also helps the family to have a better standard of living, which everyone ....(12).... for and rightly too.

### QUESTIONS

1. A. recognised B. realized
C. regarded D. looked

2. A. exclusive B. only
C. working D. one

3. A. Day by day B. Slowly
C. Later D. Gradually

4. A. on B. in
C. at D. to

5. A. finding B. seeking
C. enjoying D. sharing

6. A. distinguishing B. proving
C. mastering D. struggling

7. A. scenario B. circumstances
C. society D. culture

8. A. thinking B. finding
C. educating D. proving

9. A. excelating B. intensifying
C. changing D. escalating

10. A. registered B. recognised
C. requisite D. minimum

11. A. substituting B. segment
C. influencing D. suplement

12. A. do crave B. does crave
C. starve D. do starve

## PASSAGE-12

Importance of music especially in today's hum drum life cannot be ....(1).... . Today man is surrounded by ....(2).... worries and listening to music ....(3).... his nerves. Music acts as a ....(4).... and soothes the nerves. It is a fine art and groups of all ages ....(5).... to its sweet sound. A person gifted with aesthetic ....(6).... finds music as a food for his soul. Some of the great musicians of the world ....(7).... in high esteem ....(8).... of the kind of they produce western, oriental, classical, pop or light. These musicians ....(9).... concerts which attract people from all walks of life. If people are ....(10).... to balming music, they will definitely find life a rich and healthy ....(11)..... In this way, the importance of music is really ....(12).... .

### QUESTIONS

1. A. overstated B. understated
C. irrelevant D. relevant

2. A. varied B. innumerable
C. different D. variegated

3. A. calm B. cure
C. soothe D. please

4. A. stimulant B. catalyst
C. machinery D. device

5. A. are attracted B. get attracted
C. are pleased D. feel pleasure

6. A. beauty B. blessing
C. capabilities D. knowledge

7. A. were held B. are held
C. are taken D. are received

8. A. no matter B. considering
C. respectively D. irrespective

9. A. popularize B. organize
C. form D. propagate

10. A. forced B. brought
C. introduced D. exposed

11. A. stage B. experience
C. achievement D. thing

12. A. considerable B. unavoidable
C. imimense D. recognisable

## PASSAGE-13

There are groups of people in ....(1).... developing countries who are in poverty line and who became the victims and ....(2).... in a self-fulfilling vicious of poverty. ....(3).... of the parents in the society ....(4).... afford to send their children to school. ....(5)...., the children often go to the labour force ....(6).... in order to ....(7).... the family income and to help the economic ....(8).... of the family. The Indian Government and educational ....(9).... are taking adequate steps for their standard of living and ....(10).... opportunities for schooling with full day food and other required ...(11)... .

## QUESTIONS

1. A. each B. all C. whole D. every
2. A. engulfed B. surrounded C. trapped D. fall
3. A. line B. circle C. frame D. structure
4. A. can't B. couldn't C. cannot D. can never
5. A. Though B. Despite C. Instead D. Even so
6. A. at an early age B. in his growing stage C. in his childhood D. at his childhood
7. A. add B. supplement C. hike D. improve
8. A. servility B. survivality C. conditon D. situation
9. A. activist B. executives C. planners D. propagonist
10. A. approving B. alloting C. distributing D. providing
11. A. privileges B. facilities C. necessities D. factors

## PASSAGE-14

What is urgently, ....(1).... in our country is a proper survey and a planned assessment of what sort of jobs ....(2).... demand both in the public as well as in the private sector and there ....(3).... a controlled enrolment in institutes and institutions which should be training young men in such needed jobs. It is a ....(4).... task, no doubt, but when the government and the private agencies ....(5).... make large scale survey for so many other problems of the country why cannot this grave problem of unemployment be ....(6).... at a priority basis and money and manpower be invested and ....(7).... to make an assessment of the requirements and then the process of their fulmilment ....(8).... . What is actually needed is not only scheming and planning but actually to have a ....(9)... to find the root of the ....(10).... . Only then can the ....(11).... be found out.

## QUESTIONS

1. A. demanded B. needed C. prevalent D. lacking
2. A. are of B. are at C. are most in D. currently
3. A. needs to be B. is C. are D. shall be
4. A. labourious B. Herculean C. time taking D. stupendous
5. A. can B. could C. are out to D. readily
6. A. noticed B. surveyed C. treated D. observed
7. A. used B. employed C. organised D. treated
8. A. be worked out B. be taken up C. be decided D. be developed
9. A. spirit B. will C. motive D. strength
10. A. malady B. grievances C. curse D. paradox
11. A. treatment B. cure C. remedy D. solution

## PASSAGE-15

A sudden flood of ....(1).... dangerous toys like swords and bow and arrow make their ....(2).... in the market during the Dussehra festival. ....(3)...., eyes can and do get injured ....(4).... by these toys and ....(5)...., the victims aare innocent children. ....(6).... by the Ram Lila and similar television serials, children ....(7).... swords at each other or fire arrows from bows which ....(8).... to permanent blindness if ....(9).... to hit the eye. This happens ....(10).... if the injury is servere and not managed properly. Any injury in and around the eye ....(11).... taken seriously land managed on an emergency basis.

## QUESTIONS

1. A. potentially B. instantly C. constantly D. inevitably
2. A. arrival B. appearance C. place D. position
3. A. unknowingly B. undoubtedly C. undauntedly D. unfortunately
4. A. advertently B. inadvertently C. unfortunately D. unknowingly
5. A. almost B. almost always C. all the time D. very often

6. A. Motivated B. Inspired
C. Encouraged D. Taught

7. A. attack B. take out
C. brandish D. home

8. A. can lead B. could lead
C. would lead D. lead

9. A. it targets B. it comes
C. they happen D. they are

10. A. usually B. generally
C. commonly D. more often

11. A. are to be B. is to be
C. shall be D. may be

## PASSAGE-16

The scientist of today is a man of ....(1).... ambition. He is not contented with ....(2).... he has achieved, but wants to be a creator of new and surprising things so that the common people may ....(3).... at the marvels of his ....(4)...., feel thrilled and go away ....(5).... by his superior wisdom and his ....(6).... inventiveness. The new and challenging scientific forces now ....(7).... by him in the universe will continue to work ....(8).... in ever increasing numbers, to lead mankind to ....(9).... material progress, and to ....(10).... in its hand unlimited power for conquering ....(11).... territories of knowledge and experience.

### QUESTIONS

1. A. increasing B. elevating
C. soaring D. diversing

2. A. what B. whatever
C. those D. that

3. A. broad B. work
C. gape D. deride

4. A. invention B. genius
C. life D. achievement

5. A. impressed B. dejected
C. attracted D. motivated

6. A. enviable B. reliable
C. unavoidable D. considerable

7. A. brought B. given
C. let loose D. realised

8. A. fruitfully B. miracles
C. magic D. wonders

9. A. unscathed B. unrelenting
C. unmitigated D. unprecedented

10. A. keep B. allot
C. load D. place

11. A. greater B. varied
C. unknown D. more and more

## PASSAGE-17

Education of the future has to ....(1).... human values and see that the human factor is not neglected. The task of education is to help the individual to know himself. ....(2).... as the individual is ignorant of his ....(3)...., his potentialites and his mission of life, he ....(4).... contribute in a creative manner ....(5).... his own growth and development of the society. It is often said that, as education is the ....(6).... of the thinking elite of the nation, ....(7).... the nation's future depends on its system of education. This is true to some ....(8).... .But ....(9)...., the general outlook of society has also a strong ....(10).... on education itself so that education can only be reformed when a ....(11).... change has already begun in society.

### QUESTIONS

1. A. consider B. protect
C. care D. preserve

2. A. Till then B. So long
C. Uptill then D. Till that time

3. A. own B. credibilities
C. nature D. real self

4. A. can't B. could not
C. could never D. cannot

5. A. in B. throughout
C. to D. towards

6. A. developing process B. development
C. building up D. guidance

7. A. much of B. many of
C. mostly D. mainly

8. A. limit B. horizon
C. context D. extent

9. A. conversely B. alternately
C. actually D. outwardly

10. A. hearing B. relation
C. opposition D. affinity

11. A. consequent B. corresponding
C. subsequent D. similar

## PASSAGE-18

Every action we perform ....(1).... a result. And, naturally, we lay claim ....(2).... the results or fruits ....(3).... from that action in the ....(4).... that it is we who perform the action. This is .....(5).... ignorance because ....(6).... is it the Lord who ....(7).... the result of any action, it is by His will ....(8).... that even the action is accomplished. The will of the Lord ....(9).... whether we cooperate with His will or strive ....(10).... If God wills that an action takes place, he arranges for the ....(11).... for it to happen. It is ....(12).... experience that sometimes despite our best efforts we ....(13).... achieve the results we desire, and at other times the seemingly most ....(14).... situations mysteriously get ....(15).... . ....(16).... way man chooses to act, both the act and the outcome of the cost are dependent ....(17).... on the will of the Lord.

## QUESTIONS

**1.** A. produce B. produces
C. causes D. undergoes

**2.** A. on B. at
C. to D. for

**3.** A. occuring B. obtaining
C. deriving D falling

**4.** A. belief B. hope
C. fantasy D. folly

**5.** A. sheen B. keen
C. sheer D. sheathe

**6.** A. alone B. only that
C. not only D. for only

**7.** A. declares B. decides
C. ordains D. ornate

**8.** A. completely B. entirely
C. only D. alone

**9.** A. prevails always B. prevails everywhere
C. is prevalent D. always prevails

**10.** A. alone B. always
C. constantly D. independently

**11.** A. wherewithal B. whereabouts
C. whatsoever D. wherefore

**12.** A. usual B. general
C. universal D. common

**13.** A. does not B. may not
C. do not D. might not

**14.** A. intractable B. intangible
C. internecine D. intricate

**15.** A. subsided B. resolved
C. solved D. converted

**16.** A. Whatever B. All the
C. All those D. Whichever

**17.** A. mainly B. actually
C. entirely D. generally

## PASSAGE-19

For centuries, women not only in India but all over the world ....(1).... treated as ....(2).... secondary position to men. ....(3).... human history men ....(4).... far greater power then women to name, classify, and order the worlds in which they both live. ....(5).... studies in various parts of the world point out to a wide ....(6).... in male and female roles ....(7).... cultures and demonstrate the possibility of change in these sex-determined roles. The 20th century in particular ....(8).... the cause of gender justice by internationalizing struggles for equality ....(9).... women and other oppressed people. Women's struggles against their ....(10).... were interwined in ....(11).... degrees with ideologies and movements based on the values of freedom, self-determination, equality, democracy and justice.

## QUESTIONS

**1.** A. has been B. have been
C. had been D. were

**2.** A. occupying B. taking
C. possessing D. serving

**3.** A. All through B. Throughout
C. Since D. From

**4.** A. have B. had
C. have had D. enjoy

**5.** A. Sociological B. Anthropological
C. General D. Practical

**6.** A. concord B. repulsion
C. disagreement D. variation

**7.** A. among B. across
C. between D. of

**8.** A. developed B. envolved
C. promoted D. entertained

**9.** A. for B. to
C. among D. by

**10.** A. subsidiary B. subsequent
C. subservience D. subordination

**11.** A. various B. varying
C changing D. differeing

## PASSAGE-20

What is required today in our country is ....(1).... of a new political culture based on full respect for human liberty, on pluralism and on a better social deal for all. The major ....(2).... facing us today is to carry out democratic transformation in all the ....(3)...., social, cultural, economic and political. The events of the 20th century ....(4).... one thing absolutely clear that human ....(5)...., everywhere, specially in countries whose political structures were ....(6).... to reflect the revolutionary aspirations of the people ....(7).... not only under stress and strain but are ....(8).... vast upheavals because of the ....(9).... of democracy. At the same time it has also to be understood that democracy cannot be ....(10).... into a static mould.

## QUESTIONS

1. A. growing B. developing C. creating D. creation
2. A. development B. crisis C. challenge D. drawback
3. A. corners B. context C. realm D. spheres
4. A. have made B. has made C. had made D. made
5. A. travails B. traverse C. trapse D. transverse
6. A. supposed B. meant C. caused D. forced
7. A. were B. was C. are D. have been
8. A. developing B. evolving C. experiencing D. faced with
9. A. denial B. rebuff C. rebuttal D. absence
10. A. shaped B. flex C. frozen D. caused

## PASSAGE-21

We are living in very exciting ....(1).... . The ....(2).... change is dizzying and the impact this progress is having on our present and – more importantly – on our future is difficult to ....(3).... in its ...(4).... . This is the age of ....(5).... micro processors, sophisticated software, new hardware technology and high bandwith, high-speed networks. The PC gave us a new way to work, play and ....(6).... . In fact, it brought ....(7).... our desktops computing power, which until a few years ....(8).... had only been available to corporates. With the ....(9).... of the internet, the PC ....(10).... us the most convenient and flexible way to head on to the Net.

## QUESTIONS

1. A. periods B. days C. phase D. times
2. A. phase B. pace C. sphere D. drastic
3. A. guess B. forecast C. comprehend D. approximate
4. A. whole B. entirety C. fruition D. fullness
5. A. strong B. changing C. powerful D. sonorous
6. A. convey B. communicate C. entertain D. enjoy
7. A. onto B. to C. on D. at
8. A. back B. earlier C. behind D. before
9. A. addendum B. adherence C. afoot D. advent
10. A. allowed B. privileged C. brought D. offered

## PASSAGE-22

Visualisation is a strong ....(1).... to memory. Those persons who ...... (2) ..... a powerful memory cannot do so without taking the help of visualisaton. Such persons have developed the .o ....(3).... visualisation even in such ....(4).... tasks as remembering names and numbers. These persons have the names and numbers ....(5).... in their brain even after hearing those names and figues only once. On the other hand those who take the help of revising to memorise ....(6).... to forget it once they have ....(7).... the practice of revising ....(8).... the ones who have applied visualisation to memorise. Psychologists ....(9).... in visualisation a powerful tool for personality development. The more you visualise, the more you are ....(10).... your attitude and behaviour to the blue prints of your vision and ....(11).... more you are inching towards success.

## QUESTIONS

1. A. way B. path C. aid D. symptom
2. A. command B. master C. rule D. enjoy
3. A. use B. apply C. put D. place
4. A. trivial B. difficult C. mundane D. unscrupulous
5. A. impress B. imprinted C. impinge D. store
6. A. bent B. incline C. prone d. tend
7. A. dropped B. left C. gave up D. given up
8. A. unlike B. opposite C. contrary D. not like
9. A. found B. have found C. sees D. finds
10. A. shaping B. moulding C. making D. attuning
11. A. actually B. factually C. subsequently D. consequently

## PASSAGE-23

....(1).... people today remember the war that was fought after China invaded India in 1962. Not because the war was never really ....(2).... . Nor because it was ....(3).... almost before it began. The reason is ....(4).... that most of us were yet to be born. The main reason for the Chinese attack seems to ....(5).... to establish the ....(6).... order, expose our ....(7)...., put us in our place. The official reason, ....(8)...., was the territorial dispute, ....(9).... more than 100,000 square kilometres. ....(10).... speaking, India borders Tibet, not China. The McMohan Line ....(11).... the border with Tibet in what is now Arunachal Pradesh was the result of a 1914 treaty ....(12).... British India and Tibet. This was not ....(13).... to the Chinese the result was a .....(14)..... nose. The Chinese attack was ....(15).... fast and furious. ....(16).... brave soldiers ....(17).... down their lives, but India was simply unable to halt the ....(17).... . Panic quickly ....(18)....

### QUESTIONS

**1.** A. A few B. Few C. Fewer D. A little

**2.** A. joined B. combined C. acted D. approved

**3.** A. finished B. ceased C. over D. stopped

**4.** A. simple B. simply C. common D. commonly

**5.** A. had been B. have C. had D. have been

**6.** A. pecking B. unavoiding C. powerful D. selfish

**7.** A. projections B. pretensions C. presumption D. pretending

**8.** A. more over B. probably C. perhaps D. however

**9.** A. effecting B. causing C. affecting D. influencing

**10.** A. Formally B. Informally C. Broadly D. Technically

**11.** A. relating B. dividing C. defining D. laying

**12.** A. among B. between C. of D. by

**13.** A. favourable B. favoured C. acceptable D. accepting

**14.** A. angry B. bloody C. honed D. blitz

**15.** A. quick B. prick C. sudden D. unassuming

**16.** A. Some B. Few C. Many D. A lot of

**17.** A. onrush B. onset C. omnipotence D. omen

**18.** A. come in B. gone in C. set in D. set out

## PASSAGE-24

Man has always been ....(1).... with flying because it ....(2).... a sense of freedom, of romance and thrill-something too ....(3).... to resist. It is the task of the ....(4).... of the skies to safeguard Indian air-space from unwelcome ....(5)..... . The Indian Air Force . . .(6).... a chequered and glorious history. From its ....(7).... days of single-engine aeroplanes like Tempests and Spitfires to the state of the art multi-engine, supersonic MIG and Sukhoi fighters, the Indian Air Force ....(8).... a long way. In addition to the already existing ....(9).... of aircraft and weapon systems, plans are ....(10).... to enhance its air defence power and ....(11).... capability through upgradation and ....(12).... .

### QUESTIONS

**1.** A. fascinated B. moved C. inspired D. fancied

**2.** A. generates B. cultivates C. reaps D. evokes

**3.** A. envisaging B. impressing C. enchanting D. laudable

**4.** A. sentiness B. sedulous C. venturous D. fervid

**5.** A. emigrants B. intruders C. foreigners D. tourists

**6.** A. had B. have C. have had D. has had

**7.** A. early B. undeveloped C. growing D. embryonic

**8.** A. had come B. has come C. have come D. came

**9.** A. invention B. inventory C. mechanism D. technique

**10.** A. progressive B. afresh C. afoot D. affluent

**11.** A. combat B. increase C. intensify D. ensure

**12.** A. acquistion B. acknowledgement C. acquiescence D. accumulation

## PASSAGE-25

Libraries were never ....(1).... the place to ....(2).... They never will be. But those who've visited libraries for the ....(3).... pleasure of it will testify to the feeling of ....(4).... on entering the labyrinth ....(5).... high with books. Suddenly, a ....(6).... spent reading seems the ideal. It's a similar experience to ....(7).... in a bookshop. The difference : in the second situation, despair ....(8).... you as your eyes zoom ....(9).... on the price; in the first there is the ....(10).... that all these books are yours for the asking. Today, ....(11)...., liberary use is almost ....(12).... necessity-based. The reading room is ....(13).... full with students poring ....(14).... their books..

### QUESTIONS

1. A. realised B. seen C. recognised D. considered
2. A. hung out B. hang out C. hang out in D. hung out in
3. A. mere B. sheer C. trivial D. trifle
4. A. exhilaration B. exhaustion C. expedition D. extrapolation
5. A. going B. moving C. pik D. towering
6. A. long time B. whole life C. life time D. life long
7. A. browsing B. move about C. move D. stroll
8. A. swamps B. swab C. swoon D. swoop
9. A. at B. on C. in D. upon
10. A. idea B. surity C. certainty D. knowledge
11. A. although B. however C. in fact D. moreover
12. A. wholly B. partially C. outwardly D. purely
13. A. tight B. completely C. over crowded D. cramped
14. A. into B. onto C. over D. upon

## PASSAGE-26

The ....(1).... of a country does not depend on the abundance of its revenue but more ....(2).... by its citizens; its men of education, enlightenment and character. It is for the ....(3).... of higher learning to ....(4).... an academic environment of equity, justice and fair play where those ....(5).... in the ....(6).... task of nation building can ....(7).... their responsibilities in a spirit of sincerity, dedication and commitment. Higher education in India ....(8).... great strides after independence. The ideal of education is to ....(9).... for self-preservation but which also prepares us to recognise and ....(10).... the rights of others and to shoulder our ....(11).... as responsible citizens.

### QUESTIONS

1. A. prospects B. fortune C. protrusion D. gaiety
2. A. illustrated B. emancipated C. defined D. apprehended
3. A. institute B. centre C. college D. university
4. A. encourage B. embark C. promote D. polish
5. A. employed B. recruited C. held D. engaged
6. A. paramount B. ardous C. lucrative D. laudable
7. A. dispense B. disburse C. carry D. discharge
8. A. have taken B. had taken C. has taken D. is taking
9. A. evoke B. prepare C. encourage D. cultivate
10. A. concede B. preserve C. coddle D. clung
11. A. obligations B. obduracy C. obsequiousness D. portfolio

## PASSAGE-27

Observation is one of the key ....(1).... of modern corporate behaviour. Indeed it has long been the ....(2).... for humans and animals generally. It is essential for every corporate citizen to be able to taste the ....(3).... of what is happening around him all the time, not merely to survive but to ....(4).... . ....(5).... the corporate corridors to check which way the wind is blowing ! Know when it is appropriate to get your ....(6).... in and when it is ....(7).... to maintain a low profile. To ....(8).... a career with the ease and ....(9).... of a winner, you need to be able to ....(10).... a disaster before it happens ! You need to take an advantage before someone else ....(11).... . You need to be at the right place before someone else ....(12).... there. Observation or paying attention to what's happening around us is essential ....(13).... . We need to take the time to ....(14).... the habit of paying attention so that we can make our work ....(15).... and so that we can stand at ease! Career ....(16).... will be the happy outcome!

## QUESTIONS

1. A. approach B. method C. tactics D. means
2. A. rule B. norm C. convention D. technique
3. A. presence B. essence C. events D. problem
4. A. thrive B. throb C. fare D. blow
5. A. Sniff B. Snuffle C. Spin-off D. Splutter
6. A. shore B. oar C. objective D. ogle
7. A. correct B. right C. prudent D. prudish
8. A. carry B. initiate C. continue D. conduct
9. A. caprice B. comfort C. over-confidence D. aplomb
10. A. forecast B. apprehend C. guess D. foretell
11. A. do B. does C. takes D. gets
12. A. come B. comes C. get D. gets
13. A. everytime B. alltime C. everywhere D. forever
14. A. reap B. sow C. cultivate D. grow
15. A. easy B. easier C. easiest D. simple
16. A. advancement B. progression C. achievement D. cultivation

## PASSAGE-28

The ....(1).... Euphoria over the ....(2).... fall in the cost of domestic air travel has ....(3).... to a more realistic appraisal of what is on offer. The aggressive ....(4).... schemes offered since the beginning of July have certainly been good news for certain categories of passengers who probably value .....(5).... above anything else. For them, the heavily discounted fare ....(6).... enables them to afford air travel for the first time. In fact, the ....(7).... of the fare cut ....(8).... such that in specific instances air travel compares ....(9).... to the fares charged by the Railways for upper class travel. Obviously, it ....(10).... for a change in mindset to switch to air travel in ....(11).... to, say, rail transport in India. Economy and affordability will certainly be key ....(12).... but they must be made available ....(13).... a fairly long period. To put it differently, cheaper air travel or at least a ....(14).... fare structure ....(15).... institutionalised in the country.

## QUESTIONS

1. A. embryonic B. early C. ending D. initial
2. A. casual B. sudden C. surprising D. dramatic
3. A. raised B. caused C. given way D. gave way
4. A. lucrative B. lofty C. laudable D. promotional
5. A. expenses B. affordability C. comfort D. time
6. A. scheme B. structure C. system D. circular
7. A. portion B. ratio C. magnitude D. proportion
8. A. are B. is C. has been D. have been
9. A. very slightly B. very favourably C. specifially D. generally
10. A. causes B. calls C. invites D. lures
11. A. choice B. favour C. preference D. alternative
12. A. determinants B. detrimenetals C. performers D. issues
13. A. over B. for C. to D. through
14. A. different B. distinctive C. reducing D. differential
15. A. must be B. has to be C. ought to be D. have to be

## PASSAGE-29

"I need a break" is a common ..... (1) ..... among the ....(2).... middle and elite classes – under ....(3).... pressure to perform, to live up to their own artificial standards, to earn, and earn some more and ....(4).... some more. But in this vortex, time is at a ....(5)...., and the much needed break ....(6).... materialises because harried professionals are unable to stay away from work long enough ....(7).... from the city and breathe in some fresh air—metaphorically and literally. And weekends? They are ....(8).... lazing at home, ....(9).... on chores, or may be watching some mind numbing television programme. Because it would be hard to think of a place you ....(10).... escape to that was far enough from the city to be ....(11).... and yet close enough to ....(12).... as a weekend break.

## QUESTIONS

1. A. restrain B. refrain
C. remark D. saying
2. A. hurried B. harried
C. worried D. busy
3. A. continuous B. consequent
C. constant D. stable
4. A. even B. add
C. farther D. then
5. A. premium B. minimum
C. limitation D. restriction
6. A. never often B. often never
C. although never D. sometimes do not
7. A. to stay away B. to escape
C. to go away D. to get moved
8. A. there B. for
C. those D. some
9. A. getting B. catching
C. catching up D. catching down
10. A. can B. ever
C. would D. could
11. A. refreshed B. refreshing
C. resting D. rejoining
12. A. consider B. anticipate
C. contemplate D. meditate

## PASSAGE-30

Every monsoon I'm reminded of an incident that ....(1).... many years ago when I was a young man ....(2).... my first job in Mumbai. I was staying with my sister in those days. On one wet and windy night I ....(3).... with friends, and as it happens when you are in pleasant company, the ....(4).... . It was past ten when I finally bid goodby to my companions and moved towards my sister's house. It had rained the whole day, and it ....(5).... to drizzle again. The rain had ....(6).... people indoors earlier than usual and the dimly-lit street I was walking along was ....(7).... . I had heard that the road was ....(8).... . They said one could hear a woman calling for help on some nights. As I proceeded, I suddenly saw a figure walking ....(9).... me. A bandicoot chose to ....(10).... across my path, just then she seemed to have ....(11).... into thin air. Then I heard a faint ....(12).... for help. This frightened me and as such I turned and fled. The next morning I came to know from my sister that the bandicoot was no other but her friend who had mistakenly thought she was being ....(13).... . Out of fear she was looking behind and walking when she ....(14).... into a ditch. Now every monsoon, I'm reminded of my ....(15).... on that wet night.

## QUESTIONS

1. A. happened B. occured
C. took place D. had taken place
2. A. in B. on
C. working at D. working with
3. A. had been out B. went for outing
C. had gone D. was out
4. A. time passes B. time runs
C. time flies D. time files
5. A. has B. was
C. began D. had begun
6. A. pushed B. sent
C. send D. driven
7. A. calm B. peace
C. lonely D. deserted
8. A. mysterious B. ghostly
C. haunted D. devilish
9. A. before B. in front of
C. a head D. near
10. A. scuttle B. scurry
C. scuff D. scrouge
11. A. faded B. vanished
C. vaporised D. melted
12. A. sound B. voice
C. cry D. whisper
13. A. followed B. chased
C. pursued D. caught
14. A. fall B. stumbled
C. threw D. jumped
15. A. foolishness B. ignorance
C. confusion D. cowardice

## PASSAGE-31

Most of India's educational institutions, ....(1).... by hiring people who are ....(2).... qualified to be teachers. They are ....(3).... an unhappy group, which is ill-paid and which commands ....(4).... respect. Sadly, it is these men and women who have the enormous duty of ...(5).... tomorrow's society, a responsibility that remains ....(6).... . Children are ....(7).... in this terrifying circle : they are ....(8).... into submission, their innocence is destroyed and their lives become ....(9).... joyless. What follows is still ....(10).... . A violent childhood ....(11).... a violent adulthood. A child who faces the ....(12).... of an adult grows up ....(13).... that violence is the answer to all problems. They become ....(14).... individuals and often their intellectual development ....(15).... in the absence of congenial peace.

## QUESTIONS

1. A. get away B. manage C. run D. go away
2. A. not really B. really not C. virtually not D. not actually
3. A. commonly B. mainly C. specifically D. usually
4. A. scant B. scanty C. scarce D. rare
5. A. forming B. moulding C. framing D. making
6. A. unsatisfied B. unprecedented C. unfulfilled D. unrequited
7. A. taught B. caught C. captured D. chained
8. A. battered B. split C. squeezed D. shaped
9. A. universally B. utterly C. wholly D. complete
10. A. unfavourable B. bad C. not good D. worse
11. A. may lead to B. may grow to C. may reach to D. would develop to
12. A. consequences B. wrath C. grief D. wretch
13. A. thinking B. supposing C. infering D. believing
14. A. complex B. complicated C. rough D. sanguine
15. A. slows down B. moves slowly C. hampers D. brakes

## PASSAGE-32

Men ....(1).... the maker of their own destinies and they ....(2).... make the destiny of the society and the nation. Life is a great gift of God to men and man ....(3).... making constant efforts to live a ....(4).... life right from the stone age to the modern one. But it is man who ....(5).... to think out how to live well. The ....(6).... before mankind today is between self-preservation and self-destruction. Science has given men all the powers that they need but the new millennium ....(7).... new challenges. We are ....(8).... what nature has given us—forests are being cut down, slums are being ....(9)...., rivers are being polluted. Medical science has made great ....(10)....; but the population is growing in a geometrical ....(11).... . Our natural resources like coal and oil are being ....(12).... . Atomic energy is our only hope. The ....(13).... welcome of the new millennium lies in our determination and hope for self-preservation ....(14).... self-destruction.

## QUESTIONS

1. A. are B. have been C. being D. had been
2. A. unitedly B. ultimately C. conjointly D. co-exist to
3. A. have been B. are C. has been D. have had been
4. A. congenial B. cordial C. congregational D. congruent
5. A. have B. is C. are D. has
6. A. optional B. choice C. possibilities D. probabilities
7. A. presents B. places C. offers D. puts forth
8. A. destroying B. ignoring C. neglecting D. wasting
9. A. developed B. constructed C. created D. manufactured
10. A. advancement B. advances C. achievement D. inventions
11. A. dimension B. angle C. index D. proportion
12. A. deported B. deplored C. depleted D. disposed
13. A. actual B. real C. warm D. innate
14. A. upon B. over C. on D. above

# II. PASSAGES

**Directions:** *Read each of the following passages carefully and choose the best answer to each question out of the four alternatives and mark it in the Answer Sheet.*

## PASSAGE-1

Cyber crime is the branded stigma defacing the culture and magnanimity of computer technology. It is up keeping the flag with indomitable triumph against developing computer technology worldwide.

Modern age is striding with marching steps of technology revolution beating the past decade of ancestral belief with ultimate care. Computer invention has unfolded the mystery of quick access with the objective of minimum manpower and cutting the time consumption parameters.

As each coin has dual face of its portrait, likewise computer technology is sick of creeping virus. Synthetic manmade dilemma of site hackers activation is causing setback to the expanding anchor of revolutionary device with great loss of time, economy and data profile as suffered by consumers. A recent report from Internet security firm Websense estimates that 85.6 per cent of all the unwanted e-mails contained links to spam sites. The company's data suggests that the number of malicious sites grew 233 per cent in the last six months and saw 671 per cent growth in the number of malicious sites during the last year. In June alone, the total number of e-mails detected as containing viruses increased by 600 per cent compared to May.

Chat rooms, blogs and message boards where the users post comments have been identified as the top targets of hackers and spammers due to the high traffic these attract. According to Websense, 95 per cent of user-generated comments to blogs, chat rooms and message boards during the first half of 2009 were malicious.

It is advisable not to click on spurious links and stay away from keying in passwords at unknown sites as they are most likely to be spammed. Hackers can steal your passwords and log in to your account and access critical information like account numbers and contact details among other things.

### QUESTIONS

**1.** The above passage is:
A. an advisory for the computer users.
B. an advisory for the Internet users.
C. a warning against possible threat to the Internet users.
D. related to chat rooms, blogs and message boards.

**2.** People who use chat rooms and blogs,
A. are safe and have no threats from spam.
B. are more prone to malicious e-mails.
C. create virus and hack the accounts of others.
D. are unsafe.

**3.** According to the writer, it is not safe to:
A. log on to spurious links.
B. access one's own account frequently.
C. have essential information stored in a computer.
D. include data-stealing code.

**4.** Hackers and spammers, according to the writer, are:
A. a new threat to the Internet users and the economy.
B. only pranksters and not serious threat to the system.
C. trained, professional technocrats who are an asset.
D. not expert professionals.

**5.** Which word in the passage is synonym of *weblog*?
A. blog B. password
C. site D. e-mail

**6.** Which agency has assessed the data record with spam sites?
A. Microsoft
B. Internet security from Google
C. Websense
D. Spammers

**7.** Which month dominates the e-mails detection data record?
A. May B. June
C. Last six months D. Last year

## PASSAGE-2

South Asian tropical weather reels valuable geographical aesthetic beauty surrounded by wildlife, mountains, steep elevations with dense forest. Human sapiens has been old and innocent victim of natural calamities branded as flood, hurricane, storm, earthquake and tsunami since ages.

Biological data depicts the loss of valuable men and material suffered by mankind owing to the chain reaction by such fatal natural incidents. Global warming has turned an eyesore to the rapid glory of rising civilisation with great mystery yet to be unfolded. UNO data reveals the rate of mortality owned due to natural disaster with great sway of cruel time factor.

Of the 245 natural disasters in the first 11 months of 2009, 224 or 91.4 per cent were due to weather, a UN study has found.

Of the 58 million people affected, 55 million were affected by weather-related disasters, which accounted for $15 billion (₹ 7,05,000 crore) spent in coping with these disasters.

A study has found that half of these disasters, mainly storms and floods, have taken place in Asia, Debarati Guha Sapir of Brussels-based CRED said.

And this data does not include the loss due to drought because that takes longer to account for. Guha Sapir said, "We have found that this is due to global warming, weak political systems, urbanisation, weak infrastructure, population increase and deforestation."

"We have to cap the emissions of greenhouse gases because they produce greater risk of disasters," WMO head Michel Jerraud said. Greenhouse gases, mainly carbon dioxide, are causing the climate change that is already affecting farm output, making droughts, floods and storms more frequent and more severe, and raising the sea level.

## QUESTIONS

**1.** Mark the correct statement(s).

1. Weather is responsible for most of the natural disasters.
2. There is no need to worry about the climatic changes.
3. All the nations are trying to have a common pact to tackle natural disasters.

A. 1 is correct  B. Only 2 is correct
C. Only 3 is correct  D. 1 and 2 are correct

**2.** Which one of the following statements is not true?
A. More than 58 million people have been affected by natural disasters.
B. $15 billion have been spent in coping with these disasters.
C. Most of the natural disasters have taken place in Asia.
D. The report does not include the loss caused by droughts.

**3.** The main cause of natural disasters is :
A. global warming
B. weak political system
C. deforestation
D. all of these

**4.** The first priority before the nations and the scientists across the world is :
A. to cap the emission of greenhouse gases.
B. to reach an agreement on the nuclear weapons.
C. to help one another when natural disasters occur.
D. to find out the causes of natural disasters.

**5.** Which word in the passage means the same as *serious*?
A. Reduce  B. Severe
C. Underlined  D. Underscore

**6.** Which region is mainly affected by these disasters?
A. United Nation  B. Africa
C. Asia  D. Brussels

**7.** Which statement is true?
A. Sea level rise is an alarming incident.
B. Rapid urbanisation is a curse to the global warming.
C. Deforestation with climatic change is responsible for green house gaseous effect.
D. All of these.

## PASSAGE-3

Time has brought forth different classical and instrumental range of device that serves healing element to the aweful and mentally distressed state of affair. Temperament compatibility matching is a reasonable trend of motion adhered with the concept of body movement termed as dance therapy.

Dance has mobilised different acknowledgement of its noted culture proclaimed by experts and sensational aspirants. Vedas describe the dance origin from aryan culture to the creeping span of modern India. Archaeological Survey of India has claimed the civilsation existence issue owing to excavation of past events traced in the stone idols displayed in dance "mudra".

Dance is an art form that generally refers to movement of the body, usually rhythmic and to music, used as a form of expression, social interaction or presented in a spiritual or performance setting. Gymnastics, figure skating and synchronised swimming are sports that incorporate dance, while martial arts Kata are often compared to dances. Motion in ordinarily inanimate objects may also be described as dances (the leaves dance in the wind). Every dance, no matter what style, has something in common. It not only involves flexibility and body movement, but also physics. If the proper physics is not taken into consideration, injuries may occur. Choreography is the art of creating dances. The person who creates (*i.e.* choreographs) a dance, is known as the choreographer. Dance has certainly been an important part of ceremony, rituals, celebrations and entertainment since the birth of the earliest human civilisations. Archaeology delivers trace of dance from prehistoric times such as the 9,000 years old Rock Shelters of Bhimbetka painting in India and Egyptian tomb painting depicting dancing figures from circa 3300 BC. One of the earliest structured uses of dance may have been in the performance and in the telling of myths. Before the production of written languages, dance was one of the methods of passing these stories down from generation to generation.

## QUESTIONS

1. Dance does not necessarily involve:
   A. movement of the body.
   B. face expression.
   C. rhythmic movements.
   D. costumes.
2. According to the passage, which one of the following sports does not incorporate dance?
   A. Figure skating  B. Gymnastics
   C. Chess  D. Swimming
3. Which one, according to the passage, is not common in all the dances?
   A. Flexibility  B. Body movement
   C. Music  D. Physics
4. Physics in every dance is an important element to:
   A. master the art of dance.
   B. to perform it scientifically.
   C. to save oneself from injury.
   D. to get an award.
5. In prehistoric times dance was:
   A. a substitute of written language.
   B. a source of entertainment.
   C. a necessary ritual.
   D. not allowed in royal palaces.
6. Choreographer is a term addressed to:
   A. a sports trainer  B. a gym coach
   C. a painting teacher  D. a dance teacher
7. What does the term 'the telling of myths' refer to?
   A. Telling the beads  B. Vedic convention
   C. Spiritual recitation  D. Protest march

## PASSAGE-4

Personal sentiments exposure portray in sober class of distinct feature with fair and pleasant expression. As the cruelty can be overpowered by the amicable terms likewise, impossible review let with expression can be publically announced by either electronic device or diary writing habit. On line conversation such as chattering, message convey are the rampant tool of the time to manage in communication congestion.

Blogs, online versions of personal diaries, have been a craze for quite some time now. Some of us, before the Internet age, used to maintain a small diary to jot down random thoughts, reflections, sayings, poems and other such stuff. Their online versions, however, are much more than that. The biggest difference between a blog and a personal diary is while the latter was a very private affair accessible not even to family members, a blog is a public account. In fact the whole world connected to the internet gets to read its contents if they come across it.

What a blogger should keep in mind while blogging is that by displaying our thoughts, emotions, opinions and personal life in full public glory, we are revealing a part of our private life. We are giving outsiders, strangers, friends, colleagues and relatives a full view of what's happening inside us and without lives, something we would hesitate to do in real life. Once blogging begins, it's difficult to control, and we end up sharing our personal thoughts and emotions that we would otherwise have kept to ourselves. The blog entices us, and we fall to be bait.

Blogs don't preserve our anonymity. They let us publish our pictures, professional and personal details, physical address and locations, etc. The biggest precaution to be observed therefore is to think twice before publishing anything, and ask oneself if one would like to make such matters public. The blog readers try to judge us, understand us, get information about us and take pleasure while peeping into our private lives without realising it.

## QUESTIONS

1. Blogs are __________.
   A. diaries  B. personal diaries
   C. online diaries  D. official diaries
2. Earlier the personal diaries were not available even to family members but blog can be read by:
   A. family and friends
   B. friends only
   C. anyone who connects to the Internet
   D. relatives
3. Which one of the following statements is not true?
   A. Blogging does not affect our privacy.
   B. Blogging displays our private life in public.
   C. Blogging cannot be controlled easily.
   D. Blogging allows outsiders to peep into our personal life.
4. The writer in the above passage:
   A. favours blogging.
   B. criticises the practices.
   C. does not want the reader to become a victim of blogging.
   D. favours blogging but with some precautions.
5. Which word in the passage stands for *an account from on point of view*?
   A. version  B. block
   C. affair  D. account
6. The word Anonymity in the passage refers to:
   A. hostility  B. friendship
   C. unacknowledged  D. differences
7. What precaution is stressed by the narrator while releasing personal information?

A. Suggest Comprehensive issue only
B. Reader friendly blog appreciation
C. Hiding personal facts
D. Diary maintenance

## PASSAGE-5

Pleasure and sorrow being twin face of a coin suffers the sign of commend and condemn since long before the historic ages. Warriors outcry with victory decorated with deep throat laugh has marked the sentimental coverage of battle filed victory. Baffled war victims, war widows, dependents are the oppressed classes. They seek relief against those causing sabotage to their established settlement.

The history of literature really began long before man learned to write. Dancing was the earliest of the arts. Man danced for joy round his primitive camp fire after the defeat and slaughter of his enemy. He yelled and shouted as he danced and gradually the yells and shouts became coherent and caught the measure of the dance and thus the first war song was sung. As the idea of God developed, prayers were framed. The song and prayers became traditional and were repeated from one generation to another, each generation adding something of its own. As man slowly grew more civilsed, he was compelled to invent some method of writing by three urgent necessities. There were certain things that were dangerous to forget and which, therefore, had to be recorded.

It was often necessary to communicate with persons who were some distance away and it was necessary to protect one's property by making tools and so on, in some distinctive manner. So man taught himself to write and having learned to write purely for utilitarian reasons, he used this new method for preserving his songs and his prayers. Of course, among these ancient people, there were only a very few individuals who learned to write, and only a few could read what was written.

## QUESTIONS

**1.** Liguistic comment and condemn refers to:
A. physical grudge against sorrows
B. a temporary verbal communication
C. slip of tongue with praise and denounce
D. a communal fury against the joys

**2.** Which one of the following statements is true?
A. Study reveals the historic onslaught with cruelty only.
B. Suffers pledge to reform the existing tyranny.
C. A permanent code of sympathetic temper is sought by the suffers.
D. Language dominates with great passion during mental aggression.

**3.** Before man invented writing, ______.
A. literature was passed on by word of mouth
B. prayres were considered literature
C. literature was just singing and dancing
D. all of the above

**4.** According to the passage, dance originated from
A. literature B. yelling and shouting
C. prayers D. war

**5.** Writing was invented because
A. there were certain things which had to be remembered.
B. there were certain things which had to be communicated to the people who were away.
C. there were certain rituals which had to be preserved.
D. all of the above

**6.** Which one of the following statements is not true?
A. Since only a few individuals had learnt to write and a few could read what was written.
B. Prayers were developed after the idea of god developed.
C. People learned writing for utilitarian reasons.
D. Dancing was the earliest form of art.

**7.** Which one of the following words in the passage stands for *ancient*?
A. primitive B. traditional
C. coherent D. utilitarian

## PASSAGE-6

Quality dominates the world ahead of its spherical, classical, racial or any undue discrimination ever exercised by any individual. Physical characteristics of a produce differs its structural attribution in quality from substandard produce with richness of prolong usage features declared by the claimant. Talent Hunt initiated by quality seekers have turned the table of established brand on account of innovative additions presented by their hardships.

The simple message that quality matters because it is cheaper to do things right the first time is yet to sink into the thinking of Indian managers and workers who seem quite content to live in their cloistered world where mediocrity reigns supreme. It is only the ignorant who believe that quality consciousness is a cultural trait. Barely half a century back no one associated Japan with high quality, but today 'Made in Japan' is a symbol of assured quality. The daily drill at school is far more important than the seasonal seminar and an obsession with quality at home is the best way of convincing the world that we value good quality. Indian exports will never be recognised for quality unless Indians are known to insist on good quality at home.

Global appreciation surrounds the exceptional brand by keeping up the physical standard neatly and efficiently. It is designed to meet the international standards' numerous logos and certificates to upkeep the label of quality consciousness. It has prime motto of swaying clean chit observation to the sanctioned produce without any objection. Modern age has been proved a turning point to the old established traditional belief. They are using tiring house hold produce to industrial device responsible to deface the status of rapid development. We breath into the cool and fresh air of healthy surrounding devised by mankind monitored by quality management with rigorous span or struggle tackled with due care.

## QUESTIONS

1. The theme of the passage is:
   A. quality consciousness
   B. export promotion
   C. quality management
   D. promoting Indian culture
2. According to the passage, the Indian exports will never be recognised for quality:
   A. unless there is technical advancement.
   B. unless there is competition.
   C. unless the Indians are known to insist on good quality.
   D. unless government supports the exporters.
3. Which one of the following statements is true?
   A. Indians are known for their insistence on quality.
   B. Indians are not quality conscious.
   C. Japan is not known for its quality product.
   D. 'Made in Japan' is not a symbol of assured quality.
4. The best way to convince the world about quality is:
   A. to conduct seminars on quality control.
   B. to advertise the products.
   C. to value for quality products at home.
   D. all of the above
5. According to the passage, the main fault with the Indian managers is that:
   A. they are not hard-working.
   B. they are not quality conscious.
   C. they are not well trained in quality control.
   D. they lack technical knowledge.
6. How quality consciousness is termed as a cultural trait with the ignorant?
   A. The mature opinion of quality.
   B. Quality dominates ahead of traditional belief.
   C. Cultural trait justifies any quality standard.
   D. Quality consciousness leads to management growth.
7. Why 'Made in Japan' is a symbol of assured quality?
   A. Traditional belief
   B. Quality consciousness
   C. Age old negligence suffering
   D. High export offer

## PASSAGE-7

Creamy outlook with soft speech presentation is a prima facie attraction that brings joy on the withering faces with a mixture of sensational touch. Smile with grace is the ultimate boon to the mankind keeping away any melancholy at bay. Old age is often miscalculated as liability with little attention paid to them. Their talents and learned potential is buried alive with undue care by oblivious approach due to disfigured or deformed physical structure taken over by aged talents of the society.

It happens to us all, however hard we may try to delay the process. We grow old. Cosmetic surgery may remove the wrinkles, skin which has sagged may be tightened by means of a facelift and hair dresser may dye grey hair a more youthful colour, but we cannot remain young forever.

However, what is important is the quality of life. Some people are lucky to be taken care of at home whereas others may have to move to residential homes. The worst part of ageing is that often the mind becomes less alert. As people grow older, they experience short term memory. Later some may suffer from dementia, often in the form of Alzheimer's disease.

By no means all people are in this category. Many senior citizens are in the possession of all their faculties and see retirement as a time of freedom. Not only that if they have a generous retirement pension, they are likely to be quite well off with money to be spent on a holiday and other luxuries. Because of this, both businesses and government have a new respect for what is known as grey power.

It is unfortunate that many people regard old people as geriatrics who have one foot in the grave. Someone should remind them that they too would be old one day!

They are honoured with senior citizen label granted by the authority with due regard paid from distinct possession of living cadres. One should always bear in mind the old saying "Tit for Tat". Which denotes its symbolic regulation of periodical sufferings. The aforesaid misdoings of emotional disparity, done by striding steps is a curse to the mankind.

## QUESTIONS

1. Cosmetic surgery :
   A. helps in the retention of youth forever.
   B. cannot stop the natural process of ageing.

C. is the solution to ageing.
D. is the fancy of the rich.

**2.** While ageing man's greatest worry is :
A. his growing wrinkles.
B. his short term memory.
C. his quality of life.
D. moving to a residential home.

**3.** The government considers grey power as :
A. a liability
B. an asset
C. neither an asset nor a liability
D. a spent force

**4.** Retirement is seen as a time of freedom because people :
A. no longer have to go to office.
B. can enjoy their earnings.
C. can spend time with their families.
D. finally move into residential homes.

**5.** *geriatrics* in the passage refers to :
A. handicapped people
B. doctors for the aged
C. a branch of medicine
D. aged people

**6.** What is the theme of the passage?
A. Old is gold
B. The grey power
C. Youth domination in the society
D. Aged suffering

**7.** What does the phrase 'suffer from dementia' refer to?
A. Harmful
B. Short term memory loss
C. Lunacy
D. Paralysis

## PASSAGE-8

1. The world is teemed with different continents and oceans surrounded with settled and manless island as declared by the geographical experts of the world.

2. Pacific island dominates amongst the oceans escorted with wildlife, ecosphere and manageable resources with identified culture of scientific explorations. Man hunt for unseen spheres remains a landmark occasion yearning for lavish search with instrumental approach. Galapagos Islands remind us of such human efforts noted for spherical search with wildhunt.

3. The Galapagos Islands in the Pacific Ocean are a rocky, lonely spot, but they are also one of the most unusual places in the world. The reason is that they are the home of some of the last giant tortoises left on earth.

4. Weighing hundreds of pounds, these tortoises wander slowly around the rocks and sand of the islands. Each of these islands has its own particular kind of tortoise. There are seven different kinds of tortoises on the eight islands.

5. Hundreds of years ago, thousands of tortoises wandered around these islands. All that changed when people started landing there. When people first arrived, their ships had no refrigerators. This meant that fresh food was always a problem for the sailors on board. The giant tortoises provided a solution to his problem.

6. Ships would anchor off the islands, and crew would seize as many tortoises as they could. Once the animals were aboard the ship, the crew would roll the tortoises onto their backs and use them for soups and stews.

7. Human search never ends with seeking variable resources sustainable to their growth-oriented programme. Man hunt with crew supported by voyage turns the pages of historical map to best transformation regions discovered by his hardcore practice. How long 'wants' arrest his peace of mind with the dream of next destination is yet to know with.

## QUESTIONS

**1.** The author calls the Galapagos Islands an unusual place because :
A. they are in the Pacific Ocean.
B. the endangered giant tortoises are found there.
C. they are rocky and lonely spots.
D. they are located off the western coast of South America.

**2.** Which statement is correct?
A. There is one kind of tortoise found on the seven islands.
B. There are eight kinds of tortoises found on the eight islands.
C. There are seven kinds of tortoises found on the eight islands.
D. All the tortoises are on one island.

**3.** The giant tortoises provided a solution to the problem of not having refrigerators because :
A. the sailors went looking for refrigerators as they were starving.
B. fresh food was available in plenty as the sea was vast.
C. the fresh giant tortoise could be killed and eaten whenever the sailors were hungry.
D. the sailors seized the tortoise to store in refrigerators.

4. *Ships would anchor off the islands* means that Ships:
   A. would go off
   B. would be near the shore
   C. would be off to another land
   D. would go to another island

5. In paragraph 6 the word crew means:
   A. the new settlers.
   B. the men arriving on Galapagos Islands.
   C. the men working on the ships.
   D. the men catching the tortoises.

6. Mark the True statement which best suits the passage.
   A. Galapagos is the unusual island due to regular plains.
   B. People landed at Island duely in search of tortoises.
   C. Lack of refrigerators made crew turn to tortoises.
   D. Tortoises numbered more than crews on the Island.

7. Soups and stews refers to :
   A. soup apart with flesh.
   B. soup extracted out of tortoise cooking.
   C. tortoise fat.
   D. a synthetic process of vegetation.

## PASSAGE-9

The goal of the fair, to be held at the Cervantes Institute in the Indian capital, is to attract the largest number of students in order to present them with information on the educational programmes Spain has to offer, primarily postgraduate. Studying in Spain gives students an added advantage of living and studying in one of the world's most important economies that also aims for an internationalisation of its university system, which plays a decisive role in knowledge-based economy.

In this context, the Spanish universities, both private and public, numbering 77 in total, offer Master degrees and PhD programmes adapted to the European Higher Education Area; a harmonised space between all European countries that have opted to participate in this model. This implies that any student that obtains a postgraduate degree in a Spanish university will automatically have their studies recognised in any participating country and may continue their doctoral studies without needing to validate their degree. In addition, Spanish universities are offering more and more postgraduate degrees in English in order to attract international students. Nevertheless, it is also very common for students to come to Spain intending to complete postgraduate studies in Spanish as well. Students are offered a double advantage from, first, studying in high quality university programmes, and second, studying in a rapidly growing language, that will soon reach 500 million speakers. Spanish is also the official language in more than 20 countries and a second language in important economies such as the United States and Brazil, which gives graduates and edge when entering the workforce.

These are just a few reasons why studying in Spain is such a unique opportunity. On February 19 and 20th, Indian students are invited to visit the Cervantes Institute where they can directly ask the universities any and all questions about studying in Spain as well as get information about programmes that the universities offer.

Another incentive for students to attend will be the prize drawing for six intensive Spanish courses at Spanish universities in summer 2011. The six big winners will have air fare, accommodations, and tuition paid for while attending the month-long course.

## QUESTIONS

1. The objective of the fair is ______.
   A. to tell about Spain
   B. to tell about the courses being started in India
   C. to impart information about education in Spain
   D. none of the above

2. Decisive role means ______
   A. taking decisions B. important role
   C. key role D. minor role

3. Spanish Universities are offering programmes in English because ______.
   A. English is a global language
   B. it wants to get students from all over the world
   C. English is easy to understand
   D. it is easy to get professors to teach in English

4. One of the advantages of studying in Spain is that ______.
   A. it is a beautiful country
   B. education there is cheap
   C. courses are easy
   D. Spanish is the second language in some important countries

5. Those who attend the fair ______.
   A. will get to participate in a prize draw
   B. will be given free air ticket to Spain
   C. will get fee waiver for one term
   D. none of the above

## PASSAGE-10

An incandescent bulb lights up when electrical power heats a metal filament wire to a high temperature until it glows. You usually get them rated between 15 and 100 watts. Meanwhile, fluorescent lamps (tubes and their newer compact versions, known as CFLs) use inert gases inside to fluoresce and produce light. There are also lamps that use an array of light-emitting diodes (LEDs) working in the way electrons behave, a phenomenon called electro luminescence. Because LED lamps are costly, very few homes use them—and it's best to wait a while before buying for their prices to come down, just as you did with CFLs over the past years.

At about ₹ 20 a piece, incandescent bulbs may look cheap, but they are not. They waste some 90 per cent of the power consumed—as heat. Consumers preferred them to energy-efficient fluorescent tubes not just because they are cheaper, but also because you may place them in choice lamp shades. Or because the bluish-white illumination from tubes can seem harsh and unnatural, and may contribute to glare and eyestrain.

If you don't like the way tube lights look in the hall or bedroom, use them only in passages, verandas and the kitchen.

## QUESTIONS

**1.** Bulbs light up when ______.
A. metal filament burns
B. electricity heats up metal filament
C. electric current is in excess
D. metal comes in contact with heat

**2.** CFLs use
A. gases like Argon, Krypton, etc.
B. mercury
C. thin metal strips
D. any of the above

**3.** Electro luminescence is the process where ______.
A. electrons and protons react to emit light
B. diodes function as electrons and emit light
C. light is generated by water
D. light is generated by sun

**4.** Incandescent bulbs are costly because ______.
A. they cost ₹ 20 a piece
B. they break easily
C. their power consumption is high
D. none of the above

**5.** Bulbs are used because they ______.
A. are cheap
B. conserve energy
C. you can place them in choice lamp shades
D. none of the above

## PASSAGE-11

Conservation of water in the agricultural sector is essential since water is necessary for the growth of plants and crops. A depleting watertable and a rise in salinity due to overuse of chemical fertilisers and pesticides have made matters serious. Various methods of water harvesting and recharging have been and are being applied all over the world to tackle the problem. In areas where rainfall is low and water is scarce, the local people have used simple techniques that are suited to their region and reduce the demand for water. In India's arid and semi-arid areas, the 'tank' system is traditionally the backbone of agricultural production. Tanks are constructed either by bunding or by excavating the ground and collecting rainwater.

Rajasthan, located in the Great Indian Desert, receives hardly any rainfall, but people have adapted to the harsh conditions by collecting whatever rain falls. Large bunds to create reservoirs known as khadin, dams called johads, tanks and other methods were applied to check water flow and accumulate run-off. At the end of the monsoon season, water from these structures was used to cultivate crops. Similar systems were developed in other parts of the country. These are known by various local names *jal talais* in Uttar Pradesh, the *haveli* system in Madhya Pradesh, *ahar* in Bihar, and so on.

## QUESTIONS

**1.** There is an increase in water salinity due to ______.
A. conservation of water
B. depletion of water
C. overuse of chemical fertilisers and pesticides
D. water harvesting

**2.** 'Depleting watertable' means ______.
A. reduction in the groundwater level
B. measurement of water level
C. recharging of water level
D. usage of fertilisers and pesticides

**3.** In arid and semi-arid regions, rainwater is collected by ______.
A. using industrial methods
B. constructing tanks
C. harvesting of water
D. adapting to the harsh conditions

**4.** How much rainfall does Rajasthan, the state in the Great Indian Desert, receive?
A. plenty of rainfall B. no rainfall
C. moderate rainfall D. scanty rainfall

**5.** Where do farmers of Rajasthan get water from to cultivate their crops after the monsoon season?
A. from tanks, bunds, dams and reservoirs
B. from whatever rain that falls
C. from excess rainwater
D. from the rivers

## PASSAGE-12

Every family with two or more children often experiences sibling rivalry at one time or the other. Children in general, fight with each other for their parents' attention. They fight among themselves mostly on trivial issues. If it does not get excessive, this kind of rivalry can, in fact, be a healthy competition that trains children to share, respect one another. They will learn to deal with frustration and displeasures in the maturing process.

The firstborns generally feel that they don't have to share their parents' love and attention. But when the next baby or siblings come along, they feel neglected and that changes everything. The first child starts to feel that he/she is no longer the centre of attraction and that he/she is being sidelined because of the new one. Some children might develop negative feelings and emotional imbalance, which may lead to regressive behaviour.

Such problems could be averted if right moves are taken. One way is to explain the firstborns about the arrival of a new child. They need to establish a connection with the new baby before it is born. Older children should be trained to show a positive attitude towards their siblings. They should be involved, along with their parents, in teaching their siblings social and manual skills, which in turn, helps them to accept them. Sometimes personality differences and parental conflicts too have an impact on the children. Parents have to show patience, understand these issues and should openly communicate with their children to resolve them.

### QUESTIONS

1. Sibling rivalry means fight between ______.
   A. firstborn and second child
   B. children of same parents
   C. children born to different parents
   D. cousins and relatives
2. 'Why do firstborns feel neglected by the arrival of a new child in the family?
   A. because they have to share their parents' love and attention
   B. because of their negative attitude
   C. because they hate their siblings
   D. because parents do not love them
3. What does the word 'regressive' in para 2 mean?
   A. emotional imbalance
   B. withdraw or shy away
   C. negative feeling
   D. harsh or rude
4. How can older children develop a positive attitude towards their siblings?
   A. by developing sibling rivalry
   B. by keeping away from their siblings
   C. by their involvement in matters related to the young ones
   D. by dominating their siblings
5. What should parents do to control sibling rivalry?
   A. allow children to fight among themselves
   B. do not allow any communication between children
   C. punish the children
   D. openly communicate with children to resolve issues

## PASSAGE-13

Music can have strong consequences on our feelings. One should try to gain benefits from the power of music. Music, in general, helps one to calm down and feel revitalized. It helps to beat a bad mood or to continue a good state of mind. To cheer up or to enhance vitality, one should listen to music with beats, lots of drumming and a fast tempo. When one wants to relax after a busy day, instrumental music with less percussion and a slower rhythm can help. Listening to soothing music before stressful activities has a lot of benefits and so is always advised. A collection of preferred relaxing tunes help to combat stress at work. One can change one's frame of mind by switching from one kind of music to another. To feel refreshed, it is better to start with something tranquil and soothing and to slowly pick up the pace and the beat. But when one prefers to settle down after a busy schedule, follow the reverse style.

Music is an incredible means that people can use to communicate things, especially their feelings and emotions. When added to speech in a song, it becomes a powerful device of communication. Music generally needs special aptitude, inborn talent and rigorous practice. Also, a person needs to have fine muscular strength in order to sing in tune or play a musical instrument. Recollection of the notes demands good memory power. Besides, many people feel that music and love are connected to each other. A person tries to make an impression on his/her love by way of selecting appropriate music.

### QUESTIONS

1. Music with fast beats and lots of drumming __________.
   A. boosts up one's energy
   B. calms down one's mind
   C. is less beneficial
   D. leads to stress
2. What does 'percussion' mean?
   A. stressful condition
   B. tranquil mood

C. thumping or fast beat
D. inborn talent

3. What kind of music is preferred when a person wants to settle down?
A. music with lots of percussion
B. first upbeat music and then soothing music
C. music of string instruments
D. first gentle music and then fast music

4. Why is music considered to be a powerful means of communication?
A. because it helps people to express their emotions
B. because it is an incredible tool
C. because it reduces stress at work
D. because it enhances energy in people

5. What qualities are needed for a person to sing or play a musical instrument?
A. love, talent, speech and memory
B. aptitude, emotion, strength and love
C. knowledge, emotion, love and talent
D. aptitude, talent, practice and strength

## PASSAGE-14

In order to heal your emotional baggage and prevent it from possibly costing you yet another relationship, you must recognise the roots of your emotional pain or fears and acknolwedge your accountability in them.

According to psychologists, one should review the event or experience that you think caused you to be hurt and identity your role in the experience. "Allow yourself to learn from that and forgive yourself—often misplaced guilt can be the cause for fear. Acknowledge that your past does not have to dictate your future. Release all the emotional hurt and fears that were weighing you down and standing in the way of your seeing each individual relationship for its own merit and potential. It can be difficult to let go of the security blanket of past behaviours but assure yourself that you no longer need them. Sometimes one may require professional help to be able to identify, draw links, acknowledge, accept and forgive themselves. In the end, it all comes down to trust. Want to leave that baggage behind? Allow yourself to trust again," concludes a psychologist.

## QUESTIONS

1. It is important to understand ________.
A. pain
B. emotions
C. cause of emotional pain
D. effect of emotional pain

2. It is advised that we should ________.
A. stop feeling the pain
B. review the event
C. take rest
D. all of the above

3. We should not allow the past ________.
A. to guide our future
B. to bother us
C. actions to make today's decision
D. to affect our present

4. We should learn to let go ________.
A. pain
B. negative emotion
C. fear
D. the security of the past

5. The most important thing in life is ________.
A. trust
B. love
C. compassion
D. fear

## PASSAGE-15

Maintaining work-life balance is necessary because imbalance wreaks chaos in life. Increased pressure on one side will affect the other side too.

After all, the two cannot be completely disconnected! The first step towards this is finding the cause for the imbalance.

Some of the potential causes are—you are genuinely overloaded with work, you are incompetent, your time management skills are poor or you chase conflicting goals.

Once you identify the problem, you should admit it and work towards overcoming it. When you are better organised, your efficiency increases. Make a list of activities and prioritise them. This should be done on daily, weekly and monthly basis.

Plan in advance how you will deal with impending additional responsibilities. If you have to spend extra time at the office, inform your family about it and seek their support. If you have to take leave, inform your boss.

When your organisation is going through a change, there is a crisis or you are vying for a promotion, it can be inevitable to spend more time at work. So explore alternative ways to show your loved ones that you care. When you are with your family and friends, make the most of the time. Do not think about work at least during the 'special' time you allotted for them.

Pay attention to your health. Sleep well. Spend time on activities that can help beat fatigue. Allot time for physical exercises, yoga or sports.

## QUESTIONS

1. Chaos here means __________.
   A. disturbance  B. confusion
   C. happiness  D. calmness
2. As soon as we identify the problem we should __________.
   A. work towards overcoming it
   B. forget it
   C. overcome it
   D. none of the above
3. When there is extra work one should __________.
   A. stay up at night  B. work from home
   C. plan in advance  D. all of the above
4. When one is spending time with family __________.
   A. one should carry work also
   B. one should relax and sleep
   C. one should keep thinking about work
   D. one should not think about work
5. It is important to take care of one's health because __________.
   A. it helps to be positive and chargeable
   B. one can do more work
   C. work is worship
   D. none of the above

## PASSAGE-16

You are at a party and want to watch your weight and health. However when the appetisers are served you notice nothing looks healthy. The next thing you know, you go ahead and eat those decorative little morsels and blow your eating plan. Stop!

Those little delicious nuts in that bowl are chock-full of nutrition. They will improve your cardiovascular health; hold cancer prevention properties and help you lose weight. It's hard to believe but it's true!

The idea that something from nuts may actually help weight control seems a little counter-intuitive at first; bearing in mind the reputation nuts have for being both fatty and fattening. Nuts are nutrient-packed, healthy 'primal' food, and something that experience shows satisfy the appetite and prevent overeating at meal time. High in proteins, unsaturated fats may aid in weight loss and other disease-fighting properties.

What do nuts have that is heart-healthy? Nuts are an intensely fatty food, with about 80 per cent of the calories they offer coming from fat. But bear in mind that the type of oils found in nuts such as almonds, cashews, walnuts is predominantly the healthy monounsaturated and polyunsaturated type.

Researchers found that people who eat nuts regularly have lower risk of heart disease. In 1998, a study conducted by the Harvard School of Public Health found that women who ate nuts less than four times a week were 40 per cent less likely to die of heart disease. Further, potential heart health benefits of nuts were also found among men. In 2002, the Physician's Health Study found that men who consumed nuts two or more times per week had reduced risk of sudden cardiac death.

## QUESTIONS

1. Nuts possess __________.
   A. nutritive value
   B. fattening properties
   C. oil
   D. all of the above
2. During meal time nuts __________.
   A. add taste to the food
   B. satisfy appetite
   C. should not be consumed
   D. create an urge for water
3. Nuts contain __________.
   A. unhealthy oils  B. cholesterol
   C. healthy oils  D. none of the above
4. People who consume nuts regularly __________.
   A. are not prone to heart attacks
   B. are prone to heart attacks
   C. are not prone to kidney failure
   D. are prone to kidney failure
5. Sudden cardiac death means death due to __________.
   A. kidney failure
   B. sudden heart failure
   C. sudden brain malfunction
   D. increase in lung pressure

## PASSAGE-17

Acupuncture is an ancient form of healing that dates back to Stone Age. It is a technique of inserting and manipulating fine needles into specific points on the body to relieve pain or for therapeutic purposes. Acupuncture originated in China and is most commonly associated with traditional Chinese medicine. As per the traditional Chinese medical theory, acupuncture points are situated on meridians along which 'Qi' (pronounced as 'chee'), the vital energy, flows. Apparently, there is no known histological basis for the existence of acupuncture meridians. Different types of acupuncture such as Classical Chinese, Japanese, Tibetan, Vietnamese and Korean are practised throughout the world.

The practice of acupuncture is based on the understanding that a vital energy flows along channels or meridians throughout our bodies. When this energy becomes blocked or does not flow freely, it causes disharmony or disease. In order to correct this disharmony, the vital force must be stimulated so that it moves freely again. A set of very fine needles are used to stimulate peculiar points located on the flow of energy and the actions of the various acupuncture points to treat diseases and disharmonies in the body. Quite significantly, acupuncture is not usually painful. Acupuncture needles are tiny and are quickly inserted through the skin, where the nerves that transmit pain are located. The sensation of the insertion is like a "quick pinch". In general, there is an agreement that acupuncture is safe when administered by well-trained practitioners using sterile needles and that further research is appropriate.

## QUESTIONS

**1.** Where does vital energy flow through in human bodies?

A. through muscle cells
B. through blood cells
C. through meridians
D. through sense organs

**2.** How are acupuncture points stimulated?

A. by inserting find needles into specific points on the body
B. by knowing the histological basis
C. by flow of vital energy
D. by going to China

**3.** A person specialising in the technique of Acupuncture is called ________.

A. a practitioner
B. an acupuncturist
C. a classical Chinese
D. a medical doctor

**4.** How is a disease caused as per the traditional Chinese medical theory?

A. when one feels a quick pinch
B. when blood does not flow through the vessels
C. when needles are inserted into specific points
D. when vital energy does not flow freely through meridians

**5.** Where are the acupuncture needles inserted?

A. in the nerve cells where vital energy flows
B. on the upper part of the right or left hand
C. in the skin where the nerves transmitting pain are found
D. in the muscular part of the hip region

## PASSAGE-18

While many of India's parks have been developed from the hunting preserves of princely India, Keoladeo, popularly known as Bharatpur Wildlife Sanctuary, is perhaps the only case where the habitat has been created by a maharaja. In earlier times, Bharatpur town used to be flooded regularly every monsoon. In 1760, an earthen dam, called the Ajam Dam, was constructed, to save the town from this annual vagary of nature. The depression created by extraction of soil for the dam was cleared and this became the Bharatpur Lake.

At the beginning of this century, this lake was developed and divided into several portions. A system of small dams, dykes, sluice gates, etc., was created to control the water level in different sections. This became the hunting preserve of the Bharatpur royalty and also one of the best duck-shooting wetlands in the world. But hunting was prohibited by mid-60s and the area was then declared a national park on 10 March 1982. This was later accepted as a World Heritage site in December 1985.

The major attractions of tourists visiting this park are the numerous migratory birds, which come from as far away as Siberia and Central Asia to spend their winters in Bharatpur, before returning to their breeding grounds. The migratory birds at this bird sanctuary include several species of Cranes, Pelicans, Geese, Ducks, Eagles, Hawks, Shanks, Stints, Wagtails, Warblers, Wheatears, Fly catchers, Buntings, Larks and Pipits, etc.

## QUESTIONS

**1.** Bharatpur Wildlife Sanctuary was developed ________.

A. from the hunting preserves of princely India
B. by constructing Ajam dam
C. by the Maharaja of Bharatpur Royalty
D. from the floods of every monsoon

**2.** What is the reason behind the construction of Ajam dam?

A. to develop a hunting preserve
B. to develop a wildlife sanctuary
C. to bring an end to floods
D. to save the town from being flooded

**3.** One of the best duck-shooting wetlands of the world is ________.

A. Princely India B. Bharatpur lake
C. Ajam dam D. Bharatpur royalty

**4.** When was Bharatpur Lake given the status of a national park?

A. 10 March 1982 B. 10 January 1982
C. 10 December 1985 D. 10 October 1985

5. What are migratory birds?
   A. birds from Siberia and Central Asia
   B. birds that travel long distances during some seasons
   C. birds from Bharatpur Wildlife Sanctuary
   D. birds from the hunting preserves of India

## PASSAGE-19

*Lexicographer : a writer of dictionaries, a harmless drudge, that busies himself in tracing the original, and detailing the signification of words.* Thus said Samuel Johnson in his Dictionary, with an ironic swipe at his own work. It wasn't the first dictionary of the English language, but it continued to be regarded as an authoritative if quirky icon of language for more than two centuries. In two volumes and 2,300 pages, Johnson tried to tidy up a notoriously untidy and promiscuous language, though he knew at the same time that it was futile to attempt to straitjacket it. We tend to think of dictionaries as "anonymous" productions, but Johnson's personality is all over the work. In his bitter definition of a patron, "commonly a wretch who supports with insolence, and is paid by flattery", Johnson took care of his own patron, Lord Chesterfield, who had promised to help financially but had not delivered till too late. Since Johnson's Dictionary, which has been reprinted, abridged, and is still written about, there have been books too numerous to count on the English language: Melvyn Bragg's The Adventure of English: The Biography of a Language, the most recent (2004), Raymond Williams' Keywords: A Vocabulary of Culture and Society (1985), one of the most respected. But there are hundreds of others.

### QUESTIONS

1. Samuel Johnson made an ironic remark at his own work by calling a lexicographer __________.
   A. a harmless drudge
   B. a writer of dictionaries
   C. one who is busy in tracing the original
   D. all the above
2. Johnson's Dictionary __________.
   A. continues to be regarded as an authority on icons
   B. was one of the first dictionaries of English language
   C. was regarded a quirky icon of language
   D. has been printed for more than two centuries
3. Tick the correct statement.
   A. Since Johnson's dictionary many have been reprinted.
   B. Johnson's dictionary has been reprinted and abridged.
   C. Johnson abridged his dictionary many times.
   D. Johnson abridged Melvyn Bragg's 'The Adventure of English'.
4. Which of the following statements are true?
   (1) Johnson's dictionary has two volumes.
   (2) His dictionary defines 'patron' as commonly a wretch who supports with insolence, and is paid by flattery.
   (3) Lord Chesterfield was Johnson's patron.
   (4) Lord Chesterfield did not help Johnson financially.
   A. (1) and (3) are True, (2) and (4) are False.
   B. All are True.
   C. (1), (2) and (3) are True and (4) is False.
   D. (2), (3) and (4) are True and (1) is False.
5. Find a word in the passage that means the same as 'unsuccessful'.
   A. swipe  B. insolence
   C. straitjacket  D. futile

## PASSAGE-20

Swaminathan went to school feeling that he was the worst perjurer on earth. His conscience bothered him : he wasn't at all sure if he had been accurate in his description of Samuel. He could not decide how much of what he had said was imagined and how much of it was real. He stopped for a moment on the roadside to make up his mind about Samuel.... His cane skinned people's hands. Swaminathan cast his mind about for an instance on this. There was none within his knowledge. Years and years ago he was reputed to have skinned the knuckles of a boy in the First Standard and made him smear the blood on his face. No one had actualy seen it. But year after year the story persisted among the boys.... Swaminathan's head was dizzy with confusion in regard to Samuel's character—whether he was good or bad, whether he deserved the allegations in the letter or not.... he felt an impulse to run home and beg his father to take back the letter. But Father was an obstinate man.

As he approached the yellow building he realised that he was perjuring himself and was ruining his teacher. Probably the Headmaster would dismiss Samuel and then the police would chain him and put him in jail. For all this disgrace, humiliation and suffering who would be responsible? Swaminathan shuddered. The more he thought of Samuel, the more he grieved for him. As he felt the bulge of the letter in his pocket, he felt like an executioner.

As he entered the school gate an idea occurred to him, a sort of solution. He wouldn't deliver the letter to the Headmaster immediately, but at the end of the day—to that extent he would disobey his father and exercise his independence. There was nothing wrong in it, and Father would not know it anyway. If the letter was given at the end of the day there was a chance that Samuel might do something to justify the letter.

Swaminathan stood at the entrance to his class. Samuel was teaching arithmetic. He looked at Swaminathan for a moment, Swaminathan stood hoping that Samuel would fall on him and tear his skin off. But Samuel merely asked, 'Are you just coming to the class?'

## QUESTIONS

**1.** Swami was not comfortable going to school that day because ________.

A. he was not well

B. he had lied about his teacher Samuel

C. he had not done his home work

D. his friend was not there

**2.** He was not sure about Samuel's character because ________.

A. what he knew was all hearsay

B. what he knew was his imagination

C. other teachers had told him so

D. none of the above

**3.** Swami's father was not likely to take back the letter because

A. he believed that Samuel was a good teacher

B. his father wanted to help Swami and other children

C. he was a very stubborn man

D. all of the above

**4.** Swami decided to ________.

A. give the letter to the Headmaster

B. give the letter directly to Mr. Samuel

C. tear off the letter

D. give it to the Headmaster at the end of the school

**5.** As Swami was late to the school he expected ________.

A. Mr. Samuel to hit him

B. Mr. Samuel will allow him into the class

C. to be shouted at by Mr. Samuel

D. none of the above

## PASSAGE-21

Leadership does not exist without followership. A leader has to be accepted by the group which the former is supposed to lead. To gain acceptability the leader should cause an emotive impact on the group members. The character exhibited by leaders make them dear to their followers. A leader is one who effectively inspires employees to achieve worthwhile goals. What character of the leader motivates the followers? It is not pomp and show or flattery or sanctioning more incentives.

Pomp and show creates a sense of awe and the leader is defied rather than emulated. Flattery is unrealistic and cannot serve as a long-term motivational tool.

A leader's style should be one that can be emulated by all irrespective of cadre, class or calibre. Simplicity in one's day-to-day conduct is the only thing that can be adopted by all. When the leader is simple, he is counted as one belonging to the group of which he is the leader. That's to motivate the people. Motivation is the innate quality that enables an individual or group to contribute unlimitedly with limited means. It is the proud prerogative of enlightened human beings.

## QUESTIONS

**1.** Leadership co-exists with ________.

A. obedience B. followership

C. discipline D. incentives

**2.** The pre-requisite for the success of a leader is ________.

A. obedience by the group

B. simplicity of the leader

C. acceptability by the group he is supposed to lead

D. strict discipline of the group

**3.** The leader should cause an emotive impact on the group members as ________.

A. to ensure obedience

B. to enforce discipline

C. to control the group

D. to gain acceptability

**4.** To inspire employees to achieve long term goals, a leader should not use ________.

A. sanctioning more incentives

B. flattery

C. pomp and show

D. all of the above

**5.** Find a word having the same meaning as 'emotive' from the words given below:

A. Prerogative B. Enlightened

C. Sensitive D. Proud

## PASSAGE-22

We first became aware that something unusual was happening when one of the ship's officers came up to the Chief Engineer, who sat at one table and spoke to him on a low voice. The Chief Engineer at once stood up and with a brief excuse which told us nothing, left the dining room. At first we thought that there had been an accident or that a fire had broken out on board ship, but soon the word went round that a man had been floating in the sea. Then we noticed that the ship had slowed down and was beginning to turn round, with a rather violent motion. Some of the passengers did not wait to finish their meal, but at once rushed upon deck. Others crowded round the portholes, making it impossible for us to eat in comfort. There was such confusion in the dining room that we decided to join those who had come up on deck.

There we learnt that one of the crew had seen a man in the sea some distance from the ship. He had informed the captain who at once ordered the ship to be turned round. We were now only two hundred yards or so from the man and a life boat had already been lowered into the sea. In it there were four sailors, who were sitting ready at the oars, an officer and the ship's doctor. The officer shouted an order and the sailors began to row away the ship. But looking in the same direction as the boat was going, we were able to make out the position of the man in the water. He was clinging to a large piece of wood. At last, after what seemed to us an age the life boat reached the man and two of the sailors pulled him on the boat. This was not at all easy for the sea was rather rough. Then the sailors began to row back to the ship again. The life boat was raised out of the water and the rescued man, wrapped in a blanket was helped out on the deck. Leaning on the arm of the ship's doctor, but still able to walk, in spite of his terrible experience he was led off to the ship's hospital. As he passed along the deck everyone cheered loudly.

## QUESTIONS

1. 'We' here refers to ________.
   A. the crew members
   B. the sailors
   C. the passengers of the ship
   D. all of the above
2. The Passengers rushed to the back of the ship because ________.
   A. the ship was drowning
   B. a fire had broken out on board ship
   C. a fight had broken up
   D. the crew was trying to save a drowning man
3. It was tough for the crew to save the drowning man as ________.
   A. the weather was rough
   B. the sea was rough
   C. the man was unwilling to come along with the sailors
   D. the ship had moved ahead
4. Everyone cheered the man loudly as ________.
   A. he had saved the drowning man
   B. he had informed about the drowning man
   C. he had survived a terrible experience
   D. he was the doctor who treated the drowning man
5. The words or the phrase in the passage that means 'it came into knowledge' is ________.
   A. seem to us an age
   B. with a rather violent motion
   C. in comfort
   D. the word went round

## PASSAGE-23

In this world there is no worse nuisance than a boy at the age of fourteen. He is neither ornamental nor useful. It is impossible to shower affection on him as a smaller boy; and he is always getting in the way. If he talks with a childish lisp he is called a baby, and if in a grown-up way he is called impertinent. In fact, talk of any kind from him is resented. Then he is at the unattractive, growing age. He grows out of his clothes with indecent haste: His voice grows hoars and breaks and quivers; His face grows suddenly angular and unsightly. It is easy to excuse the shortcomings of early childhood, but it is hard to tolerate even unavoidable lapses in a boy of fourteen. He becomes painfully self-conscious, and when he talks with elderly people is either unduly forward, or else so unduly shy that he appears ashamed of his own existence.

Yet, it is at this age that in his heart of hearts, a young lad most craves recognition and love; and he becomes the devoted slave of any one who shows him consideration. But none dare openly love him, for that would be regarded as undue indulgence and therefore bad for the boy. So, what with scolding and chiding, he becomes very much like a stray dog that has lost its master.

His own name is the only paradise that a boy of fourteen can know. To live in a strange house with strange people is little short of fortune; while it is height of bliss to receive the kind looks of women and never to suffer their slights.

## QUESTIONS

1. The expression 'he is always getting in the way' means that he is ________.
   A. found/seen everywhere you go
   B. behaving in a different way from expected/desired
   C. always troubling others with his undesired ways
   D. he goes where he is asked to
2. A lad of fourteen years of age is resented because ________.
   A. he behaves too childishly
   B. he acts like a grown-up
   C. his behaviour becomes neither of a child nor of a grown-up
   D. he looks troublesome
3. A fourteen-year-old boy becomes self-conscious when ________.

A. when he is regarded neither as a young nor a grown-up
B. when he is slighted by elders
C. when he is not appreciated for his good actions
D. none of the above

**4.** The great bliss for such a boy is _________.
A. to be rewarded for his achievements
B. to receive the kind glances of women
C. to have the company of jolly friends
D. to do what he likes to do

**5.** The writer's own attitude towards the fourteen-year-old boy is _________.
A. satirical B. sympathetic
C. indifferent D. none of the above

## PASSAGE-24

For years, Fukuoka was widely known as the closest city that Japan had to Venice. It might not have enjoyed the splendid architecture, piazzas or the Basilica San Marco of the Italian city, but the people of the largest metropolis on Kyushu, Japan's most southerly main island, prided themselves on the carefully maintained network of rivers that emptied into the graceful curve of Hakata Bay and gave Fukuoka its blue credentials. Today, however, the capital of Kyushu is forging a new identity for itself as green complements the blue.

Not satisfied with pioneering a method of semi-aerobic landfill known the world over as "The Fukuoka Method", the city has gone on to implement some highly exacting rubbish-segregating standards for both homes and businesses. And it has ambitious plans to turn itself into the world's first city to be powered by hydrogen, a project that is under way and will eventually evolve into a "corridor" of homes and businesses linking Fukuoka with the larger cities of Osaka, Nagoya and eventually, the mammoth Tokyo, some 900 kilometres to the rest.

All that and yet Fukuoka is still regarded as the most pleasant place to live in Japan and among the best in the world. In its annual quality of life survey in July 2010, Britain's *Monocle* magazine ranked Fukuoka the 14th "most liveable" city on the planet, thanks in part to its air connections with the rest of Asia, its low crime rate, sub-tropical climate, excellent public transport services and cultural opportunities.

City authorities also received high marks for subsidising local residents who want to install solar-energy systems in their homes to the tune US$1.2 million. Elsewhere, funds have been invested in the creation of green spaces.

### QUESTIONS

**1.** The city of Fukuoka is considered _________.
A. closest to Venice B. different from Venice
C. Peaceful city D. close to Rome

**2.** Green complements the blue means _________.
A. green and blue do not go together
B. green and blue go well with each other
C. If we have green in a place, it is auspicious to have blue there
D. none of these

**3.** Fukuoka has set very high standards for
A. cleanliness
B. keeping city green
C. separating bash at home as well as work place
D. maintaining clean air

**4.** Fukuoka is high on the list of the most liveable cities in the world because _________.
A. there is less crime
B. environment is clean
C. excellent connectivity, within and outside the city
D. all of the above

**5.** Residents of Fukuoka who wish to install solar powered system _________.
A. Know the advantages of the same
B. will be subsidised by the state
C. are encouraged by the government
D. none of these

## PASSAGE-25

A tiger relies on stealth to catch its prey. It has excellent eyesight and hearing, which help it track animals in the dark. Tigers hunt large animals such as deer and wild pigs, which will provide food for a few days. They slink up on their prey unseen, only charging when they are within about 20m (65 ft). Tigers kill their prey by biting the back, its neck or throat, then dragging it away into thick cover to feed. When they have eaten enough, they conceal the carcass with leaves so they can return to it later on. Male tigers can eat up to 40 kg (85 lb) of meat in one meal.

Tigers love water and often bathe or cool off in rivers and pools during the heat of the day. They usually hunt at night and rest during the day. Most tigers live alone, although mothers with cubs or young siblings sometimes hunt together. A male tiger roams a territory of up to 100 sq km (60 sq. miles) in area, defining its boundaries with scent markings, droppings and scratch marks on boulders or trees. These signals tell other tigers about its sex and size as well as its territory. Tigers also communicate by roaring and moaning. They defend their territory fiercely against rival males, but will tolerate some overlap with the smaller territories of females.

### QUESTIONS

**1.** Stealth means _________.
A. by cheating

B. secret way
C. attacking from front
D. jumping at the prey

**2.** Tigers hunt big animals because ________.
A. it is easy to hunt them
B. their meat is tasty
C. the meat will last them a few days
D. they are easily available

**3.** Tigers drag their prey into the bush ________.
A. so that nobody can disturb them
B. it is cool under a bush
C. other animals may snatch their prey
D. to conceal it

**4.** During the hot summer season ________.
A. tigers like to cool by staying in water
B. tigers go off to sleep
C. tigers stay under the bush
D. tigers move to cooler areas

**5.** Tigers prefer to ________.
A. stay in small groups
B. stay alone
C. stay as a family
D. take care of their young one

## PASSAGE-26

The Kidneys of nearly five per cent of people under the age of 20 are not functioning normally, a study shows. The youngsters have albumin in the urine, which indicates that they could develop a serious kidney disease later in their lives. Doctors say that more youngsters today are at a risk of kidney malfunction due to lifestyle changes, which includes smoking, consumption of junk food and less physical activity from desk-bound jobs. On the eve of World Kidney Day, doctors are stressing on the early detection of Kidney malfunction as the only way to reduce serious complications and chronic kidney disease.

For the pilot study, the institute of nephrology at a hospital used a home detection kit that is dipped in urine to show presence of protein in the sample. During the study, 1,000 people were given the kits. A total of 265 returned them with feedback. Of this, 5% of the young population had urinary protein.

Doctors say that the main issue with kidney disease is the lack of early detection. If detected early, patients can avoid reaching the stage of dialysis, which indicates irreversible and serious kidney damage. "Simple health screening test comprising urine tests, blood test and ultrasounds are important. Early diagonsis and treatment for kidney disease can significantly delay and even prevent kidney failure and need for dialysis." said doctors. One doctor said home detection kits would help in early detection, and added that they were targeting young people in colleges and IT firms to use this kit.

## QUESTIONS

**1.** As many as ________ of youngsters have kidney problem.
A. 20%
B. 5%
C. 22%
D. 12%

**2.** This problem is mainly due to ________.
A. obesity in youngsters
B. change in lifestyle
C. poor intake of water
D. none of the above

**3.** The main problem with kidney related disease is ________.
A. it is fatal
B. it cannot be treated
C. it cannot be detected early
D. it is painful

**4.** Simple tests will help in ________.
A. preventing and delaying kidney failure
B. giving treatment
C. relieving pain
D. all of the above

**5.** Hospitals are targeting colleges and IT firms because ________.
A. youngsters need it the most
B. these places have only youngsters
C. they want to bring down kidney issue among youngsters
D. all of the above

## PASSAGE-27

Global warming this century could trigger a run away thaw of Greenland's ice sheet and other abrupt shifts such as a dieback of the Amazon rainforest, scientists say.

They urged governments to be more aware of "tripping points" in nature, tiny shifts that can bring big and almost always damaging changes such as a melt of Arctic summer sea ice or a collapse of the Indian monsoon.

"Society may be lulled into a false sense of security by smooth projections of global change," the scientists at British, German and American institutes wrote in a report saying there were many little-understood thresholds in nature.

"The greatest and clearest threat is to the Arctic with summer sea ice loss likely to occur long before, and potentially contribute to, Greenland ice sheet melt", they wrote in the journal "Proceedings" of the National Academy of Sciences. "Tipping elements in the tropics, the boreal zone, and west Antarctica are surrounded by large uncertainty", they wrote, pointing to more potential abrupt shifts than seen in a 2007 report by the UN Climate Panel.

A projected drying of the Amazon basin, linked both to logging and to global warming, could set off a dieback of the rainforest. Many of these tipping points could be closer.

Other sudden changes linked to climate change, stoked by human use of fossil fuels, included a dieback of northern pine forests, or a stronger warming of the Pacific under EI Nino weather events that can disrupt weather world-wide, they wrote.

A possible greening of parts of the Sahel and the Sahara, if monsoon rains in West Africa were disrupted, was one of the few positive abrupt shifts identified by the scientists.

Even a moderate warming could set off a thaw of Greenland's ice sheet that could then vanish in 300 years—raising sea levels by 20 ft, or 2 meters a century and threatening coasts, Pacific islands and cities from Bangkok to Buenos Aires. The UN Climate Panel foresees a rise in world sea level ranging up to about 80 cms this century and reckons that a thaw of Greenland would take hundreds of years longer.

The new study said a disappearance of Arctic sea ice in summer time could happen in coming decades—earlier than projected by the UN panel. That could stoke further global warming as dark water soaks up more heat than ice and snow.

## QUESTIONS

**1.** Global warming can cause ______.
A. thawing of green land
B. excess rain
C. severe draught
D. a green earth

**2.** Nations should be sensitive to small changes that can cause ______.
A. famine
B. melting of Arctic ice
C. decrease in sea level
D. chill in polar regions

**3.** There could be a die-back of the rainforest because of ______.
A. drying of Amazon Basin
B. water level
C. ses level
D. melting glaciers

**4.** As a result of rains in West Africa ______.
A. Sahara will turn into desert
B. Sahara will turn green
C. flood will come
D. none of these

**5.** According to a UN panel report ______ in this century.
A. sea level will decrease
B. sea level will remain same
C. sea level will rise
D. none of these

## PASSAGE-28

From time immemorial drugs have been used by humans for medical purposes. But never before had the abuse ... (A) ... narcotics caused such unprecedented worldwide concern and posed an alarming menace to the society. According to recent World Health Organization estimates, there are millions of ... (B) ... addicts and abusers of cocaine, opium, barbiturates, sedatives and tranquilizers all over the world. It is now an international problem that ... (C) ... the Indian government. Recent movies like Udta Punjab have highlighted that the consumption of drugs has affected the youth in the state of Punjab adversely. Taking a drug other than for medical reason in amount, strength, frequency or manner that ... (D) ... the physical and mental functioning is drug abuse. Drug abuse is a painful problem for the addict, for the family and for all those who touch their lives. It is mostly the youngsters that fall prey to drugs. At this stage, the youngsters are especially vulnerable to pressure from friends. The future generation is virtually being crippled under the impact of drugs. Due to intake of drugs, the person may lose will power, concentration, memory and judgement capacity. There is a need to create awareness amongst the youth as well as work towards rehabilitation of those trapped in ...(E)... abuse.

## QUESTIONS

**1.** Choose the most appropriate option for (B):
A. heroin B. heroine
C. medicine D. work

**2.** Choose the most appropriate option for (D):
A. mends B. damages
C. invigorates D. augments

**3.** Choose the most appropriate option for (E):
A. object B. environment
C. substance D. habitat

**4.** Choose the most appropriate option for (C):
A. surprises B. pleases
C. bothers D. amuses

**5.** Choose the most appropriate option for (A):
A. by B. of
C. from D. through

## PASSAGE-29

Once upon a time there was a bird. It was ignorant. It sang all right, but never recited scriptures. It hopped pretty frequently, but lacked manners. Said the Raja to himself: "Ignorance is costly at the long run. For fools consume as much food as others, and yet give nothing in return."

He called his nephews to his presence and told them that the bird must have a sound schooling. The pundits were summoned, and at once went to the root of the matter. They decided that the ignorance of the bird was due to their natural habit of living in poor nest. Therefore, according to pundits, the first thing necessary for this bird's education was a suitable cage. The pundits had their rewards and went home happily. A golden cage was built with gorgeous decorations. Crowds came to see it from all parts of the world. "Culture, captured and caged" exclaimed some, in a rapture of ecstasy and burst into tears. Others remarked: "even if culture be missed, the cage will remain, to the end, a substantial fact. How fortunate for the bird." The goldsmith filled his bag with money and lost no time in sailing homewards.

The pundits sat down to educate the bird. With proper deliberation they took their pinch of snuff, as one of them said: "Text-books can never be too many for our purpose!" The nephews brought together an enormous crowd of scribes. They copied from books, and copied from copies, till the manuscripts were piled up to an uncatchable height. Men murmured in amazement. "Oh, the tower of culture, egregiously high! The end of it lost in the clouds!" The scribes, with light hearts, hurried home, their pockets heavily laden. The nephews were furiously busy keeping the cage in proper trim. As their constant scrubbing and polishing went on, the people said with satisfaction: "This is progress indeed!" Men were employed in large numbers, and supervisors were still more numerous. These, with their cousins of all different degrees of distance, built a palace for themselves and lived there happily ever after. Whatever may be its other deficiencies, the world is never in want of fault-finders; and they went about saying that every creature remotely connected with the cage flourished beyond words, excepting only the bird.

When this remark reached the Raja's ears, he summoned his nephews before him and said: "My dear nephews, what is this that we hear?" The nephews said in answer: "Sire, let the testimony of the goldsmiths and the pundits, the scribes and the supervisors, be taken, if the truth is to be known. Food is scarce with the fault-finders, and that is why their tongues have gained in sharpness." The explanation was so luminously satisfactory that the Raja decorated each one of his nephews with his own rare jewels.

The Raja at length being desirous of seeing with his own eyes how his education department engaged itself with the little bird, made his appearance one day at the great hall of learning. From the gate rose the sounds of conch-shells and gongs, horns, bugles and trumpets, cymbals, drums and kettle drums, tom-toms, tambourines, flutes, fifes, barrel-organs and bagpipes. The pundits began chanting mantras with their topmost voices, while the goldsmiths, scribes, supervisors, and their numberless cousins of all different degrees of distance, loudly raised a round of cheers.

The nephews pleased, the Raja was about to remount his elephant, when the fault-finder from behind some bush, cried out: "Maharaja, have you seen the bird?"

"Indeed, I have not!" exclaimed the Raja. "I completely forgot about the bird. Turning back, he asked the pundits about the method they followed in instructing the bird. It was shown to him. He was immensely impressed. The method was so stupendous that the bird looked ridiculously unimportant in comparison. The Raja was satisfied that there was no flaw in the arrangements. As for any complaint from the bird itself, that simply could not be expected. Its throat was so completely choked with the leaves from the books that it could neither whistle nor whisper. It sent a thrill through one's body to watch the process.

This time, while remounting his elephant, the Raja ordered his state ear-puller to give a thorough good pull at both the ears of the fault-finder. The bird thus crawled on, duly and properly, to the verge of inanity. In fact, its proper was satisfactory in the extreme. Nevertheless, nature occasionally triumphed overt training, and when the morning light peeped into the bird's cage it sometimes fluttered its wings in a reprehensible manner. And, though it is hard to believe, it pitifully packed at its bars with its feeble break. "What impertinence!" growled the Kotwal.

The blacksmith, with his forge and hammer took his place in the Raja's Department of Education: Oh, what resounding blows! The iron chain was soon completed, and the bird's wings were clipped. The Raja's brother-in-law looked back, and shook their heads, saying: "This bird not only lacks good sense, but also gratitude!" With text-book in hand and baton in the other, the pundits gave the poor bird what may fitly be called lessons!

The Kotwal was honoured with a title for his watchfulness, and the blacksmith for skill in forging chains. The bird died.

***(A Parrot's story by Rabindra Nath Tagore)***

## QUESTIONS

**1.** The Raja wanted the bird to have sound schooling because

A. the bird was consuming the resources of the state but giving nothing in return.

B. he wanted to eventually kill the bird.

C. he wanted to show his gratitude towards the bird.

D. he wished to set before his subjects an example of love towards nature.

2. 'The tower of culture' symbolizes
   A. money  B. raja
   C. manuscripts  D. cage
3. The word 'impertinence' refers to
   A. disrespect  B. stupid
   C. loyalty  D. civility
4. The status of the 'bird' in this story can be compared today with that of a
   A. head of the school
   B. student
   C. teacher educator
   D. teacher
5. The bird died in the end because
   A. it lacked good sense
   B. its cage was dirty
   C. Its natural instincts were suppressed
   D. it was brutally beaten up by the Raja

## PASSAGE-30

Rakesh was on his way home from school when he bought the cherries. He paid fifty paise for the bunch. It took him about half-an-hour to walk home, and by the time he reached the cottage there were only three cherries left. 'Have a cherry, Grandfather,' he said, as soon as he saw his grandfather in the garden. Grandfather took one cherry and Rakesh promptly ate the other two. He kept the last seed in his mouth for some time, rolling it round and round on his tongue until all the tang had gone. Then he placed the seed on the palm of his hand and studied it. 'Are cherry seeds lucky?' asked Rakesh.

'Of course.'

'Then I'll keep it.'

'Nothing is lucky if you put it away. If you want luck, you must put it to some use.'

'What can I do with a seed?'

'Plant it.'

So, Rakesh found a small space and began to dig up a flowerbed. 'Hey, not there,' said Grandfather, 'I've sown mustard in that bed. Plant it in that shady corner, where it won't be disturbed.' Rakesh went to a corner of the garden where the earth was soft and yielding. He did not have to dig. He pressed the seed into the soil with his thumb and it went right in. Then he had his lunch, and ran off to play cricket with his friends, and forgot all about the cherry seed.

When it was winter in the hills, a cold wind blew down from the snows and went whoo-whoo-whoo in the deodar trees, and the garden was dry and bare. In the evenings Grandfather and Rakesh sat over a charcoal fire, and Grandfather told Rakesh stories and in turn Rakesh would read to him from the newspaper, Grandfather's eyesight being rather weak. Rakesh found the newspaper very dull – especially after the stories – but Grandfather wanted all the news.

One morning in the garden he bent to pick up what he thought was a small twig and found to his surprise that it was well rooted. He stared at it for a moment, then ran to fetch Grandfather, calling, 'Dada, come and look, the cherry tree has come up!' 'What cherry tree?' asked Grandfather, who had forgotten about it. 'The seed we planted last year –look, it's come up!' Rakesh went down on his haunches, while Grandfather bent almost double and peered down at the tiny tree. It was about four inches high. 'Yes, it's a cherry tree,' said Grandfather. 'You should water it now and then.' Rakesh ran indoors and came back with a bucket of water. 'Don't drown it!' said Grandfather. Rakesh gave it a sprinkling and circled it with pebbles. 'What are the pebbles for?' asked Grandfather. 'For privacy,' said Rakesh. He looked at the tree every morning, but it did not seem to be growing very fast, so he stopped looking at it except quickly, out of the corner of his eye. And, after a week or two, when he allowed himself to look at it properly, he found that it had grown – at least an inch!

The cherry tree grew quickly during monsoon. It was about two feet high when a goat entered the garden and ate all the leaves. Only the main stem and two thin branches remained. 'Never mind,' said Grandfather, seeing that Rakesh was upset. 'It will grow again; cherry trees are tough.' Towards the end of the rainy season new leaves appeared on the tree. Then a woman cutting grass scrambled down the hillside, her scythe swishing through the heavy monsoon foliage. She did not try to avoid the tree: one sweep, and the cherry tree was cut in two. When Grandfather saw what had happened, he went after the woman and scolded her; but the damage could not be repaired. 'Maybe it will die now,' said Rakesh. 'Maybe,' said Grandfather. But the cherry tree had no intention of dying. By the time summer came again, it had sent out several new shoots with tender green leaves.

One day he found a bright green praying-mantis perched on a branch, peering at him with bulging eyes. Rakesh let it remain there; it was the cherry tree's first visitor. The next visitor was a hairy caterpillar, who started making a meal of the leaves. Rakesh removed it quickly and dropped it on a heap of dry leaves. Come back when you're a butterfly,' he said.

Winter came early. The cherry tree bent low with the weight of snow. In February it was Rakesh's birthday. He was nine – and the tree was four, but almost as tall as Rakesh. One morning, when the Sun came out, Grandfather came into the garden to 'let some warmth get into my bones,' as he put it. He stopped in front of the cherry tree, stared at it for a few moments, and then called out,

'Rakesh! Come and look! Come quickly before it falls!' Rakesh and Grandfather gazed at the tree as though it had performed a miracle. There was a pale pink blossom at the end of a branch. 'There are so many trees in the forest,' said Rakesh. 'What's so special about this tree? Why do we like it so much?' 'We planted it ourselves,' said Grandfather. That's why it's special. 'Just one small seed,' said Rakesh, and he touched the smooth bark of the tree that he had grown. He ran his hand along the trunk of the tree and put his finger to the tip of a leaf. 'I wonder,' he whispered. 'Is this what it feels to be God?'

## QUESTIONS

**1.** The plot of the story revolves around the concept(s) of:

A. relation between grandfather and Rakesh
B. hope, responsibility, perseverance and pride
C. how to plant trees
D. how to feel like God

**2.** The author is an ardent lover of:

A. cherries B. grandfather stories
C. nature and animals D. reading newspaper

**3.** Why does Rakesh circle the plant with some pebbles?

A. His grandfather asked him
B. He likes to play with pebbles
C. To beautify his garden
D. For privacy

**4.** In the story, the Cherry tree symbolises:

A. beauty B. innocence
C. birth D. survival

**5.** The status of 'the cherry tree' in this story can be compared today with that of a:

A. birds B. trees
C. animals D. humans

# III. POETRY

**Directions:** *Read the following poems carefully and choose the best answer to each question out of the four alternatives and mark it in the Answer Sheet.*

## POEM-1

It is an ancient Mariner,
And he stoppeth one of three.
'By thy long grey beard and glittering eye,
Now wherefore stopp'st thou me?
The Bridegroom's doors are opened wide,
And I am next of kin;
The guests are met, the feast is set:
May'st hear the merry din.'

He holds him with his skinny hand,
'There was a ship,' quoth he.
'Hold off! unhand me, grey-beard loon!'
Eftsoons his hand dropt he.

He holds him with his glittering eye —
The Wedding-Guest stood still,
And listens like a three years' child:
The Mariner hath his will.

— ***ST Coleridge***

## QUESTIONS

**1.** What is the most potent factor with the Ancient Mariner that enables him to hold the wedding guest?

A. His glittering eye B. His skinny hand
C. His long grey-beard D. His starting words.

**2.** What is the significance of comparing the wedding guest to a three years' child?

A. A three years' child is innocent.
B. He is afraid of a strange man.
C. He is fond of listening to stories.
D. He cannot run away from a grown-up man.

**3.** Which among the following is not an argument presented by the wedding-guest?

A. The wedding-guest is a close relative of the Bridegroom.
B. His participation in some ceremonies is essential.
C. Merry-making is already going on.
D. Other guests have already arrived.

**4.** The Ancient Mariner is:

A. A young man
B. A middle-aged man
C. An old man
D. It is not clear from the text

**5.** The Mariner's story is related to:

A. A ship B. Giants
C. Fairies D. A forest

## POEM-2

Shall I hear the lament of the nightingale, submissively lending my ear?

Am I the rose to suffer its cry in silence year after year?
The fire of verse gives me courage and bids me no more to be faint.

With dust in my mouth, I am abject: to God I make my complaint.

Sometimes You favour our rivals then sometimes with us You are free,

I am sorry to say it so boldly. You are no less fickle than we.

*(Iqbal: 'Complaint to God')*

## QUESTIONS

**1.** What fault does the poet find in God?
   A. God causes misery to people.
   B. He opposes the poet and his companions and favours their opponents.
   C. He is fickle.
   D. He does not care for the poor.

**2.** What gives courage to the poet?
   A. The song of the nightingale.
   B. The power of poetry.
   C. The sweet smell of the rose.
   D. God's mercy.

**3.** What is the present mood of the poet?
   A. He is distraught.
   B. He is in a happy mood.
   C. He is in a contemplating mood.
   D. He is talking only frivolously.

**4.** Why does the poet use the word "lament" for the song of the nightingale?
   A. The nightingale is sad at poet's miserable condition.
   B. It is only teasing the poet.
   C. It seems sad to the poet only.
   D. Proverbially, the nightingale is said to sing sweet but sad songs.

**5.** In what situation is the rose placed in the poem?
   A. Very advantageous situation.
   B. Helpless situation.
   C. Confusing situation.
   D. Situation of expectation.

## POEM-3

'In vain to me the smiling mornings shine,
And reddening Phoebus lifts his golden fire;
The birds in vain and amorous descant join,
Or cheerful fields resume their green attire.
These ears, alas! for other notes repine;
"A different object do these eyes require;
My lonely anguish melts no heart but mine;
And in my breast the imperfect joys expire;"
Yet morning smiles the busy race to cheer,
And new-born pleasure brings to happier men;
The fields to all their wanted tribute bear;
To warm their little loves the birds complain.
"I fruitless mourn to him that cannot hear,
And weep the more because I weep in vain."

***— Thomas Gray***

## QUESTIONS

**1.** The poet's object in the given poem cannot hear him because:
   A. He has gone deaf.
   B. He does not care for him.
   C. He is awfully busy.
   D. He is dead.

**2.** What does nature bring to the poet?
   A. A sense of loss
   B. A feeling of joy
   C. A sense of satisfaction
   D. A feeling of charm

**3.** Why does the poet use the phrase "in vain" so many times?
   A. To tell about the uselessness of his existence.
   B. To tell about the uselessness of beauties of nature and his wails.
   C. To tell about the uselessness of birds' love.
   D. To tell about waste of morning time.

**4.** What feeling can a keenly observant reader get from a study of the first twelve lines and the last two lines?
   A. A feeling of harmony.
   B. A feeling of amplitude.
   C. A feeling of dichotomy of sense.
   D. A sense of overall satisfaction.

**5.** What does the morning bring to the "happier men"?
   A. A sense of loss.
   B. A new joy.
   C. A feeling of sorrow.
   D. A feeling of sympathy.

## POEM-4

'Turn on the prudent Ant thy heedless eyes,
Observe her labours, Sluggard, and be wise;
No stern command, no monitory voice,
Prescribes her duties, or directs her choice;
Yet, timely provident, she hastes away
To snatch the blessings of a plenteous day;
When fruitful Summer loads the teeming plain,
She crops the harvest, and she stores the grain.

How long shall sloth usurp thy useless hours,
Unnerve thy vigour, and enchain thy powers?
While artful shades thy downy couch enclose,
And soft solicitation courts repose,
Amidst the drowsy charms of dull delight,
Year chases year with unremitted flight,
Till Want now following, fraudulent and slow,
Shall spring to seize thee, like an ambush'd foe.

***— Dr Samuel Johnson***

## QUESTIONS

**1.** What can be said to be the overwhelming quality of an ant?
A. Industriousness
B. Dutifulness
C. Time-consciousness
D. Regular routine

**2.** What will finally overtake a sluggard?
A. Sloth B. Waste of time
C. Loss of energy D. Want

**3.** What does the Ant do in summer?
A. It enjoys the beauties of nature.
B. It sits in the shade of trees.
C. It fills its stores with grain.
D. It spends time eating summer fruits.

**4.** Which among the following is not the characteristic of Want?
A. Fraudulence
B. Ambush
C. Springing over the enemy.
D. Abusing the enemy.

**5.** What is the main characteristic of summer?
A. It is a very hot season.
B. It is a fruitful season.
C. It expects all to do their duties.
D. It always comes on time.

## POEM-5

On their own feet they came, or on shipboard,
Camel-back, horse-back, ass-back, mule-back,
Old civilisations put to the sword.
Then they and their wisdom went to rack;
No handiwork of Callimachus,
Who handled marble as if it were bronze,
Made draperies that seemed to rise
When sea-wind swept the corner stands:
His long lamp-chimney shaped like the stem
Of a slender palm, stood but a day;
All things fall and are built again,
And those that build them again are gay.

***— WB Yeats***

## QUESTIONS

**1.** Which of the following means of transport was not used by the destroyers of old civilizations?
A. By sea
B. By air
C. On the backs of animals
D. On foot

**2.** What is the eternal law of life?
A. Destruction and recreation
B. Destruction
C. Creation
D. Failure of art

**3.** Which of the following could Callimachus do?
A. Make a long thin lamp-chimney last long.
B. Engrave in bronze.
C. Make metallic artefacts.
D. Work with marble without breaking it.

**4.** Is there no hope for civilizations?
A. Yes, there is.
B. No, there's none.
C. The poet gives no clue to it.
D. There is only a little hope.

**5.** Who get real happiness from their activity?
A. The destroyers. B. The builders.
C. The observers. D. The sea-creatures.

## POEM-6

I lay in sorrow, deep *distressed*:
My *grief* a proud man heard;
His looks were cold, he gave me gold
But not a kindly word,
My sorrow passed—I paid him back
The gold he gave to me;
Then stood *erect* and spoke my thanks
And blessed his *Charity.*
I *lay* in *want,* in grief and pain:
A poor man passed my way;
He bound my head, he gave me *bread*
He watched me night and day.
How shall I pay him back again,
For all he did to me?

Oh, gold is great, but greater far

Is *heavenly* Sympathy!

***—Charles Mackey***

## QUESTIONS

1. The proud man heard the poet
   A. crying in sorrow B. sing in joy
   C. lying in misery D. crying due to pain
2. The proud man helped the poet by
   A. giving him comfort
   B. assisting him to lie down
   C. his cold looks
   D. giving him gold
3. The poet thanked the proud man by
   A. speaking nicely to him
   B. giving him money
   C. praising him
   D. blessing his large-heartedness
4. The poor man helped the poet by
   A. giving him comfort
   B. binding his body
   C. giving him food
   D. serving him like his own
5. The word 'heavenly' means
   A. relating to paradise
   B. like that of heaven
   C. like angels
   D. like gods

## POEM-7

The earth was green, the sky was blue;

I saw and heard one sunny *morn*

A *skylark hang* between the two,

A singing *speck* above the corn.

A stage below in gay *accord*,

White butterflies danced on wing,

And still the singing skylark *soared*,

And silent sank and soared to sing.

The *cornfield stretched* a *tender* green

To right and left beside my walks;

I knew he had a nest unseen

Somewhere among the million *stalks.*

And as I *paused* to hear his song

While swift the sunny moments *slid*,

Perhaps his *mate* sat listening long,

And listened longer than I did.

***—Christina Rossetti***

## QUESTIONS

1. The skylark sang when
   A. it rained
   B. the sun shone
   C. the earth was green and the sky without clouds
   D. there were clouds
2. The skylark while singing looked like
   A. a star B. an insect
   C. an eagle D. a small dot
3. The skylark rose upwards and upwards
   A. while flying B. while singing
   C. as it sang D. as it flew
4. The nest of the skylark was
   A. in the fields below
   B. among the numberless stems of corn
   C. beside other nests
   D. among trees
5. The word 'paused' means
   A. stopped B. stood erect
   C. flew across D. went straight

## POEM-8

The Forst *performs* its secret *ministry*,

Unhelped by any wind. The owlet's cry

Came loud—and *hark*, again! loud as before.

The *inmates* of my cottage, all at rest,

Have left me to that *solitude*, which suits

*Abstruser musings* : save that at my side

My *cradled infant slumbers* peacefully.

Tis calm indeed! so calm, that it disturbs

And *vexes meditation* with its strange

And extreme silentness ......

***—S.T. Coleridge***

## QUESTIONS

1. The 'secret ministry' of the frost is that
   A. it is falling on the ground
   B. it ministers the earth
   C. it has a secret deal with the nature
   D. it deals with the air
2. There is silence all round. This is seen in the phrase
   A. and hark, again
   B. all at rest
   C. that solitude
   D. Abstruser musings
3. Who is sleeping in the cradle?
   A. the poet's son B. the poet's child
   C. the poet's nephew D. a stranger baby

4. What disturb(s) the calm?
A. the surroundings B. nature
C. weather D. calmness
5. The word 'meditation' means
A. prayers B. thought
C. deep thought D. deep ideas

## POEM-9

She *dwelt* among the *untrodden* ways
Beside the springs of Dove,
A Maid whom there were none to praise
And very few to love :
A *violet* by a *mossy* stone
Half hidden from the eye!
—*Fair* as a star, when one
Is shining in the sky.
She lived unknown, and few could know
When Lucy *ceased* to be;
But she is in *grave,* and, oh,
The difference to me!

—***William Wordsworth***

## QUESTIONS

1. Lucy lived a lonely life because
A. no person loved her
B. no one praised her
C. there was no human population
D. she was born in nature
2. Lucy was like a
A. rose flower B. a star
C. a violet flower D. a daffodil
3. She died on unknown death because
A. no one knew her
B. no one could tell where she died
C. she was never known
D. no one knew when she died
4. That the poet is sad over Lucy's death is clear in the words :
A. she is in grave
B. oh
C. the difference to me
D. Lucy ceased to be
5. The word 'untrodden' means
A. not covered
B. unwalkable
C. not walked over
D. hard to walk

## POEM-10

I wandered lonely as cloud
That *floats* on high o'er *vales* and hills,
When all at once I saw a crowd,
A *host* of golden daffodils ;
Beside the lake, beneath the trees,
*Fluttering* and dancing in the breeze.
Continuous as the stars that shine
And *twinkle* in the milky way,
They *stretched* in never-ending line
Along the *margin* of a *bay* :
Ten thousasnd saw I at a *glance,*
*Tossing* their head in *sprightly* dance.
The waves beside them danced; but they
*Outdid* the *sparkling* waves in *glee* :
A poet could not but be gay,
In such a *jocund* company;
I *gazed*—and gazed—but little thought
What wealth the show to me had brought.
For oft, when on my couch I lie
In vacant or in *pensive* mood,
They *flash* upon that inward eye
Which is the bliss of *solitude*;
And then my heart with pleasure fills
And dances with the daffodils.

—***William Wordsworth***

## QUESTIONS

1. The poet compares himself with
A. a cloud that is rainy
B. a cloud
C. a floating cloud
D. a daffodil
2. The daffodils danced
A. like stars
B. beside the lake
C. like twinkling stars
D. in lake water
3. The daffodils made the waves shy in their
A. dancing B. shining
C. sparkling D. shaking
4. The poet's wealth from daffodils is
A. the bliss of solitude
B. their dancing
C. their bright colour
D. his joyful heart

5. The word 'sprightly' means
   A. happy B. blissful
   C. joyful D. playing

## POEM-11

Is this a holy thing to see
In a rich and fruitful land,
Babes reduc'd to *misery,*
Fed with cold and *usurous* hand?
Is that *trembling* cry a song?
Can it be a song of joy?
And so many children poor?
It is a land of poverty?
And their sun does never shine,
And their fields are *bleak and bare,*
And their ways are fill'd with thorns :
It is *eternal* winter there.
For where'er the sun does shine,
And where'er the rain does fall,
Babes can never hunger there,
Nor poverty the mind *appall.*

***—William Blake***

## QUESTIONS

1. 'Rich and fruitful land' stands for
   A. U.S.A. B. England
   C. India D. China
2. Babies there sing a song with
   A. joy B. trembling hands
   C. a trembling cry D. sadness
3. If the babies live a miserable life, that country is indeed a country of
   A. sick children B. happy children
   C. poor children D. hungry children
4. 'It is eternal winter there' means
   A. children's life is not happy
   B. children's future is bleak
   C. winter is all the year around
   D. winter is at the peak
5. The word 'usurous' means
   A. of zamindar
   B. very cruel
   C. of money lender
   D. of trader

## POEM-12

There was a family of rabbits
who lived near a *pack* of wolves.
The wolves *announced* that they did
not like the way the rabbits were
living. One night several wolves were
killed in an earthquake and this was
blamed on the rabbits, for it
is well known that rabbits *pound*
on the ground with their *hind*
legs and cause earthquakes. On
another night one of the wolves was
killed by a bolt of *lightning*
and this also was blamed on the
rabbits. The wolves *threatened* to *civilise* the
rabbits if they didn't behave, and
the rabbits decided to run away
to a desert island. But the other
animals, who lived at a great distance,
shamed then saying, "You must stay where
you are and be brave. This is no world
for escapists. If the wolves attack you,
we will come to your aid, in all
*probability."* So the rabbits continued
to live near the wolves. And one day
there was a *terrible* flood which
drowned a great many wolves. This was
blamed on the rabbits, for it is
well known that they with long
ears cause floods. The wolves *descended* on
the rabbits for their own good,
and imprisoned them in a dark *cave,*
for their own protection.
When nothing was heard about
the rabbits for some weeks, the other
animals demanded to know what
had happened to them. The wolves
replied that the rabbits had been
eaten and since they had been
eaten the affair was a purely
internal matter.
"They were trying to escape" said
the wolves, "and, as you know, this
is no world for escapists."

***—James Thurber***

## QUESTIONS

1. Rabbits do an activity that is similar to earthquakes. It is
   A. moving the soil
   B. causing earthquakes
   C. shaking their hind legs
   D. striking the ground
2. The second time wolves died due to
   A. electricity B. lightning
   C. floods D. earthquakes
3. The other animals advised the rabbits not to go away because
   A. they shouldn't be affraid of wolves
   B. there was no fear
   C. they must be brave
   D. they should oppose the wolves
4. The lesson of the incident is that those who escape
   A. can't live
   B. can't progress
   C. shall be free from danger
   D. shall lag behind
5. The word 'announced' means
   A. went away B. spoke
   C. whistled D. declared

## POEM-13

The countryside must *preserved*
(Preferably miles away from me.)
Neat hectares of the *stuff* reserved
For those in need of flower or tree.
I'll make do with *landscape* painting
Film *documentaries* on TV
And when I need to escape, *panting,*
Then open-mouthed I'll head for the sea.
Let others *stroll* and take their *leisure,*
In grasses wade upto their knees.
For I *derive* no earthly pleasure
From the green green *rash* that makes me *sneeze.*

—*Roger McGough*

## QUESTIONS

1. The poet feels that the countryside should look
   A. green
   B. covered with vegetation
   C. full of flowers
   D. good with trees
2. The poet would like to satisfy himself of his desire to see nature from
   A. films B. documentaries
   C. TV D. cable TV
3. The poet gets immense pleasure when he is far from
   A. natural beauty
   B. countryside
   C. villageside
   D. film documentaries
4. The poet hates the greenery because it makes him
   A. sick B. dissatisified
   C. a nature lover D. sneeze
5. The word 'landscape' means
   A. a scene of nature
   B. physical scene of a place
   C. nature beauty
   D. vegetation

## POEM-14

One infant grows up and becomes a *jockey;*
Another plays basketball or hockey,
This one the prize ring hates to enter
That one becomes a *tackle or center,*
I am just as glad as glad can be
That I'm not them, that they're not me.
With all my heart do I admire
Athletes who *sweat* for fun or hire,
Who take the field in *gaudy pomp,*
And *maim* each other as they *romp,*
My *limp and bashful spirit* feeds
On other people's *heroic deeds.*
Now A runs ninety yards to score,
B knocks the champion to the floor.
C risking *vertebrae and spine,*
*Lashes his steed* across the line,
You'd think my *ego* it would please
To *swap* positions with one of these.
Well, ego might be pleased enough,
But zealous athletes play so rough,
They do not ever, in their dealings
Consider one another's feelings.
I'm glad that when my struggle begins
*Twixt prudence* and ego, prudence wins.
Athletes, I'll drink to you
Or eat with you,

Or anything except compete with you,
Buy tickets worth their weight in *radium,*
To watch you *gambol* in a stadium.
And reassure myself anew
That you're not me and I'm not you.

—*Ogden Nash*

## QUESTIONS

**1.** The poet admires the sportspersons who
A. win the game
B. perspire for goals
C. beat other participants
D. enjoy playing

**2.** The poet's spirit enjoys
A. the great sport feats of the players
B. seeing them getting injured
C. knocking one another of sportspersons
D. their fighting for the goal

**3.** What makes the poet not to be a sportsperson?
A. hatred to be a player
B. wisdom to avoid playing
C. fear of injuries
D. careless playing leading to injuries

**4.** The poet will do anything
A. to see the players playing
B. to go to the stadium
C. for the sportspersons
D. for the well-being of the players

**5.** The word 'prudence' means
A. athletics B. wisdom
C. skill D. bravery

## POEM-15

The *fair breeze* blew, the white foam flew,
The *furrow* followed free;
We were the first that ever burst
Into that silent sea.
Down dropt the breeze, the sails *dropt* down,
T was sad as sad could be;
And we did speak only to break
The silence of the sea!
All in a hot and copper sky,
The bloody Sun, at noon,
Right up above the mast did stand,
No bigger than the Moon.
Day after day, day after day,
We *struck*, nor breath nor motion;
As *idle* as a painted ship
Upon a painted ocean.

—*S.T. Coleridge*

## QUESTIONS

**1.** The weather became fine and this is clear from
A. the wind blowing very fast
B. the wind blowing leisurely
C. the furrow being free
D. the white foam

**2.** But soon the weather became very bad as
A. the ship couldn't move
B. the sails couldn't gather wind
C. they became sad
D. they couldn't speak

**3.** The sky became
A. very hot
B. bloody
C. hot and copper like
D. very perspiring

**4.** The ship looked like a painted one because it
A. couldn't run B. couldn't move
C. got fully aground D. got anchored

**5.** The word 'mast' means
A. a pillar
B. sailing prop
C. upright post in a ship
D. upright post of wood in a ship

## POEM-16

The old priest Peter Gilligan
Was *weary* night and day;
For half his *flock* were in their beds,
Or under green *sods* lay.
Once while he *nodded* on a chair,
At the *moth-hour* of *eve*,
Another poor man sent for him,
And he began to *grieve.*
"I have no rest, nor joy, nor peace,
For people die and die";
And after cried he, "God forgive!
My body *spake,* not I!"
He knelt, and *leaning* on the chair
He prayed and fell asleep;
And the moth-hour went from the fields,
And stars began to *peep.*

"*Mavrone,* mavrone! The man has died
While I slept on the chair";
He *roused* his horse out of its sleep,
And rode with little care.
He rode now as he never rode,
By rocky *lane and fern*;
The sick man's wife opened the door :
"Father! You come again!"
"And is the poor man dead?" he cried.
"He died an hour ago."
The old priest Peter Gilligan
In grief *swayed to and fro.*
"When you were gone, he turned and died
As merry as a bird."
The old priest Peter Gilligan
He knelt at that word.

***—W.B. Yeats***

## QUESTIONS

**1.** Peter Gilligan was very tired because he
A. had not slept for long
B. had been serving the people day and night
C. nursed the sick
D. cared much for his own people

**2.** He worried much because
A. his people were dying
B. he had had no sleep
C. his own people were sad
D. the poor man came to him

**3.** He regretted that the man died
A. when he had slept
B. when it was midnight
C. when no one was near him
D. when he slept

**4.** Father Gilligan found when he visited the poor man's house that
A. God nad visited in his place
B. God had excused him
C. he was not wanted
D. he couldn't do anything

**5.** The word 'moth-hour' means
A. late evening  B. midnight
C. morning  D. mid-day

## POEM-17

It takes much time to kill a tree,
Not a simple *job* of the knife
Will do it. It has grown
Slowly *consuming* the earth,
Rising out of it, feeding
Upon its *crust, absorbing*
Years of sunlight, air, water,
And out of its *leprous hide*
*Sprouting* leaves.
So *hack and chop*
But this alone won't do it.
Not so much pain will do it.
The bleeding *bark* will heal
And from close to the ground
Will rise *curled green twigs,*
*Miniature boughs*
Which if unchecked will expand again
To former size.
No,
The root is to be pulled out
Out of the *anchoring* earth;
It is to be roped, tied,
And pulled out—*snapped out*
Or pulled out *entirely,*
Out from the earth-cave,
And the strength of the tree *exposed,*
The source, white and wet,
The most sensitive, hidden
For years inside the earth.
Then the matter
Of *scorching* and *choking*
In sun and air,
*Browning,* hardening,
*Twisting, withering,*
And then it is done.

***—Gieve Patel***

## QUESTIONS

**1.** The tree has come out of the earth after
A. taking breath in the atmosphere
B. using the soil
C. feeling the heat of the sun
D. absorbing the crust.

**2.** If the tree is chopped, it will still
A. live  B. wither
C. stand  D. heal

**3.** If the tree is chopped, its leaves will
A. glisten
B. grow to their former size

C. will rise from the ground
D. shine beautifully

**4.** The 'white and wet' part of a tree when uprooted is its
A. source
B. sensitive part
C. life
D. important part

**5.** The word 'hidden' means
A. clear B. obscure
C. safe D. concealed

## POEM-18

The quality of mercy is not *strain'd*;
It droppeth as the gentle rain from heaven
Upon the place beneath. It is twice blest.
It blesseth him that gives and him that takes.
T is *mightiest* in the mightiest; it *becomes*
The *throned monarch* better than his *crown*;
His *sceptre* shows the force of *temporal* power,
The *attribute* to *awe* and *majesty,*
Wherein doth sit the *dread* and fear of kings;
But mercy is above this sceptred *sway,*
It is enthroned in the hearts of kings,
It is an attribute to God himself;
And earthly power doth then show likest God's
When mercy *seasons* justice.

## QUESTIONS

**1.** Mercy is compared with
A. rain
B. king
C. monarch
D. gentle rain

**2.** Mercy adds more glory to a
A. king
B. monarch
C. monarch's crown
D. monarch sitting in his throne

**3.** When does mercy becoem God-like?
A. when it enters a king's heart
B. when it mixes with the king's grace
C. when it is seasoned with justice
D. when mercy seasons a king's justice

**4.** What shows the temporal power of a monarch?
A. his throne B. his mercy
C. sceptre D. his crown

**5.** The word 'attribute' means
A. quantity B. quality
C. absolute D. feature

## POEM-19

Whose *woods* these are I think I know,
His house is in the village thought,
He will not see me stopping here
To watch his woods fill up with snow.
My little horse must think it *queer*
To stop without a farmhouse near
Between the woods and frozen lake
The darkest evening of the year.
He gives his *harness bells* a shake
To ask if there is some mistake.
The only other sound's the sweep
Of easy wind and *downy flake.*
The woods are lovely; dark and deep,
But I have promises to keep,
And miles to go before I sleep,
And miles to go before I sleep.

## QUESTIONS

**1.** The poet is standing
A. in a village
B. on the bank of a river
C. in a forest
D. by the side of a lake

**2.** When the poet stands, the horse
A. shakes its harness bells
B. shakes the bells
C. stands silently
D. asks a question

**3.** What kind of a weather is it?
A. wet and cloudy
B. cold and snowy
C. very cold and windy
D. cold and windy

**4.** '... before I sleep' means here
A. before I sleep on my bed
B. before I die
C. before I go home and sleep
D. before I 'sleep' at one level and **before I 'die'** at another

**5.** The words 'downy flake' mean
A. soft particles of snow
B. soft snow
C. fluffy snow
D. soft and fluffy

## POEM-20

The little creature
with a hundred feet
was on its journey
to where
only it knew.
My civilised foot
dressed in polished leather
came down upon it
even so gently
there was only a soft sound
*signifying*
the end
of a creature of God
my Maker
I looked to see
if my *sole* was *spoiled*
and walked away

## QUESTIONS

1. '... with a hundred feet' actually means
   A. a hundred feet
   B. many feet
   C. about a hundred feet
   D. near about a hundred feet
2. The poet calls his foot 'civilised' because he
   A. means it otherwise
   B. is civilised
   C. is wearing polished shoes
   D. looks civilised
3. This poem can be classified as
   A. humorous B. religious
   C. satirical D. romantic
4. The poet walked away. It means he
   A. didn't bother about the death of the centipede
   B. remained indifferent towards the centipede's death
   C. regetted the centipede's death
   D. felt pity for the insect
5. The word 'signifying' here means
   A. displacing B. indicating
   C. making it important D. proving

# ANSWERS

## I. Cloze Test

### PASSAGE-1

| 1 | 2 | 3 | 4 | 5 | 6 |
|---|---|---|---|---|---|
| A | B | A | C | D | A |
| 7 | 8 | 9 | 10 | 11 | 12 |
| A | B | A | B | C | B |
| 13 | 14 | | | | |
| D | B | | | | |

### PASSAGE-2

| 1 | 2 | 3 | 4 | 5 | 6 |
|---|---|---|---|---|---|
| B | B | A | D | B | C |
| 7 | 8 | 9 | 10 | 11 | |
| C | B | A | C | A | |

### PASSAGE-3

| 1 | 2 | 3 | 4 | 5 | 6 |
|---|---|---|---|---|---|
| C | D | A | A | B | B |
| 7 | 8 | 9 | 10 | 11 | 12 |
| C | D | B | A | B | C |

### PASSAGE-4

| 1 | 2 | 3 | 4 | 5 | 6 |
|---|---|---|---|---|---|
| B | C | A | B | D | C |
| 7 | 8 | 9 | 10 | 11 | 12 |
| B | C | A | D | B | A |
| 13 | | | | | |
| D | | | | | |

### PASSAGE-5

| 1 | 2 | 3 | 4 | 5 | 6 |
|---|---|---|---|---|---|
| D | C | A | B | C | B |
| 7 | 8 | 9 | 10 | 11 | 12 |
| C | D | B | A | D | C |

### PASSAGE-6

| 1 | 2 | 3 | 4 | 5 | 6 |
|---|---|---|---|---|---|
| A | B | D | B | A | B |
| 7 | 8 | 9 | 10 | 11 | 12 |
| D | C | D | C | B | B |

### PASSAGE-7

| 1 | 2 | 3 | 4 | 5 | 6 |
|---|---|---|---|---|---|
| A | B | D | A | B | C |
| 7 | 8 | 9 | 10 | 11 | 12 |
| D | D | C | D | A | B |
| 13 | | | | | |
| D | | | | | |

**PASSAGE-8**

| 1 | 2 | 3 | 4 | 5 | 6 |
|---|---|---|---|---|---|
| C | C | B | A | D | B |
| **7** | **8** | **9** | **10** | **11** | **12** |
| D | D | C | D | A | B |

**PASSAGE-9**

| 1 | 2 | 3 | 4 | 5 | 6 |
|---|---|---|---|---|---|
| B | B | C | B | D | A |
| **7** | **8** | **9** | **10** | **11** | **12** |
| D | A | B | C | D | D |

**PASSAGE-10**

| 1 | 2 | 3 | 4 | 5 | 6 |
|---|---|---|---|---|---|
| A | D | A | D | D | C |
| **7** | **8** | **9** | **10** | **11** | **12** |
| B | B | D | A | A | B |

**PASSAGE-11**

| 1 | 2 | 3 | 4 | 5 | 6 |
|---|---|---|---|---|---|
| C | B | D | A | B | A |
| **7** | **8** | **9** | **10** | **11** | **12** |
| A | B | D | C | A | B |

**PASSAGE-12**

| 1 | 2 | 3 | 4 | 5 | 6 |
|---|---|---|---|---|---|
| A | B | C | A | B | C |
| **7** | **8** | **9** | **10** | **11** | **12** |
| B | D | B | D | B | C |

**PASSAGE-13**

| 1 | 2 | 3 | 4 | 5 | 6 |
|---|---|---|---|---|---|
| D | C | B | C | C | A |
| **7** | **8** | **9** | **10** | **11** | |
| B | B | C | D | B | |

**PASSAGE-14**

| 1 | 2 | 3 | 4 | 5 | 6 |
|---|---|---|---|---|---|
| B | C | A | D | C | C |
| **7** | **8** | **9** | **10** | **11** | |
| D | A | B | A | C | |

**PASSAGE-15**

| 1 | 2 | 3 | 4 | 5 | 6 |
|---|---|---|---|---|---|
| A | B | D | B | D | B |
| **7** | **8** | **9** | **10** | **11** | |
| C | A | C | D | B | |

**PASSAGE-16**

| 1 | 2 | 3 | 4 | 5 | 6 |
|---|---|---|---|---|---|
| C | A | C | B | A | A |
| **7** | **8** | **9** | **10** | **11** | |
| C | B | D | D | D | |

**PASSAGE-17**

| 1 | 2 | 3 | 4 | 5 | 6 |
|---|---|---|---|---|---|
| D | B | D | D | D | C |
| **7** | **8** | **9** | **10** | **11** | |
| A | D | A | A | B | |

**PASSAGE-18**

| 1 | 2 | 3 | 4 | 5 | 6 |
|---|---|---|---|---|---|
| B | C | B | A | C | C |
| **7** | **8** | **9** | **10** | **11** | **12** |
| C | D | D | D | A | D |
| **13** | **14** | **15** | **16** | **17** | |
| C | A | B | D | C | |

**PASSAGE-19**

| 1 | 2 | 3 | 4 | 5 | 6 |
|---|---|---|---|---|---|
| B | A | B | C | B | D |
| **7** | **8** | **9** | **10** | **11** | |
| B | C | D | D | B | |

**PASSAGE-20**

| 1 | 2 | 3 | 4 | 5 | 6 |
|---|---|---|---|---|---|
| D | C | D | A | A | B |
| **7** | **8** | **9** | **10** | | |
| C | C | A | C | | |

**PASSAGE-21**

| 1 | 2 | 3 | 4 | 5 | 6 |
|---|---|---|---|---|---|
| D | B | C | B | C | B |
| **7** | **8** | **9** | **10** | | |
| A | D | D | D | | |

**PASSAGE-22**

| 1 | 2 | 3 | 4 | 5 | 6 |
|---|---|---|---|---|---|
| C | A | B | C | B | D |
| **7** | **8** | **9** | **10** | **11** | |
| A | A | B | D | D | |

**PASSAGE-23**

| 1 | 2 | 3 | 4 | 5 | 6 |
|---|---|---|---|---|---|
| B | A | C | B | A | A |
| **7** | **8** | **9** | **10** | **11** | **12** |
| B | D | C | A | C | B |
| **13** | **14** | **15** | **16** | **17** | **18** |
| C | B | C | C | A | C |

**PASSAGE-24**

| 1 | 2 | 3 | 4 | 5 | 6 |
|---|---|---|---|---|---|
| A | D | C | A | B | D |
| **7** | **8** | **9** | **10** | **11** | **12** |
| D | B | B | C | A | A |

**PASSAGE-25**

| 1 | 2 | 3 | 4 | 5 | 6 |
|---|---|---|---|---|---|
| D | C | B | A | D | C |

| 7 | 8 | 9 | 10 | 11 | 12 |
|---|---|---|---|---|---|
| A | A | C | D | B | D |
| **13** | **14** | | | | |
| D | A | | | | |

**PASSAGE-26**

| 1 | 2 | 3 | 4 | 5 | 6 |
|---|---|---|---|---|---|
| A | C | B | C | D | B |
| **7** | **8** | **9** | **10** | **11** | |
| D | C | B | A | A | |

**PASSAGE-27**

| 1 | 2 | 3 | 4 | 5 | 6 |
|---|---|---|---|---|---|
| C | B | B | A | A | B |
| **7** | **8** | **9** | **10** | **11** | **12** |
| C | A | D | D | B | D |
| **13** | **14** | **15** | **16** | | |
| C | C | B | B | | |

**PASSAGE-28**

| 1 | 2 | 3 | 4 | 5 | 6 |
|---|---|---|---|---|---|
| D | D | C | D | B | B |
| **7** | **8** | **9** | **10** | **11** | **12** |
| C | C | B | B | C | A |
| **13** | **14** | **15** | | | |
| A | D | C | | | |

**PASSAGE-29**

| 1 | 2 | 3 | 4 | 5 | 6 |
|---|---|---|---|---|---|
| B | B | C | D | A | B |
| **7** | **8** | **9** | **10** | **11** | **12** |
| A | B | C | D | B | C |

**PASSAGE-30**

| 1 | 2 | 3 | 4 | 5 | 6 |
|---|---|---|---|---|---|
| B | C | A | A | D | D |
| **7** | **8** | **9** | **10** | **11** | **12** |
| D | C | C | B | B | C |
| **13** | **14** | **15** | | | |
| A | B | D | | | |

**PASSAGE-31**

| 1 | 2 | 3 | 4 | 5 | 6 |
|---|---|---|---|---|---|
| A | B | D | A | B | C |
| **7** | **8** | **9** | **10** | **11** | **12** |
| B | A | B | D | A | B |
| **13** | **14** | **15** | | | |
| D | A | A | | | |

**PASSAGE-32**

| 1 | 2 | 3 | 4 | 5 | 6 |
|---|---|---|---|---|---|
| B | C | C | A | D | B |
| **7** | **8** | **9** | **10** | **11** | **12** |
| C | A | C | B | D | C |
| **13** | **14** | | | | |
| B | B | | | | |

# II. Passages

**PASSAGE-1**

| 1 | 2 | 3 | 4 | 5 | 6 |
|---|---|---|---|---|---|
| A | D | A | A | A | C |
| **7** | | | | | |
| B | | | | | |

**PASSAGE-2**

| 1 | 2 | 3 | 4 | 5 | 6 |
|---|---|---|---|---|---|
| A | A | D | A | B | C |
| **7** | | | | | |
| D | | | | | |

**PASSAGE-3**

| 1 | 2 | 3 | 4 | 5 | 6 |
|---|---|---|---|---|---|
| D | C | D | C | A | D |
| **7** | | | | | |
| B | | | | | |

**PASSAGE-4**

| 1 | 2 | 3 | 4 | 5 | 6 |
|---|---|---|---|---|---|
| C | C | A | D | A | D |
| **7** | | | | | |
| C | | | | | |

**PASSAGE-5**

| 1 | 2 | 3 | 4 | 5 | 6 |
|---|---|---|---|---|---|
| B | D | D | B | D | C |
| **7** | | | | | |
| A | | | | | |

**PASSAGE-6**

| 1 | 2 | 3 | 4 | 5 | 6 |
|---|---|---|---|---|---|
| A | C | B | C | B | C |
| **7** | | | | | |
| B | | | | | |

**PASSAGE-7**

| 1 | 2 | 3 | 4 | 5 | 6 |
|---|---|---|---|---|---|
| B | C | C | B | D | B |
| **7** | | | | | |
| C | | | | | |

**PASSAGE-8**

| 1 | 2 | 3 | 4 | 5 | 6 |
|---|---|---|---|---|---|
| B | C | C | B | B | C |
| **7** | | | | | |
| A | | | | | |

**PASSAGE-9**

| 1 | 2 | 3 | 4 | 5 |
|---|---|---|---|---|
| C | C | B | D | A |

**PASSAGE-10**

| 1 | 2 | 3 | 4 | 5 |
|---|---|---|---|---|
| B | A | B | C | C |

**PASSAGE-11**

| 1 | 2 | 3 | 4 | 5 |
|---|---|---|---|---|
| C | A | B | D | A |

**PASSAGE-12**

| 1 | 2 | 3 | 4 | 5 |
|---|---|---|---|---|
| A | A | B | C | D |

**PASSAGE-13**

| 1 | 2 | 3 | 4 | 5 |
|---|---|---|---|---|
| A | C | B | A | D |

**PASSAGE-14**

| 1 | 2 | 3 | 4 | 5 |
|---|---|---|---|---|
| C | B | A | D | A |

**PASSAGE-15**

| 1 | 2 | 3 | 4 | 5 |
|---|---|---|---|---|
| B | A | C | D | A |

**PASSAGE-16**

| 1 | 2 | 3 | 4 | 5 |
|---|---|---|---|---|
| A | B | C | A | B |

**PASSAGE-17**

| 1 | 2 | 3 | 4 | 5 |
|---|---|---|---|---|
| C | A | B | D | C |

**PASSAGE-18**

| 1 | 2 | 3 | 4 | 5 |
|---|---|---|---|---|
| B | D | B | A | B |

**PASSAGE-19**

| 1 | 2 | 3 | 4 | 5 |
|---|---|---|---|---|
| D | C | B | C | D |

**PASSAGE-20**

| 1 | 2 | 3 | 4 | 5 |
|---|---|---|---|---|
| B | A | C | D | A |

**PASSAGE-21**

| 1 | 2 | 3 | 4 | 5 |
|---|---|---|---|---|
| B | C | D | D | C |

**PASSAGE-22**

| 1 | 2 | 3 | 4 | 5 |
|---|---|---|---|---|
| C | D | B | C | D |

**PASSAGE-23**

| 1 | 2 | 3 | 4 | 5 |
|---|---|---|---|---|
| A | C | D | B | A |

**PASSAGE-24**

| 1 | 2 | 3 | 4 | 5 |
|---|---|---|---|---|
| A | D | A | D | B |

**PASSAGE-25**

| 1 | 2 | 3 | 4 | 5 |
|---|---|---|---|---|
| B | C | D | A | B |

**PASSAGE-26**

| 1 | 2 | 3 | 4 | 5 |
|---|---|---|---|---|
| B | B | C | A | D |

**PASSAGE-27**

| 1 | 2 | 3 | 4 | 5 |
|---|---|---|---|---|
| A | B | A | B | C |

**PASSAGE-28**

| 1 | 2 | 3 | 4 | 5 |
|---|---|---|---|---|
| A | B | C | C | B |

**PASSAGE-29**

| 1 | 2 | 3 | 4 | 5 |
|---|---|---|---|---|
| A | C | A | B | C |

**PASSAGE-30**

| 1 | 2 | 3 | 4 | 5 |
|---|---|---|---|---|
| B | C | D | D | D |

## III. Poetry

**POEM-1**

| 1 | 2 | 3 | 4 | 5 |
|---|---|---|---|---|
| A | C | B | C | A |

**POEM-2**

| 1 | 2 | 3 | 4 | 5 |
|---|---|---|---|---|
| C | B | A | D | B |

**POEM-3**

| 1 | 2 | 3 | 4 | 5 |
|---|---|---|---|---|
| D | A | B | C | B |

**POEM-4**

| 1 | 2 | 3 | 4 | 5 |
|---|---|---|---|---|
| B | D | C | D | B |

**POEM-5**

| 1 | 2 | 3 | 4 | 5 |
|---|---|---|---|---|
| B | A | D | A | B |

**POEM-6**

| 1 | 2 | 3 | 4 | 5 |
|---|---|---|---|---|
| C | D | D | D | B |

**POEM-7**

| 1 | 2 | 3 | 4 | 5 |
|---|---|---|---|---|
| C | D | B | B | A |

**POEM-8**

| 1 | 2 | 3 | 4 | 5 |
|---|---|---|---|---|
| A | B | A | D | C |

**POEM-9**

| 1 | 2 | 3 | 4 | 5 |
|---|---|---|---|---|
| A | C | D | B | C |

**POEM-10**

| 1 | 2 | 3 | 4 | 5 |
|---|---|---|---|---|
| C | B | A | A | C |

**POEM-11**

| 1 | 2 | 3 | 4 | 5 |
|---|---|---|---|---|
| B | C | C | B | C |

**POEM-12**

| 1 | 2 | 3 | 4 | 5 |
|---|---|---|---|---|
| D | B | C | B | D |

**POEM-13**

| 1 | 2 | 3 | 4 | 5 |
|---|---|---|---|---|
| B | B | A | D | B |

**POEM-14**

| 1 | 2 | 3 | 4 | 5 |
|---|---|---|---|---|
| A | A | D | A | B |

**POEM-15**

| 1 | 2 | 3 | 4 | 5 |
|---|---|---|---|---|
| B | B | C | C | D |

**POEM-16**

| 1 | 2 | 3 | 4 | 5 |
|---|---|---|---|---|
| B | A | D | A | A |

**POEM-17**

| 1 | 2 | 3 | 4 | 5 |
|---|---|---|---|---|
| B | A | B | A | D |

**POEM-18**

| 1 | 2 | 3 | 4 | 5 |
|---|---|---|---|---|
| D | D | C | C | B |

**POEM-19**

| 1 | 2 | 3 | 4 | 5 |
|---|---|---|---|---|
| C | A | C | D | A |

**POEM-20**

| 1 | 2 | 3 | 4 | 5 |
|---|---|---|---|---|
| B | A | C | B | B |

# English Literature : At a Glance

## THE OLD ENGLISH PERIOD (I) (ANGLO-SAXON PERIOD) (450-1050)

**Beowulf** is probably the oldest epic of the Teutonic world. It is believed to be belonging to the first half of the sixth century.

### *Some important works of the Anglo-Saxon period (Pre-Christian Era)*

Some important works of the Anglo-Saxon period are: *The Ruined Burg, The Lover's Message. The Maiden's Complaint, The Wanderer* and *the Seafarer.*

*'The Wanderer* is also known as *'Widsith'*. The work is based on the wandering life of the gleeman.

Belonging to this period, we also have *"Deor's Lament"*, which, according to Long is, "much more poetic than *'Widsith,'* and is the one perfect lyric of the Anglo-Saxon period.

In the *Seafarer*, we have glimpses of hard sea life along with the call of the sea, which we, in our times, find more pronouncedly, but perhaps less picturesquely, in Masefield's *"Sea-Fever"*.

### *Some Christian writers of the Anglo-Saxon period*

Whereas the pagan literature of the Anglo-Saxon period was chiefly in the form of oral legends which they had brought with them from the foreign lands which they previously inhabited, the Christian writing mainly came into existence as a result of the teachings of the monks who had come under the influence of two schools—the Augustinian School (from Rome) and Northumbrian School (from Ireland).

While the former, did not produce much lasting works, the latter produced a number of good and great writers, *e.g.,* **The Venerable Bede (673-735), Caedmon (seventh century)** and **Cynewulf (eighth century)**.

Besides the poets mentioned above, we have **Alfred (848-90)** who is chiefly known as a translator.

## ANGLO-NORMAN PERIOD (1066-1350)

### *Some important works of the Anglo-Norman period*

One important work of this period is *Geoffrey's "Historic Regum Britanniae"* (1137) commonly known as *"History"*. Geoffrey is believed to have died in 1154.

Geoffrey's work which became immensely popular in his own life, is a mixture of pagan and Christian legends and is based more on lies than on real historical events.

However, the said work has its literary value for its poetry and romance pertaining to king Arthur and his Knights, and hence, it became a source of inspiration and scintillating subject matter for such illustrious authors as Malory, Shakespeare and Tennyson.

Geoffrey's work was in Latin verse. Thereafter appeared *"Layman's Brut"* (c. 1200) which has its main interest in giving Arthur's legends in (Anglo-Saxon) English itself.

Then there appeared what are known as *"Metrical Romances"* which were based on the "matter" of France, Rome and Britain.

While in the *Matter of France,* **Charlemagne's** exploits dominated and in the *Matter of Rome* Alexander's adventures and the war of Troy were the main subjects, in the *Matter of Britain*, exploits of Arthur and his knights of the Round Table were chief subject matter. There were a number of cycles pertaining to the knights of Arthur, among them being **Sir Gawain (1350)** *Quest of the Holy Grail, Death of Arthur, Merlin, etc.*

Besides the above, other works of the period included ballads, lyrics and such poems as the *Owl and the Nightingale, Ormulum, Cursor Mundi (1320), The Pearl, Patience, Cleanness, etc.* Also **Roger Bacon's** *"Opus Majus"* appeared in 1267.

## THE AGE OF CHAUCER (1340-1400)

The Hundred years war between England and France had already started in 1338 when **Chaucer** was born in **1340**.

In the earlier years of the war, England was all-powerful and under Edward III it won victories over France at Sluys in 1340 and Crecy in 1346, culminating in the capture of Calais in 1347.

Another thumping victory was won by the Black Prince, Edward III's son in 1356 by defeating the French at Poitiers.

As a result of the English victories, the English foreign trade began to flourish, particularly in the export of wool to Flanders, which filled the coffers of the English king and the people also became richer, as we notice conspicuously in **Chaucer's** *Canterbury Tales* when we consider the lot of so many characters, particularly those belonging to landed aristocracy.

This picture is also graphically depicted in **Trevelyan's** *British History of Six Centuries.*

It was unfortunate for England that in the moment of its glory it was overtaken by plague, the Black Death which took a heavy toll of life all over Europe in 1348-49.

As a result of the Black Death, most of the labourers who escaped death, left the country, and this caused an intense scarcity of the availability of essential commodities at cheap rates. To meet this menace, the Parliament tried to force the labourers to accept the same wages as they were getting before the Black Death, and it all finally precipitated into the well-known Peasants' Revolt during the reign of Richard II.

In spite of the passage of certain statutes purported to safeguard the English clergy against the undue domination of the Pope, the low simmering of wrath among the clergymen for several reasons, there emerged in the "Lollards Movement" under the leadership of the redoubtable Wyclif.

Another prominent feature, this one in the literary world, was the slow advent of the spirit of New Learning from Italy and drastic changes in the structure of the English language which had already been continuing as the inevitable outcome of the Norman conquest at Hastings in 1066.

These were the general conditions in which the most significant writers of the age—**Chaucer, Langland, Dunbar,** etc. lived and flourished, thus heralding a new age slowly, but boldly and surely.

## MAJOR AUTHORS AND THEIR WORKS OF CHAUCER'S AGE

**Sir Thomas More (1478-1535)**

*Utopia (English Version)*

**William Tyndale (1485-1536)**

*New Testament*

**Geoffrey Chaucer (1340-1400)**

*The Boke of the Duchesse*

*The Romaunt of the Rose*

*The House of Fame*

*Troylus Cryseyde*

*The Canterbury Tales*

*Legends of Good Women*

*The Parliament of Fouls*

**Wyclif (1320-1384)**

*The Bible*

**John Heywood (1564-1627)**

*Four P's*

**Thomas Sackville and Thomas Norton : (1536-1608) (1532-1584)**

*Gorboduc*

# The Seventeenth Century

## THE RENAISSANCE (1578-1625)

The Renaissance of English Literature coincides with the Age of Queen Elizabeth I. Hence, in the history of English literature, this period is also called as the *Elizabethan Age*. The inspiration for the great works of this period came from the prolific translations into English of works of ancient Rome and Greece. Thus, Plutarch's *Lives* was translated by **Sir Thomas North (1579)** from the French version. Montaigne's Essays was translated by **John Florio (1603)**. In verse, Ovid's *Metamorphoses* was translated by **Arthur Golding (1565, 1567)**. Among other works of foreign origin translated into English were Ariosto's *Orlando Furioso* by **Harrington (1591)**, and Homer's *Iliad* by **George Chapman (1598)**.

The rising English stage and the English novel borrowed from Boccaccio, Cinthio, Bandello and Straparola — the Italians. Attracted though England was to Italian art, it resisted the evil influences of debauchery, crime and passions that the Italian spirit represented. Yet, the time was ripe in England for the full development of every art and literary form. Renaissance means *a flowering again of art and culture*. It inculcated a sense of wonder in things. England also wanted to rival Spain, France and Portugal in her navigational triumphs. Thus in 1578, Sir Francis Drake circumnavigated the world, and in 1588, the English navy destroyed the Armada. The same spirit of adventure moved literature. In *Apologie for Poetrie*, Sidney described the poet — of all sciences 'the monarch'. Poets were encouraged to innovate new styles and rhythms.

## Poetry

Three great men of letters led the Renaissance in England — Spenser, Sidney and Lyly.

**Edmund Spenser (1552-1599)** wrote the *Shepheardes Calendar* (1579)—an allegory. The union of line and metre is varied and rich. In *Hymnes In honour of Love and Beautie*, he sets forth his philosophy, the conflict in his mind between paganism and Christianity. He also wrote a satire named, *Mother Hubberd's Tale* to denounce the neglect of arts and letters. His pastoral, *Colin Clout's Come Home Again* describes his stay in London in 1589. His *Amoretti* (1595) are sonnets on love and his *Epithalamion* is an ode, But his masterpiece is the *Faerie Queene* (1589, 1595), an allegory in which characters represent virtues and vices. In it his lyrical quality and colour-effects are at their best. The *Faerie Queene* is Queen Elizabeth. The nine-line stanza he used is now called the *Spenserian stanza*.

**Sir Philip Sidney (1554-1586)** was a scholar, knight and courtier. In 1580 he wrote *Arcadia* which has a blend of pastoral and heroic elements It is a romance of chivalry and love. The language is characterized by *pathetic fallacy* — endowing inanimate objects with feelings and sensations. William Shakespeare borrowed from this style. His other poem, *Astrophel and Stella* (1591) describes his lost love for the daughter of an Earl. His *Apologie for Poetrie* (1595) written in an unaffected prose, is a plea for poetry.

**John Lyly (1554-1606)** invented an artistic, flowery style called *euphuism* through his famous romance, *Euphues, the Anatomy of Wit* (1579). This style was adopted by the refined people of the Court. The style is characterized by the use of alliteration and antithesis, fantastic metaphors and similes based on mythology, and natural history of flora and fauna.

The works of these three trail-blazed many poets and sonneteers like Samuel Daniel, Michael Drayton, Thomas Watson, Henry Constable and Thomas Lodge. Notable works from 1590 to 1603 were **Samuel Daniel's (1562-1619)** *The Civil Wars* (1595) describing the *War of the Roses*, **Michael Drayton's (1563-1631)** *Id^a, the Shepherd's Garland, The Baron's Wars, England's Heroicall Epistles* (1603) and *Poly-Olbion*, a long description of England in 15,000 alexandrines or lines of twelve syllables. England came to be known as *"a nest of singing birds"* because of the great number of lyrics and poems written in this period. **Thomas Campion (1567-1620)** published an anthology called *Two Books of Ayres* (1612). Many of the best poems are found in plays by Ben Jonson, Thomas Dekker, Beaumont and Fletcher, and Webster. But those of William Shakespeare are probably the most beautiful. In his *Sonnets*, he describes his love for a married woman who betrays him. Other poems of this period are Marlowe's Hero and Leander (1598), Shakespeare's *Venus and Adonis* (1593) and *The Rape of Lucrece* (1594).

After Elizabeth's reign, in James I rule, poetry became religious and didactic. The Protestant spirit dominated the literary works. The poems of George Wither, William Browne, the Fletcher brothers and William Drummond show the influence of Spenser still.

**Ben Jonson (1573-1637)** was the greatest humanist of the time. He was mainly a playwright but wrote poems also. His poetry is found in collections like Epigrams and The Forest (1616) and The Underwoods (1640). He was a satirist and neo-classicist being influenced by the Latin classics.

**John Donne's (1573-1631)** poetry is revolut-ionary. He disobeys the laws of rhythm and uses a device called the metaphysical conceit in which strangely opposite ideas are juxtaposed.

## Prose

Much of the prose of the period is poetical, influenced by euphuism. Robert Greene, Thomas Lodge, Thomas Nashe, Thomas Deloney, and Thomas Dekker are the major writers. **Robert Greene's (1558-1592)** works include *Mamilia* and *Menaphon* and **Thomas Lodge's (1558-1625)** include *Rosalynde: Euphues Golden Legacie* (1590). **Thomas Nashe (1567-1601)** wrote pamphlets like The *Anatomie of Absurdities* and *The Terrors of the Night*. **Thomas Dekker's (1572-1632)** *The Gils Horne booke* is famous for its picturesque prose. Most of the poets and prose writers of this period were also dramatists. Shakespeare used prose for homely and humorous scenes and verse for tragic ones.

Many writers of the English Renaissance were inspired by the literary criticism of the Continent to write some themselves. Stephen Gosson's *The Schoole of Abuse* (1579) and *Sidney's Apologie for Poetrie* are good examples. Sidney eulogizes the poet as a law-giver. The period also saw works of religious prose. **Richard Hooker's (1554-1600)** pamphlet on the Marlin Marprelate controversy is a famous one. Hooker's *Of the Laws of Ecclesiastical Polity* (1594) is a masterpiece of English prose. The most seminal work of the period is the authorized version of the Bible published in 1611. The work was commissioned by James 1. A beautiful prose minus archaism is used by the revisers. The diction was to influence the English language very deeply. It is the language of daily speech, yet fresh and lofty.

Side by side with religious literature, secular and philosophical literature, mostly written by **Francis Bacon (1561-1626)**, came out. He had taken all knowledge as his province and elaborated his doctrines in his *Novum*

*Organum* (1620). His ideas influenced the formation of *The Royal Society for Improving Natural Knowledge* in 1645. His most popular work is his *Essays* written on diverse topics in a terse, epigrammatic style. The English writers quote copiously from Bacon today. His sentences are household terms. Take for example, "*He that hath wife and children hath given hostages to fortune*". "*Some books are to be tasted, others to be swallowed and some few to be chewed and digested*".

Another great prose-writer of the period was **Robert Burton (1577-1640)** whose *The Anatomy of Melancholy* (1621) is full of pedantry. He borrowed from numerous sources and is full of melancholy and jests; his style abounds in synonyms and epithets.

## Drama

Drama thrived in the Renaissance. Foreign influence, especially of Italy, predominated. Plays were written so that the public would enjoy them and applaud the stage. There was a great variety of plays written — pure tragedy, tragi-comedy, historical drama, romantic comedy, comedy of errors, farce, pastoral, etc. The stage was a simple structure, circular in form with a courtyard open to the sky. A platform projected into the courtyard. Boys played the female roles. The public consisted of groundlings and courtiers on galleries. The unities of time, place and action were disregarded. Farce and tragedy were found in succession.

Several mythological allegories were acted before the court. **John Lyly's** euphuistic romances like *Campaspe* (1584), *Sapho and Phao, Endymion* (1592), *Midas* were praises of the queen. **George Peele (1558-1598)** wrote *The Araygnement of Paris* (1584) and *The Old Wives' Tale*. There were violent plays like **Thomas Kyd's (1558-1594)** The *Spanish Tragedie* (1585) and **Christopher Marlowe's (1564-1593)** *Tamburlaine, the Great* (1587) and *Doctor Faustus* (1592). *Doctor Faustus* is an allegory on the Renaissance love of power. It shows how Doctor Faustus, the scientist, sells his soul to the devil for twenty-four years of full power to satisfy every desire. In the end his agony increases as the devil approaches to claim his soul. Marlowe also wrote *The Jew of Malta*, which shows the unbridled love for wealth, and the historical play Edward II. Marlowe crafted the blank verse (mighty line as Shakespeare called it and used). This was suited to the fiery speeches of his characters.

The towering genius of the age was certainly **William Shakespeare (1564-1616)**. He was versatile and wrote about 36 plays and 144 sonnets. "Shakespeare was not of an age but for all times" and "Poets are born not made", wrote Ben Jonson about him. He created a gallery of nearly 800 characters who typify personalities found through human history. Julius Caesar's pride and ambition, Macbeth's unbridled ambition, King Lear's dotedness, and Othello's susceptibility to suspicion against his wife — are tragic flaws that govern men even today.

Shakespeare was not educated except for a few years at a grammar school. He had 'little Latin and less Greek' and read books in translation from Latin and Greek. He adapted the stories into a World entirely his own, instinct with life and vibrancy. Shakespeare began his career by acting for the stage. Then he wrote plays and staged them, mainly to seek court patronage. His great success made him the envy of his contemporaries like Robert Greene. In his tragedies he depicts the fall of great men owing to a tragic flaw in their character. Although they had the will to change their destiny, a fate controlled them. He used the beliefs of his time like the supernatural powers and phenomena to capture the interest of his audience. Some of his historical plays are *Richard II* (1596) and *King John* (1595). Among the romantic comedies *As You Like It* (1600), *The Merchant of Venice* (1596) and *Twelfth Night* (1601) are popular. *A Midsummer Night's Dream* (1595) is a fairy play. *Romeo and Juliet* (1594) is a tragicomedy. He used prose and blank verse.

His *Henry IV* (I & 2) (1597, 1598) contain much more blank verse than his other plays. In depth of psychological insight, and power of style *Hamlet* (1601), one of Shakespeare's great tragedies, stands supreme. *The Tempest* (161I) is one of his last plays which shows the dramatist's mellowed maturity.

Even after 400 years, Shakespeare's plays are very popular, being translated into almost every important language. "*Age cannot wither her nor custom stale her infinite variety*"; Shakespeare described Cleopatra in these words. The same may be said about his plays also.

**Ben Jonson** was Shakespeare's antithesis. He borrowed the style of the classics and was very erudite. He carefully studied society and wrote about it. He took the different 'humours' or dominating characteristics of men and satirized them in *Every Man in his Humour* (1598) and *Every Man out of his Humour* (1599), *Volpone, or the Fox* (1605) and *The Alchemist* (1605). He also wrote the historical tragedies, *Sejanus His Fall* (1603)' and *Catiline His Conspiracy* (1611). The plays are very true to history. John Marston, Thomas Dekker, Thomas Heywood and Middleton were other playwrights of the age. John Webster (1580-1625) is famous for horror plays like *The White Devil* (1609-1612) and *The Duchess of Malfi* (1613-1614).

## MAJOR AUTHORS AND THEIR WORKS

**Edmund Spenser (1552-1599)**

*The Faerie Queene*

*The Shepheardes Calendar*

*Amoretti*

*Epithalamion*
*Prothalamion*
*Mother Hubberd's Tale*
*The Ruins of Time*
*The Tears of the Muses*
*Astrophel*

**Phillip Sidney (1554-1586)**

*Arcadia*
*Astrophel and Stella*
*An Apologie for Poetrie*

**Ben Jonson (1573-1637)**

*Every Man in His Humour*
*Every Man Out of His Humour*
*Volpone Or the Fox*
*Cynthia's Revels*
*The Alchemist*
*Bartholomew Fayre*
*Epicaene or the Silent Women*
*Sejanus His Fall*
*Catline His Conspiracy*
*The Poetaster*
*The Devil as an Ass*
*The Masque of Beauty*

**Samuel Daniel (1562-1619)**

*Delia*
*Civil Wars between the Two Houses of Lancaster and York*

**Michael Drayton (1563-1631)**

*The Battle of Agincourt*
*England's heroic Epistles*
*The Barons' Wars*
*Polyolbion*

**William Shakespeare (1564-1616)**

*The Two Gentlement of Verona*
*The Merry Wives of Windsor*
*Measure for Measure*
*The Comedy of Errors*
*Love's Labour's Lost*
*The Taming of the Shrew*
*All's Well that Ends Well*
*A Midsummer Night's Dream*
*The Merchant of Venice*
*Much Ado About Nothing*
*As You Like it*
*Twelfth Night*
*Romeo and Juliet*
*Macbeth*
*Hamlet*
*King Lear*
*Othello*
*Antony and Cleopatra*
*Julius Caesar*
*Timon of Athens*
*Coriolanus*
*Titus Andronicus*
*Troilus and Cressida*
*King John*
*King Richard the Second*
*King Henry the Fourth-Part First*
*King Henry the Fourth-Second Part*
*King Henry the Fifth*
*King Henry the Sixth-First Part*
*King Henry the Sixth-Second Part*
*King Henry the Sixth-Third Part*
*King Richard the Third*
*King Henry the Eighth*
*Cymbeline*
*Pericles*
*The Winter's Tale*
*The Tempest*
*Venus and Adonis and Rape of Lucrece (Narrative Poems)*
*Sonnets (154 in number).*

**Christopher Marlowe (1564-1593)**

*Tamburlaine the Great*
*Edward II*
*Doctor Faustus*
*The Jew of Malta*
*The Tragedy of Dido, Queen of Carthage.*

**George Peele (1558-1597)**

*The Araygnement of Paris*
*The Famous Chronicle of King Edward I*

**Robert Greene (1560-1592)**

*Frier Bacon and Frier Bungey*
*Orlando Furioso*
*Pandosto*

**Thomas Nashe (1567-1601)**

*The Unfortunate Traveller Or The Life of Jack Wilton*

**Thomas Lodge (1558-1625)**

*The Wounds of Civil War*
*Rosalynde*

**Thomas Kyd (1557-1595)**

*The Spanish Tragedy*

**John Lyly (1554-1606)**
*Euphues, The Anatomy of Wit*
*Euphues and His England*
*Endymion*

**Francis Bacon (1561-1626)**
*Essays*
*The Advancement of Learning*
*The New Atlantis*
*Novum Organum*

**John Webster (1580-1625)**
*The White Devil*
*The Duchess of Malfi*
*The Devil's Law Case.*

**Thomas Heywood (1575-1650)**
*A Woman Killed with Kindness*
*The English Traveller*
*The Captives*

**Robert Burton (1577-1640)**
*The Anatomy of Melancholy*

**Sir Thomas Browne (1605-1682)**
*Religio Medici*
*Vulgar Errors*
*Hydrotaphia or Urne Burriale*
*Christian Morals*

**Thomas Hobbes (1588-1679)**
*Leviathan*

**Jeremy Taylor (1613-1667)**
*The Liberty of Prophesying*
*Holy Living*
*Holy Dying*

## END OF THE RENAISSANCE (1625-1660)

### Prose

Puritanism set the trend for the literature during the reign of Charles 1. The Bible was the guiding spirit which may be best seen in Milton's works. The zealous Calvinists enforced Presbyterianism. The passionate curiosity for life which characterized the Renaissance gave place to a search for salvation. **Sir Thomas Browne (1605-1682)** was a scientist, but in his *Pseudodoxia Epidemica or Vulgar Errors* (1646), we see his belief in miracles. His *Religio Medici* (1642) speaks of the vanity of earthly life. **George Herbert's (1596-1633)** *The Country Parson* and **Jeremy Taylor's (1613-1667)** *Holy Living* (1650) and *Holy Dying* (1651) are sermons championing religious freedom. **John Milton (1608-1674)**, who is famous as a poet, wrote numerous pamphlets in favour of divorce which are models of beautiful prose. His *Areopagitica* (1644) is a speech for the liberty of unlicensed writing.

Another great prose-writer was **Thomas Hobbes (1588-1679)** whose *Leviathan* (1651) is a famous work. He was an empiricist and realist and believed that sensations and ideas are caused by physical reasons. Numerous works of ethics, sociology and history were written. *The History of the Rebellion and Civil Wars in England* was written by **Edward Hyde (1609-1674). Izaac Walton (1593-1683)** wrote the biographies of John Donne and George Herbert. *The Compleat Angler* (1653) is his famous work on the post-Civil War scene and contains descnptions of the English countryside.

### Poetry

Two types of poets existed then — the Cavaliers, who were the Royalists, and the religious or Metaphysical poets. Thomas Carew, Sir John Suckling, John Cleveland, Robert Herrick were Cavalier poets who displayed epicurean tastes. Imagination and sensuous imagery predominate their poems. Among the religious poets, Herbert, Crashaw, Vaughan and Marvell stand out. They were mystics. **George Herbert's (1593-1633)** style is simple and expresses Christian piety in his anthology The Temple (1633). His poems *The Pulley and Love* are very popular. **Richard Crashaw (1613-1649)** used fantastic conceits; e.g. he describes the maudlin St. Mary Magdalene's eyes as "walking baths, compedious oceans", **Henry Vaughan (1622-1695)** was a mystic and his poem The Retreat is a nostalgic longing for the blissful heavenly state of childhood.

John Milton's greatest achievement was his *Paradise Lost* (1667). In theme it deals with the fall of man. In form, it follows the strict unity of the classical epic. His other poems are *L'Allegro* (1632), *Il Penseroso* (1632), *Comus* (1634), *Lycidas* (1637), *Samson Agonistes* (1671), etc.

## RESTORATION LITERATURE (1620-1734)

### Prose

In 1660, Charles II returned to the throne and the Puritan republic ended. The year is also marked as the beginning of the modem literature. **John Bunyan's (1628-1688)** works, *Grace Abounding* (1666) and *The Pilgrim's Progress* (1678) are the last surviving works of Puritan faith. The Pilgrim's Progress is an allegory describing the trials and tribulations on the way to salvation as faced by a Christian. Bunyan's prose is a blend of common speech and the grandeur of the revised Bible.

The scientific spirit took over the reign. The Royal Society of London for the Improvement of Natural

Knowledge, to which Bacon and William Harvey (who discovered the circulation of blood) had contributed, now had many learned men. **Sir Isaac Newton** published Principia in 1687. He discovered the laws of gravity, of the diffraction of white light and the theory of fluxions.

**John Locke (1632-1704)** propounded a new philosophy of commonsense and intelligent reasoning in his *An Essay Concerning Human Understanding* (1690). It lays stress on development of character. It was to influence the English thought. Voltaire was one of his French disciples.

## Poetry

Restoration literature was derived from pre-Commonwealth national literature and was a reaction against Puritan oppression. It rejected severe moral codes of conduct and was chiefly satiric in nature. **Samuel Butler's (1612-1680)** poem, *Hudibras* published in three parts (1663, 1664 & 1678), is a typical work of this period. It is inspired by *Don Quixote*. He satirizes Sir Hudibras as a grotesque Presbyterian with a squire called Ralpho. It lays bare all the human follies in octosyllabic couplets. Many court poets like **Andrew Marvell (1621-1678)** and **John Oldham (1653-1683)** were veterans of the Republican era and satirize the follies of the new age.

The great poet of the period was **John Dryden (1631-1700)**. He excelled in almost every kind of composition. He wrote a series of heroic stanzas in honour of Cromwell on his death. He was a disciple of the metaphysical poets displaying their far-fetched images and conceits. In *Astraea Redux* (1660), he celebrated the return of Charles II and in *Annus Mirabilis* (1667) he commemorated the Great Fire of London and the war with Holland. He was a staunch Tory and his famous satires are *Absalom and Achitophel* (1681), *The Medal and Mac-Flecknoe*. In this last work he satirizes Shadwell, the Whig poet. *The Hind and the Panther* (1687) is an allegory on Catholicism and Anglicanism. Dryden also translated the classics, chiefly Persuis and Juvenal. He turned Virgil's *Aeneid* into brilliant couplets. His *Alexander's Feast* is an ode in honour of St. Cecilia.

## Drama

The dramatic works of the Restoration were licentious and full of cynicism. They regarded the moral code of the Puritans as a matter of ridicule. Scenery now played an important part on the stage and actresses, not boys, played the female roles. The theatre was regarded as a place of vice and evil. Shakespeare's plays were rewritten and his tragedies like *Romeo and Juliet* given happy endings. French influence dominated and extraordinary superhuman feats were described. Heroes were presented as ideals and were made to give pompous speeches.

**Dryden** wrote many plays like *Aurengzebe* or *The Great Mogul* (1675) and The Conquest of Granada (1669, 1670) which abound in rhetoric.

The tragedians were **Thomas Otway (1651-1685)**, Nathaniel Lee (1653-1692) and **Nicholas Rowe (1674-1718)**. The comedy of this period reflects the gay intrigues of the society. Caricature and farce were used and obscenity also touched it. The main aim was to amuse. **Sir George Etheredge (1635-1691)** was an innovator and **William Wycherley (1640-1715)** was a moralist playwright. **William Congreve (1670-1729)** wrote a series of masterpieces including *The Way of the World* (1700). **John Vanbrugh** (1664-1726) and **George Farquhar (1678-1707)** were other comedy writers of the period.

## Criticism

Dryden was the first English critic. *The Essay of Dramatick Poesie* (1668) is his longest single prose work and a major piece of English literary criticism. It is in the form of a discussion between four characters, one of whom is Dryden himself. It deals with topics related to theatre and evaluates the works of the Elizabethan dramatists, especially of Shakespeare.

## The Diarists of the Restoration Period

One of the sources of information and genres of prose writing during the Restoration were diaries. The important names are those of John Evelyn, Samuel Pepys and Roger North. **John Evelyn (1620-1706)** was a rich man who had cultured tastes. He was a member of the Royal Society and had wide interests in diverse fields like gardening, forestry, navigation and architecture. His *Diary* which was written almost throughout his lifetime throws a floodlight on the major social and national events of the time like the Galley Slaves and the Great Fire. It is written in a plain, graphic style. **Samuel Pepys (1633-1703)** had a chequered career. Coming from the middle classes, he joined the civil services and rose to be the secretary of the Admiralty. He also became the President of the Royal Society and a member of Parliament. His famous *Diary*, covering a period of ten years, is in the form of confessions. It was written in laconic sentences like the messages of a telegram and was in a sort of code which was deciphered only in 1825. The diary shows him to be a man of versatile interests like music, science and literature. But the most controversial aspect is the detailed confessions of his life. Nobody seemed to guess he was a libertine, a morally debauched character who could stoop to low means. When we read the diary, it seems he is writing of another person. **Roger North** belonged to an elite family. He was a Tory gentleman and was engaged in the politics of the times. His famous work is *North's Lives of the Norths* containing biographies of three relatives and an autobiography. His pen pictures and anecdotes are in colloquial style.

## MAJOR AUTHORS AND THEIR WORKS

**Robert Herrick (1591-1574)**

*Noble Numbers*

*Hesperides*

**Thomas Carew (1598-1639)**

*Poems*

*'He that loves a rosy cheek'*

**Sir John Suckling (1660-1642)**

*'Ballad upon a Wedding'*

*'Why so pale and wan, Fond Lover'?*

**Andrew Marvell (1621-1678)**

*'To His Coy Mistress'*

*'The Rehearsal Transprosed'*

*'Ode upon Cromwell's Return from Ireland'*

*New Letters (a Prose Work)*

**George Herbert (1593-1633)**

*The Temple*

*Affliction*

*Easter Wings*

*The Collar*

*Man*

**Richard Crashaw (1613-1649)**

*Carmen Deo Nostro*

*The Infant Morturs*

*Steps to the Temple*

**John Milton (1608-1674)**

*Paradise Lost (in twelve Books)*

*Paradise Regained*

*Comus*

*Lycidas*

*Samson Agonistes*

*L'Allegro*

*Ill Penseroso*

*Areopagitica (Prose Work)*

*Ode on the Morning of Christ's Nativity*

*Sonnets (including) :*

*'On His Blindness'*

*'On the Late Massacre in Piedmont'*

*'When the Assault was Intended to the City'*

*'On His Having Arrived at the Age of Twenty-three'*

*A large number of Tracts and Pamphlets in support of the Parliament*

**John Donne (1573-1631)**

*Songs and Sonnets*

*Aires and Angels*

*A Nocturnall upon Lucies Day*

*A Valediction : Forbidding Mourning*

*The Extasie*

*Devotions (Sermon in Prose)*

*Ignatius His Enclave (a Prose Work)*

*Of the Progress of the Soul*

*Death's Duell*

**Abraham Cowley (1618-1667)**

*Pyramus and Thisbe*

*The Mistress*

*The Davideis*

*Pindarique Odes*

*Constantia and Philetus*

*Discourse by Way of Vision*

*Concerning the Government of Cromwell* (a Prose Work)

**Henry Vaughan (1622-1695)**

*Poems*

*Regeneration*

*The Retreat*

*Olor Iscanus*

*Thalia Redivia*

*Silex Scintillans*

**John Dryden (1631-1700)**

*(i) Heroic Stanzas on the Death of Oliver Cromwell*

*Astraea Redux* (on the Restoration of Charles II)

*Absalom and Achitophel*

*Religio Laici*

*The Hind and the Panther*

*The Fables*

*Annus Mirabilis*

*The Medal*

*Mac Flecknoe*

*Alexander's Feast*

*Prefaces to His Plays* (in Prose)

*An Essay of Dramatic Poesy*

*(ii) Dryden's Plays*

*Tyrannic Love*

*Conquest of Granada*

*All for love*

*The Rival Ladies*

*The Indian Emperor*

*Aureng-Zeb*

*Don Sebastian*

*Cleomenes*

*Love Triumphant*

**John Vanbrugh (1664-1726)**

*The Relapse*

*The Provoked Wife*

*The Confederacy*

**George Farquhar (1678-1707)**
*The Recruiting Officer*
*The Beaux Stratagem*

**Thomas Otway (1652-1685)**
*Orphan*
*Venice Preserved*
*Don Carlos*
*Alcibiades*

**Nathaniel Lee (1653-1692)**
*Nero*
*The Rival Queens*
*Sophonisba*

**John Bunyan (1628-1688)**
*The Pilgrim's Progress*
*Grace Abounding*
*The Life and Death of Mr. Badman*
*The Holy War*

**John Locke (1632-1704)**
*Essay on the Human Understanding*
*Treatise on Government*
*Thoughts on Education*

**John Evelyn (1620-1706)**
*Diary*

**Samuel Pepys (1633-1703)**
*Diary*

# The Eighteenth Century

## THE AUGUSTAN AGE (1700-1740)

In general, the eighteenth century was the age of understanding and enlightenment. The emphasis was on the advancement of the human mind. Sensibility was the guiding principle. This age borrowed the humour and poetic technique of the previous century.

This age is generally called *The Augustan Age* or *The Age of Queen Anne* because the queen patronized the men of letters. The period is also known as the Classical Age. It Was an age of tolerance and harmony and was guided by reason. Dryden still wrote and was a contemporary of French authors Corneille, Racine and Moliere. Many English works were translated by the French. Poetry was still for aristocrats and the courts, but prose spread among the common public. People demanded instructions and information and practical hints for living. This led writers to use a simple style to be comprehensible to all.

### Poetry

**Matthew Prior (1664-1721)** began by writing a parody of The Hind and the Panther in which he expounded his opinions on politics. **Sir Samuel Garth (1661-1791)** and **Joseph Addison (1672-1719)** used the heroic couplet of Dryden. Addison described Marlborough's victory at Blenheim in his poem *The Campaign* (1704). But the poetical luminary of the period was **Alexander Pope (1688-1744)**. He polished Dryden's couplet and used it as a weapon of satire, like in the famous *An Essay on Man* (1732-1734). His *An Essay on Criticism* (1711) and *The Rape of the Lock* (1712, 1714) are other great works. The latter is in mock-heroic style and describes the anger of a lady whose lock of hair had been cut off. Pope also translated the Iliad. He wrote *The Dunciad* (1728) to castigate bad poets. His *Imitations of Horace* (1733-1737) is highly admired even today.

**Jonathan Swift,** usually known as a prose writer, also showed a gift or versification like in his poem *On the Death of Dr. Swift*. **John Gay (1685-1732)** was popular for his fables like *The Hare with Many Friends* and his songs in *The Beggar's Opera*. **Edward Young's (1683-1765)** *The Commaint, or Night Thoughts on Life, Death, and Immortality* (1742), is a poet's delight in meditation underlining the vanity of all earthly glory.

### Prose

This period saw an increasing demand for the circulation of facts and ideas among the public. **Daniel Defoe (1659-1731)** was a trail-blazer as a Journalist and his popular works are *The True-Born Englishman* (1701) and *The Shortest way with the Dissenters* (1702). Defoe wrote the first English nove! Robinson Crusoe (1719), which is a children's classic or collection of adventure stories. He cultivated the art of reporting and presented his stories as historical narratives which are precise and practical.

Steele, Addison, Swift, Arbuthnot were the other great prose-writers of the time. They introduced a style adorned by figures of speech. The periodicals of Steele and Addison contain essays which deal with practical moral questions and reflect the morals of the time.

**Richard Steele (1672-1729)** led a dissipated life and was full of remorse for it. He extols the Bible as a guide in life in his work *The Christian Hero*. He launched the journal *The Tatler* in 1709. **Joseph Addison** propagated rational and moderate ideas He collaborated with Steele on *The Tatler*. Steele then founded *The Spectator* in 1711 and

Addison again collaborated. Here they were merely the spectators of the society and its foibles. It epitomizes the whole nation. The character of Sir Roger de Coverley is a masterpiece, a comic personality with eccentricities. Other characters, Sir Andrew Freeport. Will Honeycomb, Captain Sentry capture the imagination of the readers.

**Jonathan Swift (1667-1745)** enjoyed ridicule rather than correction. He lays bare all the vices of man as something that are beyond correction. He ridiculed the modern authors in his The *Battle of the Books* (1704) and attacked the Papists and Presbyterians in *The Tale of a Tub* (1704). His most popular work is a children's classic, *Gulliver's Travels* (1726), which is also a satire on politics, religions, science and nature of man.

**John Arbuthnot (1667-1735)** was another humanist and man of wit and is known for his *The History of John Bull* (1712), an amusing allegory on the politics of the time.

During this period a number of deists like Locke, Collins and Tindal propounded a philosophy advocating reasoning rather than superstitious beliefs as advocated by orthodox Christians. Earl of Shaftesbury (1671-1713), Lord Bolingbroke (1678-1751) and Mandeville were other rationalists of the time who wrote many prose works.

## THE AGE OF TRANSITION (1740-1800)

Like all other periods of transition, this age was also disturbed and confused. Two movements can be clearly observed in the writings of the time: (*i*) the allegiance to the old order of classicism, and (*ii*) the search after the new order of Romanticism. The period was marked by new learning, new philosophy, growth of historical research and new realism.

This period is also known as the *Age of Johnson* because **Samuel Johnson (1709-1784)**, the greatest English man of letters, flourished during this period. Samuel Johnson was a versatile man of letters translator, journalist, commentator, critic, novelist, biographer and poet. He created two satirical poems, *London* (1738) and *The Vanity of Human Wishes* (1749). He had a supple style and describes his personal reflections in his essays *The Rambler* (1750-1752) and *The Idler* (1758-1760). His *Dictionary of English Language* (1747-1755) shows remarkable precision in definition and a feeling for the correct use of words. Besides the novel *Rasselas, Prince of Abyssinia* (1759) his best works are biographical and literary studies and his edition of *Shakespeare* (1765). His *Lives of the Poets* (1777-1781) is a biographical work. His admirer James Boswell's famous biography of Johnson has made him immortal. He is described here in candid details. His prejudices, excellences and demerits are all laid bare.

### Poetry

Poetry showed the influence of Dryden and Pope. It was mainly didactic and satirical and the couplet still was the major form.

**Oliver Goldsmith's (1728-1774)** *Deserted Village* (1770) is a masterpiece of the period. **James Thomson's (1700-1748)** *The Seasons* (1730) is a praise of the beauties of Nature in all her diversity. Other noteworthy poems of the period are **William Collins' (1721-1759)** *Ode to Evening*, a delightful lyric, and **Thomas Gray's (1716-1771)** *Elegy Written in a Country Churchyard* (1751).

A general belief in human liberty was seen as the French Revolution proceeded. **William Cowper** (1731-1800) who wrote *The Ballad of John Gilpin,* **George Crabbe (1754-1832)**, the Scotsman **Robert Burns (1759-1796)** and the mystic **William Blake (1757-1827)** echoed the sentiments of the period. Burns was a farmer and wrote in original racy dialect thus causing a break from convention. Blake was a visionary and his poems are collected in *Songs of Innocence* (1789) and *Songs of Experience* (1794). In *The Tyger,* he uses the Lamb as a symbol of innocence and of Jesus, and the Tiger as the symbol of evil in the world, of the evil seen in the French Revolution where thousands were sent to the guillotine.

### Novel

The period saw the development of the novel. A series of masterpieces came out. In the novel, the author could describe events in detail. Defoe's novels so far were based on strange subjects. Now they concentrated on commonplace events of family life and society. Adventure of earlier novels gave place to character portrayal. The novels were very long and filled with minute details. **Samuel Richardson (1689-1761)** wrote *Pamela, or Virtue Rewarded* (1740) and *Clarissa Harlowe* (1747-1748). **Henry Fielding (1707-1754)** is famous for *Joseph Andrews* (1742) and *Tom Jones* (1749), **Tobias Smollet (1721-1771)** wrote *The Adventures of Roderick Random* (1748) and *The Expedition of Humphry Clinker* (1771), **Laurence Sterne (1713-1768)** wrote *Tristram Shandy* (1760), and **Oliver Goldsmith** *The Vicar of Wakefield* (1766).

### Letter

There were famous letter writers also, like **Lord Chesterfield (1694-1773). Horace Walpole (1719-1797), Thomas Gray and Richardson**. Frequently, a series of letters was bound into book-form. Collections of this kind were the letters of **Lady Mary Wortley Montagu (1689-1762)**, written to Pope from Constantinople, and of Thomas Gray, from the Lake District. Chesterfield's letters to his son contain comments on political and social matters. Richardson's *Pamela* is entirely in letter-form.

## Drama

The century was the age of the great novels. Drama lost originality and talent. People saw Shakespeare's plays enacted, but what attracted them was the genius of the actors. However, there were a few good plays written. For instance, Johnson's *Irene* (1749), Fielding's *The Miser*, Goldsmith's anti-sentimental comedy *She Stoops to Conquer* (1773), and Sheridan's *The School for Scandal* (1777) and *The Rivals* (1775).

## Historical Work

Towards the last part of the century the history of England was rocked by many revolutionary changes the impact of which were felt in English literature. Till the mid-18th century Victorian England reigned supreme. She was mistress of the seas and her imperial rule covered many colonies. In 1776, America declared her independence and the British Parliament was divided on the issue. Many Britishers favoured the American claims. In 1789, the French Revolution broke out and here too the Britishers were divided into two camps. Inspired by the writings of Rousseau, many believed the Revolution was being fought for the right causes. The Parliament resounded with the speeches of the famous. Some even accused Warren Hastings for his extortion policies in India and some others were against slave-trade.

Treatises on philosophy by **David Hume (1711-1776)** and histories by **William Robertson (1721-1793)** and political economy (*Wealth of Nations*) by **Adam Smith (1723-1790)** came out.

**Edmund Burke (1729-1797)** read law and began writing to propound his views on human feelings and emotions. His language is as oratorical in Parliament at the trial of Warren Hastings as in his famous writing *A Philosophical Inquiry into the Origin of our Ideas of the Sublime and the Beautiful* (1756).

Other orators who expressed themselves in writing were Tom Painè, Godwin and Jeremy Bentham. **William Godwin (1756-1836)** advocated the elimination of government in *Enquiry Concerning Political Justice* (1793). He proscribed law, marriage, gratitude, everything that limited liberty. His monumental work is *The Decline and Fall of the Roman Empire* (1776-1788) in which he describes the growth of Christianity and his belief in reason rather than the divine. At the same time **William Paley (1743-1805)** wrote *A View of the Evidences of Christianity* (1794) to prove the existence of miracles by logic.

## MAJOR AUTHORS AND THEIR WORKS

**Alexander Pope (1688-1744)**

*Pastorals*
*An Essay on Criticism*
*Windsor Forest*
*The Rape of the Lock*
*Dunciad*
*Translation of Iliad and Odyssey*
*To Lord Bathrust*
*On the Use of the Riches*
*An Essay on Man*
*Epistle to Dr. Arbuthnot*
*Of the Knowledge and Characters of Men*
*Of the Characters of Women*
*The Messiah*
*Satires and Epistles of Horace Imitated*

**Matthew Prior (1664-1721)**

*Solomon on the Vanity of the World*
*Alma : or the Progress of the Mind*
*The Town and Country Mouse*

**John Gay (1685-1732)**

*Fables*
*The Shepherd's Week*
*The Rural Sports*
*Trivia*
*The Beggar's Opera*
*The Streets of London*

**Edward Young (1683-1765)**

*Night Thoughts*

**Dr. Samuel Johnson (1709-1784)**

*The Vanity of Human Wishes*
*London*
*The Lives of the Poets*
*Preface to Shakespeare*
*Dictionary of the English Language*
*A journey to the Western Islands of Scotland*
*The Rambler*
*Rasselas*
*Prince of Abyssinia*
*The Life of Savage*
*The Adventurer*
*The Idler*

**Daniel Defoe (1661-1731)**

*Robinson Crusoe*
*Mall Flanders*

*Colonel Jack*
*The Memoirs of a Cavalier*
*Captain Singleton*
*Journal of the Plague Year*
*Roxana*

**Jonathan Swift (1667-1745)**
*The Battle of the Books*
*A Tale of a Tub*
*Gulliver's Travels*
*Journal to Stella*
*The Drapier's Letters*
*Cadenus and Vanessa*

**Joseph Addison (1672-1719)**
*The Spectator*
*The Campaign*
*Public Credit*
*The Vision of Mirza*
*Cato*
*Rosamond*
*The Drummer*

**Richard Steele (1672-1729)**
*The Tatler*
*The Guardian*
*The Funeral*
*The Lying Lover*
*The Tender Husband*
*The Conscious Lover*

**Thomas Gray (1716-1771)**
*Elegy Written in a Country Churchyard*
*On a Distant Prospect of Eton College*
*On the Death of a Favourite Cat*
*The Bard*
*The Progress of Poesy*
*The Fatal Sisters*
*The Descent of Odin*

# The Nineteenth Century

## THE ROMANTIC AGE (1798-1830)

The eighteenth century literature of England was inspired by reason, but the nineteenth century was the age of imagination. The Preface to the *Lyrical Ballads* by William Wordsworth and Samuel Taylor Coleridge in 1798, heralds the period of English Romanticism. The authors of this work were disgusted with the excesses of the French Revolution, they condemned the Rationalist Movement. England turned away from the literature of France and transferred her sympathies to Germany. The philosophical doctrine of Romanticism was inspired by Germany. Romanticism was essentially poetic. Although poles apart in their political beliefs, Wordsworth and Shelley both considered the poet as the guide, prophet and seer of mankind.

### Poetry

For the great Romantics — Wordsworth, Shelley, Keats, Byron — the study of the wondrous world of feelings, senses, instincts, of Man' relation to Nature, were of prime importance. Romanticism is shot with *metaphysics.* As M. Lanson puts it, *tout traverse de frissons metaphysique* Alexander Pope had used poetry to depict the thoughts of the philosophers in his *Essay on Man.* The Romantics, dedicated to Romantic imagination — *the esemplastic imagination* as Coleridge called it — were convinced that what was revealed to their poetic intuitions, was right, the Truth. Mysterious forces divine in origin moved the earth, not cold rationalist cause and effect. Pope's couplet was dull and too precise governed by convention. The Romantics sought a lyrical form using unusual images and association of words. They found models for these in the Renaissance and the old popular poetry.

**William Wordsworth (1770-1850)** is aptly called the "High Priest of Nature". He saw Nature as the *'Stern Daughter of the voice of God',* man's conscience whose balmy presence never disappointed. He was born in 1770 in the picturesque Lake District of England. Here he spent happy years of his childhood in communion with God and Nature. After study at Cambridge, he went to France in 1791 and was enthused by the cause of the Revolution. But when the Reign of Terror came and thousands died at the guillotine, his fine sensibilities, his search for human equality and peace received a rude shock. He engaged himself in the philosophy of William Godwin for sometime. Finding no solution to the problem of human pain, he finally turned to the study of Nature. In the poems of the Lyrical Ballads he describes the mundane happenings of country life, the activities of humble people. He used their common dialect with its flawed grammar as his style. He decries the coming of the industrial era which mechanized English life. With no ornament, his poetry draws its power from the intensity of his feelings and imagination, In The Prelude (1805), a long poem, Wordsworth set out to look back and retrospect on his life. He follows the growth, the turnings of his poetic genius since childhood, ruminates on his errors and recalls the corrective lessons of Nature. In his great moral poem, The Excursion (1814), he uses a philosophy to refute the pessimism that the Revolution had brought.

**Samuel Taylor Coleridge (1772-1834)** was Wordsworth's "Spirits Brother". He was guided by the same philosophy of the imagination. While Wordsworth's imagination gave him a special vision of the common things of rustic life, Coleridge stirred up the supernatural. To appredíate his poetry peopled with strange, translunary beings like the Ancient Mariner, one needs *'that willing suspension of disbelief that constitutes poetic faith'*, In *The Rime of the Ancient Mariner*, Coleridge describes tne strange adventures of a sailor in a ship. Having killed an albatross, the mariner suffers from hallucinations. The poem, with strange rhythm and cadences, creates a wondrous world. Coleridge was a master of lyrical style. His other famous poems are *Christabel* (1816), and *Kubla Khan* (1816). *Kubia Khan* was written as a result of an opium dream and described the wonderful, strange palace of the Chinese king, Kubla Khan. Coleridge certainly fulfils the meaning of *'Renaissance'* as *'a renascence of wonder'*.

**Robert Southey (1774-1843)** wrote poetry based on outlandish settings and myths like *Thalaba, the Destroyer* (1801), *The Curse of Kehama* (1810), and *Roderick, the Last of the Goths* (1814). His descriptions are rich and graphic and he uses a great variety of verse forms. He wrote a number of poems in ballad form.

**Walter Scott (1771-1832)** also had an interest in ballad poetry. He translated the *Lenore* from German (1796). His *The Minstrelsy of the Scottish Border* (1802) shows a great romantic interest in the Middle Ages and the days of chivalry.

The second generation of great Romantic poets include Shelley, Keats and Byron.

**Percy Bysshe Shelley (1792-1822)** gave up his title and wealth to write poetry. His aim was to awaken mankind to the millenium, the coming future, which would remove human anguish and sorrow. His famous ode, *Ode to the West Wind* is an impassioned exhortation — *Make me thy lyre eu'n as the forest is ...... If Winter comes, can Spring be far behind?* He came under the influence of William Godwin, the philosopher. He proclaimed himself an atheist at the age of 21. His works include *Queen Mab* (1813), *Prometheus Unbound* (1818-1819), which shows human revolt against false gods, *To a Skylark, Adonais* (1821), which is an elegy to Keats, and The Cenci (1819). Shelley's style is a mixture of abstractions and visual images.

**John Keats (1795-1821)** was the most sensuous of the great Romantic poets. As we read his poems, richly laden with imagery and associations, all the senses are stirred up the visual, olfactory, auditory and tactile. It is said he tasted pepper in wine to describe certain lines. His famous odes are *To a Nightingale, To Autumn* and *On a Grecian Urn.*

**Lord George Gordon Byron (1788-1824)** was a wealthy nobleman who shunned the popular beliefs of his times. He was notorious as a dilletante. At the age of 19, he wrote Hours of Idleness (1807). With the publication of *Childe Harold's Pilgrimage* (1812) he became famous. Childe Harold was Byron himself, the figure of the disillusioned man, the hero fed up of pleasures and debauches. He lives an outlawed life and is rebellious in spirit. He took on more incarnations in his poems, *The Giaour* (1813), *The Corsair* (1814), *The Siege of Corinth* (1815). In these he displayed his own passions and eccentricities. In 1816, divorced from his wife, he retired to Switzerland and then to Italy. He wrote a number of plays — *Manfred* (1817), *Cain* (1821) and *The Deformed Transformed* (1824). The crowning work was his lyrical, satirical *Don Juan* (1819-1823). He went to Greece to fight for its independence, but died of illness. His satire is political, against England and also against English hypocrisy and cant. His licentious descriptions caused scandals. Don Juan, his magnum opus, is written in ottava rima or eight-line stanzas and is full of wit and mockery.

**Thomas Moore (1779-1852), Thomas Campbell (1777-1844), Samuel Rogers (1763-1855), Jamess Hogg (1770-1835), Walter Savage Landor (1775-1864)** and **Leigh Hunt (1784-1859)** were other poets of the time.

## Novel

Novels of terror and mystery prospered from 1800 to 1830. **Matthew Gregory Lewis** (1775-1818) wrote *Tales of Terror* (1800) and *Tales of Wonder* (1801). **Charles Lamb's (1775-1834)** *Tales from Shakespeare* (1807) is very popular even today. *Mrs Shelley,* the poet's wife, wrote the classic *Frankenstein* in which a scientist creates a monster that turns on its creator and destroys his most beloved ones. It is a novel of prophetic fear. **Miss Mary Mitford** wrote on country life and **Maria Edgeworth (1767-1849)** brought out educational novels like Belinda (1801) and *Tales of Fashionable Life* — novels for children.

**Jane Austen (1775-1817)** produced half a dozen novels which are drawing-room comedies of life. They study the passion and distress of young ladies and the life of country-folk. The novels — *Pride and Prejudice* (1813), *Sense and Sensibility* (1811), *Emma* (1816), *Persuasion* (1818), *Mansfield Park* (1814), *Northanger Abbey* (1818) — are realistic and witty, full of bracing dialogue.

**Walter Scott** was Scotland's greatest novelist recreating the past of his country's myths and ballads with rich humour. *Waverly* (1814), *Guy Mannering* (1815), *The Heart of Midlothian* (1818) contain history and direct observation. In *Ivanhoe* (1820), he describes the history of England in the days of the legendary Richard, the Lion Heart. *Kenilworth* (1821), *Quentin Dunward* (1823) were his other famous historical novels. He imbued the Romantic era with a love for the Middle Ages.

## Prose/Criticism

The Romantic Age saw a number of reviewers and critics like **Jeremy Bentham (1748-1832)**, who expounded utilitarian doctrines, **Sydney Smith (1771-1845)**, and **William Cobbett (1762-1835)**. Coleridge, the poet, interpreted the doctrines of Kant and Schelling which show the distinction between pure reason and practical reason.

Lamb, Hazlitt, De Quincey and Leigh Hunt were Romantic critics of literature. **Charles Lamb's** essays on Shakespeare's tragedies state that we cannot do justice to them by staging them since the passions which are to be felt in their intensity are torn to tatters by the gimmickry of the actors. **William Hazlitt's (1778-1830)** criticism of some of Shakespeare's characters like Falstaff — *he laughs three inches below the flesh* — is a masterpiece. Coleridge's famous work of criticism, *Biographia Literaria* (1817), marvellously analyses Wordsworth's poetry. The Romantics believed that Shakespeare's art was organic like a work of Nature and *"esemplastic"* — able to blend different elements by imagination. **Thomas De Quincey's (1785-1859)** style is penetrating and incisive when criticizing the poets in *The Confessions of an English Opium Eater* (1821).

## MAJOR AUTHORS AND THEIR WORKS

**William Wordsworth (1770-1850)**

*The Lyrical Ballads*
*The Prelude*
*The Excursion*
*Tintern Abbey*
*Ode on Intimations of Immortality*
*Michael*
*The Solitary Reaper*
*Loadamia*
*Ode to Duty*
*To Milton*
*The Leech-Gatherer*
*Upon Westminster Abbey*
*The Rainbow*
*We Are Seven*
*The World Is Too Much with Us*
*To the Cuckoo*
*The Daffodils*
*Lucy Gray*
*Simon Lee*
*Early Spring*
*Strange Fits of Passion Have I Known*

**Walter Scott (1771-1832)**

*The Bride of Lammermoor*
*Ivanhoe*
*Quentin Durward*
*The Heart of midlothian*
*Old Mortality*
*The Antiquity*
*Guy Mannering*
*Waverly*
*Rob Roy*
*Kenilworth*
*Red Gauntlet*
*The Black Dwarf*
*The Monastery*
*The Abbot*
*The Pirate*
*The Fortunes of Night*
*The Betrothed*
*The Talisman*
*Woodstock*
*Lives of the Novelists*
*Life of Napoleon*
*Tales of Grandfather*
*The Lay of the Last Minstrel*
*The Minstrelsy of the Scottish Border*
*Marmion*
*The Lady of the Lake*
*Rockeby*

**Robert Southey (1774-1843)**

*Joan of Arc*
*Wat Tyler*
*After Blenheim*
*The Holly Tree*
*The Scholar*
*A Vision of Judgement*
*Madoc*
*Life of Nelson*
*Thalaba the Destroyer*
*Roderick*
*The Curse of Kehama*

**S.T. Coleridge (1772-1834)**
*Biographia Literaria*
*Table Talk*
*Aids to Reflection*
*Christabel*
*Kubla Khan*
*The Rime of the Ancient Mariner*
*France : An Ode*
*Destiny of Nations*
*Frost at Midnight*
*Dejection : An Ode*
*Youth and Age*
*Religious Musings*

**Lord Byron (1788-1824)**
*Childe Harold's Pilgrimage*
*Don Juan*
*The Bride of Abydos*
*Manfred*
*The Giaour*
*Hours of Idleness*
*The Vision of Judgement*
*The Prisoner of Chillon*
*Lara*
*Marino Faliero*
*English Bards and Scotch Reviewers*
*The Siege of Corinth*
*The Corsair*
*Cain*

**P.B. Shelley (1792-1822)**
*On the Necessity of Atheism*
*The Revolt of Islam*
*Prometheus Unbound*
*The Mask of Anarchy*
*Hellas*
*The Cenci*
*The Witch of Atlas*
*The Indian Serenade*
*Ozymandias of Egypt*
*Epipsychidion*
*Alaster*
*Queen Mab*
*Adonais*
*Ode to the West Wind*
*The Cloud*
*Ode to a Skylark*
*O World! O Life! O Time!*
*Defence of Poetry (a Prose Work)*
*To Night*
*The Sensitive Plant*
*A Lament*

**John Keats (1795-1821)**
*Endymion*
*Lamia*
*Hyperion*
*The Eve of St. Agnes*
*Isabella*
*The Eve of St. Mark*
*La Belle Dame Sans Merci*
*Ode to a Nightingale*
*Ode to Autumn*
*Ode On a Grecian Urn*
*Ode to Psyche*
*On Melancholy*
*On First Looking into Chapman's Homer*
*Bright Star*

**Jane Austen (1775-1871)**
*Sense and Sensibility*
*Pride and Prejudice*
*Mansfield Park*
*Emma*
*Persuasion*
*Northanger Abbey*

**Charles Lamb (1775-1834)**
*Essays of Elia*
*The Last Essays of Elia*
*John Woodvil*
*Tales from Shakespeare*
*Specimens of English Dramatic Poets*
*The English Comic Writers*
*The Old Familiar Faces*

**William Hazlitt (1778-1830)**
*Characters of Shakespeare's Plays*
*The English Poets*
*The English Comic Writers*
*The Dramatic Literature of the Age of Elizabeth*
*The Round Table : A Collection of Essays*
*Table Talk on Men and Manners*
*The Spirit of the Age*

**Thomas De Quincey (1785-1859)**
*Confessions of an English Opium Eater*
*Joan of Arc*
*English Mail Coach*
*Dream Fugue*
*Murder Considered as One of the Fine Arts*
*Suspiria de Profundis*

**Samuel Rogers (1763-1855)**

*Pleasures of Memory*

*Italy*

**James Hogg (1770-1835)**

*Kilmeny*

*The Queen's Wake*

**Thomas Campbell**

*Pleasures of Hope*

*Theodoric*

*Gertrude of Wyoming*

*Lachiel*

*Lord Ullin's Daughter*

*The Last Man*

*Ye Mariners of England*

*Hohenlinden*

*The Battle of Baltic*

**Thomas Moore (1779-1852)**

*Lalla Rookh*

*Irish Melodies*

**Leigh Hunt (1784-1859)**

*Story of Rimini*

*Autobiography*

**Walter Savage Landor (1775-1864)**

*Gebir*

*Hellenics*

*Imaginary Conversations*

*The Citations of William Shakespeare*

*Pericles and Aspasia*

## THE VICTORIAN ERA (1830-1880)

During this era, the conflict between religion and science, mysticism and rationalism, became intense. There were those who, influenced by Darwin's theory of evolution as expounded in his *On the Origin of Species,* lost their faith in the biblical explanation of man's descent from Adam and Eve. They wanted to shun dogma and accept the scientific spirit. Others lamented the loss of faith and the rising consumer values. Mat thew Arnold in his poem *Dover Beach* writes:

*"The Sea of Faith was once too at the full.....*

*But now I only hear its long withdrawing melancholy roar......"*

### Prose

Carlyle and Ruskin echoed the prophecies of the Romantic era in their prose works. **Thomas Carlyle (1795-1881)**, the Scotsman, abandoned orthodoxy and came under the influence of the German writers Schiller, Novalis, Richter and Goethe. His work *Sartor Resartus* (1833-1834) is a sort of allegory based on a German professor who has written a treatise on clothes. He penetrates through the clothes to the essence of the man's being. Carlyle was also a historian. His historical works are *The French Revolution* (1837) and *The History of Frederich II of Prussia, called frederik the Great* (1858-1865). These are satirical and prophetic, expounding how man and society are organized. He was against materialism and praised the Magi and prophets of the past. He advocates strength and power.

**John Ruskin (1819-1900)** was indignant about the ugliness of existence brought in by industrialism and the machine. *Unto This Last* (1860), which influenced Gandhiji's economic theories, describes his disgust for soulless labour. He was a student of arts. *Modern Painters* (1843, 1860) is about landscape painters like Turner. He also wrote *The Seven Lamps of Architecture* (1849) and *The Stones of Venice* (1851-1853), praising Gothic art.

**Matthew Arnold (1822-1888)**, the poet, wanted his countrymen to inculcate classical qualities to become harmonious in morals and in creative works. The English must break away from their insular moorings by imbibing the teachings of Greece and the French. He is *the detector-general of the intellectual failings of his own nation*. Poetry, according to him, is important in character formation, and culture is *"the minister of the sweetness and light essential to the perfect character"*. His works include *On translating Homer, The Study of Celtic Literature and Essays in Criticism* (1865, 1889). He wrote St. Paul and Protestantism advocating that dogma should be removed from Christianity and it should adjust itself to the findings of science.

A number of philosophers, historians and scholars wrote in this period. Charles Darwin's theory of evolution dramatically affected human thought. **John Stuart Mill (1806-1873)** expounded the processes of logic and political economy. **Herbert Spencer (1820-1903)** and **Thomas Henry Huxley (1825-1895)** were scientists. **Thomas Babington Macaulay (1800-1859)** was a poet, essayist and historian who advocated English education in India. The Oxford Movement gave rise to religious writers like **John Keble (1792-1866)** and **John Henry Newman (1801-1890)**. Newman's famous work is *Apologia pro Vita Sua* (1864) in which he explains why he had converted to the Roman Church.

### Novel

The transition from Walter Scott's novels to Charles Dicken's first novel in 1836 is a great one. When Queen Victoria ascended the throne, **Frederick Marryat (1792-1848)** produced sea-stories; **Edward Bulwer Lytton (1803-1873)** wrote about Byronic heroes, attractive criminals and historical novels like *The Last Days of Pompeii* (1834); **Benjamin Disraeli** (1804-1881), the Prime Minister of England, wrote *Coningsby: or The New Generation* (1844) and *Sybil: or The Two Nations* (1845) to show that the aristocrats of the society had a duty towards the unfortunate ones. In Disraeli's novels, one finds the politics of Queen Victoria's reign.

Perhaps the greatest Victorian novelist is **Charles Dickens (1812-1870)**, whose identification with the underdog in society was unmatched by any writer. One reason for this is his own troubled childhood led in penury under the shadow of a father who was in debtor's prison. The part of his life comes through vividly in his novel *David Copperfield* (1849-1850) which is also an indictment of the cruel, unimaginative schools of his times. He was a master craftsman in character delineation. A host of characters and their dialogues have become household in the English-speaking world. Thus the incorrigible optimist Micawber, Geakle, Pickwick, Fagin and others are types of characters that may be seen all around us anywhere. Dickens had a forgiving sense of humour. He never let bitterness creep into his recreations of painful events of the past. Among his famous novels are: *Pickwick Papers* (1836; in the picaresque style), *Barnaby Rudge* (1841) and *A Tale of Two Cities* (1859; based on the French Revolution), *Oliver Twist* (1837) and *Hard Times* (1854); novels exposing social conditions. He has a picturesque style and concrete imagination.

**William Makepeace Thackeray (1811-1863)** made a penetrating analysis of upper middle class and aristocratic society. He was a master of irony. In *The Book of Snobs* (1849), he ridicules the tendency to fawn on nobility and to imitate their manners. *Vanity Fair* (1847-1848), *History of Pendennis* (1848-1850), *The Newcomes* (1853-1855), *The History of Henry Esmond* (1852) and *The Virginians* (1857-1859) are pictures of contemporary life in which he depicts human eccentricities and follies. He was adept at reproducing jargon and idiolects.

The Romantic spirit was still alive in the works of the Bronte sisters. **Charlotte Bronte (1816-1855)** wrote *Jane Eyre* (1847), the story of a governess in a terrifying house. Her sister **Emily Bronte (1818-1848)** wrote *The Wuthering Heights* (1847), set in a wild landscape. Powerful passions and characters have made this one of the greatest novels of all times.

**George Eliot (1819-1880)**, a pen-name for Mary Ann Evans, wrote Adam Bede (1859), the story of a girl who was forced to murder her own baby. *The Mill on the Floss* (1860) and *Romola* (1863) are other novels by her. In *Middlemarch, a Study of Provincial Life* (1871-1872), the novelist builds up, from the lives of a great number of deeply studied characters, the complex picture of the life of a small town.

## Poetry

The poetry of this period still shows the influence of the Romantic Era. **Alfred, Lord Tennyson (1809-1892)** was an eclectic, selecting the best of his forerunners. He was first interested in style and metre, but later on ideas started interesting him. A great many poems by him are flawlessly beautiful. If *The Lotus Eaters* is softly languorous, *Ulysses* has a striking severity. Tennyson also experienced the intellectual crisis of his times and shared its anxieties. For instance, *The Princess* (1847) is occupied with the question of feminism. *In Memoriam* (1850) is one of his most beautiful poems. It is an elegy on the premature death of his friend Arthur Hallam. It concerns itself with the belief in immortality, the conflict between the hopes of Christianity and the rationalism of science. It is composed of octosyllabic quatrains. He shows a type of Byronic revolt in Locksley Hall (1886) and Maud (1855). In *Idylls of the King* (1859, 1869, 1889) he took Arthurian legends as his theme.

**Robert Browning (1812-1889)** was famous for using the technique of dramatic monologue in his poems. Through the protagonists of his poems he gives vent to his feelings, passions and aspirations. Thus in *Paracelsus* (1835), he describes the highly ambitious hero who wanted to transform man's life. We find here Browning's views on truth and philosophy. His other poems include *Sordello* (1840), *Pippa Passes* (1841), *My Last Duchess, Porphyria's Lover* and his masterpiece, *The Ring and the Book* (1868-1869). In his works we find an excess of thought and a rare vocabulary. He uses blank verse dexterously. His brusque speech, broken syntax and uneven rhythm are in contrast to Tennyson's. As Pound and Eliot have said, Browning brought verse nearer to modem colloquial speech. Browning's characters are remote in time and culture. Some of these are Rabbi Ben Ezra, Fra Lippo Lippi and Andrea del Sarto. In *The Ring and the Book* he takes as his subject an Italian crime and explores the minds of all his characters. He strikes a note of hope in his poems. The lines *"God's in his heaven/And all's well with the world"* lay bare his beliefs. But in general, Browning is considered a difficult poet.

**Matthew Arnold (1822-1888)** was a reflective poet with a melancholic bent. A deep brooding pensiveness informs his poetry. Dover Beach shows his concern with the loss of faith in a world of science. His epic poem *Sohrab and Rustum, Tristram and Iseult, The Scholar Gypsy* are other famous works.

Dante Gabriel Rossetti, William Morris and Algernon Charles Swinburne together are known as the Pre-Raphaelite poets. They affected Raphael, the Renaissance painter, in their desire to paint sonorous wordpictures which may not have much content to conveyor any philosophy to reveal. It was in accordance with the aestheticism of Ruskin. In fact Rossetti and Morris were painters as well as poets. They worshipped beauty like John Keats did. Robert Buchanan attacked these poets as belonging to *the fleshly school of poetry.*

**Dante Gabriel Rossetti (1828-1882)** translated the Italian poet Dante's *Vita Nuova.* His *The Blessed Damozel* is an exquisite poem and his best sonnets are contained in *The House of Life* in which he extols his young and beautiful wife. They are full of rich sounds and images and mystic symbols. Rossetti was inspired by the ballads of the Middle Ages. Like the primitive Italian painters, he uses rich colours and depicts warm sensuous feelings.

**William Morris (1834-1896)** was enchanted by Gothic art of the Middle Ages. His poems drew inspiration from those of Froissart, Chaucer and Malory. He borrowed stories from Scandinavia and Iceland. His poems are like frescoes and are very lyrical in quality. The famous ones are *The Earthly Paradise* (1868-1870) and *The Life and Death of Jason* (1867). These works show rhythm and use of archaism. He strove to bring civilization back to art from the utilitarian industrialization.

**Algernon Charles Swinburne (1837-1909)** was a prodigy. He was a musician, and a sonority of rhymes filled his poetry. He took romantic themes like revolt against society, hatred of monarchy and struggle against traditional morality. His *Atalanta in Calydon* (l865) is his masterpiece and is known for its choral passages.

To these poets of the Victorian Age must be added the name of **Edward Fitzgerald (1809-1883)** whose **The Rubaiyat of Omar Khayyam (1859)** is a classic.

## MAJOR AUTHORS AND THEIR WORKS

**Alfred Lord Tennyson (1809-1892)**

*The Princess*
*In Memoriam*
*Maud*
*Enoch Arden*
*Idylls of the King*
*Queen Mary*
*Harold*
*Backet*
*Akbar's Tomb*
*Crossing the Bar*
*Locksley Hall*
*Locksley Hall Sixty Years After*
*Dora*
*Poems by Two Brothers*
*The Falcon*
*The Cup*
*Poems Chiefly Lyrical*
*Ulysses*
*Poems Chiefly Lyrical*
*Ulysses*
*The Lotos-Eaters*
*The Death of Oenone and Other Poems*

**Robert Browning (1812-1889)**

*Pauline*
*Paracelsus*
*Strafford*
*Sordello*
*Bells and Pomegranates*
*Christmas Eve and Easter Day*
*Men and Women*
*Dramatis Personae*
*The King and the Book*
*Asolando*
*Pippa Passes*
*Fra Lippo Lippi*
*Andrea del Sarto*
*King Victor and King Charles*
*Dramatic Lyrics*
*Dramatic Romances and Lyrics*

**Matthew Arnold (1822-1888)**

*Sohrab and Rustum*
*Tristram and Iseult*
*Balder Dead*
*Empedocles on Etna*
*Stanzas from the Grande Chartreuse*
*The Strayed Reveller and Other Poems*
*Dover Beach*
*Thyrsis*
*Scholar Gypsy*
*On Translating Homer*
*New Poems*
*On the Study of Celtic Literature*
*Essays in Criticism*

*Culture and Anarchy*
*Literature and Dogma*
*Mixed Essays*
*Friendship's Garland*
*God and the Bible*

**D.G. Rossetti (1828-1882)**

*The Blessed Damozel*
*World's Worth*
*Ave*
*The White Ship*
*Sister Helen*
*Eden Bower*
*The House of Life*
*Ballads and Sonnets*

**Christina Georgina Rossetti (1830-1894)**

*The Goblin Market*
*The Prince's Market*
*A Pageant and Other Poems*

**William Morris (1834-1896)**

*The Defence of Guenevere*
*The Life and Death of Jason*
*The Earthly Paradise*
*A Dream of John Bull*
*News from Nowhere*
*A Tale of the House of the Wolfings*
*The Roots of the Mountains*
*The Story of the Glittering Plain*
*The Sundering Flood*
*Hope and Fears for Art*
*Signs of Change*

**A.C. Swinburne (1837-1909)**

*Atalanta in Calydon*
*Erechtheus*
*Tristram of Lyonesse*
*Chasteland*
*Bathwell*
*Mary Stuart*
*William Blake : A Critique*
*A Study of Shakespeare*
*A Study of Ben Jonson*
*Songs Before Sunrise*

**Edward Fitzgerald (1809-1883)**

*Euphranor : A Dialogue on Youth*
*Translation of Rubaiat*

**Thomas Carlyle (1795-1881)**

*Sartor Resartus*
*The French Revolution*
*Heroes and Hero-Worship*
*Past and Present*
*The Letters and Speeches of Oliver Cromwell*
*Latter-day Pamphlets*
*Life of John Sterling*
*History of Frederick the Great*
*Chartism*

**John Ruskin (1819-1900)**

*The Modern Painters*
*Salsette and Elephanta*
*The Seven Lamps of Architectur*
*The Stones of Venice*
*The Two Paths*
*Unto This Last*
*Munera Pulveris*
*Time and Tide by Wear and Tyne*
*Fors Clavigera*
*Sesame and Lilies*
*The Crown of Wild Olive*

**T.B. Macaulay (1800-1859)**

*History of England from the Accession of James II*
*Lays of Ancient Rome*

**Charles Dickens (1812-1870)**

*Pickwick Papers*
*Nicholas Nickleby*
*Martin Chuzzlewit*
*Dombey and Son*
*David Copperfield*
*Bleak House*
*A Tale of Two Cities*
*Great Expectations*
*Our Mutual Friend*
*Edwin Drood*
*Oliver Twist*
*Little Dorrit*
*Baraby Rudge*
*The Uncommercial Traveller*
*A Christmas Carol*
*Hard Times*
*Old Curiosity Shop*

**William Makepeace Thackeray (1811-1863)**

*Vanity Fair*

*Barry Lyndon*
*Pendennis*
*Henry Esmond*
*The New Comes*
*The Virginians*
*Adventures of Philip*
*The Book of Snobs*
*The History of Pendennis*
*Lovel the Widower*
*The Round about Papers*
*The English Humorists of the Eighteenth Century*
*The Four Georges*
*Rebecca and Rowena*
*The Rose and The Ring*
*Ivanhoe—the Legend of the Rhine*

**George Meredith (1828-1909)**

*The Ordeal of Richard Feveral*
*Evan Harrington*
*Emilia in England*
*Rhoda Fleming*
*Vittoria*
*The Adventures of Harry Richmond*
*Diana of the Crossways*
*One of Our Conquerous*
*The Amazing Marriage*
*The Egoist*
*Beauchamp's Career*
*The Tragic Comedians*

**Charlotte Bronte (1816-1855)**

*Jane Eyre*
*Shirley*
*The Professor*
*Villette*

**Emily Bronte (1818-1848)**

*Wuthering Heights*

**George Eliot (1810-1880)**
**(Mary Ann Evans)**

*Adam Bede*
*The Mill on the Floss*
*Silas Marner*
*Scenes of Clerical Life*
*Life of Jesus*
*Romola*
*Fleix Holt the Radical*
*Daniel Deronda*
*Middlemarch*

**Benjamin Disraeli (1804-1881)**

*Vivian Gray*
*Sybil : Or the Two Nations*
*The Voyage of Captain Popavilla*
*Henrietta Temple*
*Coningsby : or the New Generation*
*Tancred : or the New Crusade*
*The Wondrous Tale of Alroy and the Rise of Iskander*
*Contarini Fleming : A Psychological Auto-biography*

**R.L. Stevenson (1850-1894)**

*Travels with a Donkey in the Cevennes*
*An Inland Voyage*
*Virginibus Pueresque*
*New Arabian Nights*
*Treasure Island*
*The Strange Case of Dr. Jackyll and Mr. Hyde*
*Kidnapped*
*The Black Arrow*
*The Master of Ballantrae*
*Catriona*
*Underwords*
*A Child's Garden of Verses*

**Thomas Hardy (1840-1828)**

*Under the Greenwood Tree*
*Desperate Remedies*
*A Pair of Blue Eyes*
*Two on a Tower*
*Far From the Madding Crowd*
*The Return of the Native*
*The Mayor of Casterbridge*
*Tess of the D'Urbervilles*
*Jude the Obscure*
*The Hand of Ethelberta*
*The Trumpet Major*
*The Woodlanders*
*The Well-beloved*
*A Laodicean*
*A Group of Noble Dames*
*Life's LIttle Ironies*
*Wessex Poems*
*The Dynasts*
*A Changed Man*
*Winter Words*
*The Waiting Supper and Other Tales*

# The Modern Age (1880 Onwards)

As the 20th century dawned, new values replaced the old ones and shaped the literature of Great Britain. England fast lost its imperial image as her colonies revolted and fought for independence. Industrialization progressed by leaps and bounds and the two World Wars brought economic depression. All this affected the content of literature. Writers sought new vehicles of expression. The findings of **Sigmund Freud** in the realms of psychology took novelists to the subconscious mind. A great number of writers who became famous men of letters in English came from Ireland **(G.B. Shaw, W.B. Yeats, James Joyce and Samuel Beckett)** and from America **(T.S. Eliot and Ezra Pound)**. Socialism became a practising creed and feminism raised her head. Dogmatic Christianity was more or less ignored. Although great strides were made in scientific inventions, science could not provide suitable answers to the deep questioning of the human mind resulting in ethical philosophy. The age saw the end of feudalism. Victorian reticence and prudery gave way to decadence in literature. English writers came under the influence of the French Parnassians and Symbolists. Scandinavia and Russia represented by **Ibsen** and **Tolstoy** also influenced the British men of letters. Many a poet wished to fight free from the fixed rules of versification and wrote in free verse. Many imitated the American poet **Walt Whitman**. English literature became more expansive in its concerns. The life and culture of foreign lands were depicted. Although **Kipling** was an imperialist, his works go beyond England. Being born in India, his works give a graphic view of the country. The great Celtic Revival under Yeats brought a new strain to English literature. Finally, the theatre, lying dormant for a century, now woke up with renewed vigour.

## Criticism

The Age began with scholarly works in literary history. **Leslie Stephen (1832-1904)** wrote biographical and critical essays. He produced *The English Utilitarians and the Dictionary of National Biography*. He was an agnostic and rationalist. **A.C. Bradley (1851-1935), H.J.C. Grierson (1866-1960)** and **Edward Dowden (1843-1913)** were other famous critics. Bradley is famous for his critical work on Shakespeare's tragedies.

**Walter Horatio Pater (1839-1894)** propounded the literary doctrine *Art for Art's Sake* which was a quest for the most refined pleasure. The exquisite in art came from a reflection of the past. He eulogized the accomplishments of the Renaissance. His prose style was rich, musical and classical. His works include *Studies in the History of the Renaissance* (1873) and *Marius the Epicurean* (1885).

**John Addington Symonds (1840-1893)** was another admirer of the Renaissance. **Oscar Wilde (1856-1900)**, more known as a novelist and dramatist, gave a wider dimension to the theory of Art for Art's Sake by spicing it with wit and paradox. **George Saintsbury (1845-1933)** and **Sir Walter Raleigh (1861-1922)** were other famous critics.

## Poetry

Most of the poetry written in this period are the works of those more renowned as novelists: Robert Louis Stevenson, Rudyard Kipling and Thomas Hardy. William Butler Yeats, who pioneered the Celtic Revival, Thomas Steams Eliot, whose *Wasteland* is a watershed leading to modern poetry, Gerard Manley Hopkins, the Catholic poet, are the famous poets of this period.

**Rudyard Kipling (1865-1936)** wrote on imperialist themes in *Barrack Room Ballads* (1892), *The Seven Seas* (1896) and *Five Nations* (1903). These poems were aimed by their rugged music to rouse people to protest. He combined folk-music with music-hall chorus. It had the sound of drum beats and bugle-calls and even the refinements of chamber music. The poetry of imperialism, heroism of national policy, contained slang and even biblical allusions. In fact, his popularity was that of Walt Whitman, the national poet of America. Many of his subjects were from India, like the poem *Gunga Din*.

**W.E. Henley (1849-1903)** also wrote poetry which praised Britain's colonial power. *The Song of the Sword, For England's Sake* and *London Voluntaries* are some of his better-known poems.

There were also a group of poets called the Decadents. They were aesthetes and their doctrine was 'Art for Art's Sake'. **Oscar Wilde** was the leading poet of the group. *The Ballad of Reading Gaol* (1898) is his famous work inspired by his crime and imprisonment.

A group of poets had a pessimistic view of life. **John Davidson (1857-1909), Ernest Dawson (1867-1900)** and **A.E. Housman (1859-1936)** are some of these poets. But the leading pessimist of the age was **Thomas Hardy (1840-1928)**, better known as a novelist. He published *Wessex Poems* (1898) after the novel *Jude the Obscure* failed to receive public acclaim. His poetry was musical and highly individual. He had a disillusioned view of life. From 1903 to 1908, he produced the vast poetical work *The Dynasts*, written under the background of Napoleon's struggle against Europe combining real history with symbolic flashes. His poem, *To an Unborn Pauper Child,* reveals his utter dejection with life: *'Breathe : hid heart'*, it begins.

**Francis Thompson (1859-1907)** and **Gerard Manley Hopkins (1844-1889)** were religious poets of the beginning of the twentieth century. Thompson's poem, *The Hound of Heaven* is a masterpiece. It describes God as a Heavenly Hound chasing man to capture his soul and man fleeing Him in the pleasures of life. The Jesuit, Hopkins invented a new type of verse called *'sprung rhythm'*. It was filled with strange word coinages and is difficult for the ordinary reader to understand. His poetry reflects the conflirt within him between his attraction to Roman Catholicism and his joy tor the beautiful creation. He wrote a number of religious poems of which *The Wreck of the "Deutschland"* is one of the best. It describes the death of five Franciscan nuns on board the ship, *Deutschland*.

Irish, English and Continental influences met in **W.B. Yeats (1865-1939)**. He Was born in Ireland but came to live in London. He was influenced by the strange mystical visions of William Blake, by pre-Raphaelite refinement and even the mysticism and occultism of the Orient, especially of India. His poetry is an attempt to revive Celtic mysticism and Irish mythology. Apparently it Was Yeats who introduced Rabindra Nath Tagore to the West. He also came under the influence of Verlaine, a French symbolist poet. His best poetry is in *The Wild Swans at Coole* (1919), *The Tower* (1928) and *The Winding Stair* (1933). Some of his well-known poems are: *Easter* (1916), *The Second Coming, Byzantium, A Prayer for my Daughter, Leda and Swan, Sailing to Byzantium, Meru, Lapis Lazudili, Among School Children,* etc. His progress as a poet can be assessed by comparing the beautiful but simple *Lake Isle of Innisfree* with the beautiful and profound *Byzantium*.

The towering poet of the 20th century is **Thomas Steams Eliot (1888-1965)**. Eliot came on to the scene when the West was passing through tremendous upheavals — belief in religion, especially of the Church was fading, democracy was the new experiment in politics, and many modernist trends were noticeable in literature. Eliot proclaimed himself "a royalist in politics, an Anglo-Catholic in religion and a classicist in literature". Tradition, according to him, was not the dead past but the past living in the present. In his essay *Tradition and the Individual Talent,* he states that "the talent of an artist shows itself not where he differs from the ancients but where, in his work, they assert their immortality". Eliot's poetry shows metaphysical, symbolist and imagist strains, but his individual talent shines forth unmistakeably. An eclectic philosophy, borrowed from his own Christianity and Buddhism and the Upanishads informs his poetry. His poetry, especially *The Wasteland* (1922) is a poem that describes the zeitgeist (spirit of the times) and the *angoisse metaphysique* (metaphysical anguish) of life in post-World War Europe. It begins with the sentence *"April is a cruel month"* and this sets the strain lor the whole poem. A brooding sense of futility and human inanity pervades modern life. Eliot achieves this effect by a combination of literary allusions to the past which stirs associations, and by what is called as the *objective correlative*. This last technique means that images are described which call up an emotion or a feeling. His other poems are *The Lave Song of J. Alfred Prufrock* and *Four Quartets* (1944). These lines from the *Four Quartets* may sum up the disillusionment of the times: *"Footfalls echo in the memory/Down the passage one could not take / To the door one could not open"*. Eliot was a poet of spiritual regeneration.

As the century proceeds, a host of poets make their mark **Stephen Spender (1909-1995), W.H. Auden (1907-1973), C. Day Lewis (1904-1972), Louis MacNeice (1907-1963)** — all of them wrote with a Social awareness, exposing the horror of the bourgeois culture and capitalist exploitation and the terror of totalitarianism.

We cannot end this section of the early modern twentieth century without a reference to **Rupert Brooke (1887-1915), Wilfred Owen (1893-1918)** and **Siegfried Sassoon (1886-1967)** popularly known as the "War poets". They had served the Armed Forces in the First World War, and after 1918, disillusioned by the horrors they had witnessed took their pens to write against the war. The poem *The Soldier* is one of the finest lyrics in the English language. It describes the poet's sense of impending death in battle and his love for his country: *"If I should die/Think only this of me/That there is a part of England/Buried in some foreign land"*. Another poem is Sassoon's *Everyone Sang,* which describes the exultation felt by the soldiers returning home after the General Armistice was signed. They are described as *freed birds*.

## Novel

Just like poetry, the novel of this century reflects the great passions and strivings of the age. The discoveries of **Sigmund Freud (1856-1939)** revealed the relationship of man's behaviour to his subconscious mind. The subconscious contains impressions of past experiences which influence a person's attitudes and behaviour. These discoveries led not only to new methods of psychiatric treatment but also to new dramatic techniques in the art of the novel. The stream-of-consciousness method used by James Joyce and Virginia Woolf spring from these discoveries. The modem novel is more and more concerned with an analysis of human behaviour. The focus shifts from a description of the external atmosphere to the thoughts of the characters.

**Thomas Hardy's** works are tinged with a gloomy pessimism reminiscent of Schopenhauer, and an analogy may be found in his works to Flaubert and Zola from

France. Hardy's country Dorsetshire and the surroundings become the 'Wessex' of his novels. His work is full of realistic descriptions of the countryside. The places, full of pre-historic and Roman remains, heaths, have a character, and influence the people living there. The pre-historic past presses on the life of today. He is adept at delineating rustic characters. Man is a puppet of fate and an uncontrollable destiny drives him along life. A bitter helplessness pervades his novels *Far from the Madding Crowd* (1874), *The Return of the Native* (1878), *The Mayor of Casterbridge* (1886), and *Jude the Obscure* (1895). His success reached a climax with *Tess of the d'Urbervilles* (1891). His *Tess of the D'UrberviUes* and *Jude the Obscure,* because of their frank handling of sex and religion, aroused the hostility of the reading public. These two books, however, present Hardy's most moving indictments of the human situation.

**The works of George Robert Gissing (1857-1903)** produce a sense of absolute dejection. He worked as an ill-paid hack in the poor districts of London and described these places vividly in his books. Although impressed by Charles Dickens, his writings show none of Dickens' humour. One bitter, wretched world, a miserable London, exists in his works. Thus *Demos, a Story of English Socialism* (1886) describes the futility of socialist agitation, *The Nether World* (1889), the wretchedness of the London slums, *New Grub Street* (1891), the hopeless lot of a penniless writer, and *The Odd Women* (1893), the plight of unmarried women. His style is as bare and unaffected as his ideas.

**Robert Louls Stevenson (1850-1894)** stands in contrast to Hardy and Gissing in his recreation of the life of action and adventure. Although he suffered from an incurable malady, he did not lose faith in himself. He brought out *An Inland Voyage* (1878), *Travels with a Donkey in the Cevennes* (1879), *The Silverado Squatters, Treasure Island* (1833), *Kidnapped* and *The Master of Ballantrae* (1889) among others. The last three are very popular among children the world over. He also wrote children's adventure classics like *The Treasure Island* (1883), *Dr Jekyll and Mr. Hyde* (1886) and *Kidnapped* (1886). In *Dr. Jekyll and Mr Hyde* he touches upon the dual nature of man his good and evil aspects. His style is vivid and full of interesting details.

Another great novelist was the Pole, **Joseph Conrad (1857-1924)**, who perfected his knowledge of English and wrote in a vivid style with a strong foreign accent. His experience of sailing life and work in the English merchant service gave him the ideas to write masterpieces like *The Nigger of the Narcissus* (1897), and *Lord Jim: A Tale* (1900). Like the Slavs he was preoccupied with the problem of human misery. *Lord Jim* and *The Heart of Darkness* (1902) show his anger at what the white man had done to exploit Africa and other nations. A trait of his narrative technique is the gradual picture of his character formed from fragmentary descriptions of witnesses. He has a rich, sensuous prose style full of striking imagery.

**Rudyard Kipling** wrote stories about Indian life: *Plain Tales from the Hills* (1888) and *Soldiers Three* (1888). *Plain Tales from the Hills* depicts an Englishman's encounter with the strange East. Kipling was born in Bombay and spent his early life in India. He knew the land and its customs, its people and languages. His best book is *Kim* (1901), the story of a half-Irish boy, who speaks the language of the rustics of India and accompanies a Buddhist Lama on his search for "Nirvana" or Salvation. Kipling is adept at describing the sights and smells of India and its colourful people with their racy dialects. He also wrote two animal epics entitled, *The Jungle Book* (1894) and a series of short stories for children like *Captains Courageous* (1897), just *So Stories* (1902) and *Puck of Pook's Hill* (1906). Kipling was influenced by Carlyle's doctrine of energy. As a spokesman of the Imperialist theme he believed that it was ideal for a person to sacrifice himself for his tribe. He believed that especially the white man was ordained to rule and lead nations. His works praise Britain's hegemony over her colonies.

Shortly after Kipling, came H. G. Wells and John Galsworthy who were Socialists and criticized the English society. **H.G. Wells** (1866-1946) began by writing stories with a semi-scientific flavour like *The Time Machine* (1895), *The Island of Dr Moreau* (1896), *The Invisible Man* (1897) and *The War of the Worlds* (1898). The stories are ingenuously plotted and thrill and disturb the readers. Later on Wells' interest shifted to social problems He became a member of the Fabian Society. He wrote *Mankind in the Making* (1903) describing how society would look like when reformed by socialism. He also satirized the society in *Love and Mr Lewisham* (1900), *Kipps* (1905). *Tono-Bungay* (1909) and *Marriage* (1912). He does not glorify Britain's past and he scorns the existing institutions of his country. He wrote a number of remarkable books after the outbreak of World War I in 1914. These show his restless self examining spirit. Some of these are *Mr Britling Sees it through* (1916) and *The Undying Fire* (1919).

In the works of **John Galsworthy (1867-1933)** we find an artistic conscience. Like Wells, he also attacked the concept of property and commercialism in his novels. He too exposed and criticized national prejudices, especially those existing among his own class, the landed gentry. He was widely read in Continental Literature and was especially influenced by France and Russia. Turgenev with his noble realism was his ideal. He is a detached and impartial observer of his country's decadent values. He advocates a fearless search for truth. *In The Island Pharisees* (1904) he exposes the stagnation of thought among English privileged classes. A similar theme is touched in other novels like *The Country House* (1907), *The Patrician* (1911) and *The Dark Flower* (1913) where country squires, aristocracy and artists are critically studied. *The Forsyte Saga* (1922) is his masterpiece. It is a natural history of the rich upper-middle class family. He describes their attitude to events like the Great War, the growth of socialism, unemployment and the coal strike.

**Enoch Arnold Bennett (1867-1931)** wrote a number of different types of novels presenting a detailed picture of an industrial district in the provinces. He is a realist like the French nationalists. His masterpiece is *The Old Wives' Tale* (1908).

**G.K. Chesterton (1874-1936)** was a champion of tradition and he refuted and opposed the attacks of his contemporaries against English society in *Orthodoxy* (1908), *The Napoleon of Notting Hill* (1904). He believed in tradition sanctified by ages of experience and even in the religious bond between men. His style is effective with the use of imagery and comparison and he spices it with plenty of humour.

**James Joyce (1882-1941)** pioneered a new type of novel with the *stream-of-consciousness* technique. Characters in *Ulysses* (1922) unreel themselves by a sort of interior monologue. Speech is mimicked and styles are parodied. *Ulysses* is modelled on the *Odyssey* of Homer and set in the slums of Dublin. The thousand pages of this novel cover just one day in the life of Leopold Bloom and Stephen Dedalus. Joyce coined words from several languages and was a master craftsman with wit and conceits. His other famous work is the autobiographical *A Portrait of the Artist as a Young Man* (1916) which describes his adolescence and sensuous tendencies.

**Virginia Woolf (1882-1941)** continued the stream-of-consciousness technique. Her works *To the Lighthouse* (1927) and *Mrs Dallaway* (1925) reveal the hidden inner life of her characters.

**E.M. Forster (1879-1970)** was the novelist of cultural relations. In **A Passage to India** (1924) he studies the conflict between the west and the east and takes a favourable stand for the latter. *Where Angels Fear to Tread* (1905) studies how the cultural divide between an Italian girl and her English husband leads to the ruination of their marriage and life.

**D.H. Lawrence (1885-1930)** was a prolific writer. His outspoken views on sexual relations raised much hue and cry. He considered sex the religion of the blood. His novels were dubbed pornographic. He believed in the free expression of human personality, in being guided by unrestrained primitive instincts. In *Sons and Lovers* (1913) he studies the relationship of son and mother and the social disparity of a father, a coalminer and a mother, a teacher. The novel is autobiographical. Other works by him are *The Rainbow* (1915), *Women in Love* (1921), and *The Plumed Serpent* (1926). *The Rainbow,* suppressed as obscene, treats the conflict between man and woman. *Lady Chatterley's Lover* (1928) was canned for being obscene.

**George Orwell (1903-1950)** wrote novels which were an indictment of totalitarian government: *Animal Farm* (1945) and *Nineteen Eighty-Four* (1949). **Aldous Huxley's** *Brave New World* (1932) is a prophetic book about the future of civilization in the context of scientific advancement.

## Drama

After Shakespeare, **George Bernard Shaw (1856-1950)** is the great playwright whose works enlivened the British stage. Shaw, like Ibsen, believed in drama as a vehicle for ideas. He had a rich Irish sense of humour and his plays are satires on various social and philosophical themes. His general technique was to discuss the problem of his play first in its preface. Often this preface is longer than the play itself. *Widowers' Houses* (1892) was his first play. In this he discusses the problem of Housing. In *Mrs Warren's Profession* (1894) he lays bare the profession of a prostitute. In *Arms and the Man* (1894) the theme is the chocolate-cream soldier. Shaw was an iconoclast breaking well-established idols or myths. Thus this play disillusions us of the romantic image of a soldier. He is not one who is willing to die for his country, but one who loves his life. When the enemy is weak, he attacks, but withdraws and takes to his heels if the enemy is strong. George Bernard Shaw had a keen interest in the English language and formulated a standard pronunciation for it. He studies the theme of how language can influence one's rise in the social ladder. Professor Higgins succeeds in teaching a flower-girl to rid herself of a cockney accent and to speak well enough to pass for royalty! In *Man and Superman* we see Shaw as a master conversationalist. Ideas are discussed without much action taking place in the play. *The Apple Cart* (1929) shows the weaknesses of democracy. Although an Irish man, Shaw did not write on Irish themes as such.

**Oscar Wilde** reminds one of the Restoration playwrights Sheridan and Congreve in his comedy of manners. His style is full of paradox and verbal wit. Some of his famous plays are *Lady Windermere's Fan* (1892), *A Woman of No Importance* (1893) and *The Importance of Being Ernest* (1895).

**John Galsworthy's** plays *Sfrife* (1909), *Justice* (1910) and *Loyalties* (1922) were based on the theme of class exploitation.

W.B. Yeats contributed to the Irish drama. His Celtic theme comes through in *The Countess Cathleen* (1892) and *The Land of Heart's Desire* (1894). **Sean O'Casey** (1884-1964) and **J. M. Synge** (1871-1909) were other noted Irish playwrights. The latter's plays, *The Playboy of the Western World* (1907) and *Riders to the Sea* (1904) are famous.

**T.S. Eliot's** contribution to the modern theatre were religious and moral plays. He uses the Greek "chorus" style in *Murder in the Cathedral* (1935) to heighten the dramatic effect of the murder of Thomas Becket by the Archbishop of Canterbury's men. *The Family Reunion* (1939) is a play about sin and expiation. Eliot pruned verse to sound like prose. This is done dexterously in *The Cocktail Party* (1949) and *The Confidential Clerk* (1953) where characters speak verse which sounds like prose.

A group of playwrights came to be known as the "Angry Young Men". **John Osborne (1929-1994)** was the most prominent of them. His play *Look Back in Anger* (1956) catches the mood of the frustrated youth in post-War England. In his plays, he exposes the wretchedness of the working class.

**Harold Pinter (1930-2008)** mixes comedy and horror in his plays like *The Birthday Party* (1958).

Another group of dramatists drew their inspiration from France. *The Absurd Theatre*, as it was called, began in France with Albert Camus, Jean Genet anJ Ionesco as its pioneers. In England, **Samuel Beckett (1906-1989)** was the Irish dramatist of this school. His plays *Endgame* (1955), *Krapp's Last Tape* (1958) and *Waiting For Godot* (1906) show the meaninglessness of human action and the unrelieved gloom of existence.

## MAJOR AUTHORS AND THEIR WORKS

**George Bernard Shaw (1856-1950)**

*Widowers' Houses*
*Candida*
*You Never Can Tell*
*Man and Superman*
*Back to Methuselah*
*Saint Joan*
*Heartbreak House*
*The Philanderer*
*Mrs. Warren's Profession*
*Caesar and Cleopatra*
*John Bull's Other Island*
*Major Barbara*
*The Doctor's Dilemma*
*Getting Married*
*The Apple Cart*
*Pygmalion*
*The Dark Lady of the Sonnets*
*Plays Pleasant and Unpleasant*
*The Millionaire*
*The Intelligent Woman's Guide to Socialism*
*Everybody's Political What is What*
*Cashel Byron's Profession*
*Love Among the Artists*
*Androcles and the Lion*
*The Devil's Disciple*
*The Man of Destiny*

**W.B. Yeats (1865-1939)**

*The Land of Heart's Desire*
*The Countess Cathleen*
*The Shadowy Waters*
*The Hour-glass*
*The Resurrection*
*The King's Threshold*
*On Baile's Strand*
*The Cat and the Moon*
*Ideas of Good and Evil*
*Discoveries*
*The Wind among the Reeds*
*The Wanderings of Oisin*
*The Tower*
*The Winding Stair and Other Poems*
*Lake Isle of Innisfree*
*Byzantium*

**John Galsworthy (1867-1933)**

*The Silver Box*
*Strife*
*The Skin Game*
*The Man of Property*
*Justice*
*Loyalties*
*Escape*
*The Inn of Tranquility*
*The Forsyte Saga*
*The Country House*
*Fraternity*
*The Patrician*
*The Dark Flower*
*Saint's Progress*
*Maid in Waiting*
*Flower Wilderness*

**Rudyard Kipling (1865-1936)**

*Kim*

*The Jungle Book*
*Barrack-room Ballads*
*Departmental Ditties*
*The Seven Seas*
*The Five Nations*
*Tales from the Hills*
*Soldiers Three*
*Life's Handicap*
*The Phantom Rickshaw*
*Many Inventions*
*The Day's Work*
*Just-so Stories for Little Children*
*Rewards and Fairies*
*Debits and Credits*

**H.G. Wells (1866-1946)**

*The Time Machine*
*Love and Mr. Levisham*
*Kipps*
*The History of Mr. Polly*
*Mr. Britling Sees It Through*
*Christina Albertas Father*
*The Wonderful Visit*
*The Island of Dr. Moreau*
*The Invisible Man*
*The War of the Worlds*
*The First Men in the Moon*
*The Food of the Goas*
*Marriage*
*Experiment in Autobiography*
*The Contemporary Novel*

**Joseph Conrad (1857-1924)**

*The Nigger of the 'Narcissus'*
*Typhoon*
*Lord Jim*
*Victory*
*Almayer's Folly*
*An Outcast of the Islands*
*Youth*
*Heart of Darkness*
*The Secret Agent*
*The Shadow of Line*
*Suspense-A Napoleonic Novel*

**Arnold Bennett (1867-1931)**

*The Old Wives' Tale*
*Clayhanger*
*Riceyman Steps*
*Buried Alive*
*Hilda Lessways*
*These Twain*
*Sacred and Profane Love*
*The Pretty Lady*
*The Love Match*
*The Author's Craft*

**Walter de la Mare (1873-1956)**

*Peacock Pie*
*Memoirs of a Midget*
*Songs of Childhood*
*Bells and Grass*
*The Traveller*
*Early the Morning*
*Love*

**T.S. Eliot (1888-1965)**

*The Waste Land*
*Prufrock and Other Observations*
*Gerontion*
*The Hollow Men*
*Ash Wednesday*
*Four Quartets*
*Sweeney Agonistes*
*Murder in the Cathedral*
*The Rock*
*The Family Reunion*
*The Cocktail Party*
*The Confidential Clerk*
*The Sacred Wood*
*After Strange Gods*
*The Elder Statesman*
*The Idea of a Christian Society*
*What is a Classic?*
*For Lancelot Andrews*
*The Use of Poetry and the Use of Criticism*
*Elizabethan Essays*
*Points of View*

**Virginia Woolf (1882-1941)**

*The Voyage Out*
*Jacob's Room*
*Mrs. Dalloway*
*To The Light House*
*The Waves*
*Flush*
*Orlando : A Biography*
*The Common Reader*
*Roger Fry*
*The Death of the Moth*
*Mr. Bennett and Mrs. Brown*

*A Room of One's Own*
*Between the Acts (Unfinished)*

**E.M. Forster (1879-1970)**

*Abinger Harvest*
*Two Cheers for Democracy*
*A Passage to India*
*Howard's End*
*The Hill of Devi*
*The Celestial Omnibus*
*Collected Short Stories*
*Where Angels Fear to Tread*
*The Longest Journey*
*The Story of the Siren*
*A Room with a View*
*The Eternal Moment*

**James Joyce (1882-1941)**

*Ulysses*
*Portrait of the Artist as a Young Man*
*Finnegans Wake*
*Dubliners*

**D.H. Lawrence (1885-1930)**

*Sons and Lovers*
*Woman in Love*
*Lady Chatterly's Lover*
*The Rainbow*
*The White Peacock*
*Kangaroo*
*The Plumed Serpent*

**Aldous Huxley (1894-1963)**

*Point Counter Point*
*The Burning Wheel*
*Those Barren Leaves*
*Brave New World*
*After Many a Summer*
*Eyeless in Gaza*
*Antic Hay*
*Time Must Have a Stop*
*Crome Yellow*
*The Defeat of Youth*
*The Perennial Philosophy*
*The Devils of Loudun*

**George Orwell (1903-1950)**

*The Animal Farm*
*The Road to Wigan Pier*
*Nineteen Eighty-Four*
*Burmese Days*
*Keep the Aspidistra Flying*

**Oscar Wilde (1854-1900)**

*The Sphinx*
*The Ballad of Reeding Gaol*
*The Canterville Ghost*
*De Profundis*
*The Duchess of Padua*
*The Importance of Being Earnest*
*An Ideal Husband*
*Lady Windermere's Fan*
*Salome*
*The Picture of Dorian Gray*
*The Happy Prince and the Other Tales*

**Harold Pinter (1930-2008)**

*The Birthday Party*
*The Dumb Waiter*
*The Care Taker*
*A Night Out*
*The Home Coming*
*Old Times*
*Silence*

# Indian Writing in English

## ANAND, MULKRAJ (1905-2004)

He was greatly influenced by Premchand on the one hand and Tagore on the other.

### Works

Some of his famous novels are :

1. The Village (1939)
2. Across the Black waters (1940)
3. The Sword and the sickle (1942)
4. Untouchable (1933) (his first novel)
5. Seven summers (1951)
6. Private Life of an Indian Prince (1953)
7. The Big Heart (1945)
8. Coolie (1936) (It was recast in seventies)
9. Two Leaves and a Bud (1937)
10. The Old Woman and the Cow (1960)
11. The Road (1961)
12. Death of a Hero (1963)
13. Confession of a Lover (1976)
14. Morning Face (1968)

## AUROBINDO, GHOSE (1872-1950)

- He was known as the "firebrand" of India.
- He was a poet, a saint, a philosopher, statesman, yogi and a prophet.
- He is one of the pre-Independence Titanic trio of Indian poets—Tagore, Aurobindo and Sarojini Naidu.
- He is chiefly known for his
  - *(i)* Savitri (1953) a poetic epic on a grand scale.
  - *(ii)* The Life Divine (1939-40)
  - *(iii)* Essays on Gita
- He is a great exponent and proponent of ancient Indian thought.
- According to R. K. Singh, "Aurobindo is sympathetic to the modernist trends in writing and study of poetry and, in fact, himself adopts some of the methods followed by the modern poets."
- To quote Mr. Singh again, "In Aurobindo's literary order, poetry is a means of spiritual expression that helps to open the consciousness..."

## CHATTERJEE, BANKIM CHANDRA (1838-94)

- He is generally called 'The Father of Bengali fiction.'
- Today he is most known for his patriotic bent of mind.
- In all he wrote 14 novels.
  - *(i)* Some of them are historical.
  - *(ii)* Others are social.
  - *(iii)* Still others are philosophical with stress on renunciation and non-attachment.
- Some of his novels are :
  - *(i)* *The Poison Tree (1884):* It is a story of Hindu life in Bengal of the period
  - *(ii)* Kapalkundala (1885)
  - *(iii)* Durgeshnandini (1890)
  - *(iv)* Krishnakanta's Will (1895)
  - *(v)* The Two Rings (1897)
  - *(vi)* Rajmohan's Wife (1904) (published posthumously)
  - *(vii)* Anand Math (1884)

## CHAUDHURI, NIRAD, C. (1897-1999)

- He came into limelight with the publication of his "The Autobiography of an Unknown Indian." (1951).
- His other important works are:
  - *(i)* A Passage to India (1959)
  - *(ii)* Continent of Circe (1966)
    (He received the Duff Cooper Memorial Prize).
  - *(iii)* The Intellectual in India (1967)
  - *(iv)* To Live or Not to Live (1970)
- He is known for his most correct and chaste prose for which he has earned much acclaim from the scholars and critics, including Khushwant Singh.

## DESAI, ANITA (Born-1937)

- She is a renowned novelist and short story writer.
- Some of her famous novels are :
  - *(i)* Cry, the Peacock (1963)
  - *(ii)* Voices in the City (1965)
  - *(iii)* Bye-Bye, Blackbird (1971)
  - *(iv)* Fire on the Mountain (1977)
  - *(v)* Clear Light of Day (1980)
- Her collection of short stories is captioned "Games at Twilight" (1978)

## GANDHI, M.K. (1869-1948)

1. His famous work in English is "My Experiments with Truth."
2. The work is an important autobiographical writing which is held in high esteem for its truthfulness, frankness, simplicity and directness of expression in non-ornamental effective English.

## MARKANDAYA, KAMALA (1924-2004)

1. She is one of the modern novelists and is known for her:
   - *(i)* Nectar in a Sieve (her first novel) (It is a novel on miserable rural life).
   - *(ii)* Some Inner Fury (1955)
     (It is a novel of violence and destruction)
   - *(iii)* A Silence of Desire (1960)
     (It is a novel urging the readers to speak out frankly to unburden their hearts).
   - *(iv)* Possession (1963)
     (The problem of possession is discussed in this novel).
   - *(v)* A Handful of Rice (1966)
     (It depicts the life of the poor classes in Madras).
   - *(vi)* The Coffer Danus (1969)
   - *(vii)* The Nowhere Man (1972)
   - *(viii)* Two Virgins (1973)
   - *(ix)* The Golden Honeycomb (1977)
   - *(x)* Pleasure City (1982).

## KHUSHWANT SINGH (Born-1915)

- He is known for his novels :
    - *(i)* Train to Pakistan (his masterpiece)
    - *(ii)* I Shall Not Hear the Nightingale (1959). (It describes the social life of a Sikh family during the pre-Independence period).
- "The Mark of Vishnu" is another of his well-known works.
- Some of his known stories
    - *(a)* Karma
    - *(b)* When Sikh Meets Sikh
    - *(c)* The Rape, etc.
- He is also known for his:
    - *(i)* A History of the Sikhs
    - *(ii)* Translation of Japji Sahib, etc.
- His regular columns appear weekly in some dailies, *e.g.* :
    - *(i)* 'With Malice Towards One And All'—The Hindustan Times.
    - *(ii)* 'This Above All'—The Tribune.
- Mulk Raj Anand is stated to have said that Khushwant Singh's "Train to Pakistan" is likely to last, while about his other creative literary work, one may have some doubts.
- Among his latest work is "Truth, Love and Little Malice."

## MULLER, MAX (1823-1900)

- He was a famous Indologist, German orientalist and linguist, who unearthed a lot of ancient Indian history and Sanskrit scriptures, the Rig Veda, in particular, of which he published six colossal volumes, for which he had got an assignment from the East India Company in 1847.
- Actually he was a student of Sanskrit, who started comparative study of languages and "Avesta" (in 1845) which is the renowned sacred book of the Zoroastrians.
- He gave seven lectures on Indian and ancient Indian philosophy at Cambridge University, which have now been published by Rupa & Co. under the caption: "India: What Can it Teach Us?"
- He distinguishes the highest wisdom of Greece and India by using the terms "to know ourselves" and "to know our self", respectively.
- Muller makes very appreciative comments on the Rig Veda and the Vedic Religion.

## NAIDU, SAROJINI (1879-1949)

- She is a well-known Indian English poet, who started writing poetry at a very early age and she was inspired by Edmund Gosse to choose Indian themes and scenery rather than imitating the English classics.
- She is now known as 'The Nightingale of India.'
- She took a keen interest in India's struggle for freedom.

Some of her works are :

1. The Golden Threshold (1905)
2. The Bird of Time (1912)
3. The Broken Wing (1917)
4. The Sceptred Flute (1946)
5. The Feather of the Dawn (1961) (It appeared posthumously)

Some of her famous poems are :

1. The Queen's Rival
2. Palanquin Bearers
3. To My Fairy Fancies
4. The Pardah Nashin
5. Awake
6. Village Song
7. The Soul's Prayer
8. Fishermen of Coromondel
9. It You Call Me
10. Caprice
11. Summer Woods
12. Songs of Radha
13. The Bird Sanctuary, etc.

## NANDY, PRITISH (Born-1951)

- He was the editor of the 'Illustrated Weekly of India' and has now Telecast a T.V. serial over the Doordarshan: "Hungama Unlimited."
    - *(i)* He is a prolific poet, though he is still not considered one of the best.
    - *(ii)* Most of his poetry has been dismissed by critics as mere experimental gimmickry. Such was Saleem Peeradina.
    - *(iii)* Even Nissim Ezekiel dubbed him to be a poetaster.
- Some of his works are :
    - *(i)* Gods and Olives (1967)
    - *(ii)* On Either Side of Arrogance (1968)
    - *(iii)* From the Outer Bank of the Brahmputra (1969)
    - *(iv)* Riding the Midnight River (1975)
    - *(v)* In secret Anarchy (1979), etc.
- He has written a number of anthologies and translated a number of poets including Agyeya, Amrita Pritam, Kaifi Azmi etc.
- He has also written some short stories and a verse play.

## NARAYAN, R.K. (1906-2001)

- Of the three great novelists, Narayan, Anand and Rao, it is Narayan who has won the maximum accolade both in India and abroad.
- One of his great achievements is his creation of the famous town of Malgudi like Hardy's Wessex.
- Narayan is the true master of humour, irony, realism, romance and artistry.
- Most of his novels and stories depict the life of people of South India.
- It is sometimes held that Narayan lacks true pathos, genuine depth of feeling, realistic description of poverty and misery, the elements which go in for making a novelist a great one.
- However, he has earned much popularity as a novelist, and within the range of his own art, he cannot be taken except with due regard and attention.

Some of his famous novels are :

1. Swami and Friends (1935)
2. Bachelor of Arts
3. The English Teacher
4. The Financial Expert
5. Mr. Sampath (1949)
6. The Guide (1958)
7. The Man-eater of Malgudi
8. The Dark Room (1939)
9. Waiting for the Mahatma
10. The Vendor of Sweets
11. The Painter of Signs (1976)

(He won the Sahitya Akademi Award for 'Guide' in 1961)

## R.K. NARAYAN (as a short story writer)

- Some of his stories have appeared in the following collections:
  - *(i)* Malgudi Days
  - *(ii)* Dodu and Other Stories
  - *(iii)* Cyclone and Other Stories
  - *(iv)* Gods, Demons and Others

Narayan has written a few hundred stories, most of them quite interesting and highly readable:

Some of his famous short stories are :

1. The Golden
2. A Career
3. The Snake Song
4. Man Hunt
5. A Willing Slave
6. An Astrologer's Day
7. The Doctor's word
8. God of Troubles, etc.

## NEHRU, JAWAHARLAL (1889-1964)

- He needs no introduction as a freedom fighter, statesman and first Prime Minister of India.
- Some of his literary works are :
  - *(i)* An Autobiography (1936)
  - *(ii)* Glimpses of World History (1939)
  - *(iii)* Discovery of India (1946)
- Children enjoy reading his "Letters from Father to His Daughter."
- He is known for his simple, chaste, poetic English which is a model of natural style.

## PRITAM, AMRITA (1919-2005)

- She is the most famous Punjabi Author.
- She won the Jnanpith Award for her "Kagaj Te Kenvas" in 1981.
- Her best known autobiographical work which appeared in the seventies is "Rasidi Ticket."
- *(i)* Her "Shadows of words : An Auto-biography" (a transcreation of the Hindi original by Jyoti Sabharwal) has been published by Macmillan in 2002.

  *(ii)* The book presents "an inner journey down the memory lane" presented by the author, who considers old age the best part of her life, like the last sips of tea, which are "usually the sweetest."

## RADHAKRISHAN, SARVAPALLI (1888-1975)

- He is known as an outstanding educationist and a philosopher who presented the Hindu/Indian viewpoint to the world.
- His works include
  - *(i)* An Idealist View of Life (Lectures)
  - *(ii)* Indian Philosophy (1923,1927)
  - *(iii)* The Hindu View of Life (1932)
  - *(iv)* An Idealist View of Life (1932)
  - *(v)* Eastern Religious and Western Thought (1939)
- He wrote in a very simple, intelligible prose-style.

## RAO, RAJA (1908-2006)

- His famous works are:
  - *(i)* The Serpent and the Rope (1960)
  - *(ii)* Kanthapura (1938)
  - *(iii)* The Cat and Shakespeare (1965-66)
- *(i)* He was awarded the Sahitya Akademi Award for his 'The Serpent and the Rope' in 1964.

  *(ii)* He was also decorated with Padma Bhushan in 1969.

### Raja Rao as a short story writer

- He is also a well-known short story writer.
- His first collection of short stories was "Jauni" which was published in France in 1930.
- The collection: "The Cow of the Barricades" was published in 1947

Some of his famous short stories are :

1. Akkayya
2. The Little Gram-shop
3. Kanaka Pal
4. Narsiga

## ROY, ARUNDHATI (Born-1961)

She made her debut with her novel: "The God of Small Things" which won her the Booker Prize in 1997, besides a handful amount running into crores as royalty for less than four hundred pages which comprise the said novel.

## DE, SHOBHA (Born-1948)

- She is a renowned contemporary Indian English novelist and T.V. serial script writer.
- Some of her novels are prescribed in universities in England and Australias.
- Her T.V. serial "Swabhiman" which ran into numerous episodes was telecast over the Doordarshan.
- *(i)* She has become even more popular with her serial "Kittie Party" telecast over the Zee T.V.

  *(ii)* According to the Tribune, it "is a clever insight into the mind of today's urban Indian women poised at the crossroads of modernity and tradition."

## TAGORE, RABINDRANATH (1861-1941)

Tagore was a versatile genius. He was a :

*(i)* poet
*(ii)* novelist
*(iii)* short story writer
*(iv)* dramatist
*(v)* musician
*(vi)* actor (in dramas)
*(vii)* painter
*(viii)* statesman and a host of other things.

Some of his famous novels are :

1. The House and the World (1919)
2. The Wreck (1921)
3. Gora (1923)

## VIVEKANANDA, SWAMI (1863-1902)

He is a well-known Indian seer, prophet, recluse preacher, lecturer and poet, who:

*(i)* made the ancient Indian philosophy known to the whole world at the Parliament of Religious in Chicago, USA.

*(ii)* Brought about a wave of resurgence among the Indian masses through his stirring spiritually inspired speeches which were also full of:

*(a)* patriotic fervour

*(b)* love for universal brotherhood.

*(c)* spirit of social uplight, etc.

# Glossary of Literary Terms

***Abridged edition***

Condensed or shortened version of a work.

***Absence***

1. It is a modern term which is used to explain a work of art on the basis of aspects which are absent rather than those which are manifestly present in the work.

***Acronym***

1. A word formed from the initial letters of other words, *e.g.*
   NOIDA for New Okhla Industrial Development Authority.
2. The word may be considered synonymous to 'acrostic'.

***Acrostic***

1. It is a form of literary exercise in which the first letters of each line in a poem form a word as we read downwards.
2. Here are two Acrostics by H.S. Bhatia :

*(i)* "Wait, O little child, wait!
In the wind lies thy message,
Not in the hubbub of the worldly;
Else you may repent, says the sage."
(The word formed is "WINE"

***Act***

Major division in a dramatic work.

### Adage

Maxim or proverb.

### Addendum

Addition or appendix to a book.

### Aesthetic Realism

1. *(i)* According to Hudson, "Esther Waters" by George Moore was a landmark in this movement toward aesthetic realism.
   *(ii)* This movement was the vehicle of the new realists of which Moore and Gossing were representatives.
   *(iii)* According to Hudson, "they mistook mere ugliness for frankness and "seeing life steadily and seeing it whole."

### Alexandrine

1. It is a line of six iambic feet instead of five.
2. It is not known for certain how this line originated.
3. It appears that it was evolved by Spenser by adding the Alexandrine to the eight-line stave (a b a b b c b c) of Chaucer that he used in the Monkeys Tale.

### Alienation Effect

It was a term devised by the famous German playwright, Bartolt Brecht, who wanted to bring home the need, for realization of a kind of 'alienation' of the audience and the actors from the stage during the performance of a play, as the play being a play and not a part of real life.

### Allegory

1. When the abstract or spiritual ideas are presented through living images, the result is the allegory.

***Examples of Allegorical Works***

1. The Pilgrim Progress
2. The Scarlet Letter
3. The Faery Queene
4. Morality Plays, such as "Everyman".
5. Seven Deadly Sins in Dr. Faustus, etc.

### Alliteration

1. It signifies the repetition of initial consonant sounds, *e.g.*

   The furrow followed free.

### Almanac

Book or table comprising a calendar of days, weeks and months indicating special occasions or events.

### Anagnorisis

It means Discovery or Reversal in a Tragedy.

### Anagram

Letters or word or phrase which, when re-arranged, form a new word.

### Anapaest

It comprises two unaccented syllables followed by an accented one:

*(i)* Redeploy

*(ii)* Introduce

*(iii)* Camouflage

### Androcentrism

The term implies the predominance of man in all social and intellectual activities.

### Anecdote

Brief account or story about an individual.

### 'Angry Young Men'

It was a movement which came into existence in the second half of the twentieth century, mainly as a result of Osborn's play: "Look Back In Anger."

### Annotation

Textual comment on a book.

### Anthology

Collection of poetry or prose from diverse sources.

### Anticipated Future

*See* 'Prosopopaeia'

### Antithesis

1. It signifies the setting of one thing against another, often of opposite sense *e.g.*

   'A *friend never* betrays, an *enemy always* does.
2. 'Antithesis' can be expressed in literature also by presenting two aspects (of life) side by side, *e.g.* the real and the marvellous.

### Aphorism

Short statement of a truth or dogma couched in memorable terms.

### Apostrophe

It implies an exclamatory address to a person. (usually a dead one), some inanimate object or an abstract idea, *e.g.*

"Milton! thou shouldst be living with us at this hour..."

### Archaism

It is a word or phrase which is no longer in use, *e.g.* loon, quoth, yclept, eftsoon(s), etc.

### Archetypal Approach to Criticism

1. This Approach is also called Mythological, Ritualistic or Totemic Approach.
2. It endeavours to study literature on the basis of myth.

### Areopagitica

This is the name of Milton's famous prose pamphlet, pleading for freedom, freedom of the press, in particular.

### Argot

Slang or coarse vernacular language.

### Aside

1. It is a kind of device similar to "soliloquy" (being probably comparatively brief) when a character speaks to himself.
2. The best example of an "aside" may be Shylock's words : "How like a fawning publican he looks" in Act. I sc. 3 of The Merchant of Venice.

### Assonance

Unlike the alliteration (which signifies the repetition of consonant sounds), it signifies the repetition of vowel sounds, *e.g.*

1. I *hear* him *bear* the mark of a *seer* on his head.

### Autobiography

An account of a person's life by himself or herself.

### Avant-garde

Without going into historical aspects of the word, one can say that it implies those (persons) who support or create the newest ideas, fashions (generally literary or artistic), techniques, styles, etc. in an art, piece of literature, etc.

### Ballad

1. Broadly-speaking, there are two kinds of ballads:
   *(i)* Traditional Ballads such as those pertaining to Robin Hood, Chevy Chase, etc.
   *(ii)* Modern Ballads, such as The Rime of Ancient Mariner, etc.

### Bathos

1. It is a term to denote anticlimax.
2. It is generally used when there is sudden descent or fall from the sublime to the trite or ridiculous, *e.g.*

   Delay not thine departure hence,

   For thou mightst have a hot pudding, Awaiting thee.

### Belles lettres

Essays on literary studies and the aesthetics of literature.

### Bibliography

List of works on a particular subject or author.

### Biography

An account of a person's life.

### Blank verse

Poetry with unrhymed line endings (usually written in iambic pentameters).

### Blurb

These are the words of praise or description of a book in a nutshell, inserted usually by the publisher on the cover page or jacket of the book, to attract the reader's eye.

### Bound verse

Verse based on metrical pattern.

### Burlesque

It is a way of writing which generates irony, humour and satire, *e.g.* Cervantes' Don Quixote, Samuel Butler's Hudibras, etc.

### Bowdlerize

To 'cleanse' a work by omitting or cutting out indecent passages, phrases or words.

### Cacophony

When the excessive use of high sounding words is made such that the meaning is lost or diminished in value in the sound, the result is cacophony instead of euphony.

### Cadence

Rhythm and phrasing of language.

### Caesura

1. In classical prosody, 'Caesura' means "break between words within a metrical foot." (Concise Oxford).
2. In English prosody, it means "pause about middle of line." (ibid.).
3. A Caesura "which does not immediately follow the ictus" is known as 'Feminine Caesura" (Chambers 20th century).

   (**Note :** In modern connotation, Caesura implies natural pause in a line of verse and not an unnatural or forced one)

### Canon

Collection of works established as genuine.

### Canto

Division of an epic or narrative poem.

### Caption

Short description accompanying an illustration.

### Caricature

The chief characteristics of characters are sometimes so exaggerated by the author that the characters look like some humorous or even funny creatures. The result is the creation of caricatures. This is what Dickens (more than any other author) has done.

### Catalogue

List of books or works.

### Catastrophe

1. It signifies the complete (often sudden) devastation of the fortunes of a character (often the hero and/or the heroine) in a play or piece of fiction.

### Catharsis

This is the term used for the ousting of the emotions of pity and fear in the tragedy.

### Chronicle Plays

1. These are the plays based on (English) History.
2. Such plays became very popular among the people in the sixteenth century.
3. These plays contain almost every important character, real or legendary, in the period of the times concerned.

### Cipher

Writing that employs sub-stitution or transposition of letters.

### Classic

*(i)* A classic (in reality, any book) is "the expression of man" as an individual.

*(ii)* It is also the expression of his mindset and the stance taken by him.

### Cliche

Any word, phrase or expression that has lost its real effect for having been too frequently used by authors or laymen is called a cliche which may otherwise be quite lovable, *e.g.*

*(i)* The news is too good to be true.

*(ii)* The sorrow was too deep for tears.

*(iii)* Thanking you in anticipation, etc.

### Climax

1. It is the main point of interest in a play or novel which is reached usually in the third act (or sometimes 4th of a 5 act of a play) or towards the end.
2. The resolution often takes place after the Climax or the forces for it start working or increase their intensity after it.

### Colloquial

1. In speech, we sometimes make use of certain words and phrases which are not acceptable in standard speech
2. Such colloquial expressions should be avoided in all formal speech or writing.

### Colonialism

1. The term differs from 'colonization' as the term may imply political or economic control of policies in a political unit without real annexation of land.

### Colonisation

Literarily, the most significant modernist theories in the matter of

*(i)* colonisation

*(ii)* post colonisation

*(iii)* decolonisation, and

*(iv)* neo-colonisation have been provided and practised by—

*(a)* Ngugiwa Thiong'o

*(b)* Soyinka

*(c)* Achebe Chinua, etc.

### Comedy

Humorous dramatic piece; *high comedy* has welldrawn characterization and witty dialogue; *low comedy*, or *slapstick* has absurd situations and boisterous action; *farce* is exaggerated comedy; *tragi-comedy* is a blend of the tragic and comic; *satire* uses sarcasm and wit to ridicule people's follies and vices (originally in verse).

### Comic Relief

1. It is the name given to the brief light or comic dramatic action within the performance of a regular serious play to bring about a relief to the spectators to regain their real selves, for a short while to relax their strained nerves and prepare for further action, often more serious and culminating into breath-taking, gasping climax before denouement.

### Conceit

1. A conceit is a far-fetched or highly complex and even obscure or unintelligible comparison between two, often dissimilar, persons or objects.
2. It was commonly used by the Elizabethans particularly the Metaphysical poets, especially Donne.

### Concordance

Alphabetical index of words in a work, or works by a single author.

### Confidant/Confidante

1. In a play when a character takes upon himself/herself the task of some secret or information characteristic about a character to another, the character indulging in such an activity is known as a "confidant" (mas.) or "confidante" (fem.)
2. Such information or secret is generally in the matter of love.
3. A good example of a 'confidante' is Nerissa in the Merchant of Venice.

### Connotation

1. It signifies the suggested or implied meaning of word as against the transparent or literary meaning.
2. Connotative devices are brought into play by the artists, poets in particular to enhance pleasure and acceptability conveyed by words and other expressions.
3. Poets like Keats and T.S. Eliot frequently resort to the device of suggestiveness which is akin to connotation.

### Consummation

1. When a work achieves complete satisfaction on all counts-literary as well as artistic, it is consummation that results.
2. An artist who has the knack, calibre or skill to make this achievement, is a consummate artist.

### Copyright

Protective law to prevent pirating or plagiarism of an author's work.

### Couplet

Two successive rhyming lines in poetry.

### Court Comedy

1. It is opposed to the Domestic Comedy in the sense that instead of domestic scenes it contains other elements which attract a different kind of audience, *e.g.*
   - *(i)* endless play of words
   - *(ii)* elaborate dialogues
   - *(iii)* repartees, jests, retorts, etc.

### Cycle

Group of works united by an overall theme.

### Dactyl

1. Dactyl means one accented syllable followed by two unaccented ones, e.g.
   - *(i)* Lazily
   - *(ii)* Separate
   - *(iii)* Unspoken.

### Decayed (or Constant) Metaphor

*See* Metaphor

### Deism

1. A "deist" is a theist who believes in the existence of God but rejects the idea of a revealed religion.

### Denouement

1. It is the final resolution of the problem in a piece of dramatic performance.
2. The best document comes about when it arises naturally out of the action of the play and not through the 'Deus ex machina'.

### Detonation

When a word refers to its literal meaning independent of the meaning which the author may intend to convey, it is the device of "Detonation" which is at play.

### Diabolus Ex Machina

1. The term literally means "devil out of the machine".
2. When all of a sudden a person or an event spoils the whole good game, causing unmitigated misery, it is the work of "Diabolus Ex Machina".
3. Thus, the term signifies sudden, unexpected turn of events for a plightful situation.

### Dialect

Manner of speaking pertaining to a particular class or geographical region.

### Dialectic

1. It was used originally to refer to the nature of a logical argument.
2. Later, it began to be linked to Kant, Hegel and Marx in varying forms.
3. The three generally accepted aspects of 'dialectic' are:
   - *(i) Thesis:* It is akin to the (original) idea.
   - *(ii) Antithesis:* It implies the inherent opposition in the thesis, which may operate after some time.
   - *(iii) Synthesis:* It implies the resolution of the conflict to evolve a higher (or final) truth.

### Dialogue

1. Dialogue is something very important in any poetic or prose play or a piece of prose fictions.
2. *(i)* The nature of the dialogue, including its language depends upon the kind of the play—a tragedy, comedy, romance, etc. or the kind of the scene prevailing there at the time and place of the dialogue.

(ii) Much also depends upon the taste of the spectators or audience which again is related to the spirit of the age :

### A Dialogical Novel

1. It is a kind of novel in which a number of voices, interactive in the scheme, operate in work, resulting in a kind of dialogue (or series of dialogues) as against the Monologic Presentation.

### Diary

Sequential private record of personal and other events kept by an individual.

### Diction

1. It refers to the selection, arrangement and order of words.
2. The term which has become more popular in literary world is "Poetic Diction" to which a lot of space has been devoted by Wordsworth in his "Preface to Lyrical Ballads."

### Dictionary

Book containing the words of a language, and their definitions, alphabetically; two-language dictionaries contain the corresponding words of both languages and their meanings, also alphabetically; any book that gives words and phrases about a particular subject, arranged alphabetically.

### Didactic

A work is didactic in nature when it undertakes to teach a moral, *e.g.* much of Wordsworth's poetry.

### Digest

Publication where works are abridged.

### Digression

1. When a writer, instead of carrying on the main plot or incident, starts indulging in a side story, dialogue or descriptive narration, it is digression that results.
2. Digression gives extraneous pleasure which is not inherent in or indispensable to the main story.
3. Digression can sometimes enhance the value of a work but more often it mars its spirit.

### Documentary

Form of fiction or drama based on documentary evidence provided by newspapers, recent historical reports or other contemporary or recent factual evidence.

### Doggerel

Rough, ill-constructed verse.

### Domestic Comedy

1. One of the earliest examples of the Domestic Comedies is "Gammer Gurton's Needle" (Cir. 1562)
2. It presents realistic life of the peasant class of its times.
3. It is full of fun and coarse humour.

### Double entendre

Ambiguity in a word or expression, one of whose meanings is usually bawdy or frivolous.

### Drama

Work to be performed on a stage by actors.

### Dramatic Irony

It is a device occurring in a drama when a character on the stage is unaware of a fact which the audience know and understand.

### Dramatic Monologue

1. It is a kind of drama or piece of dramatic poetry in which only one character speaks out throughout the performance and script.

### Dramatis Personae

Characters in a play.

### Duologue

Conversation between two characters in a play, story or poem.

### Edition

Total number of copies of a book printed from unchanged set of type.

### Electicism

The term implies the gleaning of facts or ideas from different sources instead of depending on just one source (or a few sources).

### Elegy

Serious meditative poem; often lamenting death.

### Empathy

In a play or novel, when the reader or spectator begins to feel like the hero/heroine or some particular character as if he/she were that character, it is "empathy" which is at play.

### Empiricism

Empiricism implies the importance of experiment and experience in the matter of gaining knowledge.

### Encyclopedia

Comprehensive work encompassing and describing many aspects of knowledge; specialist work covering comprehensively a subject or discipline.

### Epic

Long narrative poem incorporating myth, legend, folklore and history, about the deeds of heroes, warriors, important people: a grandiose treatment of an individual's or nation's story.

### Epic Style

1. It is a style which is dignified and exalted (as grand style is), as:
   *(i)* Paradise Lost by Milton
   *(ii)* Aeneid by Virgil
   *(iii)* Iliad by Homer
   *(iv)* Hyperion by Keats, etc.
2. Sometimes, it is, also referred to as 'heroic' style.'

### Epigram

1. It signifies some brief, witty word, saying or piece of writing.
2. Pope's work, for instance, is a model of "Epigrammatic" style.
3. Bacon's essays are a bundle of Epigrams.

### Epilogue

It is the last item in a work of art (as in a drama) which often declares or comments upon the conclusion of the work.

### Epistle

Direct address to another person, a 'letter' in the form of verse.

### Epitaph

Valediction to dead person or persons; inscription on a tomb or grave.

### Epithet

1. It comprises a word or group of words to describe the chief characteristics of a person, *e.g.*
   *(i)* Alexander the Great
   *(ii)* The Holy Bible.

### Eponymous

Person whose name becomes the title of the work.

### Erastianism

1. It implies the doctrine that the state should have supremacy over the church in ecclesiastical matters.
2. Erastianism was one of the doctrines which was vehemently opposed by the followers of the Oxford Movement
3. The doctrine is probably wrongly ascribed to Erastus.

### Essay

Short composition, usually in prose, discussing a topic or variety of topics.

### Euphemism

1. When an unpleasant expression has to be made in a comparatively pleasant or less harsh way, the mellowed or toned down words which are used express euphemism, *e.g.*
   *(i)* Instead of saying about a person "He acted foolishly, we can say, "He should have acted more wisely."
   *(ii)* Instead of saying about a person that he has died, we sometimes say, "God Almighty has called him" or "He has left for his heavenly abode."

### Euphony

1. It signifies the pleasant combination of words which create desirable rhythms and tonal effects without interfering with the intended meaning
2. An excessive use of such devices can lead to tautology or bombasticism and sound superficial or facile.
3. The generally accepted antonym of euphony is "Cacophony".

### Euphuism

1. An ornate, floral style of writing popularized by Lyly.

### Exposition

It signifies a way of writing where explanations are not withheld or suppressed but manifestly made clear to the reader for immediate response based on clarity.

### Fable

A short narrative in prose or verse, often with animals, that points a moral.

### Fiction

General term for an imaginative work, usually in prose.

### Figure of Speech (or of Rhetoric)

It signifies the unusual use of words to heighten their effect.

### First person

Style of novel, etc., in which narrator is a character.

### Flashback

1. When a writer while presenting a situation suddenly refers to a past situation or event, it is the device of "flashback" that he exploits.
2. Browning, T.S. Eliot and Stream of consciousness novelists, in particular, take advantage of this device.

### Folk tale

Story handed down by word of mouth from generation to generation.

### Foot

In poetry, rhythmic unit of two or three syllables.

### Foreshadowing

1. It is a device in which the author himself prepares the spectators (or readers) for the catastrophe or some important event which may be on the cards.
2. Such a device checks the readers, etc. from suffering from the malady of disbelief.
3. Shakespeare is probably one of the greatest masters of this device, and it is sometimes believed that one of the main reasons of Shakespeare's grand success was his convincing mastery over the technique of foreshadowing.

### Foreword

Short introduction to a work.

### Free verse (vers libre)

Poetry free from mechanical restrictions such as metre and rhyme, cadenced according to meaningful stress.

### Fustian

It means the use of pompous, ornate, Euphuist or bombastic language.

### Gazetteer

Geographical dictionary or index.

### Ghost writer

Person who undertakes literary work for another who takes the credit.

### Glossary

Alphabetical list of unfamiliar or uncommon words, usually appended to work in which they appear.

### Haiku

According to Oxford Dictionary, "A Haiku is a Japanese poem of seventeen syllables, in three lines of five, seven and fine traditionally evoking images of the natural world."

### Haplology

"Omission in utterance of a sound resembling a neighbouring sounds (as 'idolatry' for 'idololatry') (ibid.)

### Haplography

"The inadvertent writing once of what should have been written twice." (Chambers 20th Century Dictionary)

### Heroic Couplet

1. A couplet written in iambic pentametre is known as a 'heroic couplet'.

### Heroic verse

1. A poem written in heroic couplets is known as 'heroic verse,' *e.g.* Pope's poems such as:
   (*i*) Essay Man
   (*ii*) Essay in Criticism
   (*iii*) The Rape of the Lock, etc.

### Homily

1. It is a term pertaining to a work which instead of laying stress on artistic or aesthetic standards, undertakes to urge the readers on to a high moral life.
2. It is just like a sermon in a church.
3. Such are the most of the poems of Longfellow.

### Homograph

1. It implies a word which has the same spelling and pronunciation as another, but is different in meaning and origin from the other, *e.g.* :
   (*i*) bear (*n*) an animal
   (*ii*) bear (*v*) (to) tolerate
   (*iii*) bear (*v*) (to) carry

### Homonym

1. (*i*) It is "a word having the same sound and perhaps the same spelling as another, but a different meaning and origin" (Chambers.....)
   (*ii*) Hence, *Homonymous* means: " having the same name : having different *significations* and origin but the same sound." (ibid.)

### Hurd, Bishop

1. He aroused great interest in the Gothic and imaginative literature with his "Letters on Chivalry and Romance" (1762)

### Hyperbole

1. It is a figure of speech which expresses an exaggerated statement to heighten the effect of a rhetorical statement, *e.g.*
   (*i*) O child, may you never die!
   (*ii*) Child is Father of the Man

### Idiom

Form of expression of phrase peculiar to its language and possessing a meaning other than its literal one.

### Idolatry

1. It means the worship of an image which is believed to be the abode of a superhuman being.

### Idyll

Short pastoral poem conveying mood of happy innocence.

### Imagism

School of poetry (early 1900s) concerned with precise language, direct treatment, and freedom of form.

### Imperialism

1. It means the state policy for a country (as of England and certain other European countries, in particular during certain periods of history) to expands its area by annexing foreign lands and sub-during the natives.

### Impersonality

1. It means that the author himself should not be palpably visible in a piece of literature, in other words, the work should be done on highly objective lines.

### Indianism

When an expression is commonly used in India but is not used by the English, it is called an "Indianism," *e.g.*

*(i)* 'demise' instead of 'death'

*(ii)* 'bearer' instead of 'waiter'

*(iii)* 'left for his heavenly abode' instead of 'died,' etc.

### Interior Monologue

1. It is a device, as used by James Joyce in Ulysses, to express the thoughts, feelings and emotions of a character on usually more than one levels of consciousness.
2. It is a sort of inner debate which may or may not be conflict in essence.

### Interludes

1. Just as Miracles passed into Moralities, the latter gradually passed into Interludes, as the people wanted entertainment along with instruction.

### Introduction

Essay stating author's intention to reader.

### Inversion

It is the figure of speech (much used by Milton but ridiculed by many modern critics) in which words are presented in their unnatural order, *e.g.*

O God's glory I sing,
And to His Mercy I pray.

### Irony

1. It is a device used to convey a meaning which is the opposite of the apparent meaning, *e.g.* What a brave son of India Jai Chand was!

### Jingle

Verse or verses with strong rhyme and rhythm.

### Journal

Paper, periodical or magazine.

### Judicial Criticism

1. It is the kind of criticism which is a sort of judgement on a writer or his work of art.
2. Such kind of best example is Pope's "Essay on Criticism".

### Legend

Story about a particular person containing myth and historical fact; explanation of symbols on a map or chart.

### Lexicon

Dictionary, especially for Classical and Middle Eastern languages.

### Limerick

1. It is a kind of humorous verse written in five jingling lines.
2. The form seems to have derived "from a refrain formerly used, referring to 'Limerick' in Ireland." (Chambers 20th Century Dictionary)

### Linguistics

The scientific study of language.

### Litotes

1. It is akin to "understatement" which is sometimes used by writers to emphasise the desired meaning, *e.g.* India is not lagging in Information Technology.
2. However, more often it is an "understatement used ironically, especially using a negative to express the category as :

   'I shan't be sorry when it's over' meaning 'I shall be very glad', or 'It was no easy matter' for 'It was very difficult.'"

   (Advanced Learner's Dictionary)

### Lyric

Usually short, song-like poem in which the poet expresses personal feelings.

### Manuscript

Book or work written by hand.

### Maxim

Short statement or even sentence containing a general truth about human conduct and human nature.

### *Melodrama*

1. It was a crude form of drama which appealed to the groundings who were not much interested in the artistic minuteness such as the plot, characterization, etc.
2. They wanted only entertainment through striking scenes and absorbing movement of incidents and situations.

### *Metaphor*

1. It is a kind of simile when a comparison is suggested rather than explicitly stated, such that 'as' or 'like' is not used in such a case, *e.g.*

   *(i)* Lala Lajpat Rai was the Lion of Punjab.

   *(ii)* I see a lily on thy face.

### *Meter*

Patterns of stressed and unstressed syllables in verse.

### *Metonymy*

1. It implies the use of the name of some person or thing for another person or thing, *e.g.*

   *(i)* Have you studied 'Milton'?
   (Milton here means Milton's works).

   *(ii)* In the 'light' of these remarks:
   ('light' here means in view of....)

   *(iii)* Sceptre and Crown (i.e. monarchy)
   Must tumble down.

### *Metre*

It may not be possible or even necessary to describe it here in full detail, but we can have a cursory look at the following :

1. *Monometre :* It means a line (or verse) with a single iamb (foot)
2. *Dimetre:* It means a line with two iambs.
3. *Trimetre:* It means a line with three iambs.
4. *Tetrametre:* It means a line with four iambs.
5. *Penta metre:* It means a line with five iambs.
6. *Hexta metre:* It means a line with six iambs.
7. *Hepta metre:* It means a line with seven iambs.

### *Miracle and Mystery Plays*

1. These plays were sponsored by the church and were originally held within the premises of the church, but later, as the number of audience swelled, the boundaries of the church seemed too limited and the plays began of be held outside the church.
2. *(i)* The Miracle plays represented the lives of saints, and later for any biblical theme.

   *(ii)* The Mystery plays represented scenes from the life of Jesus Christ.

### *Mock Heroic*

When an apparent epic is presented in a light vein, it is known as a "mock heroic" poem piece of fiction, etc., *e.g.*

*(i)* The Rape of the Lock

### *Modernism*

1. Towards the close of the 20th century, a movement against such modes as realism and naturalism started in all forms of literature and art such as poetry, drama, novel, music, painting, architecture, sculpture, etc. which continued unabated during the first world war period and partly upto the middle of the century.

### *Modulation*

1. Of necessity poetry is musical.
2. As in music, to avoid poetry from falling into "monotony," there is the system of "modulation" which here means, changing the key or tone, to introduce the element of variety to give or enhance pleasure.

### *Monologue*

Single person addressing an audience alone, in drama, verse or prose. *Interior monologue*: unspoken but thought speech in verse or prose.

### *Moralities or Morality Play*

1. They were basically allegories on the same lines as Miracles, or Mysteries but without direct represent of scriptural or Christ-concerned events or personages.
2. In Moralities abstract virtues and vices like Wisdom, Goodness, Justice, Evil, Vice, Greed, Lethargy, Lust, etc. were personified and presented on stage as persons.

### *Myth*

Non-factual story that embodies explanation of how something comes to exist, usually involving supernatural or superhuman creatures.

### *Narrative*

Story or tale in prose or verse.

### *Narratology*

1. It means the study of different forms and structures of a narrative work in the matter of its various syntactical, literary and grammatical frameworks.

### *Neoclassicism*

Movement of late 17th and 18th century reviving classical values in English literature, emphasizing discipline, reason and clarity.

### Neologism

Newly-coined word.

### New Wave (la Nouvelle Vague)

Movement in literature and cinema originating in France in late 1950s that attempted to eschew fixed values, revealing a character by the way he experienced objects and events, which were often meticulously described.

### Nom de plume

Term used to indicate a fictitious name used by a writer to represent his work.

### Novel

Extended piece of prose fiction.

### Novelette

Long short story of some 15,000 words.

### Novella

Prose fiction longer than a short story, shorter than a novel (about 30,000 words), concentrating upon a single event.

### Obscurity

1. When a writer's language is not (or not easily) intelligible to the reader, the work concerned is termed as obscure.

### Ode

Lyric poem describing an event or feelings about a person, object or event *Pindaric Ode* (Greece) written for choral recitation in units of three stanzas; *Horatian Ode* (Rome) consisted of succession of stanzas following pattern of first one.

### Omniscient Author

It is a device used by some outstanding modern novelists to move freely from the objective narrative to the internal or subjective psyche of a character or characters and then comment freely and apparently unattached on the significance, possibility or outcome of any or some events.

### Onomatopoeia

When the very sound (pronunciation) of a word conveys the sense of the object producing such sound, the use of onomatopoeia becomes clear *e.g.,*

*(i)* The *lashing* of waves on the sea-shore

*(ii)* The *rustle* of leaves

*(iii)* The *hissing* of the snake

*(iv)* The *jungle* of coins

*(v)* The *clanging* of arms.

### Oxymoron

1. It is a figure of speech in which two apparently contradictory words or terms are used to convey, a paradoxical sense, e.g.

   *(i)* 'busy-idle days' (Lamb in Dream children)

   *(ii)* Life in Death (Coleridge in 'Rime.....').

### Pantomime

1. Pantomimes became popular in England particularly in the first quarter of the 18th century.
2. A Pantomime is a dramatic representation pertaining to some myth, legend or traditional tale (or it may have some fairy element in it).

### Parable

A story which conveys a moral lesson is known as a parable, as for instance, the biblical parables.

### Paradox

It is a figure of speech in which a truth is brought home through the use of self-contradictory statement, *e.g.*

*(i)* Cowards die many a time before their death.

*(ii)* Discretion is the better part of valour.

*(iii)* After death, we awake into an eternal life.

### Parallelism

1. It is a rhetorical device where balancing sentences, phrases or words are used to enhance effect, e.g.

   What is important is not what you say, but what is important is what you mean.
2. Excessive use of this device leads to monotony and superficiality.

### Parody

Comic imitation of serious words, style, sense, subject of a writer to make them appear ridiculous.

### Pastoral

Literature depicting idealized rural life.

### Pathetic Fallacy

When nature is shown as sympathising with human lot, the device used is called "pathetic fallacy," *e.g.*

*(i)* Byron's description of the battle of Waterloo in Childe Harold's Pilgrimage.

*(ii)* The behaviour of slow-moving nature in Tennyson's "Lotos-eaters".

### Pedantry

1. The term refers to the excessive display of knowledge such as:

   *(i)* Foreign words and phrases

(ii) Allusions
(iii) Archaic words
(iv) high sounding and sesquipedalian words
(v) cataloguing, etc.

when these are not strictly needed within the context of the work.

### Periodic Sentence

A sentence in which the Principal clause occurs at the end when it is preceded by one or more subordinate clauses, such that the sense is clear only when the whole sentence is read, is known as a 'periodic sentence'.

### Periodical

Magazine or journal published regularly.

### Periphrasis

1. It means a round about way of saying a thing, *e.g.* An idle singer of an empty day, etc.
2. The term is close to circumlocution and euphemism in sense and effect.

### Personification

1. It is a device where inanimate objects are shown as those having life and behaving likewise, *e.g.*

"But yonder comes the powerful *king* of day."

*—Thomson*

### Pessimists

Although in English literature, we have a number of pessimist poets or a good number of poets expressing at times pessimistic ideas or writing sometimes in a pessimistic mood, yet two of the poets are known in particular, as "Pessimists." They are:

(i) Thomas Hardy
(ii) A.E. Housman

### Philology

Study of literature. language and linguistics.

### Picaresque

Chronicle of adventures of a rogue; originated in 16-century Spain.

### Plagiarism

Wrongful appropriation and publication of another's work as one's own.

### Platitude

It means a truth or generalization which is too well-known mainly because of its overuse, *e.g.*

Truth is evergreen.

### Pleonasm

(a) It means the use of words more than those which are absolutely necessary, *e.g.*

1. He sat *down* on the ground.
2. He looked up *high* towards the sky.
3. He has got *sole* monopoly over such kind of business.

(b) In essence, it is akin to Tautology or circumlocution.

### Plot

Plan or organization of events and characters in a play, work of fiction or poem as to induce curiosity and suspense in the audience or reader.

### Poem

Literary work which may be in rhyme, blank verse or a combination of the two.

### Poetic Diction

1. Diction stands chiefly for choice of words.
2. In poetry, poetic diction is unavoidable as mere metre is not enough to make a poem a literary piece of work.
3. In other words, mere versification or combination of words in rhyme or any other verse form does not make poetry.
4. The poets resort to several devices in this regard, some of which are :

(i) Use of similes, metaphors, symbols, inversions, and other figures of speech as such as hyperbole, irony, antithesis, personification, etc.
(ii) Omission of some parts of speech or grammatical rules.
(iii) Use of archaic or uncommon words.
(iv) Change in order of words, etc.
(v) Use of picturesque phrases and expressions
(vi) Use of other ornamental devices such as epithets
(vii) Use of highly musical lies, fanciful flights etc.

### Poetic Justice

1. It means the reward or punishment handed down to the characters at the end of a work of art according to their deeds.

### Poetry

Any kind of metrical composition in a literary work.

### Pornography

Work in which there is a deliberate emphasis on the sexual behaviour of characters, in order to arouse sexual excitement.

### Potboiler

Work written essentially to gain the author a livelihood.

### Precis

Concise statement; short summary of a work.

### Preface

Introduction to a work.

### Prologue

It is often the original statement by the writer (as in a drama) which highlights the chief aim of the work which is going to be unfolded or staged.

### Propaganda

Work devoted to the dissemination of an idea or belief, usually biased.

### Prose

Writings not in verse.

### (Modern) Prose Style

1. The English prose style started by Bacon, flourished in the hands of Addison and Steele and numerous essayists and prose stylists that followed.
2. As a fine example of the latest modern prose style, Naipaul who won the Nobel Prize for Literature in 2001 deserves to be mentionéd.

### Prosody

Study of the handling of language in poetry.

### Prosopopaeia

1. This figure of speech is used when:
   *(i)* The past (called the Historic Present) is written in the present tense:
   Sohrab and Rustam clash with their full might.
   *(ii)* The (anticipated) future is written in the present tense:
   Here, we go to our new house tomorrow with all our belongings carried in a lorry and then tucked in elegant mahogany almirahs.

### Pseudonym

Name other than the true one used by an author to represent his work.

### Psychological Process

It is the process applied to the study of a piece of literature to penetrate another's mind and to study the activities, utterances, etc. of various characters, as, for instance, to arrive at the exact nature of Hamlet's madness whether there was "method" in it or not.

### Pun

1. When a word gives several meanings (often for fun) as in a play, it is the "pun" that is used.
2. Shakespeare is a great master of this device.
3. **Example :**
   *(i)* This is the *book*.
   *(ii)* It means
   *(a)* any book
   *(b)* a holy book, often the Bible.

### Realism

Literature that attempts to depict life objectively and faithfully.

### Refrain

Phrase, line or lines repeated at intervals or at the end of a stanza in poetry.

### Review

Notice or critical article on musical, artistic or literary work.

### Revue

Theatrical entertainment made up of sketches, dances, songs, recitals and improvised pieces, usually humorous, satirical or topical.

### Rhetoric

Art of using language, in speaking or writing, to persuade. The persuasive style (rather than the content) of a work.

### Rhythm

1. It signifies the measured regular beat or movement of sounded words in language.
2. Rhythm is a must in poetry as well as prose, as it introduces or enhances the element of pleasure, interest and curiosity.

### Rhyme

Echoing sound or audible similarity in two or more words, especially at endings. Device used to construct much poetry.

### Riddle

Puzzle, question or enigma; conundrum.

### Roman a clef

Novel based upon actual people under disguised names.

### Romance

Tale of chivalry, originally written in verse (Medieval times); term applied now to any wonderful or mysterious tale far removed from reality.

### Romance Languages

1. Languages which have emerged straightaway from Latin and/or Greek, are called Romance Languages.

### Romanticism

Movement originating in late 18th century as revolt against neoclassicism, emphasizing imaginative style.

### Saga

Lengthy prose work, sometimes in several parts, describing the history and events surrounding medieval kings, warriors and, recently, fictitious families.

### Satire

Any work in which wickedness, folly, vice and corruption in individuals and society is exposed by ridicule and scorn.

### Science fiction

Literature based on scientific fact or fantasy, on earth or on other worlds in space, often set in periods in the distant future.

### Semantics

Branch of linguistics dealing with meaning, and the change of meaning, in words.

### Semiology

General study or science of signs with which humans communicate with each other (including words and their use in every context).

### Sermon

Verbal instruction of some length, usually religious.

### Short story

Work of fiction usually revolving around single event.

### Sic

Included in brackets after a printed word or quoted passage to indicate that it is quoted accurately, however actually incorrect.

### Simile

1. When we draw comparison between two persons by using (usually 'like', as-so or as) it is the 'simile' that we make use of, *e.g.*
   *(i)* As red as a rose
   *(ii)* As happy as a lark
   *(iii)* She looked like a violet, half-hidden behind the rock.
2. *An Exaggerated Simile:* It is a simile in which the sense is clearly exaggerated, *e.g.*
   *(i)* He ran as fast as lightning
   *(ii)* He has in himself the force as much as there is in ten horses.

### Slang

Colourful and vernacular language of the street, marketplace, barrackroorn, workplace, sportsplace and playground.

### Soliloquy

Kind of monologue in which a stage character expresses his thoughts and feelings.

### Song

Poem or verse set to music.

### Sonnet

14-line poem of set rhyme-scheme; Elizabethan (Shakespearean) *ababcdcdefefgg*, Italian *abbaabba cdcdcd* (or *cdecde*).

### Stanza

Group of lines of verse in definite pattern, usually repeated in a poem.

### Strophe and Anti Strophe

1. Strophe is "the song sung by the chorus (in a Greek play) as it moved towards one side, answered by an exact counterpart." (Chambers 20th Century Dictionary)
2. Anti-Strophe is the term for the Strophe, "as it returned: part of any ode thus answered..." (*ibid.*)

### Style

Characteristic manner of expression in prose or verse; the way in which a thing is written by an author.

### Stock Material

Material necessary for a writer to write.

### Stock Characters

Characters that are commonly found in most of pieces of dramas or fiction.

### Stock Situations

Situations which are frequently presented byauthors in their works.

### Synthesis, Poetry of

The term "Poetry of Synthesis" is referred to by I.A. Richards, and it has been thus explained by Cleanth Brooks—

"... a poetry which does not leave out what is apparently hostile to its dominant tone, and which, because it is able to fuse the irrelevant and disordant, has come to terms with itself and invulnerable to irony."

### *Structure*

"The structure meant is a structure of meaning, evaluations and interpretations : and the principle of unity which informs it seems to one of balancing and harmonizing connotations, attitudes and meanings."

### *Tragedy of Blood (And Thunder)*

1. It was basically a melodramatic presentation of horrible, gory scenes.
2. The first famous tragedy of this kind is Kyd's "Spanish Tragedy".

### *Sublimity*

1. It is a term which is used to describe inexplicable beauty which is beyond any rules to describe or measure.

### *Symbolism*

French poetic movement of late 19th century that developed as revolt against realism, concentrating on evoking emotions by use of indirect suggestion (symbol and metaphor); flourished in Russia at turn of century as literary movement, and later in British novel.

### *Synecdoche*

1. This figure of speech is used when the understanding of one thing by means of another is employed.
2. This can be done in several ways, some of which are mentioned below :
   *(i)* When a part stands for a whole or genus, e.g. We have fifty *hands* in our factory. (hands = workers)
   *(ii)* When a whole or genus stands for a part, e.g. He belongs to a different *world* from yors (world = category, social set-up, economic status, etc.)
   *(iii)* When an individual represents a class, *e.g.*
   He is the *Nestor* of our village.
   (Nestor = the oldest man)

### *Syntax*

It means :

*(i)* The way a sentence is constructed
*(ii)* Arrangement of words in writing (or in speech) according to the rules of grammar
*(iii)* Rules pertaining to this system or arrangement.

### *Synonym*

A word similar in meaning to another.

### *Synopsis*

Outline of the main points of a work; a summary.

### *Tale*

Spoken or written narrative.

### *Tautology*

Overuse of synonyms or repetition of ideas in sentence.

### *Theme*

Central idea of a work, rather than its subject.

### *Thesis*

Long essay or treatise on a subject, usually expository; work presented to examiners for academic qualification.

### *Third person*

Style of novel, etc., in which narrator is outside action.

### *Tract*

Short printed treatise on religious or political subject.

### *Tragedy*

It is "a drama in which the principal characters are involved in desperate circumstances or led by overwhelming passions. It is invariably serious and dignified. The movement is always stately, but grows more and more rapid as it approaches the climax ; and the end is always calamitous, resulting in death or dire misfortune of the principals."

### *Tragic Flaw*

1. In Shakespeare's tragedies, in particular, we often find a particular flaw in the character of the hero which ultimately leads to the fall of his destiny, along with the fall of his state or estate.

### *Transferred Epithet*

When an epithet is transferred from a person to a thing, it is known as a 'transferred epithet', *e.g.*

*(i)* It is a *foolish* idea
*(ii)* Let *happy* days come.

### *Translation*

Rendering of a work into another language.

### *Treatise*

Formal work examining a subject and the principles underlying it.

### *Trochaic Line Metre*

1. A line in verse is known as a *"trochaic" line* when the first, third and other odd syllables in it are accented (as in the 'Iambic metre') irrespective of the length of the line.
2. A poem comprising such lines is known as having been written in the "Trochaic" metre.

### *Understatement*

1. It is practically the opposite of hyperbole and is sometimes used by the writers to emphasise indirectly the desired meaning.

### *Vade mecum*

Manual or handbook carried for frequent reference.

### *Verisimilitude*

It is the likeness of truth presented in a work of art that makes it similar to the characteristics or situation in real life and that enables the readers to accept it ungrudgingly as truth (and may be, sometimes, more than real happening in life).

### *Vernacular*

Domestic or native language.

### *Versification*

Study of how traditional verse is constructed.

### *Wit*

(*i*) Dryden defines (in "Annus Mirabilis") wit as "delightful imagining of persons, actions, passions or things."

### *Yarn*

Story or tale, sometimes improbable and far-fetched.

# Literary and Media Knowledge

## NOBEL PRIZE FOR LITERATURE 2000–2021

| Year | Laureate | Country | Language | Genre(s) |
|---|---|---|---|---|
| 2000 | Gao Xingjian | China, France | Chinese | novel, drama, literary criticism |
| 2001 | V. S. Naipaul | United Kingdom Trinidad & Tobago | English | novel, essay |
| 2002 | Imre Kertesz | Hungary | Hungarian | novel |
| 2003 | J. M. Coetzee | South Africa | English | novel, essay, translation |
| 2004 | Elfriede Jelinek | Austria | German | novel, drama |
| 2005 | Harold Pinter | United Kingdom | English | drama |
| 2006 | Orhan Pamuk | Turkey | Turkish | novel, screenplay, essay |
| 2007 | Doris Lessing | United Kingdom | English | novel, drama, poetry, short story, memoirs |
| 2008 | J. M. G. Le Clezio | France Mauritius | French translation | novel, short story, essay |
| 2009 | Herta Muller | Germany Romania | German | novel, poetry |
| 2010 | Mario Vargas Llosa | Peru Spain | Spanish drama | novel, short story, essay |
| 2011 | Tomas Transtromer | Sweden | Swedish | poetry, translation |
| 2012 | Mo Yan | China | Chinese | novel, short story |
| 2013 | Alice Munro | Canada | English | short story |
| 2014 | Patrick Modiano | France | French | novel |
| 2015 | Svetlana Alexievich | Belarus (Born in Ukrainian SSR) | Russian | history, essay |
| 2016 | Bob Dylan | United States | English | poetry, songwriting |
| 2017 | Kazuo Ishiguro | United Kingdom (born in Japan) | English | novel |
| 2018 | Olga Tokarczuk | Poland | Polish | novel |

| Year | Laureate | Country | Language | Genre(s) |
|---|---|---|---|---|
| 2019 | Peter Handke | Austria | German | novel |
| 2020 | Louise Gluck | United States | English | poetry |
| 2021 | Abdulrazak Gurnah | United Kingdom (born in Tanzania) | English | novel |

## MAN BOOKER PRIZE (2000–2021)

| Year | Winner | Book | Genre | Country |
|---|---|---|---|---|
| 2000 | Margaret Atwood | The Blind Assassin | Novel | Canada |
| 2001 | Peter Carey | True History of the Kelly Gang | Historical novel | Australia |
| 2002 | Yann Martel | Life of Pi | Fantasy novel | Canada |
| 2003 | DBC Pierre | Vernon God Little | Novel | Australia, Mexico |
| 2004 | Alan Hollinghurst | The Line of Beauty | Historical novel | United Kingdom |
| 2005 | John Banville | The Sea | Novel | Ireland |
| 2006 | Kiran Desai | The Inheritance of Loss | Novel | India |
| 2007 | Anne Enright | The Gathering | Novel | Ireland |
| 2008 | Aravind Adiga | The White Tiger | Novel | India |
| 2009 | Hilary Mantel | Wolf Hall | Historical novel | United Kingdom |
| 2010 | Howard Jacobson | The Finkler Question | Novel | United Kingdom |
| 2011 | Julian Barnes | The Sense of an Ending | Novel | United Kingdom |
| 2012 | Hilary Mantel | Bring Up the Bodies | Historical novel | United Kingdom |
| 2013 | Eleanor Catton | The Luminaries | Historical novel | New Zealand |
| 2014 | Richard Flanagan | The Narrow Road to the Deep North | Historical novel | Australia |
| 2015 | Marlon James | A Brief History of Seven Killings | Historical/ experimental novel | United Kingdom |
| 2016 | Paul Beatty | The Sellout | Satirical novel | United States of America |
| 2017 | George Saunders | Lincoln in the Bardo | Historical/ experimental novel | United States of America |
| 2018 | Anna Burns | Milkman | Novel | United Kingdom |
| 2019 | Margaret Atwood | The Testaments | Novel | United Kingdom |
| 2019 | Bernardine Evaristo | Girl, Woman, Other | Experimental Novel | United Kingdom |
| 2020 | Douglas Stuart | Shuggie Bain | Novel | United Kingdom & United States |
| 2021 | Domon Galgut | The Promise | Novel | South Africa |

## SAHITYA AKADEMI AWARDS–2021

| Name | Language | Name | Language |
|---|---|---|---|
| Anuradha Sarma Pujari | Assamese | Namita Gokhale | English |
| Bratya Basu | Bengali | Daya Prakash Sinha | Hindi |
| Mwdai Gahai | Bodo | DS Nagabhushana | Kannada |
| Raj Rahi | Dogri | Wali Mohd Aseer Kashtawari | Kashmiri |

| Name | Language | Name | Language |
|---|---|---|---|
| Sanjiv Verenkar | Konkani | Meethesh Nirmohi | Rajasthani |
| George Onakkoor | Malayalam | Vindeshwariprasad Mishr "Vinay" | Sanskrit |
| Kiran Gurav | Marathi | Niranjan Hansda | Santali |
| Chhabilal Upadhyaya | Nepali | Arjun Chawla | Sindhi |
| Hrushikesh Mallick | Odia | Ambai | Tamil |
| Khalid Hussain | Punjabi | Gorati Venkanna | Telugu |

## JNANPITH AWARD WINNERS (2000-2021)

| Award Winners | Year | Award Winners | Year |
|---|---|---|---|
| Dr. Indira Goswami (Assamese) | 2000 | Pratibha Ray (Odiya) | 2011 |
| Rajendra Keshav Lal Shah (Gujarati) | 2001 | Ravuri Bharadhwaja (Telugu) | 2012 |
| D. Jayakanthan | 2002 | Kedarnath Singh (Hindi) | 2013 |
| Vinda Karandikar (Marathi) | 2003 | Bhalchandra Nemade (Marathi) | 2014 |
| Rehman Rahi (Kashmiri) | 2004 | Raghuveer Chaudhari (Gujarati) | 2015 |
| Kunwar Narain (Hindi) | 2005 | Shankha Ghosh (Bengali) | 2016 |
| Ravindra Kelekar (Konkani) and Satyavrat Shastri (Sanskrit) | 2006 | Krishna Sobti (Hindi) | 2017 |
| O.N.V. Kurup (Malayalam) | 2007 | Amitav Ghosh (English) | 2018 |
| Akhlaq Khan Shahryar (Urdu) | 2008 | Akkitham Achuthan Namboothiri (Malayalam) | 2019 |
| Amar Kant & Shrilal Shukla (Hindi) | 2009 | Nilamani Phookan (Assamese) | 2020 |
| Chandrasekhar Kambar (Kannada) | 2010 | Damodar Mauzo (Konkani) | 2021 |

# Famous Books and Authors

| Book | Author |
|---|---|
| **A Secular Agenda** | Arun Shourie |
| **A Suitable Boy** | Vikram Seth |
| **Accession of Extinction** | D.R. Mankekar |
| **Adam Beda** | George Eliot |
| **Adhe Adhure** | Mohan Rakesh |
| **Adonis** | P.B. Shelley |
| **Adventures of Huckleberry Finn** | Mark Twain |
| **Adventures of Sherlock Holmes** | Arthur Conan Doyle |
| **Adventures of Tom Sawyer** | Mark Twain |
| **Advise and Consent** | Allen Drury |
| **Affluent Society** | J.K. Galbraith |
| **After the Dark Night** | S.M. Ali |
| **Age of Reason** | Jean Paul Sartre |
| **Agni Pariksha** | Acharya Tulsi |
| **Agni Veena** | Kazi Nazrul Islam |
| **The Agony and the Ecstasy** | Irving Stone |
| **Ain-i-Akbari** | Abul Fazal |
| **Ajat Shatru** | Jai Shankar Prasad |

| Book | Author |
|---|---|
| **Akbarnama** | Abul Fazal |
| **Alchemist, The** | Ben Jonson |
| **Alice in Wonderland** | Lewis Carroll |
| **All is Well that Ends Well** | William Shakespeare |
| **All things Bright and Beautiful** | James Herroit |
| **Amar Kosh** | Amar Singh |
| **Ambassador's Journal** | J.K. Galbraith |
| **Ambassador's Report** | Chester Bowles |
| **An American Tragedy** | Theodore Drieser |
| **An Autobiography** | Jawaharlal Nehru |
| **An Eye to China** | David Selboume |
| **An Idealist View of Life** | Dr. S. Radhakrishnan |
| **An Unknown Indian** | Nirad C. Choudhury |
| **Anandmath** | Bankim Chandra Chatterjee |
| **Ancient Mariner** | Samuel Taylor Coleridge |
| **And Quiet Flows the Don** | Mikhail Sholokhov |
| **Androcles and the Lion** | George Bernard Shaw |
| **Animal Farm, The** | George Orwell |

| Book | Author |
|---|---|
| **Anna Karenina** | Count Leo Tolstoy |
| **Another Life** | Derek Walcott |
| **Answer of History** | Mohammed Raza Pahlavi |
| **Antony and Cleopatra** | William Shakespeare |
| **Ape and Essence** | A. Huxley |
| **Apple Cart** | George Bernard Shaw |
| **Arabian Nights** | Sir Richard Burton |
| **Area of Darkness** | V.S. Naipaul |
| **Arms and the Man** | George Bernard Shaw |
| **Around the World in Eighty days** | Jules Verne |
| **Arrangement, The** | Elia Kazan |
| **Arrival and Departure** | Arthur Koestler |
| **Arrowsmith** | Sinclair Lewis |
| **Arthashastra** | Kautilya |
| **As You Like It** | William Shakespeare |
| **Ascent of the Everest** | Sir John Hunt |
| **Ashtadhyayi** | Panini |
| **Asian Drama** | Gunnar Myrdal |
| **Asia and Western Dominance** | K.M. Panikkar |
| **Atoms of Hope** | Mohan Sundara Rajan |
| **August 1914** | Alexander Solzhenitsyn |
| **August Coup, The** | Mikhail S. Gorbachev |
| **Autumn Leaves** | O. Pulla Reddi |
| **Avanti Sundari** | Dandi |
| **Babur Nama** | Zaheeruddin Mohammed Babur |
| **Babbit** | Sinclair Lewis |
| **Back of Methuselah** | George Bernard Shaw |
| **Backward Place, A** | Ruth P. Jhabwala |
| **Bandicoot Run** | Manohar Malgonkar |
| **Bang-i-Dara** | Mohammed Iqbal |
| **Bangla Desh The Unfinished Revolution** | Lawrence Liftschultz |
| **Banyan Tree, The** | Hugh Tinker |
| **Beast and Man** | Murry Midgely |
| **Beginning of the Beginning** | Acharya Rajneesh |
| **Betrayal of Pearl Harbour** | James Rusbridge and Eric Nave |
| **Bend in the Ganges, A** | Manohar Malgonkar |
| **Ben Hur** | Lewis Wallace |
| **Bermuda Triangle** | Charles Berlitz |
| **Berry Patches** | Yevgeny Yevtushenko |
| **Best and the Brightest, The** | David Halberstan |
| **Between the Lines** | Kuldip Nayar |
| **Beyond Modernisation, Beyond Self** | Sisir Kumar Ghose |
| **Bharat Bharati** | Maithili Sharan Gupta |
| **Bharatiya Parampara Ke Mool Swar** | Govind Chandra Pande |
| **Big Breach, The** | Richard Tomlinson |
| **Big Fisherman, The** | Lloyd C. Douglas |

| Book | Author |
|---|---|
| **Biopgraphia Literaria** | Samuel Taylor Coleridge |
| **Bisarjan** | Rabindra Nath Tagore |
| **Birth and Death of Sun** | George Gamow |
| **Bitter Sweet** | Noel Coward |
| **Black Arrow, The** | Robert Louis Stevenson |
| **Blind Ambitions** | John Dean |
| **Blind Beauty** | Boris Pasternak |
| **Blind Men of Hindustan ! Indo-Pak Nuclear War** | General K.S. Sundarji |
| **Bliss was it in that Dawn** | Minoo Masani |
| **Bloodline** | Sidney Sheldon |
| **Blue Bird** | Maurice Macterlink |
| **Bone People, The** | Kerl Hulme |
| **Born Free** | Joy Adamson |
| **Bread, Beauty and Revolution** | Khwaja Ahmed Abbas |
| **Breakthrough** | Gen. Moshe Dayan |
| **Bride for the Sahib and other Stories, A** | Khushwant Singh |
| **Bride's Book of Beauty, The** | Mulk Raj Anand |
| **Broken Wings** | Sarojini Naidu |
| **Brothers Karamazhov** | Fyodor Dostoevsky |
| **Bubble, The** | Mulk Raj Anand |
| **Bhudha Charitam** | Ashvaghosha |
| **Bunch of Old Letters, A** | Jawaharlal Nehru |
| **Butterfield-8** | John O' Hara |
| **By Love Possessed** | James Cozzens |
| **Caesar and Cleopatra** | George Bernard Shaw |
| **Cancer Ward** | Alexander Solzhenitsyn |
| **Candida** | George Bernard Shaw |
| **Candide** | Voltaire |
| **Canterbury Tales** | Gooffory Chaucer |
| **Cardinal, The** | Henry M. Robinson |
| **Centennial** | James Michener |
| **Chandalika** | Rabindra Nath Tagore |
| **Chemmeen** | Thakazhi Sivasankar Pillai |
| **Cherry Orchard** | Anton Chekov |
| **Chesaplake** | James A. Michener |
| **Chidambara** | Sumitra Nandan Pant |
| **Chikaveera Rajendra** | Masti Venkatesh Iyengar |
| **Children of Gebelawi** | Naguib Mahfouz |
| **Childe Herolds Pilgrimage** | Lord Byron |
| **China Passage, A** | J.K. Galbraith |
| **China's Watergate** | Leo Goodstadt |
| **Chinese Betrayal** | B.N. Mullick |
| **Chitra** | Rabindra Nath Tagore |
| **Chittirappaval** | P.V. Akilandam |
| **Chomas Drum** | K. Shivaram Karnath |
| **Chronicle of a Death Foretold** | Gabrel Garcia Marquez |
| **Class, The** | Eric Segal |
| **Climate of Treason** | Andrew Boyle |

| Book | Author |
|---|---|
| **Comedy of Errors** | William Shakespeare |
| **Common Sense** | Thomas Paine |
| **Comus** | John Milton |
| **Communist Manifesto** | Karl Marx |
| **Confessions** | J.J. Rousseau |
| **Confessions of a Lover** | Mulk Raj Anand |
| **Confessions of an Opium Eater, The** | Thomas Dequicey |
| **Confidential Clerk** | T.S. Eliot |
| **Conquest of Self** | M.K. Gandhi |
| **Conservationist, The** | Ms. Nadine Gordimer |
| **Continent of Circle** | Nirad C. Choudhury |
| **Coolie** | Mulk Raj Anand |
| **Coup, The** | John Updike |
| **Count of Monte Cristo** | Alexander Dumas |
| **Court Dancer** | Rabindra Nath Tagore |
| **Covertly Papers** | Joseph Addison |
| **Cresent Moon** | Rabindra Nath Tagore |
| **Crescent over Kashmir** | Anil Maheshwari |
| **Crime and Punishment** | Fyodor Dostoevsky |
| **Crisis into Chaos** | E..M.S. Namboodiripad |
| **Crisis in India, The** | Ronald Segal |
| **Critique of Pure Reason, A** | Immanuel Kant |
| **Crown and the Loincloth, The** | Chaman Nahal |
| **Crown of Wild Olive, The** | John Ruskin |
| **Cry My Beloved Country** | Alan Patan |
| **Culture in the Vanity Bag** | Nirad C. Choudhury. |
| **Curtain Raisers** | K. Natwar Singh |
| **Dangerous Summer, The** | Ernest Hemingway |
| **Darkness at Noon** | Arthur Keostler |
| **Dark Room, The** | R.K. Narayan |
| **Dashkumar Charitam** | Dandi |
| **Das Kapital** | Karl Marx |
| **Daughter of the East** | Benazir Bhutto |
| **David Copperfield** | Charles Dickens |
| **Day in Shadow, The** | Nayantara Sehgal |
| **Days of His Grace** | Eyvind Johnson |
| **Dean's December** | Saul Below |
| **Death of a City** | Amrita Pritam |
| **Death of a Patriot** | R.E. Harrington |
| **Death of a President** | William Manchester |
| **Death, The Supreme Friend** | Kakasaheb Kalelkar |
| **Debacle** | Emile Zola |
| **Decameron** | Giovanni Boccaccio |
| **Decline and Fall of the Roman Empire** | Edward Gibbon |
| **Decline and Fall of Indira Gandhi** | D.R. Mankekar and Kamala Mankekar |
| **Decline of the West** | O Spengier |
| **Deewan-i-Ghalib** | Mirza Ghalib |
| **Delhi** | Khushwant Singh |

| Book | Author |
|---|---|
| **Democracy Means Bread and Freedom** | Piloo Mody |
| **Democracy Redeemed** | V.K. Narsimhan |
| **Descent of Man** | Charles Darwin |
| **Deserted Village** | Oliver Goldsmith |
| **Devdas** | Sharat Chandra Chatterjee |
| **Die Blendung** | Elias Canetti |
| **Dilemma of our Time** | Harold Joseph Laski |
| **Diplomacy in Peace and War** | J.N. Kaul |
| **Discovery of India** | Jawaharlal Nehru |
| **Distant Drums** | Manohar Malgonkar |
| **Distant Neighbours** | Kuldip Nayar |
| **Divine Comedy** | A. Dante |
| **Divine Life** | Swami Sivananda |
| **Doctor's Dilemma** | George Bernard Shaw |
| **Dolls's House, A** | Ibsen |
| **Don Juan** | Lord Byron |
| **Don Quixote** | Saavedra Miguel de Cervantes |
| **Double Helix, The** | J.D. Watson |
| **Dragon's Teeth** | U.B. Sinclair |
| **Dream in Hawaii, A** | Bhabani Bhattacharya |
| **Dream of Fair to Middling Women** | Samuel Beckett |
| **Dreams Roses and Fire** | Eyvind Johnson |
| **Dr. Jekyll and Mr. Hyde** | Robert Louis Stevenson |
| **Durgesh Nandini** | Bankim Chandra Chatterjee |
| **Dynamics of Social Change** | Chandra Shekhar |
| **Earth** | Emile Zola |
| **Earth Mother, The** | Pupul Jayakar |
| **Economic Planning of India** | Ashok Mehta |
| **Economics of the Third World** | S.K. Ray |
| **Eduction of Public Man** | Hubert Humphery |
| **Eight Lives** | Raj Mohan Gandhi |
| **Elegy Written in a Country Church Yard** | Thomas Grey |
| **Emile** | J.J. Rousseau |
| **Emma** | Jane Austen |
| **End of Era** | C.S. Pandit |
| **Ends and Means** | Aldous Huxley |
| **Envoy to Nehru** | Escott Reid |
| **Essays for Poor to the Rich** | John Kenneth Galbraith |
| **Essays of Elia** | Charles Lamb |
| **Essays on Gita** | Sri Aurobindo Ghosh |
| **Eternal Himalayas** | Major H.P.S. Ahluwalia |
| **Eternal India** | Indira Gandhi |
| **Executioner's Song** | Norman Mailer |
| **Expanding Universe** | Arthur Stanley Eddington |
| **Eye of the Storm, The** | Patric White |
| **Face to Face** | Lasse & Mrs. Lisa Berg |
| **Faces of Everest** | Maj. H.P.S. Ahluwalia |
| **Facts are Facts** | Khan Abdul Wali Khan |

| Book | Author |
|---|---|
| **Fall of a Sparrow, The** | Salim Ali |
| **Family Reunion** | T.S. Eliot |
| **Far From the Madding Crowd** | Thomas Hardy |
| **Far Pavilions, The** | M.M. Kaye |
| **Faraway Music, The** | Svetlana Allilueva |
| **Farewell the Trumpets** | James Morris |
| **Farewell to Arms, A** | Ernest Hemingway |
| **Farm House** | George Orwell |
| **Father and Sons** | Ivan Turgenev |
| **Faust** | J.W. Von Goethe |
| **Fidelio** | L. Beethoven |
| **Fifth Horseman, The** | Larry Collins and Dominique Lapierre |
| **Final Days, The** | Bob Woodward and Carl Bernstein |
| **Finding a Voice-Asian Women in Britain** | Amrit Wilson |
| **Fire Next Time, The** | James Balbwin |
| **First Circle** | Alexander Solzhenitsyn |
| **Flames form the Ashes** | P.D. Tandon |
| **Flounder, The** | Gunter Grass |
| **Food Nutrition and Poverty in India** | V.K.R.V. Rao |
| **For Whom the Bell Tolls** | Ernest Hemingway |
| **Forbidden Sea, The** | Tar Ali Baig |
| **Forsyte Saga** | John Galsworthy |
| **Forty Nine Days** | Amrita Pritam |
| **Freedom At Midnight** | Larry Collins and Dominique Lapierre |
| **French Revolution** | Thomas Carlyle |
| **Friends and Foes** | Sheikh Mujibur Rehman |
| **Friends not Masters** | Ayyub Khan |
| **From Here to Eternity** | James Jones |
| **From India to America** | L. S. Chandrashekhar |
| **From Raj to Rajiv** | Mark Tully & Zaheer Masani |
| **Ganadevata** | Tara Shanker Bando-padhyay |
| **Gandhi and Stalin** | Louis Fisher |
| **Gardener** | Rabindra Nath Tagore |
| **Gathering Storm** | Winston Churchill |
| **Geeta Govinda** | Jaya Dev |
| **Ghasiram Kotwal** | Vijay Tendulkar |
| **Gita Rahasya** | Bal Gangadhar Tilak |
| **Glimpses of World History** | Jawaharlal Nehru |
| **Godan** | Munshi Prem Chand |
| **Godfather, The** | Mario Puzzo |
| **God of Small Things, The** | Arundhati Roy |
| **Gold Bat, The** | P.G. Wodehouse |
| **Golden Gate** | Vikram Seth |
| **Golden Threshold, The** | Sarojini Naidu |
| **Gone with the Wind** | Margaret Mitchel |
| **Good Earth** | Pearl S. Buck |
| **Gora** | Rabindra Nath Tagore |
| **Grammar of Politics** | Harold Joseph Laski |
| **Grapes of Wrath** | John Steinbeck |
| **Great Challenge, The** | Louis Fishcer |
| **Great Depression of 1990, The** | Ravi Batra |
| **Great Expectations** | Charles Dickens |
| **Great Gatsby** | F. Scott Fitzgerald |
| **Great Illusion** | Norman Angel |
| **Great Tragedy** | Z.A. Bhutto |
| **Guide, The** | R.K. Narayan |
| **Gulag Archipelago** | Alexander Solzhenitsyn |
| **Gul-i-Naghma** | Raghupati Sahai (Firaq) Gorakhpuri |
| **Gulistan and Bostan** | Sheikh Saadi |
| **Gulliver's Travels** | Jonathan Swift |
| **Gurusagaram** | O.P. Vijayan |
| **Hamlet** | William Shakespeare |
| **Handful of Dust, A** | Evelyn Waugh |
| **Harry Potter*** | J.K. Rowling |
| **Harsha Charita** | Ban Bhatt |
| **Heat and Dust** | Ruth P. Jhabwala |
| **Heir Apparent** | Dr. Karan Singh |
| **Henderson, the Rain King** | Saul Below |
| **Henry Esmond** | William Thackeray |
| **Hero of our Times** | Richard Hough |
| **Heroes and Hero Worship** | Thomas Carlyle |
| **Higher than Hope** | Fatima Meer |
| **Himalayan Blunder** | Brigadier J.P. Dalvi |
| **Hindu Civilization** | J.M. Barrier |
| **Hinduism** | Nirad C. Choudhury |
| **Hindu View of Life** | Dr. S. Radhakrichnan |
| **Hounds of Baskervilles, The** | Arthur Conan Doyle |
| **House Divided** | Pearl S. Buck |
| **House for Mr. Biswas, A** | V.S. Naipaul |
| **Huckieberry Finn** | Mark Twain |
| **Human Factor** | Graham Greene |
| **Humboldt's Gift, The** | Saul Bellow |
| **Humour** | Ben Johnson |
| **Hunchback of Notre Dame** | Victor Hugo |
| **Hungary Stones** | Rabindra Nath Tagore |
| **I Am Not an Island** | K.A. Abbas |
| **I Follow the Mahatma** | K.M. Munshi |
| **Idiot, The** | Fyodor Dostoevsky |
| **Idols** | Sunil Gavaskar |
| **Idylls of the King** | Alfred Teennyson |
| **If I am Assassinated** | Z.A. Bhutto |
| **Illiad** | Homer |
| **Importance of Being Earnest** | Oscar Wilde |
| **In Afghanistan's Shadow** | Salig S. Harrison |
| **In Evil Hour** | Gabriel Garcia Marquez |

| Book | Author |
|---|---|
| **In a Free State** | V.S. Naipaul |
| **In Memorium** | Alfred Lord Tennyson |
| **In Search of Gandhi** | Richard Attenbrough |
| **In Search of Identity** | Anwar-al-Sadat |
| **India A Wounded Civilization** | V.S. Naipaul |
| **India Changes** | Taya Zinkin |
| **India Discovered** | John Keay |
| **India Divided** | Rajendra Prasad |
| **India from Curzon to Nehru and After** | Durga Das |
| **India Remembered** | Percival and Margaret Spear |
| **India of Our Dreams** | M.V. Kamath |
| **India, The Critical Years** | Kuldip Nayar |
| **India Today** | Rajni Palme Dutt |
| **India We Left** | Humphry Trevelyan |
| **India Wins Freedom** | Maulana Abul Kalam Azad |
| **Indian Home Rule** | M.K. Gandhi |
| **Indian Muslims** | Mohammed Mujeeb |
| **Indian Muslims The Need For a Positive Outlook** | Wahiduddin Khan |
| **Indian Philosophy** | Dr. S. Radhakrishnan |
| **Indian War of Independence** | V.D. Savarkar |
| **India's China War** | Neville Maxwell |
| **India's Priceless Heritage** | N.A. Palkhivala |
| **India** | Magasthenes |
| **Indira's India** | S. Nihal Singh |
| **Indira Gandhi's Emergence and Style** | Nayantara Sehgal |
| **Inheritance of Loss, The** | Kiran Desai |
| **Inner Circle, The** | Jonathan Frost |
| **Inside Asia (also, Inside Europe and Inside Africa)** | John Gunter |
| **Inside Third Reich** | Albert Spencer |
| **Intimacy** | Jean Paul Sartre |
| **Invisible Man** | H.G. Wells |
| **Iron in the Soul** | Jean Paul Sartre |
| **Isabella** | John Keats |
| **Islamic Bomb** | Stev Weissman and Herbert Krounsney |
| **Island in the Steams** | Ernest Hemingway |
| **Is Paris Burning** | Larry Collins And Dominique Lapierre |
| **Ivanhoe** | Sir Walter Scott |
| **Jane Eyre** | Charlotte Bronte |
| **Jazz** | Toni Morison |
| **Jean Christopher** | Roman Rolland |
| **Jinnah-India-Partition Independence** | Jaswant Singh |
| **Jobs for Millions** | V.V. Giri |
| **Judgement, The** | Kuldip Nayar |

| Book | Author |
|---|---|
| **Judge's Miscellany, A** | M. Hidayatullah |
| **Jullius Caesar** | William Shakespeare |
| **Jungel Book** | Rudyard Kipling |
| **Justice of Peace Ke Aansu** | Janardan Prasad Singh |
| **Kadambari** | Bana Bhatt |
| **Kagaz te Kanwas** | Amrita Pritam |
| **Kali Aandhi** | Kamleshwar |
| **Kamayani** | Jai Shanker Prasad |
| **Kamasutra** | S.J. Vatsyayan |
| **Kanthapura** | Raja Rao |
| **Kapal Kundala** | Bankim Chandra Chatterjee |
| **Kashmir-Behind the Vale** | M.J. Akbar |
| **Kaya Kalp** | Munshi Prem Chand |
| **Kayar** | Thakazhi Sivasankara Pillai |
| **Ken Attendant Godot** | Samuel Backett |
| **Kenilworth** | Sir Walter Scott |
| **Khak-i-Dil** | Jan Nissar Akhtar |
| **Kidnapped** | Robert Louis Stevenson |
| **Killer Angels** | Michael Shaara |
| **Kim** | Rudyard Kipling |
| **King of Dark Chamber** | Rabindra Nath Tagore |
| **King Lear** | William Shakespeare |
| **Kipps** | H. G. Wells |
| **Kissinger Years, The** | T.N. Kaul |
| **Kitni Navon Main Kitni Bar** | S.H. Vatsyayan |
| **Kore Kagaz** | Amrita Pritam |
| **Kublai Khan** | Samuel Taylor Coleridge |
| **Kulliyat-i-Iqbal** | M. Iqbal |
| **Kumar Sambhava** | Kalidas |
| **L'Allegro** | John Milton |
| **La Divine Comedia** | A. Dante |
| **Lady Chatterley's Lover** | D.H. Lawrence |
| **Lady of the Lake** | Sir Walter Scott |
| **Lajja** | Ms. Taslima Nasreen |
| **Last Days of Pompeii** | Edward George Lytton |
| **Last Maharaja, The** | Jean Louis Nou and Jacques Pouchepadass |
| **Last Thing** | C.P. Snow |
| **Laws Versus Justice** | V.R. Krishna Iyer |
| **Lead Kindly Light** | Vincent Shean |
| **Le Contract Social (The Social Contract)** | J.J. Rousseau |
| **Leaders** | Richard Nixon |
| **Leaves of Grass** | Walt Whiteman |
| **Letters from the Field** | Margaret Mead |
| **Les Miserables** | Victor Hugo |
| **Leviathan** | Thomas Hobbes |
| **Life Divine** | Aurbindo Ghosh |
| **Life of Dr. Johnson** | James Boswell |
| **Light that Failed** | Rudyard Kipling |

| Book | Author |
|---|---|
| **Lines of Fate** | Marek Kharitonov |
| **Lipika** | Rabindra Nath Tagore |
| **Living Room** | Graham Greene |
| **Lolita** | V. Nabokov |
| **Long Walk to Freedom** | Nelson Mandela |
| **Look Back in Anger** | John Osborne |
| **Lord of the Files** | William Golding |
| **Lost Child** | Mulk Raj Anand |
| **Lost Honour** | John Dena |
| **Lotus Eaters** | A Tennyson |
| **Love Story** | Eric Segal |
| **Lycidas** | John Milton |
| **Macbeth** | William Shakespeare |
| **Magic Mountain** | Maharishi Ved Vyas |
| **Main Street** | Sinclair Lewis |
| **Major Barbara** | George Bernard Shaw |
| **Making of a Midsummer Night's Dream, The** | David Selbourne |
| **Malgudi Days** | R.K. Narayan |
| **Malti Madhav** | Bhavabhuti |
| **Malavikagnimitra** | Kalidas |
| **Man and Superman** | George Bernard Shaw |
| **Man Eaters of Kumaon** | Jim Corbett |
| **Man of Destiny** | George Bernard Shaw |
| **Mankind and Mother Earth** | Arnold Toynbee |
| **Man, The Unknown** | Lewis Carroll |
| **Man for All Seasons, A** | Robert Bolt |
| **Man for Moscow** | G. Wynne |
| **Many Worlds** | K.P.S. Menon |
| **Marriage and Morals** | Bertrand Russel |
| **Masters, The** | C.P. Snow |
| **Mati Matal** | Gopinath Mohanty |
| **Maurice** | E.M. Forster |
| **Mayor of Casterbridge** | Thomas Hardy |
| **Meghdoot** | Kalidas |
| **Mein Kampf** | Adolf Hitler |
| **Memories of Hope** | Charles de Gaulle |
| **Memories of Malgudi** | R.K. Narayan |
| **Men who Kept the Secrets** | Thomas Powers |
| **Men who Killed Gandhi, The** | Manohar Malgonkar |
| **Merchant of Venice** | William Shakespeare |
| **Middle Ground, The** | Margaret Drabble |
| **Middle March** | George Eliot |
| **Midnight's Children*** | Salman Rushdie |
| **Midsummer Night's Dream, A** | William Shakespeare |
| **Mill on the Floss** | George Eliot |
| **Miser, The** | Moliere |
| **Mistaken Identify** | Nayantara Sehgal |
| **Moby Dick** | Hermann Melville |
| **Modern Painters** | John Ruskin |
| **Moon and Six Pence** | W. Somerset Maugham |
| **Moonlight Sonata** | L Beethoven |
| **Mookhajiva Kanasugalu** | K. Shivram Karnath |
| **Mother** | Maxim Gorky |
| **Mother India** | Katherine Mayo |
| **Mountbatten and Independent India** | Larry Collins & Dominique Lapierre |
| **Mountbatten and The Partition of India** | Larry Collins & Dominique Lapierre |
| **Mrinalini** | Bankim Chandra Chatterjee |
| **Mrs. Gandhi's Second Reign** | Arun Shourie |
| **Much Ado About Nothing** | William Shakespeare |
| **Mudra Rakshasa** | Vishakhadatta |
| **Murder in the Cathedral** | V.S. Eliot |
| **Muslim Dilemma in India** | M. K. A. Baig |
| **My Days** | R.K. Narayana |
| **My Early Life** | M.K. Gandhi |
| **My Experiments with Truth** | M.K. Gandhi |
| **My India** | S. Nihal Singh |
| **My Life and Times** | V.V. Giri |
| **My Music, My Love** | Ravi Shankar |
| **My Own Boswell** | M. Hidayatullah |
| **My Presidential Years** | R.Venkata Raman |
| **My Struggles** | E.K. Nayanar |
| **My Truth** | Indira Gandhi |
| **Mysterious Universe** | James Jens |
| **Naked Came the Stranger** | Penelope Ashe |
| **Naked Face, The** | Sidney Sheldon |
| **Naked Triangle, The** | Balwant Gargi |
| **Naku Thanthi** | D.R. Bondrc |
| **Nana** | Emile Zola |
| **Nature of Mass Poverty, Thc** | J.K. Galbraith |
| **Natya Shastra** | Bharat Muni |
| **Neela Chand** | Shiv Prasad Singh |
| **Nehru Family and Sikhs** | Harbans Singh |
| **Netaji Dead or Alive** | Samar Guha |
| **New Dimensions of India's Foreign Policy** | Atal Behari Vajpayee |
| **Nine Days' Wonder** | John Mansfield |
| **Nineteen Eighty-four** | George Orwell |
| **1999-Victory Without War** | Richard Nixon |
| **Nisheeth** | Uma Shanker Joshi |
| **Niti-Sataka** | Bharatrihari |
| **Nixon in White House** | Seymour M. Hersh |
| **Non-Violence in Peace and War** | M.K. Gandhi |
| **Nuclear India** | G.G. Mirchandani and P.K.S. Namboodari |
| **O'Jerusalem** | Larry Collins and Dominique Lapierre |
| **Occasion for Loving** | Nadine Gordimer |
| **Oddakkuzal** | G. Shankara Kurup |
| **Odyssey** | Homer |

| Book | Author |
|---|---|
| **Of Human Bondage** | W. Somerset Maugham |
| **Old Man and the Sea** | Ernest Hemingway |
| **Oliver Twist** | Charles Dickens |
| **Omeros** | Derek Walcott |
| **One Day on the Life of Ivan Denisovich** | Alexander Solzhenitsyn |
| **One Hundred Years of Solitude** | Gabriel Marquez |
| **One World** | Wendell Wilkie |
| **One World to Share** | Sridath Ramphal |
| **Origin of Species** | Charles Darwin |
| **Oru Desattinte Katha** | S.K. Pottekkatt |
| **Oscar and Lucinda** | Peter Carey |
| **Othello** | William Shakespeare |
| **Other Side of Midnight, The** | Sidney Sheldon |
| **Our Films, Their Films** | Satyajit Ray |
| **Paddy Clarke Ha Ha Ha** | Roddy Doyle |
| **Pakistan Papers** | Mani Shankar Aiyer |
| **Painted Veil** | W. Somerset Maugham |
| **Painter of Signs** | R.K. Narayan |
| **Pair of Blue Eyes, A** | Thomas Hardy |
| **Pakistan Crisis** | David Loshak |
| **Pakistan Cut to Size** | D.R. Mankekar |
| **Pakistan, The Gathering Storm** | Benazir Bhutto |
| **Panchatantra** | Vishnu Sharma |
| **Paradise Lost** | John Milton |
| **Paradise Regained** | John Milton |
| **Passge to England, A** | Nirad C. Choudhury |
| **Passage to India, A** | E.M. Forster |
| **Past and Present** | Thomas Carlyle |
| **Pather Panchali** | Bibhuti Bhushan Bandhopadhayaya |
| **Patriot, The** | Pearl S. Buck |
| **Personal Adventure, A** | Theodore H. White |
| **Peter Pan** | J. M. Berrie |
| **Pickwick Papers** | Charles Dickens |
| **Pilgrim's Progress** | John Bunyan |
| **Pinjar** | Amrita Pritam |
| **Plans for Departure** | Nayantara Sehgal |
| **Portrait of India** | Ved Mehta |
| **Post Office** | Rabindra Nath Tagore |
| **Power and Glory** | Graham Greene |
| **Power That Be** | David Halberstan |
| **Pratham Pratishruti** | Ashapurna Devi |
| **Prelude** | William Wordsworth |
| **Prem Pachisi** | Munshi Prem Chand |
| **Premonitions** | P.N. Haksar |
| **Price of Power** | Kissinger |
| **Pride and Prejudice** | Jane Austen |
| **Prince** | Nicolo Machiaveli |

| Book | Author |
|---|---|
| **Principla** | Issac Newton |
| **Prison and Chocolate Cake** | Nayantara Sehgal |
| **Prison Diary** | Jaya Prakash Narayan |
| **Prisoner of Zenda** | Anthony Hope |
| **Prisoner's Scrapbook, A** | L.K. Advani |
| **Prithviraj Raso** | Chanda Bardai |
| **Professor, The** | Charlotte Bronte |
| **Promises to Keep** | Chester Bowels |
| **Pygmalion** | George Bernard Shaw |
| **Pyramids of Sacrifice** | Peter L. Berger |
| **Radharani** | Bankim Chandra Chatterjee |
| **Rage of Angels** | Sidney Sheldon |
| **Raghuvansha** | Kalidas |
| **Ragtime** | E.L. Doctorow |
| **Rainbow, The** | Pearl S. Buck |
| **Rains Came** | Louis Bromefield |
| **Rajtarangini** | Kalhana |
| **Ram Charita Manas** | Tulsidas |
| **Ramayana** | Maharishi Valmiki |
| **Rangbhoomi** | Munshi Prem Chand |
| **Rang-i-Shairi** | Raghupati Sahai (Firaq Gorakhpuri) |
| **Rape of Bangladesh** | Anthony Mascarenhas |
| **Rape of the Lock** | Alexander Pope |
| **Ratnavali** | Harsh Vardhan |
| **Razor's Edge** | W. Somerset Maugham |
| **Rebel, The** | Albert Camus |
| **Rebirth** | Leonid Brezhnev |
| **Red and Black, The** | Stendhal |
| **Red Badge of Courage** | Stephan Crane |
| **Red Star over China** | Edgar Snow |
| **Reflections of the French Revolution** | Edmund Burke |
| **Reminiscences of the Nehru Age** | M.O. Mathai |
| **Reprieve** | Jean Paul Sartre |
| **Republic** | Plato |
| **Resurrection** | Count Leo Tolstoy |
| **Return of the Native, The** | Thomas Hardy |
| **Returning to the Source** | Acharya Shree Rajneesh |
| **Revenue Stamps, The** | Amrita Pritam |
| **Rich Like Us** | Nayantara Sehgal |
| **Riding the Storm** | Harold MacMillan |
| **Rights of Man** | Thomas Paine |
| **Rise and Fall of the Great Powers** | Paul Kennedy |
| **Ritu Samhara** | Kalidas |
| **Rivals, The** | R.B. Shridan |
| **Road to Folly** | Leslie Ford |
| **Robe, The** | Lloyd C. Douglas |
| **Robinson Crusoe** | Daniel Defoe |

| Book | Author |
|---|---|
| **Romeo and Julliet** | William Shakespeare |
| **Rubaiyat** | Omar Khayyam |
| **Rubaiyat-i-Omar Khayyam** | Edward Fitzgerald |
| **Sadar-i-Riyasat** | Karan Singh |
| **Saket** | Maithili Sharan Gupta |
| **Sakha Ram Binder** | Vijay Tendulkar |
| **Samler's Planet** | Saul Bellow |
| **Sands of Time** | Sidney Sheldon |
| **Satanic Verses** | Salman Rushdie |
| **Sanctuary** | William Faulkner |
| **Satyartha Prakash** | Swami Dayanand |
| **Savitri** | Sri Aurobindo Ghosh |
| **Scarlet Letter** | Nathaniel Hawthorne |
| **Scarlet Pimpernal** | Baroness Orczy |
| **Sceptred Flute** | Sarojini Naidu |
| **Scholar Extraordinary** | Nirad C. Choudhury |
| **School for Scandal, The** | R.B. Sheridan |
| **Scope of Happiness, The** | Vijayalakshmi Pandit |
| **Search for Home, A** | Sasthi Brata |
| **Sense and Sensibility** | Jane Austen |
| **Sense of Time, A** | H.S. Vatsyayan |
| **Sesame and Lilies** | John Ruskin |
| **Seven Lamps of Architecture** | John Ruskin |
| **Seven Summers** | Mulk Raj Anand |
| **Shadow from Ladakh** | Bhabani Bhattacharya |
| **Shahnama** | Firdausi |
| **Shakuntala** | Kalidas |
| **Shalimar** | Manohar Malgonkar |
| **Shall We Tell the President** | Jeffrey Archer |
| **Shape of Things to Come** | H.G Wells |
| **Shame** | Salman Rushdie |
| **She Stoops to Conquer** | Oliver Goldsmith |
| **Ship of Fools** | Katherine Anne Porter |
| **Shivaji, The Great Patriot** | Lala Lajpat Rai |
| **Shoes of the Fisherman, The** | Morris West |
| **Silas Marner** | George Eliot |
| **Six Characters in Search of an Author** | Lugi Pirandello |
| **Slave, The** | Issac Bashevis Singer |
| **Small Land** | Leonid Brezhnev |
| **Sohrab and Rustam** | Matthew Arnold |
| **Song of India, The** | Sarojini Naidu |
| **Sonnets, The** | William Shakespeare |
| **Sons and Lovers** | D.H. Lawrence |
| **Sound and the Fury, The** | William Faulkner |
| **Soz-i-Watan** | Munshi Prem Chand |
| **Spaniard in the Works, A** | John Lennon |
| **Spirit of the Age** | William Hazlitt |
| **Spy Catcher** | Peter Wright |

| Book | Author |
|---|---|
| **St. John** | George Bernard Shaw |
| **Story of My Life** | Moshe Dayan |
| **Story of Real Man** | Nikolayev Polevol |
| **Strangers and Brothers Omnibus** | C.P. Snow |
| **Sunny Days** | Sunil Gavaskar |
| **Study of History, A** | Arnold Toynbee |
| **Swami and Friends** | R.K. Narayan |
| **Swapnavasvadatta** | Bhasa |
| **Sword and the Sickle** | Mulk Raj Anand |
| **Tale of a Tub, A** | Jonathan Swift |
| **Tale of Two Cities, A** | Charles Dickens |
| **Tales from Shakespeare** | Charles Lamb |
| **Talisman** | Sir Walter Scott |
| **Tamas** | Bhisham Sahni |
| **Tarzan of the Apes** | Edger Rice Burroughs |
| **Tears of D'Urberviles** | Thoms Huardy |
| **Tempest, The** | William Shakespeare |
| **Thank You, Jeeves** | P.G. Wodehouse |
| **The Garden of Life** | Naveen Patnaik |
| **The White Tiger*** | Arvind Adiga |
| **Thieves in the Night** | Arthur Koestler |
| **Thirteenth Sun** | Amrita Pritam |
| **Three Musketeers** | Alexander Dumas |
| **Thorn Birds** | Colleen McCollough |
| **Thousand Days, A** | Arthur M. Shlesinger |
| **Through the Indian Looking Glass** | David Selbourne |
| **Through the Looking Glass** | Lewis Carroll |
| **Times Machine** | H.G. Wells |
| **Time to be Happy** | Nayantara Sehgal |
| **To Live or not to Live** | Nirad C. Choudhury |
| **Tom Jones** | Henry Fielding |
| **Train to Pakistan** | Khushwant Singh |
| **Traveller, The** | Olive Goldsmith |
| **Treasure Island** | Robert Louis Stevenson |
| **Trial, The** | Franz Kafka |
| **Trinity** | Leon Uris |
| **Triumph** | John Kenneth Galbraith |
| **Tropic of Cancer** | Henry Miller |
| **Tryst with Destiny** | L. S. Gopalan |
| **Twelfth Night** | William Shakespeare |
| **Twenty Years After** | Alexander Dumas |
| **Two Leaves and a Bud** | Mulk Raj Anand |
| **Two Women** | Alberto Moravia |
| **Ulysses** | James Joyce |
| **Uncle Tom's Cabin** | H.B. Stowe |
| **Unhappy India** | Lala Lajpat Rai |
| **Universe Around Us** | James Jeans |
| **Unto this Last** | John Ruskin |

| Book | Author |
|---|---|
| **Untold Story** | General B.M. Kaul |
| **Upturned Soil, The** | Mikhail Sholokhov |
| **Urvashi** | Ramdhari Singh Dinkar |
| **Utopia** | Thomas More |
| **Uttar Ramcharita** | Bhava Bhuti |
| **Valley of Dolls** | Jacqueline Susann |
| **Vanity Fair** | William Thackeray |
| **Vendor of Sweets, The** | R.K. Narayan |
| **Vicar of Wakefield** | Oliver Goldsmith |
| **Victim, The** | Saul Bellow |
| **View From Delhi, A** | Chester Bowles |
| **View From the UN** | U. Thant |
| **Village by the Sea, A** | Anita Desai |
| **Village , The** | Mulk Raj Anand |
| **Vinay Patrika** | Tulsidas |
| **Virangana** | Maithili Sharan Gupta |
| **Virginians, The** | William Thackeray |
| **Vish Vriksha** | Bankim Chandra Chatterjee |
| **Voice of Conscience** | V.V. Giri |
| **Voice of Freedom , A** | Nayantara Sehgal |
| **Voice of the Voiceless** | Ruth Harring |
| **Waiting for Godot** | Thomas Becket |
| **Wake up India** | Annie Besant |
| **Walls of Glass, The** | K.A. Abbas |
| **War and Peace** | Count Leo Tolstoy |
| **War of the Worlds, The** | H.G. Wells |
| **Waste Land** | T.S. Eliot |

| Book | Author |
|---|---|
| **Way to all Flesh** | Samuel Butler |
| **Way of the World, The** | William Congreve |
| **Wealth of Nations** | Adam Smith |
| **Week With Gandhi, A** | Louis Fisher |
| **We Indians** | Khushwant Singh |
| **We, the People** | N.A. Palkivala |
| **Where the Grass is Greener** | David M. Smith |
| **White House Years** | Henry Kissinger |
| **Wings of Fire** | A.P.J. Abdul Kalam* |
| **Willhelm Meister** | J.W. Von Goethe |
| **Without Fear or Favour** | Neelam Sanjiva Reddy |
| **Witness to an Era** | Frank Moraes |
| **Woman's Life, A** | Guy de Maupassant |
| **Wonder That Was India, The** | A.L. Basham |
| **Worthy it is** | Odysseus Elytis |
| **Wreck, The** | Rabindra Nath Tagore |
| **Wuthering Heights** | Emile Bronte |
| **Yajnaseni** | Pratibha Roy |
| **Yama** | Mahadevi Verma |
| **Yashodhara** | Maithili Sharan Gupta |
| **Yayati** | V.S. Khandekar |
| **Year of the Upheaval** | Henry Kissinger |
| **Year of the Vulture, The** | Amita Malik |
| **Yesterday and Today** | K.P.S. Menon |
| **Zhivago, Dr.** | Boris Pasternak |
| **Zulfi, My Friend** | Piloo Mody |

## FAMOUS AUTHORS IN DIFFERENT LANGUAGES

| | |
|---|---|
| **English** | William Shakespeare, John Milton, Chaucer, Spenser, Lord Byron, P.B. Shelley, John Keats, Francis Bacon, T.S. Eliot, Cecil Dlay Lewis, Alduous Huxley, W.B. Yeats Bunyan, Dryden, Dr. Johnson, Alexander Pope, Robert Browning, Charles Lamb, Charles Dickens, Thomas Hardy, W.M. Thackeray, George Eliot, Alfred Tennyson, Robert Bridges, George Bernard Shaw, D.H. Lawrence, Oliver Goldsmith, Sheridan, Walter Scott, William Wordsworth, S.T. Coleridge, Henry Fielding, Somerset Maugham, J.K. Rowling. |
| **French** | Imile Zola, Gustave Flaubert, Moliere, Proudhon, Jean Paul Sartre, Le Sage, Victor Hugo, Alexander Dumas, Balzac. |
| **German** | Goethe, Hoffman, Lessing, Schelling, Schaupenhuer, Heinrich Heine, Guenter Grass |
| **Russian** | Tolstoy, Mikhail Solokhov, Turgenev, Dostoevsky, Maxim Gorky, Techov, Alexander Salzhenitsyn, Boris Pasternak |
| **Greek** | Homer, Aesop, Aristophanes, Euripedes, Herodotus, Hesoid, Theocritus, Xenophon, Aeschylus, Sophocles |
| **Latin** | Dante, Boccacio, Terence, Virgil, Ovid, Horace, Seneca |
| **Norwegian** | John Bojer, Ibsen |
| **Persian** | Ghalib, Umar Khyyam, Abul Fazal, Amir Khusro, Faiz, Firdausi, Mohd. Iqbal Saddi |
| **Spanish** | Juan Valera, Lope De Vega, Cervantes |

## FAMOUS CHARACTERS AND THEIR CREATORS

| Character | Creator | Character | Creator |
|---|---|---|---|
| Adam | Milton | Juliet | William Shakespeare |
| Alice | Lewis Carroll | Jessica | William Shakespeare |
| Ancient Mariner | Coleridge | Jean Valjin | Victor Hugo |
| Ariel | William Shakespeare | Jacques | William Shakespeare |
| Antonio | William Shakespeare | Jeeves | P.G. Wodehouse |
| Anna Karenina | Leo Tolstoy | King Arthur | Tennyson |
| Bassomio | William Shakespeare | Kim | Rudyard Kipling |
| Bertie Wooster | P.G. Wodehouse | Long John Silver | R.L. Stevenson |
| Brutus | William Shakespeare | Macbeth | William Shakespeare |
| Beatrix | Thackery | Micawber | Charles Dickens |
| Beatrice | William Shakespeare | Miranda | William Shakespeare |
| Christian | John Bunyan | Mephistopheles | J.W. Von Goethe |
| Cordelia | William Shakespeare | Mellors | D.H. Lawrence |
| Cleopatra | William Shakespeare | Malaprop | Sheridian |
| Clare | Thomas Hardy | Oliver Twist | Charles Dickens |
| Claudius | William Shakespeare | Peggotty | Charles Dickens |
| David Copperfield | Charles Dickens | Priyangbada | Kalidas |
| Dushyanta | Kalidas | Portia | William Shakespeare |
| Don Quixote | Cervantes | Pip | Charles Dickens |
| Eliza Doolittle | George Bernard Shaw | Perry Mason | Erle Stanley Gardner |
| Estella | Charles Dickens | Pickwick | Charles Dickens |
| Faust | J.W. Von Goethe | Rip Van Winkle | Washington Irving |
| Gora | Rabindranath Tagore | Sam Weller | Charles Dickens |
| Hamlet | William Shakespeare | Surpanakha | Valmiki |
| Harry Potter | J.K. Rowling | Shylock | William Shakespeare |
| Hyde | R.L. Stevenson | Sherlock Halmes | Arthur Conan Doyle |
| Hercule Poirot | Agatha Christie | Shakuntala | Kalidas |
| Hawkins | R.L. Stevenson | Sancho Panza | Cervantes Saavedra |
| Hector | Homer | Tess | Thomas Hardy |
| Ivanhoe | Sir Walter Scott | Watson | Arthur Conan Doyle |
| Iago | William Shakespeare | Zhivago | Boris Pasternak |
| James Bond | Ian Fleming | | |

## GREAT POETS

| Language | Poet |
|---|---|
| Hindi | Surdas, Tulsidas, Keshav |
| Sanskrit | Valmiki, Vedvyas, Kalidas |
| Bengali | Rabindra Nath Tagore |
| Urdu | Mirza Ghalib |
| Persian | Sheikh Saadi |
| Latin | Virgil |
| Greek | Homer |
| English | Shakespeare |
| German | Goethe |
| Italian | Dante |
| French | Sully Proudhone |
| Punjabi | Waris Shah |

## GREAT INDIAN AUTHORS AND POETS

| Language | Authors and Poets |
|---|---|
| **Assamese** | Birendra Kumar Bhattacharya; Hem Chandra Barua; Hem Chandra Goswami; Madhavkandali. |
| **Bengali** | Ashapoorna Devi; Bankim Chandra Chatterjee; Bibhuti Bhushan Bandopadhyaya; Bishnu Dey; Pramendra Mitra; Rabindra Nath Tagore; R.C. Dutt; Michael Madhusudan Datt; Kazi Nazrul Islam; Tarashankar Bandopadhyaya. |
| **English** | Kamala Das; Manohar Malgonkar; R.K. Narayan; Raja Rao; Mulk Raj Anand; Bhabani Bhatacharya; Sasthi Brata; Arun |

| Language | Authors and Poets |
|---|---|
| | Joshi; Chaman Nahal; K.A. Abbas; Anita Desai; R. Prawer Jhabwala; Kamla Markandaya; Khushwant Singh; Manoj Dass. |
| **Gujarati** | K.M. Munshi; Mirabai; Narmada Sagar; Narsingh Mehta; Govardhan Ram; Uma Shankar Joshi. |
| **Hindi** | Tulsidas; Surdas; Kesav Das; Bihari; Kabir; Sumitra Nandan Pant; Jai Shankar Prasad; Maithili Sharan Gupta; Munshi Prem Chand; Upendra Nath Ashk; Suryakant Tripathi 'Nirala', Acharya Chatursen; Mohan Rakesh; Harivansh Rai Bachchan; Mahadevi Verma; Bhagwati Charan Verma; Ramdhari Singh Dinkar. |
| **Kannada** | K.V. Puttappa; B.M. Pampan; Panna; Ramchandra Bendre; K.S. Karanth; Purandar Das. |
| **Malayalam** | C.V. Raman Pillai; S.K. Pottekkatt; G. Sankara Kurup; Thakazhi Sivasankara Pillai; O. Chandu Menon; Vallathol; Kumaran Asan. |

| Language | Authors and Poets |
|---|---|
| **Marathi** | Hari Narayan Apte. Tikaram Mahay; Tukaram; V.S. Khandekar. |
| **Oriya** | Gopalbandhu Das; Gopi Nath Mohanty; Radha Nath Roy. |
| **Punjabi** | Sheikh Farid; Bhai Veer Singh; Dhani Ram Chatrik; Amrita Pritam; Nanak Singh; Balwant Gargi; Waris Shah; Bulle Shah. |
| **Sanskrit** | Maharishi Valmiki; Maharishi Ved Vyas, Shreeharsh; Ashvaghosh; Shudrak; Bharvi; Jaidev; Bhartrihari; Kalidas; Banabhatta; Bhavabhuti; Dandi. |
| **Tamil** | P.V. Akilandam, Subramaniam Bharati; Ramalingam. |
| **Telugu** | Lakshmi Narasimhan; Triputi; V. Satyanarayana. |
| **Urdu** | Assadulla Khan 'Ghalib'; Mohammed Iqbal; Mir Taqui Mir; Prem Chand; 'Firaq' Gorakhpuri; Rajinder Singh Bedi; Krishan Chander; Qurrat-ul-Ain Hyder; Sardar Jafri; Qazi Abdul Sattar. |

## WELL KNOWN QUOTATIONS

1. A thing of beauty is a joy for ever; Its loveliness increases; It will never pass into nothingness. — *Keats: Endymion*
2. A little knowledge is a dangerous thing — *Pope*
3. Beauty is truth, truth beauty that is all. Ye know on earth, all all ye need to know — *Keats: Ode on a Grecian urn*
4. All the world is a stage and all the man and women merely players — *Shakespeare: As you like it*
5. Some books are to be tested, others to be swallowed and some few to be chewed and digested —*Bacon*
6. Better to reign in hell than serve in heaven — *Milton: Paradise lost*
7. The child is father of the man — *Wordsworth: My heart leaps up*
8. A single step for man — a giant leap for mankind — *Neil Armstrong*
9. Dilli Chalo — *Netaji Subhash Chandra Bose*
10. To be or not to be — that is the question. — *Shakespeare: Hamlet*
11. Only free men negotiate. I shall never negotiate while I am still a prisoner — *Nelson Mandela*
12. Truth and non-violence are my God — *Mahatama Gandhi*
13. Let a hundred flowers bloom and let a thousand schools of thought contend – *Mao Tse-tung*
14. Jai Jawan, Jai Kisan — *Lal Bahadur Shastri*
15. Eureka! Eureka! — *Archimedes*
16. Some are born great, some achieve greatness and some have greatness thrust upon them — *Shakespeare*
17. Where wealth accumulates, men decay — *Goldsmith*
18. Power tends to corrupt and absolute power corrupts absolutely — *Lord Acton*
19. Man is by nature a political animal — *Aristotle*
20. I have nothing to offer but blood, toil, tears and sweat — *Winston Churchill*
21. I came, I saw, I conquered — *Julius Ceaser*
22. For fools rush in where angels fear to tread — *Pope*
23. Generations to come, it may, will scarce believe that such a one as this ever in flesh and blood walked upon this earth — *Einstein*
24. Government of the people, by the people, for the people — *Lincon*
25. East is east and west is west and never the twain shall meet — *Kipling*
26. Swaraj is my birth right — *Bal Gangadhar Tilak*

**27.** Cowards die many times before their death: The valiant never taste of death but once
*— Shakespeare: Julius Ceaser*

**28.** Where ignorance is bliss, It is folly to be wise
*— Grey*

**29.** I know nothing except the fact of my ignorance
*— Socrates*

**30.** We are such stuff as dreams are made of and our little life is rounded with a sleep
*— Shakespeare: The Tempest*

**31.** What's in a name? That which we call a rose By any other name would smell as sweet
*— Shakespeare: Merchant of Venice*

**32.** Patriotism is the best refuge of a scoundrel
*— Samuel Johnson*

**33.** Reading maketh a full man; conference a ready man; and writing an exact man *— Francis Bacon*

**34.** It is excellent to love a giant's strength
but it is tyrannous to use it like a giant
*— Shakespeare: Measure to Measure*

**35.** Water, water everywhere
Not any drop to drink
*— S.T. Coleridge: The Ancient Mainer*

**36.** It is strange but true, for truth is always strange
*— Byron: Don Juan*

**37.** Virtue is its own reward *— Cicero: De Fintibus*

**38.** Frailty, thy name is woman
*— Shakespeare: Hamlet*

**39.** We don't fear to negotiate, but we do not negotiate out of fear *— J.F. Kennedy*

**40.** Give us good mothers and I shall give you good nation *— Napoleon*

**41.** The woods are lovely, dark and deep
But I have promises to keep
And miles to go before I sleep *— Robert Frost*

**42.** We have made a tryst with destiny *— Pt. Nehru*

**43.** Eli, Eli, Lamma Sabcathani (My God, my God, why last thou forsaken me)
*— Jesus Christ at the Cross*

**44.** If winter comes can spring be for behind
*— Shelley*

**45.** Man does not live by bread alone *— Bible*

**46.** Nothing is good or bad, thinking makes it so
*— Shakespeare: Hamlet*

**47.** Garibi hatao *— Indira Gandhi*

**48.** Aram haram hai *— Jawaharlal Nehru*

**49.** Quit India *— Mahatma Gandhi*

**50.** Jai Jawan, Jai Kisan, Jai Vigyan
*— Atal Behari Vajpayee*

# Multiple Choice Questions

## THE LAST LESSON
*By Alphonse Daudet*

**1. Assertion (A):** Franz was scared to go to school.

**Reason (R):** He had not learnt his homework and was late for school.

A. Both (A) and (R) are true and (R) is the correct explanation of (A)
B. Both (A) and (R) are true, but (R) is not the correct explanation of (A)
C. (A) is true, but (R) is false
D. (A) is false, but (R) is true

**2. Assertion (A):** Franz was tempted to stay out of doors.

**Reason (R):** The weather was warm, birds were chirping and Prussian soldiers were drilling.

A. Both (A) and (R) are true, but (R) is not the correct explanation of (A)
B. Both (A) and (R) are true and (R) is the correct explanation of (A)
C. (A) is true, but (R) is false
D. (A) is false, but (R) is true

**3. Assertion (A):** Usually there was a great commotion when the school began.

**Reason (R):** The noise was produced by the opening & closing of desks, lessons repeated in unison by students and the teachers' ruler rapping on the table.

A. Both (A) and (R) are true and (R) is the correct explanation of (A)
B. Both (A) and (R) are true, but (R) is not the correct explanation of (A)
C. (A) is true, but (R) is false
D. (A) is false, but (R) is true

**4. Assertion (A):** That day everything was as quiet as Sunday morning.

**Reason (R):** It was indeed a Sunday morning and no one was present in the school.

A. Both (A) and (R) are true and (R) is the correct explanation of A
B. Both (A) and (R) are true, but (R) is not the correct explanation of (A)

C. (A) is true, but (R) is false
D. (A) is false, but (R) is true

**5. Assertion (A):** M. Hamel was wearing his special dress for the last French class.

**Reason (R):** The dress comprised of beautiful green coat, frilled shirt & the little black silk cap.
A. Both (A) and (R) are true and (R) is the correct explanation of (A)
B. Both (A) and (R) are true, but (R) is not the correct explanation of (A)
C. (A) is true, but (R) is false
D. (A) is false, but (R) is true

**6. Assertion (A):** The elderly villagers occupied the back benches on the last day of French lesson.

**Reason (R):** This fact surprised Franz the most.
A. Both (A) and (R) are true and (R) is the correct explanation of (A)
B. Both (A) and (R) are true, but (R) is not the correct explanation of (A)
C. (A) is true, but (R) is false
D. (A) is false, but (R) is true

**7. Assertion (A):** The whole school seemed strange and solemn to Franz.

**Reason (R):** The order had come from Berlin to teach only German in the schools of Alsace & Lorraine. That was their last French class.
A. Both (A) and (R) are true and (R) is the correct explanation of (A)
B. Both (A) and (R) are true, but (R) is not the correct explanation of (A)
C. (A) is true, but (R) is false
D. (A) is false, but (R) is true

**8. Assertion (A):** Franz was filled with repentance and guilt on the last day of French class.

**Reason (R):** He did not study French when he had time, he wasted his time in seeking birds' eggs and sliding on the Saar.
A. Both (A) and (R) are true, but (R) is not the correct explanation of (A)
B. Both (A) and (R) are true and (R) is the correct explanation of (A)
C. (A) is true, but (R) is false
D. (A) is false, but (R) is true

**9. Assertion (A):** The elderly people occupied the back benches.

**Reason (R):** They were present for thanking M Hamel, for being sorry too for not going to school more, for showing their respect towards the country that was theirs no more.
A. Both (A) and (R) are true and (R) is the correct explanation of (A)
B. Both (A) and (R) are true, but (R) is not the correct explanation of (A)
C. (A) is true, but (R) is false
D. (A) is false, but (R) is true

**10. Assertion (A):** The teacher is also responsible for poor performance of students in studies.

**Reason (R):** He often sent them to water his flowers instead of learning their lessons, declared holidays for no reason.
A. Both (A) and (R) are true, but (R) is not the correct explanation of (A)
B. Both (A) and (R) are true and (R) is the correct explanation of (A)
C. (A) is true, but (R) is false
D. (A) is false, but (R) is true

**11. Assertion (A):** French language was the most beautiful, the clearest and the most logical of all the languages.

**Reason (R):** As long as the Frenchmen held fast to their language, they had chances of winning freedom.
A. Both (A) and (R) are true and (R) is the correct explanation of (A)
B. Both (A) and (R) are true, but (R) is not the correct explanation of (A)
C. (A) is true, but (R) is false
D. (A) is false, but (R) is true

**12. Assertion (A):** Will they make them sing in German, even the pigeons.

**Reason (R):** They had enslaved France, so they could do every impossible act.
A. Both (A) and (R) are true and (R) is the correct explanation of (A)
B. Both (A) and (R) are true, but (R) is not the correct explanation of (A)
C. (A) is true, but (R) is false
D. (A) is false, but (R) is true

**13. Assertion (A):** When it struck twelve, M. Hamel made a gesture with his hand to everyone that the school was dismissed.

**Reason (R):** He was too emotional and upset over the Berlin order to speak anything.
A. Both (A) and (R) are true, but (R) is not the correct explanation of (A)
B. Both (A) and (R) are true and (R) is the correct explanation of (A)
C. (A) is true, but (R) is false
D. (A) is false, but (R) is true

**14.** Look at the statements given below. Choose the option that correctly identifies which statements are fact and which are opinion:
(*a*) By sitting in the class, the elders of Alsace showed their respect for M. Hamel.

(*b*) The elders were regretting that they did not learn their mother tongue.
(*c*) The elders did not appreciate the faithful service of M. Hamel and were only there to bid farewell to the teacher.
(*d*) The teacher was sorrowful as he was to leave not only his students but also the school which he had nurtured.

A. Fact (*a*) and (*d*); opinion (*b*) and (*c*)
B. Fact (*b*) and (*c*); opinion (*a*) and (*d*)
C. Fact (*a*) and (*b*); opinion (*c*) and (*d*)
D. Fact (*b*) and (*d*); opinion (*a*) and (*c*)

**15. Statement I:** The narrator feels sorry for M. Hamel.
**Statement II:** Franz could not accept the fact that he won't be learning French any longer.
A. Statement I is true, but Statement II is false.
B. Statement I is false, but Statement II is true.
C. Both these statements can be inferred from the lesson.
D. Neither of the statements can be inferred from the lesson.

**Directions:** *Read each of the following passages carefully and choose the best answer to each question out of the four alternatives.*

### PASSAGE-1

I started for school very late that morning and was in great dread of a scolding, especially because M. Hamel had said that he would question us on participles, and I did not know the first word about them. For a moment, I thought of running away and spending the day out of doors. It was so warm, so bright!

**16.** Who is the author of these lines?
A. William Douglas B. Selma Lagerlof
C. Alphonse Daudet D. Anees Jung

**17.** Who was Mr Hamel?
A. Principal B. French teacher
C. Village Sarpanch D. Franz's father

**18.** Why was Franz in great dread?
A. He had not prepared his grammar lesson
B. He had bunked the class the previous day
C. He had not brought his notebook
D. None of these

**19.** What did Franz think for a moment?
A. teaching a lesson to his teacher
B. pranking the principal
C. bunking the class
D. joining the Civil movement

### PASSAGE-2

I jumped over the bench and sat down at my desk. Not till then, when I had got a little over my fright, did I see that our teacher had on his beautiful green coat, his frilled shirt, and the little black silk cap, all embroidered, that he never wore except on inspection and prize days. Besides, the whole school seemed so strange and solemn.

**20.** Who is 'I' in the given lines?
A. Franz B. M. Hamel
C. The Mayor D. The Narrator

**21.** What was unusual about M. Hamel's dress?
A. Wore clean clothes
B. Wore a brand new outfit
C. Wore a traditional French outfit
D. Wore his fancy clothes

**22.** Why was M. Hamel dressed so unusually?
A. He was retiring
B. It was his last lesson
C. He was leaving the school
D. He was going to be imprisoned

**23.** Which word in the extract would also mean 'formal and dignified'?
A. Inspection B. Strange
C. Solemn D. Fright

**24.** 'Got a little over my Fright' means:
A. a bit afraid B. a bit settled
C. being cautious D. all of these

### PASSAGE-3

"My children, this is the last lesson I shall give you. The order has come from Berlin to teach only German in the schools of Alsace and Lorraine. The new master comes tomorrow. This is your last French lesson. I want you to be very attentive." What a thunderclap these words were to me!

**25.** Why does M. Hamel want the students to be attentive?
A. Because it is his last French lesson
B. Because the order has come from Berlin
C. Because he is about to reveal the question paper
D. Because the government officer is on a visit

**26.** Which order from Berlin is called as 'thunderclap' by Franz?
A. The order of closing schools for a month
B. The order of stopping teaching French
C. The order of executing anyone in Alsace & Lorraine
D. The order of demolishing the school building

**27.** How would you describe Franz's tone when he says, "What a thunderclap these words were to me"?
A. Angry B. Gloomy
C. Perplexed D. Irritated

**28. Statement I:** M. Hamel had been subjected to mental torture with the decision to teach only German in Alsace and Lorraine.

**Statement II:** Nobody except Franz was able to realize the pain in M. Hamel's eyes.

A. Statement I is true, but Statement II is false
B. Statement I is false, but Statement II is true
C. Both Statement I & II cannot be inferred from the passage
D. Both Statement I & II can be inferred from the passage

**29.** In which of the following options can the underlined words not be replaced with 'wretch'?

A. The beggar has broken my car window.
B. Items like a stick and grenadier are now variable.
C. He is a lonely and miserable rogue.
D. Before the poor knave had time to speak, he was shot.

### PASSAGE-4

My last French lesson why I hardly knew how to write I should never learn anymore I must stop there then oh how sorry I was for not learning my lessons for seeking Birds eggs or going sliding on the Saar my books that had seemed such a nuisance a while ago so heavy to carry my grammar and my history of the saints were old friends now that I couldn't give up.

**30.** Why was it the speaker's last French lesson?

A. because his French teacher was retiring
B. because of a government order to teach only German
C. because the speaker was migrating
D. because French has become a language to be taught in higher classes

**31.** What is the speaker feeling after getting to know that it is his last French lesson?

A. sad B. regretful
C. frightened D. distraught

**32.** What did Franz do to skip his French lessons?

A. seeking bird eggs
B. going on the slides
C. working on the mill
D. both (A) and (B)

**33.** How do Franz's feelings regarding his books change?

A. He feels that they were his friends
B. He believes that they were a nuisance
C. He feels that his identity is related to his books
D. He believed that they are of no use to him

### PASSAGE-5

Poor man! It was in honour of this last lesson that, he had put on his fine Sunday clothes, and now I understood why the old men of the village were sitting there in the back of the room. It was because they were sorry, too, that they had not gone to school more. It was their way of thanking our master for his forty years of faithful service and of showing their respect for the country that was theirs no more.

**34.** Why does the narrator refer to M. Hamel as 'poor man'?

A. He empathizes with M. Hamel as he had to leave the village.
B. He believed that M Hamel's 'fine Sunday clothes' clearly reflected that he was not rich.
C. He feels sorry for M. Hamel as it was his last French lesson.
D. He thinks that M. Hamel's patriotism and sense of duty resulted in his poverty.

**35.** Which of the following idioms might describe the villagers' act of attending the last lesson most accurately?

A. too good to miss
B. too little, too late
C. too many cooks spoil the broth
D. too cool for school

**36.** Choose the option that might raise a question about M. Hamel's 'faithful service'.

A. When Franz came late M. Hamel told him that he was about to begin class without him.
B. Franz mentioned how cranky M. Hamel was and 'his great ruler rapping on the table'.
C. M Hamel often sent students to water his flowers and gave a holiday when he wanted to go fishing.
D. M Hamel permitted villagers to put their children 'to work on a farm or at the mills' for some extra money.

**37.** Choose the option that most appropriately fills in the blanks, for the following description of the given extract.

The villagers and their children sat in the class, forging with their old master a *(i)* ........ togetherness. In that moment, the class room stood *(ii)* ........ . It was France itself and the last French lesson a desperate hope to *(iii)* ........ to the remnants of what they had known and taken for granted their own *(iv)*......... .

A. *(i)* graceful *(ii)* still *(iii)* hang on *(iv)* country
B. *(i)* bygone *(ii)* up *(iii)* keep on *(iv)* education
C. *(i)* beautiful *(ii)* mesmerised *(iii)* carry on *(iv)* unity
D. *(i)* forgotten *(ii)* transformed *(iii)* hold on *(iv)* identity

### PASSAGE-6

But I got mixed up on the first words and stood there, holding onto my desk, my heart beating, and not daring to look up.

**38.** Who is I here?

A. Mr Hamel B. Franz
C. Village Sarpanch D. Not clear from the story

**39.** What was asked in the classroom from 'I'?
A. Rule of grammar
B. Addition rule
C. Multiplication table of 18
D. Essay on the language

**40.** Why did he stand holding the desk?
A. He was surprised at the question
B. He had not prepared his lesson
C. He was absent the previous day
D. He did not listen the question clearly

**41.** What was the reaction of the teacher?
A. Scolded him
B. Shouted at him
C. Sent him out of the class
D. Pitied him

### PASSAGE-7

I heard M. Hamel say to me, "I won't scold you, little Franz; you must feel bad enough. See how it is! Every day we have said to ourselves, Bah! I have plenty of time. I'll learn it tomorrow. And now you see where we have come out. That's the great trouble with Alsace; she puts off learning till tomorrow.

**42.** For what reason Franz could have been scolded?
A. For being late to school
B. for not learning participles
C. for ignoring his lessons
D. for playing all the time

**43.** Why should Franz be feeling bad?
A. his teacher was retiring
B. he would not learn French now
C. he was rusticated
D. his inability to show his command over friend

**44.** The given lines indicate how M. Hamel is feeling. Pick the option that correctly states these feelings.

| | |
|---|---|
| 1. angry | 2. regretful |
| 3. sad | 4. hatred |
| 5. Joyous | 6. sympathetic |
| A. 1 and 4 | B. 2 and 3 |
| C. 5 and 6 | D. 1 and 3 |

**45.** The story 'The Last lesson' highlights which human tendency?
A. male chauvinism B. procrastination
C. courage D. cowardice

### PASSAGE-8

M. Hamel went on to talk of the French language, saying that it was the most beautiful language in the world— the clearest, the most logical; that we must guard it among us and never forget it, because when a people are enslaved, as long as they hold fast to their language as it is as if they had the key to their prison. Then he opened a grammar book and read us our lesson. I was amazed to see how well I understood it. All he said seemed so easy, so easy.

**46.** Which of the following can be attributed to M. Hamel's declaration about the French language?
A. Subjective expertise
B. Nostalgic pride
C. Factual accuracy
D. Patriotic magnification

**47.** Read the quotes given below. Choose the option that might best describe Hamel's viewpoint.
(*a*) Those who know nothing of foreign languages know nothing of their own.
(*b*) Language is the road map of a culture. It tells you where its people come from and where they are going.
(*c*) A poor man is like a foreigner in his own country.
(*d*) The greatest propaganda in the world is our mother tongue, that is what we learn as children, and which we learn unconsciously. That shapes our perception for life.
A. option (*a*) B. option (*b*)
C. option (*c*) D. option (*d*)

**48.** "I was amazed to see how well I understood it". Select the option that does not explain why Franz found the grammar lesson 'easy'.
A. Franz was paying careful attention in class this time.
B. M. Hamel was being extremely patient and calm in his teaching.
C. Franz was inspired and had found a new meaning and purpose to learning.
D. Franz had realized that French was the clearest and most logical language.

**49.** Franz was able to understand the grammar lesson easily because he was:
A. receptive B. appreciative
C. introspective D. competitive

### PASSAGE-9

All at once, the church clock struck 12, then the Angelus. At the same moment the trumpets of the Prussians, returning from drill sounded under our windows. M. Hamel stood up very pale in his chair. I never saw him look so tall.

**50.** What is Angelus?
A. Prayers said in the morning
B. Prayers said in the middle of the day
C. Prayers said in the evening
D. All of these

**51.** Who are the Prussians?
A. Residents of Germany
B. Residents of Poland
C. Residents of some parts of Austria
D. All of these combined

**52.** Why was M. Hamel so pale?
A. He was tired by the end of the class
B. He was replaced by the German teacher
C. He was not well
D. He was tired due to the Mischief caused by the students

**53.** 'I never saw him look so tall' means:
A. Sad B. Excited
C. Lively D. seemed very confident

**PASSAGE-10**

"Viva La France!" then he stopped and leaned his head against the wall and without a word he made a gesture to us with his hand— "school is dismissed—you may go".

**54.** The reason for his stopping and leaning against the wall was:
A. because he was unwell
B. because he was emotional
C. because he wanted to teach German too
D. because the students didn't pay attention in his lecture

**55.** What does 'Viva La France' mean?
A. Good bye France B. Good living France
C. Long live France D. France is the best

**56.** The phrase 'Viva La France' indicates the speakers:
A. Enthusiasm B. Depression
C. Nostalgia D. Patriotism

**57.** Why does M. Hamel write Viva La France on the black board:
A. to show his love for French
B. to show his love for teaching
C. to show his love for his country
D. both (A) and (C)

**58.** French think, "Will they make them sing in German". What does this mean?
A. it means that nothing will be affected
B. it means that when people are deprived their surroundings are also affected
C. it means that a change will be welcome
D. it means that Franz was unaware of what was happening

**59.** Choose the statement that is not true:
A. Franz did not like going to school
B. He was scared of M Hamel
C. He was excited that he was going to learn German
D. He was regretful on the day of the last lesson

**60.** What had the narrator counted on to enter the school unnoticed?
A. he counted the leaves of a plant outside the classroom
B. he counted the blessing of God
C. he counted the number of people he met on his way
D. he counted on the hustle and bustle that was usual in the school

**61.** What did M. Hamel tell the people in the class about French language?
A. French was the most beautiful language in the world
B. French was the most illogical language in the world
C. French was the most logical language in the world
D. Both (A) and (C)

**62.** Which language was made compulsory to be taught in the schools of Alsace and Lorraine?
A. Portuguese B. French
C. German D. Spanish

**63.** For how many years had Hamel taught at the school?
A. 10 years B. 20 years
C. 30 years D. 40 years

**64.** Who were present in the class the last day?
A. all the villagers were present in the class
B. all the students and elderly villagers were present in the class
C. everyone except the teacher were present in the class
D. the Inspector from the neighbouring town was present in the class

**65.** The word 'rapping' means:
A. singing
B. slapping on the head
C. striking to attract attention
D. teaching strictly

**66.** "The birds were chirping at the edge of the woods and in the open fields back of the sawmill the Prussian soldiers were drilling."

Which of the following sentences can be said as true after reading the given lines?
A. Alsace bordered Prussia and so Franz could hear the drilling.
B. The Prussian soldiers had started to construct their official building.
C. The people of Alsace like Franz were attracted to the sound of drilling.
D. Prussia had won over Alsace and Lorraine and thus were practicing to settle their authority.

**67.** Franz saw a huge crowd assembled in front of the bulletin board, but did not stop. How would you evaluate his reaction?
A. Franz was too little to care about the news of lost battles.
B. Nobody in Franz's family was in the army, so it did not matter.

C. Bad news had become very normal, so he went about his task.
D. It was too crowded for Franz to find out what news was up on the board.

**68.** What did the blacksmith say to Franz?
A. To read the bulletin-board.
B. To get his homework completed.
C. To hurry to the school.
D. To not go so fast.

**69.** "There was usually great bustle and noise when school began, but it was all very quiet". Which of the following describes Franz's emotions most accurately?
A. Shock and awe
B. Disappointment and anxiety
C. Confusion and distress
D. Curiosity and uncertainty

**70.** Which of the statements cannot be attributed to Franz?
A. Franz did not like studying; he would rather enjoy nature.
B. Franz loved his teacher a lot.
C. Franz regretted that he did not study French at all.
D. Franz was a naughty student.

**71.** What does M. Hamel blame the parents for?
A. They preferred children to work in farms.
B. They were not strict.
C. They did not come to M. Hamel's class.
D. They did not love the French language.

**72.** "It seemed almost as if the poor man wanted to give us all he knew before going away and put it all into our heads at one stroke". Which of the following sentences does not use the phrase 'at one stroke' correctly?
A. The smoke choked the joking man at one stroke.
B. I managed to please both the buyer and the seller at one stroke.
C. Let's settle the matter at one stroke.
D. When the economy crashed, thousands lost their jobs, their homes and their pensions at one stroke.

**73.** 'They looked like little flags floating everywhere in the school room, hung from the rod at the top of our desks.' In the given sentence, which literary device has been used:
A. Alliteration B. Metaphor
C. Simile D. Both (A) and (C)

**74.** Choose the term which best matches the tone of statement: "but he had the courage to hear every lesson to the very last".
A. Acceptance B. Neglect
C. Discipline D. Regret

**75.** "I never saw him look so tall". Which of the following best captures M. Hamel on the last day of school?
A. Cranky, measurable, dedicated, resigned
B. Patient, dignified, emotional, courageous
C. Calm, nostalgic, disappointed, patriotic
D. Proud, reproachful, persistent, heroic

**76.** What do the marching soldiers under the windows represent?
A. The Dawn of Prussia and the defeat of French people
B. The defeat of Prussia
C. The victory of French
D. None of these

**77.** Pick a quote that best describes the theme of the story:
A. What is the nation without a mother tongue?
B. The rhythm of my body is the same as my mother tongue. It is in this rhythm where I find sanctity that I can return to my mother who is everywhere in the universe.
C. Language is the blood of the soil into which thoughts run and out of which they grow.
D. Poetry is the mother tongue of the human race.

**78.** What did Hauser bring?
A. Sweets B. Children
C. Friends D. Old Primer

**79.** What made Franz forget M. Hamel's ruler and crankiness?
A. Police Patrolling
B. Strange Quietness
C. Bustle on the streets
D. The idea of his going away

**80.** When people are enslaved, what key do they have to the prison, according to M. Hamel?
A. Their behaviour B. Power
C. Aggressiveness D. Mother tongue

**81.** What does the expression "in great dread of scolding" mean?
A. To be happy about it
B. Very badly scared of scolding
C. To be indifferent
D. None of these

**82.** M. Hamel is introduced as a ruler-wielding teacher. This demonstrates that:
A. he is concerned B. he is adamant
C. he is unfeeling D. he is a hard taskmaster

**83.** What is the moral that Alphonse Daudet wants to bring out?
A. Not to put off things that one can do that day
B. Old order changed to new
C. One should accept everything that happens
D. Teachers should be respected

**84.** For the last two years, where did all the bad news come from?
A. The Bulletin Board
B. Town Hall
C. School
D. M. Hamel's House

**85.** What did Mr. Hamel bring for his class on his last day in the school?
A. New pens B. New notebooks
C. Sweets D. Story books

**86.** What was Franz expected to be prepared for at school that day?
A. Song B. Dance
C. Essay writing D. Participles

**87.** Who asked Franz not to hurry to school?
A. Old Hauser B. Former Mayor
C. Former Postmaster D. Blacksmith Watcher

**88.** The story is set in the days of:
A. Franco–Prussian war (1870-71)
B. Franco–German war (1870-71)
C. Franco–Poland war (1880-81)
D. Franco–Austrian war (1880-81)

**89.** Prussia then comprised of:
A. Germany, Poland, Parts of Austria
B. Germany, Italy, Poland
C. Germany, England, France
D. France, Austria, Poland

## LOST SPRING

*By Anees Jung*

**Directions:** *Read each of the following passages carefully and choose the best answer to each question out of the four alternatives.*

### PASSAGE-1

"This morning, Saheb is on his way to the milk booth. In his hand is a steel canister. "I now work in a tea stall down the road", he says, pointing in the distance. "I am paid 800 rupees and all my meals". Does he like the job? I ask. His face, I see, has lost the carefree look. The steel canister seems heavier than the plastic bag he would carry so lightly over his shoulder. The bag was his. The canister belongs to the man who owns the tea shop. Saheb is no longer his own master!"

**90.** "His face, I see, has lost the carefree look". This means as per the assumption of the author, in his looks, Saheb is .......
A. Not burdened with responsibility
B. Burdened with responsibility
C. Burdened but without any responsibility
D. Not burdened but feels responsible

**91.** Choose the appropriate statements for "Saheb is no longer his own master!"
(*i*) Saheb carries his bag for rag picking.
(*ii*) Saheb works in a tea stall.
(*iii*) Saheb is paid 800 rupees.
(*iv*) Saheb carries canister.
A. (*i*), (*ii*) & (*iii*) B. (*i*), (*ii*) & (*iv*)
C. (*i*), (*iii*) & (*iv*) D. (*ii*), (*iii*) & (*iv*)

**92.** Read the statements given below.
Choose the correct statement to analyse the mental condition of Saheb-e-Alam.
A. He seems to be dignified working at the tea-stall.
B. He seems to be proud collecting milk from the milk booth.
C. He seems to be responsible carrying the steel canister.
D. He seems to be enjoying his freewheel at the tea-stall.

**93.** Select the option/options that does *not* explain Saheb's nature of thinking in his new job at the tea stall.
(*i*) He thinks collecting milk is a part of his new job.
(*ii*) Canister is heavy, but he thinks he should carry it for survival.
(*iii*) He is earning 800 rupees and all meals, so he should justify the job.
(*iv*) He is a servant now, he can have a carefree life.
A. Only option (*iii*)
B. Both options (*ii*) & (*iv*)
C. Both options (*i*) & (*iv*)
D. Only option (*iv*)

**94.** Choose the option that most appropriately fills in the blanks, for the following description of the given extract.
People migrate from villages to cities in search of a better life. They want to earn money so that they can lead a good life and (*i*) ________ their children in a better way. As cities have more (*ii*) ________ for work, this makes them migrate from the villages to these big cities. (*iii*) ________ all miseries and challenges of life at young age, Saheb even finds a job in a tea stall, shifting from rag picking to (*iv*) ________ his struggle for survival.
A. (*i*) give; (*ii*) scope; (*iii*) controlling; (*iv*) continue
B. (*i*) rare; (*ii*) opportunities; (*iii*) Accepting; (*iv*) prove
C. (*i*) provide; (*ii*) jobs; (*iii*) Denying; (*iv*) stop
D. (*i*) leave; (*ii*) chances; (*iii*) Chasing; (*iv*) deal

### PASSAGE-2

Savita, a young girl in a drab pink dress, sits alongside an elderly woman, soldering pieces of glass. As her hands move mechanically like the tongs of a machine, I wonder if she knows the sanctity of the bangles she helps make. It symbolises an Indian woman's suhaag, auspiciousness in marriage. It will dawn on her suddenly one day when her head is draped with a red veil, her hands dyed red with henna, and red bangles rolled onto her wrists. She will then become a bride. Like the old woman beside her who became one many years ago. She still has bangles on her wrist, but no light in her eyes. "Ek waqt ser bhar khana bhi nahin khaya", she says, in a voice drained of joy. She has not enjoyed even one full meal in her entire lifetime — that's what she has reaped! Her husband, an old man with a flowing beard, says, "I know nothing except bangles. All I have done is make a house for the family to live in." Hearing him, one wonders if he has achieved what many have failed in their lifetime. He has a roof over his head!

**95.** I know nothing except bangles. Which one of the following best speaks about the character of the old man.

A. (*i*) Cunning; (*ii*) wise; (*iii*) soft; (*iv*) obedient
B. (*i*) Intelligent; (*ii*) irresponsible; (*iii*) caring; (*iv*) simple
C. (*i*) Innocent; (*ii*) foresight (*iii*) responsible; (*iv*) caring
D. (*i*) Impeccable; (*ii*) honest; (*iii*) rude; (*iv*) simple

**96.** Which option best indicates that the old woman too has sacrificed something in her life for the sake of her family.

(*i*) The old woman has bangles on her wrist, but she can't see them.
(*ii*) She has not even enjoyed one full meal in her life time.
(*iii*) She never supported her husband in bangle making in her life.
(*iv*) She knows nothing expect making bangles which symbolise an Indian woman's suhaag.

A. (*i*) & (*iv*) B. (*ii*) & (*iii*)
C. (*iii*) & (*iv*) D. (*i*) & (*ii*)

**97.** "Ek waqt ser bhar khana bhi nahin khaya", the grand mother says. Her voice indicates that she is .......... .

A. Undergoing an emotion of great happiness.
B. Going through an emotion which lacks happiness.
C. Undergoing an emotion of anger and frustration.
D. Experiencing an emotion which reflects her fear and anxiety.

**98.** Which of these statements is *ture* about the husband of the elderly woman?

A. He says he knows nothing about making bangles in Firozabad.
B. He did not enjoy even one full meal in his entire life for the sake of his family.
C. He says he knows only bangle making and nothing else in his life.
D. All he has done in his life for the sake of his wife is making bangles for her.

**99.** "I wonder if she knows the sanctity of the bangles she helps make". In this statement, "I wonder reflects" the author's ............. .

A. Curiosity B. Anxiety
C. Embarrassment D. Restlessness

**100.** The narrator asks Saheb to go to school. What is the intension of the narrator here?

A. Narrator wants Saheb to enjoy in the school.
B. Narrator wants Saheb to go for rag picking and school as well.
C. Narrator wants Saheb to go to school instead of rag picking.
D. Narrator seriously encourages him to go to school.

**101.** "It takes longer to build a school" says the narrator to Saheb. What does the narrator really mean here?

A. There is a possibility to build a school.
B. It takes very long time to build a school.
C. There is a way to build a school.
D. There is no intention to build a school.

**102.** "After months of knowing him, I ask him his name. "Saheb-e-Alam", he announces. He does not know what it means. If he knew its meaning — lord of the universe — Saheb would have a hard time believing it" because ............... .

A. He was too poor to bear such a big name.
B. He was not suitable to bear such a big name.
C. His name was opposite to his life.
D. His life was quite suitable to his name.

**103.** "I like the game", he hums, "content to watch it standing behind the fence". The above sentence refers that Saheb ........ .

A. Is not satisfied with watching the game standing by the fence of club.
B. Is satisfied with watching the game standing by the fence of the club.
C. Wants to watch the game standing inside the fence of the club.
D. Is not allowed to watch the game even from the fence of the club.

**104.** "His dream looms like a mirage amidst the dust of streets that fill his town Firozabad, famous for its bangles". For Anees Jung, the dream of Mukesh appears as it is far away from reality. As per the circumstances, she thinks Mukesh would ........... .

A. Gradually be adjusted with the demands of his family.
B. Gradually be satisfied with his family profession.
C. Gradually be influenced by the societal pressures.
D. All the above

**105.** "It is his karam, his destiny", says Mukesh's grandmother, who has watched her own husband go blind with the dust from polishing the glass of bangles.

Which one of the following statements appropriately suits to the mind-set or lookout of Mukesh's grandmother.

A. She doesn't like her family members in the business of bangle making.
B. She wants her grandson, Mukesh to find his own destiny.
C. She thinks that her husband has gone blind due to his fate.
D. She doesn't believe in karam and destiny which play a major role in the lives of bangle makers.

**106.** "I want to be a motor mechanic", Mukesh repeats. Which one of the following best speaks about his repetition.

A. He is thinking to become a motor mechanic if everything is comfortable for him.
B. He wants to be a motor mechanic if his parents permit him.
C. He is strong in his decision of becoming a motor mechanic.
D. He wants to become a motor mechanic to impress the author.

**107.** The author asks, "Do you know anything about car driving?" Mukesh answers, "I will learn to drive a car". Choose the best efforts from the following which can help Mukesh materialise his dream of becoming a car driver.

A. His dedication and readiness to learn about car driving from the garage.
B. His mental state of uncertainty and lack of conviction to dream of cars.
C. His determination to walk to the garage which is a long way from his home.
D. All the above except (B)

**108.** **Assertion:** The children of Seemapuri are living a life of exploitation.

**Reason:** Extreme poverty forces them to lead such a life.

A. Both (A) and (R) are true and (R) is the correct explanation of (A).
B. Both (A) and (R) are true and (R) is not the correct explanation of (A).
C. (A) is true, but (R) is false.
D. (A) is false, but (R) is true.

**109.** **Assertion:** Most of the ragpickers appear walking bare foot in cities and on village roads.

**Reason:** They were caught in the web of a vicious circle of middlemen.

A. Both (A) and (R) are true and (R) is the correct explanation of (A).
B. Both (A) and (R) are true and (R) is not the correct explanation of (A).
C. (A) is true, but (R) is false.
D. (A) is false, but (R) is true.

**110.** **Assertion:** Garbage is wrapped in wonder for the elders in Seemapuri.

**Reason:** For the elders, it is a means of survival.

A. Both (A) and (R) are true and (R) is the correct explanation of (A).
B. Both (A) and (R) are true and (R) is not the correct explanation of (A).
C. (A) is true, but (R) is false.
D. (A) is false, but (R) is true.

**111.** **Assertion:** Saheb was not allowed to play tennis in the neighbourhood club.

**Reason:** He had proper shoes but no racquet to play tennis.

A. Both (A) and (R) are true and (R) is the correct explanation of (A).
B. Both (A) and (R) are true and (R) is not the correct explanation of (A).
C. (A) is true, but (R) is false.
D. Both (A) and (R) are false.

**112.** **Assertion:** Saheb is no longer his own master.

**Reason:** The tea canister which he carries is his own property.

A. Both (A) and (R) are true and (R) is the correct explanation of (A).
B. Both (A) and (R) are true and (R) is not the correct explanation of (A).
C. (A) is true, but (R) is false.
D. (A) is false, but (R) is true.

**113.** **Statement 1:** Mukesh insists on being his own master.

**Statement 2:** He has no fascination for continuing his family profession.

A. If Statement 1 is the cause, Statement 2 is the effect.
B. If Statement 1 is the effect, Statement 2 is the cause.
C. Both the statements are the effects of a common cause.
D. Both the statements are the effects of independent causes.

**114.** **Statement 1:** The children's eyes are more adjusted to the dark than to the light outside.

**Statement 2:** The boys and girls end up losing their eye sight before they become adults.

A. If Statement 1 is the cause, Statement 2 is the effect.
B. If Statement 1 is the effect, Statement 2 is the cause.
C. Both the statements are the effects of a common cause.

D. Both the statements are the effects of independent causes.

**115. Statement 1:** The young bangle makers could not organise themselves into a cooperative.

**Statement 2:** They were caught in a web of vicious circle.

A. If Statement 1 is the cause, Statement 2 is the effect.

B. If Statement 1 is the effect, Statement 2 is the cause.

C. Both the statements are the effects of a common cause.

D. Both the statements are the effects of independent causes.

**116. Statement 1:** Exemplary punishment should be given by law to those who employ the children to work in hazardous industries.

**Statement 2:** Child Labour is banned by the law.

A. If Statement 1 is the cause, Statement 2 is the effect.

B. If Statement 1 is the effect, Statement 2 is the cause.

C. Both the statements are the effects of a common cause.

D. Both the statements are the effects of independent causes.

**117. Statement 1:** Saheb's family left Bangladesh and came to India.

**Statement 2:** Saheb is no longer his own master.

A. If Statement 1 is the cause, Statement 2 is the effect.

B. If Statement 1 is the effect, Statement 2 is the cause.

C. Both the statements are the effects of a common cause.

D. Both the statements are the effects of independent causes.

## DEEP WATER

*By William Douglas*

**Directions:** *Read each of the following passages carefully and choose the best answer to each question out of the four alternatives.*

### PASSAGE-1

I had not been there long when in came a big bruiser of a boy, probably eighteen years old. He had thick hair on his chest. He was a beautiful physical specimen, with legs and arms that showed rippling muscles. He yelled, Hi, Skinny! How'd you like to be ducked?

**118.** How did the pool look like when the narrator went there?

A. Pleasant and lively.

B. Thrilling and attractive.

C. Timid and indifferent.

D. Still and clean.

**119.** Why did the narrator sit on the side of the pool?

A. To enjoy the beauty of the pool.

B. He was afraid of entering the pool alone.

C. To wait for the coach to arrive.

D. To prepare himself mentally to enter the pool.

**120.** What did the big bruiser of a boy do?

A. He flashed his rippling muscles.

B. He frightened the narrator.

C. He picked the narrator and tossed him into the deep end.

D. He took the narrator along to make him learn swimming.

**121.** The word 'bruiser' in the extract means:

A. Aggressor B. Genius

C. Gentleman D. Intelligent

### PASSAGE-2

I laughed and said, "Well, Mr. Terror, what do you think you can do to me"? It fled and I swam on.

**122.** Who is 'I' here?

A. William Doughlas B. Anees Jung

C. Khushwant Singh D. Kamala Das

**123.** Who is being addressed to as Mr. Terror?

A. Coach B. Young boy

C. Water D. None of these

**124.** Why did the narrator laugh?

A. Happy go lucky nature

B. Mocking Mr. Terror

C. Confident of defeating Mr. Terror

D. All of these

**125.** Why did Mr. Terror leave?

A. Could intimidate the narrator.

B. Could not make the narrator beg for help.

C. Could brighten up the narrator.

D. Could not frighten the narrator.

### PASSAGE-3

It had happened when I was ten or eleven years old. I had decided to learn to swim. There was a pool at the Y.M.C.A in Yakima that offered exactly the opportunity. The Yakima River was treacherous. Mother continually warned against it and kept fresh in my mind the details of each drowning in the river. But the Y.M.C.A pool was safe.

**126.** Who is 'I' in the above lines?

A. The narrator B. The coach

C. The young boy D. Father of the young boy.

**127.** Why did mother not allow 'I' to learn swimming in a river?
A. Religion did not allow this.
B. Social barriers to learn swimming.
C. Afraid about safety of her child.
D. All of these

**128.** What was reported to 'I'?
A. Coldness of water in Yakima river.
B. Coldness of water in swimming pool.
C. Drowning cases in Yakima river.
D. Drowning cases in swimming pool.

**129.** How was Y.M.C.A. a safe pool?
A. It had warm water.
B. It was open only during day time.
C. It had no water in it.
D. It was two to three feet deep at the shallow end.

**Directions:** *Choose the correct option with reference to the two statements given below:*

**130.** **Statement 1:** Douglas tried his best to jump out of water.
**Statement 2:** After a while, Douglas was not anxious in water.
A. If Statement 1 is the cause, Statement 2 is the effect.
B. If Statement 1 is the effect, Statement 2 is the cause.
C. Both the statements are the effect of a common cause.
D. Both the statements are the effects of independent causes.

**131.** **Statement 1:** The author's father laughed to mock his son's inability to swim.
**Statement 2:** The author wanted to swim just to prove to his father that he can swim.
A. Statement 1 is true, but Statement 2 is false.
B. Statement 1 is false, but Statement 2 is true.
C. Both Statement 1 and Statement 2 cannot be inferred.
D. Both Statement 1 and Statement 2 can be inferred.

**132.** **Statement 1:** Douglas had been haunted by fear for many years.
**Statement 2:** Douglas decided to learn to swim.
A. If Statement 1 is the cause, Statement 2 is the effect.
B. If Statement 1 is the effect, Statement 2 is the cause.
C. Both the statements are the effect of a common cause.
D. Both the statements are the effects of independent causes.

**133.** **Statement 1:** The narrator's mother warned him against swimming in the Yakima River.
**Statement 2:** Many people swam safely in the Yakima River.
A. Statement 1 is false, but Statement 2 is true.
B. Statement 1 is true, but Statement 2 is false.
C. Both Statement 1 and Statement 2 are true
D. Both Statement 1 and Statement 2 are false.

**134.** **Statement 1:** I crossed to oblivion.
**Statement 2:** The curtain of life fell.
A. If Statement 1 is the cause, Statement 2 is the effect.
B. If Statement 1 is the effect, Statement 2 is the cause.
C. Both the statements are the effect of a common cause.
D. Both the statements are the effects of independent causes.

**135.** **Statement 1:** The narrator was in the grip of fear of water.
**Statement 2:** This deprived him of the joys of canoeing, boating, swimming and fishing.
A. Statement 1 is false, but Statement 2 is true.
B. Statement 1 is true, but Statement 2 is false.
C. Both Statement 1 and Statement 2 are true
D. Both Statement 1 and Statement 2 are false.

**136.** **Statement 1:** At the age of ten or eleven, the narrator decided to learn to swim with water wings at the Y.M.C.A. pool.
**Statement 2:** The Y.M.C.A. pool was dangerous at the shallow end.
A. Statement 1 is false, but Statement 2 is true.
B. Statement 1 is true, but Statement 2 is false.
C. Both Statement 1 and Statement 2 are true.
D. Both Statement 1 and Statement 2 are false.

**137.** **Statement 1:** In death there is peace.
**Statement 2:** There is terror only in the fear of death.
A. If Statement 1 is the cause, Statement 2 is the effect.
B. If Statement 1 is the effect, Statement 2 is the cause.
C. Both the statements are the effect of a common cause.
D. Both the statements are the effects of independent causes.

**138** **Statement 1:** The narrator went to different lakes to swim.
**Statement 2:** He found tiny vestiges of fear still gripped him.
A. If Statement 1 is the cause, Statement 2 is the effect

B. If Statement 1 is the effect, Statement 2 is the cause

C. Both the statements are the effect of a common cause

D. Both the statements are the effects of independent causes

**139. Statement 1:** The narrator swam up & down the Warm Lake.

**Statement 2:** He could finally overcome his fear of water.

A. Statement 1 is false, but Statement 2 is true.

B. Statement 1 is true, but Statement 2 is false.

C. Both Statement 1 and Statement 2 are true.

D. Both Statement 1 and Statement 2 are false.

**140. Statement 1:** As the narrator sank into the pool, light was going out.

**Statement 2:** There was no more panic.

A. If Statement 1 is the cause, Statement 2 is the effect.

B. If Statement 1 is the effect, Statement 2 is the cause.

C. Both the statements are the effect of a common cause.

D. Both the statements are the effects of independent causes.

**141. Statement 1:** The narrator was going down into the pool.

**Statement 2:** He planned to make a big jump upwards and succeeded.

A. Statement 1 is false, but Statement 2 is true.

B. Statement 1 is true, but Statement 2 is false.

C. Both Statement 1 and Statement 2 are true.

D. Both Statement 1 and Statement 2 are false.

**Directions:** *Read each of the following passages carefully and choose the best answer to each question out of the four alternatives.*

### PASSAGE-1

Then I started down a third time. I sucked for air and got water. The yellowish light was going out. Then all effort ceased. I relaxed. Even my legs felt limp; and a blackness swept over my brain.

**142.** "Then all efforts ceased" What did the author mean by this?

A. He lost all hope.

B. He yielded himself.

C. That he gave in courage to survive

D. All of these

**143.** Which of the statement is *true* with the reference to the extract?

A. His friend was coming to help him

B. His legs were almost immobilized

C. His arms were moving unceasingly

D. He could see a great light.

**144.** Which option indicates more accurately narrator's state of mind?

A. His mind was blank

B. He was greatly terrified

C. He was excited

D. He was puzzled

**145.** Which option indicates that the poet was becoming unconscious?

A. The yellowish light was going out.

B. A blackness swept over my brain.

C. All effort ceased.

D. My legs felt limp.

### PASSAGE-2

The belt went through a pulley that ran on an overhead cable. He held on to the end of the rope, and we went back and forth, across the pool, hour after hour, day after day, week after week. On each trip across the pool a bit of the panic seized me. Each time the instructor relaxed his hold on the rope and I went under, some of the old terror returned and my legs froze. It was three months before the tension began to slack

**146.** "A 'pulley' that ran on an overhead cable". What does this mean?

A. An apparatus with a wheel

B. An apparatus with a rope

C. An apparatus without wheel

D. An apparatus with a wheel and a rope

**147.** The statement "Back and forth, across the pool" indicates:

A. Moving from one point to another

B. Moving clockwise and anticlockwise

C. Rising and falling

D. Ascending and descending

**148.** 'Tension began to slack' implies:

A. Fear started multiplying

B. Fear started increasing

C. Stress started decreasing

D. Stress started intensifying

**149.** 'Panic seized me' refers to:

A. Emancipating with joy

B. Fear gripped him

C. Boundless joy

D. Full of agony

### PASSAGE-3

The experience had a deep meaning for me, as only those who have known stark terror and conquered it can appreciate. In death there is peace. There is terror only in the fear of death, as Roosevelt knew when he said, "All we have to fear is fear itself." Because I had experienced both the sensation of dying and the terror that fear of it can produce, the will to live somehow grew in intensity. At last I felt released — free to walk the trails and climb the peaks and to brush aside fear.

**150.** "In death there is peace" choose the correct option with reference to the above:
A. End of one's existence is happiness
B. That death is solace & comfort
C. That one's final abode is uncertain
D. That there is torment in death

**151.** The phrase 'Brush aside' refers to:
A. Get closer to B. To finally get rid of
C. Take it for granted D. Not care at all

**152.** "All we have to fear is fear itself". What does the narrator learn from President Roosevelt's statement?
A. To cancel the fear B. To frighten the fear
C. To dispel the fear D. To prevent the fear

**153.** "I had experienced both the sensation of dying and terror that fear of it can produce", which of the following idioms might describe the above statement
A. "To be scared to death"
B. "Once in a blue moon"
C. "With a silver spoon"
D. "Hand to mouth"

## MY MOTHER AT SIXTY-SIX
*By Kamala Das*

**Directions:** *Read the following extract and choose the most appropriate option for each question.*

I saw my mother,
beside me, doze, open mouthed,
her face ashen like that of a corpse and realised with pain
that she was as old as she looked
but soon put that thought away,
and looked out at Young Trees sprinting,

**154.** Kamala Das turned her attention from her mother, because
A. She was feeling guilty.
B. She was shirking her responsibility.
C. She was trying to escape from pain filled emotions.
D. She didn't like the idea of her mother growing old.

**155.** The Poetic Device used in the above lines is also found in
A. Leena is the Lata Mangeshkar of Hyderabad.
B. Ayra is as cool as a cucumber to receive the heavy news.
C. The elephant is heavier than many other animals.
D. He is a tiger

**156.** The words 'doze' and 'ashen' reflect that the mother was:
A. Tired and sleepy
B. Sick and unhealthy
C. Lost strength and vigour as she had grown old
D. Hale and healthy

**157.** What did the poet realize seeing her mother beside her in the car?
A. That her mother may not survive for long
B. That her mother was suffering
C. That her mother wanted her to be with her
D. That she wanted to go with her daughter

**158.** 'Thought Away' means:
A. Diverted
B. Escaped
C. Drifted
D. Avoided

**159.** 'Trees sprinting' contains:
A. Metaphor B. Personification
C. Simile D. Alliteration

**160.** The Literary Devices used in the above extract are:
A. Simile and Refrain
B. Simile and personification
C. Simile and Alliteration
D. Only simile

**Directions:** *Read the following extract and choose the most appropriate option for each question.*

I looked again at her,
wan, pale as a late winter's moon and felt that old familiar ache,
my childhood's fear,
but all I said was, see you soon, Amma,
all I did was smile and smile and smile......

**161.** Kamala Das comparing her mother to winter moon signifies:
A. Human life is as short as that of the moon
B. Though the mother is old, she is still beautiful
C. Winter is the last season of the year
D. Mother is about to die

**162.** Though she feels painful, Kamala Das smiles on ......
A. To hide her sad feelings and emotions
B. To encourage her mother to smile and feel good
C. Not to dishearten her mother by showing her worried face
D. All the above

**163.** The tone of the poem is:
A. Pensive and sorrowful
B. Disillusioned and unhappy
C. Happy but discontented
D. Remorseful

**Directions:** *Study the two statements, in each question, labelled as Assertion (A) and Reason (R).*

**164. Assertion (A):** Kamala Das was honest and didn't have any hesitation in describing her mother's ageing face.

**Reason (R):** She compares her mother's face to a corpse.

A. Both (A) and (R) are true and (R) is the correct explanation of (A)
B. Both (A) and (R) are true, but (R) is not the correct explanation of (A)
C. (A) is true, but (R) is false
D. (A) is false, but (R) is true

**165. Assertion (A):** Kamala Das didn't like her mother growing old.

**Reason (R):** She turns her attention away from her mother.

A. Both (A) and (R) are true and (R) is the correct explanation of (A)
B. Both, (A) and (R) are true, but (R) is not the correct explanation of (A)
C. (A) is true, but (R) is false
D. (A) is false, but (R) is true

**166. Assertion (A):** The poet feels the pain of separation at the airport.

**Reason (R):** She started smiling at her.

A. Both (A) and (R) are true and (R) is the correct explanation of (A)
B. Both (A) and (R) are true, but (R) is not the correct explanation of (A)
C. (A) is true, but (R) is false
D. (A) is false, but (R) is true

**167. Assertion (A):** The poet gracefully accepts the reality of her mother growing old.

**Reason (R):** She left for her destination without much difficulty.

A. Both (A) and (R) are true and (R) is the correct explanation of (A)
B. Both (A) and (R) are true, but (R) is not the correct explanation of (A)
C. (A) is true, but (R) is false
D. Both (A) and (R) are false

**168. Assertion (A):** The poet didn't reveal her sorrow on her face in the airport.

**Reason (R):** She didn't like to create a scene there.

A. Both (A) and (R) are true and (R) is the correct explanation of (A)
B. Both (A) and (R) are true, but (R) is not the correct explanation of (A)
C. (A) is true, but (R) is false
D. (A) is false, but (R) is true

**169. Assertion (A):** Kamala Das took her mother to airport.

**Reason (R):** She wanted to spend some more time with her.

A. Both (A) and (R) are true and (R) is the correct explanation of (A)
B. Both (A) and (R) are true, but (R) is not the correct explanation of (A)
C. (A) is true, but (R) is false
D. (A) is false, but (R) is true

**170. Assertion (A):** The poet compares her mother to young trees.

**Reason (R):** Her mother was also young once.

A. Both (A) and (R) are true and (R) is the correct explanation of (A)
B. Both (A) and (R) are true, but (R) is not the correct explanation of (A)
C. (A) is true, but (R) is false
D. (A) is false, but (R) is true

**171. Assertion (A):** The poet advocates the aged parents should be taken care of by their children.

**Reason (R):** She looked after her mother by being by her side.

A. Both (A) and (R) are true and (R) is the correct explanation of (A)
B. Both (A) and (R) are true, but (R) is not the correct explanation of (A)
C. (A) is true, but (R) is false
D. Both (A) and (R) are false

**172. Assertion (A):** The poet compares her mother to a winter moon

**Reason (R):** Winter moon doesn't shine well like in other seasons.

A. Both (A) and (R) are true and (R) is the correct explanation of (A)
B. Both (A) and (R) are true, but (R) is not the correct explanation of (A)
C. (A) is true, but (R) is false
D. (A) is false, but (R) is true

**173. Assertion (A):** Kamala Das was scared of losing her mother or her company from her childhood days.

**Reason (R):** So, kamala Das was expecting this and hence ready for this to happen.

A. Both (A) and (R) are true and (R) is the correct explanation of (A)
B. Both (A) and (R) are true, but (R) is not the correct explanation of (A)
C. (A) is true, but (R) is false
D. (A) is false, but (R) is true

## AN ELEMENTARY SCHOOL CLASSROOM IN A SLUM

*By Stephen Spender*

**174. Assertion (A):** The slum children's faces are like rootless weeds and their hair unkempt.

**Reason (R):** The slum children were malnourished.

A. Both (A) and (R) are true, but (R) is the correct explanation of (A)

B. Both (A) and (R) are true, but (R) is not the correct explanation of (A)

C. (A) is false, but (R) is true

D. (A) is true, but (R) is false

**175. Assertion (A):** The stunted unlucky heir of twisted bones is reciting a father's gnarled disease.

**Reason (R):** The boy has been born with polio.

A. (A) is true, but (R) is false

B. (A) is false, but (R) is true

C. Both (A) and (R) are true, but (R) is the correct explanation of (A)

D. Both (A) and (R) are true, but (R) is not the correct explanation of (A)

**176. Assertion (A):** The small boy is dreaming of squirrel's game.

**Reason (R):** The boy is not interested in the lesson as it is boring.

A. (A) is true, but (R) is false

B. (A) is false, but (R) is true

C. Both (A) and (R) are true, but (R) is the correct explanation of (A)

D. Both (A) and (R) are true, but (R) is not the correct explanation of (A)

**177. Statement 1:** The slum children were like bottle bits of stones.

**Statement 2:** The slum children were thin and weak but look beautiful.

A. Statement 1 is true, but Statement 2 is false

B. Statement 1 is false, but Statement 2 is true

C. Both Statement 1 and Statement 2 are true, but Statement 2 is the correct explanation of Statement 1

D. Both Statement 1 and Statement 2 are true, but Statement 2 is not the correct explanation of Statement 1

**178. Assertion (A):** Ships, Sun and love tempt the children to steal

**Reason (R):** The slum children have the tendency to steal.

A. (A) is true, but (R) is false

B. (A) is false, but (R) is true

C. Both (A) and (R) are true, but (R) is the correct explanation of (A)

D. Both (A) and (R) are true, but (R) is not the correct explanation of (A)

**179. Assertion (A):** The slum children should be taken to the green fields outside.

**Reason (R):** The slum children were forced to stay inside the classroom.

A. (R) is the explanation of (A)

B. (A) is the explanation (R)

C. (A) is the problem and (R) is the solution

D. (R) is the problem while (A) is the solution

**180. Assertion (A):** The poet wants the children to break barriers and be free.

**Reason (R):** The poet doesn't want them to be superstitious.

A. Both (A) and (R) are true, but (R) is the correct explanation of (A)

B. Both (A) and (R) are true, but (R) is not the correct explanation of (A)

C. (A) is false, but (R) is true

D. (A) is true, but (R) is false

**181.** The following words show that the children suffer from 'acute malnutrition':

1. Stunted through
2. Twisted bones
3. Paper-seeming
4. Skin peeped

A. 1 and 2 are true

B. 2 and 3 are true

C. 3 and 4 are true

D. All are true

**182. Assertion (A):** The classroom walls are painted in 'sour cream':

**Reason (R):** The colour symbolizes the bleak future of the slum children.

A. Both (A) and (R) are true, but (R) is the correct explanation of (A)

B. Both (A) and (R) are true, but (R) is not the correct explanation of (A)

C. (A) is false, but (R) is true

D. (A) is true, but (R) is false

**183. Assertion (A):** The slum children consider Shakespeare wicked.

**Reason (R):** The slum children are evil and they have malice against him.

A. Both (A) and (R) are true, but (R) is the correct explanation of (A)

B. Both (A) and (R) are true, but (R) is not the correct explanation of (A)

C. (A) is false, but (R) is true

D. (A) is true, but (R) is false

**184. Statement 1:** The slum children consider map a bad example.

**Statement 2:** The world in the map has no relation to their world.

A. Statement 1 is true, but Statement 2 is false

B. Statement 1 is false, but Statement 2 is true

C. Both Statement 1 and Statement 2 are true, but Statement 2 is the correct explanation of Statement 1

D. Both Statement 1 and Statement 2 are true, but Statement 2 is not the correct explanation of Statement 1

**Directions:** *Read the extracts given below and answer the questions that follow.*

### POEM-1

Far far from gusty waves these children's faces.
Like rootless weeds, the hair torn around their pallor
The tall girl with her weighed-down head. The paper-seeming boy,
with rat's eyes.

**185.** What does the poet contrast the children's faces with?
A. Flowers B. Stars
C. Waves D. Plants

**186.** How do the faces of these children look?
A. beautiful and attractive
B. like rootless weeds
C. ugly and awkward
D. vigorous and refreshing

**187.** Why are they compared to rootless weeds?
A. because they are healthy
B. because they are malnourished
C. because they are not beautiful
D. because they are from rural background

**188.** Why is the head of the tall girl 'weighed down'?
A. because she is doing something
B. because she is depressed due to abject poverty
C. she is reading something
D. she is not interested

**189.** What figure of speech is used in the last line?
A. Alliteration B. Simile
C. Metaphor D. Personification

**190.** What does 'the paper-seeming boy' imply?
A. he eats papers
B. he sells papers
C. he is lean and thin like a paper
D. he is pure like a paper

### POEM-2

...........The stunted, unlucky heir
of twisted bones, reciting a father's gnarled disease,
His lesson, from his desk. At the back of the dim class
One unnoted, sweet and young. His eyes live in a dream
Of squirrel's game, in tree room other than this.

**191.** Why does the poet call the boy 'unlucky heir'?
A. he lost his father
B. his father left her mother
C. his father lost all money
D. he has inherited a disease of twisted bones

**192.** What is he reciting?
A. devotional songs
B. school lessons
C. his father's gnarled disease
D. folklore

**193.** Why was the boy unnoted?
A. Because he is small and sitting at the back
B. Because he is not intelligent
C. Because he is illiterate
D. Because he is not fair

**194.** What does the boy dream of?
A. beautiful world B. squirrel's game
C. owning big house D. riding a bike

**195.** What similarity do they have with respect to their physical condition?
A. all were neat and tidy
B. all were untidy
C. they were malnourished
D. all were beautiful

### POEM-3

On sour cream walls, donations, Shakespeare's head,
Cloudless at dawn, civilized dome riding all cities.
Belled, flowery, Tyrolese valley. Open-handed map
Awarding the world its world.

**196.** Why were the classroom walls called sour cream walls?
A. because they were painted bright colour
B. because they were painted light yellow colour
C. the colour is pleasant and beautiful
D. it is dark brown colour

**197.** What things were displayed on the walls of the classroom?
A. medals won by the institution
B. freedom fighters
C. philosophers
D. poets, buildings, world map and valleys

**198.** What does the world map award?
A. A lot of knowledge
B. a lot of treasure
C. Rich, beautiful world
D. experience

**199.** Why is Shakespeare called wicked?
A. Because he represents the rich world
B. Because he wrote against them
C. He does not give them happiness and comfort
D. he wrote about their lives

### POEM-4

And yet, for these
Children, these windows, not this map, their world.
Where all their future's painted with a fog,
A narrow street sealed in with a lead sky
Far far from rivers, capes, and stars of words.

**200.** What is the world of slum children?
A. Beautiful fields
B. The windows of the classroom
C. Slum
D. Mountains

**201.** Why is their future painted with fog?
A. Because they work tirelessly in dark cells
B. Because the room is filled with fog
C. Because they have no clear vision of future
D. They were denied admission

**202.** How is their world different from the world in the map?
A. Very similar to their world
B. Contrary to the world in the map
C. Not comfortable
D. Does not offer any clues

**POEM-5**

Surely, Shakespeare is wicked, the map a bad example,
With ships and sun and love tempting them to steal—
For lives that slyly turn in their cramped holes
From fog to endless night?

**203.** Why is Shakespeare wicked?
A. he wrote about love
B. he didn't write about them
C. he is very wealthy
D. they have no access to love and happiness

**204.** Why do the slum children consider map a bad example?
A. it is not showing their place
B. it doesn't help them
C. it shows a world which is quite different from their world
D. it is not visible to them

**205.** Where do the children spend their lives?
A. in foggy slums B. beautiful fields
C. villages D. cities

**206.** What do you understand by 'from fog to endless night'?
A. they travel through the fog
B. they work at night
C. they spend their entire lives in slums
D. they grope in darkness

**207.** Which word in the passage means "narrow"?
A. slyly B. steal
C. tempt D. cramped

**POEM-6**

Unless, governor, inspector, visitor,
This map becomes their window and these windows
That shut upon their lives like catacombs,

**208.** Who can change the condition of slum children?
A. school teachers
B. The Principal
C. governor, inspector and visitor
D. parents

**209.** What action does the poet want them to take?
A. to build a new school
B. to take them to the world outside
C. to provide playground
D. to give them money

**210.** What are 'catacombs'?
A. underground cemetery
B. the caterpillars
C. the mushrooms
D. edible plants

**211.** What do the 'catacombs' signify?
A. the dead condition
B. the darkness
C. the little narrow homes of the slum dwellers
D. the difficulties they face

**POEM-7**

Break O break open till they break the town
And show the children to green fields, and make their world
Run azure on gold sands, and let their tongues
Run naked into books the white and green leaves open
History theirs whose language is the sun.

**212.** What should be shown to slum children?
A. Beautiful pictures B. films
C. green fields D. historical places

**213.** What would they break?
A. buildings B. dams
C. the barriers which separate them from the world outside
D. their poor huts

**214.** How can they understand history?
A. by reading the biographies
B. by reading books
C. by observing nature
D. by viewing films

**215.** Which word in the stanza means "bright blue"?
A. naked B. sands
C. azure D. doom

## KEEPING QUIET
*By Pablo Neruda*

**216.** **Assertion (A):** The self-introspection is necessary for all literary persons.

**Reason (R):** Then only they will be able to meditate and save mankind from destruction.

A. Both (A) and (R) are correct and (R) is the correct explanation of (A).

B. Both (A) and (R) are correct, but (R) is not the correct explanation of (A).
C. (A) is true and (R) is false.
D. (A) is false and (R) is true.

**217. Assertion (A):** The poet wants everyone to remain quiet for sometime.

**Reason (R):** Silence will allow to listen to the voices of quiet and serene nature.

A. Both (A) and (R) are correct and (R) is the correct explanation of (A).
B. Both (A) and (R) are correct, but (R) is not the correct explanation of (A).
C. (A) is true and (R) is false.
D. (A) is false and (R) is true.

**218. Assertion (A):** The exercise of counting upto twelve is suggested by the poet.

**Reason (R):** It helps to sit still and achieve a sense of togetherness.

A. Both (A) and (R) are correct and (R) is the correct explanation of (A).
B. Both (A) and (R) are correct, but (R) is not the correct explanation of (A).
C. (A) is true and (R) is false.
D. (A) is false and (R) is true.

**219. Assertion (A):** Pablo Neruda desires to stop inhuman activities.

**Reason (R):** He wants to live in a peaceful atmosphere.

A. Both (A) and (R) are correct and (R) is the correct explanation of (A).
B. Both (A) and (R) are correct, but (R) is not the correct explanation of (A).
C. (A) is true and (R) is false.
D. (A) is false and (R) is true.

**220. Assertion (A):** The poet wants everyone to learn from the nature to create and not to destroy.

**Reason (R):** He wants to escape from his duty towards the mankind.

A. Both (A) and (R) are correct and (R) is the correct explanation of (A).
B. Both (A) and (R) are correct but (R) is not the correct explanation of (A).
C. (A) is true and (R) is false.
D. (A) is false and (R) is true.

**221.** Identify the tone of Pablo Neruda in the following line:

*Perhaps the Earth can teach us....*

A. Confident and clear about the future events.
B. Dramatic about the prediction he made.
C. Convinced about the sequence of events to follow.
D. Uncertain, yet hopeful about the possibility.

**222.** Based on the poem, choose the correct option with reference to the two statements given below.

**Statement 1:** The poet urges his countrymen to stop for a while.

**Statement 2:** The poet urges all men to stop for a second.

A. Statement 1 is true, but Statement 2 is false.
B. Statement 1 is false, but Statement 2 is true.
C. Both Statement 1 and Statement 2 are true.
D. Both Statement 1 and Statement 2 cannot be inferred.

**223.** Select the option that best conveys the feelings of the poet corresponding to the following:

"Fishermen in the cold sea
would not harm whales"

A. • fishermen would not kill whales because they did not need them
• fishermen would not kill whales because they were scared of them

B. • fishermen would not kill whales because they realised the damage that they were causing to the ecosystem
• fishermen would stop killing whales for commercial purposes.

C. • fishermen only wished they would not kill whales
• fishermen would not kill whales because they feared that whale population was fast dwindling

D. • fishermen would not kill whales themselves because others were doing that for them
• fishermen would not kill whales because there was a moratorium on killing whales

**224.** Based on the poem, choose the correct option with reference to the two statements given below.

**Statement 1:** The poet is in anguish at the plight of the earth and expresses hope that the situation may improve.

**Statement 2:** The poet's fears of total destruction of the earth are baseless.

A. Statement 1 is true, but Statement 2 is false.
B. Statement 1 is false, but Statement 2 is true.
C. Both Statement 1 and Statement 2 are true.
D. Both Statement 1 and Statement 2 cannot be inferred.

**225.** Read the statements given below carefully. Choose the option that best describes these statements, with reference to the poem 'Keeping Quiet'.

**Statement I:** The poem 'Keeping Quiet' calls for change as much in the individual as human society at large.

**Statement II:** The poem 'Keeping Quiet' implies that individual change will lead to bigger societal change.

**Statement III:** Neruda believes that when people come together as a community, they will be able to bring a transformation in each person.

A. Statement I is True, Statement II is False, and Statement III cannot be inferred.
B. Statement I and II cannot be inferred, Statement III is True.
C. Statement I is True, Statements II and III cannot be inferred.
D. Statement I cannot be inferred, Statement II cannot be inferred, Statement III is False.

**226.** Based on the poem 'Keeping Quiet', choose the correct option with reference to the two statements given below.

**Statement 1:** The poet cautions that one should not mistake doing nothing for total inactivity.

**Statement 2:** The poet also avers that he does not mean to associate with death.

A. Statement 1 is true, but Statement 2 is false.
B. Statement 1 is false, but Statement 2 is true.
C. Both Statement 1 and Statement 2 are true.
D. Both Statement 1 and Statement 2 cannot be inferred.

**227.** Classify (1) to (4) as fact (F) or opinion (O), based on your reading of *Keeping Quiet*.

1. The poet wants all humans to introspect themselves by observing silence.
2. The poet says there would no survivors if there were all kinds of wars.
3. The poet says that man can learn from the earth that we still can hope for life even when everything seems dead.
4. Poet says that men are threatening themselves, through their acts, with death.

A. F-1, 3, 4; O-2
B. F-1, 3; O-2, 4
C. F-2; O-1, 3, 4
D. F-3, 4; O-1, 2

**Directions (Qs. No. 228-231):** *Read the extract to attempt questions that follow:*

For once on the face of the Earth let's not speak in any language, let's stop for one second, and not move our arms so much. It would be an exotic moment without rush, without engines, we would all be together in a sudden strangeness.

**228.** The poet uses the word "let's" to _______.

A. initiate a conversation between the poet and the readers.
B. invite readers as part of the poem's larger call to humanity.
C. welcome readers into the world of the poem and its subject.
D. address readers as fellow members of the human race.

**229.** Margaret Atwood said, "Language divides us into fragments, I wanted to be whole". Choose the option that correctly comments on the relationship between Margaret Atwood's words and the line from the above extract – "let's not speak in any language"

A. Atwood endorses Neruda's call to not speak in any language.
B. Atwood justifies Neruda's request to not engage in any speaking.
C. Atwood undermines Neruda's intent to stop and not speak in any language.
D. Atwood surrenders to Neruda's desire for silence and not speak in any language.

**230.** Why do you think the poet employs words like "exotic" and "strangeness"?

A. To highlight the importance of everyone being together suddenly for once.
B. To emphasize the frantic activity and chaos that usually envelops human life.
C. To indicate the unfamiliarity of a sudden moment without rush or without engine.
D. To direct us towards keeping quiet and how we would all be together in that silence.

**231.** Choose the option that correctly matches the idioms given in Column-A with their meanings in Column-B.

| Column-A | Column-B |
|---|---|
| 1. On the face of the earth | *(i)* In existence |
| 2. What on earth something | *(ii)* To do all possible to accomplish |
| 3. Move heaven and earth | *(iii)* To express surprise or shock |
| 4. The salt of the earth | *(iv)* To be good and worthy |

| | 1 | 2 | 3 | 4 |
|---|---|---|---|---|
| A. | *(i)* | *(iv)* | *(iii)* | *(ii)* |
| B. | *(i)* | *(iii)* | *(ii)* | *(iv)* |
| C. | *(ii)* | *(i)* | *(iv)* | *(iii)* |
| D. | *(iv)* | *(ii)* | *(iii)* | *(i)* |

**Directions (Qs. No. 232-235):** *Read the extract to attempt questions that follow:*

If we were not so single-minded about keeping our lives moving, and for once could do nothing, perhaps a huge silence might interrupt this sadness of never understanding ourselves and of threatening ourselves with death.

**232.** Look at the images given below. Choose the image to which the above extract can be seen as an appropriate response.

A.  B. 

C.  D. 

**233.** What do you think is the mood of the poet in the above extract?
A. gloomy, cynical
B. reflective, inspired
C. introspective, aware
D. critical, demotivated

**234.** Pick the option that does not complete the given sentence suitably, as per the extract. Threatening ourselves with death ________.
A. feeds on the fear of death.
B. challenges finiteness of life.
C. keeps us rushing through life.
D. makes us restless and impatient.

**235.** What might the "huge silence" signify?
A. melancholy B. understanding
C. discomfort D. flexibility

**Directions (Qs. No. 236-239):** *Read the extract to attempt questions that follow:*

**236.** Choose the option that best describes these statements, with reference to the poem.

**Statement I:** The poem 'Keeping Quiet' calls for change as much in the individual as human society at large.

**Statement II:** The poem 'Keeping Quiet' implies that individual change will lead to bigger societal change.

**Statement III:** Neruda believes that when people come together as a community, they will be able to bring a transformation in each person.

A. Statement I is True, Statement II is False, and Statement III cannot be inferred.
B. Statement I and II cannot be inferred, Statement III is True.
C. Statement I is True, Statements II and III cannot be inferred.
D. Statement I cannot be inferred, Statement II cannot be inferred, Statement III is False.

**237.** "What I want should not be confused with total inactivity". Choose the option that draws the most accurate parallel.

Keeping quiet: total inactivity = ________ : ________
A. reflection and death
B. silence and chaos
C. stagnation and introspection
D. mindfulness and fear

**238.** What statement does Neruda make about wars?
A. Wars are of varied kinds – internal, green wars, wars with gas, with fire etc.
B. Wars are wasteful and cause irrecoverable loss and damage to property and life.
C. Wars never yield any winners, and the loss is far greater than what can be measured.
D. Wars are unavoidable in the enduring struggle for human dignity and power.

**239.** "Now I'll count up to twelve and you keep quiet and I will go". Why does the poet wish to go at the end of the poem?
A. The poet does not believe people will be quiet.
B. The poet has already invested enough time.
C. The poet will move on and seek to inspire others.
D. The poet is marking the end of the poem by leaving.

**Directions (Qs. No. 240-243):** *Read the extract to attempt questions that follow:*

It would be an exotic moment
without rush, without engines,
we would all be together
in a sudden strangeness.

**240.** The rhyme of the poem is:
A. aabb B. abab
C. acbc D. None of the above

**241.** The 'exotic moment' that the poet refers to is, when:
A. the whole world is destroyed
B. all the people divided
C. all the people together with oneness
D. all the people speak only in one language

**242.** Which of the following is an example of anaphora?
A. We would all be together
B. Without rush, without engines
C. It would be an exotic moment
D. All the above

**243.** The phrase 'sudden strangeness' is an example of
A. Metaphor B. Simile
C. Oxymoron D. Alliteration

**Directions (Qs. No. 244-247):** *Read the extract to attempt questions that follow:*

Those who prepare green wars,
wars with gas, wars with fire,

victory with no survivors,
would put on clean clothes
and walk about with their
brothers
in the shade, doing nothing.

**244.** According to the poet wars would result in:
A. the victory of none
B. the death of all
C. complete annihilation of the world
D. above all

**245.** The phrase 'clean clothes' symbolises:
A. Peace B. Well ironed clothes
C. New clothes D. Spotless clothes

**246.** _______ walk about in the shade ________.
A. people who hate one another, singing
B. people who love one another dancing
C. people who wage wars, doing nothing
D. none of the above

**247.** The poetic device used in the fourth line of the extract is
A. Alliteration B. Personification
C. Transferred epithet D. None of the above

**Directions (Qs. No. 248-251):** *Read the extract to attempt questions that follow:*

What I want should not be
confused
with total inactivity.
Life is what it is about;
I want no truck with death.

**248.** Which of the following is not correct?
A. The poet wants all people to be idle doing nothing
B. The poet wants all people to keep quiet to introspect
C. The poet wants all people to be like brothers
D. The poet wants all people to love one another

**249.** The phrase 'Life is what it is about' means:
A. living life miserably
B. living life licentiously
C. living life carefully
D. living life as it is

**250.** 'I want no truck with death' indicates that the poet:
A. wants a truck for death
B. does not mean that inactivity is death
C. assures people that they would not face death at all
D. does not want a truck

**251.** The above extract is taken from _______ written by _______.
A. 'Keeping Quiet' by John Keats
B. 'My Mother at Sixty Six' by Pablo Neruda
C. 'Keeping Quiet' by Pablo Neruda
D. 'My Mother at Sixty Six' by John Keats

**Directions (Qs. No. 252-254):** *Read the extract to attempt questions that follow:*

Perhaps the Earth can teach us
as when everything seems dead
and later proves to be alive.

**252.** What can we learn from the Earth?
A. No hope for life after such large scale destruction of the planet
B. Hope for life in spite of the wars of all kinds referred to by the poet
C. No scope for life on the planet
D. Hope for life on other planets, after complete destruction of the Earth

**253.** The words 'everything seems dead' refer to:
A. animals' life B. plants' life
C. flora and fauna D. none of the above

**254.** The last line of poem ends on a/an ________ note.
A. pessimistic B. optimistic
C. disillusioned D. imaginary

## THE THIRD LEVEL

*By Jack Finney*

**255.** Choose the option that correctly identifies which statements are facts and which are opinion:
(*i*) Charley is suffering from mental sickness and he is hallucinating.
(*ii*) Charley's wife is concerned and cares for her husband.
(*iii*) Charley's vivid description of the Third level shows he has a strong desire to go to Galesburg.
(*iv*) Charley's friend Sam Weiner cheated Charley and escape from the third level
A. Fact-(*i*) opinion-(*ii*) (*iii*) (*iv*)
B. Fact-(*i*) and (*ii*) opinion-(*iii*) and (*iv*)
C. Fact-(*iii*) and (*ii*) opinion-(*iv*) and (*i*)
D. Fact-(*ii*) and (*iii*) opinion-(*i*) and (*iii*)

**256. Assertion (A):** Charley wanted to go to Galesburg Illinois.

**Reason (R):** He has heard many wonderful stories about Galesburg from his grandfather.
A. Both (A) and (R) are true and (R) is the correct explanation of (A)
B. Both (A) and (R) are true, but (R) is not the correct explanation of (A)
C. A is true, but (R) is false
D. A is false, but (R) is true

**257. Statement 1:** Charley finds it very strange that only he could see the third level.

**Statement 2:** The third level according to his friend is a place in his mind.
A. Statement 1 is true, but statement 2 is false.
B. Statement 1 is false, but statement 2 is true.

C. Both statement 1 and statement 2 cannot be inferred.
D. Both statement 1 and statement 2 can be inferred.

**258. Assertion (A):** The clerk refused to accept the money offered by Charley.

**Reason (R):** He thought the currency was fake.
A. (A) is true, but (R) is false
B. (A) is false, but (R) is true
C. Both (A) and (R) are true and (R) is the correct explanation of (A)
D. Both (A) and (R) are true, but (R) is not the correct explanation of (A)

**259. Statement 1:** Sam believed Charley was unhappy and looking for an escape. Charley's stamp-collection was a proof of it.

**Statement 2:** Charley thought all in the modern world are looking for an escape and his hobby of stamp-collection has nothing to do with it.
A. Both statements 1 and 2 can be inferred.
B. Statement 2 is false, but statement 1 is true.
C. Statement 1 is false, but statement 2 is true
D. Both statements 1 and statement 2 are false.

**260. Assertion (A):** Sam could not go back to his old business in Galesburg Illinois.

He will start a hay and grain business there.

**Reason (R):** Sam can not start his psychiatric practice there as life is peaceful and no one needs a psychiatrist.
A. (A) is true, but (R) is false
B. (A) is false, but (R) is true
C. Both (A) and (R) are true, but (R) is not the correct explanation of (A)
D. Both (A) and (R) are true and (R) is the correct explanation of (A)

**261. Assertion (A):** Charley looked at the newspaper. It was The World. He realized he was in a different world.

**Reason (R):** Charley knew that the world is no longer published in the world he came from.
A. Both (A) and (R) are false, but (R) is the true explanation of (A)
B. Both (A) and (R) are true and (R) is the true explanation of (A)
C. (A) is false (R) is true
D. (A) is true, but (R) is not the true explanation of (A)

**262. Assertion (A):** Charley bought old style currency to buy two tickets to Galesburg Illinois.

**Reason (R):** He wanted to start a business there.
A. (A) is true (R) is false
B. Both (A) and (R) are true
C. (A) is false, but (R) is true explanation of (A)
D. Both (A) and (R) are true and (R) is true explanation of (A)

**263.** Suppose you visit Galesburg Illinois of 1894. Which of the following advertisement is least likely to be found there.
A. Baby food—A life begins with full nutrition.
B. Dress designer-Reclaim yourself.
C. Tea: Refreshing start of your beautiful day.
D. Yoga camp: Stress buster.

**264. Assertion (A):** Charley idolized the peaceful perfect world of Galesburg Illinois.

**Reason (R):** Galesburg Illinois of 1894 was a stark contrast to post world war modern world.
A. (A) is true (R) is false.
B. Both (A) and (R) are true and (R) is the true explanation of (A)
C. Both (A) and (R) are true, but (R) is not the true explanation of (A)
D. (R) is true (A) is false

**265. Assertion (A):** Charley noticed that lights at the station were dim and flickering.

**Reason (R):** In 1894, open gaslights were used at the railway station.
A. Both (A) and (R) are false, but (R) is the true explanation of (A)
B. (A) is true and (R) is false, but (R) is not the true explanation of (A)
C. (A) is false (R) is true
D. Both (A) and (R) are true and (R) is the true explanation of (A)

**266. Assertion (A):** Charley believed that the Third Level do exist and his friend Sam Weiner has escaped to Galesburg Illinois.

**Reason (R):** Sam has disappeared and no one knows where has he gone.
A. (A) is true, but (R) is false
B. Both (A) and (R) are true, but (R) is not the true explanation of (A)
C. Both (A) and (R) are true and (R) is the true explanation of (A)
D. (A) is true, but (R) is not the true explanation of (A)

**267. Assertion (A):** The third level refers to the third underground level of the grand central railway station.

**Reason (R):** Sam Weiner's letter states it clearly that the Third level does exist.
A. Both (A) and (R) are true, but (R) does not explain (A)
B. Both (A) and (R) are false
C. Both (A) and (R) are true and (A) can be inferred from (R)
D. (A) is true (R) is False and (A) can not be inferred from (R)

**268. Assertion (A):** Charley wanted to reach home immediately so he wanted to take a train.

**Reason (R):** Charley has been in and out of Grand central station hundreds of times.

A. Both (A) and (R) are false, but (R) does explain (A)
B. Both (A) and (R) are true, but (A) can not be inferred from (R)
C. Both (A) and (R) are true and (A) can be inferred from (R)
D. (A) is true (R) is False and (A) cannot be inferred from (R)

**269. Assertion (A):** Charley's Grandfather lived in a peaceful world in 1894.

**Reason (R):** The first word war was some 20 years off in future and the Second World War was forty years in future.

A. (A) and (R) both are true and (A) can be inferred from (R)
B. Both (A) and (R) are true, but (A) cannot be inferred from (R)
C. (A) is true, but (R) is false
D. (A) is true, but (R) is false and (A) can be inferred from (R)

**270. Assertion (A):** Charley was a common man like any other 31 years old with normal life style.

**Reason (R):** Charley wanted a peaceful life without war and stress.

A. (A) is true, but (R) is false
B. (A) is false, but (R) is true
C. Both (A) and (R) are true and (R) is the true explanation of (A)
D. Both (A) and (R) are false

**271. Statement 1:** Charley was among the many people who were suffering from mental ennui due to monotony of life.

**Statement 2:** Louisa, his wife was very happy and contented with her life.

A. Statement 1 can be inferred, but statement 2 can not be inferred
B. Statement 1 and statement 2 both can be inferred.
C. Statement 2 can be inferred, but statement 1 can not be inferred.
D. Statement 1 and 2 can not be inferred.

**272. Statement 1:** Eggs were thirteen cents a dozens in 1894.

**Statement 2:** Cost of living was comparatively less in 1894.

A. Statement 2 can be inferred, but statement 1 can not be inferred.
B. Statement 1 and 2 can not be inferred
C. Statement 1 can be inferred, but statement 2 can not be inferred
D. Statement 1 is true and statement 2 can be inferred.

**273. Assertion (A):** At the stamp and coin store I go to, I found out that Sam bought eight hundred dollars' worth of old-style currency.

**Reason (R):** That ought to set him up in a nice little hay, feed and grain business; he always said that's what Sam really wished he could do.

A. Both (A) and (R) are wrong and (R) does not explain (A)
B. Both (A) and (R) are true and (R) explains (A)
C. (A) is true, but (R) is false
D. (A) is false, but (R) is true

**274 Assertion (A):** Charley did not share his thoughts about the tunnel under the city with Sam.

**Reason (R):** Charley thought his job would be at stake if he shared these thoughts.

A. Both (A) and (R) are true, but (R) does not explain (A)
B. Both (A) and (R) are false and (R) does not explain (A)
C. (A) is true and (R) is false
D. Both (A) and (R) are false

**275.** Imagine Charley visit India on 25 th March, 2020 to India. Which of the following would be the Lead Story in Indian Newspaper?

A. Indian wins 2 Gold Medals in Japan Olympics.
B. Nifty bulls have a dominant day.
C. Telecom sector is ailing in India.
D. P.M. announces 21 days nation-wide lockdown.

**Directions:** *Read each of the following passages carefully and choose the best answer to each question out of the four alternatives.*

### PASSAGE-1

The paper inside wasn't blank. It read:

941 Willard Street
Galesburg, Illinois
July 18, 1894

Charley I got to wishing that you were right. Then I got to believing you were right. And, Charley, it's true; I found the third level! I've been here two weeks, and right now, down the street at the Daly's, someone is playing a piano, and they're all out on the front porch singing Seeing Nelly Home.' And I'm invited over for lemonade. Come on back, Charley and Louisa. Keep looking till you find the third level! It's worth it, believe me!

The note is signed Sam

"Charley I got to wishing that you were right. Then I got to believing you were right"

**276.** What does the writer wish to believe?

A. That the third level does exist.

B. That Charley was not stable.
C. That the write was there in Galesburg.
D. That the tunnel does exist under the city.

**277.** Where has the writer been for two weeks?
A. In the third level.
B. In New York.
C. In Galesburg Illinois.
D. In the future where life is peaceful.

**278.** What does the letter state about the mood of the write?
A. Anxious B. Depressed
C. Excited D. Nonchalant

**279.** Who are 'THEY' out on the front porch singing 'Seeing Nelly Home'?
A. Sam's friends.
B. People of Galesburg Illinois.
C. A Singers' group.
D. Charley's relatives.

## PASSAGE-2

"But I've never again found the corridor that leads to the third level at Grand Central Station, although I've tried often enough. Louisa was pretty worried when I told her all this, and didn't want me to look for the third level any more, and after a while I stopped; I went back to my stamps. But now we're both looking, every weekend, because now we have proof that the third level is still there. My friend Sam Weiner disappeared! Nobody knew where, but I sort of suspected because Sam's a city boy, and I used to tell him about Galesburg — I went to school there — and he always said he liked the sound of the place. And that's where he is, all right. In 1894."

**280.** Why do you think the speaker is looking for The Third Level?
A. He wanted to meet his grandfather.
B. He wanted to go to Galesburg Illinois.
C. He wanted to meet his friends in the third level.
D. He wanted to prove to everyone that Third level does exist.

**281.** What is being referred by Sam's *a city boy?*
A. Life in a city is peaceful
B. Life in a city is very challenging and stressful.
C. Boys in cities are carefree and happy
D. City boys are smart and would not believe in fantasy.

**282.** How would you describe the speaker's vision of Galesburg Illinois?
A. Wishful escapism
B. Idealized sentimentality
C. Nostalgic simplicity
D. Dream like fantasy

**283.** Which word from the following can be used in place of Suspected'?
A. Doubted B. Trusted
C. Confined D. Accused

## PASSAGE-3

Have you ever been there? It's a wonderful town still, with big old frame houses, huge lawns, and tremendous trees whose branches meet overhead and roof the streets. And in 1894, summer evenings were twice as long, and people sat out on their lawns, the men smoking cigars and talking quietly, the women waving palm-leaf fans, with the fire-flies all around, in a peaceful world. To be back there with the First World War still twenty years off, and World War II over forty years in the future... I wanted two tickets for that.

**284.** Who is speaking to whom in the given extract?
A. Charley to Louisa
B. Charley to the reader
C. Sam to Charley
D. Charley to Sam

**285.** The given extract is **NOT** an example of:
A. Analogy B. Metaphor
C. Imagery D. Allegory

**286.** "Men smoking cigars and women waving palm-leaf" refers to a society:
A. Orthodox B. Conservative
C. Liberal D. Modern

**287.** Which word from the extract is an antonym of small?
A. Huge B. Tremendous
C. Long D. Both (A) and (B)

## PASSAGE-4

Well, maybe, but my grandfather didn't need any refuge from reality; things were pretty nice and peaceful in his day, from all I hear, and he started my collection. It's a nice collection too, blocks of four of practically every U.S. issue, first-day covers, and so on. President Roosevelt collected stamps too, you know".

**288.** What collection is referred in the extract?
A. Money collection B. Coin collection
C. Toys collection D. Stamp Collection

**289.** Which word from the following is an antonym of 'Refuge'?
A. Escape B. Furnish
C. Deny D. Sanction

**290.** What does the narrator mean by 'My grandfather started my collection':
A. His grandfather helped him collect coins.
B. His grandfather was a philanthropist.
C. He picked the hobby of stamp collection from his grandfather.
D. His grandfather loved planting trees.

**291.** Which other story from your text-books has a reference to President Roosevelt.

A. Deep Water B. Lost Spring
C. Last Lesson D. None of the above

## PASSAGE-5

There were brass spittoons on the floor, and across the station a glint of light caught my eye; a man was pulling a gold watch from his vest pocket. He snapped open the cover, glanced at his watch and frowned. He wore a derby hat, a black four-button suit with tiny lapels, and he had a big, black, handlebar mustache. Then I looked around and saw that everyone in the station was dressed like eighteen-ninety-something.

**292.** What caused the glint of light?

A. The bras spittoons
B. The gold watch
C. The sun
D. The chimneys

**293.** The above extract is an example of:

A. Allusion B. Enjambment
C. Metaphor D. Imagery

**294.** The word in the extract which means 'to look angry and serious' is:

A. Frown B. Glint
C. Lapels D. Glance

**295.** Which of the following sentences uses the word 'Snap' as a noun?

A. He shifted his weight and a twig snapped.
B. I think this is too important for a snap decision.
C. He shut the book with a snap and stood up.
D. The brake pedal has just snapped off.

**296.** 'Dressed like eighteen-ninety-something' which literary device has been used here?

A. Metaphor B. Paradox
C. Anti-thesis D. Simile

## PASSAGE-6

The corridor I was in began angling left and slanting downward and I thought that was wrong, but I kept on walking. All I could hear was the empty sound of my own footsteps and I didn't pass a soul. Then I heard that sort of hollow roar ahead that means open space and people talking. The tunnel turned sharp left; I went down a short flight of stairs and came out on the third level at Grand Central Station.

**297.** The corridor angling left and slanting downward is an example of....

A. A blend
B. An intersection between time and space
C. Hallucination
D. Dizziness

**298.** What made the narrator think that he was in a 'wrong corridor'?

A. Because it was falling down.
B. Because it was wobbly.
C. Because it was behaving strange.
D. All of the above

**299.** What is meant by "I didn't pass a soul"?

A. He didn't find any other person there.
B. He didn't cross any ghost.
C. He couldn't see his shadow.
D. None of the above

**300.** Which of the following does **NOT** mean 'Hollow'?

A. Void B. Empty
C. Vacant D. Solid

## PASSAGE-7

But that's the reason, he said, and my friends all agreed. Everything points to it, they claimed. My stamp collecting, for example; that's a temporary refuge from reality.

**301.** In what context the word 'reason' is referred here?

A. That charley was hallucinating
B. That charley was day dreaming
C. That charley was unhappy and looking for an escape from reality
D. That Charley was not successful in his career.

**302.** With whom did all Charley's friends agree?

A. Psychiatrist, Sam B. Louisa, his wife
C. His grandfather D. His boss

**303.** What according to Sam and his friends was a temporary refuse from reality for Charley?

A. His day–dreaming
B. His stamp collection
C. His visits to the third level
D. His nostalgia about Galesburg.

**304.** The word 'Refuge' from the passage can be best replaced with:

A. Shade B. Rest
C. Leisure D. Shelter

## PASSAGE-8

That night, among my oldest first-day covers, I found one that shouldn't have been there. But there it was. It was there because someone had mailed it to my grandfather at his home in Galesburg; that's what the address on the envelope said. And it had been there since July 18, 1894 and I opened it

**305.** Why should this particular first day cover not be there?

A. Because it was a modern first day cover from the future.
B. Because it was an old first day cover from the past.

C. Because it was not addressed to his grandfather.
D. Because it could not have been collected by his grandfather.

**306.** Why is Charley not aware of this particular first day cover?
A. Because it appeared recently.
B. It was not meant for him.
C. It was addressed to Louisa, his wife.
D. He was forgetful.

**307.** The Picture of President Garfield indicates that the first day cover was:
A. New one B. Slightly old
C. Recent one D. Definitely old

**308.** What can be inferred from the extract regarding this first day cover?
A. That someone from the present travelled to the past.
B. That someone from the future has written this
C. That Charley was followed by secret society
D. That Charley was being tricked.

## PASSAGE-9

Now, I don't know why this should have happened to me. I'm just an ordinary guy named Charley, thirty-one years old, and I was wearing a tan gabardine suit and a straw hat with a fancy band; I passed a dozen men who looked just like me. And I wasn't trying to escape from anything; I just wanted to get home to Louisa, my wife.

**309.** What has happened to the narrator?
A. He got transported to the third level of grand central station.
B. He got transported to Galesburg Illinois
C. He got transported to the future.
D. He recently met an alien.

**310.** "I passed a dozen men just like me" indicates?
A. Modern fashion
B. Modern Life style
C. Monotony of modern life
D. Lack of variety in fashion

**311.** Why was the narrator in hurry?
A. He wanted to go for a party with his wife.
B. He wanted to go for a movie with his wife.
C. He had some important meeting.
D. He was already late from office.

**312.** Which word from the extract means a 'dust coat'?
A. Gabardine B. Straw
C. fancy D. None of the above

## PASSAGE-10

The clerk figured the fare he glanced at my fancy hatband, but he figured the fare and I had enough for two coach tickets, one way. But when I counted out the money and looked up, the clerk was staring at me. He nodded at the bills. That ain't money, mister, he said, and if you re trying to skin me, you won't get very far, and he glanced at the cash drawer beside him.

**313.** Why did the clerk glance at Charley's fancy hatband?
A. Because it was just like his own hat.
B. Because charley's hat was not an ordinary sight for him.
C. Because Charley had a star in his hat band.
D. Because Charley had a mysterious mark on his hat.

**314.** Why did Charley wanted to buy two tickets?
A. He wanted to go to Galesburg Illinois with his wife.
B. He wanted to go to meet his grandfather with Sam.
C. He wanted to escape in the past with his boss.
D. He wanted to go to the future with his wife.

**315** Which of the following does **NOT** explain the expression "If you want to skin me" from the passage.
A. If you want to trick me
B. If you want to cheat me
C. If you want to deceive me
D. If you want to fight with me

**316.** Which word from the extract means 'take a brief or hurried look'?
A. Nodded B. Stare
C. Glance D. Figure

## PASSAGE-11

"Once I got into a tunnel about a mile long and came out in the lobby of Roosevelt Hotel. Another time I came up in an office building on forty-sixth-street, three blocks away":

**317.** Which of the following statement is true in the given context?
A. The narrator knew about the tunnel and he has been exploring various places.
B. The narrator has been in and out of the third level for quite a few times.
C. The narrator has been visiting his grandfather in Galesburg Illinois frequently.
D. The narrator was aware that he has been wandering here and there quite often.

**318.** Who is 'I' in the extract?
A. Sam B. Louisa
C. Charley D. None of the above

**319.** What can be inferred by the 'tunnel' from this extract?
A. A gateway into past.
B. A portal into another planet.
C. A gateway into the future.
D. A portal into an alien world.

320. Which word from the extract means 'An Underground Passageway'?
A. Lobby B. Office
C. Tunnel D. None of the above

## PASSAGE-12

But I've never again found the corridor that leads to the third level at Grand Central Station, although I've tried often enough. Louisa was pretty worried when I told her all this, and didn't want me to look for the third level any more, and after a while I stopped; I went back to my stamps. But now we're both looking, every weekend.

321 Which corridor the speaker is looking?
A. The corridor leading to the third level.
B. The corridor which was under construction.
C. The corridor that took him to the tunnel.
D. None of the above

322. What made Louisa worried?
A. She knew that the speaker was hallucinating.
B. She was concerned about the well-being of Charley.
C. She thought Charley was fantasizing.
D. All of the above

323. Why did the speaker stop looking for the third level after some time?
A. He was not well.
B. He went to his hobby of stamp-collection.
C. All his efforts couldn't locate the third level.
D. He realized he was fantasizing.

324. 'Now we both are looking' who are WE here?
A. Charley and Louisa.
B. Charley and Sam.
C. Charley and his boss.
D. All of the above

## PASSAGE-13

He said I was unhappy. That made my wife kind of mad, but he explained that he meant the modern world is full of insecurity, fear, war, worry and all the rest of it, and that I just want to escape. Well, who doesn't? Everybody I know wants to escape, but they don't wander down into any third level at Grand Central Station.

325. He said I was Unhappy. Identify ***I*** and ***He*** in the sentence.
A. Charley and his boss.
B. Charley and his grandfather.
C. Charley and Sam.
D. Charley and his neighbour.

326. 'That made my wife kind of mad' What does ***Mad*** mean here?
A. Jealous B. Insecure
C. Crazy D. Angry

327. Why was Charley's wife angry?
A. She thought he was going crazy.
B. She thought he was unhappy because of her.
C. She thought Charley was going to Galesburg leaving her alone.
D. None of the above

328. Which of the following does **NOT** mean 'Wander'?
A. Stroll B. Roam
C. Travel D. Cease

329. What was the Third Level?
A. An imaginary discovery of the of Charley's mind.
B. A big tunnel on the grand central station
C. A time-machine on the grand central station.
D. A level in the game that charley had been playing.

330. Why did the narrator go to a psychiatrist?
A. Because he was unhappy and wanted to know why
B. Because he went through an experience no one else did
C. Because he was unhappy and wanted to know why
D. Because he was depressed

331. What is the genre of the lesson "The Third Level"?
A. Historical Fiction B. Tragedy
C. Science Fiction D. Fantasy

332. How frequently the author has been in and out of the grand central?
A. He is a regular visitor
B. He has been in and out of the grand central hundreds of times
C. The author travels every day from grand central.
D. The author visits the grand central occasionally.

333. What does Sam think of Modern Life?
A. That life if full of stress, war and fear.
B. That life is easy and enjoyable
C. That the modern world is full of wonders
D. That the modern world is a great place to be

334. What is a first day cover?
A. It's a stamp issued on the first day of the year.
B. It's a stamp issued in the name of the first citizen of a country
C. An envelope bearing a stamp postmarked on its day of issue.
D. An envelope issued on the first day of the year.

335. As a Metaphor of the title 'The Third Level' which of the following would **NOT** be an appropriate explanation?
A. The bridge between the past and present.
B. The excruciating monotony of the modern life.
C. The convergence of reality and fantasy.
D. The dire need for an alternate plane of understanding

**336.** What was the date on the newspaper?
A. June 15, 1894 B. June 11, 1894
C. June 10, 1894 D. July 13, 1894

**337.** Why did Charley visit the Library?
A. To gather more information about the third level.
B. To read more books on Time-Travel.
C. To confirm the main story of the newspaper.
D. To find a book he had seen in the third level.

**338.** How would you Sam describe Charley?
A. Escapist B. Carefree
C. Happy go lucky D. Workaholic

**339.** What is the name of Charley's wife?
A. Aliza B. Alisa
C. Louisa D. Lucia

**340.** What do you call a person who collects stamps?
A. Ticket collector B. Philatelist
C. Stamp-Collector D. Philanthropist

**341.** What was the name of the newspaper?
A. The Reuters B. The Telegraph
C. The Statesmen D. The world

**342.** What does the time table mention regarding grand central station?
A. That there are three levels
B. That there are two levels
C. That there is only one level
D. None of the above

**343.** Why did Charley decide to take sub way from Grand central station?
A. He used to take a train from there everyday
B. He wanted to go to Galesburg Illinois
C. He accidently reached there
D. He was late so he took a train to reach home fast.

**344.** Who did Charley discuss his strange visit to the third level?
A. His psychiatrist B. His friends
C. His wife D. His grandfather

**345.** How did Sam interpret charley's visit to the third level?
A. Waking wish fulfillment
B. Escape
C. Dream come true
D. Both (A) and (B)

**346.** What are some of the things Charley observe at Third Level?
A. Brass spittoons
B. Handlebar moustaches
C. Flickering chimney lights
D. All of the above

**347.** Why did Charley make a hasty retreat from the Third Level?
A. He came back because he was scared of the experience.
B. He came back hurriedly as he thought he will be arrested.
C. He came back to share this experience with his family.
D. He came back as he was concerned about his wife.

**348.** Why did Charley withdraw all his savings?
A. To get it exchanged in old style currency
B. To buy a home in Galesburg Illinois
C. To buy a gift for his wife
D. To pay fee to his psychiatrist

**349.** Why did Louisa become mad at Charley when Sam diagnosed him as unhappy?
A. She thought her husband was fantasizing.
B. She thought she was the reason for his unhappiness.
C. She thought her husband was an escapist.
D. She thought Sam was misguiding her husband.

**350.** What is Sam's take on Charley's hobby of stamp-collection?
A. Medium of escape
B. Connection between past and present
C. A good part time hobby
D. A good source of information

**351.** What business would have Sam established in Galesburg for a living?
A. Practice psychiatry
B. Become a flute player
C. Hay and grain business
D. Farming

**352.** What was the main story about on the first page of *The World?*
A. President Roosevelt
B. President Garfield
C. President Lincoln
D. President Cleveland

**353.** Why did Sam feel that Charley wanted to escape?
A. He feels charley was stressed because the modern world is full of war and worry.
B. He feels Charley was not happy with his job.
C. He feels that Charley was not happy with his wife.
D. He feels Charley's boss was very demanding.

**354. Explain:** Waking dream wish fulfillment.
A. An experience which takes one to future.
B. An experience which makes one forget the present.
C. An experience which takes one in the past.
D. An experience where one becomes forgetful.

**355.** What does Charley's letter to Sam signify?
A. A proof of time travel
B. A proof that third level does exist
C. A blend of reality with fantasy
D. A proof that Charley has been to Galesburg Illinois.

**356.** Why did Charley compare the grand central station with a tree?
A. The shape of the central station is like that of a tree.
B. Like a tree, the grand central station is very high.
C. Like a tree the grand central gives shade to its visitors.
D. Like the roots of a tree the grand central station is expanding.

**357.** Which US president was a philatelist mentioned in the story?
A. President Garfield
B. President Roosevelt
C. President Cleveland
D. President Jackson

**358.** What for Sam was invited according to the letter?
A. For a lemonade
B. For a dance party
C. For a birthday party
D. For a rain dance party

**359.** Why did the clerk at the ticket window refuse to accept Charley's money?
A. Money was insufficient
B. Money was torn
C. Money was old style
D. His money was of modern times

**360.** Which of the following is apt to justify the story 'the third level'.
A. "I like nonsense; it wakes up the brain cells. Fantasy is a necessary ingredient in living". —Dr. Seuss
B. "Fantasy is hardly an escape from reality. It's a way of understanding it". —Lloyd Alexander
C. "Stories of imagination tend to upset those without one". —Terry Pratchett
D. Fantasy and reality often overlap—Walt Disney

**361.** With regards to an intersection of time and space in the story, which of the following is **NOT** true?
A. People with side burns, handle-bar moustaches and women in sheep skin coat
B. Open gaslight and smaller booths
C. A large no of ticket windows
D. Broader Currency notes

**362.** What is the significance of 1894 in the lesson?
A. It represents a utopian world
B. It stands for the past
C. Charley's grandfather lived there
D. All of the above

**363.** Out of the following which one is the best way to overcome harsh realities of life?
A. Watching TV B. Reading good books
C. Day dreaming D. Fantasizing

## THE ENEMY
*By Pearl S Buck*

**Directions:** *Read each of the following passages carefully and choose the best answer to each question out of the four alternatives.*

### PASSAGE-1

It was at this moment that both of them saw something black come out of the mist. It was a man.

**364.** Who was watching the mist?
A. The fisherman
B. Doctor Sadao and Hana
C. Tom
D. Hana

**365.** Who came out of the mist?
A. General Takima B. The fisherman
C. Hana D. A man

**366.** The word 'both' refers to:
A. The fisherman and the police
B. Dr sadao and Hana
C. The gardener and cook
D. The enemy and General Takima

**367.** From where did the man come out from the mist?
A. From the black B. From the ocean
C. From the house D. From the tree

### PASSAGE-2

His father had taken him often to the islands of those seas, and never had failed to say to the little brave boy at his side, "Those islands yonder, they are the stepping stones to the future of Japan".

**368.** Who is referred to as "him" in the above extract?
A. Dr. Sadao Hoki B. Hana
C. The gardener D. Dr Sadao's father

**369.** Who is referred as "the little brave boy" in the above extract? What is his full name?
A. Dr Sadao Hoki B. Hana
C. The General D. Tom

**370.** Dr. Sadao was ..........
A. a psychiatrist B. an engineer
C. a professor D. a surgeon

**371.** Who is the speaker?
A. Dr. Sadao's father B. Dr. Sadao
C. Hana D. The white man

## PASSAGE-3

"A White man!" Hana whispered. Yes, it was a white man. The wet cap fell away and there was his wet yellow hair, long, as though for many weeks it had not been cut and upon his young and tortured face was a rough yellow beard.

**372.** What did Dr Sadao and Hana mean by 'white man'?
A. the man whose face appeared white due to sand
B. an American prisoner of war
C. a man wearing white shirt
D. none of these

**373.** Hana's remark "A white man!" on seeing the white man indicated what she was feeling. Pick the option that correctly States the feelings.
1. Horror 2. Shocked
3. Unfamiliar 4. Annoyed
A. 1 and 2 B. 2 and 3
C. 2 and 4 D. 1 and 4

**374.** How did the white man's face appear?
A. Young C. Fresh
B. Tortured D. Both (A) and (B)

**375.** Why didn't the white man know the presence of Dr. Sadao and Hana?
A. As he was sleeping
B. As he was pretending to be unconscious
C. As he was unconscious
D. None of these

## PASSAGE-4

"Don't faint", he said sharply. He did not put down his exploring instrument. "If I stop now, the man will surely die." She clapped her hands to her mouth and leaped up and ran out of the room. Outside in the garden he heard her retching but he went on with his work.

**376.** "Don't faint", he said. Who said these words and to whom?
A. Dr Sadao to Hana
B. The cook to the Gardener
C. Dr. Sadao to the patient
D. The patient to Dr. Sadao

**377.** Who would die? Who was retching?
1. Dr Sadao's wife 2. The General
3. The enemy Soldier 4. The old Gardener
A. 1 and 2 B. 3 and 1
C. 2 and 1 D. 3 and 4

**378.** Why did Dr. Sadao feel impatient and irritable with the prisoner?
A. It was getting late at night
B. He was tired and sleepy
C. He would not get paid
D. He could not tend to his wife

**379.** Where was the white man?
A. in the garden
B. on the beach
C. in the room of Sadao's father
D. with the general

## PASSAGE-5

"My old master's son knows very well what he ought to do," he now said, pinching a bud from a bush as he spoke. "When the man was so near death why did he not let him bleed?"

**380.** "When the man was so near-death why did he not let him bleed ?" Who said these words?
A. The cook B. Yumi
C. The gardener D. The General

**381.** What is the feeling of the speaker?
A. Sarcasm B. Sadness
C. Indignation D. Appreciative

**382.** How had the man come to be bleeding?
A. He was scratched by the brambles head first
B. He had tripped and fallen
C. His body was torn by the rocks flanking the beach
D. He had been shot

**383.** Dr. Sadao's helping the white soldier displays which qualities of his?
1. He was above the narrow prejudices.
2. He was a bit selfish when it came to his country's matter.
3. He considered his duty above all the other things.
4. He was cunning and egoist person.
A. 1 and 2 B. 2 and 3
C. 1 and 3 D. 3 and 4

## PASSAGE-6

Now Sadao remembered the wound and with his expert finger he began to search for it. Blood flowed freshly at his touch.

**384.** Who was wounded?
A. Sadao B. Hana
C. The White Soldier D. Yumi

**385.** Which word best suits 'trained' in the extract?
A. touch B. tended
C. expat D. expert

**386.** What kind of wound the man had?
A. It was a knife stab
B. It was an injury
C. It was a gun shot
D. The rock had struck the wound

**387.** What was the dilemma that Dr. Sadao faced?
A. Whether he should marry Hana or not.
B. Whether he should leave Japan and settle in another country.

C. Whether he should study further or start practice
D. Whether he should save the life of the white soldier or let him die.

**PASSAGE-7**

We must simply tell them that we intend to give him to the police— as indeed we must, Sadao

**388.** Who is the speaker of the above extract?
A. Hana B. Dr. Sadao
C. Yumi D. The General

**389.** Who is referred as them in the above extract?
A. The Police B. The Fishermen
C. The Servants D. The Officials

**390.** Which word in the extract means 'certainly'?
A. Simply B. Intend
C. Indeed D. Give

**391.** How many of them were employed at the house by the speaker of the extract?
A. Three B. Four
C. Six D. Two

**PASSAGE-8**

He stood gazing down on the motionless man. This man must have extraordinary vitality or he would have been dead by now. But then he was very young—perhaps not yet twenty five.

**392.** Who is referred as 'he' in 'he stood gazing'?
A. The police B. The gardener
C. Dr. Sadao D. The General

**393.** What was the age of the man?
A. Twenty five B. Thirty five
C. Forty five D. Fifty five

**394.** In whose bedroom the man was lying?
A. In the children's bedroom
B. In the master bedroom
C. The bedroom of the old man
D. The bedroom of the General.

**395.** Which word in the extract is the synonym of "strength"?
A. Vitality B. Extraordinary
C. Motionless D. Gazing

**PASSAGE-9**

When she saw him her thick lips folded themselves into stubbornness. "I have never washed a white man", she said, "and I will not wash so dirty a one now".

**396.** Who is referred as "she" in the above extract?
A. Hana B. The Cook
C. Yumi D. The Girl

**397.** Who is the listener of the above extract?
A. The Cook B. Hana
C. The Girl D. Yumi

**398.** Was "the White man" conscious when the above lines is spoken?
A. Yes, he was conscious
B. No, he was unconscious
C. He was sleeping
D. He was pretending sleeping

**399.** Which phrase is the antonym of "always"?
A. Thick B. Never
C. Will D. Now

**PASSAGE-10**

"Well, well" the old man said in a tone of amazement, "so I did! But you see, I suffered a good deal. The truth is, I thought of nothing but myself. In short, I forgot my promise to you".

**400.** Who is referred to as "you" in the above extract?
A. The General B. Doctor Sadao
C. The Assassins D. The Gardener

**401.** Who is referred to "The old man" in the above extract?
A. The Gardener B. Doctor Sadao
C. The General D. The Assassins

**402.** Who suffered a good deal in the above extract?
A. The General B. Doctor Sadao
C. The Assassins D. The Gardener

**403.** Who failed to keep the promise?
A. The Gardener B. Doctor Sadao
C. The General D. The Assassins

**PASSAGE-11**

"It is very unfortunate that this man should have washed up on your door step". He said irritably.

**404.** Who is the speaker of the above lines?
A. The Gardener B. Doctor Sadao
C. The General D. The Assassins

**405.** Who is the listener of the above lines?
A. The General B. Doctor Sadao
C. The Assassins D. The Gardener

**406.** Who is referred to as "the man"?
A. The General
B. Doctor Sadao
C. The White American soldier
D. The Gardener

**407.** Which word in the extract is the synonym of "Unlucky"?
A. Irritably B. Washed
C. Unfortunate D. The man

**408.** **Statement 1:** Those islands yonder, they are the 'stepping – stones' to the future of Japan.

**Statement 2:** Dr. Sadao Hoki's father had dreamt of a bright future for his son and he hadn't been disappointed.

A. Statement 1 is true, but statement 2 is false
B. Statement 1 is false, but statement 2 is true
C. Both statement 1 and statement 2 cannot be inferred
D. Both statement 1 and statement 2 can be inferred

**409. Statement 1:** Dr. Sadao had waited to fall in love with Hana until he was sure she believed in traditional Japanese values else his father would never have welcomed her.

**Statement 2:** Sadao and Hana's chance meeting had turned out to be a very fruitful relationship.
A. Statement 1 is true, but statement 2 is true
B. Statement 1 is false, but statement 2 is true
C. Both statement 1 and statement 2 cannot be inferred
D. Both statement 1 and statement 2 can be inferred

**410. Statement 1:** Doctor Sadao is not a dedicated surgeon, kind and compassionate towards people in distress.

**Statement 2:** He faced conflict of duty as a doctor and a citizen of Japan.
A. Statement 1 is true, but statement 2 is false
B. Statement 1 is false, but statement 2 is true
C. Both statement 1 and statement 2 cannot be inferred
D. Both statement 1 and statement 2 can be inferred

**411. Statement 1:** Hana was a balanced woman.

**Statement 2:** She was graceful and dignified about the servants when they were leaving the house.
A. Statement 1 is true, but statement 2 is false
B. Statement 1 is false, but statement 2 is true
C. Both statement 1 and statement 2 cannot be inferred
D. Both statement 1 and statement 2 can be inferred

**412. Statement 1:** The General was selfish by nature, thinks of his treatment only.

**Statement 2:** He had no faith in Sadao as a doctor.
A. Statement 1 is true, but statement 2 is false
B. Statement 1 is false, but statement 2 is true
C. Both Statement 1 and Statement 2 cannot be inferred
D. Both Statement 1 and Statement 2 can be inferred

**413. Statement 1:** The gardener felt that Sadao should have let the soldier to die.

**Statement 2:** He thought that the sea and the gun would take revenge if he saves the soldier.
A. Statement 1 is true, but Statement 2 is false
B. Statement 1 is true, but Statement 2 is true
C. Both Statement 1 and Statement 2 cannot be inferred
D. Both Statement 1 and Statement 2 can be inferred

**414.** Two statements (Assertion and Reasons) are given below: Choose the option from the one that follow the Statements.

**Assertion (A):** Dr. Sadao was a true Patriot.

**Reason (R):** He informed the general about the presence of the white man in his house.
A. Both (A) & (R) are true and (R) is the correct explanation of (A)
B. Both (A) & (R) are true, but (R) is not the correct explanation of (A)
C. (A) is true, but (R) is false
D. (A) is false, but (R) is true

**415. Assertion (A):** The General sent the assassins to the house of Dr. Sadao.

**Reason (R):** He himself was in pain and needed Dr. Sadao's help.
A. Both (A) & (R) are true and (R) is the correct explanation of (A)
B. Both (A) & (R) are true, but (R) is not the correct explanation of (A)
C. (A) is true, but (R) is false
D. (A) is false, but (R) is true

**416.** Who wrote *Don Juan*?
A. Shakespeare B. Tennyson
C. Byron D. T.S. Eliot

**417.** Who wrote *The Life of Johnson*?
A. Boswell B. Macaulay
C. Churchill D. Sir Walter Raleigh

**418.** *Priest's Nun's Tale* was written by:
A. Spenser B. Charles Lamb
C. Tennyson D. Chaucer

**419.** Who is said to have first used the term "Metaphysics"?
A. Matthew Arnold B. Sidney
C. Donne D. Dr. Johnson

**420.** The writer of *Volpone* is:
A. Johnson B. Milton
C. Jonson D. Shelley

**421.** Which is the correct chronological sequence?
A. Spenser—Chaucer—Milton—Donne
B. Spenser—Wordsworth—Tennyson—T.S. Eliot
C. Milton—Shakespeare—Philip Larkin—Keats
D. Auden—Eliot—Shelley—Keats

**422.** *Pilgrim's Progress* was written by:
A. Milton B. Shelley
C. Swinburne D. John Bunyan

**423.** The writer of the line : *"Stone walls do not a prison make"* is:
A. Lovelace B. Milton
C. W.B. Yeats D. T.S. Eliot

**424.** *"Monkey's Paw"* is a:
A. Poem B. Drama
C. Short story D. Novel

**425.** Lyrical Ballads appeared in:
A. 1690 B. 1798
C. 1802 D. 1800

**426.** The writer of *'A Pair of Blue Eyes'* is:
A. Thackeray B. Dickens
C. George Eliot D. Thomas Hardy

**427.** *Hard Times* was written by:
A. Thackeray B. Dickens
C. Trollope D. Marquese

**428.** Which of the following poets was most impressed by the German philosophy?
A. Chaucer B. Wordsworth
C. Coleridge D. Southey

**429.** The two cities referred to in *"A Tale of Two Cities"* are:
A. London and Paris
B. London and Rome
C. Rome and Paris
D. Moscow and Rome

**430.** *The Peasant's Bread* is a story by:
A. Maupassant B. Tagore
C. R.K. Narayan D. Tolstoy

**431.** *The Financial Express* was written by:
A. Raja Rao B. R.K. Narayan
C. Tagore D. Mulk Raj Anand

**432.** *"Negative Capability"* is a term associated with:
A. Tagore B. Shelley
C. Keats D. Coleridge

**433.** The most impressive treatment of "imagination" has been given by:
A. Coleridge B. Shelley
C. Eliot D. Yeats

**434.** *Lady Chatterley's Lover* was banned because it was considered:
A. obscene B. revolutionary
C. obscurantist D. None of these

**435.** *For Whom The Bell Tolls* was written by:
A. Marquese B. Hemingway
C. Hawthorne D. None of these

**436.** The writer of : *"A Pair of Mustachios"* is:
A. Anand B. Tagore
C. Raja Rao D. Anita Desai

**437.** The writer of *Scarlet Letter* is:
A. Henry James B. James Joyce
C. Hawthorne D. None of these

**438.** Rousseau is associated with:
A. French Revolution
B. American War of Independence
C. Russian (Bolshevik) Revolution
D. None of these

**439.** Who wrote *'Train to Pakistan'*?
A. Narayan B. Manohar Malgaon
C. Khushwant Singh D. Anand

**440.** Who is the writer of *Azadi*?
A. R.K. Narayan B. Khushwant Singh
C. Tagore D. Chaman Nahal

**441.** *"The God of Small Things"* is written by:
A. R.K. Narayan B. Hemingway
C. Graham Greene D. Arundhati Roy

**442.** Who wrote the poem *"Listeners"*?
A. Tennyson B. Thomas Hood
C. Goldsmith D. Walter de la Mare

**443.** In writing *"Canterbury Tales"* Chaucer was influenced by:
A. Decameron B. The Divine Comedy
C. The Holy Bible D. None of these

**444.** *'Animal Farm'* was written by:
A. James Joyce B. Virginia Woolf
C. George Orwell D. Hemingway

**445.** Shobha De is a:
A. poet B. dramatist
C. novelist D. an actress

**446.** Dunciad was written by:
A. Dryden B. Pope
C. Tennyson D. Shelley

**447.** Bernard Shaw got the Nobel Prize for:
A. Pygmalion B. Man and Superman
C. Saint Joan D. None of these

**448.** The Victorian Period is marked by:
A. Great political upheavals
B. Great social security
C. Great wars
D. Economic deprivation

**449.** Swift is known mainly as:
A. an essayist B. a poet
C. a satirist D. a short story writer

**450.** Who is the writer of the novel *"The Village"*?
A. Khushwant Singh B. Anita Desai
C. Mulk Raj Anand D. R.K. Narayan

**451.** The most famous writer of the heroic couplet is:
A. Dryden B. Chaucer
C. Spenser D. Pope

**452.** *Macflecknoe* is a poem written by:
A. Dryden B. Pope
C. Tennyson D. Yeats

**453.** Who wrote *'Everyman in His Humour'*?
A. Shakespeare B. Jonson
C. Milton D. Keats

**454.** *'Indian Jugglers'* is an essay by:
A. De Quincey B. Gardiner
C. Hazlitt D. Lamb

**455.** Who wrote *'The Gropes of Wrath'*?
A. Pearl Buck B. Hemingway
C. Virginia Woolf D. John Steinbeck

**456.** Who rendered into English the ancient Greek tragedy *"Atlanta in Calydon"*?
A. Swinburne B. Shelley
C. Tennyson D. Arthur Hugh Clough

**457.** *The Deserted Village* was written by:
A. Cowper B. Goldsmith
C. Keats D. Johnson

**458.** *'Savitri'* is an epic written by:
A. Tagore
B. Prem Chand
C. Aurobindo
D. Bankim Chandra Chatterjee

**459.** The anthem *"Vande Mataram"* occurs in
A. Godan B. Anand Math
C. Gora D. Train to Pakistan

**460.** *'All Fool's Day'* is an essay written by:
A. Charles Lamb B. Hazlitt
C. A.G. Gardiner D. R.C. Stevenson

**461.** The drama *Tamburlaine* is written by:
A. Shakespeare B. Marlowe
C. Lyly D. Green

**462.** The book *"Appreciations"* was written by:
A. Morris B. Arnold
C. Walter Pater D. Christina Rossetti

**463.** *"The Admirable Crichton"* was written by:
A. Steinbeck B. T.S. Eliot
C. Trollope D. James Barrie

**464.** *"The Death of a Salesman"* was written by:
A. James Barrie B. Eugene O'Neill
C. Arthur Miller D. None of these

**465.** The Restoration period is said to have started from:
A. 1660 B. 1676
C. 1625 D. 1645

**466.** Who wrote *"The Lady's Not for Burning"*?
A. Barrie B. Christopher Fry
C. Robert Bridges D. T.S. Eliot

**467.** Who wrote the poem *"Brahma"*?
A. T.S. Eliot B. Emerson
C. Whitman D. Frost

**468.** The writer of *Walden* is:
A. Tennyson B. Whitman
C. Thoreau D. Frost

**469.** In *'Sons and Lovers'* Lawrence has depicted the life of:
A. factory workers B. miners
C. farmers D. animals

**470.** Who wrote *Kim*?
A. Kipling B. Tagore
C. Lawrence D. Narayan

**471.** *'The Hairy Ape'* is a famous play by:
A. Barrie B. Eugene O'Neill
C. Christopher Fry D. T.S. Eliot

**472.** Who is the writer of *Frankenstein*?
A. George Eliot B. Jane Austen
C. Mary Shelley D. Emile Bronte

**473.** Who wrote the *'Cries of Children'*?
A. Robert Browning B. Elizabeth Barrett
C. Thomas Hood D. Cowper

**474.** Which poet is known as poet's poet?
A. Shakespeare B. Milton
C. Spenser D. Shelley

**475.** Who wrote the maximum number of sonnets?
A. Shakespeare B. Milton
C. Sidney D. Wordsworth

**476.** *Adonais* is the eulogy written on the death of:
A. Coleridge B. Byron
C. Keats D. Wordsworth

**477.** Who wrote *Mother*?
A. Tolstoy B. Maxim Gorky
C. Chekhov D. Hardy

**478.** Who is associated with *Malgudi*?
A. Narayan
B. Anand
C. Manohar Malgonkar
D. Anita Desai

**479.** The author of *Beowulf* is:
A. Bede B. Cynewulf
C. Chaucer D. Unknown

**480.** The Anglo-Saxon period is often said to be from 450 to ......
A. 900 B. 1000
C. 1050 D. 1100

**481.** *"To a Mountain Daisy"* is a poem by:
A. Wordsworth B. Shelley
C. Keats D. Burns

**482.** Who wrote: *"The Devil's Disciple"*?
A. Galsworthy B. Barrie
C. Shaw D. Fry

**483.** Who wrote *"The Decline and Fall of the Roman Empire"*?
A. Walter Raleigh B. Trollope
C. Smollett D. Edward Gibbon

**484.** Richard Hooker was a prose writer of the:
A. Victorian period B. Romantic period
C. Elizabethan period D. Chaucerian age

**485.** Alexander Dumas was:
A. an English writer B. an American writer
C. a French writer D. a German writer

**486.** Which one was not one of the Lake poets?
A. Shelley B. Wordsworth
C. Southey D. Coleridge

**487.** *The Theory of Catharsis* is associated with:
A. Plato B. Dryden
C. Aristotle D. Sidney

**488.** Who wrote *'In Defence of Poetry'*?
A. T.S. Eliot B. Yeats
C. Keats D. Shelley

**489.** *'The Playboy of the Western World'* is a play by:
A. Barrie B. Synge
C. Fry D. Eliot

**490.** *'Silent Woman'* is a play by:
A. Marlowe B. Shakespeare
C. Ben Jonson D. Lyly

**491.** The Scene of *Beowulf* is laid in:
A. England B. France
C. Spain D. None of these

**492.** *"Kidnapped"* was written by:
A. Dickens B. Thackeray
C. Hardy D. R.L. Stevenson

**493.** *'The Prisoner of Zenda'* was written by:
A. Sterne B. Trollope
C. Anthony Hope D. George Eliot

**494.** What was the full name of Cervantes?
A. Jim Cervantes
B. John Cervantes
C. Miguel de Cervantes
D. Sir Roger Cervantes

**495.** Besides being a poet, Chaucer was:
A. a trader B. a manufacturer
C. a teacher D. a diplomat

**496.** The name of William Golding's first novel is:
A. The Inheritors B. Lord of the Flies
C. Pincher Martin D. The Pyramid

**497.** The author of *Erewhon* is:
A. Hardy B. Marquese
C. Samuel Butler D. Cervantes

**498.** Which of the following is a *Comedy of Manners*?
A. The Way of the World
B. The Duchess of Malfi
C. The Lady's Not for Burning
D. The Hairy Ape

**499.** Which one among the following is not a pessimist?
A. Gissing B. Browning
C. Hardy D. Thomson

**500.** Charles Reade's drama *"Drink"* was adapted from a work of:
A. Goethe B. Zola
C. Mallarwe D. Tennyson

**501.** Which one among the following was not a utilitarian?
A. Rousseau B. James Mill
C. Ricardo D. Bentham

**502.** *'The Praise of Folly'* was written by:
A. Walter Raleigh B. Thomas Moore
C. Charles Lamb D. Ruskin

**503.** Who wrote: *"In Praise of Idleness"*?
A. Bertrand Russell B. Thomas More
C. Charles Lamb D. Hazlitt

**504.** The real name of Saki is:
A. H.H. Munro B. Samuel Butler
C. George Orwell D. The Duke

**505.** Who started: *"The Tatler"*?
A. Addison B. Swift
C. Steele D. Stevenson

**506.** The poem *'The Song of the Shirt'* was written by:
A. Mrs. Browning B. Pope
C. Shelley D. Thomas Hood

**507.** *Sir Roger* was originally the creation of:
A. Addison B. Dryden
C. Steele D. Milton

**508.** Who wrote: *"Areopagitica"*?
A. Charles Lamb B. Hazlitt
C. De Quincey D. Milton

**509.** *'The Selfish Giant'* is a story written by:
A. Tagore B. Oscar Wilde
C. Maupassant D. Tolstoy

**510.** Who wrote : *"Four Quartets"*?
A. T.S. Eliot B. W.B. Yeats
C. W.H. Auden D. Philip Larkins

**511.** Who wrote : *"Look Back in Anger"*?
A. Steinbeck B. Christopher Fry
C. John Osborne D. Barrie

**512.** Who wrote : *"The Devils of Loundun"*?
A. Bertrand Russell B. Aldous Huxley
C. J.B. Priestley D. Hazlitt

**513.** Who wrote : *"Principles of Human Knowledge"*?
A. Milton B. John Bunyan
C. Nash D. George Berkeley

**514.** Who wrote : *"Liber Amoris"*?
A. Lamb B. Hazlitt
C. Byron D. Wordsworth

**515.** *"A Railway Clerk"* is a poem by:
A. Keki N. Daruwallah B. Nissim Ezekiel
C. Shiv K. Kumar D. Jayanta Mahapatra

**516.** Who won The Booker of Bookers?
A. Arundhati Roy B. Khushwant Singh
C. Mulk Raj Anand D. Salman Rushdie

**517.** Who wrote: *"The Battle of Books"*?
A. Bacon B. Hazlitt
C. Swift D. None of these

**518.** Who wrote: *"Nectar in a Sieve"*?
A. Mulk Raj Anand
B. Manohar Malgonkar
C. Kamala Markandaya
D. Pearl S. Buck

**519.** *'The Good Earth'* was written by:
A. Raja Rao B. R.K. Narayan
C. Pearl S. Buck D. Kamala Markandaya

**520.** The writer of *'The Dove Found No Rest'* is:
A. Pearl S Buck B. Hemingway
C. Raja Rao D. Dennis Stoll

**521.** Who wrote: *"So Many Hungers"*?
A. Bhabani Bhattacharya
B. Kamala Markandaya
C. Manohar Malgonkar
D. Chaman Nahal

**522.** Who is the writer of *"The Middleman and Other Stories"*?
A. Mulk Raj Anand B. Bharati Mukherjee
C. Tagore D. Prem Chand

**523.** Cicero was a Roman:
A. philologist B. physician
C. orator D. None of these

**524.** Who is the writer of *"Gita Rahasya"*?
A. Tulsi Das B. Vivekananda
C. Shivananda D. B.G. Tilak

**525.** *'The Rubaiyat of Omar Khayyam'* was translated into English by:
A. Robert Browning B. Tennyson
C. Fitz Gerald D. Hopkins

## ANSWERS

| 1 | 2 | 3 | 4 | 5 | 6 | 7 | 8 | 9 | 10 |
|---|---|---|---|---|---|---|---|---|---|
| A | A | A | C | B | B | A | D | A | B |
| **11** | **12** | **13** | **14** | **15** | **16** | **17** | **18** | **19** | **20** |
| B | A | B | A | C | C | B | A | C | A |
| **21** | **22** | **23** | **24** | **25** | **26** | **27** | **28** | **29** | **30** |
| D | B | C | B | A | B | C | C | B | B |
| **31** | **32** | **33** | **34** | **35** | **36** | **37** | **38** | **39** | **40** |
| B | D | A | C | B | C | D | B | A | B |
| **41** | **42** | **43** | **44** | **45** | **46** | **47** | **48** | **49** | **50** |
| D | B | B | B | B | D | B | D | A | D |
| **51** | **52** | **53** | **54** | **55** | **56** | **57** | **58** | **59** | **60** |
| D | B | D | B | C | D | D | B | C | D |
| **61** | **62** | **63** | **64** | **65** | **66** | **67** | **68** | **69** | **70** |
| D | C | D | B | C | D | C | D | B | B |
| **71** | **72** | **73** | **74** | **75** | **76** | **77** | **78** | **79** | **80** |
| A | A | C | C | B | A | A | D | D | D |
| **81** | **82** | **83** | **84** | **85** | **86** | **87** | **88** | **89** | **90** |
| B | D | A | A | B | D | D | A | A | B |
| **91** | **92** | **93** | **94** | **95** | **96** | **97** | **98** | **99** | **100** |
| D | C | D | B | C | D | B | C | A | C |

| 101 | 102 | 103 | 104 | 105 | 106 | 107 | 108 | 109 | 110 |
|---|---|---|---|---|---|---|---|---|---|
| D | C | B | D | C | C | D | A | C | D |
| **111** | **112** | **113** | **114** | **115** | **116** | **117** | **118** | **119** | **120** |
| D | C | B | C | B | B | D | D | B | C |
| **121** | **122** | **123** | **124** | **125** | **126** | **127** | **128** | **129** | **130** |
| A | A | C | D | D | A | C | C | D | A |
| **131** | **132** | **133** | **134** | **135** | **136** | **137** | **138** | **139** | **140** |
| C | A | B | A | C | B | D | C | C | A |
| **141** | **142** | **143** | **144** | **145** | **146** | **147** | **148** | **149** | **150** |
| B | D | B | A | B | D | A | C | D | B |
| **151** | **152** | **153** | **154** | **155** | **156** | **157** | **158** | **159** | **160** |
| B | C | A | C | B | C | A | A | B | B |
| **161** | **162** | **163** | **164** | **165** | **166** | **167** | **168** | **169** | **170** |
| B | D | A | A | D | B | D | B | A | D |
| **171** | **172** | **173** | **174** | **175** | **176** | **177** | **178** | **179** | **180** |
| D | C | C | A | C | D | C | A | D | D |
| **181** | **182** | **183** | **184** | **185** | **186** | **187** | **188** | **189** | **190** |
| D | A | D | C | C | B | B | B | C | C |
| **191** | **192** | **193** | **194** | **195** | **196** | **197** | **198** | **199** | **200** |
| D | C | A | B | C | B | D | C | C | B |
| **201** | **202** | **203** | **204** | **205** | **206** | **207** | **208** | **209** | **210** |
| A | B | D | C | A | C | D | D | B | A |
| **211** | **212** | **213** | **214** | **215** | **216** | **217** | **218** | **219** | **220** |
| C | C | C | C | C | D | C | A | A | B |
| **221** | **222** | **223** | **224** | **225** | **226** | **227** | **228** | **229** | **230** |
| D | B | B | C | B | C | B | B | A | B |
| **231** | **232** | **233** | **234** | **235** | **236** | **237** | **238** | **239** | **240** |
| B | D | C | B | B | A | A | C | C | D |
| **241** | **242** | **243** | **244** | **245** | **246** | **247** | **248** | **249** | **250** |
| C | B | D | D | A | C | A | A | D | B |
| **251** | **252** | **253** | **254** | **255** | **256** | **257** | **258** | **259** | **260** |
| C | B | B | B | D | A | D | C | A | D |
| **261** | **262** | **263** | **264** | **265** | **266** | **267** | **268** | **269** | **270** |
| B | A | D | C | D | B | C | B | A | C |
| **271** | **272** | **273** | **274** | **275** | **276** | **277** | **278** | **279** | **280** |
| A | D | B | C | D | A | C | C | B | B |
| **281** | **282** | **283** | **284** | **285** | **286** | **287** | **288** | **289** | **290** |
| B | C | A | B | D | A | D | D | B | C |
| **291** | **292** | **293** | **294** | **295** | **296** | **297** | **298** | **299** | **300** |
| A | B | D | A | C | D | B | C | A | D |
| **301** | **302** | **303** | **304** | **305** | **306** | **307** | **308** | **309** | **310** |
| C | A | B | D | D | A | D | A | A | C |
| **311** | **312** | **313** | **314** | **315** | **316** | **317** | **318** | **319** | **320** |
| D | A | B | A | D | C | D | C | A | C |

| 321 | 322 | 323 | 324 | 325 | 326 | 327 | 328 | 329 | 330 |
|---|---|---|---|---|---|---|---|---|---|
| A | B | C | A | C | D | B | D | A | B |
| 331 | 332 | 333 | 334 | 335 | 336 | 337 | 338 | 339 | 340 |
| C | B | A | C | D | B | C | A | C | B |
| 341 | 342 | 343 | 344 | 345 | 346 | 347 | 348 | 349 | 350 |
| D | B | D | A | D | D | B | A | B | A |
| 351 | 352 | 353 | 354 | 355 | 356 | 357 | 358 | 359 | 360 |
| C | D | A | B | C | D | B | A | D | D |
| 361 | 362 | 363 | 364 | 365 | 366 | 367 | 368 | 369 | 370 |
| C | D | B | B | D | B | B | A | A | D |
| 371 | 372 | 373 | 374 | 375 | 376 | 377 | 378 | 379 | 380 |
| A | B | A | D | C | A | B | D | C | C |
| 381 | 382 | 383 | 384 | 385 | 386 | 387 | 388 | 389 | 390 |
| C | C | C | C | D | C | D | A | C | C |
| 391 | 392 | 393 | 394 | 395 | 396 | 397 | 398 | 399 | 400 |
| A | C | A | C | A | C | B | B | B | B |
| 401 | 402 | 403 | 404 | 405 | 406 | 407 | 408 | 409 | 410 |
| C | A | C | C | B | C | C | D | A | B |
| 411 | 412 | 413 | 414 | 415 | 416 | 417 | 418 | 419 | 420 |
| D | A | B | A | D | C | A | D | D | C |
| 421 | 422 | 423 | 424 | 425 | 426 | 427 | 428 | 429 | 430 |
| B | D | A | C | B | D | B | C | A | D |
| 431 | 432 | 433 | 434 | 435 | 436 | 437 | 438 | 439 | 440 |
| B | C | A | A | B | A | C | A | C | D |
| 441 | 442 | 443 | 444 | 445 | 446 | 447 | 448 | 449 | 450 |
| D | D | A | C | C | B | C | A | C | C |
| 451 | 452 | 453 | 454 | 455 | 456 | 457 | 458 | 459 | 460 |
| D | A | B | C | D | A | B | C | B | A |
| 461 | 462 | 463 | 464 | 465 | 466 | 467 | 468 | 469 | 470 |
| B | C | D | C | A | B | B | C | B | A |
| 471 | 472 | 473 | 474 | 475 | 476 | 477 | 478 | 479 | 480 |
| B | C | B | C | D | C | B | A | D | C |
| 481 | 482 | 483 | 484 | 485 | 486 | 487 | 488 | 489 | 490 |
| D | C | D | C | C | A | C | D | B | C |
| 491 | 492 | 493 | 494 | 495 | 496 | 497 | 498 | 499 | 500 |
| D | D | C | C | D | B | C | A | B | B |
| 501 | 502 | 503 | 504 | 505 | 506 | 507 | 508 | 509 | 510 |
| A | B | A | A | C | D | C | D | B | A |
| 511 | 512 | 513 | 514 | 515 | 516 | 517 | 518 | 519 | 520 |
| C | B | D | B | B | D | C | C | C | D |
| 521 | 522 | 523 | 524 | 525 | | | | | |
| A | B | C | D | C | | | | | |

# ENGLISH GRAMMAR & VOCABULARY

## Spelling Errors

The most common errors in English are of spellings of words. Even the most learned men are sometimes confused about the correct spellings of some words. One must keep and use a dictionary religiously. Never ignore and let pass a new word casually.

A number of question to test your knowledge of spellings are compiled here. Try to solve as many as you can.

## Multiple Choice Questions

**Directions:** *Find the correctly spelt word out of the four options in each question.*

**1.** A. Accompalish B. Ackmplesh C. Acomplush D. Accomplish

**2.** A. Acommodation B. Acomodation C. Accomodation D. Accommodation

**3.** A. Astonished B. Astronished C. Astoneshed D. Asstonished

**4.** A. Benefeted B. Benefitted C. Benifited D. Benefited

**5.** A. Belligerent B. Beligirent C. Belligarant D. Belligerrent

**6.** A. Chancelery B. Chancellery C. Chancellary D. Chancelary

**7.** A. Discriminate B. Discremineta C. Discrimenate D. Discriminat

**8.** A. Damage B. Dammage C. Damaige D. Dammege

**9.** A. Efficiant B. Effecient C. Efficient D. Eficient

**10.** A. Extravagant B. Extreragent C. Extreregant D. Extravegent

**11.** A. Efflorascence B. Eflorescene C. Efflloroscence D. Efflorescence

**12.** A. Equinimity B. Equanimmity C. Equannimity D. Equanimity

**13.** A. Farmament B. Farmement C. Fermament D. Fremament

**14.** A. Grieff B. Grief C. Grieef D. Grrief

**15.** A. Guarantee B. Garuntee C. Guaruntee D. Gaurantee

**16.** A. Hypocritical B. Hypocretical C. Hypocriticel D. Hypocirticel

**17.** A. Humurous B. Humorous C. Humoreus D. Humorrous

**18.** A. Itenerary B. Itinarery C. Itinarary D. Itinerary

**19.** A. Indipenseble B. Indispansible C. Indispensable D. Indipensable

**20.** A. Imprecticability B. Impracticebility C. Impracticibility D. Impracticability

**21.** A. Incradulous B. Incredulous C. Incridulous D. Incredalous

**22.** A. Juddicious B. Judiceous C. Judicious D. Judiceus

**23.** A. Kleptomonia B. Kleptemonia C. Kleptomania D. Klaptomania

**24.** A. Lackdaisical B. Lackadaisical C. Lckadaisicle D. Lackadisical

**25.** A. Licentious B. Licontious C. Licenttious D. Licientious

**26.** A. Meddicine B. Medicine C. Medicene D. Medicinne

**27.** A. Meritricious B. Merefrecious C. Meretricious D. Merritricious

**28.** A. Missunderstood B. Miesunderstood C. Misunderstood D. Misunderstod

**29.** A. Occurad B. Occurred C. Ocurred D. Occured

**30.** A. Osttentatious B. Ostentetious C. Ostentatious D. Ostenttatious

**31.** A. Obnosious B. Obnoxeous C. Obnoxious D. Obnoseous

**32.** A. Omenous B. Ominous C. Ommineous D. Omineous

**33.** A. Pecification B. Pacification C. Pecifacation D. Pecefication

**34.** A. Prograssive B. Progressive C. Progresive D. Prograsive

**35.** A. Pasiveness B. Passiveness C. Passeveniss D. Passivines

**36.** A. Polyendry B. Poliendry C. Pollyendry D. Polyandry

**37.** A. Puerille B. Puerrile C. Puerile D. Purrile

**38.** A. Pesanger B. Passenger C. Pessenger D. Pasanger

**39.** A. Querrelsome B. Quarrelsame C. Quarrelsome D. Querralsome

**40.** A. Rigourous B. Rigerous C. Rigorous D. Regerous

**41.** A. Survellance B. Surveilance C. Surveillance D. Survaillance

**42.** A. Schedule B. Schdule C. Schedale D. Schedeule

**43.** A. Sepalchrle B. Sepalchral C. Sepulchrle D. Sepulchral

**44.** A. Sympathetic B. Smypathetic C. Sympothetic D. Sympethetic

**45.** A. Sincerely B. Sencerely C. Sincerelly D. Sincerrely

**46.** A. Satellite B. Sattellite C. Satelite D. Sattelite

**47.** A. Teracherous B. Treacherous C. Treacheraus D. Treachereans

**48.** A. Uncivilized B. Uncevilized C. Uncivillized D. Uncevelized

**49.** A. Vainglorious B. Vaniglorious C. Vaniglerious D. Vaingloreus

**50.** A. Vulnarable B. Valnerable C. Velnerable D. Vulnerable

## ANSWERS

| 1 | 2 | 3 | 4 | 5 | 6 | 7 | 8 | 9 | 10 |
|---|---|---|---|---|---|---|---|---|---|
| D | D | A | B | A | C | A | A | C | A |
| **11** | **12** | **13** | **14** | **15** | **16** | **17** | **18** | **19** | **20** |
| D | D | C | B | A | A | B | D | C | D |
| **21** | **22** | **23** | **24** | **25** | **26** | **27** | **28** | **29** | **30** |
| B | C | C | B | A | B | C | C | B | C |
| **31** | **32** | **33** | **34** | **35** | **36** | **37** | **38** | **39** | **40** |
| C | B | B | B | B | D | C | B | C | C |
| **41** | **42** | **43** | **44** | **45** | **46** | **47** | **48** | **49** | **50** |
| C | A | D | A | A | A | B | A | A | D |

# Spotting Errors

The most common errors in English are of spellings, grammar and usage of words. By regular practice, the errors can be easily spotted and minimised.

## Common Errors with Nouns and Noun-Phrases

| Incorrect | Correct |
|---|---|
| 1. I have bought new *furnitures.* | I have bought new *furniture.* |
| 2. The wages of sin *are* death. | The wages of sin *is* death. |
| 3. She told these *news* to her mother. | She told her mother this *news.* |
| 4. He took *troubles* to do his work. | He took *trouble* (or pains) over his work. |
| 5. The *cattles* were grazing. | The *cattle* were grazing. |
| 6. He showered *many abuses* on me. | He showered *much abuse* on me. |
| 7. I spent the holidays with my *family members.* | I spent the holidays with my *family.* |
| 8. There is no *place* in this compartment. | There is no *room* in this compartment. |
| 9. Write this new *poetry* in your *copy.* | Write this new *poem* in your *note-book.* |
| 10. He took *insult* at this. | He took *offence* at this. |
| 11. Put your *sign* here. | Put your *signatures* here. |
| 12. She is my *cousin sister.* | She is my *cousin.* |
| 13. *Sunil's* my *neighbour's* house was burgled. | *Sunil* my *neighbour's* house was burgled. |
| 14. I lost a *ten-rupees* note. | I lost *a ten-rupee* note. |
| 15. Road closed for *repair.* | Road closed for *repairs.* |
| 16. His house is out of *repairs.* | His house is out of *repair.* |
| 17. What is the *reason* of an earthquake? | What is the *cause* of an earthquake? |
| 18. This building is made of *stones.* | This building is made of *stone.* |
| 19. I disapprove of *these kinds* of games. | I disapprove of *this kind* of games. |
| 20. Veena's and Sheela's father is ill. | Veena and Sheela's father is ill. |
| 21. His *son-in-laws* are doctors. | His *sons-in-law* are doctors. |
| 22. *Alms* is given to the *poor.* | *Alms* are given to the poor. |
| 23. He always keeps his words. | He always keeps his *word.* |
| 24. I carried the *luggages.* | I carried the *luggage.* |
| 25. *Two-third* of the work is left. | *Two-thirds* of the work is left. |

## Common Errors with Pronouns

| Incorrect | Correct |
|---|---|
| 1. Both did not go. | Neither went. |
| 2. We all did not go. | None of us went. |
| 3. Each of these boys play. | Each of these boys plays. |
| 4. Whoever does best he will get a prize. | Whoever does best will get a prize. |

| Incorrect | Correct |
|---|---|
| 5. One should not waste his time. | A man should not waste his time. |
| 6. I and she are sisters. | She and I are sisters. |
| 7. He is wiser than me. | He is wiser than I. |
| 8. Between you and I, Anil is not to be trusted. | Between you and me, Anil is not to be trusted. |
| 9. Nobody was there but I. | Nobody was there but me. |
| 10. Who is there ? It is me. | Who is there ? It is I. |
| 11. Only he and me can use this card. | Only he and I can use this card. |
| 12. Let you and I go now. | Let you and me go now. |
| 13. Everyone got one's pay. | Everyone got his pay. |
| 14. Everyone is frightened when they see a tiger. | Everyone is frightened when he sees a tiger. |
| 15. These two friends are fond of one another. | These two friends are fond of each other. |
| 16. I did not like him coming at that hour. | I did not like his coming at that hour. |
| 17. Who do you think I met? | Whom do you think I met? |
| 18. You should avail this opportunity. | You should avail yourself this opportunity. |
| 19. When you have read these books, please return the same to me. | When you have read the books, please return them to me. |
| 20. They that are humble need fear no fall. | Those that are humble need fear no fall. |

## Common Errors with Adjectives

| Incorrect | Correct |
|---|---|
| 1. These all oranges are good. | All these oranges are good. |
| 2. He held the book in the both hands. | He held the book in both hands. |
| 3. Both men have not come. | Neither man has come. |
| 4. That man should do some or other work. | That man should do some work or other. |
| 5. He is elder than I. | He is older than I. |
| 6. Shakespeare is greater than any other poets. | Shakespeare is greater than any other poet. |
| 7. He is a coward man. | He is a cowardly man. |
| 8. Many villagers cannot write his own name. | Many villagers cannot write their own name. |
| 9. Each of us loves our home. | Each of us loves his home. |
| 10. Much efforts bring their reward. | Much effort brings its reward. |
| 11. He found hundred rupees. | He found a hundred rupees. |
| 12. He had leave of four days. | He had four days leave. |
| 13. This is a worth seeing sight. | This is a sight worth seeing. |
| 14. He will spend his future life here. | He will spend the rest of his life here. |
| 15. There is a best teacher in that class. | There is a very good teacher in that class. |
| 16. Of the two plans this is the best. | Of the two plans this is the better. |
| 17. He is becoming strong every day. | He is becoming stronger every day. |
| 18. He is worst than I. | He is worse than I. |
| 19. Jaipur is hot than Delhi. | Jaipur is hotter than Delhi. |
| 20. In our library the number of books is less. | In our library the number of books is small. |

## Common Errors with Verbs

| Incorrect | Correct |
|---|---|
| 1. He asked had we taken our luggage. | He asked if we had taken our luggage. |
| 2. She asked what are you doing. | She asked what we were doing. |
| 3. Rama asked to Anil why he is angry. | Rama asked Anil why he was angry. |
| 4. He does not care for his money. | He does not take care of his money. |
| 5. He does not care for his work. | He takes no care over his work. |
| 6. No one cared for him after his mother died. | No one took care of him after his mother died. |
| 7. He got angry before I said a word. | He got angry before I had said a word. |
| 8. I met a man who was my tutor 20 years ago. | I met a man who had been my tutor twenty years ago. |
| 9. I had been for walking yesterday. | I went for a walk yesterday. |
| 10. If I shall do this I shall be wrong. | If I do this I shall be wrong. |
| 11. I have left trekking. | I have given up trekking. |
| 12. I came to know as to how he did this. | I learnt how he did this. |
| 13. I came to know why he was sad. | I found out why he was sad. |
| 14. He knows to swim. | He knows how to swim. |
| 15. The criminal's head was cut. | The criminal's head was cut off. |
| 16. I said to him to go. | I told him to go. |
| 17. I told the teacher to excuse me. | I asked the teacher to excuse me. |
| 18. He is troubling me. | He is giving me trouble. |
| 19. I have got a hurt on my leg. | I have hurt my leg. |
| 20. She gave a speech. | She made a speech. |

## Common Errors in Subject-Verb Agreement

| Incorrect | Correct |
|---|---|
| 1. The owners of this factory *is* very rich. | The owners of this factory *are* very rich. |
| 2. The pleasures of nature that one can experience at Shimla *is* beyond description. | The pleasures of nature that one can experience at Shimla *are* beyond description. |
| 3. There *is* no street lights in our colony. | There *are* no street lights in our colony. |
| 4. He and I *am* entrusted with the job. | He and I *are* entrusted with the job. |
| 5. Rice and curry *are* his favourite dish. | Rice and curry *is* his favourite dish. |
| 6. The honour and glory of our country *are* at stake. | The honour and glory of our country *is* at stake. |
| 7. Time and tide *waits* for none. | Time and tide *wait* for none. |
| 8. All the passengers with the driver *was* killed. | All the passengers, with the driver, *were* killed. |
| 9. The teacher, with her students, *were* going out. | The teacher, with her students, *was* going out. |
| 10. I as well as they *am* tired. | I as well as they *are* tired. |
| 11. Not only the soldiers but their captain also *were* captured. | Not only the soldiers but their captain also *was* captured. |
| 12. Neither you nor I *were* selected. | Neither you nor I *was* selected. |
| 13. Either of these two applicants *are* fit for the job but neither want to accept it. | Either of these two applicants *is* fit for the job but neither wants to accept it. |
| 14. One of these students are sure to stand first. | One of these students *is* sure to stand first. |
| 15. Everyone of these workers want a raise. | Everyone of these workers wants a raise. |
| 16. None of these letters has been answered so far. | None of these letters *have* been answered so far. |
| 17. None of the girls were present at the party. | None of the girls *was* present at the party. |
| 18. Many a battle were fought on Indian soil. | Many a battle *was* fought on Indian soil. |
| 19. A lot of work remain to be done. | A lot of work *remains* to be done. |
| 20. The majority of these girls likes music. | The majority of these girls *like* music. |

## Common Errors in the Use of Modals/Auxiliary Verbs

| Incorrect | Correct |
|---|---|
| 1. When I shall see him I shall tell him this. | When I *see* him, I shall tell him this. |
| 2. If I should do wrong, he would punish me. | If I *did* wrong, he would punish me. |
| 3. Until he will have confessed his fault, he will be kept in prison. | Until he *has* confessed his fault, he will be kept in prison. |
| 4. She will obey me. | She *shall* obey me. |
| 5. You would work hard. | You *should* work hard. |
| 6. You shall find him in the garden. | You *will* find him in the garden. |
| 7. He must have died of exposure, but we cannot be certain. | He *might* have died of exposure, but we cannot be certain. |
| 8. You might not show disrespect to your elders. | You *must* not show disrespect to your elders. |
| 9. You may take exercise in order to maintain good health. | You *must* take exercise in order to maintain good health. |
| 10. He must be a crook for all we know. | He *may* be a crook for all we know. |

## Common Errors in the Use of Adverbs

| Incorrect | Correct |
|---|---|
| 1. He is very much angry. | He is *very* angry. |
| 2. She was very good enough to help me. | She was *good enough* to help me. |
| 3. She runs much fast. | She runs *very* fast. |
| 4. She runs very faster than Seema. | She runs *much* faster than Seema. |
| 5. It is bitter cold today. | It is *bitterly* cold today. |
| 6. He is a much learned man. | He is a very learned man. |
| 7. She is thinking very hardly. | She is thinking very hard. |
| 8. To tell in brief the film was boring. | *In short* the film was boring. |
| 9. He told the story in details. | He told the story *in detail.* |
| 10. I did it anyhow. | I *managed to do* it somchow. |
| 11. Aeroplanes reach Europe soon. | Aeroplanes reach Europe quickly. |
| 12. Before long there were dinosaurs on the earth. | *Long ago,* there were dinosaurs on the earth. |
| 13. This book is too interesting. | This book is *very* interesting. |
| 14. He lives miserly. | He lives in *a miserly* way. |
| 15. Just I had gone when she came. | I had just gone when she came. |
| 16. He sings good. | He sings *well.* |
| 17. He sings good than I. | He sings *better* than I. |
| 18. Really speaking it is cold. | *As a matter of fact* it is cold. |
| 19. He is enough tall to reach the ceiling. | He is *tall enough* to reach the ceiling. |
| 20. He went directly to his college. | He went *direct* to his college. |

## Common Errors in the Use of Conjunctions

| Incorrect | Correct |
|---|---|
| 1. As he is fat so he runs slowly. | As he is fat *he* runs slowly. |
| 2. If he is fat then he will run slowly. | If he is fat, he will run slowly. |
| 3. Though he is fat still he runs fast. | Though he is fat, *he runs* fast. |
| 4. *As* I pulled the trigger at the sametime he shook my arm. | As I pulled the trigger, he shook my arm. |

| Incorrect | Correct |
|---|---|
| 5. No sooner I had spoken than he left. | No sooner *had* I spoken than he left. |
| 6. Not only he will go, but also he will stay there. | Not only *will he* go, but he *will also* stay there. |
| 7. Neither he comes nor he writes. | Neither *does he* come nor *does he* write. |
| 8. Scarcely he entered the room than the telephone rang. | Scarcely *had* he entered the room *when the* telephone rang. |
| 9. Hardly she had left the house than it began to rain. | Hardly *had she* left the house *when* it began to rain. |
| 10. He is the fastest runner and he comes last. | He is the fastest runner *but* he comes last. |
| 11. She is as innocent as if she looks. | She is as innocent as she looks. |
| 12. Until he does not try he must be punished. | He must be punished unless he tries. |
| 13. I want to know as to why you are late. | I want to know why you are late. |
| 14. I am fond of Chinese food as for example sweet and sour prawns. | I am fond of Chinese food, for example, sweet and sour prawns. |
| 15. He was angry therefore I ran away. | He was angry so I ran away. |
| 16. I was trying to work, at that time he was disturbing me. | While I was trying to work, he was disturbing me. |
| 17. Supposing if he is late, what will happen? | Supposing he is late (or if he is late) what will happen? |
| 18. He asked me that why I was late. | He asked me why I was late. |
| 19. Let us catch a taxi lest we should not get late. | Let us catch a taxi lest we should get late. |
| 20. She dresses herself like the teacher does. | She dresses herself as the teacher does. |
| 21. Wait while I come. | Wait *until* (or *till)* I come. |
| 22. Until, there is corruption in India, there can be little progress. | *As long* as there is corruption in India there can be little progress. |
| 23. I have never told a lie nor cheated anybody. | I have never told a lie *nor have I* cheated anybody. |
| 24. Both Mohan as well as Arun are responsible for this action. | Both Mohan *and* Arun are responsible for this action. |
| 25. Hindus and Muslims both are to blame for the riots. | *Both Hindus* and Muslims are to blame for the riots. |

## Common Errors in the Use of Prepositions

| Incorrect | Correct |
|---|---|
| 1. I will not listen him. | I will not listen *to* him. |
| 2. Copy this word by word. | Copy this word *for* word. |
| 3. He enquired from her where she lived. | He enquired *of* her where she lived. |
| 4. Sign here with ink. | Sign here *in* ink. |
| 5. Has she come in train or by foot? | Has she come *by* train or *on* foot? |
| 6. She said this at his face. | She said this *to* his face. |
| 7. Open the book on page one. | Open the book *at* page one. |
| 8. I was invited for lunch. | I was *invited to* lunch. |
| 9. I am ill since three months. | I have been *ill for* three months. |
| 10. This paper is inferior than that. | This paper is inferior *to* that. |
| 11. This resembles to that. | This *resembles* that. |
| 12. My brother is superior than you in strength. | My brother is superior *to* you in strength. |
| 13. He wrote me. | He wrote *to* me. |
| 14. I shall explain them this. | I shall explain this *to* them. |
| 15. Send this letter on my address. | Send this letter *to* my address. |
| 16. He suggested me this. | He suggested this *to* me. |
| 17. He goes *on his* work. | He goes *to his* work. |
| 18. He *reached to* Nagpur. | He *reached* Nagpur. |
| 19. He told *to me* to go. | He told *me* to go. |
| 20. The term begins *from* July 1st. | The term begins *on* July 1st. |

## Miscellaneous Errors

| *Incorrect* | *Correct* |
|---|---|
| 1. Many *homes* are lying vacant. | Many *houses* are lying vacant. |
| 2. It is cool in the *shadow* of the tree. | It is cool in the *shade* of the tree. |
| 3. She *keeps* good health. | She *enjoys* good health. |
| 4. My leg is *paining*. | *I am feeling pain* in my leg. |
| 5. *See* this word in the dictionary. | *Look up* this word in the dictionary. |
| 6. The train will arrive *just now*. | The train will arrive *shortly*. |
| 7. They are *pulling* on well. | They are *getting* on well. |
| 8. The river has *over flown* its bank. | The river has *over flown* its banks. |
| 9. He was appointed *on* the post. | He was appointed *to* the post. |
| 10. Last but not *the least,* we have to discuss the problem of over population. | Last but not *least,* we have to discuss the problem of over population. |
| 11. *Cities* after *cities* fell. | *City* after *city* fell. |
| 12. What is the use Munir going there? | What is the use of Munir going there? |
| 13. He *did many mischief.* | He *made much mischief.* |
| 14. It is exact five *in* my watch. | It is exact five *by* my watch. |
| 15. I will dine with them on *next Sunday.* | I will dine with them *Sunday next.* |
| 16. Misfortunes when faced bravely and *manly* become less troublesome. | Misfortunes when faced bravely and *manfully* become less troublesome. |
| 17. I am *laid down* with fever. | I am *laid up* with fever. |
| 18. He is habituated to smoking. | He is *addicted* to smoking. |
| 19. *According to my opinion* he is right. | *In my opinion* (or according *to me)* he is right. |
| 20. Could you please *open* this knot? | Could you please *untie* this knot? |

# Multiple Choice Questions

**Directions:** *In this section, each sentence has three parts, indicated by (A), (B) and (C). Read each sentence to find out whether there is an error. If you find an error in any one of the parts (A, B, C), indicate your response by marking the letter related to that part. If a sentence has no error, indicate this by marking '(D)' which stands for "No error". Errors may belong to grammar, usage or idiom. Ignore errors of punctuation, if any.*

**1.** (A) Beware of/(B) a fair-weather friend/(C) who is neither a friend in need nor a friend indeed/(D) No error.

**2.** (A) Copernicus proved/(B) that Earth/(C) moves round the Sun./(D) No error.

**3.** (A) Seldom we have been treated/(B) in such a rude manner/(C) by the police personnel./(D) No error.

**4.** (A) Some men are born great,/(B) some achieve greatness/(C) and some had greatness thrust on them./(D) No error.

**5.** (A) The property/(B) was divided/(C) among the two brothers./(D) No error.

**6.** (A) I am quite certain/(B) that the lady is not only greedy/(C) but miserly./(D) No error.

**7.** (A) The aircraft overloaded/(B) there was something wrong of the battery/(C) and the engine was making a queer noise/(D) No error.

**8.** (A) A thorough inquiry of the misappropriation of funds/(B) is now imperative/(C) to bring the guilty to book/(D) No error.

**9.** (A) The brilliant success in the examination/(B) as well as his record in sports/(C) deserves high praise/(D) No error.

**10.** (A) While travelling by a train/(B) on a cold winter night/(C) an argument rose between two passengers in our compartment/(D) No error.

**11.** (A) I cannot find/(B) where has he gone/(C) though I have tried may best/(D) No error.

12. (A) If I was/(B) the Prime Minister of India/(C) I would work wonders/(D) No error.

13. (A) Amit's severe bout of flu/(B) debilitated him so much/(C) that he was too tired to do for work for a week./(D) No error.

14. (A) This is the crux of the entire problem;/(B) everything centres on/(C) it being resolved./(D) No error.

15. (A) One of the major aims of the Air Force/(B) was the complete demolition of all means of transportation/(C) by the bombing of rail lines and terminals./(D) No error.

16. (A) His strong voice cut over/(B) the hum of conversation/(C) like a knife through butter./(D) No error.

17. (A) Even though they weren't expecting us/(B) they managed to knock up/(C) a marvellous meal./(D) No error.

18. (A) The celebrated singer was/(B) surrounded by the usual crowd/(C) of lackeys and hangerons./(D) No error.

19. (A) If it weren't/(B) for you,/(C) I wouldn't be alive today./(D) No error.

20. (A) He looked like a lion/(B) baulked from/(C) its prey./(D) No error.

21. (A) Widespread flooding/(B) is effecting/(C) large areas of the villages./(D) No error.

22. (A) She regards/(B) negotiating prices with customers/(C) as her special preserve./(D) No error.

23. (A) Often in political campaigns, a point is reached at which/(B) the candidates take out their gloves./(C) and start slugging with bare fists./(D) No error.

24. (A) If we really set to/(B) we can get the whole house/(C) cleaned in an afternoon./(D) No error.

25. (A) Pieces of rock plummeted/(B) down the mountainside/(C) in the ground below./(D) No error.

26. (A) Since the two parties each won/(B) the same number of seats,/(C) the minority party holds the balance of power./(D) No error.

27. (A) It's arrogant for you/(B) to assume you'll/(C)win every time./(D) No error.

28. (A) We've paid for our travel and accommod-ation,/(B) so we need only to take/(C) some pocket-money with us./(D) No error.

29. (A) There's no evidence to show/(B) that information technology secrets are more/(C) vulnerable in India than Britain or the US./(D) No error.

30. (A) It is shameful that hunting/(B) is still considered sport/(C) by some unscrupulous people in the civilized world./(D) No error.

31. (A) The Prime Minister's good looks won him/(B)the election but he has still to prove/(C) that he's not a just pretty face./(D) No error.

32. (A) The two books are the same/(B) except for the fact that this/(C) has an answer in the back./(D) No error.

33. (A) He estimated his income tax bill/(B) by extrapolation over figures/(C) submitted in previous years./(D) No error.

34. (A) The modern office block/(B) sticks out like a sore thumb/(C) among the old buildings in the area./(D) No error.

35. (A) I will try to put over/(B) some feelers to gauge/(C) people's reactions to our proposal./(D) No error.

36. (A) A major contribution of Mathura sculptors/(B)of that period were the creation and popularization/(C) of the Buddha's image in human form./(D) No error.

37. (A) Amit has been deceiving Mona/(B) for many years but she/(C) has not still tumbled to it./(D) No error.

38. (A) Mahavira was an advocate of nonviolence and vegetarianism,/(B) who revived and reorganized the Jain doctrine/(C) and established rules for their monastic order. (D) No error.

39. (A) Microwaves are the principle carriers/(B) of television, telephone and data transmissions/(C)between stations on earth and between the earth and satellites./(D) No error.

40. (A) An unit is an abstract idea,/(B) defined either by reference to/(C) a randomly chosen material standard or to a natural phenomenon./(D) No error.

41. (A) With the crisis deepening,/(B) the critics sense an opportunity/(C) about putting in place a more radical strategy./(D) No error.

42. (A) The salesman gave us/(B) a big spiel about why/(C) we should buy his product./(D) No error.

43. (A) I will need several weeks/(B) to invent the lie of the land before/(C) I can make any decision about the future of the business./(D) No error.

44. (A) You should be cautious/(B) and make a few discrete enquiries about/(C) the firm before you sign anything./(D) No error.

45. (A) Your husband doesn't/(B) believe that you are older/(C) than I./(D) No error.

46. (A) We are meeting today afternoon/(B) to discuss the matter/(C) and reach a compromise./(D) No error.

**47.** (A) Either Ram or/(B) you is responsible/(C) for this action./(D) No error.

**48.** (A) The student flatly denied/(B) that he had copied/ (C) in the examination hall./(D) No error.

**49.** (A) By the time you arrive tomorrow/(B) I have finished/ (C) my work./(D) No error.

**50.** (A) The speaker stressed repeatedly on/(B) the importance of improving/(C) the condition of the slums./(D) No error.

**51.** (A) The captain with the members of his team/(B) are returning/(C) after a fortnight./(D) No error.

**52.** (A) After returning from/(B) an all-India tour/(C) I had to describe about it/(D) No error.

**53.** (A) The teacher asked his students/(B) if they had gone through/(C) either of the three chapters included in the prescribed text./(D) No error.

**54.** (A) Although they are living in the country/(B) since they were married/(C) they are now moving to the town./(D) No error.

**55.** (A) Do you know/(B) how old were you/(C) when you came here?/(D) No error.

## ANSWERS

| 1 | 2 | 3 | 4 | 5 | 6 | 7 | 8 | 9 | 10 |
|---|---|---|---|---|---|---|---|---|---|
| D | B | A | C | C | C | B | A | D | C |
| **11** | **12** | **13** | **14** | **15** | **16** | **17** | **18** | **19** | **20** |
| B | A | C | C | B | A | A | C | C | C |
| **21** | **22** | **23** | **24** | **25** | **26** | **27** | **28** | **29** | **30** |
| C | A | A | A | C | A | A | B | D | B |
| **31** | **32** | **33** | **34** | **35** | **36** | **37** | **38** | **39** | **40** |
| C | C | C | D | A | B | C | C | A | A |
| **41** | **42** | **43** | **44** | **45** | **46** | **47** | **48** | **49** | **50** |
| C | D | D | D | C | A | B | D | B | A |
| **51** | **52** | **53** | **54** | **55** | | | | | |
| B | C | C | B | D | | | | | |

# Articles

## Definite and Indefinite Articles

(*i*) 'A' and 'an' are Indefinite Articles.

(*ii*) 'The' is Definite Article.

(*iii*) 'A' and 'an' modify a noun in a general way.

(*iv*) 'The' particularises it. *e.g.*,

Mohan has **a pen.**

**The pen** which you gave me was expensive.

## Vowel and Consonant Sounds

(*i*) 'A' is used before words starting with the sound of a consonant.

(*ii*) 'An' is used before a vowel sound (vowels a, e, i, o, u) *e.g.*,

a book, a cat, a useful thing, a European girl, a university,

but an FDR, an MA, an honest boy, an hour, an owl, an egg, an umbrella, etc.

## Use of Articles 'A' and 'An'

**A** cat mews. (*i.e.,* every cat)

**The cat** of my neighbour mews day and night. (*i.e.,* a particular cat)

He gave me **an** egg. (Here 'an' means 'one')

## Use of Article 'The'

1. 'The' is used before names of rivers, mountains, seas, oceans:

   The Himalayas, the Ganga, the Yamuna, the Bay of Bengal, the Indian Ocean, the Nile, the English Channel, *etc.*
2. Names of newspapers and magazines:

   The Times of India, the Tribune, The Sun, *etc.*
3. Names of the famous and holy books:
   The Guru Granth Sahib, The Gita, The Ramayana, *etc.*
4. Names of creations of nature:
   the sun, the earth, the moon, the sky, *etc.*
5. While using Adjectives as Nouns:
   **The poor** should be helped by **the rich.**
6. Sometimes with the Comparative Degree:
   **The more** you think, **the more** you worry.
7. With the Superlative Degree:
   She is **the most intelligent** girl in our school.
8. Before the imaginary lines and directions:

   The Latitude, The Equator, the east, the west, etc.
9. Before the names of musical instruments:
   the violin, the piano, the flute, etc.
10. While using a Proper Noun as a Common Noun:

    Mohan is **the Sachin** of our team.

## Omission of Article 'The'

1. Before some Nouns used to convey general sense, articles are not used but are used to particularise them:
   Man is mortal.
2. Before Proper Nouns:
   Rakesh is an intelligent boy.
3. With Abstract Noun:
   Childhood is the prime time of one's life.
   The childhood of Sohan was full of sorrow.
4. With Material Nouns:
   Milk is an essential food.
   The milk of the cow is sweet.
5. Usually no article is used before names of diseases:
   Cancer is a fatal disease.
   However, when we talk about a disease figuratively, we use an article before its name, *e.g.*
   Corruption is a cancer.
6. Names of games and language:
   I like football.
   I can speak Punjabi, Hindi and English.
7. Gold is a precious metal.

   **NOTE:** As you must have noted above, the definite article 'the' has been used where a noun is particularised.

## Double Use of Article 'The'

Read the following sentences carefully to understand this :

1. The poet and novelist has been honoured.
   (The same person is the poet as well as novelist)
2. The poet and the novelist have been honoured.
   (The poet and the novelist are two different persons).
3. I have a black and white dog.
   (that is, one dog)
4. I have a black and a white dog.
   (that is, two dogs)

# Multiple Choice Questions

**Directions :** *Fill in the blanks with suitable articles. Mark 'D' if no article required.*

**1.** Do you know ....... boy in white?
A. a B. an
C. the D. No article

**2.** She is ....... girl I am looking for.
A. a B. an
C. the D. No article

**3.** Have you read ....... Mahabharat?
A. a B. an
C. the D. No article

**4.** .......rich are not always happy.
A. A B. An
C. The D. No article

**5.** Oranges are sold by ....... dozen.
A. a B. an
C. the D. No article

**6.** Milk is sold by ....... litre.
A. a B. an
C. the D. No article

**7.** ....... Amazon is the longest river in the world.
A. A B. An
C. The D. No article

**8.** ....... higher you climb, the colder it gets.
A. A B. An
C. The D. No article

**9.** She is ....... untidy girl.
A. a B. an
C. the D. No article

**10.** I am ....... M.A. is English.
A. a B. an
C. the D. No article

**11.** I have already spent ....... few rupees I had.
A. a B. an
C. the D. No article

**12.** ....... English are very hard-working.
A. A B. An
C. The D. No article

**13.** April is the fourth month of ....... year.
A. a B. an
C. the D. No article

**14.** Rice is sold by ....... kilogram
A. a B. an
C. the D. No article

**15.** She is ....... best of the three girls.
A. a B. an
C. the D. No article

**16.** ....... man in the car is a friend of mine.
A. A B. An
C. The D. No article

**17.** Brevity is ....... soul of wit.
A. a B. an
C. the D. No article

**18.** ....... thing of beauty is a joy for ever.
A. A B. An
C. The D. No article

**19.** ....... little learning is a dangerous thing.
A. A B. An
C. The D. No article

**20.** ....... best sauce for food is hunger.
A. A B. An
C. The D. No article

**21.** Birds of ....... feather flock together.
A. a B. an
C. the D. No article

**22.** He makes ....... living by begging.
A. a B. an
C. the D. No article

**23.** It is ....... pity that he died so young.
A. a B. an
C. the D. No article

**24.** What ....... nuisance it is?
A. a B. an
C. the D. No article

**25.** Delhi is ....... London of India.
A. a B. an
C. the D. No article

**26.** Where is ........ will, there is a way.
A. a B. an
C. the D. No article

**27.** Her father is ....... physician and surgeon.
A. a B. an
C. the D. No article

**28.** This will benefit ........ poor.
A. an B. an
C. the D. No article

**29.** ........bird in hand is better than two in a bush.
A. A B. An
C. The D. No article

**30.** As he is hard-working, he will win ........ prize.
A. a B. an
C. the D. No article

**31.** ........ water of this well is dirty.
A. A B. An
C. The D. No article

**32.** Only ....... wearer knows where the shoe pinches.
A. a B. an
C. the D. No article

**33.** ........ action will be taken against you.
A. A B. An
C. The D. No article

**34.** ........ sun rises in the east.
A. A B. An
C. The D. No article

**35.** She was promoted to ....... highest post.
A. a B. an
C. the D. No article

**36.** Did you see ........ Taj Mahal?
A. a B. an
C. the D. No article

**37.** He is ........ one-eyed man.
A. a B. an
C. the D. No article

**38.** This is ........ useful book.
A. a B. an
C. the D. No article

**39.** Cloth is sold by ........ metre.
A. a B. an
C. the D. No article

**40.** The sun sets in ........ west.
A. a B. an
C. the D. No article

**41.** Amar bought......umbrella yesterday.
A. a B. an
C. the D. No article

**42.** Surinder is ...... honest boy.
A. a B. an
C. the D. No article

**43.** She wrote ...... book in French.
A. a B. an
C. the D. No article

**44.** ...... lion roars.
A. A B. An
C. The D. No article

**45.** ..... apple a day keeps the doctor away.
A. A B. An
C. The D. No article

**46.** John bought ...... car yesterday.
A. a B. an
C. the D. No article

**47.** His father is ..... engineer in the U.S.A.
A. a B. an
C. the D. No article

**48.** It is hard for ..... owl to fly during the day times.
A. a B. an
C. the D. No article

**49.** She had ..... rimmed hat.
A. a B. an
C. the D. No article

**50.** My uncle is ..... heart specialist.
A. a B. an
C. the D. No article

**51.** He looks as foolish as ........ ass.
A. a B. an
C. the D. No article

**52.** Did you go to ........ prison to visit him?
A. a B. an
C. the D. No article

**53.** I found ........ one-rupee note in the market.
A. a B. an
C. the D. No article

**54.** It is a pleasure to meet such ........ efficient man.
A. a B. an
C. the D. No article

**55.** The Sanyasi lived in a cave in ........ Himalayas.
A. a B. an
C. the D. No article

**56.** There is ........ union in our factory.
A. a B. an
C. the D. No article

**57.** He hit his wife on the head with ....... umbrella.
A. a B. an
C. the D. No article

**58.** I caught him by ....... collar.
A. a B. an
C. the D. No article

**59.** Child is ....... father of man.
A. a B. an
C. the D. No article

**60.** He gazed at ....... moon for two hours.
A. a B. an
C. the D. No article

## ANSWERS

| 1 | 2 | 3 | 4 | 5 | 6 | 7 | 8 | 9 | 10 |
|---|---|---|---|---|---|---|---|---|---|
| C | C | C | C | C | C | C | C | B | B |
| **11** | **12** | **13** | **14** | **15** | **16** | **17** | **18** | **19** | **20** |
| C | C | C | C | C | C | C | A | A | C |
| **21** | **22** | **23** | **24** | **25** | **26** | **27** | **28** | **29** | **30** |
| A | A | A | A | C | A | A | C | A | A |
| **31** | **32** | **33** | **34** | **35** | **36** | **37** | **38** | **39** | **40** |
| C | C | B | C | C | C | A | A | C | C |
| **41** | **42** | **43** | **44** | **45** | **46** | **47** | **48** | **49** | **50** |
| B | B | A | A | B | A | B | B | A | A |
| **51** | **52** | **53** | **54** | **55** | **56** | **57** | **58** | **59** | **60** |
| B | C | A | B | C | A | B | C | C | C |

# Prepositions

A Preposition is a word that comes before a Pronoun or a Noun and expresses the relationship between Noun or Pronoun and some part of the remaining sentence.

(*a*) He is busy **with** his work.
(*b*) The boy jumped **into** the river.
(*c*) The birds are chirping **in** the trees.

In these sentences the words **with, into** and **in** show the relationship between the verbs **busy, jumped** and **chirping** with the nouns **work, river** and **trees** respectively.

## Position of the Preposition

**A.** A Preposition usually precedes its object.
(*i*) He laughs **at** the poor.
(*ii*) He is angry **with** you.
(*iii*) She agrees **with** me.

**B.** In the case of Relative Pronouns it comes after the subject.
(*i*) This is the boy whom I was looking **for**.
(*ii*) That is the pen whose mention I was making **of**.

**C.** In the following cases, the Preposition comes after its object.
(*i*) Where is the boy you were complaining **against**?
(*ii*) What things are there you are looking **for**?
(*iii*) Who is there, you are waiting **for**?

## Omission of the Prepositon

In many cases when the sentences contain Nouns of Time or Place, the Prepositions **from, in** and **for** are often omitted.

(*i*) He walked many kilometres.
(*ii*) He came to see me last year.
(*iii*) As I could not find my puppy anywhere, I looked here and there.

Prepositions are small words that show the relationship between one word and another. Prepositions in the following sentences show the position of the paper in relation to the desk, the book, hand and the door.

The paper is **on** the desk.
The paper is **under** the book.
The paper is **in** his hand.
The paper is **by** the door.

## Common Prepositions

| | | |
|---|---|---|
| about | at | by |
| in | onto | toward |
| above | before | concerning |
| inside | out | under |
| across | behind | despite |
| into | over | until |
| after | below | down |
| like | since | up |
| against | beneath | during |
| near | through | upon |
| along | beside | except |
| of | throughout | with |
| amid | between | for |
| off | till | within |
| among | beyond | from |
| on | to | without |

# Multiple Choice Questions

**Directions:** *Select the most appropriate preposition from the given alternatives to fill in the blanks and make the sentence meaningfully complete.*

**1.** Don't try to be an advocate ..... these criminals.
A. for B. with
C. across D. in

**2.** The audience admired him ..... his sweet voice.
A. to B. on
C. for D. at

**3.** I want to check your bag ..... fake currency notes.
A. to B. for
C. upon D. on

**4.** The dew drops clung .... the blades of grass.
A. for B. on
C. to D. in

**5.** The thief was chased ..... by the police.
A. on B. after
C. into D. at

**6.** Please carry this bag ..... my room.
A. on B. for
C. to D. in

**7.** A lorry bumped ..... a car.
A. on B. over
C. into D. to

**8.** They were begging ..... food.
A. for B. on
C. to D. after

**9.** She always boasts ..... her wealth.
A. of B. for
C. on D. after

**10.** She banged ..... the door violently.
A. for B. to
C. on D. down

**11.** I applied ..... the post of a clerk.
A. for B. on
C. in D. to

**12.** I applied ..... the Principal for the post of a teacher.
A. to B. on
C. with D. for

**13.** I begged ..... him not to divulge the secret.
A. for B. of
C. with D. to

**14.** You had better borrow a pen ..... Rakesh.
A. over B. into
C. from D. by

**15.** I baked a cake ..... the guests.
A. to B. for
C. on D. of

**16.** She is confident ..... (her) success.
A. with B. on
C. of D. for

**17.** The doctor will cure you ..... malaria.
A. of B. with
C. for D. from

**18.** This law is common ..... all.
A. to B. upon
C. over D. at

**19.** She was condemned ..... her bad hand writing.
A. on B. for
C. into D. of

**20.** In summer there will be a great demand ..... desert cooler.
A. on B. with
C. for D. of

**21.** We shall wait ..... you.
A. on B. for
C. towards D. after

**22.** Tom displayed his injury ..... all his friends.
A. for B. upon
C. to D. at

**23.** She distributed the sweets ..... the two brothers.
A. among B. between
C. for D. in

**24.** Please distribute these apples ..... all.
A. among B. to
C. for D. at

**25.** It rarely happened that he defended ..... an innocent person.
A. against B. for
C. upon D. at

**26.** The parents were disappointed ..... the performance of their son.
A. on B. with
C. at D. of

**27.** Common salt dissolves ..... water.
A. for B. in
C. with D. by

**28.** This medicare is free ..... sugar.
A. on B. to
C. from D. of

**29.** The manager granted leave ..... the clerk.
A. to B. on
C. into D. for

**30.** The air was heavy ..... aroma of perfumes.
A. on B. with
C. into D. from

**31.** She had a quick glance ..... the magazine.
A. at B. from
C. into D. to

**32.** The climate of Kashmir is favourable ..... me.
A. with B. in
C. to D. for

**33.** They hate you ..... your poverty.
A. for B. on
C. in D. of

**34.** He is eligible ..... this post.
A. for B. to
C. with D. at

**35.** The smoke was emerging ..... down the foot of the hill.
A. on B. to
C. from D. at

**36.** The criminal managed to escape ..... the prison.
A. upon B. from
C. with D. of

**37.** You should educate your friends ..... the benefits of living in villages.
A. on B. towards
C. upon D. in

**38.** She made a lot of efforts ..... win the match.
A. for B. to
C. upon D. at

**39.** The new inspector will enquire ..... the murder case.
A. on B. for
C. into D. at

**40.** The retired soldiers were exempted ..... all taxes.
A. from B. to
C. on D. of

**41.** She was adept ..... journalism.
A. at B. on
C. with D. in

**42.** She is afraid ..... snakes.
A. on B. to
C. of D. with

**43.** I agree ..... your proposal.
A. for B. on
C. to D. with

**44.** The children were amazed ..... so big a python.
A. at B. on
C. in D. with

**45.** She was anxious ..... the final match.
A. about B. on
C. with D. for

**46.** He apologized ..... his being late.
A. towards B. for
C. on D. as

**47.** The children were amused ..... his jokes.
A. for B. to
C. at D. on

**48.** She is angry ..... you.
A. to B. with
C. on D. for

**49.** She is angry ..... your teasing remark.
A. at B. in
C. for D. with

**50.** A big patch of land was allocated ..... the refugees.
A. to B. for
C. in D. upon

## ANSWERS

| 1 | 2 | 3 | 4 | 5 | 6 | 7 | 8 | 9 | 10 |
|---|---|---|---|---|---|---|---|---|---|
| A | C | B | C | B | C | C | A | A | C |
| 11 | 12 | 13 | 14 | 15 | 16 | 17 | 18 | 19 | 20 |
| A | A | B | C | B | C | A | A | B | C |
| 21 | 22 | 23 | 24 | 25 | 26 | 27 | 28 | 29 | 30 |
| B | C | B | A | A | C | B | C | A | B |
| 31 | 32 | 33 | 34 | 35 | 36 | 37 | 38 | 39 | 40 |
| A | C | A | A | C | B | A | B | C | A |
| 41 | 42 | 43 | 44 | 45 | 46 | 47 | 48 | 49 | 50 |
| A | C | C | A | A | B | C | B | A | A |

# Synonyms & Antonyms

There are thousands of words in English language. No one can remember their meanings easily but with regular practice one can memorise most of them. A number of words with their Synonyms and Antonyms are compiled here. Try to learn as many as you can and answer the questions thereafter.

| *Words* | *Synonyms* | *Antonyms* |
|---|---|---|
| **Abandon** | Cease, Forsake | Continue |
| **Abhor** | Hate, Loathe, Detest | Like, Love |
| **Abiding** | Enduring, Durable | Fleeting |
| **Able** | Proficient, Competent | Incompetent, Unfit |
| **Ability** | Skill, Power | Disability, Inability |
| **Abortive** | Fruitless, Futile | Fruitful, Successful |
| **Abolish** | Destroy, Undo | Restore, Revive |
| **Abridge** | Shorten, Curtail | Lengthen, Expand |
| **Absolve** | Forgive, Pardon, Excuse | Condemn |
| **Accelerate** | Hasten | Retard |
| **Accord** | Agreement, Harmony | Discord, Disagreement |
| **Accumulate** | Collect, Store, Amass | Distribute, Scatter |
| **Adamant** | Hard, Inflexible | Flexible |
| **Adversity** | Misfortune, Distress | Prosperity |
| **Adept** | Expert, Skilful | Inexpert, Unskillful |
| **Aggravate** | Heighten, Intensify | Quell, Suppress |
| **Agile** | Nimble | Clumsy, Undeft |
| **Alert** | Vigilant | Heedless |
| **Allay** | Calm, Soothe, Assuage | Arouse |
| **Ameliorate** | Improve, Advance, Amend | Worsen, Deteriorate |
| **Ambiguous** | Vague, Unclear | Clear |
| **Amiable** | Lovable, Agreeable | Disagreeable |
| **Annihilate** | Destroy | Create |
| **Arduous** | Hard, Strenuous | Easy |
| **Attacks** | Assault | Defend |
| **Audacity** | Boldness | Cowardice |
| **Auspicious** | Favourable, Propitious, Lucky | Ominous, Inauspicious, Unlucky |
| **Austere** | Harsh, Severe, Rigorous | Easy-going |
| **Authentic** | True, Genuine | Spurious, False |
| **Avarice** | Greed | Generosity |
| **Averse** | Unwilling, Loath, Disinclined | Willing, Inclined |

| Words | Synonyms | Antonyms |
|---|---|---|
| **Aversion** | Hostility, Hatred | Affinity, Liking |
| **Base** | Low, Mean, Ignoble | Noble, Exalted |
| **Boisterous** | Noisy, Stormy | Calm, Quiet |
| **Brave** | Courageous, Daring, Bold, Plucky | Cowardly, Dastardly, Timid |
| **Brief** | Short, Concise, Laconic | Lengthy, Diffuse |
| **Bright** | Vivid, Radiant | Dull, Dark |
| **Brutal** | Savage, Cruel | Humane, Kindly |
| **Callous** | Hard, Cruel, Indifferent | Soft, Tender, Concerned |
| **Cautious** | Careful, Wary | Rash, Reckless, Foolhardy |
| **Censure (*n*)** | Blame, Condemnation | Praise |
| **Censure (*vb*)** | Blame, Condemn | Praise, Commend |
| **Circumscribed** | Restricted, Confined, Limited | Unconfined, Unrestricted |
| **Civil** | Polite, Courteous, Gracious, Urbane | Rude, Uncivil, Impolite, Ungracious |
| **Coerce** | Compel, Force | Volunteer |
| **Compassionate** | Pitiful, Sympathetic, Merciful | Unsympathetic, Merciless, Cruel |
| **Compress** | Condense, Abbreviate | Expand, Lengthen |
| **Conspicuous** | Noticeable, Manifest | Inconspicuous |
| **Constant** | Steady, Steadfast, Uniform | Inconstant, Variable |
| **Cordial** | Friendly, Warm, Hearty | Cold, Unfriendly |
| **Covert** | Hidden, Secret | Overt, Open |
| **Cruel** | Savage, Ruthless, Vicious | Kind, Gentle, Benevolent |
| **Cursory** | Rapid, Superficial | Thorough, Exhaustive, Intensive |
| **Credible** | Believable, Probable, Plausible | Incredible, Unbelievable, Fantastic |
| **Crafty** | Cunning, Sly | Artless, Simple, Ingenuous |
| **Costly** | Expensive, Dear | Cheap, Inexpensive |
| **Confidence** | Trust, Reliance | Distrust, Doubt |
| **Death** | Decease, Demise | Existence, Life |
| **Dearth** | Scarcity, Lack, Want, Paucity, Shortage | Plenty, Abundance |
| **Decay** | Dissolution, Decline, Decomposition, Disintegration | Regeneration |
| **Deference** | Respect, Reverence | Disrespect, Irreverence |
| **Deficient** | Lacking, Inadequate | Complete, Sufficient |
| **Desolate** | Lonely, Deserted | Crowded, Occupied |
| **Destitute** | Wanting, Needy | Rich, Affluent |
| **Diligence** | Industry, Perseverance | Idleness |
| **Disgrace** | Dishonour, Discredit | Honour, Credit |
| **Dwindle** | Decrease, Shrink | Grow, Increase |
| **Earthly** | Terrestrial, Mundane | Celestial, Heavenly, Unearthly |
| **Eligible** | Qualified, Suitable | Ineligible, Unsuitable |
| **Emancipate** | Liberate, Free | Enslave |
| **Excited** | Impassioned, Stimulated | Composed, Cool, Impassive |
| **Extraordinary** | Uncommon, Remarkable, Marvellous | Commonplace, Ordinary |
| **Extravagant** | Lavish, Prodigal, Wastrel, Spendthrift | Thrifty, Economical, Frugal |
| **Fabricate** | Construct, Make | Destroy |
| **Fabulous** | Fictitious, Mythical | Actual, Real |
| **False** | Untrue, Mendacious | True, Genuine |

| *Words* | *Synonyms* | *Antonyms* |
|---|---|---|
| **Famous** | Well-known, Renowned | Obscure, Unknown |
| **Fantastic** | Fanciful, Imaginative, Visionary | Practical, Down to earth |
| **Fearful** | Nervous, Anxious, Afraid, Scared | Fearless, Dauntless |
| **Felicity** | Happiness | Sorrow |
| **Gaiety** | Joyousness, Hilarity | Mourning, Dullness |
| **Garrulous** | Talkative, Loquacious | Taciturn, Silent, Reserved |
| **Generous** | Liberal, Magnanimous | Stingy, Miserly |
| **Gigantic** | Huge, Colossal | Minute, Small |
| **Graphic** | Vivid, Pictorial, Meaningful | Vague |
| **Guest** | Visitor | Host |
| **Guile** | Fraud, Trickery | Artlessness, Ingenuousness |
| **Gratitude** | Gratefulness | Ingratitude, Ungratefulness |
| **Gratuitous** | Voluntary, Spontaneous, Unwarranted | Involuntary, Forced |
| **Hamper** | Hinder, Obstruct | Facilitate, Ease |
| **Haughty** | Arrogant, Proud | Humble, Modest |
| **Hazardous** | Dangerous, Perilous | Safe, Secure Protected |
| **Headstrong** | Obstinate, Stubborn | Weak-willed, Flexible |
| **Hope** | Belief, Conviction, Expectation | Despair, Hopelessness |
| **Improvident** | Prodigal, Carelessness | Provident, Economical |
| **Incessant** | Unceasing, Continuous | Discontinuous |
| **Indolent** | Slothful, Lethargic | Active, Energetic |
| **Joy** | Delight, Pleasure | Sadness, Gloom |
| **Jolly** | Jovial, Merry | Gloomy, Sad |
| **Judicious** | Discreet, Prudent | Indiscreet, Injudicious |
| **Knowledge** | Enlightenment, Learning | Ignorance, Stupidity |
| **Laborious** | Industrious, Assiduous | Slothful, Lazy |
| **Laxity** | Slackness, Looseness | Firmness |
| **Lenient** | Mild, Forbearing | Strict, Stern |
| **Lethal** | Deadly, Fatal, Mortal | Life-giving, Vital, Vivifying |
| **Liberal** | Generous, Tolerant | Intolerant, Illiberal |
| **Liberty** | Freedom, Independence | Slavery, Bondage |
| **Lively** | Animated, Active | Dull, Listless |
| **Loyal** | Faithful, Devoted | Treacherous, Disloyal, Unfaithful |
| **Lucky** | Fortunate | Unlucky, Unfortunate |
| **Lucrative** | Profitable | Unprofitable |
| **Magnanimous** | Generous, Largehearted | Ungenerous, Stingy |
| **Malady** | Illness, Ailment | Health |
| **Manifest** | Noticeable, Obvious | Obscure, Puzzling |
| **Meagre** | Small | Plentiful, Large |
| **Mean** | Low, Abject | Noble, Exalted |
| **Mendacious** | False, Untruthful | Truthful |
| **Misery** | Sorrow, Distress | Happiness, Joy |
| **Morbid** | Sick, Diseased | Healthy |
| **Mournful** | Sorrowful, Sad | Joyful, Happy |

| Words | Synonyms | Antonyms |
|---|---|---|
| **Negligent** | Careless, Heedless | Careful |
| **Notorious** | Infamous, Disreputable | Reputable |
| **Obedient** | Submissive, Compliant, Docile | Disobedient, Recalcitrant, Wayward |
| **Obsolete** | Antiquated, Out-of-Date | Current, Modern |
| **Opportune** | Timely, Seasonable | Inopportune |
| **Opulence** | Wealth, Riches | Penury, Poverty |
| **Onerous** | Heavy, Burdensome | Light, Easy |
| **Palatable** | Tasty, Delicious | Unpalatable |
| **Pathetic** | Touching | Joyous, Cheery |
| **Persuade** | Urge, Induce | Dissuade |
| **Praise (*vb*)** | Applaud, Eulogise | Condemn |
| **Praise (*n*)** | Applause, Eulogy | Condemnation |
| **Precarious** | Risky, Uncertain | Safe, Certain |
| **Pretence** | Pretext, Excuse | Candour, Frankness |
| **Propagate** | Breed, Circulate | Terminate, Restrict |
| **Quaint** | Odd, Singular | Usual, Ordinary |
| **Quell** | Suppress, Subdue | Agitate, Arouse |
| **Rare** | Uncommon, Scarce | Common, Ordinary |
| **Refined** | Polished, Elegant | Crude, Coarse |
| **Remote** | Distant | Near, Close |
| **Renown** | Fame, Reputation | Infamy, Notoriety |
| **Rigid** | Stiff, Unyielding | Flexible, Yielding |
| **Remorseful** | Regretful, Repentant | Unrepentant |
| **Rebellion** | Revolt, Mutiny, Insurgency | Loyalty |
| **Scared** | Holy, Consecrated | Profane, Unholy |
| **Sane** | Sensible, Sound | Insane |
| **Scold** | Chide, Rebuke | Praise |
| **Serious** | Grave, Earnest | Frivolous |
| **Shy** | Bashful | Bold, Impudent |
| **Simple** | Plain, Artless | Complex, Cunning, Shrewd |
| **Solitary** | Single, Lonely, Secluded | Numerous, Multitude |
| **Shallow** | Superficial | Deep |
| **Solace** | Comfort, Relief | Discomfort, Grief |
| **Spurious** | Sham, False | Genuine, Authentic |
| **Stagnant** | Still, Motionless | Moving |
| **Surplus** | Excess | Deficit, Shortage |
| **Tame** | Gentle, Mild, Domesticated | Savage, Wild |
| **Teacher** | Instructor, Educator | Student, Pupil |
| **Tedious** | Wearisome, Monotonous | Agreeable, Lively |
| **Temporal** | Worldly, Secular | Spiritual |
| **Temperate** | Moderate | Immoderate, Intemperate |
| **Tortuous** | Winding, Circuitous | Straight, Direct |
| **Tough** | Hard, Strong | Tender, Soft, Flexible |
| **Transient** | Temporary, Fleeting | Lasting, Durable, Permanent |

| Words | Synonyms | Antonyms |
|---|---|---|
| **Truswothy** | Reliable | Unreliable, Untrustworthy |
| **Tranquil** | Calm | Agitated |
| **Ugly** | Unsightly, Repulsive | Beautiful, Attractive |
| **Useful** | Advantageous, Serviceable | Useless |
| **Vehemence** | Passion, Force | Apathy, Indifference |
| **Vindictive** | Revengeful | Forgiving |
| **Wholesome** | Healthy | Unwholesome, Morbid, Unhealthy, Diseased |
| **Wicked** | Evil, Impious | Pious, Good |
| **Wise** | Sagacious, Erudite | Foolish, Stupid |
| **Wrath** | Anger, Fury, Rage | Love, Peace, Calm |
| **Wreck** | Ruin, Destroy | Create, Construct |
| **Yield** | Surrender, Submit | Resist, Revolt |
| **Yielding** | Submissive, Supple | Inflexible, Intractable |
| **Yoke** | Oppression, Bondage | Freedom |
| **Zeal** | Passion, Fervour | Apathy, Indifference |
| **Zest** | Relish, Enthusiasm | Distaste, Disrelish |

# Multiple Choice Questions

**Directions (Qs. 1 to 50):** *In the following questions choose the word which best expresses the MEANING of the given word.*

**1.** TEPID
A. Hot B. Warm
C. Cold D. Boiling

**2.** MAYHEM
A. Jubilation B. Havoc
C. Excitement D. Defeat

**3.** TIMID
A. Fast B. Slow
C. Medium D. Shy

**4.** CANTANKEROUS
A. Quarrelsome B. Rash
C. Disrespectful D. Noisy

**5.** PRECARIOUS
A. Cautious B. Critical
C. Perilous D. Brittle

**6.** TACITURNITY
A. Dumbness B. Changeableness
C. Hesitation D. Reserve

**7.** INEBRIATE
A. Dreamy B. Stupefied
C. Unsteady D. Drunken

**8.** HARBINGER
A. Massenger B. Steward
C. Forerunner D. Pilot

**9.** INTIMIDATE
A. To hint B. Frighten
C. Bluff D. Harass

**10.** IRONIC
A. Inflexible B. Bitter
C. Good-natured D. Disguisedly sarcastic

**11.** STRINGENT
A. Tense B. Stringy
C. Strict D. Causing to shrink

**12.** ECSTATIC
A. Animated B. Bewildered
C. Enraptured D. Willful

**13.** COMMENSURATE
A. Measurable B. Proportionate
C. Beginning D. Appropriate

**14.** DESTITUTION
A. Humility B. Moderation
C. Poverty D. Beggary

**15.** ASCEND
A. Leap B. Grow
C. Deviate D. Mount

**16.** UNCOUTH
A. Ungraceful B. Rough
C. Slovenly D. Dirty

**17.** LYNCH
A. Hang B. Madden
C. Killed D. Shoot

18. LAUD
A. Lord B. Eulogy
C. Praise D. Extolled

19. CORRESPONDENCE
A. Agreements B. Contracts
C. Documents D. Letters

20. VENUE
A. Place B. Agenda
C. Time D. Duration

21. STERILE
A. Barren B. Arid
C. Childless D. Dry

22. SYNOPSIS
A. Index B. Mixture
C. Summary D. Puzzle

23. GERMANE
A. Responsible B. Logical
C. Possible D. Relevant

24. PONDER
A. Think B. Evaluate
C. Anticipate D. Increase

25. CANNY
A. Obstinate B. Handsome
C. Clever D. Stout

26. ABUNDANT
A. Ripe B. Cheap
C. Plenty D. Absent

27. CONSEQUENCES
A. Results B. Conclusions
C. Difficulties D. Applications

28. SHIVER
A. Shake B. Rock
C. Tremble D. Move

29. DILIGENT
A. Progressive B. Brilliant
C. Inventive D. Hard-working

30. DISTANT
A. Far B. Removed
C. Reserved D. Separate

31. FORAY
A. Excursion B. Contest
C. Ranger D. Intuition

32. FRUGALITY
A. Foolishness B. Extremity
C. Enthusiasm D. Economy

33. GARNISH
A. Paint B. Garner
C. Adorn D. Abuse

34. VIGOUR
A. Strength B. Boldness
C. Warmth D. Enthusiasm

35. CANDID
A. Apparent B. Explicit
C. Frank D. Bright

36. BRIEF
A. Limited B. Small
C. Little D. Short

37. GARRULITY
A. Credulity B. Senility
C. Loquaciousness D. Speciousness

38. FURORE
A. Excitement B. Worry
C. Flux D. Anteroom

39. NEUTRAL
A. Unbiased B. Non-aligned
C. Undecided D. Indifferent

40. LAMENT
A. Complain B. Comment
C. Condone D. Console

41. ADVERSITY
A. Failure B. Helplessness
C. Misfortune D. Crisis

42. TURN UP
A. Land up B. Show up
C. Crop up D. Come up

43. DEIFY
A. Flatter B. Challenge
C. Worship D. Face

44. ERROR
A. Misadventure B. Misgiving
C. Ambiguity D. Blunder

45. SHALLOW
A. Artificial B. Superficial
C. Foolish D. Worthless

46. MASSACRE
A. Murder B. Stab
C. Assassinate D. Slaughter

47. COMBAT
A. Conflict B. Quarrel
C. Feud D. Fight

48. VORACIOUS
A. Wild B. Hungry
C. Angry D. Quick

49. IMPROMPTU
A. Offhand B. Unimportant
C. Unreal D. Effective

50. RABBLE
A. Mob B. Noise
C. Roar D. Rubbish

**Directions (Qs. 51 to 100):** *In the following questions choose the word which is the exact OPPOSITE of the given words.*

**51.** STRINGENT
A. General B. Vehement
C. Lenient D. Magnanimous

**52.** FLIMSY
A. Frail B. Filthy
C. Firm D. Flippant

**53.** BUSY
A. Occupied B. Engrossed
C. Relaxed D. Engaged

**54.** ADAPTABLE
A. Adoptable B. Flexible
C. Yielding D. Rigid

**55.** LOVE
A. Villainy B. Hatred
C. Compulsion D. Force

**56.** BALANCE
A. Disbalance B. Misbalance
C. Debalance D. Imbalance

**57.** RELINQUISH
A. Abdicate B. Renounce
C. Possess D. Deny

**58.** MOUNTAIN
A. Plain B. Plateau
C. Precipice D. Valley

**59.** FICKLE
A. Courageous B. Sincere
C. Steadfast D. Humble

**60.** PERENNIAL
A. Frequent B. Regular
C. Lasting D. Rare

**61.** RARELY
A. Hardly B. Definitely
C. Frequently D. Periodically

**62.** STARTLED
A. Amused B. Relaxed
C. Endless D. Astonished

**63.** ADHERENT
A. Detractor B. Enemy
C. Alien D. Rival

**64.** QUIESCENT
A. Indifferent B. Troublesome
C. Weak D. Unconcerned

**65.** CONDENSE
A. Expand B. Distribute
C. Interpret D. Lengthen

**66.** BENIGN
A. Malevolent B. Soft
C. Friendly D. Unwise

**67.** OBSCURE
A. Implicit B. Obnoxious
C. Explicit D. Pedantic

**68.** HYPOCRITICAL
A. Gentle B. Sincere
C. Amiable D. Dependable

**69.** EVASIVE
A. Free B. Honest
C. Liberal D. Frank

**70.** INDUSTRIOUS
A. Indifferent B. Indolent
C. Casual D. Passive

**71.** EXTRICATE
A. Manifest B. Palpable
C. Release D. Entangle

**72.** LUCID
A. Glory B. Noisy
C. Obscure D. Distinct

**73.** INSIPID
A. Tasty B. Stupid
C. Discreet D. Feast

**74.** OBEYING
A. Ordering B. Following
C. Refusing D. Contradicting

**75.** VICTORIOUS
A. Defeated B. Annexed
C. Destroyed D. Vanquished

**76.** COMMISSIONED
A. Started B. Closed
C. Finished D. Terminated

**77.** VANITY
A. Pride B. Humility
C. Conceit D. Ostentious

**78.** ZENITH
A. Acme B. Top
C. Nadir D. Pinnacle

**79.** TANGIBLE
A. Ethereal B. Concrete
C. Actual D. Solid

**80.** REPRESS
A. Inhibit B. Liberate
C. Curb D. Quell

**81.** EPILOGUE
A. Dialogue B. Prelude
C. Post script D. Epigram

**82.** FRAUDULENT
A. Candid B. Direct
C. Forthright D. Genuine

**83.** LOQUACIOUS
A. Reticent B. Talkative
C. Garrulous D. Verbose

**84.** NIGGARDLY
A. Frugal B. Thrifty
C. Stingy D. Generous

**85.** PERTINENT
A. Irrational B. Irregular
C. Insistent D. Irrelevant

**86.** FAINT-HEARTED
A. Warm-hearted B. Full-blooded
C. Hot-blooded D. Stout-hearted

**87.** VIOLENT
A. Humble B. Harmless
C. Gentle D. Tame

**88.** STATIONARY
A. Active B. Mobile
C. Rapid D. Busy

**89.** HONORARY
A. Dishonourable B. Reputed
C. Paid D. Official

**90.** COMMON
A. Rare B. Small
C. Petty D. Poor

**91.** REPEL
A. Attend B. Concentrate
C. Continue D. Attract

**92.** ARTIFICIAL
A. Red B. Natural
C. Truthful D. Solid

**93.** CAPACIOUS
A. Limited B. Caring
C. Foolish D. Changeable

**94.** PROVOCATION
A. Vocation B. Pacification
C. Peace D. Destruction

**95.** METICULOUS
A. Mutual B. Shaggy
C. Meretricious D. Slovenly

**96.** ABLE
A. Disable B. Inable
C. Unable D. Enable

**97.** COMFORT
A. Uncomfort B. Miscomfort
C. Discomfort D. None of these

**98.** GAIN
A. Loose B. Fall
C. Lost D. Lose

**99.** SYNTHETIC
A. Affable B. Natural
C. Plastic D. Cosmetic

**100.** ACQUITTED
A. Freed B. Burdened
C. Convicted D. Entrusted

## ANSWERS

| 1 | 2 | 3 | 4 | 5 | 6 | 7 | 8 | 9 | 10 |
|---|---|---|---|---|---|---|---|---|---|
| B | B | D | A | B | D | D | C | B | D |
| **11** | **12** | **13** | **14** | **15** | **16** | **17** | **18** | **19** | **20** |
| C | C | B | C | D | A | C | C | D | A |
| **21** | **22** | **23** | **24** | **25** | **26** | **27** | **28** | **29** | **30** |
| A | C | D | A | C | C | A | C | D | A |
| **31** | **32** | **33** | **34** | **35** | **36** | **37** | **38** | **39** | **40** |
| A | D | C | A | C | D | C | A | A | A |
| **41** | **42** | **43** | **44** | **45** | **46** | **47** | **48** | **49** | **50** |
| C | B | C | D | B | D | D | B | A | A |
| **51** | **52** | **53** | **54** | **55** | **56** | **57** | **58** | **59** | **60** |
| C | C | C | D | B | D | C | D | C | D |
| **61** | **62** | **63** | **64** | **65** | **66** | **67** | **68** | **69** | **70** |
| D | B | B | A | C | A | C | B | B | B |
| **71** | **72** | **73** | **74** | **75** | **76** | **77** | **78** | **79** | **80** |
| D | C | A | A | A | D | B | C | A | B |
| **81** | **82** | **83** | **84** | **85** | **86** | **87** | **88** | **89** | **90** |
| B | D | B | D | D | D | C | B | C | A |
| **91** | **92** | **93** | **94** | **95** | **96** | **97** | **98** | **99** | **100** |
| D | B | A | B | D | C | C | D | B | C |

# One Word Substitutions

There are many words in English language which can be perfectly used for a number of words. These words help in expressing ideas in a short and correct manner for the right occasion. Such words not only enhance the vocabulary but also enable you to economise in the use of words to a great extent. Try to learn as many as you can.

## Denoting Numbers

- A collection of poems — *anthology*
- A number of merchant ships protected by warships (in war-time) — *convoy*
- A number of stars grouped together — *constellation*
- A number of hired applauders, *i.e.* persons paid to clap — *claque*
- A number of people at church — *congregation*
- A number of people gathered together for some common purpose — *gathering, assembly, society*
- A group of people who get together to work for some cause of common interest — *coterie*
- A number of workmen, prisoners, thieves — *gang*
- A number of sheep — *flock*
- A number of geese — *gaggle*
- A number of leopards — *leap*
- A number of lions, monkeys — *pride, troop*
- A number of herrings, mackerel — *shoal*
- A number of fish taken in a net — *catch, haul*
- A number of whales, porpoises — *school, gam*
- A number of oxen or horses (two or more) harnessed together — *team*
- A number of ships, cars, buses — *fleet*

## Denoting Places

- A place where bees are kept — *apiary*
- A place where birds are kept — *aviary*
- A place where fishes are kept — *aquarium*
- A dwelling-place of an animal underground — *burrow*
- A squirrel's home — *drey*
- A nest of a bird of prey — *eyrie, aerie*
- A place where spirituous liquors are produced — *distillery*
- A place where clothes are washed and ironed — *laundry*
- A place where Government records are kept — *archives*
- A place where treasures of art, curiosities, etc. are preserved or exhibited — *museum*
- A place where fruit trees are grown — *orchard*

## Pertaining to the Literary Sphere

- A work whose writer is unknown — *anonymous*
- A record of one's life written by oneself — *autobiography*
- The history of the life of a person — *biography*
- The heading or short description of a newspaper article, chapter of a book etc. — *caption*

- A humorous play, having a happy ending — *comedy*
- A list of books in a library — *catalogue, bibliography*
- A book in which the events of each day are recorded — *diary*
- A books containing the words of a language with their definitions, in alphabetical order — *dictionary*
- A book of names and addresses — *directory*
- A short speech by a player at the end of a play — *epilogue*
- A brief summary of a book — *epitome*
- A book containing information on all branches of knowledge — *encyclopedia*
- To remove the offensive portions of a book — *expurgate*
- A speech delivered without earlier preparation — *extempore*
- A noisy or vehement speech intended to excite passions — *harangue*
- A written account, usually in book form of the interesting and memorable experiences of one's life — *memoirs*
- A note to help the memory — *memorandum*
- A declaration of plans and promises put forward by a candidate for election, political party or a sovereign — *manifesto*
- A short speech by a player at the beginning of a play — *prologue*
- Literary theft, or passing off an author's original work as one's own — *plagiarism*
- Speaking aloud to oneself — *soliloquy*
- A play with a sad or tragic end — *tragedy*

## Pertaining to Religion

- One who believes that man can have no knowledge of God but only of natural phenomena — *agnostic*
- One who renounces his religious vows or forsakes his religious principles — *apostate*
- One who does not believe in existence of God — *atheist*
- One intolerantly devoted to a particular creed — *bigot*
- To utter profane language against God or anything holy — *blaspheme*
- A breaker of church images — *iconoclast*
- Worship of images or idols — *idiolatory*
- One who believes in God — *theist*
- One who believes in only one God — *monotheist*
- One who believes in many Gods — *polytheist*

## Pertaining to Government

- To give up a throne or other office of dignity — *abdicate*
- Absence of government — *anarchy*
- Government by Sovereign of uncontrolled authority — *autocracy, despotism*
- Government by departments of states — *bureaucracy*
- Government of the people, for the people and by the people — *democracy*
- Government by the nobility — *aristocracy*
- The right of self-government — *autonomy*
- Government by a few — *oligarchy*
- Government by the wealthy — *plutocracy*
- Government by divine guidance — *theocracy*
- To decide a political question by the direct vote of the whole electorate — *referendum*
- Sweeping governmental change — *revolution*
- The science of government — *politics*

## Pertaining to Professions

- One who attends to the diseases of the eye — *oculist*
- One who tests eyesight and sells spectacles — *optician*
- One who attends to the teeth — *dentist*
- One skilled in the care of hands and feet — *chiropodist*

- A physician who assists women at child-birth *obstetrician*
- One who drives a motorcar *chauffeur*
- One who makes or sells candles *chandler*
- One who preserves the skins of animals and mounts them so as to resemble the living animals *taxidermist*
- One who compiles a dictionary *lexicographer*
- One who writes books *author*
- One skilled in the treatment of diseases of animals *veterinarian*
- A tradesman who manages funerals *undertaker*
- One who draws up contracts and lends money on interest *scrivener*
- One who lends money and keeps goods as security *pawnbroker*
- A teacher who travels from place to place to give instruction. *peripatetic*
- One who travels from place to place selling miscellaneous articles *hawker, pedlar*
- One who collects postage stamps *philatelist*
- One who lends money at exorbitant interest *usurer*
- One who takes care of a building *janitor*
- One who sells sweets and pastries *confectioner*
- One who works in a coalmine *collier*
- One who flies an aeroplane *pilot, aviator*
- One who studies rocks and soils *geologist*
- One who shoes horses *farrier*
- A professional rider in horses races *jockey*
- One who deals in silks, cotton, woollen, and linen goods *mercer*
- One who deals in wines *vintner*
- One who deals in fish *fishmonger*
- One who deals in iron and hardware *ironmonger*
- One who sells fruits, vegetables, etc. from a barrow *costermonger*
- One who sets type in a printing office *compositor*

## Pertaining to Medicine

- A substance which destroys or weakens germs *antiseptic*
- Any medicine which produces insensibility *anaesthetic*
- A medicine to counteract poison *antidote*
- Want or poorness of blood *anaemia*
- A medicine which alleviates pain *anodyne*
- To cut off a person's body a part which is infected *amputate*
- One who is recovering from illness *convalescent*
- To be able to tell the nature of disease by its symptoms *diagnose*
- A disease affecting many persons at the same place and time *epidemic*
- A disease confined to a particular district or place *endemic*
- To disinfect by smoke *fumigate*
- Free or exempt from infection *immune*
- A person who is sick *invalid*
- A cure for all diseases *panacea*
- A disease widely epidemic *pandemic*
- Confinement to one place to avoid spread of infection *quarantine*

## Pertaining to Characteristics and Actions

- One who devotes his life to the welfare and interests of other people *altruist*
- One who can use both hands with equal ease *ambidexterous*
- One who fishes with a rod *angler*
- One who kills secretly or by surprise *assassin*
- A person who collects things belonging to ancient times *antiquary*
- One who is always finding faults *censorious*

- One living at the same time as another *contemporary*
- One who sneers at the aims and beliefs of his fellowmen *cynic*
- One who delights in speaking about oneself *egotist*
- One who exalts his own opinion *egoist*
- One who dies for a noble cause *martyr*
- One who retires from society to live a solitary life *recluse, hermit*
- One who maliciously sets fire to buildings *incendiary*
- One who is banished from his home or his country *exile*
- One who takes refuge in a foreign country *refugee, alien*
- One who runs away from justice or the law *fugitive*
- One who walks in his sleep *somnambulist*
- One who looks on the bright side of things *optimist*
- One who looks on the dark side of things *pessimist*
- A hater of mankind *misanthropist*
- One who knows everything *omniscient*
- One who is all powerful *omnipotent*
- One who is present everywhere *omnipresent*
- One who devotes his service or wealth for the love of mankind *philanthropist*
- One new to anything *novice, tyro, neophyte*
- One who engages in any pursuit for the love of it, and not for gain *amateur*
- One who journeys to a holy place *pilgrim*
- A leader of the people who can sway his followers by his oratory *demagogue*
- One who has special skill in judging art, music, tastes, etc. *connoisseur*
- One whose reasoning is clever yet false *sophist*
- One who makes a display of his learning *pedant*
- One who is indifferent to pain or pleasure *stoic*
- One who loves his country and serves it devotedly *patriot*
- One devoted to the pleasures of eating and drinking *epicure*
- One who poses to be what he is not *hypocrite, impostor*
- One who foretells events *prophet*
- One who pretends to know a great deal about everything *mountebank, charlatan, quack*
- One versed in many languages *linguist*
- One who cannot pay one's debts *insolvent*
- One who takes over after another in office or employment *successor*
- One who has been before another in office or employment *predecessor*
- One who is opposed to intellectual progress *obscurant*
- One who abstains from alcoholic drinks *teetotaller*
- One who hides away on a ship to obtain a free passage *stowaway*
- One who spends very little *miser*
- One who spends too much *spendthrift*

## Pertaining to War

- An unprovoked attack by an enemy *aggression*
- Shells, bombs, military stores *ammunition*
- A place where naval or military weapons are made or stored *ordnance*
- An agreement between belligerents to stop fighting *armistice*
- A general pardon of offenders *amnesty*
- To reduce to nothing *annihilate*
- Nations carrying on warfare *belligerents*
- To surround a place with the intention of capturing *besiege*
- To camp in the open air without tents or covering *bivouac*

- To seize for military use *commandeer*
- A person who is forced by law to become a soldier *conscript*
- An order prohibiting ships to leave the ports *embargo*
- A number of firearms being discharged continuously *fusillade*
- To make an examination or preliminary survey of enemy territory for military objectives *reconnoitre*

## Pertaining to Marriage and Children

- One who marries a second wife or husband while the legal spouse is alive *bigamist*
- One vowed to a single or unmarried life *celibate*
- One engaged to be married *fiancé, fiancee*
- A child whose parents are dead *orphan*
- A hater of marriage *misogamist*
- One who has more than two wives at a time *polygamist*

## Pertaining to Death

- Dead and decaying flesh (esp. of animals) *carrion*
- A monument set up for persons who are buried elsewhere *cenotaph*
- To preserve a dead body from putrefaction *embalm*
- Words inscribed on a tomb *epitaph*
- An examination of dead body *postmortem, autopsy*
- An account in the newspaper of the funeral of one deceased *obituary*
- The property left to someone by a will *legacy*
- Occurring after death *posthumous*
- The act of killing a human being *homicide*
- Murder of a new born child *infanticide*
- Murder of a brother *fratricide*
- Murder of a sister *sororicide*
- Murder of a mother *matricide*
- Murder of a father *patricide*
- Murder of a parent *parricide*
- Murder of a king *regicide*

## Pertaining to Sciences and Arts

- The study of all heavenly bodies and the earth in relation to them *astronomy*
- The science of land management *agronomics*
- The study of mankind *anthropology*
- The study of physical life or living matter *biology*
- The study of plants *botany*
- The art of beautiful handwriting *calligraphy*
- The science which deals with the varieties of human race *ethnology*
- The study of the origin and history of words *etymology*
- The study of coins *numismatics*
- The study of human face *physiognomy*
- The art of making fireworks *pyrotechnics*
- The study of birds *ornithology*
- The study of languages *philology*
- At home equally on land or in water *amphibious*
- The inside of a nut *kernel*
- The central or innermost part of fruit *core*
- The animals of a certain region *fauna*

- The plants and vegetation of a certain region *flora*
- Absence of rain for a long time *drought*
- To supply land with water by artificial means *irrigate*
- One who studies plant and animal life *naturalist*
- A cud-chewing animal, *e.g.* the cow *ruminant*
- A gnawing animal, *e.g.* the rat *rodent*
- A four-footed animal *quadruped*
- Animals which carry their young in a pouch, *e.g.* kangaroo *marsupials*
- Soil composed largely of decayed vegetable matter *humus*
- A preparation for killing insects *insecticide*
- A plant or animal growing on another *parasite*
- Living for many years *perennial*

## Miscellaneous

- Loud enough to be heard *audible*
- Not distinct enough to be heard *inaudible*
- Fit for food *edible*
- Unfit for human consumption *inedible*
- Fit to be chosen or selected *eligible*
- Not having the qualities for being chosen *ineligible*
- Writing that is easy to read *legible*
- Writing that is difficult to decipher *illegible*
- Able to read *literate*
- Unable to read *illiterate*
- Born of married parents *legitimate*
- Born of unmarried parents *illegitimate*
- To send back a person to his own country *repatriate*
- To banish from one's country *expatriate*
- To move from one country to another *migrate*
- One who leaves his country to settle in another *emigrant*
- One who comes into a foreign country to settle there *immigrant*
- Incapable of being redeemed from evil, *i.e.* beyond correction *incorrigible*
- That which cannot be rubbed out or blotted out *ineffaceable, indelible*
- That which cannot be conquered *invincible*
- Incapable of making errors *infallible*
- That which cannot be avoided or prevented *inevitable*
- Incapable of being burnt *incombustible*
- That which easily catches fire *inflammable, flammable*
- That which cannot be seen *invisible*
- Living for ever *immortal*
- Increase the gravity of an offence *aggravate*
- Ordinary or commonplace remark *platitude*
- That which cannot be satisfied *insatiable*
- That which cannot be repaired *irreparable*
- That which cannot be imitated *inimitable*
- Persons (or efforts) that cannot be wearied *indefatigable*
- One who eats too much *glutton*
- To destroy completely *annihilate*
- A statement open to more than one interpretation *ambiguous*
- A round about way of speaking *circumlocution*
- Cautious observation of events, etc. *circumspection*
- That which cannot be hurt *invulnerable*

# Multiple Choice Questions

**Directions:** *Below are given some statements each of which is capable of being expressed by one word only. Each statement is followed by four such words of which only one is correct. Out of the given alternatives A, B, C and D choose the correct word which very closely fits each definition.*

1. A set of papers giving information about a person or event:
   A. editorial B. agenda
   C. dossier D. clippings
2. List and explanations of technical, difficult, etc. terms:
   A. preface B. glossary
   C. bibliography D. appendix
3. One who pays too much care to his clothes and personal appearance:
   A. conscious B. dandy
   C. cynosure D. leer
4. A child born after death of father:
   A. effeminate B. immature
   C. fatherless D. posthumous
5. A person who is hard to please:
   A. insensible B. hypocrite
   C. egoist D. fastidious
6. Complete failure in something attempted:
   A. fiasco B. vain
   C. falsies D. flop
7. A word which can be interpreted in any way:
   A. confusing B. misnomer
   C. ambiguous D. precise
8. A group of persons united by common interests:
   A. society B. class
   C. clique D. coterie
9. A person who is inexperienced and easily deceived:
   A. fool B. immature
   C. blackhorn D. greenhorn
10. Instruction by question and answer:
    A. interrogatory B. catechism
    C. bulletin D. alibi
11. Record of events by someone with first hand knowledge:
    A. novice B. report
    C. memoir D. itinerary
12. A mode of talk familiar to a particular group or profession:
    A. jargon B. colloquial
    C. slang D. abuses
13. Person who is crazy:
    A. lackadaisical B. tarter
    C. scrupulous D. loony
14. A person who readily believes others:
    A. hasty B. immature
    C. credulous D. credible
15. One who eats human flesh:
    A. beast B. cannibal
    C. maneater D. carnivorous
16. Intentional destruction of racial groups:
    A. genocide B. homicide
    C. fratricide D. communal riot
17. One with weakness of mind caused by old age:
    A. dastard B. dotard
    C. fop D. philanderer
18. Study of insects:
    A. zoology B. philology
    C. entomology D. etymology
19. A critical judge of any art particularly fine arts:
    A. connoisseur B. veteran
    C. philistine D. dilettante
20. One who introduces items of an entertainment:
    A. consort B. compere
    C. director D. introducer
21. A combination of business firms:
    A. enterprise B. franchise
    C. cartel D. autonomous
22. Freeing of suppressed emotions:
    A. catastrophe B. catharsis
    C. epilogue D. chagrin
23. One who believes in the power of fate:
    A. optimist B. pessimist
    C. fearful D. fatalist
24. The murder of brother:
    A. genocide B. homicide
    C. salvage D. fratricide
25. Additional to proper payment:
    A. premium B. overtime
    C. ex-gratia D. fringe
26. A person or thing used to tempt somebody into a position of danger:
    A. decoy B. provocateur
    C. jinx D. scapegoat
27. Custom of having more than one husband at the same time:
    A. polygamy B. polyandry
    C. bigamy D. sexagenary
28. A person of refined taste in food and drink:
    A. emeritus B. epicure
    C. glutton D. gourmand

29. A tombstone inscription:
A. epithet B. encomium
C. epistle D. epitaph

30. An office which has no work but high salary:
A. fortuitous B. gratuitous
C. sinecure D. ceremonial

31. One who is indifferent to pains and pleasure of life:
A. stoic B. metaphysical
C. pessimist D. sceptic

32. List of names of persons showing duties to be performed by each in turn:
A. notice B. bulletin
C. roster D. agenda

33. Long angry speech of criticism or accusation:
A. track record B. tirade
C. taut D. outburst

34. One who is in favour of never drinking alcoholic drinks:
A. idealist B. uxorious
C. teetotaller D. unalcoholic

35. Trying to win favour by flattery and charm:
A. smarmy B. shrewish
C. toady D. loquacious

36. A decision on which one cannot go back:
A. incorrigible B. irrevocable
C. rigid D. invulnerable

37. The science that studies the varieties of human race:
A. phrenology B. physiology
C. sociology D. ethnology

38. A person who hates women:
A. philogynist B. philatelist
C. misogamist D. misogynist

39. A group of people in a particular grade in an organisation:
A. colleague B. staff
C. echelon D. commission

40. Honourably discharged from service:
A. emeritus B. latitudinarian
C. infallible D. meritorious

41. One who does not believe in the existence of God:
A. atheist B. altruist
C. agnostic D. flippant

42. The large money paid for an early retirement:
A. goldmine B. golden handshake
C. gratuity D. lion's share

43. A hater of learning and knowledge:
A. misologist B. misogynist
C. philologist D. philanthropist

44. One who lives and acts for the welfare of others:
A. misanthrope B. credulous
C. altruist D. gregarious

45. Mental weariness for want of occupation:
A. desperate B. depression
C. fatigue D. ennui

46. That which makes it difficult to recognise the presence in real of somebody or something:
A. cover B. mask
C. make-up D. camouflage

47. To bear a hand in one's new business:
A. partnership B. interfere
C. assist D. join

48. One who renounces the world and practices self-discipline in order to attain salvation:
A. devotee B. ascetic
C. theist D. parsimonious

49. A place where gambling is practiced:
A. hotel B. motel
C. casino D. stadium

50. A sad song is a:
A. dirge B. elegy
C. ditty D. knell

## ANSWERS

| 1 | 2 | 3 | 4 | 5 | 6 | 7 | 8 | 9 | 10 |
|---|---|---|---|---|---|---|---|---|---|
| C | B | B | D | D | A | C | C | D | B |
| 11 | 12 | 13 | 14 | 15 | 16 | 17 | 18 | 19 | 20 |
| C | A | D | C | B | A | B | C | A | B |
| 21 | 22 | 23 | 24 | 25 | 26 | 27 | 28 | 29 | 30 |
| C | B | D | D | D | A | B | B | D | C |
| 31 | 32 | 33 | 34 | 35 | 36 | 37 | 38 | 39 | 40 |
| A | C | B | C | A | B | D | D | C | A |
| 41 | 42 | 43 | 44 | 45 | 46 | 47 | 48 | 49 | 50 |
| A | B | A | C | D | D | C | B | C | A |

# Idioms and Phrases

- An idiom is a group of words established by usage as having a meaning different from the individual words.
- A phrase is a small group of words standing together as an idiomatic expression.

Learn and practise as may as you can.

## Idioms and Idiomatic Phrases

✦ **ABC** (basic principles)
She does not know the ABC of photography.

✦ **At one's beck and call** (ready to obey)
He had a dozen men at his beck and call.

✦ **At sixes and sevens** (in disorder)
The drawing room articles were lying at sixes and sevens on the floor.

✦ **A wet blanket** (a discouraging person)
Don't allow Rakesh to accompany you to the hunting trip because he is a wet blanket.

✦ **A big gun** (an important person)
Mr Smith is a big gun in our city.

✦ **At a stone's throw** (at a short distance from)
My school is at a stone's throw from my house.

✦ **A man of word** (a person who keeps his promise)
Mr Sharma is a man of word.

✦ **A man of a few words** (a remarkable person)
Gandhiji was a man of a few words.

✦ **At arm's length** (to keep away)
We should always keep bad boys at arm's length

✦ **A bolt from the blue** (a sudden and unexpected event)
The news of my friend's death came to me like a bolt from the blue.

✦ **A man of letters** (a scholar)
Radha Krishnan was a man of letters.

✦ **A hard nut to crack.** (a puzzling problem)
To get a win over American basket ball team is a hard nut to crack for India.

✦ **A yeoman's service** (service which is beneficial to the human beings)
He did yeoman's service through his life.

✦ **A snake in the grass** (a hidden foe)
Beware of him because he seems to be a snake in the grass.

✦ **Acid test** (hard test)
The election will be an acid test for the ruling party.

✦ **A wolf in sheep's clothing** (a hypocrite)
You should not keep company with him because he is a wolf in sheep's clothing.

✦ **At the eleventh hour** (at the last moment)
The war was about to start but fortunately at the eleventh hour a messenger came to the PM with a message of peace.

✦ **A great card** (an important person)
Mr Sood is a great card in the ministry of finance.

✦ **A fool of the first water** (one completely foolish)
Being a fool of the first water he could not solve even the simplest sum.

✦ **A bone of contention** (to be the cause of quarrel)
Kashmir is the bone of contention between India and Pakistan.

✦ **A green hand** (not very much experienced)
We shall pay a little to a green hand.

✦ **All in all** (completely)
Rajesh is all in all in this office.

✦ **A bed of roses** (a comfort)
Life is not a bed of roses.

✦ **An apple of discord** (to be the cause of)
Kashmir is an apple of discord between India and Pakistan.

✦ **A white elephant** (of no use)
This sort of glib talker always proves a white elephant in the end.

✦ **A red letter day** (An important day)
15th August is a red letter day for the Indians.

✦ **By hook or by crook** (by any means fair or foul)

✦ **Black sheep** (a traitor)
Later on Mr XYZ proved a black sheep.

✦ **By dint of** (by means of)
By dint of hard work, she earned a lot of money.

✦ **Break ones back** (to work hard to get something)
He broke his back to earn his livelihood.

✦ **Break the back of** (accomplish the hardest part of a certain job)
There is nothing to be worried about as we've already broken the back of the problem.

✦ **Beat about the bush** (to go on talking on some worthless topic)
Stop this beating about the bush, come to the main task.

✦ **Beyond one's means** (beyond one's budget)
He is living beyond his means, therefore, he is sure to get ruined.

✦ **Cut loose** (Keep away)
India should cut loose from bad politics.

✦ **Chips of the same block** (having the same taste)
They are the chips of the same block.

✦ **Cut-throat competition** (a stiff competition)
There is a cut-throat competition among the publishers in the market.

✦ **Come what may** (no matter what happens)
I'll do it come what may.

✦ **Drop someone a line** (send a letter, etc.)
Please drop me a line of your well-being.

✦ **Dull the edge of** (reduce the intensity of)
Take this pill and it will dull the edge of pain.

✦ **From hand to mouth** (without any saving)
The poor factory worker is living from hand to mouth.

✦ **Fair and square** (clean)
One must be fair and square in one's dealing.

✦ **Hard of hearing** (somewhat deaf)
She is a bit hard of hearing.

✦ **In the good books of** (be good in one's mind)
Jack is in the good books of his teachers.

✦ **In black and white** (in written)
Don't give him anything in black and white.

✦ **In cold blood** (mercilessly)
The old woman was murdered in cold blood.

✦ **In a crack** (all of a sudden or rapidly)
The thief left the place in a crack.

✦ **In full swing** (in full force)
The studies of the students are going on in full swing.

✦ **In the twinkling of an eye** (quickly)
The monkey ate up grams in the twinkling of an eye.

✦ **Keep the ball rolling** (to maintain the progress of some activity)
After the death of his father he had to take the charge of his office to keep the ball rolling.

✦ **Neck and neck** (even)
There is a neck and neck fight between the two boxers.

✦ **Once in a blue moon** (seldom)
She visits her brother once in a blue moon.

✦ **Slow and steady** (slowly but continually)
Slow and steady wins the race.

✦ **To cut a sorry figure** (present oneself in a bad way)
She cut a sorry figure on the stage.

✦ **To give a red carpet reception** (to give a warm welcome)
The PM was given a red carpet reception in America.

✦ **To dance one's tune** (to follow someone submissively)
He always dances to his brother's tune.

✦ **To turn a deaf ear to** (to disregard)
She turned a deaf ear to her parents' advice.

✦ **To call a spade a spade** (to speak the truth)
Gandhiji always called a spade a spade.

✦ **To bring to book** (to scold)
The naughty boy was brought to book by the teacher.

✦ **To cut short** (to reduce)
Smoking will cut short your life.
He wants to get money by hook or by crook.

✦ **To grease the palm of** (to bribe)
Rohit greased the palm of the clerk and got the file moved.

✦ **Through thick and thin.** (under all circumstances)
We'll stand by you through thick and thin.

✦ **To die by inches** (to die a painful death)
The old man died by inches.

✦ **To eat one's words** (to retract one's statement)
You'll have to eat your words because you have spoken without thinking.

✦ **To burn the midnight oil** (to work hard)
You'll have to burn the midnight oil if you want to get good marks.

✦ **To poke one's nose into** (to meddle with)
It is bad to poke your nose into others' affair.

✦ **To fall flat** (to have no effect)
His father's advice fell flat on him.

✦ **To make a clean breast of** (to confess)
He made a clean breast of his involvement in the bomb blast.

✦ **To get the better of** (overcome)
Anger got the better of him.

✦ **To break somebody's back** (to give too much work to him to do)

She broke his back by giving him so much hard work to do.

✦ **Throw cold water on** (to discourage)
She tried to throw cold water on his plan but he was well-determined.

✦ **The long and short of** (in brief)
The long and short of his lecture is that we should live like brothers.

✦ **To burn one's fingers** (to get oneself in trouble)
You have burnt your fingers by speaking against him.

✦ **To turn over a new leaf** (to change the course of life)
He has turned over a new leaf in his life.

✦ **To have one's own axe to grind** (to have vested interest)
He has his own axe to grind in this matter.

✦ **To take to one's heels** (to run away)
The thief took to his heels as soon as he saw the policeman.

✦ **To move heaven and earth** (to make too much effort)
The young man moved heaven and earth to find a job.

✦ **To be caught red handed** (to be caught at the time of committing a crime)
The clerk was caught red handed when he was accepting bribe from Mr ABC.

✦ **To receive with open arms** (to give a warm welcome)
The new president of the club was received with open arms by the members.

✦ **To be born with a silver spoon in one's mouth** (to be born in a rich family)
Mr. J. L. Nehru was born with a silver spoon in his mouth.

✦ **To come to light** (to be known)
A new disease has recently come to light.

✦ **To be the apple of one's eye** (be very dear)
He is the apple of his parent's eye.

✦ **To make fun of** (laugh at)
The children made fun of the waiter in the hotel.

✦ **To let the cat out of the bag** (to divulge secret)
It was Sohan who let the cat out of the bag by telling the real matter.

✦ **To open a new chapter** (to start some habit, etc.
By drinking, you've opened a new chapter in your life.

✦ **To make the flesh creep** (to terrify)
The story made my flesh creep.

✦ **To lose ground** (to retreat)
After fighting for some time the Pakistani army began to lose ground.

✦ **To bring to book** (to punish)
The student was brought to book by the teacher.

✦ **To show a clean pair of heels** (to run away)
The thief showed a clean pair of heels as soon as he saw the policeman approaching.

✦ **To gain ground** (to be established)
He gained ground in India in a few years.

✦ **To get wind of** (to get information)
I got wind of his secret plans.

✦ **Under a cloud** (be in trouble or in a state of disgrace or suspicion)
His company seemed to be under a cloud as it had no funds to pay the wages to the workers.

## Verbal Phrases

✦ **Act upon** (to follow)
I acted upon my father's advice.

✦ **Act upto** (to perform within limits)
He acted upto his conscience.

✦ **Act beyond** (to perform crossing limits)
We should not act beyond our capacity.

✦ **Act for** (to perform in place of someone else)
The vice principal acted for the principal.

✦ **Back up** (to make a queue)
The vehicles began to back up.

✦ **Back down** (withdraw claim in the presence of opposition)
The leader backed down from his previous statement.

✦ **Back off** (draw back some plan or action)
They backed off from building a flyover.

✦ **Back out** (withdraw from a promise, etc.)
The government backed out of its promise.

✦ **Break down** (stop working) My car broke down on the highway.

✦ **Break into** (enter in certain premises by breaking the door, etc.)
Last night a thief broke into my neighbour's.

✦ **Break off** (stop all of a sudden)
She broke off and began to think over about her/his hand.

✦ **Break out** (spread)
Cholera has broken out in the town.

✦ **Break out of** (escape from)
A prisoner broke out of the prison last night.

✦ **Break up** (disperse)
The cloud of fog began to break up as the sun rose.

✦ **Break something up** (Cause something to break into small pieces)
She broke up the chocolate to distribute it among the girls.

✦ **Break with** (Cut off connection after quarrelling with someone)
He has broken with his brother.

✦ **Call on** (pay a visit to somebody)
I'll call on Mohan's today.

✦ **Call out** (to start)
The workers have called out a strike.

✦ **Call off** (to stop the strike etc.)
The workers have called off the strike.

✦ **Call at** (to visit someone's house)
I called at his house yesterday.

✦ **Call in** (send for)
Please call in the doctor.

✦ **Carry on** (continue)
Please carry on your work.

✦ **Carry something out** (perform a task)
Our company is carrying out a big deal with a foreign company.

✦ **Carry something over** (postpone)
The fancy dress competition had to be carried over till Monday)

✦ **Carry someone off** (kill somebody)
Cancer carried her off on the day of her 20th birthday.

✦ **Come of age** (get established)
As our company has come of age, so, there is no problem in selling our goods.

✦ **Come of** (belong to)
She comes of a royal family.

✦ **Come over** (surmount)
We at last came over all our problems.

✦ **Come off** (to take place)
The marriage of my brother comes off in the next month.

✦ **Come round** (agree)
At last he came round to my views.

✦ **Come under** (fall in the category of)
All these animals come under the same species.

✦ **Come down with** (suffer from)
She came down with whopping cough.

✦ **Come from** (be the nature of)
She came from London.

✦ **Come about** (happen)
The explosion came about when the worker struck the match to light a cigarette.

✦ **Cut off** (die)
The princess was cut off in the prime of her life.

✦ **Cut down** (reduce)
The prices of consumer goods should be cut down.

✦ **Cut someone out** (exclude someone)
His father cut him out of his will.

✦ **Fall in**
She fell in love with the prince.

✦ **Fall down** (fail)
The deal fell down for lack of transparency.

✦ **Fall out** (quarrel)
She fell out with his elder brother.

✦ **Fall through** (fail)
The project fell through for lack of funds.

✦ **Get away** (escape)
She got away with her life.

✦ **Get by** (to accomplish something with great difficulty)
She is not rich. She has just enough to get by.

✦ **Get on** (perform)
How are you getting on with your studies?

✦ **Get out** (become known)
The news got out that the PM was paying a visit to Russia.

✦ **Get over** (overcome)
At last I got over all obstacles.

✦ **Get up** (rise)
When do you get up in the morning?

✦ **Give up** (stop)
He gave up smoking.

✦ **Give out** (emit)
Garlic gives out a pungent smell.

✦ **Give in** (collapse)
The bridge gave in under the heavy load.

✦ **Give away** (distribute)
The Principal gave away the prizes.

✦ **Give out** (announce)
It was given out that the President of India would visit the place soon.

✦ **Go off** (explode)
The gun went off suddenly.

✦ **Go on** (continue)
She went on about how she flew the aeroplane.

✦ **Go through** (examine)
I'll go through this book later on.

✦ **Go up** (be built)
The construction of the house is going up.

✦ **Grind on** (continue for a long time in a tedious way)
The discussion over political issues ground on.

✦ **Grind something out** (produce something a tedious way)
She will grind some more short stories.

✦ **Look out** (be careful)
Look out! there is a snake.

✦ **Look down upon** (hate)
We should not look down upon the poor.

✦ **Look at** (watch)
Look at the blackboard.

✦ **Look after** (take care of)
We ought to look after our old parents.

✦ **Look into** (investigate)
The new police inspector will look into the matter.

✦ **Look up** (rise)
The prices of consumer goods are looking up.

✦ **Look back** (think of the past)
It made her feel disolate when she looked back on things of the past.

✦ **Make up** (to fulfil)
I'll make up my deficiency in Mathematics.

✦ **Make out** (understand)
I could not make out what she said.

✦ **Make up one' mind** (to resolve)
I have made up my mind to settle in the USA.

✦ **Make off** (leave hurriedly)
She made off without informing anybody.

✦ **Make something over** (transfer)
She should make her property over to her sons.

✦ **Make over** (hand over)
He made over the charge of the file to Mr Robert.

✦ **Pull back** (retreat)
The government has pulled back from its previous policy.

✦ **Pull something down** (demolish)
The authorities concerned pulled down a few building which were illegally built on government land.

✦ **Pull out** (pluck)
The child pulled out a few petals of the flower.

✦ **Pull through** (recover)
The patient will pull through.

✦ **Push on** (continue a journey)
It was getting darker but we pushed on.

✦ **Push at** (exert force)
He pushed at the bell, but it did not ring.

✦ **Push for** (demand persistently)
The workers have been pushing for the installation of new machines for five years.

✦ **Put out** (extinguish)
She put out the light.

✦ **Put on** (wear)
He put on an overcoat.

✦ **Put off** (postpone)
The plan had to be put off.

✦ **Put by** (spare something for future)
We must put by some money for future.

✦ **Put up with** (stay)
Your aunt is out of town for a couple of days, you may put up with us till she comes.

✦ **Put something down** (record something)
She put a new idea down on the paper.

✦ **Take after** (resemble)
He takes after his father.

✦ **Take off** (remove)
He took off his shoes.

✦ **Take something out** (obtain)
You may take out some money from Rohit if you want to purchase this car.

✦ **Take to** (fall into the habit of)
He took to gambling.

✦ **Turn something down** (reject something)
The judge turned down his appeal.

✦ **Turn on** (attack)
The thief turned on him with a knife.

## Multiple Choice Questions

**Directions:** *Some idioms/phrases are given below with their probable meanings. Select the options with their correct meanings.*

**1. Carry out**
A. To take from one place to another
B. To continue
C. To obey
D. To make efforts

**2. In the same boat**
A. A worn out choice
B. Indifferent
C. In identical circumstances
D. Carry off

**3. In one's good book**
A. A costly book
B. A priceless treasure
C. In one's favour
D. An enchanting beauty

**4. Keep a straight face**
A. To do make up
B. To change clothes

C. Assume responsibility
D. To remain serious

**5. To be above board**
A. To have a good height
B. To be honest in any business deal
C. To have no debts
D. To try to be beautiful

**6. On the face of it**
A. To agree B. From an action
C. More than enough D. Apparently

**7. Let the bygones be bygones**
A. In one's favour B. To pretend
C. To forget the past D. Other choice

**8. To split hairs**
A. Major distinctions
B. Hair with two ends
C. To make minute distinction
D. Without distinction

**9. Bread and butter**
A. Both bread and butter
B. Something essential
C. Livelihood
D. Relevant things

**10. To bell the cat**
A. To catch a cat and tie a bell round its neck
B. To make an effort
C. To be quick
D. To face a risk

**11. Hard and fast**
A. Strict B. Solid
C. Fast moving D. Some hard surface

**12. Part and parcel**
A. The part of a parcel
B. An essential part
C. A missing parcel
D. Some part of a machine sent by parcel

**13. Null and void**
A. Something invalid
B. Something that can be avoided
C. Something that can be nullified
D. Something evil

**14. To make clean breast of**
A. To gain prominence
B. To praise oneself
C. To confess without reserve
D. To destroy before it blooms

**15. Trump card**
A. A powerful means of achieving an object
B. Resourcefulness
C. The best gamble to attain success
D. None of these

**16. Tall talk**
A. A discussion continued for a long time
B. A high sounding talk
C. A meaningful talk
D. A useless talk

**17. Small talk**
A. Gossip
B. A discussion carried on for a long time
C. A brief discussion
D. None of these

**18. Throw out of gear**
A. To replace B. Hinder, disturb
C. To decide D. Take up tune

**19. To and fro**
A. Back and forth B. Puzzled
C. Amazed D. Reprove

**20. To bell the cat**
A. To do an easy job
B. To be indifferent to
C. To undertake a difficult job
D. To clarify

**21. To be under cloud**
A. Puzzle B. Enjoy the favour
C. Talk thoughtlessly D. To be under suspicion

**22. A labour of love**
A. A tragic end
B. A funny thing
C. Not fruitful
D. Work done without payment

**23. Follow suit**
A. Follow an example B. Wear a new dress
C. Irrelevant D. A gay person

**24. Foul play**
A. Bad intentions
B. A play not well acted
C. A play not liked by the audience
D. None of these

**25. To pick holes**
A. To find some reason to quarrel
B. To destroy something
C. To criticise someone
D. To cut some part of an item

**26. To smell a rat**
A. To see signs of plague epidemic
B. To get bad smell of a dead rat
C. To suspect foul dealings
D. To be in a bad mood

**27. To put a spoke in one's wheel**
A. To encourage
B. Act without restraint

C. Risk something
D. To obstruct one's progress

**28. To pull one's leg**
A. To give up B. Take care of
C. To befool D. To know

**29. To play with fire**
A. Grasp the truth
B. To handle something dangerous
C. To ridicule
D. To flee away

**30. To reckon with**
A. Take up time B. Make an inventory
C. To deal with D. Submit to punishment

**31. To run short**
A. Talk until one is tired at
B. Apply to oneself
C. To get rid of
D. To have or be too little

**32. A man of letters**
A. A postman B. A learned man
C. A hypocrite D. An ignorant man

**33. A maiden speech**
A. A speech made in the parliament
B. A speech made before unmarried girls
C. A speech made by a political leader
D. A speech made for the first time

**34. Order of the day**
A. An order passed on a particular day
B. A current law
C. Something common or general
D. None of these

**35. To end in smoke**
A. To make completely understand
B. To ruin oneself
C. To excite great applause
D. None of these

**36. To give vent to**
A. To allow to flow forth
B. To prove a failure
C. To amass wealth
D. To evade

**37. To eat humble pie**
A. To apologise or confess
B. To order
C. To flatter
D. To get rid of

**38. A black sheep**
A. An unlucky person B. A negro
C. An ugly person D. None of these

**39. To catch a tartar**
A. To trap wanted criminal with great difficulty
B. To catch a dangerous person
C. To meet with disaster
D. To deal with a person who is more than one's watch

**40. Sit on fence**
A. To remain neutral
B. To show contempt
C. To enjoy the surroundings
D. To become fond of

**41. Pay off old scores**
A. To repay the debt B. To have revenge
C. To invite D. Secretly

**42. Turn turtle**
A. To cheat B. To be lopsided
C. To frustrate D. To dance to the tune

**43. Wash one's hands of**
A. To refuse B. To assist
C. To abuse D. To refuse to be

**44. Under duress**
A. Under compulsion
B. Willing
C. To elicit information
D. To demand

**45. To turn the tables**
A. To ruin someone
B. To turn the situation to one's own side
C. To reverse the situation
D. To move from one point to another

**46. On the cards**
A. Possibly B. Probably
C. Openly D. Likely

**47. To leave someone in the lurch**
A. To come to compromise with someone
B. Constant source of annoyance to someone
C. To put someone at ease
D. To desert someone in his difficulties

**48. To play second fiddle**
A. To be happy, cheerful and healthy
B. To reduce importance of one's senior
C. To support the role and view of another person
D. To do back seat driving

**49. To yearn for**
A. To weep for B. To remember
C. To admire D. To long for intensely

**50. Call off**
A. To finish B. To withdraw
C. To postpone D. To cry

# ANSWERS

| 1 | 2 | 3 | 4 | 5 | 6 | 7 | 8 | 9 | 10 |
|---|---|---|---|---|---|---|---|---|---|
| C | C | C | D | B | D | C | C | C | D |
| **11** | **12** | **13** | **14** | **15** | **16** | **17** | **18** | **19** | **20** |
| A | B | A | C | C | B | A | B | A | C |
| **21** | **22** | **23** | **24** | **25** | **26** | **27** | **28** | **29** | **30** |
| D | D | A | A | C | C | D | C | B | C |
| **31** | **32** | **33** | **34** | **35** | **36** | **37** | **38** | **39** | **40** |
| D | B | D | C | D | A | A | D | B | A |
| **41** | **42** | **43** | **44** | **45** | **46** | **47** | **48** | **49** | **50** |
| B | B | D | A | C | D | D | C | D | B |

# Narration

## Direct and Indirect Narration/Speech

The exact words spoken by the speaker are known as Direct Speech.

The words spoken by somebody and expressed by someone else with some modification are known as Indirect Speech.

(*a*) Ram says to me, "You do not help me."

(*b*) Ram tells me that I do not help him.

The sentence (*a*) shows the words spoken by Ram. So, it is a sentence of Direct Speech.

The sentence (*b*) shows the words spoken by Ram and expressed by someone else with certain modification. So, it is a sentence of Indirect Speech.

The following points should be noted while changing Direct Speech into Indirect speech:

**1.** The verb outside the inverted commas is called the Reporting Verb.

**2.** The verb or sentence inside the inverted commas is called the Reported Speech.

**3.** If the Reporting verb is in the Present or Future Tense, there is no change in the tense in the Reported Speech.

**4.** If the Reporting Verb is in the Past Tense, the Tense in the Reported Speech is changed.

**5.** The Reporting verb may be in any Tense, in it the Pronouns are changed as under:

(*i*) First Person according to Subject

(*ii*) Second Person according to Object

(*iii*) Third Person, No change.

**6.** If the Reporting verb is in the Past Tense the Adverb will change as under in the Indirect Speech.

| ***Direct*** | ***Indirect*** |
|---|---|
| now | then |
| here | there |
| after | before |
| today | that day |
| yesterday | the previous day |
| these | those |
| tomorrow | the next day |
| last week | the previous week |
| this | that |

**7.** Adjectives/Determiners are changed as under:

| ***Direct*** | ***Indirect*** |
|---|---|
| this | that |
| these | those |

### Rules for Change of Tense

| Reporting Verb | Reporting Speech | Change of Tense |
|---|---|---|
| Present Tense | Any Tense | No change |
| Future Tense | Any Tense | No change |
| Past Tense | Present/Future Tense | Change into corresponding Past Tense |
| Past Tense | Past Indefinite Tense | Change into Past Perfect Tense |
| Past Tense | Past Continuous Tense | Change into Past Perfect Continuous Tense |
| Past Tense | Past Perfect/Perfect Continuous Tense | No change |
| Past Tense | Universal Truth | No change |
| Past Tense | Proverb | No change |

## Transformation of Speech Based on Special Rules

### 1. Rule Related to Interrogative Sentence

- If the answer of an interrogative sentence is possible in yes-no manner.

**Illustration.**

Dhoni said to Sachin, "Will you help me?"

Dhoni asked Sachin whether he would help him.

(**Note :** The answer of R.S. is possible in yes-no manner)

**Rule of Transformation from Direct to Indirect speech**

**Step I** : Change R.V. into ask.

**Step II** : In place of comma use 'if/whether'.

**Step III** : Change interrogative sentence into assertive sentence.

- If the answer of an interrogative sentence is not possible in yes-no manner.

**Illustration:**

Sachin said to Dhoni, "What do you want?"

Sachin asked Dhoni what he wanted.

(**Note :** Only in Step II, you have to avoid comma and inverted comma and rest will be same as mentioned above).

### 2. Rule related to Imperative Sentence

- Imperative sentence is a sentence which shows Order/Advice/Request

**Illustration:**

My teacher said to me, "Go there".

My teacher ordered me to go there.

**Rule of Transformation from Direct to Indirect Speech**

**Step I** : Change R.V. as per meaning/sense of R.S. into order/request/advise.

**Step II** : In place of comma, use 'to'.

**Step III** : Rest portion will be same.

### 3. Rule related to Optative Sentence

- Optative sentence is a sentence which expresses the feeling of bless/curse/pray/wish.

**Illustration:**

Mother said to me, "May you live long!"

Mother blessed me that I might live long.

**Rule of Transformation from Direct to Indirect Speech**

**Step I** : Change R.V. as per meaning/sense of R.S. into bless/curse/pray/wish.

**Step II** : In place of comma, use 'that'.

**Step III** : Change optative sentence into assertive sentence.

### 4. Rule related to Exclamatory Sentence

- Exclamatory sentence is a sentence which takes note of exclamatory (!) mark in that sentence showing inner feeling.

**Illustration:**

She said, "Alas! I am ruined".

She exclaimed with sorrow that she was ruined.

**Rule of Transformation from Direct to Indirect Speech**

**Step I** : Change R.V. as per meaning/sense of R.S. into exclaim/exclaims/exclaimed/will or shall exclaim + joy/sorrow/anger/surprise/applause/contempt.

**Step II** : Change comma into that.

**Step III** : Change note of exclamation (!) into full stop (.)

**Step IV** : Change exclamatory sentence into assertive sentence.

## Universal, Historical Truth, etc.

If the Reported Speech expresses a Universal or Historical or Habitual truth, its Tense will not change.

1. The teacher said to the students, "The sun rises in the east."

   The teacher told the students that the sun rises in the east.

2. My father said to me, "The First Battle of Panipat was fought in 1526."

   My father told me that the First Battle of Panipat was fought in 1526.

# Multiple Choice Questions

**Directions (Qs. 1 to 13):** *Select the correct Indirect Speech for the following sentences:*

**1.** I said to him, "I shall help you."

A. I told him that I can help him.
B. I told him that I would help him.
C. I told him that I will help him.
D. I told him that I shall be helping him.

**2.** My Teacher said to me, "The earth revolves round the sun."

A. My teacher told me that the earth revolves round the sun.
B. My teacher told me that the earth revolve round the sun.
C. My teacher told me that the earth had been revolving round the sun.

D. My teacher told me that the earth has been revolving round the sun.

**3.** I said to my friend, "My father daily goes for a walk."

A. I told my friend that my father daily goes for a walk.

B. I told my friend that my father daily went for a walk.

C. I told my friend that my father has to go for a walk.

D. I told my friend that my father had gone for a walk.

**4.** He said to me, "May God bless you!"

A. He requested that God can bless me.

B. He prayed that God can bless me.

C. He prayed that God might bless me.

D. He prayed that God will bless me.

**5.** The patient said, "Thank you, doctor."

A. The patient thanked the doctor.

B. The patient requested the doctor with thanks.

C. The patient told the doctor thanks.

D. The patient suggested the doctor thanks.

**6.** Satish said, "No, I shall not talk to him."

A. Satish told that he should not talk to him.

B. Satish suggested that he would not have talked to him.

C. Satish exclaimed with sorrow that he would not talk with him.

D. Satish refused to talk to him.

**7.** The child said, "What a lovely place!"

A. The child exclaimed with sorrow that it was a lovely place.

B. The child thought that the place was lovely.

C. The child exclaimed with joy that the place was very lovely.

D. The child suggested that the place was lovely.

**8.** He said, "What a fool I have been!"

A. He told himself with sorrow that he was a fool.

B. He confessed with regret that he had been a great fool.

C. He said himself a fool.

D. He suggested that he could be a fool.

**9.** He said, "Alas! I am ruined."

A. He told me that he had been ruined.

B. He exclaimed with joy that he had been ruined.

C. He exclaimed with sorrow that he was ruined.

D. He told me that he should not be ruined.

**10.** The accused said, "I am not guilty."

A. The accused exclaimed with sorrow that I am not guilty.

B. The accused exclaimed with joy that he was not guilty.

C. The accused stated that he was not guilty.

D. The accused told me that he has not been guilty.

**11.** My teacher said, "The earth is round".

A. My teacher said that the earth was round.

B. My teacher says that the earth is round.

C. My teacher said that the earth is round.

D. My teacher ordered that the earth is round.

**12.** He said, "What a place it is!"

A. He said that it was a very fine place.

B. He said that is a very fine place.

C. He said that the place is fine.

D. He exclaimed with joy/surprise that it was a very fine place.

**13.** Ria said, "Shall I thread the needle?"

A. Ria asked if she should thread the needle.

B. Ria asked if she shall thread the needle.

C. Ria ordered if she should thread the needle.

D. Ria says that if she would thread the needle.

**Directions (Qs. 14 to 33):** *Pick out the correct alternative that completes the incomplete sentence which is changed into Indirect Narration.*

**14.** She said to me, "I shall see you as soon as I get time."
She told me:

A. that she will see me as soon as she will get time.

B. that she would see me as soon as she would get time.

C. she would see me whenever she got time.

D. that she would see me whenever she gets time.

**15.** My secretary said to me, "Your plane will leave if you do not go at once."
My secretary told me that:

A. her plane would leave if she did not go at that time.

B. her plane would leave if I do not go at once.

C. my plane would leave if I did not go at that very time.

D. my plane will leave if I did not go at that time.

**16.** My mother said to me, "Don't quarrel among yourselves".
My mother:

A. forbade me to quarrel among ourselves.

B. asked me not to quarrel among ourselves.

C. asked me that not to quarrel among ourselves.

D. asked me to quarrel not among ourselves.

**17.** Her father said to her mother, "Excuse the daughter."
Her father:

A. requested her mother to excuse the daughter.

B. asked her mother to excuse the daughter.

C. asked her mother to have excused the daughter.

D. asked her mother to have been excused.

**18.** He said to his friend, "Wait here till father comes."
He requested his friend:
A. to wait here till father had come.
B. that to wait there till his friend came.
C. to wait there till father came.
D. to wait here until his friend came.

**19.** She said to her maid, "Run and catch the thief."
She ordered her maid:
A. ran and catch the thief.
B. that to run and to catch the thief.
C. ran and caught the thief.
D. to run and catch the thief.

**20.** Anita said to Sunita, "What are you doing?"
Anita asked Sunita:
A. what she will be doing.
B. that what she is doing.
C. that what she was doing.
D. what she was doing.

**21.** She said to me, "Are you meeting me today?"
She enquired of me:
A. whether I am meeting her that day.
B. whether I was meeting her today.
C. whether I was meeting her that day.
D. I was meeting her that day.

**22.** Nitish said to me, "When did you buy this pen?"
Nitish asked me:
A. when I was to buy that pen.
B. when I would buy that pen.
C. when I had bought that pen.
D. when I was buying that pen.

**23.** She said to me, "Are you going to market?"
She enquired of me:
A. I am going to market.
B. I was going to market.
C. if I was going to market.
D. if I had been going to the market.

**24.** Damini said, "Why did not you change your clothes?"
Damini asked me:
A. why I had not changed my clothes.
B. why I did not change my clothes.
C. why I would not change my clothes.
D. why I have not been changing my clothes.

**25.** Umesh said to me, "Have you read that novel?"
Umesh asked me:
A. if he was reading that novel.
B. if he had read that novel.
C. if I had read that novel.
D. if I was reading that novel.

**26.** She said to me, "I shall forgive you."
She told me:
A. that she will forgive me.
B. that she was going to forgive me.
C. that she will not forgive me.
D. that she would forgive me.

**27.** I said to her, "It was very hot last night."
I told her:
A. that it had been very hot the previous night.
B. that it was very hot the previous night.
C. that it has been very hot the last night.
D. that it had been very hot this night.

**28.** She said to me, "I thank you for the help you have given."
She:
A. told me that she thanked me for the help I had given.
B. thanked me for the help I have given.
C. thanked to me for the help I have given.
D. thanked me for the help I had given.

**29.** Mohini said to me, "Trust in God."
Mohini advised me:
A. that I should trust in God.
B. should trust in God.
C. trusted in God.
D. to trust in God.

**30.** I said to him, "Let us go to school."
I told him:
A. we would go to school.
B. we shall go to school.
C. that we would go to school.
D. that we should go to school.

**31.** Rajni said, "May God bless you?"
Rajni:
A. exclaimed with wish that God might bless me.
B. expressed a wish that God might bless me.
C. asked God to bless me.
D. shouted with joy to bless me.

**32.** My mother said me, "Do not have so many friends."
My mother forbade me:
A. to have so many friends.
B. not to have so many friends.
C. to have been so many friends.
D. to possess so many friends.

**33.** Ram said, "Pay attention to me."
Ram asked:
A. pay attention to him.
B. paid attention to him.
C. having paid attention to him.
D. to pay attention to him.

**Directions (Qs. 34 to 50):** *In questions below, the sentences have been given in Direct/Indirect Speech. Out of the four alternatives suggested select the one which best expresses the given sentence in Indirect/Direct Speech.*

**34.** She said that her brother was getting married
A. She said, "Her brother is getting married."
B. She told, "My brother is getting married"
C. She said, "My brother is getting married".
D. She said, "My brother was married".

**35.** "Please don't go away", she said.
A. She said to please her and not go away.
B. She told me to go away.
C. She begged me not to go away.
D. She begged that I not go away.

**36.** "If you don't keep quiet I shall shoot you", he said to her in a calm voice.
A. He warned her to shoot if she didn't keep quiet calmly.
B. He said calmly that I shall shoot you if you don't be quiet.
C. He warned her calmly that he would shoot her if she didn't keep quiet.
D. Calmly he warned her that be quiet or else he will have to shoot her.

**37.** I told him that he was not working hard.
A. I said to him, "You are not working hard."
B. I told him, "You are not working hard."
C. I said, "You are not working hard."
D. I said to him, "He is not working hard."

**38.** She said that she would finish the work the next day.
A. She said, "I will finish the work the next day."
B. She said, "I will finish the work tomorrow."
C. She said, "You will finish the work tomorrow."
D. She said, "I finished the work."

**39.** She said to him, "Why don't you go today?"
A. She asked him why he did not go that day.
B. She said to him that why he don't go today.
C. She asked him not to go today.
D. She asked him why he did not go today.

**40.** "Are you alone, my son?" asked a soft voice close behind me.
A. A soft voice asked that what I was doing there alone.
B. A soft voice said to me are you alone son.
C. A soft voice from my back asked if I was alone.
D. A soft voice behind me asked if I was alone.

**41.** My cousin said, "My room-mate had snored throughout the night."
A. My cousin said that her room-mate snored throughout the night.
B. My cousin told me that her room-mate snored throughout the night.
C. My cousin complained to me that her room-mate is snoring throughout the night.
D. My cousin felt that her room-mate may be snoring throughout the night.

**42.** He asked Rama if he needed his help then.
A. He said to Rama, "Do you need my help?"
B. He told Rama, "Tell me if you need help."
C. He asked Rama, "Do I need your help?"
D. He said to Rama, "Do you need my help now?"

**43.** Nita ordered her servant to bring her a cup of tea.
A. Nita told her servant, "Bring a cup of tea."
B. Nita said, "Bring me a cup of tea."
C. Nita said to her servant, "Bring me a cup of tea."
D. Nita said to her servant, "Bring her that cup of tea."

**44.** He exclaimed with joy that India had won the Sahara Cup.
A. He said, "India has won the Sahara Cup."
B. He said, "India won the Sahara Cup."
C. He said, "How! India will win the Sahara Cup."
D. He said, "Hurrah! India has won the Sahara Cup."

**45.** The boy said, "Who dare call you a thief?"
A. The boy enquired who dared call him a thief.
B. The boy asked who called him a thief.
C. The boy told that who dared call him a thief.
D. The boy wondered who dared call a thief.

**46.** The little girl said to her mother, "Did the sun rise in the East?
A. The little girl said to her mother that the sun rose in the East.
B. The little girl asked her mother if the sun rose in the East.
C. The little girl said to her mother if the sun rises in the East.
D. The little girl asked her mother if the sun is in the East.

**47.** Dhruv said that he was sick and tired of working for that Company.
A. Dhruv said, "I am sick and tired of working for this Company."
B. Dhruv said, "He was tired of that Company."
C. Dhruv said to me, "I am sick and tired of working for this Company."
D. Dhruv said, "I will be tired of working for that Company."

**48.** He said to his father, "Please increase my pocket-money."
A. He told his father, please increase the pocket-money.
B. He pleaded his father to please increase my pocket-money.
C. He requested his father to increase his pocket-money.
D. He asked his father increase his pocket-money.

**49.** She said to her friend, "I know where is everyone."
A. She told that she knew where was everyone.
B. She told her friend that she knew where was everyone.
C. She told her friend she knew where is everyone
D. She told her friend that she knows where was everyone.

**50.** His father ordered him to go to his room and study.
A. His father said, "Go to your room and study."
B. His father said to him, "Go and study in your room."
C. His father shouted, "Go right now to your study room."
D. His father said firmly, "Go and study in your room."

## ANSWERS

| 1 | 2 | 3 | 4 | 5 | 6 | 7 | 8 | 9 | 10 |
|---|---|---|---|---|---|---|---|---|---|
| B | A | A | C | A | D | C | B | C | C |
| **11** | **12** | **13** | **14** | **15** | **16** | **17** | **18** | **19** | **20** |
| C | D | A | B | C | A | B | C | D | D |
| **21** | **22** | **23** | **24** | **25** | **26** | **27** | **28** | **29** | **30** |
| C | C | C | A | C | D | A | A | A | D |
| **31** | **32** | **33** | **34** | **35** | **36** | **37** | **38** | **39** | **40** |
| B | A | D | C | C | C | A | B | A | D |
| **41** | **42** | **43** | **44** | **45** | **46** | **47** | **48** | **49** | **50** |
| A | D | C | B | A | B | A | C | B | A |

# Voice

A sentence in active voice focuses on the person or thing doing the action. A sentence in passive voice focuses on the person or thing affected by the action. *e.g.*,

The idol was built. (Active voice)
Someone built the idol. (Passive voice)

## Transformation of Voice

- Voice and Tense are closely associated with each other.
- Tense plays an important role while transforming the voice.

On the basis of following points, voice can be transformed from active to passive voice.

## The Present Indefinite Tense

**Active voice:** Subject + $V_1$ + Object
**Passive voice:** Subject + is, am, are + $V_3$ + by + Object

1. **Active voice:** He sings sweet songs.
   **Passive voice:** Sweet songs are sung by him.
2. **Active voice:** She does not cause any hindrance in my work.
   **Passive voice:** No hindrance in my work is caused by her.
3. **Active voice:** Do they love their country?
   **Passive voice:** Is their country loved by them?

## The Present Continuous Tense

**Active voice:** Subject + is/am/are + $V_1$ + ing + Object.
**Passive voice:** Subject + is/am/are + being + $V_3$ + by + Object.

1. **Active voice:** She is cooking food.
   **Passive voice:** Food is being cooked by her.
2. **Active voice:** Rita is not knitting a sweater.
   **Passive voice:** A sweater is not being knitted by Rita.
3. **Active voice:** Is Meena baking a cake?
   **Passive voice:** Is a cake being baked by Meena?

## The Present Perfect Tense

**Active voice:** Subject + has/have + $V_3$ + Object.
**Passive voice:** Subject + has/have + been + $V_3$ + by + Object.

1. **Active voice:** I have written an essay.
   **Passive voice:** An essay has been written by me.
2. **Active voice:** They have not whitewashed the fence.
   **Passive voice:** The fence has not been whitewashed by them.
3. **Active voice:** Have you cut the cake?
   **Passive voice:** Has the cake been cut by you?

## The Past Indefinite Tense

**Active voice:** Subject + $V_2$ + Object
**Passive voice:** Subject + was/were + $V_3$ + by + Object

1. **Active voice:** He composed a new song.
   **Passive voice:** A new song was composed by him.
2. **Active voice:** He did not operate the computer.
   **Passive voice:** The computer was not operated by him.
3. **Active voice:** Did she catch a fish?
   **Passive voice:** Was a fish caught by her?

## The Past Continuous Tense

**Active voice:** Subject + was/were + $V_1$ + ing + Object
**Passive voice:** Subject + was/were + being + $V_3$ + by + Object

1. **Active voice:** The farmers were ploughing the fields.
   **Passive voice:** The fields were being ploughed by the farmers.
2. **Active voice:** He was not administering the new drug to the patient.
   **Passive voice:** The new drug was not being administered to the patient by him.
3. **Active voice:** Was she sewing a dress?
   **Passive voice:** Was a dress being sewn by her?

## The Past Perfect Tense

**Active voice:** Subject + had + $V_3$ + Object.
**Passive voice:** Subject + had + been + $V_3$ + by + Object

1. **Active voice:** He had issued me an import licence.
   **Passive voice:** I had been issued an import licence.
2. **Active voice:** We had not visited the Taj.
   **Passive voice:** The Taj had not been visited by us.
3. **Active voice:** Who had taught you English?
   **Passive voice:** By whom had you been taught English?

## The Future Indefinite Tense

**Active voice:** Subject + will/shall + $V_1$ + Object.
**Passive voice:** Subject + will/shall + be + $V_3$ + by + Object.

1. **Active voice:** He will remove the dust from the shelf.
   **Passive voice:** The dust from the shelf will be removed by him.
2. **Active voice:** He will not open the main gate.
   **Passive voice:** The main gate will not be opened by him.
3. **Active voice:** Will you help us?
   **Passive voice:** Shall we be helped by you?

## The Future Perfect Tense

**Active voice:** Subject + will/shall + have + $V_3$ + Object.
**Passive voice:** Subject + will/shall + have + been + $V_3$ + by + Object.

1. **Active voice:** They will have sold their house by then.
   **Passive voice:** Their house will have been sold by them by then.
2. **Active voice:** He will not have informed the police about it.
   **Passive voice:** The police will not have been informed about it by him.
3. **Active voice:** Will they have accepted the deal?
   **Passive voice:** Will the deal have been accepted by them?

## Imperative Sentences

1. **Active voice:** Open the window.
   **Passive voice:** You are ordered to open the window.
   ***Or***
   Let the window be opened.
2. **Active voice:** Please/kindly open the window.
   **Passive voice:** You are requested to open the window.
3. **Active voice:** Never make a noise.
   **Passive voice:** A noise should never be made.

## Infinitives

1. **Active voice:** It is time to open the shop.
   **Passive voice:** It is time for the shop to be opened.
2. **Active voice:** He begged the officer to forgive him.
   **Passive voice:** He begged the officer to be forgiven.
3. **Active voice:** He has to break the door.
   **Passive voice:** The door has to be broken by him.

## Prepositional Verb

1. **Active voice:** She laughed at the beggar.
   **Passive voice:** The beggar was laughed at by her.
2. **Active voice:** He listened to the news.
   **Passive voice:** The news was listened to by him.
3. **Active voice:** They called in the doctor.
   **Passive voice:** The doctor was called in by them.

## Double Object

1. **Active voice:** He gave me a pen.
   **Passive voice:** A pen was given to me by him.
   ***Or***
   I was given a pen by him.
2. **Active voice:** She told us a story.
   **Passive voice:** A story was told (to) us by her.
   ***Or***
   We were told a story by her.

## Use of Preposition other than 'by'

1. **Active voice:** The jug contains juice.
   **Passive voice:** Juice is contained in the jug.
2. **Active voice:** The audience thronged the hall.
   **Passive voice:** The hall was thronged with the audience.
3. **Active voice:** I know her.
   **Passive voice:** She is known to me.

## Quasi Passive Verbs

1. **Active voice:** Quinine tastes bitter.
   **Passive voice:** Quinine is bitter when tasted.
   ***Or***
   Quinine is bitter when it is tasted.
2. **Active voice:** Sugar is sweet (to taste).
   **Passive voice:** Sugar is sweet when tasted.
   ***Or***
   Sugar is sweet when it is tasted.

## Implied Sentences

1. **Active voice:** The driver drove the bus.
   **Passive voice:** The bus was driven.
2. **Active voice:** Someone read the news.
   **Passive voice:** The news was read.
3. **Active voice:** They say work is worship.
   **Passive voice:** It is said that work is worship.

# Multiple Choice Questions

**Directions (Qs. 1 to 20):** *In the following questions, a sentence has been given in Active/Passive Voice. Out of the four alternatives suggested, select the one that Best Expresses the same sentence in Passive/Active Voice.*

**1.** Circumstances will oblige me to go.
A. I will oblige the circumstances and go.
B. I shall be obliged to go by the circumstances.
C. Under the circumstances, I should go.
D. I shall be obliged by the circumstances to go.

**2.** We waste much time on trifles.
A. Much time was wasted on trifles.
B. Much time will be wasted on trifles.
C. Much time is wasted by us on trifles.
D. Much time is wasted on trifles.

**3.** Mohan gave the beggar an old shirt.
A. An old shirt was given to Mohan by the beggar.
B. An old shirt was given to the beggar by Mohan
C. The begger was gave an old shirt by Mohan.
D. An old shirt was gave to the beggar by Mohan.

**4.** They have made him a king.
A. A king has been made by him.
B. He was made a king by them.
C. They have been made kings by him.
D. He has been made a king by them.

**5.** Who taught you English?
A. By whom English was taught to you?
B. By whom you were taught English?
C. By whom was English taught to you?
D. By whom are you taught English?

**6.** Was he knocking at the door?
A. Was the door being knocked at by him?
B. Was the door being knocked by him?
C. Was the door knocked by him?
D. Was the door knocking at him?

**7.** What was Rani doing?
A. What was done by Rani?
B. What was Rani being done?
C. What was being done by Rani?
D. What was being doing Rani?

**8.** Why were you wasting your time?
A. Why was your time being wasted?
B. Why was your time being wasted by you?
C. Why was your time wasted by you?
D. Why was your time wasted?

**9.** She has laid out a small garden.
A. A small garden has been laid by her.
B. A small garden has laid her.
C. A small garden being laid by her.
D. A small garden has been laid out by her.

**10.** She had already solved all the sums.
A. All the sums had already been solved by her.
B. All the sums have already been solved by her.
C. All the sums have been solved by her.
D. All the sums are solved by her.

**11.** He will have posted the letter.
A. The letter has been posted by him.
B. The letter will be posted by him.
C. The letter will have been posted by him.
D. The letter is posted by him.

**12.** They will have sold all the books by 4 P.M.
A. All the books will be sold by 4 P.M.
B. All the books will have been sold by 4 P.M.
C. All the books were being sold by 4 P.M.
D. All the books must be sold by 4 P.M.

**13.** Do you speak English?
A. Is English spoken by you?
B. Does English spoken by you?
C. Is English being spoken by you?
D. Does English being spoken by you?

**14.** Had they seen me before?
A. Had myself been seen by them before?
B. Had me being seen by them before?
C. Had I been seen by them before?
D. Had I being seen by them before?

**15.** May I take this pen?
A. May this pen will be taken by me?
B. May this pen shall be taken by me?
C. May this pen should be taken by me?
D. May this pen be taken by me?

**16.** Can we send it by air?
A. Can this be sent by air?
B. Can it be sent by air?
C. Can it go by air?
D. Can it be send by air?

**17.** Who wrote this book?
A. By whom was this book written?
B. By whom is this book written?
C. By whom was this book being written?
D. By whom is this book being written?

**18.** What did you buy?
A. What is bought by you?
B. What is being bought by you?
C. What was bought by you?
D. What was being bought by you?

**19.** Whom do you want?
A. Who is wanted by you?
B. Who is being wanted by you?
C. You are wanted by whom?
D. You are being wanted by whom?

**20.** When will you raise this question?
A. When this question will be raised by you?
B. When will this question be raised by you?
C. When this question is being raised by you?
D. When is this question being raised by you?

**Directions (Qs. 21 to 35):** *In each of the following questions, a sentence is given in Active Voice. Below it are given four alternatives suggesting the Passive Voice form of the above sentence. Choose the correct alternative.*

**21.** Who did this?
A. This was done by whom?
B. By whom was this done?
C. Who has done this?
D. By whom this was done?

**22.** One should keep ones promises.
A. Promises should be kept.
B. Ones promises should be kept by one.
C. Promises must be kept.
D. Ones promises one should keep.

**23.** Give the order.
A. Order given.
B. Order be given.
C. Let the order be given.
D. Order may be given by you.

**24.** You will have to do it.
A. It will be done by you.
B. It will have to be done by you.
C. It has to be done by you.
D. It would have to be done by you.

**25.** Keep to the left.
A. You are ordered to keep to the left.
B. You ought to keep to the left.
C. You are advised to keep to the left.
D. You must keep to the left.

**26.** They will arrange a party.
A. A party will have to be arranged by them.
B. A party they will have to arrange.
C. A party will be arranged by them.
D. A party by them will be arranged.

**27.** Someone has picked my pocket.
A. My pocket is picked.
B. My pocket has picked.
C. My pocket has been picked.
D. My pocket was picked.

**28.** He kept me waiting.
A. I kept waiting for him.
B. I kept waiting by him.
C. I was waiting for him.
D. I was kept waiting by him.

**29.** Why do you tell a lie?
A. Why is a lie told by you?
B. Why is told a lie by you?
C. Why is told by you a lie?
D. Why has a lie been told by you?

**30.** I have written a letter.
A. A letter is written by me.
B. A letter has been written by me.
C. A letter was written by me.
D. A letter had been written by me.

**31.** They will have helped you.
A. You will have helped by them.
B. You will have been helped by them.
C. You will be helped by them.
D. You will be helped by them.

**32.** Open the door.
A. Door may be opened.
B. Let the door be open.
C. Let the door be opened.
D. Door be opened.

**33.** I am reading a book.
A. A book is read by me.
B. A book is being read by me.
C. A book has been read by me.
D. A book in been read by me.

**34.** Why did your brother write such a letter?
A. Why your brother wrote such a letter?
B. Why was by brother written such a letter?
C. Why was such a letter written by your brother?
D. Why was written such a letter by your brother?

**35.** Did you run a great risk?
A. Was a great risk run by you?
B. Was run a great risk by you?
C. Was by you run a great risk?
D. Had you run a great risk?

**Directions (Qs. 36 to 45):** *In each of the following questions, a sentence is given in Passive Voice. Below it are given four alternatives suggesting the Active Voice form of the above sentence. Choose the correct alternative.*

**36.** He was made king.
A. He became king.
B. They made him king.
C. They had made him king.
D. He has been made king.

**37.** Good news is expected by us.
A. We are expecting good news.
B. We have been expecting good news.
C. We had expected good news.
D. We expect good news.

**38.** The child must be looked after.
A. The child you must look after.
B. You must look after the child.
C. You must look the child after.
D. You may look after the child.

**39.** What is wanted by you?
A. What you want?
B. What did you want?
C. What do you want?
D. What you do want?

**40.** Your father is known to me.
A. I am known to your father.
B. I know your father.
C. I have known your father.
D. I knew your father.

**41.** She may be told the story by you.
A. The story may be told by you to her.
B. You may tell the story to her.
C. You may tell her the story.
D. You may tell to her the story.

**42.** Duty ought to be done.
A. Let duty be done.
B. One ought to do one's duty.
C. One should do his duty.
D. Do you duty.

**43.** Is English spoken by you?
A. Did you speak English?
B. Do you speak English?
C. Have you spoken English?
D. Do you know how to speak English?

**44.** Gold coins are contained in this box.
A. This box contains gold coins.
B. This box has contained gold coins.
C. This box is containing gold coins.
D. This box has gold coins.

**45.** Character is revealed by manners.
A. Manners revealed character.
B. Manners reveal character.
C. Manners have revealed character.
D. Manners do reveal character.

## ANSWERS

| 1 | 2 | 3 | 4 | 5 | 6 | 7 | 8 | 9 | 10 |
|---|---|---|---|---|---|---|---|---|---|
| D | C | B | D | C | A | C | B | D | A |
| **11** | **12** | **13** | **14** | **15** | **16** | **17** | **18** | **19** | **20** |
| C | B | A | C | D | B | A | C | A | B |
| **21** | **22** | **23** | **24** | **25** | **26** | **27** | **28** | **29** | **30** |
| B | A | C | B | C | C | C | D | A | B |
| **31** | **32** | **33** | **34** | **35** | **36** | **37** | **38** | **39** | **40** |
| B | C | B | C | A | B | D | B | C | B |
| **41** | **42** | **43** | **44** | **45** | | | | | |
| C | B | B | A | B | | | | | |

# Sentence Completion

Filling the blanks is such an exercise that starts with the primary schools and continues at the highest level of competitive examinations. One must practise it regularly to score well.

# Multiple Choice Questions

**Directions:** *Pick out the most effective word(s) from the given words to fill in the blanks and make the sentence meaningfully complete.*

**1.** One requires great ................ to teach and handle little children who are restless.
A. patience B. attitude
C. determination D. knowledge

**2.** The researchers will ................ some of the causes of increasing poverty in the state.
A. fund B. investigate
C. promote D. circulate

**3.** I usually perform ........ when nobody is watching me.
A. alone B. good
C. better D. hard

**4.** It was ................ to everyone that the minister had been drinking.
A. observed B. known
C. discovered D. realised

**5.** I would rather stay indoors ................ the rain stops.
A. so B. waiting
C. until D. usually

**6.** The process should be completed as far as possible within a week, ..... which the matter should be brought to notice of the officer concerned.
A. following B. failing
C. realizing D. referring

**7.** The officers are ..... to regular transfers.
A. free B. open
C. subject D. available

**8.** All letters received from Government should ..... be acknowledged.
A. suddenly B. obviously
C. immediately D. occasionally

**9.** Mumbai office ..... a meeting of senior officials to discuss the high incidence of frauds.
A. attended B. convened
C. reported D. registered

**10.** The note should be ..... to all the concerned departments for their consideration.
A. regulated B. requested
C. carried D. forwarded

**11.** Your present statement does not .............. what you said last week.
A. accord to B. accord in
C. accord with D. accord for

**12.** I had a vague ................ that the lady originally belonged to Scotland.
A. notion B. expression
C. imagination D. theory

**13.** The prisoner showed no .............. for his crimes.
A. hatred B. obstinacy
C. remorse D. anger

**14.** It is inconceivable that in many schools children are subjected to physical .......... in the name of discipline.
A. violation B. exercise
C. violence D. security

**15.** We have not yet fully realised the ............... consequences of the war.
A. happy B. pleasing
C. grim D. exciting

**16.** Happiness consists in being .............. what we have.
A. contented to B. contented with
C. contented for D. contented in

**17.** His rude behaviour is a ................ his organization.
A. disgrace for B. disgrace on
C. disgrace upon D. disgrace to

**18.** No child is .................. understanding. One has to wait and provide proper guidance.
A. dull to B. dull in
C. dull of D. dull for

**19.** I am fully .................. the problems facing the industry.
A. alive with B. alive to
C. alive for D. alive on

**20.** The Romans were ................ science.
A. bad in B. bad to
C. bad for D. bad at

**21.** Although I was .......... of his plans, I encouraged him, because there was no one else who was willing to help.
A. sceptical B. remorseful
C. fearful D. excited

**22.** You have no business to ......... pain on a weak and poor person.
A. inflict B. put
C. direct D. force

**23.** Her uncle died in a car accident. He was quite rich. She suddenly ........ all her uncle's money.
A. succeeded B. caught
C. gave D. inherited

**24.** There was a major accident. The plane crashed. The pilot .......... did not see the tower.
A. likely B. probably
C. scarcely D. hurriedly

**25.** The car we were travelling in ........... a mile from home.
A. broke off B. broke down
C. broke into D. broke up

**26.** What are you ......... in the kitchen cupboard?
A. looking in B. looking on
C. looking to D. looking for

**27.** I did not see the point of ........ waiting for them, so I went home.
A. hanging around B. hang on
C. hang together D. hanging up

**28.** He lost confidence and ......... of the deal at the last minute.
A. backed out B. backed on
C. backed down D. backed onto

**29.** To the dismay of all the students, the class monitor was ..... berated by the principal at a school assembly.
A. critically B. ignominiously
C. prudently D. fortuitously

**30.** All attempts to revive the fishing industry were ..... failure.
A. foredoomed to B. heading at
C. predicted for D. estimated to

**31.** There are ..... parked outside than yesterday.
A. fewer cars B. few cars
C. less cars D. a small number of cars

**32.** The minister had to ..... some awkward questions from reporters.
A. fend B. fend at
C. fend out D. fend off

**33.** The ..... of evidence was on the side of the plaintiff since all but one of the witnesses testified that his story was correct.
A. propensity B. force
C. preponderance D. brunt

**34.** Attention to detail is ..... of a fine craftsman.
A. hallmark B. stamp
C. seal of authority D. authenticity

**35.** Behaving in a ........... and serious way, even in a ............ situation, makes people respect you.
A. calm, difficult B. steady, angry
C. flamboyant, tricky D. cool astounding

**36.** Along with a sharp rise in ........, a recession would eventually result in more men, women, and children living in ........... .
A. crime, apathy B. fatalities, poor
C. deaths, slums D. unemployment, poverty

**37.** The government has ........ to provide financial aid to the ones ...... by severe floods in the city.
A. desired, troubled B. promised, havoc
C. failed, affected D. wanted, struck

**38.** An airplane with ....... passengers on board made an unscheduled ......... as the airport to which it was heading was covered with thick fog.
A. imitable, slip B. faulty, stop
C. variety, halt D. numerous, landing

**39.** Deemed universities ............ huge fees, but have not been successful in providing ............... education to our students.
A. collect, maintaining
B. pay, better
C. ask, good
D. charge, quality

**40.** If the banks desire to ........ profit, they should get rid of ........ measures.
A. lose, concentrate B. increase, populist
C. earn, unhealthy D. maximise, traditional

**41.** Leadership defines what the future should look like and ...... people with that vision.
A. aligns B. develops
C. trains D. encourages

**42.** We upset ourselves by responding in an ...... manner to someone else's actions.
A. unabashed B. irrational
C. arduous D. arguable

**43.** All the people involved in that issue feel a great ..... to his suggestion.

A. contradiction B. adherence
C. indifference D. repugnance

**44.** These elections will be remembered as much for its anti-incumbency mood as for its ...... mandate.
A. invincible B. rational
C. unprecedented D. deliberate

**45.** How do you expect us to stay in such a ...... building even if it can be hired on a nominal rent?
A. scruffy B. disperate
C. fragmented D. robust

**46.** ...... efforts from all concerned are required to raise the social and economic conditions of our countrymen.
A. Perpetual B. Dynamic
C. Massive D. Exploring

**47.** Many companies see technology as a ...... for a whole host of business problems.
A. consideration B. preference
C. linking D. panacea

**48.** Known as devout and serious person, she also has ...... sense of humour.
A. better B. plentiful
C. quick D. good

**49.** The matter would have become serious if ...... action had not been taken.
A. hasty B. fast
C. timely D. unusual

**50.** The ...... with which he is able to yield the paint brush is really remarkable.
A. ease B. practice
C. majesty D. sweep

**51.** You must ensure the correctness of the information before ................. .
A. drawing B. enabling
C. learning D. jumping

**52.** The rocket ................. the target and did not cause any casualty.
A. sensed B. reached
C. missed D. exploded

**53.** It is desirable to take ................. in any business if you want to make profit.
A. advice B. risk
C. loan D. recourse

**54.** They wasted all the money on purchase of some ................. items.
A. excellent B. important
C. significant D. trivial

**55.** When he found the wallet his face glowed but soon it faded as the wallet was ................. .
A. empty B. vacant
C. recovered D. stolen

**56.** He has served the country by ................. many significant positions.
A. appointing B. creating
C. developing D. holding

**57.** The frequent errors are a result of the student's ................. .
A. talent B. smartness
C. carelessness D. perception

**58.** The robbers eventually ................. in breaking into the house.
A. succeeded B. decided
C. caught D. trained

**59.** I finally ................. her to stay another day.
A. advised B. persuaded
C. suggested D. called

**60.** Most of the people who ................. the book exhibition were teachers.
A. witnessed B. presented
C. conducted D. attended

## ANSWERS

| 1 | 2 | 3 | 4 | 5 | 6 | 7 | 8 | 9 | 10 |
|---|---|---|---|---|---|---|---|---|---|
| A | B | C | A | C | B | C | C | B | D |
| 11 | 12 | 13 | 14 | 15 | 16 | 17 | 18 | 19 | 20 |
| C | A | C | C | C | B | D | B | B | D |
| 21 | 22 | 23 | 24 | 25 | 26 | 27 | 28 | 29 | 30 |
| B | C | C | B | C | C | D | A | B | A |
| 31 | 32 | 33 | 34 | 35 | 36 | 37 | 38 | 39 | 40 |
| A | D | D | A | A | D | C | D | C | B |
| 41 | 42 | 43 | 44 | 45 | 46 | 47 | 48 | 49 | 50 |
| A | A | D | C | A | A | D | D | C | A |
| 51 | 52 | 53 | 54 | 55 | 56 | 57 | 58 | 59 | 60 |
| A | C | B | D | A | D | C | A | B | D |

# Sentence Improvement

One may use the same words in many ways but the best way is only one that makes the perfect usage of the words and conveys the proper meaning of the expression. Try it yourself in the following questions.

# Multiple Choice Questions

**Directions:** *In these questions, a part of the sentence is bold. Below are given alternatives to the bold part at A, B and C which may improve the sentence. Choose the correct alternative. In case no improvement is needed, your answer is 'D'.*

**1.** Discreet salience **is extremely important** to create that 'irresistible-yet-unattainable' image for brands that want to take India seriously

A. was extremely important
B. is mainly important
C. was important extremely
D. No Improvement

**2.** This, over a designer outfit that he wanted for a friend's party and **that his sensitive** parents refused him.

A. which his sensitive B. which his insensitive
C. that his insensitive D. No Improvement

**3.** Goa was full of non-Goa property hunters **rushing about buying up the place** like tomorrow was an expired lease.

A. rushing in buying up the place
B. rushed about buying up the place
C. rushing about to buy up the place
D. No Improvement

**4.** Property hunting is a **tired and hungry** making business.

A. is a tiresome and hungry
B. is a tiring and hungry
C. is a tiring and waste
D. No Improvement

**5.** Cultural differences aside, **till luxury need speaks** in a manner that befits.

A. luxury still needs to speak
B. luxury still need to speak
C. luxury till need to speak
D. No Improvement

**6.** Indian food—the culinary avatar of the subcontinent's social history presented on a platter—**is without doubt the best food** in the world.

A. is undoubtedly the greatest food
B. is without doubt greatest food
C. is best food without doubt
D. No Improvement

**7.** It must retain the language of poetry. **It needed to create** stories, and not statements.

A. It needed creating
B. It needs creating
C. It needs to create
D. No Improvement

**8.** This year, Asia-Pacific has become the first region **to reach aggregate profiting** in biotech.

A. to reach aggregated profitability
B. to reach aggregate profitability
C. to reach aggregate of profit
D. No Improvement

**9.** India is deviating to embrace the West. If Western luxury brands deviate a little, **albeit selectively**, they will find rich Indian arms open far and wide.

A. though selectively
B. however selectively
C. albeit selectedly
D. No Improvement

**10.** China and India continued to attract **attention and** deals, motivated by the desire to increase access to these **largest and growing** drug markets and by the need to lower the costs of drug development.

A. larger and growing
B. large and growing
C. larger and grown
D. No Improvement

**11.** Luxury brands are **still above of the** clover curve here, with their elite (small) audiences.
A. still ahead of the
B. still in the
C. still far of the
D. No Improvement

**12.** Agencies **hence needed to be** sure of returns before investing, say admen.
A. hence needs to be
B. so needs to be
C. hence need to be
D. No Improvement

**13.** India is still a nascent market and that's the spirit everyone's **looking at it**.
A. looking for it B. looking in it
C. looking with it D. No Improvement

**14.** Questioning the state's move to allow women to serve liquor but not dance in bars **of the ground that** dancing aroused physical lust.
A. on the grounds that
B. of the grounds that
C. over the grounds that
D. No Improvement

**15.** For England the positives from their crushing series lose come in the shape of James Anderson and Kevin Pietersen, **both of which** have made significant strides up the rankings.
A. both of which B. both of whom
C. both of who D. No Improvement

**16.** International campaigns can work well for luxury here, **but context cannot be** ignored.
A. so context cannot be
B. but context cannot
C. but context couldn't
D. No Improvement

**17.** For one, the Indian luxury context, **while evolved rapidly**, still has its own meaning, and its own implications.
A. while evolved rapid
B. which evolving rapidly
C. while evolving rapidly
D. No Improvement

**18.** **But** too much of availability can compromise a luxury brand or **made it lose** its lustre.
A. make her lose B. make him lose
C. make it lose D. No Improvement

**19.** Still, it's under-the-upper **layers themselves who** are aspiring for slivers of luxury.
A. layers themselves which
B. layer itself who
C. layers themself which
D. No Improvement

**20.** It is like saying Hindi movies, with skimpily dressed dancers, would **effect public** order.
A. effect your B. affect public
C. affected public D. No Improvement

**21.** The court held that a few women being involved in prostitution was no **justice to deny other** bar girls the right to livelihood.
A. justification to declare other
B. justification to deny other
C. justice to let other
D. No Improvement

**22.** All-rounder cricketer has also made some progress **over the** player rankings.
A. above the B. at the
C. up the D. No Improvement

**23.** Former minister on Sunday **joined hands** with a suspended Lok Sabha member to float a new political outfit.
A. folded hands
B. walked hand in hand
C. shaked hands
D. No Improvement

**24.** Pakistan's former ministers will meet in London on Monday **to ask** a strategy to return home from exile.
A. to chalk out
B. to negotiate
C. to create
D. No Improvement

**25.** It's a family potboiler, medical thriller and political drama **all in one**–except that it's all too real and all too grim.
A. all 3 in one
B. all coupled into one
C. all rolled into one
D. No Improvement

**26.** India's efforts to get international support for its civil nuclear energy programme got **a go ahead on** Sunday as Germany indicated it would not come in the way of the India-US nuclear deal.
A. a life in B. a boost on
C. a boost at D. No Improvement

**27.** Is it time for old bungalows to **bite the dust**?
A. go down B. get down
C. come down D. No Improvement

**28.** The bungalows was an outward manifestation of a certain **way in life**, and with that era gone.
A. way for life B. way of life
C. way at life D. No Improvement

**29.** The builder Mittals will reportedly **raise their money**-raking high-rise behind it.
A. highten their money
B. rise their money
C. raise there money
D. No Improvement

**30.** The impatient present has usually demolished **more of the** past before we wake up to the irretrievable loss.
A. much of B. much of their
C. much of the D. No Improvement

**31.** Preservation is a romantic notion; demolition **quiet** more practical reasons.
A. has many, B. had many,
C. have many, D. No Improvement

**32.** You must get back to your **charming self** and impress the audience with your social skills.
A. own self B. main self
C. own uniqueness D. No Improvement

**33.** Stay focused on your goals and don't **get disturbed by** non-materialistic possessions.
A. get involved by
B. get betrayed by
C. get distracted by
D. No Improvement

**34.** You may appear more optimistic than your detractors **may want it to be**.
A. want you to be
B. wish yourself to be
C. seek you be
D. No Improvement

**35.** There are a number of mineral springs in the Czech territory, which **has been used** for medicinal purposes since the early 15th century.
A. have been used B. had been used
C. has being used D. No Improvement

**36.** The picturesque mountains **offer**s excellent bungee jumping spots.
A. shows B. provides
C. offer D. No Improvement

**37.** Begin your **meal with** traditional faves like potato soup, beef soup with liver dumplings or dill soup made from sour milk.
A. meals with B. meal in
C. meals of D. No Improvement

**38.** You can also **go to the** National Museum building and the famous Prague State Opera.
A. went to B. visit the
C. saw D. No Improvement

**39.** If they close the Gulf for a **length of time** to shipping, then certainly we could look at $150, probably higher.
A. larger amount of time
B. larger duration of time
C. larger amount of hours
D. No Improvement

**40.** **More of them** are owned by the state and even the privately-owned ones are open to the public.
A. Most of which B. Most of them
C. Most of all D. No Improvement

**41.** Constructed in the ninth century by the Prince Booivoj, the castle has transformed **oneself** from a wooden fortress surrounded by earthen bulwarks to the imposing form it has today.
A. himself B. herself
C. itself D. No Improvement

**42.** Apart from frequent art exhibitions, **their are also** permanent collections devoted to archaeology, anthropology, mineralogy, natural history and numismatics.
A. there is also B. there are also
C. their are also D. No Improvement

**43.** You can visit the Czech Museum of Fine Arts, **at a** permanent exhibition on Czech Kubism.
A. with a
B. for a
C. in a
D. No Improvement

**44.** Tensions **above** Iran come at a time of strong demand for energy.
A. under B. inside
C. over D. No Improvement

**45.** Because its shores line the narrow Straits of Hormuz, Iran **could quickly hit** both military and commercial shipping.
A. will quickly hit
B. shall quickly hit
C. will be quick hitting
D. No Improvement

**46.** For most people who exercise **at the** morning, there is no getting around the question: Eat and run? Or run and eat later?
A. in the B. in
C. at the time of D. No Improvement

**47.** Are ad agencies even attempting to peer into the keyhole of this indulgence sanctum to garner consumer insights **ahead of** the curve?

A. above
B. over
C. within
D. No Improvement

**48.** Too many people rush into the world of credit and don't stop to think about how **their actions could affect their** credit score and ability to qualify for credit in the future.

A. their actions may affect their
B. their actions might affect their
C. their actions will affect their
D. No Improvement

**49.** According to the report, **number of deal with** vaccines were energized by concerns around avian flu, SARS, and biodefence products, while looming patent expirations led to more deals in generics.

A. number of deals in
B. number of deal in
C. number of deals with
D. No Improvement

**50.** This is how the Bombay High Court responded to the state government's purported **moral stand which** dance bars were causing grave harm to society.

A. moral stand in
B. moral stand at
C. moral stand that D. No Improvement

**51.** If you have a high credit limit, use **at least a** third of it.

A. atleast a
B. at last a
C. utmost a
D. No Improvement

**52.** Fitness experts will say that **first eating provides** fuel for a proper workout.

A. eating in the beginning provides
B. first eat provides
C. eating first provides
D. No Improvement

**53.** One study that examined the claim directly in 1995 found that a group of people did **burned much calories from fat on days** when they exercised on an empty stomach than on days when they had a small breakfast first.

A. burn more calories from fat on days
B. burn more calorie from fat on days
C. burnt more calories from fat on days
D. No Improvement

**54.** Carefree children spent their afternoons **to run about barefoot**, their clothes dusty, and telltale twigs of the neighbour's mango tree in their hair.

A. running barefoot in the sun
B. run about barefoot in the sun
C. running about barefoot in the sun
D. No Improvement

**55.** A year ago, a 13-year-old girl attempted suicide because her mother **refuses to pay his** mobile bills.

A. refuses to pay her B. refused to pay her
C. refused to pay his D. No Improvement

## ANSWERS

| 1 | 2 | 3 | 4 | 5 | 6 | 7 | 8 | 9 | 10 |
|---|---|---|---|---|---|---|---|---|---|
| D | C | D | B | A | D | C | C | D | B |
| **11** | **12** | **13** | **14** | **15** | **16** | **17** | **18** | **19** | **20** |
| C | C | D | A | C | D | C | C | C | C |
| **21** | **22** | **23** | **24** | **25** | **26** | **27** | **28** | **29** | **30** |
| B | C | C | A | C | B | D | B | D | C |
| **31** | **32** | **33** | **34** | **35** | **36** | **37** | **38** | **39** | **40** |
| A | D | C | A | D | C | A | B | D | B |
| **41** | **42** | **43** | **44** | **45** | **46** | **47** | **48** | **49** | **50** |
| C | B | A | C | D | A | D | C | A | C |
| **51** | **52** | **53** | **54** | **55** | | | | | |
| C | C | A | C | B | | | | | |

# Reordering Words & Sentences

Different words form a sentence and convey their meaning only when arranged in a proper order. A Paragraph is formed from sentences, it will convey its true meaning and purpose only when the sentences are arranged in a proper manner. Try and practise it in this exercise.

## Multiple Choice Questions

**Directions (Qs. 1 to 20):** *In the following questions, some parts of the sentence have been jumbled up. You are required to rearrange these parts which are labelled P, Q, R and S to produce the correct sentence. Choose the option with proper sequence.*

**1.** We are doing
P : to the people
Q : to give relief
R : all we can
S : but more funds are needed
The correct sequence should be
A. P Q R S  B. R Q P S
C. Q P R S  D. S P Q R

**2.** The man
P : when he was
Q : in the office last evening
R : could not finish
S : all his work
The correct sequence should be
A. P Q R S  B. Q R S P
C. R Q P S  D. R S P Q

**3.** The people decided
P : they were going
Q : how much
R : to spend
S : on the construction of the school building
The correct sequence should be
A. Q P R S  B. P Q R S
C. P R Q S  D. S Q P R

**4.** The man said that
P : those workers
Q : would be given a raise
R : who did not go on
S : strike last month
The correct sequence should be
A. P Q R S  B. P R S Q
C. Q P R S  D. R S P Q

**5.** I think
P : the members
Q : are basically in agreement
R : of the group
S : on the following points
The correct sequence should be
A. R Q P S  B. S Q R P
C. P R Q S  D. P Q S R

**6.** While it was true that
P : I had
Q : to invest in industry
R : some lands and houses
S : I did not have ready cash
The correct sequence should be
A. P Q R S  B. P R S Q
C. S Q P R  D. Q P R S

**7.** P : But for your help
Q : to finish this work
R : it would not have been possible
S : in time
The correct sequence should be
A. P R Q S  B. S P Q R
C. R P Q S  D. P Q R S

**8.** The boy
P : in the competition
Q : who was wearing spectacles
R : won many prizes
S : held in our college

The correct sequence should be

A. P Q R S B. R P S Q

C. Q R P S D. Q P S R

**9.** About 200 years ago,

P : in the south of India

Q : an old king

R : ruled over a kingdom

S : called Rajavarman

The correct sequence should be

A. Q S R P B. P Q R S

C. Q P S R D. Q S P R

**10.** P : his land

Q : a wooden plough

R : the Indian peasant still uses

S : to cultivate

The correct sequence should be

A. R Q P S B. Q P S R

C. S R Q P D. R Q S P

**11.** He was a man,

P : even if he had to starve

Q : who would not beg

R : borrow or steal

S : from anyone

The correct sequence should be

A. P Q R S B. P R Q S

C. Q R S P D. Q P R S

**12.** P : in the progress of

Q : universities play a crucial role

R : our civilization

S : in the present age

The correct sequence should be

A. S Q P R B. Q R S P

C. Q R P S D. S Q R P

**13.** P : far out into the sea

Q : for the next two weeks there were further explosions

R : which hurled

S : ashes and debris

The correct sequence should be

A. Q R P S B. R S P Q

C. Q R S P D. S R P Q

**14.** William Shakespeare,

P : in his lifetime

Q : the great English dramatist

R : wrote thirty-five plays

S : and several poems

The correct sequence should be

A. P Q R S B. R S P Q

C. Q S R P D. Q R S P

**15.** Whenever I am,

P : with an old friend of mine

Q : in New Delhi

R : to have dinner

S : I always try

The correct sequence should be

A. S Q P R B. Q S R P

C. R P S Q D. P R Q S

**16.** P : I don't know

Q : must have thought

R : what people sitting next to me

S : but I came away

The correct sequence should be

A. R S Q P B. R Q S P

C. P Q R S D. P R Q S

**17.** P : in estimating the size of the earth

Q : but they were hampered by the lack of instruments of precision

R : ancient astronomers

S : used methods which were theoretically valid

The correct sequence should be

A. R P Q S B. P R Q S

C. R S Q P D. R P S Q

**18.** P : It is a pity that

Q : by offering a handsome dowry

R : a number of parents think that

S : they will be able to ensure the happiness of their daughters

The correct sequence should be

A. S Q R P B. P R S Q

C. P S R Q D. P R Q S

**19.** The common man

P : in nurturing

Q : a more active role

R : communal harmony

S : should play

The correct sequence should be

A. P R S Q B. S Q P R

C. S Q R P D. P R Q S

**20.** The doctor

P : able to find out

Q : what has caused

R : the food poisoning

S : has not been

The correct sequence should be

A. S P R Q B. P R Q S

C. P R S Q D. S P Q R

**Directions (Qs. 21 to 40):** *A number of sentences are given below which when properly sequenced form a coherent paragraph. Each sentence is labelled as abcdef...... Choose the most logical order of sentences from among the given choices to construct a coherent paragraph:*

**21.** (a) Parts of northern region were pounded by heavy rains today,
(b) Vehicular traffic came to a near halt.
(c) As mid and high altitude areas of Himachal Pradesh were in grip of severe cold wave with snow lashing the tribal areas and mid ranges receiving showers.
(d) As the sky remained heavily overcast with dark clouds reducing the visibility considerably.
(e) A large number of tourists were forced to buy heavy woollens and stay indoors due to inclement weather.
A. ecabd B. adecb
C. edabc D. acbde

**22.** (a) The idea is that students should be able to find employment for themselves after the course.
(b) The Central Board of Secondary Education is planning a revamp of its vocational courses.
(c) For this it is necessary to tie up with the industry as well as mobilise schools for their support.
(d) While others will be made less academic and more in tune with the needs of the industry.
(e) A number of courses have been identified as 'deadwood' and will be done away with.
A. bedac B. abcde
C. acebd D. baced

**23.** (a) Clearly, age is not a deterrent in one's choice of learning.
(b) Perhaps, it was because of her childhood desire.
(c) When Rachna came to Delhi eight years back, she had not anticipated a career in the field of art.
(d) She has been successful in the various exhibitions that she has been part of in terms of business.
(e) She had got into expressing her thoughts with the help of a brush and colours only because her daughter refused to get initiated into it.
(f) She feels that her use of colour appeals to people.
A. aedcbf B. cdefba
C. cebadf D. acdebf

**24.** (a) The rehabilitation record has been dismal.
(b) It has been two years years since the earthquake rudely rattled the people of Gujarat.
(c) And since then, life has been a constant struggle.
(d) The quake set Gujarat's clock back by 10 years.
(e) Things changed forever.
A. bedca B. bcade
C. dbace D. edcba

**25.** (a) In fact, success in exams depended on rote learning from old notes.
(b) when he was studying civil engineering in a college in Gujarat.
(c) He was detained for lack of attendance.
(d) Lectures were soporific, classes rarely worth attending and 80 per cent attendance compulsory.
(e) The college became a trap he hated.
(f) His is a plight many engineers across India would identify with.
(g) He found the going tough.
A. abcdgef B. bgdacef
C. fabcdge D. abcdefg

**26.** (a) In a country that has close to 600 recognised engineering colleges, there are only seven IITs.
(b) Barring a few exeptions, the academic atmosphere in these is moribund.
(c) The very best students usually get there.
(d) many waste themselves in frustration.
(e) Most of those who get into engineering are good students.
(f) but about 1.25 lakh others and up in the remaining colleges.
A. aecfbd B. abecdf
C. abcdef D. acfbed

**27.** (a) Whatever the job market, common wisdom says that IIT graduates will find jobs where others have failed.
(b) The IIT brand name is a ticket to success.
(c) When recruiters go headhunting, the IITs are still top of their list.
(d) Its possessor is understood to have an excellent academic record and the will to succeed.
(e) In the job market, that counts.
A. bdeac B. abcde
C. abdce D. dbace

**28.** (a) It will pave the way .........
(b) signalling a new beginning in strategic ties......
(c) for a tangible Indian economic presence in Iran and Central Asia.
(d) Iran has offered India valuable road linkages to central Asia ......
(e) aimed at promoting peace and economic cooperation in the region.
A. dbeac B. debca
C. acebd D. abced

**29.** (a) A good college is essential for a successful career and admissions are based on marks.
(b) The marks-based system followed by all the boards in the country recognises only a small percentage of students as successful.
(c) The marks one scores in the crucial board exams dictate the path his life takes.
(d) Anyone scoring below a certain percentage is automatically branded a 'failure'.
(d) So if you cannot make it into the best college, your career is over even before it has started.

A. abcde B. bcdea
C. bdcae D. abdec

30. (a) The project has already started on an experimental basis in the west district.
(b) A website is soon going to be launched where application forms can be downloaded and submitted.
(c) Standing in a queue at a government office to submit application form will be a thing of the past.
(d) A unique code will be alloted while submitting the form which will help in finding the status of the application.
A. abcd B. dabc
C. cbda D. badc

31. (a) To curb bio-terrorism is a difficult task.
(b) To check these attacks and lessen their impact, we need an impartial team of sincere, strong and dedicated men.
(c) The media can play a strong role in stopping this unnecessary spread of panic.
(d) Since bio-terrorism is not visible or easily detectable, it can be used often.
(e) Men who honour the lives of their fellow countrymen before their own.
A. abcde B. dabce
C. adbec D. acbed

32. (a) He was dying.
(b) No one was ready to touch him as even shifting him from one place to another would lead to profuse bleeding.
(c) He was a five-day old infant, premature and bleeding profusely.
(d) Even if injected one small needle, blood would ooze out and continue to flow for an hour at a stretch.
(e) This small being had haematoma, a thick blood clot in his brain.
A. edbca B. cabde
C. eacdb D. cedba

33. (a) The day I don't treat a patient, I feel .......
(b) I have enough to eat, I crave for blessings now.
(c) But if a financially weak patient gives me only ₹ 50, I don't mind.
(d) Each month I do three to four operations free of cost.
(e) I have lost something in life.
(f) My consultation fee is ₹ 300.
A. fcdeab B. dfcbae
C. fcabde D. bdfcea

34. (a) When he was rushed to the nearby Primary Health Centre after his fall, the doctor referred him to a hospital.
(b) This worsened his injury.
(c) Had a little precaution been exercised after the accident, Tarun would have continued with his gymnastic classes.
(d) He was paralysed from waist downwards when he fell from the vaulting horse while doing gymnastics.
(e) However, the doctor forgot to tell Tarun's parents to take him on a stretcher as he had suffered spinal injuries.
(f) Tarun is wheelchair bound for two years.
A. fdeabc B. abcdef
C. fdcaeb D. fdbcae

35. (a) As the temperature rises, staying hydrated can become a greater challenge for people exercising both indoors and out.
(b) Several things can influence this process, including age, gender, physical conditioning. humidity and a lack of sufficient fluids.
(c) In hot weather, individuals can lose as much as two quarts of sweat per hour.
(d) As we age, we have a lower perceived level of thirst in response to fluid loss and early stages of dehydration.
(e) If not replenished, this can lead to dehydration, heat exhaustion and even heatstroke.
A. abcde B. dbcae
C. cbdea D. acebd

36. (a) The leopard was discovered in the servant quarters of a farmhouse.
(b) The injuries appeared to have been caused by the paws of the leopard, and were not teeth wounds.
(c) It took the wild life officials, Delhi Police and Delhi zoo vets eight hours to capture the leopard that had wandered into a factory in south Delhi.
(d) The leopard then jumped into the factory where the workers managed to lock it in a small generator room before calling in the police.
(e) Before its capture, the leopard attacked two women and a man in the farmhouse.
A. aebdc B. bdaec
C. eadbc D. adbec

37. (a) Police suspect a carpenter working at John's house as he has not reported for work since the day the boy went missing.
(b) John did not return home in the afternoon.
(c) John's mother had herself put the boy on the vehicle in the morning.

(d) John smiled at him and was last seen walking up to him.
(e) His parents called the school and were told John had not been to school at all and had been marked absent.
(f) He was about to enter the school when someone called out his name.

A. cfdbea B. debfca
C. bfdaec D. abcdef

**38.** (a) However, the mayhem over the last few months is deeply shocking.
(b) Yet I do not agree with the prophets of doom who see nothing but disaster ahead.
(c) When I came back to my motherland India after a stay in Switzerland, I felt I was trading a hotbed of intense religious and political violence for peace and quiet.
(d) I think our nation is searching for an identity.
(e) And a new vision of the future will emerge from this.

A. abcde B. cabde
C. cebad D. bedca

**39.** (a) An integrated and combined approach was required to reveal the mystery of the brain —its structure, composition and function.
(b) Since the early 80's, scientists were clear that the brain would be the final frontier to conquer.
(c) The initiative was flagged off and came to be known as the Human Brain Project.
(d) But that wasn't easy because understanding the brain involved completely integrating information from the level of the gene to the level of behaviour.
(e) To fulfill this requirement a group of American scientists from various disciplines decided to work together.

A. acbed B. bdaec
C. abdec D. badec

**40.** (a) A product is something that is made in a factory, a brand is something that is bought by a consumer.
(b) The trick therefore, lies in the brand positioning.
(c) For a consumer, the satisfaction of becoming associated with a name that is the 'best' and the 'leader' is far more important and at times makes him ignore the price factor.
(d) Brands come and go.
(e) Still there are those who manage to stay and develop an affinity with consumers.

A. aebcd B. debac
C. decab D. aecdb

## ANSWERS

| 1 | 2 | 3 | 4 | 5 | 6 | 7 | 8 | 9 | 10 |
|---|---|---|---|---|---|---|---|---|---|
| B | D | A | B | C | C | A | C | A | D |
| **11** | **12** | **13** | **14** | **15** | **16** | **17** | **18** | **19** | **20** |
| C | A | C | D | B | D | C | B | B | D |
| **21** | **22** | **23** | **24** | **25** | **26** | **27** | **28** | **29** | **30** |
| D | A | C | A | B | D | A | A | C | C |
| **31** | **32** | **33** | **34** | **35** | **36** | **37** | **38** | **39** | **40** |
| C | D | B | C | D | A | A | B | B | B |

# Comprehension Passages

## Passages

**Directions:** *Read the following passages and answer the questions given below each.*

### PASSAGE-1

In the Roman times, defected enemies were generally put to death as criminals for having offended the emperor of Rome. In the middle ages, however, the practice of ransoming of returning prisoners in exchange for money became common. Though some saw this custom as a step towards a most humane society, the primary reasons behind it were economic rather than humanitarian.

In those times, rulers had only a limited ability to raise taxes. They could neither force their subject to fight nor pay them to do so. The promise of material compensation in the form of goods and ransom was therefore the only way of inducing combatants to participate in a war. In the middle ages, the predominant incentive for the individual soldiers was the expectation of spoils. Although collecting ransom clearly brought financial gain, keeping a prisoner and arranging for his exchange had its cost. Consequently, procedures were devised to reduce transaction costs.

One such device was a rule asserting that the prisoner had to assess his own value. This compelled the prisoner to establish a value *without too much distortion;* indicating too low a value would increase, the captive's chances of being killed, while indicating too high a value would either ruin him financially or create a prohibitively expensive ransom that would also result in death.

**1.** It can be inferred from the passage that a medieval soldier

A. was less likely to kill captured members of opposing armies than was a soldier of the Roman Empire

B. was similar to a 20th century terrorist in that he operated on a basically independent level and was motivated solely by economic incentives

C. had few economic options and chose to fight because it was the only way to earn an adequate living

D. was motivated to spare prisoners' lives by humanitarian rather than economic ideals

**2.** Which of the following best describes the change in policy from executing prisoners in Roman times to ransoming prisoners in the middle ages?

A. The emperors of Rome demanded more respect than did medieval rulers and thus Roman subjects went to greater lengths to defend their nation

B. It was a reflection of the lesser degree of direct control medieval ruler had over subjects

C. It became a show of strength and honour warrior of the middles ages to be able to capture and return their enemies

D. Medieval soldiers were not as hum-anitarian as their ransoming practices might have indicated

**3.** The primary purpose of the passage is to

A. discuss the economic basis of the medieval practice of exchanging prisoners for ransom

B. examine the history of the treatment of prisoner of war

C. emphasize the importance of a warrior's code of honour during the middle ages

D. explore a way of reducing the cost of ransom

**4.** The author uses the phrase *"without too much distortion"* in order to

A. indicate that prisoners would fairly assess their worth

B. emphasize the important role medieval prisoners played in determining whether they should be ransomed

C. explain how prisoners often paid more than an appropriate ransom in order to increase their chances for survival

D. suggest that captors and captives often had understanding relationships

## PASSAGE-2

The world dismisses curiosity by calling it idle or mere idle curiosity—even though curious persons are seldom idle. Parents do their best to extinguish curiosity in their children because it makes life difficult to be faced everyday with a string of unanswerable questions about what makes fire hot or why grass grows. Children whose curiosity survives parental discipline are invited to join our university. With the university, they go on asking their questions and trying to find the answers. In the eyes of a scholar, that is what a university is for. Some of the questions which the scholars ask, seem to the world to be scarcely worth asking, let alone answering. They asked questions too minute specialised for you and me to understand without years of explanation. If the world inquires of one of them why he wants to know the answer to a particular question he may say especially if he is a scientist, that the answer will in some obscure way make possible a new machine or weapon or gadget. He talks that way because he knows that the world understands and respects utility.

But to you who are now part of the university, he will say that he wants to know the answer simply because he does not know it, the way the mountain climber wants to climb a mountain, simply because it is there. Similarly a historian asked by an outsider why he studies history may come out with the argument that he has learnt to repeat on such occasions, something about knowledge of the past making it possible to understand the present and mould the future. But if you really want to know why a historian studies the past, the answer is much simpler, something happened and he would like to know what. All this does not mean that the answers which scholars find to their questions have no consequences. They may have enormous consequences but these seldom form the reason for asking the questions or pursuing the answers. It is true that scholars can be put to work answering questions for the sake of the consequences as thousands are working, now, for example, in search of a cure for cancer. But this is not the primary function of the scholars. For the consequences are usually subordinate to the satisfaction of curiosity.

**1.** According to the passage, the children make life difficult for their parents
- A. by their ceaseless curiosity
- B. by unceasing bombardment of questions
- C. by asking irrelevant questions
- D. by posing profound questions

**2.** The common people consider some of the questions that the scholars ask unimportant
- A. as they are too lazy and idle
- B. as they are too modest
- C. as it's beyond their comprehension
- D. as it is considered a waste of time

**3.** A historian really studies the past
- A. to comprehend the present and to reconstruct the future
- B. to explain the present and plan the future
- C. to understand the present and make fortune
- D. to understand the present and mould the future

**4.** Children whose curiosity survives parental discipline means
- A. children retaining their curiosity in spite of being discouraged by their parents
- B. children pursuing their mental curiosity
- C. children's curiosity subdued due to parents' intervention
- D. children being disciplined by their parents

**5.** According to the passage, parents do their best to discourage curiosity in their children
- A. because they have no time
- B. because they have no patience to answer them
- C. because they feel that their children ask stupid questions continuously
- D. because they are unable to answer all their questions

## PASSAGE-3

The factor of geographical distribution is equally, possibly even more, significant that English is spoken as first or native language in at least four continents of the world, Russian in two, Chinese and the Indian languages in one. English is without question the closest approach to a world language today. It goes without saying that no two persons ever have an identical command of their common language. Certainly, they have not precisely the same vocabulary. There are at least minor differences in pronunciation, indeed the same individual will not pronounce his vowels and consonants in absolutely identical fashion everytime he utters them. Everyone possesses, in addition, certain individual traits of grammatical form and syntactical order, constituting that peculiar and personal quality of language which we term as style. All of this is implicit in the well-known phrase, 'Style is the man.' No men are identical, no two styles are the same. If this be true of but two persons, the potential of differences resident in a language spoken by more than 200 million truly staggers imagination.

**1.** The author argues that English is the closest approach to a world language because
- A. there are more native speakers of English than of any other language
- B. English has less number of mutually unintelligible dialects
- C. the geographical distribution of English covers a much greater area
- D. other languages are much too complex to be world languages

2. The fact that the same individual will not pronounce his vowels and consonants identically everytime shows that
   A. literary style varies from person to person
   B. mutual intelligibility is a myth
   C. vocabulary varies from individual to individual
   D. no two persons speak the same language exactly the same way
3. It is evident from the passage that style is
   A. a strange type of language
   B. a language where one does not have to be particular about correctness and grammar
   C. language used in a particular way by an individual
   D. a question of grammatical and syntactic correctness
4. According to some authorities
   A. more people speak Chinese dialect than English
   B. more people speak English as an auxiliary language than as a first language
   C. more people speak English in the UK than in England
   D. about one-fourth of the world's population speaks English
5. The overall implication of the passage is that
   A. to suppose that 230 million people speak English as a native language would certainly be an underestimate
   B. the 55 million inhabitants of the British Isles speak like the 30 million inhabitants of the dominions and colonies
   C. a little less than half the native English speakers in the world live in the US
   D. about one-tenth of the total English-speaking world population lives in British dominions and colonies

## PASSAGE-4

What is the future which awaits our children? The underlying assumption of the question, that Indian children have a common future, is itself dubious. It can legitimately be asked whether a student who is well-fed, attending a boarding school in the salubrious climate of the hills and learning to use computers has any future in common with a malnourished child who goes to a school with no blackboards, if indeed he does go to school. The latter may have no worthwhile future at all. And it might be worthwhile to analyse the significance of this marginalisation of more than 75 per cent of the children of this country.

The failure to provide an infrastructure for primary education in the villages of India more than 40 years after independence is in sharp contrast with the sophisticated institutions, for technical institutes of higher education are funded by the government, which essentially means that the money to support them comes from taxes. And, since indirect taxation forms a substantial part of the taxes collected by the government, the financial burden is borne by all the people. L.K. Jha put it graphically when he observed that 25 paise of every rupee spent on educating an IIT student comes from the pockets of men and women whose children may never enter a proper classroom.

1. The author is trying to highlight which of the following?
   A. Faulty system of direct taxes
   B. The greatness of L.K. Jha
   C. Need of sophisticated education for rural poor
   D. Need to have common future for Indian children
2. Which of the following pairs have been termed as 'sharp contrast' by the author?
   (*i*) Infrastructure for technical education
   (*ii*) Lack of infrastructure for rural primary schools
   (*iii*) 25 paise of every rupee earned by Government is spent on education
   (*iv*) The financial burden of higher technical education is borne by all people
   (*v*) 75% of children have limited opportunities
   A. (*ii*) and (*iv*) B. (*ii*) and (*iii*)
   C. (*iii*) and (*iv*) D. (*i*) and (*ii*)
3. Which of the following statements is not true?
   (*i*) The author welcomes Govt.'s initiative on primary education
   (*ii*) 75% of the children have a bright future
   (*iii*) 25% cost of educating a technocrat comes from poor people
   A. Only (*i*) B. Only (*ii*)
   C. Only (*iii*) D. Only (*i*) and (*ii*)
4. According to the author, who among the following does not have a hopeful and prosperous future?
   (*i*) All students from technical institutes
   (*ii*) All students financially supported by the Government
   A. Only (*i*) B. Only (*ii*)
   C. Both (*i*) and (*ii*) D. Neither (*i*) nor (*ii*)
5. What seems to be the likely answer of the author to the question posed by him in the first sentence of the passage?
   (*i*) There is no common future for the Indian children
   (*ii*) The future is worthwhile for majority of Indian children
   (*iii*) The majority may never enter a proper classroom
   A. Only (*i*) B. Only (*ii*)
   C. Only (*iii*) D. Both (*i*) and (*ii*)
6. What seems to be the purpose of the author in writing this passage?

A. Setting goals for children of upper middle class
B. Questioning the legitimacy of public schools
C. Highlighting lack of infrastructural facilities for primary education
D. Focusing on inequality in educational opportunities

## PASSAGE-5

Cyber crime is the branded stigma defacing the culture and magnanimity of computer technology. It is upkeeping the flag with indomitable triumph against developing computer technology worldwide.

Modern age is striding with marching steps of technology revolution beating the past decade of ancestral belief with ultimate care. Computer invention has unfolded the mystery of quick access with the objective of minimum manpower and cutting the time consumption parameters.

As each coin has dual face of its portrait, likewise computer technology is sick of creeping virus. Synthetic man-made dilemma of site hackers activation is causing setback to the expanding anchor of revolutionary device with great loss of time, economy and data profile as suffered by consumers. A recent report from Internet security firm Websense estimates that 85.6 per cent of all the unwanted e-mails contained links to spam sites. The company's data suggests that the number of malicious sites grew 233 per cent in the last six months and saw 671 per cent growth in the number of malicious sites during the last year. In June alone, the total number of e-mails detected as containing viruses increased by 600 per cent compared to May.

Chat rooms, blogs and message-boards where the users post comments have been identified as the top targets of hackers and spammers due to the high traffic these attract. According to Websense, 95 per cent of user-generated comments to blogs, chat rooms and message-boards during the first half of the year were malicious.

It is advisable not to click on spurious links and stay away from keying in passwords at unknown sites as they are most likely to be spammed. Hackers can steal your passwords and log in to your account and access critical information like account numbers and contact details among other things.

**1.** The above passage is:
A. an advisory for the computer users.
B. an advisory for the Internet users.
C. a warning against possible threat to the Internet users.
D. related to chat rooms, blogs and message boards.

**2.** People who use chat rooms and blogs,
A. are safe and have no threats from spam.
B. are more prone to malicious e-mails.
C. create virus and hack the accounts of others.
D. are unsafe.

**3.** According to the writer, it is not safe to:
A. log on to spurious links.
B. access one's own account frequently.
C. have essential information stored in a computer.
D. include data-stealing code.

**4.** Hackers and spammers, according to the writer, are:
A. a new threat to the Internet users and the economy.
B. only pranksters and not serious threat to the system.
C. trained, professional technocrats who are an asset.
D. not expert professionals.

**5.** Which word in the passage is synonym of *weblog*?
A. blog B. password
C. site D. e-mail

**6.** Which agency has assessed the data record with spam sites?
A. Microsoft
B. Internet security from Google
C. Websense
D. Spammers

**7.** Which month dominates the e-mails detection data record?
A. May B. June
C. Last six months D. Last year

## PASSAGE-6

Progress in life depends a good deal on crossing one threshold after another. Some time ago, a man watched his little nephew try to write his name. It was hard work, very hard work. The little boy had arrived at an effort threshold. Today he writes his name with comparative ease. No new threshold confronts him. This is the way with all of us. As soon as we cross one threshold, as soon as we conquer one difficulty, a new difficulty appears, or should appear. Some people make the mistake of steering clear of thresholds. Anything that requires genuine thinking and use of energy, they avoid. They prefer to stay in a rut where thresholds are not met. Probably, they have been at their job a number of years. Things are easy for them. They make no effort to seek out new obstacles to overcome. Real progress stops under such circumstances.

Some middle-aged and elderly people greatly enrich their lives by continuing to cross thresholds. One man went into an entirely new business when he was past middle life and made success of it, De Morgan didn't start to write novels until he was past sixty. Psychologists have discovered that man can continue to learn throughout his life. And it is undoubtedly better to try and fail than not to try at all. There one can be placed in the category of the Swiss mountaineer of whom it was said, *"He died climbing"*. When a new difficulty arises to obstruct your path, do not complain. Accept the challenge. Determine to cross this threshold as you have crossed numerous other thresholds in your past. In the words of a poet, do not rest but strive *to pass from dream to grander dream.*

1. What obstructs real progress in life?
   A. Remaining at one and the same post
   B. Avoiding the thinking and energy
   C. Shunning every work
   D. Stopping education
2. What does progress in life depend upon?
   A. Good habits
   B. Hardwork
   C. Overcoming one difficulty after another
   D. Spirit of service and cooperation
3. What does *'He died climbing'* signify?
   A. He died when he was climbing the hill
   B. He died before getting at the top
   C. He strove hard till the last moment of life
   D. He climbed the hill and then died
4. What does *'to pass from dream to grander dream'* mean?
   A. Always having greater and greater aspiration in life
   B. Seeing one good dream and then greater aspiration in life
   C. Making plan after plan
   D. Seeing one dream after the other
5. What did the man entering a new business past middle life do of his business?
   A. He miserably failed in it
   B. He achieved partial success
   C. He dropped the business after some time
   D. He achieved good success in it
6. How can you accomplish the most difficult tasks?
   A. By mobilizing all possible resources
   B. By avoiding all obstacles
   C. By sticking to hardwork
   D. By doing it bit by bit and persisting in the effort
7. What does De Morgan's life teach?
   A. That it is futile to learn many things
   B. That one is never old in case he has vigour
   C. That it is never too late to learn
   D. That creative writing can be made even late in life
8. How do middle-aged and elderly people add brilliance to their lives?
   A. By overcoming difficulty one after another
   B. By getting sycophants to surround them
   C. By making fine speeches
   D. By acquiring resourcefulness
9. What should we do when a new difficulty obstructs our path?
   A. Run away from it
   B. Be bold and face it
   C. Manoeuvre to get it removed
   D. Enlist other people's help to get it over
10. When did De Morgan start to write novels?
    A. When he was sixty years old
    B. When he was below sixty
    C. When he studied psychology
    D. None of these

## PASSAGE-7

It is *heartening* to know that if one had not had any heart attack earlier and he stops smoking, his chances of having a heart attack *drop* to that of a non-smoker in about six months' time. Stopping of smoking is also the single most effective means of secondary prevention (recurrence of a heart attack) in heart patients.

Smoking leads to pain and stiffness in the legs while walking. No amount of drugs can help. The only remedy is to give up smoking. If women smoke during pregnancy, there is an increased risk of death of the baby in the womb or soon after birth. Even where the baby survives, there is likelihood of delayed physical and intellectual development of the baby till it reaches 11 years of age.

Still worse the fact about smoking is that passive smoking is equally dangerous. Passive smokers are those who do not smoke but being in the company of smokers have to inhale smoke exhaled by the smokers They are equally prone to heart diseases, lung cancer and bronchitis, for no fault of theirs. It is seen that the incidence of these diseases is greater among women whose husbands are *heavy* smokers As such, every non-smoker has a fundamental right to safeguard himself against the danger of passive smoking. "Your smoking is injurious to my health and I have a right to stop you from smoking" could be the slogan against passive smoking. It is a great threat to the health of the individual, the family and the society. In fact one has to choose between health and smoking including passive smoking. *One cannot have both.*

Another matter of *grave concern* about smoking is the long time interval between the start of smoking habit and the manifestation of deadly diseases like cancer, chronic bronchitis and heart attack. People are generally not aware of the link between smoking and the misery they have to undergo years later and younger people often fall victim to this menacing habit under the wrong impression that they are *immune* to its disastrous effects, not realising that they are *heading* towards catastrophe. The prolonged incubation period of many tobacco-related diseases has prevented recognition of the size of the threat and the *grim* picture of chronic and life-threatening diseases.

1. What is "passive smoking"?
A. Giving up the habit of smoking abruptly
B. Exhaling smoke by a non-smoker
C. Unintended intake of smoke exhaled by smokers
D. Smoking cigarettes which are harmless in nature

2. The effects of passive smoking are more and more prominently observed among
A. the children
B. the smokers
C. the wives of smokers
D. the non-smokers

3. Which of the following is a heartening thing, according to the author?
A. People who have had a heart attack stop smoking
B. It takes only six months for any person to quit smoking
C. The smoker carries the risk of heart attack for six months
D. None of these

4. Which of the following statements is/are false in the context of the passage?
(*i*) Passive smokers are not free from risk of heart diseases
(*ii*) Intake of certain medicines helps recover pain and stiffness in legs caused by smoking
(*iii*) Younger people are immune to the disastrous effects if their regular smoking is under control
A. (*i*) and (*ii*) only B. (*ii*) and (*iii*) only
C. (*ii*) only D. (*iii*) only

5. Which of the following is not mentioned in the passage as a likely result of smoking by women during pregnancy?
A. Death of baby before birth
B. Death of baby after birth
C. Survival of baby with some abnormality
D. Abnormal delay in the childbirth

6. Which of the following is considered by the author as a matter of "grave concern"?
A. Inordinate delay in appearance of symptoms of hazards of smoking
B. Long time required for giving up the habit of smoking
C. Manifestation of deadly diseases like cancer, bronchitis, etc.
D. Lack of awareness of people regarding the hazards of smoking

7. The youth feel that they are immune to the hazardous effects of smoking because
A. these effects of smoking are not visible within a short time span
B. they do not realise that they are heading towards disaster
C. they feel a great thrill in acquiring the habit of smoking
D. the link between smoking and its disastrous effects cannot be established

8. Which factor prevents people from realising the extent of threat of smoking hazards?
A. Their lack of awareness of civic responsibilities
B. Their firm belief that they are not immune to these hazards
C. The less disastrous effects of tobacco-related diseases
D. None of these

9. The last sentence of the third para *"One cannot have both"* means
A. active smoking and passive smoking
B. smoking and risk of heart diseases
C. threat to the individual and also to the family
D. None of these

**Directions (Qs. 10 to 12):** *Choose the word which is most nearly the **SAME** in meaning as the word given in bold capitals as used in the passage.*

10. **HEADING**
A. crowning B. marching
C. adorning D. title

11. **HEAVY**
A. excessive B. bulky
C. large D. thick

12. **DROP**
A. roll B. escape
C. remove D. reduce

**Directions (Qs. 13 to 15):** *Choose the word which is most nearly the **OPPOSITE** in meaning of the word given in bold capitals as used in the passage.*

13. **GRIM**
A. dim B. dark
C. presentable D. pleasant

14. **IMMUNE**
A. free B. vulnerable
C. powerful D. weak

15. **HEARTENING**
A. cheerful B. miserable
C. frightening D. dangerous

## PASSAGE-8

The happy man is the man who lives objectively, who has free affections and wide interests, who secures his happiness through these interests and affections and through the fact that they, in turn, make him an object of interest and affection to many others. To be the recipient of affection is a potent cause of happiness, but the man who demands affection is not the man upon whom it is *bestowed.* The man who receives affection is, speaking broadly, the man who gives it. But it is useless to attempt to give it as a calculation, in the way in which one might lend money at interest, for a calculated affection is not genuine and is not felt to be so by the recipient.

What then can a man do who is unhappy because he is encased in self? So long as he continues to think about the causes of his unhappiness, he continues to be self-centred and therefore does not get outside the vicious circle, if he is to get outside it, it must be genuine interests, not by simulated interests adopted merely as a medicine. Although this difficulty is real, there is nevertheless much that he can do if he has rightly diagnosed his trouble. If, for example, his trouble is due to a sense of sin, conscious or unconscious, he can first persuade his conscious mind that he has no reason to feel sinful and then proceed, to plant his rational conviction in his unconscious mind, concerning himself meanwhile with some more or less neutral activity. If he succeeds in *dispelling* the sense of sin, it is possible that genuine objective interests will arise spontaneously. If his trouble is self-pity, he can deal with it in the same manner after first persuading himself that there is nothing extraordinarily unfortunate in his circumstances.

If fear is his trouble, let him practise exercises designed to give courage. Courage has been recognised from time immemorial as an important virtue, and a great part of training of boys and young men has been devoted to producing a type of character capable of fearlessness in battle. But moral courage and intellectual courage have been much less studied, they also, however, have their technique. Admit to yourself everyday at least one painful truth, you will find this quite useful. Teach yourself to feel that life still be worth living even if you were not, as of course you are, immeasurably superior to all your friends in virtue and in intelligence. Exercises of this sort prolonged through several years will at last enable you to admit facts *without flinching* and will, in so doing, free you from the empire of fear over a very large field.

**1.** Who according to the passage is the happy man?
   A. who is encased in self
   B. who has free affection and wide interests
   C. who is free from worldly passions
   D. who has externally centre passions

**2.** According to the passage, calculated affection
   A. appears to be false and fabricated
   B. makes other pen-on to love you
   C. turns into permanent affection over a period of time
   D. leads to self-pity

**3.** Which of the following virtues, according to the passage, has been recognised for long as an important virtue?
   A. Patriotism B. Sacrifice
   C. Courage D. Self-consciousness

**4.** Which of the following, according to the passage, has not been studied much?
   A. Feeling of guilt and self-pity
   B. The state of mind of an unhappy man
   C. How to get absorbed in other interests
   D. Moral and intellectual courage

**5.** If a man is suffering from a sense of sin
   A. he should invite opinion of others
   B. he should admit his sin at once
   C. he should consciously realize that he has no reason to feel sinful
   D. he should develop a fearless character

**6.** What happens to a man who demands affection?
   A. His feelings are reciprocated by others
   B. He tends to take a calculated risk
   C. He becomes a victim of a viscious circle
   D. None of these

**7.** What should a man do who is suffering from the feeling of self-pity?
   A. He should control his passions and emotions
   B. He should persuade himself that everything is alright in his circumstances
   C. He should seek affection from others
   D. He should develop a feeling of fearlessness

**8.** How to get out of the viscious circle mentioned in the passage?
   A. By practicing skills of concentration
   B. By inculcating the habits of self-absorption
   C. Being true to others and one's internal circumstances
   D. None of these

**9.** Which of the following statements is not *true* in the context of the passage?
   A. Happy man has wide interests
   B. Courage has been recognized as an important virtue
   C. Unhappy man is encased in self
   D. Issue of intellectual courage has been extensively studied

**10.** Which of the following words is ***SIMILAR*** in meaning of the word **'bestowed'** as used in the passage?
   A. Conferred B. Accommodated
   C. Trusted D. Withdrawn

**11.** Which of the following statements is *true* in the context of the passage?
   A. All passions stem from unhappiness
   B. The happy man lives in subjectively

C. Any virtue has a dark side also
D. One feels happy if one receives affection

**12.** Which of the following words is ***SIMILAR*** in meaning to the word **'flinching'** as used in the passage?
A. Wincing B. Convincing
C. Explaining D. Debating

**13.** What happens when you think about cause of your unhappiness?
A. You try to introspect and look critically at yourself
B. You realize that the life can be lived in different ways
C. You try to practice exercise designed to give courage
D. You remain a self-centred person

**14.** What according to the passage is the real cause of happiness?
A. Material rewards and incentives received
B. Critical analysis of the happy state of mind
C. Affection received from others
D. Calculated risks taken

**15.** Which of the following words is ***OPPOSITE*** in meaning of the word **'dispelling'** as used in the passage?
A. Giving B. Accumulating
C. Projecting D. Scattering

## PASSAGE-9

Education, particularly higher education, is the obvious but crucially important instrument for nation building. As Confucious has said:

"If you are thinking of one year, plant rice. If you are thinking of a decade, plant trees. If you are thinking of a century, educate the people."

When we set about the task of higher education, we should be absolutely clear in our perception of the goals of education in the specific context of our nation's development. No *doubt,* one of the important aims of education would be to create the required range and nature of trained manpower assessed to be needed by different sectors of national growth. The entire educational apparatus must be geared progressively to fulfill the requirements of different phases of our growth in every sector—primary, secondary and *tertiary.* The aim must be to ensure that our country does not experience either *paucity,* or a *surfeit* of trained manpower in any specific segment of our economy. The requirements of our country, as a free, democratic, secular, socialist, nation, *aspiring* for rapid development, *entail* a specific recipe for our educational institutions. Today's educational institutions must therefore be developed accordingly and must regulate themselves to give the country the precise nature and quantum of trained manpower as projected by the requirements of our planned economy.

**1.** The author has quoted thoughts of Confucious to stress
A. importance of planting trees for human beings
B. the worthless efforts in planting rice
C. the benefits of investing in education
D. the need for assessing manpower requirement

**2.** Which statement cannot be made on the basis of the passage?
A. Higher education should keep in view the requirements of national economy
B. Higher education has not been employed for nation building
C. All levels of education have a role to play in nation's growth
D. In our country we need to have a specially planned educational system

**3.** The writer believes that
A. there are no problems related to higher education
B. investment in education is of long-range
C. higher education should be used to assess manpower needs
D. aims of higher education in India are absolutely clear

**4.** The author's expectations from higher education, are essentially
A. unrealistic B. confusing
C. critical D. vague

**5.** The writer indicates that
A. higher education did not play any role in national growth
B. primary education did not play any role in national growth
C. our nation experiences paucity of trained manpower in many sectors
D. today's higher education has no precise goals to achieve

**6.** Author has used the word 'apparatus' to indicate the
A. scientific nature of education
B. complicated organization demanded by education
C. readily visible benefits of education
D. entire equipment of education to perform particular function

**7.** Which of the following has not been conveyed by the passage?
A. Education at any level can contribute in nation building
B. Manpower needs in many areas can be fulfilled through higher education
C. Rapid development of our nation is possible through higher education
D. Present higher education does not ensure surfeit of trained manpower

8. This passage is likely to be addressed to
   A. politicians only B. scientists only
   C. students only D. cannot be said
9. Choose a suitable title to the passage:
   A. Manpower Planning in India
   B. Importance of Higher Education
   C. Demands of Higher Education
   D. Role of Higher Education in India

**Directions (Qs.10 to 12):** *Choose the word which is most nearly the **SAME** in meaning as the word given in bold capitals as used in the passage.*

10. **DOUBT**
    A. suspicion B. certain
    C. definite D. sure
11. **TERTIARY**
    A. last B. important
    C. third D. terminal
12. **ASPIRING**
    A. inquiring B. awaiting
    C. involving D. striving

**Directions (Qs.13 to 15):** *Choose the word which is most **OPPOSITE** in meaning as the word given in bold capitals as used in the passage.*

13. **PAUCITY**
    A. moderate B. enormity
    C. mediocrity D. littleness
14. **SURFEIT**
    A. abundance B. redundancy
    C. repletion D. lack
15. **ENTAIL**
    A. entitled B. ensure
    C. dismiss D. retain

## PASSAGE-10

Books are a great treasurehouse of knowledge. They are the living examples of man's *march* on the path to higher and higher civilisation. The great men who died long ago, live in their books. We feel their very personality and existence when we read their books. We feel as if they were conversing with us.

Books not only store civilization but also carry it forward. All coming generations get the light of knowledge from the books written by their ancestors and try to improve upon that knowledge. Civilization cannot make much ***headway*** in a country where there are not many *great* books. We get through books the latest knowledge in the fields of arts, science, commerce, etc. This knowledge is helpful to us and *enables* us to achieve success in the field of our choice.

Books are never failing friends. They never *desert* us, not even when all fair-weather friends have deserted us. They dispel the dark clouds of gloom from our minds and increase our happiness if we are already happy. Through the ages, the scriptures and other great books have provided immeasurable *solace* to the wounded and strife-torn humanity.

There may be books prescribed for some course or profession, but then there are books for general study. The books of literature—poetry, drama, novel, short stories, etc., are generally highly thrilling and inspiring if they are written by a good author. There may be tragic, comical or humorous books. The question is that of an individual's choice.

To be a lover of books, though not to be bookworm, is a sign of good luck. A voracious reader gets much *more pleasure* from reading books than a miser gets in hoarding money. The knowledge embedded in books is valueless; so is pleasure obtained from reading them. A good book absorbs the whole spirit of man; the reader's pleasure is indescribable.

1. Which of the following, according to the passage, is not true about books?
   A. They are source of inspiration
   B. They are source of knowledge
   C. They are source of happiness
   D. They are means of livelihood
2. How do the books help in progress of civilization?
   A. Based on the earlier books new knowledge is obtained
   B. The books provide solution to many problems
   C. The books inspire the scientists
   D. Not mentioned in the passage
3. How do the books make people more happy?
   A. They help the reader to overcome the shadows of uncertainty
   B. They help bring in joy by amusing the reader through their content
   C. They help the reader to understand the darker side of life
   D. Not mentioned in the passage
4. Which of the following is the author's view about the knowledge and pleasure derived from books?
   (*i*) We get more of knowledge and less of pleasure
   (*ii*) We get more of pleasure and less of knowledge
   (*iii*) We get knowledge and pleasure in equal measure
   A. only (*i*) B. only (*ii*)
   C. either (*i*) or (*ii*) D. only (*iii*)
5. The high quality of books produced by a country indicates:
   A. it has a high rate of literacy
   B. it has a progressive civilization
   C. it is not an industrialised nation
   D. it has learned ancestors

**6.** Why are the books, according to the passage, called never-failing friends?
A. Books do not betray individuals
B. Books are inanimate
C. Books always give companionship to the reader
D. Books are available in the market anytime unlike others

**7.** How do the books help in bringing peace in the minds of people?
A. Books provide information about the past civilization
B. Books help people learn to take correct steps with the help of the recorded information
C. Books act as a window to the minds of the great men
D. Not mentioned in the passage

**8.** Which of the following has been described as a sign of good luck?
A. Being a miser
B. Having lot of money
C. Advancing the culture
D. A passion for books

**Directions (Qs. 9 to 12):** *Choose the word which is most nearly the **SAME** in meaning as the word given in bold capitals as used in the passage.*

**9. SOLACE**
A. peace B. tranquillity
C. calmness D. console

**10. ENABLES**
A. helps B. succeeds
C. promotes D. stops

**11. HEADWAY**
A. higher B. forge
C. movement D. improve

**12. MARCH**
A. move B. progress
C. pass D. register

**Directions (Qs. 13 to 15):** *Choose the word which is most **OPPOSITE** in meaning of the word given in bold capitals as used in the passage.*

**13. GREAT**
A. small B. thin
C. short D. ordinary

**14. PLEASURE**
A. displeasure B. pain
C. happiness D. hardship

**15. DESERT**
A. waterhole B. bitter
C. accompany D. propel

## ANSWERS

**PASSAGE-1**

| 1 | 2 | 3 | 4 |
|---|---|---|---|
| A | B | A | A |

**PASSAGE-2**

| 1 | 2 | 3 | 4 | 5 |
|---|---|---|---|---|
| A | C | D | A | D |

**PASSAGE-3**

| 1 | 2 | 3 | 4 | 5 |
|---|---|---|---|---|
| A | D | C | D | A |

**PASSAGE-4**

| 1 | 2 | 3 | 4 | 5 | 6 |
|---|---|---|---|---|---|
| D | A | D | A | A | D |

**PASSAGE-5**

| 1 | 2 | 3 | 4 | 5 | 6 | 7 |
|---|---|---|---|---|---|---|
| A | D | A | A | A | C | B |

**PASSAGE-6**

| 1 | 2 | 3 | 4 | 5 |
|---|---|---|---|---|
| A | C | C | A | D |
| 6 | 7 | 8 | 9 | 10 |
| D | B | A | B | D |

**PASSAGE-7**

| 1 | 2 | 3 | 4 | 5 |
|---|---|---|---|---|
| C | C | D | B | D |
| 6 | 7 | 8 | 9 | 10 |
| A | A | D | D | B |
| 11 | 12 | 13 | 14 | 15 |
| A | D | D | B | C |

**PASSAGE-8**

| 1 | 2 | 3 | 4 | 5 |
|---|---|---|---|---|
| B | A | C | D | C |
| 6 | 7 | 8 | 9 | 10 |
| D | B | D | D | A |
| 11 | 12 | 13 | 14 | 15 |
| D | D | D | C | B |

**PASSAGE-9**

| 1 | 2 | 3 | 4 | 5 |
|---|---|---|---|---|
| D | D | C | D | D |
| 6 | 7 | 8 | 9 | 10 |
| D | A | D | B | A |
| 11 | 12 | 13 | 14 | 15 |
| C | D | B | D | C |

**PASSAGE-10**

| 1 | 2 | 3 | 4 | 5 |
|---|---|---|---|---|
| D | A | D | D | B |
| 6 | 7 | 8 | 9 | 10 |
| A | D | D | D | A |
| 11 | 12 | 13 | 14 | 15 |
| D | B | D | B | C |

YOUR SPACE

# BUSINESS STUDIES

# Nature and Significance of Management

## DEFINITIONS OF MANAGEMENT

"Management is the process of designing and maintaining an environment in which individuals, working together in groups, efficiently accomplish selected aims."

*—Harold Koontz and Heinz Weihrich*

"Management is defined as the process of planning, organising, actuating and controlling an organisation's operations in order to achieve coordination of the human and material resources essential in the effective and efficient attainment of objectives."

*—Robert L. Trewelly and M. Gene Newport*

"Management is the process of working with and through others to effectively achieve organisational objectives by efficiently using limited resources in the changing environment." *—Kreitner*

## CONCEPT

Management is a very popular term and has been used extensively for all types of activities and mainly for taking charge of different activities in any enterprise. Management aims at guiding their efforts towards achieving a common objective—a goal. Thus, management has to see that tasks are completed and goals are achieved (*i.e.*, effectiveness) with the least amount of resources at a minimum cost (*i.e.*, efficiency).

Management, has therefore, been defined as a process of getting things done with the aim of achieving goals effectively and efficiently. We need to analyse this definition. There are certain terms which require elaboration. These are (a) process, (b) effectively, and (c) efficiently.

Being effective or doing work effectively basically means finishing the given task. Effectiveness in management is concerned with doing the right task, completing activities and achieving goals. In other words, it is concerned with the end result.

But it is not enough to just complete the tasks. There is another aspect also, *i.e.*, being efficient or as we say doing work efficiently.

Efficiency means doing the task correctly and with minimum cost. There is a kind of cost-benefit analysis involved and the relationship between inputs and outputs. If by using less resources (*i.e.*, the inputs) more benefits are derived (*i.e.*, the outputs) then efficiency has increased. Efficiency is also increased when for the same benefit or outputs, fewer resources are used and less costs are incurred. Input resources are money, materials, equipment and persons required to do a particular task. Obviously, management is concerned with the efficient use of these resources, because they reduce costs and ultimately lead to higher profits.

## CHARACTERISTICS OF MANAGEMENT

The Characteristics of Management are:

(*i*) **Management is a goal-oriented process:** An organisation has a set of basic goals which are the basic reason for its existence. These should be simple and clearly stated. Different organisations have different goals. For example, the goal of a retail store may be to increase sales, but the goal of The Spastics Society of India is to impart education to children with special needs. Management unites the efforts of different individuals in the organisation towards achieving these goals.

(*ii*) **Management is all pervasive:** The activities involved in managing an enterprise are common to all organisations whether economic, social or political. A petrol pump needs to be managed as much as a hospital or a school. What managers do in India, the USA, Germany or Japan is the same. How they do it may be quite different. This difference is due to the differences in culture, tradition and history.

(*iii*) **Management is multidimensional:** Management is a complex activity that has three main dimensions. These are:

(*a*) **Management of work:** All organisations exist for the performance of some work. In a factory, a product is manufactured, in a garment store a customer's need is satisfied and in a hospital a patient is treated. Management translates this work in terms of goals to be achieved and assigns the means to achieve it. This is done in terms of problems to be solved, decisions to be made, plans to be established, budgets to be prepared, responsibilities to be assigned and authority to be delegated.

(*b*) **Management of people:** Human resources or people are an organisation's greatest asset. Despite all developments in technology "getting work done through people" is still a major task for the manager. Managing people has two dimensions:

(*i*) it implies dealing with employees as individuals with diverse needs and behaviour;

(*ii*) it also means dealing with individuals as a group of people.

The task of management is to make people work towards achieving the organisation's goals, by making their strengths effective and their weaknesses irrelevant.

(*c*) **Management of operations:** No matter what the organisation, it has some basic product or service to provide in order to survive. This requires a production process which entails the flow of input material and the technology for transforming this input into the desired output for consumption. This is interlinked with both the management of work and the management of people.

(*iv*) **Management is a continuous process:** The process of management is a series of continuous, composite, but separate functions (planning, organising, directing, staffing and controlling). These functions are simultaneously performed by all managers all the time. We may have observed that Smita at Namchi Designer Candles performs several different tasks in a single day. Some days she may spend more time in planning a future exhibition and on another day, she may spend time in sorting out an employee's problem. The task of a manager consists of an ongoing series of functions.

(*v*) **Management is a group activity:** An organisation is a collection of diverse individuals with different needs. Every member of the group has a different purpose for joining the organisation but as members of the organisation they work towards fulfilling the common organisational goal. This requires team work and coordination of individual effort in a common direction. At the same time management should enable all its members to grow and develop as needs and opportunities change.

(*vi*) **Management is a dynamic function:** Management is a dynamic function and has to adapt itself to the changing environment. An organisation interacts with its external environment which consists of various social, economic and political factors. In order to be successful, an organisation must change itself and its goals according to the needs of the environment. We probably know that McDonalds, the fast food giant made major changes in its menu to be able to survive in the Indian market.

(*vii*) **Management is an intangible force:** Management is an intangible force that cannot be seen but its presence can be felt in the way the organisation functions. The effect of management is noticeable in an organisation where targets are met according to plans, employees are happy and satisfied, and there is orderliness instead of chaos.

## IMPORTANCE OF MANAGEMENT

The following points highlight the importance of management in an organisation:

(*i*) **Management helps in achieving group goals:** Management is required not for itself but for achieving the goals of the organisation. The task of a manager is to give a common direction to the individual effort in achieving the overall goal of the organisation.

(*ii*) **Management increases efficiency:** The aim of a manager is to reduce costs and increase productivity through better planning, organising, directing, staffing and controlling the activities of the organisation.

(*iii*) **Management creates a dynamic organisation:** All organisations have to function in an environment which is constantly changing. It is generally seen that individuals in an organisation resist change as it often means moving from a familiar, secure environment into a newer and more challenging one. Management helps people adapt to these changes so that the organisation is able to maintain its competitive edge.

(*iv*) **Management helps in achieving personal objectives:** A manager motivates and leads his team in such a manner that individual members are able to achieve personal goals while contributing to the overall organisational objective. Through motivation and leadership the management helps individuals to develop team spirit, cooperation and commitment to group success.

(*v*) **Management helps in the development of society:** An organisation has multiple objectives to serve the purpose of the different groups that constitute it. In the process of fulfilling all these, management helps in the development of the organisation and through that it helps in the development of society. It helps to provide good quality products and services, creates employment opportunities, adopts new technology for the greater good of the people and leads the path towards growth and development.

## NATURE OF MANAGEMENT

Management is as old as civilisation. Although modern organisations are of recent origin, organised activity has existed since the time of the ancient civilisations. In fact, organisations may be considered the distinguishing feature that separated civilised society from uncivilised ones. The earliest management practices were a set of rules and regulations that grew out of the experiences of governmental and commercial activities. The development of trade and commerce gradually led to the development of management principles and practices.

The term 'management' today has several different connotations that highlight the different aspects of its nature. The study of management has evolved over a period of time along with the modern organisations; based both on the experience and practice of managers and a set of theoretical relationships. Over a period of time, it has grown into a dynamic subject with its own special characteristics. However, one question that needs to be addressed pertaining to the nature of management is whether it is a science or an art or both? In order to answer this let us examine the features of both science and art to see how far management fulfills them.

## MANAGEMENT AS AN ART

What is art? Art is the skillful and personal application of existing knowledge to achieve desired results. It can be acquired through study, observation and experience. Since art is concerned with personal application of knowledge some kind of ingenuity and creativity is required to practice the basic principles learnt.

The basic features of an art are as follows:

(*i*) **Existence of theoretical knowledge:** Art presupposes the existence of certain theoretical knowledge. Experts in their respective areas have derived certain basic principles which are applicable to a particular form of art. For example, literature on dancing, public speaking, acting or music is widely recognised.

(*ii*) **Personalised application:** The use of this basic knowledge varies from individual to individual. Art, therefore, is a very personalised concept. For example, two dancers, two speakers, two actors, or two writers will always differ in demonstrating their art.

(*iii*) **Based on practice and creativity:** All art is practical. Art involves the creative practice of existing theoretical knowledge. We know that all music is based on seven basic notes. However, what makes the composition of a musician unique or different is his use of these notes in a creative manner that is entirely his own interpretation.

Management can be said to be an art since it satisfies the following criteria:

(*i*) A successful manager practices the art of management in the day-to-day job of managing an enterprise based on study, observation and experience. There is a lot of literature available in various areas of management like marketing, finance and human resources which the manager has to specialise in. There is existence of theoretical knowledge.

(*ii*) There are various theories of management, as propounded by many management thinkers, which prescribe certain universal principles. A manager applies these scientific methods and body of knowledge to a given situation, an issue or a problem, in his own unique manner. A good manager works through a combination of practice, creativity, imagination, initiative and innovation. A manager achieves perfection after long practice. Students of management also apply these principles differently depending on how creative they are.

(*iii*) A manager applies this acquired knowledge in a personalised and skillful manner in the light of the realities of a given situation. He is involved in the activities of the organisation, studies critical situations and formulates his own theories for use in a given situation. This gives rise to different styles of management.

The best managers are committed and dedicated individuals; highly trained and educated, with personal qualities such as ambition, self-motivation, creativity and imagination, a desire for development of the self and the organisation they belong to. All management practices are based on the same set of principles; what distinguishes a successful manager from a less successful one is the ability to put these principles into practice.

## MANAGEMENT AS A SCIENCE

Science is a systematised body of knowledge that explains certain general truths or the operation of general laws. The basic features of science are as follows:

(*i*) **Systematised body of knowledge:** Science is a systematic body of knowledge. Its principles are based on a cause and effect relationship. For example, the phenomenon of an apple falling from a tree towards the ground is explained by the law of gravity.

(*ii*) **Principles based on experimentation:** Scientific principles are first developed through observation and then tested through repeated experimentation under controlled conditions.

(*iii*) **Universal validity:** Scientific principles have universal validity and application.

Based on the above features, we can say that management has some characteristics of science.

(*i*) Management has a systematised body of knowledge. It has its own theory and principles that have developed over a period of time, but it also draws on other disciplines such as Economics, Sociology, Psychology and Mathematics. Like all other organised activity, management has its own vocabulary of terms and concepts. For example, all of us discuss sports like cricket and soccer using a common vocabulary. The players also use these terms to communicate with each other. Similarly managers need to communicate with one another with the help of a common vocabulary for a better understanding of their work situation.

(*ii*) The principles of management have evolved over a period of time based on repeated experimentation and observation in different types of organisations. However, since management deals with human beings and human behaviour, the outcomes of these experiments are not capable of being accurately predicted or replicated. Therefore, management can be called an inexact science. Despite these limitations, management scholars have been able to identify general principles of management. For example, scientific management principles by F.W. Taylor and Functional Management principles by Henri Fayol which you will study in the next chapter.

(*iii*) Since the principles of management are not as exact as the principles of science, their application and use is not universal. They have to be modified according to a given situation. However, they provide managers with certain standardised techniques that can be used in different situations. These principles are also used for training and development of managers.

We must have understood from the foregoing discussion that management has features of both art and science. The practice of management is an art. However, managers can work better if their practice is based on the principles of management. These principles constitute the science of management. Management as an art and a science are therefore not mutually exclusive, but complement each other.

## MANAGEMENT AS A PROFESSION

A profession has the following characteristics:

(*i*) **Well-defined body of knowledge:** All professions are based on a well-defined body of knowledge that can be acquired through instruction.

(*ii*) **Restricted entry:** The entry to a profession is restricted through an examination or through acquiring an educational degree. For example, to become a chartered accountant in India a candidate has to clear a specified examination conducted by the Institute of Chartered Accountants of India.

(*iii*) **Professional association:** All professions are affiliated to a professional association which regulates entry, grants certificate of practice and formulates and enforces a code of conduct. To be able to practice in India lawyers have to become members of the Bar Council which regulates and controls their activities.

(*iv*) **Ethical code of conduct:** All professions are bound by a code of conduct which guides the behaviour of its members. All doctors, for example, take the oath of ethical practice at the time they enter the profession.

(*v*) **Service motive:** The basic motive of a profession is to serve their client's interests by rendering dedicated and committed service. The task of a lawyer is to ensure that his client gets justice.

Management does not meet the exact criteria of a profession. However, it does have some of the features of a profession:

(*i*) All over the world there is marked growth in management as a discipline. It is based on a systematic body of knowledge comprising well-defined principles based on a variety of business situations. This knowledge can be acquired at different colleges and professional institutes and through a number of books and journals. The subject of management is taught at different institutions. Some of these have been set up with the specific purpose of providing management education such as the Indian Institutes of Management (IIMs) in India. Entry to different institutes is usually through an examination.

(*ii*) There is no restriction on anyone being designated or appointed as manager in any business enterprise. Anyone can be called a manager irrespective of the educational qualifications possessed.

Unlike professions such as medicine or law which require a practicing doctor or lawyer to possess valid degrees, nowhere in the world is it mandatory for a manager to possess any such specific degree. But professional knowledge and training is considered to be a desirable qualification, since there is greater demand for those who possess degrees or diplomas from reputed institutions. Therefore, as such the second criterion has not been strictly met.

(*iii*) There are several associations of practising managers in India, like the AIMA (All India Management Association) that has laid down a code of conduct to regulate the activities of their members. There is, however, no compulsion for managers to be members of such an association nor does it have any statutory backing.

(*iv*) The basic purpose of management is to help the organisation achieve its stated goal. This may be profit maximisation for a business enterprise and service for a hospital. However, profit maximisation as the objective of management does not hold true and is fast changing. Therefore, if an organisation has a good management team that is efficient and effective it automatically serves society by providing good quality products at reasonable prices.

## LEVELS OF MANAGEMENT

Management is a universal term used for certain functions performed by individuals in an enterprise who are bound together in a hierarchy of relationships. Every individual in the hierarchy is responsible for successful completion of a particular task. To be able to fulfill that responsibility he is assigned a certain amount of authority or the right to take a decision. This authority-responsibility relationship binds individuals as superiors and subordinates and gives rise to different levels in an organisation. Generally speaking there are three levels in the hierarchy of an organisation.

### Top Management

They consist of the senior-most executives of the organisation by whatever name they are called. They are usually referred to as the chairman, the chief executive officer, chief operating officer, president and vice-president. Top management is a team consisting of managers from different functional levels, heading finance, marketing etc. For example chief finance officer, vice president (marketing). Their basic task is to integrate diverse elements and coordinate the activities of different departments according to the overall objectives of the organisation. These top level managers are responsible for the welfare and survival of the organisation. They analyse the business environment and its implications for the survival of the firm. They formulate overall organisational goals and strategies for their achievement. They are responsible for all the activities of the business and for its impact on society. The job of the top manager is complex and stressful, demanding long hours and commitment to the organisation.

### Middle Management

Middle Management is the link between top and lower level managers. They are subordinate to top managers and superior to the first line managers. They are usually known as division heads, for example production manager. Middle management is responsible for implementing and controlling plans and strategies developed by top management. At the same time they are responsible for all the activities of first line managers. Their main task is to carry out the plans formulated by the top managers. For this they need to:

(*i*) interpret the policies framed by top management,

(*ii*) ensure that their department has the necessary personnel,

(*iii*) assign necessary duties and responsibilities to them,

(*iv*) motivate them to achieve desired objectives, and

(*v*) cooperate with other departments for smooth functioning of the organisation. At the same time they are responsible for all the activities of first line managers.

### Supervisory or Operational Management

Foremen and supervisors comprise the lower level in the hierarchy of the organisation. Supervisors directly oversee the efforts of the workforce. Their authority and responsibility is limited according to the plans drawn by the top management. Supervisory management plays a very important role in the organisation since they interact with the actual work force and pass on instructions of the middle management to the workers. Through their efforts quality of output is maintained, wastage of materials is minimised and safety standards are maintained. The quality of workmanship and the quantity of output depends on the hard work, discipline and loyalty of the workers.

•••

# Business Environment

## CONCEPT & ELEMENTS OF BUSINESS ENVIRONMENT

Business Environment means a collection of all individuals, entities and other factors, which may or may not be under the control of the organisation, but can affect its performance, profitability, growth and even survival.

Every business organisation operates in a distinctive environment, as it cannot exist in isolation. Such an environment influence business and also gets affected by its activities.

### Features of Business Environment

(*i*) **Totality of External Forces:** Business environment is the sum total of all things external to business firms and, as such, is aggregative in nature.

(*ii*) **Specific and General Forces:** Business environment includes both specific and general forces. Specific forces (such as investors, customers, competitors and suppliers) affect individual enterprises directly and immediately in their day-to-day working. General forces (such as social, political, legal and technological conditions) have impact on all business enterprises and thus may affect an individual firm indirectly only.

(*iii*) **Dynamic Nature:** Business environment is dynamic in nature. It keeps on changing whether in terms of technological improvement, shifts in consumer preferences or entry of new competition in the market.

(*iv*) **Uncertainty:** Business environment is largely uncertain as it is very difficult to predict future happenings, especially when environment changes are taking place too frequently as in the case of information technology or fashion industries.

(*iv*) **Relativity:** Business environment is a relative concept since it differs from country to country and even region to region. Political conditions in the USA, for instance, differ from those in China or Pakistan. Similarly, demand for sarees may be fairly high in India whereas it may be almost non-existent in France.

(*v*) **Multi-faceted:** Business environment changes are frequent and depend on knowledge and existence of business person. Changes may be viewed differently by different individuals. It may be an opportunity for some or a threat for others.

### Importance of Business Environment

(*i*) **First Mover Advantage:** Early identification of opportunities helps an enterprise to be the first to exploit them instead of losing them to competitors. For example, Maruti Udyog became the leader in the small car market because it was the first to recognize the need of small cars in India.

(*ii*) **Identification of Threats:** Identification of possible threats helps in taking corrective and improving measures to survive the competition. For instance; if an Indian firm finds that a foreign multinational is entering the Indian market, it can meet the threat by adopting measures like, by improving the quality of the product, reducing cost of the production, engaging in aggressive advertising, and so on.

(*iii*) **Coping with Rapid Changes:** All types of enterprises are facing increasingly dynamic environment. In order to effectively cope with these significant changes, firms must understand and examine the environment and develop suitable course of action.

(*iv*) **Improving Performance:** The enterprises that continuously monitor their environment and adopt suitable business practices are the ones which not only improve their present performance but also continue to succeed in the market for a longer period.

(*v*) **Giving Direction for Growth:** The interaction with the environment leads to opening up new frontiers of growth for the business firms. It enables the business to identify the areas for growth and expansion of their activities.

## TYPES OF BUSINESS ENVIRONMENT

There are mainly two types of business environment, internal and external. A business has absolute control in the internal environment, whereas it has no control on the external environment. It is therefore, required by businesses, to modify their internal environment on the basis of pressures from external.

## Internal Environment

The internal environment has received considerable attention by firms. Internal environment contains the owner of the business, the shareholders, the managing director, the non-managers, employees, the customers, the infrastructure of the business organization, and the culture of the organization.

It includes '6 M' *i.e.*

- Man (Human Resource)
- Money (Financial Factors)
- Marketing Resources
- Machinery (Physical Assets)
- Management Structure and Nature
- Miscellaneous Factors (Research and Development, Company Image and Brand Equity, Value System, Competitive Advantage)

### *Human Resource (MAN)*

The human resource is the important factor for any organization as it contributes to the strength and weakness of any organization. The human resource in any organization must have characteristics like skills, quality, high morale, commitment towards the work, attitude, etc. The involvement and initiative of the people in an organization at different levels may vary from organization to organization. The organizational culture and over all environment have bearing on them. It is an internal factor and an organisation has absolute control on changing this factor as per the needs of the enterprise and other forces.

### *Financial Factors (MONEY)*

Factors like financial policies, financial positions and capital structure are another important internal factor which has a substantial impact on business functioning and performance. Financial facilities are required to start and operate the organisation. The sources of finance are share capital, banking and other financial institutions and unorganised capital markets. The recent changes in the Indian capital market indicate the availability of plenty of finance, both from the financial institutions as well as from the general public. The availability of finance coupled with various incentives attached is a facilitating internal factor.

### *Marketing Resources*

Resources like the organization for marketing, quality of the marketing men, brand equity and distribution network have direct impact on marketing efficiency of the company and thereby, affecting the decision making component of the management. This, in lieu has great impact on the internal environment of business.

### *Physical Assets and Facilities*

Facilities like production capacity, technology are among the factors which influences the competitiveness of the firm. The proper acquisition and working of the assets is indeed essential for efficient working of the organization. An organisation invests money in plant and machinery because it expects a positive rate of return over cost in future. The revenue from the use of plant and machinery should be sufficient so as to cover the invested money, operating costs, and generate enough profit to satisfy the organisation. The availability of plant and machinery is dependent on technological development of the country and the government's approach towards foreign technical collaboration.

### *Management Structure and Nature*

The structure of the organization also influences the business decisions. Being internal forces, the organizational structure like the composition of board of directors influences the decisions of business. The structure and style of the organization directly has an impact on the decision making decisions of a firm. These needs to be appropriately managed for smooth functioning and operations. The strategies available to an organisation are determined by its structure. Different strategies are better suited to different environments. Thus, if an organisation has to thrive, its structure must fit its business environment in which it develops. Some markets and environments change faster than others. A firm working in high technological environment, for example, needs to have a fast reaction time because its competitors are introducing new products all the time. In rapidly changing environments, organizations may find it difficult to stay up to date on all the changes and implications of their own operations and activities. Organizations in slow markets tend to have rigid, hierarchical structures, while those in changing markets are more adaptive. They can create new divisions in their management structure, to deal with emerging issues.

### *Miscellaneous Factors*

The other internal factors that contribute to the business environment are as follows:

(*i*) **Research and Development:** Though Research and Development needs are mostly outsourced from the external environment but it has a direct impact on working, operations and decision making of the organization. This aspect mainly determines the company's ability to innovate and compete. R&D mainly results in technological improvements of the Business environment. The technological environment refers to the sum total of knowledge providing ways of doing things. It may include inventions and techniques which affect the way of doing things that is, designing, producing and distributing products. A given technology affects an organisation, in the manner it is organised and faces competition.

(*ii*) **Company Image and Brand Equity:** The image of the company in the outside market has the impact on the internal environment of the company. It helps in raising the finance, making joint ventures, other alliances, expansions and acquisitions, entering sale and purchase contracts, launching new products, etc. Brand equity also helps the company in similar manner.

(*iii*) **Value System:** The principles of right and wrong that are accepted by an individual or organisation are what comprise value system. The value system of the founders and those at the helm of affairs has important bearing on the choice of business, the mission and the objectives of the organization, business policies and practices. These values helps guide the basic principles of business for a period of time which moulds an impression of positivism among people dealing with the business. The values are independent of business purposes and are integral part for success of business.

(*iv*) **Competitive Advantage:** Competitor analysis is a critical aspect of analyzing the internal business environment. Competitor's actions affect the ability of the business to make profits, because competitors will continually seek to gain an advantage over each other, by differentiating their product and service, and by seeking to provide better value for money. It involves: – identifying the actual competitors – assessing competitors' objectives, strategies, strengths & weaknesses, and reaction patterns – selecting the strategies to deal with competitors.

The internal analysis of strengths and weaknesses focuses on internal factors that give an organization certain advantages and disadvantages in meeting the needs of its target market thereby gaining the competitive edge over the competitors.

## Technological Environment

Rapid developments in technology exert a powerful influence on all the organisations and not just on those operating in a high-tech environment, say, microprocessor manufacture, pharmaceuticals, fibre-optic technology and so on. The combined impact of computer, digital technology and telecommunications affects most of private and public sector undertakings.

As rightly called by none other as Mr. J. Schumpeter "a perennial gate of creative destruction." Change of technology is both creative and destructive process in that it is responsible for building new by destroying the old. Thus, the heart of any progress is destruction.

## External Environment

The external environment of an organisation comprises of all entities that exists outside its boundaries, but have significant influence over its growth and survival. An organisation has little or no control over its external environment but needs to constantly monitor and adapt to these external changes. A proactive or reactive response leads to significantly different outcomes. There are two types of external environment

(*a*) Micro/Operating Environment

(*b*) Macro/General Environment

### *(a) Micro Environment*

The micro environment is also known as the task environment and operating environment because the micro environmental forces, though are external factors, still have a direct bearing on the operations of the firm. The micro environment consists of the factors in the company's immediate environment that affects the performance and working of the company. The micro environmental factors are more intimately linked with the company than the macro factors. The micro forces need not necessarily affect all the firms in a particular industry in the similar ways. Some of the micro factors may be particular to any given type of organisation.

Micro environmental factors, internal factors close to a business that have a direct impact on its strategy includes:

- Customers
- Employees
- Suppliers
- Shareholders
- Media
- Competitors

**Customers and Consumers:** Customers are people who buy an organization's products/services. In simple words, an organization cannot survive without customers. A consumer, on the other hand, is the ultimate user of the product/service. For example, a husband might purchase a product for his wife. In this case, the husband is the customer and the wife is the consumer.

**Competitors:** Every business has competition. Competitors are other organizations that compete with each other for both resources and markets. Hence, it is important that an organization is aware of its competitors and in a position to analyze threats from its competition. A business must be aware of its competitors, their strengths and weaknesses, and the most aggressive and powerful competitors at all times.

**Organization:** One of the most important aspects of the micro environment of an organization is the self-analysis of the organization itself. It must understand its own strengths and weaknesses, objectives and goals of the business, and resource availability. The following non-specific elements of an organization can affect its performance:

- **Owners:** People who have a major shareholding in the organization and have vested interests in the well-being of the company.
- **Board of Directors:** The board of directors is elected by the shareholders for overseeing the general management of the business and ensuring that the shareholder's interests are met.
- **Employees:** People who work in the organization are major contributors to its success. It is important that all employees embrace the organization's goals and objectives.

**Market:** The market is much more than the sum of all the customers. The organization must study the market in terms of its actual size, the potential for growth, and its attractiveness. Some important issues are:

- The cost structure of the market
- Price Sensitivity of the market
- Technological structure of the market
- The existing distribution system of the market
- The maturity of the market

**Suppliers:** Suppliers are another important component of the micro environment. Organizations depend on many suppliers for equipment, raw material, etc. to maintain their production. Suppliers can influence the cost structure of the industry and are hence a major force.

**Intermediaries:** Intermediaries are also a major determining force in business. Most customers are unaware of the manufacturer of the products they buy since they approach retailers, departmental store, chain stores or online stores for their purchase.

### *(b) Macro Environment*

Macro environment is also known as general environment and remote environment. Macro factors are generally more uncontrollable than micro environment factors. When the macro factors become uncontrollable, the success of company depends upon its adaptability to the environment. This environment has a bearing on the strategies adopted by the firms and any changes in the areas of the macro environment are likely to have a far-reaching impact on their operations.

The macro environment is primarily concerned with major issues and upcoming changes in the environment. The acronym for the macro analysis is "STEEP." The five areas of interest are:

- Socio-Cultural and Demographics
- Technology
- Economic Conditions
- Ecology and Physical Environment
- Political and Legal

## ECONOMIC ENVIRONMENT

The economic environment is the sum total of the economic conditions and the nature of the economy in which the business has to operate and compete.

This will include the nature of the economy, the direction in which it is progressing, the availability:

*(i)* **Socio Cultural and Demographics:** Societal values and lifestyles change over time, and the most important of these; directly or indirectly leave an impact on the business environment. For example, over the past generation, it has become acceptable for women to work; people are not retiring at 65; and people are more aware of the environment etc. The changes in culture and lifestyle may come from many sources: medical (smoking, healthy eating, exercises); science (global warming, going 'green'); economic (people working longer, women in the workforce); cultural diversity (music preferences, foods, living accommodations, medicine); and technologies (biodegradable plastic) are just a few examples.

These changes will be important to the industry and to the business. The social environment of business includes social factors like customs, traditions, values, beliefs, poverty, literacy, life expectancy rate etc. The social structure and the values that a society cherishes have a considerable influence on the functioning of business firms. For example, during festive seasons, there is an increase in the demand for new clothes, sweets, fruits, flower, etc. Due to increase in literacy rate, the consumers are becoming more conscious of the quality of the products. Due to change in family composition, more nuclear families with single child concepts have come up. This increases the demand for the different types of household goods. It may be noted that the consumption patterns, the dressing and living styles of people belonging to different social structures and culture vary significantly.

Demographics refer to the size, density, distribution and growth rate of population. All these factors have a bearing on the demand for various goods and services. For example, a country where population rate is high and children constitute a large section of population, and then, there will be more demand for such products. Similarly, the demand of the people of cities and towns are different than that of people of rural areas. The high rise of population indicates the easy availability of labour. These encourage the business enterprises to use labour intensive techniques of production. Moreover, availability of skilled labour in certain areas motivates the firms to set up their units in such area. For example, the business units from America, Canada, Australia, Germany, UK, are coming to India due to easy availability of skilled manpower. Thus, a firm that keeps a watch on the changes on the demographic front and reads them accurately will find opportunities knocking at its doorsteps.

*(ii)* **Technology:** Technology is understood as the systematic application of scientific or other organised knowledge to practical tasks. Technology changes fast and to keep the pace with the dynamics of business environment; organisation must be on its toes to adapt to the changed technology in their system. The business in a country is greatly influenced by the technological development. The technology adopted by the industries determines the type and quality of goods and services produced. Technological environment influences the business in terms of investment in technology, consistent application of technology and the effects of technology on markets. Technological environment include the methods, techniques and approaches adopted for production of goods and services and its distribution. The varying technological environments affect the designing of products in different countries. Technology encompasses something more than computers. Technology comes in many forms such as medical devices, new plastics, and production techniques.

*(iii)* **Economic Conditions:** The economic conditions of a country refer to a set of economic factors that have great influence on business organizations and their operations. These include gross domestic product, per capita income, markets for goods and services, availability of capital, foreign exchange reserve, growth of foreign trade, strength of capital market etc. All these help in improving the pace of economic growth.

*(iv)* **Ecology and Physical Environment:** The ecology and physical environment plays a large part in many businesses – especially for those which carry out production and manufacturing activities. Infact, business are affected on daily basis due to enviornmental and ecological changes. For example, the impact of climate change must be considered: water and fuel costs could change dramatically, if the world warms by only a couple of degrees. The natural environment includes geographical and ecological factors that influence the business operations. These factors include the availability of natural resources, weather and climatic condition, location aspect, topographical factors, etc. For example, sugar factories are set up only at those places where sugarcane can be grown. It is always considered better to establish manu-facturing unit near the sources of input. Further, government's policies to maintain ecological balance, conservation of natural resources etc. put additional responsibility on the business sector.

*(v)* **Political and Legal:** Political environment refers to three political institutions viz. legislature, executive and the judiciary in shaping, directing, developing and controlling business activities. The political environment of a country is influenced by the political organisations such as philosophy of political parties, ideology of government or party in power, nature and extent of bureaucracy influence of primary groups. The political environment of the country influences the business to a great extent. The political environment includes the political system, the government policies and their attitude towards the business community. All these aspects have a bearing on the strategies adopted by the business firms. The stability of the government also influences business and related activities to a great extent. It sends a signal of strength, confidence to various interest groups and investors. Further, ideology of the political party also influences the business organisation and its operations. Political changes are closely tied up with legal changes. Legal environment includes flexibility and adaptability of law and other legal rules governing the business. It may include the exact rulings and decision of the courts. These affect the business and its managers to a great extent. This refers to set of laws, regulations, which influence the business organisations and their operations. Every business organisation has to obey, and work within the framework of law. Additionally, an industry may have specific laws and regulations. For example, a pet store would deal with federal animal welfare and prohibited pet laws as wells as state laws concerning animal cruelty, housing, veterinary care and so on.

• • •

# Principles of Management

## PRINCIPLES AND PRACTICES OF MANAGEMENT

### PRINCIPLES OF MANAGEMENT

A principle can be defined as a fundamental statement or truth providing a guide to thought or action. The fundamental statement tells what results are expected when the principle is applied. Principles of management are to the manager as a table of materials' strengths and weaknesses is to a civil engineer. The table gives fundamental truths, expressed as quantitative data based on years of experience and testing. The engineer can predetermine the safe, allowable load for a steel girder of a building simply by using the table and analyzing the design drawings and specifications. Similarly, management principles also have been developed from years of experience and testing, in public and private, in big and small organizations.

The principles emerge based on certain qualities/characteristics that have relevance to management theory and practice. Good management principles should be:

(*i*) practical, which means they can be applied almost anytime in the organization's life and be appropriate;

(*II*) relevant to the broad forms of organizational structure;

(*iii*) consistent in the sense that for similar sets of circumstances, similar results will occur; and

(*iv*) flexible in that their application should take into account particular differences or changes in the conditions that affect the organization. For example, consider the statement: "For maximum managerial efficiency, total costs should be kept to a minimum".

Although this is usually a valid principle for most organizations, it might be reassessed or abandoned in cases of emergency such as defending our country against a nuclear attack. The use of management principles is intended to simplify, guide and facilitate management work.

Therefore, the management principles act as keys to what actions should be taken in what contexts and in what manner. They provide the benchmarks from which one can further one's understanding of the subject and they can be viewed as capsules of what is believed to be major considerations in current management thought.

Given below are the important principles of management that will help you in using them as the keys for your better understanding of the management (Kumar, 1982).

1. **Management is purposeful:** Management deals with the achievement of something specific, expressed as an objective or goal. Managerial success is commonly measured by the extent to which objectives are achieved. Management exists because it is an effective means of getting needed work accomplished. The fact that some executives have subordinates reporting to them does not *ipso facto* make them managers.
2. **Management makes things happen:** Managers, focus their attention and efforts on bringing about successful action. They know where to start, what to do to keep things moving, and how to follow through. Successful manager has an urge for accomplishment and the members of the group respect the manager and get along with people firmly expecting the best.
3. **Management is an activity, not a person or group of persons:** Management is not people; it is an activity like walking, reading, swimming, running or doing any specific activity. People involved in management can be designated as managers, members of management, or executive, leaders who actually manage a distinct activity/activities. It can be studied, and the knowledge about an activity is obtained, and skill in its application acquired.
4. **Management is accomplished by, with and through the efforts of others:** To participate in management necessitates relinquishing the normal tendency to perform all things oneself and get tasks accomplished by, with and through the efforts of group members. This is far more difficult than it sounds.

   Normally a person acquires ability in a specialized type of work and wins Concept and Theories of promotions through increasing knowledge and skill in that field of Management: Their Relevance to Extension specialization. However, the time comes when further promotion requires shifting from the role of a specialist to that of a management member. The prime measure of success becomes setting or securing agreement on the proper goals and getting all others to accomplish these goals. How successfully this deliberate shift is made determines the potential of the new manager. This characteristic merits recognition by the ambitious specialist when he turns to be a manager. Likewise, the employee with expertise in training when advanced to assistant personnel manager may continue to be a training expert, thus not succeeding in the new managerial post.

5. **Management is usual & associated with the efforts of a group:** It is common to associate management with a group. However, management is also applicable to an individuals' efforts as members of the group. For example, a person manages many personal affairs. However, the group emphasis stems from the fact that an enterprise comes into existence to attain goals, and these are achieved more readily by a group than by one person alone. People become members of an enterprise to satisfy their needs and because they feel their gains will outweigh their losses or burdens as members of a group.
6. **Management is intangible:** It has been called the unseen force, its presence evidenced by the results of its efforts - orderliness, enthusiastic employees, buoyant spirit, and adequate work output. Strange as it may seem, in some instances the identity of management is brought into focus by its absence or by the presence of its direct opposite, mismanagement. The result of mismanagement also becomes clear.
7. **Management is an idea, not replaced by the computer:** The computer is an extremely powerful tool of management. It can widen a manager's vision and sharpen insight by supplying more and faster information for making key decisions. The computer has enabled the manager to conduct analyses for beyond the normal human's analytical capacities. It has forced managers to reexamine their analytical processes and judgement in view of the almost unbelievable data processing and feedback facilities of the modern computer.

   However, a manager must supply judgement and imagination as well as interpret and evaluate what the data mean in each individual case. For example, it is doubtful that General George Washington would have crossed the Delaware River if he had relied on a computer to help him decide. The data of using leaky boats at night during a snowstorm to face a numerically superior enemy would have indicated a low probability of success. However, despite such rationale, Washington believed he could succeed, seized the initiative, assumed the large risk, and won his objective.
8. **Management is an outstanding means for exerting real impact on human life:** A manager can do much to improve the work-environment, to stimulate people to do things better, and to make favourable actions to take place. Personal frustrations and disappointments need not be accepted and may be viewed passively as inevitable. A manager can achieve progress, bring hope, and help group members acquire the better things in life.

## DEVELOPMENT OF MANAGEMENT THOUGHT

The earliest contribution to the management theories can be traced back to the periods of the Greeks, the Romans and the Egyptians. The use of the principle of specialisation and division of labour was evident in China as early as 1650 B.C. The Roman Catholic Church with its hierarchy of management has greatly contributed to the management thoughts. The development of management thought has been evolutionary in nature. The present status and position of management can, therefore, be best appreciated and understood in the light of its evolution over the years. Much of the development in this field has taken place during the last 100 years. The time periods in which different management concepts have evolved and developed can be divided into the following five segments:

1. Pre-Scientific Management Era (Before 1880)
2. Scientific Management (1880-1930)
3. Human Relations Era (1930-50)
4. Management Science Era (1950-1960)
5. Systems approach (1960-1970).
6. Contingency approach (1970 onwards).

The above time periods are only suggestive. They only signify the dominance of a management thought during a particular time period.

The main schools of management thoughts are:

1. **Management process school:** The Management Process School has developed during the scientific management era. Frederick Taylor and Henry Fayol were the founders of this school of thought. They perceived the management theory as a process of getting things done through and with people operating in organised groups. The process was considered to be universal regardless of the type of enterprise or the level in a given enterprise.

2. **Human behaviour school:** Human behaviour approach is the outcome of the Hawthorne Experiments in the early 1930 conducted by Elton Mayo and his associates. Abraham Maslow, Douglas McGregor, Keith Davis, Chester Barnard and Kurt Lewin are the other who made a significant contribution to the school. The advocates of human behaviour school viewed an organisation collectively as a social system of inter-personal and inter-group relationships.
3. **Empirical school:** The Empirical School started around 1952, *i.e.* in the social science era. Earnest Dale, the founder of this school identified management as a study of experience rather than the general principles as believed by the founders of the management process school. This approach was adopted by the Graduate School of Business Administration at the Harvard University for imparting management instruction and education to its students.
4. **Social science school:** Chester Barnard is considered to the father of the Social Science School. According to him, management is a social system, a system of co-operative relationships, and co-operation and team work among the organisational system is necessary for the achievement of organisational objectives. This approach seeks to identify the nature of cultural relationships of various social groups and attempts to integrate them into a social system.
5. **Decision theory school:** Decision theory approach revolves round the basic problem of management, *i.e.* decision-making, the selection of a suitable course of action out of the given alternatives. The major contribution to this approach was made by Herbert A. Simon. According to him, the manager is a decision-maker and the organisation is a decision-making unit. Therefore, the basic problem in managing is to make rational decisions.
6. **Quantitative school:** The Quantitative School of management thoughts is just an extension of the Decision Making Approach. This approach is also known as Operations Research School as it envisages the use of mathematical relationships, theories and models for making logical and rational decisions. The main contributors to this school of thoughts are Richard Cyert, Russel Ackoff, William Churchman and Forrester.
7. **Systems school:** Systems Approach to management views an organization as a single, unified and purposeful system which is composed of many inter-related sub-systems. It studies the organisational system as a whole and inter-relation between its various sub-systems and external environment. Kenneth Boulding, R.A. Johnson, F.E. Cast and Trist were the major contributors to the Systems Approach of Management.
8. **Contingency school:** Joan Woodward, P.R. Lawrence, Hickson and Fiedler are the major contributors to the Contingency Approach. According to them, there is no universal technique of management. The management action is contingent upon the situation. Thus, a manager's task is to identify which technique will, in a particular situation, under particular circumstances and at a particular time, best contribute to the attainment of the organisational goals.

## CONTRIBUTION OF F.W. TAYLOR

The concept of scientific management was introduced by Frederick Winslow Taylor in the USA in the beginning of 20th century. This concept was further carried on by Frank and Lillian Gilbreth, Henry Gantt, George Berth Edward Felen and others.

Scientific management was concerned essentially with improving the operational efficiency at the shop floor level.

"Scientific management is the art of knowing exactly what you want your men to do and then seeing that they do it in the best and cheapest way."—**F.W. Taylor**

Taylor joined Midvale Steel Company in the U.S.A as a worker and later on became a supervisor. During this period, he continued his studies and eventually completed his Master of Engineering (M.E.). Subsequently, he joined Bethlehem Steel Company. At both these places, he undertook several experiments in order to improve the efficiency of people at work. On the basis of his experiments, he published a book entitled as 'Scientific Management'.

Some of the major contributions of Taylor under scientific management are as follows:

1. **Time and motion study:** Time study is the art of observing and recording the time required to do each detailed element of an industrial operator. Motion study refers to the study and analysis of the movements of an operator in performing a job so that attempts can be made to remove useless movements from the process. Time and motion study together help in determining the best method of performing a job and the standard time allowed for it.
2. **Functional foremanship:** Taylor evolved the concept of functional foremanship based on the specialisation of functions. He identified eight types of foreman to direct the activities of workers. Of these, the following four foremen are concerned with planning:

   (*a*) Route clerk.

(*b*) Instruction card clerk.

(*c*) Time and cost clerk.

(*d*) Disciplinarian.

The remaining four foremen are concerned with the execution of work. These are:

(*a*) Speed boss.

(*b*) Inspector.

(*c*) Maintenance foreman.

(*d*) Gang boss.

3. **Differential payment:** Taylor introduced a new payment scheme called differential piece wage plan. Under this scheme, a worker received low price rate if he produced the standard number of pieces. On the other hand, the worker received high rate if he surpassed the standard. Workers were motivated to work hard and earn more.
4. **Reorganization of supervision:** Taylor introduced the concept of functional foremenship. Taylor suggested that the work should be planned by a foreman and not the workers. Under functional foremanship, he suggested employing four, six or eight foremen who would give orders to an individual worker depending on their specialization.
5. **Scientific selection and training:** The selection of workers by scientific methods would not alone serve the purpose, unless their placement on right jobs is earned. Appropriate training would prepare the workers to accept challenging job, and avail of promotion opportunities arising in the organisation. Taylor thought of entrusting the task of selection and training to a central personnel department.
6. **Cordial relations between management and workers:** In its essence, scientific management is a complete 'mental revolution' on the part of workers as well as management. According to Taylor, it involves an immense change in the attitude of both the sides. Both the parties must realize that their prosperity is dependent on each other and none should try to prosper at the cost of the other.

Taylor's concept of scientific management developed into a movement and dominated the industrial management science for several decades after him.

## CONTRIBUTION OF HENRY FAYOL

Henry Fayol was a French mining engineer who later turned a leading industrialist and a successful manager. His life-long experience, in the field of managing, was produced in the form of a monograph titled 'Administration Industrielleet-Generale' in 1916 in the French language. This monograph was reprinted in French several times but was never translated in English until 1929. Henry Fayol has been rightly called the 'father of administrative management' for his practical approach to management theory. He has identified fourteen fundamental principles of management. These fourteen principles are:

1. **Division of labour and specialisation:** Division of labour is a famous principle of economics, put forth by the classical economists like Adam Smith. Fayol applied this principle to management theory. Division of labour leads to specialisation, which in turn improves the efficiency of the employees.
2. **Authority and responsibility:** According to Fayol, authority and responsibility must flow in the same direction. Responsibility is the natural outcome of authority. A proper balance between authority and responsibility helps to prevent the misuse of authority and promotes a fair fixation of responsibility.
3. **Discipline:** Discipline means observation of certain rules and regulations. People in the organisation should be bound to accept certain code of conduct. The three basic requisites of discipline are disciplined supervisors at all the levels, clear and fair agreement on goals and judicious application of penalties.
4. **Unity of command:** According to this principle, an employee should receive orders only from one superior. If more than one superior exercise their authority over the same employee then the latter will always be in a state of confusion and a confused employee will never be able to perform to the best of his ability.
5. **Unity of direction:** Unity of direction is essential for achieving unity in action, in the pursuit of common goals by a group of persons. For this Fayol advocates 'one head and one plan'. Unity of direction (one head, one plan) is not same as unity of command (one employee receives orders from one superior).
6. **Subordination of individual interest to general interest:** According to this principle, the fulfilment of individual objectives in the long run is contingent upon the attainment of common objectives in the short run. Thus, in case the need arises, an individual must sacrifice, in favour of larger group objectives.
7. **Remuneration:** Remuneration is the price paid to people, managers and workers, for the services rendered by them. According to Fayol, the system of remunerating personnel should be fair and satisfactory to both the employees and employer. It should be attractive in order to employ and retain the best personnel.

8. **Centralisation:** Everything that goes to increase the importance of subordinates' role is decentralisation and everything which goes to reduce it, is centralisation. There should be a fair balance between the degree of centralisation and decentralisation in order to achieve the best results.
9. **Scalar chain:** Scalar chain refers to the line of authority from the highest to the lowest executive for the purpose of communication. However in the routine course of business, employees at the same level can communicate with each other following the principle of 'Gang Plank'.
10. **Order:** Fayol has classified order into two categories:
    (*a*) **Material order:** Material order is described as 'a place for everything and everything in its place'.
    (*b*) **Social order:** Social order demands the employment of a right person in the right place.
11. **Equity:** The principle of equity implies a sense of fairness and justice to all. Observance of equity alone makes personnel, loyal and devoted. Loyalty and devotion must be elicited from the personnel through a combination of kindness and justice while dealing with them.
12. **Stability of tenure:** An employee needs time to adjust with the new work, its environment and demonstrate efficiency. Therefore, stability of tenure is a desirable principle for ensuring efficiency. Unnecessary employees' turnover is the cause and effect of a bad management.
13. **Initiative:** Initiative is the freedom to propose and execute a plan. To have freedom in this respect is the greatest satisfaction for an intelligent person. A manager, who induces his subordinates to think and act on their own, is always better and more successful than the one who does not.
14. **Espirit-de-Corps:** Espirit-de-Corps is a French phrase which means "union is strength". It means the spirit of loyalty and devotion to the group, to which one belongs. It is the foundation of a sound organisation. This can be achieved by avoiding the dirty policy of 'divide and rule' and promoting effective communication.

These principles are flexible and require suitable adjustment and modification in the view of situational factors operating in the different enterprises.

## CONTRIBUTION OF ELTON MAYO

Human Relations Movements actually started with the series of experiments conducted by George Elton Mayo, professor of Industrial Research at the Harvard Graduate School of Business and his colleagues at the Hawthorne plant of Western Electric Company.

At the time of the experiments, there was an acute problem of employee dissatisfaction at the plant. It was also quite evident that the employees were not producing up to their fullest capability. This happened in spite of the fact that it was one of the most progressive companies with pension schemes, sickness benefit schemes, and numerous other facilities offered to its employees.

The company sought help from the group of university professors to tackle the issue when the earlier attempts of the experts produced in conclusive findings. The study continued for an extended period of time and had gone through various phases, which is briefly described here.

1. **Phase I: Illumination Experiments:** In order to test the traditional belief that better illumination will lead to higher level of productivity, two groups of employees were selected. In one, the contr l group, the illumination remained unchanged throughout the experiment while in the other the illumination was increased. As had been expected, the productivity went up in the latter or what was known as the experimental group. But what baffled the experimenters was the fact that the output of the control group also went up. The investigators then started to reduce the illumination for the test group. But in this case as well, the output went up again. Thus, the researchers had to conclude that illumination affected production only marginally and there must be some factor which produced this result.
2. **Phase II: Relay Assembly Test Room:** In this phase, apart from illumination, the possible effects of other factors such as length of the working day, rest pauses and their duration and frequency and other physical conditions were probed. It was found that the productivity and morale of the group increased consistently during the period of experiment. Surprisingly, here also the researchers found that the production of the group had no relation with the working conditions. The outcome of the group went increasing at an all-time high even when all the improvements in the working conditions were withdrawn. The researchers, thus, concluded that socio-psychological factors such as feeling of importance, recognition, attention and participation, small informal cohesive work group, non-directive supervision, etc. played a key role in increasing the productivity.
3. **Phase III: Interviewing Program:** From the Relay Assembly Test Room, the researchers for the first time became aware about the existence of informal groups and the importance of social context of the organizational life. To probe deeper into this area in

order to identify the factors responsible for human behaviour, they interviewed more than 20,000 employees. The direct questioning was later replaced by non-directive type of interviewing. The study revealed that the workers' social relationship inside the organizations has a significant influence on their attitude and behaviour. It was also found that merely giving a person an opportunity to talk and air his grievances has a beneficial effect on his morale.

4. **Phase IV: Bank Wiring Test Room:** It had been discovered that social groups in an organization have considerable influence on the functioning of the individual members. Observers noted that in certain departments, output had been deliberately restricted by the workers. Mayo decided to investigate one such department which was known as the bank wiring room where there were fourteen men working on an assembly line.

It was found that the group evolved its own production norms which were much lower than that set by the authority. This was done deliberately by the group to protect the slow workers and because of the apprehension that if the pace of production were increased, a sizeable number of the workforce would eventually be redundant. The group norm was so strictly adhered to by most of the group members that nobody dared to violate it for the fear of being ostracized by the group. An individual who had emerged as the informal leader controlled the group.

Thus, the Hawthorne study pointed out the following:

1. A business organization is a socio-technical entity, where the social interactions among its members is extremely important.
2. There is not necessarily a direct correspondence between working conditions and high production.
3. Economic motives are not the only motive for an employee. Social needs can also significantly affect their behaviour.
4. Employee-centered leaders always tend to be more effective than the task-oriented leaders.
5. The informal groups and not the individuals are the units of analysis in a group.

Later on people like Douglas McGregor, Abraham Maslow, Kurt Lewin, Chester Bernard, Rensis Likert, Chris Argyris, Warren Bennis etc. from more formal behaviour science background developed an approach which later came to be known as behavioural science approach.

However, the Human Relation movements and the Behaviourist Schools also had their share of criticisms. These are:

1. It is diagonally opposite to the classical schools. It focuses on the human side of the organization and certainly ignored other critical factors.
2. At times some hard decisions have to be taken in an organization and it is impractical to try to please every one all the time.
3. Though it is true that individuals do have other than economic motives, the importance of financial incentives cannot be ignored.
4. There is hardly any empirical support for the view 'happy workers are more productive', which seems to be the focal theme of this school.

## CONTRIBUTION OF MARY PARKER FOLLETT (1868–1933)

She was a social philosopher whose ideas had clear implications for management practice. Her contribution towards the understanding of group is of immense value. She believed that groups were the mechanisms through which people could combine their differing talents for the greater good of the organization, which she defined as the community in which managers and subordinates could work in harmony. The Mangers and workers should view themselves as partners and as a part of common group. She was convicted that the traditional and artificial distinction between the managers who give the orders and the workers who take the orders obscured their natural relationships. Manager should rely more on their expertise and knowledge to lead subordinates than on the formal authority of their position. Thus, her humanistic ideas influenced the way we look at motivation, leadership, power and authority. The Follett Behavioural Model of control being sponsored by an oriented towards the group, while self-control exercised by both individuals and the group ultimately result in both sharing the power. In the Follett Holistic Model of Control, Follett captured the interactive, integrative nature of self-control groups being influenced by the forces within the work environment.

## CONTRIBUTION OF CHESTER BARNARD (1886–1961)

**Chester Barnard,** President of Bell Telephone Company, developed theories about the functions of the manager as determined by constant interaction with the environment. Barnard saw organizations as social systems that require human cooperation. He expressed his view in his book *The Function of the Executive.* He proposed ideas that bridged classical and human resource view points. Barnard believes that organizations were made up of people with interacting social relationships. The manager's major functions were to communicate and stimulate subordinates to high level of efforts.

He saw the effectiveness of an organization as being dependent on its ability to achieve cooperative efforts from a number of employees in a total, integrated system. Barnard also argued that success depended on maintaining good relations with the people and institutions with whom the organization regularly interacted. By recognizing the organization's dependence on investors, suppliers, customers, and other external stakeholders, Barnard introduced the idea that managers had to examine the external environment and then adjust the organization to maintain a state of equilibrium. Barnard also developed set of working principles by which organizational communication systems can maintain final authority for the management team. These principles are:

- Channels of communication should be definitely known.
- Objective authority requires a definite formal channel of communication to every members of an organization.
- The line of communication must be as direct or short as possible.
- The complete line of communication should usually be used.
- Competence of the persons serving at communication centers that is officers, supervisory heads, must be adequate.
- The line of communication should not be interrupted during the time the organization is to function.

## CLASSICAL APPROACH TO MANAGEMENT THEORY

Classical management thought can be divided into three separate schools - scientific management, administrative theory and bureaucratic management. Classical theorists formulated principles for setting up and managing organizations. These views are labelled "Classical" because they form the foundation for the field of management thought. The major contributors to the three classified schools of management thought viz. scientific management, administrative theory and bureaucratic management are Frederick W. Taylor, Henry Fayol and Max Weber respectively.

### Scientific Management

**Frederick Winslow Taylor (1856–1915)** is considered to be the father of scientific management. Taylor was supported in his efforts by Henry Gantt, Frank and Lillian Gilberth and Harrington Emerson. All these disciples of Taylor became famous in their own right. Together with Taylor they revolutionised management thinking. Scientific management is the name given to the principles and practices, that grew out of the work of Frederick Taylor and his followers and that are characterised by concern for efficiency and systematisation in management. Four basic parts of a series of ideas developed by Taylor are as follows:

(*i*) Each person's job should be broken down into elements and a scientific way to perform each element should be determined.

(*ii*) Workers should be scientifically and trained to do the work in the designed and trained manner.

(*iii*) There should be good cooperation between management and workers so that tasks are performed in the designed manner.

(*iv*) There should be a division of labour between managers and workers. Managers should take over the work of supervising and setting up instructions and designing the work, and the workers should be free to perform the work themselves.

Taylor did a lot of work on improving management of production operations. He demonstrated in the classic case of the pig iron experiment at the Bethlehem Steel Company, how both output per worker and the daily pay of worker could be increased by employing scientific method.

The two major managerial practices that emerged from Taylor's approach to management are: the piece-rate incentive system, and the time-and-motion study.

- **Piece-rate incentive system:** Taylor felt that the wage system was one of the major reasons for soldiering. To resolve this problem, he advocated the use of a piece-rate incentive system. The aim of this system was to reward the workers who produced the maximum output.
- **Time and Motion study:** Taylor tried to determine the best way to perform each and every job. To do so, he introduced a method called "time-and-motion" study in which jobs are broken down into various small tasks or motions and unnecessary motions are removed to find out the best way of doing a job.

Among the other significant contributors to scientific management was Henry L Gantt. Gantt was a contemporary and an associate of Taylor. He emphasised the psychology of the worker and the importance of morale in production. Gantt insisted that willingness to use correct methods and skills in performing a task was as important as knowing the methods and having the skills. Thus he saw the importance of the human element in productivity and propounded the concept of motivation as we understand today. Gantt devised a wage-payment system and developed a charting stem or control chart for scheduling production operation which became the basis for modern scheduling techniques like CPM and PERT.

After Taylor, Frank and Lillian Gilbreth made numerous contributions to the concepts of scientific management. Frank Gilbreth (1868–1924) is considered the "father of motion study". Lillian Gilbreth (1878–1972) was associated with the research, pertaining to motion studies. Motion study involves finding out the best sequence and minimum number of motions needed to complete a task. Frank and Lillian were mainly involved in exploring neb ways for eliminating unnecessary motions and reducing work fatigue.

### *Limitations of scientific management*

Scientific management has provided many valuable insights in the development of management thought. In spite of the numerous contributions it made, there are a few limitations of scientific management. They are as follows:

- The principles of scientific management revolve round the problems at the operational level and do not focus on the management of an organization from a manager's point of view. These principles focus on the solutions of problems from an engineering point of view.
- The proponents of scientific management were of the opinion that people were rational and were motivated primarily by the desire for material gain. Taylor and his followers overlooked the social needs of workers and overemphasized their economic and physical needs.
- Scientific management theorists also ignored the human desire for job satisfaction. Since workers are more likely to go on strike over factors like working conditions and job content rather than salary, principles of scientific management, which were based on the "rational worker" model, became increasingly ineffective.

## Administrative Theory

While the proponents of scientific management developed principles that could help workers perform their tasks more efficiently, the administrative management theory focused on principles that could be used by managers to coordinate the internal activities of organizations. The most prominent of the administrative theorists was Henri Fayol.

Henry Fayol (1849–1925), a prominent European management theorist, developed a general theory of management. Fayol believed that with scientific forecasting and proper methods of management, satisfactory results were inevitable. Fayol was unknown to American managers and scholars until his most important work, "General and Industrial Management," was translated into English in 1949. Many of the managerial concepts that we take for granted today were first articulated by Fayol.

Other prominent exponents include Chester I Barnard and Colnel Lyndall Urwick (a British management expert).

### *Fayol's Unified Concept*

As the managing director of a mining company, Fayol developed a unified concept of management and broad administrative principles applicable to general and higher managerial levels. He used the word 'administration' for what we call management. Fayol focused on managerial levels and the organisation as a whole. His perspective extended beyond the shop level and the physical production processes and was macro in nature. In his French book 'Industrial and General Management', he writes that all activities of business enterprises could be divided into six groups: technical, commercial, financial, accounting, security and administrative (or managerial). He focused on the managerial activity and propounded that fundamental functions of any manager consists of planning, organising, commanding, coordinating and controlling. He emphasised that the process of management is the same at any level of an organisation and is common to all types of organisations. He also presented the following 14 principles of management as general guidelines for management practice:

(*i*) **Division of Labour:** Specialisation in the nature of work leads to division of labour. This results in efficiency in the use of labour.

(*ii*) **Authority and Responsibility:** These are directly related. Responsibility flows from authority. This authority is derived from the official position in the organisation and the personal factors such as intelligence, work attitude, personal traits, experience and the moral worth of the person holding the position.

(*iii*) **Discipline:** It is the respect for following laid down norms for achieving obedience, application, involvement as well as an outward mark of respect. Without discipline no unit can function properly. Authority, discipline and personality are closely related.

(*iv*) **Unity of Command:** This means that employees should receive orders from one superior authority only, *i.e.*, accountability to one authority only. This authority is distributed among various levels in the hierarchy of positions in the organisation.

(*v*) **Unity of Direction:** Activities in an enterprise must be organised to achieve set goals. Each group of activities with the same objective must have one authority and one plan.

(*vi*) **Subordination of Individual to Organisational Interest:** If this is not so it results in the malfunctioning of the organisation and gives rise to conflicts.

(*vii*) **Remuneration:** Employees work for remuneration; therefore, remuneration must be fair. It is an important motivating factor.

(*viii*) **Centralization:** Depending on the situation, an organization should adopt a centralized or decentralized approach to make optimum use of its personnel.

(*ix*) **Scalar chain:** This refers to the chain of authority that extends from the top to the bottom of an organization. The scalar chain defines the communication path in an organization.

(*x*) **Order:** This refers to both material and social order in organizations. Material order indicates that everything is kept in the right place to facilitate the smooth coordination of work activities. Similarly, social order implies that the right person is placed in the right job (this is achieved by having a proper selection procedure in the organization).

(*xi*) **Equity:** All employees should be treated fairly. A manager should treat all employees in the same manner without prejudice.

(*xii*) **Stability of tenure of personnel:** A high labour turnover should be prevented and managers should motivate their employees to do a better job.

(*xiii*) **Initiative:** Employees should be encouraged to give suggestions and develop new and better work practices.

(*xiv*) ***Espirit de corps:*** This means "a sense of union." Management must inculcate a team spirit in its employees.

Apart from a list of basic management principles, for achieving good organisation and dealing with the numerous facets of managing an organisation, he laid tremendous emphasis on logic, rationality and consistency. Taylor worked from the bottom of the hierarchy upward, whereas Fayol worked from the apex downwards, with 4 management centered' philosophy.

**Chester Barnard,** who held a number of important public service posts including President of New Jersey Bell Telephone, has significantly influenced the theory and practice of management for nearly half a century, through his ideas expressed in his classic book 'the functions of the executive'. He believed that the most important function of a manager is to promote cooperative effort towards goals of the organisation. Cooperation depends on effective communication and a balance between rewards to, and contributions by, each employee.

**Colonel L Urwick** was a distinguished executive and management consultant in U.K. He wrote a book entitled 'the elements of administration' in which he tried to assemble the concepts and principles of Taylor, Fayol, Mooney, Railey and other early management theorists.

Inspired by Fayol, Harold Koontz and Cyril O'Donnell propounded a new school of thought known as the management process school. They believe that management is a dynamic process of performing the functions of planning, organising, staffing, directing and controlling. These 'functions' and the principles, on which they are based, are believed to have general and universal applicability. Managers perform the same functions irrespective of their levels and the difference, if any, will be in the degree of complexity. These functions are applicable to all organisations wherever group effort is involved and the management theory is not culture bound. In other words these functions are all pervasive. For the same reason the management process approach is also called the universal approach.

### *Limitations of Administrative Management*

Like the scientific management school, the administrative management school is also criticised on some grounds. Many of the principles of this school, including those of Fayol, are contradictory and have dilemmas. These principles are no better than proverbs, which give opposite messages. For example, the principle of unity of command contradicts the principle of specialization or division of labour and the principle of limited span of control, contradicts that the number of organizational levels should be kept at a minimum.

Further the principle of specialization is internally inconsistent; for purpose, process, and place are competing modes of specialization and to secure the advantages of anyone mode, the organizer must sacrifice the advantages of the other three modes. All modes cannot be followed simultaneously while pursuing specialization.

Secondly, these principles are based on a few case studies and they are not empirically tested. Thirdly, these principles are stated as unconditional statements and valid under all circumstances, which is not practicable. More and more conditional principles of management are needed. Fourthly, these principles result in the formation of mechanistic organization structures, which are insensitive to employees' social and psychological needs. Such structures inhibit the employees' self-actualization and accentuate their dependence on superiors.

## BEHAVIOURAL APPROACH TO MANAGEMENT THEORY

The behavioural school of management emphasized what the classical theorists ignored *i.e.* the human element. While classical theorists viewed the organization from a production point of view, the behavioural theorists viewed it from the individuals point of view—their attitudes, behaviours and group process in the work place.

The behavioural approach emerged primarily as an outcome of the Howthorne studies. Mary Parker Follett, Elton Mayo and his associates, Abraham Maslow, Douglas McGregor and Chris Argyris were the major contributors to this school. They emphasized the importance of the human element. These theories could easily be applied to the management or organisations.

**Abraham H. Maslow (1908-1970),** psychologist, theorized that people were motivated by a hierarchy of needs. Maslow (1943) focused on human needs. His theory rested on three assumptions. *First,* all of us have needs which are never completely fulfilled. *Second,* through our acts we try to fulfil our unsatisfied needs. *Third,* human needs occur in the following hierarchical manner:

(*i*) physiological needs;

(*ii*) safety or security needs;

(*iii*) belonging needs or self-fulfilment needs.

According to Maslow, once needs at a specific level have been satisfied, they no longer act as motivators of behaviours. Then the individual strives to fulfill needs at the next level. Managers who accepted Maslow's hierarchy of needs attempted to change their management practices so that employees' needs could be satisfied.

## Human-Relations School

Elton Mayo is considered as the father of the human relations movement, which later become organisational behaviour. The other two important co-researchers of this school are F.J. Roethlisberger and William J Dickson. They believed that organisations always involve inter-relationships among members and that it is the manager's role to see that relationships are as conflict-free as possible, in order to accomplish the organisation's objectives. They believed that the human aspect of business organisations had been largely ignored. They felt that satisfaction of psychological needs should be the primary concern of the management.

Mayo, Roethlisberger and Dickson conducted studies, at the Hawthorne, Illinois plant of Chicago Western Electric Company, which became famous as the Hawthorne experiments or studies later. They felt that, if the best work environment could be determined (just as the best way to perform the job could be determined by scientific management), then workers would be more efficient and become less tired. They also felt the importance of evaluating the attitudes and reactions of workers to their jobs and their environment. They attempted through several experiments to determine the relationship between working conditions and productivity. They set up test groups, for which changes were made in lighting, frequency of rest periods, and working hours and control groups for which no changes were made.

Mayo and others, in their initial lighting experiment, came to the conclusion that some factors other than light were responsible for increased productivity. From a follow up interview of employees, they realised that people were not leaving their feelings, attitudes, and emotions at home, and employees were not at work simply for economic benefit. But other dimensions also affected their performance. In a final experiment they discovered that the workers had developed their own idea of the level of output that was fair. This informal standard of behaviour, called a norm, was enforced by the work group to the point that output was restricted. Any worker who produced more than that number was pressurised by coworkers to comply with the norm.

Mayo and his colleagues arrived at two important conclusions: (*i*) existence of strong informal groups (*ii*) employees' behaviour at work is affected by pan economic factors. They revealed some inadequacies of the rational and structured approaches of classical theory and the fallacy of viewing all workers as rational and economic beings. Thus evolved a social person view of employees from the Hawthorne studies.

As against the rational economic view, the social person view is that:

(*i*) individuals are motivated by social needs;

(*ii*) people obtain their sense of identity through Interpersonal relationships;

(*iii*) because of industrial progress and routinisation, the work has become dissatisfying;

(*iv*) employees are more responsive to the social forces of peer groups than to incentives and controls of management;

(*v*) employees respond to provisions for their social needs and acceptance offered by management. The social person view of human relations school has necessitated managerial strategies for improving the human skills of the supervisors, replacing individual incentive plans by group incentive plans; focusing on employees' feelings and attitudes, and their effect on productivity rather than managerial functions. The concept of social manager has evolved, and the social manager assumes the role of helper and coach, and carries out human relations programs shunning a stem and aloof attitude.

This theory, virtually, looked beyond organisational factors (*i.e.,* environmental factors) and aimed at as conflict-free inter-relationships, as possible, among members of the organisation. Drawing heavily from social psychology and individual psychology, this theory expected the manager to be a leader and supervisor of a rather tolerant (democratic and participative) type and considered every employee to be a unique socio-psychological being. The lesson of Hawthorne experiments was that the psychological needs of individuals have a significant impact on group performance and that employees often mis-state their concerns.

As a corollary it was also learnt that when employees are given special attention, output is likely to increase regardless of the actual changes in the working conditions (Hawthorne Effect). In other words, the result supported the thesis that reasonable satisfaction of the needs and desires of employees will lead to greater output.

Human relations approaches laid greater emphasis on the work group and need for better communication between supervisors and workers. The Human relations movement is looked as a trend towards power equalisation.

It is an attempt for reduction in the power and status differential between supervisors and subordinates. It is looked upon as a continuing reaction against the emphasis of programmed work, rigid hierarchical control and a high degree of specialisation of Taylorism. However, they did not reject all the classical ideas. The neoclassical writers believed that treating employees like individuals (neo-classical) would make them act according to the principles (classical). They said "treat employees as if they are important and give the workers the feeling of participation."

### *Limitations of Human Relation School*

Human relations school has several limitations as well. It is considered to be a swing in the opposite direction of classical theory. In other words, they saw only human variables as critical and ignored other variables. Every organisation is made of a number of diverse social groups with incompatible values and interests. These groups might cooperate in some spheres and compete and clash in others. It is practically impossible to satisfy everybody and turn the organisation into a big happy family.

This approach over-emphasises the importance of symbolic rewards which may not be appreciated by recipient's 'significant others' and underplays the role of material rewards. Further, the assumption about formation of informal groups is unrealistic and not very common. Informal groups can only make the worker's day more pleasant and not his repetitive, monotonous and uncreative task. Workers do not come to the organisation to seek affection and affiliation. Techniques of human relations school try to play a trick on workers to create a false sense of happiness, and are not really concerned with their real well being.

There is a difference between allowing workers to participate in making decisions and letting workers think that they are participating. In this sense, this approach is also production-oriented and not employee-oriented. The unqualified application of these techniques in all situations is not possible.

For example, where secrecy of decision is required and when decisions have to be made quickly on emergent basis, this approach may not work. This approach makes an unrealistic demand on the supervisor and expects him to give up his desire for power. The assumptions, that the satisfied workers are more productive, and that improved working conditions and human relations lead to increased output may, not always be true. Above all, human behaviour is not the total field of concern of the manager.

Human relations movement accepted scientific management's central goal of efficiency, but focused on individuals and on small-group processes rather than large organisations. It stressed communication, leadership and interpersonal relations, particularly between employees and their bosses.

Like scientific management efforts, research in human relations, focused on the lower levels of organisation rather than on the middle and upper groups, and hence lacked comprehensive scope. Behaviour scientists became interested in companies as research sites, but they tended to use their findings to build their own disciplines, or to establish a science of human relations rather than a science of management.

Thus the human relations movement accepted many of the assumptions of the scientific management thinkers, and it did not achieve a major breakthrough in management theory.

## QUANTITATIVE APPROACHES TO MANAGEMENT THEORY

The management perspective emerged during the world war II. During the war, the army (in the U.S and U.K) brought together managers, government officials and scientists to help it deploy its resources more efficiently and effectively. These experts used some of the mathematical approaches to management devised earlier by Taylor and Gantt to solve the logistical problems encountered by the army during the war.

The quantitative approach to management includes the application of statistics, optimization models, information models and computer simulation. More specifically, this approach focuses on achieving organizational effectiveness through the application of mathematical and statistical concepts. The three main branches of the quantitative approach are:

(*i*) management science,

(*ii*) operations management, and

(*iii*) management information system.

(*i*) **Management science:** The management science approach stresses the use of mathematical models and statistical methods for decision-making. It visualizes management as a logical entity, the action of which can be expressed in terms of mathematical symbols, relationships and measurement data. Another name commonly used for management science is operations research. Recent advances in computers have made it possible to use complex mathematical and statistical models in the management of organizations. Management science techniques are widely used in the following areas.

**Capital budgeting and cash flow management:** It includes the following.

- Production scheduling.
- Developing product strategies.
- Planning for human resources development programs.
- Maintenance of optimal inventory levels.
- Aircraft scheduling.

Various mathematical tools like the waiting-line theory or queering theory, linear programming, the Program Evaluation Review Technique (PERT), the critical path method (CPM), the decision theory, the stimulation theory, the probability theory, sampling, time series analysis, etc., have increased the effectiveness of managerial decision-making. To apply a quantitative approach to decision-making, individuals with mathematical, statistical, engineering, economics and business background and skills are required. Since one person cannot have all these skills the quantitative method requires a team approach to decision-making.

This approach has been criticized for its overemphasis on mathematical tools. Many managerial activities cannot be quantified because they involve human beings who are governed by many irrational elements as well.

(*ii*) **Operations Management:** Operations management is an applied form of management science. It deals with the effective management of the production process and the timely delivery of an organization's products and services. Operations management is concerned with:

(*i*) inventory management,
(*ii*) work scheduling,
(*iii*) production planning,
(*iv*) facilities location and design, and
(*v*) quality assurance.

The tools used by operations managers are forecasting, inventory analysis, materials requirement, planning systems, networking models, statistical quality control methods, and project planning and control techniques.

(*iii*) **Management information systems (MIS):** Management information system focuses on designing and implementing computer-based information systems for business organizations. In simpler term, the MIS converts raw data into information and provides the needful information to each manager at the right time in the needed form.

## MODERN APPROACHES TO MANAGEMENT THEORY

Besides the classical and behavioural approaches to management, there are certain modern approaches to management, viz. the systems theory and the contingency theory. These two approaches have significantly shaped modern management thought and are discussed below.

### System Approach

The Systems Approach to management was developed during 1950. Management thinkers such as Kenneth Boulding, Bertalanffy, R.A. Johnson and Chester Barnard made a significant contribution to the development of the Systems Approach to management.

The term 'system' may be defined as a composite entity consisting of a number of elements which as inter-dependent and inter-acting. These elements are referred to as the sub-systems. Each system is distinguished from the other systems by a boundary, which defines its outer limits. The boundary of a system is determined by the intensity of interactions and inter-dependencies of its elements. The world outside the boundary of the system is known as its environment.

Considering the relationship between a system and its environment, the systems may be classified into two categories:

1. **Closed system:** A closed system interacts least with its environment. It is self-contained and does not depend much on the other systems. It does not receive any input from the other systems. It is a non-adaptive system.
2. **Open system:** An open system actively interacts with the other systems and establishes exchange relationships. Such systems are often forced to adapt themselves with the external environment in order to survive and grow.

Under the systems approach, the management can be best described in the following way:

1. **Management is a social system:** Management is an art of getting things done through others. It is practised by the people (managers), through the people (operating staff) and for the people (consumers and the society at large). Thus, the importance of human factor in management cannot be ignored. Hence, management is a social system.
2. **Management is an open system:** Management, like any other social system, is an open system. Being an open system, it interacts with its environment. Out of this interaction, it avails various resources and allocates and combines them to produce desirable output, which is supplied to the environment.

3. **Management is an adaptive system:** Management seeks to maintain a continuous equilibrium of an enterprise with the external environment - economic, social, political, cultural and technological, in order to ensure not only the survival and growth of the enterprise but also to make it fulfil the aspirations of the society, in the best possible manner.
4. **Management is a dynamic system:** Nothing ever is permanent except change. The environment, in which management functions, is dynamic in nature. Thus, management needs to continuously adjust to the changing environment. Thus, the success of a management can be best evaluated in terms of its adaptability to the environment.
5. **Management system is probabilistic:** Management system is probabilistic and not deterministic. This is because the application of theories and principles as laid down by the management theorists will not always yield the same results. These principles do not have universal applicability, since human behaviour is dynamic and differ from person to person.
6. **Management system is multi-dimensional:** According to the systems theory, management has both, micro and macro approach. At the macro level, it can be applied to suprasystem, *i.e.,* a business system as a whole and at the micro level; it can be applied to an organisation. It can also be applied to the sub-systems of an organisation.
7. **Management is an integrated system:** Systems approach to management takes an integrated view of the function of managing. There is no simple cause effect relationship in management, rather each managerial phenomena is the result of a number of inter-related and inter-dependent factors. The management integrates these factors in order to view these phenomena in totality.

Systems approach to management provides an integrated of managing. It considers the management in its totality in relation to its environment. Thus, it permits both - analysis and synthesis, differentiation and integration - right from primary sub-system level to the macro system level. However, the systems philosophy has been criticised as being too abstract, vague and over-conceptual.

## Contingency Approach

The contingency approach, also called situational approach, was developed by managers, consultants and researchers who tried to apply the concepts of the major schools of thought to the real-life situations. When methods, highly effective, in one situation failed to work in other situations, they sought an explanation. Why did an organizational development program work brilliantly in one situation and fail miserably in another? The advocates of the contingency approach had a logical answer - results differ because situations differ; a technique that works in one case will not necessarily work in all the cases.

"When a sub-system in an organisation behaves in response to another system or sub-system, we say that response is contingent on the environment. Hence, a contingency approach is an approach where the behaviour of one sub-unit is dependent on its environmental relationship to other units or sub-units that have control over the consequences desired by that sub-unit."—Tosi and Hammer

As per the above statement, contingency approach has the following features:

1. Management action is contingent on certain action outside the system or sub-system of an organisation, as the case may be.
2. Organisational action should be based on the behaviour of action outside the system so as to integrate the organisation with its external environment.
3. Since the organisation-environment relationship is not static, no action can be universal. It varies from situation to situation.

In conclusion it can be said that the managerial action largely depends upon the total strength and weakness of the organisation and opportunities and threats which lie out in the environment of each organisation.

According to the contingency approach, a manager's task is to identify which technique will, in a particular situation, under particular circumstances and at a particular time, best contribute to the attainment of management goals. Managers have to find a "best fit' between the demands of:

1. The tasks; 2. The people; and 3. The environment.

For example, where workers need to be encouraged to increase productivity, a classical theorist may prescribe a work simplification scheme while a behavioural scientist may seek to create a psychologically motivating climate and recommend some approach like job enrichment. But the manager trained in the contingency approach will ask, "Which method will work best here?"

1. If the workers are unskilled and training facilities and resources are limited, then work simplification will be the best option.
2. On the other hand, with skilled workers driven by pride in their abilities, a job-enrichment program might be more effective.

On the whole, contingency approach represents an important turn in modern management theory, because it portrays each set of organizational relationships in its unique circumstances.

# FUNCTION OF MANAGEMENT

## PLANNING

### Introduction and Meaning

When management is reviewed as a process, planning is the first function performed by a manager. The work of a manager begins with the setting of objectives of the organization and goals in each area of the business.

Planning is a tool in the hands of a manager who wants to face problems created by change. Successful managers deal with foreseen problems and unsuccessful managers struggle with unforeseen problems. The difference lies in planning. Every enterprise which strives to survive and grow must place heavy emphasis upon planning.

A planner foresees opportunities and devises ways and means to take advantage from them. There may be cases where little bit of planning helps in achieving objectives. This may happen in favourable situations. In a competitive business world a manager cannot wait for favourable circumstances, he has to decide in the face of uncertainties. There is no place for guesswork or chance. The need is for proper planning.

Planning means looking ahead. It is deciding in advance what is to be done. Planning helps in determining the course of action to be followed for achieving various organisational objectives. It is a decision in advance; what to do, when to do, how to do and who will do a particular task. Planning is a process which involves 'thinking before doing'. It is concerned with a mental state of the manager. He thinks before undertaking a work. Other functions of management like organising, controlling and directing are also undertaken after proper planning.

In the past four decades every type of enterprise has shown a tremendous interest in planning. In the present economic, technological, political and social set up planning is essential for the survival of an enterprise. The change and growth bring new opportunities but they also bring more risks. The task of planning is to minimise risk while taking advantage of opportunities.

### Definitions

The words 'planning' and 'a plan' may also be taken as similar but their meanings are different. A plan is a commitment to particular course of actions whereas planning is an activity consisting of a process.

To clear the meaning of planning further, some definitions have been discussed:

**George Terry,** "Planning is the selecting and relating of facts and the making and using of assumptions regarding the future in the visualization and formulation of proposed activities believed necessary to achieve desired results.'' According to Terry planning is based on certain assumptions which are required to formulate policies of the business. The purpose of planning is to achieve business objectives.

**Hart,** "The determination in advance of a line of action by which certain results are to be achieved." Planning is the deciding of a course required for reaching organisational goals. The line of action is decided in advance so that actual execution becomes easy later on.

**Koontz and O'Donnell,** "The selection from among alternatives for future courses of action for the enterprise as a whole and each department with it." Although the exact future can seldom be predicted and factors beyond control may interfere with the best-laid plans, unless there is planning, events are left to chance. It is an intellectually demanding process and requires the selection of a course of action.

**Alfred and Beaty,** "Planning is the thinking process, the organised forecast, the vision based on fact and experience that is required for intelligent action." Planning is a process in which decisions are taken in advance. The pros and cons of the decisions and their implications in the future are discussed beforehand. A wrong decision may create difficulties for the management and may result in financial loss too.

**Louis A. Allen,** "Management planning involves the development of forecasts, objectives, policies, programmes, procedures, schedules and budgets." According to Allen, planning is essentially deciding about future. The ways and means required to achieve organisational goals form the essential part of planning.

**George B. Galloway,** "Planning is the opposite of improvising. In simple words, it is organised foresight plus corrective hindsight,... Conceived as a process, planning embraces a series of steps:

(*i*) the determination of objectives to be sought;

(*ii*) research to understand the problem;

(*iii*) the discovery of alternative solutions;

(*iv*) policymaking, choosing between alternatives, including the frequent choice of doing nothing;

(*v*) the detailed execution of the chosen alternative known in physical planning as layout or design."

As per this view, planning starts with setting up of objectives and leads to the execution of various policies. A good planner chooses the best method of doing a thing for achieving the desired results.

## Nature of Planning

1. **Planning is goal-oriented:** Every plan must contribute in some positive way towards the accomplishment of group objectives. Planning has no meaning without being related to goals.
2. **Primacy of Planning:** Planning is the first of the managerial functions. It precedes all other management functions.
3. **Pervasiveness of Planning:** Planning is found at all levels of management. Top management looks after strategic planning. Middle management is in charge of administrative planning. Lower management has to concentrate on operational planning.
4. **Efficiency, Economy and Accuracy:** Efficiency of plan is measured by its contribution to the objectives as economically as possible. Planning also focuses on accurate forecasts.
5. **Co-ordination:** Planning co-ordinates the what, who, how, where and why of planning. Without co-ordination of all activities, we cannot have united efforts.
6. **Limiting Factors:** A planner must recognise the limiting factors (money, manpower etc.) and formulate plans in the light of these critical factors.
7. **Flexibility:** The process of planning should be adaptable to changing environmental-conditions.
8. **Planning is an intellectual process:** The quality of planning will vary according to the quality of the mind of the manager.

## Importance of Planning

As a managerial function planning is important due to the following reasons:

1. **To manage by objectives:** All the activities of an organisation are designed to achieve certain specified objectives. However, planning makes the objectives more concrete by focusing attention on them.
2. **To offset uncertainty and change:** Future is always full of uncertainties and changes. Planning foresees the future and makes the necessary provisions for it.
3. **To secure economy in operation:** Planning involves, the selection of most profitable course of action that would lead to the best result at the minimum costs.
4. **To help in co-ordination:** Co-ordination is, indeed, the essence of management, and planning is the base of it. Without planning it is not possible to co-ordinate the different activities of an organisation.
5. **To make control effective:** The controlling function of management relates to the comparison of the planned performance with the actual performance. In the absence of plans, a management will have no standards for controlling other's performance.
6. **To increase organisational effectiveness:** Mere efficiency in the organisation is not important; it should also lead to productivity and effectiveness. Planning enables the manager to measure the organisational effectiveness in the context of the stated objectives and take Notes further actions in this direction.

## Advantages of Planning

- All efforts are directed towards desired objectives or results. Unproductive work and waste of resources can be minimised.
- Planning enables a company to remain competitive with other rivals in the industry.
- Through careful planning, crisis can be anticipated and mistakes or delays avoided.
- Planning can point out the need for future change and the enterprise can manage the change effectively.
- Planning enables the systematic and thorough investigation of alternative methods or alternative solutions to a problem. Thus we can select the best alternative to solve any business problem.
- Planning maximises the utilisation of available resources and ensures optimum productivity and profits.
- Planning provides the ground work for laying down control standards.
- Planning enables management to relate the whole enterprise to its complex environment profitably.

## Disadvantages of Planning

- Environmental factors are uncontrollable and unpredictable to a large extent. Therefore planning cannot give perfect insurance against uncertainty.
- Planning is many times very costly.
- Tendency towards inflexibility to change is another limitation of planning.
- Planning delays action.
- Planning encourages a false sense of security against risk or uncertainty.

## Planning Process

The planning process involves the following steps:

1. **Analysis of External Environment:** The external environment covers uncontrollable and unpredictable factors such as technology, market, socio-economic

climate, political conditions etc., within which our plans will have to operate.

2. **Analysis of Internal Environment:** The internal environment covers relatively controllable factors such as personnel resources, finance, facilities etc., at the disposal of the firm. Such an analysis will give an exact idea about the strengths and weakness of the enterprise.
3. **Determination of Mission:** The "mission" should describe the fundamental reason for the existence of an organisation. It will give firm direction and make out activities meaningful and interesting.
4. **Determination of Objectives:** The organisational objectives must be spelled out in key areas of operations and should be divided according to various departments and sections. The objectives must be clearly specified and measurable as far as possible. Every member of the organisation should be familiar with its objectives.
5. **Forecasting:** Forecasting is a systematic attempt to probe into the future by inference from known facts relating to the past and the present. Intelligent forecasting is essential for planning. The management should have no stone unturned in reducing the element of guesswork in preparing forecasts by collecting relevant data using the scientific techniques of analysis and inference.
6. **Determining Alternative course of Action:** It is a common experience of all thinkers that an action can be performed in several ways, but there is a particular way which is the most suitable for the organisation. The management should try to find out these alternatives and examine them carefully in the light of planning premises.
7. **Evaluating Alternative Courses:** Having sought out alternative courses and examined their strong and weak points, the next step is to evaluate them by weighing the various factors.
8. **Selecting the Best:** The next step - selecting the course of action is the point at which the plan is adopted. It is the real point of decision-making.
9. **Establishing the sequence of activities:** After the best programme is decided upon, the next task is to work out its details and formulate the steps in full sequences.
10. **Formulation of Action Programmes:** There are three important constituents of an action plan:
    - The time-limit of performance.
    - The allocation of tasks to individual employees.
    - The time-table or schedule of work so that the functional objectives are achieved within the predetermined period.
11. **Reviewing the planning process:** Through feedback mechanism, an attempt is made to secure that which was originally planned. To do this we have to compare the actual performance with the plan and then we have to take necessary corrective action to ensure that actual performance is as per the plan.

## Principles of Planning

A number of fundamental principles have been devised over the years for guiding managers undertaking planning. Some of these principles are discussed as under:

1. **Principle of Contribution to Objectives:** All types of plans are prepared to achieve the objectives of the organization. Both major and derivative plans are prepared to contribute to the objectives of the enterprise. Planning is used as a means to reach the goals.
2. **Principles of Primacy of Planning:** This principle states that planning is the first or primary function of every manager. He has to plan first and then proceed to carry out other functions. Other managerial functions are organised to reach the objectives set in planning.
3. **Principle of Planning Premises:** In order to make planning effective, some premises or presumptions have to be made on the basis of which planning has to be undertaken. Plans are, generally not properly structured the reason being that planning premises are not properly developed. This principle lays emphasis on properly analysing the situation which is going to occur in future.
4. **Principle of Alternatives:** Planning process involves developing of many alternatives and then selecting one which will help in achieving desired business goals. In the absence of various alternative, proper planning will be difficult.
5. **Principle of Timing:** Plans can contribute effectively to the attainment of business goals if they are properly timed. Planning premises and policies are useless without proper timing.
6. **Principle of Flexibility:** This principle suggests flexibility in plans if some contingencies arise. The plans should be adjusted to incorporate new situations. The dangers of flexibility should be kept in mind. The changes may upset the earlier commitments. So the cost of changes should be compared to the benefits of flexibility.
7. **Principle of Commitment:** There should be a time frame for meeting the commitments made. This will ensure the achievement of targets in time.

8. **Principle of Competitive Strategies:** While formulating own plans a manager should keep in mind the plans of competitors. The plans should be framed by thinking of what the competitors will do in similar situations.

## Types of Planning

There are three types of planning. These are identified on the following dimensions:

1. On the basis of coverage of activities
   (*i*) Corporate planning
   (*ii*) Functional planning
2. On the basis of Importance of Contents.
   (*i*) Strategic Planning.
   (*ii*) Operational Planning
3. On the basis of time period involved.
   (*i*) Long term planning.
   (*ii*) Short-term Planning

### *1. Corporate Planning and Functional Planning*

We have seen earlier that planning activity is pervasive and can be undertaken at various levels of an organization. It may be for the organization as a whole or for its different functions. Thus, based on the coverage of activities, there may be planning for the organization as a whole, known as corporate planning or for its different functions, known as functional planning.

(*a*) **Corporate Planning:** Corporate planning is undertaken at the top level, also known as corporate level, and covers the entire organizational activities. It is of integrative nature and integrates entire planning process of the organization. The basic focus of corporate planning is to determine the long-term objectives of the organization as a whole and to generate plans to achieve these objectives bearing in mind the probable changes in the environment. Corporate planning, generally, has long-term orientation and provides basis for functional planning.

(*b*) **Functional Planning:** Functional planning is of segmental nature and is undertaken for each major function of the organization like production/ operations, marketing, finance, human resource, etc. At the second level, functional planning is undertaken for subfunctions within each major function. For example, marketing planning is undertaken at the level of marketing department and to put marketing plan in action, planning at subfunctions of marketing like sales, product promotion, marketing research, etc. is undertaken.

A basic feature of functional planning is that it is derived out of corporate planning and, therefore, it should contribute to the latter. This contribution is achieved by integrating and coordinating functional planning with corporate planning.

### *2. Strategic Planning and Operational Planning*

On the basis of importance of contents, planning may be divided into strategic planning and operational planning.

(*a*) **Strategic Planning:** Strategic planning involves setting long-term direction of the organization in which it wants to proceed in future. It is the process of deciding long-term objectives of the organization and defining where the organizational resources and efforts should be put to achieve organizational objectives. Strategic planning deals with strategic issues like type of business to be undertaken, diversification of business into new lines, type of products to be offered, and so on.

This way, strategic planning encompasses all the functional areas of business and is effected within the existing and long-term framework of environmental factors. Strategic planning also involves rigorous analysis of various environmental factors to relate the organization relates to its environment.

(*b*) **Operational Planning:** Operational planning, also known as tactical planning, is the process of deciding the most effective use of the resources already allocated through strategic planning and to develop a control mechanism to ensure effective implementation of the actions so that organizational objectives are achieved. Usually operational planning covers one year or so. It aims at sustaining the organization in its production/generation and distribution of current products (goods and services) to the existing markets. Operational planning answers the questions about a particular action as follows:

(*i*) Why is the action required?
(*ii*) What action is to be taken?
(*iii*) What will the action accomplish?
(*iv*) What are the likely results of the action?
(*v*) What conditions must be met in putting the action in operation?

Operational planning is undertaken within the framework of the strategic planning. Examples of operational planning are adjustment of production within given capacity, increasing the efficiency of operating activities through analysis of past performance, budgeting future costs, specific details of future short-term operations, and so on.

### Difference between Strategic Planning and Operational Planning

Apart from the period of time involved in strategic planning and operational planning, there are certain differences between the two. The major differences between the two are as follows:

(*a*) **Range of Choice:** Strategic planning guides the choice among the broad directions in which the organization seeks to move and allocation of its financial, physical, and human resources over future specified period of time. Operational planning, on the other hand, focuses on the ways and means in which each of the individual functions may be programmed so that progress may be made towards the attainment of organizational objectives.

(*b*) **Type of Environment:** The type of environment for two types of planning is different. Strategic planning takes into account the external environment and tries to relate the organization with it. The nature of external environment, thus, is of prime concern of strategic planners. Operational planning mostly focuses on internal organizational environment so as to make the effective use of given resources.

(*c*) **Focus:** Strategic planning focuses on setting long-term trend and direction for managerial actions. Focus of operational planning is on making effective use of organizational resources allocated by strategic planning process.

(*d*) **Sequence of Formulation:** Strategic planning precedes operational planning and the latter is primarily concerned with the implementation of the former. Therefore, operational planning is based on strategic planning.

(*e*) **Level of Formulation:** Strategic planning is formulated by top-level management with the support of specified planning staff in the organization. At this level, managers can take an overall view of the organization and have necessary capability to relate the organization with its environment.

Operational planning is usually spread over a wide range within the organization and is generally performed by operating managers with the help of the subordinate staff.

### 3. Long-term Planning and Short-term Planning

Planning is concerned with future course of action. This may be of long term or short term. Thus, there are long-term planning and short-term planning

(*a*) **Long-term Planning:** Long-term planning is of strategic nature and involves more than one year period, usually 3-5 years though period of 5 years is more common in Indian context. Long-term planning usually covers all the functional areas of the business and is undertaken within the existing and long-term future environmental scenario. In the long-term planning process, high emphasis is placed on analysis of environmental factors. Sometimes, basic changes in the organization like change in organizational vision and mission, major change in organization structure, change in key personnel of the organization, etc. become the significant factor for long-term planning.

(*b*) **Short-term Planning:** Short-term planning usually covers one year. This aims at making effective use of organizational resources—financial, physical, and human resources. Short-term planning directly and immediately affects functional areas—production, marketing, finance, etc.

### Business Forecasting

In order to formulate accurate plans, managers have to find out the likely behaviour of relevant factors in future. This is done to some extent by making suitable forecast through business forecasting (simply known as forecasting) which is defined as follows:

Forecasting is the process of estimating the relevant events of future, based on the analysis of their past and present behaviour. On the basis of the definition, the following features of forecasting can be identified:

1. Forecasting is related to future events.
2. Forecasting defines the probability of happening of future events. Therefore, happening of future events can be precise only to a certain extent.
3. Forecasting is made by analyzing the past and present relevant events, that is, taking those factors which are relevant for the functioning of an organization.
4. The analysis of various factors may require the use of various statistical tools and techniques. However, personal observations can also help in the process.

## DECISION MAKING

### Meaning and Definition

The word decision has been derived from the Latin work "decider" which means "cutting off". Thus, decision involves cutting off of alternatives between those that are desirable and those that are not desirable. A decision is the selection from among alternatives. It is a solution selected after examining several alternatives and decisive because the decider foresees that the course of action he selects will be more than the others to further his goals and will be accompanied by the fewest possible objectionable consequences. Decision is a kind of choice of a desirable alternative.

A few definitions of decision making are given below:

In the words of **Ray A Killian,** "A decision in its simplest form is a selection of alternatives".

**Dr. T.G. Glover** defines decision "as a choice of calculated alternatives based on judgement".

In the words of **George R. Terry,** "Decision making is the selection based on some criteria from two or more possible alternatives".

**Felix M. Lopez** says that "A decision represents a judgement; a final resolution of a conflict of needs, means or goals; and a commitment to action made in face of uncertainty, complexity and even irrationally".

According to **Rustom S. Davar,** "Decision-making may be defined as the selection based on some criteria of one behaviour alternative from two or more possible alternatives to decide means to cut off or in practical content to come to a conclusion".

**Fremont A. Shull, Andrew L Delbecq** and **Larry L Cummings** define decision making as "a conscious human process involving both individual and social phenomenon based upon factual and value premises which concludes with a choice of one behavioural activity from among one or more alternatives with the intention of moving toward some desired state of affairs".

From the above definitions, we can conclude that, Decision Making involves the process of establishing goals, tasks and searching for alternatives for a decision problem.

## Types of Decisions

**Programmed and Non-programmed Decisions:** Herbert Simon has grouped organizational decisions into two categories based on the procedure followed. They are:

**Programmed decisions:** Programmed decisions are routine and repetitive and are made within the framework of organizational policies and rules. These policies and rules are established well in advance to solve recurring problems in the organization. Programmed decisions have short-run impact. They are, generally, taken at the lower level of management.

**Non-programmed Decisions:** Non-programmed decisions are decisions taken to meet non-repetitive problems. Non-programmed decisions are relevant for solving unique/ unusual problems in which various alternatives cannot be decided in advance. A common feature of non-programmed decisions is that they are novel and non-recurring and therefore, readymade solutions are not available. Since these decisions are of high importance and have long-term consequences, they are made by top level management.

**Strategic and Tactical Decisions:** Organizational decisions may also be classified as strategic or tactical.

**Strategic Decisions:** Basic decisions or strategic decisions are decisions which are of crucial importance. Strategic decisions a major choice of actions concerning allocation of resources and contribution to the achievement of organizational objectives. Decisions like plant location, product diversification, entering into new markets, selection of channels of distribution, capital expenditure etc. are examples of basic or strategic decisions.

**Tactical Decisions:** Routine decisions or tactical decisions are decisions which are routine Notes and repetitive. They are derived out of strategic decisions. The various features of a tactical decision are as follows:

- Tactical decision relates to day-to-day operation of the organization and has to be taken very frequently.
- Tactical decision is mostly a programmed one therefore, the decision can be made within the context of these variables.
- The outcome of tactical decision is of short-term nature and affects a narrow part of the organization.
- The authority for making tactical decisions can be delegated to lower level managers because: first, the impact of tactical decision is narrow and of short-term nature and Second, by delegating authority for such decisions to lower-level managers, higher level managers are free to devote more time on strategic decisions.

## Decision Making Process

The decision making process is presented in the figure below:

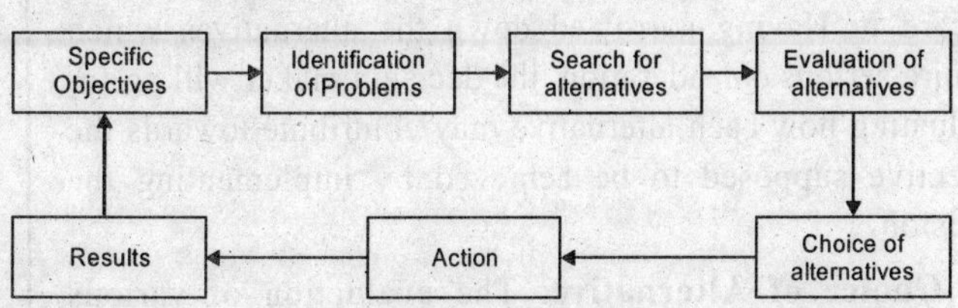


**Fig.** *Decision Making Process*

**Specific Objective:** The need for decision making arises in order to achieve certain specific objectives. The starting point in any analysis of decision making involves the determination of whether a decision needs to be made.

**Problem Identification:** A problem is a felt need, a question which needs a solution. In the words of **Joseph L Massie** "A good decision is dependent upon the recognition of the right problem". The objective of problem identification is that if the problem is precisely and specifically identified, it will provide a clue in finding a possible solution.

A problem can be identified clearly, if managers go through diagnosis and analysis of the problem.

1. **Diagnosis:** Diagnosis is the process of identifying a problem from its signs and symptoms. A symptom is a condition or set of conditions that indicates the existence of a problem. Diagnosing the real problem implies knowing the gap between what is and what ought to be, identifying the reasons for the gap and understanding the problem in relation to higher objectives of the organization.
2. **Analysis:** Diagnosis gives rise to analysis. Analysis of a problem requires:
   (*a*) Who would make decision?
   (*b*) What information would be needed?
   (*c*) From where the information is available?

Analysis helps managers to gain an insight into the problem.

**Search for Alternatives:** A problem can be solved in several ways; however, all the ways cannot be equally satisfying. Therefore, the decision maker must try to find out the various alternatives available in order to get the most satisfactory result of a decision. A decision maker can use several sources for identifying alternatives:

(*a*) His own past experiences
(*b*) Practices followed by others and
(*c*) Using creative techniques

**Evaluation of Alternatives:** After the various alternatives are identified, the next step is to evaluate them and select the one that will meet the choice criteria, the decision maker must check proposed alternatives against limits, and if an alternative does not meet them, he can discard it. Having narrowed down the alternatives which require serious consideration, the decision maker will go for evaluating how each alternative may contribute towards the objective supposed to be achieved by implementing the decision.

**Choice of Alternative:** The evaluation of various alternatives presents a clear picture as to how each one of them contribute to the objectives under question. A comparison is made among the likely outcomes of various alternatives and the best one is chosen.

**Action:** Once the alternative is selected, it is put into action. The actual process of decision making ends with the choice of an alternative through which the objectives can be achieved.

**Results:** When the decision is put into action, it brings certain results. These results must correspond with objectives, the starting point of decision process, if good decision has been made and implemented properly. Thus, results provide indication whether decision making and its implementation is proper.

## Characteristics of Effective Decisions

An effective decision is one which should contain three aspects. These aspects are given below:

1. **Action Orientation:** Decisions are action-oriented and are directed towards relevant and controllable aspects of the environment. Decisions should ultimately find their utility in implementation.
2. **Goal Direction:** Decision making should be goal-directed to enable the organization to meet its objectives.
3. **Effective in Implementation:** Decision making should take into account all the possible factors not only in terms of external context but also in internal context so that a decision can be implemented properly.

## Rationality in Decision Making

A rational decision is one that is based on logical reasons and facts. Thus, it involves appropriate means for achieving appropriate ends. In establishing means-ends relationship, two concepts may be applied: maximization and optimization. These concepts are contrasting. As a result, two models of decision making have emerged which put different emphasis on rationality in decision making. These are economic man model and administrative man model.

### *1. Economic Man Model*

The classical approach to decision making in economics uses economic man model and treats the decision maker as an economic man who is completely rational.

Decision making based on economic man model has the following features:

(*a*) The decision making is completely rational in the means-ends sense. Economic man always identifies clearly the ends to which he wants to reach and the means which are available for the purpose.
(*b*) Economic man is rational in that he can order his various preferences according to his Notes hierarchy of values and make his choice so as to maximize some desired value. In organizational context, this desired value would be equivalent to achievement of organizational objectives to the maximum extent.

(*c*) There is complete awareness of various alternatives and their outcomes. It assumes that there is no limit on the collection of information and its processing.

The economic man model is a normative model rather than a descriptive model because it is concerned with what a decision maker should do rather than what he actually does in reaching his decision. In business context, the concept of economic man model cannot be applied because of two reasons. First, the complete rationality is not possible because the decision-making condition is assumed to be certain which is seldom available. The complete certain condition does not really exist for making decisions having long-term impact. Second, even if rationality is possible, it cannot be applied because it amounts to maximization of profit which is not possible due to so many pressures from the environmental forces. Because of these reasons, economic man model is not suitable for managerial decision making.

### 2. Administrative Man Model

In contrast to economic man model which is a normative model, administrative man model is descriptive. Simon has suggested the concept of administrative man which describes the behaviour of decision maker in the context of what he actually does in making decisions. This model assumes that there is a certain amount of limit on rationality because of the conditions in which decisions are made. These conditions lack of certainty. Administrative man model of decision making is characterized by the following features:

(*a*) In choosing among alternatives, administrative man attempts to satisfy or look for the alternative which is satisfactory or good enough. Examples of satisfying criteria may be adequate market share, adequate profit, fair price, etc.

(*b*) Since administrative man believes in satisfying rather than maximizing, he can make his decisions without determining all possible alternatives.

(*c*) Administrative man is able to make decisions with relatively simple rules of thumb or tricks of trade, or from force of habit. These techniques do not make almost impossible demands upon his capacity for thought.

The basic difference between economic man and administrative man models is that the former goes for searching all the alternatives and tries to maximize out of his decision while the latter continues to search alternatives until he finds one that meets some personally determined minimum acceptable level. Beyond that, he does not search alternatives to find an even better alternative. Thus, instead of maximizing as required by complete rationality, he optimizes as required by partial rationality.

## Limits on Rationality

From the above discussions, we come to know decisions are not always fully rational. Simon has called this situation as 'bounded rationality'. There are two types of factors which put limits on rationality in decision making: decision-making mechanism and human factors involved in decision making.

### 1. Decision-making Mechanism

Rational decision making is based on the assumptions that:

(*i*) all the alternatives of choices are known;

(*ii*) the consequences of all the alternatives are known; and

(*iii*) the decision maker has a complete utility ordering for all possible consequences. These assumptions are seldom fulfilled in practice.

In practice, the decision maker does not have information about all the alternatives. Even for a single alternative, he may not have all the relevant information. In fact, major decisions which are generally non-programmed are made under the condition of partial ignorance implying that all possible alternatives are not known. Further, there is a problem in anticipating the consequences of various available alternatives on the objectives to be achieved by a decision.

### 2. Human Factors in Decision Making

A major source of limit on rationality is in the form of human factors involved in decision making. The major human factors which affect rationality in decision making are as follows:

(*a*) **Personal Value System:** Value system is a framework of personal philosophy which governs and influences the individual reactions and responses to any situation. Thus, what is good or bad is judged on the basis of personal value system. As a result, value system of the decision maker affects choice of an alternative in terms of what should be best for the organization.

(*b*) **Perception:** Problems and their solutions are quite abstract in nature. Thus, there is a likelihood that individual's perception regarding the problems and their solutions is different and consequently the way of tackling the problems may be different. This is so because people act according to what they perceive. For example, an organizational problem is generally interpreted as marketing problem by marketing people but financial problem by finance people. The perception of people is affected by several factors most of which are related with personal characteristics.

(*c*) **Political and Power Behaviour:** Political and power behaviour in an organization also affects the extent to which a decision would be rational. Since the major choices in an organization are arrived at after a lot of consultation and involvement of various people their interactions play significant part in the choice process. For example, **Mintzberg** has pointed out that many key organizational decisions are made through bargaining process where various interest groups put pressure according to their own interest. Thus, it is not necessary that the required level of rationality exists in the decisions.

(*d*) **Time Constraint:** Time factor also affects the rationality in decision making. In many cases, even though further information is needed, decisions are made only with available information because of lack of time. When one makes several decisions every day, the efficiency criteria justify making them promptly. Pressures to make decisions often require behaviour that contradicts the assumptions of rational economic man.

## ORGANIZING

Organizing is the function of management which follows planning. It is a function in which the synchronization and combination of human, physical and financial resources takes place. All the three resources are important to get results. Therefore, organizational function helps in achievement of results which in fact is important for the functioning of a concern. According to **Chester Barnard,** Organizing is a function by which the concern is able to define the role positions, the jobs related and the co-ordination between authority and responsibility. Hence, a manager always has to organize in order to get results.

### Definition of Organisation

The term 'Organisation' connotes different things to different people. Many writers have attempted to state the nature, characteristics and principles of organisation in their own way. It can be used as a group of persons working together or as a structure of relationships or as a process of management. Now, let us analyse some of the important definition of organising or organisation, and understand the meaning of organisation.

According to **Sheldon,** "Organisation is the process of so combining the work which individuals or groups have to perform with facilities necessary for its execution, that the duties so performed provide the best channels for efficient, systematic, positive and co-ordinated application of available effort."

In the words of **Chester I Barnard,** "Organisation is a system of co-operative activities of two or more persons."

**Mc Ferland** has defined organisation as, "an identifiable group of people contributing their efforts towards the attainment of goals".

According to **Louis A Allen,** "Organisation is the process of identifying and grouping the work to be performed, defining and delegating responsibility and authority, and establishing relationships for the purpose of enabling people to work most effectively together in accomplishing objectives.

According to **North Whitehead,** "Organisation is the adjustment of diverse elements, so that their mutual relationship may exhibit more pre-determined quality."

In the words of **Theo Haimann,** "Organising is the process of defining and grouping the activities of the enterprise and establishing the authority relationships among them. In performing the organising function, the manager defines, departmentalises and assigns activities so that they can be most effectively executed."

In the words of **Mooney and Railey,** "Organisation is the form of every human association for the attainment of a common purpose."

According to **John M Pfiffner** and **Frank P Sherwood,** "Organisation is the pattern of ways in which large number of people, too many to have intimate face-to-face contact with all others, and engaged in a complexity of tasks, relate themselves to each other in the conscious, systematic establishment and accomplishment of mutually agreed purposes."

In the words of **Koontz and O'Donnell,** "Organisation involves the grouping of activities necessary to accomplish goals and plans, the assignment of these activities to appropriate departments and the provision of authority, delegation and co-ordination."

According to **Northcott, C.H.,** "Organisation refers to arrangements by which tasks are assigned to men and women so that their individual efforts contribute effectively to some more or less clearly defined purpose for which they have been brought together."

In the words of **G.E. Milward,** "Organisation is a process of dividing work into convenient tasks or duties, of grouping such duties in the form of posts of delegating authority to each post and of appointing qualified staff to be responsible that the work is carried out as planned."

### Organisation Structure

An organisation structure shows the authority and responsibility relationships between the various positions in the organisation by showing who reports to whom.

Organisation involves establishing an appropriate structure for the goal seeking activities. It is an established pattern of relationship among the components of the organisation. **March** and **Simon** have stated that—"Organisation structure consists simply of those aspects of pattern of behaviour in the organisation that are relatively stable and change only slowly." The organisation is generally shown on an organisation chart. It shows the authority and responsibility while designing the relationships between various in the organization. Organistion structure, due attention should be given to the principles of organization.

## Significance of Organisation Structure

1. Properly designed organisation can help improve teamwork and productivity by providing a framework within which the people can work together most effectively.
2. Organisation structure determines the location of decision-making in the organisation.
3. Sound organisation structure stimulates creative thinking and initiative among organisational members by providing well defined patterns of authority.
4. A sound organisation structure facilitates growth of enterprise by increasing its capacity to handle increased level of authority.
5. Organisation structure provides the pattern of communication and coordination.
6. The organisation structure helps a member to know what his role is and how it relates to other roles.

## Determining the Kind of Organisation Structure

According to **Peter F Drucker,** "Organisation is not an end in itself, but a means to the end of business performance and business results. Organisation structure is an indispensable means; and the wrong structure will seriously impair business performance and may even destroy it. Organisation structure must be designed so as to make possible to attainment of the objectives of the business for five, ten, fifteen years hence".

Thus it is essential that a great deal of care should be taken while determining the organisation structure. **Peter Drucker** has pointed out three specific ways to find out what kind or structure is needed to attain the objectives of a specific business:

(*i*) **Activities Analysis:** The purpose of 'activities analysis' is to discover the primary activity of the proposed organisation, for it is around this that other activities will be built. It may be pointed out that in every organisation; one or two functional areas of business dominate. For example, designing is an important activity of the readymade garments manufacturer. After the activities have been identified and classified into functional areas, they should be listed in the order of importance. It is advisable to divide and sub-divide the whole work into smaller homogeneous units so that the same may be assigned to different individuals. Thus, in devising an organisational structure, it is important to divide the entire work into manageable units. It has rightly been said that the job constitutes the basic building block in building up an organisational structure.

(*ii*) **Decision Analysis:** At this stage, the manager finds out what kinds of decisions will need to be made to carry on the work of the organisation. What is even more important, he has to see where or at what level these decisions will have to be made and how each manager should be involved in them. This type of analysis is particularly important for deciding upon the number of levels or layers in the organisation structure.

As regards decision, analysis, **Peter Drucker,** has emphasized four basic characteristics. They are:

(*a*) the degree of futurity in the decision;

(*b*) the impact that decision has on other functions;

(*c*) the character of the decision determined by a number of qualitative factors, such as, basic principles of conduct, ethical values, social and political beliefs etc., and

(*d*) whether the decisions are periodically recurrent or rates as recurrent decisions may require a general rule whereas a rate decision is to be treated as a distinctive event.

A decision should always be made at the lowest possible level and so close to the scene of action as possible.

(*iii*) **Relations Analysis:** Relations Analysis will include an examination of the types of relationships that develop within the organisation. These relationships are vertical, lateral and diagonal. Where a superior-subordinate relationship is envisaged, it will be a vertical relationship. In case of an expert or specialist advising a manager at the same level, the relationship will be lateral. Where a specialist exercises authority over a person in subordinate position in another department in the same organisation it will be an instance of diagonal relationship. **Peter Drucker** emphasises that "the first thing to consider in defining a manager job is the contribution his activity has to make to the larger unit of which it is a part."

Thus, downward, upward and lateral (side-ways) relations must be analysed to determine the organisation structure.

## Principles of Organisation

1. **Consideration of unity of objectives:** The objective of the undertaking influences the organisation structure. There must be unity of objective so that all efforts can be concentrated on the set goals.
2. **Specialisation:** Effective organisation must include specialisation. Precise division of work facilitates specialisation.
3. **Co-ordination:** Organisation involves division of work among people whose efforts must be co-ordinated to achieve common goals. Co-ordination is the orderly arrangement of group effort to provide unity of action in the pursuit of common purpose.
4. **Clear unbroken line of Authority:** It points out the scalar principle or the chain of command. The line of authority flows from the highest executive to the lowest managerial level and the chain of command should not be broken.
5. **Responsibility:** Authority should be equal to responsibility *i.e.,* each manager should have enough authority to accomplish the task.
6. **Efficiency:** The organisation structure should enable the enterprise to attain objectives with the lowest possible cost.
7. **Delegation:** Decisions should be made at the lowest competent level. Authority and responsibility should be delegated as far down in the organisation as possible.
8. **Unity of Command:** Each person should be accountable to a single superior. If an individual has to report to only one supervisor there is a sense of personal responsibility to one person for results.
9. **Span of Management:** No superior at a higher level should have more than six immediate subordinates. The average human brain can effectively direct three to six brains (*i.e.,* subordinates).
10. **Communication:** A good communication sub-system is essential for smooth flow of information and understanding and for effective business performance.
11. **Flexibility:** The organisation is expected to provide built in devices to facilitate growth and expansion without dislocation. It should not be rigid or inelastic.

## Formal and Informal Organisation

The formal organisation refers to the structure of jobs and positions with clearly defined functions and relationships as prescribed by the top management. This type of organisation is built by the management to realise objectives of an enterprise and is bound by rules, systems and procedures.

Everybody is assigned a certain responsibility for the performance of the given task and given the required amount of authority for carrying it out. Informal organisation, which does not appear on the organisation chart, supplements the formal organisation in achieving organisational goals effectively and efficiently.

The working of informal groups and leaders is not as simple as it may appear to be. Therefore, it is obligatory for every manager to study thoroughly the working pattern of informal relationships in the organisation and to use them for achieving organisational objectives.

## Formal Organisation

**Chester I Barnard** defines formal organisation as—"a system of consciously coordinated activities or forces of two or more persons. It refers to the structure of well-defined jobs, each bearing a definite measure of authority, responsibility and accountability." The essence of formal organisation is conscious common purpose and comes into being when persons:

(*i*) Are able to communicate with each other

(*ii*) Are willing to act and

(*iii*) Share a purpose.

The formal organisation is built around four key pillars. They are:

- Division of labour
- Scalar and functional processes
- Structure and
- Span of control

Thus, a formal organisation is one resulting from planning where the pattern of structure has already been determined by the top management.

### *Characteristic Features of Formal Organisation*

1. Formal organisation structure is laid down by the top management to achieve organisational goals.
2. Formal organisation prescribes the relationships amongst the people working in the organisation.
3. The organisation structures is consciously designed to enable the people of the organisation to work together for accomplishing the common objectives of the enterprise.
4. Organisation structure concentrates on the jobs to be performed and not the individuals who are to perform jobs.

5. In a formal organisation, individuals are fitted into jobs and positions and work as per the managerial decisions.

   Thus, the formal relations in the organisation arise from the pattern of responsibilities that are created by the management.
6. A formal organisation is bound by rules, regulations and procedures.
7. In a formal organisation, the position, authority, responsibility and accountability of each level are clearly defined.
8. Organisation structure is based on division of labour and specialisation to achieve efficiency in operations.
9. A formal organisation is deliberately impersonal. The organisation does not take into consideration the sentiments of organisational members.
10. The authority and responsibility relationships created by the organisation structure; are to be honoured by everyone.
11. In a formal organisation, coordination proceeds according to the prescribed pattern.

### Advantages of Formal Organisation

1. The formal organisation structure concentrates on the jobs to be performed. It, therefore, makes everybody responsible for a given task.
2. A formal organisation is bound by rules, regulations and procedures. It thus ensures law and order in the organisation.
3. The organisation structure enables the people of the organisation to work together for accomplishing the common objectives of the enterprise.

### Disadvantages or Criticisms of Formal Organisation

1. The formal organisation does not take into consideration the sentiments of organisational members.
2. The formal organisation does not consider the goals of the individuals. It is designed to achieve the goals of the organisation only.
3. The formal organisation is bound by rigid rules, regulations and procedures. This makes the achievement of goals difficult.

## Informal Organisation

Informal organisation refers to the relationship between people in the organisation based on personal attitudes, emotions, prejudices, likes, dislikes etc. an informal organisation is an organisation which is not established by any formal authority, but arises from the personal and social relations of the people.

These relations are not developed according to procedures and regulations laid down in the formal organisation structure; generally large formal groups give rise to small informal or social groups. These groups may be based on same taste, language, culture or some other factor. These groups are not pre-planned, but they develop automatically within the organisation according to its environment.

### Characteristics Features of Informal Organisation

1. Informal organisation is not established by any formal authority. It is unplanned and arises spontaneously.
2. Informal organisations reflect human relationships. It arises from the personal and social relations amongst the people working in the organisation.
3. Formation of informal organisations is a natural process. It is not based on rules, regulations and procedures.
4. The inter-relations amongst the people in an informal organisation cannot be shown in an organisation chart.
5. In the case of informal organisation, the people cut across formal channels of communications and communicate amongst themselves.
6. The membership of informal organisations is voluntary. It arises spontaneously and not by deliberate or conscious efforts.
7. Membership of informal groups can be overlapping as a person may be member of a number Notes of informal groups.
8. Informal organisations are based on common taste, problem, language, religion, culture, etc. It is influenced by the personal attitudes, emotions, whims, likes and dislikes etc. of the people in the organisation.

### Benefits of Informal Organisation

1. It blends with the formal organisation to make it more effective.
2. Many things which cannot be achieved through formal organisation can be achieved through informal organisation.
3. The presence of informal organisation in an enterprise makes the managers plan "and act more carefully."
4. Informal organisation acts as a means by which the workers achieve a sense of security and belonging. It provides social satisfaction to group members.

5. An informal organisation has a powerful influence on productivity and job satisfaction.
6. The informal leader lightens the burden of the formal manager and tries to fill in the gaps in the manager's ability.
7. Informal organisation helps the group members to attain specific personal objectives.
8. Informal organisation is the best means of employee communication. It is very fast.
9. Informal organisation gives psychological satisfaction to the members. It acts as a safety valve for the emotional problems and frustrations of the workers of the organisation because they get a platform to express their feelings.
10. It serves as an agency for social control of human behaviour.

## Organisation Charts and Manuals

**Organisation chart:** The pattern of network of relations between the various positions in an organisation as well as between the persons who hold those positions is referred to as "Organisation chart". Organisation data are often shown in the form of graphic chart. Organisation charts are the important tool for providing information on managerial positions and relationships in an organisation.

### *Meaning of Organisation Chart*

According to **Harold Koontz** and **Cyril Donnell,** "Every organisation can be charted, for a chart is nothing more than an indication of how departments are tied together along their principal lines of authority."

In the words of **George R Terry,** "A chart is a diagrammatical form which shows important aspects of an organisation including the major functions and their respective relationships, the channels of supervision, and the relative authority of each employee who is in charge of each respective function."

According to **Louis A Allen,** "The organisation chart is a graphic means of showing organisation data. Organisation charts are snap-shots; they show only the formal organisation and depict it for only a given moment in time."

In the words of **J Batty,** "An organisation chart is a diagrammatic representation of the framework or structure of an organisation."

According to **Henry H Albens,** "An organisation chart portrays managerial positions and relationships in a company or department unit."

From the above definitions, it is clear that an organisation chart is a diagrammatical form which shows important aspects of an organisation including the major functions and their respective relationships. It is a graphic portrayed of positions in the enterprise and of the formal lines of communication among them. It enables each executive and employee to understand his position in the organisation and to know to whom he is accountable. The organisation chart has the following characteristics:

- It is a diagrammatical presentation.
- It shows principal lines of authority in the organization.
- It shows the interplay of various functions and relationships.
- It indicates the channels of communication.

The organisation chart should not be confused with the organisation structure. An organisation chart is merely a type of record showing the formal organisational relationships which management intends should prevail. It is, therefore, primarily a technique of presentation.

### *Meaning of Organisation Manual*

An organisation chart shows who has the authority over whom but does not state that extent of authority or the duties each person in the organisation is expected to perform. In order to supplement the information of this chart, an organisation may prepare a Manual or Management Guide. Manual sets down in the form of a book or booklet all the details of the organisation, its objectives and policies, authorities, functions, duties and responsibilities of each unit and all information relating thereto.

A manual can be a useful instrument of management which more than justifies the amount of work and money involved in its compilation. Where a good manual is in use, each person can determine the responsibilities of his job and its proper relationship with other jobs in the organisation.

Jurisdictional conflicts and overlapping can be avoided. A manual provides quick settlement of all misunderstandings. It relieves the manager from the botheration of repeating the same information time and again. It provides uniformity and consistency in the procedures and practices. If, a good organisation manual is in use, each personnel in the organisation can know the responsibilities of his job and its relationship with other jobs in the organisation. Good organisation manual has the following contents.

1. Nature of the enterprise
2. Objectives of the enterprise
3. Policies of the management
4. Job Descriptions
5. Duties and responsibilities of various personnel
6. Instructions relating to the performance of standard as well as non-standard jobs.

## Types of Organisation

Organisation requires the creation of structural relationship among different departments and the individuals working there for the accomplishment of desired goals. Organisation structure is primarily concerned with the allocation of tasks and delegation of authority. The establishment of formal relationships among the individuals working in the organisation is very important to make clear the lines of authority in the organisation and to coordinate the efforts of different individuals in an efficient manner. According to the different practices of distributing authority and responsibility among the members of the enterprise, several types of organisation structure have been evolved. They are:

1. Line organisation
2. Line and Staff organisation
3. Functional organisation
4. Committee organization

### *Line Organisation*

This is the simplest and the earliest form of organisation. It is also known as "Military", "Traditional", "Scalar" or "Hierarchical" form of organisation. The line organisation represents the structure in a direct vertical relationship through which authority flows. Under this, the line of authority flows vertically downward from top to bottom throughout the organisation.

The quantum of authority is highest at the top and reduces at each successive level down the hierarchy. All major decisions and orders are made by the executives at the top and handed down to their immediate subordinates who in turn break up the orders into specific instructions for the purpose of their execution by another set of subordinates. A direct relationship of authority and responsibility is thus established between the superior and subordinate. The superior exercises a direct authority over his subordinates who become entirely responsible for their performance to their commanding superior.

Thus, in the line organisation, the line of authority consists of an uninterrupted series of authority steps and forms a hierarchical arrangement. The line of authority not only becomes the avenue of command to operating personnel, but also provides the channel of communication, coordination and accountability in the organisation.

**Prof. Florence** enunciates three principles which are necessary to realise the advantages of this system and the non-observance of which would involve inefficiency.

1. Commands should be given to subordinates through the immediate superior; there should be no skipping of links in the chain of command.
2. There should be only one chain. That is, command should be received from only one immediate superior.
3. The number of subordinates whose work is directly commanded by the superior should be limited.

#### *Advantages or Merits of Line Organisation*

1. It is the easiest to establish and simplest to explain to the employers.
2. It fixes responsibility for the performance of tasks in a definite manner upon certain individuals.
3. There is clear-cut identification of authority and responsibility relationship. Employees are fully aware of the boundaries of their job.
4. It is most economical and effective.
5. It makes for unity of control thus conforming to the scalar principle of organisation.
6. It ensures excellent discipline in the enterprise because every individual knows to whom he is responsible. The subordinates are also aware of the necessity of satisfying their superior in their own interests.
7. It facilitates prompt decision-making because there is definite authority at every level.
8. As all the activities relating to one department or division are managed by one executive, Notes there can be effective coordination of activities.
9. This system is flexible or elastic, in the sense that, as each executive has sole responsibility in his own position and sphere of work, he can easily adjust the organisation to changing conditions.
10. Under this system, responsibility and authority are clearly defined. Every member of the organisation knows his exact position, to whom he is responsible and who are responsible to him. Because of the clear fixation of responsibility, no person can escape from his liability.

#### *Disadvantages or Demerits of Line Organisation*

1. With growth, the line organisation makes the superiors too overloaded with work. Since all work is done according to the wishes of one person alone, the efficiency of the whole department will come to depend upon the qualities of management displayed by the head of that department. If therefore, something happens to an Efficient manager, the future of the department and of the concern as a whole would be in jeopardy.
2. Being an autocratic system, it may be operated on an arbitrary, opinionated and dictatorial basis.
3. Under this system, the subordinates should follow the orders of their superior without expression their

opinion on the orders. That means there is limited communication.

4. There may be a good deal of nepotism and favouritism. This may result in efficient people being left behind and inefficient people getting the higher and better posts.
5. The line organisation suffers from lack of specialised skill of experts. Modern business is so complex that it is extremely difficult for one person to carry in his head all the necessary details about his work in this department.
6. Line organisation is not suitable to big organisations because it does not provide specialists in the structure. Many jobs require specialised knowledge to perform them.
7. If superiors take a wrong decision, it would be carried out without anybody having the courage to point out its deficiencies.
8. The organisation is rigid and inflexible.
9. There is concentration of authority at the top. If the top executives are not capable, the enterprise will not be successful.

### Line and Staff Organisation

In line and staff organisation, the line authority remains the same as it does in the line organisation. Authority flows from top to bottom. The main difference is that specialists are attached to line managers to advise them on important matters. These specialists stand ready with their speciality to serve line mangers as and when their services are called for, to collect information and to give help which will enable the line officials to carry out their activities better.

The staff officers do not have any power of command in the organisation as they are employed to provide expert advice to the line officers. The combination of line organisation with this expert staff constitutes the type of organisation known as line and staff organisation. The 'line' maintains discipline and stability; the 'staff' provides expert information. The line gets out the production, the staffs carries on the research, planning, scheduling, establishing of standards and recording of performance. The authority by which the staff performs these functions is delegated by the line and the performance must be acceptable to the line before action is taken.

#### *Features of Line and Staff Organisation*

1. Under this system, there are line officers who have authority and command over the subordinates and are accountable for the tasks entrusted to them. The staff officers are specialists who offer expert advice to the line officers to perform their tasks efficiently.
2. Under this system, the staff officers prepare the plans and give advice to the line officers and the line officers execute the plan with the help of workers.
3. The line and staff organisation is based on the principle of specialisation.

#### *Advantages or Merits of Line and Staff Organisation*

- It brings expert knowledge to bear upon management and operating problems. Thus, the line managers get the benefit of specialised knowledge of staff specialists at various levels.
- The expert advice and guidance given by the staff officers to the line officers benefit the entire organisation.
- As the staff officers look after the detailed analysis of each important managerial activity, it relieves the line managers of the botheration of concentrating on specialized functions.
- Staff specialists help the line managers in taking better decisions by providing expert advice. Therefore, there will be sound managerial decisions under this system.
- It makes possible the principle of undivided responsibility and authority, and at the same time permits staff specialisation. Thus, the organisation takes advantage of functional organisation while maintaining the unity of command.
- It is based upon planned specialisation.
- Line and staff organisation has greater flexibility, in the sense that new specialized activities can be added to the line activities without disturbing the line procedure.

#### *Disadvantages or Demerits of Line and Staff Organisation*

- Unless the duties and responsibilities of the staff members are clearly indicated by charts and manuals, there may be considerable confusion throughout the organization as to the functions and positions of staff members with relation to the line supervisors.
- There is generally a conflict between the line and staff executives. The line managers feel that staff specialists do not always give right type of advice, and staff officials generally complain that their advice is not properly attended to.
- Line managers sometimes may resent the activities of staff members, feeling that prestige and influence of line managers suffer from the presence of the specialists.
- The staff experts may be ineffective because they do not get the authority to implement their recommendations.

- This type of organisation requires the appointment of large number of staff officers or experts in addition to the line officers. As a result, this system becomes quite expensive.
- Although expert information and advice are available, they reach the workers through the officers and thus run the risk of misunderstanding and misinterpretation.
- Since staff managers are not accountable for the results, they may not be performing their duties well.
- Line mangers deal with problems in a more practical manner. But staff officials who are specialists in their fields tend to be more theoretical. This may hamper coordination in the organisation.

### Functional Organisation

The difficulty of the line organisation in securing suitable chief executive was overcome by F.W. Taylor who formulated the Functional type of organisation. As the name implies, the whole task of management and direction of subordinates should be divided according to the type of work involved. As far as the workman was concerned, instead of coming in contact with the management at one point only, he was to receive his daily orders and help directly from eight different bosses; four of these were located in the planning room and four in the shop.

The four specialists or bosses in the planning room are:

(*i*) Route Clerk

(*ii*) Instruction Card Clerk

(*iii*) Time and Cost Clerk

(*iv*) Shop disciplinarian

**Route Clerk:** To lay down the sequence of operations and instruct the workers concerned about it.

**Instruction Card Clerk:** To prepare detailed instructions regarding different aspects of work.

**Time and Cost Clerk:** To send all information relating to their pay to the workers and to secure proper returns of work from them.

**Shop Disciplinarian:** To deal with cases of breach of discipline and absenteeism.

The four specialists or bosses at the shop level are:

1. Gang Boss
2. Speed Boss
3. Inspector
4. Repair Boss

**Gang Boss:** To assemble and set up tools and machines and to teach the workers to make all their personal motions in the quickest and best way.

**Speed Boss:** To ensure that machines are run at their best speeds and proper tools are used by the workers.

**Repair Boss:** To ensure that each worker keeps his machine in good order and maintains cleanliness around him and his machines.

**Inspector:** To show to the worker how to do the work.

It was F. W. Taylor who evolved functional organisation for planning and controlling manufacturing operations on the basis of specialisation. But in practice, functionalisation is restricted to the top of the organisation as recommended by Taylor.

#### *Features of Functional Organisation*

The features of functional organisation are as follows:

1. The work of the enterprise is divided into different functional departments and the different functional departments are placed under different specialists.
2. The functional specialist has the authority or right to give orders regarding his function whosesoever that function is performed in the enterprise.
3. Under this system, the workers have to receive instructions from different specialists.
4. If anybody in the enterprise has to take any decision relating to a particular function, it has to be in consultation with the functional specialist.
5. Under this system, the workers have to perform a limited number of functions.

### Committee Organisation

Committee organisation as a method of managerial control has very little practical importance, because it is managed by a senior member of the committee only. But the committee organisations are widely used for the purpose of discharging advisory functions of the management. Committees are usually relatively formal bodies with a definite structure. They have their own organisation. To them are entrusted definite responsibility and authority.

According to **Hicks,** "A committee is a group of people who meet by plan to discuss or make a decision for a particular subject."

According to **Louis A Allen,** "A committee is a body of persons appointed or elected to on an organised basis for the consideration of matters brought before it."

A committee may formulate plans, make policy decisions or review the performance of certain units. In some cases, it may only have the power to make recommendations to a designated official.

Whatever may be the scope of their activities, committees have come to be recognised as an important instrument in the modern business as well as non-business organisations.

# SPAN OF MANAGEMENT

Delegation, decentralisation, and span of control are closely related terms. Span of control—often referred to as *span of management* or *span of supervision* is an important principle that states that there should be a manageable number of subordinates under one superior. While grouping activities and creating departments, the basic issue is : How many subordinates should be placed under one superior, manager, or supervisor? However, span of management is more comprehensive as it involves not only supervision or control, but also all managerial activities. The manager is responsible for all activities of subordinates working under him.

## Definitions of Span of Control

The term can be defined as:

1. Span of management (or span of control) implies the number of subordinates a superior can manage (or control) effectively. It is a key determinant of complexity of manager's job, the number of managers required, and the shape (or structure) of the organisation.
2. Span of control (or span of management) refers to the number of subordinates who can be effectively controlled (or managed) by a superior. It also denotes the number of subordinates who report to a superior.
3. Span of control (or span of management) refers to the number of subordinates who directly report to the superior, or the number of subordinates that a superior can manage effectively.

**Determination of Span of Management:** Span of control is a valid principle as any manager can effectively direct and control only a limited (or manageable) number of subordinates, However, experts do not agree on the specific number of subordinates who can be placed under one superior.

**Classical thinkers** opine that an ideal span of control ranges from three to eight subordinates. However, the number of subordinates depends on the level of management, for example, at lower level management, span of control widens, **Davis** calls managerial (higher) span of control as executive span and lower level as operative span. To him, span of control is three to nine for managerial level and as many as thirty for operative span. On the other hand, **Urwick** suggests that span of control for top management may be *four,* but for supervisory level it may be in between *eight* to *twelve.*

**V.A. Graicunas,** a French management consultant, suggested mathematical formulas to fix the number of subordinates under one superior. He Identified three types of relationships between superior and subordinates, as discussed below:

1. **Direct Single Relationships:** Such relations arise from the direct individual contact of the superior with the subordinates. If there are three subordinates, there will be three direct single relationships.
2. **Direct Group Relationships:** Such relations arise between the superior and subordinates in all possible combinations. If there are three subordinates, there will be nine possible combinations.
3. **Cross Relationships:** Such relations arise because of mutual interactions of subordinates under one superior. If there are three subordinates, there will be six relationships. Graicunas gave following formulas to find out the number of relationships with $n$ number of subordinates, which determine span of control:

   Direct single relationships = $n$

   Direct group relationships = $n(2n^{-1} - 1)$

   Cross Relationships = $n(n - 1)$

   Total Relationships = $n(2^n/2 + n - 1)$

   *Example:* If there are six subordinates, the number of total relationship will be 222 as calculated under:

   Number of total relations with six subordinates is:

   $= n(2^n/2 + n - 1)$

   $= 6(2^6/2 + 6 - 1)$

   $= 6(32 + 5)$

   $= 6 \times 37 = 222.$

## DEPARTMENTATION

### Meaning

Departmentation is the process of grouping various activities into separate units of departments. A department is a distinct section of the business establishment concerned with a particular group of business activities of like nature. The actual number of departments in which a business house can be divided depends upon the size of establishment and its nature. A big business enterprise will, usually, have more departments as compared to a small one. In the words of **Allen,** "Departmentation is a means of dividing a large and monolithic functional organisation into smaller, flexible, administrative units."

### Need and Significance of Departments

Departments comprise a framework for as organization and enable it to expand in definition.

Departmentation aims at

(*i*) specialisation of activities for efficient performance;

(*ii*) simplifying the task of management within a workable span; and

(*iii*) maintaining co-ordination and control of the various activities.

The advantages of departmentation can be summed up as:

1. It increases the efficiency of the enterprise since various activities are grouped into workable units.
2. It renders the task of fixation of accountability for results very easy since activities are well defined and responsibilities are clearly laid.
3. It provides for fixation of standards for performance appraisal and thus ensures effective control.
4. It creates opportunities for the departmental heads to take initiative and thus develop managerial facilities.

## CENTRALIZATION AND DECENTRALIZATION

### Centralization

Centralization of authority refers to the concentration of decision-making authority with the top management. It means all important executive and operational decisions are made more at the higher levels of organization. The decisions and actions at lower levels are subject to the prior approval of the higher authority in a centralized organization. Centralization points out to a higher degree of retention of authority and responsibility by the top management.

This type of organization is ideal for small organizations where there are few employees or subordinates and the top management can effectively supervise and control them.

#### *Definitions*

"Centralization is the systematic and consistent reservation of authority at central points in the organization."

**—Louis Allen**

"Centralisation is that organization where the role of subordinates is reduced." **—Henry Fayol**

#### *Advantages*

- It facilitates quick decision-making since all major decisions are made by the top management.
- It requires less number of managers or superiors and there is no duplication of work.
- It involves very few managers. This reduce paper work between the management and lower levels.
- It ensures better coordination of activities since there is unity of command and decisions are quickly communicated directly to employees.
- It is ideal for small organizations because of its low cost, greater coordination and quick decision-making.
- It brings uniformity among various departments, divisions and branches. This improves organizational efficiency productivity.
- Centralization helps to eliminate overlapping and duplications of activities and this results in considerable cost savings.

#### *Disadvantages*

- Centralization restricts the scope of delegation and decentralization which is harmful to large organizations.
- Due to centralisation, decision-making power rests with few top executives which puts a heavy burden on the top executives.
- Centralization does not provide lower level managers a scope for self-development as they have to act as per the decisions taken at the top-level.
- In centralization, decisions are imposed on lower-level as a result there is no motivation on the part of lower level workers to work hard.
- Centralization does not train subordinates for higher position.

### Decentralization

Decentralization means dispersal of decision-making power to lower-levels of the organization. It implies the distribution of managerial authority of planning, directing, coordinating, controlling etc., among executives at all levels in the organization. Linder decentralization major decision-making authority is given to the departmental heads. Decentralization is not same as delegation. Delegation means delegating authority and responsibility from one individual to another, while decentralization is a broader concept which means scattering of authority throughout the organization.

#### *Definition*

"Decentralization refers to systematic effort to delegate to the lowest levels, all authority except that which can only exercised at the central points." **—Louis A. Allen**

"Decentralization of authority is a fundamental phase of delegation to the extent that the authority is not delegated; it is decentralized." **—Koontz and O' Donnell**

#### *Factors determining degree of decentralization*

Whether to delegate or not depends upon the personal choice of individual managers as well as the philosophy of higher level management. However, some of the other factors beside the choice of manager and philosophy of management that affect decentralization are:

(*a*) **Size of organization:** Decentralisation depends upon the size of the organization. Larger the size of an organization, the more urgent is the need of decentralization. The complexities of large organization may require routine and repetitive decisions to be decentralized at the lower level of management hierarchy.

(*b*) **History of organization:** Decentralization also depends upon the way organization has been built-up over the period of time. Those organizations which grow from within, under the direction of the owner-founder, tend to be centralized, while organizations that grow through mergers and amalgamations and widespread expansion tend to be decentralized.

(*c*) **Geographical expanse:** An organisation having branches at dispersed geographical locations has no option than to decentralize.

(*d*) **Management philosophy:** Decentralization is a kind of management philosophy to regulate organizational processes. In fact, decentralisation is a way of organizational life. Some progressive managers view it as a tool of harnessing capabilities of their workforce, while some others may view it as a tool of satisfying their own ego and dominate their workforce.

(*e*) **Availability of managers:** Availability of managers directly affects the degree of decentralization. If competent and experienced managers readily available in the organization, then there are more chances of decentralization. Decentralization in such organizations is also necessary to satisfy inner sense of such managers as they like to lead rather than being led.

(*f*) **Pattern of planning:** Planning is the primary function of management. All other managerial functions are subsidiary to it. If the organisation follows participative planning. Then naturally authority in the organization will be more decentralized. However, if planning activities are centralized at the top level then authority too will be centralized.

(*g*) **Control techniques:** Controlling is necessary for ensuring performance as per pre-determined plans. If control systems in the organization are well developed and effective, more functions can be decentralized at the lower level. This is because control system puts check on the activities of lower level managers and deviations, if any, can be located easily.

(*h*) **Structure of organization:** In the organizations that practice division of labour and specialization and have a number of departments and sub-units for major activities, decentralization becomes a natural phenomenon. Authority responsibility in such organizations automatically get dispersed to a number of departmental heads, thus, larger the organization more would be decentralized.

(*i*) **Environmental influences:** Besides the various factors discussed above, most of which are internal to the organization, there are a number of external factors which either compel an organization to centralize or decentralize. Some of the factors are government policy, organizational pattern in the industry, availability of experts and professionals etc.

### *Advantages of Decentralization*

Some of the advantages of decentralization are discussed as under:

1. **It Reduces Burden of Top Executives:** Centralisation of authority over-burdens top executives. They are left with no time for planning, etc. In decentralisation decision-making power is delegated to the lower levels relieving top executives of some of their burden. Under this system, top executives will retain only that work which requires their personal attention otherwise everything is assigned to persons at appropriate levels. This will reduce the burden of top executives and they will be able to devote more time for planning, etc.

2. **It Takes Quick Decisions:** Under decentralised system, decision-making powers are delegated to the level of actual execution. Whenever there is a need for taking a decision, the concerned executive will decide the things immediately.

   There is no need to make reference to the top level for most of the work. It quickens the process of decision-making.

3. **It Facilitates Diversification:** With the expansion and diversification of activities there will be a need to delegate authority at departmental level. Decentralisation gives enough authority to persons at various levels for carrying out the required task. The centralised system of authority will not allow diversification beyond a certain level because decision-making is reserved by one man only. The organisation will become more and more complex with the addition of new products and setting up of more units. Decentralised system will be more suitable for expanding enterprises.

4. **Motivation of Subordinates:** Under decentralization, subordinates get opportunity for taking decisions independently. This fulfils the human need for power, independence and status. Subordinates will realise their importance in the organisation. They will try to put their maximum efforts so that their performance improves.

   They get a chance to take initiative and to try new ideas. The subordinates feel motivated under decentralised set-up.

5. **It is Sense of Competition:** Under decentralised system, different departments or units are made separate profit centres. The employees of different departments will compete with each other to show better results. The sense of competition will improve the performance of all departments or segments.

6. **Provides Product or Market Emphasis:** Since decision-taking is scattered and goes to lower levels of management there will be more product or market emphasis. The changing tastes and fashions require prompt decisions. The decentralised system will respond immediately to the changing situations. The persons concerned with marketing will take quick decisions as are necessary under the situation.

7. **Division of Risk:** The enterprise is divided into a number of departments under decentralisation. Management can experiment new ideas at one department without disturbing others. This will reduce the risk if things go adverse. Once the experiment is successful it can be used in other segments also. So risk element can be limited under decentralised system.

8. **Effective Control and Supervision:** With the delegation of authority, span of control will be effective. Since executives at lower levels will have the full authority to lake important decisions, they will recommend awards or punishments as per their performance. This will improve supervision and control.

### *Disadvantages of Decentralisation*

Decentralisation suffers from a number of drawbacks and some of these are discussed as follows:

1. **Lack of Co-ordination:** Under decentralisation each department, unit or section enjoys substantial powers. They have the powers to formulate their own policies and programmes. It becomes difficult to co-ordinate the activities of various segments. Moreover, every segment emphasises its own work only without bothering about others. This creates more difficulties in co-ordinating activities.

2. **Difficulty in Control:** Since different units work independently it becomes difficult to control their activities. Top management will not be able to exercise effective control because it does not remain in touch with day-to-day activities of various segments.

3. **Costly:** Decentralised system involves heavy overhead expenses. Every decentralized division has to be self-sufficient for its activities like production, marketing, accounting, personnel, etc. A number of persons will be employed to man various activities. These persons are paid higher salaries involving huge costs. Decentralised system is suitable for large scale enterprises only. Small-scale business units cannot afford to spend higher overhead expenses.

4. **Lack of Able Managers:** Decentralised system will succeed only if competent persons are employed to manage various jobs in different segments. Competent persons are not sometimes available as per the requirements. The system will fail if competent personnel are not available.

## DELEGATION

### Meaning

Delegation of authority involves giving authority to various organizational positions to get things done. All important decisions are taken at top level by Board of Directors. The execution is entrusted to Chief Executive. The Chief Executive assigns the work to departmental managers who in turn delegate the authority to their subordinates. Every superior delegates the authority to subordinates for getting a particular work done. The process goes to the level where actual work is executed.

There is a limit up to which a person can supervise the subordinates. When the number of subordinates increases beyond it then he will have to delegate his powers to others who perform supervision for him. A manager is not judged by the work he actually performs on his own but the work he gets done through others. He assigns duties and authority to his subordinates and ensures the achievement of desired organisational goals.

### Definitions

**Allen,** "The entrustment of a part of the work, or responsibility and authority to another, and the creation of accountability for performance."

**O.S. Hiner** says "Delegation takes place when one person gives another the right to perform work on his behalf and in his name, and the second person accepts a corresponding duty or obligation to do what is required of him."

**Douglas C. Basil,** "Delegation refers to a manager's ability to share his burden with others. It consists of granting authority or the right to decision-making in certain defined areas and charging subordinates with responsibility for carrying through an assigned task."

## Characteristics of Delegation

Delegation is the assignment of authority to subordinates in a defined area and making them responsible for the results. Delegation has the following characteristics:

1. Delegation takes place when a manager grants some of his powers to subordinates.
2. Delegation occurs only when the person delegating the authority himself has that authority *i.e.* a manager must possess what he wants to delegate.
3. Only a part of authority is delegated to subordinates.
4. A manager delegating authority can reduce, enhance or take it back. He exercises full control over the activities of the subordinates even after delegation.
5. It is only the authority which is delegated and not the responsibility. A manager cannot abdicate responsibility by delegating authority to subordinates.

## Need of Delegation

Delegation is a universally accepted principle. It has been practised since time immemorial and in every field. Delegation is necessary not only for a business undertaking but also for running a government. In government, legislative bodies delegate their powers to Council of Ministers who in turn delegate to officers and so on. Delegation is essential even for running a family because head of the family will have to get the help of various members for performing various tasks.

An industrial undertaking benefits by delegation in the following ways:

1. **Relieving Top Executives:** Top executives cannot perform and supervise each and every work. Moreover they are required to undertake important tasks of planning and controlling. Delegation helps executives in delegating their work to subordinate officers.
2. **Improved Functioning:** In the absence of delegation some persons may be burdened with more tasks while others may not have sufficient work to do. Delegation helps in rationalizing the functioning of an organisation. Work is divided among various persons in such a way that it is done in an efficient way. Nobody is unduly burdened and no work is left unattended.
3. **Use of Specialists:** Delegation enables the use of specialists for taking up different functions. A production manager will be assigned the task of production, a sales manager will look after sales department, a lawyer will look after legal matters and so on. The use of specialists for different functions will improve the quality of work.
4. **Helps in Employee Development:** When subordinates are given independent assignments then they will be able to use their initiative and experience. This will also give them confidence in taking up further responsibilities. Without delegation, subordinates will not get a chance to try their knowledge. Delegation of power is the best way of developing subordinates and preparing them for taking up more responsibilities in future.
5. **Helps in Expansion and Diversification:** The expansion and diversification of an enterprise needs the services of more and more persons. The assignment of various tasks to subordinates will prepare them for undertaking new assignments. If subordinates are not assigned important works earlier then it will be dangerous to give them independent tasks straight way. Delegation is very useful for undertaking expansion and diversification plans.

## Factors Influencing Degree of Delegation

Delegation of authority is a must for every organisation. The question to be decided is how much authority should be delegated to subordinate managers. The pattern to be followed for delegation should be decided on the basis of its requirements. It will be wise to check from time to time the already existing delegation of authority in order to make sure that it is appropriate and adequate.

A number of factors influence the decision about delegation. Some of these are discussed as follows:

1. **Knowledge about Company:** The history of the company influences the degree of delegation. A company grown over a period of time has a tendency to centralise powers. When a concern is small then most of the decision-making is done by the owner. With the growth of business, the tendency to centralise powers remains. On the other hand if a concern is the outcome of a merger, amalgamation or combination, there may be a great amount of decentralisation. If a company is working on a decentralised pattern it will be run in the same way

even on its acquisition. So the growth history of a concern influences the degree of delegation.

2. **Assignment of duties:** The element of delegation is linked to the availability of subordinate managers. If sufficient persons are available who can take responsibility then delegation can easily be done. Generally, managers complain that sufficient subordinate managers are not available who can be assigned important duties. Unless subordinates are delegated the powers they will not learn the art of management. With additional experience and training their judgement would be improved and they will become more capable subordinates. Many large firms push decision-making to the lower ranks of the organisation for the purpose of developing and training managerial manpower. A subordinate may be given small powers in the beginning. As he develops his managerial capabilities he can be assigned more important work. One thing should be clear that unless otherwise powers are delegated to lower levels, the concern will not be able to develop subordinate managers. The delegation process should be continually pursued so that people are trained to undertake more responsibilities.

3. **Importance and Costliness of Decisions:** The importance and costliness of decisions greatly influences the degree of delegation. Generally speaking, the costlier and more important the decision, the greater the probability of its being made at the upper level of the managerial hierarchy. Decision-making also requires various facts and figures about the issue. A manager will ensure that he gets all required information for deciding the issue. This type of information is easily available at higher levels of management. A manager knows that he can delegate authority and not responsibility. Some decisions can influence the whole organisation. Any wrong decision on such important matters can damage the enterprise beyond control.

   Such decisions are taken at higher level because these persons have the past experience of deciding such things. In a manager's career he should first be given authority to take decisions which are not too costly so that he is able to learn from his experience.

4. **Size of the Enterprise:** The extent of delegation is linked to the size of the enterprise. In a large unit more decision making is needed at various levels of management. The problems of communication and co-ordination often arise in such units. If decision-making is closer to the place of action it will save time, paper work is reduced, misunderstandings in communication can largely be eliminated. There is a tendency to decentralise in big units for avoiding many difficulties.

5. **Available Controls:** A manager delegating authority wants to be sure that it is used in accordance with his intentions and the general objectives of the organisation. In order to achieve this there must be control devices. Generally, managers hesitate to delegate due to the reason that they do not know how to control. They have a feeling that it takes more time to exercise control than exercising the authority themselves. It will be better to set up some control devices. The better the control devices, the more will be the delegation of authority.

6. **Types of Enterprise:** The degree of delegation of authority may also be influenced by the type of enterprise. If the enterprise is in an industry which is rapidly expanding, as in the electronic field, top management will have to delegate otherwise it will be over burdened with many decisions. Decentralisation of authority will take place even if the subordinate managers do not have adequate experience to exercise authority. Management should make guidelines for subordinate managers for taking proper decision.

   If the enterprise operates in a static industry then all decision-making is done at the central level. In case of banking and insurance the growth is slow and decision-making remains at the top. So delegation of authority depends upon the nature of the enterprise.

7. **Environmental Factors:** In addition to internal factors delegation may be influenced by internal factors too. These factors may be natural unions, government control over business and tax policies. Some large concerns have to deal with workers' unions at national level. All the negotiations are done and decisions are taken at national level. In such a situation the things are decided at head quarter level and are applicable at all levels. It, therefore, follows that within the area of labour relations, decision-making is decentralised. The same holds true as applied to government control over business, and tax laws.

## Difference between Decentralisation and Delegation

The words decentralisation and delegation appear to be interchangeable but it is not so. Even though both involve dispersal of authority but decentralisation is an extension of delegation.

Following are the points of distinction between the two:

| | Delegation | Decentralisation |
|---|---|---|
| 1. Nature | Delegation is individualistic. It involves two persons, superiors and subordinates. | Decentralisation is totalistic in nature. It involves delegation from top management to the department or divisional level. |
| 2. Control | Control rests with the delegator or superior. | In this system top management exercises minimum control. All powers are given to concerned departments or divisions. |
| 3. Need | Delegation is essential to get things done by others. Unless otherwise authority is delegated it will be difficult to assign responsibility. | Decentralisation is optional because it is the philosophy of management. Top management may or may not disperse authority. |
| 4. Responsibility | In delegation, responsibility remains with the delegator. He can delegate authority and not responsibility. | In decentralisation, head of the department is responsible for all activities under him. He is required to show better performance of the whole department. |

## Matrix Organization

Matrix organization structure is the combination of two complementary structures—project structure and functional structure. Project organization structure is the structure in which divisions are created on the basis of projects undertaken by an organization at a particular time. On completion of a project, the concerned division is abolished and its resources are allocated to other projects. Project organization structure is created for completing projects of large size which take sufficiently long time. Matrix organization structure is also created for completing projects but size of these projects is much smaller with shorter time duration.

### *Advantages of Matrix Organization Structure*

As compared to functional and divisional organization structures, matrix organization structure is of comparatively recent origin but its use has spread in various fields, including educational institutions which undertake multidisciplinary projects. In fact, matrix structure has been evolved to overcome the limitations of traditional hierarchical organization structures (functional and divisional). It has the following advantages:

1. Matrix organization structure focuses on resources of each project, permitting better planning and control to meet the project deadline. In project execution, time is of prime importance and, therefore, it should be completed within the specified time. However, since the organization cannot create many project divisions, matrix serves the purpose adequately.
2. It is quite flexible structure as compared to traditional hierarchical structures. Therefore, it can work very well in dynamic environment by absorbing the inevitable events that may occur as work progresses on projects.
3. It emphasizes professional competence by elaborating authority of knowledge rather than authority of position, this type of internal environment in the organization provides personnel to develop and test their professional competence and widen their scope to contribute maximum in the organization.
4. It relieves top management for taking long-term course of actions so that the organization can design its strategies suitable to environmental needs.

# COORDINATION

## Meaning

Coordination is concerned with harmonious and unified action directed toward a common objective. It ensures that all groups and persons work efficiently, economically and in harmony. Coordination requires effective channels of communication. Person to person communication is most effective for co-ordination. Co-ordination is undertaken at every level of management.

## Definition

According to **Henry Fayol,** "To Coordinate is to harmonise all the activities of a person in order to facilitate its working and its success".

According to **George Terry,** "Co-ordination deals with the task of blending efforts is order to ensure successful attainment of an objective. It is accomplished by means of planning organising, actuating, and controlling.

According to **Neoman,** "Co-ordination is a part of all phases of administration and that it is not a separate and definite activity".

## Principles of Coordination

**Mary Parker Follett,** in her discussion, has stated the following important principles of coordination:

1. **Principle of Direct Contract:** Miss Follett believes that co-ordination can be achieved more easily by direct interpersonal horizontal relationships and direct personal communications, which bring out agreement on methods, actions, and ultimate

achievement. The possibilities of conflict and misunderstanding always remain. These can be removed or sorted out by direct contact and proper communication among various persons. Direct contact even helps in creating mutual goodwill which may help in proper co-ordination.

2. **Principle of Early Beginning:** Co-ordination can be achieved more readily in the early stages of planning and policy-making. If the policies are in execution stage then co-ordination may become difficult. If the plans are executed without proper co-ordination then results may be disastrous. "If the head of the production department, while he is forming his policy, meets and discusses with the other heads, the question involved a successful co-ordination is far more likely to be achieved, that is, you cannot, with the greatest degree of success for your undertaking, make policy forming and policy adjusting two separate processes." Achieving co-ordination in the early stages of planning and policy making is essential.
3. **Principle of Reciprocal Relationship:** All the factors in a situation are reciprocally related. The work of one person is dependent on that of the other, who in turn, may be dependent on some other. For instance, A works with B and he in turn works with C and D. The relationship of all the four will be reciprocal. In the absence of co-ordination among them the work of everyone will suffer. Similarly, other factors like materials, finance, sales, production will be dependent upon one another. When members in an organisation realise that all factors are reciprocally related then co-ordination becomes easy.
4. **Principle of Continuity:** As the fourth principle of co-ordination, **Mary Follett** states that coordination is a continuing process and something which must go on all the time. It is a managerial process which is exercised every time so that the working is smooth and uninterrupted. It is not like reconciling conflicts as and when they arise. Co-ordination cannot be left to a sheer chance but management should make constant efforts to achieve it. There is a constant need for co-ordination in a business.

## Importance of Coordination

Co-ordination is essential at every level of management. It is a process of group efforts for achieving business, goals. The quality of management will depend upon the efficiency achieved in co-ordination. According to **Chester Barnard,** "the quality of co-ordination is the crucial factor in the survival of organisation." Smooth working and achievement of organisational goals will depend upon sound co-ordination.

The important benefits of coordination are stated as follows:

1. **Better Personnel Relations:** Management and staff create cordial human relations through coordination. The points of dispute or conflict among different persons, between line and staff, etc. can be settled by mutual discussions. Better personal relations are also helpful in increasing the morale of employees which ultimately leads to job satisfaction. The results of co-ordinated group efforts will be much better than the sum results of different individuals. The members will willingly and wholeheartedly contribute towards the success of the enterprise. Therefore, co-ordination is necessary to bring unity of action in the organisation.
2. **Unity of Direction:** Co-ordination helps in creating unity of direction. Different segments of the business may set different goals. The co-ordination process helps in synchronising various efforts. It motivates various employees to view their work from the standpoint of the business. In the absence of co-ordination, there may be conflicting goals and everybody may perceive the objectives in a different way. This will create confusion and chaos in the organisation. Coordination will help in reconciling conflicting views.
3. **Essential for Management:** The increase in the size of organisation has brought a number of complexities. There is a degree of specialisation, division of labour and large number of individuals. Everybody has his own personality traits and ways of working. It is essential to synchronise the work of all persons in the organisation. Co-ordination helps in bringing unity of action for achieving business goals.
4. **Efficiency and Economy:** Co-ordination promotes efficiency and economy in the organisation. By co-ordinating activities the efficiency is brought in the working. It also helps in avoiding delays and eliminating duplication of efforts. This will result in saving of time and energy, thus bringing economy to the business.
5. **Helpful in Developing and Retaining of Personnel:** Co-ordination by synchronising various activities, helps in promoting team spirit among organisational personnel. There will be no conflict or confusion in division of work and everybody will try to improve his own performance. This helps in developing potentialities of every person in the organisation. Coordination also helps in promoting job satisfaction among employees by giving them personal contentment. The concern will be able to retain the services of good employees.

# CONTROLLING

## Meaning

Controlling is an important function of management. It is the process that measures current performance and guides it towards some predetermined objectives. Under primitive management, control was undertaken only when something went wrong and the objectives of control was to reprimand the person responsible for these events and take action against him. The modern concept of control envisages a system that not only provides a historical record of what has happened to the business as a whole but also pinpoints the reasons why it has happened and provides data that enable the manager to take corrective steps, if he finds he is on the wrong track. Therefore, there is no intention to punish the person for wrongdoing, but to find out the deviations between the actual performance and the standard performance and to take steps to prevent such variances in future.

The concept of control is often confused with lack of freedom. The opposite of control is not freedom but chaos or anarchy. Control is fully consistent with freedom. In fact, they are interdependent. Without control, freedom cannot be sustained for long. Without freedom, control becomes ineffective. Both freedom and accountability are embedded in the concept of control.

## Definitions of Controlling

Control is the process through which managers assure that actual activities conform to planned activities. According to **Breach**—"Control is checking current performance against predetermined standards contained in the plans, with a view to ensuring adequate progress and satisfactory performance."

According to **George R Terry**—"Controlling is determining what is being accomplished *i.e.,* evaluating the performance and if necessary, applying corrective measures so that the performance takes place according to plans."

According to **Billy E Goetz**—"Management control seeks to compel events to conform plans".

According to **Robert N Anthony**—"Management control is the process by which managers assure that resources are obtained and used effectively and efficiently."

In the words of **Koontz and O'Donnell**—"Managerial control implies measurement of accomplishment against the standard and the correction of deviations to assure attainment of objectives according to plans."

In the words of **Haynes and Massie**—"Fundamentally, control is any process that guides activity towards some predetermined goal. The essence of the concept is in determining whether the activity is achieving the desired results".

In the words of **J.L. Massie**—"Control is the process that measures current performance and guides it towards some predetermined goals."

In the words of **Henry Fayol**—"Control consists in verifying whether everything occurs in conformity with the plan adopted, the instructions issued and the principles established. Its object is to find out the weakness and errors in order to rectify them and prevent recurrence. It operates on everything, *i.e.,* things, people and actions".

From the above definitions it is clear that the managerial function of control consists in a comparison of the actual performance with the planned performance with the object of discovering whether all is going on well according to plans and if not why. Remedial action arising from a study of deviations of the actual performance with the standard or planned performance will serve to correct the plans and make suitable changes. Controlling is the nature of follow-up to the other three fundamental functions of management. There can, in fact, be not controlling without previous planning, organising and directing. Controlling cannot take place in a vacuum.

## Characteristics of Controlling

Managerial control has certain characteristic feature. They are:

1. Control is the function of every manager. Managers at all levels have to perform this function to contribute to the achievement of organisational objectives.
2. Control leads to appraisal of past activities. The deviations in the past are revealed by the control process. Corrective actions can be initiated accordingly.
3. Control is linked with future, as past cannot be controlled. It should anticipate possible deviations and to think of corrective action for the control of such deviations in the future. It is usually preventive as presence of control system tends to minimize wastages, losses and deviations from standards.
4. Control is concerned with setting standards, measurement of actual performance, comparison of actual performance with predetermined standards and bringing to light the variations between the actual performance and the standard performance.
5. Control implies taking corrective measures. The object in checking the variations or Notes deviations is to rectify them and prevent their recurrence. It is only action which adjusts performance to predetermined standards whenever deviations occur.
6. Control can be exercised only with reference to and or the basis of plans. To quote **Mary Gushing Niles**—"Whereas planning sets the course, control observes deviations from the course or to an appropriately changed one".

7. To some people, control is opposite of freedom. This is not true. Control is based on facts and figures. Its purpose is to achieve and maintain acceptable productivity from all resources of an enterprise. Therefore, control aims at results and not at persons. It is for correcting a situation, and not for reprimanding persons.
8. Information or feedback is the guide to control. The feedback is helpful to the manager to determine how far the operations are proceeding in conformity with plans and standards, and where remedial action is called for.
9. Control involves continuous review of standards of performance and results in corrective action which may lead to change in the performance of other functions of management. This makes control a dynamic and flexible process.
10. Control is a continuous activity. It involves constant analysis of validity of standards, policies, procedures etc.

## Steps in Control Process

There are three basic steps in a control process:

A. Establishing standards.

B. Measuring and comparing actual results against standards.

C. Taking corrective action.

# CONTROL TECHNIQUES

## Meaning

A variety of tools and techniques have been used over the years to help managers control. The activities in their organization. Every management wants to ensure that the scarce resources at its disposal are effectively and productively utilised. To achieve this objective it has to devise a monitoring system which will keep the management informed about the implementation of its plans and policies. In case the plans are not properly implemented then variations in performance must come to the notice of management so that timely corrective measures are taken up. A control system should be devised to evaluate the performance of various segments of the enterprise.

There are two types of control techniques, which are as follows:

### *1. Traditional Control Techniques*

(*i*) Budgeting and Budgetary Control

(*ii*) Cost Control

(*iii*) Production Planning and Control

(*iv*) Inventory Control

(*v*) Break Even Analysis

(*vi*) Profit and Loss Control

(*vii*) Statistical Data Analysis

### *2. Modern Control Techniques*

(*i*) Return on Investment Control

(*ii*) Programme Evaluation and Review Technique (PERT)

(*iii*) Management Information System (MIS)

(*iv*) Management Audit

### *Mordern Control Techniques*

Following are the modern techniques of control which are commonly used at present:

1. **Return on Investment Control (ROI):** Profits are the measure of overall efficiency of a business. Profit earned in relation to the capital employed in a business is an important control device. If the rate of return on investment (shareholder's funds) is quite satisfactory, it will be taken as a yard-stick of good performance. The return on investment can be compared over a period of time as well as with that of other similar concerns. This comparison will show the Notes present performance in relation to earlier periods and also the level of achievement of the concern in comparison to other concerns.

   The return on investment is computed by dividing the operating net profit (before interest and tax) by the capital employed in the concern. The following formula is used for this purpose:

   **Return on Investment:** ROI is used to measure the overall efficiency of a concern. It reveals how well the resources of a concern are used, higher the return better are the results.

2. **Programme Evaluation and Review Technique (PERT):** Programme evaluation and review technique (PERT) was first developed as a management tool for coordination and early completion of Polaris Ballistic Missile Project in USA resulting in a reduction of 30 per cent time in project execution. A contemporary of PERT is CPM (Critical Path Method) and was developed in connection with maintenance and construction work. PERT is useful at several stages of project management starting from early planning stages when various alternative programmes are being considered to the scheduling phase, when time and resources schedules are laid out, to final stage in operation, when used as control device to measure actual versus planned progress. PERT uses 'network' as the basic tool of project management and is helpful in completing a project on schedule by co-ordinating different jobs involved in its completion.

3. **Management Information System (MIS):** Management information system (MIS) is an approach of providing timely, adequate and accurate information to the right person in the organisation which helps in taking right decisions. So MIS is a planned and organised approach to the transferring of intelligence within an organisation for better management. The information is furnished into useful quantums of knowledge in the form of reports. An effective system of MIS collects data from all possible sources. The information is properly processed and stored for use in future.

   **MIS is of two types:**

   (*i*) Management operating system meant for meeting the information needs of lower and middle level management. The information supplied generally relates to operations of the business.

   (*ii*) Management reporting system which supplies information to top level management for decision-making. The information is presented in a way which enables management to take quick decisions.

   An MIS should be so designed which helps management in exercising effective control over all aspects of the organisation.

4. **Management Audit:** Management audit is an investigation by an independent organization to find out whether the management is carried out most effectively or not. In case there are drawbacks at any level then recommendations should be given to improve managerial efficiency. In the words of **Leslie R. Howard,** "Management audit is an investigation of a business from the highest level downward in order to ascertain whether sound management prevails throughout, thus facilitating the most effective relationship with the outside world and the most efficient organisation and smooth running internally."

## MANAGEMENT BY OBJECTIVES (MBO)

### Meaning

MBO provides for a regular review of performance. The objectives of MBO provide guidelines for appropriate system and procedures. MBO is one of the techniques by which executives can improve organizational performance and effectiveness. The idea of MBO was contributed by Donaldson Brown and Alfred Sloan in 1920s and Edward Hagenin in 1930s. (Peter Drucker, known as father of MBO technique, coined this term in 1954. Some other authorities on the subject are Charles L. Hughes, Goal Setting (American Management Association, 1965); Dale D. Me Conkey, How to Manage by Results (American Management Association, 1967); George S. Ordiornc, Management by Objectives (Pitman, 1965); W.J. Reddin, Effective Management by Objectives (Me Graw-Hill, 1971).

### Definition of MBO

According to **George S. Odirone,** "The system of management by objectives can be described as a process whereby the superior and subordinate managers of an organisation jointly identify its common goals, define each individual's major areas of responsibility in terms of results expected of him, and use these measures as guides for operating the unit and assessing the contribution of each of its members."

According to **Koontz and Weihrich,** "Management by objectives is a comprehensive managerial system that integrates many key managerial activities in a systematic manner and that is consciously directed toward the effective and efficient achievement of organisational and individual objectives.

**S.K. Chakravarty** defines it as. "MBO is a result-centered, non-specialist, operational managerial process for the effective utilisation of material, physical, and human resources of the organisation by integrating the individual with the organisation and organisation with the environment."

According to **Terry and Franklin,** "A managerial objective is the intended goal that prescribes definite scope and suggests direction to the planning efforts of a manager." This definition states four aspects of management by objectives *i.e.,* goal, scope, definiteness, direction. From managerial point of view the target to be achieved should be identified and clear. The scope of the goals should be stated in the prescribed boundaries. The goal should also state definiteness, a vague goal will create more confusion and has no managerial value.

**Pros Reddin** says that MBO is the establishment of effectiveness areas and effectiveness standards for management positions and as produce conversion of all these into measurable time sound objectives linked vertional, and horizontally with future planning".

## STAFFING

Every organization requires a number of persons for taking up different positions. The positions are created through the process of organization and their occupants help in achieving the business objectives. The persons occupying different positions should have the ability to meet their requirements. Staffing basically involves matching jobs and individuals. It may be defined as filling and keeping filled positions in the organization structure. This may require functions like manpower planning, recruitment, selection, training, development, performance appraisal, transfers, promotions etc. It is clear that staffing must be closely linked to organizing, that is, the setting up of intentional structures of roles and positions. Staffing involves making people suitable to jobs while organizing involves creation of job. Staffing is considered to be the management of managers while personnel management involves plans, policies and procedures for operative positions. It is taken to be a separate function of management. Staffing involves specialized knowledge and approach and allows more emphasis on human resource and its proper selection, training and development. Staffing refers to the managerial function of attracting, acquiring, activating, developing and maintaining human resources for achieving organizational goals efficiently.

## Definitions

According to **McFarland,** "Staffing is the function by which managers build an organizational through the recruitment, selection and development of individuals as capable employees."

According to **Koontz and O'Donnell,** "The managerial function of staffing is defined as filling positions in the organization structure through identifying workforce requirements, inventorying the people available, recruitment, selection, placement, promotion, appraisal, compensation and training of needed people."

## Nature

1. Staffing is a basic function management.
2. It is concerned with human resource management in the organization.
3. Staffing function is performed continuously.
4. Every manager has to guide and train employees and also evaluate their performance on a continuous basis.
5. The main purpose of this function is to make optimum utilization of human resources and also to provide proper satisfaction to employees.
6. Staffing is performed by all managers.
7. In big concerns there is a separate personnel department to deal with this function, but even here this department advises line managers regarding different aspects of human resources.
8. Since staffing deals with human beings who have their own needs, emotions and aspirations, this function is different from other managerial function.

## Process

The purpose of staffing is to employ most suitable and competent persons as per the requirements of the organization. With this aim in view the following staff process is followed:

1. **Estimating manpower needs:** The first thing in staffing process is to estimate manpower needs. These needs are influenced by the type and size of the organization. Total manpower requirements are properly assessed. The requirements for human beings are compared with that of the persons already available in the organization.
2. **Recruitment and selection of staff:** Recruitment is the process of searching prospective employees and persuading them to apply in the organization. Selection is the procedure of spotting most suitable candidates out of those who are interested to get employment in the enterprise. The purpose of recruitment and selection is to employing right man for the right job.
3. **Training and development:** Training is meant to improve the skill and knowledge of employees. It is beneficial to both employer and employees. A well trained worker improves his efficiency. A formal training will avoid the risk of trial and error and will also minimize the cost and wastage involved in training. Development refers to the training of managerial staff. Through development, managerial staff does not increase its capabilities to perform the present work but also enhances their ability to meet challenges in future.
4. **Promotion and transfer:** Employees are promoted to higher ranks on the basis of their merit and seniority. Staffing also involves transfer of persons from one job to another, from one place to another place to another on the basis of their ability, competence and ability.
5. **Remuneration:** Remuneration is paid for the services of labour. Employee motivation mainly depends upon the wage and salary structure prevalent in an organization. Employees should be paid fair remuneration so that they feel encouraged to contribute maximum in their efforts.
6. **Performance appraisal:** After selecting and training an employer for a particular job, management would like to see how he performs high work. Performance appraisal is a systematic evaluation of employees contribution to the organization in performance of their jobs. Not only qualities but deficiencies are also evaluated to improve the performance of employees.

# DIRECTING

Management is the art of getting things done through others. One of the main functions of a manager is to direct subordinates effectively. Directing is concerned with carrying out the desired plans. It initiates organised and planned action and ensures effective performance by subordinates towards the accomplishment of group activities. Direction is called management in action.

## Definitions

According to **Koontz and O'Donnell,** "Directing is the interpersonal aspect of managing by which subordinates are led to understand and contribute effectively and efficiently to the attainment of enterprise's objectives."

According to **Urwick and Breach,** "Directing is the guidance, the inspiration, the leadership of those men and women that constitute the real core of the responsibilities of management."

According to **Haimann,** "Directing consists of the process and techniques utilizing in issuing instructions and making certain that operations are carried out as originally planned."

## Principles of effective direction

1. **Harmony objectives:** It is an essential function of management to make the people realize the objectives of the group and direct their efforts towards the achievement of their objectives. The principle implies harmony of personal interest and common interest.
2. **Unity of command:** This principle states that one person should receive orders from only one superior, in other words, one person should be accountable to only one boss. In the absence of unity of command, the authority is undermined, discipline weakened, loyalty divided and confusion and delays are caused.
3. **Unity of direction:** To have effective direction, there should be one head and one plan for a group of activities having the same objectives. In other words, each group of activities having the same objectives must have one plan of action and must be under the control of one supervisor.
4. **Direct supervision:** The directing function of management becomes more effective if the superior maintains direct personal contact with is subordinates. Direct supervision infuses a sense of participation among subordinates that encourages them to put in their best to achieve the organizational goals and develop an effective system of feed-back of information.
5. **Participative or democratic management:** The function of directing becomes more effective if participative or democratic style of management is followed. According to this principle, the superior must act according to the manual consent and the decisions reached after consulting the subordinates.
6. **Effective communication:** To have effective direction, it is very essential to have an effective communication system which provides for free flow of ideas, information, suggestions, complaints and grievances.
7. **Follow-up:** In order to make direction effective, a manager has to continuously direct, guide, motivate and lead his subordinates. A manager has not only to issue orders and instructions but also to follow-up the performance so as to ensure that work is being performed as desired.

## Importance of Direction

1. **Initiates action:** Direction is required to initiative action. The function of planning, organizing, staffing etc., will be taken up only when directly is given to initiate them. Decision starts the actual work for achieving enterprise objectives.
2. **Improves efficiency:** A manager tries to get maximum work from his subordinates. This will be possible only through motivation and leadership and these techniques are a part of direction.
3. **Ensures co-ordination:** Direction helps in ensuring mutual understanding and team work. The individual efforts are directed in such a way that personal performances help in achieving enterprise objectives.
4. **Helpful in implementing changes:** A business operates in a changing environment. New situations develop every now and then. A proper system of motivation will help employees in taking up new challenges.
5. **Provides stability:** Effective leadership, supervision and motivation will help in the smooth growth of an enterprise. A growing concern will provide stability to its activities.
6. **Motivation:** Motivation is an important element of direction. Motivation is a factor which encourages persons to give their best performance and help in achieving enterprise goals. A strong positive motivation will enable the increased output of employees. A key element in direction is motivation.
7. **Supervision:** Direction involves giving instructions to employees for undertaking some work. In order to see whether employees are doing the things as per targets or not there is a need for supervision. In supervision all the activities of the employees are controlled and efforts are made to ensure proper achievement of targets.
8. **Co-ordination:** Direction will be effective only when there is a proper co-ordination. In direction, different persons are asked to perform specific tasks. In order to see that efforts of every employee are in the direction of achieving organizational goals there is a need of co-ordinate various activities.

●●●

# Marketing Management

## DEFINITION OF MARKETING

Numerous definitions were offered for marketing by different authors. Some of the definitions are as follows:

1. "Marketing is the process that seeks to influence voluntary exchange transactions between a customer and a marketer."

   ***—William G. Zikmund and Michael D'Amico***

2. "Marketing is the process of discovering and translating consumer needs and wants into products and services, creating demand for these products and services and then in turn expanding this demand."

   ***—H.L. Hansen***

3. "Marketing is the business process by which products are matched with markets and through which transfer of ownership are affected."

   ***—Edward W. Cundiff***

4. "Marketing consists of the performance of business activities that direct the flow of goods and services from producers or suppliers to consumers or endusers."

   ***—American Marketing Association***

5. "Marketing is a societal process by which individuals and groups obtain what they need and want through creating, offering and freely exchanging products and services of value with others."

   ***—Philip Kotler***

6. "Marketing is the performance of activities that seek to accomplish an organizations objectives by anticipating customer or client needs and directing the flow of need satisfying goods and services from producer to customer or client."

   ***—William D. Perreault and E. Jerome McCarthy***

## MARKETING CONCEPTS

**Philip Kotler** has shown five competing concepts for carrying out marketing activity in any organisation:

1. **The Production Concept:** The philosophy holds that high production efficiency and wide distribution coverage would sell the product offered to the market. The high production efficiency means that the input-output ratio should be favourable. It will lead to economies of scale and decline in cost per unit. Thus, the concept holds that customer favours products with low offered price and products are easily available. This orientation of the organisation is mostly practised in situations where demand exceeds supply or product cost is high that can be brought down by mass production. The market situation in most of the developing countries is such that while demand for products exists, the products are not available.

   Is marketing applicable in situations where demand exceeds supply for most of the products and at most of the times? The answer is **yes**. Marketing activities can still be applied in such market situations. For example, amusement parks are very few in India. There is a lot of demand for such parks. What can be done under such a situation?

   1. Discourage demand on certain days of the week in which there is overcrowding.
   2. Raise entry and riding charges.
   3. Reduce promotion and services.
   4. Provide alternative amusement parks/places/entertainment channels to divert them (i.e., give wider customer choice).

   In other words, the solution lies in demarketing, where the purpose is not to destroy demand but reduce it to desired levels. Thus, we see that the production concept is applicable in situations where demand exceeds supply. In practice, production concept is followed by many factory owners (by count of number of units produced), government agencies like unemployment offices, telephone operators (number of calls attended per day), Traffic Inspectors (number of challans), etc. However, number of counts adds the element of impersonality and poor product or service quality and delivery. This is because the implementation of the production concept forces the field staff to behave mechanically with the target of achieving relevant number in mind.

2. **The Product Concept:** The firms following this philosophy believe that by making superior products and improving their quality over a period of time,

they will be able to attract more customers. The underlying assumption is that customer favours quality, performance and innovative features, etc. The buyer will admire such products. Given the product concept, superior products are perhaps always welcomed by the customer.

3. **The Selling Concept:** This refers to the situation where there is aggressive selling and associated promotional efforts. The consideration of this philosophy is customer buying initiative and resistance. The assumption is that customer, if left alone, would not buy enough of the company's product. This sort of customer attitude is mostly found for unsought goods like surgical goods, insurance, videophone, etc. Here hard-sell takes place. When used for sought goods like scooters, televisions, refrigerators, the easy sale takes place.
4. **The Marketing Concept:** Consumer-oriented marketing has given rise to a new philosophy in business known as 'marketing concept'. The marketing concept emphasizes the determination of the requirements of potential customers and supplying products to satisfy their requirements. Marketing should be viewed as an integrated process of identification, assessment and satisfaction of human wants. Determination of wants of the customers takes precedence over production. In other words, product is developed and produced to satisfy the needs of the customers. Thus, the emphasis is on selling satisfaction and not merely on selling goods.
5. **The Societal Marketing Concept:** Once again depending on **Philip Kotler** we may say that "the societal marketing concept holds that the organisations tasks is to determine the needs, wants, and interests of target markets and to deliver the desired satisfaction more effectively and efficiently than competitors in a way that preserves or enhances the customers and society's well-being".

## Difference between Marketing Concept and Selling Concept

The modern marketing concept is a course of business thinking, while marketing is a process or a course of business action. As shown in the following figure, marketing concept focuses on customers for earning profits through customers satisfaction and follows integrated marketing. But traditional marketing or selling focused on products to earn profits through increased sales volume and followed sales promotion techniques for this purpose. Thus, marketing concept makes a sharp distinction between marketing and selling.

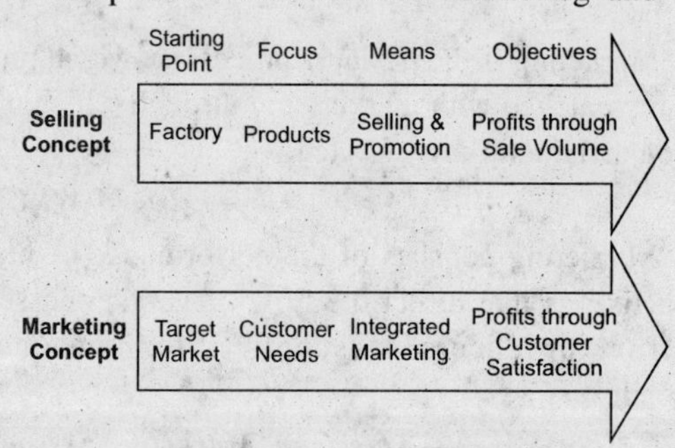


**Fig.** *Selling vs. Marketing*

**Table:** *Difference between Marketing and Selling*

| | Marketing | Selling |
|---|---|---|
| 1. | Marketing starts with customer needs and takes outside-in view of the market. | Selling starts with factory and takes inside-out view of the market. |
| 2. | Marketing focuses on customer's needs of want-satisfying products. | Selling focuses on seller's needs of converting his products into cash. |
| 3. | Emphasis is given on product planning and developments to match products with the market. | Emphasis is placed on sale of products already produced. |
| 4. | Customer is treated as a king. He is given supreme importance. | Seller/product enjoys supreme importance. |
| 5. | Marketing aims at profits through customer satisfaction. | Selling aims at profits through sales volume. |
| 6. | The principle of caveat vendor (let the seller beware) is followed. | The principle of caveat emptor (let the buyer beware) is followed. |
| 7. | Integrated approach to marketing is practised. | Fragmented approach to selling is practised. |

## APPROACHES TO THE STUDY OF MARKETING

There are different methods for viewing a subject with different perspectives. These are listed below:

1. **Product or Commodity Approach:** This approach undertakes the study of marketing on the basis of a commodity. The marketing situation of each product is studied under the following heads: sources and conditions of supply, marketing organisations and

policies, involvement of different middlemen, characteristics and the extent of the market of the product, etc. For example, when one studies the marketing of cotton, one will begin with examining the sources of supply, nature and volume of demand, the purpose for which it is required, how it is transported, the problem of storage, standardisation, packing, branding, etc. This approach is termed as 'descriptive approach' and that itself is claimed to be its advantage. In this method, the commodity serves as a focus around which organisational, institutional and managerial aspects of marketing are studied.

This approach is criticised for being repetitive and time-consuming since the emphasis is on products. The classification of products tends to create another problem. In spite of these defects, it is capable of giving a broad introductory view of marketing if it is combined with an institutional approach. For example, the study of Industrial Marketing is based on this approach.

2. **Institutional Approach:** Under this approach, the description and analysis of different institutions engaged in marketing are undertaken. It pays special attention to the problems and operations of each type of marketing institutions. The institutions normally include producers, wholesalers, agents, retailers and facilitating institutions engaged in activities such as transportation, warehousing, etc. These institutions, individually, are the 'cells' of the marketing body; and in their inter-relationships 'cells' constitute the functional part of marketing body. The activities performed by each institution form part of the whole area of marketing.

   The serious defect of this method as that it leaves one with an inadequate understanding of marketing. The approach has failed to bring out effectively the inter-relations of all the institutions.

3. **Functional Approach:** The credit for designing this approach goes to A.W. Shaw, who enumerated the functions of middlemen as follows: sharing the risk; transporting the goods; financing the operations; selling (communication of ideas about the goods); and assembling, assorting and re-shipping. Later on, I.D.H. Weld introduced some notable changes in the concept by pointing out that the above functions are not always performed by middlemen but also partly by producers and partly by consumers.

   A marketing function is a major specialised activity performed in marketing. The functional approach, therefore, splits down the field of marketing into a few functions. The purpose of such a split-up is to enable one to separate the essential from the non-essential elements. This method analyses in detail the specific functions of marketing such as buying, selling, transportation, storage, standardisation, grading, financing, risk-taking and marketing research, etc.

   But this approach is also not free from defects. *First*, an undue emphasis on functions of marketing does not permit one to know how these functions are applied in specific business operations. *Secondly*, the marketing functions are so numerous that it is difficult to eliminate the unnecessary from the necessary functions. *Finally*, this approach also is repetitive to some extent.

4. **Decision-making or Management Approach:** This approach is of recent origin. It combines certain features of the other three approaches. It is based on the fact that marketing is purely a management function. The changes in marketing are mainly due to two factors: 'controllables' and 'uncontrollables'. The uncontrollable factors include economic, sociological and political forces. These may tend to cause changes in marketing, which are beyond the control of the business firm. The controllables mean those marketing forces which are well under the control of the firm. These include adjustment in prices, advertising, personal selling, etc. Both, these factors are of great importance to the marketing decision maker.

   This approach lays emphasis on the application side of marketing problems. Therefore, it is incapable of giving an overall idea about the subject theoretically.

5. **Legal Approach:** Though fundamental and practical, this approach is a very narrow one. It concentrates only on one aspect, *i.e.,* the effect of transfer of title in a legal way. Regulatory aspects alone are studied under this approach. Under the Indian context, however, this approach has got some significance. There are numerous rules passed in our country which regulate or, to a large extent, control marketing activities. For example, Common Carriers Act, Sale of Goods Act, etc.

6. **Economic Approach:** In the economic approach, marketing is considered in a narrow sense, because the economist is concerned only with the problems of value, demand and price. It is true that value and price, and demand and supply factors are important in market mechanism. But such an approach alone is incapable of giving the whole idea of marketing.

7. **System Approach:** This is a variation or, more aptly, an advancement of the management approach. Broadly defined, the system is an organized body of

independent parts (or "sub-system") that have separate but identifiable areas of operation. For instance, business as a whole is a body, but is composed of separate functional areas, such as, production, engineering, personnel, marketing, etc. These functions could be split down further into still smaller parts (sub-sub-systems). Accordingly marketing has product planning, pricing, promotion, distribution, etc. as sub-sub-systems. Each of these functions is independent but they are interdependent also. They are continually interacting to achieve the aim of the system as a whole.

## CORE MARKETING CONCEPT

The important or core marketing concepts are shown in figure. They consist of needs, wants, and demands; marketing offers (products, services, and experiences); value and satisfaction; exchanges, transactions, and relationships; and markets. All these core marketing concepts are linked to one another, with each concept building on the one before it.

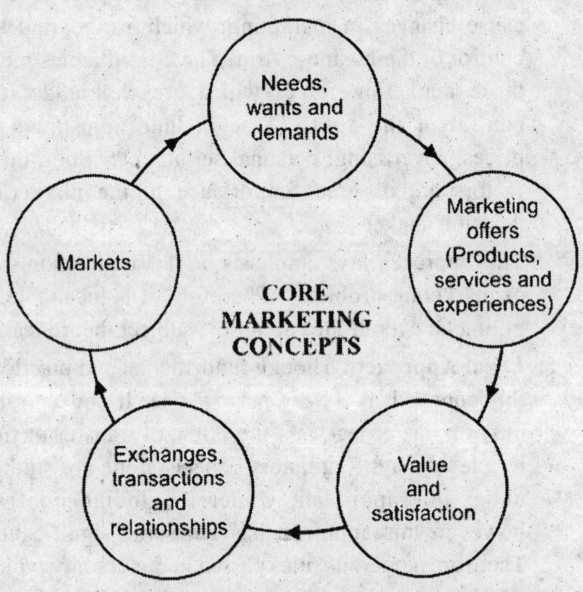


**Fig.** *Core Marketing Concepts*

### Needs

The concept of human needs is the fundamental concept underlying all marketing activities. Human needs are states of felt deprivation. They are biogenic in origin and include physiological needs for food, clothing, warmth, shelter and safety. Social needs are craving for belonging and affection. Knowledge and self-expression are the other individual needs of human beings. All these needs are basic requirements of any individual, and are not a creation by marketing people.

### Wants

Wants are the forms human needs take as they are shaped by culture and individual personality characteristics. When an American needs food, he may want a McDonald burger, or steak, French fries, and a Coke; whereas, if an Indian needs food, he may want a dosa, chapattis or rice, and coffee or tea. Wants are shaped by the society in which one lives and are described in terms of products that will satisfy needs. The only other difference between needs and wants is that while human needs are limited, wants are unlimited.

### Demand

When human wants are backed by purchasing power and willingness to buy, they become demands. Based on their needs, wants and buying capacity, consumers ask for or demand products which they feel will give them maximum value and satisfaction. Most of the marketing companies take pains to study and understand their customers' needs, wants and demands, based on which they plan their strategies for products and promotions. Consumer behaviour studies and consumer research are primarily for identifying and analyzing consumer needs, wants and the related buying behaviour.

***Example:*** Need, Want and Demand of an MBA Student

**Need:** Transportation - The MBA student has to reach college in time. Buses are not dependable.

**Want:** The student wants a motorcycle, which looks grand, has many latest features and is dependable. E.g. Bajaj or Honda.

**Demand:** Purchasing power is provided by the boy's father, who also has the willingness to buy the bike, which his son wants.

### *Maslow's Hierarchy of Needs*

Abraham Maslow, a leading psychologist, sought to explain why people are driven by particular needs at particular times.

Why does a scientist spend long hours at work in the laboratory, forgoing all other activities and pleasures?

Why does an athlete endure months of painful training in preparation for the Olympics?

Why does one person devote all efforts toward amassing a fortune?

Obviously, biological needs cannot account for the diversity and complexity of human behaviour. Maslow proposed an interesting way of classifying human motives. He assumed a hierarchy of motives ascending from the basic biological needs to more complex psychological motives that become important only after the more basic needs have been satisfied. (*See* fig.)

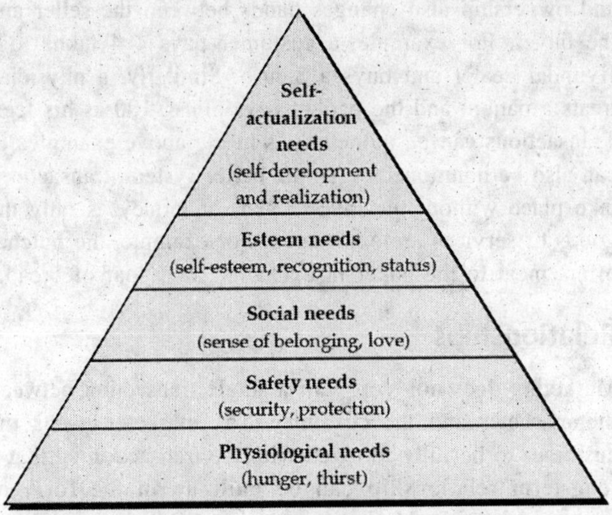


**Fig.** *Maslow's Hierarchy of needs*

- **Physiological Needs:** These are the first and foremost basic level of human needs. These needs, which are required to sustain biological life, include food, water, air, shelter, clothing, sex - all biogenic needs or primary needs. For the man who is extremely hungry, no other interest exists but food.
- **Safety Needs:** After the first level of need is satisfied, safety and security needs become the driving force behind an individual's behaviour. Health, healthcare, savings accounts, insurance policies, education and professional or vocational training satisfy the need for security.
- **Social Needs:** The third level of Maslow's hierarchy includes such needs as love, affection, belonging, and acceptance. People seek warm and satisfying human relationships with other people in the society and are motivated by love for their families.
- **Esteem Needs:** When social needs are more or less satisfied, the fourth level becomes operative. This level is concerned with esteem or egoistic needs. Need for self-acceptance, self-esteem, success, independence, and personal satisfaction with a job well done reflect esteem needs. In addition, status, reputation, and recognition from others (show off one's success) reflect egoistic needs.
- **Need for Self-Actualisation:** This need refers to the individual's desire to fulfil his or her potential (self-fulfilment)—to become everything he or she is capable of becoming. Desire to become an Olympic star, or leading singer or artist, a research scientist, a Chief Executive Officer in an MNC, etc., are examples of self-actualisation.

In the marketing context, buyer's needs are normally biogenic or physiological, and psychogenic or psychological. When they are aroused to a sufficient level of intensity, they become motives, urging the buyer to seek satisfaction through buying and using a product or service. Maslow's hierarchy of needs included physiological needs, safety needs, social needs, esteem needs and self-actualisation needs. According to Maslow, needs are satisfied according to their hierarchical priority.

The needs at one level must be at least partially satisfied before those at the next level become important motives for action. When food and safety are difficult to obtain, the satisfaction of these needs will dominate a person's actions and the motives will have little significance. Only when the satisfaction of the basic needs is easy will the individual have the time and energy for aesthetic and intellectual interests. Artistic and scientific endeavours do not flourish in societies where people must struggle for food, shelter and safety. Some buyer behaviour will be influenced by all the above-mentioned motives. Maslow's theory will help marketing people to understand how various products fit into the needs, wants, goals and lives of consumers. The hierarchy model offers a highly useful framework for marketers trying to develop appropriate advertising appeals for their products. It enables marketers to focus their advertising appeals on a need level that is likely to be shared by a large segment of the target audience. It also facilitates need-based product positioning or repositioning. The need hierarchy is often used as the basis for market segmentation with specific advertising appeals directed to one or more need-segment level.

## Marketing Offers

Marketing offers are combinations of products, services, information, or experiences offered to a market to satisfy a need or want. It is also called 'a value proposition', which is a set of benefits that marketing people promise to the consumers to satisfy their needs. The largest share of marketing offers consists of physical (tangible) products which include non-durable goods (fast moving consumer goods or FMCG) and consumer durables.

Marketing offers are not limited to physical products only. In addition to tangible products, marketing offers include services, activities or benefits offered for sale that are essentially intangible and do not result in the ownership of anything. Banking, airline, hotel, transportation, tourism and travel, consultancy, etc., are examples of such services. In addition, marketing offers also include other entities, such as persons, places, organizations, information and ideas.

## Customer Value

Consumers have a wide choice of products and services which promise satisfaction of a particular need. They normally decide on their choices based on their perceptions of the value and satisfaction that different products and services deliver, or offer. Customer value is the difference between the value the customer gains from buying and using a product and the cost of buying the product. They normally form expectations about the value of different marketing offers and buy accordingly. This involves the customers' mental process of judging the value of the product and is called customer perceived value. Customer expectations are based on past buying experiences, and the opinions of friends and family members.

The promises offered by marketers and the information about similar product offers of competitors also influence expectations.

The main task of marketing, therefore, becomes value-creation and value delivery. Marketing offers are value propositions promising benefits and value.

### Customer Satisfaction

Customer satisfaction with a purchase depends on how well the product's performance lives up to the customer's expectations. Customer satisfaction is a key influence on the future buying behaviour of the people. Satisfied customers will buy the product again and tell the others about their good buying experiences. Dissatisfied customers, on the other hand, switch to a competitor's products and also discourage others from buying the product. Marketers must be careful to set the right level of expectations. If they set expectations too low, they may satisfy those who buy but fail to attract enough customers. If they raise expectations too high, customers will be disappointed. Customer value and customer satisfaction are key building blocks for developing and managing customer relationships.

### Exchanges

Exchange is another core concept of marketing. It is the act of obtaining an object which one needs from another by offering some other thing in return. In the exchange process, two or more individuals are involved, each side possessing something that is considered to be of value to the other. Both will have the ability to discuss and agree or disagree on the terms of exchange and deliver the object after an agreement is reached. This stage of offering something and discussing the mutually beneficial and acceptable terms is the exchange process. Marketing occurs when individuals decide to satisfy needs and wants through exchange.

### Transactions

As a consequence of the exchange process, when the two parties reach an agreement on the terms of exchange, it becomes transaction. A transaction will consist of an exchange of values between the two or more parties involved, and ownership also changes hands between the seller and the buyer. For example, a customer pays ₹ 4 lakhs to a Hyundai dealer and buys a Santro. Similarly, a physician treats a patient and the patient pays him ₹ 100 as his fees. Transactions can be monetary as in the above examples or can also be nonmonetary. In the barter system, transactions take place without the involvement of money as only the goods or services are exchanged. For example, the butcher offers meat to the baker in exchange for a loaf of bread.

### Relationships

Marketing does not stop with a single transaction between the marketer and the customer. The marketer wants the customer to be fully satisfied with the transaction so that a long-term relationship can be built up in the form of customer loyalty. Marketing consists of actions taken to build and maintain desirable exchange relationships with target audiences involving a product, service, idea or other object. Beyond simply attracting new customers and creating transactions, the goal is to retain customers and grow their business with the company.

### Market

In common parlance, a market is a place where buyers and sellers meet to buy or sell products, as in the case of a fish market, vegetable market or grain market. But in marketing, a market refers to the different groups of consumers for a product or service. Market need not be a place as in the traditional sense. Here, the sellers or marketers are treated as the industry and the buyers as the market. Examples are the general consumer market, business market, global market and specific markets like teenagers' market, children's market, working women's market, insurance market, healthcare market and education market.

A market is the set of actual and potential buyers of a product. Such buyers or customers share a particular need or want that can be satisfied through exchange relationships. The size of the market will depend on the number of people who exhibit the need, have the buying power, and are willing to exchange their resources for what they want.

Marketers work to understand the needs and wants of specific markets and to select the markets that they can serve best. In turn, they develop products and services that create value and satisfaction for customers in these markets. The result is profitable long-term customer relationships.

## MARKETING MIX

The marketing manager is a mixer of ingredients, according to James Culliton, a noted marketing expert, who coined the expression, 'marketing mix'.

"The marketing mix is the set of controllable, tactical, marketing tools that the firm blends to produce the response it wants in the target market." (Philip Kotler). The marketing mix consists of the variables, product, price, place and promotion, well-known as the four Ps of marketing, as classified by McCarthy. Figure gives a complete picture of the different tools under marketing mix variables.

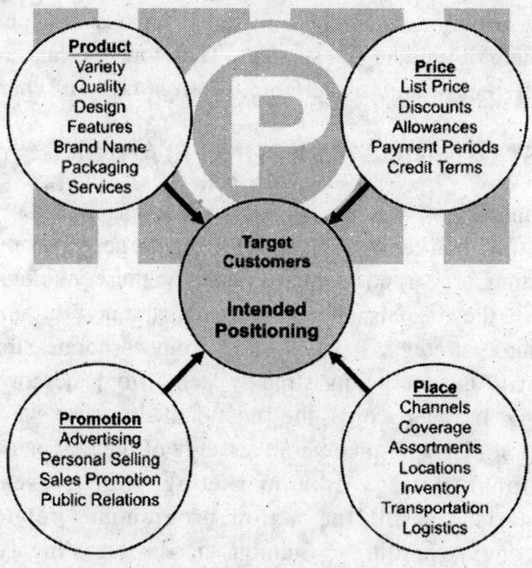


**Fig.** *The Marketing Mix Variables*

**Product** stands for the goods and services offered by a company to the target market, to satisfy needs and wants.

**Price** refers to the money value that the consumers have to pay to buy the product or service.

**Promotion** refers to activities of personal selling, advertising, and communicating product benefits and attributes to target consumers to persuade them to purchase.

**Place** stands for physical distribution activities through which the product moves from the factory to the customer. Channels of distribution, logistics, warehousing, transport, etc. come under the place variable.

To be successful, the marketing programmes have to blend the four variables into an ideal integrated action plan aimed at achieving the corporate objectives. While the four Ps concept relates to the seller's perspective of the market, there are four Cs in the consumer's view. They are:

| **Four Ps** | **Four Cs** |
|---|---|
| Product | Customer solution |
| Price | Customer cost |
| Place | Convenience |
| Promotion | Communication |

To be effective, marketing people have to consider the four Cs first and then build the four Ps based on the requirements.

## MARKETING CHANNELS

### Distribution Channels

Distribution aspect of marketing is concerned with the management of marketing channels (channels of distribution).

In broad meaning, distribution channel in marketing means, the channel through which a product of a particular manufacturer reaches customers in their place. In effect, distribution channels provide a number of options to the manufacturer to deliver the products and suggest alternative strategies to address the 'place' factor of marketing mix. According to Kotler, Bowen and Makens (2008), 'distribution system provides a steady flow of customers'. Competition, globalization, electronic distribution and the perishable nature of tourism product signify the importance of distribution channels'. Distribution aspect of marketing is concerned with the management of marketing channels (channels of distribution).

### Definition

In the words of Kotler *et al.* (2008), 'distribution channel' is a set of independent organisations involved in the process of making a product or service available to the consumer or business user'.

According to Shoemaker and Shaw (2008), 'distribution channel can be defined as a group of organisations, independent or not, that are involved in the process of making a product or service available for use of consumption'.

The definition mentions three components.

(*i*) Manufacturer (Producer of product or service)

(*ii*) Set of organisations as intermediaries (Distribution Channel)

(*iii*) End user (Consumer)

It can be explained like this; the producer manufactures the product in a factory or the supplier of the service has some benefit to offer to the needy customers. The producer/supplier depends intermediaries to reach the consumer. The end user may be living in a different place than the place of the production, hence the intermediary act as a link between the producer/supplier and the consumer to smoothen the process.

### Types of Channels

Because of the wide variety of channel arrangements that exist, it is difficult to generalise the structure of channels across all industries. However, distribution channels are usually of two types:

### *Direct Marketing Channel (or Zero Level)*

This type of channel has no intermediaries. In this distribution system, the goods go from the producer directly to the consumer, *e.g.*, Eureka Forbes.

0 Level

Producer ←→ Consumer

### *Indirect Marketing Channel*

This may further be classified into the following categories:

1. **One-level Channel:** In this type of channel there is only one intermediary between producer and consumer. This intermediary may be a retailer or a distributor.

   1 Level

   Producer → Retailer → Consumer

   If the intermediary is a distributor, this type of channel is used for speciality products like washing machines, refrigerators or industrial products.

   1 Level

   Producer → Distributor → Consumer

2. **Two-level Channel:** This type of channel has two intermediaries, namely, wholesaler/distributor and retailer.

   2 Level

   Producer → Wholesaler/Distributor → Retailer → Consumer

3. **Three-level Channel:** This type of channel has three intermediaries, namely, distributor, wholesaler and retailer. This pattern is also used for convenience products.

   3 Level

   Producer → Distributor → Wholesaler → Retailer → Consumer

4. **Four-level Channel:** This type of channel has four intermediaries, namely, agent, distributor, wholesaler and retailer. This channel is similar to the previous two. This type of channel is used for consumer durable products also.

   4 Level

   Producer → Agent → Distributor → Wholesaler → Retailer → Consumer

In addition to the above mentioned channels, some different types of channels are also possible. There is no watertight classification of channels. The use or selection of a channel also depends upon the product under consideration. Basically there are three or four types of products, viz.

(*i*) Consumer non-durables

(*ii*) Consumer durables

(*iii*) Industrial products, and

(*iv*) Agricultural products.

Distribution channels of different types also depend on the nature of product and services. Therefore, we can say that for different products, there are different types of channels.

## STRATEGIC MARKETING PLANNING

Stanton defines strategic marketing planning as the process of setting marketing goals, selecting target markets and designing a marketing mix to satisfy these markets and achieve these goals. The marketing strategy is therefore functional strategy. It is different from corporate strategy. However, the marketing strategy stems from the corporate strategy. In other words, the functional strategies should be in conformity with the overall strategy of the company. The functional strategy like marketing strategy sets the boundaries for all the action programmes related to marketing. According to Stanton, the six stages involved in strategic marketing planning process are:

1. Situational analysis—with a purpose to determine where we are and where are we going.
2. Determine the objectives—these goals should be specific and realistic
3. Select and measure target markets—identify present and potential customers
4. Design marketing mix strategies and tactics—How do we get to where we want to go?
5. Prepare annual marketing plan—the how to do it guide to yearly marketing operations.
6. Implementation and evaluation—How are we doing? Did we do what we said we would do?

Situation analysis consists of an analysis of external environmental forces and the non-marketing resources that influence an organization's marketing programmed. These factors are: political, economic, competitive, socio cultural, historical, etc. this analysis also reviews and evaluates an organization's existing marketing mix so as to identify the flaws and problems associated with them. This analysis will help an organization to know where it is and where it should reach in future, which may be called the first stage.

The second stage is to formulate the objectives. This includes both the corporate objectives as well as marketing objectives. At the time of setting the marketing objectives, care should be taken to make it specific, measurable and in conformity with the corporate objectives. It will be better to spell them out in writing so that there is no scope for confusion.

In the third stage, the organization should identify the present and potential customers. This is what is called selection of target markets. Apart from analyzing the existing market for its products, the organization should try to identify the new market for its products. For this purpose, the company has to adopt the marketing segmentation technique. Once the market is segmented, it is necessary to forecast the market for the product in each segment.

The fourth stage is to design a strategic marketing mix that enables the organization to satisfy the wants of its target markets and to achieve the marking objectives. The design and later the operation of the marketing mix components constitute the bulk of a Company's marketing effort.

In the fifth stage, the strategic marketing planning is prepared. A series of short term marketing plans are prepared. Usually a period of one year is covered. They are called annual marketing plans. It includes a statement of objectives, identification of target markets, strategies relating to the marketing mix, information regarding the budgetary support for the marketing activity.

After formulating the strategic marketing planning in the above manner, the last stage is, it should be implemented and evaluated periodically. This is done to understand how for the organization is following plan. If there are deviations, the causes and consequences of such deviations are analysed. Further, to design the future course of action, there is a need to analyze the changing marketing environment. The actual performance of the strategic plan has to be critically evaluated so as to accomplish the objectives of the company as desired and as planned. In the process of evaluation, it any defect is found, corrective measures should be incorporated immediately. It would also be wise to do this evaluation segment - wise so that the strategy developed for each segment can be perfected. It is also good to study the strategic planning of the competitor to come out with new ideas and plans.

## MARKETING SEGMENTATION, TARGETING AND POSITIONING

### Introduction

In the increasingly competitive world of today, no two consumers have similar sets of preferences. A marketer has to divide the markets and understand unique characteristics of each of them so that s/he can develop effective marketing strategies aimed to specific consumer groups. A general marketing strategy is unlikely to cater for the entire market because people differ in their tastes and preferences. The success of marketing strategy depends upon how well it is able to cater to the diverse needs of the consumers. In order to achieve this, division of markets into different segments is required. These segments need to be targeted with appropriate strategies. Product positioning is developing perceptual position of the product in the minds of the consumers. Such sets of activities are collectively known as STP - Segmentation, Targeting and Positioning strategies. These are also known as the three components of target marketing.

### Market Segmentation

Stanton has defined market segmentation as consisting of total heterogeneous market for a product and dividing it into several sub-markets or segments, each of which tends to be homogenous in all significant steps. In other words, market segmentation is a technique of dividing the customers of a product or a service into several homogenous groups. This exercise helps the marketers in understanding their specific needs and thus design their offerings accordingly. The effective segmentation can be achieved only when the market segments are measurable, accessible, large enough to be viable and have adequate potential.

There are several bases of market segmentation. In its simplest form, market can be segmented as comprising of ultimate consumers and business users. Besides this, consumer markets can be segmented on the basis of geographical, demographic, psychographic and behavioural variables.

Geographical segmentation entails dividing the market on the basis of the territory. Demographic segmen-tation is done on the basis of the demographic characteristics of the population, *e.g.*, age, gender, family life cycle, income, occupation, religion, race, social class etc. The psychographic variables often taken as a basis for segmentation are the personality characteristics, lifestyle etc. Behavioural seg-mentation divides buyers into groups on the basis of their knowledge, attitudes, responses to the products, occasions, user status, user rate, loyalty status etc.

The business markets are segmented on the basis of demographics, operating characteristics (heavy/medium/light users etc.), purchasing approaches, nature of industry, situational factors and personal characteristics of the decision makers.

The market segments are subjected to constant evaluation in terms of segment size and growth, segment structural attractiveness, objectives and resources of the company etc. After having segmented the markets, firms usually employ three marketing strategies - undifferentiated marketing, differentiated marketing and concentrated marketing, with each having its own pros and cons.

## Basis of Segmenting the Consumer Markets:

There are four major bases that may be used for segmenting the consumer markets:

1. Geographic
2. Demographic
3. Psychographic
4. Behavioural Variables

### *Geographical Segmentation*

Geographical segmentation is the process of dividing the market into different geographical units such as nations, states, regions, countries etc. A company may decide to operate in one or more geographical areas, or to operate in all areas but pay attention to geographical differences in needs and wants. This segment is very commonly used to allocate the territories to the salemen. For example: coolers are not sold in hilly areas or areas with hot and humid climate.

### *Demographic Segmentation*

Demographic segmentation consists of dividing the market into groups based on variables such as gender, family life cycle, income, occupation, education, nationality. One reasons that consumer needs, wants, and usage rates often vary with demographic variables are easier to measure than other variables.

(*i*) **Age:** Consumer needs and wants change with age, some companies use age and life cycle segmentation offering different products or using different marketing approaches for different age and life cycle stages. Companies offer different marketing producers for the customers of different age groups, *e.g.* Horlicks Junior is sold to the children of age groups upto 2 years while Horlicks is targeted for children upto 15 years.

(*ii*) **Life Cycle:** Companies segment the markets on the basis of the stage of the life cycle of their customers. While most motorcycle manufacture target unmarried trendy teenagers, Maruti positions its entry level car as a "family car". Santro seeks to capture the market of middle sized cars and targets trendy customers, living a fast life and craving for style.

(*iii*) **Gender:** Some products are specifically targeted for males, while others are for females. For examples, Axe perfume is targeted for the men, while Fa is targeted for females. Most recently, a popular brand Fair and Lovely has been launched for male consumers as there was a demand for such a product in this segment as well. Many manufacturers employ gender as a very powerful basis for segmentation. The manufacturers of garments, cosmetics, magazines etc. employ this as a basis for segments.

(*iv*) **Income:** Income segmentation is used by the marketers of products and sevices such as automobiles, boats, clothing, cosmetics and travel. Many companies target affluent consumers with luxury goods and convenience services. For example, Maruti offes its range of cars for people of different income groups. While Maruti 800 is specifically targeted for lower middle class.

(*v*) **Social Class:** Social class is measure made up of combination of demographic characteristics. This includes level of education types of occupation and type of neighbourhood a person lives in.

### *Psychographic Segmentation*

Psychographic segmentation divides buyer into different groups based on lifestyle or personality characteristics. People in the some demographic group can have different psychographic mark-ups.

(*i*) **Personality Characteristics:** Marketers also have used personality variables to segment market, giving their products, that personality that correspond to consumer personality. Market segmentation based on personality have been used for products such as cigarettes, insurance etc. For example, Cigarette manufacturer has associated its brand RED & WHITE with bravery. Similarly, Raymonds associates it clothing with personality of a man. Their slogan "The complete man" is a representative of their market strategy.

(*ii*) **Life style:** Life style relates to activities, interests and opinions. People lifestyle affect what products they buy and what brands they prefer. Marketers segment their market based on life style characteristics. Some people are used to living a fast life. Hence, they make use of convenience products. Manufacturers of fast foods, microwaves, vacuum cleaners target such market segments.

### *Behavioural Segmentation*

Behavioural segmentations divides buyers into groups on their knowledge, attitudes, use or responses to a product.

(*i*) **Occasions:** Buyers can be grouped according to occasions where they get the ideas to buy, actually make purchase or use the purchase item. Occasion segmentation can help firms build up product usage. For example, in India it is customary to paint the houses during the festival season. Marketers of paints become active during this period of the year. Event managers become active during the marriage season.

Similarly, there is a sudden increase in the demand of the products that are consumed on specific occasions, for example, crackers during Diwali, durables during Navratras, etc.

*(ii)* **User Status:** Markets can be segmented into groups of non-users, ex-users, Potential users, first time users and regular users of a product. Potential users are regular users and may require different kinds of marketing appeals.

*(iii)* **Usage Rate:** Markets also can be segmented into light, medium and heavy users groups. Heavy users are often a small percentage of markets, but account for a high percentage of total buying. The mobile companies offer differential tariffs, making the call rates more economical for those who have more usage. On the other hand, electricity companies in India charge higher rates from the heavy users of the consumers. These are some of the examples where different marketing strategies have been employed for different product usage.

*(iv)* **Loyalty status:** A market can also be segmented by consumer loyalty; consumers can be loyal to brands, stores and companies. Buyer can be divided according to degree of loyalty. Many companies have relationship programmes, loyalty bonuses, exchange offers where they reward the loyal customers and secure long term affiliations with them. Such customers become their means of publicity and bring in more sales to them.

### Segmentation Process

Mere identification of a difference between one customer group and another does not complete market segmentation. Many other steps have to be carried out for effectiveness market segmentation. The main steps involves in segmentation process are as follows:

(*a*) Assess differences between consumer groups

(*b*) Identify characteristics of each consumer groups

(*c*) De-segregate consumers into separate segments

(*d*) Develop strategies for market segments

(*e*) Estimate the possible impact of marketing strategies in each segment

(*f*) Estimate the likely levels of purchase by each segment

(*g*) Select the segment with higher potential

## TARGET MARKETING

Target marketing is the process of assessing the relative worth of different market segments and selecting one or more segments in which to compete. These become the target segments. Titan is using the target marketing strategy very effectively. German car manufacturer Mercedes target high status consumers with experience and prestigious motor cars.

According to David Cravens and others "Target market is a group of existing or potential customers within a particular product market towards which an organisation directs its marketing efforts".

### Target Marketing Strategies

- **Total market approach:** A company develops a single marketing mix and directs it at the entire market for a particular product. This approach is used when an organisation defines the total market for a particular product as its target market.
- **Concentration approach:** An organisation directs its marketing efforts toward a single market segment through a single marketing mix. The total market may consist of several segments, but the organisation selects only one of the segments as its target market.
- **Multi-segment approach:** An organisation directs its marketing efforts at two or more segments by developing a marketing mix for each segment.

### Steps in Target Marketing

It involves the following four major steps:

1. **Market segmentation:** Markets are segmented on the basis of certain characteristic such as sex, education, income, age etc.
2. **Market targeting:** It refers to evaluating each market segments attractiveness and selecting one or more of the segments to enter. Thus target marketing and market targeting are not one and the same. Market targeting is only a step in target marketing.
3. **Designing the marketing mix:** After selecting the segment, the next step is to design a suitable product and other marketing mix elements for each segment selected.
4. **Product Positioning:** Market segmentation strategy and market positioning strategy are like two sides of a coin. Target marketing begins with segmentation and ends with positioning.

## POSITIONING

Positioning is defined as an act of designing the company's offering and image to occupy a distinctive place in the target's mind. The concept was proposed by two advertisers Al Ries and Jack Trout. They proposed that well known products generally hold a distinctive position in the consumers' minds. If the marketers can understand this distinctive position, they can isolate the product attributes, or the Unique Selling Propositions (USPs) that have led to the development of such a distinct position. Accordingly, they can design a marketing strategy that can secure a favourable action from the target consumers.

The act of creating an image about a product or brand in the consumers mind is known as positioning.

In the words of Kotler, "Positioning is the act of designing the company's offer and image so that it occupies a distinct and valued place in the target consumers minds."

In short, the process of creating an image for a product in the minds of targeted customers is known as product positioning. Close-up tooth paste is looked upon by the consumers more as a mouth wash than a teeth cleaner, while 'pepsodent' has created an impression of germ killer in the consumers minds.

## Techniques of Positioning

Following technique are used in positioning a product in the market:

- Positioning by Corporate Identity: The companies that have become a tried and trusted household name. For example, Tata, Sony etc.
- **Positioning by Brand Endorsement:** Marketers use the names of company's powerful brands for line extentions or while entering another product category. E.g., Lux, Surf, Dettol etc.
- **Positioning by Product Attributes and Benefits:** It emphasize the special attributes and benefits of the product. Close-up is positioned on fresh breath and cosmetics benefits.
- **Positioning by use, Occasion and Time:** It is to find an occasion or time of use and sit on it. For example, Vicks vaporub is to be used for child's cold at night.
- **Positioning by Price and Quality:** Company position its brand by emphasizing its price and quality. Eg. Nirma detergent powder.
- **Positioning by Product Category:** Brand is perceived to be another product category. Eg. Maruti positioned its van as *omni*, family car.
- **Positioning by Product User:** Positioning the product as an exclusive product for a particular class of customers. Eg. Scooty as a two wheeler for teenagers.
- **Positioning by Competitor:** An offensive positioning strategy and is often seen in cases of comparative advertising. Eg. Tide and Rin.
- **Positioning by Symbols:** Some companies use some symbols for positioning their products. Eg. Vodafone symbol.

● ● ●

# Financial Management

## MEANING OF BUSINESS FINANCE

Money required for carrying out business activities is called business finance. Almost all business activities require some finance. Finance is needed to establish a business, to run it, to modernise it, to expand, or diversify it. It is required for buying a variety of assets, which may be tangible like machinery, factories, buildings, offices; or intangible such as trademarks, patents, technical expertise, etc. Also, finance is central to running the day-to-day operations of business, like buying material, paying bills, salaries, collecting cash from customers, etc. needed at every stage in the life of a business entity. Availability of adequate finance is, thus, very crucial for the survival and growth of a business.

## FINANCIAL MANAGEMENT

All finance comes at some cost. It is quite imperative that it needs to be carefully managed. Financial Management is concerned with optimal procurement as well as the usage of finance. For optimal procurement, different available sources of finance are identified and compared in terms of their costs and associated risks. Similarly, the finance so procured needs to be invested in a manner that the returns from the investment exceed the cost at which procurement has taken place. Financial Management aims at reducing the cost of funds procured, keeping the risk under control and achieving effective deployment of such funds. It also aims at ensuring availability of enough funds whenever required as well as avoiding idle finance. Needless to emphasise, the future of a business depends a great deal on the quality of its financial management.

**Importance:** The role of financial management cannot be overemphasised, since it has a direct bearing on the financial health of a business. The financial statements, such as Balance Sheet and Profit and Loss Account, reflect a firm's financial position and its financial health. Almost all items in the financial statements of a business are affected directly or indirectly through some financial management decisions. Some prominent examples of the aspects being affected could be as under:

*(i)* **The size and the composition of fixed assets of the business:** For example, a capital budgeting decision to invest a sum of ₹ 100 crores in fixed assets would raise the size of fixed assets block by this amount.

*(ii)* **The quantum of current assets and its break-up into cash, inventory and receivables:** With an increase in the investment in fixed assets, there is a commensurate increase in the working capital requirement. The quantum of current assets is also influenced by financial management decisions. In addition, decisions about credit and inventory management affect the amount of debtors and inventory which in turn affect the total current assets as well as their composition.

*(iii)* **The amount of long-term and short-term funds to be used:** Financial management, among others, involves decision about the proportion of long-term and short-term funds. An organisation wanting to have more liquid assets would raise relatively more amount on a long-term basis. There is a choice between liquidity and profitability. The underlying assumption here is that current liabilities cost less than long term liabilities.

*(iv)* **Break-up of long-term financing into debt, equity etc:** Of the total long-term finance, the proportions to be raised by way of debt and/or equity is also a financial management decision. The amounts of debt, equity share capital, preference share capital are affected by the financing decision, which is a part of financing management.

*(v)* **All items in the Profit and Loss Account, e.g., Interest, Expense, Depreciation, etc.:** Higher amount of debt means higher interest expense in future. Similarly, use of higher equity may entail higher payment of dividends. Similarly, an expansion of business which is a result of capital budgeting decision is likely to affect virtually all items in the profit and loss account of the business.

It can, thus, be stated that the financial statements of a business are largely determined by financial management decisions taken earlier. Similarly, the future financial statements would depend upon past as well as current financial decisions. Thus, the overall financial health of a business is determined by the quality of its financial management. Good financial management aims at mobilisation of financial resources at a lower cost and deployment of these in most lucrative activities.

## FINANCIAL DECISIONS

Financial management is concerned with the solution of three major issues relating to the financial operations of a firm corresponding to the three questions of investment, financing and divident decision. In a financial context, it means the selection of best financing alternative or best investment alternative. The finance function, therefore, is concerned with three broad decisions which are explained below:

### Investment Decision

A firm's resources are scarce in comparison to the uses to which they can be put. A firm, therefore, has to choose where to invest these resources, so that they are able to earn the highest possible return for their investors. The investment decision, therefore, relates to how the firm's funds are invested in different assets.

Investment decision can be long-term or short-term. A long-term investment decision is also called a Capital Budgeting decision. It involves committing the finance on a long-term basis. For example, making investment in a new machine to replace an existing one or acquiring a new fixed asset or opening a new branch, etc. These decisions are very crucial for any business since they affect its earning capacity in the long run. The size of assets, profitability and competitiveness are all affected by capital budgeting decisions. Moreover, these decisions normally involve huge amounts of investment and are irreversible except at a huge cost.

Therefore, once made, it is often almost impossible for a business to wriggle out of such decisions. Therefore, they need to be taken with utmost care. These decisions must be taken by those who understand them comprehensively. A bad capital budgeting decision normally has the capacity to severely damage the financial fortune of a business. Short-term investment decisions (also called working capital decisions) are concerned with the decisions about the levels of cash, inventory and receivables. These decisions affect the day-to-day working of a business. These affect the liquidity as well as profitability of a business. Efficient cash management, inventory management and receivables management are essential ingredients of sound working capital management.

#### *Factors affecting Capital Budgeting Decision*

A number of projects are often available to a business to invest in. But each project has to be evaluated carefully and, depending upon the returns, a particular project is either selected or rejected. If there is only one project, its viability in terms of the rate of return, viz., investment and its comparability with the industry's average is seen.

There are certain factors which affect capital budgeting decisions.

(*a*) **Cash flows of the project:** When a company takes an investment decision involving huge amount it expects to generate some cash flows over a period. These cash flows are in the form of a series of cash receipts and payments over the life of an investment. The amount of these cash flows should be carefully analysed before considering a capital budgeting decision.

(*b*) **The rate of return:** The most important criterion is the rate of return of the project. These calculations are based on the expected returns from each proposal and the assessment of the risk involved. Suppose, there are two projects, A and B (with the same risk involved), with a rate of return of 10 per cent and 12 per cent, respectively, then under normal circumstance, project B should be selected.

(*c*) **The investment criteria involved:** The decision to invest in a particular project involves a number of calculations regarding the amount of investment, interest rate, cash flows and rate of return. There are different techniques to evaluate investment proposals which are known as capital budgeting techniques. These techniques are applied to each proposal before selecting a particular project.

### Financing Decision

This decision is about the quantum of finance to be raised from various long-term sources. Short-term sources are studied under the 'working capital management'.

It involves identification of various available sources. The main sources of funds for a firm are shareholders' funds and borrowed funds. The shareholders' funds refer to the equity capital and the retained earnings. Borrowed funds refer to the finance raised through debentures or other forms of debt. A firm has to decide the proportion of funds to be raised from either sources, based on their basic characteristics. Interest on borrowed funds have to be paid regardless of whether or not a firm has earned a profit. Likewise, the borrowed funds have to be repaid at a fixed time. The risk of default on payment is known as financial risk which has to be considered by a firm likely to have insufficient shareholders to make these fixed payments. Shareholders' funds, on the other hand, involve no commitment regarding the payment of returns or the repayment of capital. A firm, therefore, needs to have a judicious mix of both debt and equity in making financing decisions, which may be debt, equity, preference share capital, and retained earnings.

The cost of each type of finance has to be estimated. Some sources may be cheaper than others. For example, debt is considered to be the cheapest of all the sources, tax deductibility of interest makes it still cheaper. Associated risk is also different for each source, e.g., it is necessary to pay interest on debt and redeem the principal amount on maturity. There is no such compulsion to pay any dividend on equity shares. Thus, there is some amount of financial risk in debt financing. The overall financial risk depends upon the proportion of debt in the total capital. The fund raising exercise also costs something. This cost is called floatation cost. It also must be considered while evaluating different sources. Financing decision is, thus, concerned with the decisions about how much to be raised from which source. This decision determines the overall cost of capital and the financial risk of the enterprise.

### Factors Affecting Financing Decisions

The financing decisions are affected by various factors. Important among them are as follows:

(*a*) **Cost:** The cost of raising funds through different sources are different. A prudent financial manager would normally opt for a source which is the cheapest.

(*b*) **Risk:** The risk associated with each of the sources is different.

(*c*) **Floatation Costs:** Higher the floatation cost, less attractive the source.

(*d*) **Cash Flow Position of the Company:** A stronger cash flow position may make debt financing more viable than funding through equity.

(*e*) **Fixed Operating Costs:** If a business has high fixed operating costs (e.g., building rent, Insurance premium, Salaries, etc.), It must reduce fixed financing costs. Hence, lower debt financing is better. Similarly, if fixed operating cost is less, more of debt financing may be preferred.

(*f*) **Control Considerations:** Issues of more equity may lead to dilution of management's control over the business. Debt financing has no such implication. Companies afraid of a takeover bid would prefer debt to equity.

(*g*) **State of Capital Market:** Health of the capital market may also affect the choice of source of fund. During the period when stock market is rising, more people invest in equity. However, depressed capital market may make issue of equity shares difficult for any company.

## Dividend Decision

The third important decision that every financial manager has to take relates to the distribution of dividend. Dividend is that portion of profit which is distributed to shareholders. The decision involved here is how much of the profit earned by company (after paying tax) is to be distributed to the shareholders and how much of it should be retained in the business. While the dividend constitutes the current income re-investment as retained earning increases the firm's future earning capacity. The extent of retained earnings also influences the financing decision of the firm. Since the firm does not require funds to the extent of re-invested retained earnings, the decision regarding dividend should be taken keeping in view the overall objective of maximising shareholder's wealth.

### Factors Affecting Dividend Decision

How much of the profits earned by a company will be distributed as profit and how much will be retained in the business is affected by many factors. Some of the important factors are discussed as follows:

(*a*) **Amount of Earnings:** Dividends are paid out of current and past earning. Therefore, earnings is a major determinant of the decision about dividend.

(*b*) **Stability Earnings:** Other things remaining the same, a company having stable earning is in a better position to declare higher dividends. As against this, a company having unstable earnings is likely to pay smaller dividend.

(*c*) **Stability of Dividends:** Companies generally follow a policy of stabilising dividend per share. The increase in dividends is generally made when there is confidence that their earning potential has gone up and not just the earnings of the current year. In other words, dividend per share is not altered if the change in earnings is small or seen to be temporary in nature.

(*d*) **Growth Opportunities:** Companies having good growth opportunities retain more money out of their earnings so as to finance the required investment. The dividend in growth companies is, therefore, smaller, than that in the non-growth companies.

(*e*) **Cash Flow Position:** The payment of dividend involves an outflow of cash. A company may be earning profit but may be short on cash. Availability of enough cash in the company is necessary for declaration of dividend.

(*f*) **Shareholders' Preference:** While declaring dividends, managements must keep in mind the preferences of the shareholders in this regard. If the shareholders in general desire that at least a certain amount is paid as dividend, the companies are likely to declare the same. There are always some shareholders who depend upon a regular income from their investments.

(*g*) **Taxation Policy:** The choice between the payment of dividend and retaining the earnings is, to some extent, affected by the difference in the tax treatment of dividends and capital gains. If tax on dividend is higher, it is better to pay less by way of dividends. As compared to this, higher dividends may be declared if tax rates are relatively lower. Though the dividends are free of tax in the hands of shareholders, a dividend distribution tax is levied on companies. Thus, under the present tax policy, shareholders are likely to prefer higher dividends.

(*h*) **Stock Market Reaction:** Investors, in general, view an increase in dividend as a good news and stock prices react positively to it. Similarly, a decrease in dividend may have a negative impact on the share prices in the stock market.

Thus, the possible impact of dividend policy on the equity share price is one of the important factors considered by the management while taking a decision about it.

(*i*) **Access to Capital Market:** Large and reputed companies generally have easy access to the capital market and, therefore, may depend less on retained earning to finance their growth. These companies tend to pay higher dividends than the smaller companies which have relatively low access to the market.

(*j*) **Legal Constraints:** Certain provisions of the Companies Act place restrictions on payouts as dividend. Such provisions must be adhered to while declaring the dividend.

(*k*) **Contractual Constraints:** While granting loans to a company, sometimes the lender may impose certain restrictions on the payment of dividends in future. The companies are required to ensure that the dividend does not violate the terms of the loan agreement in this regard.

## FINANCIAL PLANNING

Financial planning is essentially the preparation of a financial blueprint of an organisation's future operations. The objective of financial planning is to ensure that enough funds are available at right time. If adequate funds are not available the firm will not be able to honour its commitments and carry out its plans.

On the other hand, if excess funds are available, it will unnecessarily add to the cost and may encourage wasteful expenditure. It must be kept in mind that financial planning is not equivalent to, or a substitute for, financial management. Financial management aims at choosing the best investment and financing alternatives by focusing on their costs and benefits. Its objective is to increase the shareholders' wealth. Financial planning on the other hand aims at smooth operations by focusing on fund requirements and their availability in the light of financial decisions. For example, if a capital budgeting decisions is taken, the operations are likely to be at a higher scale. The amount of expenses and revenues are likely to increase. Financial planning process tries to forecast all the items which are likely to undergo changes.

It enables the management to foresee the fund requirements both the quantum as well as the timing. Likely shortage and surpluses are forecast so that necessary activities are taken in advance to meet those situations.

Thus, financial planning strives to achieve the following twin objectives.

(*a*) **To ensure availability of funds whenever required:** This include a proper estimation of the funds required for different purposes such as for the purchase of long-term assets or to meet day-to-day expenses of business etc. Apart from this, there is a need to estimate the time at which these funds are to be made available. Financial planning also tries to specify possible sources of these funds.

(*b*) **To see that the firm does not raise resources unnecessarily:** Excess funding is almost as bad as inadequate funding. Even if there is some surplus money, good financial planning would put it to the best possible use so that the financial resources are not left idle and don't unnecessarily add to the cost.

Thus, a proper matching of funds requirements and their availability is sought to be achieved by financial planning. This process of estimating the fund requirement of a business and specifying the sources of funds is called financial planning. Financial planning takes into consideration the growth, performance, investments and requirement of funds for a given period. Financial planning includes both short-term as well as long-term planning. Long-term planning relates to long term growth and investment. It focuses on capital expenditure programmes. Short-term planning covers short-term financial plan called budget.

Typically, financial planning is done for three to five years. For longer periods it becomes more difficult and less useful. Plans made for periods of one year or less are termed as budgets. Budgets are example of financial planning exercise in greater details. They include detailed plan of action for a period of one year or less.

Financial planning usually begins with the preparation of a sales forecast. Let us suppose a company is making a financial plan for the next five years. It will start with an estimate of the sales which are likely to happen in the next five years. Based on these, the financial statements are prepared keeping in mind the requirement of funds for investment in the fixed capital and working capital. Then the expected profits during the period are estimated so that an idea can be made of how much of the fund requirements can be met internally *i.e.,* through retained earnings (after dividend payouts).

This results in an estimation of the requirement for external funds. Further, the sources from which the external funds requirement can be met are identified and cash budgets are made, incorporating these factors.

## CAPITAL STRUCTURE

One of the important decisions under financial management relates to the financing pattern or the proportion of the use of different sources in raising funds. On the basis of ownership, the sources of business finance can be broadly classified into two categories viz., 'owners' funds' and 'borrowed funds'. Owners' funds consist of equity share capital, preference share capital and reserves and surpluses or retained earnings. Borrowed funds can be in the form of loans, debentures, public deposits etc. These may be borrowed from banks, other financial institutions, debentureholders and public.

Capital structure refers to the mix between owners and borrowed funds. These shall be referred as equity and debt in the subsequent text. It can be calculated as debt-equity ratio *i.e.,* $\left(\frac{\text{Debt}}{\text{Equity}}\right)$ or as the proportion of debt out of the total capital *i.e.,* $\left(\frac{\text{Debt}}{\text{Debt + Equity}}\right)$.

Debt and equity differ significantly in their cost and riskiness for the firm. The cost of debt is lower than the cost of equity for a firm because the lender's risk is lower than the equity shareholder's risk, since the lender earns an assured return and repayment of capital and, therefore, they should require a lower rate of return.

Additionally, interest paid on debt is a deductible expense for computation of tax liability whereas dividends are paid out of after-tax profit. Increased use of debt, therefore, is likely to lower the over-all cost of capital of the firm provided that the cost of equity remains unaffected. Impact of a change in the debt-equity ratio upon the earning per share is dealt with in detail later in this chapter.

Debt is cheaper but is more risky for a business because the payment of interest and the return of principal is obligatory for the business. Any default in meeting these commitments may force the business to go into liquidation. There is no such compulsion in case of equity, which is therefore, considered riskless for the business. Higher use of debt increases the fixed financial charges of a business. As a result, increased use of debt increases the financial risk of a company.

Financial risk is the chance that a firm would fail to meet its payment obligations.

Capital structure of a company, thus, affects both the profitability and the financial risk. A capital structure will be said to be optimal when the proportion of debt and equity is such that it results in an increase in the value of the equity share. In other words, all decisions relating to capital structure should emphasise on increasing the shareholders' wealth.

The proportion of debt in the overall capital is also called financial leverage.

Financial leverage is computed as $\frac{D}{E}$ or $\frac{D}{D+E}$ when D is the Debt and E is the Equity. As the financial leverage increases, the cost of funds declines because of increased use of cheaper debt but the financial risk increases.

### Factors affecting the Choice of Capital Structure

Deciding about the capital structure of a firm involves determining the relative proportion of various types of funds. This depends on various factors. For example, debt requires regular servicing. Interest payment and repayment of principal are obligatory on a business.

In addition a company planning to raise debt must have sufficient cash to meet the increased outflows because of higher debt. Similarly, important factors which determine the choice of capital structure are as follows:

1. **Cash Flow Position:** Size of projected cash flows must be considered before borrowing. Cash flows must not only cover fixed cash payment obligations but there must be sufficient buffer also. It must be kept in mind that a company has cash payment obligations for (*i*) normal business operations; (*ii*) for investment in fixed assets; and (*iii*) for meeting the debt service commitments *i.e.,* payment of interest and repayment of principal.
2. **Interest Coverage Ratio (ICR):** The interest coverage ratio refers to the number of times earnings before interest and taxes of a company covers the interest obligation. This may be calculated as follows:

$$\text{ICR} = \frac{\text{EBIT}}{\text{Interest}}$$

The higher the ratio, lower shall be the risk of company failing to meet its interest payment obligations. However, this ratio is not an adequate measure. A firm may have a high EBIT but low cash balance. Apart from interest, repayment obligations are also relevant.

3. **Debt Service Coverage Ratio (DSCR):** Debt Service Coverage Ratio takes care of the deficiencies referred to in the Interest Coverage Ratio (ICR). The cash profits generated by the operations are compared with the total cash required for the service of the debt and the preference share capital. It is calculated as follows:

$$\frac{\text{Profit after tax + Depreciation + Interest + Non Cash exp.}}{\text{Pref. Div + Interest + Repayment obligation}}$$

A higher DSCR indicates better ability to meet cash commitments and consequently, the company's potential to increase debt component in its capital structure.

4. **Return on Investment (RoI):** If the RoI of the company is higher, it can choose to use trading on equity to increase its EPS, *i.e.,* its ability to use debt is greater.

5. **Cost of Debt:** A firm's ability to borrow at a lower rate increases its capacity to employ higher debt. Thus, more debt can be used if debt can be raised at a lower rate.

6. **Tax Rate:** Since interest is a deductible expense, cost of debt is affected by the tax rate. The firms in our examples are borrowing @ 10%. Since the tax rate is 30%, the after tax cost of debt is only 7%. A higher tax rate, thus, makes debt relatively cheaper and increases its attraction vis-à-vis equity.

7. **Cost of Equity:** Stock owners expect a rate of return from the equity which is commensurate with the risk they are assuming. When a company increases debt, the financial risk faced by the equity holders, increases. Consequently, their desired rate of return may increase. It is for this reason that a company can not use debt beyond a point. If debt is used beyond that point, cost of equity may go up sharply and share price may decrease inspite of increased EPS. Consequently, for maximisation of shareholders' wealth, debt can be used only upto a level.

8. **Floatation costs:** Process of raising resources also involves some cost. Public issue of shares and debentures requires considerable expenditure. Getting a loan from a financial institution may not cost so much. These considerations may also affect the choice between debt and equity and hence the capital structure.

9. **Risk Consideration:** Financial risk refers to a position when a company is unable to meet its fixed financial charges namely interest payment, preference dividend and repayment obligations. Apart from the financial risk, every business has some operating risk (also called business risk). Business risk depends upon fixed operating costs. Higher fixed operating costs result in higher business risk and vice-versa. The total risk depends upon both the business risk and the financial risk. If a firm's business risk is lower, its capacity to use debt is higher and vice-versa.

10. **Flexibility:** If a firm uses its debt potential to the full, it loses flexibility to issue further debt. To maintain flexibility, it must maintain some borrowing power to take care of unforeseen circumstances.

11. **Control:** Debt normally does not cause a dilution of control. A public issue of equity may reduce the managements' holding in the company and make it vulnerable to takeover. This factor also influences the choice between debt and equity especially in companies in which the current holding of management is on a lower side.

12. **Regulatory Framework:** Every company operates within a regulatory framework provided by the law e.g., public issue of shares and debentures have to be made under SEBI guidelines. Raising funds from banks and other financial institutions require fulfillment of other norms. The relative ease with which these norms can, be met or the procedures completed may also have a bearing upon the choice of the source of finance.

13. **Stock Market Conditions:** If the stock markets are bullish, equity shares are more easily sold even at a higher price. Use of equity is often preferred by companies in such a situation. However, during a bearish phase, a company, may find raising of equity capital more difficult and it may opt for debt. Thus, stock market conditions often affect the choice between the two.

14. **Capital Structure of other Companies:** A useful guideline in the capital structure planning is the debt-equity ratios of other companies in the same industry. There are usually some industry norms which may help. Care however must be taken that the company does not follow the industry norms blindly. For example, if the business risk of a firm is higher, it can not afford the same financial risk. It should go in for low debt. Thus, the management must know what the industry norms are, whether they are following them or deviating from them and adequate justification must be there in both cases.

## FIXED AND WORKING CAPITAL

### Meaning

Every company needs funds to finance its assets and activities. Investment is required to be made in fixed assets and current assets. Fixed assets are those which remains in the business for more than one year, usually for much longer, e.g., plant and machinery, furniture and fixture, land and building, vehicles, etc.

Decision to invest in fixed assets must be taken very carefully as the investment is usually quite large. Such decisions once taken are irrevocable except at a huge loss. Such decisions are called capital budgeting decisions.

Current assets are those assets which, in the normal routine of the business, get converted into cash or cash equivalents within one year, e.g., inventories, debtors, bills receivables, etc.

### Management of Fixed Capital

Fixed capital refers to investment in long-term assets. Management of fixed capital involves allocation of firm's capital to different projects or assets with long-term implications for the business. These decisions are called investment decisions or capital budgeting decisions and affect the growth, profitability and risk of the business in the long run. These long-term assets last for more than one year.

It must be financed through long-term sources of capital such as equity or preference shares, debentures, long-term loans and retained earnings of the business. Fixed Assets should never be financed through short-term sources.

Investment in these assets would also include expenditure on acquisition, expansion, modernisation and their replacement. These decisions include purchase of land, building, plant and machinery, launching a new product line or investing in advanced techniques of production. Major expenditures such as those on advertising campaign or research and development programme having long term implications for the firm are also examples of capital budgeting decisions. The management of fixed capital or investment or capital budgeting decisions are important for the following reasons:

(*i*) **Long-term growth:** These decisions have bearing on the long-term growth. The funds invested in long-term assets are likely to yield returns in the future. These will affect the future prospects of the business.

(*ii*) **Large amount of funds involved:** These decisions result in a substantial portion of capital funds being blocked in long-term projects. Therefore, these investments are planned after a detailed analysis is undertaken. This may involve decisions like where to procure funds from and at what rate of interest.

(*iii*) **Risk involved:** Fixed capital involves investment of huge amounts. It affects the returns of the firm as a whole in the long-term. Therefore, investment decisions involving fixed capital influence the overall business risk complexion of the firm.

(*iv*) **Irreversible decisions:** These decisions once taken, are not reversible without incurring heavy losses. Abandoning a project after heavy investment is made is quite costly in terms of waste of funds. Therefore, these decisions should be taken only after carefully evaluating each detail or else the adverse financial consequences may be very heavy.

### Factors affecting the Requirement of Fixed Capital

1. **Nature of Business:** The type of business has a bearing upon the fixed capital requirements. For example, a trading concern needs lower investment in fixed assets compared with a manufacturing organisation; since it does not require to purchase plant and machinery, etc.
2. **Scale of Operations:** A larger organisation operating at a higher scale needs bigger plant, more space etc. and therefore, requires higher investment in fixed assets when compared with the small organisation.
3. **Choice of Technique:** Some organisations are capital intensive whereas others are labour intensive. A capital-intensive organisation requires higher investment in plant and machinery as it relies less on manual labour. The requirement of fixed capital for such organisations would be higher. Labour intensive organisations on the other hand require less investment in fixed assets. Hence, their fixed capital requirement is lower.
4. **Technology Upgradation:** In certain industries, assets become obsolete sooner. Consequently, their replacements become due faster. Higher investment in fixed assets may, therefore, be required in such cases. For example, computers become obsolete faster and are replaced much sooner than say, furniture. Thus, such organisations which use assets which are prone to obsolescence require higher fixed capital to purchase such assets.
5. **Growth Prospects:** Higher growth of an organisation generally requires higher investment in fixed assets. Even when such growth is expected, a company may choose to create higher capacity in order to meet the anticipated higher demand quicker. This entails larger investment in fixed assets and consequently larger fixed capital.

6. **Diversification:** A firm may choose to diversify its operations for various reasons. With diversification, fixed capital requirements increase e.g., a textile company is diversifying and starting a cement manufacturing plant. Obviously, its investment in fixed capital will increase.
7. **Financing Alternatives:** A developed financial market may provide leasing facilities as an alternative to outright purchase. When an asset is taken on lease, the firm pays lease rentals and uses it. By doing so, it avoids huge sums required to purchase it. Availability of leasing facilities, thus, may reduce the funds required to be invested in fixed assets, thereby reducing the fixed capital requirements. Such a strategy is specially suitable in high risk lines of business.
8. **Level of Collaboration:** At times, certain business organisations share each other's facilities. For example, a bank may use another's ATM or some of them may jointly establish a particular facility. This is feasible if the scale of operations of each one of them is not sufficient to make full use of the facility. Such collaboration reduces the level of investment in fixed assets for each one of the participating organisations.

## WORKING CAPITAL

Apart from the investment in fixed assets every business organisation needs to invest in current assets. This investment facilitates smooth day-to-day operations of the business. Current assets are usually more liquid but contribute less to the profits than fixed assets. Examples of current assets, in order of their liquidity, are as under.

1. Cash in hand/Cash at Bank
2. Marketable securities
3. Bills receivable
4. Debtors
5. Finished goods inventory
6. Work in progress
7. Raw materials
8. Prepaid expenses

These assets, as noted earlier, are expected to get converted into cash or cash equivalents within a period of one year. These provide liquidity to the business. An asset is more liquid if it can be converted into cash quicker and without reduction in value. Insufficient investment in current assets may make it more difficult for an organisation to meet its payment obligations. However, these assets provide little or low return. Hence, a balance needs to be struck between liquidity and profitability.

Current liabilities are those payment obligations which are due for payment within one year; such as bills payable, creditors, outstanding expenses and advances received from customers, etc.

### Factors Affecting The Working Capital Requirements

1. **Nature of Business:** The basic nature of a business influences the amount of working capital required. A trading organisation usually needs a smaller amount of working capital compared to a manufacturing organisation. This is because there is usually no processing. Therefore, there is no distinction between raw materials and finished goods. Sales can be effected immediately upon the receipt of materials, sometimes even before that. In a manufacturing business, however, raw material needs to be converted into finished goods before any sales become possible. Other factors remaining the same, a trading business requires less working capital. Similarly, service industries which usually do not have to maintain inventory require less working capital.
2. **Scale of Operations:** For organisations which operate on a higher scale of operation, the quantum of inventory and debtors required is generally high. Such organisations, therefore, require large amount of working capital as compared to the organisations which operate on a lower scale.
3. **Business Cycle:** Different phases of business cycles affect the requirement of working capital by a firm. In case of a boom, the sales as well as production are likely to be larger and, therefore, larger amount of working capital is required. As against this, the requirement for working capital will be lower during the period of depression as the sales as well as production will be small.
4. **Seasonal Factors:** Most business have some seasonality in their operations. In peak season, because of higher level of activity, larger amount of working capital is required. As against this, the level of activity as well as the requirement for working capital will be lower during the lean season.
5. **Production Cycle:** Production cycle is the time span between the receipt of raw material and their conversion into finished goods. Some businesses have a longer production cycle while some have a shorter one. Duration and the length of production cycle, affects the amount of funds required for raw materials and expenses. Consequently, working capital requirement is higher in firms with longer processing cycle and lower in firms with shorter processing cycle.

6. **Credit Allowed:** Different firms allow different credit terms to their customers. These depend upon the level of competition that a firm faces as well as the credit worthiness of their clientele. A liberal credit policy results in higher amount of debtors, increasing the requirement of working capital.
7. **Credit Availed:** Just as a firm allows credit to its customers it also may get credit from its suppliers. To the extent it avails the credit on purchases, the working capital requirement is reduced.
8. **Operating Efficiency:** Firms manage their operations with varied degrees of efficiency. For example, a firm managing its raw materials efficiently may be able to manage with a smaller balance. This is reflected in a higher inventory turnover ratio. Similarly, a better debtors turnover ratio may be achieved reducing the amount tied up in receivables. Better sales effort may reduce the average time for which finished goods inventory is held. Such efficiencies may reduce the level of raw materials, finished goods and debtors resulting in lower requirement of working capital.
9. **Availability of Raw Material:** If the raw materials and other required materials are available freely and continuously, lower stock levels may suffice. If, however, raw materials do not have a record of un-interrupted availability, higher stock levels may be required. In addition, the time lag between the placement of order and the actual receipt of the materials (also called lead time) is also relevant. Larger the lead time, larger the quantity of material to be stored and larger shall be the amount of working capital required.
10. **Growth Prospects:** If the growth potential of a concern is perceived to be higher, it will require larger amount of working capital so that it is able to meet higher production and sales target whenever required.
11. **Level of Competition:** Higher level of competitiveness may necessitate larger stocks of finished goods to meet urgent orders from customers. This increases the working capital requirement. Competition may also force the firm to extend liberal credit terms discussed earlier.
12. **Inflation:** With rising prices, larger amounts are required even to maintain a constant volume of production and sales. The working capital requirement of a business thus, become higher with higher rate of inflation. It must, however, be noted that an inflation rate of 5%, does not mean that every component of working capital will change by the same percentage. The actual requirement shall depend upon the rates of price change of different components (e.g., raw material, finished goods, labour cost,) Finished goods as well as their proportion in the total requirement.

•••

# Financial Markets

## CONCEPT OF FINANCIAL MARKET

A business is a part of an economic system that consists of two main sectors – households which save funds and business firms which invest these funds. A financial market helps to link the savers and the investors by mobilizing funds between them. In doing so it performs what is known as an allocative function. It allocates or directs funds available for investment into their most productive investment opportunity. When the allocative function is performed well, two consequences follow:

- The rate of return offered to households would be higher.
- Scarce resources are allocated to those firms which have the highest productivity for the economy.

There are two major alternative mechanisms through which allocation of funds can be done: via banks or via financial markets. Households can deposit their surplus funds with banks, who in turn could lend these funds to business firms. Alternately, households can buy the shares and debentures offered by a business using financial markets. The process by which allocation of funds is done is called financial intermediation. Banks and financial markets are competing intermediaries in the financial system, and give households a choice of where they want to place their savings.

A financial market is a market for the creation and exchange of financial assets. Financial markets exist wherever a financial transaction occurs. Financial transactions could be in the form of creation of financial assets such as the initial issue of shares and debentures by a firm or the purchase and sale of existing financial assets like equity shares, debentures and bonds.

## FUNCTIONS OF FINANCIAL MARKET

Financial markets play an important role in the allocation of scarce resources in an economy by performing the following four important functions.

1. **Mobilisation of Savings and Channeling them into the most Productive Uses:** A financial market facilitates the transfer of savings from savers to investors. It gives savers the choice of different investments and thus helps to channelise surplus funds into the most productive use.
2. **Facilitating Price Discovery:** You all know that the forces of demand and supply help to establish a price for a commodity or service in the market. In the financial market, the households are suppliers of funds and business firms represent the demand. The interaction between them helps to establish a price for the financial asset which is being traded in that particular market.
3. **Providing Liquidity to Financial Assets:** Financial markets facilitate easy purchase and sale of financial assets. In doing so they provide liquidity to financial assets, so that they can be easily converted into cash whenever required. Holders of assets can readily sell their financial assets through the mechanism of the financial market.
4. **Reducing the Cost of Transactions:** Financial markets provide valuable information about securities being traded in the market. It helps to save time, effort and money that both buyers and sellers of a financial asset would have to otherwise spend to try and find each other. The financial market is thus, a common platform where buyers and sellers can meet for fulfillment of their individual needs.

Financial markets are classified on the basis of the maturity of financial instruments traded in them. Instruments with a maturity of less than one year are traded in the money market. Instruments with longer maturity are traded in the capital market.

## MONEY MARKET

The money market is a market for short term funds which deals in monetary assets whose period of maturity is upto one year. These assets are close substitutes for money. It is a market where low risk, unsecured and short term debt instruments that are highly liquid are issued and actively traded everyday. It has no physical location, but is an activity conducted over the telephone and through the internet. It enables the raising of short-term funds for meeting the temporary shortages of cash and obligations and the temporary deployment of excess funds for earning returns. The major participants in the market are the Reserve Bank of India (RBI), Commercial Banks, Non-Banking Finance Companies, State Governments, Large Corporate Houses and Mutual Funds.

## Money Market Instruments

1. **Treasury Bill:** A Treasury bill is basically an instrument of short-term borrowing by the Government of India maturing in less than one year. They are also known as Zero Coupon Bonds issued by the Reserve Bank of India on behalf of the Central Government to meet its short-term requirement of funds. Treasury bills are issued in the form of a promissory note. They are highly liquid and have assured yield and negligible risk of default. They are issued at a price which is lower than their face value and repaid at par. The difference between the price at which the treasury bills are issued and their redemption value is the interest receivable on them and is called discount. Treasury bills are available for a minimum amount of ₹ 25,000 and in multiples thereof.

   *Example:* Suppose an investor purchases a 91 days Treasury bill with a face value of ₹ 1,00,000 for ₹ 96,000. By holding the bill until the maturity date, the investor receives ₹ 1,00,000. The difference of ₹ 4,000 between the proceeds received at maturity and the amount paid to purchase the bill represents the interest received by him.

2. **Commercial Paper:** Commercial paper is a short-term unsecured promissory note, negotiable and transferable by endorsement and delivery with a fixed maturity period. It is issued by large and creditworthy companies to raise short-term funds at lower rates of interest than market rates. It usually has a maturity period of 15 days to one year. The issuance of commercial paper is an alternative to bank borrowing for large companies that are generally considered to be financially strong. It is sold at a discount and redeemed at par. The original purpose of commercial paper was to provide short-terms funds for seasonal and working capital needs. For example companies use this instrument for purposes such as bridge financing.

   *Example:* Suppose a company needs long-term finance to buy some machinery. In order to raise the long term funds in the capital market the company will have to incur floatation costs (costs associated with floating of an issue are brokerage, commission, printing of applications and advertising, etc.). Funds raised through commercial paper are used to meet the floatation costs. This is known as Bridge Financing.

3. **Call Money:** Call money is short term finance repayable on demand, with a maturity period of one day to fifteen days, used for inter-bank transactions. Commercial banks have to maintain a minimum cash balance known as cash reserve ratio. The Reserve Bank of India changes the cash reserve ratio from time to time which in turn affects the amount of funds available to be given as loans by commercial banks. Call money is a method by which banks borrow from each other to be able to maintain the cash reserve ratio. The interest rate paid on call money loans is known as the call rate. It is a highly volatile rate that varies from day-to-day and sometimes even from hour-to-hour. There is an inverse relationship between call rates and other short-term money market instruments such as certificates of deposit and commercial paper. A rise in call money rates makes other sources of finance such as commercial paper and certificates of deposit cheaper in comparison for banks raise funds from these sources.

4. **Certificate of Deposit:** Certificates of deposit (CD) are unsecured, negotiable, short-term instruments in bearer form, issued by commercial banks and development financial institutions. They can be issued to individuals, corporations and companies during periods of tight liquidity when the deposit growth of banks is slow but the demand for credit is high. They help to mobilise a large amount of money for short periods.

5. **Commercial Bill:** A commercial bill is a bill of exchange used to finance the working capital requirements of business firms. It is a short-term, negotiable, self-liquidating instrument which is used to finance the credit sales of firms. When goods are sold on credit, the buyer becomes liable to make payment on a specific date in future. The seller could wait till the specified date or make use of a bill of exchange. The seller (drawer) of the goods draws the bill and the buyer (drawee) accepts it. On being accepted, the bill becomes a marketable instrument and is called a trade bill. These bills can be discounted with a bank if the seller needs funds before the bill matures. When a trade bill is accepted by a commercial bank it is known as a commercial bill.

## CAPITAL MARKET

The term capital market refers to facilities and institutional arrangements through which long-term funds, both debt and equity are raised and invested. It consists of a series of channels through which savings of the community are made available for industrial and commercial enterprises and for the public in general. It directs these savings into their most productive use leading to growth and development of the economy. The capital market consists of development banks, commercial banks and stock exchanges.

An ideal capital market is one where finance is available at reasonable cost. The process of economic development is facilitated by the existence of a well functioning capital market. In fact, development of the financial system is seen as a necessary condition for economic growth. It is essential that financial institutions are sufficiently developed and that market operations are free, fair, competitive and transparent.

The capital market should also be efficient in respect of the information that it delivers, minimise transaction costs and allocate capital most productively.

The Capital Market can be divided into two parts:

(*a*) Primary Market

(*b*) Secondary Market.

## Primary Market

The primary market is also known as the new issues market. It deals with new securities being issued for the first time. The essential function of a primary market is to facilitate the transfer of investible funds from savers to entrepreneurs seeking to establish new enterprises or to expand existing ones through the issue of securities for the first time. The investors in this market are banks, financial institutions, insurance companies, mutual funds and individuals.

A company can raise capital through the primary market in the form of equity shares, preference shares, debentures, loans and deposits. Funds raised may be for setting up new projects, expansion, diversification, modernisation of existing projects, mergers and takeovers etc.

### *Methods of Floatation*

There are various methods of floating new issues in the primary market:

1. **Offer through Prospectus:** Offer through prospectus is the most popular method of raising funds by public companies in the primary market. This involves inviting subscription from the public through issue of prospectus. A prospectus makes a direct appeal to investors to raise capital, through an advertisement in newspapers and magazines. The issues may be underwritten and also are required to be listed on at least one stock exchange. The contents of the prospectus have to be in accordance with the provisions of the Companies Act and SEBI disclosure and investor protection guidelines.
2. **Offer for Sale:** Under this method securities are not issued directly to the public but are offered for sale through intermediaries like issuing houses or stock brokers. In this case, a company sells securities enbloc at an agreed price to brokers who, in turn, resell them to the investing public.
3. **Private Placement:** Private placement is the allotment of securities by a company to institutional investors and some selected individuals. It helps to raise capital more quickly than a public issue. Access to the primary market can be expensive on account of various mandatory and non-mandatory expenses. Some companies, therefore, cannot afford a public issue and choose to use private placement.
4. **Rights Issue:** This is a privilege given to existing shareholders to subscribe to a new issue of shares according to the terms and conditions of the company. The shareholders are offered the 'right' to buy new shares in proportion to the number of shares they already possess.
5. **e-IPOs:** A company proposing to issue capital to the public through the on-line system of the stock exchange has to enter into an agreement with the stock exchange. This is called an Initial Public Offer (IPO). SEBI registered brokers have to be appointed for the purpose of accepting applications and placing orders with the company. The issuer company should also appoint a registrar to the issue having electronic connectivity with the exchange. The issuer company can apply for listing of its securities on any exchange other than the exchange through which it has offered its securities. The lead manager coordinates all the activities amongst intermediaries connected with the issue.

## Secondary Market

The secondary market is also known as the stock market or stock exchange. It is a market for the purchase and sale of existing securities. It helps existing investors to disinvest and fresh investors to enter the market. It also provides liquidity and marketability to existing securities. It also contributes to economic growth by channelising funds towards the most productive investments through the process of disinvestment and reinvestment. Securities are traded, cleared and settled within the regulatory framework prescribed by SEBI. Advances in information technology have made trading through stock exchanges accessible from anywhere in the country through trading terminals. Along with the growth of the primary market in the country, the secondary market has also grown significantly during the last ten years.

**Primary and Secondary Markets — A Comparison**

| Primary Market (New Issue Market) | Secondary Market (Stock Exchange) |
|---|---|
| (i) There is sale of securities by new companies or further (new issues of securities by existing companies to investors). | (i) There is trading of existing shares only. |
| (ii) Securities are sold by the company to the investor directly (or through an intermediary). | (ii) Ownership of existing securities is exchanged between investors. The company is not involved at all. |
| (iii) The flow of funds is from savers to investors, *i.e.* the primary market directly promotes capital formation. | (iii) Enhances encashability (liquidity) of shares, *i.e.*, the secondary market indirectly promotes capital formation. |
| (iv) Only buying of securities takes place in the primary market, securities cannot be sold there. | (iv) Both the buying and the selling of securities can take place on the stock exchange. |
| (v) Prices are determined and decided by the management of the company. | (v) Prices are determined by demand and supply for the security. |
| (vi) There is no fixed geographical location. | (vi) Located at specified places. |

## STOCK EXCHANGE

A stock exchange is an institution which provides a platform for buying and selling of existing securities. As a market, the stock exchange facilitates the exchange of a security (share, debenture etc.) into money and vice versa. Stock exchanges help companies raise finance, provide liquidity and safety of investment to the investors and enhance the credit worthiness of individual companies.

### Meaning of Stock Exchange

According to Securities Contracts (Regulation) Act 1956, stock exchange means any body of individuals, whether incorporated or not, constituted for the purpose of assisting, regulating or controlling the business of buying and selling or dealing in securities.

### Functions of a Stock Exchange

The efficient functioning of a stock exchange creates a conducive climate for an active and growing primary market for new issues. An active and healthy secondary market in existing securities leads to positive environment among investors. The following are some of the important functions of a stock exchange.

1. **Providing Liquidity and Marketability to Existing Securities:** The basic function of a stock exchange is the creation of a continuous market where securities are bought and sold. It gives investors the chance to disinvest and reinvest. This provides both liquidity and easy marketability to already existing securities in the market.
2. **Pricing of Securities:** Share prices on a stock exchange are determined by the forces of demand and supply. A stock exchange is a mechanism of constant valuation through which the prices of securities are determined. Such a valuation provides important instant information to both buyers and sellers in the market.
3. **Safety of Transaction:** The membership of a stock exchange is well-regulated and its dealings are well defined according to the existing legal framework. This ensures that the investing public gets a safe and fair deal on the market.
4. **Contributes to Economic Growth:** A stock exchange is a market in which existing securities are resold or traded. Through this process of disinvestment and reinvestment savings get channelised into their most productive investment avenues. This leads to capital formation and economic growth.
5. **Spreading of Equity Cult:** The stock exchange can play a vital role in ensuring wider share ownership by regulating new issues, better trading practices and taking effective steps in educating the public about investments.
6. **Providing Scope for Speculation:** The stock exchange provides sufficient scope within the provisions of law for speculative activity in a restricted and controlled manner. It is generally accepted that a certain degree of healthy speculation is necessary to ensure liquidity and price continuity in the stock market.

### Dematerialisation and Depositories

All trading in securities is now done through computer terminals. Since all systems are computerised, buying and selling of securities are settled through an electronic book entry form. This is mainly done to eliminate problems like theft, fake/forged transfers, transfer delays and paperwork associated with share certificates or debentures held in physical form.

This is a process where securities held by the investor in the physical form are cancelled and the investor is given an electronic entry or number so that she/he can hold it as an electronic balance in an account. This process of holding securities in an electronic form is called dematerialisation. For this, the investor has to open a demat account with an organisation called a depository. In fact, now all Initial Public Offers (IPOs) are issued in dematerialisation form and more than 99% of the turnover is settled by delivery in the demat form.

The Securities and Exchange Board of India (SEBI) has made it mandatory for the settlement procedures to take place in demat form in certain select securities. Holding shares in demat form is very convenient as it is just like a bank account. Physical shares can be converted into electronic form or electronic holdings can be reconverted into physical certificates (rematerialisation). Dematerialisation enables shares to be transferred to some other account just like cash and ensures settlement of all trades through a single account in shares. These demat securities can even be pledged or hypothecated to get loans. There is no danger of loss, theft or forgery of share certificates. It is the broker's responsibility to credit the investor's account with the correct number of shares.

## Working of the Demat System

1. A depository participant (DP), either a bank, broker, or financial services company, may be identified.
2. An account opening form and documentation (PAN card details, photograph, power of attorney) may be completed.
3. The physical certificate is to be given to the DP along with a dematerialisation request form.
4. If shares are applied in a public offer, simple details of DP and demat account are to be given and the shares on allotment would automatically be credited to the demat account.
5. If shares are to be sold through a broker, the DP is to be instructed to debit the account with the number of shares.
6. The broker then gives instruction to his DP for delivery of the shares to the stock exchange.
7. The broker then receives payment and pay the person for the shares sold.
8. All these transactions are to be completed within 2 days, *i.e.*, delivery of shares and payment received from the buyer is on a T+2 basis, settlement period.

## National Stock Exchange of India (NSE)

The National Stock Exchange is the latest, most modern and technology driven exchange. It was incorporated in 1992 and was recognised as a stock exchange in April, 1993. It started operations in 1994, with trading on the wholesale debt market segment. Subsequently, it launched the capital market segment in November 1994 as a trading platform for equities and the futures and options segment in June 2000 for various derivative instruments. NSE has set up a nationwide fully automated screen based trading system.

The NSE was set up by leading financial institutions, banks, insurance companies and other financial intermediaries. It is managed by professionals, who do not directly or indirectly trade on the exchange. The trading rights are with the trading members who offer their services to the investors. The Board of NSE comprises senior executives from promoter institutions and eminent professionals, without having any representation from trading members.

### *Objectives of NSE*

NSE was set up with the following objectives:

(*a*) Establishing a nationwide trading facility for all types of securities.

(*b*) Ensuring equal access to investors all over the country through an appropriate communication network.

(*c*) Providing a fair, efficient and transparent securities market using electronic trading system.

(*d*) Enabling shorter settlement cycles and book entry settlements.

(*e*) Meeting international benchmarks and standards.

Within a span of ten years, NSE has been able to achieve its objectives for which it was set up. It has been playing a leading role as a change agent in transforming the Indian capital market.

NSE has been able to take the stock market to the door step of the investors. It has ensured that technology has been harnessed to deliver the services to the investors across the country at the lowest cost. It has provided a nation wide screen based automated trading system with a high degree of transparency and equal access to investors irrespective of geographical location.

### *Market Segments of NSE*

The Exchange provides trading in the following two segments.

(*i*) **Whole Sale Debt Market Segment:** This segment provides a trading platform for a wide range of fixed income securities that include central government securities, treasury bills, state development loans, bonds issued by public sector undertakings, floating rate bonds, zero coupon bonds, index bonds, commercial paper, certificate of deposit, corporate debentures and mutual funds.

(*ii*) **Capital Market Segment:** The capital market segment of NSE provides an efficient and transparent platform for trading in equity, preference, debentures, exchange traded funds as well as retail Government securities.

## BSE (Bombay Stock Exchange Ltd.)

BSE Ltd (formerly known as Bombay Stock Exchange Ltd) was established in 1875 and was Asia's first Stock Exchange. It was granted permanent recognition under the Securities Contract (Regulation) Act, 1956. It has contributed to the growth of the corporate sector by providing a platform for raising capital. It is known as BSE Ltd but was established as the Native Share Stock Brokers Association in 1875. Even before the actual legislations were enacted, BSE Ltd already had a set of Rules and Regulations to ensure an orderly growth of the securities market. BSE is one such exchange set up as a corporate entity with a broad shareholder base. It has the following objectives:

(*a*) To provide an efficient and transparent market for trading in equity, debt instruments, derivatives, and mutual funds.

(*b*) To provide a trading platform for equities of small and medium enterprises.

(*c*) To ensure active trading and safeguard market integrity through an electronically-driven exchange.

(*d*) To provide other services to capital market participants, like risk management, clearing, settlement, market data, and education.

(*e*) To conform to international standards.

Besides having a nation-wide presence, BSE has a global reach with customers around the world. It has stimulated innovation and competition across all market segments. It has established a capital market institute, called the BSE Institute Ltd, which provides education on financial markets and vocational training to a number of people seeking employment with stock brokers. The exchange has about 5000 companies listed from all over the country and outside, and has the largest market capitalisation in India.

## Securities and Exchange Board of India (SEBI)

The Securities and Exchange Board of India was established by the Government of India on 12 April, 1988 as an interim administrative body to promote orderly and healthy growth of securities market and for investor protection. It was to function under the overall administrative control of the Ministry of Finance of the Government of India. The SEBI was given a statutory status on 30 January, 1992 through an ordinance. The ordinance was later replaced by an Act of Parliament known as the Securities and Exchange Board of India Act, 1992.

### Reasons for the Establishment of SEBI

The capital market has witnessed a tremendous growth during 1980's, characterised particularly by the increasing participation of the public.

This ever expanding investors population and market capitalisation led to a variety of malpractices on the part of companies, brokers, merchant bankers, investment consultants and others involved in the securities market.

The glaring examples of these malpractices include existence of self-styled merchant bankers unofficial private placements, rigging of prices, unofficial premium on new issues, non-adherence of provisions of the Companies Act, violation of rules and regulations of stock exchanges and listing requirements, delay in delivery of shares etc.

These malpractices and unfair trading practices have eroded investor confidence and multiplied investor grievances.

The Government and the stock exchanges were rather helpless in redressing the investor's problems because of lack of proper penal provisions in the existing legislation. In view of the above, the Government of India decided to setup a separate regulatory body known as Securities and Exchange Board of India.

### Purpose and Role of SEBI

The basic purpose of SEBI is to create an environment to facilitate efficient mobilisation and allocation of resources through the securities markets. It also aims to stimulate competition and encourage innovation. This environment includes rules and regulations, institutions and their interrelationships, instruments, practices, infrastructure and policy framework.

This environment aims at meeting the needs of the three groups which basically constitute the market, viz, the issuers of securities (Companies), the investors and the market intermediaries.

- To the issuers, it aims to provide a market place in which they can confidently look forward to raising finances they need in an easy, fair and efficient manner.
- To the investors, it should provide protection of their rights and interests through adequate, accurate and authentic information and disclosure of information on a continuous basis.
- To the intermediaries, it should offer a competitive, professionalised and expanding market with adequate and efficient infrastructure so that they are able to render better service to the investors and issuers.

### Objectives of SEBI

The overall objective of SEBI is to protect the interests of investors and to promote the development of, and regulate the securities market. This may be elaborated as follows:

1. To regulate stock exchanges and the securities industry to promote their orderly functioning.
2. To protect the rights and interests of investors, particularly individual investors and to guide and educate them.
3. To prevent trading malpractices and achieve a balance between self regulation by the securities industry and its statutory regulation.
4. To regulate and develop a code of conduct and fair practices by intermediaries like brokers, merchant bankers etc., with a view to making them competitive and professional.

### Functions of SEBI

Keeping in mind the emerging nature of the securities market in India, SEBI was entrusted with the twin task of both regulation and development of the securities market. It also has certain protective functions.

### Regulatory Functions

1. Registration of brokers and sub-brokers and other players in the market.
2. Registration of collective investment schemes and Mutual Funds.
3. Regulation of stock brokers, portfolio exchanges, underwriters and merchant bankers and the business in stock exchanges and any other securities market.
4. Regulation of takeover bids by companies.
5. Calling for information by undertaking inspection, conducting enquiries and audits of stock exchanges and intermediaries.
6. Levying fee or other charges for carrying out the purposes of the Act.
7. Performing and exercising such power under Securities Contracts (Regulation) Act 1956, as may be delegated by the Government of India.

### Development Functions

1. Training of intermediaries of the securities market.
2. Conducting research and publishing information useful to all market participants.
3. Undertaking measures to develop the capital markets by adapting a flexible approach.

### Protective Functions

1. Prohibition of fraudulent and unfair trade practices like making misleading statements, manipulations, price rigging etc.
2. Controlling insider trading and imposing penalties for such practices.
3. Undertaking steps for investor protection.
4. Promotion of fair practices and code of conduct in securities market.

### The Organisation Structure of SEBI

As SEBI is a statutory body there has been a considerable expansion in the range and scope of its activities. Each of the activities of the SEBI now demands more careful, closer, co-ordinated and intensive attention to enable it to attain its objectives. Accordingly, SEBI has been restructured and rationalised in tune with its expanded scope. It has decided its activities into five operational departments. Each department is headed by an executive director. Apart from its head office at Mumbai, SEBI has opened regional offices in Kolkata, Chennai, and Delhi to attend to investor complaints and liaise with the issuers, intermediaries and stock exchanges in the concerned region.

The SEBI also formed two advisory committees. They are the Primary Market Advisory Committee and the Secondary Market Advisory Committee. These committees consist of the market players, the investors associations recognised by the SEBI and the eminent persons in the capital market. They provide important inputs to the SEBI's policies.

The objectives of the two Committees are as follows:

(*a*) To advise SEBI on matters relating to the regulation of intermediaries for ensuring investors protection in the primary market.

(*b*) To advise SEBI on issues related to the development of primary market in India.

(*c*) To advise SEBI on disclosure requirements for companies.

(*d*) To advise for changes in legal framework to introduce simplification and transparency in the primary market.

(*e*) To advise the board in matters relating to the development and regulation of the secondary market in the country.

The committees are however non-statutory in nature and the SEBI is not bound by the advise of the committee. These committees are a part of SEBI's constant endeavor to obtain a feedback from the market players on various issues relating to the regulations and development of the market.

# Consumer Protection

## IMPORTANCE OF CONSUMER PROTECTION

The concept of consumer protection is to safeguard the interests of the consumers. It adopts measures to protect consumers from unethical malpractices by businesses and provide a swift redressal of their grievances with regard to:

1. Sale of adulterated goods such as adding inferior substances to the product being sold.
2. Sale of counterfeit goods such as selling a product of lesser value than the real product.
3. Sale of sub-standard goods such as the sale of products that do not meet the prescribed quality standards.
4. Sale of duplicate goods.
5. Use of malfunctioning weights and measures that lead to underweight of products.
6. Black marketing and hoarding that eventually leads to scarcity of the product and well as a rise in the price of the same.
7. Overcharging a product, i.e., charging a product above its Maximum Retail Price.
8. Supplying of defective goods.
9. Advertisements that are misleading, *i.e.,* advertisements that falsely claim a product or a service to be shown as superior quality, grade or standard when not in real.
10. Supply of inferior services, *i.e.,* quality of service lesser than the condition agreed.

### Need for Consumer Protection

The need for consumer protection arises from the need to protect consumers from the loss or injury or other prevailing malpractices and to ensure:

1. Physical safety of a consumer.
2. Access to information.
3. Corporate Social Responsibility to provide quality and quantity of goods at fair prices.
4. Consumer satisfaction.
5. Social Justice and Trusteeship.
6. Survival and the Growth of businesses.

### From Consumers' point of view

The importance of consumer protection from the consumers' point of view can be understood from the following points:

(*i*) **Consumer Ignorance:** In the light of widespread ignorance of consumers about their rights and reliefs available to them, it becomes necessary to educate them about the same so as to achieve consumer awareness.

(*ii*) **Unorganised Consumers:** Consumers need to be organised in the form of consumer organisations which would take care of their interests. Though, in India, we do have consumer organisations which are working in this direction, adequate protection is required to be given to consumers till these organisations become powerful enough to protect and promote the interests of consumers.

(*iii*) **Widespread Exploitation of Consumers:** Consumers might be exploited by unscrupulous, exploitative and unfair trade practices like defective and unsafe products, adulteration, false and misleading advertising, hoarding, black-marketing, etc. Consumers need protection against such malpractices of the sellers.

### From the point of view of Business

A business must also lay emphasis on protecting the consumers and adequately satisfying them. This is important because of the following reasons:

(*i*) **Long-term Interest of Business:** Enlightened businesses realise that it is in their long-term interest to satisfy their customers. Satisfied customers not only lead to repeat sales but also provide good feedback to prospective customers and thus, help in increasing the customer-base of business. Thus, business firms should aim at long-term profit maximisation through customer satisfaction.

(*ii*) **Business uses Society's Resources:** Business organisations use resources which belong to the society. They, thus, have a responsibility to supply such products and render such services which are in public interest and would not impair public confidence in them.

(*iii*) **Social Responsibility:** A business has social responsibilities towards various interest groups. Business organisations make money by selling goods and providing services to consumers.

Thus, consumers form an important group among the many stakeholders of business and like other stakeholders, their interest has to be well taken care of.

(*iv*) **Moral Justification:** It is the moral duty of any business to take care of consumer's interest and avoid any form of their exploitation. Thus, a business must avoid unscrupulous, exploitative and unfair trade practices like defective and unsafe products, adulteration, false and misleading advertising, hoarding, black marketing, etc.

(*v*) **Government Intervention:** A business engaging in any form of exploitative trade practices would invite government intervention or action. This can impair and tarnish the image of the company. Thus, it is advisable that business organisations voluntarily resort to such practices where the customers' needs and interests will well be taken care of.

## THE CONSUMER PROTECTION ACT, 2019

The Consumer Protection Act, 2019 seeks to protect and promote the consumers' interest through speedy and inexpensive redressal of their grievances. It extends to the whole of India.

It is applicable to all types of businesses whether a manufacturer or a trader and whether supplying goods or providing services including e-commerce firms. The Act confers certain rights to consumers with a view to empowering them and to protect their interests.

### Who is a consumer?

A 'consumer' is generally understood as a person who uses or consumes goods or avails of any service. Under the Consumer Protection Act 2019, a consumer is a person who buys any goods or avails services for a consideration, which has been paid or promised, or partly paid and partly promised, or under any scheme of deferred payment. It includes any user of such goods or beneficiary of services if such use is made with the approval of the buyer. It applies to both offline and online transactions through electronic means or by teleshopping or direct selling or multilevel marketing.

However, any person who obtains goods or avails services for resale or commercial purpose is not treated as a consumer and is outside the scope of Consumer Protection Act, 2019.

## CONSUMER RIGHTS

The Consumer Protection Act, 2019 provides for six rights of consumers. These rights include the following:

1. **Right to Safety:** The consumer has a right to be protected against goods and services which are hazardous to life, health and property. For example, electrical appliances which are manufactured with substandard products or do not conform to the safety norms might cause serious injury. Thus, consumers are educated that they should use electrical appliances which are ISI marked as this would be an assurance of such products meeting quality specifications.
2. **Right to be informed:** The consumer has a right to have complete information about the product he intends to buy including its ingredients, date of manufacture, price, quantity, directions for use, etc. It is because of this reason that the legal framework in India requires the manufactures to provide such information on the package and label of the product.
3. **Right to be assured:** The consumer has the freedom to access variety of products at competitive prices. This implies that the marketers should offer a wide variety of products in terms of quality, brand, prices, size, etc. and allow the consumer to make a choice from amongst these.
4. **Right to be heard:** The consumer has a right to file a complaint and to be heard in case of dissatisfaction with a good or a service. It is because of this reason that many enlightened business firms have set up their own consumer service and grievance cells. Many consumer organisations are also working towards this direction and helping consumers in redressal of their grievances.
5. **Right to seek redressal:** The consumer has a right to get relief against unfair trade practice of restrictive trade practices or unscrupulous exploitation in case the product or a service falls short of his expectations. The Consumer Protection Act, 2019 provides for redressal to the consumers including replacement of the product, removal of defect in the product, compensation paid for any loss or injury suffered by the consumer, etc.
6. **Right to Consumer Education:** The consumer has a right to acquire knowledge and to be a well informed consumer throughout life. He should be aware about his rights and the reliefs available to him in case of a product or service falling short of his expectations. Many consumer organisations and some enlightened businesses are taking an active part in educating consumers in this respect.

## CONSUMER RESPONSIBILITIES

The Consumer Protection Act empowers the consumer to fight against any unscrupulous, exploitative and unfair, restrictive trade practices adopted by sellers. Consumer rights, by themselves, cannot be effective in achieving the objective of consumer protection. Consumer protection can, in effect, be achieved only when the consumers also understand their responsibilities.

A consumer should keep in mind the following responsibilities while purchasing, using and consuming goods and services—

(*i*) Be aware about various goods and services available in the market so that an intelligent and wise choice can be made.

(*ii*) Buy only standardised goods as they provide quality assurance. Thus, look for ISI mark on electrical goods, FPO mark on food products, Hallmark on jewelry, etc.

(*iii*) Learn about the risks associated with products and services, follow manufacturer's instructions and use the products safely.

(*iv*) Read labels carefully so as to have information about prices, net weight, manufacturing and expiry dates, etc.

(*v*) Assert yourself to ensure that you get a fair deal.

(*vi*) Be honest in your dealings. Choose only from legal goods and services and discourage unscrupulous practices like black-marketing, hoarding, etc.

(*vii*) Ask for a cash memo on purchase of goods or services. This would serve as a proof of the purchase made.

(*viii*) File a complaint in an appropriate consumer forum in case of a shortcoming in the quality of goods purchased or services availed. Do not fail to take an action even when the amount involved is small.

(*ix*) Form consumer societies which would play an active part in educating consumers and safeguarding their interests.

(*x*) Respect the environment. Avoid waste, littering and contributing to pollution.

## WAYS AND MEANS OF CONSUMER PROTECTION

A consumers' awareness about their rights and responsibilities is just one of the ways in which the objective of consumer protection can be achieved. There are other ways in which this objective may be achieved.

1. **Self-regulation by Business:** Socially responsible firms follow ethical standards and practices in dealing with their customers Good and ethical practices encourage firms to realise that it is in their long-term interest to serve the customers in a rightful manner. Many firms have set up their customer service and grievance cells to redress the problems and grievances of their consumers.
2. **Business Associations:** The associations of trade, commerce and business like Federation of Indian Chambers of Commerce of India (FICCI) and Confederation of Indian Industries (CII) have laid down their code of conduct which lay down for their members the guidelines in their dealings with the customers.
3. **Consumer Awareness:** A consumer, who is well-informed about his rights and the reliefs available to him, would be in a position to raise his voice against any unfair trade practices or unscrupulous exploitation. In addition to this, an understanding of his responsibilities would also enable a consumer to safeguard his interests. In this regard, the Department of Consumer Affairs, GOI, has been undertaking *Jago Grahak Jago* campaign, for generating awareness among consumers.
4. **Consumer Organisations:** Consumer organisations play an important role in educating consumers about their rights and providing protection to them. These organisations can force business firms to avoid malpractices and exploitation of consumers.
5. **Government:** The government can protect the interests of the consumers by enacting various measures. For example, the GOI has set up a toll-free National Consumer Helpline Number 1800114000 for this purpose. The legal framework in India encompasses various legislations which provide protection to consumers. The most important of these regulations is the Consumer Protection Act, 2019. The Act provides for a central authority to regulate matters relating to violation of rights of consumers, unfair trade practices and false or misleading advertisements which are prejudicial to the interests of consumers. This is known as Central Consumer Protection Authority (CCPA). A three-tier machinery at the district, state and national levels for redressal of consumer grievances.

## REDRESSAL AGENCIES UNDER THE CONSUMER PROTECTION ACT

For the redressal of consumer grievances, the Consumer Protection Act, 2019 provides for setting up of a three-tier enforcement machinery at the District, State, and the National levels, known as the District Consumer Disputes Redressal

Commission, State Consumer Disputes Redressal Commission, and the National Consumer Disputes Redressal Commission. They are briefly referred to as the 'District Commission', 'State Commission', and the 'National Commission', respectively. While the National Commission is set up by the Central Government, the State Commissions and the District Forums are set up, by the State Government. The Figure on redressal agencies shows the hierarchical structure of this three-tire machinery.

The consumer grievances are redressed by the three tire machinery:

### District Commission

District commission has a jurisdiction to entertain complaints where value of goods or services paid as consideration does not exceed one crore rupees. Either on the first hearing or at any later stage, it appears to district commission that there exists elements of settlement which may be acceptable to the parties, it may direct them to give their consent for settlement of dispute through mediation within five days. In case the parties agree for settlement by mediation and give written consent, the district commission refers the matter for mediation and the provisions relating to mediation shall apply.

However, in the event of failure of settlement by mediation proceeds with the complaint. If the complaint alleges defect in goods which cannot be determined without proper analysis or test of goods, the commission obtains the sample of goods, seal it and refer to the appropriate authority for analysis.

In case of services, the dispute is settled based on the basis of evidence brought to its notice by the complainant and can ask for any required information document or records from the service provider for settlement.

If any of the parties are not satisfied by the order of District Commission can appeal against such order to the State Commission on the grounds of facts or law within a period of forty five days from the date of order.

### State Commission

It is established by the respective state government and ordinarily function at the state capital. State Commission has a jurisdiction to entertain complaints where value of goods and services paid as consideration exceeds one crore but does not exceed ten crore rupees. If any of the parties are not satisfied by the order of State Commission can appeal against such order to the National Commission within a period of thirty days of such order.

### National Commission

The National Commission has territorial jurisdiction over the whole country. National Commission has a jurisdiction to entertain complaints where value of goods or services paid as consideration exceeds ten crores of rupees. If any of the parties are not satisfied by the order of National Commission can appeal against such order to the Supreme Court of India within a period of thirty days of such order.

## ENTREPRENEURSHIP DEVELOPMENT

The terms 'entrepreneur,' 'entrepreneurship' and 'enterprise' can be understood by drawing an analogy with the structure of a sentence in English language. Entrepreneur is the person (the subject), entrepreneurship is the process (the verb) and enterprise is the creation of the person and the output of the process (the object).

Entrepreneurs play important roles both in relation to economic development and in relation to the enterprise. In relation to economic development, entrepreneurs contribute to growth in GDP, capital formation and employment generation besides creating business opportunities for others and bringing about an improvement in the quality of life in the community in which they operate. In relation to the enterprise, they perform a number of roles right from the conception of a business idea, examining its feasibility and mobilisation of resources for its eventual realisation as a business firm. They bear the uncertainties and risks associated with the business activity, introduce product, market, technological and a host of other innovations. In the developing country context they also assume the responsibility for the day-to-day management of the enterprise.

Given its critical role in economic development at a broader level and business start-ups at the micro level, it is imperative that a conscious effort be made to popularise entrepreneurship as a career option. In this regard, EAPs and EDPs can play an important role. Besides, there is a need to create an entrepreneurship friendly environment. Since, entrepreneurship is the outcome of a dynamic interaction between the person and the environment, there is need also for developing entrepreneurial competencies, motivations, values and attitudes.

•••

# Multiple Choice Questions

1. 'Doing the task with minimum cost" name the term associated with management?
   A. Efficiency B. Effective
   C. Both D. Management

2. The objective of the Marketing Department of 'KOTEX Ltd.' is to increase sales by 10 per cent by offering discounts. But, the finance department may not approve of such discounts as it means loss of revenue. These kinds of conflict arise in organizations because each department performing activities in isolation from others and barriers between departments are becoming more rigid. Identify the point of importance of coordination to which this case is related:
   A. Growth in size
   B. Functional differentiation
   C. Specialization
   D. None of these

3. Policy formulation is the function of:
   A. Top level Managers
   B. Middle level Managers
   C. Operational Management
   D. None of the above

4. Goal setting is the function of:
   A. CEO B. Foreman
   C. Supervisor D. Superintendent

5. How does a manager want to achieve his objectives?
   A. Efficiently
   B. Effectively
   C. Efficiently and effectively
   D. None of the above

6. Successful organizations do not achieve goals by chance but by following a deliberate process known as:
   A. Planning B. Co-ordination
   C. Controlling D. Management

7. Which one of the following sequences of process of management is correct?
   A. Planning, Directing, Controlling, Organising, Staffing
   B. Directing, Staffing, Planning, Organising, Controlling
   C. Planning, Organising, Staffing, Directing, Controlling
   D. Organising, Planning, Staffing, Controlling, Directing

8. Which degree is compulsory to become a manager?
   A. B.B.A.
   B. M.Com.
   C. M.B.A.
   D. No compulsion of degree

9. In which of the following occupation, no minimum qualification is prescribed?
   A. Manager B. Doctor
   C. Lawyer D. Chartered Accountant

10. Managing Director will be considered under which level of management?
    A. Top-level B. Middle-level
    C. Lower-level D. None of these

11. Foreman will be considered under which level of management?
    A. Lower-level B. Middle-level
    C. Top-level D. None of these

12. Management is essential for the organizations which are:
    A. Non-profit organizations
    B. Service organizations
    C. Social organizations
    D. All of the above

13. Successful management ensures that:
    A. Goals are achieved with least cost
    B. Timely achievement of goals
    C. Both of the above
    D. None of the above

14. Ravi works as a production manager in Rosy Private Limited. He has been given the task of getting 10000 units of hand woven table mats manufactured at the cost of ₹ 150 per unit, within 100 days. In order to be acknowledged as an effective manager, he must ensure that:
    A. The cost of production does not exceed ₹ 150 per unit
    B. The work is completed within 100 days even at higher cost per unit
    C. The cost of production is less than ₹ 150 per unit
    D. All of the above

15. Management is said to be poor if it is:
    A. Efficient but ineffective
    B. Effective but inefficient

C. Both inefficient and ineffective
D. All of the above

**16.** Suzy Enterprises Limited is planning to increase its sales by 25% in the next year. Identify the feature of management being highlighted in the given statement:
A. Management is all pervasive
B. Management is a goal oriented process
C. Management is a continuous process
D. All of the above

**17.** Keeping in view, the changes in the consumer demands and preferences, 'Royal Bakery' has reduced the sugar and fat content in its products. This approach of business shows that management is:
A. An intangible force
B. A group activity
C. A dynamic function
D. A multidimensional activity

**18.** Management is considered to be an art because:
A. The principles of management have universal validity
B. The principles of management have universal application
C. Different principles of management are brought into effect differently by different managers
D. It is not important for the practicing managers to be a member of a professional association.

**19.** 'Corrective action' comes under which function of management?
A. Planning B. Organising
C. Directing D. Controlling

**20.** Match the concept of management in Column-I with their respective meaning in Column-II:

| Column-I | Column-II |
|---|---|
| (*a*) Effectiveness | (*i*) doing the task correctly with minimum cost. |
| (*b*) Efficiency | (*ii*) finishing the task on time. |
| (*c*) Process | (*iii*) The primary functions or activities that management performs to get. |

| | (*a*) | (*b*) | (*c*) |
|---|---|---|---|
| A. | (*i*) | (*ii*) | (*iii*) |
| B. | (*ii*) | (*i*) | (*iii*) |
| C. | (*iii*) | (*ii*) | (*i*) |
| D. | (*i*) | (*iii*) | (*ii*) |

**21.** Match the objective of management in Column-I with their respective definition in Column-II:

| Column-I | Column-II |
|---|---|
| (*a*) Survival | (*i*) Increase in the number of employees, the number of products or increase in the capital investment, etc. |
| (*b*) Profit | (*ii*) A vital Incentive for the continued successful operation of the enterprise. |
| (*c*) Growth | (*iii*) An organisation must earn enough revenues to cover costs. |

| | (*a*) | (*b*) | (*c*) |
|---|---|---|---|
| A. | (*i*) | (*ii*) | (*iii*) |
| B. | (*ii*) | (*i*) | (*iii*) |
| C. | (*ii*) | (*iii*) | (*i*) |
| D. | (*i*) | (*iii*) | (*ii*) |

**Directions (Qs. No. 22-29):** *Read the following statements—Assertion (A) and Reason (R), and select the correct alternative in each case:*
A. Both Assertion (A) and Reason (R) are true.
B. Both Assertion (A) and Reason (R) are false.
C. Assertion (A) is true and Reason (R) is false.
D. Assertion (A) is false and Reason (R) is true.

**22. Assertion (A) :** There is a kind of cost-benefit analysis involved and the relationship between inputs and outputs.
**Reason (R) :** If by using less resources (*i.e.,* the inputs) more benefits are derived (*i.e.,* the outputs) then effectiveness has increased.

**23. Assertion (A) :** Coordination is not an exclusive function of the top management.
**Reason (R) :** Coordination is the responsibility of all managers—top, middle and operational levels.

**24. Assertion (A) :** Management is a full-fledged profession.
**Reason (R) :** Management meets the exact criteria of a profession.

**25. Assertion (A) :** Management is a series of continuous interrelated functions.
**Reason (R) :** The process of management is a series of continuous, interrelated, but separate functions (planning, organising, directing, staffing and controlling). These functions are simultaneously performed by all managers all the time.

**26. Assertion (A) :** Planning cannot prevent problems.
**Reason (R) :** Planning can only predict the problems and prepare contingency plans to deal with then if and when they occur.

**27. Assertion (A) :** Management is a dynamic function.
**Reason (R) :** An organisation interacts with its external environment which consists

of various social, economic and political factors. In order to be successful, an organisation must change itself and its goals according to the needs of the environment.

**28. Assertion (A) :** Management is a tangible force and its presence can be felt in the way the organization functions.

**Reason (R) :** The effect of management is noticeable in an organisation where targets are met according to plan, employees are happy and satisfied, and there is orderliness instead of chaos.

**29. Assertion (A) :** Coordination is an all pervasive function.

**Reason (R) :** Coordination is required at all levels of management due to the inter-dependent nature of activities.

**Directions (Qs. No. 30-33):** *Read the following statements—Assertion (A) and Reason (R), and select the correct alternative in each case:*

A. Both Assertion (A) and Reason (R) are True and Reason (R) is the correct explanation of Assertion (A).
B. Both Assertion (A) and Reason (R) are True, but Reason (R) is not the correct explanation of Assertion (A).
C. Assertion (A) is True, but Reason (R) is False.
D. Assertion (A) is False, but Reason (R) is true.

**30. Assertion (A) :** Social objective of management involve creation of benefits or economic values to the society.

**Reason (R) :** Now a days, profit maximization is the only objective of management.

**31. Assertion (A) :** Management is an exact science.

**Reason (R) :** It is based on human behaviour. It is neither precise nor as comprehensive as the pure science like physics or chemistry.

**32. Assertion (A) :** Satisfaction of personnel objectives is very important in an organisation.

**Reason (R) :** Employees are one of the most valuable resources for an organization.

**33. Assertion (A) :** Management principles are developed through observation and repeated experimentation.

**Reason (R) :** Outcomes of management principles can be predicted accurately.

**Directions (Qs. No. 34-37):** *These questions are based on the following CASE.*

Anu is a well-known face in the field of publishing. She owes the success of her business to her own education in business management and her team of certified management consultants. Therefore, she decides to send both her children Shreya and Darshal abroad to acquire degrees in the field of business management in their individual areas of expertise. She feels that all over the world there is marked growth in management as a discipline, but still it is not considered to be a full-fledged profession for certain reasons.

On the basis of the above case:

**34.** If Anu considers management as a discipline, identify the reason:
A. a lot of literature is available
B. it is a skillful activity
C. requires regular practice
D. has a code of conduct

**35.** Identify the concept of management in the above case:
A. science
B. both Art & Science
C. profession
D. art

**36.** Every manager applies his personal skill and knowledge in the day-to-day functioning of an enterprise. It is proved because:
A. management is an art
B. management is a science
C. management is a profession
D. None of these

**37.** Identify the features of management as a profession:
A. systematic body of knowledge
B. restricted entry
C. service motive
D. All of the above

**Directions (Qs. No. 38-42):** *Read the following and answer the questions on the basis of the same:*

Alcargo Ltd. is a operating its business on large scale. Co. realizes that human resources are the most important assets of its business. So HRM Department is set up to show a developmental path to the employees through proper training modules and job enrichment. Time to time incentives and awards are given to employees which was based on their performance, which keeps the employees highly motivated. Ravi, just a graduate in humanities is appointed as the Plant superintendent in the company. Ravi knew that there are certain theories and principles of management based on deep observation and experimentation. So, he studied various theories and principles of management before joining the Company. Ravi is very energetic and he likes to deal with severe situations. On August 20th, He informed his boss that the goal he had been assigned had been achieved and the quality was also very good. The best part is that there is one day left for the deadline, which is August 21. However, his boss was dissatisfied because the expenses incurred by his team to complete the project exceeded the upper limit (norms).

**38.** Which objective of management is pursued by management of Alcargo Ltd.:
A. Organizational objectives
B. Social objectives
C. Personal objectives
D. None of these

**39.** Identify the feature of profession which is not applicable here—"Ravi, just a graduate in humanities is appointed as the Plant superintendent in the company.'
A. Well defined body of knowledge
B. Restricted Entry
C. Ethical code of conduct
D. Service Motive

**40.** Which aspect of management is violated by Ravi in above case?
A. Planning B. Efficiency
C. Effectiveness D. Controlling

**41.** Identify the nature of management highlighted in this line—"Ravi knew that there are certain theories and principles of management based on deep observation and experimentation."
A. Management as Profession
B. Management as Science
C. Management as an Art
D. None of the above

**42.** Which aspect of management is followed by Ravi in above case?
A. Planning B. Efficiency
C. Effectiveness D. Controlling

**Directions (Qs. No. 43 and 44):** *Answer the following questions, based on the above case studies.*

Mr Mukesh used to manufacture shoes by employing labour who were easily available. When his son after completion is MBA joined the business. He analysed that if we use capital intensive method by using a machine it will reduce the cost and the quality of shoes will also improve.

**43.** Which technique of scientific management is used by his son?
A. Fatigue study B. Motion study
C. Method study D. Work study

**44.** What is the objective of that technique?
A. Finding the best way of doing thing
B. Finding the rest interval
C. Finding the minimum cost
D. All of the above

**Directions (Qs. No. 45 and 46):** *Answer the following questions, based on the above case studies.*

Mr Rajiv is the owner of "Laxmi Diary". He is producing various milk products. He always tests various ways of producing different products and chooses the best and most economical way of production. He is also very particular about fixing a place for everything and he makes sure that all the employees are given a fixed place so that there is no wastage of time and delay in production.

**45.** Which technique of scientific management is applied by Mr. Rajiv?
A. Motion study B. Fatigue study
C. Method study D. None of the above

**46.** Which principle of Henry Fayol is followed by him?
A. Principle of equity B. Principle of order
C. Principle of discipline D. All of the above.

**Directions (Qs. No. 47 and 48):** *Answer the following questions based on the above case studies.*

Principles of Taylor and Fayol are mutually complementary. One believed that the management should share the gain with the workers while the other suggested that employee's compensation should depend upon the earning capacity of the company and should give them a reasonable standard of living.

**47.** Which principle of Fayol is applied here?
A. Remuneration B. Discipline
C. Equity D. Esprit the corps

**48.** Which principle of Taylor is applied here?
A. Harmony not discord
B. Cooperation not individualism
C. science not rule of thumb
D. None of the above

**49.** Manager of ABC Ltd. does not allocate work as per the capability of workers. Which principle is violated by them?
A. Principle of equity
B. Principle of discipline
C. Principle of order
D. Principle of Division of work

**50.** The salesman of ABC Ltd. could not achieve his sales target of 1000 units, on enquiry it was found that he was not allowed to take decision related to give discount or credit to any of his customer. State the principle of Management violated in this case.

A. Principle of Division of work
B. Principle of order
C. Principle of authority and responsibility
D. None of these

**51.** Suraj was engaged in the business of carpet making. Since company was making handmade carpet as well as machine made carpet. There were lot of overlapping of activities, so the Production manager advised there should be two separate division for both of them. Where in each division should have its own incharge plans and execution.

Identify the principle of management insisted by Production Manager.

A. Unity of command B. Unity of direction
C. Order D. Equity

**52.** Mr. Malhotra, Finance Manager of ABC Ltd. Applied for leave to attend a family function in Amritsar. The director of the company requested him to cancel his leave as there is an important meeting schedule on that date. Mr. Malhotra immediately agreed and cancelled his trip as he thought attending meeting is more import for company's benefit.

Which principle of Fayol is applied by Mr. Malhotra?

A. Principle of subordination of individual interest to general interest
B. Principle of equity
C. Principle of order
D. Principle of Discipline

**53.** The principles of management are said to be flexible as:

A. They aim at influencing behaviour of human beings.
B. They are general guidelines to action, but do not provide readymade solutions to management problems.
C. They can be modified by the manager when the situation so demands.
D. Their application is dependent upon the prevailing situation at a particular point of time.

**54.** "Management principles are not as rigid as principles of pure science." Which of the following best describes the given statement?

A. Management principles deal with human behaviour and, thus, are to be applied creatively given the demands of the situation.
B. Principles of management are formed after research in work situations, which are technical in nature.
C. Principles of management contribute towards the development of management both as a science and as an art.
D. None of the above

**55.** The principles are guidelines to action but do not provide readymade, straitjacket solutions to all managerial problems. This is so because.

A. The applications of principles has to be changed as per requirements.
B. Real business situations are very complex and dynamic and are a result of many factors.
C. Principles are like different tools serving different purposes, the manager has to decide which tool to use under what circumstances.
D. All the above

**56.** "The principles of management are not rigid prescriptions, which have to be followed absolutely." Which of the following best describes the given statement?

A. Management principles aim at influencing behaviour of human beings.
B. Management principles enable a better understanding of the relationship between human and material resources in accomplishing organisational purposes.
C. Management principles are flexible and can be modified by the manager when the situation so demands.
D. None of the above

**57.** The application of principles has to be changed as per requirements. For example, employees deserve fair and just remuneration. But what is just and fair is determined by multiple factors. They include contribution of the employee, paying capacity of the employer and also prevailing wage rate for the occupation under consideration.

Identify the nature of principles of management highlighted above.

A. General Guidelines B. Flexible
C. Mainly Behavioural D. Contingent

**58.** A manager should have the right to punish a subordinate for wilfully not obeying a legitimate order but only after sufficient opportunity has been given to a subordinate for presenting her/his case. Identify the principle of management highlighted above.

A. Authority and Responsibility
B. Discipline
C. Equity
D. Stability of Personnel

**59.** According to Fayol, discipline requires _______.

A. Good superiors at all levels
B. clear and fair agreements
C. Judicious application of penalties
D. All of these

60. _______ is an extension of the principle of division of work and specialization to the shop floor; and it violates the principle of Unity of command.
A. Cooperation, not individualism
B. Functional foremanship
C. Unity of Direction
D. Standardisation and Simplification of work

61. Which of the following technique of scientific management violate's the principle of Equity?
A. Functional foremanship
B. Standardisation and Simplification of work
C. Differential Piece Wage System
D. Method Study

62. A worker directly contacts the CEO of the company with a complaint regarding working conditions in the factory. Which of the following principles is being violated here?
A. Unity of Command
B. Discipline
C. Scalar Chain
D. Unity of Direction

63. Same battery can be used in different mobile phones of a particular brand. This is an example of which of the following techniques of scientific management?
A. Standardisation of work
B. Method Study
C. Simplification of work
D. Functional Foremanship

64. "She/he keeps machines, materials, tools etc., ready for operations by concerned workers'.
Whose work is described by this sentence under functional foremanship?
A. Route Clerk B. Repair Boss
C. Gang Boss D. Instruction Card Clerk

65. Which one of the following statements best describes 'Mental Revolution' as described by F.W. Taylor?
A. It implies change of attitude.
B. The management and workers should not play the game of one upmanship.
C. Both management and workers require each other.
D. Workers should be paid more wages..

66. In an organisation, each person should be scientifically selected. Then work assigned should suit his physical, mental and intellectual capabilities. To increase efficiency, they should be given the required training. Efficient employees would produce more and earn more. Which of the following principle of management is highlighted above?
A. Science, not rule of thumb
B. Division of work
C. Development of each and every person to his/her greatest efficiency and prosperity
D. Remuneration of employees

67. According to this principle of management, there should be obedience to organisational rules and contract of employment, clear and fair decisions and judicious application of penalties which are necessary for the working of the organisation.

The principle of management referred to above is:
A. Authority and Responsibility
B. Discipline
C. Unity of Command
D. Subordination of Individual Interest to General Interest

68. Sanak and Gagan started their career in Wales Limited (a printing press) after going through a rigorous recruitment process. Since they had no prior work experience, the firm decided to give them one year to prove themselves. The principle of management followed by Wales Limited is:
A. Authority and Responsibility
B. Discipline
C. Equity
D. Stability of Personnel

69. Match the principle of management in Column-I with their respective explanation in Column-II:

| Column-I | Column-II |
|---|---|
| (*a*) Scalar chain | (*i*) When no division of the company has a separate plan of action. |
| (*b*) Subordination of individual interest to general interest | (*ii*) When a manager awards contract for supply of raw material to a particular party, which happens to be owned by his relative ignoring other parties, who can supply the same at a cheaper rate. |
| (*c*) Unity of direction | (*iii*) When a subordinate habitually contacts higher authorities in the company by passing his/her immediate superior. |
| (*d*) Equity | (*iv*) When the manager grants one month medical leave to a supervisor with pay and only one week medical leave to accountant. |

| | (*a*) | (*b*) | (*c*) | (*d*) |
|---|---|---|---|---|
| A. | (*i*) | (*ii*) | (*iii*) | (*iv*) |
| B. | (*ii*) | (*i*) | (*iii*) | (*iv*) |
| C. | (*iii*) | (*ii*) | (*i*) | (*iv*) |
| D. | (*iii*) | (*i*) | (*ii*) | (*iv*) |

**70.** Match the technique of scientific management in Column-I with their respective explanation in Column-II:

| | |
|---|---|
| (*a*) Time study | (*i*) Each specialist is to be assigned work according to her/his qualities. For example, those with technical mastery, intelligence and grit may be given planning work. Those with energy and good health may be assigned execution work. |
| (*b*) Method study | (*ii*) Devising new varieties instead of the existing ones and eliminating unnecessary diversity of products. |
| (*c*) Functional foremanship | (*iii*) Fixing the standard time taken to perform a well-defined job so as to determine the number of workers to be employed; frame suitable incentive schemes and determine labour costs. |
| (*d*) Standardisation and simplification of work | (*iv*) Finding out one best way of doing the job to minimise the cost of production and maximizethe quality and satisfaction of the customer. |

| | (*a*) | (*b*) | (*c*) | (*d*) |
|---|---|---|---|---|
| A. | (*iii*) | (*ii*) | (*i*) | (*iv*) |
| B. | (*ii*) | (*i*) | (*iii*) | (*iv*) |
| C. | (*iii*) | (*iv*) | (*i*) | (*ii*) |
| D. | (*i*) | (*iii*) | (*ii*) | (*iv*) |

**71.** Match the technique of scientific management in Column-I with their respective explanation in Column-II:

| | |
|---|---|
| (*a*) Standardisation of work | (*i*) Separation of planning and execution functions |
| (*b*) Simplification of work | (*ii*) Setting benchmarks for every business activity which must be adhered to during production |
| (*c*) Method study | (*iii*) Eliminating superfluous varieties, sizes and dimensions. |
| (*d*) Functional foremanship | (*iv*) Minimising the cost of production and maximise the quality and satisfaction of the customer |

| | (*a*) | (*b*) | (*c*) | (*d*) |
|---|---|---|---|---|
| A. | (*i*) | (*ii*) | (*iii*) | (*iv*) |
| B. | (*ii*) | (*iii*) | (*iv*) | (*i*) |
| C. | (*ii*) | (*iv*) | (*i*) | (*iii*) |
| D. | (*i*) | (*iii*) | (*ii*) | (*iv*) |

**72.** Match the technique of scientific management in Column-I with their respective explanation in Column-II:

| | |
|---|---|
| (*a*) Method Study | (*i*) To reduce a given line or product to fixed types, sizes and characteristic |
| (*b*) Time Study | (*ii*) Devising new varieties of the existing ones |
| (*c*) Standardisation of work | (*iii*) To find out one best way of doing the job |
| (*d*) Simplification of work | (*iv*) To determine the number of workers to be employed; frame suitable incentive schemes and determine labour costs |

| | (*a*) | (*b*) | (*c*) | (*d*) |
|---|---|---|---|---|
| A. | (*iii*) | (*iv*) | (*i*) | (*ii*) |
| B. | (*i*) | (*ii*) | (*iii*) | (*iv*) |
| C. | (*ii*) | (*iv*) | (*i*) | (*iii*) |
| D. | (*iii*) | (*i*) | (*ii*) | (*iv*) |

**Directions (Qs. No. 73-80):** *In the given questions a statement of assertion followed by a statement of reason is given. Choose the correct answer out of the following choices.*

A. Both Assertion (A) and Reason (R) are true and Reason (R) is the correct explanation of Assertion (A).

B. Both Assertion (A) and Reason (R) are true, but Reason (R) is not correct explanation of Assertion (A)

C. Assertion (A) is true, but reason (R) is false

D. Assertion (A) is false, but reason (R) is true

**73. Assertion (A) :** Taylor's technique of functional foremanship is based on fayol's principle of division of work.

**Reason (R) :** Taylor advocated separation of planning and execution functions of a foreman through a planning and production in-charge under him. Each of the in-charge will have four personnel working under him according to their specialisation.

**74. Assertion (A) :** A principle refers to a statement which reflects the fundamental truth about some phenomenon based on cause and effect relationship.

**Reason (R) :** Management principles are broad and general guidelines for decision marking and behaviour of managers.

**75. Assertion (A) :** Managerial Principles are guidelines for managerial action.

**Reason (R) :** Values are not guidelines for human behaviour.

**76. Assertion (A) :** Management principle can not be applied differently under different conditions.

**Reason (R) :** Some changes can be made in application of principles according to the requirement of the company.

**77. Assertion (A) :** Management principles provide managers with useful insight into reality.

**Reason (R) :** Management principles improve knowledge, ability and understanding of managers under various managerial situations.

**78. Assertion (A) :** Fayol suggested that employees in the organisation must be given an opportunity to take some initiative in making and execution a plan.

**Reason (R) :** It does not help to develop feeling of belongingness in the employees.

**79. Assertion (A) :** Taylor insists that each job performed in the organisation should be based on intuition and not on scientific enquiry.

**Reason (R) :** Taylor insists that standard time for a job should be set up scientifically by performing time study in the organisation and then the day's target should be fixed.

**80. Assertion (A) :** Technique of "Simplification of Work" eliminate superfluous verities. Sizes and dimensions of products.

**Reason (R) :** Technique of "Simplification of work" reduced inventories, fuller utilisation of equipment and increased turnover to reduce cost.

**Directions (Qs. No. 81-84):** *Answer the Question, based on below paragraph.*

Rajat joined as a CEO of Bharat Ltd. a firm manufacturing computer hardware. On the first day he addressed the employees. He said that he believed that a good company should have an employee suggestion system and he wished to minimize employee turnover to maintain organisational efficiency. He informed all employees that he would ensure that all agreements were clear, fair and there was judicious application of penalties. However, he said that he believed that lazy personnel should be dealt with sternly to send the message that everyone was equal in the eyes of management. Also that he would want to promote a team spirit of unity and harmony among employees, which would give rise to a spirit of mutual trust and belongingness among team members and eventually minimize need for using penalties. He told all present that the interests of the organization should take priority over the interests of any one individual employee.

**81.** Identify the principle of management in the following line. "He said that he believed that a good company should have an employee suggestion system"

A. Unity of command B. Unity of direction
C. Discipline D. Initiative

**82.** Identify the principle of management in following line. "He wished to minimize employee turnover to maintain organizational efficiency."

A. Stability of personnel
B. Discipline
C. Centralization and Decentralization
D. Remuneration of employees

**83.** Identify the principle of management in the following lines. "He informed all employees that he would ensure that all agreements were clear, fair and there was judicious application of penalties."

A. Initiative B. Equity
C. Discipline D. Esprit de corps

**84.** Identify the principle of management in the following lines. "Which would give rise to a spirit of mutual trust and belongingness among team members.

A. Discipline B. Unity of command
C. Initiative D. Esprit de corps

**Directions (Qs. No. 85-88):** *Answer the question based on below paragraph.*

Radhika opens a jewellery showroom in Jaipur after completing a course in jewellery designing. She has employed eleven persons in her showroom. For greater productivity, she divides the work into small tasks and each employee is trained to perform his/ her specialised job. The sales persons are allowed to close a deal with a buyer by giving a maximum of 10% discount, whereas the decision to give any further discounts rests with Radhika as the final authority. In the earlier days of starting of the business, five of her employees were asked the put in extra hours of work. In return she had promised to give them a special incentive within a year. Therefore, after six months when the business was doing well, she awarded a cash bonus to each of these employees to honour her commitment. However, when it comes to settling the conflicts among her employees, she tends to be more biased towards her female employees.

**85.** Identify the principle of management in "She divided the work into small tasks and each employee is trained to perform his/her specialised job."

A. Unity of command B. Unity of direction
C. Division of work D. Discipline

**86.** Identify the principle "The sales persons are allowed to close a deal with a buyer by giving a maximum of 10% discount, whereas the decision to give any further discount rests with Radhika as the final authority".
A. Division of work
B. Discipline
C. Initiative
D. Centralisation and decentralisation

**87.** Identify the principle of management in the following lines. "Therefore after six months when the business was doing well, she awarded a cash bonus to each of these employees to honour her commitment.
A. Discipline B. Initiative
C. Scalar chain D. Remuneration

**88.** Which principle is violated in the following lines. "However when it comes to setting the conflicts among her employees, she tends to be more biased towards her female employees."
A. Discipline B. Equity
C. Division of work D. Justice

**Directions (Qs. No. 89-92):** *Answer the question based on below paragraph.*

As students of a management course Karan and Kunal were asked to prepare a project report on applicability of principles of management in real business situations. In order to conduct the survey Kunal had selected an outlet of a popular chain of fast food restaurant whereas Karan visited a nearby department store. When Kunal presented his report to class, Karan realised that their observations were matching on various grounds. In both the business units, work is divided into small tasks and each is performed by a trained employee. A set of rules are predetermined and communicated to employees for compliance and these is a fixed place for every thing and all employees have been allotted individual space. Moreover, the manager encourage a spirit of mutual trust and belongingness among the employees so that need for imposing penalties is reduced.

**89.** Identify the principle of management in the following lines "work is divided into small tasks and each is performed by a trained employee."
A. Unity of direction B. Unity of command
C. Division of work D. Initiative

**90.** Identify the principle of management in following lines "A set of rules are predetermined and communicated to the employees for compliance."
A. Discipline B. Scalar chain
C. Unity of command D. Unity of direction

**91.** Identify the principles of management in the following lines: "There is a fixed place for everything and all employees have been allotted individual space".
A. Unity of direction B. Order
C. Scalar chain D. Equity

**92.** Identify the principle of management in the following lines: "Managers encourage a spirit of mutual trust and belongingness among the employees."
A. Unity of command B. Order
C. Equity D. Esprit de corps

**93.** Business environment is the sum total of all the factors and forces.........to a business.
A. Internal B. Specific
C. External D. All of these

**94.** Investors, customers, competitors and suppliers come under.......forces.
A. General B. Specific
C. General and Specific D. None of the above

**95.** Specific attitudes that elected government representatives hold towards business is called............ environment.
A. Legal B. Social
C. Technological D. Political

**96.** Which of the following best indicates the importance of business environment?
A. Identification
B. Improvement in performance
C. Coping with rapid changes
D. All of the above

**97.** "There is a great demand for reservation in jobs for economically weaker sections of the society." Identify the type of dimension of business environment mentioned.
A. Technological environment
B. Political environment
C. Legal environment
D. Social environment

**98.** WhatsApp was the first application for mobile chat. Afterwards, many other applications came but still whatsapp is No.1 in mobile chat. Which importance of Business Environment is highlighted here?
A. Helps in tapping resources
B. Helps in policy making
C. Identifying threat and getting warning signal
D. Helps to identify opportunities and getting first mover advantages

**99.** The government of India proposed to encourage e-transactions by encouraging the use of plastic money (through debit, credit and gift cards) or net banking by allowing deductions in usage charges, fees and income tax exemptions. Which component of business environment does it represent?
A. Economic environment
B. Political environment

C. Legal environment
D. Social environment

**100.** The court issued the order that for vehicles to be smokeless was most essential and that any one violating this order shall have to pay a heavy fine. Identify the dimension of Business environment?
A. Economic environment
B. Political environment
C. Legal environment
D. Social environment

**101.** Which of the following is an example of social environment?
A. Money supply in the economy
B. Consumer Protection Act
C. The Constitution of the country
D. Composition of family

**102.** Match the following

| | Column-I | | Column-II |
|---|---|---|---|
| (*a*) | Stock Market indicates | (*i*) | Political environment |
| (*b*) | Customs and traditions | (*ii*) | Social environment |
| (*c*) | New techniques of operating business | (*iii*) | Technological environment |
| (*a*) | General stability and peace in the country | (*iv*) | Economic environment |

Find the correct option:

| | (*a*) | (*b*) | (*c*) | (*d*) |
|---|---|---|---|---|
| A. | (*iv*) | (*iii*) | (*i*) | (*ii*) |
| B. | (*ii*) | (*iii*) | (*iv*) | (*i*) |
| C. | (*iii*) | (*iv*) | (*ii*) | (*i*) |
| D. | (*iv*) | (*ii*) | (*iii*) | (*i*) |

**103.** Which of the following dimensions of business environment includes legislations passed by the government administrative orders issued by government authorities?
A. Technological environment
B. Political environment
C. Legal environment
D. Social environment

**104.** Which of the following is a component of economic environment?
A. Concern with quality of life
B. Rates of saving and investment
C. Extent of government intervention in business
D. Birth and death rate

**105.** Banking sector reform has led to many attractive schemes of deposits and lending money. The banks are offering loans at very nominal rate of interest and with minimum formalities to be completed.
Identify the dimension of Business environment highlighted here?
A. Political B. Social
C. Economical D. Technical

**106.** Under which environment effect, IBM and Coca-Cola had to leave India?
A. Political B. Social
C. Economical D. Technical

**107.** Introduction of mobile phones have negatively effected the business of cameras and watches it is related to:
A. Technological environment
B. Political environment
C. Legal environment
D. Social environment

**108.** ......... is considered a major element of the economic environment.
A. Public debt
B. The nature of relationship of our country with foreign countries
C. Birth and death rate
D. Literacy rates

**109.** Non-discriminatory employment practices is the part of which dimension of business environment?
A. Political B. Social
C. Economical D. Legal

**110.** 'Threats to law and order' is an example of ______ environment of business.
A. Political B. Social
C. Economical D. Legal

**111.** The trend of Yoga as a result of COVID -19 relates to:
A. Social B. Political
C. Technological D. Legal

**112.** It is very difficult to predict the changes of Business environment. No one can predict business environment 100% accurately. Which of the following feature of the business environment is highlighted by this point?
A. Uncertainty B. Dynamic
C. Relativity D. Complexity

**Directions (Qs. No. 113-117):** *There are two statements marked as Assertion (A) and Reason (R). Read the statements and choose the appropriate option from the options given below:*
A. Both Assertion (A) and Reason (R) is the correct explanation of Assertion (A)
B. Both Assertion (A) and Reason (R) are true, but reason (R) is not the correct explanation of Assertion (A)

C. Assertion (A) is true, but Reason (R) is false
D. Assertion (A) is false, but Reason (R) is true

**113. Assertion (A) :** Entry of new firms in the market may make an enterprise think afresh about how to deal with the situations
**Reason (R) :** Business environment assist in planning and policy formulation.

**114. Assertion (A) :** Demand for sarees may be fairly high in India whereas it may be almost non existent in America.
**Reason (R) :** Business environment consists of numerous inter-related and dynamic conditions of forces which arise from different sources.

**115. Assertion (A) :** Turbulent market conditions, less brand loyalty, division and sub-division of market are just a few of the images to describe business environment.
**Reason (R) :** Business environment is getting dynamic where changes are taking place at a slow pace.

**116. Assertion (A) :** Manufacturers have now flexible manufacturing systems.
**Reason (R) :** Agricultural and industrial production trends are the economic dimensions of the environment which affect the business environment.

**117. Assertion (A) :** Reservation of jobs for backward classes as per the constitution of India affects the business environment.
**Reason (R) :** Various elements of legal dimensions affect the business environment.

**Directions (Qs. No. 118-122):** *Read the following text and answer the questions on the basis of the same.*

Neel and Aakash after finishing their graduation under vocational stream decide to start their own travel agency which will book rail tickets and air tickets on commission basis. They also thought of providing tickets within 10 minutes through the use of internet. They discussed the idea with their professor Mr. Singh who liked the idea and suggested them to first analyse the business environment which consist of investors, competitors and other forces like social, political, etc., that may affect their business directly or indirectly. He further told them about the technological improvements and shifts in customer preferences that were taking place and hence, they should be aware of the environmental trends and changes which may hinder their business performance. He emphasised on making plans keeping in mind the threats posed by the competitors so that they can deal with the situation effectively. This alignment of business operations with the business environment will result in better performance.

**118.** Identify the components of business environment highlighted in the above paragraph
A. economic environment
B. social environment
C. technological environment
D. political environment

**119.** Identify the features of business environment as discussed by Professor Singh with Neel and Akash.
A. specific and general forces
B. inter-relatedness
C. dynamic nature
D. uncertainty

**120.** Identify the points of importance of business environment as stated by Professor Singh in the above situation.
A. It enables the firm to identify opportunities and getting the first mover advantage
B. It helps the form to identify threats and early warning signals
C. It helps in tapping useful resources
D. It helps in assisting in planning and policy formulation.

**121.** Which of the following is not an element of legal environment?
A. Court judgement
B. The extent and nature of government intervention in business
C. Government regulations
D. Administrative orders issued by the government authorities.

**122.** Neel and Aakash after finishing their graduation under vocational stream decided to start their own travel agency which will book rail tickets and air tickets on commission basis which dimension of business environment highlighted here.
A. Economical B. Political
C. Legal D. social

**Directions (Qs. No. 123-127):** *Read the following text and answer the questions on the basis of the same.*

The government all over the world are becoming more and more cautious towards the environment. To ensure the same, recently, many state governments passed an order to ban polythene bags since these are non biodegradable. As a result, the government also decided to give a subsidy to jute industry (bags). The minister said in the statement that they believe it will be helpful as income of people are rising and people can afford jute bag. After this subsidy,

Aman saw great potential in jute multi-pocket bags business which was not established yet in India but had been flourishing in UK where he studied during his graduation. He launched the product and his business started to boom. So, more companies entered into the market with other articles and improvisations.

**123.** Which business dimension is highlighted in the line, "As a result, the government also decided to give a subsidy to jute industry (bags)."

A. Legal B. Political
C. Economic D. Social

**124.** Which business dimension is highlighted in the line, "The Minister said in the statement that he believes it will be helpful as income of people are rising and people can afford jute bags."?

A. Legal B. Political
C. Economic D. Social

**125.** Which merit of business environment is highlighted in the lines, "After the subsidy Aman saw great potential in jute multi-pocket bags business which was not established yet in India but had been flourishing in UK where he studied during his graduation."

A. Identify opportunities
B. Tapping useful resources
C. Coping with rapid changes
D. Assisting in planning

**126.** Which merit of business environment is highlighted in the lines, "He launched the product and his business started to boom. So, more companies entered into the market with other articles and improvisations."

A. Identify opportunities
B. Identified threats
C. Assisting in planning
D. Coping with rapid changes

**127.** Which dimension of business environment is highlighted in the given lines, "To ensure the same, many state government passed an order to ban polythene bags since these are non biodegradable."?

A. Political
B. Legal
C. Technological
D. Economic

**Directions (Qs. No. 128-132):** *Read the following text and answer the questions on the basis of the same.*

Yogesh Agro Limited started a new venture for distribution of harmful and chemical free fertilizers vegetables they conducted a survey to find out customer preferences for such vegetables. They found out that most of the customers were concerned about the harmful chemicals being used in growing the vegetables. They found out that 90% of the households were searching for alternatives. The company connected a group of agriculture experts to lay down the procedure for growing the vegetables by the farmers. They decided to train the farmers in new technology to grow chemical free vegetables according to new innovative methods. The experts also suggested soil management techniques through which farmers would be able to create an abundant and lasting harvest. Due to increased awareness for healthcare, demand for products of Yogesh Agro Limited increased and thus the business flourished.

**128.** "They found that most of the customers were concerned about the harmful chemicals being used in growing the vegetables. They found out that 90% of the households searching for alternative."

Identify the dimension of business environment highlighted above.

A. Economic environment
B. Social environment
C. Technological environment
D. Political environment

**129.** "They decided to train the farmers in new technology to grow chemical-free vegetable according to new innovative methods."

Identity the dimension of business environment highlighted above.

A. Economic environment
B. Social environment
C. Technological environment
D. Political environment

**130.** "Due to increased awareness for healthcare demand for products of Yogesh Agro Limited increased and thus the business flourished."

What feature/ characteristic of business environment is highlighted above?

A. Specific and general forces
B. Inter-relatedness
C. Dynamic nature
D. Relativity

**131.** Which of the following is not a component of economic environment?

A. Balance of payments and changes in foreign exchange reserves
B. The nature of relationship of our country with foreign countries
C. Expansion of transportation and communication facilities
D. Volume of imports and exports of different items.

**132.** "The experts also suggested soil management techniques through which farmers would be able to create an abundant and lasting harvest." Which dimension of business environment is highlighted here?

A. Technological B. Legal
C. Political D. Social

**133.** Radha Rani is the C.E.O. of 'Radhika Sales Pvt. Ltd.' Besides other managerial activities, she is an expert in planning. While planning for her company, she noticed that at first several options are gathered, then their evaluation is done and finally the most suitable option is selected. Once she was confronted with such a problem as had only one option available for its solution. To select this very option was her compulsion. Now, for the first time she realized that the necessity of planning is there only when several options are available.

Identify the feature of planning in the event stated above.

A. Planning is continuous
B. Planning is futuristic
C. Planning involves decision making
D. Planning is pervasive

**134.** Saurabh decided to start a chocolates manufacturing business. He set the target of earning 10% profit on sales in the first year. As a good businessman, he was concerned about the future of the business, which was uncertain. He gathered information that the demand for chocolates is increasing day by day. He used this information as the base for future planning and shared it with his team. On the basis of the gathered information, he scheduled a meeting in the following week to find innovative ways to achieve the objectives. Identify one out of the two steps, which have been followed by Saurabh that are related to the process of one of the functions of management.

A. Follow up action
B. Selecting an alternative
C. Developing Premises
D. Evaluating alternative courses

**135.** In a business organization, the manager is busy in making plans for the coming year. The company has launched so many new products in the market. The main question before the company is how to advertise the new products. In the answer to this question, the planners collected several suggestions; namely, the job of advertisement should be done by the company itself; for advertisement the help of outsourcing of services should be taken; some of the work of advertisement should be done by the company itself and for some of it the outsourcing should be depended on. Still, other answers to this question are being looked for.

Which particular stage of the 'Planning Process' in the above event is being completed by the managers?

A. Setting objectives
B. Developing premises
C. Identifying alternative courses of action
D. Evaluating alternative courses

**136.** Suhani a home science graduate from a reputed college has recently done a cookery course. She wished to start her own venture with a goal to provide 'health food' at reasonable price. She discussed her idea with her teacher (mentor) who encouraged her. After analyzing various options for starting her business venture, they shortlisted the option to sell readymade and 'ready to make' vegetable shakes and sattu milk shakes. Then they both weighed the pros and cons of both the shortlisted options. Name the function of management being discussed above.

A. Planning B. Organizing
C. Directing D. Controlling

**Directions (Qs. No. 137-139):** *Read extract given below and answer the questions on the basis of the same.*

The CEO of ABC Limited, automobile enterprise dreams of his company becoming the best player in future for which he sets the objectives, forecast the future and develops various courses of action. He has also made a statement indicating sales volume for the next financial year to achieve the desired sales as highlighted in the statement. He decided to advertise in all the leading newspapers is in every state of India for the next six months, so he also wants to train his employees for achieving his sales target.

As a part of the training programme for newly appointed sales executive, CEO fixes responsibility of sales managers as mentors to take the executives for visit to their existing customers and help them learn on the job.

**137.** Which function of management is highlighted in the first line of the given extract?

A. Planning B. Controlling
B. Staffing D. None of these

**138.** Changes and events cannot be eliminated but they can be anticipated and managerial response to them can be developed. Which importance of planning is highlighted in the above statement?

A. Planning provides direction.
B. Planning reduces overlapping and wasteful activities.
C. Planning reduces the risk of uncertainty.
D. Planning facilitates decision making.

**139.** Sales Forecasting is the basis on which a business firm prepares its annual plan for production and sales. Which feature of planning is highlighted in the above case?

A. Planning focuses on achieving objectives.
B. Planning is continuous.
C. Planning is the primary function of management.
D. Planning is futuristic.

**Directions (Qs. No. 140-143):** *Read extract given below and answer the questions on the basis of the same.*

Mona inherited a 30-acres ancestral land from her grandparents. She decided to venture into agriculture, for this purpose she set out specific goals, objectives. Everything was a challenge because she was not aware about farming. She learned every activity and, in the process, thought of assisting other farmers as well. She eventually launched her own company Agro Limited. She wanted to be sure that the activities effectively met the best interest of the company and the farmers. Hence, she prepared an annual plan for production, sales and marketing, through sales forecasting she'll I realized that farmers were growing only one or two crops. On account of this the land remained idle for the rest of the year. She identified and evaluated different alternatives through which the farms could be utilized throughout the year. She used her foresight and systematic thinking, based on analysis of all fixed analysis of all the facts and examined and evaluated all the alternatives. She presented a plan to the Farmers Union, where after harvesting the primary crops, seasonal vegetables and foods could be grown.

**140.** Hence she prepared an annual plan for production sales and marketing through sales forecasting. Which feature of planning is depicted in this statement?

A. Planning is continuous
B. Planning is futuristic
C. Planning involves decision-making
D. Planning is a mental exercise

**141.** For this purpose she set out specific goals objectives and activities which feature of planning is depicted in this statement?

A. Planning focuses on achieving objectives
B. Planning is a primary function of management
C. Planning involves decision-making
D. Planning is a mental exercise

**142.** Thus, she identified and evaluated different alternatives through which the farms could be utilized throughout the year. Which feature of planning is depicted here?

A. Planning is pervasive
B. planning is continuous
C. planning his futuristic
D. planning involves decision-making

**143.** She used her foresight and logical and systematic thinking based on analysis of all facts and examined and evaluated all the alternatives. Which feature of planning is depicted here?

A. Planning focuses on achieving objectives
B. Planning is a primary function of management
C. Planning is mental exercise
D. Planning involves decision-making

**144.** Identify the statement which is not correct:

A. Planning is required a top-level management only.
B. Planning facilitates decision-making
C. Planning is a time consuming process
D. All are correct.

**145.** _______ are the anticipated environments in which plans are expected to operate.

A. Planning premises
B. Forecasting
C. Objectives
D. None of these

**146.** Mr. Ram is the C.E.O. in 'Ram Lakhan General Pvt. Ltd.' He is the head of the team making plans for the company also. He gave a number of suggestions to the team out of which the two main suggestions were: First, Mr. Ram said that they had to face a lot of problem in getting the main raw material used in the company, but in the next year it was possible that they could get it easily. Secondly, in the second coming year the rate of bank interest was most likely to increase, which would affect the company's costs. He laid emphasis on this matter that both of his remarks should be kept in view while preparing the plans. Clarify to which stage of the planning process the above event is related.

A. Setting objectives
B. Developing premises
C. Identifying alternative courses of action
D. Evaluating alternative courses

**147.** Mrs. Madhvi Bhire is working as a manager in 'Taarik and Company'. She is involved in a problem related to a particular product. She is unable to decide whether she should produce that product in her own company or she should buy it from the market. She studied both the options deeply with the help of specialists. In order to maintain the company's impression on the minds of the customers, she decided to produce the product in the company itself. She is hopeful of the complete success of this decision. Identify the stage of the 'planning process' on which Mrs. Madhvi reached the final decision.

A. Evaluating alternative courses
B. Selecting an alternative
C. Implementing the plan
D. Follow-up action

**148.** During partition, Kundan Lal came to Mumbai from Lahore with a lot of wealth. Keeping in view his innate ability to visualize and create things, he decided to work as a junior assistant in a film studio. Over a period of time, as he gained experience and his work was well acclaimed, he decided to set up his own film studio. Initially he was himself looking into every aspect of the business, but as his work increased manifolds and his own productivity reduced with age, he hired Jimmy as manager. Jimmy being immature in his work started giving bookings for the studio haphazardly. He would never decide anything in advance or do any kind of forecasting of events. This led to lot of confusions and conflicts. As a result, the goodwill earned by Kundan Lal over the years began to decline.

In context of the above case. Identify and explain the function of management which Jimmy failed to perform by quoting lines form the paragraph.

A. Planning
B. Directing
C. Controlling
D. Staffing

**149.** Rakhi Dua is employed at the middle level management of 'Punjab Food Suppliers'. Working in her department she noticed that they are asked to implement the plans prepared by the top management without making any change. Many a time, even though wishing to do so, she cannot make any change in them. As a result of it, the initiative and creativity of the managers at the middle level management, gets killed. Not only this, several times, even opportunities of advantage slip out of hand. Rakhi is very unhappy with this state of affairs of the company, and she is thinking of shifting to some other company at the earliest.

Identify the 'limitation of planning' in the above event.

A. Planning leads to rigidity
B. Planning may not work in a dynamic environment.
C. Planning reduces creativity
D. None of these

**150.** Super Fine Rice Ltd. has the largest share of 55% in the market. The company's policy is to sell only for cash. In 2015, for the first time company's number one position in the industry has been threatened because other companies started selling rice on credit also. But the managers of Super Fine Rice Ltd. continued to rely on its previously tried and tested successful plans which didn't work because the environment is not static. This led to decline in sales of Super Fine Rice Ltd.

The above situation is indicating two 'limitations of planning' which led to decline in it sales. Identify one of them.

A. Planning creates rigidity
B. Planning reduces creativity
C. Planning involves huge costs
D. Planning does not guarantee success

**151.** Planning is futuristic.

A. False
B. True
C. Both
D. None of these

**152.** Allother managerial functions are performed within the framework of the plans drawn. Identify the related feature of planning.

A. Planning focuses on achieving objectives
B. Planning is pervasive
C. Planning is futuristic
D. Planning is primary function of management

**153.** Planning requires logical and systematic thinking rather than guess work or wishful thinking. Identify the related feature of planning

A. Planning is futuristic
B. Planning is a mental exercise
C. Planning establishes standards for controlling
D. Planning focuses on achieving objectives

**154.** Planning cannot foresee everything, and thus, there may be obstacles to effective planning. Identify the related limitation of planning.

A. Planning leads to rigidity
B. Planning may not work in a dynamic environment
C. Planning does not guarantee success
D. Planning reduces creativity

**155.** Identify the correct sequence of steps involved in the planning process.

A. Evaluating alternative courses, Identifying alternative course of actions, Setting objectives, Developing premises
B. Setting objectives, Identifying alternative course of actions, Evaluating alternative courses, Developing premises
C. Setting objectives, Developing premises, Identifying alternative course of actions, Evaluating alternative courses
D. Setting objectives, Developing premises, Identifying alternative course of actions, Evaluating alternative courses

**156.** By comparing ______ with standards manager can know whether the goals are achieved or not.

A. Risk
B. Ideas
C. Actual performance
D. Costs

**157.** Planning provides direction is a:
A. Importance of planning
B. Limitation of planning
C. Characteristics of planning
D. Method

**158.** Pervasiveness of planning indicates that planning:
A. is a top management function
B. extends throughout the organization
C. is a future-oriented activity
D. is the first element of management process

**159.** _______ is a feature of planning also referred to as primacy of planning.
A. Pervasive
B. Primary function of management
C. Continuous
D. Integrating

**160.** Which of the following quality a manager must possess to succeed in planning?
A. Reflective Thinking
B. Imagination
C. Farsightedness
D. All of these

**161.** Planning requires logical and systematic thinking rather than guess work or wishful thinking.
Identify the related feature of planning.
A. Planning is futuristic
B. Planning is a mental exercise
C. Planning establishes standards for controlling
D. Planning focuses on achieving objectives

**162.** Planning results in decreasing:
A. Coordination
B. Proper use of resource
C. Future uncertainties
D. Control

**163.** Making assumptions for future is called
A. Making derivative plans
B. Making policy
C. Setting planning premises
D. All of the above

**Directions (Qs. No. 164 and 165):** *Read the extract given below and answer the questions on the basis of the same.*

After completing a diploma in Bakery and Patisserie, Julie sets up a small outlet at Goa Airport to provide a healthy food option to the travellers. To begin with, she has decided to sell five types of patties, three types of pizzas and low sugar muffins in four flavours. Thus, by deciding in advance what to do and how to do, she is able to reduce the risk of uncertainty and avoid overlapping and wasteful activities. But sometimes her planning does not work due to some unavoidable circumstances like cancellation of flights due to bad weather conditions, government alert etc. which adversely affects her business.

**164.** Identify points highlighting the importance of planning mentioned in the above paragraph.
A. Reduces the risk of uncertainty
B. Avoiding overlapping and wasteful activities
C. A and B
D. None of these

**165.** The limitation of planning which adversely affects Payal's business is:
A. Planning may not work in a dynamic environment
B. Planning may not guarantee success
C. Planning involves huge costs
D. None of these

**Directions (Qs. No. 166-169):** *Read the following text and answer the following questions on the basis of the same.*

Simplex limited had been taken over by Mundhra Group immediately following India's independence. Since then, it enjoys a rich record of industry presence and experience. In 2005, with the aim to accelerate growth the company had gone through several rounds of meetings and discussions before launching ERP system to attract large projects. The management had done effective forecast and critical thinking regarding allocation resources to reduce wastage. For this purpose, the company had laid down multiple courses of action to meet the challenge of adverse situations. In 2008, the company suffered loss in many projects due to the great recession despite taking many cost cutting measures. The management had taken utmost care regarding the possible outcome and timely review of the plans to achieve the set target during that hard time. In 2010, the system implemented successfully which subsequently helped the company to execute numerous projects with precision and timeliness.

**166.** "In 2005, with the aim to accelerate growth the company had gone through several rounds of meetings and discussions." What is the objective mentioned here according to the process stated here?
A. Developing Premises
B. Growth & Development
C. Launching IT enabled system
D. Cost cutting.

**167.** "In 2008, the company suffered loss in many projects due to the great recession despite taking many cost cutting measures." Which limitation of the management process is indicated here?
A. It fails to cope with sudden changes
B. It involves huge cost
C. It requires critical thinking
D. Economic Environment

**168.** State whether the given statement is True or False:

"The management had done effective forecast and critical thinking regarding allocation of resources to reduce wastage."

A. True B. False
C. Both D. None of these

**169.** "The management had taken utmost care regarding the possible outcome and timely review of the Plans to achieve the set target during that hard time." Which is the last step of the Process mentioned here?

A. Implementation of plan
B. Timely execution of projects
C. Follow up
D. To prepare alternative course of action

**170.** Match the following:

| Column-I | Column-II |
|---|---|
| (*a*) Mental exercise | (*i*) Looking ahead and regarded as forward looking. |
| (*b*) Futuristic | (*ii*) Intellectual activity of thinking rather than doing. |
| (*c*) Continuous | (*iii*) Need for a new plan based on future requirements and needs. |

| | (*a*) | (*b*) | (*c*) |
|---|---|---|---|
| A. | (*ii*) | (*i*) | (*iii*) |
| B. | (*i*) | (*iii*) | (*ii*) |
| C. | (*iii*) | (*ii*) | (*i*) |

D. None of these

**171.** Mr Reeshabh Bhandari is the chief manager in 'Bhandari Pustak Parkashans'. He is fond of continuing to present innovative ideas while planning for his business. His ideas are usually very significant. It has been observed several times that these very ideas take the form of concrete plans. This is the very reason that Mr Bhandari's contribution to the growth and prosperity of the company continues to be quite great. Identify the 'importance of planning' described above.

A. Planning provides direction
B. Planning reduces the risk of uncertainty
C. Planning reduces overlapping and wasteful activities
D. Planning promotes innovative ideas

**172.** Generally, it is thought that planning is related to the planning cycle. It means that a plan is framed, it is implemented and it is followed by another plan and so on.

The above statement is related to a feature of planning, identify it.

A. Planning is continuous
B. Planning is futuristic
C. Planning involves decision making
D. Planning is pervasive

**173.** Name the process which co-ordinates human efforts, assembles resources and integrates both into a unified whole to be utilized for achieving specified objectives:

A. Management B. Planning
C. Organising D. Directing

**174.** It refers to the number of subordinates that can be effectively managed by a superior:

A. Organisational structure
B. Informal organisation
C. Span of management
D. None of the above

**175.** As the span of management increases in an organisation, the number of levels of management in the organisation

A. Increases B. Decreases
C. Remains unaffected D. None of the above

**176.** Uranus Limited is a company dealing in metal products. The work is mainly divided into functions including production, purchase, marketing, accounts and personnel. Identify the type of organisational structure followed by the organisation.

A. Functional structure B. Relational structure
C. Divisional structure D. None of the above

**177.** Under this type of organisational structure, manpower is grouped on the basis of different products manufactured.

A. Divisional structure B. Functional structure
C. Network structure D. Matrix structure

**178.** Rishabh has joined as a Creative Head in an entertainment company. He always ensures that the work has been divided into small and manageable activities and also the activities of similar nature are grouped together. Identify the related step in organising process being mentioned in the above lines.

A. Identification and division of work
B. Departmentalisation
C. Assignment of duties
D. Establishing reporting relationships

**179.** Identify the correct sequence of steps to be followed in an organising process.

A. Departmentalisation, Establishing reporting relationships, Assignment of duties, Identification and division of work
B. Identification and division of work, Departmentalisation, Assignment of duties, Establishing reporting relationships
C. Identification and division of work, Assignment of duties, Departmentalisation, Establishing reporting relationships
D. Identification and division of work, Establishing reporting relationships, Departmentalisation, Assignment of duties

**180.** It is the obligation of a subordinate to properly perform the assigned duty.
A. Responsibility B. Authority
C. Accountability D. All of the above

**181.** Which of the following is not a demerit of functional structure?
A. It places more emphasis on the objectives pursued by a functional head than on overall enterprise objectives.
B. It may lead to conflict of interests among departments due to varied interests.
C. It leads to occupational specialisation.
D. It may lead to difficulty in co-ordination among functionally differentiated departments.

**182.** When decision-making authority is retained organisation is said to be by higher management levels, an:
A. Decentralised B. Centralised
C. Fragmented D. None of the above

**183.** Which of the following cannot be delegated?
A. Authority B. Responsibility
C. Accountability D. None of these

**184.** Which of the following is not an element of delegation?
A. Authority B. Accountability
C. Responsibility D. None of these

**185.** Harshit Ltd. has grown in size. It was a market leader but with changes in business environment and with the entry of MNCs, its market share is declining. To cope up with the situation CEO starts delegating some of his authority to the General Manager, who also felt himself overburdened and with the approval of CEO disperses some of his authority to various levels throughout the organisation. Identify the concept of management discussed above.
A. Delegation B. Organising
C. Decentralisation D. Centralisation

**186.** In which situation the divisional structure happens to be appropriate?
A. Where the number of major products is more than one
B. Where the size of the organisation is quite large
C. Both (A) and (B)
D. Where primarily only one product is sold

**187.** In order to successfully realize the objectives of an organisation, first of all it is ensured which activities will have to be performed. In the list of activities, all the activities, both big and small, are included. But it is not possible to set up separate departments for all the activities. Some similar activities are put together in the same department. In this way some necessary departments are set up. The reason for doing so is to exercise control over unnecessary administrative expenses. Identify the concept of management under which similar activities are put together and departments are set up.
A. Departmentalisation
B. Delegation
C. Decentralisation
D. Centralisation

**188.** The accountability flows:
A. In all directions B. Downwards
C. Upwards D. None of the above

**189.** Which of the following is not a merit of divisional structure?
A. It promotes product specialisation
B. It ensures that different functions get due attention
C. It promotes flexibility and faster decision making
D. It facilitates expansion and growth as new divisions

**190.** Centralisation refers to:
A. Retention of decision-making authority
B. Dispersal of decision-making authority
C. Creating divisions as profit centres
D. Opening new centres or branches

**191.** Match the following on the basis of meaning of the content (remembering)

| | |
|---|---|
| (*a*) Divisional structure | (*i*) formation is based on functions |
| (*b*) Functional structure | (*ii*) number of subordinates that can be managed by superiors |
| (*c*) Span of management | (*iii*) product specialization |

| | (*a*) | (*b*) | (*c*) |
|---|---|---|---|
| A. | (*i*) | (*ii*) | (*iii*) |
| B. | (*i*) | (*iii*) | (*ii*) |
| C. | (*iii*) | (*i*) | (*ii*) |
| D. | (*ii*) | (*i*) | (*iii*) |

**192.** Match the following on the basis of demerits of the content:

| | |
|---|---|
| (*a*) Divisional structure | (*i*) Difficult for a multi-product company |
| (*b*) Functional structure | (*ii*) Difficult to fix responsibility |
| | (*iii*) Non economical |

| | (*a*) | (*b*) |
|---|---|---|
| A. | (*i*) | (*ii*) |
| B. | (*ii*) | (*i*) |
| C. | (*iii*) | (*i*) |
| D. | (*ii*) | (*iii*) |

**193.** Match the following on the basis of features:

| | | |
|---|---|---|
| (*a*) Divisional structure | (*i*) | Occupational specialization |
| (*b*) Functional structure | (*ii*) | Perfect control |
| | (*iii*) | Business Environment |

| | (*a*) | (*b*) |
|---|---|---|
| A. | (*i*) | (*ii*) |
| B. | (*ii*) | (*i*) |
| C. | (*iii*) | (*i*) |
| D. | (*ii*) | (*iii*) |

**194.** Match the following:

| | | |
|---|---|---|
| (*a*) Departmentalization | (*i*) | Dividing the work as per plan |
| (*b*) Assignment of duties | (*ii*) | Allocation of responsibility |
| (*c*) Division of Work | (*iii*) | The activities which are of similar nature |

| | (*a*) | (*b*) | (*c*) |
|---|---|---|---|
| A. | (*i*) | (*ii*) | (*iii*) |
| B. | (*i*) | (*iii*) | (*ii*) |
| C. | (*iii*) | (*i*) | (*ii*) |
| D. | (*iii*) | (*ii*) | (*i*) |

**195.** Match the following by choosing the correct option:

| Column-I | | Column-II |
|---|---|---|
| (*a*) Leads to specialization | (*i*) | Delegation |
| (*b*) Functional and divisional | (*ii*) | Step of organising process |
| (*c*) It has narrow scope | (*iii*) | Importance of organization |
| (*d*) Establishing reporting relationships | (*iv*) | Types of organisation structure |

| | (*a*) | (*b*) | (*c*) | (*d*) |
|---|---|---|---|---|
| A. | (*i*) | (*ii*) | (*iii*) | (*iv*) |
| B. | (*ii*) | (*iv*) | (*i*) | (*iii*) |
| C. | (*iii*) | (*iv*) | (*i*) | (*ii*) |
| D. | (*iv*) | (*i*) | (*ii*) | (*iii*) |

**196.** Match the following:

| | | |
|---|---|---|
| (*a*) Authority | (*i*) | Arises from formal position |
| (*b*) Accountability | (*ii*) | Arises from delegation of authority |
| (*c*) Responsibility | (*iii*) | Arises from responsibility |

| | (*a*) | (*b*) | (*c*) |
|---|---|---|---|
| A. | (*i*) | (*ii*) | (*iii*) |
| B. | (*i*) | (*iii*) | (*ii*) |
| C. | (*iii*) | (*i*) | (*ii*) |
| D. | (*iii*) | (*ii*) | (*i*) |

**197.** Match the steps in the process of organising in Column-I with the appropriate 'explanation' in Column-II:

| Column-I | | Column-II |
|---|---|---|
| (*a*) Identification and division of work activities | (*i*) | Dividing work into manageable |
| (*b*) Departmentalisation | (*ii*) | Establishing a hierarchal structure |
| (*c*) Assignment of duties | (*iii*) | Grouping similar activities together |
| (*d*) Establishing authority & reporting relationships | (*iv*) | Allocating jobs to the members of each department |

| | (*a*) | (*b*) | (*c*) | (*d*) |
|---|---|---|---|---|
| A. | (*i*) | (*ii*) | (*iii*) | (*iv*) |
| B. | (*i*) | (*iii*) | (*iv*) | (*ii*) |
| C. | (*iii*) | (*iv*) | (*i*) | (*ii*) |
| D. | (*iv*) | (*i*) | (*ii*) | (*iii*) |

**Directions (Qs. No. 198-202):** *There are two statements marked as Assertion (A) and Reason (R). Read the statements and choose the appropriate option from the options given below:*

A. Both (A) and (R) are true and (R) is the correct explanation of (A)
B. Both (A) and (R) are true and (R) is not the correct explanation of (A)
C. (A) is true, but (R) is false
D. (A) is false, but (R) is true

**198. Assertion (A) :** Identification and division of work is the first step in the process of organising.

**Reason (R) :** Organising involves identifying and dividing the work that has to be done in accordance with previously determined plans.

**199. Assertion (A) :** Organising provides a clear description of jobs and related duties.

**Reason (R) :** Organising stimulates creativity amongst the managers.

**200. Assertion (A) :** Functional Organization helps in increasing managerial and operational efficiency and this results in increased profit.

**Reason (R) :** Functional Organization promotes efficiency in utilisation of manpower as employees perform similar tasks within a department and are able to improve performance.

**201. Assertion (A) :** Organising helps management in implementing the principle of initiative among employees.

**Reason (R)** : Organising satisfies the subordinate's need for recognition and provides them with opportunities to develop and exercise initiative.

**202. Assertion (A) :** Authority determines the superior subordinate relationship wherein the superior communicates his decision to the subordinate, expecting compliance from him and the subordinate executes the decision as per the guidelines of the superior.

**Reason (R)** : Accountability is the obligation of a subordinate to properly perform the assigned duty.

**203. Assertion (A) :** The span of management at the upper level is generally narrow while at the lower level span is wide.

**Reason (R)** : The task allocated to subordinates at the lower level of management are more specific and precise and thus making supervision easy and simple.

A. (A) is correct, but (R) is wrong
B. (A) is wrong, but (R) is correct
C. Both (A) and (R) are correct
D. Both (A) and (R) are wrong

**Directions (Qs. No. 204-212):** *There are two statements marked as Assertion (A) and Reason (R). Read the statements and choose the appropriate option from the options given below:*

A. Both Assertion (A) and reason (R) are true
B. Both Assertion (A) and reason (R) are false
C. Assertion (A) is true and reason (R) is false
D. Assertion (A) is false and reason (R) is true

**204. Assertion (A) :** Delegation helps a manager to extend his area of operations as without it, his activities would be restricted to only what he himself can do.

**Reason (R)** : A manager, no matter how capable he is, cannot manage to do every task on his own. The volume of work makes it impractical for him to handle it all by himself.

**205. Assertion (A) :** Delegation does not mean abdication.

**Reason (R)** : A manager is under obligation to perform the delegated task.

**206. Assertion (A) :** Responsibility is derived from authority and accountability is derived from responsibility.

**Reason (R)** : Responsibility is the obligation of a subordinate to properly perform the assigned duty, for which he/she has been delegated authority by his/her superior. Once authority has been delegated and responsibility accepted, one cannot deny accountability.

**207. Assertion (A) :** A large sized organisation can be totally decentralised.

**Reason (R)** : As an organisation grows in size and complexity, there is a tendency to move towards decentralised decision-making. Complete centralisation would imply concentration of all decision making functions at the apex of the management hierarchy.

**208. Assertion (A) :** Decentralisation must always be balanced with centralisation in areas of major policy decisions.

**Reason (R)** : Decentralisation recognises the decision maker's need for autonomy. The management, however, needs to carefully select those decisions which will be pushed down to lower levels and those that will be retained for higher levels.

**209. Assertion (A) :** Decentralisation should be applied with caution by the top management.

**Reason (R)** : It can lead to organisational disintegration if the departments start to operate on their own guidelines which may be contrary to the interest of the organisation.

**210. Assertion (A) :** Organisation structure is the outcome of the planning process.

**Reason (R)** : The organising process leads to the creation of an organisation structure which includes the designing of roles to be filled by suitably skilled people and defining the inter-relationship between these roles so that ambiguity in performance of duties can be eliminated.

**211. Assertion (A) :** The need for an adequate organisation structure is felt by an enterprise whenever it grows in size or complexity.

**Reason (R)** : As an organisation grows, coordination becomes difficult due to the emergence of new functions and increase in structural hierarchies. Thus, for an organisation to function smoothly and face environmental changes, it becomes necessary to pay attention to its structure.

**212. Assertion (A) :** Organisation structure is an indispensable means; and the wrong structure will seriously impair business performance and even destroy it.

**Reason (R) :** A proper organisation structure is essential to ensure a smooth flow of communication and better control over the operations of a business enterprise. It specifies the relationships between people, work and resources.

**Directions (Qs. No. 213-216):** *Read the extract given below and answer the questions on the basis of the same:*

Mohit, the owner of 'Ravi Constructions' decided to begin a campaign in order to create awareness among the residents for creating a clean and safe environment. In an effort to develop clean surroundings in the area, he formed a team of 30 members to list the different ways that can be adopted for keeping the area clean. Different people had different suggestions, someone suggested to take the help of local residents including young children, one suggestion was to involve unemployed youth. The idea to take the help of volunteers was also given. A combination of the most effective strategies after evaluating all options was selected for implementation. To achieve the desired goals and objectives, various activities were identified like:

(*i*) Purchase of essential items like dustbins, garbage bags, brooms, phenyl, etc.

(*ii*) Door-to-door collection of garbage.

(*iii*) Recycling of garbage.

(*iv*) Disposal of garbage, etc.

Thus, an organisational design was chosen which grouped similar activities together in order to minimise duplication of effort. After identification and grouping of these activities, the work was allocated among the different members.

**213.** "After identification of different activities the work was allocated to different members."

Which step does this represent in the process of organising?

A. Identification and division of work
B. Departmentalisation
C. Assignment of duties
D. Establishing reporting relationships

**214.** "Thus, an organisational design was choosen which grouped similar activities together in order to minimise duplication of effort."

Which step under the process of organising is being referred to in this line?

A. Identification and division of work
B. Departmentalisation
C. Assignment of duties
D. Establishing reporting relationships

**215.** "Thus, an organisational design was chosen which grouped similar activities together in order to minimise duplication of effort."

Which step under the process of organising is being referred to in this line?

A. Identification and division of work
B. Departmentalisation
C. Assignment of duties
D. Establishing reporting relationships

**216.** "Thus, an organisational design was choosen which grouped similar activities together in order to minimize duplication of effort."

Which organisational design is being referred to in this line?

A. Functional B. Formal
C. Divisional D. Informal

**Directions (Qs. No. 217-220):** *Read the extract given below and answer the questions on the basis of the same:*

Aman decided to start a business of manufacturing toys. He identified the following main activities which he has to perform: (*i*) purchase of raw materials, (*ii*) purchase of machinery, (*iii*) production of toys; (*iv*) arrangement of finance; (*v*) sale of toys; (*vi*) identifying the areas where they can sell their toys; (*vii*) selection of employees. In order to facilitate the work he thought that four managers should be appointed to look after: (*a*) production (*b*) finance (*c*) marketing (*d*) personnel.

As planned, all this was executed and the business started doing well. But the manager of production department is overburdened with routine work and is unable to concentrate on core issues of the department. To overcome this problem, he entrusted some of his responsibility and authority to his immediate subordinate.

**217.** Identify the function of management involved in the above mentioned paragraph.

A. Planning B. Organising
C. Directing D. Controlling

**218.** Which concept/process is used by the production manager?

A. Decentralisation B. Delegation
C. Training D. Coordination

**219.** Name the step in the process of planning which is considered "the real point of decision making".
A. Setting objectives
B. Selecting the best alternative
C. Evaluating alternatives
D. Developing premises

**220.** Who will be accountable finally if the subordinate is unable to complete the task accordingly within time?
A. The Manager B. The Subordinate
C. Both (A) and (B) D. None of these

**221.** With which element is exchange mechanism related?
A. Publicity B. Marketing
C. Advertising D. Branding

**222.** Which one of the following is a marketing management philosophy?
A. Societal marketing concept
B. Distribution concept
C. Direct marketing concept
D. Channel concept

**223.** Which one of the following is not a marketing mix?
A. Product B. Physical distribution
C. Product pricing D. Production process

**224.** Marketing is called a ______ process because it involves interaction of buyers and sellers.
A. Economic B. Social
C. Legal D. Political

**225.** _______ is the marketing function which is concerned with informing the customers about the firm's products.
A. Transportation B. Selling
C. Advertising D. Public Relations

**226.** Hena is planning to set up a small manufacturing unit for manufacturing eco-friendly packaging material. She has decided to market her products through the conventional channel of distribution, which involves wholesalers and retailers. Identify the channel of distribution being adopted by the company.
A. Zero level channel
B. One level channel
C. Two level channel
D. Three level channel

**227.** Within 2 years of it's inception, Bhavishya Limited has created a very positive reputation about itself and its products in the eyes of general public by participating extensively in various social welfare programs. Identify the component of promotion mixing described in the given lines.
A. Advertising B. Personal selling
C. Public relation D. Sales promotion

**228.** Harshit is planning a start up a venture for offering mobile pet care services at door step. He has decided to charge ₹ 1000 for heated hydrobath & blow dry of a pet and ₹ 500 for shampoo and conditioning. Identify the element of marketing mix which is not being described in the above case.
A. Product B. Place
C. Price D. None of the above

**229.** Guneet went to a shop and expressed her desire to buy a copper water bottle only of Prestige company. Identify the component related to branding being described in the above case.
A. Trademark B. Generic name
C. Brand name D. Brand mark

**230.** Karam Limited is offering a travel package for 15 destinations worldwide with a free insurance on the bookings for the month of December, 2019. Identify the feature of marketing being described in the above lines.
A. Needs and wants
B. Creating a market offering
C. Customer value
D. Exchange mechanism

**231.** Agile Limited has launched a new range of air conditioners in order to add value to the usability of the product. The new range of air conditioners have an inbuilt air purifier and are available in attractive colours. Identify the type of marketing philosophy being described in the above lines.
A. Product concept
B. Production concept
C. Marketing concept
D. Societal marketing concept

**232.** Sujhav Limited is a company dealing in various types of fire extinguishers. Considering the fact that people generally don't buy fire extinguishers, the company undertakes aggressive sales promotion efforts in order to create and maintain demand for the product. Identify the type of marketing philosophy being described in the given case:
A. Product concept
B. Selling concept
C. Marketing concept
D. Societal marketing concept

**233.** Madhubala is planning to launch an online education portal. In order to understand the varied needs of the students, she conducted an online survey. Based on the feedback of the survey, she has decided to offer educational packages to the prospective buyers. Identify the type of marketing concept being described in the given lines.

A. Product concept
B. Production concept
C. Marketing concept
D. Societal marketing concept

**234.** Pragati Limited has chalked out an action plan in order to increase its market share in the international market by 20% in the next one year. The action plan contains the details about how the production levels will be increased, promotional activities will be carried out and so on. Identify the type of marketing function being described in the given lines.
A. Gathering and analysing market information
B. Marketing planning
C. Product designing and development
D. Packaging and labelling

**235.** What does the symbol given below denote?

TM ®

A. Brand name
B. Brand mark
C. Trademark
D. Generic name

**236.** Sugandha purchased a pack of crayons for her daughter from a nearby stationery shop. She noticed that the crayons were packed in a portable transparent plastic bag. Identify the level of packaging being described in the above lines.
A. Primary package
B. Secondary packaging
C. Transportation packaging
D. None of the above

**237.** On visiting a supermarket to buy a pack of moisturizer, Harsha noticed that the packaging of most of the beauty products exhibited a photograph of a celebrity. Identify the related function of packaging being described in the given case.
A. Facilitates the use of product
B. Assists in promotion of the product
C. Helps in product identification
D. Provides protection to the product

**238.** The labelling of a pack of oats cookies explains how the product is beneficial in adding fibre to the diet and the other related health benefits. Identify the related function of labelling being described in the given case.
A. Describes the product and specifies its content
B. Identification of the product or brand
C. Grading of products
D. Helps in promotion of the products

**239.** Identify the related function of labelling being depicted below as given on the pack of the chips.

A. Describes the product and specifies its content
B. Grading of products
C. Helps in promotion of the products
D. Identification of the product or brand

**240.** Mehak Limited has hired 300 salesmen who will be assigned the task of contacting prospective buyers and creating awareness about the new range of organic incenses introduced by the company. Identify the element of promotion been described in the given lines.
A. Advertising B. Sales promotion
C. Personal selling D. Public relation

**Directions (Qs. No. 241-260):** *Read the following cases carefully and answer these questions.*

**Case-1**

"Time Line" watch manufacturing company is a renowned company marketing watches. It performs various activities like, market analysis, product designing or merchandising, packaging, warehousing, branding, pricing, promotion and selling. The company maintains good customer relations through various follow up activities. This helps the company in procuring repeat sales orders.

**241.** Name the concept related to the activities mentioned in the above paragraph.
A. Marketing B. Selling
C. Industry D. Packaging

**242.** Which concept of marketing is used to develop good relations with customers?
A. Branding B. sales promotion
C. labelling D. public relation

**Case-2**

"Every time I travelled, people asked me to bring them chips, khakra and pickles from all over the country," says Anoushka. Finally, she and her colleague, Sumeet, decided to make a business out of it. They launched a Facebook page, asked people what they wanted, and they came up with a list of about 100 places and tied-up with two dozen vendors to begin with. They were servicing people from Jaipur who wanted spices from Kerala, people from Panipat who wanted halwa from Jammu and people from Delhi who ordered fresh tea leaves from Darjeeling. Through their business, they wished to bridge the gap between sellers and buyers. The business is now worth millions.

**243.** Which function of marketing was performed by both friends while acquiring information about people's choice through facebook page?

A. Gathering and analysing marketing information
B. Marketing planning
C. Branding
D. None of these

**244.** Which promotional tool is suitable for them?

A. Advertising B. Personal selling
C. Publicity D. Sales promotion

**245.** Important element of marketing mix that Anouskha and Sumeet will have to be involved in for making the goods available to customers at the right place, in the right quantity and at the right time is:

A. Product B. Price
C. Promotion D. Place

**Case-3**

Radhika was a student of Business Studies of Class XII. Her father was a farmer who grew different varieties of rice and was well-versed in the various aspects of rice cultivation. He was also selected by the government for a pilot-project on rice cultivation. As a project work in Business Studies, she decided to study the feasibility of marketing good quality rice at a reasonable price. Her father suggested her to use the Internt to gather customers' views and opinions. She found that there was a huge demand for packaged organic rice. She knew that there were no predetermined specifications in case of rice because of which it was difficult to achieve uniformity in the output. To differentiate the product from its competitors, she gave it the name of 'Malabari Organic Rice' and classified it into three different varieties, namely — Popular, Classic and Supreme, based on the quality. She felt that these names would help her in product differentiation.

**246.** Radhika has given a special name to her product, what does this name refer to?

A. Brand name B. Brand Mark
C. Generic name D. Trade mark

**247.** Radhika has classified her product into different varieties, which function of marketing has been performed by Radhika in this step?

A. Gathering and analysing marketing information
B. Standardisation and Grading
C. Product designing and development
D. None of these

**248.** Radhika's father suggested her to use internet for acquiring information about people's taste and preferences. Why is it necessary to know about taste and preferences of customers in marketing

A. It is essence of marketing
B. Customers are required for profit making.
C. Customer is called king of market
D. Customer satisfaction is main objective of marketing.

**Case-4**

Haryaram is a famous chain selling a large variety of products in the Indian market. Their products include chips, biscuits, sweets and squashes. It charges a comparatively higher price than its competitors as it sells quality products. Besides, it offers regular discounts to its customers and easy credit terms to its retailers. It has five of its own retail shops. It also sells its products through various grocery stores so that the products are made available to customers at the right place, in the right quantity and at the right time. It regularly uses different communication tools to increase its sales.

**249.** Which type of products are sold by Haryaram?

A. Consumer goods B. Producer goods
C. Services D. None of the above

**250.** Which philosophy of marketing management is being used by Haryaram?

A. Production concept B. Product concept
C. Selling concept D. Marketing concept

**251.** Which promotional tool is being used by offering discounts to customers ?

A. Advertising B. Personal selling
C. Sales promotion D. Public relations

**252.** Haryaramis selling goods through grocery store, which channel of distribution is being used by Haryaram?

A. Direct channel B. One level
C. Two level D. None of these

**Case-5**

As a project work in Business Studies, the Commerce students of Himachal Public School, Himachal Pradesh thought of preparing apple jam from the apples grown in their school premises and sell it in the school annual fete. They approached the Principal who not only appreciated the students but also gave her consent for the same. The school decided to donate 50% of the revenue generated from the sale to a nearby orphanage. After the school fete, the school also decided to extend this project by providing employment to visually challenged and disadvantaged sections of society on regular basis.

**253.** Product-related decisions which the students had to take to identify product in the market:

A. Branding B. Labelling
C. Packaging D. None of these

**254.** Label of jam should be:

A. Brand label B. Grade label
C. Descriptive label D. None of the above

### Case-6

Unilever has found a new way to make ice creams by using an ingredient called 'ice structuring protein' which is widely found in nature especially, in fishes which allows them to survive in freezing arctic waters. Combining ISP with stabiliser technology allows to make ice creams that don't melt so easily thereby making it more convenient for small children and consumers in hot countries.

**255.** The component of marketing mix being taken into consideration by the company.
A. Product B. Price
C. Place D. Promotion

**256.** The function of marketing highlighted here:
A. Gathering and analysing marketing information
B. Marketing planning
C. Product designing and development
D. Branding

### Case-7

As the number of people making online purchases has increased manifolds, there is a growing concern about the disposal and management of packaging waste. Every item bought is delivered with excess packaging and sometimes even non-biodegradable materials are used.

**257.** Name the levels of packaging that the marketers uses for extra protection besides the immediate package.
A. Primary packaging
B. Secondary packaging
C. Transportation packaging
D. None of these

### Case-8

Suraj is a small entrepreneur involved in the manufacturing of hair wax. He finds that cost of production of 100 gm of hair wax is ₹ 250. He has decided to keep a margin of 15% as profit. Moreover, he has assessed that there is a free competition in this product segment.

**258.** Identify the function of marketing being performed by Suraj.
A. Pricing B. Branding
C. Labelling D. Promotion

### Case-9

In today's world, through social media, news spread in a flash. Moreover, if it is bad news, it acquires a speed that is virtually impossible to stop. Hence, all corporates are more susceptible to a tarnished image today than in any other day and age. The loss of goodwill may lead to decreased revenue, loss of clients or suppliers and fall in market share. Over the years, therefore, most of the companies have set up a separate department to manage the public opinions about them. The department works in close coordination with the various interest groups like consumers, government, suppliers etc. and strives to handle effectively if any controversies arise.

**259.** Identify the element of promotion mix being referred to in the above lines.
A. Advertising B. Publicity
C. Personal selling D. Public relations

**260.** Which department is formed for this promotional tool?
A. Marketing department
B. Finance department
C. Human resource department
D. Public relations department

**261.** An automobile company is a leading manufacturing company in its segment. The company has decided to launch fully solar charged vehicles. This technology will cost the company ₹ 2000 crores annually. When the relationship manager of the company was asked about the reason of bearing so much extra cost he replied that the company considered environmental friendly techniques as the only solution to increasing pollution. The company feels by bearing extra cost it is fulfilling its responsibility. Which concept of marketing management is being followed?
A. production concept
B. product concept
C. selling concept
D. social marketing concept

**Directions (Qs. No. 262-276):** *There are two statements marked as Assertion (A) and Reason (R). Read the statements and choose the appropriate option from the options given below:*
A. Both are correct and (R) is the correct explanation of (A)
B. Both are correct but, (R) is not the correct explanation of (A)
C. Both statements are incorrect
D. (A) is correct, but (R) is incorrect

**262. Assesrion (A) :** Exchange mechanism is known as essence of marketing.
**Reason (R) :** Customer receives goods and services and producer receives price for product through procees of exchange.

**263. Assertion (A) :** The purpose of marketing is to generate customer value at a profit.
**Reason (R) :** Marketing is the process of satisfying needs and wants of customers through the process of exchange.

**264. Assertion (A) :** Selling focuses on profit maximization through maximization of sales.
**Reason (R) :** Selling is considered as a part of marketing.

**265. Assertion (A) :** Production concept focuses on increasing scale of production to reduce price of products.

**Reason (R) :** Production concept is used where demand is more than supply.

**266. Assertion (A) :** Social marketing concept is followed generally by marketers in present time.

**Reason (R) :** Social responsibility is considered as an important aspect to get success in the business.

**267. Assertion (A) :** Production mix is the combination of all decisions taken by marketers regarding product.

**Reason (R) :** Product mix covers only tangible attributes of products.

**268. Assertion (A) :** Brand is used to identify a product in market by customers.

**Reason (R) :** Brand provides a specific name to a product.

**269. Assertion (A) :** Packaging is known as a silent salesman.

**Reason (R) :** Attractive and innovative package can attract a lot of customers to purchase the product.

**270. Assertion (A) :** A firm sets lower price per unit to increase profit in long run.

**Reason (R) :** Lower price increases demand for the product and market area to earn greater profit through sales.

**271. Assertion (A) :** There should be a balance in level of inventory maintained in warehouse.

**Reason (R) :** Higher level will increase the cost of carrying inventory and lower level will make difficult to fulfill demand.

**272. Assertion (A) :** Advertising is called paid form of impersonal communication.

**Reason (R) :** Advertising covers a large market area with low cost.

**273. Assertion (A) :** Personal selling is called a dialogue.

**Reason (R) :** Personal selling is possible through face to face contact and communication with customers.

**274. Assertion (A) :** Sales promotion activities are occasionally used.

**Reason (R) :** Sales promotion activities are short term incentives offered to customers for making immediate purchase.

**275. Assertion (A) :** Expenditure on advertisement is not a waste but a profitable investment.

**Reason (R) :** Advertisements increases sales of products in the long run and increases profit for the business.

**276. Assertion (A) :** Industrial products are easily sold through personal selling.

**Reason (R) :** Queries of customers can be easily solved in personal selling.

**277.** Match the column-I with column-II:

| **Statement** | **Marketing concept** |
|---|---|
| (*a*) Scale of production | (*i*) Product concept |
| (*b*) Quality of product | (*ii*) Selling concept |
| (*c*) Promotional activities | (*iii*) Production concept |
| (*d*) Customer satisfaction | (*iv*) Marketing concept |

| | (*a*) | (*b*) | (*c*) | (*d*) |
|---|---|---|---|---|
| A. | (*i*) | (*ii*) | (*iv*) | (*iii*) |
| B. | (*i*) | (*iii*) | (*iv*) | (*ii*) |
| C. | (*iii*) | (*i*) | (*ii*) | (*iv*) |
| D. | (*iii*) | (*i*) | (*iv*) | (*ii*) |

**278.** Match the column-I with column-II:

| **Statement** | **Marketing mix** |
|---|---|
| (*a*) Combination of tangible and intangible attributes of products | (*i*) Place mix |
| (*b*) It is related to deciding about pricing of product | (*ii*) Promotion mix |
| (*c*) It is related to providing information and persuading customer | (*iii*) Price mix |
| (*d*) Providing product to customer at the right time, at the right quantity and at the right place | (*iv*) Product mix |

| | (*a*) | (*b*) | (*c*) | (*d*) |
|---|---|---|---|---|
| A. | (*i*) | (*iii*) | (*iv*) | (*ii*) |
| B. | (*iv*) | (*iii*) | (*ii*) | (*i*) |
| C. | (*iii*) | (*iv*) | (*ii*) | (*i*) |

D. None of the above

**279.** Match the column-I with column-II:

| **Statement** | **Components of product mix** |
|---|---|
| (*a*) Process of preparing a name, sign or symbol for a product | (*i*) Packaging |
| (*b*) Process of preparing an wrapper or container for product | (*ii*) Labelling |
| (*c*) Procees of preparing a slip used to describe information about product | (*iii*) Branding |

| | (*a*) | (*b*) | (*c*) |
|---|---|---|---|
| A. | (*ii*) | (*i*) | (*iii*) |
| B. | (*iii*) | (*i*) | (*ii*) |
| C. | (*i*) | (*iii*) | (*ii*) |
| D. | (*iii*) | (*ii*) | (*i*) |

**280.** Match the column-I with column-II:

| Statement | Elements of promotion mix |
|---|---|
| (*a*) It is paid form of personal communication | (*i*) Advertising |
| (*b*) It is made through identified sponsor | (*ii*) Sales promotion |
| (*c*) These are short term incentives | (*iii*) Personal selling |
| (*iv*) It is non sale communication | (*iv*) Public relations |

| | (*a*) | (*b*) | (*c*) | (*d*) |
|---|---|---|---|---|
| A. | (*iii*) | (*i*) | (*ii*) | (*iv*) |
| B. | (*ii*) | (*iii*) | (*iv*) | (*i*) |
| C. | (*iii*) | (*i*) | (*iv*) | (*ii*) |
| D. | (*iv*) | (*ii*) | (*i*) | (*iii*) |

**281.** Which of the following does not apply to Principles of Management?

A. Applicable in large firms
B. Formed by practice and experimentation
C. Flexible
D. Contingent

**282.** The principles of management are said to be flexible as:

A. They aim at influencing behaviour of human beings.
B. They are general guidelines to action, but do not provide readymade solutions to management problems.
C. They can be modified by the manager when the situation so demands.
D. Their application is dependent upon the prevailing situation at a particular point of time.

**283.** "Management principles are not as rigid as principles of pure science." Which of the following best describes the given statement?

A. Management principles deal with human behaviour and thus, are to be applied creatively given the demands of the situation.
B. Principles of management are formed after research in work situations, which are technical in nature.
C. Principles of management contribute towards the development of management both as a science and as an art.
D. None of the above

**284.** The application of principles has to be changed as per requirements. For example, employees deserve fair and just remuneration. But what is fair and just is determined by multiple factors. They include contribution of employee, paying capacity of the employer and also prevailing wage rate for the occupation under consideration. Identify the nature of principles of management highlighted above.

A. General guidelines  B. Flexible
C. Mainly Behavioral  D. Contingent

**285.** _______ is an extension of the principle of division of work and specialization to the shop floor and it violates the principle of Unity of Command.

A. Cooperation not individualism
B. Functional foremanship
C. Unity of Direction
D. Standardization and simplification of work

**286.** Gang Plank is a term associated with which principle of Fayol?

A. Equity  B. Order
C. Scalar Chain  D. Initiative

**287.** Jeevan Ltd. is a company manufacturing garments under the brand name 'Apsara'. The management of the company does not give the workers reasonable time to show results. Even the management does not promote a team spirit of unity and harmony among workers. The workers often have to work under two superiors at the same time. Identify the principles of management overlooked in the above case.

A. Stability of Personnel B. Esprit De Corps
C. Unity of Command  D. All of these

**288.** _______ principle of management is being violated if management does not fulfill its promise to increase wages of workers after the mission is accomplished.

A. Order  B. Equity
C. Discipline  D. Initiative

**289.** Which one of the following is not an objective of standardization of work?

A. To reduce a given line or product to fixed types, sizes and characteristics
B. To establish interchange ability of manufactured parts and products
C. To establish standards of excellence and quality in material
D. None of the above

**290.** Shiv and Karthik started their career in Wales Limited (a printing press) after going through a rigorous recruitment process. Since they had a no prior work experience, the firm decided to give them one year to prove themselves. The principle of management followed by Wales Limited is _______ .

A. Authority and Responsibility
B. Discipline
C. Equity
D. Stability of Personnel

**291.** In one of the principles of scientific management, Taylor emphasizes that there should be equal division of work and responsibility between workers and management and management should work almost side by side with workers helping and smoothing the way for them. Identify the principle.

A. Science not rule of thumb

B. Harmony not discord
C. Cooperation, not individualism
D. Development of each and every person to his/her greatest efficiency and prosperity

**292.** In order to fix a standard target of performance for workers, it was necessary for Shiv Ltd. to fix standard time for workers to perform a particular job. For this Mr. Ganesh, the Production Manager of the company observed the workers when they are performing the job. He used a stop watch in hand and noted down the average time taken by the workers for completion of the job. He repeated the same observation for 100 times and then calculated average time for the performance of the job. This was fixed as standard time on the basis of which efficient and inefficient workers were distinguished. Identify the technique of scientific management followed by Mr. Ganesh.
A. Time study B. Method study
C. Motion study D. Fatigue study

**293.** A manager should have the right to punish a subordinate for wilfully not obeying a legitimate order but only after sufficient opportunity has been given to a subordinate for presenting her/his case. Identify the principle of management highlighted above.
A. Discipline
B. Order
C. Authority and Responsibility
D. Unity of Command

**294.** Which of the following statements is true with reference to principles of management?
A. The principles of management have evolved
B. The principles of management are yet to be evolved
C. The principles of management are in the continuous process of evolution
D. None of the above

**295.** 'Rule of thumb' refers to:
A. Use of personal judgement in handling management issues
B. Adopting a hit-and-trial approach to resolve management problems
C. Both (A) and (B)
D. None of the above

**296.** According to this principle of scientific management, "Scientific management has for its foundation the firm conviction that true interest of the management and workers are one and the same; the prosperity for the employer cannot exist for a long time unless it is accompanied by prosperity for the employees and vice versa."
A. Science, not rule of thumb
B. Cooperation, not individualism
C. Harmony, not discord
D. All of the above

**297.** Instruction card clerk is responsible for:
A. Getting task completed accurately and on time
B. Drafting instructions for workers
C. Preparing time and cost sheet
D. Checking quality of work

**298.** Differential piece wage system:
A. Ensures job satisfaction among workers
B. Motivates workers
C. Increased productivity
D. All the above

**299.** Esprit de Corps means:
A. Unity in direction B. Unity in strength
C. Unity of authority D. None of the above

**300.** According to the technique of Scientific management "Differential Piece Wage system" How much more will a worker making 60 units earn as compared to a worker making 49 units? If the standard output per day is 50 units and those who make standard output or more than standard get ₹ 75 per unit and those below get ₹ 65 per unit.
A. ₹ 4500 B. ₹ 3185
C. ₹ 1315 D. ₹ 325

**301.** 'For you' was in the business of cosmetic products. The business was doing well and the company was consistently meeting its objectives. Encouraged by the good track record, the top management kept a target of 15% increase in sales in the next year. The next year, two competitors entered in the market and because of which the company could not meet its target. Identify the limitations of one of the functions of management because of which the company was not able to achieve its objectives.
A. Planning does not guarantee success
B. Planning leads to rigidity
C. Planning may not work in dynamic environment
D. None of the above

**302.** Name the function of management which bridges the gap between where we are and where we want to go.
A. Planning B. Staffing
C. Organising D. Directing

**303.** Which feature of planning says that planning is a forward-looking function?
A. Planning is continuous
B. Planning is pervasive
C. Planning is futuristic
D. Planning is rigid

**304.** Select the feature of planning from the following
A. Planning is futuristic B. Provides direction
C. It is pervasive D. All the above

**305.** ABC Ltd sets objectives prepares strategies and other plans keeping the internal and external forces in mind, enabling all individuals working in the organisation

to decide what action should be taken and in which direction. Identify the importance of planning highlighted in the statement.
A. Planning provides direction
B. Planning reduces uncertainty
C. It reduces overlapping
D. It facilitates decision making

**306.** A bag manufacturer prepares next year's production plan after forecasting the demand. Identify the feature of planning
A. Planning is a mental exercise
B. Planning is futuristic
C. It is continuous
D. Expensive

**307.** Changes and events cannot be eliminated but can be anticipated and managerial response to them can be developed. Which importance of planning is highlighted in the above statement.
A. Planning provides direction
B. Planning reduces overlapping and wasteful activities
C. Planning reduces the risk of uncertainty
D. It facilitates decision making

**308.** It requires application of mind involving foresight, intelligence, imagination and sound judgement. Which feature of planning is indicated here?
A. It is futuristic
B. It involves decision making
C. It is mental exercise
D. It is continuous

**309.** Planning is required at all levels of management as well as in all departments of the organisation. It is not an exclusive function of top management nor of any particular department. Identify the feature of planning highlighted above.
A. Planning is continuous
B. Planning is futuristic
C. Planning involves decision making
D. Planning is pervasive

**310.** Match the following:

| **Column-I** | **Column-II** |
|---|---|
| (*a*) Anticipate changes | (*i*) Provides direction |
| (*b*) Planning states in advance how work is to be done | (*ii*) Reduces the risk of uncertainty |
| (*c*) Establishes standards for controlling | (*iii*) Promotes innovation |
| (*d*) Planning encourages new ideas | (*iv*) Provides the goals against which actual performance is being measured. |

| | (*a*) | (*b*) | (*c*) | (*d*) |
|---|---|---|---|---|
| A. | (*ii*) | (*i*) | (*iv*) | (*iii*) |
| B. | (*ii*) | (*i*) | (*iii*) | (*iv*) |
| C. | (*i*) | (*iii*) | (*iv*) | (*ii*) |
| D. | (*iii*) | (*ii*) | (*iv*) | (*i*) |

## ANSWERS

| 1 | 2 | 3 | 4 | 5 | 6 | 7 | 8 | 9 | 10 |
|---|---|---|---|---|---|---|---|---|---|
| A | B | A | A | C | D | C | D | A | A |
| 11 | 12 | 13 | 14 | 15 | 16 | 17 | 18 | 19 | 20 |
| A | D | C | B | C | B | C | C | D | B |
| 21 | 22 | 23 | 24 | 25 | 26 | 27 | 28 | 29 | 30 |
| C | C | A | B | A | A | A | D | A | C |
| 31 | 32 | 33 | 34 | 35 | 36 | 37 | 38 | 39 | 40 |
| A | A | C | A | C | A | A | C | B | B |
| 41 | 42 | 43 | 44 | 45 | 46 | 47 | 48 | 49 | 50 |
| B | C | C | A | C | B | A | A | D | C |
| 51 | 52 | 53 | 54 | 55 | 56 | 57 | 58 | 59 | 60 |
| B | A | C | A | B | C | D | A | A | B |
| 61 | 62 | 63 | 64 | 65 | 66 | 67 | 68 | 69 | 70 |
| C | C | A | C | C | C | B | D | C | C |
| 71 | 72 | 73 | 74 | 75 | 76 | 77 | 78 | 79 | 80 |
| B | A | A | B | C | D | A | C | D | A |
| 81 | 82 | 83 | 84 | 85 | 86 | 87 | 88 | 89 | 90 |
| D | A | C | D | C | D | A | B | C | B |

| 91 | 92 | 93 | 94 | 95 | 96 | 97 | 98 | 99 | 100 |
|---|---|---|---|---|---|---|---|---|---|
| B | D | C | D | D | D | D | D | A | C |
| 101 | 102 | 103 | 104 | 105 | 106 | 107 | 108 | 109 | 110 |
| D | D | C | B | C | A | A | A | B | D |
| 111 | 112 | 113 | 114 | 115 | 116 | 117 | 118 | 119 | 120 |
| A | A | A | B | C | B | B | C | A | B |
| 121 | 122 | 123 | 124 | 125 | 126 | 127 | 128 | 129 | 130 |
| B | A | B | C | A | B | B | B | C | B |
| 131 | 132 | 133 | 134 | 135 | 136 | 137 | 138 | 139 | 140 |
| B | A | C | C | C | A | A | B | D | B |
| 141 | 142 | 143 | 144 | 145 | 146 | 147 | 148 | 149 | 150 |
| A | D | C | A | A | B | B | A | C | D |
| 151 | 152 | 153 | 154 | 155 | 156 | 157 | 158 | 159 | 160 |
| B | D | B | B | C | C | A | B | B | D |
| 161 | 162 | 163 | 164 | 165 | 166 | 167 | 168 | 169 | 170 |
| B | C | C | C | A | B | A | A | C | A |
| 171 | 172 | 173 | 174 | 175 | 176 | 177 | 178 | 179 | 180 |
| D | A | C | C | B | A | A | B | B | A |
| 181 | 182 | 183 | 184 | 185 | 186 | 187 | 188 | 189 | 190 |
| C | B | C | D | C | C | C | D | B | A |
| 191 | 192 | 193 | 194 | 195 | 196 | 197 | 198 | 199 | 200 |
| C | C | B | D | C | B | B | A | B | A |
| 201 | 202 | 203 | 204 | 205 | 206 | 207 | 208 | 209 | 210 |
| A | C | C | A | C | A | D | A | A | D |
| 211 | 212 | 213 | 214 | 215 | 216 | 217 | 218 | 219 | 220 |
| A | A | C | B | B | A | B | B | B | A |
| 221 | 222 | 223 | 224 | 225 | 226 | 227 | 228 | 229 | 230 |
| B | A | D | B | C | C | C | D | C | C |
| 231 | 232 | 233 | 234 | 235 | 236 | 237 | 238 | 239 | 240 |
| A | C | C | B | C | A | B | D | C | C |
| 241 | 242 | 243 | 244 | 245 | 246 | 247 | 248 | 249 | 250 |
| A | D | A | A | D | A | B | D | A | B |
| 251 | 252 | 253 | 254 | 255 | 256 | 257 | 258 | 259 | 260 |
| C | B | A | C | A | C | B | A | D | D |
| 261 | 262 | 263 | 264 | 265 | 266 | 267 | 268 | 269 | 270 |
| D | A | B | B | B | A | D | A | A | A |
| 271 | 272 | 273 | 274 | 275 | 276 | 277 | 278 | 279 | 280 |
| A | B | A | A | A | A | C | B | B | A |
| 281 | 282 | 283 | 284 | 285 | 286 | 287 | 288 | 289 | 290 |
| A | C | A | D | B | C | D | C | D | D |
| 291 | 292 | 293 | 294 | 295 | 296 | 297 | 298 | 299 | 300 |
| C | A | C | C | C | C | B | D | C | C |
| 301 | 302 | 303 | 304 | 305 | 306 | 307 | 308 | 309 | 310 |
| C | A | C | D | A | B | C | C | D | A |

●●●

# MATHEMATICS

CHAPTER

# 1

# ALGEBRA

## SETS

A set is a collection of well defined objects. The objects of a set are taken as distinct only on the ground of simplicity.

The objects that comprises of the set are called elements. Number of objects in a set can be finite or infinite.

*For example,* a set of chairs, the set of Nobel laureates in the worlds, the set of integers, the set of natural numbers less than 10, the set of points in the plane.

The number of elements in a set is called the cardinality of the set. (If S is a set the cardinality is denoted by |S|).

Usually a set is represented by its list of elements separated by comma, between two curly brackets.

*For example,* {1, 2, 3, 4, 5} is the list of integers bigger than 0 and lesser than or equal to 5.

## TYPES OF SETS

In sets theory, there are many types of sets. Some of them are discussed below.

### Singleton Set

A set contains only one element. *For example:* A = {3} and B = {pencil}. Here A and B are containing only one element so both are singleton sets.

### Empty Set/Null Set

An empty set is a set with no element. It is denoted by A = { } or A = ?.

### Proper Set

If A and B are two sets, then A is a proper subset of B if $A \subseteq B$ but $A \neq B$.

*For example,* If B = {$x$, $y$, $z$} then A = {$x$, $z$} is a proper subset of B.

### Power Set

The collection of all subsets of a set is the power set of that set. If A is the set then P(A) is denoted as its power set.

The number of elements contained by any power set can be calculated by $n[P(A)] = 2^n$ where $n$ is the number of elements in set A.

*For example,* If A = {$x$, $y$} then, P(A) = {∅, {$x$}, {$y$}, {$x$, $y$}}

Number of elements in P(A) = $2^2 = 4$.

### Universal Set

Any set which is a superset of all the sets under consideration and usually it is denoted as S or U.

*For example,* Let P = {$a$, $b$, $c$} and Q = {$x$, $b$, $z$} then we take S − {$a$, $b$, $c$, $x$, $z$} as universe set.

### Equal Sets

Two sets P and Q are equal if both are a subset of each other.

Mathematically: If $P \subseteq Q$ and $Q \subseteq P$ then P = Q.

For example, P = {3, 6, 8} and Q = {6, 3, 8}

## RELATION

A relation is a set of ordered pairs. Any set of ordered pairs is, therefore, a relation. The set of first components of the ordered pairs is called the domain and the set of second component is called the range, *e.g.,* in the relation, {(5, 7), (2, 9), (1, 4), (0, 1)}, the domain is {5, 2, 1, 0} and the range is {7, 9, 4, 1}.

**Notation for relation :** The letter 'R' is used to designate a relation. *For example,*

(*i*) R = {(2, 9), (3, 8), (4, 7), (6, 10)}

(*ii*) R = {($x$, $y$) : $x, y \in W$, $y = x^2$}.

**The notation xRy:** If $(x, y)$ is a member of a relation R, then the symbol $x$R$y$ is also used and read '$x$ is the relation R to $y$, *i.e.*, $(x, y) \in R \Rightarrow xRy$.

## Some Particular Relations on a Set

Let A be any (non-empty) set:

(*i*) **Empty relation:** As $\phi \subset A \times A$, $\phi$ is a relation on A. This relation is called the empty relation on A.

*For example:* Consider the relation R on the set A = (1, 2, 3) given by

$$R = \{(a, b) : a, b \in A, a + b = 10\}$$

Here A × A = {(1, 1), (1, 2), (1, 3), (2, 1), (2, 2), (2, 3), (3, 1), (3, 2), (3, 3)} and we note that no pair $(a, b)$ in A × A satisfies the condition $a + b = 10$, so R is empty set. Therefore, R is the empty relation.

(*ii*) **Universal relation:** As $A \times A \subset A \times A$, A × A is a relation on A. This relation is called the universal relation on A.

*For example:* Consider the relation R on the set A = {1, 2, 3} given by

$$R = \{(a, b) : a, b \in A, |a - b| \geq 0\}$$

We note that all pairs $(b, a)$ in A × A satisfy $|a - b| \geq 0$, so R is the whole set A × A. Therefore, R is the universal relation.

Both the empty relation and the universal relation are sometimes called trivial relations.

(*iii*) **Identity relation:** The relation $I_A = \{(a, a); \text{for all } a \in A\}$ is called the identity relation on A. Note that in identity relation every element is related to itself only.

*For example:* If A = (1, 2, 3), then the identity relation on A is given by $I_A = \{(1, 1), (2, 2), (3, 3)\}$.

## TYPES OF RELATIONS ON A SET

Let R be a relation on a (non-empty) set A, then R is called *a*

(*i*) reflexive relation iff $a$ R $a$ *i.e.*, $(a, a) \in R$ for all $a \in A$

(*ii*) symmetric relation iff $a$ R $b$ implies $b$ R $a$ *i.e.*, $(a, b) \in R$ implies $(a, c) \in R$ for all $a, b \in A$.

(*iii*) transitive relation iff $a$ R $b$, $b$ R $c$ implies $a$ R $c$ *i.e.*, $(a, b) \in R$, $(b, c) \in R$ implies $(b, a) \in R$ for all $a, b, c \in A$.

### Equivalence Relation

A relation R on a (non-empty) set A is called on equivalence relation iff it is:

(*i*) reflexive (*ii*) symmetric and (*iii*) transitive *i.e.*, iff

(*i*) $a$ R $a$ for all $a \in A$

(*ii*) $a$ R $b$ implies $b$ R $a$ for all $a, b \in A$ and

(*iii*) $a$ R $b$, $b$ R $c$ implies $a$ R $c$ for all $a, b, c \in A$

## FUNCTIONS

A function is simply used to represent the dependence of one quantity on the other and easily defined with the help of the concept of mapping. In simple words, a function is a relation which derives one output for each input.

The set A is called the domain of the function and the set B is called co-domain of the function. The set C of all members of B associated to members of A by the function is called the range of the function. Thus, in the function displayed in Fig.

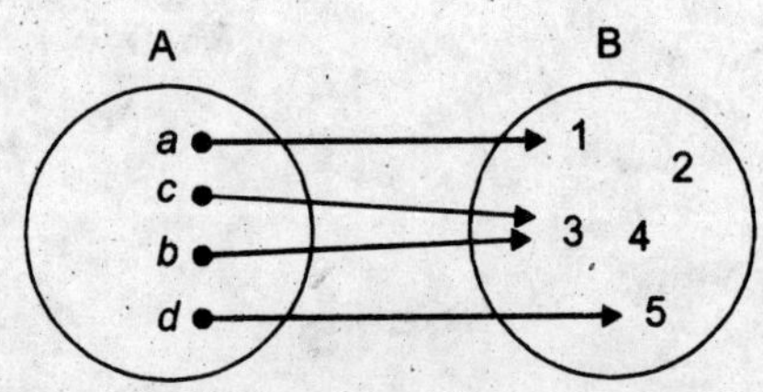


***Fig.***

Domain = $\{a, b, c, d\}$, Codomain = {1, 2, 3, 4, 5}, Range = {1, 3, 5}.

**Note:** Obviously, the range is the subset of co-domain.

## TYPES OF FUNCTIONS

1. **One-one function:** A function '$f$' from X to Y is called one-one (or injective) iff different elements of X have different images in Y *i.e.*, iff $x_1 \neq x_2 \Rightarrow f(x_1) \neq f(x_2)$ for all $x_1, x_2 \in x$, or equivalently, $f(x_1) = f(x_2) \Rightarrow x_1 = x_2$ for all $x_1, x_2 \in X$.
2. **Many-one function:** A function '$f$' from X to Y is called many-one iff two or more elements of X have same image in Y. In other words, a function '$f$' from X to Y is called many-one iff it is not one-one.
3. **Onto function:** A function '$f$' from X to Y is called onto (or surjective) iff each elements of Y is the image of at least one element of X i.e., iff codomain of $f$ = range of $f$ *i.e.* iff $Y = f(X)$.
4. **Into function:** A function '$f$' from X to Y is called into iff there exists at least one element in Y which is not the image of any element of X i.e., iff range of $f$ is a proper subset of codomain of $f$. In other words, a function '$f$' from X to Y is called into iff it is not onto.
5. **One-one correspondence:** A function '$f$' from X to Y is called a one-one correspondence (or bijective) iff $f$ is both one-one and onto.

### Even and Odd Functions

A real function $f$ is called an even function iff $f(-x) = f(x)$ for all $x \in D_f$ and $f$ is called an odd function iff $f(-x) = -f(x)$ for all $x \in D_f$.

## DE MORGAN'S LAW

The complement of the union of two sets is the intersection of their complements and the complement of the intersection of two sets is the union of their complements. These are called De Morgan's laws.

(*i*) $(A \cup B)' = A' \cap B'$

(*ii*) $(A \cap B)' = A' \cup B'$

## APPLICATION OF SET THEORY

If A is a finite set, then the number of elements in A is denoted by $n(A)$.

If A and B are two finite sets, then two cases arise:

**Case 1:** If A and B are disjoint, then there is no common element in A and B.

Therefore, $n(A \cup B) = n(A) + n(B)$

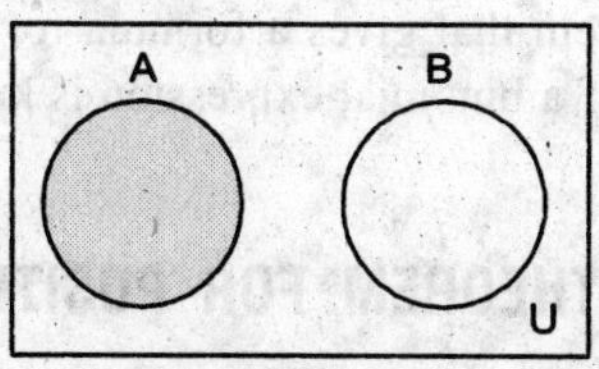


**Case 2:** If A and B are not disjoint, then there are common elements in A and B. We have

(*i*) $n(A \cup B) = n(A) + n(B) - n(A \cap B)$

(*ii*) $n(A \cup B) = n(A - B) + n(B - A) + n(A \cap B)$

(*iii*) $n(A) = n(A - B) + n(A \cap B)$

(*iv*) $n(B) = n(B - A) + n(A \cap B)$

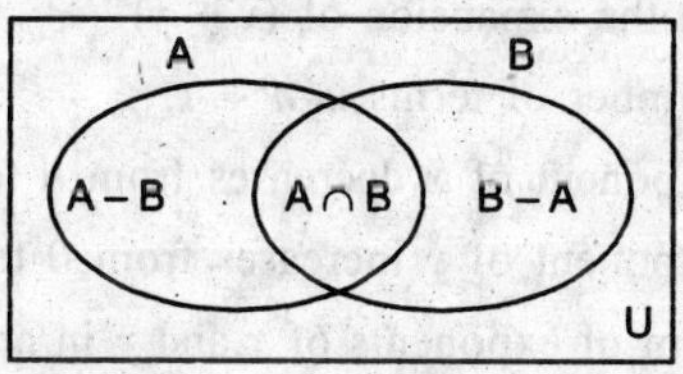


## INVERSE FUNCTION

In mathematics, the inverse function of a function $f$ is a function that undoes the operation of $f$. The inverse of $f$ exists if and only if $f$ is bijective, and if it exists, is denoted by $f'\{-1\}$.

## PEANO AXIOMS

Peano axioms, also known as Peano's postulates, in number theory, five axioms introduced in 1889 by Italian mathematician Giuseppe Peano.

The five Peano axioms are:

1. Zero is a natural number.
2. Every natural number has a successor in the natural numbers.
3. Zero is not the successor of any natural number.
4. If the successor of two natural numbers is the same, then the two original numbers are the same.
5. If a set contains zero and the successor of every number is in the set, then the set contains the natural numbers.

## INDICES

When a number 'P' is multiplied by itself '$n$' time, then the product is called $n$th power of 'P' and is written as $P^n$. Here, P is called the base and $n$ is known as the index of the power. Therefore, $P^n$ is the exponential expression. $P^n$ is read as 'P raised to the power $n$' or 'P to the power $n$'.

## LAWS OF INDICES

Let P, Q be two real numbers and $m$, $n$ be two positive integers, then

(*i*) $P^m \times P^n = P^{m+n}$ (*ii*) $\frac{P^m}{P^n} = P^{m-n}$

(*iii*) $(P^m)^n = P^{mn}$ (*iv*) $(PQ)^n = P^n \times Q^n$

(*v*) $\left(\frac{P}{Q}\right)^n = \frac{P^n}{Q^n}$ (*vi*) $P^0 = 1$

(*vii*) $P^{-n} = \frac{1}{P^n}$

## SURDS

When root of a non-negative rational number (*i.e.*, quantities of type $\sqrt[n]{a}$, $a$ being a rational number) does not provide an exact solution, then this root is called a surd. *For example,* $\sqrt{2}, \sqrt{5}, 3\sqrt{8}, a+\sqrt{b}$, etc.

- All surds are irrational numbers.
- All irrational numbers are not surds.

## LAWS OF SURDS

Let P, Q be two positive rational numbers and $m$, $n$ be two positive integers, then

(*i*) $\sqrt[m]{P} = P^{1/m}$

(*ii*) $\sqrt[m]{PQ} = \sqrt[m]{P} \times \sqrt[m]{Q}$

(*iii*) $m\sqrt{\frac{P}{Q}} = \frac{\sqrt[m]{P}}{\sqrt[m]{Q}}$

(*iv*) $\left(\sqrt[m]{P}\right)^m = P$

(*v*) $\left(\sqrt[m]{P}\right)^n = (P^{1/m})^n = P^{n/m} = \sqrt[m]{P^n}$

## PROGRESSIONS

There are three types of progressions, which are as follow:

### Arithmetic Progression (AP)

The progression of the form $a$, $a + d$, $a + 2d$, $a + 3d$,... is known as an arithmetic progression with first term $a$ and common difference $d$. We have,

(*i*) $n$th term, $T_n = a + (n - 1)d$

(*ii*) Sum of $n$ terms of AP, $S_n = \frac{n}{2}[2a+(n-1)d]$

(*iii*) Sum of $n$ terms, $S_n = \frac{n}{2}[a+l]$, where, $l$ = last term

### Geometric Progression (GP)

The progression of the form $a$, $ar$, $ar^2$, $ar^3$, ... is known as a geometric progression with first term $a$ and common ratio $r$. We have,

(*i*) $n$th term of GP, $T_n = ar^{n-1}$

(*ii*) Sum of $n$ terms of GP, $S_n = \frac{a(1-r^n)}{(1-r)}$, where $r < 1$

(*iii*) Sum of $n$ terms of GP, $S_n = \frac{a(r^n-1)}{r-1}$, where $r > 1$

(*iv*) Sum of an infinite GP, $S_\infty = \frac{a}{1-r}$

### Harmonic Progression (HP)

A series of quantities $a_1, a_2, a_3, a_4, ...., a_n$ is said to be in HP when their reciprocals $\frac{1}{a_1}, \frac{1}{a_2}, \frac{1}{a_3}, ...., \frac{1}{a_n}$ are in AP.

- The converse is also true.
- Simply, there is no general formula for the sum of any number of quantities in HP. All questions in HP are generally solved by inverting the terms and making use of the properties of the corresponding AP.

## PARTIAL FRACTIONS

When a rational expression is split into the sum of two or more rational expressions, the rational expressions that are a part of the sum are called partial fractions. This is referred to as splitting the given algebraic fraction into partial fractions. The denominator of the given algebraic expression has to be factorized to obtain the set of partial fractions.

| Factor in denominator | Term in partial fraction decomposition |
|---|---|
| $ax + b$ | $\frac{A}{ax+b}$ |
| $(ax + b)^k$ | $\frac{A_1}{ax+b}+\frac{A_2}{(ax+b)^2}+...+\frac{A_k}{(ax+b)^k}$ |
| $ax^2 + bx + c$ | $\frac{Ax+B}{ax^2+bx+c}$ |
| $(ax^2 + bx + c)^k$ | $\frac{A_1x+B_1}{ax^2+bx+c}+\frac{A_2x+B_2}{(ax^2+bx+c)^2}+...+\frac{A_kx+B_k}{(ax^2+bx+c)^k}$ |

## BINOMIAL EXPRESSION

An algebraic expression consisting of two terms is called a binomial expression.

e.g., $(x + y)$, $(2x - 3y)$, $\left(x+\frac{1}{3x}\right)$, $\left(\frac{5}{6}-\frac{4}{x^2}\right)$ etc.

The theorem that gives a formula for the expansion of some power of a binomial expression is known as binomial theorem.

## BINOMIAL THEOREM FOR POSITIVE INTEGRAL INDEX

**Theorem:** If $x$ and $y$ are real numbers, then for all $n \in N$,

$$(x + y)^n = {}^nC_0x^ny^0 + {}^nC_1x^{n-1}y^1 + {}^nC_2x^{n-2}y^2 + ...... + {}^nC_{n-1}x^1y^{n-1} + {}^nC_nx^0y^n$$

### Some Observation in a Binomial Expansion

For $n \in N$, in the expansion of $(x + y)^n$

(*i*) the number of terms is $n + 1$.

(*ii*) the exponent of $x$ decreases from $n$ to 0.

(*iii*) the exponent of $y$ increases from 0 to $n$.

(*iv*) the sum of exponents of $x$ and $y$ in any terms is $n$.

(*v*) ${}^nC_0, {}^nC_1, {}^nC_2, .... {}^nC_n$ are called binomial coefficients.

Since ${}^nC_r = {}^nC_{n-r}$

we have ${}^nC_0 = {}^nC_n$, ${}^nC_1 = {}^nC_{n-1}$, ${}^nC_2 = {}^nC_{n-2}$, ....

### Important Particular Cases of the Binomial Expansion

(*i*) $(x - y)^n = {}^nC_0x^ny^0 - {}^nC_1x^{n-1}y^1 + {}^nC_2x^{n-2}y^2 - .... + (-1)^n\,{}^nC_nx^0y^n$.

(*ii*) $(1 + x)^n = {}^nC_0\,1^nx^0 + {}^nC_1\,1^{n-1}x^1 + {}^nC_2\,1^{n-2}x^2 + .... + {}^nC_n\,1^0x^n = 1+nx+\frac{n(n-1)}{2!}x^2+....+x^n$.

(*iii*) $(1 - x)^n = (1 + (-x))^n = {}^nC_0\,1^n(-x)^0 + {}^nC_1\,1^{n-1}(-x)^1 + {}^nC_2\,1^{n-2}(-x)^2 + .... + {}^nC_n\,1^0(-x)^n$

$$= 1-nx+\frac{n(n-1)}{2!}x^2+....+(-1)^nx^n.$$

(*iv*) The general term or the $(r+1)^{th}$ term in the expansion of $(x+y)^n$ is given by

$$T_{r+1} = {}^nC_r x^{n-r}.\ y^r$$

(*v*) The middle term(s) is the expansion of $(x+y)^n$ is (are):

(*a*) If $n$ is even, there is only one middle term which is given by:

$$T_{(n+2)/2} = {}^nC_{n/2}.x^{n/2}\ y^{n/2}$$

(*b*) If $n$ is odd, there are two middle terms which are:

$$T_{(n+1)/2}\ \&\ T_{[(n+1)/2]+1}$$

(*vi*) Term independent of $x$ contains no $x$; Hence find the value of $r$ for which the exponent of $x$ is zero.

(*vii*) To find the numerically greatest term is the expansion of $(1+x)^n$, $n \in N$ find $\frac{T_{r+1}}{T_r} = \frac{{}^nC_r x^r}{{}^nC_{r-1}x^{r-1}} = \frac{n-r+1}{r}x.$ Put the absolute value of $x$ and find the value of $r$ Consistent with the inequality $\frac{T_{r+1}}{T_r} > 1.$

Note that the numerically greatest term in the expansion of $(1-x)^n$, $x > 0$, $n \in N$ is the same as the greatest term in $(1+x)^n$.

## Binomial Coefficients

(*i*) $C_0 + C_1 + C_2 + .... + C_n = 2^n$

(*ii*) $C_0 + C_2 + C_4 + .... = C_1 + C_3 + C_5 + .... = 2^{n-1}$

(*iii*) $C_0^2 + C_1^2 + C_2^2 + .... + C_n^2 = {}^{2n}C_n = \frac{(2n)!}{n!n!}$

(*iv*) $C_0.C_r + C_1.C_{r+1} + C_2.C_{r+2} + ... + C_{n-r}.C_n = \frac{(2n)!}{(n+r)(n-r)!}$

**Remember:** $(2n)! = 2^n.n!\ [1.\ 3.\ 5\ ....\ (2n-1)]$

## Exponential Series

(*i*) $e^x = 1 + \frac{x}{1!} + \frac{x^2}{2!} + \frac{x^3}{3!} + ....\infty$; where $x$ may be any real or complex & $e = \underset{a\to\infty}{\text{Limit}}\left(1+\frac{1}{n}\right)^a$

(*ii*) $a^x = 1 + \frac{x}{1!}\ln a + \frac{x^2}{2!}\ln^2 a + \frac{x^3}{3!}\ln^3 a + ....\infty$ where $a > 0$

**Note:** (*a*) $e = 1 + \frac{1}{1!} + \frac{1}{2!} + \frac{1}{3!} + ....\infty$

(*b*) $e$ is an irrational number lying between 2.7 & 2.8. Its value correct upto 10 places of decimal is 2.7182818284.

(*c*) $e + e^{-1} = 2\left(1 + \frac{1}{2!} + \frac{1}{4!} + \frac{1}{6!} + ....\infty\right)$

(*d*) $e - e^{-1} = 2\left(1 + \frac{1}{3!} + \frac{1}{5!} + \frac{1}{7!} + ....\infty\right)$

(*e*) Logarithms to the base '$e$' are known as the Napierian system, so named after Napier, their inventor. They are also called Natural Logarithm.

## Logarithmic Series

(*i*) $\ln(1+x) = x - \frac{x^2}{2} + \frac{x^3}{3} - \frac{x^4}{4} + ....\infty$

where $-1 < x \le 1$

(*ii*) $\ln(1-x) = -\ x - \frac{x^2}{2} - \frac{x^3}{3} - \frac{x^4}{4} + ....\infty$

where $-1 \le x < 1$

(*iii*) $\ln\frac{(1+x)}{(1-x)} = 2\left(x + \frac{x^3}{3} + \frac{x^5}{5} + ....\infty\right) |x| < 1$

**Remember:** (*a*) $1 - \frac{1}{2} + \frac{1}{3} - \frac{1}{4} + ....\infty = \ln 2$

(*b*) $e^{\ln x} = x$ (*c*) $\ln 2 = 0.693$ (*d*) $\ln 10 = 1$

# DETERMINANTS

To every square matrix $A = [a_{ij}]$ of order $n$, we can associate a number (real or complex) called determinant of the matrix A, written as det A, where $a_{ij}$ is the $(i, j)$th element of A.

If $A = \begin{bmatrix} a & b \\ c & d \end{bmatrix}$, then determinant of A, denoted by $|A|$ (or det A), is given by

$$|A| = \begin{vmatrix} a & b \\ c & d \end{vmatrix} = ad - bc.$$

## Remarks

(*i*) Only square matrices have determinants.

(*ii*) For a matrix A, $|A|$ is read as determinant of A and not, as modulus of A.

## Properties of Determinants

For any square matrix A, $|A|$ satisfies the following properties.

(*i*) $|A'| = |A|$, where A′ = transpose of matrix A.

(*ii*) If we interchange any two rows (or columns), then sign of the determinant changes.

(*iii*) If any two rows or any two columns in a determinant are identical (or proportional) then the value of the determinant is zero.

(*iv*) Multiplying a determinant by $k$ means multiplying the elements of only one row (or one column) by $k$.

(*v*) If we multiply each element of a row (or a column) of a determinant by constant $k$, then value of the determinant is multiplied by $k$.

(*vi*) If elements of a row (or a column) in a determinant can be expressed as the sum of two or more elements, then the given determinant can be expressed as the sum of two or more determinants.

## System of Linear Equations

(*i*) Consider the equations:

$$a_1x + b_1y + c_1z = d_1$$
$$a_2x + b_2y + c_2z = d_2$$
$$a_3x + b_3y + c_3z = d_3$$

In matrix form, these equations can be written as AX = B, where

$$A = \begin{bmatrix} a_1 & b_1 & c_1 \\ a_2 & b_2 & c_2 \\ a_3 & b_3 & c_3 \end{bmatrix}, X = \begin{bmatrix} x \\ y \\ z \end{bmatrix} \text{ and } B = \begin{bmatrix} d_1 \\ d_2 \\ d_3 \end{bmatrix}$$

(*ii*) Unique solution of equation AX = B is given by $X = A^{-1}B$, where $|A| \neq 0$.

(*iii*) A system of equations is consistent or inconsistent according as its solution exists or not.

(*iv*) For a square matrix A in matrix equation AX = B.

(*a*) If $|A| \neq 0$, then there exists unique solution.

(*b*) **If $|A| = 0$ and (*adj* A) B $\neq 0$, then there exists no solution.**

(*c*) **If $|A| = 0$ and (*adj* A) B $= 0$, then system may or may not be consistent.**

## MATRICES

**Matrices are the ordered rectangular array of numbers, which are used to express linear equations. A matrix has rows and columns. We can also perform the mathematical operations on matrices such as addition, subtraction, multiplication of matrix. Suppose the number of rows is *m* and columns is *n*, then the matrix is represented as $m \times n$ matrix.**

## INVERSE OF A MATRIX

**Inverse of a matrix is defined usually for square matrices. For every $m \times n$ square matrix, there exists an inverse matrix. If A is the square matrix, then $A^{-1}$ is the inverse of matrix A and satisfies the property:**

**$AA^{-1} = A^{-1}A = I$, where I is the Identity matrix.**

**Also, the determinant of the square matrix here should not be equal to zero.**

## MULTIPLE CHOICE QUESTIONS

1. If $f : [0, \infty) \to [0, \infty)$ and $f(x) = \dfrac{x}{1+x}$, then *f* is:

A. one-one and onto

B. one-one but not onto

C. onto but not one-one

D. neither one-one nor onto

2. For the sets of real numbers given by:

$R_1 = \{(x, y) : x \in R, y \in R, x^2 + y^2 \leq 25\}$

$R_2 = \{(x, y) : x \in R, y \in R, 9y \geq 4x^2\}$,

$R_1 \cap R_2$ is:

A. one-to-one B. onto

C. one-to-one and onto D. None of these

3. Given $f(x) = \ln\dfrac{1+x}{2-x}$ and $g(x) = \dfrac{3x+x^3}{1+3x^2}$. Then $f(g(x))$ is equal to:

A. $-f(x)$ B. $3f(x)$

C. $[f(x)]^2$ D. None of these

4. If a function satisfies the condition $f\left(x+\dfrac{1}{x}\right) = x^2 + \dfrac{1}{x^2}$, $x \neq 0$, then domain of $f(x)$ is:

A. $[-2, 2]$ B. $(-\infty, -2] \cup [2, \infty)$

C. $(0, \infty)$ D. None of these

**5. For $|x - 1| + |x - 2| + |x - 3| \leq 6$, *x* belongs to:**

A. $0 \leq x \leq 4$ B. $x \leq 0$ or $x \geq 4$

C. $x \leq -2$ or $x \geq 4$ D. none of these

**6. If $f(x) + 2f(1 - x) = x^2 + 2 \ \forall \ x \in R$, then $f(x)$ is given as:**

A. $\dfrac{(x-2)^2}{3}$ B. $x^2 - 2$

C. 1 D. None of these

**7. Let $f : N \to N$ be defined as**

$$f(n) = \begin{cases} \dfrac{n+1}{2} & \text{if } n \text{ is odd} \\ \dfrac{n}{2} & \text{if } n \text{ is even} \end{cases}$$. Then *f* is :

A. one-to-one B. one-to-one and onto

C. onto D. None of these

**8. Let the positive numbers *a, b, c, d* be in A.P. Then *abc, abd, acd, bcd* are:**

A. Not in A.P./G.P./H.P. B. in A.P.

C. in G.P. D. in H.P.

**9. The harmonic mean of the roots of the equation**

$$\left(5+\sqrt{2}\right)x^2 - \left(4+\sqrt{2}\right)x + 8 + 2\sqrt{2} = 0 \text{ is:}$$

A. 2 B. 4
C. 6 D. 8

**10.** If cos $(x - y)$, cos $x$ and cos $(x + y)$ are in H.P., then value of $\cos x \sec(y/2)$ is:

A. $\pm\sqrt{2}$ B. $\pm\sqrt{3}$
C. $\pm 2$ D. $\pm 1$

**11.** For a positive integer $n$,

let $a(n) = 1+\frac{1}{2}+\frac{1}{3}+\frac{1}{4}+...+\frac{1}{(2^n)-1}$. Then

A. $a(200) > 100$ B. $a(100) < 100$
C. $a(50) < 25$ D. None of these

**12.** Let $S = \frac{4}{19}+\frac{44}{19^2}+\frac{444}{19^3}+...$ upto $\infty$. Then S is equal to:

A. $\frac{38}{81}$ B. $\frac{4}{19}$
C. $\frac{36}{171}$ D. None of these

**13.** If $a, b, c, ...$ are in G.P., and $a^{1/x} = b^{1/y} = c^{1/z} = ...$, then $x, y, z, ......$ are in:

A. H.P. B. G.P.
C. A.P. D. None of these

**14.** If $a^x = b^y = c^z = d^u$ and $a, b, c, d$ are in G.P., then $x, y, z, u$ are in:

A. A.P. B. G.P.
C. H.P. D. None of these

**15.** If $a, b, c, d$ and $p$ are distinct real numbers such that $(a^2 + b^2 + c^2)p^2 - 2(ab + bc + cd)p + (b^2 + c^2 + d^2) \le 0$, then $a, b, c, d$ are in:

A. A.P. B. G.P.
C. H.P. D. None of these

**Directions (Qs. No. 16-18):** In the expansion of $\left(x^3 - \frac{1}{x^2}\right)^n$, where $n$ is a positive integer, the sum of the coefficients of $x^5$ and $x^{10}$ is 0.

**16.** What is $n$ equal to?

A. 5 B. 10
C. 15 D. None of these

**17.** What is the value of the independent term?

A. 5005 B. 7200
C. – 5005 D. – 7200

**18.** What is the sum of the coefficients of the two middle terms?

A. 0 B. 1
C. –1 D. None of these

**19.** If the matrix $A = \begin{bmatrix} 2-x & 1 & 1 \\ 1 & 3-x & 0 \\ -1 & -3 & -x \end{bmatrix}$ is singular, then what is the solution set S?

A. S = {0, 2, 3} B. S = {–1, 2, 3}
C. S = {1, 2, 3} D. S = {2, 3}

**20.** If $l + m + n = 0$, then the system of equations $-2x + y + z = l$, $x - 2y + z = m$, $x + y - 2z = n$ has:

A. a trivial solution
B. no solution
C. a unique solution
D. infinitely many solutions

**21.** If $y(k) = \left(k^3 - \frac{1}{k}\right)^{2p} + \left(k^3 + \frac{1}{k}\right)^{2p}$, then function $y(k)$ is:

A. Even function
B. Odd function
C. Periodic function
D. Neither even nor odd function

**22.** The number of dissimilar terms in the expansion of $(a + b)^n$ is $n + 1$, therefore number of dissimilar terms in the expansion of $(a + b + c)^{12}$ is

A. 36 B. 91
C. 56 D. 48

**23.** Find the ratio of coefficient of $x^{-37}$ and $x^8$ in the expansion of $\left(x^5 - \frac{1}{x^4}\right)^{16}$:

A. $\frac{(8!)^2}{3!(13)!}$ B. $\frac{13!3!}{8!5!}$
C. $-\frac{(8!)^2}{3!(13)!}$ D. None of these

**24.** If the ratio of coefficient of three consecutive term in the binomial expansion of $(1 + k)^p$ is 182:84:30. Then the average of these three consecutive terms are:

A. 18 B. 13
C. 12 D. 14

**25.** If the number $N = (13^{99} - 19^{93})$ is completely divisible by integer $r$. Then value $r$ is:

A. 84 B. 172
C. 162 D. 144

**26.** In the expansion of $\left(\frac{x^3}{y} - \frac{y^3}{x}\right)^{12}$, find the ratio of the coefficient of the term independent of $x$ and the coefficient of the term independent of $y$.

A. 3 B. 1
C. 12/7 D. None of these

**27.** Find the term independent of $x$ in $\left(1+\frac{1}{x}\right)^p (1+x)^q$ is:

A. ${}^{p+q}c_{p-q}$  B. ${}^{p+q}c_p$
C. ${}^{p+q}c_q$  D. None of these

**28.** The coefficient of $x^6$ in the expansion of: $(1 - x - x^2 + x^3)^9$ is

A. 162  B. 605
C. 2430  D. None of these

**29.** If $(1 - 3x^2 + 2x^3)^6 = 1 + a_1x + a_2x^2 + .... + a_{18}x^{18}$, then $a_2 + a_4 + a_6 .... + a_{18}$

A. 2048  B. – 1811
C. – 2048  D. 2084

**30.** Find the numerical value of highest term in the expansion of $(p + q)^{15}$, where $p = 2$ and $q = 3$.

A. ${}^{15}c_6 3^9 2^6$  B. ${}^{15}c_9 2^9.3^6$
C. ${}^{15}c_8 3^8 2^7$  D. None of these

**31.** For the given system of equations $3\alpha x + 6y - 6z = 2$, $12x + 6\alpha y - 3z = 4$, $18x + 18y + 3\alpha z = 5$ has a unique solution, then $\alpha$ is not equal to:

A. 1  B. 4
C. 3  D. None of these

**32.** If $m, n \neq 0$, and $f(k) = m^k + n^k$ and

$$\begin{bmatrix} 3 & 1+f(1) & 1+f(2) \\ 1+f(1) & 1+f(2) & 1+f(3) \\ 1+f(2) & 1+f(3) & 1+f(3) \end{bmatrix} = a(1-m)^2(1-n)^2(m-n)^2,$$

then $a$ is equal to

A. –1  B. 1
C. $m.n$  D. $\frac{1}{m.n}$

**33.** If $K(a) = \begin{bmatrix} \cos a & -\sin a \\ \sin a & \cos a \end{bmatrix}, [K(-b) = ?]$

Then which of the following are correct?

I. $K(a) \times K(-b) = - K(a - b)$

II. $K(a) \times K(-b) = K(a - b)$

III. The determinant of $K(a)$ is a cubic number.

A. Only I  B. II and III
C. I and III  D. I, II and III

**34.** Find the value of the determinant given below

$$\begin{bmatrix} \log a_n & \log a_{n+1} & \log a_{n+2} \\ \log a_{n+3} & \log a_{n+4} & \log a_{n+5} \\ \log a_{n+6} & \log a_{n+7} & \log a_{n+8} \end{bmatrix}$$

Here, $a_1, a_2, a_3, ..., a_n$ are in G.P.

A. 4  B. 0
C. –2  D. None of these

**35.** The system of equations

$k - rm - qn = 0$
$m - pn - rk = 0$
$n - qk - pm = 0$

Where $k, m, n$ are not all zero, then

A. $p^2 + q^2 + r^2 - 2pqr = 1$
B. $p^2 + q^2 + r^2 + 2pqr = 1$
C. $p^2 + q^2 + r^2 + 2pqr = 0$
D. None of these

**36.** Let $P = \begin{bmatrix} 1 & 2 & 3 \\ 2 & 5 & 7 \\ -2 & -4 & -5 \end{bmatrix}$ and $Q = \begin{bmatrix} 3 & -2 & -1 \\ -4 & 1 & \beta \\ 2 & 0 & 1 \end{bmatrix}$.

If Q is the inverse of matrix P, then $\beta$ is:

A. 5  B. –1
C. 2  D. –2

**37.** Equations $x + y + z = 6$, $x + 2y + 3z = 10$ and $x + 2y + \gamma z = \delta$ have infinite solutions.

Then which of the following are correct?

I. Product $(\gamma + \delta) * (\delta - \gamma)$ gives a number multiple of 8.

II. Product $(\gamma + \delta) * (\delta - \gamma)$ = L.C.M. of $(\gamma, \delta)$

III. Number $(\gamma + \delta)$ and $(\delta - \gamma)$ are prime number.

A. Only I  B. Only II
C. Only III  D. I, II and III

**38.** Consider the system of simultaneous linear equations $p + 2aq + a = 0$, $p + 3bq + b = 0$ and $p + 4cq + c = 0$ has a non-zero solution, then $a, b, c$ are in

A. A.P.
B. G.P.
C. H.P.
D. $3a + 2b + c = 0$

**39.** Consider the system of linear simple equations $x + 8ay - 2az = 0$, $x + 6by - 2bz = 0$ and $x + 4cy - 2cz = 0$. The relation among $a$, $b$ and $c$ for which the given equations are consistent are :

A. Satisfy $a + 2b - 3c = 0$
B. in A.P.
C. in G.P.
D. in H.P.

**40.** If $\Delta_k = \begin{bmatrix} \sin^2(n+1) & \sin^2(n^2) & \sin^2(n) \\ 2k-1 & c_k^{2n+1} & 1 \\ n^2-1 & 2^{2n} & n+1 \end{bmatrix}$ then value of $\sum_{k=0}^{n} \Delta_k$ is

A. 4  B. 3
C. 2  D. 0

# ANSWERS

| 1 | 2 | 3 | 4 | 5 | 6 | 7 | 8 | 9 | 10 |
|---|---|---|---|---|---|---|---|---|---|
| B | D | B | B | A | A | C | D | B | A |
| **11** | **12** | **13** | **14** | **15** | **16** | **17** | **18** | **19** | **20** |
| A | A | C | A | B | C | C | A | A | D |
| **21** | **22** | **23** | **24** | **25** | **26** | **27** | **28** | **29** | **30** |
| A | B | C | D | C | B | C | A | C | A |
| **31** | **32** | **33** | **34** | **35** | **36** | **37** | **38** | **39** | **40** |
| D | B | B | B | B | B | C | C | D | D |

# EXPLANATORY ANSWERS

**1.** The given function is $f(x) = \frac{x}{1+x} = 1 - \frac{1}{1+x}$.
Hence its range is [0, 1) which is a subset of [0, ∞).
Also the function is one-one.

**2.** Here $x^2 + y^2 \le 25$ are the elements of $R_1$ lying with in and on the circle $x^2 + y^2 - 25$, where as $4x^2 \le 9y$ are the elements of $R_2$ lying with in and on the parabola $4x^2 = 9y$.
Hence relation $R_1 \cap R_2$ is not a function.

Hence (D) is the correct answer.

**3.** $$f(g(x)) = \ln\frac{1+g(x)}{1-g(x)} = \ln\frac{1+\frac{3x+x^3}{1+3x^2}}{1-\frac{3x+x^3}{1+3x^2}}$$

$$= \ln\frac{(1+x)^3}{(1-x)^3} = 3\ln\frac{1+x}{1-x}$$

$$= 3f(x)$$

Hence (B) is the correct answer.

**4.** $$f\left(x+\frac{1}{x}\right) = \left(x+\frac{1}{x}\right)^2 - 2$$

$$\Rightarrow \quad f(y) = y^2 - 2,$$

where $\quad y = x + \frac{1}{x}$

for $x > 0$, $\quad y = x + \frac{1}{x} \ge 2$

and for $x < 0$, $\quad y = x + \frac{1}{x} \le -2$

**5.** We have,
$|x - 1 + x - 2 + x - 3| \le |x - 1| + |x - 2| + |x - 3| \le 6$
$\Rightarrow |3x - 6| \le 6 \Rightarrow -6 \le 3x - 6 \le 6 \Rightarrow 0 \le x \le 4.$

**6.** By replacing $x$ with $(1 - x)$ in the given expression, we get

$$f(1-x) + 2f(1-1+x) = (1-x)^2 + 2$$

$$\Rightarrow \quad f(1-x) + 2f(x) = (1-x)^2 + 2$$

Now, $\quad f(x) + 2f(1-x) - 2(f(1-x) + 2f(x))$

$$= x^2 + 2 - 2((1-x)^2 + 2)$$

$$\Rightarrow \quad -3f(x) = x^2 + 2 - 2(3 - 2x + x^2)$$

$$\Rightarrow \quad 3f(x) = x^2 - 4x + 4$$

$$\Rightarrow \quad f(x) = \frac{(x-2)^2}{3}.$$

**7.** Here, $f(3) = 2$, $f(4) = 2$
Hence $f$ is not one-to-one. Also
$f(1) = 1$, $f(2) = 1$, $f(3) = 2$, $f(4) = 2$, $f(5) = 3$, $f(6) = 3$, .... $f(2n = 1) = n$
and $\quad f(2n) = n \Rightarrow$ Range of $f$ = N.
Hence (C) is correct answer.

**8.** $a, b, c, d$ are in A.P.

$\Rightarrow \frac{1}{a}, \frac{1}{b}, \frac{1}{c}, \frac{1}{d}$ are in H.P. $\Rightarrow \frac{1}{d}, \frac{1}{c}, \frac{1}{b}, \frac{1}{a}$ are in H.P.

Now multiply each term by $abcd$.

We ge, $\frac{abcd}{d}, \frac{abcd}{c}, \frac{abcd}{b}, \frac{abcd}{a}$ are in H.P.

or, $abc$, $abd$, $acd$, $bcd$ are in H.P.

**9.** $$\alpha + \beta = \frac{4+\sqrt{2}}{5+\sqrt{2}},$$

$$\alpha\beta = \frac{8+2\sqrt{2}}{5+\sqrt{2}}$$

$$\text{H.M.} = \frac{2\alpha\beta}{\alpha+\beta} = \frac{16+4\sqrt{2}}{4+\sqrt{2}} = 4$$

**10.** $$\frac{2}{\cos x} = \frac{1}{\cos(x-y)} + \frac{1}{\cos(x+y)}$$

$$\Rightarrow \quad 2(\cos^2 x - \sin^2 y) = 2\cos x \cos x \cos y$$

$$\Rightarrow \quad \cos^2 x\,(1 - \cos y) = \sin^2 y = 1 - \cos^2 y$$

$$\Rightarrow \quad \cos^2 x = 1+\cos y = 2\cos^2\left(\frac{y}{2}\right)$$

$$\Rightarrow \quad \cos x \sec\left(\frac{y}{2}\right) = \pm\sqrt{2}.$$

**11.** $$a(2n) = 1+\frac{1}{2}+\frac{1}{3}+\frac{1}{4}+...+\frac{1}{2^{2n}-1}$$

$$>1+\frac{1}{2}+\left(\frac{1}{3}+\frac{1}{4}\right)+\left(\frac{1}{5}+\frac{1}{6}+\frac{1}{7}+\frac{1}{8}\right)+...$$

$$+\left(\frac{1}{2^{2n-1}+1}+...+\frac{1}{2^{2n}}\right)-\frac{1}{2^{2n}}$$

$$>\frac{1}{2}+\frac{1}{2}+\frac{2}{4}+\frac{4}{8}+...+\frac{2^{2n-1}}{2^{2n}}+\left(\frac{1}{2}-\frac{1}{2^{2n}}\right)>\frac{n}{2} \text{ if } n>1$$

$$\therefore \quad a(200) > 100.$$

**12.** $$S = \frac{4}{19}+\frac{44}{19^2}+\frac{444}{19^3}+... \quad ...(1)$$

$$\frac{1}{19}S = \frac{4}{19^2}+\frac{44}{19^3}+... \quad ...(2)$$

Subtracting (2) from (1), we get

$$\left(\frac{18}{19}\right)S = \frac{4}{19}+\frac{40}{19^2}+\frac{400}{19^3}+...$$

$$= \frac{4/19}{1-10/19}=\frac{4}{9}$$

$$\Rightarrow \quad S = \frac{19}{18}\times\frac{4}{9}=\frac{38}{81}$$

**13.** $a^{1/x} = b^{1/y} = c^{1/z} = ... = k$(say)

$$\Rightarrow \quad \frac{\log a}{x} = \frac{\log b}{y}=\frac{\log c}{z} = .... \log k,$$

As, $a$, $b$, $c$ are in G.P.

then, $b^2 = ac$

$2 \log b = \log a + \log c$

Now, use $\log a$, $\log b$, $\log c$ ... are in A.P.

$x$, $y$ and $z$ are in A.P.

**14.** $$a^x = b^y = c^z = d^u$$

$$\Rightarrow \quad x \log a = y \log b = z \log c = u \log d$$

$$\Rightarrow \quad \frac{\log a}{1/x} = \frac{\log b}{1/y}=\frac{\log c}{1/z}=\frac{\log d}{1/u}$$

Now, use $\log a$, $\log b$, $\log c$, $\log d$ are in A.P.

**15.** $(a^2p^2 - 2abp + b^2) + (b^2p^2 - 2bcp + c^2) + (c^2p^2 - 2cdp + d^2) \le 0$

$\Rightarrow (ap - b)^2 + (bp - c)^2 + (cp - d)^2 \le 0$

As $a$, $b$, $c$, $d$ and $p$ are real this is possible if and only if:

$$ap - b = 0,$$
$$bp - c = 0,$$
$$cp - d = 0$$

$$\Rightarrow \quad \frac{b}{a} = \frac{c}{b}=\frac{d}{c}$$

$\Rightarrow$ $a$, $b$, $c$, $d$ are in G.P.

**17.** For the independent term,

put, $3n - 5r = 0$

$\Rightarrow \quad 5r = 3n = 3 \times 15 \qquad [\because n = 15]$

$\therefore \quad r = 9$

Now, put the value of $r$ in eq.

We get, $T_{9+1} = {}^{15}C_9(-1)^9 . x^{(3\times 15 - 5\times 9)}$

$$\Rightarrow \quad T_{10} = -{}^{15}C_9 . x^0 = -{}^{15}C_9 = -\frac{15!}{6!9!}$$

$$= -5005$$

So, the value of independent term is $-5005$.

**18.** Since, $n = 15$

$\therefore$ Total term in the expansion of

$\left(x^3 - \frac{1}{x^2}\right)^{15}$ is 16.

So, middle term $=\left(\frac{16}{2}\right)$th term and $\left(\frac{16}{2}+1\right)$th term

= 8th term and 9th term

Now, the sum of the coefficients of the two middle terms

$$= {}^{15}C_7(-1)^7 + {}^{15}C_8(-1)^8$$
$$= -{}^{15}C_7 + {}^{15}C_8$$
$$= -{}^{15}C_7 + {}^{15}C_7 \qquad [\because {}^nC_r = {}^nC_{n-r}]$$
$$= 0$$

**19.** For the singular matrix.

$$\begin{vmatrix} 2-x & 1 & 1 \\ 1 & 3-x & 0 \\ -1 & -3 & -x \end{vmatrix} = 0$$

$\Rightarrow (2 - x)[x(x - 3)] - [-x] + [-3 + (3 - x)] = 0$

$\Rightarrow \quad x(x - 3)(x - 2) = 0$

$\Rightarrow \quad x = 0, 2, 3$

So, the solution set is, S = {0, 2, 3}

**20.** $$\Delta = \begin{bmatrix} -2 & 1 & 1 \\ 1 & -2 & 1 \\ 1 & 1 & -2 \end{bmatrix}$$

$$= -2(4 - 1) - 1(-2 - 1) + 1 + 2 = 0$$

$$\Delta = \begin{bmatrix} l & 1 & 1 \\ m & -2 & 1 \\ n & 1 & -2 \end{bmatrix} = \begin{bmatrix} l+m+n & 0 & 0 \\ m & -2 & 1 \\ n & 1 & -2 \end{bmatrix}$$

$[R_1 \rightarrow R_1 + R_2 + R_3]$
$[\because l + m + n = 0]$

$= 0$

Similarly, $\Delta_2 = \Delta_3 = 0$

Hence, the given system of equations has infinitely many solutions.

**21.** Given function $y(k) = \left(k^3 - \frac{1}{k}\right)^{2p} + \left(k^3 + \frac{1}{k}\right)^{2p}$

Binomial expansion of $\left(k^3 - \frac{1}{k}\right)^{2p}$

$$= {}^{2p}c_0(k^3)^{2p} - {}^{2p}c_1(k^3)^{2p-1}\left(\frac{1}{k}\right)$$
$$+ {}^{2p}c_2(k^3)^{2p-2}\left(\frac{1}{k}\right)^2 \ldots\ldots {}^{2p}c_{2p}\left(\frac{1}{k}\right)^{2p} \quad \ldots(1)$$

And, Binomial expansion of $\left(k^3 + \frac{1}{k}\right)^{2p}$

$$= {}^{2p}c_0(k^3)^{2p} + {}^{2p}c_1(k^3)^{2p-1}\left(\frac{1}{k}\right)$$
$$+ {}^{2p}c_2(k^3)^{2p-2}\left(\frac{1}{k}\right)^2 \ldots\ldots {}^{2p}c_{2p}\left(\frac{1}{k}\right)^{2p} \quad \ldots(2)$$

On adding (1) and (2), we get

$$y(k) = 2\left[{}^{2p}c_0(k^3)^{2p} + {}^{2p}c_2(k^3)^{2p-2}\left(\frac{1}{k}\right)^2 \ldots\ldots {}^{2p}c_{2p}\left(\frac{1}{k}\right)^{2p}\right]$$

On putting $k = -k$,

$$y(-k) = 2\left[{}^{2p}c_0(-k^3)^{2p} + {}^{2p}c_2(-k^3)^{2p-2}\left(-\frac{1}{k}\right)^2 \ldots\ldots {}^{2p}c_{2p}\left(-\frac{1}{k}\right)^{2p}\right]$$

Here, we see, in all term exponents of $k$ is even term,

$$\therefore\ y(-k) = 2\left[{}^{2p}c_0(k^3)^{2p} + {}^{2p}c_2(k^3)^{2p-2}\left(\frac{1}{k}\right)^2 \ldots\ldots {}^{2p}c_{2p}\left(\frac{1}{k}\right)^{2p}\right]$$

Hence, $y(k) = y(-k)$. Thus the given function is even function.

**22.** Number of term in the expansion of $(a + b + c)^n$ is given by ${}^{n+2}C_2$.

Thus for $n = 12$; ${}^{n+2}C_2 = 14C_2 = \frac{14 \times 13}{2} = 91$.

Also, $(a + b + c)^{12} = [(a + b) + c]^{12}$

$= 12c_o\,(a + b)^{12} + 12c_1(a + b)^{11}\,c + \ldots + 12c_{12}c^{12}$

The R.H.S. contains, $13 + 12 + 11 + \ldots\ldots + 1$ terms

$$= \frac{13(13+1)}{2} = 91 \text{ terms}$$

**23.** Given expression : $\left(x^5 - \frac{1}{x^4}\right)^{16}$

Let $r^{th}$ term have variable term $x^{-37}$, then

$${}^{16}c_r\left(x^5\right)^{16-r}\left(\frac{1}{x^4}\right)^r(-1)^r = k.x^{-37}$$

Where $k$ = coefficient of the term

$\therefore\quad (x^5)^{16-r} \times x^{-4r} = x^{-37}$

$\Rightarrow\quad 80 - 9r = -37 \Rightarrow r = 13$

Now, coefficient of the term $(r = 13)$

$= {}^{16}c_{13}(-1)^{13} = -\,{}^{16}c_{13}$

Again, let $t^{th}$ term have variable term $x^8$, then

$80 - 9t = 8 \Rightarrow t = 8$

Coefficient of the term $(t = 8) = {}^{16}c_8(-1)^8 = {}^{16}c_8$

$$\therefore \text{ Required Ratio} = -\frac{{}^{16}c_{13}}{{}^{16}c_8} = -\frac{(8!)^2}{3!(13)!}$$

**24.** Let the ratio of coefficient of three consecutive terms $n^{th}$, $(n + 1)^{th}$ and $(n + 2)^{th}$ is 182 : 84 : 30

Then, $$\frac{{}^pc_{n-1}}{{}^pc_n} = \frac{182}{84} = \frac{13}{6}$$

$$\frac{n}{p+1-n} = \frac{13}{6}$$

$$6n = 13p - 13n + 13$$

$\Rightarrow\quad 19n = 13p + 13 \quad \ldots(i)$

Similarly, $$\frac{{}^pc_n}{{}^pc_{n+1}} = \frac{84}{30} = \frac{14}{5}$$

$$\frac{\dfrac{p!}{(n)!(p-n)!}}{\dfrac{p!}{(n+1)!(p-n-1)!}} = \frac{14}{5}$$

$$\frac{n+1}{p-n} = \frac{14}{5}$$

$\Rightarrow\quad 5n + 5 = 14p - 14n$

$\Rightarrow\quad 19n = 14p - 5 \quad \ldots(ii)$

From (*i*) and (*ii*), we get $p = 18$ and $n = 13$

Then, three consecutive terms are $13^{th}$, $14^{th}$ and $15^{th}$ terms

And Average $= \frac{13+14+15}{3} = 14$

**25.** $13 = (1 + 3 \times 4)$ and $19 = (1 + 9 \times 2)$

Now, $13^{99} - 19^{93} = (1 + 3.4)^{99} - (1 + 9.2)^{93}$

$= \{{}^{99}c_0 + {}^{99}c_1(3 \times 4) + {}^{99}c_2(3 \times 4)^2 + \ldots.\}$

$- \{{}^{93}c_0 + {}^{93}c_1(9 \times 2) + {}^{93}c_2\,(9 \times 2)^2 \ldots.\}$

$= \{1 + 99 \times 12 + {}^{99}c_2(12)^2 + \ldots\}$

$- \{1 + 93 \times 18 + {}^{93}c_2(18)^2 \ldots\}$

$= (99 \times 12 - 93 \times 18) + {}^{99}c_2(12)^2$
$+ {}^{99}c_3(12)^3 + 81 \times K$ (where $k$ = Integer)
$= -486 + 144(99.49 + 9.98.97.2) + 81\ K$
$= -162 \times 3 + 8 \times 162(11 \times 49 + 11 \times 98 \times 97 \times 2) + 81\ K$

Now, we know that, Odd Number – Odd Number = Even number

So, K must be a even number. Thus 81 K must be a multiple of 162

So, $13^{99} - 19^{93} = -162 \times 3 + 8 \times 162(11 \times 49 + 11 \times 98 \times 97 \times 2) + 162\ m$

(Where $m$ = Integer)

$= 162(-3 + 8(11 \times 49 + 11 \times 98 \times 97 \times 2) + m)$

Hence, $N = 13^{99} - 19^{93}$ is completely divisible by $r = 162$

**26.** Given expression : $\left(\frac{x^3}{y} - \frac{y^3}{x}\right)^{12}$

Let $(r + 1)^{th}$ term is independent from $x$.

$$(r+1)^{th} \text{ term} = {}^{12}c_r\left(\frac{x^3}{y}\right)^{12-r} \cdot \left(\frac{y^3}{x}\right)^r (-1)^r$$

As coefficient of $x = 0$,

$3(12 - r) - r = 0 \rightarrow r = 9$

Coefficient of term $(r = 9) = {}^{12}c_9(-1)^9 = -{}^{12}c_3$

Again, let $(t + 1)^{th}$ term is independent of $y$

$$(t+1)^{th} \text{ term} = {}^{12}c_t\left(\frac{x^3}{y}\right)^{12-t} \cdot \left(\frac{y^3}{x}\right)^t (-1)^t$$

As coefficient of $y = 0$, $t - 12 + 3t = 0$, $t = 3$

Coefficient of term $(t = 3) = {}^{12}c_3\,(-1)^3 = -{}^{12}c_3$

Now, Ratio of the coefficient $= \frac{-{}^{12}c_3}{-{}^{12}c_3} = 1$

**27.** Given Expression:

$$\left(1+\frac{1}{x}\right)^p (1+x)^q = \left(\frac{x+1}{x}\right)^p (1+x)^q$$
$$= \frac{(x+1)^{p+q}}{x^p} = x^{-p}(x+1)^{p+q}$$

Now, exponent of $x$ in a term independent of variable $x = 0$

$\therefore$ Co-efficient of term independent of $x$ in $x^{-p}(x + 1)^{p+q}$
= Co-efficient of $x^p$ in $(x + 1)^{p+q}$

Expansion of $(x + 1)^{p+q} = {}^{p+q}c_0 x^{p+q} + {}^{p+q}c_1 x^{p+q-1} + \ldots + {}^{p+q}c_q x^{p+q-q} + \ldots\ {}^{p+q}c_{p+q}$

Now, Coefficient of $x^p = {}^{p+q}c_q$

Hence, coefficient of term independent of $x$ in ${}^{p+q}c_q$

**28.** We have, $(1 - x - x^2 + x^3)^9$
$= (1 - x)^9 (1 - x^2)^9$
$= (1 - 9c_1x + 9c_2x^2 - 9c_3x^3 + \ldots - 9c_9x^9)$
$\times (1 - 9c_1x^2 + 9c_2x^4 - 9c_3x^6 + \ldots - 9c_9x^{18})$

The terms which give $x^6$ are

$9c_6x^6 + 9c_2x^2.9c_2x^4 - 9c_4.x^4.9c_1.x^2 - 9c_3x^6$

Hence the coefficient of $x^6$ is

$9c_6 + 9c_2.9c_2 - 9c_4.9c_1 - 9c_3$

$$= \frac{9\times 8x7}{1.2.3} + \frac{9\times 8}{1.2} \times \frac{9\times 8}{1.2} - \frac{9\times 8x7x6}{4.3.2.1} \times 9 - \frac{9\times 8x7}{1.2.3}$$

$= 1296 - 1134 = 162.$

**29.** Given expression

$(1 - 3x^2 + 2x^3)^6 = 1 + a_1x + a_2x^2 + \ldots + a_{18}x^{18}$

Putting $x = 1$, we get

$0 = 1 + a_1 + a_2 + \ldots + a_{18}$ ...(1)

Putting $x = -1$, we get

$4096 = 1 - a_1 + a_2 - \ldots + a_{18}$ ...(2)

Adding (1) and (2), we get

$-4096 = 2(a_1 + a_3 + a_5 + \ldots + a_{17})$

$\therefore a_1 + a_3 + a_5 + \ldots + a_{17} = -2048$

**30.** Given expression : $(p + q)^{15}$

Now, $\frac{t_r}{t_{r+1}} = \frac{{}^{15}c_{r-1}p^{16-r}q^{r-1}}{{}^{15}c_r p^{15-r}q^r}$

$= \frac{15!}{(r-1)!(16-r)!} \cdot \frac{r!(15-r)!}{15!} \cdot \frac{p}{q}$

$= \frac{r}{16-r} \cdot \frac{2}{3}$

Now, $t_r \le t_{r+1}$ when $\frac{r}{16-r} \cdot \frac{2}{3} \le 1$

or $2r \le 3(16 - r)$

or $r \le \frac{48}{5}$

$\therefore$ for $r = 1, 2, 3 \ldots 9$ we get $t_{r+1} \ge t_r$

For $r = 10, 11, 12, 13, 14, \ldots$, we get, $t_r \ge t_{r+1}$

$\therefore t_1 < t_2 < t_3 < \ldots t_9 < t_{10} > t_{11} > t_{12} > \ldots$

$\therefore t_{10}$ is the greatest term

Greatest term $t_{10} = {}^{15}c_9 2^6.3^9 = {}^{15}c_6 3^9 2^6$

**31.** The given system of equation can be written in a single matrix equation:

$$\begin{bmatrix} 3\alpha & 6 & -6 \\ 12 & 6\alpha & -3 \\ 18 & 18 & 3\alpha \end{bmatrix}\begin{bmatrix} x \\ y \\ z \end{bmatrix} = \begin{bmatrix} 2 \\ 1 \\ 3 \end{bmatrix}$$

The given system of equations will have unique solution if and only if the coefficient matrix is non-singular *i.e.* if

$$\begin{bmatrix} 3\alpha & 6 & -6 \\ 12 & 6\alpha & -3 \\ 18 & 18 & 3\alpha \end{bmatrix} \neq 0$$

$\Rightarrow 3\alpha(18\alpha^2 - 36) + 6(-54 - 36\alpha) - 6(216 - 90\alpha) \neq 0$

or $\quad 3(\alpha^3 + 11\alpha - 30) \neq 0$

$\Rightarrow \quad (\alpha^3 + 11\alpha - 30) \neq 0$

or $\quad (\alpha - 2)(\alpha^2 + 2\alpha + 15) \neq 0$

or $\quad \alpha \neq 2$

**32.** $\begin{bmatrix} 3 & 1+f(1) & 1+f(2) \\ 1+f(1) & 1+f(2) & 1+f(3) \\ 1+f(2) & 1+f(3) & 1+f(3) \end{bmatrix}$

$$= \begin{bmatrix} 1+1+1 & 1+m+n & 1+m^2+n^2 \\ 1+m+n & 1+m^2+n^2 & 1+m^3+n^3 \\ 1+m^2+n^2 & 1+m^3+n^3 & 1=m^4+n^4 \end{bmatrix}$$

$$= \begin{bmatrix} 1 & 1 & 1 \\ 1 & m & n \\ 1 & m^2 & n^2 \end{bmatrix} \times \begin{bmatrix} 1 & 1 & 1 \\ 1 & m & n \\ 1 & m^2 & n^2 \end{bmatrix}$$

$$= \begin{bmatrix} 1 & 1 & 1 \\ 1 & m & n \\ 1 & m^2 & n^2 \end{bmatrix}^2$$

$= [(1 - m)(1 - n)(m - n)]^2$ [Need to add one more step.]

So, $\quad a = 1$

**33.** $K(a)\,K(-b) = \begin{bmatrix} \cos a & -\sin a \\ \sin a & \cos a \end{bmatrix} \times \begin{bmatrix} \cos b & \sin b \\ -\sin b & \cos b \end{bmatrix}$

$$= \begin{bmatrix} \cos a.\cos b + \sin a.\sin b & \cos a.\sin b - \sin a.\cos b \\ \sin a.\cos b - \cos a \sin b & \sin a.\sin b + \cos a.\cos b \end{bmatrix}$$

$$= \begin{bmatrix} \cos(a-b) & -\sin(a-b) \\ \sin(a-b) & \cos(a-b) \end{bmatrix} = K(a - b)$$

Also, determinant of $K(a) = 1$ and 1 is cubic number.

Hence, statements II and III are correct.

**34.** Let $r$ be the common ratio, then

$$\begin{bmatrix} \log a_n & \log a_{n+1} & \log a_{n+2} \\ \log a_{n+3} & \log a_{n+4} & \log a_{n+5} \\ \log a_{n+6} & \log a_{n+7} & \log a_{n+8} \end{bmatrix}$$

$$= \begin{bmatrix} \log a_1 r^{n-1} & \log a_1 r^n & \log a_1 r^{n+1} \\ \log a_1 r^{n+2} & \log a_1 r^{n+3} & \log a_1 r^{n+4} \\ \log a_1 r^{n+5} & \log a_1 r^{n+6} & \log a_1 r^{n+7} \end{bmatrix}$$

$$= \begin{bmatrix} \log a_1 + (n-1)\log r & \log a_1 + n\log r & \log a_1 + (n+1)\log r \\ \log a_1 + (n+2)\log r & \log a_1 + (n+3)\log r & \log a_1 + (n+4)\log r \\ \log a_1 + (n+5)\log r & \log a_1 + (n+6)\log r & \log a_1 + (n+7)\log r \end{bmatrix}$$

$$= \begin{bmatrix} \log a_1 & \log a_1 & \log a_1 \\ \log a_1 & \log a_1 & \log a_1 \\ \log a_1 & \log a_1 & \log a_1 \end{bmatrix} + \begin{bmatrix} (n-1)\log r & (n)\log r & (n+1)\log r \\ (n+2)\log r & (n+3)\log r & (n+4)\log r \\ (n+5)\log r & (n+6)\log r & (n+7)\log r \end{bmatrix}$$

$$= 0 + \begin{bmatrix} (n-1)\log r & (n)\log r & (n+1)\log r \\ (n+2)\log r & (n+3)\log r & (n+4)\log r \\ (n+5)\log r & (n+6)\log r & (n+7)\log r \end{bmatrix}$$

$$= 0 + 0 \quad \left[\text{Apply } c_2 - c_2 - \frac{1}{2}c_1 - \frac{1}{2}c_3\right]$$

**35.** We have,

$$k - rm - qn = 0$$
$$rk + pn - m = 0$$
$$qk + pm - n = 0$$

Since, $k$, $m$, $n$ are not all zero. So, the equations will have a non-trivial solution.

Therefore,

$$\begin{bmatrix} 1 & r & -q \\ r & -1 & p \\ q & p & -1 \end{bmatrix} = 0$$

$\Rightarrow 1(1 - p^2) + r(-r - pq) - q(pr + q) = 0$

$\Rightarrow p^2 + q^2 + r^2 + 2pqr = 1$

**36.** Here, $\Rightarrow Q = \begin{bmatrix} 3 & -2 & -1 \\ -4 & 1 & \beta \\ 2 & 0 & 1 \end{bmatrix}$

Also since, $Q = P^{-1} \Rightarrow P.Q = 1$

$$\Rightarrow \begin{bmatrix} 1 & 2 & 3 \\ 2 & 5 & 7 \\ -2 & -4 & -5 \end{bmatrix} \cdot \begin{bmatrix} 3 & -2 & -1 \\ -4 & 1 & \beta \\ 2 & 0 & 1 \end{bmatrix} = \begin{bmatrix} 1 & 0 & 0 \\ 0 & 1 & 0 \\ 0 & 0 & 1 \end{bmatrix}$$

$$\Rightarrow \begin{bmatrix} 1 & 0 & 2\beta+2 \\ 0 & 1 & 5+5\beta \\ 0 & 0 & -4\beta-3 \end{bmatrix} = \begin{bmatrix} 1 & 0 & 0 \\ 0 & 1 & 0 \\ 0 & 0 & 1 \end{bmatrix}$$

$\Rightarrow 2\beta + 2 = 0 \Rightarrow \beta = -1$

**37.** For infinitely many solutions,

D = 0 and $D_1 = D_2 = D_3 = 0$

$$D = \begin{bmatrix} 1 & 1 & 1 \\ 1 & 2 & 3 \\ 1 & 2 & \gamma \end{bmatrix} = 1(2\gamma - 6) - 1(\gamma - 3) + 1(2 - 2)$$

$$= 2\gamma - 6 - \gamma + 3 = \gamma - 3$$

Now D = 0, $\therefore \gamma - 3 = 0$, or $\gamma = 3$.

$$D_1 = \begin{bmatrix} 6 & 1 & 1 \\ 10 & 2 & 3 \\ \delta & 2 & 3 \end{bmatrix}$$

$$= 6(6 - 6) - 1(30 - 3\delta) + 1(20 - 2\delta)$$

$$= -30 + 3\delta + 20 - 2\delta = \delta - 10$$

As, $D_1 = 0 \therefore \delta = 0$

$$D_2 = \begin{bmatrix} 1 & 6 & 1 \\ 1 & 10 & 3 \\ 1 & \delta & 3 \end{bmatrix}$$

$$= 1(30 - 3\delta) - 6(3 - 3) + 1(\delta - 10)$$

$$= 30 - 3\delta + \delta - 10 = 20 - 2\delta$$

As, $D_2 = 0 \Rightarrow \delta = 10$

$$D_3 = \begin{bmatrix} 1 & 1 & 6 \\ 1 & 2 & 10 \\ 1 & 2 & \delta \end{bmatrix}$$

$$= 1(2\delta - 20) - 1(\delta - 10) + 6(2 - 2)$$

$$= 2\delta - 20 - \delta + 10 = \delta - 10$$

As, $D_3 = 0 \Rightarrow \delta = 10$

$\therefore$ For infinite solutions $\gamma = 3$ and $\delta = 10$

Now, $(\gamma + \delta)$ and $(\delta - \gamma)$ are $(3 + 10) = 13$ and $(10 - 3) = 7$. Here, 7 and 13 both are prime number.

**38.** For the given homogeneous system to have non-zero solution, determinant of the coefficient matrix should be zero, *i.e.*

$$\begin{bmatrix} 1 & 2a & a \\ 1 & 3b & b \\ 1 & 4c & c \end{bmatrix} = 0$$

$$\begin{bmatrix} 1 & 0 & a \\ 1 & b & b \\ 1 & 2c & c \end{bmatrix} = 0$$

[Applying $c_2 \to c_2 - 2c_3$]

$$\begin{bmatrix} 1 & 0 & a \\ 0 & b & b-a \\ 0 & (2c-b) & c-b \end{bmatrix} = 0$$

[Applying $R_2 \to R_2 - R_1$, and $R_3 \to R_3 - R_2$]

$b(c - b) - (b - a)(2c - b) = 0$

$bc - 2bc + 2ac - ab = 0 \Rightarrow 2ac = ab + bc$

On dividing both sides by $abc$, we get,

$$\frac{2}{b} = \frac{1}{a} + \frac{1}{c}$$

$\therefore a, b, c$ are in Harmonic progression.

**39.** Given equations : $x + 8ay - 2az = 0$, $x + 6by - 2bz = 0$ and $x + 4cy - 2cz = 0$

Since system of equation is consistent, we have

$$\Delta = \begin{bmatrix} 1 & 8a & -2a \\ 1 & 6b & -2b \\ 1 & 4c & -2c \end{bmatrix} = 0$$

Or, $1(-12bc + 8bc) + 8a(2c - 2b) - 2a(4c - 6b) = 0$

Or, $-4bc + 16ac - 16ab - 8ac + 12ab = 0$

Or, $bc - 2ac + ab = 0$ or $bc + ab = 2ac$,

$$\therefore \quad \frac{1}{a} + \frac{1}{c} = \frac{2}{b}$$

Thus $a, b, c$, are in H.P.

**40.**
$$\Delta_k = \begin{bmatrix} \sin^2(n+1) & \sin^2(n^2) & \sin^2(n) \\ 2k-1 & c_k^{2n+1} & 1 \\ n^2-1 & 2^{2n} & n+1 \end{bmatrix}$$

$$\sum_{k=0}^{n} c_k = \begin{bmatrix} \sin^2(n+1) & \sin^2(n^2) & \sin^2(n) \\ \sum_{k=0}^{n} 2k-1 & \sum_{k=0}^{n} c_k^{2n+1} & \sum_{k=0}^{n} 1 \\ n^2-1 & 2^{2n} & n+1 \end{bmatrix}$$

$$= \begin{bmatrix} \sin^2(n+1) & \sin^2(n^2) & \sin^2(n) \\ n^2-1 & 2^{2n} & n+1 \\ n^2-1 & 2^{2n} & n+1 \end{bmatrix}$$

$$= 0$$

CHAPTER

# 2

# PROBABILITY

Probability measures how much chance is there for my expected result to happen.

Probability = (no. of favourable outcome)/(total no. of outcomes)

**Sample space:** Set of all possible outcomes of a random experiment is called Sample space. It is denoted by S.

**Event:** It is the set of favourable outcome.

**Example:** If you throw a coin and if you are looking for head, then head is the favourable outcome.

**Mutually Exclusive events:** Two events are said to be mutually exclusive if there is no common element between them.

**Exhaustive events:** The given events are Exhaustive if when I take the elements in those events forms the given sample space.

## Addition Theorem of Probability

If A and B are any two events, then

$$P(A \cup B) = P(A) + P(B) - P(A \cap B)$$

If A, B and C are any three events, then

$$P(A \cup B \cup C) = P(A) + P(B) + P(C) - P(A \cap B) - P(B \cap C) - P(A \cap C) + (A \cap B \cap C)$$

## Multiplication Theorem (Rule) of Probability

Let A and B be two events associated with a sample space S. Then,

$$P(A \cap B) = P(A) \cdot P(B/A) = P(B) \cdot P(A/B),$$

provided $P(A) \neq 0$ and $P(B) \neq 0$

If A, B and C are three events associated with a random experiment, then

$$P(A \cap B \cap C) = P(A).P(B/A).P(C/A \cap B)$$

Similarly, if $A_1$, $A_2$ ...., $A_n$ are $n$ events related to a random experiment, then

$$P(A_1 \cap A_2 \cap A_3 \cap .... A_n) = P(A_1).P(A_2/A_1).P(A_3/A_1 \cap A_2) ..... P(A_n/A_1 \cap A_2 \cap A_3 \cap ....A_{n-1})$$

## Probability of Independent Events

If A and B are independent events, then P(A/B) is precisely the same as P(A) since A is not affected by B, *i.e.* P(A/B) = P(A). Similarly, P(B/A) = P(B). Now by multiplication rule of probability, we have,

$$P(A \cap B) = P(A).P(B/A) = P(B).P(A/B)$$

$$\Rightarrow P(A \cap B) = P(A).P(B)$$

(Known as multiplication rule for independent events)

Conditional event (or dependent event) : If the probability of the happening of other is dependent or influenced by the previous happening, then other event is said to be dependent or conditional on one. It is denoted by A/B (A occurs after occurrence of B). The concept of dependent events gives rise to the concept of conditional probability.

## Conditional Probability

Let A and B be two events, then the probability of the occurrence of A under the condition that B has already occurred and $P(B) \neq 0$, is called the conditional probability of A given B and is written as P(A/B).

## MULTIPLE CHOICE QUESTIONS

**1.** A coin is tossed twice. Then, the probability that at least one tail occurs is:

A. $\frac{1}{4}$  B. $\frac{1}{2}$
C. $\frac{1}{3}$  D. $\frac{3}{4}$

**2.** Let S be a sample space containing outcomes $\omega_1, \omega_2, \omega_3, .... \omega_n$ *i.e.*, $S = \{\omega_1, \omega_2, ...., \omega_n\}$,

Then, which of the following is true?

I. $0 \le P(\omega_i) \le 1$ for each $\omega_i \in S$
II. $P(\omega_1) + P(\omega_2) + .... + P(\omega_n) = 1$
III. For any event A, $P(A) = \Sigma P(\omega_i), \omega_i \in A$

A. Only I  B. Only II
C. Only III  D. All of these

**3.** Three dice are thrown together. The probability of getting a total of at least 6 is:

A. $\frac{101}{108}$  B. $\frac{103}{108}$
C. $\frac{105}{108}$  D. $\frac{107}{108}$

**4.** If A, B and C are three mutually exclusive and exhaustive events of an experiment such that $4P(A) = 2P(B) = P(C)$, then P(A) is equal to .... K .... . Here, K refers to:

A. $\frac{1}{7}$  B. $\frac{2}{7}$
C. $\frac{5}{7}$  D. $\frac{6}{7}$

**5.** In an essay competition, the odds in favour of competitors P, Q, R and S are 1 : 2, 1 : 3, 1 : 4 and 1 : 5 respectively. Then, the probability that one of them wins the competition, is:

A. $\frac{112}{120}$  B. $\frac{113}{120}$
C. $\frac{114}{120}$  D. $\frac{115}{120}$

**6.** A card is drawn from a well-shuffled deek of cards. The probability of getting a queen of club or king of heart is:

A. $\frac{1}{52}$  B. $\frac{1}{26}$
C. $\frac{1}{13}$  D. $\frac{1}{56}$

**7.** If A and B are two events such that P(A) = 0.42, P(B) = 0.48 and $P(A \cap B) = 0.16$, then $P(A \cup B)$ is equal to:

A. 0.11  B. 0.54
C. 0.52  D. 0.74

**8.** If A and B are mutually exclusive events, then

A. $P(A) \le P(\bar{B})$  B. $P(A) \ge P(\bar{B})$
C. $P(A) < P(\bar{B})$  D. None of these

**9.** If $P(B) = \frac{3}{4}$, $P(A \cap B \cap \bar{C}) = \frac{1}{3}$ and $P(\bar{A} \cap B \cap \bar{C}) = \frac{1}{3}$, then $P(B \cap C)$ equals:

A. $\frac{1}{12}$  B. $\frac{1}{6}$
C. $\frac{1}{15}$  D. $\frac{1}{9}$

**10.** If $2P(A) = P(B) = \frac{5}{13}$ and $P(A/B) = \frac{2}{5}$, then $P(A \cup B)$ is equal to:

A. $\frac{11}{26}$  B. $\frac{13}{25}$
C. $\frac{11}{24}$  D. $\frac{11}{21}$

**11.** If $P(A) = \frac{1}{2}$, $P(B) = 0$, then $P\left(\frac{A}{B}\right)$ is:

A. zero  B. $\frac{1}{2}$
C. not defined  D. 1

**12.** If A and B are two events and $A \ne \phi$, $B \ne \phi$, then:

A. $P\left(\frac{A}{B}\right) = P(A) \cdot P(B)$  B. $P\left(\frac{A}{B}\right) = \frac{P(A \cap B)}{P(B)}$
C. $P\left(\frac{A}{B}\right) \cdot P\left(\frac{B}{A}\right) = 1$  D. $P\left(\frac{A}{B}\right) = \frac{P(A)}{P(B)}$

**13.** If card is drawn from an ordinary pack of 52 cards and a gambler bets that, it is a spade or an ace. The odds against his winning this bet is:

A. 4 : 9  B. 9 : 4
C. 3 : 8  D. 8 : 3

**14.** If $P(A) = \frac{3}{10}$, $P(B) = \frac{2}{5}$ and $P(A \cup B) = \frac{3}{5}$, then $P\left(\frac{B}{A}\right) + P\left(\frac{A}{B}\right)$ equals to:

A. $\frac{1}{4}$  B. $\frac{1}{3}$
C. $\frac{5}{12}$  D. $\frac{7}{12}$

**15.** Bag I contains 3 black and 2 white balls, bug II contains 2 black and 4 white balls. A bag and a ball is selected at random. The probability of selecting a black ball is:

A. $\frac{4}{15}$ B. $\frac{7}{15}$

C. $\frac{8}{15}$ D. None of these

**16.** Of cigarette smoking population 70% are men and 30% are women, 10% of these men and 20% of these women smoke Wills. The probability that a person seen smoking a Will to be men is:

A. $\frac{1}{5}$ B. $\frac{7}{13}$

C. $\frac{5}{13}$ D. $\frac{7}{10}$

**17.** An observed event B can occur after one of the three events $A_1$, $A_2$, $A_3$. If $P(A_1) = P(A_2) = 0.4$, $P(A_3) = 0.2$ and $P\left(\frac{B}{A_1}\right) = 0.25$, $P\left(\frac{B}{A_2}\right) = 0.4$, $P\left(\frac{B}{A_3}\right) = 0.125$, what is the probability of $A_1$ after observing B?

A. $\frac{1}{3}$ B. $\frac{6}{19}$

C. $\frac{20}{57}$ D. $\frac{2}{5}$

**18.** An insurance company insured 2000 scooter drivers, 4000 car drivers and 6000 truck drivers. The probabilities of an accident involving a scooter driver, car driver and a truck driver are 0.01, 0.03 and 0.15, respectively. One of the insured persons meets with an accident. The probability that the person is a scooter driver, is:

A. $\frac{1}{52}$ B. $\frac{3}{52}$

C. $\frac{15}{52}$ D. $\frac{19}{52}$

**19.** Suppose a girl throws a die. If she gets 1 or 2, she tosses a coin three times and notes the number of tails. If she gets 3, 4, 5 or 6, she tosses a coin once and notes whether a 'head' or 'tail' is obtained. If she obtained exactly one 'tail', what is the probability that she threw 3, 4, 5 or 6 with the die?

A. $\frac{5}{11}$ B. $\frac{6}{11}$

C. $\frac{7}{11}$ D. $\frac{8}{11}$

**20.** A drawer contains 50 bolts and 150 unts. Half of the bolts and half of the nuts are rusted. If one item is chosen at random, the probability that it is rusted or is a bolt, is:

A. $\frac{3}{8}$ B. $\frac{1}{2}$

C. $\frac{5}{8}$ D. None of these

**21.** A bag contains 3 red and 7 black balls. Two balls are selected at random without replacement. If the second selected ball is given to be red, the probability that the first selected ball is also red, is:

A. $\frac{4}{9}$ B. $\frac{2}{9}$

C. $\frac{9}{2}$ D. None of these

**22.** You are given a box with 20 cards in it. 10 of these cards have the letter I printed on them. The other ten have the letter T printed on them. If you pick up 3 cards at random and keep them in the same order, the probability of making the word IIT is:

A. $\frac{9}{80}$ B. $\frac{1}{8}$

C. $\frac{4}{27}$ D. $\frac{5}{38}$

**23.** A man is known to speak truth 3 out of 4 times. He throw a dics and reports that it is six. The probability that it is actually six is:

A. $\frac{3}{8}$ B. $\frac{1}{5}$

C. $\frac{3}{5}$ D. None of these

**24.** A bag contains 10 mangoes out of which 4 are rotten, two mangoes are taken out together. If one of them is found to be good, the probability that other is also good is:

A. $\frac{1}{3}$ B. $\frac{8}{15}$

C. $\frac{5}{18}$ D. $\frac{2}{3}$

**25.** In a certain town, 40% of the people have brown hair, 25 % have brown eyes and 15% have both brown hair and brown eyes. If a person selected at random from the town, has brown hair, the probability that he also has brown eyes is:

A. $\frac{1}{5}$ B. $\frac{3}{8}$

C. $\frac{1}{3}$ D. $\frac{2}{3}$

**26.** The probabilities that a student passes in Mathematics, Physics and Chemistry are *m*, *p* and *c*, respectively. Of these subjects, the student has a 75% chance of passing in at least one, a 50% chance of passing in at least two, and a 40% chance of passing in exactly two. Which of the following relations are true?

A. $p+m+c=\frac{19}{20}$ B. $p+m+c=\frac{27}{20}$

C. $pmc=\frac{1}{10}$ D. $pmc=\frac{1}{4}$

**27.** The number of dissimilar terms in the expansion of $(a+b)^n$ is $n+1$, therefore number of dissimilar terms in the expansion of $(a+b+c)^{12}$ is:

A. 13 B. 39

C. 78 D. 91

**28.** If '*n*' positive integer and three consecutive coefficient in the expansion of $(1+x)^n$ are in the ratio 6 : 33 : 110, then *n* is equal to:

A. 9 B. 6

C. 12 D. 16

**29.** The value of *x* in the expression $|x + x\log_{10x}|$ if the third term in the expansion is 1000000 is:

A. 10, $10^{-3/2}$ B. 100 or $10^{-3/2}$

C. 10 or $10^{-5/2}$ D. None of these

**30.** If *x* is so small that $x^3$ and higher powers of *x* may be neglected, then $\frac{(1+x)^{\frac{3}{2}}-\left[1+\frac{1}{2}x\right]}{(1+x)^{\frac{1}{2}}}$ may be approximated as:

A. $1-\frac{3}{8}x^2$ B. $3x+\frac{3}{8}x^2$

C. $-\frac{3}{8}x^2$ D. $\frac{x}{2}-\frac{3}{8}x^2$

**31.** The term independent of *x* in $(1+x)^m\left[1+\frac{1}{x}\right]^n$ is:

A. $m + n_{cm}$ B. $m + n_{cn}$

C. $m + n_{cm-n}$ D. None of these

**32.** The coefficient of $x^4$ in the expansion of $(1+x+x^2+x^3)^{11}$ is:

A. 990 B. 605

C. 810 D. None of these

**33.** If $(1+x-2x^2)^6 = 1 + a\,1^x + a_2x^2 + .... + a_{12}x^{12}$, then $a_2 + a_4 + a_6 .... + a_{12}$

A. 21 B. 11

C. 31 D. None of these

**34.** If $P(A\cap B)=\frac{1}{2}$, $P(A\cap B)=\frac{1}{2}$ and $2P(A) = P(B) = P$, then the value of P, is equal to:

A. $\frac{1}{2}$ B. $\frac{2}{3}$

C. $\frac{1}{4}$ D. $\frac{1}{3}$

**35.** A student is given a true false exam with 10 questions. If he gets 8 or more correct answers he passes the exam. Given that he guesses at the answer to each question, the probability that he passes the exam, is:

A. $\frac{6}{128}$ B. $\frac{9}{128}$

C. $\frac{7}{128}$ D. None of these

## ANSWERS

| 1 | 2 | 3 | 4 | 5 | 6 | 7 | 8 | 9 | 10 |
|---|---|---|---|---|---|---|---|---|---|
| D | D | B | A | C | B | D | A | A | A |
| 11 | 12 | 13 | 14 | 15 | 16 | 17 | 18 | 19 | 20 |
| C | B | B | D | B | B | C | A | D | C |
| 21 | 22 | 23 | 24 | 25 | 26 | 27 | 28 | 29 | 30 |
| B | D | A | C | B | B, C | D | C | C | D |
| 31 | 32 | 33 | 34 | 35 | | | | | |
| B | A | C | B | C | | | | | |

## EXPLANATORY ANSWERS

**1.** The sample space is S = {HH, HT, TH, TT}

Let E be the event of getting at least one tail

E = {HT, TH, TT}

∴ Required probability P

$$= \frac{\text{Number of favourable outcomes}}{\text{Total number of outcomes}}$$

$$= \frac{n(E)}{n(S)} = \frac{3}{4}$$

**2.** Let S be a sample space containing outcomes $\omega_1, \omega_2, \ldots \omega_n$, *i.e.*, $S = \{\omega_1, \omega_2, \ldots \omega_n\}$

If follows from the axiomatic definition of probability that

(*i*) $0 \le P(\omega_i) \le 1$ for each $\omega_i \in S$

(*ii*) $P(\omega_1) + P(\omega_2) + \ldots + P(\omega_n) = 1$

(*iii*) For any event A, $P(A) = \Sigma P(\omega_i)\ \omega_i \in A$.

**3.** The total number of elementary events

$$= 6 \times 6 \times 6 = 216$$

Let A be the event of getting a total of at least 6.

Then, $\bar{A}$ denotes the event of getting a total of less than 6 *i.e.* 3, 4, 5.

$\therefore$ $\bar{A} = \{(1, 1, 1), (1, 1, 2), (1, 2, 1), (2, 1, 1), (1, 1, 3), (1, 3, 1), (3, 1, 1), (1, 2, 2), (2, 1, 2), (2, 2, 1)\}$

So, $n(\bar{A}) = 10$

$\therefore$ $P(\bar{A}) = \dfrac{10}{216}$

$\therefore$ $P(A) = 1 - P(\bar{A}) = 1 - \dfrac{10}{216} = \dfrac{103}{108}$

**4.** Let $4P(A) = 2P(B) = P(C) = p$,

which gives $P(A) = \dfrac{p}{4}$, $P(B) = \dfrac{p}{2}$ and $P(C) = p$

Now, since A, B, C are mutually exclusive and exhaustive events, we have,

$$P(A) + P(B) + P(C) = 1 \Rightarrow p = \frac{4}{7}$$

Hence, $P(A) = \dfrac{p}{4} = \dfrac{1}{7}$

**5.** Let A, B, C and D be the events that the competitors P, Q, R and S respectively win the competition.

Then, $P(A) = \dfrac{1}{3}$, $P(B) = \dfrac{1}{4}$, $P(C) = \dfrac{1}{5}$ and $P(D) = \dfrac{1}{6}$

Since, only one competitors can win the competition.

Therefore, A, B, C, D are mutually exclusive events.

$\therefore$ Required probability $= P(A \cup B \cup C \cup D)$

$$= P(A) + P(B) + P(C) + P(D)$$

$$= \frac{1}{3} + \frac{1}{4} + \frac{1}{5} + \frac{1}{6} = \frac{114}{120}$$

**6.** Here, $n(S) = 52$, $n(E_1) = 1$, $n(E_2) = 1$, $n(E_1 \cap E_2) = \phi$

$\therefore$ $P(E_1 \cup E_2) = P(E_1) + P(E_2) - P(E_1 \cap E_2)$

$$= \frac{1}{52} + \frac{1}{52} - 0 = \frac{1}{26}$$

**7.** Given, $P(A) = 0.42$, $P(B) = 0.48$ and $P(A \cap B) = 0.16$

$\therefore$ $P(A \cup B) = P(A) + P(B) - P(A \cap B)$

$$= 0.42 + 0.48 - 0.16$$

$$= 0.90 - 0.16 = 0.74$$

**8.** Given that, A and B are two mutually exclusive events.

Then, $P(A \cup B) = P(A) + P(B)$ $[\because (A \cap B) = \phi]$

$$P(A) + P(B) \le 1$$

$$P(A) + 1 - P(\bar{B}) \le 1$$

$$P(A) \le P(\bar{B})$$

**9.** We have, $P(\bar{A} \cap B \cap \bar{C}) = \dfrac{1}{3}$

$\Rightarrow$ $P((B \cap \bar{C}) \cap \bar{A}) = \dfrac{1}{3}$

$\Rightarrow$ $P(B \cap \bar{C}) - P((B \cap \bar{C}) \cap A) = \dfrac{1}{3}$

$$[\because P(X \cap \bar{Y}) = P(X) - P(X \cap Y)]$$

$\Rightarrow$ $P(B \cap \bar{C}) - P(A \cap B \cap \bar{C}) = \dfrac{1}{3}$

$\Rightarrow$ $P(B \cap \bar{C}) - \dfrac{1}{3} = \dfrac{1}{3}$

$\Rightarrow$ $P(B \cap \bar{C}) = \dfrac{2}{3}$

$\Rightarrow$ $P(B) - P(B \cap C) = \dfrac{2}{3}$

Now, $P(B \cap C) = P(B) - \dfrac{2}{3} = \dfrac{3}{4} - \dfrac{2}{3} = \dfrac{1}{12}$

**10.** Given, $2P(A) = P(B) = \dfrac{5}{13}$

$\Rightarrow$ $P(A) = \dfrac{5}{26}$ and $P(B) = \dfrac{5}{13}$

Now, $P\left(\dfrac{A}{B}\right) = \dfrac{P(A \cap B)}{P(B)}$

$\Rightarrow$ $\dfrac{2}{5} = \dfrac{P(A \cap B)}{\frac{5}{13}}$

$\Rightarrow$ $P(A \cap B) = \dfrac{2}{5} \times \dfrac{5}{13} = \dfrac{2}{13}$

Again, $P(A \cup B) = P(A) + P(B) - P(A \cap B)$

$$= \frac{5}{26} + \frac{5}{13} - \frac{2}{13}$$

$$= \frac{5 + 10 - 4}{26} = \frac{11}{26}$$

**11.** It is given that $P(A) = \dfrac{1}{2}$ and $P(B) = 0$

$$P\left(\frac{A}{B}\right) = \frac{P(A \cap B)}{P(B)} = \frac{P(A \cap B)}{0} = \infty$$

Therefore, $P\left(\dfrac{A}{B}\right)$ is not defined.

**12.** If $A \neq \phi$ and $B \neq \phi$, then

$$P\left(\frac{A}{B}\right) = \frac{P(A \cap B)}{P(B)}$$

**13.** Let A be the event of getting a spade or an ace from a pack of 52 cards.

Then, total number of possible outcomes

$$= {}^{52}C_1 = 52$$

$\because$ There are 13 spade cards with 1 ace card of spade and three ace other than spade card.

$\therefore$ Number of favourable outcomes $= {}^{16}C_1 = 16$

$$\therefore \quad P(A) = \frac{16}{52} = \frac{4}{13}$$

Hence, odds against A are

$$P(\bar{A}) : P(A) = \frac{9}{13} : \frac{4}{13} = 9 : 4$$

**14.** Here, $P(A) = \frac{3}{10}$, $P(B)\frac{2}{5}$ and $P(A \cup B) = \frac{3}{5}$

$$P\left(\frac{B}{A}\right) + P\left(\frac{A}{B}\right) = \frac{P(B \cap A)}{P(A)} + \frac{P(A \cap B)}{P(B)}$$

$$= \frac{P(A) + P(B) - P(A \cup B)}{P(A)} + \frac{P(A) + P(B) - P(A \cup B)}{P(B)}$$

$$= \frac{\frac{3}{10} + \frac{2}{5} - \frac{3}{5}}{\frac{3}{10}} + \frac{\frac{3}{10} + \frac{2}{5} - \frac{3}{5}}{\frac{2}{5}} = \frac{\frac{1}{10}}{\frac{3}{10}} + \frac{\frac{1}{10}}{\frac{2}{5}} = \frac{1}{3} + \frac{1}{4} = \frac{7}{12}$$

**15.** Let $E_1$ = Bag I is selected

$E_2$ = Bag II is selected

and A = Black ball is drawn

Then, $P(E_1) = P(E_2) = \frac{1}{2}$, $P\left(\frac{A}{E_1}\right) = \frac{3}{5}$,

$$P\left(\frac{A}{E_2}\right) = \frac{2}{6},$$

$$\because \quad P(A) = P(E_1) \times P\left(\frac{A}{E_1}\right) + P(E_2) \times P\left(\frac{A}{E_2}\right)$$

$$= \frac{1}{2} \times \frac{3}{5} + \frac{1}{2} \times \frac{2}{6}$$

$$= \frac{3}{10} + \frac{1}{6} = \frac{9+5}{30} = \frac{14}{30} = \frac{7}{15}$$

**16.** Let $E_1$ and $E_2$ denote the cigarette smoking population of men and women, respectively.

Given, $P(E_1) = 0.7$, $P(E_2) = 0.3$

$$P\left(\frac{A}{E_1}\right) = 0.1, \quad P\left(\frac{A}{E_2}\right) = 0.2$$

Using Baye's theorem,

$$P\left(\frac{E_1}{A}\right) = \frac{P(E_1)\, P\left(\frac{A}{E_1}\right)}{P(E_1) \times P\left(\frac{A}{E_1}\right) + P(E_2) P\left(\frac{A}{E_2}\right)}$$

$$= \frac{0.7 \times 0.1}{0.7 \times 0.1 + 0.3 \times 0.2}$$

$$= \frac{0.07}{0.07 + 0.06} = \frac{0.07}{0.13} = \frac{7}{13}$$

**17.** Required probability $= P\left(\frac{A_1}{B}\right)$

$$= \frac{P(A_1)\, P\left(\frac{B}{A_1}\right)}{P(A_1)\, P\left(\frac{B}{A_1}\right) + P(A_2) P\left(\frac{B}{A_2}\right) + P(A_3) P\left(\frac{B}{A_3}\right)}$$

$$= \frac{0.4 \times 0.25}{0.4 \times 0.25 + 0.4 \times 0.4 + 0.2 \times 0.125}$$

$$= \frac{0.1}{0.1 + 0.16 + 0.025} = \frac{0.1}{0.285} = \frac{20}{57}$$

**18.** Let $\quad P(A) = P(\text{scooter}) = \frac{2000}{12000} = \frac{1}{6}$

$$P(B) = P(\text{car}) = \frac{4000}{12000} = \frac{1}{3}$$

and $\quad P(C) = P(\text{truck}) = \frac{6000}{12000} = \frac{1}{2}$

Let E = Event that person meets with accident.

Then, $P\left(\frac{E}{A}\right) = \frac{1}{100}$, $P\left(\frac{E}{B}\right) = \frac{3}{100}$, $P\left(\frac{E}{C}\right) = \frac{15}{100}$

$\therefore$ Required probability

$$P\left(\frac{A}{E}\right) = \frac{P(A) \cdot P\left(\frac{E}{A}\right)}{P(A) \cdot P\left(\frac{E}{A}\right) + P(B) \cdot P\left(\frac{E}{B}\right) + P(C) \cdot P\left(\frac{E}{C}\right)}$$

$$= \frac{\frac{1}{6} \times \frac{1}{100}}{\frac{1}{6} \times \frac{1}{100} + \frac{1}{3} \times \frac{3}{100} + \frac{1}{2} \times \frac{15}{100}} = \frac{\frac{1}{6}}{\frac{1}{6} + 1 + \frac{15}{2}}$$

$$= \frac{\frac{1}{6}}{\frac{1+6+45}{6}} = \frac{1}{52}$$

**19.** Let $E_1$ be the event that the girl gets 1 or 2. $E_2$ be the event that the girl gets 3, 4, 5 or 6, and A be the event that the girl gets exactly a 'tail'.

Then, $P(E_1) = \frac{2}{6} = \frac{1}{3}$

and $P(E_2) = \frac{4}{6} = \frac{2}{3}$

$P\left(\frac{A}{E_1}\right) = P$ (getting exactly one tail when a coin is tossed three times) $= \frac{3}{8}$

$P\left(\frac{A}{E_2}\right) = P$ (getting exactly a tail when a coin is tossed once) $= \frac{1}{2}$

Now, required probability

$$P\left(\frac{E_2}{A}\right) = \frac{P(E_2)\cdot P\left(\frac{A}{E_2}\right)}{P(E_1)\cdot P\left(\frac{A}{E_1}\right) + P(E_2)\cdot P\left(\frac{A}{E_2}\right)}$$

$$= \frac{\frac{2}{3}\cdot\frac{1}{2}}{\frac{1}{3}\cdot\frac{3}{8}+\frac{2}{3}\cdot\frac{1}{2}} = \frac{\frac{1}{3}}{\frac{1}{8}+\frac{1}{3}} = \frac{8}{11}$$

**20.** Let A : Item chosen a rusted.
B : Item chosen is bolt.
Here A and B are non – mutually exclusive events.
$A \cap B$ : Item is a rusted bolt.

Total number of bolts = 50

∴ Number of rusted bolts = 25

Total number of nuts = 150

∴ Number of rusted nuts = 75

Total number of rusted items = 25 + 75 = 100

$$P(A \cup B) = P(A) + P(B) - P(A \cap B)$$

$$\frac{100}{200}+\frac{50}{200}-\frac{25}{200} = \frac{100+50-25}{200} = \frac{125}{200} = \frac{5}{8}.$$

**21.** Let 'A' = {a red ball is selected at first draw}
'B' = {a red ball is selected at second draw}

Then $P(A \cap B) = P$ (Red ball and Red ball)

$$= \frac{3}{10}\times\frac{2}{9} = \frac{1}{5}$$

$P(B) = P$ (Red ball and Red ball or Black ball and Red ball)

$= P$ (Red ball and Red ball) + P (Black ball and Red ball)

$$= \frac{3}{10}\times\frac{2}{9}+\frac{7}{10}\times\frac{3}{9} = \frac{3}{10}$$

$$\therefore P\left(\frac{A}{B}\right) = \frac{P(A\cap B)}{P(B)} = \frac{\frac{1}{5}}{\frac{3}{10}} = \frac{10}{3\times 15} = \frac{2}{9}.$$

**22.** Required probability
= P(I in Ist draw) × P(I in 2nd draw) × P(T in 3rd draw)

$$= \frac{^{10}c_1}{^{20}c_1}\times\frac{^{9}c_1}{^{19}c_1}\times\frac{^{10}c_1}{^{18}c_1}\times = \frac{10}{20}\times\frac{9}{19}\times\frac{10}{18} = \frac{5}{38}$$

**23.** Let A denotes the event that a six occurs and B the event that the man reports that it is a six.

Then the probability that it is actually a six is given by

$$P\left(\frac{A}{B}\right) = \frac{P(A\cap B)}{P(B)}$$

Now $P(A \cap B) = \frac{1}{6}\times\frac{3}{4} = \frac{3}{24}$

$P(B) = P(A \cap B) + P(A \cap B)$

$$= \frac{1}{6}\times\frac{3}{4}+\frac{5}{6}\times\frac{1}{4} = \frac{8}{24}$$

Hence $P\left(\frac{A}{B}\right) = \frac{\frac{3}{24}}{\frac{8}{24}} = \frac{3}{8}.$

**24.** Number of ways of selecting 2 good mangoes

$= {}^6c_2 = 15$

The number of ways that at least one of the two selected mangoes is to be good

$= {}^6c_1 \times {}^9c_1 = 6 \times 9 = 54$

Required probability $= \frac{15}{54} = \frac{5}{18}.$

**25.** $P(A) = \frac{40}{100} \cdot P(B) = \frac{25}{100}$

$P(A \cap B) = \frac{15}{100}$

$$P\left(\frac{B}{A}\right) = \frac{P(A\cap B)}{P(A)} = \frac{\frac{15}{100}}{\frac{40}{100}} = \frac{15}{40} = \frac{3}{8}.$$

**26.** According to the problem,

$$m + p + c - mp - mc - pc + mpc = \frac{3}{4} \quad ...(1)$$

$$mp\ (1 - c) + mc\ (1 - p) + pc\ (1 - m) = \frac{2}{5}$$

$$\text{or } mp + mc + pc - 3\ mpc = \frac{2}{5} \quad ...(2)$$

$$\text{Also, } pm + pc + mc - 2mpc = \frac{1}{2} \quad ...(3)$$

$$(2) \text{ and } (3) \Rightarrow mpc = \frac{1}{2} - \frac{2}{5} = \frac{1}{10}$$

$\therefore \quad mp + mc + pc = \frac{2}{5}+\frac{3}{10}=\frac{7}{10}$

$\therefore \quad m + p + c = \frac{3}{4}+\frac{7}{10}-\frac{1}{10}$

$= \frac{15+14-2}{20}=\frac{27}{20}$

**27.** $(a + b + c)^{12} = [(a + b) + c]^{12}$

$= {}^{12}c_o (a + b)^{12} + {}^{12}c_1 (a + b)^{11}c + ... + {}^{12}c_{12}c^{12}$

The R.H.S. contains, 13 + 12 + 11 + .... + 1 terms

$= \frac{13(13+1)}{2}$ = terms

Also no. of term in the expansion of $(a + b + c)^n$ is given by $n + {}^2c_2$.

Thus for $n = 12$; $n + {}^2c_2 = n + {}^{14}c_2 = \frac{14\times13}{2}=91.$

**28.** Let $(r + 1)$th, $(r + 2)$th and $(r + 3)$th be three consecutive terms.

Then, ${}^nC_r : {}^nC_{r+1} : {}^nC_{r+2} = 6 : 33 : 110$

Now, $\frac{{}^nC_r}{{}^nC_{r+1}} = \frac{6}{33}=\frac{2}{11}$

$\Rightarrow \quad \frac{r+1}{n-r} = \frac{2}{11}$

$\Rightarrow \quad 2n - 2r = 11r + 11$

$\Rightarrow \quad 2n - 13r = 11 \quad ....(i)$

and, $\frac{{}^nC_{r+1}}{{}^nC_{r+2}} = \frac{33}{110}=\frac{3}{10}$

$\Rightarrow \quad \frac{r+2}{n-r-1} = \frac{3}{10}$

$\Rightarrow \quad 3n - 3r - 3 = 10r + 20$

$\Rightarrow \quad 3n - 13r = 23 \quad ...(ii)$

Solving (*i*) and (*ii*), we get $n = 12$.

**30.** (D)

**31.** We have,

$$(1+x)^m\left[1+\frac{1}{x}\right]^n = (1+x)^m\left[\frac{x+1}{x}\right]^n$$

$$= \frac{(1+x)^{m+n}}{x^n} = x^{-n} (1 + x)^{m+n}$$

$\therefore$ Required term independent of $x$ = coefficient of $x^0$ in

$x^{-n} (1 + x)^{m+n}$ = coefficient of $x^n$ in $(1 + x)^{m+n}$ $= m + n_{cn}$.

**32.** We have,

$(1 + x + x^2 + x^3)^{11} = (1 + x)^{11} (1 + x^2)^{11}$

$= (1 + 11c_1x + 11c_2x^2 + 11c_3x^3 + 11c_4x^4 + ...)$
$\times (1 + 11c_1x^2 + 11c_2x^4 + ....)$

The terms, which give $x^4$ are:

1. $11c_2x^4 + 11c_2x^2.11c_1x^2 + 11c_4.x^4.1$

Hence the coefficient of $x^4$ is

$11c_2 + 11c_2 \times 11c_1 + 11c_4$

$= \frac{11\times10}{1.2}+\frac{11\times10}{1.2}\times\frac{11}{1}+\frac{11\times10\times9\times8}{4.3.2.1}$

$= 55 + 605 + 330 = 990.$

**33.** Given

$(1 + x - 2x^2)^6 = 1 + a\,1^x + a_2x^2 + .... + a_{12}x^{12}$

Putting $x = 1$, we get

$0 = 1 + a_1 + a_2 + ... + a_{12} \quad ...(1)$

Putting $x = -1$, we get

$64 = 1 - a_1 + a_2 - ... + a_{12} \quad ....(2)$

Adding (1) and (2), we get

$64 = 2(1 + a_2 + a_4 + ....)$

$\therefore a_2 + a_4 + a_6 + a_{12} ... = 31$

**34.** $P(A \cap B) \Rightarrow P(A \cup B) = 1 - P(A \cup B)$

$\Rightarrow \quad \frac{1}{2} = 1 - P(A \cup B)$

$\Rightarrow \quad P(A \cup B) = \frac{1}{2}$

Also $\quad P(A \cup B) = \frac{1}{2}$

Now $\quad P(A \cup B) = P(A) + P(B) - P(A \cap B)$

$\therefore \quad \frac{1}{2} = \frac{p}{2}+p-\frac{1}{2}$

$\therefore \quad \frac{3p}{2} = 1, \therefore P = \frac{2}{3}.$

**35.** $n$ = total no. of ways = $2^{10}$ = 1024.

Since each answer can be true or false.

And $m$ = favourable number of ways.

$= 10c_8 + 10c_9 + 10c_{10}$
$= 45 + 10 + 1 = 56.$

Since to pass the exam, he must give 8 or 9 or 10 true answers.

Hence, $\quad p = \frac{m}{n}=\frac{56}{1024}=\frac{7}{128}.$

CHAPTER

# 3

# TRIGONOMETRY

## TRIGONOMETRIC IDENTITY

An equation involving trigonometric functions which is true for all those angles for which the functions are defined is called a trigonometric identity.

### Conditional Trigonometric Identities

If A + B + C = 180° (or $\pi$), or A, B, C are angles of a triangle.

Then,

(a) $\sin (A + B) = \sin (\pi - C) = \sin C$, etc.

(b) $\sin\left(\frac{A}{2}+\frac{B}{2}\right) = \sin\left(\frac{\pi}{2}-\frac{C}{2}\right) = \cos\frac{C}{2}$, etc

(c) $\sin A + \sin B + \sin C = 4\cos\frac{A}{2}\cos\frac{B}{2}\sin\frac{C}{2}$

(d) $\cos A + \cos B + \cos C = 1 + 4\sin\frac{A}{2}\sin\frac{B}{2}\sin\frac{C}{2}$

(e) $\tan A + \tan B + \tan C = \tan A \tan B \tan C$

(f) $\cot A \cot B + \cot B \cot C + \cot C \cot A = 1$

(g) $\tan\frac{A}{2}\tan\frac{B}{2} + \tan\frac{B}{2}\tan\frac{C}{2} + \tan\frac{C}{2}\tan\frac{A}{2} = 1$

### Periodic Properties of Trigonometric Functions

(a) $\sin x$, $\cos x$, $\sec x$ and $\text{cosec}x$ are periodic functions with fundamental period $2\pi$.

(b) $\tan x$ and $\cot x$ are periodic functions with fundamental period $\pi$.

(c) $|\sin x|$, $|\cos x|$, $|\tan x|$, $|\cot x|$, $|\text{sex}\, x|$, $|\text{cosec}\, x|$ are periodic functions with fundamental period $\pi$.

(d) $\sin^n x$, $\cos^n x$, $\sec^n x$, $\text{cosec}^n x$ are periodic functions with fundamental period $2\pi$ or $\pi$ according as $n$ is odd or even.

(e) $\tan^n x$ and $\cot^n x$ are periodic function with fundamental period $\pi$ whether $n$ is odd or even.

### Properties of Triangle

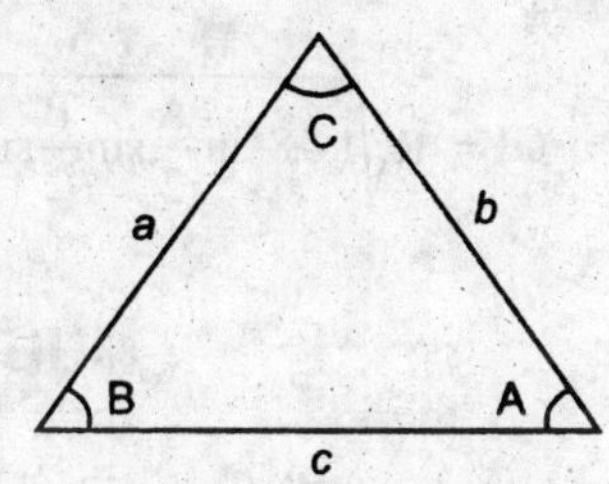


(a) Sine Rule : $\frac{a}{\sin A} = \frac{b}{\sin B} = \frac{c}{\sin C}$

(b) Consine Rule : $\cos A = \frac{b^2 + c^2 - a^2}{2bc}$

(c) Projection formula

(i) $a = b \cos C + c \cos B$

(ii) $b = c \cos A + a \cos C$

(iii) $c = a \cos B + b \cos A$

(d) Tangent Rule:

$$\tan\left(\frac{B-C}{2}\right) = \frac{b-c}{b+c}\tan\left(\frac{B+C}{2}\right) = \frac{b-c}{b+c}\cot\frac{A}{2}$$

(e) Half angle formula:

(i) $\sin\frac{A}{2} = \sqrt{\frac{(s-b)(s-c)}{bc}}$

(ii) $\cos\frac{A}{2} = \sqrt{\frac{s(s-a)}{bc}}$

(*iii*) $\tan\frac{A}{2} = \sqrt{\frac{(s-b)(s-c)}{s(s-a)}}$

(*f*) Area of a triangle:

$$\Delta = \frac{1}{2}bc\sin A = \frac{1}{2}ca\sin B = \frac{1}{2}ab\sin C$$

## Orthocentre of the Triangle and Pedal Triangle

(*a*) The distances of the orthocentre of the triangle from the vertices are 2R cos A, 2R cos B, 2R cos C and its distances from the sides are 2R cos B cos C, 2R cos C cos A, 2R cos A cos B.

(*b*) Circumradius of the pedal triangle = $\frac{R}{2}$

(*c*) Area of the pedal triangle = 2Δ cos A cos B cos C.

(*d*) Circumcentre O, centroid G and orthocentre O′ are collinear and G divides OO′ in the ratio 1 : 2.

(*e*) Distance between the circumcentre O and the incentre I is

$$OI = R\sqrt{1 - 8\sin\frac{A}{2}\sin\frac{B}{2}\sin\frac{C}{2}}$$

## Heights and Distances

(*a*) The angle of elevation or depression is the angle between the line of observation and the horizontal line according as the object is at a higher or lower level than the observer.

(*b*) The angle of elevation or depression is always measured from horizontal line through the point of observation.

## Trigonometric Equations

The general solution of some trigonometrical equations

| | Trigonometric equation | General solution |
|---|---|---|
| (*i*) | $\sin\theta = \sin\alpha$ | $\theta = n\pi + (-1)^n\alpha,\ n \in Z$ |
| (*ii*) | $\cos\theta = \cos\alpha$ | $\theta = 2n\pi \pm \alpha\quad n \in Z$ |
| (*iii*) | $\tan\theta = \tan\alpha$ | $\theta = n\pi + \alpha\quad n \in Z$ |
| (*iv*) | $\sin^2\theta = \sin^2\alpha$ | $\theta = n\pi \pm \alpha\quad n \in Z$ |
| (*v*) | $\cos^2\theta = \cos^2\alpha$ | $\theta = n\pi \pm \alpha\quad n \in Z$ |
| (*vi*) | $\tan^2\theta = \tan^2\alpha$ | $\theta = n\pi \pm \alpha\quad n \in Z$ |

Since all the trigonometrical ratios are periodic, the equations of the form sin θ = *k*, cos θ = *k*, or tan θ = *k* etc., can have infinite number of angles satisfying it.

## MULTIPLE CHOICE QUESTIONS

**1.** If (1 + sin A) (1 + sin B) (1 + sin C) = (1 − sin A) (1 − sin B) (1 − sin C), then each side is equal to:

A. ± sin A sin B sin C  B. tan A tan B tan C
C. ± cot A cot B cot C  D. ± cos A cos B cos C

**2.** If $T_n = \sin^2 5n° - \cos^2 5n°$, the value of $T_1 + T_2 + ... + T_{18}$ is:

A. 18  B. 1
C. 0  D. None

**3.** If $m\tan(\theta - 30°) = n\tan(\theta + 120°)$, then $\frac{m+n}{m-n}$ equals:

A. 2 cos2θ  B. $\frac{1}{2}\cos 2\theta$
C. sin2θ  D. $\frac{1}{2}\sin 2\theta$

**4.** If S = tan 9° − tan 27° − tan 63° + tan 81°, T = tan 9° + cot 9° − tan 27° − cot 27°, R = cosec 18° − cosec 54°, then

A. S = R = T  B. S = R = 2T
C. 2S = R = T  D. S = 2R = T

**5.** If $H = \frac{\cot 3x}{\cot x}$, then

A. $H \in \left[1, \frac{1}{2}\right]$  B. $H \notin \left[\frac{1}{3}, 3\right]$
C. $H \in \left[\frac{1}{3}, \frac{1}{2}\right]$  D. None

**6.** The greatest value of cos2*x* + 3sin *x* is:

A. $\sqrt{10}$  B. 9
C. $\frac{17}{8}$  D. $\frac{15}{4}$

**7.** The period of which of the functions is not $\frac{\pi}{2}$:

A. |cos2*x*|  B. $\sin^6 x + \cos^6 x$
C. sin4*x*  D. None

**8.** $\tan\theta + \tan 2\theta + \sqrt{3}\tan\theta\tan 2\theta = \sqrt{3}$ has how many solutions in the interval (0, 2π):

A. 2  B. 4
C. 6  D. 8

**9.** The general solution of $\sqrt{2}\sec\theta + \tan\theta = 1$ is:

A. $\theta = n\pi + \frac{\pi}{4}$  B. $\theta = 2n\pi - \frac{\pi}{4}$
C. $\theta = n\pi \pm \frac{\pi}{4}$  D. $\theta = n\pi + (-1)^n\frac{\pi}{4}$

**10.** If $e^{\cos x} - e^{-\cos x} - 4 = 0$, then which of the following is true?

A. has two real solutions in $(0, \pi)$
B. has two real solutions in $\{0, 2\pi)$
C. has no real solution
D. has exactly one real solution

**11.** The solution of the equation $\cos^{58}x + \sin^{40}x = 1$

A. $x = n\pi$ B. $n = \frac{n\pi}{2}$

C. $x = \frac{n\pi}{2} \pm \frac{\pi}{4}$ D. None

**12.** If $32\tan^8\theta = 2\cos^2\alpha - 3\cos\alpha$, and $3\cos 2\theta = 1$ the general value of $\theta$ is:

A. $\alpha = n\pi \pm \frac{\pi}{3}$ B. $\alpha = 2n\pi \pm \frac{2\pi}{3}$

C. $\alpha = \frac{n\pi}{2} \pm \pi$ D. None

**13.** $\cot^{-1}7 + \cot^{-1}8 + \cot^{-1}18 =$

A. $\tan^{-1}3$ B. $\cot^{-1}\frac{1}{3}$

C. $\sin^{-1}\left(\frac{1}{\sqrt{10}}\right)$ D. None

**14.** $\tan^{-1}\left(\frac{a-b}{1+ab}\right) + \tan^{-1}\left(\frac{b-c}{1+bc}\right) + \tan^{-1}\left(\frac{c-a}{1+ca}\right) =$

A. 0 B. $\tan^{-1}\left(\frac{a+b+c}{1-ab-bc-ca}\right)$

C. $\tan^{-1}(a+b+c)$ D. None

**15.** $\tan^{-1}\left(\frac{c_1x - y}{c_1y + x}\right) + \tan^{-1}\left(\frac{c_2 - c_1}{1 + c_2c_1}\right) + \tan^{-1}\left(\frac{c_3 - c_2}{1 + c_3c_2}\right) + \ldots$ $n$ terms $= \tan^{-1}\frac{Y}{x} - \tan^{-1}(k)$ then $k$ is equal to:

A. $\frac{1}{c_n}$ B. $c_n$

C. $c_{n-1}$ D. $\frac{1}{c_{n-1}}$

**16.** The number of real solutions of the equation $\tan^{-1}(x-1) + \tan^{-1}x = \tan^{-1}(x+1) = \tan^{-1}(3x)$ is:

A. 0 B. 1
C. 2 D. 3

**17.** $\lim\limits_{n\to\infty} \sum_{1}^{\infty} \tan^{-1}\left(\frac{1}{n^2+n+1}\right) =$

A. 0 B. 1

C. $\frac{\pi}{4}$ D. $\frac{\pi}{2}$

**18.** If $\cos^{-1}\left(\frac{x}{2}\right) + \cos^{-1}\left(\frac{y}{3}\right) = \theta$, the value of $9x^2 - 12xy \cos\theta + 4y^2$ is:

A. $9\sin^2\theta$ B. $36\sin^2\theta$
C. $18\cos^2\theta$ D. $\cos^2\theta$

**19.** If the angles of a triangle are in the ratio 3 : 4 : 5, the least and the greatest sides are in the ratio:

A. $\sqrt{3}-1:1$ B. $\sqrt{3}:2+\sqrt{3}$

C. $\sqrt{2}:1+\sqrt{3}$ D. $1:\sqrt{3}+1$

**20.** The angle of elevation of a ladder leaning against a wall is 60° and the foot of the ladder is 4.6 m away from the wall. The length of the ladder is:

A. 2.3 m B. 4.6 m
C. 7.8 m D. 9.2 m

## ANSWERS

| 1 | 2 | 3 | 4 | 5 | 6 | 7 | 8 | 9 | 10 |
|---|---|---|---|---|---|---|---|---|---|
| D | B | A | D | B | C | D | C | B | C |
| **11** | **12** | **13** | **14** | **15** | **16** | **17** | **18** | **19** | **20** |
| B | B | C | A | A | D | C | B | A | D |

## EXPLANATORY ANSWERS

**1.** Multiplying both sides by $(1 - \sin A)(1 - \sin B)(1 - \sin C)$, we have $(1 - \sin^2 A)(1 - \sin^2 B)(1 - \sin^2 C) = (1 - \sin A)^2 (1 - \sin B)^2 (1 - \sin C)^2$:

*i.e.*, $\cos^2 A \cos^2 B \cos^2 C$

$= (1 - \sin A)^2 (1 - \sin B)^2 (1 - \sin C)^2$

$\Rightarrow (1 - \sin A)(1 - \sin B)(1 - \sin C)$

$= \pm \cos A \cos B \cos C$

$\therefore$ each side is equal to $\pm \cos A \cos B \cos C$

**2.** Here $T_n = -(\cos^2 5n° - \sin^2 5n°) = -\cos 10n°$

$T_1 + T_2 + \ldots + T_{18}$

$= -[\cos 10° + \cos 20° + \ldots + \cos 180°]$

$= -[\cos 10° + \cos 20° + \ldots + \cos 160° + \cos 170° + \cos 180°]$

$= [\cos 180°]$ $(\because \cos\theta + \cos(180 - \theta) = 0)$

$= -(-1) = 1.$

**3.** $$\frac{m}{n} = \frac{\tan(\theta+120°)}{\tan(\theta-30°)} = \frac{-\cot(\theta+30°)}{\tan(\theta-30°)}$$

$$\Rightarrow \frac{m}{n} = \frac{\cos(\theta+30°)\cos(\theta-30°)}{-\sin(\theta+30°)\sin(\theta-30°)}$$

$$\Rightarrow \frac{m}{n} = \frac{\cos^2\theta-\sin^2 30°}{\sin^2 30°-\sin^2\theta}$$

Applying componendo and dividendo, we have

$$\frac{m+n}{m-n} = \frac{\cos^2\theta-\sin^2\theta}{\cos^2\theta+\sin^2\theta-2\sin^2 30°} = 2\cos 2\theta.$$

**4.** S = $\tan 9° - \tan 27° - \tan 63° + \tan 81°$

$= \tan 9° - \tan 27° - \tan(90° - 27°) + \tan(90° - 9°)$

$= \tan 9° - \tan 27° - \cot 27° + \cot 9°$

$= (\tan 9° + \cot 9°) - (\tan 27° + \cot 27°)$ (= T)

$$= \left(\frac{\sin 9°}{\cos 9°}+\frac{\cos 9°}{\sin 9°}\right)-\left(\frac{\sin 27°}{\cos 27°}+\frac{\cos 27°}{\sin 27°}\right)$$

$$= \frac{\sin^2 9°+\cos^2 9°}{\sin 9°\cos 9°}-\left(\frac{\sin^2 27°+\cos^2 27°}{\sin 27°\cos 27°}\right)$$

$$= \frac{2}{\sin 18°}-\frac{2}{\sin 54°} \ (= 2R) = \frac{2(\sin 54°-\sin 18°)}{\sin 18°\sin 54°}$$

$$= \frac{2.2\cos 36°\cdot\sin 18°}{\sin 18°\sin(90°-36°)} = \frac{4\cos 36°}{\cos 36°} = 4$$

**5.** Let $$y = \frac{\cot 3x}{\cot x} = \frac{\tan x}{\tan 3x} = \frac{\tan x(1-3\tan^2 x)}{3\tan x-\tan^3 x}$$

$\Rightarrow (3 - \tan^2 x)y = 1 - 3\tan^2 x$

$$\Rightarrow \tan^2 x = \frac{1-3y}{3-y}$$

but $\tan^2 x > 0 \therefore \frac{1-3y}{3-y} > 0$

$\Rightarrow (3 - y), (1 - 3y) > 0$

(multiplying by $(3 - y)^2$ on both sides)

$(y - 3)(3y - 1) > 0$

$$\Rightarrow y < \frac{1}{3} \text{ or } y > 3 \Rightarrow y \notin \left[\frac{1}{3}, 3\right]$$

**6.** Let $\cos 2x + 3\sin x = y$, then

$$y = 1 - 2\sin^2 x + 3\sin x$$

$$= 1-2\left\{\left(\sin x-\frac{3}{4}\right)^2-\frac{9}{16}\right\}$$

$$= \frac{17}{8}-2\left(\sin x-\frac{3}{4}\right)^2$$

$y$ is greatest, when $\left(\sin x-\frac{3}{4}\right)^2$ is least.

$\therefore$ for $\sin x = \frac{3}{4}$, we get the maximum value of $y$.

**7. Note:** (*i*) The period of $\cos ax$ or $\sin ax$ is $\frac{2\pi}{a}$

(*ii*) The period of $|\cos ax|$ or $|\sin ax|$ is $\frac{\pi}{a}$

Here the period of $|\cos 2x|$ is $\frac{\pi}{2}$ and period of $\sin 4x$ is $\frac{\pi}{2}$.

Also $\sin^6 x + \cos^6 x = (\sin^2 x + \cos^2 x)^3 - 3\sin^2 x\cos^2 x (\sin^2 x + \cos^2 x)$

$$= 1-\frac{3}{4}(2\sin x\cos x)^2 = 1-\frac{3}{4}\sin^2 2x$$

$$= 1-\frac{3}{4}(1-\cos 4x) = \frac{1}{4}+\frac{3}{4}\cos 4x,$$

which is a periodic function of period $\frac{\pi}{2}$.

**8.** $\tan\theta + \tan 2\theta = \sqrt{3}(1 - \tan\theta\tan 2\theta)$

$$\Rightarrow \frac{\tan\theta+\tan 2\theta}{1-\tan\theta\tan 2\theta} = \sqrt{3}$$

$$\Rightarrow \tan 3\theta = \tan\frac{\pi}{3}.$$

$$\Rightarrow 3\theta = n\pi+\frac{\pi}{3}$$

$$\Rightarrow \theta = \frac{(3n+1)\pi}{9} \text{ for all } n \in Z$$

for $n = 0, 1, 2, 3, 4, 5, \theta \in (0, 2\pi)$

**9.** We have $\frac{\sqrt{2}}{\cos\theta}+\frac{\sin\theta}{\cos\theta} = 1$

$$\Rightarrow \cos\theta - \sin\theta = \sqrt{2}$$

$$\Rightarrow \frac{1}{\sqrt{2}}\cos\theta-\frac{1}{\sqrt{2}}\sin\theta = 1$$

$$\Rightarrow \cos\left(\theta+\frac{\pi}{4}\right) = 1 = \cos\theta$$

$$\Rightarrow \theta+\frac{\pi}{4} = 2n\pi$$

$$\Rightarrow \theta = 2n\pi-\frac{\pi}{4} \text{ for all } n \in Z.$$

**10.** We have $(e^{\cos x})^2 - 4e^{\cos x} - 1 = 0$

$$\Rightarrow e^{\cos x} = \frac{4\pm\sqrt{20}}{2} = 2\pm\sqrt{5}$$

Since $e^{\cos x} > 0$, we have $e^{\cos x} = 2 + \sqrt{5}$

$\therefore \cos x = \log_e\left(2+\sqrt{5}\right) > 1$ and $2+\sqrt{5} > e$

Hence the given equation has no real solution.

**11.** **Case I:** If $\cos^2 x < 1$, $\sin^2 x < 1$,
We have $(\cos^2 x)^{29} + (\sin^2 x)^{20} < \cos^2 x + \sin^2 x = 1$
not possible.
**Case II:** If $\cos^2 x = 1$, $\sin^2 x = 0$, then $x = n\pi$.
**Case III:** If $\sin^2 x = 1$, $\cos^2 x = 0$, then $x = n\pi \pm \frac{\pi}{2}$.
Thus combining Case (II) and Case (III),
We get the solution $x = \frac{n\pi}{2}, n \in Z$.

**12.** $\cos 2\theta = \frac{1}{3} \Rightarrow \frac{1-\tan^2\theta}{1+\tan^2\theta} = \frac{1}{3}$

$\tan^2\theta = \frac{1}{2} \Rightarrow \tan^8\theta = \frac{1}{16}$

$\therefore \quad 2\cos^2\alpha - 3\cos\alpha = 32\tan^8\theta = 2$

$\Rightarrow \quad 2\cos^2\alpha - 3\cos\alpha - 2 = 0$

$\Rightarrow (2\cos\alpha + 1)(\cos\alpha - 2) = 0$

$\Rightarrow \quad \cos\alpha = -\frac{1}{2} \quad (\because \cos\alpha \neq 2)$

$\Rightarrow \quad \alpha = 2n\pi \pm \frac{2\pi}{3}, n \in Z$

**14.** $\tan^{-1}a - \tan^{-1}b + \tan^{-1}(b) - \tan^{-1}c + \tan^{-1}c - \tan^{-1}a = 0$

**15.** $\tan^{-1}\left(\frac{c_1 x - y}{c_1 y - x}\right) + \tan^{-1}\left(\frac{c_2 - c_1}{1 + c_2 c_1}\right) + \ldots + \tan^{-1}\left(\frac{c_n - c_{n-1}}{1 + c_n c_{n-1}}\right)$

$= \tan^{-1}\left(\frac{\frac{x}{y} - \frac{1}{c_1}}{1 + \frac{x}{y}\cdot\frac{1}{c_1}}\right) + \tan^{-1}\left(\frac{\frac{1}{c_1} - \frac{1}{c_2}}{1 + \frac{1}{c_1}\cdot\frac{1}{c_2}}\right) + \ldots + \tan^{-1}\left(\frac{\frac{1}{c_{n-1}} - \frac{1}{c_n}}{1 + \frac{1}{c_{n-1}}\cdot\frac{1}{c_n}}\right)$

$= \tan^{-1}\frac{x}{y} - \tan^{-1}\frac{1}{c_1} + \tan^{-1}\frac{1}{c_1} - \tan^{-1}\frac{1}{c_2} +$

$\ldots + \tan^{-1}\frac{1}{c_{n-1}} - \tan^{-1}\left(\frac{1}{c_n}\right)$

$= \tan^{-1}\frac{x}{y} - \tan^{-1}\left(\frac{1}{c_n}\right)$.

**16.** $\tan^{-1}(x-1) + \tan^{-1}(x+1) = \tan^{-1}3x - \tan^{-1}x$

$\Rightarrow \tan^{-1}\left(\frac{(x-1)+(x+1)}{1-(x-1)(x+1)}\right) = \tan^{-1}\left(\frac{3x - x}{1 + 3x\cdot x}\right)$

$\Rightarrow \quad x(1 + 3x^2) = (2 - x^2)x$

$\Rightarrow \quad x(4x^2 - 1) = 0$

$\Rightarrow \quad x = 0, x = \pm\frac{1}{2}$

**17.** $S_n = \sum_1^\infty \tan^{-1}\left(\frac{1}{n^2+n+1}\right)$

$= \sum_1^\infty \tan^{-1}\left(\frac{(n+1)-n}{1+(n+1)n}\right)$

$= \sum_1^\infty \left[\tan^{-1}(n+1) - \tan^{-1}n\right]$

$= [\tan^{-1}2 - \tan^{-1}1] + [\tan^{-1}3 - \tan^{-1}2] + \ldots$

$+ [\tan^{-1}(n+1) - \tan^{-1}n]$

$= \tan^{-1}(n+1) - \tan^{-1}(1)$

$= \tan^{-1}(n+1) - \frac{\pi}{4}$

$\therefore \lim_{n\to\infty} S_n = \lim_{n\to\infty}\left\{\tan^{-1}(n+1) - \frac{\pi}{4}\right\} = \frac{\pi}{2} - \frac{\pi}{4} = \frac{\pi}{4}$

**18.** Let $\cos^{-1}\left(\frac{x}{2}\right) = A$, $\cos^{-1}\left(\frac{y}{3}\right) = B$,

Thus $A + B = \theta$.

$\Rightarrow \quad \cos(A + B) = \cos\theta$

$\Rightarrow \cos A \cos B - \sin A \sin B = \cos\theta$

$\Rightarrow \quad \frac{x}{2}\times\frac{y}{3} - \cos\theta = \sqrt{1-\cos^2 A}\sqrt{1-\cos^2 B}$

$\Rightarrow \quad xy - 6\cos\theta = \sqrt{4-x^2}\sqrt{9-y^2}$

squaring both sides, we have

$x^2y^2 - 12xy\cos\theta + 36\cos^2\theta = (4-x^2)(9-y^2)$

$\Rightarrow \quad 9x^2 - 12xy\cos\theta + 4y^2 = 36(1 - \cos^2\theta)$

$\Rightarrow \quad 9x^2 - 12xy\cos\theta + 4y^2 = 36\sin^2\theta$

**19.** Let $A = 3\theta$, $B = 4\theta$, $c = 5\theta$

$A + B + C = \pi \Rightarrow 12\theta = 180° \Rightarrow \theta = 15°$

thus the angles are $A = 45°$, $B = 60°$, $C = 75°$

$\therefore$ $a$ and $c$ are the least and greatest sides opposite to the smallest and greatest angle A and C, respectively.

By sine rule,

$\frac{a}{c} = \frac{\sin A}{\sin C} = \frac{\sin 45°}{\sin 75°} = \frac{\sin 45°}{\sin(30°+45°)}$

$= \frac{2}{\sqrt{3}+1} = \frac{2(\sqrt{3}-1)}{(\sqrt{3}+1)(\sqrt{3}-1)} = \frac{\sqrt{3}-1}{1}$

**20.** Let AB be the wall and BC be the ladder.

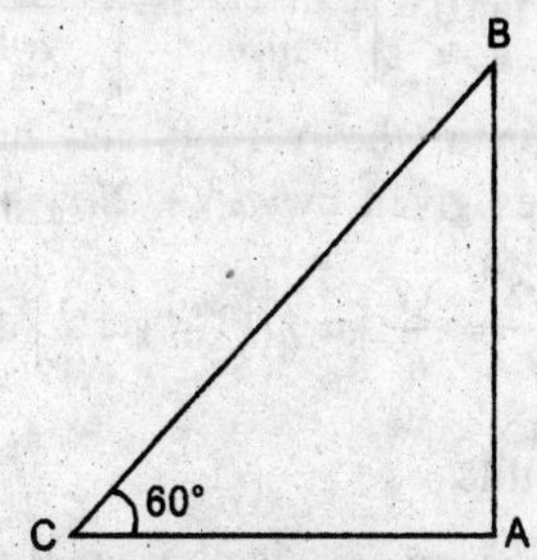


Then, $\angle ACB = 60°$ and $AC = 4.6$ m.

$\frac{AC}{BC} = \cos 60° = \frac{1}{2}$

$\Rightarrow \quad BC = 2 \times AC = (2 \times 4.6)\text{ m} = 9.2\text{ m}$

CHAPTER

4

# CO-ORDINATE GEOMETRY

## PAIR OF STRAIGHT LINES

An equation of the type

$$ax^2 + 2hxy' + by^2 = 0 \quad ...(1)$$

is a homogeneous equation of second degree.

[Note that the sum of the powers of $x$ and $y$ in every term is the same and equal to 2]

The homogeneous equation of the second degree always represents a pair of straight lines passing through the origin.

If $ax^2 + 2hxy + by^2 = 0$ represents the pair of lines $y = m_1x$ and $y = m_2x$. Then

$$ax^2 + 2hxy + by^2 = b(y - m_1x)(y - m_2x) \quad ...(2)$$

Comparing the coefficients we get

$$m_1 + m_2 = -\frac{2h}{b} \text{ and } m_1m_2 = \frac{a}{b} \quad ...(3)$$

If the equation $ax^2 + 2hxy + by^2 = 0$ represents the straight lines $y = m_1x$ and $y = m_2x$, then the acute angle $\theta$, between the lines is given by

$$\tan\theta = \left|\frac{m_1 - m_2}{1 + m_1m_2}\right| = \left|\frac{2\sqrt{h^2 - ab}}{a+b}\right|$$

The equation of the pair of lines bisecting the angle between the lines given by $ax^2 + 2hxy + by^2 = 0$ is

$$\frac{x^2 - y^2}{a-b} = \frac{xy}{h} \text{ or } h(x^2 - y^2) - (a - b)xy = 0.$$

### Important Results

(*a*) Two lines are coincident if $\tan\theta = 0$
*i.e.*, if $h^2 - ab = 0$

(*b*) Two lines are perpendicular of $\tan\theta = \infty$
*i.e.*, if $a + b = 0$

$\therefore$ The equation of a pair of perpendicular straight lines can be given by $ax^2 + 2hxy - ay^2 = 0$

[Substituting $b = -a$]

or $x^2 + 2pxy - y^2 = 0$, where $2p = \frac{2h}{a}$.

(*c*) If the lines given by the equation $ax^2 + 2hxy + by^2 = 0$ are equally inclined to axes, then the coordinate axes are the bisectors, *i.e.*, the equation of pair of bisector must be $xy = 0$. Therefore $h = 0$.

(*d*) If two pairs of straight lines are equally inclined to one another, then both must have the same pair of bisectors.

(*e*) Since coeff. of $x^2$ + coeff. of $y^2 = 0$. Therefore two bisectors are always perpendicular. (The original lines may or may not be perpendicular)

## CIRCLE

If centre of the circle is $(h, k)$ and radius is $a$ then equation of circle will be $(x - h)^2 + (y - k)^2 = a^2$.

The general equation of circle is $x^2 + y^2 + 2gx + 2fy + c = 0$ whose centre is $(-g, -f)$ and radius is $\sqrt{g^2 + f^2 - c}$.

If the ends of diameter of circle and $(x_1, y_1)$ and $(x_2, y_2)$ then equation of circle will be $(x - x_1)(x - x_2) + (y - y_1)(y - y_2) = 0$.

The equation of tangent to the circle $x^2 + y^2 = a^2$ at the point $(x_1, y_1)$ is $xx_1 + yy_1 = a^2$.

The equation of tangent to the circle $x^2 + y^2 + 2gx + 2fy + c = 0$ at the point $(x_1, y_1)$ is $xx_1 + yy_1 + g(x + x_1) + f(y + y_1) + c = 0$.

Line $y = mx + c$, will touch the circle $x^2 + y^2 = a^2$, if $c^2 = a^2(1 + m^2)$.

# CONIC SECTION (Parabola, Ellipse and Hyperbola)

## PARABOLA

The equation of Parabola is $y^2 = 4ax$, whose vertex is (0, 0) and focus is $(a, 0)$.

Equation of directrix is $x = -a$ and axis is $y = 0$

Length of latus rectum for all forms of parabola is $= 4a$.

Equation of tangent of parabola $y^2 = 4ax$ at the point $(x_1, y_1)$ is:

$$yy_1 = 2a\,(x + x_1)$$

Line $y = mx + c$, will touch the parabola $y^2 = 4ax$ if $c = \frac{a}{m}$.

The equation of any tangent of parabola $y^2 = 4ax$ is $y = mx + \frac{a}{m}$ which touches the parabola at the point $\left(\frac{a}{m^2}, \frac{2a}{m}\right)$.

Equation of normal of parabola at the point $(x_1, y_1)$ is $(y - y_1) = -\left(\frac{y_1}{2a}\right)(x - x_1)$.

Equation of normal to parabola at the point $(am^2, -2am)$ is

$$y = mx - 2am - am^3.$$

## ELLIPSE

The equation of ellipse is $\frac{x^2}{a^2}+\frac{y^2}{b^2}=1$, where $b^2 = a^2(1 - e^2)$, eccentricity $(e)$, centre (0, 0), vertex $(\pm a, 0)$, foci $(\pm ae, 0)$ and equations of directrix are $x = \pm\left(\frac{a}{e}\right)$.

Latus rectum of ellipse $= \frac{2b^2}{a}$.

Equation of tangent of ellipse $\frac{x^2}{a^2}+\frac{y^2}{b^2}=1$, at the point $(x_1, y_1)$ is $\frac{xx_1}{a^2}+\frac{yy_1}{b^2}=1$

Line $y = mx + c$, will touch an ellipse $\frac{x^2}{a^2}+\frac{y^2}{b^2}=1$, if

$$c^2 = a^2m^2 + b^2$$

Equation of any tangent of ellipse is:

$$y = mx + \sqrt{(a^2m^2 + b^2)}.$$

Equation of normal of ellipse $\frac{x^2}{a^2}+\frac{y^2}{b^2}=1$, at the point $(x_1, y_1)$ is $\frac{x - x_1}{\frac{x_1}{a^2}} = \frac{y - y_1}{\frac{y_1}{b^2}}$.

Equation of auxillary circle of ellipse

$$\frac{x^2}{a^2}+\frac{y^2}{b^2}=1 \text{ is } x^2 + y^2 = a^2.$$

Equation of chord of contact of tangents drawn on ellipse $\frac{x^2}{a^2}+\frac{y^2}{b^2}=1$ at the point $(x_1, y_1)$ is

$$\frac{xx_1}{a^2}+\frac{yy_1}{b^2}=1.$$

Equation of diameter of ellipse $\frac{x^2}{a^2}+\frac{y^2}{b^2}=1$ is

$$y = -\left(\frac{b^2}{a^2m}\right)x$$

Conjugate diameter : $y = m_1x$ and $y = m_2x$ are conjugate diameters of ellipse $\frac{x^2}{a^2}+\frac{y^2}{b^2}=1$ if

$$m_1m_2 = -\left(\frac{b^2}{a^2}\right)$$

Equation of that chord of ellipse $\frac{x^2}{a^2}+\frac{y^2}{b^2}=1$ whose mid-point is $(x_1, y_1)$ is:

$$\frac{xx_1}{a^2}+\frac{yy_1}{b^2}=\frac{x_1^2}{a^2}+\frac{y_1^2}{b^2}$$

## HYPERBOLA

Let $\qquad \frac{x^2}{a^2} - \frac{y^2}{b^2} = 1 \qquad$ ...(1)

be the equation of a hyperbola,

where $\qquad b^2 = a^2(e^2 - 1) \qquad$ ...(2)

(*a*) **Transverse Axis:** Intercept of the hyperbola on the axis (AA′) is called its transverse axis, the transverse axis, AA′ = 2*a*.

(*b*) **Conjugate Axis:** Length BB′ = 2*b*, on *y*-axis is called conjugate axis of the hyperbola.

[Note that the hyperbola does not intersect the *y*-axis].

(*c*) **Eccentricity:** $e = \sqrt{1+\frac{b^2}{a^2}} = \sqrt{1+\left(\frac{\text{conjugate axis}}{\text{transverse axis}}\right)^2}$

(*d*) **Focal Difference:** Let $P(x_1, y_1)$ be any point on the hyperbola, then

$$SP = ePM = e\left(x_1 - \frac{a}{e}\right) = ex_1 - a$$

and
$$S'P = ePM' = e\left(x_1 + \frac{a}{e}\right) = ex_1 + a$$

The difference of the focal distances

$$|S'P - SP| = 2a = \text{transverse axis}$$

∴ The difference of the focal distances of any point on the hyperbola is a constant, equal to transverse axis.

## MULTIPLE CHOICE QUESTIONS

**1.** The straight line $(2x + 3y + 4) + \lambda(6x - y + 12) = 0$ will be parallel to $y$-axis, if the value of $\lambda$ is:
A. 1 B. 2
C. 3 D. 4

**2.** If the portion of a straight line intercepted between the co-ordinate axes is bisected at (2, 2), then the equation of the line is:
A. $x + y = 4$ B. $x + 2y = 6$
C. $2x + y = 6$ D. $3x - y = 4$

**3.** The locus of a point, whose abscissae and ordinates are always equal, is:
A. $x - y = 0$ B. $x - y = 1$
C. $x + y = 0$ D. $x + y = 1$

**4.** If there is a triangle whose vertices are A(3, –5), B(7, 3) and C(–5, 5), then the equation $6x - y = 23$ represents
A. the line AB
B. The line joining the mid-points of BC and AC
C. the median through A
D. altitudes from A to BC

**5.** Area of the parallelogram formed by the lines $y = mx$, $y = mx + 1$, $y = nx$ and $y = nx + 1$ equals
A. $\frac{|m+n|}{(m-n)^2}$ B. $\frac{2}{|m+n|}$
C. $\frac{1}{|m+n|}$ D. $\frac{1}{|m-n|}$

**6.** The value of $k$ so that the equation
$3y^2 - 8xy - 3x^2 - 29x + ky - 18 = 0$
represents a pair of straight lines is:
A. 3 B. –1
C. 1 D. 8

**7.** The lines given by the equation
$x^2 + 6xy + 9y^2 + 4x + 12y - 5 = 0$ are
A. perpendicular B. parallel
C. coincident D. None of these

**8.** The angle between the two straight lines represented by the equation
$6x^2 + 5xy - 4y^2 + 7x + 13y - 3 = 0$ is
A. $\tan^{-1}\frac{3}{5}$ B. $\tan^{-1}\frac{11}{2}$
C. $\tan^{-1}\frac{2}{11}$ D. $\tan^{-1}\frac{5}{3}$

**9.** The point of intersection of the straight lines given by the equation
$3y^2 - 8xy - 3x^2 - 29x + 3y - 18 = 0$ is
A. $\left(-\frac{3}{2}, -\frac{5}{2}\right)$ B. (1, –1)
C. (2, 1) D. (–1, 1)

**10.** The pair of straight lines joining the origin to the intersection of the straight line $y = mx + c$ and the curve $x^2 + y^2 = a^2$ are at right angles if:
A. $a^2(1 - m^2) = c^2$
B. $a^2(1 + m^2) = 2c^2$
C. $a^2(1 - m^2) = 2c^2$
D. $a^2(1 + m^2) = c^2$

**11.** If the pair of straight lines
$x^2 - 2pxy - y^2 = 0$ and $x^2 - 2qxy - y^2 = 0$
be such that each pair bisects the angle between the other pair, then:
A. $pq = 1$ B. $p = q$
C. $p + q = 0$ D. $pq = -1$

**12.** If a straight line touches both the circle $x^2 + y^2 = 2$ and the parabola $y^2 = 8x$, then its equation is:
A. $y = \pm(x + 1)$ B. $y = \pm(2x + 1)$
C. $y = \pm(x + 2)$ D. $y = \pm x$

**13.** The normal to the circle $(x - 2)^2 + y^2 = 4$ at the point (4, 0) meets the circle again at:
A. (0, 4) B. (0, 2)
C. (0, 0) D. (2, 0)

**14.** The possible value of $p$ for which the line $x \cos \alpha + y \sin \alpha = p$ is a tangent to the circle $x^2 + y^2 - 2qx \cos \alpha - 2qy \sin \alpha = 0$, is/are:

A. 0 and $q$ B. $q$ and $2q$
C. 0 and $2q$ D. $q$

**15.** The equation $x^2 + y^2 + 2gx + 2fy + c = 0$ represents a circle of non-zero radius if

A. $g^2 + f^2 > c$ B. $g^2 + f^2 < c$
C. $g^2 + f^2 = c$ D. None of these

**16.** The length of the intercept made by the circle $x^2 + y^2 - 7x + 6 = 0$ on the $x$-axis is:

A. 5 B. 7
C. 6 D. $-6$

**17.** Consider the line $2x - y - 2 = 0$ and the circles $x^2 + y^2 - 6x + 2y + 5 = 0$ and $5x^2 + 5y^2 = 4$. The line is a tangent to:

A. the first circle but not to the second
B. the second circle but not to the first
C. Both the circles
D. Neither of the circles

**18.** If the two circles $(x - 1)^2 + (y - 3)^2 = r^2$ and $x^2 + y^2 - 8x + 2y + 8 = 0$ intersect in two distinct points, then

A. $r > 2$ B. $r < 2$
C. $r = 2$ D. None of these

**19.** If the circles $x^2 + y^2 + 2x + 2ky + 6 = 0$ and $x^2 + y^2 + 2ky + k = 0$ intersect orthogonally, then $k$ is:

A. 2 or $-\frac{3}{2}$ B. $-2$ or $-\frac{3}{2}$
C. 2 or $\frac{3}{2}$ D. $-2$ or $\frac{3}{2}$

**20.** The equations of the tangents drawn from the origin to the circles $x^2 + y^2 - 2rx - 2hy + h^2 = 0$, are

A. $x = 1$
B. $y = 0$
C. $(h^2 - r^2) x - 2rhx = 0$
D. $(h^2 - r^2) x + 2rhy = 0$

**21.** The tangent to the circle $x^2 + y^2 = 5$ at $(1, -2)$ touches the circle $x^2 + y^2 - 8x + 6y + 20 = 0$ at the point:

A. $(2, -1)$ B. $(3, -1)$
C. $(4, -1)$ D. $(5, -1)$

**22.** The length of the intercept made by the circle $3x^2 + 3y^2 + 4x + 2y + 1 = 0$ on the $x$-axis is:

A. $\frac{2}{3}$ B. $-\frac{2}{3}$
C. less than 1 D. more than $-1$

**23.** The focus of the parabola $x^2 + 8y = 0$ at:

A. $(0, -2)$ B. $(0, 2)$
C. $(2, 0)$ D. $(-2, 0)$

**24.** The eccentricity of the ellipse $\frac{x^2}{25} + \frac{y^2}{9} = 1$ is:

A. $\frac{9}{25}$ B. $\frac{5}{4}$
C. $\frac{25}{9}$ D. $\frac{4}{5}$

**25.** Consider the equation

$y^2 - 8x - 2y - 7 = 0$

and the following statements:

I. It represents a parabola.
II. Its vertex is $(-1, 1)$.
III. Its focus is $(0, 0)$.
IV. It has $x = -3$ as the directrix.

Of these statements:

A. I, III and IV are correct
B. I, II and III are correct
C. I, II and IV are correct
D. I, II, III and IV are correct

**26.** The locus of a variable point whose distance from $(-2, 0)$ is $\frac{2}{3}$ times its distance from the line $x = -\frac{9}{2}$ is:

A. ellipse B. parabola
C. hyperbola D. None of these

**27.** Let E be the ellipse of $\frac{x^2}{9} + \frac{y^2}{4} = 1$ and C be the circle $x^2 + y^2 = 9$. Let P and Q be the points (1, 2) and (2, 1) respectively, then

A. Q lies inside C bus outside E.
B. Q lies outside both C and E.
C. P lies inside both C and E.
D. P lies inside C but outside E.

**28.** The equation $2x^2 + 3y^2 - 8x - 18y + 35 = k$ represents:

A. no locus if $k > 0$
B. an ellipse if $k < 0$
C. a point if $k = 0$
D. a hyperbola if $k > 0$

**29.** Diameter of a circle which passes through the focus of an ellipse $\frac{x^2}{16} + \frac{y^2}{9} = 1$, whose centre is at (0, 3) is:

A. 3 B. 12
C. 8 D. 2

**30.** The equation $y^2 - 2x - 2y + 5 = 0$ represents:

A. a circle with centre (1, 1).
B. a parabola with focus (1, 2).
C. a parabola with directrix $x = \frac{3}{2}$.
D. a parabola with directrix $x = -\frac{1}{2}$.

## ANSWERS

| 1 | 2 | 3 | 4 | 5 | 6 | 7 | 8 | 9 | 10 |
|---|---|---|---|---|---|---|---|---|---|
| C | A | D | * | D | A | B | B | A | B |
| **11** | **12** | **13** | **14** | **15** | **16** | **17** | **18** | **19** | **20** |
| D | C | C | C | A | A | C | D | A | C |
| **21** | **22** | **23** | **24** | **25** | **26** | **27** | **28** | **29** | **30** |
| B | A | A | D | C | A | A | C | C | C |

## EXPLANATORY ANSWERS

**2.** Suppose the equation of the line is $\frac{x}{a}+\frac{y}{b}=1$

Since AB is bisected at (2, 2).

$$\therefore \quad 2 = \frac{a+0}{2},\ 2 = \frac{0+b}{2}$$

or $\quad a = 4,\ b = 4$

Hence, the equation of the line is

$$\frac{x}{4}+\frac{y}{4} = 1 \text{ or } x + y = 4$$

**4.** Equation of the line AB is

$$y - 3 = \frac{3+5}{7-3}(x-7)$$

or $\quad 2x - y = 11 \qquad (\neq 6x - y = 23)$

Equation of the line joining the mid-points of BC (1, 4) and AC (–1, 0) is

$$y - 0 = \frac{0-4}{-1-1}(x+1)$$

or $\quad 2x - y = -2 \qquad (\neq 6x - y = 23)$

Equation of the median through A is:

$$\frac{y+5}{x-3} = -\frac{1}{\frac{5-3}{-5-7}} = 6 \text{ or } 6x - y = 23 \text{ (same)}$$

**5.** Here $\quad y = \frac{m}{m-n}$ or $\frac{n}{n-m}$

Depending on which one of $n$ or $m$ is greater.

$$\text{Area of parallelogram} = 2\times\left[\frac{1}{2}\times 1\times\frac{1}{|m-n|}\right] = \frac{1}{|m-n|}.$$

**17.** The line $2x - y - 2 = 0$ will touch the circle

$$x^2 + y^2 - 6x + 2y + 5 = 0$$

If perpendicular distance from its centre (3, –1) on the line is equal to its radius $= \sqrt{9+1-5} = \sqrt{5}$

*i.e.*, if $\quad \frac{|2\times 3-(-1)-2|}{\sqrt{4+1}} = \sqrt{5}$

*i.e.*, if $\quad \frac{5}{\sqrt{5}} = \sqrt{5}$ which is true.

Similarly, for the second circle

$$\frac{|-2|}{\sqrt{4+1}} = \frac{2}{\sqrt{5}} \text{ which is true.}$$

**18.** Here, $c_1 = (1, 3),\ r_1 = r;\ c_2 = (4, -1),\ r_2 = 3$

In case they intersect in two distinct points, then

$$c_1c_2 < r_1 + r_2 \text{ and } c_1c_2 > r_1 - r_2$$

or $\quad 5 < r + 3$ and $5 > r - 3$

or $\quad r > 2$ and $r < 8$

*i.e.*, $\quad 2 < r < 8$

**19.** Since the units intersect orthogonally,

$\therefore\ 2 \times 1 \times 0 + 2 \times k \times k = 6 + k$

or $\quad 2k^2 = k + 6$ or $2k^2 - k - 6 = 0$

or $\quad (k - 2)(2k + 3) = 0$ or $k = 2,\ k = -\frac{3}{2}$

**20.** The joint equation of the pair of tangents OA and OB can be obtained by making the equation (*i*) of the circle homogeneous with the help of the equation (*ii*). Thus, we get it as:

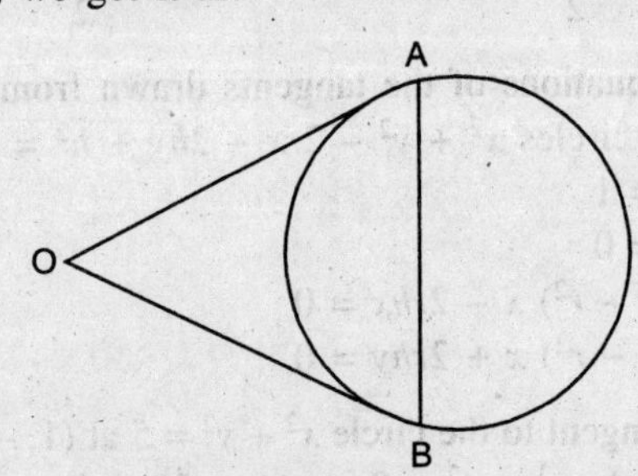


$$x^2 + y^2 - 2(rx+hy)\cdot\frac{(rx+hy)}{h^2} + h^2\cdot\left(\frac{rx+hy}{h^2}\right)^2 = 0$$

or $\quad h^2(x^2 + y^2) = (rx + hy)^2$

or $\quad h^2x^2 + h^2y^2 = r^2x^2 + h^2y^2 + 2rhxy$

or $\quad x^2(h^2 - r^2) - 2rhx = 0 \Rightarrow x = 0$

or $\quad x(h^2 - r^2) - 2rhy = 0$

**21.** The tangent to the circle,

$$x^2 + y^2 = 5 \text{ at } (1, -2) \text{ is } x(1) + y(-2) - 5 = 0$$

or $\quad x - 2y - 5 = 0 \qquad$ ...(1)

Suppose it touches the circle

$x^2 + y^2 - 8x + 6y + 20 = 0$ at $(x_1, y_1)$ ...(*i*)

Also, the equation of tangent at

$(x_1, y_1)$ is $x(x_1 - 4) + y(y_1 + 3) - 4x_1 + 3y_1 + 20 = 0$ ...(*ii*)

Since (*i*) and (*ii*) represent the same lines

$$\frac{x_1 - 4}{1} = \frac{y_1 + 3}{-2} = \frac{-4x_1 + 3y_1 + 20}{-5}$$

Solving these, $x_1 = 3$, $y_1 = -1$.

**22.** Intersection of the circle $3x^2 + 3y^2 + 4x + 2y + 1 = 0$ with the $x$-axis ($y = 0$) is given by $3x^2 + 4x + 1 = 0$ or $(3x + 1)(x + 1) = 0$

$$\therefore \quad x_1 = -\frac{1}{3}, \; x_2 = -1$$

Hence, length of intercept on $x$-axis

$$= |x_1 - x_2| = \left|-\frac{1}{3} + 1\right| = \left|\frac{2}{3}\right| = \frac{2}{3}$$

**23.** The focus of the parabola $x^2 + 8y = 0$

or $\quad x^2 = -8y = -(4 \times 2)y$

is at $\quad (0, -a) = (0, -2)$.

**24.** Eccentricity, $e$ of the given ellipse with $a = 5$, $b = 3$ is given by,

$$b^2 = a^2(1 - e^2)$$

or $\quad 9 = 25(1 - e^2)$ or $1 - e^2 = \frac{9}{25}$

or $\quad e^2 = 1 - \frac{9}{25} = \frac{16}{25}$ or $e = \frac{4}{5}$.

**25.** $\quad y^2 - 8x - 2y - 7 = 0$

or $y^2 - 2y + 1 = 8x + 7 + 1 = 8x + 8$

or $\quad (y - 1)^2 = 8(x + 1)$

which can be put as $Y^2 = 8X = 4 \times 2X$

where $\quad Y = y - 1$, $X = x + 1$

This clearly represents a parabola, whose

(*a*) Vertex is at $X = 0$, $Y = 0$ or $x + 1 = 0$, $y - 1 = 0$
or $\quad x = -1$, $y = 1$

(*b*) Focus is at $X = 2$, $Y = 0$ or $x + 1 = 2$, $y - 1 = 0$
or $\quad x = 1$, $y = 1$

(*c*) Directrix is $X = -2$ or $x + 1 = -2$
or $\quad x = -3$

**27.** Since distance between P(1, 2) and centre of circle

$$C(0, 0) = \sqrt{(1-0)^2 + (2-0)^2} = \sqrt{5} < 9.$$

Therefore P lies inside the circle C.

Similarly, as $\sqrt{(2-0)^2 + (1-0)^2} = \sqrt{5} < 9$, therefore Q also lies inside the circle C.

Next, side for the ellipse $4x^2 + 9y^2 - 36 = 0$, at P(1, 2), $4(1)^2 + 9(2)^2 - 36 = 4 > 0$ at Q(2, 1), $4(2)^2 + 9(1)^2 - 36 = -11 < 0$, Q lies inside the ellipse and P lies outside E.

Hence, Q lies inside C but outside E.

**28.** When $\quad k = 0$, the equation becomes

$$2x^2 + 3y^2 - 8x - 18y + 35 = 0$$

or $\quad 2(x - 2)^2 + 3(y - 3)^2 = 0$

Since the sum of two positive numbers is zero, $\therefore$ each must be zero.

or $\sqrt{2}(x-2) = 0$ and $\sqrt{3}(y-3) = 0$

$\Rightarrow \quad x = 2$, $y = 3$

Hence, when $k = 0$, given equation represents a point, *viz*, (2, 3).

**30.** Given equation is $y^2 - 2x - 2y + 5 = 0$

or $y^2 - 2y + 1 = 2x - 4$ or $(y - 1)^2 = 2(x - 2)$

Shifting the origin to (2, 1), the equation becomes

$$Y^2 = 4 \cdot \frac{1}{2} X$$

which represents a parabola whose directrix is

$$X = -\frac{1}{2} \text{ or } x - 2 = -\frac{1}{2} \text{ or } x = \frac{3}{2}$$

CHAPTER

# 5

# CALCULUS

Calculus is the branch of mathematics that deals with continuous change. It helps us to understand the changes between the values which are related by a function. Calculus Math mainly focused on some important topics such as differentiation, integration, limits, functions, and so on.

## LIMIT

If $f(x)$ approaches to a real number $l$, when $x$ approaches to $a$ *i.e.*, if $f(x) \to l$ when $x \to a$, then $l$ is called the limit of the function $f(x)$. In symbolic form, it can be written as:

$$\lim_{x\to a} f(x) = l$$

### LEFT HAND AND RIGHT HAND LIMIT

$$\text{LHL} = \lim_{x\to a^-} f(x) = l_1$$

$$\text{RHL} = \lim_{x\to a^+} f(x) = l_2$$

### Formulae for Limits

(*a*) $\lim_{x\to 0} \frac{\sin x}{x} = 1 = \lim_{x\to 0} \frac{x}{\sin x}$

(*b*) $\lim_{x\to 0} \frac{\tan x}{x} = 1 = \lim_{x\to 0} \frac{x}{\tan x}$

(*c*) $\lim_{x\to 0} \frac{\sin^{-1} x}{x} = 1 = \lim_{x\to 0} \frac{x}{\sin^{-1} x}$

(*d*) $\lim_{x\to 0} \frac{\tan^{-1} x}{x} = 1 = \lim_{x\to 0} \frac{x}{\tan^{-1} x}$

(*e*) $\lim_{x\to 0} \frac{a^x - 1}{x} = \log_e a, a > 0$

(*f*) $\lim_{x\to 0} \frac{e^x - 1}{x} = 1$

(*g*) $\lim_{x\to 0} \frac{\log_e(1+x)}{x} = 1$

(*h*) $\lim_{x\to a} \frac{x^n - a^n}{x - a} = na^{n-1}$

(*i*) $\lim_{x\to 0} (1+kx)^{1/x} = e^k$, where $k$ is any constant

(*j*) $\lim_{x\to \infty} \frac{\log_a(1+x)}{x} = \log_a e, a > 0 \neq 1$

(*k*) $\lim_{x\to \infty} \frac{\sin x}{x} = \lim_{x\to \infty} \frac{\cos x}{x} = 0$

(*l*) $\lim_{x\to \infty} \cos x = 1$

## CONTINUITY AT A POINT

A function $f(x)$ is continuous at a point $x = a$, were $a \in$ domain of $f(x)$, if

$$\lim_{x\to a^-} f(x) = f(a) = \lim_{x\to a^+} f(x)$$

where, $\lim_{x\to a^-} f(x)$ is Left Hand Limit (LHL) of $f(x)$ at $x = a$

$\lim_{x\to a^+} f(x)$ is Right Hand Limit (RHL) of $f(x)$ at $x = a$

and $f(a)$ is the value of $f(x)$ at $x = a$.

## DIFFERENTIABILITY

Let $f(x)$ be defined at any point $c$ in the interval $(a, b)$. Then $f(x)$ is said to be differentiable at $x = c$ if the function has a derivative at this point, *i.e.*, if $f'(c)$ exists. Hence, if

$\lim_{h\to 0} \frac{f(c+h)-f(c)}{h}$ exists, then the function $f(x)$ is called differentiable at point $x = c$.

For the existence of this limit it is necessary that when $h \to 0$, the *left-hand* and *right-hand* limits both must exist and they must be equal.

The Right Hand Derivative (RHD) of $f(x)$ at the point $x = c$ is defined as

$$Rf'(c) = \lim_{h\to 0^+} \frac{f(c+h)-f(c)}{h}, h > 0$$

Similarly, the Left Hand Derivative (LHD) of $f(x)$ at $x = c$ is defined as

$$Lf'(c) = \lim_{h\to 0^-} \frac{f(c+h)-f(c)}{h}, h > 0$$

or $$Lf'(c) = \lim_{h\to 0} \frac{f(c-h)-f(c)}{-h}, h > 0$$

Hence, function $f(x)$ is differentiable at $x = c$ iff

$$Rf'(c) = Lf'(c).$$

## TANGENT AND NORMAL LINES

In calculus, the tangent line touches the curve at exactly one point and this line has the same slope as the curve at that point. The line which is perpendicular to the tangent line is called the normal line. These two lines can be shown as given in the below figure:

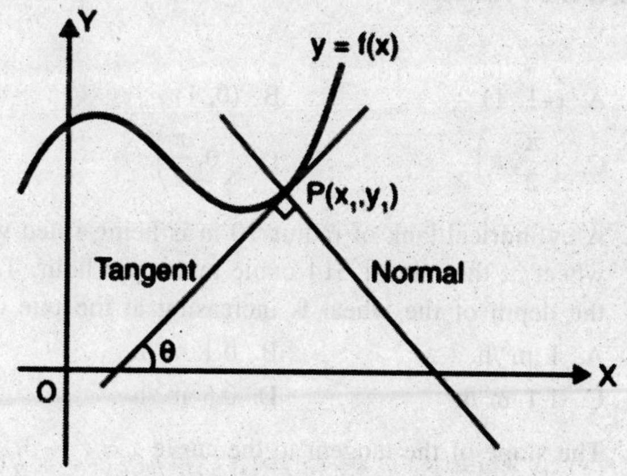


For a function $y = f(x)$, the slope of the tangent line is given by $dy/dx$.

## MAXIMA AND MINIMA

Maxima and minima are known as the extrema of a function. Maxima and minima are the maximum or the minimum value of a function within the given set of ranges.

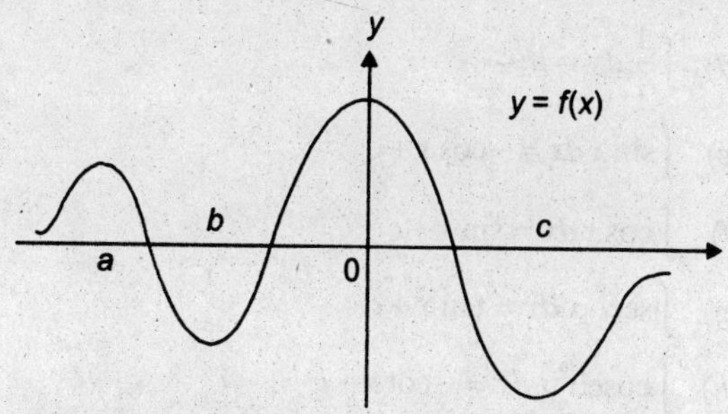


There are two types of maxima and minima that exist in a function, which are:

- Local Maxima and Minima
- Absolute or Global Maxima and Minima

A second-order derivative test for maxima and minima tests whether the slope is equal to 0 at the critical point $x = c(f'(c) = 0)$, at which point we find the second derivative of the function. Within the given range, if the second derivative of the function is present:

- **Local maxima :** If $f''(c) < 0$
- **Local Minima :** If $f''(c) > 0$
- **Test fails :** If $f''(c) = 0$

## INTEGRATION

### INTEGRATION BY SUBSTITUTION

Let $f$ be a continuous function of $u$ and $u$ be a continuously differentiable function of $x$ on $[a, b]$. Then

$$\int f(u)du = \int f(u(x))u'(x)\,dx$$

Integration by parts is the inverse of the product rule.

### INTEGRATION BY PARTS

Let $f$ and $g$ be continuously differentiable functions on $[a, b]$. Then

$$\int_a^b f(x)g'(x)dx = f(x)g(x)\Big|_a^b - \int_a^b g(x)f'(x)dx$$

This rule is often written with differentials in the form $\int u\,dv = uv - \int v\,du$.

### Standard Formulas for Indefinite Integration

(a) $\int x^n dx = \frac{x^{n+1}}{n+1} + c$

(b) $\int a^x dx = \frac{a^x}{lna} + c$

(c) $\int e^x dx = e^x + c$

(d) $\int \frac{1}{x} dx = \ln x + c$

(e) $\int \sin x\, dx = -\cos x + c$

(f) $\int \cos x\, dx = \sin x + c$

(g) $\int \sec^2 x\, dx = \tan x + c$

(h) $\int \text{cosec}^2 x\, dx = -\cot x + c$

(i) $\int \sec x \tan x\, dx = \sec x + c$

(j) $\int \text{cosec}\, x \cot x\, dx = -\text{cosec}\, x + c$

(k) $\int \frac{1}{\sqrt{1-x^2}} dx = \sin^{-1} x + c$

(l) $\int \frac{1}{\sqrt{1-x^2}} dx = -\cos^{-1} x + c$

(m) $\int \frac{1}{1+x^2} dx = \tan^{-1} x + c$

(n) $\int \frac{1}{1+x^2} dx = -\cot^{-1} x + c$

(o) $\int \frac{1}{x\sqrt{x^2-1}} dx = \sec^{-1} x + c$

(p) $\int \frac{1}{x\sqrt{x^2-1}} dx = -\text{cosec}^{-1} x + c$

## DIFFERENTIAL EQUATIONS WITH VARIABLE SEPARABLE

**We know that the first order, first degree differential equation is of the form:**

$$\frac{dy}{dx} = F(x, y) \quad ...(i)$$

**If F(x, y) is expressed as the product of $g(x)\, h(y)$, where $g(x)$ is the function of $x$ and $h(y)$ is the function of $y$, then the differential equation is said to be of variable separable type. Thus, the differential equation (i) takes the form:**

$$\frac{dy}{dx} = g(x).h(y) \quad ...(ii)$$

**If $h(y) \neq 0$, and separating the variables, equation (ii) becomes**

$$(1/h(y))\, dy = g(x)\, dx \quad ...(iii)$$

**Now, integrate the equation (iii) on both sides, we get**

$$\int (1/h(y))dy = \int g(x)dx \quad ...(iv)$$

**Hence, equation (iv) provides the solution for the differential equation in the form:**

$$H(y) = G(x) + C$$

**Where H(y) and G(x) are the antiderivatives of $1/h(y)$ and $g(x)$, respectively and C is called the arbitrary constant.**

## MULTIPLE CHOICE QUESTIONS

**1. The rate of change of the area of a circle with respect to its radius $r$ at $r$ = 6 cm is:**

A. 10 π B. 12 π
C. 8 π D. 11 π

**2. For all real values of $x$, the minimum value of $\frac{1-x+x^2}{1+x+x^2}$ is:**

A. 0 B. 1
C. 3 D. $\frac{1}{3}$

**3. The maximum value of $[x(x-1)+1]^{\frac{1}{3}}, 0 \le x \le 1$ is:**

A. $\left(\frac{1}{3}\right)^{\frac{1}{3}}$ B. $\frac{1}{2}$
C. 1 D. 0

**4. On which of the following intervals is the function $f$ given by $f(x) = x^{100} + \sin x - 1$ strictly decreasing?**

A. (–1, 1) B. (0, 1)
C. $\left(\frac{\pi}{2}, \pi\right)$ D. $\left(0, \frac{\pi}{2}\right)$

**5. A cylindrical tank of radius 10 m is being filled with wheat at the rate of 314 cubic metre per hour. Then the depth of the wheat is increasing at the rate of:**

A. 1 m³/h B. 0.1 m³/h
C. 1.1 m³/h D. 0.5 m³/h

**6. The slope of the tangent to the curve $x = t^2 + 3t - 8$, $y = 2t^2 - 2t - 5$ at the point (2, –1) is:**

A. $\frac{22}{7}$ B. $\frac{6}{7}$
C. $\frac{7}{6}$ D. $\frac{-6}{7}$

**7. The line $y = mx + 1$ is a tangent to the curve $y^2 = 4x$ if the value of $m$ is:**

A. 1 B. 2
C. 3 D. $\frac{1}{2}$

**8.** The normal at the point (1, 1) on the curve $2y + x^2 = 3$ is:

A. $x + y = 0$  B. $x - y = 0$
C. $x + y + 1 = 0$  D. $x - y + 1 = 0$

**9.** The function $f : R \to R$ given by $f(x) = -|x - 1|$ is:

A. continuous as well as differentiable at $x = 1$
B. not continuous but differentiable at $x = 1$
C. continuous but not differentiable at $x = 1$
D. neither continuous nor differentiable at $x = 1$

**10.** The function $f(x) = \cot x$ is discontinuous on the set:

A. $\{x = n\pi : n \in Z\}$
B. $\{x = 2n\pi : n \in Z\}$
C. $\left\{x = (2n+1)\frac{\pi}{2};\ n \in Z\right\}$
D. $\left\{x = \frac{n\pi}{2};\ n \in Z\right\}$

**11.** The function $f(x) = \dfrac{x-1}{x(x^2-1)}$ is discontinuous at:

A. exactly one point
B. exactly two points
C. exactly three points
D. no point

**12.** If $f(x) = x^2 \sin\frac{1}{x}$, where $x \neq 0$, then the value of the function $f$ at $x = 0$, so that the function is continuous at $x = 0$, is:

A. 0  B. −1
C. 1  D. None of these

**13.** The value of $c$ in Rolle's theorem for the function $f(x) = x^3 - 3x$ in the interval $\left[0, \sqrt{3}\right]$ is:

A. 1  B. −1
C. $\frac{3}{2}$  D. $\frac{1}{3}$

**14.** If $y = \log\sqrt{\tan x}$, then the value of $\frac{dy}{dx}$ at $x = \frac{\pi}{4}$ is:

A. 0  B. 1
C. $\frac{1}{2}$  D. $\infty$

**15.** If $y = \sqrt{\sin x + y}$, then $\frac{dy}{dx}$ is equal to:

A. $\dfrac{\cos x}{2y-1}$  B. $\dfrac{\cos x}{1-2y}$
C. $\dfrac{\sin x}{1-2y}$  D. $\dfrac{\sin x}{2y-1}$

**16.** What is the value of the given limit, $\lim\limits_{x\to 0}\dfrac{2x}{x}$?

A. 2  B. 0
C. $\frac{1}{2}$  D. $\frac{2}{3}$

**17.** The value of $\lim\limits_{x\to 0}\dfrac{8^x - 4^x}{4x}$ is:

A. $\frac{1}{2}\ln 2$  B. $\frac{1}{4}\ln 2$
C. 0  D. $\ln 2$

**18.** $\lim\limits_{x\to\frac{\pi}{2}}\left[x\tan x - \frac{\pi}{2}\sec x\right] =$

A. 0  B. 1
C. −1  D. $\frac{\pi}{2}$

**19.** If $y = Ae^{5x} + Be^{-5x}$, then $\frac{d^2y}{dx^2}$ is equal to:

A. $25y$  B. $5y$
C. $-25y$  D. $15y$

**20.** $x = at^2$, $y = 2at$, then $\frac{d^2y}{dx^2}$ at $t = 2$ is:

A. $\frac{1}{4}$
B. $\frac{-1}{4}$
C. $\frac{1}{16a}$
D. $\frac{-1}{16a}$

## ANSWERS

| 1 | 2 | 3 | 4 | 5 | 6 | 7 | 8 | 9 | 10 |
|---|---|---|---|---|---|---|---|---|---|
| B | D | C | D | A | B | A | B | C | A |
| **11** | **12** | **13** | **14** | **15** | **16** | **17** | **18** | **19** | **20** |
| C | A | A | B | A | A | B | C | A | D |

## EXPLANATORY ANSWERS

**1.** Area of circle (A) = $\pi r^2$

The rate of change of area w.r.t. its radius $r = \dfrac{dA}{dr}$

Now, A = $\pi r^2$

$$\therefore \quad \frac{dA}{dr} = 2\pi \times 6$$

$$= 12\pi \text{ cm}^2\text{/radius.}$$

**2.** Let $y = \dfrac{1-x+x^2}{1+x+x^2}$

$$\frac{dy}{dx} = \frac{(-1+2x)(1+x+x^2)-(1-x+x^2)(1+2x)}{(1+x+x^2)^2}$$

Numerator of $\dfrac{dy}{dx} = 2(x-1)(x+1)$,

$$\therefore \quad \frac{dy}{dx} = \frac{2(x-1)(x+1)}{(x^2+x+1)^2}, \ \frac{dy}{dx} = 0 \text{ at } x = 1, -1$$

At $x = 1$, $\dfrac{dy}{dx}$ changes sign from –ve to +ve

$\therefore$ $y$ is minimum at $x = 1$

Minimum value of $\dfrac{1-x+x^2}{1+x+x^2} = \dfrac{1-1+1}{1+1+1} = \dfrac{1}{3}$.

**3.** Let $y = [x(x-1)+1]^{1/3}$

$$\therefore \quad \frac{dy}{dx} = \frac{(2x-1)}{3[x(x-1)+1]^{2/3}}, \ \frac{dy}{dx} = 0 \text{ at } x = \frac{1}{2}$$

$\dfrac{dy}{dx}$ changes sign from –ve to +ve at $x = \dfrac{1}{2}$

$\therefore$ $y$ is minimum at $x = \dfrac{1}{2}$

Value of $y$ at $x = 0$, $(0+1)^{1/3} = 1^{1/3} = 1$

Value of $y$ at $x = 1$, $(0+1)^{1/3} = 1^{1/3} = 1$

$\therefore$ The maximum value of $y$ is 1.

**4.** Let $f(x) = x^{100} + \sin x - 1$

$\therefore$ $f(x) = 100\, x^{99} + \cos x$

(A) for (–1, 1) *i.e.*, $-1 < x < 1$, $-1 < x^{99} < 1$

$\Rightarrow -100 < 100\, x^{99} < 100$

Also $0 < \cos x < 1$

$\Rightarrow f'(x)$ can either be +ve or –ve on (–1, 1)

$\therefore$ $f(x)$ is neither increasing nor decreasing on (–1, 1).

(B) For (0, 1) *i.e.*, $0 < x < 1$, $x^{99}$ and $\cos x$ are both +ve

$\therefore$ $f(x) > 0$

$\Rightarrow f(x)$ is increasing on (0, 1).

(C) For $\left(\dfrac{\pi}{2}, \pi\right)$ *i.e.*, $\dfrac{\pi}{2} < x < \pi$, $x^{99}$ is +ve and $-1 < \cos x < 0$

$\therefore$ $f'(x) > 0$

$\Rightarrow f(x)$ is increasing on $\left(\dfrac{\pi}{2}, \pi\right)$

(D) For $\left(0, \dfrac{\pi}{2}\right)$, *i.e.*, $0 < x < \dfrac{\pi}{2}$, $x^{99}$ and $\cos x$ are both –ve

$\therefore$ $f'(x) < 0$

$\Rightarrow f(x)$ is decreasing on $\left(0, \dfrac{\pi}{2}\right)$.

**5.** Let $h$ be the height of the cylindrical tank at any instant.

Volume of cylindrical tank = $\pi r^2 h = \pi(10)^2 h$,

$\therefore$ $v = 100\, \pi h$

Rate of change of volume

$$\therefore \quad \frac{dv}{dt} = 100\pi\frac{dh}{dt} \quad \text{...}(i)$$

The tank is filled at the rate of 314 cubic metre per hour *i.e.*,

$\dfrac{dv}{dt} = 314$ from (*i*) $314 = 100\pi\dfrac{dh}{dt}$

$$\therefore \quad \frac{dh}{dt} = \frac{314}{100\pi} = \frac{314}{100 \times 3.14} = 1$$

Hence, the depth of the tank changes at 1 cubic m/h.

**6.** The curve is $x = t^2 + 3t - 8$, $y = 2t^2 - 2t - 5$ ...(*i*)

Put $x = 2$,

$\Rightarrow \quad (t+5)(t-2) = 0$

Put $t = 2$ in $y = 2t^2 - 2t - 5 = 8 - 4 - 5 = -1$

At $x = 2$, $y = -1$, $t = 2$

Differentiating (*i*)

$$\frac{dx}{dt} = 2t + 3$$

$$\frac{dy}{dx} = 4t - 2$$

$\therefore \quad \dfrac{dy}{dx} = \dfrac{dy}{dt} \times \dfrac{dt}{dx}$

$= \dfrac{4t-2}{2t+3}$

At $t = 2$, $\quad \dfrac{dy}{dx} = \dfrac{4 \times 2 - 2}{2 \times 2 + 3}$

$= \dfrac{6}{7}$.

**7.** The equation of the curve is $y^2 = 4x$

Differentiating w.r.t. $x$

$\therefore \dfrac{dy}{dx} = \dfrac{4}{2y} = \dfrac{2}{y}$

Slope of tangent $= \dfrac{2}{y} = m$

$\therefore y = \dfrac{2}{m}$ ...(*i*)

$(x_1, y_1)$ lies on $y^2 = 4x$, $y_1^2 = 4x_1$ ...(*ii*)

Equation of tangent at $(x_1, y_1)$

or $\quad y = mx + y_1 - mx_1$ ...(*iii*)

$y = mx + 1$ ...(*iv*)

Comparing (*iii*) & (*iv*)

$y_1 - mx_1 = 1$ ...(*v*)

from (*i*) & (*ii*) $m = \dfrac{2}{y_1}$

$x_1 = \dfrac{y_1^2}{4}$

$\therefore$ Put these values in (*v*)

or $\quad y_1 - \dfrac{y_1}{2} = \dfrac{y_1}{2} = 1$

$\therefore y_1 = 2$

$\therefore m = \dfrac{2}{y_1} = \dfrac{2}{2} = 1$

**8.** The equation of the curve $2y + x^2 = 3$

Differentiating,

$\therefore \quad \dfrac{dy}{dx} = -x$

$\dfrac{dy}{dx}$ at $(1, 1) = -1 =$ slope of tangent

Since slope of normal $= \dfrac{-1}{\text{Slope of tangent}} = 1$

$\therefore$ The equation of the normal is

$y - y_1 =$ (slope of normal) $(x - x_1)$

$y - 1 = 1\ (x - 1)$

or $x - y = 0$.

**9.** We have,

$$f(x) = -|x-1| = \begin{cases} x-1, & \text{if } x \le 1 \\ -(x-1), & \text{if } x > 1 \end{cases}$$

At $x = 1$

LHL $= \lim\limits_{h \to 0} f(1-h)$

$= \lim\limits_{h \to 0} (1-h) - 1$

$= 0$

RHL $= \lim\limits_{h \to 0} f(1+h)$

$= \lim\limits_{h \to 0} -(1+h-1)$

$= 0$

$f(1) = 1 - 1 = 0$

$\therefore$ LHL = RHL = $f(0)$

$\Rightarrow f(x)$ is continuous everywhere

Now, at $x = 1$

LHD $= \dfrac{d}{dx}(x-1) = 1$

RHD $= \dfrac{d}{dx}\{-(x-1)\} = -1$

LHD $\neq$ RHD

$\therefore f(x)$ is not differentiable of $x = 1$.

**10.** We know that, $f(x) = \cot x$ is continuous in $R - \{n\pi : n \in Z\}$

Since, $\quad f(x) = \cot x = \dfrac{\cos x}{\sin x}$

[Since, $\sin x = 0$ at $\{n\pi, n \in Z\}$]

Hence, $f(x) = \cot x$ is discontinuous on the set $\{x = n\pi : n \in Z\}$.

**11.** We have,

$f(x) = \dfrac{x-1}{x(x^2-1)}$

$\therefore f(x)$ is discontinuous when $x(x^2 - 1) = 0$

$\Rightarrow \quad x = 0, x = \pm 1$

$\therefore f(x)$ is discontinuous

at $\quad x = 0, -1, 1$

*i.e.*, exactly at three points.

**12.** $\because \ f(x) = x^2 \sin\left(\dfrac{1}{x}\right)$,

where $x \neq 0$

$\because \lim\limits_{x \to 0} f(x) = 0$

Hence, value of the function $f$ at $x = 0$, so that it is continuous at $x = 0$ is 0.

**13.** $\because \quad f'(c) = 0 \quad [\because f'(x) = 3x^2 - 3]$

$\Rightarrow \quad 3c^2 - 3 = 0$

$\Rightarrow \quad c^2 = \frac{3}{3} = 1$

$\Rightarrow \quad c = \pm 1$

where $1 \in (0, \sqrt{3})$

$\Rightarrow \quad c = 1.$

**14.** We have, $y = \log \sqrt{\tan x}$

$$\therefore \quad \frac{dy}{dx} = \frac{1}{\sqrt{\tan x}} \times \frac{1}{2\sqrt{\tan x}} \times \sec^2 x$$

$$\Rightarrow \quad \frac{dy}{dx} = \frac{\sec^2 x}{2\tan x}$$

$$\Rightarrow \quad \left.\frac{dy}{dx}\right|_{\text{at } x=\frac{\pi}{4}} = \frac{(\sqrt{2})^2}{2 \times 1} = \frac{2}{2} = 1.$$

**15.** $\because \quad y = (\sin x + y)^{1/2}$

$$\frac{dy}{dx} = \frac{1}{2}(\sin x + y)^{-1/2}.\frac{d}{dx}(\sin x + y)$$

$$= \frac{1}{2}.\frac{1}{(\sin x + y)^{1/2}}.\left(\cos x + \frac{dy}{dx}\right)$$

$$\Rightarrow \quad \frac{dy}{dx} = \frac{1}{2y}\left(\cos x + \frac{dy}{dx}\right) \quad [\because (\sin x + y)^{1/2} = y]$$

$$\Rightarrow \frac{dy}{dx}\left(1 - \frac{1}{2y}\right) = \frac{\cos x}{2y}$$

$$\Rightarrow \quad \frac{dy}{dx} = \frac{\cos x}{2y}.\frac{2y}{2y-1}$$

$$= \frac{\cos x}{2y-1}.$$

**16.** Given $\lim_{x \to 0} \frac{2x}{x}$

Using L'Hospital's Rule, by differentiating both the numerator and denominator with respect to $x$,

$$\lim_{x \to 0} \frac{2}{1} = 2.$$

**17.** $\lim_{x \to 0} \frac{8^x - 4^x}{4x} \left[\frac{0}{0} \text{ form}\right]$

Applying L'Hospital's Rule,

$$= \lim_{x \to 0} \frac{8^x \ln 8 - 4^x \ln 4}{4}$$

$$= \frac{1}{4}(\ln 8 - \ln 4) = \frac{1}{4}\ln\frac{8}{4}$$

$$= \frac{1}{4}\ln 2.$$

**18.** $\lim_{x \to \frac{\pi}{2}} \left[x \tan x - \frac{\pi}{2}\sec x\right]$

$$= \lim_{x \to \frac{\pi}{2}} \left[\frac{x \sin x - \frac{\pi}{2}}{\cos x}\right] \left(\frac{0}{0} \text{ form}\right)$$

By L'Hospital's Rule,

$$\lim_{x \to \frac{\pi}{2}} \left[\frac{x \cos x + \sin x}{-\sin x}\right] = -1$$

**19.** $y = Ae^{5x} + Be^{-5x}$

$$\Rightarrow \quad \frac{dy}{dx} = 5Ae^{5x} - 5Be^{-5x}$$

$$\Rightarrow \quad \frac{d^2y}{d^2x} = 25Ae^{5x} + 25Be^{-5x}$$

$$= 25y.$$

**20.** $\frac{dx}{dt} = 2at, \frac{dy}{dt} = 2a$

$$\frac{dy}{dx} = \frac{2a}{2at} = \frac{1}{t}$$

$$\frac{d^2y}{dx^2} = \frac{-1}{t^2} \times \frac{dt}{dx}$$

$$= \frac{-1}{t^2} \times \frac{1}{2at}$$

$$\left(\frac{d^2y}{dx^2}\right)_{x=2} = \frac{-1}{2a \times 2^3}$$

$$= \frac{-1}{16a}.$$

CHAPTER

6

# VECTORS

A vector is an object which has both magnitudes and direction. It is usually represented by an arrow which shows the direction (→) and its length shows the magnitude. The arrow which indicates the vector has an arrowhead and its opposite end is the tail. It is denoted as → V.

## MAGNITUDE AND DIRECTION OF VECTORS

### Magnitude of a Vector

The magnitude of a vector $\overrightarrow{PQ}$ is the distance between the initial point P and the end point Q. In symbols the magnitude of $\overrightarrow{PQ}$ is written as $\left|\overrightarrow{PQ}\right|$.

or $$\left|\overrightarrow{PQ}\right| = \sqrt{(x_2 - x_1)^2 + (y_2 - y_1)^2}$$

### Direction of a Vector

The direction of a vector is the measure of the angle it makes with a horizontal line. One of the following formulas can be used to find the direction of a vector:

$\tan\theta = \dfrac{y}{x}$, where $x$ is the horizontal change and $y$ is the vertical change

or $\tan\theta = \dfrac{y_2 - y_1}{x_2 - x_1}$, where $(x_1, y_1)$ is the initial point and $(x_2, y_2)$ is the terminal point.

## VECTOR ALGEBRA

Just like in usual algebra, we also perform arithmetic operations such as addition, subtraction, multiplication on vectors. However, in the case of multiplication, vectors have two terminologies, such as dot product and cross product.

The vector addition follows two important laws, which are:

1. Commutative Law: P + Q = Q + P
2. Associative Law : P + (Q + R) = (P + Q) + R
3. P – Q = P + (–Q)

### Dot Product

The dot product is often called a scalar product. It is represented using a dot(.) between two vectors. The dot product for both the vectors is given by:

- P.Q. = |P| |Q| cos θ

  If P and Q are both in the same direction, *i.e.* θ = 0°, then
- P.Q. = |P| |Q|

  If P and Q are both orthogonal, *i.e.*, θ = 90°, then
- P.Q. = 0 [since cos 90° = 0]

### Cross Product

A cross product is denoted by the multiplication sign(x) between two vectors. It is a binary vector operation, defined in a three-dimensional system.

It is represented by;

- P × Q = |P| |Q| sin θ

### Vector Algebra Formulas

Apart from the addition, subtraction and multiplication, there are some other formulas of vectors in algebra. They are:

- Let P($x$, $y$, $z$) be a point. The position vector of P is $\vec{OP} = \vec{r} = x\hat{i} + y\hat{j} + z\hat{k}$ and the magnitude of this vector is given by $\left|\vec{OP}\right| = \left|\vec{r}\right| = \sqrt{x^2 + y^2 + z^2}$.

- Suppose for any vector, $r$ is the magnitude, $(l, m, n)$ are the direction cosines and $(a, b, c)$ are the direction ratios, then:

$$l = a/r,\ m = b/r,\ n = c/r$$

- Let $|\vec{a}|$ be any vector, then the unit vector in the direction of $|\vec{a}|$ is given by $\hat{a} = \dfrac{\vec{a}}{|\vec{a}|}$.

- The position vector of a point P dividing a line segment joining the points A and B whose position vectors are $|\vec{a}|$ and $|\vec{b}|$ respectively, in the ratio $m : n$ internally is given by $\dfrac{n\vec{a} + m\vec{b}}{m+n}$

- In the case of external division, the formula becomes:

$$\frac{m\vec{b} + n\vec{a}}{m-n}$$

- Matrix representation of the cross product of two vectors is given by:

$$\vec{a} \times \vec{b} = \begin{vmatrix} \hat{i} & \hat{j} & \hat{k} \\ a_1 & b_1 & c_1 \\ a_2 & b_2 & c_2 \end{vmatrix}$$

## MULTIPLE CHOICE QUESTIONS

**1. Magnitude of the vector $\vec{a} = \frac{1}{\sqrt{3}}\hat{i} + \frac{1}{\sqrt{3}}\hat{j} + \frac{1}{\sqrt{3}}\hat{k}$ is:**

A. 1 B. 1.5
C. 0.5 D. $\sqrt{3}$

**2. Find the unit vector in the direction of vector $\overrightarrow{PQ}$, where P and Q are the points (1, 2, 3) and (4, 5, 6), respectively:**

A. $\frac{1}{\sqrt{3}}\hat{i} + \frac{1}{\sqrt{3}}\hat{j} - \frac{1}{\sqrt{3}}\hat{k}$ B. $\frac{1}{\sqrt{3}}\hat{i} - \frac{1}{\sqrt{3}}\hat{j} + \frac{1}{\sqrt{3}}\hat{k}$

C. $-\frac{1}{\sqrt{3}}\hat{i} + \frac{1}{\sqrt{3}}\hat{j} + \frac{1}{\sqrt{3}}\hat{k}$ D. $\frac{1}{\sqrt{3}}\hat{i} + \frac{1}{\sqrt{3}}\hat{j} + \frac{1}{\sqrt{3}}\hat{k}$

**3. If $P_1(x_1, y_1, z_1)$ and $P_2(x_2, y_2, z_2)$ are any two points, then the vector joining $P_1$ and $P_2$ is the vector $P_1P_2$. Magnitude of the vector $\overrightarrow{P_1P_2}$ is:**

A. $\sqrt{(x_2 - x_1)^2 + (y_2 - y_1)^2 + (z_2 + z_1)^2}$

B. $\sqrt{(x_2 + x_1)^2 + (y_2 - y_1)^2 + (z_2 - z_1)^2}$

C. $\sqrt{(x_2 - x_1)^2 + (y_2 + y_1)^2 + (z_2 - z_1)^2}$

D. $\sqrt{(x_2 - x_1)^2 + (y_2 - y_1)^2 + (z_2 - z_1)^2}$

**4. Find the scalar and vector components of the vector with initial point (2, 1) and terminal point (–5, 7).**

A. –7 and 6; $7\hat{i}$ and $-6\hat{j}$

B. –7 and 6; $-7\hat{i}$ and $6\hat{j}$

C. 7 and 6; $7\hat{i}$ and $6\hat{j}$

D. –7 and –6; $-7\hat{i}$ and $-6\hat{j}$

**5. Find a vector in the direction of the vector $5\hat{i} - \hat{j} + 2\hat{k}$ which has a magnitude of 8 units:**

A. $\frac{40}{\sqrt{30}}\hat{i} - \frac{8}{\sqrt{30}}\hat{j} - \frac{16}{\sqrt{30}}\hat{k}$

B. $\frac{40}{\sqrt{30}}\hat{i} - \frac{8}{\sqrt{30}}\hat{j} + \frac{16}{\sqrt{30}}\hat{k}$

C. $-\frac{40}{\sqrt{30}}\hat{i} - \frac{8}{\sqrt{30}}\hat{j} + \frac{16}{\sqrt{30}}\hat{k}$

D. $\frac{40}{\sqrt{30}}\hat{i} + \frac{8}{\sqrt{30}}\hat{j} + \frac{16}{\sqrt{30}}\hat{k}$

**6. Find $|\vec{a} \times \vec{b}|$, if $\vec{a} = 3\hat{i} + \hat{j} + 2\hat{k}$ and $\vec{b} = 2\hat{i} - 2\hat{j} + 4\hat{k}$**

A. $17\sqrt{2}$ B. $19\sqrt{3}$
C. $8\sqrt{3}$ D. $19\sqrt{5}$

**7. If $\vec{a}, \vec{b}$ and $\vec{c}$ are any three vectors then the correct expression for distributivity of scalar product over addition is:**

A. $\vec{a}\cdot(\vec{b}+\vec{c}) \neq \vec{a}\cdot\vec{b} + \vec{a}\cdot\vec{c}$

B. $\vec{a}\cdot(\vec{b}+\vec{c}) > \vec{a}\cdot\vec{b} + \vec{a}\cdot\vec{c}$

C. $\vec{a}\cdot(\vec{b}+\vec{c}) = \vec{a}\cdot\vec{b} + \vec{a}\cdot\vec{c}$

D. $\vec{a}\cdot(\vec{b}+\vec{c}) < \vec{a}\cdot\vec{b} + \vec{a}\cdot\vec{c}$

**8. Find the direction cosines of the vector $\hat{i} + 2\hat{j} + 3\hat{k}$**

A. $\frac{1}{\sqrt{14}}, -\frac{2}{\sqrt{14}}, \frac{3}{\sqrt{14}}$ B. $-\frac{1}{\sqrt{14}}, \frac{2}{\sqrt{14}}, \frac{3}{\sqrt{14}}$

C. $\frac{1}{\sqrt{14}}, \frac{2}{\sqrt{14}}, \frac{3}{\sqrt{14}}$ D. $\frac{1}{\sqrt{14}}, \frac{2}{\sqrt{14}}, -\frac{3}{\sqrt{14}}$

**9.** Find a unit vector perpendicular to each of $\vec{a}+\vec{b}$ and $\vec{a}-\vec{b}$, where $\vec{a}=3\hat{i}+2\hat{j}+2\hat{k}$ and $\vec{b}=\hat{i}+2\hat{j}-2\hat{k}$

A. $\pm\frac{2}{3}\hat{i}\pm\frac{2}{3}\hat{j}\mp\frac{1}{3}\hat{k}$  B. $\pm\frac{2}{3}\hat{i}\mp\frac{2}{3}\hat{j}\mp\frac{1}{3}\hat{k}$

C. $\pm\frac{2}{3}\hat{i}\pm\frac{2}{3}\hat{j}\pm\frac{1}{3}\hat{k}$  D. $\mp\frac{2}{3}\hat{i}\mp\frac{2}{3}\hat{j}\mp\frac{1}{3}\hat{k}$

**10.** Find the sum of the vectors $\vec{a}=\hat{i}-2\hat{j}+\hat{k}$, $\vec{b}=-2\hat{i}+4\hat{j}+5\hat{k}$ and $\vec{c}=\hat{i}-6\hat{j}-7\hat{k}$

A. $-4\hat{j}-\hat{k}$  B. $\hat{i}-4\hat{j}-\hat{k}$

C. $-\hat{i}+4\hat{j}-\hat{k}$  D. $-\hat{i}-4\hat{j}-\hat{k}$

**11.** Find the direction cosines of the vector joining the points A(1, 2, –3) and B(–1, –2, 1), directed from A to B.

A. $\frac{1}{3},-\frac{2}{3},\frac{2}{3}$  B. $-\frac{1}{3},\frac{2}{3},\frac{2}{3}$

C. $-\frac{1}{3},-\frac{2}{3},\frac{2}{3}$  D. $-\frac{1}{3},-\frac{2}{3},-\frac{2}{3}$

**12.** If a unit vector $\vec{a}$ makes angles $\frac{\pi}{3}$ with $\hat{i}\,\frac{\pi}{4}$ with $\hat{j}$ and an acute angle θ with $\hat{k}$, then find θ

A. $\frac{\pi}{10}$  B. $\frac{\pi}{5}$

C. $2\frac{\pi}{3}$  D. $\frac{\pi}{3}$

**13.** Write down a unit vector in XY-plane, making an angle of 30° with the positive direction of $x$-axis.

A. $-\frac{\sqrt{3}}{2}\hat{i}-\frac{1}{2}\hat{j}$  B. $\frac{\sqrt{3}}{2}\hat{i}-\frac{1}{2}\hat{j}$

C. $\frac{\sqrt{3}}{2}\hat{i}+\frac{1}{2}\hat{j}$  D. $-\frac{\sqrt{3}}{2}\hat{i}+\frac{1}{2}\hat{j}$

**14.** Find the angle between two vectors $\vec{a}$ and $\vec{b}$ with magnitudes $\sqrt{3}$ and 2, respectively, having $\vec{a}\cdot\vec{b}=\sqrt{6}$

A. $\frac{\pi}{3}$  B. $\frac{\pi}{2}$

C. $\frac{\pi}{5}$  D. $\frac{\pi}{4}$

**15.** If a unit vector $\vec{a}$ makes angles $\frac{\pi}{3}$ with $\hat{i}$, $\frac{\pi}{4}$ with $\hat{j}$ and an acute angle θ with $\hat{k}$, then the components of $\vec{a}$ are:

A. $\frac{1}{2},\frac{1}{\sqrt{2}},\frac{1}{3}$  B. $\frac{1}{3},\frac{1}{\sqrt{2}},\frac{1}{2}$

C. $\frac{1}{3},\frac{1}{\sqrt{3}},\frac{1}{2}$  D. $\frac{1}{2},\frac{1}{\sqrt{2}},\frac{1}{2}$

**16.** If $a$ and $b$ are two vectors such that $a \cdot b = 0$ and $a \times b = 0$, which one of the following is correct?

A. $a$ is parallel to $b$

B. $a$ is perpendicular to $b$

C. Either $a$ or $b$ is a null vector

D. None of the above

**17.** If the vectors $-i - 2xj - 3yk$ and $i - 3xj - 2yk$ are orthogonal to each other, what is the locus of the point $(x, y)$?

A. A straight line  B. An ellipse

C. A parabola  D. A circle

**18.** If $c$ is the unit vector perpendicular to both the vectors $a$ and $b$, what is another unit vector perpendicular to both the vectors $a$ and $b$?

A. $c \times a$  B. $c \times b$

C. $-\frac{(a \times b)}{|a \times b|}$  D. $\frac{(a \times b)}{|a \times b|}$

**19.** For what value of $m$ are the points with position vectors $10i + 3j$, $12i - 5j$ and $mi + 11j$ collinear?

A. – 8  B. 4

C. 8  D. 12

**20.** Magnitude of the vector

$$\hat{k}=\frac{2}{\sqrt{6}}\hat{i}-\frac{2}{\sqrt{6}}\hat{j}-\frac{1}{6}\hat{k}$$

A. $\sqrt{6}$  B. $\frac{2}{\sqrt{3}}$

C. $\frac{\sqrt{6}}{2}$  D. None of these

## ANSWERS

| 1 | 2 | 3 | 4 | 5 | 6 | 7 | 8 | 9 | 10 |
|---|---|---|---|---|---|---|---|---|---|
| A | D | D | B | B | C | C | C | B | A |
| **11** | **12** | **13** | **14** | **15** | **16** | **17** | **18** | **19** | **20** |
| C | D | C | D | D | C | D | C | C | C |

# EXPLANATORY ANSWERS

**1.** $\vec{a} = \frac{1}{\sqrt{3}}\hat{i} + \frac{1}{\sqrt{3}}\hat{j} + \frac{1}{\sqrt{3}}\hat{k}$, then

$$|\vec{a}| = \sqrt{\left(\frac{1}{\sqrt{3}}\right)^2 + \left(\frac{1}{\sqrt{3}}\right)^2 + \left(\frac{1}{\sqrt{3}}\right)^2}$$

$$= \sqrt{\frac{1}{3} + \frac{1}{3} + \frac{1}{3}}$$

$$= \sqrt{\frac{3}{3}} = 1$$

**2.** $\overrightarrow{PQ} = 3\hat{i} + 3\hat{j} + 3\hat{k}$

$$\widehat{PQ} = \frac{\overrightarrow{PQ}}{|\overrightarrow{PQ}|} = \frac{3\hat{i} + 3\hat{j} + 3\hat{k}}{\sqrt{3^2 + 3^2 + 3^2}}$$

$$= \frac{3\hat{i} + 3\hat{j} + 3\hat{k}}{\sqrt{27}}$$

$$= \frac{3(\hat{i} + \hat{j} + \hat{k})}{3\sqrt{3}}$$

$$= \frac{1}{\sqrt{3}}\hat{i} + \frac{1}{\sqrt{3}}\hat{j} + \frac{1}{\sqrt{3}}\hat{k}$$

**3.** If $P_1(x_1, y_1, z_1)$ and $P_2(x_2, y_2, z_2)$ are any two points, then the vector joining $P_1$ and $P_2$ is the vector $P_1P_2$, then;

$$|\overrightarrow{P_1P_2}| = \sqrt{(x_2 - x_1)^2 + (y_2 - y_1)^2 + (z_2 - z_1)^2}$$

**4.** The scalar and vector components of the vector with initial point (2, 1) and terminal point (–5, 7) is given by: (–5 –2) *i.e.*, –7 and (7 – 1) *i.e.* 6. Therefore, the scalar components are –7 and 6, and vector components are $-7\hat{i}$ and $6\hat{j}$.

**5.** Let $\vec{a} = 5\hat{i} - \hat{j} + 2\hat{k}$

then, $8\hat{a} = 8\cdot\frac{\vec{a}}{|\vec{a}|}$

$$= 8\cdot\frac{5\hat{i} - \hat{j} + 2\hat{k}}{\sqrt{5^2 + (-1)^2 + 2^2}}$$

$$= \frac{8(5\hat{i} - \hat{j} + 2\hat{k})}{\sqrt{30}}$$

$$= \frac{40}{\sqrt{30}}\hat{i} - \frac{8}{\sqrt{30}}\hat{j} + \frac{16}{\sqrt{30}}\hat{k}$$

**6.**

$$\vec{a} \times \vec{b} = \begin{vmatrix} \hat{i} & \hat{j} & \hat{k} \\ 3 & 1 & 2 \\ 2 & -2 & 4 \end{vmatrix} = 8\hat{i} - 8\hat{j} - 8\hat{k}$$

$$\therefore \quad |\vec{a} \times \vec{b}| = \sqrt{8^2 + (-8)^2 + (-8^2)} = 8\sqrt{3}$$

**7.** If $\vec{a}, \vec{b}$ and $\vec{c}$ are any three vectors then the correct expression for distributivity of scalar product over addition is $\vec{a}\cdot(\vec{b} + \vec{c}) = \vec{a}\cdot\vec{b} + \vec{a}\cdot\vec{c}$

**8.** Let $\vec{a} = \hat{i} + 2\hat{j} + 3\hat{k}$, Then,

$$\hat{a} = \frac{\vec{a}}{|\vec{a}|} = \frac{\hat{i} + 2\hat{j} + 3\hat{k}}{\sqrt{1^2 + 2^2 + 3^2}}$$

$$= \frac{i + 2\hat{j} + 3\hat{k}}{\sqrt{14}}$$

Therefore, the D.C.'s of vector *a* are:

$$\frac{1}{\sqrt{14}}, \frac{2}{\sqrt{14}}, \frac{3}{\sqrt{14}}.$$

**9.** It is given that:

$$\vec{a} = 3\hat{i} + 2\hat{j} + 2\hat{k} \text{ and } \vec{b} = \hat{i} + 2\hat{j} - 2\hat{k}$$

$$\therefore \quad \vec{a} + \vec{b} = 4\hat{i} + 4\hat{j} \text{ and } \vec{a} - \vec{b} = 2\hat{i} + 4\hat{k}$$

$$\therefore \quad (\vec{a} + \vec{b}) \times (\vec{a} - \vec{b}) = \begin{vmatrix} \hat{i} & \hat{j} & \hat{k} \\ 4 & 4 & 0 \\ 2 & 0 & 4 \end{vmatrix}$$

$$= 16\hat{i} - 16\hat{j} - 8\hat{k}$$

$$\Rightarrow |(\vec{a} + \vec{b}) \times (\vec{a} - \vec{b})| = \sqrt{576} = 24$$

Therefore, the unit vector perpendicular to both the vectors $(\vec{a} + \vec{b})$ and $(\vec{a} - \vec{b})$ is given by:

$$= \pm\frac{(16\hat{i} - 16\hat{j} - 8\hat{k})}{24}$$

$$= \pm\frac{1}{3}(2\hat{i} - 2\hat{j} - \hat{k})$$

**10.** We have,

vectors $\vec{a} = \hat{i} - 2\hat{j} + \hat{k}, \vec{b} = -2\hat{i} + 4\hat{j} + 5\hat{k}$

and $\vec{c} = \hat{i} - 6\hat{j} - 7\hat{k}$

$$\Rightarrow \vec{a} + \vec{b} + \vec{c} = \hat{i} - 2\hat{j} + \hat{k} + (-2\hat{i} + 4\hat{j} + 5\hat{k}) + \hat{i} - 6\hat{j} - 7\hat{k}$$

$$\Rightarrow \vec{a} + \vec{b} + \vec{c} = 0\hat{i} - 4\hat{j} - \hat{k}$$

**11.** We have: $\overline{AB} = -2\hat{i} - 4\hat{j} + 4\hat{k}$

then, $\widehat{AB} = \dfrac{\overline{AB}}{|\overline{AB}|}$

$= \dfrac{-2\hat{i} - 4\hat{j} + 4\hat{k}}{\sqrt{(-2)^2 + (-4)^2 + 4^2}}$

$= \dfrac{-2\hat{i} - 4\hat{j} + 4\hat{k}}{\sqrt{36}}$

$= \dfrac{-2\hat{i}}{6} - \dfrac{4\hat{j}}{6} + \dfrac{4\hat{k}}{6}$

$= \dfrac{-1}{3}\hat{i} - \dfrac{2}{3}\hat{j} + \dfrac{2}{3}\hat{k}$

Therefore, the D.C.'s of vector AB are given by:

$-\dfrac{1}{3}, -\dfrac{2}{3}, \dfrac{2}{3}$

**12.** Let, $\vec{a} = a_1\hat{i} + a_2\hat{j} + a_3\hat{k}$,

It is given that

$|\vec{a}| = 1$

then,

$\Rightarrow \quad a_1^2 + a_2^2 + a_3^2 = 1 \quad ...(i)$

$\therefore \quad \vec{a}\cdot\hat{i} = (a_1\hat{i} + a_2\hat{j} + a_3\hat{k})\cdot\hat{i}$

$\Rightarrow \quad |\vec{a}||\hat{i}|\cos\dfrac{\pi}{3} = a_1 \Rightarrow a_1 = \dfrac{1}{2}$

$\therefore \quad \vec{a}\cdot\hat{j} = (a_1\hat{i} + a_2\hat{j} + a_3\hat{k})\cdot\hat{j}$

$|\vec{a}||\hat{j}|\cos\dfrac{\pi}{4} = a_2 \Rightarrow a_2 = \dfrac{1}{\sqrt{2}}$

$\therefore \quad \vec{a}\cdot\hat{k} = (a_1\hat{i} + a_2\hat{j} + a_3\hat{k})\cdot\hat{k}$

$\Rightarrow \quad |\vec{a}||\hat{k}|\cos\theta = a_3 \Rightarrow a_3 = \cos\theta$

Putting these values in (1), we get

$\dfrac{1}{4} + \dfrac{1}{2} + \cos^2\theta = 1$

$\Rightarrow \quad \dfrac{3}{4} = 1 - \cos^2\theta \Rightarrow \sin^2\theta = \dfrac{3}{4}$

$\Rightarrow \quad \sin\theta = \dfrac{\sqrt{3}}{2} \Rightarrow \theta = 60°$

**13.** Let $\vec{r} = x\hat{i} + y\hat{j}$ be a unit vector in XY plane

$x = \dfrac{\sqrt{3}}{2}; y = \dfrac{1}{2}, \quad (\because |\vec{r}| = 1)$

$\therefore \quad \vec{r} = \dfrac{\sqrt{3}}{2}\hat{i} + \dfrac{1}{2}\hat{j}$ is the required vector.

**14.** $|\vec{a}| = \sqrt{3}, |\vec{b}| = 2, \vec{a}\cdot\vec{b} = \sqrt{6}$,

$\Rightarrow \quad \vec{a}\cdot\vec{b} = |\vec{a}|\cdot|\vec{b}|\cos\theta$

$= 2\sqrt{3}\cos\theta$

$\Rightarrow \quad \cos\theta = \dfrac{1}{\sqrt{2}} \Rightarrow \theta = \dfrac{\pi}{4}$

**15.** Let $\vec{a} = a_1\hat{i} + a_2\hat{j} + a_3\hat{k}$, it is given that left $|\vec{a}| = 1$, then

$\Rightarrow \quad a_1{}^2 + a_2{}^2 + a_3{}^2 = 1 \quad ...(i)$

$\therefore \quad \vec{a}\cdot\hat{i} = (a_1\hat{i} + a_2\hat{j} + a_3\hat{k})\cdot\hat{i}$

$\Rightarrow \quad |\vec{a}||\hat{i}|\cos\dfrac{\pi}{3} = a_1 \Rightarrow a_1 = \dfrac{1}{2}$

$\therefore \quad \vec{a}\cdot\hat{j} = (a_1\hat{i} + a_2\hat{j} + a_3\hat{k})\cdot\hat{j}$

$\Rightarrow \quad |\vec{a}||\hat{j}|\cos\dfrac{\pi}{4} = a_2 \Rightarrow a_2 = \dfrac{1}{\sqrt{2}}$

$\therefore \quad \vec{a}\cdot\hat{k} = (a_1\hat{i} + a_2\hat{j} + a_3\hat{k})\cdot\hat{k}$

$\Rightarrow \quad |\vec{a}||\hat{k}|\cos\theta = a_3 \Rightarrow a_3 = \cos\theta$

Putting these values in (*i*), we get

$\dfrac{1}{4} + \dfrac{1}{2} + \cos^2\theta = 1$

$\Rightarrow \quad \dfrac{3}{4} = 1 - \cos^2\theta \Rightarrow \sin^2\theta = \dfrac{3}{4}$

$\Rightarrow \quad \sin\theta = \dfrac{\sqrt{3}}{2} \Rightarrow \theta = 60°$

$\therefore \quad a_3 = \cos 60° = \dfrac{1}{2}$

$\Rightarrow \quad \vec{a} = \dfrac{1}{2}\hat{i} + \dfrac{1}{\sqrt{2}}\hat{j} + \dfrac{1}{2}\hat{k}$

**16.** If $a.b = 0 \Rightarrow a \perp b$

and $a \times b = 0 \Rightarrow a \parallel b$

But both conditions can't exist simultaneously. The one possible way for both conditions to exist simultaneously is that either of $a$ and $b$ is a null vector.

**17.** Let $a = -\hat{i} - 2x\hat{j} - 3y\hat{k}$

and $b = \hat{i} - 3x\hat{j} - 2y\hat{k}$

The both the vectors are orthogonal to each other, then

$a\cdot b = 0$

$\Rightarrow (-\hat{i} - 2x\hat{j} - 3y\hat{k})\cdot(\hat{i} - 3x\hat{j} - 2y\hat{k}) = 0$

$\Rightarrow \quad -1 + 6x^2 + 6y^2 = 0$

$\Rightarrow \quad 6x^2 + 6y^2 = 1$

$\Rightarrow \quad x^2 + y^2 = \frac{1}{6}$

Which is the equation of a circle.

**18.** If $c$ is perpendicular to both vectors $a$ and $b$, then

$$c = a \times b$$

But $c$ is the unit vector.

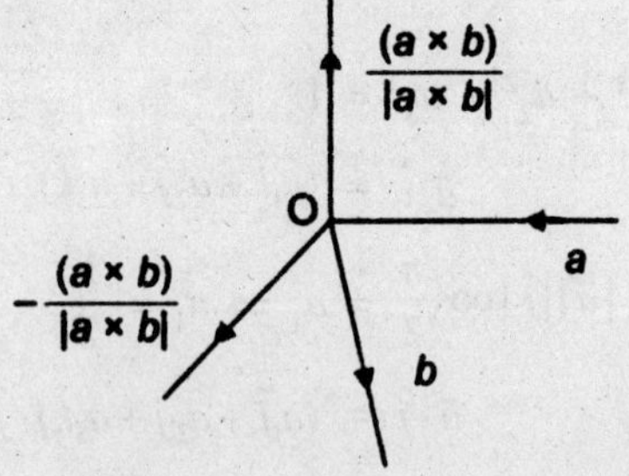


Then, $c = \frac{a \times b}{|a \times b|}$ in the vertical upper direction and the other perpendicular unit vector $c$ on both vectors $a$ and $b$ is:

$$c = -\frac{(a \times b)}{|a \times b|}$$

which is vertically below direction.

**19.** Let $\quad OA = 10\hat{i} + 3\hat{j}$

$\quad OB = 12\hat{i} - 5\hat{j}$

and $\quad OC = m\hat{i} + 11\hat{j}$

Since, A, B and C are collinear.

We have, $\quad AB = \lambda BC$

$\Rightarrow \quad (OB - OA) = \lambda(OC - OB)$

$\Rightarrow \quad (2\hat{i} - 8\hat{j}) = \lambda\{(m-12)\hat{i} + 16\hat{j}\}$

On comparing the coefficients of $\hat{i}, \hat{j}$ and $\hat{k}$ we get

$\lambda(m - 12) = 2 \quad$ ...(*i*)

and $\quad 16\lambda = -8$

$\Rightarrow \quad \lambda = -\frac{1}{2}$

From Eq. (*i*),

$-\frac{1}{2}(m-12) = 2$

$\Rightarrow \quad m - 12 = -4$

$\Rightarrow \quad m = 8$

**20.** Magnitude of vector

$$|\vec{k}| = \sqrt{\left(\frac{2}{\sqrt{6}}\right)^2 + \left(-\frac{2}{\sqrt{6}}\right)^2 + \left(-\frac{1}{\sqrt{6}}\right)^2}$$

$$= \sqrt{\frac{4}{6} + \frac{4}{6} + \frac{1}{6}}$$

$$= \sqrt{\frac{9}{6}} = \sqrt{\frac{3}{2}} = \frac{\sqrt{6}}{2}$$

CHAPTER

# 7

# THREE DIMENSIONAL GEOMETRY

**Direction Cosines:** Let $\alpha, \beta, \gamma$ be the angles which a directed line makes with the positive directions of the axes of $x$, $y$ and $z$ respectively then $\cos\alpha, \cos\beta, \cos\gamma$ are called the direction cosines of the line.

The direction cosines are usually denoted by $< l, m, n >$. Then $l = \cos\alpha$, $m = \cos\beta$, $n = \cos\gamma$.

**Direction Ratios:** Let $a, b, c$ be proportional to the d.c.'s $l, m, n$, then $a, b, c$ are called the direction ratios.

**Position of a Point in Terms of Radius Vector and d.c.'s:** Let $P(x, y, z)$ be any point and $OP = r$. Then $\cos\alpha = x/r$, $\cos\beta = y/r$, $\cos\gamma = z/r$. Then $x, y, z$ are direction ratios of OP and coordinates of P are $(r\cos\alpha, r\cos\beta, r\cos\gamma)$, *i.e.*, $(lr, mr, nr)$.

**Relation Between Direction Cosines:**

$$OP^2 = [x^2 + y^2 + z^2]$$

$$\Rightarrow \quad r^2 = r^2(\cos^2\alpha + \cos^2\beta + \cos^2\gamma)$$

$$= r^2(l^2 + m^2 + n^2)$$

$$\therefore \quad l^2 + m^2 + n^2 = 1$$

**D.R.'s and D.C.'s:** Let $a, b, c$ be d.r.'s and $l, m, n$ the d.c.'s of a line, then

$$\frac{a}{l} = \frac{b}{m} = \frac{c}{n} = r \text{ (say)}$$

$$\therefore a^2 + b^2 + c^2 = r^2(l^2 + m^2 + n^2) = r^2$$

$$\therefore r = \sqrt{[a^2 + b^2 + c^2]}$$

$\therefore$ Direction cosines $l, m, n$ are given by

$$l = \frac{a}{r}, m = \frac{b}{r}, n = \frac{c}{r}, \text{ where } r = \sqrt{[(a^2 + b^2 + c^2)]}$$

**D.C.'s of Axes:** Since the positive $x$-axes makes angle 0°, 90° with axes of $x$, $y$ and $z$ respectively, $\therefore$ d.c.'s of $x$-axes are 1, 0, 0. Similarly, for $y$ and $z$-axes.

$\therefore$ D.C.'s of $x$-axis are 1, 0, 0
D.C.'s of $y$-axis are 0, 1, 0
D.C.'s of $z$-axis are 0, 0, 1

**Direction Ratios of the Line Joining two Points:** Let $A(x_1, y_1, z_1)$ and $B(x_2, y_2, z_2)$ be two points, then d.r.'s of AB are $x_2 - x_1, y_2 - y_1, z_2 - z_1$, and d.c.'s of AB are $\frac{1}{r}(x_2 - x_1)$, $\frac{1}{r}(y_2 - y_1)$, $\frac{1}{r}(z_2 - z_1)$ where $r = \sqrt{[\Sigma(x_2 - x_1)^2]}$.

**Projection of a Line on Another Line:** Let PQ be a line segment with $P(x_1, y_1, z_1)$ and $Q(x_2, y_2, z_2)$ and let L be a straight line whose d.c.'s are $l, m, n$. Note that $l, m, n$ are d.c.'s of line L, not d.r.'s. Then the length of projection of PQ on the line L is

$$\text{Projection} = |l(x_2 - x_1)| + m(y_2 - y_1) + n(z_2 - z_1)|.$$

**Angle Between Two Lines:** Let $\theta$ be the angle between the lines with d.c.'s $l_1, m_1, n_1$ and $l_2, m_2, n_2$, then

$$\cos\theta = l_1 l_2 + m_1 m_2 + n_1 n_2.$$

Also $\sin^2\theta = \Sigma(l_1 m_1)^2$

**Perpendicularity and Parallelism:** Let the two lines have their d.c.'s given by $l_1, m_1, n_1$ and $l_2, m_2, n_2$ respectively then they are perpendicular if $\theta = 90°$ *i.e.*, $\cos\theta = 0$

$$\text{if } l_1 l_2 + m_1 m_2 + n_1 n_2 = 0$$

Also the two lines are parallel if $\theta = 90°$, *i.e.*, $\sin\theta = 0$.

*i.e.*, $\frac{l_1}{l_2} = \frac{m_1}{m_2} = \frac{n_1}{n_2}$

**Example 1:**

What is the angle between the lines whose direction cosines are proportional to (2, 3, 4) and (1, –2, 1), respectively?

A. 90° B. 60°
C. 45° D. 30°

**Solution:** (A) $l_1 = 2$, $l_2 = 1$, $m_1 = 3$, $m_2 = -2$, $n_1 = 4$, $n_2 = 1$

We know that,

$\cos\theta = l_1l_2 + m_1m_2 + n_1n_2$

$\cos\theta = 2 \times 1 + 3 \times (-2) + 4 \times 1$

$\cos\theta = 0$

or $\theta = \frac{\pi}{2}$ or $90^\circ$.

**The Plane:** A geometrical locus is a plane if it is such that if P and Q are any two points on the locus, then every point on the line PQ is also a point on the locus.

**Equation of a Plane:** The equation of every plane is of the first degree, *i.e.*, of the form $ax + by + cz + d = 0$, in which $a, b, c$ are constants, where $a^2 + b^2 + c^2 \neq 0$ (*i.e.*, $a, b, c \neq 0$ simultaneously).

**Planes Parallel to the Coordinate Planes:**

(*a*) Equation of *y-z* plane is $x = 0$

(*b*) Equation of *z-x* plane is $y = 0$

(*c*) Equation of *x-y* plane is $z = 0$

(*d*) Equation of the plane parallel to *x-y* plane at a distance $c$(if $c > 0$, towards positive *z*-axis) is $z = c$. Similarly, planes parallel to *y-z* plane and *z-x* plane are $x = c$ and $y = c$ respectively.

**Equation of Planes Parallel to the Axes:** If $a = 0$, the plane is parallel to *x*-axis, *i.e.*, equation of the plane parallel to *x*-axis is

$$by + cz + d = 0$$

Similarly, equations of planes || to *y*-axis and || to *z*-axis are $ax + cz + d = 0$ and $ax + by + d = 0$, respectively.

**Equation of Plane Through Origin:**

Equation of plane passing through origin is $ax + by + cz = 0$.

**Equation of a Plane Through a given Point:** Let the plane $ax + by + cz + d = 0$ passes through the point $(x_1, y_1, z_1)$, then $ax_1 + by_1 + cz_1 + d = 0$.

∴ Subtracting, we get $a(x - x_1) + b(y - y_1) + c(z - z_1) = 0$ which is the required equation.

**Equation of a Plane in Intercept Form:** Equation of the plane which cuts off intercepts *a, b, c* from the axes is

$$\frac{x}{a} + \frac{y}{b} + \frac{z}{c} = 1.$$

**Equation of a Plane in Normal Form:** If the length of the perpendicular distance of the plane from the origin is *p* and direction cosines of this perpendicular are (*l, m, n*), then the equation of the plane is $lx + my + nz = p$.

**Transformation of the Equation of a Plane to the Normal Form:** To reduce any equation to the normal form, first write the constant term on the right-hand side and make it positive, then divide each term by $\sqrt{(a^2 + b^2 + c^2)}$, where *a, b, c* are coefficients of *x, y* and *z* respectively.

*e.g.*, $$\frac{ax}{\pm\sqrt{(a^2+b^2+c^2)}} + \frac{by}{\pm\sqrt{(a^2+b^2+c^2)}} + \frac{cz}{\pm\sqrt{(a^2+b^2+c^2)}} = \frac{d}{\pm\sqrt{(a^2+b^2+c^2)}}$$

where + sign is to be taken if $d > 0$

and − sign is to be taken if $d < 0$.

**Equation of a Plane Through Three Points:** The equation of the plane through three non-collinear points $(x_1, y_1, z_1)$, $(x_2, y_2, z_2)$, $(x_3, y_3, z_3)$ is

$$\begin{vmatrix} x & y & z & 1 \\ x_1 & y_1 & z_1 & 1 \\ x_2 & y_2 & z_2 & 1 \\ x_3 & y_3 & z_3 & 1 \end{vmatrix} = 0$$

**Angle Between Two Planes:** Consider two planes $ax + by + cz + d = 0$ and $a'x + b'y + c'z + d' = 0$. Angle between these planes is the angle between their normals. Since direction ratios of their normals are *a, b, c* and *a', b', c'* respectively and θ, the angle between them is given by

$$\cos\theta = \frac{aa'+bb'+cc'}{\sqrt{(a^2+b^2+c^2)}\sqrt{(a'^2+b'^2+c'^2)}}$$

∴ Planes are perpendicular if $aa' + bb' + cc' = 0$ and they are parallel if $a/a' = b/b' = c/c'$.

**Planes Parallel to a given Plane:** Equation of a plane parallel to the plane $ax + by + cz + d = 0$ is $ax + by + cz + d' = 0$.

*d'* is to be found by other given condition.

**Example 2:**

What is the accute angle between the planes $x + y + 2z = 3$ and $-2x + y - z = 11$?

A. $\frac{\pi}{5}$ B. $\frac{\pi}{4}$

C. $\frac{\pi}{6}$ D. $\frac{\pi}{3}$

**Solution:** (D) We are given that the equation of planes are $x + y + 2z = 0$ and $-2x + y - z = 11$.

We know that the angle between two planes $a_1x + b_1y + c_1z + d_1 = 0$ and $a_2x + b_2y + c_2z + d_2 = 0$ is given by,

$$\cos\theta = \left|\frac{a_1a_2 + b_1b_2 + c_1c_2}{\sqrt{a_1^2 + b_1^2 + c_1^2}\sqrt{a_2^2 + b_2^2 + c^2}}\right|$$

Here,

$a_1 = 1$, $b_1 = 1$, $c_1 = 2$, $a_2 = -2$, $b_2 = 1$ and $c_2 = -1$

Therefore,

$$\cos\theta = \left|\frac{1\times(-2)+1\times1+2\times(-1)}{\sqrt{1+1+4}\sqrt{4+1+1}}\right|$$

$$\cos\theta = \left|\frac{-3}{\sqrt{6}\sqrt{6}}\right|$$

$$\cos\theta = \frac{3}{6}$$

$$\cos\theta = \frac{1}{2}$$

or $\theta = \frac{\pi}{3}$.

**A Plane Through the Line of Intersection of Two given Planes:** Consider two planes

$u = ax + by + cz + d = 0$ and

$v = a'x + b'y + c'z + d' = 0.$

The equation $u + \lambda v = 0$, $\lambda$ a real parameter, represents the plane passing through the line of intersection of given planes and if planes are parallel, this represents a plane parallel to them.

**Bisectors of Angles Between Two Planes:** Let the equations of the two planes be

$ax + by + cz + d = 0$ and $a_1x + b_1y + c_1z + d = 0$.

Then equations of bisectors of angles between them are given by

$$\frac{ax+by+cz+d}{\sqrt{(a^2+b^2+c^2)}} = \pm\frac{a_1x+b_1y+c_1z+d_1}{\sqrt{(a_1^2+b_1^2+c_1^2)}}$$

**Area of a Triangle:** Let $A(x_1, y_1, z_1)$, $B(x_2, y_2, z_2)$, $C(x_3, y_3, z_3)$ be the vertices of a triangles ABC and $l, m, n$ be the d.c.'s of the normal.

Let $\Delta_x$ = projection of $\Delta$ ABC on $y$-$z$ plane $\Delta_x = \Delta.l$. Similarly,

$\Delta_y$ = projection of $\Delta$ ABC on $z$-$x$ plane $\Delta.m$

$\Delta_z$ = projection of $\Delta$ ABC on $x$-$y$ plane $\Delta.n$

$\therefore\ \Delta_x^2 + \Delta_y^2 + \Delta_z^2 = \Delta^2 (l^2 + m^2 + n^2) = \Delta^2.$

$\therefore\ \Delta = \sqrt{(\Delta_x^2 + \Delta_y^2 + \Delta_z^2)}.$

Also it is obvious that

$$\Delta_x = \frac{1}{2}\begin{vmatrix} y_1 & z_1 & 1 \\ y_2 & z_2 & 1 \\ y_3 & z_3 & 1 \end{vmatrix}, \Delta_y = \frac{1}{2}\begin{vmatrix} z_1 & x_1 & 1 \\ z_2 & x_2 & 1 \\ z_3 & x_3 & 1 \end{vmatrix}$$

$$\text{and } \Delta_x = \frac{1}{2}\begin{vmatrix} x_1 & y_1 & 1 \\ x_2 & y_2 & 1 \\ x_3 & y_3 & 1 \end{vmatrix}$$

**Volume of a Tetrahedron:** Volume of the tetrahedron with vertices $A(x_1, y_1, z_1)$, $B(x_2, y_2, z_2)$, $C(x_3, y_3, z_3)$ and $D(x_4, y_4, z_4)$ is given by

$$V = \frac{1}{6}\begin{vmatrix} x_1 & y_1 & z_1 & 1 \\ x_2 & y_2 & z_2 & 1 \\ x_3 & y_3 & z_3 & 1 \\ x_4 & y_4 & z_4 & 1 \end{vmatrix}$$

If $ax^2 + by^2 + cz^2 + 2fyz + 2gzx + 2hxy = 0$ represents a pair of planes, then the angle between the planes is given by

$$\tan\theta = \frac{2\sqrt{f^2+g^2+h^2-ab-bc-ca}}{a+b+c}$$

**Straight Lines:** A straight line in space is characterised by the intersection of two planes which are not parallel and therefore, the equation of a straight line is present as a solution of the system constituted by the equation of the two planes:

$a_1x + b_1y + c_1z + d_1 = 0$
$a_2x + b_2y + c_2z + d_2 = 0$

This form is also known as unsymmetrical form.

Some particular straight lines:

| *Straight Lines* | *Equation* |
|---|---|
| *(i)* Through the origin | $y = mx, z = nx$ |
| *(ii)* $x$-axis | $y = 0, z = 0$ |
| *(iii)* $y$-axis | $x = 0, z = 0$ |
| *(iv)* $z$-axis | $x = 0, y = 0$ |
| *(v)* ‖ to $x$-axis | $y = p, z = q$ |
| *(vi)* ‖ to $y$-axis | $x = h, z = q$ |
| *(vii)* ‖ to $z$-axis | $x = h, y = p$ |

**Equation of a Straight Line in Symmetrical Form:**

*(a) One point form:* Let $A(x_1, y_1, z_1)$ be a given point on the straight line and $l, m, n$ the d.c.'s of the line, then its equation is

$$\frac{x-x_1}{l} = \frac{y-y_1}{m} = \frac{z-z_1}{n} = r \text{ (say)}$$

It should be noted that $P(x_1 + lr, y_1 + mr, z_1 + nr)$ is a general point on this line at a distance $r$ from the point $A(x_1, y_1, z_1)$, *i.e.*, AP = $r$. One should note that for AP = $r$, $l, m, n$ must be d.c.'s not d.r.'s. If $a, b, c$ are direction ratios of the line, then equation of the line is

$$\frac{x-x_1}{l} = \frac{y-y_1}{m} = \frac{z-z_1}{n} = r, \text{ but here AP} \neq r.$$

*(b)* Equation of the line through two points $A(x_1, y_1, z_1)$ and $B(x_2, y_2, z_2)$ is

$$\frac{x-x_1}{x_2-x_1} = \frac{y-y_1}{y_2-y_1} = \frac{z-z_1}{z_2-z_1}.$$

**Example 3:**

The line passing through (1, 2, 3) and having direction ratios given by <1, 2, 3> cuts the $x$-axis at a distance $k$ from origin. What is the value of $k$?

A. 0 B. 1
C. 2 D. 3

**Solution:** **(A)** The equation of line which passes through (1, 2, 3) having direction ratios <1, 2, 3> is given by,

$$\frac{x-1}{1} = \frac{y-2}{2} = \frac{z-3}{3} = a \text{ (say)}$$

or $x - 1 = a$

$y - 2 = 2a$, $z - 3 = 3a$

$y = 2a + 2$ and $z = 3a + 3$

At $x$ axis, $y = 0$ and $z = 0$

Therefore,

$2a + 2 = 0$ and $3a + 3 = 0$

$a = -1$ and $a = -1$

Hence, $x = (-1) + 1 = 0$.

**Angle Between a Line and a Plane:** Let equations of the line and plane be

$$\frac{x-x_1}{l} = \frac{y-y_1}{m} = \frac{z-z_1}{n},$$

and $ax + by + cz + d = 0$ respectively and $\theta$ be the angle which line makes with the plane. Then $(\pi/2 - \theta)$ is the angle between the line and the normal to the plane. So,

$$\sin\theta = \frac{al+bm+cn}{\sqrt{(a^2+b^2+c^2)}\sqrt{(l^2+m^2+n^2)}}$$

Line is parallel to plane if $\theta = 0$

*i.e.*, if $al + bm + cn = 0$

Line is $\perp$ to the plane if line is parallel to the normal of the plane, *i.e.*, if $\frac{a}{l} = \frac{b}{m} = \frac{c}{n}$.

**Condition in Order that the Line may Lie on the given Plane:** The line $\frac{x-x_1}{l} = \frac{y-y_1}{m} = \frac{z-z_1}{n}$ will lie on the plane $Ax + By + Cz + D = 0$ if

(*a*) $Al + Bm + Cn = 0$ and

(*b*) $Ax_1 + By_1 + Cz_1 + D = 0$

**Shortest Distance Between Two Skew Straight Lines:** Shortest distance between two skew lines is perpendicular to both.

**Magnitude and Equation to the Shortest Distance:**

**Ist method (Projection method):** Suppose the equation of the lines are

$$\frac{x-\alpha}{l} = \frac{y-\beta}{m} = \frac{z-\gamma}{n} \qquad \text{...(1)}$$

and $$\frac{x-\alpha'}{l'} = \frac{y-\beta'}{m'} = \frac{z-\gamma'}{n'} \qquad \text{...(2)}$$

Let $\lambda$, $\mu$, $\nu$, be d.c.'s of the shortest distance. Since shortest distance is perpendicular to each of the given lines, therefore $l\lambda + m\mu + n\nu = 0$; and $l'\lambda + m'\mu + n'\nu = 0$.

Now solving these, we get

$$\frac{\lambda}{mn'-m'n} = \frac{\mu}{nl'-n'l} = \frac{\nu}{lm'-l'm} = \frac{1}{\sqrt{\Sigma(mn'-m'n)^2}}$$

$$\therefore \quad \lambda = \frac{mn'-m'n}{\sqrt{\Sigma(mn'-m'n)^2}}, \ \mu = \frac{nl'-n'l}{\sqrt{\Sigma(mn'-m'n)^2}},$$

$$\nu = \frac{lm'-l'm}{\sqrt{\Sigma(mn'-m'n)^2}}$$

$P(\alpha, \beta, \gamma)$ is a point on line (1) and $Q(\alpha', \beta', \gamma')$ is a point on line (2). Shortest distance will be the projection of the line PQ, joining these points on the line whose d.c.'s are $\lambda$, $\mu$, $\nu$.

$\therefore$ Shortest distance $= (\alpha - \alpha')\lambda + (\beta - \beta')\mu + (\gamma - \gamma')\nu$

$$= \frac{(\alpha-\alpha')(mn'-m'n)+(\beta-\beta')(nl'-n'l)+(\gamma-\gamma')(lm'-l'm)}{\sqrt{\{\Sigma(mn'-m'n)^2\}}}$$

$$= \begin{vmatrix} \alpha-\alpha' & \beta-\beta' & \gamma-\gamma' \\ l & m & n \\ l' & m' & n' \end{vmatrix} \div \sqrt{\{\Sigma(mn'-m'n)^2\}}$$

Equation to the plane containing line (1) and the shortest distance is

$$\begin{vmatrix} x-\alpha & y-\beta & z-\gamma \\ l & m & n \\ \lambda & \mu & \nu \end{vmatrix} = 0 \qquad \text{...(3)}$$

Equation to the plane containing the line (2) and the shortest distance is

$$\begin{vmatrix} x-\alpha' & y-\beta' & z-\gamma' \\ l' & m' & n' \\ \lambda & \mu & \nu \end{vmatrix} = 0 \qquad \text{...(4)}$$

Equation (3) and (4) will represent the shortest distance between the given lines (1) and (2).

**2nd method (Foot method):** A point on (1) is $P(lr + \alpha, mr + \beta, nr + \gamma)$ and a point on (2) is $Q(l's + \alpha', m's + \beta', n's + \gamma')$

If P and Q are the points of intersections of shortest distance with the given line, then PQ is perpendicular to both the lines. If $\lambda$, $\mu$, $\nu$ be the d.r.'s of shortest distance, then $\lambda = lr + \alpha - l's - \alpha'$, $\mu = mr + \beta - m's - \beta'$ and $\nu = nr + \gamma - n's - \gamma'$

$\therefore$ $l\lambda - m\mu + n\nu = 0$ and $l'\lambda - m'\mu + n'\nu = 0$.

Solving these equations, we can find $r$ and $s$ and then P and Q.

Now, we can find S.D. which is PQ, its equation is the equation through P and Q.

**3rd method (Vector method):** Since $l$, $m$, $n$ and $l'$, $m'$, $n'$ are d.c.'s of the lines, unit vectors in their direction are

$\hat{e} = l\hat{i} + m\hat{j} + n\hat{k}$ and $= \hat{e}' = l'i + m'j + n'k$.

Let RS be the S.D., then $\overrightarrow{RS}$ is $\perp$ to both.

So, RS = projection of PQ on RS $= \frac{\overrightarrow{PQ}.(\hat{e}\times\hat{e}')}{|\hat{e}\times\hat{e}'|}$.

**Sphere:** A sphere is the locus of a point which remains at a constant disance from a fixed point. The constant distance is called the radius and the fixed point, the centre of the sphere.

**Equation of a Sphere:** Let $(a, b, c)$ be the centre and $r$ be the radius of a given sphere. Then the equation of the sphere is

$$(x - a)^2 + (y - b)^2 + (z - c)^2 = r^2.$$

**General Equation of a Sphere:** The equation

$$x^2 + y^2 + z^2 + 2ux + 2vy + 2wx + d = 0$$

represents a sphere with centre at $(-u, -v, -w)$ and radius $\sqrt{(u^2 + v^2 + w^2 - d)}$ if $u^2 + v^2 + w^2 - d > 0$.

**Sphere with a given Diameter:** The equation of the sphere described on the segment joining points $A(x_1, y_1, z_1)$ and $B(x_2, y_2, z_2)$ as a diameter is

$$(x - x_1)(x - x_2) + (y - y_1)(y - y_2) + (z - z_1)(z - z_2) = 0$$

**Equation of Sphere Through Four Points:** Equation of the sphere passing through four non-coplanar points $(x_1, y_1, z_1)$, $(x_2, y_2, z_2)$, $(x_3, y_3, z_3)$ and $(x_4, y_4, z_4)$ is

$$\begin{vmatrix} x^2+y^2+z^2 & x & y & z & 1 \\ x_1^2+y_1^2+z_1^2 & x_1 & y_1 & z_1 & 1 \\ x_2^2+y_2^2+z_2^2 & x_2 & y_2 & z_2 & 1 \\ x_3^2+y_3^2+z_3^2 & x_3 & y_3 & z_3 & 1 \\ x_4^2+y_4^2+z_4^2 & x_4 & y_4 & z_4 & 1 \end{vmatrix} = 0$$

## MULTIPLE CHOICE QUESTIONS

**1.** The ratio in which the line joining (2, 4, 5), (3, 5, –4) is divided by the Y-Z plane is

A. 2 : 3 B. 3 : 2
C. –2 : 3 D. 4 : –3

**2.** A straight line which makes an angle of 60° with each of $y$ and $z$ axes, is inclined with $x$-axis at an angle

A. 45° B. 30°
C. 75° D. 60°

**3.** The projection of line joining (3, 4, 5) and (4, 6, 3) on the line joining (–1, 2, 4) and (1, 0, 5) is

A. 4/3 B. 2/3
C. 8/3 D. 1/3

**4.** The coordinates of a point P are (3, 12, 4) with respect to the origin O. Then the direction cosines of OP are

A. 3, 12, 4
B. 1/4, 1/3, 1/2
C. $3/\sqrt{(13)}, 1/\sqrt{(13)}, 2/\sqrt{(13)}$
D. 3/13, 12/13, 4/13

**5.** The graph of the equation $y^2 + z^2 = 0$ in three dimensional space is

A. $x$-axis B. $y$-axis
C. $z$-axis D. $yz$-plane

**6.** A line makes angles $\alpha, \beta, \gamma, \delta$ with the four diagonals of a cube, then $\cos^2 \alpha + \cos^2 \beta + \cos^2 \gamma + \cos^2 \delta$ has the value

A. 0 B. 2
C. 4/3 D. 5/3

**7.** The straight lines whose direction cosines are given by $al + bm + cn = 0$, $fmn + gnl + hlm = 0$ are perpendicular if

A. $\frac{f}{a} + \frac{g}{b} + \frac{h}{c} = 0$
B. $\sqrt{(a/f)} + \sqrt{(b/g)} + \sqrt{(c/h)} = 0$
C. $\sqrt{(af)} = \sqrt{(bg)} = \sqrt{(ch)}$
D. $\sqrt{(a/f)} = \sqrt{(b/g)} = \sqrt{(c/h)}$

**8.** A line segment (vector) has length 21 and direction ratios (2, –3, 6). If the line makes an obtuse angle with $x$-axis, the components of the line (vector) are

A. 6, – 9, 18 B. 2, – 3, 6
C. – 18, 27, – 54 D. – 6, 9, – 18

**9.** Direction cosines of the line which is perpendicular to the lines whose direction ratios are 1, – 1, 2 and 2, 1, – 1, are given by

A. $[-1/\sqrt{(35)}, 5/\sqrt{(35)}, 3/\sqrt{(35)}]$
B. $[-1/\sqrt{(35)}, -5/\sqrt{(35)}, 3/\sqrt{(35)}]$
C. $[1/\sqrt{(35)}, 5/\sqrt{(35)}, -3/\sqrt{(35)}]$
D. None of these

**10.** The angle between pair of lines whose direction ratios are 1, 1, 2 and $\sqrt{3} - 1, -\sqrt{3} - 1, 4$ is

A. 30° B. 45°
C. 60° D. 90°

**11.** If centroid of the tetrahedron OABC, where A, B and C are given by $(a, 1, 2)$, $(2, b, 1)$ and $(3, 2, c)$ respectively, be (1, 2, 3), then distance of $P(a, b, c)$ from origin is equal to

A. $\sqrt{(107)}$ B. $\sqrt{(14)}$
C. $\sqrt{(107/4)}$ D. None of these

**12.** The three lines drawn from O with direction ratios $[1, -1, k]$, $[2, -3, 0]$ and $[1, 0, 3]$ are coplanar. Then $k = ?$

A. 1 B. 0
C. no such $k$ exists D. None of these

**13.** The foot of the perpendicular from (0, 2, 3) to the line $\frac{x+3}{5} = \frac{y-1}{2} = \frac{z+4}{3}$ is

A. (–2, 3, 4) B. (2, – 1, 3)
C. (2, 3, – 1) D. (3, 2, – 1)

**14.** The equation of the plane passing through the point (– 2, – 2, 2) and containing the line joining the points (1, 1, 1) and (1, – 1, 2) is

A. $x + 2y - 3z + 4 = 0$
B. $3x - 4y + 1 = 0$
C. $5x - 2y - 3z - 17 = 0$
D. $x - 3y - 6z + 8 = 0$

**15.** If the plane $x - 2y + 3z = 0$ is rotated through a right angle about its line of intersection with the plane $2x + 3y - 4z - 5 = 0$, then the equation of plane in its new position is

A. $28x - 17y + 9z = 0$
B. $22x + 5y - 4z - 35 = 0$

C. $25x + 17y + 52z - 25 = 0$
D. $x + 35y - 10z - 70 = 0$

**16.** If from a point P(*a, b, c*) perpendiculars PA,PB are drawn to YZ and ZX planes, then the equation of the plane OAB is
A. $bcx + cay + abz = 0$
B. $bcx + cay - abz = 0$
C. $bcx - cay + abz = 0$
D. $-bcx + cay + abz = 0$

**17.** A plane meets the coordinate axes in A, B, C and (α, β, γ) is the centroid of the Δ ABC. Then the equation of the plane is
A. $x/\alpha + y/\beta + z/\gamma = 3$
B. $x/\alpha + y/\beta + z/\gamma = 1$
C. $3x/\alpha + 3y/\beta + 3z/\gamma = 1$
D. $\alpha x + \beta y + \gamma z = 1$

**18.** Equation of the plane perpendicular to the plane $x - 2y + 5z + 1 = 0$ which passes through the points (2, – 3, 1) and (– 1, 1, – 7) is given by
A. $4x - 4y + z + 7 = 0$
B. $4x + 7y + 2z + 11 = 0$
C. $2x + y - z = 0$
D. None of these

**19.** The volume of the terahedron included between the plane $2x - 3y + 4z - 12 = 0$ and the three coordinate planes is
A. $3\sqrt{(29)}$ B. $6\sqrt{(29)}$
C. 12 D. None of these

**20.** Equation of the plane through P(2, 3 –1) at right angle to OP is
A. $2x + 3y - z = 14$ B. $2x + 3y - z = \sqrt{(14)}$
C. $2x + y - z = 14$ D. None of these

**21.** Equation of the plane that passes through the point (2, –3, 1) and is perpendicular to the line joining the points (3, 4, – 1) and (2, – 1, 5) is given by
A. $x + 5y - 6z + 19 = 0$ B. $x - 5y + 6z - 23 = 0$
C. $x + 5y - 6z = 19$ D. None of these

**22.** The coordinates of the point of intersection of the line $\frac{x+1}{1} = \frac{y+3}{3} = \frac{z+2}{-2}$ with the plane $3x + 4y + 5z = 5$ are
A. (5, 15, – 14) B. (3, 4, 5)
C. (1, 3, – 2) D. (3, 12, – 10)

**23.** The direction cosines of two lines at right angles are $l_1, m_1, n_1$ and $l_2, m_2, n_2$.
Then the d.c.'s of a line ⊥ to both the given lines are
A. $m_1n_2 - m_2n_1, n_1l_2 - n_2l_1, l_1m_2 - l_2m_1$
B. $l_1 + l_2, m_1 + m_2, n_1 + n_2$
C. $l_1 - l_2, m_1 - m_2, n_1 - n_2$
D. None of these

**24.** The line $\frac{x-2}{3} = \frac{y-3}{4} = \frac{z-4}{5}$ is parallel to the plane
A. $2x + y - 2z = 0$
B. $3x + 4y - 5z = 7$
C. $x + y + z = 2$
D. $2x + 3y + 4z = 0$

**25.** If the line $x = ay + b, z = cy + d$ and the line $x = a'y + b', z = c'y + d'$ are perpendicular, then
A. $aa' + bb' = 1$ B. $aa' + cc' = -1$
C. $aa' + bb' = 0$ D. None of these

**26.** The coordinates of the foot of the perpendicular from the point (1, 3, 4) upon the plane $2x - y + z = 0$ are
A. (1, 1, – 4) B. (4, – 3, 1)
C. (1, – 3, 4) D. (– 1, 4, 3)

**27.** The angle between the lines $x = 1, y = 2$ and $y = -1$ and $z = 0$ is
A. 90° B. 30°
C. 60° D. 0°

**28.** P is a fixed point (*a, a, a*) on a line through the origin equally inclined to the axes, then any plane through P ⊥ to OP, makes intercepts on the axes, the sum of whose reciprocals is equal to
A. *a* B. 3/2*a*
C. 3*a*/2 D. None of these

**29.** The equations of the projection of the line
$$\frac{x-1}{2} = \frac{y-2}{1} = \frac{z-3}{3}$$
on the plane $x + y + z - 1 = 0$ are
A. $x + y + z - 1 = 0 = 2x - y - z + 3$
B. $x + y - z - 1 = 0 = x + 2y - z - 3$
C. $2x - y + 3z - 1 = 0 = x + y + z + 1$
D. $x + 2y - 3z = 0 = x + y + z - 1$

**30.** A straight line passes through the point (2, – 1, – 1). It is parallel to the plane $4x + y + z + 2 = 0$ and is perpendicular to the line $x/1 = y/(-2) = (z - 5)/1$. The equation of the straight line are
A. $(x - 2)/4 = (y + 1)/1 = (z + 1)/1$
B. $(x + 2)/4 = (y - 1)/1 = (z - 1)/3$
C. $(x - 2)/(-1) = (y + 1)/1 = (z + 1)/3$
D. $(x + 2)/(-1) = (y - 1)/1 = (z - 1)/3$

**31.** The distance of the point (3, 8, 2) from the line $\frac{x-1}{2} = \frac{y-3}{4} = \frac{z-2}{3}$ measured parallel to the plane $3x + 2y - 2z + 5 = 0$ is
A. 2 B. 3
C. 5 D. None of these

**32.** The angle between the lines in which the planes $3x - 7y - 5z = 1$, $5x - 13y + 3z + 2 = 0$ cut the plane $8x - 11y + 2z = 0$ is
A. $\pi/3$ B. $\pi$
C. $\pi/2$ D. $2\pi/3$

**33.** The shortest distance between the lines

$$\frac{x-1}{2}=\frac{y-2}{3}=\frac{z-3}{4} \text{ and } \frac{x-2}{3}=\frac{y-4}{4}=\frac{z-5}{5} \text{ is}$$

A. 1/6 B. $1/\sqrt{6}$
C. $(1/\sqrt{3})$ D. 1/3

**34.** The image of the point (1, 3, 4) w.r.t. the plane $2x - y + z + 3 = 0$ is
A. (– 1, 4, 3) B. (– 3, 5, 2)
C. (1, 3, 4) D. None of these

**35.** A plane passes through a fixed point $(a, b, c)$. The locus of the foot of the perpendicular drawn to it from the origin is
A. $x^2 + y^2 + z^2 + ax + by + cz = 0$
B. $x^2 + y^2 + z^2 - ax - by - cz = 0$
C. $x^2 + y^2 + z^2 + 2ax + 2by + 2cz = 0$
D. $x^2 + y^2 + z^2 + 2ax - 2by - 2cz = 0$

**36.** A sphere of constant radius $2k$ passes through the origin and meets the axis in A, B, C. The locus of the centroid of the tetrahedron OABC is
A. $x^2 + y^2 + z^2 = 4k^2$
B. $x^2 + y^2 + z^2 = k^2$
C. $2(x^2 + y^2 + z^2) = k^2$
D. None of these

**37.** The equation of the sphere with centre at (2, 3, – 4) and touching the plane $2x + 6y - 3z + 15 = 0$ is
A. $x^2 + y^2 + z^2 - 4x - 6y + 8z - 20 = 0$
B. $x^2 + y^2 + z^2 + 4x - 6y - 8z - 20 = 0$
C. $x^2 + y^2 + z^2 - 4x - 6y + 8z + 20 = 0$
D. None of these

**38.** A sphere $x^2 + y^2 + z^2 = 9$ is cut by the plane $x + y + z = 3$. The radius of the circle so formed is
A. $\sqrt{6}$ B. $\sqrt{3}$
C. 3 D. 6

**39.** The plane $2x - 2y + z + 12 = 0$ touches the sphere $x^2 + y^2 + z^2 - 2x - 4y + 2z - 3 = 0$ at the point
A. (1, – 4, – 2) B. (– 1, 4, – 2)
C. (– 1, – 4, 2) D. (1, 4, – 2)

## ANSWERS

| **1** | **2** | **3** | **4** | **5** | **6** | **7** | **8** | **9** | **10** |
|---|---|---|---|---|---|---|---|---|---|
| C | A | A | D | A | C | A | D | A | C |
| **11** | **12** | **13** | **14** | **15** | **16** | **17** | **18** | **19** | **20** |
| D | A | C | D | B | B | A | B | C | A |
| **21** | **22** | **23** | **24** | **25** | **26** | **27** | **28** | **29** | **30** |
| A | C | A | A | B | D | A | D | A | C |
| **31** | **32** | **33** | **34** | **35** | **36** | **37** | **38** | **39** | |
| D | C | B | B | B | B | A | A | B | |

## EXPLANATORY ANSWERS

**1.** Let the required ratio be λ : 1.
Then the point is

$$\frac{3\lambda+2}{\lambda+1}, \frac{5\lambda+4}{\lambda+1}, \frac{-4\lambda+5}{\lambda}$$

It lies on YZ plane, so its $x$-coordinate = 0
*i.e.,* $\lambda = -2/3$ ∴ Ratio is – 2: 3
*i.e.,* – 2 : 3 externally.

**2.** Let α be the angle. Then the d.c.'s of the line are cos α, 1/2, 1/2.
∴ $\cos^2 \alpha + 1/4 + 1/4 = 1$, *i.e.,* $\cos^2 \alpha = 1/2$ or $\alpha = 45°$.

**3.** Direction ratios of the line joining (– 1, 2, 4) and (1, 0, 5) are 2, – 2, 1 so its d.c.'s are 2/3, – 2/3, 1/3.
∴ Length of projection of the line segment joining points (3, 4, 5) and (4, 6, 3)
$= |(1/3)[(4 - 3)2 + (6 - 4)(-2) + (-2)(1)]|$
$= |(1/3)[2 - 4 - 2]| = 4/3.$

**4.** $OP = \sqrt{(3^2 + 12^2 + 4^2)} = 13 = r$ (say)
Let d.c.'s of OP be $l, m, n$
∴ $x = lr, y = mr, z = nr$
⇒ $l = x/r, n = y/r, n = z/r,$
*i.e.,* $l = 3/13, m = 12/13, n = 4/13.$

**5.** $y^2 + z^2 = 0 \Rightarrow y = 0, z = 0.$
In three dimensional space, $y = 0, z = 0$ represents $x$-$z$ plane, $x$-$y$ plane respectively whose intersection is $x$-axis.

**6.**

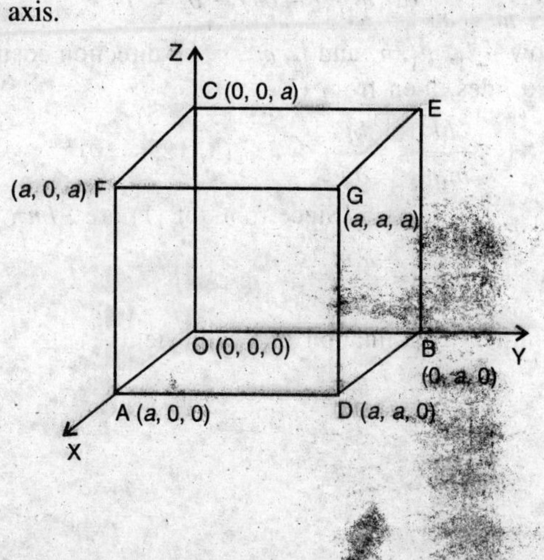

The four diagonals of the cube are OG, AE, BF and DC.

The direction ratios of these diagonals are as follows:

d.r.'s of OG are $a - 0$, $a - 0$, $a - 0$, *i.e.*, $a, a, a$

d.r.'s of AE are $0 - a$, $a - 0$, $a - 0$, *i.e.*, $-a, a, a$

d.r.'s of BF are $a - 0$, $0 - a$, $a - 0$, *i.e.*, $a, -a, a$

d.r.'s of DC are $0 - a$, $0 - a$, $a - 0$, *i.e.*, $-a, -a, a$

Let d.r.'s of the given line be $x, y, z$.

Let given line makes angles $\alpha, \beta, \gamma, \delta$ with the diagonals OG, AE, BF and DC respectively.

Then $\cos\alpha = \dfrac{xa + ya + za}{\sqrt{a^2 + a^2 + a^2}\sqrt{x^2 + y^2 + z^2}}$

$= \dfrac{xa + ya + za}{\sqrt{3a^2}\sqrt{x^2 + y^2 + z^2}} = \dfrac{x + y + z}{\sqrt{3}\sqrt{x^2 + y^2 + z^2}}$

$\therefore \quad \cos^2\alpha = \dfrac{(x + y + z)^2}{3(x^2 + y^2 + z^2)}$

Similarly,

$\cos^2\beta = \dfrac{(-x + y + z)^2}{3(x^2 + y^2 + z^2)}$

$\cos^2\gamma = \dfrac{(x - y + z)^2}{3(x^2 + y^2 + z^2)}$

$\cos^2\delta = \dfrac{(-x - y + z)^2}{3(x^2 + y^2 + z^2)}$

Thus $\cos^2\alpha + \cos^2\beta + \cos^2\gamma + \cos^2\delta$

$= \dfrac{1}{3(x^2 + y^2 + z^2)}[(x + y + z)^2 + (-x + y + z)^2 + (x - y + z)^2 + (-x - y + z)^2]$

$= 4/3.$

**7.** From the first relation

$n = -\dfrac{al + bm}{c}$

Putting it in second relation

$fm\left(-\dfrac{al + bm}{c}\right) + gl\left(-\dfrac{al + bm}{c}\right) + hlm = 0,$

or $afml + bfm^2 + agl^2 + bglm - chlm = 0,$

$ag\dfrac{l^2}{m^2} + \dfrac{l}{m}(af + bg - ch) + bf = 0 \qquad \text{...(1)}$

Now if $l_1, m_1, n_1$ and $l_2, m_2, n_2$ be direction cosines of two lines, then from (1)

$\dfrac{l_1l_2}{m_1m_2} = \dfrac{bf}{ag},$

[Since roots of (1) are $l_1/m_1$, $l_2/m_2$]

or $\dfrac{l_1l_2}{f/a} = \dfrac{m_1m_2}{g/b}$

Similarly, elimination of $l$ will yield

$\dfrac{m_1m_2}{g/b} = \dfrac{n_1n_2}{h/c}$

$\therefore \quad \dfrac{l_1l_2}{f/a} = \dfrac{m_1m_2}{g/b} = \dfrac{n_1n_2}{h/c} = q$ (say)

We know that the lines are perpendicular if

$l_1l_2 + m_1m_2 + n_1n_2 = 0,$

*i.e.*, if $(f/a)q + (g/b)q + (h/c)q = 0,$

*i.e.*, if $f/a + g/b + h/c = 0.$

**8.** Let components of the vector (line segment) be $a, b, c$.

Then $a^2 + b^2 + c^2 = 21^2 = 441$

$\dfrac{a}{2} = \dfrac{b}{-3} = \dfrac{c}{6} = \lambda$ (say)

and $a < 0$

$\therefore \quad \lambda^2 [4 + 9 + 36] = 441 \Rightarrow \lambda^2 = 9$

Since $a = 2\lambda < 0$, $\lambda = -3$

$\therefore$ Components are $-6, 9, -18$.

**9.** If $l, m, n$ are the d.c.'s of the line which is perpendicular to the given lines, then

$1.l - 1.m + 2.n = 0$

and $2.l + 1.m - 1.n = 0$

$\therefore \quad \dfrac{l}{1-2} = \dfrac{m}{4+1} = \dfrac{n}{1+2}$

*i.e.*, $\dfrac{l}{-1} = \dfrac{m}{5} = \dfrac{n}{3} = \dfrac{\sqrt{(l^2 + m^2 + n^2)}}{\sqrt{(1 + 25 + 9)}} = \dfrac{1}{\sqrt{35}}$

$\Rightarrow l = -1/\sqrt{(35)},\ m = 5/\sqrt{(35)},\ n = 3/\sqrt{(35)}.$

**10.** D.c.'s of the line are $1/\sqrt{6}, 1/\sqrt{6}, 2/\sqrt{6}$ and $(\sqrt{3} - 1)/2\sqrt{6}$, $(-\sqrt{3} - 1)2\sqrt{6}$, $4/2\sqrt{6}$

$\therefore \quad \sqrt{(1^2 + 1^2 + 2^2)} = \sqrt{6}$

and $\sqrt{[(\sqrt{3} - 1)^2 + (-\sqrt{3} - 1)^2 + 4^2]} = \sqrt{(24)} = 2\sqrt{6}.$

If $\theta$ is the angle between the lines then

$\cos\theta = l_1l_2 + m_1m_2 + n_1n_2$

$= \dfrac{1}{\sqrt{6}}\cdot\dfrac{\sqrt{3} - 1}{2\sqrt{6}} + \dfrac{1}{\sqrt{6}}\cdot\dfrac{-\sqrt{3} - 1}{2\sqrt{6}} + \dfrac{2}{\sqrt{6}}\cdot\dfrac{4}{2\sqrt{6}} = \dfrac{1}{2}$

$\Rightarrow \quad \theta = 60°.$

**11.** Coordinates of the centroid, say G of tetrahedron OABC are

$\left(\dfrac{0 + a + 1 + 2}{4}, \dfrac{0 + 2 + b + 1}{4}, \dfrac{0 + 3 + 2 + c}{4}\right)$

*i.e.*, $[(a + 3)/4, (b + 3)/4, (c + 5)/4]$.

If the centroid is (1, 2, 3) then

$(a + 3)/4 = 1,\ (b + 3)/4 = 2,\ (c + 5)/4 = 3$

$\Rightarrow \quad a = 1, b = 5, c = 7$

$\therefore$ Coordinates of P are $(a, b, c)$, *i.e.*, (1, 5, 7)

$\therefore \quad PG = \sqrt{\{(1 - 1)^2 + (5 - 2)^2 + (7 - 3)^2\}} = 5.$

**12.** If lines are coplanar and $l, m, n$ are d.c.'s of the normal on the plane, then

$1.l - 1.m + k.n = 0$

$2.l - 3.m + 0.n = 0$

$1.l + 0.m + 3.n = 0$

$$\Rightarrow \begin{vmatrix} 1 & -1 & k \\ 2 & -3 & 0 \\ 1 & 0 & 3 \end{vmatrix} = 0 \Rightarrow k = 1.$$

**13.** Any point on the given line is $(5r - 3, 2r + 1, 3r - 4)$. If it is the foot of the perpendicular from (1, 2, 3), then

$5(5r - 3 - 0) + 2(2r + 1 - 2) + 3(3r - 4 - 3) = 0$

*i.e.,* $38r = 38$, *i.e.,* $r = 1$

$\therefore$ Foot of perpendicular is (2, 3, – 1).

**14.** Equation of a plane through (–2, –2, 2) is given by

$a(x + 2) + b(y + 2) + c(z - 2) = 0$

It contains the line joining the points (1, 1, 1) and (1, –1, 2), so these points also lie in the plane.

$\therefore$ $3a + 3b - c = 0,$

$3a + b + 0.c = 0$

$\therefore$ $\frac{a}{1} = \frac{b}{-3} = \frac{c}{-6} = r$ (say)

or $a = r, b = -3r, c = -6r$

$\therefore$ Equation of the plane is

$x - 3y - 6z + 8 = 0.$

**15.** The equation of the given plane is

$x - 2y + 3z = 0$ ...(1)

Equation of plane through the line of intersection of plane (1) and plane $2x + 3y - 4z - 5 = 0$, can be taken as

$(x - 2y + 3z) + \lambda(2x + 3y - 4z - 5) = 0$

*i.e.,* $(1 + 2\lambda)x + (-2 + 3\lambda)y + (3 - 4\lambda)z - 5\lambda = 0$ ...(2)

If angle between planes (1) and (2) is 90°, then

$1.(1 + 2\lambda) - 2.(-2 + 3\lambda) + 3.(3 - 4\lambda) = 0$

$\Rightarrow$ $\lambda = 7/8$

Putting in (2) the equation of the plane in the new position is $22x + 5y - 4z - 35 = 0$.

**16.** A and B, foot of perpendicular from P(*a, b, c*) to *y-z* plane and *z-x* plane, are given by A(0, *b, c*) and (*a*, 0, *c*). A plane through origin (0, 0, 0) is

$px + qy + rz = 0$ ...(1)

It passes through A and B, so

$0p + bq + cr = 0$

and $ap + 0q + cr = 0$

$\therefore$ $\frac{p}{bc} = \frac{q}{ac} = \frac{r}{-ab} = \lambda$ (say)

$\therefore$ The equation of the plane OAB is

$bcx + cay - abz = 0.$

**17.** Let the equation of the plane be

$x/a + y/b + z/c = 1$ ...(1)

Plane (1) meets the axes at A(*a*, 0, 0), B(0, *b*, 0) and C(0, 0, *c*).

If $(\alpha, \beta, \gamma)$ is the centroid of the $\Delta$ ABC, then

$\alpha = (a + 0 + 0)/3,$

$\beta = (0 + b + 0)/3,$

$\gamma = (0 + 0 + c)/3$

*i.e.,* $a = 3\alpha, b = 3\beta, c = 3\gamma$

Putting in (1), the equation of the required plane is

$x/\alpha + y/\beta + z/\gamma = 3.$

**18.** Equation of a plane through (2, – 3, 1) is

$a(x - 2) + b(y + 3) + c(z - 1) = 0$ ...(1)

It passes through (– 1, 1, – 7), so

$-3a + 4b - 8c = 0$ ...(2)

It is perpendicular to the plane

$x - 2y + 5z + 1 = 0,$

so $a - 2b + 5c = 0$ ...(3)

Solving (2) and (3), we get

$\frac{a}{4} = \frac{b}{7} = \frac{c}{2} = \lambda$

Putting these values of *a, b, c* in (1), equation of the required plane is

$4x + 7y + 2z + 11 = 0.$

**19.** Vertices of the tetrahedron are (0, 0, 0), (6, 0, 0), (0, – 4, 0), (0, 0, 3)

$$\therefore \quad \text{Volume} = \frac{1}{6}\begin{vmatrix} 0 & 0 & 0 & 1 \\ 6 & 0 & 0 & 1 \\ 0 & -4 & 0 & 1 \\ 0 & 0 & 3 & 1 \end{vmatrix} = 12.$$

**20.** Coordinates of the given point P are (2, 3, – 1)

OP is normal to the required plane so direction ratios of the normal to the plane are 2, 3, – 1.

Equation of the plane through P(2, 3, –1) is $a(x - 2) + b(y - 3) + c(z + 1) = 0$

Since, the direction ratios of the normal to the plane are 2, 3, – 1,

so, we have $a/2 = b/3 = c/(-1)$ and hence the equation of the required plane is

$2(x - 2) + 3(y - 3) - 1(z + 1) = 0$

or $2x + 3y - z = 14.$

**21.** Direction ratios of the line joining the point A(3, 4, – 1), B(2, – 1, 5) are

3 – 2, 4 + 1, – 1 – 5, *i.e.,* 1, 5, – 6.

Equation of the plane through P(2, –3, 1) is

$a(x - 2) + b(y + 3) + c(z - 1) = 0$ ...(1)

The plane is perpendicular to the line AB so the direction ratios of the normal to the plane (1) are 1, 5, – 6 and hence, we have

$\frac{a}{1} = \frac{b}{5} = \frac{c}{-6},$

therefore the equation of the required plane is

$1(x - 2) + 5(y + 3) - 6(z - 1) = 0.$

or $x + 5y - 6z + 19 = 0.$

**22.** Equation of the line is

$\frac{x+1}{1} = \frac{y+3}{3} = \frac{z-2}{-2} = r$ (say) ...(1)

Any point on it can be written as

$(r - 1, 3r - 3, - 2r + 2)$

If this point is the point of intersection of the line (1) and plane

$3x + 4y + 5z = 5$ ...(2)

Then, this point should lie on the plane (2),

so $3(r - 1) + 4(3r - 3) + 5(- 2r + 2) = 5$

*i.e.,* $5r - 5 = 5$ or $r = 2$

$\therefore$ Required point of intersection is (1, 3, – 2).

**23.** Let $l, m, n$ be the direction cosines of the line $\perp$ to both. Therefore

$$ll_1 + mm_1 + nn_1 = 0,$$

and $ll_2 + mm_2 + nn_2 = 0$

$$\therefore \quad \frac{l}{m_1n_2 - m_2n_1} = \frac{m}{n_1l_2 - n_2l_1} = \frac{n}{l_1m_2 - l_2m_1}$$

$$= \frac{\sqrt{[l^2 + m^2 + n^2]}}{\sqrt{\Sigma(m_1n_2 - m_2n_1)^2}}$$

Now $l^2 + m^2 + n^2 = 1$ and

$\sqrt{\Sigma}(m_1n_2 - m_2n_1)^2 = \sin\theta = \sin 90 = 1$

[$\because$ given lines are $\perp$]

$\therefore$ d.c.'s are

$m_1n_2 - m_2n_1,\ n_1l_2 - n_2l_1,\ l_1m_2 - l_2m_1.$

**24.** The line $\dfrac{x-\alpha}{l} = \dfrac{y-\beta}{m} = \dfrac{z-\lambda}{n}$ is parallel to the plane

$ax + by + cz + d = 0$

If the line is $\perp$ to the normal to the plane, *i.e.,*

$al + bm + cn = 0$

In this question, this condition is satisfied by the plane $2x + y - 2z = 0$.

**25.** The equation of the two lines can be written as

$$\frac{x-b}{a} = \frac{y-0}{1} = \frac{z-d}{c}$$

and $$\frac{x-b'}{a'} = \frac{y-0}{1} = \frac{z-d'}{c'}$$

$\therefore$ The lines are perpendicular if

$a.a' + 1.1 + c.c' = 0$, *i.e.,* $aa' + cc' = - 1$.

**26.** Perpendicular to the plane is parallel to the normal to the plane, so d.r.'s of the line $\perp$ to the plane

$2x - y + z + 3 = 0$ are 2, – 1, 1

$\therefore$ Equation of $\perp$ drawn through the point (1, 3, 4) is

$$\frac{x-1}{2} = \frac{y-3}{-1} = \frac{z-4}{1} = r \text{ (say)}$$

Any point on it is $(2r + 1, - r + 3, r + 4)$. If this is the foot of the $\perp$, then it should lie on the plane.

$\therefore$ $2(2r + 1) - (- r + 3) + (r + 4) + 3 = 0$

*i.e.,* $6r + 6 = 0$, *i.e.,* $r = - 1$

So, foot of the perpendicular is (– 1, 4, 3).

**27.** The lines are

$$x = 1,\ y = 2,\ \textit{i.e.,}\ \frac{x-1}{0} = \frac{y-2}{0} = \frac{z}{1}$$

and $y = - 1, z = 0$ *i.e.* $\dfrac{x}{1} = \dfrac{y+1}{0} = \dfrac{z}{0}$

$\therefore$ If $\theta$ is the angle between them, then

$\cos\theta = 0.1 + 0.0 + 1.0 = 0$

*i.e.,* $\theta = 90°$.

**28.** Since the line is equally inclined to the axes, and passes through the origin, its direction cosines are 1, 1, 1. So its equation is

$$\frac{x}{1} = \frac{y}{1} = \frac{z}{1}$$

A point P on it is given by $(a, a, a)$. So equation of the plane through

P$(a, a, a)$ and $\perp$ to OP is

$1.(x - a) + 1.(y - a) + 1.(z - a) = 0$

[$\because$ OP is normal to the plane]

*i.e.,* $x + y + z = 3a$

or $$\frac{x}{3a} + \frac{y}{3a} + \frac{z}{3a} = 1$$

Intercepts on axes are $3a, 3a, 3a$, whose reciprocals are $1/3a, 1/3a, 1/3a$

$\therefore$ Sum of reciprocals of these intercepts

$$= \frac{1}{3a} + \frac{1}{3a} + \frac{1}{3a} = \frac{3}{3a} = \frac{1}{a}.$$

**29.** The projection of the line

$$\frac{x-1}{2} = \frac{y-2}{1} = \frac{z-3}{3} \quad ...(1)$$

on the plane $x + y + z - 1 = 0$ ...(2)

is the line of intersection of the plane (2) and the plane perpendicular to the plane (2) and containing the line (1).

Now, equation of the plane through line (1) can be taken as

$A(x - 1) + B(y - 2) + C(z - 3) = 0$ ...(3)

where $2.A + 1.B + 3.C = 0$ ...(4)

If plane (3) is perpendicular to the plane (2), then

$1.A + 1.B + 1.C = 0$ ...(5)

from (4) and (5)

$\Rightarrow A/(- 2) = B/1 = C/1 = k$ (say).

$\therefore$ $A = - 2k, B = k, C = k$

Putting in (3), we get

$2x - y - z + 3 = 0$ ...(6)

Hence the required projection is given by planes (2) and (6).

**30.** Let $a, b, c$ be the d.r.'s of the required line.

$\therefore$ Line is $\parallel$ to the plane $4x + y + z + 2 = 0$ and $\perp$ to the line $x/1 = y/(- 2) = (z - 5)/1$

$\therefore$ $4a + 1.b + 1.c = 0$ ...(1)

and $1.a - 2.b + 1.c = 0$ ...(2)

$\Rightarrow$ $a/3 = b/(-3) = c/(-9) = k$ (say)

$\therefore$ Equation of the required line is

$$\frac{x-2}{a} = \frac{y+1}{b} = \frac{z+1}{c}$$

*i.e.,* $(x-2)/3 = (y+1)/(-3) = (z+1)/(-9)$

*i.e.,* $(x-2)/(-1) = (y+1)/1 = (z+1)/3$.

**31.** Let the line through the point (3, 8, 2), say A and parallel to the plane

$3x + 2y - 2z + 5 = 0$ ...(1)

meet the line

$$\frac{x-1}{2} = \frac{y-3}{4} = \frac{z-2}{3} \quad ...(2)$$

at the point P $(1 + 2r, 3 + 4r, 2 + 3r)$

$\therefore$ d.r.'s of line AP are

$1 + 2r - 3, 3 + 4r - 8, 2 + 3r - 2$

*i.e.,* $2r - 2, 4r - 5, 3r$

$\because$ AP is parallel to the plane (1)

$\therefore$ $3(2r - 2) + 2(4r - 5) - 2(3r) = 0 \Rightarrow r = 2$

$\therefore$ Coordinates of P are (5, 11, 8)

$\therefore$ Required distance = AP = 7.

**32.** Let $l_1, m_1, n_1$ and $l_2, m_2, n_2$ be the d.r.'s of the lines in which the planes

$3x - 7y - 5z = 1$ and $5x - 13y + 3z + 2 = 0$ cut the plane $8x - 11y + 2z = 0$, then

$3l_1 - 7m_1 - 5n_1 = 0$

$8l_2 - 11m_2 + 2n_2 = 0$

$\therefore$ $l_1/(-69) = m_1/(-46) = n_1/23$

and $5l_2 - 13m_2 + 3n_2 = 0$

$8l_2 - 11m_2 + 2n_2 = 0$

$\therefore$ $l_2/7 = m_2/14 = n_2/49$.

If $\theta$ is the angle between the two lines, then

$$\cos\theta = \frac{l_1l_2 + m_1m_2 + n_1n_2}{\sqrt{(l_1^2 + m_1^2 + n_1^2)}\sqrt{(l_2^2 + m_2^2 + n_2^2)}} = 0$$

$\therefore$ $\theta = \pi/2$.

**33.** Shortest distant between the lines

$$\frac{x-\alpha}{l} = \frac{y-\beta}{m} = \frac{z-\gamma}{n}$$

and $\dfrac{x-\alpha'}{l'} = \dfrac{y-\beta'}{m'} = \dfrac{z-\gamma'}{n'}$ is given by

$$\text{Shortest distant} = \begin{vmatrix} \alpha-\alpha' & \beta-\beta' & \gamma-\gamma' \\ l & m & n \\ l' & m' & n' \end{vmatrix} \div \sqrt{\Sigma(mn' - m'n)^2}$$

Here lines are $\dfrac{x-1}{2} = \dfrac{y-2}{3} = \dfrac{z-3}{4} = r$ (say)

and $\dfrac{x-2}{3} = \dfrac{y-4}{4} = \dfrac{z-5}{5} = s$ (say)

$\therefore$ $\Sigma(mn' - m'n)^2 = \sqrt{(-1)^2 + (2)^2 + (1)^2} = \sqrt{6}$

$$\therefore \text{ Shortest distant} = \begin{vmatrix} 1 & 2 & 2 \\ 2 & 3 & 4 \\ 3 & 4 & 5 \end{vmatrix} \div \sqrt{6} = \frac{1}{\sqrt{6}}.$$

**34.** Equation of the line through A(1, 3, 4) are perpendicular to the plane

$2x - y + z + 3 = 0$ is

$$\frac{x-1}{2} = \frac{y-3}{-1} = \frac{z-4}{1} = r \text{ (say)}$$

Any point P on it is $(2r + 1, -r + 3, r + 4)$.

If this point is the image of (1, 3, 4), then mid-point of AP should lie on the plane.

$$\therefore 2\left(\frac{2r+1+1}{2}\right) - \left(\frac{-r+3+3}{2}\right) + \left(\frac{r+4+4}{2}\right) + 3 = 0$$

or $4r + 4 + r - 6 + r + 8 + 6 = 0$ or $r = -2$

$\therefore$ Image of (1, 3, 4) is $(-3, 5, 2)$.

**35.** Equation of plane through the point $(a, b, c)$ is

$\alpha(x - a) + \beta(y - b) + \gamma(z - c) = 0$. ...(1)

Equation of the perpendicular from origin (0, 0, 0) to this plane is

$$\frac{x}{\alpha} = \frac{y}{\beta} = \frac{z}{\gamma} = r \text{ (say)} \quad ...(2)$$

Let $P(x_1, y_1, z_1)$ be the foot of the perpendicular. Then it lies on (2) and plane (1), so

$x_1 = \alpha r, y_1 = \beta r, z_1 = \gamma r$

$$\therefore \frac{x_1}{r}(x_1 - a) + \frac{y_1}{r}(y_1 - b) + \frac{z_1}{r}(z_1 - c) = 0$$

*i.e.,* $x_1^2 + y_1^2 + z_1^2 - ax_1 - by_1 - cz_1 = 0$

Hence locus of P is

$x^2 + y^2 + z^2 - ax - by - cz = 0$.

**36.** Let OA = $a$, OB = $b$ and OC = $c$.

$\therefore$ Equation of sphere through O(0, 0, 0), A($a$, 0, 0), B(0, $b$, 0), C(0, 0, $c$) is

$x^2 + y^2 + z^2 - ax - by - cz = 0$ ...(1)

Radius of this sphere

$= \sqrt{(a^2/4 + b^2/4 + c^2/4)} = 2k$

$\Rightarrow$ $a^2 + b^2 + c^2 = 16k^2$ ...(2)

If $(f, g, h)$ is the centroid of the tetrahedron OABC, then $f = a/4$, $g = b/4$, $h = c/4$

*i.e,* $a = 4f$, $b = 4g$, $c = 4h$

Putting in (2), we get

$f^2 + g^2 + h^2 = k^2$

$\therefore$ Locus of centre $(f, g, h)$ is $x^2 + y^2 + z^2 = k^2$.

**37.** The centre of the sphere is given as (2, 3, – 4).

∴ Radius of the sphere

= length of perpendicular from the centre (2, 3, – 4) to the plane

$$2x + 6y - 3z + 15 = 0$$

$$= \frac{2.2 + 6.3 - 3(-4) + 15}{\sqrt{[2^2 + 6^2 + (-3)^2]}} = 7$$

∴ The equation of the required sphere is

$$(x - 2)^2 + (y - 3)^2 + (z + 4)^2 = (7)^2$$

*i.e.,* $x^2 + y^2 + z^2 - 4x - 6y + 8z - 20 = 0.$

**38.** For sphere $x^2 + y^2 + z^2 = 9$, centre C is (0, 0, 0) and radius CA = 3.

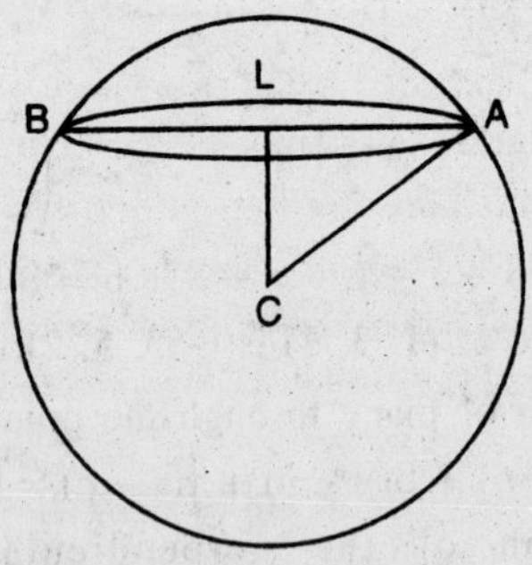


Now, CL = length of ⊥ from C on plane

$$x + y + z = 3$$

$$= \frac{3}{\sqrt{(1+1+1)}} = \sqrt{3}$$

In Δ ACL, AL = √(CA² – CL²) = √6.

**39.** Centre of the sphere

$x^2 + y^2 + z^2 - 2x - 4y + 2z - 3 = 0$ is

(1, 2, – 1) and radius is √(1 + 4 + 1 + 3) = 3

⊥ distance of centre from the plane

$2x - 2y + z + 12 = 0$

= (2.1 – 2.2 – 1 + 12)/√(4 + 4 + 1) = 3 = radius

∴ Plane touches the sphere.

Now point of contact is the foot of perpendicular drawn from the centre to the plane. Equation of line ⊥ to the plane from centre (1, 2, – 1) is

$$\frac{x-1}{2} = \frac{y-2}{-2} = \frac{z+1}{1} = r \text{ (say)}$$

Any point on it is $(2r + 1, -2r + 2, r - 1)$

This should lie on the plane

∴ $2(2r + 1) - 2(-2r + 2) + (r - 1) + 12 = 0$

or $r = -1$

∴ Point of contact is (– 1, 4, – 2).

CHAPTER

# 8

# LINEAR PROGRAMMING

## INTRODUCTION

Linear programming deals with the optimization (maximization or minimization) of a function of variables known as *objective function*, subject to a set of linear equalities and/or inequalities known as *constraints*. The objective function may be profit, cost, production capacity or any other measure of effectiveness, which is to be obtained in the best possible or optimal manner. The constraints may be imposed by different sources such as market demand, production processes and equipment, storage capacity, raw material availability, etc. By linearity is meant a mathematical expression in which the variables do not have powers.

### Requirements for a Linear Programming Problem

All organizations, big or small, have at their disposal, men, machines, money and materials, the supply of which may be limited. If the supply of these resources were unlimited, the need for management tools like linear programming would not arise at all. Supply of resources being limited, the management must find the best allocation of its resources in order to maximize the profit or minimize the loss or utilize the production capacity to the maximum extent. However, this involves a number of problems which can be overcome by quantitative methods, particularly the linear programming.

Generally speaking, linear programming can be used for optimization problems if the following conditions are satisfied:

1. There must be a well defined objective function (profit, cost or quantities produced) which is to be either maximized or minimized and which can be expressed as a linear function of decision variables.
2. There must be constraints on the amount or extent of attainment of the objective and these constraints must be capable of being expressed as linear equalities or inequalities in terms of variables.
3. There must be alternative courses of action. For example, a given product may be processed by two different machines and problem may be as to how much of the product to allocate to each machine.
4. Another necessary requirement is that decision variables should be interrelated and non- negative. The non-negativity condition shows that linear programming deals with real life situations for which negative quantities are generally illogical.
5. As stated earlier, the resources must be in limited supply. For example, if a firm starts producing greater number of a particular product, it must make smaller number of other products as the total production capacity is limited.

### Some Important Inferences

It is important to see what the assumption of linearity implies. Intuitively it means that powers of variables (*e.g.*, $x_{12}^3$, $x_{13}^{5/2}$), their products (*e.g.*, $x_{11}\ x_{12}$) and their combinations (*e.g.*, $a_{11}x_{11} + a_{12} \log x_{12}$) are not permissible in the objective function equation as well as constraints.

More generally, linearity can be characterised by certain *additive* and *multiplicative properties*. For example, if a machine processes job A in 5 hours and job B in 10 hours, then time taken to process both job A and B is 5 + 10 = 15 hours. This, however, is true only when the change-over time from Job A to B is negligible. Some processes may not behave this way. For instance, when several liquids of different chemical compositions are mixed, the resulting volume may not be equal to the sum of the volumes of the individual liquids. Here, the property of additivity does not hold.

The multiplicative property implies: If a product yields a profit of ₹ 10, the profit earned from the sale of 12 such products will be ₹ (10 × 12) = ₹ 120. This may not be always true because of quantity discounts. Further, even if the sale price is constant, the manufacturing cost per unit may vary with the number of units produced and so may vary the profit per unit. The real world situations may not be strictly linear. However, the assumed linearity represents their close approximation and provides very useful answers.

In most linear programming problems the decision variables are permitted to take any non-negative values that satisfy the constraints. However, there are problems wherein variables are restricted to have integral values only. Though such problems, strictly speaking, are not linear programming problems, they are frequently solved by linear programming techniques and the values are then rounded off to nearest integers to satisfy the constraints. This approximation, however, is valid only if the variables have large optimal values.

The objective function does not involve any constant term, *i.e.*, we do not write

$$\text{maximize (or minimize) } Z = \sum_{j=1}^{n} c_j x_j + c.$$

The reason for this is simple: the optimal values of $x_j$ are just independent of any constant $c$. This constant $c$, if present, is ignored during the process of optimization and can be added to the optimal value of the objective function after the solution to the problem is obtained.

Mathematically, the constraints that restrict the decision variables to be non-negative do not differ from other constraints. However, since while solving the problems they are handled differently from the other constraints, they have been termed as *non-negativity restrictions* and the term *constraints* has been used to represent constraints other than the non-negativity restrictions and this terminology will be continued throughout the text.

## Examples on the Applications of Linear Programming

In this section we illustrate the application of linear programming to various situations with the help of examples. The objective is to familiarize the reader with some of the areas where this technique may be applied. In these examples the stress is laid on the analysis of the situation and formulation of the L.P. model rather than its solution. The solution of such problems is discussed separately.

## EXAMPLE 1. (Production Allocation Problem)

A firm produces three products. These products are processed on three different machines. The time required to manufacture one unit of each of the three products and the daily capacity of the three machines are given in the table below.

**Table 1**

| Machine | Time per unit (minutes) | | | Machine capacity (minutes/day) |
|---|---|---|---|---|
| | Product 1 | Product 2 | Product 3 | |
| $M_1$ | 2 | 3 | 2 | 440 |
| $M_2$ | 4 | — | 3 | 470 |
| $M_3$ | 2 | 5 | — | 430 |

It is required to determine the daily number of units to be manufactured for each product. The profit per unit for product 1, 2 and 3 is ₹ 4, ₹ 3 and ₹ 6 respectively. It is assumed that all the amounts produced are consumed in the market.

## Formulation of Linear Programming Model

**Step 1**

From the study of the situation find the *key-decision* to be made. In this connection, looking for variables helps considerably. In the given situation key decision decides the extent of products 1, 2 and 3, as the extents are permitted to vary.

**Step 2**

Assume symbols for variable quantities noticed in step 1. Let the extents (amounts) of products, 1, 2 and 3 manufactured daily be $x_1$, $x_2$ and $x_3$ respectively.

**Step 3**

Express the *feasible alternatives* mathematically in terms of variables. Feasible alternatives are those which are physically, economically and financially possible. In the given situation feasible alternatives are sets of values of $x_1$, $x_2$ and $x_3$,

$$\text{where } x_1, x_2, x_3 \geq 0, \quad \text{...(1)}$$

since negative production has no meaning and is not feasible.

**Step 4**

Mention the *objective* quantitatively and express it as a linear function of variables. In the present situation, objective is to maximize the profit.

$$\text{i.e., maximize} \quad Z = 4x_1 + 3x_2 + 6x_3. \quad \text{...(2)}$$

**Step 5**

Put into words the *influencing factors* or *constraints*. These occur generally because of constraints on availability (resources) or requirements (demands). Express these constraints also as linear equalities/inequalities in terms of variables.

Here, constraints are on the machine capacities and can be mathematically expressed as

$$\begin{aligned} 2x_1 + 3x_2 + 2x_3 &\leq 440, \\ 4x_1 + 0x_2 + 3x_3 &\leq 470, \quad \text{...(3)} \\ 2x_1 + 5x_2 + 0x_3 &\leq 430. \end{aligned}$$

## EXAMPLE 2. (Production Planning Problem)

A factory manufactures a product each unit of which consists of 5 units of part A and 4 units of part B. The two part A and B require different raw materials of which 120 units and 240 units respectively are available. These parts can be manufactured by three different methods. Raw material requirements per production run and the number of units for each part produced are given below.

**Table 2**

| Method | Input per run (units) | | Output per run (units) | |
|---|---|---|---|---|
| | Raw material 1 | Raw material 2 | Part A | Part B |
| 1 | 7 | 5 | 6 | 4 |
| 2 | 4 | 7 | 5 | 8 |
| 3 | 2 | 9 | 7 | 3 |

Determine the number of production runs for each method so as to maximize the total number of complete units of the final product.

## Formulation of Linear Programming Model

**Step 1**

The *key-decision* to be made is to determine the number of production runs for each method.

**Step 2**

Let $x_1$, $x_2$, $x_3$ represent the number of production runs for method 1, 2 and 3 respectively.

**Step 3**

*Feasible alternatives* are the sets of values of

$$x_1, x_2 \ \& \ x_3, \quad \text{where } x_1, x_2, x_3 \geq 0, \qquad ...(1)$$

since negative number of production runs has no meaning and is not feasible.

**Step 4**

The objective is to maximize the total number of units of the final product. Now, the total number of units of part A produced by different methods is $6x_1 + 5x_2 + 7x_3$ and for part B is $4x_1 + 8x_2 + 3x_3$. Since each unit of the final product requires 5 units of part A and 4 units of part B, it is evident that the maximum number of units of the final product cannot exceed the smaller value of

$$\frac{6x_1+5x_2+7x_3}{5} \quad \text{and} \quad \frac{4x_1+8x_2+3x_3}{4}$$

Thus the objective is to maximize

$$Z = \text{Min}\left(\frac{6x_1+5x_2+7x_3}{5}, \frac{4x_1+8x_2+3x_3}{4}\right). \qquad ...(2)$$

**Step 5**

*Constraints* are on the availability of raw materials. They are, for

$$\text{raw material 1, } 7x_1 + 4x_2 + 2x_3 \leq 120,$$
$$\text{and raw material 2, } 5x_1 + 7x_2 + 9x_3 \leq 240. \qquad ...(3)$$

The above formulation violates the linear programming properties since the objective function is non-linear. (Linear relationship between two or more variables is the one in which the variables are directly and precisely proportional). However, the above model can be easily reduced to the generally acceptable linear programming format.

$$\text{Let } y = \text{Min}\left(\frac{6x_1+5x_2+7x_3}{5}, \frac{4x_1+8x_2+3x_3}{4}\right)$$

$$\text{It follows that } \frac{6x_1+5x_2+7x_3}{5} \geq y$$

$$\text{and } \frac{4x_1+8x_2+3x_3}{4} \geq y.$$

*i.e.*, $6x_1 + 5x_2 + 7x_3 - 5y \geq 0$,

and $4x_1 + 8x_2 + 3x_3 - 4y \geq 0$.

## EXAMPLE 3. (Advertising Media Selection Problem)

An advertising company wishes to plan its advertising strategy in three different media—television, radio and magazines. The purpose of advertising is to reach as large a number of potential customers as possible. Following data has been obtained from market survery:

**Table 3**

| | Television | Radio | Magazine I | Magazine II |
|---|---|---|---|---|
| Cost of an advertising unit | ₹30,000 | ₹20,000 | ₹15,000 | ₹10,000 |
| No. of potential customers reached per unit | 2,00,000 | 6,00,000 | 1,50,000 | 1,00,000 |
| No. of female customers reached per unit | 1,50,000 | 4,00,000 | 70,000 | 50,000 |

The company wants to spend not more than ₹ 4,50,500 on advertising. Following are the further requirements the must be met:

(*i*) at least 1 million exposures take place among female customers,

(*ii*) advertising on magazines be limited to ₹ 1,50,000,

(*iii*) at least 3 advertising units be bought on magazine I and 2 units on magazine II, and

(*iv*) the number oof advertising units on television and radio should each be between 5 and 10.

Formulate an L.P. model for the problem.

## Formulation of Linear Programming Model

**Step 1**

The *key decision* to be made is to determine the number of advertising units to be bought in television, radio, magazine I and magazine II.

**Step 2**

Let $x_1$, $x_2$, $x_3$, $x_4$ represent the number of these advertising units in television, radio, magazine I and magazine II respectively.

**Step 3**

*Feasible alternatives* are sets of values of $x_1$, $x_2$, $x_3$, $x_4$, where $x_1$, $x_2$, $x_3$, $x_4$, all $\geq 0$.

**Step 4**

The *objective* is to maximize the total number of potential custome₹

*i.e.,* maximize $Z = 10^5(2x_1 + 6x_2 + 1.5x_3 + x_4)$.

**Step 5**

*Constraints* are on the advertising budget:

$$30{,}000x_1 + 20{,}000x_2 + 15{,}000x_3 + 10{,}000x_4 \leq 4{,}50{,}000$$

or $30x_1 + 20x_2 + 15x_3 + 10x_4 \leq 450$

on number of female customers reached by the advertising campaign:

$$1{,}50{,}000x_1 + 4{,}00{,}000x_2 + 70{,}000x_3 + 50{,}000x_4 \geq 10{,}00{,}000$$

or $15x_1 + 40x_2 + 7x_3 + 5x_4 \geq 100$,

on expenses on magazine advertising:

$$15{,}000x_3 + 10{,}000x_4 \leq 1{,}50{,}000$$

or $15x_3 + 10x_4 \leq 150$,

on no. of units on magazines:

$$x_3 \geq 3,$$
$$x_4 \geq 2,$$

on no. of units on television:

$$5 \leq x_1 \leq 10,$$

on no. of units on radio:

$$5 \leq x_2 \leq 10.$$

## GRAPHICAL METHOD

An LPP with only two variables presents a simple case, for which the solution can be derived using a graphical method. The graphical technique provides a pictorial representation of the solution and one gets insight into the basic concepts used in solving large L.P.P.

### Working Procedure

To solve a linear programming problem graphically:

**Step 1**

Formulate the given problem as a linear programming problem.

**Step 2**

Plot the given constraints as equalities on $x_1 \sim x_2$ coordinate plane and determine the convex region formed by them.

**Step 3**

Determine the vertices of the convex region and find the value of objective function at each vertex. The vertex which gives the optimal (maximum or minimum) value of the objective function gives the desired optimal solution to the problem.

Otherwise, draw the dotted line through the origin representing the objective function with $z = 0$. As $z$ is increased from zero, this line moves to the right remaining parallel to itself. We go on sliding this line (parallel to itself), till it is farthest away from the origin and passes through only one vertex of the convex region. This is the vertex where the maximum value of $z$ is attained.

When it is required to minimize $z$, the value of $z$ is increased till the dotted line passes through the nearest vertex of the convex region.

**Example 1:** Maximize $Z = 3x_1 + 4x_2$ ...(*i*)

subject to $4x_1 + 2x_2 \leq 80$ ...(*ii*)

$2x_1 + 5x_2 \leq 180$ ...(*iii*)

$x_1, x_2 \geq 0$ ...(*iv*)

**Solution:** Consider $x_1 - x_2$ coordinate system as shown in Fig. 1. The non-negativity restrictions (*iv*) imply that the values of $x_1$, $x_2$ lie in the first quadrant only.

We plot the lines $4x_1 + 2x_2 = 80$ and $2x_1 + 5x_2 = 180$.

Then any point on or below $4x_1 + 2x_2 = 80$ satisfies (*ii*) and any point on or below $2x_1 + 5x_2 = 180$ satisfies (*iii*). This shows that the desired point $(x_1, x_2)$ must be somewhere in the shaded convex region OABC. This region is called the *solution space* or *region of feasible solutions* for the given problem. Its vertices are O(0, 0), A(20, 0), B(2.5, 35) and C(0, 36).

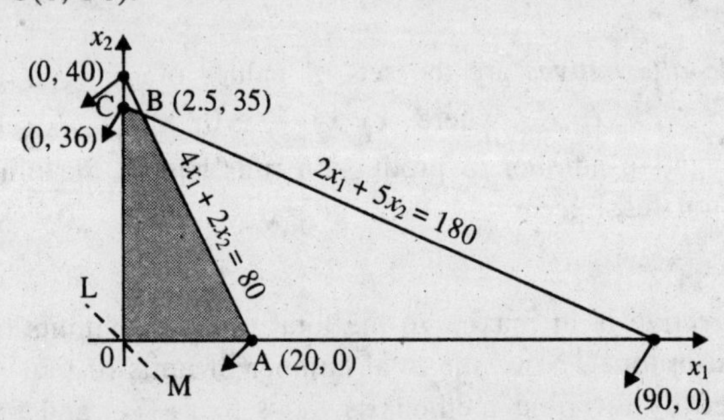


**Fig. 1**

The values of the objective function (*i*) at these points are

$$Z(O) = 0,\ Z(A) = 60,\ Z(B) = 147.5,\ Z(C) = 144.$$

Thus the maximum value of Z is 147.5 and it occurs at B. Hence the optimal solution to the problem is

$$x_1 = 2.5\ x_2 = 35 \text{ and } Z_{max} = 147.5.$$

**NOTE:** Our aim is to find the point (or points) in the solution space which maximizes the profit function Z. To do this, we observe that on making $Z = 0$, (*i*) becomes $3x_1 + 4x_2 = 0$ which is represented by the dotted line LM through O. As the value of Z is increased, the line LM starts moving parallel to itself towards the right. Larger the value of Z, more will be the company's profit. In this way, we go on sliding LM till it is farthest away from the origin and passes through one of the corners of the convex region. This is the point where the maximum value of Z is attained. Just possible, such a line may be one of the edges of the solution space. In that case every point on that edge gives the same maximum value of Z.

Here $Z_{max}$ is attained at B(2.5, 35). Hence the optimal solution is $x_1 = 2.5$, $x_2 = 35$ and $Z_{max} = 147.5$.

**Example 2:** Find the maximum value of $Z = 2x + 3y$ subject to the constraints: $x + y \le 30$, $y \ge 3$, $0 \le y \le 12$, $x - y \ge 0$, and $0 \le x \le 20$.

**Solution:** Any point $(x, y)$ satisfying the conditions $x \ge 0$, $y \ge 0$ lies in the first quadrant only. Also since $x + y \le 30$, $y \ge 3$, $y \le 12$, $x \ge y$ and $x \le 20$, the desired point $(x, y)$ lies within the convex region ABCDE (shown shaded in Fig. 2). Its vertices are A(3, 3), B(20, 3), C(20, 10), D(18, 12) and E(12, 12).

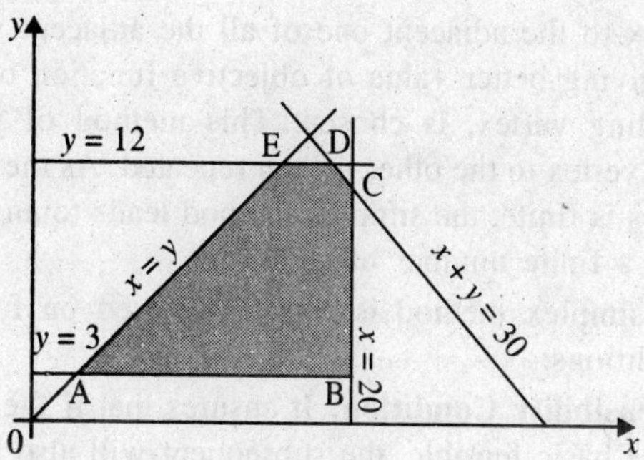


**Fig. 2**

The values of Z at these five vertices are Z(A) = 15, Z(B) = 49, Z(C) = 70, Z(D) = 72, and Z(E) = 60.

Since the maximum value of Z is 72 which occurs at the vertex D, the solution to the L.P.P. is $x = 18$, $y = 12$ and maximum Z = 72.

**Example 3:** A company manufactures two types of cloth, using three different colours of wool. One yard length of type a cloth requires 4 *oz* of red wool, 5 *oz* of green wool and 3 *oz* of yellow wool. One yard length of type B cloth requires 5 *oz* of red wool, 2 *oz* of green wool and 8 *oz* of yellow wool. The wool available for manufacture is 1000 *oz* of red wool, 1000 *oz* of green wool and 1200 *oz* of yellow wool. The manufacturer can make a profit of ₹ 5 on one yard of type A cloth and ₹ 3 on one yard of type B cloth. Find the best combination of the quantities of type A and type B cloth which gives him maximum profit by solving the L.P.P. graphically.

**Solution:** Let the manufacturer decide to produce $x_1$ yards of type A cloth and $x_2$ yards of type B cloth. Then the total income in rupees, from these units of cloth is given by

$$Z = 5x_1 + 3x_2 \quad ...(i)$$

To produce these units of two types of cloth, he requires

red wool = $4x_1 + 5x_2$ oz,

green wool = $5x_1 + 2x_2$ oz,

and yellow wool = $3x_1 + 8x_2$ oz.

Since the manufacturer does not have more than 1000 oz of red wool, 1000 oz of green wool and 1200 oz of yellow wool, therefore

$$4x_1 + 5x_2 \le 1000 \quad ...(ii)$$

$$5x_1 + 2x_2 \le 1000 \quad ...(iii)$$

$$3x_1 + 8x_2 \le 1200 \quad ...(iv)$$

Also $x_1 \ge 0, x_2 \ge 0. \quad ...(v)$

Thus the given problem is to maximize Z subject to the constraints (*ii*) to (*v*).

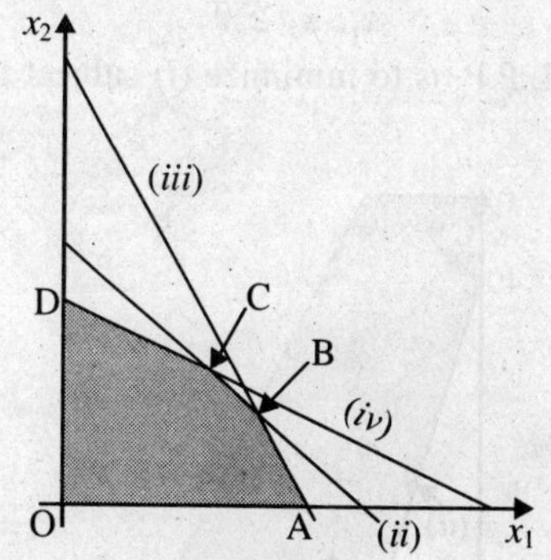


**Fig. 3**

Any point satisfying the condition (*v*) lies in the first quadrant only. Also the desired point satisfying the constraints (*ii*) to (*iv*) lies in the convex region OABCD (Fig. 3). Its vertices are O(0, 0), A(200, 0), B(3000/17, 1000/17), C(2000/17, 1800/17) and D(0, 150).

The values of Z at these vertices are given by Z(O) = 0, Z(A) = 1000, Z(B) = 1057.6, Z(C) – 905.8 and Z(D) = 450.

Since the maximum value of Z is 1058.8 which occurs at the vertex B, the solution to the given problem is $x_1 = 3000/17$, $x_2 = 1000/17$ and max. Z = 1058.8.

Hence the manufacturer should produce 176.5 yards of type A cloth 58.8 yards of type B cloth, so as to get the maximum profit of ₹ 1058.8.

**Example 4:** A company making cold drinks has two bottling plants located at towns $T_1$ and $T_2$. Each plant produces three drinks A, B and C and their production capacity per day is shown below:

| *Cold drinks* | *Plant at* | |
|---|---|---|
| | $T_1$ | $T_2$ |
| A | 6,000 | 2,000 |
| B | 1,000 | 2,500 |
| C | 3,000 | 3,000 |

The marketing department of the company forecasts a demand of 80,000 bottles of A, 22,000 bottles of B and 40,000 bottles of C during the month of June. The operating costs per day of plants at $T_1$ and $T_2$ are ₹ 6,000 and ₹ 4,000 respectively. Find (graphically) the number of days for which each plant must be run in June so as to minimize the operating costs while meeting the market demand.

**Solution:** Let the plants at $T_1$ and $T_2$ be run for $x_1$ and $x_2$ days. Then the objective is to minimize the operation costs *i.e.*

$$\text{min. } Z = 6000x_1 + 4000x_2 \qquad ...(i)$$

Constraints on the demand for the three cold drinks are:

for A, $6,000x_1 + 2,000x_2 \geq 80,000$

or $\qquad 3x_1 + x_2 \geq 40 \qquad ...(ii)$

for B, $1,000x_1 + 2,500x_2 \geq 22,000$

or $\qquad x_1 + 2.5x_2 \geq 22 \qquad ...(iii)$

for C, $3,000x_1 + 3,000x_2 \geq 40,000$

or $\qquad x_1 + x_2 \geq 40/3 \qquad ...(iv)$

Also $\qquad x_1, x_2 \geq 0 \qquad ...(v)$

Thus the L.P.P. is to minimize (*i*) subject to constraints (*ii*) to (*v*).

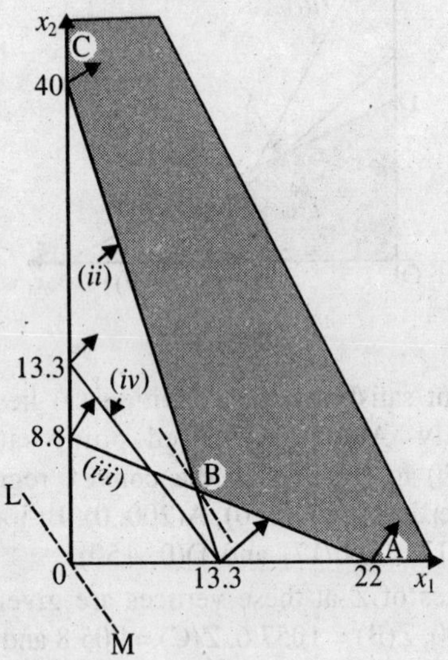


**Fig. 4**

The solution space satisfying the constraints (*ii*) to (*v*) is shown shaded in Fig. 4. As seen from the direction of the arrows, the solution space is unbounded. The constraint (*iv*) is dominated by the constraints (*ii*) and (*iii*) and hence does not affect the solution space. Such a constraint as (*iv*) is called the *redundant constraint.*

The vertices of the convex region ABC are A(22, 0), B(12, 4) and C(0, 40).

Values of the objective function (*i*) at these vertices are

Z(A) = 132000, Z(B) = 88,000, Z(C) = 160,000.

Thus the minimum value of Z is ₹ 88,000 and it occurs at B. Hence the solution to the problem is $x_1$ = 12 days, $x_2$ = 4 days, $Z_{min}$ = ₹ 88,000.

**Otherwise:** Making Z = 0, (*i*) becomes $3x_1 + 2x_2 = 0$ which is represented by the dotted line LM through O. As Z is increased, the line LM moves parallel to itself, to the right. Since we are interested in finding the minimum value of Z, value of Z is increased till LM passes through the vertex nearest to the origin of the shaded region, *i.e.* B(12, 4).

Thus the operating cost will be minimum for $x_1$ = 12 days, $x_2$ = 4 days and $Z_{min}$ = 6000 × 12 + 4000 × 4 = ₹ 88,000.

**Remarks.** The dotted line parallel to the line LM is called the *iso-cost line* since it represents all possible combinations of $x_1$, $x_2$ which produce the same total cost.

## SIMPLEX METHOD

Solving as LPP Graphically, the region of feasible solutions was found to be convex, bounded by vertices and edges joining them. The optimal solution occurred at some vertex. If the optimal solution is not unique, the optimal points were on an edge. These observations also hold true for the general LPP *i.e.*, the essential problem of an LPP is that of finding the particular vertex of the convex region which corresponds to the optimal solution. The most commonly used method for locating the optimal vertex is the simplex method. This method consists in moving step-by-step from one vertex to the adjacent one of all the adjacent vertices, the one giving better value of objective function over that of preceding vertex, is chosen. This method of jumping from one vertex to the other is then repeated. As the number of vertices is finite, the simplex method leads to an optimal vertex in a finite number of steps.

The simplex method is primarily based on following two conditions:

**1. Feasibility Condition:** It ensures that if the starting solution is basic feasible, the subsequent will also be basic feasible.

**2. Optimality Condition:** It ensures that only improved solutions will be obtained.

Now, we shall elaborate the above terms in relation to the general linear programming problem in standard form, i.e.

Maximize $Z = c_1x_1 + c_2x_2 + .... + c_nx_n$

subject to $\sum_{j=1}^{n} a_{ij}x_j + s_i = b_i, = 1, 2, .... m$

and $x_j \geq 0$, $s_i \geq 0$, $j = 1, 2, .... n$.

(*i*) **Solution:** $x_1, x_2, ...., x_n$ is a solution of the general L.P.P., if it satisfies the constraint.

(*ii*) **Feasible solution:** $x_1, x_2, .... x_n$ is a feasible solution of the general L.P.P. if it satisfies both the constraints and the non-negativity restrictions. The set of all feasible solution is called the feasible region. A linear programme is said to be infeasible when the set is empty.

(*iii*) **Basic solution** is the solution of the *m* basic variables when each of the *n* non-basic variables is equated to zero.

(*iv*) **Basic feasible solution** is that basic solution which also optimizes the objective function and satisfying the constraint and non-negative criteria.

(*v*) **Optimal solution** is that to basic feasible solution which also optimizes the objective function while satisfying constraints and non-negativity criteria.

(*vi*) **Non-degenerate basic feasible solution** is that basic feasible solution which contains exactly *m* non-zero basic variables. If any of the basic variables becomes zero, it is called a degenerate basic solution.

## MULTIPLE CHOICE QUESTIONS

**1.** Using the Hungarian method, the optimal value of the assignment problem whose cost matrix is given by

| | | | |
|---|---|---|---|
| 5 | 23 | 14 | 8 |
| 10 | 25 | 1 | 23 |
| 35 | 16 | 15 | 12 |
| 16 | 23 | 11 | 7 |

is

A. 29　　B. 52
C. 26　　D. 44

**2.** Let a primal linear programming problem admit an optimal solution. Then the corresponding dual problem

A. does not have a feasible solution
B. has a feasible solution but does not have any optimal solution
C. does not have a convex feasible region
D. has an optimal solution

**3.** Consider the Linear Programming Problem

Max. $z = x_1 + 5x_2 + 3x_3$

subject to $2x_1 - 3x_2 + 5x_3 \le 3$
$3x_1 + 2x_3 \le 5$
$x_1, x_2, x_3 \ge 0$

Then the dual of this Linear Programming Problem

A. has a feasible solution, but does not have a basic feasible solution
B. has a basic feasible solution
C. has infinite number of feasible solution
D. has no feasible solution

**4.** The unit cost $c_{ij}$ of producing product *i* at plant *j* is given by the matrix:

$$\begin{bmatrix} 14 & 12 & 16 \\ 21 & 9 & 17 \\ 9 & 7 & 5 \end{bmatrix}$$

The total cost of optimal assignment is

A. 20　　B. 22
C. 25　　D. 28

**5.** Consider the following Linear Programming Problem (LPP).

Minimize $z = 2x_1 + 3x_2 + x_3$

subject to $x_1 + 2x_2 + 2x_3 - x_4 + x_5 = 3$
$2x_1 + 3x_2 + 4x_3 + ... + x_6 = 6$
$x_i \ge 0, \ i = 1, 2, ... 6$

A non degenerate basic feasible solution $(x_1, x_2, x_3, x_4, x_5, x_6)$ is

A. (1, 0, 1, 0, 0, 0)　B. (1, 0, 0, 0, 0, 7)
C. (0, 0, 0, 0, 3, 6)　D. (3, 0, 0, 0, 0, 0)

**6.** If the cost matrix for an assignment problem is given by

$$\begin{bmatrix} a & b & c & d \\ b & c & d & a \\ c & d & a & b \\ d & a & b & c \end{bmatrix}$$

where *a*, *b*, *c*, *d* > 0 then the value of the assignment problem is

A. $a + b + c + d$
B. min $\{a, b, c, d\}$
C. max $\{a, b, c, d\}$
D. 4 min $\{a, b, c, d\}$

**7.** Consider the transportation problem given below. The bracketted elements in the table indicate a feasible solution and the elements on the left hand corner are the costs $c_{ij}$.

| | | | | $a_i$ |
|---|---|---|---|---|
| | 2 (1) | 5 | 1 | 1 |
| | 1 | 3 (1) | 4 (1) | 2 |
| $b_j$ | 1 | 1 | 1 | 3 |

A. this solution is a basic feasible solution
B. this solution can be made basic feasible
C. this is an optimal solution
D. the problem does not have an optimal solution

**8.** Which of the following is a correct statement?

A. If the primal problem is in its standard form, dual variables will be non-negatives.
B. Dual simplex method always leads to generate basic feasible solution.
C. Dual simplex method is applicable to an LPP, if initial basic feasible solution is not optimum.
D. If the number of primal variables is very small and the number of constraints is very large, then it is more efficient to solve the dual rather than the primal problem.

**9.** When we solve a system of simultaneous linear equations by using two-phase simplex method, the values of decision variables may be

A. Positive
B. Negative
C. Non-negative
D. Positive or Negative

**10.** The primal LPP is
Max $z = 7x_1 - 3x_2$
subject to $x_1 + x_2 \geq 3,\ 8x_1 + 4x_2 \leq 16,$
$5x_1 + 3x_2 \geq 15,\ x_1, x_2 \geq 0$
then dual of this problem has
A. Unique feasible and optimal solution
B. No feasible solution
C. Infinite number feasible solution but not any optimal solution
D. Degenerate optimal solution

**11.** The LPP
Max $z = 2x_1 + 3x_2 + x_3$
subject to $-2x_1 + 3x_2 + 5x_3 \geq 5$
$-x_1 + 2x_2 + 3x_3 \leq 4$
$x_1, x_2, x_3 \geq 0$ has
A. Optimal solution
B. Unbounded solution
C. No feasible solution
D. No solution

**12.** If the primal problem is given by
Min $z = 2x_2 + 5x_3$
subject to $x_1 + x_2 \geq 2$
$2x_1 + x_2 + 6x_3 \leq 6$
$x_1 - x_2 + 3x_3 = 4$
$x_1, x_2, x_3 \geq 0$
then its dual is
A. Max $z' = 2w_1 + 6w_2 - 4w_3$
subject to $w_1 + 2w_2 - w_3 \leq 0$
$w_1 + w_2 + w_3 \leq 2$
$-6w_2 - 3w_3 \leq 5$
$w_1, w_2 \geq 0$ and $w_3$ unrestricted
B. Max $z' = 2w_1 - 6w_2 + 4w_3$
subject to $w_1 - 2w_2 + w_3 \leq 0$
$w_1 - w_2 - w_3 \leq 2$
$-6w_2 + 3w_3 \leq 5$
$w_1, w_2 \geq 0$ and $w_3$ unrestricted
C. Max $z' = 2w_1 - 6w_2 - 4w_3$
subject to $w_1 - 2w_2 - w_3 \leq 0$
$w_1 - w_2 + w_3 \leq 2$
$-6w_2 - 3w_3 \leq 5$
$w_1, w_2, w_3 \geq 0$
D. None of these

**13.** The primal LPP is
Max $z = 7x_1 - 3x_2$
subject to $x_1 + x_2 \geq 3,\ 8x_1 + 4x_2 \leq 16,$
$5x_1 + 3x_2 \geq 15,\ x_1, x_2 \geq 0$
Then dual of this problem has
A. Unique feasible and optimal solution
B. No feasible solution
C. Infinite number of feasible solution but not any optimal solution
D. Degenerate optimal solution

**14.** Consider the Linear Programming Problem
Maximize $z = 3x + 9y$
subject to $x + 4y \leq 8$
$x + 2y \leq 4,\ x, y \geq 0$
The maximum value of $z$ is
A. 6 B. 15
C. 18 D. 21

**15.** Consider the following transportation problem

| | A | B | C | D | **Demand** |
|---|---|---|---|---|---|
| I | 21 | 16 | 25 | 13 | 11 |
| II | 17 | 18 | 14 | 23 | 13 |
| III | 32 | 27 | 18 | 41 | 19 |
| **Requirement** | 6 | 10 | 12 | 15 | 43 |

Then the optimal cost of the above problem is
A. 796 B. 804
C. 812 D. 820

**16.** The number of basic feasible solution of the LPP.
$2x_1 + 3x_2 - x_3 + 4x_4 = 8,$
$x_1 - 2x_2 + 6x_3 - 7x_4 = -3,$
$x_1, x_2, x_3, x_4 \geq 0$
with respect to objective function
Max $z = 2x_1 + 3x_2 + 4x_3 + 7x_4$
A. 2 B. 3
C. 4 D. 6

**17.** In the above problem, the value of $z$ for the optimal solution
A. 25.4 B. 27.2
C. 28.9 D. 30.4

## ANSWERS

| 1 | 2 | 3 | 4 | 5 | 6 | 7 | 8 | 9 | 10 |
|---|---|---|---|---|---|---|---|---|---|
| A | D | B | D | C | A | B | D | D | C |
| **11** | **12** | **13** | **14** | **15** | **16** | **17** | | | |
| A | B | B | C | A | C | C | | | |

# EXPLANATORY ANSWERS

**1.** The given assignment cost matrix is

| | | | |
|---|---|---|---|
| 5 | 23 | 14 | 8 |
| 10 | 25 | 1 | 23 |
| 35 | 16 | 15 | 12 |
| 16 | 23 | 11 | 7 |

Apply the Hungarian method (*i.e.* substracting the minimum cost of each row to the other element of the same row)

then

| | | | |
|---|---|---|---|
| 0 | 18 | 9 | 3 |
| 9 | 24 | 0 | 22 |
| 23 | 4 | 3 | 0 |
| 9 | 16 | 4 | 0 |

As the second column does not any zero, apply the Hungarian rule for second column, we get

| | | | |
|---|---|---|---|
| ~~0~~ | 14 | 9 | 3 |
| 9 | 20 | ~~0~~ | 22 |
| 23 | ~~0~~ | 3 | 0 |
| 9 | 12 | 4 | ~~0~~ |

*i.e.* Hence the optimal cost = 5 + 1 + 16 + 7 = 29.

**3.** The given LPP is

Maximum $Z = x_1 + 5x_2 + 3x_3$

Subject to $2x_1 - 3x_2 + 5x_3 \leq 3.$

$3x_1 + 2x_3 \leq 5$

$x_1, x_2, x_3.$

As the number of variables are 3 and the number of constraints are 2.

Hence the basic solution can be obtained by making any one of the three variables equating to zero.

**Case I:** When $x_1 = 0$

then the constraints becomes

$$-3x_2 + 5x_3 = 3$$

$$2x_3 = 5 \Rightarrow x_3 = \frac{5}{2}$$

*i.e.* $$-3x_2 + \frac{25}{2} = 3$$

or $$3x_2 = \frac{25}{2} - 3 = \frac{19}{2}$$

$\Rightarrow$ $$x_2 = \frac{19}{6}$$

*i.e.* the basic solution in this case is

$$x_1 = 0, x_2 = \frac{19}{6}, x_3 = \frac{5}{2}.$$

**Case II:** When $x_2 = 0$, then the constraints become

$$2x_1 + 5x_3 = 3 \times 3$$
$$3x_1 + 2x_3 = 5 \times 2$$

$\Rightarrow$ $(15 - 4)x_3 = 9 - 10$

$\Rightarrow$ $$x_3 = \frac{-1}{11} \text{ (not a basic solution)}$$

**Case III:** When $x_3 = 0$, then the constraint becomes

$$2x_1 - 3x_2 = 3$$

$$3x_1 = 5 \Rightarrow x_1 = \frac{5}{3}$$

$\Rightarrow$ $$\frac{10}{3} - 3x_2 = 3 \Rightarrow x_2 = \frac{1}{9}$$

*i.e.* the basic solution in this case is

$$x_1 = \frac{5}{3}, x_2 = \frac{1}{9}, x_3 = 0$$

*i.e.* given LPP has basic feasible solution.

**4.** The given assignment cost matrix is

| | | |
|---|---|---|
| 14 | 12 | 16 |
| 21 | 9 | 17 |
| 9 | 7 | 5 |

using the Hungarian method, (*i.e.* substracting the minimum cost of each row to the other element of the same row).

Then

| | | |
|---|---|---|
| 2 | 0 | 4 |
| 12 | 0 | 8 |
| 4 | 2 | 0 |

(as the first column does not have any zero, apply the Hungarian rule for the first column, we get).

| | | |
|---|---|---|
| [0] | ~~0~~ | 4 |
| 10 | [0] | 8 |
| 2 | 2 | [0] |

Hence the optimal assignment cost

= 14 + 9 + 5 = 28.

**6.** The given cost matrix of the assignment problem is

$$\begin{bmatrix} a & b & c & d \\ b & c & d & a \\ c & d & a & b \\ d & a & b & c \end{bmatrix}$$

if let *a* is the minimum among the *a, b, c, d,* then apply the Hungarian method for the given cost matrix, we get

$$\begin{bmatrix} 0 & b-a & c-a & d-a \\ b-a & c-a & d-a & 0 \\ c-a & d-a & 0 & b-a \\ d-a & 0 & b-a & c-a \end{bmatrix}$$

clearly all the rows and column consist exactly one zero element. Hence it will be the minimum cost matrix.

*i.e.* The optimal cost in this case

$$= a + a + a + a = 4a.$$

Similarly when $b$ is the minimum among the $a, b, c, d$, then by the Hungarian method, the optimal cost in this case $= b + b + b + b = 4b$.

*i.e.* The required optimal cost = $4.\min\{a, b, c, d\}$.

**12.** The given primal problem is

$$\text{Min } Z = 2x_2 + 5x_3$$

Subject to $x_1 + x_2 \geq 2$

$$2x_1 + x_2 + 6x_3 \leq 6$$

$$x_1 - x_2 + 3x_3 = 4.$$

As the given objective function is of minimization type. Hence all the constraint should be made to $\geq$ type.

*i.e.* The given primal problem can be changed to

$$\text{Min } Z = 0 \cdot x_1 + 2 \cdot x_2 + 5 \cdot x_3$$

Subject to $x_1 + x_2 \geq 2$

$$-2x_1 - x_2 - 6x_3 \geq -6$$

$$x_1 - x_2 + 3x_3 \geq 4$$

$$-x_1 + x_2 - 3x_3 \geq -4.$$

Now converting the above primal into dual by duality principle then objective function is of maximization type.

*i.e.* $\text{Max } Z' = 2w_1 - 6w_2 + 4(w_3' - w_3'')$

Subject to

$$w_1 - 2w_2 + (w_3' - w_3'') \leq 0$$

$$w_1 - w_2 + (w_3' - w_3'') \leq 2$$

$$0.w_1 - 6w_2 + 3(w_3' - w_3'') \leq 5.$$

Writting $w_3 = w_3' - w_3''$ the above inequalities can be rewritten as max $Z' = 2w_1 - 6w_2 + 4w_3$.

Subject to $w_1 - 2w_2 + w_3 \leq 0$

$$w_1 - w_2 + w_3 \leq 2$$

$$-6w_2 + 3w_3 \leq 5$$

where $w_1, w_2 \geq 0$ and $w_3$ is unrestricted.

**13.** The given primal LPP is

$$\max Z = 7x_1 - 3x_2$$

subject to

$$x_1 + x_2 \geq 3,\ 8x_1 + 4x_2 \leq 16,\ 5x_1 + 3x_2 \geq 15$$

as primal LPP is of maximization type, converting all the inequalities into ($\leq$) type. We get

$$\max Z = 7x_1 - 3x_2$$

subject to $-x_1 - x_2 \leq -3$

$$8x_1 + 4x_2 \leq 16$$

$$-5x_1 - 3x_2 \leq -15.$$

Now by the duality principle, we get

$$\text{Min } Z' = -3y_1 + 16y_2 - 15y_3$$

subject $-y_1 + 8y_2 - 5y_3 \geq 7$

$$-y_2 + 4y_2 - 3y_3 \geq -3$$

for determining the basic solution, we make any one out of three equal to zero, case by case.

**Case I:** When $y_1 = 0$

then $8y_2 - 5y_3 = 7$

$$4y_2 - 3y_3 = -3$$

$$\Rightarrow \quad -5y_3 + 6y_3 = 13$$

$$\Rightarrow \quad y_3 = 13$$

$$\Rightarrow \quad 8y_2 = 7 + 65 = 72$$

$$y_2 = \frac{72}{8} = 9.$$

*i.e.* $y_1 = 0,\ y_2 = 9,\ y_3 = 13.$

**Case II:** When $y_2 = 0$

then $-y_1 - 5y_3 = 7$

$$-y_1 - 3y_3 = -3$$

$$\Rightarrow -2y_3 = 10 \quad y_3 = -5 \text{ (not basic)}$$

**Case III:** When $y_3 = 0$

$$-y_1 + 8y_2 = 7$$

$$-y_1 + 4y_2 = -3$$

$$\Rightarrow 4y_2 = 10$$

$$y_2 = \frac{5}{2}$$

$$-y_1 + 10 = -3$$

$$\Rightarrow \quad y_1 = 13.$$

**14.** The given LPP is

$$\max Z = 3x + 9y$$

subject to $x + 4y \leq 8$

$$x + 2y \leq 4$$

$$x, y \geq 0$$

Solution space is shown in the given by the shaded region of the plotted graph.

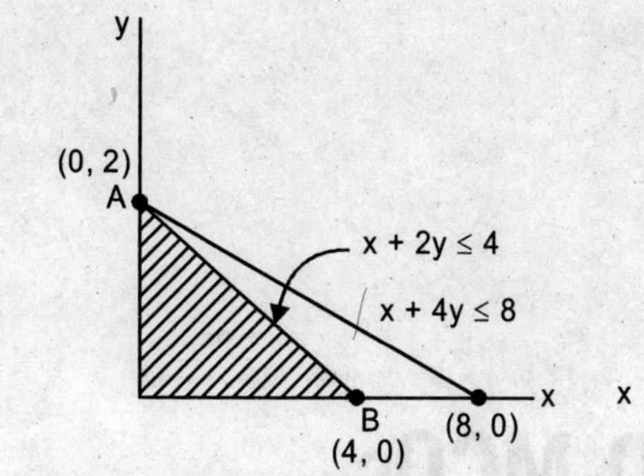


The optimum value of the objective function is obtained at the boundary of the region *i.e.* either at A(0, 2) or at B(4, 0).

Now at $Z(A) = 3.0 + 9.2 = 18$

and $Z(B) = 3.4 + 9.0 = 12$.

Hence the maximum value of Z is at the point A.

*i.e.* $Z_{max} = 18$.

**15.**

| | A | B | C | D | Demand |
|---|---|---|---|---|---|
| I | 21 | 16 | 25 | 13 | 11 |
| II | 17 | 18 | 14 | 23 | 13 |
| III | 32 | 27 | 18 | 41 | 19 |
| | 6 | 10 | 12 | 15 | 43 |

Apply the Vogel's Approximation method, for the initial basic feasible solution.

| | | | (11) | | |
|---|---|---|---|---|---|
| 21 | 16 | 25 | 13 | 11 | [3] |
| 17 | 18 | 14 | 23 | 13 | [3] |
| 32 | 27 | 18 | 41 | 19 | [9] |
| 6 | 10 | 12 | 15 | 43 | |
| [4] | [2] | [4] | [10] | | |

(6)

| | | | | | |
|---|---|---|---|---|---|
| 17 | 18 | 14 | 23 | 13 | [3] |
| 32 | 27 | 18 | 41 | 19 | [9] |
| 6 | 10 | 12 | 4 | 32 | |
| [15] | [9] | [4] | [18] | | |

| | | (4) | | |
|---|---|---|---|---|
| 18 | 14 | 23 | 7 | [4] |
| 27 | 18 | 41 | 19 | [9] |
| 10 | 12 | 4 | | |
| [9] | [4] | [18] | | |

(3)

| | | | |
|---|---|---|---|
| 18 | 14 | 3 | [4] |
| 27 | 18 | 19 | [9] |
| 10 | 12 | | |
| [9] | [4] | | |

| (7) | (12) | |
|---|---|---|
| 27 | 18 | 19 |
| 7 | 12 | |

Hence the initial basic solution is given as

| | | | | |
|---|---|---|---|---|
| 21 | 16 | 25 | (11) 13 | 11 |
| (6) 17 | (3) 18 | 14 | (4) 23 | 13 |
| (7) 32 | (12) 27 | 18 | 41 | 19 |
| 6 | 10 | 12 | 15 | |

the optimal cost $= 11 \times 13 + 17 \times 6 + 18 \times 3 + 23 \times 4 + 27 \times 7 + 12 \times 18 = 796$.

CHAPTER

# 9

# PASSAGE BASED MCQs

## PASSAGE-1

A general election of Lok Sabha is a gigantic exercise. About 911 million people were eligible to vote and voter turnout was about 67%, the highest ever.

Let I be the set of all citizens of India who were eligible to exercise their voting right in general election held in 2019. A relation 'R' is defined on I as follows:

$R = \{(V_1, V_2) : V_1, V_2 \in I$ and both use their voting right in general election – 2019}

**1.** Two neighbors X and Y $\in$ I. X exercised his voting right while Y did not cast her vote in general election – 2019. Which of the following is true?

A. $(X, Y) \in R$ B. $(Y, X) \in R$

C. $(X, X) \notin R$ D. $(X, Y) \notin R$

**2.** Mr. 'X' and his wife 'W' both exercised their voting right in general election-2019,

Which of the following is true?

A. both (X, W) and (W, X) $\in$ R

B. (X,W) $\in$ R but (W, X) $\notin$ R

C. both (X, W) and (W, X) $\notin$ R

D. (W, X) $\in$ R but (X, W) $\notin$ R

**3.** Three friends $F_1$, $F_2$ and $F_3$ exercised their voting right in general election-2019, then which of the following is true?

A. $(F_1, F_2) \in R$, $(F_2, F_3) \in R$ and $(F_1, F_3) \in R$

B. $(F_1, F_2) \in R$, $(F_2, F_3) \in R$ and $(F_1, F_3) \notin R$

C. $(F1, F_2) \in R$, $(F_2, F_2) \in R$ but $(F_3, F_3) \notin R$

D. $(F_1, F_2) \notin R$, $(F_2, F_3) \notin R$ and $(F_1, F_3) \notin R$

**4.** The above defined relation R is ..................

A. Symmetric and transitive but not reflexive

B. Universal relation

C. Equivalence relation

D. Reflexive but not symmetric and transitive

**5.** Mr. Shyam exercised his voting right in General Election-2019, then Mr. Shyam is related to which of the following?

A. All those eligible voters who cast their votes

B. Family members of Mr.Shyam

C. All citizens of India

D. Eligible voters of India

## PASSAGE-2

Sherlin and Danju are playing Ludo at home during Covid-19. While rolling the dice, Sherlin's sister Raji observed and noted the possible outcomes of the throw every time belongs to set {1, 2, 3, 4, 5, 6}. Let A be the set of players while B be the set of all possible outcomes.

$A = \{S, D\}$, $B = \{1, 2, 3, 4, 5, 6\}$

**1.** Let $R : B \to B$ be defined by $R = \{(x, y): y$ is divisible by $x\}$ is;

A. Reflexive and transitive but not symmetric

B. Reflexive and symmetric and not transitive

C. Not reflexive but symmetric and transitive

D. Equivalence

**2.** Raji wants to know the number of functions from A to B. How many number of functions are possible?

A. $6^2$ B. $2^6$

C. 6! D. $2^{12}$

**3.** Let R be a relation on B defined by R = {(1, 2), (2, 2), (1, 3), (3, 4), (3, 1), (4, 3), (5, 5)}. Then R is:

A. Symmetric B. Reflexive

C. Transitive D. None of these three

**4.** Raji wants to know the number of relations possible from A to B. How many numbers of relations are possible?

A. $6^2$ B. $2^6$

C. 6! D. $2^{12}$

5. Let R : B → B be defined by R = {(1, 1), (1, 2), (2, 2), (3, 3), (4, 4), (5, 5),(6, 6)}, then R is:
   A. Symmetric
   B. Reflexive and Transitive
   C. Transitive and symmetric
   D. Equivalence

## PASSAGE-3

An organization conducted bike race under 2 different categories-boys and girls. Totally there were 250 participants. Among all of them finally three from Category 1 and two from Category 2 were selected for the final race. Ravi forms two sets B and G with these participants for his college project.

Let B = $\{b_1, b_2, b_3\}$ G = $\{g_1, g_2\}$ where B represents the set of boys selected and G the set of girls who were selected for the final race.

Ravi decides to explore these sets for various types of relations and functions.

1. Ravi wishes to form all the relations possible from B to G. How many such relations are possible?
   A. $2^6$ B. $2^5$
   C. 0 D. $2^3$
2. Let R: B → B be defined by R = {(x, y): x and y are students of same sex}, Then this relation R is ..........
   A. Equivalence
   B. Reflexive only
   C. Reflexive and symmetric but not transitive
   D. Reflexive and transitive but not symmetric
3. Ravi wants to know among those relations, how many functions can be formed from B to G?
   A. $2^2$ B. $2^{12}$
   C. $3^2$ D. $2^3$
4. Let R : B → G be defined by R = $\{(b_1, g_1), (b_2, g_2), (b_3, g_1)\}$, then R is ..............
   A. Injective
   B. Surjective
   C. Neither Surjective nor Injective
   D. Surjective and Injective
5. Ravi wants to find the number of injective functions from B to G. How many numbers of injective functions are possible?
   A. 0 B. 2!
   C. 3! D. 0!

## PASSAGE-4

Students of Grade 9, planned to plant saplings along straight lines, parallel to each other to one side of the playground ensuring that they had enough play area. Let us assume that they planted one of the rows of the saplings along the line $y = x - 4$. Let L be the set of all lines which are parallel on the ground and R be a relation on L.

Answer the following using the above information.

1. Let relation R be defined by R = $\{(L_1, L_2): L_1 \parallel L_2$ where $L_1, L_2$ € L$\}$ then R is ........ relation
   A. Equivalence
   B. Only reflexive
   C. Not reflexive
   D. Symmetric but not transitive
2. Let R = $\{(L_1, L_2) : L_1 \perp L_2$ where $L_1, L_2$ € L$\}$ which of the following is true?
   A. R is Symmetric but neither reflexive nor transitive
   B. R is Reflexive and transitive but not symmetric
   C. R is Reflexive but neither symmetric nor transitive
   D. R is an Equivalence relation
3. The function $f$ : R → R defined by $f(x) = x - 4$ is ................
   A. Bijective
   B. Surjective but not injective
   C. Injective but not Surjective
   D. Neither Surjective nor Injective
4. Let $f$ : R → R be defined by $f(x) = x - 4$. Then the range of $f(x)$ is ..............
   A. R B. Z
   C. W D. Q
5. Let R = $\{(L_1, L_2) : L_1$ is parallel to $L_2$ and $L_1 : y = x - 4\}$ then which of the following can be taken as $L_2$?
   A. $2x - 2y + 5 = 0$ B. $2x + y = 5$
   C. $2x + 2y + 7 = 0$ D. $x + y = 7$

## PASSAGE-5

Raji visited the Exhibition along with her family. The Exhibition had a huge swing, which attracted many children. Raji found that the swing traced the path of a Parabola as given by $y = x_2$.

Answer the following questions using the above information.

1. Let $f$ : R → R be defined by $f(x) = x^2$ is ................
   A. Neither Surjective nor Injective
   B. Surjective
   C. Injective
   D. Bijective
2. Let $f$ : N → N be defined by $f(x) = x^2$ is ................
   A. Surjective but not Injective
   B. Surjective
   C. Injective
   D. Bijective

3. Let $f : \{1, 2, 3, ......\} \to \{1, 4, 9, ....\}$ be defined by $f(x) = x^2$ is ............

A. Bijective

B. Surjective but not Injective

C. Injective but Surjective

D. Neither Surjective nor Injective

4. Let : $N \to R$ be defined by $f(x) = x^2$. Range of the function among the following is ............

A. $\{1, 4, 9, 16, .....\}$

B. $\{1, 4, 8, 9, 10, .....\}$

C. $\{1, 4, 9, 15, 16, .....\}$

D. $\{1, 4, 8, 16, .....\}$

5. The function $f : Z \to Z$ defined by $f(x) = x^2$ is .........

A. Neither Injective nor Surjective

B. Injective

C. Surjective

D. Bijective

## PASSAGE-6

Two men on either side of a temple of 30 meters high observe its top at the angles of elevation α and β respectively. (as shown in the figure below). The distance between the two men is $40\sqrt{3}$ meters and the distance between the first person A and the temple is $30\sqrt{3}$ meters.

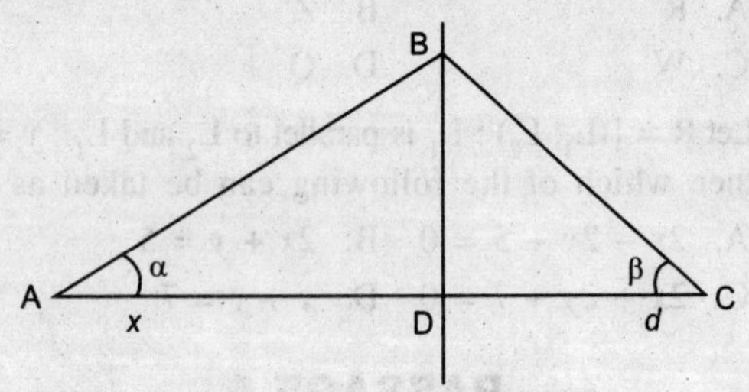


Based on the above information answer the following:

1. $\angle CAB = \alpha =$

A. $\sin^{-1}\left(\frac{2}{\sqrt{3}}\right)$  B. $\sin^{-1}\left(\frac{1}{2}\right)$

C. $\sin^{-1}(2)$  D. $\sin^{-1}\left(\frac{\sqrt{3}}{2}\right)$

2. $\angle CAB = \alpha =$

A. $\cos^{-1}\left(\frac{1}{5}\right)$  B. $\cos^{-1}\left(\frac{2}{5}\right)$

C. $\cos^{-1}\left(\frac{\sqrt{3}}{2}\right)$  D. $\cos^{-1}\left(\frac{4}{5}\right)$

3. $\angle BCA = \beta =$

A. $\tan^{-1}\left(\frac{1}{2}\right)$  B. $\tan^{-1}(2)$

C. $\tan^{-1}\left(\frac{1}{\sqrt{3}}\right)$  D. $\tan^{-1}\left(\sqrt{3}\right)$

4. $\angle ABC =$

A. $\frac{\pi}{4}$  B. $\frac{\pi}{6}$

C. $\frac{\pi}{2}$  D. $\frac{\pi}{3}$

5. Domain and Range of $\cos^{-1}x =$

A. $(-1, 1), (0, \pi)$  B. $[-1, 1], (0, \pi)$

C. $[-1, 1], [0, \pi]$  D. $(-1,1)\left[-\frac{\pi}{2}, \frac{\pi}{2}\right]$

## PASSAGE-7

The Government of India is planning to fix a hoarding board at the face of a building on the road of a busy market for awareness on COVID-19 protocol. Ram, Robert and Rahim are the three engineers who are working on this project. "A" is considered to be a person viewing the hoarding board 20 metres away from the building, standing at the edge of a pathway nearby. Ram, Robert and Rahim suggested to the firm to place the hoarding board at three different locations namely C, D and E. "C" is at the height of 10 metres from the ground level. For the viewer A, the angle of elevation of "D" is double the angle of elevation of "C" The angle of elevation of "E" is triple the angle of elevation of "C" for the same viewer. Look at the figure given and based on the above information answer the following:

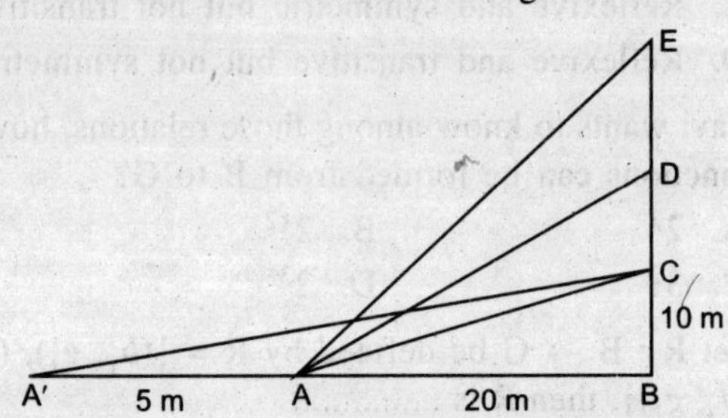


1. Measure of $\angle CAB =$

A. $\tan^{-1}(2)$  B. $\tan^{-1}\left(\frac{1}{2}\right)$

C. $\tan^{-1}(1)$  D. $\tan^{-1}(3)$

2. Measure of $\angle DAB =$

A. $\tan^{-1}\left(\frac{3}{4}\right)$  B. $\tan^{-1}(3)$

C. $\tan^{-1}\left(\frac{4}{3}\right)$  D. $\tan^{-1}(4)$

3. Measure of $\angle EAB =$

A. $\tan^{-1}(11)$  B. $\tan^{-1}3$

C. $\tan^{-1}\left(\frac{2}{11}\right)$  D. $\tan^{-1}\left(\frac{11}{2}\right)$

**4.** A′ Is another viewer standing on the same line of observation across the road. If the width of the road is 5 meters, then the difference between ∠CAB and ∠CA′B is:

A. $\tan^{-1}\left(\frac{1}{2}\right)$ B. $\tan^{-1}\left(\frac{1}{8}\right)$

C. $\tan^{-1}\left(\frac{2}{5}\right)$ D. $\tan^{-1}\left(\frac{11}{21}\right)$

**5.** Domain and Range of $\tan^{-1}x$ =

A. $R^+, \left(-\frac{\pi}{2},\frac{\pi}{2}\right)$ B. $R^-, \left(-\frac{\pi}{2},\frac{\pi}{2}\right)$

C. $R, \left(-\frac{\pi}{2},\frac{\pi}{2}\right)$ D. $R, \left(0,\frac{\pi}{2}\right)$

## PASSAGE-8

A manufacture produces three stationery products Pencil, Eraser and Sharpener which he sells in two markets. Annual sales are indicated below:

| Market | Products (in numbers) | | |
|---|---|---|---|
| | *Pencil* | *Eraser* | *Sharpener* |
| A | 10,000 | 2000 | 18,000 |
| B | 6000 | 20,000 | 8,000 |

If the unit Sale price of Pencil, Eraser and Sharpener are ₹ 2.50, ₹ 1.50 and ₹ 1.00 respectively, and unit cost of the above three commodities are ₹ 2.00, ₹ 1.00 and ₹ 0.50 respectively, then,

Based on the above information answer the following:

**1.** Total revenue of market A

A. ₹ 64,000 B. ₹ 60,400

C. ₹ 46,000 D. ₹ 40,600

**2.** Total revenue of market B

A. ₹ 35,000 B. ₹ 53,000

C. ₹ 50,300 D. ₹ 30,500

**3.** Cost incurred in market A

A. ₹ 13,000 B. ₹ 30,100

C. ₹ 10,300 D. ₹ 31,000

**4.** Profit in market A and B respectively are

A. (₹ 15,000, ₹ 17,000)

B. (₹ 17,000, ₹ 15,000)

C. (₹ 51,000, ₹ 71,000)

D. (₹ 10,000, ₹ 20,000)

**5.** Gross profit in both market

A. ₹ 23,000 B. ₹ 20,300

C. ₹ 32,000 D. ₹ 30,200

## PASSAGE-9

Amit, Biraj and Chirag were given the task of creating a square matrix of order 2. Below are the matrices created by them. A, B, C are the matrices created by Amit, Biraj and Chirag respectively.

$$A = \begin{bmatrix} 1 & 2 \\ -1 & 3 \end{bmatrix} \quad B = \begin{bmatrix} 4 & 0 \\ 1 & 5 \end{bmatrix} \quad C = \begin{bmatrix} 2 & 0 \\ 1 & -2 \end{bmatrix}$$

If $a = 4$ and $b = -2$, based on the above information answer the following:

**1.** Sum of the matrices A, B and C, A + (B + C) is:

A. $\begin{bmatrix} 1 & 6 \\ 2 & 7 \end{bmatrix}$ B. $\begin{bmatrix} 6 & 1 \\ 2 & 7 \end{bmatrix}$

C. $\begin{bmatrix} 7 & 2 \\ 1 & 6 \end{bmatrix}$ D. $\begin{bmatrix} 2 & 1 \\ 7 & 6 \end{bmatrix}$

**2.** $(A^T)^T$ is equal to:

A. $\begin{bmatrix} 1 & 2 \\ -1 & 3 \end{bmatrix}$ B. $\begin{bmatrix} 2 & 1 \\ 3 & -1 \end{bmatrix}$

C. $\begin{bmatrix} 1 & -1 \\ 2 & 3 \end{bmatrix}$ D. $\begin{bmatrix} 2 & 3 \\ -1 & 1 \end{bmatrix}$

**3.** $(bA)^T$ is equal to:

A. $\begin{bmatrix} -2 & -4 \\ 2 & -6 \end{bmatrix}$ B. $\begin{bmatrix} -2 & 2 \\ -4 & -6 \end{bmatrix}$

C. $\begin{bmatrix} -2 & 2 \\ -6 & -4 \end{bmatrix}$ D. $\begin{bmatrix} -6 & -2 \\ 2 & 4 \end{bmatrix}$

**4.** AC-BC is equal to:

A. $\begin{bmatrix} -4 & -6 \\ -4 & 4 \end{bmatrix}$ B. $\begin{bmatrix} -4 & -4 \\ 4 & -6 \end{bmatrix}$

C. $\begin{bmatrix} -4 & -4 \\ -6 & 4 \end{bmatrix}$ D. $\begin{bmatrix} -6 & 4 \\ -4 & -4 \end{bmatrix}$

**5.** $(a + b)$B is equal to:

A. $\begin{bmatrix} 0 & 8 \\ 10 & 2 \end{bmatrix}$ B. $\begin{bmatrix} 2 & 10 \\ 8 & 0 \end{bmatrix}$

C. $\begin{bmatrix} 8 & 0 \\ 2 & 10 \end{bmatrix}$ D. $\begin{bmatrix} 2 & 0 \\ 8 & 10 \end{bmatrix}$

## PASSAGE-10

Three schools DPS, CVC and KVS decided to organize a fair for collecting money for helping the flood victims. They sold handmade fans, mats and plates from recycled material at a cost of ₹ 25, ₹ 100 and ₹ 50 each respectively. The numbers of articles sold are given as:

| School/Article | DPS | CVC | KVS |
|---|---|---|---|
| Handmade fans | 40 | 25 | 35 |
| Mats | 50 | 40 | 50 |
| Plates | 20 | 30 | 40 |

Based on the information given above, answer the following questions:

1. What is the total money (in Rupees) collected by the school DPS?
   A. 700 B. 7,000
   C. 6,125 D. 7875

2. What is the total amount of money (in Rs.) collected by schools CVC and KVS?
   A. 14,000 B. 15,725
   C. 21,000 D. 13,125

3. What is the total amount of money collected by all three schools DPS, CVC and KVS?
   A. ₹ 15,775 B. ₹ 14,000
   C. ₹ 21,000 D. ₹ 17,125

4. If the number of handmade fans and plates are interchanged for all the schools, then what is the total money collected by all schools?
   A. ₹ 18,000 B. ₹ 6,750
   C. ₹ 5,000 D. ₹ 21,250

5. How many articles (in total) are sold by three schools?
   A. 230 B. 130
   C. 430 D. 330

## PASSAGE-11

On her birth day, Seema decided to donate some money to children of an orphanage home. If there were 8 children less, everyone would have got Rs.10 more. However, if there were 16 children more, everyone would have got Rs. 10 less. Let the number of children be x and the amount distributed by Seema for one child be y (in Rs.).

Based on the information given above, answer the following questions:

1. The equations in terms $x$ and $y$ are:
   A. $5x - 4y = 40$, $5x - 8y = -80$ B. $5x - 4y = 40$, $5x - 8y = 80$
   C. $5x - 4y = 40$, $5x + 8y = -80$ D. $5x + 4y = 40$, $5x - 8y = -80$

2. Which of the following matrix equations represent the information given above?
   A. $\begin{bmatrix} 5 & 4 \\ 5 & 8 \end{bmatrix}\begin{bmatrix} x \\ y \end{bmatrix} = \begin{bmatrix} 40 \\ -80 \end{bmatrix}$
   B. $\begin{bmatrix} 5 & -4 \\ 5 & -8 \end{bmatrix}\begin{bmatrix} x \\ y \end{bmatrix} = \begin{bmatrix} 40 \\ 80 \end{bmatrix}$
   C. $\begin{bmatrix} 5 & -4 \\ 5 & -8 \end{bmatrix}\begin{bmatrix} x \\ y \end{bmatrix} = \begin{bmatrix} 40 \\ -80 \end{bmatrix}$
   D. $\begin{bmatrix} 5 & 4 \\ 5 & -8 \end{bmatrix}\begin{bmatrix} x \\ y \end{bmatrix} = \begin{bmatrix} 40 \\ -80 \end{bmatrix}$

3. The number of children who were given some money by Seema, is:
   A. 30 B. 40
   C. 23 D. 32

4. How much amount is given to each child by Seema?
   A. ₹ 32 B. ₹ 30
   C. ₹ 62 D. ₹ 26

5. How much amount Seema spends in distributing the money to all the students of the Orphanage?
   A. ₹ 609 B. ₹ 960
   C. ₹ 906 D. ₹ 690

## PASSAGE-12

Two farmers Ramakishan and Gurucharan Singh cultivate only three varieties of rice namely Basmati, Permal and Naura. The sale (in rupees) of these varieties of rice by both the farmers in the month of September and October are given by the following matrices A and B.

September sales (in Rupees)

$$A = \begin{bmatrix} 10,000 & 20,000 & 30,000 \\ 50,000 & 30,000 & 10,000 \end{bmatrix} \begin{matrix} \text{Ramakishan} \\ \text{Gurucharan} \end{matrix}$$

October sales (in Rupees)

$$B = \begin{bmatrix} 5,000 & 10,000 & 6,000 \\ 20,000 & 10,000 & 10,000 \end{bmatrix} \begin{matrix} \text{Ramakishan} \\ \text{Gurucharan} \end{matrix}$$

1. The total sales in September and October for each farmer in each variety can be represented as ............ .
   A. A + B B. A – B
   C. A > B D. A < B

2. What is the value of $A_{23}$?
   A. 10000
   B. 20000
   C. 30000
   D. 40000

3. The decrease in sales from September to October is given by ................ .
   A. A + B B. A – B
   C. A > B D. A < B

4. If Ramkishan receives 2% profit on gross sales, compute his profit for each variety sold in October.
   A. ₹ 100, ₹ 200 and ₹ 120
   B. ₹ 100, ₹ 200 and ₹ 130
   C. ₹ 100, ₹ 220 and ₹ 120
   D. ₹ 110, ₹ 200 and ₹ 120

5. If Gurucharan receives 2% profit on gross sales, compute his profit for each variety sold in September.
   A. ₹ 100, ₹ 200, ₹ 120
   B. ₹ 1000, ₹ 600, ₹ 200
   C. ₹ 400, ₹ 200, ₹ 120
   D. ₹ 1200, ₹ 200, ₹ 120

## PASSAGE-13

Manjit wants to donate a rectangular plot of land for a school in his village. When he was asked to give dimensions of the plot, he told that if its length is decreased by 50 m and breadth is increased by 50 m, then its area will remain same, but if length is decreased by 10m and breadth is decreased by 20m, then its area will decrease by 5300 $m^2$.

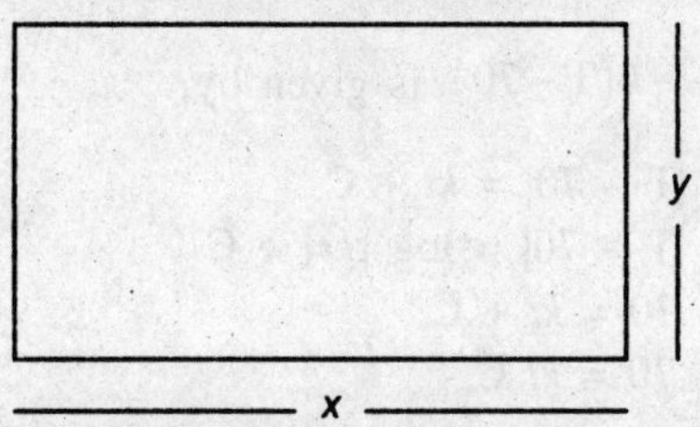


Based on the information given above, answer the following questions:

**1.** The equations in terms of X and Y are

A. $x - y = 50, 2x - y = 550$

B. $x - y = 50, 2x + y = 550$

C. $x + y = 50, 2x + y = 550$

D. $x + y = 50, 2x + y = 550$

**2.** Which of the following matrix equation is represented by the given information

A. $\begin{bmatrix} 1 & -1 \\ 2 & 1 \end{bmatrix}\begin{bmatrix} x \\ y \end{bmatrix} = \begin{bmatrix} 50 \\ 550 \end{bmatrix}$

B. $\begin{bmatrix} 1 & 1 \\ 2 & 1 \end{bmatrix}\begin{bmatrix} x \\ y \end{bmatrix} = \begin{bmatrix} 50 \\ 550 \end{bmatrix}$

C. $\begin{bmatrix} 1 & 1 \\ 2 & -1 \end{bmatrix}\begin{bmatrix} x \\ y \end{bmatrix} = \begin{bmatrix} 50 \\ 550 \end{bmatrix}$

D. $\begin{bmatrix} 1 & 1 \\ 2 & 1 \end{bmatrix}\begin{bmatrix} x \\ y \end{bmatrix} = \begin{bmatrix} -50 \\ -550 \end{bmatrix}$

**3.** The value of $x$ (length of rectangular field) is

A. 150 m  B. 400 m

C. 200 m  D. 320 m

**4.** The value of $y$ (breadth of rectangular field) is

A. 150 m  B. 200 m

C. 430 m  D. 350 m

**5.** How much is the area of rectangular field?

A. 60000 sq. m.  B. 30000 sq. m.

C. 30000 m  D. 3000 m

## PASSAGE-14

The Relation between the height of the plant ($y$ in cm) with respect to exposure to sunlight is governed by the following equation $y = 4x - \frac{1}{2}x^2$ where x is the number of days exposed to sunlight.

**1.** The rate of growth of the plant with respect to sunlight is ..............

A. $4x - \frac{1}{2}x^2$  B. $4 - x$

C. $x - 4$  D. $x - \frac{1}{2}x^2$

**2.** What is the number of days it will take for the plant to grow to the maximum height?

A. 4  B. 6

C. 7  D. 10

**3.** What is the maximum height of the plant?

A. 12 cm  B. 10 cm

C. 8 cm  D. 6 cm

**4.** What will be the height of the plant after 2 days?

A. 4 cm  B. 6 cm

C. 8 cm  D. 10 cm

**5.** If the height of the plant is $\frac{7}{2}$ cm, the number of days it has been exposed to the sunlight is .............

A. 2  B. 3

C. 4  D. 1

## PASSAGE-15

$P(x) = - 5x^2 + 125\,x + 37500$ is the total profit function of a company, where x is the production of the company.

**1.** What will be the production when the profit is maximum?

A. 37500  B. 12.5

C. –12.5  D. –37500

**2.** What will be the maximum profit?

A. ₹ 38,28,125

B. ₹ 38281.25

C. ₹ 39,000

D. None

**3.** Check in which interval the profit is strictly increasing.

A. $(12.5, \infty)$

B. for all real numbers

C. for all positive real numbers

D. $(0, 12.5)$

**4.** When the production is 2units what will be the profit of the company?

A. 37500  B. 37,730

C. 37,770  D. None

**5.** What will be production of the company when the profit is ₹ 38250?

A. 15

B. 30

C. 2

D. data is not sufficient to find

## PASSAGE-16

A potter made a mud vessel, where the shape of the pot is based on $f(x) = |x - 3| + |x - 2|$, where $f(x)$ represents the height of the pot.

**1.** When $x > 4$ What will be the height in terms of $x$?
A. $x - 2$  B. $x - 3$
C. $2x - 5$  D. $5 - 2x$

**2.** Will the slope vary with $x$ value?
A. Yes
B. No

**3.** What is $\frac{dy}{dx}$ at $x = 3$
A. 2
B. −2
C. Function is not differentiable
D. 1

**4.** When the $x$ value lies between (2, 3) then the function is:
A. $2x - 5$  B. $5 - 2x$
C. 1  D. 5

**5.** If the potter is trying to make a pot using the function $f(x) = [x]$, will he get a pot or not? Why?
A. Yes, because it is a continuous function
B. Yes, because it is not continuous
C. No , because it is a continuous function
D. No , because it is not continuous

## PASSAGE-17

A Veterinary doctor was examining a sick cat brought by a pet lover. When it was brought to the hospital, it was already dead. The pet lover wanted to find its time of death. He took the temperature of the cat at 11.30 pm which was 94.6°F. He took the temperature again after one hour; the temperature was lower than the first observation. It was 93.4°F. The room in which the cat was put is always at 70°F. The normal temperature of the cat is taken as 98.6°F when it was alive. The doctor estimated the time of death using Newton law of cooling which is governed by the differential equation: $\frac{dT}{dt} \propto (T - 70)$, where 70°F is the room temperature and T is the temperature of the object at time $t$.

Substituting the two different observations of T and $t$ made, in the solution of the differential equation $\frac{dT}{dt} - k(T - 70)$ where k is a constant of proportion, time of death is calculated.

1. State the degree of the above given differential equation.
2. Which method of solving a differential equation helped in calculation of the time of death?
A. Variable separable method
B. Solving Homogeneous differential equation
C. Solving Linear differential equation
D. all of the above
3. If the temperature was measured 2 hours after 11.30 pm, will the time of death change? (Yes/No)
4. The solution of the differential equation $\frac{dT}{dt} - k(T - 70)$ is given by,
A. $\log |T - 70| = kt + C$
B. $\log |T - 70| = \log |kt| + C$
C. $T - 70 = kt + C$
D. $T - 70 = kt\ C$

**5.** If $t = 0$ when T is 72, then the value of $c$ is
A. −2  B. 0
C. 2  D. Log 2

## PASSAGE-18

Polio drops are delivered to 50 K children in a district. The rate at which polio drops are given is directly proportional to the number of children who have not been administered the drops. By the end of 2nd week half the children have been given the polio drops. How many will have been given the drops by the end of 3rd week can be estimated using the solution to the differential equation $\frac{dy}{dx} = k(50 - y)$ where $x$ denotes the number of weeks and $y$ the number of children who have been given the drops.

1. State the order of the above given differential equation.
2. Which method of solving a differential equation can be used to solve $\frac{dy}{dx} = k(50 - y)$?
A. Variable separable method
B. Solving Homogeneous differential equation
C. Solving Linear differential equation
D. all of the above

**3.** The solution of the differential equation $\frac{dy}{dx} = k(50 - y)$ is given by,
A. $\log |50 - y| = kx + C$
B. $-\log |50 - y| = kx + C$
C. $\log |50 - y| = \log |kx| + C$
D. $50 - y = kx + C$

**4.** The value of c in the particular solution given that $y(0) = 0$ and $k = 0.049$ is.
A. log 50  B. log 1/50
C. 50  D. − 50

5. Which of the following solutions may be used to find the number of children who have been given the polio drops?
   A. $y = 50 - e^{kx}$
   B. $y = 50 - e^{-kx}$
   C. $y = 50\ (1 - e^{-kx})$
   D. $y = 50\ (e^{-kx} - 1)$

## PASSAGE-19

A coach is training 3 players. He observes that the player A can hit a target 4 times in 5 shots, player B can hit 3 times in 4 shots and the player C can hit 2 times in 3 shots

From this situation answer the following:

1. Let the target is hit by A, B: the target is hit by B and, C: the target is hit by A and C. Then, the probability that A, B and, C all will hit, is
   A. 4/5 B. 3/5
   C. 2/5 D. 1/5
2. Referring to (*i*), what is the probability that B, C will hit and A will lose?
   A. 1/10 B. 3/10
   C. 7/10 D. 4/10
3. With reference to the events mentioned in (*i*), what is the probability that 'any two of A, B and C will hit?
   A. 1/30 B. 11/30
   C. 17/30 D. 13/30
4. What is the probability that 'none of them will hit the target'?
   A. 1/30 B. 1/60
   C. 1/15 D. 2/15
5. What is the probability that at least one of A, B or C will hit the target?
   A. 59/60 B. 2/5
   C. 3/5 D. 1/60

## PASSAGE-20

The reliability of a COVID PCR test is specified as follows: Of people having COVID, 90% of the test detects the disease but 10% goes undetected. Of people free of COVID, 99% of the test is judged COVID negative but 1% are diagnosed as showing COVID positive. From a large population of which only 0.1% have COVID, one person is selected at random, given the COVID PCR test, and the pathologist reports him/her as COVID positive.

Based on the above information, answer the following:

1. What is the probability of the 'person to be tested as COVID positive' given that 'he is actually having COVID?
   A. 0.001 B. 0.1
   C. 0.8 D. 0.9
2. What is the probability of the 'person to be tested as COVID positive' given that 'he is actually not having COVID'?
   A. 0.01 B. 0.99
   C. 0.1 D. 0.001
3. What is the probability that the 'person is actually not having COVID?
   A. 0.998 B. 0.999
   C. 0.001 D. 0.111
4. What is the probability that the 'person is actually having COVID given that 'he is tested as COVID positive'?
   A. 0.83
   B. 0.0803
   C. 0.083
   D. 0.089
5. What is the probability that the 'person selected will be diagnosed as COVID positive'?
   A. 0.1089 B. 0.01089
   C. 0.0189 D. 0.189

## PASSAGE-21

In answering a question on a multiple choice test for class XII, a student either knows the answer or guesses. Let 3/5 be the probability that he knows the answer and 2/5 be the probability that he guesses. Assume that a student who guesses at the answer will be correct with probability 1/3. Let $E_1$, $E_2$, E be the events that the student knows the answer, guesses the answer and answers correctly respectively.

Based on the above information, answer the following

1. What is the value of $P(E_1)$?
   A. 2/5 B. 1/3
   C. 1 D. 3/5
2. Value of $P(E \mid E_1)$ is
   A. 1/3 B. 1
   C. 2/3 D. 415
3. $\sum_{k=1}^{k=2} P(E|E_k)P(E_k)$ equals
   A. 11/15 B. 4/15
   C. 1/5 D. 1
4. Value of $\sum_{k=1}^{k=2} P(E_k)$
   A. 1/3 B. 1/5
   C. 1 D. 3/5
5. What is the probability that the student knows the answer given that he answered it correctly?
   A. 2/11 B. 5/3
   C. 9/11 D. 13/3

# ANSWERS

## PASSAGE-1

| 1 | 2 | 3 | 4 | 5 |
|---|---|---|---|---|
| D | A | A | C | A |

## PASSAGE-2

| 1 | 2 | 3 | 4 | 5 |
|---|---|---|---|---|
| A | A | D | D | B |

## PASSAGE-3

| 1 | 2 | 3 | 4 | 5 |
|---|---|---|---|---|
| A | A | D | B | A |

## PASSAGE-4

| 1 | 2 | 3 | 4 | 5 |
|---|---|---|---|---|
| A | A | A | A | A |

## PASSAGE-5

| 1 | 2 | 3 | 4 | 5 |
|---|---|---|---|---|
| A | C | A | A | A |

## PASSAGE-6

| 1 | 2 | 3 | 4 | 5 |
|---|---|---|---|---|
| B | C | D | C | C |

## PASSAGE-7

| 1 | 2 | 3 | 4 | 5 |
|---|---|---|---|---|
| B | C | D | B | C |

## PASSAGE-8

| 1 | 2 | 3 | 4 | 5 |
|---|---|---|---|---|
| C | B | D | A | C |

## PASSAGE-9

| 1 | 2 | 3 | 4 | 5 |
|---|---|---|---|---|
| C | A | B | C | C |

## PASSAGE-10

| 1 | 2 | 3 | 4 | 5 |
|---|---|---|---|---|
| B | A | C | D | D |

## PASSAGE-11

| 1 | 2 | 3 | 4 | 5 |
|---|---|---|---|---|
| A | C | D | B | B |

## PASSAGE-12

| 1 | 2 | 3 | 4 | 5 |
|---|---|---|---|---|
| A | A | B | A | B |

## PASSAGE-13

| 1 | 2 | 3 | 4 | 5 |
|---|---|---|---|---|
| B | A | C | A | B |

## PASSAGE-14

| 1 | 2 | 3 | 4 | 5 |
|---|---|---|---|---|
| B | A | C | B | D |

## PASSAGE-15

| 1 | 2 | 3 | 4 | 5 |
|---|---|---|---|---|
| B | B | D | B | A |

## PASSAGE-16

| 1 | 2 | 3 | 4 | 5 |
|---|---|---|---|---|
| C | A | C | C | D |

## PASSAGE-17

| 1 | 2 | 3 | 4 | 5 |
|---|---|---|---|---|
| Degree is 1 | A | No | A | D |

## PASSAGE-18

| 1 | 2 | 3 | 4 | 5 |
|---|---|---|---|---|
| Order is 1 | A | B | B | C |

## PASSAGE-19

| 1 | 2 | 3 | 4 | 5 |
|---|---|---|---|---|
| C | A | D | B | A |

## PASSAGE-20

| 1 | 2 | 3 | 4 | 5 |
|---|---|---|---|---|
| D | A | B | C | B |

## PASSAGE-21

| 1 | 2 | 3 | 4 | 5 |
|---|---|---|---|---|
| D | B | A | C | C |

# ACCOUNTANCY/ BOOK KEEPING

# 1

# ACCOUNTING FOR NOT-FOR-PROFIT ORGANISATION

## MEANING AND CHARACTERISTICS OF NOT-FOR-PROFIT ORGANISATION

Not-for-Profit Organisations refer to the organisations that are for used for the welfare of the society and are set up as charitable institutions which function without any profit motive. Their main aim is to provide service to a specific group or the public at large. Normally, they do not manufacture, purchase or sell goods and may not have credit transactions.

Hence they need not maintain many books of account (as the trading concerns do) and Trading and Profit and Loss Account. The funds raised by such organisations are credited to capital fund or general fund. The major sources of their income usually are subscriptions from their members donations, grants-in-aid, income from investments, etc.

The main objective of keeping records in such organisations is to meet the statutory requirement and help them in exercising control over utilisation of their funds. They also have to prepare the financial statements at the end of each accounting period (usually a financial year) and ascertain their income and expenditure and the financial position, and submit them to the statutory authority called Registrar of Societies.

**The main characteristics of such organisations are:**

- The main sources of income of such organisations are: (*i*) subscriptions from members, (*ii*) donations (general). (*iii*) legacies(general). (*iv*) grant-in-aid, (*v*) income from investments, etc.
- Such organisations are formed for providing service to a specific group or public at large such as education, health care, recreation, sports and so on without any consideration of caste, creed and colour.
- The surplus generated in the form of excess of income over expenditure is not distributed amongst the members.
- The accounting information provided by such organisations is meant for the present and potential contributors and to meet the statutory requirement.
- The Not-for-Profit Organisations earn their reputation on the basis of their contributions to the welfare of the society rather than on the customers' or owners' satisfaction.
- The funds raised by such organisations through various sources are credited to capital fund or general fund.
- Their affairs are usually managed by a managing/ executive committee elected by its members.
- These are organised as charitable trusts/societies and subscribers to such organisation are called members.

## ACCOUNTING RECORDS OF NOT-FOR-PROFIT ORGANISATIONS

The main sources of their income are subscriptions from members, donations, financial assistance from government and income from investments. Most of their transactions are in cash or through the bank. These institutions are required by law to keep proper accounting records and keep proper control over the utilization of their funds. This is why they usually keep a cash book in which all receipts and payments are duly recorded. They also maintain a ledger containing the accounts of all incomes, expenses, assets and liabilities which facilitates the preparation of financial statements at the end of the accounting period. In addition, they are required to maintain a stock register to keep complete record of all fixed assets and the consumables.

**Final Accounts or Financial Statements:** The Not-for-Profit Organisations are also required to prepare financial statements at the end of the each accounting period. Although these organisations are non-profit making entities and they are not required to make Trading and Profit & Loss Account but it is necessary to know whether the income during the year was sufficient to meet the expenses or not. Not only that they have to provide the necessary financial information to members, donors, and contributors and also to the Registrar of Societies.

For this purpose, they have to prepare their final accounts at the end of the accounting period and the general principles of accounting are fully applicable in their preparation as stated earlier, the final accounts of a 'not-for-profit organisation' consist of the following:

- Receipt and Payment Account
- Income and Expenditure Account, and
- Balance Sheet.

The Receipt and Payment Account is the summary of cash and bank transactions which helps in the preparation of Income and Expenditure Account and the Balance Sheet. Besides, it is a legal requirement as the Receipts and Payments Account has also to be submitted to the Registrar of Societies along with the Income and Expenditure Account, and the Balance Sheet.

Income and Expenditure Account is akin to Profit and Loss Account. The Not-for-Profit Organisations usually prepare the Income and Expenditure Account and a Balance Sheet with the help of Receipt and Payment Account.

## RECEIPT AND PAYMENT ACCOUNT

It is prepared at the end of the accounting year on the basis of cash receipts and cash payments recorded in the cash book. It is a summary of cash and bank transactions under various heads.

**Illustration:**

**Silver Cricket Club Cash Book (Columnar)**

*Dr.* *Cr.*

| Date 2014 | Receipts | L.F. | Bank Amount (₹) | Office Amount (₹) | Date 2014 | Payments | L.F. | Bank Amount (₹) | Office Amount (₹) |
|---|---|---|---|---|---|---|---|---|---|
| April 1 | Balance b/d | | 35,000 | 20,000 | April 15 | Insurance premium | | 15,000 | |
| April 10 | Subscriptions | | 1,20,000 | | May 12 | Printing and stationery | | 10,750 | |
| April 10 | Entrance fees | | 13,000 | | May 20 | Postage and courier fees | | | 430 |
| May 20 | Life membership fees | | 12,000 | | June 16 | Telephone expenses | | | 810 |
| June 12 | Locker rent | | | 42,000 | July 10 | Wages and salaries | | | 22,000 |
| July 23 | Life membership fees | | 8,000 | | July 15 | Rates and Taxes | | 17,000 | |
| Aug. 20 | Donation for building | | 60,000 | | July 30 | Govt. securities | | 1,00,000 | |
| Sept. 13 | Subscriptions (2013-14) | | 30,000 | | Aug. 13 | Printing and stationery | | 15,000 | |
| Sept. 13 | Subscription | | 45,000 | | Aug. 15 | Postage and courier service | | | 480 |
| Sept. 14 | Entrance fees | | 10,000 | | Sept. 10 | Lighting | | 12,250 | |
| Nov. 9 | Subscription | | 35,000 | | Sept 13 | Telephone expenses | | | 830 |
| Nov. 9 | Subscription (2015-16) | | 10,000 | | Oct. 1 | Wages and salaries | | 10,000 | 12,000 |
| **2015** | | | | | Oct. 18 | Printing and stationery | | 13,000 | |
| Feb. 07 | Subscription | | 25,000 | | Oct. 31 | Govt. securities | | 1,00,000 | |
| Mar. 28 | Interest on government securities | | 18,000 | | Dec. 31 | Wages and Salaries | | 22,000 | |
| | | | | | **2015** | | | | |
| | | | | | Jan. 21 | Courier charges | | | 240 |
| | | | | | Feb. 2 | Telephone expenses | | | 960 |
| | | | | | Mar. 10 | Postage and Courier fees | | | 850 |
| | | | | | Mar. 27 | Lighting | | 14,000 | |
| | | | | | Mar. 27 | Wages and Salaries | | 22,000 | |
| | | | | | Mar. 31 | Balance c/d | | 70,000 | 23,400 |
| | | | **4,21,000** | **62,000** | | | | **4,21,000** | **62,000** |

**Part A**

Item wise Aggregation of various Receipts

**Subscriptions (2014–2015)**

| Date | Amount (₹) |
|---|---|
| April 10, 2014 | 1,20,000 |
| Sept. 13, 2014 | 45,000 |
| Nov. 9, 2014 | 35,000 |
| Feb. 7, 2015 | 25,000 |
| **Total** | **2,25,000** |

**Subscriptions (2013–14)**

| Date | Amount (₹) |
|---|---|
| Sept. 13, 2014 | 30,000 |
| **Total** | **30,000** |

**Subscription (2015–16)**

| Date | Amount (₹) |
|---|---|
| Nov. 9, 2014 | 10,000 |
| **Total** | **10,000** |

**Entrance Fees**

| Date | Amount (₹) |
|---|---|
| April 10, 2014 | 13,000 |
| Sept.14, 2014 | 10,000 |
| **Total** | **23,000** |

**Locker Rent**

| Date | Amount (₹) |
|---|---|
| June 12, 2014 | 42,000 |
| **Total** | **42,000** |

**Life Membership fee**

| Date | Amount (₹) |
|---|---|
| May 20, 2014 | 12,000 |
| July 23, 2014 | 8,000 |
| **Total** | **20,000** |

**Donation for Buildings**

| Date | Amount (₹) |
|---|---|
| Aug. 20, 2014 | 60,000 |
| **Total** | **60,000** |

**Interest on Government securities**

| Date | Amount (₹) |
|---|---|
| March 28, 2015 | 18,000 |
| **Total** | **18,000** |

**Part B**

Item wise Aggregation of various Payments

**Insurance Premium**

| Date | Amount (₹) |
|---|---|
| April 15, 2014 | 15,000 |
| **Total** | **15,000** |

**Printing and Stationery**

| Date | Amount (₹) |
|---|---|
| May 12, 2014 | 10,750 |
| Aug. 13, 2014 | 15,000 |
| Oct. 18, 2014 | 13,000 |
| **Total** | **38,750** |

**Lighting**

| Date | Amount (₹) |
|---|---|
| Sept. 10, 2014 | 12,250 |
| March 27, 2015 | 14,000 |
| **Total** | **26,250** |

**Telephone Expenses**

| Date | Amount (₹) |
|---|---|
| June 16, 2014 | 810 |
| Sept. 13, 2014 | 830 |
| Feb. 2, 2015 | 960 |
| **Total** | **2,600** |

**Rates and Taxes**

| Date | Amount (₹) |
|---|---|
| July 15, 2014 | 17,000 |
| **Total** | **17,000** |

**Government Securities**

| Date | Amount (₹) |
|---|---|
| July 30, 2014 | 1,00,000 |
| Oct. 31, 2014 | 1,00,000 |
| **Total** | **2,00,000** |

**Wages and Salaries**

| Date | Amount (₹) |
|---|---|
| July 10, 2014 | 22,000 |
| Oct. 1, 2014 | 22,000 |
| Dec. 31, 2014 | 22,000 |
| March 27, 2015 | 22,000 |
| **Total** | **88,000** |

**Postage and Courier Service**

| Date | Amount (₹) |
|---|---|
| May 20, 2014 | 430 |
| Aug. 15, 2014 | 480 |
| Jan. 21, 2015 | 240 |
| March 10, 2015 | 850 |
| **Total** | **2,000** |

The above data can also be shown in the form of the respective accounts in the ledger. A detailed illustrative list of items of receipts and payments is given in table below.

| Receipts | Payments |
|---|---|
| 1. Donations | 1. Purchase of Fixed Assets |
| (a) General | 2. Purchase of Sports Material |
| (b) Specific purpose | 3. Investment in Securities |
| 2. Entrance Fees | 4. Printing and Stationery |
| 3. Legacies | 5. Postage and Courier Charges |
| 4. Sale of Investments | 6. Advertisements |
| 5. Sale of Fixed Assets | 7. Wages and Salary |
| 6. Subscriptions from Members | 8. Honorarium |
| 7. Life Membership Fees | 9. Telephone Charges |
| 8. Sale of old Newspapers | 10. Electricity and Water Charges |
| 9. Sale of Old Sports Material | 11. Repairs and Renewals |
| 10. Interest on Fixed Deposits | 12. Upkeep of Play Ground |
| 11. Interest/ Dividend on Investments | 13. Conveyance Charges |
| 12. Proceed from Charity Shows | 14. Subscription for Periodicals |
| 13. Sale of Scrap | 15. Audit Fees |
| 14. Grant-in-aid | 16. Entertainment Expenses |
| 15. Interest/Dividend on Specific Fund Investments | 17. Municipal Taxes |
|  | 18. Charity |
| 16. Miscellaneous Receipts. | 19. Insurance |

**Receipt and Payment Account for the year ending ...............**

| Receipts | Amount (₹) | Payments | Amount (₹) |
|---|---|---|---|
| Balance b/d |  | Balance b/d (Bank overdraft) | xxx |
| Cash in Hand | xxx | Wages and Salaries | xxx |
| Cash at Bank | xxx | Rent | xxx |
| Subscriptions | xxx | Rates and Taxes | xxx |
| General Donations | xxx | Insurance | xxx |
| Sale of newspaper/ periodicals/waste paper | xxx | Printing and Stationery | xxx |
|  |  | Postage and courier | xxx |
| Sale of old sports materials | xxx | Advertisement | xxx |
| Interest on fixed deposits |  | Sundry expenses | xxx |
| Interest/Dividend on general investments | xxx | Telephone charges | xxx |
| Locker Rent | xxx | Entertainment expenses | xxx |
| Sale of scraps | xxx | Audit fees | xxx |
| Proceeds from charity show | xxx | Honorarium | xxx |
| Miscellaneous receipts | xxx | Repair and Renewals | xxx |
| Grant-in-aid | xxx | Upkeep of ground | xxx |
| Legacies | xxx | Conveyance | xxx |
| Specific Donations | xxx | Newspapers and Periodicals | xxx |
| Sale of Investments | xxx | Purchases of Assets | xxx |
| Sale of Fixed Assets | xxx | Purchase of Investments | xxx |
| Life membership fees | xxx | Balance c/d | xxx |
| Entrance fees | xxx | Cash in hand | xxx |
| Receipts on account of specific purpose funds | xxx | Cash at Bank* | xxx |
| Interest on specific funds' investments | xxx |  |  |
| Balance b/d (Bank Overdraft)* | xxx |  |  |
|  | xxxxx |  | xxxxx |

***Format of Receipt and Payment Account***

*There will be either of the two amounts i.e., each at bank or bank overdraft, not both.

It may be noted that the receipts side of the Receipt and Payment Account gives a list of revenue receipts (for past, current and future periods) as well as capital receipts. Similarly, the payments side of the Receipts and Payments Account lists the Revenue Payments (for past, current and future periods) as well as Capital Payments.

### *Steps in the Preparation of Receipt and Payment Account*

- Take the opening balances of cash in hand and cash at bank and enter them on the debit side. In case there is bank overdraft at the begining of the year, enter the same on the credit side of this account.
- Show the total amounts of all receipts on its debit side irrespective of their nature (whether capital or revenue) and whether they pertain to past, current and future periods.
- Show the total amounts of all payments on its credit side irrespective of their nature (whether capital or revenue) and whether they pertain to past, current and future periods.
- None of the receivable income and payable expense is to be entered in this account as they do not involve inflow or outflow of cash.
- Find out the difference between the total of debit side and the total of credit side of the account and enter the same on the credit side as the closing balance of cash/bank. In case, however, the total of the credit side is more than that of the total of the debit side, show the difference on the debit as bank overdraft and close the account.

From the following information based on the data assimilated from the cash book given in example, the Receipt and Payment Account of Silver Cricket Club for the year ended on March 31, 2015 will be prepared as follows:

**Summary of Cash Book**

| Details | | Amount (₹) |
|---|---|---|
| Cash in hand as on April 1, 2014 | | 20,000 |
| Cash at bank as on April 1, 2014 | | 35,000 |
| Subscription: | ₹ | |
| 2013-14 | 30,000 | |
| 2014-15 | 2,25,000 | |
| 2015-16 | 10,000 | 2,65,000 |
| Donation for Building | | 60,000 |
| Entrance fees | | 23,000 |
| Life membership fee | | 20,000 |
| Printing and Stationery | | 38,750 |
| Lighting | | 26,250 |
| Rates and Taxes | | 17,000 |
| Telephone charges | | 2,600 |
| Postage and courier | | 2,000 |
| Wages and Salaries | | 88,000 |
| Insurance Premium | | 15,000 |
| Interest on government securities | | 18,000 |
| Locker rent | | 42,000 |
| Purchase of government securities | | 2,00,000 |
| Cash in hand as on March 31, 2015 | | 23,400 |
| Cash at bank as on March 31, 2015 | | 70,000 |

**Receipt and Payment Account for the year ending March 31, 2015**

Dr. Cr.

| Receipts | | Amount (₹) | Payments | Amount (₹) |
|---|---|---|---|---|
| Cash in hand as on April 1, 2014 | | 20,000 | Printing and Stationery | 38,750 |
| | | | Lighting | 26,250 |
| Cash at bank as on April 1, 2014 | | 35,000 | Rates and Taxes | 17,000 |
| | | | Telephone charges | 2,600 |
| Subscription: | | | Postage and Courier | 2,000 |
| 2013–14 | 30,000 | | Wages and Salaries | 88,000 |
| 2014–15 | 2,25,000 | | Insurance Premium | 15,000 |
| 2015–16 | 10,000 | 2,65,000 | Purchase of govt. securities | 2,00,000 |
| Donation for building | | 60,000 | Cash in hand as on March 31, 2015 | 23,400 |
| Entrance fees | | 23,000 | | |
| Life membership fee | | 20,000 | Cash at bank as on March 31, 2015 | 70,000 |
| Interest on investment in Government securities | | 18,000 | | |
| Locker rent | | 42,000 | | |
| | | **4,83,000** | | **4,83,000** |

## INCOME AND EXPENDITURE ACCOUNT

It is the summary of income and expenditure for the accounting year. It is just like a profit and loss account prepared on accrual basis in case of the business organisations. It includes only revenue items and the balance at the end represents surplus or deficit. The Income and Expenditure Account serves the same purpose as the profit and loss account of a business organisation does. All the revenue items relating to the current period are shown in this account, the expenses and losses on the expenditure side and incomes and gains on the income side of the account. It shows the net operating result in the form of surplus (i.e. excess of income over expenditure) or deficit (i.e. excess of expenditure over income), which is transferred to the capital fund shown in the balance sheet.

**Difference between Income and Expenditure Account and Receipt and Payment Account**

| Basis of distinction Account | Income and Expenditure | Receipt and Payment Account |
|---|---|---|
| Nature | It is like as profit and loss account. | It is the summary of the cash book. |
| Nature of Items | It records income and expenditure of *revenue* nature only. | It records receipts and payments of revenue as well as capital nature. |
| Period | Income and expenditure items relate only to the current period. | Receipts and payments may also relate to preceding and succeeding periods. |
| Debit side | Debit side of this account records expenses and losses. | Debit side of this account records the receipts. |
| Credit side | Credit side of this account records income and gains. | Credit side of this account records the payments. |
| Depreciation | Includes depreciation. | Does not includes depreciation. |
| Opening Balance | There is no opening balance. | Balance in the beginning represents cash in hand/ cash at bank or overdraft at the beginning. |
| Closing Balance | Balance at the end represents excess of income over expenditure or vice-versa. | Balance at the end represents cash in hand at the end and bank balance (or bank overdraft). |

## BALANCE SHEET

'Not-for-Profit' Organisations prepare Balance Sheet for ascertaining the financial position of the organisation. The preparation of their Balance Sheet is on the same pattern as that of the business entities.

It shows assets and liabilities as at the end of the year. Assets are shown on the right hand side and the liabilities on the left hand side.

However, there will be a Capital Fund or General Fund in place of the Capital and the surplus or deficit as per Income and Expenditure Account which is either added to/ deducted from the capital fund, as the case may be. It is also a common practice to add some of the capitalised items like legacies, entrance fees and life membership fees directly in the capital fund.

Besides the Capital or General Fund, there may be other funds created for specific purposes or to meet the requirements of the contributors/donors such as building fund, sports fund, etc. Such funds are shown separately in the liabilities side of the balance sheet.

Some times it becomes necessary to prepare Balance Sheet as at the beginning of the year in order to find out the opening balance of the capital/general fund.

### Some Peculiar Items

Some of the common peculiar items are explained as under:

- **Subscriptions:** Subscription is a membership fee paid by the member on annual basis. This is the main source of income of such orgnisations. Subscription paid by the members is shown as receipt in the Receipt and Payment Account and as income in the Income and Expenditure Account.
- Donations: It is a sort of gift in cash or property received from some person or organisation. It appears on the receipts side of the Receipts and Payments Account. Donation can be for specific purposes or for general purposes.
  - (*i*) **Specific Donations:** If donation received is to be utilised to achieve specified purpose, it is called Specific Donation.
  - (*ii*) **General Donations:** Such donations are to be utilised to promote the general purpose of the organisation. These are treated as revenue receipts as it is a regular source of income hence, it is taken to the income side of the Income and Expenditure Account of the current year.

**Balance Sheet of as on ..............**

| Liabilities | Amount (₹) | Assets | Amount (₹) |
|---|---|---|---|
| Capital fund: | | | |
| Opening Balance | ...... | Cash in hand and /or Cash at Bank | ...... |
| Add: Surplus | | | |
| OR | | Outstanding Incomes | ...... |
| Less: Deficit | | Prepaid Expenses | ...... |
| Add: Capitalised Income of the Current | ...... | Stock of Consumable Items: | |
| Year on account of: | | Previous Balance | |
| Legacies | ...... | Add: Purchases in the current period | |
| Entrance Fees | ...... | | |
| Life Membership Fees | ...... | Less: Value consumed during the period | ...... |
| Closing Balance | ...... | | |
| *Special Fund/Donations:* | | Previous Balance | ...... |
| Previous Balance (If any ) | | Add: Purchases in the current period | |
| Add: Receipts for the item during the period | | Less: Book Value of the Asset sold/disposed off | |
| Add: Income earned on fund/ Donations' Investments | | Closing Balance | ...... |
| Less: Expenses paid out of fund/ Donations | | | |
| Net Balance | ...... | | |
| Creditors for Purchases and/or supplies | ...... | | |
| Bank Overdraft | ...... | | |
| Outstanding Expenses: | | | |
| Income received in Advance | ...... | | |
| | ...... | | ...... |

- **Legacies:** It is the amount received as per the will of a deceased person who may or may not specify the use of the amount. Legacies, use of which is specified are specific legacy and is shown in the balance sheet as liability. If the use is not specified it is considered as revenue nature and credited to income and expenditure account.
- **Life Membership Fees:** Some members prefer to pay lump sum amount as life membership fee instead of paying periodic subscription. Such amount is treated as capital receipt and credited directly to the capital/ general fund.
- **Entrance Fees:** Entrance fee also known as admission fee is paid only once by the member at the time of becoming a member.

  In case of organisations like clubs and some charitable institutions, is limited and the amount of entrance fees is quite high. Hence, it is treated as non-recurring item and credited directly to capital/ general fund.
- **Sale of old asset:** Receipts from the sale of an old asset appear in the Receipts and Payments Account of the year in which it is sold. But any gain or loss on the sale of asset is taken to the Income and Expenditure Account of the year.
- **Sale of Periodicals:** It is an item of recurring nature and shown as the income side of the Income and Expenditure Account.
- **Sale of Sports Materials:** Sale of sports materials (used materials like old balls, bats, nets, etc) is the regular feature with any Sports Club. It is usually shown as an income in the Income and Expenditure Account.
- **Payments of Honorarium:** It is the amount paid to the person who is not the regular employee of the institution. Payment to an artist for giving performance at the club is an example of honorarium. This payment of honorarium is shown on the expenditure side of the Income and Expenditure Account.

- **Endowment Fund:** It is a fund arising from a bequest or gift, the income of which is devoted for a specific purpose.
- **Government Grant:** Schools, colleges, public hospitals, etc. depend upon government grant for their activities. The recurring grants in the form of maintenance grant is treated as revenue receipt (i.e. income of the current year) and credited to Income and Expenditure account.
- **Special Funds:** The Not-for-Profit Organisations office create special funds for certain purposes/activities such as 'prize funds', 'match fund' and 'sports fund', etc.
- **Stationery:** Normally expenses incurred on stationary, a consumable items are charged to Income and Expenditure Account.

  But in case stock of stationery (opening and/or closing) is given, the approach would be make necessary adjustments in purchases of stationery and work out cost of stationery consumed and show that amount in Income and Expenditure Account and its stock in the balance sheet.

## MULTIPLE CHOICE QUESTIONS

1. The Receipt and Payment account of a Non-Profit Organisation is a:
   A. Nominal Account
   B. Real Account
   C. Income Statement Account
   D. Financial Statements

2. In regard to Rent expenses paid in advance of a non-profit organisation which of the following classification is correct:
   A. Expense B. Liability
   C. Equity D. Assets

3. Income & Expenditure Account is based on:
   A. Cash Accounting
   B. Accrual Accounting
   C. Government Accounting
   D. Management Accounting

4. Which of the following is regarded as apt to show purchase of fixed asset for a non profit organisation:
   A. Income & Expenditure Account
   B. Profit & Loss Account
   C. Balance Sheet
   D. None of the above

5. Which of the following is to be recorded in an income and expenditure Account:
   A. Purchase of a fixed Asset
   B. Capital Expenditure incurred on a fixed asset
   C. Profit on the sale of a fixed asset
   D. Sale of a fixed asset

6. XYZ club has a bar that maintains a separate trading account for its trading activities. Which of the following is the treatment of profit or loss on bar trading activities?
   A. Profit or loss is directly shown in the Balance Sheet
   B. Profit or loss is to be presented in income and expenditure account
   C. Profit and loss is credited in income statement.
   D. Profit or loss is added to accumulated fund

7. Which of the following is the accounting equation for a non-profit organisation?
   A. Asset = Capital + Liabilities
   B. Capital + Liabilities = Assets
   C. Accumulated Fund + Liabilities = Assets
   D. Liabilities = Assets + Accumulated Fund

8. Subscription received but not yet earned is considered as:
   A. Asset B. Liability
   C. Income D. Expenditure

9. On What basis receipts and payments account is made:
   A. Cash basis
   B. Accrual basis
   C. Both Cash & Accrual basis
   D. None of these

10. The control of non trading concern rest in the hand of:
    A. Directors B. Managing Agents
    C. Governing body D. Promoters

11. If debit side of receipt and payment account exceeds the credit side, it represents:
    A. Deficit Balance B. Surplus Balance
    C. Cash at Bank D. Bank Overdraft

12. Deficit balance can be shown in balance Sheet as:
    A. Liability B. Assets
    C. Owner's equity D. None of these

13. Receipt and Payment account includes:
    A. Revenue items
    B. Cash items
    C. Revenue & Cash items
    D. None of the above

14. Which should be considered as capital receipt of a club:
    A. Donation B. sale of newspaper
    C. sale of bar items D. sale of furniture

**15.** At the beginning of an accounting year a club has assets of ₹ 19,000 and liabilities of ₹ 5,000. ₹ 1,800 is the debit balance of the income & expenditures account. The opening capital fund is:

A. ₹ 18,000 B. ₹ 11,200
C. ₹ 15,800 D. ₹ 24,800

**16.** The opening balance of the Prize fund of a sports club was ₹ 6,400. Further donations towards this fund received during the accounting year amounted to ₹ 4,300. During the year, ₹ 3,500 was spent on prizes and ₹ 400 was received as interest on investment of the Prize Fund. The closing balance of the Prize fund is:

A. ₹ 1,900 B. ₹ 10,200
C. ₹ 10,600 D. ₹ 7,600

**17.** Salaries payable for the current year amount to ₹ 8,500 at the end of the year. Outstanding salaries amounted to ₹ 300. Salaries paid in advance last year pertaining to the current year amounted to ₹ 500. Prepaid salaries for the next year amount to ₹ 250. Total amount paid for salaries during the year is:

A. ₹ 7,550 B. ₹ 7,500
C. ₹ 7,950 D. ₹ 6,500

**18.** Second hand furniture worth ₹ 6,000 was purchased. It was repaired for ₹ 600 and installed by workmen to whom ₹ 200 was paid as wages. The furniture should be capitalised for:

A. ₹ 6,200 B. ₹ 6,800
C. ₹ 6,600 D. ₹ 6,000

**19.** Fixed assets fund is:

A. Endowment Fund
B. Current restricted Fund
C. Current unrestricted fund
D. Meant for accounting of asses and depreciation

**20.** Donations received for special purpose should be:

A. Credited to a separate fund account and shown in the Balance Sheet
B. Treated as revenue
C. Treated as revenue unless the amount is large
D. Not recorded at all

**21.** Amount received from the sale of old furniture by a club is treated as:

A. Revenue Receipt B. Capital Receipt
C. Asset D. Liability

**22.** Receipt & Payment Account shows:

A. A debit balance B. A credit balance
C. Surplus or deficit D. Capital fund

**23.** Subscription received in advance during the accounting year is:

A. an income B. an expense
C. Asset D. Liability

**24.** Receipts and Payments Account generally shows:

A. A Debit balance B. A Credit balance
C. Surplus or Deficit D. Capital Fund

**25.** Income and Expenditure Account records transactions of:

A. Revenue nature only
B. Capital nature only
C. Both revenue and capital nature
D. Income of only revenue nature and expenditure of revenue and capital nature

**26.** Income and Expenditure Account reveals:

A. Surplus or Deficiency B. Cash in Hand
C. Net Profit D. Capital Account

**27.** The amount of 'Subscription received from members' by a Non-profit organisation is shown in which of the following?

A. Debit side of Income and Expenditure Account
B. Credit side of Income and Expenditure Account
C. Liability side of Balance Sheet
D. Assets side of Balance Sheet

**28.** Donation received for a special purpose:

A. Should be credited to Income and Expenditure Account
B. Should be credited to separate account and shown in the Balance Sheet
C. Should be shown on the assets side
D. Should not be recorded at all.

**29.** Subscription received by a school for organising annual function is treated as:

A. Capital Receipt (i.e., Liability)
B. Revenue Receipt (i.e., Income)
C. Asset
D. Earned Income

**30.** The amount of 'Entrance Fees' received by a Non-profit organisation (if it is received regularly) is shown in which of the following?

A. Liability side of Balance Sheet
B. Assets side of Balance Sheet
C. Debit side of Income and Expenditure Account
D. Credit side of Income and Expenditure Account

**31.** Out of following items, which one is shown in the Receipts and Payments Account?

A. Outstanding Salary B. Depreciation
C. Life Membership Fees D. Accrued Subscription

**32.** Not-for-profit organisations prepare:

A. Trading Account
B. Trading & Profit and Loss Account
C. Income and Expenditure Account
D. All of the above

33. The Receipts and Payments Account is a summary of:
A. Debit and Credit balance of Ledger Accounts
B. Cash Receipts and Payments
C. Expenses and Incomes
D. Assets and Liabilities

34. Receipts and Payments Account is a:
A. Personal Account
B. Real Account
C. Nominal Account
D. Real and Nominal Account, both

35. Income and Expenditure Account is a:
A. Personal Account
B. Real Account
C. Nominal Account
D. Real and Nominal Account, both

36. Credit side balance in Income & Expenditure Account reveals:
A. Excess of cash receipts overpayments
B. Excess of cash payments over receipts
C. Excess of expenditure over income
D. Excess of income over expenditure

37. Source of income for a not-for-profit organisation is:
A. Subscription from Members
B. Donation
C. Entrance Fees
D. All of the above

38. Which of the following represent capital receipt:
A. Life Membership Subscription
B. Donation
C. Subscription
D. Interest on Investments

39. Amount received from sale of grass by a club should be treated as:
A. Capital Receipt B. Revenue Receipt
C. Asset D. Earned Income

40. The amount received for sale of old sports materials by a Non-profit organisation is shown in which of the following?
A. Debit side of Income and Expenditure Account
B. Liability side of Balance Sheet
C. Credit side of Income and Expenditure Account
D. Assets side of Balance Sheet

41. If there is a 'Match Fund', then match expenses and incomes are transferred to:
A. Income and Expenditure A/c
B. Assets side of Balance Sheet
C. Liabilities side of Balance Sheet
D. Both Income and Expenditure A/c and to Balance Sheet

42. Subscription received in advance during the current year is:
A. an income B. an asset
C. a liability D. None of these

43. Subscription received in cash during the year amounted to ₹ 40,000; subscription outstanding at the end of previous year was ₹ 1,500 and outstanding at the end of current year was ₹ 2,000. Subscription received in advance for next year was ₹ 800. The amount credited to Income & Expenditure Account will be:
A. ₹ 38,700 B. ₹ 39,700
C. ₹ 40,300 D. ₹ 41,300

44. Subscription received in cash during the year amounted to ₹ 5,00,000; subscription outstanding at the end of previous year was ₹ 20,000 and outstanding at the end of current year was ₹ 25,000. Subscription received in advance for next year was ₹ 8,000 and received in advance during previous year was ₹ 7,000. The amount credited to Income & Expenditure Account will be:
A. ₹ 5,04,000 B. ₹ 5,06,000
C. ₹ 4,96,000 D. ₹ 4,94,000

45. Subscription received in cash during the year amounted to 760,000; subscription received in advance for next year was 73,000 and received in advance during previous year was 72,000. Subscription in arrear at the end of current year was 75,400. The amount credited to Income & Expenditure Account will be:
A. ₹ 53,600 B. ₹ 66,400
C. ₹ 55,600 D. ₹ 64,400

46. Subscription received in cash during the year amounted to ₹ 300000; subscription received in advance for next year was ₹ 10,000 and received in advance during previous year was ₹ 8,000. Subscription in arrear at the end of previous year was ₹ 18000 and subscription in arrear at the end of current year was ₹ 12000. The amount credited to Income & Expenditure Account will be:
A. ₹ 2,96,000 B. ₹ 3,04,000
C. ₹ 2,92,000 D. ₹ 3,08,000

47. What amount will be credited to the Income and Expenditure Account for the year ending 31st March, 2021 on the basis of the following information?

| | 31-3-2020 | 31-3-2021 |
|---|---|---|
| Outstanding Subscription | 10,000 | 25,000 |
| Advance Subscription | 3,000 | 2,000 |

Subscriptions received during the year 2020-21 were ₹ 4,00,000.
A. ₹ 3,84,000 B. ₹ 4,16,000
C. ₹ 3,86,000 D. ₹ 4,14,000

**48.** There are 200 members, each paying an annual subscription of 71,000; subscription received during the year 71,95,000; subscriptions received in advance at the beginning of the year 73,000 and at the end of the year 72,000. Amount shown in Income & Expenditure Account will be:

A. ₹ 2,00,000 B. ₹ 1,96,000
C. ₹ 1,94,000 D. ₹ 1,84,000

**49.** The opening balance of Prize Fund was ₹ 32,800. During the year, donations received towards this fund amounted to ₹ 15,400; amount spent on prizes was 712,300 and interest received on prize fund investment was ₹ 4,000. The closing balance of Prize Fund will be:

A. ₹ 56,500 B. ₹ 64,500
C. ₹ 39,900 D. ₹ 31,900

**50.** Salary paid in cash during the current year was ₹ 80,000; Outstanding salary at the end was ₹ 4,000; Salary paid in advance last year pertaining to the current year was ₹ 3,200; paid in advance during current year for next year was ₹ 5,000. The amount debited to Income and Expenditure Account will be:

A. ₹ 85,800 B. ₹ 77,800
C. ₹ 82,200 D. ₹ 74,200

**51.** Salary paid in cash during the current year was ₹ 30,000; Outstanding salary at the end of previous year was ₹ 2,000 and outstanding salary at the end of current year was ₹ 3,000. Salary paid in advance during current year for next year was ₹ 2,600. The amount debited to Income and Expenditure Account will be:

A. ₹ 33,600 B. ₹ 26,400
C. ₹ 31,600 D. ₹ 28,400

**52.** Salary paid for the year ended 31st March, 2021 amounted to ₹ 75,000. How much amount will be recorded in Income and Expenditure Account in the following case?

| | 31-3-2020 | 31-3-2021 |
|---|---|---|
| Outstanding Salary | 6,500 | 6,000 |
| Prepaid Salary | 1,200 | 1,000 |

A. ₹ 75,700 B. ₹ 74,300
C. ₹ 75,300 D. ₹ 74,700

**53.** How much amount will be shown in Income and Expenditure Account in the following case?

| | 1-4-2020 | 31-3-2021 |
|---|---|---|
| Creditors for Stationery | 8,000 | 6,000 |
| Stock of Stationery | 3,000 | 3,200 |

During 2020-21 payment made for Stationery was ₹ 60,000.

A. ₹ 57,800 B. ₹ 62,200
C. ₹ 61,800 D. ₹ 58,200

**54.** How much amount will be shown in Income and Expenditure Account in the following case?

| | 31-3-2020 | 31-3-2021 |
|---|---|---|
| Unpaid for Medicines | 10,000 | 12,000 |
| Stock of Medicines | 8,000 | 13,000 |

Payment made for medicines during 2020-21 was ₹ 2,50,000.

A. ₹ 2,53,000 B. ₹ 2,47,000
C. ₹ 2,57,000 D. ₹ 2,43,000

**55.** If a General Donation of huge amount is received by a school, that donation is treated as:

A. Revenue Receipt (Income)
B. Capital Receipt (Liability)
C. Assets
D. Earned Income

**56.** If a general donation of smaller amount is received by a school, that donation will be shown in:

A. Liability Side
B. Asset Side
C. Debit side of Receipt and Payment A/c
D. Credit side of Receipt and Payment A/c

**57.** Out of the billowing items, which one is shown in the 'Receipts and Payments Account" of a not for profit organisation?

A. Accrued subscription B. Outstanding salary
C. Depreciation D. None of these

**58.** Out of the following items, which is not shown in the 'Receipts and Payments A/c' of a not for profit organisation?

A. Subscription received in advance
B. Subscription due
C. Last year subscription received
D. All of the above

**59.** Out of the following items, which is shown in the 'Receipts and Payments A/c' of a not for profit organisation?

A. Subscription received in advance
B. Last year subscription received
C. Current year subscription received
D. All of the above

**60.** A not-for-profit organisation has all of the following characteristics, except that it will:

A. operate for purposes other than to provide goods or service at a profit
B. have a positive fund balance
C. not possess ownership interests like a corporation
D. receive significant contributions from provides who do not expect returns

61. Excess of income over expenditure is in the balance sheet capital fund:
A. added to B. deducted from
C. not added to D. not deducted from

62. On what basis receipts and payments account is made:
A. Cash basis
B. Accrual basis
C. Both Cash & Accrual basis
D. None of these

63. A not for profit organisation prepares:
A. Receipts and Payments Account
B. Trading Account
C. Income and Expenditure Account
D. Both (A) and (C)

64. Subscription received by a school for organising annual function is treated as:
A. Capital receipt (i.e. Liability)
B. Revenue receipt (i.e. income)
C. Assets
D. Earned income

65. Capital Receipts are represented in:
A. Balance Sheet
B. Trading Account
C. Profit and Loss Account
D. Manufacturing Account

66. Receipt and payment account is a summary of:
A. income and expenses
B. cash receipts and payments
C. balances of various ledger accounts
D. None of these

67. Choose NPO from the following:
A. Reliance Industries Limited
B. Indian Hoc Important Federation
C. Infosys Lt(d)
D. Private Hospital

68. Donation received for a special purpose:
A. Should be credited to Income and Expenditure Account
B. Should be credited to separate account and shown in the Balance Sheet
C. Should be shown on the assets side
D. Should not be recorded at all

69. The receipt and payment account is a—account in nature.
A. nominal B. real
C. personal D. None of these

70. A not for profit organisation includes:
A. Religious Organisations
B. Trade unions
C. Clubs
D. Educational institutions

71. All receipts of capital nature are as shown in:
A. Income and Expenditure A/c
B. Balance Sheet
C. Profit & Loss A/c
D. None of these

72. Subscription receives during the year ₹ 5,00000....

Subscriptions outstanding at the end of the year ₹ 80,000; Subscrition outstanding at the beginning of the year ₹ 60,000 Net Income from subscription will be:
A. 4,80,000 B. 6,40,000
C. 5,20,000 D. 3,60,000

73. In non-profit accounting, sal. of old newspapers is generally considered as a/an:
A. income B. expenses
C. capital receipt D. None of these

74. Income and expenditure account is based on:
A. cash accounting B. accrual accounting
C. Both (A) and (B) D. Neither (A) nor (B)

75. At the beginning of an accounting year a club has assets of ₹ 19,000 and liabilities of ₹ 5,000. ₹ 1,800 is the debit balance of the income & expenditures account. The opening capital fund is:
A. ₹ 18,000 B. ₹ 11,200
C. ₹ 15,800 D. ₹ 24,800

76. No cash transaction will be excluded form:
A. Balance Sheet
B. Profit & Loss A/c
C. Receipts and Payments
D. Income and Expenditure A/c

77. Subscription received during the year 2019-20: ₹ 1,50,000. Outstanding Subscription as on 31st March, 2019: ₹ 1,00,000. The amount shown as subscription receipt will be:
A. ₹ 50,000 B. ₹ 1,50,000
C. ₹ 1,00,000 D. ₹ 1,25,000

78. Out of the following, which is Unrestricted Fund?
A. Annuity Fund B. Sports Fund
C. Capital Fund D. Endowment Fund

79. Which of the following is an example of not-profit-organisation:
A. Public hospitals B. Corporations
C. Audit firm D. Insurance companies

80. The Receipts and Payments Account is a summary of:
A. Debit and Credit balance of Ledger Accounts
B. Cash Receipts and Payments
C. Expenses and Incomes
D. Assets and Liabilities

**81.** Identify capital receipt from the following:
A. Life Membership Fees B. Rent Receipt
C. Entrance fees D. Sports expenses

**82.** Salary paid in cash during the current year was ₹ 80,000; Outstanding salary at the end was ₹ 4,000; Salary paid in advance last year pertaining to the current year was ₹ 3,200; paid in advance during current year for next year was ₹ 5,000. The amount debited to Income and Expenditure Account will be:
A. ₹ 85,800 B. ₹ 77,800
C. ₹ 82,200 D. ₹ 74,200

**83.** How much amount will be shown in income and Expenditure Account in the following case? 1-4-2019 31-3-2020 Creditors for Stationery 8,000 6,000 Stock of Stationery 3,000 3,200 during 2019-20 payment made for Stationery was ₹ 60,000.
A. ₹ 57,800 B. ₹ 62,200
C. ₹ 61,800 D. ₹ 58,200

**84.** Income and Expenditure Account is prepared on:
A. Cash Basis B. Accrual Basis
C. Both (A) and (B) D. Sales Basis

**85.** Main source of Income for a Not-for-Profit Organistion is:
A. Rent
B. Salaries
C. Donations and Subscriptions
D. Sale of Assets

**86.** Credit purchase of stationery is ₹ 64,000, which is 80% of total purchase, compute cash purchase of stationery.
A. ₹ 16,000 B. ₹ 24,000
C. ₹ 8,000 D. ₹ 40,000

**87.** Subscription received in advance during the current year is:
A. an income B. an asset
C. a liability D. None of these

**88.** Receipts and Payments Account is prepared on:
A. Cash Basis B. Time Basis
C. Accrual Basis D. Sales Basis

**89.** Amount received from sale of grass by a club should be treated as:
A. Capital Receipt B. Revenue Receipt
C. Asset D. Earned Income

**90.** Legacy Donation received by NPO to be used for specific purpose is accounted as:
A. Revenue Receipt
B. Capital Receipt
C. an Asset
D. is decided by the Mangement

## ANSWERS

| 1 | 2 | 3 | 4 | 5 | 6 | 7 | 8 | 9 | 10 |
|---|---|---|---|---|---|---|---|---|---|
| B | D | B | C | C | B | C | B | A | C |
| **11** | **12** | **13** | **14** | **15** | **16** | **17** | **18** | **19** | **20** |
| C | B | C | D | C | D | C | B | D | A |
| **21** | **22** | **23** | **24** | **25** | **26** | **27** | **28** | **29** | **30** |
| B | A | D | A | A | A | B | B | A | D |
| **31** | **32** | **33** | **34** | **35** | **36** | **37** | **38** | **39** | **40** |
| C | C | B | B | C | D | D | A | B | C |
| **41** | **42** | **43** | **44** | **45** | **46** | **47** | **48** | **49** | **50** |
| C | C | B | A | D | C | B | A | C | C |
| **51** | **52** | **53** | **54** | **55** | **56** | **57** | **58** | **59** | **60** |
| D | D | A | B | B | C | D | B | D | B |
| **61** | **62** | **63** | **64** | **65** | **66** | **67** | **68** | **69** | **70** |
| A | A | D | B | A | B | B | B | B | A |
| **71** | **72** | **73** | **74** | **75** | **76** | **77** | **78** | **79** | **80** |
| B | C | A | B | C | C | A | C | A | B |
| **81** | **82** | **83** | **84** | **85** | **86** | **87** | **88** | **89** | **90** |
| A | C | A | B | C | A | C | A | B | B |

# 2

# ACCOUNTING FOR PARTNERSHIP

A partnership consists of more than one owner. It is formed by individuals who contribute capital, skill and administrative ability, and agree to share profits and losses of the business.

According to Section 4 of the Partnership Act 1932, partnership means "the relationship between persons who have agreed to share the profits of a business carried on by all or any of them acting for all".

The persons who come together to form partnership are individually known as 'partners' and collectively a 'firm'.

**Essential Features of Partnership:**

- **Agreement:** Partnership is created by an agreement and not by operation of law as in case of Hindu Undividual Family [HUF]. The agreement forms the basis of their mutual relationship.
- **Number of Persons:** There must be at least two persons to form a partnership. The maximum number of persons constituting a partnership must not exceed 10 in the case of banking business and 20 in any other business.
- **Business:** The agreement should be to carry on some business so as to make profits. A joint ownership of some property does not constitute partnership.
- **Sharing Profits and Losses:** The agreement must be to share the profits and losses of the business. An agreement entered into by individuals for a charitable purpose will not treated as a partnership.
- **Mutual Agency:** the business may be carried on by all the partners or any of them acting for all. Thus, each partner acts in two capacities, one as an agent and the other as a principal. He can bind the firm and its other partners by his acts and he is also bound by the acts of other partners with regard to the business of the firm.

## PARTNERSHIP DEED

A partnership comes into existence by an agreement among the partners. This agreement can be either oral or in writing. The law does not stipulate the partners to have a written agreement. But in order to avoid the disputes that are likely to arise in the conduct of business, a written agreement is preferred. A written document containing the terms and conditions of the conduct of partnership business is called 'partnership deed'. The partners are free to incorporate any provision in the deed subject to the Indian Partnership Act, 1932. A partnership deed generally consists of particulars relating to the following:

- Name of the firm and place of business
- Names and addresses of all the partners
- Nature of business and its duration
- The amount of capital to be contributed by each partner
- The accounting period of the firm
- The bank where the money is to be deposited and the authority of the partners to sign the cheques or documents
- Profit and loss sharing ratio
- Rate of interest both on capitals and drawings
- The maximum amount and period of drawings
- Loans from partners and the rate of interest on such loans
- Conditions regarding the payment of salary and commission to the partners
- Rights, duties and liabilities of partners
- Methods of maintaining accounts, their audit, and revaluation of assets and liabilities at the time of admission of a new partners or retirement of any partner
- Valuation and treatment of goodwill in the case of admission of a new partner or retirement or death of an existing partner

- Treatment of loss arising out of insolvency of one or more partners
- Method of settling the dues of deceased partner to his legal representatives
- Method of settling disputes among the partners
- Procedure for the dissolution and settlement of accounts after the dissolution
- Any other matter relating to the conduct of business

## PROVISIONS AFFECTING PARTNERSHIP ACCOUNTS

In the absence of any written or oral agreement among the partners, the following provisions of the Partnership Act shall apply.

- **Profit Sharing:** Partners share the profits and losses of the firm equally irrespective of their capital contribution.
- **Interest on Capital:** No partner is entitled to claim any interest on the amount of capital contributed. Where, however, the agreement provides for interest on capital it is payable only out of the profits of the business. In other words, if there are losses, interest on capital will not be allowed even if the agreement so provides.
- **Interest on Loan:** If any partner, apart from his share of capital, advances loan to the firm, he is entitled to receive interest at the rate of 6 per cent per annum.
- **Interest on Drawings:** No interest will be charged on drawings made by the partners.
- **Remuneration to Partners:** No salary or commission will be paid to any of the partners for participating in the business of the firm.

## Special Aspects of Partnership Accounts

Accounting treatment for partnership firm is similar to that of a sole proprietorship business with the exception of the following aspects:

- Maintenance of Partners' Capital Accounts;
- Distribution of Profit and Loss among the partners;
- Adjustments for Wrong Appropriation of Profits in the Past;
- Reconstitution of the Partnership Firm; and
- Dissolution of Partnership Firm.

## Maintenance of Capital Accounts of Partners

There are two methods by which the capital accounts of partners can be maintained. These are:

- **Fixed Capital Method:** Under the fixed capital method, the capitals of the partners shall remain fixed unless additional capital is introduced or a part of the capital is withdrawn as per the agreement among the partners. All items like share of profit or loss, interest on capital, drawings, interest on drawings, etc. are recorded in a separate accounts, called Partner's Current Account.
- **Fluctuating Capital Method:** Under the fluctuating capital method, only one account, i.e. capital account is maintained for each partner. All the adjustments such as share of profit and loss, interest on capital, drawings, interest on drawings, salary or commission to partners, etc are recorded directly in the capital accounts of the partners. This makes the balance in the capital account to fluctuate from time to time. That's the reason why this method is called fluctuating capital method.

**Difference between Fixed and Fluctuating Capital Accounts**

| Basis of Distinction | Fixed Capital | Fluctuating Capital |
|---|---|---|
| Number of accounts | Under this method, two separate accounts are maintained for each partner viz., 'capital account' and 'current account'. | Each partner has one account, i.e. capital account, under this method |
| Items related to deed | Drawings, salary, interest on capital, etc. are posted (transferred) in the current accounts and not in the capital accounts. | All adjustments for drawings, salary interest on capital, etc., are posted (transfered) in the capital accounts, |
| Fixed balance | The capital account balance remain unchanged unless there is addition to or withdrawal of capital. | The balance of the capital account fluctuates from year to year |
| Credit balance | The capital accounts always show a credit balance. | The capital account may sometimes show a debit balance. |

## Distribution of Profit among Partners

The profits and losses of the firm are distributed among the partners in an agreed ratio. However, if the partnership deed is silent, the firm's profits and losses are to be shared equally by all the partners.

- **Profit and Loss Appropriation Account:** Profit and Loss Appropriation Account is merely an extension of the Profit and Loss Account of the firm. It shows how the profits are appropriated or distributed among the partners.
- **Interest on Capital:** No interest is allowed on partners' capitals unless it is expressly agreed among

the partners. When the Deed specifically provides for it, interest on capital is credited to the partners at the agreed rate with reference to the time period for which the capital remained in business during a financial year. Interest on capital is generally provided for in two situations: (*i*) when the partners contribute unequal amounts of capitals but share profits equally, and (*ii*) where the capital contribution is same but profit sharing is unequal.

- **Interest on Drawings:** The partnership agreement may also provide for charging of interest on money withdrawn out of the firm by the partners for their personal use. As stated earlier, no interest is charged on the drawings if there is no express agreement among the partners about it. However if the partnership deed so provides for it, the interest is charged at an agreed rate, for the period for which drawings have been made. Remained outstanding from the partners during an accounting year. Charging interest on drawings discourages excessive amounts of drawings by the partners.

## GUARANTEE OF PROFIT TO A PARTNER

Sometimes a partner is admitted into the firm with a guarantee of certain minimum amount by way of his share of profits of the firm. Such assurance may be given by all the old partners in a certain ratio or by any of the old partners, individually to the new partner. The minimum guaranteed amount shall be paid to such new partner when his share of profit as per the profit sharing ratio is less than the guaranteed amount.

**Illustration:**

Vinod and Sanjeev share profits and losses in the ratio of 2 : 1. From January 01, 2014 they admit Rakesh into their firm who is to be given a share of 1/10 of the profits with a guaranteed minimum of ₹ 25,000. Vinod and Sanjeev continue to share profits as before but agree to bear any deficiency on account of guarantee to Rakesh in the ratio of 3 : 2 respectively. The profits of the firm for the year ending December 31, 2015 amounted to ₹ 1,20,000. Prepare Profit and Loss Appropriation Account.

**Books of Vinod and Sanjeev**
**Profit and Loss Appropriation Account**
**for the year ending .....**

Dr. Cr.

| Particulars | | Amount (₹) | Particulars | Amount (₹) |
|---|---|---|---|---|
| Capital Accounts: (for share of profit) | | | Net profit | 1,20,000 |
| Vinod 6/10 × 1,20,000 | 72,000 | | | |
| Less: Deficiency share | 7,800 | 64,200 | | |
| Sanjeev 3/10 × 1,20,000 | 36,000 | | | |
| Less: Deficiency share | 5,200 | 30,800 | | |
| Rakesh | 12,000 | | | |
| Add: Share of Deficiency from | | | | |
| Vinod | 7,800 | | | |
| Sanjeev | 5,200 | 25,000 | | |
| | | **1,20,000** | | **1,20,000** |

**Working Notes:**

New profit sharing Ratio will be calculated as follows:

Rakesh to share $\frac{1}{10}$ of the profits. The remaining profit $\frac{9}{10}$ will be shared by Vinod and Sanjeev in the ratio of 2 : 1.

Vinod's share in profit will be $\frac{2}{3}\times\frac{9}{10}=\frac{3}{10}$

Sanjeev's share will be $\frac{1}{3}\times\frac{9}{10}=\frac{3}{10}$

The New ratio becomes $\frac{3}{5}:\frac{3}{10}:\frac{1}{10}$ or 6 : 3 : 1.

Vinod's share in profit = $1,20,000\times\frac{6}{10}$ = ₹ 72,000

Sanjeev's share in profit = ₹ 36,000,

Rakesh's share in profit = ₹ 12,000.

Deficiency of Rakesh (₹ 13,000) will be shared by Vinod and Sanjeev in the ratio of 3 : 2.

Vinod will bear 3/5 of 13,000, *i.e.*, ₹ 7,800 and Rakesh, 2/5 of ₹ 13,000, *i.e.*, ₹ 5,200.

Thus, the profits of the firm will be shared as follows.

Vinod will get ₹ 72,000 – ₹ 7,800 = ₹ 64,200.

Sanjeev will get ₹ 36,000 – ₹ 5,200 = ₹ 30,800

Rakesh will get ₹ 12,000 + ₹ 7,800 + ₹ 5,200 = ₹ 25,000.

## Past Adjustments

Sometimes a few omissions or errors in the recording of transactions or the preparation of summary statements are found after the final accounts have been prepared and the profits distributed among the partners. The omission may be in respect of interest on capitals, interest on drawings, interest on partners' loan, partner's salary, partner's commission or outstanding expenses. There may also be some changes in the provisions of partnership deed or system of accounting having impact with retrospective effect. All these acts of omission and commission need adjustments for correction of their impact. Instead of altering old accounts, necessary adjustments can be made either; (a) through 'Profit and Loss Adjustment Account', or (b) directly in the capital accounts of the concerned partners.

**Illustration:**

Rohan, Sohan and Mohan are partners sharing profits and losses in the ratio of 5 : 3 : 2. The partnership deed provides for charging interest on drawing's @ 10% p.a. The drawings of Rohan, Sohan and Mohan during the year ending March 31, 2015 amounted to ₹ 20,000, ₹ 15,000 and ₹ 10,000 respectively. After the final accounts have been prepared, it was discovered that interest on drawings has not been taken into consideration. Give necessary adjusting journal entry.

**Statement showing Net Effect of Omitting Interest on Drawings**

| Particulars | Rohan (₹) | Sohan (₹) | Mohan (₹) | Total |
|---|---|---|---|---|
| Amount which should have been debited by way of interest on drawings | 2,000 (Dr) | 1,500 (Dr) | 1,000 (Dr) | 4,500 |
| Amount that should have been credited by way of share of profit | 2,250 (Cr.) | 1,350 (Cr.) | 900 (Cr.) | 4,500 |
| Required Adjustment | Cr. 250 (Short) | Cr. 150 (Excess) | Cr.100 (Excess) | |

Journal Entry for adjustment of interest on drawings would be:

| | | | |
|---|---|---|---|
| Sonu's Capital A/c | Dr. | 150 | |
| Himesh's Capital A/c | Dr. | 100 | |
| To Nusrat's Capital A/c | | | 250 |
| (Adjustment for omission of interest on drawings) | | | |

## MULTIPLE CHOICE QUESTIONS

**1.** Rent to a partner is shown in:
A. Dr. side of Profit And Loss Appropriation A/c
B. Cr. side of Profit And Loss Appropriation A/c
C. Dr. side of Profit And Loss A/c
D. Cr. side of Profit And Loss A/c

**2.** Which of the following items will be shown in Partner's Capital A/c under Fixed Capital method?
A. Drawings from profits
B. Drawings from capital
C. Interest on drawings
D. All of the above

**3.** Interest on Partner's Loan will be credited to:
A. Partner's Loan A/c
B. Partner's Capital A/c
C. Profit and Loss A/c
D. None of the above

**4.** Which one of the following items is not an appropriation out of profits?
A. Interest on capital
B. Salary to a partner
C. Commission to a partner
D. Interest on partner's loan

**5.** Following are essential elements of a partnership firm except:
A. Atleast two persons
B. There is an agreement between all partners
C. Equal share of profits and losses
D. Partnership agreement is for some lawful business activity

6. Which one of the following is not a right of a partner?
   A. Right to inspect the books of the firm
   B. Right to take part in the affairs of the company
   C. Right to share the profits/losses of the firm
   D. Right to receive salary at the end of each month

7. The relation of partner with the firm is that of:
   A. An owner
   B. An agent
   C. An owner and agent both
   D. A manager

8. Pick the odd one out:
   A. Rent to a partner
   B. Manager's commission
   C. Interest on partner's loan
   D. Interest on partner's capital

9. Articles of partnership are also known as:
   A. Partnership prospectus
   B. Partnership deed
   C. Principles of partnership
   D. None of these

10. In case of partnership, the act of any partner is:
   A. Binding on all partners
   B. Binding on that partner only
   C. Binding on all partners except that particular partner
   D. None of these

11. Interest on capital will be paid to the partners if provided for in the partnership deed but only out of:
   A. Profits B. Reserves
   C. Accumulated profits D. Goodwill

12. What is the minimum number of partners in a partnership firm?
   A. 50 B. 100
   C. 2 D. None of these

13. Current accounts of partners are maintained under which method?
   A. Fluctuating Capital method
   B. Fixed Capital method
   C. Both of the above
   D. None of these

14. Limited Liability Partnerships came into existence in India after the enactment of:
   A. Indian Partnership Act, 1932
   B. Limited Liability Partnership Act, 1932
   C. Limited Liability partnership Act, 2008
   D. Indian companies Act, 2013

15. A and B are partners sharing profits and losses equally. They admitted C as a partner with an equal share giving him a guarantee of minimum ₹ 50,000 profit p.a. The profit for the year after C's admission was ₹ 1,20,000. What will be the net amount that will be credited to A's Capital A/c?
   A. ₹ 50,000 B. ₹ 40,000
   C. ₹ 35,000 D. ₹ 80,000

16. If a partner withdraws an equal amount in the beginning of each month for a period of 10 months, what will be the average period for calculation of Interest on Drawings?
   A. 6.5 months B. 7.5 months
   C. 6 months D. 5.5 months

17. X and Y are partners sharing profits and losses in the ratio of 3 : 2 with capitals ₹ 5,00,000 each. According to partnership deed, interest on capital is allowed @ 10% p.a. The profit for the year is ₹ 50,000. What amount will be credited to X and Y in such condition?
   A. ₹ 50,000 to A and B each
   B. ₹ 25,000 to A and B each
   C. ₹ 30,000 to A and ₹ 20,000 to B
   D. None of these

18. P and Q are partners sharing profits and losses in the ratio of 2 : 1 with capitals ₹ 1,00,000 and ₹ 80,000 respectively. The interest on capital has been provided to them @ 8% instead of 10%. In the rectifying adjustment entry, Q will be:
   A. Debited by ₹ 400 B. Credited by ₹ 400
   C. Debited by ₹ 1600 D. Credited by ₹ 1600

19. Akhil and Ravi are partners sharing profits and losses in the ratio of 7 : 3 with capitals of ₹ 8,00,000 and ₹ 6,00,000 respectively. According to partnership deed interest on capital is to be provided @ 8% p.a. and is to be treated as a charge. Profit for the year is ₹ 80,000. Choose the correct option:
   A. A will be credited by ₹ 64,000 and B will be credited by ₹ 48,000.
   B. A will be credited by ₹ 56,000 and B will be credited by ₹ 24,000.
   C. A will be credited by ₹ 22,400 and B will be credited by ₹ 9,600.
   D. A will be credited by ₹ 41,600 and B will be credited by ₹ 38,400

20. X, Y and Z are partners sharing profits and losses equally. Their capitals on March 31, 2021 are ₹ 80,000; ₹ 60,000; ₹ 40,000 respectively. Their personal assets are worth as follows: X-₹ 20,000; Y-₹ 15,000 and Z-₹ 10,000. The extent of their liability in the firm would be:
   A. X-₹ 80,000; Y-₹ 60,000; Z-₹ 40,000
   B. X-₹ 20,000; Y-₹ 15,000; Z-₹ 10,000
   C. X-₹ 1,00,000; Y-₹ 75,000; Z-₹ 50,000
   D. Equal

**21.** A and B are partners. B draws a fixed amount at the end of every month. Interest on drawings is charged @15% p.a. At the end of the year interest on B's drawings amounted to ₹ 8,250. Drawings of B were:

A. ₹ 12,000 p.m.
B. ₹ 10,000 p.m.
C. ₹ 9,000 p.m.
D. ₹ 8,000 p.m.

**22.** Mohit and Rohit were partners in a firm with capitals of ₹ 80,000 and ₹ 40,000 respectively. The firm earned a profit of ₹ 30,000 during the year. Mohit's share in the profit will be:

A. ₹ 20000 B. ₹ 15000
C. ₹ 10000 D. ₹ 18000

**23.** R and S are partners sharing profits in the ratio of 2 : 1. S has advanced a loan of ₹ 1,00,000 to the firm on 1st October, 2020. The net profit earned by the firm for the year ending 31st March, 2021 is ₹ 90,000. What amount will be credited to S's capital account?

A. ₹ 60,000 B. ₹ 30,000
C. ₹ 29,000 D. ₹ 32,000

**24.** Match List-I with List-II:

| List-I | List-II |
|---|---|
| (*a*) Interest on Capital | (*i*) Cr. Side of Profit and Loss Appropriation A/c |
| (*b*) Interest on Drawings | (*ii*) Dr. Side of Profit and Loss Appropriation A/c |
| (*c*) Interest on Partner's Loan | (*iii*) Dr. side of Profit and Loss A/c |

| | (*a*) | (*b*) | (*c*) |
|---|---|---|---|
| A. | (*i*) | (*ii*) | (*iii*) |
| B. | (*ii*) | (*i*) | (*iii*) |
| C. | (*iii*) | (*ii*) | (*i*) |
| D. | (*ii*) | (*iii*) | (*i*) |

**25.** Which of these is not a duty of partnership?

A. To act outside authority
B. Use property of firm for official purposes
C. Devote time to business of the partnership
D. To indemnity for the less caused by his/her neglect

**26.** Match List-I with List-II:

| List-I | List-II |
|---|---|
| (*a*) Maximum number of partners | (*i*) 6% p.a. |
| (*b*) Partnership Deed | (*ii*) 50 |
| (*c*) Interest on partner's loan | (*iii*) Written agreement |

| | (*a*) | (*b*) | (*c*) |
|---|---|---|---|
| A. | (*i*) | (*ii*) | (*iii*) |
| B. | (*ii*) | (*i*) | (*iii*) |
| C. | (*iii*) | (*ii*) | (*i*) |
| D. | (*ii*) | (*iii*) | (*i*) |

**27.** Match List-I with List-II:

| List-I | List-II |
|---|---|
| (*a*) Drawings in the beginning of each quarter | (*i*) 4.5 |
| (*b*) Drawings in the beginning of each month | (*ii*) 6.5 |
| (*c*) Drawings in the end of each quarter | (*iii*) 7.5 |

***Codes:***

| | (*a*) | (*b*) | (*c*) |
|---|---|---|---|
| A. | (*i*) | (*ii*) | (*iii*) |
| B. | (*ii*) | (*i*) | (*iii*) |
| C. | (*iii*) | (*ii*) | (*i*) |
| D. | (*ii*) | (*iii*) | (*i*) |

**28.** Match List-I with List-II:

| List-I | List-II |
|---|---|
| (*a*) One who takes part in business activities | (*i*) Dormant partner |
| (*b*) One who does not take part in business activities | (*ii*) Nominal partner |
| (*c*) One who lends his name to a partnership firm but actually is not a partner of the firm | (*iii*) Active partner |

| | (*a*) | (*b*) | (*c*) |
|---|---|---|---|
| A. | (*i*) | (*ii*) | (*iii*) |
| B. | (*ii*) | (*i*) | (*iii*) |
| C. | (*iii*) | (*ii*) | (*i*) |
| D. | (*iii*) | (*i*) | (*ii*) |

**Directions (Q.No. 29-33):** *Read the following information carefully and answer the questions that follow.*

X and Y are partners in 3 : 2. Their capital balances as on 1st April 2020 amounting to ₹ 2,00,000 each.

On 1st February, 2021, X contributed an additional capital of ₹ 1,00,000. Following are the terms of deed:

(*a*) Interest on capital @ 6% per annum

(*b*) Interest on drawings @ 8% per annum

(*c*) Salary to X ₹ 1500 per month

(*d*) Commission to Y @10% on net profit after charging interest on capital, salary and his commission.

Drawings of the partners were ₹ 20,000 and ₹ 30,000 respectively during the year. Net profit earned by the firm was ₹ 2,08,000.

**29.** What is the amount of Interest on capitals of X and Y:

A. ₹ 12,000 each
B. ₹ 12,000 to X and ₹ 13,000 to Y
C. ₹ 13,000 to X and ₹ 12,000 to Y
D. None of these

**30.** What is the amount of interest on drawings of X and Y:

A. ₹ 1200 and ₹ 1800 respectively
B. ₹ 800 and ₹ 1200 respectively
C. ₹ 1200 and ₹ 800 respectively
D. ₹ 1600 ₹ 2400 respectively

**31.** What is the amount of commission payable to Y?

A. ₹ 15000 B. ₹ 16500
C. ₹ 20800 D. None of these

**32.** What is X's share in the net divisible profit?

A. ₹ 124400 B. ₹ 83600
C. ₹ 91200 D. ₹ 60800

**33.** What will be the closing capital of X after all adjustments?

A. ₹ 422200 B. ₹ 401400
C. ₹ 300000 D. ₹ 423000

**Directions (Qs. No. 34-43):** *The following questions consist of two statements—Assertion (A) and Reason (R). Answer these questions selecting the appropriate option given below:*

Give Answer—

A. Both (A) and (R) are true and (R) is the correct explanation of (A)
B. Both (A) and (R) are true and (R) is not the correct explanation of (A)
C. (A) is true, but (R) is false
D. (A) is false, but (R) is true

**34. Assertion (A) :** In the absence of Partnership deed profits and losses are divided equally among the partners.

**Reason (R)** : This rule is applicable according to Indian partnership Act, 1932.

**35. Assertion (A) :** Personal properties of a partner may also be used to pay off the firm's debts.

**Reason (R)** : All partners have limited liability in the firm.

**36. Assertion (A) :** Partnership firm is a form of organisation where two or more persons carry on business activity on the basis of agreement among them.

**Reason (R)** : The profit or loss arising from the partnership business is shared by the partners in the agreed ratio.

**37. Assertion (A) :** Maximum number of partners in a partnership firm is 50.

**Reason (R)** : Maximum number of partners in a partnership firm is prescribed in Companies Act, 2013.

**38. Assertion (A) :** A partnership deed covers all matters relating to mutual relationship among the partners.

**Reason (R)** : But in the absence of partnership deed, provisions of the Indian partnership Act, 1932 shall apply for accounting purposes.

**39. Assertion (A) :** Rent to partner is not shown in Profit and Loss Appropriation Account.

**Reason (R)** : Rent to a partner is a charge against profit.

**40. Assertion (A) :** Interest on Partner's capital may be shown in Profit and Loss Account.

**Reason (R)** : If Partners treat interest on capital as a charge.

**41. Assertion (A) :** Rent payable to partner is credited to Partner's Capital account.

**Reason (R)** : Rent is payable to partner for letting the firm use his personal property for business.

**42. Assertion (A) :** For calculating Interest on Drawings, product method is used.

**Reason (R)** : Partners withdraw different amounts of money at different intervals of time.

**43. Assertion (A) :** Guarantee of minimum profit may be given to a partner.

**Reason (R)** : It is compulsory as per Indian Partnership Act, 1932.

**44.** Features of a partnership firm are:

A. Two or more persons are carrying common business under an agreement.
B. They are sharing profits and losses in the fixed ratio.
C. Business is carried by all or any of them acting tor all as an agent.
D. All of the above.

**45.** Following are essential elements of a partnership firm except:

A. At least two persons
B. There is an agreement between all partners
C. Equal share of profits and losses
D. Partnership agreement is for some business.

**46.** In case of partnership the act of any partner is:

A. Binding on all partners
B. Binding on that partner only
C. Binding on all partners except that particular partner
D. None of the above

**47.** Which of the following statement is true?
A. a minor cannot be admitted as a partner
B. a minor can be admitted as a partner, only into the benefits of the partnership
C. a minor can be admitted as a partner but his rights and liabilities are same of adult partner
D. None of the above

**48.** Ostensible partners are those who:
A. do not contribute any capital but get some share of profit for lending their name to the business
B. contribute very less capital but get equal profit
C. do not contribute any capital and without having any interest in the business, lend their name to the business
D. contribute maximum capital of the business

**49.** The relation of partner with the firm is that of:
A. An Owner
B. An Agent
C. An Owner and an Agent
D. Manager

**50.** What should be the minimum number of persons to form a Partnership:
A. 2 B. 7
C. 10 D. 20

**51.** Number of partners in a partnership firm may be :
A. Maximum Two
B. Maximum Ten
C. Maximum One Hundred
D. Maximum Fifty

**52.** Liability of partner is:
A. Limited
B. Unlimited
C. Determined by Court
D. Determined by Partnership Act

**53.** Which one of the following is NOT an essential feature of a partnership?
A. There must be an agreement
B. There must be a business
C. The business must be carried on for profits
D. The business must be carried on by all the partners

**54.** Every partner is bound to attend diligently to his in the conduct of the business.
A. Rights B. Meetings
C. Capital D. Duties

**55.** Forming a Partnership Deed is:
A. Mandatory
B. Mandatory in Writing
C. Not Mandatory
D. None of the Above

**56.** Partnership Deed is also called:
A. Prospectus
B. Articles of Association
C. Principles of Partnership
D. Articles of Partnership

**57.** Which of the following is not incorporated in the Partnership Act?
A. profit and loss are to be shared equally
B. no interest is to be charged on capital
C. all loans are to be charged interest @6% p.a.
D. all drawings are to be charged interest

**58.** When is the Partnership Act enforced?
A. when there is no partnership deed
B. where there is a partnership deed but there are differences of opinion between the partners
C. when capital contribution by the partners varies
D. when the partner's salary and interest on capital are not incorporated in the partnership deed

**59.** In the absence of partnership deed, the following rule will apply:
A. No interest on capital
B. Profit sharing in capital ratio
C. Profit based salary to working partner
D. 9% p.a. interest on drawings

**60.** In the absence of agreement, partners are not entitled to:
A. Salary B. Commission
C. Equal share in profit D. Both (A) and (B)

**61.** Which one of the following items cannot be recorded in the profit and loss appropriation account?
A. Interest on capital B. Interest on drawings
C. Rent paid to partners D. Partner's salary

**62.** If any loan or advance is provided by partner then, balance of such Loan Account should be transferred to:
A. B/S Assets side B. B/S Liability Side
C. Partner's Capital A/c D. Partner's Current A/c

**63.** On 1st June 2018 a partner introduced in the firm additional capital ₹ 50,000. In the absence of partnership deed, on 31st March 2019 he will receive interest:
A. ₹ 3,000 B. Zero
C. ₹ 2,500 D. ₹ 1,800

**64.** A partner introduced additional capital of ₹ 30,000 and advanced a loan of ₹ 40,000 to the firm at the beginning of the year. Partner will receive year's interest:
A. ₹ 4,200 B. ₹ 2,400
C. Nil D. ₹ 1,800

**65.** In the absence of partnership deed, partners share profits or losses:
A. In the ratio of their Capitals
B. In the ratio decided by the court
C. Equally
D. In the ratio of time devoted

**66.** In the absence of Partnership Deed :
A. Interest will not be charged on partner's drawings
B. Interest will be charged @. 5% p.a. on partner's drawings
C. Interest will be charged @ 6% p.a. on partner's drawings
D. Interest will be charged @ 12% p.a. on partner's drawings

**67.** In the absence of express agreement, interest @ 6% p.a. is provided:
A. On opening balance of partner's capital accounts
B. On closing balance of partner's capital accounts
C. On loan given by partners to the firm
D. On opening balance of partner's current accounts

**68.** Which of the following items are recorded in the Profit & Loss Appropriation Account of a partnership firm?
A. Interest on Capital  B. Salary to Partner
C. Transfer to Reserve  D. All of the above

**69.** Is rent paid to a partner appropriation of profits?
A. It is appropriation of profit
B. It is not appropriation of profit
C. If partner's contribution as capital is maximum
D. If partner is a working partner.

**70.** Net profit of a firm is ₹ 49,500. Manager is entitled to a commission of 10% on profits before charging his commission. Manager's Commission will be:
A. ₹ 4,950  B. ₹ 4,500
C. ₹ 5,500  D. ₹ 495

**71.** Which of the following statement is true?
A. Fixed capital account will always have a credit balance
B. Current account can have a positive or a negative balance
C. Fluctuating capital account can have a positive or a negative balance
D. All of the above

**72.** Which accounts are opened when the capitals are fixed?
A. Only Capital Accounts
B. Only Current Accounts
C. Capital Accounts as well as Current Accounts
D. Either Capital Accounts or Current Accounts

**73.** Which accounts are opened when the capitals are fluctuating?
A. Only Capital Accounts
B. Only Current Accounts
C. Capital Accounts as well as Current Accounts
D. Either Capital Accounts or Current Accounts

**74.** Balance of partner's current accounts are:
A. Debit balance
B. Credit balances
C. Debit or Credit balances
D. Neither Debit nor credit balances

**75.** Which item is recorded on the credit side of partner's current accounts:
A. Interest on Fanner's Capitals
B. Salaries of Partners
C. Share of profits of Partners
D. All of the Above

**76.** If the Partners' Capital Accounts are fixed 'salary payable to partner' will be recorded :
A. On the debit side of Partners' Current Account
B. On the debit side of Partners' Capital Account
C. On the credit side of Partners' Current Account
D. None of the above

**77.** It the Partner's Capital Accounts are fixed, interest on capital will be recorded:
A. On the credit side of Current Account
B. On the credit side of Capital Account
C. On the debit side of Current Account
D. On the debit side of Capital Account

**78.** If the Partner's Capital Accounts are fluctuating, in that case following item/items will be recorded in the credit side of capital accounts:
A. Interest on capital
B. Salary of partners
C. Commission of partners
D. All of the above

**79.** Interest on partner's capitals will be debited to:
A. Profit and Loss Account
B. Profit and Loss Appropriation Account
C. Partner's Capital Accounts
D. None of the Above

**80.** Interest on partner's capitals will be credited to:
A. Profit and Loss Account
B. Profit and Loss Appropriation Account
C. Interest Account
D. Partner's Capital Accounts

**81.** For the firm interest on drawings is:
A. Capital Payment  B. Expenses
C. Capital Receipt  D. Income

**82.** Interest on Partner's drawings will be debited to:
A. Profit and Loss Account
B. Profit and Loss Appropriation Account
C. Partner's Current Account
D. Interest Account

**83.** When partners' capital accounts are floating, which one of the following items will be written on the credit side of the partners' capital accounts:
A. Interest on drawings
B. Loan advanced by partner to the firm
C. Partner's share in the firm's loss
D. Salary to the active partners

**84.** When partners' capital accounts are fixed, which one of the following items will be written in the partner's capital account:
A. Partner's Drawings
B. Additional capital introduced by the partner in the firm
C. Loan taken by partner from the firm
D. Loan Advanced by partner to the firm

**85.** Interest on partner's drawings will be credited to
A. Profit and Loss Account
B. Profit and Loss Appropriation Account
C. Partner's Capital Accounts
D. None of the Above

**86.** For the firm interest on capital is:
A. Capital Payment  B. Capital Receipt
C. Loss  D. Income

**87.** Partners are suppose to pay interest on drawing only when by the:
A. Provided, Agreement
B. Permitted, Investors
C. Agreed, Partners
D. 'A' & 'C' above

**88.** Where will you record interest on drawings:
A. Debit Side of Profit & Loss Appropriation Account
B. Credit Side of Profit & Loss Appropriation Account
C. Credit Side of Profit & Loss Account
D. Debit Side of Capital/Current Account only

**89.** How would you close the Partner's Drawing Account:
A. By transfer to Capital or Current Account Debit Side.
B. By transfer to Capital Account Credit Side.
C. By transfer to Current Account Credit Side.
D. Either 'B' or 'C'.

**90.** If date of drawings of the partner's is not given in the question, interest is charged for how much time:
A. 1 month
B. 3 months
C. 6 months
D. 12 months

## ANSWERS

| 1 | 2 | 3 | 4 | 5 | 6 | 7 | 8 | 9 | 10 |
|---|---|---|---|---|---|---|---|---|---|
| C | B | A | D | C | D | C | D | B | A |
| **11** | **12** | **13** | **14** | **15** | **16** | **17** | **18** | **19** | **20** |
| A | C | B | C | C | D | B | B | D | B |
| **21** | **22** | **23** | **24** | **25** | **26** | **27** | **28** | **29** | **30** |
| B | B | C | B | A | D | C | D | C | B |
| **31** | **32** | **33** | **34** | **35** | **36** | **37** | **38** | **39** | **40** |
| A | C | B | A | C | B | C | B | A | A |
| **41** | **42** | **43** | **44** | **45** | **46** | **47** | **48** | **49** | **50** |
| D | A | C | D | C | A | B | C | C | A |
| **51** | **52** | **53** | **54** | **55** | **56** | **57** | **58** | **59** | **60** |
| D | B | D | D | C | D | D | A | A | D |
| **61** | **62** | **63** | **64** | **65** | **66** | **67** | **68** | **69** | **70** |
| C | B | B | B | C | A | C | D | B | A |
| **71** | **72** | **73** | **74** | **75** | **76** | **77** | **78** | **79** | **80** |
| D | C | A | C | D | C | A | D | B | D |
| **81** | **82** | **83** | **84** | **85** | **86** | **87** | **88** | **89** | **90** |
| D | C | D | B | B | C | D | B | A | C |

●●●

# 3

# RECONSTITUTION OF A PARTNERSHIP

Partnernership is an agreement between two or more persons (called partners) for sharing the profits of a business carried on by all or any of them acting for all. Any change in the existing agreement amounts to reconstitution of the partnership firm.

## MODES OF RECONSTITUTION OF A PARTNERSHIP FIRM

Reconstitution of a partnership firm usually takes place in any of the following ways:

- **Admission of a New Partner:** A new partner may be admitted when the firm needs additional capital or managerial help. According to the provisions of Partnership Act 1932 unless it is otherwise provided in the partnership deed a new partner can be admitted only when the existing partners unanimously agree for it.
- **Change in the Profit Sharing Ratio Among the Existing Partners:** Sometimes the partners of a firm may decide to change their existing profit sharing ratio. This may happen an account of a change in the existing partners' role in the firm.
- **Retirement of an Existing Partner:** It means withdrawal by a partner from the business of the firm which may be due to his bad health, old age or change in business interests. In fact a partner can retire any time if the partnership is at will.
- **Death of a Partner:** Partnership may also stand reconstituted on death of a partner, if the remaining partners decide to continue the business of the firm as usual.

## ADMISSION OF A NEW PARTNER

According to the Partnership Act 1932, a new partner can be admitted into the firm only with the consent of all the existing partners unless otherwise agreed upon. With the admission of a new partner, the partnership firm is reconstituted and a new agreement is entered into to carry on the business of the firm.

A newly admitted partner acquires two main rights in the firm–

1. Right to share the assets of the partnership firm; and
2. Right to share the profits of the partnership firm.

Following are the other important points which require attention at the time of admission of a new partner:

1. New profit sharing ratio;
2. Sacrificing ratio;
3. Valuation and adjustment of goodwill;
4. Revaluation of assets and Reassessment of liabilities;
5. Distribution of accumulated profits (reserves); and
6. Adjustment of partners' capitals.

### New Profit Sharing Ratio

When new partner is admitted he acquires his share in profits from the old partners. In other words, on the admission of a new partner, the old partners sacrifice a share of their profit in favour of the new partner. But, what will be the share of new partner and how he will acquire it from the existing partners is decided mutually among the old partners and the new partner.

**Illustration:**

Rajiv and Raman are partners sharing profits in the ratio of 3 : 2. They admit Nikhil as a new partner for 1/5th share in the future profits of the firm which he gets equally from Rajiv and Raman. Calculate new profit sharing ratio of Rajiv, Raman and Nikhil.

**Solution**

$$\text{Nikhil's share} = \frac{1}{5} \text{ or } \frac{2}{10}$$

$$\text{Rajiv's share} = \frac{3}{5} - \frac{1}{10} = \frac{5}{10}$$

$$\text{Raman's share} = \frac{2}{5} - \frac{1}{10} = \frac{3}{10}$$

New profit sharing ratio between Rajiv, Raman and Nikhil will be 5 : 3 : 2.

## Sacrificing Ratio

The ratio in which the old partners agree to sacrifice their share of profit in favour of the incoming partner is called sacrificing ratio.

The sacrifice by a partner is equal to:

Old Share of Profit – New Share of Profit

**Illustration:**

Naresh and Suresh are partners in a firm sharing profits in the ratio of 4 : 3.

They admitted Rajesh as a new partner. The profit sharing ratio of Naresh, Suresh and Rajesh will be 2 : 3 : 1. Calculate the gain or sacrifice of old partner.

**Solution**

$$\text{Naresh's old share} = \frac{4}{7}$$

$$\text{Naresh's new share} = \frac{2}{6}$$

$$\text{Naresh's sacrifice} = \frac{4}{7} - \frac{2}{6} = \frac{10}{42}$$

$$\text{Suresh's new share} = \frac{3}{6}$$

$$\text{Suresh's old share} = \frac{3}{7}$$

$$\text{Suresh's gain} = \frac{3}{6} - \frac{3}{7} = \frac{3}{42}$$

$$\text{Rajesh's share} = \frac{1}{6} \text{ or } \frac{7}{42}$$

Admission of a Partner

Naresh sacrifice = Suresh's gain + Rajesh's gain

$$= \frac{3}{42} + \frac{7}{42} = \frac{10}{42}$$

In this case, the whole sacrifice is by Naresh alone.

## Goodwill

Goodwill is also one of the special aspects of partnership accounts which requires adjustment (also valuation if not specified) at the time of reconstitution of a firm viz., a change in the profit sharing ratio, the admission of a partner or the retirement or death of a partner.

In simple words, goodwill can be defined as "the present value of a firm's anticipated excess earnings" or as "the capitalised value attached to the differential profit capacity of a business". Thus, goodwill exists only when the firm earns super profits. Any firm that earns normal profits or is incurring losses has no goodwill.

### *Factors Affecting the Value of Goodwill*

The main factors affecting the value of goodwill are as follows:

- **Nature of business:** A firm that produces high value added products or having a stable demand is able to earn more profits and therefore has more goodwill.
- **Location:** If the business is centrally located or is at a place having heavy customer traffic, the goodwill tends to be high.
- **Efficiency of management:** A well-managed concern usually enjoys the advantage of high productivity and cost efficiency. This leads to higher profits and so the value of goodwill will also be high.
- **Market situation:** The monopoly condition or limited competition enables the concern to earn high profits which leads to higher value of goodwill.
- **Special advantages:** The firm that enjoys special advantages like import licences, low rate and assured supply of electricity, long-term contracts for supply of materials, well-known collaborators, patents, trademarks, etc. enjoy higher value of goodwill.

### *Methods of Valuation of Goodwill*

The important methods of valuation of goodwill are as follows:

1. Average Profits Method
2. Super Profits Method
3. Capitalisation Method

#### *1. Average Profits Method*

Under this method, the goodwill is valued at agreed number of 'years' purchase of the average profits of the past few years. It is based on the assumption that a new business will not be able to earn any profits during the first few years of its operations. Hence, the person who purchases a running business must pay in the form of goodwill a sum which is equal to the profits he is likely to receive for the first few years. The goodwill, therefore, should be calculated by multiplying the past average profits by the number of years during which the anticipated profits are expected to accrue.

**Illustration:**

The profit for the five years of a firm are as follows – year 2013 ₹ 4,00,000; year 2014 ₹ 3,98,000; year 2015 ₹ 4,50,000; year 2016 ₹ 4,45,000 and year 2017 ₹ 5,00,000. Calculate goodwill of the firm on the basis of 4 years purchase of 5 years average profits.

**Solution**

| Year | Profit (₹) |
|---|---|
| 2013 | 4,00,000 |
| 2014 | 3,98,000 |
| 2015 | 4,50,000 |
| 2016 | 4,45,000 |
| 2017 | 5,00,000 |
| **Total** | **21,93,000** |

$$\text{Average Profit} = \frac{\text{Total Profit of Last 5 Years}}{\text{No. of years}}$$

$$= ₹\frac{21,93,000}{5}$$

$$= ₹\ 4,38,600$$

Goodwill = Average Profits × No. of Years Purchased

= ₹ 4,38,600 × 4

= ₹ 17,54,400

The above calculation of goodwill is based on the assumption that no change in the overall situation of profits is expected in the future.

### 2. Super Profits Method

The basic assumption in the average profits (simple or weighted) method of calculating goodwill is that if a new business is set up, it will not be able to earn any profits during the first few years of its operations. Hence, the person who purchases an existing business has to pay in the form of goodwill a sum equal to the total profits he is likely to receive for the first 'few years'.

But it is contended that the buyer's real benefit does not lie in total profits; it is limited to such amounts of profits which are in excess of the normal return on capital employed in similar business. Therefore, it is desirable to value, goodwill on the basis of the excess profits and not the actual profits. The excess of actual profits over the normal profits is termed as super profits.

$$\text{Normal Profit} = \frac{\text{Firm's Capital} \times \text{Normal Rate Return}}{100}$$

Firms capital includes partners capital and reserves and surplus but excludes fictitious assets and goodwill.

**Illustration:**

The books of a business showed that the firm's capital employed on December 31, 2015, ₹ 5,00,000 and the profits for the last five years were: 2010–₹ 40,000: 2012-₹ 50,000; 2013-₹ 55,000; 2014-₹ 70,000 and 2015-₹ 85,000. You are required to find out the value of goodwill based on 3 years purchase of the super profits of the business, given that the normal rate of return is 10%.

**Solution**

$$\text{Normal Profit} = \frac{\text{Firm's Capital} \times \text{Normal Rate Return}}{100}$$

$$= ₹\frac{5,00,000 \times 10}{100}$$

$$= ₹\ 50,000$$

Average Profits:

| Year | Profit (₹) |
|---|---|
| 2011 | 40,000 |
| 2012 | 50,000 |
| 2013 | 55,000 |
| 2014 | 70,000 |
| 2015 | 85,000 |
| **Total** | **3,00,000** |

$$\text{Average Profit} = ₹\frac{3,00,000}{5} = ₹\ 60,000$$

Super Profit = ₹ 60,000 – 50,000 = ₹ 10,000

Goodwill = ₹ 10,000 × 3 = ₹ 30,000.

### 3. Capitalisation Method

Under this method the goodwill can be calculated in two ways: (*a*) by capitalizing the average profits, or (*b*) by capitalising the super profits.

(*a*) **Capitalisation of Average Profits:** Under this method, the value of goodwill is ascertained by deducting the actual firm's capital in the business from the capitalized value of the average profits on the basis of normal rate of return. This involves the following steps:

(*i*) Ascertain the average profits based on the past few years' performance.

(*ii*) Capitalize the average profits on the basis of the normal rate of return to ascertain the capitalised value of average profits as follows: Average Profits × 100/Normal Rate of Return

(*iii*) Ascertain the actual firm's capital (net assets) by deducting outside liabilities from the total assets (excluding goodwill and ficticious assets).

Firms' Capital = Total Assets (excluding goodwill) – Outside Liabilities Where outside Liabilities include both long term and short term Liabilities.

(*iv*) Compute the value of goodwill by deducting net assets from the capitalised value of average profits, i.e. (*ii*) – (*iii*).

(*b*) **Capitalisation of Super Profits:** Goodwill can also be ascertained by capitalising the super profit directly. Under this method there is no need to work out the capitalised value of average profits. It involves the following steps.

(*i*) Calculate capital of the firm, which is equal to total assets (excluding goodwill and ficticious assets) *minus outside liabilities.*

(*ii*) Calculate normal profits on capital employed.

(*iii*) Calculate average profit for past years, as specified.

(*iv*) Calculate super profits by deducting normal profits from average profits.

(*v*) Multiply the super profits by the required rate of return multiplier, that is,

Goodwill = Super Profits × 100 Normal Rate of Return

In other words, goodwill is the capitalised value of super profits. The amount of goodwill worked out by this method will be exactly the same as calculated by capitalising the average profits.

## Treatment of Goodwill

The incoming partner who acquires his share in the profits of the firm from the existing partners brings in additional amount to compensate them for loss of their share in super profits. It is termed as his share of goodwill (also called premium for goodwill).

### 1. When the new Partner brings goodwill in cash

The amount of premium brought in by the new partner is shared by the existing partners in their ratio of sacrifice. If this amount is paid to the old partners directly (privately) by the new partner, no entry is passed in the books of the firm. But, when the amount is paid through the firm, which is generally the case, the following journal entries are passed:

(*i*) Bank A/c Dr.
To Premium for Goodwill A/c
(Amount brought by new partner as premium)

(*ii*) Goodwill A/c Dr.
To Sacrificing Partners Capital A/c
(Individually)(Goodwill distributed among the existing partners' in their sacrificing ratio).

Alternatively, it is credited to the new partner's capital account and then adjusted in favour of the existing partners in their sacrificing ratio. In that case the journal entries will be as follows:

(*i*) Bank A/c Dr.
To New Partner's Capital A/c
(Amount brought by new partner for his share of goodwill).

(*ii*) New Partner's Capital A/c Dr.
To Sacrificing Partner's Capital A/c's
(Individually)
(Goodwill brought by new partners distributed among the existing partners in their sacrificing ratio)

If the partners decide that the amount of premium for goodwill credited to their capital accounts should be retained in business, an additional entry is not passed. If, however, they decide to withdraw their amounts, (in full or in part) the following additional entry will be passed:

Existing Partner's Capital A/c (Individually) Dr.
To Bank A/c
(The amount of goodwill withdrawn by the existing partners)

**Illustration:**

Vijay and Sanjay are partners in a firm sharing profits and losses in the ratio of 3 : 2. They admitted Ajay into partnership with 1/4 share in profits. Ajay brings in ₹ 30,000 for capital and the requisite amount of premium in cash. The goodwill of the firm is valued at ₹ 20,000. The new profit sharing ratio is 2 : 1 : 1. Vijay and Sanjay withdraw their share of goodwill. Give necessary journal entries.

**Solution**

(a) Ajay will bring ₹ 5,000 (1/4 of ₹ 20,000) as his share of goodwill (premium)

(b) Sacrificing Ratio is 2 : 3 as calculated below:
For Vijay, old ratio is 3/5 and the new ratio is 2/4, hence, his sacrificing ratio is

$$= \frac{3}{5} - \frac{2}{4}$$

$$= \frac{12-10}{20}$$

$$= \frac{2}{20}$$

For Sanjay, old ratio is 2/5 and the new ratio is 1/4, hence, his sacrificing ratio is:

$$= \frac{2}{5} - \frac{1}{4} = \frac{8-5}{20}$$

$$= \frac{3}{20}$$

**Books of Vijay and Sanjay**

**Journal**

| Date | Particulars | | L.F. | Debit (₹) | Credit (₹) |
|---|---|---|---|---|---|
| 1. | Bank A/c | Dr. | | 35,000 | |
| | To Ajay's Capital A/c | | | | 30,000 |
| | To Premium for Goodwill A/c | | | | 5,000 |
| | (The amount of capital and goodwill brought by Ajay) | | | | |
| 2. | Premium for Goodwill A/c | Dr. | | 5,000 | |
| | To Vijay's Capital A/c | | | | 2,000 |
| | To Sanjay's Capital A/c | | | | 3,000 |
| | (the amount of goodwill brought by Ajay shared by Vijay and Sanjay in their sacrificing ratio) | | | | |
| 3. | Vijay's Capital A/c | Dr. | | 2,000 | |
| | Sanjay's Capital A/c | Dr. | | 3,000 | |
| | To Bank A/c | | | | 5,000 |
| | (Cash withdrawn by Vijay and Sanjay for their share of goodwill) | | | | |

Note: Alternatively, journal entries (1) and (2) could be as follows:

**Books of Vijay and Sanjay**

**Journal**

| Date | Particulars | | L.F. | Debit (₹) | Credit (₹) |
|---|---|---|---|---|---|
| 1. | Bank A/c | Dr. | | 35,000 | |
| | To Ajay's Capital A/c | | | | 35,000 |
| | (Ajay brought in ₹ 30,000 for capital and ₹ 5,000 as goodwill) | | | | |
| 2. | Ajay's Capital A/c | Dr. | | 5,000 | |
| | To Vijay's Capital A/c | | | | 2.000 |
| | To Sanjay's Capital A/c | | | | 3,000 |
| | (Amount of goodwill brought in by Ajay shared by Vijay and Sanjay in their sacrificing in the ratio of 2 : 3) | | | | |

When goodwill already exists in books: Goodwill, if existing in the books of the firm, it is written off at the time of admission of a partner.

For example, in the goodwill of the firm is valued at ₹ 20,000 and Ajay who is admitted to 1/4 share in its profits, brings in ₹ 5,000 as his share of goodwill. Suppose, goodwill already appeared in books at ₹ 10,000 the following additional journal entry shall be passed for writing off the existing amount of goodwill.

| Date | Particulars | | L.F. | Debit (₹) | Credit (₹) |
|---|---|---|---|---|---|
| | Vijay's Capital A/c | Dr. | | 6,000 | |
| | Sanjay's Capital A/c | Dr. | | 4,000 | |
| | To Goodwill A/c | | | | 10,000 |
| | (Goodwill written-off in old ratio) | | | | |

***When the new partner does not bring goodwill in cash, partly or fully***

Goodwill not brought by the new partner will be debited to current account of new partner while sacrificing partners' capital accounts will be credited for their respective shares.

When the new partner does not bring the share of goodwill, there exists two possibilities :

(*a*) **Goodwill does not exist in the books:** When goodwill does not exist in the books, sacrificing partners are credited with their share of goodwill and new partner is debited by the amount of goodwill not brought by him. The journal entry in this case is:

Incoming (New) Partners Current A/c Dr.
To Sacrificing Partners Capital A/c (individually)
(Account of goodwill not brought in by new partner)

Sometimes the new partner brings part of premium for goodwill in cash. In such a situation, new partners current account will be debited by the amount not brought by new partner.

(*b*) **When goodwill exist in the books:** Goodwill appearing in the books will be written-off by debiting old partners' capital accounts in their old profit sharing ratio. Thereafter new value of goodwill will be given effect by crediting sacrificing partners' capital accounts and debiting new partners' current account.

The journal entries will be as under:

(*i*) When the valve of goodwill appears in the books and is written - off
Partners capital A/c (old) Dr.
(In profit sharing ratio)
To Goodwill A/c
(Goodwill appearing in the books written-off)

(*ii*) For new value of goodwill :
Incoming partners' current A/c. Dr.
To Sacrificing partners capital A/c. [In sacrificing (individually) ratio)

### *2. Hidden Goodwill*

Sometimes the value of goodwill is not given at the time of admission of a new partner. In such a situation it has to be inferred from the arrangement of the capital and profit sharing ratio.

## ADJUSTMENT FOR ACCUMULATED PROFITS AND LOSSES

Sometimes a firm may have accumulated profits not yet transferred to capital accounts of the partners. These are usually in the form of general reserve, reserve and/or Profit and Loss Account. The new partner is not entitled to have any share in such accumulated profits. These are distributed among the partners by transferring it to their capital current accounts in old profit sharing ratio. Similarly, if there are some accumulated losses in the form of a debit balance of profit and loss account and/or deferred revenue expenditure appearing in the balance sheet of the firm.

## REVALUATION OF ASSETS AND REASSESSMENT OF LIABILITIES

At the time of admission of a new partner, it is always desirable to ascertain whether the assets of the firm are shown in books at their current values. In case the assets are overstated or understated, these are revalued. Similarly, a reassessment of the liabilities is also done so that these are brought in the books at their correct values. At times there may also be some unrecorded assets and liabilities of the firm. These also have to be brought into the books of the firm. For this purpose the firm has to prepare the Revaluation Account. The gain or loss on revaluation of each asset and liability is transferred to this account and finally its balance is transferred to the capital accounts of the old partners in their old profit sharing ratio.

The journal entries recorded for revaluation of assets and reassessment of liabilities are as follows:

(i) For increase in the value of an asset
Asset A/c Dr.
To Revaluation A/c (Gain)

(ii) For reduction in the value of an asset
Revaluation A/c Dr.
To Asset A/c (Loss)

(iii) For appreciation in the amount of a liability
Revaluation A/c Dr.
To Liability A/c (Loss)

(iv) For reduction in the amount of a liability
Liability A/c Dr.
To Revaluation A/c (Gain)

(v) For an unrecorded asset
Asset A/c Dr.
To Revaluation A/c (Gain)

(vi) For an unrecorded liability
Revaluation A/c Dr.
To Liability A/c (Loss)

(vii) For transfer of gain on Revaluation if credit balancc
Revaluation A/c Dr.
To Old Partners Capital A/cs (Old ratio)
(individually)

(viii) For transferring loss on revaluation
Old partner's Capital A/cs Dr.
(Individually) (Old ratio)
To Revaluation A/c

**Note:** Entries (i), (ii), (iii) and (iv) are recorded only with the amount increase and decrease in the value of assets and liabilities.

## ADJUSTMENT OF CAPITALS

Sometimes, at the time of admission, the partners agree that their capitals should also be adjusted so as to be proportionate to their profit sharing ratio. In such a situation, if the capital of the new partner is given, the same can be used as a base for calculating the new capitals of the old partners. The capitals thus ascertained should be compared with their old capitals after all adjustments relating to goodwill reserves and revaluation of assets and liabilities, etc. have been made; and then the partner whose capital falls short, will bring in the necessary amount to cover the shortage and the partner who has a surplus, will withdraw the excess amount of capital.

## MULTIPLE CHOICE QUESTIONS

**1.** The partners whose share decrease as a result of change in profit sharing ratio are known as:
A. Sacrificing Partners B. Gaining Partners
C. Sleeping Partners D. None of these

**2.** The partners whose share increase as a result of change in profit sharing ratio are known as:
A. Gaining Partners B. Sacrificing Partners
C. Sleeping Partners D. None of these

**3.** Gaining ratio is the ratio with which the profit share of the partners:
A. Increase B. Decrease
C. Both D. None of these

**4.** Sacrificing Partners is the ratio with which the profit share of the partners:
A. Increase B. Decrease
C. Both D. None of these

**5.** Profit of the firm that have not been distributed among the partners, called:
A. Super Profit B. Average Profit
C. Accumulated Profits D. None of these

**6.** What adjustment are required when existing partners decide to change their profit sharing ratio?
A. Adjustment for Goodwill
B. Adjustment of Reserve
C. Accumulated Profits & Losses
D. All of the above

**7.** A firm is reconstituted, whenever there is a:
A. Admission of a new partner
B. Retirement of Existing Partner
C. Death of a partner
D. All of the above

**8.** How can the gaining partner compensate the sacrificing partner in case of change in profit sharing ratio:
A. By Paying Goodwill B. By Paying Profit
C. By Paying Losses D. None of these

**9.** Employees Provident Fund is:
A. Distributed among the partners
B. Not distributed among the partners
C. Distributed in profit sharing ratio
D. None of these

**10.** New Profit sharing ratio is the ratio in which all the partners, including the new partner, share future:
A. Profits of the firm
B. Losses of the firm
C. Profits & Losses of the firm
D. None of these

**11.** Profit & loss adjustment account, which:
A. Increase value of the assets
B. Decrease Value of Liablities
C. Both (A) and (B)
D. None of these

**12.** General reserve at the time of admission of a partner is transferred to:
A. Revaluation account
B. Old partners capital account
C. Both (A) and (B)
D. None of these

**13.** Z is admitted to a firm for 1/4 share in the profits for which he brings in ₹ 10000 towards premium for goodwill, it will be taken by the old partners in
A. The new profit sharing ratio
B. The old Profit sharing ratio
C. The Sacrificing ratio
D. None of the options

**14.** Revaluation A/c (alternatively Profit & Loss Adjustment account) is a:
A. Real Account
B. Nominal Account
C. Personal Account
D. None of these

**15.** The balance in the investment fluctuation fund, after meeting the loss on revaluation of investments, at the time of admission of a partner will be transferred to:
A. Personal Account
B. The revaluation Account
C. Old partners capital Account
D. None of these

**16.** If the incoming partner is to bring in premium for goodwill in cash and also a balance exists in the goodwill account, then this goodwill account is written of among the old partners in:
A. The new profit sharing ratio
B. The old profit sharing ratio
C. The sacrificing ratio
D. None of these

**17.** When A and B , sharing profits and losses in the ratio of 3 : 2, Admit C as a partner giving him 1/5th share of profits, this will be given by A and B:
A. In the ratio of their profits
B. Equally
C. In the ratio of their capitals
D. None of these

**18.** If the adjustment in the values of assets at the time of the admission of a partner shows profits, the same should be credited to the capital accounts of:
A. All partners in their old profit sharing ratio
B. The old partners in their new profit sharing ratio
C. The old partners in their old profit sharing ratio
D. None of these

**19.** The new partner get the right of:
A. Share Future profit B. Share in the assets
C. Both (A) and (B) D. None of these

**20.** New Profit sharing ratio is:
A. New Share + Old Share
B. Old Share + Acquire Share
C. Old Share – Acquire share
D. None of these

**21.** Gaining ratio is:
A. New Ratio – Profit Sharing ratio
B. New Ratio + Old ratio
C. New Ratio – Old ratio
D. None of these

**22.** At the time of retirement of a partner, if goodwill appears in the balance sheet, it must be written off, the capital accounts of all partners are debited in:
A. The old profit sharing ratio
B. The new profit sharing ratio
C. The capital ratio
D. None of these

**23.** In the event of death of a partner, the amount of general reserve is transferred to partners capital accounts in:
A. The old profit sharing ratio
B. The new profit sharing ratio
C. The capital ratio
D. None of these

**24.** According to the partnership Act ( SEC-37), the interest payable to the deceased partner on the amount left by him will be:
A. 6% P.A. B. 10% P.A.
C. 12% P.A. D. None of these

**25.** The share of goodwill of the retiring partner is debited to remaining partners in their:
A. Gaining Ratio
B. New Profit sharing ratio
C. Old Profit sharing ratio
D. None of these

**26.** Decrease in the value of Liabilities on reconstitution of the partnership firm results into:
A. Neither Gain of loss to Existing partner
B. Loss to the Existing Partner
C. Gain to the Existing Partner
D. None of these

**27.** On the admission of a new partner, increase in the value of assets is debited to:
A. Assets Account
B. Revaluation A/c
C. Profit & Loss Account
D. None of these

**28.** Change in profit sharing ratio of existing partners result in:
A. Reconstitution of firm
B. Revaluation firm
C. Amalgamation firm
D. None of these

**29.** Change in the partnership agreement results in:
A. Reconstitution of firm
B. Dissolution of firm
C. Amalgamation firm
D. None of these

**30.** Change in partnership agreement:
A. Changes in the relationship among the partner
B. Results in end of partnership business
C. Dissolved the partnership firm
D. None of these

**31.** Goodwill is:
A. tangible asset B. intangible asset
C. fictitious asset D. Both (B) and (C)

**32.** Which of the following is not the reconstittuion of partnership?
A. Admission of a Partner
B. Dissolution of Partnership
C. Change in Profit Sharing Ratio
D. Retirement of a Partner

**33.** At the time of admission of a partner, Employees Provident Fund is:
A. Distributed to partners in the old profit sharing ratio
B. Distributed to partners in the new profit sharing ratio
C. Adjusted through gaining ratio
D. None of these

**34.** On the admission of a new partner:
A. Old partnership is dissolved
B. Both old partnership and firm are dissolved
C. Old firm is dissolved
D. None of the above

**35.** What are super profits?
A. Actual profit – Normal Profit
B. Normal profit – Actual profit
C. Actual profit + Normal profit
D. None of the above

36. Gaining ratio is used to distribute ______ in case of retirement of a partner.
A. Goodwill
B. Revaluation Profit or Loss
C. Profit and Loss Account (Credit Balance)
D. Both (B) and (C)

37. Which of the following does not result into reconstitution of a firm?
A. Dissolution of partnership firm
B. Dissolution of partnership
C. Change in profit sharing ratio of existing partners
D. Death of partner

38. Which of the following is/are required at the time of change in profit sharing ratio among partners?
A. Accounting treatment of goodwill
B. Revaluation of assets and reassessment of liabilities
C. Accounting treatment of Accumulated Profit
D. All of the above

39. Change in profit sharing ratio among partners results in:
A. Sacrifice of share in profit by one or more partners
B. Gain of share in profit by one or more partners
C. Both (A) and (B)
D. None of the above

40. Which of the following does not result in the change in the profit sharing ratio?
A. When one or more partners acquire an interest in the business from another partner or partners
B. When a partner is admitted in the firm
C. When a partner goes on a vacation
D. When a partner dies

41. At the time of change in profit sharing ratio, it is important to determine the ______ and ______ of partners.
A. Sacrificing ratio, gaining ratio
B. Profit, loss
C. Goodwill, Profit
D. Capital, Profit

42. Any change in the relationship of existing partners which results in an end of the existing agreement and enforces making of new agreement is called:
A. Revaluation of partnership
B. Reconstitution of partnership
C. Realisation of partnership
D. None of the above

43. The ratio in which a partner surrenders his share in favour of a partner is known as:
A. New profit-sharing ratio
B. Sacrificing Ratio
C. Gaining Ratio
D. Capital Ratio

44. The ratio in which a partner receives a rise in his share of profits is known as:
A. New Ratio B. Sacrificing Ratio
C. Capital Ratio D. Gaining Ratio

45. Reserves and accumulated profits are transferred to partners' capital accounts at the time of reconstitution in:
A. Old profit-sharing ratio
B. Sacrificing Ratio
C. Gaining ratio
D. New profit-sharing ratio

46. Increase and decrease in the value of assets and liabilities are recorded through:
A. Partners' Capital Account
B. Revaluation Account
C. Profit and Loss Appropriation a/c
D. Balance Sheet

47. In which of the following case, revaluation account is debited?
A. Increase in value of asset
B. Decrease in value of asset
C. Decrease in value of liability
D. No change in value of assets

48. In which of the following cases, revaluation account is credited?
A. Decrease in value of liability
B. Increase in value of liability
C. Decrease in value of asset
D. No change in value of liability

49. Partner's capital account is credited when there is:
A. Profit on revaluation
B. transfer of general reserve
C. transfer of accumulated profits
D. All of the above

50. Sacrificing ratio is the difference between :
A. New ratio and old ratio
B. Old ratio and new ratio
C. New ratio and gaining ratio
D. Old ratio and gaining ratio

51. A and B are partners in a firm sharing profits in the ratio of 3 : 2. They decided to share future profits equally. Calculate A's gain or sacrifice
A. 2/10 (sacrifice) B. 5/10 (gain)
C. 1/10 (gain) D. 1/10 (sacrifice)

52. In case of change in profit-sharing ratio, the gaining partner must compensate the sacrificing partners by paying the proportional amount of
A. capital B. cash
C. goodwill D. None of these

**53.** In case of change in profit-sharing ratio, the accumulated profits are distributed to the partners in

A. new ratio B. old ratio
C. sacrificing ratio D. equal ratio

**54.** X, Y and Z are partners sharing profits and losses in the ratio of 5 : 3 : 2. They decide to share the future profits in the ratio of 3 : 2 : 1. Workmen compensation reserve appearing in the balance sheet on the date if no information is available for the same will be:

A. Distributed among the partners in old profit sharing ratio
B. Distributed among the partners in new profit sharing ratio
C. Distributed among the partners in capital ratio
D. Carried forward to new balance sheet without any adjustment

**55.** A, B and C were are partners in a firm sharing profits in the ratio of 3 : 4 : 1. They decided to share profits equally w.e.f from 1-4-2019. On that date the profit and loss account showed the credit balance of 96,000. instead of closing the profit and loss account, it was decided to record an adjustment entry reflecting the change in profit sharing ratio. In the journal entry:

A. Dr. A by 4,000; Dr. B by 16,000; Cr C by 20,000
B. Cr. A by 4,000; Cr. B by 16,000; Dr C by 20,000
C. Cr. A by 16,000; Cr. B by 4,000; Dr C by 20,000
D. Dr. A by 16,000; Dr. B by 4,000; Cr C by 20,000

**56.** Match the following items:

| | |
|---|---|
| *(i)* Ratio in which Partners share profit and loss before reconstitution of firm | *(a)* New profit sharing ratio |
| *(ii)* Ratio in which Partners surrender their share of profit in favour of other partner's | *(b)* Gaining ratio |
| *(iii)* Ratio in which all the Partners share the future profit and losses | *(c)* Sacrificing ratio |
| *(iv)* Ratio in which Partners acquire the share from other | *(d)* Old ratio |

***Codes:***

| | *(i)* | *(ii)* | *(iii)* | *(iv)* |
|---|---|---|---|---|
| A. | *(d)* | *(c)* | *(a)* | *(b)* |
| B. | *(a)* | *(c)* | *(d)* | *(b)* |
| C. | *(d)* | *(b)* | *(c)* | *(a)* |
| D. | *(c)* | *(b)* | *(d)* | *(a)* |

**57.** Match the following items:

| | |
|---|---|
| *(i)* Old ratio – New ratio | *(a)* Gaining ratio |
| *(ii)* Goodwill | *(b)* Fixed Assets |
| *(iii)* General reserve | *(c)* Credit Balance |
| *(iv)* New ratio - Old ratio | *(d)* Sacrificing Ratio |

***Codes:***

| | *(i)* | *(ii)* | *(iii)* | *(iv)* |
|---|---|---|---|---|
| A. | *(d)* | *(b)* | *(c)* | *(a)* |
| B. | *(a)* | *(c)* | *(d)* | *(b)* |
| C. | *(a)* | *(b)* | *(c)* | *(d)* |
| D. | *(c)* | *(b)* | *(d)* | *(a)* |

**58.** Which of the following is NOT true in relation to goodwill?

A. It is an intangible asset
B. It is fictitious assets
C. It has a realisable value
D. None of the above

**59.** When Goodwill is not purchased goodwill account can:

A. Never be raised in the book
B. Be raised in the book
C. Be partially raised in the books
D. Be raised as per the agreement of the partners.

**60.** The goodwill of the firm is NOT affected by;

A. Location of the firm
B. Reputation of firm
C. Better customer service
D. None of the above

**61.** For which of the following situations, the old profit-sharing ratio of partners is used at the time of admission of a new partner?

A. When new partner brings only a part of his share of goodwill.
B. When new partner is not able to bring his share of goodwill.
C. When, at the time of admission, goodwill already appears in the balance sheet.
D. When new partner brings his share of goodwill in cash.

**62.** A and B are partners in a firm having a capital of ₹ 54,000 and ₹ 36,000 respectively. They admitted C for 1/3rd share in the profits C brought proportionate amount of capital. The Capital brought in by C would be:

A. ₹ 90,000 B. ₹ 45,000
C. ₹ 5,400 D. ₹ 36,00

**63.** A, B and C are partner's in a firm. If D is admitted as a new partner:

A. old firm is dissolved
B. old firm and old partnership is dissolved
C. old partnership is reconstituted
D. None of the above.

**64.** On the admission of a new partner increase in the value of assets is debited to
A. Profit and Loss Adjustment account
B. Assets account
C. Old partner's capital account
D. None of the above

**65.** At the time of admission of a partner, undistributed profits appearing in the balance sheet of the old firm is transferred to the capital account of:
A. old partners in old profit sharing ratio
B. old partners in new profit sharing ratio
C. all the partner in the new profit sharing ratio
D. None of these

**66.** A, B and C are partners sharing profits in the ratio of 3 : 2 : 1. They agree to admit D into the firm. A, B and C agreed to give1/3rd,1/6th,1/9th share of their profit. The share of Profit of D will be:
A. 1/10 B. 11/54
C. 12/54 D. 13/54

**67.** A and B are in partnership sharing profits in the ratio of 3 : 2. they take C as a new Partner. Goodwill of the firm is valued at ₹ 3,00,000 and C brings ₹ 30,000 as his Share of goodwill In cash which is entirely credited to the Capital Account of A. New Profit sharing ratio will be:
A. 3 : 2 : 1 B. 6 : 3 : 1
C. 5 : 4 : 1 D. 4 : 5 : 1

**68.** A and B are partners sharing profit in the ratio of 3 : 2. They admit C as a partner by giving him 1/3 share in future profits. The new ratio will be:
A. 12 : 8 : 5 B. 8: 12 : 5
C. 5 : 5 : 12 D. None of these

**69.** A and B are partners sharing profits and losses in the ratio of 7 : 5. They agree to admit C, their manager, into partnership who is to get 1/6th share in the profits. He acquires this share as 1/24th from A and 1/8th from B, The new profit sharing ratio will be:
A. 13 : 7 : 4 B. 7 : 13 : 4
C. 7 : 5 : 6 D. 5 : 7 : 6

**70.** A and B are partners in a business sharing profits and losses in the ratio of 7 : 3 respectively. They admit C as a new partner. A sacrificed 1/7th share of his profit and B sacrificed 1/3rd of his share in favour of C. The new profit sharing ratio of A, B and C will be:
A. 3 : 1 : 1 B. 2 : 1 : 1
C. 2 : 2 : 1 D. None of the above

**71.** Which of the following items are added to previous year's profits for finding normal profits for valuation of goodwill?
A. Loss on sale of fixed assets
B. Loss due to fire, earthquake etc.
C. Undervaluation of closing stock
D. All of the above

**72.** Revaluation account or Profit & Loss adjustment account is:
A. Real Account B. Nominal Account
C. Personal Account D. None of the above

**73.** Under which method of valuation of goodwill, normal rate of return is not considered?
A. Loss on sale fixed assets
B. Loss due to fire, earthquake etc.
C. Undervaluation of closing stock
D. All of the above

**74.** The partners whose share increase as a result of change in profit sharing ratio are known as:
A. Gaining Partners
B. Sacrificing Partners
C. Sleeping Partners
D. None of the above

**75.** Following are the methods of calculating goodwill except:
A. Super profit method
B. Average profit method
C. Weighted Average profit method
D. Capital profit method

**76.** A, B and C are partners in a firm, if D is admitted as a new partner:
A. Old firm is dissolved
B. Old firm and old partnership is dissolved
C. Old partnership is reconstituted
D. None of the above

**77.** Revaluation Account is a ______ Account.
A. Real B. Nominal
C. Personal D. Liability

**78.** The excess amount which the firm can get on selling its assets over and above the saleable value of its assets is called:
A. Surplus B. Super profits
C. Reserve D. Goodwill

**79.** A firm is reconstituted, whenever there is a:
A. Death of a partner
B. Retirement of Existing Partner
C. All of the options
D. Admission of a new partner

**80.** When Goodwill is not purchased goodwill account can:
A. Never be raised in the books
B. Be raised in the books
C. Be partially raised in the books
D. Be raised as per the agreement of the partners

**81.** The goodwill of the firm is not affected by:
A. Location of the firm
B. Reputation of the firm
C. Better customer services
D. None of the above

**82.** Weighted average profit method of calculating goodwill is used when:
A. Profits are not equal B. Profits show a trend
C. Profits are fluctuating D. None of the above

**83.** When the balance sheet is prepared after retirement (subsequent to preparation of Revaluation Account), ______ values are shown in it.
A. Historical B. Realisable
C. Market D. Revalued

**84.** Balance in the Investment Fluctuation Reserve, after meeting the loss on Revaluation of Investments, as the time of admission of a partner will be transferred to:
A. Old Partners' Capital Accounts
B. Revaluation Account
C. Sacrificing Ratio
D. None of the above

**85.** If at the time of retirement, there some unrecorded asset, it will be ______ to Account.
A. Debited, Revaluation
B. Credited, Revaluation
C. Debited, Goodwill
D. Credited, Partners' Capital

**86.** When goodwill is withdrawn by old partners ______ a/c is credited.
A. cash/bank
B. capital
C. revaluation
D. Profit and Loss Adjustment

**87.** Revaluation Account for Profit and Loss Adjustment A/c is a:
A. Real Account B. Personal Account
C. Nominal Account D. Asset Account

**88.** There is a change in profit sharing ratio of existing partners and the question is silent about investment fluctuation reserve, then it is distributed among partners in:
A. Old Ratio B. New Ratio
C. Sacrificing Ratio D. Gaining Ratio

**89.** Under the capitalisation method, the formula for calculating the goodwill is:
A. Super Profits multiplied by the rate of return
B. Average Profits multiplied by the rate of return
C. Super Profits divided by the normal rate of return
D. Average Profits divided by the rate of return

**90.** Which of the following is true in relation to goodwill?
A. Goodwill is a fictitious asset
B. Goodwill is a current asset
C. Goodwill is a wasting asset
D. Goodwill is an intangible asset

**91.** The partner whose share has increased as a result of change is called:
A. Sacrificing partner
B. Sacrificing ratio
C. Gaining partner
D. Gaining ratio

**92.** Under Super Profit Method, goodwill is calculated by:
A. Number of years' Purchase × Average Profit
B. Number of years' Purchases × Super Profit
C. Super Profit × Normal Rate of Return
D. Super Profit × Normal Profit

**93.** The excess amount which the firm can get on selling its assets over and above the saleable value of its assets is called:
A. Surplus B. Super Profits
C. Reserve D. Goodwill

**94.** Retiring partner is compensated for parting with the firm's future profit in favour of remaining partners. The remaining partners contribute to such compensation amount in:
A. Gaining Ratio
B. Sacrificing Ratio
C. Capital Ratio
D. Profit Sharing Ratio

**95.** If any asset is taken over by partner from the firm ______ account will be debited.
A. asset
B. revaluation
C. capital
D. Profit and Loss Adjustment

**96.** At the time of admission of a new partner, the balance of Workmen Compensation Reserve will be transferred to:
A. Old partners in the Old profit sharing ratio
B. Sacrificing partners in the sacrificing ratio
C. Revaluation Account
D. All partners in the new profit sharing ratio

**97.** Which statement is true with respect to AS-26?
A. Purchased goodwill can be shown in the Balance Sheet
B. Revalued goodwill can be shown in the Balance Sheet
C. Both purchased goodwill and revalued can be shown in the Balance Sheet
D. None of the above

**98.** In case of admission of a partner, the profit or loss on revaluation of assets and liabilities is shared by ______ partners.

A. all B. none of these
C. new D. old

**99.** The account which is prepared to adjust the increase or decrease in the value of assets at the time of admission of partner is called:

A. Realisation Account
B. Revaluation Account
C. Profit and Loss Account
D. None of the above

**100.** Decrease in the value of Liabilities on reconstitution of the partnership firm result into:

A. Gain to the Existing partner
B. Loss to the Existing partner
C. Netiher Gain of loss to Existing partner
D. None of the above

## ANSWERS

| 1 | 2 | 3 | 4 | 5 | 6 | 7 | 8 | 9 | 10 |
|---|---|---|---|---|---|---|---|---|---|
| A | A | A | B | C | D | D | A | B | C |
| **11** | **12** | **13** | **14** | **15** | **16** | **17** | **18** | **19** | **20** |
| C | B | C | B | C | B | C | C | C | B |
| **21** | **22** | **23** | **24** | **25** | **26** | **27** | **28** | **29** | **30** |
| C | A | A | A | C | C | B | A | B | A |
| **31** | **32** | **33** | **34** | **35** | **36** | **37** | **38** | **39** | **40** |
| B | B | D | A | A | A | A | D | C | C |
| **41** | **42** | **43** | **44** | **45** | **46** | **47** | **48** | **49** | **50** |
| A | B | B | D | A | B | B | A | D | B |
| **51** | **52** | **53** | **54** | **55** | **56** | **57** | **58** | **59** | **60** |
| D | C | B | A | B | A | A | B | A | D |
| **61** | **62** | **63** | **64** | **65** | **66** | **67** | **68** | **69** | **70** |
| C | B | C | B | A | D | C | D | A | A |
| **71** | **72** | **73** | **74** | **75** | **76** | **77** | **78** | **79** | **80** |
| D | B | C | A | D | C | B | D | C | A |
| **81** | **82** | **83** | **84** | **85** | **86** | **87** | **88** | **89** | **90** |
| B | B | D | A | B | A | C | A | C | D |
| **91** | **92** | **93** | **94** | **95** | **96** | **97** | **98** | **99** | **100** |
| C | B | D | A | C | A | A | D | B | A |

●●●

# 4

# DISSOLUTION OF PARTNERSHIP FIRM

According to Section 39 of the partnership Act 1932, the dissolution of partnership between all the partners of a firm is called the dissolution of the firm. That means the Act recognises the difference in the breaking of relationship between all the partners of a firm and between some of the partners; and it is the breaking or discontinuance of relationship between all the partners which is termed as the dissolution of partnership firm.

## DISSOLUTION OF PARTNERSHIP

The dissolution of partnership may take place in any of the following ways:

- Change in existing profit sharing ratio among partners;
- Admission of a new partner;
- Retirement of a partner;
- Death of a partner;
- Insolvency of a partner;
- Completion of the venture, if partnership is formed for that; and
- Expiry of the period of partnership, if partnership is for a specific period of time;

## DISSOLUTION OF A FIRM

Dissolution of a firm takes place in any of the following ways:

- **Dissolution by Agreement:** A firm is dissolved:
  (*a*) with the consent of all the partners or
  (*b*) in accordance with a contract between the partners.
- **Compulsory Dissolution:** A firm is dissolved compulsorily in the following cases:
  (*a*) when all the partners or all but one partner, become insolvent, rendering them incompetent to sign a contract;
  (*b*) when the business of the firm becomes illegal; or
  (*c*) when some event has taken place which makes it unlawful for the partners to carry on the business of the firm in partnership, e.g., when a partner who is a citizen of a country becomes an alien enemy because of the declaration of war with his country and India.
- **On the Happening of Certain Contingencies:** Subject to contract between the partners, a firm is dissolved:
  (*a*) if constituted for a fixed term, by the expiry of that term;
  (*b*) if constituted to carry out one or more ventures, by the completion thereof;
  (*c*) by the death of a partner;
  (*d*) by the adjudication of a partner as an insolvent.
- **Dissolution by Notice:** In case of partnership at will, the firm may be dissolved if any one of the partners gives a notice in writing to the other partners, signifying his intention of seeking dissolution of the firm.
- **Dissolution by Court:** At the suit of a partner, the court may order a partnership firm to be dissolved on any of the following grounds:
  (*a*) when a partner becomes insane;
  (*b*) when a partner becomes permanently incapable of performing his duties as a partner;
  (*c*) when a partner is guilty of misconduct which is likely to adversely affect the business of the firm;
  (*d*) when a partner persistently commits breach of partnership agreement;
  (*e*) when a partner has transferred the whole of his interest in the firm to a third party;
  (*f*) when the business of the firm cannot be carried on except at a loss; or
  (*g*) when, on any ground, the court regards dissolution to be just and equitable.

**Difference between Dissolution of Partnership and Dissolution of Firm**

| Basis | Dissolution of Partnership | Dissolution of Firm |
|---|---|---|
| Termination of business | The business is not terminated. | The business of the firm is closed. |
| Settlement of assets and liabilities | Assets and liabilities are revalued and new balance sheet is drawn. | Assets are sold and liabilities are paid-off. |
| Court's intervention | Court does not intervene because partnership is dissolved by mutual agreement. | A firm can be dissolved by the court's order. |
| Economic relationship | Economic relationship between the partners continues though in a changed form. | Economic relationship between the partners comes to an end. |
| Closure of books | Does not require because the business is not terminated. | The books of account are closed. |

## SETTLEMENT OF ACCOUNTS

In case of dissolution of a firm, the firm ceases to conduct business and has to settle its accounts. For this purpose, it disposes off all its assets for satisfying all the claims against it. In this context it should be noted that, subject to agreement among the partners, the following rules as provided in Section 48 of the Partnership Act 1932 shall apply.

(*a*) **Treatment of Losses**

Losses, including deficiencies of capital, shall be paid:

(*i*) first out of profits,

(*ii*) next out of capital of partners, and

(*iii*) lastly, if necessary, by the partners individually in their profit sharing ratio.

(*b*) **Application of Assets**

The assets of the firm, including any sum contributed by the partners to make up deficiencies of capital, shall be applied in the following manner and order:

(*i*) In paying the debts of the firm to the third parties;

(*ii*) In paying each partner proportionately what is due to him/her from the firm for advances as distinguished from capital (i.e. partner's loan);

(*iii*) In paying to each partner proportionately what is due to him on account of capital; and

(*iv*) The residue, if any, shall be divided among the partners in their profit sharing ratio.

### Private Debts and Firm's Debts

Where both the debts of the firm and private debts of a partner co-exist, the following rules, as stated in Section 49 of the Act, shall apply.

(*a*) The property of the firm shall be applied first in the payment of debts of the firm and then the surplus, if any, shall be divided among the partners as per their claims, which can be utilised for payment of their private liabilities.

(*b*) The private property of any partner shall be applied first in payment of his private debts and the surplus, if any, may be utilised for payment of the firm's debts, in case the firm's liabilities exceed the firm's assets.

It may be noted that the private property of the partner does not include the personal properties of his wife and children.

Thus, if the assets of the firm are not adequate enough to pay off firm's liabilities, the partners have to contribute out of their net private assets (private assets minus private liabilities).

## ACCOUNTING TREATMENT

When the firm is dissolved, its books of account are to be closed and the profit or loss arising on realisation of its assets and discharge of liabilities is to be computed.

For this purpose, a Realisation Account is prepared to ascertain the net effect (profit or loss) of realisation of assets and payment of liabilities which may be is transferred to partner's capital accounts in their profit sharing ratio.

Hence, all assets (other than cash in hand bank balance and fictitious assets, if any), and all external liabilities are transferred to this account.

It also records the sale of assets, and payment of liabilities and realisation expenses. The balance in this account is termed as profit or loss on realisation which is transferred to partners' capital accounts in the profit sharing ratio.

**Realisation Account**

Dr. Cr.

| Particulars | Amount (₹) | Particulars | Amount (₹) |
|---|---|---|---|
| Intangible Assets | xxx | Bank Loan Mortgage | xxx |
| Land and Building | xxx | Sundry creditors | xxx |
| Plant and Machinery | xxx | Bills payables | xxx |
| Furniture and Fittings | xxx | Bank overdraft | xxx |
| Loan to other parties | xxx | Outstanding expenses | xxx |
| Bills receivables | xxx | Provision for doubtful debts | xxx |
| Sundry debtors | xxx | Cash/Bank (sale of assets) | xxx |
| Cash/Bank (payment of liabilities) | xxx | Partner's capital account (assets taken by the partner) | xxx |
| Cash/Bank (payment of unrecorded liabilities) | xxx | Loss (transferred to partners' capital accounts) | xxx |
| Partner's capital account | xxx | Loss (transferred to partners) | xxx |
| Investments (liability assumed by the partner) | xxx | Investment Fluctuation Fund | xxx |
| Profit (transferred to partners' capital account's in their profit sharing ratio) | xxx | | |
| **Total** | **xxxxx** | **Total** | **xxxxx** |

**Format of Realisation Account**

## JOURNAL ENTRIES

**1. For trnasfer of assets**

All asset accounts excluding cash, bank and the fictitious assets, if any are closed by transfer to the debit of Realisation Account at their book values.

Realisation A/c Dr.
 To Assets (Individually) A/c

**2. For transfer of liabilities**

All external liability accounts including provisions, if any, are closed by transferring them to the credit of Realisation account.

Liabilities (individually) Dr.
 To Realisation A/c

**3. For sale of assets**

Bank A/c Dr.
 To Realisation A/c

[with the same value]

**4. For an asset taken over by a partner**

Partner's Capital A/c Dr.
 To Realisation A/c

[with the amount assets are taken over]

**5. For payment of liabilities**

Realisation A/c Dr.
 To Bank A/c

[with the amount at which settled]

**6. For a liability which a partner takes responsibility to discharge**

Ralisation A/c Dr.
 To Partner's Capital A/c

**7.** For settlement with the creditor through transfer of assets when a creditor accepts an asset in full and final settlement of his account, no journal entry needs to be recorded. But, if the creditor accepts an asset only as part payment of his/her dues, the entry will be made for cash payment only.

Realisation A/c Dr.
 To Bank A/c

However, when a creditor accepts an asset whose value is more than the due amount he/she pay cash to the firm for the difference for which the entry will be:

Bank A/c Dr.
 To Realisation A/c

**8. For payment of realisation expenses**

(*a*) When some expenses are incurred and paid by the firm in the process of realisation of assets and payment of liabilities:

Realisation A/c Dr.
To Bank A/c

(*b*) When realisation expenses are paid by a partner on behalf of the firm:

Realisation A/c Dr.
To Partner's Capital A/c

(*c*) When a partner has agreed to bear the realisation expenses:

(*i*) if payment of realisation expenses is made by the firm

Partner's Capital A/c Dr.
To Bank A/c

(*ii*) if the partner himself pays the realisation expenses, no entry is required

**Note:** In the absence of information about who is paying the expenses, it is implied that expenses are paid by the partner who has agreed to bear expenses.

**9. For agreed remuneration** to such partner who agrees to undertake the dissolution work.

Realisation A/c Dr.
To Partner's Capital A/c

**10. For realisation of any unrecorded assets including goodwill,** if any

Bank A/c Dr.
To Realisation A/c

**11. For settlement of any unrecorded liability**

Realisation A/c Dr.
To Bank A/c

**12. For transfer of profit and loss on realisation** (Cr. Blance)

(*a*) In case of profit on realisation

Realisation A/c Dr.
To Partners' Capital A/c (individually) A/c

(*b*) In case of loss on realisation

Partners' Capital A/c (individually) Dr.
(Dr. Blance)
To Realisation A/c

**13. For settlement of loan by a firm to a partner:**

Bank A/c Dr.
To loan to partners A/c

**14. For transfer of accumulated profits in the form of general reserve to partners' capital accounts in their profit sharing ratio:**

General Reserve A/c Dr.
To Partners' Capital A/c (individually)

**15. For transfer of fictitious assets, if any, to partners' capital accounts in their profit sharing ratio:**

Partners' Capital A/c (individually) Dr.
To Fictitious Asset A/c

**16. For payment of loans due to partners**

Partner's Loan A/c Dr.
To Bank A/c

**17. For settlement of partners' accounts**

If the partner's capital account shows a debit balance after posting of rebount entries firms. He brings in the necessary cash for which the entry will be:

Bank A/c Dr.
To Partner's Capital A/c

The balance is paid to partners whose capital accounts show a credit balance and the following entry is recorded.

Partners' Capitals A/c (individually) Dr.
To Bank A/c

It may be noted that the aggregate amount finally payable to the partners must equal to the amount available in bank and cash accounts. Thus, all accounts of a firm are closed in case of dissolution.

**Illustration:**

Sonu and Ashu sharing profits as 3 : 1 and they agree upon dissolution. The Balance Sheet as on March 31, 2017 is as under:

**Balance Sheet of Sonu and Ashu as on March 31, 2017**

| Liabilities | | Amount (₹) | Assets | Amount (₹) |
|---|---|---|---|---|
| Loan | | 12,000 | Cash at bank | 15,000 |
| Creditors | | 18,000 | Stock | 45,000 |
| Capital | | | Furniture | 16,000 |
| Sonu | 1,10,000 | | Debtors | 70,000 |
| Ashu | 68,000 | 1,78,000 | Plant and Machinery | 52,000 |
| | | | Loan to Ashu | 10,000 |
| | | **2,08,000** | | **2,08,000** |

Sonu took over plant and machinery at an agreed value of ₹ 60,000. Stock and Furniture were sold for ₹ 42,000 and ₹ 13,900 respectively. Debtors were taken over by Ashu at ₹ 69,000. Creditors were paid subject to discount of ₹ 900. Sonu agrees to pay the loans. Realisation expenses were ₹ 1,600. Prepare Realisation Account, Bank Account and Capital Accounts of the Partners.

***Solution***

**Books of Sonu and Ashu Realisation Account**

Dr. Cr.

| Particulars | | Amount (₹) | Particulars | | Amount (₹) |
|---|---|---|---|---|---|
| Stock | | 45,000 | Loan | | 12,000 |
| Furniture | | 16,000 | Creditors | | 18,000 |
| Debtors | | 70,000 | Sonu's capital (plant & machinery) | | 60,000 |
| Plant and Machinery | | 52,000 | Ashu's capital (debtors) | | 69,000 |
| Bank (creditors) | | 17,100 | Bank: | | |
| Sonu's capital (loan) | | 12,000 | Stock | 42,000 | |
| Bank (realisation expenses) | | 1,600 | Furniture | 13,900 | 55,900 |
| Profit transferred to: | | | | | |
| Sonu's capital | 900 | | | | |
| Ashu's capital | 300 | 1,200 | | | |
| | | 2,14,900 | | | 2,14,900 |

**Partners Capital Accounts**

Dr. Cr.

| Date 2017 | Particulars | J.F. | Sonu (₹) | Ashu (₹) | Date 2017 | Particulars | J.F. | Sonu (₹) | Ashu (₹) |
|---|---|---|---|---|---|---|---|---|---|
| | Realisation [plant and machinery] | | 60,000 | | | Balance b/d | | 1,10,000 | 68,000 |
| | | | | | | Realisation [loan] | | 12,000 | |
| | Realisation [debtors] | | | 69,000 | | Realisation [profit] | | 900 | 300 |
| | Bank | | 62,900 | | | Bank | | | 700 |
| | | | 1,22,900 | 69,000 | | | | 1,22,900 | 69,000 |

**Bank Account**

Dr. Cr.

| Date 2017 | Particulars | J.F. | Amount (₹) | Date 2017 | Particulars | J.F. | Amount (₹) |
|---|---|---|---|---|---|---|---|
| | Balance b/d | | 15,000 | | Realisation [creditor] | | 17,100 |
| | Realisation (assets realised) | | 55,900 | | Realisation [expenses] | | 1,600 |
| | Loan to Ashu | | 10000 | | Sonu's capital | | 62,900 |
| | Ashu's capital | | 700 | | | | |
| | | | 81,600 | | | | 81,600 |

## MULTIPLE CHOICE QUESTIONS

**1.** Dissolution of the firm means:
A. Liabilities paid
B. Business of the firms ends
C. Assets Sold
D. All of the options

**2.** The modes by which a firm may be dissolved are:
A. By Notice
B. By Mutual Agreement
C. Compulsory Dissolution
D. All of the options

3. Why is realisation account prepared:
A. For profit sharing B. Opening the account
C. Closing the accounts D. None of these

4. How will goodwill account appearing in the balance sheet be treated in case of dissolution of the firm
A. By transferring to realisation A/c (Cr. Side)
B. By transferring to realisation A/c (Dr. Side)
C. Both Side
D. None of these

5. What will be the accounting treatment of balance of the realisation account:
A. Transferred to partners Capital A/c in their old ratio
B. Transferred to partners Capital A/c in their profit sharing ratio
C. Transferred to partners Capital A/c in their new ratio
D. None of these

6. At the time of dissolution of the firm, if goodwill appears in the balance sheet, it is transferred to:
A. Realisation A/c B. Revaluation A/c
C. Capital A/c D. Current Account

7. At the time of dissolution of firm, loan from partner is:
A. Not transferred to realisation A/c
B. Transferred to realisation A/c
C. Transferred to partners capital A/c
D. None of these

8. Where it is agreed that a partner will be paid a lump sum amount for dissolution, if the payment is made by the firm, the payment is debited to:
A. All the partners capital Account
B. Realisation Account
C. Concerned partners capital Account
D. None of these

9. Unrecorded assets when realised is credit to:
A. Partners capital A/c B. Realisation A/c
C. Current Account D. None of these

10. Unrecorded Liabilities when paid are debited to:
A. Realisation A/c B. Partners capital A/c
C. Current Account D. None of these

11. Why a new partner is admitted in the firm?
A. For Increase the Capital of the firm.
B. For Increase the Number of partners
C. For Increase the Profit sharing Ratio
D. None of these

12. Which is the main right of a partner?
A. Share the old profits of the firm
B. Stop other partners for drawings.
C. Share the Profits of the firm.
D. All of the options

13. According to Section 30 of Partnership Act 1932:
A. A Minor can be admitted as a partner by the consent of all partners for the time being.
B. New partner will bring capital and goodwill in cash
C. New partner will inspect the books of accounts
D. New partner is allowed to share old profits

14. The incoming partner cannot acquire his share of profits:
A. From the old partners in their old profit sharing ratio
B. From the old partners in their new profit sharing ratio
C. From one or more partners, (not from all partners)
D. From the old partners in some agreed ratio

15. At the time of admission of a new partner, the new partner acquires his share from the old partners in the:
A. Old ratio B. New Ratio
C. Both A and B D. Sacrificing ratio

16. Sacrifice ratio is used only for:
A. Revaluation of Assets
B. Revaluation profit
C. Distribution of Reserve
D. Distribution of Premium for goodwill

17. Section ____ of the Indian Partnership Act provides that a new partner shall not be inducted into a firm without the consent of all existing partners
A. 40 B. 35
C. 31 D. 45

18. When a new partner is admitted he acquires his share of profits from the old partners, this will ____ the old partners shares in profits:
A. Reduce B. Remain same
C. No change D. Decrease

19. Is admission of a new partner a reconstitution of partnership firm:
A. Yes
B. No
C. It is dissolution of firm
D. It is called merger

20. Why new profit ratio is determined even for old partners?
A. Change in the agreement among all partners
B. No change in agreement
C. Due to change in external environment
D. All of the options

21. Sacrificing ratio is calculated for
A. new partners
B. old partners
C. all partners (including new)
D. None of the options

**22.** Revaluation Account is also known as ________.
A. Profit and Loss Adjustment Account
B. Asset Account
C. Profit and Loss Account
D. Only profit

**23.** Gaining Ratio is Applicable for:
A. For Revaluation
B. For the distribution of Reserves and profits
C. For the Calculation of profit
D. Retiring partners share of goodwill only

**24.** Why there is need to calculate New profit share ratio
A. After retirement of a partner, there will be change in the continuing partners ratio.
B. After retirement of a partner, there is no change in the continuing partners ratio.
C. To settle the loan amount due to outgoing partner
D. All of the options

**25.** Except outgoing partner, which other partner can be credited at the time of settlement of goodwill amount?
A. Gaining partner B. Sacrificing partner
C. All the partners D. None of the options

**26.** Retirement or death of a partner will create a situation for the continuing partners, which is known as:
A. Reconstitution of Firm B. Dissolution of firm
C. Amalgamation D. None of the options

**27.** New Ratio Old Ratio is called:
A. Gaining Ratio B. Profit Sharing ratio
C. Sacrificing ratio D. None of the options

**28.** How sacrificing ratio is differ from gaining ratio on the basis of mode of calculation:
A. calculated by taking difference between old and gaining ratio
B. calculated by taking difference between new and old ratio
C. calculated by taking difference between old and new ratio
D. None of the options

**29.** Only in Balance Sheet at the time of retirement of a partner, general reserve given in the balance sheet should be credited to all the partners (including outgoing partner) in their old profit sharing ratio.
A. Credit side of Capital account of all the partners
B. Debit side of Capital account of all the partners
C. Both (A) and (B)
D. None of the options

**30.** Which of the following is prepared at the time of retirement of a partner?
A. Revaluation Account
B. Profit and Loss Suspense Account
C. Both (A) and (B)
D. None of the options

**31.** Which of the following item is not shown in the credit side of deceased partners capital account?
A. Share of profit B. Share of loss
C. Revaluation profit D. All of the options

**32.** Bad debts recovered will be recorded in:
A. Cr. Side of revaluation account
B. Dr. Side of revaluation account
C. Both (A) and (B)
D. None of the options

**33.** At the time of dissolution of firm, at which stage the balance of partner's capital accounts is paid?
A. After making the payment to third party's loans
B. Before making the payment of partners in respect of their loans
C. After making the payment to third party for their loans as well as partners loans
D. None of the above.

**34.** On firm's dissolution, which one of the following account should be prepared at the last?
A. Realisation Account
B. Partner's Capital Accounts
C. Cash Account
D. Partner's Loan Account

**35.** On dissolution of a firm, a partner paid ₹ 700 for firm's realisation expenses. Which account will be debited?
A. Cash Account
B. Realisation Account
C. Capital Account of the Partner
D. Profit & Loss A/c

**36.** On taking responsibility of payment of realisation expenses by a partner, the account credited will be:
A. Realisation Account
B. Cash Account
C. Capital Account of the Partner
D. None of the Above

**37.** On dissolution of a firm, an unrecorded furniture of the value of ₹ 5,000 was taken up by a partner for ₹ 4,300. Which Account will be credited and by how much amount?
A. Cash Account by ₹ 4,300
B. Realisation Account by ₹ 700
C. Partner's Capital Account by ₹ 5,000
D. Realisation Account by ₹ 4,300

**38.** On the basis of following data, final payment to a partner on firm's dissolution will be made:

Debit balance of Capital Account ₹ 14,000; Share of his profit on realisation ₹ 43,000; Firm's asset taken over by him for ₹ 17,000.
A. ₹ 31,000 B. ₹ 29,000
C. ₹ 12,000 D. ₹ 60,000

**39.** On payment of expenses of dissolution, account will be debited:

A. Realisation Account B. Cash Account
C. Profit & Loss Account D. None of the Above

**40.** Investments valued ₹ 2,00,000 were not shown in the books. One of the creditors took over these investments in full satisfaction of his debt of ₹ 2,20,000. How much amount will be deducted from creditors?

A. ₹ 20,000 B. ₹ 2,20,000
C. ₹ 4,20,000 D. ₹ 2,00,000

**41.** If opening capitals of partners are A: ₹ 3,00,000, B: ₹ 2,00,000 and C: ₹ 1,00,000 and their drawings during the year are A: ₹ 50,000, B: ₹ 40,000 and C: ₹ 30,000 and creditors are ₹ 60,000, what will be the amount of assets of the firm?

A. ₹ 5,40,000 B. ₹ 4,20,000
C. ₹ 4,80,000 D. ₹ 6,60,000

**42.** On dissolution of a firm, partners' capital accounts balance was ₹ 63,000; creditors balance was ₹ 12,000 and profit & loss account debit balance was ₹ 6,000. Profit on realisation of assets was ₹ 7,800. Total amount realised from assets was:

A. ₹ 81,000 B. ₹ 76,800
C. ₹ 70,800 D. None of these

**43.** Anu, Bina and Charan are partners. The firm had given a loan of ₹ 20,000 to Bina. They decided to dissolve the firm. In the event of dissolution, the loan will be settled by

A. transferring it to debit side of Realisation Account.
B. transferring it to credit side of Realisation Account.
C. transferring it to debit side of Bina's Capital Account.
D. Bina paying Anu and Charan privately.

**44.** Rohit, a partner is to carry out dissolution and he gets ₹ 50,000 as remuneration. Realisation Expenses were ₹ 25,000. Realisation Account will be debited with

A. ₹ 50,000 B. ₹ 75,000
C. ₹ 25,000 D. ₹ 1,00,000

**45.** Amount received from sale of unrecorded asset at the time of dissolution of the firm is credited to:

A. Partners' Capital Accounts
B. Profit and Loss Account
C. Realisation Account
D. Cash Account

**46.** Court can make an order to dissolve the firm when:

A. Some partner has become fully mad
B. Partnership deed is fully followed
C. Continued future profits are expected
D. Firm is running legal business

**47.** On dissolution of a firm, realisation account is debited with

A. Cash received on sale of assets
B. All outside liabilities of the firm
C. All assets to be realised
D. Any asset taken over by one of the partners

**48.** On dissolution of a firm, out of the proceeds received from the sale of assets ........... will be paid first of all.

A. Partner's Capital
B. Partner's Loan to Firm
C. Partner's additional capital
D. Outside Creditors

**49.** On firm's dissolution, on realisation of goodwill (which was shown in Balance Sheet) will be credited to:

A. Cash A/c B. Realisation A/c
C. Profit & Loss A/c D. None of the A/c

**50.** Which of the following is not the mode of dissolution of the firm?

A. By mutual agreement
B. On happening of an event
C. Dissolution by court
D. Retirement of a partner

## ANSWERS

| 1 | 2 | 3 | 4 | 5 | 6 | 7 | 8 | 9 | 10 |
|---|---|---|---|---|---|---|---|---|---|
| D | D | C | B | B | A | A | C | B | A |
| **11** | **12** | **13** | **14** | **15** | **16** | **17** | **18** | **19** | **20** |
| A | C | A | B | D | D | C | A | A | C |
| **21** | **22** | **23** | **24** | **25** | **26** | **27** | **28** | **29** | **30** |
| B | A | D | A | B | A | A | C | A | A |
| **31** | **32** | **33** | **34** | **35** | **36** | **37** | **38** | **39** | **40** |
| B | B | C | C | B | C | D | C | A | B |
| **41** | **42** | **43** | **44** | **45** | **46** | **47** | **48** | **49** | **50** |
| A | B | C | B | C | A | C | D | B | D |

# 5

# ACCOUNTING FOR SHARE AND DEBENTURE CAPITAL

Before going through this chapter, it is advisable to go through the salient features of the companies as well as the Companies Act (both explained in this book in detail) to get a full idea of the functioning of the companies and its salient features.

## SHARE CAPITAL

A company is a legal entity separate from its owners. But as far as the accounting is concerned, the basic rules are same whether it is a company or a firm. Though there are some peculiarities in the company accounts which we shall discuss as we go along, the basic difference is that unlike in the partnership where there are few owners, in companies the owners may run into thousands. All of them hold share in the company. The various divisions of share capital are as follows :

- **Authorized or Nominal Capital :** It is the capital mentioned in the Capital clause of the Memorandum of Association of the company with which the company is registered. The company cannot issue shares more than the authorized capital unless Capital clause is altered.
- **Issued Capital :** It is that portion of authorized capital which is offered to the public for subscription. The remaining part of the Authorized capital is known as the 'Unissued Capital' which can be issued later on..
- **Subscribed Capital :** Out of the issued capital, the portion for which public subscribe to the shares of the company is called subscribed capital.
- **Called up Capital :** It is that portion of the subscribed capital which has been called up by the company from the shareholders. Capital is generally called on allotment as well as through various instalments known as 'Calls'.
- **Paid up Capital :** It represents that portion of the Called up capital with regard to which the company has received call money from the shareholders.
- **Reserve Capital :** According to Section 99 of the Companies Act a company may, by a special resolution determine that a portion of its uncalled capital should not be called up, except in the event of winding up of the company.

## ISSUE OF SHARES

When the company issues shares to the public, the journal entries in respect of various transactions are explained as below:

| TRANSACTION | ACCOUNTING ENTRY | |
|---|---|---|
| | DEBIT | CREDIT |
| (1) Receipt of application money | Bank A/c | Share Application A/c |
| (2) Application money in respect of shares allotted | Share Application A/c | Share Capital A/c |
| (3) Refund for rejected applications | Share Application A/c | Bank A/c |
| (4) Adjustment of excess application money towards allotment | Share Application A/c | Share allotment A/c |
| (5) Adjustment of excess application money towards calls-in-advance | Share Application A/c | Calls-in-advance A/c |

| TRANSACTION | ACCOUNTING ENTRY | |
|---|---|---|
| | DEBIT | CREDIT |
| (6) When allotment is made and money is due | Share Allotment A/c | Share Capital A/c |
| (7) Receipt of allotment money | Bank A/c | Share allotment A/c |
| (8) Where a call is made for the call money due | Share call A/c | Share Capital A/c |
| (9) Adjustment of money in calls-in-advance towards the call account | Calls-in-advance A/c | Share Call A/c |
| (10) Receipt of call money | Bank A/c | Share Call A/c |

When the company receives applications for shares more than it wants to issue, it gives pro-rata allotment to the applicants. For example, if the company wants to allot 1000 shares and number of shares applied are 3000, the company will allot only 1/3rd of the shares applied by the applicants. The balance amount on application is either adjusted as calls in advance or is refunded to the applicants.

### Calls-in-advance and Arrears

When the applicant sends more money than required, the excess money is called calls-in-advance. Such a calls-in-advance can be accepted only when the company is so authorized by its Articles of Association. If the company has adopted Table A, then it is required to pay 6% interest on such amount. The shareholder is not entitled to any dividend on the amount paid as calls-in-advance.

On the other hand, if shareholder makes default in sending call money according to conditions, then money not so sent is called calls-in-arrear. It is a liability of the shareholder and default to pay this may lead to forfeiture of shares.

### Issue of Shares for Consideration other Than Cash

Shares are sometimes issued to certain persons for consideration other than cash. For example issue of shares to a vendor who sells some asset to the company or to the promoters for their services. In the first case, the treatment is simple. In place of making payment by cheque, the payment is made in the form of shares and hence the share capital account will be credited in place of bank account. But, when the shares are issued to the promoters, the following accounting entry is made :

Goodwill A/c Dr.

To Share Capital A/c

The amount is debited to Goodwill account because it is considered that without the work of the promoters, it would not have been possible to create the company.

### Issue of Shares At Premium

When a share is issued at a price which is above its face value, then it is said that it has been issued at premium. Share premium is often charged by the company at the time of allotment of shares.

As per the Companies Act, 1956, such premium whether received in cash of in kind must be credited to a separate account called "Share Premium Account".

Under Section 78 of Companies Act, the amount to the credit of this account may be used wholly or in part for following purposes :

1. Paying up un-issued shares of the company to be issued to members of the company as fully paid bonus shares.
2. Writing off the preliminary expenses of the company.
3. Writing off the expenses of, or the commission paid or discount allowed on any shares or of any debentures of the company.
4. Providing for the premium payable on the redemption of any redeemable preference shares or of any debentures of the company.

### Issue of Shares At Discount

When a share is issued at a price which is less than its face value then it is said that it has been issued at discount. A Company can issue share at discount on fulfilling the conditions of Section 79 of the Companies Act. Discount on issue of shares being a loss of capital nature, is shown on the asset side of the balance sheet and is amortised(written off) over a period of time decided by the company.

## FORFEITURE OF SHARES

In case a member fails to pay any call on the day appointed for payment, the directors may, either by the adoption of Table A or by an express provision in its Articles, proceed to forfeit the shares held by such a defaulting shareholder. On forfeiture, the name of the shareholder is removed from the register of the company.

But, before forfeiting shares, a proper notice requiring payment of the calls with interest should be served to the shareholder. It may be noted that share capital account, on forfeiture, is debited with the called up amount(excluding the share premium called and paid by the shareholder) and not with the face value of the share.

### Forfeiture of Shares Issued at Premium/ Discount

When shares issued at premium are forfeited, the share premium which was due and not paid by the shareholder should be cancelled by giving a debit entry to the share premium account. But, the share premium which was due and paid by the shareholder should not be cancelled. This is according to Sec. 78 of Companies Act that share premium once collected cannot be cancelled even if the shares are forfeited. On the other hand, discount on issue of shares is a loss and is debited at the time of issue of shares. When these shares are forfeited, the discount on issue of shares account is credited to cancel the effect of earlier debit entry.

### Re-issue of Forfeited Shares

Shares forfeited on the non-payment of calls can be re-issued by the company as and when company finds it suitable and convenient. But, the amount collected on re-issue together with the amount already paid before the share were forfeited should not be less than the amount credited as paid up on re-issue of shares. When the shares forfeited are re-issued at a discount, such discount is to be debited to forfeited shares account. After setting off the amount earlier received on shares, if still there is some balance, it should be transferred to Capital Reserve Account. The accounting entries on re-issue of shares are similar to those at the time of issue of fresh shares.

### Value of Right Share

In case a company makes a further issue of shares to its existing shareholders, it is known as a Right Issue. The existing shareholders may accept or reject the offer of shares. They can even sell these right shares in the market. In such a situation it is important to know the value of the share being offered by the company as right. The following method is employed.

### Issue of Bonus Shares

Bonus shares are those shares which are allotted to the existing equity shareholders of the company without any consideration, either in cash or in kind. In other words, these are free shares issued by the company to the existing shareholders in some ratio of their existing shareholding. Bonus shares can be issued subject to the provisions of the Articles of Association and the Companies Act, 1956. Issue of bonus shares result into the capitalization of profits and reserves of the company. According to the SEBI guidelines, following conditions must be observed while making any bonus issue :

1. Bonus issue should be made out of free reserves built out of genuine profits or share premium collected in cash only.
2. Reserves created out of revaluation of fixed assets should not be capitalized.
3. The bonus issue cannot be made unless the partly paid shares, if any, are made fully paid up.
4. The company has not defaulted in payment of interest or principal in respect of fixed deposits or debentures.
5. Consequent to the issue of bonus shares, if the subscribed and paid up capital exceeds the authorized share capital, resolution shall be passed by the company at its general meeting for increasing the authorized capital.

### Brokerage

Brokerage is merely the act of procuring subscriptions for shares or debentures without any responsibility. The company pays brokerage to the broker on the shares subscribed through him and he has no obligation to take up the shares that may remain unsold.

## REDEMPTION OF PREFERENCE SHARES

According to Section 80, the following are the rules for redemption of preference shares :

(*a*) The shares to be redeemed should be fully paid up.

(*b*) They can be redeemed either out of the profits of the company which would otherwise be available for dividend or out of the proceeds of a fresh issue of shares (may be equity but not debentures) made for the purpose of redemption.

(*c*) The premium payable on redemption must be provided either out of accumulated profits of the company or the Share Premium account before the shares are redeemed.

(*d*) When the shares are redeemed out of the profits, an amount equal to the nominal value of the shares so redeemed should be transferred from the profits to a reserve account called **Capital Redemption Reserve** account which may be used in issuing the fully paid bonus shares by the company.

(*e*) Redemption of preference shares does not amount to reduction in the authorized capital of the company.

It is to be noted that in "Proceeds of fresh issue of shares" as mentioned above, only the nominal value of shares issued should be considered for determining the amount to be credited to Capital Redemption Reserve Account. It means that any premium received on issue of shares should be disregarded. But if the shares are issued at discount, the actual proceeds of the issue (Discounted price of shares) should be deducted from the face value of preference shares to be redeemed to arrive at the amount to be transferred to CRR A/c. The following journal entries are passed by the company on redemption of preference shares:

(*a*) If the company makes fresh issue of shares

Bank A/c Dr.

To Share Capital A/c

To Share Premium Account

(if issued on premium)

(*b*) When preference shares are redeemed at premium

Share premium A/c Dr.

Profit and Loss A/c Dr.

To Premium on Redemption A/c

(*c*) Transferring the amount to the CRR A/c

Profit & Loss A/c Dr.

General Reserve A/c Dr.

To CRR A/c

(Face value of shares to be redeemed - Face value of fresh issue of shares)

(*d*) Transferring the capital to the shareholders A/c

Preference shares A/c Dr.

Premium on Redemption A/c Dr.

To preference shareholders A/c

(*e*) When payment is made to the shareholders

Preference shareholders A/c Dr.

To Bank A/c

**Illustration 1:** A company has to redeem 1,000 preference shares of ₹ 100 each at ₹ 103. For this purpose, it issues 500 equity shares of ₹ 100 each at a premium of 10%.

The following figures will be important:

| | |
|---|---|
| Total amount to be redeemed (103 × 1000) | 1,03,000 |
| Share premium on equity shares (10 × 500) | 5,000 |
| Amount to be transferred to CRR A/c | |
| (1,00,000 – 50,000) | 50,000 |

The premium to be paid on redemption will be adjusted against the premium received from the new issue. The balance amount of premium by the new issue will not be considered for determining the amount to be transferred to the CRR A/c. If the fresh issue of shares is to be determined according to the divisible profit available with the company, the minimum possible number of shares to be issued has to be determined. This can be arrived at by applying the following equation:

Face value of preference shares + Premium on redemption = Share Premium account in the balance sheet + Divisible profit available (including reserves) + Fresh shares to be issued (say 'X' ) + Premium on issue of fresh shares.

**Illustration 2 :** Preference shares of ₹ 20,000 are to be redeemed at 10% premium and the Balance of Profit and Loss account and General Reserves is ₹ 4,000 and ₹ 6000 respectively. Share premium accounts balance is ₹ 1,000. Fresh issue of shares is to be made at 10% premium.

Applying the formula, the company needs to issue shares of ₹ 10,000.

## ISSUE AND REDEMPTION OF DEBENTURES

The accounting entries for issue of debentures are same as that of equity shares. The only difference is that after the issue of debentures, the company has to make regular payment of interest to the debenture holders. It should be kept in mind that the amount of interest payable to the debenture holders is calculated at the rate of interest those debentures are carrying multiplying it with the face value of debentures irrespective of the fact that the debentures may have been issued at par, or at premium or at discount. Also first interest is payable from the date of issue of debentures to the date of payment of interest (quarterly, half yearly or yearly).

**Illustration 3 :** A company has issued 1000, 8% debentures of ₹ 100 each at ₹ 95 to be repayable at ₹ 105 each to be repayable after 5 years. The interest is payable half yearly. The interest to be paid at the end of each half year will be (1,000 × 100 × 8% / 2) = 4,000.

Another point is that if the debentures are issued at discount and to be redeemed at premium, the total loss on discount as well as the premium is booked at the time of issue itself by debiting the total amount to 'Loss on issue of debentures' A/c.

This loss is considered as Deferred Revenue expenditure and is written off over the period of tenure of the debentures equally. If the debentures are repayable in installments, the amount is written off based on the proportion of the debentures outstanding at the end of each year.

**Illustration 4 :** In the above example, the total loss on issue of debentures is ₹ 10,000 (1,000 × 10). This loss will be written off over a period of 5 years i.e. ₹ 2,000 per year. If the debentures are to be redeemed in 5 installments starting from the end of the first year, the use of funds in 5 years will be ₹ 1,00,000, 80,000, 60,000, 40,000 and 20,000 respectively. So, the loss of ₹ 10,000 will be written off in the ratio of 5 : 4 : 3 : 2 : 1.

### Cum-interest and Ex-interest Purchase of Debentures

Debentures may be purchased either on cum-interest basis or on ex-interest basis. If the debentures are purchased on cum-interest basis, it means that the price of the debenture includes the next installment of interest payable by the company. So, the purchaser of the debentures is entitled to the interest from the date of purchase. On the other hand, in ex-interest purchase, the next interest installment is received by the seller only and thereafter all the interests are received by the purchaser. So, ex-interest price of debentures is always lower than the cum-interest price.

### Manner of Redemption of Debentures

The debentures can be redeemed in any of the following ways:

1. One time payment on maturity
2. Payment in Instalments
3. Purchase of debentures in open market

As regards, the first two manners, the accounting entries are simple. Complications arise in case debentures are redeemed by way of purchase in open market. Under this method also, the debentures may be purchased for two purposes :

(*a*) Purchase of debentures for redemption

(*b*) Purchase of debentures for investment

### Purchase of Debentures for Redemption

In this case, the company purchases debentures in the open market some time before the debentures are due for redemption. The purchased debentures are redeemed once the due date arrives and hence no payment need be made to the outsiders. In this case, the debentures may be purchased cum-interest or ex-interest.

**Illustration 5:** A company buys on 1-10-2004 own debentures of ₹ 10,000 of ₹ 100 each at ₹ 98 ex-interest for cancellation. Interest is payable @6% on 30th June and 31st December. The accounting entry will be

| | | | |
|---|---|---|---|
| 6% Debentures A/c | Dr. | 10,000 | |
| Interest on Debentures A/c | Dr. | 150 | |
| To Bank A/c | | | 9950 |
| To Profit on Redemption A/c | | | 200 |

(Since the debentures were purchased ex-interest, original holder is entitled to the interest for the whole 6 months. On 31st December, since the debentures are held by the company, no interest will be paid. So, the interest will be paid to the original debenture holder for 3 months at the time of purchase and rest 3 months' interest is included in the purchase price. So interest will be debited only for 3 months instead of 6 months.)

In the same case, had the debentures been purchased on cum-interest, the company would have got the benefit of interest from October to December and hence the purchase price would have been only ₹ 98 and consequently, the profit would have been ₹ 350.

### Purchase of Debentures as Investment

Often, companies buy their own debentures as investment to save the interest which would otherwise have been payable. Such debentures are kept alive and can be disposed off again in the market. The accounting treatment is done like any other investment. When a company buys its own debentures as investment, an account called 'Own Debentures Account' will be debited with the amount actually paid, disregarding the nominal value of debentures purchased. When own debentures are bought and kept as investment, the interest on such debentures should be credited to the P&L account, the debit being given to the Interest on debentures account. In this manner, the interest on debentures account will show the full amount due on outstanding debentures. The credit to the P&L account shows the gain made by the purchase of own debentures.

The profit made by the company on redemption through open market purchase is a capital profit(which is considered when the debentures are cancelled).

Any loss on issue of debentures may be written off against such profit. The balance of profit, if any should be transferred to Capital Reserve A/c.

**Illustration 6 :** A company issued 1000, 6% debentures of ₹ 1000 each. Interest is paid half yearly on 30th Sept. and 31st March. On February 1, 2004, the company purchased 20 of its own debentures as investment at ₹ 970. The journal entry will be as below:

| | | | |
|---|---|---|---|
| Own Debentures A/c | Dr. | 19,400 | |
| Interest on Debentures A/c | Dr. | 400 | |
| To Bank A/c | | | 19,800 |

(Debentures purchased ex-interest, interest for 4 months being payable extra)

OR

| | | | |
|---|---|---|---|
| Own Debentures A/c | Dr. | 19,000 | |
| Interest on Debentures A/c | Dr. | 400 | |
| To Bank A/c | | | 19,400 |

(Debentures purchased cum-interest, interest for 4 months included in the price)

| | | | |
|---|---|---|---|
| Interest on Debentures A/c | Dr. | 200 | |
| To Profit & Loss A/c | | | 200 |

(Being the interest on debentures held by the company for 2 months)

| | | | |
|---|---|---|---|
| 6% Debentures A/c | Dr. | 20,000 | |
| To Own Debentures A/c | | | 19,400 |
| To Profit on Redemption A/c | | | 600 |

(Being the cancellation of the debentures purchased ex-interest. In case of cum-interest debentures, profit would be ₹ 1000)

### Redemption at Premium of Debentures Issued At Discount

Sometimes, to attract the investors, the company may issue the debentures on the discount and in addition promise to redeem the debentures at premium. In such a case, since both the losses are known at the time of issue of debentures, they are taken into the accounts and is written off over a period of time.

### Debenture Redemption Reserve/Sinking Fund

When debentures are to be redeemed, the company has to arrange a large amount of cash for payment. This may affect the company's working capital. To avoid such a situation and to pay the debentures out of the profits, the company creates Debenture Redemption Reserve. Every year, the company transfers some part of its profit to this account and this amount is invested by the company in some liquid assets. The transfer made every year and the income on such investments keeps on accumulating and when the debentures are to be redeemed, the company sells this investment and repays the debentures. The following journal entries are made in this respect :

1. When amount is transferred to the reserve
   P&L Appropriation A/c Dr.
   To Debenture Redemption Reserve A/c
2. When the amount is invested
   DRR Investment A/c Dr.
   To Bank A/c
3. Interest on investment is received
   Bank A/c Dr.
   To DRR A/c
4. When investing the total amount including the interest received
   DRR Investment A/c Dr.
   To Bank A/c
5. On sale of investment
   Bank A/c Dr.
   To DRR Investment A/c
6. Transferring the loss/profit on sale of investment
   DRR Investment A/c (if Profit) Dr.
   To DRR A/c
7. Transfer of balance in DRR A/c
   DRR A/c Dr.
   To General Reserve A/c

**Note :** The above entries are similar to those made for creation of sinking fund for replacement of a fixed asset.

## FORM OF BALANCE SHEET

Every company has to follow the form of balance sheet as given in Schedule VI of Companies Act which has been reproduced as below:

| PARTICULARS | AMOUNT | PARTICULARS | AMOUNT |
|---|---|---|---|
| **SHARE CAPITAL**<br>Authorised shares of ₹ ------each Issued: (distinguishing between various classes of capital) ----- shares of ₹ ------ each Subscribed : ------- shares of ₹ ------ each<br>Of the above shares, ----- shares are allotted as fully paid up pursuant to a contract without payment being received in cash.<br>Of the above shares,-----shares are allotted as fully paid up by way of bonus shares.<br>Less : Calls unpaid :<br>(a) My managing agent or secretaries<br>(b) By Directors<br>(c) By others.<br>Add :Forfeited shares (amount originally paid up)<br>(any capital profit on reissue of forfeited shares should be transferred to Capital Reserve)<br>**RESERVES AND SURPLUS**<br>1. Capital Reserves<br>2. Capital Redemption Reserve<br>3. Share Premium Account<br>4. Other Reserves specifying the nature of each reserve and the amount in respect thereof. | | **FIXED ASSETS**<br>Distinguishing expenditure upon :<br>(a) Goodwill<br>(b) Land<br>(c) Buildings<br>(d) Leaseholds<br>(e) Plant and Machinery<br>(f) Furniture and fittings<br>(g) Patents, trademarks, and design<br>(h) Livestock<br>(i) Vehicles<br>Under each of the assets, the original cost, additions and deductions during the year and total depreciation provided should be mentioned.<br>If any amount is written off on reduction of capital, the balance sheet for the first 5 years after reduction shall also show the amount of reduction made.<br>**INVESTMENTS**<br>1. Investment in Govt. or trust securities<br>2. Investment in shares, debentures etc.<br>3. Immovable properties<br>4. Inv. In capital of partnership firm | |

| PARTICULARS | AMOUNT | PARTICULARS | AMOUNT |
|---|---|---|---|
| Less : Debit balance in profit and loss account (if any)<br>5. Surpluses i.e. balance in profit and loss account<br>6. Proposed additions to reserves<br>7. Sinking Funds.<br>(The word 'Fund' in relation to any reserve should be used only where such reserve is specifically represented by earmarked investments)<br>**SECURED LOANS:**<br>(a) Debentures<br>(b) Loans and advances from bank<br>(c) Loans and advances from subsidiaries<br>(d) Other loans and advances<br>(Loans from directors, secretaries, manager should be shown separately)(In case of debenture, terms of redemption or conversion is to be stated with the earliest date of redemption or conversion)<br>**UNSECURED LOANS:**<br>1. Fixed Deposits<br>2. Loans and advances from subsidiaries<br>3. Short term loans from :<br>(a) Banks<br>(b) Others<br>(Short term loans include those which are due for not more than 1 year as at the date of balance sheet)<br>Other loans and advances<br>**CURRENT LIABILITIES AND PROVISIONS:**<br>**CURRENT LIABILITIES**<br>(a) Acceptances (Bills Payable)<br>(b) Sundry Creditors<br>(c) Subsidiary Companies<br>(d) Advance payments and unexpired discounts for the portion for which value has still to be given<br>(e) Unclaimed Dividends<br>(f) Other liabilities<br>(g) Interest accrued but not due on loans<br>**PROVISIONS**<br>1. Provision for Taxation<br>2. Proposed dividends<br>3. For Contingencies<br>4 For Provident Fund scheme<br>5. For insurance, pension and other benefits<br>6. Other provisions.<br>A foot note to the balance sheet may be added to show separately:<br>(a) Claims against the company not acknowledged as debts<br>(b) Uncalled liability on shares partly paid<br>(c) Arrears of fixed cumulative dividends<br>(d) Estimated amount of contracts remaining to be executed on capital account<br>(e) Other moneys for which the company is contingently liable | | Aggregate amount of the company's quoted investments and also the market value thereof shall be shown.<br>**CURRENT ASSETS, LOANS AND ADVANCES**<br>**(A) Current Assets**<br>(a) Interest accrued on investment<br>(b) Stores and spare parts<br>(c) Loose tools<br>(d) Stock in trade<br>(e) Work in progress<br>(f) Sundry debtors (less : provision)<br>Debts outstanding for more than 6 months should be stated separately.<br>(g) Cash balance in hand<br>(h) Bank balance<br>**(B) Loans and Advances**<br>1. Advances and loans to subsidiaries<br>2. Bills of exchange<br>**MISCELLANEOUS EXPENDITURE AND LOSSES NOT WRITTEN OFF**<br>(a) Preliminary expenses<br>(b) Expenses of commission or underwriting on issue of shares and debentures<br>(c) Discount allowed on the issue of shares and debentures<br>(d) Interest paid out of capital during construction<br>(e) Development expenditure not adjusted<br>(f) Debit balance of Profit and Loss account | |

**Note :** Now the companies have to disclose the names of all small scale industrial undertakings to whom the company owes any sum together with interest outstanding for more than 30 days in the balance sheet under the heading 'Current Liabilities and Provisions'.

## MULTIPLE CHOICE QUESTIONS

1. Name the head of Capital Clouse of Memorundum of Association of a company in which maximum amount of share capital mentioned is called _____.
   A. Reserve Capital B. Subscribed Capital
   C. Authorised Capital D. Issued Capital

2. The part of un-called capital, to be called only in the liquidation of a company is called:
   A. Un-reserved Capital B. Reserve Capital
   C. Capital Reserve D. Calls-in Arrears

3. A shareholder allotted to whom 9,000 shares of ₹ 10 per share failed to pay first & final of ₹ 2 per share. ₹ 18,000 to be recorded in the books of company with _____.
   A. Dr. to Calls-in Arrears A/c
   B. Dr. to Share Forfeiture A/c
   C. Cr. to Calls-in Arrears A/c
   D. Cr. to Share Forfeiture A/c

**Directions (Qs. No. 4 and 5):** *Read the following statement carefully and give the answer for the questions.*

Golden Firework Ltd is authorised to issue shares 5,00,000 of ₹ 100 each. Company raised the capital by issue of 2,00,000 shares through e-IPO. As per the decision Managing Board of Directors of company, company issued 75,000 shares to their parent company and 40,000 shares issued to existing employees of company as per their choice and option at the below price than the market price.

4. "Company issued 75,000 shares to their parent company" is an example of _____.
   A. Public Issue B. Private Placement
   C. ESOP D. Issue other than cash

5. "40,000 shares issued to existing employees of company as per their choice and option at the below price than the market price." Is an example of _______
   A. Public Issue B. Private Placement
   C. ESOP D. Issue other than cash

**Directions (Qs. No. 6-9):** *Read the following statement carefully and give the answer for the questions.*

X Ltd issued 2,00,000 shares of ₹ 100 each. Amount to be paid on Application ₹ 30 per share; on allotment ₹ 40 per share and on first & final call ₹ 30 per share. All money was duly subscribed and paid towards the nominal value of shares except on 9,000 shares who failed to pay allotment and calls money. These shares were forfeited. 5,000 shares were re-issued at ₹ 80 per share fully paid.

6. Which amount of the following will be shown into the Balance Sheet of the company under the sub-head "Share Capital"?
   A. ₹ 1,96,00,000 B. ₹ 1,97,20,000
   C. ₹ 2,00,00,000 D. ₹ 1,97,70,000

7. Which amount the following will be called paid up share capital?
   A. ₹ 1,96,00,000 B. ₹ 1,97,20,000
   C. ₹ 2,00,00,000 D. ₹ 1,97,70,000

8. Which amount of the following, balance in Share Forfeiture Account?
   A. ₹ 4,00,000 B. ₹ 1,50,000
   C. ₹ 1,20,000 D. ₹ 50,000

9. Which amount of the following will be transferred to Capital Reserve?
   A. ₹ 4,00,000 B. ₹ 1,50,000
   C. ₹ 1,20,000 D. ₹ 50,000

10. Which one of the following is a permanent representative personal account of share-holders?
    A. Share Application A/c
    B. Share Allotment A/c
    C. Share Application & Allotment A/c
    D. Share Capital A/c

11. Which of the following is a temporary representative personal account of shareholders?
    A. Share Application A/c
    B. Share Allotment A/c
    C. Share Application & Allotment A/c
    D. All of these

12. A shareholder failed to pay share allotment money on 12,000 shares @ ₹ 30 per share. Which one of the following account will be taken into account?
    A. Debited to Share Capital A/c
    B. Debited to Calls-in Arrears A/c
    C. Credited to Calls-in Arrears A/c
    D. Credited to Share Capital A/c

13. Received share application money towards application & allotment of shares will be credited to which of the following account?
    A. Share Application & Allotment A/c
    B. Share Application A/c
    C. Share Capital A/c
    D. None of these

14. Ashok a shareholder of a company allotted shares to whom 12,000 of ₹ 100 each, failed to pay allotment ₹ 30 per share and first & final call ₹ 30 per share. Ashok had paid only application money. Pro-rata allotment proportion is 5 : 6. What will be the amount of calls-in arrears on allotment, from the following:
    A. ₹ 3,60,000 B. ₹ 2,64,000
    C. ₹ 96,000 D. None of these

**15.** The allowed amount of discount on re-issue of shares will be _______ .
A. @ 10% of issue price
B. Up to the amount of forfeited money
C. Could not issue at discount
D. None of these

**16.** Once, forfeited shares reissued, balance of share forfeiture money will be transferred to _______.
A. General Reserve
B. Capital Reserve
C. Reserve Capital
D. Securities Premium Reserve

**17.** 12,000 shares of ₹ 100 each forfeited due to non-payment of ₹ 40 per share. First & final call of ₹ 30 per share not yet made. These shares were reissued at ₹ 80 per share for ₹ 70 per share.

Which of the following journal entry is correct for the forfeiture of shares?

A. Share Capital A/c Dr. 12,00,000
  To Calls-in Arrears A/c 8,40,000
  To Share Forfeiture A/c 3,60,000
B. Share Capital A/c Dr. 12,00,000
  To Calls-in Arrears A/c 3,60,000
  To Share Forfeiture A/c 8,40,000
C. Share Capital A/c Dr. 8,40,000
  To Calls-in Arrears A/c 3,60,000
  To Share Forfeiture A/c 4,80,000
D. Share Capital A/c Dr. 8,40,000
  To Calls-in Arrears A/c 4,80,000
  To Share Forfeiture A/c 3,60,000

**18.** 12,000 shares of ₹ 100 each forfeited due to non-payment of ₹ 40 per share. First & final call of ₹ 30 per share not yet made. These shares were reissued at ₹ 80 per share for ₹ 70 per share.

Which of the following journal entry is correct for the re-issue of forfeiture of shares?

A. Bank A/c Dr. 9,60,000
  To Share Capital A/c 9,60,000
B. Bank A/c Dr. 8,40,000
  To Share Capital A/c 8,40,000
C. Bank A/c Dr. 9,60,000
  To Share Capital A/c 8,40,000
  To Securities Premium Reserve A/c 1,20,000
D. Bank A/c Dr. 9,60,000
  Share Foreiture A/c Dr. 2,40,000
  To Share Capital A/c 12,00,000

**19.** 12,000 shares of ₹ 100 each forfeited due to non-payment of ₹ 40 per share. First & final call of ₹ 30 per share not yet made. These shares were reissued at ₹ 80 per share for ₹ 70 per share.

Which of the following forfeited amount will be transferred to Capital Reserve A/c?
A. 4,80,000 B. 3,60,000
C. 1,20,000 D. None of these

**20.** 12,000 shares of ₹ 100 each forfeited due to non-payment of allotment of ₹ 40 per share and first & final call of ₹ 30 per share. Out of the forfeited shares, 9,000 shares were reissued at ₹ 80 per share fully paid.

Which of the following amount of share forfeiture account will be transferred to Capital Reserve Account?
A. 90,000 B. 1,80,000
C. 3,60,000 D. 2,70,000

**21.** If the premium on forfeited shares has already been received, then securities premium reserve account should be:
A. Credited
B. Debited
C. No treatment
D. Transferred to Capital Reserve A/c

**22.** A company issued 40,000 preference shares of ₹ 100 per share at par payable as under:
On Application : 20%
On Allotment : 40%
On First & Final Call : balance
Applications were received for 50,000 shares. Allotment was made on pro-rata basis. How much amount will be received in cash on allotment?
A. 14,00,000 B. 16,00,000
C. 18,00,000 D. 20,00,000

**Directions (Qs. No. 23-27):** *Read the following statement carefully and give the answer for the questions.*

AB Ltd issued 3,00,000 shares of ₹ 100 each at 20% premium through e-IPO, payable as under:

On Application : ₹ 40 (including 10% premium) per share

On Allotment : ₹ 40 (excluding 10% premium) per share

On First & Final Call : Balance

Share was subscribed for 5,00,000 shares. 50,000 share applications were rejected with letter of regret and pro-rata allotment was made to remaining share applicants. All money was duly received except from Raghav, allotted to whom 15,000 shares failed to pay allotment and calls.

These shares were forfeited and out of which 9,000 shares reissued at ₹ 75 per share fully paid.

**23.** What the amount was called in first & final call per share?
A. ₹ 20 per share B. ₹ 40 per share
C. ₹ 30 per share D. None of these

24. Which of the following amount received on allotment of shares?

A. ₹ 1,50,00,000 B. ₹ 90,00,000
C. ₹ 45,00,000 D. ₹ 85,50,000

25. Which of the following amount will be debited to calls-in arrears account on allotment?

A. ₹ 6,00,000 B. ₹ 4,50,000
C. ₹ 3,00,000 D. ₹ 7,50,000

26. Which of the following Journal entry is correct for the forfeiture of shares?

A. Share Capital A/c Dr. 15,00,000
Securities Premium Reserve A/c Dr. 1,50,000
To Calls-in Arrears A/c 9,00,000
To Share Forfeiture A/c 7,50,000

B. Share Capital A/c Dr. 15,00,000
Securities Premium Reserve A/c Dr. 3,00,000
To Calls-in Arrears A/c 9,00,000
To Share Forfeiture A/c 9,00,000

C. Share Capital A/c Dr. 15,00,000
To Calls-in Arrears A/c 7,50,000
To Share Forfeiture A/c 7,50,000

D. Share Capital A/c Dr. 15,00,000
To Calls-in Arrears A/c 9,00,000
To Share Forfeiture A/c 6,00,000

27. Which of the following amount will be transferred to Capital Reserve Account?

A. ₹ 7,50,000 B. ₹ 6,00,000
C. ₹ 4,50,000 D. ₹ 2,25,000

28. Match the columns with reference to share capital of a company:

| Column I | Column II |
|---|---|
| (*a*) Capital Reserve | (*i*) Memorandum of Association |
| (*b*) Minimum Subscription | (*ii*) Allotment / Calls due but did not receive |
| (*c*) Calls-in Arrears | (*iii*) Reserves & Surplus |
| (*d*) Authorised Capital | (*iv*) SEBI Guidelines |

| | (*a*) | (*b*) | (*c*) | (*d*) |
|---|---|---|---|---|
| A. | (*iii*) | (*iv*) | (*ii*) | (*i*) |
| B. | (*ii*) | (*iv*) | (*i*) | (*iii*) |
| C. | (*ii*) | (*i*) | (*iii*) | (*iv*) |
| D. | (*i*) | (*ii*) | (*iii*) | (*iv*) |

29. Golden Fire Works Ltd took over assets worth ₹ 10,00,000 and liabilities of ₹ 3,00,000 of a company. Out of the purchase consideration of ₹ 12,00,000; ₹ 2,00,000 of bill payable accepted and the balance paid by issue of shares of ₹ 100 each at 25% premium. How much amount will be credited to Securities Premium Reserve A/c?

A. ₹ 1,75,000 B. ₹ 2,50,000
C. ₹ 3,00,000 D. ₹ 2,00,000

30. A, B and C are partners sharing profits in the ratio of 3:2:1. They are agreed to admit D into the partnership for 1/4th share. An extract of their balance sheet on 1st April, 2021 is as follows:

| Liabilities | Amt. in ₹ | Assets | Amt. in ₹ |
|---|---|---|---|
| Investment Fluctuation Fund | 20,000 | Investments (Cost) | 4,00,000 |

If the market value of Investments is ₹ 4,20,000 then the Investment Fluctuation Fund will be shown in the Balance Sheet of reconstituted firm at ₹ ______.

A. 40,000 B. 20,000
C. Zero D. None of these

31. AB Ltd purchased a Machinery from XY Ltd for ₹ 4,50,000. AB Ltd immediately paid ₹ 90,000 by Bank Draft and the balance by issue of preference share of ₹ 100 each at 20% premium for the purchase consideration of Machinery to XY Ltd. Shares issued by AB Ltd?

A. 3,000 preference shares
B. 30,000 preference shares
C. 3,600 preference shares
D. 36,000 preference shares

32. X Ltd takeover the business of Y Ltd with the following assets and liabilities:

Sundry Assets : ₹ 6,50,000; Other Liabilities : ₹ 50,000

X Ltd immediately paid ₹ 1,50,000 by promissory note for two months and the balance by issue of 5,000 equity shares of ₹ 100 each for purchase consideration of running business to Y Ltd.

Which of the following journal entry is correct for the purchase of running business of Y Ltd?

A. Sundry Assets A/c Dr. 6,50,000
To Other Liabilities A/c 50,000
To Promissory Note A/c 1,50,000
To Y Ltd A/c 4,50,000

B. Sundry Assets A/c Dr. 6,50,000
To Other Liabilities A/c 50,000
To Promissory Note A/c 1,50,000
To Capital Reserve A/c 1,50,000
To Y Ltd A/c 3,00,000

C. Sundry Assets A/c Dr. 6,50,000
Goodwill A/c Dr. 50,000
To Other Liabilities A/c 50,000
To Promissory Note A/c 1,50,000
To Y Ltd A/c 5,00,000

D. None of these

**Directions (Qs. No. 33-36):** *There are two statements marked as Assertion (A) and Reason (R). Read the statements and choose the appropriate option from the options given below for the question.*

A. Both Assertion (A) and Reason (R) are true and Reason (R) is the correct explanation of Assertion (A)
B. Both Assertion (A) and Reason (R) are true, but Reason (R) is not the correct explanation of Assertion (A)
C. Assertion (A) is false, but Reason (R) is true
D. Assertion (A) is true, but Reason (R) is false

**33. Assertion (A) :** Received amount of securities premium will not debited to securities premium reserve account, on forfeiture of shares.

**Reason (R) :** Received amount of securities premium will be debited while writing off of certain type of capital loss or expenditure.

**34. Assertion (A) :** Equity shares does not carry fixed rate of dividend and they are the ultimate risk bearer.

**Reason (R) :** Equity share-holders are getting dividend from residual part of profits and in the case of windup of the company, invested money will be refunded at the last.

**35. Assertion (A) :** Cumulative preference share capital is the share capital in which unpaid amount of dividend to be paid in the next year along with unpaid amount of dividend of previous year.

**Reason (R) :** Participative preference share capital holders have right to participate in the decision making activities relating to their interest.

**36. Assertion (A) :** A company must receive minimum subscription on public issue of shares.

**Reason (R) :** In default to receive minimum subscription, company could not allot its shares.

**37.** 6,000 shares of ₹ 100 each (applied for 7,500 shares) forfeited due to non-payment of allotment ₹ 40 per share. First & final call was not yet made. Company received only application money at ₹ 50 per share including premium of ₹ 20 per share.

Which of the following amount will be forfeited by the company?

A. ₹ 3,75,000 B. ₹ 3,00,000
C. ₹ 2,55,000 D. ₹ 1,80,000

**38.** Debenture holders are:
A. Owners of the Company
B. Debtors of the Company
C. Creditors of the Company
D. Promoters of the Company

**39.** Debentures represent the:
A. Long-term Borrowings of a Company
B. The Investment of Equity-Shareholders
C. Directors' shares in a company
D. Short-term Borrowings of a Company

**40.** Zero Coupon Bonds are issued:
A. At Zero Interest Rate
B. With Specified Rate of Interest
C. Without Specified Rate of Interest
D. None of These

**41.** Interest payable on debentures is:
A. an appropriation of profits of the company
B. a charge against profits of the company
C. transferred to sinking fund investment account
D. transferred to general reserve

**42.** A debenture holder is entitled to:
A. Fixed dividend
B. Share in profits
C. Voting rights in the company
D. Interest at the fixed rate

**43.** On liquidation of company, principal amount of debentures is returned:
A. First of All
B. Last of All
C. Before Equity Capital
D. After Equity Capital

**44.** Which of the following statements is false?
A. Debenture is a form of public borrowing.
B. It is customary to prefix debentures with the agreed rate of interest.
C. Debenture interest is a charge against profits.
D. The issue price and redemption value of debentures cannot differ.

**45.** Which of the following is not a characteristic of Bearer Debentures?
A. They are treated as negotiable instruments.
B. Their transfer requires a deed of transfer.
C. They are transferable by mere delivery.
D. The interest on it is paid to the holder irrespective of identity.

**46.** Which of the following statements is false?
A. At maturity, debenture holders get back their money.
B. Debentures can be forfeited for non-payment of call money.

C. In company's balance sheet, debentures are shown under the head Long term Borrowings.
D. Interest on debentures is a charge against profits.

**47.** Which of the following statements is false:
A. A Company can issue redeemable debentures.
B. A Company can issue debentures with voting rights.
C. A Company can issue convertible debentures.
D. A Company can buy its own debentures and shares.

**48.** The Principal amount of debentures will be repaid by the company either at the end of a specified period or by instalments during the life time of the company. Such types of debentures are called:
A. Redeemable Debentures
B. Irredeemable Debentures
C. Convertible Debentures
D. Bearer Debentures

**49.** The debentures whose principal amount is not repayable by the company during its life time, but the payment is made only at the time of Liquidation of the company, such debentures are called:
A. Bearer Debentures
B. Redeemable Debentures
C. Irredeemable Debentures
D. Non-Convertible Debentures

**50.** Debenture Application Account is in the natutre of:
A. Real Account B. Personal Account
C. Nominal Account D. None of the above

**51.** Discount on issue of Debentures is in the nature of:
A. Revenue loss
B. Capital loss
C. Deferred Revenue Expenditure
D. None of the above

**52.** Premium received on issue of debentures may be utilised for:
A. For writing off discount allowed on issue of shares
B. For writing off premium allowed on redemption of debentures
C. For writing off preliminary expenses
D. All of the Above

**53.** Debentures of a Company can be issued:
A. For Cash
B. For Consideration other than Cash
C. As a Collateral Security
D. Any of the above

**54.** On issue of debentures as a collateral security, which account is credited?
A. Debentures Account
B. Bank Loan Account
C. Debenture Holdings Account
D. Debenture Suspense Account

**55.** Debentures issued as collateral security will be debited to:
A. Bank Account
B. Debentures Suspense Account
C. Debentures Account
D. Bank Loan Account

**56.** Interest on debentures issued as a collateral security is paid on:
A. Nominal value of debentures
B. No interest is paid
C. Face value of debentures
D. Paid up value of debentures

**57.** Loss on Issue of Debentures is written off:
A. In the year of the issue of debentures
B. During the life of the debentures
C. Within 3 years of the issue of debentures
D. In the year of redemption of debentures

**58.** When debentures are to be redeemed at premium an extra entry has to be made at the time of issue of debentures, which a/c should be credited in this entry?
A. Loss on issue of debentures A/c
B. Debenture redemption premium A/c
C. Bank A/c
D. Debenture holder's A/c

**59.** Premium on Redemption of Debentures Account is:
A. Personal Account B. Real Account
C. Nominal Account D. All of the Above

**60.** Shares may be issued:
A. At per value B. At a premium
C. Both (A) and (B) D. None of these

**61.** Which of the following statements is false?
A. A company can redeem its preference shares
B. Preference shareholders are creditors of a company
C. The part of the authorized capital which can be called up only in the event of liquidation of a company is called reserve capital
D. Capital redemption reserve can be utilized for issuing fully paid bonus shares

**62.** Share premium cannot be used to:
A. Issue Bonus shares
B. Redeem Preference shares
C. Write-off Preliminary expenses
D. Write-off discount on issue of shares

**63.** A company cannot issue redeemable preference shares for a period exceeding:
A. 6 years B. 7 years
C. 8 years D. 20 years

**64.** Which of the following cannot be used for the purpose of creation of capital redemption reserve account?

A. Profit and loss account (Credit balance)
B. General Reserve account
C. Dividend equalization reserve account
D. Unclaimed dividends account

**65.** P Ltd. issued 5,000, 12% debentures of ₹ 100 each at a premium of 10%, which are redeemable after 10 years at a premium of 20%. The amount of loss on redemption of debentures to be written off every year = ?
A. ₹ 80,000 B. ₹ 40,000
C. ₹ 10,000 D. ₹ 8,000

**66.** Which of the following is true with regard to 10% Debentures issued at a discount of 20%?
A. The carrying amount of debentures gets reduced each year at a rate of 20%
B. Issue price and the carrying amount of debentures are equal
C. At the time of redemption, the debenture holder will be paid the issue price
D. The face value and the carrying amount of debentures are equal

**67.** Which of the following is false?
A. Equity is owner's stake and the debenture is a debt
B. Rate of interest on debenture is fixed
C. Debenture holders get preferential treatment over the equity holders at the time of liquidation
D. Interest on debentures is an appropriation of profits

**68.** Discount on issue of debentures is a:
A. Revenue loss to be charged in the year of issue
B. Capital loss to be written off from capital reserve
C. Capital loss to be written off over the tenure of the debentures
D. Capital loss to be shown as goodwill

**69.** Which of the following is false with respect to debentures?
A. They can be issued for cash
B. They can be issued for consideration other than cash
C. They can be issued as collateral security
D. They can be issued in lieu of dividends

**70.** Which of the following is not a characteristics of Bearer Debentures?
A. They are treated as negotiable instruments
B. The transfer requires a deed of transfer
C. They are transferable by mere delivery
D. The interest on it is paid to the holder irrespective of identity

## ANSWERS

| 1 | 2 | 3 | 4 | 5 | 6 | 7 | 8 | 9 | 10 |
|---|---|---|---|---|---|---|---|---|---|
| C | B | A | B | C | B | A | C | D | D |
| **11** | **12** | **13** | **14** | **15** | **16** | **17** | **18** | **19** | **20** |
| D | B | A | B | B | B | D | C | B | A |
| **21** | **22** | **23** | **24** | **25** | **26** | **27** | **28** | **29** | **30** |
| C | A | C | D | B | A | D | A | B | C |
| **31** | **32** | **33** | **34** | **35** | **36** | **37** | **38** | **39** | **40** |
| A | C | A | A | B | B | C | C | A | C |
| **41** | **42** | **43** | **44** | **45** | **46** | **47** | **48** | **49** | **50** |
| B | D | C | D | B | B | B | A | C | B |
| **51** | **52** | **53** | **54** | **55** | **56** | **57** | **58** | **59** | **60** |
| B | D | D | A | B | B | A | B | A | C |
| **61** | **62** | **63** | **64** | **65** | **66** | **67** | **68** | **69** | **70** |
| B | B | D | D | C | D | D | C | D | B |

•••

# 6

# ANALYSIS OF FINANCIAL STATEMENTS

## FINANCIAL STATEMENTS

Any business organization prepares various statements for different information and purposes. The income statement report what has actually happened to earnings during the given period. The balance sheet presents a summary of financial position of the company at a given point of time. Both of them are known as financial statements.

The analysis and interpretation of these statements is the job of a manager. This can be done in many ways. The important methods of analysis and interpretation of financial statements are as below:

(*a*) Comparative statement

(*b*) Common size statement

(*c*) Ratio analysis

(*d*) Funds flow analysis

(*e*) Cash flow analysis

### Comparative Statement

A financial statement gives a lot of information about the entity. But, the information is more useful and more clear to a lay man if it is given in a comparative form. The data of the current year is compared with that of last year or last few years. This can be done by showing the figures for more than one year for all items in the balance sheet or profit and loss account side by side. It can also be done by showing the actual figure for the current year and giving the difference from the previous year in rupees or in percentage. The following is an illustration of comparative profit and loss account and balance sheet.

**Illustration 1:**

**Comparative Balance Sheet**

| Particulars | For the period | | Increase / Decrease | |
|---|---|---|---|---|
| | 2007 | 2008 | Absolute | Percentage |
| Share capital | 1,00,000 | 1,00,000 | Nil | ----- |
| Debentures | 2,00,000 | 1,50,000 | (-) 50,000 | (-) 25% |
| Sundry creditors | 60,000 | 72,000 | 12,000 | 20% |
| TOTAL LIABILITIES | 3,60,000 | 3,22,000 | (-) 38,000 | (-) 10.5% |
| Plants and Machinery | 1,00,000 | 1,50,000 | 50,000 | 50% |
| Investments | 80,000 | 72,000 | (-) 8,000 | (-) 10% |
| Sundry debtors | 80,000 | 70,000 | (-) 10,000 | (-) 12.33% |
| Cash at hand | 1,00,000 | 30,000 | (-) 70,000 | (-) 70% |
| TOTAL ASSETS | 3,60,000 | 3,22,000 | (-) 38,000 | (-) 10.5% |

**Comparative Income Statement**

| Particulars | For the period | | Increase / Decrease | |
|---|---|---|---|---|
| | 2007 | 2008 | Absolute | Percentage |
| Sales | 12,00,000 | 15,00,000 | 3,00,000 | 25% |
| Purchases | 8,00,000 | 9,60,000 | 1,60,000 | 20% |
| Closing stock | 30,000 | 25,000 | (-) 5,000 | (-) 16.67% |
| GROSS PROFIT | 2, 45,000 | 3,50,000 | 1,05,000 | 43% |
| Operating expenses | 1,00,000 | 1,50,000 | 50,000 | 50% |
| Non-operating expenses | 80,000 | 72,000 | (-) 8,000 | (-) 10% |
| **NET PROFIT** | **65,000** | **1,28,000** | **63,000** | **98%** |

### *Benefits Of Comparative Statements*

Comparative statements are very useful for the financial statement analysis in the following ways:

(*a*) It reveals trend of the item concerned

(*b*) It helps the management to know the inefficiency in any part of the operations, if any

(*c*) It shows how the business has performed with respect to the last year

(*d*) It is also useful for comparing performance in the same year as compared to other firms placed similarly.

## Common Size Statements

It is a method in which various items of a financial statement are compared to each other in terms of their weightage in the concerned financial statement. In this method, one figure of the statement is taken as base figure which is assumed as 100%.

All other figures are then arrived at in percentage as a portion of the base figure. For example, in balance sheet the total of the statement is taken as 100 and all the assets and liabilities are expressed as a percentage with respect to total. Similarly, in profit and loss account, the base figure is taken as Sales.

This is called 'Vertical analysis' and when the same type of statement is prepared for a number of years to show the trend, it is called 'Horizontal analysis'.

**Illustration 2 :** Taking the above figures, the common size statements may also be prepared :

**Comparative Balance Sheet**

| Particulars | 2007 | | 2008 | |
|---|---|---|---|---|
| | Amount | % of Total | Amount | % of Total |
| Share capital | 1,00,000 | 27.8% | 1,00,000 | 31.06% |
| Debentures | 2,00,000 | 55.6% | 1,50,000 | 46.58% |
| Sundry creditors | 60,000 | 16.6% | 72,000 | 22.36% |
| TOTAL LIABILITIES | 3,60,000 | 100% | 3,22,000 | 100% |
| Plants and Machinery | 1,00,000 | 27.8% | 1,50,000 | 46.58% |
| Investments | 80,000 | 22.2% | 72,000 | 22.36% |
| Sundry debtors | 80,000 | 22.2% | 70,000 | 21.74% |
| Cash at hand | 1,00,000 | 27.8% | 30,000 | 09.32% |
| **TOTAL ASSETS** | **3,60,000** | **100%** | **3,22,000** | **100%** |

**Comparative Balance Sheet**

| Particulars | 2007 | | 2008 | |
|---|---|---|---|---|
| | Amount | % of Total | Amount | % of Total |
| Sales | 12,00,000 | 100% | 15,00,000 | 100% |
| Purchases | 8,00,000 | 67% | 9,60,000 | 64% |
| Closing stock | 30,000 | 2.5% | 25,000 | 01.67% |
| GROSS PROFIT | 2,45,000 | 20.42% | 3,50,000 | 23.33% |
| Operating expenses | 1,00,000 | 08.33% | 1,50,000 | 10.0% |
| Non-operating expenses | 80,000 | 06.7% | 72,000 | 04.8% |
| **NET PROFIT** | **65,000** | **05.42%** | **1,28,000** | **08.53%** |

Now, it is easy for a lay man also to analyse that the gross profit margin has increased due to reduction in the cost of purchases. Also, thought there is an increase in the operating expenses, due to reduction in non-operating expenses the net profit margin has increased.

While preparing the above statement, the figures are expressed in terms of percentage of the base figure like to find the percentage of cash for 2007 we took

1,00,000 / 3,60,000 × 100 = 27.8%

Similarly, to find the percentage for purchases in 2008

9,60,000 / 15,00,000 × 100 = 64%

## RATIO ANALYSIS

Ratio analysis is a very powerful analytical tool for measuring performance of an organization. The ratio analysis concentrates on the inter-relationship among the figures appearing in the above mentioned and various other statements. It helps the management to analyze the past performance of the firm and to make further projections. Ratio analysis allows interested parties like shareholders, investors, creditors, government and analysts to make an evaluation of certain aspects of a firm's performance.

The calculation of ratios is a relatively easy and simple task but the proper analysis and interpretation of ratios can be made only by skilled analyst. While interpreting the financial information, the analyst has to be careful about limitations imposed by the accounting concepts and methods of valuation. Information of non-financial nature will also be taken into consideration before a meaningful analysis is made.

Ratio analysis pinpoints the strengths and weaknesses of the business mainly in two ways. Firstly, by comparing current performance with that of past and secondly by comparing the performance of the business with that of the industry as whole or other firms in the industry.

### Interpretation of Ratio

A ratio may be interpreted in many ways depending upon the purpose of the ratio.

1. It may be interpreted individually or as a stand alone ratio. For example, a ratio of 20% net profit on the sales shows a good margin in itself.
2. It may be interpreted by doing comparison between the ratio over a period of time. For example, if the same ratio is compared with the last year which was 30%, it means that margin have fallen this year.
3. It may also be interpreted by comparing with similar firms in the same industry. If the same ratio of a comparable firm is 16%, the margins of company under consideration is very good.
4. It may be interpreted by taking it together with other ratios. For example, in this case the margins are good but the return on capital employed is only 5%. It means the sales is very less but margins are high because of higher prices.

### Types of Ratios

There are various ratios used in analysis. For the convenience of understanding, they can be divided into the following broad categories :

A. Long Term Solvency Ratios
B. Short Term Solvency Ratios
C. Turnover Ratios
D. Profitability Ratios
E. Operating Ratios
F. Market Test Ratios

We shall discuss various ratios under all the above categories.

### *A. Long Term Solvency Ratios*

The long term financial stability of the firm may be considered as dependent upon its ability to meet all its liabilities, including those not currently payable. The following are important ratios measuring the long term solvency:

1. **Debt-Equity Ratio:** Capital is derived from two sources : shares and loans. Every company has to raise equity capital. The effect of raising loan is to introduce an element of gearing or leverage into the capital structure of the company.

$$\text{Debt-Equity ratio} = \frac{\text{Long term debt}}{\text{Shareholders' Fund}}$$

Shareholders' fund is equal to the share capital plus reserves and surpluses less preliminary expenses, if any. This ratio indicates the relationship between loan funds and net worth of the company, which is known as gearing. A debt-equity ratio of 2 : 1 is accepted norm. Higher the ratio, higher is the gearing and higher is the risk of long term insolvency. As a general rule, gearing should be low in those industries where demand is volatile and profits are subject to fluctuations. Usually, in calculating the ratio, the preference share capital is excluded from debt, but if the ratio is to show effect of use of fixed interest sources on earnings available to the shareholders then it is to be included. On the other hand, if the ratio is to examine financial solvency, then preference shares shall form part of the capital.

The ratio may also be calculated as below:

$$\text{Debt-Equity ratio} = \frac{\text{Long term debt}}{\text{Shareholders' Fund} + \text{Long term Debt}}$$

2. **Capital Gearing Ratio:** It is the proportion of fixed interest bearing funds to equity shareholders' funds.

$$\text{Capital Gearing Ratio} = \frac{\text{Fixed Interest Bearing Funds}}{\text{Equity Shareholders' Funds}}$$

The fixed interest bearing funds include debentures, long term loans, and preference share capital. This ratio indicates the degree of vulnerability of earnings available for equity shareholders.

3. **Fixed Assets To Long Term Funds Ratio:**

$$\text{F/A to L/T Funds Ratio} = \frac{\text{Fixed Assets}}{\text{Long Term Funds}}$$

Fixed assets represent the gross fixed assets minus depreciation till the date of calculation. The closeness of the ratio to 1 indicates that fixed assets are financed by long term funds. If the ratio is significantly less than 1, it means that long term funds are being used to finance current assets also. A very high ratio is dangerous for short term solvency as it implies that short term funds are also used to finance long term assets.

4. **Proprietary Ratio:** It expresses the relationship between net worth and total assets.

$$\text{Proprietary Ratio} = \frac{\text{Net Worth}}{\text{Total Assets}}$$

Net worth = equity capital + Preference share capital + Reserves – Fictitious assets

Total assets = Fixed assets + Current assets

Reserves earmarked specifically for a particular purpose should not be included in calculation of net worth. A high proprietary ratio is indicative of strong financial position of the business.

5. **Dividend Cover:**

$$\text{Dividend Cover} = \frac{\text{Net Profit after Tax}}{\text{Dividend}}$$

This ratio indicates the number of times the dividends are covered by net profit. This highlights the amount retained by a company for financing of future operations.

6. **Interest Cover:**

Interest Cover

$$= \frac{\text{Profit before Interest, Depreciation and Tax (PBDIT)}}{\text{Interest}}$$

It shows how many times interest charges are covered by funds that are available for payment of interest. Here, PBDIT is used because interest is paid before payment of tax and depreciation is non-cash expense. In the dividend cover ratio as shown above, since the dividend is paid on PAT, PAT is in numerator. A high interest cover indicates that the firm is conservative in using debt and a very low ratio indicates excessive use of debt.

7. **Debt Service Coverage Ratio:** It indicates whether the business is earning sufficient profits to pay not only the interest charges, but also the installments due to the 'principal' amount. This ratio is widely used by banks for analyzing the profitability of a project before financing it.

$$\text{DSCR} = \frac{\text{Profit before Interest and Tax}}{\text{Interest + Loan Installments}}$$

### *B. Short Term Solvency Ratios*

These ratios measure the liquidity of the firm and its ability to meet its maturing short term obligations. Liquidity is defined as the ability to realise value in money, which is the most liquid of all assets. It refers to the ability to pay in cash, the obligations that are due. Excess liquidity, though a guarantor of solvency would reflect lower profitability. On the other hand, too little liquidity may lead to risk of insolvency. The important ratios to measure short term solvency are :

1. **Current Ratio:**

Current ratio

$$= \frac{\text{Current Assets (including loans and advanced}}{\text{Current Liabilities (including Provision)}}$$

The ratio measures the solvency of the company in the short term. Current assets are those assets which can be converted into cash within a year. Current liabilities are those liabilities that are payable within a year. A current ratio of 1.33 : 1 is considered good. A very high ratio will have adverse impact on the profitability of the organization. To know the reason of high current ratio the next ratio is used.

2. **Quick Ratio/Liquid Ratio:** This ratio shows whether high current ratio is due to piling up of inventory. If the difference between current ratio and quick ratio is significant, then the organization is carrying high inventory.

Quick ratio =

$$\frac{\text{Quick Assets (Current Assets – Inventories – Prepaid Expenses)}}{\text{Quick Liabilities (Current Liabilities – Bank Overdraft)}}$$

It is also known as Acid-test ratio. It is used along with the current ratio.

3. **Absolute Liquidity Ratio:**

$$\text{Absolute Liquidity Ratio} = \frac{\text{Cash + Marketable Securities}}{\text{Current Liabilities}}$$

Absolute liquidity ratio is a subsequent innovation in ratio analysis. It eliminates uncertainty of receipts attached to the bills receivables. Therefore, this ratio excludes bills receivables also. The Absolute Liquidity Ratio only tests short-term liquidity in terms of cash and marketable securities.

### C. Turnover Ratios

Turnover or activity ratios measure how effectively the firm employs its resources. These ratios involve comparison between the level of sales and investment in various assets - inventories, debtors, fixed assets etc. Activity ratios are used to measure the speed with which various accounts are converted into sales or cash. The following activity ratios are important:

**1. Inventory Turnover Ratio:**

$$\text{Inventory turnover ratio} = \frac{\text{Cost of goods sold}}{\text{Average Inventory}}$$

Average inventory is average of opening and closing stock. If the cost of goods sold is not available, sales figure is used. It shows how many times the company's inventory has been sold during the year. Higher the ratio, higher is the efficiency of the business.

**2. Debtor Turnover Ratio:**

$$\text{Debtor turnover ratio} = \frac{\text{Total Credit Sales}}{\text{Average Debtors}}$$

This ratio indicates the number of times of sales as compared to debtors. In other words, it shows the duration of credit given to debtors. The inverse of this ratio is Average collection period.

$$\text{ACP} = \frac{\text{Average Debtros}}{\text{Total Credit Sales}} \times 365$$

It shows in how many days the company receives payment for its credit sales. The actual collection period can be compared with the stated terms of the company. Higher this ratio(or lower the turnover ratio), lower is the efficiency in collection.

**3. Creditors Turnover Ratio:** Similar to above ratios, the Creditor's turnover ratio or the Average payment period is:

$$\text{Creditors' Turnover ratio} = \frac{\text{Total Credit Purcases}}{\text{Average Creditors}}$$

$$\text{Average Payment Period} = \frac{\text{Average Creditors}}{\text{Credit Purchases}} \times 365$$

**4. Fixed Asset Turnover Ratio:**

$$\text{F/A turnover ratio} = \frac{\text{Sales}}{\text{Fixed Assets}}$$

This measures the company's ability to generate sales revenue in relation to the size of the investment. A high ratio indicates efficient utilization of fixed assets in generating sales and a low ratio indicates otherwise.

### D. Profitability Ratios

The purpose of study and analysis of profitability ratios are to help assess the adequacy of profits earned by the company and also to discover whether profitability is increasing or declining. These ratios show the combined effects of liquidity, asset management and debt management. They are measured with reference to various items as below:

**1. Return On Capital Employed:** ROCE or Return on Investment (ROI) is one of the fundamental ratios.

$$\text{ROI} = \frac{\text{Net Profit before interest and tax}}{\text{Capital Employed}} \times 100$$

Here, capital employed is equal to capital of the company (equity plus loan) less any fictitious assets and debit balance of Profit and Loss Account. This ratio encourages managers to obtain assets that will provide a satisfactory return on investment and to dispose of assets that are not providing an acceptable return.

**2. Earning Per Share (Eps):** It is one of the most widely used ratios to determine the market value of the firm.

$$\text{EPS} = \frac{\text{Profit after Tax - Preference dividend}}{\text{No. of equity shares}}$$

Higher EPS means better capital productivity. Growth in EPS is more relevant than the absolute value for pricing of share. It should be kept in mind that higher EPS does not necessarily lead to higher dividend payout.

**3. Gross Profit Margin:**

$$\text{G/P Ratio} = \frac{\text{Gross profit (Sales-Cost of goods sold)}}{\text{Sales}} \times 100$$

Gross profit, as shown is calculated before taking into consideration the administrative and marketing expenses. It measures, the company's manufacturing or trading efficiency.

**4. Net Profit Margin:** It is calculated as above after deducting the administrative and marketing expenses but before deducting interest and taxes.

$$\text{N/P Ratio} = \frac{\text{Net Profit after Tax (PAT)}}{\text{Sales}} \times 100$$

**5. Return On Net Worth:**

$$\text{Return on Net worth} = \frac{\text{Net Profit after Tax}}{\text{Net worth}} \times 100$$

This ratio indicates the efficiency of utilization of assets in generating revenue.

### *E. Operating Ratios*

The ratios of all operating expenses (material, labour, factory overheads, administration and selling expenses) to sales is the operating ratio. A comparison of the operating ratio would indicate whether the cost content is high or low in the figure of sales. If the annual comparison shows that the ratio has increased, the management would be naturally interested to know as to which element of the cost has gone up. It is not necessary that the management should be concerned only when the operating ratio goes up. If the operating ratio has fallen, though the unit selling price has remained the same, still the position needs analysis as it may be the sum total of efficiency in certain departments and inefficiency in others. An effective management is interested in making a complete analysis. It is therefore, necessary to break up the operating ratio into various cost ratios. They are :

$$\text{Material cost ratio} = \frac{\text{Material consumed}}{\text{Sales}} \times 100$$

$$\text{Labour cost ratio} = \frac{\text{Labour cost}}{\text{Sales}} \times 100$$

$$\text{Factory overheads ratio} = \frac{\text{Factory Expenses}}{\text{Sales}} \times 100$$

Administrative expenses ratio

$$= \frac{\text{Administrative Expenses}}{\text{Sales}} \times 100$$

Selling and Distribution Overhead ratio

$$= \frac{\text{Selling and Distribution Expenses}}{\text{Sales}} \times 100$$

$$\text{Operating ratio} = \frac{\text{Cost of Goods Sold}}{\text{Sales}} \times 100$$

### *F. Market Test Ratios*

These ratios relate to the firm's stock price to its earnings and book value. They give management an indication of what investors think of the company's past performance and future prospectus. Market test ratios are as follows:

**1. Dividend Payout Ratio:**

$$\text{Dividend payout ratio} = \frac{\text{Dividend per share}}{\text{Earnings per share (EPS)}}$$

This ratio indicates the extent of the net profits distributed to the shareholders as dividend.

A high payout signifies a liberal distribution policy and a low payout reflects conservative distribution policy.

**2. Dividend Yield:**

$$\text{Dividend Yield} = \frac{\text{Dividend per share}}{\text{Market price of share}} \times 100$$

This ratio reflects the percentage yield that an investor receives on his investment at the current market price of the share.

**3. Book Value:**

$$\text{Book value} = \frac{\text{Net Worth}}{\text{No. of equity shares}}$$

This ratio indicates the net worth per equity share. It is reflection of past earning and distribution policy of the company. A high book value indicates that the company has huge reserves and is a potential candidate for issue of bonus. Book value is considered as less relevant for market price as compared to EPS.

**4. Price Earning (P/E) Ratio:**

$$\text{P/E ratio} = \frac{\text{Market Price of Share}}{\text{EPS}}$$

This ratio indicates the number of times the earnings of the latest year at which the share price of a company is quoted. A low P/E ratio as compared to industry reflects under valuation of the price of the share. It is considered as barometer of market sentiment.

## Importance of The Rate of Return on Investment

Return on investment (ROI) is one of the most important ratios used by managers while making an investment. As already explained:

$$\text{ROI} = \frac{\text{Net Profit before Interst and Tax}}{\text{Capital Employed}} \times 100$$

But, there is no unanimity over the use of capital employed or the profit taken. Managers may take net profit after tax, net profit before interest and tax, net profit after interest but before tax etc.

For the purpose of simplicity, it is often taken as ROI

$$= \frac{\text{Net Profit}}{\text{Capital Employed}}$$

American company DuPont has given a chart which shows how the Return on investment can be broken into various ratio and form this one ratio the whole analysis of the performance of the organization can be done.

The chart is as below:

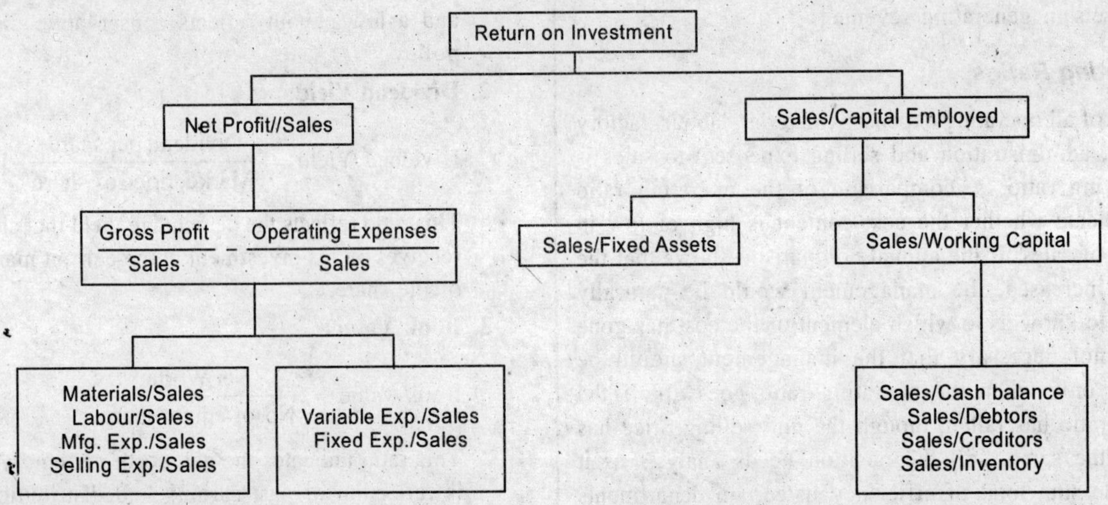


As the above chart shows that one single ratio may give a broad picture of the performance of the organization. Here, capital employed can be taken as Fixed assets and Net working capital, and operating expenses can be broken into various expenses. In the above chart, Sales/Capital employed is also known as 'Capital Turnover Ratio'.

**Illustration 3:** From the following P&L A/c and Balance sheet calculate various ratios.

| | | | |
|---|---|---|---|
| To opening Stock | 10000 | By Sales | 100000 |
| To Purchases | 55000 | By Closing Stock | 15000 |
| To Gross Profit | 50000 | | |
| | 115000 | | 115000 |
| To Administration expenses | 15000 | By Gross profit | 50000 |
| To Interest | 3000 | | |
| To Selling expenses | 12000 | | |
| To Net profit | 20000 | | |
| | 50000 | | 50000 |

**Balance Sheet**

| | | | |
|---|---|---|---|
| Capital | 100000 | Land and Building | 50000 |
| Profit and Loss A/c | 20000 | Plant and Machinery | 30000 |
| Creditors | 25000 | Stock | 15000 |
| Bills payable | 15000 | Debtors | 15000 |
| | | Furniture | 20000 |
| | | Bills receivable | 12500 |
| | | Cash at bank | 17500 |
| | **160000** | | **160000** |

1. Inventory Turnover Ratio = Cost of goods sold / Average Stock

   Average Stock = Opening Stock + Closing stock / 2 = 10000 + 15000 / 2 = 12500

   Cost of goods sold = Opening stock + Purchases – Closing stock = 10000 + 55000 – 15000 = 50000

   Stock / Inventory Turnover ratio = 50000 / 12500 = 4 times

2. Current Ratio = Current Assets / Current Liabilities

   Current assets = 60000 (Stock, Debtors, Bills and Cash)

   Current Liabilities = 40000 ( Creditors and Bills)

   So, Current Ratio = 60000 / 40000 = 1.5 : 1

3. Net Profit Margin/Ratio = $\frac{\text{Net Profit}}{\text{Net Sales}} \times 100$ ;

$$\frac{2000 \times 100}{100000} \times 100 = 20\%$$

4. Liquid Ratio = Liquid Assets / Current Liabilities

Liquid Assets = 45000 (Current assets – Stock)

Current Liabilities = 40000

Liquid Ratio = 45000 / 40000 = 1.125 : 1

5. Proprietary Ratio = $\frac{\text{Shareholders' Funds}}{\text{Total Assets}} \times 100$;

$$\frac{120000\,(\text{Capital} + \text{Profit})}{160000} \times 100 = 75\%$$

**Illustration 4 :**

| | | | |
|---|---|---|---|
| Current Ratio | 2.5 | Bank Overdraft | 10000 |
| Liquid Ratio | 1.5 | Working Capital | 60000 |

From the above information, find out the value of inventory and creditors

If current ratio is 2.5, means Current assets and Current liabilities are in the ratio of 2.5 : 1

Working capital = Current assets – Current liabilities

So, 60000 = 2.5 Current Liabilities – Current Liabilities (since C/A = 2.5 C/L)

60000 = 1.5 Current Liabilities

Current Liabilities = 40000

Since, no information is given, it is considered that current liabilities comprise only Bank overdraft and creditors.

So, Creditors = 40000 – 10000 = 30000

Current Assets = 2.5 (40000) = 100000

Liquid Ratio is 1.5 and liquid liability is only creditors i.e. 30000

Therefore, Liquid Assets = 1.5 (30000) = 45000

Inventory = Current Assets – Liquid Assets

= 100000 – 45000

= 55000

## Limitations of Ratio Analysis

1. It is based on financial statements which are themselves subject to severe limitations. Therefore, any ratio analysis based on a mis-statement suffers from the similar limitations.
2. In case of inter-firm comparison, no two firms are similar in age, size and product unit. Therefore, any comparison of ratios of two such firms must take these factors into account.
3. Both, the inter-period and inter-firm comparisons are affected by price level changes. A change in the price level can affect the validity of ratios calculated for different time periods.
4. The ambiguity in defining terms like gross profit, capital employed, operating profit, current assets etc. also leads to distortions in the ratio analysis and ratios based on different concepts can be misleading.
5. Any decision cannot be taken based on a single ratio. The analyst has to use various ratios and other forms of accounting analysis before taking any decision.
6. Conclusions from analysis of statements are not sure indicators of bad or good management.
7. Ratio analysis is only a tool and is helpful to spot out the symptoms. The analyst has to carry out further investigations and exercise his judgement in arriving at a correct diagnosis.

## MULTIPLE CHOICE QUESTIONS

**1.** Which of the following is not the limitation of financial statement analysis?

A. Ignores price level changes
B. window dressing
C. Qualitative aspect ignored
D. Inter firm comparisons

**2.** Current maturities of long-term debt are shown under:

A. Long term Provisions
B. Long term Borrowings
C. Short term Borrowings
D. Other Current liabilities

**3.** Indicate the item which appears as short-term provisions:

A. Provision for doubtful debts
B. Provision for gratuity
C. Employee's Provident fund
D. Securities premium reserve

**4.** Which of the following are the sub headings of Current Liabilities?

(*i*) Short term borrowings
(*ii*) Trade payables
(*iii*) Short term provisions
(*iv*) Short term Investment
(*v*) Other current liabilities
(*vi*) Short term loans and advances

Select the correct code:

A. (*i*), (*ii*), (*iii*), (*v*) B. (*i*), (*iv*), (*v*), (*vi*)
C. (*iii*), (*iv*), (*v*), (*vi*) D. (*ii*), (*iv*), (*v*), (*vi*)

**5.** Which of the following is not included in sub heading 'Inventory'?
A. Stock of finished goods
B. Work in progress
C. Stores and spares
D. Cheques in hand

**6.** Which of the following is not included in sub heading 'Cash and cash equivalents?
A. Cash in hand B. Marketable securities
C. Cash at Bank D. Cheques in hand

**7.** Main objective of Common size statement:
A. To present composition of various items
B. To provide common base for comparison
C. To establish relationship between various items
D. All of the above

**8.** Match the following:

| | | | |
|---|---|---|---|
| 1. | Short term loan | (*i*) | Other current liabilities |
| 2. | Short term loans and advances | (*ii*) | Short term borrowing |
| 3. | Debentures | (*iii*) | Long term borrowings |
| 4. | Debentures redeemable during current year | (*iv*) | Current investments |

Select the correct code:

| | 1 | 2 | 3 | 4 |
|---|---|---|---|---|
| A. | (*iii*) | (*ii*) | (*iv*) | (*i*) |
| B. | (*iii*) | (*iv*) | (*ii*) | (*i*) |
| C. | (*ii*) | (*iv*) | (*iii*) | (*i*) |
| D. | (*i*) | (*ii*) | (*iii*) | (*iv*) |

**9.** Fixed assets of a company increased from ₹ 3,00,000 to ₹ 4,00,000. The percentage change is:
A. 25% B. 20%
C. 33.33% D. 40%

**10.** Balance Sheet of company is required to be prepared in the format given in:
A. Schedule II Part II B. Schedule III Part III
C. Schedule III Part I D. Table A

**11.** As per Companies Act, the Balance Sheet of a company is required to be in:
A. Horizontal Form
B. Vertical Form
C. Either Horizontal or Vertical
D. Neither of the above

**12.** According to prescribed order of assets in a Company's Balance Sheet which asset should be shown first of all:
A. Non-Current Assets
B. Current Assets
C. Current Investments
D. Loans and Advances

**13.** Calls in Arrears appear in a Company's Balance Sheet under:
A. Reserve & Surplus B. Shareholders Funds
C. Contingent Liabilities D. Short-term Borrowings

**14.** Goodwill appears in a Company's Balance Sheet under:
A. Current Assets
B. Non-Current Assets
C. Long-term Provisions
D. Long-term Borrowing

**15.** Securities Premium Reserve appears in a Company's Balance Sheets:
A. Share Capital B. Long-term Provision
C. Reserve & Surplus D. Contingent Liability

**16.** Provision for Tax appears in a Company's Balance Sheet under Sub-head:
A. Short-term Provisions
B. Reserves and Surplus
C. Long-term Provisions
D. Other Current Liabilities

**17.** Which of the following items is shown under the head 'Non-Current Assets' while preparing the Balance Sheet of a company:
A. Underwriting Commission
B. Current Investment
C. Inventory
D. Patents

**18. Assertion (A):** 'Interest accrued but not due on borrowings' is shown under 'Other current liabilities'.

**Reason (R):** All liabilities, of which payment is expected to be made within 12 months from the date of Balance Sheet, shall be treated as Current.
A. Both Assertion (A) and Reason (R) are true and Reason (R) is the correct explanation of Assertion (A)
B. Both Assertion (A) and Reason (R) are true, but Reason (R) is not the correct explanation of Assertion (A)
C. Assertion (A) is false, but Reason (R) is true
D. Assertion (A) is true, but Reason (R) is false

**19.** Revenue from Operations 4,00,000; Cost of Revenue from Operations 60% of Revenue from Operations; Operating expenses 30,000 and rate of income tax is 40%. What will be amount of profit after tax:
A. 64,000 B. 78,000
C. 52,000 D. 96,000

**20.** Which of the following items are included in 'Revenue from operations' for a financial company:
(*i*) Dividend received
(*ii*) Sales
(*iii*) Sale of scrap

(iv) Interest earned
(v) Profit on sale of fixed asset
(vi) Profit on sale of investments
(vii) Refund of income tax

Select the correct code:

A. (i), (iv), (v), (vi) B. (i), (v), (vi), (vii)
C. (iii), (iv), (v), (vii) D. (ii), (iv), (v), (vi)

**21.** Which of the following profits of capital nature may be transferred to capital reserve:

(i) Profit on redemption of debentures
(ii) Securities Premium Reserve
(iii) Debenture redemption reserve
(iv) Surplus in statement of profit and loss
(v) Profit on sale of fixed assets
(vi) Profit on purchase of running business
(vii) Profit on reissue of forfeited shares

Select the correct code:

A. (i), (ii), (iv), (v) B. (i), (v), (vi), (vii)
C. (iii), (iv), (v), (vii) D. (ii), (iv), (v), (vi)

**Directions (Qs. No. 22-26):** *From the following case study choose the correct alternatives of question.*

Lenovo ltd. has authorized share capital of ₹ 1,00,00,000 divided into 10,00,000 equity shares of ₹ 10 each. It has existing issues and paid-up capital of ₹ 25,00,000. It further issued to public 2,50,000 equity shares at a premium of 20% for subscription payable as under:

On applications: ₹ 3

On allotment: ₹ 6; and

On call: Balance Amount

The issue was fully subscribed and allotment was made to all the applicants. The company did not make the call during the year.

**22.** Which of the following amount will be shown into the balance sheet of the company under the subhead 'Share Capital'?

A. ₹ 50,00,000 B. ₹ 42,50,000
C. ₹ 1,00,00,000 D. ₹ 10,00,000

**23.** Which of the following amount will be shown as 'paid-up capital'?

A. ₹ 50,00,000 B. ₹ 42,50,000
C. ₹ 1,00,00,000 D. ₹ 10,00,000

**24.** The amount of securities premium reserve will be:

A. ₹ 5,00,000 B. ₹ 42,50,000
C. ₹ 1,50,000 D. ₹ 10,00,000

**25.** Which of the following amount will be called as 'subscribed but not fully paid capital'?

A. ₹ 50,00,000 B. ₹ 42,50,000
C. ₹ 17,50,000 D. ₹ 25,00,000

**26.** Securities premium reserve will be shown under which sub-heading of the balance sheet?

A. Reserve & Surplus
B. Securities premium reserve
C. Shareholders' funds
D. Capital reserve

**27.** The part of un-called capital, to be called only in the liquidation of a company is called:

A. Un-reserved Capital
B. Reserve Capital
C. Capital Reserve
D. Calls-in Arrears

**28.** Match the following:

| | |
|---|---|
| 1. Capital Reserve | (i) Cash & Cash equivalents |
| 2. Calls in Advance | (ii) Intangible fixed assets |
| 3. Licenses & franchise | (iii) Reserves & Surplus |
| 4. Marketable Securities | (iv) Other current liabilities |

| | 1 | 2 | 3 | 4 |
|---|---|---|---|---|
| A. | (iii) | (ii) | (iv) | (i) |
| B. | (iii) | (iv) | (ii) | (i) |
| C. | (ii) | (iv) | (iii) | (i) |
| D. | (i) | (ii) | (iii) | (iv) |

**29.** Match the following:

| | |
|---|---|
| 1. Mortgage loan | (i) Other income |
| 2. Premium on redemption of debentures | (ii) Capital work in progress |
| 3. Building under construction | (iii) Long term borrowings |
| 4. Interest received | (iv) Other long term liabilities |

| | 1 | 2 | 3 | 4 |
|---|---|---|---|---|
| A. | (iii) | (ii) | (iv) | (i) |
| B. | (iii) | (iv) | (ii) | (i) |
| C. | (ii) | (iv) | (iii) | (i) |
| D. | (i) | (ii) | (iii) | (iv) |

**30. Assertion (A):** The objective of financial statement analysis is to measure the earning capacity and financial strength of a business and to facilitate comparative study.

**Reason (R):** Financial statements of a company are to be prepared as per format prescribed in Schedule III of the Indian Companies Act, 2013.

A. Both Assertion (A) and Reason (R) are true and Reason (R) is the correct explanation of Assertion (A)
B. Both Assertion (A) and Reason (R) are true, but Reason (R) is not the correct explanation of Assertion (A)
C. Assertion (A) is false, but Reason (R) is true
D. Assertion (A) is true, but Reason (R) is false

**31. Assertion (A) :** In vertical analysis financial statements for a single year or on a particular date are reviewed and analyzed with the help of proper devices like ratios.

**Reason (R) :** Such type of analysis is based on data of a single year. As such it is also called static analysis.

A. Both Assertion (A) and Reason (R) are true and Reason (R) is the correct explanation of Assertion (A)
B. Both Assertion (A) and Reason (R) are true, but Reason (R) is not the correct explanation of Assertion (A)
C. Assertion (A) is false, but Reason (R) is true
D. Assertion (A) is true, but Reason (R) is false

**32.** The mathematical expression that provides a measure of the relationship between two figures is called:
A. Conclusion B. Ratio
C. Model D. Decision

**33.** The _________ is a measure of liquidity which excludes ________, generally the least liquid asset:
A. current ratio, trade receivable
B. liquid ratio, trade receivable
C. current ratio, inventory
D. liquid ratio, inventory

**34.** Proportion of shareholder's funds to total assets is called
A. Proprietary ratio
B. Capital gearing ratio
C. Debt equity ratio
D. Current ratio

**35.** Current liabilities ₹ 40,000; Current assets ₹ 1,00,000; Inventory ₹ 20,000. Quick ratio is
A. 1 : 1 B. 2.5 : 1
C. 2 : 1 D. 1 : 2

**Directions (Qs. No. 36-45):** *There are two statements marked as Assertion (A) and Reason (R). Read the statements and choose the appropriate option from the options given below for the question.*
A. Both (A) and (R) are true and (R) is the correct explanation of (A)
B. Both (A) and (R) are true and (R) is not the correct explanation of (A)
C. (A) is true, but (R) is false
D. (A) is false, but (R) is true

**36. Assertion (A) :** Higher proportion of shareholders' funds in financing the assets is a positive feature as it provides security to creditors

**Reason (R) :** Proprietary ratio expresses relationship of proprietor's (shareholders) funds to net assets.

**37. Assertion (A) :** Total long term debt includes Debentures, long term loans from banks and financial institutions.

**Reason (R) :** Shareholders funds includes Equity share capital, Preference share capital, Reserves and surplus.

**38. Assertion (A) :** Ratio analysis is one of the tools employed to know the financial health of a concern.

**Reason (R) :** Ratio analysis is not the only technique available to take investment decision.

**39. Assertion (A) :** Capital employed means the long-term funds employed in the business and includes shareholders' funds, debentures and long-term loans

**Reason (R) :** Capital employed may be taken as the total of non-current assets and working capital.

**40. Assertion (A) :** Activity Ratio are known as efficiency ratios.

**Reason (R) :** Higher turnover ratio means better utilisation of assets and signifies improved efficiency and profitability.

**41. Assertion (A) :** Profitability ratios are calculated to analyse the earning capacity of the business which is the outcome of utilisation of resources employed in the business.

**Reason (R) :** Ratio analysis is helpful to take investment decision.

**42. Assertion (A) :** A low current ratio endangers the business and puts it at risk of facing a situation where it will not be able to pay its short-term debt on time.

**Reason (R) :** Current Ratio = Current Assets (Excluding Inventory and Prepaid Expenses)/Current Liabilities

**43. Assertion (A) :** Due to cash sale of a computer(a fixed asset), the current ratio will increase without any change in the current liabilities.

**Reason (R) :** Current Ratio = Current Assets/Current Liabilities

**44. Assertion (A) :** A high operating ratio indicates a favourable position.

**Reason (R) :** A high operating ratio leaves a high margin to meet non-operating expenses.

**45. Assertion (A) :** If debt component of the total long-term funds employed is small, outsiders feel more secure.

**Reason (R) :** A high Debt-Equity Ratio is considered risky as it may put the firm into difficulty in meeting its obligations to outsiders.

**Directions (Qs. No. 46-49):** *Read the following information and answer the given questions.*

| Year Amount | 2020 In (₹) | 2019 In (₹) | 2018 In (₹) |
|---|---|---|---|
| Outstanding expenses | 50,000 | 40,000 | 25,000 |
| Prepaid Expenses | 3,00,000 | 2,50,000 | 3,50,000 |
| Trade Payables | 18,00,000 | 16,00,000 | 14,00,000 |
| Inventory | 12,00,000 | 10,00,000 | 11,00,000 |
| Trade Receivables | 11,00,000 | 8,00,000 | 10,00,000 |
| Cash in Hand | 17,00,000 | 12,00,000 | 15,00,000 |
| Revenue from operations | 24,00,000 | 18,00,000 | 20,00,000 |
| Gross Profit Ratio | 12% | 15% | 18% |

**46.** Current Ratio for the year 2020 will be ______ .

A. 2 : 1 B. 1.8 : 1
C. 2.32 : 1 D. 2.4 : 1

**47.** Quick Ratio for the year 2018 will be ______ .

A. 1.75 : 1 B. 1.8 : 1
C. 0.94: 1 D. 1.25 : 1

**48.** Inventory Turnover Ratio for the year 2018 will be ______.

A. 1.62 : 1 B. 1.82 : 1
C. 1.55 : 1 D. 1.92 : 1

**49.** Cost of Revenue from Operations for the year 2020 would be ______ .

A. ₹ 21,12,000 B. ₹ 21,13,000
C. ₹ 21,15,000 D. ₹ 21,17,000

**Directions (Qs. No. 50-53):** *Consider the following data and answer the following:*

| Particulars | ₹ |
|---|---|
| Revenue From Operations | 12,00.000 |
| Cost of Revenue from Operations | 9,00,000 |
| Operating Expenses | 15,000 |
| Inventory | 20,000 |
| Other Current Assets | 2,00,000 |
| Current Liabilities | 75,000 |
| Paid up Share Capital | 4,00,000 |
| Statement of Profit & Loss (Dr.) | 47,500 |
| Total Long Term Debt | 2,50,000 |

**50.** The Operating ratio is ______.

A. 75.62% B. 75%
C. 76.25% D. 76%

**51.** The Liquid ratio is ______.

A. 2.67 : 1 B. 2.17 : 1
C. 2 : 1 D. 3 : 1

**52.** Debt-Equity ratio is ______.

A. 0.75 : 1 B. 1 : 1
C. 2 : 1 D. 0.63 : 1

**53.** Working Capital Turnover Ratio is ______.

A. 8 times B. 8.28 times
C. 7.28 times D. 8.78 times

**54.** Match List-I with List-II and select the correct answer using the options given blow:

| List-I | List-II |
|---|---|
| (*a*) Current ratio | 1. Liquidity |
| (*b*) Net profit ratio | 2. Efficiency |
| (*c*) Debt-Equity ratio | 3. Long term solvency |
| (*d*) Inventory turnover ratio | 4. profitability |

| | (*a*) | (*b*) | (*c*) | (*d*) |
|---|---|---|---|---|
| A. | 1 | 4 | 3 | 2 |
| B. | 1 | 3 | 4 | 2 |
| C. | 2 | 4 | 3 | 1 |
| D. | 4 | 3 | 1 | 2 |

**55.** Match List-I with List-II and select the correct answer using the options given blow:

| List-I | List-II |
|---|---|
| (*a*) Inability to pay interest | 1. Current ratio |
| (*b*) Liquidity crisis | 2. Debtor turnover ratio |
| (*c*) Inefficient collection of receivable | 3. Interest Coverage Ratio |
| (*d*) This ratio measures the degree of indebtedness of an enterprise and gives an idea to the long-term lender regarding extent of security of the debt | 4. Debt-Equity ratio |

| | (*a*) | (*b*) | (*c*) | (*d*) |
|---|---|---|---|---|
| A. | 3 | 1 | 2 | 4 |
| B. | 3 | 1 | 4 | 2 |
| C. | 1 | 4 | 3 | 2 |
| D. | 4 | 3 | 1 | 2 |

**56.** Match List-I with List-II and select the correct answer using the options given blow

| List-I | List-II |
|---|---|
| (*a*) Test of activity | 1. Acid test ratio |
| (*b*) Test of liquidity | 2. Debt-equity ratio |
| (*c*) Test of Profitablility | 3. Debtor's Turnover Ratio |
| (*d*) Test of Solvency | 4. ROI |

| | (a) | (b) | (c) | (d) |
|---|---|---|---|---|
| A. | 3 | 1 | 2 | 4 |
| B. | 3 | 4 | 1 | 2 |
| C. | 1 | 4 | 3 | 2 |
| D. | 3 | 1 | 4 | 2 |

**57.** To test the liquidity of a concern, which of the following ratios are useful?
(*i*) Quick Ratio
(*ii*) Net Profit Ratio
(*iii*) Debt-Equity Ratio
(*iv*) Current Ratio

Select the correct answer from the following options:
A. (*i*) and (*ii*) B. (*i*) and (*iv*)
C. (*ii*) and (*iii*) D. (*ii*) and (*iv*)

**58.** Which of the following is not correctly matched?
A. Liquid Ratio — Proportion
B. Inventory Turnover Ratio — Proportion
C. Debt-Equity Ratio — Proportion
D. Liquid Ratio — Proportion

**59.** When current ratio is 2 : 1 then equal increase in current assets and current liabilities would result in:
A. no change in current ratio
B. increase in current ratio
C. decrease in current ratio
D. current ratio will be double

**60.** Which one of the following statements is not true?
A. Conversation of debentures into preference shares will decrease debt-equity ratio
B. Long-term liabilities due for payment within a year should be treated as current liabilities
C. Higher operating ratio indicates higher profits
D. Cost of sales is a better numerator than sales while calculating stock turnover.

**61.** Higher the ratio, the more favourable it is, doesn't stand true for:
A. Operating ratio
B. Liquidity Ratio
C. Net Profit Ratio
D. Stock turnover Ratio

**62.** The ideal level of liquid ratio is:
A. 1 : 1
B. 2 : 2
C. 3 : 3
D. All of the above

**63.** Collection of debtors:
A. Decreases current ratio
B. Increases current ratio
C. Has no effect on current ratio
D. None of the above

**64.** Which of the following are limitations of ratio analysis?
(*a*) Ratio analysis may result in false results if variations in price levels are not considered.
(*b*) Ratio analysis ignores qualitative factors
(*c*) Ratio Analysis ignores quantitative factors
(*d*) Ratio Analysis is historical analysis.

Chose the correct option from following:
A. (*a*), (*b*) and (*d*) B. (*a*), (*c*) and (*d*)
C. (*a*), (*b*) and (*c*) D. (*a*), (*b*), (*c*), (*d*)

**65.** Liquid ratio is also known as:
(*a*) Quick ratio
(*b*) Acid test ratio
(*c*) Working capital ratio
(*d*) Stock turnover ratio

Chose the correct option from following:
A. (*a*) and (*b*) B. (*a*) and (*c*)
C. (*c*) and (*b*) D. (*c*) and (*d*)

**66.** To know the return on investment, by capital employed we mean:
A. Net Fixed Assets
B. Current Asset – Current Liabilities
C. Gross Block
D. Fixed Assets + Current Assets – Current Liabilities

**67.** If sales is 74,20,000, sales returns is 7,20,000 and cost of goods sold 73,20,000, gross profit ratio will be:
A. 20% B. 25%
C. 15% D. 10%

**68.** The following groups of ratios primarily measure risk:
A. Liquidity, activity and profitability
B. Liquidity, activity and common stock
C. Liquidity, activity and debt
D. Activity, debt and profitability

**69.** Which of the following is an operating' income?
A. Sale of Merchandise
B. Interest Income
C. Dividend Income
D. Profit on the sale of old car

**70.** Current Ratio is 3.5 : 1. Working Capital is ₹ 90,000. Calculate the amount of Current Assets and Current Liabilities
A. Current Asset = ₹ 1,26,000; Current Liability = ₹ 26,000
B. Current Asset = ₹ 1,16,000; Current Liability = ₹ 36,000
C. Current Asset = ₹ 1,26,000; Current Liability = ₹ 36,000
D. Current Asset = ₹ 1,36,000; Current Liability = ₹ 16,000

**71.** A technique that is used in comparative analysis of financial statement is:
A. graphical analysis
B. preference analysis
C. common size analysis
D. returning analysis

**72.** The low price for earnings ratio is the result of:
A. low riskier firms B. high riskier firms
C. low dividends paid D. high marginal rate

**73.** The formula such as, net income available for common stockholders divided by total assets is used to calculate:
A. return on total assets B. return on total equity
C. return on debt D. return on sales

**74.** The price per ratio is divided by cash flow per share ratio, is used for calculating:
A. dividend to stock ratio
B. sales to growth ratio
C. cash flow to price ratio
D. price to cash flow ratio

**75.** The techniques which are used to identify financial statements trends include:
A. common size analysis
B. per cent change analysis
C. returning ratios analysis
D. Both (A) and (B)

**76.** A formula such as net income available to common stockholders divided by common equity is used to calculate:
A. return on earnings power
B. return on investment
C. return on common equity
D. return on interest

**77.** The companies that help to set benchmarks are classified as:
A. competitive companies
B. benchmark companies
C. analytical companies
D. return companies

**78.** The total assets divided by common equity is a formula used for calculating:
A. equity multiplier B. graphical multiplier
C. turnover multiplier D. stock multiplier

**79.** The price per share divided by earnings per share is the formula for calculating:
A. price earnings ratio B. earnings price ratio
C. pricing ratio D. earnings ratio

**80.** The profit margin multiply assets turnover equity multiplier is used to calculate:
A. return on turnover B. return on stock
C. return on assets D. return on equity

## ANSWERS

| 1 | 2 | 3 | 4 | 5 | 6 | 7 | 8 | 9 | 10 |
|---|---|---|---|---|---|---|---|---|---|
| D | B | A | B | D | B | D | C | C | C |
| **11** | **12** | **13** | **14** | **15** | **16** | **17** | **18** | **19** | **20** |
| B | A | B | B | C | A | D | A | D | A |
| **21** | **22** | **23** | **24** | **25** | **26** | **27** | **28** | **29** | **30** |
| B | B | B | A | C | A | B | B | B | A |
| **31** | **32** | **33** | **34** | **35** | **36** | **37** | **38** | **39** | **40** |
| A | B | D | A | C | A | B | B | B | A |
| **41** | **42** | **43** | **44** | **45** | **46** | **47** | **48** | **49** | **50** |
| A | C | A | B | B | C | A | D | A | C |
| **51** | **52** | **53** | **54** | **55** | **56** | **57** | **58** | **59** | **60** |
| A | D | B | A | A | D | B | B | C | C |
| **61** | **62** | **63** | **64** | **65** | **66** | **67** | **68** | **69** | **70** |
| A | D | A | A | A | D | A | D | A | C |
| **71** | **72** | **73** | **74** | **75** | **76** | **77** | **78** | **79** | **80** |
| C | A | A | D | D | C | B | A | A | D |

●●●

# 7

# STATEMENT OF CHANGES IN FINANCIAL POSITION

## CONCEPT OF FLOW STATEMENT

A balance sheet is a snapshot view of the status of a firm's funds at one instance of time. But it does not give a picutre of from where the funds have come and how funds from various sources were received and utilised during the year. A flow statement explains the changes that took place in a balance sheet account or group of accounts during the period between the dates of two balance sheets. Income statement is also a flow statement.

Similarly two flow statements cash flow and fund flow are widely used. It contains all the details of the financial resources which have become available during an accounting period and the ways in which those resources have been used up.

The term fund has been defined differently be different authors. But, in general, it means 'working capital' which is excess of current assets over current liabilities.

### Preparation of Funds Flow Statement

The funds flow statement is not prepared alone. To take a holistic view, three statements are prepared:

(*i*) **Funds Flow Statement.** It is also known as Statement of Sources and Application of funds. This statement summarizes all the areas from which funds were received and the areas in which funds were used.

The format of the statement is as below:

| Sources | Amount | Application | Amount |
|---|---|---|---|
| Funds from Operations (Adjusted P&L A/c) | | Funds lost in Operations | |
| Issue of share capital Issue of Debentures | | Redemption of preference shares/Debentures | |
| Raising Long term loans | | Repayment of long term loans | |
| Receipt of calls on shares | | Purchase of fixed assets/Investments | |
| Sale of Fixed assets or Investments | | Non-trading payments like dividends/Tax | |
| Decrease in Working capital | | Net increase in working capital | |
| Non-trading receipts like dividends | | | |

This statement is like Cash account. All the receipts are considered as sources and all the payments are considered as application of funds.

(*ii*) **Statement of Changes in Working Capital.** The primary purpose of this statement is to determine the net changes in the working capital and that figure appears in the Funds flow statement as shown above. In this statement, all current assets and liabilities are individually listed. The acquisition of current assets and repayment of current liabilities will result into application of funds or increase in working capital. On the other hand, decrease in current assets and increase in current liabilities results in decrease in working capital and hence sources of funds.

(*iii*) **Adjusted Profit and Loss Account.** This is also called as Statement showing Funds generated from Operations. In this statement, we start with the profit/loss as shown in the profit and loss account. Then we exclude all the revenues and expenditures which do not pertain to the basic operations of the firm or are incidental losses and revenue. We add all the non-operational expenses and deduct all the non-operational revenues.

The items are: Depreciation, Amortisation of fictitious assets, Appropriation of retained earnings, Loss/profit on sale of fixed assets, Payment or receipt of dividend, Taxation, Appreciation in value of fixed assets etc.

## FUNDS FROM OPERATIONS

Funds from operations show the amount generated by the business activities. It is important to note that net profit as shown by the P&L account does not always mean the funds from operation. For this purpose only, adjusted P&L account is prepared as shown in the above example. The reasons for difference in net profit and funds from operations are many. One of them is there are certain expenses for which no payment is made like depreciation which does not affect the working capital. So, to arrive at the funds generated from operations, the following adjustments are made in the Profit and Loss Account.

**ADD :** Following items are added to the Net Profit as shown in P&L account :

1. Depreciation on fixed assets
2. Written off fictitious and intangible items like goodwill, preliminary expenses, discount on issue of shares etc.
3. Loss on sale of fixed assets
4. Appropriation of profits like transfer to general reserve or sinking funds.
5. Dividend on shares

**DEDUCT :** Following items are deducted from net profit:

(*a*) Profit on sale of fixed assets

(*b*) Profit on revaluation of fixed assets

(*c*) Non-operating incomes like dividend, interest on investment, ret received etc.

In case there is net loss in the profit and loss account, the first set of items are deducted and the second set of items are added to the net loss to arrive at the figure of funds from operations.

**Illustration 1 :** Calculate funds from operations from the following P&L account :

| | | | |
|---|---|---|---|
| To Expenses paid and outstanding | 1,50,000 | By Gross Profit | 2,25,000 |
| To Depreciation | 35,000 | By gain on sale of land | 30,000 |
| To loss on sale of machine | 2,000 | | |
| To Discount | 100 | | |
| To Goodwill written off | 10,000 | | |
| To Net Profit | 57,900 | | |
| | **2,55,000** | | **2,55,000** |

Calculation of funds from operations :

| | | |
|---|---|---|
| Net Profit (as given) | | 57,900 |
| *Add :* Non-operating items debited to P&L A/c | | |
| Depreciation | 35,000 | |
| Loss on sale of machine | 2,000 | |
| Goodwill written off | 10,000 | 47,000 |
| | | 1,04,900 |
| *Less :* Non-operating items credited to P&L A/c | | |
| Gain on sale of land | 30,000 | 30,000 |
| FUNDS FROM OPERATIONS | | 74,900 |

### Treatment of Specific Items

There are certain accounts which need specific treatment while calculating the funds flow.

1. **Provision For Taxation.** While preparing funds flow statement, the provision for taxation may be treated either as appropriation of profit or as current liability. If it is treated as current liability, it is considered while preparing the statement of changes in working capital and showing it as current liability. If it is treated as appropriation of profit, no effect will be given on funds flow when the provision is made. But, the payment of tax is shown as application of funds. The amount of tax paid is calculated by opening Provision for Taxation account as follow:

| | |
|---|---|
| To Bank A/c | By Opening balance |
| (Tax paid i.e. application of money) | By P&L Appropriation A/c |
| To Closing balance | (Provision made during the year) |

2. **Proposed Dividend.** This account can also be treated either as current liability or as appropriation of profit. When treated as current liability, like provision of taxation, it is also taken as current liability in the preparation of statement of changes in the working capital.

   In case it is treated as the appropriation of profit, the proposed dividend for the year is added back to the profit and proposed dividend for the last year is deducted form the profit while calculating the funds form operations.

3. **Interim Dividend.** Interim dividend paid is shown as an application of fund in the funds flow statement. It is also added back in the net profit for calculating the funds from operations, if it has already been debited to P&L account.

**Illustration 2 :** From the following balance sheet, prepare funds flow statement :

| Liabilities | 2007 | 2008 | Assets | 2007 | 2008 |
|---|---|---|---|---|---|
| Share Capital | 30,000 | 40,000 | Goodwill | 11,500 | 9,000 |
| Preference shares | 15,000 | 10,000 | Land & Building | 20,000 | 7,000 |
| General reserve | 4,000 | 7,000 | Plant | 8,000 | 20,000 |
| Profit and Loss A/c | 3,000 | 4,800 | Debtors | 16,000 | 20,000 |
| Proposed dividend | 4,200 | 5,000 | Stock | 7,700 | 10,900 |
| Creditors | 5,500 | 8,300 | Bills Receivable | 2,000 | 3,000 |
| Bills Payable | 2,000 | 1,600 | Cash in hand | 1,500 | 1,000 |
| Provision for Taxation | 4,000 | 5,000 | Cash at bank | 1,000 | 800 |
| | **67,700** | **81,700** | | **67,700** | **81,700** |

1. Depreciation of ₹ 2,000 on L&B and ₹ 1,000 on Plant has been charged in 2008.
2. Interim Dividend of ₹ 2,000 has been paid in 2008.
3. Income tax of ₹ 3,500 has been paid during the year 2008.

**Statement of Changes in Working Capital**

| Particulars | 2007 | 2008 | Effect (+/-) on Working capital |
|---|---|---|---|
| CURRENT ASSETS | | | |
| Debtors | 16,000 | 20,000 | (+) 4,000 |
| Stock | 7,700 | 10,900 | (+) 3,200 |
| Bills receivable | 2,000 | 3,000 | (+) 1,000 |
| Cash in hand | 1,500 | 1,000 | (-) 500 |
| Cash at bank | 1,000 | 800 | (-) 200 |
| TOTAL CURRENT ASSETS | **28,200** | **35,700** | |
| CURRENT LIABILITIES | | | |
| Creditors | 5,500 | 8,300 | (-) 2,800 |
| Bills payable | 2,000 | 1,600 | (+) 400 |
| Provision for taxation | 4,000 | 5,000 | (-) 1,000 |
| Proposed dividend | 4,200 | 5,000 | (-) 800 |
| TOTAL CURRENT LIABILITIES | **15,700** | **19,900** | |
| NET WORKING CAPITAL (Application of Funds) | **12,500** | **15,800** | **(+) 3,300** |

**Adjusted Profit and Loss Account**

| Particulars | Amount | Particulars | Amount |
|---|---|---|---|
| To Depreciation on | | By Opening balance | 3,000 |
| Plant | 1,000 | By Funds from Operations | 12,300 |
| Building | 2,000 | (Balance figure) | |
| To Goodwill Written off | 2,500 | | |
| To Transfer to G.R. | 3,000 | | |
| To Interim dividend | 2,000 | | |
| To Closing balance | 4,800 | | |
| | **15,300** | | **15,300** |

**Funds Flow Statement**

| Sources of Funds | Amount | Application of Funds | Amount |
|---|---|---|---|
| Issue of Equity shares | 10,000 | Redemption of Preference shares | 5,000 |
| Sale of building | 1,000 | Purchase of plant | 13,000 |
| Funds from operations | 12,300 | Dividend paid | 2,000 |
| | | Net increase in working capital | 3,300 |
| | 23,300 | | 23,300 |

**Note :**

1. Sale of building figure has been calculated as ( 20,000 – 2,000 – 17,000 = 1,000)
2. Purchase of plant has been calculated as (1,000 + 20,000 – 8,000 = 13,000)

## CASH FLOW ANALYSIS

It is very similar to Funds flow analysis. The major difference between the two is that cash flow statement analyses the receipts and application of cash only (which is a part of working capital) whereas funds flow statement analyses movement in the funds as a whole. According to SEBI guidelines, are listed companies have to present their cash flow statement in the Annual Report of the company. Cash flow statement during a period is classified into three categories

A. Operating activities

B. Investing activities

C. Financing activities

Operating activities are defined as all transactions that are not investing or financing activities. These transactions include the cash inflows associated with sales, interest and dividend revenues and outflows associated with purchases, operating expenses, interest, taxes etc. In nutshell, if we consider the format of the balance sheet, transactions occurring in current assets and current liabilities and transaction of profit and loss account fall under this category. While calculating cash from operations, all non-cash as well as non-operating incomes and expenditures are excluded.

Investing activities include acquiring or disposing off long term assets such as plants and equipments, securities, lending money etc. Increase or decrease in accounts receivables and inventory are not treated as investment activities; they are included in operating activities. In this category falls the transaction under the heads Fixed assets and Investments.

Financing activities include the borrowing of funds and issue of securities, their repayments etc. Transaction coming under the heads Capital and Reserves and surplus, Secured and Unsecured loans are financing activities.

### Benefits of Cash Flow Statement

A cash flow statement, when used in conjunction with the other financial statements, provides information that enables users to evaluate the changes in net assets of an enterprise, its financial structure, including solvency and liquidity, and its ability to affect the amount and timing of cash flows in order to adapt to changing circumstances and opportunities. Cash flow information is useful in assessing the ability of the enterprise to generate cash and cash equivalents and enable users to develop models to assess and compare the present value of the future cash flows of different enterprises. It also enhances the comparability of the reporting of operating performance by different enterprises because it eliminates the effects of using different accounting treatments for the same transactions and events.

### Cash From Operations

Finding out cash from operations is similar to that finding out funds from operations with one change. In funds flow analysis, we prepare three statement viz., Adjusted P&L account, Statement of changes in working capital account and Funds flow account. But in cash flow analysis only two accounts are prepared i.e. Adjusted P&L account and Cash from operations.

So, while finding out the cash from operations, the adjustment regarding changes in the working capital is also made.

Hence, to find out cash from operations, two steps are followed :

1. Find out the funds from operations as shown before
2. Add or deduct the net changes in working capital.

### Funds Flow Analysis v/s Cash Flow Analysis

(*a*) Funds flow statement is based on accrual system while in preparing cash flow statement, only cash or cash equivalent items are considered.

(*b*) Funds flow analysis is more useful for long range financial planning. Cash flow analysis is more useful for identifying and correcting the current liquidity problem of the firm.

(*c*) Funds flow statement is a broader concept as cash itself is part of funds.

(*d*) Funds flow statement tallies the funds generated from various sources with various uses to which they are put. Cash flow statement starts with the opening balance of cash and reach to the closing balance of cash by proceeding through sources and uses.

(*e*) Cash flow statement is to be presented with the annual report of a company statutorily. Preparation of funds flow statement is not legally binding.

(*f*) In cash flow statement, the changes in the working capital are incorporated in the cash flow from operating activities.

**Illustration 3 :** From the following information, calculate cash from operations.

| Particulars | 2008 | 2008 |
|---|---|---|
| Debtors | 50,000 | 47,000 |
| Bills receivable | 10,000 | 12,500 |
| Creditors | 20,000 | 25,000 |
| Bills payable | 8,000 | 6,000 |
| Outstanding Expenses | 1,000 | 1,200 |
| Prepaid Expenses | 800 | 700 |
| Accrued Income | 600 | 750 |
| Income received in Advance | 300 | 2,501 |
| Profit made during the year | | 1,30,000 |

**Cash from Operations:**

| | | | | |
|---|---|---|---|---|
| Profit made during the year | | | 1,30,000 | |
| Add : Decrease in Debtors | | | 3,000 | |
| Increase in Creditors | | | 5,000 | |
| Increase in outstanding expenses | | | | 200 |
| Decrease in Prepaid expenses | | | 100 | |
| | | | 1,38,300 | |
| Less : Increase in Bills receivable | 2,500 | | | |
| Increase in accrued Income | 150 | | | |
| Decrease in Bills payable | | 2,000 | | |
| Decrease in Income received in Advance | | 50 | | 4,700 |
| **Cash from Operations** | 1,33,600 | | | |

**Illustration 4 :**

From following information prepare the cash flow statement for the year 2008. (Amounts in '000)

| | | | |
|---|---|---|---|
| Net Profit | 25,000 | Interest Expenses | 10,000 |
| Dividend paid | 8,535 | Interest paid during the year | 10,520 |
| Provision for Income-tax | 5,000 | Increase in Working capital (except cash) | 56,075 |
| Income tax paid during the year | 4,248 | Purchase of Fixed asset | 14,560 |
| Loss on sale of asset | 40 | Investment in Joint Venture | 3,850 |
| Book value of asset sold | 185 | Expenditure on work-in-progress | 34,740 |
| Depreciation | 20,000 | Proceeds from calls in arrear | 2 |
| Amortisation of capital grant | 6 | Receipt of grant for capital project | 12 |
| Profit on sale of investment | 100 | Receipt from long term borrowings | 25,980 |
| Book value of investment sold | 27,765 | Receipt from short term borrowings | 20,575 |
| Interest income on investment | 2,506 | Opening cash balance | 5,003 |
| Closing cash balance | 6,988 | | |

**Cash Flow Statement for the Year 2008**

| | | |
|---|---|---|
| CASH FLOW FROM OPERATING ACTIVITIES | | |
| Net profit before taxation (25000 + 5000) | 30,000 | |
| Adjustment for : | | |
| Depreciation | 20,000 | |
| Loss on sale of asset | 40 | |
| Amortisation of capital grant | (6) | |
| Profit on sale of investment | (100) | |
| Interest income on investment | (2506) | |
| Interest expenses | 10,000 | |
| Operating profit before working capital changes | 57,428 | |
| Changes in working capital (Increase) | (56075) | |
| Cash generated from Operations | 1,353 | |
| Income tax paid | (4248) | |
| Net cash used in operating activities | | (2,895) |
| **CASH FLOW FROM INVESTING ACTIVITIES** | | |
| Sale of assets | 145 | |
| Sale of investments (27765 + 100) | 27,865 | |
| Interest income from investments | 2,506 | |
| Purchase of fixed assets | (14560) | |
| Investment in Joint Venture | (3850) | |
| Expenditure on work-in-progress | (34740) | |
| Net cash used in Investing activities | | (22,634) |
| **CASH FLOW FROM FINANCING ACTIVITIES** | | |
| Proceeds from calls in arrear | 2 | |
| Receipt of grant for capital project | 12 | |
| Receipt from long term borrowings | 25,980 | |
| Receipt from short term borrowings | 20,575 | |
| Interest paid | (10520) | |
| Dividend paid | (8535) | |
| Net cash from financing activities | | 27,514 |
| Net increase in cash and cash equivalent | 1,985 | |
| Cash balance at the beginning of the period | 5,003 | |
| Cash balance at the end of the period | 6,988 | |

## MULTIPLE CHOICE QUESTIONS

**1.** Statement of cash flows includes:
A. Financing Activities B. Operating Activities
C. Investing Activities D. All of the Above

**2.** In cash flows, when a firm invests in fixed assets and short-term financial investments results in
A. Increased Equity B. Increased Liabilities
C. Decreased Cash D. Increased Cash

**3.** A firm that issues stocks and bonds to raise funds results in
A. Decreases Cash B. Increases Cash
C. Increases Equity D. Indian Overseas Bank

**4.** The purchase value of assets over its serviceable life is categorised as
A. Appreciated Liabilities

B. Appreciated Assets
C. Depreciation
D. Appreciation

**5.** The basic financial statements include:
A. Statement of Cash Flows
B. Income Statement
C. Balance Sheet
D. All of the Above

**6.** The statement of cash flow clarifies cash flows according to:
A. Operating and Non-operating Flows
B. Inflow and Outflow
C. Investing and Non-operating Flows
D. Operating, Investing, and Financing Activities

**7.** Cash flow example from a financing activity is:
A. Payment of Dividends
B. Receipt of Dividend on Investment
C. Cash Received from Customers
D. Purchase of Fixed Asset

**8.** Cash flow example from an investing activity is:
A. Issue of Debenture
B. Repayment of Long-term Loan
C. Purchase of Raw Materials for Cash
D. Sale of Investment by Non-Financial Enterprise

**9.** Cash flow example from an operating activity is:
A. Purchase of Own Debenture
B. Sale of Fixed Assets
C. Interest Paid on Term-deposits by a Bank
D. Issue of Equity Share Capital

**10.** Which item comes under financial activities in cash flow?
A. Redemption of Preference Share
B. Issue of Preference Share
C. Interest Paid
D. All the above

**11.** As per Accounting Standard-3, Cash Flow is classified into
A. Operating activities and investing activities
B. Investing activities and financing activities
C. Operating activities and financing activities
D. Operating activities, financing activities and investing activities

**12.** Cash Flow Statement is also known as:
A. Statement of Changes in Financial Position on Cash basis
B. Statement accounting for variation in cash
C. Both (A) and (B)
D. None of the above

**13.** The objectives of Cash Flow Statement are
(*a*) Analysis of cash position
(*b*) Short-term cash planning
(*c*) Evaluation of liquidity
(*d*) Comparison of operating Performance
A. Both (*a*) and (*b*) B. Both (*a*) and (*c*)
C. Both (*b*) and (*d*) D. (*a*), (*b*), (*c*), (*d*)

**14.** In cash flow statement, the item of interest is shown in:
(*a*) Operating Activities
(*b*) Financing Activities
(*c*) Investing Activities
A. Both (*a*) and (*b*) B. Both (*a*) and (*c*)
C. Both (*b*) and (*c*) D. (*a*), (*b*), (*c*)

**15.** Cash Flow Statement is based upon:
A. Cash basis of accounting
B. Accrual basis of accounting
C. Credit basis of accounting
D. None of the above

**16.** Which of the following statements are false?
(*a*) Cash Flow Statement is helpful in the formation of policies.
(*b*) Cash Flow Statement is useful for external analysis
(*c*) Cash Flow Statement is helpful in estimating future cash flow
A. Both (*a*) and (*b*) B. Both (*a*) and (*c*)
C. Both (*b*) and (*c*) D. None of the above

**17.** Which of the following statements are true?
(*a*) Cash flow reveals only the inflow of cash
(*b*) Cash flow reveals only the outflow of cash
(*c*) Cash flow is a substitute for income statement
(*d*) Cash flow statement is not a replacement of funds flow statement.
A. Only (*a*) B. Only (*b*)
C. Both (*b*) and (*c*) D. Only (*d*)

**18.** As per AS-3, Cash Flow Statement is mandatory for
(*a*) All enterprises
(*b*) Companies listed on a stock exchange
(*c*) Companies with a turnover of more than Rs 50 crores
A. Both (*a*) and (*b*) B. Both (*a*) and (*c*)
C. Both (*c*) and (*b*) D. Only (*a*)

**19.** In the case of financial enterprises, the cash flow resulting from interest and dividend received and interest paid should be classified as cash flow from
A. Operating activities B. Financing activities
C. Investing activities D. None of the above

**20.** In case of other enterprises cash flow arising from interest paid should be classified as cash flow from ________ while dividends and interest received should be stated as cash flow from ____.
A. Operating activities, financing activities
B. Financing activities, investing activities

C. Investing activities, operating activities
D. None of the above

**21.** When a fixed asset is bought as hire purchase, interest element is classified under ______ and loan element is classified under________.
A. Operating activities, financing activities
B. Financing activities, investing activities
C. Investing activities, operating activities
D. None of the above

**22.** Which of the following statements are false?
(*a*) Old Furniture written off doesn't affect cash flow.
(*b*) Cash flow statement is a substitute for cash account.
(*c*) Appropriation of retained earnings is not shown in Cash flow statement.
(*d*) Net cash flow during a period can never be negative.
A. (*a*), (*b*), (*c*) B. (*b*), (*c*), (*d*)
C. (*c*), (*d*), (*a*) D. None of the above

**23.** Which of the following is not a cash inflow?
A. Decrease in debtors B. Issue of shares
C. Decrease in creditors D. Sale of fixed assets

**24.** Which of the following is not a cash outflow?
A. Increase in Prepaid expenses
B. Increase in debtors
C. Increase in stock
D. Increase in creditors

**25.** Cash flow statement is prepared for financial planning of:
A. Long range B. Medium range
C. Short range D. Very Long range

**26.** Which of the following is source of cash?
A. Cash deposited into Bank
B. Cash withdrawn from Bank
C. Sale of Goods costing ₹ 10,000 for ₹ 8,000
D. Sale of marketable securities for cash

**27.** Which of the following is not source of cash?
A. Issue of shares B. Purchase of Machinery
C. Sale of Asset D. Dividend received

**28.** Which of the following is not application of cash?
A. Increase in Debtors
B. Increase in Inventory
C. Increase in Bills Payable
D. Increase in Prepaid Expenses

**29.** If a machine whose original cost is ₹ 40,000 having accumulated depreciation ₹ 12,000, were sold for ₹ 34,000 then while preparing Cash Flow Statement its effect on cash flow will be :
A. Cash flow from financing activities ₹ 34,000
B. Cash flow from financing activities ₹ 6,000
C. Cash flow from investing activities ₹ 34,000
D. Cash flow from investing activities ₹ 6,000

**30.** If 6% Pref. share capital ₹ 2,00,000 were redeemed at a premium of 5%, while preparing Cash Flow Statement its effect on cash flow will be:
A. Cash used from financing activities ₹ 2,12,000
B. Cash received from financing activities ₹ 2,12,000
C. Cash used (Payment) from financial activities ₹ 2,10,000
D. Cash used (Payment) from financial activities ₹ 2,00,000

**31.** If the amount of goodwill is ₹ 40,000 at the beginning of a year and ₹ 48,000 at the end of that year then while preparing cash flow statement its effect on cash flow will be:
A. Cash used (Payment) in Investing Activities ₹ 8,000
B. Cash received from operating activities ₹ 8,000
C. Cash used (Payment) from Operating Activities ₹ 8,000
D. Cash used (Payment) from Financial Activities ₹ 8,000

**32.** How will you deal increase in the balance of 'Securities Premium Reserve' while preparing a Cash Flow Statement?
A. Cash Flow from Operating Activities
B. Cash Flow from Investing Activities
C. Cash Flow from Financing Activities
D. Cash Equivalent

**33.** A Ltd., engaged in the business of retailing of two wheelers, invested ₹ 50,00,000 in the shares of a manufacturing company. Dividend received on this investment will be:
A. Cash Flow from Operating Activities
B. Cash Flow from Investing Activities
C. Cash Flow from Financing Activities
D. Cash Equivalent

**34.** How will you treat payment of dividend in a Cash flow statement?
A. Cash Flow from Operating Activities
B. Cash Flow from Investing Activities
C. Cash Flow from Financing Activities
D. Cash Equivalent

**35.** How will you treat Bank Overdraft in a Cash Flow Statement?
A. Cash Flow from Operating Activities
B. Cash Flow from Investing Activities
C. Cash Flow from Financing Activities
D. Cash Equivalent

**36.** Where will you show purchase of Goodwill in a Cash Flow Statement?

A. Cash Flow from Operating Activities
B. Cash Flow from Investing Activities
C. Cash Flow from Financing Activities
D. Cash Equivalent

**37.** How will you treat payment of 'Interest on Debentures' while preparing a Cash Flow Statement?
A. Cash Flow from Operating Activities
B. Cash Flow from Investing Activities
C. Cash Flow from Financing Activities
D. Cash Equivalent

**38.** State whether cash deposited in bank will be classified under which kind of activity?
A. Cash Flow from Operating Activities
B. Cash Flow from Investing Activities
C. Cash Flow from Financing Activities
D. No Cash Flow

**39.** A company has to prepare its balance sheet once in:
A. Six months B. Two years
C. A year D. As and when it needs

**40.** Income statement of a business shows:
A. Net profit
B. Net operating result of specified period
C. Net loss
D. None of these

**41.** The statement which shows the periodical increase or decrease of funds is called __________ statement.
A. Funds flow B. Cash flow
C. Income D. Working capital

**42.** Fund flow statement is based on the concept of:
A. Business entity B. Accounting period
C. Going concern D. All of the above

**43.** Funds means...
A. Money
B. Cash
C. Machinery
D. Any form of financial resources

**44.** Excess of current assets over current liabilities is called:
A. Net working capital B. Net current assets
C. Free current assets D. All of the above

**45.** Which of the following is the component of current assets?
A. Stock
B. Prepaid expenses
C. Income earned but not received
D. All of the above

**46.** The term flow of funds refers to:
A. Change in funds
B. Change in working capital
C. Both
D. None of these

**47.** Transaction between________ may cause the flow of funds.
A. Current assets and fixed assets
B. Current assets and long term liabilities, and capital
C. Current liabilities and fixed assets
D. All of the above

**48.** The term current account refers to:
A. Current assets
B. Current liabilities
C. Both (A) and (B)
D. None of these

**49.** The term non-current account refers to:
A. Capital
B. Liabilities
C. Long term liabilities
D. Both (A) & (C)

**50.** Share premium, share forfeited, profit and loss account, balance of profit are the examples of:
A. Current assets
B. Permanent liabilities
C. Fixed assets
D. Current liabilities

**51.** The funds flow analysis is of primary importance to:
A. Personnel management
B. Financial management
C. Quality control management
D. Auditing

**52.** Basically, the funds flow statement is considered a tool for:
A. Cost control B. Financial analysis
C. Performance analysis D. None of these

**53.** Who uses the funds flow statement widely?
A. Financial institutions
B. Financial managers
C. Analysts
D. All of the above

**54.** Basically, the funds flow statement shows the causes for changes of ________ during a period.
A. Assets B. Liabilities
C. Both (A) and (B) D. None of these

**55.** The sources of side of funds flow statement shows the______ sources of funds of a firm.
A. Internal B. External
C. Both (A) and (B) D. None of these

**56.** Funds flow statement is a substitute for:
A. Income statement
B. Balance sheet
C. Both (A) and (B)
D. None of these

**57.** Which of following are original statements?
A. Funds flow statement
B. Financial statement
C. Cash flow statement
D. Working capital statement

**58.** Which of the following statement is dynamic in nature?
A. Balance sheet B. Funds flow
C. Both (A) and (B) D. Income statement

**59.** Funds flow statement is complementary to:
A. Balance sheet B. Income statement
C. Both (A) and (B) D. None of these

**60.** Which of the following is the source of funds?
A. Issue of shares
B. Raising long term loans
C. Sale of fixed assets
D. All of these

## ANSWERS

| 1 | 2 | 3 | 4 | 5 | 6 | 7 | 8 | 9 | 10 |
|---|---|---|---|---|---|---|---|---|---|
| D | C | B | C | D | D | A | D | C | D |
| 11 | 12 | 13 | 14 | 15 | 16 | 17 | 18 | 19 | 20 |
| D | C | D | C | A | D | D | C | A | B |
| 21 | 22 | 23 | 24 | 25 | 26 | 27 | 28 | 29 | 30 |
| B | B | C | D | C | C | B | C | C | C |
| 31 | 32 | 33 | 34 | 35 | 36 | 37 | 38 | 39 | 40 |
| A | C | B | C | C | B | C | D | C | B |
| 41 | 42 | 43 | 44 | 45 | 46 | 47 | 48 | 49 | 50 |
| A | C | D | D | D | C | D | C | D | B |
| 51 | 52 | 53 | 54 | 55 | 56 | 57 | 58 | 59 | 60 |
| B | B | D | C | C | D | B | B | C | D |

●●●

# 8

# OVERVIEW OF COMPUTERISED ACCOUNTING SYSTEM

## COMPUTERISED ACCOUNTING SYSTEM (CAS)

Computerised Accounting System refers to the processing of accounting transaction through the use of hardware and software in order to produce accounting records and reports.

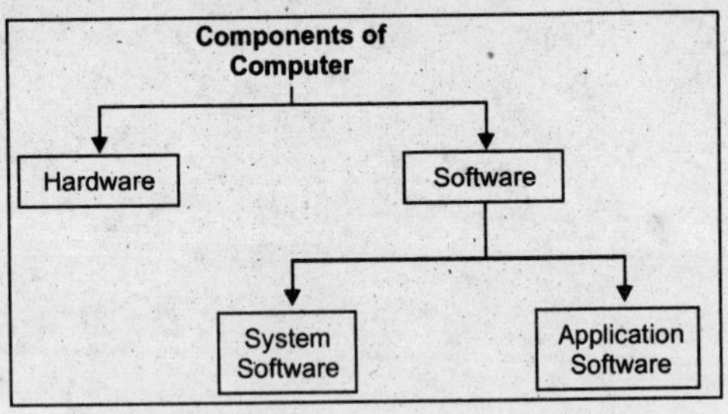


**Fig.** *Components of Computer*

CAS takes accounting transactions as inputs that are processed through Accounting Software to generate the following reports:

- Day books/Journals
- Ledger
- Trial Balance
- Position Statement (Balance Sheet)
- Statement of Profit and Loss (Profit and Loss Account)

### Basic flow of Accounting Transaction

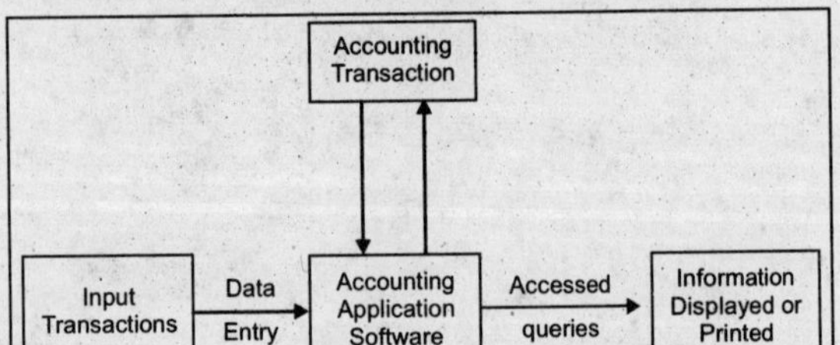


**Fig.** *Data to Information by Business Application Software*

### Data and Information

Various elements (items) of accounting transactions are essentially the data items, which are processed through an accounting software to generate different sets of information in the form of accounting reports such as journals, ledger, etc. A data-item (data element) is the smallest named unit of data in the information system. In accounting, a transaction consists of four data elements, such as name of account, accounting code, date of transaction and amount.

### Components of CAS

The manual system of accounting is traditionally most popular method of keeping records of financial transactions of an organisation. Financial statements are the end products of the accounting process, which are prepared in accordance with Generally Accepted Accounting Principles (GAAP). The accounting cycle means the processes involved in identifying, measuring and communicating the information. The basic phases of the cycle are as follows:

(*i*) Business transactions are analysed.

(*ii*) The transactions are recorded in the journal.

(*iii*) Journal entries are posted to the ledger accounts.

(*iv*) A trial balance is prepared from balances of accounts.

(*v*) Accounts are reviewed and the necessary adjustments made.

(*v*) Adjustments are posted in the ledger to prepare adjusted trial balance.

(*vi*) Adjusted trial balance is used to prepare the balance sheet and profit and loss account.

(*vii*) Financial Statements are prepared from the finally adjusted ledger and balancing the accounts.

The above accounting cycle can be processed through the use of computers.

### Salient Features of CAS

Following are the salient features required for CAS software:

- **Simple and Integrated:** CAS is designed to automate and integrate all the business operations, such as sales, finance, purchase, inventory and manufacturing. CAS is integrated to provide accurate, up-to-date business information rapidly. The CAS may be integrated with enhanced MIS (Management Information System), Multi-lingual and Data Organisation capabilities to simplify all the business processes of the organisation easily and cost-effectively.
- **Transparency and Control:** CAS provides sufficient time to plan, increases data accessibility and enhances user satisfaction. With computerised accounting, the organisation will have greater transparency for day-to-day business operations and access to the vital information.
- **Accuracy and Speed:** CAS provides user-definable templates (data entry screens or forms) for fast, accurate data entry of the transactions. It also helps in generalising desired documents and reports.
- **Scalability:** CAS enables in changing the volume of data processing in tune with the change in the size of the business. The software can be used for any size of the business and type of the organisation.
- **Reliability:** CAS makes sure that the generalised critical financial information is accurate, controlled and secured.

### Using Software of CAS

There are two basic activities in using software of CAS – One time activitics and recurring activites. One time activities include creation of Organisation details, accounting year, type of ledger (also called "creation of master files"), etc. While reccuring activities include entry of transactions and generation of reports. The transactions are recorded on the basis of Cash Vouchers, Bank Vouchers, Purchase Vouchers, Sales Vouchers, Journal Vouchers, etc. Reports include generation of Day books, Ledgers, Trial Balance, Statement of Profit and Loss, Position Statement and Cash Flow Statement.

#### *Security Features of Cas Software*

Every accounting software ensures data security, safety and confidentiality. Therefore every, software provides the following:

- **Password Security:** Password is a mechanism, which enables a user to access a system including data. The system facilitates defining the user rights according to organisation policy. Consequently, a person in an organisation may be given access to a particular set of a data while he may be denied access to another set of data.
- **Data Audit:** This feature enables one to know as to who and what changes have been made in the original data thereby helping and fixing the responsibility of the person who has manipulated the data and also ensures data integrity. Basically, this feature is similar to Audit Trail.
- **Data Vault:** Software provides additional security through data encryption. Encryption essentially scrambles the information so as to make its interpretation extremely difficult (almost impossible). Thus, Encryption ensures security of data even if it lands in wrong hands, because the receiver of data will not be able to decode and interpret it.

### Advantages of CAS

Following are the advantages of Computerised Accounting System (CAS):

- Timely generation of reports and information in desired format.
- Efficient record keeping.
- Ensures effective control over the system.
- Economy in the processing of accounting data.
- Confidentiality of data is maintained.

### Limitations of CAS

Following are the limitation of CAS software:

- Faster obsolescence of technology necessitates investment in shorter period of time.
- Data may be lost or corrupted due to power interruptions.
- Data are prone to hacking.
- Un-programmed and un-specified reports cannot be generated.

## ACCOUNTING INFORMATION SYSTEM (AIS)

Accounting Information System (AIS) and its various subsystems may be implemented through Computerised Accounting System. The subsystems of AIS are briefly described below:

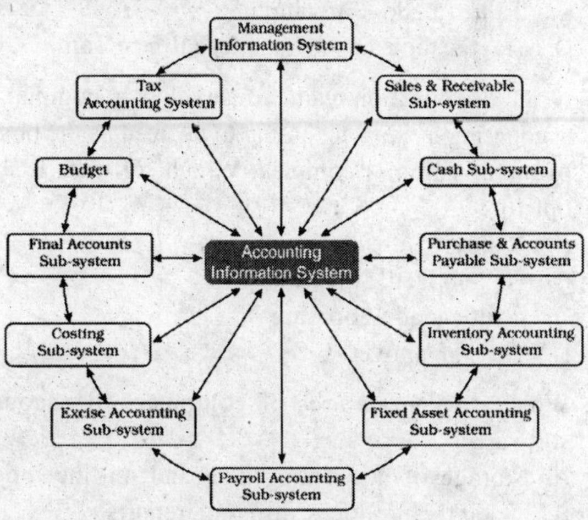


**Fig.** *The sub-systems of Accounting Information System*

## MULTIPLE CHOICE QUESTIONS

**1.** What are the features of a computerized accounting system?
A. It facilitates off-line input and storage of accounting data
B. This system never fails
C. It generates a print-out of purchase and sale invoices
D. None of the above

**2.** What is not an advantage of a computerized accounting system?
A. High Speed B. High Reliability
C. Reduced training cost D. None of the above

**3.** What are the types of a computerized accounting system?
A. Ready to use Software B. Customized Software
C. Tailor-made Software D. All of the above

**4.** What are the advantages of tailor-made software?
A. These are ready-made softwares
B. Low cost
C. High secrecy of data
D. None of the above

**5.** What are the factors to be considered while source accounting software?
A. Flexibility
B. Adaptability
C. Interest of management
D. Both (A) & (B)

**6.** Ram want to install a computerised accounting system but his budget is low. Which software he should opt for?
A. Ready to use Software
B. Customized Software
C. Tailor-made Software
D. He can buy any of above, all cost same

**7.** If an organisation want to develop a computerised accounting system according to its need as the business of organisation is complex. Which software it should opt for?
A. Ready to use Software
B. Customized Software
C. Tailor-made Software
D. Any of above

**8.** What are the features of computerized accounting software?
A. storage of accounting data and on-line input
B. instantly produces different reports
C. group different account
D. All of the above

**9.** The ..........of a vendor is also an important factor to consider while opting for a computerized accounting software.
A. Level of profit B. Honesty
C. Capability D. None of the above

**10.** Software must be easy to.......
A. Install B. Adapt
C. Understand D. All of the above

**11.** Accounting Packages are developed on the basis of:
A. Accounting concepts
B. Accounting conventions
C. Both Accounting concepts and Conventions
D. None of the above

**12.** What type of Software is an Accounting Package?
A. System Software
B. Application Software
C. Utility Software
D. Basic

**13.** The components of computerised accounting system are:
A. Data, Report, Ledger, Software, Hardware
B. Software, Hardware, People, Procedure, Data
C. Data, Coding, Procedure, Objective, Output
D. People, Procedure, Hard ware, software

**14.** Grouping of Accounts means the classification of data from:
A. Assets, Capital, and Liabilities
B. Assets, Capital, Liabilities, Revenues & Expenses
C. Assets, Owners equity, Revenue & Expenses
D. Capital, Liabilities, Revenues & Expenses

**15.** Codification of Accounts required for the purpose of:
A. Hierarchical relationship between groups and components
B. Data processing faster and preparing of final accounts
C. Keeping data and information secured
D. None of the above

**16.** Method of codification should be:
A. Such that it leads to grouping of accounts
B. An identification mark
C. Easy to understand and leads to grouping of accounts
D. None of the above

**17.** Final account subsystem in Accounting Information System (AIS) deals with:
A. Preparation of budgets
B. Preparation of Pay Roll
C. Preparation of Final Accounts
D. None of the above

**18.** Pick the odd one out:
A. Password security B. Data Audit
C. Data Bank D. Data vault

**19.** Which among the following is an example of mnemonic codes?
A. AS03, AS04, AS05
B. 1925, 1926, 1927, 1928
C. ACC, ECO, ENG, MAL
D. 001-100, 101-200, 201-300, 301-400

**20.** Which among the following deals with generation of reports that are vital for management decision making?
A. Costing sub system
B. Pay Roll Accounting Sub system
C. Budget Sub System
D. Management Information System

**21.** The need of codification is:
A. Easy to process data
B. Keeping proper records
C. The generation of block codes
D. The encryption of data

**22.** Choose the correct pair:
A. Cash and Bank sub system – Deals with receipts and payments of cash
B. Inventory subsystem – deals with recording of sales
C. Payroll Accounting sub system – deals with the preparation of final accounts
D. Accounts receivable sub system – deals with expenses

**23.** It refers to the system of recording, organising, summarising, analysing, interpreting and communicating the financial data of a business.
A. Manual Accounting
B. Computerised Accounting
C. Auditing
D. Human Resource Accounting

**24.** Following businesses generally require customised software:
A. Banking
B. Medical
C. Retail or point of Sale
D. All of the above

**25.** Features of computerised accounting system:
A. Complete visibility
B. Fast, powerful, simple and integrated
C. Accuracy and speed
D. All of the above

**26.** When different accounts are clubbed on the basis of some common characteristics that are shared by them, the concept is known as________.
A. Asset B. Liability
C. Income D. Grouping

**27.** _________ is the systematic assignment of number to items to classify and organise them.
A. Codification B. Coding
C. Grouping D. Recording

**28.** Most organisations use ______ for coding their accounts.
A. Block code B. Block number
C. Block group D. Block section

**29.** Computers can be used in accounting in different number of ways:
A. Utility in batch processing
B. Utility in Online/Interactive Processing
C. Utility in Wage/Payroll System
D. All of the above

**30.** Such systems also generate reports which allow the accounting professionals to have a proper view of different transactions in a comprehensive manner.
A. Enterprise Resource Planning software
B. Pre-packaged accounting software
C. Spreadsheet software
D. Customised accounting packages

**31.** This software is a package which is used for managing the entire organisation in a comprehensive.
A. Enterprise Resource Planning software
B. Pre-packaged accounting software
C. Spreadsheet software
D. Customised accounting packages

**32.** The individual field in the sheet is known as a ______.
A. Row B. Cell
C. Column D. Group

**33.** Such kind of software offers various functionalities such as cell content, pivot table, formulas and macros:
A. Enterprise Resource Planning software
B. Pre-packaged accounting software
C. Spreadsheet software
D. Customised accounting packages

**34.** The software may also allow for graphical rendering of data, which is useful for carrying out analysis:
A. Enterprise Resource Planning software
B. Spreadsheet software
C. Pre-packaged accounting software
D. Customised accounting packages

**35.** This is the kind of software which is specifically designed for meeting the requirements of a particular business:
A. Enterprise Resource Planning software

B. Customised accounting packages
C. Pre-packaged accounting software
D. Spreadsheet software

**36.** The components of Computerised Accounting System are:
A. Data, Report, Ledger, Hardware, Software
B. Data, People, Procedure, Hardware, Software
C. People, Procedure, Ledger, Data, Chart of Accounts
D. Data, Coding, Procedure, Rules, Output

**37.** The Computerised Accounting System refers to:
A. Printing of Balance Sheet and Profit and Loss Accounts using computer
B. Processing of accounting transaction through computer and produce records and reports
C. Processing of accounting related data and printing reports
D. None of the above

**38.** The components of Computerised Accounting System refers to:
A. Business transactions are analysed, transactions recorded, prepare trial balance, preparation of balance sheet and profit and loss account
B. From data entry to preparation of final statements
C. Transformation of manual accounting system to CAS
D. None of the above

**39.** The CAS should be:
A. Simple and integrated, transparent, accurate, scalability, reliability
B. Complex, Accurate, Transparent, Faster to work
C. Able to transform the manual accounting system to computerised accounting system
D. None of the above

**40.** 44. Where do we record all type of adjustment entry in Tally?
A. F5 : Payment B. F6 : Receipt
C. F7 : Journal D. F4 : Contra

**41.** Control unit works as __________ of the computer.
A. Monitor B. Brain
C. Component D. Part

**42.** Accounting standards issued by ICAI are mandatory in India:
A. True B. False
C. Both (A) and (B) D. None of these

**43.** Which shortcut key is used in Company Feature's screen to use Accounting Features in Tally?
A. F1 B. F2
C. F3 D. F4

**44.** Which of the following is true statement for computerised accounting system?
(*a*) The computer accounting system is based on the concept of database.
(*b*) Computer accounting system does not away with the concept of creating and maintaining journals, ledger etc.
A. Only (*a*) B. Only (*b*)
C. Both (*a*) and (*b*) D. None of the above

**45.** Which shortcut key is used in 'Company Features' screen to use Inventory Features in Tally?
A. F1 B. F2
C. F3 D. F4

**46.** Which shortcut key is pressed to display Part No. for automobile industries?
A. F1 B. F2
C. F11 D. F12

**47.** Application softwares:
A. Can operate on its own
B. Cannot operate without Operating Software
C. Both (A) and (B)
D. None of these

**48.** Accounting software requires:
A. Transactions to be entered once
B. Transactions to be entered at each stage *i.e.* recording and posting into accounts
C. Both (A) and (B)
D. None of the above

**49.** Accounting softwares available are:
A. Readymade or off-the-shelf software
B. Tailor-made software
C. Customised Software
D. All of these

**50.** Which of the following software is not operating software?
A. MS DOS B. Windows XP
C. MS Word D. None of these

**51.** What type of application software is Tally?
A. Statistics Package
B. Spreadsheet Package
C. Accounting Package
D. All of these

**52.** Tally package is developed by:
A. Peutronics B. Tally Solutions
C. Coral Softwares D. Vedika Softwares

**53.** Which option is used to place data taken in pen drive or CD to Appropriate place in Tally?
A. Backup B. Restore
C. Split Company Data D. None of these

**54.** Which option is used in Tally to close opened Company?
A. Alter B. Shut Company
C. Create Company D. Select Company

**55.** Which shortcut key is used to take print of any report in Tally?
A. Ctrl + P B. Shift + P
C. Alt + P D. Alt + Ctrl + P

**56.** Which shortcut key is used to export data of any company in Microsoft Excel spreadsheet or in any other company?
A. Alt + P B. Alt + E
C. Alt + O D. Alt + S

**57.** Which submenu is used to create new ledgers, groups and voucher types in Tally?
A. Account Info. B. Inventory Info.
C. Accounting Vouchers D. Inventory Vouchers

**58.** Which submenu is used for voucher entry in Tally?
A. Vouchers B. Account Vouchers
C. Accounts Info D. None of these

**59.** Which option is used to view list of Primary and Secondary groups in Tally?
A. List of Accounts B. Accounts
C. List D. None of these

**60.** Which ledger is created by Tally automatically as soon as we create a new company?
A. Cash B. Profit & Loss A/c
C. Capital A/c D. (A) and (B) both

**61.** Which option is used to make changes in created Groups of Ledgers in Tally?
A. Create B. Display
C. Alter D. Change

**62.** Which voucher type is used to transfer amount from one bank to another?
A. Contra B. Payment
C. Receipt D. Post-Dated

**63.** Where do we record transactions of salary, rent or interest paid?
A. Contra B. Journal
C. Receipt D. Payment

**64.** Where do we record credit purchase of furniture in Tally?
A. Purchase B. Payment
C. Receipt D. Journal

**65.** Where do we record purchase return, sales return, depreciation, bad debts etc. in Tally?
A. Journal B. Payment
C. Contra D. Receipt

## ANSWERS

| 1 | 2 | 3 | 4 | 5 | 6 | 7 | 8 | 9 | 10 |
|---|---|---|---|---|---|---|---|---|---|
| C | C | D | C | D | A | C | D | C | D |
| **11** | **12** | **13** | **14** | **15** | **16** | **17** | **18** | **19** | **20** |
| C | B | B | B | A | C | C | C | C | D |
| **21** | **22** | **23** | **24** | **25** | **26** | **27** | **28** | **29** | **30** |
| D | A | B | D | D | D | B | A | D | B |
| **31** | **32** | **33** | **34** | **35** | **36** | **37** | **38** | **39** | **40** |
| A | B | C | B | B | B | B | A | A | C |
| **41** | **42** | **43** | **44** | **45** | **46** | **47** | **48** | **49** | **50** |
| B | A | A | A | B | D | B | A | D | C |
| **51** | **52** | **53** | **54** | **55** | **56** | **57** | **58** | **59** | **60** |
| C | A | B | B | C | B | A | B | A | D |
| **61** | **62** | **63** | **64** | **65** | | | | | |
| C | A | D | D | A | | | | | |

●●●

# 9

# USING COMPUTERISED ACCOUNTING SYSTEM

## USE OF COMPUTERS IN MANAGERIAL APPLICATIONS

### What is a Computer

The word "Computer" comes from the word compute which means to calculate. So a computer is normally considered to be a calculating device that can perform arithmetic operation at an enormous speed. But more accurately, a computer may be defined as a device that operates upon data. Data can be anything, like bio-data of several applicants when the computer is used to assist us for recruiting personnel. Similarly, the data can be the details of passengers such as name, age, etc. when the computer is employed for making airline or railway reservations.

The two basic types of computers are the analog and the digital. The analog computer handles or process information which is of a physical nature, as for example, temperature, pressure, etc. The digital computer process information which is essentially in a binary or two-state form namely, zero and one. When talking about computers, we mostly refer to the **digital** type electronic machines.

Digital computers fall into ranges called microcomputers, minicomputers, mainframes, and supercomputers classified in ascending order of size—small, medium, large and very large.

### Characteristics of Computers

Computer display the following characteristics depending on their type of use:

(*a*) The ability to perform calculations at a fast speed and to store that information for future retrieval or use.

(*b*) The ability to take in information and to store that information for future retrieval or use.

(*c*) The ability to take in and store a small variety of instructions for computers to obey.

(*d*) The ability to use simple logical rules to make decisions for their own internal control or for the control of some external activity.

(*e*) The ability to communicate with other computer systems.

(*f*) To carry out calculations accurately and speedily.

### Applications of Computers

Computers may be used in the following fields/institutions:

**(*a*) Office Uses:** The work done in offices is generally, the preparation of letters, reports, memoranda, copy of advertisement, publicity, minutes, contracts, forms, notes etc. All these tasks can be performed by computers more efficiently. Small offices, organizations and institutions can afford to have a personal computer because of its low price. A high end PC personal computer costs in the range of ₹ 35,000 to ₹ 50,000. This type of computer can help user in reports preparation, storing and retrieving and displaying of test. Word processing package like Microsoft Office 2000, Word Perfect, Word Pro etc. are available that help users to write, edit, manipulate, store, retrieving, display, and print the text. The paperless office needs much less office space and lesser number of workers to do the same job more smartly.

**(*b*) Publication of Books (Desktop Publications):** Authors prepare manuscripts of books using Word processing programs. Tests is stored on a floppy disk and formatted by specialized personnel called type-setters. These are then printed using laser printers. Laser printers produce high quality print and the final copy is called the camera ready copy (CRC). These prints are sent to the offset press for printing purposes and then binding is done at the binding centres. The cover page of the books are made by artists or they are also designed using another graphic software such as corel DRAW. The cover is then sent for printing in another type of printing press which is specialized only in colour printing. Illustrations, pictures and tables are also created on specialized softwares such as Auto CAD. Such figures and diagrams are then imported and pasted in the text of the book using a word processor. These jobs are done very fast. Thus book publishing is revolutionized by computers.

**(c) Data Analysis:** Special software called spreadsheet program are used for data analysis. Data are entered in rows and columns in a spreadsheet. Using spreadsheet program one can tabulated results, and carry out interpolation of results such as the likely profits of the company based on the sales and expenses. These results are then compared by the actual results and corrections are accordingly applied from time to time. One can prepare product sales, profit, investment. Similarly, statistical packages are available for any kind of computation for data analysis. They have functions to calculate average, maximum and minimum, mean, mode and median values etc. They can accept data from other files and sort, merge and manipulate data as needed.

**(d) Graphics:** Computers are being used to make drawings, graphics and pictures. Corel DRAW, Harvard Graphics and Freelance Plus for Windows are some such software packages which help an artist in increasing his drawing capability. Preparation of drawings is a time consuming task if it is done by draftsman. But computers can draw sophisticated drawings in minutes. It can produce three-dimensional pictorial views. Graphics such as bar graphs, pie charts and line graphs are plotted from spreadsheet data and other tabulated form of stored data. Graphics packages are also used to recognize picture, process images, draw pictures etc.

**(e) Computer Aided Manufacture:** Computers are used to control production of engineering items, chemical processes etc. Designers use Computer Aided Design softwares to design machines and machine parts which are likely to be manufactured in large numbers. Computers are also used to control manufacturing machines such as lathes, drill or milling machines. Integrated approach of Computer Aided Design (CAD) and Computer Aided Manufacture (CAM) is used in automated factories. The designers design new machines using CAD. There are softwares packages to get design information from the CAD design database and convert them automatically into other programs which activate and control manufacturing machines such as lathes, drills, milling machines etc. A series of computer-controlled machines perform the whole task of production. Maruti Udyog in Gurgaon (Haryana) in India for the manufacturing and assembly Maruti Cars.

**(f) Database Management:** Computers are used to handle files which store a variety of information. The terms database is used to refer to one or more related files. Information can be seen on the computer screen. To handle files, database management packages are widely used. Let us suppose a computer stores information in a file regarding students, e.g. name of the students, roll number, marks subject wise, total percentage of marks subject wise, percentage of total, division awarded etc. If one asks computer to print the list of students who have secured total marks 75% and above, computer will be able to do so very easily. One can also ask it to print the names of the students who have secured the highest marks in different subjects. A database management system can provide information from more than one related files.

A user would like to have certain information which is not in a single file. The program will search all the required information from different files and supply it to user. Take an example of records maintained by an advocate. He maintains two files. One file contains the records of different clients. It may be named as client file. It records client number, client identification number, name of the client, address, phone number, amount due etc. He maintains another file which keeps the records of different cases. It may be named as the case file. It records case number, identification number of the client of different cases, attorney, court, judge, opening date, court date etc. Suppose the advocate wants information about which cases are to be taken up on a particular date, the details of the cases and details of clients to obtain information requires searching both the files—client files as well as case file. The software package will collect information from both the files. The case file gives the information about the cases that are due on a particular date. It also gives the identification numbers of the client corresponding to each case. For these identification numbers the details of clients are obtained from the client file. The information so retrieved is given to the user in a very short time.

**(g) Project Management:** A project work has a series of tasks which must be completed in scheduled time. Computers can be used to manage project work to plan, schedule and control man power, material and other resources needed to complete the project work in time at reasonable cost. What are the tasks to be performed, the sequence in which tasks are to be performed, time required to complete each task and the starting data—all this information should be supplied to the computer. The project management package shows the longest sequence of events in the project called critical path. It calculates total project time. In case a project lags behind the schedule, speed can be increased to reduce the time of completion of one or more tasks on the critical path to catch up the schedule. Project management package will show the impact of the delay. It will quickly show the modified schedule. It will also show the increased man power required for completing project in time.

(*h*) **Communications:** Computers are extensively used in sending and receiving information over long distances. For communication purposes one must have a computer, a data communication package and a modulator and demodular (modem). Telephone line is designate to transmit analog signals. On the other hand, a computer processes digital signals consisting of pulse or no pulse *i.e.*, presence or absence of an electrical voltage. Digital signals can not be transmitted over existing telephone lines which have been designed to transmit analog signals.

The Modulators/demodulators (Modem) are needed to convert or modulate digital signals to analog signals and vice versa to use existing telephone lines. The modem receives data from a computer or a terminal and converts (modulates) the digital signals into analog signals which can be transmitted over, telephone lines. The modem at the other end receives data from telephone lines and converts (or demodulates) the received analog signals into digital signals. These digital signals are processed by a computer at the receiving end. They are thereafter reproduced as the original information. Data can be transmitted in both directions. When data is being transmitted from one end, the modem placed at the other end performs demodulation. When data is received at the other end, the modem placed at this end performs demodulation. Computer communications are being used in electronic mail, video conference, banking, brokerage and to get information services etc.

(*i*) **Education:** In educational institutions computers are used as teaching aid, research tool and analysing system. When computer is used as a teaching aid it is referred to as computer—assisted instruction (CAI). The computer asks questions to test the students's ability to understand the subject. When a student gives an answer, the computer gives some comments to indicate that answer is right or wrong. If the answer is not correct, the computer gives some error signal. The CAI programs can be prepared in a variety of modes, such as tutorial, discovery, problem solving, modelling, and drill and practice. In tutorial mode the computer presents new ideas followed by text questions. In discovery mode the computer presents information and asks students to draw conclusions. In problem solving mode computer allows students to apply their concept in solving a problem. In modelling mode a process or a system is presented mathematically to make its analysis. Computers can also repeat the presentation of the material as many times as desired. This helps students make certain concepts clear if they are not clear in earlier attempts. Question bank may be prepared and stored in computer's memory. Test questions may be stored so that students can manage their examination to test their knowledge.

(*j*) **Medical Field:** Computers are widely used in hospitals to help doctors in diagnosis, get information on patients, diseases treatments, drugs etc. They are also used in administration of the hospital and in keeping patient records Doctors can discuss with colleagues about the diagnosis of a diseases using tele-conferencing. Doctors are taking help of expert system in the diagnosis and treatment of patients.

Presently expert systems are helping doctors but such systems are not the substitute for doctors. They are useful primarily in aiding doctors in diagnosis and treatment. Computers are also used in pathological laboratories also.

(*k*) **Airways and Railways Ticket Reservations:** The computer is capable of storing all necessary information in connection with ticket reservation, such as train number, stations in route, distance, number of seats available for each train in each class, fare etc. If seats are available, computer prints and issues ticket. Computer also prints reservation charts. It also gives information regarding train timings.

(*l*) **Industrial Control and Instrumentation:** Computers are extensively used in automatic control of temperature of a furnace, speed of a motor, generators voltage and power boiler's pressure, testing of products etc. Microprocessor based system have been developed for industrial control and instrumentation.

(*m*) **Military:** Computers are extensively used in defence. Modern tanks, torpedoes, missiles etc. employ computerized control systems. A guided missile uses internal computer for its own control. They can fly into dangerous zones without the risk of pilot's life. Communications. Radar systems employ computers for processing data and display images. Computerized control systems provide information about range, height, etc. of the target.

(*n*) **Banks:** Banks use computers to provide on line service to customers and to answer customer's enquiry regarding their bank balance, etc. To handle cash, banks use cash dispensing machines. With the use of a computer electronic transfer of funds from one account to another has become possible. A customer from his home, office or store can insert his identification number and type the transaction details on the terminal details on the terminal's keyboard. Immediately the amount he specifies will move out of his account and enter another's account.

(*o*) **Design and Research Work:** Design of bridges, towers, building, generators, motors, etc. need very complex calculations. In some cases, massive data are to be processed particularly in statistical analysis. Computers are suitable for both complex computations as well as processing of massive amount of data. Nowadays computers are a must for this type of work.

(*p*) **Other Applications:** Microprocessors which can control engine operations such as air fuel mixture, ignition timing etc. are available in the market for efficient operations. Computers also control door locks, air conditioning, braking, skidding and speed of the car. Smart watches are also in the market. Any smart product contains an embedded microprocessor. A microprocessor gives time, data, month etc. A number of smart products such as smart crane, smart material handler, smart camera, smart TV, smart thermostat, smart taxi meter etc. are available. The user can program a smart product to perform certain tasks as he desires.

Personal computers are also used in home for playing games, communicating with data base services, processing, computer aided education, home management, accounting etc. Computers are used in automatic electronic telephone exchange.

An exchange can handle larger number of customers in faster and efficient manner. Many types of communications are controlled by computers. The computer-controlled telescope are able to detect and track satellites beyond radar range.

## DATA PROCESSING

Manipulation of facts to the advantage of the users is called data processing. It may be done using manual or electronic methods. The main purpose of Electronic Data Processing (EDP) is to do complex job at incredible speed and accuracy.

Sometimes, a part of the data processing job may be done using manual methods. As an example, your class teacher may prepare the list of marks obtained by you in various tests and examinations manually. However, further processing into grades and merit may be done using electronic computers because electronic machines are faster and more accurate and calculations will not go wrong. Since electronic machines are faster in operation and reasonable affordable, one may prefer them over manual systems. Different cycle is which data processed electronically is given below:

I. **Input Cycle:** In this phase, data is prepared in some convenient form and on a medium most suitable for entry into a processing machine. For example, in a manual system, we may prefer to write data in a tabular form on a sheet of paper such as the marks sheet of students of a class. We do so, because it is very convenient to read the marks written in tabular form. In case of electronic data processing machines, we may record data on a magnetic tape or floppy disk.

II. **Processing Cycle:** In this cycle, we manipulate or combine the inputted data with other data as per the instructions. For example, in a manual processing cycle, a class teacher adds the marks secured by each student in different subjects. She divides this aggregate by the maximum marks and calculates the percentage of marks. She can also award a grade, based on the percentage of marks. In an electronic data processing system, these actions are performed automatically in accordance with a series of instructions called a program, which is stored in the computer. The computer will do exactly the same job as is told to it by the set of instructions or program.

III. **Output Cycle:** Once data are processed, the results need to be brought out in a form most suitable for the user. This is called the output cycle. For example, in the marks processing case, the marks of each student in each subject are transferred to printed report cards. Remarks like pass/fail are also recorded on this report along with the merit and the grades. This job is done by a class teacher in a manual data processing system and by a computer printer in an electronic data processing system. A block diagram of the three cycle is shown in the following Fig. 1.

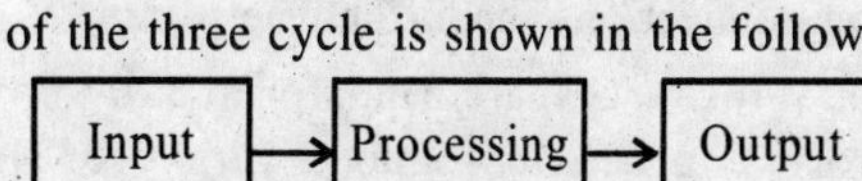


**Fig. 1.** *Block Diagram of a Basic Data Processing Cycle*

## INFORMATION SYSTEM

### What is an Information System

An information system can be any organized combination of people, hardware, software, communications networks, and data resources that collects, transforms and disseminates information in an organization. People have relied on informa-tion system to communicate with each other using a variety of physical devices (hardware), information processing instructions and procedures (software), communications and channels (networks), and stored data (data resources) since the down of civilization. The following figure 2 represents the information systems :

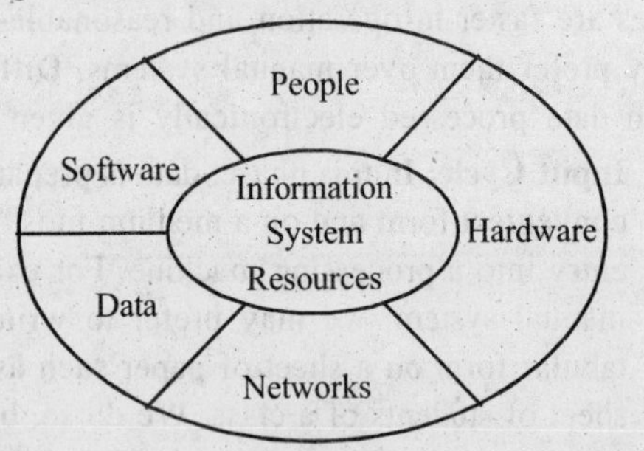


**Fig. 2**

### Components of Information System

An information system depends on:

- The resources of people (end users and IS Specialists)
- Hardware (machines and media)
- Software (programs and procedures)
- Data (data and knowledge bases), and
- Networks (communications media and network support) to perform input, processing, output, storage, and control activities that convert data resources into information products.

The information system model highlights the relationship among the components and activities of information systems (see Fig. 3). It provides a framework that emphasizes four major concepts that can be applied to all types of information system:

- People, hardware, software, data, and networks are the five basic resources of information systems.
- People resources include end users and IS specialists hardware resources consist of machines and media, software resources include both programs and procedures, data resources can include data and knowledge bases, and network resources include communications media and networks.
- Data resources are transformed by information processing activities into a variety of information products for end users.
- Information processing consists of input, processing, output, storage, and control activities.

## MIS AND DECISION MAKING

Management Information System (MIS) provide information in the form of reports and displays to managers and many business professionals. For example, sales managers may use their networked computers and Web browsers to get instantaneous displays about the sales results of their products and to access their corporate intranet for daily sales analysis reports that evaluate sales made by each sales-person.

MIS is one of the part of management support systems.

As MIS produces information products that support many of the day-to-day decision making needs of managers and business professionals. Reports, displays, and responses produced by such management support systems provide information that these decision makers have specified in advance as adequately meeting their information needs. Such predefined information products satisfy the information needs of decision makers at the operational and tactical levels of the organization who are faced with more structured typed of decision situations.

For example, sales managers rely heavily on sales analysis reports to evaluate differences in performance among sales people who sell the same type of products to the same type of customers. They have a pretty good idea of the kinds of information about sales results they need to manage sales performance effectively.

Managers and other decision makers use an MIS to request information at their networked workstations that supports their decision making activities. This information takes the form of periodic, exception and demand reports and immediate responses to inquiries. Web browsers, application programs, and database management software provide access to information in the intranet and other operational databases of the organization. Remember, operational databases are maintained by transactions processing systems. Data about the business environment are obtained from Internet or extranet databases when necessary.

Management Information systems provide a variety of information products to managers. Four major reporting alternatives are provided by such systems:

1. **Periodic Scheduled Reports:** This traditional form of providing information to managers users a prespecified format designed to provide managers with informational on a regular basis. Typical examples of such periodic scheduled reports are daily or weekly sales analysis reports and monthly financial statement.

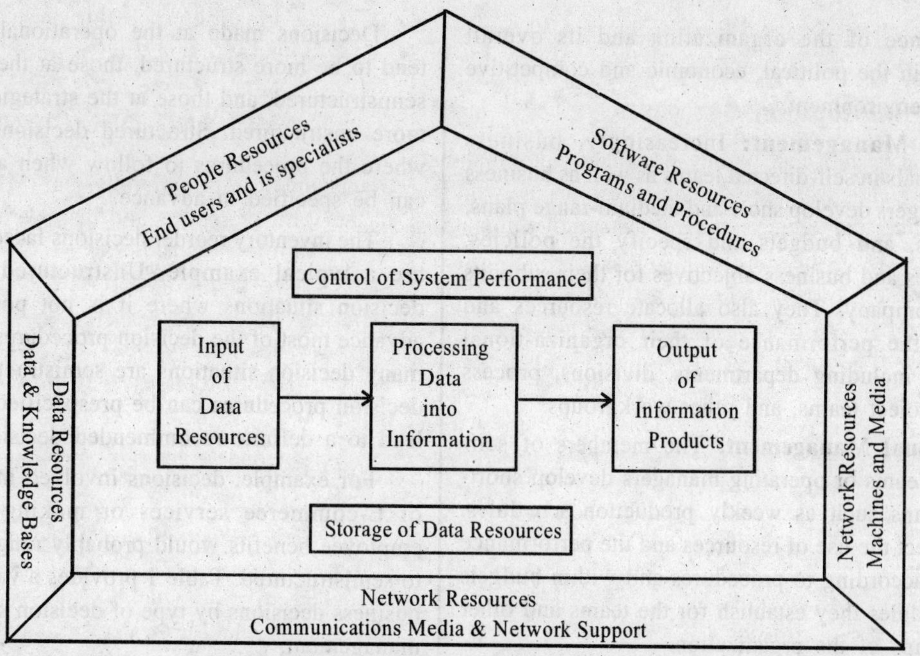


**Fig. 3.** *The Components of Information System*

2. **Exception Reports:** In some cases, reports are produced only when exceptional conditions occur. In other cases, reports are produced periodically but contain information only about these exceptional conditions. For example, a credit manager can be provided with a report that contains only information on customers who exceed their credit limits. Exception reporting reduces information overload, instead of overwhelming decision makers with periodic detailed reports of business activity.
3. **Demand Reports and Responses:** Information is available whenever a manager demands it. For example, Web browsers and DBMS query languages and report generators enable managers at PC workstations to get immediate responses or find and obtain customized reports as a result of their requests for the information they need. Thus, manager do not have to wait for periodic reports to arrive as scheduled.
4. **Push Reporting:** Information is pushed to a manager's networked workstation. Many companies are using webcasting software to selectively broadcast reports and other information to the networked PCs of managers and specialists over their corporate intranets.

## Decision Making Process

A process of intelligence, design, and choice activities that result in the selection of a particular course of action.

Information requirements of decision makers are depicted in the following Fig. 4.

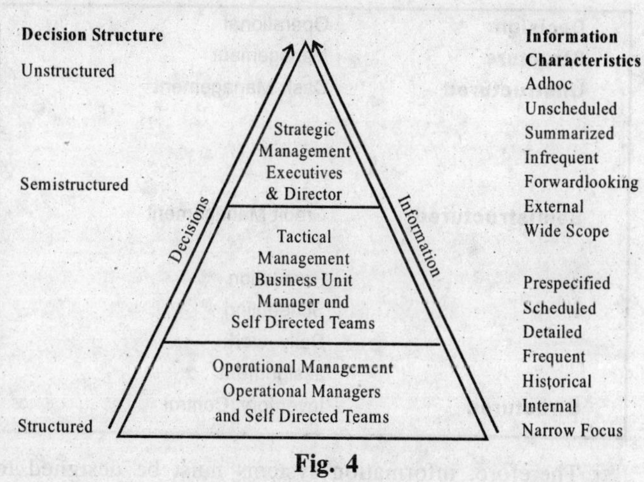


**Fig. 4**

The type of information required by decision makers in a company is directly related to the level of management decision making and the amount of structure in the decision situations they face. The framework of the classic managerial pyramid shown in the Fig. 4 applies even in today's down sized organizations and flattened or non hierarchical organizational structures. Levels of management decision making still exist, but their size, shape and participants continue to change as today's fluid organizational structures evolve. Thus, the levels of managerial decision making that must be supported by information technology in a successful organization are:

- **Strategic Management:** Typically, a board of directors of an executive committee of the CEO and top executives develop overall organizational goals, strategies, policies and objectives as part of a strategic planning process. They also monitor the strategic performance of the organization and its overall direction in the political, economic and competitive business environment.

- **Tactical Management:** Increasingly, business professionals in self-directed teams as well as business unit managers develop short-and medium-range plans, schedules, and budgets and specify the policies, procedures and business objectives for their subunits of the company. They also allocate resources and monitor the performance of their organiza-tional subunits, including departments, divisions, process teams, project teams, and other workgroups.
- **Operational Management:** The members of self-directed teams or operating managers develop short-range plans such as weekly production schedules. They direct the use of resources and the performance of tasks according to procedures and within budgets and schedules they establish for the teams and other workgroups of the organization.

Decisions made at the operational management level tend to be more structured, those at the tactical level more semistructured, and those at the strategic management level more unstructured. Structured decisions involve situations where the procedures to follow when a decision is needed can be specified in advance.

The inventory reorder decisions faced by most businesses are a typical example. Unstructured decisions involve decision situations where it is not possible to specify in advance most of the decision procedures to follow. At most, many decision situations are semistructured. That is, some decision procedures can be prespecified, but not enough to lead to a definite recommended decision.

For example, decisions involved in starting a new line of E-commerce services or making major changes to employee benefits would probably range from unstructured to semistructured. Table 1 provides a variety of examples of business decisions by type of decision structure and level of management.

**Table 1**

| Decision Structure | Operational Management | Tactical Management | Strategic Management |
|---|---|---|---|
| **Unstructured** | Cash Management | Business process reengineering<br>Work Group performance analysis | New E-commerce initiatives Company reorganization |
| **Semistructured** | Credit Management | Employee performance appraisal | Product Planning |
| | Production Scheduling | Capital budgeting | Mergers and acquisitions |
| | Daily work assignment | Program budgeting | Site location |
| **Structured** | Inventory Control | Program Control | |

Therefore, information systems must be designed to produce a variety of information products to meet the changing needs of decision makers throughout an organization. For example, decisions makers at the strategic management level require more summarized, ad hoc, unscheduled reports, forecasts, and external intelligence to support their more unstructured planning and policy making responsibilities. Decision makers at the operational management level, on the other hand, may require more prespecified internal reports emphasizing detailed current and historical data comparisons that support their more structure responsibilities in day-to-day operations.

## SYSTEMS ANALYSIS AND DESIGNS

### Systems

The term system is derived from the Greek word systema, which means an organized relationship among functioning units or components. A system exists because it is designed to achieve one or more objectives. We come into daily contact with the transportation system, the telephone system, the accounting system, the production system, computer system etc.

A system is an orderly grouping of interdependent components linked together according to a plan to achieve a specific objectives. System analysis and design are the application of the systems approach to problem solving generally using computers. To reconstruct a system the analyst must consider its elements—outputs and inputs, processors, control, feedback and environment.

Systems fall into three classifications :

(*a*) Physical (tangible entitles) or abstract, such as models or formulas.

(*b*) Open (allowing inputs and providing outputs) or closed, which isolates it from the environment.

(*c*) Man made such as information systems.

A system may be schematic (two dimensional), a flow system to abstract the real world (e.g., PERT Chart), a static (exhibiting one relationship such as Gnatt Chart) or a dynamic system model that approximates the business organization.

An information system is an open system that allows inputs and facilitates interaction with the user. The main characteristics of an open system are input from outside, processing, output, operating in cycles through feedback, differentiation, and equifinality.

There are three levels of information in organizations that require a special type of information system :

(*a*) Strategic information relates to long range planning policies and upper management. It is achieved with the aid of decision support systems.

(*b*) Managerial information middle management and department heads in policy implementation and control. It is maintained with the aid of management information systems.

(*c*) Operational information is daily information needed to operate the business. It is established by data processing systems.

The nature of information and managerial levels is related to whether decision making is structured or unstructured. A relatively closed stable, and mechanistic business tends to develop a more structured information process for planning and control. Open, dynamic organizations are associated with uncertain environments where more unstructured rather than structured decisions are made to cope with uncertainty.

The informal communications network of employees in the organization is a useful source for examining systems, since computers cannot provide all the information user staff support is important.

Managerial levels determine the kind of information needed to solve a problem. Lower-level management needs detailed information to make day-to-day structured decisions. Higher-level management requires summarized information to attain goals. MIS is combination of information for various managerial levels.

The key element of MIS is the data base-ideally, a nonredundant collection of interrelated data items that are processed through application programs. The data base offers several advantageous to end users and is the wave of the future. The historical nature of MIS reports and the need to deal with unstructured problem situations prompted the introduction of Decision Support System (DSS). The concept is future oriented, emphasizing decision making in problem situations, not information processing; it requires a computer aided environment and accentuates a combined "mean", machine, and decision environment.

System analysis and design are keyed to the life cycle. The stages are :

(*a*) Recognition of the need for change

(*b*) Feasibility study

(*c*) Analysis of the present system

(*d*) Design of a candidate system

(*e*) Testing and implementation of the system

(*f*) Post implementation

The idea for change originates in the environment (government, consumers, union, etc.) or from within the firm (user, analyst, etc.). Once the problem is verified, an initial investigation is conducted to determine whether change is feasible. If the answer is yes, a feasibility study is authorized.

Analysis is a detailed study of the various operations performed by a system. This involves gathering information and using structured tools for analysis.

System design refers to the technical specifications that will be applied in implementing the candidate system. This involves input/output, file, and processing design.

Implementation is concerned with detail—the physical creation of the candidate system. The key point is actual operation and user acceptance testing before the system is released to the user.

After implementation, maintenance begins. This includes enhancement, modifications, or any change from the original specifications. This phase terminates the system development life cycle.

In deciding on the project to design, a number of factors are considered: technical (availability of qualified specialists), operational (user's experience with similar projects), and economic (cost effectiveness of the proposed system). Political considerations also play a role in the final selection.

To ensure the success of the system, careful and often extensive planning is required. This work falls under project management, where a project is organized into work unit levels involving tasks (lowest level), activities, phases and milestones. The overall management process is crucial to the successful completion of systems.

A system analyst is a person who conducts a study, identifies activities and objectives and determines a procedure to achieve the objectives. Systems analysis is that a history dating back to Taylor. Early analysts worked in factories, specializing in improving work methods and setting time standards for production. With the advent of the computer, the analyst assumed the role of a problem solver and a specialist in developing computer applications.

Success in systems analysis requires interpersonal and technical skills. Interpersonal skills emphasize communication and interface with the user, whereas technical skills include creativity, problem solving, and managing the overall project. During analysis, there is greater need for interpersonal skills, but during design there is greater emphasis on technical skills. During implementation, both skills are needed.

A career in system analysis requires academic preparation, experience, and good interpersonal relations. The person must be familiar with the innerworkings of business and competent in system tools and methodologies. The personal qualities include creativity and communications skills and being systematic and sensitive.

Analyst perform a multitude of sales—as change agent, investigator, architect, psychologist, salesperson, and motivator. They also need to understand politics.

An important aspect of system development is the viability of the relationship between the analyst and the user. Research indicates that the probability of system failure increases without a good interface.

Three behavioural issues are related to system success:
1. establishing user motivation,
2. narrowing analyst/user differences, and
3. neutralizing political factors.

Related to system success also is the extent of the commitment to avoid future conflict. Therefore, coordination of people's ideas for system design is important for system development.

The analyst is the key member of the MIS organization. An MIS facility consists of four major areas :

(*a*) Administration, which handles user liaison, long-range planning, budget planning and control, and personnel.

(*b*) Systems analysis and design, which is organized as project oriented, pool oriented or functional.

(*c*) Programming, which is structured around applications, software, and maintenance. It is organized on a pool or a team basis.

(*d*) Operations, which deals with job scheduling, supplies inventory and the data library.

Of all the managerial and administration positions in the MIS area the position of the analyst is perhaps the most crucial. The job carries considerable responsibility, high status, and attractive pay.

The tasks that make up system development are changing. To perform them well, assistance is becoming available from paraprofessionals. Although less experienced than the systems analyst, they perform general support tasks and specific system development tasks such as drafting data flow diagrams and maintaining data dictionaries. Care must be taken to determine what tasks should be assigned to the paraprofessional.

Another new position in systems work is the technical writer, who is brought to when the candidate system is near completion. The main contribution is quality documentation.

Under the System Development Life Cycle following stages have been followed :

1. Recognition of need
2. Feasibility study
3. Analysis
4. Design
5. Implementation
6. Post-implementation and maintenance

## INFORMATION TECHNOLOGIES

Under the topic Information Technologies generally we studied about Major Concepts, developments, and management issues in information technology—that is, hardware, software, networks, data resource management, and many Internet-based technologies.

Business professionals rely on many types of information system. Some information systems use simple manual (paper-and-pencil) hardware devices and informal (word-of-mouth) communication channels. However, in this text, we will concentrate on computer based information systems that use computer hardware and software, the Internet and other telecommunications networks, computer based data resource management techniques, and many other information technologies to transform data resources into an endless variety of information products for consumers and business professionals.

### Basic Strategies in the Business Use of Information Technology

#### *Lower Costs*

- Use IT to substantially reduce the cost of business processes.
- Use IT to lower the costs of customers of suppliers.

#### *Differentiate*

- Develop new IT features to differentiate products and services.
- Use IT features to reduce the differentiation advantages of competitors.
- Use IT features to reduce the differentiation advantage of competitors
- Use IT features to focus products and services at selected market niches.

#### *Innovate*

- Create new products and services that include IT components.

- Develop unique new markets or market niches with the help of IT.
- Make radical changes to business processes with IT that dramatically cut costs, improve quality, efficiency, or customer service, or shorten time to market.

***Promote Growth***

- Use IT to manage regional and global business expansion.
- Use IT to diversify and integrate into other products and services.

***Develop Growth***

- Use IT to create organisations of business partners.
- Develop interenterprise information systems linked by the Internet and extranets that support strategic business relationships with customers, suppliers, subcontractors, and others.

With the help of information technology the business enterprises cut their costs and maximize the benefits.

Information technology plays a major role in reengineering most business process. The speed, information processing capabilities, and connectivity of computers and Internet technologies can substantially increase the efficiency of business processes, as well as communications and collaboration among the people responsible for their operation and management. For example, the order management process illustrated in the following Fig. 5 is vital to the success of most companies. Many of them are reengineering this process with enterprise resource planning software and Web-enabled electronic business and Commerce systems.

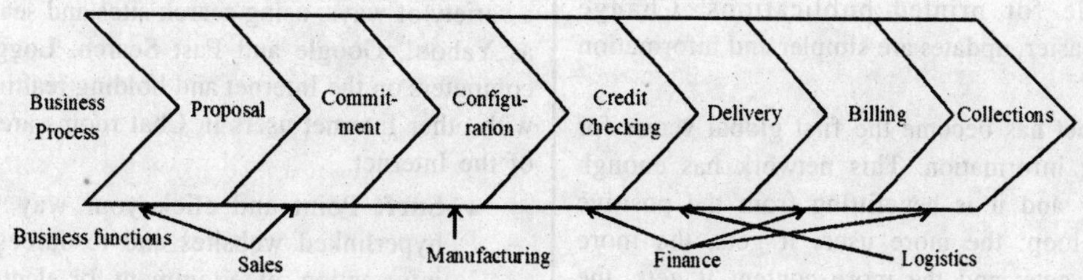


**Fig. 5**

The order management process consists of several business processes and crosses the boundaries of traditional business functions.

**Examples of information technologies that support re-engineering the sales and order management processess:**

- Customer relationship management systems using corporate intranets and the internet.
- Supplier managed inventory systems using the internet and extranet.
- Cross functional EROP software for integrating manufacturing, distribution, finance, and human resource processes.
- Customer-accessible E-Commerce websites for order entry, status checking, payment, and service.
- Customer, product, and order status databases accessed via intranets and extranets by employees and suppliers.

## INTERNET

The Internet is a worldwide network of networks. It is a conglomeration of smaller networks and other connected machines spanning the entire globe. It consists of over 30,000 networks in 71 countries. Around the world, each country has at least one backbone network that operates at a very high speed and carries the bulk of the traffic. Other smaller networks are connects to that backbone. As on 31st August 2008 there are 355 Licenses for provision of internet services. Based on reports received from Internet Service Providers, there are approx. 11.05 million internet subscriber in India as on March 2008.

The Internet has no central authority—networks on the Internet simply agree to cooperate with each other. Individual computers on these networks can share files and transmit information. Various networks connected to Internet format messages with Internet Protocol (IP). IP is often used in conjunction with TCP (Transmission Control Protocol). The Combination of TCP/IP has made the Internet robust and flexible.

### Purpose of Internet

The Internet has revolutionized the communication methods around the world. Sitting at a workstation or PC, one can get any kind of information one wants.

The latest technological advances have enabled it to be used as a business tool as well, with the result that companies are today spending considerable amount of money on Internet research. The amalgamation of computer and communication technologies has resulted in the integration of data, sound and video on the Internet, which in turn has made it a powerful tool for re-engineering business process the world over.

One can use the Internet for the following purpose :

(*a*) To exchange electronic mail with friends all over the globe for a small price.

(*b*) To participate in group discussions on topics of interest, through public news groups.

(*c*) To find educational tools. Universities around the world, book stores, and libraries are sharing on line-information.

(*d*) To shop-commercial electronic store fronts are growing in number in the USA and Europe. One can order different products over the Internet.

(*e*) In the case of business one can get technical support for products one is using. One can publish information such as technical or marketing literature.

(*f*) Because the Internet is electronic, one can make changes to reflect late breaking news that would be impossible for printed publications. Change becomes easier, updates are simpler and information is instant.

(*g*) The Internet has become the first global venue for publishing information. This network has enough users now and it is benefitting from the positive feedback loop: the more users it gets, the more content it gets; and the more content it gets, the more users it gets.

(*h*) Internet's main asset is freedom. An alternative to controlling its freedom is to train and educate the user.

Typical applications of Internet are as follows:

1. Internet connectivity
2. Electronic mail server
3. Corporate communications
4. Database services
5. Remote job applications
6. Travel reservations
7. Electronic fund transfer
8. Credit and verifications

The most popular internet applications are E-mail, browsing the sites on the World Wide Web, and participating in newsgroups and chat rooms. Internet E-mail messages usually arrive in seconds or a few minutes anywhere in the world, and can take the form of data, text, fax and video files. Internet browser software like Netscape Navigator and Microsoft Explorer enables millions of users to surf the World Wide Web by clicking their way to the multimedia information resources stored on the hyperlinked pages of business, government, and other websites. Websites offer information and entertainment, and are the launch sites for electronic commerce transactions between businesses and their suppliers and customers.

The Internet provides electronic discussion forums and bulletin board systems formed and managed by thousands of special interest newsgroups. You can participate in discussions or post messages on thousands of topics for other users with the same interests to read and respond to. Other popular applications include downloading software and information files and accessing databases provided by thousands of business, government, and other organizations. You can make online searches for information at websites in a variety of ways, using search sites and search engines such as Yahoo!, Google and Fast Search. Logging on to other computers on the Internet and holding realtime conversations with other Internet users in Chat rooms are so popular uses of the Internet.

- **Surf:** Point and click your way to thousands of hyperlinked websites and resources for multimedia information, entertainment, or electronic commerce.
- **E-mail:** Exchange electronic mail with millions of Internet users.
- **Discuss:** Participate in discussion forums or post message on bulletin board systems formed by thousands of special-interest newsgroups.
- **Chat:** Hold realtime text conversations in website chat rooms with Internet users around the world.
- **Buy and Sell:** You can buy and sell practically anything via E-Commerce retailers, wholesalers, service providers, and online auctions.
- **Download:** Transfer data files, software, reports, articles, pictures, music, videos, and other types of files to your computer system.
- **Compute:** Log on to and use thousands of Internet computer systems around the world.
- **Other Uses:** Make long-distance phone calls, hold desktop video conferences, listen to radio programs, watch television, play video games, explore virtual worlds, etc.

## MULTIPLE CHOICE QUESTIONS

**1.** Who is the marketer of Tally?

A. Tally Package Pvt. Ltd.
B. Tally Gold Pvt. Ltd.
C. Tally Solutions Pvt. Ltd.
D. None of the above

**2.** Who is the developer of Tally?

A. Wally Feurzeig
B. John G. Kemeny
C. Nandan M. Nilekani
D. Shyam Sundar Goenka

**3.** What is the Short-cut key for quitting tally?
A. Alt + Ctrl + Q B. Alt + Q
C. Ctrl + Q D. Alt + F2 + Q

**4.** What does tally run on?
A. Windows B. Tally Solutions
C. ERP Module D. Tally Gold Edition

**5.** What is Short-cut key for selecting company?
A. Alt + F1 B. F1
C. Ctrl + F1 D. Alt + Ctrl + F1

**6.** What are the two ledgers that is by default provided by tally?
A. Cash A/c & Bank A/c
B. Bank A/c & P/L A/c
C. Cash A/c & P/L A/c
D. None of the above

**7.** How to activate calculator in tally anywhere?
A. Alt + C B. Ctrl + N
C. Ctrl + Alt + N D. Ctrl + R

**8.** What are the languages required for tally?
A. C B. C++
C. C & C++ D. None of the above

**9.** What is Primary Key?
A. A primary key is a maximal set of attributes in a table that uniquely identifies tuples in that table.
B. A primary key is a minimal set of attributes in a table that uniquely identifies tuples in that table.
C. A primary key is a unique identifier.
D. Both (B) & (C)

**10.** What is the short-cut key for back-up?
A. Shift + Tab
B. Alt + Tab
C. Shift + Ctrl + Tab
D. None of the above

**11.** What is the short-cut to copy text from Tally?
A. Ctrl + Alt + C B. Alt + C
C. Ctrl + Shift + C D. Alt + Shift + C

**12.** What is the short-cut to paste text from Tally?
A. Ctrl + Shift + V B. Alt + V
C. Ctrl + Alt + V D. Alt + Shift + V

**13.** What is the benefit of income tax return file?
A. Claim Tax Refund
B. Income & Address Proof
C. Avoid Penalty and Prosecution
D. All of the above

**14.** What is the due date of submission of return for an individual?
A. 31st July B. 31st August
C. 30th September D. 31st October

**15.** What is the due date of submission of return for a company?
A. 31st July B. 31st August
C. 30th September D. 31st October

**16.** What is the Short-cut key for Payments in Tally?
A. F3 B. F4
C. F5 D. F6

**17.** What is the short-cut key for Receipts (transaction for direct cash) in Tally?
A. F4 B. F5
C. F6 D. F7

**18.** Which Shortcut key is used to create a new company in Tally?
A. Ctrl + F3 B. Alt + F3
C. Ctrl + F4 D. Alt + F4

**19.** Create a new company in Tally from Company Info. menu is possible by selecting:
A. New Company B. Start Company
C. Create D. Create Company

**20.** The option used in Tally to close opened Company is:
A. Alter Company B. Close Company
C. Shut Company D. Exit Company

**21.** Which one from the following options is the acknowledgement of filing the return of income?
A. ITR4 B. ITR – V
C. Form26AS D. Form 26QB

**22.** Which sub menu is used to create new ledger, groups and voucher types in tally
A. Account Info B. Accounting Vouchers
C. Inventory Vouchers D. Inventory Info

**23.** Related fields in a database are grouped to form a:
A. Data file B. Data record
C. Bank D. Menu

**24.** A report generator is used to:
A. Delete files B. Print files on paper
C. Data entry D. Update files

**25.** Which option is used in Tally to make changes in created company?
A. Shut Company B. Select Company
C. Alter D. None of these

**26.** Salary Account comes under which head:
A. Indirect Incomes B. Indirect Expenses
C. Direct Incomes D. Direct Expenses

**27.** To creating voucher, step after GOT is:
A. Accounts info.
B. Accounting vouchers
C. Inventory vouchers
D. Inventory info.

**28.** Which menu appears after starting tally for the first time?
A. Gateway of Tally B. Company Info
C. Display D. None of these

**29.** Which shortcut key is used in Company Features screen to use Inventory features in Tally?
A. F1 B. F2
C. F4 D. F3

**30.** Which shortcut key to zoom in Tally?
A. Alt + P B. Alt + Z
C. Alt + Ctrl + Z D. None of these

**31.** Which shortcut key is used in company for statutory and taxation in Tally?
A. F11 And Then F3 B. F12 And Then F3
C. Alt + F11 D. Alt + Ctrl + F11

**32.** Where do we record transactions of Salary, Rent paid?
A. Contra B. Journal
C. Receipt D. Payment

**33.** In Tally functions of F3 button:
A. To close the company
B. To select the different company
C. To change the current date
D. To select the company

**34.** All payments are entered under Accounting Voucher in Tally through:
A. F5 B. F6
C. F7 D. F8

**35.** For Bad Debt Recovery which group required to be selected:
A. Indirect income B. Direct income
C. Direct expenses D. Indirect expenses

**36.** Tally ERP 9 Logo is displayed at:
A. Left of the bottom pane
B. Right of the bottom pane
C. Middle of the bottom pane
D. None of the above

**37.** Find out which is not a Default Ledger in Tally:
A. Profit and Loss B. Cash in Hand
C. Capital Account D. None of these

**38.** Choose the right option to change the Company Information:
A. Company info > Back up
B. Company info > Alter
C. Company info > split Company Data
D. None of these

**39.** Multiple godown are activated from:
A. F11 B. F11 > F1
C. F11 > F2 D. F11 > F3

**40.** To print a voucher from Tally pressing:
A. Ctrl + P B. Shift + P
C. Alt + P D. Ctrl + Alt + P

**41.** In Tally to make journal entry select the right option:
A. F7 B. F10
C. F11 D. Alt + F7

**42.** Select Credit Note Voucher with shortcut key:
A. Alt + F8
B. Ctrl + F8
C. Shift + F8
D. None of the above

**43.** For Reconciliation of Bank in bank ledger press:
A. F3 B. F5
C. F10 D. F12

**44.** To record purchase of Fixed Assets in credit, pass the entry from:
A. Payment mode B. Receipt Mode
C. Journal Mode D. Contra Mode

**45.** To get Payroll Reports choose:
A. Gateway of Tally > Display
B. Gateway of Tally > Display > Statement of Accounts
C. Gateway of Tally > Display > Statement of Payroll
D. Gateway of Tally > Display > Payroll Reports

**46.** TDS deduction entry can be made through:
A. Payment Voucher B. Journal Voucher
C. Receipt Voucher D. All of the above

**47.** Which shortcut key is pressed to create a new Ledger during voucher entry?
A. Alt + C B. Alt + X
C. Alt + D D. Alt + A

**48.** To register and create account for e filing of Income Tax which is the required documents:
A. Permanent Account Number
B. Tax Deduction Account Number
C. TDS Certificate
D. Form 16

**49.** Following is an annual statement maintained for disclosing the details of tax credit in a tax-payer's account as per the database of the I-T Department:
A. 234C B. 26AS
C. ITR V D. None of the above

**50.** Transfer of materials from one godown to another godown, use:
A. Manufacturing Journal
B. Stock Journal
C. Purchase Journal
D. Both (A) & (B)

**51.** CRM stands for _______.
A. Collective Relationship Management
B. Clients Relationship Management
C. Customer Relationship Module
D. Customer Relationship Management

**52.** Financial Accounting Module is considered as the _______ module of ERP.
A. Secondary B. Supporting
C. Most important D. Passive

**53.** Management of quality in the different processes of the organisation is usually managed by the ______ of the ERP system.
A. Quality Assurance Module
B. Quality Management Module
C. Quality Control Module
D. Quality Improvement Module

**54.** ETL stands for _______.
A. Extract, Transmit, Load
B. Exchange, Transform, Load
C. Exchange, Transmit, Load
D. Extract, Transform, Load

**55.** Which of the following are the two major approaches of creating a data warehouse?
A. Managerial, Application
B. Top down, Bottom up
C. Centralized, Decentralized
D. Addition, Substitution

**56.** In top-down approach of data warehouse creation, there is _______ view of data.
A. Narrow B. Restricted
C. Enterprise D. Collective

**57.** _______ is the process of analyzing data to find previously unknown trends and pattern so to make informed business decisions.
A. Big Data
B. Data Warehouse
C. Data Mining
D. Data Analysis

**58.** XBRL uses _______ as its backbone.
A. HTTPs Technology
B. Cryptography Technology
C. XML Technology
D. HTML Technology

**59.** Which of the following is not a criterion that is needed to be ensured in MIS Report?
A. Relevant B. Timely
C. Accessible D. Structured

**60.** Which of the following kind of data analysis is like a detective work?
A. Exponential Data Analysis
B. Big Data Analysis
C. Exploratory Data Analysis
D. Confirmatory Data Analysis

## ANSWERS

| 1 | 2 | 3 | 4 | 5 | 6 | 7 | 8 | 9 | 10 |
|---|---|---|---|---|---|---|---|---|---|
| C | D | B | A | B | C | B | C | D | A |
| **11** | **12** | **13** | **14** | **15** | **16** | **17** | **18** | **19** | **20** |
| A | C | D | A | C | C | C | B | D | C |
| **21** | **22** | **23** | **24** | **25** | **26** | **27** | **28** | **29** | **30** |
| B | A | B | B | C | B | A | B | B | B |
| **31** | **32** | **33** | **34** | **35** | **36** | **37** | **38** | **39** | **40** |
| A | D | B | A | A | A | C | B | C | C |
| **41** | **42** | **43** | **44** | **45** | **46** | **47** | **48** | **49** | **50** |
| A | B | B | C | D | B | A | A | B | B |
| **51** | **52** | **53** | **54** | **55** | **56** | **57** | **58** | **59** | **60** |
| D | C | B | D | B | C | C | C | C | C |

• • •

# 10

# ACCOUNTING USING DATABASE MANAGEMENT SYSTEM (DBMS)

## DATABASE

A database is a collection of data for generating useful and decision worthy information. It consists of an organized collection of interrelated data for one or more users, in a digital form. We find several examples of databases in our daily life like a database for school or a bank, library, bus/railway reservation system etc. Database Management System offers a logical way of storing data in a systematic manner which overcomes the several limitations such as data redundancy and inconsistency, data duplicity, difficulty in accessing data, data isolation, and data security problems. These difficulties, among others, prompted the development of database systems which represents data into the relational tables for the logical view of the database. In order to understand how data is stored in a database to produce reliable and meaningful information, let us take an hypothetical case of an accounting database for maintaining data relating to accounting transactions of a business firm named Unique Electronics.

The core of any database management system is the data itself. Another important aspect regarding DBMS is the difference between data and information.

**Data:** It is the unorganised facts which need to be compiled to form meaningful information.

**Information:** Once the data is processed and made into a structured context, it is called information.

### Types of DBMS

A collection of information which is managed such that it can be updated and easily accessed is called a database. A software package which can be used to manipulate, validate and retrieve this database is called a Database Management System.

For example, Airlines use this software package to book tickets and confirm reservations which are then managed to keep a track of the schedule.

There are majorly four types of database:

- **Network Database:** When the details of multiple members can be linked to the files of multiple owners and vice versa, it is called a network database.
- **Hierarchical Database:** When the data stored in the form of records and is connected to each other through links is called hierarchical database. Each record comprises fields and each field comprises only one value.
- **Relational Database:** When the data is organised as a set of tables comprising rows and columns with a pre-defined relationship with one another, it is called a relational database.
- **Object-oriented Database:** The information is represented as objects, with different types of relationships possible between two or more objects. Such databases use an object-oriented programming language for development.

### Components of Database Management Software

There four main components on which the working of a DBMS depends. This includes:

- **Data:** The main component is the data. The entire database is set based on the data and the information processed based on it. This data acts as a bridge between the software and hardware components of DBMS. This can further be divided into three varieties:
    - **User Data:** The actual data based on which the work is done.

- **Metadata:** This is the data of the data, *i.e.*, managing the data required to enter the information.
- **Application MetaData:** This is the structure and format of the queries.

To simplify it, in a table, the information given in each table is the User Data, the number of tables, rows and columns is the MetaData the structure we choose is the Application MetaData.

- **Hardware:** These are the general hardware devices which help us save and enter the data like hard disks, magnetic tapes, etc.
- **Software:** The software acts as a medium of communication between the user and the database. Based on the user's requirement, the database can be modified and updated. To perform operations on the data, query languages like SQL are used.
- **Users:** No function can be performed without the Users. Thus, they form the fourth most important component of DBMS. The information entered into a database is used by the User or the administrator to perform their business operations and responsibilities.

## MICROSOFT ACCESS AND ITS COMPONENTS

It is one of the popularly used database management system (DBMS) to create, store and manage database. It is also popularly called MS ACCESS.

Every component that is created using Access is an object and several such similar objects constitute a class. Access which is available with the following seven-object classes.

Each of these object classes is capable of creating their respective object replicas.

1. **Tables:** This objective class allows a database designer to create the data tables with their respective fieldnames, data types and properties.
2. **Queries:** This object is used to create the SQL compatible query statement with or without the help of graphic users Interface (GUI) to define tables. Stone data and retriene both data and information.
3. **Forms:** This object class allows the designer to create an appropriate user interface to formally interact with the back end database, defined by the tables and queries.
4. **Pages:** This object class is meant to create Data access pages, which can be posted on a website of an organisation using internet or sent via e-mail to someone of the organisation's network.
5. **Macros:** In macro programming, the objects using individual instructions called macro-oriented actions are manipulated. A macro is a list of macro-oriented actions that run as a unit. Access provides for such macro programming.
6. **Modules:** These are foundations of any application and allow the designer to create a set of programming instructions, called functions or sub-routines that can be used throughout the application.

## Designing and Creating Simple Tables, Forms, Queries and Reports in the Context of Accounting System

M.S. Access is a popular method which is used in creating, storing and managing database. It is popularly known as 'ACCESS'; Afters the following features in order to enable us to manage our data:

(*i*) Tables
(*ii*) Forms
(*iii*) Queries
(*iv*) Reports

### *Creation of Tables*

A table is created to store the data related to each type of information. Data tables are created with respective filled names, data types and properties. For accounting purposes there are five data tables:

Employees, Accounts, Vouchers, Support and Account type Tables.

### *Components of Table*

(*i*) Byte
(*ii*) Data
(*iii*) Record
(*iv*) Table

### *Selecting the Table Contents and Properties*

(*i*) Field Names
(*ii*) Field Type or Data Types
(*iii*) Field Size
(*iv*) Field Properties
(*v*) Primary Key

Three options are available to create a table:

(*a*) Create table in design view
(*b*) Create table by using Wizard
(*c*) Create table by entering data

### *Creation of Forms*

MS Access provides for creation of a form. There are two options available to create a form:

(*a*) In design view and

(*b*) By using Wizard

This can be achieved by double clicking at the data base file, immediately the window appears which is vertically devided into two parts:

- **Left Hand Side displays:** List of data base objects such as tables, queries, forms, reports, pages, macros and modules
- **Right hand side displays:** The various objects created under each of the classes of objects.

### *Creation of Queries*

An accounting information that is presented in an accounting report is generated by creating and executing various queries using DBMS. A query is a statement that gives a filtered data according to ove's conditions and specifications. A query may be created to find and retrieve the exact data the meet the specific conditions.

Various queries that can be created in MS Accesss:

(*a*) Select Queries

(*b*) Parameter Queries

(*c*) Summary Queries

(*d*) Action Queries

(*e*) SQL Queries

There are three ways to create a query

(*a*) Through Wizard

(*b*) Design view and

(*c*) SQL

### *Reports*

The outout of accounting system takes the form of accounting reports. MS Access affairs a great flexibility in designing and generating customised reports. Reports presents data in printed format. Every report is collection of related information for a particular need and purpose. The main purpose of reports is to provide output from the database on paper.

The process of generating accounting reports involves three steps:

(*i*) Designing the report

(*ii*) Identifying the accounting information queries and

(*iii*) Creating an accounting report by using such queries

There are three ways of creating a report:

**(*a*) Auto Report:** With columnar and tabular formats.

**(*b*) By using the Report Wizard:** To choose the fields from multiple tables alongwith specifications.

**(*c*) Design View:** In this method, the report is designed by assembling and embedding various components from report tool box.

## Applications of DBMS

- **Railway Reservation System:** The railway reservation system database plays a very important role by keeping record of ticket booking, train's departure time and arrival status and also gives information regarding train late to people through the database.
- **Library Management System:** Now-a-days it's become easy in the Library to track each book and maintain it because of the database. This happens because there are thousands of books in the library. It is very difficult to keep a record of all books in a copy or register. Now DBMS used to maintain all the information related to book issue dates, name of the book, author and availability of the book.
- **Banking:** Banking is one of the main applications of databases. We all know there will be a thousand transactions through banks daily and we are doing this without going to the bank. This is all possible just because of DBMS that manages all the bank transactions.
- **Universities and colleges:** Now-a-days examinations are done online. So, the universities and colleges are maintaining DBMS to store Student's registrations details, results, courses and grade all the information in the database. For example, telecommunications. Without DBMS there is no telecommunication company. DBMS is most useful to these companies to store the call details and monthly postpaid bills.
- **Credit card transactions:** The purchase of items and transactions of credit cards are made possible only by DBMS. A credit card holder has to know the importance of their information that all are secured through DBMS.
- **Social Media Sites:** By filling the required details we are able to access social media platforms. Many users sign up daily on social websites such as Facebook, Pinterest and Instagram. All the information related to the users are stored and maintained with the help of DBMS.
- **Finance:** Now-a-days there are lots of things to do with finance like storing sales, holding information and finance statement management etc. these all can be done with database systems.
- **Military:** In military areas the DBMS is playing a vital role. Military keeps records of soldiers and it has so many files that should be kept secure and safe. DBMS provides a high security to military information.
- **Online Shopping:** Now-a-days we all do Online shopping without wasting the time by going

shopping with the help of DBMS. The products are added and sold only with the help of DBMS like Purchase information, invoice bills and payment.

- **Human Resource Management:** The management keeps records of each employee's salary, tax and work through DBMS.
- **Manufacturing:** Manufacturing companies make products and sell them on a daily basis. To keep records of all those details DBMS is used.
- **Airline Reservation system:** Just like the railway reservation system, airlines also need DBMS to keep records of flights arrival, departure and delay status.

So finally, we can clearly conclude that the DBMS is playing a very important role in each and every field.

## ADVANTAGES AND DISADVANTAGES OF DATABASE SYSTEMS

### Advantages of Database Systems

The DBMS (Database Management System) is preferred ever the conventional file processing system due to the following advantages:

#### *1. Controlling Data Redundancy*

In the conventional file processing system, every user group maintains its own files for handling its data files. This may lead to:

- Duplication of same data in different files.
- Wastage of storage space, since duplicated data is stored.
- Errors may be generated due to updation of the same data in different files.
- Time in entering data again and again is wasted.
- Computer Resources are needlessly used.
- It is very difficult to combine information.

#### *2. Elimination of Inconsistency*

In the file processing system information is duplicated throughout the system. So changes made in one file may be necessary be carried over to another file. This may lead to inconsistent data. So we need to remove this duplication of data in multiple file to eliminate inconsistency.

#### *3. Better service to the users*

- A DBMS is often used to provide better services to the users. In conventional system, availability of information is often poor, since it normally difficult to obtain information in a timely manner because our existing systems are not capable to produce the same.
- Once several conventional systems are combined to form one centralized database, the availability of information and its updateness is likely to improve since the data can now be shared and DBMS makes it easy to respond to anticipated information requests.
- Centralizing the data in the database also means that user can obtain new and combined information easily that would have been impossible to obtain otherwise.
- Also use of DBMS should allow users that don't know programming to interact with the data more easily, unlike file processing system where the programmer may need to write new programs to meet every new demand.

#### *4. Flexibility of the System is Improved*

- Since changes are often necessary to the contents of the data stored in any system, these changes are made more easily in a centralized database than in a conventional system.
- Applications programs need not to be changed on changing the data in the database.

#### *5. Integrity can be improved*

- Since data of the organization using database approach is centralized and would be used by a number of users at a time, it is essential to enforce integrity-constraints.
- In the conventional systems because the data is duplicated in multiple files so updating or changes may sometimes lead to entry of incorrect data in some files wherever it is applicable.

#### *6. Standards can be enforced*

- Standards are easier to enforce in database systems because all the data in database is access through centralized DBMS.
- Here standards may relate to the naming of data, structure of data, format of the data etc.
- Standardizing stored data formats is usually desirable for the purpose of data interchange or migration between systems.

#### *7. Security can be improved*

- In conventional systems, applications are developed in an adhoc manner. Often different system of an organization would access different components of the operational data, in such an environment enforcing security can be quiet difficult.

#### *8. Organization's requirement can be easily identified*

- All organizations have sections and departments and each of these units often consider the work of their unit as the most important and therefore consider their need as the most important.

- Once a database has been setup with centralized control, it will be necessary to identify organization's requirement and to balance the needs of the competition units.

### *9. Data Model must be developed*

- Perhaps the most important advantage of setting up of database system is the requirement that an overall data model for an organization be build. In conventional systems, it is more likely that files will be designed as per need of particular applications demand.
- The overall view is often not considered. Building an overall view of an organization's data is usual cost effective in the long terms.

### *10. Provides backup and Recovery*

- Centralizing a database provides the schemes such as recovery and backups from the failures including disk crash, power failures, software errors which may help the database to recover from the inconsistent state to the state that existed prior to the occurrence of the failure, though methods are very complex.

## Disadvantages of Database Systems

The following are the disadvantages of Database Systems

1. **Database Complexity:** The design of the database system is complex, difficult and is very time consuming task to perform.
2. **Substantial hardware and software start-up costs:** Huge amount of investment is needed to setup the required hardware and the softwares needed to run those applications.
3. **Damage to database affects virtually all applications programs:** If one part of the database is corrupted or damaged because of the hardware or software failure, since we don't have many versions of the file, all the application programs which are dependent on this database are implicitly affected.
4. **Extensive conversion costs in moving form a file-based system to a database system:** If you are currently working on file based system and need to upgrade it to database system, then large amount of cost is incurred in purchasing different tools, adopting different techniques as per the requirement.
5. **Initial training required for all programmers and user:** Large amount of human efforts, the time and cost is needed to train the end users and application programmers in order to get used to the database systems.

## MULTIPLE CHOICE QUESTIONS

**1.** The data dictionary of a D2BMS is called:
A. DBMS directory B. DBMS Catalog
C. System Catalogue D. All of the above

**2.** __________ implement specifications developed by the system analysts in the form of programs?
A. Application analysts
B. Application Programmers
C. System analysts
D. All of the above

**3.** __________ is used to specify the user views and their mapping to the conceptual schema?
A. Data definition language
B. Data Manipulation language
C. View definition language
D. All of the above

**4.** _______ presents users with the list of options.
A. Menu-based interface
B. Form-based interface
C. Graphical user interface
D. All of the above

**5.** _______ use both forms and menus.
A. Menu-based interface
B. Form-based interface
C. Graphical user interface
D. All of the above

**6.** System contains privileged commands only for:
A. System analysts B. Parametric users
C. DBA staff D. All of the above

**7.** __________ is combinations of both object oriented concepts and relational concepts.
A. Object-oriented model
B. Relational model
C. Object-relational model
D. All of the above

**8.** __________ supports applications like image retrieval, searching, multimedia etc.
A. Object-oriented model
B. Relational model
C. Object-relational model
D. All of the above

**9.** DML commands from an application program written in a host programming language is extracted from a ________.
A. Programmer
B. DBA
C. System analysts
D. Pre-compiler

**10.** Primary storage devices are ______ storage.
A. Volatile B. Non-volatile
C. Both (A) and (B) D. None of these

**11.** Secondary storage devices are ______ storage.
A. Volatile B. Non-volatile
C. Both (A) and (B) D. None of these

**12.** Disks are made up of:
A. Glass material B. Plastic material
C. Magnetic material D. None of these

**13.** For disk packs of magnetic disks, the tracks with the same diameter on the various surfaces are called:
A. Parallel tracks B. Surface tracks
C. Disk tracks D. Cylinder

**14.** The data stored on the same cylinder can be retrieved __________ than if it distributed among different cylinders.
A. Faster B. Medium
C. Slower D. None of these

**15.** The hardware address of a block contains:
A. Surface number B. Track number
C. Block number D. All of the above

**16.** The seek time and rotational delay are ______ than the block transfer time.
A. Larger B. Medium
C. Smaller D. None of these

**17.** ______________ are sequential access devices.
A. Magnetic Disks B. Magnetic tapes
C. Both (A) and (B) D. None of these

**18.** __________ permits continuous reading and writing on consecutive disk bocks.
A. Searching B. Buffering
C. Double buffering D. None of these

**19.** A file is a sequence of:
A. Blocks B. Tracks
C. Records D. None of these

**20.** Disadvantage of ______________ is that we must use linear search or binary search to locate the desired record?
A. Direct file organization
B. Sequential file organization
C. Both (A) and (B)
D. None of these

**21.** Insert can violate any of the four types of constraints:
A. Modify Constraints, Key Constraints, Entity Constraints, Referential Integrity
B. Domain Constraints, Key Constraints, Entity Constraints, Referential Integrity
C. Domain Constraints, Key Constraints, Modify Constraints, Referential Integrity
D. Domain Constraints, Key Constraints, Entity Constraints, Modify Constraints

**22.** Amongst the following which are the types of attributes?
A. Entity Attributes, Composite Attributes, Derived Attributes, Null Attributes
B. Simple Attributes, Entity Attributes, Derived Attributes, Null Attributes
C. Simple Attributes, Composite Attributes, Derived Attributes, Null Attributes
D. Simple Attributes, Composite Attributes, Entity Attributes, Null Attributes

**23.** When two transactions run concurrently types of problems encounter are:
A. Data delete Problem, Dirty read problem, Incorrect summary problem
B. Lost update problem, Dirty read problem, Incorrect summary problem
C. Lost update problem, Data delete Problem, Incorrect summary problem
D. Lost update problem, Dirty read problem, Data delete Problem

**24.** Locking Technique for Concurrency Control are:
A. Binary Locks, Shared Locks, Exclusive Locks
B. Decimal Locks, Shared Locks, Exclusive Locks
C. Binary Locks, Decimal Locks, Exclusive Locks
D. Binary Locks, Shared Locks, Decimal Locks

**25.** There are three types of fragmentation:
A. Cross Fragmentation, Vertical Fragmentation, Mixed Fragmentation
B. Horizontal Fragmentation, Cross Fragmentation, Mixed Fragmentation
C. Horizontal Fragmentation, Vertical Fragmentation, Cross Fragmentation
D. Horizontal Fragmentation, Vertical Fragmentation, Mixed Fragmentation

**26.** Amongst the following persons which person group belongs to a DBMS?
A. DBA, Database Designers, End Users, System Analysts, Tool Developer
B. DBA, Database Designers, Project Manager, System Analysts, Tool Developer
C. DBA, Database Designers, Application Programmer, System Analysts, Tool Developer
D. DBA, Database Designers, End Users, System Analysts, Application Programmer

**27.** The name of the very first microprocessor chip available commercially was:
A. Intel 4004 B. Intel 639
C. Intel 308 D. Motorola 33

**28.** A collection of related data:
A. Information B. Valuable Information
C. Database D. Metadata

**29.** DBMS manages the interaction between ______ and database.
A. Users B. Clients
C. End Users D. Stake Holders

**30.** IMS stands for:
A. Information Mastering System
B. Instruction Management System
C. Instruction Manipulating System
D. Information Management System

**31.** A model developed by Hammer and Mc Leod in 1981:
A. SDM B. OODBM
C. DDM D. RDM

**32.** DBMS is a set of ______ to access the data.
A. Codes B. Programs
C. Information D. Metadata

**33.** Which of the following isn't a level of abstraction?
A. physical B. logical
C. user D. view

**34.** A level that describes how a record is stored:
A. physical B. logical
C. user D. view

**35.** The ______ level helps application programs hide the details of data types.
A. physical B. logical
C. user D. view

**36.** A logical structure of the database:
A. Schema B. Attribute
C. Parameter D. Instance

**37.** The actual content in the database at a particular point:
A. Schema B. Attribute
C. Parameter D. Instance

**38.** Which of the following is not an object-based logical model?
A. ER B. Network
C. Semantic D. Functional

**39.** SQL is ______ .
A. Relational B. Network
C. IMS D. Hierarchical

**40.** A level that describes data stored in database and the relationships among the data:
A. physical B. logical
C. user D. view

**41.** Ted is creating a database for several customers. What is the data type for the field customer name?
A. Yes/No B. Data
C. Number D. Currency

**42.** A secondary key is:
A. A second way to open the Lab door
B. A second table in a database
C. Two columns with the same data in a database
D. A candidate key until the primary key is selected

**43.** Table Rows are called:
A. fields B. records
C. table D. entry

**44.** What does this SQL line mean: WERE PUPIL.candidate Number = SUBJECT.candidateNumber?
A. Makes a link between the PUPIL and SUBJECT tables
B. 2 Candidates must be equal to each other
C. PUPIL and SUBJECT are fields in the candidate Number table
D. Ask your teacher if you do not know

**45.** Which datatype is suitable for your date of birth?
A. TEXT B. NUMBER
C. DATE D. TIME

**46.** In a database form, the blanks in which information is entered are called:
A. Fields B. Record
C. Query D. Database

**47.** Which of the following is NOT an example of a database?
A. telephone book
B. real estate listing
C. online library catalog
D. DVD

**48.** Mr. Cheek needs a printout of students arranged by age from oldest to youngest. This is an example of which type of sort?
A. Ascending
B. Descending
C. Primary Sort
D. Secondary Sort

**49.** Which are disadvantages of distributed databases?
A. If data is stored and updated in more than one place there is an increased chance of data inconsistency
B. Increased costs due to expensive communication lines
C. There are security issues if sensitive personal data is being transferred
D. The company is not dependent on one central database

**50.** Which of the following is DDL command?
A. Insert B. Roll back
C. Create D. Update

**51.** A graphical interface that allows users to query a database by filling in information on the form:
A. Table B. Query
C. Form D. Report

**52.** A collection of fields related or associated with a focal point is called?
A. File B. Database
C. Field D. Record

**53.** I am a snapshot in time of the database that can be printed, sorted and grouped. I may be printed to look at monthly sales:
A. Form B. Report
C. Query D. Filter

**54.** What is an example of a database?
A. My best friend B. Play Station
C. The Television D. Phone Contacts

**55.** Find out the templates available in Access:
A. Contacts B. Nutrition Tracking
C. Call Tracker D. All of the above

**56.** This feature ensures records deleted in the Parent table will result in any related records deleted in the Child table:
A. Referential Integrity B. Cascade Delete
C. Cascade Updated D. Cascade amend

**57.** An element of ERD where anything about which data are to be collected and stored:
A. entity B. attribute
C. relationship D. constraint

**58.** All of the following could be attributes of an ENTITY called PERSON, except which one?
A. Gender B. Natacha Hansen
C. Weight D. Haircolour

**59.** Which feature of a DBMS enables a database to be interrogated based on specific criteria?
A. Query B. Report
C. Form D. Relationship

**60.** Another name for a record:
A. Field B. Table
C. Tuple D. Attribute

**61.** ______ offers the ability to query the data and insert, alter and delete tuples.
A. Transaction Control Language (TCL)
B. Data Control Langauge (DCL)
C. Data Definition Language (DDL)
D. Data Manipulation Language (DML)

**62.** We can add or remove the user IDs using which of these fixed roles?
A. db_setupadmin B. db_securityadmin
C. db_accessadmin D. db_sysadmin

**63.** Section (sect name, wing, expenses) and Student (student_ID, name, sec name, fees).

Here in both of these relations, the sect_name attribute appears commonly. In this case, using common attributes in the relation schema is a way in which we can relate the ______ relations.
A. Tuple of common
B. Attributes of common
C. Attributes of distinct
D. Tuple of distinct

**64.** Fifth Normal form is concerned with:
A. Join dependency
B. Domain-key
C. Multivalued dependency
D. Functional dependency

**65.** The ______ system does not require a password to travel across the internet.
A. Response B. Challenge-response
C. Manipulation D. Readable

**66.** When recovering from a failure:
A. examination of each pair of physical blocks occurs
B. examination of a specified pair of physical blocks occurs
C. examination of the first pair of physical blocks occurs
D. None of the above

**67.** The Optical disk technology utilises:
A. RAID B. A laser beam
C. DAT D. Helical scanning

**68.** The node pointing towards another node in a B+ tree is known as:
A. External node B. Leaf node
C. Internal node D. Final node

**69.** A transaction enters into its ______ state when it finishes the final statement.
A. Abort state
B. Partially committed state
C. Committed state
D. Active state

**70.** In crabbing, the protocol locking goes:
A. down the tree, back up
B. up the tree, back down
C. down the tree, releases
D. up the tree, releases

## ANSWERS

| 1 | 2 | 3 | 4 | 5 | 6 | 7 | 8 | 9 | 10 |
|---|---|---|---|---|---|---|---|---|---|
| C | B | C | A | C | C | C | C | D | A |
| **11** | **12** | **13** | **14** | **15** | **16** | **17** | **18** | **19** | **20** |
| B | C | D | A | D | A | B | C | C | B |
| **21** | **22** | **23** | **24** | **25** | **26** | **27** | **28** | **29** | **30** |
| B | C | B | A | D | A | A | C | C | D |
| **31** | **32** | **33** | **34** | **35** | **36** | **37** | **38** | **39** | **40** |
| A | B | C | A | D | A | D | B | A | B |
| **41** | **42** | **43** | **44** | **45** | **46** | **47** | **48** | **49** | **50** |
| B | D | B | A | C | A | D | B | A | C |
| **51** | **52** | **53** | **54** | **55** | **56** | **57** | **58** | **59** | **60** |
| C | D | B | D | D | B | A | B | A | C |
| **61** | **62** | **63** | **64** | **65** | **66** | **67** | **68** | **69** | **70** |
| D | C | D | A | B | A | A | C | B | A |

• • •

# 11

# ACCOUNTING APPLICATIONS OF ELECTRONIC SPREADSHEET

## ELECTRONIC SPREADSHEET

Electronic Spreadsheet is a combination of rows and columns. Visually, the spreadsheet looks like any other matrix with rows and columns. It is also known as a worksheet. This worksheet is so large that the human eye cannot view all its rows and columns at a point of time. Therefore, user focuses on few rows and columns and keeps changing the focus to the required part of the worksheet, as and when required. It is normally used for calculations and comparison of numerical or financial data for arriving at the desired information for reporting.

An electronic spreadsheet is a computer program that allows the user to add and process data. The concept of electronic spreadsheet can well be understood with the help of MS Excel, which is one of the MS office software.

### Basics and Features of Spreadsheet

A spreadsheet is characterized by certain features, given as under:

- **Grid:** By definition, a spreadsheet is seen as grid structured by number of rows and columns. Each row is sequentially assigned number such as 1, 2, 3.... And every column is assigned an alphabet for identification. First 26 columns are assigned alphabets beginning A to Z and thereafter, the columns begins with AA followed by AB till the last column is assigned alphabets.
- **Element:** Each element of spreadsheet is defined by a point of intersection between a particular row and column. It is therefore, addressed by referring to the relevant row and column.
- **Lens View:** Spreadsheet allows the user to view and concentrate on a limited number of rows and columns to work with.
- **Functions:** Spreadsheet is supported by a large number of functions capable of performing difficult and lengthy calculations in fractions of seconds.
- **Formatting:** Spreadsheet has text formatting capabilities. This enables the generated report to be saved, printed and exported to other applications for use.
- **Save, Print and Export:** Spreadsheet is saved as a file so that it can be opened for additions and alterations as per the need arisen. It can also be printed by selecting a part of the entire sheet. It can also be sent to mail recipient as an attachment.

## MICROSOFT EXCEL

### *Starting EXCEL*

To start up the program:

1. Open the Windows **Start** menu
2. Choose **All Programs** then **Microsoft Office** followed by Microsoft Office Excel 2007

**Tip:** To create a shortcut to this software on the Desktop, right click on **Microsoft Office Excel 2007** then choose Send To followed by Desktop (create shortcut).

we'll then be able to load Excel using the icon on the Desktop.

### *The Excel Screen*

We will then be presented with an empty worksheet, as below, ready to enter your data:

Let us familiarize some of the key commands and resources in Excel Window:

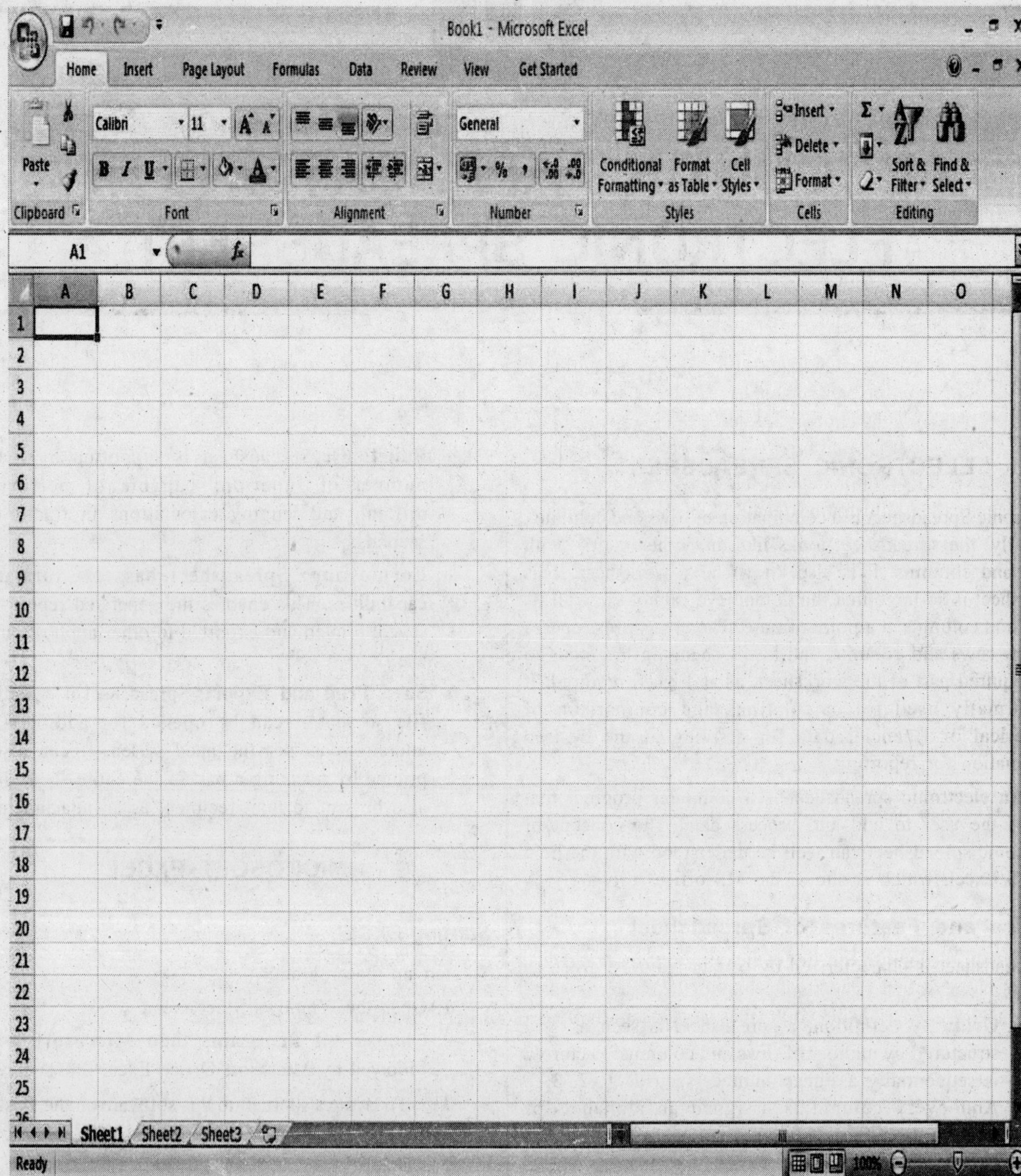


### *The Microsoft Office Button*

It is the button in the upper-left corner of the Excel Window. When you click on the button, it displays a menu that can be used to create a new workbook, open an existing workbook, save a workbook, print and perform many other tasks.

### *The Quick Access Toolbar*

It is present next to the Microsoft Office Button on the top. It provides you access to the commands you frequently use. By default Following appear on the Quick Access Toolbar:

- **Save:** To save your file (you may also press keyboard button (Ctrl + S).
- **Undo:** To rollback the action that you last took (Ctrl + Z).
- **Redo:** To reapply the action you rolled back or to repeat an action (Ctrl + Y).

### The Title Bar

It is next to the Quick Access toolbar at the top. It displays the title of the workbook on which you are currently working. By default, the first new workbook is named as Book1. For each additional workbook you open, the number increases by one. You may save the workbooks by any legal filename you want.

### The Ribbon

The Ribbon is the panel at the top portion of the document, right below the Title Bar. To begin with it has following seven tabs:

- **Home:** It has basic commands for creating, formatting and editing the spreadsheets. It has controls for working with the clipboard, fonts, alignment, number, styles, cells and editing.
- **Insert:** It has commands for inserting tables, pictures, shapes, other illustrations, links, charts, header, footer, etc.
- **Page Layout:** The commands here help to set the layout of the spreadsheet, apply a theme to set the overall look, set the margins, orientation, size, backgrounds, etc.
- **Formulas:** It has commands that help you use different formulas and functions.
- **Data:** Has commands to import, query, view data from external sources, sort, filter or manage data.
- **Review:** Has commands to add comments, protect sheet, protect workbook, share workbook, etc.
- **View:** Helps to change the display of the worksheet area.

Besides these basic tabs, additional tabs appear from time to time, depending on the context we are working in. These tabs are called contextual tabs. For example, if you select a chart, a Chart Tools contextual tab appears that has commands to help we design and format the chart. These contextual tabs appear in a different colour to make them easy to spot.

The commands on each tab are organized into groups. Hence, a group is a collection of logically related command buttons that you can use to manage a Worksheet. Commonly used featuresare displayed on the Ribbon and additional options can be accessed through the dialog box launcher at the bottom-right corner of each group.

### The Formula Bar

The formula bar is divided into three sections:

- **Name Box:** Located on the left most side of the formula bar, it displays the address of the current cell.
- **Formula Bar Buttons:** Middle section of the formula bar with indented circle on the left (to increase or decrease the size of the name box) and function wizard (labeled fx) on the right. When you start entering data in the cell, Cancel (*) and Enter (^) buttons also appear.
- **Cell Contents:** Right side of the formula bar displays the cell entries.
- **The Worksheet Area:** The worksheet area displays all the cells. It is in the cells that you enter, format or edit your data.

### The Status Bar

The Status Bar appears at the very bottom of the Excel window and provides such information as the sum, average, minimum, and maximum value of selected numbers. We can change what displays on the Status bar by right-clicking on the Status Bar and selecting the options you want from the Customize Status Bar menu. You click a menu item to select it. You click it again to deselect it. A check mark next to an item means the item is selected.

## MULTIPLE CHOICE QUESTIONS

**1.** In a spreadsheet, letters are used to represent ______ .

A. Cells B. Rows
C. Columns D. Blocks

**2.** A numeric data analysis tool that allows us to create a computerized ledger:

A. Word processing package
B. Mathematical package
C. Graphics package
D. Spread Sheet Package

**3.** Spreadsheets cannot:

A. do calculations B. create graphics
C. plot graphs D. plot charts

**4.** An easier way to set up complicated calculations:

A. Functions B. Fractions
C. Booleans D. Fractions

**5.** ______________ help us to see patterns.

A. Charts B. Graphs
C. Spreadsheets D. Calculations

**6.** In a computer spreadsheet, to choose built in function we used is:

A. defined function B. function finder
C. built in function D. paste function

7. In a computer spreadsheet, tool used to construct formulas is called:
A. formula bar B. filter
C. auditing toolbar D. format printer

8. Computer spreadsheet cell that is highlighted with a heavy border is a:
A. active cell
B. cell containing a formula
C. locked cell
D. cell

9. Vertical dimension of a computer spreadsheet is called:
A. row B. column
C. record D. field

10. Which of the following isn't a part of a spreadsheet?
A. row number B. column number
C. column letter D. cell address

11. The placement of information within a cell at the left edge, right edge, or centered is:
A. Indentation B. Placement
C. Identification D. Alignment

12. In a computer spreadsheet, block of cells is called:
A. range B. column
C. workbook D. function

13. In computer spreadsheet, a workbook is a group of:
A. many rows
B. many columns
C. worksheet
D. least number of column

14. Faster way to change horizontal alignment in a computer document is:
A. align left B. center
C. align right D. all of these

15. A block of cells is called:
A. Function B. Calculation
C. Formula D. Range

16. Title bar in MS-Excel displays name of the:
A. worksheet B. workbook
C. formula D. location

17. In a computer, cell's address that is included in range C5:E7 is:
A. C8 B. D6
C. E4 D. D9

18. In a computer, correct row address is:
A. AA B. 25
C. 3B D. C5

19. In a computer spreadsheet, a pre programmed Formula is basically a:
A. function B. cell
C. graph D. rang

20. In a computer, page orientation is changed through:
A. page setup dialog box
B. setup dialog box
C. paper dialog box
D. print dialog box

21. In a computer, graphics representation of data is named as:
A. chart B. graphics
C. picture D. figure

22. Which of the following isn't a part of a spreadsheet?
A. row number B. column number
C. column letter D. cell address

23. The cell that is in use:
A. Active cell B. Highlighted cell
C. Main cell D. Formula cell

24. A change in the appearance of a value or label in a cell:
A. Alteration B. Format
C. Indentation D. Design

25. An entry in a spreadsheet cell representing wages or test scores is most likely a:
A. label B. value
C. formula D. calculation

26. Computer spreadsheet capability to allow a pie chart to be generated from data in spreadsheet cells is termed as:
A. decoration B. data appearance
C. functions D. charting

27. In a computer, element which is not a part of chart is:
A. plot area B. fill handler
C. series D. chart area

28. In a computer spreadsheet, first part of number format describes:
A. text values B. negative number
C. positive number D. zero values

29. Cell in a computer spreadsheet that contain a formula or function will show:
A. formula or function
B. cell's address
C. resulting display value
D. range

30. In a computer spreadsheet, function which is used to count numbers of entries in given range is called:
A. length B. counter
C. counting D. count

31. Main window in a computer spreadsheet is called:
A. work sheet B. work
C. account book D. work book

32. In a computer, fourth part of number format describes:
A. text values B. positive number
C. negative number D. zero values

33. In a computer spreadsheet, each cell contain a:
A. formula B. value
C. label D. all of these

34. In a computer spreadsheet, SUM, AVERAGE, MIN and MAX are examples of:
A. functions B. calculations
C. formulas D. relative addressing

35. Actual working area of computer's Microsoft Excel is:
A. worksheet B. workbook
C. notebook D. None of these

36. An entry in a spreadsheet cell like "Monthly Wages" or "Final Approval Rating" would most likely to be a:
A. calculation B. value
C. label D. formula

37. In a computer spreadsheet, number of arguments in SQRT function are:
A. equal to column no B. equal to range
C. one D. two

38. The tool used for constructing a formula is called:
A. Formula Filter B. Formula Painter
C. Formula Bar D. Formula Wizard

39. Which was the first electronic Spreadsheet?
A. Slide rule
B. Software
C. Quantum Pro
D. Visible calculator

40. Spreadsheets are made up of:
A. Rows B. Columns
C. Cells D. Rows and columns

41. Which company has introduced **Quattro pro**?
A. Microsoft International
B. Borland International
C. Sun Micro Systems
D. AT&T Corporation

42. 4 VisiCalc is a:
A. Analysis B. Inventory control
C. Financial analysis D. Program

43. StarCalc is a powerful:
A. Table B. Project
C. Spreadsheet program D. Worksheet program

44. Who invented VisiCalc for Apple?
A. Dan Bricklin and Bob Frankston
B. Bob Frankston
C. J.H. Biurd
D. Dan Bricklin

45. Which one of the following is a Spreadsheet?
A. Star Office Writer B. Star Office
C. Star Office Calc D. Star Office base

46. Graphic representations of numbers are known as:
A. Cells B. Charts
C. Bar diagrams D. Graphs

47. How many columns are there in a VisiCalc Spreadsheet?
A. 62 B. 63
C. 64 D. 72

48. How many icons appear in the floating tool bar?
A. 3 B. 5
C. 6 D. 7

49. Maximum width of a cell is:
A. 128 characters B. 240 characters
C. 480 characters D. 1024 characters

50. Values, entered in a cell, are always:
A. Centred B. Left aligned
C. Right aligned D. Not aligned at all

51. To create a worksheet, it is:
A. Not important to be knowledgeable about the task to be done
B. Important to understand a programming language
C. Important to be knowledgeable about the spreadsheet
D. Both (A) and (B)

52. If cell D1 contains 20, cell D2 contains 30, and cell D3 contains the formula +D1+D2, then cell D3 display 50. If cell D1 has its value changed to 12, then cell D3 will now display:
A. +D1+D2 B. 12
C. 30 D. 42

53. In the Subtotal dialog box, the __________ box is used to select the column on which you want to add the Subtotal to.
A. group by B. consolidate by
C. filter by D. update by

54. In order to group sheets, while holding the _________ key, click on the Sheets tab you want to group.
A. Alt B. Shift
C. Ctrl D. Tab

55. The comments that are added while creating a scenario is displayed in the ___________ while using scenario.
A. preview pane B. navigator box
C. comment window D. None of these

56. In Goal seek dialog box, in the ___________ we enter the reference of the cell that contains the value to be changed.
A. variable cell B. changing cell
C. modifying cell D. replacing cell

57. Default name of first scenario created in Sheet1 of Calc is:
A. Sheet_1_Scenario B. Sheet_Scenario_1
C. Sheet1_Scenario_1 D. None of these

58. We can rename a new sheet in Calc:
A. After inserting a new sheet
B. While inserting a new sheet
C. Both (A) and (B)
D. None of these

59. To start the macro recorder, which of the following command is used?
A. Tools → Macros → Record Macro
B. Tools → Record → Record Macro
C. Data → Macros → Record
D. None of these

60. Cell referencing can be done by using a as well:
A. keyboard, windows menu
B. keyboard, mouse
C. windows menu, mouse
D. None of these

61. To create the link from one document to another, both the documents should be:
A. opened B. closed
C. Both (A) and (B) D. None of these

62. In case, another user is trying to save the shared worksheet and resolve conflicts, you see a message that the shared spreadsheet file is due to a merge in progress.
A. stopped B. locked
C. Both (A) and (B) D. None of these

63. Internally for each recorded macro, some code is generated, which is stored inside ________ and ____________ clause.
A. Sub, End Sub
B. Section, End Section
C. Function, End Function
D. None of these

64. To create a hyperlink to a webpage, FTP server of Telnet connection, click on the icon:
A. internet explorer B. Internet
C. Hyperlink D. Document

65. Aparna has made four spreadsheets containing marks of 5 subjects of all the students of her class. She has to prepare a sheet that contains the total marks of all the subjects of her class. Name the option that can be used to perform this task:
A. Subtotal B. Average
C. Goal Seek D. Scenario

## ANSWERS

| 1 | 2 | 3 | 4 | 5 | 6 | 7 | 8 | 9 | 10 |
|---|---|---|---|---|---|---|---|---|---|
| A | D | B | A | A | D | A | A | B | B |
| **11** | **12** | **13** | **14** | **15** | **16** | **17** | **18** | **19** | **20** |
| D | A | C | D | D | B | B | B | A | A |
| **21** | **22** | **23** | **24** | **25** | **26** | **27** | **28** | **29** | **30** |
| A | B | A | B | B | D | B | C | C | C |
| **31** | **32** | **33** | **34** | **35** | **36** | **37** | **38** | **39** | **40** |
| D | A | D | A | A | C | C | C | D | D |
| **41** | **42** | **43** | **44** | **45** | **46** | **47** | **48** | **49** | **50** |
| B | A | C | A | C | B | B | D | B | C |
| **51** | **52** | **53** | **54** | **55** | **56** | **57** | **58** | **59** | **60** |
| C | D | A | C | B | A | C | C | A | B |
| **61** | **62** | **63** | **64** | **65** | | | | | |
| A | B | A | B | A | | | | | |

• • •

# 12

# MISCELLANEOUS QUESTIONS

1. Profits can be fraudulently inflated by:
   A. Suppression of sales returns
   B. Treating capital expenditure as revenue
   C. Overestimation of liabilities
   D. Omission of prepaid expenses

2. A credit sale of goods to Shivendra should be debited to:
   A. Sales Account B. Goods Account
   C. Shivendra Account D. Purchase Account

3. Which of the following assets does not depreciate?
   A. Machinery and equipment
   B. Patents
   C. Land
   D. Furniture

4. Valuing the stock in trade at market price or cost price which is less is an example of the convention of:
   A. consistency B. disclosure
   C. knowing the value D. None of these

5. Double entry principle means:
   A. Having debit for every credit and similarly credit for each debit.
   B. Writing all the entries twice in the book.
   C. Maintaining the double account for all business transactions.
   D. Writing two times the same entry.

6. A sale of goods to Vaibhav Deep for cash should be debited to:
   A. Vaibhav's A/c B. Cash A/c
   C. Sale of goods A/c D. None of these

7. A withdrawal of cash from business by the proprietor of the firm should be credited to:
   A. Capital Account B. Cash Account
   C. Drawing Account D. Proprietor's Account

8. The preparation of a trial balance helps in:
   A. Locating errors of principle
   B. Locating errors of omission
   C. Locating clerical errors
   D. Locating compensatory errors

9. A cheque received and deposited in the bank on the same day is recorded in the:
   A. Cash column of the cash book
   B. Bank column of the cash book
   C. Credited in the cash book
   D. Debited in the cash book

10. Petty cash may be used to pay:
    A. the expenses relating to postages and conveyance
    B. salaries and wages to the final staff
    C. for the purchase of furniture and fittings
    D. None of these

11. A reserve is charge against:
    A. Trading account
    B. Profit and loss account
    C. Profit and loss appropriation account
    D. None of these

12. The payment side of cash book is under cost by ₹ 200 when overdraft as per pass book is the starting point:
    A. ₹ 200 will be deducted
    B. ₹ 200 will be added
    C. No effect will be in the pass book
    D. None of these

13. An amount of ₹ 300 is debited twice in the pass book when overdraft as per the cash book is the starting point:
    A. ₹ 600 will be added
    B. ₹ 500 will be deducted
    C. No effect will be in the cash book
    D. None of these

**14.** Expenditure incurred by a publisher for acquiring copy rights is a:
A. Capital expenditure
B. Revenue expenditure
C. Deferred revenue expenditure
D. None of these

**15.** Immediately after purchasing a new truck ₹ 1,000 is paid to have the name of the company and other advertising material painted on the truck. This ₹ 1,000 is a:
A. Capital expenditure
B. Deferred revenue expenditure
C. Revenue expenditure
D. None of these

**16.** A return Inwards book is kept to record:
A. return of goods sold
B. returns of anything purchased
C. returns of goods purchased
D. returns of anything sold

**17.** Bill Receivable Book is a part of the:
A. Ledger
B. Balance sheet
C. Journal
D. Profit and Loss Account

**18.** A sales of ₹ 2000 wrongly entered in the purchase book:
A. decreases the gross profit by ₹ 2000
B. increases the gross profit by ₹ 2000
C. increases the gross profit by ₹ 4000
D. None of these

**19.** Which of the following are current assets?
A. Bank loan for three years
B. Account receivable
C. Long-term investments
D. Debentures sinking fund investments

**20.** Insurance unexpires accounts is a:
A. Real account B. Personal account
C. Nominal account D. None of these

**21.** Goodwill account is a:
A. Nominal Account B. Real Account
C. Personal Account D. None of these

**22.** Bank overdraft account is a:
A. Personal Account B. Real Account
C. Nominal Account D. All of these

**23.** Contingent liability is shown due to:
A. Convention of full disclosure
B. Convention of conservatism
C. Convention of materiality
D. Dual aspect concept

**24.** Which item is shown on the debit side of a trial balance?
A. Rent outstanding
B. Prepaid Expenses
C. Purchases
D. Excess of income over expenses by the firm

**25.** Purchase for office furniture on account is recorded in:
A. General Journal B. Cash book
C. Purchase book D. Sales book

**26.** Sales on account is recorded in:
A. Cash book B. Journal
C. Sales book D. General Journal

**27.** The credit balance in the bank account is:
A. Capital B. a liability
C. an asset D. an expense

**28.** Cash sales are recorded in:
A. Sales book B. Cash book
C. Journal D. Purchase book

**29.** Error of commission do not permit:
A. The trial balance to agree
B. Correct the total of balance sheet
C. Correct totalling of trial balance
D. None of these

**30.** An item of ₹ 72 has been debited to a personal account as ₹ 27, is an error of:
A. Commission B. Omission
C. Principle D. None of these

**31.** Sales to Shyam of ₹ 500 not recorded in the books would affect:
A. Shyam's account B. Cash account
C. Sales account D. None of these

**32.** Which of the following accounts is increased by credit entries?
A. Bank Overdraft B. Purchases Account
C. Goodwill Account D. Sales Return Account

**33.** Profit and loss account of business shows the:
A. Net profit earned
B. Gross profit earned
C. Balance of all accounts
D. Capital employed in business

**34.** If a receipt of ₹ 200 from Rajesh out debtor has not been recorded in the books the profit would show:
A. an increase of ₹ 200
B. a decrease of ₹ 200
C. neither an increase nor a decrease
D. None of these

**35.** Closing stock is valued at:
A. Market price
B. Cost price

C. Cost price or market price whichever is lower
D. Cost price or market price whichever is higher

**36.** Unearned income account is:
A. an liability B. a liability
C. an expernse D. an income

**37.** Depreciation is provided on:
A. Current Assets B. Liquid Assets
C. Fictitious Assets D. Fixed Assets

**38.** A bill of exchange is drawn by a:
A. Creditor B. Debtor
C. Shareholder D. Debenture holder

**39.** Bills receivable account is:
A. a revenue Account B. an expense Account
C. a liability Account D. None of these

**40.** When goods are purchased for the joint venture out of joint bank A/C the amount is debited to:
A. Joint bank A/C B. Joint venture A/C
C. Purchases account D. None of these

**41.** Bills receivable endorsed are debited to:
A. Debtor's Account
B. Creditor's Account
C. Bills payable Account
D. Bills receivable Account

**42.** Subscription received during the year were ₹ 800 for the current year. ₹ 100 for the previous year and ₹ 100 for the next year. In the receipts and payments account the receipts from subscriptions would appear at:
A. ₹ 700 B. ₹ 800
C. ₹ 900 D. ₹ 1000

**43.** Any donation received for a specific purpose is a:
A. Liability B. Assets
C. Revenue receipts D. Capital receipts

**44.** The convention of conservatism will have the effect of:
A. Over statement of assets
B. Under statement of assets
C. Under statement of liabilities
D. Under statement of provision for bad and doubtful debts

**45.** Expenditure incurred by a publisher for acquiring copyright is a:
A. Capital expenditure
B. Revenue expenditure
C. Deferred revenue expenditure
D. None of these

**46.** Expenses incurred on resarch and development is an example of:
A. Capital expenditure
B. Revenue expenditure
C. Deferred revenue expenditure
D. None of these

**47.** Amount spent on increasing the seating capacity in a cinema hall is:
A. Capital expenditure
B. Revenue expenditure
C. Deferred revenue expenditure
D. None of these

**48.** Which of the following is not capital expenditure?
A. Cost of issuing shares and debentures
B. Wages paid for construction of building
C. Repairs on a second-hand machinery newly purchased
D. Purchase of new spark plug at a cost of ₹ 8.50 for a two-year old car

**49.** Window dressing is prohibited due to:
A. Convention of conservatism
B. Convention of disclosure
C. Convention of materiality
D. Accrual concept

**50.** Quantitative transactions are not recorded in accounts due to:
A. dual concept
B. accrual concept
C. money measurement concept
D. None of these

**51.** Concept of Realisation implies:
A. When cash is received from debtors
B. When goods are delivered to customer
C. When order is received
D. None of these

**52.** Which of the following are not current liabilities?
A. Bank overdraft
B. Redeemable debentures
C. Provision for doubtful debts
D. Accounts payable

**53.** Provision for doubtful debts account is a:
A. Personal account
B. Real account
C. Nominal account
D. None of these

**54.** LIFO inventory method was used in year I, FIFO in year II and weighted average in year III. Which accounting principle is violated?
A. Cost principle
B. Consistency
C. Materiality
D. No principle of accounting is violated

**55.** Land was reported at its selling price which is substantially higher than its cost. The increase in value was included in the income statement, which accounting principle is violated?

A. Cost principle B. Going concern concept
C. Entity concept D. Conservatism

**56.** The cost of three small files (of ₹ 4 each) was charged to expenses when purchased even though they had a useful life of several years. This was done according to the:

A. Cost principle B. Conservatism principle
C. Full disclosure D. Materiality

**57.** The amount spent on unsuccessful patent rights is a:

A. Capital expenditure
B. Deferred revenue expenditure (if the amount is large)
C. Revenue expenditure (even though the amount is large)
D. None of these

**58.** Double entry system of book keeping refers to a system where:

A. the number of accounts with a debit balance must agree with the number of accounts with the credit balance
B. each transaction is recorded twice, once in journal and then in ledger
C. equal debit and credit entries are made for each transaction
D. each transaction is recorded in two set of account books

**59.** An entry of ₹ 500 was wrongly posted to wages account instead of machinery account, as wages are to be capitalised. It is an error of:

A. Commission B. Omission
C. Principle D. Clerical error

**60.** Which of the following statements best explains the relationship between journal and ledger?

A. First recording in journal and then posting to ledger completes the double entry of the transaction.
B. The journal is the book of original entry where as the ledger is the book of second entry.
C. The journal is the book for analytical record and ledger is the book for chronological record.
D. The process of recording, in the journal is called journalising, the process of recording in the ledger is called posting.

**61.** In order to determine the amount of sales, to which of the following records one should refer?

A. Sales book B. Sales account
C. Journal D. Total debtors account

**62.** Which of the following errors is revealed by trial balance?

A. Wrong amount entered in the book of original entry
B. Wrong amount entered in a ledger account
C. Complete ommission of an entry from the book of original entry
D. All of these

**63.** Which of the following errors are revealed by trial balance?

A. Omission of an amount from the trial balance
B. Posting of the wrong amount
C. Wrong totalling of the book of original entry
D. None of these

**64.** Which of the following errors will cause the trial balance to be out of balance?

A. The total of the purchase book is ₹ 1000 short
B. Good received back from Mahesh, ₹ 250 have not been entered in the Returns inward book
C. Office furniture purchased from Ravi and Co. ₹ 950 has been entered in the purchase book
D. A purchase of ₹ 251 from Gopal and Co. has been entered in the purchase book as ₹ 215.

**65.** Which of the following errors will not cause the trial balance to be out of order?

A. ₹ 590 received from P. Das has been debited to ₹ 10 Das
B. A purchase of ₹ 258 from Lekhi has been debited to his account as ₹ 285
C. The total of the discount column of the cash book (cr.) is ₹ 20 short
D. An invoice for ₹ 460 is entered in the sales book as ₹ 640

**66.** Which of the following errors will not cause the trial balance to be out of balance?

A. ₹ 310 for goods sold, was posted to the credit of charges
B. Purchases returns book for December 1978 was overcast by ₹ 220
C. Sales book carried forward ₹ 2400 instead of ₹ 2004
D. All of these

**67.** An invoice of ₹ 560 is entered in the sales book as ₹ 650. The total of the debit side of the trial balance is ₹ 21,440. Assuming no other error what is the total of the credit side of the trial balance?

A. ₹ 21,240
B. ₹ 21,350
C. ₹ 21,330
D. None of these

**68.** Which of the following books should be used to record purchase of a typewriter on account?
A. Cash books B. Purchase book
C. Sales book D. Journal

**69.** Which of the following books should be used to record purchase of merchandise an account?
A. Cash book B. Purchase book
C. Sales book D. Journal

**70.** Agreement of the trial balance may not indicate that:
A. no error remains undetected
B. double entry has been completed
C. arithmetic accuracy is reasonably proved
D. all ledger accounts have been correctly posted

**71.** Networking capital of a firm is the:
A. Effective capital of the company when the business is in full swing.
B. Capital borrowed from banks.
C. Difference between the current assets and current liabilities.
D. Capital provided by shares holders only.

**72.** If sales are ₹ 60,000; gross profit 1/3 on cost. Purchases are ₹ 49,000 and the closing stock is ₹ 9,000. The opening stock will be:
A. Nil B. ₹ 5,000
C. ₹ 20,000 D. ₹ 49,000

**73.** A company has inadvertently overstated its ending inventory. This will:
A. Increase the income of the succeeding year.
B. Decrease the income of the current year.
C. Have no effect on the income of the succeeding year.
D. Decrease the income of the succeeding year.

**74.** Modern Leasing Co. Ltd. has debt equity ratio 8 : 1. It has decided to issue bonus shares in the ratio of 1 : 1. The debt-equity ratio after the issue would be:
A. 8 : 1 B. 4 : 1
C. 1 : 8 D. 1 : 4

**75.** Which one of the following ratio is the indicator of the long term solvency of the firm?
A. Acid test ratio
B. Debt-equity ratio
C. Time interest earned ratio
D. None of these

**76.** To test the liquidity of a concern which of the following ratios are useful?
A. Acid test ratio
B. Capital turnover ratio
C. Bad debts to sales ratio
D. Inventory turnover ratio

**77.** A low inventory turnover ratio may be the result of:
I. Obsolescence of some of the stock
II. Slow moving inventory
III. Frequent stock-outs
IV. Fast moving inventory
Of these statements:
A. I and II are correct B. II alone is correct
C. IV alone is correct D. II and III are correct

**78.** If earning per share of X limited is ₹ 15 and the price-earnings ratio of other similar companies is ₹ 10, then the market value of the share of ₹ X Ltd. will be:
A. ₹ 300 B. ₹ 150
C. ₹ 75 D. ₹ 25

**79.** Which one of the following is least suited for measuring return on investment?
A. Income invested capital
B. Net operating income before interest and taxes average total assets
C. Operating income ratio total assets turnover
D. Net income after interest but before taxes average total share holder equity

**80.** Given in the following table is data for various companies in the same industry:

| | A | B | C | D |
|---|---|---|---|---|
| Current Assets | 150 | 140 | 100 | 120 |
| A/c Receivable | 60 | 50 | 50 | 70 |
| Turnover Ratio | 6.5 | 5.0 | 5.5 | 5.0 |
| Current Liabilities | 100 | 120 | 80 | 130 |

The two firms which appear to be having better liquidity position are:
A. A and B B. B and C
C. A and C D. B and D

**81.** While calculating the Net Present Value under discounted cash flow method of return on Investment analysis the operations involved are:
I. Cash out flow
II. Discounted net cash flow
III. Cash inflow
IV. Net present value

The correct sequence of these operations is:
A. I, II, III, IV B. I, III, II, IV
C. IV, I, III, II D. III, I, IV, II

**82.** Rate of return on investment is meaningful to:
I. Shareholder
II. Creditors
III. Management
Of the statements given above:
A. I alone is true B. I and III are true
C. II and III are true D. I, II and III are true

**83.** Purchase of machinery and equipment for cash by firm:
A. Increase the total assets
B. Keeps total assets unchanged
C. Decreases the total assets
D. Increases the liability of the firm

**84.** Which of the following is an operating expense?
A. Depreciation of plant B. Expired insurance
C. None of the above D. All of these

**85.** Which of the following are current assets?
A. Bank loan for three years
B. Account Receivable
C. Long-term investments
D. Debentures sinking fund investments

**86.** Purchase of office equipment results in:
A. Decrease in liability B. Decrease in capital
C. Increase in capital D. Increase in fixed Assets

**87.** Payment of a liability results in:
A. Increase in total Assets
B. Decrease in total Assets
C. No change in total Assets
D. None of these

**88.** Which one of the following is correct about 'margin of safety' ratio?
A. Capital employ/net worth
B. Contribution/sales volume
C. Operating profit/contribution
D. Contribution/sales of BEP

**89.** If the profit is 25% of the cost price, then it is:
A. 20% of the sale price B. 25% of the sale price
C. 30% of the sale price D. 33% of the sale price

**90.** Repayment of loan results into:
A. Source of fund B. Application of fund
C. No flow of fund D. All of these

**91.** Sale of building results into:
A. Source of fund B. No flow of fund
C. Application of fund D. None of these

**92.** The term 'funds' as used in funds flow statement means:
A. Cash
B. Current assets
C. Current liabilities
D. Current Assets minus current liabilities

**93.** Payment of interim dividend is a:
A. Source of fund B. Application of fund
C. No flow of fund D. All of these

**94.** If the rate of gross profit is 25% on cost of goods sold and the sales are ₹ 200000 the amount of profit will be:
A. ₹ 50000 B. ₹ 40000
C. ₹ 45000 D. None of these

**95.** Quick ratio is a good indicator of the liquid position of a concern. The ideal quick ratio is:
A. 2 : 1 B. 1 : 1
C. 3 : 1 D. 4 : 1

**96.** When current ratio is 4 : 1 and the amount of current liabilities ₹ 12,000. What is the amount assets?
A. ₹ 12,000 B. ₹ 4,000
C. ₹ 48,000 D. ₹ 60,000

**97.** Which of the following is a non–operating income?
A. Profit on the sale of used plant in manufacturing company.
B. Revenue from sales in a trading concern.
C. Dividends received by an investment company.
D. Premiums received by an insurance company.

**98.** Which of the following is correct?
A. Cost of goods sold + closing stock – opening stock = Purchases
B. Cost of goods sold – closing stock + opening stock = Purchases
C. Opening stock + closing stock – cost of goods sold = Purchases
D. Closing stock – cost of goods sold + opening stock = Purchases
E. None of these

**99.** Which of the following is not correct?
A. Purchases + Opening stock – Cost of goods sold = Closing stock
B. Opening stock + Purchases – Closing stock = Cost of goods sold
C. Closing stock + Cost of goods sold – Purchase = Opening stock
D. Cost of goods sold – Closing stock – Purchases = Opening stock

**100.** The equation for the Debt Equity Ratio is:
A. Long-term debt/Equity capital
B. Liquid Assets/current liability
C. Current Assets/current liabilities
D. Net profits/net sales

**101.** Opening stock – ₹ 15,000, Purchases – ₹ 40,000; cost of goods sold – ₹ 52,000; Sales – ₹ 57,000 what is the amount of gross profit or loss?
A. ₹ 12,000
B. ₹ 5,000
C. ₹ 5,000 (Loss)
D. ₹ 7,000

**102.** Sales return – 2,500; Sales – ₹ 12,800; Purchases – ₹ 8,400; Gross profit ₹ 2,100
What is the amount of cost of goods sold?
A. ₹ 10,700 B. ₹ 10,500
C. ₹ 8,200 D. ₹ 6,300

**103.** For the purpose of final accounts, stock is valued according to:
A. Cost or market value whichever is less
B. First–in first–out basis
C. Last–in first–out basis
D. Any of these

**104.** The works manager gets commission of 10% on the profits after charging such commission. If the profit is ₹ 2,200 what is the amount of his commission:
A. ₹ 220 B. ₹ 200
C. ₹ 240 D. ₹ 244.44

**105.** If profits are 25% of selling price, what is the percentage of profit to cost?
A. 20% B. 25%
C. 30% D. 33%

**106.** In which of the following methods, inventory is valued at the latest prices prevailing in the market?
A. Last-in first-out (LIFO)
B. First-in first-out (FIFO)
C. Replacement price method
D. Weighted average method

**107.** In ABC Analysis, which category represents those items which are used in largest quantity but their value is not high?
A. 'A' items B. 'B' items
C. 'C' items D. None of these

**108.** FIFO is advisable in case of:
A. Rising prices B. Falling prices
C. Constant prices D. All of these

**109.** Which of the following methods results in lower valuation of inventory and lower income when prices are rising?
A. FIFO B. LIFO
C. Simple average D. Weighted average

**110.** When current ratio is 2 : 1, an equal increase in current assets and current liabilities would:
A. Increase the current ratio
B. Decrease the current ratio
C. Not change the current ratio
D. Will affect some other ratio

**111.** When the current ratio is 2 : 5, and the amount of current liabilities is ₹ 25,000 what is the amount of current assets?
A. ₹ 62,500 B. ₹ 12,500
C. ₹ 10,000 D. None of these

**112.** When quick ratio is 1.5 : 1 and the amount of quick assets ₹ 30,000 what is the amount of quick liabilities?
A. ₹ 20,000 B. ₹ 50,000
C. ₹ 45,000 D. ₹ 30,000

**113.** Which of the following items is not taken into account while computing current ratio?
A. Sundry creditors B. Sundry debtors
C. Furniture D. Bank over draft

**114.** Which of the following items is not an operating expense?
A. Advertising
B. Depreciation of office equipment
C. General management salaries
D. Power consumed

**115.** When net sales for the year are ₹ 2,50,000 and debtors ₹ 50,000, the average collection period is (assuming year of 360 days):
A. 60 days B. 45 days
C. 42 days D. 72 days

**116.** Given-fixed long term liabilities ₹ 5,50,000, fixed assets ₹ 12,00,000, capital ₹ 8,50,000, current liabilities ₹ 2,50,000, current assets ₹ 4,00,000, solvency ratio is:
A. 5 : 12 B. 8 : 16
C. 15 : 17 D. 10 : 15

**117.** If the cost of goods sold is ₹ 1 lakh, the value of opening and closing stock is ₹ 20,000 and ₹ 30,000 respectively, the stock turnover ratio will be:
A. 3.3 times B. 4 times
C. 5 times D. 6 times

**118.** Dividing net sales by average debtors would yield:
A. Acid test ratio B. Return on sales ratio
C. Debtors turnover ratio D. None of these

**119.** Which of the following transactions change the current ratio?
A. Purchase of goods for cash
B. Plant acquired on account
C. Sold goods on credit
D. Debentures converted into equity capital

**120.** When the operating ratio is 91.5, the ratio of operating profit to sales:
A. Will be 91.5%
B. Will be 8.5%
C. Cannot be known from the given information
D. None of these

**121.** In calculating the Earning per Shares (EPS), the net profit is dividend by:
A. Number of equity shares
B. Number of preference shares
C. Number of equity plus preference shares
D. Total liabilities

**122.** Given net profit ₹ 1,50,000, preference dividend ₹ 25,000, taxes ₹ 10,000. What is the Earning per Shares (EPS), If there are 1 lac shares?
A. ₹ 1.50 B. ₹ 1.25
C. ₹ 1.15 D. None of these

**123.** Accounting information given by a company:

| | |
|---|---|
| Total assets turnover | 3times |
| Net profit margin | 10% |
| Total assets | ₹ 1,00,000 |

The net profit is:

A. ₹ 10,000 B. ₹ 15,000
C. ₹ 25,000 D. ₹ 30,000

**124.** Given that Assets ₹ 20,00,000

| | |
|---|---|
| Tax | ₹ 25,000 |
| Profit before tax | ₹ 2,25,000 |
| Net worth | ₹ 10,00,000 |

What is the Return on Investment (ROI)?

A. 10% B. 12.5%
C. 20% D. 25%

**125.** The immediate solvency ratio is:

A. Quick ratio B. Current ratio
C. Stocks turn ratio D. Debtors turnover ratio

**126.** Pay out ratio means:

A. Ratio of debtors to creditors
B. Ratio of earning that are distributed through dividends
C. Ratio of profit distributed to profit retained
D. Ratio of profit to capital

**127.** Current ratio is increased by:

I. Cash received from debtors
II. Issue of redeemable debentures
III. Selling the old machine for cash
IV. Converting debentures into equity capital

A. I, II and III B. II and III
C. I and III D. III and IV

**128.** ROI takes into account:

A. Share holders investment
B. Interest on working capital
C. Interest on fixed assets
D. All of these

**129.** Match the following:

| | |
|---|---|
| I. Test of liquidity | (*a*) ROI |
| II. Test of profitability | (*b*) Debtors turnover |
| III. Test of solvency | (*c*) Acid test ratio |
| IV. Test of activity | (*d*) Debt equity ratio |

***Codes:***

| | I | II | III | IV |
|---|---|---|---|---|
| A. | (*a*) | (*d*) | (*b*) | (*c*) |
| B. | (*d*) | (*a*) | (*c*) | (*b*) |
| C. | (*b*) | (*c*) | (*a*) | (*d*) |
| D. | (*c*) | (*a*) | (*d*) | (*b*) |

**130.** A person interested in investing for growth in the market price of shares should invest in a company with:

A. High net profit ratio B. High gross profit ratio
C. High payout ratio D. Low payout ratio

**131.** Given Current ratio = 2.5 : 1
Net working capital = ₹ 30,000

What is the amount of current liabilities?

A. ₹ 20,000 B. ₹ 30,000
C. ₹ 50,000 D. ₹ 60,000

**132.** In Computing Debt/Equity ratio, debt means:

A. Debentures only
B. Short-term creditors
C. Short-term as well as long-term creditors
D. All of these

**133.** Which of the following liabilities are taken into account for acid test ratio?

I. Trade creditors II. Bank overdraft
III. Bills payable IV. Outstanding expenses
V. Redeemable debentures

***Codes:***

A. I, II, III, IV and V B. I, III and IV
C. I, II, III, and IV D. I, III, IV and V

**134.** Which of the following results in the flow of funds?

A. Creditors issued bills payable
B. Loss on the sale of machinery
C. Transfer to general reserve
D. Building sold on credit

**135.** A transaction results in the flow of fund when:

A. Non-current asset is purchased out of a current asset
B. Debentures are redeemed
C. Preference share capital is issued
D. All of these

**136.** Which of the following is not a source of fund?

A. Purchase of machinery
B. Profit earned during the year
C. Issue of share capital
D. Long term loan raised

**137.** If net profit is ₹ 25,000 after writing off preliminary expenses of ₹ 5,000 then the funds from operation will be:

A. ₹ 25,000 B. ₹ 30,000
C. ₹ 20,000 D. ₹ 22,000

**138.** Which of the following items is not added to net profit for computing the amount of funds from operations?

A. Depreciation on machinery
B. Profit on sale of machinery
C. Goodwill written off
D. Loss on sale of furniture

**139.** When net profit is ₹ 23,000 and profit on the sale of a fixed asset is ₹ 2,000, what is the fund from operations?

A. ₹ 23,000 B. ₹ 21,000
C. ₹ 25,000 D. ₹ 24,000

**140.** Plant and machinery on 1st January 1982 is ₹ 50,000 and on 31st December 1982 it is ₹ 80,000. Depreciation of ₹ 10,000 was provided during the year. This has resulted in:

A. Source of funds of ₹ 30,000
B. Application of funds of ₹ 30,000
C. Application of funds of ₹ 40,000
D. Source of funds of ₹ 40,000

**141.** While preparing 'Annual financial statements' 'Credit Balance' shown by the Bank pass Book should be treated as:

A. A liability
B. An income
C. An excess of payments over receipts
D. An asset

**142.** The joint life policy a account received on the death of a partner is credited to the:

A. Joint life policy reserve account
B. Capital accounts of all the partners in their profit sharing ratio
C. General ratio
D. Profit and loss account

**143.** Consider the following activities connected with the accounting information system:

I. Preparation of the table of accounting.
II. Communication of accounting information
III. Preparation of accounting information report.
IV. Collection of accounting data.

The correct sequence of these activities is:

A. IV, I, III, II  B. I, IV, III, II
C. IV, III, I, II  D. I, II, IV, III

**144.** A cooperative store having a turnover of ₹ 10 lakh and profit of ₹ 50, 000 purchased locks costing ₹ 300 for use in the shop. The accountant charged it in the P & L A/c of current year, but the auditor raised an objection saying that it should be capitalised. On which one of the following conventions could the accountant be defended?

A. Disclosure  B. Materiality
C. Conservatism  D. Consistency

**145.** Consider the following statements:

Notes forming part of accounts of companies invariably display significant Accounting Policies

I. as per the requirement of SEBI guidelines for disclosure and investor protection.
II. because it is a mandatory requirement under the Companies Act, 1956.
III. as required by As-I-disclosure of accounting policies, which is mandatory.
IV. as it is required under the listing agreement with the stock exchanges.

Which of the above statements are correct?

A. I, II, and III  B. II, and III
C. II, III and IV  D. I and IV

**146.** Match List-I with List-II and select the correct answer using the codes given below the Lists:

| List-I | List-II |
|---|---|
| I. Showing joint life policy at surrender value | (a) Concept of consistency |
| II. Team spirit and dedication of cost employees are not recorded in the books of accounts | (b) Concept of cost |
| III. Methods of depreciation and inventory valuation should not be changed frequently | (c) Concept of conservatism |
| IV. Fixed assets are recorded at 'cost less depreciation' | (d) Concept of money measurement |

***Codes:***

| | I | II | III | IV |
|---|---|---|---|---|
| A. | (c) | (d) | (a) | (b) |
| B. | (c) | (d) | (b) | (a) |
| C. | (d) | (c) | (a) | (b) |
| D. | (d) | (c) | (b) | (a) |

**147.** If depreciation is calculated on the basis of the formula, $\frac{n(n+1)}{2}$, then which one of the following methods is adopted?

A. Dinininshing value method
B. Annuity method
C. Sum of years Digits Method
D. Sinking Fund Method

**148.** Consider the following methods of inventory valuation:

I. Simple Average  II. First-in-first-out
III. Last-in-first-out  IV. Weighted Average

Which of these methods do not match current cost with current revenues?

A. I and III  B. I, II and III
C. I, II, and IV  D. II, III and IV

**149.** Consider the following fundamental assumptions:

I. Prudence  II. Going concern
III. Accrual  IV. Consistency

As per Accounting standard-1, which of these assumptions are taken into consideration while preparing financial statements?

A. I and IV  B. II and III
C. I, II, III and IV  D. II, III, and IV

**150.** Which one of the following statements is correct?

A. Preliminary expenses are revenue expenses
B. Cost of issuing shares and debentures and rising

loans, such as legal expenses and under writing commission are capital expenditure

C. Interest on loan is a capital expenditure

D. Cost of machinery purchased is a revenue expenditure

**151.** The ending balance of owner's equity is ₹ 21,000. During the years the owner contributed ₹ 6,000 and withdrew ₹ 4,000. If the firm had ₹ 8,000 net income for the year, what was the owner's equity at the beginning?

A. ₹ 23,000 B. ₹ 21,000
C. ₹ 19,000 D. ₹ 11,000

**152.** The ending balance of the accounts receivable amount was ₹ 12,000. Services billed to customers for the period were ₹ 21,500 and collection on account from customers was ₹ 23,600. The beginning balance of account receivable was:

A. ₹ 33,500 B. ₹ 14,100
C. ₹ 9,800 D. ₹ 33,300

**153.** Which one of the following is a capital expenditure?

A. Compensation paid for breach of a contract of supply of goods
B. Interest on borrowings during the period of construction of works
C. Loss of stock by fire
D. Loss due to embezzlement by the Manager

**154.** A company issued 14% debentures of ₹ 10,00,000 at a discount of 10%. The discount allowed will be treated in the account books as:

A. Capital expenditure
B. Revenue expenditure
C. Deferred revenue expenditure
D. Capital loss

**155.** A building standing in the books at ₹ 30,000 was sold for ₹ 45,000. The gain on the sale of building was transferred to profit and loss account thus taking the net profit to ₹ 1,70,000. The fund from operation will be:

A. ₹ 2,15,000 B. ₹ 1,17,000
C. ₹ 1,55,000 D. ₹ 2,00,000

**156.** Match List-I with List-II and select the correct answer using the codes given below the Lists:

| List-I | List-II |
|---|---|
| I. Lease hold property | (*a*) Depreciation Fund Method |
| II. Mines, quarries, etc. | (*b*) Annuity Method |
| III. The interest lost on the acquisition of an asset | (*c*) Fixed Instalment Method |
| IV. To provide for replacement of asset at the end of its useful life | (*d*) Depletion Method |

***Codes:***

| | I | II | III | IV |
|---|---|---|---|---|
| A. | (*b*) | (*a*) | (*d*) | (*c*) |
| B. | (*c*) | (*d*) | (*a*) | (*b*) |
| C. | (*c*) | (*d*) | (*b*) | (*a*) |
| D. | (*d*) | (*c*) | (*a*) | (*b*) |

**157.** Following are the extracts from the Trial Balance of a firm:

| Particulars | ₹ Dr. | ₹ Cr. |
|---|---|---|
| Sundry debtors | 50,000 | – |
| Provision for doubtful debts | – | 5,000 |
| Bad debts | 3,000 | – |
| Additional Information: | | |

I. Additional bad debts ₹ 3,000.
II. Keep the provision for bad debts @ 10% on debtors.

The net amount of bad debts that will appear in the Profit and Loss Account will be:

A. ₹ 8,000 B. ₹ 7,500
C. ₹ 5,700 D. ₹ 4,500

**158.** A and B sharing profits in the ratio of 3 : 2 and having capitals of ₹ 30,000 and ₹ 15,000 respectively decided to dissolve the firm. After paying off all liabilities, they realised from various assets is ₹ 15,000. This amount will be distributed between A and B as:

A. ₹ 9,000 and ₹ 6,000 respectively
B. ₹ 10,000 and ₹ 5,000 respectively
C. ₹ 7,500 and ₹ 7,500 respectively
D. ₹ 12,000 and ₹ 3,000 respectively

**159.** A, B and C are partners sharing profits in the ratio of 6 : 3 : 1. They dicided to dissolve the firm when their capitals were ₹ 8,000, ₹ 3,000 and ₹ (–1) 1,000 respectively other liabilities and assets were-Bank over draft ₹ 3,500; A's advance to the firm ₹ 500; sundry creditors ₹ 2,500; plant and machinery ₹ 7,500; stock-in trade ₹ 2,500; Sundry debtors ₹ 6,000 and Cash ₹ 500. Plant and machinery realised at 20% less, stock-in trade at 25% less and sundry debtors at 30% less than their respective book value. Expenses of dissolution amounted to ₹ 250. C become insolvent and his private estate yielded ₹ 100 only. What is the loss on realisation?

A. ₹ 4,125 B. ₹ 4,150
C. ₹ 4,175 D. ₹ 4,225

**160.** A, B and C are the partners in a business firm sharing their profits in the ratio of 4 : 3 : 2. A new partner D enters the firm. The new profit sharing ratio for A, B, C and D is 5 : 4 : 2 : 1. D contributes a goodwill of ₹ 36,000. This good-will is to be allocated among A, B and C. Which one of the following will be the correct allocation?

| | A | B | C |
|---|---|---|---|
| | ₹ | ₹ | ₹ |
| A. | 16,000 | 12,000 | 8,000 |
| B. | 12,000 | 8,000 | 16,000 |
| C. | 12,000 | Nil | 24,000 |
| D. | 24,000 | Nil | 12,000 |

**161.** A, B and C are equal partners in a firm with capital of ₹ 16,800, ₹ 12,600 and ₹ 6,000 respectively with bills payable ₹ 3,300; creditors ₹ 6,000; cash ₹ 600; debtors ₹ 10,800; stocks ₹ 11,400; furniture ₹ 2,400 and building ₹ 19,500. E is admitted to the firm and brings ₹ 9,000 as goodwill and ₹ 15,000 as capital. Half the goodwill is withdrawn by old partners, and stock and furniture is depreciated by 10%. A provision of 5% on debtors is created and value of building is taken at ₹ 27,000. The profit on revaluation will be:

A. ₹ 5,500 B. ₹ 5,580
C. ₹ 5,400 D. ₹ 5,680

**162.** A and B are partners in a firm sharing profits in the ratio of 3 : 2. They admit C as a new partner for 1/3 share in the profits of the firm. The new profit-sharing ratio of A, B and C is:

A. 3 : 2 : 1 B. 3 : 2 : 2
C. 3 : 2 : 3 D. 6 : 4 : 5

**163.** Under the net worth method, the basis of ascertaining profit is the:

A. Difference between the liabilities on two dates.
B. Difference between the gross assets on two dates.
C. Difference between the capital on two dates.
D. Increase in net worth before adjusting for drawings and additions to capital.

**164.** A non-performing asset with a financial institution denotes an asset on which:

A. Regular dividend is not being received
B. Interest is on default for two quarters or more
C. Repayment of capital appears difficult
D. There is no earning of profit

**165.** A company forfeited 100 shares of ₹ 10 each owing to the default in the payment of share call money of ₹ 5 each. These shares were issued at ₹ 9 each, payable at ₹ 2 on application, ₹ 2 on allotment and the balance of ₹ 5 on call. The shares were then reissued to another share holder at a price of ₹ 6 per share.
The amount to be debited to forfeited shares account on account of discount on reissue of shares would be:

A. ₹ 100 B. ₹ 300
C. ₹ 400 D. ₹ 500

**166.** The issue of bonus shares must be in accordance with the guidelines issued by the:

A. Company Law Board
B. Controller of Capital Issues
C. Securities and Exchange Board of India
D. Registrar of Companies

**167.** Consider the following statements:

I. Obsolescence of some of the stock
II. Slow-moving inventory
III. Frequent stock-outs
IV. Fast-moving inventory

Which of the above statement (s) is/are correct?

A. I and II B. IV alone
C. II alone D. II and III

**168.** Consider the following ratios:

I. Acid test ratio
II. Capital turnover ratio
III. Bad debts to sales ratio
IV. Inventory turnover ratio

Which of these ratios are more appropriate for testing the liquidity of a concern?

A. I and III B. I and IV
C. II and IV D. II and III

**169.** Consider the given data:

I. Proprietary ratio = 0.75
II. Current ratio = 2 : 1
III. Proprietary fund = ₹ 60,000
IV. Fixed assets = ₹ 50.000

The working capital will be computed as:

A. ₹ 10,000 B. ₹ 15,000
C. ₹ 20,000 D. ₹ 25,000

**170.** Consider the following Balance sheet of ABC Company Limited as on March 31, 2008:

| Liabilities | ₹ | Assets | ₹ | ₹ |
|---|---|---|---|---|
| Equity Shares Capital | 20,00,000 | Fixed assets | 60,00,000 | |
| Preference Share Capital | 10,00,000 | Less depreciation | 20,00,000 | 40,00,000 |
| General reserve | 5,00,000 | | | |
| 10% Debentures | 11,00,000 | Debtors | | 10,00,000 |
| Creditors | 7,00,000 | Stock | | 6,00,000 |
| Outstanding expenses | 3,00,000 | Cash | | 1,00,000 |
| Profit & Loss A/c | 1,05,000 | Formation Expenses | | 5,000 |
| | **57,05,000** | | | **57,05,000** |

The current ratio of ABC Company is:

A. 2.00 B. 1.90
C. 1.85 D. 1.70

**171.** Match List-I with List-II and select the correct answer using the codes given below the Lists:

| List-I | List-II |
|---|---|
| I. Current assets ÷ Current liabilities | (*a*) Performance of equity capital |
| II. Fixed assets ÷ Long-term funds | (*b*) Short-term solvency |
| III. Debt Equity | (*c*) Capital structure |
| IV. Earnings after interest and taxes ÷ Number of shares issued | (*d*) Over all performance |

***Codes:***

| | I | II | III | IV |
|---|---|---|---|---|
| A. | (*b*) | (*e*) | (*c*) | (*d*) |
| B. | (*a*) | (*b*) | (*c*) | (*d*) |
| C. | (*b*) | (*e*) | (*d*) | (*c*) |
| D. | (*a*) | (*b*) | (*d*) | (*c*) |

**Directions (Qs. No. 172 & 173):** *These questions are based on the following Balance-sheet of Messrs A Limited as on 31st Dec., 2008:*

| Liabilities | ₹ (in lakhs) | Assets | ₹ (in lakhs) |
|---|---|---|---|
| Owned funds | 25.00 | Fixed assets | 27.00 |
| Long term debt | 1.50 | Current assets | 6.10 |
| Current liabilities | 5.00 | Other assets | 0.40 |
| Unclaimed dividends | 0.20 | | |
| Provisions | 1.80 | | |
| | **33.50** | | **33.50** |

Study the Balance sheet carefully and attempt the following questions:

**172.** 'Owned funds' would be:
A. ₹ 25 lakh
B. ₹ 8.50 lakh
C. ₹ 25.20 lakh
D. ₹ 27 lakh

**173.** The 'margin of safety'. *i.e.*, the cushion of protection for creditors is:
A. 4.06 : 1
B. ₹ 4.60 lakh
C. 0.20 : 1
D. ₹ 22 lakh

**174.** If the management of A Limited want to evaluate the general efficiency, which one of the following additional information is required?
A. Sales and earnings after income-tax and interest.
B. Break-up of owned funds into share capital, reserves and surpluses, etc.
C. Earnings before income-tax and interest.
D. Operating expenses and sales.

**175.** Financial indicators of four companies are as follows:

| Company | Current ratio | Debt equity ratio | Rate of return on investment | Fixed assets turnover |
|---|---|---|---|---|
| A | 2.0 : 1 | 2.5 : 1 | 10% | 5 |
| B | 2.5 : 1 | 3.0 : 1 | 25% | 4 |
| C | 1.5 : 1 | 4.0 : 1 | 20% | 3 |
| D | 1.0 : 1 | 3.5 : 1 | 15% | 2 |

In general, which of the above companies would fall in the highest risk class?
A. A and B
B. B and C
C. C and D
D. A and D

**176.** Consider the particulars given below:

Sales = ₹ 60,000
Variable cost = ₹ 25,000
Fixed cost = ₹ 30,000

Based on these data, the operating leverage shall be:
A. 5
B. 7
C. 8
D. 9

**177.** Consider the following statements:

Redeemable preference shares of a company can be redeemed out of
I. Profits of the company which would otherwise be available for dividend.
II. Company's share premium account.
III. Fresh issue of shares made for the purpose of redemption.

Which of the above statements are correct?
A. I and II
B. I and III
C. II and III
D. I, II and III

**178.** The main purpose of depreciation accounting is to:
A. Charge the cost of asset.
B. Allocate the cost of the asset over its estimated useful life.
C. Provide replacement of the asset on the expiry of its useful life.
D. Value the assets on the closing date of the year.

**179.** Which one of the following pairs is not correctly matched?
A. Increase in working capital – Application of fund
B. Increase in current liability – Source of fund
C. Issue of shares – Source of fund
D. Issue of bonus shares – Source of fund

**180.** Consider the following statements:
I. Operational loss is a source of funds.
II. Decrease in working capital is a source of funds.
III. Additions to fixed assets are an application of funds.
IV. Fresh introduction of capital is an application of funds.

Which of the above statements are applicable while preparing the funds flow statements?
A. I and II
B. I and III
C. II and III
D. I, III and IV

**181.** A company's reported current profit is ₹ 70,000 after incorporating the following: Loss on sale of investments ₹ 10,000; Premium on redemption of debentures ₹ 1,500; Depreciation on machinery and plant ₹ 20,000; Goodwill and preliminary expenses written off ₹ 30,000; Gain from sale of non current assets ₹ 40,000. The net inflow of funds from the operation would be:

A. ₹ 91,500 B. ₹ 80,000
C. ₹ 70,000 D. ₹ 59,500

**182.** For the purpose of analysing changes in financial position, enterprises prepare:

A. Balance sheet and Profit and Loss A/c.
B. Cash flow statement and funds flow statement.
C. Statement of cash from Operations and Balance sheet.
D. Statement of changes in working capital and statement of cash from operations.

**183.** Materiality in accounting is decided:

A. By the size of an item.
B. By the knowledge as to whether an individual item is having a significant influence on financial statement.
C. Solely by the discretion of the accountant.
D. By the physical volume of the transaction.

**184.** Match List-I (Event) with List-II (Result) and select the correct answer using the codes given below the Lists:

| List-I | List-II |
|---|---|
| I. Collusion between two or more persons | (*a*) Payments of dividends otherwise not possible |
| II. Falsification of accounts to increase apparent profits | (*b*) Error of principle committed |
| III. Operation of an effective system of internal check | (*c*) Trial balance may agree |
| IV. Purchase of raw materials is debited to Loose tools and concealed | (*d*) Frauds perpetrated and account |
| | (*e*) Possiblility of errors and frauds is considerably reduced |

***Codes:***

| | I | II | III | IV |
|---|---|---|---|---|
| A. | (*c*) | (*d*) | (*e*) | (*b*) |
| B. | (*d*) | (*a*) | (*e*) | (*b*) |
| C. | (*d*) | (*a*) | (*b*) | (*e*) |
| D. | (*b*) | (*d*) | (*a*) | (*c*) |

**185.** Accounting is the process of matching:

A. Benefits and costs
B. Revenues and costs
C. Cash inflows and outflows.
D. Potential and real performance.

**186.** A had started business with ₹ 20,000 in the beginning of the year. During the year he borrowed ₹ 10,000 from B. He further Introduced ₹ 20,000 in the business. He also gave ₹ 5,000 as loan to his son. Goods given away as charity by him was ₹ 2,000. Profits earned by him was ₹ 25,000. He also withdrew ₹ 3,000 from the business. His capital at the end of the year would be:

A. ₹ 50,000 B. ₹ 40,000
C. ₹ 62,000 D. ₹ 48,000

**187.** Match List-I with List-II and select the correct answer using the codes given below the list:

| List-I | List-II |
|---|---|
| I. A long term debt instrument on which interest is accumulated and paid on maturity | (*a*) Mutual fund |
| II. A debt instrument on which rebate is available under the Income Tax Act | (*b*) Deep Discount Bond |
| III. Pooling together the money of different investors and investing it in diversified securities | (*c*) Infrastructure Bond |
| IV. Buying the right but not the obligation to sell a security for a specific price | (*d*) Put option |

***Codes:***

| | I | II | III | IV |
|---|---|---|---|---|
| A. | (*d*) | (*a*) | (*b*) | (*c*) |
| B. | (*b*) | (*c*) | (*a*) | (*d*) |
| C. | (*c*) | (*a*) | (*b*) | (*d*) |
| D. | (*c*) | (*a*) | (*d*) | (*b*) |

**188.** To guard against the dangers of excess payment arising out of double insurance or over-insurance made by the insured, insurance companies provide in their agreement:

A. Average clause B. Subrogation clause
C. Risk clause D. Indemnity clause

**189.** A person insured his property worth ₹ 10,000 against fire for ₹ 8,000. His actual loss by fire is ₹ 5,000 and there is an average clause in the policy. His claim will be:

A. ₹ 10,000 B. ₹ 8,000
C. ₹ 5,000 D. ₹ 4,000

**190.** In the Balance sheet, under the sub-heading 'current liabilities and provisions', disclosure of the name (s) of small-scale industries/undertakings is required if the company owes a sum:

A. Exceeding ₹ 1 lakh as outstanding for more than 6 months.

B. Not exceeding ₹ 1 lakh as outstanding for more than 6 months.

C. Exceeding ₹ 1 lakh as outstanding for more than 30 days.

D. Exceeding ₹ 50,000 as outstanding for more than 2 months.

**Directions (Qs. No. 191-205):** *These questions consist of two statements, one labelled the Assertion (A) and the other labelled the Reason (R). You are to examine these two statements carefully and decide if the Assertion (A) and the Reason (R) are individually true and if so, whether the Reason is a correct explanation of the Assertion. Select your answers to these items using the codes.*

**191. Assertion (A) :** Management accounting provides management with information for decision making.

**Reason (R) :** Management accounting is a branch of cost accounting.

*Codes:*

A. Both (A) and (R) are true, and (R) is the correct explanation of (A).

B. Both (A) and (R) are true, but (R) is not a correct explanation of (A).

C. (A) is true, but (R) is false.

D. (A) is false, but (R) is true.

**192. Assertion (A) :** Under diminishing balance method of depreciation, the charge for depreciation keeps on diminishing year after year in all subsequent years.

**Reason (R) :** Under diminishing balance method, the rate per cent at which depreciation is written off goes on diminishing from year to year.

*Codes:*

A. Both (A) and (R) are true, and (R) is the correct explanation of (A).

B. Both (A) and (R) are, true, but (R) is not a correct explanation of (A).

C. (A) is ture, but (R) is false.

D. (A) is false, but (R) is true.

**193. Assertion (A) :** No item of capital expenditure finds its place in the Trading and Profit & Loss Account or some other form of revenue accounts.

**Reason (R) :** Capital expenditure consists of expenditure, the benefit of which is not fully consumed in one accounting period but is spread over several periods.

*Codes:*

A. Both (A) and (R) are true, and (R) is the correct explanation of (A).

B. Both (A) and (R) are true, but (R) is not a correct explanation of (A).

C. (A) is true, but (R) is false.

D. (A) is false, but (R) is true.

**194. Assertion (A) :** Now-a-days many companies prepare their Balance sheet in a vertical form rather than in the traditional horizontal form.

**Reason (R) :** Part IV of schedule IV to the Companies Act, 1956 permits both the forms.

*Codes:*

A. Both (A) and (R) are true and (R) is the correct explanation of (A).

B. Both (A) and (R) are true, but (R) is not a correct explanation of (A).

C. (A) is true, but (R) is false.

D. (A) is false, but (R) is true.

**195. Assertion (A) :** When pro-rata allotment of shares is made, the surplus application money is transferred to share allotment A/c.

**Reason (R) :** The company is not required to pay any interest on such surplus application money.

*Codes:*

A. Both (A) and (R) are true, and (R) is the correct explanation of (A).

B. Both (A) and (R) are true, but (R) is not a correct explanation of (A).

C. (A) is true, but (R) is false.

D. (A) is false, but (R) is true.

**196. Assertion (A) :** One single primary ratio, that measures the financial outcome of all recorded business activities, is ROI.

**Reason (R) :** In practice, however, variations are also found in the ratio because capital and return are subject to different interpretations by firms.

*Codes:*

A. Both (A) and (R) are true, and (R) is the correct explanation of (A).

B. Both (A) and (R) are true, (R) is not a correct explanation of (A).

C. (A) is true, but (R) is false.

D. (A) is false, but (R) is true.

**197. Assertion (A) :** ROI is the index to study management efficiency.

**Reason (R) :** Earning power in relation to total investment is measured by ROI.

*Codes:*
A. Both (A) and (R) are true, and (R) is the correct explanation of (A).
B. Both (A) and (R) are true, but (R) is not a correct explanation of (A).
C. (A) is true, but (R) is false.
D. (A) is false, but (R) is true.

**198. Assertion (A) :** For a company, every debt is not a loan, but every loan is a debt.

**Reason (R) :** In the case of deposit of money with the company, it is the depositor who is the prime mover, where as in the case of loan it is the company who is the prime mover.

*Codes:*
A. Both (A) and (R) are true, and (R) is the correct explanation of (A).
B. Both (A) and (R) are true, but (R) is not a correct explanation of (A).
C. (A) is true, but (R) is false.
D. (A) is false, but (R) is true.

**199. Assertion (A) :** A company is accountable to the society since it makes use of community owned assets and other infrastructural facilities and concessions provided by the state from the tax payers' money.

**Reason (R) :** The best way of social responsibility reporting is to prepare a Value-Added Statement (VAS) which shows the income earned by share holders.

*Codes:*
A. Both (A) and (R) are true, and (R) is the correct explanation of (A).
B. Both (A) and (R) are true, but (R) is not a correct explanation of (A).
C. (A) is true, but (R) is false.
D. (A) is false, but (R) is true.

**200. Assertion (A) :** The matching concept requires that costs be recognised as expenses in the period in which revenue is realised.

**Reason (R) :** There may not be a match between expenditure and expenses over a short period.

*Codes:*
A. Both (A) and (R) are true, and (R) is the correct explanation of (A).
B. Both (A) and (R) are true, but (R) is not a correct explanation of (A).
C. (A) is true, but (R) is false.
D. (A) is false, but (R) is true.

**201. Assertion (A) :** According to International Accounting Standards Committee, fixed production expenses should be included in inventory valuation on the basis of normal capacity. According to the Institute of Chartered Accountants of India, it is for the management to decide the Question.

**Reason (R) :** The Question to be decided is whether the fixed production expenses be excluded from inventory valuation and charged wholly to the revenue of that year or whether these expenses be included on the basis of normal level of production. The former method, is called 'marginal costing' and the latter 'absorption costing?

*Codes:*
A. Both (A) and (R) are true, and (R) is the correct explanation of (A).
B. Both (A) and (R) are true, but (R) is not a correct explanation of (A).
C. (A) is true, but (R) is false.
D. (A) is false, but (R) is true.

**202. Assertion (A) :** The fixed assets in the balance sheet of a limited company are required to be shown at cost less depreciation.

**Reason (R) :** The balance sheet and profit and loss account are to disclose a true and fair view.

*Codes:*
A. Both (A) and (R) are true, and (R) is the correct explanation of (A).
B. Both (A) and (R) are true, but (R) is not a correct explanation of (A).
C. (A) is true, but (R) is false.
D. (A) is false, but (R) is true.

**203. Assertion (A) :** Share premium amount can be refunded in cash to equity share holders.

**Reason (R) :** Share premium is usually collected when the market price of the shares is higher than the face value of the share.

*Codes:*
A. Both (A) and (R) are true, and (R) is the correct explanation of (A).
B. Both (A) and (R) are true, but (R) is not a correct explanation of (A).
C. (A) is true, but (R) is false.
D. (A) is false, but (R) is true.

**204. Assertion (A) :** Conventionally, a newly-started company should adopt a low geared capital structure where the share of equity capital and reserves is higher than the share of fixed interest bearing securities.

**Reason (R)** : During initial years, the profit is low and the company tries to strengthen its financial position.

*Codes:*

A. Both (A) and (R) are true, and (R) is the correct explanation of (A).
B. Both (A) and (R) are true, but (R) is not a correct explanation of A.
C. (A) is true, but (R) is false.
D. (A) is false, but (R) is true.

**205. Assertion (A)** : A new firm can be profitable and yet not be able to pay its debts as they become due.

**Reason (R)** : New firms often have the problem of having increased investments in inventory and fixed assets at an amount which exceeds cash generated from operations.

*Codes:*

A. Both (A) and (R) are true, and (R) is the correct explanation of (A).
B. Both (A) and (R) are true, but (R) is not a correct explanation of (A).
C. (A) is true, but (R) is false.
D. (A) is false, but (R) is true.

**206.** Which one of the following routines best describes the chronology of steps taken in the selling process?
A. Receipt of order, invoicing, processing order, shipment of goods.
B. Invoicing, processing order, shipment of goods, accounting for sale.
C. Receipt of order, processing order, accounting for sale, shipment of goods
D. Processing order, invoicing, shipment of goods, accounting for sale.

**207.** When prices show a rising trend, which one of the following methods of inventory valuation will result in lower income and lower valuation of inventory?
A. FIFO
B. LIFO
C. Simple average method
D. Weighted average method

**208.** Under which one of the following methods of depreciation is the amount of the assets never reduced to zero?
A. Straight line method
B. Diminishing balance method
C. Sum of years digit method
D. Annuity method

**209.** Consider the following statements:
Secret reserves serve the purpose of
I. enabling the directors to tide over unfavourable items
II. meeting exceptional losses
III. increasing the working capital
Of these statement:
A. I and II are correct
B. II and III are correct
C. I and III are correct
D. I, II and III are correct

**210.** ABC analysis is a:
A. System of profit and loss appropriation
B. technique of financial planning
C. technique of inventory control
D. technique of profit determination

**211.** A sum of ₹ 50,000 was spent by a factory in over – hauling its existing plant and machinery and it enhanced its working life by five years.

The aforesaid expenditure is:
A. Capital expenditure
B. Partly capital and partly revenue expenditure
C. Revenue loss
D. Deferred revenue expenditure

**212.** Match List-I (Items of Expenditure and Receipt) with List-II (Nature of Expenditure and Receipt) and select the correct answer using the codes given below the lists:

| List-I | List-II |
|---|---|
| I. Replacement cost of an old asset | (*a*) Revenue expenditure |
| II. Special repairing charges of an asset | (*b*) Capital receipt |
| III. Huge advertisement expenses | (*c*) Deferred revenue expenditure |
| IV. Sale value of an old motorcar | (*d*) Capital expenditure |

*Codes:*

| | I | II | III | IV |
|---|---|---|---|---|
| A. | (*d*) | (*a*) | (*c*) | (*b*) |
| B. | (*d*) | (*a*) | (*b*) | (*c*) |
| C. | (*a*) | (*d*) | (*c*) | (*b*) |
| D. | (*a*) | (*d*) | (*b*) | (*c*) |

**213.** Which one of the following is not a capital expenditure?
A. Legal expenses incurred in raising a debenture loan
B. Compensation paid to a dismissed employee
C. Brokerage paid to the broker at the time of purchase of land
D. Expenses for pulling down an old structure

**214.** Out standing wages is an item of:
A. Current asset
B. Current liability
C. Non-current asset
D. Non-current liability

**215.** A and B partners sharing profits and losses in the ratio of 3 : 1. They have agreed to admit C into the partnership firm. C is given 1/4 th share of future profits which he acquires in the ratio 2 : 1 from A and B. The new profit sharing ratio would be:

A. 4 : 3 : 1  B. 7 : 2 : 3
C. 3 : 1 : 7  D. 7 : 3 : 2

**216.** A, B, C were partners sharing profits in the proportion of 1/2, 1/3 and 1/6 respectively. On 31st March, 1997 their capital stood as follows:

A = ₹ 4,00,000
B = ₹ 3,00.000
C = ₹ 2,50,000

A sum of ₹ 1,20,000 also appeared as reserve fund in their balance sheet on this date. B retires on this date when the goodwill of the firm was valued at ₹ 1,80,000.

Profit and loss adjustment account prepared on that date without taking goodwill and reserve fund into consideration showed a net profit of ₹ 28500. The net amount payable to B will be:

A. ₹ 3,82,500  B. ₹ 4,09,500
C. ₹ 3,63,800  D. ₹ 4,04,000

**217.** X and Y are partners sharing profits in the ratio of 1 : 1. They admit Z for 1/5 th share who contributed ₹ 25,000 for his share of goodwill. The total value of the goodwill of the firm will be:

A. ₹ 25,000  B. ₹ 50,000
C. ₹ 1,00,000  D. ₹ 1,25,000

**218.** On the death of a partner, the amount of joint life policy should be credited to the capital accounts of:

A. all partners including the deceased partner in their profit-sharing ratio.
B. remaining partners in the new profit sharing ratio.
C. remaining partners equally.
D. all partners including the deceased partners in their capital ratio.

**219.** In the absence of any contract to the contrary, capital profit or arising on dissolution of a partnership firm is credited to the partners' capital account in:

A. Equal proportion
B. Capital ratio
C. Profit-sharing ratio
D. Proportion to assets realised

**220.** Writing off the expired cost of an intangible asset is called:

A. Amortisation
B. Capitalisation
C. Depletion
D. Depreciation

**221.** The debt : equity ratio of a company is 8 : 1. It was decided to issue bonus shares in the ratio of 1 : 2. The debt : equity ratio after the issue of bonus shares would be:

A. 8 : 1  B. 4 : 1
C. 1 : 8  D. 1 : 4

**222.** Profit prior to incorporation is an example of:

A. Revenue reserve  B. Secret reserve
C. Capital reserve  D. General reserve

**223.** Interest on calls in arrears is charged according to Table A of schedule I to the Companies Act, 1956 at the rate of:

A. 5% p.a.  B. 6% p.a.
C. 12% p.a.  D. 10% p.a.

**224.** The ratios which measure the relative contribution of financing by owners and financing provided by outsiders are called:

A. Liquidity ratios  B. Leverage ratios
C. Activity ratios  D. Profitability ratios

**225.** Right's shares are the shares that are offered to the:

A. Directors of the company
B. Debenture holders
C. Existing share holders
D. Creditors of the company

**226.** Unpaid calls are shown in the balance sheet of a company:

A. By adding it to the share capital
B. By deducting it from the called-up share capital
C. Under the head 'current assets'
D. Under the head 'current liabilities'

**227.** Pro-rata allotment of shares means allotment of shares:

A. Equally amongst the applicants
B. At the discretion of the directors
C. To all the applicants in proportion to the shares applied for
D. To only a few selected applicants

**228.** Match List-I with List-II and select the correct answer using the codes given below the Lists:

| List-I | List-II |
|---|---|
| I. Acid test ratio | (*a*) Liquidity ratio |
| II. Gearing ratio | (*b*) Profitability ratio |
| III. Working capital turnover ratio | (*c*) Leverage ratio |
| IV. Return on capital employed | (*d*) Long-term solvency ratio |
| | (*e*) Activity ratio |

***Codes:***

| | I | II | III | IV |
|---|---|---|---|---|
| A. | (*a*) | (*c*) | (*e*) | (*b*) |
| B. | (*b*) | (*e*) | (*a*) | (*c*) |
| C. | (*a*) | (*e*) | (*d*) | (*b*) |
| D. | (*e*) | (*c*) | (*d*) | (*a*) |

**229.** Which of the following transaction(s) will improve the Current Ratio?

I. Bills receivable dishonored.
II. Cash collected from customers.
III. Issue of new shares.
IV. Payment of preliminary expenses by way of equity shares.

Select the correct answer using the codes given below:

***Codes:***

A. I, II and III
B. IV alone
C. III alone
D. II and IV

**230.** In the case of a particular depreciation method, the periodic depreciation is smaller than the asset's actual annual depreciation cost. The annual net incidence on profit and loss account remains constant due to incorporation of only fixed depreciation. The periodic depreciation is not recorded through the asset account. The depreciation method used in this case is:

A. Sinking fund method
B. Diminishing balance method
C. Annuity method
D. Sum-of-years digits method

**231.** X Ltd. forfeited 30 shares of ₹ 10 each fully called up for non-payment of allotment money of ₹ 3 per share and call money of ₹ 4 per share. These shares are reissued for ₹ 8 per share fully paid. What is the amount to be transferred to capital Reserve Account?

A. ₹ 300 B. ₹ 60
C. ₹ 30 D. ₹ 90

**232.** Credit sales of a company during the year are ₹ 1,20,000, Debtors ₹ 20,000 and Bills Receivable ₹ 10,000. The average collection period is:

A. 3 Months B. 4 Months
C. 5 Months D. 6 Months

**233.** Collection of sundry debtors would:

A. Increase current ratio
B. Decrease current ratio
C. Have no effect on current ratio
D. Increase debtors' turnover

**234.** Which one of the following statements is not correct? A high gross profit margin ratio is the result of:

A. higher sales price, cost of goods sold remaining constant
B. lower cost of goods sold, sales price remaining constant
C. an increase in the proportionate volume of higher margin items
D. increase in the sales return, cost of goods sold remaining the same

**235.** A company with a paid-up capital of 5000 equity shares of ₹ 10 each has a turnover of four times with a margin of 8% on sales. The ROI of the company will be:

A. 28% B. 32%
C. 35% D. 42%

**236.** The best definition of 'Capital employed' in calculating the rate of return on investment is:

A. Current assets + gross fixed assets
B. Current assets + net fixed assets
C. Working capital + gross fixed assets
D. Working capital + net fixed assets

**237.** While calculating the net present value under discounted cash flow method of return on investment analysis, the calculations involved are:

I. Cash outflow
II. Discounted net cash flow
III. Cash inflow
IV. Net present value

The correct sequence of these calculations is:

A. IV, I, III, II B. I, III, II, IV
C. I, II, III, IV D. III, I, IV, II

**238.** Patents and copyrights fall under the category of:

A. Current assets B. Liquid assets
C. Intangible assets D. Nominal assets

**239.** Match List-I (Balance sheet items) with the List-II (Classification) and select the correct answer using the codes given below the Lists:

| List-I | List-II |
|---|---|
| I. Discount on debenture | (*a*) Current liability |
| II. Forfeited shares | (*b*) Non-current asset account |
| III. Income tax payable | (*c*) Current asset. |
| IV. Debtors' acceptance | (*d*) Non-current liability |

***Codes:***

| | I | II | III | IV |
|---|---|---|---|---|
| A. | (*b*) | (*d*) | (*a*) | (*c*) |
| B. | (*d*) | (*b*) | (*c*) | (*a*) |
| C. | (*b*) | (*d*) | (*c*) | (*a*) |
| D. | (*d*) | (*b*) | (*a*) | (*c*) |

**240.** Ajoy Ltd. makes a net profit of ₹ 1,00,000, after providing for depreciation on assets amounting to ₹ 20.000 and writing off preliminary expenses amounting to ₹ 10,000 and gain of ₹ 5,000 on sale of a piece of machinery. Funds from operation of Ajoy Ltd. would be:

A. ₹ 1,00,000 B. ₹ 1,20,000
C. ₹ 1,25,000 D. ₹ 1,35,000

**241.** According to the Principle of Subrogation:

A. The insured must take all necessary steps to minimise the loss

B. The actual amount of loss, not exceeding the amount of the policy, shall be paid
C. The actual amount of loss should be distributed among the different insurers of the same risk
D. On making good the loss, the insured to succeed to all the rights of the insured regarding the subject matter of insurance

**242.** The persons who agree to insure cargo, hull or freight are called:
A. undertakers B. caretakers
C. underwriters D. bookkeepers

**Directions (Q. 243-245):** *In the given context of the statement, mark the answer according to the following codes.*
***Codes:***
A. Both (A) and (R) are true, and (R) is the correct explanation of (A)
B. Both (A) and (R) are true, but (R) is not a correct explanation of (A)
C. (A) is true, but (R) is false.
D. (A) is false, but (R) is true.

**243. Assertion (A) :** The liability of shareholders in a private limited company is limited to the amount unpaid on shares.
**Reason (R) :** The number of shareholders of a private limited company is limited to fifty.

**244. Assertion (A) :** High capital gearing leads to greater speculation.
**Reason (R) :** Proportion of equity the share capital in relation to the total capital comprising the other securities is small leading to capitalisation being highly geared.

**245. Assertion (A) :** Special rules and procedures are followed in the import and export trade.
**Reason (R) :** The need for import and export trade is explained by the principles of comparative Cost Theory.

**246.** Partnership is a form of business organisation in which business debts can be recovered:
A. the managing partners
B. all the managers and partners
C. the firm and the managers
D. the firm and all the partners

**247.** Of the following organisations the easiest to wind up is the:
A. Public Limited Company
B. Multinational Corporation
C. Private Limited Company
D. Partnership Firm

**248.** Match List-I with List-II and select the correct answer using the codes given below the lists:

| List-I | List-II |
|---|---|
| I. Partners and Firms | (*a*) agent and principal relationship |
| II. Sole Proprietorship | (*b*) prospectus |
| III. Public Limited company | (*c*) personal supervision |
| IV. Nominal partnership | (*d*) firm image |

***Codes:***

| | I | II | III | IV |
|---|---|---|---|---|
| A. | (*a*) | (*b*) | (*c*) | (*d*) |
| B. | (*b*) | (*c*) | (*a*) | (*d*) |
| C. | (*a*) | (*c*) | (*b*) | (*d*) |
| D. | (*d*) | (*b*) | (*a*) | (*c*) |

**249.** The main object of stock exchange is to:
A. Provide facilities for speculation
B. Safeguard the interest of investors
C. Help in the capital formation the country
D. Provide a ready market for securities

**250.** Fishing has been classified as:
A. Extractive Industry
B. Genetic Industry
C. Manufacturing Industry
D. None of these

**251.** 'Fishing Culture' is classified in:
A. Extractive Industry B. Genetic Industry
C. Construction Industry D. None of these

**252.** If a partnership firm is not registered with the Registrar of firms:
A. it has to pay penalty for non-registration
B. the members can file suits against the third party
C. the members can enforce their rights among themselves
D. None of these

**253.** Which of the following is not an economic activity?
A. A doctor practising
B. A lawyer practising law
C. A professional cricketer playing cricket
D. A student playing cricket

**254.** In order an activity may be called business which of the following condition need not be satisfied?
A. There should be exchange or transfer of goods or services
B. There should be continuity of dealings
C. Dealings may be either in goods or services
D. There should be certainty of profit

**255.** Fish culture, should be classified as:
A. extractive industry
B. genetic industry
C. manufacturing industry
D. construction industry

**256.** In a private business enterprise profit should be regarded as:
A. the legitimate reward for honest end labour
B. the supreme objective of business
C. the sole objective of business
D. subsidiary to service motive

**257.** Which of the following should be regarded as the most important factor for deciding the form of business organisation?
A. Types of business, trading manufacturing, etc
B. Expected volume of business
C. Financial requirements
D. Area of operations

**258.** An establishment insured its property worth ₹ 50 lacs for ₹ 30 lacs against fire. The actual loss due to fire was ₹ 40 lacs. The firm can get:
A. ₹ 50 lacs B. ₹ 40 lacs
C. ₹ 30 lacs D. None of these

**259.** The liability of a sole proprietor is:
A. limited to the extent of his capital invested in the business
B. limited to the extent of the value of business assets
C. limited to the extent of the value of business assets and his all private assets
D. None of these

**260.** The maximum number of partners in a firm for a general business is:
A. 7 B. 10
C. 50 D. 20

**261.** The agreement of partnership:
A. must be in oral
B. must be in writing
C. can be either oral or in writing
D. must be in writing on a stamp paper

**262.** Liability of partners in respect of the firm's debts is:
A. limited up to the amount of his capital in the business
B. unlimited
C. limited up to the amount of guarantee given by the partner
D. limited up to the amount of his capital and loan to the firm if any

**263.** Partnership may come into existence:
A. by the operation of law
B. by an express agreement only
C. by an express or implied agreement only
D. by inheritance of property

**264.** A partner has an implied authority to:
A. acquire immovable property on behalf of the firm
B. enter into a partnership on behalf of the firm
C. to borrow money on behalf of the firm
D. to compromise or relinquish any claim or portion of a claim by the firm

**265.** If a firm is not registered with the registrar of firms:
A. it has to pay penalty for non-registration
B. it introduces certain disabilities which make registration necessary at one time or the other
C. the members of the unregistered firm can enforce their rights between themselves
D. the members of the unregistered firm can file suit against third parties

**266.** Dissolution of firm takes place:
A. by the death or insolvency of any one partner
B. the retirement of any one partner
C. by the expiry of the term
D. by the insolvency of all but one partner

**267.** Registration of Joint Stock Company is:
A. compulsory
B. optional
C. compulsory for public companies and optional for private company
D. compulsory for companies with liabilities limited by shares and optional for companies with liabilities limited by guarantee

**268.** The minimum number of member require for registration of a co-operative society is:
A. two B. seven
C. ten D. twenty

**269.** Co-operative and public companies are similar in respect of:
A. the liability of members
B. the minimum number of members required for registration
C. the maximum number of members
D. None of these

**270.** Profits earned by a co-operative society are distributed:
A. to members in the ratio of capital held by them
B. to member in the ratio of purchases made by them
C. by providing a nominal rate of interest on capital contribution by members and remaining in the ratio of purchases made by members
D. by declaring divided at a specific rate and remaining transferring to general reserves

**271.** Management of a co-operative organisation is in the hands of:
A. persons nominated by the Registrar of co-operative societies
B. an elected body by the members
C. some persons nominated by Registrar of co-operative societies and other selected by the member
D. the promoters of the co-operative organisation

**272.** Which of the following is an example of a company incorporated by a special act of parliament?
A. Delhi Cloth Mills Ltd.
B. Tata Iron and Steel Co. Ltd.
C. Industrial Finance Corporation.
D. Swadeshi Cotton Mills Ltd.

**273.** Which of the following documents need not be prepared and Registered with the Registrar of companies in Public limited companies?
A. Memorandum of Association
B. Articles of Association
C. Statutory Declaration
D. Directors of undertaking to take up and pay for qualification shares

**274.** The term, 'capitalisation' is used in relation to:
A. sole-proprietorship
B. partnership
C. joint stock companies
D. co-operative societies

**275.** Which of the following methods provide a better basis of capitalisation for an established concern?
A. Add up the cost of fixed assets and working capital required
B. Add up the cost of fixed assets, working capital and cost of promotion etc.
C. Capitalise the profits to be earned
D. Estimate on the basis of financial position of other similar companies

**276.** Watered capital means:
A. over-capitalistation
B. under capitalistation
C. excessive capital
D. part of the capital not represented by assets

**277.** Over capitalisation may be remedied by:
A. increasing the number of equity shares
B. increasing the per value of shares
C. issuing additional preference shares
D. redemption of debentures

**278.** Under Capitalisation can be remedied by:
A. issue of bonus shares
B. redemption of preference shares
C. redemption of debentures
D. reduction of interest of debentures

**279.** Capital gearing means:
A. proper capitalisation
B. watered capital
C. fixation of a proper ratio between two or more types of securities
D. trading on equity

**280.** A company is said to be low geared when the proportion of:
A. equity capital to the total capital is small
B. preference capital to the total capital is small
C. debentures capital to the total capital is small
D. both preference and debentures capital to the total is small

**281.** Working capital can be used for the purchase of:.
A. machinery B. goodwill
C. land and building D. raw material

**282.** Which of the following sources is not used for medium term financing?
A. Issue of equity shares
B. Issue of preference shares
C. Issue of debentures
D. Terms loan from banks

**283.** Working capital is represented by:
A. current liabilities
B. current assets minus current liabilities
C. total assets minus current liabilities
D. cash-in-hand plus stock-in-trade

**284.** Participating preference shares are those which participate:
A. in the voting
B. in the general meeting of the company
C. in the management of the company
D. in the profits over and above their fixed dividend

**285.** In which of the following, rate of interest/dividends is not fixed?
A. equity capital B. debentures
C. preference capital D. public deposits

**286.** To which of the following types of companies, debentures suit as a source of finance?
A. companies with fluctuating earnings
B. campanies which stable earnings
C. companies which cannot earn a rate of profit higher than the rate of interest, payable on debentures.
D. All of these

**287.** First debentures are those:
A. which are issued before share capital
B. which are repayable before other debentures
C. which are secured by a floating charges
D. which are secured by a fixed charges

**288.** Underwriters are persons who:
A. purchase the shares and debentures of a company
B. work as agents of the company for the sale of shares and debentures
C. manage the issue of shares and debentures
D. undertake to buy those shares and debentures not subscribed for by the public

**289.** Which of the following institutions undertake underwriting of shares and debentures of companies?
A. Unit Trust of India
B. Industrial Development Bank of India
C. State Finance Corporations
D. All of these

**290.** Which of the following sources of finance do not pose a burden on the company?
A. Public deposits
B. Debentures
C. Loans from financial institutions
D. Retained earnings

**291.** Which of the following is not a component of the new issue market?
A. Stock Exchange
B. Unit Trust of India
C. Financial Institution of India like IFC, IDBI
D. LIC

**292.** When an existing company offers its shares for sale to the existing shareholders, it is known as:
A. private placing B. bonus issue
C. rights issue D. offer for sale

**293.** The first stock exchange was set up in India in:
A. Kolkata B. Mumbai
C. Delhi D. Chennai

**294.** The first stock exchange was set up in India in:
A. 1887 B. 1905
C. 1908 D. 1923

**295.** Which of the speculators expects the price of securities to rise in the near future?
A. bull B. bear
C. stag D. lame duck

**296.** Which of the following speculative activities is based on disparity in quote prices in different markets?
A. Option dealings B. Arbitrage
C. Margin trading D. Blank transfers

**297.** Contango charge is paid by a:
A. bull speculator to bear speculator
B. bear speculator to bull speculator
C. lame duck to bull speculator
D. bull to lame duck speculator

**298.** Listing of securities in a stock exchange for the purpose of trading indicates that:
A. at the time of listing, the company is financially sound
B. at the time of listing, the company is legally organised
C. the stock exchange guarantees about the financial soundness of the company
D. All of these

**299.** An existing company raising additional capital:
A. must offer the new shares to the existing shareholders
B. need not offer the new shares to the existing shareholders
C. issues share to debenture holders
D. issue shares to preference share holders

**300.** Stock exchange deals with the:
A. second hand securities
B. issues of equity shares
C. issue of preference shares
D. issue of debentures

**301.** One of the impelling causes of business combination is:
A. desire for bigness B. wasteful competition
C. influence of tariffs D. rationalisation

**302.** When a cement mill, a steel mill and a chemical company combine, it is a case of?
A. horizontal combination
B. vertical combination
C. diagonal combination
D. circular combination

**303.** Which of the following is an example of vertical integration?
A. One small steel mill combines with a big steel mill
B. Two steel mills of the same combine
C. Iron ore firm combines with iron melting firm
D. Paper mill combines with a publishing company

**304.** Combination of plants at the same stage of production or in the same trade or commerce is called a:
A. horizontal combination
B. vertical combination
C. diagonal combination
D. allied combination

**305.** One of the main advantages of vertical combination is that.
A. it helps in avoiding competition
B. it helps in controlling the market
C. it helps in controlling the quality of raw material and finished output
D. it brings about coordination between activities of combining units

**306.** Pools are a type:
A. horizontal combinations
B. vertical combinations
C. allied combinations
D. None of these

**307.** Cartel is a type of:
A. horizontal combination
B. vertical combination
C. allied combination
D. mixed combination

**308.** FICCI was formed in the year:
A. 1920 B. 1925
C. 1926 D. 1951

**309.** Business combinations are formed to derive the advantages of:
A. enabling the units to join hands and establish a monopoly
B. avoiding wasteful competition
C. enabling business units to withstand the rigors of a depression
D. All of these

**310.** Match the following:

| List-I | List-II |
|---|---|
| I. Trust | (a) Company A holds more than 51% share capital of the company B |
| II. Merger | (b) Existing companies A and B are merged into company C |
| III. Holding Company | (c) Business of number of firms is entrusted to the care of Board of Trustees |
| IV. Amalgamation | (d) Company A takes over Company B |

Select the correct answer from the code given below:
***Codes:***

| | I | II | III | IV |
|---|---|---|---|---|
| A. | (b) | (c) | (a) | (d) |
| B. | (a) | (b) | (c) | (d) |
| C. | (c) | (d) | (a) | (b) |
| D. | (b) | (a) | (d) | (c) |

**311.** MRTP Act came into force in:
A. 1969 B. 1970
C. 1971 D. 1980

**312.** Resale price maintenance is a:
A. Restrictive trade practice
B. Monopolistic trade practice
C. None of these
D. Both of these

**313.** When custom duty is levied according to the value of the goods, it is known as:
A. revenue duty B. excise duty
C. specific duty D. ad-valorem duty

**314.** When custom duty is levied according to the weight of good, it is known as:
A. revenue duty B. excise duty
C. specific duty D. ad-valorem duty

**315.** Import procedure begins with:
A. mate's receipt
B. marine insurance
C. indent
D. shipping bill

**316.** Shipping order is issued by the owner of the ship when:
A. whole of the ship is hired
B. major part of the ship is hired
C. freight is reserved for the exporter
D. ship starts its journey

**317.** A shipping bill is prepared when:
A. goods are damaged in the ship.
B. goods reach their destination in satisfactory condition.
C. goods are not cleared by the custom authorities.
D. None of these

**318.** Entrepot trade means:
A. import trade
B. export trade
C. foreign trade
D. goods imported for re-export

**319.** A letter of credit means:
A. a letter sent by importer to exporter sanctioning credit deal.
B. a letter sent by exporter to importer sanction credit deal.
C. a letter containing conditions of credit purchase or sale.
D. a bank agreeing to accept and pay on due date.

**320.** A bill of loading transferable to another person by:
A. mere delivery
B. endorsement and delivery
C. any of the above
D. this one is not transferable

**321.** Charter party means:
A. an agreement by which the ship owner agrees to place the entire or part of the ship at the disposal of the merchant.
B. the party who works as a middle man between shipper and shipping company.
C. the party who performs loading or unloading operations on the ship.
D. the party working as a middleman between importer and exporter.

**322.** State Trading Corporation of India was established:
A. by a special Act of Parliament
B. under the companies Act, 1956 as a private limited company.
C. under the companies Act, 1956 as a public limited company.
D. as departmental undertaking.

**323.** Which of the following is not a subsidiary of the State Trading Corporation of India?
A. Indian Motion Picture Export Corporation of India

B. Handicraft and a Handlooms Export Corporation of India Ltd.
C. Project and Equipment Corporation of India Ltd.
D. All of these

**324.** Mate's receipt is issued by:
A. the exporter
B. the importer
C. the captain of the ship or his assistant
D. the bank

**325.** Under which of the following principles of insurance, parties to the contract must disclose and material facts known to them?
A. Indemnity
B. Utmost good faith
C. Subrogation
D. Insurable interest

**326.** A person can insure:
A. any body's property
B. only his own property
C. only that property in which he is interested
D. only that property in which he has financial interest

**327.** In the case of fire insurance, the insured must have insurable interest in the thing insured at the time:
A. when policy is taken
B. when loss is incurred
C. through out the period of contract of insurance
D. both when policy is taken and when loss is incurred

**328.** In marine insurance, the insured must have insurable interest at the time:
A. when policy is taken.
B. when the event happens.
C. when policy is taken as well as event happens.
D. when throughout the period of contract of insurance.

**329.** A person had insured his goods worth ₹ 10,000 for ₹ 8,000 against fire and his loss by fire was ₹ 9,000. His claims is:
A. ₹ 8,000
B. ₹ 9,000
C. ₹ 10,000
D. None of these

**330.** A person insured his property worth ₹ 10,000 against fire for ₹ 8,000 only. His actual loss by fire is ₹ 5,000 and there is average clause in the policy. His is claim is:
A. ₹ 10,000
B. ₹ 8,000
C. ₹ 5,000
D. ₹ 4,000

**331.** According to the principle of cause proximate the insured can recover the loss from the insurer:
A. if it is proximity caused by any of the perils insured against
B. if it is caused by any of the remote cause
C. if it is caused by any reason, what so ever
D. All of these

**332.** The principle of subrogation applies to:
A. all types of insurance
B. fire insurance only
C. marine insurance only
D. fire and marine insurance

**333.** The principle of contribution applies when:
A. there is two or more insurance on one risk
B. the insured does not take necessary steps to mitigate the loss
C. the insured insures the same risk partly with other insurers
D. the premium is not paid by the insured

**334.** Surrender value of a life policy is the amount payable by Life Insurance Corporation when:
A. the life policy matures by death.
B. the life policy matures after the expiry of the policy period.
C. the life policy is withdrawn before its maturity.
D. the payment of premiums is discontinued and the amount is payable at the maturity of the policy.

**335.** Principle of subrogation states that:
A. the actual amount of loss should be distributed among the differenced insurers of the same risk.
B. on making good the loss, the insurers is entitled to succeed to all the rights of the insured regarding the subject matter of insurance.
C. the insured must take all necessary steps to minimise the loss.
D. the actual amount of loss, exceeding the amount of the policy, shall be paid.

**336.** Average clause in a fire policy is inserted in order to check mainly:
A. under-insurance
B. over-insurance
C. both other-insurance and under-insurance
D. All of these

**337.** X mortgages certain property with Y who has insurable interest in property:
A. only X
B. only Y
C. both X and Y
D. None of these

**338.** Principle of insurable interest applies to:
A. life insurance only
B. fire insurance only
C. fire and marine insurance only
D. all types of insurance

**339.** In which of the following kinds of insurance, insurable interest should be present only at the time of loss subject-matter:
A. life insurance
B. fire insurance
C. marine insurance
D. All of these

**340.** Unless the marine policy otherwise provides, insurer is liable:

A. if the loss is caused by ordinary wear and tear.
B. if the loss is caused by peril insured against.
C. if the loss is caused by ordinary leakage and breakage.
D. if the loss is caused by inherent nature of the subject-matter.

**341.** Which one of the following defines co-ordination?

A. Actuating force which inspires a person to put his best for the fulfillment of a task
B. Orderly arranged of group effort to provide unity of action in the pursuit of a common purpose.
C. Process of transmitting information from one person to another or from one unit to another.
D. Process of determining what is to be accomplished and what has been accomplished and if necessary applying corrective measures.

**342.** Consider the following basic steps involved in the process of control:

I. Identifying the strategic control points
II. Establish the standards
III. Measuring performance against standards
IV. Correcting deviations from the standards

The correct sequence of the above steps in the process of control is:

A. I, IV, III, II
B. IV, III, II, I
C. II, I, IV , III
D. II, III, I, IV

**343.** Match List-I with List-II and select the correct answer using the codes given below the lists:

| List-I (Management thinkers) | List-II (Contribution/work) |
|---|---|
| I. Elton Mayo | (*a*) Importance of integrating the company's and employee's goal |
| II. Frederic W. Taylor | (*b*) Social problems of Industrial Civilisation |
| III. Henri Fayol | (*c*) General and Industrial Management. |
| IV. Mary Parker Follet | (*d*) Principles of Scientific Management |

***Codes:***

| | I | II | III | IV |
|---|---|---|---|---|
| A. | (*a*) | (*d*) | (*c*) | (*b*) |
| B. | (*d*) | (*c*) | (*b*) | (*a*) |
| C. | (*b*) | (*d*) | (*c*) | (*a*) |
| D. | (*c*) | (*d*) | (*a*) | (*b*) |

**344.** An organisation structure is effective if it enables individuals to contribute to the objectives of the enterprise. This is known as:

A. Scalar Principle
B. Principle of functional definition
C. Principle of unity of objectives
D. None of these

**345.** Which one of the following orders indicates the correct logical order of managerial functions?

A. Organising, planning, directing, staffing, coordination and control.
B. Planning, organising, staffing, directing, coordination and control.
C. Planning, directing, organising, staffing, control and coordination.
D. Organising, planning, staffing, directing, control and coordination.

**346.** Effective direction does NOT depend on the:

A. Communication process
B. Forces at the subordinate level
C. Ability of the manager
D. Deployment of human resources

**347.** Planning refers to:

A. Looking backward
B. Looking forward
C. Looking forward and backward
D. Looking and actual performance to decide action to be taken

**348.** Which one of the following formulae is used calculate "Cross relationship" under span of control?

A. n (n–1)
B. $n(2^n/_2 -1)$
C. $n(2^n/_2 + n-1)$
D. None of these

**349.** V.A. Graicunas has identified three sets of superior subordinate relationships, which are: Direct single relationship, Direct group relationship and cross relationship. Now if there are two, three, four and five subordinates respectively under one superior then in this context which one of the following Pairs is correctly matched?

| | Number of the subordinates | Total number of relationships |
|---|---|---|
| A. | 2 | 8 |
| B. | 3 | 18 |
| C. | 4 | 48 |
| D. | 5 | 98 |

**350.** Leadership is a function of all the following factors except:

A. Workgroup
B. Product or service
C. Leader
D. Situation

**351.** The main difference between delegation and decentralisation is that:

A. delegation refers primarily to transfer of authority from one individual to another while decentralisation refers to systematic delegation of authority to all units in an organisation.

B. delegation of authority can take place without decentralisation where as there cannot be decentralisation without delegation of authority.
C. delegation represents sharing of excessive burden of key managerial personnel while decentralisation refers to division of top managerial operations.
D. delegation may take place due to administrative, technical and routine reasons while decentralisation involves deliberate action for the smooth functioning of the organisation.

**352.** Management by exception introduces:
A. selective, responsibility oriented reporting
B. reporting of significant variances
C. requirement of full reports on performance
D. computation of actual in different spheres of performance

**353.** Consider the following office equipments used in various offices:

| | |
|---|---|
| I. Fax | II. Typewriter |
| III. Dictaphone | IV. Letter opener |

The correct order in which they are used is:

| | |
|---|---|
| A. I, II, III, IV | B. IV, III, II, I |
| C. II, IV, III, I | D. III, II, IV, I |

**354.** Control refers to:
I. Establishment of standards
II. Measurement of actual performance against the set standards
III. Correction for deviation from standards

Of these statements:
A. I alone is correct
B. III alone is correct
C. I and II are correct
B. I, II, and III are correct

**355.** Which one of the following is not related to the trait theory of leadership?
A. Physical factors such as height
B. Intelligence and extroversion
C. Self confidence and ambition
D. Training and experience of employees

**356.** Match List-I with List-II and select the correct answer from the codes given below the lists:

| List-I | List-II |
|---|---|
| I. Planning | (*a*) Training |
| II. Staffing | (*b*) Forecasting |
| III. Directing | (*c*) Evaluating |
| IV. Controlling | (*d*) Motivating |
| | (*e*) Grouping |

***Codes:***

| | I | II | III | IV |
|---|---|---|---|---|
| A. | (*c*) | (*a*) | (*d*) | (*e*) |
| B. | (*c*) | (*e*) | (*a*) | (*b*) |
| C. | (*b*) | (*a*) | (*d*) | (*c*) |
| D. | (*b*) | (*e*) | (*a*) | (*c*) |

**357.** Decentralisation of an organization is commended on account of which of the following advantages?
I. Reduced burden on top executives
II. Executive development
III. Improvement of morale
IV. Solves problems of coordination

Select the correct answer from the codes given below and mark your answer sheet accordingly:

***Codes:***

| | |
|---|---|
| A. II and III | B. I, II and IV |
| C. I, II and III | D. III and IV |

**358.** In a functional organisation:
A. There are no advisers, the executives alone having the authority and competence
B. There are specialist advisers having no authority
C. The entire organisation is divided into functions with specific role for specialists
D. The organisation is divided into functions with specialists having authority

**359.** The process of grouping activities into units for the purpose of administration may be referred to as:

| | |
|---|---|
| A. Departmentalisation | B. Decentralisation |
| C. Co-ordination | D. Specialisation. |

**360.** Span of control means that:
A. an organisation consists of various departments
B. each person's authority is clearly defined
C. every subordinate has one superior
D. a manager can supervise only a limited number of subordinates

**361.** If a general manager asks the sales manager to recruit some sales men on his behalf, it is an instance of:
A. division of authority
B. decentralisation of authority
C. delegation of authority
D. delegation of responsibility

**362.** Which one of the following principles states that recurring decisions should be handled in a routine manner by lower level managers whereas problems involving unusual matters only should be referred to higher levels?
A. Principle of unity of command
B. Scalar principle
C. Principle of exception
D. Principle of commitment

**363.** MBO is a technique which requires that the objectives of the enterprise:
A. be written and defined in broad terms
B. lay down the time period for achieving the results
C. include a plan of action for achieving the desired results
D. be defined in terms of measurable results

**Directions (Qs. No. 364 and 365):** *In the given context of the statement, mark the answer using the given codes:*

*Codes:*

A. Both (A) and (R) are true, and (R) is the correct explanation of (A).
B. Both (A) and (R) are true, but (R) is not a correct explanation of (A).
C. (A) is true, but (R) is false.
D. (A) is false, but (R) is true.

**364. Assertion (A) :** Management is a continuous operation or process involving the interaction of all functions.

**Reason (R) :** Managers first plan, then organize and finally perform the function of controlling.

**365. Assertion (A) :** When the span of control is wide, coordination and control becomes difficult.

**Reason (R) :** In a narrow span levels of authority decrease.

**366.** In the field of management some of the important techniques, relate to budgeting, cost accounting, planning and control are through:
A. Operational research
B. PERT & CPM
C. Budgetary control
D. Financial Administration

**367.** Which of the following management functions are closely related?
A. Planning and organising
B. Staffing and control
C. Planning and control
D. Planning and staffing

**368.** "Human Relations Approach" to management was originated by:
A. Henery Fayol B. Winslow Taylor
C. Elton Mayo D. Peter F. Drucker

**369.** The famous book "The Philosophy of Management" was written by:
A. Henery Fayol B. Oliver Sheldon
C. F.W. Taylor D. Urwick

**370.** Policy making is an important part of the process of:
A. Planning
B. Co-ordinating
C. Organising
D. Motivating

**371.** A firm has these characteristics : It is involved in the manufacture of custom built machinery, its products have shorter life span, the products are processed through different specialists and the products have a rigid time schedule to be met. In such a circumstance, which one of the following would be the form of organisation best suited to achieve the objectives?
A. Functional organisation
B. Line and staff organisation
C. Project (Matrix) organisation
D. Line organisation

**372.** The managerial function of organising is:
A. to review and adjust plan in the light of changing conditions
B. to establish a programme for the accomplishment of objections
C. to create a structure of functions and duties to be performed by a group of people
D. to get things done through and with the help of people

**373.** Span of management means:
A. A good organisation should consist of departments
B. Authority of each person must be clearly defined
C. Each subordinate should have one superior
D. A manager can supervise a limited number of executives

**374.** Which of the following is the oldest type of organisation?
A. Functional organisation
B. Line organisation
C. Line and staff organisation
D. Committee organisation

**375.** 'Unity of command' principle of effective direction means:
A. Subordinates should be responsible to one superior
B. Boosting the morale of the subordinates
C. decreasing the productivity of subordinates
D. All of these

**376.** In line organisation:
A. the organisation is divided according to the skill required to perform a work.
B. the organisation is divided according to the type of work involve.
C. the authority flows from the man at the top to the lowest man vertically.
D. each worker serves a number of supervisors.

**377.** The function of 'staff' in 'line and staff' organisation is to:
A. take advice from the line
B. advice the line
C. hold authority and responsibility
D. fix responsibility for performance of tasks in a definite manner upon certain individuals

**378.** Control function of management implies:
A. to bring harmony in various activities
B. to keep the work force constant
C. taking corrective course of action
D. to provide sufficient finance

**379.** The main advantage of line and staff organisation is:
A. Simplicity
B. Specialisation
C. Availability of expert advice
D. Speedy decision making

**380.** The terms speed boss, route clerk etc. are used in relation to:
A. Line organisation
B. Line and staff organisation
C. Functional organisation
D. None of these

**381.** General manager has delegated authority to production Manager for achieving budgeted production. Who is responsible for low production to Board of Directors?
A. Production Supervisors
B. Production Manager
C. General Manager
D. None of these

**382.** Delegation can be:
A. upward B. downward
C. side ward D. All of these

**383.** Unity of command is violated under:
A. Line organisation
B. Line and staff organisation
C. Functional organisation
D. None of these

**384.** 'Theory Y' states that:
A. Workers prefer to be directed
B. Workers exercise self-direction and self control
C. Workers have inherent disliking for work and will avoid it if they can
D. None of these

**385.** 'Theory X' and 'Theory Y' is given by:
A. Maslow B. Herzberg
C. Mc Gregor D. Norman

**386.** The Need – Hierarchy Theory of Motivation is given by:
A. Maslow B. Herzberg
C. Vroom D. Mc Gregor

**387.** Under the Need – Hierarchy Theory, when UDC designation is changed into 'Assistant', it is an example of:
A. Social needs
B. Esteem needs
C. Self-actualisation needs
D. All of these

**388.** Maslow's Need – Hierarchy Theory of Motivation has classified the human needs into five categories as follows:
I. Safety needs
II. Esteem needs
III. Social needs
IV. Physiological needs
V. Self-actualisation needs

What is the sequence of domination of these needs?
A. I, IV, III, II, V B. IV, I, III, II, V
C. V, III, II, IV, I D. IV, I, III, II, V

**389.** Under Expectancy Theory of Motivation, increase in motivation results when:
A. Valence increases
B. Valence decreases
C. No effect on valence
D. None of these

**390.** Which one of the following is a motivating factor as per Herzberg's Theory?
A. Salary and allowances
B. Job design
C. Working conditions
D. None of these

**391.** Match List I with List-II and select the correct answer using the codes given below the lists:

| List-I (Company Issue) | List-II (Company Documents) |
|---|---|
| I. Affirmation of compliance with the registration formalities | (a) Incorporation Certificate |
| II. Classes of shares in which share capital is divided | (b) Statutory declaration |
| III. Rules for forfeiture of shares | (c) Memorandum of association |
| IV. Name and address of the company auditor | (d) Articles of association |
| | (e) Prospectus |

*Codes:*

| | I | II | III | IV |
|---|---|---|---|---|
| A. | (a) | (d) | (c) | (e) |
| B. | (e) | (d) | (c) | (a) |
| C. | (b) | (c) | (d) | (e) |
| D. | (d) | (a) | (e) | (b) |

**392.** A special resolution for the alteration of the objects clause of the memorandum of association of a company having been passed, the aeration is to be confirmed by the:
A. Court concerned
B. Central government

C. Company law board
D. Creditors of the company

**393.** Which one of the following statements is NOT connected with the conversion of share into stock and reconversion into shares?
A. Only shares that are fully paid up can be converted into stock
B. Articles of association shall permit such conversion through a special resolution
C. Conversion can take place by passing an ordinary resolution as provided in the articles
D. Memorandum of association shall permit such conversion

**394.** Under the Indian companies Act 1956, a person can be a director in:
A. 7 companies
B. 10 companies
C. 20 companies
D. 25 companies

**395.** When a person transacts with a company on a matter which is beyond the power of the company, the person will be governed by the doctrine of:
A. Indoor management
B. Self assessment
C. Constructive notice
D. Management by exception

**396.** Which one of the following statements illustrates the doctrine of indoor management?
A. Persons dealing with the company are bound to inquire into the regularity of the internal proceedings
B. Persons dealing with the company are bound to inquire as to whether the general meeting of the shares holders was convened on proper notice
C. Persons dealing with the company are entitled to assume that what has been done has been regularly done by the company and therefore they can hold the company liable even if the internal formalities are found not to have been completed
D. Persons dealing with the company can easily assume that all acts done are introverts the company

**397.** According to Section 2 (45) of the Companies Act (as amended in 1974), a company secretary must possess the qualifications prescribed from time to time by the:
A. Company Law Board
B. Central Government
C. Registrar of Companies
D. Parliament

**398.** The company secretary files copies of resolution passed in an extraordinary general meeting with the Registrar of Companies under section:
A. 173 B. 192
C. 193 D. 208

**399.** The first annual general meeting of a company must be held within:
A. One month from the date of its incorporation
B. Six months from the date of its incorporation
C. 12 months from the date of its incorporation
D. 18 months from the date of its incorporation

**400.** Which one of the following statements relating to a company secretary is not correct?
A. He is not likely to perform duties towards shareholders
B. He is the mouth piece of the Board of Directors
C. He may be considered to be the head of the administrative section of a company
D. He is to arrange for Board meetings

**401.** The last page of the record of proceeding of each meeting in minutes book shall be dated and signed by the chairman of the same meetings within a period of 30 days of the conclusion of the meeting or in the event of death or inability of the chairman within that period by:
A. The managing director
B. A director
C. A director duly authorised by the Board for that purpose
D. The secretary

**402.** Which of the following statements are correct?
I. Minutes are not required to be read at a subsequent general meeting
II. Confirmation of minutes is not an item of agenda in general meetings
III. The chairman may disallow any matter within his opinion is detrimental to the interests of the company from being included in the minutes
IV. Members cannot obtain copies of minutes though they can inspect them during business hours

Select the correct answer using the codes given below:
***Codes:***
A. I and II B. I, II and III
C. I, III and IV D. II, III and IV

**403.** The agenda of the first Board meeting of a limited company generally consists of the following items:
I. Election of chairman
II. Approval of draft prospectus
III. Appointment of officers, *viz.*, the secretary, the manager and the accountant

IV. Incorporation of the company and the legal adviser to report on the same

The correct order in which the above items of the agenda usually appear is:

*Codes:*

A. I, II, III, IV B. IV, III, II, I
C. III, IV, I, II D. IV, I, III, II

**404.** Keeping the company's register of charges and making it available for inspection is a:

A. Contractual duty of the secretary
B. Duty of the secretary general
C. Statutory duty of the secretary
D. Duty delegated to the secretary by the Board

**405.** The maximum period for which the register of members can be closed at a time after giving 7 days pre-notice is:

A. 7 days B. 15 days
C. 30 days D. 45 days

**406.** The company secretary may be held liable for not holding the statutory meeting:

A. On the resolution of the general body
B. On the resolution of the Board of Director
C. Under section 165 of the companies Act
D. On the petition of the creditors

**407.** The minutes book containing the proceedings of general body meeting shall, at the registered office of company:

A. Be kept for inspection for 10 days
B. Be kept for inspection for one day
C. Be kept for inspection for two hours per day
D. Not be kept for inspection

**408.** Perpetuity and separate legal entity are the two most important distinctive features of:

A. Sole proprietorship form of business
B. Partnership
C. Company
D. Joint Hindu Family Firm

**409.** Partnership is a form of business organisation in which business debts can be recovered from:

A. The managing partners
B. All the managers and partners
C. The firm and the managers
D. The firm and all the partners

**410.** Of the following organisation, the easiest to wind up is the:

A. Public Limited Company
B. Multinational Corporation
C. Private Limited Company
D. Partnership Firm

**411.** Match List-I with List-II. Select the answer from the codes given below the lists:

| List-I | List-II |
|---|---|
| I. Partners and firm | (*a*) Agent and principal relationship |
| II. Sole proprietorship | (*b*) Prospectus |
| III. Public limited company | (*c*) Personal supervision |
| IV. Nominal partnership | (*d*) Firm image |

*Codes:*

| | I | II | III | IV |
|---|---|---|---|---|
| A. | (*a*) | (*c*) | (*b*) | (*d*) |
| B. | (*b*) | (*c*) | (*a*) | (*d*) |
| C. | (*d*) | (*b*) | (*c*) | (*a*) |
| D. | (*a*) | (*b*) | (*d*) | (*c*) |

**412.** Qualification share is a requirement prescribed for:

A. The officers of the company
B. Creditors of the company
C. Directors of the company
D. Auditors of the company

**413.** Most of the public sector enterprises in India are joint stock companies because this enable the:

A. Company to earn high profits
B. Government to enter any business
C. Government to exercise greater control
D. Management to work with high operational autonomy

**414.** The contracts signed by the promoters of a company:

A. Are legally binding upon the company after it is formed
B. Can be ratified by the company after its incorporation
C. Cease to be the personal liability of the promoters after the company is formed
D. Continue to be personal liability of the promoters

**415.** Doctrine of indoor management is reflected in:

A. Royal British Bank vs Turquands case
B. Solomon vs Solomon Ltd.
C. Daimler Ltd. vs Continental Tyre and Rubber Co. Ltd.
D. Kindston Cotton Mills case

**416.** The liability of share holders of a public company is limited to the extent of:

A. Paid up value of the share
B. The face value of the share
C. Called up value of the share
D. All of these

**417.** A company is called an artificial person because:

A. It does not have the shape of a normal man
B. It cannot be sued in the sort of law

C. It is invisible and intangible
D. It exists only in contemplation of law

**418.** Which of the following is the top administrative organ of the company?
A. Shareholders
B. Managing Director
C. General Manager
D. Board of Directors

**419.** The Board of Directors has to call the general body meeting giving a constructive notice of M days to all members entitled to attend the meeting. Here M stands for:
A. 7 B. 11
C. 14 D. 21

**420.** The doctrine by which an outsider is presumed to have a prior knowledge of the contents of memorandum and articles of association of a company is technically known as:
A. Doctrine of constructive notice
B. Doctrine of indoor management
C. Doctrine of retrospective notice
D. *Ignorantia legis haud excus at*

**421.** Converting Public Company into a Private Ltd. Company requires:
A. Special resolution
B. Central governmentt approval
C. Special resolution and central government approval
D. Special resolution and Company Law Board approval

**422.** The first directors of a public company are appointed by the:
A. Public B. Shareholders
C. Promoters D. Government

**423.** Rules concerning meetings and report of a joint stock company are contained in its:
A. Prospectus
B. Memorandum of Association
C. Articles of Association
D. Bye-Laws

**424.** Consider the following statements:
I. A letter of credit eliminates the risk of payment in foreign trade
II. Revolving letter of credit and circular letter of credit are two different entities
III. Revocable letter of credit is a confirmatory letter of credit
A. I only
B. II and III
C. I and III
D. I, II and III

**425.** Consider the following statements:
I. A public limited company can commence business only after getting the certificate of commencement of business
II. In a public limited company, directors can not borrow from the company without the approval of the Central Government
A. I only
B. III only
C. Both I and II
D. Neither I nor II

**426.** Consider the following statements:
I. Sole-proprietorship type of business unit is not governed by the Contract Act.
II. A private limited company is governed by the partnership act where as a public limited company is governed by the Companies Act.
A. I only
B. II only
C. Both I and II
D. Neither I nor II

**427.** A change in the exchange rate will change the amount of local currency receivable on a bill denominated in a foreign currency. The risk involved is called:
A. Foreign exchange risk
B. Import risk
C. Transaction risk
D. Monetary risk

**428.** The marine policy which insures incidental in land risks along with the marine perils is called:
A. Block policy
B. Currency policy
C. Blanket policy
D. Voyage policy

**429.** Which of the following does not meant the Qualified Institutional Buyer (QIB) under the SEBI (Disclosure & Investor Protection) guidelines as amended by the recent DIP circular?
A. Mutual funds
B. Pension fund with a corpus below ₹ 20 crore
C. Pension funds with minimum corpus of ₹ 25 crore
D. Provident funds with minimum corpus of ₹ 25 crore

**430.** When can an Annual general meeting be called after giving shorter notice than that specified?
A. If consent is accorded to by all the memebers entitled to vote
B. If consent is accorded to by 30 % of the members entitled to vote
C. If Board of Directors takes a majority decision in this regard
D. If the company secretary so wishes

**431.** Debit means:
A. Decrease in asset
B. Increase in liability
C. An entry on the left hand side of an account
D. Moderate increase in liability

**432.** Drawings account is related to:
A. Nominal account
B. Personal account
C. Real account
D. Company drawings account

**433.** Which of the following is related to nominal account?
A. Bank account
B. Commission account
C. Furniture account
D. Interest received account

**434.** Goodwill account is related to:
A. Nominal account B. Personal account
C. Real account D. Tangible account

**435.** Prepaid insurance is:
A. Nominal account B. Personal account
C. Real account D. Prepaid account

**436.** According to the going concern concept, a business entity is assumed to have:
A. a long life B. a very short life
C. an indefinite life D. a medium life

**437.** Contingent liability is shown in the balance sheet because of:
A. Convention of consistency
B. Convention of materiality
C. Convention of disclosure
D. Convention of adventure

**438.** Revenue is considered as being earned when:
A. cash is received B. production is done
C. sale is effected D. purchase is done

**439.** Accounting does not record non-financial transactions because of:
A. Entity concept
B. Accrual concept
C. Measurement concept
D. Double entry concept

**440.** According to which of the following concepts even the owner of the business who provides capital treated as a creditor of the business?
A. Entity concept
B. Cost concept
C. Money measurement concept
D. Convention of disclosure

**441.** In book-keeping posting means:
A. to record the transactions from the journal to ledger
B. to record the transactions in the journal
C. to record the transactions in the subsidiary books
D. to record the transactions in the cash book

**442.** The basic rule of book-keeping, debit the receiver and credit the giver is applicable to:
A. nominal account B. real account
C. personal account D. drawing account

**443.** Goods of the value of ₹ 1500 taken by the proprietor for his personal use should be debited to:
A. drawing account
B. sales account
C. purchases account
D. stock account

**444.** Goods destroyed by fire should be credited to:
A. purchases account
B. sales account
C. loss of goods by fire account
D. insurance account

**445.** The credit balance of bank account indicates:
A. amount payable by the bank
B. amount payable to the bank
C. cash at bank
D. loan from bank

**446.** Which of the following accounts will invariably have a debit balance?
A. Bank account
B. Accounts receivable account
C. Accounts payable account
D. Loan account

**447.** Which of the following accounts will invariably have a credit balance?
A. Discount account
B. Account payable account
C. Cash account
D. Purchases account

**448.** Which of the following accounts have only credit balance?
A. Accounts payable account
B. Salaries outstanding account
C. Reserve fund account
D. All of the above accounts

**449.** Which of the following accounts may have a debit or credit balance?
A. Discount received account
B. Sales account
C. Trade expenses account
D. Loan account

**450.** Which of the following books should be used to record purchase of furniture on credit?
A. Cash book B. Journal proper
C. Purchases book D. Sales book

## ANSWERS

| | | | | | | | | | |
|---|---|---|---|---|---|---|---|---|---|
| 1 A | 2 C | 3 C | 4 D | 5 A | 6 B | 7 B | 8 C | 9 B | 10 A |
| 11 C | 12 B | 13 B | 14 A | 15 C | 16 A | 17 C | 18 D | 19 B | 20 B |
| 21 B | 22 B | 23 A | 24 B | 25 A | 26 C | 27 C | 28 B | 29 A | 30 A |
| 31 C | 32 A | 33 A | 34 C | 35 C | 36 B | 37 D | 38 A | 39 B | 40 B |
| 41 B | 42 D | 43 D | 44 B | 45 A | 46 C | 47 A | 48 D | 49 A | 50 C |
| 51 B | 52 B | 53 B | 54 B | 55 B | 56 D | 57 C | 58 C | 59 C | 60 D |
| 61 C | 62 B | 63 C | 64 A | 65 D | 66 D | 67 B | 68 D | 69 B | 70 D |
| 71 C | 72 B | 73 D | 74 B | 75 B | 76 A | 77 A | 78 B | 79 C | 80 C |
| 81 B | 82 B | 83 B | 84 B | 85 B | 86 D | 87 B | 88 D | 89 A | 90 B |
| 91 A | 92 D | 93 B | 94 B | 95 B | 96 C | 97 A | 98 A | 99 D | 100 A |
| 101 B | 102 C | 103 D | 104 B | 105 A | 106 C | 107 C | 108 A | 109 B | 110 B |
| 111 C | 112 A | 113 C | 114 B | 115 D | 116 B | 117 B | 118 C | 119 B | 120 B |
| 121 A | 122 C | 123 D | 124 C | 125 A | 126 C | 127 B | 128 A | 129 D | 130 A |
| 131 A | 132 A | 133 C | 134 D | 135 D | 136 A | 137 B | 138 B | 139 B | 140 C |
| 141 D | 142 B | 143 A | 144 B | 145 B | 146 A | 147 C | 148 C | 149 D | 140 B |
| 151 D | 152 B | 153 B | 154 C | 155 C | 156 C | 157 C | 158 D | 159 C | 160 C |
| 161 B | 162 D | 163 D | 164 D | 165 B | 166 C | 167 C | 168 A | 169 B | 170 D |
| 171 A | 172 A | 173 D | 174 D | 175 C | 176 B | 177 B | 178 B | 179 D | 180 C |
| 181 A | 182 B | 183 B | 184 B | 185 B | 186 C | 187 B | 188 D | 189 D | 190 C |
| 191 C | 192 C | 193 A | 194 A | 195 C | 196 B | 197 A | 198 A | 199 C | 200 C |
| 201 C | 202 A | 203 C | 204 A | 205 A | 206 D | 207 B | 208 B | 209 A | 210 C |
| 211 A | 212 A | 213 D | 214 B | 215 B | 216 B | 217 D | 218 A | 219 A | 220 A |

| | | | | | | | | | |
|---|---|---|---|---|---|---|---|---|---|
| 221 | 222 | 223 | 224 | 225 | 226 | 227 | 228 | 229 | 230 |
| A | C | A | B | C | B | C | A | C | A |
| 231 | 232 | 233 | 234 | 235 | 236 | 237 | 238 | 239 | 240 |
| C | A | C | D | B | D | B | C | A | C |
| 241 | 242 | 243 | 244 | 245 | 246 | 247 | 248 | 249 | 250 |
| D | A | B | D | B | D | D | C | B | A |
| 251 | 252 | 253 | 254 | 255 | 256 | 257 | 258 | 259 | 260 |
| B | D | D | D | B | D | D | D | C | D |
| 261 | 262 | 263 | 264 | 265 | 266 | 267 | 268 | 269 | 270 |
| C | B | C | C | B | D | A | C | A | D |
| 271 | 272 | 273 | 274 | 275 | 276 | 277 | 278 | 279 | 280 |
| B | C | B | C | C | D | D | A | D | D |
| 281 | 282 | 283 | 284 | 285 | 286 | 287 | 288 | 289 | 290 |
| D | A | B | D | A | B | B | D | D | D |
| 291 | 292 | 293 | 294 | 295 | 296 | 297 | 298 | 299 | 300 |
| A | C | B | A | A | B | A | B | A | A |
| 301 | 302 | 303 | 304 | 305 | 306 | 307 | 308 | 309 | 310 |
| B | D | C | A | C | A | A | C | D | C |
| 311 | 312 | 313 | 314 | 315 | 316 | 317 | 318 | 319 | 320 |
| D | A | D | C | C | C | D | D | A | C |
| 321 | 322 | 323 | 324 | 325 | 326 | 327 | 328 | 329 | 330 |
| A | B | D | C | B | D | D | B | A | D |
| 331 | 332 | 333 | 334 | 335 | 336 | 337 | 338 | 339 | 340 |
| A | D | A | C | B | A | C | D | C | B |
| 341 | 342 | 343 | 344 | 345 | 346 | 347 | 348 | 349 | 350 |
| B | B | D | C | B | C | D | A | B | B |
| 351 | 352 | 353 | 354 | 355 | 356 | 357 | 358 | 359 | 360 |
| A | B | B | D | D | C | C | D | A | D |
| 361 | 362 | 363 | 364 | 365 | 366 | 367 | 368 | 369 | 370 |
| C | C | D | A | C | B | C | C | B | A |
| 371 | 372 | 373 | 374 | 375 | 376 | 377 | 378 | 379 | 380 |
| C | C | D | B | A | C | B | A | C | D |
| 381 | 382 | 383 | 384 | 385 | 386 | 387 | 388 | 389 | 390 |
| C | B | C | A | B | A | B | D | A | C |
| 391 | 392 | 393 | 394 | 395 | 396 | 397 | 398 | 399 | 400 |
| C | C | D | C | C | C | B | C | D | A |
| 401 | 402 | 403 | 404 | 405 | 406 | 407 | 408 | 409 | 410 |
| C | C | D | C | C | C | C | C | D | A |
| 411 | 412 | 413 | 414 | 415 | 416 | 417 | 418 | 419 | 420 |
| A | C | D | D | A | B | D | D | A | A |
| 421 | 422 | 423 | 424 | 425 | 426 | 427 | 428 | 429 | 430 |
| C | C | C | A | C | D | D | C | B | A |
| 431 | 432 | 433 | 434 | 435 | 436 | 437 | 438 | 439 | 440 |
| C | B | B | C | B | A | C | C | C | A |
| 441 | 442 | 443 | 444 | 445 | 446 | 447 | 448 | 449 | 450 |
| A | C | A | A | B | B | B | D | D | B |

●●●

# GENERAL INTELLIGENCE & REASONING

# VERBAL

CHAPTER 1

# Analogies

## NUMBER ANALOGY

In number analogy also, the relationship between the given numbers is detected and then applied to the second part to find the missing numbers. This relationship between the numbers can be based on any of the following patterns : *(i)* numbers can be odd/even/prime numbers; *(ii)* numbers can be multiples of one number; *(iii)* numbers can be squares/cubes of different numbers; *(iv)* some numbers can be added to/subtracted from/multiplied to/divided into the first number to get the second number; *(v)* the second number can be the sum/product/difference of the digits of first number; and *(vi)* combinations of any mathematical calculations given above can apply to the relationship between the two given numbers.

### SOLVED EXAMPLES

**Directions :** *Which number will come in the place of question mark?*

**1.** 25 : 81 : : 36 : ?

(*a*) 121 (*b*) 93 (*c*) 65 (*d*) 103

**Ans. (*a*) :** All the numbers are squares of different numbers.

| 25 | 81 | :: | 36 | 121 |
|---|---|---|---|---|
| ↓ | ↓ | | ↓ | ↓ |
| $5^2$ | $9^2$ | | $6^2$ | $11^2$ |

**2.** 36 : 18 : : 72 : ?

(*a*) 164 (*b*) 134 (*c*) 94 (*d*) 14

**Ans. (*d*) :** The second number is the product of digits of the first number.

36 : 18 : : 72 : 14

$3 \times 6$ $7 \times 2$

### MULTIPLE CHOICE QUESTIONS

**Directions :** *In the following questions, select the number from the given options which follows the same relationship as shared between the first two numbers.*

**1.** 1 : 11 : : 2 : ?

(*a*) 20 (*b*) 22
(*c*) 24 (*d*) 44

**2.** 18 : 27 : : 22 : ?

(*a*) 42 (*b*) 39
(*c*) 33 (*d*) 54

**3.** 14 : 20 : : 16 : ?

(*a*) 23 (*b*) 10
(*c*) 48 (*d*) 32

**4.** 8 : 27 : : 64 : ?

(*a*) 277 (*b*) 125
(*c*) 250 (*d*) 99

**5.** 0.16 : 0.0016 : : 1.02 : ?

(*a*) 10.20 (*b*) 0.102
(*c*) 0.0102 (*d*) 1.020

**6.** $\frac{1}{7} : \frac{1}{14} :: \frac{1}{9} : ?$

(a) $\frac{1}{88}$ (b) $\frac{1}{80}$

(c) $\frac{1}{81}$ (d) $\frac{1}{18}$

**7.** 5 : 24 : : 8 : ?

(a) 65 (b) 63

(c) 62 (d) 64

**8.** 23 : 53 : : 8 : ?

(a) 66 (b) 57

(c) 27 (d) 19

**9.** 6 : 9 : : 7 : ?

(a) 4 (b) 14

(c) 10 (d) 28

**10.** 7 : 28 : : 2 : ?

(a) 8 (b) 16

(c) 24 (d) 12

## EXPLANATORY ANSWERS

**1. (b) :** The first number is repeated to obtain the second number.

**2. (c) :** In the given set, the numbers are multiples of 9 and in the second set, multiples of 11.

18 : 27 : : 22 : 33

↓ ↓ ↓ ↓

$9 \times 2$ $9 \times 3$ $11 \times 2$ $11 \times 3$

**3. (a) :** The relationship between the numbers is :

14 : 20 : : 16 : 23

↓ ↓ ↓ ↓

$7 \times 2$ $(7 \times 3) - 1$ $8 \times 2$ $(8 \times 3) - 1$

**4. (b) :** The numbers are cubes of different numbers.

8 : 27 : : 64 : 125

↓ ↓ ↓ ↓

$2^3$ $3^3$ $4^3$ $5^3$

**5. (c) :** The decimals are divided by 100.

**6. (d) :** The first fraction is multiplied by half to obtain the second fraction.

$\frac{1}{7} : \frac{1}{14} :: \frac{1}{9} : \frac{1}{18}$

$\times\frac{1}{2}$ $\times\frac{1}{2}$

**7. (b) :** The second number is square of first number minus 1.

5 : 24 : : 8 : 63

$(5^2) - 1$ $(8^2) - 1$

**8. (d) :** All the numbers are prime numbers.

**9. (c) :** The second number is three more than the first number.

6 : 9 : : 7 : 10

+3 +3

**10. (a) :** The second number is four times the first.

7 : 28 : : 2 : 8

×4 ×4

## LETTER ANALOGY

In this type of analogy the relationship between two given set of letters is established and then applied to the other set to obtain the required set of letters as the answer. These letters can be moved some steps backward or forward; reversed in whole or in sections or have some common identity between each other.

## SOLVED EXAMPLES

**Directions :** *Which set of letters will come in the place of question mark?*

**1.** JILK : KLIJ : : MNPQ : ?

(a) QNPM (b) MPQN (c) QPNM (d) PNMQ

**Ans. (c) :** The letters are written in reverse order to get the related set of letters.

J I L K : K L I J : : M N P Q : Q P N M

**2.** FLO : DOL : : RDP : ?

(*a*) PGM (*b*) MGP (*c*) GMP (*d*) MPG

**Ans. (*a*) :** The first and third letters are moved two and three steps backwards respectively and the second letter three steps forward.

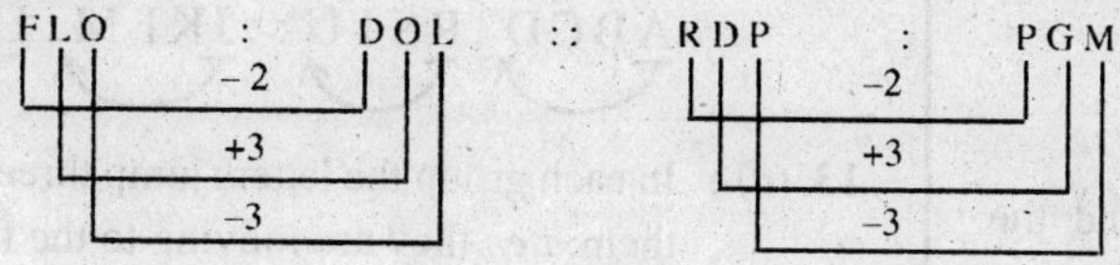


## MULTIPLE CHOICE QUESTIONS

**Directions :** *In the questions given below one term is missing. Based on the relationship of the two given terms find the missing term from the given options.*

**1.** GFC : CFG : : RPJ : ?
(*a*) JRP (*b*) JPR
(*c*) PJR (*d*) RJP

**2.** BCF : DEG : : MNQ : ?
(*a*) OPR (*b*) PQS
(*c*) OPP (*d*) QRT

**3.** NATION : ANITNO : : HUNGRY : ?
(*a*) HNUGRY (*b*) UNHGYR
(*c*) YRNGUH (*d*) UHGNYR

**4.** SSTU : MMNO : : AABC : ?
(*a*) GGHH (*b*) IJKK
(*c*) XXYZ (*d*) NOOP

**5.** ACE : FGH : : LNP : ?
(*a*) QRS (*b*) PQR
(*c*) QST (*d*) MOQ

**6.** UVW : SXU : : LMN : ?
(*a*) JOL (*b*) KNM
(*c*) JKL (*d*) MLO

**7.** EIGHTY : GIEYTH : : OUTPUT : ?
(*a*) UTOPTU (*b*) UOTUPT
(*c*) TUOUTP (*d*) TUOTUP

**8.** TSR : FED : : WVU : ?
(*a*) CAB (*b*) MLK
(*c*) PQS (*d*) GFH

**9.** CJDL : FMGR : : IKJR : ?
(*a*) OQPT (*b*) RSTU
(*c*) OQRT (*d*) KRMO

**10.** BOQD : ERTG : : ANPC : ?
(*a*) DQSF (*b*) FSHU
(*c*) SHFU (*d*) DSQF

**11.** BaBy : TaTa : : LiLy : ?
(*a*) PooL (*b*) ROse
(*c*) HaNd (*d*) DoWN

**12.** BCDA : STUR : : KLMJ : ?
(*a*) VWXU (*b*) EFHG
(*c*) SRTU (*d*) QSRP

**13.** AEI : LPT : : CGK : ?
(*a*) OSV (*b*) RUY
(*c*) TXC (*d*) FJN

**14.** RUX : TRP : : BEH : ?
(*a*) SQN (*b*) QON
(*c*) QOM (*d*) QNL

**15.** CART : ART : : FOUR : ?
(*a*) RUN (*b*) TWO
(*c*) QUE (*d*) OUR

## EXPLANATORY ANSWERS

**1. (*b*) :** The letters of the first group are reversed.

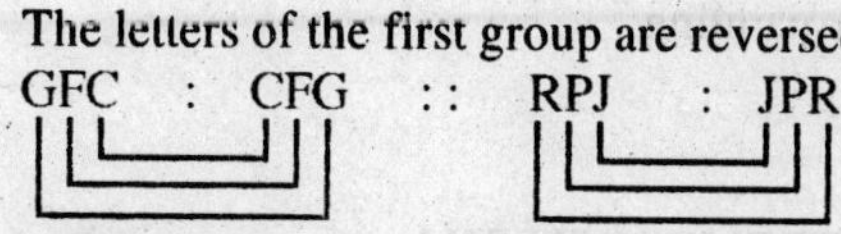


**2. (*a*) :** The three letters are moved 2, 2 and 1 steps forward respectively.

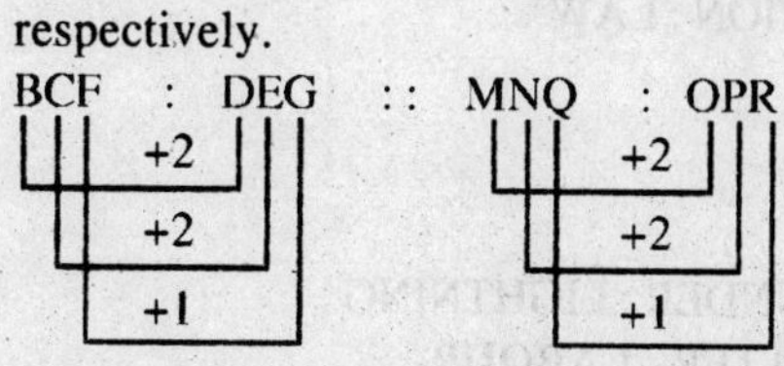


**3. (*d*) :** The word is divided in sections of two letters and the letters are reversed.

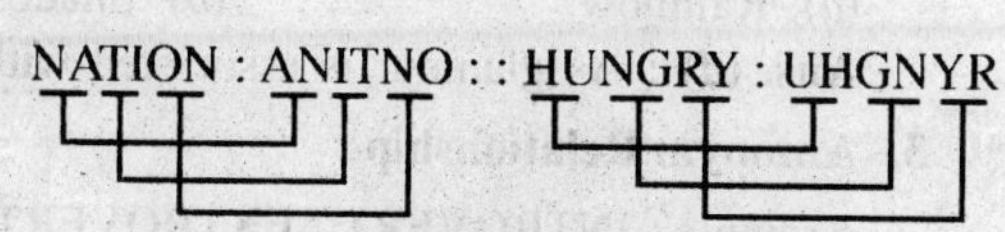


**4. (*c*) :** The first letter in each group is repeated and followed by two consecutive letters.

**5. (*a*) :** The three letters are moved 5, 4, and 3 steps forward respectively.

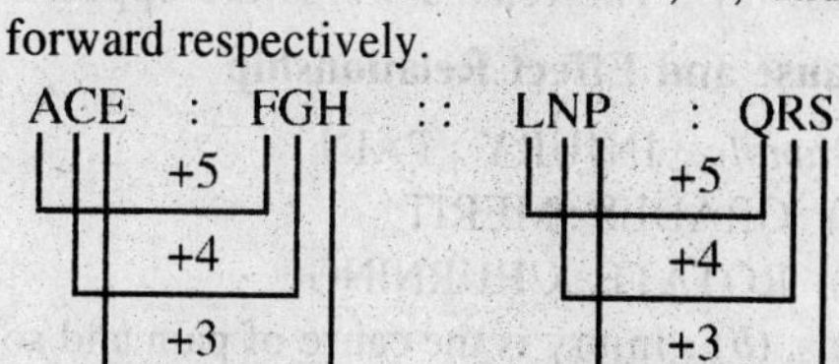

**6. (a) :** The three letters are moved –2, +2 and –2 steps respectively.

UVW : SXU : : LMN : JOL

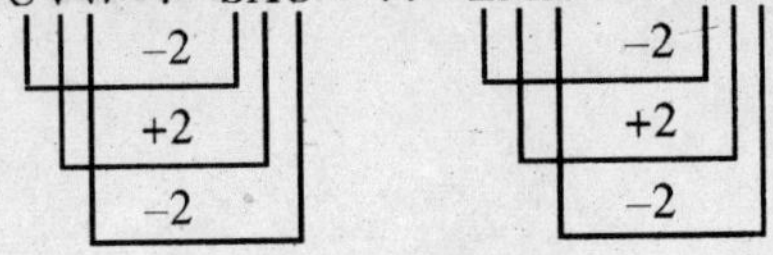


**7. (d) :** The word is divided into two sections and the letters are written backwards.

EIGHTY : GIEYTH : : OUTPUT : TUOTUP

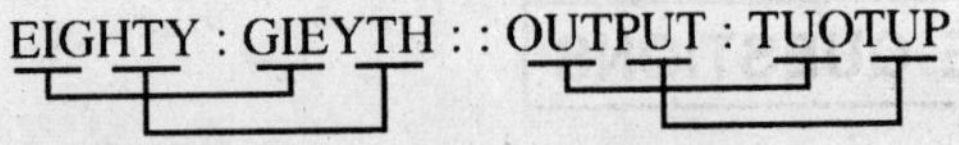

**8. (b) :** The letters are consecutive and written in reverse order.

**9. (a) :** In each set of letters, the 1st and 3rd letters are consecutive.

CJDL : FMGR : : IKJR : OQPT

**10. (a) :** In each group, the first and fourth letters are jumping one letter and the second and third letters are also jumping one letter.

BOQD : ERTG : : ANPC : DQSF

**11. (c) :** In each group the alternate letters are capitals.

**12. (a) :** In each group the first three letters are consecutive and they follow the fourth letter.

ABCD : RSTU : : JKLM : UVWX

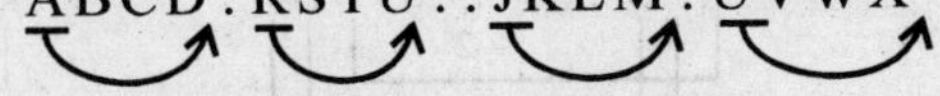

**13. (d) :** In each group the letters jump three letters between them, *i.e.*, they are moving to the fourth letter.

AEI : LPT : : CGK : FJN

**14. (c) :** The letters in first set are jumping two letters, *i.e.*, moving three steps forward and in the second they are jumping one letter, *i.e.* moving two steps backward.

RUX : TRP : : BEH : QOM

**15. (d) :** The first set of letters drop the first letter to get the second set.

CART : ART : : FOUR : OUR

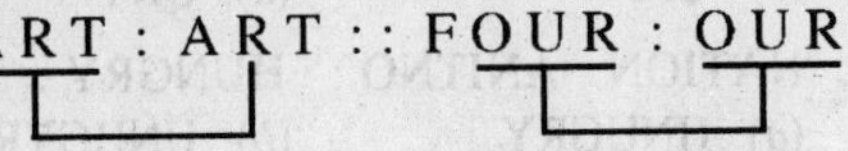

## SEMANTIC ANALOGY

In Analogy Tests the relationship between two given words is established and then applied to the other words. The type of relationship may vary, so while attempting such questions the first step is to identify the type of relationship, which can be any one of the following.

### SOLVED EXAMPLES

**1. Action Object Relationship**

*Example :* Shoot is to Gun as Eat is to.....

(*a*) Hunger (*b*) Thirst (*c*) Dinner (*d*) Fruit

**Ans. (*d*) :** The relationship between the given words is that 'shoot' is the action and 'Gun' is the specified object of action. Similarly 'eat' is the action and 'fruit' is the specified object.

**2. Association Relationship**

*Example* : Glamour is to Stardom as Colour is to.....

(*a*) Rainbow (*b*) Shades (*c*) Art (*d*) Painting

**Ans. (*d*) :** As glamour is associated with stardom so is colour with painting.

**3. Antonym Relationship**

*Example* : INTROVERT : EXTROVERT

(*a*) ANGLE : TANGENT (*b*) EXTREME : INTERIM

(*c*) AGAINST : FAVOUR (*d*) ACTION : LAW

**Ans. (*c*) :** The related words are opposite in meaning.

**4. Cause and Effect Relationship**

*Example :* INJURY : PAIN

(*a*) GRADES : MERIT (*b*) THUNDER : LIGHTNING

(*c*) ROTATE : CHURNING (*d*) MATTER : LABOUR

**Ans. (*b*) :** Injury is the cause of pain and so is thunder the cause of lightning.

**5. Degree Relationship**

*Example* : Tepid is to Hot as... is to Wail.

(*a*) Sob (*b*) Shout (*c*) Smile (*d*) Calm

**Ans. (*a*) :** Tepid is less hot and so also the lower degree of wail is sob.

**6. Grammatical Relationship**

*Example:* Clever is to Beautiful as Sour is to ...

(*a*) Lemon (*b*) Cunning (*c*) Loathing (*d*) Taste

**Ans. (*b*) :** The related words are Adjectives.

**7. Obvious Relationship**

*Example :* Mt. EVEREST : NEPAL

(*a*) MEXICO : SOUTH AMERICA (*b*) K2 : CHINA

(*c*) BIG BEN : RUSSIA (*d*) AHMEDABAD : GUJARAT

**Ans. (*d*) :** Mt. Everest is in Nepal and so is Ahmedabad in Gujarat.

**8. Part Whole Relationship**

*Example :* MAN : MAMMAL

(*a*) HAIL : SNOW (*b*) NATIVE : INHABITANT

(*c*) OFFSPRING : FAMILY (*d*) LIBERTY : LITERATE

**Ans. (*c*) :** Man is a part of the whole species of mammal so is an offspring of the whole family.

**9. Purpose Relationship**

*Example :* INSTITUTION : EDUCATION

(*a*) WAR : PEACE (*b*) HEALTH : OBESITY

(*c*) MEDICATION : RECUPERATION (*d*) BUILDING : URBANISM

**Ans. (*c*) :** The purpose of institution is to impart education and the purpose of medication is quick recuperation (recovery).

**10. Sequence Relationship**

*Example :* ........ is to Dusk as Summer is to Monsoon.

(*a*) Evening (*b*) Dawn (*c*) Night (*d*) Noon

**Ans. (*a*) :** Summer season is immediately followed by monsoon (rainy season) and evening is immediately followed by dusk.

**11. Synonym Relationship**

*Example :* INDENT : REQUEST

(*a*) REPLICA : CHEAT (*b*) DOLE : ALMS

(*c*) DISMAL : DUNCE (*d*) EXACT : CHECK

**Ans. (*b*) :** The related words have the same meaning.

**12. Volume Relationship**

*Example :* GALLONS : SWIMMING POOL

(*a*) SPECTATORS : AUDITORIUM (*b*) CURRENCY : SHARES

(*c*) DUST : MOUNTAIN (*d*) BOOKS : CATALOGUE

**Ans. (*a*) :** Gallons of water is needed to fill a swimming pool and large number of spectators can be admitted into an auditorium.

## MULTIPLE CHOICE QUESTIONS

**Directions :** *In the questions given below establish the relationship between the two words. Then from the given options select one which has the same relationship as of the given two words.*

**1.** HUNGER : FOOD : : THIRST : ?

(*a*) Water (*b*) Drink

(*c*) Tea (*d*) Coffee

**2.** HUNTER : GUN : : WRITER : ?

(*a*) Book (*b*) Pen

(*c*) Poem (*d*) Page

**3.** WOOL : SHEEP : : SILK : ?

(*a*) Saree

(*b*) String

(*c*) Silkworm

(*d*) Moth

**4.** FOOD : STOMACH : : FUEL : ?
(*a*) Engine (*b*) Automobile
(*c*) Rail (*d*) Aeroplane

**5.** WATER : SAND : : OCEAN : ?
(*a*) Island (*b*) River
(*c*) Desert (*d*) Waves

**6.** ADULT : BABY : : FLOWER : ?
(*a*) Seed (*b*) Bud
(*c*) Fruit (*d*) Butterfly

**7.** WRITER : READER : : PRODUCER : ?
(*a*) Creator (*b*) Contractor
(*c*) Creature (*d*) Consumer

**8.** ENTRANCE : EXIT : : LOYALTY : ?
(*a*) Treachery (*b*) Patriotism
(*c*) Fidelity (*d*) Reward

**9.** MOTHER : MATERNAL : : FATHER : ?
(*a*) Eternal (*b*) Detrimental
(*c*) Paternal (*d*) Formidable

**10.** PEARL : NECKLACE : : FLOWER : ?
(*a*) Plant (*b*) Garden
(*c*) Petal (*d*) Bouquet

**11.** ALPHABET : WORD : : WORD : ?
(*a*) Sound (*b*) Music
(*c*) Sentence (*d*) Dictionary

**12.** LIFE : DEATH : : HOPE : ?
(*a*) Cry (*b*) Pain
(*c*) Despair (*d*) Sad

**13.** GOOD : BAD : : VIRTUE : ?
(*a*) Blame (*b*) Sin
(*c*) Despair (*d*) Vice

**14.** BIRD : FLY : : SNAKE : ?
(*a*) Timid (*b*) Clatter
(*c*) Crawl (*d*) Hole

**15.** CAT : MOUSE : : BIRD : ?
(*a*) Cage (*b*) Trap
(*c*) Eagle (*d*) Worm

**16.** STATE : EXILE
(*a*) Police : Arrest
(*b*) Judge : Convict
(*c*) Constitution : Amendment
(*d*) Church : Excommunicate

**17.** CAPRICIOUSNESS : RELIABILITY
(*a*) Extemporaneous : Predictability
(*b*) Unreliable : Inhuman
(*c*) Tenacious : Practicality
(*d*) Arbitrary : Whimsical

**18.** LOATH : COERCION
(*a*) Detest : Caressing (*b*) Irritate : Caressing
(*c*) Irate : Antagonism (*d*) Reluctant : Persuasion

**19.** SCALES : FISH
(*a*) Lady : Dress (*b*) Tree : Leaves
(*c*) Bird : Feather (*d*) Skin : Man

**20.** TREE : SAPLING
(*a*) Hut : Mansion (*b*) Giant : Dwarf
(*c*) Horse : Foal (*d*) Ant : Elephant

## EXPLANATORY ANSWERS

**1. (*a*) :** Hunger is satiated by food, thirst by water.

**2. (*b*) :** Weapon of a hunter is a gun, weapon of a writer is a pen.

**3. (*c*) :** Wool is obtained from sheep, silk is obtained from silkworm.

**4. (*a*) :** Food is consumed in stomach, fuel is consumed in engine.

**5. (*c*) :** The related words are near opposites.

**6. (*b*) :** The youngone of an adult is a baby and that of a flower is a bud.

**7. (*d*) :** A writer aims to please the readers by his writings, a producer aims to please the consumers by his products.

**8. (*a*) :** The related words are opposites.

**9. (*c*) :** Relations on the mother's side are maternal and on the father's side paternal.

**10. (*d*) :** Many pearls make a necklace, many flowers make a bouquet.

**11. (*c*) :** More than one alphabet make a word, more than one word make a sentence.

**12. (*c*) :** The related words are opposites.

**13. (*d*) :** The related words are opposites.

**14. (*c*) :** Birds fly, snakes crawl.

**15. (*d*) :** Cat chases the mouse, bird chases the worm.

**16. (*d*) :** Punishment of leaving the State is exile, punishment of leaving the Church is excommunication.

**17. (*c*) :** The related words are antonyms

**18. (*d*) :** Loathing is the result of constant coersion, reluctance is the result of constant persuasion.

**19. (*d*) :** Covering of the fish is scales, covering of man is skin.

**20. (*c*) :** Young tree is a sapling, young horse is a foal.

CHAPTER 2

# Number Classification

## ODD ONE OUT—NUMBERS

In this type of classification, different numbers are given as options. These numbers have some commonness; except one which is the odd one. One has to identify the similarity and then strike the odd one out as answer option. The number can be odd/even/consecutive, prime numbers, multiple of some number, single, square or cubes of different numbers, plus/minus of some other number or combinations of any mathematical calculation.

### SOLVED EXAMPLES

**Directions :** *Find the odd number from the given options.*

**1.** (*a*) 62 (*b*) 121 (*c*) 36 (*d*) 256

**Ans. (*a*)** : The other numbers are squares of : 11, (= 121), 6 (= 36) and 16 (= 256)

**2.** (*a*) 27 (*b*) 132 (*c*) 93 (*d*) 154

**Ans. (*d*)** : All other numbers are divisible by 3.

### MULTIPLE CHOICE QUESTIONS

**Directions :** *In each of the following questions, there are four options. Three numbers, in these options, are alike in certain manner. Only one number does not fit in. Choose the one which is different from the rest.*

**1.** (*a*) 1948 (*b*) 2401 (*c*) 966 (*d*) 1449

**2.** (*a*) 182 (*b*) 169 (*c*) 130 (*d*) 158

**3.** (*a*) 129 (*b*) 130 (*c*) 131 (*d*) 132

**4.** (*a*) 3215 (*b*) 9309 (*c*) 4721 (*d*) 2850

**5.** (*a*) 1776 (*b*) 2364 (*c*) 1976 (*d*) 3776

**6.** (*a*) 64 (*b*) 84 (*c*) 16 (*d*) 36

**7.** (*a*) 24 (*b*) 90 (*c*) 54 (*d*) 36

**8.** (*a*) 7658 (*b*) 1234 (*c*) 9876 (*d*) 6543

**9.** (*a*) 3 (*b*) 9 (*c*) 5 (*d*) 7

**10.** (*a*) 6450 (*b*) 1776 (*c*) 2392 (*d*) 3815

**11.** (*a*) 24 (*b*) 48 (*c*) 42 (*d*) 12

**12.** (*a*) 616 (*b*) 252 (*c*) 311 (*d*) 707

**13.** (*a*) 18 (*b*) 12 (*c*) 30 (*d*) 20

**14.** (*a*) 3730 (*b*) 6820 (*c*) 5568 (*d*) 4604

## EXPLANATORY ANSWERS

1. (*a*) : Other numbers are divisible by 7.
2. (*d*) : Other numbers are multiples of 13.
3. (*c*) : 131 is a prime number.
4. (*b*) : In other numbers, no digit is repeated.
5. (*b*) : In other numbers the last two digits are same.
6. (*b*) : All other numbers are perfect squares.
7. (*a*) : In other numbers, the sum of both the digits is 9.
8. (*a*) : In others, the digits are consecutive in natural or reverse series.
9. (*b*) : All others are prime numbers.
10. (*d*) : All other numbers are divisible by 2.
11. (*c*) : All other numbers are multiples of 12.
12. (*c*) : In other numbers, the first and last digits are same.
13. (*a*) : The other numbers are $3^2 + 3 = 12$, $5^2 + 5 = 30$, $4^2 + 4 = 20$, $6^2 + 6 = 42$
14. (*b*) : In all other numbers, two digits are same.

# ODD ONE OUT—LETTERS

In this classification of letters, four groups of letters or a series of letters is given as options. One has to select the option as answer which does not share the commonness of the others.

## SOLVED EXAMPLES

**Directions :** *Find the odd one out in the following letters :*

1. (*a*) NOP (*b*) RTU (*c*) JKL (*d*) EFG

**Ans. (*b*) :** In each group the letters are consecutive. In this option the first two letters jump one letter (S) inbetween.

2. (*a*) RUX (*b*) CFI (*c*) BDG (*d*) FIL

**Ans. (*c*) :** In each group, the difference between the letters is same. In this option B and D jump one letter and D and G jump two letters.

## MULTIPLE CHOICE QUESTIONS

**Directions :** *In each of the following questions, four out of five alternatives contain alphabet placed in a particular form. Find the one that does not belong to the group.*

1. (*a*) BXCW (*b*) OTPS (*c*) GQHR (*d*) JNKM
2. (*a*) BVPS (*b*) OLMZ (*c*) RPSR (*d*) XTCD
3. (*a*) RNJH (*b*) SOKG (*c*) QMIE (*d*) MIEA
4. (*a*) QLJS (*b*) GVTI (*c*) KRPM (*d*) ONMP
5. (*a*) PEAR (*b*) TORE (*c*) REAP (*d*) TEAR
6. (*a*) ECA (*b*) JHF (*c*) OMK (*d*) UWY
7. (*a*) ACE (*b*) PRT (*c*) UWY (*d*) MNO
8. (*a*) WVU (*b*) NML (*c*) HGF (*d*) DBA
9. (*a*) ABD (*b*) FGI (*c*) LMO (*d*) STU
10. (*a*) CDE (*b*) JKL (*c*) PQS (*d*) TUV

## EXPLANATORY ANSWERS

1. (*c*) : In all other groups, first and third letters are consecutive and second and fourth letters are in reverse alphabetical order.
2. (*c*) : No letter is repeated in any other group.
3. (*a*) : In all other groups, there is a gap of three letters between two consecutive letters.
4. (*d*) : In all other groups, first and third letters are moved two steps forward to obtain fourth and second letters respectively.
5. (*b*) : All other groups contain E, A and R.
6. (*d*) : All other groups contain alternate letters from right to left.

**7. (*d*) :** All other groups contain alternate letters from left to right.

**8. (*d*) :** In all others, the three letters are consecutive but in reverse order.

**9. (*d*) :** In all others, the first two letters are consecutive and third letter is obtained by skipping one letter from the second.

**10. (*c*) :** In all other, the three letters are consecutive.

## ODD ONE OUT—WORDS

In this type of classification, five words are given out of which four are almost same in matter or meaning and only one word is different from the common four. One has to find out the word which is different from the rest.

### SOLVED EXAMPLES

**Directions :** *In the following questions spot the odd one out.*

**1.** (*a*) Father (*b*) Mother (*c*) Friend (*d*) Brother

**Ans. (*c*) :** All other are blood relations.

**2.** (*a*) Water (*b*) Jelly (*c*) Lemonade (*d*) Coffee

**Ans. (*b*) :** All other are liquids.

### MULTIPLE CHOICE QUESTIONS

**Directions :** *In each of the following questions, four words are alike in some manner. Spot the odd one out.*

**1.** (*a*) Green (*b*) Red (*c*) Colour (*d*) Orange

**2.** (*a*) Stable (*b*) Hole (*c*) Canoe (*d*) Sty

**3.** (*a*) Nose (*b*) Eyes (*c*) Skin (*d*) Teeth

**4.** (*a*) Venus (*b*) Moon (*c*) Pluto (*d*) Mars

**5.** (*a*) Happy (*b*) Gloomy (*c*) Lively (*d*) Cheerful

**6.** (*a*) Cone (*b*) Circle (*c*) Triangle (*d*) Rectangle

**7.** (*a*) Lead (*b*) Mercury (*c*) Copper (*d*) Iron

**8.** (*a*) Kite (*b*) Bird (*c*) Radar (*d*) Jet

**9.** (*a*) Knee (*b*) Shoulder (*c*) Ankle (*d*) Palm

**10.** (*a*) Deluge (*b*) Calamity (*c*) Catastrophe (*d*) War

**11.** (*a*) Cub (*b*) Chicken (*c*) Pig (*d*) Pup

**12.** (*a*) Rabbit (*b*) Crocodile (*c*) Earthworm (*d*) Snail

**13.** (*a*) Tree (*b*) Leaf (*c*) Bush (*d*) Herb

**14.** (*a*) Doctor (*b*) Teacher (*c*) Engineer (*d*) Diver

**15.** (*a*) Trot (*b*) Equestrian (*c*) Derby (*d*) Grunt

### EXPLANATORY ANSWERS

**1. (*c*) :** All others are types of colour.

**2. (*c*) :** Canoe is a boat. Others are resting places of birds/animals.

**3. (*d*) :** All others are sense organs.

**4. (*b*) :** All others are planets.

**5. (*b*) :** All others are expressions of joy

**6. (*a*) :** All others are geometrical figures.

**7. (*b*) :** All others are solid metals.

**8. (*c*) :** All others are flying objects. Radar traces the objects in sky.

**9. (*d*) :** All others are joints in human body.

**10. (*d*) :** All others are nature-bound. Only war is man-made.

**11. (*c*) :** All others are young ones of animals.

**12. (*a*) :** All others are crawling animals.

**13. (*b*) :** All others are types of vegetation.

**14. (*d*) :** All others are professions, but only Diver's profession comprises of diving under water.

**15. (*d*) :** All other terms are related with activities of a horse.

CHAPTER 3

# Small & Capital Letters/ Numbers Coding-Decoding and Classification

## TYPE - I

Coding is a secretive language which is used to change the representation of the actual term/word/value. This coded language can be framed by *(i)* moving the letters one or more steps forward or backward; *(ii)* substituting numbers for letters and vice–versa; *(iii)* writing the letters of the given word in reverse order in part or in whole; and *(iv)* replacing the letters in their natural series by the same positioned letters in their reverse series.

Alphabet in natural series are :

A B C D E F G H I J K L M N O P Q R S T U V W X Y Z

| A | E | J | O | T | Y |
|---|---|---|---|---|---|
| ↓ | ↓ | ↓ | ↓ | ↓ | ↓ |
| 1st | 5th | 10th | 15th | 20th | 25th |

Alphabet in reverse series are :

Z Y X W V U T S R Q P O N M L K J I H G F E D C B A

| Z | V | Q | L | G | B |
|---|---|---|---|---|---|
| ↓ | ↓ | ↓ | ↓ | ↓ | ↓ |
| 1st | 5th | 10th | 15th | 20th | 25th |

**Note :** On reaching Z, the series restarts from A and on reaching A, it restarts from Z.

## SOLVED EXAMPLES

**1.** If FACE is coded as GBDF, then BADE will be coded as :

(*a*) CBEF (*b*) CEBF (*c*) CFBE (*d*) CBFE

**Ans. (*a*) :** The word is coded by moving the letters one step forward.

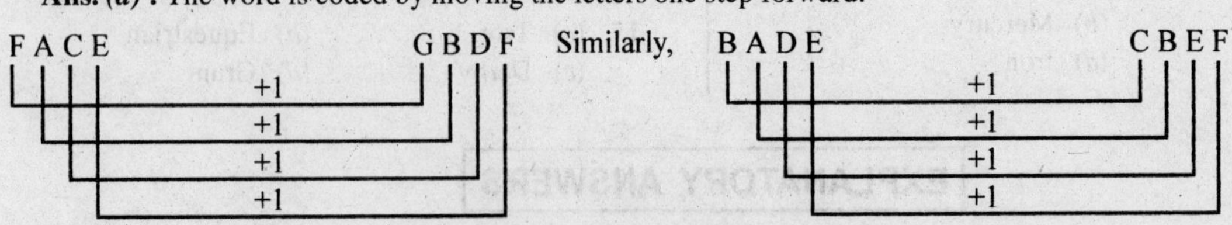


**2.** If RESULT is coded as 798206, LET will be coded as :

(*a*) 680 (*b*) 092 (*c*) 096 (*d*) 086

**Ans. (*c*) :** The letters are coded by numbers, and to code the given word, select the respective coded numbers.

R E S U L T → letters
7 9 8 2 0 6 → code

So, code for LET will be

L E T → letters
0 9 6 → code

## MULTIPLE CHOICE QUESTIONS

**Directions :** *In the following questions select the right option which indicates the correct code for the word or letter given in the question.*

1. If CHAIR is coded as FKDLU then RAID is coded as :
   (*a*) ULGD (*b*) ULKG
   (*c*) ULDG (*d*) UDLG

2. If CONDEMN is coded as CNODMEN, then TEACHER is coded as :
   (*a*) TEACHER (*b*) TAEECHR
   (*c*) TCAEEHR (*d*) TAECEHR

3. In a code language COME is written as XLNV and ABLE as ZYOV. How will MOLLY be written in that code?
   (*a*) NLOBO (*b*) NLBOO
   (*c*) LNOOB (*d*) NLOOB

4. In a certain code PROFESSION is written as EFORPNOISS. In the same code DICTIONARY will be written as :
   (*a*) YRANOITCID (*b*) ITCIDYRANO
   (*c*) ITCIDYRNAO (*d*) ITCDIYARNO

5. JUNE is coded as NXPF, how will STAY be coded in the same manner?
   (*a*) WWCZ (*b*) WVCZ
   (*c*) WWDB (*d*) VWZC

6. If in a certain code GENIUS is coded as IGPKWU, then IDIOT will be written in the same code as :
   (*a*) JEJPU (*b*) KFKQV
   (*c*) LGLRW (*d*) HCHNS

7. If ACTION is coded as ZXGRLM, then HEALTH will be coded in the same way as :
   (*a*) SVZOGS (*b*) TVZOGT
   (*c*) RUZPGR (*d*) QVGOZQ

8. If THOUSAND is coded as SGNTRZMC, then FUMING will be coded as :
   (*a*) GVNJOH (*b*) ETHLMF
   (*c*) EVLJMH (*d*) ETLHMF

9. If EARTHQUAKE is coded as MOGPENJOSM, then EQUATE will be coded as :
   (*a*) MENOPM (*b*) MENOMP
   (*c*) MJOGPM (*d*) MNJOPM

10. In a certain code language HJIZT code is deciphered as MONEY, in the same way NOVGZ will be deciphered as :
   (*a*) STUMP (*b*) STALE
   (*c*) STICK (*d*) SPIRE

11. If in a certain code JOSEPH is coded as FKOALD, then GEORGE will be coded in the same way as :
   (*a*) CBJNCA (*b*) CANKCA
   (*c*) CAKNCA (*d*) CAKCNA

12. If COUNTRY is coded in a certain way as EMWLVPA, ELECTORATE will be coded in the same manner as :
   (*a*) CJCEVQPYWC (*b*) GJGERQTYVG
   (*c*) CNCERQPCRG (*d*) GJGAVMTYVC

13. In a certain code PORTUGESE is written as ESEGUTROP, MALAYALAM will be written in the same code as :
   (*a*) MALAYALAM (*b*) MALYALAM
   (*c*) MALAYALM (*d*) MALAYLAM

14. If PHILOSOPHY is coded as HPLISOPOYH, ORNAMENTAL will be coded as :
   (*a*) ROANEMNTLA (*b*) ONRAMNEALT
   (*c*) ROANEMTNLA (*d*) ROANEMNATL

15. If SABOTAGE is coded as UADOVAIE, how will EMERGENCY be coded in the same manner?
   (*a*) GMGRIEPCA (*b*) GMGRGEPCA
   (*c*) BNBQFDOBZ (*d*) EOETGGNEY

## EXPLANATORY ANSWERS

**1. (*d*) :** The word is coded by moving the letters three steps forward.

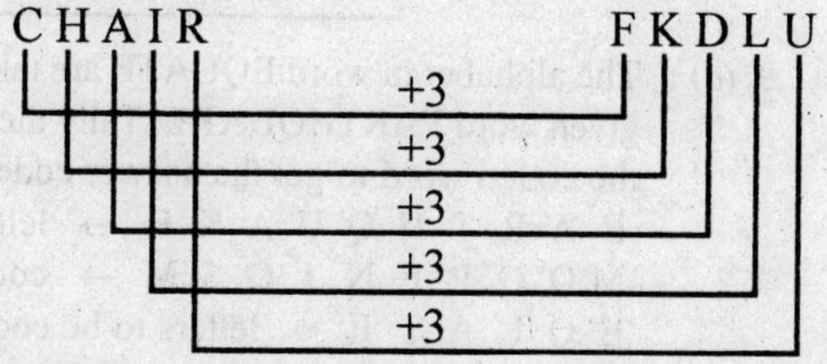


Similarly,

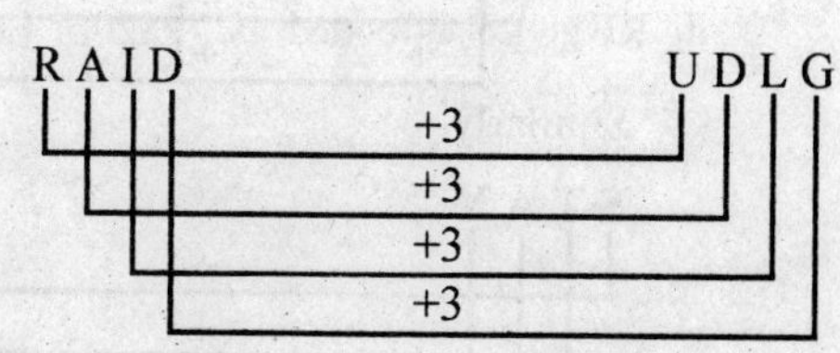


**2. (*d*) :** In this word, the second and third letters interchange their places and the fifth and sixth letters do the same. Other letters retain their position.

CONDEMN → CNODMEN

Similarly,

TEACHER → TAECEHR

**3. (d) :** The letters of the word are coded by their represented letters in the reverse series.

C O M E → letters in natural series
X L N V → letters in reverse series
↓ ↓ ↓ ↓
3rd 15th 13th 5th → position of letters

A B L E → letters in natural series
Z Y O V → letters in reverse series
↓ ↓ ↓ ↓
1st 2nd 12th 5th → position of letters

Similarly,

M O L L Y → letters in natural series
N L O O B → letters in reverse series
↓ ↓ ↓ ↓ ↓
13th 15th 12th 12th 25th → position of letters

**4. (b) :** The word is divided into two equal parts and the letters of each part are written backwards.

PROFE SSION → EFORP NOISS

Similarly,

DICTI ONARY → ITCID YRANO

**5. (a) :** The word is coded by moving the letters +4, +3, +2, and +1 steps respectively.

JUNE → NXPF (+4, +3, +2, +1)

Similarly,

STAY → WWCZ (+4, +3, +2, +1)

**6. (b) :** The word is coded by moving the letters two steps forward, *i.e.*,

GENIUS → IGPKWU (+2, +2, +2, +2, +2, +2)

Similarly,

IDIOT → KFKQV (+2, +2, +2, +2, +2)

**7. (a) :** The letters of the word are coded by their represented letters in the reverse series.

A C T I O N → letters in natural series
Z X G R L M → letters in reverse series
↓ ↓ ↓ ↓ ↓ ↓
1st 3rd 20th 9th 15th 14th → position of letters

Similarly,

H E A L T H → letters in natural series
S V Z O G S → letters in reverse series
↓ ↓ ↓ ↓ ↓ ↓
8th 5th 1st 12th 20th 8th → position of letters

**8. (d) :** The word is coded by moving the alphabet one step backwards, *i.e.*,

THOUSAND → SGNTRZMC (−1, −1, −1, −1, −1, −1, −1, −1)

Similarly,

FUMING → ETLHMF (−1, −1, −1, −1, −1, −1)

**9. (d) :** The alphabet in word EQUATE are taken from the given word EARTHQUAKE. Tally the letters from the coded word to get the answer code.

E A R T H Q U A K E → letters
M O G P E N J O S M → codes
E Q U A T E → letters to be coded
M N J O P M → answer codes

**10.** *(b)* **:** The coded alphabet are deciphered by moving five steps forward, *i.e.,*

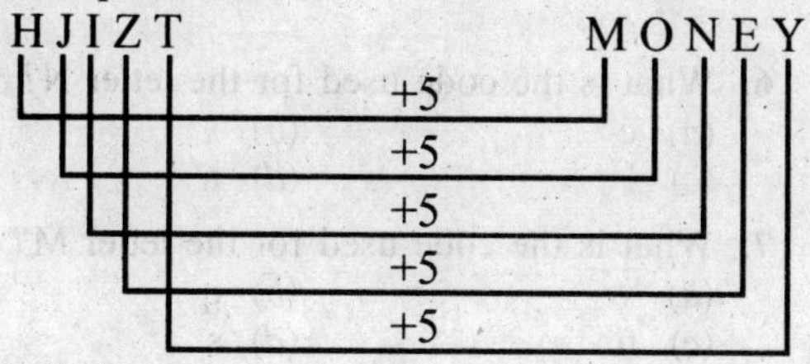


Similarly,

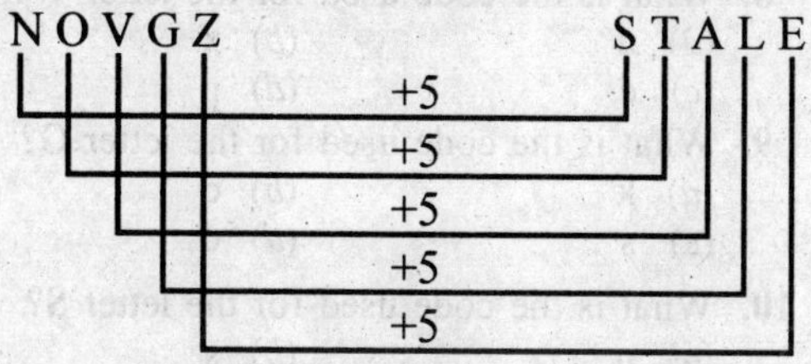


**11.** *(c)* **:** The word is coded by moving the alphabet four steps backward, *i.e.,*

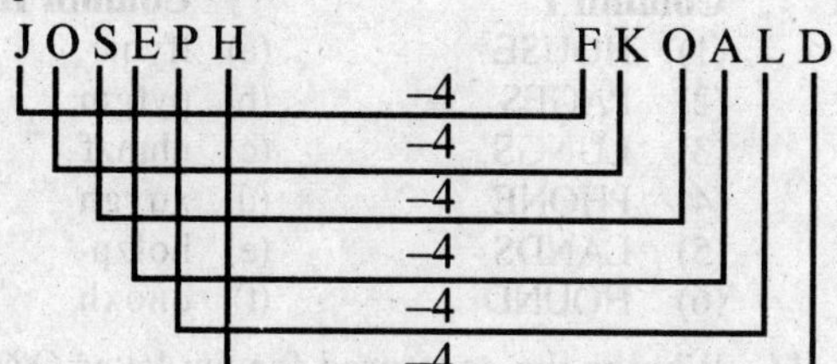


Similarly,

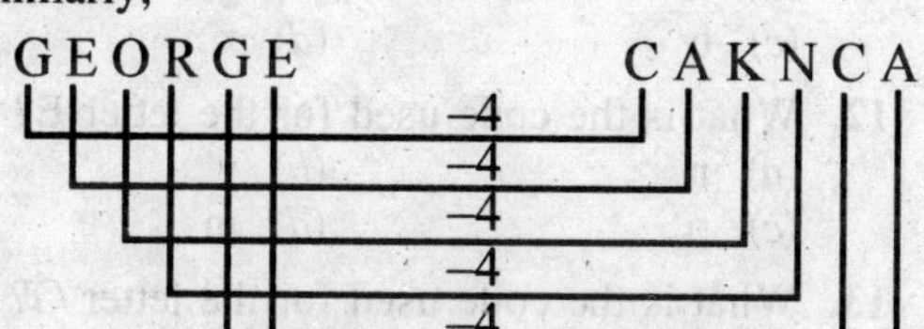


**12.** *(d)* **:** The word is coded by moving the alphabet two steps forward and two steps backward alternately, *i.e.,*

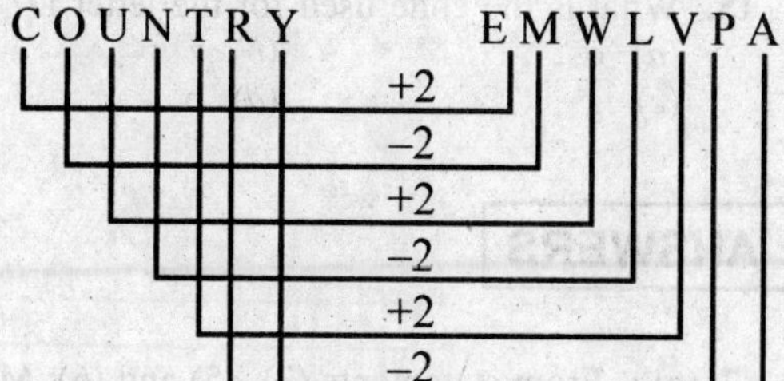


Similarly,

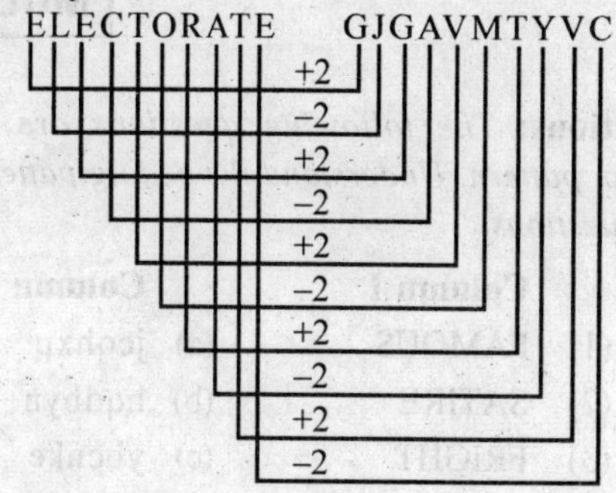


**13.** *(a)* **:** The coded word is the alphabet of the word written backwards.

Similarly,

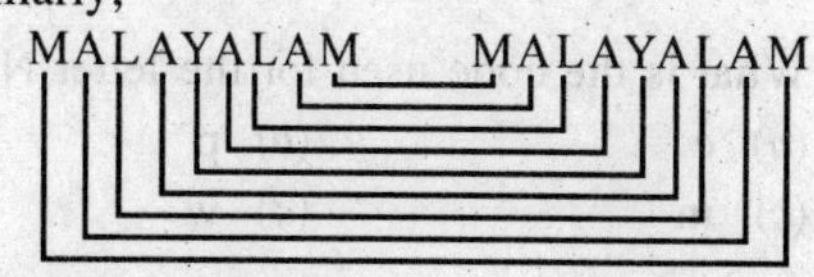


**14.** *(c)* **:** The places of two consecutive letters in the word are interchanged to form the coded word.

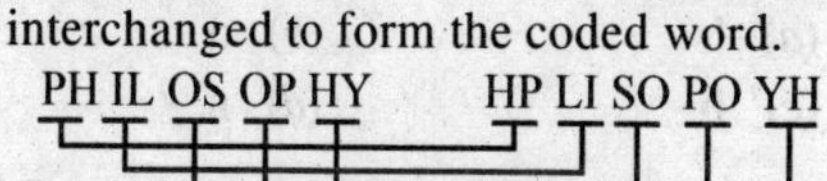


Similarly,

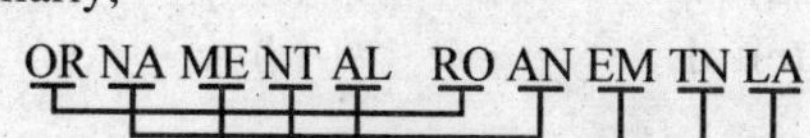


**15.** *(a)* **:** The word is coded by moving only the alphabet at odd positions two steps forward.

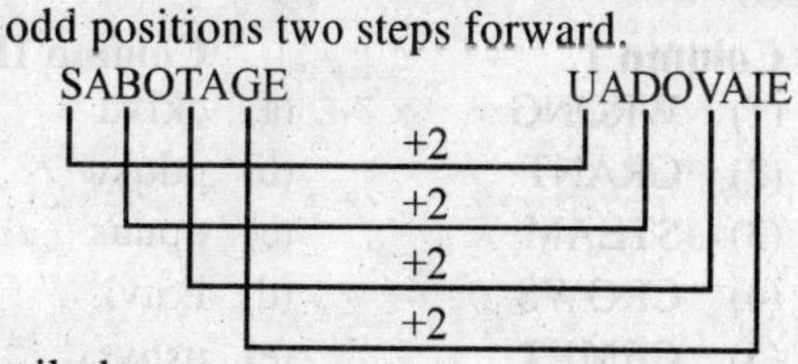


Similarly,

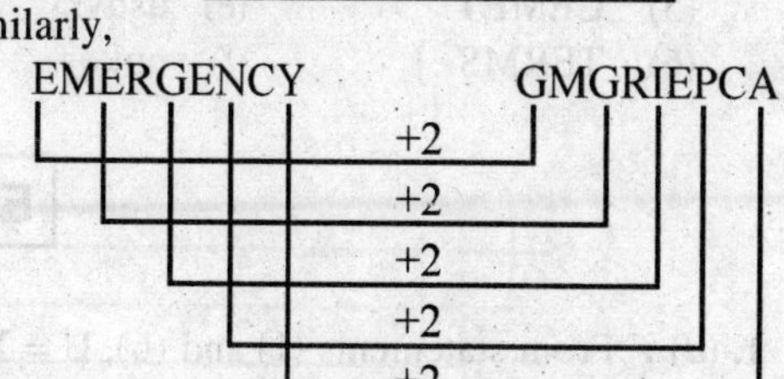


## TYPE - II

Column coding is a very complex form of coding. It needs a lot of attention and swift eye movement to decode the code for each letter of the given words. Proper words in capital letters are given in one column and the codes in small letters are given in another column. Based on the information given in both columns the candidate has to arrive at the correct answer option.

## MULTIPLE CHOICE QUESTIONS

**Directions:** *The following questions are based on the column pattern. Understand the coding pattern and answer the questions.*

| | Column I | | Column II |
|---|---|---|---|
| (1) | FAMOUS | (a) | jcqhxp |
| (2) | SATIRE | (b) | hqdbyn |
| (3) | FRIGHT | (c) | ybcnke |
| (4) | TANGLE | (d) | zewhnd |
| (5) | ROVING | (e) | epbmyw |
| (6) | HUNTER | (f) | wdnbxk |

1. What is the code used for the letter U?
(*a*) d (*b*) n
(*c*) b (*d*) x

2. What is the code used for the letter N?
(*a*) e (*b*) p
(*c*) m (*d*) w

3. What is the code used for the letter A?
(*a*) h (*b*) q
(*c*) b (*d*) n

4. What is the code used for the letter F?
(*a*) w (*b*) p
(*c*) d (*d*) c

5. What is the code used for the letter E?
(*a*) d (*b*) n
(*c*) b (*d*) k

| | Column I | | Column II |
|---|---|---|---|
| (1) | WRONG | (a) | cklxd |
| (2) | GRANT | (b) | pdqkc |
| (3) | STEAM | (c) | qpuns |
| (4) | CROWS | (d) | lxnvk |
| (5) | CEMET | (e) | usqvs |
| (6) | TERMS | (f) | nukqs |

6. What is the code used for the letter N?
(*a*) c (*b*) x
(*c*) l (*d*) n

7. What is the code used for the letter M?
(*a*) v (*b*) q
(*c*) u (*d*) s

8. What is the code used for the letter W?
(*a*) d (*b*) x
(*c*) c (*d*) p

9. What is the code used for the letter G?
(*a*) k (*b*) c
(*c*) s (*d*) d

10. What is the code used for the letter S?
(*a*) n (*b*) s
(*c*) d (*d*) k

| | Column I | | Column II |
|---|---|---|---|
| (1) | HOUSE | (a) | lfyqx |
| (2) | PAGES | (b) | pyfgm |
| (3) | LUNGS | (c) | nhmzf |
| (4) | PHONE | (d) | xqygh |
| (5) | LANDS | (e) | hofzp |
| (6) | HOUND | (f) | qnoxh |

11. What is the code used for the letter O?
(*a*) h (*b*) g
(*c*) q (*d*) x

12. What is the code used for the letter E?
(*a*) n (*b*) y
(*c*) p (*d*) m

13. What is the code used for the letter G?
(*a*) p (*b*) o
(*c*) f (*d*) m

14. What is the code used for the letter N?
(*a*) l (*b*) y
(*c*) x (*d*) h

15. What is the code used for the letter D?
(*a*) o (*b*) z
(*c*) g (*d*) p

## EXPLANATORY ANSWERS

**1. (*d*) :** From statements (1) and (6), U = X.

**2. (*d*) :** From statements (5) and (6), RN = bw. From statement (4), N = w.

**3. (*a*) :** From statements (2) and (4), ATE = hdn. From statement (6), TE = dn. Therefore, A = h.

**4. (*d*) :** From statements (1) and (3), F = c.

**5. (*a*) :** From statements (2) and (4), ATE = hdn. From statement (6), TE = dn. From statement (3), T = n. Hence E = d.

**6. (*a*) :** From statements (1) and (2), N = C.

**7. (*c*) :** From statements (3), (5) and (6), M = u.

**8. (*b*) :** From statements (1) and (4), W = x.

**9. (*d*) :** From statements (1) and (2), G = d.

**10. (*a*) :** From statements (3), (4) and (6), S = n.

**11. (*d*) :** From statements (1), (4) and (6), O = x.

**12. (*b*) :** From statements (1), (2) and (4), E = y.

**13. (*d*) :** From statements (2) and (3), G = m.

**14. (*d*) :** From statements (3), (4), (5) and (6), N = h.

**15. (*a*) :** From statements (5) and (6), D = o.

## TYPE - III

There is variety in ways of coding. Coding language is not only for words and numbers but also for hiding a group of words, statements or even sentences. This form of coding pattern may appear to be confusing but after solving only a few questions it is very easy to understand. Questions based on this coding pattern require no moving of steps or straining efforts of calculations, but only quick tallying or comparing ability. The codes can be letters or numbers.

## SOLVED EXAMPLE

In a certain code 'ra mei ket' means 'he is rich'; 'rui pha jeu' means 'run for money'; and 'pha rui ket' means 'money for rich'. Which of the following is the code for 'rich'?

(*a*) ra (*b*) pha
(*c*) ket (*d*) jeu

**Ans. (*c*) :** The given information is :

| | *Code* | *Sentence* |
|---|---|---|
| 1. | ra mei *ket* | he is *rich* |
| 2. | rui pha jeu | run for money |
| 3. | pha rui *ket* | money for *rich* |

After comparing codes and sentences 1 and 3, it is clear that word 'rich' is common and so is the code 'ket'.

## MULTIPLE CHOICE QUESTIONS

**Directions :** *In the following questions study the coded patterns and then select the right option from the given alternatives.*

**1.** In a certain language, (a) 'go ju mi' stands for 'plenty of money'; (b) pao ju go nei vu' for 'money creates lots of problems'; (c) 'kol vu nei' for 'problems create tension'; and (d) 'sol tun ju haw' for 'still money is needed'. Which of the following words stand for 'money'?

(*a*) nei (*b*) ju
(*c*) haw (*d*) go

**2.** In a certain language, (a) 'FOR' stands for 'old is gold'; (b) 'ROT' stands for 'gold is pure'; (c) 'ROM' stands for 'gold is costly'. How will 'pure old gold is costly' be written?

(*a*) TFROM (*b*) FOTRM
(*c*) FTORM (*d*) TOMRF

**3.** In a certain code '415' means 'milk is hot'; '18' means 'hot soup'; and '895' means 'soup is tasty'. What number will indicate the word 'tasty'?

(*a*) 9 (*b*) 8
(*c*) 5 (*d*) 4

**4.** In a certain code '643' means 'she is beautiful', '593' means 'he is handsome', and '567' means 'handsome meets beautiful'. What number will indicate the word 'meets'?

(*a*) 5 (*b*) 3
(*c*) 7 (*d*) 6

**5.** In a certain code language, (a) 'dugo hui mul zo' stands for 'work is very hard'; (b) 'hui dugo ba ki' for 'Bingo is very smart'; (c) 'nano mul dugo' for 'cake is hard', and (d) 'mul ki qu' for 'smart and hard'. Which of the following words stand for 'Bingo'?

(*a*) jalu (*b*) dugo
(*c*) ki (*d*) ba

**6.** In a certain code language, (a) 'pic vic nic' stands for 'winter is cold'; (b) 'to nic re' for 'summer is hot'; (c) 're pic boo' for 'winter and summer' and (d) 'vic tho pa' for 'nights are cold'. Which of the following word is the code for 'summer'?

(*a*) nic (*b*) boo
(*c*) to (*d*) re

**7.** In a certain language, (a) 'mx das sci' means 'good little frock'; (b) 'jm coz sci' means 'girl behaves good'; (c) 'ngv drs coz' means 'girl makes mischief'; and (d) 'das gp coz' means 'little girl fell'. What is the code for 'frock' in this language?

(*a*) mx (*b*) das
(*c*) sci (*d*) gp

**8.** In a certain language 'mu mit es' means 'who is she' and 'elb mu es' means 'where is she'. What is the code for 'where' in this language?

(*a*) es (*b*) elb
(*c*) mu (*d*) mit

**9.** In a certain code language '069' means 'grapes are sweet', '476' means 'very sweet fruit' and '509' means 'grapes are ripe'. Which of the following digits means 'ripe' in that language?

(*a*) 0 (*b*) 5
(*c*) 9 (*d*) 7

**10.** In a certain code language 'roi ja kyo twa' means 'Moody is writing letters', 'pok ju ja twa' means 'Woody is writing cards', 'trn kyo pos un' means 'they are writing letters', and 'koi rus pok' means 'gifts and cards'. What is the code word for 'Moody'?

(*a*) ja (*b*) twa
(*c*) roi (*d*) kyo

## EXPLANATORY ANSWERS

**1. (*b*) :**

| | Code | Sentence |
|---|---|---|
| 1. | go *ju* mi | plenty of *money* |
| 2. | pao *ju* go nei vu | *money* creates lots of problems |
| 3. | kol vu nei | problems create tension |
| 4. | sol tun *ju* haw | still *money* is needed |

In 1st, 2nd and 4th codes and their sentences the word 'ju' is repeated and so is 'money'.

**2. (*a*) :**

| | Code | Sentence |
|---|---|---|
| 1. | FOR | old is gold |
| 2. | ROT | gold is pure |
| 3. | ROM | gold is costly |

Therefore,

F stands for old
O stands for is
R stands for gold
T stands for pure
M stands for costly

So, 'pure old gold is costly' will be written as 'TFROM'.

**3. (*a*) :**

| | Code | Sentence |
|---|---|---|
| 1. | 415 | milk is hot |
| 2. | 18 | hot soup |
| 3. | 895 | soup is *tasty* |

From 3rd code and its sentence neither number '9' is repeated nor the word 'tasty'.

**4. (*c*) :**

| | Code | Sentence |
|---|---|---|
| 1. | 643 | she is beautiful |
| 2. | 593 | he is handsome |
| 3. | 567 | handsome *meets* beautiful |

From 3rd code and its sentence, neither number '7' nor the word 'meets' is repeated.

**5. (*d*) :**

| | Code | Sentence |
|---|---|---|
| 1. | *dugo hui* mul zo | work *is very* hard |
| 2. | *hui dugo* **ba** *ki* | **Bingo** *is very smart* |
| 3. | nano mul *dugo* | cake is *hard* |
| 4. | mul *ki* qu | *smart* and hard |

From 2nd code and its sentence, neither 'ba' nor 'Bingo' is repeated.

(Words repeated are in italics)

**6. (*d*) :**

| | Code | Sentence |
|---|---|---|
| 1. | pic vic nic | winter is cold |
| 2. | to nic *re* | *summer* is hot |
| 3. | *re* pic boo | winter and *summer* |
| 4. | vic tho pa | nights are cold |

The word 'summer' is common in 2nd and 3rd sentences and so is the code 're'.

**7. (*a*) :**

| | Code | Sentence |
|---|---|---|
| 1. | **mx** *das sci* | *good little* **frock** |
| 2. | jm coz *sci* | girl behaves *good* |
| 3. | ngv drs coz | girl makes mischief |
| 4. | *das* gp coz | *little* girl fell |

Word 'frock' is only in the 1st sentence. The code word 'das' is repeated in 4th sentence and 'sci' in 2nd sentence. So, 'mx' is the code for 'frock'.

**8. (*b*) :**

| | Code | Sentence |
|---|---|---|
| 1. | *mu* mit *es* | who *is she* |
| 2. | **elb** *mu* es | **where** *is she* |

The code words 'mu' and 'es' are repeated in Ist sentence. The only code left is 'elb' which means 'where'.

**9. (*b*) :**

| | Code | Sentence |
|---|---|---|
| 1. | 069 | *grapes are* sweet |
| 2. | 476 | very sweet fruit |
| 3. | 509 | *grapes are* **ripe** |

The code numbers '0' and '9' are repeated in 1st and 3rd sentences. The only code remaining is '5' which stands for 'ripe'.

**10. (*c*) :**

| | Code | Sentence |
|---|---|---|
| 1. | **roi** *ja kyo twa* | **Moody** *is writing letters* |
| 2. | pok ju *ja twa* | Woody *is writing* cards |
| 3. | trn *kyo* pos un | they are writing *letters* |
| 4. | koi rus pok | gifts and cards |

'Moody' is in 1st sentence only. The code words 'ja' and 'twa' are repeated in 2nd sentence and 'kyo' in 3rd sentence. Only code word 'roi' remains which stands for 'Moody'.

CHAPTER 4

# Semantic Series

## MULTIPLE CHOICE QUESTIONS

**1.** ADG, XVT, BEH, WUS, ?
(*a*) VTR (*b*) CFI
(*c*) DFJ (*d*) STU

**2.** GMSY, IOUA, KQWC, ?
(*a*) MSYE (*b*) NSYE
(*c*) MTYE (*d*) MSYF

**3.** ADG, GJM, ?, SVY
(*a*) MPS (*b*) MQR
(*c*) MQS (*d*) SPM

**4.** KNQ, TWZ, CFI, ?
(*a*) KOR (*b*) LOR
(*c*) MNQ (*d*) JLM

**5.** AEI, BFJ, CGK, ?
(*a*) DLH (*b*) EGF
(*c*) EFL (*d*) DHL

**6.** CFI, IKM, OPQ, ?
(*a*) UUU (*b*) UST
(*c*) VUS (*d*) TUV

**7.** LAZ, NEX, PIV, ?
(*a*) SLS (*b*) QNS
(*c*) RMT (*d*) RMS

**8.** DED, EFE, FGF, ?
(*a*) HGH (*b*) GHG
(*c*) EFE (*d*) FHF

**9.** XYZ, UVW, ?, OPQ
(*a*) RST (*b*) STU
(*c*) QRS (*d*) TUV

**10.** VCL, UEI, TGF, ?
(*a*) SJC (*b*) THI
(*c*) SIC (*d*) RHD

**11.** ABC, EFG, HIJ, ?
(*a*) IJK (*b*) KLM
(*c*) LMN (*d*) JKL

**12.** PQR, HIJ, DEF, ?
(*a*) DEF (*b*) CDE
(*c*) ABC (*d*) BCD

**13.** KNQ, TWZ, CFI, ?
(*a*) MNQ (*b*) LOR
(*c*) LPR (*d*) KOR

**14.** JOBS, KMEO, LKHK, ?, NGNC
(*a*) MJLH (*b*) LIKG
(*c*) MIKG (*d*) MNGM

**15.** ABC, ACE, ADG, ?
(*a*) AEG (*b*) AFH
(*c*) AFG (*d*) AEI

**16.** IOU, JKL, PQR, ?
(*a*) UVW (*b*) XYZ
(*c*) TUV (*d*) VWX

**17.** AZ, GT, MN, ?, YB
(*a*) KF (*b*) TS
(*c*) RX (*d*) SH

**18.** BMY, DNW, FOU, ?
(*a*) HPT (*b*) HPS
(*c*) HQS (*d*) GPS

**19.** ADG, GJM, MPS, ?
(*a*) SVW (*b*) SVY
(*c*) SUW (*d*) SWY

**20.** AZ, CX, EV, ?
(*a*) HU (*b*) GS
(*c*) GT (*d*) HT

## EXPLANATORY ANSWERS

**1. (*b*) :** There are two alternate series.

ADG XVT BEH WUS CFI

*Series I* : ADG BEH CFI

+1 +1

+1 +1

+1 +1

*Series II* : XVT WUS

–1

–1

–1

**2. (*a*) :** The series is formed by moving each letter two steps forward from one group to the next.

GMSY IOUA KQWC MSYE

+2 +2 +2

+2 +2 +2

+2 +2 +2

+2 +2 +2

(The series restarts from A on reaching Z)

**3. (*a*) :** In each group of three letters the alphabet is in the succession of +3. The next group begins with the last alphabet of the previous group.

A D G G J M M P S S V Y

+3 +3 +3 +3 +3 +3 +3 +3

**4. (*b*) :** All the alphabet in this group series is in succession of +3. The alphabetical series repeat from 'A' on reaching 'Z'.

K N Q T W Z C F I L O R

+3 +3 +3 +3 +3 +3 +3 +3 +3 +3 +3

**5. (*d*) :** Each of the three alphabet in one group corresponds to the alphabet in the next group in the succession of +1, *i.e.*,

AEI BFJ CGK DHL

+1 +1 +1

+1 +1 +1

+1 +1 +1

**6. (*a*) :** The three alphabet in one group correspond to the alphabet in the next group in the manner +6, +5, +4 respectively, *i.e.*,

CFI IKM OPQ UUU

+6 +6 +6

+5 +5 +5

+4 +4 +4

**7. (*c*) :** The three alphabet in one group correspond to the alphabet in the next group in the manner +2, +4, –2 respectively, *i.e.*,

LAZ NEX PIV RMT

+2 +2 +2

+4 +4 +4

–2 –2 –2

**8. (*b*) :** The alphabet from one group to the next are in succession of +1, *i.e.*,

DED EFE FGF GHG

+1 +1 +1

+1 +1 +1

+1 +1 +1

**9. (*a*) :** The alphabet from one group to the next are in recession of –3, *i.e.*,

XYZ UVW RST OPQ

–3 –3 –3

–3 –3 –3

–3 –3 –3

**10. (*c*) :** The alphabet in one group correspond to the alphabet in the next group in the manner –1, +2, –3 respectively, *i.e.*,

VCL UEI TGF SIC

–1 –1 –1

+2 +2 +2

–3 –3 –3

**11. (*d*) :** The difference between the last letter of the preceding group of alphabet and the first letter of the next group is decreasing by 1, *i.e.*,

ABC EFG HIJ JKL

+2 +1 +0

Otherwise the three letters in each group are in their natural order.

**12. (*d*) :** The letters in each group of alphabet are in the recession of –8, –4, –2 respectively.

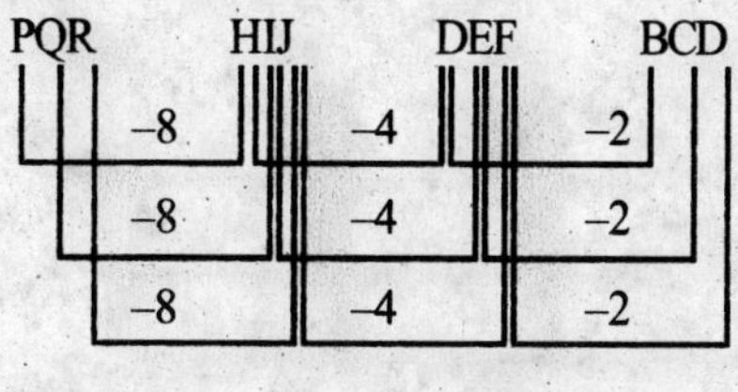


**13. (*b*) :** The letters in each group correspond to the letter in next group in the succession of +9.

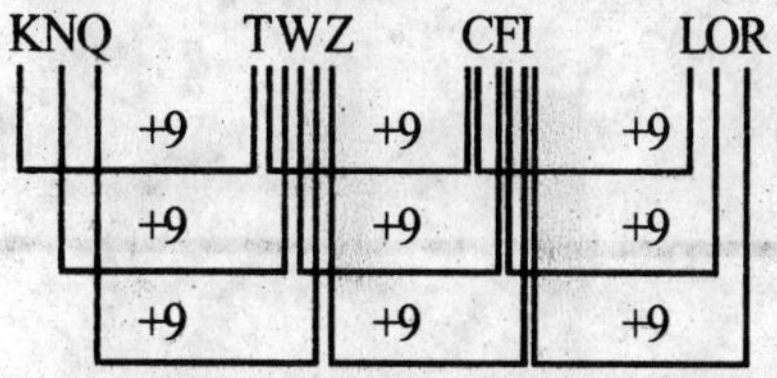


**14. (*c*) :** The alphabets in each group follow the pattern +1, –2, +3 and –4 respectively from one group to the next group.

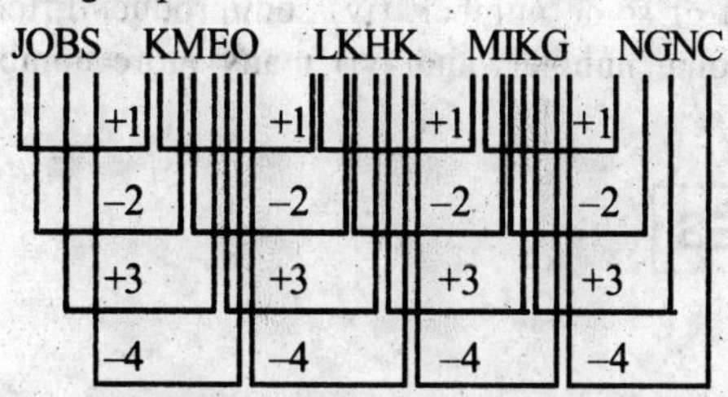


**15. (*d*) :** The difference between the letters in each group is increased by one.

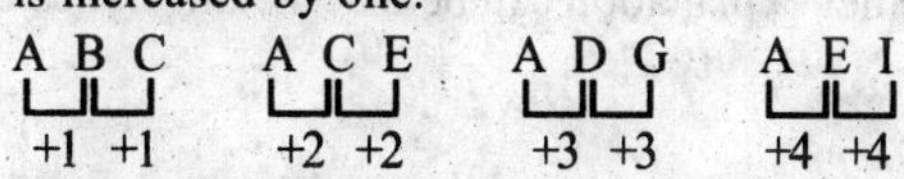


**16. (*d*) :** The series is formed in this manner :

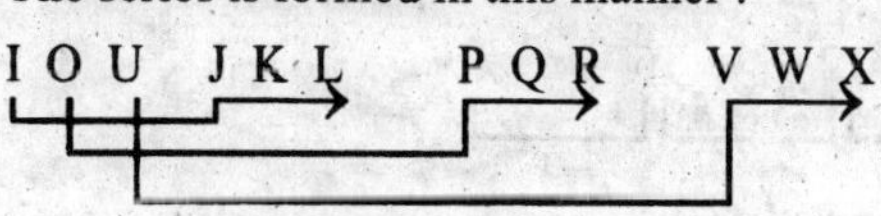


Three consecutive letters to each letter in the first group forms the other groups in the series.

**17. (*d*) :** The letters in one group correspond to the letters in the next group in the manner +6, –6 respectively, *i.e.*,

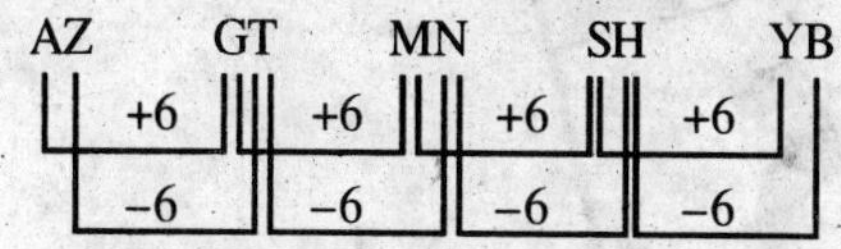


**18. (*b*) :** The letters in one group correspond to the letters in the next group in the manner +2, +1, -2 respectively, *i.e.*,

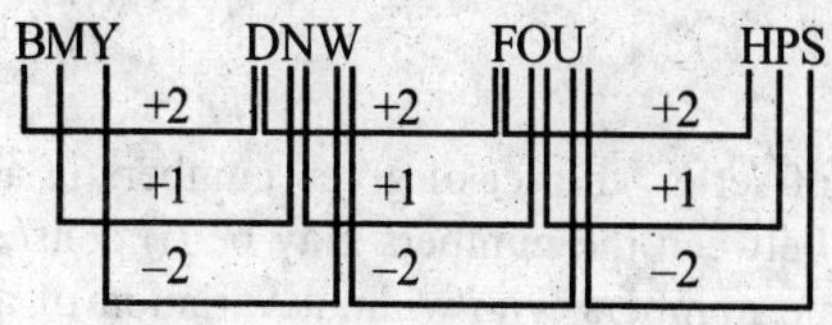


**19. (*b*) :** The letters in each group are moved six steps forward, *i.e.*,

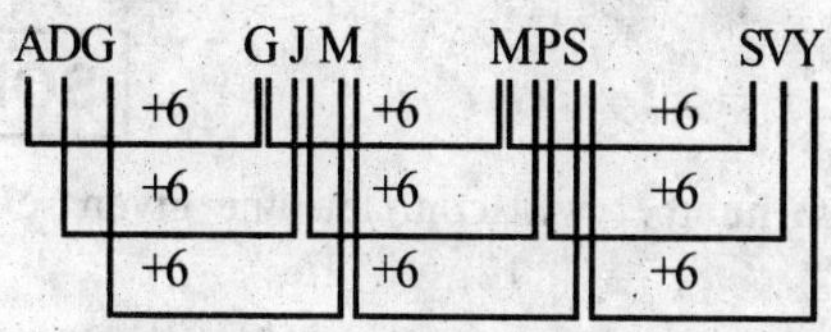


**20. (*c*) :** The letters in each group correspond to the letters in the next group in the manner +2, –2 respectively, *i.e.*,

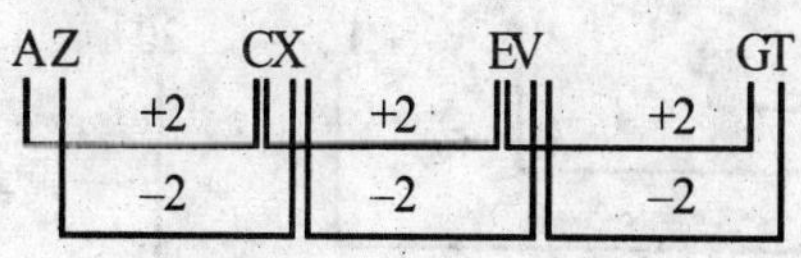

CHAPTER 5

# Number Series

In this type of series, the set of given numbers in a series are related to one another in a particular pattern or manner. The relationship between the numbers may be (i) consecutive odd/even numbers; (ii) consecutive prime numbers; (iii) squares/cubes of some numbers with/without variation of addition or subtraction of some number; (iv) sum/product/difference of preceding numbers; (v) addition/subtraction/multiplication/division by some number; and (vi) many more combinations of the relationships given above.

## SOLVED EXAMPLES

**1.** Which number will complete the given series?

4, 8, 12, 16, ?

(*a*) 18 (*b*) 20 (*c*) 22 (*d*) 24

**Ans. (*b*):** The series is made of numbers which are multiples of 4. Other explanation can be that the difference between the two consecutive numbers is 4.

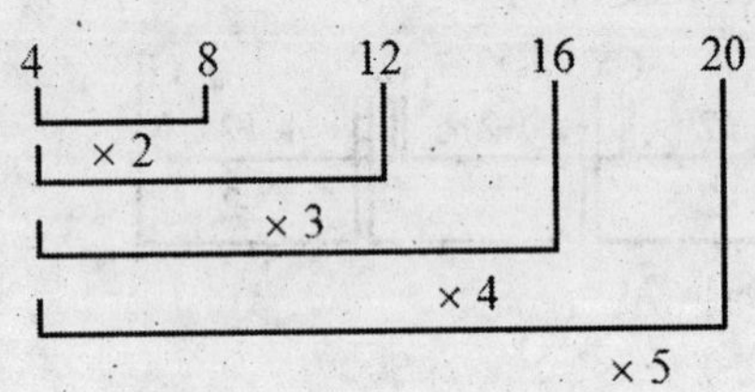


Or

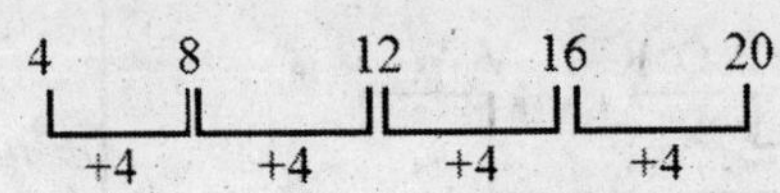


**2.** Complete the given series.

2, 14, 98, 686, ?

(*a*) 1976 (*b*) 2548 (*c*) 980 (*d*) 4802

**Ans. (*d*) :** The numbers are multiplied by 7 to obtain the next numbers.

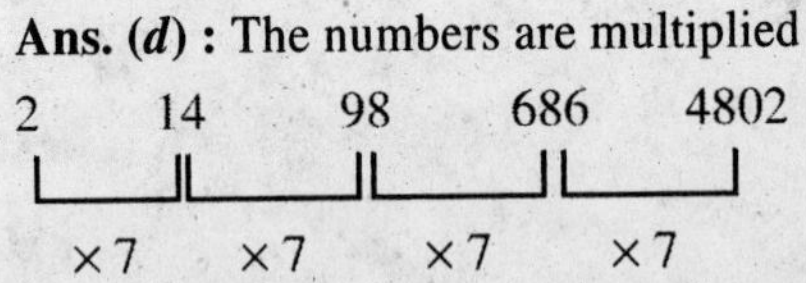


***The given series may also comprise of two alternate series merged as one.***

## MULTIPLE CHOICE QUESTIONS

**Directions:** *In the following questions, select the number(s) from the given options for completing the given series.*

**1.** 3, 9, 27, 81, 243, ?

(*a*) 486 (*b*) 729

(*c*) 972 (*d*) 359

**2.** 1, 6, 12, 19, 27, ?

(*a*) 38 (*b*) 35

(*c*) 36 (*d*) 54

**3.** 2, 6, 14, 30, 62, ?

(*a*) 126 (*b*) 128

(*c*) 120 (*d*) 130

**4.** 8, 48, 16, 96, 32, ?
(*a*) 192 (*b*) 150
(*c*) 64 (*d*) 288

**5.** 2, 8, 14, 24, 34, 48, ?
(*a*) 66 (*b*) 62
(*c*) 58 (*d*) 64

**6.** 4, 9, 19, 34, 54, ?, 109
(*a*) 89 (*b*) 84
(*c*) 74 (*d*) 79

**7.** 3, 15, 35, 63, 99, ?
(*a*) 144 (*b*) 143
(*c*) 121 (*d*) 169

**8.** 2, 3, 6, 18, 108, ?
(*a*) 1944 (*b*) 1658
(*c*) 648 (*d*) 1008

**9.** 1, 2, 3, 2, 3, 5, 4, 5, ?
(*a*) 9 (*b*) 6
(*c*) 10 (*d*) 7

**10.** 7776, 1296, 216, 36, 6, ?
(*a*) 6 (*b*) 0
(*c*) 3 (*d*) 1

**11.** 1, 8, 27, 64, 125, ?
(*a*) 172 (*b*) 176
(*c*) 216 (*d*) 189

**12.** 2, 3, 5, 7, 11, 13, ?
(*a*) 19 (*b*) 57
(*c*) 31 (*d*) 17

**13.** 80, 64, 48, 32, 16, ?
(*a*) 4 (*b*) 0
(*c*) 8 (*d*) 1

**14.** 3, 8, 13, 24, 41, ?
(*a*) 65 (*b*) 75
(*c*) 70 (*d*) 80

**15.** 9, 81, 90, 810, 819, ?
(*a*) 7371 (*b*) 900
(*c*) 8100 (*d*) 1638

**16.** 0, 8, 24, 48, 80, ?
(*a*) 110 (*b*) 96
(*c*) 120 (*d*) 140

**17.** 2, 4, 8, 3, 9, 27, 4, 16, ?
(*a*) 64 (*b*) 32
(*c*) 48 (*d*) 24

**18.** 27, 28, 25, 25, 23, 22, 21, ?
(*a*) 20 (*b*) 21
(*c*) 19 (*d*) 18

**19.** 80, 63, 72, 72, 64, 81, 56, ?
(*a*) 96 (*b*) 98
(*c*) 89 (*d*) 90

**20.** 0, 5, 22, 57, ?, 205
(*a*) 198 (*b*) 116
(*c*) 172 (*d*) 92

## EXPLANATORY ANSWERS

**1. (*b*) :** The numbers in the series are multiplied by 3 to get the next numbers.

**2. (*c*) :** The difference between the numbers in the series increases by 1, after beginning from 5, *i.e.*,

1 6 12 19 27 36
+5 +6 +7 +8 +9

**3. (*a*) :** The difference between the numbers in the series doubles each time, after beginning from 4, *i.e.*,

2 6 14 30 62 126
+4 +8 +16 +32 +64

**4. (*a*) :** *Explanation I* : The sequence in the series is × 6, ÷ 3 which is repeated.

8 48 16 96 32 192
×6 ÷3 ×6 ÷3 ×6

*Explanation II* : There are two alternate series and the numbers are multiplied by 2.

×2 ×2
8 48 16 96 32 192
×2 ×2

*Series I* : 8, 16, 32
*Series II* : 48, 96, 192

**5. (*b*) :** The sequence in the series is :

2 8 14 24 34 48 62
+6 +6 +10 +10 +14 +14

The difference increases by 4 at alternate step.

**6. (*d*) :** The difference between the numbers increases by 5, after beginning from 5, *i.e.*,

4 9 19 34 54 79 109
+5 +10 +15 +20 +25 +30

**7. (*b*) :** The series follows the sequence of the squares of even numbers beginning from 2, minus 1.

**8. (*a*) :** Every third number in the series is the product of previous two numbers.

2 3 6 18 108 1944
2 × 3
3 × 6
6 × 18
18 × 108

**9. (a) :** In this series three numbers form a set. The first two numbers of each set are in natural order and the third number is the sum of first and second numbers. The first number of the next set begins with double the first number of the previous set.

×2 ×2

1 2 3 2 3 5 4 5 9

1 + 2 2 + 3 4 + 5

**10. (d) :** The numbers in this sequence are divided by 6 each time.

**11. (c) :** The sequence in the series is cube of numbers in their natural order.

**12. (d) :** The series consists of prime numbers in increasing order.

**13. (b) :** The numbers in the series are decreasing with the difference of 16 at each step.

**14. (c) :** The sequence in the series is (number + next number) + addition of natural number increasing by 1 at each step, after beginning from 2.

3 8 13 24 41 70

(3+8) + 2

(8 + 13) + 3

(13 + 24) + 4

(24 + 41) + 5

**15. (a) :** The sequence in the series is × 9, + 9 which is repeated.

**16. (c) :** The sequence of the series consists of the product of 2 even numbers in natural order, *i.e.*,

| 0 | 8 | 24 | 48 | 80 | 120 |
|---|---|---|---|---|---|
| ↓ | ↓ | ↓ | ↓ | ↓ | ↓ |
| (0 × 2) | (2 × 4) | (4 × 6) | (6 × 8) | (8 × 10) | (10 × 12) |

**17. (a) :** In this series 3 numbers form a set. The first number is in natural order. The second number is the square of above number. The third number is the cube of first number.

**18. (c) :** There are two alternate series :

−2 −2 −2

27 28 25 25 23 22 21 19

−3 −3 −3

*Series I* : 27, 25, 23, 21 (following −2 pattern)

*Series II* : 28, 25, 22, 19 (following −3 pattern)

**19. (d) :** There are two alternate series :

−8 −8 −8

80 63 72 72 64 81 56 90

+9 +9 +9

*Series I* : 80, 72, 64, 56 (following −8 pattern)

*Series II* : 63, 72, 81, 90 (following +9 pattern)

**20. (b) :** The series follows this sequence : cube of natural numbers starting from 1 minus odd numbers starting from 1.

| 0 | 5 | 22 | 57 | 116 | 205 |
|---|---|---|---|---|---|
| ↓ | ↓ | ↓ | ↓ | ↓ | ↓ |
| $1^3-1$ | $2^3-3$ | $3^3-5$ | $4^3-7$ | $5^3-9$ | $6^3-11$ |

CHAPTER 6

# Arithmatical Reasoning

## MULTIPLE CHOICE QUESTIONS

**Directions (1–5) :** *The following questions are based on the information given below :*

Data of 450 candidates, who took part in an examination in Social Science, Mathematics and Science is given below:

| | |
|---|---|
| Passed in all the subject | 167 |
| Failed in all the subject | 60 |
| Failed in Mathematics | 199 |
| Failed in Social Science | 175 |
| Failed in Science | 191 |
| Passed in Science only | 52 |
| Passed in Mathematics only | 48 |
| Passed in Social Science only | 62 |

**1.** How many passed in at least one subject?
(*a*) 450 (*b*) 390
(*c*) 304 (*d*) 167
(*e*) None of these.

**2.** How many failed in two subjects only?
(*a*) 56 (*b*) 61
(*c*) 152 (*d*) 162
(*e*) None of these.

**3.** How many passed in Mathematics and at least in one more subject?
(*a*) 210 (*b*) 203
(*c*) 170 (*d*) 94
(*e*) None of these.

**4.** How many failed in Social Science only?
(*a*) 15 (*b*) 21
(*c*) 30 (*d*) 42
(*e*) None of these.

**5.** How many failed in one subject only?
(*a*) 152 (*b*) 144
(*c*) 61 (*d*) 56
(*e*) None of these

**6.** A, B, C, D and E play a game of cards. A says to B, ''If you give me three cards, you will have as many as E has and if I give you three cards, you will have as many as D has.'' A and B together have 10 cards more than what D and E together have. If B has two cards more than what C has and the total number of cards be 133, how many cards does B have?
(*a*) 22 (*b*) 35
(*c*) 25 (*d*) 23
(*e*) None of these

**7.** A bus starts from city X. The number of women in the bus is half of the number of men. In the city Y, 10 men left the bus and five women entered. Now, number of men and women is equal. In the beginning, how many passenger entered the bus?
(*a*) 15 (*b*) 30
(*c*) 36 (*d*) 45
(*e*) None of these

**8.** I have a few sweets to be distributed. If I keep 2, 3 or 4 in a pack, I am left with one sweet. If I keep 5 in a pack, I am left with none. What is the minimum number of sweets I can have to pack and distributed?
(*a*) 25 (*b*) 37
(*c*) 54 (*d*) 65
(*e*) None of these

**9.** A, B, C, D and E play a game of cards. A says to B, ''If you give me 3 cards, you will have as many as I have at this moment while if D takes 5 cards from you, he will have as many as E has'', A and C together have twice as many cards as E has B and D together also have the same number of cards as A and C taken together. I all together they have 150 cards, how many cards has C got.
(*a*) 28 (*b*) 29
(*c*) 31 (*d*) 35
(*e*) None of these

**10.** At the end of a business conference, ten people present shake hands with each other once. How many handshakes will be there all together?
(*a*) 20 (*b*) 45
(*c*) 90 (*d*) 55
(*e*) None of these.

**11.** Jayesh is as much younger to Anil as he is older to Prashant. If the sum of the ages of Anil and Prashant is 48 years. What is the age of Jayesh?
(*a*) 30 years
(*b*) 24 years
(*c*) 20 years
(*d*) Can't be determined
(*e*) None of these.

**12.** Five years ago Vinay's age was one-third of the age of Vikash and now Vinay's age is 17 years. What is the present age of Vikash?
(*a*) 9 years (*b*) 36 years
(*c*) 41 years (*d*) 51 years

**13.** The sum of ages of a father and son is 45 years. Five years ago the product of their ages was 4 times the father's age at that time. The present age of the father and son respectively are.
(*a*) 25 years, 10 years (*b*) 36 years, 9 years
(*c*) 39 years, 6 years (*d*) None of these.

**14.** Out of a total 120 musicians in a club, 5% can play all the three instruments – guitar, violin and flute. It so happens that the number of musicians who can play any two and only two of the above instruments is 30. The number of musicians who can play the guitar alone is 40. What is the total number of those who can play violin alone or flute alone?
(*a*) 30 (*b*) 38
(*c*) 44 (*d*) 45
(*e*) None of these.

**15.** In a group of persons travelling in a bus, 6 persons can speak Tamil, 15 can speak Hindi and 6 can speak Gujarati. In that group, none can speak any other language. If 2 persons in the group can speak two languages and one person can speak all the three languages, then how many persons are there in the group?
(*a*) 21 (*b*) 22
(*c*) 23 (*d*) 24
(*e*) None of these.

**16.** There are 50 students admitted to a nursery class. Some students can speak only English and some can speak only Hindi. Ten students can speak both English and Hindi. If the number of students who can speak English is 21, then how many students can speak Hindi, how many can speak only Hindi and how many can speak only English?
(*a*) 39, 29 and 11 respectively.
(*b*) 37, 27 and 13 respectively.
(*c*) 28, 18 and 22 respectively.
(*d*) 21, 11 and 29 respectively.

**17.** A shephard had 17 sheep. All but nine died. How many was he left with?
(*a*) Nil (*b*) 17
(*c*) 9 (*d*) 8
(*e*) None of these.

**18.** 10 years ago, Chandravati's mother was 4 times older than her daughter. After 10 years, the mother will be twice older than the daughter. The present age of Chandravati is:
(*a*) 5 years (*b*) 10 years
(*c*) 20 years (*d*) 30 years
(*e*) None of these.

**19.** Pushpa is twice as old as Rita was two years ago. If difference between their ages be 2 years, how old is Pushpa today?
(*a*) 6 years (*b*) 8 years
(*c*) 10 years (*d*) 12 years

**20.** Mr. Sohan Lal is four times as old as his son. Four years later sum of their age will be 43 years. The present age of the son is:
(*a*) 5 years (*b*) 7 years
(*c*) 8 years (*d*) 10 years
(*e*) None of these.

**21.** 15 years ago the difference between the age of two persons is 10 years. The elder one was twice as old as the younger one. The present age of the elder person is:
(*a*) 15 years (*b*) 35 years
(*c*) 65 years (*d*) 45 years
(*e*) None of these.

**22.** Consider the diagram given below:

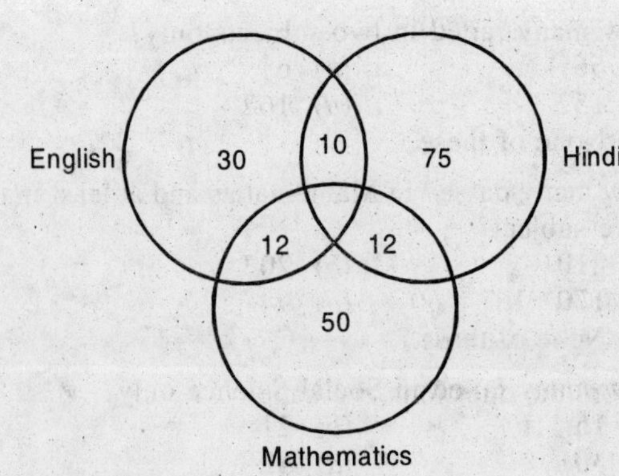


Five hundred candidates appeared in the examination conducted for the tests in English, Hindi and Mathematics. The diagram gives the number of candidates who failed in different tests. What is the percentage of candidates who failed in at least two subjects?

(*a*) 0.078 (*b*) 1.0
(*c*) 6.8 (*d*) 7.8
(*e*) None of these.

**23.** The sum of the ages of a son and father is 56 years. After four years, the age of the father will be three times that of the son. Their ages respectively are:
(*a*) 12 years, 44 years (*b*) 18 years, 36 years
(*c*) 16 years, 42 years (*d*) 16 years, 48 years
(*e*) None of these.

**24.** The number of boys in a class are three times the number of girls. Which one of the following numbers cannot represent the total number of children in the class?
(*a*) 48 (*b*) 44
(*c*) 42 (*d*) 46
(*e*) None of these.

**25.** In 10 years, A will be twice as old as B was 10 years ago. If at present A is 9 years older than B, the present age of B is:
(*a*) 19 years (*b*) 29 years
(*c*) 39 years (*d*) 49 years
(*e*) None of these.

## EXPLANATORY ANSWERS

**1.** (*b*) : Candidates passed at least in one subject = (Candidates passed in only one subjects) + (Candidates passed in only two subjects) + (Candidates passed in only all subjects).
(Candidates failed in only two subjects) + (Candidates failed in only one subject) + (Candidates passed in all the subject) = 162 + 61 + 167 = 390.

**2.** (*d*) : Candidates failed in two subjects only = Candidates passed in one subjects only = 62 + 48 + 52 = 162.

**3.** (*b*) : Candidates failed in science only =191 – (62 + 60 + 48) = 21
Candidates failed in one social science only = 15
Therefore, candidates passed in maths and at least one more subject
= (21 + 15 + 167) =203

**4.** (*a*) : Candidates failed in social science only = (candidates failed in social science) – (candidates failed in all subjects + candidates passed in science only + candidates passed in maths only)
= 175 – (60 + 52 + 48 ) = 175 – 160 = 15.

**5.** (*c*) : Candidates failed in one subject only
= (total number of candidates) – (candidates passed in all subjects + candidates failed in all the subjects + candidates passed in one subject only)
= 450 – (167 + 60 + 62 + 48 + 52)
= 450 – 389 = 61.

**6.** (*c*) : From the questions, we have
B – 3 = E ...... (i)
B + 3 = D ...... (ii)
A + B = D + E + 10 ...... (iii)
B = C + 2 ...... (iv)
A + B + C + D + E = 133 ...... (v)
From (i) and (ii)
B – E = D – B ⇒ E + D = 2 B ...... (vi)
From (iii) and (vi)
A + B = 2B + 10 ⇒ B = A – 10
or, A = B + 10 ...... (vii)
From (v), (vi), (iv) and (vii) we have
(B + 10) + (B) + (B – 2) + 2B = 133
5B = 133 – 8 = 125
= 25.

**7.** (*d*) : In the city X let the number of men be $x$
Then the number of women be $\frac{x}{2}$.
In the city $y$, $x-10=\frac{x}{2}+5$
or, $\frac{x}{2}=15$ or, $x=30$ and $y=15$.
Therefore, total number of passenger at the beginning were 30 + 15 = 45.

**8.** (*a*) : The required number will be obtained by taking LCM of 2, 3 and 4 and adding 1 into it. The number so obtained is 25.

**9.** (*a*) : From the questions it is clear that
B – 3 = A ...... (1)
D + 5 = E ...... (2)
A + C = 2 E ...... (3)
A + C = B + D ...... (4)
A + B + C + D + E = 150 ...... (5)
From (3), (4) and (5) we get
5E = 150 ∴ E = 30
Now from (2) D = 30 – 5 = 25
and from (4) A = 32
Now from (3) 32 + C = 2 × 30
C = 60 – 32 = 28.

**10.** (*b*) : Total number of handshakes = ( 9 + 8 + 7 + 6 + 5 + 4 + 3 + 2 + 1) = 45

**11.** (*b*) : Let the age of Anil and Prashant be $x$ and (48 – $x$) years.
Let the age of Jayesh be y years then
$(x - y) = y - (48 - x)$
$x - y = y - 48 + x$
$2y = 48$, $y = 24$ years
So, Age of Jayesh is 24 years.

**12.** (*c*) : Vinay's present age is 17 years.
Five years ago Vinay's age was 12 years. and that of Vikash = 36 years
Present age of Vikash = 36 + 5 = 41 years.

**13.** (*b*) : Let the present age of father be $x$ years and that of son be $(45 - x)$ years.
Five years ago the age of son was $(45 - x - 5) = (40 - x)$.
and that of father $(x - 5)$ years

$(x - 5)(40 - x) = 4(x - 5)$
$40x - x^2 - 200 + 5x = 4x - 20$
or, $41x - x^2 - 180 = 0$
$x = 36.$
$x^2 - 41x - 180 = 0$
$x^2 - (36 + 5)x + 180 = 0$
or, $x^2 - 36x - 5x + 180 = 0$
$x(x - 36) - 5(x - 36) = 0$
$(x - 36)(x - 5) = 0$
$x = 36 \mid x = 5$ unacceptable

Therefore, the present age of father and son are 36 years and 9 years respectively.

**14.** (*c*) : Let the circles x, y, z represent the musicians who can play guitar, violin and flute respectively.
P + Q + R + S + T + U + V = 120 ...... (1)
Number of musicians who can play all the three instruments = S = 5% of 120 = 6
S = 6 ...... (2)
Number of musicians who can play guitar only = P = 40 ...... (3)
Number of musicians who can play any two and only two of the instruments
= Q + T + U = 30 ...... (4)
Now, from equations (1), (2), (3) and (4) we get
P + Q + R + S + T + U + V = 120
P + (Q + T + U) + S + R + V = 120
40 + 30 + 6 + R + V = 120
R + V = 120 − 76
= 44
Total number of musicians who can play violin alone or flute alone
= (R + V)
= 44

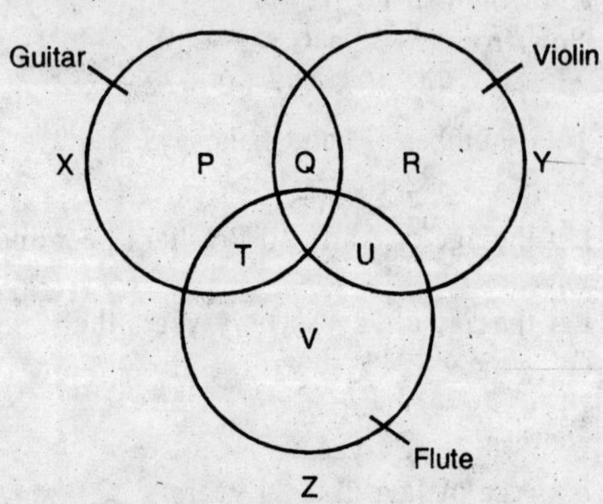


**15.** (*c*) : Let circles x, y and z represent persons who can speak Tamil, Hindi and Gujarati respectively.
Persons who speak Tamil
= A + B + D + E = 6 ... (1)
Persons who speak Hindi
= B + C + E + F = 15 ... (2)
Persons who speak Gujarati
= D + E + F + G = 6 ... (3)
Persons who speak two languages

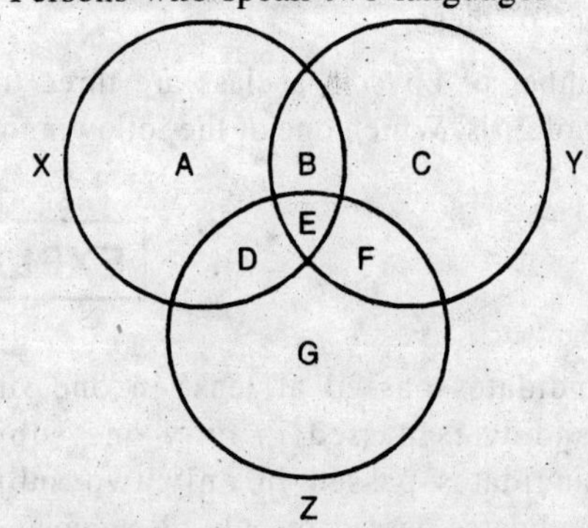


= B + D + F = 2 ... (4)
Persons who speak all the three language
= E = 1 ... (5)
Substituting the value of E in equations (1), (2) and (3) we get
A + B + D = 5 ... (6)
B + C + F = 14 ... (7)
D + F + G = 5 ... (8)
Subtracting (4) from (6), we get
A − F = 3 ... (9)
Adding (7) and (8) we get
B + C + 2F + D + G = 19 ... (10)
Adding (9) and (10) we get
A + B + C + D + F + G = 22 ... (11)
Adding (5) and (11) we get
A + B + C + D + E + F + G = 23 ... (12)
Therefore, total number of person = 23.

**16.** (*a*) :

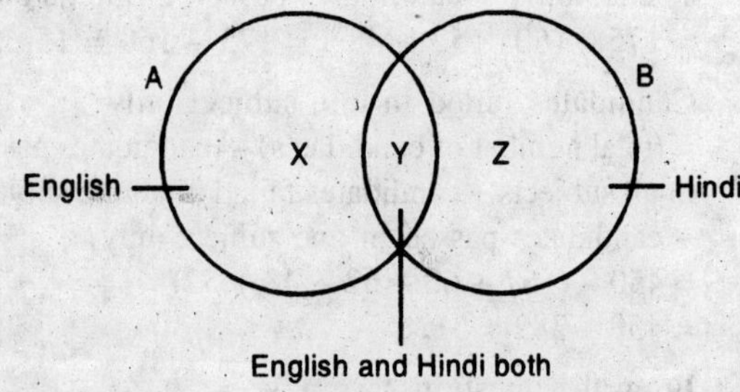


Circle A and B represent the students who speak English and Hindi respectively. Now as per information given in the question total number of students
$= x + y + z = 50$ ... (1)
$y = 10$ ... (2)
$x + y = 21$ ... (3)
From (2) and (3) $x = 11$
Number of students who can speak Hindi is $(y + z)$

From (1) we get

$y + z = 50 - 11 = 39$ ... (4)

Now, number of students who can speak Hindi only is $z$.

From (4), $y + z = 39$, $z = 39 - y = 39 - 10 = 29$

Therefore, number of the students speaking Hindi = 39, number of students speaking Hindi only = 29 and number of students speaking English only = 11.

**17.** (*c*) : 'All but nine died' means 'All except nine died'. It means that nine sheep remained alive and other died.

**18.** (*c*) : Let Chandravati's age 10 years ago be $x$ year mother's age 10 yeags ago was $4x$ year.

After ten year, or after 20 years when Chandravati's age was 10 years.

$(4x + 20) = 2(x + 20)$

$4x + 20 = 2x + 40$

$2x = 20$

or, $x = 10$ years

Present age of Chandravati = 20 years.

**19.** (*b*) : Let the present age of Pushpa be $x$ year. The present age of Rita would be $(x - 2)$ year.

Now as per question, $x = 2(x - 2 - 2)$

or, $x = 2x - 8$

or, $x = 8$

Therefore, present age of Pushpa is 8 years.

**20.** (*b*) : Let the present age of the son be $x$ years then, the age of Sohanlal would be $4x$ years. Four years later their age would be $(x + 4)$ and $(4x + 4)$ years.

Now, as per questions,

$(x + 4) + (4x + 4) = 43$ years

$5x + 8 = 43$ years

$5x = 35$ years

or, $x = 7$ years.

Therefore, the present age of son is 7 years.

**21.** (*b*) : Let the present age of the elder persons be $x$ years.

then, the present age of the younger person $= (x - 10)$ years.

$(x - 15) = 2(x - 10 - 15)$

or, $x = 35$ years.

$\therefore$ The present age of the elder person is 35 years.

**22.** (*d*) : From the diagram it is clear that number of candidates who failed in at least two subjects = number of candidates who failed in two or more subjects.

$= (10 + 12 + 12 + 5) = 39$

Therefore, required percentage

$$\left(\frac{39}{500} \times 100\right)\% = 7.8\%$$

Therefore, option (*d*) is our answer.

**23.** (*a*) : Let the age of the father be $x$, then the age of the son would be $(56 - x)$.

After four years, the age of father would be $(x + 4)$ and that of son would be $(56 - x + 4)$

Now from the information given in the questions. We have

$(x + 4) = 3(56 - x + 4)$

$x + 4 = 168 - 3x + 12$

$4x = 168 + 12 - 4 = 176$

$x = 44$ years

Therefore, the age of father and son is 44 years and 12 years respectively.

**24.** (*c*) : Let the number of girls be $x$, then from the question it is clear that number of boys are $3x$.

Therefore, total number of students

= Number of Boys + Numbers of girls

$= x + 3x = 4x$.

Now, the total number of children in the class must be a multiple of 4.

Out of the four options (c) does not qualify this condition. Hence 42 does not represent the total number of children in the class.

**25.** (*c*) : Let the present age of B be $x$ years

The present age of A would be $(x + 9)$ years.

After ten years the age of A would be $(x + 9 + 10) = (x + 19)$ years. and before ten years the age of B was $(x - 10)$ years.

Now from the information given in the question,

$(x + 19) = 2(x - 10)$

$x + 19 = 2x - 20$

$x = 19 + 20 = 39$ years.

CHAPTER 7

# Problem Solving

Number problems consists of number sequences, problems with algebraic expressions, mathematical calculations and other compatiable problems.

## SOLVED EXAMPLES

**1.** How many such 7s are there in the following number sequence which are immediately followed by 4 but not immediately preceded by 8?

5 4 7 8 9 7 4 3 8 7 5 7 4 8 7 4 1 2 7 4 5 7 9 4

(*a*) Two (*b*) Three (*c*) Four (*d*) Five (*e*) None of these

**Ans. *(b)* :** Number of 7s which are immediately followed by 4 but not immediately preceded by 8 are :

5478974387574874127457 94

1 2 3

**2.** A number is 9 times twice the other number. The sum of two numbers is 133. The two numbers are :

(*a*) 9, 124 (*b*) 11, 122 (*c*) 17, 166 (*d*) 7, 126 (*e*) 27, 136

**Ans. *(d)* :** If the smaller number is $x$, then

$$x + (2x \times 9) = 133$$
$$x + 18x = 133$$
$$19x = 133$$
$$x = 133 \div 19 = 7$$

If one number is 7, the other number is :

$$133 - 7 = 126$$

**3.** If all the numbers from 1 to 28 which are exactly divisible by 3 are arranged in descending order, which would come at the sixth place from the top?

(*a*) 12 (*b*) 21 (*c*) 15 (*d*) 18 (*e*) 24

**Ans. *(a)* :** The numbers divisible by 3 in descending order are : 27, 24, 21, 18, 15, 12, 9, 6, 3 and the number at the sixth place is 12.

## MULTIPLE CHOICE QUESTIONS

**1.** How many 6's are there in the following series of numbers which are preceded by 7 but not immediately followed by 9?

6 7 9 5 6 9 7 6 8 7 6 7 8 6 9 4 6 7 7 6 9 5 7 6 3

(*a*) One (*b*) Two

(*c*) Three (*d*) Four

**2.** In a chess tournament each of six players will play every other player exactly once. How many matches will be played during the tournament?

(*a*) 12 (*b*) 15

(*c*) 30 (*d*) 36

**3.** How many 4's are there in the following series which are preceded by 7, but are not preceded by 8?

3 4 5 7 4 3 7 4 8 5 4 3 7 4 9 8 4 7 2 7 4 1 3 6

(*a*) 1 (*b*) 2
(*c*) 3 (*d*) 4

**4.** How many even numbers are there in the following series of numbers, each of which is immediately preceded by an odd number, but not immediately followed by an even number?

5 3 4 8 9 7 1 6 5 3 2 9 8 4 3 5

(*a*) Nil (*b*) 1
(*c*) 2 (*d*) 3

**5.** If all the numbers from 1 to 51 which are exactly divisible by 3 are arranged in descending order, which of the following numbers will come at the seventh and tenth places from the top?

(*a*) 33 & 27 (*b*) 33 & 21
(*c*) 21 & 30 (*d*) 33 & 24

**6.** Nitin was counting down from 32. Shasank was counting upwards, the numbers starting from 1 and he was calling out only the odd numbers. Which common number will they call out at the same time if they were calling out at the same speed?

(*a*) 21
(*b*) 22
(*c*) 19
(*d*) They will not call out the same number

**7.** In the following list of numerals, how many 3s are followed by 3, but NOT preceded by 3?

2 4 6 3 3 1 5 7 8 3 3 3 4 6 2 3 3 3 3 9 7 2 3

(*a*) 1 (*b*) 2
(*c*) 3 (*d*) 4

**8.** If in a given number 5 8 9 4 3 2 7 6 1 4, we interchange the first and the second digits, the third and the fourth, the fifth and the sixth and so on, then counting from the right end, which digit will be sixth?

(*a*) 3 (*b*) 2
(*c*) 4 (*d*) 5

**9.** Aparna cuts a cake into two halves and cuts one-half into smaller pieces of equal size. Each of the small pieces is twenty grams in weight. If she has seven pieces of the cake in all with her, how heavy was the original cake?

(*a*) 140 grams (*b*) 280 grams
(*c*) 240 grams (*d*) 120 grams

**10.** In the following number sequence how many such even numbers are there which are exactly divisible by its immediate preceding number but not exactly divisible by its immediate following number?

3 8 4 1 5 7 2 8 3 4 8 9 3 9 4 2 1 5 8 2

(*a*) Two (*b*) Three
(*c*) Four (*d*) More than four

**11.** How many 7s are there in the following series which are not immediately followed by 3 but immediately preceded by 8?

8 9 8 7 6 2 2 6 3 2 6 9 7 3 2 8 7 2 7 7 8 7 3 7 7 9 4

(*a*) Nil (*b*) One
(*c*) Two (*d*) Three

**12.** How many 9's are there in the following sequence which are neither preceded by 6 nor immediately followed by 3?

9 3 8 6 9 9 5 9 3 7 8 9 9 9 3 9 6 3 9

(*a*) One (*b*) Two
(*c*) Three (*d*) Four

**13.** If a number is five times as great as another number which is four less than forty, then the number is :

(*a*) 220 (*b*) 180
(*c*) 144 (*d*) 200

**14.** If 2/3rd of a number is 96, what will be the 3/4th of that number?

(*a*) 108 (*b*) 198
(*c*) 128 (*d*) 48

**15.** If such numbers which are divisible by 5, and also those which have 5 as one of the digits are eliminated from the numbers 1 to 60, how many numbers would remain?

(*a*) 53 (*b*) 47
(*c*) 40 (*d*) 45

**16.** How many 8's are there in the following number series which are exactly divisible by its immediately preceding and also exactly divisible by immediately succeeding numbers?

8 2 4 5 1 7 2 8 4 8 4 2 2 8 2 6 9 8 4 5 4 8 3 2 8 4 3 1 8 3

(*a*) 1 (*b*) 2
(*c*) 3 (*d*) 4

**17.** Jagan was to either get one-seventh of a milk chocolate or one-fourteenth of a bigger fruit chocolate. Which chocolate would give him the larger piece if the fruit chocolate is three times as large as the milk chocolate?

(*a*) Milk chocolate
(*b*) Fruit chocolate
(*c*) The pieces will be of the same size
(*d*) Information inadequate

**18.** How many such 3's are there in the following number sequence which are immediately preceded by an odd number and immediately followed by an even number?

5 3 8 9 4 3 7 2 3 8 1 3 8 4 2 3 5 7 3 4 2 3 6

(*a*) One (*b*) Two
(*c*) Three (*d*) Four

**19.** Count each 7 which is not immediately preceded by 5 but is immediately followed by either 2 or 3. How many such 7's are there?

5 7 2 6 5 7 3 8 3 7 3 2 5 7 2 7 3 4 8 2 6 7 8

(*a*) 2 (*b*) 3
(*c*) 4 (*d*) 5

**20.** A number is four less than two times the other number. If their difference is 21, what is the greater number?

(*a*) 50 (*b*) 46
(*c*) 31 (*d*) 21

## EXPLANATORY ANSWERS

**1. (*c*) :** 679569768767869467769576 3
1 2 3

**2. (*b*) :** When all the players have to play with each other then the method of calculating the number of matches to be played is $\frac{n(n-1)}{2}$ where '*n*' is the number of players playing the match. So, the number of matches played will be :
$(6 \times 5) \div 2 = 30 \div 2 = 15$

**3. (*d*) :** 3 4 5 7 4 3 7 4 8 5 4 3 7 4 9 8 4 7 2 7 4 1 3 6
1 2 3 4

**4. (*c*) :** 5 3 4 8 9 7 1 6 5 3 2 9 8 4 3 5
1 2

**5. (*d*) :** The numbers divisible by 3 in descending order are:
51, 48, 45, 42, 39, 36, 33, 30, 27, 24, 21,
7th 10th
18, 15, 12, 9, 6, 3.

**6. (*d*) :** When Nitin is on count 22, Shasank is on 21 and when Nitin is on count 21, Shasank is on 23.

**7. (*c*) :** 2 4 6 3 3 1 5 7 8 3 3 3 4 6 2 3 3 3 3 9 7 2 3
1 2 3

**8. (*b*) :** The new number after interchanging the digits is :
8 5 4 9 2 3 6 7 4 1
6th

**9. (*c*) :** There is one bigger piece and six smaller pieces. One small piece weighs 20 gm. Total weight of six smaller speices is 120 gm.
∴ Weight of the bigger piece = 120 gm
∴ Weight of the original cake = 240 gm

**10. (*a*) :** 3 8 4 1 5 7 2 8 3 4 8 9 3 9 4 2 1 5 8 2
1 2

**11. (*c*) :** 898762263269732872778737794
1 2

**12. (*d*) :** 9 3 8 6 9 9 5 9 3 7 8 9 9 9 3 9 6 3 9
1 2 3 4

**13. (*b*) :** Number four less than forty is $40 - 4 = 36$
Five times the number is $= 36 \times 5 = 180$

**14. (*a*) :** If the number is *x*, then

$$\frac{2}{3}x = 96$$

$$x = \frac{96 \times 3}{2} = 144$$

$\frac{3}{4}$ th of the number is $144 \times \frac{3}{4} = 108$

**15. (*c*) :** The eliminated twenty numbers are : 5, 10, 15, 20, 25, 30, 35, 40, 45 and 50 to 60. The remaining numbers are $60 - 20 = 40$.

**16. (*d*) :** 8 2 4 5 1 7 2 8 4 8 4 2 2 8 2 6 9 8 4 5 4 8
1 2 3
3 2 8 4 3 1 8 3
4

**17. (*b*) :** If fruit chocolate (F) is equal to three times as milk chocolate (M) then —

$$F = 3M$$

or $$\frac{F}{M} = 3$$

$$\therefore \frac{1/14\ F}{1/7\ M} = \frac{3/14}{1/7}$$

When 3/14 > 1/7, then F (Fruit chocolate) will give him the larger piece.

**18. (*c*) :** 5 3 8 9 4 3 7 2 3 8 1 3 8 4 2 3 5 7 3 4 2 3 6
1 2 3

**19. (*a*) :** 5 7 2 6 5 7 3 8 3 7 3 2 5 7 2 7 3 4 8 2 6 7 8
1 2

**20. (*b*) :** If smaller number is *x*, then

$$(2x - 4) - x = 21$$
$$2x - x = 21 + 4$$
$$x = 25$$

The greater number is

$$(25 \times 2) - 4 = 46$$

CHAPTER 8

# Numerical Operations/ Symbol Substitution

Questions in this category are easy to attempt. Candidates must be quick in substituting symbols and calculations. The common pattern of questions asked are given below.

## SOLVED EXAMPLES

**1.** If '+' stands for '×'; '×' stands for '÷'; '÷' stands for '–' and '–' stands for '+' then
$2 - 8 \times 2 + 6 \div 7 = ?$
(*a*) 32 (*b*) 19 (*c*) 23 (*d*) 9

**Ans. (*b*) :** After substituting the symbols in the given expression the new expression will be :
$2 + 8 \div 2 \times 6 - 7$

The solving steps will be :
$2 + 4 \times 6 - 7$
$2 + 24 - 7$
$26 - 7 = 19$

**2.** If ▲ stands for '+'
■ stands for '–'
● stands for '÷'
✱ stands for '×' then
13 ▲ 5 ✱ 20 ● 10 ■ 9 = ?
(*a*) 26 (*b*) 37 (*c*) 14 (*d*) 55

**Ans. (*c*) :** After substituting the symbols the new expression will be :
$13 + 5 \times 20 \div 10 - 9$

The solving steps will be :
$13 + 5 \times 2 - 9$
$13 + 10 - 9$
$23 - 9 = 14$

## MULTIPLE CHOICE QUESTIONS

**Directions :** *Each of the following questions is followed by four alternatives. Select the most appropriate answer.*

**1.** If "+" means "–"; "–" means "×"; "×"means "÷" and "÷" means "+", then
$15 \times 5 \div 10 + 5 - 3 = ?$
(*a*) 9.5 (*b*) 0
(*c*) – 2 (*d*) 24

**2.** If "+" means "–"; "–" means "×"; "×"means "÷" and "÷" means "+", then
$15 \times 3 \div 15 + 5 - 2 = ?$
(*a*) 0 (*b*) 10
(*c*) 20 (*d*) 6

**3.** If "+" means "÷"; "×" means "–"; "÷"means "+" and "–" means "×", then
$16 \div 8 \times 6 - 2 + 12 = ?$
(*a*) 22 (*b*) 24
(*c*) 23 (*d*) 20

**4.** If "+" means "×"; "–" means "÷"; "÷"means "+" and "×" means "–", then what will be the value of $20 \div 40 - 4 \times 5 + 6 = ?$

(*a*) 60 (*b*) 1.67
(*c*) 150 (*d*) 0

**5.** If "+" means "×"; "–" means "÷"; "×"means "–" and "÷" means "+", then
$5 + 8 - 4 \times 2 \div 9 = ?$

(*a*) 15 (*b*) 13
(*c*) 17 (*d*) 11

**6.** If × stand for addition, ÷ stands for subtraction, + stands for multiplication and – stands for division, then $(20 \times 6 \div 6 \times 4)$ is equal to

(*a*) 5 (*b*) 24
(*c*) 25 (*d*) 80

**7.** If "+" means "×"; "÷" means "–"; "×"means "÷" and "–" means "+", what will be the value of the following expression?
$4 + 11 \div 5 - 50 = ?$

(*a*) 79 (*b*) –11
(*c*) 91 (*d*) 89

**8.** If "+" means "÷"; "÷" means "–"; "–"means "×" and "×" means "+", then
$10 \div 2 - 15 + 3 \times 5 = ?$

(*a*) 10 (*b*) 15
(*c*) 25 (*d*) 5

**9.** If A stands for add, B for subtract, C for multiply and D for divide, then for what does 4A 3B 3A 2 stand?

(*a*) 2 (*b*) 4
(*c*) 6 (*d*) 8

**10.** If × stands for add, *y* stands for subract, *z* stands for divide and *p* stands for multiply, then what is the the value of (7 p 3) y 6 × 5?

(*a*) 5 (*b*) 10
(*c*) 15 (*d*) 20

**11.** If "+" means "÷"; "÷" means "–"; "–"means "×" and "×" means "+", what will be the value of $8 + 2 \div 3 - 4 \times 6 = ?$

(*a*) –2 (*b*) $-15\frac{1}{3}$
(*c*) 12 (*d*) 15

**12.** If "+" means "÷"; "×" means "–"; "÷"means "×" and "–" means "+", what will be the value of the following expression?
$9 + 3 \div 4 - 8 \times 2 = ?$

(*a*) $6\frac{3}{4}$ (*b*) $-1\frac{3}{4}$
(*c*) $-6\frac{1}{4}$ (*d*) 18

**13.** If "–" means "÷"; "+" means "×"; "÷"means "–" and "×" means "+", then which of the following must be true?

(*a*) $1 \div 2 + 3 \times 6 - 8 = 12$
(*b*) $2 + 3 - 5 \times 8 \div 4 = 7$
(*c*) $5 + 6 \times 8 - 2 \div 3 = 31$
(*d*) $6 \div 1 + 2 - 8 \times 4 = 31$

**14.** If "÷" means "+"; "+" means "×"; "–"means "÷" and "×" means "–", then
$5 + 8 - 4 \times 2 \div 9 = ?$

(*a*) 13 (*b*) 15
(*c*) 11 (*d*) 17

## EXPLANATORY ANSWERS

**1. (*c*) :** $15 \div 5 + 10 - 5 \times 3$
$3 + 10 - 15 = -2$

**2. (*b*) :** $15 \div 3 + 15 - 5 \times 2$
$5 + 15 - 10 = 10$

**3. (*c*) :** $16 + 8 - 6 \times 2 \div 12$
$16 + 8 - 1 = 23$

**4. (*d*) :** $20 + 40 \div 4 - 5 \times 6$
$20 + 10 - 30 = 0$

**5. (*c*) :** $5 \times 8 \div 4 - 2 + 9$
$10 - 2 + 9 = 17$

**6. (*b*) :** $20 + 6 - 6 + 4 = 24$

**7. (*d*) :** $4 \times 11 - 5 + 50$
$44 - 5 + 50 = 89$

**8. (*d*) :** $10 - 2 \times 15 \div 3 + 5$
$10 - 10 + 5 = 5$

**9. (*c*) :** $4 + 3 - 3 + 2 = 6$

**10. (*d*) :** $(7 \times 3) - 6 + 5$
$21 - 6 + 5 = 20$

**11. (*a*) :** $8 \div 2 - 3 \times 4 + 6$
$4 - 12 + 6 = -2$

**12. (*d*) :** $9 \div 3 \times 4 + 8 - 2$
$12 + 8 - 2 = 18$

**13. (*c*) :** (*a*) $1 - 2 \times 3 + 6 \div 8 = 12 \Rightarrow \frac{-17}{4} = 12$

(*b*) $2 \times 3 \div 5 + 8 - 4 = 7 \Rightarrow \frac{26}{5} = 7$

(*c*) $5 \times 6 + 8 \div 2 - 3 = 31 \Rightarrow 31 = 31$

(*d*) $6 - 1 \times 2 \div 8 + 4 = 31 \Rightarrow \frac{-39}{4} = 31$

**14. (*d*) :** $5 \times 8 \div 4 - 2 + 9$
$10 - 2 + 9 = 17$

CHAPTER 9

# Word Building

These are spellings, word order and dictionary related questions. The candidate is given a word and asked to select the word that can/cannot be formed from its spellings. He/she may be asked to decide the meaningful order of the given words. He/she may also be asked to arrange the given words in the sequence in which they occur in the dictionary.

## MULTIPLE CHOICE QUESTIONS

**Directions (Qs. No. 1 to 12):** *From the given alternatives select the word which* ***cannot*** *be formed using the letters of the given word.*

**1.** REPUBLICAN
(*a*) CLIP (*b*) PURE
(*c*) ANKLE (*d*) BANE

**2.** ESTRANGE
(*a*) GENERATE (*b*) SERGEANT
(*c*) REAGENTS (*d*) GREAT

**3.** DETERMINATION
(*a*) DETENTION (*b*) DESTINATION
(*c*) TERMINATE (*d*) DOMINATE

**4.** CHRISTMAS
(*a*) CHRIST (*b*) SMART
(*c*) CRUST (*d*) HARM

**5.** LEGALIZATION
(*a*) ALERT (*b*) ALEGATION
(*c*) GALLANT (*d*) NATAL

**6.** CHARACTER
(*a*) CRATE (*b*) CHARTER
(*c*) HEARTY (*d*) TRACER

**7.** ADMINISTRATION
(*a*) Station (*b*) Minister
(*c*) Ration (*d*) Mind

**8.** ORGANISATION
(*a*) ORGAN (*b*) ORGANISE
(*c*) NATION (*d*) ORATION

**9.** PERAMBULATOR
(*a*) RAMPANT
(*b*) LABOUR
(*c*) MARBLE
(*d*) RAMBLE

**10.** POSSESSION
(*a*) SESSION
(*b*) POSE
(*c*) POISE
(*d*) OBSESS

**11.** PRINTINGS
(*a*) SAINT (*b*) PRINT
(*c*) STING (*d*) RINGS

**12.** QUALIFICATION
(*a*) LIAR (*b*) FIAT
(*c*) LION (*d*) FICTION

**13.** From the given alternatives select the word which can be formed using the letters given in the word.
ULTRANATIONALISM
(*a*) ULTRAMONTANE
(*b*) ULTRAMODERN
(*c*) ULTRAIST
(*d*) ULULATE

**14.** A meaningful word starting with R is made from the first, second, fourth, fifth and eighth letters of the word CREATIVE. Which of the following is the middle letter of the word?
(*a*) E (*b*) T
(*c*) C (*d*) A

**Directions (Qs. No. 15 to 18):** *Which one of the given responses would be a meaningful order of the following words?*

**15.** 1. Amoeba 2. Oyster
3. Worm 4. Cow
(*a*) 1, 3, 2, 4 (*b*) 1, 2, 3, 4
(*c*) 4, 3, 2, 1 (*d*) 3, 2, 4, 1

**16.** 1. Birth 2. Death
3. Childhood 4. Infancy
5. Adolescence 6. Adulthood
7. Old age
(*a*) 2, 6, 7, 5, 4, 3, 1 (*b*) 1, 4, 3, 5, 6, 7, 2
(*c*) 1, 4, 3, 6, 5, 7, 2 (*d*) 2, 7, 6, 4, 5, 3, 1

**17.** 1. Police 2. Punishment
3. Crime 4. Judge
4. Judgement
(*a*) 3, 1, 2, 4, 5
(*b*) 1, 2, 4, 3, 5
(*c*) 5, 4, 3, 2, 1
(*d*) 3, 1, 4, 5, 2

**18.** 1. Orange 2. Indigo
3. Red 4. Blue
5. Green 6. Yellow
7. Violet
(*a*) 7, 2, 4, 5, 6, 1, 3 (*b*) 7, 2, 4, 6, 5, 1, 3
(*c*) 7, 2, 6, 4, 5, 1, 3 (*d*) 7, 2, 6, 4, 1, 5, 3

**Directions (Qs. Nos. 19 and 24):** *Arrange the given words in the sequence in which they occur in the dictionary.*

**19.** 1. Clone 2. Climate
3. Clutter 4. Create
5. Clapped
(*a*) 52143 (*b*) 51234
(*c*) 52134 (*d*) 53124

**20.** 1. Lasted 2. Loop
3. Lake 4. Litter
5. Listed
(*a*) 31542 B. 31254
(*c*) 31245 (*d*) 31452

**21.** 1. Intricate 2. Interview
3. Intransigent 4. Interrogation
5. Intravenous
(*a*) 2, 4, 5, 3, 1 (*b*) 5, 3, 1, 2, 4
(*c*) 4, 2, 3, 5, 1 (*d*) 3, 5, 2, 1, 4

**22.** 1. Forge 2. Forget
3. Forgo 4. Forgive
5. Format
(*a*) 1, 2, 4, 3, 5
(*b*) 5, 2, 4, 3, 1
(*c*) 1, 4, 3, 2, 5
(*d*) 3, 4, 5, 2, 1

**23.** 1. Forecast 2. Forget
3. Foreign 4. Forsook
5. Force
(*a*) 3, 5, 1, 2, 4 (*b*) 5, 1, 3, 2, 4
(*c*) 5, 1, 3, 4, 2 (*d*) 5, 1, 2, 3, 4

**24.** 1. Fenestration 2. Feather
3. Feed head 4. Feature
5. Feminine
(*a*) 2, 4, 3, 5, 1 (*b*) 4, 2, 3, 1, 5
(*c*) 2, 4, 1, 5, 3 (*d*) 4, 2, 3, 5, 1

**25.** Arrange the given words in the sequence in which they occur in the Dictionary and locate the last word.
(*a*) Frankenstein (*b*) Frankincense
(*c*) Frankalmoign (*d*) Frauendienst

**26.** Grouping of words are given. Choose the next word in the series from the given options.
AFGHAN, INDEFINITELY, SYNOPSIS, STUPENDOUS, BURST
(*a*) GLACIAL (*b*) COMPANION
(*c*) RESCRIPT (*d*) HIJACKER

## ANSWERS

| 1 | 2 | 3 | 4 | 5 | 6 | 7 | 8 | 9 | 10 |
|---|---|---|---|---|---|---|---|---|---|
| (*c*) | (*a*) | (*b*) | (*c*) | (*a*) | (*c*) | (*b*) | (*b*) | (*a*) | (*d*) |
| **11** | **12** | **13** | **14** | **15** | **16** | **17** | **18** | **19** | **20** |
| (*a*) | (*a*) | (*c*) | (*d*) | (*a*) | (*b*) | (*d*) | (*a*) | (*c*) | (*d*) |
| **21** | **22** | **23** | **24** | **25** | **26** | | | | |
| (*c*) | (*a*) | (*b*) | (*a*) | (*d*) | (*d*) | | | | |

CHAPTER 10

# Relationship Concept

While attempting questions on blood relations, one should be clear of all the relation patterns that can exist between any two individuals. These type of questions are given mainly to test one's relationship ability.

Very well known relations are :

| | |
|---|---|
| Mother | Grandmother |
| Father | Grandfather |
| Son | Grandson |
| Daughter | Granddaughter |
| Brother | Brother-in-law |
| Sister | Sister-in-law |
| Niece | Father-in-law |
| Nephew | Mother-in-law |
| Uncle | Son-in-law |
| Aunt | Daughter-in-law |
| Husband | Cousin |
| Wife | |

The patterns of some relationships which help in solving questions in these tests are :

| | | |
|---|---|---|
| Father's *or* Mother's Father | — | Grandfather (Paternal *or* Maternal) |
| Father's *or* Mother's Mother | — | Grandmother (Paternal *or* Maternal |
| Father's *or* Mother's Son | — | Brother |
| Father's *or* Mother's Daughter | — | Sister |
| Father's Brother | — | Paternal Uncle |
| Father's Sister | — | Paternal Aunt |
| Mother's Brother | — | Maternal Uncle |
| Mother's Sister | — | Maternal Aunt |
| Uncle *or* Aunt's Son *or* Daughter | — | Cousin |
| Son's Wife | — | Daughter-in-law |
| Daughter's Husband | — | Son-in-law |
| Husband's *or* Wife's Brother | — | Brother-in-law |
| Husband's *or* Wife's Sister | — | Sister-in-law |
| Brother's Wife | — | Sister-in-law |
| Sister's Husband | — | Brother-in-law |
| Brother's Son | — | Nephew |
| Brother's Daughter | — | Niece |

## MULTIPLE CHOICE QUESTIONS

**Directions :** *In each of the following questions keenly study the relationship mentioned between the persons, and then from the given options select the right relationship as the answer.*

**1.** 'A' is the father of 'B' and 'C'. 'B' is the son of 'A' but 'C' is not the son of 'A'. What is 'C's' relation with 'A'?
(*a*) Daughter (*b*) Son
(*c*) Niece (*d*) Nephew

**2.** A lady said, "The person standing there is my grandfather's only son's daughter". How is the lady related to the standing person?
(*a*) Sister (*b*) Mother
(*c*) Aunt (*d*) Cousin

**3.** Ravi is the brother of Amit's son's son. What is Amit's relation to Ravi?
(*a*) Cousin (*b*) Father
(*c*) Grandfather (*d*) Son

**4.** Mayank said, "My mother is the sister of Rajat's brother." What is Rajat's relation with Mayank?
(*a*) Cousin (*b*) Maternal uncle
(*c*) Uncle (*d*) Brother-in-law

**5.** Introducing Lily, Raghav said, "Her father is my mother's only son". How is Lily related to Raghav?
(*a*) Aunt (*b*) Daughter
(*c*) Mother (*d*) Sister

**6.** Ajay is the brother of Vijay. Mili is the Sister of Ajay. Sanjay is the brother of Rahul and Mehul is the daughter of Vijay. Who is Sanjay's Uncle?
(*a*) Rahul (*b*) Ajay
(*c*) Mehul (*d*) Data inadequate

**7.** Adity is Bhavi's brother, Bharat is Jayant's father. Ella is Bhavi's mother. Aditya and Jayant are brothers. What is Ella's relationship with Bharat?
(*a*) Sister (*b*) Mother
(*c*) Daughter (*d*) Wife

**8.** A man introduced the boy coming with him as "He is son of the father of my wife's daughter". What relation did the boy bear to the man?
(*a*) Son-in-law (*b*) Son
(*c*) Brother (*d*) Father

**9.** A and B are two brothers. C is sister of B. D is sister of E. E is son of A. Who is D's uncle?
(*a*) D (*b*) E
(*c*) B (*d*) C

**10.** Varun said pointing towards Arun, "He is my sister's only brother's son". How is Arun related to Varun?
(*a*) Son (*b*) Brother
(*c*) Nephew (*d*) Data insufficient

**11.** Pointing to a man, a lady said, "His brother's father is my grandfather's only son." How is the lady related to the man?
(*a*) Mother (*b*) Sister
(*c*) Daughter (*d*) Aunt

**12.** Vidya is the wife of Gopi and Gopi is the brother of Akhil. Akhil is the uncle of Vijay. What is Vijay's relation with Vidya?
(*a*) Son (*b*) Nephew
(*c*) Brother-in-law (*d*) Brother

**13.** If Amit's father is Billoo's father's only son and Billoo has neither a brother nor a daughter, what is the relationship between Amit and Billoo?
(*a*) Uncle - Nephew
(*b*) Father- Daughter
(*c*) Father - Son
(*d*) Cousins

**14.** A is the sister of B. B is the son of C, and E is the daughter of D, and sister of A. What is D to C?
(*a*) Brother (*b*) Husband
(*c*) Wife (*d*) Data is inadequate

**15.** A Man said to a lady, "Fagu's mother is the only daughter of your father". How is the lady related to Fagu?
(*a*) Daughter (*b*) Sister
(*c*) Wife (*d*) Mother

**16.** Pointing to a man, a woman said, "He is the only son of my mother's mother". How is the woman related to the man?
(*a*) Aunt (*b*) Daughter
(*c*) Niece (*d*) Sister

**17.** If B's mother was A's mother's daughter, how was A related to B?
(*a*) Uncle (*b*) Aunt
(*c*) Sister (*d*) Data is insufficient

**18.** Pointing to a woman in the photograph a man said, "She is the daughter of my grandmother's only son. How is the woman related to the man?
(*a*) Mother (*b*) Daughter
(*c*) Sister-in-law (*d*) Sister

**19.** A man and a woman are sitting in a room. Man's mother-in-law and woman's mother-in-law are mother and daughter respectively. Man is the ................ of the woman.
(*a*) Father (*b*) Father-in-law
(*c*) Uncle (*d*) Grandfather-in-law

**20.** Pointing to Suman, Amit said, "He is my sister's only brother's son". How is Suman related to Amit?
(*a*) Grandson
(*b*) Son
(*c*) Nephew
(*d*) Cannot be determined

## EXPLANATORY ANSWERS

**1. (*a*) :**

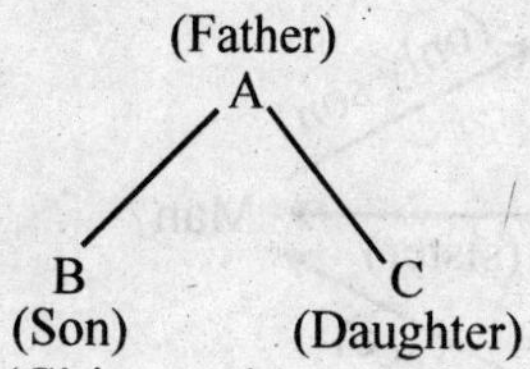


'C' is not the son of 'A', but 'A' is the father of 'C'. So, 'C' is the daughter of 'A'.

**2. (*a*) :**

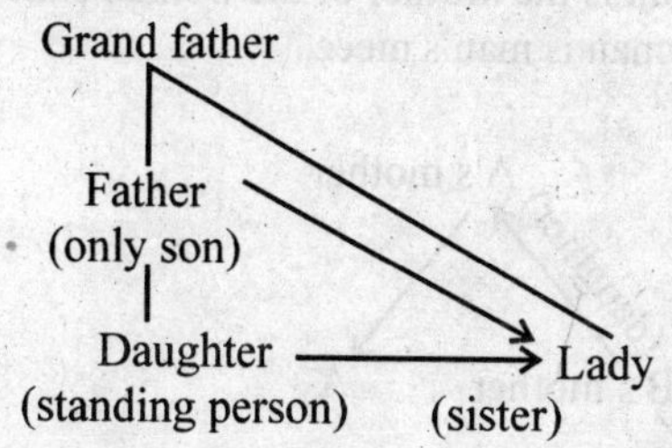


Lady's grandfather's son is lady's father and father's daughter will only be lady's sister.

**3. (*c*) :**

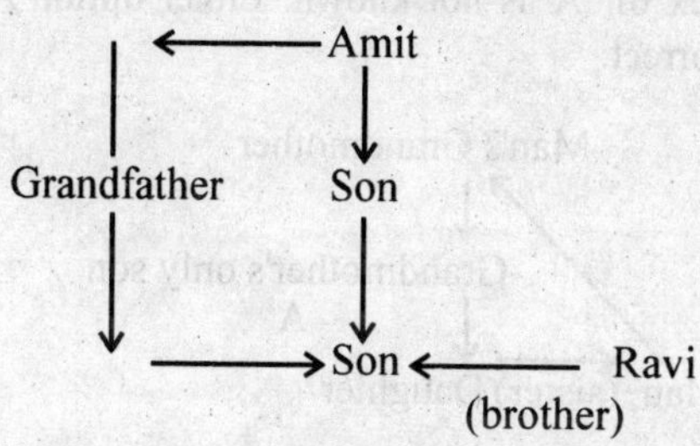


Amit's son's son is Amit's grandson. Ravi is the brother of Amit's son's son. So, Amit is also the grandfather of Ravi.

**4. (*b*) :**

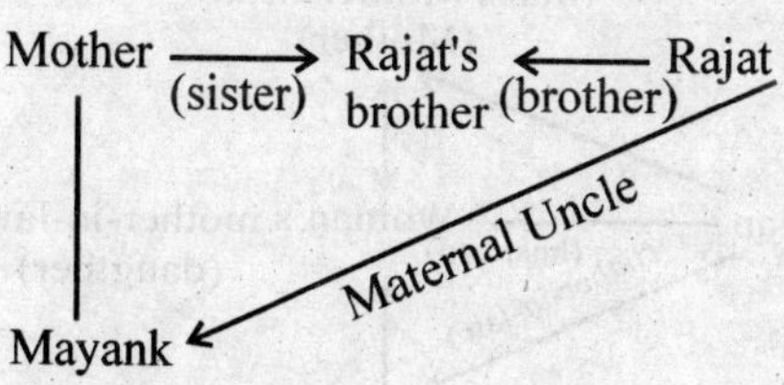


Mayank's mother is the sister of Rajat's brother. So Rajat is also the brother of Mayank's mother. Relation of the brother with his sister's child is maternal. So Rajat is Mayank's maternal uncle.

**5. (*b*) :** The relation is :

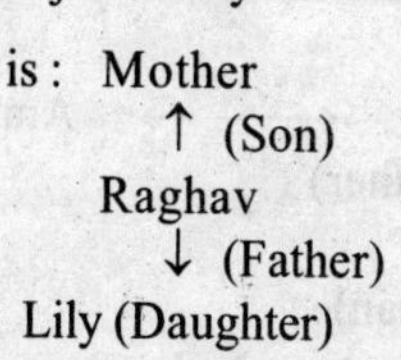


'My mother's only son' means Raghav himself. 'Her father' means Lily's father; *i.e.* Raghav and so, Lily is Raghav's daughter.

**6. (*d*) :**

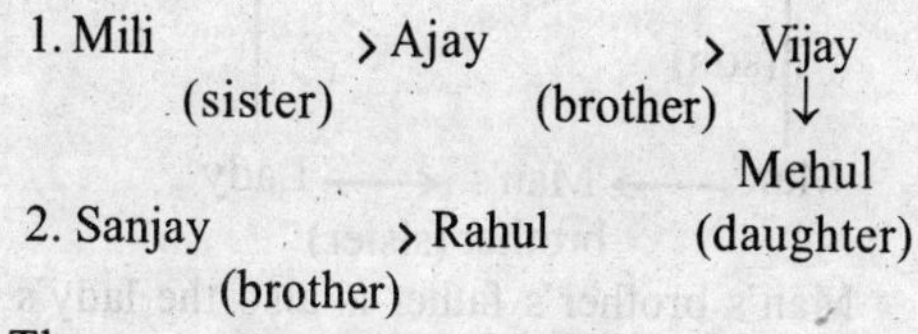


There are two sets of relationship. Information given is incomplete and no relation can be established between the two sets.

**7. (*d*) :** The relationship chart based on problem is :

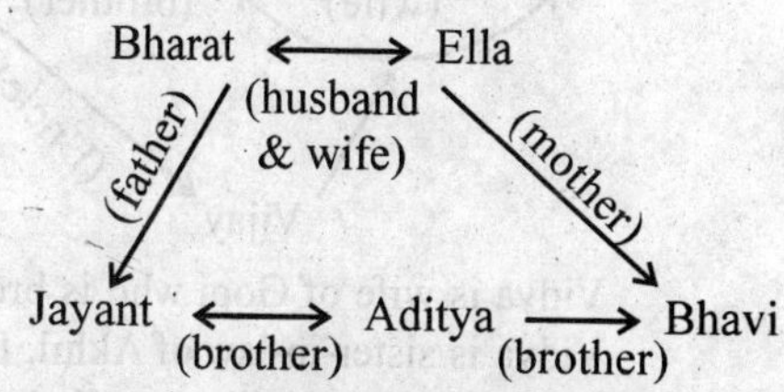


Jayant and Aditya are brothers. If Aditya is Bhavi's brother, then Jayant is also Bhavi's brother. If Bharat is Jayant's father, then he is also the father of Aditya and Bhavi. If Ella is Bhavi's mother, then she is also the mother of Aditya and Jayant. This means Bharat and Ella are husband and wife and the parents of three.

**8. (*b*) :** The relationship chart based on problem is :

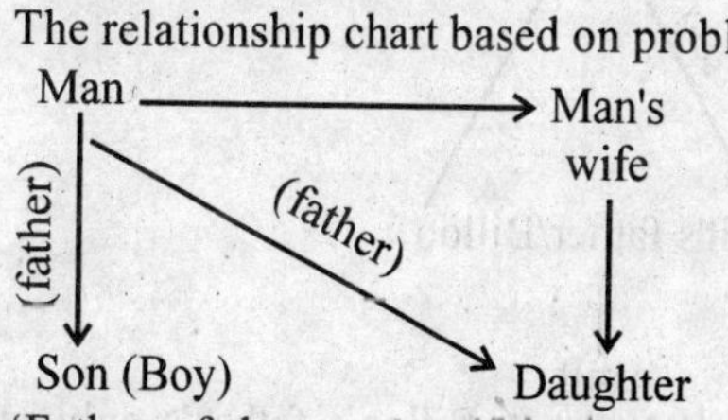


'Father of the man's wife's daughter' is the man himself and the boy in question is the man's son.

**9. (*c*) :** The relationship chart based on the problem is :

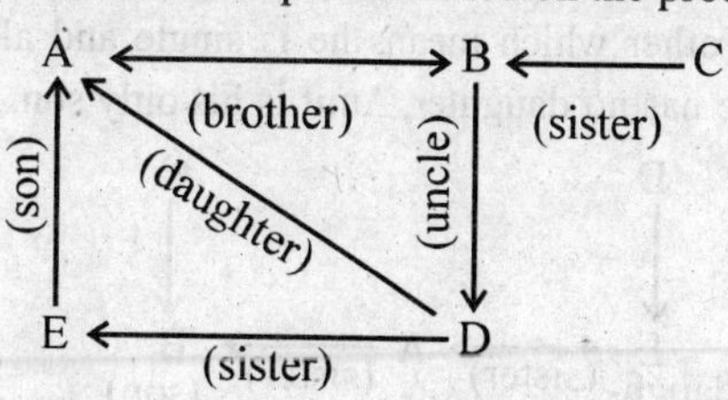


When D is sister of E, who is son of A then D is daughter of A. Brother of A is B and so, B is D's uncle.

**10. (*a*) :**

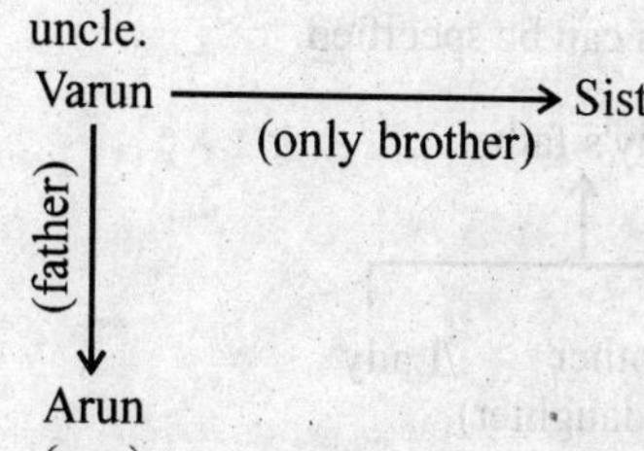


Varun's sister's only brother is Varun himself and Arun is his son.

**11. (*b*) :**

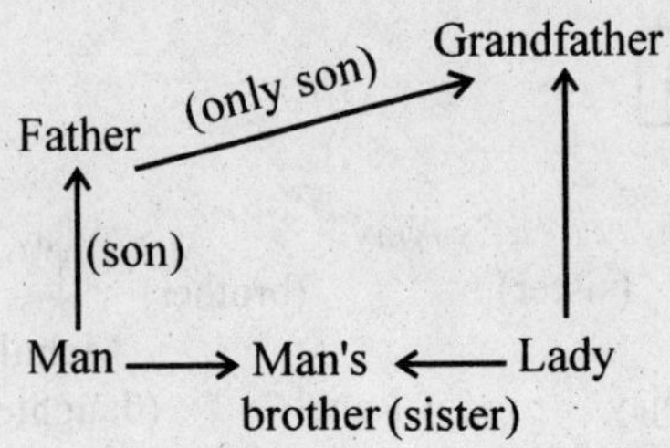


Man's brother's father is also the lady's father as he is the only son of lady's grandfather. So, the lady is man's sister.

**12. (*b*) :** The relationship chart based on problem is :

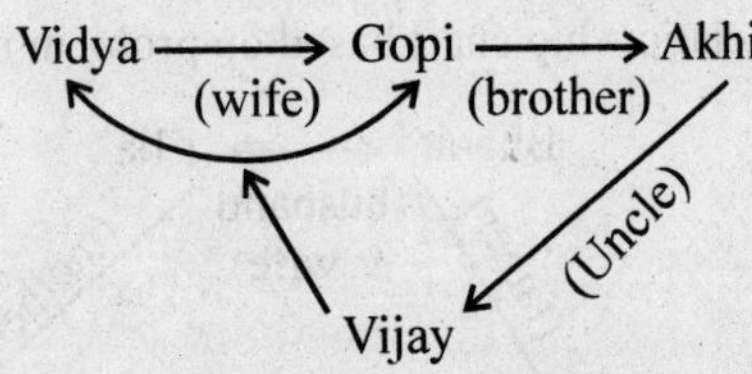


Vidya is wife of Gopi who is brother of Akhil. So, Vidya is sister-in-law of Akhil. If Akhil is uncle of Vijay then Gopi will naturally be the uncle of Vijay as it is not specified that any of the mentioned persons are Vijay's parents. Now, when Vijay is Gopi's nephew then he will also be Vidya's nephew.

**13. (*c*) :** The relationship chart based on problem is :

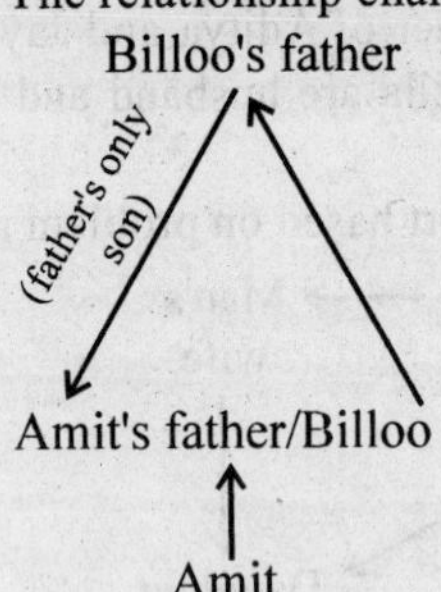


Amit's father is Billoo's father's only son means Billoo is the only son in question also, he is the father of Amit. It must be noted that Billoo has no brother which means he is single and also, when he has no daughter, Amit is his only son.

**14. (*d*) :**

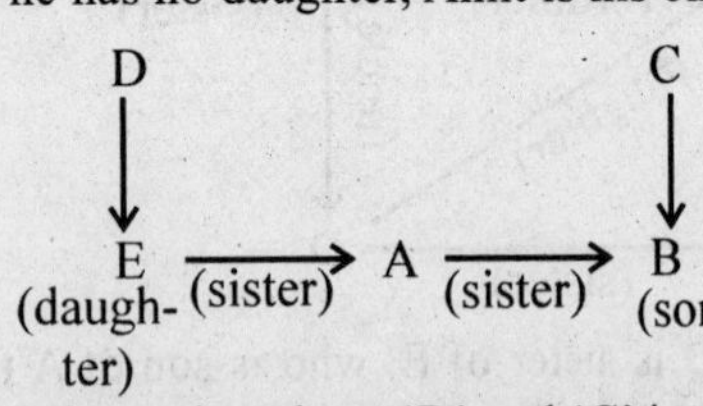


Information about 'D' and 'C' is not given as such no relation can be specified.

**15. (*d*) :**

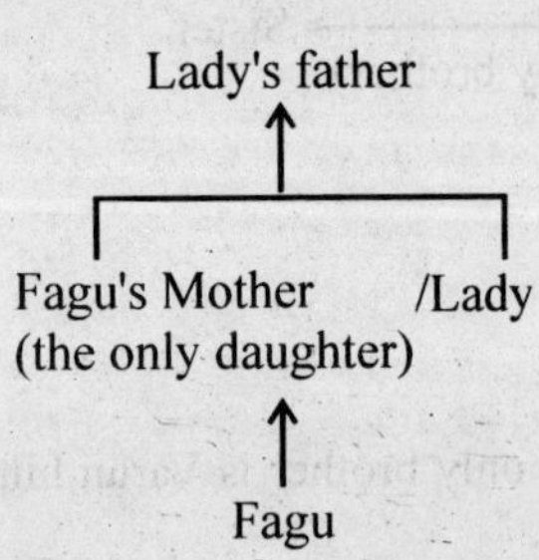


The only daughter of Lady's father is Fagu's mother.

**16. (*c*) :**

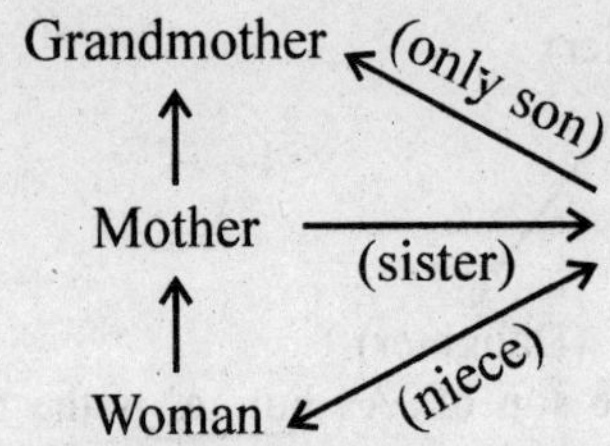


The man is the brother of the woman's mother. So, the woman is man's niece.

**17. (*d*) :**

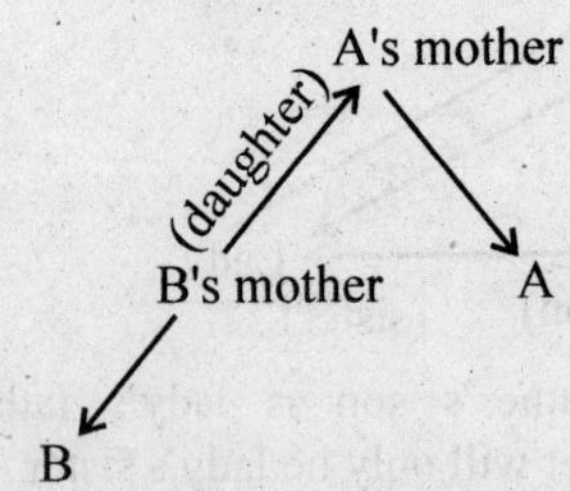


Sex of 'A' is not known. Either option A or B is correct.

**18. (*d*) :**

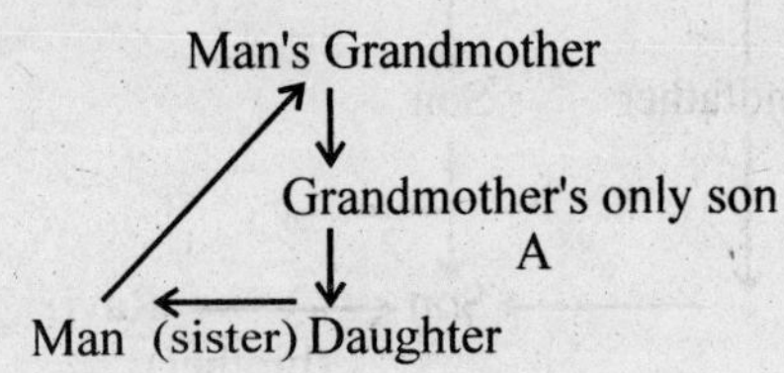


'My grandmother's only son' is the father of the man, and 'daughter of my grand-mother's only son' is the sister of the man.

**19. (*b*) :**

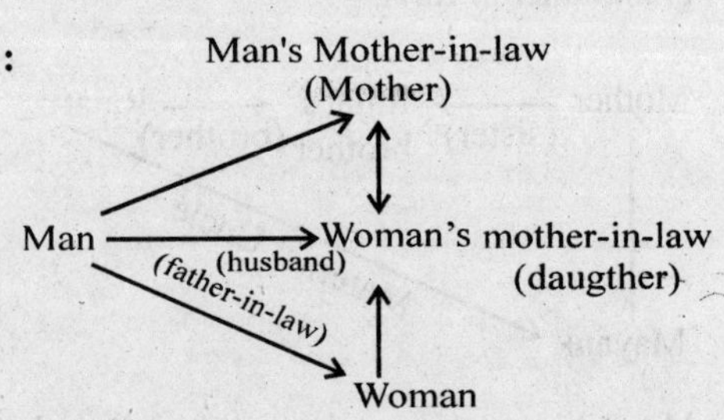


Woman's mother-in-law is the daughter of Man's mother-in-law. So, the man is the husband of woman's mother-in-law and the father-in-law of the woman.

**20. (*b*) :**

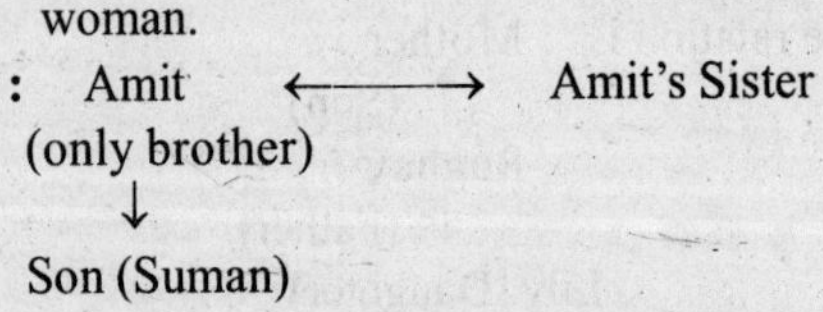


'My sister's only brother's is Amit himself and 'Sister's only brother's son' is the son of Amit *i.e.*, Suman is the son of Amit.

CHAPTER 11

# Analysis

In these type of questions, a few statements are given. Certain facts are broken up and mentioned in these statements. What is required is to analyse the statements, arrange and sort out the given facts and then answer the questions related to the given statements.

## SOLVED EXAMPLES

**1.** Icecream is as cold as snow. Ice is not as cold as hail. Flakes are not as cold as ice but colder than icecream. What is the coldest?

(*a*) Hail (*b*) Icecream (*c*) Flakes (*d*) Ice (*e*) Snow

**Ans. (*a*)** : The order showing an increase in coldness, is Icecream/Snow, Flakes, Ice, Hail.

**2.** *Read the following statements and answer the questions a and b.*

Five men Heavy, Fat, Thin, Short and Tall are running one behind the other. Of the Heavy and the Tall man one is an Artist and the other is Talkative. Thin man who is a Genius is in the centre. Short man is not Dark and the one who is Fair is ahead of Thin man. The Heavy man, who is not an Artist, is in front of the Fat man.

**a.** Who is Fair?

(*a*) Tall man (*b*) Fat man (*c*) Short man (*d*) Heavy man (*e*) Thin man

**Ans. (*b*)**

**b.** What is the Tall Man?

(*a*) Genius (*b*) Talkative (*c*) Artist (*d*) Dark (*e*) Fair

**Ans. (*c*)**

The chart of the characteristics of five men is :

Heavy man is Talkative.
Fat man is Fair.
Thin man is Genious.
Short man is not Dark.
Tall man is the artist.

## MULTIPLE CHOICE QUESTIONS

**1.** Among five friends, A is heavier than B; C is lighter than D; B is lighter than D but heavier than E. Who among them is the heaviest?

(*a*) B (*b*) C
(*c*) A (*d*) Can't say

**2.** Pune is bigger than Jhansi, Sitapur is bigger than Chittor. Raigarh is not as big as Jhansi, but is bigger than Sitapur. Chittor is not as big as Sitapur. Which is the smallest?

(*a*) Jhansi (*b*) Pune
(*c*) Chittor (*d*) Sitapur

**3.** Ajay works more than Ram. Alok works as much as Raju. Pankaj works less than Alok. Ram works more than Alok. Who works the most of all?

(*a*) Ajay (*b*) Ram
(*c*) Alok (*d*) Raju

**4.** Vipul is taller than Hans. Hans is taller than Anand. Alok is taller than Ashok. Ashok is taller than Hans. Who among them is the tallest?
(*a*) Vipul (*b*) Alok
(*c*) Ashok (*d*) Cannot be determined

**5.** Pramod is taller than Gopal. Gopal is shorter than Madhu. To find out who among them is the tallest, which of the following further informations is necessary?
(*a*) Madhu is taller than Gopal.
(*b*) Madhu is shorter than Pramod's brother
(*c*) Pramod is taller than Madhu.
(*d*) Pramod is taller than Madhu's brother.

**6.** Among five friends P, Q, R, S and T, who is the youngest? To arrive at the answer which of the following information given in the statements (A) and (B) is sufficient?
(A) R is younger than P and T.
(B) S is younger than Q.
(*a*) Only A alone is sufficient
(*b*) Either A or B is sufficient
(*c*) Both A and B together are needed
(*d*) Both A and B together are not sufficient

**7.** Sushma is richer than Rashmi whereas Anand is richer than Priya. Arun is as rich as Rashmi. Shoba is richer than Sushma.
Which of the following statements is correct according to the above propositions?
(*a*) Rashmi is poorer than Priya.
(*b*) Priya is richer than Arun
(*c*) Arun is poorer than Sushma.
(*d*) Anand is richer than Rashmi

**8.** A is elder to B while C and D are elder to E who lies between A and B. If C be elder to B, which one of the following statements is necessarily true?
(*a*) E is elder to B (*b*) A is elder to C
(*c*) C is elder to D (*d*) D is elder to C

**9.** Vikram is taller than Rajan but shorter than Annie. Jamal is taller than Annie. Sita is taller than Vikram. Rajan is shorter than Sita. Who is the shortest of all in the group?
(*a*) Sita (*b*) Rajan
(*c*) Vikram (*d*) Cannot be determined

**10.** Suresh is as much older than Kamal as he is younger than Prabodh. Navin is as old as Kamal. Which of the following statements is wrong?
(*a*) Suresh is older than Navin
(*b*) Kamal is younger than Suresh
(*c*) Prabodh is not the oldest
(*d*) Navin is younger than Prabodh

**11.** Ashok is heavier than Gopal. Mahesh is lighter than Jayesh. Prashant is heavier than Jayesh but lighter than Gopal. Who among them is the heaviest?
(*a*) Gopal
(*b*) Jayesh
(*c*) Prashant
(*d*) Ashok

**12.** Subodh's marks in English are as much more than Gopal's marks in History as less than Pramod's marks in English. To find out Subodh's marks in English, which of the following informations given in the statements (A) and (B) is/ are sufficient?
(A) Gopal's marks in History.
(B) Pramod's marks in History.
(*a*) Both A and B together are needed
(*b*) Only B is sufficient
(*c*) Either A or B is sufficient
(*d*) Both A and B together are not sufficient

**13.** Pramod is older than Jayesh and Sudhir. Vikas is younger than Anil. To find out who among them is the oldest, which of the following further information will be required, if any?
(*a*) Sudhir is older than Jayesh
(*b*) Anil is older than Jayesh
(*c*) Vikas is older than Pramod
(*d*) Vikas is younger than Pramod

**14.** Ashok is younger than Prabir and Gopal. Sohan is younger than Prabir but older than Gopal. Which of the following statements is definitely true?
(*a*) Ashok is older than Sohan
(*b*) Sohan is the oldest among them
(*c*) Gopal is younger than Ashok
(*d*) Gopal is next to the youngest among them

**15.** Among five boys, Vasant is taller than Manohar, but not as tall as Raju. Jayant is taller than Datta, but shorter than Manohar. Who is the tallest in their group?
(*a*) Raju
(*b*) Manohar
(*c*) Vasant
(*d*) Cannot be determined

**16.** A and D study in the same class. K and L study in the same class. In which class does D study? To answer the above question, which of the following informations given in the statements A and B is/are necessary?
(A) D studies one standard below L.
(B) A's elder brother studies with K.
(*a*) Both A and B together are not sufficient
(*b*) Both A and B together are needed
(*c*) Only A is sufficient
(*d*) Only B is sufficient

**Directions (Qs. 17-18) :** *(A) Gopal is shorter than Ashok but taller than Kuhav; (B) Navin is shorter than Kuhav; (C) Jayesh is taller than Navin; (D) Ashok is taller than Jayesh.*

**17.** Who among them is the tallest?
(*a*) Gopal (*b*) Ashok
(*c*) Jayesh (*d*) Navin

**18.** Which of the following informations is not necessary to answer the above question?
(*a*) A (*b*) B
(*c*) C (*d*) D

**Directions (Qs. 19-20) :** *Five men A, B, C, D and E read a newspaper. The one who reads first gives it to C. The one who reads last had taken from A. E was not the first or last to read. There were two readers between B and A.*

**19.** B passed the newspaper to whom?
(*a*) E (*b*) B
(*c*) A (*d*) None of these

**20.** Who read the newspaper last?
(*a*) E (*b*) B
(*c*) D (*d*) Cannot be determined

## EXPLANATORY ANSWERS

**1. (*d*) :** The five friends in descending order of weight are : A/D, B/C, E or A/D, B, C/E. Either A or D is the heaviest.

**2. (*c*) :** The order of cities in descending order of size is : Pune, Jhansi, Raigarh, Sitapur, Chittor.

**3. (*a*) :** On the basis of doing work, the descending order will be : Ajay, Ram, Alok/Raju, Pankaj.

**4. (*d*) :** On the basis of height, the descending order will be Vipul/Alok, Ashok, Hans, Anand. Either Vipul or Alok is the tallest.

**5. (*c*) :** According to the information both Pramod and Madhu are taller than Gopal. Option (c) decides who is the tallest.

**6. (*d*) :** Statements are not inter-related.

**7. (*c*) :** On the basis of wealth, the descending order will be :
1. Shobha, Sushma, Rashmi/Arun
2. Anand, *and* Priya
(The two statements are not inter-related.)

**8. (*a*) :** The order in descending seniority will be : A/C/D, E, B.

**9. (*b*) :** On the basis of height the descending order will be :
Jamal/Sita, Annie, Vikram, Rajan.
or
Jamal, Sita/Annie, Vikram, Rajan.

**10. (*c*) :** On the basis of age the descending order will be : Prabodh, Suresh, Kamal/Navin.

**11. (*d*) :** On the basis of weight, the descending order will be : Ashok, Gopal, Prashant, Jayesh, Mahesh.

**12. (*d*) :** Comparison in marks do no clarify Subodh's marks in a subject.

**13. (*c*) :** On the basis of age the descending order will be :
1. Pramod, Jayesh/ Sudhir
*and*
2. Anil, Vikas
Option (c) connects these two statements.

**14. (*d*) :** On the basis of age the descending order will be : Prabir, Sohan, Gopal, Ashok.

**15. (*a*) :** The boys in descending order of height will be: Raju, Vasant, Manohar, Jayant, Datta.

**16. (*a*) :** There is no useful information in either of the two statements.

**17. (*b*) :** On the basis of height the descending order will be :
Ashok, Gopal/Jayesh, Kuhav, Navin
or
Ashok, Gopal, Kuhav/Jayesh, Navin.

**18. (*c*)**

**19. (*d*) :** The men read the newspaper in this order : B, C, E, A, D, and B passed the newspaper to C.

**20. (*c*) :** See answer 19 explanation.

CHAPTER 12

# Judgement

## MULTIPLE CHOICE QUESTIONS

**1.** Eileen is planning a special birthday dinner for her husband's 35th birthday. She wants the evening to be memorable, but her husband is a simple man who would rather be in jeans at a baseball game than in a suit at a fancy restaurant. Which restaurant below should Eileen choose?

(*a*) Alfredo's offers fine Italian cuisine and an elegant Tuscan decor. Patrons will feel as though they've spent the evening in a luxurious Italian villa.

(*b*) Pancho's Mexican Buffet is an all-you-can-eat family style smorgasbord with the best tacos in town.

(*c*) The Parisian Bistro is a four-star French restaurant where guests are treated like royalty. Chef Dilbert Olay is famous for his beef bourguignon.

(*d*) Marty's serves delicious, hearty meals in a charming setting reminiscent of a baseball clubhouse in honor of the owner,Marty Lester, a former major league baseball all-star. Answer & Explanation

**2.** The film director wants an actress for the lead role of Lucy who perfectly fits the description that appears in the original screenplay. He is not willing to consider actresses who do not resemble the character as she is described in the screenplay, no matter how talented they are. The screenplay describes Lucy as an average-sized, forty something redhead, with deep brown eyes, very fair skin, and a brilliant smile. The casting agent has four actresses in mind.

1. Actress #1 is a stunning red-haired beauty who is 5'9" and in her mid-twenties. Her eyes are brown and she has an olive complexion.
2. has red hair, big brown eyes, and a fair complexion. She is in her mid-forties and is 5'5".
3. is 5'4" and of medium build. She has red hair, brown eyes, and is in her early forties.
4. is a blue-eyed redhead in her early thirties. She's of very slight build and stands at 5'.

(*a*) 1, 2 (*b*) 2, 3

(*c*) 1, 4 (*d*) 2, 4

**3.** The school principal has received complaints from parents about bullying in the school yard during recess. He wants to investigate and end this situation as soon as possible, so he has asked the recess aides to watch closely. Which situation should the recess aides report to the principal?

(*a*) A girl is sitting glumly on a bench reading a book and not interacting with her peers.

(*b*) Four girls are surrounding another girl and seem to have possession of her backpack.

(*c*) Two boys are playing a one-on-one game of basketball and are arguing over the last basket scored.

(*d*) Three boys are huddled over a handheld video game, which isn't supposed to be on school grounds. Answer & Explanation

**4.** Mrs. Carson took a taxi to meet her three friends for lunch. They were waiting for her outside the restaurant when she pulled up in the car. She was so excited to see her friends that she left her tote bag in the taxi. As the taxi pulled away, she and her friends took notice of the license plate number so they would be able to identify the car when they called the taxi company.

1. The four women seem to agree that the plate starts out with the letter J.
2. Three of them agree that the plate ends with 12L.
3. Three of them think that the second letter is X, and a different three think that the third letter is K.

The four license plate numbers below represent what each of the four women thinks she saw. Which one is most likely the license plate number of the taxi?

(*a*) JXK 12L (*b*) JYK 12L
(*c*) JXK 12I (*d*) JXX 12L

**5.** Zachary has invited his three buddies over to watch the basketball game on his wide-screen television. They are all hungry, but no one wants to leave to get food. Just as they are arguing about who should make the food run, a commercial comes on for a local pizze-ria that delivers. The phone number flashes on the screen briefly and they all try to remember it. By the time Zachary grabs a pen and paper, each of them recollects a different number.

1. All of the men agree that the first three numbers are 995.
2. Three of them agree that the fourth number is 9.
3. Three agree that the fifth number is 2.
4. Three agree that the sixth number is 6; three others agree that the seventh number is also 6.

Which of the numbers is most likely the telephone number of the pizzeria?

(*a*) 995-9266 (*b*) 995-9336
(*c*) 995-9268 (*d*) 995-8266

**6.** Mark is working with a realtor to find a location for the toy store he plans to open in his town. He is looking for a place that is either in, or not too far from, the center of town and one that would attract the right kind of foot traffic. Which of the following locations should Mark's realtor call to his attention?

(*a*) a storefront in a new high-rise building near the train station in the center of town whose occupants are mainly young, childless professionals who use the train to commute to their offices each day.
(*b*) a little shop three blocks away from the town's main street, located across the street from an elementary school and next door to an ice cream store
(*c*) a stand-alone storefront on a quiet residential street ten blocks away from the town's center
(*d*) a storefront in a small strip mall located on the outskirts of town that is also occupied by a pharmacy and a dry cleaner

**7.** The neighborhood block association has received many complaints about people knocking on doors and soliciting money for an unknown charity organization even though door-to-door solicitation is prohibited by local laws. Three residents have provided descriptions individuals who have come to their door asking for money.

Solicitor #1 is a white male, 20-25 years old, 5'9", 145 pounds, with very short brown hair. He was wearing a dark blue suit and carrying a brown leather briefcase.

Solicitor #2 is a white male, 25-30 years old, 6'2", 200 pounds, with a shaved-head. He was wearing a red T-shirt and jeans.

Solicitor #3 is a white male, approximately 23 years old, 5'10", slight build, with short brown hair. He was wearing a blue suit.

Three days after the block association meet- ing, a resident noticed a man knocking on doors in the neighborhood and phoned the police to report the illegal activity. This solic- itor was described as follows:

Solicitor #4 is a white male, 22 years old, 140 pounds, about 5'10", with short brown hair. He was carrying a briefcase and wearing a dark suit.

Based on this description, which of the three solicitations was also likely carried out by Solicitor #4?

(*a*) #1, #2, and #3
(*b*) #1, but not #2 and #3
(*c*) #1 and #3, but not #2
(*d*) #1 and #2, but not #3

**8.** Rita, an accomplished pastry chef who is well known for her artistic and exquisite wedding cakes, opened a bakery one year ago and is surprised that business has been so slow. A consultant she hired to conduct market research has reported that the local population doesn't think of her shop as one they would visit on a daily basis but rather a place they'd visit if they were celebrating a special occasion. Which of the following strategies should Rita employ to increase her daily business?

(*a*) making coupons available that entitle the coupon holder to receive a 25% discount on wedding, anniversary, or birthday cakes
(*b*) exhibiting at the next Bridal Expo and having pieces of one of her wedding cakes available for tasting
(*c*) placing a series of ads in the local newspaper that advertise the wide array of breads
(*d*) moving the bakery to the other side of town

**9.** Dr. Miller has a busy pediatric dentistry practice and she needs a skilled, reliable hygienist to keep things running smoothly. The last two people she hired were recommended by top dentists in the area, but they each lasted less than one month. She is now in desperate need of a hygienist who can competently handle the specific challenges of her practice. Which one of the following candidates should Dr. Miller consider most seriously?

(*a*) Marilyn has been a hygienist for fifteen years, and her current employer, who is about to retire, says she is the best in the business. The clientele she has worked with consists of some of the wealthiest and most powerful citizens in the county.

(*b*) Lindy recently graduated at the top of her class from one of the best dental hygiene programs in the state. Prioı to becoming a dental hygienist, Lindy spent two years working in a day care center.

(*c*) James has worked as a dental hygienist for three years in a public health clinic. He is very interested in securing a position in a private dental office.

(*d*) Kathy is an experienced and highly recommended dental hygienist who is also finishing up a degree in early childhood education, which she hopes will get her a job as a preschool teacher. She is eager to find a job in a pediatric practice, since she has always wanted to work with children.

**10.** Mrs. Jansen recently moved to Arizona. She wants to fill her new backyard with flowering plants. Although she is an experienced gardener, she isn't very well-versed in what plants will do well in the Arizona climate. Also, there is a big tree in her backyard making for shady conditions and she isn't sure what plants will thrive without much direct sunlight. Her favorite gardening catalog offers several backyard seed packages. Which one should Mrs. Jansen choose?

(*a*) The Rainbow Collection is ideal for North-east gardens. It includes a variety of colorful perennials that thrive in cool, moist conditions.

(*b*) The Greenhouse Collection will blossom year after year if planted in brightly lit locations and watered regularly.

(*c*) The Treehouse Collection will provide lush green plants with delicate colorful flowers that thrive in shady and partially shady locations.

(*d*) The Oasis Collection includes a variety of perennials that thrive in dry climates and bright sunlight.

## EXPLANATORY ANSWERS

**1.(*d*) :** Since Eileen's husband does not enjoy fancy restaurants, choices a and c can be ruled out. Choice b, although casual, doesn't sound as though it would be the kind of special and memorable evening that Eileen is looking for. Choice d, which is owned by a former baseball star and is described as "charming" and "reminiscent of a baseball clubhouse", sounds perfect for Eileen's husband, who is described as a baseball fan and a man with simple tastes.

**2.(*b*) :** 2 and 3 possess most of the required traits. They both have red hair and brown eyes, are average-sized, and are in their forties. 1 is very tall and is only in her mid-twenties. She also has an olive complexion. 4 is of very slight build and is in her early thirties. She also has blue eyes.

**3.(*b*) :** Seeing four girls surrounding another girl, while in possession of her backpack, is the most suspicious of the incidents described.

**4.(*a*) :** The four women seem to agree that the plate starts out with the letter J. Three of them agree that the plate ends with 12L. Three of them think that the second letter is X, and a different three think that the third letter is K. The plate description that has all of these common elements is "Option A".

**5.(*a*) :** All of the men agree that the first three numbers are 995. Three of them agree that the fourth number is 9. Three agree that the fifth number is 2. Three agree that the sixth number is 6; three others agree that the seventh number is also 6. "Option A" is the best choice because it is made up of the numbers that most of the men agree they saw.

**6.(*b*) :** This option is both near the center of town and in a location (near a school and an ice cream store) where children and their parents are sure to be around. This is the only option that meets both of Mark's requirements.

**7.(*c*) :** The solicitor described as #2 has a shaved head and is much taller and heavier than the solicitors described as #1 and #3. Therefore, choices a and d, which include #2, can be ruled out. Solicitors #1, #3, and #4 have such similar descriptions that the correct answer is clearly choice c.

**8.(*c*) :** This is the only option that would encourage people to think of the bakery as a shop they would visit regularly and not just on special occasions.

**9.(*b*) :** The situation described indicates that Dr. Miller's practice presents some specific challenges, namely that it is a busy environment with a child clientele. There is also some indication that even highly recommended, experienced hygienists might not be cut out for Dr. Miller's office. There is nothing to suggest that Marilyn (choice a) or James (choice c) would be a good fit for Dr. Miller's practice. Kathy (choice d) has experience and she is also interested in working with children. However, the fact that she hopes to become a preschool teacher in the not-too-distant future indicates that she might not be the kind of committed, long-term employee that Dr. Miller needs. Lindy (choice b), with her hands-on experience working with children as well as a degree from a prestigious dental hygiene program, is the most attractive candidate for the position based on the situation described

**10.(c) :** The Treehouse Collection is the only package that can thrive in shady locations. Choice a requires a Northeastern climate. Choices b and d require bright sunlight.

In this type of tests certain categories of information are given followed by certain criteria. Further, the candidates are given a few cause that needs to be analysed. They are required to take the right decision, from the given options, after comparing the information in each case with the given information and criteria.

# DECISION MAKING

## MULTIPLE CHOICE QUESTIONS

**Directions (Qs. 1 to 5) :** *Read the following information carefully and answer the questions given below it.*

Following are the criteria for admitting a student in the first year engineering course in a college.

The student must—

*(i)* have passed XII standard examination in science with at least 80% marks.

*(ii)* not be more than 20 years old as on 1. 8. 1998.

*(iii)* have secured at least 90 marks in the entrance test out of a total of 150 marks.

*(iv)* be able to pay Rs. 15,000 as tuition fees for the first semester and Rs. 5,000 admission charges at the time of taking admission.

In the case of a candidate, who satisfies all other criteria exccpt at—

*(a)* *(iv)* above but can pay at least 60% of the stipulated fees, the case may be referred to the Admission Committee.

*(b)* *(iii)* above but has secured more than 95% marks in the XIIth standard examination, the case may be referred to Chairman–Admissions.

You are given the following cases as on 1. 8. 1998. Depending upon the information provided in each case and based on the criteria mentioned above, recommend your decision. You are not to assume anything. If the information provided is not adequate to take a decision, mark 'Data inadequate' as the answer.

**1.** Subodh Mohaptara was 19 years old as on 20th December, 1997. He has secured 98% marks in XIIth standard examination with science and 80 marks in the entrance test. He can pay the requisite tuition fees and admission charges.

*(a)* Admit
*(b)* Refer to Admission Committee
*(c)* Data inadequate
*(d)* Do not admit
*(e)* Refer to Chairman–Admissions

**2.** Reema Jaiswal was born on 20th July, 1978. She has secured 85% and 75% marks in XIIth standard with science and entrance test respectively. She can pay the requisite tuition fees and admission charges.

*(a)* Refer to Chairman–Admission
*(b)* Refer to Admission Committee
*(c)* Data inadequate
*(d)* Do not admit
*(e)* Admit

**3.** Ashok Dubey was born on 27th November, 1978. He has secured 90% marks in the XIIth standard examination with science and 95 marks in the entrance test. He can pay Rs. 10,000 tuition fees and Rs. 3,500 admission charges.

*(a)* Admit
*(b)* Data inadequate
*(c)* Refer to Admission Committee
*(d)* Do not admit
*(e)* Refer to Chairman–Admissions

**4.** Sudha Mirchandani has secured 95% marks in XIIth standard science stream and 70% marks in the entrance test. She can pay only 65% of the requisite tuition fees and admission charges.

*(a)* Do not admit
*(b)* Admit
*(c)* Data inadequate
*(d)* Refer to Chairman–Admissions
*(e)* Refer to Admission Committee

**5.** Salil Malhotra was born on 25th September in 1979. He has secured 85% and 95% marks in the XIIth standard examination in science stream and entrance test respectively. He can pay the requisite tuition fees and admission charges.

*(a)* Admit
*(b)* Do not admit
*(c)* Refer to Chairman–Admissions
*(d)* Refer to Admission Committee
*(e)* Data inadequate

**Directions (Qs. 6 to 12) :** *Read the following information to answer the given questions :*

Following are the criteria for selecting candidates for Research Fellowship :

The candidate must—

*(i)* be a post–graduate with minimum of 65% marks.

*(ii)* not be more than 30 years as on 15. 10. 1993.

*(iii)* have at least 3 years research experience.

*(iv)* have diploma in Statistics.

*(v)* have secured at least 50% marks in the entrance test.

*(vi)* have finalised the topic for research.

However, in case a candidate who fulfills all other criteria except

*(a)* *(iii)* above, but has M. Phil degree, should be referred to Dean.

*(b)* *(iv)* above, should be referred to Chairman.

*(c)* *(i)* above, but has at least 55% marks in post–graduation and 65% in the entrance test, should be given fellowship.

*(d)* *(v)* above, but has at lest 45% marks, should be wait–listed.

Based on these criteria and information provided below, decide the course of action in each case. You are not to assume anything. If the data provided is not adequate to decide the given course of action, your answer will be "data inadequate". These cases are given to you as on 15. 10. 1993.

**6.** 26 years old, Mamta Deo is a post graduate with 58%. She has got four years' research experience and has finalised topic for research. She got 70% marks in diploma in Statistics and 54% marks in the entrance examination.

*(a)* Fellowship not to be granted
*(b)* Refer to Dean
*(c)* Refer to Chairman
*(d)* Grant Fellowship
*(e)* Data inadequate

**7.** Shushila Nair has 65% marks in her post–graduation and is M. Phil. She has 5 years research experience. She has secured 65% in the entrance test and has finalised the research topic. Her date of birth is 11. 8. 65.

*(a)* Grant fellowship
*(b)* Wait–list
*(c)* Refer to Dean
*(d)* Refer to Chairman
*(e)* Data inadequate

**8.** Ameer Khan has got 58% in the entrance test. He has 68% in his post-graduation and 55% in M. Phil. He has got diploma in Statistics and has also finalised the topic for research.

*(a)* Grant Fellowship
*(b)* Refer to Dean
*(c)* Refer to Chairman
*(d)* Wait-list
*(e)* Data inadequate

**9.** 28 years old Neetu Singh is M. Phil with 60% marks. She has secured 70% marks in entrance examination and has finalised the topic for research. She has also got diploma in Statistics.

*(a)* Grant Fellowship
*(b)* Fellowship not to be granted
*(c)* Refer to Chairman
*(d)* Refer to Dean
*(e)* Data inadequate

**10.** Sadhana Suman has got diploma in Statistics with 60% marks and post-graduation with 56% marks. Her date of birth is 12. 12. 1968. She has got one year research experience and is still doing her M. Phil. She has secured 65% marks in entrance exam and has also finalised the research topic.

*(a)* Grant Fellowship
*(b)* Fellowship not to be granted
*(c)* Refer to Dean
*(d)* Data inadequate
*(e)* Wait-list

**11.** Amar Sikka is 28 years old and has got 65% marks in post-graduation and 60% marks in M. Phil. He has got 65% marks in entrance examination and has finalised the topic for research. He also has a diploma in Statistics.

*(a)* Grant Fellowship
*(b)* Fellowship not to be granted
*(c)* Refer to Dean
*(d)* Refer to Chairman
*(e)* Data inadequate

**12.** Madan Paul has got 5 years' research experience and has finalised the research topic. He has got 56% marks in post-graduation. His date of birth is 15. 2. 1966. He has also got diploma in Statistics. He got 70% marks in the entrance test.

*(a)* Grant Fellowship
*(b)* Fellowship not to be granted
*(c)* Refer to Dean
*(d)* Data inadequate
*(e)* None of these

**Directions (Qs. 13 to 19) :** *Read the following information to answer the given questions :*

Following are the conditions for selecting candidates for Research Fellowship :

The candidate must—

*(i)* be a post-graduate with minimum of 60% marks.

*(ii)* not be more than 30 years as on 1. 9. 1993.

*(iii)* have at least 3 years' research experience.

(*iv*) have diploma in statistics.

(*v*) have secured at least 55% marks in the entrance test.

(*iv*) have finalised the topic for research.

However, in the case of a candidate who fulfills all other criteria except—

(*a*) (*iii*) above but has M. Phil degree, should be given fellowship.

(*b*) (*iv*) above should be referred to Dean.

(*c*) (*i*) above but has atleast 55% marks in post–graduation, should be wait-listed.

(*d*) (*v*) above but has atleast 50% marks, should be referred to Chairman.

Based on these criteria and information provided below, decide the course of action in each case. You are not to assume anything. If the data provided is not adequate to decide the given course of action, your answer will be "data inadequate". These cases are given to you as on 1. 9. 1993.

**13.** Vijay Gupta is 24 years old and has got 58% marks in the entrance examination. He has secured 63% marks in his post-graduation and 55% marks in M. Phil. He has got diploma in Statistics and has also finalised the topic for research.

(*a*) Grant Fellowship
(*b*) Refer to Dean
(*c*) Refer to Chairman
(*d*) Wait-list
(*e*) Data inadequate

**14.** Ajoy Dwivedi has secured 65% marks in the post-graduation and has secured 5 years research experience. He has secured 65% marks in the entrance test and has finalised the research topic. His date of birth is 11. 8. 1965.

(*a*) Grant Fellowship
(*b*) Wait-list
(*c*) Refer to Dean
(*d*) Data inadequate
(*e*) None of these

**15.** Madan Soren has got diploma in Statistics with 60% marks and post-graduation with 56% marks. His date of birth is 12. 12. 1968. He has got 1 year research experience and is still doing his M. Phil. He has secured 60% marks in the entrance exam and has also finalised the research topic.

(*a*) Grant fellowship
(*b*) Fellowship not to be granted
(*c*) Refer to Dean
(*d*) Data inadequate
(*e*) Wait-list

**16.** 26 years old Mamta Kulkarni is M. Phil with 60% marks. She has secured 70% marks in the entrance examination and has finali-sed the topic for research. She has also got diploma in Statistics.

(*a*) Grant Fellowship
(*b*) Fellowship not to be granted
(*c*) Refer to Chairman
(*d*) Refer to Dean
(*e*) Data inadequate

**17.** Chander Manoj has got 5 years' research experi-ence and has finalised the research topic. He has got 56% marks in post-graduation and 60% marks in the entrance test. His date of birth is 15. 2. 1966. He has also got diploma in Statistics.

(*a*) Grant Fellowship
(*b*) Fellowship not to be granted
(*c*) Refer to Dean
(*d*) Data inadequate
(*e*) None of these

**18.** Raman Hooda is 28 years old and has got 65% marks in Post-graduation and 60% marks in M. Phil. He has got 65% marks in the entrance examination and has finalised the topic for research. He also has a diploma in Statistics.

(*a*) Grant Fellowship
(*b*) Fellowship not to be granted
(*c*) Refer to Dean
(*d*) Refer to Chairman
(*e*) Data inadequate

**19.** 26 years old Janaki Deo is a post-graduate with 58% marks. She has got four years research experience and has finalised the topic for research. She got 70% marks in the diploma in Statistics and 54% marks in the entrance examination.

(*a*) Fellowship not to be granted
(*b*) Refer to Dean
(*c*) Refer to Chairman
(*d*) Grant Fellowship
(*e*) Data inadequate

**Directions (Qs. 20 to 27) :** *Read the following information carefully and answer the questions given below :*

Following are the criteria of promotion from Junior Officer's Cadre to Senior Officer's Cadre in an organi-sation :

The candidate must—

(*a*) have completed atleast 5 years in the organisation.

(*b*) have secured 65% marks in the written test for promotion.

(*c*) have secured 60% marks in the Group Discussion.

(*d*) have secured 70% marks in the interview.

(*e*) have good record of his work performance.

(*f*) have good communication skill and get along well with his colleagues.

(*g*) not be more than 40 years and less than 30 years as on 1. 9. 93.

(h) have good academic record with an average of at least 65% marks.

However, in the case of a candidate who—

(i) satisfies all other conditions except (d) above but has secured 75% marks in the written test and 65% marks in he Group Discussion, the case is to be referred to the General Manager (Personnel)–GM(P) for the decision.

(j) satisfies all other criteria except (h) above but has secured an average of more than 60% marks, the case is to be referred to the Managing Director (MD) of the organisation.

Now read the information provided in the case of each candidate in each of the questions given below and decide on the basis of the information provided and based on the above conditions, which of the courses of action you would suggest. These cases are given as on 5. 9. 1993. (Remember you are not to assume anything which is not provided in the question). If complete information is not provided, the answer would be Data inadequate.

**20.** 38 years old Rajesh has secured 65% marks in the written test for promotion, 73% marks in interview and 62% marks in Group Discussion. He has good record of his work performance, good communication skills and gets along well with his colleagues. He has good academic record with an average of 61% marks and has completed 7 years in the organisation.

(a) Refer to GM(P)
(b) Refer to MD
(c) Promote
(d) Do not promote
(e) Data inadequate

**21.** 34 years old Sudha has secured 60% marks in the written test for promotion, 72% marks in interview and 69% marks in Group discussion. She has good communication skill and gets along well with her colleagues. Her record of work performance is good and she has completed 6½ years in the organisation.

(a) Refer to MD
(b) Do not promote
(c) Refer to GM(P)
(d) Promote
(e) Data inadequate

**22.** Surekha has secured 70% marks in written test for promotion, 69% marks in Group Discussion and 72% marks in the interview. She has a good academic record with an average of 67% marks. She has good record of work performance and gets along well with her colleagues. She has good communication skill and has completed 7 years in the organisation.

(a) Do not promote
(b) Promote
(c) Refer to GM(P)
(d) Refer to MD
(e) Data inadequate

**23.** 39 years old Pawan has secured 66% marks in written promotion test and has a good academic record with an average of 62% marks. He has secured 65% marks in Group Discussion and 72% marks in interview. He has good record of his work performance, communication skill and gets along well with his colleagues. He has completed 6 years in the organisation.

(a) Do not promote
(b) Refer to MD
(c) Refer to GM(P)
(d) Promote
(e) Data inadequate

**24.** 34 years old Sudhir has secured 76% marks in the written test for promotion, 66% marks in Group Discussion and 67% marks in interview. He has good academic record with an average of 68% marks, good communication skill and gets along well with his colleagues. His work performance is good and he has completed 6 years in the organisation.

(a) Promote
(b) Refer to MD
(c) Refer to GM(P)
(d) Do not promote
(e) Data anadequate

**25.** 32 years old Manjula has good academic record with an average of 66% marks. She has secured 67% marks in Group Discussion, 75% marks in interview and 60% marks in written test for promotion. She has good communication skill and gets along well with her colleagues. She has good record of her work performance and has completed 7 years in the organisation.

(a) Do not promote
(b) Refer to MD
(c) Promote
(d) Refer to GM(P)
(e) Data inadequate

**26.** 31 years old Krishna secured 65% marks in written test for promotion, 72% marks in interview and 62% marks in Group Discussion. He has good academic record with an average of 67% marks and good communication skill. He has completed 9 years in the organisation. He gets easily annoyed and irritated with his colleagues and his record of work performance since the last two years is just average.

(a) Promote (b) Refer to GM(P)
(c) Refer to MD (d) Do not promote
(e) Data inadequate

**27.** 33 years old Neelima has secured 63% marks in Group Discussion, 71% marks in interview and 66% marks in written test for promotion. She hase good academic record with an average of 68% marks and has good communication skill. She gets along well with her colleagues and has good record of her work performance. She has completed 6 years in the organisation.

(*a*) Refer to GM(P)
(*b*) Do not promote
(*c*) Promote
(*d*) Refer to MD
(*e*) Data inadequate

## EXPLANATORY ANSWERS

**1. (*e*) :** Criterion *(iii)* is not satisfied but Criterion *(b)* gives the decision.

**2. (*d*) :** Both Criterion *(iii)* and Criterion *(b)* are not satisfied.

**3. (*c*) :** Criterion *(iv)* is not satisfied but Criterion *(a)* gives the decision.

**4. (*c*) :** Criterion *(ii)* is not given.

**5. (*a*)**

**6. (*a*) :** Both Criterion *(i)* and Criterion *(c)* are not satisfied.

**7. (*d*) :** Criterion *(iv)* is not given but Criterion *(b)* gives the decision.

**8. (*e*) :** Both Criteria *(ii)* and *(iii)* are not given and Criterion *(a)* alone cannot give the decision.

**9. (*e*) :** Both Criterion *(i)* and Criterion *(iii)* are not given and criterion *(a)* alone cannot give the decision.

**10. (*b*) :** Both Criterion *(iii)* and Criterion *(a)* are not satisfied.

**11. (*c*) :** Criterion *(iii)* is not satisfied but Criterion *(a)* gives the decision.

**12. (*a*) :** Criterion *(i)* is not satisfied but Criterion *(c)* gives the decision.

**13. (*a*) :** Criterion *(iii)* is not satisfied but Criterion *(a)* gives the decision.

**14. (*c*) :** Criterion *(iv)* is not satisfied but Criterion *(b)* gives the decision.

**15. (*b*) :** Both Criterion *(iii)* and Criterion *(a)* are not satisfied.

**16. (*e*) :** Criterion *(i)* is not given and Criterion *(c)* is not satisfied.

**17. (*e*) :** Criterion *(i)* is not satisfied but Criterion *(c)* gives the decision of "wait–list." This option is not given.

**18. (*a*) :** Criterion *(iii)* is not satisfied but Criterion *(a)* gives the decision.

**19. (*a*) :** Both Criterion *(i)* and Criterion *(iii)* are not satisfied, Criterion *(c)* and Criterion *(d)* gives different decisions.

**20. (*b*) :** Criterion *(h)* is not satisfied but Criterion *(j)* gives the decision.

**21. (*b*) :** Criterion *(b)* is not satisfied.

**22. (*e*) :** Criterion *(g)* is not given.

**23. (*b*) :** Criterion *(h)* is not satisfied but Criterion *(j)* gives the desicion.

**24. (*c*) :** Criterion *(d)* is not satisfied but Criterion *(i)* gives the decision.

**25. (*a*) :** Criterion *(b)* is not satisfied.

**26. (*d*) :** Both Criterion *(e)* and Criterion *(f)* are not satisfied.

**27. (*c*) :**

CHAPTER 13

# Statement Conclusion

In this reasoning pattern, a statement is given followed by two conclusions. The statement is to be taken as the fact. Then based on it one has to decide which of the conclusion(s) definitely follows or does not follow from the given statement.

## MULTIPLE CHOICE QUESTIONS

**Directions (Qs. 1 to 20):** *In the following questions, each question has a statement followed by two conclusions. Taking the statement to be true, decide which of the given conclusions definitely follows from the given statement. Indicate your answer as (a) if only I follows; (b) if only II follows; (c) either I or II follows; (d) if neither I nor II follows; and (e) if both I and II follow.*

**1.** *Statement* : The Principal humiliated the teacher in the presence of students.

*Conclusions I:* The Principal did not like the teacher.

*II:* The teacher was not popular amongst his students.

**2.** *Statement* : Good health is dependent on right eating habits. Most of the people do not follow any rule regarding eating.

*Conclusions I:* Most of the people have poor health.

*II:* People are ignorant of proper eating habits.

**3.** *Statement* : Until our country achieves economic equality and political freedom, democracy would be meaningless.

*Conclusions I:* Political freedom and democracy go hand in hand.

*II:* Economic equality leads to real political freedom and democracy.

**4.** *Statement* : Black cloud follows thunder. Rains follow thunder.

*Conclusions I:* Thunder is the cause of rain.

*II:* Black cloud is the cause of thunder.

**5.** *Statement* : Practice is better than precept. Most doctors are heavy smokers.

*Conclusions I:* Most doctors cannot advise people not to smoke.

*II:* Doctors do not regard smoking as injurious.

**6.** *Statement* : Workers feel highly motivated when they get sense of involvement by participating in the management of companies.

*Conclusions I:* Workers should be motivated to produce more.

*II:* Workers should be allowed to participate in the management of companies.

**7.** *Statement* : Industrial revolution which first of all started in Europe has brought about modern age.

*Conclusions I:* Disparity between rich and poor results in revolution.

*II:* Revolution overhauls society.

**8.** *Statement* : America's defence secretary reiterated that they would continue to supply arms to Pakistan.

*Conclusions I:* Pakistan is incapable of manufacturing arms.

*II:* It would ensure peace in the region.

**9.** *Statement* : Poor people are more trust-worthy as compared to the rich. They can do wonders if they are taken into confidence.

*Conclusions I:* Poor people are wonderful people.

*II:* By and large rich people are not trustworthy.

**10.** *Statement* : Government has spoiled many top ranking financial institutions by appointing bureaucrats as Directors of these institutions.

*Conclusions I:* Government should appoint Directors of the financial institutes taking into consi-deration the expertise of the person in the area of finance.

*II:* The Director of the financial institute should have exper-tise commensurate with the financial work carried out by the institute.

**11.** *Statement* : The Constitutional amendment carried out just last month prohibits the employment of child labour in any organisation.

*Conclusions I:* The employers must now abide by this amendment to the Constitution.

*II:* Children below 14 years will now be engaged in acquiring education.

**12.** *Statement* : People who speak too much against the dowry are those who had taken it themselves.

*Conclusions I:* It is easier said than done.

*II:* People have double standards.

**13.** *Statement* : Vegetable prices are soaring in the market.

*Conclusions I:* Vegetables are becoming a rare commodity.

*II:* People cannot eat vegetables.

**14.** *Statement* : As far as the rate of literacy is concerned, there is hardly any difference between the States of Kerala and West Bengal, but one is ahead of the other in respect of the percentage of population unemployed.

*Conclusions I:* Unemployment is more in Kerala than in West Bengal.

*II:* West Bengal has higher unemployment than Kerala.

**15.** *Statement* : He tirelessly argues for the replacement of the present system of allocating work to the teaching staff in the department by another system which will give the teachers higher job satisfaction.

*Conclusions I:* No system is free from problems and therefore there should be no system.

*II:* Any system you may evolve but it should give higher job satisfaction to the teachers.

**16.** *Statement* : The unequal allocation of funds by the Government for literacy and employment generation programmes stands out clearly when we analyse the attitude of government towards these two areas.

*Conclusions I:* Government has more favourable attitude towards literacy programmes than employment generation progra-mmes.

*II:* Government has more favourable attitude towards employment generation programmes than literacy programmes.

**17.** *Statement* : Amul chocolates sold enough in comparison to all other chocolate brands in India.

*Conclusions I:* No other chocolate is sold in India.

*II:* The selling data of every chocolate brand is available in India.

**18.** *Statement* : Wearing Khadi is not only good for our health but also for our nation.

*Conclusions I:* Economy of India also depends upon Khadi sector.

*II:* It is difficult to maintain Khadi clothes.

**19.** *Statement* : Ideas given by our ancestors that were once discarded as uneconomical and unviable, turn out to be as functional and inevitable in present circumstances.

*Conclusions I:* In ancient period ideas were considered either completely functional or totally infeasible.

*II:* Ideas cannot change from time-to-time.

**20.** *Statement* : The Supreme Court gave a judgement that the maintenance of old age parents is the responsibility of the married girls, if they do not have brothers.

*Conclusions I:* Constitution is always interpreted to help oppressed people out.

*II:* Before the Supreme Court gave its verdict, a married girl must have denied to pay for the maintenance of her parents.

**Directions (Qs. 21 to 25):** *In the following questions, the symbols* $*$, $\overset{*}{=}$ ,=, @ *and* $\underset{=}{@}$ *are used with the following meanings :*

(*a*) * (*b*) means (*a*) is greater than (*b*),

(*a*) $\overset{*}{=}$ (*b*) means (*a*) is either greater than or equal to (*b*).

(*a*) = (*b*) means (*a*) is equal to (*b*).

(*a*) @ (*b*) means (*a*) is smaller than (*b*) and

(*a*) $\underset{=}{@}$ (*b*) means (*a*) is either smaller than or equal to (*b*).

Answer is given as:

(*a*) If only conclusion I is true;

(*b*) If only conclusion II is true;

(*c*) If either I or II is true;

(*d*) If neither I nor II is true;

(*e*) If both I and II are true.

**21.** *Statements* : $T \underset{=}{*} P, P @ S, P = M$

*Conclusions* : *I.* $S * M$ *II.* $T @ S$

**22.** *Statements* : $R \underset{=}{@} M, M * P, R \underset{=}{*} L$

*Conclusions* : *I.* $M = L$ *II.* $P = L$

**23.** *Statements* : $M = T, T \underset{=}{@} Z, S * M$

*Conclusions* : *I.* $Z * M$ *II.* $Z = M$

**24.** *Statements* : $L @ C, C * Z, Z \underset{=}{@} F$

*Conclusions* : *I.* $C * F$ *II.* $F = C$

**25.** *Statements* : $Z @ B, N \underset{=}{*} S, B @ N$

*Conclusions* : *I.* $B = Z$ *II.* $S \underset{=}{@} B$

## EXPLANATORY ANSWERS

**1. (*a*) :** Only conclusion I follows. Conclusion II is not confirmed by the given statement.

**2. (*a*) :** Conclusion I definitely follows. Conclusion II is not confirmed by the given statement.

**3. (*b*) :** Only conclusion II follows. Conclusion I cannot be drawn from the given statement.

**4. (*b*) :** Only conclusion II follows. Conclusion I is wrong as rains are the cause of thunder.

**5. (*e*) :** Both conclusion I and conclusion II follow from the statements as the doctors who are heavy smokers indicate that they do not regard smoking as injurious and thus, cannot advise people not to smoke.

**6. (*e*) :** Both conclusions I and II follow from the statement as involvement of workers boosts production and benefits the companies.

**7. (*b*) :** Only conclusion II follows. Conclusion I is not related the statement.

**8. (*d*) :** Neither conclusion I nor conclusion II follows. Both the conclusions are unrelated to the statement.

**9. (*b*) :** Only conclusion II follows. Conclusion I is not related to the statement.

**10. (*e*) :** Both conclusion I and conclusion II follow.

**11. (*a*) :** Only conclusion I follows. Conclusion II is not related to the statement.

**12. (*e*) :** Both conclusion I and conclusion II follow as people who talk too much often do not practise what they say.

**13. (*d*) :** Neither conclusion I nor conclusion II is confirmed by the statement.

**14. (*d*) :** Neither conclusion I nor conclusion II follows as the precentage of unemployment in each state is not mentioned.

**15. (*b*) :** Only conclusion II follows. Conclusion I runs counter to the statement as a system is necessary.

**16. (*d*) :** Neither conclusion I nor conclusion II is confirmed by the statement.

**17. (*b*) :** Only conclusion II follows as the data of every chocolate brand shows the comparision of Amul chocolates with other brands. Coclusion I is not confirmed by the statement.

**18. (*a*) :** Only conclusion I follows. Conclusion II is not related to the statement.

**19. (*d*) :** Neither conclusion I, nor conclusion II follows; both the conclusions are unrelated.

**20. (*b*) :** Only conclusion II follows, because the Supreme Court judgement must have come in such a case and not in vacuum.

**21. (*a*) :** $T \geq P, P < S, P = M$

$\therefore S > M$

**22. (*d*) :** $R \leq M, M > P, R \geq L$

$\therefore L \leq R \leq M$

**23. (*c*) :** $M = T, T \leq Z, Z = M$

If $T = Z$, then $Z = M$

If $T < Z$, then $Z > M$

**24. (*d*) :** $L < C, C > Z, Z \leq F$

No relation can be established between C and F.

**25. (*d*) :** $Z < B, N \geq S, B < N$

No relation can be established between B, S and Z.

CHAPTER 14

# Syllogistic Reasoning

In this reasoning pattern two statements are followed by few conclusions drawn. Four options (*a*), (*b*), (*c*) & (*d*) are given as answers. Based on the statement the candidate has to select the right answer in each question.

## MULTIPLE CHOICE QUESTIONS

**Directions (Q. 1–10) :** *In each question given below two statements are followed by four conclusions numbered I, II, III and IV. You have to take the two given statements to be true even if they seem to be at variance from commonly known facts. Read the statements and conclusions and decide which of the conclusions logically follows from the two given statements, disregarding commonly known facts.*

**1. Statements:** All the phones are scales. All the scales are calculators.

**Conclusions:**

I. All the calculators are scales.
II. All the phones are calculators.
III. All the scales are phones.
IV. Some calculators are phones.

(*a*) Only I and IV (*b*) Only III and IV
(*c*) Only II and IV (*d*) Only I and II

**2. Statements:** No door is dog. All the dogs are cats.

**Conclusions:**

I. No door is cat.
II. No cat is door.
III. Some cats are dogs.
IV. All the cats are dogs.

(*a*) Only II and IV (*b*) Only I and III
(*c*) Only III and IV (*d*) Only III

**3. Statements:** Some tables are T.V. Some T.V. are radios.

**Conclusions:**

I. Some tables are radios.
II. Some radios are tables.
III. All the radios are T.V.
IV. All the T.V. are tables.

(*a*) Only II and IV (*b*) Only I and III
(*c*) Only IV (*d*) None of the four

**4. Statements:** All men are vertebrates. Some mammals are vertebrates.

**Conclusions:**

I. All men are mammals.
II. All mammals are men.
III. Some vertebrates are mammals.
IV. All vertebrates are men.

(*a*) Only IV (*b*) Only II
(*c*) Only III (*d*) Only I

**5. Statements:** All green are blue. All blue are white.

**Conclusions:**

I. Some blue are green.
II. Some white are green.
III. Some green are not white.
IV. All white are blue.

(*a*) Only I and II (*b*) Only I and III
(*c*) Only I and IV (*d*) Only II and IV

**6. Statements:** Some pens are books. Some books are pencils.

**Conclusions:**

I. Some pens are pencils.
II. Some pencils are pens.
III. All pencils are pens.
IV. All books are pens.

(*a*) Only I and III (*b*) Only II and IV
(*c*) All the four (*d*) None of the four

**7. Statements:** All the research scholars are psychologists. Some psychologists are scientists.

**Conclusions:**

I. All the research scholars are scientists.
II. Some research scholars are scientists.
III. Some scientists are psychologists.
IV. Some psychologists are research scholars.

(*a*) Only III and IV (*b*) None of the four
(*c*) All the four (*d*) Only III

**8. Statements:** All the goats are tigers. All the tigers are lions.

**Conclusions:**

I. All the goats are lions.
II. All the lions are goats.
III. Some lions are goats.
IV. Some tigers are goats.

(*a*) All the four (*b*) Only I, II and III
(*c*) Only I, III and IV (*d*) Only II, III and IV

**9. Statements:** All members are students. No student is a girl.

**Conclusions :**

I. All students are members.
II. No members is a girl.
III. Some students are members.
IV. Some members are girls.

(*a*) Only I follows (*b*) Only I, II and III follow
(*c*) All follows (*d*) Only II and III follows

**10. Statements :** All soaps are clean. All clean are wet.

**Conclusions :**

I. Some clean are soaps.
II. No clean is soap.
III. Some wet are soaps.
IV. All wet are soaps.

(*a*) Only I follows
(*b*) Only I and II follow
(*c*) Only either III and IV follow
(*d*) Only I and III follow

**Directions (Q. 11–15) :** *Every question below has a few statements, followed by four conclusions numbered I, II, III and IV. You have to consider every given statement as true, even if it does not conform to the well known facts. Read the conclusions and then decide which of the conclusions can be logically derived.*

**11. Statements:** Some keys are staplers. Some staplers are stickers. All the stickers are pens.

**Conclusions:**

I. Some pens are staplers.
II. Some stickers are keys.
III. No sticker is key.
IV. Some staplers are keys.

(*a*) Only I and II
(*b*) Only II and IV
(*c*) Only II and III
(*d*) Only I and IV and either II or III

**12. Statements:** All the locks are keys. All the keys are bats. Some watches are bats.

**Conclusions:**

I. Some bats are locks.
II. Some watches are keys.
III. All the keys are locks.
IV. Some keys are locks.

(*a*) Only I and II (*b*) Only I and IV
(*c*) Only II and III (*d*) Only I and III

**13. Statements:** All the papers are books. All the bags are books. Some purses are bags.

**Conclusions:**

I. Some papers are bags.
II. Some books are papers.
III. Some books are purses.
IV. Some papers are purses.

(*a*) Only I and IV (*b*) Only II and III
(*c*) Only I and II (*d*) Only I and III

**14. Statements:** All the bottles are boxes. All the boxes are bags. Some bags are trays.

**Conclusions:**

I. Some bottles are trays.
II. Some trays are boxes.
III. All the bottles are bags.
IV. Some trays are bags.

(*a*) Only III and IV (*b*) Only I and II
(*c*) Only II and III (*d*) Only I and IV

**15. Statements:** Some rats are cats. Some cats are dogs. No dog is cow.

**Conclusions:**

I. No cow is cat.
II. No dog is rat.
III. Some cats are rats.
IV. Some dogs are cats.

(*a*) Only I and IV (*b*) Only I and II
(*c*) Only I and III (*d*) Only III and IV

## EXPLANATORY ANSWERS

**1.** (*c*)

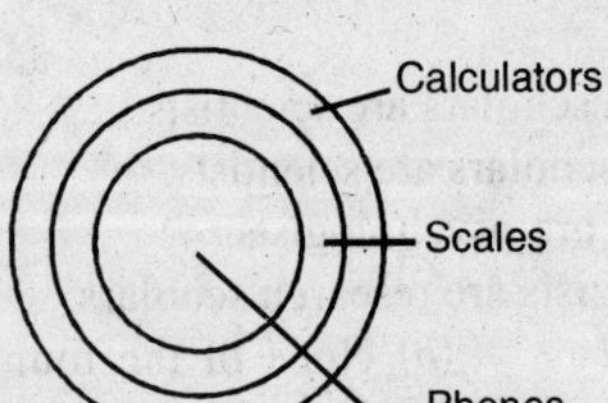


**2.** (*d*)

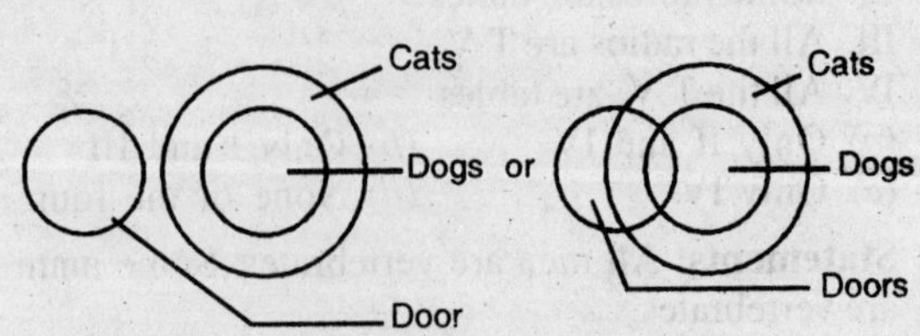

**3.** (*d*)

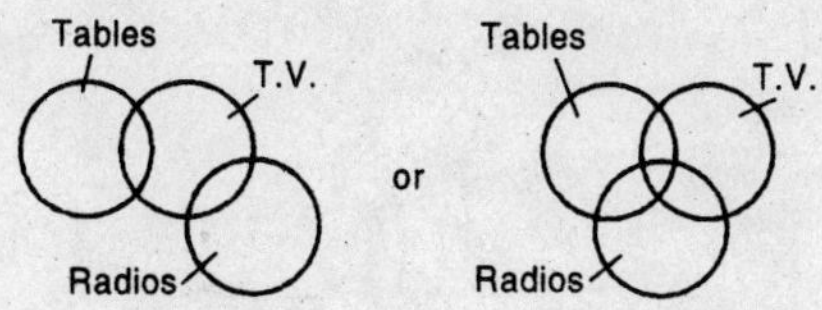


**4.** (*c*)

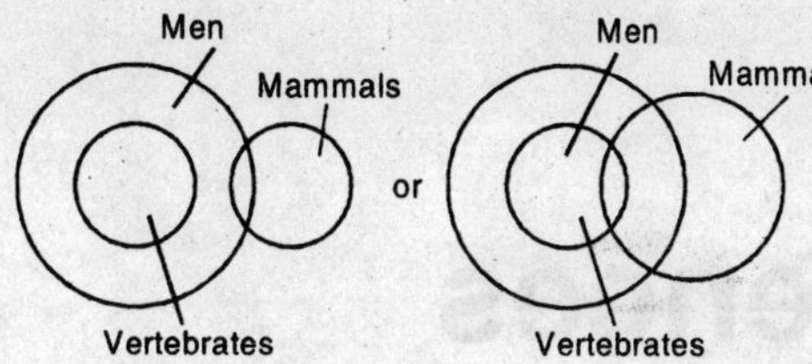


**5.** (*a*)

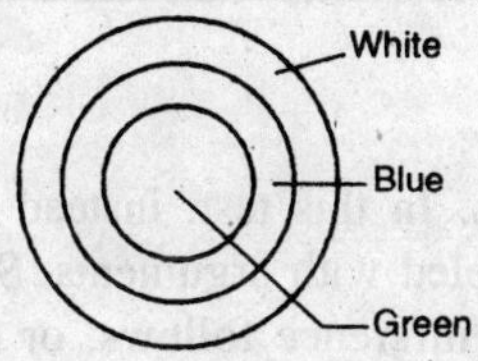


**6.** (*d*)

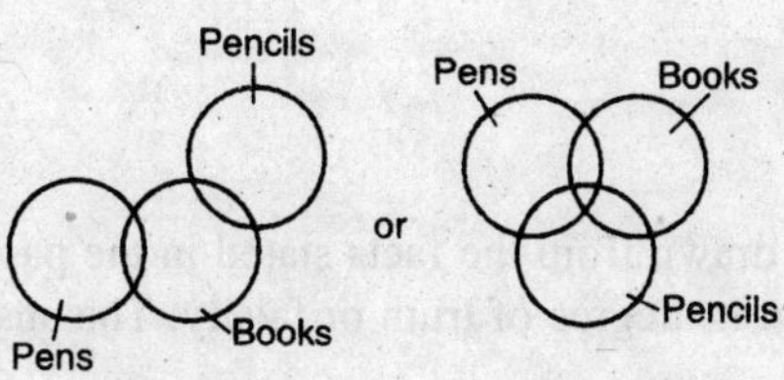


**7.** (*a*)

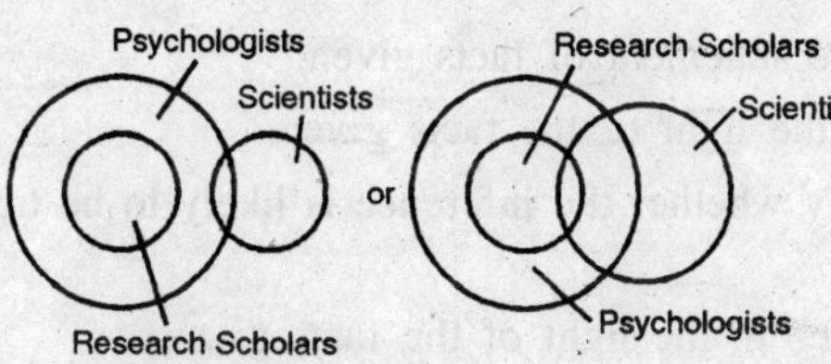


**8.** (*c*)

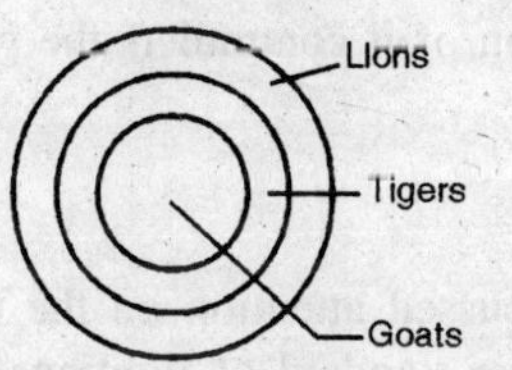


**9.** (*d*)

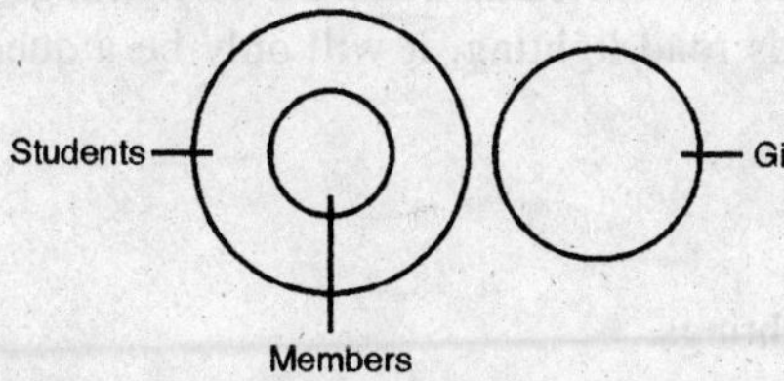


Since Members and Girls are disjoint, it follows that no members is girl. Since Members and Students have a common area, it follows that some student are members.

**10.** (*d*)

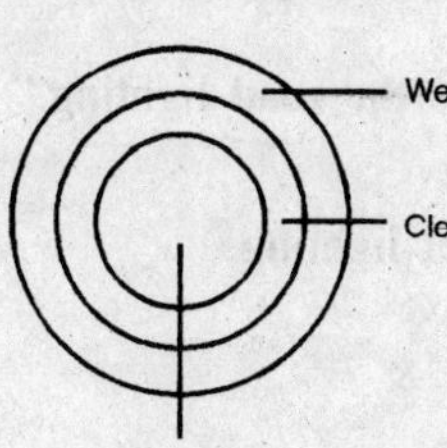


According to diagram, Clean and Soaps have a common area. So, some clean are soaps. Also wet and soaps have a common area. So, some wet are soaps.

**11.** (*d*)

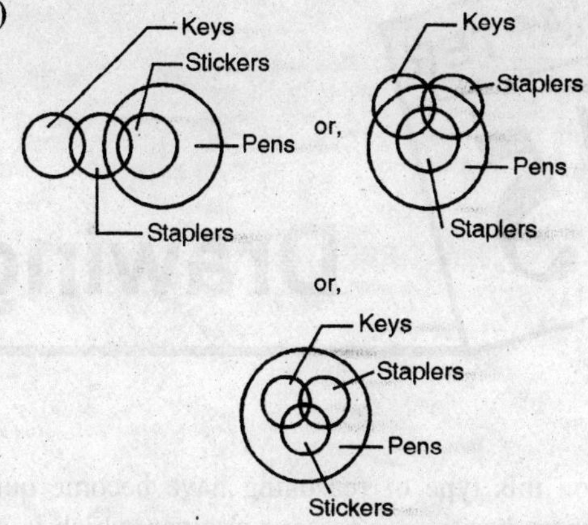


**12.** (*b*)

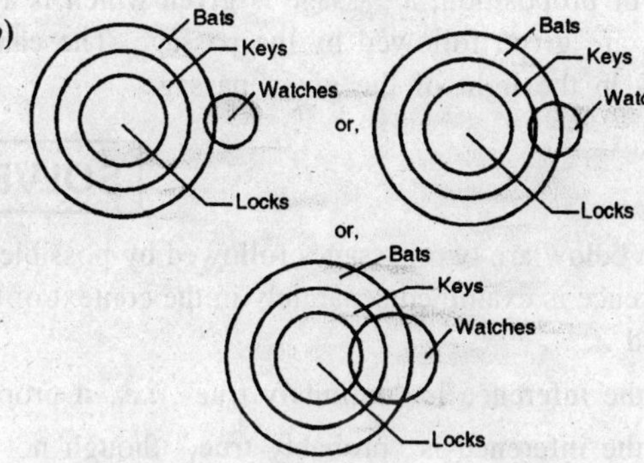


**13.** (*b*)

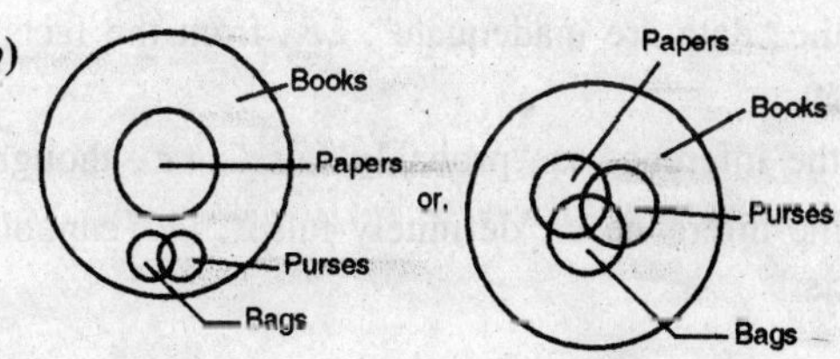


**14.** (*a*)

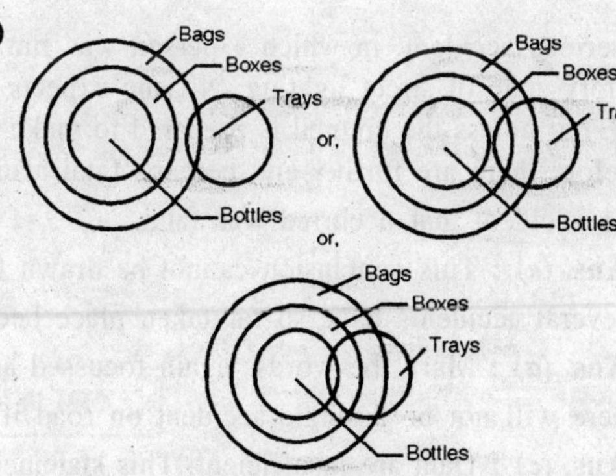


**15.** (*d*)

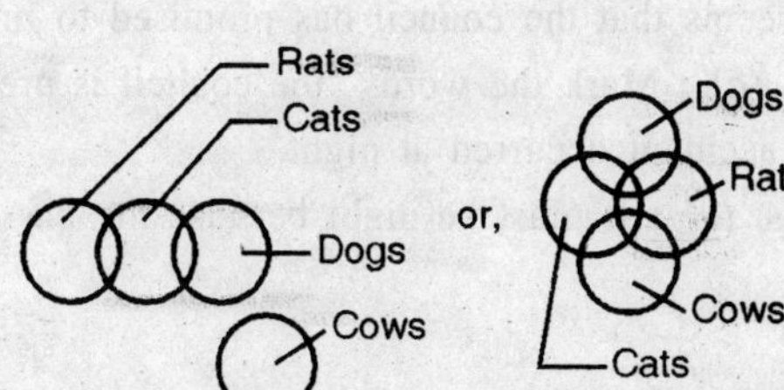

CHAPTER 15

# Drawing Inferences

Questions on this type of reasoning have become quite common in competitive examinations. In this test, instead of a statement or proposition, a passage is given which is a congregation of many propositions coupled with arguments. Some inferences are given followed by the passage. The candidate has to decide whether the given inference follows, or does not follow in the light of the given passage.

## SOLVED EXAMPLES

Given below are two passages followed by possible inferences which can be drawn from the facts stated in the passage. Each inference is examined separately in the context of the passage to decide upon its degree of truth or falsity. The answers are marked . . . .

(*a*) if the inference is "definitely true", *i.e.,* it properly follows from the statement of facts given.

(*b*) if the inference is "probably true," though not "definitely true" in the light of the facts given.

(*c*) if the "data are inadequate", *i.e.,* from the facts given you cannot say whether the inference is likely to be true or false.

(*d*) if the inference is "probably false", *i.e.,* though not "definitely false" in the light of the facts given.

(*e*) if the inference is "definitely false", *i.e.,* cannot possibly be drawn from the facts given or it contradicts the given facts.

### PASSAGE I

The serious accident, in which a person was run over by a car yesterday, has again focussed attention on the most unsatisfactory state of street lighting. No one expects side roads to be provided with the same standard of lightings as a main road, but unless the council is prepared to make good its promise as regards road lighting, it will only be a question of time before there are further and perhaps fatal accidents.

**1.** The accident that occurred was fatal.

**Ans. (*e*) :** This conclusion cannot be drawn from the facts given.

**2.** Several accidents have so far taken place because of unsatisfactory lightings.

**Ans. (*a*) :** Mark the words 'again focussed attention on the most . . . lighting'.

**3.** There will not be a single accident on road if they are satisfactorily illuminated.

**Ans. (*c*) :** Data are insufficient. This statement is not confirmed by the paragraph.

**4.** It seems that the council has promised to improve the state of lighting on side roads.

**Ans. (*a*) :** Mark the words "the council is prepared to make good its promise as regards the road lighting."

**5.** The accident occurred at night.

**Ans. (*a*) :** It must be night because the passage deals with unsatisfactory state of street lighting.

## MULTIPLE CHOICE QUESTIONS

**Directions :** *Below are given some passages followed by several possible inferences which can be drawn from the facts stated in each passage. You have to examine each inference separately in the context of the passage and decide upon its degree of truth or falsity.*

| Mark Answers | If you think... |
|---|---|
| *(a)* "Definitely True" | the inference properly follows from the statement of facts given. |
| *(b)* "Probably True" | the inference may be true in the light of the facts given but not definitely true. |
| *(c)* "Data Inadequate" | from the facts given it cannot be said whether the inference is likely to be true or false. |
| *(d)* "Probably False" | the inference is probably false in the light of the facts given though not definitely false. |
| *(e)* "Definitely False" | the inference cannot possibly be drawn from the facts given or it contradicts the given facts. |

### PASSAGE 1

Indian granite industry is in peril in the absence of a uniform policy from the state governments, despite the thrust given by liberalisation policies of the union government. Compared to the remarkable progress in the field during the last three years, the absence of matching policies by state governments had put granite quarry owners and others involved in the industry on the verge of collapse in the international market. The policies differed from state to state, had created problems as far as loyalty, dead rent and duration of lease were concerned.

1. Each state having granite quarry has set up its own rules which are contrary to the interest of the industry.
2. Till three years ago, granite production in India was not profitable.
3. The granite production is largely controlled by individuals.
4. The granite produced in India does not match with the quality of international level.
5. The union government's liberalisation policy became applicable to granite industry only during the last three years.

### PASSAGE 2

Steel production has always been burdened with costs much higher than in comparable plants overseas. On the one hand custom duty on almost all steel imports has been reduced, on the other excise duty has been raised. Domestic steel products are now uncompetitive which in turn has led to the demand that both the custom and excise rates should be reviewed to prevent sickness in the industry.

6. The steel industry in general is making losses as a fall out of the government policy.
7. The cost of production of steel in other countries is less than that in India.
8. India can compete with the foreign countries in re gard to the price of steel with a favourable government policy.
9. Foreign steel has become cheaper comparative to domestic steel.
10. The government is considering lowering of excise duty on steel products.

### PASSAGE 3

The annual domestic consumption of plastics in India is expected to grow between 2.5 and 3 million tonnes by the end of the Ist balls of the century from the current level of about one million tonnes. The global consumption of plastics now stands at 100 million tonnes. To sustain the present growth pattern, India would need two additional polymer plants of 1,000 tonnes every year till the turn of the Ist half of this century. Entrepreneurs should now think in lines of globalisation and promote projects of international capacity and they would have to look at technology transfer as well as upgradation and strategic and creative alliances.

11. The total domestic consumption of plastics in India is about one per cent of the global consumption.
12. At present India does not import plastics.
13. India lacks in technological capabilities in producing plastics.
14. There is an expected growth of about .2 per cent in the plastic consumption every year.
15. Potentially India can be one of the major players in the production of plastics in the international market.

## EXPLANATORY ANSWERS

**1.** *(a)* **:** The policies differed from state to state.

**2.** *(c)* **:** Remarkable progress during the last three years is mentioned in the paragraph but nothing suggests that the production was not profitable.

**3.** *(a)* **:** There is absence of a uniform policy from the state Governments.

**4.** *(c)* **:** According to the paragraph, absence of matching policies had put the quarry owners and others involved in the industry on the verge of collapse in the international market. Nothing is mentioned about the granite quality produced in India or of the international level.

**5. *(e)*:** The inference does not relate to the facts given in the statement.

**6. *(d)*:** Government policy alone may not be responsible for the losses. Cost or quality factor may also be responsible.

**7. *(c)*:** The paragraph mentions that steel production in India has always been burdened with costs much higher than in comparable plants overseas. But nowhere in the paragraph it is mentioned that the cost of production of steel is less in other countries.

**8. *(a)*:** If the government reviews its policy, India can definitely compete with the foreign countries in regard to the steel price.

**9. *(a)*:** Customs duty on almost all steel products has been reduced.

**10. *(b)*:** There is a demand that both the customs and excise rates should be reviewed.

**11. *(a)*:** The global consumption of plastics is 100 million tonnes and current level of consumption in India is 1 million tonnes.

**12. *(c)*:** The paragraph does not mention about the import or export of plastics.

**13. *(a)*:** Entrepreneurs would have to look at technology transfer as well as upgradation and strategic and creative alliances.

**14. *(a)*:** The expected growth by end of the Ist half of this century is between 2.5 and 3 million tonnes. India needs 2 additional polymer plants of 1,000 tonnes per year.

**15. *(a)*:** By thinking in lines of globalisation and promoting projects of international capacity India can be one of the major players in the production of plastics in the international market.

# CHAPTER 16 Trends

This type of questions are asked to assess the thinking pattern or mental trends of the candidate. These are simple questions but should be answered honestly and carefully.

## MULTIPLE CHOICE QUESTIONS

**Directions :** *In the questions given below four alternatives have been given below each one of them. You have to select the right alternative according to your mind and mark it in your answer sheet.*

**1.** I like pre-defined rules and regulations.
(*a*) Sometimes (*b*) No
(*c*) Yes (*d*) No idea

**2.** I found a purse full of money in college premise. I:
(*a*) donated the amount among poor
(*b*) gave it to the principal
(*c*) offered it at temple
(*d*) None of these

**3.** I am punctual regarding
(*a*) going to bed (*b*) time
(*c*) meals (*d*) dating

**4.** I was travelling on a boat which capsized. Firstly, I:
(*a*) rescued others (*b*) saved myself
(*c*) closed my eyes (*d*) cursed my luck

**5.** When someone asks you for help in odd situations then:
(*a*) you give him/her all possible help
(*b*) you promise him/her help
(*c*) you do not help him/her
(*d*) you turn a deaf ear

**6.** In case my wristwatch is out of order, I:
(*a*) would try to repair it myself
(*b*) would give it to watchmaker
(*c*) would buy a new watch
(*d*) would throw it away

**7.** Often I change my opinion in the last moment.
(*a*) Yes (*b*) No
(*c*) Sometimes (*d*) No idea

**8.** Generally I am extrovert and well behaved.
(*a*) Yes (*b*) No
(*c*) Sometimes (*d*) No idea

**9.** I like to use new technique of work.
(*a*) Yes (*b*) No
(*c*) Sometimes (*d*) No idea

**10.** When someone considers you wrong then:
(*a*) you do not react
(*b*) you consider him/her wrong
(*c*) you try to ward off the misunderstanding on proper occasion.
(*d*) you pick a fight

**11.** The secret of my success is:
(*a*) hard labour (*b*) awakening in night
(*c*) gossiping (*d*) luck

**12.** If you are a female and you are talking with a male:
(*a*) You hide your age
(*b*) You are afraid
(*c*) You talk without hesitation
(*d*) You avoid talks

**13.** I do like rules and regulations.
(*a*) Yes (*b*) No
(*c*) Sometimes (*d*) No idea

**14.** Excellent ideas come to my mind:
(*a*) while working alone
(*b*) while working in a group
(*c*) while in sleep
(*d*) while in bathroom

**15.** Whenever my little baby cries loudly, then I
(*a*) beat him/her
(*b*) feed milk to him/her
(*c*) make him/her sleep
(*d*) ask my husband to handle him/her

**16.** When I see a mad person, I :
(*a*) approach towards him/her
(*b*) maintain distance from him/her
(*c*) throw stone at him/her
(*d*) start laughing at him/her

**17.** While driving my car I offer lift to people who ask for lift.
(*a*) Always (*b*) Sometimes
(*c*) Never (*d*) If she is a girl

**18.** When someone tries to convince you then:
(*a*) You get convinced
(*b*) You do not get convinced
(*c*) You hear him/her passionately
(*d*) You turn a deaf ear

**19.** Whenever someone knocks on my closed door then firstly I
(*a*) open the door
(*b*) peep through the lens fitted in the door
(*c*) do not open the door
(*d*) yell at him/her

**20.** I speak to others about my expectation and dreams.
(*a*) Rarely (*b*) Often
(*c*) Sometimes (*d*) Never

**21.** Any dispute can be solved by :
(*a*) quarrelling (*b*) court
(*c*) dialogue (*d*) money

**22.** When I do any foolish work then :
(*a*) I feel ashamed (*b*) I feel proud of myself
(*c*) Nothing happens (*d*) I weep

**23.** If I were correspondent of any newspaper then I would write on the following subject :
(*a*) Cinema and theatre
(*b*) Political events
(*c*) Sports
(*d*) Stock market

**24.** If I were not human being then :
(*a*) I wish to be a bird (*b*) I wish to be a horse
(*c*) I wish to be God (*d*) Can't say

**25.** Suppose, you have worn a new shirt and your friend passed a comment that it is not looking good on you. You :
(*a*) will change the shirt immediately
(*b*) will take it lightly as it is your style
(*c*) will not change the shirt but feel offended
(*d*) will start quarrelling

**26.** I wish to live alone always.
(*a*) Yes (*b*) No
(*c*) Sometimes (*d*) Never

**27.** I want to spend my spare (extra) time :
(*a*) in reading interesting books
(*b*) in reading comics
(*c*) in viewing films
(*d*) in gossiping

**28.** Before doing any work I ask myself 'Is it appropriate'?
(*a*) Yes (*b*) No
(*c*) Sometimes (*d*) Never

**29.** If I see the GOD, I will ask for
(*a*) huge wealth (*b*) honesty
(*c*) love (*d*) heaven

**30.** People call you selfish.
(*a*) Always (*b*) Sometimes
(*c*) Never (*d*) No idea

**31.** While talking to friends I do not like to express my very personal matters.
(*a*) Yes (*b*) No
(*c*) Sometimes (*d*) Never

**32.** Consultation with others helps me to take a decision.
(*a*) Yes (*b*) No
(*c*) Sometimes (*d*) Never

**33.** After failure:
(*a*) One repents
(*b*) One tries again to succeed
(*c*) Nothing special is happened
(*d*) Nothing in life remains

**34.** I want to be convinced by arguments.
(*a*) Yes (*b*) No
(*c*) Sometimes (*d*) Never

## ANSWERS

| 1 | 2 | 3 | 4 | 5 | 6 | 7 | 8 | 9 | 10 |
|---|---|---|---|---|---|---|---|---|---|
| (*c*) | (*b*) | (*b*) | (*b*) | (*a*) | (*b*) | (*b*) | (*a*) | (*a*) | (*c*) |
| **11** | **12** | **13** | **14** | **15** | **16** | **17** | **18** | **19** | **20** |
| (*a*) | (*c*) | (*a*) | (*a*) | (*b*) | (*b*) | (*b*) | (*a*) | (*b*) | (*a*) |
| **21** | **22** | **23** | **24** | **25** | **26** | **27** | **28** | **29** | **30** |
| (*c*) | (*a*) | (*c*) | (*a*) | (*b*) | (*c*) | (*a*) | (*a*) | (*c*) | (*c*) |
| **31** | **32** | **33** | **34** | | | | | | |
| (*c*) | (*a*) | (*b*) | (*a*) | | | | | | |

# CHAPTER 17 Critical

In this type of reasoning, a statement is given and assumptions are drawn from it. An assumption is something assumed, supposed and taken for granted. The implicity of the two assumptions is in question. The implication means the hidden meaning, something which is derived from and as such based upon the statement.

## MULTIPLE CHOICE QUESTIONS

**Directions (Qs. 1 to 6):** *In each question below are given two statements followed by two conclusions numbered I and II. You have to take the two given statements to be true even if they seem to be at variance from commonly known facts and then decide which of the given conclusions logically follows from the two given statements, disregarding commonly known facts. Read both the statements and—*

*Give answer (a) if only conclusion I follows; give answer (b) if only conclusion II follows; give answer (c) if either I or II follows; give answer (d) if neither I nor II follows and give answer (e) if both I and II follows.*

**1.** *Statements* *I*: All tomatoes are red.
*II*: All grapes are tomatoes.
*Conclusions* *I*: All grapes are red.
*II*: Some tomatoes are grapes.

**2.** *Statements* *I*: All painters are smilling.
*II*: Some authors are painters.
*Conclusions* *I*: All smiling authors are painters.
*II*: Some authors are smiling.

**3.** *Statements* *I*: All peons in this office are efficient.
*II*: Ramu is not efficient.
*Conclusions* *I*: Ramu is not peon in this office.
*II*: Ramu should be more efficient.

**4.** *Statements* *I*: All weavers are hard working.
*II*: No hard working men are foolish.
*Conclusions* *I*: No weavers are foolish.
*II*: Some foolish are weavers.

**5.** *Statements* *I*: All fishes are cars.
*II*: All cars are vegetables.
*Conclusions* *I*: Some vegetables are cars.
*II*: Some vegetables are fishes.

**6.** *Statements* *I*: Some dogs are pups.
*II*: All horses are pups.

**Directions (Qs. 7 to 10):** *In each question below is given a statement followed by three assumptions number I, II and III. An assumption is something supposed or taken for granted. You have to consider the statement along with the assumptions and decide which of the assumptions is implicit in the statement. Then decide which of the alternatives is the correct answer.*

**7.** *Statement :*
"Use Riya Cold Cream for fair complexion"—an advertisement.
*Assumptions :*
*I.* People like to use cream for fair complexion.
*II.* People are easily fooled.
*III.* People respond to advertisements.
(*a*) Only I is implicit.
(*b*) Only II is implicit.
(*c*) Only I and III are implicit.
(*d*) Only I and II are implicit.
(*e*) All are implicit.

**8.** *Statement :*
"Slogans against smoking in office should be put on the notice board"—an employee in an office suggests.
*Assumptions :*
*I.* The employee felt that his suggestion will be considered.
*II.* People smoke in the office.
*III.* Some people will stop smoking after reading the slogans.
(*a*) Only I is implicit.
(*b*) Only I and II are implicit.
(*c*) Only II and III are implicit.

(*d*) None is implicit.
(*e*) All are implicit.

**9.** *Statement :*
"I want to present him a book on techniques of yoga on his birthday"—A tells B.
*Assumptions :*
*I.* A and B will be invited for the birthday celebrations.
*II.* The person to whom the book is to be presented, is not keeping good health.
*III.* Book is the best gift for birthdays.
(*a*) Only I and II are implicit.
(*b*) Only II and III are implicit.
(*c*) Only I and III are implicit.
(*d*) None is implicit.
(*e*) All are implicit

**10.** *Statement :*
Keeping in view the financial constraint, the management institution has decided to charge at the time of providing employment in various organisations, a placement fee of ₹ 25000 from the organisation in which the student will be provided the employment.
*Assumptions :*
*I.* It will help in increasing the demand of the students belonging to the management institution.
*II.* The amount collected in this way will be purposeful.
*III.* It may be possible that the organisation providing employment may select less number of students in future.
(*a*) None follows.
(*b*) Only II and III follow.
(*c*) Only I follows.
(*d*) Only I and II follow.
(*e*) None of these

## EXPLANATORY ANSWERS

**1. (*e*) :** When all tomatoes are red and all grapes are tomatoes, then all grapes are also red. When all grapes are tomatoes, then some tomatoes must be grapes. Therefore, both conclusions I and II are correct.

**2. (*b*) :** When all painters are smiling and some authors are painters, then some authors are smiling. Therefore, only conclusion II is correct.

**3. (*a*) :** When all the peons of the office are efficient, then Ramu cannot be a peon in this office. Therefore, only conclusion I is correct.

**4. (*a*) :** When all weavers are hardworking and no hardworking men are foolish, then no weavers are foolish. Therefore, only conclusion I is correct.

**5. (*e*) :** When all fishes are cars and all cars are vegetables, then all fishes will naturally be vegetables. This means that some vegetables are fishes. And when all cars are vegetables, then some vegetables will be cars naturally. Therefore, both the conclusions I and II are correct.

**6. (*d*) :** No relationship can be established between the two statements. Therefore, neither conclusion I nor conclusion II is correct.

**7. (*c*) :** The advertisement itself denotes that people like to use cream for fair complexion and they do respond to advertisements. Advertisements are for awareness of the product not for fooling people.

**8. (*e*) :** Suggestion for putting up the notice is made because some people must be smoking in office. Notice board is read by people in office and some may stop smoking after reading the slogans.

**9. (*c*) :** According to A presents are best gifts for birthdays and when A has bought the book he expects to be invited for the birthday celebration. Nothing is mentioned about health of the birthday person.

**10. (*b*) :** The amount collected will lessen the financial constraint and there is every possibility for selecting less number of students because of the fee charged.

CHAPTER 18

# Emotional Intelligence

Emotional intelligence (EI) refers to the ability to perceive, control, and evaluate emotions. Emotional intelligence (EI) is the area of cognitive ability involving traits and social skills that facilitate interpersonal behaviour. Intelligence can be broadly defined as the capacity for goal-oriented adaptive behaviour; emotional intelligence focuses on the aspects of intelligence that govern self-knowledge and social adaptation.

Emotional Intelligence that is also called Emotional Intelligence Quotient or (EQ) narrates the capability, capacity, or deftness to understand. It evaluates and manages one's emotions.

## MULTIPLE CHOICE QUESTIONS

**Directions:** *Answer the following questions by selecting the appropriate option.*

**1.** In my group of friends, I am generally aware of how each person feels about the other people in our social circle.
(*a*) Strongly Agree (*b*) Agree
(*c*) Disagree (*d*) Strongly Disagree

**2.** When I am upset, I can usually pinpoint exactly why I am distressed.
(*a*) Strongly Agree (*b*) Agree
(*c*) Disagree (*d*) Strongly Disagree

**3.** While there are some things that I would like to change, I generally like who I am.
(*a*) Strongly Agree (*b*) Agree
(*c*) Disagree (*d*) Strongly Disagree

**4.** When I make mistakes, I often berate and criticize myself and my abilities.
(*a*) Often (*b*) Sometimes
(*c*) Rarely (*d*) Almost Never

**5.** I feel uncomfortable in emotionally charged situations.
(*a*) Strongly Agree (*b*) Agree
(*c*) Disagree (*d*) Strongly Disagree

**6.** I tend to avoid confrontations. When I am involved in a confrontation, I become extremely anxious.
(*a*) Strongly Agree (*b*) Agree
(*c*) Disagree (*d*) Strongly Disagree

**7.** I am generally aloof and detached until I really get to know a person.
(*a*) Strongly Agree (*b*) Agree
(*c*) Disagree (*d*) Strongly Disagree

**8.** I tend to overreact to minor problems.
(*a*) Often (*b*) Somtimes
(*c*) Rarely (*d*) Almost Never

**9.** I feel confident about my own skills, talents, and abilities.
(*a*) Strongly Agree (*b*) Agree
(*c*) Disagree (*d*) Strongly Disagree

**10.** I would describe myself as a good judge of character.
(*a*) Strongly Agree (*b*) Agree
(*c*) Disagree (*d*) Strongly Disagree

**11.** When I am facing an unpleasant task, I tend to:
(*a*) Make a plan and work on it a little each day
(*b*) Get it over with as soon as possible
(*c*) Put it off until the last minute
(*d*) Don't do it at all

**12.** During a heated argument, I am more likely to:
(*a*) Stop the fight and agree to a short break before resuming the discussion.
(*b*) Shut down and stop responding to the other person.
(*c*) Give in and apologize in order to quickly end the argument.
(*d*) Start insulting the other person.

**13.** When making an important decision, I tend to:
(*a*) Follow my instincts
(*b*) Rely on direction from other people
(*c*) Go with the easiest option
(*d*) Guess randomly

**14.** Which of the following statements best describes you?
(*a*) I have an easy time making friends and getting to know new people.
(*b*) I get along well with others, but I have to really get to know someone before they become a true friend.
(*c*) I find it difficult to meet people and make friends.
(*d*) I cannot make friends.

**15.** You have invested a lot of time and energy into a project for one of your classes. While you feel confident about your work, your instructor gives you a C+ on the project. How do you deal with this situation?
(*a*) Decide the class is stupid and stop putting forth your best efforts.
(*b*) Berate and criticize your own work.
(*c*) Confront the instructor and ask for a better grade.
(*d*) Think about ways you could improve the project and apply these ideas to future schoolwork.

**16.** One of your best friends has suffered a miscarriage. How do you respond?
(*a*) Allow your friend to express her feelings and offer your support.
(*b*) Spend time with her, but avoid talking about her loss.
(*c*) Convince her to go out with some friends to get her mind off it.
(*d*) Give her some time to herself.

**17.** One of your co-workers has a habit that annoys you. The problem seems to be getting worse each day. How do you respond?
(*a*) Tell your co-worker what is bothering you.
(*b*) Make a complaint about the behaviour to your supervisor.
(*c*) Talk about your co-worker behind his back.
(*d*) Suffer in silence.

**18.** You've been feeling stressed out at work and haven't finished projects as quickly as you should. When your boss suddenly assigns you another large project, how do you feel?
(*a*) Anxious about getting all the work done.
(*b*) Overwhelmed by the task before you.
(*c*) Angry that your boss hasn't noticed how overworked you are.
(*d*) Depressed and sure that you can never finish it all.

**19.** If I am scheduled to meet a loved one at a certain time and that person is late, I get worried and eventually start to panic:
(*a*) Frequently (*b*) Sometimes
(*c*) Rarely (*d*) Never

**20.** Others do not want to spend time with me in public because my behaviour embarrasses them.
(*a*) Frequently (*b*) Sometimes
(*c*) Rarely (*d*) Never

**21.** I prevent being in situations where I need to show compassion and affection because I feel uncomfortable comforting others.
(*a*) Frequently (*b*) Sometimes
(*c*) Rarely (*d*) Never

**22.** When I am angry, I do not care about what I say or do and end up saying and doing things I regret later and need to apologize for.
(*a*) Frequently (*b*) Sometimes
(*c*) Rarely (*d*) Never

**23.** I feel frequently depressed and unhappy without really knowing why.
(*a*) Frequently (*b*) Sometimes
(*c*) Rarely (*d*) Never

**24.** If others point out my mistakes or give me negative feedback about myself, I feel ashamed, embarrassed and then become offensive and angry.
(*a*) Frequently (*b*) Sometimes
(*c*) Rarely (*d*) Never

**25.** Crying makes me feel better so I frequently cry when I am angry, ashamed, or embarrassed.
(*a*) Frequently (*b*) Sometimes
(*c*) Rarely (*d*) Never

## ANSWERS

| 1 | 2 | 3 | 4 | 5 | 6 | 7 | 8 | 9 | 10 |
|---|---|---|---|---|---|---|---|---|---|
| (*b*) | (*b*) | (*a*) | (*b*) | (*d*) | (*d*) | (*c*) | (*d*) | (*a*) | (*b*) |
| **11** | **12** | **13** | **14** | **15** | **16** | **17** | **18** | **19** | **20** |
| (*a*) | (*a*) | (*a*) | (*a*) | (*d*) | (*a*) | (*a*) | (*a*) | (*c*) | (*d*) |
| **21** | **22** | **23** | **24** | **25** | | | | | |
| (*d*) | (*d*) | (*d*) | (*d*) | (*d*) | | | | | |

CHAPTER 19

# Social Intelligence

Questions on social intelligence are asked to assess the common sense of the candidate in various social situations.

## MULTIPLE CHOICE QUESTIONS

**Directions :** *Each of the following questions is followed by four alternatives. Select the most appropriate answer.*

**1.** In the examination hall, you find that your question paper is too tough to be answered satisfactorily by you. The best thing you can do is:
(*a*) try cheating from your neighbouring candidate.
(*b*) leave the paper and walk out.
(*c*) try attempting those questions first of which you know something.
(*d*) complain to the examiner about the toughness of the question paper.

**2.** Your best friend is annoyed with you for certain reasons. You will :
(*a*) try your best to reason out your friend's annoyance.
(*b*) go out and make new friends.
(*c*) show indifference.
(*d*) remind the friend of your good friendship.

**3.** You were invited to a party, but on the day of the party you are informed that the party has been cancelled. You will :
(*a*) try to find out the reason for its cancellation.
(*b*) decide that you will never go to that place ever again.
(*c*) not discuss the matter with anyone.
(*d*) hold the party at your place instead.

**4.** You find that the cooking gas cylinder is leaking. The first thing you would do is :
(*a*) switch off the light.
(*b*) close the knob of the cylinder.
(*c*) call the fire brigade for help.
(*d*) alert all the members at home.

**5.** While returning home from a far away place you find that your pocket has been picked. You will :
(*a*) try to hitch-hike to home.
(*b*) hire a taxi and pay on reaching home.
(*c*) go to the nearest police station and lodge an FIR.
(*d*) call home and ask someone to pick you from the place you made the phone call.

**6.** Your friend has not invited you to his marriage party, you will :
(*a*) ignore the whole affair.
(*b*) send him your best wishes.
(*c*) attend the ceremony.
(*d*) hold it against him.

**7.** You are interviewed for a new job. Which of the following questions is most important to you?
(*a*) Remuneration you will be paid.
(*b*) Opportunities for promotion.
(*c*) Scope to develop your ideas and use them to improve the working of the organisation.
(*d*) All the above are equally important.

**8.** You are walking down the street and suddenly you see two hundred-rupee notes on the pavement. What action will you take?
(*a*) Give the money to beggar.
(*b*) Pocket it yourself.
(*c*) Deposit it in the nearest police station.
(*d*) Leave it as it is.

## ANSWERS

| 1 | 2 | 3 | 4 | 5 | 6 | 7 | 8 |
|---|---|---|---|---|---|---|---|
| (*c*) | (*a*) | (*a*) | (*b*) | (*b*) | (*b*) | (*d*) | (*c*) |

## INDEXING ADDRESS MATCHING

**Directions :** *In each question below a combination of name and address is given in the first column at the left, followed by four such combinations, one each under the columns (a), (b), (c) and (d). You have to find out the combination which is exactly the same as the combination in the first column. The number of that column which contains that combination is the answer. If all the combinations are different, the answer is '(e)'.*

**1.** Triveni Atma
Opp Lal Banglow
Varanasi -221002

(*a*) Triveni Atma
Opp Lal Bangalow
Varanasi -221002

(*b*) Triveni Atma
Opp Lal Banglow
Varanasi -220012

(*c*) Triveni Atma
Opp Lal Banglow
Varanasi -221002

(*d*) Triveni Athma
Opp Lal Banglow
Varanasi -221002

**2.** Tara Lal Appa
Javagal street
Calicat 673005

(*a*) Tara Lal Appa
Javagal Street
Calicat 673005

(*b*) Tara Lal Appa
Javagal street
Calicut 673005

(*c*) Tara Lal Appa
Javagal street
Calicat 670035

(*d*) Tara Lal Appa
Javagal streat
Calicat 673005

**3.** Iqbal Rehman
Bhandri Gali
Post Box No -3097

(*a*) Iqbal Rehman
Bhandri Ghali
Post Box No -3097

(*b*) Iqbal Rehman
Bhandri Gali
Post Box No -3097

(*c*) Iqbal Rehman
Bhandri Gali
Post Box no -3097

(*d*) Iqbal Rahman
Bhandri Gali
Post Box No -3097

**4.** Jaganpa Shinde
Christ phot co.
Tel no -27363

(*a*) Jaganpa Shinde
Christ photo co.
Tel no -27363

(*b*) Jaganpa Shinde
Christ phot co.
Tel no -27363

(*c*) Jaganpa Shinde
Christ phot co.
Tel no -273633

(*d*) Jaganna Shinde
Christ phot co.
Tel no -27363

**5.** N.R. Savitri
Giri Girls hostal
Anapuram-167951

(*a*) N.R. Savitri
Giri Girls hostal
Anapuram-167951

(*b*) N.R. Savitri
Giri Girls hostel
Anapuram-167951

(*c*) N.R. Savitri
Giri Girls hostal
Anapuram-167851

(*d*) N.R. Savithri
Giri Girls hostal
Anapuram-167951

**6.** Madam Brulopher
Jung villa
Banjaram Hills

(*a*) Madam Bruloper
Jung villa
Banjaram Hills

(*b*) Madam Brulopher
Jung villa
Banjaram Hill

(*c*) Madam Brulopher
Jung Villa
Banjaram Hills

(*d*) Madam Brulopher
Jung villa
Banjaram Hills

**7.** Samartha sen
C 20/05 Guftga Bldg
B. No. - 1631

(*a*) Samartha sen
C 20/05 Guftga Blg
B. No. - 1631

(*b*) Samartha sen
C 200 Guftga Bldg
B. No. - 1631

(*c*) Samartha sen
C 20/05 Guftga Bldg
B. No. - 1631

(*d*) Samartha sen
C 20/05 Guflga Bldg
B. No. - 1631

**8.** Phiroz Gerabl
Harmit palace
Samaita nagar

(*a*) Phiroz Gerabi
Harmit palace
Samaita nagar

(*b*) Phiroz Gerabl
Harmit place
Samaita nagar

(*c*) Phiroz Gerabl
Harmit palace
Samaita nager

(*d*) Phiroz Gherabl
Harmit palace
Samaita nagar

**9.** Nitu gajadhar
Shersing Haveli
Jaipur -302006

(*a*) Nitu gajadhar
Shersing Haveli
Jaipur -302006

(*b*) Nitu gajadar
Shersing Haveli
Jaipur -302006

(*c*) Nitu gajadhar
Shersing Haveli
Jaipur -303006

(*d*) Nitu Gajadhar
Shersing Haveli
Jaipur -302006

## ANSWERS

| 1 | 2 | 3 | 4 | 5 | 6 | 7 | 8 | 9 |
|---|---|---|---|---|---|---|---|---|
| (*c*) | (*a*) | (*b*) | (*b*) | (*a*) | (*d*) | (*c*) | (*d*) | (*a*) |

CHAPTER 20

# Venn Diagrams

In these type of questions diagrammatic representation presents a logical illustration of particular class or statements based on which the questions are asked. A clear view of the diagram makes the concept clear for attempting such questions.

## SOLVED EXAMPLE

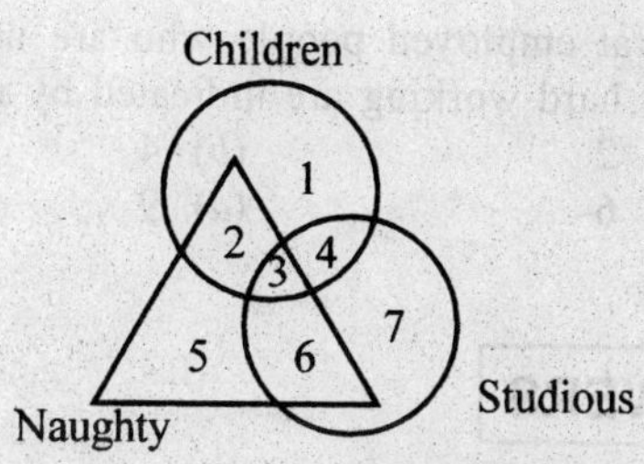


Study the above diagram and specify the region representing children who are naughty as well as studious.

(*a*) 3 and 6 (*b*) 2 and 4
(*c*) only 3 (*d*) only 4

**Ans. (*c*) :** The explanation depicting children who are naughty as well as studious will be :

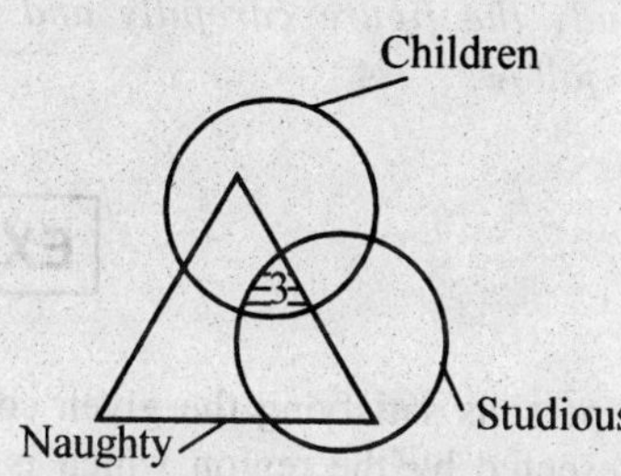


It is now clear that only region 3 represents all the three classes.

## MULTIPLE CHOICE QUESTIONS

**Directions (Qs. 1–3) :** *In the following diagram, there are three figures interlocking each other – a rectangle, a square and a triangle. Each figure represents the class mentioned against it.*

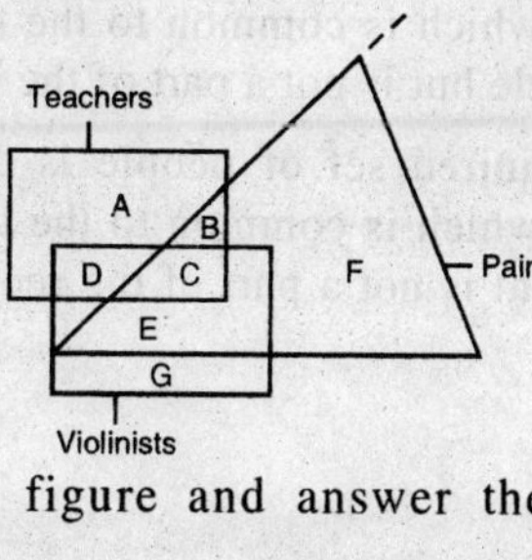


Study the figure and answer the questions that follows.

**1.** Teachers who are painters but not violinists are represented by

(*a*) B (*b*) C
(*c*) D (*d*) F

**2.** The region which represents painters and violinists but not teachers, is denoted by

(*a*) B (*b*) D
(*c*) E (*d*) F

**3.** Which letter represents teachers who are painters as well as violinists?

(*a*) B (*b*) C
(*c*) D (*d*) E

**Directions (Qs. 4–6) :** *In the figure given below, there are three interesting circles each representing certain section of people. Different regions are marked a-g. Read the statements in each of the following questions and choose the letter of the region which correctly represents the statements?*

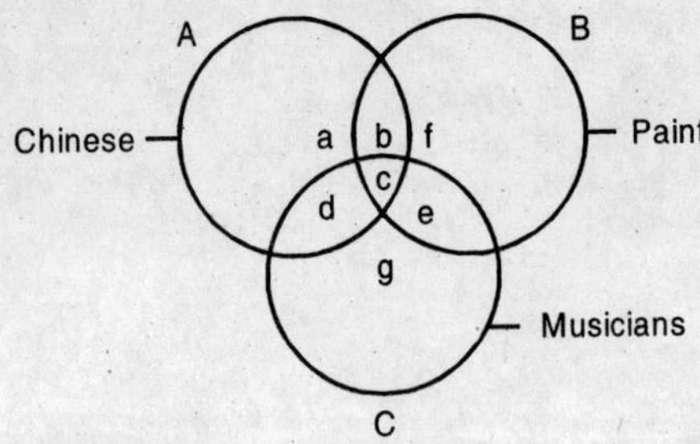


4. Chinese who are painters but not musicians?
   (*a*) b (*b*) c
   (*c*) d (*d*) g

5. Chinese who are musicians but not painters.
   (*a*) d (*b*) c
   (*c*) b (*d*) a

6. Painters who are neither Chinese nor musicians.
   (*a*) b (*b*) c
   (*c*) f (*d*) g

**Directions (Qs. 7–10) :** *In the following figure, the circle stands for employed, the square stands for hard-working, the triangle stands for rural and the rectangle stands for intelligent. Study the figure carefully and answer the questions that follow.*

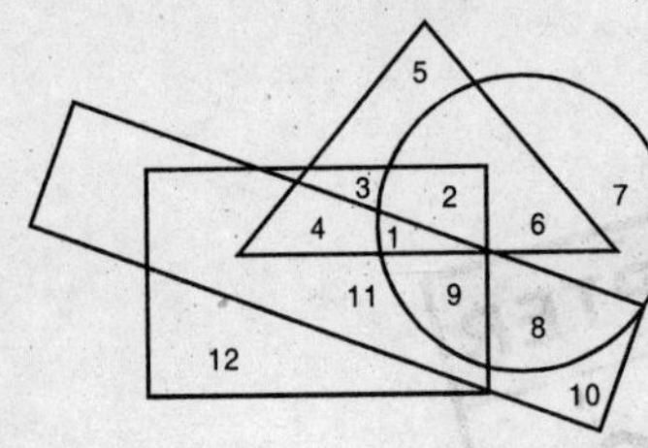


7. Rural employed people who are neither intelligent nor hard-working are indicated by region.
   (*a*) 10 (*b*) 9
   (*c*) 6 (*d*) 4

8. Unemployed rural hard-working and intelligent people are indicated by region.
   (*a*) 1 (*b*) 2
   (*c*) 3 (*d*) 4

9. Rural people who are hard-working and employed but not intelligent are indicated by region.
   (*a*) 1 (*b*) 2
   (*c*) 3 (*d*) 4

10. Rural employed people who are neither intelligent nor hard-working are indicated by region.
    (*a*) 2 (*b*) 4
    (*c*) 6 (*d*) 9

## EXPLANATORY ANSWERS

**1. (*a*) :** The persons satisfying the given conditions are represented by the region which is common to the rectangle and the triangle but not the square i.e. B.

**2. (*c*) :** The persons satisfying the given conditions are represented by the region which is common to the triangle and the square but is not a part of the rectangle i.e. E.

**3. (*b*) :** The required set of persons is represented by the letter denoting the region common to the rectangle, triangle and the square i.e. C.

**4. (*a*) :** The required region is the one which is common to the circles A and B and lies outside circle C i.e. b.

**5. (*a*) :** The required region is the one which is common to the circles A and C but is not a part of circle B i.e. d.

**6. (*c*) :** The required region is the one which lies inside the circle B but is not a part of either circle A or circle C i.e. f.

**7. (*c*) :** The required set of people is represented by the region which is common to the triangle and circle but is not a part of either the rectangle or the square i.e. 6.

**8. (*d*) :** The required set of people is represented by the region which lies outside the circle and is common to the triangle, square and rectangle i.e. 4.

**9. (*b*) :** The required set of people is represented by the region which is common to the triangle, square and circle but is not a part of the rectangle i.e. 2.

**10. (*c*) :** The required set of people is denoted by the region which is common to the triangle and the circle but is not a part of the rectangle i.e. 2.

NON-VERBAL

CHAPTER 1

# Series/Figural Series

## MISSING SERIES

This form of series is almost identical to the one mentioned earlier. Here too are given two sets of figures, the Problem Figures and the Answer Figures. The problem figures follow a particular pattern of movement which constitute the series. The only difference from the earlier mentioned set of series is that instead of depicting the last figure that continues the pattern here one of the middle figures needs to be depicted from-the answer figures. This type needs a little more concentration and brain work as the continuity is broken and has to be set right. Understand the set up of elements, pattern and figures in each set and try different styles and rules to find the answer.

## SOLVED EXAMPLES

In each question below there are two sets of figures, first problem figures and then follows the answer figures. One of the answer figures should fit into the box where a question mark is placed in the set of problem figures. The letter of the answer figure which should be considered as forming the series and should be placed in the question marked box is the answer.

**1. Problem Figures**

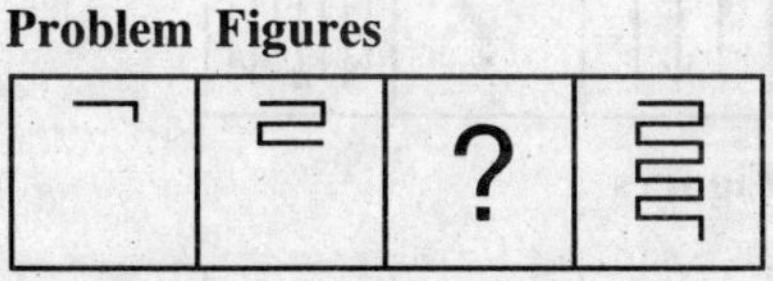


**Answer Figures**

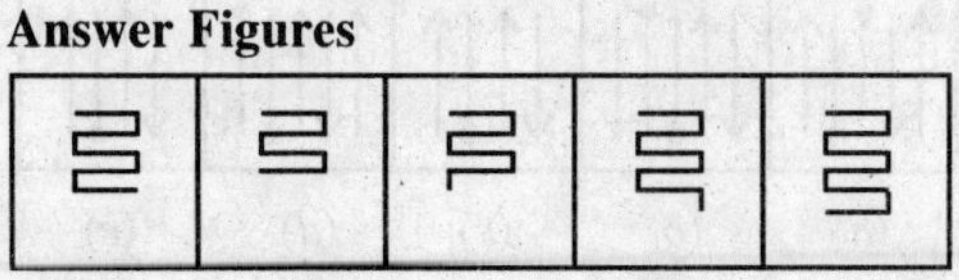

(a) (b) (c) (d) (e)

**Answer (*a*) :** Observe the set of problem figures. The design made of straight lines is becoming bigger at each step. In first figure there are two lines segments and in second figure three lines segments are increased. To continue the pattern four line segments should be increased so that further five line segments added in the last figure can complete the series. Answer figure (*a*) contains four more line segments and hence, is the right answer.

**2. Problem Figures**

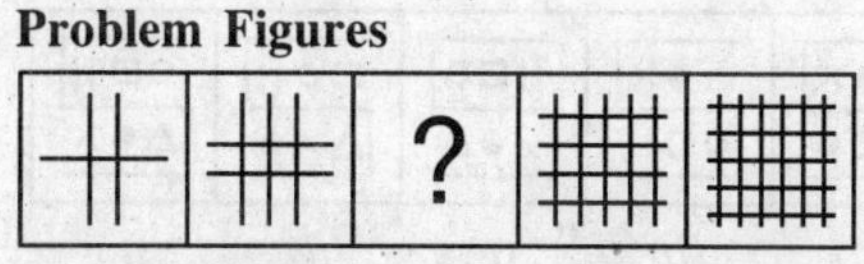


**Answer Figures**

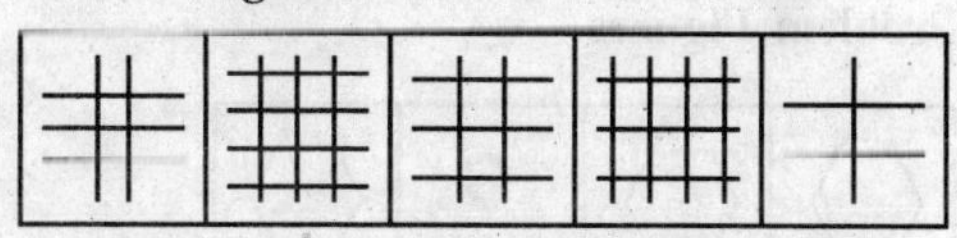

(a) (b) (c) (d) (e)

**Answer (*d*) :** Observe that at each step one vertical and one horizontal line is added. By this rule answer figure (*a*) fits in the question marked space. Note that answer figure (*b*) can also be considered in absence of option (*d*), but here the point to be noted is that the number of horizontal lines is one more than the number of vertical lines. So, answer figure (*d*), is the answer.

**3. Problem Figures**

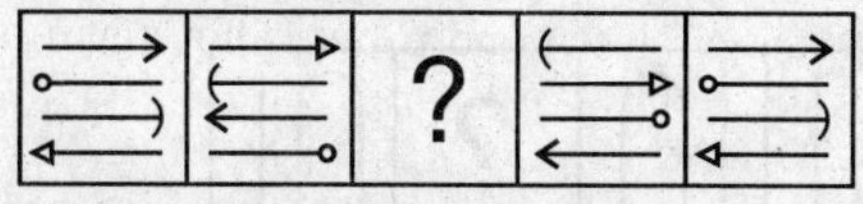


**Answer Figures**

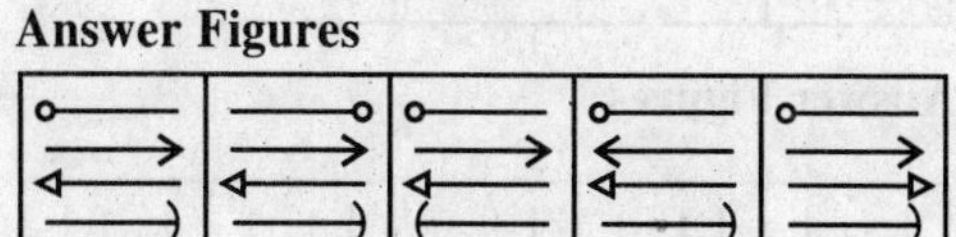

(a) (b) (c) (d) (e)

**Answer (*a*) :** Note that the fourth or the bottom element is made the first or the topmost element in the next figure. Similarly, the third element is made the second, the second element made the fourth and the first element made the third. Also, the direction of the elements is changed at each step. By the process mentioned above, answer figure A is the right choice to be considered as forming the series.

## MULTIPLE CHOICE QUESTIONS

**Directions :** *In each of these questions, there are two sets of figures. The figures placed first are Problem Figures, and those follows are Answer Figures indicated by the letters (a), (b), (c), (d) and (e). A series is established if one of the five Answer Figures is placed at the question-marked space. Figures form a series if they change from left to right according to some specific rule. The letter of the Answer Figure which should be placed in the question-marked space is the answer. All the figures, i.e. three Problem Figures and one Answer Figure placed in the question-marked space should be considered as forming the series.*

**1. Problem Figures**

**Answer Figures**

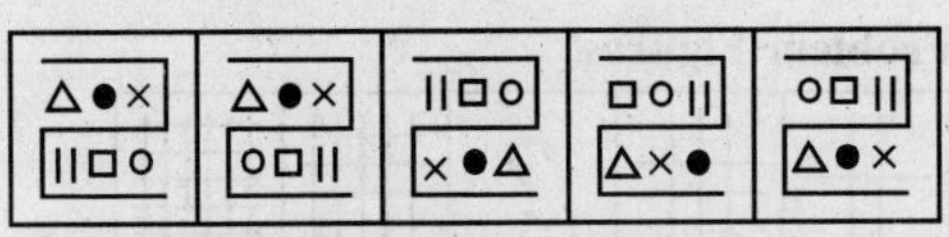

(*a*) (*b*) (*c*) (*d*) (*e*)

**2. Problem Figures**

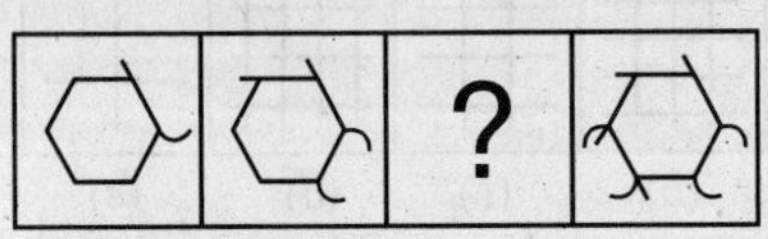

**Answer Figures**

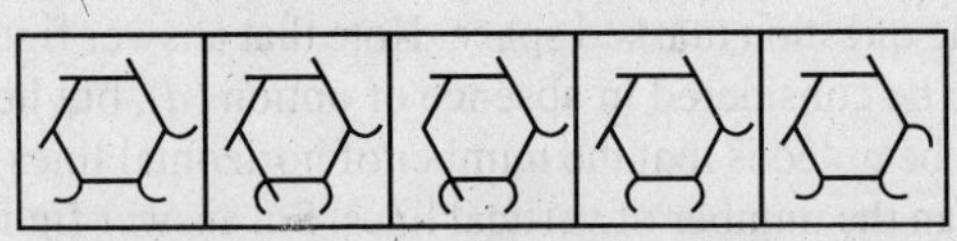

(*a*) (*b*) (*c*) (*d*) (*e*)

**3. Problem Figures**

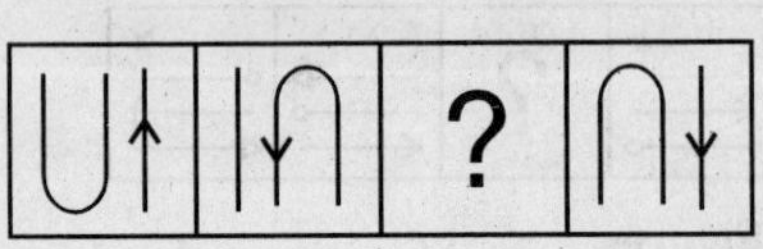

**Answer Figures**

(*a*) (*b*) (*c*) (*d*) (*e*)

**4. Problem Figures**

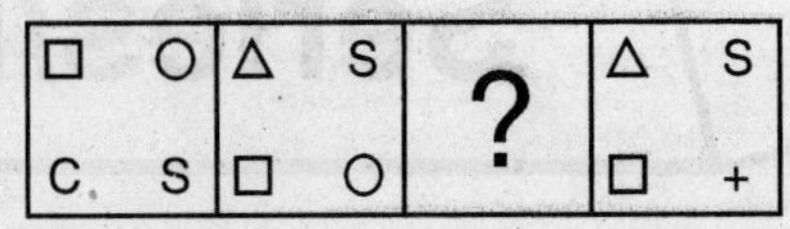

**Answer Figures**

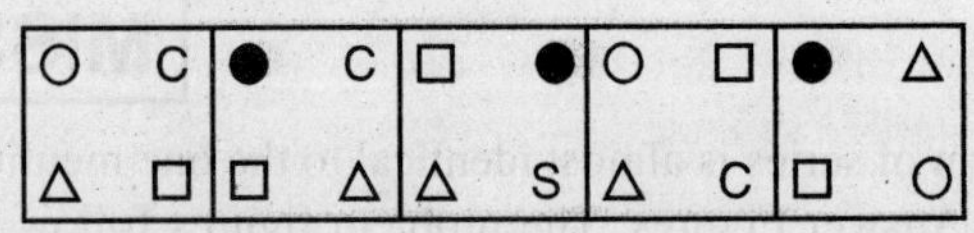

(*a*) (*b*) (*c*) (*d*) (*e*)

**5. Problem Figures**

**Answer Figures**

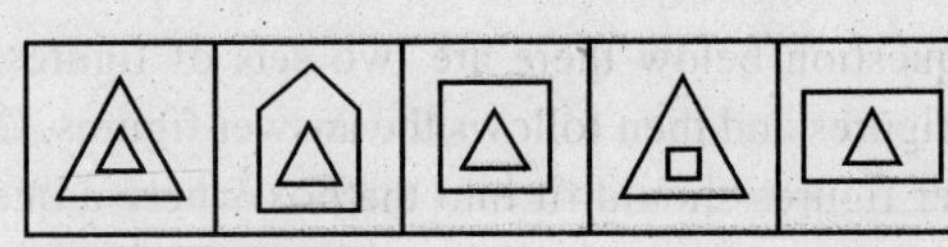

(*a*) (*b*) (*c*) (*d*) (*e*)

**6. Problem Figures**

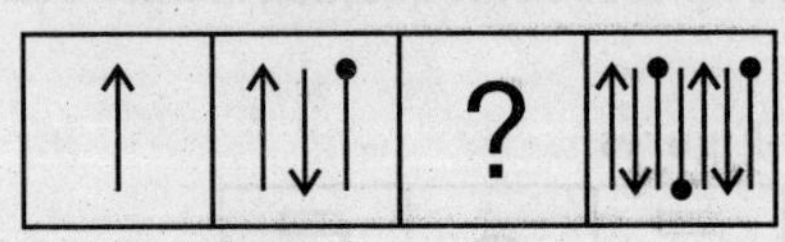

**Answer Figures**

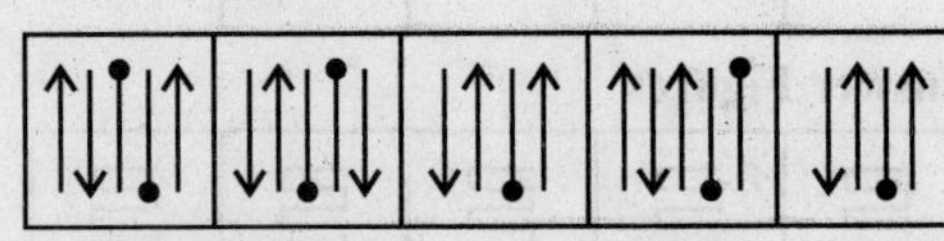

(*a*) (*b*) (*c*) (*d*) (*e*)

**7. Problem Figures**

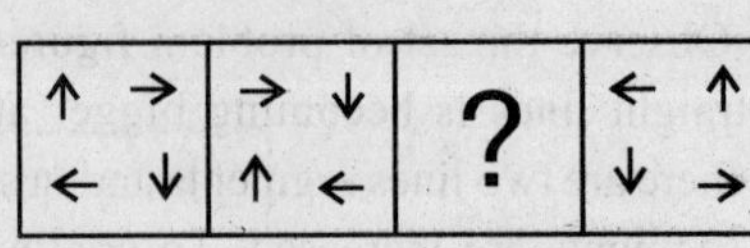

**Answer Figures**

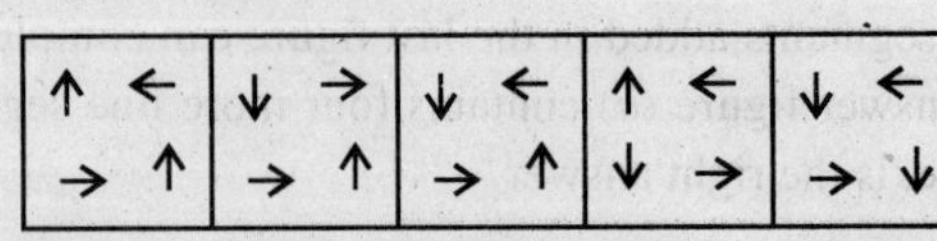

(*a*) (*b*) (*c*) (*d*) (*e*)

**8. Problem Figures**

**Answer Figures**

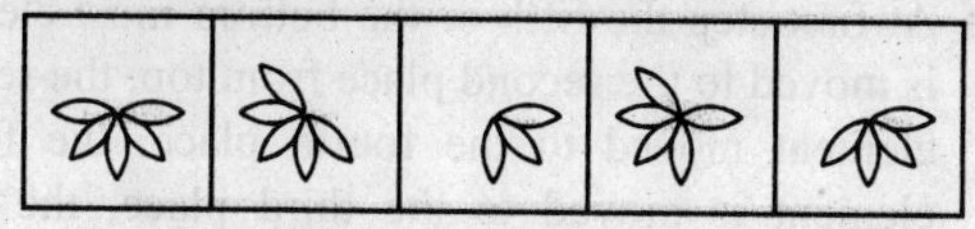

(a) (b) (c) (d) (e)

**9. Problem Figures**

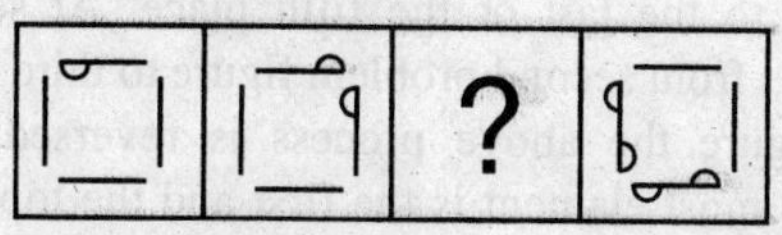

**Answer Figures**

(a) (b) (c) (d) (e)

**10. Problem Figures**

**Answer Figures**

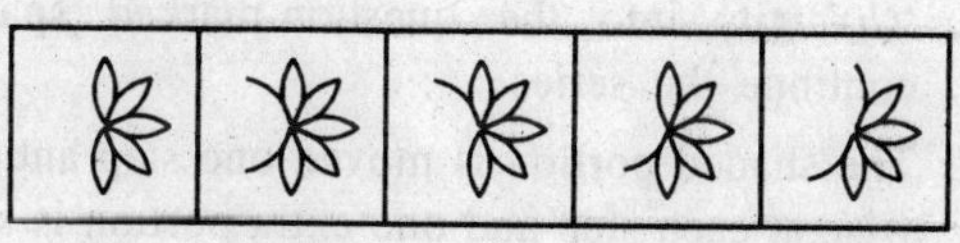

(a) (b) (c) (d) (e)

**11. Problem Figures**

**Answer Figures**

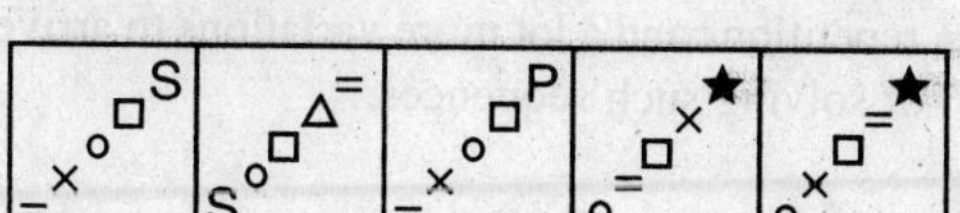

(a) (b) (c) (d) (e)

**12. Problem Figures**

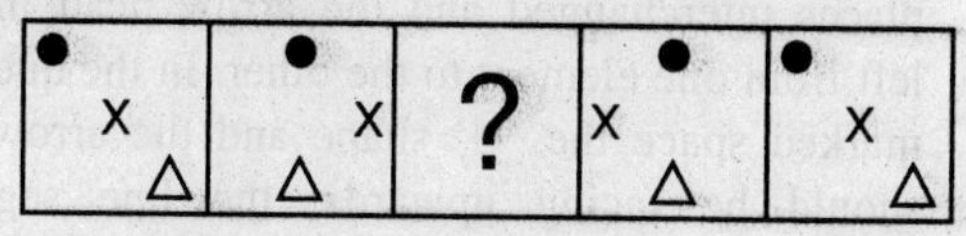

**Answer Figures**

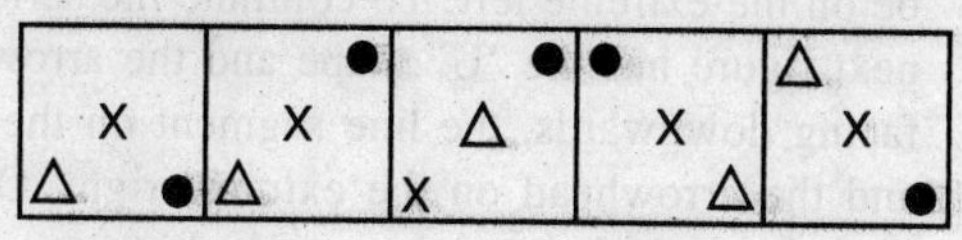

(a) (b) (c) (d) (e)

**13. Problem Figures**

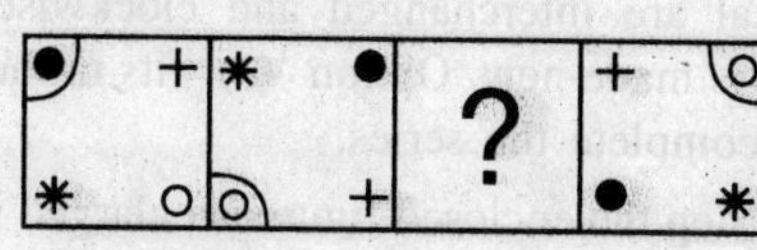

**Answer Figures**

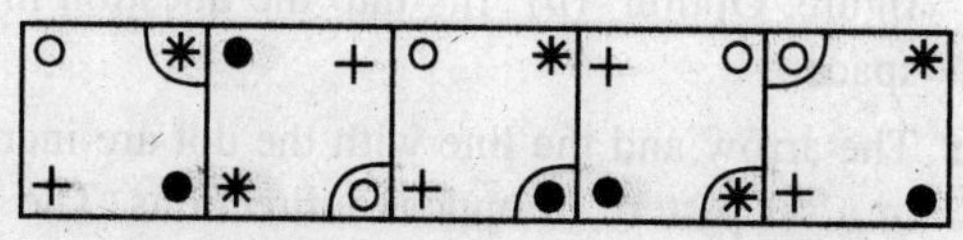

(a) (b) (c) (d) (e)

**14. Problem Figures**

**Answer Figures**

(a) (b) (c) (d) (e)

**15. Problem Figures**

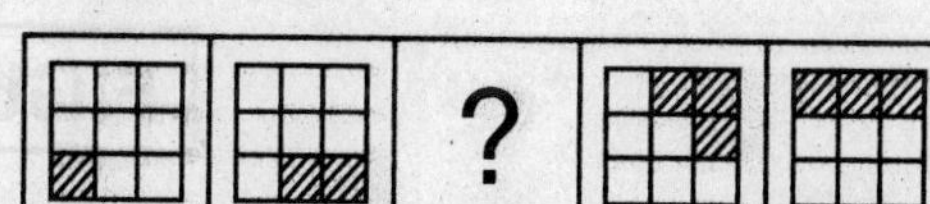

**Answer Figures**

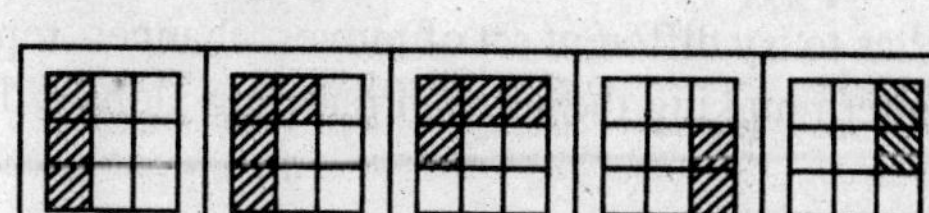

(a) (b) (c) (d) (e)

## EXPLANATORY ANSWERS

**1.** (*c*) : From first problem figure to the second the elements on the top are shifted down and vice versa. In fourth problem figure there are three elements which, as per rule, are also shifted. So, in question marked space only option '(*c*)' can be considered as forming the series.

**2.** (*d*) : Anticlockwise one of the sides of the hexagon is extended and clockwise one arc is added. The direction of the arc is changed at each step. Answer figure 'D' is the right answer.

**3. (*e*) :** Both the elements are turned upside down, their places interchanged and the arrow head moved left from one element to the other. In the question marked space the 'U' shape and the arrowhead should be facing upwards, the line segment should be on the right and the arrowhead should be on the extreme left. To continue the series the next figure has the 'U' shape and the arrowhead facing downwards, the line segment on the right and the arrowhead on the extreme right. Option '(*e*)' fits into the question marked space.

**4. (*c*) :** At each step the places of two elements on the horizontal are interchanged and clockwise one element is made new. Option '(*c*)' fits in the pattern to complete the series.

**5. (*b*) :** At each step the enclosed figure is enlarged in the next and a new figure is placed inside the enlarged figure. Option '(*b*)' fits into the question marked space.

**6. (*a*) :** The arrow and the line with the dot are increased in a set pattern in opposite directions. The series they form is two arrows and two lines with the dot which is repeated. Answer figure '(*a*)' is the right choice.

**7. (*c*) :** Each arrow is turned 90° clockwise at each step. Option '(*c*)' fits into the question marked space.

**8. (*a*) :** The number of petals removed at each step is increased by one, i.e., the petals are removed in the order of one, two and three, leaving only two petals in the last figure option '(*a*)' is the right answer.

**9. (*e*) :** The lines are moved clockwise. First a semicircle is added to the adjacent line. Then the semicircles on the opposite sides are added one by one on the two lines. Answer figure '(*e*)' fits into the question-marked space.

**10. (*c*) :** Each time one petal is removed and the half petal is clockwise and anticlockwise alternately. Answer figure '(*c*)' completes the series.

**11. (*a*) :** At first step the fifth or the bottom most element is moved to the second place from top, the second element moved to the fourth place, the fourth element is moved to the third place, the third element is moved to the first or the topmost place and the element on the top which is made new is moved to the last or the fifth place. At second step i.e., from second problem figure to third problem figure the above process is reversed. The bottom most element is the first and the top most element is the last or fifth. Hereafter, the process is repeated from the beginning. Option '(*a*)' is the right answer.

**12. (*b*) :** The three elements are moved half step everytime-first till they reach the extreme right position and then back to the left. Answer figure '(*b*)' fits into the question-marked space.

**13. (*c*) :** The four elements are moved one step clockwise and the arc one step anti-clockwise. Option '(*c*)' is the right answer.

**14. (*b*) :** The smaller design is enlarged in the next and a new smaller design is placed in its centre. Option '(*b*)' fits into the question-marked space to continue the series.

**15. (*d*) :** The shaded portion is moved one step anticlockwise at each step and one extra portion is shaded alternately.

# FIGURAL SERIES

In this form of non-verbal series, which are the most common, four or five consecutive problem figures form a definite sequence and one is required to select the one figure from the given set of Answer Figures that will continue the same sequence.

One has to try different set of moves, changes, replacements, rotations, repetitions and a lot more variations to arrive at the logical pattern making the series. Practising alone will sharpen one's skill of solving such sequences.

## SOLVED EXAMPLES

In each of the questions given below, which one of the answer figures should come after the problem figure if the sequence were continued?

**1. Problem Figures**

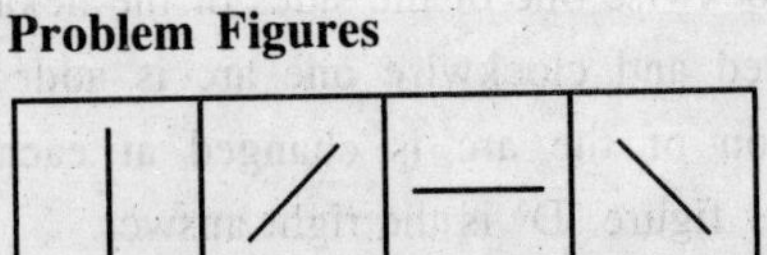

**Answer Figures**

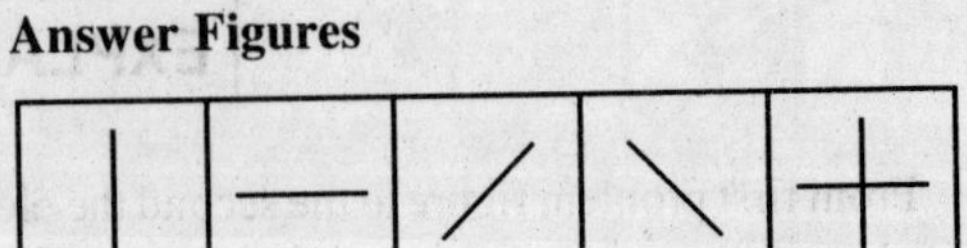

(*a*) (*b*) (*c*) (*d*) (*e*)

**Answer (*a*) :** All the figures are simple straight lines of the same size. Their directions and positions have changed.

In the first figure, the line is in a vertical position, in the second, the line has moved 45° clockwise, in the third, the line has further moved 45° clockwise, and in the fourth, the line has further moved 45° clockwise. Thus, two facts are brought out: *(i)* the line moves clockwise, and *(ii)* the line moves 45° at each step.

Now the fourth figure (Problem Figures) should be moved 45° clockwise. It will be a vertical line. Thus, the next figure to continue the series will be a vertical straight line.

## MULTIPLE CHOICE QUESTIONS

**Directions :** *In each of the following questions which one of the five answer figures given below should come after the problem figures if the sequence are continued?*

**Problem Figures**

1. 

**Answer Figures**

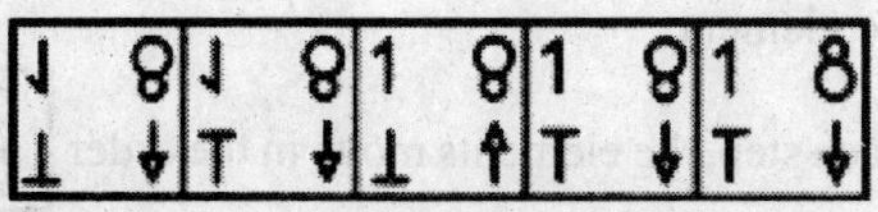

(*a*) (*b*) (*c*) (*d*) (*e*)

**Problem Figures**

2. 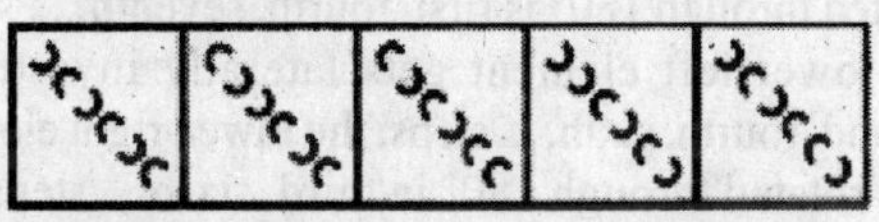

**Answer Figures**

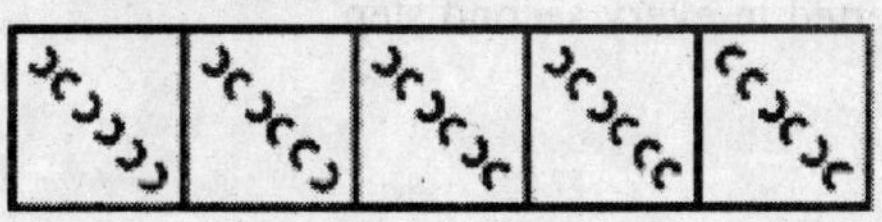

(*a*) (*b*) (*c*) (*d*) (*e*)

**Problem Figures**

3. 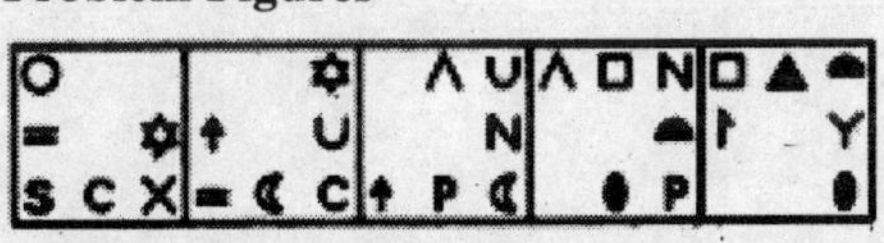

**Answer Figures**

(*a*) (*b*) (*c*) (*d*) (*e*)

**Problem Figures**

4. 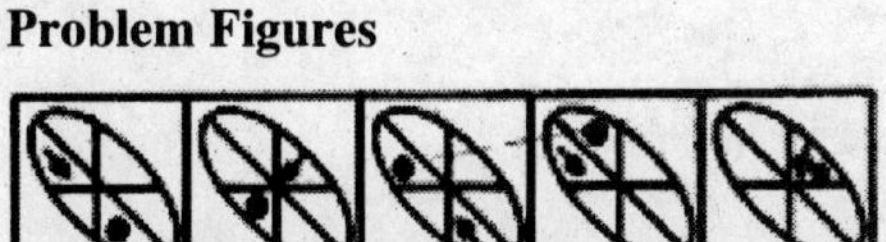

**Answer Figures**

(*a*) (*b*) (*c*) (*d*) (*e*)

**Problem Figures**

5. 

**Answer Figures**

(*a*) (*b*) (*c*) (*d*) (*e*)

**Problem Figures**

6. 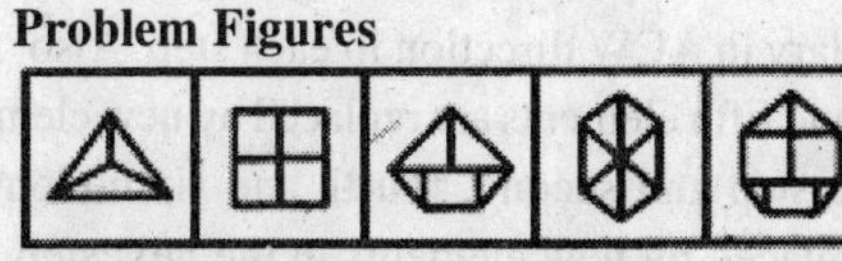

**Answer Figures**

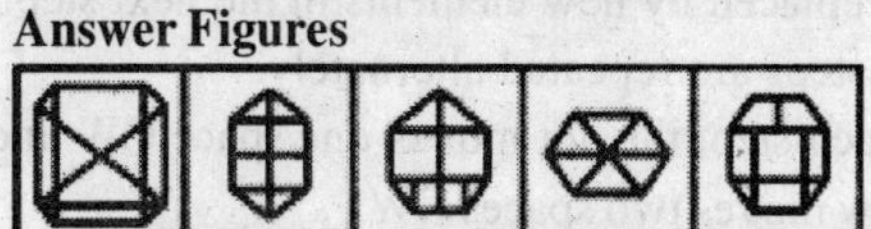

(*a*) (*b*) (*c*) (*d*) (*e*)

**Problem Figures**

7. 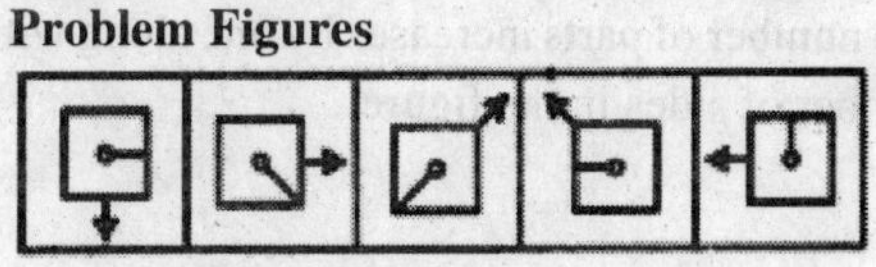

**Answer Figures**

(*a*) (*b*) (*c*) (*d*) (*e*)

**Problem Figures**

8. 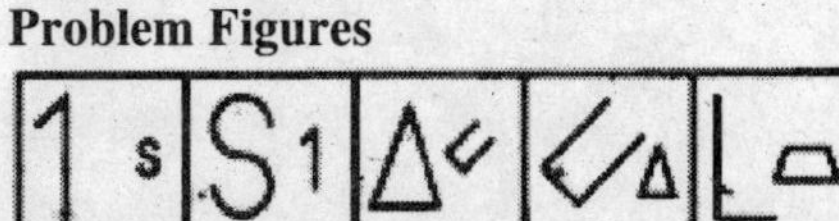

**Answer Figures**

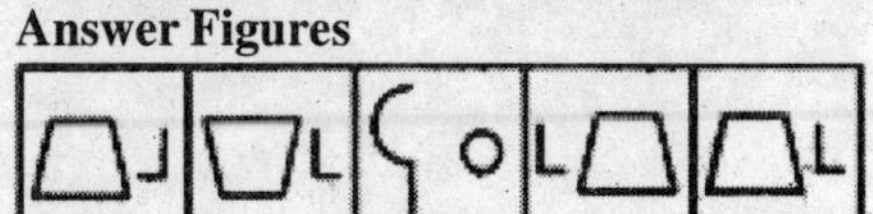

(*a*) (*b*) (*c*) (*d*) (*e*)

**Problem Figures**

9. 

**Answer Figures**

(*a*) (*b*) (*c*) (*d*) (*e*)

**Problem Figures**

10. 

**Answer Figures**

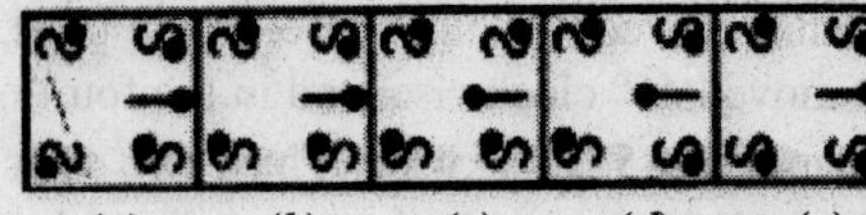

(a) (b) (c) (d) (e)

## EXPLANATORY ANSWERS

**1. (d) :** In each step, all the elements move to the adjacent corner (of the square boundary) in a CW direction and the element that reaches the upper-left corner gets vertically inverted.

**2. (c) :** We can label the arcs as shown . The arcs get inverted in the sequence (1 & 2), (3, 4 & 5), (6 & 1), (2, 3 & 4), (5 & 6), .............

**3. (d) :** All the elements move half-a-side of the square boundary in ACW direction in each step. Also, first, third and fifth elements are replaced by new elements in one step and second, fourth and sixth elements are replaced by new elements in the next step. The two steps are repeated alternately.

**4. (a) :** In each step, the dot moves one space CW and the arrow moves two spaces CW.

**5. (c) :** One arc and four arcs get inverted alternately.

**6. (e) :** The number of parts increases by one along with the number of sides in the figure.

**7. (c) :** The pin rotates 45°CW and 90°CW alternately and moves one space (each space is equal to half-a-side of the square) and two spaces CW alternately. The arrow rotates 90°ACW and 45°ACW alternately and moves two spaces and one space.

**8. (e) :** In one step, the two elements interchange positions and the smaller element gets enlarged while the larger element gets reduced in size. In the next step, the smaller element is replaced by a new small element and the larger element is replaced by a new large element.

**9. (c) :** In each step, the elements move in the order .

**10. (b) :** The upper-left element gets laterally inverted in first, third, fifth. .... steps; the upper-right element gets rotated through 180° is first, fourth, seventh,.... steps; the lower-left element gets laterally inverted in second, fourth, sixth, ... steps; the lower-right element gets rotated through 180° in third, sixth,... steps and the pin at the middle-right position gets laterally inverted in every second step.

CHAPTER 2

# Semantic Classification

Classification means arranging the given content in groups or classes having qualities of same kind. In classification type questions, the figures or items are sorted out in groups on the basis of their similarities in qualities in shapes, size, pattern, structure, genus, order, species, grade, style, constituents and other specifications, and thus the answer is found out.

## TYPE-I

Classification of this type does not have two sets of figures known as Problem Figures and Answer Figures; instead they have only one set of four or five figures known as Problem Figures. One of these Problem Figures is not like the other four figures. In other words, three or four of the Answer Figures belong to a class while one which is the odd figures, does not belong to it.

### MULTIPLE CHOICE QUESTIONS

**Directions :** *In each of the following questions one of the figures is different from the rest. Spot the figure.*

1. 

(a) (b) (c) (d) (e)

2. 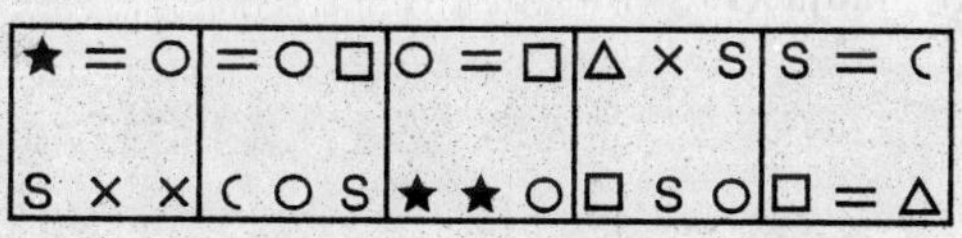

(a) (b) (c) (d) (e)

3. 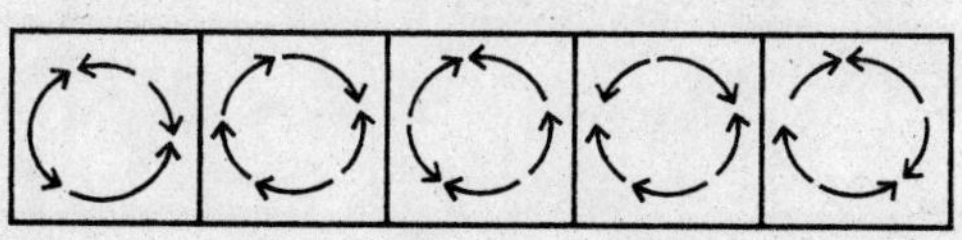

(a) (b) (c) (d) (e)

4. 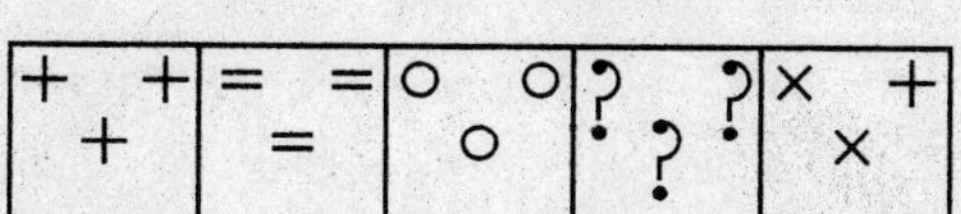

(a) (b) (c) (d) (e)

5. 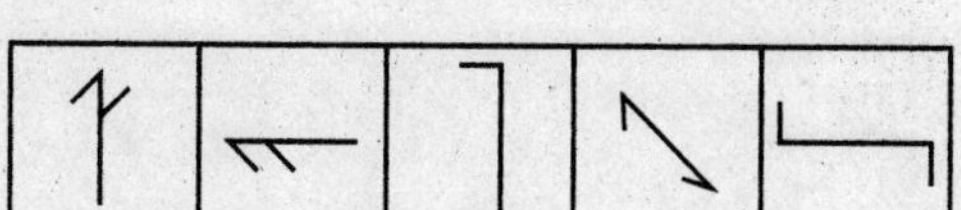

(a) (b) (c) (d) (e)

6. 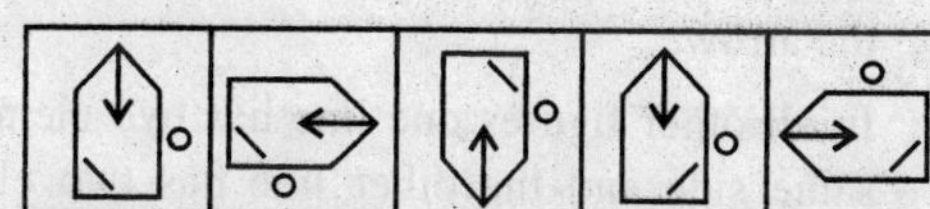

(a) (b) (c) (d) (e)

7. 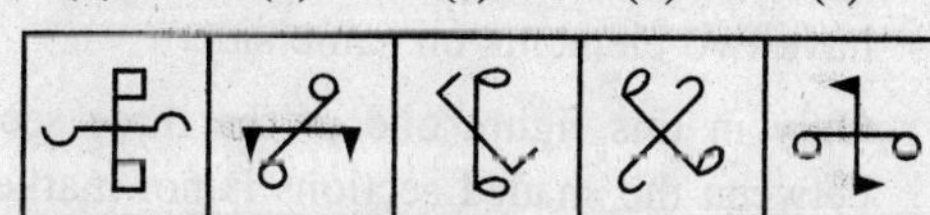

(a) (b) (c) (d) (e)

8. 

(a) (b) (c) (d) (e)

9. 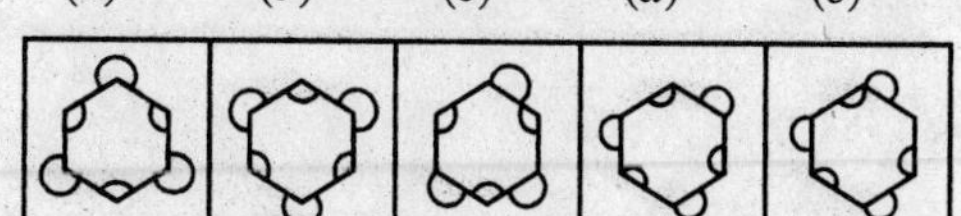

(a) (b) (c) (d) (e)

10. 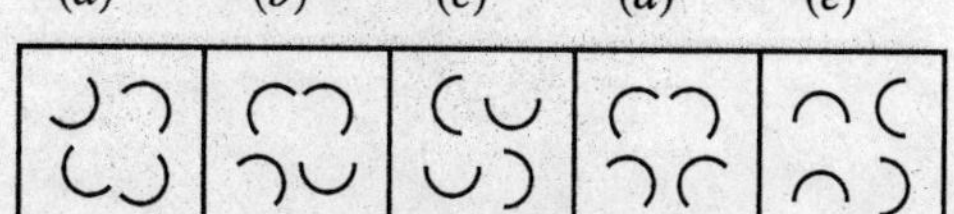

(a) (b) (c) (d) (e)

11. 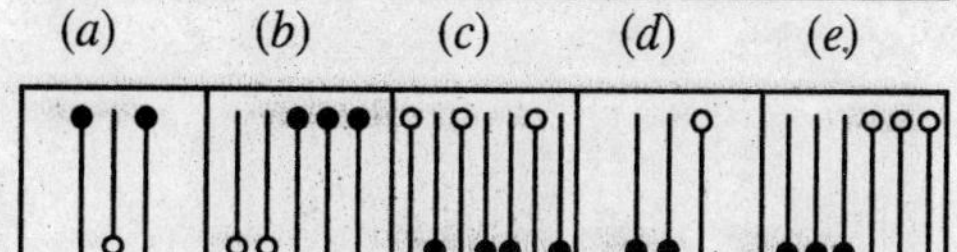

(a) (b) (c) (d) (e)

12. 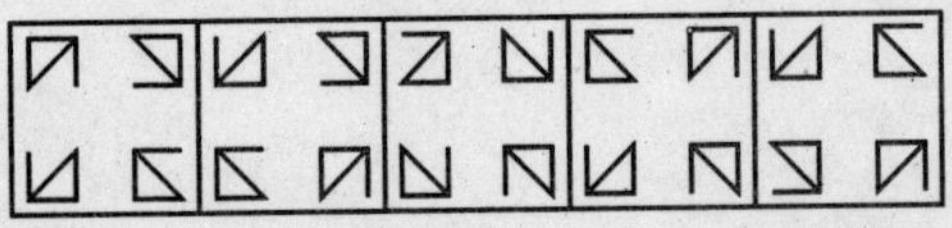

(a) (b) (c) (d) (e)

13. 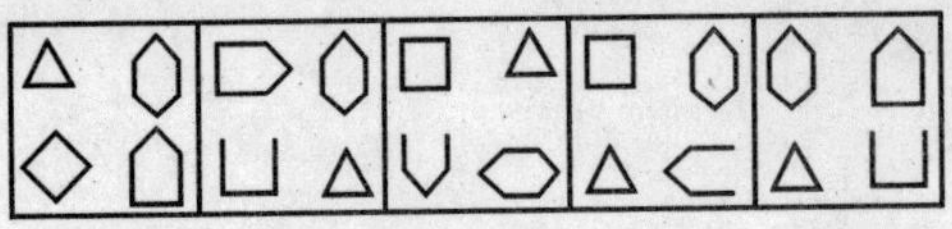

(a) (b) (c) (d) (e)

14. 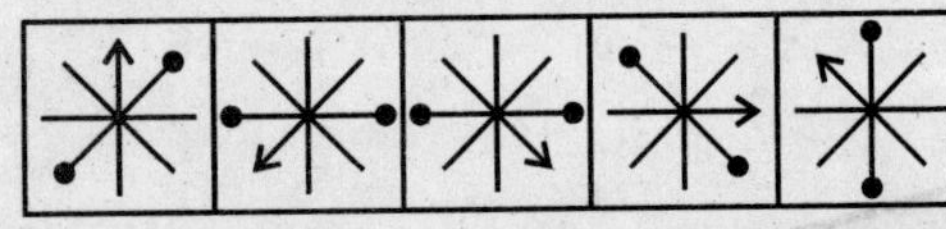

(a) (b) (c) (d) (e)

15. 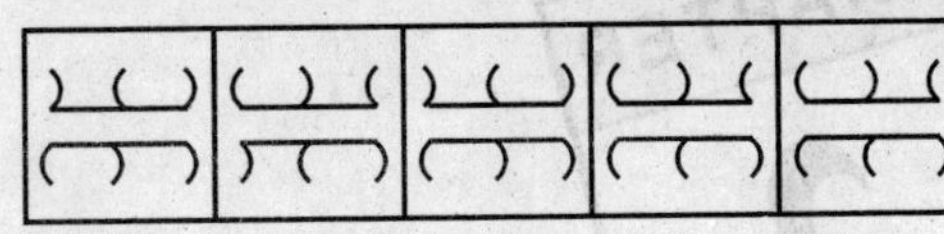

(a) (b) (c) (d) (e)

## EXPLANATORY ANSWERS

**1.** **(*d*)** : Only in this figure all the lines making the hands and legs of the human shape are drawn downwards.

**2.** **(*c*)** : In all other figures only one set of elements is identical.

**3.** **(*b*)** : Only in this figure four arrows are pointing in same direction, and one arrow in its opposite direction. In other figures three arrows are in same direction and two in the opposite direction.

**4.** **(*e*)** : All other figures have three identical elements.

**5.** **(*d*)** : In all other figures two lines are parallelly drawn.

**6.** **(*c*)** : In all other figures the circle is on the left side of the arrow.

**7.** **(*c*)** : In all other figures one line has two elements on same side and the other line has two elements, one on either side. In this figure both the lines have two elements on same side.

**8.** **(*d*)** : Only in this figure one of the three sections in between the shaded sections is not marked.

**9.** **(*e*)** : In all other figures the elements inside as well as outside the hexagon are placed at equal distance. In this figure the outside element at the top is wrongly placed (It should be near the other corner of the same line).

**10.** **(*d*)** : In all other figures two elements are in same direction and the other two elements are opposite to each other.

**11.** **(*e*)** : Only in this figure the two types of elements are equal in number.

**12.** **(*c*)** : In all other figures the diagonal line in all other elements is drawn from the right end.

**13.** **(*a*)** : In all other figures one of the four elements has one open side.

**14.** **(*c*)** : In all other figures the arrow is to the left of the dot.

**15.** **(*b*)** : In all other figures two of the three curves on one of the lines are in the same direction and are adjacent.

CHAPTER 3

# Figural Analogy

Figural Analogy is a process of reasoning between two parallel cases. It relates to agreement or correspondence in certain respects between two things. It is a process whereby the underlying relationship that exists between two figures, designs or patterns is determined. Under the process, one has to discover the features common to the two figures or designs. This common feature is a model or base. The question seeks solution on the basis of this model or base.

In non-verbal analogy questions, there are two sets of figures which are known as *(i)* Problem Figures, and *(ii)* Answer Figures. The Problem Figures are divided into two parts. The Answer Figures are given below the Problem Figures.

## MULTIPLE CHOICE QUESTIONS

**Directions :** *The second figure in the first unit of the Problem Figures bears a certain relationship to the first figure. Similarly, one of the figures in the Answer Figures bears the same relationship to the first figure in the second unit of the Problem Figures. Locate the figure which would fit the question mark.*

**1. Problem Figures**

**Answers Figures**

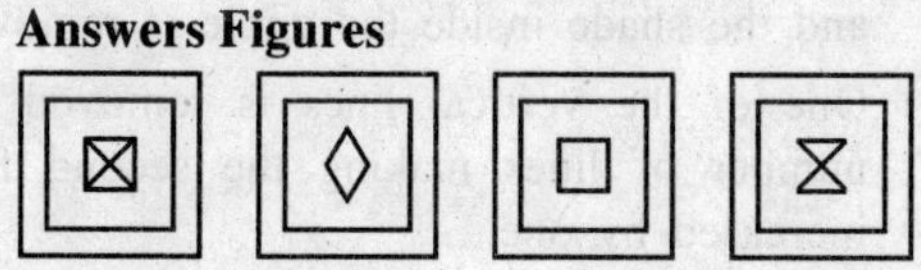

*(a)* *(b)* *(c)* *(d)*

**2. Problem Figures**

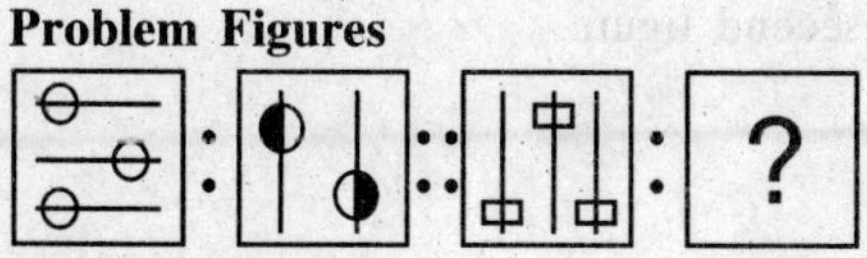

**Answer Figures**

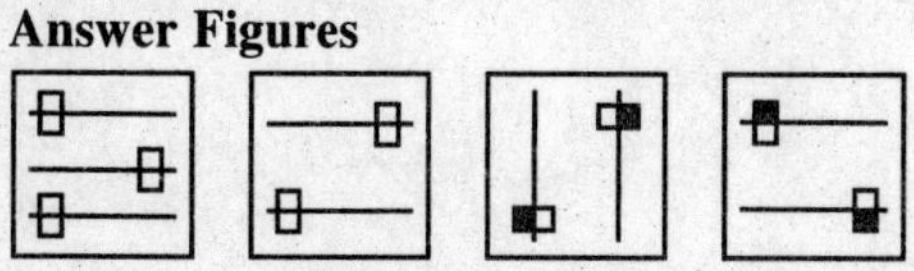

*(a)* *(b)* *(c)* *(d)*

**3. Problem Figures**

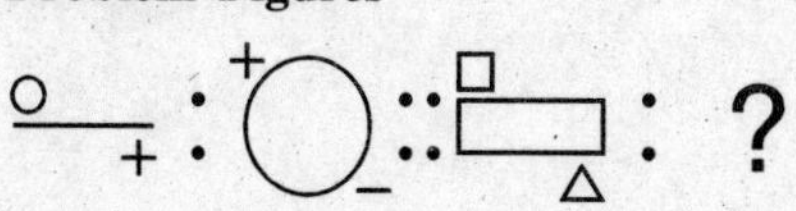

**Answer Figures**

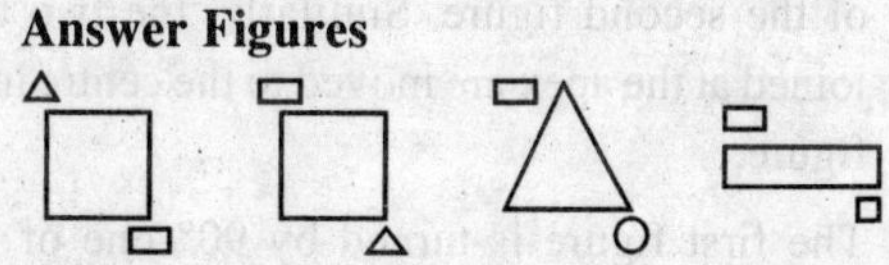

*(a)* *(b)* *(c)* *(d)*

**4. Problem Figures**

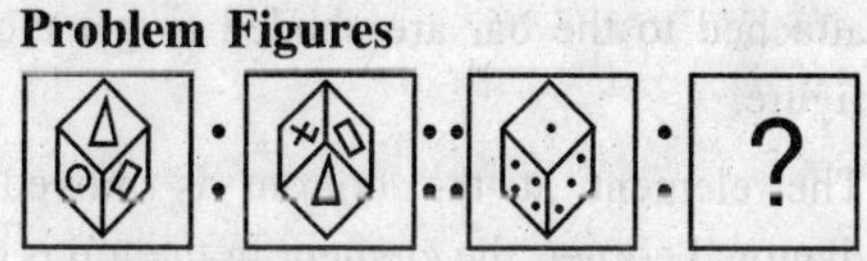

**Answer Figures**

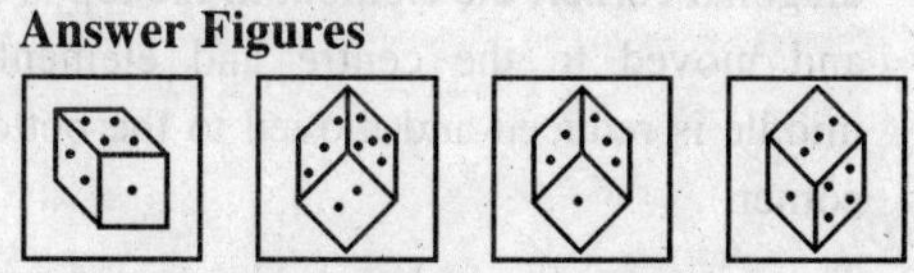

*(a)* *(b)* *(c)* *(d)*

**5. Problem Figures**

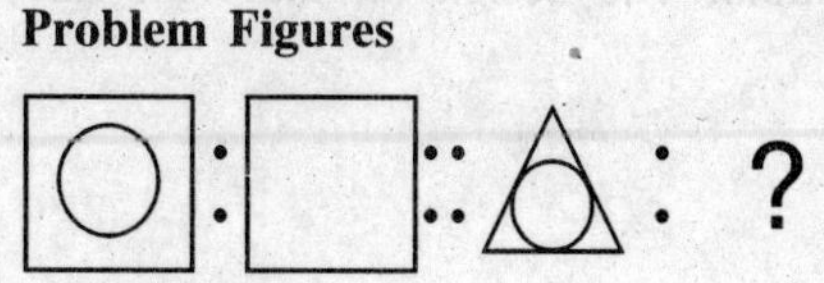

**Answer Figures**

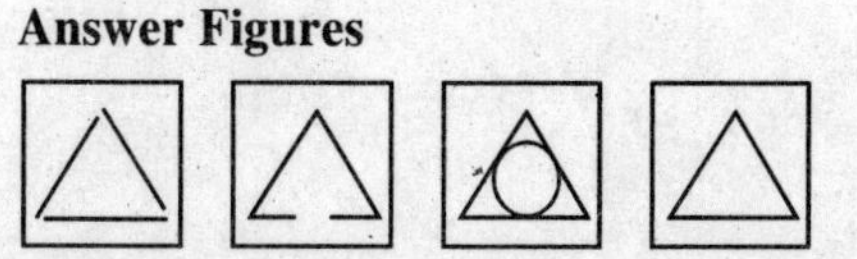

*(a)* *(b)* *(c)* *(d)*

**6. Problem Figures**

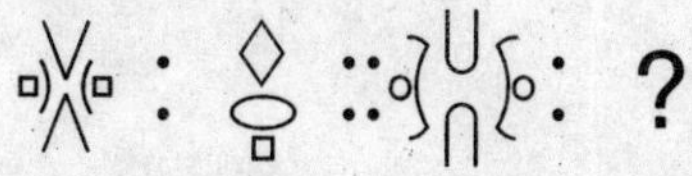

**Answer Figures**

(a) (b) (c) (d)

**7. Problem Figures**

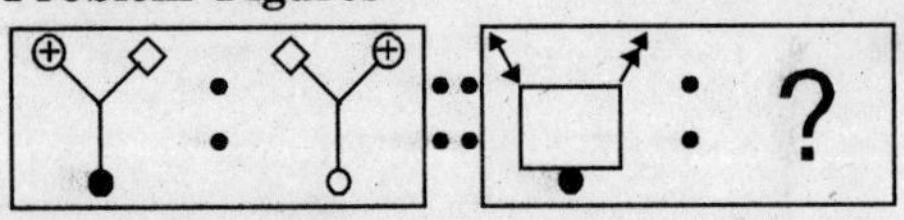

**Answer Figures**

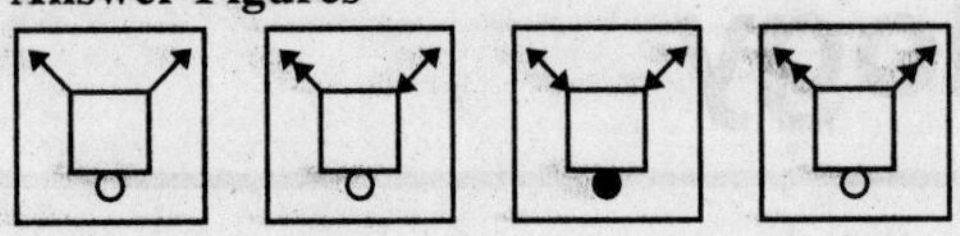

(a) (b) (c) (d)

**8. Problem Figures**

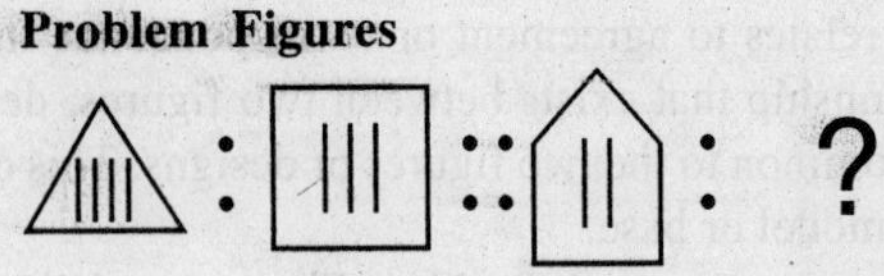

**Answer Figures**

(a) (b) (c) (d)

**9. Problem Figures**

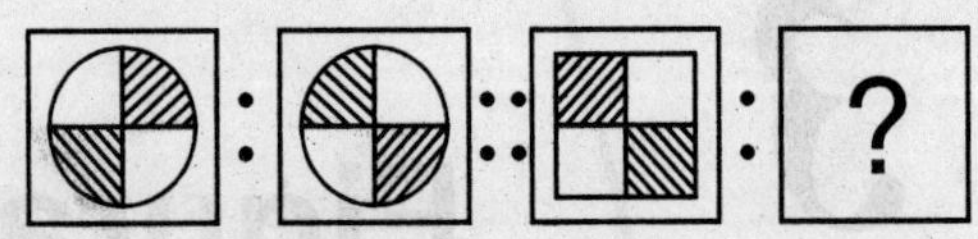

**Answer Figures**

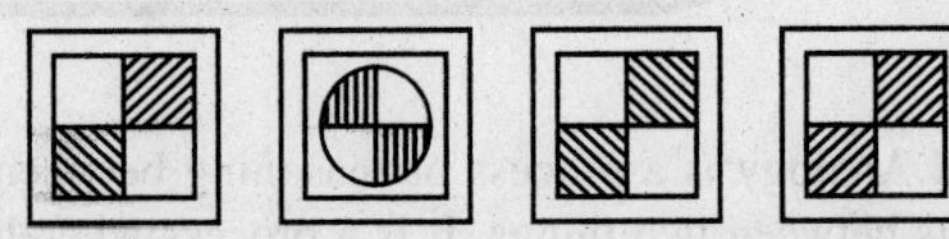

(a) (b) (c) (d)

## EXPLANATORY ANSWERS

**1. (*d*) :** The triangle in the first figure is moved to the centre of the second figure. Similarly, the two triangles joined at the apex are moved to the centre in answer figure.

**2. (*d*) :** The first figure is turned by 90° one of the bars is removed and opposite sides of the element attached to the bar are shaded to get the second figure.

**3. (*a*) :** The element at the bottom is moved to the diagonal corner, the element in the top is enlarged and moved to the centre and element in the middle is reduced and moved to the bottom right corner.

**4. (*c*) :** The view of the cube is changed from top to bottom. The design on the right side remains unchanged while the design on the left side is changed.

**5. (*d*) :** The inner shape in the first figure is removed to get the second figure.

**6. (*b*) :** The two half shapes placed vertically are turned upside down and joined, and this new shape is moved to the top. The two curved shapes placed horizontally are joined and this new shape is moved to the centre. One of the two remaining corner shapes is moved to the bottom.

**7. (*b*) :** The places of elements on the top are interchanged and the shade inside the circle is removed.

**8. (*a*) :** One of the vertical lines is removed and the number of lines making the second figure is increased by one.

**9. (*a*) :** First figure is rotated 90° anticlockwise to get the second figure.

# CHAPTER 4

# Spatial Visualization

In such questions, cut-out pieces are given alongwith the whole figure, that is the figure out of which the figures have been cut. By looking at the cut-out figures one has to find out the figure which may be constituted by putting the pieces together, i.e., one has to find out the figure of which the pieces have been cut. One has to be very imaginative and has to use space perception in finding out the solution. The whole process is mental and requires special skill in visualising different spatial patterns. It is not easy to develop this skill overnight but it can certainly be cultivated by practice and the method of trial and error.

## MULTIPLE CHOICE QUESTIONS

**Directions (Qs. 1-5) :** *Which one figure can be made out of given paper cut-outs?*

**1.**

(a) (b) (c) (d)

**2.**

(a) (b) (c) (d)

**3.**

(a) (b) (c) (d)

**4.**

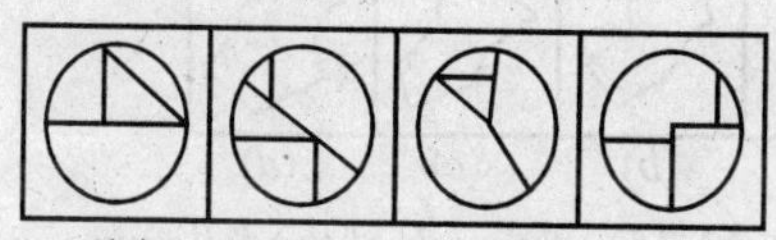

(a) (b) (c) (d)

**5.**

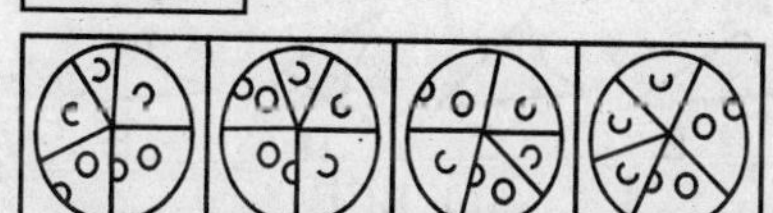

(a) (b) (c) (d)

**Direction (Qs. 6-10) :** *In each of the following questions an irregular piece of paper has been cut into two pieces. One piece has been shown on the left while the other piece has been given as one of the four alternatives against it. Find the correct alternative:*

**6.**

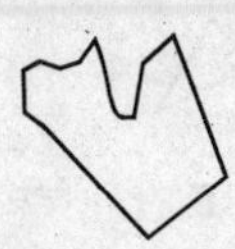

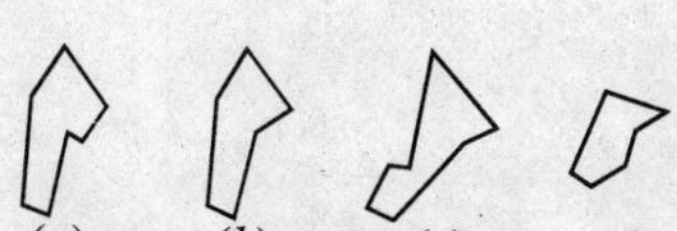

(a) (b) (c) (d)

**7.**

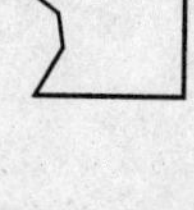

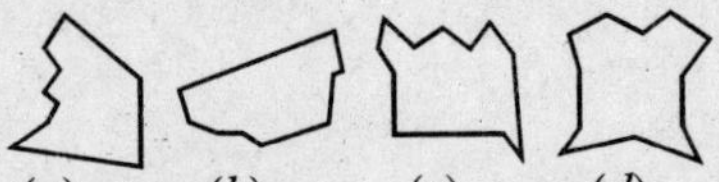

(a) (b) (c) (d)

**8.** 

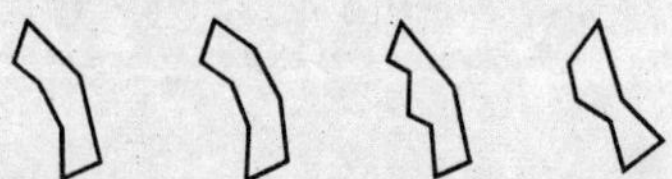

(a) (b) (c) (d)

**9.** 

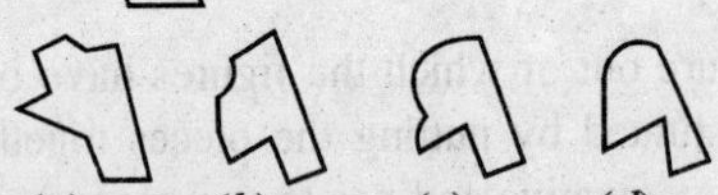

(a) (b) (c) (d)

**10.** 

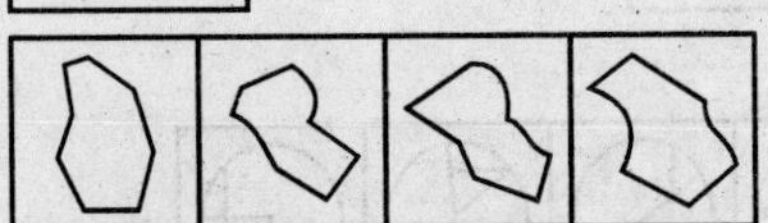

(a) (b) (c) (d)

**Directions (Qs. 11-15) :** *In each of the following questions five diagrams marked A to E are given. Three of these when put together form an equilateral triangle and have been given as one of the four alternatives under the question. Find the correct alternative in each case.*

**11.** 

A B C D E

(a) ABE (b) BCE
(c) ADE (d) BDE

**12.** 

A B C D E

(a) ABC (b) BCD
(c) CDE (d) BDE

**13.** 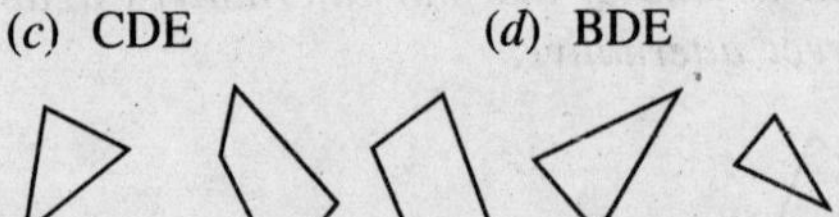

A B C D E

(a) BCD (b) CDE
(c) ABD (d) ABE

**14.** 

A B C D E

(a) ABD (b) ACD
(c) BDE (d) CDE

**15.** 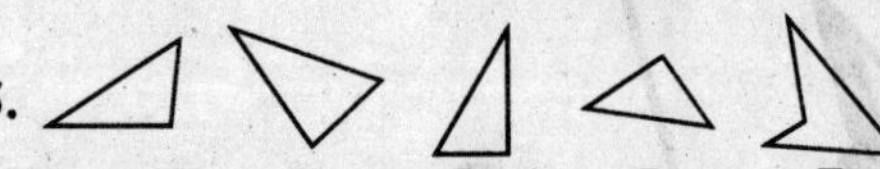

A B C D E

(a) ABC (b) ACE
(c) BDE (d) CDE

**Directions (Qs. 16-20) :** *In each of the following questions five diagrams A, B, C, D and E have been given. Three of these diagrams make a complete square which have been given as one of the four alternatives under it. Find the correct alternative in each case.*

**16.** 

A B C D E

(a) ABC (b) BDE
(c) CDE (d) BCD

**17.** 

A B C D E

(a) ACD (b) BDE
(c) BCE (d) CDE

**18.** 

A B C D E

(a) ACD (b) BCD
(c) ACE (d) CDE

**19.** 

A B C D E

(a) ABC (b) ACE
(c) ADE (d) CDE

**20.** 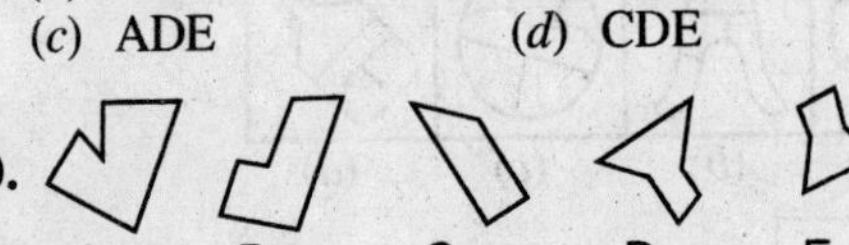

A B C D E

(a) BDE (b) ABC
(c) ACD (d) BCD

## ANSWERS

| 1 | 2 | 3 | 4 | 5 | 6 | 7 | 8 | 9 | 10 |
|---|---|---|---|---|---|---|---|---|---|
| (b) | (d) | (c) | (a) | (b) | (b) | (c) | (a) | (d) | (c) |
| 11 | 12 | 13 | 14 | 15 | 16 | 17 | 18 | 19 | 20 |
| (c) | (d) | (d) | (b) | (b) | (d) | (b) | (c) | (c) | (d) |

CHAPTER 5

# Space Visualization

In these type of questions, a template or a layout of a cube, dice or a box is given, which can be folded to produce different patterns. To solve these questions what is required is a clear study of the given layout and the selection of one figure, from the alternative patterns which can be made from the given layout. To attempt such problems understand the unfolded patterns given below:

**Layout 1.** 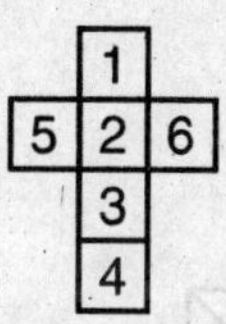

or 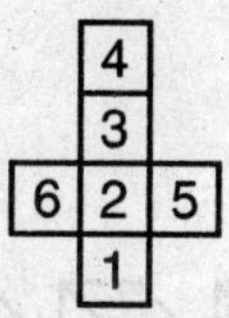


The opposite sides are :
1—3, 2 — 4 and 5 — 6

**Layout 2.** 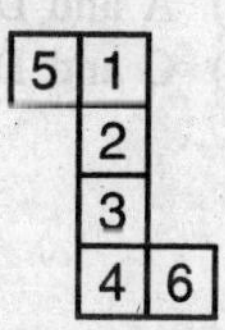

or 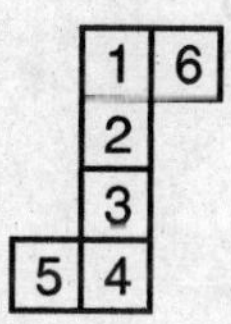


The opposite sides are :
1 — 3, 2 — 4 and 5 — 6

**Layout 3.** 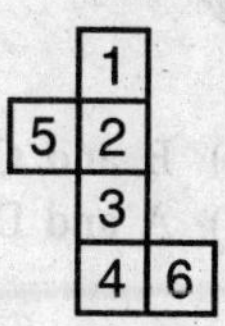

or 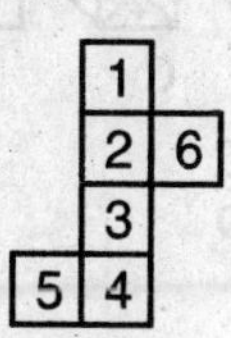


The opposite sides are :
1 — 3, 2 — 4 and 5 — 6.

**Layout 4.** 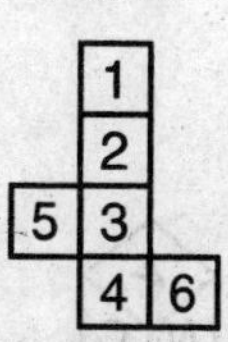

or 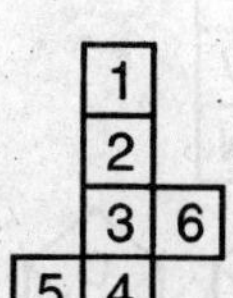


The opposite sides are :
1 — 3, 2 — 4 and 5 — 6

**Layout 5.** 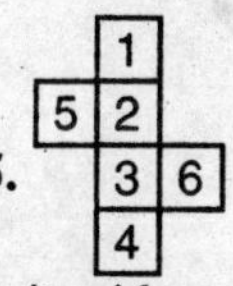

or 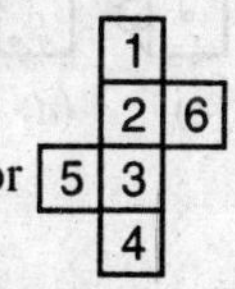


The opposite sides are :
1 — 3, 2 — 4 and 5 — 6

**Layout 6.** 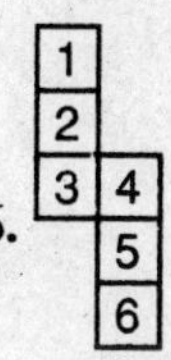

or 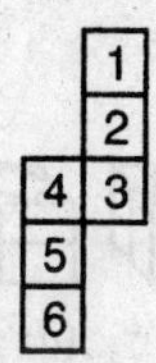


The opposite sides are :
1 — 3, 2 — 5 and 4 — 6

**Layout 7.** 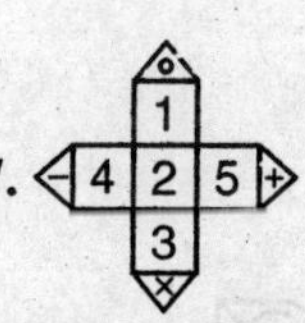


The opposite sides are :

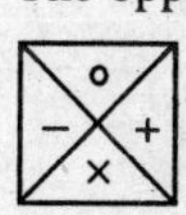 — 2, 1 — 3 and 4 — 5. Here, side 6 is divided into four parts

**Layout 8.** 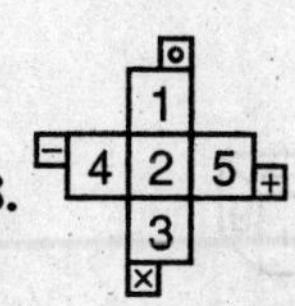


The opposite sides are

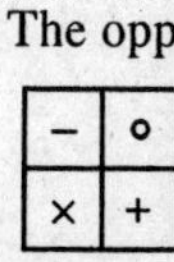 — 2, 1 — 3 and 4 — 5. Here, side 6 is divided into four parts.

Observe from the above layouts that all sides except the opposite side are adjacent sides. Also keep in mind that the three visible sides of the option figures are one of the opposite sides of each opposite pair.

## MULTIPLE CHOICE QUESTIONS

**Directions :** *The figure is folded to produce different box patterns. Study the pattern to know if they can be produced from given figure and select the answer from the alternatives.*

1. 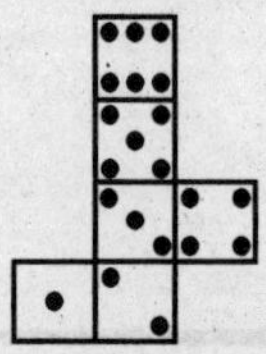

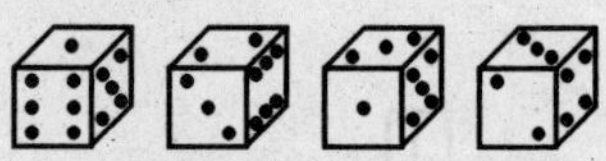

(a) (b) (c) (d)

2. 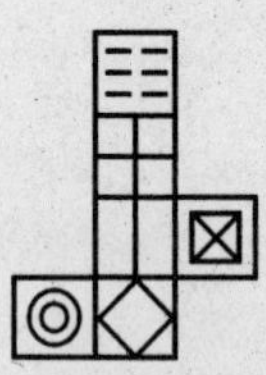

(a) (b) (c) (d)

3. 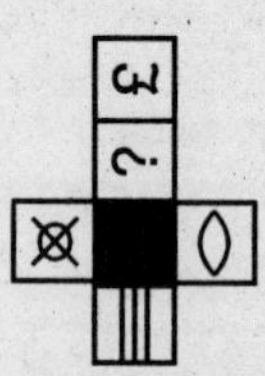

(a) (b) (c) (d)

4. 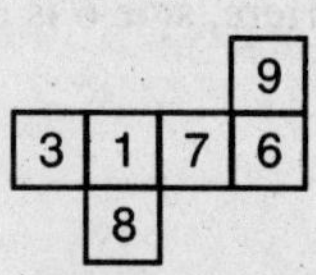

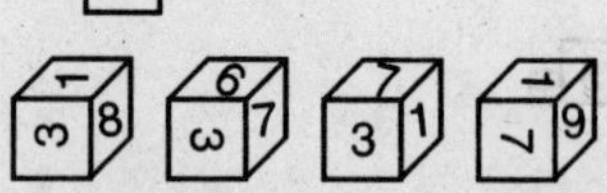

(a) (b) (c) (d)

5. 

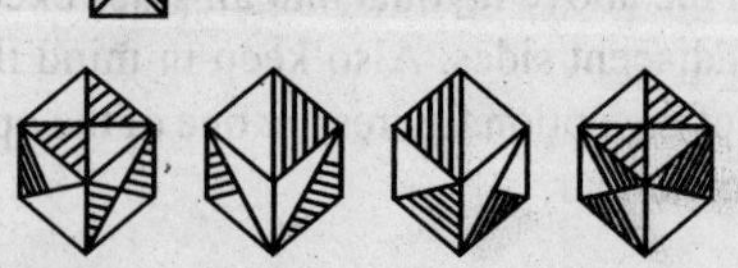

(a) (b) (c) (d)

6. 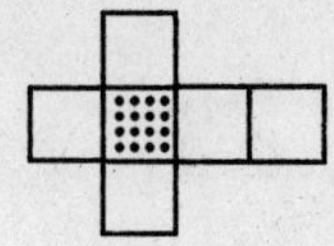

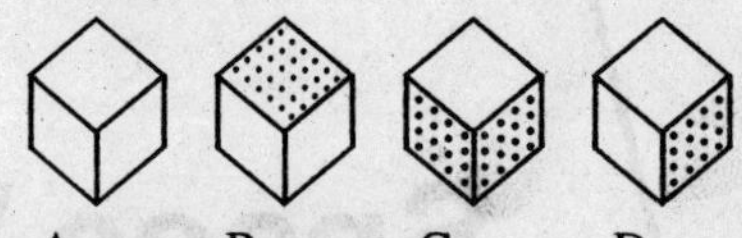

A B C D

(a) A, B and D (b) B and D
(c) B, C and D (d) A and D

7. 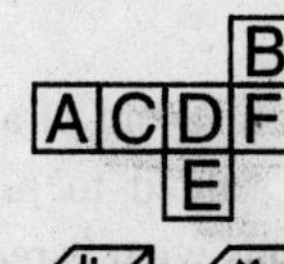

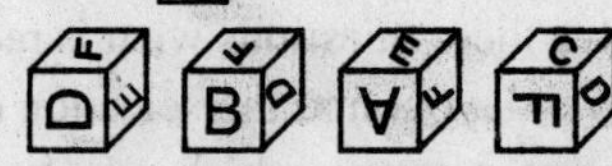

A B C D

(a) A and B (b) A and D
(c) B and C (d) All four

8. 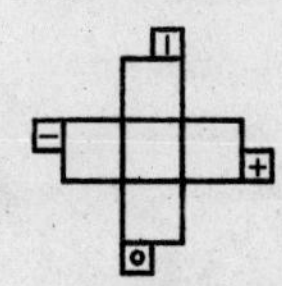

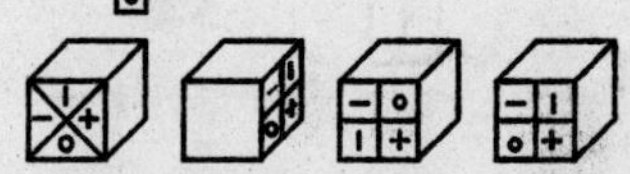

A B C D

(a) B and D (b) A and D
(c) B and C (d) C and D

9. 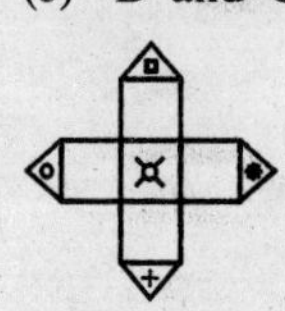

A B C D

(a) A and C (b) B and C
(c) B and D (d) A and D

10. 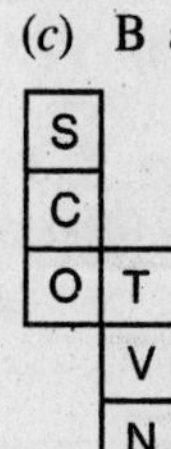

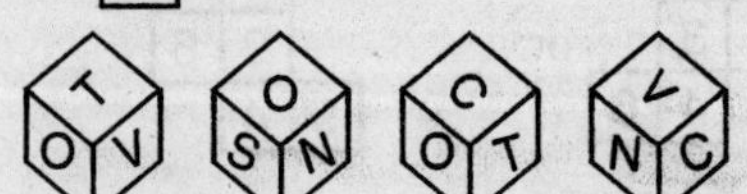

A B C D

(a) B and C (b) A and D
(c) A and C (d) All four

**11.**

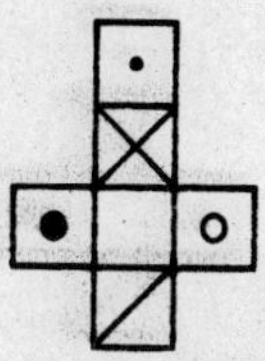

A B C D

(*a*) A and D (*b*) B, C and D

(*c*) All four (*d*) None of the above

**12.**

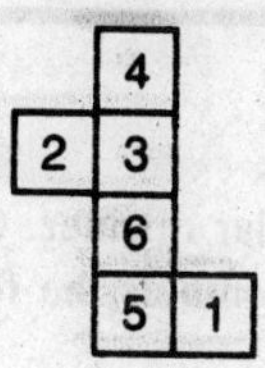


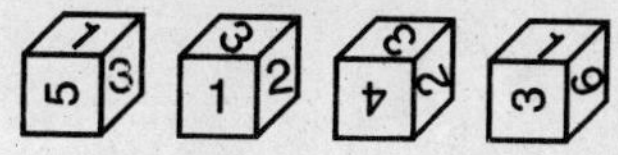

A B C D

(*a*) A and C (*b*) C and D

(*c*) B and C (*d*) B and D

**13.**

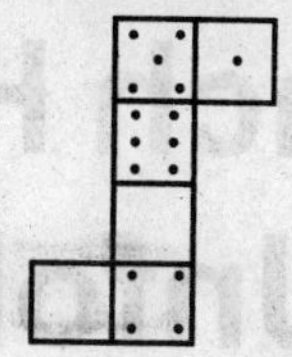

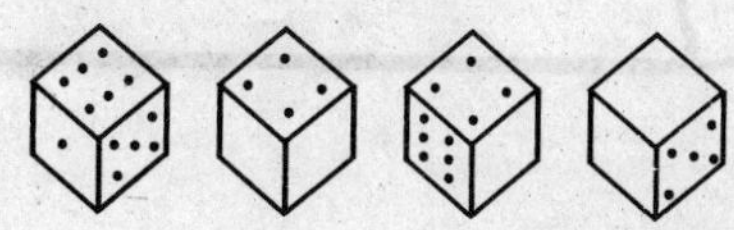

A B C D

(*a*) A and C (*b*) A and B

(*c*) B and C (*d*) B and D

## EXPLANATORY ANSWERS

**(All answers are based on number pattern of the sides as in the layout given in the beginning of this section)**

**1. (*d*) :** The given figure is same as layout 4. The sides adjacent to top side 3 are in order 2, 5, 4, 6 — of these sides, 4 and 6 are seen on left and right sides respectively.

**2. (*b*) :** The given figure is same as layout 4. The sides adjacent to top side 5 are in order 4, 3, 2, 1 —of these sides 1 and 4 are seen on left and right sides respectively.

**3. (*d*) :** The given figure is same as layout 1. The sides adjacent to top side 5 are in order 4, 3, 2, 1 — of these sides 2 and 1 are seen on left and right sides respectively.

**4. (*a*) :** The given figure is same as layout 3. The sides adjacent to top side 2 are in order 1, 5, 3, 6 — of these sides 1 and 5 are seen on left and right sides respectively.

**5. (*c*) :** The given figure is same as layout 1. The sides adjacent to top side 6 are in order 1, 2, 3, 4 — of these sides 2 and 3 are seen on left and right sides respectively.

**6. (*a*) :** The given figure is same as layout 1. The top, left and right sides in figure option (a) are 1, 4 and 5 respectively (other combinations of sides for this figure are also possible); in figure option (b) 2, 1 and 5 respectively (other combination of sides for this figure are also possible; and in figure option (d) 1, 5 and 2 respectively (other combinations of sides for this figure are also possible).

**7. (*a*) :** The given figure is same as layout 4. In option figure (a) the top side 4 has side 3 on left and side 5 on right. In option figure (b) the top side 4 has side 6 on its left and side 3 on right.

**Note :** in option figure (c) the sides are correct but the printing of letter on right side is incorrect.

**8. (*a*) :** The given figure is same as layout 8. Option figures (b) and (d) contain the correct joints of side 6.

**9. (*b*) :** The given figure is same as layout 7. Option figures (a) and (c) contain the correct joints of side 6.

**10. (*c*) :** The given figure is same as layout 6. In option figure (a) the top side 4 has side 3 on left and side 5 on right. In option figure (c) the top side 2 has side 3 on left and side 4 on right.

**11. (*d*) :** The given figure is same as layout 1. None of the figure options can be made from the given figure.

**12. (*b*) :** The given figure is same as layout 3. In option figure (c) the top side 2 has side 1 on left and side 5 on right. In option figure (d) the top side 6 has side 2 on left and side 3 on right.

**13. (*b*) :** The given figure is same as layout 2. In option figure (a) the top side 2 has side 6 on left and side 1 on right. In option figure (b) the top side 4 has side 3 on left and side 5 on right.

CHAPTER

6

# Pinch Hole/Paper Folding & Unfolding

These type of questions are based on a piece of paper which is folded and cut or punched in a particular manner. One of the option figures either resembles the pattern that would be formed when the paper is unfolded or resembles the form in which the paper is folded and cut or punched.

## MULTIPLE CHOICE QUESTIONS

**Directions (Qs. 1-5) :** *In each one of the following problems, a square transparent sheet with a pattern is given. Figure out from amongst the four alternatives as to how the pattern would appear when the transparent sheet is folded at the dotted line.*

1. 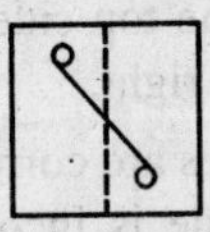

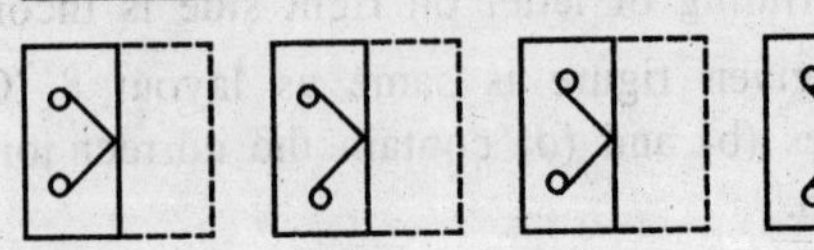

(a) (b) (c) (d)

2. 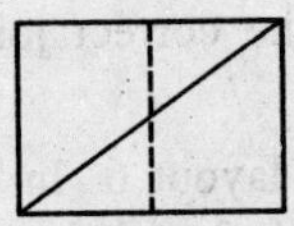

(a) (b) (c) (d)

3. 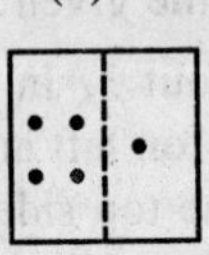

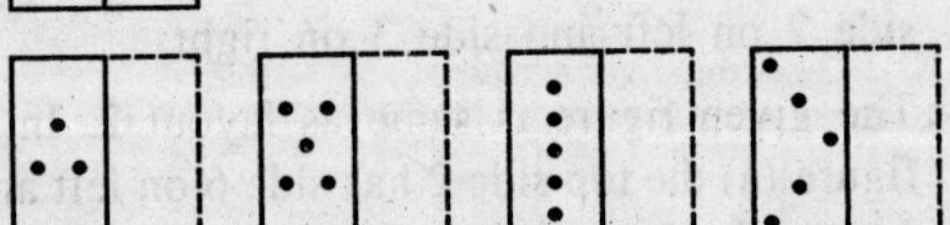

(a) (b) (c) (d)

4. 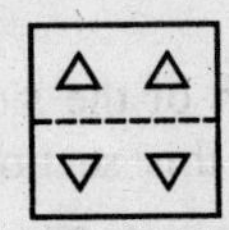

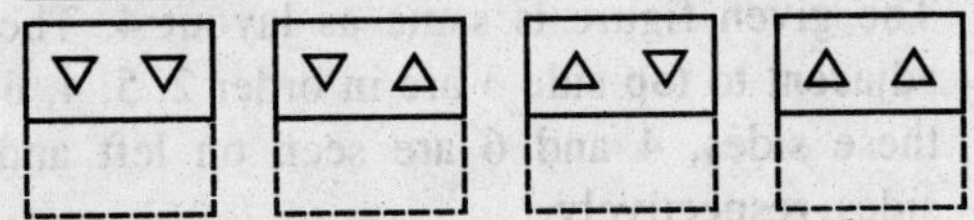

(a) (b) (c) (d)

5. 

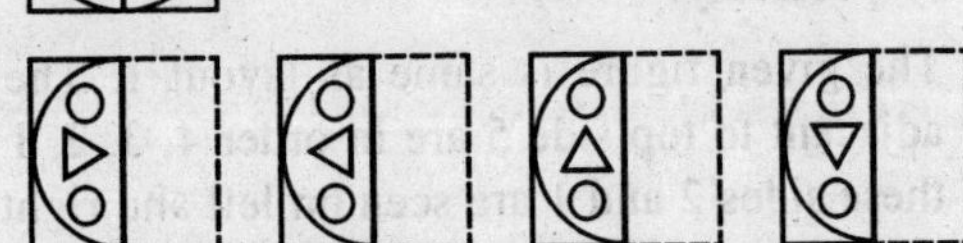

(a) (b) (c) (d)

**Directions (Qs. 6-13) :** *In each of the following questions a piece of paper has been folded and then punched. From the given options figure out the correct response which shows how it will appear when opened.*

6. 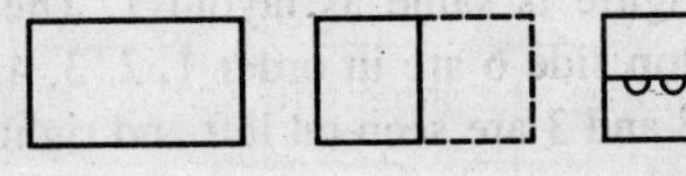

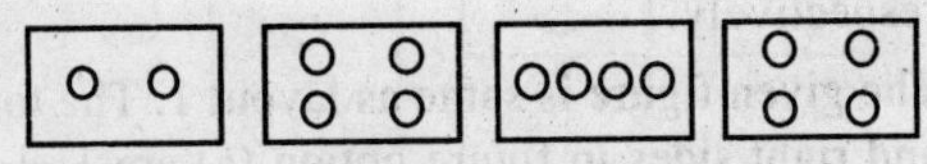

(a) (b) (c) (d)

7. 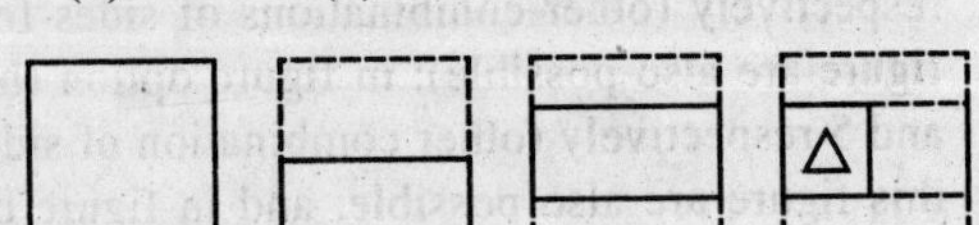

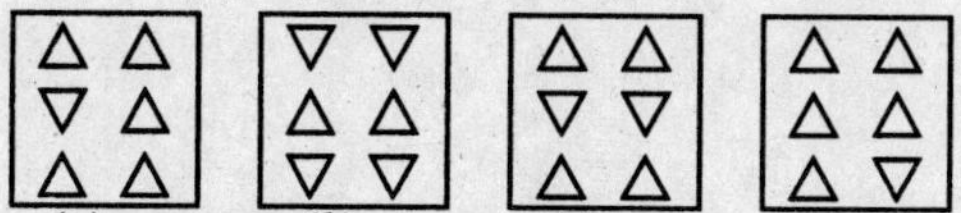

(a) (b) (c) (d)

8.

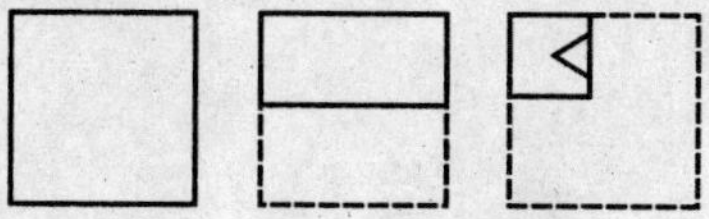

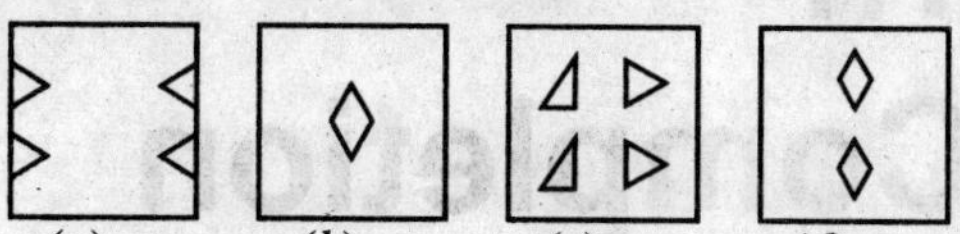

(a) (b) (c) (d)

9.

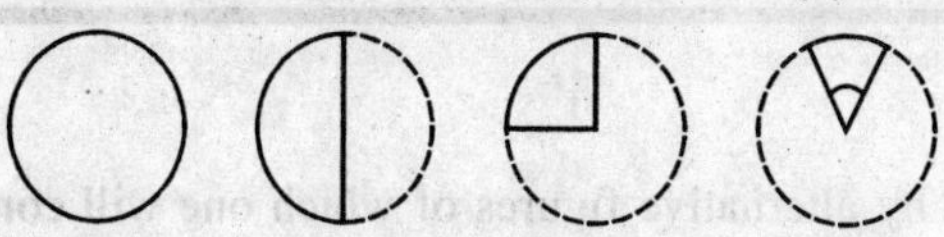

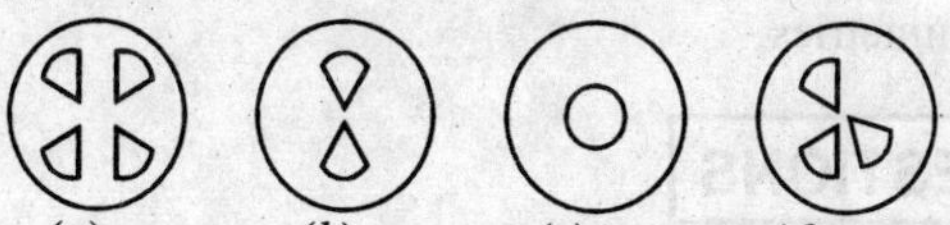

(a) (b) (c) (d)

10.

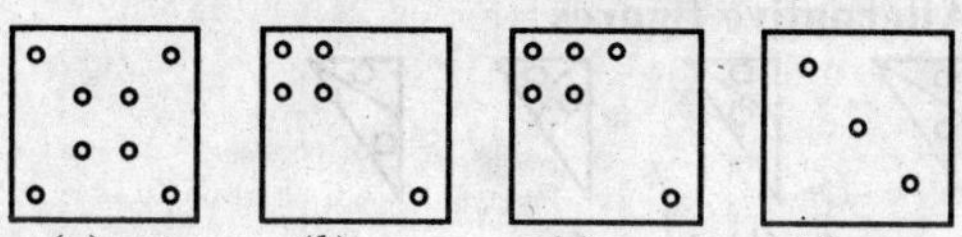

(a) (b) (c) (d)

11.

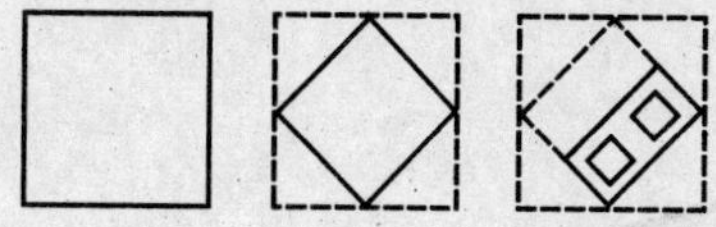

(a) (b) (c) (d)

12.

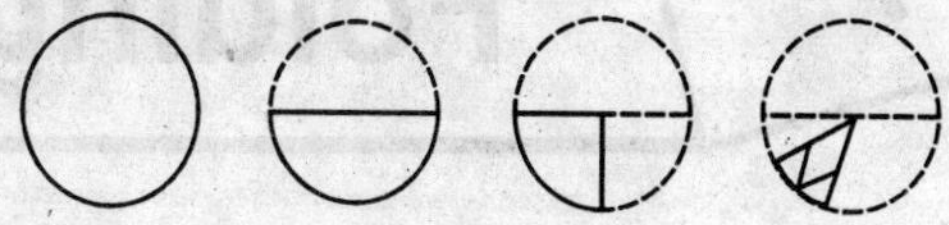

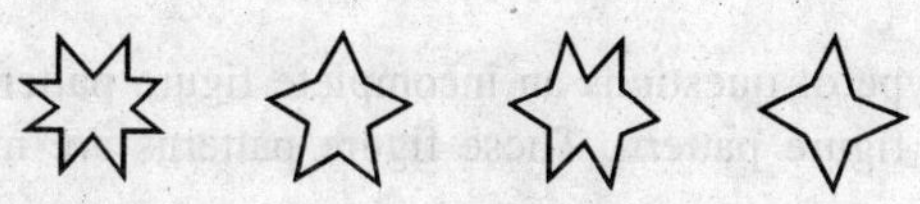

(a) (b) (c) (d)

13.

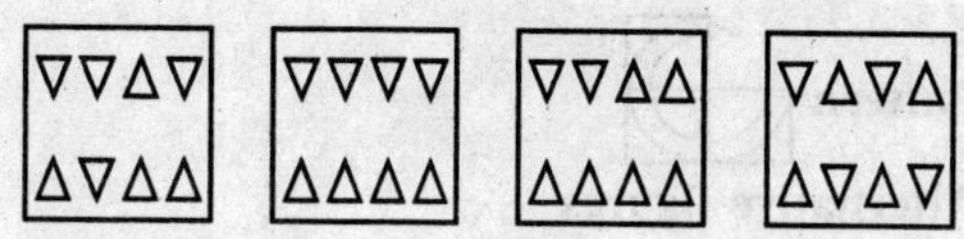

(a) (b) (c) (d)

## EXPLANATORY ANSWERS

**1.** (*d*)

**2.** (*c*)

**3.** (*b*)

**4.** (*d*)

**5.** (*b*)

**6.** (*c*) : When unfolding, the steps will be :

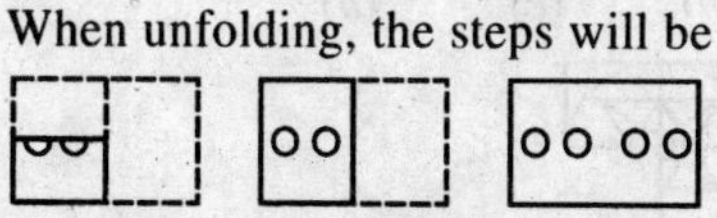

**7.** (*b*) : When unfolding, the steps will be :

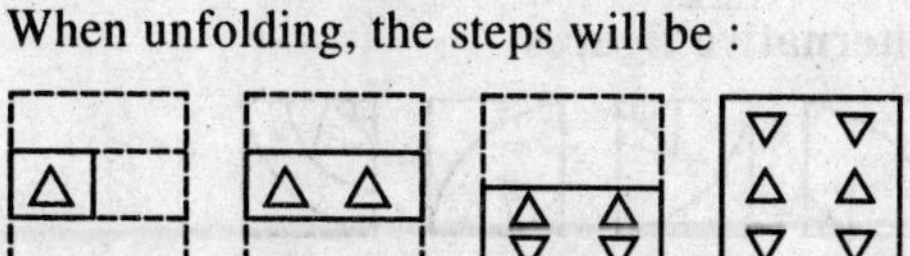

**8.** (*d*) : When unfolding, the steps will be :

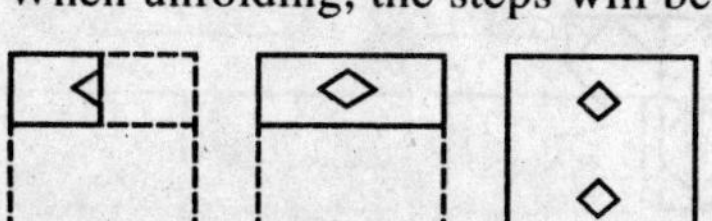

**9.** (*c*) : When unfolding, the steps will be :

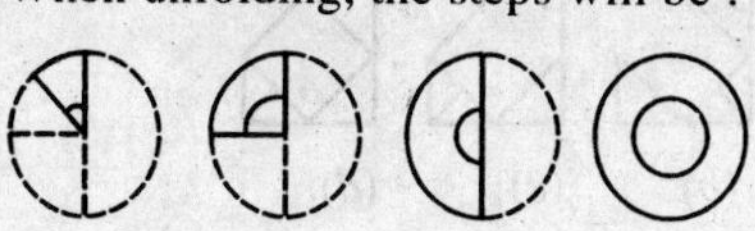

**10.** (*a*) : When unfolding, the steps will be :

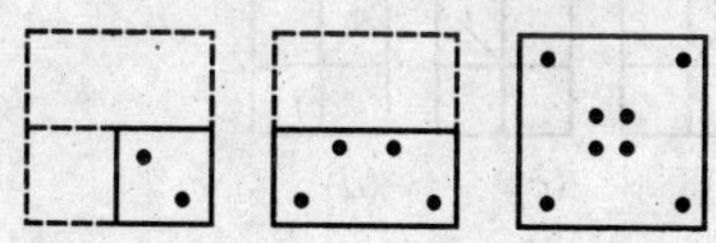

**11.** (*d*) : When unfolding, the steps will be :

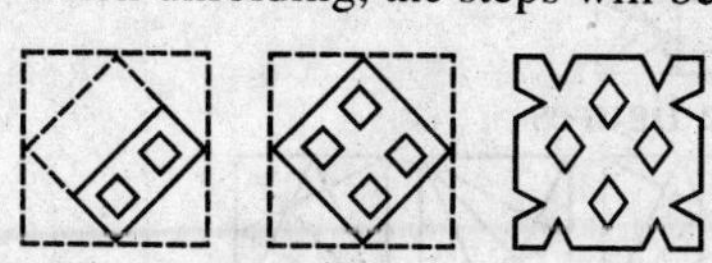

**12.** (*a*) : When unfolding, the steps will be :

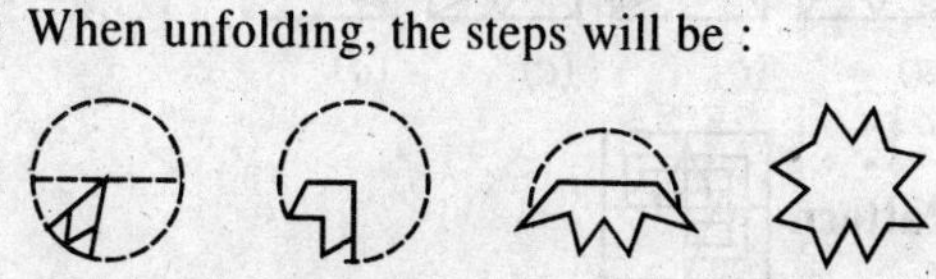

**13.** (*b*) : When unfolding, the steps will be :

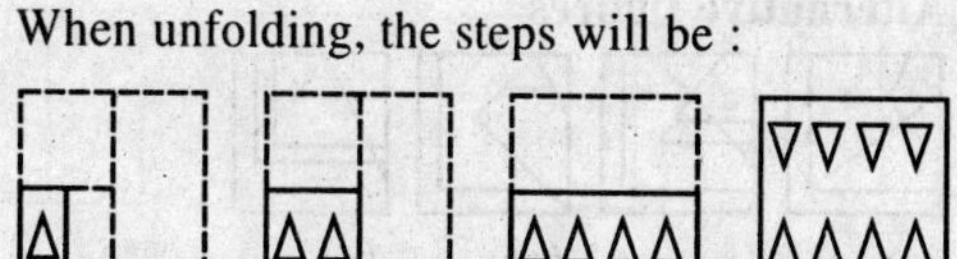

CHAPTER 7

# Figural Pattern Folding and Completion

In these type of questions an incomplete figure pattern is given followed by alternative figures of which one will **complete** the given figure pattern. These figure patterns are mainly based on symmetries.

## MULTIPLE CHOICE QUESTIONS

**Directions :** *In each question, which one of the alternative figures will complete the given figure pattern?*

**1. Pattern** 

**Alternative figures**

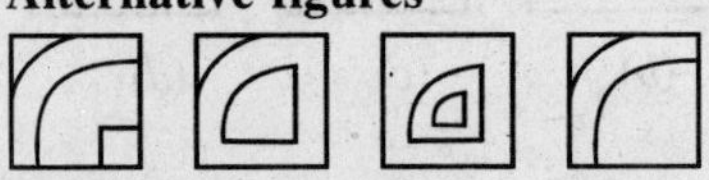

(*a*) (*b*) (*c*) (*d*)

**2. Pattern** 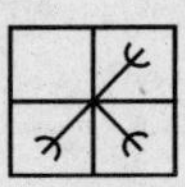

**Alternative figures**

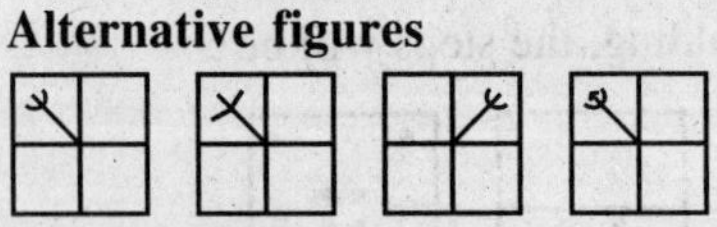

(*a*) (*b*) (*c*) (*d*)

**3. Pattern** 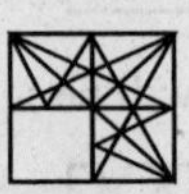

**Alternative figures**

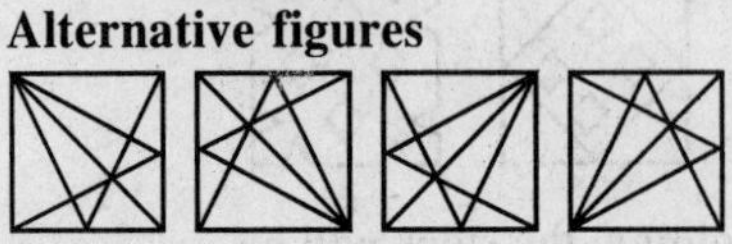

(*a*) (*b*) (*c*) (*d*)

**4. Pattern** 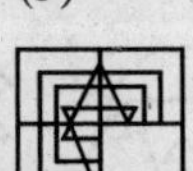

**Alternative figures**

(*a*) (*b*) (*c*) (*d*)

**5. Pattern** 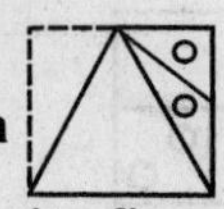

**Alternative figures**

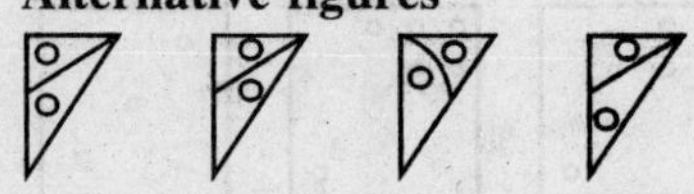

(*a*) (*b*) (*c*) (*d*)

**6. Pattern** 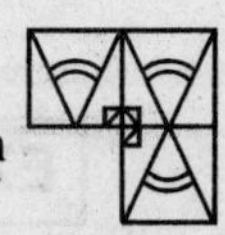

**Alternative figures**

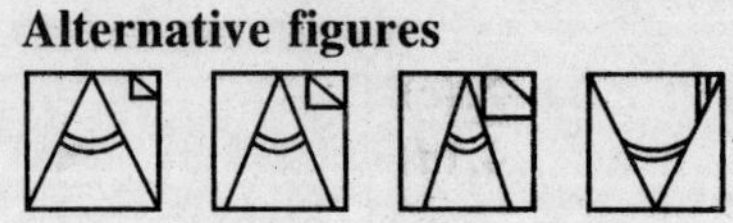

(*a*) (*b*) (*c*) (*d*)

**7. Pattern** 

**Alternative figures**

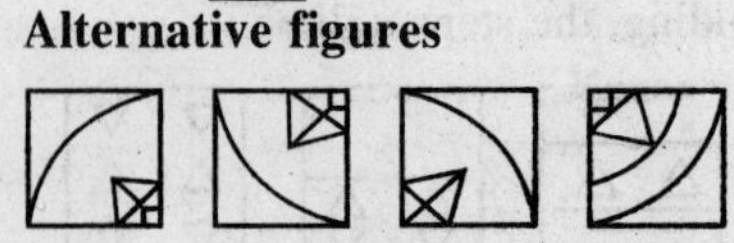

(*a*) (*b*) (*c*) (*d*)

**8. Pattern** 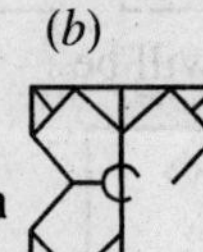

**Alternative figures**

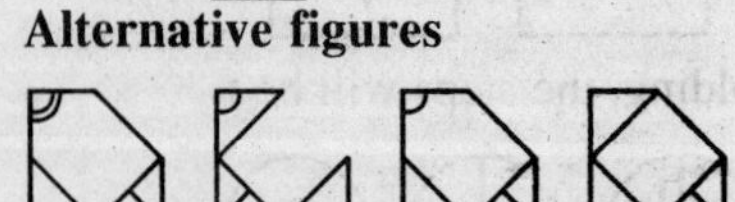

(*a*) (*b*) (*c*) (*d*)

**9. Pattern** 

**Alternative figures**

(*a*) (*b*) (*c*) (*d*)

**10. Pattern** 

**Alternative figures**

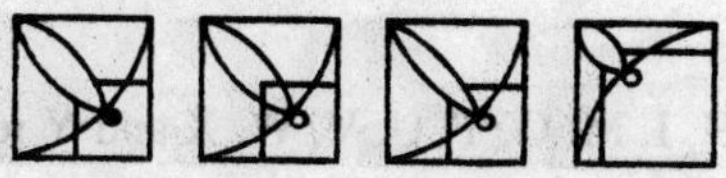

(*a*) (*b*) (*c*) (*d*)

**11. Pattern** 

**Alternative figures**

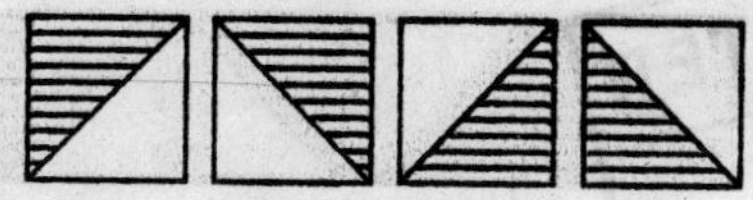

(*a*) (*b*) (*c*) (*d*)

**12. Pattern** 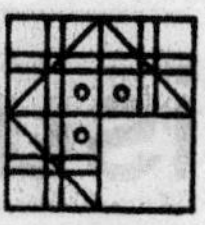

**Alternative figures**

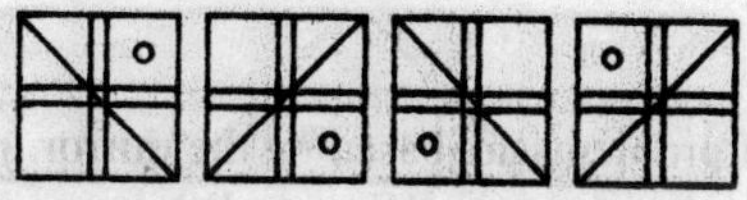

(*a*) (*b*) (*c*) (*d*)

## EXPLANATORY ANSWERS

All the completed figures will look like this:

**1. (*b*) :** 

**2. (*a*) :** 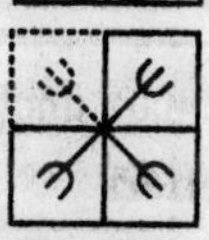

**3. (*d*) :** 

**4. (*d*) :** 

**5. (*a*) :** 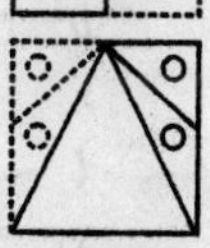

**6. (*a*) :** 

**7. (*b*) :** 

**8. (*c*) :** 

**9. (*a*) :** 

**10. (*b*) :** 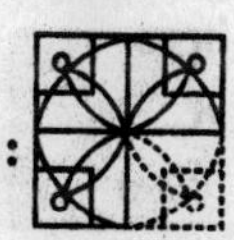

**11. (*a*) :** 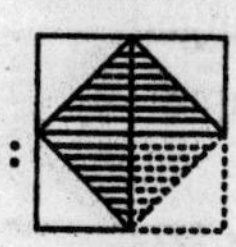

**12. (*d*) :** 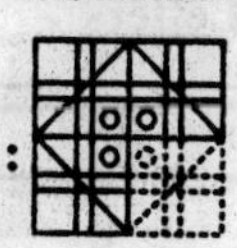

CHAPTER 8

# Visual Memory

These type of problems are based on the mirror images or reflections of number, letters and figures. While attempting such questions one must be able to visualise clearly the questioned reflections, be they on vertical plane or on horizontal plane. Study the chart and information given below. The visualisation of letters and numbers is easier than the visualisation of figures for the simple reason that the figures have many forms and all cannot be summed up.

**Horizontal Mirror Images (HMI) of Numbers**

| *Number* | *HMI* | *Number* | *HMI* |
|---|---|---|---|
| 0 | 0 | 5 | ꙅ |
| 1 | ı | 6 | ɘ |
| 2 | ƨ | 7 | ٢ |
| 3 | Ɛ | 8 | 8 |
| 4 | ߂ | 9 | ᑫ |

**Note :** HMI of 0 and 8 remain unchanged

**Vertical Mirror Images (VMI) of Numbers**

| Numbers : | 0 | 1 | 2 | 3 | 4 | 5 | 6 | 7 | 8 | 9 |
|---|---|---|---|---|---|---|---|---|---|---|
| VMI : | 0 | I | ᘔ | 3 | ᔭ | ς | ϱ | ˩ | 8 | 6 |

**Note :** VMI of 0, 3 and 8 remain unchanged.

Exceptions in style need caution. Example 3 will be 3, or 8 will be 8.

**Horizontal Mirror Images of Capital Letters**

| Letter | HMI | Letter | HMI | H letter | HMI |
|---|---|---|---|---|---|
| A | A | J | Ⴑ | S | Ƨ |
| B | ᗺ | K | ꓘ | T | T |
| C | Ɔ | L | ⅃ | U | U |
| D | ᗡ | M | M | V | V |
| E | Ǝ | N | И | W | W |
| F | ꟻ | O | O | X | X |
| G | Ә | P | ꟼ | Y | Y |
| H | H | Q | Ọ | Z | Ƶ |
| I | I | R | Я | | |

**Note :** HMI of A, H, I, M, O, T, U, V, W, X and Y remain unchanged.

Exceptions in style need caution. Example : A will be A, or X will be X.

**Vertical Mirror Images of Capital Letters**

| Letters : | A | B | C | D | E | F | G | H | I | J | K | L | M |
|---|---|---|---|---|---|---|---|---|---|---|---|---|---|
| VMI : | ∀ | B | C | D | E | Ŀ | ⅁ | H | I | ſ | K | Ⅎ | W |

| Letters : | N | O | P | Q | R | S | T | U | V | W | X | Y | Z |
|---|---|---|---|---|---|---|---|---|---|---|---|---|---|
| VMI : | N | O | b | Ó | ꓤ | S | ⊥ | ∩ | Λ | M | X | ⅄ | Z |

**Note :** VMI of C, D, E, H, I, K, O and X remain unchanged.

**Horizontal Mirror Images of Small Letters**

| Letter | HMI | Letter | HMI | Letter | HMI |
|---|---|---|---|---|---|
| a | ɒ | j | ꞁ | s | ƨ |
| b | d | k | ʞ | t | ɟ |
| c | ɔ | l | l | u | u |
| d | b | m | m | v | v |
| e | ɘ | n | n | w | w |
| f | ꟻ | o | o | x | x |
| g | ǫ | p | q | y | y |
| h | ʜ | q | p | z | z |
| i | i | r | ɿ | | |

**Note :** HMI of o, v, w and x remain unchanged.

**Vertical Mirror Images of Small Letters**

| Letter : | a | b | c | d | e | f | g | h | i | j | k | l | m |
|---|---|---|---|---|---|---|---|---|---|---|---|---|---|
| VMI : | ɐ | p | c | q | ɕ | ƪ | ƃ | ɥ | ! | ɾ | ʞ | l | ɯ |

| Letter : | n | o | p | q | r | s | t | u | v | w | x | y | z |
|---|---|---|---|---|---|---|---|---|---|---|---|---|---|
| VMI : | u | o | b | d | ɹ | s | ʇ | n | ʌ | ʍ | x | ʎ | z |

**Note :** VMI of c, o and x remain unchanged. Letter l has exceptions: if it is a straight vertical line – l then it remains unchanged.

## MULTIPLE CHOICE QUESTIONS

**Directions (Qs. 1 to 15) :** *In each question below which is the exact horizontal mirror image?*

1. DuST
   (a) ꓕƧuᗡ (b) ᗡnƧT
   (c) TƧuᗡ (d) ᗡuƧT
2. CHAIR
   (a) ЯIHAƆ (b) ЯIAHƆ
   (c) ЯIAHC (d) ƆHAIЯ
3. WHOM
   (a) MOHW (b) WOHM
   (c) ꟽHOꟽ (d) ꟽOHꟽ
4. plaque
   (a) ǝupɒlq (b) ǝuqblp
   (c) qlapue (d) ǝnqɐlp
5. brows
   (a) dɿowƨ (b) drows
   (c) ƨwoɿd (d) ƨword
6. flying
   (a) ƃniyl⅂ (b) gnilʎɟ
   (c) gniyl⅂ (d) ɟlyinƃ
7. 4379
   (a) 9ꓘƐ4 (b) 4379 (mirrored)
   (c) 9ꓘ34 (d) 4376 (mirrored)
8. 57182
   (a) ƧꓘI8Ƨ (b) 57I82 (mirrored)
   (c) Ƨ8IꓘƧ (d) 57182 (mirrored)
9. 69430
   (a) 0Ɛ496 (b) 0ꟼ496
   (c) 0Ɛ496 (d) 0Ɛ496
10. 2JKS
    (a) ƧKႱƧ (b) ƧKJ2
    (c) ƧKႱ2 (d) ƧKJƧ
11. P9Yf3
    (a) ƐfY9ꟼ (b) ƐfY9P
    (c) ƐꟻY9ꟼ (d) ƐꟻY9P
12. GZ5QRh
    (a) hЯQƧZG (b) hЯQ5ZG
    (c) hЯQƧZG (d) hЯQ5ZG
13. 2$%CH
    (a) HC%$Ƨ (b) HC%$2
    (c) HC%$2 (d) HC%$2
14. 7↑FN8
    (a) 8ИꟻↀƧ (b) 8NꟻↀƧ
    (c) 8ИF↑7 (d) 8NF↑7
15. yk19G
    (a) Ә9Ikʏ (b) G91ky
    (c) Ә91ky (d) G91ky

## ANSWERS

| 1 | 2 | 3 | 4 | 5 | 6 | 7 | 8 | 9 | 10 |
|---|---|---|---|---|---|---|---|---|---|
| (c) | (b) | (a) | (a) | (c) | (d) | (b) | (a) | (d) | (c) |
| **11** | **12** | **13** | **14** | **15** | | | | | |
| (d) | (b) | (c) | (a) | (d) | | | | | |

CHAPTER 9

# Discrimination

In these problems one has to count the geometrical figures in a given complex figure. A little bit of systematic approach is needed to get the correct number of the asked figure. The shapes of all geometrical figures must be clear in mind.

## SOLVED EXAMPLES

**1.** How many straight lines are used to make the figure given below?

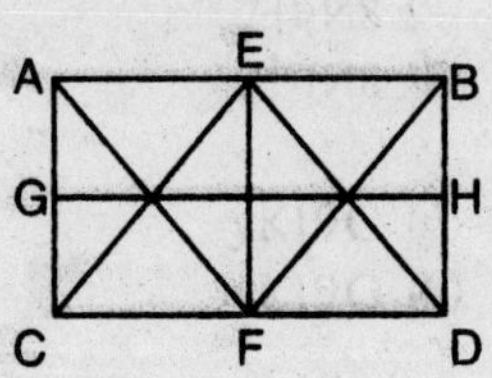


(*a*) 8 (*b*) 6
(*c*) 10 (*d*) 12

**Answer (*c*) :** The method of counting is given below.

The horizontal lines are AB, GH and CD i.e. – 3 lines, the vertical lines are AC, EF and BD i.e. – 3 lines, the diagonal lines are CE, FB, AF and ED i.e. – 4 lines, therefore the total number of straight lines is

3 + 3 + 4 = 10

**2.** How many square are there is this figure?

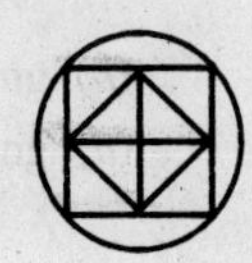

(*a*) 4 (*b*) 6
(*c*) 8 (*d*) 5

**Answer (*b*) :** The squares are counted in this manner.

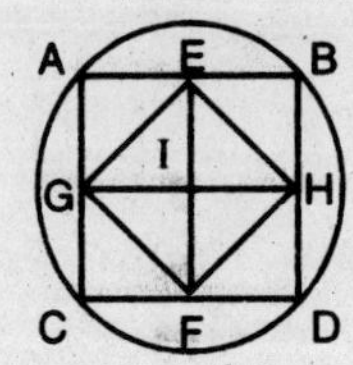


There is one main square ABCD divided into four parts by lines EF and GH. So, all the 5 squares are ABCD, AEGI, GICF, EBIH and IHFD. The square in the middle is EGHF. The total number of squares are 5 + 1 = 6

## MULTIPLE CHOICE QUESTIONS

**1.** How many triangles are there in the figure given below?

(*a*) 24 (*b*) 27
(*c*) 25 (*d*) 26

**2.** How many parallelograms are there in this figure?

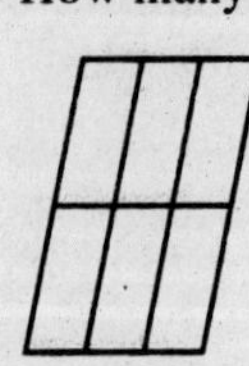

(*a*) 9 (*b*) 13
(*c*) 15 (*d*) 18

**3.** How many triangles are there in this figure?

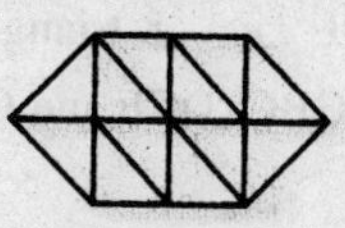

(*a*) 16 (*b*) 17
(*c*) 18 (*d*) 19

**4.** The number of rectangles in this figure are.

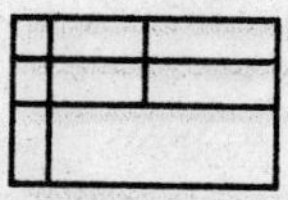

(*a*) 21 (*b*) 24
(*c*) 23 (*d*) 25

**5.** How many squares are hidden in this figure?

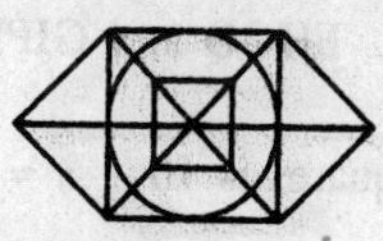

(*a*) 7 (*b*) 8
(*c*) 9 (*d*) 10

**6.** The number of triangles in this figure are.

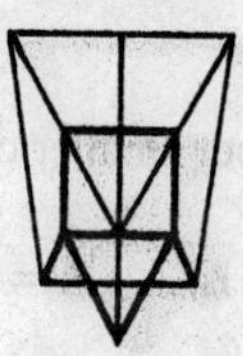

(*a*) 19 (*b*) 16
(*c*) 21 (*d*) 15

**7.** How many squares are there in the figure given below?

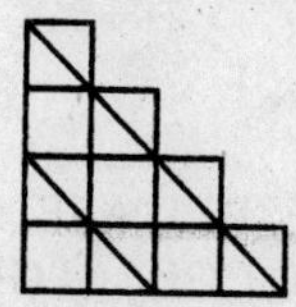

(*a*) 10 (*b*) 11
(*c*) 13 (*d*) 14

**8.** The number of circles in this figure is

(*a*) 6 (*b*) 5
(*c*) 2 (*d*) 3

**9.** How many triangles are there in the figure given below?

(*a*) 28 (*b*) 36
(*c*) 24 (*d*) 32

**10.** How many straight lines are needed to draw the figure in question 9?

(*a*) 10 (*b*) 12
(*c*) 11 (*d*) 13

## EXPLANATORY ANSWERS

**1. (*a*) :**

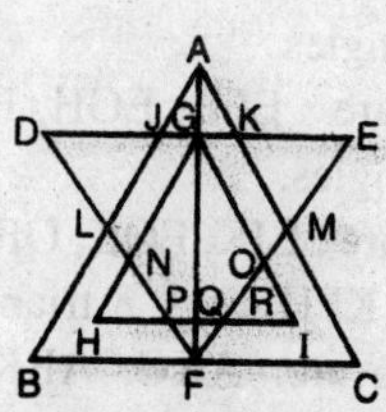

- The main triangles making the figure are ABC, DEF and GHI *i.e.,* – 3 triangles
- The simplest triangles are AJG, AGK, KEM, DJL, NHP, PQF, QFR and ORI *i.e.,* – 8 triangles
- The triangles formed by the bisecting line AF are ABF, AFC, GHQ, GQI, DGF and GFE *i.e.,* – 6 triangles
- The triangles formed inbetween the three triangles AJK, ALF, AMF, DGN, DGF, LBF, MFC, GEO, GNF and GOF – *i.e.,* 10 triangles
- So, the total number of triangles is 3 + 8 + 6 + 10 = 27

**2. (*d*) :**

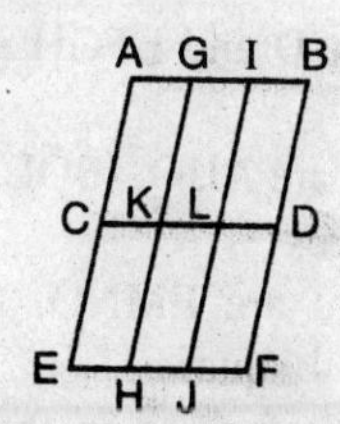

- The main parallelogram is ABEF *i.e.,* 1 parallelogram
- When divided into half by line CD the main figure has ABCD and CDEF *i.e.,* 2 parallelograms
- When further lines GH and IJ are drawn, the parallelograms are AGEH, GIJH and IBJF *i.e.,* – 3 parallelograms.
- The simplest parallelogram are AGCK, CKEH, GIKL, KLHJ, IBLD and LDJF *i.e.* – 6 parallelograms

Other parallelograms are AICL, CLEJ, GBKD, KDHF, AIEJ and GBHF – *i.e.,* 6 parallelograms

So, the total number of parallelograms is

1 + 2 + 3 + 6 + 6 = 18

**3. (a) :**

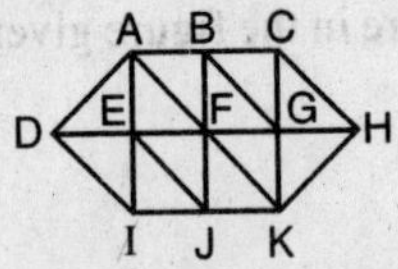


The simplest triangles are ADE, DEI, AEF, ABF, EIJ, EFJ, BFG, BCG, FJK, FGK, CGH and GHK – *i.e.,* – 12 triangles

The bisected triangles are ADI and CHK – *i.e.* – 2 triangles

Other triangles are AIK and ACK *i.e.,* – 2 triangles

So, the total number of triangles is
12 + 2 + 2 = 16

**4. (c) :**

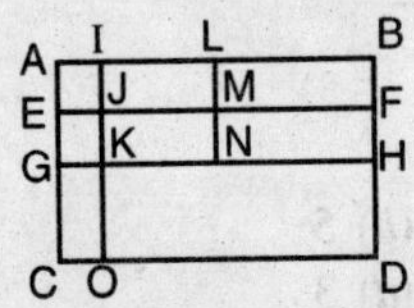


The main rectangle is ABCD – *i.e.,* – 1 rectangle

The simplest rectangles are AIEJ, ILJM, LBMF, EJGK, JMKN, MFNH, GKCO and KHOD *i.e.* – 8 rectangles.

The rectangles which have two parts are ALEM, IBJF, EMGN, JFKH, AIGK, IKLN, LBNH, EJCO and GHCD *i.e.* – 9 rectangles.

The rectangles which have three parts are AICO, ABEF and EFGH *i.e.* – 3 rectangles

The rectangles which have four parts are ALGN and IBKH *i.e.* – 2 rectangles

So, the total number of rectangles
1 + 8 + 9 + 3 + 2 = 23

**5. (d) :**

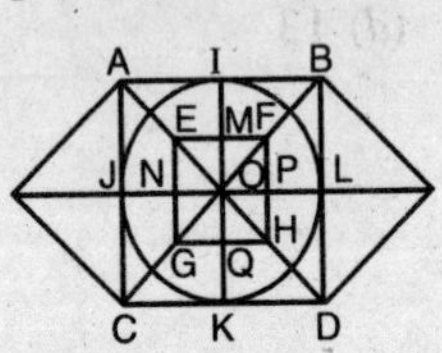


The main squares are ABCD and EFGH *i.e.,* – 2 squares

The simplest outer squares are AIJO, IBOL, JOCK and OLKD *i.e.,* – 4 squares

The simplest inner square are EMNO, NOGQ, MFOP and OPQH *i.e.,* – 4 squares

There are no other squares formed in the figure

So, the total number of squares is
2 + 4 + 4 = 10

**6. (b) :**

The main triangles are : ABC, DEF, LNF, and HJC *i.e.* 4 triangles

The simplest triangles are : HIC, IJC, HDC, JCE, DKL, LMF, MFN and NOE *i.e.* – 8 triangles

Other triangles are : AGC, GBC, DCF and CEF – *i.e.* 4 triangles

So, the total number of triangles is 4 + 8 + 4 = 16

**7. (c) :**

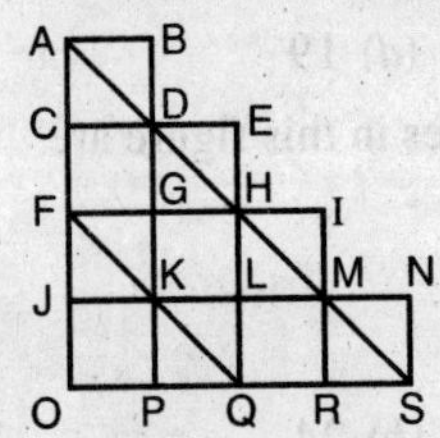


The simplest squares are : ABCD, CDFG, DEGH, FGJK, GHKL, HILM, JKOP, KLPQ, LMQR and MNRS *i.e.* – 10 squares.

Other squares are : CEJL, FHOQ and GIPR *i.e.* – 3 squares

So, the total number of squares is 10 + 3 = 13

**8. (a) :**

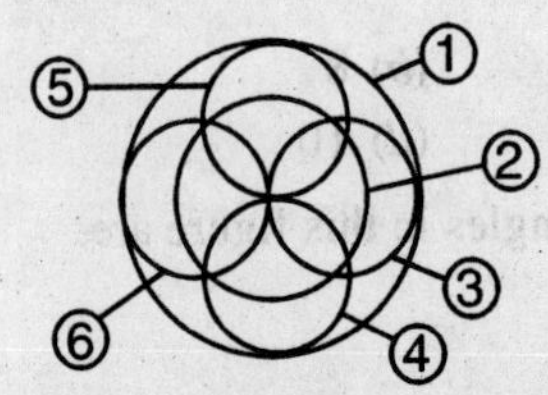


There are two main circles and four smaller circles intersecting each other.

So, the total number of circles is 2 + 4 = 6

**9. (d) :**

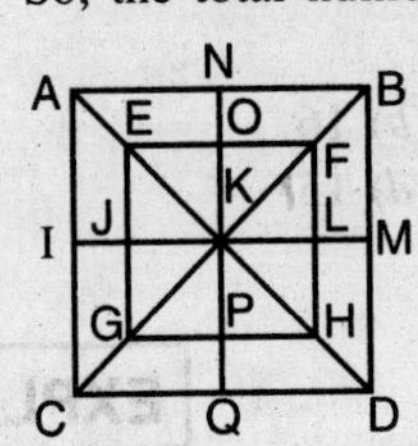


The larger triangles are : ABC, BCD, ABD and ACD *i.e.* – 4 triangles

The smaller triangles are : EFH, EGH, EFG and FGH *i.e.* – 4 triangles.

The simplest triangles are : EJK, EOK, OFK, JKG, FKL, KLH, KGP and KPH *i.e.* – 8 triangles

The bisected triangles are: AKC, ABK, CKD, KBD, EKG, EKF, KHG, KHF, i.e., –8 triangle.

Other triangles are : ANK, NKB, KBM, KMD, KQD, KQC, KCI, IKA *i.e.* – 8 triangles.

So, the total number of triangles is
4 + 4 + 8 + 8 + 8 = 32

**10. (b) :** The horizontal lines are : AB, EF, KL, GH and CD *i.e.* – 5 lines.

The vertical lines are AC, EG, IJ, FH and BD *i.e.* – 5 lines.

The diagonal lines are : AD and BC *i.e.* – 2 lines.

So, the total number of lines used to draw this figure is 5 + 5 + 2 = 12

CHAPTER

10

# Embedded Figures

In these type of questions a figure form is given followed by alternative figures. In one of these figure options the given form is embedded. Practice of visualisation comes handy in attempting such easy questions.

## MULTIPLE CHOICE QUESTIONS

**Directions (Qs. 1 to 6) :** *In the questions given below a figure is given. From the given alternatives select the one in which the given figure is embedded.*

**1.**

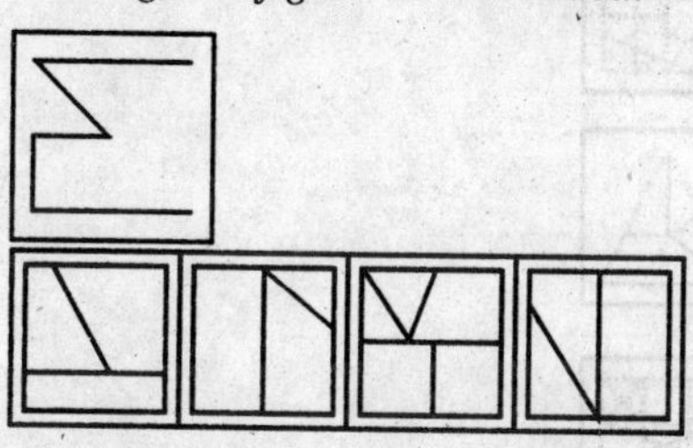

(a) (b) (c) (d)

**2.**

(a) (b) (c) (d)

**3.**

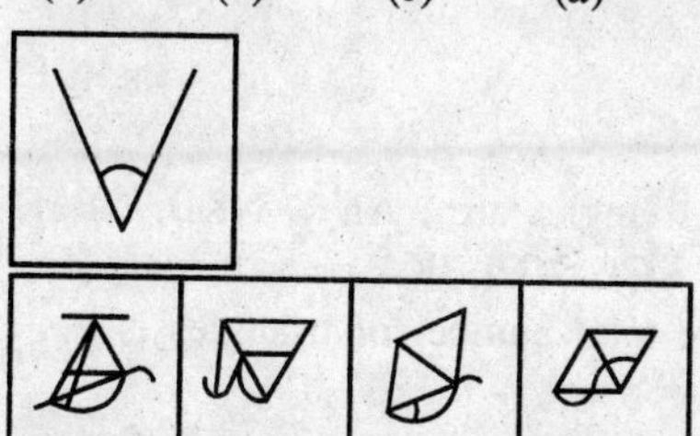

(a) (b) (c) (d)

**4.**

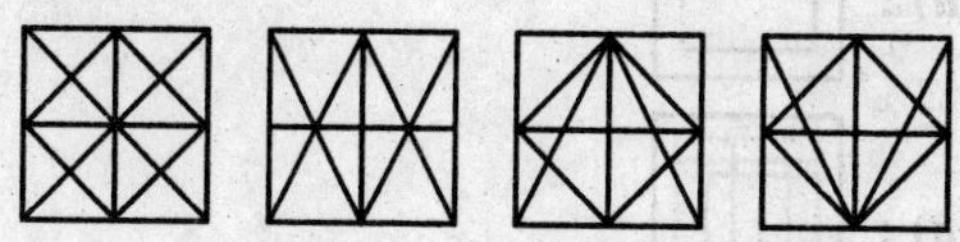

(a) (b) (c) (d)

**5.**

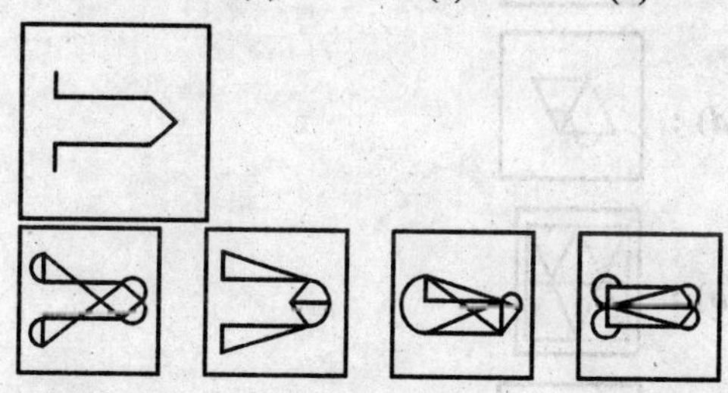

(a) (b) (c) (d)

**6.**

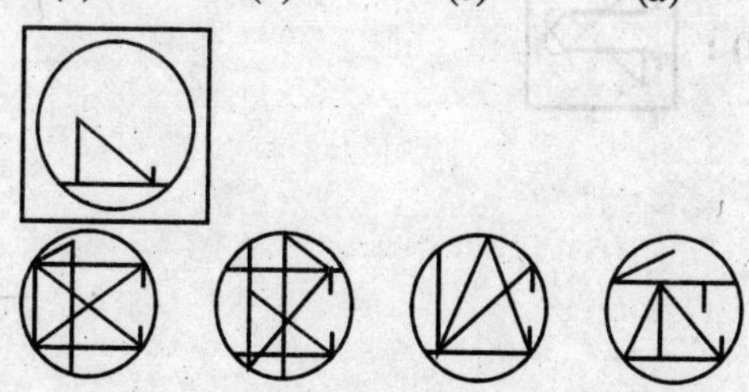

(a) (b) (c) (d)

**Directions (Qs. 7 to 10) :** *In each question given below find the figure form which is embedded in the given pattern.*

**7.**

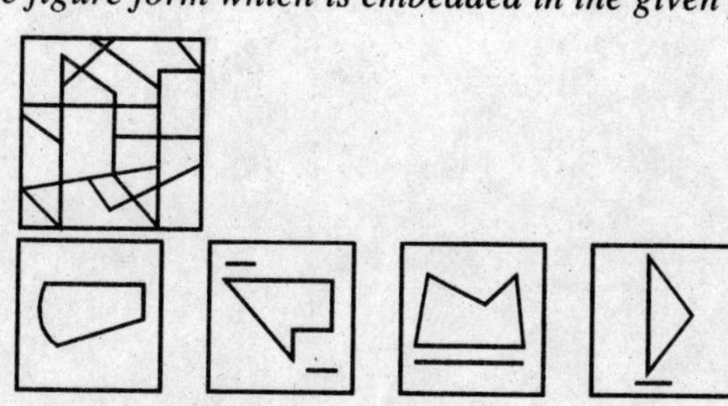

(a) (b) (c) (d)

8. 

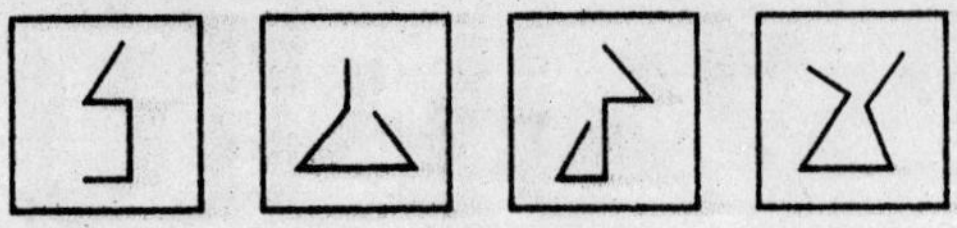

(a) (b) (c) (d)

9. 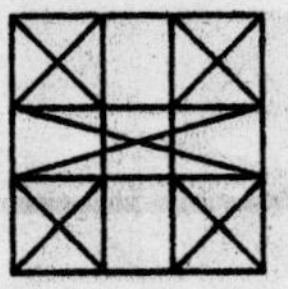

(a) (b) (c) (d)

10. 

(a) (b) (c) (d)

## EXPLANATORY ANSWERS

1. (a) : 

2. (a) : 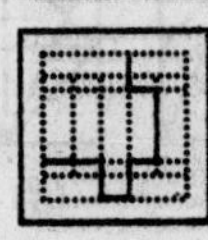

3. (d) : 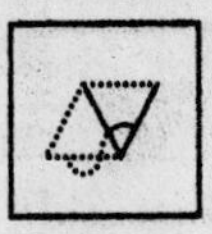

4. (b) : 

5. (a) : 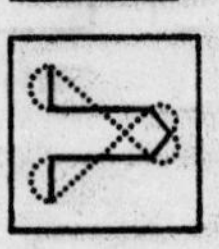

6. (b) : 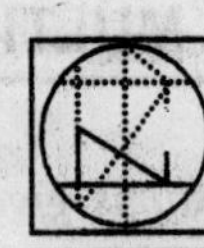

7. (d) : 

8. (b) : 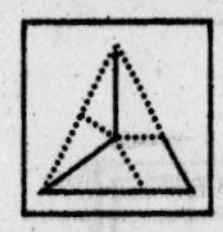

9. (c) : 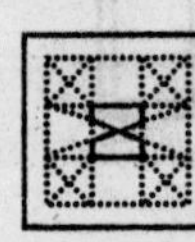

10. (d) : 

2008

# QUANTITATIVE APTITUDE

CHAPTER 1

# Numbers System

## Whole Numbers

In our System of numeration, numbers are written by using the symbols 0, 1, 2, 3, 4, 5, 6, 7, 8 and 9 with each symbol getting a value depending on the place it occupies. These symbols are called digits. A number related to the objects in a collection gives an idea of how many objects are there in the collection.

The number 789345126 can be represented as:

| Ten crores | Crores | Ten Lacs (Millions) | Lacs | Ten Thousands | Thousands | Hundreds | Tens | Units |
|---|---|---|---|---|---|---|---|---|
| $10^8$ | $10^7$ | $10^6$ | $10^5$ | $10^4$ | $10^3$ | $10^2$ | $10^1$ | $10^0$ |
| 7 | 8 | 9 | 3 | 4 | 5 | 1 | 2 | 6 |

This number can be read as: "Seventy-eight crores, ninety-three lacs, forty-five thousands, one hundred twenty six".

1. **Natural Numbers or Positive Integers (N = 1, 2, 3, 4, 5 .....):** These are also called counting numbers. When two natural numbers are added or multiplied together, the result is always a natural number. Therefore, all positive integers, used for counting objects, are always **natural numbers** whereas zero together with negative integers and fractional numbers are not natural numbers.
2. **Whole Numbers: (W = 0, 1, 2, 3, 4, 5, .......):** The number '0' together with the natural numbers gives us the numbers which are called **whole numbers,** e.g., 0, 1, 2, 3, 4 ..... etc. whereas –10, –15, –12 ..... or $\frac{1}{5}, \frac{2}{9}, \frac{4}{5}$..... etc. are not whole numbers.
3. **Integers: (I = ........, –5, –4, –3, –2, –1, 0, 1, 2, 3, 4, 5, ........):** The negative numbers together with the whole numbers are called integers. The numbers –1, –2, –3, –4, –5, ..... are called negative integers and 1, 2, 3, 4, 5, ....., *i.e.,* natural numbers are called positive integers. The number 0 is simply an integer, *i.e.,* it is neither positive nor negative.
4. **Rational Numbers:** A rational number is a number that can be put in the form $\frac{p}{q}$ where $p$ and $q$ are both integers and $q \neq 0$, e.g., 8, $-\frac{7}{5}$, $-\frac{3}{4}$, $\frac{1}{7}$, 0 ..... are all rational numbers i.e. a rational number may be positive, zero or negative.
5. **Irrational Numbers:** An irrational number is a number that can not be put in the form $\frac{p}{q}$ where $p$ and $q$ are both integers and $q \neq 0$, e.g., $\sqrt{5}, \sqrt{11}, \sqrt{15}$, $3 + \sqrt{5}$ .... etc. are all irrational numbers.
6. **Real Numbers:** All those numbers which are either rational or irrational, are called real numbers, e.g., $\frac{11}{17}$, $\frac{19}{21}$, $-\frac{7}{8}$, $\sqrt{7}$, $8 + \sqrt{3}$ etc. are real numbers.
7. **Even Numbers:** All those numbers which are exactly divisible by 2, are called 'even numbers', e.g., 2, 8, 14, 28, 52 etc. are even numbers.
8. **Odd Numbers:** All those numbers which are not exactly divisible by 2, are called 'odd numbers', e.g., 1, 3, 5, 7, 9, 19 etc. are odd numbers.

9. **Composite Numbers:** The numbers which are divisible not only by 1 or themselves, but by some other numbers also, are called the 'composite numbers'. In other words, the numbers which have more than two factors are called 'composite numbers.', e.g., 4, 9, 15, 18, 27, .... etc. are composite numbers.
10. **Prime Numbers:** The numbers which have only two factors, 1 and the number itself are called 'prime numbers', e.g., 2, 5, 11, 19, 23, 31, ..... etc. are prime numbers.
11. **Co-primes:** Two numbers which have only 1 as the common factor are called 'co-primes'. 5 and 7 are co-primes. So are 15 and 16.
12. **Twin Primes:** Two prime numbers which differ by 2, are called 'twin primes', e.g., 3, 5; 5, 7; 11, 13; 71, 73 are some pairs of twin primes.
13. **Consecutive Numbers:** The numbers which are following or coming after other numbers in regular order, are called consecutive numbers. 4, 6, 8, 10 are consecutive even numbers and 9, 11, 13, 15 are consecutive odd numbers. 3, 4, 5, 6, 7 ..... etc. are consecutive numbers in the natural order of the number series.

## TESTS FOR DIVISIBILITY OF NUMBERS

1. **Divisibility by 2:** A number is divisible by 2, if its units digit is 0, 2, 4, 6 or 8. For example, each of the numbers 130, 244, 566, 278, ... etc. is divisible by 2.
2. **Divisibility by 3:** A number is divisible by 3, if the sum of its digits is a multiple of 3. For example, each of the numbers 312, 213, 456 is divisible by 3 since sum of digits in each of these numbers is (3 + 1 + 2 = 6), (2 + 1 + 3 = 6) and (4 + 5 + 6 = 15) respectively, each of which is a multiple of 3.
3. **Divisibility by 4:** A number is divisible by 4, if the number formed by its digits in ten's and unit's places is divisible by 4. For example, numbers formed by ten's and unit's digits of 1132, 1312, 1400 and 1348 are 32, 12, 00 and 48 respectively which are divisible by 4. Hence, these numbers also are divisible by 4.
4. **Divisibility by 5:** A number is divisible by 5, if its unit's digit is either 0 or 5. For example, each of the numbers 100, 205, 315, 435 is divisible by 5 since unit's digit in each of these numbers is either 0 or 5.
5. **Divisibility by 6:** A number is divisible by 6, if it is divisible by both 2 and 3.
6. **Divisiblity by 8:** A number is divisible by 8, if the number formed by its digits in hundred's, ten's and unit's places is divisible by 8. For example, numbers formed by hundred's, ten's and unit's digits of 1864, 1024, 2008 and 5000 are 864, 024, 008 and 000 respectively which are divisible by 8. Hence, these numbers also are divisible by 8.
7. **Divisibility by 9:** A number is divisible by 9, if the sum of its digits is a multiple of 9. For example, each of the numbers 23409, 454554, 66636 is divisible by 9 since sum of digits in each of these numbers is (2 + 3 + 4 + 0 + 9 = 18), (4 + 5 + 4 + 5 + 5 + 4 = 27) and (6 + 6 + 6 + 3 + 6 = 27) respectively, each of which is a multiple of 9.
8. **Divisibility by 10:** A number is divisible by 10, if its unit's digit is zero. For example, each of the numbers 50, 80, 1310, 1400 is divisible by 10 since unit's digit in each of these numbers is 0.
9. **Divisibility by 11:** A number is divisible by 11, if the difference of the sum of its digits in even places and the sum of its digits in odd places (starting from unit's place) is either 0 or a multiple of 11. For example, each of the numbers 909183, 540045 and 184712 is divisible by 11 since in each of the numbers difference of the sum of digits in even places and sum of the digits in odd places is [(9 + 9 + 8) – (0 + 1 + 3) = 22], [(5 + 0 + 4) – (4 + 0 + 5) = 0] and [(8 + 7 + 2) – (1 + 4 + 1) = 11] respectively, each of which is either '0' or a multiple of '11'.
10. **Divisibility by 12:** A number is divisible by 12, if it is divisible by 3 and 4 both.

    For example, take a number 769824

    (*i*) Sum of digits = 7 + 6 + 9 + 8 + 2 + 4 = 36, it is divisible by 3.

    (*ii*) The number has 24 as its last two digits, which is divisible by 4.

    Hence, 769824 is divisible by 3 and 4 both, so it is divisible by 12.
11. **Divisibility by 14:** A number is divisible by 14, if it is divisible by 2 and 7 both.
12. **Divisibility by 15:** A number is divisible by 15, if it is divisible by 3 and 5 both.
13. **Divisibility by 16:** A number is divisible by 16, if the number formed by its last four digits is divisible by 16.

    For example, take a number 9877856, the number formed by its last four digits is 7856, which is divisible by 16. Hence, the number 9877856 is divisible by 16.
14. **Divisibility by 24:** A number is divisible by 24, if it is divisible by 3 and 8 both.
15. **Divisibility by 40:** A number is divisible by 40, if it is divisible by 5 and 8 both.
16. **Divisibility by 80:** A number is divisible by 80, if it is divisible by 5 and 16 both.

[**Note:** If a number is divisible by two co-primes separately, then the number will be also divisible by the product of co-primes.]

## EXERCISE

**1.** The difference between the squares of two consecutive numbers is 25. The numbers are—
A. 11, 12 B. 12, 13
C. 15, 14 D. 14, 13

**2.** The sum of two digits of a number is 15. If 9 is added to the number, the digits are reversed. The number is—
A. 78 B. 87
C. 69 D. 96

**3.** A number which when multiplied by 11 is as much above 180 as it was originally below it. The number is—
A. 25 B. 30
C. 40 D. 45

**4.** Divide ₹ 53 among X, Y, Z so that X may receive ₹ 7 more than Y, and Y may receive ₹ 8 more than Z.
A. 10, 15, 18 B. 18, 10, 25
C. 20, 12, 27 D. 25, 18, 10

**5.** If $a = 16$ and $b = 15$, then what is the value of $\frac{a^2+b^2+ab}{a^3-b^3} = ?$
A. $\frac{1}{2}$ B. $\frac{1}{3}$
C. 1 D. 2

**6.** Find the number which when multiplied by 16 is increased by 225.
A. 13 B. 14
C. 15 D. 16

**7.** What is the largest number of four digits which is exactly divisible by 88?
A. 9999 B. 9988
C. 9944 D. 9998

**8.** If $\frac{a}{b} = \frac{4}{3}$, then $\frac{3a+2b}{3a-2b} = ?$
A. 2 B. 3
C. 4 D. 5

**9.** If $\frac{x}{y} = \frac{3}{4}$, then the value of $\frac{6}{7}+\frac{y-x}{y+x} = ?$
A. 1 B. 2
C. 3 D. 4

**10.** If the number $(10^n - 1)$ is divisible by 11, then $n$ is—
A. odd number B. even number
C. any number D. multiple of 11

**11.** $\left(1-\frac{1}{3}\right)\left(1-\frac{1}{4}\right)\left(1-\frac{1}{5}\right)...\left(1-\frac{1}{n}\right) = ?$
A. $\frac{42}{29}$ B. $\frac{n-1}{n}$
C. $\frac{2}{n}$ D. 0

**12.** $\left(2-\frac{1}{3}\right)\left(2-\frac{3}{5}\right)\left(2-\frac{5}{7}\right)...\left(2-\frac{997}{999}\right) = ?$
A. $\frac{997}{999}$ B. $\infty$
C. $\frac{997}{3}$ D. $\frac{1001}{3}$

**13.** Divide 48 into two parts such that 7 times the first part added to 5 times the second part is 246. Find the first part.
A. 2 B. 3
C. 4 D. 5

**14.** The sum of a number and its reciprocal is thrice the difference of the number and its reciprocal. Find the number.
A. $\sqrt{2}$ B. $\sqrt{3}$
C. $\sqrt{5}$ D. $\sqrt{7}$

**15.** What should be added to the product of four consecutive odd numbers to make it a perfect square?
A. 13 B. 14
C. 15 D. 16

**16.** A boy was asked to find $\frac{7}{9}$ of a fraction. He made a mistake of dividing the fraction by $\frac{7}{9}$ and so got an answer which exceeded the correct answer by $\frac{8}{21}$. Find the correct answer.
A. 2/3 B. 5/7
C. 7/12 D. 7/15

**17.** If 40% of a number is 360, what will be 15% of 15% of that number?
A. 11.5 B. 20.25
C. 15.5 D. 21.75

**18.** The sum of two numbers is 25 and the difference of their square is 75. Find the difference between the numbers.
A. 2 B. 3
C. 4 D. 5

**19.** Ram eats 8 bananas in the morning, 5 in the afternoon and 2 in the evening. How many dozens of bananas does he eat in a day.
A. $1\frac{1}{4}$ B. $\frac{1}{4}$
C. $\frac{3}{13}$ D. $14\frac{17}{30}$

**20.** $47^{7.5} \div 47^{\frac{3}{2}} \times 47^{-3} = \left(\sqrt{47}\right)^{?}$ What should come in place of the question mark (?) in the following equation?
A. 5 B. 6
C. 7 D. 8

## ANSWERS

| 1 | 2 | 3 | 4 | 5 | 6 | 7 | 8 | 9 | 10 |
|---|---|---|---|---|---|---|---|---|---|
| B | A | B | B | C | C | C | B | A | B |
| **11** | **12** | **13** | **14** | **15** | **16** | **17** | **18** | **19** | **20** |
| C | D | B | A | D | C | B | B | A | B |

## EXPLANATORY ANSWERS

**1.** Let the numbers are $x$ and $(x + 1)$

$$\therefore \quad (x+1)^2 - x^2 = 25$$
$$\Rightarrow \quad x^2 + 1 + 2x - x^2 = 25$$
$$\Rightarrow \quad 2x + 1 = 25$$
$$\Rightarrow \quad 2x = 25 - 1 = 24$$
$$\therefore \quad x = \frac{24}{2} = 12$$
$$\therefore \quad x + 1 = 12 + 1 = 13$$

Hence, the numbers are 12, 13.

**2.** Let $x$ be the digit in units place. Digit in ten's place is then $15 - x$.

$\therefore$ The number $= 10(15 - x) + x$

The new number with reverse digits

$$= 10 \times x + (15 - x)$$
$$\therefore \quad 10(15 - x) + x + 9 = 10x + 15 - x$$
$$\Rightarrow \quad 150 - 10x + x + 9 = 9x + 15$$
$$\Rightarrow \quad 18x = 144$$
$$x = \frac{144}{18} = 8$$

The digit of ten's place $= 15 - 8 = 7$

$\therefore$ The required number = 78.

**3.** Let the number is $x$

$$\therefore \quad 180 - x = 11x - 180$$
$$\Rightarrow \quad 180 + 180 = 11x + x$$
$$\Rightarrow \quad 360 = 12x,$$
$$\Rightarrow \quad x = \frac{360}{12} = 30.$$

**4.** Let Y receives ₹ $a$. Then X receives ₹ $(a + 7)$ and Z receives ₹ $(a - 8)$

But, $a + 7 + a + a - 8 =$ ₹ 53

$$\Rightarrow \quad 3a - 1 = 53,$$
$$\Rightarrow \quad 3a = 53 + 1$$
$$\Rightarrow \quad 3a = 54,$$
$$\therefore \quad a = \frac{54}{3} = ₹\ 18. = \text{Y's share}$$

X's share $= a + 7 = 18 + 7 =$ ₹ 25

Z's share $= a - 8 = 18 - 8 =$ ₹ 10.

**5.** Given $a = 16$ and $b = 15$, then $\frac{a^2+b^2+ab}{a^3-b^3}$

$$= \frac{a^2+b^2+ab}{(a-b)(a^2+b^2+ab)} = \frac{1}{a-b} = \frac{1}{16-15} = 1$$

**6.** Let the required no. $= x$

then, $\quad 16x - x = 225$

$\Rightarrow \quad 15x = 225 \therefore x = 15$

**7.** The greatest no. of 4 digit = 9999

Now, after dividing 9999 by 88, we get Remainder = 55

Hence, the largest 4 digit no. = 9999 – 55 = 9944

**8.** $$\frac{3a+2b}{3a-2b} = \frac{3\frac{a}{b}+2}{3\frac{a}{b}-2} = \frac{3\times\frac{4}{3}+2}{3\times\frac{4}{3}-2} = \frac{6}{2} = 3$$

**9.** $$\frac{6}{7}+\frac{y-x}{y+x} = \frac{6}{7}+\frac{1-x/y}{1+x/y} = \frac{6}{7}+\frac{1-3/4}{1+3/4} = \frac{6}{7}+\frac{1}{7} = 1$$

**10.** $n$ is even number.

**11.** $$\frac{2}{3}\times\frac{3}{4}\times\frac{4}{5}\times\ldots\times\frac{n-1}{n} = \frac{2}{n}$$

**12.** $$\frac{5}{3}\times\frac{7}{5}\times\frac{9}{7}\times\ldots\times\frac{1001}{999} = \frac{1001}{3}$$

**13.** Let the first part $= x$

then 2nd part $= (48 - x)$

By question, $\quad 7x + 5(48 - x) = 246$

$\Rightarrow \quad 2x = 246 - 240 \therefore x = 3$

**14.** Let the no. $= x$

then its reciprocal $= \frac{1}{x}$

By the question, $\left(x+\frac{1}{x}\right) = 3\left(x-\frac{1}{x}\right)$

$$\Rightarrow \quad \frac{x^2+1}{x} = \frac{3(x^2-1)}{x}$$
$$\Rightarrow \quad x^2 + 1 = 3x^2 - 3$$
$$\Rightarrow \quad 3x^2 - x^2 = 3 + 1 \therefore x = \sqrt{2}.$$

**15.** Let the four consecutive odd numbers be $(2x - 3)$, $(2x - 1)$, $(2x + 1)$ and $(2x + 3)$

$\therefore$ Their product $= (2x - 1)(2x + 1)(2x - 3)(2x + 3)$

$= (4x^2 - 1)(4x^2 - 9) = 16x^4 - 40x^2 + 9$

$= (4x^2 - 5)^2 - 16$

Hence, on adding 16, the result will be a perfect square.

**16.** Let the required fraction = $x$

then, by the question $x \div \frac{7}{9} - x \times \frac{7}{9} = \frac{8}{21}$

$\Rightarrow \quad x \times \frac{9}{7} - \frac{7x}{9} = \frac{8}{21} \Rightarrow \frac{32x}{63} = \frac{8}{21}$

$\Rightarrow \quad x = \frac{8}{21} \times \frac{63}{32} = \frac{3}{4}$

Hence, the correct answer = $\frac{3}{4} \times \frac{7}{9} = \frac{7}{12}$.

**17.** Let a number be $x$

then 40% of $x$ = 360

$\Rightarrow \quad \frac{40}{100} \times x = 360$

$\therefore \quad x = 360 \times \frac{100}{40} = 900$

Now by the question,

15% of 15% of 900 = $\frac{15}{100} \times \frac{15}{100} \times 900 = \frac{81}{4} = 20.25.$

**18.** Let two numbers are $a$ and $b$

Given, $a + b = 25$

and $a^2 - b^2 = 75$

$\Rightarrow \quad (a + b)(a - b) = 75$

$\Rightarrow \quad (a - b) = \frac{75}{(a+b)} = \frac{75}{25} = 3.$

**19.** Total dozen of bananas Ram eats in a day

$= \frac{8}{12} + \frac{5}{12} + \frac{2}{12} = \frac{15}{12} = 1\frac{1}{4}$

**20.** $47^{7.5} \div 47^{\frac{3}{2}} \times 47^{-3} = \left(\sqrt{47}\right)^{?}$

Let ? = $x$

then $(47)^{\frac{15}{2}} \div (47)^{\frac{3}{2}} \times (47)^{-3} = (47)^{\frac{x}{2}}$

$\Rightarrow \quad (47)^{\frac{15}{2} - \frac{3}{2} - 3} = (47)^{\frac{x}{2}}$

$\Rightarrow \quad (47)^{\frac{6}{2}} = (47)^{\frac{x}{2}}$

$\therefore \quad x = 6.$

# Decimal Fraction

## FRACTION

The relation to represent some part of the body to the whole body is known *Fraction*. For example $\frac{2}{5}$ is a fraction where 2 is the numerator and 5 is the denominator.

***Important Facts :***

*(i)* A fraction is also called a rational number.

*(ii)* A fraction is unity when its numerator and denominator are equal.

*(iii)* When a fraction is reduced in its lowest term, its numerator and denominator are prime to each other, *i.e.*, they have no common factor.

*(iv)* The value of fraction is not altered by multiplying or dividing the numerator and the denominator by the same number.

**Vulgar or Common Fraction :** The fraction such as $\frac{2}{9}, \frac{7}{11}, \frac{3}{10}, \frac{9}{100}$ are called vulgar fraction.

**Decimal Fraction :** Fractions in which denomi-nators are power of 10 are called decimal fractions.

**For example :** $\frac{1}{10}, \frac{1}{100}, \frac{7}{1000}$ etc.

Here, $\frac{1}{10}$ is 1 tenths, written as .1

$\frac{1}{100} = .01$

$\frac{7}{1000} = .007$

$\frac{13}{100} = .13$ and so on.

### Converting a Decimal into a Vulgar Fraction

First of all write down the given number as numerator without the decimal point, and for the denominator write 1 followed by as many zeros as many are there figures after the decimal point. Now reduce the fraction to its lowest terms.

**Ex :** *(i)* 0.63 $= \frac{63}{100}$

*(ii)* 3.013 $= 3\frac{013}{1000} = 3\frac{13}{1000}$

### Addition and Subtraction of Decimal Fractions

First of all write down the numbers under one another. Other than the decimal point lies in one column. After arranging in this way, we add or subtract in usual fashion.

**An example :** Add 521 + 52.1 + 5.21 + 0.521

**Sol :** 521.000
52.100
5.210
0.521 After adding we get 578.831

### Multiplication of decimal fraction

**1.** To multiply by 10, 100, 1000, etc

**Example :** *(i)* 63.02 × 10 = 630.2

(ii) 63.02 × 100 = 6302

(iii) 63.02 × 1000 = 63020

**2.** To multiply of two or more decimal fractions.

**An example :** *(i)* 5.91 × 13 = 76.83

*(ii)* 6.32 × 0.59 = 3.7288

*(iii)* 63.2 × 0.01 = 0.632

***Conclusion:*** First of all multiply the given numbers assuming them without the decimal point. Now mark off the decimal point from extreme right in the product as many places of decimal as is the sum of the number of decimal places in the given numbers.

## DIVISION OF DECIMALS

**1. When the divisor is a counting number**

**Example :** *(i)* 4.309 ÷ 10 = 0.4309

*(ii)* 0.0182 ÷ 14 = 0.0013

*(iii)* 9.586 ÷ 100 = 0.09586

*(iv)* 0.05 ÷ $10^3$ = 0.00005

*(v)* 0.49 ÷ 7 = 0.07

***Conclusion*** **:** *(i)* When divisor is the power of 10, then shift the decimal point to the left by as many places of decimal as is the power of 10, prefixing zero if necessary.

*(ii)* When divisor is other than power of 10, then divide as in the case of integers, and in quotient, put the decimal point to give as many places of decimal as are there in the dividend.

**2. When the divisor is a decimal**

**Example:**

*(i)* $0.00066 \div 0.11 = \frac{0.00066}{0.11} = \frac{0.066}{11} = 0.006$

*(ii)* $42 \div 0.07 = \frac{42}{0.07} = \frac{4200}{7} = 600$

*(iii)* $32.5 \div 0.0064 = \frac{32.5}{0.0064} = \frac{325000}{64} = 5078.125$

**Recurring Decimal :** If in a decimal number a digit or a set of digits is repeated again and again, the decimal is known as recurring decimal.

**For example:**

*(i)* 2.666... = $2.\dot{6}$

*(ii)* 1.363636... = $1.\dot{3}\dot{6}$ or $1.\overline{36}$

*(iii)* 7.3424242... = $7.3\dot{4}\dot{2}$ or $7.3\overline{42}$

Recurring decimal numbers are of two types:

*(i)* **Pure recurring decimals :** A decimal fraction in which all the figures after the decimal point are repeated is called a pure recurring decimal. For example, $0.\overline{3}$, $0.\overline{37}$, $3.\overline{4579}$ etc

*(ii)* **Mixed recurring decimals :** A decimal fraction in which at least one figure after the decimal point is not repeated is called a mixed recurring decimal. For example, $0.3\overline{59}$, $0.29\overline{54}$, $0.2\overline{7}$ etc.

### *Conversion of Recurring into Vulgar Fraction*

**1.** Pure recurring decimals

**Rule :** Put as many 9's in the denominator at the number of digits under recurring and delete the recurring sign.

For example, $0.\overline{5} = \frac{5}{9}$

$0.\overline{35} = \frac{35}{99}$

$0.\overline{24} = \frac{24}{99} = \frac{8}{33}$

**2.** Mixed Recurring Decimals

For example,

*(i)* $0.1\overline{8}$

Here, numerator = 18 − 1 = 17

and denominator = 9 × 10 = 90

$\therefore \quad 0.1\dot{8} = \frac{18-1}{90} = \frac{17}{90}$

*(ii)* $0.2\dot{7}\dot{9}$

Here, numerator = 279 − 2 = 277

and denominator = 99 × 10 = 990

$\therefore \quad 0.2\overline{79} = \frac{279-2}{990} = \frac{277}{990}$

*(iii)* $0.3\overline{56} = \frac{356-3}{99 \times 10} = \frac{353}{990}$

*(iv)* $2.5\dot{3}\dot{6} = 2 + \frac{536-53}{9 \times 100} = 2 + \frac{483}{900}$

$= 2 + \frac{161}{300} = 2\frac{161}{300}$

*(v)* $0.43\overline{213} = \frac{43213-43}{999 \times 100}$

$= \frac{43170}{99900} = \frac{4317}{9990}$

### *Addition and Subtraction of recurring decimals*

**Example :** *(i)* Add $3.\overline{76}$ and $1.4\overline{576}$ and subtract also.

| | | | |
|---|---|---|---|
| 3.7 | 676767 | 67 | |
| 1.4 | 576576 | 57 | |
| (+) 5.2 | 253344 | 24 | ⇒ $5.2\overline{253344}$ |
| (−) 2.3 | 100191 | 10 | ⇒ 2.3100191 |

*(ii)* Subtract $3.\overline{75}$ from $25.5\overline{473}$

| | | |
|---|---|---|
| 25.5 | 473473 | 47 |
| 3.7 | 575757 | 57 |
| 21.7 | 897715 | 90 |

Hence, the required subtract = $21.7\overline{897715}$

### Multiplication and Division of Recurring Decimal

**Example 1:**

(*i*) $7.\overline{63} \times 11 = 7\frac{63}{99} \times 11$

$= 7\frac{7}{11} \times 11 = \frac{84}{11} \times 11 = 84$

(*ii*) $0.\overline{09} \times 7.\overline{3} = \frac{9}{99} \times 7\frac{3}{9}$

$= \frac{1}{11} \times \frac{66}{9} = \frac{6}{9} = 0.\overline{6}$

(*iii*) $0.\overline{6} \times 7.\overline{3} = \frac{6}{9} \times 7\frac{3}{9}$

$= \frac{6}{9} \times \frac{66}{9} = \frac{44}{9} = 4.\overline{8}$

(*iv*) $0.\overline{06} \div 100 = 0.060606... \div 100 = 0.00\overline{06}$

(*v*) $0.7\overline{32} \div 0.02\overline{7} = 0.73\overline{23} \div 0.027\overline{7}$

$= \frac{7323 - 73}{99 \times 100} \div \frac{277 - 2}{99 \times 100}$

$= \frac{7250}{9900} \div \frac{275}{9900} = \frac{7250}{275} = \frac{290}{11} = 26.\overline{36}$.

## EXERCISE

**1.** Which of the following is equivalent to $\frac{15}{25}$?

A. $\frac{150}{25}$ B. $\frac{15}{250}$
C. $\frac{3}{5}$ D. $\frac{60}{75}$

**2.** If $\frac{9*3}{3*7}$ is equivalent to $\frac{9}{7}$, the sign * is replaced by

A. ÷ B. ×
C. + D. –

**3.** $\frac{5}{6}$ of an hour is equal to

A. half an hour B. 40 minutes
C. 50 minutes D. 55 minutes

**4.** An aircraft uses 2/5 of its fuel in flying 1,250 kilometres. The distance travelled on remaining fuel is

A. 1875 km B. 2125 km
C. 250 km D. 475 km

**5.** If $\frac{4}{3} * \frac{3}{4} = \frac{16}{9}$, then * means

A. + B. –
C. × D. ÷

**6.** Which of the following is the largest fraction?

$\frac{3}{15}, \frac{5}{20}, \frac{8}{64}, \frac{25}{1000}$

A. $\frac{3}{15}$ B. $\frac{5}{20}$
C. $\frac{8}{64}$ D. $\frac{25}{1000}$

**7.** Six times $x$ increased by 12 is equal to

A. $\frac{x}{2}$ B. $2x$
C. $6x + 12$ D. $12x + 6$

**8.** Five times $y$ diminished by 20 is equal to

A. $5y - 20$ B. $5y + 20$
C. $y/4$ D. $4y$

**9.** The number less than 15 by 7 is

A. $15x - 7$ B. 15/7
C. 15 D. 8

**10.** If 21 is add to four times a number, the result is 57. The number is

A. 7 B. 8
C. 9 D. 10

**11.** A number, the sum of whose fourth and fifth parts exceeds their third part by 28, is

A. 120 B. 240
C. 220 D. 160

**12.** Which fraction should be added to the sum of $5\frac{3}{4}$, $4\frac{4}{5}$ and $7\frac{3}{8}$ to make the result a whole number?

A. $\frac{1}{40}$ B. $\frac{2}{40}$
C. $\frac{3}{40}$ D. $\frac{4}{40}$

**13.** $\frac{1}{15} + \frac{3}{15} + \frac{5}{15} + \frac{6}{15} = ?$

A. $\frac{10}{15}$ B. $\frac{3}{5}$
C. $\frac{4}{5}$ D. 1

**14.** A number one-sixth of which exceeds its one-ninth by 100 is

A. 600 B. 900
C. 1500 D. 1800

**15.** The sum of 1/2, 1/4 and 1/8 of a number is 28. The number is

A. 28 B. 32
C. 36 D. 42

**16.** The sum of 1/9, 1/3, 1/6 and 7/18 of a number is 150. The number is

A. 120 B. 130
C. 140 D. 150

17. Which is the greatest?

.999, .1011, .1995, .9985

A. .999 B. .1011

C. .1995 D. .9985

18. In decimal system, $9\frac{1}{8}$ may be represented as

A. 9.18 B. 9.125

C. 9.025 D. 9.225

19. $2.205 \div 0.15 = ?$

A. 1.47 B. 14.7

C. 147 D. 0.147

20. G.C.M. of .24, 3.2 and 16.0 is

A. 80 B. 8

C. .8 D. .08

## ANSWERS

| 1 | 2 | 3 | 4 | 5 | 6 | 7 | 8 | 9 | 10 |
|---|---|---|---|---|---|---|---|---|---|
| C | B | C | A | D | B | C | A | D | C |
| **11** | **12** | **13** | **14** | **15** | **16** | **17** | **18** | **19** | **20** |
| B | C | D | D | B | D | A | B | B | D |

## EXPLANATORY ANSWERS

1. $\frac{15}{25} = \frac{3\times 5}{5\times 5} = \frac{3}{5}$

2. $\frac{9*3}{3*7} = \frac{9}{7}$, or, $\frac{9\times 3}{7\times 3} = \frac{9}{7}$, $\therefore$ The sign * is ×.

3. $\frac{5}{6}$ of 1 hr. $= \frac{5}{6}\times 60$ minutes $= 50$ minutes.

4. Remaining fuel $= 1-\frac{2}{5} = \frac{5-2}{5} = \frac{3}{5}$

Distance flown by $\frac{2}{5}$ of fuel = 1250 km.

Distance flown by full fuel $= \frac{1250}{2/5} = \frac{1250\times 5}{2}$ km.

Distance flown by $\frac{3}{5}$ of fuel

$= \frac{1250\times 5\times 3}{2\times 5} = 1875$ km.

6. $\frac{3}{15} = \frac{1}{5}, \frac{8}{64} = \frac{1}{8}, \frac{5}{20} = \frac{1}{4}, \frac{25}{1000} = \frac{1}{40}$

Now, the fractions are $\frac{1}{5}, \frac{1}{4}, \frac{1}{8}, \frac{1}{40}$

$\therefore$ The largest fraction is $\frac{1}{4} = \frac{5}{20}$

7. $x \times 6 + 12 = 6x + 12$

8. $5 \times y - 20 = 5y - 20$

9. $15 - 7 = 8$

10. Let the number be $x$

$\therefore \quad 4x + 21 = 57$ or, $4x = 57 - 21 = 36$

Hence, $x = \frac{36}{4} = 9$

11. Let the number be $x$

$\therefore \quad \frac{x}{4}+\frac{x}{5} = \frac{x}{3}+28$

$\Rightarrow \quad \frac{9x}{20} = \frac{x}{3}+28 \Rightarrow \frac{9x}{20}-\frac{x}{3} = 28$

$\Rightarrow \quad \frac{27x-20x}{60} = 28 \therefore x = \frac{28\times 60}{7} = 240.$

12. $5\frac{3}{4}+4\frac{4}{5}+7\frac{3}{8} = \frac{23}{4}+\frac{24}{5}+\frac{59}{8} = \frac{717}{40}$

717/40 becomes whole number when 3/40 is added to it, *i.e.*,

$\frac{717}{40}+\frac{3}{40} = \frac{720}{40} = 18$ which is a whole number.

13. $\frac{1}{15}+\frac{3}{15}+\frac{5}{15}+\frac{6}{15} = \frac{1+3+5+6}{15} = \frac{15}{15} = 1$

14. Let the number be $x$

$\frac{x}{6} = \frac{x}{9}+100$

$\Rightarrow \quad \frac{x}{6}-\frac{x}{9} = 100, \Rightarrow \frac{x}{18} = 100$

$\therefore \quad x = 100 \times 18 = 1800.$

15. Let the number be $x$

$\therefore \quad \frac{x}{2}+\frac{x}{4}+\frac{x}{8} = 28 \Rightarrow \frac{7x}{8} = 28$

$\therefore \quad x = \frac{28\times 8}{7} = 32.$

16. Let the number be $x$,

$\therefore \quad \frac{x}{9}+\frac{x}{3}+\frac{x}{6}+\frac{7x}{18} = 150$

$\Rightarrow \quad \frac{2x+6x+3x+7x}{18} = \frac{18x}{18} = 150 \therefore x = 150.$

17. .999 is the greatest.

18. $9\frac{1}{8} = 9+\frac{1}{8} = 9 + .125 = 9.125$

19. $2.205 \div 0.15 = \frac{2.205}{.15} = \frac{2205}{1000}\times\frac{100}{15} = \frac{2205}{150} = 14.7.$

20. G.C.M. of .24, 3.2 and 16.0

$=$ G.C.M. of $\frac{24, 320 \text{ and } 1600}{100} = \frac{8}{100} = 0.08$

# Relation Between Numbers

Simplification is a mathematical operation by which a complex expression of numbers or fractions is converted into a simpler or less difficult form. It is erroneous to solve this type of questions on random basis and a very appropriate method is to apply BODMAS Rule for arriving at the solution of such problems. Each of the letters of the word 'BODMAS' when explained serially, has following implications:

1. B → Bracket [{ (‾) } ]
2. O → of — of
3. D → Division — ÷
4. M → Multiplication — ×
5. A → Addition — +
6. S → Subtraction — –

Therefore, for simplification, we should remove the brackets first. Thereafter operation for 'of', then for 'division', after that the operation for 'multiplication' and thereafter for 'addition' and at last operation for 'subtraction' should be carried out.

**Important Notes**

A. In mathematical operations the word 'of' indicates multiplication.

B. While removing brackets, first of all bar bracket '‾' and after that small bracket '( )' is removed. Thereafter the curly bracket '{ }' and at last square bracket [ ] is removed.

## EXERCISE

**1.** The value of 51 ÷ 17 ÷ 3 is:
A. 9 B. 4
C. 3 D. 1

**2.** What will be the value of
40 × 2 ÷ 10 + 5 – 4?
A. 5 B. 8
C. 11 D. 9

**3.** The value of 28 × 104 ÷ (18 + 6) + 3 is:
A. $124\frac{1}{3}$ B. $104\frac{1}{3}$
C. $125\frac{1}{3}$ D. 128

**4.** If $75^2 - 65^2 = 2x$, then value of $x$ is:
A. 715 B. 700
C. 688 D. 711

**5.** The value of 99 × 14 ÷ 11 ÷ 0.7 is:
A. 2.9 B. 1.6
C. 1.8 D. 2.8

**6.** If 45 – [28 – {37 – (15 – ?) }] = 58, then which of the following should replace the sign of interrogation (?)?
A. 18 B. 17
C. 13 D. 19

**7.** The value of $8\frac{1}{3}+5\frac{1}{4}\times13\frac{1}{5} \div 6\frac{3}{5}$ is:
A. $19\frac{1}{3}$ B. $18\frac{5}{6}$
C. $21\frac{1}{3}$ D. $22\frac{1}{2}$

**8.** The value of $\frac{14}{3}$ of $\frac{5}{8}$ of 72 is:
A. 209 B. 217
C. 210 D. 199

**9.** What will be the value of
10 × 10 × 10 ÷ (20 ÷ 10 × 10 – 10) + 6?
A. 108 B. 111
C. 106 D. 114

**10.** What will be the value of $\frac{\frac{1}{3}\times 20 \div 4}{\frac{1}{4}\times 25 \div 5}$?
A. 7/3 B. 4/3
C. 5/3 D. 10/3

**11.** Which of the following is the standard form of $\frac{(24\times13)+(28\div7)}{(24+13)-\left(\frac{14}{3}\text{ of }\frac{5}{8}\right)}$?
A. $\frac{3792}{409}$ B. $\frac{4792}{309}$
C. $\frac{3792}{411}$ D. $\frac{3092}{409}$

**12.** If $\frac{144+32\div ?-8}{35\div\frac{1}{2}\text{ of }\frac{1}{2}} = 1$, then which of the following should replace the sign of interrogation?
A. 7 B. 6
C. 10 D. 8

**13.** What is the value of $\frac{2.70\times2.70+4.30\times4.30+8.60\times2.70}{2.70+4.30}$?
A. 6.8 B. 7.0
C. 7.6 D. 8.5

**14.** What will be the value of $\frac{\left(\sqrt{6}+\frac{1}{\sqrt{6}}\right)^2}{\frac{1}{2}\text{ of }18+4}+\frac{2}{3}$?
A. 101/78 B. 104/71
C. 101/88 D. 99/57

**15.** 1150 ÷ 50 ÷ 23 + 15 = ?
A. 16 B. 20
C. 22 D. 18

## ANSWERS

| 1 | 2 | 3 | 4 | 5 | 6 | 7 | 8 | 9 | 10 |
|---|---|---|---|---|---|---|---|---|---|
| D | D | A | B | C | D | B | C | C | B |
| **11** | **12** | **13** | **14** | **15** | | | | | |
| A | D | B | A | A | | | | | |

## EXPLANATORY ANSWERS

**1.** $\because 51 \div 17 \div 3 = \frac{51}{17} \div 3 = 3 \div 3 = \frac{3}{3} = 1$

**2.** $\because 40 \times 2 \div 10 + 5 - 4$

$= 40 \times \frac{2}{10} + 5 - 4 = 8 + 5 - 4 = 9.$

**3.** $\because 28 \times 104 \div (18 + 6) + 3$

$= 28 \times 104 \div 24 + 3$

$= 28 \times \frac{104}{24} + 3 = 28 \times \frac{13}{3} + 3$

$= \frac{364}{3} + 3 = \frac{373}{3} = 124\frac{1}{3}$

**4.** $\because 75^2 - 65^2 = 2x$

$\Rightarrow (75 + 65)(75 - 65) = 2x$

$[\because a^2 - b^2 = (a + b)(a - b)]$

$\Rightarrow 140 \times 10 = 2x \Rightarrow x = 70 \times 10 = 700$

$\therefore$ Value of $x$ is 700.

**5.** $\because .99 \times 14 \div 11 \div 0.7$

$= .99 \times \frac{14}{11} \div 0.7 = \frac{.99 \times 14}{11 \times 0.7} = 1.8$

**6.** $\because 45 - [28 - \{37 - (15 - ?)\}] = 58$

$\Rightarrow 45 - [28 - \{37 - 15 + ?\}] = 58$

$\Rightarrow 45 - [28 - \{22 + ?\}] = 58$

$\Rightarrow 45 - [28 - 22 - ?] = 58$

$\Rightarrow 45 - 28 + 22 + ? = 58$

$\Rightarrow 39 + ? = 58$

$\Rightarrow ? = 58 - 39 = 19$

Therefore, the interrogation sign should be replaced by 19.

**7.** $\because 8\frac{1}{3} + 5\frac{1}{4} \times 13\frac{1}{5} \div 6\frac{3}{5}$

$= \frac{25}{3} + \frac{21}{4} \times \frac{66}{5} \div \frac{33}{5} = \frac{25}{3} + \frac{21}{4} \times \frac{66}{5} \times \frac{5}{33}$

$= \frac{25}{3} + \frac{21}{2} = \frac{50 + 63}{6} = \frac{113}{6} = 18\frac{5}{6}$

**8.** $\because \frac{14}{3}$ of $\frac{5}{8}$ of $72 = \frac{14 \times 5 \times 72}{3 \times 8} = 210$

**9.** $10 \times 10 \times 10 \div (20 \div 10 \times 10 - 10) + 6$

$= 10 \times 10 \times 10 \div \left(\frac{20}{10} \times 10 - 10\right) + 6$

$= 10 \times 10 \times 10 \div (20 - 10) + 6$

$= 10 \times 10 \times 10 \div 10 + 6$

$= 10 \times 10 \times \frac{10}{10} + 6$

$= 10 \times 10 \times 1 + 6 = 100 + 6 = 106$

**10.** $\because \dfrac{\frac{1}{3} \times 20 \div 4}{\frac{1}{4} \times 25 \div 5} = \dfrac{\frac{1}{3} \times 5}{\frac{1}{4} \times 5} = \dfrac{\frac{5}{3}}{\frac{5}{4}} = \frac{4}{3}$

**11.** $\because \dfrac{(24 \times 13) + (28 \div 7)}{(24 + 13) - \left(\frac{14}{3} \text{ of } \frac{5}{8}\right)} = \dfrac{312 + 4}{37 - \frac{35}{12}} = \dfrac{316}{\frac{409}{12}} = \frac{3792}{409}$

**12.** If $\dfrac{144 + 32 \div ? - 8}{35 \div \frac{1}{2} \text{ of } \frac{1}{2}} = 1 \Rightarrow \dfrac{144 + \frac{32}{?} - 8}{35 \div \frac{1}{4}} = 1 \Rightarrow \dfrac{136 + \frac{32}{?}}{\frac{35}{\frac{1}{4}}} = 1$

$\Rightarrow 136 + \frac{32}{?} = 35 \times 4 = 140$

$\Rightarrow \frac{32}{?} = 140 - 136 = 4 \Rightarrow ? = \frac{32}{4} = 8$

$\therefore$ Sign of interrogation (?) will be replaced by 8.

**13.** $\dfrac{2.70 \times 2.70 + 4.30 \times 4.30 + 8.60 \times 2.70}{2.70 + 4.30}$

$= \dfrac{(2.70)^2 + (4.30)^2 + 2 \times 4.30 \times 2.70}{2.70 + 4.30}$

$= \dfrac{(2.70 + 4.30)^2}{2.70 + 4.30} \quad [\because a^2 + b^2 + 2ab = (a + b)^2]$

$= 2.70 + 4.30 = 7.00$

**14.** $\therefore \dfrac{\left(\sqrt{6} + \frac{1}{\sqrt{6}}\right)^2}{\frac{1}{2} \text{ of } 18 + 4} + \frac{2}{3} = \dfrac{(\sqrt{6})^2 + \left(\frac{1}{\sqrt{6}}\right)^2 + 2.\sqrt{6}\,\frac{1}{\sqrt{6}}}{9 + 4} + \frac{2}{3}$

$= \dfrac{6 + \frac{1}{6} + 2}{13} + \frac{2}{3} = \dfrac{\frac{49}{6}}{13} + \frac{2}{3} = \frac{49}{78} + \frac{2}{3} = \frac{101}{78}$

**15.** $1150 \div 50 \div 23 + 15$

$= \frac{1150}{50} \div 23 + 15 = 23 \div 23 + 15 = \frac{23}{23} + 15$

$= 1 + 15 = 16.$

CHAPTER 2

# Comparing Quantities

## Percentage

The word 'per cent' or 'percentage' means 'for every one hundred'. In other words, it gives an indication of rate per hundred. It is denoted by the symbol %.

For example, 5% means 5 out of one hundred or $\frac{5}{100}$.

**Remember:**

(*i*) For converting a per cent into a fraction, divide it by 100.

(*ii*) For converting a fraction into a per cent, multiply it by 100.

(*iii*) For converting a per cent into a decimal, shift the decimal point two places to the left.

(*iv*) For converting one given quantity (*x*) as a percentage of another given quantity (*y*), find $\frac{x}{y} \times 100$.

(*v*) There is no unit of percentage.

**Important Facts**—For quickly solving the problems related to percentage, remember following rules:

**Rule 1:**

(***a***) Of the given two numbers if the first is $x\%$ more than the second, then the second will be $\left(\frac{100 \times x}{100+x}\right)\%$ less than the first.

(***b***) Of the given two numbers if the first is $x\%$ less than the second, then the second will be $\left(\frac{100 \times x}{100-x}\right)\%$ more than the first.

(***c***) If two numbers are respectively $x\%$ and $y\%$ more than a third number, then the first number will be $\left(\frac{100+x}{100+y} \times 100\right)\%$ of the second.

(***d***) If two numbers are respectively $x\%$ and $y\%$ less than a third number, then the first number will be $\left(\frac{100-x}{100-y} \times 100\right)\%$ of the second.

**Rule 2:**

(***a***) If a number or quantity is increased by $x\%$ then in order to restore its original value it must be decreased by $\left[\frac{100 \times x}{100+x}\right]\%$.

(***b***) If a number or quantity is decreased by $x\%$ then in order to restore its original value it must be increased by $\left[\frac{100 \times x}{100-x}\right]\%$.

**Rule 3:**

(***a***) If a number is successively increased by $x\%$ and $y\%$ then a single equivalent increase in that number will be $\left(x+y+\frac{xy}{100}\right)\%$

(***b***) If two successive discounts of $x\%$ and $y\%$ are allowed on a particular amount, then a single discount that is equivalent to the two successive discounts will be $\left(x+y-\frac{xy}{100}\right)\%$

(***c***) If a number is successively increased by $x\%$, $y\%$ and $z\%$, then a single equivalent increase in that number will be

$$\left[(x+y+z)+\left(\frac{xy+yz+zx}{100}\right)+\frac{(xyz)}{10000}\right]\%$$

(***d***) If three successive discounts of $x\%$, $y\%$ and $z\%$ are allowed on an amount, then a single discount that is equivalent to the three successive discounts will be

$$\left[x+y+z-\frac{(xy+yz+zx)}{100}+\frac{xyz}{10000}\right]\%$$

**Rule 4:**

(***a***) If a number is increased by $x\%$ and thereafter reduced by $x\%$, then the number will be reduced by $\left(\frac{x^2}{100}\right)$ per cent.

(*b*) If a number is reduced by $x\%$ and thereafter increased by $x\%$ then the number will be reduced by $\left(\frac{x^2}{100}\right)$ per cent.

(*c*) If due to an increase of $x\%$ in the selling price of certain commodity the sell/consumption of the commodity decreases by $y\%$, then gross receipts on account of sale of that commodity will be increased or decreased by $\left(x-y-\frac{xy}{100}\right)\%$, where $x > y$ and will be decreased by $\left(y-x+\frac{xy}{100}\right)\%$, where $y > x$.

## EXERCISE

**1.** In the expression $xy^2$, the values of both variables $x$ and $y$ are decreased by 20%. By this, the value of the expression is decreased by

A. 40% B. 48.8%
C. 51.2% D. 80%

**2.** 15 litres of mixture contains 20% alcohol and rest water. If 3 litres of water be mixed in it, the percentage of alcohol in the new mixture will be:

A. 15 B. $16\frac{2}{3}$
C. 17 D. $18\frac{1}{2}$

**3.** The difference between 70% and 55% of a number is 72. The number is:

A. 370 B. 460
C. 480 D. 520

**4.** 20% of a number is 10% of:

A. half the number
B. double the number
C. ten times the number
D. twenty times the number

**5.** 75% of what area is 15 sq. metres?

A. 10 sq. metres B. 15 sq. metres
C. 20 sq. metres D. 25 sq. metres

**6.** In an examination 80% of the students passed in Mathematics and 70% passed in English, while 10% students failed in both the subjects. If 360 students passed in both the subjects, find the total number of students who appeared in the examination.

A. 400 B. 600
C. 630 D. 640

**7.** In an election, there are two candidates. A candidate secured 57% of the total votes polled and elected by a margin of 2100 votes. Find the total number of votes polled.

A. 15000 B. 17500
C. 18000 D. 21000

**8.** Electric tax is increased by 20% and its consumption is decreased by 20%. The change in the expenditure is:

A. 4% decrease B. 4% increase
C. 5% decrease D. 5% increase

**9.** A man loses 10% of his money, after spending 20% of the remainder he is left with ₹ 2160. Initially the man had:

A. ₹ 1800 B. ₹ 2500
C. ₹ 3000 D. ₹ 3200

**10.** In a school 55% of the students are below 9 years of age and the remaining 153 above 9 years of age. The total number of students in the school is:

A. 296 B. 300
C. 340 D. 1000

**11.** The selling price of certain commodity was reduced by 25%. As a result of it, the sales increased by 30%. What was the effect of it on cash collected by daily sales?

A. 2.5% decrease B. 2.5% increase
C. 5% decrease D. 5% increase

**12.** A cooler marked at ₹ 1500 is offered at ₹ 1350 due to off-season discount. Find the rate of off-season discount offered.

A. 9.5% B. 10%
C. 10.5% D. 12%

**13.** The number of Gypsy-cars sold in 2008 was 16,500 and that sold in 2007 was 16580. How much was the percentage decrease in sales of the Gypsy-cars from 2007 to 2008?

A. less than 1 per cent
B. more than 1 per cent
C. zero per cent
D. cannot be determined

**14.** A company decided to sell ₹ 50,000 T.V. set for ₹ 48,000 as a world cup offer. What is the percentage discount offered by the company?

A. 6.5 B. 7
C. 7.5 D. 4

**15.** 9% of a number is $\frac{81}{200}$, what is $\frac{2}{7}$ of that number?

A. $1\frac{1}{5}$ B. $1\frac{2}{7}$
C. $2\frac{1}{7}$ D. $2\frac{1}{5}$

## ANSWERS

| 1 | 2 | 3 | 4 | 5 | 6 | 7 | 8 | 9 | 10 |
|---|---|---|---|---|---|---|---|---|---|
| B | B | C | B | C | B | A | A | C | C |
| 11 | 12 | 13 | 14 | 15 | | | | | |
| A | B | A | D | B | | | | | |

## EXPLANATORY ANSWERS

**1.** Decrease in expression

$= xy^2 - \frac{80}{100} \times x \left(\frac{80}{100} y\right)^2 = xy^2 - \frac{64}{125} xy^2 = \frac{61xy^2}{125}$

Hence, decrease per cent

$= \frac{61xy^2}{125 \times xy^2} \times 100 = 48.8\%$

**2.** Amount of alcohol $= \frac{20}{100} \times 15 = 3$ litre

Hence, required percentage $= \frac{3}{18} \times 100 = 16\frac{2}{3}\%$

**3.** Let the number be $x$; then

$(70 - 55) \times \frac{1}{100} \times x = 72$

$\therefore \quad x = \frac{100 \times 72}{15} = 480$

**4.** Let number be 100, then 20% and 10% of the number be 20 and 10 respectively.

Hence, 20% of a number is 10% of double the number.

**5.** Let required area be $x$ sq. metre; then

$\frac{75}{100} \times x = 15$

$\therefore \ x = \frac{15 \times 100}{75} = 20$ sq metre

**6.** Here, percentage of students failed in Mathematics and English be 30% and 20% respectively.

Percentage of students failed either one or both subjects $= 30 + 20 - 10 = 40\%$

Hence, percentage of pass students $= 100 - 40 = 60\%$

Now, $\quad 60\% = 360$

$\therefore \quad 100\% = \frac{360}{60} \times 100 = 600$

**7.** Let total number of votes be $x$; then

$(57 - 43) \times \frac{1}{10} x = 2100$

$\therefore \quad x = \frac{100 \times 2100}{14} = 15000$

**8.** Let initially electric tax is ₹ 100 and consumption = 100 units

Decrease in consumption

$= 100 \times 100 - 120 \times 80 =$ ₹ 400

Hence, decrease percentage $= \frac{400 \times 100}{100 \times 100} = 4\%$

**9.** Let initally the man had ₹ $x$, then

amount of money loses $= \frac{10}{100} \times x =$ ₹$\frac{x}{10}$

Remaining amount of money $= x - \frac{x}{10} =$ ₹$\frac{9x}{10}$

Money spent $= \frac{20}{100} \times \frac{9x}{10} =$ ₹$\frac{9x}{50}$

Now, $\quad \frac{9x}{10} - \frac{9x}{50} = 2160 \Rightarrow \frac{36x}{50} = 2160$

$\therefore \ x = \frac{2160 \times 50}{36} =$ ₹ 3000

**10.** Let total number of students be $x$, then

$\frac{45}{100} \times x = 153 \ \therefore \ x = \frac{100 \times 153}{45} = 340$

**11.** Let the selling price of a commodity be ₹ 100 and number of salcs = 100 units

Decrease in daily cash

$= 100 \times 100 - 75 \times 130 =$ ₹ 250

Hence, decrease percentage $= \frac{250 \times 100}{100 \times 100} = 2.5\%$

**12.** Discount per cent

$= \frac{1500 - 1350}{1500} \times 100 = \frac{150}{1500} \times 100 = 10\%$

**13.** Required decrease percentage

$= \frac{16580 - 16500}{16580} \times 100 = \frac{80}{16580} \times 100 = 0.48\%$

**14.** Discount per cent $= \frac{2000}{50{,}000} \times 100 = 4\%$

**15.** Let the number be $x$; then

$\frac{9}{100} \times x = \frac{81}{200} \ \therefore \ x = \frac{100 \times 81}{9 \times 200} = \frac{9}{2}$

Hence, $\frac{2}{7} x = \frac{2}{7} \times \frac{9}{2} = \frac{9}{7} = 1\frac{2}{7}$.

# Discount

**Market Price (M.P.)**—The attached price is called the market price (M.P.) or list price (L.P.) of the article and the reduction allowed in the price is called the **discount**.

(*i*) Discount = M.P. – S.P.

(*ii*) $\text{Discount \%} = \dfrac{\text{Discount} \times 100}{\text{M.P.}}$

(*iii*) $\text{S.P.} = \text{M.P.} - \dfrac{\text{Discount\%} \times \text{M.P.}}{100}$

(*iv*) $\text{S.P.} = \text{M.P.} \times \left(1 - \dfrac{\text{Discount\%}}{100}\right)$

(*v*) $\text{M.P.} = \dfrac{100 \times \text{S.P.}}{100 - \text{Discount\%}}$

$\text{S.P.} = \text{M.P.}\left(\dfrac{100 - \text{Discount\%}}{100}\right)$

$\text{M.P.} - \text{S.P.} = \dfrac{\text{M.P.} \times \text{Discount\%}}{100}$

$\text{Discount\%} = \left(\dfrac{\text{M.P.} - \text{S.P.}}{\text{M.P.}}\right) \times 100$

## EXERCISE

**1.** A cloth merchant offers 15% festival discount on every saree sold. If a certain saree is sold for ₹ 680, what is its marked price?

A. ₹ 800 B. ₹ 900
C. ₹ 1250 D. ₹ 1300

**2.** A shopkeeper offers 10% discount on an article and still makes a profit of 20%. What is the C.P. of the article if the marked price is ₹ 350?

A. ₹ 259.20 B. ₹ 262.50
C. ₹ 265.75 D. ₹ 272.5

**3.** A manufactures marks his goods in such a way that after allowing 20% discount, he makes a profit of 18%. What is the marked price of an item which costs him ₹ 200?

A. ₹ 295 B. ₹ 310
C. ₹ 315 D. ₹ 375

**4.** The marked price of a brand of coffee is ₹ 35 for 100g. But the shopkeeper gives a cup costing ₹ 7.50 free with it. Even then he gets a gain of 10%. What is the cost price of 100g of coffee?

A. ₹ 15 B. ₹ 25
C. ₹ 35 D. ₹ 65

**5.** A car is marked at ₹ 2,25,000. The manufacturer gives a discount of 10%. The dealer also gives a discount of 5%. What is the S.P. of the car?

A. ₹ 1,72,369 B. ₹ 1,64,370
C. ₹ 1,52,393 D. ₹ 1,92,375

**6.** A cycle merchant allows 25% commission on his advertised price and still makes a profit of 20%. If he gains ₹ 60 over the sale of one cycle. What is his advertised price?

A. ₹ 290 B. ₹ 310
C. ₹ 480 D. ₹ 520

**7.** The marked price of a shirt was ₹ 165 and it was at a discount of 12%. What the selling price of the shirt?

A. ₹ 145.20 B. ₹ 155.30
C. ₹ 165.20 D. ₹ 175.25

**8.** A trader marks his goods 40% above the cost price and gives a discount of 20% on the marked price. What is his gain per cent?

A. 8% B. 9%
C. 12% D. 15%

**9.** How much per cent more than the C.P. should a manufacturer mark his goods so that after allowing a discount of 20% on the marked price, he gains 10%.

A. 34.5% B. 27.5%
C. 37.5% D. 38.5%

**10.** A shopkeeper allows a discount of 10% to his customers and still gains 20%. What is the marked price of an article which costs ₹ 450 to the shopkeeper?

A. ₹ 600 B. ₹ 700
C. ₹ 800 D. ₹ 900

## ANSWERS

| 1 | 2 | 3 | 4 | 5 | 6 | 7 | 8 | 9 | 10 |
|---|---|---|---|---|---|---|---|---|---|
| A | B | A | B | D | C | A | C | C | A |

## EXPLANATORY ANSWERS

**1.** S.P. = ₹ 680, Discount = 15%

$$\text{M.P.} = \frac{100 \times \text{S.P.}}{100 - \text{Discount\%}} = \frac{100 \times 680}{100 - 15} = \frac{100 \times 680}{85} = ₹\ 800$$

**2.** C.P. = ₹ $x$, 120% of $x$ = 350 – 350 × 10%

$$\frac{120}{100} \times x = 350 - 35 = 315.$$

$$x = \frac{315 \times 5}{6} = \frac{525}{2}, \text{ C.P.} = ₹\ 262.50.$$

**3.** Let M.P. = ₹ $x$

$80\%\ x = 118\%$ of 200

$$\frac{80}{100}\times x = \frac{118}{100}\times 200 \Rightarrow x = \frac{236\times 5}{4} = ₹\ 295.$$

**4.** Let C.P. of 100 gm coffee = ₹ $x$

$110\%$ of $x = 35 - 7.50 = 27.50$

$$\frac{110}{100}\times x = 27.50$$

$$x = \frac{27.50\times 100}{110\times 100}$$

C.P. = ₹ 25.

**5.** M.P. = ₹ 225000

$$\text{1st S.P.} = 225000 - 225000\times\frac{10}{100}$$

$= 225000 - 22500 = 202500$

$$\text{2nd S.P.} = 202500 - 202500\times\frac{5}{100}$$

$= 202500 - 10125 =$ ₹ 192375

**6.** Let M.P. = 100

Commission = 25%

S.P. = 100 – 25 = 75

Profit = 20%

$$\text{C.P.} = \frac{100}{120}\times 75 = \frac{375}{6} = 62.50$$

Gain = 75 – 62.50 = ₹ 12.50

$$\text{M.P.} = \frac{100}{12.50}\times 60 = ₹\ 480$$

**7.** $$\text{S.P.} = \frac{\text{M.P.}(100-\text{Discount})}{100}$$

$$= \frac{165\times(100-12)}{100} = \frac{165\times 88}{100}$$

$= 33 \times 4.4 =$ ₹ 145.20

**8.** Let C.P. = 100, M.P. = 140, Discount = 20%

$$\text{S.P.} = 140 - 140\times\frac{20}{100} = 140 - 28 = 112$$

Profit = 112 – 100 = 12

$$\text{Profit }\% = \frac{12\times 100}{100} = 12\%$$

**9.** Let C.P. = ₹ $x$, S.P. = 110% of $x = \frac{110}{100}\times x = \frac{11}{10}x.$

Discount = 20%

$$\text{M.P.} = \frac{100\times\frac{11}{10}x}{100-20} = \frac{100\times\frac{11}{10}x}{80} = \frac{11}{8}x.$$

$$\text{Required }\% = \frac{\frac{11x}{8}-x}{x}\times 100 = \frac{3x\times 100}{8x} = 37.5\%$$

**10.** C.P. = 450, Gain = 20%

$$\text{S.P.} = 450 + 450\times\frac{20}{100} = 450 + 90 = 540$$

Discount = 10%

$$\text{M.P.} = \frac{100\times\text{S.P.}}{100-\text{Discount}} = \frac{100\times 540}{100-10}$$

$$= \frac{100\times 540}{90} = ₹\ 600$$

# Profit & Loss

A consumer who goes to the market and buys certain goods. The buyer is called a customer and the shopkeeper who sells the goods to him is called a retailer. The retailer purchases goods in turn in bulk from a wholesaler who keeps a large stock of good and in this case, the retailer becomes the customer.

1. **Cost price (C.P.):** Cost price is that price at which a particular article is bought. Profit and loss both are marked at cost price.
2. **Selling Price (S.P.):** Selling price is that price at which a particular article is sold.
3. **Overheads:** The expenses incurred on transportation, maintenance, packaging, advertise-ments and the like are included as *Overhead.* These overheads and the profit when added to the cost price determine the selling price.
4. **Profit or Gain** : Whenever a person sells an article at price greater than the cost price he is said to have made a profit or gain.
   Profit or Gain = S.P. – C.P.
5. **Loss :** If S.P. is less than the C.P. there is loss.
   Loss = C.P – S.P

**Some Basic Formulae:**

*(i)* Gain = S.P. – C.P.

*(ii)* Loss = C.P. – S.P.

*(iii)* $\text{Gain }\% = \frac{\text{Gain}\times 100}{\text{C.P.}}$

*(iv)* $\text{Loss }\% = \frac{\text{Loss}\times 100}{\text{C.P.}}$

From these we can write direct expressions for S.P. and C.P.

*(v)* $\text{S.P.} = \left(\frac{100+\text{Gain}\%}{100}\right)\times\text{C.P.}$ in case of gain or profit

*(vi)* $\text{S.P.} = \left(\frac{100-\text{Loss}\%}{100}\right)\times\text{C.P.}$ in case of loss

These can be rewritten as

$$\text{C.P.} = \frac{100}{100+\text{Gain}\%}\times\text{S.P. in case of profit}$$

$$\text{C.P.} = \frac{100}{100-\text{Loss}\%}\times\text{S.P. in case of loss}$$

*(vii)* If the C.P. of $x$ goods = S.P. of $y$ goods, then

*(a)* Gain % $= \frac{x-y}{y} \times 100$ [In case of $x > y$]

*(b)* Loss % $= \frac{y-x}{y} \times 100$ [In case of $y > x$]

*(viii)* When a man sells two things at the same price each and in this process his loss on first things is $x$% and gain on second things is $x$%, then in such a type question, there is always a loss.

$$\text{Loss \%} = x\% \text{ of } x = \frac{x^2}{100} = \left(\frac{x}{10}\right)^2.$$

$$\text{and Loss} = \frac{2 \times \text{S.P.}}{\left(\frac{100}{x}\right)^2 - 1}$$

*(ix)* An article is sold at a profit of $x$%. Had it been sold for ₹ $a$ some more, $y$% would have gained. Then, C.P. of an article =

$$\frac{\text{More gain} \times 100}{\text{Difference in percentage profit}}$$

*(x)* A dishonest shopkeeper prefers to sell goods at his cost price but uses a false weight of $x$ grams for each kilogram. Then his gain per cent,

$$\text{gain \%} = \frac{\text{Error}}{\text{True value} - \text{Error}} \times 100$$

$$= \frac{1000 - x}{x} \times 100$$

$$\text{or, gain \%} = \frac{\text{True weight} - \text{False weight}}{\text{False weight}} \times 100.$$

## EXERCISE

**1.** Ashok bought 25 kg of rice at the rate of ₹ 6 per kg and 35 kg of rice at the rate of ₹ 7 per kg. He mixed the two and sold the mixture at the rate of ₹ 6.75 per kg. What was his gain or loss in the transaction?
A. ₹ 16 gain B. ₹ 16 loss
C. ₹ 10 gain D. None of these

**2.** A horse and a cow were sold for ₹ 12000 each. The horse was sold at a loss of 20% and the cow at a gain of 20%. The entire transaction resulted in
A. no loss no gain B. loss of ₹ 1000
C. gain of ₹ 1000 D. loss of ₹ 2000

**3.** Profit after selling a commodity for ₹ 425 is same as loss after selling it for ₹ 355. The cost of the commodity is :
A. ₹ 285 B. ₹ 390
C. ₹ 295 D. ₹ 400

**4.** Bhajan Singh purchased 120 reams of paper at ₹ 80 per ream. He spent ₹ 280 on transportation, paid octroi at the rate of 40 paise per ream and paid ₹ 72 to the coolie. If he wants to have a gain of 8%, what must be the selling price per ream?
A. ₹ 86 B. ₹ 86.48
C. ₹ 79 D. ₹ 90

**5.** Ram bought 4 dozen apples at ₹ 12 per dozen and 2 dozen at ₹ 16 per dozen. He sold all of them to earn 20%. At what price per dozen did he sell the apples?
A. ₹ 14.40 B. ₹ 16.00
C. ₹ 16.80 D. ₹ 16.20

**6.** Jimmy bought paper sheets for ₹ 7200 and spent ₹ 200 in transport. Paying ₹ 600 he had 330 boxes made, which he sold at ₹ 28 each. What is his profit percentage?
A. 15.5 B. 40
C. 50 D. None of these

**7.** A owns a house worth ₹ 10000. He sells it to B at a profit of 10% based on the worth of the house. B sells the house back to A at a loss of 10%. In this transaction A gets:
A. no profit no loss B. profit of ₹ 1000
C. profit of ₹ 1100 D. profit of ₹ 1200

**8.** At what price must Kantilal sell a mixture of 80 kg sugar at ₹ 6.75 per kg with 120 kg at ₹ 8 per kg to gain 20%?
A. ₹ 7.50 per kg B. ₹ 8.20 per kg
C. ₹ 8.35 per kg D. ₹ 9 per kg

**9.** Subhash purchased a taperecorder at $\frac{9}{10}$ of its selling price and sold it at 8% more than its S.P. His gain is:
A. 8% B. 10%
C. 18% D. 20%

**10.** A dealer marks his goods 20% above cost price. He then allows some discount on it and makes a profit of 8%. The rate of discount is :
A. 12% B. 10%
C. 6% D. 4%

**11.** A trader lists his articles 20% above C.P. and allows a discount of 10% on cash payment. His gain per cent is :
A. 10% B. 8%
C. 6% D. 4%

**12.** Tarun bought a T.V. with 20% discount on the labelled price. Had he bought it with 25% discount, he would have saved ₹ 500. At what price did he buy the T.V.?
A. ₹ 5000 B. ₹ 8000
C. ₹ 10000 D. ₹ 12000

**13.** While selling a watch, a shopkeeper gives a discount of 5%. If he gives a discount of 7%, he earns ₹ 15 less as profit. The marked price of the watch is :

A. ₹ 697.50 B. ₹ 712.50
C. ₹ 787.50 D. None of these

**14.** Kabir buys an article with 25% discount on its marked price. He makes a profit of 10% by selling it at ₹ 660. The marked price is :

A. ₹ 600 B. ₹ 700
C. ₹ 800 D. ₹ 885

**15.** A person bought an article and sold it at a loss of 10%. If he had bought it for 20% less and sold it for ₹ 55 more, he would have had a profit of 40%. The C.P. of the article is :

A. ₹ 200 B. ₹ 225
C. ₹ 250 D. None of these

## ANSWERS

| 1 | 2 | 3 | 4 | 5 | 6 | 7 | 8 | 9 | 10 |
|---|---|---|---|---|---|---|---|---|---|
| C | B | B | D | B | A | C | D | D | B |
| **11** | **12** | **13** | **14** | **15** | | | | | |
| B | B | D | C | C | | | | | |

## EXPLANATORY ANSWERS

**1.** C.P. of 60 kg mixture = ₹ (25 × 6 + 35 × 7) = ₹ 395

S.P. of 60 kg mixtire = ₹ (60 × 6.75) = ₹ 405

∴ Gain = ₹ (405 − 395) = ₹ 10

**2.** $\text{Loss \%} = \left(\frac{20}{10}\right)^2 = (2)^2 = 4\%$

Total S.P. = ₹ 24000

and Total C.P. = $₹\left(\frac{100}{96} \times 24000\right) = ₹\ 25000$

∴ Loss = ₹ (25000 − 24000) = ₹ 1000

**3.** Let C.P. = ₹ $x$, Then, $425 - x = x - 355$

⇒ $2x = 780$ ∴ $x$ = ₹ 390

**4.** $\text{C.P. of 1 ream} = 80 + \frac{280}{120} + \frac{72}{120} + 0.40$

$= 80 + \frac{7}{3} + \frac{3}{5} + \frac{2}{5} = ₹\ \frac{250}{3}$

∴ S.P. of 1 ream = $₹\left(\frac{108}{100} \times \frac{250}{3}\right) = ₹\ 90$

**5.** C.P. of 6 dozen apples = ₹ (12 × 4 + 16 × 2) = ₹ 80

∴ S.P. = $₹\left(\frac{120}{100} \times 80\right) = ₹\ 96$

∴ S.P. per dozen = $₹\left(\frac{96}{6}\right) = ₹\ 16$

**6.** $\text{C.P. of 1 box} = \frac{7200+200+600}{330} = ₹\ \frac{800}{33}$

Hence, $\text{Gain\%} = \frac{28 - \frac{800}{33}}{800/33} \times 100 = \frac{124}{800} \times 100 = 15.5\%$

**7.** Final C.P. for A = $\frac{110}{100} \times \frac{90}{100} \times ₹\ 10000 = ₹\ 9900$

Hence, profit for A

$= \frac{10}{100} \times ₹\ 10{,}000 + ₹\ (10{,}000 - 9900) = ₹\ 1100$

**8.** C.P. of 1 kg sugar = $\frac{80 \times 6.75 + 120 \times 8}{200} = ₹\ 7.50$

∴ S.P. of 1 kg = $₹\left(\frac{120}{100} \times 7.50\right) = ₹\ 9$ per kg

**9.** Let S.P. = ₹ 100;

C.P. for Subhash = $\frac{9}{10} \times 100 = ₹\ 90$ and S.P. = ₹ 108

Hence, gain % for Subhash = $\frac{108-90}{90} \times 100 = 20\%$

**10.** Let C.P. be ₹ 100; then Marked price = ₹ 120 and S.P. = ₹ 108

∴ Discount = $\left(\frac{12}{120} \times 100\right)\% = 10\%$

**11.** Let C.P. be ₹ 100

Then, marked price = ₹ 120

S.P. = $₹\left(\frac{90}{100} \times 120\right) = ₹\ 108$

∴ Gain % = $\left(\frac{8}{100} \times 100\right)\% = 8\%$

**12.** Here, 5% = 500

∴ $100\% - \frac{500}{5} \times 100 = ₹\ 10{,}000$

Hence, labelled price = ₹ 10,000

∴ S.P. = $\frac{80}{100} \times ₹\ 10{,}000 = ₹\ 8000$

**13.** Let the marked price = ₹ $x$

Then, $\frac{7x}{100} - \frac{5x}{100} = 15 \Rightarrow \frac{x}{50} = 15$ ∴ $x$ = ₹ 750

**14.** C.P. = $\frac{100}{110} \times 660 = ₹\ 600$

Hence, M.P. = $\frac{100}{75} \times 600 = ₹\ 800.$

# Simple Interest

*Interest* is the money paid for the use of money borrowed, *i.e.*, extra money paid for using other's money is called *interest.*

The sum borrowed is called the principal. The sum of interest and principal is called the *Amount*.

If the interest on a certain sum borrowed for a certain period is reckoned uniformly, then it is called simple interest, denoted by S.I.

Thus, if A = Amount, P = Principal,

I = Interest, T = Time (in year),

R = Rate per cent per annum, then

(*a*) $I = \frac{P \times R \times T}{100}$ (*b*) $P = \frac{100 \times I}{R \times T}$

(*c*) $T = \frac{100 \times I}{P \times R}$ (*d*) $R = \frac{100 \times I}{P \times T}$

(*e*) $P = \frac{100\,A}{100 + RT}$ (*f*) A = P + I.

## EXERCISE

**1.** If the simple interest on a certain sum of money at 6% per annum for 3 years is ₹ 90, the sum will be:

A. ₹ 500 B. ₹ 450
C. ₹ 525 D. ₹ 560

**2.** If the simple interest on ₹ 1 for 1 month is 1 paise, the rate per cent p.a. will be :

A. 10% B. 8%
C. 12% D. 6%

**3.** A sum of money doubles itself in 20 years. In how many years will it triple itself at the same rate of simple interest?

A. 30 years B. 50 years
C. 40 years D. 45 years

**4.** If the simple interest on ₹ 500 for 4 years is ₹ 40, find the rate per cent p.a.

A. 3½% B. 2%
C. 2½% D. 3%

**5.** After what time will the sum of ₹ 2000 become ₹ 2240 at 4% per annum simple interest?

A. 3 years B. 2 years
C. 5 years D. 4 years

**6.** The simple interest on a certain sum of money is $\frac{25}{64}$ of the sum and the number of years equals the rate per cent p.a. The rate per cent p.a. will be :

A. $7\frac{1}{2}\%$ B. $5\frac{1}{4}\%$
C. $6\frac{3}{4}\%$ D. $6\frac{1}{4}\%$

**7.** A sum of money amounts to ₹ 1150 in 3 years and to ₹ 1250 in 5 years at a certain rate per cent p.a. simple interest. The rate per cent p.a. will be :

A. 5% B. 8%
C. 7% D. 6%

**8.** The simple interest on a sum of ₹ 892 lent out at 6% p.a. for 8 months will be :

A. ₹ 36.68 B. ₹ 35.68
C. ₹ 48.58 D. ₹ 33.38

**9.** If the simple interest on a certain sum of money at 6% p.a. for 4½ years is ₹ 81, the sum will be:

A. ₹ 325 B. ₹ 225
C. ₹ 300 D. ₹ 340

**10.** A sum of ₹ 1850 lent out for 5 years at 3% p.a. simple interest will amount to:

A. ₹ 2227.75 B. ₹ 2127.50
C. ₹ 2137.50 D. ₹ 2086.50

**11.** A lent a sum of ₹ 1250 to B at a certain rate of interest for 3 years and a sum of ₹ 1500 to C at the same rate of interest for 2 years. If he was paid total ₹ 258.75 as interest in both cases, find the rate of interest at which money was lent by him.

A. $4\frac{1}{6}\%$ B. $6\frac{1}{4}\%$
C. $2\frac{1}{7}\%$ D. $3\frac{5}{6}\%$

**12.** A invested ₹ 5000 at a certain rate of simple interest and ₹ 4000 for the same period at 1% higher rate of interest. If the interest in both cases is same, the former rate of interest is :

A. 3% B. 4%
C. 6% D. 5%

**13.** A man lends ₹ 500 for 4 years and ₹ 600 for 3 years at a certain rate of simple interest. If he gets total ₹ 190 as interest in both cases, the rate per cent per annum is:

A. 8% B. 5%
C. 10% D. 4%

**14.** What annual instalment should be paid to clear the debt of ₹ 645 in 4 years at the rate of 5% p.a. simple interest?

A. ₹ 160 B. ₹ 185
C. ₹ 180 D. ₹ 190

**15.** If a certain sum of money at simple interest amounts to ₹ 1900 in 3 years and to ₹ 2050 in 5 years, the rate per cent per annum is:

A. 4½% B. 3½%
C. 2½% D. 5¼%

## ANSWERS

| 1 | 2 | 3 | 4 | 5 | 6 | 7 | 8 | 9 | 10 |
|---|---|---|---|---|---|---|---|---|---|
| A | C | C | B | A | D | A | B | C | B |
| 11 | 12 | 13 | 14 | 15 | | | | | |
| D | B | B | C | A | | | | | |

## EXPLANATORY ANSWERS

**1.** $P = \frac{90 \times 100}{6 \times 3} = ₹\ 500$

**2.** $\text{Rate} = \frac{1 \times 100}{100 \times \frac{1}{12}} = 12\%.$

**3.** Let principal = ₹ $x$; Amount = ₹ $2x$;
then I = $2x - x$ = ₹ $x$

$\therefore R = \frac{x \times 100}{x \times 20} = 5\%$

Again, if principal = ₹ $x$;
Amount = ₹ $3x$; then I = $3x - x$ = ₹ $2x$

Hence, $T = \frac{2x \times 100}{x \times 5} = 40$ years

**4.** $\text{Rate} = \frac{40 \times 100}{500 \times 4} = 2\%$

**5.** Here, I = 2240 − 2000 = ₹ 240

$\therefore \quad T = \frac{240 \times 100}{2000 \times 4} = 3$ years

**6.** Let, R = T = $x$; then

$\frac{25}{64}P = \frac{P \times x \times x}{100} \Rightarrow x^2 = \frac{25 \times 100}{64}$

$\therefore \quad x = \frac{5 \times 10}{8} = \frac{25}{4};\ R = 6\frac{1}{4}\%$

**7.** Here, Simple interest for 2 years
= ₹ 1250 − ₹ 1150 = ₹ 100

$\therefore$ Simple interest for 3 years = $\frac{100 \times 3}{2}$ = ₹ 150

Hence, P = ₹ 1150 − ₹ 150 = ₹ 1000

$\therefore \quad \text{Rate} = \frac{50 \times 100}{1000 \times 1} = 5\%$

**8.** Here, $I = \frac{892 \times 6 \times \frac{2}{3}}{100}$ = ₹ 35.68

**9.** $P = \frac{81 \times 100 \times 2}{6 \times 9}$ = ₹ 300

**10.** $I = \frac{1850 \times 3 \times 5}{100}$ = ₹ 277.50

$\therefore$ Amount = ₹ 1850 + ₹ 277.50
= ₹ 2127.50

**11.** $\frac{1250 \times R \times 3}{100} + \frac{1500 \times R \times 2}{100} = 258.75$

$\Rightarrow \quad 6750\ R = 25875$

$\therefore \quad R = \frac{25875}{6750} = \frac{23}{6} = 3\frac{5}{6}\%$

**12.** Here, $\frac{5000 \times R \times T}{100} = \frac{4000 \times (R+1) \times T}{100}$

$\Rightarrow \quad 5R = 4R + 4 \therefore\ R = 4\%$

**13.** Here, $\frac{500 \times R \times 4}{100} + \frac{600 \times R \times 3}{100} = 190$

$\Rightarrow \quad 38R = 190$

$\therefore \quad R = \frac{190}{38} = 5\%.$

**14.** Let annual instalment be ₹ $x$; then

$x + \frac{x \times 3 \times 5}{100} + x + \frac{x \times 2 \times 5}{100} + x + \frac{x \times 1 \times 5}{100} + x = 645 + \frac{645 \times 4 \times 5}{100}$

$\Rightarrow \quad 4x + \frac{3x}{10} = 774 \Rightarrow \frac{43x}{10} = 774$

$\therefore \quad x = \frac{774 \times 10}{43}$ = ₹ 180

**15.** Simple interest for 2 years
= ₹ 2050 − ₹ 1900 = ₹ 150

$\therefore$ Simple interest for 1 year

= ₹ $\frac{150}{2}$ = ₹ 75

Since simple interest for 3 years
= ₹ 75 × 3 = ₹ 225

$\therefore$ Principal = ₹ 1900 − ₹ 225 = ₹ 1675

Hence, $\text{Rate} = \frac{75 \times 100}{1675 \times 1} = 4½\%$

# Compound Interest

In business transaction if interest as it becomes due is not paid to the lender but is added on to the principal, the money is said to be lent at *compound interest* and the total sum owed after a given time is called the amount at compound interest for that time.

After a certain period, the difference between the amount and the original principal is called the compound Interest (C.I.).

**Some Important Formulae :**

Let Principal = P, Time = $n$ years

Rate = $r$% p.a.

then, the amount,

(*a*) when interest is compounded annually:

then, $\text{Amount} = P\left(1+\frac{r}{100}\right)^n$

(*b*) when interest is compounded half yearly:

then, $\text{Amount} = P\left(1+\frac{r/2}{100}\right)^{2n}$

(*c*) when interest is compounded quarterly :

then, $\text{Amount} = P\left(1+\frac{r/4}{100}\right)^{4n}$

(*d*) when time is fraction of a year, say $4\frac{1}{3}$ years,

then, $\text{Amount} = P\left(1+\frac{r}{100}\right)^4 \times \left(1+\frac{\frac{1}{3}r}{100}\right)$

(*e*) when rates are $r_1$%, $r_2$% and $r_3$% for Ist, IInd and IIIrd year respectively; then,

$\text{Amount} = P\left(1+\frac{r_1}{100}\right)\left(1+\frac{r_2}{100}\right)\left(1+\frac{r_3}{100}\right)$

## EXERCISE

**1.** What will be the compound interest on ₹ 8000 for 3 years at 5% p.a.?
A. ₹ 1361 B. ₹ 1261
C. ₹ 1260 D. ₹ 1250

**2.** What will be the amount if a sum of ₹ 2500 is invested for 1 year at 4% per annum compound interest, interest being compounded half-yearly?
A. ₹ 2625 B. ₹ 2601
C. ₹ 2830 D. ₹ 2901

**3.** Find the compound interest on ₹ 2560 for ½ year at 12½% per annum, interest payable quarterly.
A. ₹ 3720.50 B. ₹ 2722.50
C. ₹ 2752.50 D. ₹ 2250.50

**4.** After how many years will ₹ 3375 become ₹ 4096 at $6\frac{2}{3}$% per annum compound interest?
A. 4 years B. 2 years
C. 2½ years D. 3 years

**5.** A certain sum of money placed at compound interest amounts to ₹ 110 in 1 year and to ₹ 121 in 2 years. The rate of interest per annum is :
A. 5% B. 10%
C. 8% D. 4%

**6.** The present population of a city is 80,000. If the rate of growth is 5% per year, find its population after 3 years.
A. 88,100 B. 95,600
C. 92,610 D. 84,600

**7.** First year's interest on a sum of money placed at compound interest at the rate of 8% per annum is ₹ 72. What will be interest for the second year?
A. ₹ 77.76 B. ₹ 78.66
C. ₹ 85.66 D. ₹ 78.76

**8.** The difference between compound and simple interest on a certain sum of money for 2 years at 5% per annum is ₹ 21. Find the sum.
A. ₹ 7200 B. ₹ 8400
C. ₹ 9200 D. ₹ 8500

**9.** In how many years will a sum of ₹ 19200 placed at 10% per annum compound interest yield an interest of ₹ 4032?
A. 1½ years B. 2½ years
C. 2 years D. 3 years

**10.** The compound interest on a certain sum of money invested for 3 years at 5% per annum is ₹ 1891.50. What will be the simple interest on the same sum at the same rate for 2 years?
A. ₹ 1700 B. ₹ 1200
C. ₹ 1500 D. ₹ 2100

**11.** The simple interest on a sum of ₹ 4800 for 2 years is ₹ 768. What will be the compound interest on the same sum at the same rate and for the same period?
A. ₹ 798.72 B. ₹ 870.75
C. ₹ 920.69 D. ₹ 884.20

**12.** A sum of money lent out at a certain rate of simple interest amounts to ₹ 6600 in 2 years and to ₹ 6900 in 3 years. What will be the compound interest on the same sum of money if lent out at the same rate for 2 years?
A. ₹ 605 B. ₹ 715
C. ₹ 615 D. ₹ 595

**13.** If the first year's interest on a certain sum of money placed at 5% p.a. compound interest is ₹ 1200, what will be the interest for the third year?

A. ₹ 1220 B. ₹ 1323
C. ₹ 1423 D. ₹ 1330

**14.** If a certain sum of money placed at compound interest amounts to ₹ 960 in 3 years and to ₹ 1000 in 4 years, find the rate of compound interest.

A. $4\frac{1}{6}\%$ B. $5\frac{1}{6}\%$
C. $2\frac{1}{3}\%$ D. 3%

**15.** What would be the compound interest on ₹ 3200 at 25% per annum for 3 years?

A. ₹ 2050 B. ₹ 2775
C. ₹ 3050 D. ₹ 3180

## ANSWERS

| 1 | 2 | 3 | 4 | 5 | 6 | 7 | 8 | 9 | 10 |
|---|---|---|---|---|---|---|---|---|---|
| B | B | B | D | B | C | A | B | C | B |
| **11** | **12** | **13** | **14** | **15** | | | | | |
| A | C | B | A | C | | | | | |

## EXPLANATORY ANSWERS

**1.** ∴ $\text{C.I.} = 8000\left[\left(1+\frac{5}{100}\right)^3-1\right]$

$= 8000\left[\left(\frac{21}{20}\right)^3-1\right] = \frac{8000\times1261}{8000} = ₹\ 1261$

**2.** $A = 2500\left(1+\frac{2}{100}\right)^2 = 2500\left(\frac{51}{50}\right)^2 = \frac{2500\times51\times51}{50\times50}$

= ₹ 2601.

**3.** Amount $= 2560\left(1+\frac{25}{8\times100}\right)^2 = \frac{2560\times33\times33}{32\times32}$

= ₹ 2722.50

**4.** Here, $4096 = 3375\left(1+\frac{20}{3\times100}\right)^n$

$\Rightarrow \frac{4096}{3375} = \left(1+\frac{1}{15}\right)^n \Rightarrow \left(\frac{16}{15}\right)^3 = \left(\frac{16}{15}\right)^n$

∴ $n$ = 3 years

**5.** Here, simple interest of ₹ 110 for 1 year

= 121 − 110 = ₹ 11

Hence, rate $= \frac{11\times100}{110\times1} = 10\%$.

**6.** Population of the city after 3 years

$= 80{,}000\left(1+\frac{5}{100}\right)^3 = 80{,}000\times\frac{21}{20}\times\frac{21}{20}\times\frac{21}{20} = 92610$

**7.** Second year's interest = 72 + 8% of 72

$= 72+\frac{72\times8}{100} = 72 + 5.76 = ₹\ 77.76$

**8.** Here, $P\left[\left(1+\frac{5}{100}\right)^2-1\right]-\frac{P\times5\times2}{100} = 21$

$\Rightarrow P\left[\frac{441}{400}-1\right]-\frac{P}{10} = 21$

$\Rightarrow P\left[\frac{41}{400}-\frac{1}{10}\right] = 21 \Rightarrow P\times\frac{1}{400} = 21$

∴ $P = 21 \times 400 = ₹\ 8400$

**9.** Amount = ₹ 19200 + ₹ 4032 = ₹ 23232

Now, $23232 = 19200\left(1+\frac{10}{100}\right)^n$

$\Rightarrow \frac{23232}{19200} = \left(\frac{11}{10}\right)^n \Rightarrow \frac{121}{100} = \left(\frac{11}{10}\right)^n$

$\Rightarrow \left(\frac{11}{10}\right)^2 = \left(\frac{11}{10}\right)^n$

∴ $n$ = 2 years

**11.** Rate $= \frac{768\times100}{4800\times2} = 8\%$

∴ $\text{C.I.} = 4800\left[\left(1+\frac{8}{100}\right)^2-1\right]$

$= 4800\left[\left(\frac{27}{25}\right)^2-1\right] = \frac{4800\times104}{625} = ₹\ 798.72$

**13.** Required interest

$= 1200\left(1+\frac{5}{100}\right)^2 = 1200\times\frac{21}{20}\times\frac{21}{20} = ₹\ 1323$

**14.** Here, simple interest of ₹ 960 for 1 year

= 1000 − 960 = ₹ 40

Hence, Rate $= \frac{40\times100}{960\times1} = \frac{25}{6} = 4\frac{1}{6}\%$

**15.** Compound interest

$= 3200\left[\left(1+\frac{25}{100}\right)^3-1\right] = 3200\left[\left(\frac{5}{4}\right)^3-1\right]$

$= \frac{3200\times61}{64} = ₹\ 3050.$

●●●

CHAPTER 3

# Ratio and Proportion

## RATIO

In ratio we compare two quantities of the same kind and consider what multiple, part or parts one is of the other. In comparing 8 with 4, observe that it is 2 times 4. This comparison can be represented as $8 \div 4$ or $\frac{8}{4}$.

Hence, *ratio is that relation between two numbers which is expressed by the fraction, the numerator is which is the measure of the first quantity and denominator is the measure of the second quantity.*

If the terms of a ratio be multiplied or divided by the same quantity the value of the ratio remains unaltered.

Thus, 3 : 4 is the same as 9 : 12 and 9 : 12 is the same as 3 : 4.

## PROPORTION

The equality of two ratio is called proportion.

Consider the two ratios:

| Ist ratio | 2nd ratio |
|---|---|
| 5 : 15 | 7 : 21 |

Since, 5 is one-third of 15 and 7 is one-third of 21, the two ratios are equal. The equality of two ratios is called proportion and the numbers 5, 15, and 7, 21 are said to be in **proportion.**

The proportion may be written as 5 : 15 : : 7 : 21 (5 is to 15 as 7 is to 21)

$\Rightarrow \quad 5 : 15 = 7 : 21$

$\Rightarrow \quad \frac{5}{15} = \frac{7}{21}$

The numbers 5, 15, 7 and 21 are called the terms. 5 is the first term, 15 the second, 7 the third, and 21 the fourth.

The first and fourth terms, *i.e.*, 5 and 21 are called extremes (end terms), and the second and the third terms, *i.e.*, 15 and 7 are called the **means** (middle terms), 21 is called the fourth proportional.

***Some Important Facts:***

**1.** If $a$ and $b$ are two quantities, then

(*a*) Duplicate ratio of $a : b = a^2 : b^2$

(*b*) Sub-duplicate ratio of $a : b = \sqrt{a} : \sqrt{b}$

(*c*) Triplicate ratio of $a : b = a^3 : b^3$

(*d*) Sub-triplicate ratio $a : b = \sqrt[3]{a} : \sqrt[3]{b}$

(*e*) Inverse or reciprocal ratio of $a : b = \frac{1}{a} : \frac{1}{b}$

(*f*) Third proportional to '$a$' and '$b$' $= \frac{b^2}{a}$

**2.** If A : B = $x : y$ and B : C = $p : q$, then

(*a*) $A : C = \frac{x \times p}{y \times q}$

(*b*) A : B : C = $px : py : qy$

**3.** In what *ratio* the two kinds of tea must be mixed together one at ₹ $x$ per kg and another at ₹ $y$ per kg, so that the mixture may cost ₹ $z$ per kg?

$$\text{Ratio} = \frac{z - y}{x - z}$$

**4.** A grey hound persues a hare as takes $J_1$ leaps for every $J_2$ leaps of the hare. If $K_1$ leaps of the hound are equal to $K_2$ leaps of the hare, then the Ratio of speeds of the hound and hare is

$$\frac{J_2 \times K_1}{J_1 \times K_2}$$

**5.** The incomes of two persons are in the ratio of $a : b$ and their expenditure are in the ratio of $x : y$. If the saving of each person is ₹ $s$, then income of each is

₹ $\frac{as(y - x)}{ay - bx}$ and ₹ $\frac{bs(y - x)}{ay - bx}$ respectively.

**6.** In a mixture of $z$ litre, the ratio of milk and water is $x : y$. If another $p$ litres of water is added to the mixture, the ratio of milk and water in the resulting mixture $= \frac{xz}{yz + p(x + y)}$

**7.** There are four members $a$, $b$, $c$ and $d$, then formula for

(a) What should be added to each of these numbers so that the remaining numbers may be proportional $= \frac{ad - bc}{(b + c) - (a + d)}$

(b) What should be subtracted from each of these numbers so that the remaining numbers may be proportional $= \frac{ad - bc}{(a + d) - (b + c)}$

**8.** In a mixture the ratio of milk and water is $a : b$. If in this mixture another K litre of water is added, then the ratio of milk and water in the resulting mixture becomes $a : m$. Then the quantity of milk in the original mixture $= \frac{ak}{m - b}$ and quantity of water $= \frac{bk}{m - b}$

## EXERCISE

**1.** If A : B = 6 : 7 and B : C = 8 : 9, then A : B : C is:
A. 24 : 28 : 63 B. 48 : 28 : 63
C. 48 : 56 : 63 D. None of these

**2.** The sum of two numbers is 20 and their difference is $2\frac{1}{2}$. What is the ratio of the numbers?
A. 11 : 7 B. 9 : 11
C. 9 : 7 D. None of these

**3.** If 0.7 of one number is equal to 0.075 of another, what is the ratio of the two numbers?
A. 6 : 14 B. 3 : 28
C. 5 : 7 D. None of these

**4.** If 10% of $x$ is the same as 20% of $y$, then $x : y$ is equal to :
A. 1 : 2 B. 2 : 1
C. 5 : 1 D. 10 : 1

**5.** Two numbers are in the ratio 3 : 5. If each number is increased by 10, the ratio becomes 5 : 7. The numbers are:
A. 3, 5 B. 7, 9
C. 13, 22 D. 15, 25

**6.** The mean proportional between 0.32 and 0.02 is:
A. 0.34 B. 0.3
C. 0.16 D. 0.08

**7.** The sum of three numbers is 98. If the ratio between the first and second be 2 : 3 and that between the second and third be 5 : 8, then what is the second number?
A. 20 B. 30
C. 10 D. 40

**8.** One man adds 3 litres of water to 12 litres of milk and another 4 litres of water to 10 litres of milk. What is the ratio of the strenghts of the milk in the two mixtures?
A. 15 : 25 B. 25 : 28
C. 28 : 25 D. None of these

**9.** ₹ 425 is divided among 4 men, 5 women and 6 boys such that the share of a man, a woman and a boy may be in the ratio of 9 : 8 : 4. What is the share of a woman?
A. ₹ 34 B. ₹ 24
C. ₹ 44 D. None of these

**10.** A vessel contains liquids P and Q in the ratio 5 : 3. If 6 litres of the mixture are removed and the same quantity of liquid $q$ is added, the ratio becomes 3 : 5. What quantity does the vessel hold?
A. 40 litres B. 50 litres
C. 30 litres D. None of these

**11.** A bucket contains a mixture of two liquids P and Q in the proportion 7 : 5. If 9 litres of the mixture is replaced by 9 litres of liquid Q, then the ratio of the two liquid becomes 7 : 9. How much of the liquid P was there in the bucket?
A. 11 litres B. 21 litres
C. 31 litres D. None of these

**12.** Three glasses P, Q and R with their capacities in the ratio 2 : 3 : 4 are filled with a mixture of spirit and water. The ratio of spirit to water in P, Q and R is 1 : 5, 3 : 5 and 5 : 7 respectively. If the contents of these glasses are mixed together, what is the ratio of spirit to water in the mixture?
A. 14 : 27 B. 23 : 47
C. 25 : 47 D. None of these

**13.** A and B are two alloys of gold and copper prepared by mixing metals in proportions 7 : 2 and 7 : 11 respectively. If equal quantities of the alloys are melted to form a third alloy C, the proportion of gold and copper in C will be
A. 5 : 9 B. 5 : 7
C. 7 : 5 D. 9 : 5

**14.** Gold is 19 times as heavy as water and copper 9 times as heavy as water. The ratio in which these two metals be mixed so that the mixtures is 15 times as heavy as water is:
A. 1 : 2 B. 2 : 3
C. 3 : 2 D. 19 : 135

**15.** The contents of two vessels containing water and milk are in the ratio 1 : 2 and 2 : 5 are mixed in the ratio 1 : 4. The resulting mixture will have water and milk in the ratio:

A. 21 : 54 B. 31 : 74
C. 27 : 74 D. None of these

**16.** One year ago, the ratio between Mahesh and Suresh's salaries was 3 : 5. The ratio of their individual salaries of last year and present year are 2 : 3 and 4 : 5 respectively. If their total salaries for the present year are ₹ 4300, what is the present salary of Mahesh?
A. ₹ 1800 B. ₹ 1900
C. ₹ 1600 D. None of these

**17.** The ratio of P's and Q's income last year was 3 : 4. The ratio of their own incomes of last year and this year is 4 : 5 and 2 : 3 respectively. If the total sum of their present income is ₹ 4160. What is the present income of P?
A. ₹ 1500 B. ₹ 1400
C. ₹ 1600 D. None of these

**18.** The monthly salary of A, B, C is in the proportion of 2 : 3 ; 5. If C's monthly salary is ₹ 1200 more than that of A, then B's annual salary is:
A. ₹ 14400 B. ₹ 24000
C. ₹ 1200 D. ₹ 2000

**19.** ₹ 1050 is divided among P, Q and R. The share of P is $\frac{2}{5}$ of the combined share of Q and R. Thus P gets:
A. ₹ 200 B. ₹ 300
C. ₹ 400 D. ₹ 420

**20.** The ratio between Sumit's and Prakash's age at present is 2 : 3. Sumit is 6 years younger than Prakash. The ratio of Sumit's age to Prakash's age after 6 years will be:
A. 1 : 2 B. 2 : 3
C. 3 : 4 D. 3 : 8

## ANSWERS

| 1 | 2 | 3 | 4 | 5 | 6 | 7 | 8 | 9 | 10 |
|---|---|---|---|---|---|---|---|---|---|
| C | C | B | B | D | D | B | C | A | A |
| **11** | **12** | **13** | **14** | **15** | **16** | **17** | **18** | **19** | **20** |
| B | C | C | C | B | A | C | C | B | C |

## EXPLANATORY ANSWERS

**1.** A : B = 6 : 7
B : C = 8 : 9
∴ A : B : C = 6 × 8 : 7 × 8 : 7 × 9 = 48 : 56 : 63

**2.** Ratio $= \frac{20+\frac{5}{2}}{20-\frac{5}{2}} = \frac{22.5}{17.5} = \frac{225}{175} = \frac{9}{7} = 9:7$

**3.** We have, $0.7x = 0.075\,y$

$\frac{x}{y} = \frac{0.075}{0.7} = \frac{75}{700} = \frac{3}{28} = 3:28$

**4.** 10% of $x$ = 20% of $y$

$\Rightarrow \frac{10}{100}x = \frac{20}{100}y$

$\therefore \frac{x}{10} = \frac{y}{5} \Rightarrow \frac{x}{y} = \frac{10}{5} = \frac{2}{1} \Rightarrow x:y = 2:1$

**5.** Let the number be $3x$ and $5x$.

Then, $\frac{3x+10}{5x+10} = \frac{5}{7} \Rightarrow 7(3x+10) = 5(5x+10)$

$\Rightarrow 21x + 70 = 25x + 50 \Rightarrow 4x = 20 \Rightarrow x = 5$

So, the numbers are 15, 25.

**6.** Mean proportional $= \sqrt{0.32 \times 0.02} = \sqrt{0.0064} = 0.08$

**7.** The ratio among the three numbers is
2 : 3
5 : 8
and 10 : 15 : 24

∴ The second number $= \frac{98}{10+15+24} \times 15 = 30$

**8.** Strength of milk in the first mixture $= \frac{12}{12+3} = \frac{12}{15}$

Strength of milk in the second mixture $= \frac{10}{10+4} = \frac{10}{14}$

∴ The ratio of their strengths $= \frac{12}{15} : \frac{10}{14}$

$= 12 \times 14 : 15 \times 10 = 28 : 25$

**9.** The ratio of shares of group of men, women and boys
$= 9 \times 4 : 8 \times 5 : 4 \times 6 = 9 : 10 : 6$

∴ Share of 5 women $= \frac{425}{9+10+6} \times 10 =$ ₹ 170

∴ Share of 1 woman $= \frac{170}{5} =$ ₹ 34

**10.** Let the vessel contains $5x$ litres and $3x$ litres of liquid P and Q respectively. The removed quantity contains

$\frac{16}{5+3} \times 5 = 10$ litres of P

and 16 – 10 = 6 litres of Q.

Now, $(5x - 10) : (3x - 6 + 16) = 3 : 5$

$\Rightarrow \frac{5x-10}{3x+10} = \frac{3}{5} \Rightarrow 25x - 50 = 9x + 30$

$\Rightarrow 16x = 80 \Rightarrow x = 5$

∴ Vessel contains $8x = 8 \times 5 = 40$ litres.

**11.** Let the two liquids P and Q are $7x$ litres and $5x$ litres repectively.

Now, when 9 litres of mixture are taken out, P remains

$$7x - 9\left(\frac{7}{7+5}\right) = 7x - \frac{9\times 7}{12} = \left(7x - \frac{21}{4}\right) \text{ litres}$$

and Q remains

$$5x - 9\left(\frac{5}{7+5}\right) = 5x - \frac{9\times 5}{12} = \left(5x - \frac{15}{4}\right) \text{ litres}$$

Now, when 9 litres of liquid Q are added,

$$\left(7x - \frac{21}{4}\right) : \left(5x - \frac{15}{4} + 9\right) = 7 : 9$$

$$\Rightarrow \frac{7x - \frac{21}{4}}{5x - \frac{15}{4} + 9} = \frac{7}{9}$$

$$\Rightarrow 63x - \frac{189}{4} = 35x + \frac{147}{4}$$

$$\Rightarrow 28x = \frac{189}{4} + \frac{147}{4} = \frac{336}{4} = 84$$

$$\Rightarrow x = \frac{84}{28} = 3 \Rightarrow 7x = 7 \times 3 = 21 \text{ litres.}$$

**12.** P : Q : R

2 : 3 : 4

Spirit : Water = 1 : 5, 3 : 5 and 5 : 7

When they are mixed, the ratio of spirit to water

$$= \left(2\times\frac{1}{1+5} + 3\times\frac{3}{3+5} + 4\times\frac{5}{5+7}\right) : \left(2\times\frac{5}{1+5} + 3\times\frac{5}{3+5} + 4\times\frac{7}{5+7}\right)$$

$$= \left(\frac{1}{3} + \frac{9}{8} + \frac{5}{3}\right) : \left(\frac{5}{3} + \frac{15}{8} + \frac{7}{3}\right) = \frac{25}{8} : \frac{47}{8} = 25 : 47$$

**13.** Gold in C $= \left(\frac{7}{9} + \frac{7}{18}\right) = \frac{21}{18} = \frac{7}{6}$

Copper in C $= \left(\frac{2}{9} + \frac{11}{18}\right) = \frac{15}{18} = \frac{5}{6}$

$\therefore$ Gold : Copper $= \frac{7}{6} : \frac{5}{6} = 7 : 5$

**14.** Let 1 gm of gold be mixed with $x$ gm of copper to give $(1 + x)$ gm of mixture.

Now, 1G = $19w$

and 1C = $9w$

and mixture = $15w$

Now, 1 gm gold + $x$ gm copper = $(1 + x)$ gm mixture

$\therefore 19w + 9w \times x = (1 + x) \times 15w$

Thus, $4w = 6wx$

$$\Rightarrow x = \frac{4w}{6w} = \frac{4}{6} = \frac{2}{3}$$

So, the required ratio is $1 : \frac{2}{3}$, *i.e.*, 3 : 2.

**15.**

| | *Water* | *Milk* |
|---|---|---|
| Vessel I | $\frac{1}{3}$ | $\frac{2}{3}$ |
| Vessel II | $\frac{2}{7}$ | $\frac{5}{7}$ |

From vessel I, $\frac{1}{5}$ is taken and from vessel II, $\frac{4}{5}$ is taken. Therefore, the ratio of water to milk in the new vessel

$$= \left(\frac{1}{3}\times\frac{1}{5} + \frac{2}{7}\times\frac{4}{5}\right) : \left(\frac{2}{3}\times\frac{1}{5} + \frac{5}{7}\times\frac{4}{5}\right)$$

$$= \left(\frac{1}{15} + \frac{8}{35}\right) : \left(\frac{2}{15} + \frac{20}{35}\right) = \frac{31}{105} : \frac{74}{105} = 31 : 74$$

**16.** The ratio of Mahesh's salary for the two years = 2 : 3

The ratio of Suresh's salary for the two years = 4 : 5

We have also given that the ratio of their salary during the last year = 3 : 5

Now, we change the antecedents (2 and 4) of the first two ratios so that the antecedents in the first becomes 3 (antecedent of the third ratio) and the antecedent in the second becomes 5 (consequent of the third ratio).

Thus, $2 : 3 = 3 : \frac{9}{2}$ and $4 : 5 = 4\left(\frac{5}{4}\right) : 5\left(\frac{5}{4}\right) = 5 : \frac{25}{4}$

Now, it is clear that the ratio of their salaries for the present year is $\frac{9}{2} : \frac{25}{4} = 18 : 25$

$\therefore$ The present salary of Mahesh

$$= \frac{4300}{18+25} \times 18 = ₹\ 1800$$

**17.** The ratio of present incomes

$$= 3\times\frac{5}{4} : 4\times\frac{3}{2} = \frac{15}{4} : \frac{12}{2} = 30 : 48 = 5 : 8$$

$\therefore$ P's present income $= \frac{4160}{5+8} \times 5 = ₹\ 1600$

**18.** Let the monthly salary of A, B, C be $2x$, $3x$ and $5x$

Then, $5x - 2x = 1200$

or, $3x = 1200$

$\therefore$ $x = 400$

B's monthly salary = $3x = 3 \times 400$ = ₹ 1200

**19.** P : (Q + R) = 2 : 5

$\therefore$ P's share $= ₹\left(1050 \times \frac{2}{7}\right) = ₹\ 300$

**20.** Let their ages be $2x$ and $3x$ years.

$\Rightarrow$ $3x - 2x = 6 \Rightarrow x = 6$

Sumit's age = 12 years

Prakash's age = 18 years

After 6 years, Sumit's age = 18 years and Prakash's age = 24 years

$\therefore$ Ratio of their ages = 18 : 24 = 3 : 4

●●●

CHAPTER 4

# Algebra

## Square Roots

### ☛ Points To Remember

- A number $n$ is a perfect square number, if $n = m^2$
- A perfect square number is never negative.
- A square number never ends in 2, 3, 7 or 8.
- The number of zeros at the end of a perfect square is even.
- The square of an even number is even.
- The square of an odd number is odd.
- There are no natural number $p$ and $q$ such that $p^2 = 2q^2$.
- A number $m$ is a square root of $n$, if $n = m \times m = m^2$.
  Positive square root of $n$ is written as $\sqrt{n}$.
- If $p$ and $q$ are perfect squares $(q \neq 0)$, then
  (*i*) $\sqrt{p \times q} = \sqrt{p} \times \sqrt{q}$
  (*ii*) $\sqrt{\dfrac{p}{q}} = \dfrac{\sqrt{p}}{\sqrt{q}}$
- A perfect squares leaves remainder 0 or 1 on division by 3.
  The following table gives the possible remainders for some other prime divisors.

| Divisor | Possible Remainders |
|---|---|
| 3 | 0, 1 |
| 5 | 0, 1, 4 |
| 7 | 0, 1, 2, 4 |
| 11 | 0, 1, 3, 4, 5, 9 |
| 13 | 0, 1, 3, 4, 9, 10, 12 |

- The unit's digit of the square of a natural number is the unit's digit of the square of the digit at unit's place of the given natural number.

| Unit's digit of the number | Unit's digit of the square of the number |
|---|---|
| 0 | 0 |
| 1 or 9 | 1 |
| 2 or 8 | 4 |
| 3 or 7 | 9 |
| 4 or 6 | 6 |
| 5 | 5 |

- For every natural number $n$,
  $(n + 1)^2 - n^2 = (n + 1) + n$
  *e.g.;* $9^2 - 8^2 = 9 + 8 = 17$
  $19^2 - 18^2 = 19 + 18 = 37$
- The square of a natural number $n$ is equal to the sum of first $n$ odd natural numbers.
  *e.g.;* $2^2 = 1 + 3$
  $4^2 = 1 + 3 + 5 + 7 = 16$
  $n^2$ = Sum of first $n$ odd natural numbers.
- A triplet $(m, n, p)$ of three natural numbers $m$, $n$ and $p$ is called a pythagorean triplet if $m^2 + n^2 = p^2$
- The square root of a perfect square number can be obtained by :
  (*i*) the prime factorization. (*ii*) the division method.
- If $n$ is not a perfect square, then $\sqrt{n}$ is not a rational number.
- Squares of natural numbers having all digits 1 have a following pattern:
  $1^2 = 1$
  $11^2 = 1\,\mathbf{2}\,1$
  $111^2 = 1\,2\,\mathbf{3}\,2\,1$
  $1111^2 = 1\,2\,3\,\mathbf{4}\,3\,2\,1$

$11111^2 = 1\,2\,3\,4\,\mathbf{5}\,4\,3\,2\,1$

$111111^2 = 1\,2\,3\,4\,5\,\mathbf{6}\,5\,4\,3\,2\,1$

⋮ ⋮ ⋮

$111111111^2 = 1\,2\,3\,4\,5\,6\,7\,8\,\mathbf{9}\,8\,7\,6\,5\,4\,3\,2\,1$

In this pattern the sum of the digits of every number on the right hand side is a perfect square at given below:

$1 + 2 + 1 = 4 = 2^2$

$1 + 2 + 3 + 2 + 1 = 9 = 3^2$

$1 + 2 + 3 + 4 + 3 + 2 + 1 = 16 = 4^2$

....................................

$1 + 2 + 3 + 4 + 5 + 6 + 7 + 8 + 9 + 8 + 7 + 6 + 5 + 4 + 3 + 2 + 1 = 81 = 9^2$.

- Observe the following pattern

$11^2 = 121$

$101^2 = 10201$

$1001^2 = 1002001$

$10001^2 = 100020001$

- Observe the following pattern

$11^2 = 121$

$101^2 = 10201$

$10101^2 = 102030201$

$1010101^2 = 1020304030201$

$101010101^2 = 10203040504030201$

- **Short Cut Method to find Squares Column Method**

Using $(a + b)^2 = a^2 + 2ab + b^2$.

Make three columns: What is square of 86

$a = 8$, $b = 6$

| Step | Column I $(a^2)$ | Column II $2ab$ | Column III $b^2$ |
|---|---|---|---|
| I | $(8)^2 = 64$ | $2 \times 8 \times 6 = 96$ | $(6)^2 = 36$ |
| II | 64 | 96 + 3 = **99** | **36** |

| Step | Column I $(a^2)$ | Column II $2ab$ | Column III $b^2$ |
|---|---|---|---|
| III | 64 + 9 = **73** | 96 + 3 = **99** | **36** |

The bold digits give the required square $86^2 = 7396$.

## Square Root

Square root of a given number is that number which is multiplied by itself is equal to the given number.

For example, square root of 81 is 9 because

$92 = 9 \times 9 = 81$.

### *Methods of Finding the square root*

**(a) Prime Factorization Method**

(i) Prime Factorization Method

(ii) Group the Factors in Paris

(iii) Take one number from each pair of factors and then multiply them together.

**Example:** Find the square root of 4761?

**Solution:** $4761 = \underbrace{23 \times 23} \times \underbrace{3 \times 3}$

$\therefore \sqrt{4761} = 23 \times 3 = 69$.

**(b) Method of Division:** This method is used when the number is large and the factors cannot be easily determined.

**Exar:ple:** Find the square root of 226576?

**Solution:**

```
          476
      4 | 226516
          16
     87 | 665
      7 | 609
    946 | 5676
      6 | 5676
             ×
```

$\sqrt[2]{226576} = 476$.

## EXERCISE

**1.** $\sqrt{53824} = ?$

A. 202 B. 232
C. 242 D. 332

**2.** The value of $\sqrt{10+\sqrt{25+\sqrt{108+\sqrt{154+\sqrt{255}}}}}$ is:

A. 4 B. 6
C. 8 D. 10

**3.** Evaluate : $\sqrt{41-\sqrt{21+\sqrt{19-\sqrt{9}}}}$.

A. 3 B. 5
C. 6 D. 6.4

**4.** $\left(\frac{\sqrt{625}}{11} \times \frac{14}{\sqrt{25}} \times \frac{11}{\sqrt{196}}\right)$ is equal to:

A. 5
B. 6
C. 8
D. 11

**5.** If $x * y = x + y + \sqrt{xy}$, the value of 6*24 is:

A. 41 B. 42
C. 43 D. 44

**6.** $\sqrt{\frac{25}{81}-\frac{1}{9}} = ?$

A. $\frac{2}{3}$ B. $\frac{4}{9}$

C. $\frac{16}{81}$ D. $\frac{25}{81}$

**7.** The value of $\sqrt{0.01}+\sqrt{0.81}+\sqrt{1.21}+\sqrt{0.0009}$ is:

A. 2.03 B. 2.1

C. 2.11 D. 2.13

**8.** If $\sqrt{18225} = 135$, then the value of $\left(\sqrt{182.25}+\sqrt{1.8225}+\sqrt{0.018225}+\sqrt{0.00018225}\right)$ is:

A. 1.49985 B. 14.9985

C. 149.985 D. 1499.85

**9.** If $\sqrt{3^n} = 729$, then the value of $n$ is:

A. 6 B. 8

C. 10 D. 12

**10.** If $\sqrt{1+\frac{x}{169}} = \frac{14}{13}$, then $x$ is equal to:

A. 1 B. 13

C. 27 D. None of these

**11.** If $\sqrt{1+\frac{55}{729}} = 1+\frac{x}{27}$, then the value of $x$ is:

A. 1 B. 3

C. 5 D. 7

**12.** The value of $\frac{\sqrt{80}-\sqrt{112}}{\sqrt{45}-\sqrt{63}}$ is:

A. $\frac{3}{4}$ B. $1\frac{1}{3}$

C. $1\frac{7}{9}$ D. $1\frac{3}{4}$

**13.** Given $\sqrt{2} = 1.414$. The value of $\sqrt{8}+2\sqrt{32}-3\sqrt{128}+4\sqrt{50}$ is:

A. 8.426 B. 8.484

C. 8.526 D. 8.876

**14.** $\sqrt{\frac{0.081\times0.324\times4.624}{1.5625\times0.0289\times72.9\times64}}$ is equal to:

A. 0.024 B. 0.24

C. 2.4 D. 24

**15.** The value of $\sqrt{\frac{(0.03)^2+(0.21)^2+(0.065)^2}{(0.003)^2+(0.021)^2+(0.0065)^2}}$ is:

A. 0.1 B. 10

C. $10^2$ D. $10^3$

**16.** The square root of $(7+3\sqrt{5})(7-3\sqrt{5})$ is:

A. $\sqrt{5}$ B. 2

C. 4 D. $3\sqrt{5}$

**17.** $\left(\sqrt{3}-\frac{1}{\sqrt{3}}\right)^2$ simplifies to:

A. $\frac{3}{4}$ B. $\frac{4}{\sqrt{3}}$

C. $\frac{4}{3}$ D. None of these

**18.** $\left(\sqrt{2}+\frac{1}{\sqrt{2}}\right)^2$ is equal to :

A. $2\frac{1}{2}$ B. $3\frac{1}{2}$

C. $4\frac{1}{2}$ D. $5\frac{1}{2}$

**19.** If $3a = 4b = 6c$ and $a + b + c = 27\sqrt{29}$, then $\sqrt{a^2+b^2+c^2}$ is:

A. $3\sqrt{29}$

B. 81

C. 87

D. None of these

**20.** The square root of $0.\overline{4}$ is:

A. $0.\overline{6}$ B. $0.\overline{7}$

C. $0.\overline{8}$ D. $0.\overline{9}$

## ANSWERS

| 1 | 2 | 3 | 4 | 5 | 6 | 7 | 8 | 9 | 10 |
|---|---|---|---|---|---|---|---|---|---|
| B | A | C | A | B | B | D | B | D | C |
| **11** | **12** | **13** | **14** | **15** | **16** | **17** | **18** | **19** | **20** |
| A | B | B | A | B | B | C | C | C | A |

# EXPLANATORY ANSWERS

**1.**

| | |
|---|---|
| 2 | $\overline{5}\,\overline{38}\,\overline{24}$ (232 |
| | 4 |
| 43 | 138 |
| | 129 |
| 462 | 924 |
| | 924 |
| | × |

$\therefore \sqrt{53824} = 232.$

**2.** Given exp. = $\sqrt{10+\sqrt{25+\sqrt{108+\sqrt{154+15}}}}$

$= \sqrt{10+\sqrt{25+\sqrt{108+\sqrt{169}}}}$

$= \sqrt{10+\sqrt{25+\sqrt{108+13}}} = \sqrt{10+\sqrt{25+\sqrt{121}}}$

$= \sqrt{10+\sqrt{25+11}} = \sqrt{10+\sqrt{36}}$

$= \sqrt{10+6} = \sqrt{16} = 4$

**3.** Given exp. = $\sqrt{41-\sqrt{21+\sqrt{19-3}}}$

$= \sqrt{41-\sqrt{21+\sqrt{16}}} = \sqrt{41-\sqrt{21+4}}$

$= \sqrt{41-\sqrt{25}} = \sqrt{41-5} = \sqrt{36} = 6$

**4.** Given exp. = $\frac{25}{11}\times\frac{14}{5}\times\frac{11}{14} = 5$

**5.** $6*24 = 6 + 24 + \sqrt{6\times 24} = 30+\sqrt{144} = 30+12 = 42$

**6.** $\sqrt{\frac{25}{81}-\frac{1}{9}} = \sqrt{\frac{25-9}{81}} = \sqrt{\frac{16}{81}} = \frac{\sqrt{16}}{\sqrt{81}} = \frac{4}{9}$

**7.** Given exp.

$= \sqrt{\frac{1}{100}}+\sqrt{\frac{81}{100}}+\sqrt{\frac{121}{100}}+\sqrt{\frac{9}{10000}}$

$= \frac{1}{10}+\frac{9}{10}+\frac{11}{10}+\frac{3}{100}$

$= 0.1 + 0.9 + 1.1 + 0.03 = 2.13$

**8.** Given exp.

$= \sqrt{\frac{18225}{10^2}}+\sqrt{\frac{18225}{10^4}}+\sqrt{\frac{18225}{10^6}}+\sqrt{\frac{18225}{10^8}}$

$= \frac{\sqrt{18225}}{10}+\frac{\sqrt{18225}}{10^2}+\frac{\sqrt{18225}}{10^3}+\frac{\sqrt{18225}}{10^4}$

$= \frac{135}{10}+\frac{135}{100}+\frac{135}{1000}+\frac{135}{10000}$

$= 13.5 + 1.35 + 0.135 + 0.0135 = 14.9985$

**9.** $\sqrt{3^n} = 729 = 3^6$

$\Leftrightarrow \left(\sqrt{3^n}\right)^2 = (3^6)^2$

$\Leftrightarrow 3^n = 3^{12}$

$\Leftrightarrow n = 12$

**10.** $\sqrt{1+\frac{x}{169}} = \frac{14}{13} \Rightarrow 1+\frac{x}{169} = \frac{196}{169}$

$\Rightarrow \frac{x}{169} = \left(\frac{196}{169}-1\right) = \frac{27}{169}$

$\Rightarrow x = 27.$

**11.** $\sqrt{1+\frac{55}{729}} = 1+\frac{x}{27}$

$\Rightarrow \sqrt{\frac{784}{729}} = \frac{27+x}{27}$

$\Rightarrow \frac{28}{27} = \frac{27+x}{27}$

$\Rightarrow 27 + x = 28 \quad \Rightarrow x = 1$

**12.** $\frac{\sqrt{80}-\sqrt{112}}{\sqrt{45}-\sqrt{63}} = \frac{\sqrt{16\times 5}-\sqrt{16\times 7}}{\sqrt{9\times 5}-\sqrt{9\times 7}}$

$= \frac{4\sqrt{5}-4\sqrt{7}}{3\sqrt{5}-3\sqrt{7}} = \frac{4\left(\sqrt{5}-\sqrt{7}\right)}{3\left(\sqrt{5}-\sqrt{7}\right)} = \frac{4}{3} = 1\frac{1}{3}$

**13.** Given exp.

$= \sqrt{4\times 2}+2\sqrt{16\times 2}-3\sqrt{64\times 2}+4\sqrt{25\times 2}$

$= 2\sqrt{2}+8\sqrt{2}-24\sqrt{2}+20\sqrt{2}$

$= 6\sqrt{2} = 6 \times 1.414 = 8.484$

**14.** Given exp. = $\sqrt{\frac{81\times 324\times 4624}{15625\times 289\times 729\times 64}}$

$= \frac{9\times 18\times 68}{125\times 17\times 27\times 8} = \frac{3}{125} = 0.024$

**15.** Given exp. = $\sqrt{\frac{(0.03)^2+(0.21)^2+(0.065)^2}{\left(\frac{0.03}{10}\right)^2+\left(\frac{0.21}{10}\right)^2+\left(\frac{0.065}{10}\right)^2}}$

$= \sqrt{\frac{100\ [(0.03)^2+(0.21)^2+(0.065)^2]}{(0.03)^2+(0.21)^2+(0.065)^2}}$

$= \sqrt{100} = 10$

16. $\sqrt{(7+3\sqrt{5})(7-3\sqrt{5})} = \sqrt{(7)^2-(3\sqrt{5})^2}$

$= \sqrt{49-45} = \sqrt{4} = 2$

17. $\left(\sqrt{3}-\frac{1}{\sqrt{3}}\right)^2 = \left(\sqrt{3}\right)^2 + \left(\frac{1}{\sqrt{3}}\right)^2 - 2\times\sqrt{3}\times\frac{1}{\sqrt{3}}$

$= 3+\frac{1}{3}-2 = 1+\frac{1}{3} = \frac{4}{3}$

18. $\left(\sqrt{2}+\frac{1}{\sqrt{2}}\right)^2 = \left(\sqrt{2}\right)^2 + \left(\frac{1}{\sqrt{2}}\right)^2 + 2\times\sqrt{2}\times\frac{1}{\sqrt{2}}$

$= 2+\frac{1}{2}+2 = 4+\frac{1}{2} = 4\frac{1}{2}$

19. $4b = 6c \Rightarrow b = \frac{3}{2}c$ and $3a = 4b$

$\Rightarrow \quad a = \frac{4}{3}b = \frac{4}{3}\left(\frac{3}{2}c\right) = 2c$

$a + b + c = 27\sqrt{29}$

$2c+\frac{3}{2}c+c = 27\sqrt{29}$

$\Rightarrow \quad \frac{9}{2}c = 27\sqrt{29}$

$\Rightarrow \quad c = 6\sqrt{29}$

$\therefore \sqrt{a^2+b^2+c^2}$

$= \sqrt{(a+b+c)-2(ab+bc+ca)}$

$= \sqrt{\left(27\sqrt{29}\right)^2-2\left(2c\times\frac{3}{2}c+\frac{3}{2}c\times c+c\times 2c\right)}$

$= \sqrt{(729\times 29)-2\left(3c^2+\frac{3}{2}c^2+2c^2\right)}$

$= \sqrt{(729\times 29)-2\times\frac{13}{2}c^2}$

$= \sqrt{(729\times 29)-13\times\left(6\sqrt{29}\right)^2}$

$= \sqrt{29(729-468)}$

$= \sqrt{29\times 261} = \sqrt{29\times 29\times 9}$

$= 29 \times 3 = 87$

20. $\sqrt{0.\bar{4}} = \sqrt{\frac{4}{9}} = \frac{2}{3} = 0.666.... = 0.\bar{6}$.

# Basic Algebraic Identities of School Algebra & Elementary Surds

## Algebric Identies

**Some Important Formula**

(i) $(a + b)^2 = a^2 + 2ab + b^2$

(ii) $(a - b)^2 = a^2 - 2ab + b^2$

(iii) $a^2 - b^2 = (a - b)(a + b)$

(iv) $(a + b + c)^2 = a^2 + b^2 + c^2 + 2ab + 2bc + 2ca$

(v) $(a + b - c)^2 = a^2 + b^2 + c^2 + 2ab - 2bc - 2ca$

(vi) $(a - b + c)^2 = a^2 + b^2 + c^2 - 2ab - 2bc + 2ca$

(vii) $(-a + b + c)^2 = a^2 + b^2 + c^2 - 2ab + 2bc - 2ca$

(viii) $(a + b)^3 = a^3 + b^3 + 3ab(a + b)$ or

$= a^3 + b^3 + 3a^2b + 3ab^2$

(ix) $(a - b)^3 = a^3 - b^3 - 3ab(a - b)$ or

$= a^3 - b^3 - 3a^2b + 3ab^2$

(x) $a^3 + b^3 = (a + b)(a^2 + b^2 - ab)$ or

$= (a + b)^3 - 3ab(a + b)$

(xi) $a^3 - b^3 = (a - b)(a^2 + b^2 + ab)$ or

$= (a - b)^3 + 3ab(a - b)$

(xii) $a^3 + b^3 + c^3 - 3abc$

$= (a + b + c)(a^2 + b^2 + c^2 - ab - bc - ca)$

If $a + b + c = 0$

$a^3 + b^3 + c^3 = 3abc$

(xiii) $(x + a)(x + b) = x^2 + (a + b)x + ab$

(xiv) $(a + b)^2 + (a - b)^2 = 2(a^2 + b^2)$

(xv) $(a + b)^2 - (a - b)^2 = 4ab$

(xvi) $(a + b)^3 + (a - b)^3 = 2(a^3 + 3ab^2)$

(xvii) $(a + b)^3 - (a - b)^3 = (2(b^3 + 3a^2b)$

(xviii) If $x+\frac{1}{x} = t$ Then, $x^2+\frac{1}{x^2} = t^2-2$

(xix) If $x-\frac{1}{x} = t$ Then, $x^2+\frac{1}{x^2} = t^2+2$

(xx) $x^3+\frac{1}{x^3} = \left(x+\frac{1}{x}\right)^3 - 3\left(x+\frac{1}{x}\right)$

(xxi) $x^2-\frac{1}{x^3} = \left(x-\frac{1}{x}\right)^3 + 3\left(x-\frac{1}{x}\right)$

(xxii) $x+\frac{1}{x} = \sqrt{x^2+\frac{1}{x^2}+2}$

(xxiii) $x-\frac{1}{x} = \sqrt{x^2+\frac{1}{x^2}-2}$

## Factorization of Algebraic Expressions

**Factorization :** The process of writing an algebraic expression as the product of two or more algebraic expressions is called factorization.

**Factors :** The algebraic expressions that may be multiplied to obtain the given algebraic expressions are called factors of the given expression.

**Factor Theorem :** If $f(x)$ is completely divisible by $(x - a)$ then $f(a) = 0$, $(x - a)$ is called factor of $f(x)$, if and only if $f(a) = 0$

**Remainder Theorem :** If an expression $f(x)$ is divided by $(x - a)$ then the remainder is $f(a)$.

*e.g.*, $f(x) = ax^3 + bx + cx + d$

$f(a) = a \,.\, a^3 + b \,.\, a + c \,.\, a + d$ is known as remainder of the given polynomials.

## Surds

Given a number, it is not always possible to find some whole number which when multiplied by itself will give the given number. In other words all given numbers are not perfect square numbers. For example, square root of 9, *i.e.*, $\sqrt{9}$ is 3, which is a whole number. But square root of 15, *i.e.*, $\sqrt{15}$ = 3.873, which is not a whole number.

Hence square roots of natural numbers which are not perfect squares are not rational numbers. These are irrational numbers and are called **Surds**.

For example, $\sqrt{3}$, $\sqrt{7}$, $2+\sqrt{11}$, $4+\sqrt{13}$ ..... etc. are Surds.

Given below are a few formulas which are quite helpful in solving the problems related to surds:

**1.** $\sqrt{a} \times \sqrt{a} = a$

**2.** $\sqrt{a} \times \sqrt{b} = \sqrt{ab}$

**3.** $\left(\sqrt{a}+\sqrt{b}\right)^2 = a + b + \sqrt[2]{ab}$

**4.** $\left(\sqrt{a}-\sqrt{b}\right)^2 = a + b - \sqrt[2]{ab}$

**5.** $x\sqrt{a} + x\sqrt{b} = x\left(\sqrt{a}+\sqrt{b}\right)$

**6.** $\dfrac{1}{\sqrt{a}+\sqrt{b}} = \dfrac{1}{\sqrt{a}+\sqrt{b}} \times \dfrac{\sqrt{a}-\sqrt{b}}{\sqrt{a}-\sqrt{b}} = \dfrac{\sqrt{a}-\sqrt{b}}{a-b}$

**7.** $\dfrac{1}{\sqrt{a}-\sqrt{b}} = \dfrac{1}{\sqrt{a}-\sqrt{b}} \times \dfrac{\sqrt{a}+\sqrt{b}}{\sqrt{a}+\sqrt{b}} = \dfrac{\sqrt{a}+\sqrt{b}}{a-b}$

**8.** $a + \sqrt{b} = c + \sqrt{d} \Rightarrow a = c$ and $b = d$

**9.** $\sqrt{2}$ = 1.41421, $\sqrt{3}$ = 1.73205, $\sqrt{5}$ = 2.23607,

$\sqrt{6}$ = 2.4494 $\sqrt{7}$ = 2.64575, $\sqrt{8}$ = 2.82842,

$\sqrt{10}$ = 3.16227, $\sqrt{11}$ = 3.31662

## EXERCISE

**1.** $(28)^3 + (-15)^3 + (-13)^3 = ?$

A. 16380 B. 16250
C. 16420 D. 16280

**2.** If $x + \dfrac{1}{x} = 5$, What is the value of $x^3 + \dfrac{1}{x^3}$:

A. 120 B. 210
C. 110 D. 105

**3.** If $x^2 + \dfrac{1}{x^2} = 83$, what is the value of $x^3 - \dfrac{1}{x^3} = ?$

A. 756 B. 754
C. 856 D. 932

**4.** $23^3 - 17^3 = ?$

A. 7254 B. 7153
C. 7271 D. 7154

**5.** If $x + \dfrac{1}{x} = 15$, then the value of $x^2 + \dfrac{1}{x^2}$ will be:

A. 228 B. 230
C. 323 D. 223

**6.** If $x = 12$ and $y = 4$, the value of $(x+y)^{x/y}$ will be:

A. 4096 B. 3896
C. 4196 D. 5086

**7.** If $x + y = 2z$, then the value of $\left(\dfrac{x}{x-z} + \dfrac{z}{y-z}\right)$ will be:

A. 1 B. 4
C. 3/2 D. 2

**8.** If $x + y + z = 0$, then the value of $\dfrac{(x+y)(y+z)(z+x)}{xyz}$ will be:

A. –3 B. –2
C. 0 D. –1

**9.** If $x + \dfrac{1}{x} = 3$, the value of $x^4 + \dfrac{1}{x^4}$ will be:

A. 49 B. 47
C. 37 D. 42

**10.** If $\left(x + \dfrac{1}{x}\right)^2 = 0$, then the value of $\left(x^2 + \dfrac{1}{x^2}\right)$ will be:

A. 1 B. –1
C. 2 D. –2

**11.** If $\left(a + \dfrac{2}{a}\right) = 3$, then the value of $\left(a - \dfrac{2}{a}\right)$ will be:

A. ± 4 B. ± 5
C. ± 2 D. ± 1

**12.** If $\sqrt{a}+\frac{1}{\sqrt{a}} = 4$, then the value of $a^2 + \frac{1}{a^2}$ will be:

A. 194 B. 199

C. 178 D. 192

**13.** Factors of $x^2 - 25$ are:

A. $(x - 1)(x - 25)$

B. $(x + 25)(x - 1)$

C. $(x + 5)(x - 5)$

D. $(x - 5)(x - 5)$

**14.** Square of $\left(x-\frac{1}{x}\right)$ will be

A. $x^2 - 2 - \frac{1}{x^2}$ B. $x^2 - 2 + \frac{1}{x^2}$

C. $x^2 - 4 - \frac{1}{x^2}$ D. $x^2 - 2 + \frac{1}{x}$

**15.** Factors of $36 - 9x^2$ will be:

A. $(6 + 3x)(6 - 3x)$ B. $(3x - 6)(6 - 3x)$

C. $(3x + 6)(3x - 6)$ D. $(12x - 3x)(3 + 3x)$

## ANSWERS

| 1 | 2 | 3 | 4 | 5 | 6 | 7 | 8 | 9 | 10 |
|---|---|---|---|---|---|---|---|---|---|
| A | C | A | A | D | A | A | D | B | D |
| 11 | 12 | 13 | 14 | 15 | | | | | |
| D | A | C | B | A | | | | | |

## EXPLANATORY ANSWERS

**1.** Let $a = 28$, $b = -15$ and $c = -13$. Then

$$a + b + c = 28 - 15 - 13 = 0$$

$$a^3 + b^3 + c^3 = 3abc$$

$$(28)^3 + (-15)^3 + (-13)^3 = 3 \times 28 \times (-15) \times (-13)$$

$$= 16380$$

**2.** $$x^3+\frac{1}{x^3} = \left(x+\frac{1}{x}\right)^3 - 3\left(x+\frac{1}{x}\right)$$

$$= (5)^3 - 3 \times 5 = 125 - 15 = 110.$$

**3.** If $x^2+\frac{1}{x^2} = 83$, what is the value of $x^3-\frac{1}{x^3} = ?$

$$\left(x-\frac{1}{x}\right)^2 = x^2+\frac{1}{x^2}-2$$

$$x-\frac{1}{x} = \sqrt{83-2} = \sqrt{81}$$

$$x-\frac{1}{x} = 9$$

$$\therefore \quad \left(x^3-\frac{1}{x^3}\right) = \left(x-\frac{1}{x}\right)^3 + 3\left(x-\frac{1}{x}\right)$$

$$= (9)^3 + 3 \times 9 = 729 + 27 = 756$$

**4.** $23^3 - 17^3 = (20 + 3)^3 - (20 - 3)^3 = 2(3^3 + 3 \times 20^2 \times 3)$

$[\because (a + b)^3 - (a - b)^3 = 2(b^3 + 3a^2b)]$

$= 2(27 + 3600) = 54 + 7200 = 7254$

**5.** $\because x+\frac{1}{x} = 15 \Rightarrow \left(x+\frac{1}{x}\right)^2 = (15)^2$

$$\Rightarrow x^2+\frac{1}{x^2}+2.x\frac{1}{x} = 225$$

$$\therefore \quad x^2+\frac{1}{x^2} = 225 - 2 = 223.$$

**6.** $(x+y)^{x/y} = (12+4)^{12/4} = (16)^3 = 4096.$

$[\because x = 12, y = 4]$

**7.** $\because x + y = 2z \Rightarrow x - z = z - y = -(y - z)$

$$\therefore \quad \frac{x}{x-z}+\frac{z}{y-z} = \frac{x}{-(y-z)}+\frac{z}{y-z} = \frac{z-x}{y-z} = 1.$$

$[\because x - z = z - y]$

**8.** $\because \quad x + y + z = 0 \Rightarrow x + y = -z$

$x + y + z = 0 \Rightarrow y + z = -x$

and $x + y + z = 0 \Rightarrow z + x = -y$

$$\therefore \quad \frac{(x+y)(y+z)(z+x)}{xyz} = \frac{(-z)(-x)(-y)}{xyz}$$

$$= -1.$$

**9.** $\because x+\frac{1}{x} = 3 \Rightarrow \left(x+\frac{1}{x}\right)^2 = (3)^2$

$$\Rightarrow \quad x^2+\frac{1}{x^2}+2.x.\frac{1}{x} = 9$$

$$\Rightarrow \quad x^2+\frac{1}{x^2} = 9 - 2 = 7$$

$$\because \quad x^2+\frac{1}{x^2} = 7 \Rightarrow \left(x^2+\frac{1}{x^2}\right)^2 = (7)^2$$

$$\Rightarrow \quad x^4+\frac{1}{x^4}+2.x^2.\frac{1}{x^2} = 49$$

$$\therefore \quad x^4+\frac{1}{x^4} = 49 - 2 = 47.$$

**10.** $\left(x+\frac{1}{x}\right)^2 = 0 \Rightarrow x^2+\frac{1}{x^2}+2x.\frac{1}{x} = 0$

$$\Rightarrow \quad x^2+\frac{1}{x^2} = -2.$$

11. $\because \left(a-\frac{2}{a}\right)^2 = \left(a+\frac{2}{a}\right)^2 - 4.a.\frac{2}{a} = (3)^2 - 8 = 9 - 8 = 1$

$\therefore \left(a-\frac{2}{a}\right) = \pm\sqrt{1} = \pm 1.$

12. $\because \sqrt{a}+\frac{1}{\sqrt{a}} = 4 \Rightarrow \left(\sqrt{a}+\frac{1}{\sqrt{a}}\right)^2 = (4)^2$

$\Rightarrow a + \frac{1}{a} + 2.\sqrt{a}.\frac{1}{\sqrt{a}} = 16 \because \left(a+\frac{1}{a}\right) = 14$

$\Rightarrow \left(a+\frac{1}{a}\right)^2 = (14)^2 \Rightarrow a^2 + \frac{1}{a^2} + 2.a.\frac{1}{a} = 196$

$\therefore \quad a^2 + \frac{1}{a^2} = 196 - 2 = 194.$

13. $x^2 - 25 = (x)^2 - (5)^2$, [which is of the form $a^2 - b^2$]

$= (x + 5)(x - 5).$

14. According to question:

Square of $\left(x-\frac{1}{x}\right) = \left(x-\frac{1}{x}\right)^2$

$= x^2 - 2.x.\frac{1}{x} + \left(\frac{1}{x}\right)^2$

$= x^2 - 2 + \frac{1}{x^2}.$

15. $36 - 9x^2 = (6)^2 - (3x)^2$ [which is of the form $a^2 - b^2$]

$= (6 + 3x)(6 - 3x).$

# Graphs of Linear Equations

## Linear Equation in One Variable

**Definition:** A linear equation in one variable is an equation of the form $ax + b = 0$ or, $ax = c$ where, $a, b, c$ are real numbers, $a \neq 0$ and $x$ is a variable. Its graph is a straight line.

(*i*) If equation is on X-axis, then Y = 0

(*ii*) If equation is on Y-axis, then X = 0

## Linear Equation in Two Variables

**Definition:** An equation of the form $ax + by + c = 0$ or, $ax + by = c$ where, $a, b, c$ are real numbers, $a \neq 0, b \neq 0$ and $x, y$ are variables, is called a linear equation in two variables.

For example: (*i*) $2x + 3y - 12$ (*ii*) $x + 2y = 8$

## The System of Equations

$a_1x + b_1y + c_1 = 0$ and $a_2x + b_2y + c_2 = 0$ may be either unique solution or no solution or infinitely many solutions.

Unique solution is known as consistent or not parallel. No solution is known as inconsistent or parallel, while many solutions are known as coincident or dependent.

(*a*) **For unique solution:** $\frac{a_1}{a_2} \neq \frac{b_1}{b_2}$

(*b*) **For no solution:** $\frac{a_1}{a_2} = \frac{b_1}{b_2} \neq \frac{c_1}{c_2}$

(*c*) **For many solutions:** $\frac{a_1}{a_2} = \frac{b_1}{b_2} = \frac{c_1}{c_2}$

## Graph of linear equations

Graph of a linear equation in two variables $x$ and $y$ *i.e.*, the graph of the equation of the form

$ax + by + c = 0, a \neq 0, b \neq 0$

we consider the equation,

$2x + y = 6$

then, $y = 6 - 2x$

We find different values of this equation

| $x$ | 0 | 1 | 2 | 3 |
|---|---|---|---|---|
| $y$ | 6 | 4 | 2 | 0 |

Now, we plot these points $(x, y)$ on a graph paper and then join these points

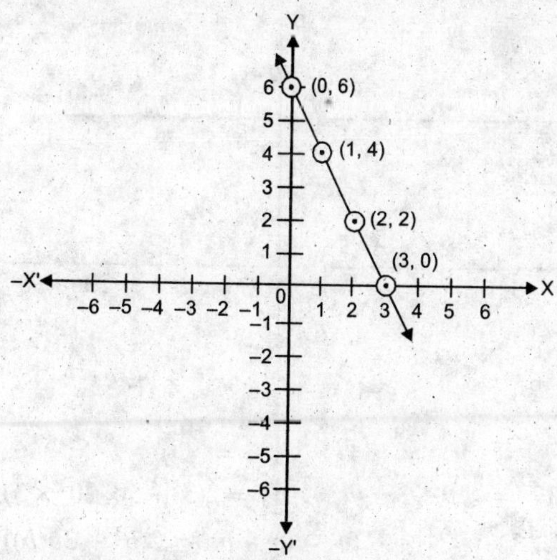


Hence, the line $l$ is called the graph of the equation

$2x + y = 6$

**Example 1:** Draw the graph:

(*i*) $x = 2$, (*ii*) $y = 3$, (*iii*) $y = 0$

**Solution:** (*i*) The given equation, $x = 2$ does not contain $y$

Table of values

| $x$ | 2 | 2 | 2 | fixed |
|---|---|---|---|---|
| $y$ | 1 | 3 | 4 | any value |

ploting the points (2, 1), (2, 3) and (2, 4) and joining them

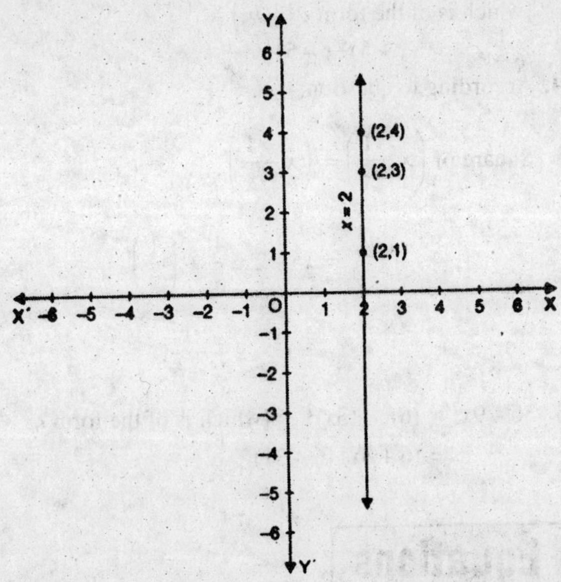


Hence, the graph of the given equation is a line parallel to y-axis

(*ii*) The given equation $y = 3$ does not contain $x$

Table of values

| $x$ | 1 | 2 | 4 | any value |
|---|---|---|---|---|
| $y$ | 3 | 3 | 3 | fixed |

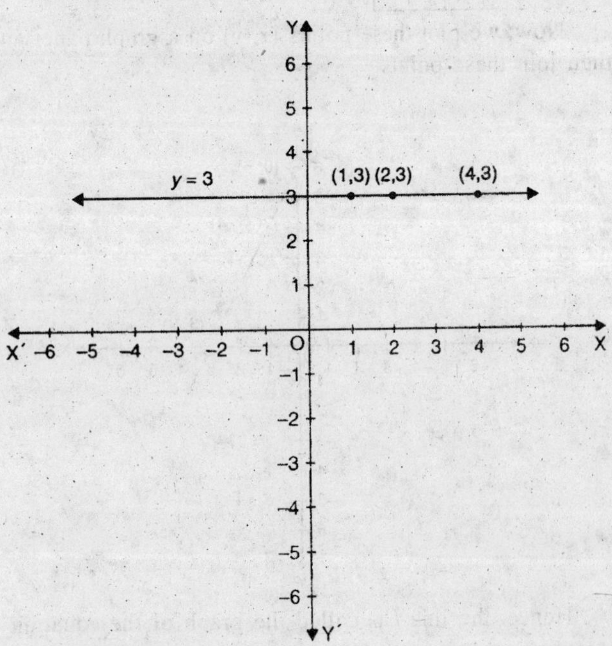


Hence, the graph of the given equation is a line parallel to $x$-axis.

(*iii*) The given equation is $y = 0$

Table of values

| $x$ | 1 | 2 | 3 | any value |
|---|---|---|---|---|
| $y$ | 0 | 0 | 0 | fixed |

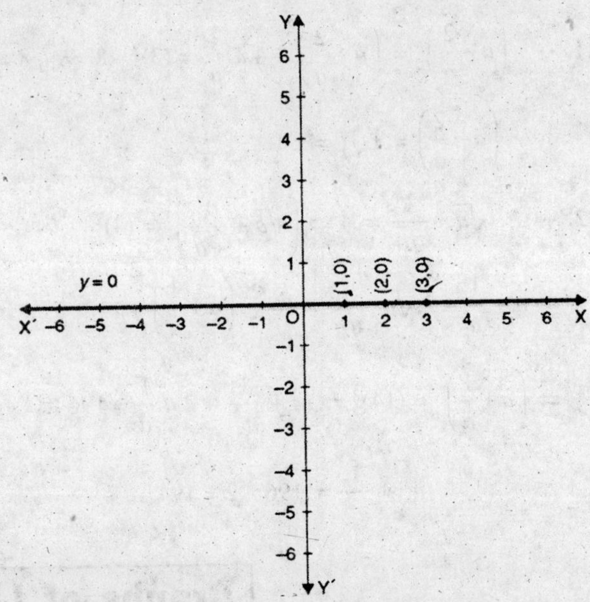


Hence, $y = 0$ is the equation of $x$-axis.

**Example 2.** Draw the graph of the line $x - 2y = 3$. From the graph find co-ordinates of the points when (*i*) $x = -5$, (*ii*) $y = 0$

**Solution:** The given equation is $x - 2y = 3$

Table of value

| $x$ | 3 | 5 | 1 |
|---|---|---|---|
| $y$ | 0 | 1 | −1 |

$\because \quad 2y = x - 3$

$\therefore \quad y = \dfrac{x-3}{2}$

Plotting the points (3, 0), (5, 1) and (1, −1) on the graph paper and joining these points.

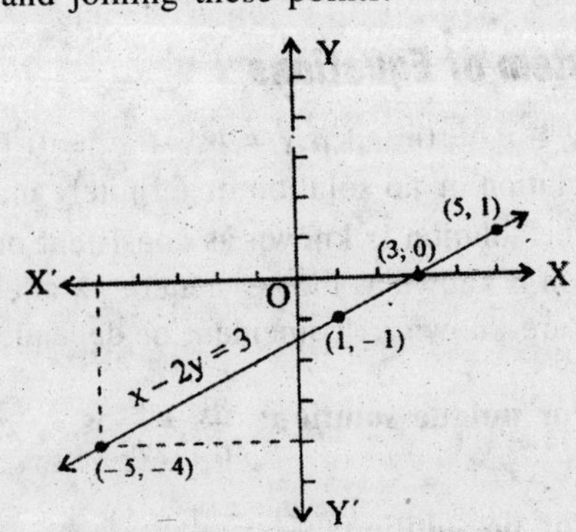


From the graph,

(*i*) when $x = -5$, then $y = -4$

(*ii*) when $y = 0$, then $x = 3$

**Example 3.** Draw the graph of the equations

$5x + 3y = 4.$

**Solution:** The given equation is $5x + 3y = 4$

$\Rightarrow \quad y = \dfrac{4-5x}{3}$

Table of values

| $x$ | –1 | 2 | 5 |
|---|---|---|---|
| $y$ | 3 | –2 | –7 |

Plot the points (–1, 3), (2, –2) and (5, –7) on the graph paper and join these points.

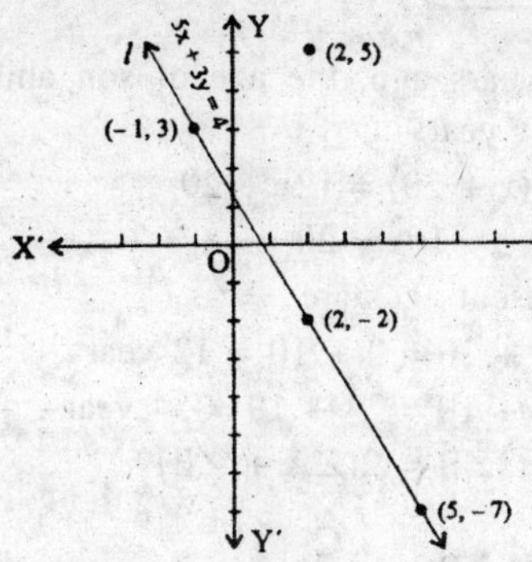


Hence, the line $l$ is called the graph of the equation,

$$5x + 3y = 4$$

**Example 4.** Draw the graph of the equation

$$2x - 3y = -11.$$

**Solution:** The given equation is

$$2x - 3y = -11$$

$$\Rightarrow \quad 3y = 2x + 11$$

$$\Rightarrow \quad y = \frac{2x+11}{3}$$

Table of values

| $x$ | –1 | 2 | –4 |
|---|---|---|---|
| $y$ | 3 | 5 | 1 |

plot the points (–1, 3), (2, 5) and (–4, 1) on the graph paper and join these points

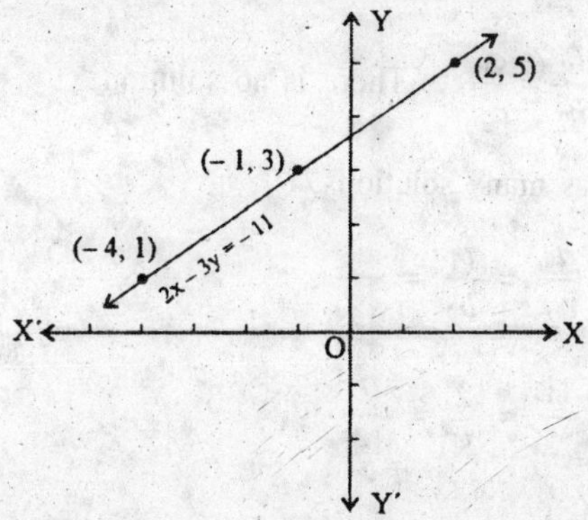


Hence, this line $l$ is called the graph of the equation $2x - 3y = -11$.

## EXERCISE

**1.** The system of linear equations $2x + 3y = 7$ and $4x + 6y = 10$ has:
A. no solution
B. unique solution
C. infinite solution
D. no conclusion can be drawn

**2.** The value of $k$ for which the system of equations $x + 2y + 7 = 0$ and $2x + ky + 14 = 0$ will have infinitely many solutions is:
A. 2 B. 4
C. 6 D. 8

**3.** For what value of α, the system of equations $\alpha x + 3y = \alpha - 3$ and $12x + \alpha y = \alpha$ will have a unique solution?
A. $\alpha \neq \pm 6$ B. $\alpha \neq \pm 3$
C. $\alpha \neq +6$ D. None of these

**4.** For what value of $k$, the system of equations will represent the coincident lines $x+5y-7=0$ and $4x+20y+k=0$?
A. 28 B. –28
C. –26 D. None of these

**5.** A lady has 50 paise and ₹ 1 coins in her purse. If in all, she has 40 coins totally ₹ 25.50 how many of each type of coins does she have?
A. 26, 11 B. 11, 29
C. 29, 11 D. None of these

**6.** A father is three times as old as his son. After twelve years his age will be twice as the age of his son. Find their present ages in years.
A. 12, 26 B. 24, 36
C. 36, 12 D. None of these

**7.** Ten years ago, father was twelve times as old as his son. Ten years after, he will be twice as old as his son will be. Find their present ages in years.
A. 12, 36 B. 12, 24
C. 12, 34 D. None of these

**8.** The present age of a father is 3 years more than three times the age of son. Three years hence father's age will be 10 years more than twice the age of son. Determine their present ages in years.
A. 10, 33 B. 33, 10
C. 10, 30 D. None of these

**9.** In a triangle $ABC$, $\angle C = 3\angle B = 2(\angle A + \angle B)$. Find three angles in degrees.
A. 20°, 50°, 120° B. 30°, 40°, 120°
C. 20°, 40°, 120° D. None of these

**10.** The fraction becomes 2 when 1 is added to both the numerator and the denominator, and it becomes 3 when 1 is subtracted from both the numerator and denominator. The given fraction is :
A. 7/3 B. 4/7
C. 3/7 D. 7/4

## ANSWERS

| 1 | 2 | 3 | 4 | 5 | 6 | 7 | 8 | 9 | 10 |
|---|---|---|---|---|---|---|---|---|---|
| A | B | A | B | C | C | C | A | C | A |

## EXPLANATORY ANSWERS

**1.** $\frac{2}{4} = \frac{3}{6} \neq \frac{7}{10} \Rightarrow \frac{1}{2} = \frac{1}{2} \neq \frac{7}{10}$

$\frac{a_1}{a_2} = \frac{b_1}{b_2} \neq \frac{c_1}{c_2}$ ∴ There is no solution.

**2.** Since, it has many solutions.

∴ $\frac{a_1}{a_2} = \frac{b_1}{b_2} = \frac{c_1}{c_2}$

$\frac{1}{2} = \frac{2}{K} = \frac{7}{14}$

$\frac{1}{2} = \frac{2}{K} \Rightarrow K = 4.$

**3.** Since, the given equations have unique solution.

∴ $\frac{a_1}{a_2} \neq \frac{b_1}{b_2}$

$\frac{\alpha}{12} \neq \frac{3}{\alpha}$

$\Rightarrow \quad \alpha^2 \neq 36 \Rightarrow \alpha \neq \pm 6$

**4.** Since, the given set of equations represent coincident lines.

then, $\frac{1}{4} = \frac{5}{20} = \frac{-7}{K} \Rightarrow K = -28$

**5.** Let, $x$ be the number of 50 paise coins and $y$ be the number of ₹ 1 coins.

According to the question,

$x + y = 40$ ...(*i*)

and $\frac{x}{2} + y = 25.50$

$\Rightarrow \quad x + 2y = 51$ ...(*ii*)

Subtracting equation (*i*) from (*ii*) and solving

we get, $x = 29,\ y = 11$

**6.** Let, age of son = $x$ years.

∴ age of father = $3x$ years.

According to the question,

$2(x + 12) = 3x + 12 \Rightarrow x = 12$

∴ Son's age = 12 years; Father's age = 36 years.

**7.** Let ten years ago, the age of son and father were $x$ and $12x$ years.

Then, $2(x + 20) = 12x + 20$

$\Rightarrow \quad 10x = 20 \Rightarrow x = 2$

Their present ages are

$x + 10 = 2 + 10 = 12$ years

$12x + 10 = 24 + 10 = 34$ years.

**9.** ∴ $\angle C = 3\angle B = 2(\angle A + \angle B)$

$\angle A + \angle B = \frac{\angle C}{2}$

We have, $\angle A + \angle B + \angle C = 180°$

(Sum of angles of a triangle is 180°)

$\frac{\angle C}{2} + \angle C = 180°$

$3\angle C = 2 \times 180°$

$\angle C = \frac{2 \times 180°}{3} = 120°$

$3\angle B = \angle C$

$\angle B = \frac{\angle C}{3} = \frac{120°}{3} = 40°$

∴ $\angle A = 180° - (120° + 40°) = 180° - 160° = 20°.$

**10.** Let the fraction be $\frac{x}{y} \Rightarrow \frac{x+1}{y+1} = 2$

$\Rightarrow \quad x + 1 = 2y + 2$

$\Rightarrow \quad x - 2y = 1$ ...(*i*)

Again $\frac{x-1}{y-1} = 3$

$\Rightarrow \quad x - 1 = 3y - 3$

$\Rightarrow \quad x - 3y = -2$ ...(*ii*)

from (*i*) and (*ii*)

$x - 2y = 1$

$x - 3y = -2$

$-\quad +\quad +$

$y = 3$

Putting the value of $y$ in (*i*) then we get, $x = 7$

∴ fraction $= \frac{x}{y} = \frac{7}{3}$

CHAPTER

# 5 Average

The average of any number of quantities of the same kind can be found by dividing their sum by their number.

Thus,

$$\text{Average} = \frac{\text{Sum of quantities}}{\text{No. of quantities}}$$

Sum of quantities = Their average × Their number

$$\text{Number of quantities} = \frac{\text{Sum of quantities}}{\text{Their average}}$$

When a body coveres the same distance at two different speeds $p$ km/hr and $q$ km/hr, then its average speed for the whole journey is $\frac{2pq}{p+q}$ km/hr.

## EXERCISE

**1.** The average of the fractions $1\frac{1}{2}$, $2\frac{1}{3}$, $3\frac{1}{3}$ and $4\frac{5}{6}$ is:

A. 2 B. $2\frac{1}{2}$
C. 3 D. 4

**2.** The average of first nine multiples of 3 is

A. 12.0 B. 12.5
C. 15.0 D. 18.5

**3.** The average of 13 numbers is 68, the average of first 7 numbers is 63 and the average of last 7 numbers is 70. What is the 7th number?

A. 43 B. 45
C. 47 D. 49

**4.** One-third of a certain journey was covered at the rate of 25 km per hour, one-fourth at the rate of 30 km per hour and the rest at the 50 km per hour. What is the average speed per hour for whole journey?

A. $33\frac{1}{3}$ kmph B. $44\frac{1}{4}$ kmph
C. $22\frac{1}{2}$ kmph D. 33 kmph

**5.** Nine men went to a hotel. Eight of them spent ₹ 3 for each over their meals and the ninth spent ₹ 2 more than the average expenditure of all the nine. What is the total money spent by them?

A. ₹ 29.25 B. ₹ 29.50
C. ₹ 29 D. ₹ 30

**6.** An establishment is permitted an average monthly contingency expenditure of ₹ 500 per month during the financial year. When a trial check was made at the end of the first nine months of the year it was found that the average monthly contingency expenditure worked out to be ₹ 511. What average monthly expenditure for the next three months should be aimed at in order to attain the permissible average of ₹ 500 per month for the whole year?

A. ₹ 567 B. ₹ 467
C. 367 D. ₹ 667

**7.** Average age of 8 persons increased by 2 years, when two men whose ages are 20 and 24 years are replaced by two women. What is the average age of women?

A. 30 years B. 31 years
C. 28 years D. 33 years

**8.** A man had seven children. When their average age was 12 years, the child who was 6 years of age died. What was the average of the surviving children 5 years after the death of the child?

A. 15 years B. 16 years
C. 17 years D. 18 years

**9.** The weight of a body, calculated as the average of seven different experiments is 53.735 grams. The average of the first three is 54.005 grams, the fourth was greater than the fifth by 0.004 gram, while the average of the sixth and seventh was 0.010 gram less

than the average of the first three. What is the weight of the body as obtained by the fourth experiment?
A. 53.068 gm B. 53.078 gm
C. 53.086 gm D. 53.072 gm

**10.** A batsman has a certain average of runs for 16 innings. In the 17th innings, he makes a score of 85 runs thereby increasing his average by 3. What is the average after the 17th inning?
A. 33 runs B. 34 runs
C. 37 runs D. 36 runs

**11.** The average of 50 numbers is 38. If two numbers namely 45 and 55 are discarded, the average of the remaining numbers is
A. 36.5 B. 37
C. 37.5 D. 37.52

**12.** The average of 6 observations is 12. A new seventh observation is included and the new average is decreased by 1. The seventh observation is
A. 1 B. 3
C. 5 D. 6

**13.** A man whose bowling average is 12.4 takes 5 wickets for 26 runs and thereby decreases his average by 0.4. The number of wickets, taken by him, before his last match, is
A. 85 B. 78
C. 72 D. 64

**14.** The average of marks obtained by 120 candidates was 35. If the average of marks of passed candidates was 39 and that of failed candidates was 15, the number of candidates who passed the examination is
A. 100 B. 110
C. 120 D. 150

**15.** The average of three numbers is 42. The first is twice the second and the second is twice the third. The difference between the largest and the smallest number is
A. 18 B. 36
C. 54 D. 72

## ANSWERS

| 1 | 2 | 3 | 4 | 5 | 6 | 7 | 8 | 9 | 10 |
|---|---|---|---|---|---|---|---|---|---|
| C | C | C | A | A | B | A | D | D | C |
| **11** | **12** | **13** | **14** | **15** | | | | | |
| C | C | A | A | C | | | | | |

## EXPLANATORY ANSWERS

**1.** Average $= \frac{1}{4}\left(\frac{3}{2}+\frac{7}{3}+\frac{10}{3}+\frac{29}{6}\right)$

$= \left(\frac{9+14+20+29}{24}\right) = \frac{72}{24} = 3$

**2.** Average $= \frac{3(1+2+3+4+5+6+7+8+9)}{9} = \frac{135}{9}$

$= 15$

**3.** Average of 13 numbers = 68

$\therefore$ Total of 13 numbers = 13 × 68 = 884

Average of last 7 numbers = 70

$\therefore$ Total of last 7 numbers = 7 × 70 = 490

$\therefore$ Average of first 6 numbers

= 884 − 490 = 394

$\therefore$ Average of first 7 numbers = 63

$\therefore$ Total of first 7 numbers = 63 × 7 = 441

$\therefore$ 7th number = 441 − 394 = 47

**4.** Let the total distance covered during journey = 60 km

$\frac{1}{3}$ of the distance covered during journey

$= 60 \times \frac{1}{3} = 20$ km

$\frac{1}{4}$ of the distance covered during journey

$= \frac{1}{4} \times 60 = 15$ km

$\therefore$ The distance covered during the rest of journey = 60 − (20 + 15) = 25 km

Time taken to cover 20 km at 25 km/h

$= \frac{20}{25}$ hours $= \frac{4}{5}$ hour

Time taken to cover 15 km at 30 km/h

$= \frac{15}{30}$ hours $= \frac{1}{2}$ hour

Time taken to cover 25 km at 50 km/h

$= \frac{25}{50}$ hours $= \frac{1}{2}$ hour

Total time taken $= \frac{4}{5}+\frac{1}{2}+\frac{1}{2} = \frac{9}{5}$ hours

Hence average speed per hour

$= 60 \div \frac{9}{5} = \frac{60 \times 5}{9}$

$= \frac{100}{3}$ km/h $= 33\frac{1}{3}$ km/h

**5.** Let the average expenditure of all the nine
$= ₹\ x$

Now amount spent by eight
$= ₹\ 3 \times 8 = ₹\ 24$

and total spent by the ninth $= ₹\ x + 2$

$\Rightarrow \quad \frac{26 + x}{9} = x$

$\therefore$ Average amount spent by nine $= \frac{26 + x}{9}$

Total amount spent by nine $= 24 + x + 2 = 26 + x$

$\Rightarrow \quad 9x = 26 + x$

or, $\quad 8x = 26$

$\Rightarrow \quad x = \frac{26}{8} = ₹\ 3.25$

Hence total money spent
$= ₹\ (3.25 \times 9) = ₹\ 29.25$

**6.** Average monthly expenditure permitted $= ₹\ 500$

Total expenditure permitted for 12 months
$= ₹\ 500 \times 12 = ₹\ 6000$

Expenditure incurred during the first nine months
$= ₹\ 511 \times 9 = ₹\ 4{,}599$

Expenditure for the last three month
$= ₹\ (6000 - 4599) = ₹\ 1{,}401$

$\therefore$ Average monthly expenditure for the three months
$= ₹\ \frac{1401}{3} = ₹\ 467$

**7.** Total increase in the age of 8 persons
$= 2 \times 8 = 16$ years

Total age of two men being replaced
$= 20 + 24 = 44$ years

Total of the age of two women $= 44 + 16 = 60$ years

$\Rightarrow$ The average age of women
$= \frac{60}{2} = 30$ years.

**8.** Average age of 7 children $= 12$ years

Total ages of 7 children $= 12 \times 7 = 84$ years

Age of 1 child who died $= 6$ years

Total ages of remaining 6 children
$= 84 - 6 = 78$ years

$\therefore$ Average age of 6 children $= \frac{78}{6} = 13$ years

$\therefore$ Average age of 6 children after 5 years
$= 13 + 5 = 18$ years

**9.** Total weight of 7 experiments
$= 53.735 \times 7 = 376.145$ gm

Total weight of first three
$= 54.005 \times 3 = 162.015$ gm

The average of the 6th and 7th was 0.010 gm less than that of the first three.

$\therefore$ Average of the 6th and 7th
$= 54.005 - 0.010 = 53.995$ gm

$\therefore$ Total of the 6th and 7th $= 53.995 \times 2 = 107.990$ gm

Thus, total of 4th and 5th
$= 376.145 - (162.015 + 107.990) = 106.140$ gm

The fourth was greater than the fifth by 0.004 gm

$\therefore \quad$ The fifth $= (106.140 - 0.004) \times \frac{1}{2} = \frac{106.136}{2}$
$= 53.068$ gm

Hence, the fourth $= 53.068 + 0.004$
$= 53.072$ gm

**10.** Average increase in the score of 17 innings
$= 3$ runs

Total increase in the score of 17 innings
$= 3 \times 17 = 51$ runs

$\therefore$ His average of 16 innings
$= 85 - 51 = 34$ runs

Hence, average after the 17th innings
$= 34 + 3 = 37$ runs

**11.** Total of 50 numbers $= 50 \times 38 = 1900$

Total of 48 numbers
$= 1900 - (45 + 55) = 1800$

$\therefore \quad$ Average $= \frac{1800}{48} = 37.5$

**12.** Seventh observation
$= (7 \times 11 - 6 \times 12) = 5$

**13.** Suppose the number of wickets taken before the last match $= x$

$\Rightarrow \quad \frac{12.4x + 26}{x + 5} = 12$

$\Rightarrow \quad 12.4x + 26 = 12x + 60$

$\Rightarrow \quad x = 85$

**14.** Let the number of candidates who passed $= x$

$\Rightarrow \quad 39 \times x + 15 \times (120 - x) = 120 \times 35$

$\Rightarrow \quad 24x = 4200 - 1800$

$\therefore \quad x = \frac{2400}{24} = 100$

**15.** Let the third number $= x$

Then, second number $= 2x$ and first number $= 4x$

$\therefore \quad \frac{x + 2x + 4x}{3} = 42$

$\Rightarrow \quad \frac{7x}{3} = 42 \Rightarrow x = \frac{42 \times 3}{7}$

$\Rightarrow \quad x = 18$

So, (largest) $-$ (smallest) $= (4x - x) = 3x = 54$

●●●

CHAPTER 6

# Partnership Business

When two or more than two persons agree to invest money to run a business jointly, this association or deal is called *partnership* and those who invest money are called *pertners.* The total investment is called the *capital.*

**Kind of partners :** There are two kinds of partners.

1. **Working or active partner :** When a partner devotes his time for the business in addition to invest his money, he is called a working partner.
   With mutual agreement, the active partners get some fixed percentage of profit as *working allowance.*
2. **Sleeping or non-active partner :** A partner who simply invests money, but does not attend to the business is called a sleeping partner.

**Kind of partnership :**

(*i*) **Simple partnership :** If the capitals of several partners are invested for the same period, it is called a simple partnership.

(*ii*) **Compound or complex partnership :** If the capitals of the partners are invested for diffrent intervals of time, the partnership is called compound or complex.

## EXERCISE

**1.** A and B started a business with the investment of ₹ 80000 and ₹ 60000 respectively. At the end of the year total profit in the business will be divided between them in the ratio of :

A. 2 : 3 B. 3 : 4
C. 2 : 1 D. 4 : 3

**2.** A and B started a business in partnership with the investment of ₹ 4000 and ₹ 6000 respectively. If at the end of the year total profit is ₹ 2250, what will each of them get?

A. ₹ 900, ₹ 1350
B. ₹ 800, ₹ 1450
C. ₹ 1000, ₹ 1250
D. ₹ 1200, ₹ 1050

**3.** Sonu, Monu and Mohit together start a business with the investment of ₹ 1800, ₹ 1500 and ₹ 1600 respectively. If at the end of the year, Monu gains a profit of ₹ 900 the total profit in the business is :

A. ₹ 2880 B. ₹ 2940
C. ₹ 3200 D. ₹ 3240

**4.** Omdutt started a business with a capital of ₹ 8000. After six months, Sanjay joined him with investment of some capital. If at the end of the year each of them gets equal amount as profit, how much did Sanjay invest in the business?

A. ₹ 18000 B. ₹ 17500
C. ₹ 16000 D. ₹ 16500

**5.** A, B and C buy a farm for ₹ 100000. A contributes ₹ 40000 in it. They sell it, and from the profit B gets ₹ 2750 and C gets ₹ 1750. What would be the profit of A?

A. ₹ 2780 B. ₹ 3000
C. ₹ 3280 D. ₹ 2785

**6.** A and B jointly invest ₹ 2100 and ₹ 3100 respectively in a firm. A is an active partner and hence he gets 25% of the profit separately. If their business yields them total ₹ 1040 as profit, what will be the gain of each of them?

A. ₹ 415, ₹ 625 B. ₹ 575, ₹ 465
C. ₹ 515, ₹ 525 D. ₹ 560, ₹ 480

**7.** Two partners invested ₹ 12500 and ₹ 8500 respectively in a business and decided that 60% of the profit incurred from the business will be equally divided between them while remaining profit will be assumed as interest on their capitals. If one of the partners gets ₹ 300 more profit than the other, what is the total profit in the business?

A. ₹ 3937.50 B. ₹ 4940.50
C. ₹ 3936.50 D. ₹ 4156

**8.** Neeraj and Birju are partners in a business. They divide between them the profit incurred in the business in such a proportion that $\frac{2}{5}$th portion of the profit gained by Neeraj is equal to $\frac{1}{3}$rd portion of the profit gained by Birju. If total profit in the business is ₹ 1210, find the profit earned by Birju.

A. ₹ 780 B. ₹ 660
C. ₹ 680 D. ₹ 590

**9.** A, B and C together took under lease a pasture ground for ₹ 888. If in this pasture ground A put his 20 sheep out to graze for 2½ months, B put his 30 sheep out to graze for 4 months and C put his 36 sheep out to graze for 3½ months, find the lease amount paid by each of them.

A. ₹ 205, ₹ 315, ₹ 378 B. ₹ 150, ₹ 360, ₹ 378
C. ₹ 170, ₹ 360, ₹ 358 D. ₹ 228, ₹ 360, ₹ 300

**10.** A, B and C started a business with the investment of ₹ 5000, ₹ 6000 and ₹ 4000 respectively. A is an active partner and therefore he gets 30% of the profit separately. Rest of the profit is divided in the ratio of their capitals. If at the end of year, A's profit is ₹ 200 more than the sum of the profits made by B and C, find the profit made by each of them.

A. ₹ 1620, ₹ 1242, ₹ 1178
B. ₹ 1720, ₹ 1252, ₹ 1228
C. ₹ 1510, ₹ 1187, ₹ 1133
D. ₹ 1600, ₹ 840, ₹ 560

**11.** Premchand, Nanak and Prabhat together rented a house for 2 years and settled to pay ₹ 1368 as rent. They lived together in this house for 5 months. Then Prabhat left the house and went away. 8 months after Nanak also went away and left the house for Premchand to live alone. How much did Premchand pay as rent of this house?

A. ₹ 1025 B. ₹ 950
C. ₹ 880 D. ₹ 780

**12.** A started a business with an investment of ₹ 4000. B joined him after 4 months and C joined him after 5 months. At the end of year they get profit in the ratio of 3 : 4 : 7. Find the ratio of capitals invested in the business by B and C.

A. 1 : 2 B. 2 : 1
C. 3 : 2 D. 1 : 3

**13.** Amit, Sumeet and Suresh started a business with capitals in the ratio of 2 : 3 : 4. Amit took back half of his investment after 3 months and Sumeet took back one-third portion of his investment after 4 months. If at the end of year, Suresh gets a profit of ₹ 3200, what is the total profit in the business?

A. ₹ $6076\frac{2}{3}$ B. ₹ $6066\frac{2}{3}$
C. ₹ 8000 D. ₹ $8333\frac{1}{3}$

**14.** A, B and C started a business in partnership. A invested ₹ 4000 for 8 months and ₹ 6000 for 4 months. B invested ₹ 3000 for 6 months and ₹ 5000 for next 6 months of the year while C invested ₹ 3000 for whole of the year. If at the end of year, total profit is ₹ 7000, what will be the shares of A, B and C in the profit?

A. ₹ 2800, ₹ 2400, ₹ 1800
B. ₹ 2500, ₹ 2600, ₹ 1900
C. ₹ 2600, ₹ 2500, ₹ 1900
D. ₹ 2000, ₹ 2700, ₹ 2300

**15.** A, B and C started a business in partnership with respective investment of ₹ 20000, ₹ 18000 and ₹ 12000. A and B are active partners and therefore they get an additional profit of 12% and 8% respectively for supervision and other related work they do for improvement of the trade. Rest of the profit is divided among them in the proportion of their capitals. If profit made by A is ₹ 648 more than B, find the profit earned by each of them.

A. ₹ 3960, ₹ 3312, ₹ 1728
B. ₹ 4960, ₹ 3312, ₹ 1728
C. ₹ 3690, ₹ 3132, ₹ 1820
D. ₹ 5960, ₹ 3600, ₹ 1750

**16.** Three labourers work for 5 hours, 6 hours and 7 hours respectively in a field and get wages in the proportion of time of working in the field. Three days after they increase their working hours by 1 hour. 4 days after they increase their working hours, work in the field gets finished. If their total wages is ₹ 276, find the share of wages earned by each of them.

A. ₹ 78, ₹ 92, ₹ 106 B. ₹ 88, ₹ 87, ₹ 101
C. ₹ 80, ₹ 90, ₹ 106 D. ₹ 81, ₹ 95, ₹ 100

**17.** A, B and C together took a pasture ground on rent at ₹ 16 per month with a view to graze their sheep in this ground. A, B and C owned 70, 50 and 40 sheep respectively. After 4 months A sold $\frac{2}{7}$th portion of his sheep to B and 3 month after that C sold $\frac{2}{5}$th portion of his sheep to A. How much will each of them pay as rent after the end of a year?

A. ₹ 70, ₹ 70, ₹ 52 B. ₹ 76, ₹ 76, ₹ 40
C. ₹ 80, ₹ 76, ₹ 36 D. ₹ 40, ₹ 76.30, ₹ 76

**18.** Samir and Saurabh started a joint firm. Samir's investment was thrice the investment of Saurabh and the period of his investment was two times the period of investment of Saurabh. If Saurabh got ₹ 4000 as profit, then their total profit is:

A. ₹ 16000 B. ₹ 20000
C. ₹ 24000 D. ₹ 28000

**19.** A, B and C together start a business. The amounts invested by A and B are in the ratio of 4 : 3 whereas the ratio of investments of B and C is 2 : 3. If the total profit earned is ₹ 46000, what is C's share in the profit?

A. ₹ 14000 B. ₹ 15000
C. ₹ 16000 D. ₹ 18000

**20.** Rani and Nisha started a business initially with ₹ 5100 and ₹ 6600 respectively. If the total profit is ₹ 2730, what is the Rani's share in the profit?

A. ₹ 1190 B. ₹ 1200
C. ₹ 1530 D. ₹ 1540

## ANSWERS

| 1 | 2 | 3 | 4 | 5 | 6 | 7 | 8 | 9 | 10 |
|---|---|---|---|---|---|---|---|---|---|
| D | A | B | C | B | B | A | B | B | D |
| **11** | **12** | **13** | **14** | **15** | **16** | **17** | **18** | **19** | **20** |
| B | A | B | A | A | A | B | D | D | A |

## EXPLANATORY ANSWERS

**1.** Ratio between their profits = 80000 : 60000 = 4 : 3.

**2.** Ratio of capitals of A and B = 4000 : 6000 = 2 : 3

A's share in the profit = $\frac{2}{5} \times 2250$ = ₹ 900

B's share in the profit = $\frac{3}{5} \times 2250$ = ₹ 1350

**3.** Ratio of their capitals
= 1800 : 1500 : 1600 = 18 : 15 : 16
Sum of proportionals = 18 + 15 + 16 = 49
Monu's profit = ₹ 900

∴ Total profit in the business = $\frac{900}{15} \times 49$ = ₹ 2940

**4.** Investment by Omdutt for 1 month
= ₹ 8000 × 12 = ₹ 96000
Let Sanjay invested ₹ $x$ for 6 months
∴ Capital of Sanjay for 1 month = ₹ $x \times 6$ = ₹ $6x$
Now, $6x = 96000$
∴ $x$ = ₹ 16000

**5.** Here, ratio of capitals of A and (B + C)
= 40000 : 60000 = 2 : 3
Profit of (B + C) = 2750 + 1750 = ₹ 4500

Hence, A's profit = $\frac{4500}{3} \times 2$ = ₹ 3000

**6.** Separate profit for A = $\frac{1040 \times 25}{100}$ = ₹ 260

Remaining profit = ₹ (1040 – 260) = ₹ 780
Ratio of capitals of A and B = 2100 : 3100 = 21 : 31

A's profit = $\frac{21}{52} \times 780$ = ₹ 315

B's profit = $\frac{31}{52} \times 780$ = ₹ 465

Total profit of A = ₹ (315 + 260) = ₹ 575
Therefore A and B will make profit of ₹ 575 and ₹ 465 respectively.

**7.** Ratio of their capitals = 12500 : 8500 = 25 : 17
Hence, sum of their ratios = 25 + 17 = 42 and difference of ratios = 25 – 17 = 8
Now total profit taken as interest

= $\frac{300}{8} \times 42$ = ₹ 1575

Hence, total profit in the business

= $\frac{100}{40} \times 1575$ = ₹ 3937.50

**8.** Let shares of Neeraj and Birju in profit are ₹ $x$ and ₹ $y$ respectively; then,

$\frac{2}{5}x = \frac{1}{3}y \quad \therefore x : y = 5 : 6$

Hence, share of Birju = $\frac{6}{11} \times 1210$ = ₹ 660

**9.** Ratio of their shares = (20 × 5/2) : (30 × 4) : (36 × 7/2) = 25 : 60 : 63
Sum of proportionals = 25 + 60 + 63 = 148
Total lease amount = ₹ 888

∴ Amount paid by A = $\frac{25}{148} \times 888$ = ₹ 150

Amount paid by B = $\frac{60}{148} \times 888$ = ₹ 360

Amount paid by C = $\frac{63}{148} \times 888$ = ₹ 378

**10.** Ratio of capitals of A, B and C = 5000 : 6000 : 4000
= 5 : 6 : 4
Let total profit in the business = ₹ $x$; then

$$\frac{30x}{100} + \frac{5}{15} \times \frac{70x}{100} - \frac{(6+4)}{15} \times \frac{70x}{100} = 200$$

$$\Rightarrow \frac{8x}{15} - \frac{7x}{15} = 200 \quad \therefore x = ₹\ 3000$$

Hence, A's profit = $\frac{8 \times 3000}{15}$ = ₹ 1600;

B's profit = $\frac{6}{15} \times \frac{7 \times 3000}{10}$ = ₹ 840;

C's profit = $\frac{4}{15} \times \frac{7 \times 3000}{10}$ = ₹ 560

**11.** Rent for 1 month = $\frac{1368}{24}$ = ₹ 57

Total rent paid by Premchand

$= 5 \times \frac{57}{3} + 8 \times \frac{57}{2} + 11 \times 57$

= 95 + 228 + 627 = ₹ 950.

**12.** Let, B and C invest ₹ $x$ and ₹ $y$ respectively

∴ Ratio of their capitals = 48000 : $8x$ : $7y$

But given ratio of the profits = 3 : 4 : 7

$8x : 7y = 4 : 7 \Rightarrow \frac{x}{y} = \frac{1}{2}$

Hence, $x : y = 1 : 2$

**13.** Ratio of capitals of Amit, Sumeet and Suresh

= (2 × 3 + 1 × 9) : (3 × 4 + 2 × 8) : (4 × 12)

= 15 : 28 : 48

Sum of the ratios = 15 + 28 + 48 = 91

∴ Total profit in the business

$= \frac{91}{48} \times 3200 =$ ₹ $6066\frac{2}{3}$

**14.** Ratio of their capitals

= (4000 × 8 + 6000 × 4) : (3000 × 6 + 5000 × 6) : (3000 × 12)

= 56000 : 48000 : 36000 = 14 : 12 : 9

Sum of proportionals = 14 + 12 + 9 = 35

Share of A in the profit = $\frac{14}{35} \times 7000$ = ₹ 2800

Share of B in the profit = $\frac{12}{35} \times 7000$ = ₹ 2400

Share of C in the profit = $\frac{9}{35} \times 7000$ = ₹ 1800

**15.** Ratio of their capitals

= 20000 : 18000 : 12000 = 10 : 9 : 6

Let total profit in the business = ₹ $x$; then

$$\left(\frac{12x}{100} + \frac{10}{25} \times \frac{80x}{100}\right) - \left(\frac{8x}{100} + \frac{9}{25} \times \frac{80x}{100}\right) = 648$$

$$\Rightarrow \frac{11x}{25} - \frac{46x}{125} = 648 \Rightarrow \frac{9x}{125} = 648$$

$$\therefore \quad x = \frac{648 \times 125}{9} = ₹\ 9000$$

Hence, share of A = $\frac{11x}{25} = \frac{11 \times 9000}{25}$

= ₹ 3960;

Share of B = $\frac{46x}{125} = \frac{46 \times 9000}{125}$ = ₹ 3312

Share of C = $\frac{6}{25} \times \frac{80x}{100} = \frac{6}{25} \times \frac{4}{5} \times 9000$ = ₹ 1728

**16.** Ratio of their working hours

= (5 × 3 + 6 × 4) : (6 × 3 + 7 × 4) : (7 × 3 + 8 × 4)

= 39 : 46 : 53

Sum of proportionals = 39 + 46 + 53 = 138

∴ Wages for the 1st labourer = $\frac{39}{138} \times 276$ = ₹ 78

Wages for the 2nd labourer = $\frac{46}{138} \times 276$ = ₹ 92

Wages for the 3rd labourer = $\frac{53}{138} \times 276$ = ₹ 106

**17.** Number of sheep of A for 1 month

$= [70 \times 4 + (70 - \frac{2}{7} \times 70) \times 3 + (70 - \frac{2}{7} \times 70 + \frac{2}{5} \times 40) \times 5]$

= 280 + 150 + 330 = 760

Number of sheep of B for 1 month

$= [50 \times 4 + (50 + \frac{2}{7} \times 70) \times 8] = 200 + 560 = 760$

Number of sheep of C for 1 month

$= [40 \times 7 + (40 - \frac{2}{5} \times 40) \times 5] = 280 + 120 = 400$

Hence, ratio of their sheep

= 760 : 760 : 400 = 19 : 19 : 10

Sum of proportionals = 19 + 19 + 10 = 48

1 year's rent of the pasture ground = 16 × 12 = ₹ 192

∴ Rent to be paid by A = $\frac{19}{48} \times 192$ = ₹ 76

Rent to be paid by B = $\frac{19}{48} \times 192$ = ₹ 76

Rent to be paid by C = $\frac{10}{48} \times 192$ = ₹ 40

**18.** Ratio of Capitals of Samir and Saurabh

= (3 × 2) : (1 × 1) = 6 : 1

Saurabh's profit = ₹ 4000

Hence, total profit in the business

= 7 × ₹ 4000 = ₹ 28000

**19.** A : B = 4 : 3 and B : C = 2 : 3,

Therefore, A : B : C = 8 : 6 : 9

Hence, C's profit = $\frac{9}{23} \times 46000$ = ₹ 18000

**20.** Ratio of their Capitals = 5100 : 6600 = 17 : 22

Hence, Rani's profit = $\frac{17}{39} \times 2730$ = ₹ 1190

CHAPTER 7

# Mixture and Alligation

**Alligation** deals with calculation of values or properties of a mixture. Alligation is the rule that enables us—

(1) to find the proportion in which the two or more ingredients at the given prices must be mixed to yield a mixture at the given price. This is termed as "Alligation Alternate".

(2) to calculate the average or mean value of a mixture when the prices of two or more ingredients which are to be mixed together and proportion in which they are to be mixed are given. This is termed as "Alligation Medial".

**1. Rule of Alligation:**

$$\frac{\text{Amount of Cheaper ingredient}}{\text{Amount of Dearer ingredient}} = \frac{\text{Cost price of Dearer} - \text{Mean Price}}{\text{Mean Price} - \text{Cost Price of Cheaper}}$$

Here cost price of unit quantity of the mixture is called the *Mean Price.*

The above rule may be represented schematically as under:

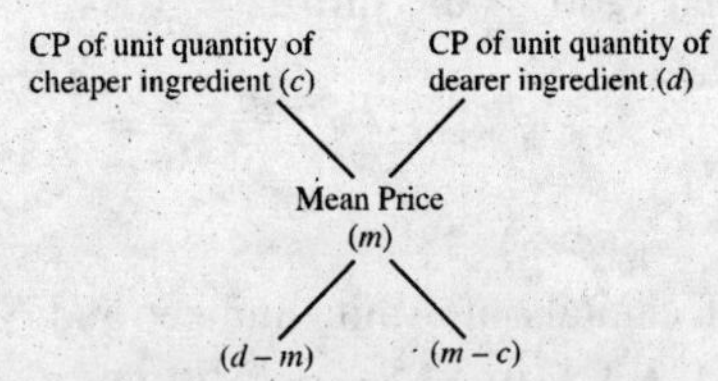


(Cheaper quantity) : (Dearer quantity) $= (d - m) : (m - c)$

This relationship is very helpful in solving problems on mixture involving percentage values, rates, prices, speeds etc.

**2.** $m$ gm of sugar solution has $x$ % sugar in it. To increase the sugar content in the solution to $y$ %, quantity of sugar need to be added $= \dfrac{m(y-x)}{100-y}$

**3.** A vessel contains $x$ litres of liquid A. $y$ litres are withdrawn and replaced by liquid B. Next $y$ litres of the mixture is withdrawn and again replaced by liquid B. This operation is repeated $n$ times.

$$\frac{\text{Quantity of liquid A left after } n\text{th operation}}{\text{Whole quantity of liquid A initially present}} = \left(\frac{x-y}{x}\right)^n \text{ or } \left(1-\frac{y}{x}\right)^n$$

## EXERCISE

**1.** In what proportion must tea at ₹ 62 per kg be mixed with tea at ₹ 72 per kg in order to obtain the mixture worth ₹ 65 per kg?

A. 4 : 6 B. 7 : 3
C. 2 : 3 D. 4 : 7

**2.** Find the quantity of rice @ ₹ 10 per kg. which should be mixed with 25 kgs of rice @ ₹ 8 per kg, so that on selling the mixture @ 15 per kg there is 80% profit.

A. 6 kgs B. 7 kgs
C. 3 kgs D. 5 kgs

**3.** A shopkeeper buys 26 kgs of milk @ ₹ 16 per kg. He also buys from another source an inferior quality of milk @ ₹ 10 per kg. How much quantity of the latter should he buy to mix it with the former so that he can sell the mixture @ ₹ 14 per kg without making any loss?

A. 13 kgs B. 12 kgs
C. 14 kgs D. 16 kgs

**4.** Two vessels A and B contain milk and water in the ratio 7 : 5 and 17 : 7 respectively. In what ratio mixtures from two vessels should be mixed to get a new mixture containing milk and water in the ratio 5 : 3?

A. 1 : 2 B. 2 : 1
C. 2 : 3 D. 3 : 2

**5.** Two vessels A and B contain mixture of milk and water in the ratio 4 : 1 and 9 : 11 respectively. They are mixed in the ratio of 3 : 2. Find the ratio of milk : water in the resulting mixture.
A. 34 : 16 B. 33 : 17
C. 16 : 34 D. 17 : 33

**6.** A person has two solutions of sugar with 30% and 50% concentration respectively. In what proportion should he mix two solutions to get 45% concentration in the resulting mixture?
A. 1 : 3 B. 3 : 1
C. 2 : 3 D. 3 : 2

**7.** 6 litres of milk and water mixture has 75% milk in it. How much milk should be added to the mixture to make it 90% pure?
A. 8 litres B. 9 litres
C. 10 litres D. 12 litres

**8.** In what ratio must water be added to spirit to gain 25% by selling it at cost price?
A. 1 : 4 B. 4 : 1
C. 3 : 4 D. 4 : 3

**9.** A shopkeeper has 50 kgs of rice. He sells a part of it at 20% profit and the rest at 40% profit. If he gains 25% on the whole, find the quantity of each part.
A. 12.5 kgs and 37.5 kgs B. 37.5 kgs and 12.5 kgs
C. 23.5 kgs and 21.5 kgs D. 21.5 kgs and 23.5 kgs

**10.** A shopkeeper has 100 kgs of tea. He sells a part of it at 20% profit and the rest at 5% loss. If his overall profit is 10%, find the quantity for each part.
A. 20 kgs B. 25 kgs
C. 30 kgs D. 40 kgs

**11.** A merchant has 160 kgs of wheat. He sells a part of it at 10% profit and the rest of 6% loss. If he incurs 4% loss on the whole, find the quantity for each part.
A. 120 kgs B. 140 kgs
C. 150 kgs D. 160 kgs

**12.** A man bought a certain quantity of sugar for ₹ 8000. He sells one-fourth of it at 20% loss. At what per cent profit should he sell the remainder stock so as to make an overall profit of 20%?
A. 20% B. 30%
C. 35% D. 40%

**13.** A person has ₹ 5000. He invests a part of it at 3% per annum and the remainder at 8% per annum simple interest. His total income in 3 years is ₹ 750. Find the sum invested at different rates of interest.
A. ₹ 2000 and ₹ 3000 B. ₹ 2500 and ₹ 2500
C. ₹ 3000 and ₹ 2000 D. ₹ 2750 and ₹ 2250

**14.** A person covers a dista2nce of 100 kms in 10 hours, partly by walking at 7 km/hr and rest by running at 12 km/hr. Find the distance covered in each part.
A. 48 kms B. 72 kms
C. 108 kms D. 124 kms

**15.** The average monthly salary of employees, consisting of officers and workers, of an organisation is ₹ 3000. The average salary of an officer is ₹ 10,000 while that of a worker is ₹ 2000 per month. If there are total 400 employees in the organisation, find the number of officers and workers separately.
A. 300, 100 B. 50, 350
C. 250, 150 D. 310, 90

**16.** The average daily wages of staff, consisting of supervisors and labourers, of a company is ₹ 50. The average wages of supervisors is ₹ 150 while that of labourers is ₹ 40 per day. If the number of supervisors is 15, find the number of labourers in the company.
A. 150 B. 175
C. 180 D. 200

**17.** ₹ 675 was divided among 75 boys and girls. Each boy gets ₹ 20 whereas a girl gets ₹ 5. Find the number of boys and girls.
A. 20, 55 B. 15, 60
C. 25, 50 D. 30, 45

**18.** A sum of ₹ 70 is divided among 10 children. Each boy gets ₹ 10 whereas a girl gets ₹ 5. If the number of boys is 4, find the number of girls.
A. 6 B. 7
C. 8 D. 9

**19.** From a cask of wine containing 25 litres, 5 litres are withdrawn and the cask is refilled with water. The process is repeated a second and then a third time. Find the quantity of wine left in the cask and also the ratio of wine to water in the resulting mixture.
A. 61 : 64 B. 16 : 46
C. 46 : 16 D. 64 : 61

**20.** A vessel contains 80 litres of milk. 16 litres of milk was taken out of the vessel and replaced by water. Then 16 litres of mixture was withdrawn and again replaced by water. The operation was repeated for third time. How much milk is now left in the vessel?
A. 96.40 litres B. 50.36 litres
C. 40.96 litres D. 32.76 litres

## ANSWERS

| 1 | 2 | 3 | 4 | 5 | 6 | 7 | 8 | 9 | 10 |
|---|---|---|---|---|---|---|---|---|---|
| B | D | A | B | B | A | B | A | B | D |
| **11** | **12** | **13** | **14** | **15** | **16** | **17** | **18** | **19** | **20** |
| B | B | C | B | B | A | A | A | D | C |

# EXPLANATORY ANSWERS

**1.** 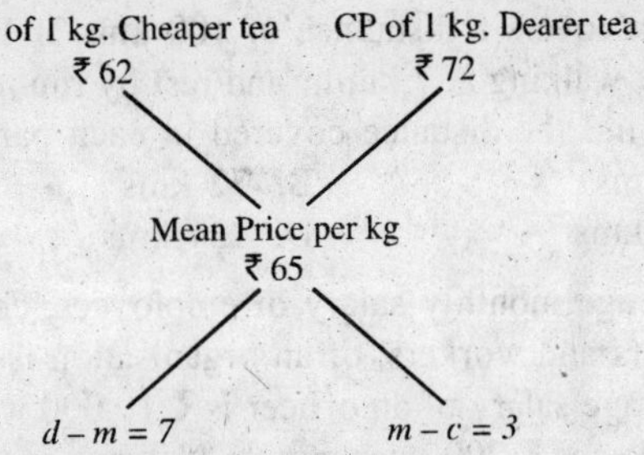


Using Alligation rule,

$$\frac{\text{Quantity of cheaper tea}}{\text{Quantity of dearer tea}} = \frac{d-m}{m-c} = \frac{7}{3}$$

Therefore, they must be mixed in the ratio of 7 : 3.

**3.** 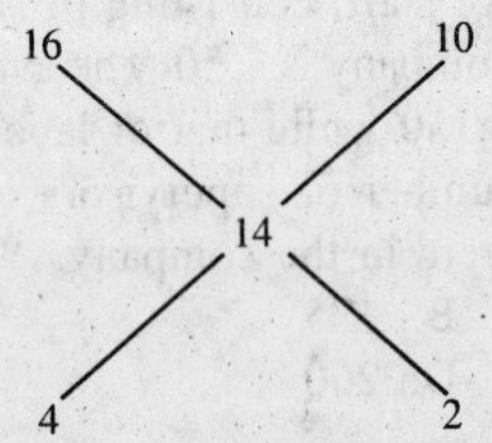


or 2 : 1 $\dfrac{\text{Quantity of milk @ ₹ 10 per kg}}{\text{Quantity of milk @ ₹ 16 per kg}} = \dfrac{1}{2}$

So, quantity of milk @ ₹ 10 per kg. $= \dfrac{26}{2} = 13$ kgs.

**5.** Fraction is *Milk* *Water*

A : $\dfrac{4}{5}$ $\dfrac{1}{5}$

B : $\dfrac{9}{20}$ $\dfrac{11}{20}$

$(3A + 2B) = A$ and $B : \left(\dfrac{12}{5}+\dfrac{9}{10}\right) \left(\dfrac{3}{5}+\dfrac{11}{10}\right)$

$\dfrac{33}{10}$ $\dfrac{17}{10}$

So, Ratio of milk : water in the resulting mixture = 33 : 17.

**6.** 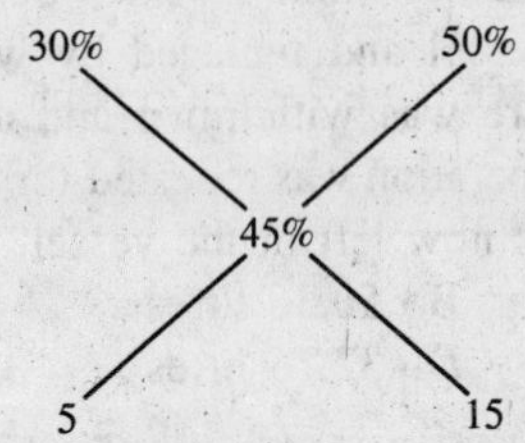


He should mix 30% and 50% in the ratio 5 : 15 or 1 : 3.

$\dfrac{\text{30\% Solution}}{\text{50\% Solution}} = \dfrac{1}{3}$ or 1 : 3

**7.** The given solution has 75% milk.

Milk to be added has 100% milk.

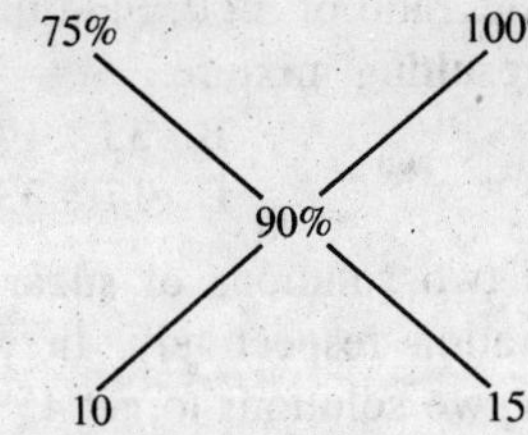


Milk should be added to the given mixture in the ratio 15 : 10 or 3 : 2.

$\therefore$ Quantity of milk to be added $= \dfrac{3}{2} \times 6 = 9$ litres.

**8.** Let cost price of spirit be ₹ 1 per litre.

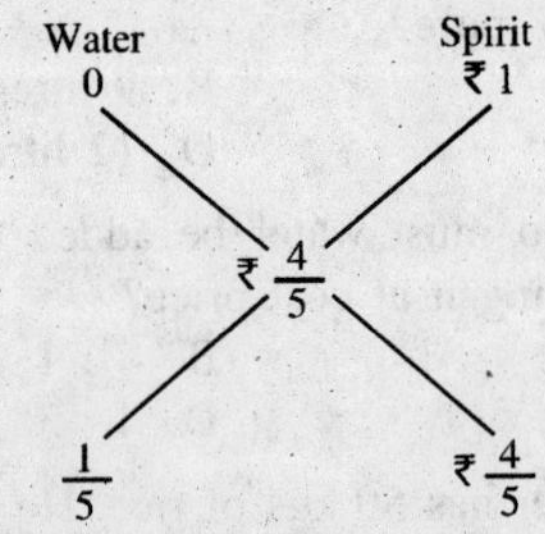


Then SP of mixture = ₹ 1 per litre

Gain = 25%

So, CP of mixture $= 1 \times \dfrac{100}{125} =$ ₹ $\dfrac{4}{5}$

We assume that CP of water is zero.

Using alligation rule on cost price,

Water should be mixed to spirit in the ratio $\dfrac{1}{5} : \dfrac{4}{5}$ or 1 : 4.

**9.** 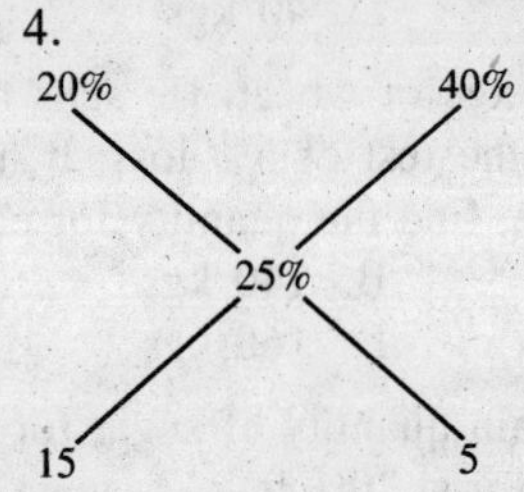


or 3 : 1

Quantity sold at 20% profit $= \dfrac{3}{3+1} \times 50 = 37.5$ kgs.

Quantity sold at 40% profit = (50 – 37.5) = 12.5 kgs.

**10.** 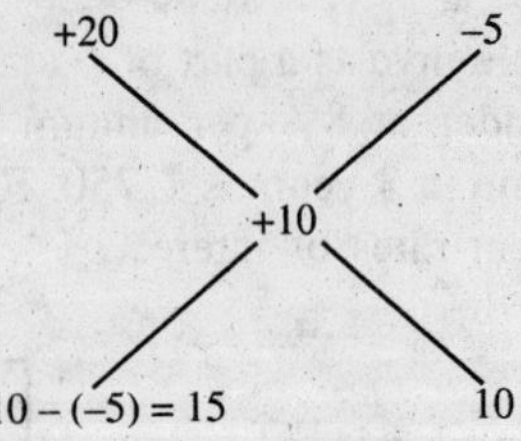


or 3 : 2

Quantity sold at 20% profit $= \dfrac{3}{3+2} \times 100 = 60$ kgs.

Quantity sold at 5% loss = (100 – 60) = 40 kgs.

**11.**

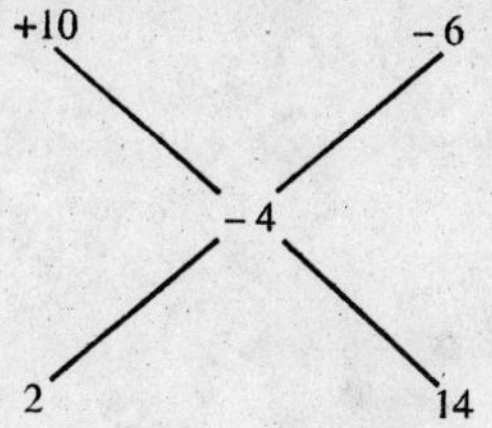


or 1 : 7

Quantity sold at 10% profit = $\frac{1}{1+7} \times 160 = 20$ kgs.

Quantity sold at 6% loss = 160 − 20 = 140 kgs.

**12.** Let the remainder stock be sold at $x\%$ profit.

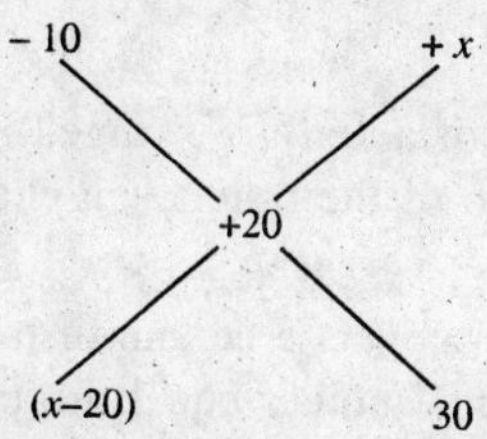


$\frac{x-20}{30} = \frac{1/4}{3/4}$ or $x - 20 = 30 \times \frac{1}{3}$

or $x = 20 + 10$, $x = 30\%$ profit.

**13.** Average rate of interest

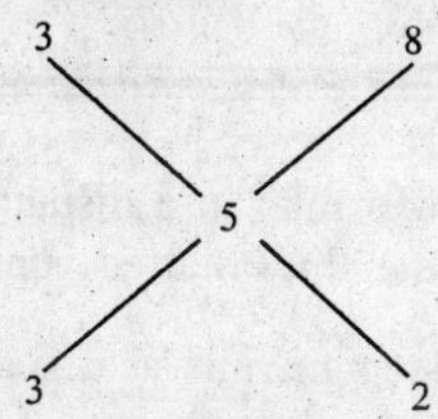


$= \frac{100 \times 750}{5000 \times 3} = 5\%$ per annum

Investment at 3% per annum = $\frac{3}{3+2} \times 5000 =$ ₹ 3000

Investment at 8% per annum = $\frac{2}{3+2} \times 5000 =$ ₹ 2000.

**14.** Average speed = $\frac{100}{10} = 10$ km/hr.

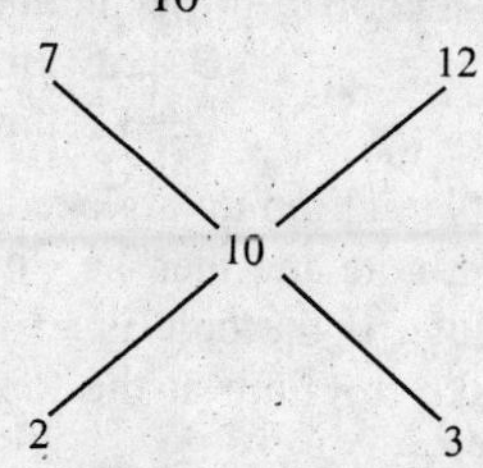


Ratio of time taken at 7 km/hr to 12 km/hr = 2 : 3

Time taken at 7 km/hr = $\frac{2}{2+3} \times 10 = 4$ hrs.

Distance covered at 7 km/hr = 7 × 4 = 28 km.

Distance covered at 12 km/hr = 100 − 28 = 72 km.

**15.**

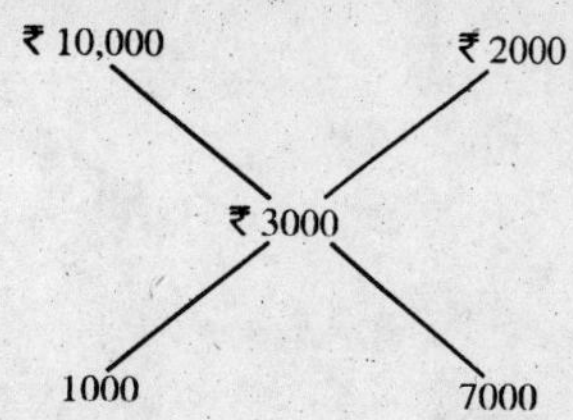


$\frac{\text{Number of officers}}{\text{Number of workers}} = \frac{1000}{7000} = \frac{1}{7}$

No. of officers = $\frac{1}{1+7} \times 400 = 50$

No. of workers = 400 − 50 = 350

**16.**

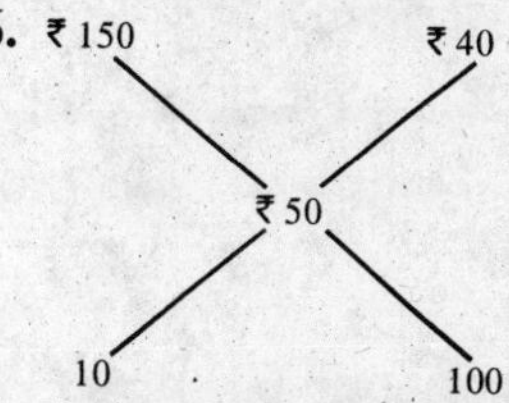


$\frac{\text{Number of supervisors}}{\text{Number of labourers}} = \frac{10}{100} = \frac{1}{10}$

Total number of labourers

= Total no. of supervisors × 10

= 15 × 10 = 150.

**18.**

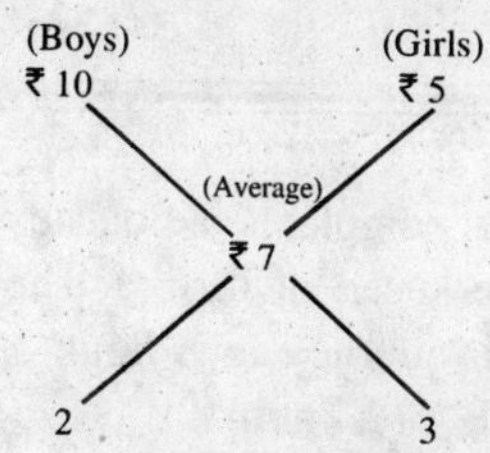


$\frac{\text{Number of girls}}{\text{Number of boys}} = \frac{3}{2}$

Number of girls = $\frac{3}{2} \times 4 = 6$

**19.** Here, quantity of wine left after third operation

$= \left(1 - \frac{5}{25}\right)^3 \times 25$

$= \left(\frac{4}{5}\right)^3 \times 25 = \frac{64}{125} \times 25 = \frac{64}{5} = 12\frac{4}{5}$ litres.

Final ratio of wine to water

$= \frac{(64/125)}{(1-64/125)} = \frac{64/125}{61/125}$

Wine : Water = $\frac{64}{61}$.

**20.** Amount of milk left

$= 80\left(1 - \frac{16}{80}\right)^3 = 80\left(\frac{4}{5}\right)^3 = 80 \times \frac{64}{125}$

= 40.96 litres.

●●●

CHAPTER

# 8 Time and Distance

**Important Formulae:**

1. Speed = Distance ÷ Time
2. Distance = Time × Speed
3. Time = Distance ÷ Speed
4. $x$ km/hr = $\left(x \times \frac{5}{18}\right)$ m/sec
5. $x$ metres/sec = $\left(x \times \frac{18}{5}\right)$ km/hr.
6. If the speed of a body is changed in the ratio $m : n$, then the ratio of the time taken changes in the ratio $n : m$.
7. When a man covers a certain distance with a speed of $x$ km/h and another equal distance at the rate of $y$ km/h, then for the whole journey, the average speed is given by

$$\text{Average speed} = \frac{2xy}{x+y} \text{ km/h.}$$

## EXERCISE

**1.** A car moving at 48 km/hr completes a journey in 10 hours. By how much the speed of this car should be increased so as to do this journey in 8 hours?

A. 8 km/hr. B. 12 km/hr
C. 10 km/hr D. 15 km/hr

**2.** Starting from a point at a speed of 4 km/hr a man reaches at a cerain place and returns back to the point from where he had started journey on bicycle at the speed of 16 km/hr. His average speed during the entire journey will be:

A. 6.4 km/h B. 8.4 km/h
C. 5.4 km/h D. 10 km/h

**3.** A motorist covers a certain distance at a average speed of 48 km/h in 45 minutes. What speed in km/h he must maintain to cover the same distance in 30 minutes?

A. 66 km/h B. 79 km/h
C. 80 km/h D. 72 km/h

**4.** Two points A and B are 150 km apart. A man completes his onward journey from A to B in 3 hours 20 minutes and return journey from B to A in 4 hours 10 minutes. His average speed during the entire journey will be less than his average speed during the journey from A to B by:

A. 5 km/h B. 7.5 km/h
C. 9 km/h D. 3 km/h

**5.** A policeman saw a thief at a distance of 200 m. The policeman and the thief started running at the same time. If the policeman runs at a speed of $4\frac{1}{6}$ m per second and the thief at a speed of $3\frac{1}{3}$ m per second, after what time the policeman will catch the thief?

A. 12 min B. 10 min
C. 9 min D. 4 min

**6.** Kanchan walks from her home at 4 kms per hour and reaches her school 5 minutes late. If she walks at 5 kms per hour, she reaches the school 2½ minutes earlier. How far is the school from her home?

A. 3.5 kms B. 2.5 kms
C. 2.75 kms D. 3.2 kms

**7.** A monkey wants to climb up a glazed pole. He climbs 12 metres in 1 minute and then he slips back 3 metres in the next minute. If the pole is 63 metre high, how long does he take to climb at the top of the pole?

A. $11\frac{1}{4}$ min B. $12\frac{1}{2}$ min
C. $12\frac{3}{4}$ min D. $14\frac{3}{4}$ min

**8.** A and B start walking at the same time on a circular path with circumference 35 metre. If they walk in the same direction at 4 km/hr and 5 km/hr respectively, after what time will they meet together?

A. 35 hours B. 27 hours
C. 24 hours D. 40 hours

**9.** While walking at $\frac{3}{5}$ of his usual speed Kamalkant reaches at his destination late by 30 minutes. His usual time consumed in reaching to his destination is:
A. 32 min B. 40 min
C. 45 min D. 42 min

**10.** The distance between two stations A and B is 300 km. A train leaves the station A with a speed of 40 km/hr. At the same time another train departs from the station B with a speed of 50 km/hr. How much time will these two trains take to cross each other?
A. 3 hrs 40 min B. 3 hrs 20 min
C. 2 hrs 20 min D. 3 hrs 45 min

**11.** Gulshan starts from a place P at 2 p.m. and walks to Q at 5 km per hour. Tarun starts from P at 3 p.m. and follows Gulshan on bicycle at 10 km per hour. By when Tarun will catch Gulshan?
A. At 5.30 p.m. B. At 4.00 p.m.
C. At 4.30 p.m. D. At 6.00 p.m.

**12.** Nilesh goes to school from his village at the speed of 4 km/hr and returns from school to village at the speed of 2 km/hr. If he takes 6 hours in all, then what is the distance between the village and the school?
A. 8 km B. 6 km
C. 5 km D. 4 km

**13.** A school bus covers a distance from a village to school at the speed of 12 km/hr and reaches the school 8 minute late. The next day the bus covers the same distance at the speed of 20 km/hr and reaches the school 10 minutes early. What is the distance between village and the school?
A. 6 km B. 9 km
C. 12 km D. 15 km

**14.** By increasing the speed of the bus by 10 km/hr the time of journey for 72 km is reduced by 36 minutes. What was the original speed of the bus?
A. 30 km/hr B. 35 km/hr
C. 40 km/hr D. 45 km/hr

**15.** A car completes a fixed journey in 8 hours. It covers half distance at the speed of 40 km/hr and rest at the 60 km/hr, the distance of the journey is:
A. 400 km B. 420 km
C. 384 km D. 350 km

**16.** A car covers four consecutive extensions of 3 km each at the speeds of 10 km/hr, 20 km/hr, 30 km/hr and 60 km/hr. Its average speed of journey is:
A. 30 km/hr B. 25 km/hr
C. 20 km/hr D. 10 km/hr

**17.** A girl rides her bicycle 10 km at an average speed of 12 km/hr and another 12 km at an average speed of 10 km/hr. Her average speed for the entire journey is approximately:
A. 12.2 km/hr B. 11.2 km/hr
C. 10.8 km/hr D. 10.4 km/hr

**18.** Raman drove from home to a neighbouring town at the speed of 50 km/hr and on his returning journey, he drove at the speed of 45 km/hr and also took an hour longer to reach home. What distance did he cover each way?
A. 900 km B. 500 km
C. 450 km D. 225 km

**19.** A man takes 6 hours 35 minutes in walking to a certain place and riding back. He would have taken 2 hours less by riding both ways. What would be the time he would take to walk both ways?
A. 10 hours B. 8 hours 35 minutes
C. 8 hours 25 minutes D. 8 hrs

**20.** A man covers a distance of 6 km at the rate of 4 km/hr and other 4 km at 3 km/hr this average speed is
A. $3\frac{5}{9}$ km/hr B. $3\frac{9}{17}$ km/hr
C. $5\frac{9}{17}$ km/hr D. $9\frac{3}{17}$ km/hr

## ANSWERS

| 1 | 2 | 3 | 4 | 5 | 6 | 7 | 8 | 9 | 10 |
|---|---|---|---|---|---|---|---|---|---|
| B | A | D | A | D | B | C | A | C | B |
| **11** | **12** | **13** | **14** | **15** | **16** | **17** | **18** | **19** | **20** |
| B | A | B | A | C | C | C | C | B | B |

## EXPLANATORY ANSWERS

**1.** Let he has to increase his speed by $x$ km/hr for given condition; then,

$$(48 + x) \times 8 = 48 \times 10$$

$$\Rightarrow \quad 48 + x = 60 \therefore x = 12 \text{ km/hr}$$

**2.** Average speed during the entire journey

$$= \frac{2xy}{x+y} = \frac{2 \times 4 \times 16}{4+16} = \frac{8 \times 16}{20} = 6.4 \text{ km/hr.}$$

**3.** Let required speed be $x$ km/hr; then

$$x \times \frac{1}{2} = 48 \times \frac{3}{4} \therefore x = 48 \times \frac{3}{4} \times 2 = 72 \text{ km/hr}$$

**4.** During onward journey from A to B:

$$\text{Average speed} = \frac{150}{10/3} = \frac{150 \times 3}{10} = 45 \text{ km/hr.}$$

During entire jouney:

Average speed = $\frac{300}{\frac{10}{3}+\frac{25}{6}} = \frac{300 \times 6}{45}$ = 40 km/hr.

Hence, difference of average speed
= 45 – 40 = 5 km/hr.

**5.** Suppose the policeman will catch the thief after $t$ sec

then, $\left(\frac{25}{6}-\frac{10}{3}\right)t = 200 \Rightarrow \frac{5}{6}t = 200$

$\therefore\ t = \frac{200 \times 6}{5}$ = 240 sec = 4 min.

**6.** Suppose the distance between her house to the school = $x$ km

Difference of time = $\frac{5}{2} - (-5) = \frac{15}{2}$ min = $\frac{1}{8}$ hr.

$\frac{x}{4} - \frac{x}{5} = \frac{1}{8} \Rightarrow \frac{x}{20} = \frac{1}{8}\ \therefore\ x = \frac{20}{8}$ = 2.5 km

**7.** The monkey climbs 12 metres in 1 minute and then he slips back 3 metres in the next minute

∴ The monkey climbs in the first 2 minutes = 12 – 3 = 9 metres

∴ In the first 12 minutes the monkey climbs = 9 × 6 = 54 metres

Remaining height of the pole to be covered by the monkey = 63 – 54 = 9 metre

∴ The monkey will climb the height of 9 metres in the 13th minute

∵ The monkey climbs 12 metres in 1 minute

∴ The monkey will climb 9 metres in

$\frac{1}{12} \times 9 = \frac{3}{4}$ minute

∴ Time spent in climbing at the top of the pole

$= \left(12+\frac{3}{4}\right)$ minutes = $12\frac{3}{4}$ minutes

**8.** The two persons walk in the same direction

∴ Their relative speed = 5 – 4 = 1 km/hr

Distance covered in 1 round on the circular path = 35 km

∴ They will meet after $\frac{35}{1}$ = 35 hours.

**9.** Suppose usual speed of Kamalkant is $v$ km/hr and his destination is at a distance of $x$ kms; then usual time taken = $\frac{x}{v}$ hours.

$\frac{x}{3v/5} - \frac{x}{v} = \frac{1}{2} \Rightarrow \frac{2x}{3v} = \frac{1}{2}\ \therefore\ \frac{x}{v} = \frac{3}{4}$ hour = 45 min.

**10.** The two trains are moving in the opposite directions

∴ Relative speed = 40 + 50 = 90 km/hr.

∴ Time taken to cross each other

$= \frac{300}{90} = 3\frac{1}{3}$ hours or, 3 hours 20 minutes.

**11.** Let Tarun will catch Gulshan after $t$ hours the starting of Tarun; then, $10t = 5(t + 1)$

$\Rightarrow 5t = 5\ \therefore\ t = 1$ hr

Hence, required time = 3 p.m. + 1 hr. = 4 p.m.

**12.** Let $x$ km be the distance between village and the school; then

$\frac{x}{4} + \frac{x}{2} = 6 \Rightarrow \frac{3x}{4} = 6\ \therefore\ x = \frac{6 \times 4}{3}$ = 8 km

**13.** Let $x$ km be the distance from village to school, then

$\frac{x}{12} - \frac{x}{20} = [8 - (-10)] \times \frac{1}{60}$

$\Rightarrow \frac{x}{30} = \frac{18}{60}\ \therefore\ x = \frac{18}{60} \times 30$ = 9 km

**14.** Let original speed of the bus be $x$ km/hr; then

$\frac{72}{x} - \frac{72}{x+10} = \frac{36}{60} \Rightarrow \frac{72(x+10-x)}{x^2+10x} = \frac{3}{5}$

$\Rightarrow\ 1200 = x^2 + 10x$

$\Rightarrow x^2 + 10x - 1200 = 0$

$\Rightarrow (x + 40)(x - 30) = 0$

$\therefore\ x = 30$ or $x = -40$

Taking positive value only, so speed of the bus = 30 km/hr.

**15.** Let the distance of the journey be $x$ km, then,

$\frac{x}{2 \times 40} + \frac{x}{2 \times 60} = 8 \Rightarrow \frac{5x}{240} = 8$

$\therefore\ x = 8 \times 48$ = 384 km

**16.** Total distance of the journey = 4 × 3 km = 12 km

Total time taken = $\frac{3}{10} + \frac{3}{20} + \frac{3}{30} + \frac{3}{60} = \frac{36}{60} = \frac{3}{5}$ hr.

Hence, average speed = $\frac{12}{3/5} = \frac{12 \times 5}{3}$ = 20 km/hr.

**17.** Average speed

$= \frac{10+12}{\frac{10}{12}+\frac{12}{10}} = \frac{22}{61/30} = \frac{22 \times 30}{61} = \frac{660}{61}$ = 10.8 km/hr

**18.** Let his distance of journey of each way be $x$ km; then

$\frac{x}{45} - \frac{x}{50} = 1 \Rightarrow \frac{x}{450} = 1$

$\therefore\ x = 450$ km

**19.** Here, Walking to a certain place + riding back = 6 hrs 35 min. ...(*i*)

2 × riding the same distance = 4 hrs 35 min. ...(*ii*)

Multiplying equation (*i*) × 2 and subtracting (*ii*) we get

Time taken in walking both ways = 13 hrs 70 min – 4 hrs. 35 min = 8 hrs. 35 min.

**20.** His average speed = $\frac{6+4}{\frac{6}{4}+\frac{4}{3}} = \frac{10}{17/6} = \frac{60}{17} = 3\frac{9}{17}$ km/hr

●●●

CHAPTER 9

# Time and Work

**IMPORTANT FACTS:**

1. If A can do a piece of work in $n$ days, then work done by A in 1 day $= \frac{1}{n}$.
2. If work done by A in 1 day $= \frac{1}{n}$; then A can finish the whole work in $n$ days.
3. If A is twice as good a workman as B then; Ratio of work done by A and B = 2 : 1
   Ratio of times taken by A and B to finish a work = 1 : 2.

## EXERCISE

1. 12 boys can do a piece of work in 16 days. In how many days can 6 boys do the same work?
   A. 16 days B. 32 days
   C. 23 days D. 24 days

2. A can do a piece of work in 8 days while B can do the same work in 16 days. If they start working together, how long would they take to complete half portion of this work?
   A. $2\frac{2}{3}$ days B. $3\frac{5}{7}$ days
   C. $4\frac{1}{2}$ days D. $3\frac{1}{2}$ days

3. A can do a piece of work in 4 days. B is 50% more efficient than A. How long would B alone take to finish this work?
   A. $3\frac{1}{3}$ days B. $5\frac{1}{4}$ days
   C. $2\frac{2}{3}$ days D. $1\frac{2}{3}$ days

4. A and B working together complete a work in 35 days. If A takes 60 days to complete it, how long would B alone take to complete it?
   A. 64 days B. 72 days
   C. 81 days D. 84 days

5. A few children working together can do a piece of work in 18 days. If the number of children employed on the work is made double, how long would they take to complete half of the work?
   A. $4\frac{1}{2}$ days B. $2\frac{1}{3}$ days
   C. $8\frac{3}{4}$ days D. $6\frac{1}{2}$ days

6. 10 men or 18 boys can do a piece of work in 15 days. In how many days would 25 men and 15 boys complete the same work working together?
   A. $5\frac{1}{2}$ days B. $4\frac{1}{2}$ days
   C. $6\frac{2}{3}$ days D. $2\frac{1}{3}$ days

7. A can do a piece of work in 40 days. He starts working, but having some other engagements he drops out after 5 days. Thereafter B completes this work in 21 days. How many days would A and B take to complete this work working together?
   A. 15 days B. 16 days
   C. 17 days D. 11 days

8. Two persons A and B can complete a piece of work in 8 hours and 16 hours respectively. If they work at it alternately for an hour, A starting first, in how many hours will the work be finished?
   A. $9\frac{1}{3}$ hours B. $10\frac{1}{2}$ hours
   C. $11\frac{1}{2}$ hours D. $8\frac{1}{2}$ hours

**9.** 15 men can complete a work in 210 days. They started the work but at the end of 10 days 15 additional men, with double efficiency, were inducted. How many days, in whole, did they take to finish the work?

A. $76\frac{2}{3}$ days  B. $84\frac{3}{4}$ days
C. $72\frac{1}{2}$ days  D. 70 days

**10.** A and B working together can complete a piece of work in 12 days and B and C working together can complete the same work in 16 days. A worked at it for 5 days and B worked at it for 7 days. C finished the remaining work in 13 days. How many days would C alone take to complete it?

A. 10 days  B. 24 days
C. 32 days  D. 40 days

**11.** A cistern is filled by a tap in $3\frac{1}{2}$ hours. Due to a leak in the bottom of the cistern, it takes half an hour longer to fill the cistern. If the cistern is full, how long will it take the leak to empty it?

A. 28 hours  B. 29 hours
C. $31\frac{1}{3}$ hours  D. 38 hours

**12.** A is twice as good a workman as B and thrice as good a workman as C. If C alone can do a piece of work in 24 days, how long would the three persons take to finish the work working together?

A. $3\frac{3}{11}$ days  B. $4\frac{4}{7}$ days
C. $4\frac{4}{11}$ days  D. $3\frac{4}{11}$ days

**13.** Two pipes can fill a tank in 8 hours and 12 hours respectively whereas an escape pipe can empty it in 6 hours. If the three pipes are opened at 1 p.m., 2 p.m. and 3 p.m. respectively, at what time will the tank be filled?

A. 7.00 a.m.  B. 8.00 a.m.
C. 5.00 a.m.  D. 7.30 a.m.

**14.** Working 7 hours daily 24 men can complete a piece of work in 27 days. In how many days would 14 men complete the same piece of work working 9 hours daily?

A. 32 days  B. 31 days
C. 36 days  D. 39 days

**15.** A, B and C undertake to do a piece of work for ₹ 529. If A and B working together do $\frac{19}{23}$ work and B and C working together do $\frac{8}{23}$ work, how should the money be divided among them?

A. ₹ 345, ₹ 102, ₹ 82
B. ₹ 345, ₹ 92, ₹ 92
C. ₹ 330, ₹ 107, ₹ 92
D. ₹ 330, ₹ 92, ₹ 107

## ANSWERS

| 1 | 2 | 3 | 4 | 5 | 6 | 7 | 8 | 9 | 10 |
|---|---|---|---|---|---|---|---|---|---|
| B | A | C | D | A | B | A | B | A | B |
| **11** | **12** | **13** | **14** | **15** | | | | | |
| A | C | A | C | B | | | | | |

## EXPLANATORY ANSWERS

**1.** ∵ 12 boys can do a piece of work in 16 days.
∴ 1 boy will do the same piece of work in 16 × 12 days.
∴ 6 boys will do the same piece of work in

$\frac{16\times12}{6}$ days = 32 days.

**2.** (A + B)'s 1 day's work $= \frac{1}{8}+\frac{1}{16}=\frac{3}{16}$

Hence, (A + B) will do the whole work in $\frac{16}{3}$ days

So, they will do the half portion of the work in

$\frac{16}{3\times2}$ days $= \frac{8}{3} = 2\frac{2}{3}$ days.

**3.** A's 1 day's work $=\frac{1}{4}$;

Hence, B's 1 day's work $= \frac{150}{100}\times\frac{1}{4}=\frac{3}{8}$

So, B will do the whole work in $\frac{8}{3}=2\frac{2}{3}$ days.

**4.** (A + B)'s 1 day's work $= \frac{1}{35}$

and also, A's 1 day's work $= \frac{1}{60}$

Hence, B's 1 day's work

$= \frac{1}{35}-\frac{1}{60}=\frac{5}{420}=\frac{1}{84}$

So, B will do the whole work in 84 days.

**5.** Let number of children be $x$;
Now $x$ children can do the work in 18 days.

Hence, $2x$ children will do $\frac{1}{2}$ of the work in

$\frac{18 \times x}{2x \times 2} = \frac{9}{2}$ days $= 4\frac{1}{2}$ days.

**6.** 10 men $\equiv$ 18 boys; 25 men $\equiv \frac{18}{10} \times 25 = 45$ boys

Hence, 25 men + 15 boys = 45 + 15 = 60 boys

Now, 18 boys can do a piece of work in 15 days.

Hence, 60 boys will do a piece of work in

$\frac{15 \times 18}{60} = \frac{9}{2}$ days $= 4\frac{1}{2}$ days.

**7.** A's 5 days' work $= 5 \times \frac{1}{40} = \frac{1}{8}$

Remaining work $= 1 - \frac{1}{8} = \frac{7}{8}$, which is done by B in 21 days.

Hence, B's 1 day's work $= \frac{7}{8 \times 21} = \frac{1}{24}$

Now, (A + B)'s 1 day's work $= \frac{1}{40} + \frac{1}{24} = \frac{8}{120} = \frac{1}{15}$

Hence, (A + B) will complete the work in 15 days.

**8.** In 2 hours the part of work $= \frac{1}{8} + \frac{1}{16} = \frac{3}{16}$ will be completed.

Hence, in 5 pairs of hours the part of work

$= 5 \times \frac{3}{16} = \frac{15}{16}$ will be completed

Remaining work $= 1 - \frac{15}{16} = \frac{1}{16}$ which will be done by A.

Time taken by A to complete the $\frac{1}{16}$ work

$= \frac{1/16}{1/8} = \frac{1}{2}$ hour.

Hence, required number of hours

$= 10 + \frac{1}{2} = 10\frac{1}{2}$ hours.

**9.** 15 men's 10 days' work $= 10 \times \frac{1}{210} = \frac{1}{21}$

Remaining work $= 1 - \frac{1}{21} = \frac{20}{21}$

Now, (15 men + 15 men having double efficiency)'s 1 day's work $= \frac{1}{210} + \frac{2}{210} = \frac{3}{210} = \frac{1}{70}$

Hence, number of days

$= \frac{20/21}{1/70} = \frac{20}{21} \times 70 = \frac{200}{3} = 66\frac{2}{3}$ days

So, required number of total days

$= 10 + 66\frac{2}{3} = 76\frac{2}{3}$ days.

**10.** Here, A worked for 5 days, B for 7 days and C for 13 days $\equiv$ (A + B) worked for 5 days, (B + C) for 2 days and C for 11 days.

Let C will complete the work in $x$ days,

Now, (A + B)'s 5 days' work + (B + C)'s 2 days' work + C's 11 days' work

$= \frac{5}{12} + \frac{2}{16} + \frac{11}{x} = \frac{13}{24} + \frac{11}{x}$

Again, $\frac{13}{24} + \frac{11}{x} = 1 \Rightarrow \frac{11}{x} = \frac{11}{24} \quad \therefore x = 24$

Hence, C would alone complete the work in 24 days.

**11.** In 1 hour $\frac{2}{7}$ cistern is filled by the tap.

Hence, in $\frac{1}{2}$ hour $\frac{2}{14} = \frac{1}{7}$ cistern is filled by the tap.

So, $\frac{1}{7}$ cistern is emptied by the leakage in 4 hours.

So, 1 cistern will be emptied by the leakage in 28 hours.

**13.** Let tank will be filled up after $t$ hours of starting of pipe A;

Then, $t \times \frac{1}{8} + (t-1) \times \frac{1}{12} - (t-2) \times \frac{1}{6} = 1$

$\Rightarrow t\left(\frac{1}{8} + \frac{1}{12} - \frac{1}{6}\right) - \frac{1}{12} + \frac{1}{3} = 1$

$\Rightarrow t \times \frac{1}{24} = 1 - \frac{1}{4}$

$\therefore t = \frac{3}{4} \times 24 = 18$ hours

Hence, required time = 1 p.m. + 18 hours = 7 a.m.

**14.** Working 7 hours a day 24 men can do the work is 27 days.

Hence, working 9 hours a day 14 men will do the work in $\frac{27 \times 24 \times 7}{9 \times 14} = 36$ days.

**15.** The part of work is done by B

$= \frac{19}{23} + \frac{8}{23} - 1 = \frac{4}{23}$

The part of work is done by A $= \frac{19}{23} - \frac{4}{23} = \frac{15}{23}$

The part of work is done by C $= \frac{8}{23} - \frac{4}{23} = \frac{4}{23}$

Hence, share of A $= \frac{15}{23} \times$ ₹ 529 = ₹ 345

share of B $= \frac{4}{23} \times$ ₹ 529 = ₹ 92

share of C $= \frac{4}{23} \times$ ₹ 529 = ₹ 92

So, Their shares are ₹ 345, ₹ 92 and ₹ 92.

CHAPTER 10

# Geometry

## Triangle and Its Various Kinds of Centres

There are 4 very important ways of viewing the center of a triangle. We can look at its CENTROID, ORTHOCENTER, CIRCUMCENTER, and the INCENTER.

### Centroid

The centroid is the first center and is obtained by locating the intersection of the three medians of the triangle. The median of a triangle is obtained by joining each vertex with the midpoint of the opposite side.

- It is the point of the intersection of the three median of the triangle. It is denoted by G.
- A centroid divides the area of the triangle in exactly three parts.

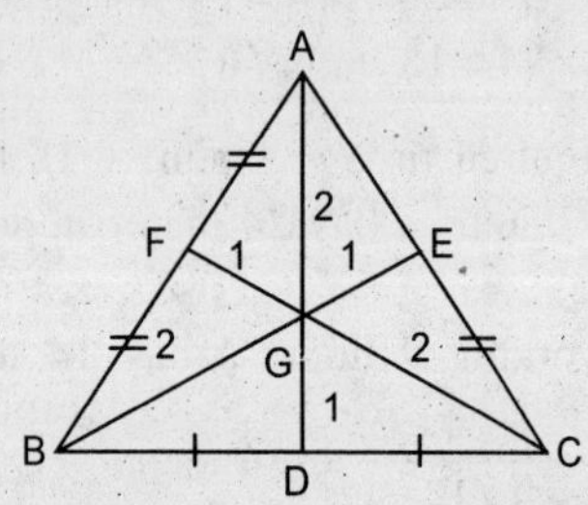


**Medians:**

- A line segment joining the midpoint of the side with the opposite vertex is called median.
- Median bisects the opposite side as well as divide the area of the triangle in two equal parts.

### Orthocenter

The second center of a triangle is the orthocenter. It is obtained by finding the intersection of the 3 altitudes of the triangle. An altitude is found by joining each vertex with the point on the opposite side that creates a perpendicular line with the opposite side.

It is the point of intersection of all the three altitudes of the triangle.

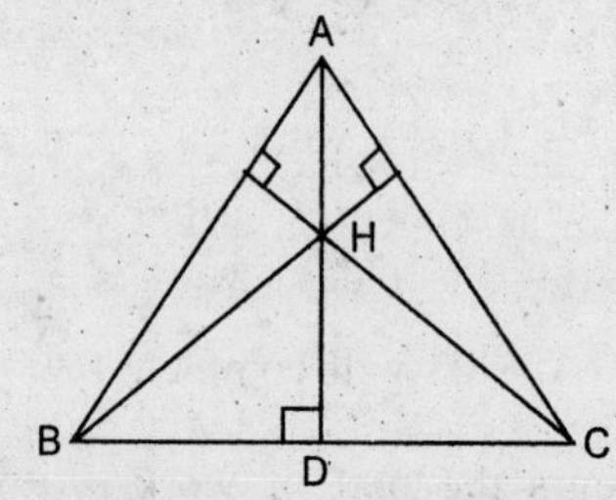


$\angle BHC = 180 - \angle A$

$\angle AHB = 180 - \angle C$

$\angle AHC = 180 - \angle B$

**Position of orthocentre inside the triangle:**

**Acute angled triangle:** lies inside the triangle.

**Obtuse angle triangle:** lies outside the triangle on the backside of the obtuse angle. Orthocentre and circumcentre lie opposite to each other in obtuse angle triangle.

### Circumcenter

The third center is the circumcenter. The circumcenter is the intersection of the perpendicular bisectors of each side of the triangle. We can also think of this center as the point that is equidistant from each of the vertices. Since it is equidistant from each vertex, we can also construct a circle that passes through each vertex with the center being the circumcenter.

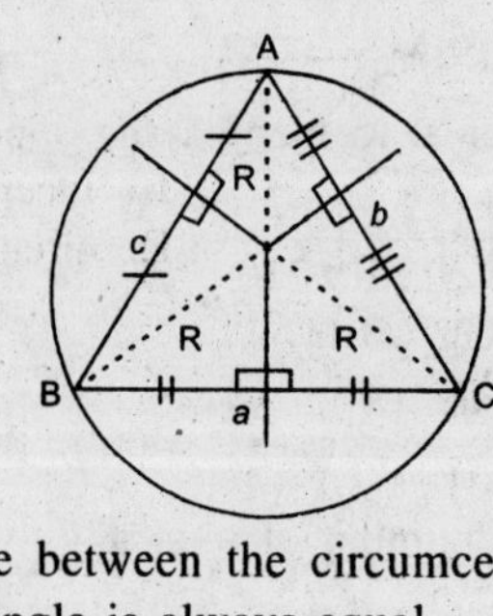


The distance between the circumcentre and the three vertices of a triangle is always equal.

OA = OB = OC = R (circumradius) = $abc/4A$

$\angle BOC = 2\angle A$

$\angle AOC = 2\angle B$

$\angle AOB = 2\angle C$

**Location of circumcentre in various types of triangle:**

**Acute angle triangle:** Lies inside the triangle

**Obtuse angle triangle:** Lies outside the triangle

**Right angle triangle:** Lies at the midpoint of the hypotenuse.

## Incenter

The last center is the incenter. The incenter is found by first constructing the angle bisectors of each of the three angles. The incenter is the intersection of these 3 segments.

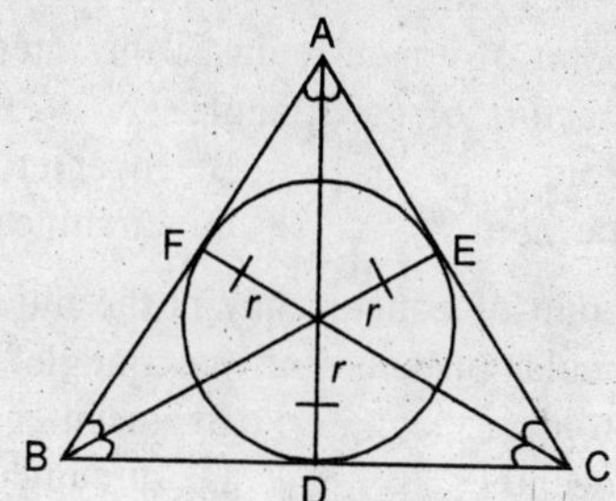


The distance of the in-centre from the all the three sides is equal (ID = IE = IF = inradius "$r$")

In-radius ($r$) = Area of triangle/Semiperimetre = A/S

$\angle BIC = 90 + \angle A/2$

$\angle AIC = 90 + \angle B/2$

$\angle AIB = 90 + \angle C/2$

## EXERCISE

1. In a triangle, a segment connecting the midpoints of two sides of the triangle is called a ______.
   A. shortcut  C. centroid
   B. midsegment  D. vertex

2. Point Q represents which point of concurrency?

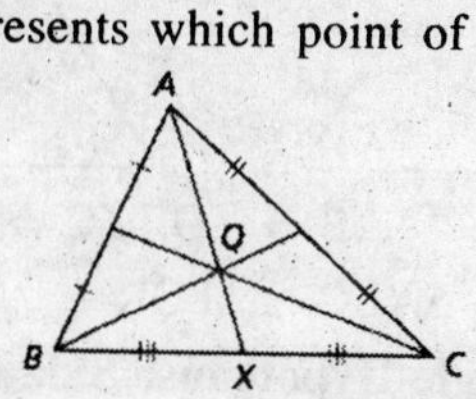


   A. centroid  C. orthocenter
   B. incenter  D. circumcenter

3. Point P represents which point of concurrency?

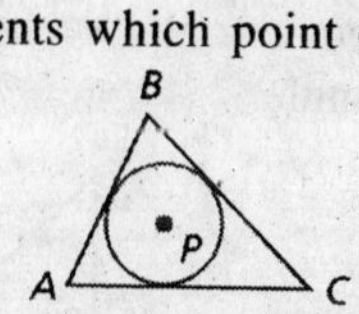


   A. centroid  C. orthocenter
   B. incenter  D. circumcenter

4. Point P represents which point of concurrency?

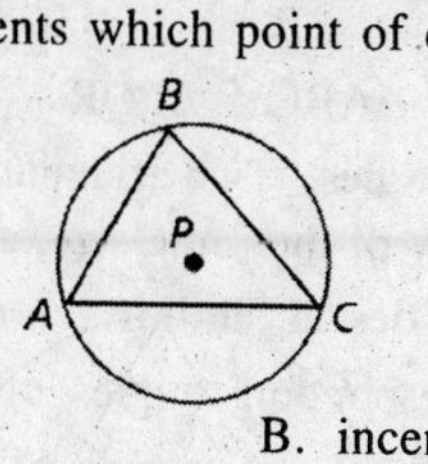


   A. centroid  B. incenter
   C. orthocenter  D. circumcenter

5. Point T represents which point of concurrency?

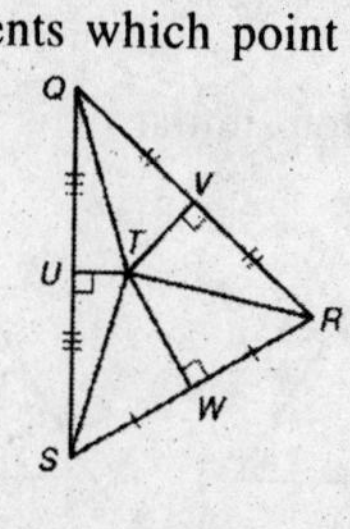


   A. centroid  B. incenter
   C. orthocenter  D. circumcenter

6. Point M represents which point of concurrency?

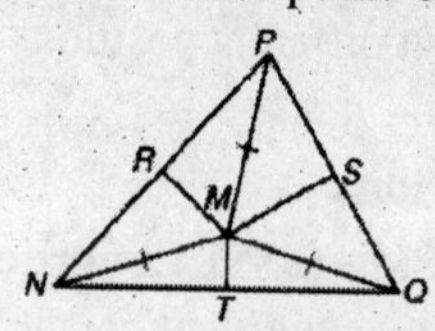


   A. centroid  B. incenter
   C. orthocenter  D. circumcenter

7. Point M represents which point of concurrency?

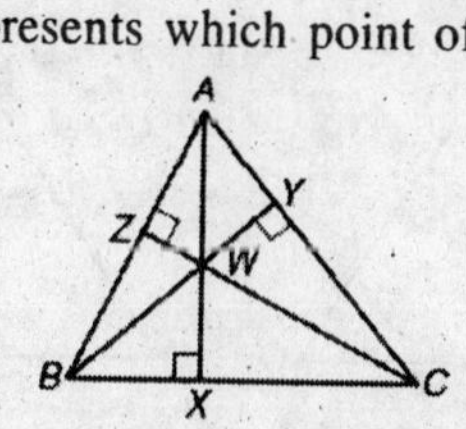


   A. centroid  B. incenter
   C. orthocenter  D. circumcenter

8. Point L represents which point of concurrency?

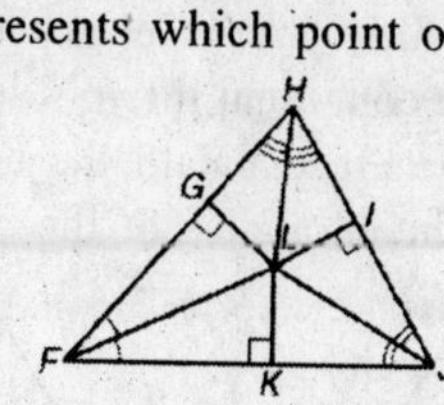


   A. centroid  B. incenter
   C. orthocenter  D. circumcenter

9. Which point of concurrency is the intersection of the medians of the triangle?
   A. centroid  B. incenter
   C. orthocenter  D. circumcenter

10. Which point of concurrency is the intersection of the altitudes of the triangle?
   A. centroid  B. incenter
   C. orthocenter  D. circumcenter

**11.** Which point of concurrency is the intersection of the angle bisectors of the triangle?
A. centroid B. incenter
C. orthocenter D. circumcenter

**12.** Which point of concurrency is the intersection of the perpendicular bisectors of the triangle?
A. centroid B. incenter
C. orthocenter D. circumcenter

**13.** Which point of concurrency is equidistant from the three sides of a triangle?
A. centroid B. incenter
C. orthocenter D. circumcenter

**14.** Which point of concurrency is equidistant from the three verticies of a triangle?
A. centroid B. incenter
C. orthocenter D. circumcenter

**15.** Which point of concurrency is the center of gravity of a triangle?
A. centroid B. incenter
C. orthocenter D. circumcenter

## ANSWERS

| 1 | 2 | 3 | 4 | 5 | 6 | 7 | 8 | 9 | 10 |
|---|---|---|---|---|---|---|---|---|---|
| B | A | B | D | D | D | C | B | A | C |
| 11 | 12 | 13 | 14 | 15 | | | | | |
| B | D | B | D | A | | | | | |

# Congruence and Similarity of Triangles

**Congruence of triangle:** Two triangles having same shape and measurement but different positions are called congruent triangle.

**Congruence criterion**

(*i*) **Side-Side-Side (SSS) Congruence criterion:** Two triangles are congruent if the three sides of one triangle are equal to the three sides of the other triangle.

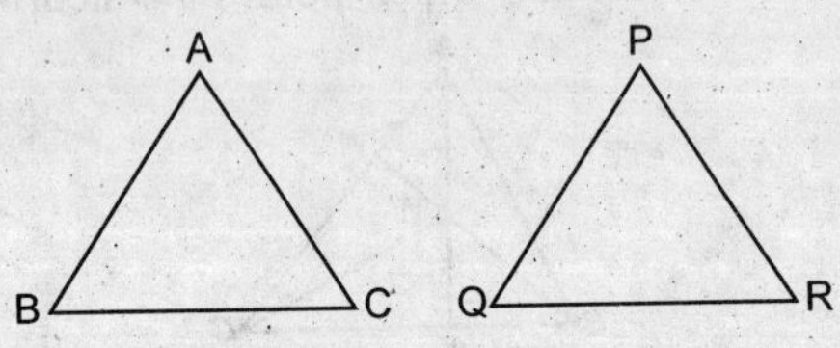


Here, AB = PQ, BC = QR and AC = PR

$\therefore$ $\Delta ABC \cong \Delta PQR$

(*ii*) **Side-Angle-Side (SAS) Congruence criterion:** Two triangles are congruent if two sides and the included angle of one are equal to the corresponding sides and the included angles of the other.

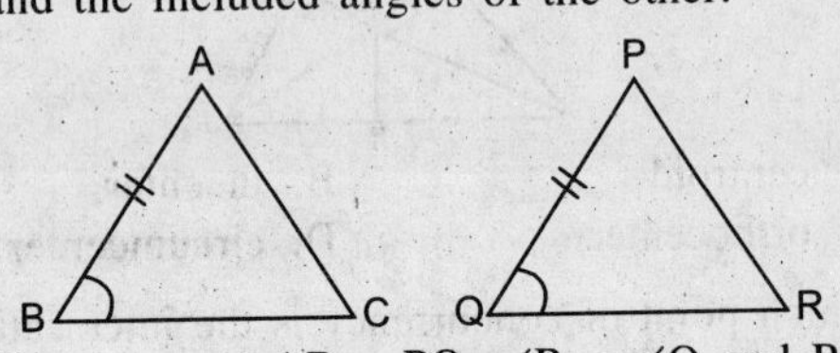


Here, AB = PQ, $\angle B = \angle Q$ and BC = QR

$\therefore$ $\Delta ABC \cong \Delta PQR$

(*iii*) **Angle-Side-Angle (ASA) Congruence criterion:** Two triangles are congruent if two angles and the included side of one triangle are equal to the corresponding two angles and the included side of the triangle.

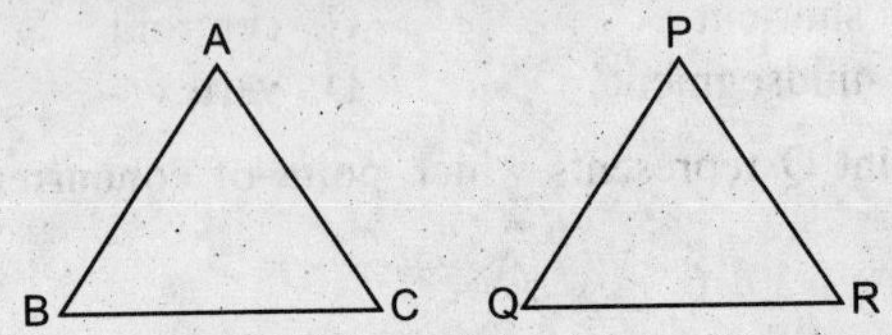


$\because$ $\angle B = \angle Q$, $\angle C = \angle R$ and BC = QR

$\therefore$ $\Delta ABC \cong \Delta PQR$

(*iv*) **Right Angle-Hypotenuse-Side (RHS) congruence criterion:** Two right triangles are congruent. If the hypotenuse and one side of one triangle are respectively equal to the hypotenuse and one side of the other triangle.

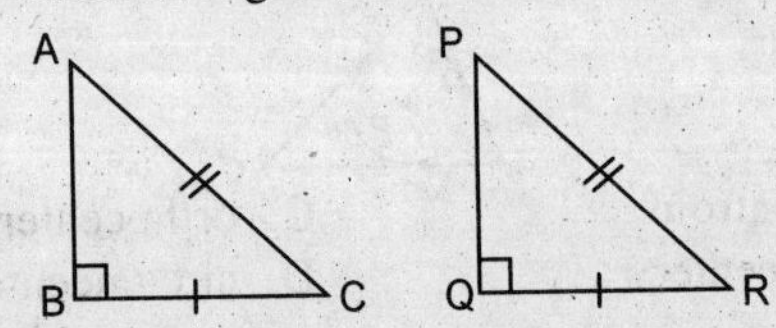


$\because$ $\angle B = \angle Q = 90°$, AC = PR, BC = QR

$\therefore$ $\Delta ABC \cong \Delta PQR$.

**Similar Triangles:** Two triangles having same shape but not necessarily of the same size, called similar triangle.

**Basic properties of similar triangles:**

(*i*) The corresponding angles of similar triangles are equal.

(*ii*) The corresponding sides of similar triangles are proportional.

The symbol for similar or is similar to is ~.

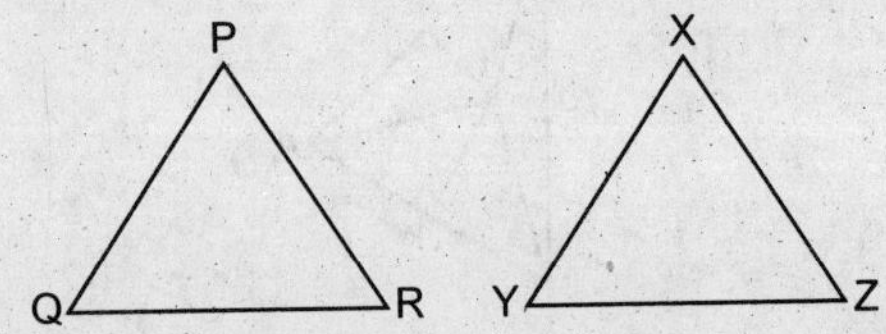

$\angle P = \angle X$, $\angle Q = \angle Y$ and $\angle R = \angle Z$

Then, $\frac{PQ}{QR} = \frac{XY}{YZ}$ or, $\frac{PR}{PQ} = \frac{XZ}{XY}$

Thus, $\Delta PQR \sim \Delta XYZ$

→ Congruent triangles are always similar but similar triangles may or may not be congruent.

→ Any two equilateral triangles are always similar triangles.

## SOME IMPORTANT THEOREMS

### Basic Proportionality Theorem: (Thalse Theorem)

**Theorem 1:** *In a triangle, a line drawn parallel to one side to intersect the other sides in distinct points divides the two sides in the same ratio.*

**Given:** A $\Delta ABC$ in which DE is drawn parallel to side BC.

To prove. $\frac{AD}{DB} = \frac{AE}{EC}$.

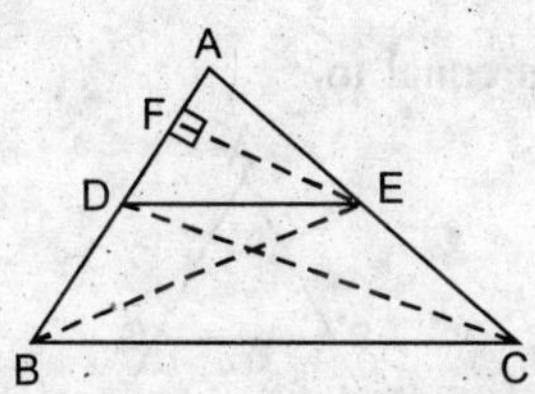


**Const.:** Join BE and CD. Draw $EF \perp AB$.

**Proof:** ar.($\Delta BDE$) = ar.($\Delta CDE$) ...(1)

[∵ $\Delta s$ on the same base DE and between the same parallels are equal in area]

$$\frac{ar.(\Delta ADE)}{ar.(\Delta BDE)} = \frac{\frac{1}{2} \times AD \times EF}{\frac{1}{2} \times BD \times EF}$$

[∵ Area of $\Delta = \frac{1}{2}$ base × height]

$$\Rightarrow \frac{ar.(\Delta ADE)}{ar.(\Delta BDE)} = \frac{AD}{DB} \quad ...(2)$$

Similarly, $\frac{ar.(\Delta ADE)}{ar.(\Delta CDE)} = \frac{AE}{EC}$ ...(3)

$$\therefore \frac{ar.(\Delta ADE)}{ar.(\Delta BDE)} = \frac{AE}{EC}$$

[from (1) and (3)] ...(4)

$$\therefore \frac{AD}{DB} = \frac{AE}{EC} \quad \text{[from (2) and (4)]}$$

**Corollary 1:** $\frac{AD}{DB} = \frac{AE}{EC}$

Adding 1 to both sides, we get

$$\frac{AD}{DB} + 1 = \frac{AE}{EC} + 1$$

$$\Rightarrow \frac{AD + DB}{DB} = \frac{AE + EC}{EC}$$

**Corollary 2:** $\frac{AD}{DB} = \frac{AE}{EC}$

$$\Rightarrow \frac{DB}{AD} = \frac{EC}{AE}$$

Adding 1 to both sides, we get

$$1 + \frac{DB}{AD} = 1 + \frac{EC}{AE}$$

$$\Rightarrow \frac{AD + DB}{AD} = \frac{AE + EC}{AE}$$

$$\Rightarrow \frac{AB}{AD} = \frac{AC}{AE}.$$

### Converse of Basic Proportionality Theorem

**Theorem 2:** *If a line divides any two sides of a triangle in the same ratio, prove that it is parallel to the third side.*

**Given:** A $\Delta ABC$, DE is st. line such that

$$\frac{AD}{DB} = \frac{AE}{EC}$$

To Prove. DE ∥ BC

**Const.:** If DE is not ∥ BC, draw BK ∥ DE meeting AC produce in.

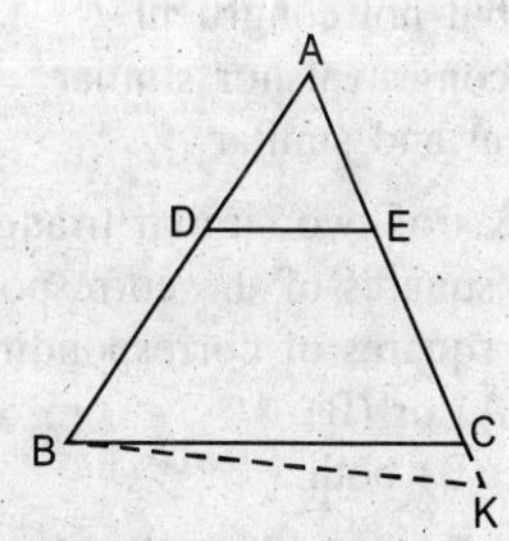


**Proof:** In DABK, DE ∥ BK

$$\therefore \frac{AD}{DB} = \frac{AE}{EK} \quad ...(1)$$

[∵ A line drawn ∥ to one side of a $\Delta$ divides the other two sides in the same ratio]

But, $\frac{AD}{DB} = \frac{AE}{EC}$ (given) ...(2)

From (1) and (2), we get

$$\frac{AE}{EK} = \frac{AE}{EC} \text{ or, } EK = EC$$

which is possible only when C and K coincides.

Hence, DE ∥ BC.

## EXERCISE

**1.** Two similar triangles have
A. equal sides B. equal areas
C. equal angles D. None of these

**2.** Two congruent triangles have
A. proportional sides
B. equal sides
C. equal corresponding sides
D. equal corresponding angles

**3.** Which of the following is false for two congruent triangles?
A. Corresponding angles are equal.
B. Two sides and included angles are equal.
C. Corresponding sides are equal.
D. Two angles and one side are equal.

**4.** If the sides of a triangle are 8 cm, 12 cm and 15 cm then the angle is
A. Right angle B. Obtuse angle
C. Acute angle D. None of these

**5.** If two triangles are on the same base and between the parallel lines then they will be
A. equilaterals B. right angled
C. equal in area D. congruent

**6.** If the three heights of a traingle are equal then it is
A. right angled triangle B. obtuse angled triangle
C. equilateral triangle D. None of these

**7.** If two corresponding sides and the angle between them of a traingle are equal to another triangle. Then the angles are :
A. congruent but not similar
B. similar but not congruent
C. neither congruent nor similar
D. congruent and similar.

**8.** Ratio of areas of two similar triangles is equal to :
A. ratio of squares of the corresponding altitudes
B. ratio of squares of corresponding medians.
C. Either (A) or (B)
D. (A) and (B) both

**9.** If the areas of two similar triangles are equal then the triangles :
A. are congruent
B. have equal length of corresponding sides
C. (A) and (B)
D. None of these

**10.** Two isosceles triangles have equal vertical angles and their areas are in the ratio of 9 : 25 then the ratio between their corresponding heights is :
A. 5 : 3 B. 25 : 9
C. 3 : 5 D. 16 : 9

**11.** If in a $\Delta$ DEF, GH || EF and DG : EG = 2 : 3 then the value of $\frac{ar(\Delta DGH)}{ar(\Delta DEF)}$ is :

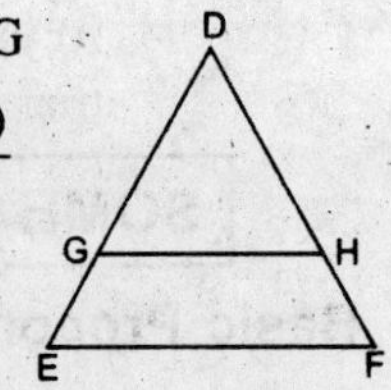


A. $\frac{2}{15}$ B. $\frac{4}{15}$
C. $\frac{4}{25}$ D. $\frac{2}{25}$

**12.** Sides of two similar triangles are in the ratio of 5 : 11 then ratio of their areas is :
A. 25 : 11 B. 25 : 121
C. 125 : 121 D. 121 : 25

**13.** If $\Delta ABC \sim \Delta ADE$ and ar ($\Delta$ ADE) = 9 ar ($\Delta$ ABC) then $\frac{BC}{DE}$ is equal to :

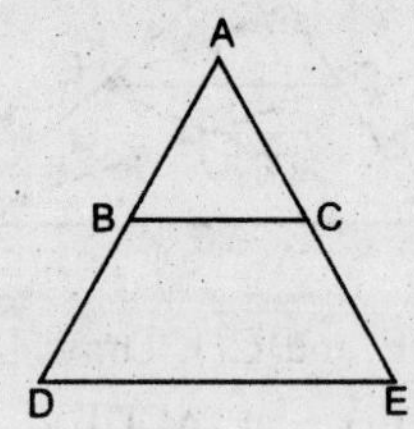


A. $\frac{1}{3}$ B. $\frac{1}{9}$
C. $\frac{3}{4}$ D. None of these

**14.** In a triangle a line is drawn from the mid-point of one side of and parallel to another side then
A. the line bisects the whole traingle
B. bisects the third side
C. bisects the opposite angle
D. None of these

**15.** If in a $\Delta ABC$, $\angle B = \angle C$ and BD = CE then which of the following is true
A. $DE = \frac{1}{2}BC$ B. DE || BC
C. (A) and (B) D. None of these

### ANSWERS

| 1 | 2 | 3 | 4 | 5 | 6 | 7 | 8 | 9 | 10 |
|---|---|---|---|---|---|---|---|---|---|
| C | C | D | C | C | C | C | D | C | C |
| **11** | **12** | **13** | **14** | **15** | | | | | |
| C | B | A | B | B | | | | | |

# EXPLANATORY ANSWERS

**10.** According to equestion

$\angle A = \angle D$ and $\dfrac{ar(\Delta ABC)}{ar(\Delta DEF)} = \dfrac{9}{25}$

Since, AB = AC (given) ....(*i*)

DE = DF (given) ....(*ii*)

Dividing (i) by (ii)

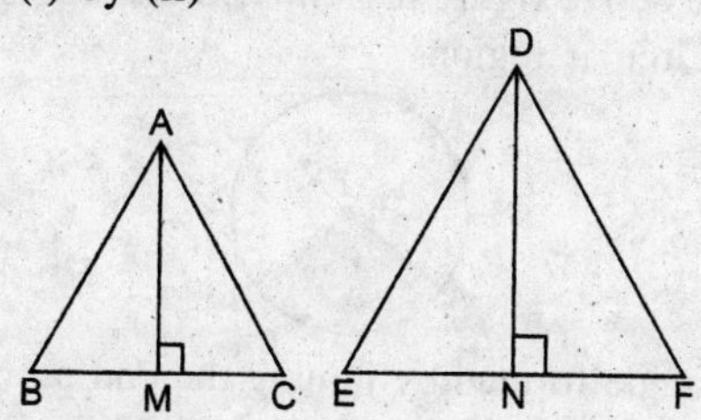

$$\frac{AB}{DE} = \frac{AC}{DF} \quad ...(iii)$$

Hence, $\Delta ABC \sim \Delta DEF$

[By SAS criterion of similar $\Delta s$]

In $\Delta AMC$ and $\Delta DNF$

$\angle AMC = \angle DNF = 90°$

$\angle C = \angle F$ (because $\Delta ABC \sim \Delta DEF$)

$\therefore \angle AMC \sim DNF$

(By AA Criterion of similar $\Delta s$)

$$\therefore \frac{AC}{DF} = \frac{AM}{DN}$$

and, $$\frac{ar(\Delta ABC)}{ar(DEF)} = \frac{AC^2}{DF^2} = \frac{AM^2}{DN^2}$$

$$\therefore \frac{AM^2}{DN^2} = \frac{9}{25}$$

$$\Rightarrow \frac{AM}{DN} = \frac{3}{5}$$

Hence required ratio = 3 : 5

**11.** $\dfrac{DG}{EG} = \dfrac{2}{3} \therefore \dfrac{DG}{DE} = \dfrac{2}{2+3} = \dfrac{2}{5}$

In $\Delta$ DGH and $\Delta$ DEF, $\angle D = \angle D$

$\angle DGH = \angle DEF$

(Since, GH || EF and DE is the transversal among corresponding angles)

$\therefore \Delta DGH \sim \Delta DEF$

(By AA criterion of similar triangles)

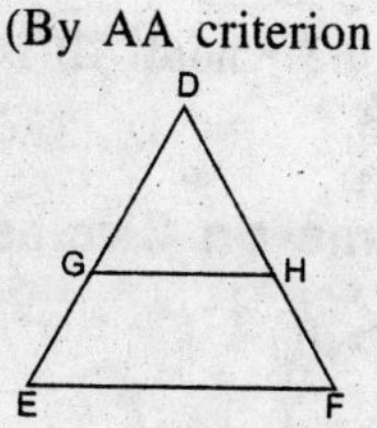

$$\therefore \frac{ar(\Delta DGH)}{ar(\Delta DEF)} = \frac{DG^2}{DE^2} = \frac{2^2}{5^2} = \frac{4}{25}$$

**12.** Since, ratio of area of two similar traingles = ratio of square of corresponding sides

ratio of sides = 5 : 11

$\therefore$ ratio of their areas = $(5)^2 : (11)^2 = 25 : 121$.

**13.** From question,

$ar(\Delta ADE) = 9\ ar(\Delta ABC)$

or, $$\frac{ar(\Delta ABC)}{ar(\Delta ADE)} = \frac{1}{9} = \frac{BC^2}{DE^2}$$

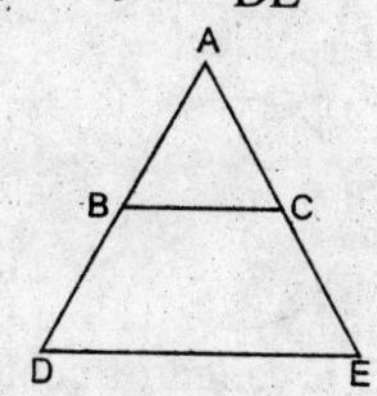

Hence, $$\frac{BC}{DE} = \sqrt{\frac{1}{9}} = \frac{1}{3}$$

**14.** From question, In $\Delta ABC$, D is the mid-point of AB and DE is drawn parallel to BC and it meets at E on AC.

Since, DE || BC (By B.P. Theorem)

$$\frac{AD}{DB} = \frac{AE}{EC} \quad ...(i)$$

also, AD = DB ($\because$ D is mid-point)

$$\therefore \frac{AD}{DB} = 1$$

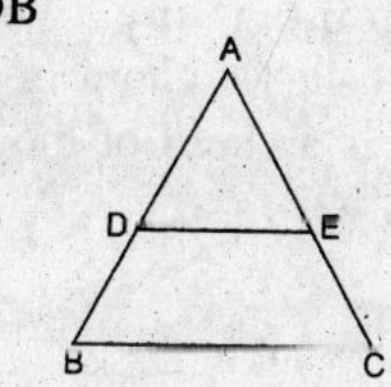

Now, $\dfrac{AE}{EC} = 1$ (From ...(*i*))

$\Rightarrow$ AE = EC

Hence, the line bisects the third line

**15.** According to questions, $\angle B = \angle C$ (given)

$\Rightarrow$ AB = AC (*i*)

and, BD = CE (*ii*)

Subtracting (*ii*) from (*i*), AB – BD = AC – CE

$\Rightarrow$ AD = AE (*iii*)

Dividing (*iii*) by (*ii*)

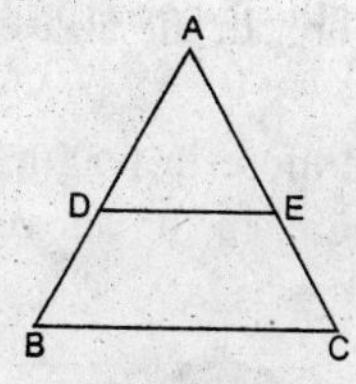

$$\frac{AD}{BD} = \frac{AE}{CE}$$

$\therefore$ DE || BC [By converse of BP Theorem]

Hence, option (B) is true.

# Circle and Its Chord

A circle is a set of those points in a plane that are at a given constant distance from a given fixed point in the plane. The fixed point is called the **centre of the circle** and the constant distance of every point on the circle from its centre of called the **radius of the circle**.

## Things to Remember

1. Locus of a point moving in a plane such that its distance from a fixed point in the same plane remains constant is called a circle.

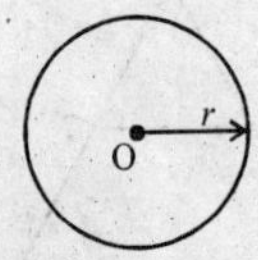


2. The fixed point O is called its centre and the constant distance $r$ is called the radius.
3. The path traced by the moving point as described above is called the circumference of the circle.
4. The part of the plane containing the circle that consists the circle and its interior is called the circular region.

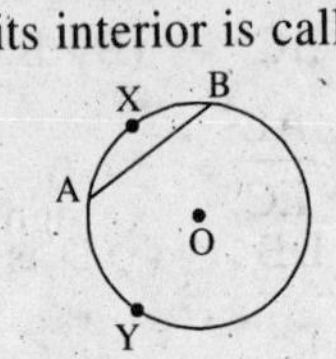


5. Line segment joining any two points on the circumference is called a chord of the circle. In the above figure AB is a chord of the circle.

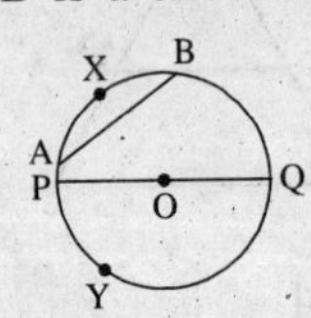


6. The chord passing through the centre of the circle is called its diameter.
   In the above figure PQ is a diameter of the circle.
7. Diameter is the longest chord of the circle.
8. Any fraction of the circumference is called an arc of the circle.
9. The remaining part of the circumference is called the alternate segment of the circle with respect to the arc.
10. An arc of a circle smaller in length than the semicircle is called a minor arc. In the above figure arc AXB is a minor arc.
11. An arc of a circle more in length than the semicircle is called a major arc. In the above figure arc AYB is a major arc.

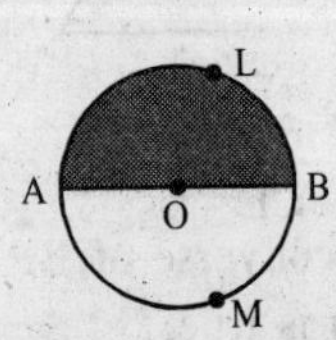


12. Diameter of a circle divides its circumference into two equal arcs. Each of them is called a semicircle.
13. The part of the plane containing the semicircle that consists the semi-circle, the enclosing diameter and its interior is called the semicircular region.
    In the above figure region ALB and region BMA are semicircular regions.

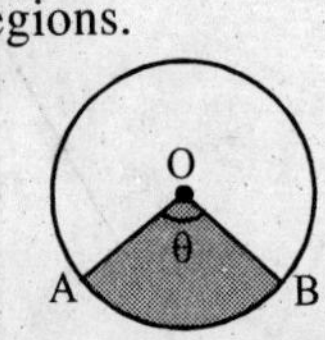


14. The angle formed by joining the end points of an arc to the centre of the circle is said to be the angle subtended by an arc at the centre of the circle. In the above figure, $\theta$ is the degree measure of arc AB.
15. The part of the plane containing the circle that consists of the arc enclosing radii and its interior is called the sector of the circle. In the above figure AOB is sector of the circle.
16. A chord of the circle other than a diameter divides the circular region into two unequal parts.
    Each of these parts is called a segment. The larger part is called the major segment and the smaller is called the minor segment.

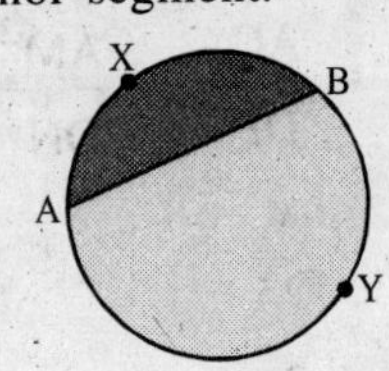


    In the above figure segment AXB is a minor segment and segment BYA is the major segment.
17. Two circles in a plane are said to be concentric if they have same centre but different radii.
18. The chord formed by joining the end points of an arc of a circle is called its corresponding chord.

    In the given figures chord AB is the corresponding chord of arc AB.

## Important Theorems on Circles

1.

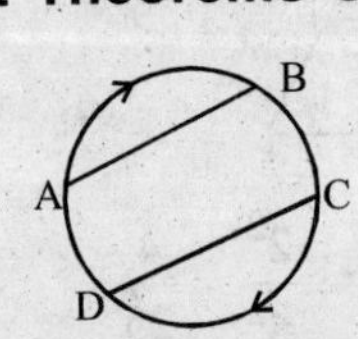

(*a*) If two arcs of a circle are equal then their corresponding chords are also equal.
AB = CD
$\Leftrightarrow$ arcAB = arcCD.

(*b*) If two chords of a circle are equal then their corresponding arcs are also equal.

**2.**

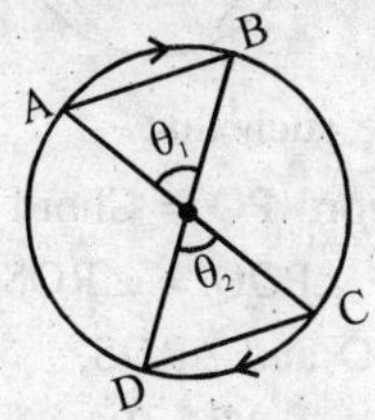


(*a*) If two chords of a circle are equal then they subtend equal angles at the centre of the circle.

(*b*) If two chords of a circle subtend equal angles at the centre of a circle then they are equal

$AB = CD \Leftrightarrow \theta_1 = \theta_2$

**3.**

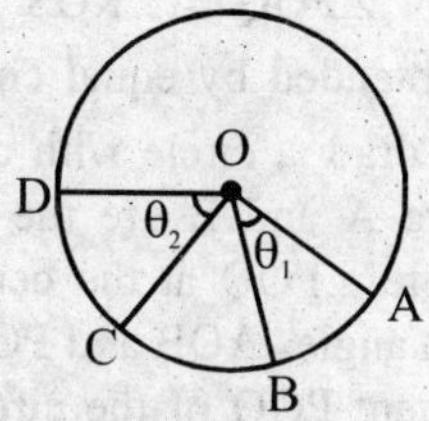


(*a*) If two arcs of a circle have same degree measure then they are equal.
arc AB = arc CD
$\Leftrightarrow \theta_1 = \theta_2$

(*b*) If two arcs of a circle are equal then their degree measures are also equal.

**4.**

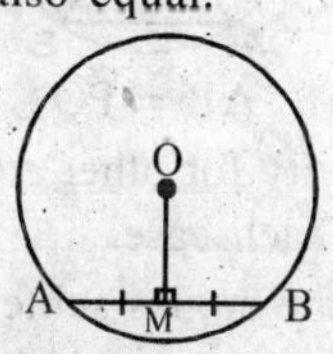


(*a*) Perpendicular to a chord from the centre of the circle bisects the chord.

(*b*) Line segment joining the centre of the circle to the mid point of the chord is perpendicular to the chord.

OM ⊥ AB $\Leftrightarrow$ M is the mid point of AB.

**5.**

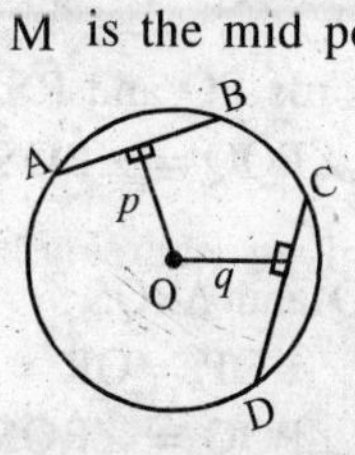


(*a*) If two chords of a circle are equidistant from the centre of the circle, they are equal.

(*b*) If two chords of a circle are equal then they are equidistant from the centre of the circle
$AB = CD \Leftrightarrow p = q$

**6.**

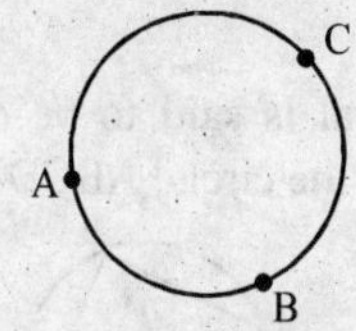


Through any three non collinear points, passes one and only one circle. A, B and C are three non-collinear points in a plane then one and only one circle passes through them.

**7.** Perpendicular bisector of a chord of a circle passes through the centre of the circle.

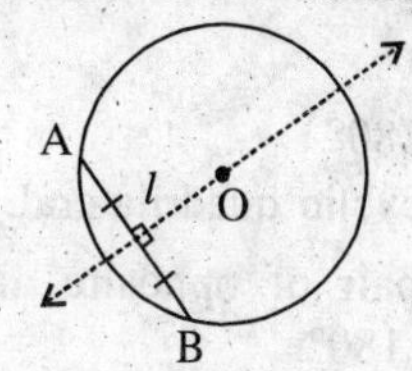


*l* is the ⊥ bisector of AB $\Leftrightarrow$ *l* passes through O.

**8.**

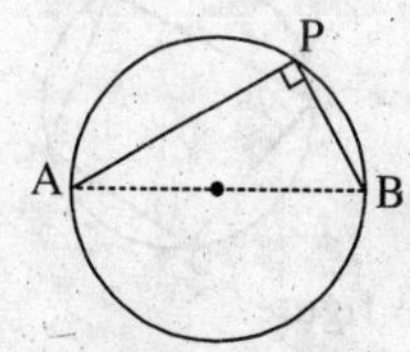


(*a*) **Theorem of Thales:** Angle in a semicircle is a right angle.

(*b*) If an arc subtends a right angle at any point in its alternate segment then it is a semi-circle.

$\overparen{APB}$ is a semicircle $\Leftrightarrow \angle APB = 90°$

**9.** Angles in the same segment of a circle are equal

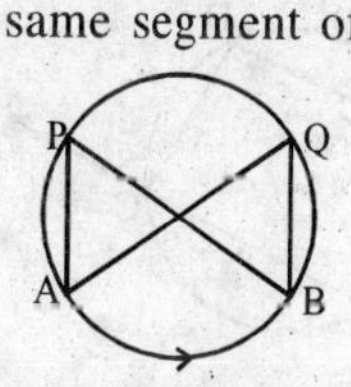


In the above figure $\angle APB = \angle AQB$

**10.**

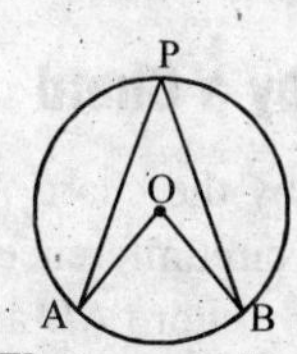


**Degree Measure Theorem :** Degree measure of an arc is twice the angle subtended by it at any point on the alternate segment of the circle with respect to the arc. In the above figure $\angle AOB = 2\angle APB$

**11.** If a line segment joining two points subtends equal angles at two other points on same side of the line containing the two points then the four points are concyclic.

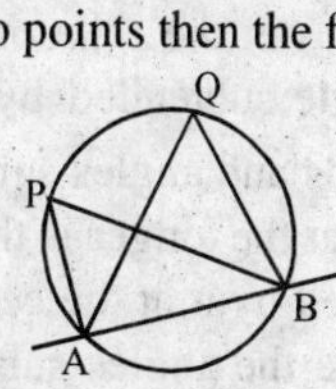


In the above figure $\angle APB = \angle AQB$, then A,B,Q and P are concylic.

**Definition**

A quadrilateral is said to be cyclic if all of its four vertices lie on the circle, ABCD is a cyclic quadrilateral.

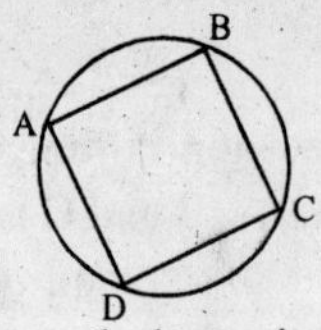


**12.** If in a quadrilateral the pair of opposite angles is supplementary then the quadrilateral is cyclic.

In the above figure

$\angle A + \angle C = 180°$

or $\angle B + \angle D = 180°$.

$\Rightarrow$ ABCD is cyclic quadrilateral.

**13.** Sum of each pair of opposite angles of a cyclic quadrilateral is 180°.

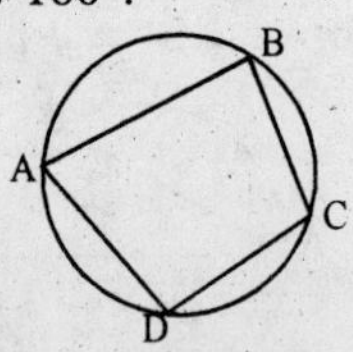


In the above figure

ABCD is cyclic quadrilateral

$\Rightarrow \angle A + \angle C = 180°$

and $\angle B + \angle D = 180°$.

**14.** Exterior angle of a cyclic quadrilateral is equal to its opposite interior angle.

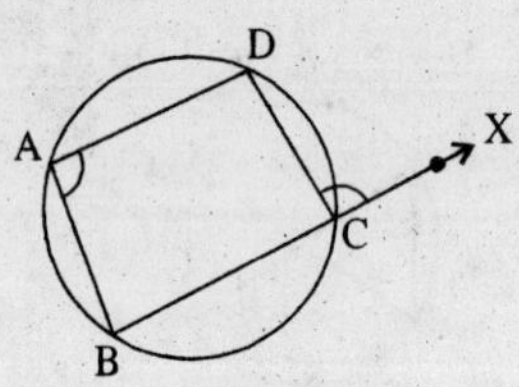


In the above figure, $\angle DCX = \angle A$

## Angle subtended by a Chord

The angle subtended by the chord AB at a point C (not on the chord AB) on the circumference of the circle is $\angle ACB$. The angle subtended by chord AB at the centre O is $\angle AOB$.

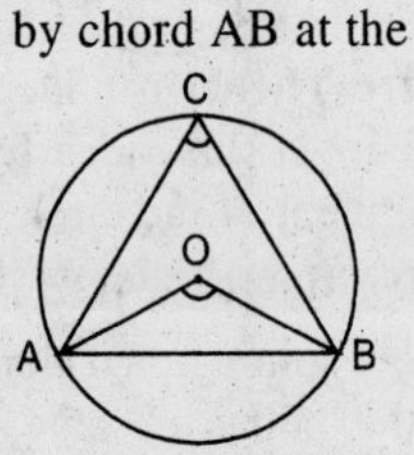


**Activity:** Let us find out the relation between the size of the chord and the angle subtended by it at the centre.

We draw many chords and angles subtended by them at the centre. We observe that the longer is the chord the bigger will be the angle subtended by it at the centre. We draw two equal chords and measure the angles subtended by them at the centre. We find that the angles subtended by them at the centre are equal.

**Theorem 1.** Equal chords of a circle subtend equal angles at the centre.

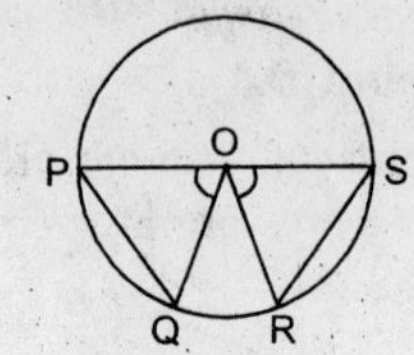


**Given.** A circle such that

Chord PQ = Chord RS

**To prove,** $\angle POQ = \angle ROS$

**Proof.** In $\Delta POQ$ and $\Delta ROS$,

$PQ = RS$

$OP = OS$ = radius

$OQ = OR$ = radius

$\therefore \Delta POQ \cong \Delta ROS$

(By SSS Theorem of congruence)

$\Rightarrow \angle POQ = \angle ROS$ (C.P.C.T.)

$\Rightarrow$ Angles subtended by equal chords are equal.

**Activity,** We draw a circle with centre O and draw an angle AOB, where A and B are the points on the circle. Draw another angle $\angle POQ$ at the centre equal to $\angle AOB$. Separate these two angles AOB and POQ. If we put segment AOB on the segment POQ of the circle, we find that they cover each other.

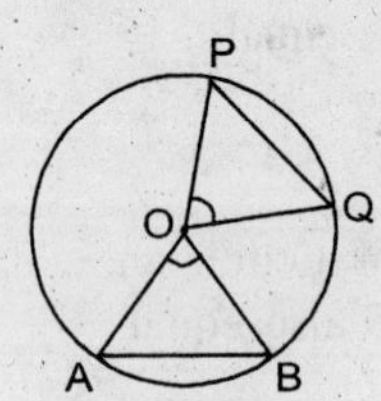


So, $AB = PQ$

Repeat this activity for other equal angles. We find the chords are equal in each case.

**Theorem 2.** If the angles subtended by the two chords at the centre of a circle are equal, then the chords are equal.

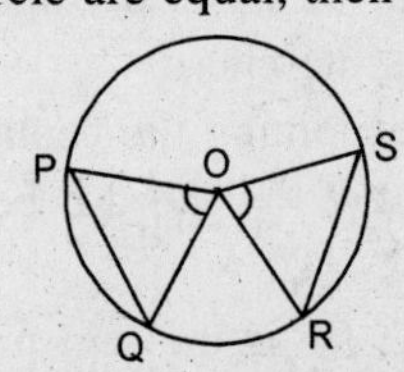


**Given.** Two chords PQ and RS of a circle in which,

$\angle POQ = \angle ROS$; $PQ = RS$

**To prove.**

**Proof.** In $\Delta POQ$ and $\Delta ROS$

$OP = OR$ = radius

$\angle POQ = \angle ROS$

$OQ = OS$ = radius

$\therefore \Delta POQ \cong \Delta ROS$

[By SAS Theorem of congruence]

$\Rightarrow PQ = RS$ (C.P.C.T.)

Hence, Chords are equal.

## EXERCISE

**1.** AB and CD are two parallel chords of a circle such that AB = 5 cm and CD = 11 cm. If distance between them is 3 cm then radius of the circle is

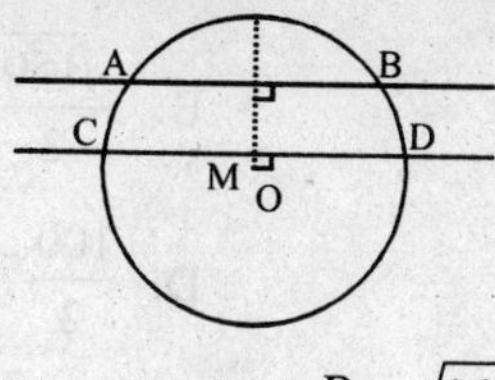

A. $2\sqrt{146}$ cm B. $\sqrt{146}$ cm
C. $\frac{\sqrt{146}}{2}$ cm D. None of these

**2.** The maximum number of common tangents to any pair of circles in the same plane is :
A. 4 B. 5
C. 2 D. 3

**3.** Find the length of a chord which is at a distance of 3 cm from the centre of a circle of radius 5 cm.
A. 2 cm B. 6 cm
C. 8 cm D. 10 cm

**4.** If AB and AC are two chords of a circle of radius 5 cm such that AB = AC = $4\sqrt{5}$ cm then the length of the chord BC is :
A. 8 cm B. 8.4 cm
C. 9 cm D. None of these

**5.** In the given figure AB is the diameter of the circle, PM bisects ∠APB then the measure of ∠ABM is :

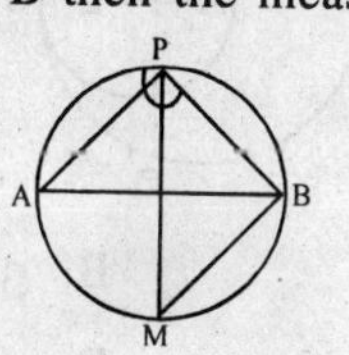

A. 45° B. 30°
C. 15° D. 60°

**6.** Determine the value of $x$ in the figure given below.

A. 53° B. 106°
C. 26.5° D. 100°

**7.** Determine the value of $x$ in the figure given below.

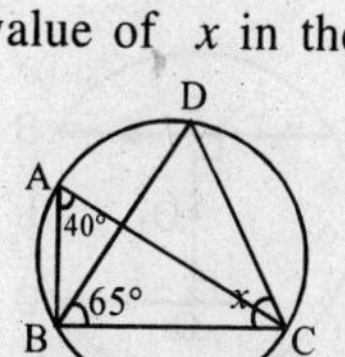

A. 40° B. 75°
C. 65° D. 105°

**8.** Determine the value of $x$ in the figure given below.

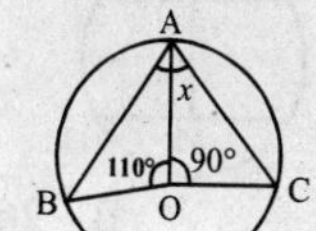

A. 80° B. 100°
C. 90° D. 110°

**9.** PQ is a diameter and PQRS is a cyclic quadrilateral. If ∠PSR = 150°, then measure of ∠RPQ is :

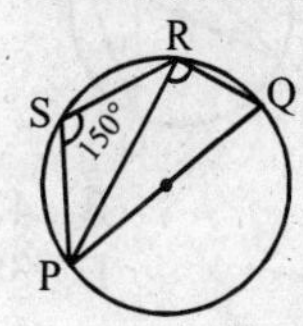

A. 90° B. 60°
C. 30° D. None of these

**10.** Determine the value of $x$ in the figure given below.

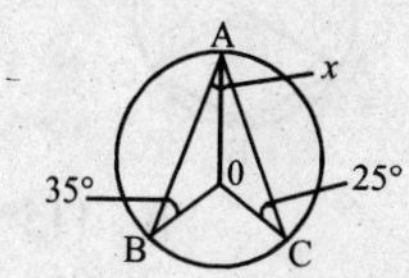

A. 35° B. 25°
C. 30° D. 60°

**11.** Determine the value of $x$ in the figure given below.

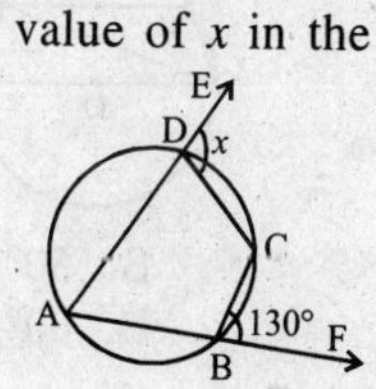

A. 65° B. 60°
C. 50° D. 80°

**12.** Chords AB and CD of a circle meet inside the circle at D. If PA = 4 cm, AB = 7 cm and PD = 6 cm then length of CD is :

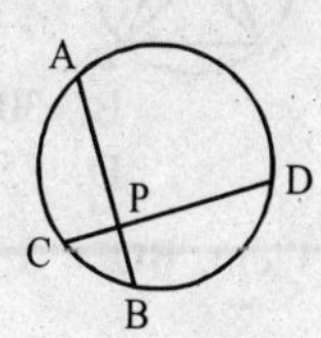

A. 8 cm B. 6 cm
C. 2 cm D. None of these

**13.** Chords AB and CD of a circle when product meet out side the circle at P, If AB = 4 cm; BP = 3 cm and CP = 14 cm then the length of CD is

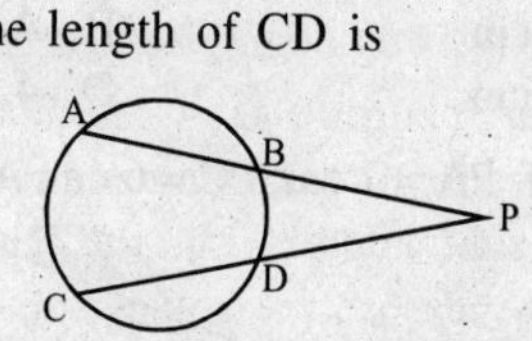

A. 3 cm B. 4.5 cm
C. 6 cm D. None of these

**14.** AB and CD are two parallel chords of circle such that AB = 10 cm and CD = 24 cm. If LM = 17 cm then the diameter of the circle is

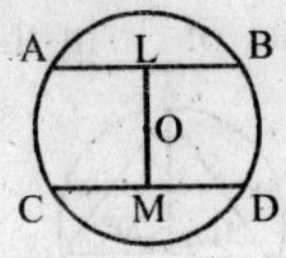


A. 13 cm  B. 26 cm
C. 14 cm  D. None of these

**15.** In the given figure determine the value of $x$.

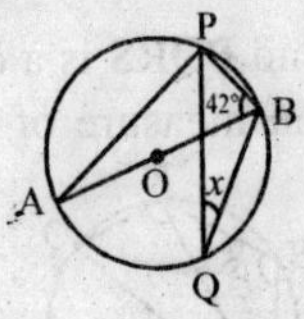


A. 48°  B. 42°
C. 60°  D. 38°

**16.** In the given figure determine the value of $x$.

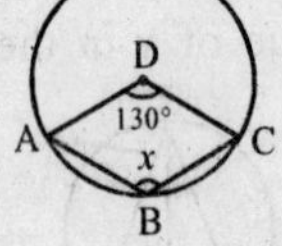


A. 90°  B. 115°
C. 130°  D. 65°

**17.** Find $x$

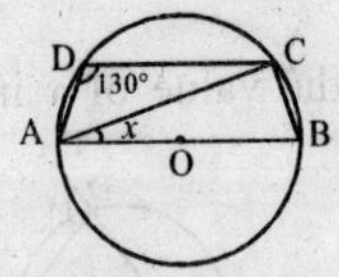


A. 40°  B. 50°
C. 30°  D. 60°

**18.** If O is the centre of the circle and ΔAOB is an equilateral triangle, then the measure of ΔACB is

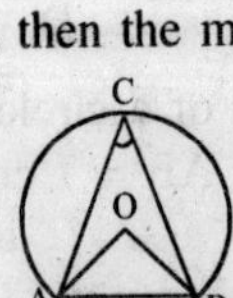


A. 60°  B. 30°
C. 90°  D. 75°

**19.** Find $x$ if AO = 8.1 cm, BO = 5 cm, OC = 9 cm and OD = $x$ cm.

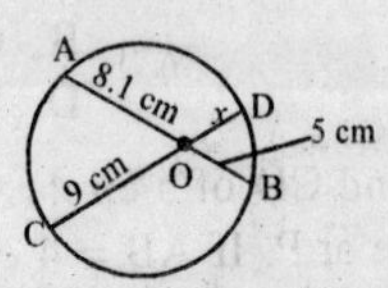


A. 4.1 cm  B. 4.1 cm
C. 4.2 cm  D. 4.5 cm

**20.** Find $x$ if PA = 7 cm, PC = 6 cm, AB = 9 cm and CD = $x$

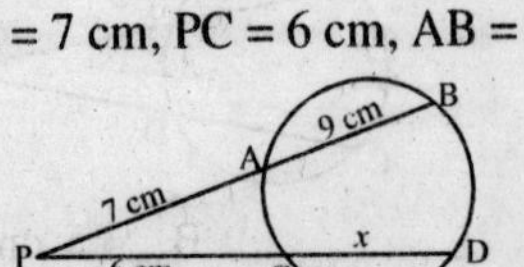


A. 12.0 cm  B. 12.6 cm
C. 12.66 cm  D. 12.67 cm

**21.** Two chords AB, CD of lengths 5 cm, 11 cm respectively of a circle are parallel. If the distance between AB and CD is 3 cm, find the radius of the circle.

A. $\frac{\sqrt{146}}{2}$  B. $\frac{\sqrt{150}}{2}$

C. $\frac{150}{3}$  D. $\frac{100}{2}$

**22.** O is the centre of the circle of radius 5 cm, OP ⊥ AB, OQ ⊥ CD, AB ∥ CD, AB = 6 cm and CD = 8 cm. Determine PQ.

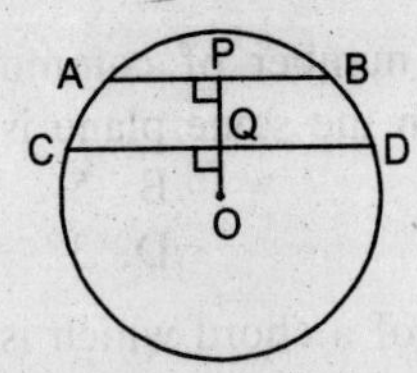


A. 5 cm  B. 10 cm
C. 1 cm  D. 2 cm

**23.** Two circle with centres A and B and of radii 5 cm and 3 cm, respectively touch each other internally. If the perpendicular bisector of segment AB meets the bigger circle in P and Q. Find the length of PQ.

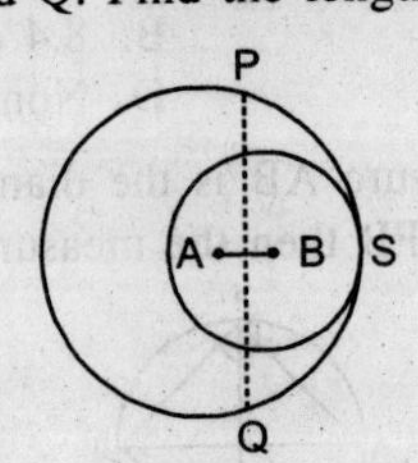


A. $4\sqrt{6}$ cm  B. $3\sqrt{2}$ cm
C. $5\sqrt{4}$ cm  D. $3\sqrt{5}$ cm

**24.** AB and CD are two parallel chords of a circle, which are an opposite sides of the centre, such that AB = 10 cm, CD = 24 cm and the distance between AB and CD is 17 cm. Find the radius of the circle.

A. 15 cm  B. 13 cm
C. 14 cm  D. 20 cm

**25.** O is the centre of the circle with radius 5 cm. OP ⊥ AB, OQ ⊥ CD, AB ∥ CD, AB = 8 cm and CD = 6 cm. Determine PQ.

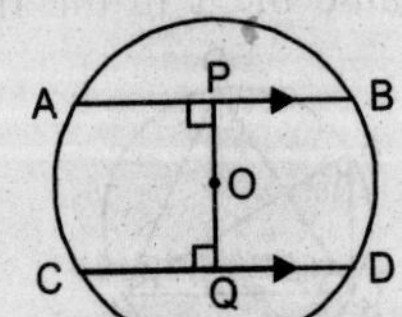


A. 3 cm  B. 4 cm
C. 5 cm  D. 7 cm

## ANSWERS

| 1 | 2 | 3 | 4 | 5 | 6 | 7 | 8 | 9 | 10 |
|---|---|---|---|---|---|---|---|---|---|
| C | A | C | A | A | A | B | A | B | D |
| **11** | **12** | **13** | **14** | **15** | **16** | **17** | **18** | **19** | **20** |
| C | A | D | B | A | B | A | B | D | C |
| **21** | **22** | **23** | **24** | **25** | | | | | |
| A | C | A | B | D | | | | | |

## EXPLANATORY ANSWERS

**1.** Let OM = $x$

Then $x^2+\left(\frac{11}{2}\right)^2=r^2$ and $(x+3)^2+\left(\frac{5}{2}\right)^2=r^2$

Then, $x^2+6x+9+\frac{25}{4}=x^2+\frac{121}{4}$

$\Rightarrow$ $6x = 15 \Rightarrow x = 2.5$ cm

Thus, $r^2=(2.5)^2+\frac{121}{4}=\frac{146}{4} \Rightarrow r=\frac{\sqrt{146}}{2}$ cm

**3.** Length of chord = $2.\sqrt{5^2-3^2}=8$ cm.

**4.** Let OP = $x$ and BP = $y$

Then $x^2+y^2=25$ and $(5+x)^2+y^2=80$

Solving these two, we get, $y$ = BP = 4 cm

Thus, BC = 8 cm.

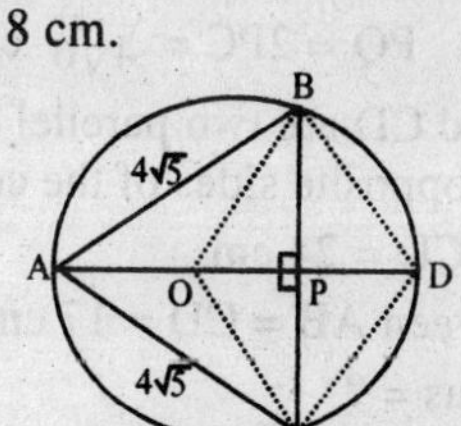


**5.** $\angle ABM=\angle APM=\frac{1}{2}\angle APB=\frac{1}{2}\times 90°=45°$

**6.** As angle in the same segment are equal.

$x = 53°$

**7.** $x+65°+40°=180°$

$x = 75°$

**8.** $x=\frac{1}{2}[(180°-110°)+(180°-90°)]$

$=\frac{1}{2}(70°+90°)=80°$

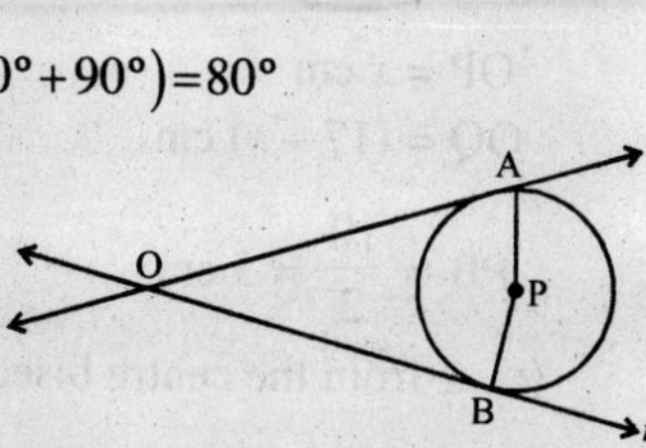


Let P be the centre of a circle touching $l$ and $m$. Clearly, AP = BP.

Hence, P lies on angle bisector of $\angle$ AOB. Hence, locus of P will be the angle bisectors of the angles formed by these intersecting lines.

**9.** $\angle PQR=180°-150°=30°$

$\angle PRQ=90°$ (Angle of a semicircle)

$\angle RPQ+90°+30°=180°$

$\Rightarrow \angle RPQ=60°$

**10.** $\angle OAB=\angle OBA(\because OA=OB)$

$\angle OAB=35°$

Similarly, $\angle AOC=25°$

$\therefore\ \angle x=35°+25°=60°$

**12.** Use $PA\times PB=PC\times PD$

4 × (7 – 4) = 6 × PC

$\Rightarrow$ PC = 2 cm

CD = PC + PD = 2 + 6 = 8 cm.

**13.** Use $PA\times PB=PC\times PD$

$\Rightarrow (4+3)\times 3=14\times PD \Rightarrow PD=1.5$ cm

$\Rightarrow CD=PC-PD=14-1.5=12.5$ cm.

**14.** Let OL = $x$.

Then $OM(17-x)$

Also LB = 5 cm,

MD = 12 cm.

Then $x^2+25=r^2$ and $(17-x)^2+144=r^2$

Solving these we get

$x$ = 12 cm and $r$ = 13 cm

Thus, diameter = 2 × 13 = 26 cm.

**15.** $x+42°+90°=180° \Rightarrow x=48°$

**18.** $\angle ACB=\frac{1}{2}\angle AOB=\frac{1}{2}\times 60°=30°$

**21.** Given, chord AB = 5 cm, chord CD = 11 cm and AB ∥ CD

Perpendicular distance ML between AB and CD = 3 cm

To find. Radius of the circle.

Construction, Join OB, OD and draw perpendicular bisectors OL of AB and OM of CD

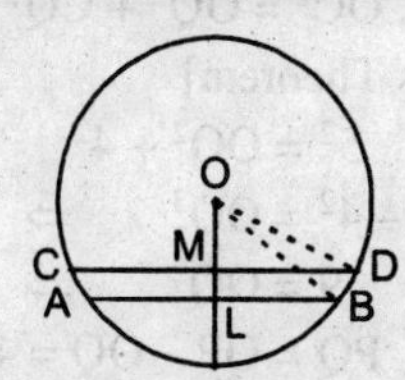

Procedure. In rt. $\Delta OMD$,

$$OD^2 = MD^2 + OM^2$$

(By Pythagoras Theorem)

Let, $OM = x$ cm

$$\therefore \quad r^2 = \left(\frac{11}{2}\right)^2 + x^2 \quad ...(1)$$

And In rt. $\Delta OLB$, $OB^2 = BL^2 + OL^2$

$$\Rightarrow \quad r^2 = \left(\frac{5}{2}\right)^2 + (3+x)^2 \quad ...(2)$$

From (1) and (2), we get,

$$r^2 = \left(\frac{11}{2}\right)^2 + x^2 = \left(\frac{5}{2}\right)^2 + (3+x)^2$$

$$\Rightarrow \quad \frac{121}{4} + x^2 = \frac{25}{4} + 9 + x^2 + 6x$$

$$\Rightarrow \quad x^2 - x^2 + 6x = \frac{121}{4} - \frac{25}{4} - 9$$

$$\Rightarrow \quad 6x = \frac{121 - 25 - 36}{4} = \frac{60}{4} = 15$$

$$\Rightarrow \quad x = \frac{15}{6} \text{ cm} = \frac{5}{2} \text{ cm}$$

From (1), $$r^2 = \left(\frac{11}{2}\right)^2 + \left(\frac{5}{2}\right)^2 = \frac{121+25}{4} = \frac{146}{4}$$

or $$r = \frac{\sqrt{146}}{2} \text{ cm.}$$

**22.** Given. A circle with centre O, such that chord AB = 6 cm, chord CD = 8 cm

AB || CD and radius of the circle = 5 cm

OP ⊥ AB and OQ ⊥ CD

To find. PQ

Construction. Join OA and OC

Procedure. AP = 1/2, AB = 3 cm, CQ = 1/2, CD = 4 cm

[Perpendicular from the centre of the circle bisects the chord]

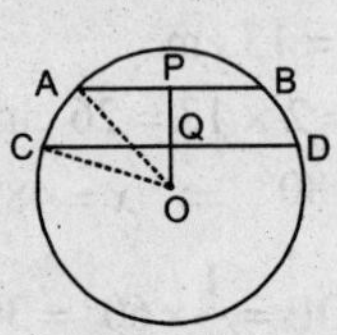


In right Δ OPA, $OA^2 = OP^2 + AP^2$

[By Pythagoras Theorem]

$$\Rightarrow \quad 5^2 = OP^2 + 3^2$$

$$\Rightarrow \quad 5^2 - 3^2 = OP^2 \quad \Rightarrow \quad 25 - 9 = OP^2$$

$$\Rightarrow \quad 16 = OP^2 \quad \Rightarrow \quad 4 = OP$$

In right $\Delta OQC$, $OC^2 = OQ^2 + CQ^2$

[By Pythagoras Theorem]

$$5^2 = OQ^2 + 4^2$$

$$\Rightarrow \quad 5^2 - 4^2 = OQ^2 \quad \Rightarrow \quad 25 - 16 = OQ^2$$

$$\Rightarrow \quad 9 = OQ^2 \quad \Rightarrow \quad 3 = OQ$$

$$\therefore \quad PQ = OP - OQ = 4 - 3 = 1 \text{ cm.}$$

**23.** Given. Two circles touch internally at S, A and B be the centres of the bigger and smaller circles, respectively. The perpendicular bisector PQ bisects AB and meets the circle at P and Q.

To find PQ

Construction. Join PA, ABS

Procedure. With given radii, we find

AS = 5 cm

BS = 3 cm

AB = 5 – 3 = 2 cm and AC = 1 cm

[⊥ bisector bisects the chord]

PA = radius of bigger circle = 5 cm

In the right triangle ACP,

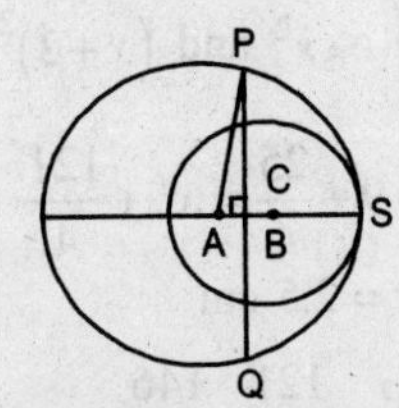


$$PC^2 = PA^2 - AC^2$$

[By Pythagoras Theorem]

$$\Rightarrow \quad PC^2 = (5)^2 - (1)^2$$

$$\Rightarrow \quad PC^2 = 25 - 1 = 24$$

$$\Rightarrow \quad PC = \sqrt{24} \Rightarrow PC = 2\sqrt{6}$$

$$\therefore \quad PQ = 2PC = 4\sqrt{6} \text{ cm.}$$

**24.** Given, AB and CD are two parellel chords of a circle, which are on opposite sides of the centre.

AB = 10 cm, CD = 24 cm

Distance between AB = CD = 17 cm

To find. Radius = ?

Construction. Draw OP ⊥ AB and OQ ⊥ CD. Join OB and OD.

Procedure. Since AB || CD and OP ⊥ AB, OQ ⊥ CD

∴ Points P, O and Q are collinear.

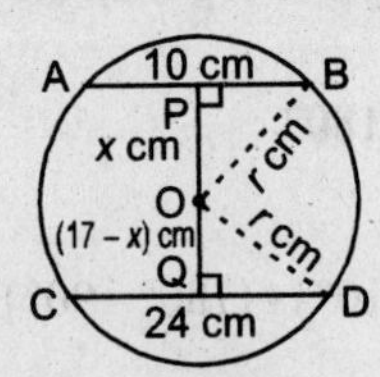


Let, $OP = x$ cm

Then, $OQ = (17 - x)$ cm

$$PB = \frac{10}{2} = 5 \text{ cm}$$

(∵ ⊥ from the centre bisects the chord)

$$QD = \frac{24}{2} = 12 \text{ cm}$$

(∵ ⊥ from the centre bisects the chord)

In rt. ΔOPB, $r^2 = x^2 + 5^2$ ...(1)

(By Pythagoras Theorem)

In rt. $\Delta OQD$, $r^2 = (17 - x)^2 + 12^2$ ...(2)

From (1) and (2), we have

$$x^2 + 25 = (17 - x)^2 + 12^2$$

$$\Rightarrow x^2 + 25 = 289 + x^2 - 34x + 144$$

$$\Rightarrow x^2 - x^2 + 34x = 289 + 144 - 25$$

$$\Rightarrow 34x = 408$$

$$\Rightarrow x = 12 \text{ cm}$$

Using the value of $x$ in (1), we get,

$$r^2 = 12^2 + 5^2 = 144 + 25 = 169$$

$\therefore$ Radius, $r = 13$ cm. ($\because$ radius can't be –ve)

**25.** Given, AB and CD are two parallel chords. AB = 8 cm, CD = 6 cm, radius = 5 cm.

To find. PQ

Construction. Join OA, OC, where O is the centre of the circle

Procedure. AP = PB = 4 cm ...[$\because$ AB = 8 cm]

CQ = QD = 3 cm ...[$\because$ CD = 6 cm]

[$\because \perp$ from the centre of a circle on any chord of the circle bisects it]

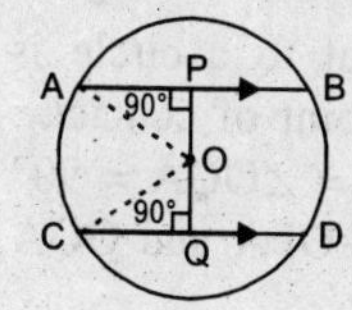


In rt. $\Delta OAP$, OA = OC = radii of the circle = 5 cm

$OP^2 = OA^2 - AP^2$ [By Pythagoras Theorem]

$= (5)^2 - (4)^2 = 25 - 16 = 9$

$\Rightarrow$ OP = 3

In rt. $\Delta OCQ$, $OQ^2 = OC^2 - CQ^2$ [By Pythagoras Theorem]

$(5)^2 - (3)^2 = 25 - 9 = 16$

$\Rightarrow$ OQ = 4

$\therefore$ PQ = PO + OQ = 3 + 4 = 7 cm.

# Tangent

### Secant

A line which interesects a circle in two distinct points is called a **secant** of the circle. In the fig. the line $l$ intersects the circle in two distinct points A and B. The line $l$ is a secant to the circle.

### Tangent

A tangent to a circle is a line that intersects the circle at exactly one point. The point at which it meets the circle is called its point of contact and the line (tangent) is said to touch the circle at this point. In the figure, the line $l$ meets the circle at only point A. Here A is the point of contact.

## Some Important theorems on tangent

**Theorem 1:** *A tangent to a circle is perpendicular to the radius throught the point of contact.*

**Given:** A tangent AB to a circle C(O, $r$) with the point P as its point of contact.

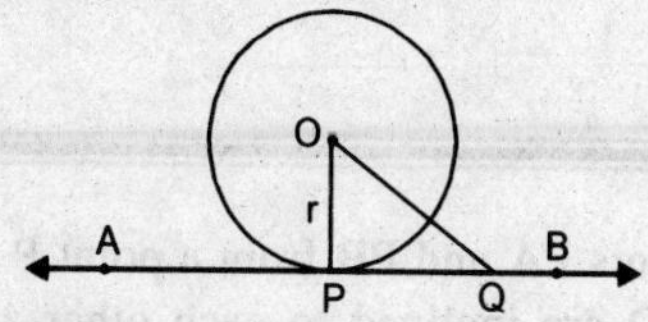


**To prove:** OP $\perp$ AB.

**Construction:** Let Q be any point other that P, an AB. join OQ.

**Proof:** $\because$ Q is a point on the tangent AB other than the point of contact P.

$\therefore$ Q lies in the exterior of the circle.

$\therefore$ OQ > OP

i.e., OP < OQ

Thus, of all the segments that can be drawn from the centre O to any point on the line AB, OP is the shortest.

We know that the shortest segment that can be drawn from a given point to a given line perpendicular from the given point to the given line.

Hence OP $\perp$ AB.

**Theorem 2: (Converse of theorem 1)**

*A line drawn through the end of a radius and perpendicular on it is tangent to the circle.*

**Given:** A radius OP of a circle C(O, $r$) and a line APB perpendicular to OP.

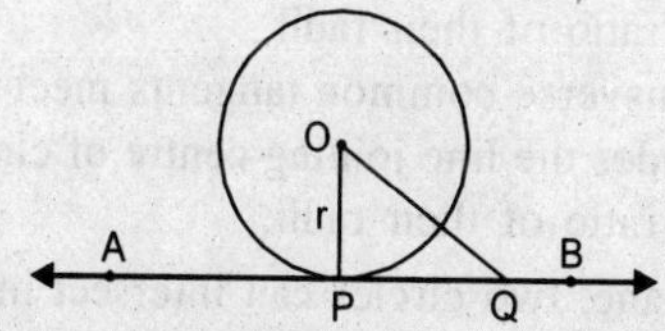


**To prove:** AB is the tangent to the circle at A.

**Proof:** Take a point Q, different from P, on line AB, since OP $\perp$ AB, OQ > OP.

$\therefore$ The point Q lies outside the circle (since OP is the shortest line segment from O to AB).

Thus every point on the line AB, other P, lies outside the circle and therefore AB meets the circle only at the point P. Hence AB is a tangent to the circle.

**Theorem 3:** *The lengths of the two tangents drawn from an external point to a circle are equal.*

**Given:** A is an external point to the circle C(O, r). AP and AQ are two tangent segments from A to the circle.

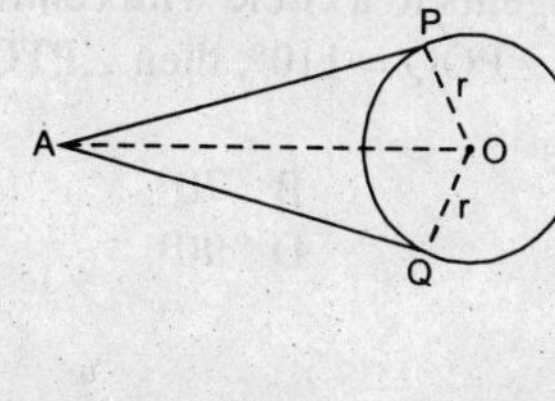

**To prove:** AP = AQ.

**Construction:** Draw line segments AP, OP and OQ.

**Proof:** A tangent to a circle is perpendicular to the radius through the point of contact.

$\therefore$ $\angle OPA = \angle OQA = 90°$

Now in right $\Delta$s OPA and OQA,

OP = OQ [each = r]

OA = OA [common]

$\therefore$ $\Delta OPA \cong \Delta OQA$ [by RHS congruence rule]

$\therefore$ AP = AQ [c.p.c.t.c.]

## Common Tangents to Two circles

(*i*) Where the two circles neither intersect nor touch each other, there are FOUR common tangents, two of them are transverse & the others are direct common tangents.

(*ii*) When they intersect there are two common tangents, both of them being direct.

(*iii*) When they touch each other:

(*a*) **Externally:** there are three common tangents, two direct and one is the tangent at the point of contact.

(*b*) **Internally:** only one common tangent possible at their point of contact.

(*iv*) Length of an external common tangent & internal common tangent to the two circles is given by:

$$L_{ext} = \sqrt{d^2 - (r_1 - r_2)^2} \ \& \ L_{int} = \sqrt{d^2 - (r_1 + r_2)^2}$$

Where $d$ = distance between the centres of the two circles. $r_1$ & $r_2$ are the radii of the two circles.

(*v*) The direct common tangents meet at a point which divides the line joining centre of circles externally in the ratio of their radii.

Transverse common tangents meet at a point which divides the line joining centre of circles internally in the ratio of their radii.

In a plane, two circles can intersect in two points, one point, or no points. Coplanar circles that intersect in one point are called **tangent circles.** Coplanar circles that have a common center are called **concentric.**

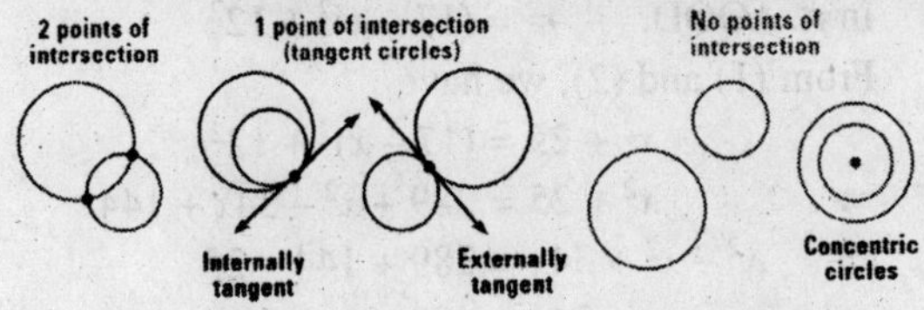


A line or segment that is tangent to two coplanar circles is called a **common tangent.** A *common internal tangent* intersects the segment that joins the centers of the two circles. A *common external tangent* does not intersect the segment that joins the centers of the two circles.

**Example:** Tell whether the common tangents are internal or external.

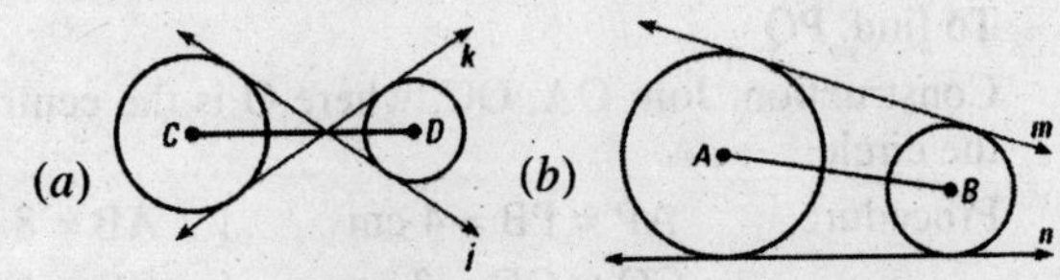


***Solution:*** (*a*) The lines *j* and *k* intersect $\overline{CD}$, so they are common internal tangents.

(*b*) The lines m and n do not intersect $\overline{AB}$, so they are common external tangents.

In a plane, the **interior of a circle** consists of the points that are inside the circle. The **exterior of a circle** consists of the points that are outside the circle.

**Example:** Give the center and the radius of each circle. Describe the intersection of the two circles and describe all common tangents.

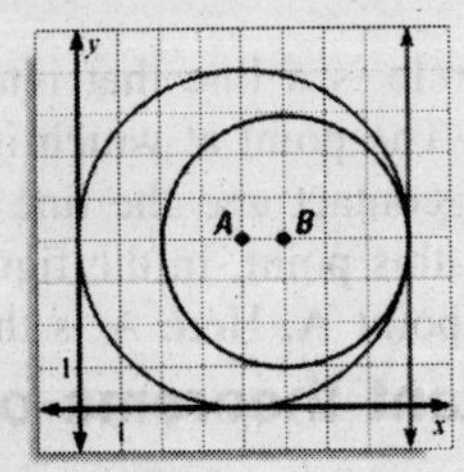


***Solution:*** The center of $\odot$A is A(4, 4) and its radius is 4. The center of $\odot$B is B(5, 4) and its radius is 3. The two circles have only one point of intersection. It is the point (8, 4). The vertical line x = 8 is the only common tangent of the two circles.

## EXERCISE

1. From a point Q, the length of the tangent to a circle is 24 cm and the distance from the centre is 25 cm. The radius of the circle is

A. 7 cm  B. 12 cm
C. 15 cm  D. 24.5 cm

2. In the given figure, if TP and TQ are the two tangents to a circle with centre O and that $\angle POQ = 110°$, then $\angle PTQ$ is equal to

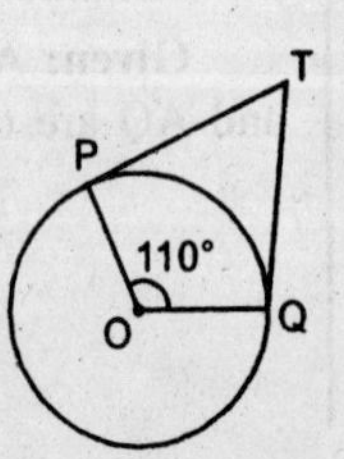


A. 60°  B. 70°
C. 80°  D. 90°

3. If tangents PA and PB from a point P to a circle with centre O are inclined to each other at angle of 80°, then $\angle POA$ is equal to

A. 50°  B. 60°
C. 70°  D. 80°

4. In Fig., a circle touches all the four sides of a quadrilateral ABCD whose sides AB = 6 cm, BC = 7 cm and CD = 4 cm. Find AD

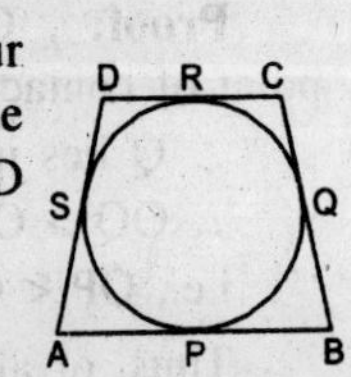


A. 2 cm  B. 5 cm
C. 3 cm  D. 4 cm

**5.** If AB, AC, PQ are tangents in the figure and AB = 5 cm. The perimeter of $\Delta APQ$ is

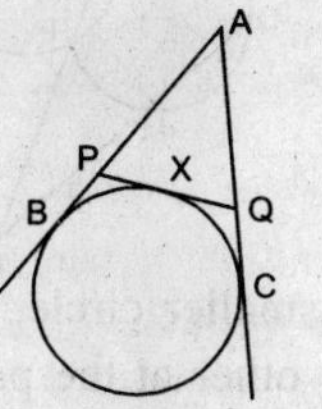


A. 8 cm  B. 6 cm
C. 10 cm  D. 5 cm

**6.** In Fig., a circle is inscribed within a quadrilateral ABCD. Given that BC = 38 cm, BQ = 27 cm and DC = 25 cm and that AD is perpendicular to DC. The radius of the circle is

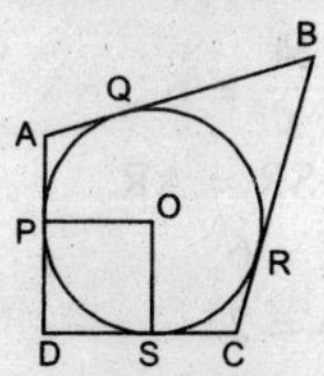


A. 10 cm  B. 14 cm
C. 8 cm  D. 12 cm

**7.** Two tangents are drawn to a circle from an external point A, touching the circle at the points P and Q. A third tangent intersects segment AP at B and segment AQ at C and touches the circle at R. If AQ = 10 units, then the perimeter of $\Delta ABC$ (in units) is

A. 22.0  B. 20.5
C. 20.0  D. 40.0

**8.** In Fig., two circles intersect each other at points P and Q. From A on line PQ, secant AMD for one circle and secant ASR for the second one are drawn. If AM = 3, MD = 5 and AS = 4, determine SR.

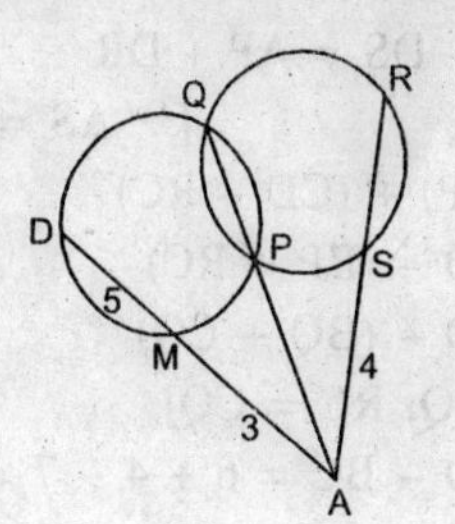


A. 2 cm  B. 4 cm
C. 3 cm  D. 1 cm

**9.** In the figure, KLMN is a cyclic quadrilateral and PQ is a tangent to the circle at K. If LN is a diameter of the circle. $\angle KLN = 30°$ and $\angle MNL = 60°$. Determine $\angle QKN$

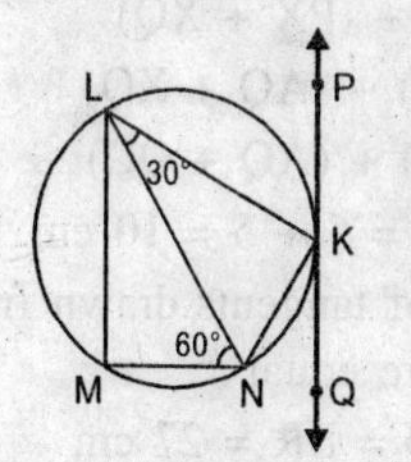


A. 30°  B. 60°
C. 90°  D. 100°

**10.** In the given Fig., PQ is tangent and O is the centre of the circle. Find EP is OP = 21, OQ = 9 and OM $\sqrt{80}$.

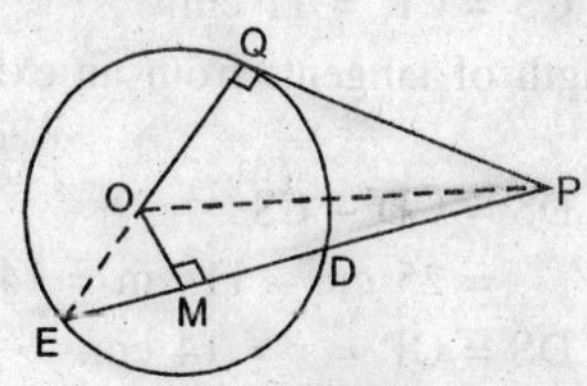


A. 10  B. 20
C. 30  D. 40

## ANSWERS

| 1 | 2 | 3 | 4 | 5 | 6 | 7 | 8 | 9 | 10 |
|---|---|---|---|---|---|---|---|---|---|
| A | B | A | C | C | B | C | A | A | B |

## EXPLANATORY ANSWERS

**1.** In rt. $\angle d$ $\Delta OTQ$,

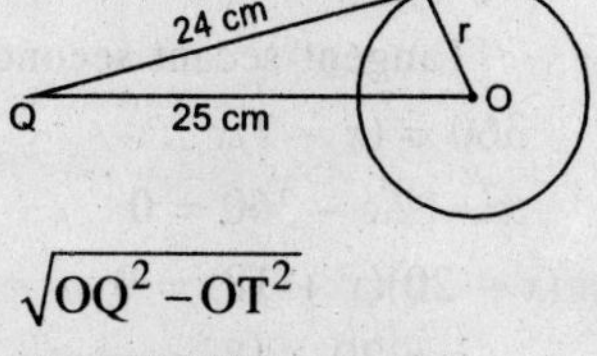


$$OT = \sqrt{OQ^2 - OT^2}$$

$$= \sqrt{25^2 - 24^2} = \sqrt{625 - 576} = \sqrt{49} = 7 \text{ cm.}$$

**2.** Since $\angle POQ + \angle PTQ = 180°$

$[\because \angle OPT = 90°, \angle OQT = 90°]$

$\Rightarrow$ $110° + \angle PTQ = 180°$

$\Rightarrow$ $\angle PTQ = 180° - 110° = 70°.$

**3.** Since $\angle APB = 80°$

$\angle AOB = 180° - 80° = 100°$

$\angle PAO = \angle PBO = 90°$

Since OP bisects $\angle AOB$

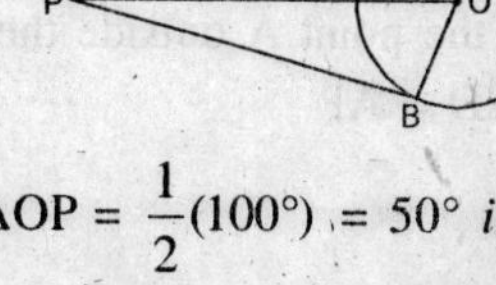


$$\angle AOP = \frac{1}{2}(100°) = 50° \text{ i.e. } \angle POA = 50°.$$

**4.** AD = AS + DS = AP + DR

[∵ AS = AP and DS = DR]

= (AB – BP) + (CD – RC)

= AB + CD – (BP + RC)

= AB + CD – (BQ + CQ)

[∵ BP = BQ, RC = CQ]

= AB + CD – BC = 6 + 4 – 7 = 3 cm.

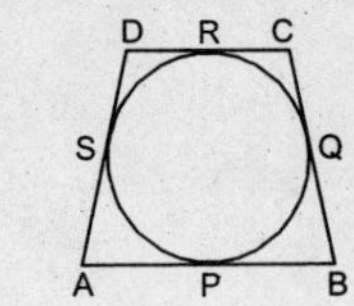


**5.** Since AB and AC are the tangents from the same point A

∴ AB = AC = 5 cm

Similarly, BP = PX and XQ = QC

Perimeter of ΔAPQ

= AP + AQ + PQ

= AP + AQ + (PX + XQ)

= (AP + PX) + (AQ + XQ)

= (AP + BP) + (AQ + QC)

= AB + AC = 5 + 5 = 10 cm.

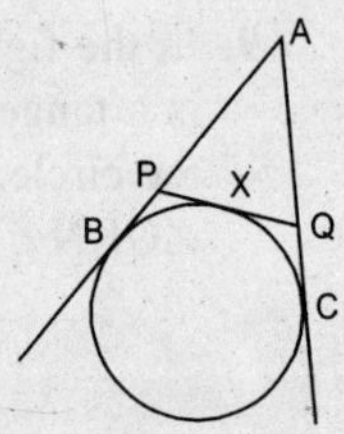


**6.** ∵ Lengths of tangents drawn from an external point to a circle are equal

∴ BQ = BR = 27 cm

Let $x$ be the radius of the circle

∴ OP = OS = PD = $x$

CR = BC – BR

= 38 – 27 = 11 cm

Now CS = CR = 11 cm

[∵ Length of tangents from an external point to a circle are equal]

∴ DS = CD – CS

= 25 cm – 11 cm = 14 cm

But DS = OP = $x$ = 14 cm.

Hence radius = OP = 14 cm.

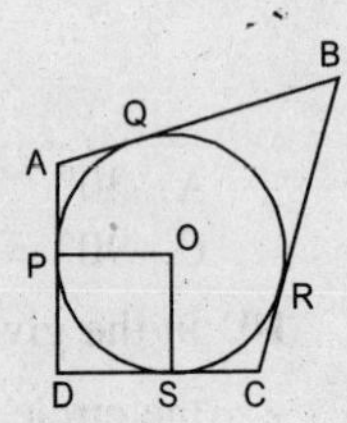


**7.** Since the tangents to a circle from an external point are equal in length

AP = AQ = 10 units

and BP = BR, CQ = CR

Adding these, we get,

BP + CQ = BR + CR = BC

Adding AB and AC to both sides, we get

BP + CQ + AB + AC = BC + AB + AC

⇒ (BP + AB) + (CQ + AC) = AB + BC + AC

⇒ AP + AQ = Perimeter of ΔABC

⇒ (10 + 10) units = Perimeter of ΔABC

∴ Perimeter of ΔABC = 20 units.

∴ (*iii*) is the correct answer.

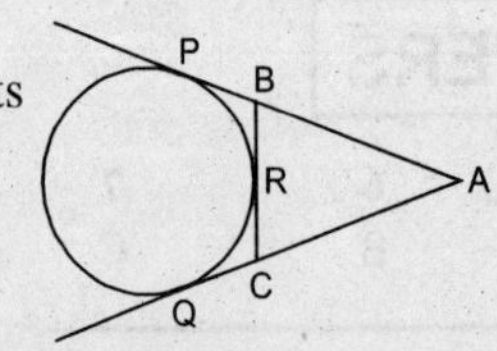


**8.** In the larger circle, chord QP and chord DM intersect each other at the point A outside the circle

∴ AM × AD = AP ...(1)

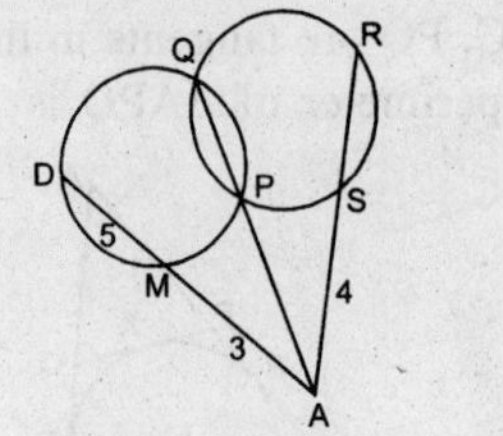


Again in the smaller circle, chord QP and chord RS intersect each other at the point A outside the circle.

∴ AS × AR = AP × AQ ...(2)

∴ AM × AD = AS × AR ...(3)

[From (1) and (2)]

Now AD = AM + MD

= 3 + 5 = 8

∴ From (3), 3 × 8 = 4 × AR

⇒ $AR = \frac{24}{4} = 6$

But AS + SR = AR

∴ 4 + SR = 6,

SR = 6 – 4 = 2.

**9.** KN is a chord through the point of contact K.

∴ ∠QKN = ∠KLN = 30°

[∠s in the alt. segment are equal]

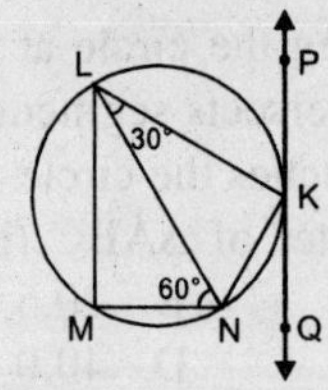


**10.** Join OQ and OE

In ΔOPQ, $m$ ∠OQP = 90°

∴ $OQ^2 + QP^2 = OP^2$ [By Pythagoras Theorem]

⇒ $(9)^2 + QP^2 = (21)^2$

⇒ $QP^2 = (21)^2 - (9)^2 = 360$

In rt. ∠*d* ΔOME,

$OM^2 + EM^2 = OE^2$

⇒ $80 + (EM)^2 = (9)^2$

⇒ $EM^2 = 81 - 80 = 1$

⇒ $EM = +\sqrt{1} = 1$

∴ ED = 2EM = 2 × 1 = 2

Let EP = $x$

Then $PQ^2 = PD \times PE$

[Tangent secant second point theorem]

∴ $360 = (x - 2)x$

⇒ $x^2 - 2x - 360 = 0$

⇒ $(x - 20)(x + 18) = 0$

⇒ $x = 20, -18$

But $x \neq -18$

Hence EP = 20.

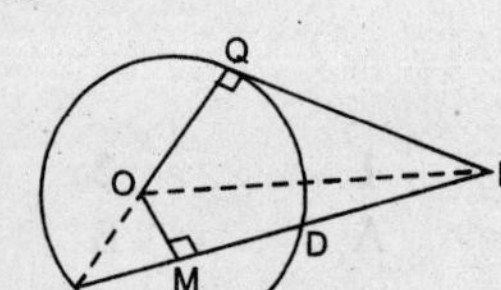


●●●

CHAPTER 11

# Mensuration

## Triangle, Quadrilaterals, Regular Polygons

In mensuration we often have to deal with the problem of finding the areas and perimeters of plane figures.

### Triangle

1. Perimeter = 3 × side

2. Area = $\frac{1}{2} \times \text{base} \times \text{height}$, or

Area = $\sqrt{s(s-a)(s-b)(s-c)}$

where $a$, $b$, $c$, are the lengths of the sides of triangle and $s = \frac{a+b+c}{2}$

**Right Angled Triangle :** It is one where one of the angles is right angle, i.e., 90°.

1. $(\text{Hypotenuse})^2 = (\text{Perpendicular})^2 + (\text{Base})^2$

2. Area = $\frac{1}{2} \times \text{Base} \times \text{Perpendicular}$

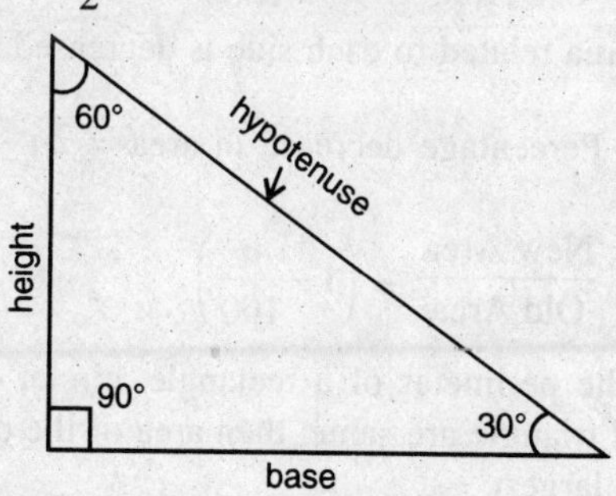


**N.B. :** 30-60-90 triangle is a special case of right angled triangle, where the three angles are equal to 30°, 60° and 90°.

Here,

3. Side opposite to the angle 30°

$= \frac{1}{2} \times \text{Hypotenuse}$

4. Side opposite to the angle 60°

$= \frac{\sqrt{3}}{2} \times \text{Hypotenuse}$

**Equilateral Triangle :** All three sides are equal in length and all three angles are equal to 60°

1. Area = $\frac{\sqrt{3}}{4} \times (\text{Side})^2$  2. Area = $\frac{(\text{Height})^2}{\sqrt{3}}$

3. Height = $\frac{\sqrt{3}}{2} \times \text{side}$  4. Perimeter = 3 × side

**Isosceles Triangle :** Two sides are equal in lengths.

1. Area = $\frac{b}{4}\sqrt{4a^2 - b^2}$

where $a$ = lengths of opposite sides

$b$ = length of unequal side

2. In an isosceles right triangle,

(*a*) Hypotenuse = $\sqrt{2} \times \text{congruent side (a)}$

(*b*) Area = $\frac{1}{2} \times a^2$

(*c*) Perimeter = $\sqrt{2} \times a(\sqrt{2}+1)$

### Quadrilaterals

**Rectangle:**

1. Area = length($l$) × breadth($b$)
2. Perimeter = $2(l + b)$
3. Diagonal = $\sqrt{l^2 + b^2}$
4. Area of the path (inside of the rectangle) $= 2x\ (l + b - 2x)$

   where, $x$ is the width of path.
5. Area of the path (Outside of the rectangle) = $2x\ (l + b + 2x)$

**Square:**

1. Area = $(\text{Side})^2$
2. Perimeter = 4 × side
3. Diagonal = side × $\sqrt{2}$
4. Area of path (outside of square) = $4x \times (a + x)$ [where $a$ = side, $x$ = width of path]
5. Area of path (inside of square) = $4x \times (a - x)$

**Parallelogram:** In parallelogram opposite sides are parallel and equal. The two diagonals are not always equal but they bisect each other at the point of intersection.

Area = Base × Height.

**Trapezium :** It is a quadrilateral whose one pair of opposite sides is parallel. Other two opposite sides are oblique.

1. Area = $\frac{1}{2} \times \text{Height} \times (\text{Sum of parallel sides})$. Here, height is the distance between the two parallel sides.
2. Median = $\left(\frac{1}{2} \times \text{Sum of parallel side}\right)$. Here, median is the segment joining the midpoints of oblique sides.
3. Height = $\frac{2}{K}\sqrt{s(s-k)(s-c)(s-d)}$ (where $k = a - b$, *i.e.*, the difference between the parallel sides and $c$ and $d$ are the two non-parallel sides.)

   Also $s = \frac{k+c+d}{2}$

**Rhombus :** It is parallelogram whose all sides are equal and diagonals are bisect each other at right angle.

1. Area = $\frac{1}{2} \times \text{Product of diagonals}$
2. Side = $\sqrt{\left(\frac{d_1}{2}\right)^2 + \left(\frac{d_2}{2}\right)^2}$, where $d_1$ and $d_2$ are diagonals
3. Perimeter = 4 × side
4. Area of a rhombus (with one side and one diagonal given)

   $= \text{diagonal} \times \sqrt{(\text{side})^2 - \left(\frac{\text{diagonal}}{2}\right)^2}$
5. Other diagonal

   $= 2 \times \sqrt{(\text{side})^2 - \left(\frac{\text{diagonal}}{2}\right)^2}$

**Quadrilateral :** Area = $\frac{1}{2} \times$ One diagonal ×

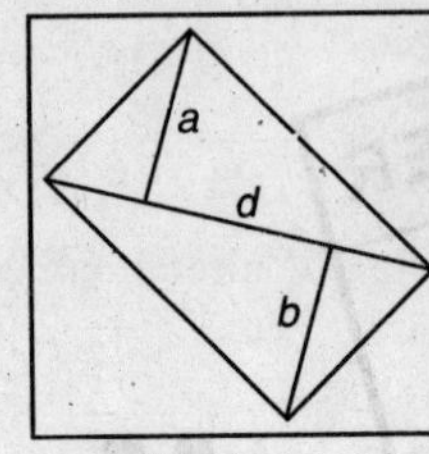


(Sum of perpendicular to it from the opposite vertices)

$= \frac{1}{2} \times d \times (a+b)$

**Circle :**

1. Diameter = 2 × Radius
2. Area = $\pi r^2 = \frac{\pi}{4} d^2$

   [where $d$ = diameter = $\sqrt{\frac{4A}{\pi}}$
3. Circumference = $2\pi r = \pi d$
4. Radius = $\frac{\text{Circumference}}{2\pi} = \frac{\sqrt{\text{Area}}}{\pi}$
5. Length of an Arc = $\frac{\theta}{360°} \times 2\pi r$
6. Area of sector = $\frac{\theta}{360°} \times \pi r^2 = \frac{1}{2} \times \text{Arc} \times r$
7. Area of the ring or circular path = $\pi (R + r)(R - r)$

***Remember some tricks for plane figures.***

(*i*) If area related each side is increased by $a\%$, then

(*a*) Percentage increase in the area $= 2a + \frac{a^2}{100}$

(*b*) $\frac{\text{New Area}}{\text{Old Area}} = \left(1 + \frac{a}{100}\right)^2$

(*ii*) If area related to each side is decreased by $a\%$, then

(*a*) Percentage decrease in area = $2a - \frac{a^2}{100}$

(*b*) $\frac{\text{New Area}}{\text{Old Area}} = \left(1 - \frac{a}{100}\right)^2$

(*iii*) If the perimeter of a rectangle, circle, quadrilateral and triangle are same, then area of the circle will be the largest.

## Polygon

1. Interior angle + Exterior angle = 180°
2. Each interior angle = $\left(\frac{2n-4}{n}\right) \times 90°$ where $n$ = number of sides
3. Sum of Exterior angles = 360°
4. Perimeter = Number of sides × Length of side.

5. For an equilateral triangle of side '$a$' (a) radius of inscribed circle = $\frac{a}{2\sqrt{3}}$ and side of the triangle = $2\sqrt{3}r$, (b) radius of circumcircle = $\frac{a}{\sqrt{3}}$

6. Area of regular polygon = $\frac{1}{2}$(No. of sides) (Radius of the incribed circle)

7. Area of regular hexagon

$= \frac{3\sqrt{3}}{2}(\text{side})^2 = 2.598\ (\text{side})^2$

8. Area of a regular octagon

$= 2\left(\sqrt{2}+1\right)(\text{side})^2 = 4.828\ (\text{side})^2$

9. Area of cyclic quadrilateral A

$= \sqrt{s(s-a)(s-b)(s-c)(s-d)}$

where, $s = \frac{a+b+c+d}{2}$ and,

$\angle A + \angle C = \angle B + \angle D = 180°$

10. For circum-circle, if $a$ is the length of each side of a regular polygon and R is the circum-radius, then

(a) $R = \frac{a}{2}\operatorname{cosec}\left(\frac{180°}{n}\right)$

(b) Area of the polygon = $\frac{1}{4}na^2\cot\left(\frac{180°}{n}\right)$, or

(c) Area of the polygon

$= nR^2\sin\left(\frac{180°}{n}\right)\cos\left(\frac{180°}{n}\right)$

(d) Area of the circum-circle of $n$-sided regular polygon

$= \frac{\pi}{4}a^2\operatorname{cosec}^2\left(\frac{180°}{n}\right)$

11. For in-circle, if $a$ is the length of a side of a regular polygon and $r$ is the radius of the in-circle, then

(a) $r = \frac{a}{2}\cot\left(\frac{180°}{n}\right)$

(b) Area of the polygon = $\pi r^2\cot\left(\frac{180°}{n}\right)$

(c) Area of the in-circle of an $n$-sided regular polygon

$= \frac{\pi}{4}a^2\cot^2\left(\frac{180°}{n}\right)$

(d) Radius of the in-circle of a regular hexagon = $\frac{\sqrt{3}}{4}\times a^2$

(e) Area of the in-circle = $\frac{3}{4}\pi a^2$

## EXERCISE

1. A rectangle measures 50 cm × 25 cm. Its area is
   A. 1150 sq. cm B. 1250 sq. cm
   C. 1275 sq. cm D. 1280 sq. cm

2. A field is in the form of a square whose perimeter is 580 m. Area of this field is
   A. 20025 sq. m B. 20225 sq. m
   C. 30025 sq. m D. 19975 sq. cm

3. Find the area of the square whose each side measures 20 cm.
   A. 300 sq. cm B. 380 sq. cm
   C. 360 sq. cm D. 400 sq. cm

4. Area of a circle is 154 sq. cm. Its circumference will be
   A. 44 cm B. 48 cm
   C. 54 cm D. 68 cm

5. The base and the height of a triangle is 8 cm and 10 cm respectively. Its area will be
   A. 40 sq. cm B. 20 sq. cm
   C. 49 sq. cm D. 64 sq. cm

6. If it is given that the parallel sides of a trapezium are 15 m and 25 m while the distance between them is 10 m. its area will be
   A. 150 sq. m B. 225 sq. m
   C. 200 sq. m D. 270 sq. m

7. Perimeter of a rectangular field is 760 m and its length and breadth are in the ratio 11 : 8. Area of this rectangular field is
   A. 35200 sq. m B. 34700 sq. m
   C. 35600 sq. m D. 45200 sq. m

8. If side of a square is reduced by 50%, its area will be reduced by
   A. 50% B. 75%
   C. 80% D. 60%

9. If area of a square is equal to the area of a rectangle 6.4 m long and 2.5 m wide, then each side of this square measures
   A. 8 m B. 5.4 m
   C. 3.8 m D. 4 m

10. If perimeter of a right angled triangle is six times its smallest side, then the three sides of this triangle are in the ratio of
    A. 13 : 5 : 12 B. 13 : 12 : 5
    C. 12 : 5 : 13 D. 13 : 5 : 10

11. The perimeter of a square is 24 m and that of another is 32 m. Find the perimeter of a third square area of which is equal to sum of the areas of these two squares
    A. 40 m B. 51 m
    C. 37 m D. 42 m

**12.** If each side of a square is doubled, its area will become
A. double B. four times
C. three times D. eight times

**13.** The difference between the areas of two squares is 225 sq. metres and each side of the bigger square is 25 metres. The side of the smaller square is
A. 18 m B. 21 m
C. 20 m D. 22 m

**14.** If the perimeter of an equilateral triangle is 72 cm, its area will be
A. $144\sqrt{3}$ sq. cm B. $142\sqrt{3}$ sq. cm
C. $154\sqrt{2}$ sq. cm D. $144\sqrt{2}$ sq. cm

**15.** The radii of two circles are 5 cm and 12 cm respectively. Find the radius of a circle which is equal in area to these two circles.
A. 15 cm B. 13 cm
C. 10 cm D. 8 cm

**16.** If the circumference of a circle is equal to the perimeter of a square, then their areas are in the ratio of
A. 14 : 11 B. 7 : 8
C. 14 : 13 D. 13 : 11

**17.** Three sides of a triangle are in the ratio of 17 : 15 : 8. If the perimeter of this triangle is 40 m, find its area
A. 50 sq. m B. 49 sq. m
C. 60 sq. m D. 69 sq. m

**18.** If the length of a rectangle is increased by 20% and width is decreased by 15%, then its area
A. decreased by 4% B. increases by 2%
C. decreases by 2% D. increases by 3%

## ANSWERS

| 1 | 2 | 3 | 4 | 5 | 6 | 7 | 8 | 9 | 10 |
|---|---|---|---|---|---|---|---|---|---|
| B | A | D | A | A | C | A | B | D | B |
| 11 | 12 | 13 | 14 | 15 | 16 | 17 | 18 | | |
| A | B | C | A | B | A | C | B | | |

## EXPLANATORY ANSWERS

**1.** Area of the rectangle
$= l \times b = 50 \times 25 = 1250$ sq. cm

**2.** Perimeter of the square = 4 × side
**According to question :**
$4 \times \text{side} = 580 \Rightarrow \text{side} = \frac{580}{4} = 145$ m
$\therefore$ Area = $(\text{side})^2 = (145)^2 = 20025$ sq. m.

**3.** Area of the square = $(\text{side})^2 = (20)^2 = 400$ sq. cm.

**4.** Area of the circle= $\pi r^2$
$\therefore \quad \pi r^2 = 154$
$\Rightarrow \quad r^2 = \frac{154 \times 7}{22}$
$\Rightarrow \quad r^2 = 7 \times 7 \Rightarrow r = 7$ cm
$\therefore$ Circumference of the circle
$= 2\pi r = 2 \times \frac{22}{7} \times 7 = 44$ cm.

**5.** Area of the triangle
$= \frac{1}{2} \times \text{base} \times \text{height} = \frac{1}{2} \times 8 \times 10 = 40$ sq. cm.

**6.** Area of the trapezium
$= \frac{1}{2} \times (\text{sum of the parallel sides}) \times \text{distance between them}$
$= \frac{1}{2} \times (15 + 25) \times 10 = \frac{1}{2} \times 40 \times 10 = 200$ sq. m.

**7.** Suppose length and breadth of the rectangular field are $11x$ m and $8x$ m.
$\therefore$ Perimeter of the field
$= 2(11x + 8x) = 2 \times 19x = 38x$ m.

**According to question :**
Perimeter of the field = 760 m
$\therefore \quad 38x = 760 \Rightarrow x = \frac{760}{38} = 20$
$\therefore$ Length of the field = 11 × 20 = 220 m
Breadth of the field = 8 × 20 = 160 m
$\therefore$ Area of the field = 220 × 160 = 35200 sq.m.

**8.** Suppose side of the square = $x$ m
**In the first case :**
Area of the square = $x^2$ sq. m.
**In the second case :**
On effecting 50% reduction in the side of the square,
Side of the new square = $x - 50\%$ of $x = \frac{x}{2}$ m
$\therefore$ Area of the new square = $\left(\frac{x}{2}\right)^2 = \frac{x^2}{4}$ sq.m.
$\therefore$ Reduction in area of the square
$= x^2 - \frac{x^2}{4} = \frac{3x^2}{4}$ sq. m.
$\therefore$ Percentage reduction = $\frac{3x^2/4}{x^2} \times 100 = 75\%$
Hence, area of the square will be reduced by 75%.

**9.** Area of the rectangle = 6.4 × 2.5 = 16.00 sq.m.
**According to question :**
Area of the square = Area of the rectangle
$\therefore$ Area of the square = 16 sq. m.
$\therefore$ Side of the square = $\sqrt{16} = \sqrt{4 \times 4} = 4$ m.

**10.** Suppose, the three sides of the triangle are $a$, $b$ and $c$ and $a$ is the largest while $c$ is the smallest side of the triangle.

$\therefore \quad a^2 = b^2 + c^2 \quad ...(i)$

Perimeter of the triangle = $a + b + c$

**According to question :**

$(a + b + c) = c \times 6$

$\Rightarrow \quad a + b = 5c \quad ...(ii)$

From equation $(i)$, $a^2 - b^2 = c^2$

$\Rightarrow (a + b)(a - b) = c^2$

$\Rightarrow \quad 5c(a - b) = c^2$

$\Rightarrow \quad a - b = \frac{c}{5} \quad [\because a + b = 5c] \quad ...(iii)$

From equation $(ii)$ and $(iii)$,

$a + b = 5c,\ a - b = \frac{c}{5}$

$\Rightarrow \quad 2a = 5c + \frac{c}{5}$

$= \frac{26c}{5} \Rightarrow a = \frac{26c}{10} = \frac{13}{5}c$

$\Rightarrow \quad a : c = 13 : 5$

on substituting the value of a in equation $(ii)$

$b = 5c - \frac{13c}{5} = \frac{12c}{5}$

$\Rightarrow \quad b : c = 12 : 5$

$\therefore \quad a : b : c = 13 : 12 : 5$

Hence, the three sides of the right angled triangle are in the ratio of 13 : 12 : 5.

**11.** Perimeter of the 1st square = 24 m

$\therefore$ Side of the 1st square $= \frac{24}{4} = 6$ m

Perimeter of the 2nd square = 32 m

$\therefore$ Side of the 2nd square $= \frac{32}{4} = 8$ m

**According to question :**

Area of the third square = Area of the first two squares

$\therefore$ Area of the third square = Areas of the 1st square + Area of the 2nd square

$= 6^2 + 8^2 = 36 + 64 = 100$ sq. m.

$\therefore$ Side of the third square $= \sqrt{100} = 10$ m

$\therefore$ Perimeter of the third square

$= 4 \times \text{side} = 4 \times 10 = 40$ m.

**12. In the first case:**

Side of the square = $x$ m

$\therefore$ Area of the square = $x^2$ sq. m

**In the second case:**

Side of the square = $2x$ m.

$\therefore$ Area of the square = $(2x)^2 = 4x^2$ sq. m

Hence, it is clear that if side of a square is doubled, its area becomes four times.

**13.** Suppose side of the smaller square = $x$ m

$\because$ Area of the bigger square = $(25)^2 = 625$ sq. m

And area of the smaller square = $x^2$ sq. m

**According to question :**

Differene between the areas of two squares

= 225 sq. m

$\therefore \quad 625 - x^2 = 225$

$\Rightarrow \quad x^2 = 625 - 225 = 400$

$\Rightarrow \quad x = \sqrt{400} = 20$ m

$\therefore$ Side of the smaller side = 20 m.

**14.** Suppose side of the equilateral triangle = $x$ cm

$\therefore$ Perimeter of the triangle = $3x$ cm

**According to question :**

$3x = 72 \Rightarrow x = \frac{72}{3} = 24$ cm.

$\therefore$ Area of the equilateral triangle

$= \frac{\sqrt{3}}{4} \times x^2 = \frac{\sqrt{3}}{4} \times (24)^2$

$= 144\sqrt{3}$ sq. cm.

**15.** $\because$ Radius of the first circle = 5 cm

$\therefore$ Area of the first circle $= \pi \times 5^2 = 25\pi$ sq. cm and

Radius of the second circle = 12 cm

$\therefore$ Area of the second circle

$= \pi \times 12^2 = 144\pi$ sq. cm

**According to question :**

Area of the new circle

= Sum of the areas of the two circles

$\therefore$ Area of the new circle

$= 25\pi + 144\pi = 169\pi$ sq. cm $= \pi(13)^2$ sq. cm

Hence, it is clear that the radius of the new circle will be 13 cm.

**16.** Suppose radius of the circle = R cm

And side of the square = $x$ cm

$\therefore$ Circumference of the circle = $2\pi$R cm

and Perimeter of the square = $4x$ cm

**According to question :**

$2\pi R = 4x \Rightarrow R = \frac{2x}{\pi}$

$\therefore$ Ratio between the areas of the circle and the square

$= \pi R^2 : x^2$

$\Rightarrow x \times \left(\frac{2x}{\pi}\right)^2 : x^2 \Rightarrow \frac{4x^2}{\pi} : x^2 \Rightarrow 4 : \pi : \Rightarrow 4 : \frac{22}{7}$

$\Rightarrow \quad 14 : 11.$

**18.** Suppose the length and the width of the rectangle are $x$ metre and $y$ metre respectively.

$\therefore$ Area of the rectangle = $xy$ sq. metre

**According to question :**

On effecting 20% increase in the length and 15% decrease in the width :

Length of the new rectangle

$= x + 20\%$ of $x = 1.2\ x$ metre

Width of the new rectangle

$= y - 15\%$ of $y = .85\ y$ metre

$\therefore$ Area of the new rectangle

$= 1.2x \times .85y = 1.020\ xy$ sq. metre

# Prism; Right Circular Cone; Right Circular Cylinder; Sphere; Hemisphere; Right Pyramid; Rectangular Parallelepiped

In mensuration we often have to deal with the problem of finding the volume of solid figure.

**Cuboid :** A cuboid has six faces, each one a ractangle. It has 12 edges. For example, a rectangular brick.

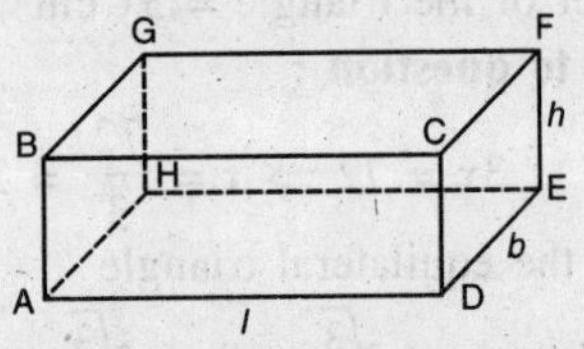


Let length = $l$, Breadth = $b$ and height = $h$, then,

1. Volume = (Length × Breadth × Height)
2. Whole surface = $2(lb + bh + lh)$
3. Diagonal = $\sqrt{l^2+b^2+h^2}$
4. Area of 4 walls of a room = $2 \times h\ (l + b)$

**Cube :** In a cube, Length = Breadth = Height

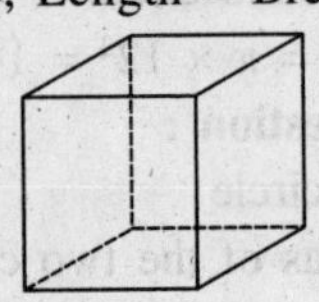

1. Volume = $(l)^3$
2. Length = $\sqrt[3]{\text{Volume}}$
3. Whole Surface area = $6\ l^2$
4. Diagonal = $l \times \sqrt{3}$
5. Lateral surface area = $4\ l^2$

**Cylinder :**

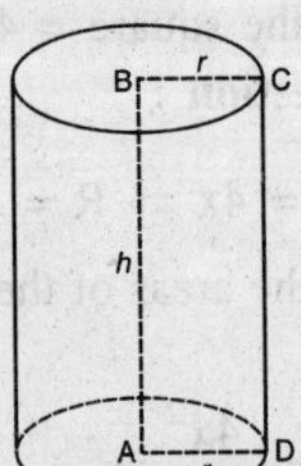


1. Volume = $\pi r^2 h$
2. Curved surface Area = $2\pi rh$
3. Total surface area = $2\pi r(r + h)$
   where $r$ = radius, $h$ = height
4. Curved surface of hollow cylinder
   $= 2\pi h\ (r_1 + r_2)$
5. Total surface of hollow cylinder
   $= 2\pi h\ (r_1 + r_2) + 2\pi\ (r_1^2 - r_2^2)$
6. Volume of hollow cylinder
   $= \pi h\left(r_1^2 - r_2^2\right)$
   where $r_1$ = outer radius
   $r_2$ = inner radius

**Spherical Cell :**

1. Volume = $\frac{4}{3}\pi\left(R^3 - r^3\right)$
2. Total surface area = $4\pi(R^2 - r^2)$
   where R = Outer radius
   $r$ = Inner radius

**Sphere**

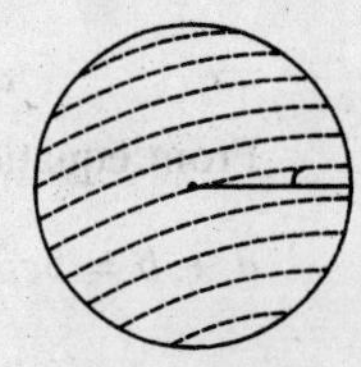


1. Volume = $\frac{4}{3}\pi r^3$
2. Surface area = $4\pi r^2$

**Semi-Sphere**

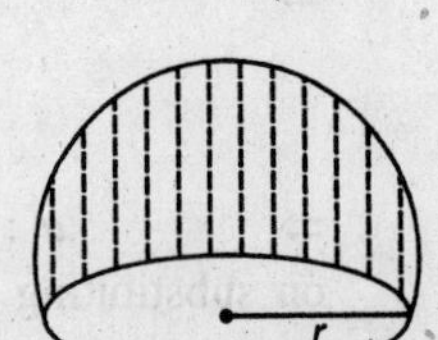


1. Volume = $\frac{2}{3}\pi r^3$
2. Curved surface area = $2\pi r^2$
3. Total surface area = $3\pi r^2$

**Cone :**

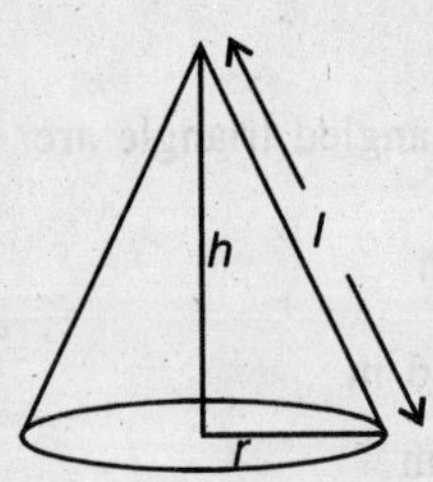


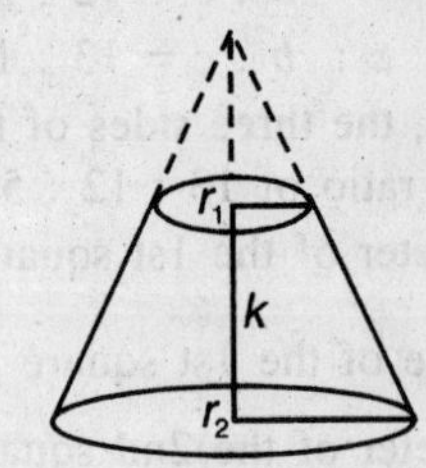


1. Slant height $(l)$ = $\sqrt{r^2+h^2}$
2. Volume = $\frac{1}{3}\pi r^2 h$
3. Curved surface area = $\pi rl$
4. Total surface area = $\pi r\ (l + r)$
5. If the thickness of the frustum of a cone be $k$ and the radii of its ends are $r_1$ and $r_2$, then
   *(i)* Slant height of the frustum of a cone
   $= \sqrt{K^2+(r_1-r_2)^2}$
   *(ii)* Curved surface of the frustum = $\pi(r_1 + r_2)\ l$.
   *(iii)* Volume = $\frac{\pi K}{3}\left(r_1^2+r_1r_2+r_2^2\right)$

**Right Pyramid**

1. Volume = $\frac{1}{3}(\text{area of the base})\times\text{height}$
2. Lateral surface area
   $= \frac{1}{2}(\text{Perimeter of the base})\times\text{Slant height}$
3. Total surface area = 2 (Area of one end) + Lateral surface area

**Right Prism**

1. Volume = Area of the base × Height
2. Lateral surface Area = Perimeter of the Base × Height
3. Total surface Area = 2 (Area of one end) + Lateral surface area.

## Rectangular Parallelepiped

Sometimes also referred to as "Rhomboid", a parallelepiped is a 3-D shape moulded by 6 parallelograms. If observed more carefully, as a cube relates to a square, a cuboid relates to a rectangle, the same way a parallelepiped is related to parallelogram.

We have the following formula for finding out the volume, lateral surface area and surface area of rectangular parallelepiped.

The formulas are:

Volume = abc

Surface area = 2ab + 2bc + 2ac

Diagonal = $\sqrt{a^2 + b^2}$

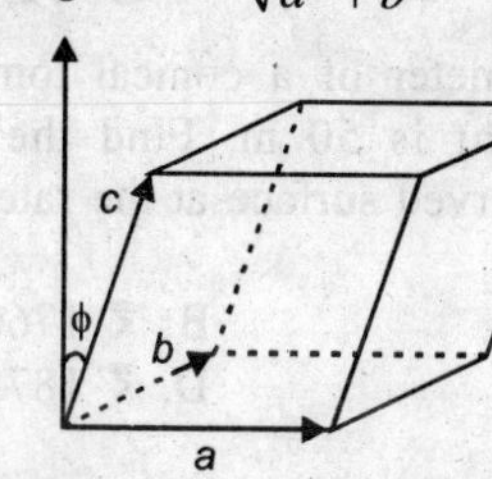


**Example:** Counting 38 cu. ft. of coal to a ton, how many tons will a coal bin 19 ft. long, 6 ft. wide, and 9 ft. deep contain, when level full?

**Solution:** The volume of a rectangular parallelepiped is given by the formula

V = L × W × H

Substitute the values of length, width and height of a tin, we have

V = L × W × H

V = (19ft) (6R.) (9 ft.)

V = 1026 $R^3$

The density of a substance is given by the formula

$$\rho = \frac{W}{V}$$

where, ρ is the density, W is the weight, and V is the volume of a substance respectively.

W = V × ρ

Therefore, the weight of a coal in a bin is:

$$W = (1026 R^3)\left(\frac{1 \text{ ton}}{38 n^3}\right)$$

W = 27 tons.

**Example:** The base face of a parallelepiped has opposite sides measuring 5 inches and 10 inches. The height of the parallelepiped is 4 inches. Find the cost of painting its walls from outside at a cost of INR 1.5 per square inch.

**Solution:** We need to find the lateral surface area first, therefore;

LSA = Perimeter of base × height

LSA = 2 (5 + 10) + 6

LSA = 180 sq. inch

Cost of painting = Lateral surface area × cost per square inch

Cost of painting the walls = 180 × 1.5 = ₹ 270.

## EXERCISE

**1.** A solid in the form of a cuboid is 4 cm × 3 cm × 2 cm. Its volume will be

A. 20 cu cm B. 22 cu cm
C. 28 cu cm D. 24 cu cm

**2.** A reservoir is 3 m long, 2 m wide and 1 m deep. Its capacity in litres is

A. 8000 litres B. 10000 litres
C. 6500 litres D. 6000 litres

**3.** Surface area of a cube is 1014 sq. cm. Its volume will be

A. 2197 cu cm B. 2297 cu cm
C. 2179 cu cm D. 2117 cu cm

**4.** If the volumes of two cubical blocks are in the ratio of 8 : 1, what will be the ratio of their edges?

A. 1 : 2 B. 2 : 1
C. 4 : 1 D. 2 : 3

**5.** Two spheres have their surface areas in the ratio 9 : 16. Their volumes are in the ratio of

A. 64 : 27 B. 27 : 64
C. 16 : 27 D. 11 : 27

**6.** The length of the longest rod that can be place in a room 12 m long, 9 m broad and 8 m high is

A. 17 m *(b)* 18 m
C. 25 m D. 16 m

**7.** The radius and the height of a right circular cone are in the ratio of 3 : 5. If its volume is 120π cu m, its slant height is

A. $3\sqrt{34}$m B. $2\sqrt{28}$m
C. $2\sqrt{44}$m D. $2\sqrt{34}$m

**8.** Circumference of the base of a cylinder is 88 cm and height of the cylinder is 42 cm. Its volume is

A. 25872 cu cm B. 28572 cu cm
C. 25870 cu cm D. 22584 cu cm

**9.** It fwo cubes each of 10 cm side are kept close to each other, then the cuboid so formed will have surface area equal to

A. 1200 sq. cm B. 5000 sq. cm
C. 1000 sq. cm D. 1250 sq. cm

**10.** A rectangular piece of paper is 30 cm long and 20 cm wide. How many ways can be adopted if one wants to give this rectangular piece of paper a cylindrical form?
A. Three B. Two
C. One D. Four

**11.** In the above question, the cylinders formed will have their volumes in the ratio of
A. 2 : 3 B. 3 : 1 : 1
C. 3 : 2 D. 1 : 3 : 1

**12.** If a solid sphere of 3 cm radius is melted and recast into a right circular cone whose base radius is same as that of the sphere, the height of the cone will be
A. 8 cm B. 12 cm
C. 6 cm D. 5 cm

**13.** Diameter of a roller is 2.4 m and it is 1.68 m long. If it takes 1000 complete revolutions once over to level a field, the area of the field is
A. 12672 sq. m B. 12671 sq. m
C. 12762 sq. m D. 11768 sq. m

**14.** If each edge of a cube is increased by 10%, then by how much percent will the surface area of this cube be increased?
A. 21% B. 18%
C. 15% D. 20%

**15.** Height and base radius of a solid cylinder are 14 m and 4 m respectively. It is melted and recast into a solid cone of the same base radius as that of the cylinder, what will be the height of the cone?
A. 21 m B. 42 m
C. 48 m D. 54 m

**16.** A room is in the form of a cube of side 10 m. How many bales of cotton can be kept in it if each bale covers 5 cu m space?
A. 100 B. 175
C. 200 D. 225

**17.** Three cubes having side 2 cm, 3 cm respectively are melted together to form a new cube. The side of the new cube will be
A. 3.526 cm B. 4.628 cm
C. 4.626 cm D. 4.528 cm

**18.** If base diameter of a cylinder is increased by 50%, then by how much percent its height must be decreased so as to keep its volume unaltered?
A. 45.56% B. 55.56%
C. 50.16% D. 62.33%

**19.** The surface area of a cube is 600 sq. m. Its diagonal is
A. $10\sqrt{3}$ cm B. $5\sqrt{3}$ cm
C. $4\sqrt{2}$ cm D. $10\sqrt{2}$ cm

**20.** The base diameter of a conical tomb is 28 m and its slant height is 50 m. Find the cost of white-washing its curved surface at the rate of 80 paise per sq. m?
A. ₹ 1860 B. ₹ 1760
C. ₹ 1950 D. ₹ 1875

## ANSWERS

| 1 | 2 | 3 | 4 | 5 | 6 | 7 | 8 | 9 | 10 |
|---|---|---|---|---|---|---|---|---|---|
| D | D | A | B | B | A | D | A | C | B |
| **11** | **12** | **13** | **14** | **15** | **16** | **17** | **18** | **19** | **20** |
| C | B | A | A | B | C | C | B | A | B |

## EXPLANATORY ANSWERS

**1.** Volume of the cuboid
$= l \times b \times h = 4 \times 3 \times 2 = 24$ cu. cm.

**2.** Volume of the reservoir
$= l \times b \times h = 3 \times 2 \times 1 = 6$ cu. cm
($\because$ 1 cu m = 1000 litre)
$\therefore$ Capacity of the reservoir
$= 6 \times 1000 = 6000$ litre.

**3.** Surface area of a cube = $6 \times (\text{side})^2$
$\therefore \quad 6 \times (\text{side})^2 = 1014$
$\Rightarrow \quad (\text{side})^2 = \dfrac{1014}{6} = 169$
$\Rightarrow \quad \text{side} = \sqrt{169} = 13$ cm
$\therefore$ Volume of the cube = $(\text{side})^3 = (13)^3$
$= 2197$ cu cm.

**4.** Suppose sides of the two cubical blocks are $a_1$ and $a_2$ respectively
$\therefore$ Volume of the two cubical blocks will be $(a_1)^3$ and $(a_2)^3$ rspectively
**According to question :**
$$a_1^3 : a_2^3 = 8 : 1$$
$$\therefore \quad \frac{a_1^3}{a_2^3} = \frac{8}{1}$$
$$\therefore \quad \left(\frac{a_1}{a_2}\right)^3 = \left(\frac{2}{1}\right)^3 \Rightarrow a_1 : a_2$$
$$= 2 : 1$$
Therefore ratio of their edges = 2 : 1.

**5.** Suppose radii of the two spheres are $r_1$ and $r_2$ respectively.

$\therefore$ Surface areas of the two spheres are $4\pi r_1^2$ and $4\pi r_2^2$ respectively

**According to question :**

$4\pi r_1^2 : 4\pi r_2^2 = 9 : 16 \Rightarrow r_1^2 : r_2^2 = 9 : 16$

$$\Rightarrow \quad \frac{r_1^2}{r_2^2} = \frac{9}{16} \Rightarrow \left(\frac{r_1}{r_2}\right)^2 = \left(\frac{3}{4}\right)^2$$

$$\Rightarrow \quad r_1 : r_2 = 3:4 \Rightarrow \left(\frac{r_1}{r_2}\right)^3 = \left(\frac{3}{4}\right)^3$$

$$\Rightarrow \quad \frac{r_1^3}{r_2^3} = \frac{27}{64} \Rightarrow r_1^3 : r_2^3 = 27 : 64.$$

Therefore ratio of their volumes

$$= \frac{4}{3}\pi r_1^3 : \frac{4}{3}\pi r_2^3 = r_1^3 : r_2^3 = 27 : 64$$

**6.** The longest rod that can be placed in the cuboidal room = Length of the diagonal =

$$\sqrt{l^2 + b^2 + h^2} = \sqrt{(12)^2 + (9)^2 + (8)^2}$$

$$= \sqrt{144 + 81 + 64} = \sqrt{289} = 17 \text{ m}$$

**7.** Suppose the base radius and the height of the right circular cone are $3x$ m and $5x$ m respectively.

$\therefore$ Volume of the cone

$$= \frac{1}{3}\pi r^2 h = \frac{1}{3}\pi (3x)^2 \times 5x \text{ cu m}$$

**According to question :**

Volume of the cone = $120\pi$ cu m (given)

$$\therefore \quad \frac{1}{3}\pi \times 9x^2 \times 5x = 120\pi$$

$$\Rightarrow \quad x^3 = \frac{120 \times 3}{9 \times 5}$$

$$\Rightarrow \quad x^3 = 8 \Rightarrow x^3 = (2)^3$$

$$\Rightarrow \quad x = 2 \text{ m}$$

$\therefore$ The radius and the height of the cone will be $3 \times 2 = 6$ m and $5 \times 2 = 10$ m respectively.

$\therefore$ Slant height of the cone

$$= \sqrt{r^2 + h^2} = \sqrt{(6)^2 + (10)^2}$$

$$\doteq \sqrt{36 + 100} = \sqrt{136} = 2\sqrt{34} \text{m}.$$

**8.** Suppose the base radius of the cylinder = $r$ cm

$\therefore$ Circumference of the base of the cylinder = $2\pi r$ cm

**According to question :**

$$2\pi r = 88$$

$$\therefore \quad r = \frac{88}{2\pi} = \frac{88 \times 7}{2 \times 22} = 14 \text{ cm}$$

$\therefore$ Volume of the cylinder

$$= \pi r^2 h = \frac{22}{7} \times (14)^2 \times 42$$

$$= 22 \times 2 \times 14 \times 42$$

$$= 25872 \text{ cu cm.}$$

**9.** Candidates should note that in such type of questions where two cubes of equal edges are kept close to each other, only the length of the cuboid so form increases and breadth and height of the cuboid remain same as that of the cube.

$\therefore$ Length of the cuboid = Edge of the first cube + Edge of the second cube

$$= 10 + 10 = 20 \text{ cm}$$

$\therefore$ Surface area of the cuboid

$= 2(20 \times 10 + 10 \times 10 + 10 \times 20)$

$$= 2(200 + 100 + 200)$$

$$= 5 \times 500 = 1000 \text{ sq. cm.}$$

**10.** Obviously, two ways can be adopted if one wants to give the rectangular piece of paper a cylindrical form, *i.e.*,

1. *When the paper is bent towards its length.* In this case, the circumference of the base of the cylinder will be equal to the length of the rectangular piece of paper and the height of the cylinder will be equal to the breadth of the rectangular piece of paper.
2. *When the paper is bent towards its breadth.* In this case, the circumference of the base of the cylinder will be equal to the breadth of the rectangular piece of paper and the height of the cylinder will be equal to the length of the rectangular piece of paper.

**11. In the first case :**

$$2\pi r = 30$$

$$r = \frac{15}{\pi} \text{ cm and } h = 20 \text{ cm}$$

$\Rightarrow$ volume $(v_1) = \pi r^2 h$

$$= \frac{15 \times 15 \times 20}{\pi} = \frac{4500}{\pi} \text{ cu cm}$$

**In the second case :**

$$2\pi r = 20 \Rightarrow r = \frac{10}{\pi} \text{ cm and } h = 30 \text{ cm}$$

$\therefore$ Volume $(v_2) = \pi r^2 h$

$$= \frac{10 \times 10 \times 30}{\pi} = \frac{3000}{\pi} \text{ cu cm}$$

$\therefore$ Ratio of the two volumes

$$= v_1 : v_2 = \frac{4500}{\pi} : \frac{3000}{\pi} = 3 : 2$$

**12.** Volume of the sphere of radius 3 cm

$$= \frac{4}{3}\pi (3)^3 = \frac{4}{3}\pi \times 27 \text{ cu cm}$$

Suppose the height of the cone = $h$ cm

∴ Volume of the cone having base radius equal to that of the sphere = $\frac{1}{3}\pi(3)^2 \times h$

∵ Volume of the cone = Volume of the sphere

∴ $\frac{1}{3}\pi(3)^2 \times h = \frac{4}{3}\pi \times 27 \Rightarrow h = 12$ cm

∴ Height of the cone = 12 cm.

**13.** Diameter of the roller = 2.4 m

∴ Radius of the roller = 1.2 m

And height (length) of the roller = 1.68 m

∴ Surface area of the roller

$= 2\pi rh = 2 \times \frac{22}{7} \times 1.2 \times 1.68 = 12.672$ sq. m

∴ In one complete revolution, the roller covers 2.672 sq. m.

∴ It will cover in 1000 revolutions = 12.672 × 1000 = 12672 sq. m

∴ Area of the field = 12672 sq. m.

**14.** The two edges which are included in surface area of the cube are increased by 10%.

∴ $x\% = y\% = 10\%$

and in case of percentage increase, values of $x$ and $y$ are positive

∴ Percentage increase in the surface area of the cube

$= \left(x + y + \frac{xy}{100}\right)\%$

$= \left(10 + 10 + \frac{10 \times 10}{100}\right)\% = 21\%.$

**15.** Volume of the solid cylinder

$= \pi r^2 h = \pi r^2 \times 14$ cu m

**According to question :**

Radius of the cone = Radius of the cylinder

= $r$ m = 4 m

and volume of the cone

= Volume of the cylinder

∴ $\frac{1}{3}\pi r^2 \times \text{height} = \pi r^2 \times 14$

∴ Height = 14 × 3 = 42 m

∴ Height of the cone = 42 m.

**16.** Volume of the cubical room

$= (10)^3 = 1000$ cu m

Number of cotton bales which can be placed in the room

$= \frac{\text{Volume of the room}}{\text{Volume of each cotton bale}} = \frac{1000}{5} = 200.$

**17.** Edges of the three cubes are 2 cm, 3 cm and 4 cm respectively

∴ Their volumes will be $(2)^3 = 8$ cu cm, $(3)^3 = 27$ cu cm and $(4)^3 = 64$ cu cm respectively.

Volume of the new cube = Total volume of the three cubes

∴ Volume of the new cube

= 8 + 27 + 64 = 99 cu cm

∴ Side of the new cube = $\sqrt[3]{99} = 4.626$ cm.

**18.** Suppose the height of the cylinder should be decreased by H%

∵ Volume of a cylinder comprises two radii (*i.e.*, two edges) and one height (as the third edge). Radius is increased by 50%.

It means $x\% = y\% = 50\%$ and percentage decrease in the third edge (*i.e.*, height) = H%.

Therefore, z% = H% and in case of percentage decrease value of $z$ will be negative.

∴ Change in the volume of the cylinder

$= \left(x + y + (-z) + \frac{xy + y(-z) + (-zx)}{100} + \frac{xy(-z)}{100^2}\right)\%$

Since volume of the cylinder remains unchanged.

∴ Change = 0%

∴ $\left(50 + 50 + (-H) + \frac{50 \times 50 - 50H - 50H}{100} + \frac{50 \times 50 \times (-H)}{100^2}\right)\%$

∴ 100 – H + 25 – H – .25H = 0

⇒ 2.25H = 125

⇒ $H = \frac{125}{2.25} = 55.56$

∴ Height of the cylinder should be decreased by 55.56%.

**19.** ∵ Surface area of the cube = 6 × (side)$^2$

∴ 6 × (side)$^2$ = 600

⇒ side$^2$ = 100

⇒ side = $\sqrt{100}$ = 10 cm

∴ Diagonal of the cube

$= \sqrt{3} \times \text{side} = \sqrt{3} \times 10 = 10\sqrt{3}$ cm.

**20.** ∵ Area of the curved surface of the cone = $\pi rl$

(where $r$ = radius of the cone and $l$ = slant height of the cone)

∴ Area of the curved surface of the cone

$= \frac{22}{7} \times \frac{28}{2} \times 50 = 2200$ sq. m.

∴ Cost of whitewashing at 80 paise per sq. m

$= 2200 \times \frac{80}{100} = ₹\ 1760.$

●●●

CHAPTER 12

# Trigonometry

## Trigonometrical Ratios; Degree and Radian Measures; Standard Identities; Complementary Angles

**Measurement of Angles:** In general, the angles are measured in degrees or in radians which are defined as follows:

*(a)* ***Degrees*:** A right angle is divided into 90 equal parts and each part is called a degree. Thus a right angle is equal to 90 degrees. One degree is denoted by $1^\circ$.

A degree is divided into sixty equal parts and each part is called a minute and is denoted by $1'$.

A minute is divided into sixty equal parts and each part is called a second and is denoted by $1''$.

Thus, we have

1 right angle = $90^\circ$ (read as 90 degrees)

$1^\circ = 60'$ (read as 60 minutes)

$1' = 60''$ (read as 60 seconds)

*(b)* ***Radians*:** A radian is the angle subtended at the centre of a circle by an arc equal in length to the radius of the circle.

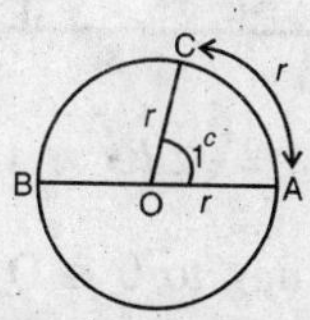


In the adjacent figure OA = OC = arc AC = $r$ = radius of the circle, then measurement of $\angle$ AOC is one radian and is denoted by $1^c$. Thus $\angle$ AOC = $1^c$.

**A Constant Number π:** The ratio of the circumference to the diameter of a circle is always equal to a constant and this constant is denoted by the Greek letter $\pi$.

Thus $\pi$ = circumference/diameter.

$\therefore$ If $r$ is the radius of a circle, then its circumference $= 2\pi\, r$.

The constant $\pi$ is an irrational number and its approximate value is taken as 22/7.

**Relation Between an Arc and an Angle:** If $s$ is the length of an arc of a circle of radius $r$, then the angle $\theta$ (in radians) subtended by this arc at the centre of the circle is given by $\theta = s/r$ or $s = r\,\theta$

*i.e.,* arc = radius × angle in radians

Given in the figure,

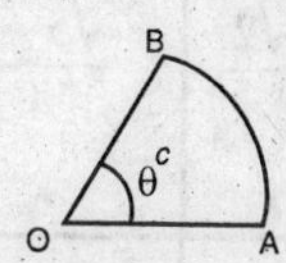


$$\angle \text{AOB} = \frac{\text{arc ACB}}{r} \text{ (in radians)}$$

$$= \frac{\pi r}{r} = \pi \text{ radians.}$$

Thus we have, $\pi$ radians = $180^\circ$ = 2 right angles

or 1 radian $= \dfrac{180}{\pi}$ degrees $= \dfrac{180}{22} \times 7$ degrees $= 57^\circ\ 17'\ 44.8''$ (Appr.)

**Sectorial Area:** Let OAB be a sector having central angle $\theta^c$ and radius $r$. Then area of the sector OAB is given by $\dfrac{1}{2} r^2\, \theta$.

**Trigonometrical Ratios:** In a right angled triangle ABC, if $\angle$ CAB = $\theta$, then BC = side opposite to the angle $\theta$ = Perpendicular = $p$ (say), AC = side opposite to the right angle = Hypotenuse = $h$ (say) and AB = $b$ (say).

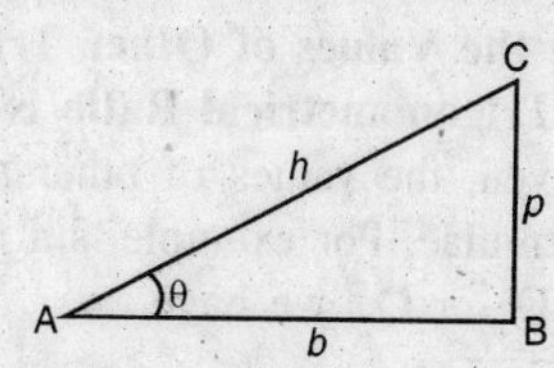

The six trigonometrical ratios are given as follows:

$\sin\theta = p/h$, $\cos\theta = b/h$, $\tan\theta = p/b$.

(Also $\tan\theta = \sin\theta/\cos\theta$, $\operatorname{cosec}\theta = 1/\sin\theta$ ,

$\sec\theta = 1/\cos\theta$, $\cot\theta = 1/\tan\theta$,)

***Basic Formulae Connecting Six Trigonometrical Ratios***

The formulae connecting the six trigonometrical ratios are:

(*i*) $\sin^2\theta + \cos^2\theta = 1$ or $\cos^2\theta = 1 - \sin^2\theta$ or $\sin^2\theta = 1 - \cos^2\theta$.

(*ii*) $1 + \tan^2\theta = \sec^2\theta$ or $\sec^2\theta - \tan^2\theta = 1$

(*iii*) $1 + \cot^2\theta = \operatorname{cosec}^2\theta$ or $\operatorname{cosec}^2\theta - \cot^2\theta = 1$.

***Sign of Trigonometrical Ratios:***

1st quadrant $0 < \theta < 90°$,

all trigonometrical ratios +ve,

2nd quadrant $90° < \theta < 180°$,

only $\sin\theta$ and $\operatorname{cosec}\theta$, +ve

3rd quadrant $180° < \theta < 270°$,

only $\tan\theta$ and $\cot\theta$, +ve

4th quadrant $270° < \theta < 360°$,

only $\cos\theta$ and $\sec\theta$, +ve.

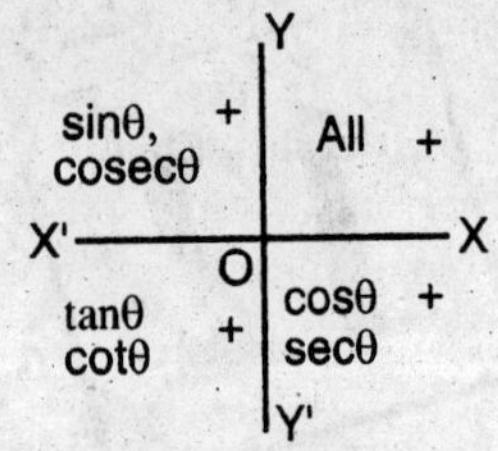


***Trigonometrical Ratios of Related Angles:***

$\sin(-\theta) = -\sin\theta$

$\sin(90° - \theta) = \cos\theta$

$\cos(90° - \theta) = \sin\theta$

$\tan(90° - \theta) = \cot\theta$

$\sin(90° + \theta) = \cos\theta$

$\cos(90° + \theta) = -\sin\theta$

$\tan(90° + \theta) = -\cot\theta$

$\cos(-\theta) = \cos\theta$

$\sin(180° + \theta) = -\sin\theta$

$\cos(180° + \theta) = -\cos\theta$

$\tan(180° + \theta) = \tan\theta$

$\sin(270° - \theta) = -\cos\theta$

$\cos(270° - \theta) = -\sin\theta$

$\tan(270° - \theta) = \cot\theta$

$\tan(-\theta) = -\tan\theta$

$\sin(270° + \theta) = -\cos\theta$

$\cos(270° + \theta) = \sin\theta$

$\tan(270° + \theta) = -\cot\theta$

$\sin(360° + \theta) = \sin\theta$

$\cos(360° + \theta) = \cos\theta$

$\tan(360° + \theta) = \tan\theta$

***Table giving sine, cosine and tangent of some angles less than 90°:***

| | 0° | 15° | 18° | 22.5° | 30° | 36° | 45° | 60° | 67.5° | 90° |
|---|---|---|---|---|---|---|---|---|---|---|
| sin | 0 | $\frac{\sqrt{6}-\sqrt{2}}{4}$ | $\frac{\sqrt{5}-1}{4}$ | $\frac{\sqrt{2-\sqrt{2}}}{2}$ | $\frac{1}{2}$ | $\frac{\sqrt{10-2\sqrt{5}}}{4}$ | $\frac{1}{\sqrt{2}}$ | $\frac{\sqrt{3}}{2}$ | $\frac{\sqrt{\sqrt{2}+1}}{\sqrt{(2\sqrt{2})}}$ | 1 |
| cos | 1 | $\frac{\sqrt{6}+\sqrt{2}}{4}$ | $\frac{\sqrt{10+2\sqrt{5}}}{4}$ | $\frac{\sqrt{\sqrt{2}+1}}{\sqrt{(2\sqrt{2})}}$ | $\frac{\sqrt{3}}{2}$ | $\frac{\sqrt{5}+1}{4}$ | $\frac{1}{\sqrt{2}}$ | $\frac{1}{2}$ | $\frac{\sqrt{2-\sqrt{2}}}{2}$ | 0 |
| tan | 0 | $2-\sqrt{3}$ | $\frac{\sqrt{25-10\sqrt{5}}}{5}$ | $\sqrt{2}-1$ | $\frac{1}{\sqrt{3}}$ | $\sqrt{5-2\sqrt{5}}$ | 1 | $\sqrt{3}$ | $\sqrt{2}+1$ | not defined |

**Bounds of T-Ratios:** Since $\sin^2\theta + \cos^2\theta = 1$, the absolute values of $\sin\theta$ and $\cos\theta$ can never be greater than 1.

Thus $0 \le |\sin\theta| \le 1$, $0 \le |\cos\theta| \le 1$,

*i.e.*, $-1 \le \sin\theta$; $\cos\theta \le 1$, or $0 \le \sin^2\theta$; $\cos^2\theta \le 1$.

Also $\sec\theta$; $\operatorname{cosec}\theta \ge 1$ or $\le -1$

*i.e.*, $\sec\theta$, $\operatorname{cosec}\theta$ can never lie between –1 and 1.

It should be noted that $-\infty < \tan\theta$; $\cot\theta < \infty$.

**To Determine the Values of Other Trigonometrical Ratios when one Trigonometrical Ratio is given:** If one of the *t*-ratio is given, the values of other *t*-ratios can be found by using formulae. For example, $\sin\theta = 1/3$. Since sine is positive in $Q_1$ or $Q_2$, we have

$\cos\theta = \sqrt{1-(1/9)}$

or $-\sqrt{1-(1/9)}$, *i.e.*, $2\sqrt{2}/3$

or $-2\sqrt{2}/3$ according to $\theta \in Q_1$ or $\theta \in Q_2$.

We can also find other ratios by forming right angled triangle, *e.g.*, Let $\tan\theta = 1/2$, $\pi < \theta < 3\pi/2$, then since $\theta$ in $Q_3$, sine and cosine both are negative,

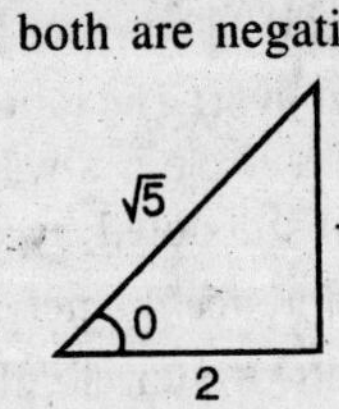


$\therefore$ We have $\sin\theta = -1/\sqrt{5}$,

$\cos\theta = -2/\sqrt{5}$.

**Approximate Values of sin θ, cos θ and tan θ when θ is Small:** Let $\theta$ be small and measured in radians, then sin

$\theta \approx \theta$, cos ≈ 1, $\tan\theta \approx \theta$. These are first degree approximations. The second degree approximations are given by

$\sin\theta \simeq \theta$, $\cos\theta \simeq 1 - \frac{1}{2}\theta^2$, $\tan\theta = \theta$.

**Increasing and Decreasing Behaviour of Trigonometrical Ratios:** When $-\pi/2 < \theta < \pi/2$, $\sin\theta$ increases in $Q_1$ and $Q_4$ with angle while in $Q_2$, $Q_3$, $\sin\theta$ decreases from 1 to –1.

Thus $\theta_1 < \theta_2$

$\Rightarrow \sin\theta_1 < \sin\theta_2$ ($\theta_1, \theta_2 \in Q_1$ or $Q_4$)

$\Rightarrow \sin\theta_1 > \sin\theta_2$ ($\theta_1, \theta_2 \in Q_2$ or $Q_3$)

We can decide the behaviour of other ratios in a similar manner. If we denote ↑ for increasing and ↓ for decreasing, we have the following chart:

y

| | | | |
|---|---|---|---|
| sin | ↓ | sin | ↑ |
| cos | ↓ | cos | ↓ |
| tan | ↑ | tan | ↑ |
| cot | ↓ | cot | ↓ |
| sec | ↑ | sec | ↑ |
| cosec | ↑ | cosec | ↓ |
| x' | O | | x |
| sin | ↓ | sin | ↑ |
| cos | ↑ | cos | ↑ |
| tan | ↑ | tan | ↑ |
| cot | ↓ | cot | ↓ |
| sec | ↓ | sec | ↓ |
| cosec | ↑ | cosec | ↓ |

y'

## EXERCISE

**1.** The angles of a triangle are in A.P. and the radian measure of the smallest to the degree measure of the mean is π : 200. The greatest angle in radians is:
A. (11/30)π B. π/3
C. π/2 D. None of these

**2.** The moon's distance from the earth is 3,50,000 kilometres and its diameter subtends an angle of 31' at the eye of the observer. The diameter of the moon is:
A. 3157 (11/27) km B. 315 (11/27) km
C. 3050 (11/27) km D. None of these

**3.** If sin θ = – 3/5 and θ lies in the third quadrant, then the value of cos (θ/2) is:
A. 1/5 B. –1/√(10)
C. 1/5 D. 1/√(10)

**4.** If tan θ = – 4/3, then sin θ is:
A. – 4/5 but not 4/5 B. –4/5 or 4/5
C. 4/5 but not – 4/5 D. None of these

**5.** If the angle θ is in the third quadrant and tan θ = 3, then the value of sin θ is:
A. 1/√(10) B. –1/√(10)
C. –3/√(10) D. 3/√(10)

**6.** If (sec α + tan α) (sec β + tan β) (sec γ + tan γ) = tan α tan β tan γ, then (sec α – tan α) (sec β – tan β) (sec γ – tan γ) = ?
A. cot α cot β cot γ
B. tan α tan β tan γ
C. cot α + cot β + cot γ
D. tan α + tan β + tan γ

**7.** Which of the following is correct?
A. sin 1° > sin 1
B. sin 1° < sin 1
C. sin 1° = sin 1
D. sin 1° = (π/180) sin 1

**8.** Which of the following is correct?
A. tan 1 > tan 2 B. tan 1 = tan 2
C. tan 1 < tan 2 D. tan 1 = 1

**9.** The value of log tan 1° + log tan 2° + ..... + log tan 89° is:
A. 0 B. 1
C. ∞ D. None of these

**10.** The value of cos 105° + sin 105° is:
A. 0 B. $\sqrt{(3/2)}$
C. $1/\sqrt{2}$ D. $(\sqrt{3}+1)/2$

**11.** The value of $\sin\left(67\frac{1}{2}°\right)\sin\left(22\frac{1}{2}°\right)$ is:
A. $-2\sqrt{2}$ B. $2\sqrt{2}$
C. $1/2\sqrt{2}$ D. $-1/2\sqrt{2}$

**12.** The value of (1 + cosπ/8) (1 + cos3π/8) (1 + cos5π/8) (1 + cos7π/8) is:
A. 1/2 B. 1/4
C. 1/8 D. 1/16

**13.** The valuc of $\sin^2\frac{2\pi}{15} - \sin^2\frac{\pi}{30}$ is:
A. $(\sqrt{5}-1)/4$ B. $(\sqrt{5}-1)/8$
C. $(\sqrt{5}+1)\sqrt{3}/2$ D. $(\sqrt{5}-1)\sqrt{3}/2$

**14.** The value of sin 50° – sin 70° + sin 10° is:
A. 0 B. 1
C. 2 D. None of these

**15.** The value of $\left(\sqrt{3}\,\text{cosec}\,20° - \sec 20°\right)$ is:
A. 2 B. $2\sqrt{3}$
C. 4 D. $\sqrt{8}/2$

# ANSWERS

| 1 | 2 | 3 | 4 | 5 | 6 | 7 | 8 | 9 | 10 |
|---|---|---|---|---|---|---|---|---|---|
| A | A | B | B | C | A | B | A | A | C |
| **11** | **12** | **13** | **14** | **15** | | | | | |
| C | C | B | A | C | | | | | |

# EXPLANATORY ANSWERS

**1.** Let the angles in degrees in A.P. be taken as $A = \theta - \phi,\ B = \theta,\ C = \theta + \phi$

$\therefore \quad A + B + C = 180° = 3\theta$

$\Rightarrow \quad B = \theta = 60°$

Now $\dfrac{\pi}{200} = \dfrac{\text{A in radian}}{\text{B in degrees}}$

$= \dfrac{(60-\phi)(\pi/180)}{60}$

$\Rightarrow \quad \phi = 6°$

$\therefore$ Greatest angle $C = \theta + \phi = 66°$

$= 66 \times (\pi/180)$

$= (11/30)\ \pi$ radians.

**2.** Let $l$ be the diameter of moon and $a$ its distance from the earth. If the moon subtends an angle $\theta$ at the eye of the observer, then

$l = a\theta = 350000 \times \left(\dfrac{31}{60} \times \dfrac{\pi}{180}\right)$

$= \dfrac{3500 \times 31}{6 \times 18} \times \dfrac{22}{7} = 3157\dfrac{11}{27}$ km.

**3.** $\because$ $\theta$ lies in the third quadrant

$\because$ $\cos\theta$ is –ve

$\because$ $\sin\theta = -3/5$

$\Rightarrow \quad \cos\theta = -\sqrt{(1-\sin^2\theta)} = -4/5$

Now, $\cos^2\dfrac{1}{2}\theta = \dfrac{1}{2}(1 + \cos\theta)$

$= \dfrac{1}{2}(1 - 4/5) = 1/10$

$\Rightarrow \quad \cos\dfrac{1}{2}\theta = +1/\sqrt{(10)}$

But given that, $180° < \theta < 270°$

$\Rightarrow 90° < \theta/2 < 135°$

*i.e.,* $\theta/2$ lies in the second quadrant

$\Rightarrow \cos\dfrac{1}{2}\theta$ is –ve

Hence $\cos\dfrac{1}{2}\theta = -1/\sqrt{10}$.

**4.** $\tan\theta = -4/3$

$\Rightarrow$ $\theta$ lies in 2nd or 4th quadrant.

$\therefore$ $\sin\theta$ is positive or negative according as $\theta$ lie in 2nd or 4th quadrant respectively, *i.e.,* $\sin\theta$ may be positive or negative.

Now $\quad \sin\theta = \tan\theta/\sqrt{(1 + \tan^2\theta)} = 4/5$

Hence $\quad \sin\theta = -4/5$ or $4/5$.

**5.** $\because$ $\theta$ is in the third quadrant,

$\because \sin\theta < 0$.

Thus $\quad \sin\theta = -\tan\theta/\sqrt{(1 + \tan^2\theta)}$

$= -3/\sqrt{(10)}$.

**6.** Multiplying both sides of the given expression by (secα – tanα). (secβ – tanβ). (secγ – tanγ), we get; 1.1.1 = (secα – tanα) . (sec β – tan β). (sec γ – tan γ). tan α tan β tan γ

$\Rightarrow$ (sec α – tan α).(sec β – tan β).(sec γ – tan γ) = cot α.cot β.cot γ.

**7.** 1 radian = (180/π) Degrees = 57° (appr.)

$\therefore \sin 1° < \sin 57° \Rightarrow \sin 1° < \sin 1$.

**8.** 1 radian = 57° (appr.)

which lie in first quadrant. $\therefore \tan 1 > 0$,

and 2 radians = 114° (appr.), which lie in second quadrant $\therefore \tan 2 < 0$

Hence $\tan 1 > \tan 2$.

**9.** $\log\tan 1° + \log\tan 2° + ... + \log\tan 89°$

$= \log\left[\tan 1°.\tan 2°...\tan 45°...\tan 88°.\tan 89°\right]$

$= \log\left[\tan 1°.\tan 2°...\tan 45°...\tan(90°-2°)\tan(90°-1°)\right]$

$= \log\left[\tan 1°.\cot 1°.\tan 2°.\cot 2°...1\right]$

$= \log 1 = 0$

**10.** $\cos 105° + \sin 105°$

$= \cos(60° + 45°) + \sin(60° + 45°)$

$= \cos 60° \cos 45° - \sin 60° \sin 45°$

$\quad + \sin 60° \cos 45° + \cos 60° \sin 45°$

$= \dfrac{1}{2}.\dfrac{1}{\sqrt{2}} - \dfrac{\sqrt{3}}{2}.\dfrac{1}{\sqrt{2}} + \dfrac{\sqrt{3}}{2}.\dfrac{1}{\sqrt{2}} + \dfrac{1}{2}.\dfrac{1}{\sqrt{2}}$

$= \dfrac{2}{2\sqrt{2}} = \dfrac{1}{\sqrt{2}}$

**11.** $\sin\left(67\frac{1^\circ}{2}\right)\sin\left(22\frac{1^\circ}{2}\right)$

$= \sin\left(45^\circ+22\frac{1^\circ}{2}\right)\sin\left(45^\circ-22\frac{1^\circ}{2}\right)$

$= \sin^2 45^\circ - \sin^2 22\frac{1^\circ}{2} = \left(\frac{1}{\sqrt{2}}\right)^2 - \frac{1-\cos 45^\circ}{2}$

$= \frac{1}{2} - \frac{1}{2}\left(1-\frac{1}{\sqrt{2}}\right) = \frac{1}{2}\left(1-1+\frac{1}{\sqrt{2}}\right) = \frac{1}{2\sqrt{2}}$

**12.** $\left(1+\cos\frac{\pi}{8}\right)\left(1+\cos\frac{3\pi}{8}\right)\left(1+\cos\frac{5\pi}{8}\right)\left(1+\cos\frac{7\pi}{8}\right)$

$= (1+\cos\pi/8)(1-\cos\pi/8)$

$(1+\cos 3\pi/8)(1-\cos 3\pi/8)$

$= \sin^2 \pi/8.\ \sin^2 3\pi/8 = \frac{1}{4}\left(2\sin\frac{3\pi}{8}.\sin\pi/8\right)^2$

$= \frac{1}{4}\left[\cos\frac{\pi}{4}-\cos\frac{\pi}{2}\right]^2 = \frac{1}{4}\left(\frac{1}{\sqrt{2}}-0\right)^2 = \frac{1}{4}\times\frac{1}{2}=\frac{1}{8}$

**13.** $\sin^2\frac{2\pi}{5}-\sin^2\frac{\pi}{30} = \sin\left(\frac{2\pi}{15}+\frac{\pi}{30}\right)\sin\left(\frac{2\pi}{15}-\frac{\pi}{30}\right)$

$= \sin\frac{\pi}{6}.\sin\frac{\pi}{10} = \frac{1}{2}\times\frac{\sqrt{5}-1}{4} = \frac{1}{8}\left(\sqrt{5}-1\right)$

**14.** $\sin 50^\circ - \sin 70^\circ + \sin 10^\circ$

$= 2\cos 60^\circ \sin(-10)^\circ + \sin 10^\circ$

$= 2 \times \frac{1}{2} \times -\sin 10^\circ + \sin 10^\circ$

$= -\sin 10^\circ + \sin 10^\circ = 0$

**15.** $\sqrt{3}\ \text{cosec}\ 20^\circ - \sec 20^\circ$

$= \tan 60^\circ\ \text{cosec} 20^\circ - \sec 20^\circ$

$= \frac{\sin 60^\circ}{\cos 60^\circ}.\frac{1}{\sin 20^\circ} - \frac{1}{\cos 20^\circ}$

$= \frac{\sin 60^\circ \cos 20^\circ - \cos 60^\circ \sin 20^\circ}{\cos 60^\circ.\sin 20^\circ \cos 20^\circ}$

$= \frac{\sin(60^\circ-20^\circ)}{\frac{1}{2}.\frac{1}{2}(2\sin 20^\circ\cos 20^\circ)} = 4.\frac{\sin 40^\circ}{\sin 40^\circ} = 4$

# Heights and Distance

**Angle of Elevation and Depression:** Let O and P be two points such that P is at higher level than O. Let PQ, OX be horizontal lines through P and O, respectively.

If an observer (or eye) is at O and the object is at P, then ∠XOP is called the angle of elevation of P as seen from O.

This angle is also called the angular height of P from O.

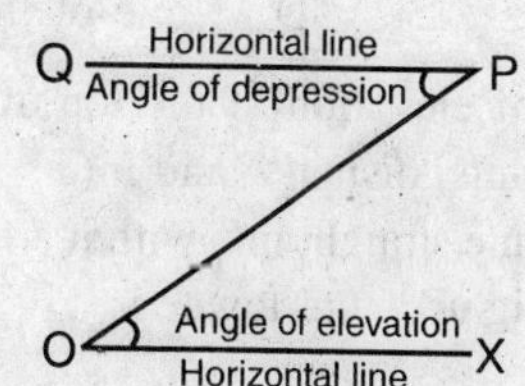


If an observer (or eye) is at P and the object is at O, then ∠QPO is called the angle of depression of O as seen from P.

## EXERCISE

**1.** A person standing on the bank of a river observes that the angle subtended by a tree on the opposite bank is 60°, when he retires 40 metres from the bank he finds the angle to be 30°. Then the breadth of the river is:

A. 40 m  B. 60 m
C. 20 m  D. 30 m

**2.** At a point on a level plane a tower subtends an angle $\theta$ and a flag-staff $a$ ft. in length at the top of the tower subtends an angle $\phi$. The height of the tower is:

A. $\frac{a\sin\theta\cos\phi}{\cos(\theta+\phi)}$  B. $\frac{a\sin\theta\cos(\theta+\phi)}{\sin\phi}$

C. $\frac{a\cos(\theta+\phi)}{\sin\theta\sin\phi}$  D. None of these

**3.** The angle of elevation of the top of a tower standing on a horizontal plane from a point A is $\alpha$. After walking a distance $a$ towards the foot of the tower the angle of elevation is found to be $\beta$. The height of the tower is:

A. $\frac{a\sin\alpha\sin\beta}{\sin(\beta-\alpha)}$  B. $\frac{a\sin\alpha\sin\beta}{\sin(\alpha-\beta)}$

C. $\frac{a\sin(\beta-\alpha)}{\sin\alpha\sin\beta}$  D. $\frac{a\sin(\alpha-\beta)}{\sin\alpha\sin\beta}$

**4.** The angle of elevation of the top of a TV tower from the three points A, B, C in a straight line (in the horizontal plane) through the foot of the tower are $\alpha$, $2\alpha$, $3\alpha$ respectively. If AB = $a$, the height of the tower is:

A. $a\tan\alpha$  B. $a\sin\alpha$
C. $a\sin 2\alpha$  D. $a\sin 3\alpha$

5. The height of the centre of the round balloon of radius $r$, which subtend an angle $\alpha$ at the eye of an observer and the elevation of whose centre from the eye is $\beta$, is given by:

A. $r \sin \alpha \sin \beta$ B. $r \operatorname{cosec} \frac{1}{2} \alpha \sin \beta$

C. $r \operatorname{cosec} \alpha \sin \beta$ D. None of these

6. ABCD is a square plot. The angle of elevation of the top of a pole standing at D from A or C is 30° and that from B is $\theta$, then $\tan \theta$ is equal to:

A. $\sqrt{6}$ B. $1/\sqrt{6}$
C. $\sqrt{3}/\sqrt{2}$ D. $\sqrt{2}/\sqrt{3}$

7. The angle of elevation of the top of two vertical towers as seen from the middle point of the line joining the foot of the towers are 60° and 30° respectively. The ratio of the heights of the towers is:

A. 2 : 1 B. $\sqrt{3}$ : 1
C. 3 : 2 D. 3 : 1

8. ABC is a triangular park with AB = AC = 100 metres. A clock tower is situated at the mid-point of BC. The angles of elevation of the top of the tower of A and B are $\cot^{-1}(3.2)$ and $\operatorname{cosec}^{-1}(2.6)$ respectively. The height of the tower in metres is:

A. 25/2 B. 25
C. 50 D. None of these

9. The angles of elevation of the top of a vertical tower from two points, distant $a$ and $b$ $(a > b)$ from the base and in the same straight line with it are complementary. Then the height of the tower is:

A. $\sqrt{(ab)}$ B. $\sqrt{(a^2+b^2)}$
C. $\sqrt{(a^2-b^2)}$ D. $\sqrt{a(a-b)}$

10. From the top of a $h$ metre high cliff the angles of depression of the top and the bottom of a tower are observed to be 30° and 60° respectively. The height of the tower is:

A. $h\sqrt{3}$ B. $2h\sqrt{3}$
C. $h/3$ D. $2h/3$

11. A vertical pole is 75m high. Find the angle subtended by the pole a point 75 m away from its base.

A. 30° B. 45°
C. 60° D. 90°

12. A person standing on the bank of river finds that the angle of elevation of the top of a tower on opposite side bank is 45°. Which of the following statement is correct?

A. Breadth of the river is half of the height of the tower
B. Breadth of the river and the height of the tower are equal
C. Breadth of the river is twice the height of the tower
D. None of these

13. The angles of depression of two ships from the top of a light house are 45° and 30° towards east. If the ships are 200 m apart, find the height of the light house.

A. 100 m B. 173 m
C. 200 m D. 273 m

14. A man 2 m high, walks at a uniform speed of 6 m/min away from a lamp post, 5 m high. Find the rate at which the length of his shadow increases.

A. 4 m/min B. 8 m/min
C. 9 m/min D. 14 m/min

15. Two ships leave a port at the same instant. One sails at 30 km/hr in the direction N 32°E while the other sails at 20 km/hr in the direction S 58° E. After two hours the ships are distant from each other by:

A. $15\sqrt{6}$ km B. 36.5 km
C. $20\sqrt{13}$ km D. 100 km

## ANSWERS

| 1 | 2 | 3 | 4 | 5 | 6 | 7 | 8 | 9 | 10 |
|---|---|---|---|---|---|---|---|---|---|
| C | B | A | C | B | B | D | B | A | D |
| **11** | **12** | **13** | **14** | **15** | | | | | |
| B | B | D | A | C | | | | | |

## EXPLANATORY ANSWERS

1. Let A be the position of a person on the bank of a river and OP the tree on the opposite bank and $\angle OAP$ = 60°. When the person retires to the position B, s.t.

$$AB = 40 \text{ m then } \angle OBP = 30°$$

Let OA = $x$ m and OP = $h$ m

In $\Delta$ OAP, OP = OA tan 60° = $x\sqrt{3}$

and in $\Delta$ OBP, OP = OB tan 30° = $(x + 40)/\sqrt{3}$

$\therefore$ $(x + 40)/\sqrt{3} = x\sqrt{3} \Rightarrow x = 20$ m

2. Let OP be the tower of height $h$ (say) and PQ the flag-staff of height $a$, such that

$$\angle OAP = \theta \text{ and } \angle PAQ = \phi$$

In $\Delta$OAP and $\Delta$OAQ

$$OA = OP \cot \theta = h \cot \theta$$

and $$OA = OQ \cot (\theta + \phi) = (h + a) \cot (\theta + \phi)$$

$\therefore$ $$h \cot \theta = (h + a) \cot (\theta + \phi)$$

$$\Rightarrow h = \frac{a \cot(\theta+\phi)}{\cot\theta - \cot(\theta+\phi)} = \frac{a \sin\theta \cos(\theta+\phi)}{\sin\phi}.$$

**3.** Let OP be the tower of height $h$ (say) and A and B be the two positions on the horizontal line through O, such that

$\angle$ OAP = $\alpha$, $\angle$ OBP = $\beta$ and OB = $x$

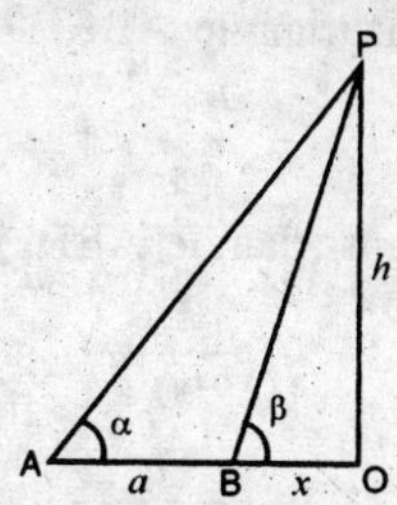


In $\Delta$OBP, OB = $x$ = $h$ cot $\beta$, and

in $\Delta$OAP, OA = $a + x$ = $h$ cot $\alpha$

$\therefore a = h(\cot\alpha - \cot\beta)$

$\Rightarrow h = a \sin\alpha \sin\beta / \sin(\beta - \alpha)$

**4.** OP is vertical tower. The elevations of the top of P from A, B, C are $\alpha$, $2\alpha$, $3\alpha$ respectively

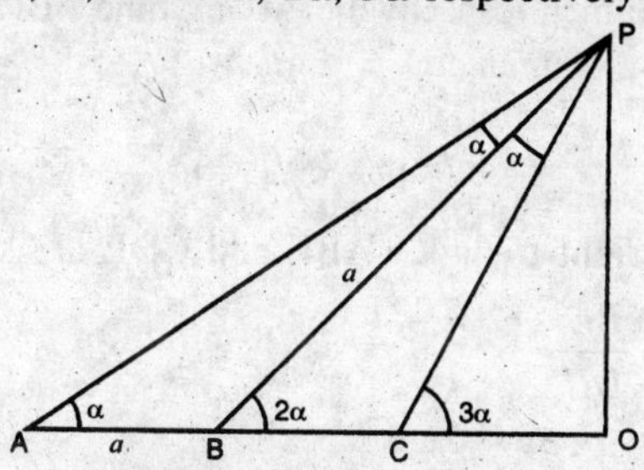


$\angle OAP = \angle APB = \alpha$

$\therefore$ AB = PB = $a$

In $\Delta$OBP, OP = PB sin $2\alpha$ = $a$ sin $2\alpha$

**5.** Let O be the centre of the balloon of radius $r$ which subtend an angle $\alpha$ at the eye of an observer at E.

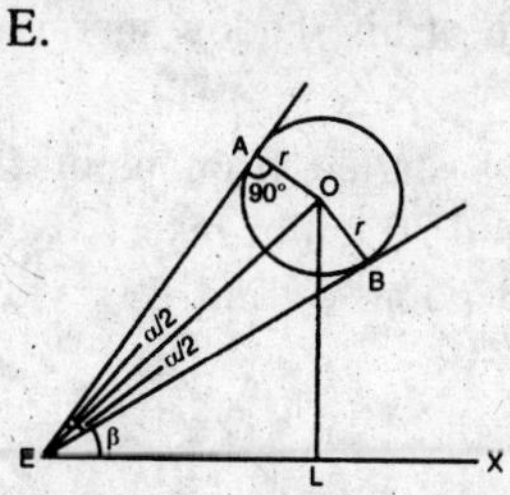


If EA and EB are the tangents to the balloon,

then $\angle OEA = \angle OEB = \dfrac{\alpha}{2}$

In $\Delta$OAE, $\sin \dfrac{1}{2}\alpha$ = OA/OE $\therefore$ OE = $r$ cosec $\dfrac{1}{2}\alpha$

In $\Delta$OEL, height of the centre of the balloon

= $h$ = OE sin $\beta$ = $r$ cosec $\dfrac{1}{2}\alpha$ sin $\beta$.

**6.** Let $a$ be the length of a side of square plot ABCD and $h$, the height of the pole standing at D. Since elevations of P from A or C is 30° and that from B is $\theta$,

$\therefore$ In $\Delta$PCD, tan 30° = $h/a$

*i.e.*, $h/a = 1/\sqrt{3}$

And in $\Delta$PBD,

tan $\theta$ = PD/BD

$= h/(a\sqrt{2})$

$= 1/\sqrt{6}$

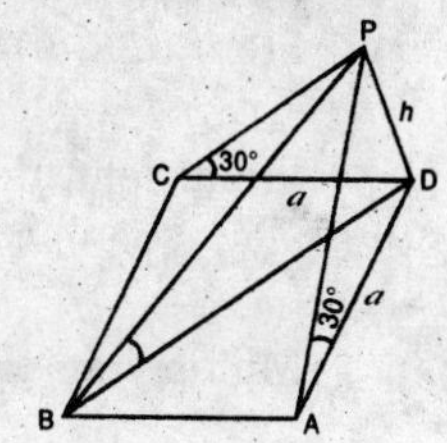


$\therefore$ BD = $\sqrt{(AB^2 + AD)^2} = a\sqrt{2}$.

**7.** Let AB and CD be two towers of heights $h_1$ and $h_2$ respectively and O the mid-point of the line joining the foots A and C of the towers.

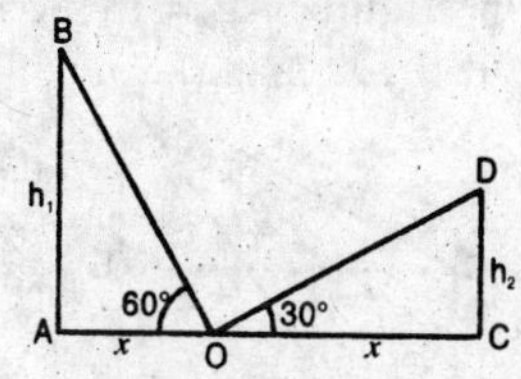


Let OA = OC = $x$

Then $h_1 = x \tan 60° = x\sqrt{3}$

and $h_2 = x \tan 30° = x/\sqrt{3}$

$\therefore \dfrac{h_1}{h_2} = \dfrac{3}{1}$, Hence, $h_1 : h_2 = 3 : 1$.

**8.** Given $\alpha = \cot^{-1}(3.2)$, $\beta = \text{cosec}^{-1}(2.6)$

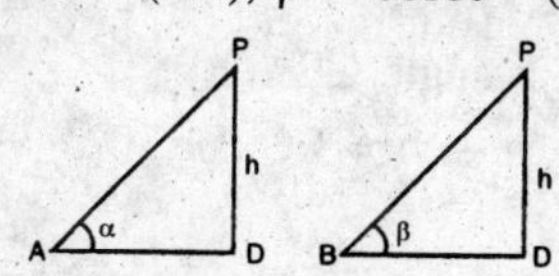


In $\Delta$PAD, AD = $h$ cot $\alpha$,

In $\Delta$PBD, BD = $h$ cot $\beta$

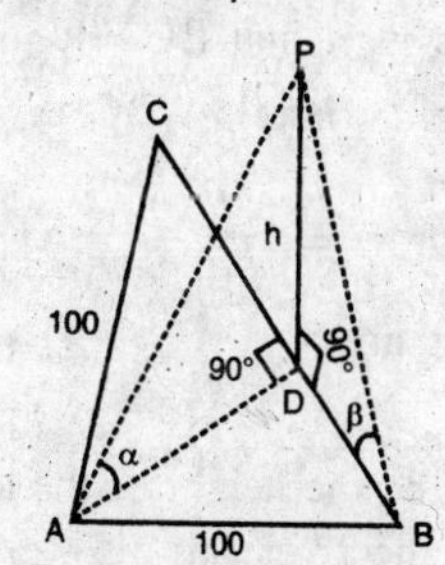


In $\Delta$ABD, $AB^2 = AD^2 + BD^2$

$= h^2(\cot^2\alpha + \cot^2\beta)$

$\Rightarrow 100^2 = h^2\{\cot^2\alpha + (\text{cosec}^2\beta - 1)\}$

$\Rightarrow 100^2 = h^2[(3.2)^2 + (2.6)^2 - 1] = 16h^2$

$\Rightarrow h = 25$ m.

**9.** Let CD = $h$ unit be the height of the tower and A and B be the two points on the ground, such that DA = $a$; DB = $b$; $\angle$ DAC = $\alpha$ and $\angle$ DBC = 90° − $\alpha$

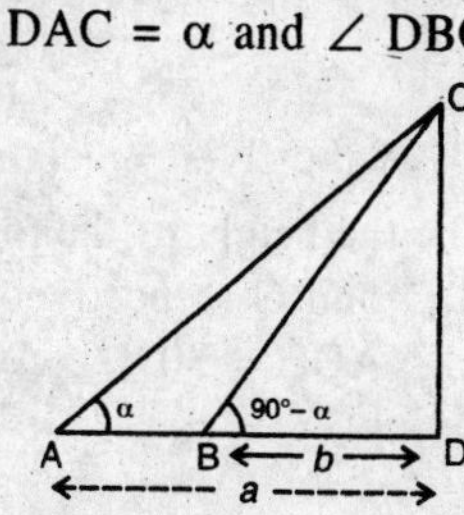

From right triangle ADC,

$$CD = h = a \tan\alpha \quad ...(i)$$

From right triangle BDC,

$$CD = h = b \tan(90° - \alpha)$$
$$= b \cot\alpha \quad ...(ii)$$

Multiplying equations *(i)* and *(ii)*, we get

$$h^2 = a \tan\alpha \,.\, b\cot\alpha$$

Hence, $h = \sqrt{ab}$

**10.** Let AB = $h$ m be the height of cliff and CD = $x$ m be the height of the tower and also ∠ADB = 60° and ∠ACE = 30°.

Now, from the figure, AE = $(h - x)$m

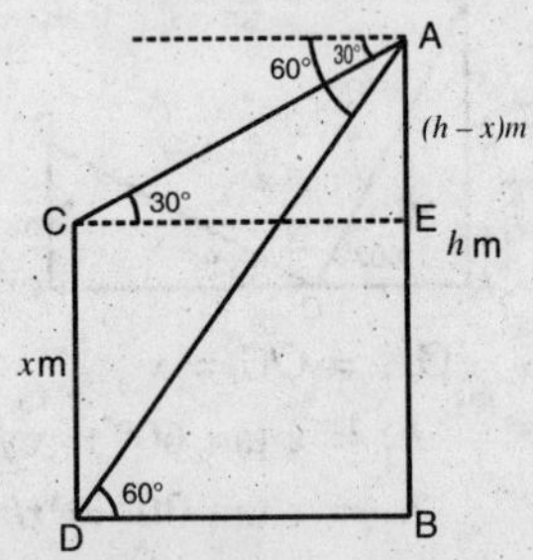


From right triangle ABD,

$$BD = h\cot 60° = \frac{h}{\sqrt{3}} \text{ m}$$

From right triangle CEA,

$$(h - x) = EC \tan 30° = BD \tan 30°$$

$$\Rightarrow \quad h - x = \frac{h}{\sqrt{3}}.\frac{1}{\sqrt{3}} \quad \therefore x = h - \frac{h}{3} = \frac{2h}{3} m$$

**11.** Let AB = 75m be the height of pole and C is a point on the ground such that BC = 75m

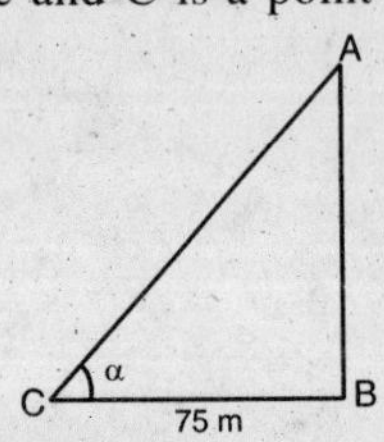


Now, from right triangle ABC,

$$\tan\alpha = \frac{AB}{BC} = \frac{75}{75}$$

$$\Rightarrow \quad \tan\alpha = 1$$

$$\therefore \quad \alpha = 45°$$

**12.** Let AB = $h$ m be the height of the tower; BC = $x$ m be the breadth of the river and also ∠ACB = 45°

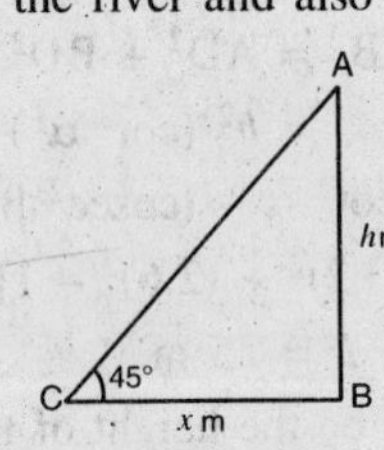


Now from right triangle ABC

$$\tan 45° = \frac{h}{x} \Rightarrow 1 = \frac{h}{x} \quad \therefore x = h$$

Hence, breadth of the river = height of the tower

**13.** Let AB = $h$m be the height of the tower and two ships are situated at D and C respectively; such that, CD = 200 m; ∠ ADC = 30°; ∠ ACB = 45° and BC = $x$m (say)

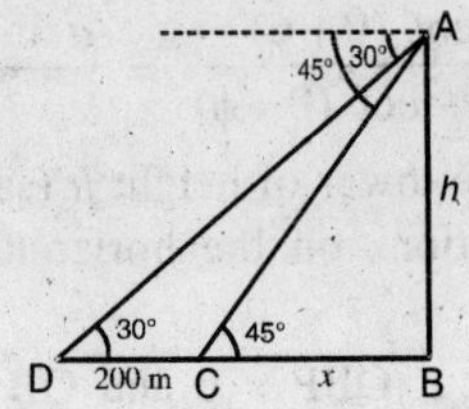


Now from right triangle ABC,

$$\tan 45° = \frac{h}{x} \Rightarrow 1 = \frac{h}{x} \quad \therefore x = h$$

Again from right triangle ABD,

$$\tan 30° = \frac{h}{200 + x}$$

$$\Rightarrow \quad \frac{1}{\sqrt{3}} = \frac{h}{200 + h} \quad (\because x = h)$$

$$\Rightarrow \quad \sqrt{3}h - h = 200$$

$$\Rightarrow \quad h(1.732 - 1) = 200$$

$$\therefore \quad h = \frac{200}{0.732} = 273.2 \text{ m} \sim 273 \text{ m}$$

**14.** Let AB = 5m and CD = 2m be the heights of a lamp post and the men respectively. At any time $t$ BD = $x$ m and shadow of man ED = $y$ m.

Then, $\frac{dx}{dt} = 6$m/min

Now, right triangles ABE and CDE are similar; then

$$\frac{AB}{CD} = \frac{BE}{DE} \Rightarrow \frac{5}{2} = \frac{x + y}{y}$$

$$\Rightarrow \quad 5y - 2y = 2x$$

$$\Rightarrow \quad 3y = 2x$$

$$\Rightarrow 3.\frac{dy}{dt} = 2.\frac{dx}{dt}$$

$$\Rightarrow 3.\frac{dy}{dt} = 2 \times 6 \;\therefore\; \frac{dy}{dt} = 4$$

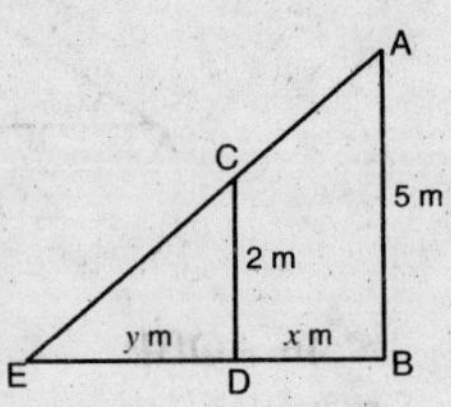


Hence, length of his shadow increases at the rate of 4 m/min.

**15.** Let two ships started from point O at the speed of 30 km/hr 0 and 20 km/hr respectively, after two hours they reach at points A and B.

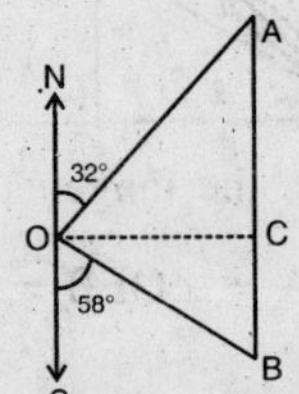


Now, ∠ NOA = 32° and ∠ SOB = 58°,

Then, ∠ AOB = 180° – (32° + 58°) = 90°

Since Δ AOB is a right triangle in which OA = 2 × 30 = 60 km and OB = 2 × 20 = 40 km

$$\text{Since, } AB = \sqrt{OA^2 + OB^2} = \sqrt{(60)^2 + (40)^2}$$
$$= \sqrt{5200} = 20\sqrt{13} \text{ km}$$

●●●

CHAPTER 13

# Data Handling

## Histogram; Frequency Polygon; Bar Diagram & Pie-Chart

### Graphical Representation of Statistical Data

One of the most convincing and appearing ways in which statistical result may be presented is through diagrams and graphs. The impressions created by diagrams last much longer than those created by the figures presented in a tabular form.

*Rather than present data numerically in the form of a table it can sometimes be better to illustrate the information through the use of graphs, charts, diagrams and so on.*

The frequency distribution of a discrete value is best represented by a bar diagram. The height of the bars is proportional to the frequency of each variate-value. The bars must be kept distinct to show that the variate-values are distinct.

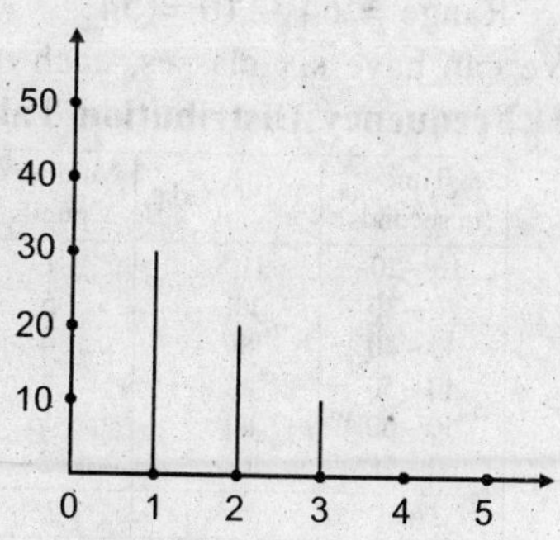


A simple bar chart is used to illustrate a frequency distribution. The lengths of the bars are proportional to the frequency and the bars are of equal width.

**Some Important Types of Diagrams and Graphs**

The different types of Diagrams and Graphs

(1) Bar diagram

(2) Histogram

(3) Frequency circle

(4) Cumulative frequency curve of the ogive

(5) Pie diagram.

### Bar Diagram

Bar diagram is the easiest and most adaptable general purpose chart. In this, bars or rectangles of uniform width are drawn with equal spaces in between on the axis. Along the $y$-axis is shown, the scale of the height of the rectangles.

Thickness of bars is not taken into account, they should be so constructed that they look attractive and beautiful. This can be done by colouring them or by preparing designs in them.

However, the colour or designs of all bars representing one type of data should be identical. The bars may be vertical or horizontal. Some of the main bar diagrams are:

(*i*) Simple Bar-Diagram

(*ii*) Sub-divided Bar-Diagram

(*iii*) Multiple Bar-Diagram

**The following Examples of Illustrate :**

**Example:** The following table gives the population of India (in millions). Draw a bar diagram of the data:

**Population (in million) of India 1931-1971**

| Year | Population (*in millions*) |
|---|---|
| 1931 | 275.5 |
| 1941 | 312.1 |
| 1951 | 356.9 |
| 1961 | 439.9 |
| 1971 | 546.9 |

**Solution:** The above data is represented by a simple bar diagram as follows :

Simple Bar Diagram Showing Population (in Millions)

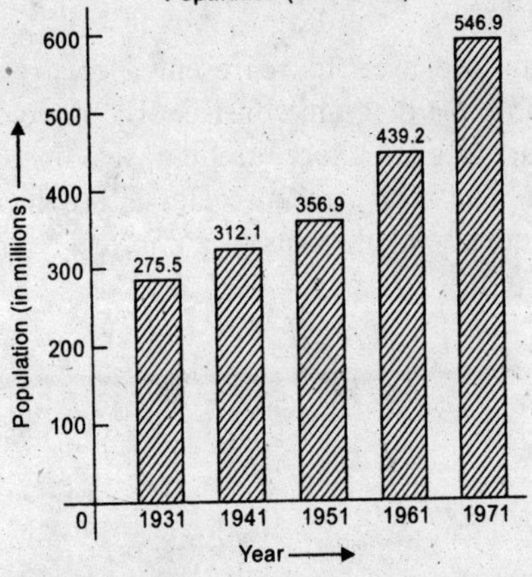


Here years are denoted on the $x$-axis and population (in millions) on the $y$-axis. The length of each bar corresponds to the number representing population on the $y$-axis.

## Sub-Divided or Component Bar Diagram

The sub-divided bar diagram is used where the total magnitude of the given variable is to be divided into various parts or sub-classes. The bars are drawn proportional in length to the total and divided in the ratios of their components. Different colours, shades, designs, etc. are used to distinguish the various components.

**Example:** Represent the following data of sex-wise distribution of students in a school by a bar diagram.

| Year | No. of Students | | Total |
|---|---|---|---|
| | *Male* | *Female* | |
| 1978 | 800 | 250 | 1050 |
| 1979 | 900 | 300 | 1200 |
| 1980 | 950 | 375 | 1325 |
| 1981 | 1000 | 400 | 1400 |
| 1982 | 1150 | 450 | 1600 |

**Solution:** The above data are represented by a sub-divided bar diagram, as follows.

Sub-Divided Bar Diagram showing Sex-wise Distribution of Students

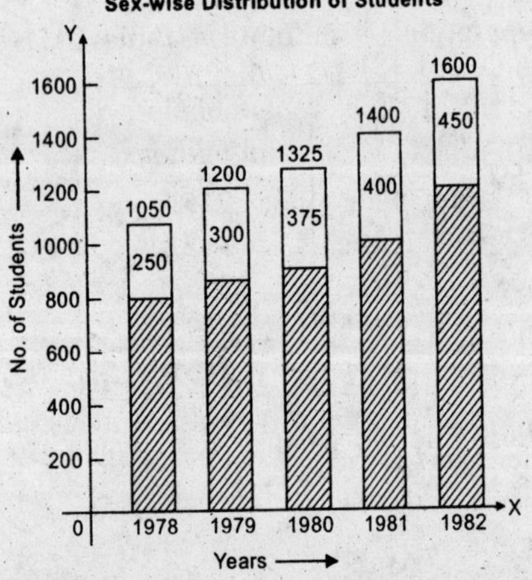


In a multiple bar diagram two or more sets of inter-related data are presented. The technique of drawing such a diagram is basically the same as that of simple bar diagram.

## Histograms

The histogram is most popularly used for graphical presentation of a frequency distribution. A histogram is a graph that represents the class frequencies in a frequency distribution by vertical adjacent rectangles. After choosing a convenient scale on the axes, mark off the class intervals along $x$-axis and the frequencies of the respective class intervals along $y$-axis. Then construct rectangles with each class intervals as breadth and the respective frequency of the class interval as height. The set of the all adjacent rectangles so constructed form a histogram.

**Note :** A histogram is a development of the bar chart but remember when drawing a histogram it is the Area of each bar which is proportional to the frequency and there are no gaps between the bars because the classes are usually arranged so that there are no gaps.

**The following Examples of Illustrates:**

**Example:** The time taken, in seconds, to solve a problem by each of 25 pupils is as follows: 16, 20, 26, 27, 28, 30, 33, 37, 38, 40, 42, 42, 43, 46, 46, 48, 49, 50, 53, 58, 59, 60, 64, 52, 20.

(*a*) Construct a frequency distribution for these data, using a class interval of 10 seconds.

(*b*) Draw a histogram to represent the frequency distribution.

**Solution:**

(*a*) Lowest observation = 10

Highest observation = 64

Range = 64 − 10 = 54

We can have six classes, each of width 10.

**Frequency Distribution Table**

| Time (in seconds) | Tally marks | Number of pupils |
|---|---|---|
| 10 – 20 | I | 1 |
| 20 – 30 | IIII̸ | 5 |
| 30 – 40 | IIII | 4 |
| 40 – 50 | IIII̸ III | 8 |
| 50 – 60 | IIII̸ | 5 |
| 60 – 70 | II | 2 |
| Total | | 25 |

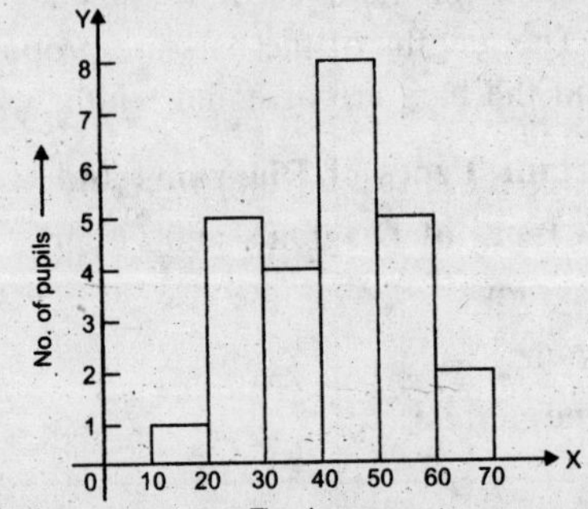

## Frequency Polygon

A frequency polygon is a graph of frequency distribution. The steps constructing a frequency polygonal are:

1. Draw a suitable histogram keeping in view all the basic principles.
2. Get the mid-points of the upper horizontal side of each rectangle.
3. Join these mid-points of the adjacent rectangles of the histogram by straight lines taken in order, they form a polygon called frequency polygon.
4. End of frequency polygon preferably extended to the base line.

In a frequency polygon the variables or individuals of each class are assumed to be concentrated at the class-intervals.

**Note:** If only frequency polygon is to be drawn, first represent the class-marks ($x_i$) on the $x$-axis and corresponding frequencies ($f_i$) on $y$-axis. Plot all the points ($x_i$, $f_i$). Then join these points by line segments. The figure so obtained is known as the frequency polygon. The polygon should be brought down at the ends to the $x$-axis at each and of the drawn.

**The following Examples of Illustrate:**

**Example:** In a city the following weekly observations were made in a study on cost of Living Index for the year 1970–71.

| Cost of Living Index | No. of weeks |
|---|---|
| 140 – 150 | 5 |
| 150 – 160 | 10 |
| 160 – 170 | 20 |
| 170 – 180 | 9 |
| 180 – 190 | 6 |
| 190 – 200 | 2 |

Draw a histogram and frequency polygon on the same scale.

**Solution:**

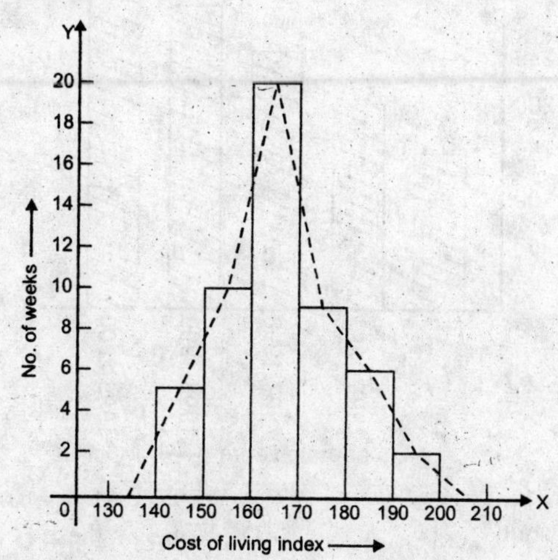


## Pie Diagram

Pie-diagrams are used to represent a relative frequency distribution. A pie diagram consists of a circle divided into as many sectors as there are classes in a frequency distribution. The area of each sector is proportional to the relative frequency of the class.

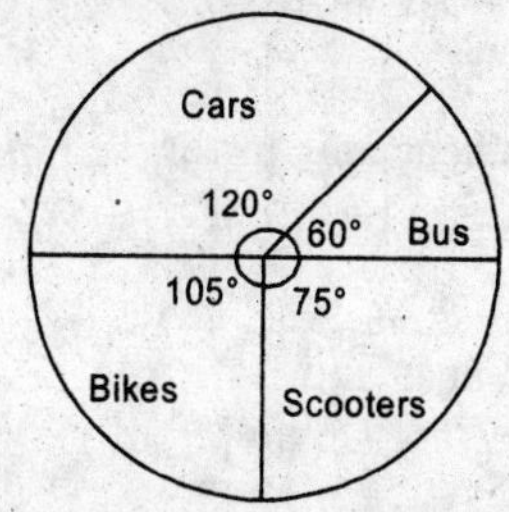


Now we make angles at the centre proportional to the relative frequencies. And in order to get the angles of the disired sectors, we divide 360° in the proportion of the various relative frequencies, *i.e.*,

$$\text{Central angle} = \left[\frac{\text{Frequency} \times 360°}{\text{Total frequency}}\right]$$

**Example :** The pie-chart provided below gives the distribution of land (in a village) under various food crops. Study the pie-chart carefully and answer the questions that follow.

**Distribution of Areas (in Acre) Under various Food Crops**

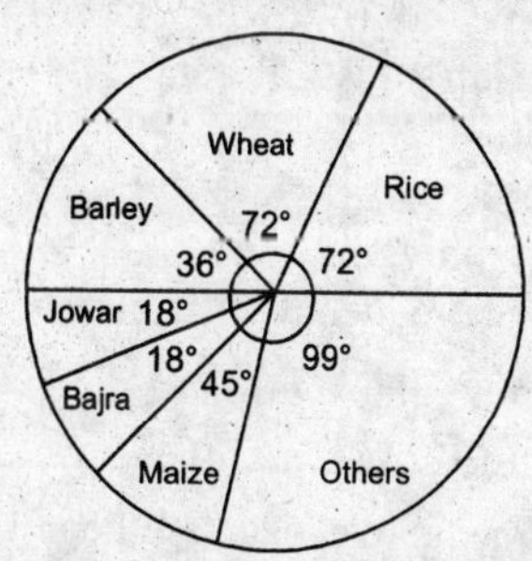


1. Which combination of three crops contribute to 50% of the total area under the food crops?
   (*a*) Wheat, Barley and Jowar
   (*b*) Rice, Wheat and Jowar
   (*c*) Rice, Wheat and Barley
   (*d*) Bajra, Maize and Rice
2. If the total area under jowar was 1.5 million acres, then what was the area (in million acres) under rice?
   (*a*) 6 (*b*) 7.5
   (*c*) 9 (*d*) 4.5
3. If the production of wheat is 6 times that of barley, then what is the ratio between the yield per acre of wheat and barley?
   (*a*) 3 : 2 (*b*) 3 : 1
   (*c*) 12 : 1 (*d*) 2 : 3

**Solution:**

**1 (c):** The total of the central angles corresponding to the three crops which cover 50% of the total area, should be 180°. Now, the total of the central angles for the given combinations are:

(*i*) Wheat, Barley and Jowar
$= (72° + 36° + 18°)$
$= 126°$

(*ii*) Rice, Wheat and Jowar
$= (72° + 72° + 18°)$
$= 162°$

(*iii*) Rice, Wheat and Barley
$= (72° + 72° + 36°)$
$= 180°$

(*iv*) Bajra, Maize and Rice
$= (18° + 45° + 72°)$
$= 135°$

Clearly, (*iii*) is the required combination.

**2 (a):** The area under any of the food crops is proportional to the central angle corres-ponding to that crop.

Let, the area under rice production be $x$ million acres.

Then, $18 : 72 = 1.5 : x$

$$\Rightarrow x = \left(\frac{72 \times 1.5}{18}\right) = 6.$$

Thus, the area under rice production = 6 million acress

**3 (b):** Let, the total production of barley be T tonnes and let Z acres of land be put under barley production. Then, the total production of wheat = (6T) tonnes. Also, area under wheat production = (2Z) areas.

$$\left[\because \frac{\text{Area under Wheat production}}{\text{Area under Barley production}} = \frac{72°}{36°} = 2 \text{ and therefore, Area under wheat} = 2 \times \text{Area under barley} = (2Z) \text{ acres}\right]$$

Now, yield per acre for wheat

$$= \left(\frac{6T}{2Z}\right) \text{ tonnes/acre} = \left(\frac{3T}{Z}\right) \text{ tonnes/acre}$$

and yield per acre for barley

$$= \left(\frac{T}{Z}\right) \text{ tonnes/acre.}$$

$$\therefore \text{ Required Ratio} = \left(\frac{3T/Z}{T/Z}\right) = 3:1.$$

## EXERCISE

**1.** Which one of the following is not the graphical representation of statistical data?
A. Bar graph
B. Histogram
C. Frequency polygon
D. Cumulative frequency distribution

**2.** In a frequency distribution, ogives are graphical representation of:
A. Frequency
B. Relative frequency
C. Cumulative frequency
D. Raw data

**3.** A frequency polygon is constructed by plotting frequency of the class interval and the:
A. upper limit of the class
B. lower limit of the class
C. mid value of the class
D. any values of the class

**4.** In a histogram the area of each rectangle is proportional to:
A. the class mark of the corresponding class interval
B. the class size of the corresponding class interval
C. frequency of the corresponding class interval
D. cumulative frequency of the corresponding class interval

**5.** In a histogram, each class rectangle is constructed with base as:
A. frequency B. class-intervals
C. range D. size of the class

**6.** Read the bar graph shown in figure and answer the following question:

In which year is the increase of students maximum?

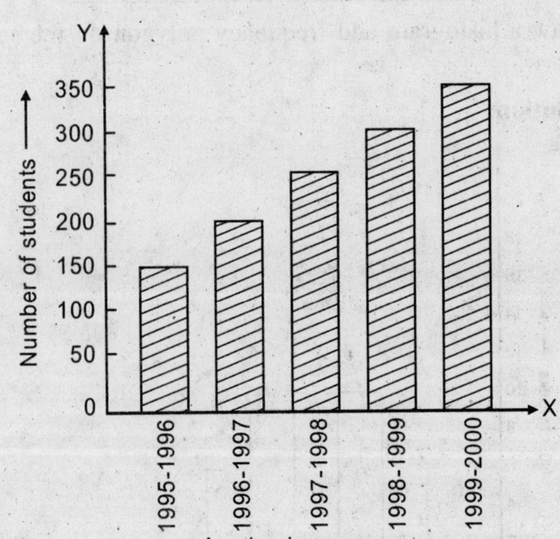


A. 1996-1997 B. 1997-1998
C. 1999-2000 D. None of these

**Directions (Qs. 7 to 9) :** *Read the following bar graph shown in figure and answer the following questions:*

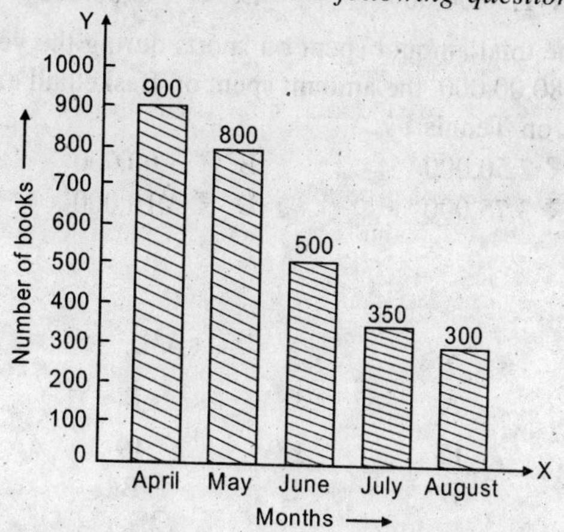


**7.** In which month was the sale of the books maximum?

A. April B. May
C. June D. August

**8.** In which month was the sale of the books minimum?

A. April B. May
C. July D. August

**9.** What is the total sale during these five months?

A. 3800 copies B. 2850 copies
C. 2800 copies D. 2950 copies

**Directions (Qs. 10 to 12) :** *Read the following bar graph given in figure and answer the following questions:*

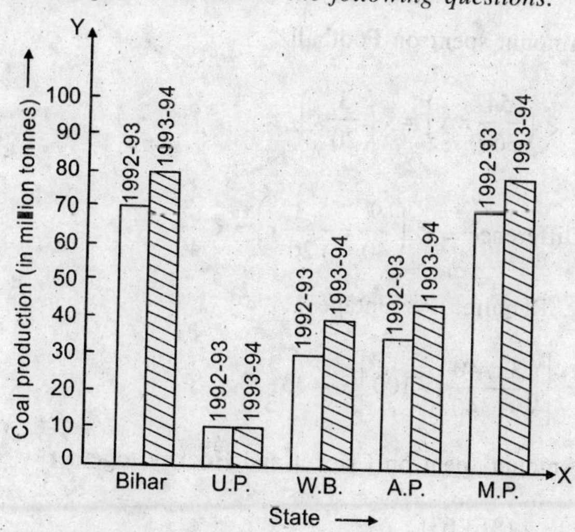


**10.** Which two states have same production in 1993-94?

A. M.P. and Bihar
B. M.P. and U.P.
C. U.P. and Bihar
D. W.B. and U.P.

**11.** Which state has same production in both the years?

A. M.P. B. Bihar
C. U.P. D. W.B.

**12.** Which state has minimum production?

A. M.P. B. A.P.
C. W.B D. U.P.

**Directions (Qs. 13 to 15) :** *The following bar graph shows the results of an annual examination in a secondary school. Read the bar graph and choose the correct alternative in each of the following.*

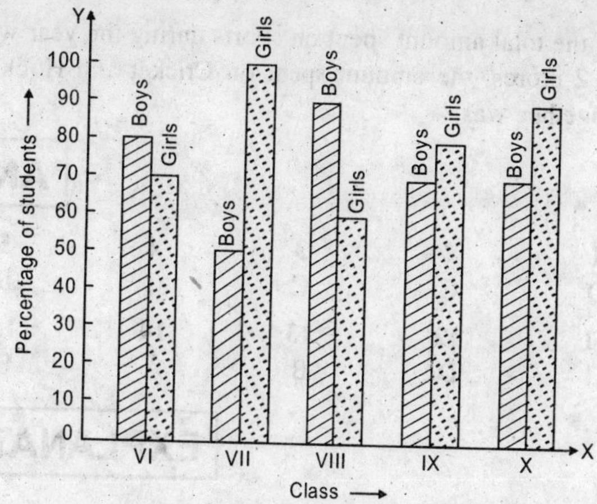


**13.** The pair of classes in which the results of boys and girls are inversely proportional are:

A. VI, VIII B. VI, IX
C. VIII, IX D. VIII, X

**14.** The class having the lowest failure rate of girls is:

A. VII B. X
C. IX D. VIII

**15.** The class having the lowest pass rate of boys is:

A. VI B. VII
C. VIII D. IX

**Directions (Qs. 16 to 20) :** *The circle-graph given here shows the spendings of a country on various sports during a particular year. Study the graph carefully and answer the questions given below it.*

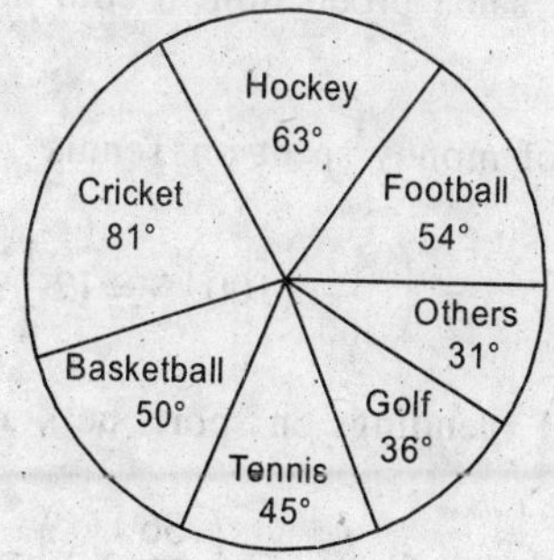


**16.** What per cent of the total spendings is spent on Tennis?

A. $12\frac{1}{2}\%$ B. $22\frac{1}{2}\%$
C. 25% D. 45%

**17.** How much per cent more is spent on Hockey than that on Golf?

A. 27% B. 35%
C. 37.5% D. 75%

**18.** How much per cent less is spent on Football than that on Cricket?

A. $22\frac{2}{9}\%$ B. 27%

C. $33\frac{1}{3}\%$ D. $37\frac{1}{2}\%$

**19.** If the total amount spent on sports during the year was ₹ 2 crores, the amount spent on Cricket and Hockey together was:

A. ₹ 8,00,000 B. ₹ 80,00,000

C. ₹ 1,20,00,000 D. ₹ 1,60,00,000

**20.** If the total amount spent on sports during the years be ₹ 1,80,00,000, the amount spent on Basketball exceeds that on Tennis by:

A. ₹ 2,50,000 B. ₹ 3,60,000

C. ₹ 3,75,000 D. ₹ 4,10,000

## ANSWERS

| 1 | 2 | 3 | 4 | 5 | 6 | 7 | 8 | 9 | 10 |
|---|---|---|---|---|---|---|---|---|---|
| D | C | C | C | B | D | A | D | B | A |
| **11** | **12** | **13** | **14** | **15** | **16** | **17** | **18** | **19** | **20** |
| C | D | B | A | B | A | D | C | B | A |

## EXPLANATORY ANSWERS

**6.** The increase in the number of students is uniform as the increase in the heights of bars is uniform. Hence, in this case the increase is not maximum in any of the year.

**7.** The sale of the books was maximum in the month of April as the height of the rectangle corresponding to April month is maximum.

**8.** The sale of the books was minimum in the month of August as the height of the corresponding rectangle is minimum.

**9.** Total sale of the books during 5 months.

(900 + 800 + 500 + 350 + 300) = 2850 copies.

**10.** M.P. and Bihar have same production in 1993-1994.

**11.** U.P. has the same production in both the years.

**12.** U.P.

**16.** Percentage of money spent on Tennis

$$= \left(\frac{45}{360} \times 100\right)\% = 12\frac{1}{2}\%$$

**17.** Let the total spendings on sports be ₹ $x$. Then,

Amount spent on Golf = ₹ $\left(\frac{36}{360} \times x\right) = ₹\frac{x}{10}$

Amount spent on Hockey

$$= ₹\left(\frac{63}{360} \times x\right) = ₹\frac{7}{40}x.$$

Difference = ₹ $\left(\frac{7}{40}x - \frac{x}{10}\right) = ₹\frac{3x}{40}$

∴ Required Percentage

$$= \left[\left(\frac{3x/40}{x/10}\right) \times 100\right]\% = 75\%$$

**18.** Let the total spendings on sports be ₹ $x$. Then,

Amount spent on Cricket

$$= ₹\left(\frac{81}{360} \times x\right) = ₹\left(\frac{9}{40}x\right)$$

Amount spent on Football

$$= ₹\left(\frac{54}{360} \times x\right) = ₹\left(\frac{3}{20}x\right)$$

Difference = ₹ $\left(\frac{9}{40}x - \frac{3}{20}x\right) = ₹\frac{3}{40}x$

∴ Required Percentage

$$= \left[\left(\frac{3x/40}{9x/40}\right) \times 100\right]\% = 33\frac{1}{3}\%$$

**19.** Amount spent on Cricket and Hockey together

$$= ₹\left[\frac{(81+63)}{360} \times 2\right] \text{ crores}$$

= ₹ 0.8 crores = ₹ 8000000.

**20.** Amount spent on Basketball exceeds that on Tennis by :

$$= ₹\left[\frac{(50-45)}{360} \times 18000000\right] = ₹\ 250000.$$

●●●

# GENERAL KNOWLEDGE & GENERAL AWARENESS

# INDIAN HISTORY

## ANCIENT INDIA

### INDUS VALLEY CIVILISATION (2500-1750 BC)

- The earliest excavations in the Indus valley were done at Harappa in the West Punjab and Mohenjodaro in Sindh. Both places are now in Pakistan.

**Important Sites**

- The most important sites are Kot Diji in Sindh, Kalibangan in Rajasthan, Ropar in the Punjab, Banawali in Haryana, Lothal, Surkotada and Dhaulavira, all the three in Gujarat.
- Mohenjodaro is the largest of all the Indus cities and it is estimated to have spread over an area of 200 hectares.

**Indus Valley Civilisation : An Objective Study**

| *Major Sites* | *Excavators* | *Year* | *River* | *Location* | *Important Findings* |
|---|---|---|---|---|---|
| 1. Harappa | D.R. Sahni | 1921 | Ravi | West Punjab (Pakistan) | Granaries, Virgin Goddess, Cemetery, Stone symbol of Lingam and Yoni |
| 2. Mohenjodaro | R.D. Banerjee | 1922 | Indus | Sindh (Pakistan) | Great Bath, Great Granary, Assem bly Hall, Proto-Shiva, Brick Kilns, Meso-potamian seals |
| 3. Chanhudaro | N.G. Mazumdar | 1931 | Indus | Sindh (Pakistan) | Bronze toy cart, Ink-pot, Lipstick, City without a citadel |
| 4. Kalibangan | B.B. Lal & B.K. Thapar | 1953 | Ghaggar | Ganganagar (Rajasthan) | Decorated bricks, ploughed field surface, Firealtars |
| 5. Lothal | S.R. Rao | 1957 | Bhogwa | Ahmedabad (Gujarat) | Dockyard, Rice husk, Fire altars, Double burial |
| 6. Banawali | R.S. Bist | 1973 | Ghaggar | Hissar (Haryana) | Toy plough, Gridiron pattern of Town planning. |
| 7. Dholavira | R.S. Bist | 1990 | Luni | Kutchh (Gujarat) | A Large well & a bath, A stadium |
| 8. Surkotada | J. Joshi | 1964 | — | Gujarat | Bones of Horse, Pot burials |

**Salient Features of the Harappan Culture**

- The Harappan Civilization was primarily Urban.
- Mohenjodaro and Harappa were the planned cities.
- The large-scale use of burnt bricks in almost all kinds of constructions are the important characteristics of the Harappan culture.
- Another remarkable feature was the underground drainage system connecting all houses to the street drains which were covered by stone slabs or bricks.
- The most important public place of Mohenjodaro is the Great Bath measuring 39 feet length, 23 feet breadth and 8 feet depth.
- Agriculture was the most important occupation. In the fertile soils, farmers cultivated two crops a year. They were the first who had grown paddy.
- Wheat and barley were the main crops grown besides sesame, mustard and cotton.
- Animals like sheep, goats and buffalo were domesticated. The use of horse is not yet firmly established.
- Bronze and copper vessels are the outstanding examples of the Harappan metal craft.
- A large number of seals numbering more than 2000 have been discovered.

### Social Life

- Jewelleries such as bangles, bracelets, fillets, girdles, anklets, ear-rings and finger rings were worn by women. These ornaments were made of gold, silver, copper, bronze and semi precious stones.
- Fishing was a regular occupation while hunting and bull fighting were other pastimes.
- Manufacture of terracotta (burnt clay) was a major industry of the people.
- Figures of animals such as sacred bull and dove were discovered. The figures of Mother Goddesses were used for religious purposes.
- Most of the inscriptions were engraved on seals. It is interesting to note that the Indus script has not yet been deciphered.
- The Pipal tree was used as a religious symbol.
- The origin of the '*Swastika*' symbol can be traced to the Harrapan Civilization.
- The chief male deity was Pasupati, (proto-Siva) represented in seals as sitting in a yogic posture with three faces and two horns.

## THE VEDIC PERIOD

### RIG VEDIC AGE (1500 - 1000 B.C.)

- The Early Vedic period is known from the *Rig Veda*.
- The *Rig Veda* refers to Saptasindhu or the land of seven rivers. This includes the five rivers of the Punjab, namely, Jhelum, Chenab, Ravi, Beas and Sutlej along with the Indus and Saraswati.
- Historians view that the Aryans came from Central Asia. They entered India through the Khyber pass between 2000 B.C. and 1500 B.C. They first settled in seven places in the Punjab region which they called Sapta Sindhu. Slowly, they moved towards the Gangetic Valley.
- The Aryan Civilisation was a rural civilisation.

### Vedic Literature

- The word 'Veda' is derived from the root 'vid', which means to know and signifies 'superior knowledge'.
- The Vedic literature consists of the four Vedas – Rig, Yajur, Sama and Atharva.
- The *Rig Veda* is the earliest of the four Vedas divided into 10 mandalas and it consists of 1028 hymns. The hymns were sung by *Hotri* in praise of various gods.
- The *Yajur Veda* consists of various details of rules to be observed at the time of sacrifice. Its hymns were recited by *Adharvayus*.
- The *Sama Veda* is set to tune for the purpose of chanting during sacrifice. It is called the book of chants and the origins of Indian music are traced in it. Its hymns were recited by *Udgatri*.
- The *Atharva Veda* contains details of rituals.
- Besides the Vedas, there are other sacred works like the Brahmanas, the Aranyakas, the Upanishads, and the epics Ramayana and Mahabharata.

### Political Organisation

- During this period, the kingdom was tribal in character. Each tribe formed a separate kingdom.
- The basic unit of political organisation was *kula* or family.
- The highest political unit was called *jana* or tribe.
- There were several tribal kingdoms during the Rig Vedic period such as Bharatas, Matsyas, Yadus and Purus. The head of the kingdom was called as *rajan* or king.
- There were two popular bodies called the *Sabha* and *Samiti*. The former seems to have been a council of elders and the latter, a general assembly of the entire people.

### Social Life

- Family was the basis of the society.
- The head of the family was known as *grihapathi*.

### Economic Condition

- The Rig Vedic Aryans were pastoral people and their main occupation was cattle rearing. Their wealth was estimated in terms of their cattle.
- Carpentry was another important profession.

### RELIGION

- The important Rig Vedic gods were Prithvi (Earth), Agni (Fire), Vayu (Wind), Varuna (Rain) and Indra (Thunder).
- Indra was the most popular among them during the early Vedic period.
- There were also female gods like Aditi and Ushas. There were no temples and no idol worship during the early Vedic period.

**Rigvedic Rivers**

| River | Name in Rigveda |
|---|---|
| Indus | Sindhu |
| Jhelum | Vitasta |
| Chenab | Asikni |
| Ravi | Parushini |
| Beas | Vipasa |
| Sutlej | Sutudri |
| Gomati | Gomal |
| Saraswati | Sarasvati |
| Ghaggar | Prishadavati |

### LATER VEDIC PERIOD (1000–600 B.C.)

- This age is also called as the Epic Age because the two great epics the Ramayana and Mahabharata were written during this period.

- The Sama, Yajur, Atharva Vedas, Brahmanas, Aranyakas, Upanishads and the two epics are the sources of information for this period.

### Political Organisation

- Larger kingdoms were formed during the later Vedic period.
- The king performed various rituals and sacrifices to strengthen his position. They include Rajasuya (consecration ceremony), Asvamedha (horse sacrifice) and Vajpeya (chariot race).
- Kingship became hereditary.
- Kings assumed titles like Ekrat, Samrat and Sarvabhauma.

### Economic Condition

- Iron was used extensively in this period and this enabled the people to clear forests and to bring more land under cultivation. Agriculture became the chief occupation.
- Taxes like Bali, Sulk and Bhaga were collected from the people.
- Wealth was calculated in terms of cows.

### Social Life

- The four divisions of society (Brahmins, Kshatriyas, Vaisyas and Sudras) or the Varna system was thoroughly established during the Later Vedic period.
- The Ashrama system was formed to attain 4 purusharthas. They were *Dharma*, *Artha*, *Kama* and *Moksha*.

### Religion

- Gods of the Early Vedic period like Indra and Agni lost their importance. Prajapathi (the creator), Vishnu (the protector) and Rudra (the destroyer) became prominent during the Later Vedic period.

## JAINISM AND BUDDHISM

### JAINISM

- Jainism originated in the 6th century B.C. It rejected Vedic religion and avoided its rituals.
- Founded by Rishabha Deva. Rishabha Deva was succeeded by 23 Thirthankaras (prophets). Mahavira was the 24th Thirthankara.

### Vardhamana Mahavira (540-468 B.C.)

- Vardhamana was born in a village called Kundagrama near Vaishali in Bihar.
- His father was *Siddhartha*. He was the head of a famous Kshatriya clan.
- His mother was *Trisala*. She was a princess of the Lichchhavi clan. She was the sister of the ruler of Vaishali.
- Vardhamana was married to *Yasoda*, a princess. They had a daughter.
- At the age of 30, he left his home and family. He became an ascetic (monk). He wandered from place-to-place in search of truth for 12 years.
- In the 13th year of his penance, he attained the highest spiritual knowledge called Kevalya or Jnana. Thereafter, he was called Mahavira and Jina. His followers were called Jains and his religion Jainism.
- He died at the age of 72 in 468 B.C. at a place called Pavapuri near modern Rajgir in Bihar.

### Teachings of Jainism

- The three principles of Jainism, also known as Triratnas (three gems), are:
  1. right faith.
  2. right knowledge.
  3. right conduct.
- Mahavira preached his disciples to follow the five principles. They are:
  1. Ahimsa—not to injure any living beings
  2. Satya—to speak the truth
  3. Asteya—not to steal
  4. Tyag—not to own property
  5. Brahmacharia—to lead a virtuous life.

### Spread of Jainism

- Mahavira preached his religion in Prakrit language which was the language of the masses.
- Chandragupta Maurya, Kharavela of Kalinga and the royal dynasties of south India such as the Gangas, the Kadambas, the Chalukyas and the Rashtrakutas patronised Jainism.
- Jainism was divided into two sects after Vallabhi Council, namely *Svetambaras* (wearing white dresses) under Sthulbhadra and *Digambaras* (naked) under Bhadrabahu.
- The first Jain Council was convened at Pataliputra by Sthulabahu, the leader of the *Digambaras*, in the beginning of the 3rd century B.C.
- The second Jain Council was held at Vallabhi in 5th century A.D. The final compilation of Jain literature called *Twelve Angas* was completed in this council.

### BUDDHISM

### Gautama Buddha (563-483 B.C.)

- Buddha's original name was *Siddhartha*.
- Siddhartha was born in the Lumbini Garden near Kapilavastu in Nepal. His father was Suddhodana. He was a Sakya chief of Kapilavastu. His mother, Mayadevi, died when Siddhartha was only seven days old. He was brought up by his step mother Mahaprajapati Gauthami.
- At the age of sixteen Siddhartha, married Yasodhara and gave birth to a son, Rahul.
- The sight of an old man, a diseased man, a corpse and an ascetic turned him away from worldly life. He left home at the age of twenty-nine in search of Truth.
- He wandered for seven years and at last, he sat under a bodhi tree at Bodh Gaya in Bihar and did intense penance, after which he got Enlightenment (Nirvana) at the age of

thirty-five. Since then, he became known as the Buddha or 'the Enlightened One'.

- Buddha delivered his first sermon at Sarnath near Banaras (now Varanasi).
- He died at the age of 80 in 483 B.C. at Kushinagar in Uttar Pradesh.

### Teachings of Buddha

- The Four Noble Truths of Buddha are:
  1. The world is full of suffering.
  2. The cause of suffering is desire.
  3. If desires are get rid off, suffering can be removed.
  4. This can be done by following the Eightfold Path.
- The Eightfold Path consists of:
  1. Right Thought.
  2. Right Belief.
  3. Right Speech.
  4. Right Action.
  5. Right Living.
  6. Right Efforts.
  7. Right Knowledge.
  8. Right Meditation.

### Buddhist Literature

- In Pali language.
- Buddhist scriptures in Pali are commonly referred to as *Tripitakas, i.e.*, 'Three Baskets'.
- ***Vinaya Pitaka:*** Rules of discipline in Buddhist monasteries.
- ***Sutta Pitaka:*** Largest, contains collection of Buddha's sermons.
- ***Abidhamma Pitaka:*** Explanation of the philosophical principles of the Buddhist religion.

**Main Buddhist Councils**

| Buddhist Council | Time | Place | Chairman | Patron |
|---|---|---|---|---|
| First | 483 BC | Rajagriha | Mahakashyapa | Ajatasatru |
| Second | 383 BC | Vaishali | Sabakamuni | Kalashoka |
| Third | 250 BC | Patliputra | Moggaliputta Tissa | Ashoka |
| Fourth | AD 72 | Kundalvana | Vasumitra, Ashwaghosa | Kanishka |

**The Mahajanapadas**

| Mahajanapadas | Capital |
|---|---|
| 1. Kashi | Varanasi |
| 2. Kosala | Shravasti |
| 3. Anga | Champanagri |
| 4. Magadh | Girivraj or Rajgriha |
| 5. Vajji | Vaishali |
| 6. Malla | Kushinagar and Pavapuri |
| 7. Chedi | Shuktimati |
| 8. Vatsa | Kaushambi |
| 9. Kuru | Hastinapur, Indraprastha and Isukara |
| 10. Panchal | Ahichhatra and Kampilya |
| 11. Matsya | Viratnagar |
| 12. Surasen | Mathura |
| 13. Asmaka | Paudanya |
| 14. Avanti | Ujjaini |
| 15. Gandhara | Taxila |
| 16. Kamboj | Rajpur (Hatak) |

## DYNASTIES OF ANCIENT INDIA

### HARYANKA DYNASTY

- Bimbisara was the founder of Haryanka Dynasty.
- He was a contemporary of both Vardhamana Mahavira and Gautama Buddha.
- During his rule, Darius I, the Achaemenian emperor, conquered the Indus Valley area.
- Ajatasatru imprisoned his father Bimbisara.
- The first Buddhist Council was convened by Ajatasatru at Rajgir.
- The immediate successor of Ajatasatru was Udayin.
- Udayin laid the foundation of the new capital at Pataliputra situated at the confluence of the two rivers, the Ganges and the Sone.
- Shishunaga was the founder of Shishunaga dynasty.
- After Shishunaga, the mighty empire began to collapse. His successor was Kakavarman or Kalasoka. During his reign, the second Buddhist Council was held at Vaishali.
- Kalasoka was killed by the founder of the Nanda dynasty.

### NANDAS

- The fame of Magadha scaled new heights under the Nanda dynasty.
- Mahapadmananda was the founder of Nanda rule in Magadha.
- The last Nanda ruler was Dhana Nanda. Alexander invaded India during his rule.

# MAURYAN EMPIRE

## CHANDRAGUPTA MAURYA (322–298 B.C.)

- Chandragupta Maurya was the founder of the Mauryan Empire. He overthrew Nanda dynasty with the help of Chanakya.
- Chandragupta defeated Seleukos Nikator, the Greek general of Alexander, in a battle in 305 B.C.
- Seleukos sent Megasthenes as Greek Ambassador to the Court of Chandragupta. Megasthenes wrote *Indica*.
- Chandragupta was a follower of Jainism.
- He came to Sravana Belgola, near Mysore with a Jain monk called Bhadrabahu. The hill in which he lived until his death is called Chandragiri.
- Chanakya served as prime minister during the reigns of Chandragupta and Bindusara.

## BINDUSARA (298–273 B.C.)

- Chandragupta Maurya was succeeded by his son Bindusara.
- Bindusara was called by the Greeks as "*Amitraghatha*" meaning, slayer of enemies.

## ASHOKA (273–232 B.C.)

- Ashoka was the most famous ruler of the Mauryan dynasty.
- The most important event of Ashoka's reign was his victorious war with Kalinga in 261 B.C.
- Ashoka convened the Third Buddhist Council at Pataliputra around 250 B.C. in order to strengthen the *Sangha*. It was presided over by Moggaliputta Tissa.
- Ashoka's edicts and inscriptions were deciphered by James Prinsep in 1837.
- The last Mauryan king, Brahadratha was killed by his minister Pushyamitra Sunga. It put an end to the Mauryan Empire.

## SUNGAS

- The founder of the Sunga dynasty was *Pushyamitra Sunga*, who was the commander-in-chief under the Mauryas.
- He ascended the throne of Magadha in 185 B.C.
- Pushyamitra was a staunch follower of Brahmanism. He performed two asvamedha sacrifices.
- After the death of Pushyamitra, his son Agnimitra became the ruler.
- Agnimitra was a great conqueror. He was also the hero of the play *Malavikagnimitram* written by Kalidasa.

## KANVA

- The last Sunga ruler was Devabhuti, who was murdered by his minister Vasudeva Kanva, the founder of the *Kanva dynasty*.
- The Kanva dynasty ruled for 45 years. After the fall of the Kanvas, the history of Magadha was a blank until the establishment of the Gupta dynasty.

## SATAVAHANAS

- The founder of the Satavahana dynasty was Simuka.
- The greatest ruler of the Satavahana dynasty was *Gautamiputra Satakarni.*
- The greatest port of the Satavahanas was Kalyani on the west Deccan. Gandakasela and Ganjam on the east coast were the other important seaports.
- The fine painting at Amaravathi and Nagarjunakonda caves belong to this period.

# SANGAM AGE (300 B.C. TO A.D. 300)

- The Sangam Age constitutes an important chapter in the history of South India.
- According to Tamil legends, there existed three Sangams (Academy of Tamil poets) in ancient Tamil Nadu popularly called Muchchangam. These Sangams flourished under the royal patronage of the Pandyas.
- *The first Sangam*, held at then Madurai, chaired by Agastya.
- *The second Sangam* was held at Kapadapuram, chaired by Tolkappiyar.
- *The third Sangam* at Madurai was founded by Mudathirumaran.

## Political History

- The Tamil country was ruled by three dynasties namely the Chera, Chola and Pandyas during the Sangam Age.

## CHERAS

- The Cheras ruled over parts of modern Kerala. Their capital was Vanji and their important seaports were Tondi and Musiris.
- The greatest Chera King was *Senguttuvan*.

## CHOLAS

- The Chola kingdom of the Sangam period extended from modern Tiruchi district to southern Andhra Pradesh.
- Their capital was first located at Uraiyur and then shifted to Puhar. Kaveripattinam served as their port.

# GUPTA PERIOD

- The Gupta period is considered as the *Golden Age* in the history of India because this period witnessed all round developments in Religion, Literature, Science, Art and Architecture.

## CHANDRAGUPTA I (320-334 A.D.)

- In the beginning of the 4th Century A.D., Sri Gupta established a small Kingdom at Pataliputra. He is considered as the founder of the Gupta dynasty.

- The first notable ruler of the Gupta dynasty was Chandragupta I. He assumed the title *Maharajadhiraja*. The Meherauli Iron Pillar inscription mentions his extensive conquests.
- Chandragupta I is considered to be the founder of the Gupta era which starts with his accession in A.D. 320.

### SAMUDRAGUPTA (335-380 A.D.)

- Samudragupta was the greatest of the rulers of the Gupta dynasty. The Allahabad Pillar inscription provides a detailed account of his reign.
- Because of his military achievements, Samudragupta was hailed as '*Indian Napoleon*'.

### CHANDRAGUPTA II (380-414 A.D.)

- Samudragupta was succeeded by his son Chandragupta II Vikramaditya.
- The greatest of the military achievements of Chandragupta II was his war against the Saka *satraps* of western India.
- The famous Chinese pilgrim, Fahien visited India (A.D. 399 - A.D. 414) during the reign of Chandragupta II.

### SUCCESSORS OF CHANDRAGUPTA II

- Kumaragupta (415-455) was the son and successor of Chandragupta II. His reign was marked by general peace and prosperity.
- Kumaragupta was the founder of the Nalanda University.
- Kumaragupta was followed by *Skandagupta* who ruled from A.D. 456 to A.D. 468.
- After Skandagupta's death, many of his successors like Purugupta, Narasimhagupta, Buddhagupta and Baladitya could not save the Gupta empire from the Huns. Ultimately, the Gupta power totally disappeared due to the Hun invasions and later by the rise of Yasodharman in Malwa.

## PUSHYABHUTI DYNASTY (600 - 647 A.D.)

- The greatest king was *Harshavardhana*, son of Prabhakar Vardhana of Thaneshwar. He shifted the capital to *Kannauj*.
- *Hieun Tsang* visited during his reign.
- He established a large monastery at Nalanda. Banabhata adorned his court, wrote Harshacharita and Kadambari. Harsha himself wrote three plays–Priyadarshika, Ratnawali and Nagananda.

### PALLAVAS

- The Pallavas established their kingdom in Tondaimandalam by Simhavishnu with its capital at Kanchipuram.
- Other great Pallava rulers were Mahendravarman I, Narasimhavarman I, and Narasimhavarman II.
- The *Kailasanatha temple* at Kanchipuram is the greatest architectural masterpiece of the Pallava art.

### CHALUKYAS (543-755 A.D.)

- Pulakesin I was the founder of the Chalukya dynasty. He established a small kingdom with Vatapi or Badami as its capital.
- The structural temples of the Chalukyas exist at Aihole, Badami and Pattadakal (Virupaksha temple). Cave temple architecture was also famous under the Chalukyas. Their cave temples are found in Ajanta, Ellora and Nasik.

### RASHTRAKUTAS (755-975 A.D.)

- The art and architecture of the Rashtrakutas were found at Ellora and Elephanta.

### CHOLAS

- Cholas became prominent in the ninth century and established an empire comprising the major portion of South India. Their capital was Tanjore.
- The founder of the Chola kingdom was Vijayalaya.
- Rajaraja Chola built the famous Brihadeeswara temple at Tanjore.
- *Dancing Figure of Shiva* (Nataraja) belong to Chola period.

# MEDIEVAL INDIA

## ARAB CONQUEST OF SIND

- In 712 A.D., Muhammad bin Quasim invaded Sind. Quasim defeated Dahir, the ruler of Sind and killed him in a well-contested battle.

### Mahmud of Ghazni

- In 1024, Mahmud marched from Multan across Rajaputana, defeated the Solanki King Bhimadeva I, plundered Anhilwada and sacked the famous temple of Somanatha. This was his last campaign in India. Mahmud died in 1030 A.D.
- Mahmud patronized art and literature. *Firdausi* was the poet-laureate in the court of Mahmud.

### Muhammad Ghori

- Prithviraj Chauhan defeated Ghori in the first battle of Tarain near Delhi in 1191 A.D.
- In the Second Battle of Tarain in 1192, Muhammad Ghori thoroughly routed the army of Prithiviraj, who was captured and killed.
- After his brilliant victory over Prithviraj at Tarain, Muhammad Ghori returned to Ghazni leaving behind his

favourite general Qutb-ud-din Aibak to make further conquests in India.

## SULTANATE PERIOD

## SLAVE DYNASTY (1206-1290)

- The Slave dynasty was also called Mamluk dynasty. Mamluk was the Quranic term for slave.

### Qutb-ud-din Aibak

- Qutb-ud-din Aibak was a slave of Muhammad Ghori, who made him the Governor of his Indian possessions.
- After the death of Ghori in 1206, Aibak declared his independence. He assumed the title Sultan and made Lahore his capital.
- Muslim writers call Aibak Lakh Baksh or giver of lakhs because he gave liberal donations to them.
- He built the famous Quwat-Ul-Islam mosque at Delhi. He began the construction of the famous Qutb Minar at Delhi but did not live long to complete it. It was later completed by Iltutmish.

### Iltutmish (1210-1236 A.D.)

- Iltutmish belonged to the Ilbari tribe and hence his dynasty was named as Ilbari dynasty.
- He shifted his capital from Lahore to Delhi.
- He organised the *Iqta system* and introduced reforms in civil administration and army.

### Raziya (1236-1240 A.D.)

- She appointed an Abyssinian slave Yakuth as Master of the Royal Horses.
- In 1240, Altunia, the governor of Bhatinda revolted against her. She went in personally to suppress the revolt but Altunia killed Yakuth and took Raziya prisoner.
- Bahram Shah, son of Iltutmish killed her.

### Balban (1266-1286 A.D.)

- Balban introduced rigorous court discipline and new customs such as prostration and kissing the Sultan's feet to prove his superiority over the nobles.
- He also introduced the Persian festival of *Nauroz* to impress the nobles and people with his wealth and power.
- He established a separate military department - *diwan-i-arz* – and reorganized the army.

## KHILJI DYNASTY (1290-1320 A.D.)

- The founder of the Khilji dynasty was Jalaluddin Khilji.
- Ala-ud-din Khilji was the greatest ruler of the Khilji Dynasty.
- He was the first Muslim ruler to extend his empire right upto Rameshwaram in the South.
- The Sultan had built a new city called Siri near Delhi.
- Amir Khusrau the great Persian poet, patronised by Balban, continued to live in Ala-ud-din Khilji's court also.
- He introduced the system of *dagh* (branding of horses) and prepared *huliya* (descriptive list of soldiers).
- Ala-ud-din Khilji maintained a large permanent standing army and paid them in cash from the royal treasury.

## TUGHLAQ DYNASTY

- Ghiyas-ud-din Tughlaq was the founder of the Tughlaq dynasty.
- To have the capital at the centre of the empire and safe from the Mongol raids, Tughlaq chose Devagiri as his new capital in A.D. 1327. The Sultan renamed the new capital Daulatabad.
- In 1329-30, Muhammad-bin-Tughlaq introduced a token currency.
- Firoz Shah Tughlaq became Sultan after the death of Muhammad-bin-Tughlaq in A.D. 1351.
- He was the first Sultan to impose irrigation tax.
- He had built new towns of Firozabad, Jaunpur, Hissar and Firozpur.
- Timur—Mongol leader of Central Asia, ordered general massacre in Delhi (AD 1398) at the time of Nasiruddin Mahmud (later Tughlaq king).

## SAYYID DYNASTY

- Before his departure from India, Timur appointed Khizr Khan as governor of Multan. He captured Delhi and founded the Sayyid dynasty in 1414.
- Mubarak Shah, Mohammed Shah and Alam Shah were some of the other important noteworthy rulers of Sayyid Dynasty.

## LODHI DYNASTY

- The Lodhis were Afghans.
- Bahlol Lodhi was the first Afghan ruler while his predecessors were all Turks. He died in 1489 and was succeeded by his son, Sikandar Lodhi.
- In 1504, Sikandar Lodhi founded the city of Agra and transferred his capital from Delhi to Agra.
- Babar marched against Delhi and defeated and killed Ibrahim Lodhi in the first battle of Panipat (1526).

# BAHMANI AND VIJAYANAGAR KINGDOMS

- The break up of the Delhi Sultanate provided an opportunity for the rise of a number of kingdoms in the Deccan.
- After the decline of the Tughlaqs, there arose two important kingdoms in the Deccan. They were the Bahmani and Vijayanagar kingdoms.

## VIJAYANAGAR EMPIRE

- The Vijayanagar Kingdom was set up in A.D. 1336. Its aim was to check the spread of Muslim power and protect Hindu Dharma in South India.
- Four dynasties – Sangama, Saluva, Tuluva and Aravidu – ruled Vijayanagar from A.D. 1336 to 1672.
- Vijayanagar was founded in 1336 by Harihara and Bukka of the Sangama dynasty.
- The Moroccan traveller, Ibn Batuta, Venetian traveller Nicolo de Conti, Persian traveller Abdur Razzak and the Portuguese traveller Domingo Paes were among them who left valuable accounts on the socio-economic conditions of the Vijayanagar Empire.
- The Hampi ruins and other monuments of Vijayanagar provide information on the cultural contributions of the Vijayanagar rulers.

## KRISHNA DEVA RAYA (1509-1530)

- The Tuluva dynasty was founded by Vira Narasimha.
- The greatest of the Vijayanagar rulers, Krishna Deva Raya belonged to the Tuluva dynasty.
- Krishna Deva Raya himself authored a Telugu work, *Amukthamalyadha* and Sanskrit works, *Jambavati Kalyanam* and *Ushaparinayam*.
- He built the famous *Vittalaswamy* and *Hazara Ramaswamy* temples at Vijayanagar.
- Krishna Deva Raya renovated Virupaksha temple in A.D. 1510.
- After his death the enemies of Vijayanagar joined together and defeated the Vijayanagar ruler in the battle of Talaikota.

## BAHMANI KINGDOM

- The founder of the Bahmani kingdom was Alauddin Bahman Shah also known as Hasan Gangu in 1347. Its capital was Gulbarga.
- Ahmad Wali Shah shifted the capital from Gulbarga to Bidar.
- *Gol Gumbaj* was built by *Muhammad Adil Shah*; it is famous for the so called '*Whispering Gallery*'.
- *Quli Qutub Shah* built the famous *Golcunda Fort*.

# MUGHAL EMPIRE (1526-1707 AD)

## BABAR (1526-1530 AD)

- Babar was the founder of the Mughal Empire in India.
- On 21st April, 1526 the first Battle of Panipat took place between Babar and Ibrahim Lodhi, who was killed in the battle.
- Babar was the first one to use guns or artillery in a battle on the Indian soil.
- Babar defeated Rana Sanga of Mewar in the battle of Kanwah in A.D. 1527.
- Babar was a soldier-scholar and wrote his own autobiography called Babar Nama in Turkish language.

## HUMAYUN (1530-1556 AD)

- Sher Shah defeated Humayun at Chausa in A.D. 1539 and again at Kannauj in A.D. 1540.
- After losing his kingdom, Humayun became an exile for the next fifteen years.
- In 1555, Humayun defeated the Afghans and recovered the Mughal throne. After six months, he died in 1556 due to his fall from the staircase of his library.
- *Gulbadan Begum*, Humayun's half-sister wrote *Humayun-nama*.

## SHER SHAH SURI

- The founder of the Sur dynasty was Sher Shah, whose original name was Farid.
- Sher Shah became the ruler of Delhi in 1540.
- Sher Shah organized a brilliant administrative system. The central government consisted of several departments.
- He built a new city on the banks of the river Yamuna near Delhi. Now the old fort called Purana Quila and its mosque is alone surviving.
- He built a Mausoleum at Sasaram, which is considered as one of the master pieces of Indian architecture.

## AKBAR (1556-1605 AD)

- When Akbar ascended the throne in A.D. 1556 he was only 14 years old. His guardian Bairam Khan served him as a faithful minister and tutor.
- Bairam Khan, along with Akbar met Hemu in the second Battle of Panipat in 1556. Hemu was initially successful, but lost his consciousness after an arrow hit him. Akbar killed him.
- The Battle of Haldighati was fought between Rana Pratap of Mewar and Mughal army led by Man Singh and Asif Khan. Some historian say that this battle was indecisive but some say that Rana Pratap was defeated by Akbar.
- Akbar abolished the pilgrim tax and in 1562, he abolished Jaziya.
- Akbar evolved a new faith called Din-i-Illahi or Divine Faith.

## JAHANGIR (1605-1627 AD)

- When Akbar died, Prince Salim succeeded with the title Jahangir (Conqueror of World) in 1605.
- Jahangir's eldest son, Khusrau, rebelled against him. He was arrested and put into prison. *Guru Arjun Dev, the fifth Sikh Guru* was executed by Jahangir.
- In 1611, Jahangir married Mehrunnisa who was known as Nurjahan (Light of World).
- Jahangir died in A.D. 1627.

### SHAHJAHAN (1628-1658 AD)

- The reign of Shahjahan is generally considered as the *Golden Age* of the Mughal period.
- Shahjahan is called as the *Prince of Builders*. He had built the Jama Masjid and Red Fort in Delhi and Taj Mahal in Agra.
- Fine arts like painting, music and literature reached high level of development during Shahjahan's time.

### AURANGAZEB (1658-1707 AD)

- Aurangazeb was the last great Mughal ruler. He ascended the throne after killing his three brothers Dara, Shuja and Murad in a fratricidal war.
- Aurangazeb defeated Sikandar Shah of Bijapur and annexed his kingdom.
- Aurangazeb was against the Sikhs and he executed the ninth Sikh Guru Tegh Bahadur.
- He was called *Darvesh* or a *Zinda Pir*. He forbade *Sati*. Conquered Bijapur (AD 1686) and Golconda (AD 1687) and reimposed Jaziya and Pilgrim tax in AD 1679.
- He built *Biwi ka Makbara* on the tomb of his queen *Rabaud-Durani* at Aurangabad; *Moti Masjid* within Red Fort, Delhi; and the Jami or Badshahi Mosque at Lahore.
- Aurangazeb died in A.D. 1707.

### LATER MUGHALS / FALL OF THE MUGHALS

#### Bahadur Shah (1707-1712)

- Assumed the title of *Shah Alam I*.

#### Jahandar Shah (1712-1713)

- First puppet Mughal emperor. He abolished *jaziya*.

#### Farrukhslyar (1713-1719)

#### Mohammad Shah (1719-1748)

- Nadir Shah (*of Iran*) defeated him in the Battle of Karnal (1739) and took away *Peacock throne* and *Kohinoor diamond*.

#### Ahmad Shah (1748-1754)

#### Alamgir II (1754-1759),

#### Shah Alam II (1759-1806)

#### Akbar II (1806-1837)

- He gave Ram Mohan Roy the title '*Raja*'. He sent Raja Ram Mohan Roy to London to seek a raise in his allowance.

#### Bahadur Shah II (1837-1857)

- He was confined by the British to the Red Fort. During the revolt of 1857, he was proclaimed the Emperor by the rebels. He was deported to Rangoon after that.

### Literature of Mughal Period

| Author | Work |
|---|---|
| Babar | Tuzuk-i-Babari |
| Abul Fazal | Ain-i-Akbari, Akbarnamah |
| Jahangir | Tuzuk-i-Jahangiri |
| Hamid | Padshahnama |
| Darashikoh | Majm-ul-Bahrain |
| Mirza Md Qasim | Alamgirnama |

## THE MARATHAS

### SHIVAJI (1627-1680 AD)

- Shivaji was born at Shivner in 1627. His father was Shahji Bhonsle and mother Jija Bai.
- His religious teacher was Samarth Ramdas and guardian was Dadaji Kondadev.
- In 1674, Shivaji crowned himself at Raigarh and assumed the title Chatrapathi.
- *Ashtapradhan* (eight ministers) helped in administration. These were Peshwas, Sar-i-Naubat (Military), Mazumdar or Amatya (Accounts); Waqenavis (Intelligence); Surnavis (Corres-pondence); *Dabir* or *Sumanta* (Ceremonies); *Nyayadhish* (Justice); and *Panditrao* (Charity).
- Successors of Shivaji were Shambhaji, Rajaram and *Shahu* (fought at Battle of Khed in AD 1708).

### THE PESHWAS

- Balaji Vishwanath was the first Peshwa. He began his career as a small revenue official and became Peshwa in 1713.
- Baji Rao I was the eldest son of Balaji Vishwanath. He was considered as the "greatest exponent of guerilla tactics after Shivaji".
- It was during reign of Balaji Baji Rao (Nanasaheb) when the Marathas lost the Third Battle of Panipat.
- Baji Rao II ( last Peshwa) was the first Maratha to have fled from the British attacks instead of fighting with them. Baji Rao II surrendered to Sir John Malcom.

### THE SIKH

- Guru Nanak Dev was the founder of Sikhism, the religion that draws its elements from both Hinduism and Islam.
- Name of the ten Sikh Gurus and their works are given below:
  1. **Guru Nanak Dev (1469-1539AD):** The founder of Sikhism.
  2. **Guru Angad Dev (1504-1552AD):** Developed Gurmukhi.
  3. **Guru Amar Das (1479-1574AD):** Struggled against Sati system and Purdah system.
  4. **Guru Ram Das (1534-1581AD):** Founded Amritsar, the holy city of Sikhism.

5. **Guru Arjun Dev (1563-1606AD):** He built the *Swarn Mandir* (Golden Temple).
6. **Guru Hargobind (1595-1644 AD):** Established Akal Takht.
7. **Guru Har Rai (1630-1661 AD)**
8. **Guru Har Krishan (1656-1664 AD)**
9. **Guru Tegh Bahadur (1621-1675 AD)**
10. **Guru Gobind Singh (1666-1708 AD):** Founded the Khalsa and Sikh baptism, composed many poems, and nominated the Sikh sacred text as the final and enduring Guru.

# MODERN INDIA

## THE ADVENT OF THE EUROPEANS

### THE PORTUGUESE

- Vasco-da-Gama, a Portuguese explorer, sailed through the route of Cape of Good Hope and reached near Calicut on 20th May 1498 A.D. during the reign of King Zamorin (Hindu King of Calicut).
- Vasco-da-Gama founded a factory at Cannanore on his second visit to India in 1501. In due course, Calicut, Cochin and Cannanore became the Portuguese trading centres.
- Francisco Almeida came to India in 1505. He was the first Governor of Portuguese possessions in India.
- The real founder of Portuguese power in India was *Alfonso de Albuquerque*. He captured Goa from the rulers of Bijapur in 1510. It was made their headquarters.

### THE DUTCH

- The United East India Company of the Netherlands founded a factory at Masulipatnam in 1605. They built their first fort on the main land of India at Pulicut in 1609, near Madras (Chennai). They captured Nagapattinam from the Portuguese.
- They made Agra, Surat, Masulipatnam and Chinsura in Bengal as their trading centres.

### THE DANES

- The Danish East India Company was established in 1616 in Denmark.
- They came to South India and founded a factory at Tranquebar (Tharangambadi) in 1620. They also made settlements at Serampore near Calcutta (Kolkata).

### THE ENGLISH

- The English East India Company was formed in 1599 under a charter granted by Queen Elizabeth in 1600.
- The East India Company sent Sir William Hawkins to the court of the Mughal Emperor Jahangir in 1609 to obtain permission to erect a factory at Surat.
- In 1615, Sir Thomas Roe, another British merchant, came to Jahangir's court. He stayed for three years and succeeded in getting permission to set up their trading centres at Agra, Surat, Ahmedabad and Broach.
- In 1690, the British got permission from Aurangazeb to build a factory on the site of Calcutta. In 1696 a fort was built at that place. It was called Fort William.

### THE FRENCH

- The French East India Company was established in 1664 under the inspiring and energetic leadership of Colbert, the economic adviser of the French King Louis XIV.
- In 1667, the first French factory was established at Surat by Francis Caron who was nominated as Director-General.
- French were defeated by English in the *Battle of Wandiwash* (1760).

## EAST INDIA COMPANY

- After the Battle of Plassey in 1757 and the Battle of Buxar in 1764, the East India Company became a political power.
- India was under the East India Company's rule till 1858 when it came under the direct administration of the British Crown.
- Robert Clive was the first Governor of Fort William under the Company's rule.

### GOVERNOR-GENERALS OF BENGAL

#### Warren Hastings (1772-85 AD)

- In 1772, the Company appointed Warren Hastings as the Governor of Fort William.
- The Dual System introduced by Robert Clive was abolished by Warren Hastings.
- Warren Hastings was known for his expansionist policy. His administration witnessed the Rohilla War, the First Anglo-Maratha War and the Second Anglo-Mysore War.
- Pitt's India Act (1784) was passed.

#### Lord Cornwallis (1786-93 AD)

- Cornwallis inaugurated the policy of making appointments mainly on the basis of merit thereby laying the foundation of the Indian Civil Service.
- Lord Cornwallis introduced Permanent Revenue Settlement.
- Tipu Sultan signed the Treaty of Srirangapatnam in 1792 with the British.

### Sir John Shore (1793-98 AD)

- Played an important role in the introduction of Permanent Settlement.
- *Battle of Kharda* between the Nizams and the Marathas (1795).

### Wellesley (1798-1805)

- Wellesley came to India with a determination to launch a forward policy that he adopted to achieve his object is known as the 'Subsidiary Alliance'.
- The Fourth Anglo-Mysore War started in 1799. The war was short and decisive. Tipu fought till his capital Srirangapatnam was captured and he himself was shot dead.
- Peshwa Baji Rao II signed the *Treaty* of *Bassein* with the British in 1802. It was a subsidiary treaty and the Peshwa was recognized as the head of the Maratha kingdom.
- The Treaty of Deogaon(1803) was signed between Bhonsle and Wellesley.

### Lord Minto (1807-1813)

- Lord Minto concluded the Treaty of Amritsar with Ranjit Singh of Punjab in 1809.
- The Charter Act of 1813 was passed during this period.

### Lord Hastings (1813-1823)

- Anglo Nepal War (1814-1816) and Treaty of Sugauli (1816).
- Third Maratha War (1817-18), dissolution of Maratha confederacy and creation of Bombay Presidency.
- He encouraged the freedom of the Press and abolished the censorship introduced in 1799.

## GOVERNOR-GENERALS OF INDIA

### Lord William Bentinck (1828-1835)

- Charter Act of 1833 was passed and he was made the first Governor-General of India. Before him, the designation was Governor-General of Bengal.
- The social reforms of William Bentinck made his name immortal in the history of British India. These include the abolition of *Sati*, the suppression of Thugs and the prevention of female infanticide.
- The Government Resolution in 1835 made English the official and literary language of India.

### Lord Metcalfe (1835-36 AD)

- Known as liberator of press in India.

### Lord Auckland (1836-42 AD)

- First Afghan War (1838-42), a disaster for the English.

### Lord Ellenborough (1842-44 AD)

- Brought an end to Afghan war. War with Gwalior (1843), *Annexation of Sind* by Charles Napier (1843).

### Lord Hardinge (1844-48 AD)

- First Anglo-Sikh War (1845-46) and Treaty of Lahore (1846). Gave preference to English educated persons in employment.

### Lord Dalhousie (1848-1856)

- The Doctrine of Lapse was applied by Dalhousie.
- The first railway line connecting Bombay with Thane was opened in 1853.

## VICEROYS OF INDIA

### Lord Canning (1856-62 AD)

- Lord Canning became the first Viceroy of India in 1858.
- Revolt of 1857, Mutiny took place. Indian Penal Code 1860 was passed.

### Lord Elgin (1862 AD)

- Wahabi Movement.

### Lord John Lawrence (1864-69 AD)

- Established the *High Courts* at Calcutta, Bombay and Madras in 1865.
- Telegraphic communication was opened with Europe. Created the Indian Forest Department.

### Lord Northbrooke (1872-76 AD)

- Kuka Rebellion in Punjab, Famine in Bihar.

### Lord Lytton (1876-80)

- In 1878, the Vernacular Press Act was passed. This Act empowered a Magistrate to secure an undertaking from the editor, publisher and printer of a vernacular newspaper that nothing would be published against the English Government. This Act crushed the freedom of the Indian press.
- In 1878, the Arms Act was passed. This Act prevented the Indians to keep arms without appropriate license.
- Lord Lytton also held a Darbar at Delhi in 1877 in which Queen Victoria was declared as the Empress of India. This extravagant Darbar cost millions of ruppes.
- In 1878, the Statutory Civil Service was established exclusively for Indians.

### Lord Ripon (1880-84 AD)

- Lord Ripon repealed the Vernacular Press Act and earned much popularity among Indians.
- Ripon appointed a Commission in 1882 under the chairmanship of Sir William Hunter.
- The Commission came to be known as the Hunter Commission. The Commission recommended for the expansion and improvement of the elementary education of the masses.

- Ripon was founder of local self-government in modern India.

### Lord Dufferin (1884-88 AD)

- *Third Burmese War* (1885-86 AD). Establishment of the Indian National Congress in 1885.

### Lord Lansdowne (1888-94 AD)

- Factory Act of 1891 granted weekly holiday and stipulated working hours for women and children.

### Lord Elgin II (1894-99 AD)

- Southern uprisings of 1899. Great famine of 1896-1897 and Lyall Commission on famine was established.

### Lord Curzon (1899-1905 AD)

- Curzon instituted in 1902, a Universities Commission to go into the entire question of university education in the country.
- On the basis of the findings and recommendations of the Commission, Curzon brought in the Indian Universities Act of 1904, which brought all the universities in India under the control of the government.

### Lord Minto (1905-10 AD)

- Swadeshi Movement (1905-08); foundation of Muslim League (1906); Surat Session and split in the Congress (1907). Morley-Minto Reforms (1909).

### Lord Hardinge (1910-16 AD)

- Capital shifted from Calcutta to Delhi (1911); Delhi Durbar; Partition of Bengal was cancelled. The Hindu Mahasabha was founded in 1915 by Pandit Madan Mohan Malaviya.

### Lord Chelmsford (1916-21 AD)

- Gandhi returned to India (1915) and founded the Sabarmati Ashram (1916), Champaran Satyagraha, Satyagraha at Ahmedabad (1981), Kheda Satyagraha (1918).
- Rowlatt Act (March, 1919) and the Jallianwala Bagh Massacre (13th April, 1919).
- Khilafat Committee was formed and Khilafat Movement started (1919-20).
- Non-Cooperation Movement started (1920-22).

### Lord Reading (1921-26)

- Moplah Rebellion (1921) took place. *Kakori Train* Robbery on 1st August, 1925. *Communal Riots* of 1923-25 in Multan, Amritsar, Delhi etc.

### Lord Irwin (1926-31 AD)

- Lahore Session of Congress and *Poorna Swaraj* Declaration (1929).
- Simon Commission visited India in 1927.
- Dandi March (12th March, 1930). Civil Disobedience Movement (1930).
- First Round Table Conference was held in England in 1930. Gandhi-Irwin Pact.

### Lord Willingdon (1931-36 AD)

- *Second Round Table Conference* in London in 1931 and *third* in 1932.

### Lord Linlithgow (1936-43 AD)

- Congress Ministries resignation celebrated as '*Deliverance Day*' by the Muslim League (1939), the Lahore Resolution (23rd March, 1940) of the Muslim League demanding separate state for the Muslims. (It was at this session that Jinnah propounded his Two-Nation Theory). Outbreak of World War II in 1939. Cripps Mission in 1942. Quit India Movement (8th August, 1942).

### Lord Wavell (1943-47 AD)

- Cabinet Mission Plan (16th May, 1946).
- First meeting of the Constituent Assembly was held on 9th December, 1946.
- Arranged the Shimla Conference on 25th June, 1945 with Indian National Congress and Muslim League but failed.

### Lord Mountbatten (March to Aug, 1947)

- Last viceroy of British India and the first Governor-General of free India.
- Partition of India decided by the 3rd June Plan or Mountbatten Plan.

## NATIONAL MOVEMENT (1885-1947)

### INDIAN NATIONAL CONGRESS (1885)

- Allan Octavian Hume, a retired civil servant in the British Government took the initiative to form an all-India organization. Thus, the Indian National Congress was founded and its first session was held at Bombay in 1885. W.C. Banerjee was its first president. It was attended by 72 delegates from all over India.
- The second session was held in Calcutta in 1886 and the third in Madras in 1887.
- Between 1885 and 1905, the Congress leaders were moderates. The Moderates had faith in the British justice and goodwill. They were called moderates because they adopted peaceful and constitutional means to achieve their demands.
- In 1905, Gopal Krishna Gokhale founded the Servants of India Society to train Indians to dedicate their lives to the cause of the country.

### Partition of Bengal (1905)

- By Lord Curzon on 16th October, 1905 through a royal proclamation, reducing the old province of Bengal in size by creating East Bengal and Assam out of the rest of Bengal.

- The partition of Bengal in 1905 provided a spark for the rise of extremism in the Indian National Movement.
- Curzon's real motives behind this partition were:
  - To break the growing strength of Bengali nationalism since Bengal was the base of Indian nationalism.
  - To divide the Hindus and Muslims in Bengal.
  - To show the enormous power of the British Government in doing whatever it liked.

### Swadeshi Movement (1905)

- The Swadeshi Movement involved programmes like the boycott of government service, courts, schools and colleges and of foreign goods. It was both a political and economic movement.
- Lal, Bal, Pal and Aurobindo Ghosh played an important role.

### Muslim League (1906)

- In December 1906, Muslim delegates from all over India met at Dacca for the Muslim Educational Conference.
- Taking advantage of this occasion, Nawab Salimullah of Dacca proposed the setting up of an organisation to look after the Muslim interests. The proposal was accepted.
- The All-India Muslim League was finally set up on December 30, 1906.

### Minto Morley Reforms (1909)

- Minto, the Viceroy and Morley, the Secretary of State for India jointly proposed reforms to the Indian Councils. An Act, called the Indian Councils Act or the Minto-Morley Reforms Act was passed in 1909.
- A separate communal electorate was introduced for the Muslims.

### The Lucknow Pact (1916)

- During the 1916 Congress session at Lucknow two major events occurred. The divided Congress became united. An understanding for joint action against the British was reached between the Congress and the Muslim League and it was called the Lucknow Pact.
- The signing of the Lucknow Pact by the Congress and the Muslim League in 1916 marked an important step in the Hindu-Muslim unity.

### The Home Rule Movement (1916)

- Two Home Rule Leagues were established, one by B.G. Tilak at Poona in April 1916 and the other by Mrs. Annie Besant at Madras in September 1916.
- While Tilak's Movement concentrated on Maharashtra, Annie Besant's Movement covered the rest of the country.

### August Declaration

- On 20 August, 1917, Montague, the Secretary of State in England, promised the gradual development of self-governing institutions in India.
- This August Declaration led to the end of the Home Rule Movement.

### Rowlatt Act (1919)

- In 1917, a committee was set up under the presidentship of Sir Sydney Rowlatt to look into the militant Nationalist activities. On the basis of its report the Rowlatt Act was passed in March 1919 by the Central Legislative Council. As per this Act, any person could be arrested on the basis of suspicion. No appeal or petition could be filed against such arrests.
- This Act was called the Black Act and it was widely opposed. An all-India hartal was organized on 6 April, 1919.

### Jallianwala Bagh Massacre (13 April, 1919)

- On 13th April, the Baisakhi day (harvest festival), a public meeting was organized at the Jallianwala Bagh (garden). Gen. Dyer marched in and without any warning opened fire on the crowd. The firing continued for about 10 to 15 minutes and it stopped only after the ammunition exhausted.
- According to official report 379 people were killed and 1137 wounded in the incident. There was a nationwide protest against this massacre and Rabindranath Tagore renounced his knighthood as a protest.

### Khilafat Movement (1920)

- The chief cause of the Khilafat Movement was the defeat of Turkey in the First World War.
- The Muslims in India were upset over the British attitude against Turkey and launched the Khilafat Movement.
- Ali brothers, *Mohd Ali* and *Shaukat Ali* started this movement. It was jointly led by the Khilafat leaders and the Congress.

### Non-Co-operation Movement (1920-22)

- Mahatma Gandhi announced his plan to begin Non-Cooperation with the government as a sequel to the Rowlatt Act, Jallianwala Bagh massacre and the Khilafat Movement. It was approved by the Indian National Congress at the Nagpur session in December, 1920.
- The Congress observed the Non-Co-operation movement in 1920. The main aim of this movement was to attain Swaraj through non-violent and peaceful means.
- The whole movement was abruptly called off on 11th February, 1922 by Gandhi following the Chauri-Chaura incident in the Gorakhpur district of U.P. Many top leaders of the country were stunned at this sudden suspension of the Non-Co-operation Movement.

- On 5th February an angry mob set fire to the police station at *Chauri-Chaura* and twenty two police men were burnt to death.

### Swaraj Party

- Leaders like Motilal Nehru and Chittranjan Das formed a separate group within the Congress known as the Swaraj Party on 1 January, 1923.
- The Swarajists wanted to contest the council elections and wreck the government from within.

### Simon Commission (1927)

- The Act of 1919 included a provision for its review after a lapse of ten years. However, the review commission under the chairmanship of Sir John Simon was appointed by the British Government two years earlier of its schedule in 1927.
- Indian leaders opposed the commission, as there were no Indians in it, they cried *Simon Go Back*.
- The government used brutal repression and at Lahore, *Lala Lajpat Rai* was severely beaten in lathi-charge.

### Nehru Report (1928)

- The Secretary of State, Lord Birkenhead, challenged the Indians to produce a Constitution that would be acceptable to all. The challenge was accepted by the Congress, which convened an all party meeting on 28 February, 1928.
- A committee consisting of eight was constituted to draw up a blueprint for the future Constitution of India. It was headed by Motilal Nehru. The Report published by this Committee came to be known as the Nehru Report.

### Lahore Session (1929)

- On Dec. 19, 1929, under the Presidentship of J.L. Nehru, the INC, as its Lahore session, declared Poorna Swaraj (Complete Independence) as its ultimate goal.
- On Dec. 31, 1929, the newly adopted tricolour flag was unfurled and Jan. 26, 1930 was fixed as the First Independence Day, which was to be celebrated every year.

### Dandi March (1930)

- On 12th March, 1930, Gandhi began his famous March to Dandi with his chosen 79 followers to break the salt laws. He reached the coast of Dandi on 5 April, 1930 after marching a distance of 200 miles and on 6 April formally launched the Civil Disobedience Movement by breaking the salt laws.

### Civil Disobedience Movement

- Countrywide mass participation by women.
- The Garhwal soldiers refused to fire on the people at Peshawar.

### Round Table Conference

- The first Round Table Conference was held in November 1930 at London and it was boycotted by the Congress.
- On 8th March, 1931 the Gandhi-Irwin Pact was signed. As per this pact, Mahatma Gandhi agreed to suspend the Civil-Disobedience Movement and participate in the Second-Round Table Conference.
- In September 1931, the Second Round Table Conference was held at London. Mahatma Gandhi participated in the Conference but returned to India disappointed.
- In January 1932, the Civil-Disobedience Movement was resumed.

### Poona Pact (1932)

- The idea of separate electorate for the depressed classes was abandoned, but seats reserved for them in the provincial legislature were increased.
- Thus, Poona Pact agreed upon a joint electorate for upper and lower castes.

### Demand for Pakistan

- *Chaudhary Rehmat Ali* gave the term *Pakistan* in 1933.
- In March 1940, the Muslim League demanded the creation of Pakistan.

### Cripps Mission (1942)

- The British Government in its effort to secure Indian co-operation in the Second World War sent Sir Stafford Cripps to India on 23 March, 1942. This is known as Cripps Mission.
- The main recommendations of Cripps was the promise of Dominion Status to India.
- Congress rejected it. Gandhi called Cripp's proposals as a "Post-dated Cheque".

### Quit India Movement (1942-1944)

- The All India Congress Committee met at Bombay on 8th August, 1942 and passed the famous Quit India Resolution. On the same day, Gandhi gave his call of 'do or die'.
- On 8th and 9th August, 1942, the government arrested all the prominent leaders of the Congress. Mahatma Gandhi was kept in prison at Poona. Pandit Jawaharlal Nehru, Abul Kalam Azad, and other leaders were imprisoned in the Ahamednagar Fort.
- Quit India Movement was the final attempt for country's freedom.

### Indian National Army (INA)

- On July 2, 1943, Subhash Chandra Bose reached Singapore and gave the rousing war cry of *'Dilli Chalo'*. He was made the President of Indian Independence League and soon became the supreme commander of the Indian National Army. He gave the country the slogan of *Jai Hind.*
- INA had three fighting brigades named after Gandhi, Azad and Nehru. Rani of Jhansi Brigade was an exclusive women force. INA headquarters were at Rangoon and Singapore.

### Cabinet Mission (1946)

- The Cabinet Mission put forward a plan for solution of the constitutional problem. A proposal was envisaged for setting up an Interim Government, which would remain in office till a new government was elected on the basis of the new Constitution framed by the Constituent Assembly.
- Elections were held in July 1946 for the formation of a Constituent Assembly.
- Muslim league observed the *Direct Action Day* on 16 August, 1946.
- An Interim Government was formed under the leadership of Jawaharlal Nehru on 2 September, 1946.

### Mountbatten Plan (1947)

- On 20 February 1947, Prime Minister Atlee announced in the House of Commons the definite intention of the British Government to transfer power to responsible Indian hands by a date not later than June 1948.
- Lord Mountbatten armed with vast powers became India's Viceroy on 24 March, 1947. The partition of India and the creation of Pakistan appeared inevitable to him.
- After extensive consultation Lord Mountbatten put forth the plan of partition of India on 3 June, 1947. The Congress and the Muslim League ultimately approved the Mountbatten Plan.

### Indian Independence Act, 1947

- The salient features of this Act was the partition of the country into India and Pakistan would come into effect from 15 August, 1947.
- On 15th August, 1947 India, and on the 14th August Pakistan came into existence as two independent states.
- Lord Mountbatten was made the first Governor General of Independent India, whereas Mohammad Ali Jinnah became the first Governor General of Pakistan.
- C. Rajagopalachari became the first and last Indian Governor-General of India. When India became a Republic on 26 January, 1950 Dr. Rajendra Prasad became the first President of our country.

## Socio-Religious Movements and Organisation

| *Name of the Organisation* | *Founder* | *Year* | *Place* |
|---|---|---|---|
| Atmiya Sabha | Ram Mohan Roy | 1815 | Calcutta |
| Brahmo Samaj | Ram Mohan Roy | 1828 | Calcutta |
| Dharma Sabha | Radhakanta Dev | 1829 | Calcutta |
| Tattvabodhini Sabha | Debendranath Tagore | 1839 | Calcutta |
| Nirankaris | Dayal Das, Darbara Singh, Rattan Chand etc. | 1840 | Punjab |
| Manav Dharma Sabha | Durgaram Manchharam | 1844 | Surat |
| Paramhansa Mandli | Dadoba Pandurung | 1849 | Bombay |
| Namdharis | Ram Singh | 1857 | Punjab |
| Radha Swami Satsang | Tulsi Ram | 1861 | Agra |
| Brahmo Samaj of India | Keshab Chandra Sen | 1866 | Calcutta |
| Dar-ul-Ulum | Maulana Hussain Ahmed | 1866 | Deoband |
| Prarthna Samaj | Atmaram Pandurung | 1867 | Bombay |
| Arya Samaj | Swami Dayanand Saraswati | 1875 | Bombay |
| Theosophical Society | Madam H.P. Blavatsky and Col. H.S. Olcott | 1875 | New York (USA) |
| Sadharan Brahmo Samaj | Anand Mohan Bose | 1878 | Calcutta |
| Deccan Education Society | G.G. Agarkar | 1884 | Pune (Poona) |
| Muhammadan Educational Conference | Syed Ahmad Khan | 1886 | Aligarh |
| Indian National Conference | M.G. Ranade | 1887 | Bombay |
| Deva Samaj | Shivnarayan Agnihotri | 1887 | Lahore |
| Nadwah-ul-Ulama | Maulana Shibli Numani | 1894 | Lucknow. |
| Ramakrishna Mission | Swami Vivekananda | 1897 | Belur |
| Servents of Indian Society | Gopal Krishna Gokhale | 1905 | Bombay |
| Poona Seva Sadan | Mrs. Ramabai Ranade and G.K. Devadhar | 1909 | Pune (Poona) |
| Social Service League | N.M. Joshi | 1911 | Bombay |
| Seva Samiti | H.N. Kunzru | 1914 | Allahabad |

## Newspapers and Journals

- *Bengal Gazette* (1780) (India's first newspaper)—James Augustus Hikky
- *Kesari*—B.G. Tilak
- *Maratha*—B.G. Tilak
- *Sudharak*—G.K. Gokhale

- *Amrit Bazar Patrika*—Shishir Kumar Ghosh and Motilal Ghosh
- *Yugantar*—Bhupendranath Datta and Birender Kumar Ghosh
- *Bombay Chronicle*—Firoze Shah Mehta
- *New India (Daily)*—Annie Besant

## Books and Authors

- *Causes of the Indian Mutiny*—Sir Syed Ahmed Khan
- *Ghulam Giri*—Jyotiba Phule
- *Anandmath*—Bankim Chand Chatterjee
- *Satyarth Prakash*—Swami Dayanand
- *Unhappy India*—Lala Lajpat Rai
- *India Divided*—Dr. Rajendra Prasad
- *The Discovery of India*—J.L. Nehru
- *Neel Darpan*—Dinbandhu Mitra
- *Hind Swaraj*—M.K. Gandhi
- *What Congress and Gandhi have done to the untouchables*—Dr. B.R. Ambedkar

## Important Sayings

- *'Back to Vedas'*—Dayanand Saraswati
- *'Dilli Chalo!'*—Subhash Chandra Bose's battle cry of *Azad Hind Fauj*
- *'Do or Die'*—Mahatma Gandhi (while launching Quit India movement in 1942)
- *'Give me blood and I will give you freedom'*—Subhash Chandra Bose (in his address to soldiers of *Azad Hind Fauj)*
- *'My ultimate aim is to wipe every tear from every eye'*—Jawaharlal Nehru
- *'Swaraj is my birthright and I will have it'*—Bal Gangadhar Tilak
- *'Inqualab Zindabad'*—Bhagat Singh
- *'Jai Jawan, Jai Kisan'*—Lal Bahadur Shastri
- *'Sarfaroshi ki tamanna Ab Hamare Dil mein Hai'*—Ram Prasad Bismill
- *'Saare Jahan Se Achcha,* Hindustan Hamara'—Dr. Mohammed Iqbal
- *'Hindi, Hindu, Hindustan'*—Bhartendu Harishchandra
- *'Vande Mataram'*—Bankim Chandra Chatterjee

❑❑❑

# GEOGRAPHY

## WORLD GEOGRAPHY

### THE UNIVERSE

- Existing matter and energy are together known as **Universe.**

### GALAXY

- A galaxy is a huge system of billions of stars and clouds of dust and gases.
- Our solar system is a part of *Milky Way* galaxy.
- There are millions of galaxies that make the Universe.

### STARS

- Stars account for 98 per cent of the matter in a galaxy. The stars nearest to the earth are *Proxima Centauri, Alpha Centauri, Barnard's Star, Sirius* and so on. Of these, *Sirius* is the brightest.

### LIGHT YEAR

- Light year is the distance travelled by light in one year at a speed of 2,99,792.5 km. per second.

### SOLAR SYSTEM

- The Sun, eight planets, satellites and some other celestial bodies known as asteroids and meteoroids form the solar system.

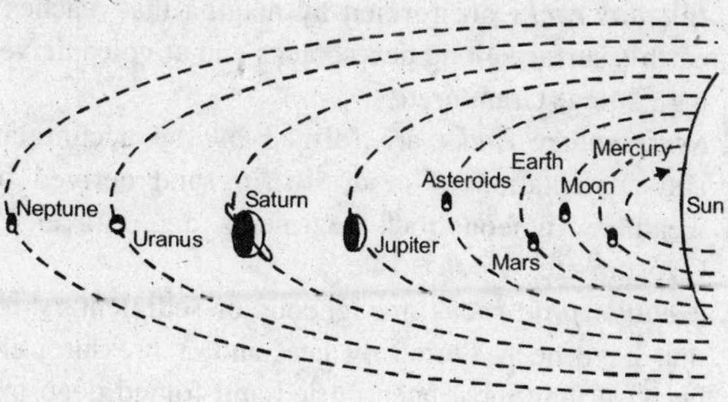


### SUN

- The Sun is in the centre of the solar system.
- The Sun is a mixture of gases. It consists of 92% hydrogen, 7.8% helium and 0.2% other gases.
- The Sun is about 150 million km away from the earth.
- The sun is an ultimate source of energy for life on Earth.
- Sunlight takes 8 min 16.6 sec to reach earth.

**Facts about Sun**

| | |
|---|---|
| **Diameter** | — $1.392 \times 10^6$ km |
| **Volume** | — 1.304 × 106 times the volume of earth |
| **Temperature** | — 6000°C at surface and 15 million degree C at the centre |
| **Relative density** | — 1.4 |
| **Gravitational Pull** | — 28 times the gravitational pull of the earth |

**Facts about Planets**

| | |
|---|---|
| Closest to Sun | *Mercury* |
| Farthest from Sun | *Neptune* |
| Heaviest | *Jupiter* |
| Hottest | *Venus* |
| Inner | *Mercury, Venus, Earth, Mars* |
| Largest | *Jupiter* |
| Smallest | *Mercury* |
| Moons, None | *Mercury, Venus* |
| Moon; Largest | *Ganymede (Jupiter), larger than Mercury* |
| Nearest to Earth | *Venus* |
| Orbits; Order | *Mercury (closest to Sun), Venus, Earth, Mars, Jupiter, Saturn, Uranus, Neptune.* |
| Rings/largest number | *Saturn* |
| Spin; Backwards | *Venus (East to West)* |

### COMETS

- It has a head and a tail. Its tail originates only when it gets closer to the sun. The tail can be 20-30 million km long. It always point away from the sun because of the force exerted by solar wind and radiation on the cometory material.

### THE EARTH

- The earth is the third nearest planet to the Sun.
- From the outer space, the earth appears blue because its two-thirds surface is covered by water. It is, therefore, called a blue planet.
- It is the densest of all planets.
- Rotation is the movement of the earth on its axis. Due to this rotation, day and night occur.
- The earth takes about 23 hours 56 minutes and 4 seconds to complete one rotation around its axis.
- Earth takes 365¼ days (one year) to revolve around the sun.

## THE EARTH: FACTS AND FIGURES

- *Mass of Earth*—5.972 × $10^{21}$ tonnes
- *Density of Earth*—5.517 times that of water
- *Volume of Earth*—1.083 × $10^{11}$ cubic km
- *Equatorial circumference*—4.007 × 104 km
- *Polar Diameter*—12,714 km
- *Equatorial Diameter*—12756 km
- *Polar or Meridional circumference*—4.0 × $10^4$ km
- *Estimated Age*—At least 4600 million years
- *Land Surface*—148,951,000 sq km
- *Water Surface*—361,150,000 sq km (71 per cent of total area)
- *Highest Point of the land surface*—Mt. Everest (8,848 metres)
- *Lowest point of the land surface*—Shores of the Dead Sea (396 metres below the sea level)
- *Greatest Ocean depth*—Mariana Trench, East of Philippines (11,033 metres below the sea level)

## THE MOON

- Earth has only one satellite, that is, the moon.
- Its diameter is only one-quarter that of the earth. It is about 3,84,400 km away from us.
- The moon moves around the earth in about 27 days. It takes exactly the same time to complete one spin. As a result, only one side of the moon (only 59% of its surface) is visible to us on the earth.
- Moonlight takes 1.3 sec. to reach earth.

## LATITUDE

- Imaginary lines drawn parallel to the equator. Measured as an angle whose apex is at the centre of the earth.
- The equator represents 0° latitude, while the North Pole is 90°N and the South Pole 90°S.
- 23½°N represents Tropic of Cancer while 23½°S represents Tropic of Capricorn.

## LONGITUDE

- It is the angular distance measured from the centre of the earth. On the globe the lines of longitude are drawn as a series of semicircles that extend from the North Pole to the South Pole through the equator. They are also called meridians.
- The distance between any two meridians is not equal. At the equator, 1 degree = 111 km. At 30°N or S, it is 96.5 km. It goes on decreasing this way until it is zero at the poles.

## INTERNATIONAL DATE LINE

- It is the 180° meridian running over the Pacific Ocean, deviating at Aleutian Islands, Fiji, Samoa and Gilbert Islands.
- Travellers crossing the Date Line from west to east repeat a day and travellers crossing it from east to west lose a day.

## INDIAN STANDARD TIME (IST)

- Indian Standard Time is calculated on the basis of 82.5°E longitude which passes through Uttar Pradesh, Madhya Pradesh, Odisha, Chattisgarh and Andhra Pradesh.

## ECLIPSES

- Sun is the only source of light for both the Earth and Moon. Eclipses occur when the light thus received is either blocked by the earth or by the Moon.
- Eclipses occur when either the Earth moves behind the Moon's shadow or the Moon moves behind the Earth's shadow.

## LUNAR ECLIPSE

- Lunar eclipse occur only when the following conditions are met.
  1. The Sun, Earth and Moon must be aligned in a straight line.
  2. The Earth must be positioned between the Sun and the Moon.
  3. The Moon must be in its full phase (Full Moon).

## SOLAR ECLIPSE

- Solar eclipses occur only when the following conditions are met.
  1. The Sun, Earth and Moon must be aligned in a straight line.
  2. The Moon must be positioned between the Sun and the Earth.
  3. Must be a New Moon day.

## ROCKS

- Rocks are composed of many minerals such as silica, aluminium, iron and magnesium. The nature of the rock is determined by the presence of its minerals.
- Rocks can be classified into three types:
  1. ***Igneous rocks*** are formed by magma that reaches the earth's surface along deep cracks and at volcanic vents. e.g., Mica, Granite etc.
  2. ***Sedimentary rocks*** are formed by the accumulation and cementation of mud, silt, or sand derived from weathered igneous rock frag-ments. e.g., Gravel, Peat, Gypsum etc.
  3. ***Metamorphic rocks*** are igneous or sedimentary rocks that have been altered by heat and/or pressure, either because they have been buried and folded deep in the crust, or because they have come into contact with molten igneous rock, e.g., Gneiss, Marble, Quartzite etc.

## VOLCANOES

Sudden eruption of hot magma (molten rock), gases, ash and other material from inside the Earth to its surface.

- ***Active*** which erupts frequently, e.g., Mauna Loa (Hawaii), Etna (Sicily), Vesuvius (Italy), Stromboli (Mediterranean Sea).

- ***Dormant*** Not erupted for quite sometime, e.g., Fujiyama (Japan), Krakatoa (Indonesia), Barren Island (Andamans).
- ***Extinct*** Not erupted for several centuries, e.g., Arthur's Seat, Edinburgh, Scotland.

### EARTHQUAKES

- Earthquakes are a form of wave energy that is transferred through bedrock. It is transmitted from the point of the earthquake focus, as spherical seismic waves. They travel in all directions outward.
- The intensity of earthquake waves is recorded by *Seismograph*.

## LANDFORMS

- There are three major landforms: mountains, plateaus and plains.

### MOUNTAINS

- A mountain can be defined as an area of land that rises abruptly from the surrounding region.
- There are three types of mountains- *Fold Mountains, Block Mountains* and the ***Volcanic Mountains***.
- Himalayas, Alps, Andes, Rockies, Atlas, etc are examples of Fold Mountains.
- The Aravali range in India is one of the oldest **fold mountain** systems in the world.
- The Rhine valley and the Vosges mountain in Europe are examples of such mountain systems.
- Volcanic mountains are formed due to volcanic activity.
- Mt. Kilimanjaro in Africa and Mt. Fujiyama in Japan are examples of such mountains.

**Major Mountain Ranges of the World**

| Range | Location | Highest Peak (m) | Length (km) |
|---|---|---|---|
| Andes | South America | 6,960 | 7,200 |
| Himalayas-Karakoram-Hindukush | South Central Asia | 8,848 | 4,800 |
| Rockies | North America | 4,401 | 4,800 |
| Great Dividing Range | East Australia | 2,228 | 3,600 |
| Western Ghat | Western India | 2,637 | 1,610 |
| Caucasus | Europe | 5,642 | 1,200 |
| Alaska | USA | 6,194 | 1,130 |
| Alps | Europe | 4,808 | 1,050 |
| Apennines | Europe | 2,912 | — |
| Ural | Asia | 1,895 | — |
| Atlas | North West Africa | — | 1,930 |

### PLATEAUS

- A plateau is an elevated flat land. It is a flat-topped table land standing above the surrounding area.

**Principal Mountain Peaks of the World**

| Mountains | Height in Metres |
|---|---|
| 1. Mount Everest | 8,848 |
| 2. K-2 (Godwin Austen) | 8,611 |
| 3. Kanchenjunga | 8,597 |
| 4. Lhotse | 8,511 |
| 5. Makalu I | 8,481 |
| 6. Dhaulagiri I | 8,167 |
| 7. Mansalu I | 8,156 |
| 8. Chollyo | 8,153 |
| 9. Nanga Parbat | 8,124 |
| 10. Annapurna I | 8,091 |
| 11. Gasherbrum I | 8,068 |
| 12. Broad Peak I | 8,047 |
| 13. Gasherbrum II | 8,034 |
| 14. Shisha Pangma (Gosainthan) | 8,014 |
| 15. Gasherbrum III | 7,952 |

### PLAINS

- A relatively low-lying and flat land surface with least difference between its highest and lowest points is called a Plain.

## OCEANS

- Oceans of the world is classified into four groups: the Pacific, the Atlantic, the Arctic and the Indian.
- The Pacific is the largest ocean, being twice the size of the Atlantic. It covers about a third of the Earth's surface, and contains more than half the water on the planet.

**Oceans of the World**

| Names | Area (Sq. Km.) | Greatest Depth |
|---|---|---|
| Pacific | 166,240000 | Mariana Trench |
| Atlantic | 86,560000 | Puerto Rico Trench |
| Indian | 73430000 | Java Trench |
| Arctic | 13230000 | — |

## Major Rivers of the World

| River | Origin | Falls in | Length (Km.) |
|---|---|---|---|
| Nile | Victoria lake | Mediterranean Sea | 6,650 |
| Amazon | Andes (Peru) | Atlantic Ocean | 6,428 |
| Yangtze | Tibetan Kiang Plateau | China Sea | 6,300 |
| Mississippi Missouri | Itaska lake (USA) | Gulf of Mexico (USA) | 6,275 |
| Yenisei | Tannu-Ola Mts. | Arctic Ocean | 5,539 |
| Hoang Ho | Kunlun Mts. | Gulf of Chibli | 5,464 |
| Ob | Altai Mts., Russia | Gulf of Ob | 5,410 |
| Congo | Lualaba & Luapula rivers | Atlantic Ocean | 4,700 |
| Amur | Northeast China | Sea of Okhotsk | 4,444 |
| Lena | Baikal Mts | Laptev Sea | 4,400 |
| Mekong | Tibetan Highlands | South China Sea | 4,350 |
| Mackenzie | Great Slave Lake | Beaufort Sea | 4,241 |
| Niger | Guinea | Gulf of Guinea | 4,200 |

## Major Gulfs of the World

| Names | Area (Sq. Km.) | Names | Areas (Sq. Km.) |
|---|---|---|---|
| Gulf of Mexico | 15,44,000 | Gulf of St. Lawrence | 2,37,000 |
| Gulf of Hudson | 12,33,000 | Gulf of California | 1,62,000 |
| Arabian Gulf | 2,38,000 | English Channel | 89,900 |

## Important Straits of the World

| Straits | Water Bodies joined | Area |
|---|---|---|
| Bab-al-Mandeb | Red Sea & Arabian Sea | Arabia & Africa |
| Bering | Arctic Ocean & Bering Sea | Alaska & Asia |
| Bosphorus | Black Sea & Marmara Sea | Turkey |
| Dover | North Sea & Atlantic Ocean | England & Europe |
| Florida | Gulf of Mexico & Atlantic Ocean | Florida & Bahamas Islands |
| Gibralter | Mediterranean Sea & Atlantic Ocean | Spain & Africa |
| Malacca | Java Sea & Bay of Bengal | India & Indonesia |
| Palk | Bay of Bengal & Indian Ocean | India & Sri Lanka |
| Magellan | South Pacific & South Atlantic Ocean | Chile |
| Sunda | Java Sea & Indian Ocean | Indonesia |

## Important Lakes of the World

| Lake | Location | Area (Sq. Km.) |
|---|---|---|
| Caspian | Russia and CIS | 371000 |
| Superior | Canada and USA | 82414 |
| Victoria | Tanzania (Africa) | 69485 |
| Huron | Canada and USA | 59596 |
| Michigan | USA | 58016 |
| Tanganyika | Africa | 32892 |
| Baikal | Russia (CIS) | 31502 |
| Great Bear | Canada | 31080 |
| Malawi | Malawi (Tanzania) | 30044 |
| Great Slave | Canada | 28438 |

## Highest Waterfalls of the World

| Name(s) (Foreign) | Location |
|---|---|
| Angel (Salto Angel) | Canaima Nat'l Park, Venezuela |
| Tugela | Natal Nat'l Park, South Africa |
| Utigord (Utigordsfoss) | Norway |
| Monge (Mongefoss) | Marstein, Norway |
| Gocta Cataracts | Chachapoyas, Peru |
| Mutarazi (Mtarazi) | Nyanga Nat'l Park, Zimbabwe |
| Yosemite | Yosemite Nat'l Park, California, U.S. |
| Espelands (Espelandsfoss) | Hardanger Fjord, Norway |
| Lower Mar Valley (Ostra Mardolafoss) | Eikesdal, Norway |
| Tyssestrengene | Odda, Norway |

## Important Cities on River Banks (World)

| City | Country | River |
|---|---|---|
| Adelaide | Australia | Torrens |
| Amsterdam | Netherlands | Amsel |
| Alexandria | Egypt | Nile |
| Ankara | Turkiye | Kazil |
| Bangkok | Thailand | Chao Praya |
| Basra | Iraq | Eupharates and Tigris |
| Baghdad | Iraq | Tigris |
| Berlin | Germany | Spree |
| Bonn | Germany | Rhine |
| Budapest | Hungary | Danube |
| Bristol | UK | Avon |
| Buenos Aires | Argentina | Laplata |
| Chittagong | Bangladesh | Majyani |
| Canton | China | Si-Kiang |
| Cairo | Egypt | Nile |
| Chung King | China | Yang-tse-kiang |
| Cologne | Germany | Rhine |
| Dandzing | Germany | Vistula |
| Dresden | Germany | Elbe |
| Dublin | Ireland | Liffy |
| Hamburg | Germany | Elbe |
| Kabul | Afghanistan | Kabul |
| Karachi | Pakistan | Indus |
| Khortoum | Sudan | Confluence of Blue & White Nile |
| Lahore | Pakistan | Ravi |
| Leningrad | Russia | Neva |
| Lisbon | Portugal | Tagus |
| Liverpool | England | Messey |
| London | England | Thames |
| Moscow | Russia | Moskva |
| Montreal | Canada | St. Lawrence |
| Nanking | China | Yang-tse-kiang |
| New Orleans | U.S.A. | Missisipi |
| New York | U.S.A. | Hudson |
| Ottawa | Canada | Ottawa |
| Paris | France | Seine |
| Philadelphia | U.S.A | Delaware |
| Perth | Australia | Swan |
| Prague | Czech Republic | Vitava |
| Quebec | Canada | St. Lawrence |
| Rome | Italy | Tiber |
| Rotterdam | The Netherlands | New Moss |
| Stalingrad | Russia | Volga |
| Shanghai | China | Yang-tse-kiang |
| Sidney | Australia | Darling |
| Saint Louis | U.S.A | Mississippi |
| Tokyo | Japan | Arakava |
| Vienna | Austria | Danube |
| Warsaw | Poland | Vistula |
| Washington D.C. | U.S.A. | Potomac |
| Yangoon | Myanmar | Irawaddy |

## World's Geographical Surnames

*City of Sky-scrapers*—New York
*City of Seven Hills*—Rome
*City of Dreaming Spires*—Oxford
*City of Golden Gate*—San Francisco
*City of Magnificent Buildings*—Washington D.C.
*City of Eternal Springs*—Quito (S. America)
*China's Sorrow*—Hwang Ho
*Cockpit of Europe*—Belgium
*Dark Continent*—Africa
*Emerald Isle*—Ireland
*Eternal City*—Rome
*Empire City*—New York
*Garden City*—Chicago
*Gate of Tears*—Strait of Bab-el-Mandeb
*Gift of the Nile*—Egypt
*Granite City*—Aberdeen (Scotland)
*Hermit Kingdom*—Korea
*Herring Pond*—Atlantic Ocean
*Holy Land*—Jerusalem
*Island Continent*—Australia
*Islands of Cloves*—Zanzibar
*Isle of Pearls*—Bahrein (Persian Gulf)
*Key to the Mediterranean*—Gibralter
*Land of Cakes*—Scotland
*Land of Golden Fleece*—Australia
*Land of Maple Leaf*—Canada
*Land of Morning Calm*—Korea
*Land of Midnight Sun*—Norway
*Land of the Thousand Lakes*—Finland
*Land of the Thunderbolt*—Bhutan
*Land of White Elephant*—Thailand
*Land of Thousand Elephants*—Laos
*Land of Rising Sun*—Japan
*Loneliest Island*—Tristan De Gunha (Mid-Atlantic)
*Manchester of Japan*—Osaka
*Pillars of Hercules*—Strait of Gibraltar
*Pearl of the Antilles*—Cuba
*Playground of Europe*—Switzerland
*Quaker City*—Philadelphia
*Queen of the Adriatic*—Venice
*Roof of the World*—The Pamirs, Central Asia
*Sugar bowl of the world*—Cuba
*Venice of the North*—Stockholm

*Windy City*—Chicago
*Whiteman's grave*—Guinea Coast of Africa
*Yellow River*—Huang Ho (China)
*Sickman of Europe*—Turkiye

## Important Boundaries

| | |
|---|---|
| **Durand Line** | Pakistan & Afghanistan |
| **MacMohan Line** | India & China |
| **Radcliff Line** | India & Pakistan |
| **Maginot Line** | France & Germany |
| **Oder Niesse Line** | Germany & Poland |
| **Hindenberg Line** | Poland & Germany (at the time of First World War) |
| **38th Parallel** | North & South Korea |
| **49th Parallel** | USA & Canada |

## Continents: Some Facts

| Continent | Biggest Counrty | Highest Peak | Longest River |
|---|---|---|---|
| Asia | China | Mt. Everest (8848 m) | Yangtze Kiang |
| Africa | Algeria | Mt. Kilimanjaro (5895 m) | Nile |
| North America | Canada | Mt. Mckinley (6194 m) | Mississippi Missouri |
| South America | Brazil | Mt. Acancagua (6960 m) | Amazon |
| Europe | Russia | Mt. Elbrus (5642 m) | Ob |
| Australia | Australia | Mt. Coscuisco (2228 m) | Darling |
| Antarctica | — | Vinson Massif (5140 m) | — |

# INDIAN GEOGRAPHY

## AREA AND LOCATION

- India is in the southern parts of the Asian continent. In the west of India lies the Arabian Peninsula while in the east lies the Indo-China Peninsula.
- India extends between 8°4' N and 37°6' N latitudes and between 68°7' E and 97°2' E longitudes.
- India, has a total geographic area of 32,87,263 sq. km. This is only 2.42 % of the total geographic area of the world but holds 17 per cent of the world's population.
- The 23½°N, which is the Tropic of Cancer, runs across the country.
- India has a length of 3214 km from north to south and 2933 km from east to west. It has a land frontier of 15200 km.
- The total length of the coastline of the mainland, Lakshadweep Islands and Andaman and Nicobar Islands is 7,516.6 km.
- India ranks seventh among the countries of the world, in terms of the geographical extent.
- India is bordered on three sides by water and on one by land, it is also a peninsula.
- India shares its common border with Afghanistan and Pakistan in the north-west, China and Bhutan in the north, and Bangladesh in the east. In the south, Sri Lanka is separated from India by a strait, known as the Palk Strait.
- 82°30' E longitude is considered as the Indian Standard Meridian. The local time of this longitude is taken as the Indian Standard Time (IST). This is 5½ hours ahead of the Greenwich Mean Time.

### THE INDIAN STATES ON INTERNATIONAL BOUNDARIES ARE:

- ***Bordering Pakistan:*** Jammu and Kashmir, Punjab, Rajasthan, Gujarat.
- ***Bordering China:*** Ladakh, Himachal Pradesh, Uttarakhand, Sikkim, Arunachal Pradesh.
- ***Bordering Nepal:*** Bihar, Uttarakhand, UP, Sikkim, West Bengal.
- ***Bordering Bangladesh:*** West Bengal, Mizoram, Meghalaya, Tripura, Assam.
- ***Bordering Bhutan:*** West Bengal, Sikkim, Arunachal Pradesh, Assam.
- ***Bordering Myanmar:*** Arunachal Pradesh, Nagaland, Manipur, Mizoram.
- ***Bordering Afghanistan:*** Jammu and Kashmir (Pakistan-occupied area).

## Important Passes

| | |
|---|---|
| • Jammu and Kashmir | Burzi-La, Joji-La |
| • Himachal Pradesh | Bara La, Cha-La, Shipki-La |
| • Uttarakhand | Niti-La, Lipu-Lekh-La |
| • Sikkim | Jelep-La, Nathu-La |
| • Arunachal Pradesh | Bomdi-La |

## Heighest Mountain Peaks of India

| Peaks | Elevation• (in mts.) |
|---|---|
| Godwin Austin (K2) | 8611* |
| Kanchenjunga | 8598 |
| Nanga Parvat | 8126 |
| Gasherbrum | 8068* |
| Broad Peak | 8047* |
| Dastegil | 7885* |
| Masherbrum (East) | 7821 |
| Nanda Devi | 7817 |
| Masherbrum (West) | 7806* |
| Rakoposhi | 7788* |
| Kamet | 7756 |
| Saser Kangdi | 7672 |

• *Above mean sea level in metres.*

* *Situated in Pak occupied Kashmir (PoK).*

## Towns at River Banks

| Town | River |
|---|---|
| Agra | Yamuna |
| Allahabad | Confluence of the Ganges and the Yamuna |
| Ayodhya | Saryu |
| Badrinath | The Ganges |
| Kolkata | Hooghly |
| Cuttuck | Mahanadi |
| Delhi | Yamuna |
| Dibrugarh | Brahmaputra |
| Ferozepur | Satluj |
| Guwahatl | Brahmaputra |
| Hardwar | The Ganges |
| Hyderabad | Musi |
| Jabalpur | Narmada |
| Kanpur | The Ganges |
| Kota | Chambal |
| Kurnool | Tungbhadra |
| Lucknow | Gomti |
| Ludhiana | Sutlej |
| Nasik | Godavari |
| Pandharpur | Bhima |
| Patna | The Ganges |
| Sambalpur | Mahanadi |
| Srinagar | Jhelum |
| Srirangapattam | Cauveri |
| Surat | Tapti |
| Varanasi | The Ganges |
| Vijaywada | Krishna |

## Famous Waterfalls of India

| Waterfall | Hgt (Mt.) | River | State |
|---|---|---|---|
| Kunchikal | 455 | Varahi | Karnataka |
| Dudhsagar | 310 | Mandvi | Goa |
| Jog/Gersoppa | 255 | Sharavati | Karnataka |
| Rakim Kund | 168 | Gaighat | Bihar |
| Chachai | 127 | Bihad | Madhya Pradesh |
| Kevti | 98 | Mahanadi | Madhya Pradesh |
| Sivasamudram | 90 | Cauveri | Karnataka |

## Important Lakes of India

| Name of lake | State/UT |
|---|---|
| Pulicat Lake | Tamil Nadu & Andhra Pradesh Border |
| Sambhar Lake | Rajasthan |
| Tso Moriri Lake | Jammu & Kashmir |
| Vembanad Lake | Kerala |
| Wular & Dal Lakes | Jammu and Kashmir |
| Chilka Lake | Odisha |
| Kolleru Lake | Andhra Pradesh |
| Loktak Lake | Manipur |
| Lonar Lake | Maharashtra |
| Pangong Lake | Ladakh |

## Rivers of India

| Name | Originates From | Falls Into |
|---|---|---|
| Yamuna | Yamunotri | Ganga |
| Chambal | Singar Chouri Peak, Vindhyan escarpment | Yamuna |
| Ghaghara | Matsatung Glacier | Ganga |
| Kosi | Near Gosain Dham Peak | Ganga |
| Sabarmati | Aravalis | Gulf of Khambat |
| Krishna | Western Ghats | Bay of Bengal |
| Godavari | Nasik district in Maharashtra | Bay of Bengal |
| Caurey | Brahmagir Range of Western Ghats | Bay of Bengal |
| Tungabharda | Western Ghats | Krishna |
| Ganges | Combines Sources | Bay of Bengal |

| Name | Originates From | Falls Into |
|---|---|---|
| Sutlej | Mansarovar Rakas lakes | Chenab |
| Indus | Near Mansarovar Lake | Arabian Sea |
| Ravi | Kullu Hills near Rohtang Pass | Chenab |
| Beas | Near Rohtang Pass | Sutlej |
| Jhelum | Verinag in Kashmir | Chenab |
| Son | Amarkantak | Ganga |
| Brahmaputra | Near Mansarovar Lake | Bay of Bengal |
| Narmada | Amarkantak | Gulf of Khambat |
| Tapti | Betul District in Madhya Pradesh | Gulf of Khambat |
| Mahanadi | Raipur District in Chhattisgarh | Bay of Bengal |
| Luni | Aravallis | Rann of Kuchchh |
| Ghaggar | Himalayas | Near Fatehabad |
| Betwa | Vindhyanchal | Yamuna |

## Geographical Surnames

| | |
|---|---|
| Bengal's Sorrow | Damodar River |
| City of Palaces | Kolkata |
| Gateway of India | Mumbai |
| Pink City | Jaipur |
| Paris of India | Jaipur |
| Manchester of India | Ahmedabad |
| Kashmir of South | Kerala |
| Son of Sea | Lakshadweep |
| Queen of Mountains | Mussourie |
| Iron City | Jamshedpur |
| Hollywood of India | Mumbai |
| Scotland of East | Meghalaya |
| City of Nababs | Lucknow |
| City of Temples & Ghats | Varanasi |
| Land of Five Rivers | Punjab |
| City of Golden Temple | Amritsar |
| Garden of India | Bangaluru |
| Spice Garden of India | Kerala |
| City of Lakes | Srinagar |
| Twin City | Hyderabad-Secunderabad |
| City of Seven Islands | Mumbai |
| Diamond Harbour | Kolkata |
| Switzerland of India | Kashmir |
| Rice Bowl | Chhattisgarh |
| Fruit Bowl | Himachal Pradesh |
| Ganga of South | Cauvery |
| Pitsburg of India | Jamshedpur |
| City of Bridges | Srinagar |
| Residence of God | Allahabad |
| A Cross-road (Quadrivial) of National Highways | Kanpur |
| Heart of India | Delhi |
| Black River | Sharda |
| City of Festivals | Madurai |
| Queen of Deccan | Pune |
| Sorrow of Bihar | Kosi River |

## Some Major Irrigational and Multipurpose Projects

| S.No. | Name of Project | Related State | River |
|---|---|---|---|
| 1. | Bargi Project | Madhya Pradesh | Bargi |
| 2. | Beas | Joint Venture of Haryana, Punjab and Rajasthan | Beas |
| 3. | Bhadra | Karnakata | Bhadra |
| 4. | Bhakra Nangal | Haryana, Punjab and Rajasthan | Sutluj |
| 5. | Bhima I | Maharashtra | Pawana |
| 6. | Bhima II | Maharashtra | Krishna |
| 7. | Chambal | Joint Project of M.P. and Rajasthan | Chambal |
| 8. | Damodar Valley Project | West Bengal and Bihar | Damodar |
| 9. | Dulhasti Power Project | Jammu and Kashmir | Chenab |
| 10. | Farakka | West Bengal | Hooghly |

| S.No. | Name of Project | Related State | River |
|---|---|---|---|
| 11. | Gandak | Bihar and U.P. | Gandak |
| 12. | Ghataprabha | Karnataka | Ghataprabha |
| 13. | Hasdeo Bango Project | Madhya Pradesh, Chhattisgarh | Hasdeo |
| 14. | Hirakud | Odisha | Mahanadi |
| 15. | Jayakwadi | Maharashtra | Godavari |
| 16. | Kakrapara | Gujarat | Tapti |
| 17. | Kangsbati | West Bengal | Kangsbati and Kumari |
| 18. | Karjan | Gujarat | Karjan |
| 19. | Kosi | Bihar | Kosi |
| 20. | Koyana | Maharashtra | Koyana |
| 21. | Krishna Project | Maharashtra | Krishna |
| 22. | Kukadi | Maharashtra | Kukadi |
| 23. | Left Bank Ghagra Canal | Uttar Pradesh | Ghagra |
| 24. | Madhya Ganga Canal | Uttar Pradesh | Ganga |
| 25. | Mahanadi Delta Scheme | Odisha | (The irrigation scheme will utilise releases from Hirakund Reservoir) |
| 26. | Mahi | Gujarat | Mahi |
| 27. | Malaprabha | Karnataka | Malaprabha |
| 28. | Mayurakshi | West Bengal | Mayurakshi |
| 29. | Nagarjunasagar | Andhra Pradesh | Krishna |
| 30. | Panam | Gujarat | Panam |
| 31. | Parambikulam Aliyar | Tamil Nadu and Kerala | Perimbikulam |
| 32. | Pochampad | Andhra Pradesh | Godavari |
| 33. | Pong Dam | Punjab | Beas |
| 34. | Ramganga | Uttarakhand | Ramganga |
| 35. | Ranjit Sagar Dam (Thein Dam) | Punjab | Ravi |
| 36. | Rihand | Uttar Pradesh | Rihand |
| 37. | Sabarmati | Gujarat | Sabarmati |
| 38. | Sharda Sahayak | U.P. | Ghagra |
| 39. | Sone High Level Canal | Bihar | Sone |
| 40. | Tawa | Madhya Pradesh | Tawa |
| 41. | Tehri Dam | Uttarakhand | Bhagirathi |
| 42. | Tungabhadra | Andhra Pradesh and Karnataka | Tungabhadra |
| 43. | Ukai | Gujarat | Tapti |
| 44. | Upper Krishna | Karnataka | Krishna |
| 45. | Upper Penganga | Maharashtra | Penganga |
| 46. | Uri Power Project | Jammu and Kashmir | Jhelum |

## Major Indian Crops

| Crops | Temp(°c) | Water(cm) | States where Produced |
|---|---|---|---|
| Wheat | 15°-25° | 60-90 | Uttar Pradesh, Madhya Pradesh, Punjab, Haryana. |
| Rice | 24°-26° | 80-200 | West Bengal, Uttar Pradesh, Punjab, Andhra Pradesh, Bihar |
| Maize | 18°-21° | 50-60 | Karnataka, Madhya Pradesh, Maharashtra |
| Jowar | 20°-35° | 40-60 | Maharashtra, Madhya Pradesh, Karnataka |
| Soyabean | 25°-27° | 50-120 | Maharashtra, Madhya Pradesh, Rajasthan |
| Cotton | 20°-30° | 80-150 | Gujarat, Maharashtra, Telangana, Karnataka, Madhya Pradesh |
| Tobacco | 20°-25° | 75-80 | Andhra Pradesh, Madhya Pradesh, Gujarat, Karnataka, Maharashtra, Uttar Pradesh |
| Tea | 24°-30° | 100-200 | Assam, West Bengal, Kerala, Tamil Nadu, Uttar Pradesh |
| Ground Nut | 15°-25° | 60-130 | Gujarat, Maharashtra |

## Mineral Wealth at a Glance (Metallic Minerals)

| Mineral | Chief Producers |
|---|---|
| Bauxite | Odisha, Gujarat, Jharkhand |
| Chromite | Odisha, Karnataka |
| Coal | Jharkhand, Odisha |
| Copper | Rajasthan, Madhya Pradesh |
| Diaspore | Uttar Pradesh, Madhya Pradesh |
| Gold | Karnataka |
| Iron | Odisha, Karnataka, Goa |
| Lead | Rajasthan, Andhra Pradesh |
| Lignite | Tamil Nadu, Jammu & Kashmir |
| Manganese | Odisha, Karnataka |
| Natural Gas | Gujarat, Assam |
| Petroleum | Gujarat, Assam, Andhra Pradesh |
| Silver | Rajasthan, Jharkhand, Gujarat |
| Tungsten | Rajasthan |
| Zinc | Rajasthan, Maharashtra |

## Zones and Headquarters of Indian Railways

| S.No. | Zone | Headquarters |
|---|---|---|
| 1. | Central | Mumbai |
| 2. | Eastern | Kolkata |
| 3. | Northern | New Delhi |
| 4. | North-Eastern | Gorakhpur |
| 5. | North-East Frontier | Maligaon, Guwahati |
| 6. | Southern | Chennai |
| 7. | South-Central | Secunderabad |
| 8. | South-Eastern | Kolkata |
| 9. | Western | Mumbai |
| 10. | East Coast | Bhubaneswar |
| 11. | East Central | Hajipur |
| 12. | North Central | Prayagraj |
| 13. | North Western | Jaipur |
| 14. | South Western | Hubballi (Hubli) |
| 15. | West Central | Jabalpur |
| 16. | South East Central | Bilaspur |
| 17. | Metro Railway | Kolkata |
| 18. | South Coast Railway | Vishakhapatnam (Proposed) |

## Major National Highways

| N H | Connects |
|---|---|
| NH 44 | Srinagar to Kanyakumari |
| NH 27 | Porbandar to Silchar |
| NH 48 | Delhi to Chennai |
| NH 52 | Sangrur to Ankola |
| NH 30 | Sitarganj to Ibrahimpatnam |
| NH 6 | Jorabat to Seling |
| NH 53 | Hazira to Paradip |
| NH 16 | East Coast (West Bengal) to Chennai |
| NH 66 | Panvel to Kanyakumari |
| NH 19 | Delhi to Kolkata |

**Major Ports of Country**

1. Syama Prasad Mookerjee (Kolkata)
2. Mumbai
3. J.L. Nehru Port (Nhava Sheva)
4. V.O. Chidambaranar (Tuticorin)
5. Chennai
6. Mormugao
7. New Mangalore
8. Paradeep
9. Deendayal (Kandla)
10. Vishakhapatnam
11. Cochin
12. Kamarajar Port Limited (Ennore).

## Major International Airports in India

| International Airports | City |
|---|---|
| Indira Gandhi International Airport | Delhi |
| Anna International Airport | Chennai |
| Sri Guru Ram Dass Ji International Airport | Amritsar |
| Rajiv Gandhi International Airport | Hyderabad |
| Calicut International Airport | Kozhikode |
| Chhatrapati Shivaji International Airport | Mumbai |
| Kempegowda International Airport | Bengaluru |
| Goa Airport in Vasco di Gama City | Goa |
| Netaji Subash Chandra Bose International Airport | Kolkata |
| Thriuvananthapuram International Airport | Thiruvananthapuram |
| Lokpriya Gopinath Bordoloi International Airport | Guwahati |
| Sardar Vallabhbhai Patel International Airport | Ahmedabad |

❒❒❒

# INDIAN POLITY

## INDIAN CONSTITUTION

- Demand for a Constituent Assembly composed of the people of India officially asserted by the Congress for the first time in 1935.
- The election for Indian Constitution Assembly held in 1946 according to the *Cabinet Mission Plan*.
- The first session of the Assembly was held in New Delhi on December 9, 1946. *Sachidanand Sinha* was elected provisional chairman of the session.
- On December 11, 1946, Dr. Rajendra Prasad was elected as the Permanent Chairman of the Constituent Assembly.
- The Constitution was framed by the Constituent Assembly of India, set-up in December 1946, in accordance with the Cabinet Mission Plan, under the Chairmanship of Sachidanand Sinha, initially.
- The total membership of Constituent Assembly after partition was 299, among them 70 were representatives from the Indian states and others from British India.
- The Chairman of the Drafting Committee was **Dr. BR Ambedkar**, also called the Father of the Constitution.
- The Constituent Assembly took 2 years, 11 months and 18 days to complete the Constitution.
- The Constitution, adopted on 8th November, 1949, contained 395 Articles and Schedules.
- The Constitution was delayed till 26th January because, in 1929, on this day Indian National Congress demanded Poorna Swaraj in Lahore Session under JL Nehru.
- Indian Constitution is a comprehensive document and it is the lengthiest written Constitution in the World.

## THE PREAMBLE

- ***The Preamble of the Constitution:*** "Wc the people of India, having solemnly resolved to Constitute India into a Sovereign, Socialist, Secular Democratic Republic and to secure to all its citizen:

  ***Justice,*** Social, economic and political;

  ***Liberty*** of thought, expression, belief, faith and worship;

  ***Equality*** of status and of opportunity; and to promote among them all;

  ***Fraternity*** assuring the dignity of the individual and the unity and integrity of the nation;

  In our Constituent Assembly, this twenty-sixth day of November, 1949, do hereby adopt, enact and give to ourselves this constitution."

### Foreign Sources of Indian Constitution

| ***Foreign Sources*** | ***Subject*** |
|---|---|
| Britain | Parliamentary system, collective responsibilities of Cabinet |
| America | Fundamental right, Independent Judiciary, Judicial review |
| Canada | Division of powers |
| Ireland | Directive principles |
| Germany | Emergency provisions |
| Russia | Fundamental duties |
| Australia | Concurrent list |

## IMPORTANT ARTICLES

**PART - I**

**UNION AND ITS TERRITORIES** (ARTICLE 1 - 4)

- The Constitution says, "India, that is Bharat, shall be a Union of States".
- Parliament has the power to create any State, reduce it, change the name of boundaries of any State.

**PART - II**

**CITIZENSHIP** (ARTICLE 5 - 11)

- The Constitution provides for a single Citizenship.
- ***Indian Citizenship can be acquire:***
  1. by birth
  2. by descent
  3. by registration
  4. by naturalisation
  5. by incorporation of territory
- ***Indian Citizenship can be lost by:***
  1. renunciation;
  2. termination — it takes place if a citizen of India voluntary acquires the citizenship of another country; and
  3. deprivation — if the Government terminates the citizenship.

## PART - III

## FUNDAMENTAL RIGHTS (ARTICLE 12 - 35)

- Following fundamental rights are enjoyed by every Indian citizen, irrespective of caste, colour, creed and sex:
  1. ***Right to Equality:*** No special privileges, no distinction on grounds of religion, caste, creed and sex.
  2. ***Right to Freedom:*** The right to freedom of expression and speech, the right to choose one's own profession, the right to reside in any part of the Indian Union.
  3. ***Right to Freedom to Religion:*** Except when it is in the interest of public order, morality, health or other conditions, everybody has the right to profess, practice and propagate his religion freely.
  4. ***Cultural and Educational Rights:*** The Constitution provides that every community can run its own institutions to preserve its own culture and language.
  5. ***Right against Exploitation:*** Traffic in human beings and forced labour and the employment of children under 14 years in factories or mines, are punishable offences.
  6. ***Rights to Constitutional Remedies:*** When a citizen finds that any of his fundamental rights has been encroached upon, he can move the Supreme Court, which has been empowered to safeguard the fundamental rights of a citizen (Article 32).

## PART - IV

## DIRECTIVE PRINCIPLES OF STATE POLICY (ARTICLE 36 - 51)

- Directive principles are not enforceable through courts. Main aim of Directive principles is to provide social and economic base of a genuine democracy.

***Some Important Directive Principles:***

- Provisions for adequate means of livelihood for all citizens (Art. 39).
- Right to work (Art. 41).
- Right to human condition of work and maternity relief (Art. 42).
- Right to a living wage and condition of work ensuring decent standard of life of worker (Art. 43).
- Common Civil Code (Art. 44).
- Prohibit consumption of liquor (Art. 47).
- Prevent slaughter of useful cattle (Art. 48).
- Organise Panchayati Raj (Art. 40).
- Separate the judiciary from the executive (Art. 50).
- Protect and maintain places of historic monuments (Art. 49).
- International peace (Art. 51).

## PART - IV A

## FUNDAMENTAL DUTIES (ARTICLE 51A)

- The fundamental duties for the Indian citizens have been incorporated in the Constitution through the Constitution (42nd) Amendment Act, 1976. These duties are:

1. to abide by the Constitution and respect its ideals and institutions, the National Flag and the National Anthem;
2. to cherish and follow the noble deeds which inspired our national struggle for freedom;
3. to uphold and protect the sovereignty, unity and integrity of India;
4. to defend the country and render national service when called upon to do so;
5. to promote harmony and the spirit of common brotherhood amongst all the people transcending religious, regional or sectional diversities and to renounce practices derogatory to the dignity of women;
6. to value and preserve the rich heritage of our composite culture;
7. to protect and improve natural environment including forests, lakes, rivers and wildlife, and to have compassion for living creatures;
8. to develop the scientific temper, humanism and the spirit of inquiry and reform;
9. to safeguard public property and to abjure violence;
10. to strive towards excellence in all spheres of individual and collective activity so that the nation constantly rises to higher levels of endeavour and achievement.
11. who is parent or guardian to provide opportunities for education to his child or, as the case may be, ward between age of six and fourteen years.

## PART - V

## UNION (ARTICLE 52 - 151)

### THE PRESIDENT

- The President is the Constitutional head of the Republic of India. He is more or less the titular head of the executive.
- He is the constitutional head but not the real executive. The real power is vested in the hands of the Council of Ministers.
- President is the first citizen of India.
- ***Qualifications:*** (i) Indian citizen, (ii) age not less than 35 years, (iii) should have qualification for election to Lok Sabha, (iv) should not hold any office of profit, (v) should not be a Member of Parliament or State Legislature.
- ***Election:*** Indirectly elected through Electoral College consisting of elected members of both the Houses of the Parliament and elected members of the Legislative Assemblies of the States.
- According to the 70th Amendment Act, 1992, the expression 'States' include the National Capital Territory of Delhi and the Union Territory of Puducherry. Members of the Legislative Councils have no right to vote in the Presidential election.

- ***Powers:*** He makes appointments to all the constitutional posts.
- He can address either House of Parliament and dissolve Lok Sabha.
- All Bills passed by Parliament must receive his assent to become an Act.
- He issues ordinances when Parliament is not in session. No Money Bill can be introduced in Lok Sabha without his recommendation.
- He appoints 12 members of special repute in the Rajya Sabha.
- He has the power of *Pardon* to a criminal in special cases.
- The President holds the office for a period of five years. He is eligible for re-election.
- He draws a fix salary per month with various allowances.
- He is also entitled to rent free official residence called Rashtrapati Bhawan.

## VICE-PRESIDENT

- ***Article 63*** of the Constitution stipulates a Vice-President for India.
- The Vice-President acts as the ex-officio Chairman of the Council of States (Rajya Sabha).
- He is elected by an electoral college consisting of the members of both Houses of Parliament in accordance with the system of proportional represen-tation by means of the single trans-ferable vote. He must be a citizen of India, not less than 35 years of age, and should be eligible for election as a member of the Council of States.
- Disputes in connection with election of a president or a vice-president are to be a dealt with in accordance with Article-71. Such disputes shall be decided by the Supreme Court.

## COUNCIL OF MINISTERS

- The Constitution of India provides for a parliament system of government under which the President is only Constitutional ruler and the real power is exercised by the Council of Ministers, headed by the Prime Minister.
- Council of Ministers is composed of all Union Ministers—the Prime Minister, Cabinet Ministers and Ministers of State.
- The Council of Ministers is Collectively responsible to the Lok Sabha.
- The Prime Minister is a link between the President and the Council of Ministers.

## PRIME MINISTER

- The Prime Minister is the leader of the majority party in the Parliament.
- He is appointed by the President. Other Ministers are appointed by the president on his advice.
- The Prime Minister is the head of the Government and the head of the Council of Ministers.
- Jawaharlal Nehru was the first Prime Minister and the longest serving so far.

## UNION LEGISLATURE

- The Legislature of the Union, which is called 'Parliament' consists of the President and the two Houses of Parliament known as the Council of states (Rajya Sabha) and the House of the People (Lok Sabha).

### RAJYA SABHA

- The Rajya Sabha is the Upper House of the Parliament and it is constituted of representatives from the States or the Constituent units of the Indian Union.
- It is a permanent body, one third of its members retiring after every two years.
- Its maximum strength is 250. Out of these, twelve members are nominated by the President from well-known personalities in the realm of Science, Art, Literature and Social Service. Rest of 238 representatives of the States and Union Territories are elected.
- Currently, the strength of the Rajya Sabha is 245.

### LOK SABHA

- The Lok Sabha whose life is five years, is the Lower House of Parliament and comprises of members directly elected by the people.
- The House of the people (Lok Sabha) at present consists of 543 directly elected members from the states and Union Territories.
- Two members of Anglo-Indian Community were nominated by the President, but by the 104th amendment of the constitution this provision have been abolished.
- The House of the People shall continue for five years (unless sooner dissolved) from the date of its meeting and no longer and the expiry of the said period of 5 years shall operate as dissolution of the House.

## PARLIAMENTARY COMMITTEES

- There are several Parliamentary Committees to assist the Parliament in its deliberations.
- These are appointed or elected by the respective Houses of Lok Sabha and Rajya Sabha on a motion made or are nominated by their presiding officers.
- Among the Standing Committees, three are financial Committees:

  (*i*) Public Account Committee;

  (*ii*) Estimate Committee;

  (*iii*) Public undertaking Committee.

### Speaker of Lok Sabha

- Speaker is elected by the Lok Sabha from among its members.
- The Speaker will have the final power to maintain order within the House of the People and to interpret its rules of procedure.
- A Deputy-Speaker is also elected to officiate in absence of the Speaker.
- *G.V. Mavlankar* was the first Speaker of the Lok Sabha (1952-1956).

### Supreme Court

- The Constitution provides for the Supreme Court, which consists of Chief Justice and 33 judges. They are appointed by the President of India.

#### QUALIFICATION AND TENURE

- Eligibility conditions for a judge of the Supreme Court are that he must be : (i) a citizen of India; (ii) a judge of a high court for a minimum period of 5 years; or (iii) an advocate of a high court for at least ten years or a distinguished jurist.
- Judges hold office till the age of 65.
- They can resign earlier or can be removed by the President on the recommendation of the two Houses of the Parliament by 2/3rd majority of the members present and voting.

#### Powers

- *Original jurisdiction:* Cases involving Government of India and the states or cases involving the enforcement of Fundamental Rights fall under original jurisdiction.
- *Appellate Jurisdiction:* In cases which are brought to it in the form of appeals against the judgement of the lower courts—It hears appeals in civil and criminal cases.
- *Advisory functions:* the Supreme Court advises the President on the constitutionality of a particular legal matter. However, its advice is not binding on the President.

***Other Powers:***

1. it is a court of record and can punish for contempt of itself;
2. it can make rules for regulating the practice and procedure of courts with the approval of the President; and
3. it can recommend to the President the removal of chairman and members of the UPSC. Supreme Court enjoys the power of judicial review (right of the court which declares as unconstitutional, the laws passed by the legislature and orders issued by executive) though it is not specifically mentioned in the Constitution.

- The first Chief Justice of India was H.J. Kania (1950-51).

#### COMPTROLLER AND AUDITOR GENERAL (CAG) (ARTICLE 148-151)

- The Comptroller and Auditor General of India is guardian of the public purse.
- It is his duty to see that not a *paisa* is spent out of consolidated fund of India or of a state without the authority of the appropriate legislature.
- He is appointed by President of India.
- A person with long administrative experience and knowledge of accounts is appointed.
- Holds office for 6 yrs or till 65 yrs of age.
- The President can remove him only on the recommendation of the 2 houses of Parliament (as in case of judge of Supreme Court).
- The CAG submits its reports to the President (in case of accounts relating to the Union Government) or to the State Governors (for State Government Accounts).
- The first CAG of India was *V Narahari Rao* (1948-1954).
- The CAG is not eligible for further office under the Union or State Governments. The expenses of the office of the CAG is charged to the Consolidated Fund of India.

#### ATTORNEY GENERAL OF INDIA

- The Attorney General of India is the first law officer of the Government of India.
- Though he is not a member of cabinet he has the right to speak in the House of Parliament, but he has no right to vote.
- The Attorney General of India shall be appointed by the President and shall hold office during his pleasure.
- His duty shall be to give advice on such legal matter from time-to-time as may be referred to him by the President.
- To be appointed as Attorney General, a candidate must be qualified to be appointed as a Judge of the Supreme Court.
- The Attorney General can participate in proceedings of the Parliament without the Right to Vote (Article 88).
- The first Attorney General of Independent India was MC Setalvad (1950-1963).

## PART - VI

## THE STATES (ARTICLE 152 - 237)

### The Governor

- The Governor is appointed by the President and holds office during the pleasure of the President.
- Apart from the power to appoint the council of ministers, if the governor finds that the government of state cannot be carried on in accordance with the provisions of the constitution (Art. 356), he may send his report to the President who may assume to himself the functions of the government of the state. (This is popularly known as 'President's Rule').
- Article 161 gives the Governor the power to grant pardons, reprieves, remission of punishment to persons convicted under the state law.

- Article 171 states that the States where Legislative Councils exists, the Governor can nominate some members from amongst those distinguished in literature, science, arts, cooperative movement and social service.

**STATES LEGISLATURE** (ARTICLE 168 - 212)

- The state legislature consists of Governor and legislative assembly.
- In some state like *Bihar, Maharashtra, Andhra Pradesh, Karnataka, Uttar Pradesh and Telangana* have a legislative council.
- The membership of the council should not be more than *one-third* of the legislative assembly but not less than 40.
- The legislative assembly of each state shall be composed of members chosen by direct election on the basis of adult suffrage and the number of members shall not be more than 500 or less than 60.
- The assembly of Sikkim, Goa, Puducherry and Mizoram have less than 60 members.

**HIGH COURTS** (ARTICLE 214-232)

- The High Court stands at the apex of the State Judiciary.
- As per the Constitution, there shall be a High Court in each State. But there may be a common High Court for two or more States and Union Territory, if it is provided by a law of the Parliament. For example, the Madras High Court has its Jurisdiction over the State of Tamil Nadu and the Union Territory of Puducherry.
- The State Government has no control over it.
- There are 25 High Courts in India.
- The Calcutta High Court, established in 1862, is the oldest High Court in India.

**THE PANCHAYATS** (ARTICLE 243-243 O)

- Panchayati Raj was introduced in India with a view to associate the people with administration at grass-root level.
- It is a three-tier system as recommended by Balwant Rai Mehta Committee.
- Introduced by the 73rd Amendment Act, 1992 which envisaged a three tier system of local governance.

*These are:*

1. Gram Panchayat at the village level
2. Panchayat Samiti at the block level
3. Zila Parishad at the district level.

**Jurisdiction and Seat of High Courts**

| Name | Territorial Jurisdiction | Seat |
|---|---|---|
| Allahabad | Uttar Pradesh | Prayagraj (Bench at Lucknow) |
| Bombay | Maharashtra, Goa, Dadar and Nagar Haveli and Daman and Diu | Mumbai (Benches at Nagpur, Panaji and Aurangabad) |
| Calcutta | West Bengal and Andaman & Nicobar | Kolkata (Circuit Benchs at Port Blair and Jalpaiguri) |
| Chhattisgarh | Chhattisgarh | Bilaspur |
| Delhi | Delhi | Delhi |
| Gauhati | Assam, Nagaland, Mizoram and Arunachal Pradesh | Guwahati (Benches at Kohima, Aizawl and Itanagar) |
| Gujarat | Gujarat | Ahmedabad |
| Himachal Pradesh | Himachal Pradesh | Shimla |
| Jammu & Kashmir and Ladakh | Jammu & Kashmir, Ladakh | Srinagar and Jammu |
| Jharkhand | Jharkhand | Ranchi |
| Karnataka | Karnataka | Bengaluru (Circuit Benches at Dharwar and Gulbarga) |
| Kerala | Kerala & Lakshadweep | Ernakulam |
| Madhya Pradesh | Madhya Pradesh | Jabalpur (Benches at Gwalior and Indore) |
| Madras | Tamil Nadu & Puducherry | Chennai (Bench at Madurai) |
| Orissa | Odisha | Cuttack |
| Patna | Bihar | Patna |
| Punjab and Haryana | Punjab, Haryana and Chandigarh | Chandigarh |
| Rajasthan | Rajasthan | Jodhpur (Bench at Jaipur) |
| Sikkim | Sikkim | Gangtok |
| Uttarakhand | Uttarakhand | Nainital |
| Tripura | Tripura | Agartala |
| Meghalaya | Meghalaya | Shillong |
| Manipur | Manipur | Imphal |
| Telangana | Telangana | Hyderabad |
| Andhra Pradesh | Andhra Pradesh | Amravati |

## THE MUNICIPALITIES (ARTICLE 243 P-243 ZG)

- Big cities have municipal corporations headed by the elected Mayor.
- For small towns there are elected boards or councils, in turn, elect their Presidents.
- Introduced by the 74th Amendment Act, 1993 which envisages three types of urban local bodies, namely, municipality (nagar palika), city council (nagar panchayat).
- Municipal governance in India was first introduced in Madras in 1688.

### PART - XIII

## (ARTICLE 301 - 307)

- In this part from Article 301-307 trade, commerce and intercourse within the territory of India are given.

### PART - XIV

## (ARTICLE 308 - 323)

- In this part services under the union and the states are given.
- ***Article 312:*** *All India Services* and ***Article 315:*** Public Service Commissions for the Union and for the States.
- The first Public Service Commission was set up in 1926, on the recommendations of the Lee Commission.

## UNION PUBLIC SERVICE COMMISSION (UPSC)

- This Commission is responsible for:
  1. recruitment to all civil services and posts, under the Union Government by written examinations, interviews and promotions, and
  2. advising the Government on all matters relating to methods of recruitment, principles to be followed in making promotions and transfers. Its Chairman is appointed by the President.

## STAFF SELECTION COMMISSION (SSC)

- The Union Government has constituted a Staff Selection Commission for recruitment to non-technical Class III posts in the central government and in subordinate offices.
- The Administrative Reforms Commission had recommended the setting up of such a Commission.
- The Commission has also been entrusted with the responsibility of making recruitment to Group 'B' services like Assistants' and Stenographers Grade 'C'.
- The Commission has a chairman and two members.

## ELECTIONS (ARTICLE 324-329)

- The Constitution provides for an independent election commission to ensure free and fair election to the Parliament, the State legislature and the offices of President and Vice-President.
- Consists of Chief Election Commissioner +2 Election Commissioners. They all enjoy equal powers.
- The Chief Election Commissioner and other Election Commissioners are appointed by the President.
- Election Commissioners are appointed for a term of 5 yrs.
- They are not eligible for re-appointment. Also, they cannot hold any office of profit after their retirement.
- The Election Commission was established on 25th January, 1950 under Article 324 of the Constitution.
- The first Chief Election Commissioner was *Sukumar Sen.*

### Functions

- Preparation of electoral rolls and keeping voters list updated.
- Recognition of various political parties and allotment of election symbols.

## NITI AAYOG

- The Indian government has replaced Planing Commission with a new institution named **NITI Aayog (National Institution for Transforming India).**
- The Niti Aayog will comprise the following:
  1. Prime Minister of India as the Chairperson.
  2. Governing Council comprising the Chief Ministers of all the States and Lt. Governors of Territories.
  3. Regional Councils will be formed to address specific issues and contingencies impacting more than one state or a region. These will be formed for a specified tenure. The Regional Councils will be convened by the Prime Minister and will comprise of the Chief Ministers of States and Lt. Governors of Territories in the region. These will be chaired by the Chairperson of the NITI Aayog or his nominee.
  4. Experts, specialists and practitioners with relevant domain knowledge as special invitees nominated by the Prime Minister.
- The full-time organizational framework will comprise of, in addition to the Prime Minister as the Chairperson:
  1. Vice-Chairperson : To be appointed by the Prime Minister.
  2. Members : Full-time. : 3
  3. Part-time members : Maximum of 2 from leading universities research organizations and other relevant institutions in an ex-officio capacity. Part time members will be on a rotational basis.
  4. Ex Officio members : Maximum of 4 members of the Council of Ministers to be nominated by the Prime Minister.
  5. Chief Executive Officer : To be appointed by the Prime Minister for a fixed tenure, in the rank of Secretary to the Government of India.
  6. Secretariat as deemed necessary.

## FINANCE COMMISSION

- The constitution of the Finance Commission is laid down in Art. 280.
- The chairman must be a person having experience in public affairs; and the other four members also having wide experience in financial matters.
- It consists of Chairman and 4 other members.
- It shall be the duty of the Finance Commission to advice the President on matters such as the distribution between the Union and States of the net proceeds of taxes that is required to be shared.
- The Finance Commission is not a permanent body. It is dissolved after it has submitted its recommendations.

## Important Amendments to the Constitution

| | |
|---|---|
| **First Amendment, 1951** | : Added Ninth Schedule. |
| **Twenty-second Amendment, 1969** | : Formation of Meghalaya within the state of Assam was facilitated. |
| **Twenty-sixth Amendment, 1971** | : The privy and privileges of the former rulers of Indian States were abolished. |
| **Thirty-first Amendment, 1973** | : The upper limit of representation of states was raised from 500 to 525. The upper limit for representation of the UTs was reduced from 25 to 20. |
| **Thirty-sixth Amendment, 1975** | : Sikkim was made a full-fledged state of Indian Union and it was included in the First Schedule. |
| **Thirty-eight Amendment, 1975** | : This act led to the amendment of Article 123, Article 213 and Article 352 which stated that the satisfaction of President or of Governor contained in these Articles would be called in question in any court of law. |
| **Forty-second Amendment, 1976** | : This amendment was done in accordance with the recommendations of Swaran Singh Committee and included a number of amendments. |
| **Forty-third Amendment, 1977** | : It provided for the restoration of the Jurisdiction of the Supreme Court and High Courts, curtailed by the enactment of the Constitution (Forty-Second Amendment) Act, 1976. |
| **Forty-fourth Amendment, 1978** | : The right to property was deleted as Fundamental Right and was made a legal right. |
| **Fifty-third Amendment, 1986** | : The Act grants statehood to the Union Territory of Mizoram, thus making it the 23rd State of the Indian Unions. |
| **Fifty-sixth Amendment, 1987** | : The UT of Goa converted into Goa state through this amendment whereas Daman and Diu were organised under a new UT. |
| **Seventy-third Amendment, 1992** | : It is concerning Panchayati Raj. |
| **Seventy-fourth Amendment, 1992** | : It is regarding Municipal Boards and Corporations. |
| **Eighty-ninth Amendment, 2003** | : It provides for constitution of a separate National Commission for Scheduled Tribes. (Earlier, there was a combined National Commission for both SC/STs). |
| **Ninety-first Amendment, 2003** | : It is regarding restricting the total number of Ministers including Prime Minister/ Chief Minister in Lok Sabha and State Legislatures to 15% of the total number of the Union or State Legislatures. |
| **Ninety-ninth Amendment, 2015** | : The amendment is in toto quashed by Supreme Court on 16 October, 2015. |
| **One hundredth Amendment, 2015** | : Exchange of certain enclave territories with Bangladesh and conferment of citizenship rights to residents of enclaves consequent to signing of Land Boundary Agreement (LBA) Treaty between India and Bangladesh. |
| **One hundredth and first Amendment, 2016** | : The act amends the Constitution to introduce "The Goods and Services Tax (GST)." |
| **One hundredth and Third Amendment, 2019** | : The Act providing 10 per cent reservation in government jobs and educational institutions to Economically Weaker Sections (EWS) of General Category, came into effect on January 14, 2019. |
| **One hundredth and Fourth Amendment, 2019** | : This Act ceased the reservation of seats for Anglo-Indians in the Lok Sabha and State Legislative assemblies and extended reservations for SCs and STs for up to ten years. |
| **One hundredth and Fifth Amendment, 2021** | : This Act restores the power of State Governments to identify and specify Socially and Economically Backward Classes (SEBCs). |
| **One hundredth and Sixth Amendment, 2023** | : This Act provides 33% reservation for women in Lok Sabha and State Legislative Assemblies. |

## NATIONAL SYMBOLS

### STATE EMBLEM

- State Emblem of India is an adaptation from the Sarnath Lion Capital of Ashoka. It was adopted by the Government of India on January 26, 1950. In the adapted form, only three lions are visible, the fourth being hidden from the view.
- The wheel (Dharma Chakra) appears in relief in the centre of the abacus with a bull on the right and a horse on the left.
- The bell-shaped lotus has been omitted. The words ''Satyameva Jayate'' meaning ''Truth alone triumphs'' are inscribed below the Emblem in Devanagari script.

### NATIONAL FLAG

- The National Flag of India is a horizontal tricolour of deep saffron (Kesari), white and dark green in equal proportion.
- In the centre of the white band there is a wheel in navy blue colour. It has 24 spokes.
- The ratio of the length and the breadth of the flag is 3 : 2. Its design was adopted by the Constituent Assembly of India on July 22, 1947.

### NATIONAL ANTHEM

- Rabindranath Tagore's song 'Jana-gana-mana' was adopted by the Constituent Assembly as the National Anthem of India on January 24, 1950.

*Jana-gana-mana-adhinayaka jaya he,*
*Bharata-bhagya-vidhata*
*Punjab-Sindh-Gujarat-Maratha-*
*Dravida-Utkala-Banga*
*Vindhya-Himachala-Yamuna-Ganga*
*Uchhala-jaladhi-taranga.*
*Tava subha name jage,*
*Tava subha asisa mange,*
*Gahe tava jaya gatha,*
*Jana-gana-mangala-dayak,*
*jaya he Bharata bhagya vidhata,*
*Jaya he, jaya he, jaya he,*
*Jaya jaya jaya, jaya he.*

### NATIONAL SONG

- Bankim Chandra Chatterji's 'Vande Mataram' which was a source of inspiration to the people in their struggle for freedom, has been adopted as National Song. It has an equal status with the National Anthem.

*Vande Mataram*
*Sujalam, suphalam, malayaja-shitalam,*
*Shasya shyamalam, Mataram*
*Shubhrajyotsna, pulkita yaminim,*
*Phulla kusumita drumadalashobhinim,*
*Subhasinim sumadhura—bhashinim,*
*Sukhadam, Varadam, Mataram.*

- **National Bird and Animal of India:** Peacock and Tiger.
- **National Aquatic Animal:** Dolphin
- **National Flower:** Lotus
- **National Calendar:** It was adopted on March 22, 1957. It has 365 days in the year and the first month of the year is Chaitra.

❑❑❑

# GENERAL SCIENCE

## PHYSICS

### PHYSICAL QUANTITIES

- Physical quantities may be divided in two classes:
  1. Scalar Quantities 2. Vector Quantities
- A scalar quantity is one which has only magnitude.
- A vector quantity has both magnitude and direction.
- Force, Velocity, Momentum, Acceleration are examples of vector quantities.
- Mass, length, time, volume, speed, energy, work are examples of scalar quantities.

### UNITS

- All measurements in physics require standard units.
- In 1960, the General Conference of Weights and Measures recommended that a metric system of measurements called the International System of Units, abbreviated as SI units, be used.

**Some Important Units**

| S.No. | Units | Quantity |
|---|---|---|
| 1. | Metre | Length |
| 2. | Kilogram | Mass |
| 3. | Second | Time |
| 4. | Ampere | Electric Current |
| 5. | Candela | Luminous Intensity |
| 6. | Newton | Force |
| 7. | Joule | Workdone |
| 8. | Watt | Power |
| 9. | Coulomb | Electric Charge |
| 10. | Volt | Potential Difference |
| 11. | Ohm | Electrical Resistance |
| 12. | Farad | Capacitance |
| 13. | Henry | Inductance |
| 14. | Lumen | Luminous Flux |

- Very small distances are measured in micro-meters or (microns) (μm), angstroms (Å), nanometers (nm) and femtometres (fm).

### MOTION

- When a body changes its position with respect to something else as time goes on, we say the body is in motion.
- There are two types of motion—translational (linear) and rotational (spin).
- The motion of a car on a road is translational whereas the motion of a top, spinning on its axis is rotational.

### SPEED

- It is a scalar form of velocity and is defined as the distance travelled in one second.
- $\text{Speed} = \dfrac{\text{distance travelled}}{\text{time required}}$
- SI unit of speed is m/s.

### VELOCITY

- The distance covered by an object in a specified direction in unit time interval is called velocity.
- The SI unit of velocity is m/s.
- Velocity is a vector quantity.

### ACCELERATION

- The velocity of a body changes due to change in its speed or direction or both. The rate of change of the velocity of a body is called its acceleration.
- $\text{Acceleration} = \dfrac{\text{change in velocity}}{\text{time taken}}$

## FORCE AND MOTION

### GRAVITATIONAL FORCE

- It is the force of attraction between two masses.
- It is gravitational force that holds the moon in its orbit round the earth and the earth in its orbit round the sun.
- *Newton's Law of Universal Gravitation* states that every particle in the universe attracts every other particle with a force that is directly proportional to the product of their masses and inversely proportional to the square of the distance between them.
- The value of G is $6.67 \times 10^{-11}$ SI units.

### CENTRIPETAL FORCE

- The force acting towards the centre on a particle executing uniform circular motion is called centripetal force and is given by

$$F = \frac{mv^2}{r}$$

where, $m$ = Mass of the object

$v$ = Speed

$r$ = Radius of the Circular Path

- In case of the moon, gravitational force between the earth and the moon acts as the centripetal force.
- Centripetal force always acts on the particle performing circular motion.

## CENTRIFUGAL FORCE

- The pseudo force that balances the centripetal force in uniform circular motion is called centrifugal force.
- Centrifugal force is directed away from the centre along the radius.
- The centrifugal force is zero exactly at the poles and maximum at the equator.

## WEIGHT

- The weight of a body is the force with which the earth attracts the body towards its centre.
- The mass of a body is a constant quantity whereas its weight varies slightly from place-to-place on the earth.
- The weight of a body is maximum at the poles and minimum at the equator. This variation in weight is due to:

  1. the shape of the earth.
  2. the rotation of the earth about its axis.
- The weight of an object is less at high elevations than at sea level.
- At the centre of the earth, the weight of a body would be zero.
- On the surface of the moon the value of the acceleration due to gravity is nearly one-sixth of that on earth and, therefore, an object on the moon would weigh only one-sixth its weight on the earth. The mass of an object on the moon would be the same as on earth.
- The weight of a body would be more if the earth stopped rotating. Conversely, if the speed of rotation were higher, the weight would be less.
- A person weighs more in a lift, which is accelerating upward.
- An astronaut feels weightless in a spaceship because he is not pushing against anything.

## FRICTION

- Friction is the force which opposes the relative motion of two surfaces in contact.
- It is friction between the ground and the soles of our shoes that makes walking possible and it is lack of friction that makes our feet slip on highly polished surfaces.
- Friction in machines wastes energy and also causes wear and tear. This friction is reduced by using (1) lubricants, and (2) ball bearings.

## NEWTON'S LAWS OF MOTION

### First Law

- Every object continues in its state of rest or of uniform motion in a straight line if no net force acts upon it. It is also known as *law of inertia*.
- **Examples:** 1. An unwary passenger in a fast-moving bus falls forward when it stops suddenly. This happens because the feet of the passenger come to rest suddenly whereas his upper part of body continues to be in motion. 2. A person getting down from a moving bus has to run some distance, in the direction of the bus, before stopping. If he does not run he is bound to fall because his feet come to rest whereas his body continues to be in motion.

### Momentum

- The momentum of a body is defined as the product of its mass and velocity.

### Second Law

- This law states that "the rate of change of momentum of a body is proportional to the applied force and takes place in the direction of the force."
- If we express force (F) in Newtons, mass ($m$) in kilograms and acceleration ($a$) in metres per second squared, we can write the second law as; F = $ma$.
- In travelling the same distance, a car consumes more fuel on a crowded road than on a free road. This happens because the car has to stop and start quite often on a crowded road. The repeated acceleration requires a force (second law), which ultimately comes from the fuel. On a free road the car runs at almost uniform speed requiring fewer accelerations and hence less fuel consumption.

### Third Law

- This law states that "to every action there is an equal and opposite reaction."
- When a bullet is fired from a gun, equal and opposite forces are exerted on the bullet and the gun.
- The engine in a jet aeroplane works on the same principle as a rocket but there is a difference in the method of obtaining the high velocity as jet.

## IMPULSE

- If a force acts on a body for a very short time, then the product of force and time is called the impulse.

  Impulse= Change in momentum

  = Force × Time

### Application of Impulse

1. A cricket player draws his hand back while catching.
2. A person jumping on hard cement floor receives more injuries than a person jumping on muddy or sandy floor.

## WORK, POWER AND ENERGY

### WORK

- Whenever a force acting on a body displaces it, work is said to be done.

  Work = Force × Distance moved in the direction of force.
- Work is a scalar quantity and its SI unit is Joule (J).

### POWER

- Power is defined as the rate of doing work.

$$\text{Power} = \frac{\text{Work done}}{\text{Time taken}}$$

- The SI unit of power is Watt (W) and is also measured in horse power.

  1 HP = 746 W

### ENERGY

- Energy is defined as the capacity to do work.

### Kinetic Energy

- The energy possessed by an object due to its motion is called kinetic energy and is described by the expression

  $KE = \frac{1}{2}mv^2$; where, m = mass of the object

  v = speed

### Potential Energy

- Potential energy is the energy possessed by the body by virtue of its position, configuration or any condition of stress or strain.
- There are many examples of potential energy. A stone held at some height above the ground has potential energy. Water in an elevated reservoir possesses potential energy.

**Transformation of Energy**

| S.No. | Equipment | Transformation |
|---|---|---|
| 1. | Dynamo | Mechanical energy into electrical energy |
| 2. | Microphone | Sound energy into electrical energy |
| 3. | Loud Speaker | Electrical energy into sound energy |
| 4. | Electric Bulb | Electrical energy into light and heat energy |
| 5. | Battery | Chemical energy into electrical energy |
| 6. | Electrical Motor | Electrical energy into mechanical energy |

### CENTRE OF GRAVITY

- The centre of gravity of a body is the point where the whole weight of the body can be considered to act.
- Racing cars are build low and with wide wheel bases to reduce the risk of overturning at sharp bends.
- While crossing a river in a boat, passengers are not allowed to stand. This keeps the CG of the system (boat and passengers) low and ensures stability.

### ARTIFICIAL SATELLITES

- In the case of a satellite, the centripetal force is provided by the gravitational pull of the earth.
- If the speed of a satellite is more than 11.2 km/s or 25,000 miles/hour, the satellite would escape the earth entirely and would never come back. This is called escape velocity.
- The existence of gaseous atmosphere on the earth is due to the high value of its escape velocity.

### Geostationary Satellites

- Geostationary satellites are stationary with respect to an observer on the earth. Their time period is 24-hour. There height above the surface of earth is 36,000 km. They are always in equatorial plane and their orbits are circular. They are also called parking orbits.

## DENSITY AND RELATIVE DENSITY

### DENSITY

- The mass per unit volume of a substance is called its density.

$$\text{Density} = \frac{\text{Mass}}{\text{Volume}}$$

- The SI unit of density is kilogram per metre cubed ($kg/m^3$).
- The relative density of a substance is the ratio of the density of the substance to the density of water.
- Relative density has no unit.

### PRESSURE

- Pressure is defined as force acting per unit area.

$$\text{Pressure} = \frac{\text{Force}}{\text{Area}}$$

- The SI unit of pressure is newton per metre squared or pascal.
- Broad wooden sleepers are placed below the rails to reduce the pressure exerted by the weight of a train.
- The pressure of water increases with depth, therefore bottom of a dam is made much thicken than the top.
- The pressure exerted on an enclosed liquid at one place is transmitted equally throughout the liquid. This is called Pascal's Principle.
- Hydraulic presses, hydraulic brakes, hydraulic door closers, etc. are applications of the Pascal's Principle.
- At high attitudes where atmosphere pressure is less nose bleeding may occur due to the greater pressure of blood.

- In an aircraft flying at high altitude, normal atmospheric pressure is maintained by the use of air pumps. If this were not done, the crew and passengers would experience difficulty in breathing and consequently face dangers.
- Atmospheric pressure is measured with an instrument called the *Barometer*.

## ARCHIMEDE'S PRINCIPLE

- This principle states that when a body is wholly or partially immersed in a fluid, it experiences an upthrust (upward force) equal to the weight of the fluid displaced.
- An iron nail sinks in water whereas a ship made of iron and steel floats. This is due to the fact that a ship is hollow and contains air and, therefore, its density is less than that of water.
- The density of sea water is more than that of river water, due to this a ship sinks less in sea water. It is for this reason that a ship rises a little when it enters a sea from a river.
- It is because of the higher density of sea water that it is easier to swim in the sea.
- A balloon filled with a light gas, such as hydrogen, rises because the average density of the balloon and the gas is less than that of air. The balloon cannot rise indefinitely because the density of the air decreases with increasing altitude. At a certain height, where the density of air is equal to the average density of the balloon, it ceases to rise and drifts sideways with the wind.
- When an ice block floats in water the water level will remain the same when all the ice melts into water.
- A *hydrometer* is an instrument used for measuring the relative density of liquids.
- A special type of a hydrometer called *Lactometer* is used for testing milk by measuring its density.

## SURFACE TENSION

- Surface tension is that property of liquids owing to which they tend to acquire minimum surface area.
- Surface tension is caused by molecular attractions.
- When a paint brush is dipped in water all its hair spread out but when it is taken out it is covered with a thin film of water which contracts due to surface tension and pulls the hair together.
- Liquid drops, such as raindrops, oildrops, drops of molten metals, dewdrops etc. are all spherical because their surface tend to contract in order to have minimum surface area. For a given volume, a sphere has the minimum surface area.
- Soaps and detergents lower the surface tension of water. This increases the wetting power of water or its ability to detach dirt particles from clothes and untensils.
- The force of attraction between unlike molecules is called **adhesion** and that between like molecules **cohesion.**
- The melted wax of a candle is drawn up into the wick by capillary action. Oil rises up a lamp wick for the same reason.
- If one end of a sugar cube is dipped into tea, the entire cube is quickly wet on account of capillary action.

## VISCOSITY

- The force which opposes the relative motion between different layers of liquid or gases is called viscous force.
- Viscosity is the property of liquids and gases both.

## BERNOULLI'S THEOREM

- According to Bernoulli's theorem, in case of streamline flow of incompressible and non-viscous fluid (ideal fluid) through a tube, total energy (sum of pressure energy, potential energy and kinetic energy) per unit volume of fluid is same at all points.

  1. When a bowler spins a ball, it changes its direction (swings) in the air due to unequal pressure acting on it.

# HEAT

- Heat is that form of energy which flows from one body to other body due to difference in temperature between the bodies. The amount of heat contained in a body depends upon the mass of the body.

## TEMPERATURE

- The temperature of a body is the quantity that tells how hot or cold it is with respect to some standard body.

## MEASUREMENT OF TEMPERATURE

- Temperature is measured by a thermometer.
- A thermometer may be graduated in following scales—
  1. The upper and lower points of centigrade scale are 100°C and 0°C.
  2. The upper and lower points of Fahrenheit scale are 212°F and 32°F.
  3. The upper and lower points of Reaumur scale are 80°R and 0°R.
  4. The upper and lower points of Kelvin scale are 373K and 273K.
  5. The upper and lower points of Rankine scale are 672° Ra and 460° Ra.
- At –40 degrees both celsius and Fahrenheit scales will show identical readings.
- Water cannot be used in a thermometer becaues it freezes at 0°C and also because of its irregular expansion.

## THERMAL EXPANSION

- Solids, liquids and gases generally expand when heated and contract when cooled.
- Gaps have to be left in railway tracks to make allowance for expansion, otherwise the rails will buckle. Allowance

is made for the expansion of long steel bridges. One end of such bridge is fixed while the other rests on rollers.

- Telephone wires sag more in summer than in winter due to thermal expansion.

### EXPANSION OF WATER

- Water has its minimum volume and maximum density at 4°C.

### TRANSMISSION OF HEAT

- There are three ways of heat transmission: 1. Conduction; 2. Convection; 3. Radiation.

#### Conduction

- In this process, heat is transferred from one place to other place by the successive vibration of the particles of the medium without bodily movement of the particles of the medium.
- Conduction takes place mainly in solids.
- Air is a very bad conductor of heat. The good insulating properties of wool, cotton, etc. are mainly due to the air spaces they contain.

#### Convection

- In this process, heat is transferred by the actual movement of particles of the medium from one place to other place.
- In liquids and gases heat is transmitted by convection.

#### Radiation

- In this mode of heat transmission heat is transferred from one place to another without effecting the intervening medium.

### HEAT CAPACITY

- The heat capacity of a body is defined as the heat required to raise the temperature of the body by 1K. Its SI unit is J/K.

### SPECIFIC HEAT CAPACITY

- The specific heat capacity of a substance is the heat required to raise the temperature of a unit mass of the substance by 1K.
- Its SI unit is J/kg K.
- It is because of its high specific heat capacity that water is used as a cooling liquid in car engine.

### LATENT HEAT

- It is defined as the amount of heat absorbed or given out by a body during the change of state.
- Each gram of ice that melts absorbs 336 J of heat.

### EVAPORATION

- Water can change into the vapour state either by boiling or by evaporation at lower temperatures.
- When sweat evaporates from the skin it draws much heat from the body and produces a cooling sensation.
- In summer, water is stored in pitchers for cooling. Water oozes out of the pores of the pitchers and cools on evaporation.
- The rate of evaporation increases with increase in temperature.

### REFRIGERATOR

- In a refrigerator, cooling is produced by the evaporation of a volatile liquid, freon, inside a copper coil (evaporator), which surrounds the freezer.
- The cooling unit (freezer) in a refrigerator is fitted near the top to cool the whole of the interior.

### RELATIVE HUMIDITY

- Relative humidity is defined as the ratio of the mass of water vapour in a given volume of air to the mass required for saturating the same volume of air at the same temperature.
- Relative humidity is measured with an instrument called the hygrometer.

### PRESSURE COOKER

- The boiling point of a liquid depends on external pressure.
- When the atmospheric pressure is 76 cm of mercury, water boils at 100°C. But when the pressure is increased, the boiling point of water is raised.
- In a pressure cooker, water boils at temperatures higher than 100°C due to increased pressure. The increased boiling temperature allows water to hold more heat which cooks food faster.
- At higher altitudes, atmospheric pressure is reduced. This lowers the boiling point of water and food takes much longer to cook.

## WAVE MOTION

- Wave motion may be defined as the transfer of energy without the net transfer of matter.
- If the particles of the medium vibrate perpendicular to the direction of propagation of wave, the wave is called transverse wave.
- Light waves are transverse waves.
- If the particles of the medium vibrate in the direction of propagation of wave, the wave is called longitudinal wave.
- Sound waves are longitudinal waves.

### ELECTROMAGNETIC WAVE

- Electromagnetic waves include an enormous range of frequencies—from radio waves with frequencies less than $10^5$ Hz to gamma rays having frequencies greater than $10^{20}$ Hz.

- All electromagnetic wave have the same speed ($3 \times 10^8$ m/s) in vacuum. The relation $v = n\lambda$ holds good for all electromagnetic waves.

### RADIO AND TELEVISION TRANSMISSION

- Radio waves sent out by radio stations are reflected by the ionosphere and can be received anywhere on the earth.
- At night the radio reception improves because the layers of the ionosphere are not exposed to sunlight and are more settled.
- Radar (Radio detection and ranging) employs high frequency radio waves for detecting objects like ships and aeroplanes.
- In microwave oven, when the waves fall on the food, these are absorbed by water, fats, sugars and certain other molecules whose consequent vibrations produce heat. Since heating occurs inside the food, without warming the surrounding air, the cooking time is greatly reduced.
- In microwave oven, food cannot be cooked in metal vessels because the metal blocks out the microwaves.

## LIGHT

- Light is a form of energy which is propagated as electromagnetic waves.
- Light is a transverse wave.
- Speed of light in vacuum is $3 \times 10^8$ m/s.
- Light takes 8 minute 16.6 second to reach from sun to earth.

### REFLECTION

- When light is incident upon a surface, part of it is reflected. But certain surfaces like mirrors and polished metals reflect almost all the light incident upon them.
- The law of reflection states that the angle of incidence is equal to the angle of reflection.
- To see full image in a plane mirror, a person requires a mirror of at least half of his height.

### INCLINED MIRROR (NO. OF IMAGES)

- When an object is placed between two inclined mirrors, several images of the object are formed.

### CURVED MIRRORS

- There are two types of curved spherical mirrors—1. Concave Mirror, 2. Convex Mirror.
- Concave mirror can concentrate the sun's radiation falling on it at one point, it can be used as a burning glass.
- Concave mirrors are also used in solar cookers.
- Large concave mirrors are used in reflecting telescopes for observing and photographing distant stars and other heavenly bodies.
- Concave mirror is also used as a shaving or make-up mirror.
- Small concave mirrors are used by dentists for examining teeth.
- Concave parabolic mirrors are used in searchlight and headlamps of cars.
- Convex mirrors are also used as rear view mirrors in vehicles.

### REFRACTION

- When a ray of light passes from one medium to other it suffers a change in direction at the boundary of separation of two media. This phenomenon is called refraction.
- When a ray passes from one medium to another optically denser medium, e.g., from air to water or glass, it bends towards the normal. Conversely, a ray passing from water or glass into air is bent away from the normal.
- Rivers appear shallow, coin in a beaker filled with water appears raised, due to refraction.
- Another effect of refraction is the apparent upward bending of the immersed portion of a stick when dipped in water.
- It is due to refraction, produced by the earth's atmosphere, that the sun is visible for several minutes after it has set below the horizon. Thus, atmospheric refraction tends to lengthen the day.
- When the sun (or moon) is near the horizon, it appears elliptical, i.e., with the vertical diameter less than the horizontal diameter. This happens because rays from the lower edge of the sun are bent more than those from the upper edge (Atmospheric Refraction).
- One of the most interesting effects of atmospheric refraction and Mirage is a combined effect of atmospheric refraction and total internal reflection.

### DISPERSION

- White light consists of seven colours—violet, indigo, blue, green, yellow, orange and red. These colours are called the spectrum of the white light.
- Violet has the minimum wavelength (or maximum frequency) and red the maximum wavelength (or minimum frequency).
- Due to different speeds, the colours are refracted through different angles and therefore, when a narrow beam of white light passes through a glass prism, it is split up into its constituent colours. This separation of light into colours is called dispersion.

### COLOUR OF OBJECTS

- We see objects because of the light they reflect.
- When a rose is viewed in white light, its petals appear red and the leaves appear green, because the petals reflect the red part of the white light and leaves reflect the green part. The remaining colours are absorbed. When the same rose is viewed in green light, the petals will appear black

and the leaves green. In blue or yellow light both the petals and leaves will appear black.

- Red, blue and green are primary colours.

## LENSES

- There are mainly two types of lenses:
  1. Convex or Converging Lens
  2. Concave or Diverging Lens
- Converging or convex lens is used as a magnifying glass.
- Power of a lens is its capacity to deviate a ray. Power of a lens is measured as the reciprocal of the focal length.

$$P = \frac{1}{f}$$

- SI unit of power of lens is dioptre (D).
- The power of a converging lens is positive and that of a diverging lens is negative.
- For all positions of the object, the images formed by diverging (concave) lens are virtual, erect and diminished.

## EYE

- The light entering the eye is focused by the eye-lens to form an image on the retina.
- In front of the eye, lens is the coloured part of eye, called the iris, which automatically adjusts the size of the pupil to the intensity of light falling on it.
- In bright light the iris automatically shuts tighter, reducing the amount of light entering the pupil. This protects the retina from getting damaged.
- When a person enters a dark room after being in bright light, he is not able to see clearly for a while because the iris is unable to dilate the pupil immediately.
- Least distance of distinct vision is 25 cm.

## DEFECTS OF VISION

- A person suffering from long sight (hyper-metropia) can clearly see objects at infinity but cannot see near objects clearly. This defect is caused by the eyeball being too short and can be corrected by wearing converging lenses.
- In the case of a person suffering from short sight (myopia), the eye ball is too long and distant objects are focused in front of the retina. This defect can be corrected by wearing diverging lenses.
- ***Astigmatism:*** Curvature of cornea becomes irregular and image is not clear. Cylindrical lens is used.

## SCATTERING OF LIGHT

- When light falls on atoms and molecules, it is scattered in all directions.
- Scattering of light is maximum for violet colour and minimum for red colour.
- Blue colour of sky is due to scattering of light.
- In the evening, the sun is lower in the sky and its light has to traverse a longer path through the atmosphere to reach an observer. Thus, at sunset, blue, green and other colours having been scattered only red and some orange light reach us and the sun appears a deep orange-red.
- In outerspace, *i.e.*, beyond the atmosphere, there is nothing to scatter the sunlight and therefore the sky appears dark and stars are visible even in the presence of the sun.

## INTERFERENCE OF LIGHT

- The superposition of two (or more) waves of the same kind that pass the same point in space at the same time is called interference.
- Beautiful colours seen in soap bubbles and oil films on water are produced due to the interference of white light reflected by these surfaces.
- LASER (Light Amplification by Stimulated Emission of Radiation) is an optical device which produces an intense beam of coherent monochromatic light.
- Examples of Interference of Light: Holography, Laser.

## DIFFRACTION OF LIGHT

- When a beam of light passes through a narrow slit or an aperture, it spreads out to a certain extent into the region of geometrical shadow. This is an example of diffraction, *i.e.*, of the failure of light to travel in a straight line.

# SOUND

- Sound waves are longitudinal and cannot travel in vacuum. The transmission of sound requires a medium : air, liquid or solid.
- The longitudinal mechanical waves which lie in the frequency range 20 Hz to 20,000 Hz are called audible or sound waves. These waves are sensitive to human ear.
- The longitudinal mechanical waves having frequencies less than 20 Hz are called Infrasonic. These waves are produced by sources of bigger size such as earthquakes, volcanic eruptions, ocean waves etc.
- The longitudinal waves having frequencies greater than 20,000 Hz are called ultrasonic waves. Human ear cannot detect these waves. But some animals such as cats, dogs, bats can detect these waves.

## PITCH

- The pitch (shrillness of a sound) depends on its frequency.
- A sound of higher frequency has a higher pitch.
- The pitch of a woman's voice is higher than that of a man.

## LOUDNESS

- The relative loudness of a sound is measured in decibels (db).
- All stringed instruments, such as the violin, sitar, guitar, etc. have sound boxes attached to increase the loudness.

## SPEED OF SOUND

- The presence of water vapour in the air increases the speed of sound.
- Sound travels faster through warm air than through cold air. The speed of sound is higher on a hot day than on a cold day.
- Thunder is heard much after the flash of lightning is seen because of the wide difference in the speeds of light and sound.

## REFLECTION OF SOUND

- When a sound wave is reflected by a distant obstacle, such as a wall or a cliff, an echo is heard.
- To hear echo, the minimum distance between the observer and reflector should be 17 m.
- Exploration of underwater gas and oil is done by detecting the echoes of shock waves produced by explosions on the water surface.
- Bats emit ultrasonic waves of frequencies up to 80,000 Hz and use the reflection of these waves (echoes) to determine the presence and distance of objects on their way and from them respectively.

## DOPPLER EFFECT

- The Doppler effect is the change in frequency of a wave (sound or light) due to the motion of the source or observer.
- It is due to the Doppler effect that the whistle of a train appears shriller when it approaches a listener than when it moves away from him.

# ELECTRICITY

- Electricity produced by friction between two dissimilar objects is known as static electricity. Depending on the nature of the objects, one acquires a positive charge and the other an equal negative charge. For example, if a glass rod is rubbed with silk, the rod acquires positive charge and the silk an equal negative charge.
- *Lightning* is a gigantic electric discharge occurring between two charged clouds or between a charged cloud and the earth.

## CONDUCTOR

- Conductors are those materials which allow electricity (charge) to pass through themselves.
- Metals conduct electricity because they have a large number of conduction or free electrons.

## INSULATORS

- Insulators are those materials which do not allow electricity to flow through themselves. Insulators have no free electrons.

## SUPER CONDUCTORS

- The resistance of metals to flow of electricity reduces with decreasing temperature. At temperatures near absolute zero, metals have almost zero resistance and became super conductors.

## SEMI-CONDUCTORS

- Certain materials, such as silicon and germanium, have electrical resistivity intermediate between those of conductors and insulators. These materials are termed as semi-conductors.
- Semi-conductors are good insulators in their pure crystalline form but their conductivity increases when small amounts of impurities are added to them.

## ELECTRIC CURRENT

- Electric current is simply the flow of electric charge. In solid conductors the flow of electrons and in fluids the flow of ions as well as electrons constitute the current.
- SI units of electric current is Ampere (A).

## ELECTRICAL RESISTANCE

- When electric current flows through a conductor, e.g., a metallic wire, it offers some obstruction to the current. This obstruction offered by the wire is called its electrical resistance.
- SI unit of Resistance is ohm.

## OHM'S LAW

- If physical conditions like temperature, intensity of light etc. remains unchanged then electric current flowing through a conductor is directly proportional to the potential difference across its ends.

## ELECTRIC MOTOR

- In an electric motor, electrical energy is converted into mechanical energy.
- Electric fans, mixers, washing machines, etc. work on electric motors.

## INVERTER

- An inverter is a device which converts DC to AC. The inverters used in homes and offices are specially designed to:
  1. Convert DC from a battery to AC, and
  2. Charge the battery.

## FUSE

- Electric fuse is a protective device used in series with an electric appliance to save it from being damaged due to high current.
- A fuse is a short piece of wire made of a tin-lead alloy, which has a low melting point.
- Fuses are always connected in the live wire in series.

## COST OF ELECTRICITY

- The consumption of electrical energy in a house is measured in the unit kWh.
- Kilowatt hour is equal to the energy consumed in the circuit at the rate of 1 kilowatt for 1 hour.

# MAGNETISM

- A magnet attracts and holds pieces of iron but does not attract pieces of copper.
- Iron, cobalt, nickel and certain alloys are strongly magnetic whereas copper, wood, glass, etc. are non-magnetic.
- Our earth behaves as a powerful magnet whose south pole is near the geographical north pole and whose north pole is near the geographical south pole.

# ATOMIC & NUCLEAR PHYSICS

- Atom consists of three fundamental particles electron, proton and neutron. All the protons and neutrons are present in the central core of atom called nucleus. Electrons revolve around the nucleus.
- The total number of protons in the nucleus is called atomic number (Z).
- The total number of proton and neutrons in the nucleus is called mass number (A).
- Ernest Rutherford, discovered nucleus by the scattering of $\alpha$-particles from gold foil.

## RADIOACTIVITY

- Henry Bacquerel (1896) observed that a photographic plate blackened, when placed near double sulphate of potassium and uranium. He further observed that uranium emitted special kind of rays. They were called Becqueral rays.
- Pierre and Marie Curie observed that the radiation from pitchblende was four times stronger than uranium. In 1898, they finally discovered two new substances—Polonium and Radium. These newly discovered substances were called radioactive substances and this property of these substances was named radioactivity.
- No radioactive substance emits both $\alpha$ and $\beta$ particles simultaneously.

## X-RAYS

- X-rays are electromagnetic radiations having wavelength from a fraction of an Angestrom to about 100Å. They were discovered by Rontgen during his studies on the electrical discharge phenomena in gases—he found that an unknown radiation was produced when electrons collided with the walls of the tubes.

## ATOMIC ENERGY

- India today ranks sixth in the atomic energy programmes. It has developed the required know-how and expertise to manufacture nuclear weapons, but it believes in the peaceful uses of atomic power. The Atomic Energy Commission was set-up in the country in 1948 under the Chairmanship of Dr. H. J. Bhabha.
- ***Bhabha Atomic Research Centre (BARC):*** The Bhabha Atomic Research Centre at Trombay near Mumbai (Maharashtra) has four research reactors: (*i*) APSARA—It is the first atomic reactor in Asia; (*ii*) CIRUS—It is a joint Indo-Canadian project; (*iii*) PURNIMA II—a zero energy fast reactor, and (*iv*) DHRUVA—a high power completely indigenous nuclear research reactor with most advanced laboratories in the world. Another fast breeder reactor KAMINI at Kalpakkam has been constructed. Today India is the seventh country in the world and the first developing nation to have mastered the fast breeder reactor technology.
- **Nuclear Power:** Under Nuclear Power Corporation of India Limited (NPCIL) there are seven nuclear power stations in operation in six States:
  (*i*) Tarapur—Maharashtra, (*ii*) Rawatbhata —Rajasthan, (*iii*) Kalpakkam—Tamil Nadu, (*iv*) Narora—U.P., (*v*) Kakrapara—Gujarat, (*vi*) Kaiga—Karnataka and (*vii*) Kudankulam—Tamil Nadu.
- **Heavy Water:** Heavy water is one of the essential input for Pressurised Heavy Water Reactors (PHWRs) used both as a coolant and moderator. The first heavy water plant was set-up in 1962 in Nangal. Subsequently 7 more plants have been set-up at (*i*) Baroda, (*ii*) Tuticorin, (*iii*) Kota, (*iv*) Talcher, (*v*) Thal, (*vi*) Hazira and (*vii*) Manuguru.
- **Research and Development Centres:** Four research centres namely (*i*) Bhabha Atomic Research Centre, Trombay (Maharashtra), (*ii*) Indira Gandhi Centre for Atomic Research, Kalpakkam (Tamil Nadu), (*iii*) Centre for Advanced Technology, Indore (Madhya Pradesh), (*iv*) Variable Energy Cyclotron Centre at Kolkata (West Bengal) are focal points of research and development work in nuclear energy and related discipline.
- **India's Nuclear Explosions:** On May 18, 1974 India conducted her first underground nuclear explosion at Pokhran (Rajasthan) in the Thar desert, 20 km. away from Jaisalmer, at a depth of more than 100 metres. The successful explosion made India the sixth nuclear nation in the world.
- India conducted 5 nuclear explosion tests at Pokhran in two phases on May 11 and May 13, 1998 and became a nuclear power state.

## IMPORTANT INVENTIONS

| Name of Invention | Inventor | Nationality | Year |
|---|---|---|---|
| Aeroplane | Orville & Wilbur Wright | U.S.A. | 1903 |
| Ball-Point Pen | John J. Loud | U.S.A. | 1888 |
| Barometer | Evangelista Torricelli | Italy | 1644 |
| Bicycle | Kirkpatrick Macmillan | Britain | 1839-40 |
| Bifocal Lens | Benjamin Franklin | U.S.A. | 1780 |
| Car (Petrol) | Karl Benz | Germany | 1888 |
| Celluloid | Alexander Parkes | Britain | 1861 |
| Cinema | Nicolas & Jean Lumiere | France | 1895 |
| Clock (mechanical) | I-Hsing & Liang Ling-Tsan | China | 1725 |
| Diesel Engine | Rudolf Diesel | Germany | 1895 |
| Dynamo | Hypolite Pixii | France | 1832 |
| Electric Lamp | Thomas Alva Edison | U.S.A. | 1879 |
| Electric Motor (DC) | Zenobe Gramme | Belgium | 1873 |
| Electric Motor (AC) | Nikola Tesla | U.S.A. | 1888 |
| Electro-magnet | William Sturgeon | Britain | 1824 |
| Electronic Computer | Dr. Alan M. Turing | Britain | 1943 |
| Film (moving outlines) | Louis Prince | France | 1885 |
| Film (musical sound) | Dr. Le de Forest | U.S.A. | 1923 |
| Fountain Pen | Lewis E. Waterman | U.S.A. | 1884 |
| Gramophone | Thomas Alva Edison | U.S.A. | 1878 |
| Helicopter | Etienne Oehmichen | France | 1924 |
| Jet Engine | Sir Frank Whittle | Britain | 1937 |
| Laser | Charles H. Townes | U.S.A. | 1960 |
| Lift (Mechanical) | Elisha G. Otis | U.S.A. | 1852 |
| Locomotive | Richard Trevithick | Britain | 1804 |
| Machine Gun | James Puckle | Britain | 1718 |
| Microphone | Alexander Graham Bell | U.S.A. | 1876 |
| Microscope | Z. Janssen | Netherlands | 1590 |
| Motor Cycle | G. Daimler | Germany | 1885 |
| Photography (on film) | John Carbutt | U.S.A. | 1888 |
| Printing Press | Johann Gutenberg | Germany | c.1455 |
| Razor (safety) | King C. Gillette | U.S.A. | 1895 |
| Refrigerator | James Harrison & Alexander Catlin | U.S.A. | 1850 |
| Safety Pin | Walter Hunt | U.S.A. | 1849 |
| Sewing machine | Barthelemy Thimmonnier | France | 1829 |
| Ship (steam) | J.C. Perier | France | 1775 |
| Ship (turbine) | Hon. Sir C. Parsons | Britain | 1894 |
| Skyscraper | W. Le Baron Jenny | U.S.A. | 1882 |
| Slide Rule | William Oughtred | Britain | 1621 |
| Steam Engine (condenser) | James Watt | Britain | 1765 |
| Steel Production | Henry Bessemer | Britain | 1855 |
| Steel (stainless) | Harry Brearley | Britain | 1913 |
| Submarine | David Bushnell | U.S.A. | 1776 |
| Tank | Sir Ernest Swinton | Britain | 1914 |
| Telegraph | M. Lammond | France | 1787 |
| Telegraph Code | Samuel F.B. Morse | U.S.A. | 1837 |
| Telephone (perfected) | Alexander Graham Bell | U.S.A. | 1876 |
| Television (mechanical) | John Logie Baird | Britain | 1926 |
| Television (electronic) | P.T. Farnsworth | U.S.A. | 1927 |
| Thermometer | Galileo Galilei | Italy | 1593 |
| Transformer | Michael Faraday | Britain | 1831 |
| Transistor | Bardeen, Shockley & Brattain | U.S.A. | 1948 |
| Washing Machine (elec.) | Hurley Machine Co. | U.S.A. | 1907 |
| Zip-Fastener | W.L. Judson | U.S.A. | 1891 |

## Important Discoveries

| *Discovery* | *Discoverer* | *Nationality* | *Year* |
|---|---|---|---|
| Aluminium | Hans Christian Oerstedt | Denmark | 1827 |
| Atomic number | Henry Moseley | England | 1913 |
| Atomic structure of matter | John Dalton | England | 1803 |
| Chlorine | C.W. Scheele | Sweden | 1774 |
| Electromagnetic induction | Michael Faraday | England | 1831 |
| Electromagnetic waves | Heinrich Hertz | Germany | 1886 |
| Electromagnetism | Hans Christian Oersted | Denmark | 1920 |
| Electron | Sir Joseph Thomson | England | 1897 |
| General theory of relativity | Albert Einstein | Switzerland | 1915 |
| Hydrogen | Henry Cavendish | England | 1766 |
| Law of electric conduction | Georg Ohm | Germany | 1827 |
| Law of electromagnetism | Andre Ampere | France | 1826 |
| Law of falling bodies | Galileo | Italy | 1590 |
| Laws of gravitation & motion | Isaac Newton | England | 1687 |
| Laws of planetary motion | Johannes Kepler | Germany | 1609-10 |
| Magnesium | Sir Humphry Davy | England | 1808 |
| Neptune (Planet) | Johann Galle | Germany | 1846 |
| Neutron | James Chadwick | England | 1932 |
| Nickel | Axel Cronstedt | Sweden | 1751 |
| Nitrogen | Daniel Rutherford | England | 1772 |
| Oxygen | Joseph Priestly, C.W. Scheele | England, Sweden | 1772 |
| Ozone | Christian Schonbein | Germany | 1839 |
| Pluto | Clyde Tombaugh | U.S.A | 1930 |
| Plutonium | G.T. Seaborg | U.S.A | 1940 |
| Proton | Ernest Rutherford | England | 1919 |
| Quantum Theory | Max Planck | Germany | 1900 |
| Radioactivity | Antoine Bacquerel | France | 1896 |
| Radium | Pierre & Marie Curie | France | 1898 |
| Silicon | Jons Berzelius | Sweden | 1824 |
| Special theory of relativity | Albert Einstein | Switzerland | 1905 |
| Sun as centre of solar system | Copernicus | Poland | 1543 |
| Uranium | Martin Klaproth | Germany | 1789 |
| Uranus (Planet) | William Herschel | England | 1781 |
| X-rays | Wilhelm Roentgen | Germany | 1895 |

## Scientific Instruments

| *Name of Instrument* | *Used for* |
|---|---|
| Altimeter | measuring altitude |
| Ammeter | measuring strength of an electric current |
| Anemometer | measuring the velocity of wind |
| Audiometer | measuring level of hearing |
| Barometer | measuring atmospheric pressure |

| Name of Instrument | Used for |
|---|---|
| Callipers | measuring the internal and external diameters of tubes |
| Calorimeter | measuring quantity of heat |
| Compass | finding out direction |
| Dynamo | converting mechanical energy into electrical energy |
| Galvanometer | detecting and determining the strength of small electric currents |
| Hydrometer | measuring specific gravity of a liquid |
| Hygrometer | measuring the humidity in the atmosphere |
| Lactometer | measuring the purity of milk |
| Manometer | measuring the gaseous pressure |
| Micrometer | measuring minute distances, angles, etc. |
| Microscope | seeing magnified view of very small objects |
| Photometer | measuring intensity of light from distant stars |
| Pyrometer | measuring high temperatures |
| Radar | detecting and finding the presence and location of moving objects like aircraft, missile, etc. |
| Radiometer | measuring the emission of radiant energy |
| Rain Gauge | measuring the amount of rainfall |
| Seismograph | measuring and recording the intensity and origin of earthquake shocks |
| Sextant | measuring altitude and angular distances between two objects or heavenly bodies |
| Spectrometer | measuring the refractive indices |
| Spherometer | measuring the curvature of spherical objects/surface |
| Sphygmomanometer | measuring blood pressure |
| Stethoscope | ascertaining the condition of heart and lungs by listening to their function |
| Stroboscope | viewing objects that are moving rapidly with a periodic motion as if they were at rest |
| Tachometer | measuring the rate of revolution or angular speed of a revolving shaft |
| Telescope | viewing magnified images of distant objects |
| Thermocouple | measuring the temperature inside furnaces and jet engines |
| Thermometer | measuring human body temperature |
| Thermostat | regulating constant temperature |
| Ultrasonoscope | measuring utrasonic sounds |
| Viscometer | measuring the viscosity of a fluid |
| Voltmeter | measuring potential difference between two points. |

# CHEMISTRY

## ELEMENTS

- An element may be defined as a substance which is made by same type of atoms and it can neither be broken into, nor built from two or more simpler substances by any known physical or chemical methods, e.g., copper, silver, hydrogen, carbon, oxygen, nitrogen, gold, iron etc.

## COMPOUNDS

- A compound may be defined as a substance which contains two or more elements combined in some fixed proportion by weight and which can be decomposed into two or more elements by any suitable method.
- The properties of a compound are entirely different from those of the elements from which it is made.
- Some common examples of compounds are water, sugar, salt, aspirin, chloroform, alcohol and ether.

## MIXTURES

- A material containing two or more elements or compounds in any proportion is a mixture.
- The components of a mixture can be separated by physical means like filtration, sublimation and distillation.

## ATOMIC STRUCTURE

### ATOM

- Atom is the smallest part of the element that takes part in a chemical reaction. Atom of an element can not be changed into that of another element by a chemical or physical means. It does not exist in free state.

### MOLECULE

- A molecule is the smallest part of an element or compound that is capable of existing independently.

### ATOMIC WEIGHT (OR ATOMIC MASS)

- The atomic mass of an element is the number of times its atom is heavier than 1/12th of the mass of carbon ($C^{12}$) atom.
- The unit used to measure atomic mass is called atomic mass unit, *i.e.*, amu.

### ELECTRON

- The electron is a fundamental particle of an atom which carries a unit negative charge. It was discovered by J.J. Thomson in 1897.

### PROTON

- It is a fundamental particle of an atom carrying a unit positive charge. It was discovered by Rutherford and Goldstein in 1886.

### NEUTRON

- It is a fundamental particle of an atom carrying no charge. It was discovered by Chadwick in 1932.

### ISOTOPES

- The atoms of the same element having different mass numbers are called isotopes.

### ISOBARS

- Elements having the same atomic mass but differ in atomic number are called isobars.

### ISOTONES

- Elements having the same number of neutrons are called isotones.

## OXIDATION AND REDUCTION

- Oxidation is a process in which a substance adds on oxygen or loses hydrogen. In modern terms, oxidation is the process in which a substance loses electrons.
- Reduction is a process in which a substance adds on hydrogen or loses oxygen. In modern terms, reduction is the process in which a substance gains electrons.
- Oxidation and reduction always occur simultaneously. If one substance is oxidised, another is reduced. The reaction in which this oxidation-reduction process occurs is called a redox reaction.
- Oxidising agents are substances which bring about the oxidation of other substances, e.g., Potassium Permanganate, Potassium Dichromate, Nitric Acid, Hydrogen Peroxide, etc.
- Reducing agents are substances which bring about the reduction of other substances, e.g., hydrogen sulphide, hydrogen, carbon, sulphur dioxide, etc.

## ACIDS, BASES AND SALTS

### ACID

- An acid is any compound that can react with a base to form a salt, the hydrogen of the acid being replaced by positive metallic ion. According to modern theory, an acid is a compound which yields hydrogen ions (protons) to a base in a chemical reaction. In a water solution, an acid tastes sour, turns blue litmus red and produces free hydrogen ions.

| Acid | Sources |
|---|---|
| Citric Acid | Lemons or Oranges (Citrus Fruits) |
| Lactic acid | Sour milk |
| Tartaric acid | Grapes |
| Acetic acid | Vinegar |
| Maleic acid | Apples |
| Oxalic acid | Tomato |
| Formic acid | Red ants |

### BASES

- Such compounds which gives salt and water with acid known as bases. Bitter in taste, turns red litmus paper into blue, contains replaceable hydroxyl group.
- Some important bases are sodium hydroxide, potassium hydroxide, sodium carbonate and ammonium hydroxide.
- All alkalies are bases but all bases are not alkalies because all bases are not soluble in water.

### SALTS

- Salts are ionic compounds containing a positive ion (cation) and a negative ion (anion).
- When an acid reacts with a base, a salt and water are formed. This reaction is called neutralization since the acid and base neutralize each other's effect.

### ELECTROLYSIS

- The process of decomposition of an electrolyte by the passage of an electric current through its molten state or its aqueous solution is called electrolysis.
- Device through which electric current is passed known as electrodes.

## METALLURGY

- Metals occur in nature, in the native (in free state) as well as in the combined state.
- Naturally occurring materials containing metals are called minerals.
- A mineral from which a given metal is obtained economically is called an ore.
- The process of extraction of a metal in a pure state on a large scale from its ore by Physical and Chemical means is called metallurgy.
- The rocky and siliceous matter that associated with the ore is known as gangue.
- Substance that is added to ore to remove the gangue is known as flux.

- The process of removal of gangue from the ore is known as concentration.
- Calcination is the heating of the ore in the absence of air. This method is employed for obtaining the metal oxides from carbonates and hydroxides.
- Roasting is the heating of the ore in the presence of air. On roasting, part of the ore is oxidised to form an oxide. This oxide is then reduced to the metal.
- The industrial reduction process for obtaining metal from the treated ore is called smelting.

### AMALGUM

- An alloy in which one of the component metals is mercury is known as amalgum.

### IRON AND STEEL

- Iron is extracted from its ores by the blast furnace process.
- Iron obtained from blast furnace is called pig iron or cast iron containing about 5% carbon.
- Pure iron is called wrought iron which does not contain carbon more than 0.2%, or any other impurities or constituents.
- Steel contains 0.25% – 2% carbon and varying amounts of other elements.

## CARBON AND ITS COMPOUNDS

### ALLOTROPY

- Such substances which having the same chemical properties, but differ in physical properties, known as allotropes and this property is called allotropy.

### DIAMOND

- Diamond is the purest form of carbon.
- It is non-conductor of heat and electricity.
- It is the hardest natural substance.
- It burns in air at 900°C and gives out $CO_2$.

### GRAPHITE (BLACK LEAD)

- It is good conductor of heat and electricity.
- Graphite is used in making lead pencils.
- Graphite is also used as electrodes, lubricant, moderators, electrotyping and carbon arc.

### AMORPHOUS FORMS OF CARBON

1. Wood Charcoal – Obtained from wood
2. Sugar Charcoal – Obtained from cane sugar
3. Bone or Animal Charcoal – Obtained from animal bones
4. Coke Charcoal – Obtained from coal

### CARBON MONOXIDE (CO)

- Carbon monoxide is an active poison and is very dangerous as it is a colourless and odourless gas and can not, therefore, be easily detected.
- The extremely poisonous nature of carbon monoxide is a result of its combining with the haemoglobin of the blood to form carbo-xyhaemoglobin, which is not decompassed by any of the processes in the body.

### HYDROCARBONS

- Compounds of carbon and hydrogen are called hydrocarbon.
- A natural source of hydrocarbon is petroleum obtained from sedimentary rocks.
- Compounds having the same molecular formula but differ in properties due to different structural formula known as isomers and this property is called isomerism.

### SATURATED HYDROCARBONS (ALKANES)

- Containing single covalent bonds only.
- Such compounds are, in general, called alkanes for instance, Methane, Ethane, Propane, Butane.

### UNSATURATED HYDROCARBONS

- Containing multiple bonds.
- Compounds with double bonds are called alkenes, e.g. ethylene, propyene etc. and triple bond containing compounds are called alkynes, e.g. acetylene, propyne etc.
- Benzene is an unsaturated cyclic hydrocarbon with the structure.
- Compounds derived from benzene are called aromatic compounds.

### FUELS

#### Solid Fuels

- These contain carbon and, during combustion, form mainly carbon dioxide and carbon monoxide with a large amount of heat.
- Examples of solid fuels are wood, coal, coke and paraffin wax.

#### Liquid Fuels

- These are basically mixtures of several hydrocarbons. During combustion, they form carbon dioxide and water.
- Liquid fuels are obtained as different fractions during the distillation of petroleum.
- Examples of liquid fuels are kerosene oil, petrol, diesel oil and alcohol.

#### Gaseous Fuels

- Gaseous fuels do not leave ash on burning and have high content of heat.
- The main gaseous fuels are liquefied petroleum gas (LPG, mainly a mixture of propane and butane and used in homes for cooking, water gas ($CO + H_2$), producer gas ($CO + N_2$), coal gas (mixture of hydrogen, methane, ethylene, carbon monoxide, nitrogen, oxygen and carbon dioxide) and natural gas (mixture of methane, ethane, propane and butane with traces of higher hydrocarbons obtained from oil well, above petroleum).

## PETROLEUM AND NATURAL GAS

- Natural gas contains about 80% methane and 10% ethane, the remaining 10% being a mixture of higher gaseous hydrocarbons.
- Compressed Natural Gas (CNG) is natural gas filled in cylinders under high pressure.
- The quality of petrol for use in car engines is denoted by their anti-knock properties.
- To increase octane number, tetra ethyl lead (TEL) is added to petrol.

## HEAVY WATER

- Chemically heavy water is deuterium oxide.
- Heavy water is used in nuclear reactors as a moderator because it slows the fast moving neutrons.

### Hard and Soft Water

- Water which produces lather with soap solution readily is called soft water.
- Water which does not produce lather with soap solution readily is called hard water.
- The hardness of water is due to presence of the bicarbonates, chlorides and sulphates of calcium and magnesium.
- Temporary hardness of water is due to the presence of bicarbonates of calcium and magnesium.
- Permanent hardness of water is due to presence of sulphates, chlorides, nitrates of calcium and magnesium.

## GLASS

- Ordinary glass is solid mixture of silica, sodium silicate and calcium silicate.
- Soft glass is a soda-lime silicate glass. It melts at low temperature. It is used in manufacturing of bottles, test tubes etc.
- Hard glass is potash lime silicate and melts at high temperature in comparison to soft glass and is used in manufacturing of flask etc.
- Flint glass is a lead potash silicate and is used in manufacturing of prism, lens and optical instruments.
- Pyrex glass is a mixture of sodium aluminium borosilicates. It is used in manufacturing of high quality equipments in laboratory because it does not melt at very high temperature.
- Safety glass is prepared by placing a layer of transparent plastic glass between two layers of glass by means of a suitable adhesive. It is used in making wind screen of automobiles, aeroplanes, trains etc.

## CEMENT

- The approximate composition of Portland cement is:
  1. Calcium Oxide → 62%
  2. Silica → 22%
  3. Alumina → 7.5%
  4. Magnesia → 2.5%
  5. Ferric Oxide → 2.5%
- A small amount of gypsum is added to slow down the setting of cement.
- Cement containing excess amount of lime cracks during setting while cement containing less amount of lime is weak in strength.
- Cement containing no iron is white but hard to burn.

## POLYMERS AND PLASTICS

- A polymer is a large molecule, built up from many hundreds of thousands of small unit called monomeric units or monomers.
- The process of formation of polymers from monomers is called polymerization.
- Plastics are cross-linked polymers and very tough.
- Some examples of plastics are — Celluloid, Bakelite and Vinyl Plastics.

## RUBBER

- Natural and Synthetic rubbers are examples of polymers.
- Natural rubber is isomer of isoprene.
- When the natural rubber is heated along with sulphur called vulcanisation. The resulting rubber is elastic, hard and strong.
- Synthetic rubbers are made by polymerisation of chloroprene, styrene and butadiene mixtures and isobutylene.

## SOAPS

- The soaps are sodium salts of higher fatty acids. They are useful only in soft water as they form an insoluble precipitate in hard water. This precipitate consists of salts of calcium and magnesium of higher fatty acids. No lather or emulsion is formed and washing is not possible.

**Some Importants Alloys**

| *Alloys* | *Composition* |
|---|---|
| Brass | Cu, Zn |
| Bronze | Cu, Sn |
| Gun metal | Cu, Sn, Zn |
| Bel metal | Cu, Sn |
| German silver | Cu, Zn, Ni |
| Dutch metal | Cu, Zn |
| Aluminium | Al, Cu |
| Nichrome | Ni, Fe, Cr, Mn |
| Chromium steel | Cr, C, Fe |

## Chemical Formulae, Commercial Name of Chemical Compounds

| Commercial Name | Chemical Compounds | Chemical formulae |
|---|---|---|
| Common salt | Sodium chloride | $NaCl$ |
| Baking soda | Sodium bicarbonate | $NaHCO_3$ |
| Washing soda | Sodium carbonate | $Na_2CO_3 . 10H_2O$ |
| Caustic soda | Sodium hydroxide | $NaOH$ |
| Chilli salt peter | Sodium nitrate | $NaNO_3$ |
| Soda ash | Sodium carbonate | $Na_2CO_3$ |
| Hypo | Sodium thiosulphate | $Na_2S_2O_3 . 5H_2O$ |

# BIOLOGY

## BRANCHES OF BIOLOGY

(a) **Anthropology:** Deals with the scientific study of man and the mankind.

(b) **Agronomy:** Deals with the management of farms and science of crop production.

(c) **Apiculture:** Deals with the process of bee keeping for commercial purposes.

(d) **Entomology:** Deals with the structure, habits and classification of insects.

(e) **Eugenics:** Deals with improving the human race.

(f) **Pathology:** Deals with the nature of disease, their causes, symptoms, effects, their cure and control.

(g) **Physiotherapy:** Deals with the treatment of diseases, body weakness or defects with the help of massage and exercise etc.

(h) **Sericulture:** Deals with the production of raw silk from silkworm.

(i) **Pharmacology:** Deals with the knowledge and manufacture of drugs.

(j) **Occupational therapy:** Deals with treating the physically handicapped or injured persons through exercise etc.

(k) **Psychology:** Deals with the study of human mind, its behaviour and mental qualities.

(l) **DNA finger printing:** Technique to help identify a person on the basis of genes.

## ANIMALS/PLANTS

- The organisms that closely resemble one another are placed in one group, the groups which have similarities are combined together into larger groups, and these into still larger ones. The most inclusive category is kingdom. Other major categories, in descending order are: phylum, class, order, family, genus, and species. Man belongs to Animal kingdom, chordata division or phylum, Mammalia class, Primates order, Hominidae family, Homo genus and Sapiens species.

## CELL THEORY

- Cell is the basic unit of structure of all living organisms. According to the cell theory, all organism are composed of cells and cell products and growth and development results from the division and differentiation of cells.
- Cells membrane surrounds all living cells.
- Nucleus is the most important cell organelle which controls and coordinates all cell activities and also concerned with the transmission of heredity characters.
- Mitochondria, ribosomes, lysosomes and dictyosomes are present in plant and animal cells.
- Only plant cells have cell wall, chloroplast and vacuole.
- Viruses constitute a difficulty since in many ways they are intermediate between living and dead matter.
- The cell is said to be made up of a substance called Protoplasm which has two main constituents cytoplasm and nucleus, and is bounded by a cell membrane on outside.
- Cells take up the raw materials for metabolism through the cell membrane from extracellular fluid surrounding them.
- Cytoplasm inside is responsible for maintaining the internal distribution of organelles and also for free cell movements.
- Mitochondria inside provides energy for reactions inside the cell. Ribosomes are responsible for the synthesis of proteins.
- The Endoplasmic Reticulum helps in addition of other sugar units to proteins and their transportation to other parts of the cell.

## FOOD

- It is a nutritive substance taken by an organism for growth, work, repair and maintaining life processes. It provides energy to do work and maintain body heat, provides materials for the growth of the body, makes necessary materials for reproduction and provides materials for the repair of damaged cells and tissues of our body.

- **Carbohydrates:** For a normal person, 400 to 500 gms of carbohydrates are required daily but for sportspersons, growing children and nursing mothers, it is on higher side.
- **Proteins:** They are complex organic compounds made up of carbon, hydrogen, oxygen and nitrogen. The building blocks of Protein are Amino acids and there are large number of amino acids.
- Proteins are essential for the growth of children and teenagers, and for maintenance and making good the wear and tear of the body tissues in adults.
- An adult needs about 1 gm of protein per kg of body weight.
- **Fats:** They are esters of long chain fatty acids and an alcohol called glycerol. Fats also contain atoms of carbon, hydrogen and oxygen.
- The main function of fats in the body is to provide a steady source of energy and for this purpose, they are deposited within the body.
- One gm of fat gives 37 kilojoules of energy which is more than double of that given by carbohydrates.
- Fats, the richest source of energy to our body, can be stored in the body for subsequent use. Fats, soluble in organic solvents and insoluble in water, also supply fat-soluble vitamins to our body.
- **Minerals:** Some of the important minerals needed by our body are — iron, iodine, calcium, phosphorus, sodium, potassium, zinc, copper, magnesium, chloride, fluoride and sulphur.
- We get most of the minerals in combined form from plant sources. Deficiency of these minerals causes many diseases.
- **Energy Requirements:** The energy requirement of a body varies according to age, sex, lifestyle, occupation, climate and special situations like pregnancy and lactation.

| Age | Energy requirements |
|---|---|
| 5 years | 6000 kJ per day |
| 11 years | 9000 kJ per day |
| 18 years | 11000 kJ per day |
| Adult (normal work) | 9600 kJ per day |
| Adult (heavy work) | 12000 kJ per day |
| Adult (very heavy work) | 16000 kJ per day |

- **Vitamins:** They act as catalysts in certain chemical reactions of metabolism in our body.
- They don't provide energy to our body nor form body tissues.
- More than 15 types of vitamins are known and only 2 vitamins — D and K can be formed in our body.

| Vitamin | Necessity | Source |
|---|---|---|
| Vitamin A | For maintaining healthy eyesight, normal skin and hair | Cod liver oil, fish, eggs, milk, carrot, leafy vegetables. |
| Vitamin $B_1$ | For growth, carbohydrate metabolism, functioning of heart, nerves and muscles. | Milk, soya-food, meat, whole cereals, green vegetables. |
| Vitamin C | For keeping teeth, gums and joints healthy, for increasing resistance of body to infection | Citrus fruits, guava, tomatoes. |
| Vitamin D | For normal growth of bones and teeth | Milk, eggs, butter, cod liver oil, sun light. |
| Vitamin E | For normal reproduction, functioning of muscles and protection of liver | Green leafy vegetables, milk, butter, tomato. |
| Vitamin K | For normal clotting of blood and normal functioning of liver | Green leafy vegetables, soyabean, tomato. |

- **Roughage:** Though it does not provide any energy to the body, yet keeps the digestive system in order, by helping in retaining water in the body and preserving constitution.
- The main source of roughage are salads, cabbage, corn cob, porridge, vegetables and fruits with stems.

## DISEASES

### COMMUNICABLE DISEASES

- They are the diseases which can be transmitted from reservoirs of infection or infected person to the healthy but susceptible persons.
- The disease causing agent or the pathogen can be transmitted directly or indirectly.

### DEFICIENCY DISEASES

- These occur due to deficiency of some nutrients in the diet or some hormone due to hypo activity or damage to endocrine glands.

| Diet Deficiency | Disease |
|---|---|
| Protein | Kwashiorkor |
| Protein-energy malnutrition | Marasmus |
| Vitamin A | Night-blindness, Xerophthalmia |
| Vitamin $B_1$ | Beri-Beri |
| Vitamin $B_2$ | Cheilosis |
| Vitamin $B_5$ | Pellagra |
| Vitamin C | Scurvy |

| | |
|---|---|
| Vitamin D | Rickets (in children), (in adult) Osteomalacia |
| Vitamin K | Hypothrombinemia |
| Iron | Anaemia |
| Iodine | Goitre |
| Fluoride | Dental caries |
| Calcium and phosphorus | Affects formation of bones and teeth |

| *Hormone Deficiency* | *Disease* |
|---|---|
| Insulin | Diabetes |
| Thyroxine | Cretinism (child), Goitre |
| STH | Dwarfism, Gigantism |

## ALLERGIC DISEASE

- In these diseases, body becomes hypersensitive to some foreign agents, allergens, which cause inflammation when come in contact with the body or enter inside the body.
- Foreign agents can be dust, pollens, certain-foods, serum, certain drugs or fabrics.
- The unfavourable response of the body to allergens is called allergic reaction. Asthma and hay fever are allergic diseases.

## BACTERIAL DISEASES

- Bacteria are minute organisms which are known to cause a number of diseases:

| Disease | Incubation period | Spread through |
|---|---|---|
| Tuberculosis | 2-10 weeks | Air-borne,droplet infection |
| Diptheria | 2-6 days | Air-borne droplet infection |
| Cholera | 6 hours to 2-3 days | Contaminated food and water. House flies are the vectors |
| Leprosy | Upto 5 years | Prolonged and intimate contact |
| Whopping cough | 7-14 days | Droplet infection |
| Tetanus | 3-21 days | Entry of cysts through any wound made by sharp object, dog bite or fall on the road |
| Typhoid | 1-3 weeks | Directed and Contact |
| Plague | 2-6 days | Rats and bed-bugs transmit the germs |
| Pneumonia | 1-3 days | Air-borne |

## VIRAL DISEASES

| Disease | Incubation period | Spread through |
|---|---|---|
| Chicken-pox | 12-20 days | Direct contact with infected persons or infected objects |
| Smallpox | 12 days | Droplet infection |
| Poliomyalitis | 7-14 days | Direct and oral |
| Measles | 10 days | Droplet infection |
| Mumps | 12-26 days | Droplet infection |
| Rabies | 1-3 months | Bite of rabied animal like dogs, monkeys, cats |
| Influenza | 24-28 hours | Air-borne |

## DISEASES CAUSED BY PROTOZOA

- Amoebiasis (Amoebic dysentery), Malaria, Kala-azar, Trypanosomiasis and Giardiasis are main diseases caused by Protozoans.
- Malaria is a parasitic infection.

# SYSTEM OF HUMAN BODY

## DIGESTIVE SYSTEM

- The digestive system consists of alimentary canal and digestive glands. Alimentary canal is about 8-10 meters long tube of varying diameter. Food is taken in through mouth.
- The tongue helps in ingestion, chewing, tasting and swallowing of food and mixing of food and saliva.
- Salivary glands secret saliva which helps in digestion of starch. Gastric glands present in the mucosa of the stomach, provide acidic medium for the food digestion.
- Liver, the largest sized, reddish brown gland of body, secrets bile. Liver is present in the right upper part of the abdomen. The bile secreted by the liver is stored in gall bladder. It helps in the emulsification and digestion of fats.
- Pancreas is the second largest gland in human body and secretes pancreatic juices. Intestine also secret juices.

## RESPIRATORY SYSTEM

- Oxygen is needed for the oxidation and expelling of carbon dioxide is necessary to avoid its-accumulation. This process of exchange of gases between the environment and the body, is called respiration.
- In some unicellular organisms like aerobic bacteria, amoeba, hydra, etc. there is direct exchange of gases between the carbon dioxide of the body and oxygen of water.
- There is no blood for transport of gases. However, in larger and complex form of animals, specialised respiratory organs are developed.
- Amphibians respire through skin, fishes through gills and mammals, birds and reptiles through lungs.
- A normal adult inspires or expires about 500 ml of gas with each breath and about 72 breathes per minutes.

## CIRCULATORY SYSTEM

- Main components of the circulatory system are heart, blood vessels and blood.
- Heart is a thick, muscular, contractile and automatic pumping organ. In birds and mammals, heart is divided into four chambers.

- Arteries are thick walled blood vessels which always carry the blood away from the heart to various body parts.
- Veins are thin walled blood vessels which always carry the blood from various parts generally to the heart.
- In an adult healthy person, the normal rate of heart beat at rest is about 70-72 times per minute.

## BLOOD

- It is red, opaque, somewhat sticky and viscous fluid in the body of animals.
- It is slightly alkaline (pH = 7.4), heavier than water (sp gr = 1.05) and five times more viscous than distilled water.
- Blood forms 6 to 10% of the body weight.
- An adult, on average, has about 6.8 litres of blood.
- Blood contains plasma and blood corpuscles with the former occupying 55-60% of the volume.
- Plasma transports food components, metabolic wastes and hormones; keeps constant level of pH of blood, maintains body temperature and helps in blood clotting.
- Erythrocytes or red blood corpuscles (RBCs), leukocytes or white blood corpuscles (WBCs) and blood platelets are other parts of the blood.
- Due to the presence of iron containing pigment haemoglobin, RBCs are red in colour. The RBCs are crucial for ex-change of oxygen and carbon dioxide. WBCs are nucleated and non-pigmented cells. They are larger in size than RBCs but far less in number (1 : 600).
- WBCs play an important role in immune system of the body. Blood platelets cause the coagulation of blood and clot formation to prevent excessive bleeding.
- Human blood is divided into four main Groups—A, B, AB and O.
- The plasma of Group A blood contains an anti-B factor and vice-versa, so that people of Groups A and B cannot accept each other's blood.
- Group AB contains neither anti-A nor anti-B factor and people with this group can receive transfusions from both but can give to neither.
- Group O contains both anti-A and anti-B and can receive blood only from Group O but can donate blood to all Groups. Group O is called universal donor because they can donate to all the Groups.
- Group AB is called universal acceptor because they can accept blood from all Groups.

## SKELETON SYSTEM

- The frame or the hard structure of the human body is composed from the bones and the organs of making such frame are called skeleton system.

### Bones

- Bone is the hardest tissue of the body and form the largest section of the body weight.
- Bones contain organic as well as inorganic matters. With advancing age, the inorganic matter's share increases, causing the bones to become more brittle.
- Long bones such as humerus and femur are hollow while small bones are solid.

## EXCRETORY SYSTEM

- In men, excretory system is formed of one pair of kidneys, one pair of ureters, a urinary bladder and a urethra. Kidney is about 10 cm long, bean shaped, dark-red and slightly flattened structure.
- Sweet glands, oil glands, lungs and liver also act as additional excretory organ.
- In case of kidney failure, a man can treated by hemodialysis or transplantation of a kidney from a donor's body.

## NERVOUS SYSTEM

- The system which controls and coordinates the body functions, retains memory and receives and sends signals, is called the nervous system.
- The nervous system comprises brain, spinal cord, nerves and nerve fibres.
- Human brain weighs about 1200 to 1400 gm. Main parts of the brain are cerebrum, cerebellum and medulla oblongata.
- Cerebrum controls voluntary function and is site of intelligence, will power, emotions, etc.
- Cerebellum controls involuntary functions like heart beat, respiration, etc.
- Spinal cord is about 45 cm long and about 35 gm in weight. It conducts impulses to and from the brain and controls reflex actions of the body.
- Various cranial (arising from ending into brain) and spinal nerves (arising from spinal cord) control smell, vision, movements of body parts, taste and hearing.

## REPRODUCTION SYSTEM

- In this type of reproduction, there is formation and fusion of sex cells, called gametes.
- Organism develops from the zygote through embryo formation.
- It generally involves two parents — male and female.
- The offsprings are different from the parent as variations appear due to new combinations of genes. So, it plays an important role in evolution.
- All higher plants and animals reproduce sexually.

## CHROMOSOMES

- Plants and animals have fixed number of chromosomes per cell.
- Genes are located on chromosomes and are responsible for transfer of characteristics from one cell to the next either in the same organism or from parents to offspring.

- Man has 23 pairs of chromosomes, of which one pair is sex chromosomes.
- Males child inherits X chromosomes from the female parent and Y from the male parent.
- Female child receives a X chromosome each from either of its parents.
- Mendel was the first scientist to explain transmission of units from reproductive cells of the parents to the off-springs.

### CLONING

- It is the process of producing genetically identical copies of a biological material, starting from a single cell. The original genes are transplanted and thus one can produce organisms of known and desirable characteristics.

### GENETIC ENGINEERING

- It is the method of artificial synthesis of new genes and their subsequent transplantation or methods of correcting the defective genes.
- It has helped in producing plants and animals with specific characters.
- So, crippling hereditary diseases can also be cured like hemophilia etc.

### DNA FINGERPRINTING

- It consists of examining repetitive DNA in the genome for variations in the length of restriction fragments.
- Every individual has his own pattern, so that fingerprinting can match blood to a particular person, and patterns are inherited from parent to child, allowing the method to identify relationships between individuals.

### IN-VITRO FERTILIZATION

- When a sperm and an egg are made to fertilize outside a living body (usually a test tube), it is called in-vitro fertilization.
- This process has been used to impregnate several females who could not do so through natural means.

### Diseases and the Parts of Body they Affect

| | |
|---|---|
| *AIDS*—Immune system of body | *Gout*—Joints of bone |
| *Arthritis*—Inflammation of joints | *Jaundice*—Liver |
| *Asthma*—Lungs | *Meningitis*—Brain or spinal cord |
| *Cataract*—Eyes | *Pleurisy*—Pleura (inflammation of) |
| *Conjunctivitis*—Eyes | *Polio*—motor neurons |
| *Diabetes*—Pancreas | *Pneumonia*—Lungs |
| *Diphtheria*—Throat | *Pyorrhoea*—Sockets of teeth |
| *Glaucoma*—Eyes | *Tuberculosis*—Lungs |
| *Eczema*—Skin | *Typhoid*—Intestine |
| *Goitre*—Front of the neck (due to enlargement of thyroid gland) | *Malaria*—Spleen |
| | *Leukaemia*—Blood |
| | Rickets—Bones |

## SPACE RESEARCH

### First in Space

| | |
|---|---|
| ✶ First creator of rules regarding space research | Isaac Newton |
| ✶ First artificial satellite launched in space | Sputnik-1 (1957) |
| ✶ First living being sent in space | Louika (a dog) |
| ✶ Firstever manned spacecraft | Vostok-I |
| ✶ First man in space | Yuri Gagarin U.S.S.R. (1961) |
| ✶ First woman in space | Valentina Tereshkova U.S.S.R. (June 1963) |
| ✶ First man who moved in space out of the spacecraft | Alexi Livonov U.S.S.R. (June 1965) |
| ✶ First person to land on moon | Neil Armstrong, America (21st July, 1969) |
| ✶ First fourwheeled carriage without human being on moon | Leunokhev-I U.S.S.R. (1970) |
| ✶ First space lab in orbit | Skylab (America, 1973) |
| ✶ First space shuttle | Columbia (America, 1981) |
| ✶ First Indian (man) in space | Squadron leader—Rakesh Sharma (13th April, 1984) |
| ✶ First Indian (Woman) in space | Kalpana Chawla (19th Nov., 1997) |
| ✶ First American woman in space | Sailyride (1983) |
| ✶ First spacecraft on Mars | Pathfinder (6 July, 1997) |
| ✶ First woman who lead spacecraft | Allin Collis (America) |
| ✶ First spacecraft without man | Shenzoo, China (20th Nov. 1999) |

## Indian Space Programme : At a Glance

| Satellite | Date | Type | Launch Vehicle | Result |
|---|---|---|---|---|
| Aryabhatta | 19-04-75 | Scientific | Cosmos | successful |
| Bhaskara I | 07-06-79 | Geosurvey | Cosmos | successful |
| Rohini | 10-08-79 | Geosurvey | S.L.V.3 | unsuccessful |
| Rohini D-1 | 18-07-80 | Geosurvey | S.L.V.3 | successful |
| Rohini | 31-05-81 | Scientific | S.L.V.3 | successful |
| Apple | 19-06-81 | Communication | Ariane | successful |
| Bhaskara II | 20-11-81 | Geosurvey | Cosonos | successful |
| INSAT-1A | 10-04-82 | Multipurpose | Delta | unsuccessful |
| Rohini | 17-04-83 | Scientific | S.L.V.3 | successful |
| INSAT-1B | 30-08-83 | Multipurpose | Space Shuttle | successful |
| SROSS I | 24-03-87 | Technical | ASLV-D1 | unsuccessful |
| IRS-1A | 17-03-88 | Remote sensing | Vostok | successful |
| SROSS II | 17-07-88 | Technical | ASLV-D2 | unsuccessful |
| INSAT-1C | 21-07-88 | Multipurpose | Ariane-4 | unsuccessful |
| INSAT-1D | 12-06-90 | Multipurpose | Delta | successful |
| IRS-1B | 29-08-91 | Remote sensing | Vostok | successful |
| INSAT-2A | 10-07-92 | Multipurpose | Ariane | successful |
| IRS-ID | 29-09-97 | Remote sensing | PSLV | successful |
| INSAT-3B | 22-03-2000 | Multipurpose | Ariane | successful |
| G-SAT-1 | 18-04-2001 | Multipurpose | GSLV-D | successful |
| MAT SAT | 12-09-2002 | Meteorology | PSLVC-4 | successful |
| INSAT-3E | 28-09-2003 | Communication | Ariane-5 | successful |
| Cartosat-1 & hamsat | 05-05-2005 | Maping and Communication | PSLV-C6 | successful |
| CARTOSAT-2 | 10-01-2007 | Communication | PSLV-C7 | successful |
| Cartosat-2A | 28-04-2008 | Communication | PSLV-C9 | successful |
| Chandrayaan-I | 22-10-2008 | Maping and Scientific | PSLV-C11 | successful |
| Oceansat-2 | 24-09-2009 | Remote Sensing | PSLV-C14 | successful |
| CARTOSAT-2B | 12-07-2010 | Communication | PSLV-C15 | successful |
| RESOURCESAT-2 | 20-04-2011 | Remote Sensing | PSLV-C16 | successful |
| GSAT-12 | 15-07-2011 | Communication | PSLV-C17 | successful |
| Megha-Tropiques | 12-10-2011 | Maping and Scientific | PSLV-C18 | successful |
| RISAT-1 | 26-04-2012 | Remote Sensing | PSLV-C19 | successful |
| Spot-6 | 09-09-2012 | Remote Sensing | PSLV-C21 | successful |
| Saral | 25-02-2013 | Scientific | PSLV-C20 | successful |
| GSAT-7 | 30-08-2013 | Defence | Ariane-5 | successful |
| MOM | 5-11-2013 | Mapping | PSLV-C25 | successful |
| GSAT-14 | 05-01-2014 | Communication | GSLV-D5 | successful |
| IRNSS-1B | 04-04-2014 | Mapping and Scientific | PSLV-C24 | successful |
| Spot-7 | 30-06-2014 | Remote Sensing | PSLV-C23 | successful |
| GSAT-16 | 07-12-2014 | Communication | Ariane-5 | successful |
| IRNSS-1D | 28-03-2015 | Mapping and Scientific | PSLV-C27 | successful |
| GSAT-6 | 27-08-2015 | Communication | GSLV-D6 | successful |
| Astrosat | 28-09-2015 | Mapping and Scientific | PSLV-C30 | successful |
| GSAT-15 | 11-11-2015 | Communication | Ariane-5 | successful |
| TELEOS-1 | 16-12-2015 | Mapping and Scientific | PSLV-C29 | successful |
| IRNSS-1E | 20-01-2016 | Mapping and Scientific | PSLV-C31 | successful |
| IRNSS-1F | 10-03-2016 | Mapping and Scientific | PSLV-C32 | successful |
| IRNSS-1G | 28-04-2016 | Mapping and Scientific | PSLV-C33 | successful |
| Cartosat-2 & others | 22-06-2016 | Mapping and Scientific | PSLV-C34 | successful |

| Satellite | Date | Type | Launch Vehicle | Result |
|---|---|---|---|---|
| insat-3DR | 08-09-2016 | Meteorology | GSLV-F05 | successful |
| Scatsat-1 & others | 26-09-2016 | Multipurpose | PSLV-C35 | successful |
| RESOURCESAT-2A | 07-12-2016 | Remote Sensing | PSLV-C36 | successful |
| CARTOSAT-2 & 103 others | 15-02-2017 | Multipurpose | PSLV-C37 | successful |
| CARTOSAT-2E | 23-06-2017 | Earth observation Satellite | PSLV-C38 | successful |
| GSAT-17 | 29-06-2017 | Earth observation Satellite | Ariane-5 ECA | successful |
| Cartosat-2F & others | 12-01-2018 | Multipurpose | PSLV-C40 | successful |
| GSAT-6A | 29-03-2018 | Communication | GSLV-F08 | successful |
| GSAT-7A | 19-12-2018 | Military Satellite | GSLV-MK-II-F11 | successful |
| Chandrayaan-2 | 22-07-2019 | Lunar Exploration | GSLV MK-III M01 | — |
| Cartosat-3 | 27-11-2019 | Earth Imagine Satellite | PSLV-C47 | successful |
| GSAT-30 | 17-01-2020 | Communication | Ariane-5 | successful |
| EOS-01 | 07-11-2020 | Earth Observation | PSLV-C49 | successful |
| Amezonia & 19 others | 28-02-2021 | Communication | PSLV-C51 | successful |
| EOS-04 | 14-02-2022 | Earth Observation | PSLV-C52 | successful |
| Oceansat-3 & 8 others | 26-11-2022 | Earth Observation | PSLV-C54 | successful |
| EOS-07 | 10-02-2023 | Earth Observation | SSLV-02 | successful |
| Chandrayaan-3 | 14-07-2023 | Lunar Exploration | LVM-3 | successful |
| Aditya-L1 | 02-09-2023 | Solar Mission | PSLV-C57 | successful |
| XPoSat | 01-01-2024 | Earth Observation | PSLV-C58 | successful |

# COMPUTER

- The computer is the system of that electronic device through which various informations are processed on the basis of a definite set of instructions called program and mathematical (numerical) and non-mathematical both types of informations are processed.
- The first mechanical computer was composed or fabricated by Blaise Pascal in 1642 and it is called Pascalene.
- But in 1833, Charles Babbage first time conceived an automatic calculator or computer.
- Charles Babbage is called the father of modern computer.
- Herman made an electronic tabulating machine based on punch cards which operates automatically.
- In 1937, first mechanical computer Mark-I was fabricated by Howard Akeen.
- The most outstanding contribution in the development of modern computer goes to John Wan Newmaan who brought the 2nd revolution in the area of computer in 1951.
- He discovered EDVAC (Electronic Discrete Variable Automatic Computer) and utilised the stored program and the binary number system in the computer.

## FUNCTIONS OF COMPUTER

- 1. Collection and composition (input) of datas;
  2. Storage of datas.
  3. Processing of datas.
  4. Retrieval or output of the proccessed informations and datas.

## UNITS OF COMPUTER

1. Input unit.
2. Central processing unit–CPU.
3. External Memory unit.
4. Output unit.

- The CPU of the computer is called brain of the computer and sometimes CPU is also called Micro Processor of the computer.
- The data is entered through the input unit in the computer and through the central processing unit with the help of External Memory Unit datas are arranged and processed.
- Ultimately by the output unit these datas or informations are issued or released.

## PARTS OF COMPUTER

- **Monitor :** The monitor of the computer is like a television in which the picture appears in the form of doted points on the screen and these are called pixels.
- **Hard Disc and Floppy Disc :** The Hard Disc is the permanent disc in the computers while the Floppy Disc is the disc utilised when datas or informations are to be transferred from one computer to another.
- **Mouse :** The mouse of the computer is like the remote control of TV through which computer is directly regulated or controlled without utilising the key-board.
- **Printer :** The printer is a device which prints any documents or processed informations of the computer.

## SOME HIGH LEVEL LANGUAGES

1. **FORTRAN :** This language was developed for solving the mathematical formulae very quickly and conveniently.
2. **COBOL :** This language was developed for the commerical purposes. For the processing of this

language a group of sentences is selected called paragraph and all paragraphs composed are called a section, while all sections composed are called a division.

3. **BASIC :** In basic a definite part of the prescribed instruction is only inserted in the computer.
4. **ALGOL :** This was basically fabricated and designed for the complex algebraic calculations.
5. **PASCAL :** It is an amplified and modified form of ALGOL.
6. **COMAL :** This computer language is used for the students of secondary level.
7. **LOGO :** This language is used for children and kids for drawing Graphic line diagrams.
8. **PROLOG :** This language is developed in 1973 in France and is used for Artificial Intelligence which is capable and equivalent to the logical program.
9. **FORTH :** This language was invented by Charles Mure which is frequently used in all types of the works in the computer.

## COMPUTER VIRUS

- The computer virus is an electronic code which is used to abolish or erradicate the inclusive informations or programs of the computer.
- Some important computer viruses are Micheleanjalo, Dork Avangor, kilo, filip, Macmug, Scores, Casecade, Jeruslem, Date crime, Coloumbs crime, Internet virus, Pachcom, Pach EXE, COM-EXE, Marizuana, C-brain, bloody, Chenge Mungu and Desi etc.

## COMPUTER NETWORKING

- There are two types of networkings which are usually occur—Local Area Networking (LAN) and Wide Area Networking (WAN).

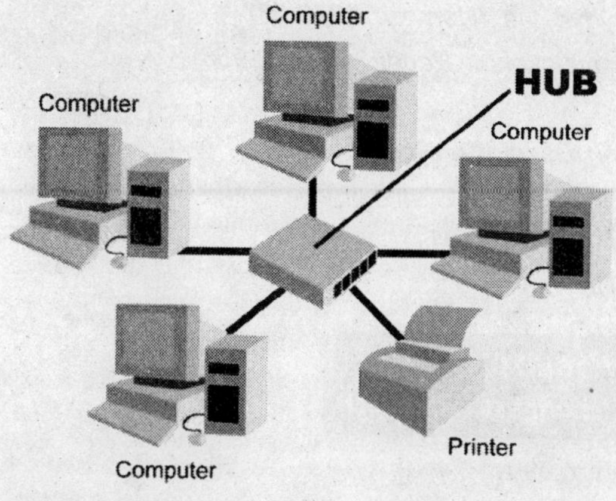


- By LAN all the computers of the same buildings are connected like the computers of university premises, computers of offices etc.
- By WAN all the comptuers of a large area are connected like the computers of all the offices of a city or town etc.
- In India a very large computer network namely INDONET has been installing through which all the main towns and cities has to be interlinked.

## COMPUTER TERMINOLOGY

- **Bit :** The bit is a unit of measurement of the electronic data. One bit is either 0 or 1 but not both. On composing 8 bits, 1 byte is formed.
- **Bug :** The Bug is the error in the computer program or system and its eradication is called Debug.
- **Byte :** Total eight bits compose a byte. Thus 8 bits = 1 byte.
- **CD-ROM :** A CD like of music CD in which data can be stored substantially called CD-ROM. In a CD with comparison to floppy extremely more datas can be stored but one problem in it is that one time recorded data can not be deleted or modified.
- **Chip :** It is a thin slice on which by a special mechanism a circuit is designed which is normally made from Silicon.
- **Memory System :** The place where computer data and program are temporarily kept is called Memory system. Usually memory is implied from RAM.
- **Modem :** The device which converts digital signals into analogue signals and vice-versa is called Modem.
- **RAM :** It is Random Access Memory (a place) where datas to be processed are kept temporarily and it is unstable memory.
- **ROM :** It is Read Only Memory and it is stable or Non-valatile memory which doesn't ended after power off.
- **Scanner :** It is a device through which graphic image is transformed to digital image and the scanners are of usually two types one desktop and another hand operating.

## PROGRAMING

- Computers perform phenomenal feats of calculation, but they do not do so in a complicated way.
- They actually carry out very simple operations, such as addition and subtraction.
- They achieve their fantastic computing power by carrying out these operations at incredible speed.
- The programme, or set of instructions for operating the computer, is therefore written as a sequence of very simple steps.

  Several computer languages have been developed for different applications, including BASIC, COBOL, FORTRAN and PASCAL. Writing programmes is very skilled and time-consuming work.
- But for most typical computer applications ready-written programmes are available, called "packages".

❒ ❒ ❒

# GENERAL KNOWLEDGE

## FIRST IN THE WORLD

| | |
|---|---|
| ✶ First Chinese visitor to India | *Fahien* |
| ✶ First foreign invader of India | *Alexander, the Great (Greek)* |
| ✶ First person to climb Mt. Everest | *Tenzing Norgay (India) and Edmund Hillary (New Zealand) (1953)* |
| ✶ First atom bomb dropped at | *Hiroshima (Japan)* |
| ✶ First man in the space | *Yuri Gagarin (former USSR)* |
| ✶ First woman in the space | *Valentina Tereshkova (former USSR)* |
| ✶ First person to walk in the space | *Alexei Leonov (former USSR)* |
| ✶ First person to land on the moon | *Neil Armstrong (USA)* |
| ✶ First and the only woman to have climbed Mt. Everest twice | *Santosh Yadav (Indian; May 12, 1992; May 10, 1993)* |
| ✶ First person on Mt. Everest without oxygen | *Phu Dorjee (Indian; May 9, 1984)* |
| ✶ First person to climb Mt. Everest twice | *Nawang Gombu* |
| ✶ First President of the USA | *George Washington* |
| ✶ First woman Prime Minister | *Sirimavo Bandaranaike (Sri Lanka)* |
| ✶ First person to swim across English Channel | *Mathew Webb* |
| ✶ First woman to swim across English Channel | *Gertrude Caroline Ederle* |
| ✶ First woman to climb Mt. Everest | *Junko Tabei (Japan)* |
| ✶ First woman to climb Mt. Everest alone and without oxygen supplies | *Alison Hargreaves (Britain: May 13, 1995)* |
| ✶ First Aeroplane to fly around the world without refuelling | *Voyager (Dec. 1986)* |
| ✶ First test-tube Baby | *Louise Brown (UK; 1978)* |
| ✶ First all-talking Film | *Jaz Singer (1927)* |
| ✶ First Secretary-General of the UN | *Trygve Lie (Norway: 1946-53)* |
| ✶ First woman President of the UN General Assembly | *Vijayalakshmi Pandit (India: 1953)* |
| ✶ First woman to reach North Pole | *Ann Bancroft (1986)* |
| ✶ First person to reach North Pole | *Robert Peary* |
| ✶ First person to reach South Pole | *Amundsen (1911)* |
| ✶ First woman to command Spacecraft in Space | *Ellin Collins* |

## SUPERLATIVES (WORLD)
### *(The Largest, Biggest, Smallest, Longest, Highest)*

| | | |
|---|---|---|
| **Animal,** | *Tallest* | Giraffe (Average height 6.09 m) |
| | *Largest and Heaviest* | Blue Whale (190 tonnes) |
| | *Longest recorded* | Boot lace Worm (55 m) |
| | *Fastest* | Cheetah (Approximately 100 km/hr) |

| | | |
|---|---|---|
| **Bay,** | *With max. shore line* | Hudson Bay (Canada: 12268 km) |
| | *With maximum area* | Bay of Bengal (India: 217 million hc) |
| **Building,** | *Tallest* | Burj Khalifa (Dubai, 818 meter) |
| **Canal,** | *Big ship (longest)* | Suez Canal (160 km) |
| | *Busiest* | Kiel Canal (North Sea) |
| **City,** | *Largest in Area* | Jiuquan Gansu, China (Area 1,67,996 Sq km) |
| **Continent,** | *biggest* | Asia |
| | *Smallest* | Australia Mainland |
| **Country,** | *Largest in Population* | China (over 137 crore) |
| | *Largest in Area* | Russia (17,075,400 sq. km) |
| | *With largest electorate* | India (over 90 crores) |
| | *Smallest independent* | State of Vatican City (0.44 $km^2$) |
| **Delta,** | *Largest* | Sundarban's Ganga-Brahmaputra delta (1,05,000 sq. km) |
| **Desert,** | *Largest* | Sahara (N. Africa; maximum length 5,150 km EW; maximum width 3,200 km NS) |
| **Dome,** | *Largest* | Singapore National Stadium (310 m) |
| **Epic,** | *Longest* | Mahabharata |
| **Film,** | *Most Oscars* | Ben Hur (11 Oscars–1959); Titanic (11 Oscars–1998); The Lord of Rings : The Return of the King (11 Oscars—2003). |
| **Fruit,** | *Most nutritive* | Avocado (Vitamins A, C, E and Proteins; Central and South America) |
| | *Least nutritive* | Cucumber |
| **Gulf,** | *Largest* | Gulf of Mexico (1,544,000 sq. km) |
| **Island,** | *Biggest* | Greenland (now known as Kalaatdlit Nunaat–2,175,000 sq km) |
| **Lake,** | *Largest* | Caspian Sea (Azerbaijan, Russia, Iran border: 37.18 lakh $km^2$) |
| | *Deepest* | Baikal (Siberia) |
| | *Largest (fresh water)* | Superior Lake (USA–Canada border: 82,350 $km^2$) |
| **Library,** | *Biggest* | United States Library of Congress (Washington D.C. founded in 1800, contains 101 million items) |
| | *Biggest non-statutory* | New York Public Library |
| **Mountain,** | *Highest peak* | Mt. Everest (8848 m; Nepal) |
| | *Highest range* | Himalayas, Asia (upto 4200 m) |
| | *Greatest mountain range* | Himalaya-Karakoram (96 out of 109 peaks over 7315 m are here) |
| **Ocean,** | *Largest and Deepest* | The Pacific (Area: 166,240,000 $km^2$; Depth: 10,924 m) |
| **Peninsula,** | *Largest* | Arabia (3.25 million sq. km) |
| **Planet,** | *Biggest* | Jupiter (equatorial diameter 142984 km) |
| | *Brightest, hottest and nearest to Earth* | Venus |
| | *Nearest to Sun* | Mercury |
| **Plateau,** | *Highest* | Tibetan Plateau (Central Asia: 4900 m) |
| **Religion,** | *Oldest* | Hinduism |
| **Religion,** | *Largest* | Christianity |
| **Rivers,** | *Longest* | (i) Nile (6650 km) (ii) Amazon (6437 km) |
| **Sea,** | *Largest* | South China Sea (2,974,600 sq. km) |
| | *Largest (inland)* | Mediterranean |
| **Star,** | *Brightest* | Sirius A (also called Dog Star) |
| **Statue,** | *Tallest* | Statue of Unity (India) 182 m. |

| | | |
|---|---|---|
| **Swimming course,** | *Longest recognised* | English Channel |
| **Temple,** | *Largest* | Angkor Vat (Cambodia: 402 acres) |
| **Waterfall,** | *Highest* | Salto-Angel (in Venezuela on a branch of river Carrao, depth 807 m.) |

## IMPORTANT CITIES, PLACES, BUILDINGS OF THE WORLD

- **Angkor Vat:** It is a large group of old Hindu temples in Cambodia; a remnant of the Khmer civilisation. The temples were constructed in the first half of the 12th century.
- **Big Ben:** A clock on the tower of the British Parliament building, installed in 1856.
- **Bethlehem:** A town in Jordan; birth place of Christ; a place of pilgrimage.
- **Cape Canaveral:** Situated in Florida (U.S.A.), it is America's spaceship launching centre. Formerly it was known as *Cape Kennedy.*
- **Eiffel Tower:** A tower in Paris (985 ft high); the principal landmark of the city; designed by a French Engineer for the Paris Exposition 1889.
- **Fleet Street:** A street in London, where offices of newspapers are situated.
- **Golden Gate Bridge (U.S.A.):** One of the world's longest suspension bridges, built in 1933-37 across the entrance (Golden Gate) of San Francisco Bay in California. It has a length of 9266 ft.
- **Harappa:** Situated near Montgomery (Pakistan). The famous ruins throw light on 5000-year-old Indus Valley Civilisation.
- **Hiroshima:** A city in Japan; it was the target of the first atom bomb ever dropped on a city (by U.S.A. on August 6, 1945); casualities numbered nearly 1,30,000 and ninety per cent of the city was levelled.
- **India Office Library (London):** A museum of Indian historical works, collected by the British. The library consists of about 3,00,000 books, a large number of manuscripts in Sanskrit, Urdu, Persian and Arabic.
- **Kaaba:** The inner shrine of the great Mosque at Mecca in Saudi Arabia. It is the most sacred place. Muslims face the Kaaba when praying.
- **Karakoram Highway:** It is a 800-km all weather road linking border of China's Sinkiang province with Pakistan.
- **Leaning Tower of Pisa:** A white marble monument (179 feet high) built in the 14th Century in Italy. It is inclined to one side.
- **Mohenjodaro:** Situated in the Larkana District of Sind (Pakistan); ancient ruins throw light on 5,000-year-old Indus Valley Civilisation.
- **Oval, Leeds and Lords (England):** Famous for cricket matches.
- **Panama Canal:** Canal connecting the Atlantic and Pacific Oceans. The canal is 50 miles long and has 12 locks. It was opened to traffic in August, 1914. The canal is administered by the U.S.A.
- **Pentagon (Washington, USA):** It is a five-sided building housing the US Defence Department offices.
- **Burj Khalifa:** It is a 162 storeyed structure built in Dubai having a height of 818 meter. It is now the highest structure of the world. Taipei 101 (508 meter) is now the second highest structure of the world.
- **Pyramids:** Gigantic stone buildings built by the ancient Egyptians in 2700 B.C.; among the seven wonders of the world. The great pyramid at Giza is the largest. These pyramids were tombs for the pharaohs and other important people.
- **Scotland Yard:** Headquarters of the Criminal Investigation Department in London. It is known all over world for its efficient working.
- **Sandhurst (England):** Famous military training institution.
- **Sphinx:** Mythical beast of ancient Egypt; usually represented in art as having a human head and the body of a lion. The most famous one is the great Sphinx, a colossal stone figure at Gizah built in the 26th Century BC.
- **Stonehenge:** Prehistoric monument near Salisbury, England built in between 1800 B.C. and 1500 B.C.
- **Suez Canal:** This canal is an important link between the Mediterranean Sea and the Red Sea. It is about 160 km long and was constructed in 1869 by a French Engineer. It has shortened the distance between Southampton (England) and Bombay (now Mumbai) by about 4,000 miles. The canal was nationalised by Col. Nasser on July 26, 1956. Port Said is the famous port at the entry from Mediterranean Sea.
- **Vatican:** Official residence of the Pope (in Rome). The smallest country. It enjoys a separate entity in the world. (Area 109 acres).
- **Wall Street (New York):** Famous stock exchange market.

## CAPITAL & CURRENCIES

| Country | Capital | Currency |
|---|---|---|
| ✶ Afghanistan | Kabul | Afghani |
| ✶ Albania | Tirana | Lek |
| ✶ Algeria | Algiers | Dinar |
| ✶ Angola | Luanda | New Kwanza |
| ✶ Argentina | Buenos Aires | Peso |
| ✶ Armenia | Yeravan | Dram |
| ✶ Australia | Canberra | Dollar |
| ✶ Austria | Vienna | Euro |
| ✶ Azerbaijan | Baku | Manat |
| ✶ Bahrain | Manama | Dinar |
| ✶ Bangladesh | Dhaka | Taka |
| ✶ Barbados | Bridgetown | Dollar |
| ✶ Belarus | Minsk | Ruble |
| ✶ Belgium | Brussels | Euro |
| ✶ Benin | Porto Novo | Franc |
| ✶ Bhutan | Thimphu | Ngultrum[1] |
| ✶ Bolivia | La paz | Dollar |
| ✶ Botswana | Gaborone | Pula |
| ✶ Brazil | Brasilia | Real |
| ✶ Bosnia Herzegovina | Sarajevo | Dinar |
| ✶ Bulgaria | Sofia | Lev |
| ✶ Cambodia | Phnom-Penh | Riel |
| ✶ Canada | Ottawa | Dollar |
| ✶ Chile | Santiago | Peso |
| ✶ China | Beijing | Yuan |
| ✶ Colombia | Bogota | Peso |
| ✶ Congo | Brazzaville | Franc |
| ✶ Croatia | Zagrcb | Kuna |
| ✶ Cuba | Havana | Peso |
| ✶ Cyprus | Nicosia | Euro |
| ✶ Czech Republic | Prague | Koruna |
| ✶ Denmark | Copenhagen | Krone |
| ✶ Ecuador | Quito | Sucre |
| ✶ Egypt | Cairo | Pound |
| ✶ Estonia | Tallinn | Euro |
| ✶ Ethiopia | Addis Ababa | Birr |
| ✶ Fiji | Suva | Dollar |
| ✶ Finland | Helsinki | Euro |
| ✶ France | Paris | Euro |
| ✶ Georgia | Tbilisi | Lari |
| ✶ Germany | Berlin | Euro |
| ✶ Ghana | Accra | Cedi |
| ✶ Greece | Athens | Euro |
| ✶ Guatemala | Guatemala City | Quetzal |
| ✶ Guyana | George Town | Dollar |
| ✶ Hungary | Budapest | Forint |

| Country | Capital | Currency |
|---|---|---|
| ✶ Iceland | Reykjavik | Krona |
| ✶ India | New Delhi | Rupee |
| ✶ Indonesia | Jakarta | Rupiah |
| ✶ Iran | Teheran | Rial |
| ✶ Iraq | Baghdad | Dinar |
| ✶ Ireland | Dublin | Euro |
| ✶ Israel | Jerusalem | Shekel |
| ✶ Italy | Rome | Euro |
| ✶ Jamaica | Kingston | Dollar |
| ✶ Japan | Tokyo | Yen |
| ✶ Jordan | Amman | Dinar |
| ✶ Kazakhstan | Akmola | Tenge |
| ✶ Kenya | Nairobi | Shilling |
| ✶ Korea (S) | Seoul | Won |
| ✶ Korea (N) | Pyongyang | Won |
| ✶ Kyrgyzstan | Bishkek | Som |
| ✶ Kuwait | Kuwait City | Dinar |
| ✶ Laos | Vientiane | Kip |
| ✶ Latvia | Riga | Euro |
| ✶ Lebanon | Beirut | Pound |
| ✶ Liberia | Monrovia | Dollar |
| ✶ Libya | Tripoli | Dinar |
| ✶ Lithuania | Vilnius | Litas |
| ✶ Luxembourg | Luxembourg | Euro |
| ✶ Macedonia | Skopje | Dinar |
| ✶ Malawi | Lilongwe | Kwacha |
| ✶ Malaysia | Kuala Lumpur | Ringgit |
| ✶ Maldives | Male | Rufiyaa |
| ✶ Mali | Bamako | Franc |
| ✶ Mauritius | Port Louis | Rupee |
| ✶ Mexico | Mexico City | Peso |
| ✶ Moldavia | Chisinau | Leu |
| ✶ Mongolia | Ulan Bator | Tugrik |
| ✶ Morocco | Rabat | Dirham |
| ✶ Mozambique | Maputo | Metical |
| ✶ Myanmar | Nay Pyi Taw | Kyat |
| ✶ Namibia | Winohoek | Dollar |
| ✶ Nepal | Kathmandu | Rupee |
| ✶ Netherlands | Amsterdam | Euro |
| ✶ New Zealand | Wellington | Dollar |
| ✶ Nigeria | Abuja | Naira |
| ✶ Norway | Oslo | Krone |
| ✶ Oman | Muscat | Rial |
| ✶ Pakistan | Islamabad | Rupee |
| ✶ Panama | Panama City | Balboa |
| ✶ Peru | Lima | New Sole |
| ✶ Philippines | Manila | Peso |
| ✶ Poland | Warsaw | Zloty |

| Country | Capital | Currency |
|---|---|---|
| ✶ Portugal | Lisbon | Euro |
| ✶ Qatar | Doha | Riyal |
| ✶ Romania | Bucharest | Leu |
| ✶ Russia | Moscow | Ruble |
| ✶ Saudi Arabia | Riyadh | Rial |
| ✶ Senegal | Dakar | Franc |
| ✶ Slovakia | Bratislava | Euro |
| ✶ Spain | Madrid | Euro |
| ✶ Sri Lanka | Colombo | Rupee |
| ✶ Sudan | Khartoum | Dinar |
| ✶ Suriname | Paramaribo | Guilder |
| ✶ Sweden | Stockholm | Krona |
| ✶ Switzerland | Berne | Swiss Francs |
| ✶ Syria | Damascus | Pound |
| ✶ South Africa | Capetown (Legislative) Pretoria *(Administrative)* | Rand |
| ✶ Tadzhikistan | Dushanbe | Ruble |
| ✶ Taiwan | Taipei | Dollar |
| ✶ Tanzania | Dodoma | Shilling |
| ✶ Thailand | Bangkok | Baht |
| ✶ Tunisia | Tunis | Dinar |
| ✶ Turkiye | Ankara | Lira |
| ✶ Turkmania | Ashikabad | Manat |
| ✶ Uganda | Kampala | Shilling |
| ✶ Ukraine | Kiev | Hyrvnia |
| ✶ United Arab Emirates | Abu Dhabi | Dirham |
| ✶ U.K. | London | Pound Sterling |
| ✶ U.S.A. | Washington | Dollar |
| ✶ Uruguay | Montevideo | Peso |
| ✶ Uzbekistan | Tashkent | Som |
| ✶ Venezuela | Caracas | Bolivar |
| ✶ Vietnam | Hanoi | Dong |
| ✶ Yemen | Sana'a | Rial |
| ✶ Zimbabwe | Harare | Dollar |
| ✶ Congo | Kinshasa | Franc |
| ✶ Zambia | Lusaka | Kwacha |

## GEOGRAPHICAL EXPLORATIONS/DISCOVERIES

| Place | Explorer/Discoverer | Nationality | Year |
|---|---|---|---|
| America | Christopher Columbus | Italy | 1492 |
| Hawaii Islands (Sandwich Islands) | Captain James Cook | England | 1778 |
| Newfoundland | John Cabot | England | 1497 |
| New Zealand | Abel Janszoon Tasman | Holland | 1642 |
| North Pole | Robert Peary | USA | 1909 |
| Sea Route to India (via Cape of Good Hope) | Vasco da Gama | Portugal | 1498 |
| South Pole | Roald Amundsen | Norway | 1911 |

## NATIONAL MONUMENTS OF SOME FAMOUS COUNTRIES

| Monument | Country | Monument | Country |
|---|---|---|---|
| Great Wall of China | China | Pyramid (Giza) | Egypt |
| Taj Mahal (Agra) | India | Kinder Disk | Denmark |
| Emperial Palace (Tokyo) | Japan | Leaning Tower of Pisa | Italy |
| Opera House (Sydney) | Australia | Statue of Liberty (New York) | USA |
| Eiffel Tower (Paris) | France | Kremlin (Moscow) | Russia |

## INTELLIGENCE AGENCIES OF SOME PROMINENT COUNTRIES

| Country | Intelligence Agency |
|---|---|
| ✶ India | *Research & Analysis Wing (RAW), Intelligence Bureau (I.B.), Central Bureau of Investigation (C.B.I.)* |
| ✶ Pakistan | *Inter Service Intelligence (I.S.I.)* |
| ✶ U.S.A. | *Central Intelligence Agency (CIA), Federal Bureau of Investigation (FBI)* |
| ✶ Britain | *Military Intelligence (M.I.)-5 and 6, Special Branch, Ultra, Joint Intelligence Organisation* |

| | |
|---|---|
| ✶ Israel | *Mosad* |
| ✶ Egypt | *Mukhabarat* |
| ✶ Japan | *Nicho* |
| ✶ Russia | *K.G.B. (Komitel Gosudarstvennoy Bezopasnosty) (Committee for State Security)* |
| ✶ Canada | *Security Intelligence Service (SIS)* |
| ✶ S. Africa | *Bureau of State Security (BSS)* |
| ✶ Iran | *Sabak* |
| ✶ Iraq | *Al-Mukhabarat* |
| ✶ Australia | *Australian Security and Intelligence Organisation (ASIO)* |
| ✶ France | *S.D.E.C.E.* |
| ✶ Spain | *C.E.S.I.D.* |

## MAJOR LANGUAGES OF THE WORLD AND THEIR SPEAKERS

Listing the languages spoken by approximately 1% of humankind (those spoken by more than 60,000,000 people), this table enumerates speakers of each tongue as a primary language.

| Language | Speakers (millions) |
|---|---|
| ✶ Chinese | 1,322.8 |
| ✶ Spanish | 471.4 |
| ✶ English | 369.9 |
| ✶ Arabic | 349.3 |
| ✶ Hindi | 342.2 |
| ✶ Bengali | 228.7 |
| ✶ Portuguese | 232.4 |
| ✶ Russian | 153.7 |
| ✶ Japanese | 126.3 |
| ✶ Lahnda | 99.6 |
| ✶ Marathi | 83.1 |
| ✶ Telugu | 82.6 |
| ✶ Turkish | 82.2 |
| ✶ Malay | 81.6 |
| ✶ Korean | 81.5 |

| Language | Speakers (millions) |
|---|---|
| ✶ French | 79.6 |
| ✶ Tamil | 77.5 |
| ✶ Vietnamese | 76.1 |
| ✶ German, Standard | 76.5 |
| ✶ Urdu | 69.0 |
| ✶ Javanese | 68.3 |
| ✶ Persian | 65.7 |
| ✶ Italian | 64.8 |
| ✶ Gujarati | 56.9 |
| ✶ Pushto | 53.1 |
| ✶ Bhojpuri | 52.3 |
| ✶ Hausa | 48.6 |
| ✶ Kannada | 43.6 |
| ✶ Yoruba | 41.0 |
| ✶ Polish | 40.0 |

***(Source:** The World Almanac-2022)*

## NAME OF PARLIAMENTS OF SOME COUNTRIES

| Country | Name of Parliament |
|---|---|
| Afghanistan | Shora |
| Argentina | National Congress |
| Australia | Federal Parliament |
| Austria | National Assembly |
| Bangladesh | Jatiya Sansad |
| India | Lok Sabha and Rajya Sabha |
| Bhutan | Tshogdu (National Assembly) |
| Britain | House of Commons and House of Lords |
| Canada | House of Commons and Senate |
| China | National People Congress |
| Denmark | Folketing |
| Iran | Majlis (Islamic Consultative Assembly) |
| Israel | Knesset |
| Japan | Diet |
| Myanmar | Pyithu Hluttaw (People's Assembly) |
| Nepal | Rashtriya Panchayat |
| The Netherlands | States-General |
| Norway | Storting |

| Country | Name of Parliament |
|---|---|
| Poland | Sejm |
| Russia | Federal Assembly (Council of the Federation and State Duma |
| South Africa | National Assembly and Senate |
| Spain | Cortes Generales |
| Sweden | Riksdag |
| Switzerland | Federal Assembly (Nationalrat and Standerat) |
| North Korea | Supreme People's Assembly |
| South Korea | National Assembly |
| U.S.A. | Congress (Senate and House of Representatives) |
| Ethiopia | Federal Council and House of Representatives |
| Iceland | Alpingi |
| Bulgaria | National Assembly |
| Cuba | National Assembly of People's Power |

## IMPORTANT NEWS AGENCIES OF THE WORLD

| Agency | Country | Agency | Country |
|---|---|---|---|
| PTI, UNI, UNIVARTA | India | Reuters, NAFEN | United Kingdom |
| Antara | Indonesia | Angence France Press (AFP) | France |
| Tanjug | Serbia | TASS | Russia |
| Associated Press (AP) | America | | |

## LARGEST AND SMALLEST COUNTRIES (Top 5)

| Largest Country (Area-wise) | Largest Country (Population-wise) | Smallest Country (Area-wise) | Smallest Country (Population-wise) |
|---|---|---|---|
| Russia | China | Vatican City | Vatican City |
| Canada | India | Monaco | Tuvalu |
| China | USA | Nauru | Palau |
| United States | Indonesia | Tuvalu | San Marino |
| Brazil | Brazil | San Marino | Liechstein |

## RELIGIONS OF THE WORLD

| Religion | Member | Percentage | Religion | Member | Percentage |
|---|---|---|---|---|---|
| Christianity | 2.5 billion | 32.2% | Buddhism | 545 million | 6.9% |
| Islam | 1.9 billion | 24.7% | Sikhism | 27 million | 0.4% |
| Hinduism | 1.07 billion | 13.5% | | | |

## NATIONAL EMBLEMS OF IMPORTANT COUNTRIES

| Country | National Emblem | Country | National Emblem |
|---|---|---|---|
| America | Golden Rod | Australia | Kangaroo |
| Ireland | Shamrock | Italy | White Lily |
| Israel | Candelabrum | Iran | Rose |
| Canada | White Lily | Great Britain | Rose |
| Chile | Candor and Huemul | Germany | Corn Flower |
| Japan | Chrysanthemum | Zimbabwe | Zimbabwe Bird |
| Denmark | Beach | Turkey | Crescent and Star |
| The Netherlands | Lion | New Zealand | Kiwi, Fern Southern Cross |
| Norway | Lion | Nepal | Kukri |
| Pakistan | Crescent | Poland | Eagle |
| France | Lily | Belgium | Lion |
| Bangladesh | Water Lily | Mongolia | The Soyombo |
| Russia | Double headed eagle | Lebanon | Cedar Tree |
| Sudan | Secretary Bird | Syria | Eagle |
| India | Lioned Capital | | |

## FIRST IN INDIA

- The first Indian to get the Nobel Prize for Literature — *Rabindra Nath Tagore*
- The first Indian to get the Nobel Prize for Physics — *C.V. Raman*
- The first Indian to get the Nobel Prize for Peace — *Mother Teresa*
- The first Indian to get the Nobel Prize for Economics — *Amartya Sen*
- The first Indian to get Special Oscar award (1992) — *Satyajit Ray*

| | |
|---|---|
| ✶ The first and the last Indian Governor-General of free India | *C. Rajagopalachari* |
| ✶ The first woman to become the Governor of a State | *Smt. Sarojini Naidu* |
| ✶ The first Indian Commander-In-Chief | *General K.M. Cariappa* |
| ✶ The first ever woman to become the Chief Minister of a State | *Smt. Sucheta Kripalani* |
| ✶ The first Indian woman President of UN General Assembly | *Smt. Vijaylakshmi Pandit* |
| ✶ The first Indian to become the President of International Court of Justice | *Dr. Nagendra Singh* |
| ✶ The first Indian woman to swim across the English Channel | *Ms. Aarti Saha* |
| ✶ The first Indian girl to become Miss Universe | *Miss Sushmita Sen* |
| ✶ The first Indian girl to become Miss World | *Rita Faria* |
| ✶ The first Indian to swim across the English Channel | *Mihir Sen* |
| ✶ The first Field Marshal | *S.H.F.J. Manekshaw* |
| ✶ The first Indian recipient of Victoria Cross | *Khudadad Khan* |
| ✶ The first Indian to conquer Mt. Everest | *Sherpa Tenzing (May 29, 1953)* |
| ✶ The first Indian Cosmonaut (man) | *Rakesh Sharma (April 3, 1984)* |
| ✶ The first Indian Cosmonaut (woman) | *Kalpana Chawla (Nov. 19, 1997)* |
| ✶ The first woman to climb Mt. Everest | *Miss Bachendri Pal (May 23, 1984)* |
| ✶ The first ICS | *Satyendranath Tagore* |
| ✶ The first to address the UN General Assembly in Hindi | *Atal Bihari Vajpayee* |
| ✶ The first Newspaper | *Bengal Gazette (Jan 27, 1780)* |
| ✶ The first Postage Stamp issued | *In 1852* |
| ✶ The first Telegraph line laid | *In 1851 (Calcutta-Diamond Harbour)* |
| ✶ The first Railways run | *April 16, 1853 (Bombay-Thane)* |
| ✶ The first Electric Train run | *1925 (Bombay-Kurla)* |
| ✶ The first Atomic Power Station | *Tarapore (Maharashtra)* |
| ✶ The first passenger-cum-cargo ship made in India | *Harshavardhan* |
| ✶ The first Satellite | *Aryabhatta (1975)* |
| ✶ The first President of the Indian National Congress | *W.C. Banerjee* |
| ✶ The first President of Indian Republic | *Dr. Rajendra Prasad* |
| ✶ The first woman judge of the Supreme Court | *Ms Fatima Bibi* |
| ✶ The first to climb Everest without oxygen | *Phu Dorjee (1987)* |
| ✶ The first film (movie) | *Raja Harishchandra* |
| ✶ The first film (talkie) | *Alam Ara* |
| ✶ The first Metro Railway | *Calcutta Metro Railway* |
| ✶ The first Test-tube baby, scientifically documented | *Born on August 6, 1986 at K.E.M. Hospital, Bombay* |
| ✶ The first TV Centre | *At Delhi* |
| ✶ The first Indian to get an Oscar | *Bhanu Athaiya* |
| ✶ The first woman pilot in IAF | *Ms Harita Kaur Deol* |
| ✶ The first woman to get Olympic Medal | *Karnam Malleswari* |
| ✶ The first woman Foreign Secretary | *Chokila Iyer* |
| ✶ First Chief of Defence Staff (CDS) | *General Bipin Rawat* |

## SUPERLATIVES (INDIA)

*Highest, Biggest, Largest and Longest in India*

| | |
|---|---|
| ✶ Award for Gallantry, highest | *Param Vir Chakra* |
| ✶ Award, highest civilian | *Bharat Ratna* |
| ✶ Bank, with largest number of branches | *State Bank of India* |

| | |
|---|---|
| ∗ Road Bridge, Longest | *Bhupen Hazarika Bridge, Assam (9.15 km)* |
| ∗ Road and Rail Bridge, Longest | *Bogibeel Bridge, Brahmaputra River, Assam* |
| ∗ Cattle Fair, Largest | *Sonepur (Bihar)* |
| ∗ City, Most Populous | *Mumbai metropolis* |
| ∗ Corridor, Longest | *Rameshwaram Temple corridor (4,000 ft.)* |
| ∗ Desert, Largest | *Thar (Rajasthan)* |
| ∗ Dam, Longest | *Hirakud Dam (Odisha)* |
| ∗ Delta, Largest | *Sunderban's Delta* |
| ∗ Dome, Largest | *Gol Gumbaj (Bijapur)* |
| ∗ Dam, Highest | *Tehri Dam (260 m)* |
| ∗ Gateway, Highest | *Buland Darwaja at Fatehpur Sikri (176 ft.)* |
| ∗ Fresh Water Lake, Largest | *Wular Lake (Kashmir)* |
| ∗ Literacy, Highest | *Kerala (94%)* |
| ∗ Museum, Largest | *Indian Museum (Kolkata)* |
| ∗ Mosque, Biggest | *Jama Masjid (Delhi)* |
| ∗ Peak, Highest** | *K-2 (Pak-Occupied Kashmir)* |
| ∗ Platform, Longest | *At Shree Siddharoodha Swamiji Railway Station Hubballi, Karnataka, SW Railway (1507 mtrs)* |
| ∗ Railway Bridge, longest | *Vembanad Bridge, Kerala (4.6 km)* |
| ∗ River, Longest*** | *The Ganges (2525 Km)* |
| ∗ Rainfall, Highest (annual mean) | *Mowsynram near Cherrapunji (1178 cm)* |
| ∗ Road Longest | *Grand Trunk Road (1,500 miles)* |
| ∗ State, with maximum forest cover | *Madhya Pradesh* |
| ∗ State, with maximum density of population | *Bihar* |
| ∗ Telescope, Largest in Asia | *Vainu Bappu Telescope (at Kavalur: Chennai) 2.34m* |
| ∗ Tunnel, Longest (Road) | *Dr. Shyama Prasad Mukherjee Tunnel (9.28 kms, J & K)* |
| ∗ Tunnel, Longest (Railway) | *T-50 Tunnel, Khari-Sumber section (12.77 kms) Jammu & Kashmir.* |
| ∗ Tallest Minaret | *Qutub Minar (Delhi 72.5 m.)* |
| ∗ Waterfall, Highest | *Kunchikal Waterfall (Karnataka: 455 m)* |
| ∗ Zoo, Largest | *Zoological Gardens (Kolkata)* |

** *Highest peak in the world is Mount Everest, which is in Nepal. K-2 is the second highest peak in the world. It is 8,611 metres high.*
*** *Indus and Brahmaputra (each 2900 km). Both of them, however, cover a long distance outside India.*

## TABLE OF PRECEDENCE

1. President
2. Vice-President
3. Prime Minister
4. Governors of States within their respective states
5. Former Presidents

5A. Deputy Prime Minister

6. Chief Justice of India, Speaker of Lok Sabha
7. Cabinet Ministers of the Union, Chief Ministers of States within their respective States
   Deputy Chairman NITI Aayog, former Prime Ministers
   Leaders of opposition in Rajya Sabha and Lok Sabha

7A. Holders of the Bharat Ratna Decoration

8. Ambassadors Extraordinary and Plenipotentiary and High Commissioners of Commonwealth Countries accredited to India, Chief Ministers of States outside their respective States
9. Judges of the Supreme Court
10. Deputy Chairman Rajya Sabha, Deputy Chief Minister of States, Deputy Speaker Lok Sabha, Members of the NITI Aayog, Minister of State of the Union and Other Minister in the Ministry of Defence.

## BOOKS AND AUTHORS

### FOREIGN

| Book | Author |
|---|---|
| * As You Like It | *William Shakespeare* |
| * A Tale of Two Cities | *Charles Dickens* |
| * Ben Hur | *Lewis Wallace* |
| * Das Kapital | *Karl Marx* |
| * David Copperfield | *Charles Dickens* |
| * Hamlet | *William Shakespeare* |
| * Iliad | *Homer* |
| * Inferno | *A. Dante* |
| * In Memoriam | *Lord Tennyson* |
| * Ivanhoe | *Walter Scott* |
| * Julius Caesar | *William Shakespeare* |
| * Lady Chatterley's Lover | *D.H. Lawrence* |
| * Lajja | *Taslima Nasreen* |
| * Les Miserable | *Victor Hugo* |
| * Leviathan | *Thomas Hobbes* |
| * Lolita | *V. Nobokov* |
| * Lycidas | *John Milton* |
| * Mein Kampf | *Adolf Hitler* |
| * Moor's Last Sigh | *Salman Rushdie* |
| * Mother | *Maxim Gorky* |
| * Mother India | *Katherine Mayo* |
| * Nana | *Emile Zola* |
| * Odyssey | *Homer* |
| * Origin of Species | *Charles Darwin* |
| * Othello | *William Shakespeare* |
| * Paradise Lost | *John Milton* |
| * Paradise Regained | *John Milton* |
| * Path to Power | *Margaret Thatcher* |
| * Pickwick Papers | *Charles Dickens* |
| * Razor's Edge | *Somerset Maugham* |
| * Republic | *Plato* |
| * The Tempest | *William Shakespeare* |
| * Time Machine | *H.G. Wells* |
| * Tom Sawyer | *Mark Twain* |
| * Treasure Island | *R.L. Stevenson* |
| * Twelfth Night | *William Shakespeare* |
| * Unto This Last | *John Ruskin* |
| * Utopia | *Thomas More* |
| * Wealth of Nations | *Adam Smith* |
| * Wonder that was India | *A.L. Basham* |

### INDIAN

| Book | Author |
|---|---|
| * Ain-i-Akbari | *Abul Fazal* |
| * Anand Math | *Bankim Chandra Chatterjee* |
| * Arthashastra | *Kautilya* |
| * A Suitable Boy | *Vikram Seth* |
| * Bhagwat Gita | *Ved Vyas* |
| * Chidambara | *Sumitranandan Pant* |
| * Devdas | *Sarat Chandra Chatterjee* |
| * Discovery of India | *Jawaharlal Nehru* |
| * Ganadevata | *Tarashankar Bandopadhyaya* |
| * Geet Govind | *Jaya Dev* |
| * Geetanjali | *R. N. Tagore* |
| * Glimpses of World History | *Jawaharlal Nehru* |
| * Godaan | *Prem Chand* |
| * Gul-e-Nagma | *Firaq Gorakhpuri* |
| * Harsh Charita | *Bana Bhatta* |
| * India Divided | *Dr. Rajendra Prasad* |
| * Justice of Peace ke Aansu | Janardan Prasad Singh |
| * The Judgement | *Kuldip Nayyar* |
| * Kadambari | *Bana Bhatta* |
| * Kagaz Te Kanwas | *Amrita Pritam* |
| * Kamayani | *Jai Shankar Prasad* |
| * Kitni Nawon Mein Kitni Bar | *S. H. Vatsyayan* |
| * Kumar Sambhav | *Kalidas* |
| * Mahabharata | *Ved Vyas* |
| * Malgudi Days | *R.K. Narayan* |
| * Meghdoot | *Kalidas* |
| * Mritunjaya | *B.K. Bhattacharya* |
| * Mudrarakshasa | *Vishakhadatta* |
| * Prison Diary | *Jaya Prakash Narayan* |
| * Raghuvansha | *Kalidas* |
| * Rajtarangini | *Kalhana* |
| * Ramayana | *Balmiki* |
| * Ramcharit Manas | *Tulsidas* |
| * Rukh Te Rishi | *Harbhajan Singh* |
| * Satyarth Prakash | *Swami Dayanand* |
| * Sur Sagar | *Surdas* |
| * The Guide | *R.K. Narayan* |

## IMPORTANT DATES AND DAYS OF THE YEAR

* **JANUARY**

**5-11** Road Safety Week
**12** National Youth Day
**15** Army Day
**15-21** Pin Code Week
**23** National Day of Patriotism
**26** Republic Day
**30** Martyr's Day

* **FEBRUARY**

**1-14** Oil Conservation Fortnight

14 Valentine's Day

* **MARCH**

4 National Safety Day
8 International Women's Day
15 Consumers' Day
16 Immunisation Day
21 World Forest Day
22 World Day for Water
24 World Meteorological Day
1-7 Preservation of Blindness Week

* **APRIL**

7 World Health Day
7-13 Handloom Week
14-20 Fire Service Week
18 World Heritage Day
22 World Earth Day

* **MAY**

1 May Day
5 National Labour Day
8 World Red Cross Day
11 National Technology Day
15 International Day of the Family
17 World Telecommunication Day
24 Commonwealth Day
31 World No-Tobacco Day

* **JUNE**

5 World Environment Day
21 World Yoga Day
26 International Day against Drug Abuse and Illicit Trafficking

* **JULY**

11 World Population Day

* **AUGUST**

1-7 World Breast feeding Week
10 Sanskrit Divas
15 Independence Day
20 Sadbhavana Divas

* **SEPTEMBER**

1-7 National Nutrition Week
5 Teachers' Day
8 International Literary Day
14 Hindi Diwas
23 World Deaf Day
27 World Tourism Day

* **OCTOBER**

2 Gandhi Jayanti
International Day of Non Violence
Anti-Leprosy Day
4 World Animal Day
6 World Habitat Day *(Ist Monday)*
8 Indian Air Force Day
14 World Standard Day
15 International Day of Rural Women
16 World Food Day
24 United Nations Day
27 Infantry Day
28 World Thrift Day
31 Anti-Terrorism Day

* **NOVEMBER**

2 All Saints Day
14 Children's Day
15-21 National Cooperative Week
19-25 Quami Ekta Week
20 Child Rights Day
26 Constitution Day

* **DECEMBER**

1 World AIDS Day
3 World Day for the Disabled
4 Naval Day
7 Flag Day
8 SMRC Day
10 Human Rights Day
14 National Energy Conservation Day

## INDIAN DEFENCE

- The Supreme Command of the Armed Forces is vested in the hands of the President of the Country.
- The responsibility for national defence, however, rests with the Cabinet. All important questions having a bearing on defence are decided by the Cabinet Committee on Political Affairs, which is presided over by the Prime Minister.
- The Defence Minister is responsible to Parliament for all matters concerning the Defence Services.
- All the administrative and operational control of Armed Forces are exercised by the Ministry of Defence. The three services—Army, Navy and Air Force function through their respective service head-quarters headed by the chief of Staff.
- The post of Chief of Defence Staff (CDS) was created in 2019.

### Indian Army Commands

| *Command* | *HQ Location* |
|---|---|
| Eastern Command | Kolkata |
| Western Command | Chandigarh |
| Northern Command | Udhampur |
| Southern Command | Pune |
| Central Command | Lucknow |
| Training Command | Shimla |
| South-Western Command | Jaipur |

## Indian Air Force Commands

| Command | HQ Location |
|---|---|
| Western Air Command | New Delhi |
| Sout-Western Air Command | Gandhinagar |
| Central Air Command | Prayagraj |
| Eastern Air Command | Shillong |
| Southern Air Command | Thiruvananthapuram |
| Training Command | Bengaluru |

## Indian Navy Commands

| Command | HQ Location |
|---|---|
| Eastern Naval Command | Vishakhapatnam |
| Western Naval Command | Mumbai |
| Southern Naval Command | Kochi |

## Commissioned Ranks in Defence Services

| Army | Navy | Air Force |
|---|---|---|
| General | Admiral | Air Chief Marshal |
| Lieutenant-General | Vice-Admiral | Air Marshal |
| Major-General | Rear-Admiral | Air Vice-Marshal |
| Brigadier | Commodor | Air Commodor |
| Colonel | Captain | Group Captain |
| Lieutenant-Colonel | Commander | Wing Commander |
| Major | Lt.Commander | Squadron Leader |
| Captain | Lieutenant | Flight Lieutenant |
| Lieutenant | Sub-Lieutenant | Flying Officer |

## Internal Security Organisations of India

| S. No. | Name of Organisation | Year of Creation | Headquarters |
|---|---|---|---|
| 1. | Assam Rifles (A.R.) | 1835 | Shillong |
| 2. | Central Reserve Police Force (CRPF) | 1939 | New Delhi |
| 3. | Territorial Army | 1948 | In different States |
| 4. | Indo-Tibetan Border Police | 1962 | New Delhi |
| 5. | Home Guard | 1962 | In different States |
| 6. | Coast Guard | 1978 | New Delhi |
| 7. | Border Security Force (B.S.F.) | 1965 | New Delhi |
| 8. | Central Industrial Security Force (CISF) | 1969 | New Delhi |
| 9. | National Security Guard | 1984 | New Delhi |
| 10. | Police | — | In different States |

## Army Institutes

| | | |
|---|---|---|
| 1. | Sainik Schools | 33 places in India |
| 2. | Rashtriya Indian Military College (prepare for entrance to N.D.A.) | Dehradun |
| 3. | National Defence Academy (three services) | Khadakwasla, Pune |
| 4. | Indian Military Academy (Army) | Dehradun |
| 5. | Officers Training Academy (3 services) Short Courses | Chennai |
| 6. | National Defence College | New Delhi |
| 7. | The College of Combat | Mhow |
| 8. | The College of Military Engineering | Kirkee |
| 9. | Military College of Telecommunication Engineering | Mhow |
| 10. | The Armoured Corps Centre and School | Ahmed Nagar |
| 11. | The School Artillery | Deolali |
| 12. | The Infantry School | Mhow and Belgaum |
| 13. | College of Material Management | Jabalpur |

## Air Force Institutions

|  |  |
|---|---|
| ∗ Air Force Academy | Hyderabad |
| ∗ Flying Instructors School | Tambaram, Chennai |
| ∗ Air Force Administrative College | Coimbatore |
| ∗ Helicopter Training School | Hakimpet |
| ∗ The College of Air Warfare | Secunderabad |
| ∗ Air Force Technical College | Jalahalli |

# UNITED NATIONS ORGANISATION (UNO)

- The United Nations (UN) is an association of states which have pledged themselves to maintain international peace and security and cooperate in solving international political, economic, social cultural and humanitarian problems towards achieving this end.
- Trygve Lie of Norway (1946-52) was the first Secretary-General of the UN.
- ***Origin:*** UN Charter was signed by 50 members on June 26, 1945. Poland signed the charter later to become one of the original 51 member-states. It officially came into existence on October 24, 1945.
- ***UN Charter:*** The Charter is the Constitution of the UNO and contains its aims and objectives and rules and regulations for its functioning.
- ***Aims and Objectives:*** They are security, welfare and human rights.
- ***Headquarters:*** New York.
- ***Flag:*** The flag is light blue in colour, and emblazoned in white, in its centre is the UN symbol—a polar map of world embraced by twin olive branches open at the top.
- ***Official Languages:*** The official languages of the UN are: English, French, Chinese, Russian, Arabic and Spanish. However, working languages are English and French only.
- ***Present Membership:*** At present 193 countries are members of the UNO. South Sudan is the latest entrant to this world organisation.
- ***Main Organs of the UNO:*** There are six main organs:
  1. General Assembly
  2. Security Council
  3. Economic and Social Council
  4. Trusteeship Council
  5. International Court of Justice, and
  6. Secretariat.

1. *General Assembly:* It consists of representative of all members of the UN. Each member country has only one vote. It meets once a year and passes UN Budget. It is the main place for discussions and policy making in the UN.
2. *Security Council:* It is the Executive body of the UN and is mainly responsible for maintaining international peace and security. It has 15 members, 5 of which (USA, UK, France, Russia and China) are permanent members. The 10 non-permanent members are elected by General Assembly for two-year term and are not eligible for immediate re-election.
3. *Economic and Social Council:* It has 54 members elected by General Assembly.
4. *Trusteeship Council:* It looks after interest of the people in areas not yet independent and leads them towards self-government.
5. *International Court of Justice:* It has 15 judges, no two of whom may be nationals of the same state. They are elected by General Assembly and Security Council for a term of 9 years. The Court elects its President and Vice-President for a 3-year term.
6. *Secretariat:* It is the Secretariat of the UN and is headed by the Secretary General.

## Some Important UN Agencies

| UN Agencies | Headquarters | Year of Establishment |
|---|---|---|
| ∗ United Nations Organisations (U.N.O.) | New York | 1945 |
| ∗ International Monetary Fund (I.M.F.) | Washington | 1945 |
| ∗ World Health Organisation (W.H.O.) | Geneva | 1948 |
| ∗ Food & Agricultural Organisation (FAO) | Rome | 1943 |
| ∗ International Labour Organisation (ILO) | Geneva | 1919 |
| ∗ UNESCO | Paris | 1946 |
| ∗ Universal Postal Union (UPU) | Berne | 1874 |
| ∗ UNIDO | Vienna | 1967 |
| ∗ International Atomic Energy Agency (IAEA) | Vienna | 1957 |

| | | |
|---|---|---|
| * United Nations Development Programme (UNDP) | New York | 1965 |
| * UNICEF | New York | 1946 |
| * International Maritime Organisation (IMO) | London | 1948 |
| * World Meteorological Organisation (WMO) | Geneva | 1951 |
| * International Telecommunication Union (ITU) | Geneva | 1947 |
| * World Trade Organisation (WTO) | Geneva | 1995 |
| * International Development Association (IDA) | Washington D.C. | 1960 |
| * World Intellectual Property Organisation (WIPO) | Geneva | 1967 |

## Famous International Organisations

| International Organisations | Headquarters | Year of Establishment |
|---|---|---|
| * International Court of Justice | The Hague | 1945 |
| * International Civil Aviation Organisation (ICAO) | Montreal | 1947 |
| * International Finance Corporation (IFC) | Washington | 1956 |
| * Arab League | Cairo | 1945 |
| * Commonwealth of Nations | London | 1931 |
| * International Bank for Reconstruction and Development (IBRD) | Washington D.C. | 1944 |
| * Organisation of Islamic Cooperation (OIC) | Jeddah (Saudi Arabia) | 1971 |
| * European Economic Community (EEC) | Geneva | 1957 |
| * Red Cross | Geneva | 1863 |
| * Interpol | Lyons | 1923 |
| * Asian Development Bank (ADB) | Manila | 1966 |
| * North Atlantic Treaty Organisation (NATO) | Brussels | 1949 |
| * Association of South East Asian Nations (ASEAN) | Jakarta | 1967 |
| * South Asian Association for Regional Cooperation (SAARC) | Kathmandu | 1985 |
| * Asia-Pacific Economic Cooperation (APEC) | Singapore | 1989 |
| * Organisation for Economic Cooperation and Development (OECD) | Paris | 1961 |
| * Organisation of Petroleum Exporting Countries (OPEC) | Vienna | 1960 |
| * Commonwealth of Independent States (CIS) | Minsk | 1991 |
| * International Olympic Committee (IOC) | Switzerland | 1894 |
| * European Union (EU) | Brussels | Changed form of EEC Established in 1958 |
| * Amnesty International (AI) | London | 1961 |
| * Shanghai Cooperation Organisation (SCO) | Beijing | 2001 |
| * BRICS Development Bank | Shanghai | 2014 |

# AWARDS AND HONOURS

## NATIONAL AWARDS

### BHARAT RATANA

- Bharat Ratna is India's highest Civilian Award. It was first awarded in 1954.
- The actual award is designed in the shape of a *peepal* leaf with Bharat Ratna inscribed in Devanagri script in the Sun Figure.
- This is India's highest civilian award. It is given for exceptional work on art, literature, science and recognition of public service of the highest order.
- The emblem, the Sun and the rim are of platinum. The inscriptions are in burnished bronze.
- Government servants are not eligible for it. The table shows the recipients of the award:

## Bharat Ratna Award Winners

| No. | Name | Year |
|---|---|---|
| 1. | Dr. S. Radhakrishnan | 1954 |
| 2. | C. Rajagopalachari | 1954 |
| 3. | Dr. C.V. Raman | 1954 |
| 4. | Dr. Bhagwan Das | 1955 |
| 5. | Dr. M. Visvesvaraya | 1955 |
| 6. | Jawahar Lal Nehru | 1955 |
| 7. | Govind Ballabh Pant | 1957 |
| 8. | Dr. D.K. Karve | 1958 |
| 9. | Dr. Bidhan Chandra Roy | 1961 |
| 10. | Purushottam Das Tandon | 1961 |
| 11. | Dr. Rajendra Prasad | 1962 |
| 12. | Dr. Zakir Hussain | 1963 |
| 13. | Dr. Pandurang Vaman Kane | 1963 |
| 14. | Lal Bahadur Shastri | 1966 |
| 15. | Indira Gandhi | 1971 |
| 16. | V.V. Giri | 1975 |
| 17. | K. Kamraj | 1976 |
| 18. | Mother Teresa | 1980 |
| 19. | Acharya Vinoba Bhave | 1983 |
| 20. | Khan Abdul Ghaffar Khan | 1987 |
| 21. | M.G. Ramachandran | 1988 |
| 22. | Dr. B.R. Ambedkar | 1990 |
| 23. | Dr. Nelson R. Mandela | 1990 |
| 24. | Rajiv Gandhi | 1991 |
| 25. | Sardar Vallabhbhai Patel | 1991 |
| 26. | Morarji R. Desai | 1991 |
| 27. | Maulana Abul Kalam Azad | 1992 |
| 28. | Jehangir Ratanji Dadabhai Tata | 1992 |
| 29. | Satyajit Roy | 1992 |
| 30. | Shri Gulzari Lal Nanda | 1997 |
| 31. | Mrs. Aruna Asaf Ali | 1997 |
| 32. | Dr. A.P.J. Abdul Kalam | 1998 |
| 33. | M.S. Subbalakshmi | 1998 |
| 34. | C. Subramaniam | 1998 |
| 35. | Jaya Prakash Narayan | 1999 |
| 36. | Prof. Amartya Sen | 1999 |
| 37. | Pt. Ravi Shankar | 1999 |
| 38. | Gopinath Bardoloi | 1999 |
| 39. | Lata Mangeshkar | 2001 |
| 40. | Bismillah Khan | 2001 |
| 41. | Bhimsen Joshi | 2009 |
| 42. | C.N.R. Rao | 2014 |
| 43. | Sachin Tendulkar | 2014 |
| 44. | Pt. Madan Mohan Malaviya | 2015 |
| 45. | Atal Bihari Vajpayee | 2015 |
| 46. | Pranab Mukherjee | 2019 |
| 47. | Bhupen Hazarika | 2019 |
| 48. | Nanaji Deshmukh | 2019 |
| 49. | Karpoori Thakur | 2024 |
| 50. | L.K. Advani | 2024 |
| 51. | Charan Singh | 2024 |
| 52. | P.V. Narasimha Rao | 2024 |
| 53. | M.S. Swaminathan | 2024 |

## REPUBLIC DAY AWARDS

### Padma Awards

They fall in line after the Bharat Ratna. They are also discontinued in 1977 along with the Bharat Ratna and award was started again in 1980.

There are three Padma Awards:

- ***Padma Vibhushan:*** This award is given for exceptional and distinguished service in any field, including service rendered by Govt. servants.
- ***Padma Bhushan:*** This award is given for distinguished service of a high order in any field, including service rendered by Govt. servants.
- ***Padma Shri:*** This award is given for distinguished service in any field, including service rendered by Government servants.

### Gallantry Awards

- ***Param Vir Chakra:*** The highest award for bravery or some daring and pre-eminent act of valour or self-sacrifice in the presence of the enemy, whether on land, at sea or in the air.
- ***Mahavir Chakra:*** It is the second highest decoration and is awarded for acts of conspicuous gallantry in the presence of the enemy, whether on land, at sea or in the air.
- ***Vir Chakra:*** It is the third in order of awards given for acts of gallantry in the presence of enemy, whether on land, at sea or in the air.
- ***Ashok Chakra:*** This medal is awarded for the most conspicuous bravery or some daring or pre-eminent act of valour or self-sacrifice on land, at sea or in the air but not in the presence of enemy.
- ***Vishishta Sewa Medal:*** It is awarded to personnel of all the three Services in class I, II and III in recognition of distinguished service of the "most exceptional" and "exceptional" and a "high" order respectively. Prefixes Parma and Ati are added before first two categories of medals respectively.
- ***Jeewan Raksha Padak:*** Awarded for meritorious acts or a series of acts of a human nature displayed in saving life from drowning, fire and rescue operations in mines etc.

## OTHER NATIONAL AWARDS

### SAHITYA AKADEMI AWARDS

- These prizes are awarded annually to the authors of the most outstanding books of literary merit published in each of the 22 languages specified in the Eighth Schedule of the Constitution.
- There are also two awards for Rajasthani and English. The award, in form of a casket containing an inscribed copper plate and a cheque of ₹ 1 lakh is given to the author or his/her heir.

### DADA SAHEB PHALKE AWARD

- The award carries a cash prize of ₹ 10 lakh, a Shawl and Swarna Kamal.
- Mrs Devika Rani Roerich was the first person to receive Dadasaheb Phalke Award in 1969.

- The award for 2021 has been given to bollywood actress Waheeda Rehman.

### BHARATIYA JNANPITH AWARD

- Instituted in 22nd May, 1961, carries a cash prize of ₹ 11 lakh, a citation and a bronze replica of Vagdevi (Saraswati).
- Instituted by a literary organisation in India.

### SARASWATI SAMMAN

- Given for outstanding literary works, value ₹ 15 lakh.

### KALINGA PRIZE

- This award is given each year by the UNESCO and founded by former Odisha Chief Minister late Shri Biju Patnaik for popularisation of science.

## INTERNATIONAL AWARDS

### NOBEL PRIZES

- These Prizes were instituted in 1901 by a Swedish scientist, Dr. Alfred Nobel; the discoverer of Dynamite.
- Six prizes are awarded annually for (i) Chemistry, (ii) Physics, (iii) Medicine, (iv) Literature, (v) Peace and (vi) Economics —started since 1969.
- Indians Honoured with Nobel Prize: So far, following Indians have been honoured with these prizes. Their names are (*i*) Rabindra Nath Tagore for Literature, for his book 'Gitanjali', in 1913, (*ii*) Dr. C.V. Raman for Physics in 1930, for his discovery of 'Raman Effect', (*iii*) Mother Teresa for Peace in 1979, (*iv*) Prof. Amartya Sen in 1998 for Economics and (*v*) Kailash Satyarthi for Peace in 2014. In addition, four non-resident Indians have also been awarded the Nobel Prize. They are: (*i*) Hargobind Khurana for Medicine in 1968, (*ii*) Subramanian Chandrasekhar for Physics in 1983, (*iii*) Venkatraman Ramkrishnan for Chemistry in 2009, (*iv*) Abhijit Vinayak Banerjee for Economics in 2019.

### GANDHI PEACE PRIZE

- The government instituted this ₹ 1 crore prize on the lines of the Nobel Peace Prize in 1995.
- It is the highest Civilian International award by the Govt. of India. The award of 2021 have been given to Gita Press, Gorakhpur.

### MAN BOOKER PRIZE 2023

- On November 26, 2023, Irish author Paul Lynch won 2023 Booker Prize for his novel, 'Prophet Song' published by Oneworld. He received 50,000 Pound sterling and the Iris Trophy for his award winning novel.

### INDIRA GANDHI PRIZE FOR PEACE, DISARMAMENT AND DEVELOPMENT

- The award was instituted in the memory of Mrs. Indira Gandhi to foster creative cooperation among nations of the world.

### Highest Honours of Some Countries

| *Country* | *Highest Honour* |
|---|---|
| India | Bharat Ratna |
| Pakistan | Nishan-e-Pakistan |
| Kuwait | Mubarak-Al-kabir Medal |
| Saudi Arabia | Shah Abdul Aziz Medal |
| Argentina | The Order of Sona Martin |
| Nicaragua | Augusto-Caesar Sandino Order |
| Vietnam | The Order of the Golden Star |
| Hungary | The Order of Banner |
| Britain | Member of British Empire, Victoria Cross |
| Japan | Order of Moulovenice Sun |
| Denmark | Order of Diana Brog |
| France | Legend of Honour |
| America | Presidential Medal of Freedom |
| Germany | Pore Lee Merit Iron Cross |
| The Netherlands | Netherlands Lion |

## SPORTS

### OLYMPICS

- First of all these games were held by the Greeks in 776 B.C. on Mount Olympus in honour of the Greek God Zeus. In this way, the history of Olympic Games is about twenty eight hundred years old. These games continued to be held every four years until 394 A.D. when these games were stopped by a royal order of the emperor of Rome.
- The modern Olympic Games which started in Athens in 1896, are the result of the devotion and dedication of a French educator Baron Pierre de Coubertin and the first Olympic meet in the modern series was held in 1896 in Athens, the Capital of Greece. Since then, they are being held every four years except for breaks during world wars.
- The Olympic flag is white in colour with five coloured rings, each ring symbolic of a continent. Summer as well as Winter Olympics are held in the same year.
- The 2020 Olympic Games was held at Tokyo in 2021.
- The official Olympic Motto is *Citius, Altius, Swifter, Higher, Stronger*. The Head Office of International Olympic Committee (IOC) is at Lausanne (Switzerland).

## COMMONWEALTH GAMES

- The Commonwealth Games are held every four years, in the year in which Asian Games are held. All the Commonwealth Countries (former colonies of Britain) can take part in it.
- The first Commonwealth Games were held in 1930 at Hamilton (Canada).
- There are currently 56 members of the Commonwealth of Nations, and 72 teams participated in the games.
- The 2022 Commonwealth Games officially known as the XXII Commonwealth Games or Birmingham 2022, held in Birmingham, England, between 28 July to 8 August 2022.

## ASIAN GAMES

- After the Second World War, most of the Asian Countries gained independence. On the lines of Olympic Games, Asian Games were planned every four years.
- India hosted the first Asian Games in 1951.

## WORLD CUP CRICKET

- The first Cricket World Cup was organised in England in 1975. A separate women's Cricket World Cup has been held every 4 years since 1973.

**List of Cricket World Cup**

| Year | Venue | Winner/Runner |
|---|---|---|
| 1975 | England | *West Indies beat Australia* |
| 1979 | England | *West Indies beat England* |
| 1983 | England | *India beat West Indies* |
| 1987 | India & Pakistan | *Australia beat England* |
| 1992 | Australia | *Pakistan beat England* |
| 1996 | India, Pakistan & Sri Lanka | *Sri Lanka beat Australia* |
| 1999 | England | *Australia beat Pakistan* |
| 2003 | South Africa | *Australia beat India* |
| 2007 | West Indies | *Australia beat Sri Lanka* |
| 2011 | India, Sri Lanka, Bangladesh | *India beat Sri Lanka* |
| 2015 | Australia, New Zealand | *Australia beat New Zealand* |
| 2019 | England | *England beat New Zealand* |
| 2023 | India | *Australia beat India* |

## HOCKEY WORLD CUP

- The first Hockey World Cup was organised in Barcelona (Spain) in 1971. Women's Hockey World Cup has been held since 1974.

## FOOTBALL WORLD CUP

- The Football World Cup is organised by FIFA (Federation of International Football Association). The World Cup is called 'Jules Rimet Cup' named after the name of FIFA President Jules Rimet. The first Football World Cup was organised in Uruguay in 1930.
- In 1942 and 1946, the Football World Cup was not played due to World War II.
- Brazil is the only nation to have participated in every World Cup so far. The 2022 Football World Cup held in Qatar. Argentina on December 18, 2022 emerged Champion of the FIFA World Cup 2022 as it prevailed over France 4-2 on penalties.

## IMPORTANT CUPS & TROPHIES

### International

- ∗ *American Cup* : Yacht Racing
- ∗ *Ashes* : Cricket
- ∗ *Davis Cup* : Lawn Tennis
- ∗ *Derby* : Horse Race
- ∗ *Grand National* : Horse Streple Chase Race
- ∗ *Jules Rimet Trophy* : World Soccer Cup
- ∗ *King's Cup* : Air Races
- ∗ *Merdeka Cup* : Football
- ∗ *Swaythling Cup* : Table Tennis (Men)
- ∗ *Ryder Cup* : Golf
- ∗ *Thomas Cup* : Badminton
- ∗ *U. Thant Cup* : Tennis
- ∗ *Walker Cup* : Golf
- ∗ *Wightman Cup* : Lawn Tennis
- ∗ *Rothman's Trophy* : Cricket
- ∗ *European Champions Cup* : Football
- ∗ *Grand Prix* : Table Tennis
- ∗ *Edgbaston Cup* : Lawn Tennis
- ∗ *Grand Prix* : Lawn Tennis

### National

- ∗ *Agha Khan Cup* : Hockey
- ∗ *Beighton Cup* : Hockey
- ∗ *Bombay Gold Cup* : Hockey
- ∗ *C.K. Naydu Trophy* : Cricket
- ∗ *Deodhar Trophy* : Cricket

* *Duleep Trophy* : Cricket
* *Durand Cup* : Football
* *Dhyan Chand Trophy* : Hockey
* *Dr. B.C. Roy Trophy* : Football (Junior)
* *Ezra Cup* : Polo
* *Guru Nanak Cup* : Hockey
* *Holkar Trophy* : Bridge
* *Irani Trophy* : Cricket
* *Indira Gold Cup* : Hockey
* *Murugappa Gold Cup* : Hockey
* *Nehru Trophy* : Hockey
* *Nixan Gold Cup* : Football
* *Rani Jhansi Trophy* : Cricket
* *Ranji Trophy* : Cricket
* *Rangaswami Cup* : Hockey
* *Ramanujan Trophy* : Table Tennis
* *Rene Frank Trophy* : Hockey
* *Rohinton Baria Trophy* : Cricket
* *Rovers Cup* : Football
* *Santosh Trophy* : Football
* *Subroto Cup* : Football

## SPORTS TERMS

* ***Badminton:*** Mixed doubles; Deuce; Drop; Smash; Let; Foot work; Setting.
* ***Base Ball:*** Pitcher; Put out, Strike; Home; Bunt.
* ***Billiards:*** Cue; Jigger; Pot; Break; In Baulk; In Off; Cannons.
* ***Boxing:*** Upper cut; Round; Punch; Bout; Knock down; Hitting below the belt; Ring.
* ***Bridge:*** Finesse; Dummy; Revoke; Grand Slam; Little Slam; No Trump; Rubber.
* ***Chess:*** Bishop, Gambit; Checkmate; Stalemate.
* ***Cricket:*** L.B.W. (leg before wicket); Creases, Popping-creases; Stumped; Bye; Leg-Bye; Googly; Hattrick; Maiden over; Drive; Bowling; Duck; Follow-on; No ball; Leg Break; Silly point; Cover point; Hit-wicket; Late-cut; Slip; Off-spinner; In-swing.
* ***Football:*** Off Side; Block; Drop-kick; Penalty-kick (or goal kick); Corner-kick; Free-kick; Dribble; Thrown-in; Foul.
* ***Golf:*** Boggy; Foursome; Stymic; Tee; Put; Hole; Niblic; Caddie; Links; The green; Bunker.
* ***Hockey:*** Carried; Short Corner; Bully; Sticks; Off side; Roll in; Striking Circle; Under-cutting; Dribble.
* ***Horse racing:*** Jockey; Punter.
* ***Polo:*** Bunker; Chukker; Mallet.
* ***Tennis:*** Back hand drive; Volley; Smash; Half-volley; Deuce; Service; Let; Grand Slam.

## Stadiums and Places Associated with Sports

| Name of Stadium | Sports | Place |
|---|---|---|
| Arun Jaitley Stadium | Cricket | Delhi |
| Jawaharlal Nehru Stadium | Athletics | Delhi |
| Shivajee Stadium | Hockey | Delhi |
| National Stadium | Hockey etc. | Delhi |
| Ambedkar Stadium | Football | Delhi |
| Brabourne Stadium | Cricket | Mumbai |
| Wankhede Stadium | Cricket | Mumbai |
| Narendra Modi Stadium | Cricket | Ahmedabad |
| Eden Garden | Cricket | Kolkata |
| Green Park Stadium | Cricket | Kanpur |
| Keenan Stadium | Cricket | Jamshedpur |
| Nehru (Chepauk) Stadium | Cricket | Chennai |
| Barabati Stadium | Cricket | Cuttack |
| Lords, Oval, Leeds | Cricket | Britain |
| Hedingle Manchester | Cricket | Britain |
| Black Heath | Rugby Football | London |
| Henley | Boat race | England |
| Wimbledon | Lawn Tennis | London |
| Wembley Stadium | Football | London |
| White City | Dog-race | England |
| Aintree | Horse-race | England |
| Tentbridge | Cricket | England |
| Patnee Martlake | Boat-race | England |
| Tibankham | Rugby Football | England |
| Sandy Lodge | Golf | Scotland |
| Forest Hill | Tennis | New York |
| Brooklyn | Baseball | New York |
| Melbourne | Cricket | Australia |

## Name of Playing Compound of Different Games

| Name of Compound | Related Sports |
|---|---|
| Court | Lawn Tennis, Badminton, Netball, Hand ball, Volleyball, Squash, Kho-Kho, Kabaddi |
| Diamond | Baseball |
| Ring | Boxing, Skating, Wrestling, Circus, Riding display |
| Course | Golf |
| Board | Table Tennis |
| Pool | Swimming |
| Alley | Bowling |
| Mat | Judo, Karate II |
| Arena | Horse Riding |
| Vellodrum | Cycling |
| Field | Polo, Football, Hockey |
| Track | Athletics |
| Pitch | Cricket, Rugby |
| Rink | Ice Hockey |

❐❐❐

# Multiple Choice Questions

**1.** Match List-I with List-II and select the correct answer from the codes given below the lists:

**List-I**

(*a*) Napoleon Bonaparte
(*b*) Jean Jacques Rousseau
(*c*) Croce
(*d*) Madame Roland

**List-II**

1. 'A history is contemporary history'
2. 'Liberty what crimes are committed in thy name'
3. 'Man is born free but everywhere he is in chains.'
4. 'I am the Child of Revolution'

**Codes :**

| | (*a*) | (*b*) | (*c*) | (*d*) |
|---|---|---|---|---|
| A. | 1 | 2 | 3 | 4 |
| B. | 4 | 3 | 1 | 2 |
| C. | 3 | 4 | 2 | 1 |
| D. | 3 | 4 | 1 | 2 |

**2.** Abraham Lincon was elected the President of United States in:
A. 1862 B. 1860
C. 1875 D. 1855

**3.** Who was known as the 'Prince of Humanists'?
A. Francisco Petrarch B. Dante
C. Boccacio D. Erasmus

**4.** D-Day is the day when:
A. Germany declared war on Britain
B. US dropped the atom bomb on Hiroshima.
C. Allied Troops landed in Normandy
D. Germany surrendered to the allies

**5.** Whose teachings inspired the French Revolution?
A. Locke
B. Rousseau
C. Hegel
D. Plato

**6.** At a time when empires in Europe were crumbling before the might of Napoleon which one of the following Governor-Generals kept the British flag flying high in India?
A. Warren Hastings B. Lord Cornwallis
C. Lord Wellesley D. Lord Hastings

**7.** Which one of the following statements regarding Fascism in Italy is *not* true?
A. The Fascists came to power as a result of popular uprising
B. In 1926, all political parties except Mussolini's party were banned
C. The Fascists suppressed the Socialist movement
D. The Fascists were hostile to the Communists

**8.** The fall of Czar Nicholas-II is known as:
A. Bloody Sunday
B. Bolshevik Revolution
C. February Revolution
D. October Revolution

**9.** Industrial Revolution took place first in:
A. France B. Germany
C. United Kingdom D. Japan

**10.** The British Prime Minister at the outbreak of World War II was :
A. Churchill B. Baldwin
C. Attlee D. Chemberlain

**11.** The 'Great Depression' (1929) economic crisis was met by adopting the policy of
A. Stimulus B. Marshall Plan
C. New Deal D. Open Door

**12.** The slogan "No taxation without representation" was raised during the:
A. American War of Independence
B. Russian Revolution
C. French Revolution
D. Indian Freedom struggle

**13.** In the nineteenth century the people of Europe started moving from the villages to the cities due to the impact of :
A. Epidemics
B. War
C. Industrialisation
D. Population explosion in villages

**14.** The important cause of the Civil War in America was:
A. Abolition of slavery
B. Quest for freedom
C. Industrialisation
D. Rebellion by the native Americans

**15.** Industrial Revolution could not have come about without:
A. Merchant capitalism
B. The Enclosure Movement
C. The services of the proletariat class
D. An agricultural revolution

16. Consider the following statements :
The French Revolution came about mainly due to the :
1. Extreme poverty of the people
2. Impact of the works of great writers
3. Cruelty of the rulers
4. Impact of impulsive reaction
Which of the above statements are correct?
A. 1, 2 and 4 B. 2 and 3
C. 1, 3 and 4 D. 1, 2, 3 and 4

17. Asia's oldest and largest Buddhist monastery is situated in :
A. Tawang (Arunachal Pardesh)
B. Lhasa (Tibet)
C. Trincomallee (Sri Lanka)
D. Ulan Bator (Mongolia)

18. Who was the main architect of the Russian Revolution?
A. Karl Marx B. Lenin
C. Stalin D. Tolstoy

19. V.I. Lenin is associated with :
A. Russian Revolution of 1917
B. Chinese Revolution of 1949
C. German Revolution
D. French Revolution of 1789

20. Which one of the following statements is *not* correct?
A. Voltaire believed in Natural Religion
B. Rousseau wrote *Social Contract*
C. Montesquieu authored *The Spirit of Laws*
D. Necker believed in 'General Will'

21. 6th April, 1930 is well known in the history of India because this date is associated with...........
A. Dandi March by Mahatma Gandhi
B. Quit India Movement
C. Partition of Bengal
D. Partition of India

22. Which ruler enforced the system of 'Price Control' in India?
A. Mohammad Tughlak
B. Razia Begum
C. Alauddin Khilji
D. Sher Shah Suri

23. The concept of 'Din-e-Elahi' was founded by which king?
A. Dara Shikoh B. Akbar
C. Sher Shah Suri D. Shahjahan

24. Who are supposed to be the earliest inhabi-tants of India? Where did they come from?
A. Aryans from Central Asia
B. Dravidians from Mediterranean
C. Negroids from Africa
D. Bhils and the Santhals from West Asia

25. The one chief characteristic of temple architecture of the Gupta Age was :
A. Absence of dome
B. Huge size
C. Beautiful carvings
D. absence of a covered courtyard for the gathering of worshippers

26. The Rigveda consists of :
A. 1000 hymns B. 2028 hymns
C. 1028 hymns D. 1038 hymns

27. The central point in Ashoka's dharma was :
A. royalty to kings
B. peace and non-violence
C. respect to elders
D. religious tolerance

28. The social evil which was conspicuously absent during ancient India was :
A. *Sati*-System B. *Devadasi*-System
C. Polygamy D. *Purdah*-System

29. Which, among the following, can be accepted as a novelty introduced by Mughal emperors to their buildings?
A. Domes B. Minarets
C. Arches D. Attached gardens

30. The first ruler of India who defeated Muhammud of Ghur was :
A. Mularaja II of Gujarat
B. Prithviraja Chauhan of Delhi
C. Jayachand of Kannauj
D. Parmaldeva of Bundelkhand

31. What important event happened in India in 1911?
A. Bengal was partitioned
B. Non-Cooperation movement was launched
C. India's capital was shifted from Calcutta to Delhi
D. Mahatma Gandhi presided over the Congress session

32. The first phase of the Congress Party (1885-1905) was characterized by its efforts to secure:
A. limited independence
B. complete freedom
C. Indianization of services
D. constitutional reforms

33. The Muslim League demanded a separate homeland for the Indian Muslims openly for the first time at its annual session held in Lahore in the year :
A. 1931 A.D. B. 1936 A.D.
C. 1940 A.D. D. 1941 A.D.

34. Under whose governorship did the East India Company secure the Diwani Rights in Bengal, Bihar and Odisha from Emperor Shah Alam?
A. Lord Cornwallis
B. Lord William Bentinck
C. Lord Clive
D. Lord Wellesley

**35.** The Simon Commission was generally boycotted by the Indian political parties. What was the reason for this general non-cooperation?
A. the Commission aimed at dividing the people
B. it was an 'all white' Commission
C. it came after the Jallianwala Bagh carnage
D. it was an eye wash

**36.** Aligarh Muslim University was founded by :
A. Dr. Saifuddin Kitchlu
B. Mohammad Ali Jinnah
C. Sir Syed Ahmed Khan
D. Maulana Mohammad Ali

**37.** Ibn Batutah was an African traveller visiting India during the time of :
A. Alivardi Khan
B. Ala-ud-din Khalji
C. Iltutmish
D. Mohammad-bin-Tughlaq

**38.** The battle of Wandiawash was fought in :
A. 1726 B. 1760
C. 1818 D. 1857

**39.** The abolition of *Sati* by government regulation was at the time of :
A. Warren Hastings B. Lord Wellesley
C. Lord Bentinck D. Lord Ahmerst

**40.** Pick out the wrong combination :
A. Dilwara Temple : Mt. Abu
B. Pashupati Temple : Kathmandu
C. Padmanabh Temple : Bangalore
D. Minakshi Temple : Madurai

**41.** Match the following:
(*a*) Chanhudaro (*b*) Kalibangan
(*c*) Lothal (*d*) Surkotada
1. Alleged discovery of the skeleton of horse.
2. Bead making.
3. Traces of a dock and ship on seal.
4. Evidence of ploughing the fields.
The Correct code is :

| | (*a*) | (*b*) | (*c*) | (*d*) |
|---|---|---|---|---|
| A. | 2 | 4 | 3 | 1 |
| B. | 2 | 1 | 3 | 4 |
| C. | 1 | 2 | 3 | 4 |
| D. | 2 | 1 | 4 | 3 |

**42.** Match the Harappan settlements with the banks of rivers on which they were located :
(*a*) Harappa 1. Ravi
(*b*) Mohenjodaro 2. Indus
(*c*) Ropar 3. Sutlej
(*d*) Kalibangan 4. Ghaggar
(*e*) Lothal 5. Bhogava

**Codes :**

| | (*a*) | (*b*) | (*c*) | (*d*) | (*e*) |
|---|---|---|---|---|---|
| A. | 1 | 2 | 3 | 4 | 5 |
| B. | 1 | 2 | 3 | 5 | 4 |
| C. | 2 | 1 | 3 | 5 | 4 |
| D. | 2 | 1 | 4 | 3 | 5 |

**43.** The Goddess 'Kannagi' whose many temples were erected during the 'Sangam Age' was the goddess of :
A. Chastity B. Love
C. Prowess D. Wisdom

**44.** The Jain goal of life is to attain deliverance from the fetters of mudane existence, the way to which lies through three jewels. Which one of the following was not included among the 'three jewels' of Jainism?
A. Right faith B. Right action
C. Right knowledge D. Right conduct

**45.** The most striking feature of the Ashokan pillar is polish. Name the Ashokan pillar which is considered to be the most graceful of all Ashokan pillars.
A. Sarnath
B. Rampurva
C. Laurya-Nandangarh
D. Rummindei

**46.** Which are the correct statements?
1. The land grants, started in Satavahana period, paved the way for feudal developments in India.
2. Silk and spices were the Chief Indian export articles of Indo-Roman trade.
3. The Guptas issued the largest number of gold coins in ancient India.
4. The first memorial of a 'SATI' dated 510 A.D. is found at Eran in Madhya Pradesh.
A. 1 and 2 B. 1, 3, and 4
C. 1 and 4 D. 1, 2, 3 and 4

**47.** Who among the following patronised the 'Gandhara' (Indo-Greek style) School of Art?
A. Ashoka, the Great
B. Harsha Vardhana
C. Kanishka
D. Chandragupta Vikramaditya

**48.** The Sultanate of Delhi had five ruling dynasties. The dynasty having longest and shortest period were :
A. Ilbari and Khalji
B. Tughlaq and Khalji
C. Tughlaq and Sayyid
D. Ilbari and Lodis

**49.** Which one of the following events took place at the last during reign of Muhammad-bin-Tughlaq?
A. Introduction of token currency
B. Increase of land-revenue in Doab
C. Transfer of Capital from Delhi to Devagiri.
D. Conquest of Khurasan and Iraq

**50.** The most learned medieval Muslim ruler who was well versed in various branches of learning including astronomy, mathematics and medicine was :
A. Jalaluddin Khilji
B. Sikander Lodi
C. Ghiyasuddin Tughlaq
D. Muhammad-bin-Tughlaq

**51.** The 'Sufis' had 12 silsilas. They propounded the idea of Union with God through:
A. Love B. Rituals
C. Fasts D. Prayers

**52.** Match the following:

| | | | |
|---|---|---|---|
| (a) Peshwa | 1. Foreign affairs | | |
| (b) Panditrao | 2. Audit and accounts | | |
| (c) Amatya | 3. Providing grants to scholars | | |
| (d) Sumant | 4. General supervision | | |
| | 5. Military affairs | | |

*Select the correct code* :

| | (a) | (b) | (c) | (d) |
|---|---|---|---|---|
| A. | 2 | 3 | 4 | 5 |
| B. | 4 | 1 | 2 | 3 |
| C. | 4 | 3 | 2 | 1 |
| D. | 3 | 1 | 4 | 2 |

**53.** The Regulating Act of 1773 can be regarded as the first measure to :
A. assert the right of British Parliament to legislate for India
B. separate the legislature from the executive
C. separate the judiciary from the executive
D. centralise law-making

**54.** What was the exact constitutional status of the Indian Republic on 26th January, 1950?
A. A Democratic Republic
B. A Sovereign, Democratic Republic
C. A Sovereign, Secular, Democratic Republic
D. A Sovereign, Socialist, Secular, Democratic Republic

**55.** When the British obtained the grant of Diwani of Bengal, Bihar and Odisha they acquired the right to :
A. maintain law and order in these territories
B. administer civil justice and collect revenue in these territories
C. collect revenue and establish revenue administration in these territories
D. militarily defend these territories

**56.** Which of the following were responsible for the growth of nationalism in India during the British rule?
1. Economic exploitation of India.
2. Impact of western education.
3. Role of the Press.
Select the correct answer using the codes given below :

**Codes:**
A. 1, 2 and 3 B. 1 and 2
C. 2 and 3 D. 1 and 3

**57.** Which one of the following nationalist leaders has been described as being radical in politics but conservative on social issues?
A. G.K. Gokhale
B. B.G. Tilak
C. Lala Lajpat Rai
D. Madan Mohan Malviya

**58.** Provincial Autonomy in British India was envisaged by the :
A. Act of 1909 B. Act of 1919
C. Act of 1935 D. Act of 1947

**59.** Dyarchy means :
A. double government
B. a government in which the centre is very powerful
C. a government based on division of power between centre and provinces
D. None of the above

**60.** The Indian National Congress observed 'Independence Day' for the first time on 26th January in :
A. 1920 B. 1925
C. 1930 D. 1947

**61.** ............is situated near the banks of Sabarmati River
A. Bhavnagar B. Aurangabad
C. Ahmedabad D. Rajkot

**62.** Sericulture is:
A. science of the various kinds of serum
B. artificial rearing of fish
C. art of silkworm breeding
D. study of various cultures of a community

**63.** The most abundant constituents of earth's crust are:
A. Igneous rocks
B. Sedimentary rocks
C. Metamorphic rocks
D. Granite

**64.** Indian Standard Time is based on:
A. 80°E longitude B. 82½°E longitude
C. 110°E longitude D. 25°E longitude

**65.** Tides in the oceans are caused by :
A. Gravitational pull of the moon on the earth's surface including sea water
B. Gravitational pull of the sun on the earth's surface only and not on the sea water
C. Gravitational pull of the moon and the sun on the earth's surface including the sea water
D. None of these

**66.** Nagarjunasagar Project is situated on the river:
A. Tungabhadra B. Cauvery
C. Krishna D. Godavari

67. The difference between the Indian Standard Time and the Greenwich Mean Time is:
A. – 3½ hours B. + 3½ hours
C. – 5½ hours D. + 5½ hours

68. Which of the following dams is not on Narmada river?
A. Indira-Sagar Project
B. Maheshwar Hydel Power Project
C. Jobat Project
D. Koyna Power Project

69. Which of the following statements is **not true** about the availability of water on the earth, the crisis for which is going to increase in the years to come?
A. About 97.5 per cent of the total volume of water available on the earth is salty
B. 80 per cent of the water available to us for use comes in bursts as monsoons
C. About 2.5 per cent of the total water available on the earth is polluted water and cannot be used for human activities
D. Possibility is that some big glaciers will melt in the coming ten-fifteen years and sea level will rise by 3-4 metres all over the earth

70. Which of the following is **not** a cash crop?
A. Jute B. Paddy
C. Cashewnut D. Sugarcane

71. Through which States does Cauvery River flow?
A. Gujarat, M.P., Tamil Nadu
B. Karnataka, Kerala, Tamil Nadu
C. Karnataka, Kerala, Andhra Pradesh
D. M.P., Maharashtra, Tamil Nadu

72. Indian Standard Time is the local time of 82½°E which passes through :
A. Guntur B. Delhi
C. Allahabad D. Kolkata

73. The 17th parallel defines the boundary between:
A. North and South Korea
B. USA and Canada
C. North and South Vietnam
D. China and Russia

74. During the period of south-west monsoon, Tamil Nadu remains dry because:
A. the winds do not reach this area
B. there are no mountains in this area
C. it lies in the rain shadow area
D. the temperature is too high to let the winds cool down

75. Which country does top in producing cocoa?
A. Ivory Coast B. Brazil
C. Japan D. Nigeria

76. The biggest reserves of thorium are in :
A. India B. China
C. The Soviet Union D. U.S.A.

77. The Girnar Hills are situated in which of the following states?
A. Gujarat B. Karnataka
C. Madhya Pradesh D. Maharashtra

78. During December 22nd the sun is vertically over:
A. Tropic of Cancer B. Tropic of Capricorn
C. The Equator D. None of the above

79. Photosphere is described as the :
A. Lower layer of atmosphere
B. Visible surface of the sun from which radiation emanates
C. Wavelength of solar spectrum
D. None of the above

80. Broadly, there are three layers of the earth of the crust, the mantle and the core. The crust forms what percentage of the volume of the earth?
A. 0.5% B. 2.5%
C. 7.5% D. 12.5%

81. The grassland of Argentina is known as :
A. Pampas B. Campos
C. Savanna D. None of the above

82. Different seasons are formed because :
A. Sun is moving around the earth
B. of revolution of the earth around the Sun on its orbit
C. of rotation of the earth around its axis
D. All of the above

83. Eskers and Drumlins are features formed by:
A. underground water
B. running water
C. the action of wind
D. glacial action

84. Match List-I and List-II and select the correct answer using the codes given below the Lists :

| List-I *(Rivers)* | List-II *(Towns)* |
|---|---|
| (*a*) Ghaghara | 1. Lucknow |
| (*b*) Brahmaputra | 2. Hoshangabad |
| (*c*) Narmada | 3. Ahmedabad |
| (*d*) Sabarmati | 4. Guwahati |
| | 5. Ayodhya |

| | (*a*) | (*b*) | (*c*) | (*d*) |
|---|---|---|---|---|
| A. | 4 | 5 | 1 | 2 |
| B. | 5 | 4 | 2 | 3 |
| C. | 5 | 4 | 3 | 1 |
| D. | 3 | 5 | 2 | 1 |

85. Which of the statements as regards the consequences of the movement of the earth is not correct?
A. Revolution of the earth is the cause of the change of seasons.
B. Rotation of the earth is the cause of days and nights.

C. Rotation of the earth causes variation in the duration of days and nights.
D. Rotation of the earth effects the movement of winds and ocean currents.

**86.** The world is divided into :
A. 12 time zones B. 20 time zones
C. 24 time zones D. 36 time zones

**87.** The 'Kiel' canal links the :
A. Pacific and Atlantic Oceans
B. Mediterranean Sea and Red Sea
C. Mediterranean Sea and Black Sea
D. North Sea and Baltic Sea

**88.** Match the following :

| List-I | List-II |
|---|---|
| (*a*) Himadri | 1. Outer Himalayas |
| (*b*) Shivalik | 2. Inner Himalayas |
| (*c*) Himanchal | 3. Middle Himalayas |
| (*d*) Sahyadri | 4. Western Ghats |

**Codes:**

| | (*a*) | (*b*) | (*c*) | (*d*) |
|---|---|---|---|---|
| A. | 1 | 2 | 3 | 4 |
| B. | 4 | 2 | 3 | 1 |
| C. | 2 | 1 | 3 | 4 |
| D. | 1 | 2 | 3 | 4 |

**89.** The term 'Regur' refers to:
A. Laterite soils
B. Black Cotton soils
C. Red Soils
D. Deltaic Alluvial Soils

**90.** Location of sugar industry in India is shifting from north to south because of:
A. cheap labour
B. expanding regional market
C. cheap and abundant supply of power
D. high yield and high sugar content in sugarcane

**91.** Consider the following statements :
1. Ozone is found mostly in the Stratosphere.
2. Ozone layer lies 55-75 km above the surface of the earth.
3. Ozone absorbs ultraviolet radiation from the Sun.
4. Ozone layer has no significance for life on the earth.

Which of the above statements are correct?
A. 1 and 3 B. 2 and 4
C. 2 and 3 D. 1 and 4

**92.** Match List-I with List-II and select the correct answer using the codes given below the Lists :

| List-I (*Crops*) | List-II (*Producer*) |
|---|---|
| (*a*) Banana | 1. Brazil |
| (*b*) Cocoa | 2. Cote d'Ivoire |
| (*c*) Coffee | 3. India |
| (*d*) Tea | 4. China |

**Codes :**

| | (*a*) | (*b*) | (*c*) | (*d*) |
|---|---|---|---|---|
| A. | 2 | 3 | 1 | 4 |
| B. | 3 | 2 | 1 | 4 |
| C. | 3 | 2 | 4 | 1 |
| D. | 2 | 3 | 4 | 1 |

**93.** Darjeeling and Dharamsala would be the right places to visit if one wanted to get a clear view respectively of :
A. Kanchanjunga and Dhauladhar ranges
B. Nandadevi and Dhauladhar ranges
C. Kanchanjunga and Nandadevi ranges
D. Nandadevi and Nanga Parvat

**94.** Atmosphere exists because:
A. The Gravitational force of the Earth
B. Revolution of the Earth
C. Rotation of the Earth
D. Weight of the gases of atmosphere

**95.** Victoria lake is located in the continent:
A. Africa
B. Asia
C. North America
D. South America

**96.** The famous Lagoon Lake of India is :
A. Dal Lake B. Chilka Lake
C. Pulicat Lake D. Mansarover

**97.** Where are most of the earth's active volcanoes concentrated?
A. Indian Ocean B. Pacific Ocean
C. Aral Sea D. Atlantic Ocean

**98.** Through which of the following states does the river Chambal flow?
A. U.P., M.P., Rajasthan
B. M.P., Gujarat, U.P.
C. Rajasthan, M.P., Bihar
D. Gujarat, M.P., U.P.

**99.** Which country is called the sugar bowl of the world?
A. Cuba B. India
C. Argentina D. USA

**100.** The area covered by forest in India is about:
A. 46% B. 33%
C. 21.71% D. 28%

**101.** A closed economy is the one which :
A. does not permit emigration or immigration
B. permits emigration but no immigration
C. engages in no foreign trade
D. engages in no foreign and domestic trade or transit

**102.** In a developed economy the major share of employment originates in the :
A. primary sector B. tertiary sector
C. secondary sector D. any of the above

**103.** The Economic and Social Commission for Asia and Pacific (ESCAP) is located at :
A. Bangkok B. Kuala Lumpur
C. Manila D. Singapore

**104.** Commercial vehicles are not produced by which of the following companies in India?
A. TELCO B. Ashok Leyland
C. DCM Daewoo D. Birla Yamaha

**105.** What is 'Stagflation'?
A. Inflation with growth
B. Deflation with growth
C. Inflation after deflations
D. Inflation with depression

**106.** The main argument advanced in favour of small scale and cottage industries in India is that:
A. cost of production is low
B. they require small capital investment
C. they advance the goal of equitable distribution of wealth
D. they generate a large volume of employment

**107.** The most serious economic problems of India are:
A. Poverty and unemployment
B. Stagnation, not poverty
C. Unemployment, not poverty
D. Underdevelopment, not poverty

**108.** Which of the following is not one of the three central problems of an economy?
A. What to produce
B. How to produce
C. When to produce
D. For whom to produce

**109.** Gender Responsive Budgeting has been adopted in India in the year:
A. 2017 B. 2004
C. 2014 D. 2005

**110.** In which of the following industries in India are the maximum number of workers employed?
A. Sugar B. Jute
C. Textiles D. Iron and Steel

**111.** Terrace Cultivation is practiced mostly:
A. in urban areas
B. on slopes of mountains
C. on tops of hills
D. in undulating tracts

**112.** Which of the following is a Selective Credit Control method?
A. Bank Rate
B. RBI directives
C. Cash Reserve Ratio
D. Open market operations

**113.** Which of the following taxes is not shared by the Central Government with the States?
A. Union excise duties
B. Customs duty
C. Income tax
D. Estate duty

**114.** ICICI is the name of a:
A. Financial Institution
B. Chemical Industry
C. Cotton Industry
D. Chamber of Commerce and Industry

**115.** Structural Unemployment arises due to
A. Deflationary conditions
B. Heavy industry bias
C. Shortage of raw material
D. Inadequate productive capacity

**116.** The rate at which RBI gives short-term loan to Commercial banks is called:
A. Reverse Repo Rate
B. Bank Rate
C. Repo Rate
D. Cash Reserve Rate

**117.** The largest public sector bank in India is:
A. Central Bank of India
B. Punjab National Bank
C. State Bank of India
D. Indian Overseas Bank

**118.** Which of the following statements best explains the term contraband goods?
A. Goods produced only for exports
B. Goods produced in joint sector only
C. Goods for the trading of which licence is not required
D. Goods that are forbidden, from export, import or even possession, by law

**119.** Price in the market is fixed by:
A. Stock exchange rates
B. The demand and supply ruling in the market at a particular time
C. The Finance Minister
D. None of the above

**120.** Devaluation of currency helps to promote:
A. National Income
B. Savings
C. Imports at lower cost
D. Exports

**121.** Balanced economic growth can be achieved only if:
A. All the sectors of economy grow at the same rate
B. Population growth is arrested
C. All the inter dependent sectors grow in harmony
D. Basic and heavy industries are assigned highest priority

**122.** 'Blue Revolution' is related to:
A. Fishries B. Poultry
C. Space Research D. Drinking Water

**123.** What is "hotline"?
A. A telecommunication link
B. An electric wire
C. Hard disk
D. Modem

**124.** Which of the following banks has launched 'No Q' App?
A. ICICI Bank B. SBI Bank
C. AXIS Bank D. None of the above

**125.** The term 'devaluation' means:
A. Reducing the value of a currency in terms of another currency
B. Increasing the value of a currency
C. Revising the value of a currency
D. None of the above

**126.** Per capita net availability of pulses has shown a tendency of:
A. Increase over time
B. Decrease over time
C. Constant over time
D. First increase then decrease

**127.** National Income is the same as:
A. Net national product at market price
B. Net domestic product at market price
C. Net national product at factor cost
D. Net domestic product at factor cost

**128.** Which one of the following is not an example of indirect tax?
A. Sales tax B. Excise duty
C. Customs duty D. Expenditure tax

**129.** The major aim of devaluation is to:
A. encourage imports
B. encourage exports
C. encourage both exports and imports
D. discourage both exports and imports

**130.** Structural unemployment arises due to:
A. deflationary conditions
B. heavy industry bias
C. shortage of raw materials
D. inadequate productive capacity

**131.** When was the Family Planning Programme officially started in India?
A. 1950 B. 1952
C. 1956 D. 1962

**132.** When was the Reserve Bank of India nationalised?
A. 1947 B. 1949
C. 1950 D. 1951

**133.** Which of the following is *not* a feature of the Indian economy?
A. High rate of population growth
B. Disguised unemployment
C. Lowest rate of adult literacy
D. High rate of exports

**134.** The 'Relative Deprivation' approach for measuring poverty has been adopted by:
A. developing countries
B. developed countries
C. under-developed countries
D. None of the above

**135.** One of the main factors that led to rapid expansion of Indian exports is:
A. Imposition of import duties
B. Liberalisation of the economy
C. Recession in other countries
D. Diversification of exports

**136.** Sustainable economic development means an increase in the rate of growth of real:
A. total and per capita product
B. total and per capita product and level of literacy rate
C. total and per capita product and life expectancy at birth
D. total and per capita product, taking into account the cost of degradation of the quality of environment in this process

**137.** Functional unemployment occurs when:
A. unemployed have no qualification for job
B. people frequently change their job
C. people were thrown out from job due to recession
D. None of these

**138.** Which among the following does **not** have a 'free trade zone'?
A. Kandla B. Mumbai
C. Visakhapatnam D. Thiruvanantpuram

**139.** Sun Belt of USA is important for which one of the following industries?
A. Cotton textile
B. Petrochemicals
C. Hi-tech electronics
D. Food Processing

**140.** Commercial banking system in India is
A. unit banking B. branch banking
C. mixed banking D. None of the above

**141.** Who gives recognition to political parties in India?
A. Parliament B. President
C. Supreme Court D. Election Commission

**142.** The Quorum of the Legislative Council is :
A. one-fourth of its total membership

B. one-third of its membership
C. one-tenth of its membership
D. 25

**143.** The Indian Constitution is:
A. federal
B. unitary
C. a happy mixture of the federal and unitary
D. federal in normal times and unitary in times of emergency

**144.** Universal adult franchise implies a right to vote to all:
A. adult residents of the State
B. adult male citizens of the State
C. residents of the State
D. adult citizens of the State

**145.** When a resolution prefering a charge against the President has been passed by a specified majority in the House, it is sent to the other House for investigation. If, as a result of such an investigation, a resolution is passed through a specified majority by the other House, declaring that the charge has been sustained, the President shall leave his office. The specified special majority must not be less than :
A. two-third of the members present and voting
B. one-third of the members present and voting
C. three-fourth of the members present and voting and two-third of the total membership
D. two-third of the total membership

**146.** Which one of the following judicial powers of the President of India has been *wrongly* listed?
A. he appoints the Chief Justice and other judges of the Supreme Court
B. he can remove the judges of the Supreme Court on grounds of misconduct
C. he can consult the Supreme Court on any question of law or fact which is of public importance
D. he can grant pardon, reprieves and respites to persons punished under Union Law

**147.** The Vice-president of India can be removed from his office before the expiry of his term if :
A. the Rajya Sabha passes a resolution by a majority of its members and the Lok Sabha agrees with the resolution
B. if the Supreme Court of India recommends his removal
C. the President so desires
D. None of the above

**148.** The Chief Justice of a High Court in India is appointed by the :
A. Governor of the State
B. Prime Minister of India
C. Chief Justice of the Supreme Court
D. President of India

**149.** Which of the following statements is constitu-tionally not true about the passing of the Union Budgets and Finance Bill in India?
1. Under the law, Finance Bill should be adopted by both the Houses of the Parliament within 45 days of its introduction.
2. If the Finance Bill is not adopted within specified period, the government loses its authority to levy the taxes proposed in the budgets.
3. In the absence of full budget, a vote-on-account gives the power to the government to spend.
4. Government cannot raise revenues without a proper approval of the Finance Bill

A. Only 2 B. Only 3
C. Only 4 D. Only 1, 2 and 3

**150.** Normally, on whose advice the President's Rule is imposed in a State?
A. Chief Minister
B. Legislative Assembly
C. Governor
D. Chief Justice of High Court

**151.** Which Article of the Indian Constitution deals with Amendment procedure?
A. Article 368 B. Article 358
C. Article 367 D. All of these

**152.** Government is the agency through which the will of :
A. the state is expressed
B. the people is expressed
C. the head of the state is expressed
D. the majority is expressed

**153.** In a unitary system of government :
A. The centre is all powerful
B. The centre is weaker than the states
C. The centre and states stand at par
D. The states and centre are supreme in their respective spheres

**154.** In Cabinet System of Government the real executive authority rests with :
A. The Council of Ministers
B. The Prime Minister
C. The Constitution
D. The Parliament

**155.** The Head of the State under a parliamentary government:
A. is an elected representative
B. is a hereditary person
C. is a nominated person
D. may be any one of the above

**156.** In the event of a ministerial proposal being defeated on the floor of the legislature, under the parliamentary system :
A. the government waits for a general no-confidence motion

B. the minister concerned is taken to task by the Prime Minister
C. the minister is forced to resign
D. the whole Council of Ministers resign

**157.** The "due process of law" is an essential characteristic of the judicial system of:
A. UK B. France
C. USA D. India

**158.** Under the Constitution it is :
A. obligatory for the President to accept the advice of the Council of Ministers but is not obliged to follow it
B. obligatory for the President to accept the advice of the Council of Ministers
C. not obligatory for the President to seek or accept the advice of the Council of Ministers
D. obligatory for the President to seek the advice of the Council of Ministers if his own party is in power

**159.** Which one of the following statements is correct?
A. the Presiding Officer of Rajya Sabha is elected every year
B. the Presiding Officer of Rajya Sabha is elected for a term of two years at a time
C. the Presiding Officer of Rajya Sabha is elected for a term of six years
D. the Vice-President of India is the ex-officio Presiding Officer of Rajya Sabha

**160.** The introduction of "no confidence" motion in the Lok Sabha requires the support of at least:
A. 50 members B. 70 members
C. 60 members D. 80 members

**161.** The High Court comes under :
A. State List B. Union List
C. Concurrent List D. None of the above

**162.** Which one of the following has been wrongly listed as a Fundamental Duty of the Indian citizens?
A. to develop scientific temper, humanism and spirit of inquiry and reform
B. to work for raising the prestige of the country in the international sphere
C. to protect and improve the natural environment
D. to strive towards excellence in all spheres of individual and collective activity

**163.** Which one of the following is not a Fundamental Duty as outlined in Article 51A of the Constitution?
A. to abide by the Constitution and respect its ideals
B. to defend the country and render national service when called upon to do so
C. to work for the moral upliftment of the weaker sections of society
D. to preserve the rich heritage

**164.** The main characteristics of the Directive Principles of State Policy given in the Indian Constitution are :
A. not enforceable by any court
B. fundamental in the governance of the country
C. 'Like instruments, instructions, political manifesto and a code of moral precepts which have to guide governors of the country'
D. no law can be passed, which is opposed to these principles

**165.** Of the following which are true?
A. In a State, the Legislative Council is dominant with regard to non-financial bills and the Legislative Assembly with regard to financial (money) bills
B. Vidhan Parishad can virtually block legisla-tion even if the same is passed by the Vidhan Sabha
C. In case of a tie between the two Houses, the Governor is duty-bound to call a joint session of the two Houses to have the issue settled on a majority verdict
D. If a Bill is twice approved by the Vidhan Sabha, it becomes law even if rejected by the Vidhan Parishad

**166.** Which one of the following types of emergency can be declared by the President?
A. Emergency due to threat of war and external aggresion
B. Emergency due to break-down of constitu-tional machinery in a State
C. Financial emergency on account of threat to the financial credit of India
D. all the three emergencies

**167.** The chairman of which of the following parliamentary committees is invariably from the members of ruling party?
A. Committee on public undertakings
B. Public accounts committee
C. Estimates committee
D. Committee on delegated legislation

**168.** Which of the following is not a formally prescribed device available to the members of parliament?
A. Question hour
B. Zero hour
C. Half-an-hour discussion
D. Short duration discussion

**169.** Which of the following is not a tool of executive control over public administration?
A. Power of appointment and removal
B. Line agencies
C. Appeal to public opinion
D. Civil services code

**170.** If the Speaker of the State Legislative Assembly decides to resign, he should submit his resignation to the:
A. Judges of the High Court
B. Deputy Speaker
C. Chief Minister
D. Finance Minister

**171.** Which tax can be levied by Gram Panchayat?
A. Sales Tax
B. Custom Duty
C. Land Revenue
D. Tax on Local Fairs

**172.** India is a Federal State because of:
A. dual judiciary
B. dual citizenship prevalent here
C. share of power between the Centre and the States
D. rigid Constitution

**173.** Residuary Subjects are those subjects which are:
A. contained in the State list
B. contained in the Union list
C. contained in the Concurrent list
D. not covered by any of the three lists

**174.** Which of the following writs can be issued, by the Supreme Court, to enforce Fundamental Rights?
A. Writ of Habeas Corpus
B. Writ of Mandamus
C. Writ of Quo Warranto
D. All of these

**175.** When the offices of both the President and the Vice-President of India are vacant, who will discharge their functions?
A. Prime Minister
B. Home Minister
C. Chief Justice of India
D. The Speaker

**176.** The Supreme Court tenders advice to the President of India on a matter of law or fact:
A. on its own
B. only when such advice is sought
C. only if the matter relates to some basic issue
D. only if the issue poses a threat to the unity and integrity of the country

**177.** Six months shall **not** intervene between two sessions of the Indian Parliament because :
A. it is the customary practice
B. it is the British convention followed in India
C. it is an obligation under the Constitution of India
D. None of the above

**178.** The States of the Indian Union can be recognised or their boundaries altered by:
A. the Union Parliament by a simple majority in the ordinary process of legislation
B. two-thirds majority of both the Houses of Parliament
C. two-thirds majority of both the Houses of Parliament and the consent of the legisla-tures of concerned States
D. an executive order of the Union government with the consent of the concerned State governments

**179.** The Basic Feature theory of the Constitution of India was propounded by the Supreme Court in the case of :
A. Minerva Mills Vs. Union of India
B. Golaknath Vs. State of Punjab
C. Maneka Gandhi Vs. Union of India
D. Keshavananda Vs. State of Kerala

**180.** Which one of the following writs is issued by a court in case of illegal detention of a person?
A. Habeas corpus B. Mandamus
C. Certiorari D. Quo-warranto

**181.** Name the instrument with the help of which a sailor in a submarine can see the objects on the surface of the sea.
A. Telescope B. Periscope
C. Gycroscope D. Stereoscope

**182.** 'HEMOPHILLIA' is the disease of ...........
A. liver B. blood
C. brain D. bones

**183.** Vitamin A is abundantly found in ...........
A. Brinjal B. Tomato
C. Carrot D. Cabbage

**184.** ........... is not soluble in water.
A. Vitamin A B. Vitamin B
C. Vitamin C D. None of these

**185.** The blood vessels with the smallest diameter are called ...........
A. capillaries B. arterioles
C. venules D. lymphatics

**186.** Out of the following ........... has the greatest elasticity.
A. steel B. rubber
C. aluminium D. annealed copper

**187.** Cooking gas is a mixture of which of the following two gases?
A. Carbon Dioxide and Oxygen
B. Butane and Propane
C. Carbon Monoxide and Carbon Dioxide
D. Methane and Ethylene

**188.** The substance most commonly used as a food preservative is:
A. sodium carbonate B. tartaric acid
C. acetic acid D. benzoic acid

**189.** Normally, the substances that fight against diseases in human systems are known as:
A. dioxyribonucleic acids
B. carbohydrates
C. enzymes
D. antibodies

**190.** The SI unit of temperature is ...........
A. Kelvin B. Celsius
C. Fahrenheit D. None of the above

**191.** One of the common fungal diseases of man is :
A. plague B. ringworm
C. cholera D. typhoid

**192.** A clear sky is blue because:
A. red light is scattered more than blue
B. ultraviolet light has been absorbed
C. blue light is scattered more than red
D. blue light has been absorbed

**193.** Jenner introduced the method of making people immune to :
A. small pox B. rabies
C. cholera D. polio

**194.** The largest cell in the human body is :
A. Nerve cell B. Live cell
C. Muscle cell D. Kidney cell

**195.** What is the device that steps up or steps down the voltage?
A. Dynamo B. Conductor
C. Inductor D. Transformer

**196.** The protein deficiency disease is known as :
A. Kwashiorker B. Cirrhosis
C. Eczema D. Clycoses

**197.** Iron deficiency causes :
A. rickets B. anaemia
C. cirrhosis D. goitre

**198.** Blood group of an individual is controlled by :
A. Haemoglobin B. Shape of RBC
C. Shape of WBC D. Genes

**199.** In a normal man the amount of blood pumped out by the heart per minute is about :
A. 1 litre B. 3 litres
C. 4 litres D. 5 litres

**200.** Red/green colour blindness in man is known as :
A. Protanopia
B. Deutetanopia
C. Both A and B above
D. Marfan's syndrome

**201.** The blue colour of the water in the sea is due to :
A. Reflection of the blue light by the impurities in sea water
B. Reflection of the blue sky by sea water and scattering of blue light by water molecules
C. Absorption of other colours by water molecules
D. None of the above

**202.** The image formed on the retina of the eye is:
A. upright and real
B. larger than the object
C. small and inverted
D. enlarged and real

**203.** Unit of loudness of sound is:
A. bel B. decibel
C. phon D. none of these

**204.** Oil rises up the wick in a lamp :
A. because oil is volatile
B. due to the capillary action phenomenon
C. due to the surface tension phenomenon
D. because oil is very light

**205.** The 'stones' formed in human kidney consist mostly of :
A. calcium oxalate
B. sodium acetate
C. magnesium sulphate
D. calcium

**206.** We hear the sound later, while the light is seen earlier:
A. because light's speed is more than that of sound
B. because lights travel in a straight direction while sound in a zigzag direction
C. because sound's frequency is lower than light
D. All of the above

**207.** Which part of an eye is transplanted?
A. Cornea B. Retina
C. Iris D. Sciera

**208.** The Universal donor group of blood is:
A. O B. A
C. B D. AB

**209.** The green colour of the leaf is due to :
A. Presence of Chloroplast
B. Presence of Chromium
C. Presence of Nicoplast
D. Presence of excess of oxygen

**210.** Voice of a child is more shrill than that of an elderly person because:
A. the pitch of the child's voice is higher than that of the person
B. the pitch is lower
C. the child is more energetic
D. None of the above

**211.** Camel uses its hump for :
A. storing water
B. storing fat
C. for balancing the body
D. temperature regulation

**212.** A man standing in a free falling lift releases a ball from his hand. The ball would be :
A. moving down
B. moving up
C. stationary
D. moving up and down

**213.** To change the quality of sound produced by an instrument we need to vary the:
A. pitch B. loudness
C. amplitude D. number of overtonnes

**214.** The disease caused by Asbestos is:
A. Emphysema B. Paralysis
C. Diarrhoea D. Dysentery

**215.** Sweetness of a sound depends upon its
A. wavelength
B. frequency
C. amplitude
D. periodicity and regularity

**216.** Bats can fly in the dark because :
A. they have a better vision in the dark
B. the pupils of their eyes are very big
C. they are guided by ultrasonic waves produced by them
D. any bird can do so

**217.** Blood is formed in the human adult by the :
A. heart B. spleen
C. kidney D. bone marrow

**218.** Pencil 'lead' is made up of:
A. graphite B. charcoal
C. lead oxide D. lampblack

**219.** The deficiency of which one of the following vitamins leads to bleeding of gums and loosening of teeth?
A. Vitamin D B. Vitamin C
C. Vitamin B D. Vitamin A

**220.** How much blood does a normal person have in his body?
A. 8 litres B. 4 to 5 litres
C. 10 litres D. 2 litres

**221.** Match List-I with List-II and select the correct answer using the codes given below the Lists :

| List-I | List-II |
|---|---|
| (*a*) Visakhadatta | 1. Mrichhakatika |
| (*b*) Shudraka | 2. Ritusamhara |
| (*c*) Kalidasa | 3. Kamasutra |
| (*d*) Vatsyayana | 4. Devichandraguptam |

**Codes :**

| | (*a*) | (*b*) | (*c*) | (*d*) |
|---|---|---|---|---|
| A. | 1 | 4 | 2 | 3 |
| B. | 4 | 1 | 3 | 2 |
| C. | 1 | 4 | 3 | 2 |
| D. | 4 | 1 | 2 | 3 |

**222.** In which one of the following langauges is the *Dalit* writing more conspicuous?
A. Punjabi B. Assamese
C. Marathi D. Odiya

**223.** The first writer to use Urdu as the medium of poetic expression was:
A. Amir Khusrau
B. Mirza Ghalib
C. Bahadur Shah Zafar
D. Faiz

**224.** The religious text of the Zoroastrians is named as:
A. Torah B. The Analects
C. Tripatika D. Zend Avesta

**225.** Name the music duo which composed music for Raj Kapoor's film 'Bobby'?
A. Laxmikant Pyarelal B. Shankar Jaikishen
C. Kalyanji Anandji D. Nadeem Shravan

**226.** Raja Harishchandra, an early Indian film, was produced by :
A. D.G. Phalke B. Ashok Kumar
C. Ardeshir Irani D. None of the above

**227.** All films are certified by ........ before they are publicly exhibited.
A. Films Division
B. National Film Development Corporation (NFDC)
C. Directorate of Advertising and Visual Publicity (DAVP)
D. Central Board of Film Certificate (CBFC)

**228.** Who among the following was the director of the film 'Taal'?
A. Gulzar B. Shekhar Kapoor
C. Satish Shah D. Subhash Ghai

**229.** Who amongst the following actresses has played the leading role in the film Elizabeth?
A. Gwyneth Paltrow B. Cate Blanchett
C. Simi Garewal D. Kim Basinger

**230.** The film 'Train to Pakistan' is based on the novel of the same name, written by:
A. Bhishma Sahani
B. Khushwant Singh
C. Amrita Pritam
D. Khwaja Ahmed Abbas

**231.** Which of the following is a folk dance form of Jharkhand?
A. Pali B. Jhumar
C. Nati D. Chhau

**232.** The first feature film (talkie) to be produced in India was:
A. Hatimtai B. Alam Ara
C. Pundalik D. Raja Harishchandra

**233.** Who directed the film "Bombay"?
A. Shyam Benegal B. Meera Nair
C. Shekhar Kapoor D. Mani Ratnam

**234.** Late Pankaj Udhas was famous in which of the following fields?
A. Singing B. Acting
C. Music D. Literature

**235.** Who among the following is the director of the film 'The Kashmir Files'?
A. Subhash Ghai B. Shekhar Kapoor
C. Ramesh Sippy D. Vivek Agnihotri

**236.** The character played by Jim Carrey in the movie *Man on Moon* is based on:
A. Andy Kaufman B. Edwin Aldrin
C. John Glenn D. Neil Armstrong

**237.** A popular Hindi film-based on the famous Sanskrit play *Mrichhakatika*, was titled:
A. Meghadoot B. Amrapali
C. Utsav D. Shakuntala

**238.** Who composed the song 'Zara Yad Karo Kurbani'?
A. Javed Akhtar
B. Pradeep
C. Nusrat Fateh Ali Khan
D. Raghupati Sahay 'Firaq'

**239.** Who was the producer of the serial 'Mahabharat'?
A. Shyam Benegal B. B.R. Chopra
C. Ramanand Sagar D. Mani Ratnam

**240.** Which of the following is a folk dance of Rajasthan?
A. Garba B. Dandya
C. Jhumar D. Kathak

**241.** 'The Colonel' is the nickname of which Indian Test Cricketer?
A. Colonel C.K. Naidu
B. Rahul Dravid
C. Mohinder Amarnath
D. Dilip Vengsarkar

**242.** The term 'Grandmaster' is used in which of these games?
A. Judo B. Chess
C. Bridge D. Karate

**243.** The term "Derby" is related with which of the following?
A. Polo B. Swimming
C. Racing D. Horse Racing

**244.** With which game is Geet Sethi associated?
A. Basketball B. Chess
C. Snooker D. Tennis

**245.** Beighton Cup is related with which of the following?
A. Hockey B. Polo
C. Cricket D. Soccer

**246.** Match List-I with List-II and select the correct answer using the codes given below the Lists :

| List-I | List-II |
|---|---|
| (a) Basketball | 1. Lob |
| (b) Bridge | 2. Revoke |
| (c) Golf | 3. Pivot |
| (d) Tennis | 4. Bunker |

**Codes :**

| | (a) | (b) | (c) | (d) |
|---|---|---|---|---|
| A. | 2 | 3 | 1 | 4 |
| B. | 2 | 3 | 4 | 1 |
| C. | 3 | 2 | 1 | 4 |
| D. | 3 | 2 | 4 | 1 |

**247.** The head office of the International Cricket Council (ICC) is situated in :
A. Zimbabwe B. Australia
C. South Africa D. UAE

**248.** Match the following :

| List-I | List-II |
|---|---|
| (a) Deodhar Trophy | 1. Volleyball |
| (b) Durand Cup | 2. Football |
| (c) Davis Cup | 3. Cricket |
| | 4. Tennis |

**Codes:**

| | (a) | (b) | (c) |
|---|---|---|---|
| A. | 3 | 2 | 4 |
| B. | 3 | 1 | 4 |
| C. | 2 | 3 | 1 |
| D. | 1 | 2 | 4 |

**249.** Which of the following is called 'Grand Slam'?
A. Winning the highest number of medals in the Olympic games
B. Winning the men's singles title in Wimbledon Championship
C. Winning the Wimbledon Singles title successively for two years
D. Winning all the four championships Australian, French, Wimblendon and US

**250.** With which game is the term 'butterfly stroke' associated?
A. Swimming B. Cricket
C. Gliding D. Skiing

**251.** Who is the first Indian to win the 'International Grand Master' title in Chess?
A. Anupama Abhayankar
B. Bhagyashree Sathe Thipsay
C. Vishwanathan Anand
D. D.V. Prasad

**252.** The XXII Commonwealth Games were held in 2022 in :
A. Kuala Lumpur B. Bangkok
C. Victoria D. Birmingham

**253.** The term 'Tee' is associated with which of the following sports?
A. Golf B. Table Tennis
C. Polo D. Judo

**254.** The famous woman Tennis player who was stabbed during a match, is
A. Steffi Graf B. Monica Seles
C. Mary Pierce D. Martina Navratilova

**255.** The term 'Baseline' is related to which of the following?
A. Golf B. Hockey
C. Badminton D. Polo

**256.** In which Indian State did the game of Polo originate?
A. Manipur B. Rajasthan
C. Gujarat D. West Bengal

**257.** Viswanathan Anand is associated with which sport?
A. Tennis B. Badminton
C. Chess D. Mountaineering

**258.** Rafael Nadal is the well-known player associated with:
A. Hockey B. Cricket
C. Tennis D. Chess

**259.** Neeraj Chopra is the well-known player associated with :
A. Javelin Throw B. Golf
C. Table Tennis D. Chess

**260.** Eden Garden, a famous Cricket stadium, is located in :
A. Kanpur B. Kolkata
C. Jamshedpur D. Pune

**261.** Maharaja Ranjit Singh Trophy is associated with :
A. Golf B. Hockey
C. Soccer D. Tennis

**262.** Jaspal Rana is a distinguished athlete in which of the following games?
A. Swimming B. Weightlifting
C. Shooting D. Archery

**263.** Cricket was an Olympic event at which of the following Olympics?
A. London, 1908 B. Amsterdam, 1928
C. Paris, 1900 D. Melbourne, 1956

**264.** WISPA competitions are associated with :
A. Squash B. Yatching
C. Boxing D. Billiards

**265.** Ryder Cup is the famous trophy of :
A. Golf B. Chess
C. Boxing D. Polo

**266.** Davis Cup is associated with the sport of :
A. Cricket B. Football
C. Tennis D. Hockey

**267.** 'Volley', 'Chop' and 'Drive Spine' are the term associated with :
A. Lawn Tennis B. Badminton
C. Table Tennis D. Golf

**268.** Lal Bahadur Shastri Stadium is located at :
A. Hyderabad B. Chennai
C. Ahmedabad D. Varanasi

**269.** The first winner of "Rajiv Gandhi Khel Ratna Award" (Now Major Dhyanchand Khel Ratna Award) was :
A. Geet Sethi
B. Sachin Tendulkar
C. Viswanathan Anand
D. Karnam Malleswari

**270.** The winner of 2023 Cricket World Cup is:
A. Australia B. Sri Lanka
C. India D. England

**271.** The first team event introduced in 1900 at Paris Olympics was :
A. Hockey B. Football
C. Cricket D. Baseball

**272.** Which of the following international tennis tournaments is held on grass court?
A. US Open B. French Open
C. Wimbledon D. Australian Open

**273.** Which cricketer is nicknamed as the pied piper of Punjab?
A. Yuvraj Singh
B. Harbhajan Singh
C. Mohinder Amarnath
D. Navjot Singh Sidhu

**274.** 'Merdeka Cup' is associated with ..........
A. Golf B. Football
C. Squash D. Hockey

**275.** The first time athletes marched into the stadium behind their nation's flag in Olympics:
A. at St. Louis 1904 B. at London 1908
C. at Antwerp 1920 D. at Paris 1924

**276.** The "Dronacharya Award" is associated with:
A. Eminent Surgeons B. Famous Sports Person
C. Sport Coaches D. Expert Engineers

**277.** Which cricketer is nicknamed as 'Jumbo'?
A. Venkatesh Prasad B. Anil Kumble
C. Glenn McGrath D. Shane Warne

**278.** The first time the Olympic Games were organised by a private company at:
A. Montreal, 1976 B. Los Angeles, 1984
C. Atlanta, 1996 D. Rome, 1960

**279.** In which Asian Games Cricket was played first?
A. Guangzhou, 2010 B. Doha, 2006
C. Busan, 2002 D. Seoul, 1986

**280.** The term 'Penalty cick' is used in :
A. Hockey B. Football
C. Baseball D. Golf

**281.** Which of the following countries is not a member of North Atlantic Treaty Organisation (NATO)?
A. Norway B. United Germany
C. Portugal D. Australia

**282.** Khmer Rouge is a dictatorial party of :
A. Cambodia B. Indonesia
C. Malaysia D. Thailand

**283.** Which country is not a member of SAARC?
A. Russia B. Bangladesh
C. Nepal D. Pakistan

**284.** The headquarters of WTO is located at :
A. Geneva B. Paris
C. The Hague D. Washington

**285.** The main function of the World Trade Organisation (WTO) is:
A. enforcing of Uruguay Round Agreements

B. facilitating multi-lateral trade relations of member countries and reviewing trade policies
C. administering trade dispute settlement procedures
D. None of the above

**286.** The Secretary-General of the UNO is appointed by the:
A. General Assembly
B. Security Council
C. Trusteeship Council
D. World Bank

**287.** The United Nations officially came into existence in 1945 on :
A. November 24 B. October 14
C. October 24 D. November 14

**288.** Which one of the following is true of the International Court of Justice?
A. The Judges of the Court are appointed according to the discretion of the Secretary General
B. No two Judges may belong to the same country
C. The Court consists of 20 Judges
D. The statute of the International Court of Justice is not an integral part of the UN Charter

**289.** Which of the following was not among the six founding countries of the European Community?
A. Belgium B. France
C. Germany D. UK

**290.** The smallest country in South America is:
A. Ecuador B. Guyana
C. Surinam D. Uruguay

**291.** In which year "Human Rights Resolution" was adopted by the U.N.?
A. 1945 B. 1946
C. 1947 D. 1948

**292.** Where is the headquarters of INTERPOL located?
A. Berlin B. California
C. Lyons D. Montreal

**293.** Parliament of which of the following countries is known as Great People's Khural?
A. Malaysia B. Mongolia
C. Thailand D. Indonesia

**294.** Numbers of major organs of United Nations are:
A. 3 B. 4
C. 5 D. 6

**295.** When is the UN Day celebrated?
A. October 24 B. January 24
C. June 24 D. September 24

**296.** Which one of the following organ of United Nations is known as the 'Policeman of the World'?
A. Security Council
B. International Court of Justice
C. The Secretariat
D. General Assembly

**297.** The members of the NAFTA include:
A. USA, Canada and Mexico
B. USA, Canada, Mexico and UK
C. USA, UK, Russia and Mexico
D. USA, Canada and Brazil

**298.** The sits of International Court of Justice is located at :
A. Vienna B. Paris
C. Hague D. New York

**299.** Which of the following is known as the Constitution of the UN?
A. UN Charter
B. UN Assembly
C. UN Security Council
D. UN Secretariat

**300.** The Headquarters of the Amnesty International is located at :
A. New York B. London
C. Geneva D. Addis-Ababa

**301.** Who is the author of the book 'PRISON DIARY'?
A. Bal Gangadhar Tilak
B. Rajendra Prasad
C. Jai Prakash Narayan
D. Jawahar Lal Nehru

**302.** Who is the author of 'Satanic Verses'?
A. Lewis Carrol B. Salman Rushdie
C. Parry Mason D. Mulk Raj Anand

**303.** Who wrote 'Gitanjali'?
A. Kalidas
B. Gopal Das 'Neeraj'
C. Rabindra Nath Tagore
D. Jawahar Lal Nehru

**304.** Who, among the following, scholars flourishing during the Gupta Age, was the author of *Dasakumara-Charita?*
A. Asanga B. Dignaga
C. Dandina D. Bhattin

**305.** The author of *Gitagovinda* was:
A. Halayudha B. Jayadeva
C. Kalhana D. Jona-raja

**306.** "Ingenious Pain" is a book/novel written by:
A. Andrew Miller B. Santa Monica
C. Ben Johnson D. Bill Gates

**307.** Who amongst the following is the author of the famous book "An Equal Music"?
A. Salman Rushdie B. Shasthivrata
C. Vikram Seth D. Kamla Markandeya

**308.** The famous Moorti Devi Award is given for excellence in which of the following fields?
A. Medicine
B. Science & Technology
C. Social Service
D. Literature

309. Who has written "Devdas"?
A. Tarasankar Bandyopadhyay
B. Bankim Chandra Chattopadhyay
C. Rabindranath Tagore
D. Sarat Chandra Chattopadhyay

310. "Ain-i-Akbari" is written by:
A. Todar Mal B. Abul Fazal
C. Sheikh Saadi D. Mirza Ghalib

311. "Alice in Wonderland" is written by :
A. Lewis Carrol B. Chester Bowles
C. Charles Dickens D. Jonathan Swift

312. "Mrichchhakatikam" is written by :
A. Vishakhadatta B. Vatsyayana
C. Sudraka D. Bana Bhatt

313. "My Experiments with Truth" is written by :
A. Jawaharlal Nehru
B. M.K. Gandhi
C. Abul Kalam Azad
D. Rajendra Prasad

314. Who wrote the book "India Wins Freedom"?
A. Maulana Abul Kalam Azad
B. Mahatma Gandhi
C. Sir Mohammad Iqbal
D. Abdul Gaffar Khan

315. Match List-I with List-II and select the correct answer using the codes given below the Lists :

| List-I | List-II |
|---|---|
| (a) *Emma* | 1. Graham Greene |
| (b) *Mother India* | 2. E.M. Forster |
| (c) *Human Factor* | 3. Jane Austen |
| (d) *Passage to India* | 4. Katherine Mayo |

**Codes :**

| | (a) | (b) | (c) | (d) |
|---|---|---|---|---|
| A. | 2 | 1 | 4 | 3 |
| B. | 3 | 4 | 1 | 2 |
| C. | 3 | 1 | 2 | 4 |
| D. | 4 | 2 | 1 | 3 |

316. 'Poverty and Un British Rule in India' is written by:
A. R.C. Dutt B. J.L. Nehru
C. D.B. Naoroji D. S.N. Sen

317. Name the author of the book *A Passage to England.*
A. E.M. Forster
B. Nirad C. Choudhuri
C. Vikram Seth
D. Eric Segal

318. The author of the book 'The Struggle in My Life' is:
A. Mandela B. J.L. Nehru
C. Tilak D. Gokhale

319. The Shanti Swarup Bhatnagar Award is given by which of the following organisations?
A. Council for Scientific and Industrial Research
B. Indian Council for Agricultural Research
C. Indian National Science Academy
D. Indian Space Research Organisation

320. Which of the following books is not written by Salman Rushdie?
A. The Satanic Verses
B. Shame
C. Naked Face
D. Midnight's Children

321. The different schools of modern socialism derive their strength primarily from the writings of ..........?
A. Joseph Stalin B. Leo Tolstoy
C. Mao Tse-tung D. Karl Marx

322. Baba Amte is famous as a ..........
A. Painter B. Singer
C. Politician D. Social Worker

323. Central Government says that ............ was received well by citizens as 'imandari ka utsav'.
A. Demonetization
B. Goods and Services Tax
C. E-NAM
D. All of the above

324. Mr. Yehudi Menuhin, was a famous:
A. Sitarist B. Cartoonist
C. Journalist D. Violinist

325. Sundarlal Bahuguna, a famous environ-mentalist, is associated with :
A. Chipko Movement
B. Narmada Bachao Andolan
C. Satyagraha Movement
D. Anti-corruption Movement

326. Mother Teressa's native place was :
A. Albania B. France
C. Greece D. Italy

327. The live polio vaccine which can be taken by mouth was developed by :
A. Albert Sabin B. Edward Jenner
C. Jonas Salk D. Selman Waksman

328. Which one of the following authors put forth the theory of the Drain of India's resources to England?
A. Raja Rammohan Roy
B. Bankim Chandra Chatterjee
C. G.G. Agarkar
D. Dadabhai Naoroji

329. The "Last Supper" is a famous renaissance painting. It was a masterpiece of :
A. Michael Angelo B. Leonardo da Vinci
C. Titian D. Raphael

**330.** Dhyanchand is associated with which sports?
A. Badminton B. Hockey
C. Tennis D. Football

**331.** 'Man is born free, yet every where he is in chains'. This was said by:
A. Voltaire B. John Stuart Mill
C. Rousseau D. Karl Marx

**332.** Who among the following was a prominent social reformer?
A. Baba Gurmukh Singh
B. Raja Mahendra Pratap
C. Bipin Chandra Pal
D. Jotiba Govind Phule

**333.** Whose real name was Gadadhar Chhattopa-dhyaya?
A. Swami Vivekanand
B. Ram Krishna Paramhansa
C. Dayanand Saraswai
D. Raja Ram Mohan Rai

**334.** Who was known as "Man of Destiny"?
A. Napoleon B. Nehru
C. Hitler D. Mussolini

**335.** Who discovered that mosquito served as a carrier of malaria?
A. Jonas Salk B. Ronald Ross
C. Louis Pasteur D. Robert Koch

**336.** Who was the first woman Governor of an Indian State?
A. Sushila Nayar
B. Sucheta Kripalani
C. Sarojini Naidu
D. Sulochana Modi

**337.** Who among the following founded the Bhartiya Jana Sangh?
A. Deen Dayal Upadhyaya
B. Veer Savarkar
C. Dr. Ram Manohar Lohia
D. Dr. Shyama Prasad Mukherjee

**338.** Who among the following President of India held his office for two successive terms?
A. V.V. Giri
B. Dr. Rajendra Prasad
C. Dr. S. Radhakrishnan
D. None of these

**339.** Ustad Amjad Ali Khan is an exponent of:
A. Flute B. Sitar
C. Sarod D. Tabla

**340.** Who is the first non-Indian to receive the Bharat Ratna?
A. Martin Luther King
B. Zubin Mehta
C. Mother Teressa
D. Khan Abdul Ghaffar Khan

## ANSWERS

| 1 | 2 | 3 | 4 | 5 | 6 | 7 | 8 | 9 | 10 |
|---|---|---|---|---|---|---|---|---|---|
| B | C | D | C | B | C | A | C | C | D |
| **11** | **12** | **13** | **14** | **15** | **16** | **17** | **18** | **19** | **20** |
| C | A | C | A | A | D | A | B | A | D |
| **21** | **22** | **23** | **24** | **25** | **26** | **27** | **28** | **29** | **30** |
| A | C | B | C | D | C | B | D | D | B |
| **31** | **32** | **33** | **34** | **35** | **36** | **37** | **38** | **39** | **40** |
| C | D | C | C | B | C | D | B | C | C |
| **41** | **42** | **43** | **44** | **45** | **46** | **47** | **48** | **49** | **50** |
| A | A | A | B | C | D | C | B | B | D |
| **51** | **52** | **53** | **54** | **55** | **56** | **57** | **58** | **59** | **60** |
| A | C | A | B | B | A | B | C | A | C |
| **61** | **62** | **63** | **64** | **65** | **66** | **67** | **68** | **69** | **70** |
| C | C | B | B | C | C | D | D | D | B |
| **71** | **72** | **73** | **74** | **75** | **76** | **77** | **78** | **79** | **80** |
| B | C | C | C | A | A | A | B | B | A |
| **81** | **82** | **83** | **84** | **85** | **86** | **87** | **88** | **89** | **90** |
| A | B | D | B | C | C | D | C | B | D |
| **91** | **92** | **93** | **94** | **95** | **96** | **97** | **98** | **99** | **100** |
| A | B | A | A | A | B | B | A | A | C |
| **101** | **102** | **103** | **104** | **105** | **106** | **107** | **108** | **109** | **110** |
| C | B | A | D | D | D | A | C | D | C |

| 111 | 112 | 113 | 114 | 115 | 116 | 117 | 118 | 119 | 120 |
|---|---|---|---|---|---|---|---|---|---|
| B | B | B | A | D | C | C | D | B | D |
| 121 | 122 | 123 | 124 | 125 | 126 | 127 | 128 | 129 | 130 |
| C | A | A | B | A | D | C | D | B | D |
| 131 | 132 | 133 | 134 | 135 | 136 | 137 | 138 | 139 | 140 |
| B | B | D | A | B | D | B | D | D | C |
| 141 | 142 | 143 | 144 | 145 | 146 | 147 | 148 | 149 | 150 |
| D | C | D | D | D | B | A | D | C | C |
| 151 | 152 | 153 | 154 | 155 | 156 | 157 | 158 | 159 | 160 |
| A | B | A | A | A | D | C | B | D | A |
| 161 | 162 | 163 | 164 | 165 | 166 | 167 | 168 | 169 | 170 |
| B | B | C | B | D | D | C | B | B | B |
| 171 | 172 | 173 | 174 | 175 | 176 | 177 | 178 | 179 | 180 |
| D | C | D | D | C | B | C | A | D | A |
| 181 | 182 | 183 | 184 | 185 | 186 | 187 | 188 | 189 | 190 |
| B | B | C | A | A | A | B | D | D | A |
| 191 | 192 | 193 | 194 | 195 | 196 | 197 | 198 | 199 | 200 |
| B | C | A | A | D | A | B | D | D | A |
| 201 | 202 | 203 | 204 | 205 | 206 | 207 | 208 | 209 | 210 |
| B | B | B | B | A | A | A | A | A | A |
| 211 | 212 | 213 | 214 | 215 | 216 | 217 | 218 | 219 | 220 |
| B | A | A | A | D | C | D | A | B | B |
| 221 | 222 | 223 | 224 | 225 | 226 | 227 | 228 | 229 | 230 |
| D | C | A | D | A | A | D | D | B | B |
| 231 | 232 | 233 | 234 | 235 | 236 | 237 | 238 | 239 | 240 |
| D | B | D | A | D | D | C | B | B | C |
| 241 | 242 | 243 | 244 | 245 | 246 | 247 | 248 | 249 | 250 |
| D | B | D | C | A | D | D | A | D | A |
| 251 | 252 | 253 | 254 | 255 | 256 | 257 | 258 | 259 | 260 |
| C | D | A | B | C | A | C | C | A | B |
| 261 | 262 | 263 | 264 | 265 | 266 | 267 | 268 | 269 | 270 |
| B | C | C | A | A | C | C | A | C | A |
| 271 | 272 | 273 | 274 | 275 | 276 | 277 | 278 | 279 | 280 |
| B | C | A | B | A | C | B | B | A | B |
| 281 | 282 | 283 | 284 | 285 | 286 | 287 | 288 | 289 | 290 |
| D | A | A | A | B | A | C | B | D | C |
| 291 | 292 | 293 | 294 | 295 | 296 | 297 | 298 | 299 | 300 |
| D | C | B | D | A | A | A | C | A | B |
| 301 | 302 | 303 | 304 | 305 | 306 | 307 | 308 | 309 | 310 |
| C | B | C | C | B | A | C | D | D | B |
| 311 | 312 | 313 | 314 | 315 | 316 | 317 | 318 | 319 | 320 |
| A | C | B | A | B | C | B | A | A | C |
| 321 | 322 | 323 | 324 | 325 | 326 | 327 | 328 | 329 | 330 |
| D | D | A | D | A | A | C | D | B | B |
| 331 | 332 | 333 | 334 | 335 | 336 | 337 | 338 | 339 | 340 |
| C | D | B | A | B | C | D | B | C | D |

□□□

# CURRENT AFFAIRS

1. Who is the first Indian to receive an honorary Knighthood under King Charles III?
   A. Ratan Tata B. Sachin Tendulkar
   C. Sunil Bharti Mittal D. Narendra Modi
2. What is the name of India's first human spaceflight program?
   A. Chandrayaan B. Aditya-1
   C. Gaganyaan D. LVM3
3. What is the literal meaning of the word "Gaganyaan" in Sanskrit?
   A. Lunar Chariot B. Celestial Vehicle
   C. Solar Probe D. Orbital Station
4. Who among the following have been awarded the Bharat Ratna in 2024?
   *(i)* Karpoori Thakur *(ii)* M.S. Swaminathan
   *(iii)* Ch. Charan Singh *(iv)* P.V. Narasimha Rao
   *(v)* L.K. Advani
   A. *(i)*, *(ii)* & *(iii)*
   B. *(iii)*, *(iv)* & *(v)*
   C. *(ii)*, *(iv)* & *(v)*
   D. *(i)*, *(ii)*, *(iii)*, *(iv)* & *(v)*
5. Who has been appointed as the new Lokpal of India?
   A. Justice Lingappa Narayana Swamy
   B. Justice AM Khanwilkar
   C. President Droupadi Murmu
   D. Sushil Chandra
6. When will the provisions of Bharatiya Nagarik Suraksha Sanhita, 2023, Bharatiya Nyaya Sanhita, 2023, and Bharatiya Sakshya Adhiniyam, 2023 come into force?
   A. July 1, 2023 B. July 1, 2024
   C. January 1, 2023 D. December 31, 2023
7. What is the name of India's first septic tank cleaning robot?
   A. Swachhata Atom B. Homosep Atom
   C. RoboCleaner 1.0 D. Sanitech Pro
8. Bharat Tex 2024 event, inaugurated by PM Modi in Feb 2024 in New Delhi is related to which sector:
   A. Technology B. Agriculture
   C. Textiles D. Tourism
9. What is the name of the country's longest signature stayed bridge, recently inaugurated by Prime Minister Narendra Modi in Gujarat?
   A. Bharati Setu B. Sudarshan Setu
   C. Dwarka Bridge D. Vishwa Setu
10. What is the name of the first private spacecraft to land on the Moon?
    A. Apollo 11 B. Odyssey
    C. Odysseus D. Artemis
11. Who emerged as the most popular global leader with a 78% approval rating by Morning Consult 2024?
    A. President of Mexico
    B. Prime Minister Narendra Modi
    C. President of Argentina
    D. US President Joe Biden
12. What is the theme of the 2024 edition of the Raisina Dialogue?
    A. "Tech Frontiers: Regulations & Realities"
    B. "Peace with the Planet: Invest & Innovate"
    C. "Chaturanga: Conflict, Contest, Cooperate, Create"
    D. "Decolonising Multilateralism: Institutions & Inclusion"
13. Who won the women's Badminton Asia Team Championships title 2024?
    A. India B. Thailand
    C. China D. Indonesia
14. Who has been honored with the 58th Jnanpith Award?
    A. Gulzar
    B. Jagadguru Rambhadracharya
    C. Both A and B
    D. None of the above
15. Who has been confirmed as the captain of the Indian cricket team for the 2024 T20 World Cup?
    A. Virat Kohli B. Rohit Sharma
    C. Ajinkya Rahane D. KL Rahul
16. Where is the 2024 T20 World Cup scheduled to be held?
    A. India and Sri Lanka
    B. Australia and New Zealand
    C. Caribbean and the USA
    D. South Africa and Zimbabwe
17. What is the significance of the BAPS Mandir in Abu Dhabi?
    A. It is the largest Hindu temple in the Middle East.
    B. It is the first traditional Hindu stone temple in the Middle East.
    C. It is a modern architectural marvel.
    D. It is dedicated to promoting unity in the Indian community.

**18.** Who emerged victorious in the Tennis Chennai Open ATP Challenger finale held on February 11, 2024?
A. Prajnesh Gunneswaran
B. Roger Federer
C. Luca Nardi
D. Sumit Nagal

**19.** Which country won the 2024 Under-19 Men's ODI Cricket World Cup?
A. India B. Australia
C. South Africa D. England

**20.** What is the primary objective of the Aadi Mahotsav 2024?
A. To promote urban art and culture
B. To showcase the rich diversity of India's tribal heritage
C. To celebrate international cuisines
D. To focus on modern technological advancements

**21.** Which Indian Prime Minister, also having served as Deputy Prime Minister, Chief Minister of Uttar Pradesh, and Union Minister for Home Affairs and Finance?
A. P.V. Narasimha Rao
B. Dr. M.S. Swaminathan
C. Chaudhary Charan Singh
D. Narendra Modi

**22.** Who won the SAFF U-19 Women's Championship in 2024?
A. Bangladesh B. Nepal
C. Bhutan D. India

**23.** Who introduced the Finance Bill, 2024, in the Lok Sabha?
A. Prime Minister Narendra Modi
B. Home Minister Amit Shah
C. Finance Minister Nirmala Sitharaman
D. Minister of State for Finance Pankaj Chaudhary

**24.** Who is the current Prime Minister of Guyana visiting India in February 2024?
A. Justin Trudeau B. Droupadi Murmu
C. Mark Phillips D. Boris Johnson

**25.** What is the name of the brand launched by government to provide subsidized rice directly to consumers in February 2024?
A. Bharat Grains B. Bharat Rice
C. Bharat Essentials D. Bharat Food

**26.** With which award will LK Advani be conferred in February 2024?
A. Padma Bhushan B. Bharat Ratna
C. Padma Vibhushan D. Param Vir Chakra

**27.** What is the name of the woman robot astronaut that will fly into space ahead of ISRO's "Gaganyaan" mission?
A. Vyomnaut B. Gaganyaatri
C. Vyommitra D. Astronautila

**28.** What is the theme of World Wetlands Day 2024?
A. Wetlands and Climate Change
B. Wetlands and Sustainable Use
C. Wetlands and Human Wellbeing
D. Wetlands and Economic Development

**29.** What is the fiscal deficit target set in the interim budget for FY 2024-25?
A. 3.5% of GDP B. 4.5% of GDP
C. 5.1% of GDP D. 6.0% of GDP

**30.** What is the status of income tax slabs or rates in the interim budget 2024-2025?
A. Increased rates B. Decreased rates
C. No changes D. Abolished

**31.** Which two countries participated in the joint military exercise SADA TANSEEQ in January 2024 in Rajasthan?
A. India and China
B. India and Pakistan
C. India and Saudi Arabia
D. India and Nepal

**32.** Which pair won the Australian Open Men's Doubles tennis championship in 2024?
A. Rohan Bopanna and Simone Bolelli
B. Matt Ebden and Andrea Vavassori
C. Rohan Bopanna and Matt Ebden
D. Simone Bolelli and Andrea Vavassori

**33.** Who emerged victorious in the men's singles final of the Australian Open tennis championship 2024?
A. Daniil Medvedev B. Novak Djokovic
C. Jannik Sinner D. Rafael Nadal

**34.** What is the name of the Indian cricketer who won the ICC ODI Player of the Year award in 2023?
A. Rohit Sharma B. Virat Kohli
C. Shikhar Dhawan D. Hardik Pandya

**35.** Who was the Chief Guest at the Republic Day parade in 2024?
A. Narendra Modi
B. Droupadi Murmu
C. Emmanuel Macron
D. Virat Kohli

**36.** What were the twin themes of the Republic Day parade in 2024?
A. Unity in Diversity and Military Strength
B. Viksit Bharat and Bharat – Loktantra ki Matruka
C. Cultural Heritage and Economic Progress
D. Nari Shakti and Global Diplomacy

**37.** Which countries participated in Exercise Desert Knight alongside the Indian Air Force in January 2024?
A. France and USA B. France and UAE
C. USA and UAE D. France and China

**38.** Who led the Pran Pratishtha ceremony of Ramlalla in Ayodhya on January 22, 2024?
A. UP Governor Anandiben Patel
B. CM Yogi Adityanath
C. Prime Minister Narendra Modi
D. RSS Chief Mohan Bhagwat

**39.** Who is the President of the 78th Session of the United Nations General Assembly?
A. Dennis Francis B. Narendra Modi
C. Antonio Guterres D. Joe Biden

**40.** Who won the gold medal at the Asian Marathon Championships 2024?
A. Huang Yongzheng B. Tiapkin Ilya
C. Man Singh D. Ashvini Jadhav

**41.** Who lost in the finals of the men's doubles at the India Open Badminton 2024?
A. Satwiksairaj Rankireddy and Chirag Shetty
B. Seo Seung-jae and Kang Min-hyuk
C. Shi Yu Qi and Lee Cheuk Yiu
D. Tai Tzu Ying and Chen Yu Fei

**42.** Which state is hosting the Khelo India Youth Games 2024?
A. Punjab B. Tamil Nadu
C. Karnataka D. Maharashtra

**43.** Where will 'Bharat Parv 2024' take place as part of the Republic Day celebrations?
A. India Gate, Delhi
B. Red Fort, Delhi
C. Rajpath, Delhi
D. Feroz Shah Kotla, Delhi

**44.** Where did the Wings India 2024 event hold in January 2024?
A. Mumbai Airport
B. Begumpet Airport, Hyderabad
C. Palam Airport, New Delhi
D. Safdarjung Airport, New Delhi

**45.** Who won The Best FIFA Men's Player award at the FIFA Football Awards ceremony in January 2024?
A. Kylian Mbappe B. Erling Haaland
C. Lionel Messi D. Aitana Bonmati

**46.** Which female football player received the Best FIFA Women's Player Award at the Award ceremony in January 2024?
A. Mary Earps B. Aitana Bonmati
C. Sarina Wiegman D. Kylian Mbappe

**47.** When does the Pran Pratishtha program for Ram Lala Virajman at Shri Ram Janmabhoomi complex begin?
A. January 21, 2024 B. January 16, 2024
C. January 22, 2024 D. January 15, 2024

**48.** What is the theme of the 54th annual meeting of the World Economic Forum?
A. Global Challenges
B. Rebuilding Trust
C. Technological Advancements
D. Economic Prosperity

**49.** Who succeeded Queen Margrethe II as the new King of Denmark on January 14, 2024?
A. Crown Prince Christian
B. Prince Frederik X
C. King Christian IX
D. Prince Mette Frederiksen

**50.** Which terrorist group captured a United Nations helicopter in Somalia in January 2024?
A. Taliban B. Al-Shabab
C. ISIS. D. Boko Haram

**51.** Who participated as the Chief Guest in the Vibrant Gujarat Global Summit 2024?
A. President of the Nepal
B. President of the United States
C. Prime Minister of Israel
D. President of the United Arab Emirates

**52.** Where is the KG-DWN-98/2 block located, where the ONGC starts oil production from Cluster-2 project in January 2024?
A. Arabian Sea B. Bay of Bengal
C. Indian Ocean D. Andaman Sea

**53.** What was the cause of the nosedive in India-Maldives relations in December 2023?
A. Trade disputes
B. Disparaging remarks about PM Modi's visit to Lakshadweep
C. Military conflicts
D. Economic sanctions

**54.** Which institute has initiated the country's first smart lab in its OPD block?
A. PGI Chandigarh B. AIIMS New Delhi
C. Apollo Hospitals D. Fortis Healthcare

**55.** When will the 2024 T20 Men's Cricket World Cup be held in the West Indies and the United States?
A. June 1 to June 15, 2024
B. June 1 to June 29, 2024
C. July 1 to July 15, 2024
D. July 1 to July 29, 2024

**56.** What is Jain Deemed to be University in Bengaluru awarded for in the Rashtriya Khel Protsahan Puruskar 2023?
A. Encouragement to Sports through CSR
B. Nurturing budding and young talent
C. Promotion of sports at the State level
D. Corporate Social Responsibility initiatives

57. Where is the 16th edition of the India International Jewellery Trade Show taking place?
A. Chennai B. Pune
C. Mumbai D. New Delhi

58. Who received the M.S. Swaminathan Award in 2024?
A. Prof. B.R. Kamboj
B. Thawar Chand Gehlot
C. Chaudhary Charan Singh
D. Rajmata Vijayaraje Scindia

59. What is the name of the Joint Military Exercise conducted between India and UAE in Rajasthan in January 2024?
A. Desert Storm 2024
B. Desert Thunder 2024
C. Desert Cyclone 2024
D. Desert Mirage 2024

60. Who are the new members set to join the Brics group on January 1, 2024?
A. Argentina, Brazil, South Africa
B. Egypt, Ethiopia, Iran, Saudi Arabia, and the United Arab Emirates
C. Mexico, Australia, Turkey
D. Canada, Japan, Germany

61. Which Indian player has been named as FIH Players of the Year 2023?
A. Hardik Singh B. Suraj Karkera
C. SP Raveendran D. Uttam Singh

62. Which state hosted the National Conference on Adventure Tourism in December 2023?
A. Rajasthan B. Maharashtra
C. Madhya Pradesh D. Gujarat

63. Which nation hosted the Indian Ocean Naval Symposium (IONS) Conclave of Chiefs in December 2023?
A. India B. Sri Lanka
C. Myanmar D. Thailand

64. Who has been selected to be conferred with the Major Dhyan Chand Khel Ratna award 2023?
A. Satwiksairaj Rankireddy
B. Chirag Shetty
C. Neeraj Chopra
D. Both (A) & (B)

65. Who was announced as the winner of Sahitya Akademi Award 2023 in Hindi language?
A. Vijay Verma B. Sanjeev
C. Rajasekaran D. Neelam Saran Gour

66. Which nation's space agency has been awarded the Leif Erikson Lunar Prize 2023?
A. USA B. Russia
C. India D. Japan

67. Which state has recently launched the SAANS campaign 2023-24?
A. Assam B. Gujarat
C. Manipur D. Meghalaya

68. UN has declared which year as the 'Year of Camelids'?
A. 2023 B. 2024
C. 2025 D. 2026

69. Which of the following was honoured with Bhutan's National Order of Merit recently?
A. Poonam Khetrapal B. Shambu Prasad Acharya
C. Ruchira Kamboj D. Vikram Doraiswami

70. Which of the following book is the winner of Gaja Capital Business Book Prize 2023?
A. Against All Odds B. Winning Middle India
C. Courting India D. Both (A) & (B)

71. Which team won the U-19 Asia Cup 2023?
A. Sri Lanka B. India
C. Bangladesh D. Nepal

72. Which state has been ranked Second in the latest Agri-marketing reforms Index 2023?
A. Andhra Pradesh B. Tamil Nadu
C. Uttar Pradesh D. Gujarat

73. Which nation was the largest recipient of remittances in 2023?
A. USA B. India
C. China D. Canada

74. Which team won the Vijay Hazare Trophy 2023-24?
A. Tamil Nadu B. Kerala
C. Haryana D. Jharkhand

75. Who won the title of Miss India USA 2023?
A. Rijul Maini B. Nandini Gupta
C. Sheynnis Palacios D. Sini Shetty

76. Prime Minister Narendra Modi inaugurated Diamond Bourse building in which state?
A. Gujarat B. Rajasthan
C. West Bengal D. Odisha

77. Which team won the inaugural edition of Khelo India Para Games in December 2023?
A. Madhya Pradesh B. Rajasthan
C. Maharashtra D. Haryana

78. Which of the following became the first Asian men to be inducted in the International Tennis Hall of Fame?
A. Vijay Amritraj B. Leander Paes
C. Both (A) & (B) D. Rohan Bopanna

79. Which Indian wrestler was named as UWW's 'Rising Star of the Year 2023'?
A. Priya Malik B. Antim Panghal
C. Deepak Punia D. Sakshi Mallik

**80.** Which of the following is the Oxford's word of the year 2023?
A. AI B. Authentic
C. Hallucinate D. Rizz

**81.** Which of the following was named as the ICC Women's Player of the month for November 2023?
A. Ashley Gardner B. Nahida Akhtar
C. Smriti Mandhana D. Harmanpreet Kaur

**82.** As per Southeast Asia Opium Survey 2023, which nation became the largest producer of Opium?
A. Afghanistan B. Laos
C. Indonesia D. Myanmar

**83.** Which nation's centre was recently awarded with the International Gender Equality Prize 2023?
A. Finland B. Afghanistan
C. Pakistan D. Iran

**84.** India's largest state-of-the-art Sports Science Centre was inaugurated in which state?
A. Telangana B. West Bengal
C. Tamil Nadu D. Odisha

**85.** Who was named as 'World Athlete of the Year' 2023?
A. Faith Kipyegon B. Noah Lyles
C. Armand Duplantis D. All of these

**86.** How many grandmasters are there in India as of December 2023?
A. 80 B. 81
C. 82 D. 84

**87.** How many medals did India win at the IBA Junior World Boxing Championship 2023?
A. 10 medals B. 16 medals
C. 17 medals D. 19 medals

**88.** Who was chosen as CEO of The Year 2023 by TIME's magazine?
A. Christiano Ronaldo B. Sam Altman
C. Mary Kom D. Sheetal devi

**89.** Which nation launched world's first portable hospital in December 2023?
A. China B. Russia
C. India D. USA

**90.** What was the theme of World Soil Day 2023?
A. Soil and Water: a source of life
B. Soils: Where food begins
C. Halt soil salinization, enhance soil production
D. Keep soil alive, protect soil biodiversity

**91.** Which of the following topped the Forbes list of 'World's 100 Most Powerful Women' of 2023?
A. Nirmala Sitharaman
B. Christine Lagarde
C. Ursula Von Der Leyen
D. Kamala Harris

**92.** Who won the 35th Jimmy George Foundation award?
A. Avinash Sable B. Chirag Shetty
C. Murali Sreeshankar D. Tejaswin Shankar

**93.** Which city hosted the 1st Asian Ranger Forum in December 2023?
A. Guwahati B. Pune
C. Delhi D. Ranchi

**94.** Which union ministry has recently released the AI based 'Gajraj system'?
A. Ministry of Education
B. Ministry of Home Affairs
C. Ministry of Environment
D. Ministry of Railways

**95.** As per NSO, what was the GDP growth rate for second quarter (Q2) for FY 2023-24?
A. 7.4% B. 7.2%
C. 6.4% D. 7.6%

**96.** Who has been appointed as the chairman of World Radio Communication Conference 2023?
A. Sultan Al Jaber B. Mohammad Al Ramsi
C. Zurab Pololikashvili D. Gilbert Houngbo

**97.** Which city is the host of the 1st Asian Ranger Forum in December 2023?
A. Shillong B. Imphal
C. Guwahati D. Pune

**98.** Which city is the host of Men's Volleyball Club World Championship 2023?
A. Bengaluru B. Hyderabad
C. Kolkata D. Imphal

**99.** How many Indians are there in the Forbes list of 'World's 100 Most Powerful Women' of 2023?
A. 1 B. 2
C. 3 D. 4

**100.** IBA Junior World Boxing Championship 2023 was held in which country?
A. Armenia B. Argentina
C. New Zealand D. South Korea

**101.** Which team won the ICC Cricket World Cup in 2023?
A. Australia B. West Indies
C. England D. India

**102.** Who was the highest run scorer in ICC Cricket World Cup 2023?
A. Virat Kohli B. Quinton de Kock
C. Rohit Sharma D. Rachin Ravindra

**103.** Who took the highest wickets in the ICC Cricket World Cup 2023?
A. Adam Zampa B. Shaheen Afridi
C. Mohammed Shami D. Dilshan Madushanka

**104.** Which cricketer holds the record for the most sixes in the ICC Cricket World Cup 2023?
A. David Warner B. Rohit Sharma
C. Glenn Maxwell D. Shreyas Iyer

105. Which two teams played in the ICC Cricket World Cup Finale of 2023?
A. India and South Africa
B. India and Pakistan
C. India and Australia
D. South Africa and Australia

06. Which stadium served as the primary venue for the ICC Cricket World Cup Finale 2023?
A. Lord's Cricket Ground
B. Melbourne Cricket Ground
C. Eden Gardens
D. Narendra Modi Stadium

107. Which player among the following earned the title of the "Player of the Tournament" in the ICC Cricket World Cup 2023?
A. Mohammed Shami B. Quinton de Kock
C. Virat Kohli D. Glenn Maxwell

108. What is the total number of medals that India won at the Asian Para Games 2023 in Hangzhou, China?
A. 82 B. 111
C. 303 D. 15

109. Indian Military is conducting the joint military exercise 'Exercise KAZIND-2023' with which country?
A. China B. Kazakhstan
C. Russia D. United States

110. What is the primary purpose of the Asian Women's Hockey Champion's Trophy 2023 that began on October 17, 2023 in Ranchi?
A. To determine the world champion in women's hockey
B. To qualify teams for the upcoming Paris Olympics
C. To promote women's hockey in Asia
D. To raise funds for hockey development

111. Who won the women's singles title at the Abu Dhabi Masters 2023 Badminton tournament on October 24, 2023?
A. Samiya Imad Farooqui
B. Unnati Hooda
C. Saina Nehwal
D. P.V. Sindhu

112. Which film has been selected as the Opening Feature Film of the 54th International Film Festival of India (IFFI) 2023?
A. "Ardhangini" (Bengali)
B. "Aattam" (Malayalam)
C. "Dhai Aakhar" (Hindi)
D. "Kantara" (Kannada)

113. Who received the Dadasaheb Phalke Lifetime Achievement Award at the 69th National Film Awards?
A. R Madhavan B. Waheeda Rehman
C. Vivek Agnihotri D. Pankaj Tripathi

114. Which film was awarded the Best Feature Film for the year 2021 at the 69th National Film Awards?
A. Ek Tha Gaon
B. Rocketry : The Nambi Effect
C. Iravin Nizhal
D. Komuram Bheemudo

115. Which director's film, "Ek Tha Gaon," received the Best Non-Feature Film award?
A. R. Madhavan B. Srishti Lakhera
C. Vivek Agnihotri D. Allu Arjun

116. Which edition of the ASEAN Summit was held in 2023 and in which city?
A. 43rd, Singapore B. 20th, Bangkok
C. 43rd, Jakarta D. 18th, Manila

117. For the assessment year [AY] 2023-24, CBDT has reduced the time taken to process income tax returns to how many days?
A. 41 days B. 52 days
C. 18 days D. 10 days

118. ISRO used which launch vehicle to successfully launch its Solar mission Aditya L1 in September 2023?
A. PSLV C-55 B. PSLV C-54
C. PSLV C-56 D. PSLV C-57

119. Which team has won the 2023 Durand Cup?
A. Kerala Blasters
B. Mohun Bagan Super Giant
C. Indian Army
D. East Bengal

120. Which player has won the 2023 Tata Steel Chess India Women's Rapid Tournament?
A. Divya Deshmukh B. Dronavalli Harika
C. Koneru Humpy D. Vantika Agrawal

121. Which of the following city the G20 summit held in 2023?
A. Brisbane (Australia) B. Osaka (Japan)
C. Antalya (Turkey) D. Delhi (India)

122. What was the inspiration for G20 2023 logo?
A. India's national flag B. Russia's national flag
C. France's national flag D. None of the above

123. What was the theme of the G20 summit 2023 held in India?
A. Shaping an Interconnected World
B. Fighting poverty with rigidity
C. "One Earth-One Family-One Future"
D. Making the world together

124. In which city, India's first 500 Kilo-volt-amperes (kVA) Underground Power Transformer Station was inaugurated in September 2023?
A. Kadapa, Andhra Pradesh
B. Jodhpur, Rajasthan
C. Chennai, Tamil Nadu
D. Bengaluru, Karnataka

**125.** Which country's Navy, along with Indian Navy (IN) has recently (in September, 2023) conducted a Passage Exercise (PASSEX)?
A. Indonesia B. Sri Lanka
C. Bangladesh D. France

**126.** When was the United Nations (UN) International Day of Clean Air for Blue Skies 2023 observed across the globe with the theme of 'Together for Clean Air'?
A. 3rd September 2023 B. 4th September 2023
C. 5th September 2023 D. 7th September 2023

**127.** In which city India's 1st Solar City was inaugurated in September 2023?
A. Chandrapur, Maharashtra
B. Tuni, Andhra Pradesh
C. Churu, Rajasthan
D. Sanchi, Madhya Pradesh

**128.** Which Railway Station has recently (in September, 2023) certified as "Green Railway Station" with the highest rating of Platinum by IGBC (Indian Green Building Council)-Confederation of Indian Industry (CII)?
A. Mumbai Central Railway Station
B. Vijayawada Railway Station
C. Guwahati Railway Station
D. Chandigarh Railway Station

**129.** In which state/UT, President Droupadi Murmu unveiled a 12-foot-high statue of the Father of the Nation, 'Mahatma Gandhi' and inaugurated a 'Gandhi Vatika'?
A. Uttar Pradesh B. Maharashtra
C. Gujarat D. Delhi

**130.** In September 2023, the Indian Men's Hockey Team won the 1st Edition of Men's Hockey Asia Cup Salalah 2023 by defeating (country) in the final held in Salalah, Oman.
A. Bangladesh B. Oman
C. Malaysia D. Pakistan

**131.** Heath Hilton Streak, Former captain of the ______ (country) Cricket team, passed away in September 2023.
A. Australia B. New Zealand
C. Zimbabwe D. England

**132.** In August 2023, Neeraj Chopra finished ______ in the men's javelin throw event with ______ metres at the Zurich Diamond League 2023 held in Zurich, Switzerland.
A. 2nd; 84.92 B. 1st; 86.23
C. 2nd; 85.71 D. 1st; 84.92

**133.** Who has been recently (in August, 2023) appointed as the 1st Women Chairperson & Chief Executive Officer (CEO) of Railway Board?
A. Jaya Varma Sinha B. Madhabi Puri Buch
C. Rekha Sharma D. Mamta Kumari

**134.** In August 2023, the Indian Women's Hockey Team won the inaugural Women's Hockey Asia Cup by defeating ________ (country) held in Salalah, Oman.
A. Bangladesh B. Indonesia
C. Thailand D. Malaysia

**135.** The _____ National Sports Day (Rashtriya Khel Divas) 2023 was observed across India on 29th August 2023.
A. 16th B. 12th
C. 14th D. 15th

**136.** In August 2023, Emmerson Mnangagwa was re-elected as the President of ________ (country) for the second term of 5 years.
A. Rwanda B. Zimbabwe
C. Tanzania D. Ghana

**137.** In August 2023, Jayanta Mahapatra, who was the first recipient of Sahitya Akademi award for ______ (language) poetry in 1981, passed away.
A. Gujarati B. Malayalam
C. Kannada D. English

**138.** In which state/UT India's first Artificial Intelligence (AI) school was inaugurated in August 2023?
A. Kerala B. Andhra Pradesh
C. Karnataka D. Delhi

**139.** What was the theme of World Water Week 2023 that was observed across the globe on 20th to 24th August 2023?
A. Water and Climate Change
B. Building Resilience Faster
C. Seeds of Change: Innovative Solutions for a Water-Wise World
D. Seeing the Unseen: The Value of Water

**140.** In August 2023, Vinai Kumar Saxena, Delhi Lieutenant Governor (LG) launched Blockchain Technology in the ICJS for electronic-forensic application (eforensic app). What does 'S' stand for in ICJS?
A. Software B. System
C. Storage D. Secondary

**141.** In August 2023, ________ (state) became the 1st state in India to provide free In Vitro Fertilisation (IVF) therapy.
A. Tamil Nadu
B. Telangana
C. Karnataka
D. Goa

**142.** In August 2023, Ali Mahaman Lamine Zeine was appointed as the transitional Prime Minister (PM) of ________ (country).
A. Niger B. Guinea
C. Senegal D. Ghana

**143.** Which of the following cities is set to establish India's first Integrated Theatre Commands (ITC)- South Western Command & Central Command in August 2023?
A. Patna, Bihar
B. Jaipur, Rajasthan
C. Lucknow, Uttar Pradesh
D. Both (B) & (C)

**144.** Which city topped the 'Swachh Vayu Sarvekshan 2023 Clean Air Survey'?
A. Indore
B. Mysore
C. Kochi
D. Panjim

**145.** Which country's central bank Governors topped the 'Global Finance Central Banker Report Cards 2023'?
A. India
B. Sri Lanka
C. USA
D. UK

**146.** What is the estimated tiger population in India, as per the report released by the Minister of State for Environment, Forest and Climate Change on Global Tiger Day on 29 July, 2023?
A. 2,500
B. 3,167
C. 3,682
D. 3,925

**147.** What is the purpose of the 'Meri Mati Mera Desh' campaign ahead of Independence Day 2023?
A. To celebrate Independence Day
B. To honour the martyred men and women
C. To organize Amrit Mahotsav celebrations
D. To build the National War Memorial

**148.** Which team won the 100th Anniversary Spanish Hockey Federation—International Tournament in July, 2023?
A. England
B. Spain
C. India
D. Germany

**149.** What is the primary payload of ISRO's PSLV-C56 rocket launched from Sriharikota on 30 June, 2023?
A. DS-SAR satellite
B. VELOX-AM microsatellite
C. ARCADE microsatellite
D. ST Engineering payload

**150.** Nisha Biswal, an Indian-American policy expert, has been confirmed to serve as the Deputy Chief Executive Officer (CEO) of which US finance agency?
A. World Bank
B. United States International Development Finance Corporation
C. International Monetary Fund (IMF)
D. Federal Reserve System

**151.** The main objective of Chandrayaan-3 is to:
A. Establish a human colony on the moon
B. Study the surface and mineralogy of the Moon
C. Conduct a comprehensive study of Mars' atmosphere
D. None of these

**152.** Who is the director of the Chandrayaan-3 mission?
A. K. Sivan
B. M. Vanitha
C. J.J. Robinson
D. Ritu Karidhal

**153.** The Chandrayaan-3 mission's rover known is:
A. Vikram
B. Pragyaan
C. Dhruv
D. Aditya

**154.** What is the estimated tiger population in India, as per the report released by the Minister of State for Environment, Forest and Climate Change on Global Tiger Day on 29 July 2023?
A. 2,500
B. 3,167
C. 3,682
D. 3,925

**155.** What is the purpose of the 'Meri Mati Mera Desh' campaign ahead of Independence Day 2023?
A. To celebrate Independence Day
B. To honour the martyred men and women
C. To organize Amrit Mahotsav celebrations
D. To build the National War Memorial

**156.** Which team won the 100th Anniversary Spanish Hockey Federation – International Tournament in July 2023?
A. England
B. Spain
C. India
D. Germany

**157.** What is the primary payload of ISRO's PSLV-C56 rocket launched from Sriharikota on 30 June 2023?
A. DS-SAR satellite
B. VELOX-AM microsatellite
C. ARCADE microsatellite
D. ST Engineering payload

**158.** What is the objective of the Khelo India campaign?
A. To enhance sports infrastructure only
B. To nurture and support talented athletes only
C. To provide a platform for identifying talented players and enhance sports infrastructure
D. To provide platforms for different sports competitions

**159.** The PM SHRI Scheme focuses on nurturing students to become ________ .
A. Wealthy entrepreneurs
B. Engaged, productive, and contributing citizens
C. Government employees
D. Members of the armed forces

**160.** At the ISSF Junior Shooting World Championships 2023, which country finished in 2nd place on the medals tally?
A. South Korea
B. India
C. United States
D. China

**161.** Which organization celebrated its 85th Raising Day on 27th July 2023?
A. Indian Army
B. CRPF (Central Reserve Police Force)
C. BSF (Border Security Force)
D. IAF (Indian Air Force)

**162.** In which city is the Asian Youth and Junior Weightlifting Championships 2023 being held?
A. Greater Noida B. Mumbai
C. New Delhi D. Kolkata

**163.** According to the latest report by the International Monetary Fund (IMF), what is the projected Gross Domestic Product (GDP) growth rate for India in the current fiscal year (2023-2024)?
A. 5.9 per cent B. 6.1 per cent
C. 6.3 per cent D. 6.5 per cent

**164.** Which operation is celebrated as Kargil Vijay Diwas, observed on July 26 every year?
A. Operation Cactus B. Operation Meghdoot
C. Operation Vijay D. Operation Pawan

**165.** What is the approved interest rate on deposits under the Employees Provident Fund scheme for the financial year 2022-23?
A. 8.10 per cent B. 8.15 per cent
C. 8.20 per cent D. 8.05 per cent

**166.** What is the recent change made by Twitter in its branding?
A. Changed its name to X Corp.
B. Replaced its blue bird logo with an X.
C. Introduced a new social media platform.
D. Acquired a competitor company.

**167.** Where will the event "Semicon India 2023" take place from 28th to 30th July 2023?
A. New Delhi B. Bengaluru
C. Hyderabad D. Gandhinagar

**168.** Who received the National Geoscience Award 2022 for Lifetime Achievement?
A. Dr. Om Narain Bhargava
B. Dr. Amiya Kumar Samal
C. President Droupadi Murmu
D. Banaras Hindu University

**169.** Which centralized facility was inaugurated by Union Home Minister Amit Shah on July 22, 2023, to address security challenges for 66 civil airports under the CISF's security cover?
A. Central Security Monitoring Centre (CSMC)
B. Air Traffic Control Centre (ATCC)
C. Aviation Security Control Centre (ASCC)
D. Security Operations Command Centre (SOCC)

**170.** Who won the Korea Open 2023 Badminton men's doubles title in Yeosu?
A. Fajar Alfian and Muhammad Rian Ardianto
B. Liang Wei Keng and Wang Chang
C. Satwiksairaj Rankireddy and Chirag Shetty
D. None of the above

**171.** The Bhoomi Samman 2023 awards were presented to individuals and teams who excelled in which program?
A. Digital India Education Enhancement Program
B. Digital India Land Records Modernization Programme
C. Digital India Healthcare Access Initiative
D. Digital India Skill Development Scheme

**172.** Who is the President of the Asian Cricket Council (ACC)?
A. Jay Shah B. Sourav Ganguly
C. Ehsan Mani D. David Richardson

**173.** Which name has been given to the alliance formed by the opposition parties to contest the 2024 Lok Sabha election?
A. National Democratic Alliance (NDA)
B. Indian National Developmental Inclusive Alliance (INDIA)
C. Congress National Alliance (CNA)
D. Democratic Opposition Front (DOF)

**174.** Which state in India registered the highest decline in the number of poor according to the National Multidimensional Poverty Index released by NITI Aayog in July 2023?
A. Bihar B. Madhya Pradesh
C. Uttar Pradesh D. Odisha

**175.** Who did Carlos Alcaraz defeat to win the Men's title at the Wimbledon championship 2023?
A. Roger Federer B. Rafael Nadal
C. Novak Djokovic D. Andy Murray

**176.** Parul Chaudhary, won a gold medal in which event at the Asian Athletics Championships 2023?
A. Women's 3000 m steeplechase
B. Women's 100 m sprint
C. Women's long jump
D. Women's shot put

**177.** During his visit to France in July 2023, Prime Minister Narendra Modi announced an agreement to use which flagship instant payment system in France?
A. NEFT (National Electronic Funds Transfer)
B. RTGS (Real Time Gross Settlement)
C. UPI (Unified Payments Interface)
D. IMPS (Immediate Payment Service)

**178.** Which was the launch site for the LVM3-M4 rocket that carried Chandrayaan-3 to the moon on July 14, 2023?
A. Satish Dhawan Space Centre, Sriharikota
B. Thumba Equatorial Rocket Launching Station
C. Abdul Kalam Island
D. Indian Space Research Organisation, Bengaluru

**179.** Which rank did the Indian Team secure in the 64th International Mathematical Olympiad (IMO) 2023 out of 112 participating countries?
A. 1st B. 5th
C. 9th D. 12th

**180.** Which ship, known as India's first indigenously built Guided Missile Destroyer, participated in the seventh edition of the Japan-India Maritime Exercise (JIMEX 23)?
A. INS Delhi B. INS Kamorta
C. INS Shakti D. INS Vikrant

**181.** Who has been selected as the recipient of the prestigious Lokmanya Tilak Award for 2023?
A. Rajnath Singh B. Dr. Dipak Tilak
C. Amit Shah D. Narendra Modi

**182.** What is the purpose of the NCC Integrated Software launched in July 2023?
A. To provide debit card facilities to NCC cadets
B. To digitalize the entire process from enrollment to alumni registration
C. To establish an all-India database of Defense Ministry personnel
D. To promote physical fitness among NCC cadets

**183.** Which state has achieved 100% Open Defecation Free (ODF) plus status?
A. Assam B. Sikkim
C. Manipur D. Meghalaya

**184.** What is the name of the launch vehicle for Chandrayaan 3?
A. GSLV Mark II B. PSLV-C50
C. GSLV Mark III D. ISRO-XL

**185.** Which day was recorded as the World's hottest day according to data from the U.S. National Centers for Environmental Prediction?
A. 5 August 2016 B. 3 July 2023
C. 21 August 2022 D. 22 June 2019

**186.** Which country will host the next meeting of the SCO Council of Heads of State in 2024?
A. China B. Russia
C. India D. Kazakhstan

**187.** Which Team won the SAFF Championship 2023?
A. Kuwait B. India
C. Lebanon D. Pakistan

**188.** Where is India's first indigenously developed 700 MW nuclear power reactor, KAPP-3, located?
A. Rawatbhata, Rajasthan
B. Kakrapar, Gujarat
C. Chutka, Madhya Pradesh
D. Gorakhpur, Haryana

**189.** Who won the Lausanne Diamond League 2023 title in javelin throw?
A. Neeraj Chopra B. Julian Webber
C. Jakub Vadlech D. Shivpal Singh

**190.** Who won the gold medal in the Asian Mixed Doubles Squash Tournament in June 2023?
A. Dipika Pallikal and Ramit Tandon
B. Harinder Pal Sandhu and Sunayna Kuruvilla
C. Sunayna Kuruvilla and Ramit Tandon
D. Dipika Pallikal and Harinder Pal Sandhu

**191.** Who has been appointed as the Director of the United Nations Office for Outer Space Affairs (UNOOSA) in Vienna?
A. Antonio Guterres B. Simonetta Di Pippo
C. Aarti Holla-Maini D. None of the above

**192.** Where will the final match of the ICC Men's Cricket World Cup 2023 be played?
A. Chennai B. Mumbai
C. Kolkata D. Ahmedabad

**193.** Which city hosted the Special Olympics World Games 2023?
A. Berlin, Germany
B. Delhi, India
C. London, United Kingdom
D. Tokyo, Japan

**194.** Which Indian women's doubles pair won the World Table Tennis, (WTT) Contender tournament 2023 in Tunis?
A. Sutirtha Mukherjee and Ayhika Mukherjee
B. Sowjanya Bavisetti and Rutuja Bhosale
C. Riya Bhatia and Rutuja Bhosale
D. Sutirtha Mukherjee and Riya Bhatia

**195.** Diksha Dagar wins Czech Ladies Open 2023 Golf Title. She has overcome which unique challenge or condition?
A. Vision impairment B. Hearing impairment
C. Physical disability D. Language barrier

**196.** Which Egypt's highest state honor was conferred upon Prime Minister Narendra Modi by President Sisi during his visit to Egypt?
A. Order of the Nile B. Order of Merit
C. Order of Excellence D. Order of the Pharaoh

**197.** Who won the Bal Sahitya Puraskar 2023 in the Hindi language category?
A. Eknath Avhad B. Suryanath Singh
C. Vishakha Vishwanath D. Sudha Murthy

**198.** Which company is planning to invest in a chip assembly and testing facility in Gujarat in June 2023?
A. Intel B. Samsung
C. Micron D. TSMC

**199.** Which country will host the world's fastest motorbike race 'Moto GP' 2023?
A. England B. India
C. Nepal D. Australia

**200.** Which country blocked the proposal to designate Sajid Mir as a global terrorist at the United Nations on 20th June?
A. China B. United States
C. Pakistan D. India

**201.** Where was North India's first Skin Bank inaugurated on 20th June 2023?
A. Safdarjung Hospital, New Delhi
B. AIIMS, New Delhi
C. Rajiv Gandhi Hospital, New Delhi
D. Sir Ganga Ram Hospital, New Delhi

**202.** Who led the yoga session at the United Nations Headquarters in New York on 9th International Yoga Day?
A. Donald Trump B. Angela Merkel
C. Narendra Modi D. Justin Trudeau

**203.** On 20th June, Who has taken charge as the Chief Executive Officer (CEO) of the Unique Identification Authority of India (UIDAI)?
A. Amit Agarwal B. Subodh Kumar Singh
C. Rupinder Singh D. Akash Tripathi

**204.** Which Indian athlete has created a new Asian shotput record at the Inter-State Championships in Bhubaneswar, on 19th June 2023?
A. Vikas Gowda
B. Jugraj Singh
C. Tajinderpal Singh Toor
D. Mohd Yasser

**205.** Which Indian player became the first Indian to win a bronze medal at the Asian Fencing Championships 2023 in China?
A. Karan Singh B. Bhavani Devi
C. Taniksha Khatri D. None of the above

**206.** Who has been appointed as the chief of the country's external intelligence agency RAW in June 2023?
A. Satyendranath Tagore B. Rameshwar Nath Kao
C. Ravi Sinha D. Vikram Sood

**207.** Who was confirmed as the first Muslim woman to serve as a federal judge in June 2023?
A. Nusrat Jahan Choudhury
B. Fathima Beevi
C. Nadia Kahf
D. None of the above

**208.** Which country won the Intercontinental Cup 2023?
A. Lebanon B. Korea
C. India D. None of the above

**209.** Who has been selected as the recipient of the Gandhi Peace Prize for the year 2021?
A. Geeta Press B. Orient Press
C. Replika Press D. Thomson Press India

**210.** Which pair won the Indonesia Open 2023 men's doubles title in Badminton?
A. Aaron Chia and Soh Wooi Yik
B. Satwiksairaj Rankireddy and Chirag Shetty
C. Kento Momota and Lee Zii Jia
D. Viktor Axelsen and Anders Antonsen

**211.** What is the theme of Yoga Day in 2023?
A. Yoga for Swaasthe and Kalyaan
B. Yoga for Peace and Harmony
C. Yoga for Sustainable Development
D. Yoga for Vasudhaiva Kutumbakam

**212.** What is the title of the song created through the collaboration between Prime Minister Narendra Modi and Grammy Award-winning Indian-American singer Falu?
A. "Millets and Global Hunger"
B. "Harvesting Hope: The Millet Anthem"
C. "Abundance of Millets"
D. "Modi's Melody for Feeding the World"

**213.** Which state receive the first prize in the best state category in the fourth National Water Awards, 2022?
A. Madhya Pradesh B. Odisha
C. Telangana D. Bihar

**214.** When was the Pradhanmantri Sangrahalaya, showcasing the journey of all Prime Ministers, opened to the public?
A. 21st April 2022 B. 25th November 2018
C. 01st April 2020 D. 07th April 2019

**215.** How many gold medals did India win in the U-17 Asian Wrestling Championships 2023 in Bishkek, Kyrgyzstan?
A. One B. Two
C. Three D. Four

**216.** 'Kheer Bhawani Mela' is a festival celebrated in which Indian state/UT?
A. Kerala B. Ladakh
C. Chhattisgarh D. Jammu and Kashmir

**217.** Which fintech company has launched "Turbo UPI" in partnership with Axis Bank and the National Payments Council of India (NPCI)?
A. Paytm B. PhonePe
C. Google Pay D. Razorpay

**218.** Maharashtra government has named which Indian cricketer as 'Smile Ambassador' under the state medical education & drug department's 'Swachh Mukh Abhiyan'?
A. Saurav Ganguly B. Virat Kohli
C. Sachin Tendulkar D. Rohit Sharma

**219.** Which state government has recently launched Namo Shetkari Mahasanman Yojana?
A. Kerala B. Gujarat
C. Maharashtra D. Rajasthan

**220.** Which state government launched a new scheme, Mo Ghara (My Home) - a credit-linked housing scheme for rural poor in the state?
A. Assam B. Odisha
C. Chhattisgarh D. Madhya Pradesh

221. Which state government has launched the 'Artificial Intelligence for Youth' initiatives in the state?
A. Kerala B. Tamil Nadu
C. Odisha D. Madhya Pradesh

222. Jude Bellingham has been named Bundesliga Player of the Season for his incredible campaign in season 2022/23. He is associated with which sports?
A. Cricket B. Football
C. Hockey D. Badminton

223. Who has bagged the gold medal in the women's 100 m hurdles event in the T-Meeting 2023 athletics meet in Tilburg, Netherlands?
A. Hima Das B. Dutee Chand
C. Kavita Tungar D. Jyothi Yarraji

224. Rail company Alstom will manufacture 100 aluminum-bodied Vande Bharat trains with sleeper facilities, after bidding the lowest for the tender at a price of Rs 150.9 crores per train. Alstom is the company of which country?
A. France B. Germany
C. Sweden D. Switzerland

225. The Indian G20 Presidency is organizing the third Employment Working Group (EWG) meeting in which city?
A. Geneva B. Paris
C. Berlin D. London

226. Which insurance company has launched a term insurance plan for Type 2 diabetics?
A. SBI General Insurance
B. Bharti AXA General Insurance
C. Bajaj Allianz General Insurance
D. Cholamandalam MS General Insurance

227. Ahmednagar district will be named after warrior queen Ahilyabai Holkar. Ahmednagar is district of which state?
A. Madhya Pradesh B. Gujarat
C. Rajasthan D. Maharashtra

228. Which Card launched country's first mobile-based expense management card?
A. IndusInd Card B. Karbon Card
C. LIC Card D. Citibank Card

229. Which Group has signed an MoU with the Gujarat government to set up a first-ever lithium-ion cell manufacturing gigafactory in Gujarat?
A. Adani Group B. Mahindra Group
C. Aditya Birla Group D. Tata Group

230. Who has been appointed as the first woman Secretary General of the World Meteorological Organisation?
A. Soumya Swaminathan B. Kristalina Georgieva
C. Petteri Taalas D. Celeste Saulo

231. Which Country to host world's largest Conservation Conference in 2025?
A. UAE B. India
C. Bangladesh D. United States

232. Who has launched the Unified Registration Portal for 'GOBARdhan'?
A. Ashwini Vaishnaw
B. Amit Shah
C. Narendra Singh Tomar
D. Gajendra Singh Shekhawat

233. Indian UPI Transactions Reach Record High of How many Trillions in May 2023?
A. ₹ 12.7 Trillion B. ₹ 14.3 Trillion
C. ₹ 15.6 Trillion D. ₹ 16.9 Trillion

234. Which medium-range ballistic missile was successfully test-fired from APJ Abdul Kalam Island?
A. Agni-1 B. Agni-2
C. Agni-3 D. Agni-4

235. India defeated which team to win the Men's Hockey Junior Asia Cup title?
A. Sri Lanka B. Pakistan
C. Nepal D. Bangladesh

236. Prime Minster Street Vendor's AtmaNirbhar Nidhi (PM SVANidhi) Scheme has recently successfully completed how many years?
A. 2 B. 3
C. 4 D. 5

237. Which state police has recently launched a massive state-wide operation named "OP Clean"?
A. Haryana B. Punjab
C. Uttar Pradesh D. Madhya Pradesh

238. Which of the following country has launched its first commercial-grade satellite?
A. North Korea B. South Korea
C. Iran D. Saudi Arabia

239. Which AIIMS has becomes the first of all AIIMS to receive the National Accreditation Board for Hospitals and Healthcare Providers (NABH) accreditation?
A. AIIMS Nagpur B. AIIMS Patna
C. AIIMS Chennai D. AIIMS Bengaluru

240. By which year the city will get the 'Smart City' tag under the Srinagar Smart City Project?
A. 2025 B. 2026
C. 2027 D. 2024

241. Which of the following country has hosted the meeting of BRICS Foreign Ministers?
A. Brazil B. Russia
C. South Africa D. India

242. Who has been appointed as the new Chairman and Managing Director of Steel Authority of India Ltd (SAIL)?
A. Ajit Kumar Saxena B. Amarendu Prakash
C. Rajesh Kumar D. Rajiv Dixit

**243.** Who has become the first woman from Tamil Nadu to climb the world's highest peak, Mount Everest?
A. Premlata Agarwal B. Krushnaa Patil
C. Malavath Purna D. Muthamizh Selvi

**244.** The third G20 Health Working Group meeting begins in which city?
A. Bengaluru B. Hyderabad
C. New Delhi D. Mumbai

**245.** Union Minister for Health and Family Welfare, Dr. Mansukh Mandaviya has inaugurated the state of-the-art National Training Centre for Food Safety and Standards Authority of India (FSSAI) in which city?
A. Patna B. Ghaziabad
C. Visakhapatnam D. Gurugram

**246.** According to a new report by Standard Chartered, India is set to remain UAE's largest export destination by which year?
A. 2025 B. 2026
C. 2030 D. 2028

**247.** Who has won the Thailand Open 2023 Women's Singles Title?
A. Iga Swiatek B. Karolína Plíšková
C. Monica Seles D. Ann Se-young

**248.** Who is the author of the book titled "The Power of One Thought : Master Your Mind"?
A. Zuni Chopra B. Durjoy Dutta
C. BK Shivani D. Samhita Arni

**249.** Who received 'Climate And Health' award at UITP Awards 2023, Barcelona?
A. CESC Limited
B. Brihanmumbai Electric Supply and Transport (BEST)
C. Indian Railway Catering and Tourism Corporation (IRCTC)
D. Uttar Haryana Bijli Vitran Nigam (UHBVN)

**250.** President Droupadi Murmu has been awarded the country's highest civilian award Grand Order of the Chain of the Yellow Star. It is the highest civilian award in which country?
A. Fiji B. Nigeria
C. Suriname D. Mauritius

**251.** Dennis Francis has been elected as the President of the 78th UN General Assembly (UNGA). He is from which country?
A. Trinidad and Tobago B. Suriname
C. Guatemala D. Costa Rica

**252.** Which state government has announced the launch of 'Mukhyamantri Seekho Aur Kamao' scheme?
A. Madhya Pradesh B. Uttar Pradesh
C. Assam D. Bihar

**253.** Who has launched a Financial Inclusion Dashboard 'ANTARDRISHTI'?
A. Urjit Patel B. Shaktikanta Das
C. Nirmala Sitharaman D. Droupadi Murmu

**254.** 'Mission Vatsalya', which was seen in the news, is a scheme implemented by which Union Ministry?
A. Ministry of Rural Development
B. Ministry of Housing and Urban Affairs
C. Ministry of Youth Affairs and Sports
D. Ministry of Women and Child Development

**255.** The 6th edition of the annual naval exercise 'Ektha' was held between India and which country?
A. Egypt B. UAE
C. Maldives D. Sri Lanka

**256.** According to the report titled "Tracking SDG7: The Energy Progress 2023", approximately how many people around the world are still using polluting fuels and techniques for cooking?
A. 2.9 billion B. 3.1 billion
C. 2.3 billion D. 1.8 billion

**257.** Who launched the Girl Empowerment Mission (GEM)-2023?
A. NHPC B. GAIL
C. Coal India D. NTPC Kanti

**258.** Which of the following has launched the "Addiction Free Amrit Kaal" campaign to promote a healthier & addiction-free India?
A. National Commission for Protection of Child
B. Central Bureau of Investigation
C. National Commission for Women
D. Ministry of Health and Family Welfare

**259.** Who will inaugurate the integrated Water Resources Action Plan-2023-25 under the Amrit Jal Kranti initiative?
A. Narendra Modi B. Piyush Goyal
C. Nirmala Sitharaman D. Manohar Lal

**260.** Which company has recently launched a new 'voice chat' feature to its Al-powered Bing Chat on the desktop?
A. Google B. IBM
C. Microsoft D. Tesla

**261.** Who has inaugurated the first-ever National Training Conclave at the International Exhibition and Convention Centre at Pragati Maidan in New Delhi?
A. Nirmala Sitharaman B. Draupadi Murmu
C. Narendra Modi D. Rajnath Singh

**262.** Who has released the report highlighting the significant impacts of 'Har Ghar Jal' program on public health and economic savings?
A. World Health Organization
B. World Intellectual Property Organization
C. International Maritime Organization
D. World Meteorological Organization

**263.** Which Countries Forge 'Atlantic Declaration' to Boost Economic Ties?
A. US and UK B. US and UAE
C. UK and India D. US and Australia

**264.** Which of the following has approved the First Loss Default Guarantee (FLDG) framework, allowing fintech to partner with banks and non-Banking financial companies (NBFCs)?
A. RBI B. SEBI
C. SIDBI D. IRDAI

**265.** WBIDC, Amazon and FICCI join hands to promote e-commerce exports from Which State?
A. West Bengal B. Gujarat
C. Tamil Nadu D. Maharashtra

**266.** Which company has successfully launched pilot study on vehicles using E27 fuel and Ethanol Blended Diesel Fuel?
A. Coal India Limited
B. Bharat Heavy Electricals Limited
C. Steel Authority of India Limited
D. Hindustan Petroleum Corporation Limited

**267.** Who was given the 'Governor of the Year' award by Central Banking in London?
A. C. Rangarajan B. Urjit Ravindra Patel
C. Shaktikanta Das D. Bimal Jalan

**268.** Which railway station was recently awarded the 'Eat Right Station' certificate?
A. Varanasi Railway Station
B. Guwahati Railway Station
C. Patna Railway Station
D. Ahmedabad Railway Station

**269.** India will host the 2025 International Institute of Administrative Sciences (IIAS) Annual Conference at Which State?
A. Gujarat B. Telangana
C. Uttar Pradesh D. Kerala

**270.** Which has launched mission EVOLVE (Electric Vehicle Operations and Lending for Vibrant Ecosystem) in association with NITI Aayog to finance MSMEs in the EV space?
A. SEBI B. RBI
C. SIDBI D. NABARD

**271.** A Book titled Rebels Against the Raj : Western Fighters for India's Freedom has won the Elizabeth Longford Prize for Historical Biography 2023. Who is the author of this book?
A. Jhumpa Lahiri B. Vikram Seth
C. Aravind Adiga D. Ramchandra Guha

**272.** Who joined hands to drive citizen awareness 'G20-Stay Safe Online' campaign?
A. Google and MeitY B. Meta and MeitY
C. Amazon and MeitY D. Microsoft and MeitY

**273.** NTPC Barauni has achieved a significant milestone by securing the first rank in the Best Industry Category at the 4th National Water Awards. NTPC Barauni is situated in which state?
A. Jharkhand B. Bihar
C. Chhattisgarh D. Rajasthan

**274.** Which country will rejoin UNESCO in July 2023 four years after leaving due to allegations of bias against Israel?
A. Russia B. Germany
C. Japan D. United States

**275.** In which country Indian Army is participating in 'Exercise Khan Quest 2023'?
A. France B. Japan
C. Mongolia D. Russia

**276.** Which state's chief minister has inaugurated "The Tribune Real Estate Expo 2023" in the state?
A. Rajasthan B. Madhya Pradesh
C. Himachal Pradesh D. Uttarakhand

**277.** Which state's hockey team won the Hockey India Junior Men's National Championship 2023?
A. Uttar Pradesh B. Madhya Pradesh
C. Haryana D. Punjab

**278.** Which Indian company is included in the list of 100 most influential companies released by 'Time' magazine?
A. Tata Group B. Reliance Industries
C. Bharti Airtel D. NPCI

**279.** Which City has set a new Guinness World Record in the Yoga event 21st June 2023?
A. Pune B. Surat
C. Indore D. Bengaluru

**280.** Who organized the 'Ocean Ring of Yoga' on 21st June 2023?
A. US Navy B. Australia Navy
C. Indian Navy D. Indian Coast Guard

**281.** Who was sworn in as the Central Vigilance Commissioner (CVC)?
A. Praveen Kumar Srivastava
B. Jagdeep Dhankhar
C. Jai Prakash Singh
D. RK Vishwakarma

**282.** Which player won the Orange Cap in IPL 2023?
A. Nishant Sindhu B. Hardik Pandya
C. Rashid Khan D. Shubman Gill

**283.** Who has been re-elected as the External Auditor of the World Health Organisation (WHO)?
A. Jim Yong Kim B. Anshula Kant
C. Ajay Banga D. Girish Chandra Murmu

**284.** Which team won Indian Premier League (IPL) 2023?
A. Chennai Super Kings B. Mumbai Indians
C. Gujarat Titans D. Kolkata Knight Riders

**285.** Who won the Malaysia Masters badminton title 2023 in men's singles?
A. Priyanshu Rajawat B. Lakshya Sen
C. Sameer Verma D. HS Prannoy

**286.** Which company carried out the construction of the new Parliament House?
A. Reliance Infrastructure Ltd.
B. Sadbhav Engineering Ltd.
C. Tata Projects Ltd.
D. Dilip Buildcon Ltd.

**287.** Where was the International Climate Research Meeting (ICRC-2023) held?
A. IIT Kanpur B. IIT Delhi
C. IIT Madras D. IIT Bombay

**288.** OpenAI launched which app in India for iPhone users on 18 May, 2023?
A. ChatGPT app
B. GPT-3.5 architecture
C. Language model training
D. OpenAI research initiative

**289.** Who recently took charge as the director of the Central Bureau of Investigation (CBI)?
A. Praveen Sood B. Alok Kumar Verma
C. Rishi Kumar Shukla D. Anil Sinha

**290.** What was the rank of AI supercomputer "AIRAWAT", in the 61st edition of the Top 500 Global Supercomputing list?
A. 61st B. 75th
C. 80th D. 55th

**291.** Which author won the 2023 International Booker Prize for his novel "Time Shelter"?
A. Nicl Gaiman B. Salman Rushdie
C. Georgi Gospodinov D. None of the above

**292.** Which team did the Indian junior hockey team defeat in their first match at the Men's Asia Cup 2023?
A. Australia B. Chinese Taipei
C. Japan D. South Korea

**293.** Who won the gold medal in the men's long jump event at the International Jumping Meeting athletics 2023?
A. Sandeep Singh Maan B. Sanjay Kumar Rai
C. Murali Sreesankar D. Ankit Sharma

**294.** Where was the 3rd Forum on India-Pacific Islands Cooperation (FIPIC Summit) held?
A. Australia B. New Zealand
C. Papua New Guinea D. Fiji

**295.** Who is the first Arab female astronaut to go into space?
A. Rayyana Barnawi B. Anousheh Ansari
C. Sara Sabry D. Marsha Ivins

**296.** In which district of Uttar Pradesh did the 3rd Khelo India University Games start?
A. Agra B. Allahabad
C. Ghaziabad D. Gautam Buddha Nagar

**297.** Who conferred Fiji's highest honour, the Companion of the Order of Fiji, to Prime Minister Narendra Modi?
A. President of Fiji
B. Prime Minister of Fiji
C. Governor-General of Fiji
D. None of these

**298.** On 22 May, 2023, who became the world No. 1 player in the men's javelin throw rankings?
A. Anderson Peters B. Rohit Yadav
C. Arshad Nadeem D. Neeraj Chopra

**299.** In the Italian Open 2023, which player won his first clay court title?
A. Novak Djokovic B. Rafael Nadal
C. Daniil Medvedev D. Holger Roon

**300.** Which Indian sportsperson won the bronze medal in the women's long jump event at the Golden Grand Prix 2023 Athletics Meet?
A. Shaili Singh B. Reeth Abraham
C. Anju Bobby George D. B Aishwarya

## ANSWERS

| 1 | 2 | 3 | 4 | 5 | 6 | 7 | 8 | 9 | 10 |
|---|---|---|---|---|---|---|---|---|---|
| C | C | B | D | B | B | B | C | B | C |
| 11 | 12 | 13 | 14 | 15 | 16 | 17 | 18 | 19 | 20 |
| B | C | A | C | B | C | B | D | B | B |
| 21 | 22 | 23 | 24 | 25 | 26 | 27 | 28 | 29 | 30 |
| C | D | C | C | B | B | C | C | C | C |
| 31 | 32 | 33 | 34 | 35 | 36 | 37 | 38 | 39 | 40 |
| C | C | C | B | C | B | B | C | A | C |
| 41 | 42 | 43 | 44 | 45 | 46 | 47 | 48 | 49 | 50 |
| A | B | B | B | C | B | C | B | B | B |

| 51 | 52 | 53 | 54 | 55 | 56 | 57 | 58 | 59 | 60 |
|---|---|---|---|---|---|---|---|---|---|
| D | B | B | B | B | B | C | A | C | B |
| 61 | 62 | 63 | 64 | 65 | 66 | 67 | 68 | 69 | 70 |
| A | D | D | D | B | C | C | B | A | D |
| 71 | 72 | 73 | 74 | 75 | 76 | 77 | 78 | 79 | 80 |
| C | C | B | C | A | A | D | C | B | D |
| 81 | 82 | 83 | 84 | 85 | 86 | 87 | 88 | 89 | 90 |
| B | D | B | D | D | D | C | B | C | A |
| 91 | 92 | 93 | 94 | 95 | 96 | 97 | 98 | 99 | 100 |
| C | C | A | D | D | B | C | A | D | A |
| 101 | 102 | 103 | 104 | 105 | 106 | 107 | 108 | 109 | 110 |
| A | A | C | B | C | D | C | B | B | B |
| 111 | 112 | 113 | 114 | 115 | 116 | 117 | 118 | 119 | 120 |
| B | B | B | B | B | C | D | D | B | A |
| 121 | 122 | 123 | 124 | 125 | 126 | 127 | 128 | 129 | 130 |
| D | A | C | D | B | D | D | B | D | D |
| 131 | 132 | 133 | 134 | 135 | 136 | 137 | 138 | 139 | 140 |
| C | C | A | C | B | B | D | A | C | B |
| 141 | 142 | 143 | 144 | 145 | 146 | 147 | 148 | 149 | 150 |
| D | A | D | A | A | D | B | C | A | B |
| 151 | 152 | 153 | 154 | 155 | 156 | 157 | 158 | 159 | 160 |
| B | D | B | D | B | C | A | C | B | B |
| 161 | 162 | 163 | 164 | 165 | 166 | 167 | 168 | 169 | 170 |
| B | A | B | C | B | B | D | A | C | C |
| 171 | 172 | 173 | 174 | 175 | 176 | 177 | 178 | 179 | 180 |
| B | A | B | C | C | A | C | A | C | A |
| 181 | 182 | 183 | 184 | 185 | 186 | 187 | 188 | 189 | 190 |
| D | B | B | C | B | D | B | B | A | D |
| 191 | 192 | 193 | 194 | 195 | 196 | 197 | 198 | 199 | 200 |
| C | D | A | A | B | A | B | C | B | A |
| 201 | 202 | 203 | 204 | 205 | 206 | 207 | 208 | 209 | 210 |
| A | C | A | C | B | C | A | C | A | B |
| 211 | 212 | 213 | 214 | 215 | 216 | 217 | 218 | 219 | 220 |
| D | C | A | A | A | D | D | C | C | B |
| 221 | 222 | 223 | 224 | 225 | 226 | 227 | 228 | 229 | 230 |
| C | B | D | A | A | C | D | B | D | D |
| 231 | 232 | 233 | 234 | 235 | 236 | 237 | 238 | 239 | 240 |
| A | D | B | B | B | B | B | B | A | D |
| 241 | 242 | 243 | 244 | 245 | 246 | 247 | 248 | 249 | 250 |
| C | B | D | B | B | C | D | C | B | C |
| 251 | 252 | 253 | 254 | 255 | 256 | 257 | 258 | 259 | 260 |
| A | B | B | D | C | C | D | A | D | C |
| 261 | 262 | 263 | 264 | 265 | 266 | 267 | 268 | 269 | 270 |
| C | A | A | A | A | D | C | B | D | C |
| 271 | 272 | 273 | 274 | 275 | 276 | 277 | 278 | 279 | 280 |
| D | A | B | D | C | C | B | D | B | C |
| 281 | 282 | 283 | 284 | 285 | 286 | 287 | 288 | 289 | 290 |
| A | D | D | A | D | C | D | A | A | B |
| 291 | 292 | 293 | 294 | 295 | 296 | 297 | 298 | 299 | 300 |
| C | B | C | C | A | D | B | D | C | A |

●●●